D1271517

DUS Ushaw College, Durham
DW Dr. Williams' Library, Dublin
DWL Worth Library, Dublin

E Edinburgh University
EC Eton College
ECP Royal College of Physicians, Edinburgh
ECS Royal College of Surgeons, Edinburgh
EH Huntly House, Edinburgh
ELY Ely Cathedral
EN National Library of Scotland (Advocates'),
Edinburgh
ENC New College, Edinburgh
EO Royal Observatory, Edinburgh
ER General Register House, Edinburgh
ES Signet, Edinburgh
EU United Free Church College, Edinburgh

FARM Farm Street Church, London
FM University of Miami, Miami, Fla.
FSF (mostly in EN) F. S. Ferguson, London
FU University of Florida, Gainesville

GB Baillie's Institution, Glasgow
GF United Free Church College, Glasgow
GH Hunterian Museum, Glasgow
GK Sir Geoffrey Keynes, London
GM Mitchell Library, Glasgow
GU Glasgow University

HC Cushing Library, Yale Medical School,
New Haven, Conn.
HEYTHROP Heythrop College, London
HG Gray Library, Haddington
HH Haigh Hall, Wigan (Crawford Library)
HR Royal Library, The Hague
HUTH Huth Sale Catalogue

I Innerpeffray, Perthshire, Scotland
IAU University of Iowa, Iowa City
IE Earlham College, Richmond, Indiana
INU Indiana University, Bloomington
IU University of Illinois, Urbana

JF Fulton Library, Yale Medical School, New
Haven, Conn.

KIRK Rudolf Kirk, San Marcos, Texas
KT Transylvania College, Lexington, Ky.

KU University of Kansas, Lawrence
KYU University of Kentucky, Lexington

L British Museum, London
LAD Admiralty, London
LAI Royal Art Institution, London
LAS Royal Agricultural Society, London
LB Baptist Union, London
LBS British and Foreign Bible Society, London
LC Library of Congress, Washington, D.C.
LCH Chemical Society, London
LCL Congregational Library, London
LCP Royal College of Physicians, London
LCS Royal College of Surgeons, London
LE Leicester Central Library
LF Friends' Library, London
LFEA Lough Fea Library, Ireland
LG Guildhall, London
LGI Gray's Inn, London
LI Inner Temple, London
LIB Royal Institute of British Architects, London
LIC Liverpool Cathedral
LIL Incorporated Law Society, London
LIU Liverpool University
LL Lincoln's Inn, London
LLL London Library
LLP Lambeth Palace, London
LM Medical Society, London
LMT Middle Temple, London
LN National Laboratory of Psychic Research,
London
LNC Lincoln Cathedral
LNH British Museum (Natural History), London
LP St. Paul's Cathedral, London
LPC Privy Council Office, London
LPM Peel Meeting, London
LPO Patent Office, London
LPR Public Record Office, London
LR Royal Society, London
LS Society of Antiquaries, London
LSC Sion College, London
LSE London School of Economics
LSG Society of Genealogists, London
LSL Royal Society of Literature, London
LSM Royal Society of Medicine, London
LT Thomason Collection, British Museum,
London

FOR REFERENCE

NOT TO BE TAKEN FROM THE ROOM

Z 2002.W5 1972 V.1

a31187 007208182b

UNIVERSITY OF WATERLOO

LIBRARY

CALL No.

SHORT-TITLE CATALOGUE

OF BOOKS PRINTED IN ENGLAND, SCOTLAND, IRELAND,
WALES, AND BRITISH AMERICA
AND OF ENGLISH BOOKS PRINTED IN OTHER COUNTRIES
1641-1700

Compiled by Donald Wing of the Yale University Library
Second edition, revised and enlarged

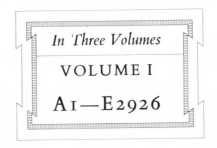

In Three Volumes

VOLUME I

A1—E2926

Withdrawn
University of Waterloo

PUBLISHED BY THE INDEX COMMITTEE OF THE
MODERN LANGUAGE ASSOCIATION OF AMERICA
NEW YORK, 1972

COPYRIGHT 1945, THE INDEX SOCIETY

Copyright © 1972
by the Modern Language Association of America

LIBRARY OF CONGRESS CATALOG CARD NO.: 70-185211

ISBN 0-87352-044-0

GENERAL INTRODUCTION

WHEN the first volume of this great reference work was published in 1945 after wartime delays, Benjamin C. Nangle emphasized in the Introduction that Donald Wing and the Index Society offered the work as a preliminary step towards a "full-dress catalogue" far in the future. Happily, thanks to Dr. Wing's single-minded dedication of purpose, this goal has now been reached. The first edition proved to be an indispensable tool of scholarship and a stimulus to research in seventeenth-century studies. This new edition adds information acquired in the past twenty-seven years. During this period scarcely a day has passed which has not produced several entries to be recorded in Dr. Wing's interleaved copy of the volumes in his Yale Library office. A thousand entries have been added in the letter A alone.

Like any comprehensive reference work these volumes are "dangerous for anyone to handle lazily." The user must always bear in mind that it is a *short-title* catalogue: in dealing with nearly 120,000 publications the editor cannot be expected to become an expert on the bibliographical niceties of each individual volume. The user of these volumes should consult Dr. Wing's discussion of "Scope and Method" before he announces to the world that he has found an item "not in Wing." In almost all such cases the "discovery" is merely evidence of the user's failure to employ the volumes intelligently. Booksellers are especially prone to such claims, which on investigation turn out to be listed in the proper places, or are found to be items such as periodicals which properly have been excluded. Another boast, "only three known copies", shows ignorance of the geographical distribution intended by the listings, for the British Museum or any great library may own several copies of a rare book.

Apropos, of booksellers, the suggestion has been made half-facetiously that the Antiquarian Booksellers' Association should put up a statue to Dr. Wing. Certainly his volumes have been a boon to the book trade, enabling dealers to price books according to their rarity. No less certainly should the learned world do so, for scholars working on seventeenth-century subjects can find in Wing's vast treasure-house information about books previously unknown or unavailable. Moreover, in contrast to most great compendia, Wing's *Short-Title Catalogue* is the single-handed work of one man and not the production of a team or editorial "factory." Nor has he enjoyed financial help, aside from a Guggenheim Fellowship, one sabbatical leave, and, after retirement, a modest grant for typing the printer's copy. We are reminded that two centuries ago, when Dr. Johnson published his *Dictionary of the English Language*, "the world contemplated with wonder so stupendous a work achieved by one man, while other countries had thought such undertakings fit only for whole academies." Or, what was written of another achiever, "*Si monumentum requiris, circumspice.*"

The publication of the first edition in 1945 was a "blessed event" for the newly-founded but unendowed group organized as the Index Society. The purpose of this publishing society was to bring into existence tool-books which publishers, both commercial and university-sponsored, then looked at askance. Guided by the Editorial Committee (Benjamin C. Nangle, Harold W. Bentley, George Sherburn, Wallace Notestein, Lawrence C. Wroth and myself) the infant Index Society received the enlightened understanding of Frederick Coykendall, then Director of Columbia University Press. His confidence in the value of the Society's program made possible the publication of Wing's *Catalogue*, as it did the Brown-Robbins *Index of Middle English Verse* which reached the public in 1943. Other tool-books followed as income from subscriptions built up a revolving fund. Never did the Index Society receive a penny of subsidy or subvention, aside from the unpaid services of its officers who even contributed necessary postage costs.

In 1966 before embarking on joint publication with the Clarendon Press of Margaret Crum's *First-Line Index of English Poetry 1500–1900 in Manuscripts of the Bodleian Library*, the officers of the Index Society decided that its future would best be assured by merging into the Modern Language Association of America. This transformation involved turning over the Society's assets and becoming the Index Committee of the MLA. Thus the revised edition of Wing's monumental work is published under MLA sponsorship. We hope and trust that other important tool-books will follow it. Whether any future publication will equal Wing's volumes in usefulness, or in adding to the revolving fund, is doubtful, now that the era of computers has superseded the age of giants.

James M. Osborn
Chairman, Index Committee,
Modern Language Association

THE INDEX COMMITTEE OF THE
MODERN LANGUAGE ASSOCIATION OF AMERICA

RALPH W. BALDNER, 1967–70
University of Victoria, Canada

HAROLD W. BENTLEY, 1962–
University of Utah (CHAIRMAN, 1962–70)

CURT F. BÜHLER, 1962–66
The Pierpont Morgan Library

DAVID V. ERDMAN, 1966–69
The New York Public Library

OTIS H. GREEN, 1962–67
University of Pennsylvania

BENJAMIN C. NANGLE, 1962–
Yale University

JAMES M. OSBORN, 1962–
Yale University (CHAIRMAN, 1970–)

STEPHEN M. PARRISH, 1967–
Cornell University

ROBERT F. ROEMING, 1970–
University of Wisconsin, Milwaukee

WILLIAM B. TODD, 1969–72
University of Texas

PREFACE TO THE REVISED EDITION

EVEN before publication of the first volume of this catalogue in 1945 the need for a new edition became apparent. By the time the sheets were printed off a hundred further locations and several additional entries were waiting for inclusion. Any publication on such a scale will encounter the problems of choosing a stopping-point. The possibility of pleasing everyone is abandoned, the hope of pleasing anyone seems vain. Once again the printer's deadline has been met, this time with some expectation that a minimum of additional information will be forthcoming.

As it was my pleasant duty in the Preface to the first edition to give credit to the John Simon Guggenheim Foundation for a fellowship to allow me to spend a year in English libraries, so for this new edition I wish to acknowledge the grant of a sabbatical leave – the first ever awarded to a librarian – from Yale University, which enabled me to journey twice to England and once to Scotland in order to verify new entries and locations. In the four decades of work which culminate in this new edition I have discovered no substitute for seeing each book before including it in these pages. Too frequently in the past I found that description in booksellers' lists (and even some in library catalogues) echoed the errors of their predecessors.

A GALLERY OF GHOSTS

Soon after the Index Society became transformed into the Index Committee of the Modern Language Association of America, they published a volume of two hundred and twenty-five pages titled *The Gallery of Ghosts*. Here I listed about five thousand titles of works which I had various reasons for believing did exist, but whose existence failed to materialize in the two hundred libraries examined. Many of these titles had been listed in early auction catalogues; others had been offered by dealers more recently. My hope was that as many as five hundred of these problems might be settled, either as proved errors in dating or spelling, or as additions with locations for the new edition of this *Short-Title Catalogue*. To my great surprise I can report that since April 1967 no less than 1375 are now accounted for: 700 books have been located, and equally important, another 675 have proved to be ghosts.

SCOPE AND METHOD

Scope

The ground rules of this new edition remain the same as for the parent volume of 1945-51. I have tried to list all "English" books printed between 1641 and 1700 inclusive which exist today. By "English" is meant all works printed in England, Scotland, Ireland, Wales, and British America, as well as all works printed anywhere else in English. Works by English authors printed in other languages outside these limits are not included. In general, then, this definition follows the proven practice of Pollard and Redgrave in their *Short Title Catalogue, 1475-1640* (1926). The only other exclusion is periodical literature. To include periodicals (for example the myriad beginning with the word *Mercurius*) would require a companion volume with collations to distinguish them by issues and dates.

Method

Except for conventional phrases, such as "By the King", the opening words of every title have been retained. Any abridgement carries ellipsis marks to indicate an omission. London is assumed as place of publication. Anonymous pieces provide problems for the casual users of the catalogue; their titles should usually be searched under the opening words *not an article*. Many otherwise anonymous works will be found under England Parliament, Scotland Estates, the names of kings, Oxford and Cambridge Universities, the Churches of England and Scotland, and almanacs.

NUMBER OF COPIES LISTED

In general only one copy is located in any one city; duplicate copies in any one library are not recorded. Where "L, O, C" in the earlier *S.T.C.* was intended to designate a relatively common book, it has resulted in countless claims of "only three known copies." My practice has been to locate every common book in ten libraries – five in Great Britain, five in the United States. Locations in private libraries follow those in public libraries. In the British locations I have attempted to list one copy in Scotland and one in Ireland as well as in London, Oxford, and Cambridge. The American locations try to give as wide a sweep geographically as possible, listing copies in California, Chicago, New England, New York, Texas and Washington for the volumes most frequently found.

Because a library is included it does not follow that *all* that library's holdings are listed. *This is not a census of copies*, but only a guide to inform scholars where a given entry may most conveniently be consulted. Only when less than five copies are located in either British or American libraries can any deduction be drawn of an entry's rarity. However, *all copies known* are listed and available in the editor's manuscript in the Yale University Library. (Inquiries should be addressed to the Reference Librarian, Beinecke Rare Book Library.)

ANONYMOUS WORKS AND PSEUDONYMS

All anonymous works should be looked for under the beginning of the title. If not found, a cross-reference to the attributed author will usually be given there. As should be obvious, I assume no responsibility for authority of attributions; wherever possible the British Museum catalogue has been followed. Pseudonyms are not treated as authors, but where one pseudonym has been used exclusively by a known author, a cross-reference will be found from the pseudonym to the author's name.

SYMBOLS OF LOCATION

Names of libraries and of the symbols used to denote them follow in two lists at the end of this Preface; for convenience to users of this catalogue the symbol list is also printed on the end-papers of each volume. A semi-colon divides the British libraries from those located outside Britain.

Instead of listing libraries in the same city by number, I have used letters exclusively. This practice will, I trust, make reference to the list of symbols less often necessary. To me the symbol LL, for instance, is more suggestive of "London – Lincoln's Inn" than was L²² in the earlier *S.T.C.*

ENTRY NUMBERS

Main entries are numbered consecutively within each letter of the alphabet, with the alphabetical letter prefixed to the number; for example E227. This procedure has been adopted to avoid the necessity of using nearly eighty thousand numbers of five digits each. This radical departure from the method of the earlier *S.T.C* is, I think, justified by the fact that E227 provides a simpler reference than, say, 27,839. However in retaining as far

as possible the numbers of my first edition it has necessitated the frequent use of letters. In the first edition added letters usually denoted a late addition. A thousand entries have since been added to the letter A – at least eleven on the first page – and the result may frighten some casual users. I hope A3AB will prove useful and less prone to error than A3.7. Where entries have been withdrawn, "Entry cancelled" stands to mark the omission.

SHORT PAMPHLETS AND BROADSIDES

An asterisk has been inserted to indicate pamphlets of less than fifty pages. This is to help scholars who may wish to order photostats and films. Broadsides are always described as "brs". In the case of broadside ballads, where two are printed on opposite sides of the leaf, each is given a separate entry. "Cap. 4°." designates a quarto volume without title-page but with a caption title.

MINOR POINTS

When bibliographical differences exist beyond the title-page in variant issues of a book or pamphlet without altering its format, they have been disregarded. For example, there are two issues of Otway's *Titus and Berenice* with page 17 containing sometimes 39 lines and sometimes 41. This kind of difference belongs to descriptive bibliography; here we are concerned solely with enumerative bibliography. The editor, further, does not pretend to decide which of two issues of the same year is earlier, even though one necessarily precedes the other.

Hebrew and Arabic type have not been used. Works beginning with such titles have "[Hebrew]" or "[Arabic]" and then the subtitle.

When the author's name does not appear on the title page, it has been placed within brackets.

Parts of books, even with new title-pages, have been omitted. Only when pagination and signatures begin is the title entered. This allows entry for a few books which are called for on other title pages; they are included here because they seem also to have been issued separately.

In a few cases (as under Æsop) the editions have been listed chronologically by language rather than by the quite arbitrary beginnings of title page. Where this occurs there is an explanatory note.

To my surprise I find more than twenty lists have been published using my first edition. Most of these employ my numbers. They range in size from the "Addenda" of the Bibliographical Society of Virginia's *Secretary's News Sheet* to the *Catalogue of the Plume Library* in Maldon, Essex.

1 Mary Isabel Fry & Godfrey Davis, "Supplements to the Short-Title Catalogue 1641–1700." *Huntington Library Quarterly*, Vol. XVI, No. 4. Aug. 1953.

2 Joseph E. Tucker. "Wing's 'Short-Title Catalogue' and Translations from the French." *The Papers of the Bibliographical Society of America*. Vol. 49. First Quarter, 1955.

3 John Wyllie. "Wing Addenda." *Secretary's News Sheet*, Bibliographical Society of the University of Virginia, No. 33. June, 1955.

4 John Alden. Bibliographia Hibernica: Additions and Corrections to Wing. Charlottesville, Bibliographical Society of the University of Virginia, 1955.

5 W. G. Hiscock. The Christ Church Supplement to Wing's Short-Title Catalogue, 1641–1700. Oxford, 1956.

6 John Alden. Wing Addenda and Corrigenda: Some Notes on Materials in the British Museum. University of Virginia, Bibliographical Society, Charlottesville, Virginia, 1958.

7 Bristol Reference Library, A Catalogue of Books . . . 1641–1700. Bristol, 1958.

8 S. G. Deed [assisted by Jane Francis]. Catalogue of the Plume Library, Maldon, 1959.

9 Edwin Wolf, 2nd. Wing Books in Library Company of Philadelphia. Philadelphia, 1959.

10 Elizabeth Wrigley. Wing Numbers in the library of the Francis Bacon Foundation, Incorporated. Pasadena, Calif., 1959. Supplement. Claremont, Calif., 1967.

11 W. J. Cameron & Pamela Brand. "Books Printed in England before 1700: A Tentative Check-list of STC & Wing Items in St. John's College, Auckland." *New Zealand Libraries*, Vol. 33, No. 8. September 1960.

12 David G. Esplin. "STC and Wing STC Books in Dunedin." *New Zealand Libraries*, 1960.

13 W. J. Cameron. "John Dryden in New Zealand." 1960. Wellington Library School, National Library Service, Bulletin No. 1.

14 W. J. Cameron. "Books Printed . . . 1641–1700 held in Australian Libraries." *Studies in Australian Bibliography*, No. 11. Sydney, 1962.

15 W. R. LeFanu. English Books Printed Before 1701 in the Library of the Royal College of Surgeons of England. London, 1963.

16 A Catalogue of Petyt Library in Skipton, Yorkshire. Gargrave, 1964.

17 A Catalogue of Printed Books in the Wellcome Historical Medical Library. Vol. II Books Printed From 1641–1850. London, 1966.

18 Wing Titles, Buffalo & Erie County Public Library, Buffalo. Buffalo, 1966.

19 A List of Books Printed . . . Before 1701 in Guildhall Library. London, 1966. 2 v.

20 A List of the Books, Pamphlets, Broadsides, and Leaflets in the Constance Meade Memorial Collection . . . between 1640 and 1701. Oxford, 1966.

21 Liverpool Cathedral, Radcliffe Library. Short Title Catalogue of Books Printed Before 1801. Liverpool, 1968.

22 William J. Cameron & Brian J. McMullin. The HPB (Hand Printed Books: A Cumulative Short-Title Catalogue of Books Printed Before 1801) Project: Phase I. London, Ontario, 1968.

That this new edition of the continuation of Pollard and Redgrave's *S.T.C.* is bigger, corrected, and improved is thanks in large part to the continuing interest of scholars. More than three hundred different people have sent in additions and corrections. I hope in the following list of acknowledgments no one has been omitted. To all I take this opportunity of saying thank you once more.

D.G.W.

Acknowledgments

H. M. Adams
Peter W. Adams
Thomas R. Adams
Janet Agnew
John Alden
C. G. Allen
Robin Alston
Charles M. Andrews*
Gertrude L. Annan

H. Richard Archer
Gabriel Austin

James T. Babb*
Elizabeth Baer
Roland H. Bainton
P. J. Baldwin
James F. Ballard
Julius P. Barclay

Robert J. Barry
Henrietta Bartlett*
Ralph A. Beals
William Beattie
Elizabeth A. Beck
Frank Benger
J. A. W. Bennett
G. E. Bentley, Jr.
Harold W. Bentley

Arthur B. Berthold
Sir Robert Birley
William Warner Bishop*
John B. Blake
William H. Bond
Harold Bowditch
Fredson Bowers
Leicester Bradner
J. R. B. Brett-Smith
Clarence S. Brigham
Roger P. Bristol
C. F. Tucker Brooke*
Lloyd A. Brown*
Christian F. Brun
W. Hamilton Bryson
Jacqueline Bull
Elizabeth H. Butler*
John Buxton

Henry J. Cadbury
Herbert Cahoon
John Callard
William J. Cameron
Bonnie Campbell
R. J. F. Carnon
Elizabeth Cass
John P. Chalmers
Derek A. Charles
C. H. Chaubard
James B. Childs
Thomas H. Clancy
Ethel B. Clark
E. A. Clough
Donald Coney
F. R. Cowell
J. Stevens Cox
John L. Cox
Marjorie L. Crandall
The Earl of Crawford & Balcarres
John Creasey
H. R. Creswick
Theodore Cunnion
Harvey Cushing*
John D. Cushing

Godfrey Davies*
Edna C. Davis

Giles E. Dawson
John M. Dawson
Vinton A. Dearing
Robert Donaldson
R. B. Downs
Thomas E. Drake
Paul S. Dunkin

H. W. Edwards
Ruth Eisenhart
Martha W. England
Arundell Esdaile*
Carol Evans

F. S. Ferguson*
Stanley Fienberg
Margaret C. Flower
Charles Fox
David F. Foxon
Sir Frank Francis
Joseph Frank
J. Milton French*
Maurice Frost
Mary Isabel Fry
Henry Fuller*
John F. Fulton*
Herman H. Fussler

Kenneth S. Gapp
K. J. Garrett
K. Garth
Willia K. Garver
Philip Gaskell
Robert Gathorne-Hardy
Sarah Geist
J. Gerritsen
Strickland Gibson*
Stanley G. Gilliam
Joseph A. Glaser
Martha T. Gnudi
Walter Goldwater
C. A. Gordan
Charles F. Gosnell
R. Gow
Ian R. Grant
W. S. Greaves
Reginald H. Griffith*
David M. Griffiths

Dikran Y. Hadidian
Ralph Hagedorn
Emily H. Hall*
H. A. N. Hallam
Mason G. Hamlyn
Jane Harding
Cyril Hargreaves
Dorothy G. Harris
Katharine K. Hasson
Benton Hatch
R. J. Hayes
Allen T. Hazen
Edward A. Henry
Philip Hepworth
Anna B. Hewitt
Lawrence Heyl
Peter Murray Hill*
R. H. Hill*
Mildred Hirsch
W. G. Hiscock*
K. J. Höltgen
J. R. B. Horden
J. K. Horsefield
Henry Horwitz
Henrietta Howell
Warren Howell
Maxwell Hunley
Maurice Hussey
H. Stanley Hyland
Ella M. Hymans

James S. Irvine

William A. Jackson*
Robin Jeffs
David Jenkins
John Jenson
John Johnson*
Richard C. Johnson

Lyle H. Kendall, Jr.
Andrew Keogh*
Sir Geoffrey Keynes
Rudolf Kirk
Bernard Knollenberg
Edwin B. Knowles*

Elizabeth Lamb

James N. Lawton
W. R. LeFanu
G. Legman
Paul Lewis
Wilmarth S. Lewis
Herman W. Liebert
Dorothy F. Livingston
Sir Richard Livingstone*
Melvin Loos*
Albert E. Lownes
Margaret D. Ludington

Jean Macalister
William H. McCarthy*
Hugh Macdonald*
Helen McIntyre
D. J. Mackenzie
R. B. McKerrow*
James G. McManaway
Archibald Malloch*
G. B. Mangan*
Mabel Martin
Katharine Martyn
Alexandra Mason
Wilmer G. Mason
C. D. Massey
William Matheson
Francis Mattson
A. Homer Mattlin
Paul Mellon
A. Miller
C. William Miller
Charles Mish
Henry A. Moe
Anna M. Monrad*
Paul Morgan
Paul G. Morrison
Howard Mott
Arnold Muirhead
A. N. L. Munby

Benjamin C. Nangle
Ronald P. Naylor
Paul Needham
John L. Nickalls
Charles C. Nickerson
Philip G. Nordell
Michael Norton

Wallace Notestein*
Simon Nowell-Smith

Corwin H. Olds
Charles D. O'Malley*
James M. Osborn

Herbert Packer
Katharine Pantzer
Michael Papantonio
Stanley Pargellis*
H. W. Parke
William R. Parker*
Stephen R. Parks
Douglas G. Parsonage
L. M. Payne
Noel R. Peattie
Ted-Larry Pebworth
Albert Peel
Ruth Pennybaker
N. M. Penzer
G. R. Pettit
Walter Pforzheimer
J. W. Phillips
Eleanor Pitcher*
Dorothy A. Plum
John E. Pomfret
W. A. Potter
Laurence C. Powell
Sir D'Arcy Power*
Eugene B. Power
Anna S. Pratt*

Otto H. Ranschburg
Doris Ranson
Howard C. Rice, Jr.
Stevens Rice
Warner G. Rice
Colin Richardson
Mary L. Richmond
Katharine C. Ricks
R. J. Roberts
Lionel Robinson
William W. Rockwell*
Rutherford D. Rogers
Carl P. Rollins*
Leona Rostenberg

M. Ray Sanborn*
Cora Sanders
Edward L. Saslow
Emily R. Schwaner
George A. Schwegmann, Jr.
S. R. Shapiro
Stanley A. Shepard
George Sherburn*
Clifford K. Shipton
E. G. Simpkin
S. M. Simpson
Paul A. Slack
William Sloane
Jeri S. Smith
Wilbur J. Smith
Wayne Somers
C. John Sommerville
Niels Sonne
Thomas M. Spaulding
H. C. Stanford
Madeline Stanton
D. T. Starnes
Edward C. Starr
G. William Stuart, Jr.
Charles E. Surman
Bradford F. Swan

James Tanis
P. J. Taplin
Charles B. Taylor
Henry C. Taylor*
Lorene Taylor
D. Thickett
Page Thomas
Godfrey Thompson
Lawrence S. Thompson
Robert A. Tibbetts
Chauncey B. Tinker*
James E. Tobin*
William B. Todd
Mary M. Tolman
Daniel Tower
Charles W. Traylen
Roland Tree*
Joseph E. Tucker
Decherd Turner

Eleanor S. Upton*
Margaret Uridge

Jane Van Arsdale
Willis Van Devanter
Jacob Viner*

David Wagstaff*
Alexander Wainwright
John M. Wallace
Peter J. Wallis
Elizabeth H. Weeks

Helen M. Welch
Neda M. Westlake
Evelyn Whelden
H. A. White
Thomas M. Whitehead
Brooke Whiting
James A. Wiley
Franklin B. Williams, Jr.
William P. Williams
Edwin E. Willoughby
Bernard E. Wilson
Edwin Wolf, 2nd
James O. Wood

Gertrude L. Woodward
Richard S. Wormser
Louis B. Wright
Lyle H. Wright
William S. Wright
Willia Wright
Wyllis E. Wright
Elizabeth S. Wrigley
Lawrence C. Wroth*
John Cook Wyllie

Curt A. Zimansky

* *deceased*

SYMBOLS AND LIBRARIES

A Abbotsford, Scotland
AB Blairs College, Aberdeen
AC Aberdeen City Charter Room
AM Marischal College, Aberdeen
AN National Library of Wales, Aberystwyth
AU Aberdeen University

BAMB Bamborough Castle
BB Baptist College, Bristol
BBE Buffalo and Erie Historical Society, Buffalo N.Y.
BBN Bevan-Naish Library, Birmingham
BC Birmingham Central Reference Library
BCN Benjamin C. Nangle, Woodbridge, Conn.
BF First Congregational Library, Belfast
BIU Birmingham University
BL Bibliothèque de l'Université de Louvain
BM Bristol Museum
BML Bath Municipal Library
BN Bibliothèque Nationale, Paris
BP Bedford Public Library
BQ Queen's University, Belfast
BR Bristol Reference Library
BSM St. Mary's College, Birmingham (Oscott College)
BU Buffalo University, Buffalo, N.Y.
BUTE Marquis of Bute

C Cambridge University Library
CA Cambridge University Archives
CC Coventry Central Library
CCA Gonville and Caius College, Cambridge
CCC Claremont Colleges Library, Claremont, Calif.
CCH Christ's College, Cambridge
CCL Clare College, Cambridge
CCO Corpus Christi College, Cambridge
CD Cashiel Diocesan Library
CDC Downing College, Cambridge
CE Emmanuel College, Cambridge
CF Fitzwilliam Museum, Cambridge
CH Henry E. Huntington Library, San Marino, Calif.
CHS Connecticut Historical Society, Hartford
CHW Watkinson Library, Hartford, Conn.
CJ Jesus College, Cambridge

CJC John Crerar Library, Chicago, Ill.
CK King's College, Cambridge
CL Loyola University, Chicago, Ill.
CLC William A. Clark Library, Los Angeles, Calif.
CLM University of California, Los Angeles, Biomedical Library
CM Magdalene College, Cambridge
CN Newberry Library, Chicago, Ill.
CNM Northwestern University Medical School, Chicago, Ill.
CP Peterhouse, Cambridge
CPA Pathology Laboratory, Cambridge
CPB Francis Bacon Foundation, Pasadena, Calif.
CPE Pembroke College, Cambridge
CPL Cardiff Public Library
CQ Queen's College, Cambridge
CS St. John's College, Cambridge
CSB University of California, Santa Barbara
CSE Selwyn College, Cambridge
CSL California State Library, Sacramento
CSS Sutro Branch, California State Library, San Francisco
CSSX Sidney Sussex College, Cambridge
CSU Stanford University, Stanford, Calif.
CT Trinity College, Cambridge
CU University of Chicago
CUC University College, Cardiff

D Dundee University
DC Dulwich College
DCH Chatsworth House, Derbyshire
DI Royal Irish Academy, Dublin
DK King's Inn, Dublin
DM Marsh's Library, St. Patrick's, Dublin
DMC Municipal Corporation, Dublin
DML Municipal Library, Dublin
DN National Library, Dublin
DOWNSIDE Downside School, Stratton on the Fosse, Bath, Somerset
DPR Public Record Office, Dublin
DRS Royal Dublin Society
DT Trinity College, Dublin
DU Durham University
DUC Durham Cathedral

DUS Ushaw College, Durham
DW Dr. Williams' Library, Dublin
DWL Worth Library, Dublin

E Edinburgh University
EC Eton College
ECP Royal College of Physicians, Edinburgh
ECS Royal College of Surgeons, Edinburgh
EH Huntly House, Edinburgh
ELY Ely Cathedral
EN National Library of Scotland (Advocates'),
    Edinburgh
ENC New College, Edinburgh
EO Royal Observatory, Edinburgh
ER General Register House, Edinburgh
ES Signet, Edinburgh
EU United Free Church College, Edinburgh

FARM Farm Street Church, London
FM University of Miami, Miami, Fla.
FSF (mostly in EN) F. S. Ferguson, London
FU University of Florida, Gainesville

GB Baillie's Institution, Glasgow
GF United Free Church College, Glasgow
GH Hunterian Museum, Glasgow
GK Sir Geoffrey Keynes, London
GM Mitchell Library, Glasgow
GU Glasgow University

HC Cushing Library, Yale Medical School,
    New Haven, Conn.
HEYTHROP Heythrop College, London
HG Gray Library, Haddington
HH Haigh Hall, Wigan (Crawford Library)
HR Royal Library, The Hague
HUTH Huth Sale Catalogue

I Innerpeffray, Perthshire, Scotland
IAU University of Iowa, Iowa City
IE Earlham College, Richmond, Indiana
INU Indiana University, Bloomington
IU University of Illinois, Urbana

JF Fulton Library, Yale Medical School, New
    Haven, Conn.

KIRK Rudolf Kirk, San Marcos, Texas
KT Transylvania College, Lexington, Ky.

KU University of Kansas, Lawrence
KYU University of Kentucky, Lexington

L British Museum, London
LAD Admiralty, London
LAI Royal Art Institution, London
LAS Royal Agricultural Society, London
LB Baptist Union, London
LBS British and Foreign Bible Society, London
LC Library of Congress, Washington, D.C.
LCH Chemical Society, London
LCL Congregational Library, London
LCP Royal College of Physicians, London
LCS Royal College of Surgeons, London
LE Leicester Central Library
LF Friends' Library, London
LFEA Lough Fea Library, Ireland
LG Guildhall, London
LGI Gray's Inn, London
LI Inner Temple, London
LIB Royal Institute of British Architects, London
LIC Liverpool Cathedral
LIL Incorporated Law Society, London
LIU Liverpool University
LL Lincoln's Inn, London
LLL London Library
LLP Lambeth Palace, London
LM Medical Society, London
LMT Middle Temple, London
LN National Laboratory of Psychic Research,
    London
LNC Lincoln Cathedral
LNH British Museum (Natural History), London
LP St. Paul's Cathedral, London
LPC Privy Council Office, London
LPM Peel Meeting, London
LPO Patent Office, London
LPR Public Record Office, London
LR Royal Society, London
LS Society of Antiquaries, London
LSC Sion College, London
LSE London School of Economics
LSG Society of Genealogists, London
LSL Royal Society of Literature, London
LSM Royal Society of Medicine, London
LT Thomason Collection, British Museum,
    London

LU University of London
LUC University College, London
LUG University of London, Goldsmith's Library
LUS Royal United Service Institution, London
LV Victoria and Albert Museum, London
LVD Dyce Collection, Victoria and Albert Museum, London
LVF Forster Collection, Victoria and Albert Museum, London
LW Dr. Williams' Library, London
LWL Wellcome Library, London

M Arnold Muirhead, St. Albans
MA University of Massachusetts, Amherst
MAB Baptist College, Manchester
MAH Maryland Historical Society, Baltimore
MAU Manchester University
MB Boston Public Library, Boston, Mass.
MBA Boston Athenaeum, Boston, Mass.
MBC Bowdoin College, Brunswick, Maine
MBJ Johns Hopkins University, Baltimore, Md.
MBP Peabody Institute, Baltimore, Md.
MBS Massachusetts Archives, Boston
MC Chetham Library, Manchester
MCL Congregational Library, Boston, Mass.
MH Harvard University, Cambridge, Mass.
MHL Harvard Law School, Cambridge, Mass.
MHO Massachusetts Horticultural Society, Boston
MHS Massachusetts Historical Society, Boston
MIU University of Minnesota, Minneapolis
MM Redpath Library, McGill University, Montreal
MMO Osler Library, McGill University, Montreal
MP Manchester Free Public Library
MR John Rylands Library, Manchester
MRL Manchester Free Reference Library
MSK Kendall Whaling Museum, Sharon, Mass.
MU University of Michigan, Ann Arbor
MWA American Antiquarian Society, Worcester, Mass.
MZ Zealand Academy, Middleburg, Netherlands

NA American Institute of Electrical Engineers, New York
NAM New York Academy of Medicine, New York
NBL Library Company, Burlington, N.J.
NC Columbia University, New York
NCL Central Library, Norwich

NCM Castle Museum, Norwich
NCU University of North Carolina, Chapel Hill
NE Newcastle Public Library
NF Fordham University, New York
NG Grolier Club, New York
NGC Guilford College, Guilford, N.C.
NGT General Theological Seminary, New York
NHC Colgate University, Hamilton, N.Y.
NHS New York Historical Society, New York
NIA St. Mark's Church, Niagara, Canada
NIC Cornell University, Ithaca, N.Y.
NJH New Jersey Historical Society, Newark
NL Lamport Hall, Northampton
NM Midland Baptist College, Nottingham
NMM Metropolitan Museum of Art, New York
NN New York Public Library
NNM J. Pierpont Morgan Library, New York
NO Norfolk and Norwich Literary Institution, Norwich
NOT Nottingham University
NP Princeton University, Princeton, N.J.
NPL Norwich Public Library
NPT Princeton Theological Seminary, Princeton, N.J.
NR Rutgers University, New Brunswick, N.J.
NS New York State Library, Albany
NSA Newcastle Society of Antiquaries
NSU Union College, Schenectady, N.Y.
NU Union Theological Seminary, New York

O Bodleian Library, Oxford
OA Oxford University Archives
OB Balliol College, Oxford
OBL Blackfriars Priory, Oxford
OBR Brasenose College, Oxford
OC Christ Church, Oxford
OCC Corpus Christi College, Oxford
OCI University of Cincinnati
OE Exeter College, Oxford
OG Greyfriars Priory, Oxford
OH Hertford College, Oxford
OJ Jesus College, Oxford
OL Lincoln College, Oxford
OM Magdalen College, Oxford
OME Merton College, Oxford
ON New College, Oxford
OP Oxford University Press
OPE Pembroke College, Oxford

OQ Queen's College, Oxford
OR Radcliffe Camera, Oxford
ORP Regent's Park, Oxford
OS St. John's College, Oxford
OSA St. Anne's College, Oxford
OW Worcester College, Oxford
OWA Wadham College, Oxford
OWC College of Wooster, Wooster, Ohio

P Plume Library, Maldon, Essex
PAP American Philosophical Society, Philadelphia, Pa.
PAPANTONIO Michael Papantonio, New York
PBL Lehigh University, Bethlehem, Pa.
PBM Bryn Mawr College, Bryn Mawr, Pa.
PC Peterborough Cathedral
PFL Philadelphia Free Library
PGN Philip G. Nordell, Philadelphia, Pa.
PH Haverford College, Haverford, Pa.
PHS Historical Society of Pennsylvania, Philadelphia
PJB P. J. Baldwin, Toronto
PL Library Company of Philadelphia
PMA Allegheny College, Meadville, Pa.
PPT Pittsburg Theological Seminary
PRF Rosenbach Foundation, Philadelphia, Pa.
PS Preussische Staats-Bibliothek, Berlin
PSC Swarthmore College, Swarthmore, Pa.
PSCO Pennsylvania State University, University Park, Pa.
PT Temple University, Philadelphia, Pa.
PU University of Pennsylvania, Philadelphia
PUL University of Pennsylvania, Law School, Philadelphia
PW Westtown School, Westtown, Pa.

R Rothamsted Agricultural Experiment Station
RB Baptist College, Rawdon
RBU Brown University, Providence, R.I.
RE Renishaw, Derbyshire
RIPON Ripon Cathedral
RNR Redwood Library, Newport, R.I.
RPJ John Carter Brown Library, Providence, R.I.
RPL Reigate Public Library

SA St. Andrews University
SC Salisbury Cathedral

SCU University of South Carolina, Columbia
SE Essex Institute, Salem, Mass.
SP Petyt Library, Skipton, Yorkshire
SR Royal Library, Stockholm
SS William Salt Library, Stafford
SW Washington University, St. Louis, Mo.
SYON Syon Abbey, South Brent, Devon

TAYLOR Robert Taylor, New York
TO University of Toronto
TSM Southern Methodist University, Dallas, Texas
TU University of Texas, Austin

UCLA University of California, Los Angeles

V University of Virginia, Charlottesville
VC Vassar College, Poughkeepsie, N.Y.
VH Hofbibliothek, Vienna

W Donald G. Wing, Woodbridge, Conn.
WARE Ware College, Armwell End, Ware, Hertfordshire
WBE United States, Bureau of Education
WC Wellesley College, Wellesley, Mass.
WCA St. George's Chapel, Windsor Castle
WCL Chapin Library, Williams College, Williamstown, Mass.
WDA United States, Department of Agriculture
WES Wesleyan University, Middletown, Conn.
WF Folger Library, Washington, D.C.
WG Georgetown University, Washington, D.C.
WGS United States, Geological Survey
WM Wandsworth Meeting
WPO United States, Patent Office
WSC Washington State University, Pullman
WSG U.S. National Library of Medicine, Washington, D.C.
WSL Wilmarth S. Lewis, Farmington, Conn.
WU University of Wisconsin, Madison
WWC Washington Cathedral Library, Washington, D.C.

Y Yale University, New Haven, Conn.
YB Birkbeck Library, York
YD Yale Divinity School, New Haven, Conn.
YL Yale Law School, New Haven, Conn.
YM York Minster
YS York Subscription Library

LIBRARIES AND SYMBOLS

Abbotsford, Scotland: A
Aberdeen City Charter Room: AC
Aberdeen University: AU
Admiralty, London: LAD
Allegheny College, Meadville, Pa.: PMA
American Antiquarian Society, Worcester, Mass.: MWA
American Institute of Electrical Engineers, New York: NA
American Philosophical Society, Philadelphia, Pa.: PAP

Baillie's Institution, Glasgow: GB
Bailliol College, Oxford: OB
Baldwin, P. J., Toronto: PJB
Bamborough Castle: BAMB
Baptist College, Bristol: BB
Baptist College, Manchester: MAB
Baptist College, Rawdon: RB
Baptist Union, London: LB
Bath Municipal Library: BML
Bedford Public Library: BP
Bevan-Naish Library, Birmingham: BBN
Bibliothèque de l'Université de Louvain: BL
Bibliothèque Nationale, Paris: BN
Birkbeck Library, York: YB
Birmingham Central Reference Library: BC
Birmingham University: BIU
Blackfriars Priory, Oxford: OBL
Blairs College, Aberdeen: AB
Bodleian Library, Oxford: O
Boston Athenaeum, Boston, Mass.: MBA
Boston Public Library, Boston, Mass.: MB
Bowdoin College, Brunswick, Maine: MBC
Brasenose College, Oxford: OBR
Bristol Museum: BM
Bristol Reference Library: BR
British and Foreign Bible Society, London: LBS
British Museum, London: L
British Museum (Natural History), London: LNH
Brown University, Providence, R.I.: RBU
Bryn Mawr College, Bryn Mawr, Pa.: PBM
Buffalo and Erie Historical Society, Buffalo, N.Y.: BBE
Buffalo University, Buffalo, N.Y.: BU
Bute, Marquis of: BUTE

California State Library, Sacramento: CSL

Cambridge University Library: C
Cambridge University Archives: CA
Cardiff Public Library: CPL
Cashel Diocesan Library: CD
Castle Museum, Norwich: NCM
Central Library, Norwich: NCL
Chapin Library, Williams College, Williamstown, Mass.: WCL
Chatsworth House, Derbyshire: DCH
Chemical Society, London: LCH
Chetham Library, Manchester: MC
Christ Church, Oxford: OC
Christ's College, Cambridge: CCH
Clare College, Cambridge: CCL
Claremont Colleges Library, Claremont, Calif.: CCC
Colgate University, Hamilton, N.Y.: NCH
College of Wooster, Wooster, Ohio: OWC
Columbia University, New York: NC
Congregational Library, Boston, Mass.: MCL
Congregational Library, London: LCL
Connecticut Historical Society, Hartford: CHS
Cornell University, Ithaca, N.Y.: NIC
Corpus Christi College, Cambridge: CCO
Corpus Christi College, Oxford: OCC
Coventry Central Library: CC
Cushing Library, Yale Medical School, New Haven, Conn.: HC

Dr. Williams' Library, Dublin: DW
Dr. Williams' Library, London: LW
Downing College, Cambridge: CDC
Downside School, Stratton on the Fosse, Bath, Somerset: DOWNSIDE
Dulwich College: DC
Dundee University: D
Durham Cathedral: DUC
Durham University: DU
Dyce Collection, Victoria and Albert Museum, London: LVD

Earlham College, Richmond, Ind.: IE
Edinburgh University: E
Ely Cathedral: ELY
Emmanuel College, Cambridge: CE

Essex Institute, Salem, Mass.: SE
Eton College: EC
Exeter College, Oxford: OE

Farm Street Church, London: FARM
Ferguson, F. S., London: FSF (mostly in EN)
First Congregational Library, Belfast: BF
Fitzwilliam Museum, Cambridge: CF
Folger Library, Washington, D.C.: WF
Fordham University, New York: NF
Forster Collection, Victoria and Albert Museum, London: LVF
Francis Bacon Foundation, Pasadena, Calif.: CPB
Friends' Library, London: LF
Fulton Library, Yale Medical School, New Haven, Conn.: JF

General Register House, Edinburgh: ER
General Theological Seminary, New York: NGT
Georgetown University, Washington, D.C.: WG
Glasgow University: GU
Goldsmith's Library, University of London: LUG
Gonville and Caius College, Cambridge: CCA
Gray Library, Haddington: HG
Gray's Inn, London: LGI
Greyfriars Priory, Oxford: OG
Grolier Club, New York: NG
Guildhall, London: LG
Guilford College, Guilford, N.C.: NGC

Haigh Hall, Wigan (Crawford Library): HH
Harvard Law School, Cambridge, Mass.: MHL
Harvard University, Cambridge, Mass.: MH
Haverford College, Haverford, Pa.: PH
Henry E. Huntington Library, San Marino, Calif.: CH
Hertford College, Oxford: OH
Heythrop College, London: HEYTHROP
Historical Society of Pennsylvania, Philadelphia: PHS
Hofbibliothek, Vienna: VH
Hunterian Museum, Glasgow: GH
Huntly House, Edinburgh: EH
Huth Sale Catalogue: HUTH

Incorporated Law Society, London: LIL
Indiana University, Bloomington: INU
Inner Temple, London: LI
Innerpeffray, Perthshire, Scotland: I

J. Pierpont Morgan Library, New York: NNM
Jesus College, Cambridge: CJ
Jesus College, Oxford: OJ
John Carter Brown Library, Providence, R.I.: RPJ
John Crerar Library, Chicago, Ill.: CJC
John Rylands Library, Manchester: MR
Johns Hopkins University, Baltimore, Md.: MBJ

Kendall Whaling Museum, Sharon, Mass.: MSK
Keynes, Sir Geoffrey, London: GK
King's College, Cambridge: CK
King's Inn, Dublin: DK
Kirk, Rudolf, San Marcos, Texas: KIRK

Lambeth Palace, London: LLP
Lamport Hall, Northampton: NL
Lehigh University, Bethlehem, Pa.: PBL
Leicester Central Library: LE
Lewis, Wilmarth S., Farmington, Conn.: WSL
Library Company, Burlington, N.J.: NBL
Library Company, Philadelphia, Pa.: PL
Library of Congress, Washington, D.C.: LC
Lincoln Cathedral: LNC
Lincoln College, Oxford: OL
Lincoln's Inn, London: LL
Liverpool Cathedral: LIC
Liverpool University: LIU
London Library: LLL
London School of Economics: LSE
Lough Fea Library, Ireland: LFEA
Loyola University, Chicago, Ill.: CL

Magdalen College, Oxford: OM
Magdalene College, Cambridge: CM
Manchester Free Public Library: MP
Manchester Free Reference Library: MRL
Manchester University: MAU
Marischal College, Aberdeen: AM
Marsh's Library, St. Patrick's, Dublin: DM
Maryland Historical Society, Baltimore: MAH
Massachusetts Archives, Boston: MBS
Massachusetts Historical Society, Boston: MHS
Massachusetts Horticultural Society, Boston: MHO
Medical Society, London: LM
Merton College, Oxford: OME
Metropolitan Museum of Art, New York: NMM
Middle Temple, London: LMT

Midland Baptist College, Nottingham: NM
Mitchell Library, Glasgow: GM
Muirhead, Arnold, St. Albans: M
Municipal Corporation, Dublin: DMC
Municipal Library, Dublin: DML

Nangle, Benjamin C., Woodbridge, Conn.: BCN
National Laboratory of Psychic Research, London: LN
National Library, Dublin: DN
National Library of Scotland (Advocates'), Edinburgh: EN
National Library of Wales, Aberystwyth: AN
New College, Edinburgh: ENC
New College, Oxford: ON
New Jersey Historical Society, Newark: NJH
New York Academy of Medicine, New York: NAM
New York Historical Society, New York: NHS
New York Public Library: NN
New York State Library, Albany: NS
Newberry Library, Chicago, Ill.: CN
Newcastle Public Library: NE
Newcastle Society of Antiquaries: NSA
Nordell, Philip G., Philadelphia, Pa.: PGN
Norfolk and Norwich Literary Institution, Norwich: NO
Northwestern University Medical School, Chicago, Ill.: CNM
Norwich Public Library: NPL
Nottingham University: NOT

Osler Library, McGill University, Montreal: MMO
Oxford University Archives: OA
Oxford University Press: OP

Papantonio, Michael, New York: PAPANTONIO
Patent Office, London: LPO
Pathology Laboratory, Cambridge: CPA
Peabody Institute, Baltimore, Md.: MBP
Peel Meeting, London: LPM
Pembroke College, Cambridge: CPE
Pembroke College, Oxford: OPE
Pennsylvania State University, University Park, Pa.: PSCO
Peterborough Cathedral: PC
Peterhouse, Cambridge: CP
Petyt Library, Skipton, Yorkshire: SP
Philadelphia Free Library: PFL
Pittsburg Theological Seminary: PPT
Plume Library, Maldon, Essex: P
Preussische Staats-Bibliothek, Berlin: PS

Princeton Theological Seminary, Princeton, N.J.: NPT
Princeton University, Princeton, N.J.: NP
Privy Council Office, London: LPC
Public Record Office, Dublin: DPR
Public Record Office, London: LPR

Queen's College, Oxford: OQ
Queen's University, Belfast: BQ
Queen's College, Cambridge: CQ

Radcliffe Camera, Oxford: OR
Redpath Library, McGill University, Montreal: MM
Redwood Library, Newport, R.I.: RNR
Regent's Park, Oxford: ORP
Reigate Public Library: RPL
Renishaw, Derbyshire: RE
Ripon Cathedral: RIPON
Rosenbach Foundation, Philadelphia, Pa.: PRF
Rothamsted Agricultural Experiment Station: R
Royal Agricultural Society, London: LAS
Royal Art Institution, London: LAI
Royal College of Physicians, Edinburgh: ECP
Royal College of Physicians, London: LCP
Royal College of Surgeons, Edinburgh: ECS
Royal College of Surgeons, London: LCS
Royal Dublin Society: DRS
Royal Institute of British Architects, London: LIB
Royal Irish Academy, Dublin: DI
Royal Library, Stockholm: SR
Royal Library, The Hague: HR
Royal Observatory, Edinburgh: EO
Royal Society, London: LR
Royal Society of Literature, London: LSL
Royal Society of Medicine, London: LSM
Royal United Service Institution, London: LUS
Rutgers University, New Brunswick, N.J.: NR

St. Andrews University: SA
St. Anne's College, Oxford: OSA
St. George's Chapel, Windsor Castle: WCA
St. John's College, Cambridge: CS
St. John's College, Oxford: OS
St. Mark's Church, Niagara, Canada: NIA
St. Mary's College, Birmingham (Oscott College): BSM
St. Paul's Cathedral, London: LP
Salisbury Cathedral: SC
Selwyn College, Cambridge: CSE

Sidney Sussex College, Cambridge: CSSX
Signet, Edinburgh: ES
Sion College, London: LSC
Society of Antiquaries, London: LS
Society of Genealogists, London: LSG
Southern Methodist University, Dallas, Texas: TSM
Stanford University, Stanford, Calif.: CSU
Sutro Branch, California State Library, San Francisco: CSS
Swarthmore College, Swarthmore, Pa.: PSC
Syon Abbey, South Brent, Devon: SYON

Taylor, Robert, New York: TAYLOR
Temple University, Philadelphia, Pa.: PT
Thomason Collection, British Museum, London: LT
Transylvania College, Lexington, Ky.: KT
Trinity College, Cambridge: CT
Trinity College, Dublin: DT

Union College, Schnectady, N.Y.: NSU
Union Theological Seminary, New York: NU
United Free Church College, Edinburgh: EU
United Free Church College, Glasgow: GF
United States, Bureau of Education: WBE
United States, Department of Agriculture: WDA
United States, Geological Survey: WGS
United States, National Library of Medicine, Washington, D.C.: WSG
United States, Patent Office: WPO
University College, Cardiff: CUC
University College, London: LUC
University of California, Los Angeles: UCLA
University of California, Los Angeles, Biomedical Library: CLM
University of California, Santa Barbara: CSB
University of Chicago: CU
University of Cincinnati: OCI
University of Florida, Gainesville: FU
University of Illinois, Urbana: IU
University of Iowa, Iowa City: IAU
University of Kansas, Lawrence: KU
University of Kentucky, Lexington: KYU
University of London: LU

University of Massachusetts, Amherst: MA
University of Miami, Miami, Fla.: FM
University of Michigan, Ann Arbor: MU
University of Minnesota, Minneapolis: MIU
University of North Carolina, Chapel Hill: NCU
University of Pennsylvania, Philadelphia: PU
University of Pennsylvania, Law School, Philadelphia: PUL
University of South Carolina, Columbia: SCU
University of Texas, Austin: TU
University of Toronto: TO
University of Virginia, Charlottesville: V
University of Wisconsin, Madison: WU
Ushaw College, Durham: DUS

Vassar College, Poughkeepsie, N.Y.: VC
Victoria and Albert Museum, London: LV

Wadham College, Oxford: OWA
Wandsworth Meeting: WM
Ware College, Armwell End, Ware, Hertfordshire: WARE
Washington Cathedral Library, Washington, D.C.: WWC
Washington State University, Pullman: WSC
Washington University, St. Louis, Mo.: SW
Watkinson Library, Hartford, Conn.: CHW
Wellcome Library, London: LWL
Wellesley College, Wellesley, Mass.: WC
Wesleyan University, Middletown, Conn.: WES
Westtown School, Westtown, Pa.: PW
William A. Clark Library, Los Angeles, Calif.: CLC
William Salt Library, Stafford: SS
Wing, Donald G., Woodbridge, Conn.: W
Worcester College, Oxford: OW
Worth Library, Dublin: DWL

Yale Divinity School, New Haven, Conn.: YD
Yale Law School, New Haven, Conn.: YL
Yale University, New Haven, Conn.: Y
York Minster: YM
York Subscription Library: YS

Zealand Academy, Middleburg, Netherlands: MZ

SHORT-TITLE CATALOGUE

OF BOOKS PRINTED IN ENGLAND, SCOTLAND, IRELAND, WALES, AND BRITISH AMERICA AND OF ENGLISH BOOKS PRINTED IN OTHER COUNTRIES

1641-1700

A

A. Collection of the brave exploits. 1686. *See* D'Assigny, Samuel.

1 —A defence of true Protestants. *For N.P., sold by Rich. Janua,* 1680. 4°.* L, O, CT, HH; CH, PL.

1A —[Anr. ed.] *For Nathaniel Ponder,* 1680. 4°.* T.C.I 430. C, CT, HH; NU, WF.

—Dialogue between A. and B. 1694. *See* Irvine, Alexander.

2 —An exact copy of a letter sent to William Laud. *For H. W. & T.B.,* 1641. 4°.* LT; NU, TU, Y.

A., A. Animadversions upon Dr. Sherlock's book. 1693. *See* South, Robert.

—Letter which was sent. 1689. *See* N., N.

—No peace. Oxford, 1645. *See* Arnway, John.

2A —The sad estate and condition of Ireland. *For Richard Baldwin,* 1689. 4°.* L, O, C, LFEA; CH, WF, Y.

—Tritheism charged. 1695. *See* South, Robert.

A., B. Buds and blossoms. 1691. *See* Antrobus, Benjamin.

—Civill rights of tythes. 1653. *See* Elderfield, Christopher.

2B —The sick-man's rare jewel. 1674. 8°. LCS.

2BA **A., C.** A catechism for the use of His Royal Highness. 1692. O.

2BB —A congratulatory poem to Her Royal Highness. colop: *By Nat. Thompson,* 1682. brs. CH, MH, Y.

2BC —A congratulatory poem to His Royal Highness. *For Samuel Walsall,* 1688. fol.* Y.

—Fasciculus praeceptorum. Oxoniæ, 1660. *See* Airay, Christopher.

2C —Protestantism reviv'd. *For S. Walsall,* 1688, brs. MH, Y.

A., D. Moral discourse. 1694. *See* Abercromby, David.

3 —The present state of the German and Turkish empires. *For D. Brown and T. Goodwin,* 1684. 8°. T.C.II 44. CT, EN; LC, MH, PBM, Y.

3A —The whole art of converse. *For Joseph Hindmarsh,* 1683. 12°. T.C.II 19. L, O, SP; CH, WCL, WF, Y.

A., E. Catalogue of all the peers. 1661. *See* Ashmole, Elias.

—Elegy on her Grace. 1684. *See* Arwaker, Edmund.

3B —A fuller relation of the great victory obtained. *For Laurance Blaiklock,* 1644. 4°.* LT, O; CH, CLC, Y.

3C —The great venture. *For Hen. Million,* 1668. 4°.* L.

4 —A letter from his Majesties quarters at Newcastle. *By E. G.,* 1646. 4°.* LT, O, HH; CN, WF, Y.

5 —Medico-mastix or, a pill for the doctor. [*London*], *printed,* 1645. 4°.* LT.

6 —The Presbiterian brother and sister. [*London*], *printed,* 1645. 4°.* LT, O, OC, DT.

7 **A., F.** A letter from a gentleman in Grayes-Inn. [*London*], *printed,* 1662. 4°.* O, BR, DT; MB, NU, WF.

8 **A., G.** No post from heaven. *Printed at Oxford,* 1643. 4°.* MADAN 1342. LT, O, CT, EN, DT; CH, CN, NU, WF, Y.

—Orthodox plea. 1669. *See* Alsop, George.

A., H. Artis logicæ. Oxon, 1696. *See* Aldrich, Henry.

—Christian physician. 1683. *See* Atherton, Henry.

—Communion of saints. Amsterdam, 1642. *See* Ainsworth, Henry.

—Counter poyson. 1642. *See* Ainsworth, Henry.

—Court convert. [*London?* 1700.] *See* Waring, Henry.

9 —Mirabile pecci: or, the non-such wonder of the peak in Darby shire. *For T. Parkhurst and G. Calvert,* 1669. 8°. T.C.I 10. L, O, OC; WF.

9A **A., I.** The good womans champion. *For Francis Grove,* [1650?] 8°.* L.

10 —A manifest and briefe discovery. *By T. W. for Joshua Kirton,* 1646. 4°.* LT, LW, DC, GU, DT; CH, NU, OWC, WF.

—Sacro-sancta regum. Oxford, 1644. *See* Maxwell, John, abp.

11 **A., J.** Advice touching chusing directors. [*London?,* 1697.] cap., fol.* HH; MH.

11A —Animadversions on George Keith's account of a national church. *Printed,* 1700. 4°.* MBA, PH, PL, Y.

—Apology for a younger brother. Oxford, 1641. *See* Ap-Robert, John.

[1]

—Brief apologie for the sequestred. [*n.p.*], 1649. *See* Allington, John.

—Call to all bishops. [*n.p.*], 1670. *See* Anderdon, John.

—Continuation of the grand conspiracy. [*n.p.*, 1660]. *See* Allington, John.

12 —The dæmon of Burton. *For C. W.*, 1671. 4°.* L; CH.

—Directions concerning the matter. 1671. *See* Arderne, James.

—Examination of Dr. Woodward's. 1697. *See* Arbuthnot, John.

13 —A funerall elegie on the unfortunate death of . . . Major Edward Grey. *For I. W.*, 1644. brs. L, LVF, HH.

—Gospel physitian. 1655. *See* Anthony, John.

—Historicall narration. 1645. *See* Ailward, John.

—Judicial astrologers. 1659. *See* Allen, John.

—Liquor alchahest. 1675. *See* Starkey, George.

—Lvcas redivivus. 1655. *See* Anthony, John.

—New prognostication. Edinburgh, 1667. *See* Almanacs.

—Postscript to a word. 1660. *See* Anderdon, John.

—Proposal to supply the defect of money. London, 1700. *See* Armour, James.

14 Entry cancelled.

—Remarks upon a letter. 1699. *See* Anderson, John.

—Secret and family prayers. *Cambridge*, 1677. *See* Armstrong, John.

—Soul's worth and danger. *Cambridge*, 1677. *See* Armstrong, John.

15 —A supply of considerable things. [*n.p.*, 1682.] cap., 4°. OC, DT; CH, WF.

—Upon the late lamentable fire in London. 1667. *See* Allison, John.

—Vindication of the Roman catholicks. 1660. *See* Caron, Redmond.

—Visitation in love. 1660. *See* Anderdon, John.

—Younger brother. Oxford, 1671. *See* Ap-Robert, John.

16 —Entry cancelled.

17 **A., M.** Cataplus: or Æneas his descent to Hell. *For Maurice Atkins, sold by William Hinchman*, 1672. 4°. T.C.I. 118. O; CLC, CN, MH, WF, Y.

—Merlinus Anglicus. 1650. *See* Almanacs.

18 —Sober and useful reflections upon a treatise of Mr. Richard Baxter's. *For Richard Chiswell*, 1680. 4°. O, C, OC, SA; MH, WF, Y.

19 —Speculum Baxterianum: or, Baxter against Baxter. *For Richard Chiswell*, 1680. 4°. T.C.I. 413. O, C, YM, E, DT; CH, NU, PL.

—Warning to the inhabitants. [*n.p.*], 1676. *See* Adams, Mary.

20 **A., N.** A true and perfect account of the discovery of a barbarous and bloody plot. *For R. T.*, 1679. 4°.* L, O, C; CH, CN, WF, Y.

20A — —[Anr. ed.] [*Dublin*], reprinted, 1678. 4°.* DIX 162. C, DK.

20B **A., P.** The character of an honest man. *For Randal Taylor*, 1683. fol.* L, O, OC, CT, LVF; CH, CN, Y.

21 —Christian charity, or seasonable advice. *Printed and are to be sold by J. Wells*, 1699. 8°. O.

22 —Christian charity to poor prisoners. 1696. 8°. O, CT.

23 —Considerations and exhortations to the serious and religious observation. *For John Nutt*, 1700. 8°. O, CT, P; CH.

—A discourse concerning Puritans. 1641. *See* Ley, John.

24 —An essay towards a character of His Sacred Majesty, King James the Second. [*n.p.*, 1685.] brs. HH.

25 —A letter of advice to the Londoners to forewarn them. [*n.p.*, 1643.] brs. LT; MIU.

25A —A new-year's gift; or, advice to a god-son. *By J.L. for Luke Meredith*, 1696. 12°. OC.

26 —Sober and serious considerations occasioned by the death of . . . King Charles II. *By John Leake for Luke Meredith* 1685. 4°.* T.C.II 129. L, O, C; CH, MBA, WF.

26A — —Second edition. *For Luke Meredith*, 1686. 4°.* T.C.II 165. OC.

—Vox clamantis. 1684. *See* Ayres, Philip.

—Voyages and adventures. 1684. *See* Ayres, Philip.

A., R. Best of remedies. 1667. *See* Alleine, Richard.

—Brief history of transubstantiation. 1674. *See* Allen, Richard.

26B —A caution against suretiship. *By B. Griffin, for Samuel Heyrick* 1688. 8°. L, BR; WF.

—Χειροθεσια. 1661. *See* Alleine, Richard.

26C —A congratulatory poem, on the safe arrival of the Scots African . . . fleet. [*Edinburgh*], 1699. brs. RPJ.

—Devotions. 1655. *See* Aylett, Robert.

27 —An elogie on the death of the learned and honourable Sir George Mackenzie. [*Edinburgh?* 1691.] brs. ALDIS 2999. E, EN.

—England's distempers. 1677. *See* Allen, Richard.

—Godly-fear. 1674. *See* Alleine, Richard.

—Godly mans portion. 1663. *See* Alleine, Richard.

—Heaven opened. 1665. *See* Alleine, Richard.

—Insulae fortunatae. 1675. *See* Allen, Richard.

—Placita Latinè. 1660. *See* Aston, Robert.

—Rebuke to backsliders. 1677. *See* Alleine, Richard.

27A —The reformed gentleman. *For T. Salusbury*, 1693. 8°. T.C.II 441. L, O, OB; CH, Y.

—Scala sancta: or the exaltation. 1692. *See* Allestree, Richard.

28 —A treatise of civil bonds. *For T. Salusbury*, 1688. 8°. T.C.II 383. EN; LC.

—Trial of our church-forsakers. 1663. *See* Abbot, Robert.

—Valiant Welshman. 1663. *See* Arnim, Robert.

—Vindiciæ pietatis. 1663. *See* Alleine, Richard.

—Wife, not ready made. 1653. *See* Aylett, Robert.

—World conquered. 1668. *See* Alleine, Richard.

A., S. Dying infants. 1699. *See* Acton, Samuel.

—Modest reply humbly offered. 1692. *See* Acton, Samuel.

28A —The virgin saint. *For Jonathan Robinson*, 1673. 8°. T.C.I 148. L.

A., T. Candle in the dark. [*n.p.*, 1656.] *See* Ady, Thomas.

—Carolina. 1682. *See* Ash, Thomas.

29 —The case of ministring at the communion-table. *By Ralph Holt, for Obadiah Blagrave*, 1683. 4°.* T.C.II 59. L, O, CJ, EC; CH, NU, PPT.

—Χειρεξοχη: the excellency. 1665. *See* Allen, Thomas.

30 —A declaration of severall observations to the reader. *For Jane Coe*, 1646. brs. LT, LG.

—Law of obligations. 1693. *See* Ashe, Thomas.

31 —Parish churches turn'd into conventicles. 1683. 4°. O, LP; CN.

32 —Religio clerici. *For Henry Brome*, 1681. 12°. T.C.I 420. L, O, OB, CT, GK; CH, MB, MH, MMO, WF, HC.

33 ——[Anr. ed.] *Printed, and are to be sold by Randal Taylor*, 1689. 12°. O, OB, LW, DT.

34 —Rump rampant. [*London?* 1660.] brs. L, O; MH.

—Some reflections upon a late pamphlet. *See* Ashenden, Thomas.

—Ταπειναινος, humble praise. 1660. *See* Arnold, Thomas.

35 —May the 14, 1642. A true relation of the chiefe passages in Ireland. *For Ed. Blackmore*, 1642. 4°.* LT, O, C, EC; CH, CN, Y.

.A., V. Duty and interest united. 1695. *See* Alsop, Vincent.

A., W. An answer to Mr. J. G. his xl queries. 1653. *See* Allen, William.

—Apology for the East-India Company. 1690. *See* Atwood, William.

—Catholicism. 1683. *See* Allen, William.

—Certaine queries touching. 1647. *See* Aspinwall, William.

—Christians justification. 1678. *See* Allen, William.

—Discourse of divine assistance. 1679. *See* Allen, William.

—Discourse of the nature, series. 1689. *See* Allen, William.

—Ευασμος Βασιλικος. 1662. *See* Ayleway, William.

—Fundamental constitution of the English. 1690. *See* Atwood, William.

—Grand errour. 1680. *See* Allen, William.

—Killing, no murder. [*n.p.*], 1698. *See* title.

—Legislative power. 1656. *See* Aspinwall, William.

—Lord Chief Justice Herbert's account. 1689. *See* Atwood, William.

35A —The necessity of altering the present oath. *For J. Salusbury*, [1690?] fol.* C.

—Of the state. 1680. *See* Allen, William.

—Perswasive to peace. 1680. *See* Allen, William.

—Practical discourse of humility. 1681. *See* Allen, William.

—Present state of the United Provinces. 1669. *See* Aglionby, William.

35B —Queries touching the ordination of ministers. *By Matthew Simmons for Henry Overton, sold by J. Pounce*, 1647. 4°.* LT.

—Serious and friendly address. 1676. *See* Allen, William.

—Thunder from Heaven. 1655. *See* Aspinwall, William.

A., William. Medulla historiae Scoticae. 1685. *See* Alexander, William.

36 The A, B, C; or, a catechisme. [*London*], *printed*, 1644. 8°.* EN.

36A The ABC with the catechism. *For the company of stationers*, 1677. 8°. OC.

37 —[Anr. ed.] *Printed*, 1680. 8°.* O.

38 —[Anr. ed.] *For the company of stationers*, 1683. 8°.* O.

38A —[Anr. ed.] —, 1687. 12°. C.

38B —[Anr. ed.] —, 1698. 12°. L.

39 The A.B.C. with the shorter catechism. *Edinburgh by George Mosman*, 1696. 8°.* O, EN.

40 —[Anr. ed.] *Glasgow, by Robert Sanders*, 1698. 8°.* ALDIS 3720. NNM.

A ha! Christmas. 1647. *See* H., T.

A tous ceulx. 1655. *See* Fox, George.

A tous governeurs. [*London?* 1661]. *See* Fox George.

41 A la mode. The cities profound policie. [*London*], *printed*, 1647. brs. L.

41A The alamode musician. [*London*], *sould by Henry Playford*, 1698. fol.* T.C.III 79. L.

42 Aarons cry to Moses. [*London*], *printed*, 1661. brs. L.

43 Aaron's rod blossoming. *For Richard Butler*, 1680. 4°.* T.C.I 414. L, O, CCH, SC; CH, MH, NU, WF, Y.

44 Aron's rod: or, a scourge. [*London*, 1690?] cap., 4°.* CLC, Y.

[Aarssens, François.] Journey into Spain. 1670. *See* Brunel, Antoine de.

45 Abbadie, Jacques. The art of knowing one-self. *Oxford, by Leonard Lichfield, for Henry Clements, and John Howell*, 1695. 12°. L, O, LW, P; CH, NU, WF, Y.

46 ——[Anr. ed.] *For R. Bentley*, 1696. 12°. T.C.II 591. L, LW, E; MU, WF, Y.

47 ——[Anr. ed.] *By E. J. for R. Bentley*, 1696. 12°. T.C.III 16. MU.

48 ——[Anr. ed.] *Oxford by L. Lichfield for Thomas Leigh, London*, 1698. 12°. T.C.III 82. L, O; CH, Y.

49 [—] Defense de la nation britannique. 1692. *Ches la vesve Mallet*. 8°. L, O, C, LW; INU, PL.

50 [—] L'esprit du Christianisme. *Par B. Griffin, pour la veuve Pean*, 1694. 4°.* L, LW.

51 [—] Histoire de la dernière conspiration d'Angleterre. *Par W. Redmayne*, 1696. 8°. L, O; BN, CLC, LC, Y.

52 [—] The history of the late conspiracy. *For Daniel Brown and Tho. Bennett*, 1696. 8°. L, O, EN; CH, CU, MH, WF, Y.

53 Entry cancelled.

54 [—] La mort du juste. *Par B. Griffin, pour la veuve Pean*, 1693. 4°.* L; Y.

55 —A new French grammar. *Oxford, by H. Hall for J. Crosley*, 1676. 8°. MADAN 3093. T.C.I 219. L [t.p. only], O.

56 —A panegyric on our late sovereign Lady Mary. *For Hugh Newman*, 1695. 4°.* T.C.II 560. L, O, CT, AU, LCL; CH, CN, MH, NU, WF, Y.

56A —Panegyrique de Marie. *Par B. Griffin, pour la veuve Pean*, 1695. 4°.* LW; CU, WF, Y.

57 —Traité de la verité de la religion chrétienne. *A Rotterdam, chez Reinier Leers*, 1684. *Et à Londres, chez Jean Beaulieu*. 12°. L; CU, MWA, NPT, V.

58 —A vindication of the truth of Christian religion. *For Jonathan Robinson, John Taylor, John Wyat, and Richard Wilkin*, 1694. 8°. T.C.II 491. L, O, C, E, DT; CH, CU, MH, NPT, Y.

59 ——Part II. *For J. Wyat, and R. Wilkin*, 1698. 8°. L, O, C, EN, DT; CU, MH, NPT.

Abby and other church-lands. [1688.] *See* Willes, John.

60 Abbot, George, *abp.* A briefe description of the whole world. *By B. Alsop for J. M., to be sold by William Sheares*, [1642]. 12°. CT, DT, E; IU, WF, Y.

61 — —[Anr. ed.] *For W. Sheares, 1656.* 12°. SP; CN, PBL, Y.

62 — —Fifth edition. *For Margaret Sheares, and John Playfere, 1664.* 12°. L, O, LV; LC, NPT.

63 [–] Cheap-side crosse censured . . . As also a remarkable passage. *By A. N. for I. R., 1641.* 4°.* MADAN 979. LT, O, LVF, LG, LP; LC, MH, NU, Y.

64 — —[Anr. ed.] . . . as also some divine arguments. *By A. N. for I. R., 1641.* 4°.* L, O, LG; LC, MH, Y.

65 **Abbot, George,** *religious writer.* Brief notes upon . . . Psalms. *By William Bentley, to be sold by John Williams, and Francis Eglesfield, 1651.* 8°. LT, C, E, GU; CH, CLC, NU.

66 —Vindiciae Sabbathi, or, an ansvver. *By I. D. for Henry Overton, 1641.* 4°. L, O, CT, CE, ENC; MBP, NU, WF, Y.

67 **Abbot, John.** Devovt rhapsodies. *By Thomas Harper for Daniel Frere, [1647].* 4°. LT, O, P; CH, MH, WF.

67A — —[Anr. ed.] *1648.* 4°. O, DC, DT; WF.

68 **Abbot, Robert.** A Christian family bvilded by God. *By J. L. for Philemon Stephens, 1653.* 8°. LT, O, LW; CLC, NU, WF.

69 —Milk for babes. *By John Legatt for Philemon Stephens, 1646.* 8°. L, O, LSC, YM; CLC, NU, Y.

69A —The trial of our church-forsakers. *Printed, 1663.* 8°. Y.

69B —The young mans warning-piece. *By J. L. for P. Stephens, 1652.* 8°. CLC.

70 — —[Anr. ed.] *For Philemon Stephens, 1657.* 8°.* L, LW; CLC.

70A — —[Anr. ed.] *For I. Williams, 1671.* 8°. O.

70B **Abbott, Margaret.** A testimony against the false teachers. *[London? 1659.]* 4°.* LT, OC, BBN; WF.

70C The abdicated bishops letters, to the abdicated King. *[London? 1691].* brs. HH; CH, PL, TU.

71 The abdicated prince: or, the adventures of four years. *For John Carterson, 1690.* 4°.* T.C.II 313. L, O, LVD, EN, AU; CH, CN, LC, MH, TU, Y.

71A — —Second edition. *–, 1690.* 12°. O; LC, MH, WF, Y.

Abel redevivus. 1651. *See* Fuller, Thomas.

72 **Abell, William.** A dialogue or accidental discourse betwixt Mr. Alderman Abell. *[London], printed, 1641.* 4°.* LT, O, LG, LVG; MH, TU, Y.

73 —The last discourse betwixt Master Abel and Master Richard Kilvert. *[London], printed, 1641.* 4°.* LT, O, LG, LVG; CH, NU, WF, Y.

74 —To the honourable the committee of Parliament for prisons . . . The humble petition of. *[London, 1654.]* cap., 4°.* NC.

Abendano, Isaac. *See* Almanacs.

75 Entry cancelled.

76 **Abercrombie, Alexander.** Disputatio juridica. *Edinburgi, apud haeres & successores Andreæ Anderson, 1694.* 4°.* EN.

77 **Abercromby, Christopher.** A short instruction for the better . . . prayer. *Paris, L. Sevestre, 1691.* sixes. L, DOWN-SIDE; CN.

78 **Abercromby, David.** Academia scientiarum: or, the academy. *By H. C. for J. Taylor, L. Meredith, T. Bennet, R. Wilde, 1687.* 8°. L, O, C, E, AU; NC, PL, WF, JF.

79 —Ars artium; or, The art of divine converse. *For the author, and sold by Samuel Smith, 1683.* 8°.* T.C.II 2. O.

80 —Davidis Abercrombii, M.D. De variatione, ac varietate pulsus. *Impensis Samuelis Smith, 1685.* 8°.* T.C.II 128. L, O, CS, E, AU; BN, CLC, NAM, NPT, WSG, JF.

81 —A discourse of wit. *For John Weld, 1685.* 12°. T.C.II 137. L, CT, ES; CH, CN, MH, NC, JF.

81A — —[Anr. ed.] *W. Leake, 1685.* 12°. CT.

82 — —[Anr. ed.] *For John Weld, 1686.* 12°. L, O, CK, E, EN; CLC, VC, Y.

83 —A moral discourse. *By Tho. Hodgkin for the author, to be sold by John Taylor: and may be had at Mr. Trehern's, 1690.* 8°. T.C.II 338. L, RPL, E; CLC, NC, WF.

84 — —Second edition. *For Dorman Newman, 1691.* 8°. T.C.II 352. L, O, C, BR.

85 —Davidis Abercrombii, M.D. Opuscula medica. *Impensis Samuelis Smith, 1687.* 8°. T.C.II 179. C, LCP, LCS; BN, WF.

86 —Protestancy to be embrac'd. *For the author by Thomas Hodgkin, 1682.* 12°. T.C.II 34. L, O, C, E, CT; NP, NU.

87 [–]Scolding no scholarship. *[Douai?], for the author, 1669.* 12°. L, ON, HH, AU, GU; NU, TU.

88 —Tuta, ac efficax luis venereæ. *Impensis Samuelis Smith, 1684.* 8°.* T.C.II 93. L, OR, E, AM; BN, CLC, MIU, WSG, HC.

89 **Aberdeen Committee of War.** Proclamation, 13 June. *[Aberdeen, Raban, 1646.]* brs. AU.

90 **Aberdeen University.** Augustissimo . . . Carolo. *[Aberdeen, Brown], 1660.* brs. ALDIS 1624. O.

91 —Information for the new Colledge of Aberdeen. *[Aberdeen, John Forbes, 1699.]* brs. ALDIS 3858. AU.

91A **Aberdeen University. Marischal College.** Illustrissimo . . . heroe. *[Aberdeen], typographeo Joannis Forbesii junioris, 1670.* brs. Y [on silk].

91B —To his Grace, His Majesties High Commissioner. *Edinburgh, 1695.* brs. EN.

92 —[Same title] —, *1696.* brs. EN.

93 —To the Right Honourable the Lord Præses. *[Aberdeen, John Forbes, 1698.]* brs. AU.

94 Aberdeen the 24 of Ianuary 1698. Orders . . . for the constables. *[Aberdeen, Forbes,] 1698.* brs. ALDIS 3721. AC.

Aberdeen's new almanack. 1682. *See* Almanacs.

95 **Abernethie, Thomas.** A vvorthy speech, by. *By T. H., 1941 [i.e., 1641].* 4°.* LT, O, C, HH, ES; CH, MH, TU, WF, Y.

96 The abhorrence, or Protestant observations. *Dublin, for Jas. Malone, 1689.* brs. DIX 235. OM; MH.

Abingtons and Alisburies. [1642]. *See* H., G.

97 The abolishing of the Booke of common prayer. *[London], reprinted, and are to be sold by Samvel Satterthvvaite, 1641.* 4°.* LT, O, CT, EN, DT; CLC, MH, NU, WF, Y.

97A About mending the coyn. colop.: *By F. Collins, 1695.* brs. NC.

98 About the East-India trade. *[1692.]* brs. HR, MH.

99 About the 7th of March, 1655. Master Whiting and Master Spelman came to Richard Hodgkinsonne. *[n.p., 1658.]* brs. LT.

100 **Abraham, f. Chanania Jagel.** [Hebrew] Catechismus Judæorum. *Typis A. Godbid & J. Playford, pro Sam. Carr, 1679.* 8° OC, CS, EC, P, DT; CH.

100A [–]The Jews catechism. *For Benjamin Harris, 1680.* 8°. WF.

Abraham in arms. Boston, 1678. *See* Nowell, Samuel.

Abridgment of Christian doctrine. Doway, 1678. *See* Turbervill, Henry.

101 An abridgment of military discipline. *Edinburgh, by the heir of Andrew Anderson*, 1686. 8°. ALDIS 2624. A, FSF.

Abridgment of Mr. Locke's essay. 1696. *See* Wynne, John.

101A An abridgment of the case of the cities. [*London?* 1691.] brs. LG.

102 The abridgement of the charter of the city of London. *Printed*, 1680. 4°. L, O, LG; WF, U.

Abridgement of the English history. 1660. *See* G., W.

102A An abridgment of the English military discipline. *By the assigns of John Bill and Christopher Barker*, 1676. 8°. OC.

102B —[Anr. ed.] —, 1678. 8°. L.

103 —[Anr. ed.] *Dublin, Benjamin Tooke*, 1678. 12°.* DIX 166. DI.

104 —[Anr. ed.] *By the assigns of John Bill, and by Henry Hills and Thomas Newcomb*, 1682. 8°. CH, Y.

104A —[Anr. ed.] —, 1684. 8°. CLC, MIU.

105 —[Anr. ed.] —, 1685. 8°. T.C.I 510. L, C; CN, Y.

106 —[Anr. ed.] *By Charles Bill, Henry Hills and Thomas Newcomb*, 1686. 8°. L, O, AN; CH, MU, PL, WF.

107 An abridgment of the late remonstrance. *For Laurence Blaiklocke*, 1648. 4°.* LT, C, HH; MH, NU, WF, Y.

107A An abridgment of the late reverend Assemblies shorter catechism. [*London?* 1675]. CH.

Abridgment of the life of S. Francis Xaverius. S. Omers, 1667. *See* B., W.

108 An abridgment of the prerogatives of St. Ann. *For Ric. Chiswell*, 1688. 4°.* T.C.II 277. O, CT, LCL, EN, DT; CH, MH, NU, WF, Y.

Abridgment of the statutes. 1661. *See* England. Laws.

—1663. *See* Hughes, William.

Abridgment or summarie. Edinburgh, 1650. *See* Monipennie, John.

Absalom and Achitophel. 1681. *See* Dryden, John.

Absalom et Achitophel. Oxon, 1682, *See* Dryden, John.

Absalom senior. 1682. *See* Settle, Elkanah.

109 Absalom's conspiracy. colop: *Printed*, 1680. brs. L, O, C, EN, MC; CH, MH, WF, Y.

110 Absolon's IX worthies: or, a key. [*London*, 1682.] brs. L, O, OC; CH, CLC, MH, WF.

111 Absalom's rebellion. *Oxford, by Leonard Lichfield*, 1645. 4°.* MADAN 1821. LT, O, DT; TU, WF, Y.

Absolute impossibility. 1688. *See* Johnson, Samuel.

112 The absolute necessity of standing by. *For Richard Baldwin*, 1689. 4°. T.C.II 260. OC, CT, AU; CH, NU, VC.

Absolution of a penitent. 1696. *See* J., P. H.

113 Abstersæ lachrymæ. The poet buffoon'd. *Printed and are to be sold by Randal Taylor*, 1694. 4°.* L, O, C, EN; MH, Y.

113A An abstract and brief illustration of the proposal . . . land-credit. colop: *Printed and sold by T. Sowle*, 1697. brs. NC.

114 An abstract containing the substance of the rules. . . New-Colledge of Cobham. *Reprinted*, 1687. 4°.* O; Y.

115 An abstract from Yorke. *For Benjamine* [*sic*] *Allen, July the fifth*, 1642. 4°.* LT, O, EC, YM.

116 An abstract of a case, shewing how East-India manufacturers are prejudicial. [*n.p., c.* 1699–1700.] brs. LL.

117 An abstract of a letter from a bishop of this land. [*London*, 1641.] cap., 4°.* L; NU.

118 Entry cancelled.

Abstract of a letter from a person. Edinburgh, 1698. *See* Paterson, William.

Abstract of a treatise. [*n.p.*], 1641. *See* Walton, Brian, *bp.*

Abstract of all the penal-laws. 1679. *See* England. Laws.

Abstract of all the statue laws. 1675. *See* England. Laws.

119 An abstract of answers given in to the Lords. [*London*], *for N. Butter*, 1641. 4°. L, O, SC.

Abstract of certain depositions. 1642. *See* Puttock, Roger.

Abstract of common principles. 1700. *See* Stephens, Edward.

Abstract of proceedings of the House. [*n.p.*, 1698.] *See* England. Parliament. House of Commons.

119A An abstract of St. Pauls late deanery. [*London*, 1653.] brs. MH.

120 An abstract of several examinations taken upon oath. *For J. C. by John Gain*, 1680. fol.* L, O, CT, EN; CH, MBA, PL, WF, Y.

121 An abstract of severall letters from Hull. *For Ben. Allen, August 2*, 1642. 4°.* LT, C, EC, DT; MH.

121A An abstract of several records. [*London?* 1694]. brs. OP.

122 The abstract of Sir Charles Holt's case. [*n.p.*], 1693/4. brs. L, LL.

123 An abstract of some few of those barbarous, cruell massacres. *For Robert Ibbitson*, 1652. fol.* LT.

123A —[Anr. ed.] *For the author*, [1662]. 4°.* L, C; CH.

Abstract of some late characters. 1643. *See* Crauford, James.

Abstract of some letters. 1679. *See* E., E.

124 An abstract of some letters sent from Dorchester. *For Henry Overton*, 1642. 4°.* LT, BR, AN; CLC.

Abstract of such parts. [1699.] *See* England. Laws.

Abstract of the act [1700]. *See* Orme, Thomas.

124A An abstract of the articles of agreement between the creditors of Sir Robert Vyner. [*London?* 1690]. brs. L.

Abstract of the bill. [1664.] *See* England. Parliament.

124B An abstract of the bloody massacre in Ireland. *Printed*, 1668. 8°. OC, A.

124C An abstract of the bloody massacres there. 1667. 4°.* O.

An abstract of the book. 1680 I. *See* Pennyman. John.

125 An abstract of the case of Francis Rockley. [1666?] brs. MH.

125A The abstract of the case of Richard Reed the younger. [*London?* 1685]. brs. L.

126 An abstract of the case of the City of Londonderry. [*London ?*1699.] brs. L, LL.

126A An abstract of the catechism. *Printed at Basel*, 1681. 8°. OWC.

127 An abstract of the charter to the governor . . . of the Bank of England. [*London ?*1694.] fol.* O, HH; MH.

128 The abstract of the claims of all persons. *Dublin, John Crook*, 1663. fol.* DIX 120. L.

129   An abstract of the commission for Greenwich Hospital. colop: *By Charles Bill, and the executrix of Thomas Newcomb, 1695.* cap., fol.* O.

130   An abstract of the consultations and debates. *Printed,* 1695. 4°.* L, LUG, GH; MH, WF, Y.

131   An abstract of the contents of several letters relating to the management of affairs with Rome. [*London ?*1679.] cap., fol.* L, O, CT, HH, EN; CH, MH, NC, WF, Y.

       Abstract of the discourse. 1694. *See* Briscoe, John.

131A   An abstract of the Dovay catechism. 1682. 8°. CN.

131B   —[Anr. ed.] 1688. 8°. YM.

132   —[Anr. ed.] *Douay, by M. Mairesse,* 1697. 12°. NU.

133   An abstract of the duties laid upon salt. colop: *For E. Whitlock,* [1696]. brs. L, LUG.

134   An abstract of the forfeitures and penalties. [*London?* 1670.] brs. L.

       Abstract of the laws. [1688.] *See* England. Laws.

135   Entry cancelled.

       Abstract of the lives. 1684. *See* Whiting, John.

136   An abstract of the moneys pay'd by Mr. Pearse. [*n.p.*], 1693. fol.* LL.

137   An abstract of the most deplorable case of Samuel White. [*London,* 1689]. brs. C.

137A   An abstract of the most material interlocutors. *Edinburgh, for the strangers,* 1682. fol.* ALDIS 2321. EN.

138   An abstract of the orders to be observed by the carmen of the city of London. [*London ?*1670.] brs. L.

138A   An abstract of the orphans accounts. [*London,* 1694?] cap., fol.* MH.

       Abstract of the penal laws. 1698. *See* England. Laws.

138B   An abstract of the present state of His Majesty's revenues. 1651. 4°.* O.

139   An abstract of the present state of the mines. [*n.p.,* 1700.] cap., fol.* L, LUG; CH, INU, MH, Y.

139A   —[Anr. ed.] *Printed,* 1700. 8°.* MH, NC, Y.

140   An abstract of the present state of the Protestants. colop: *For Iohn Whitlock,* 1682. brs. L, O, OM, HH, EN; CH.

141   An abstract of the procedure of France. *For M. Gillyflower and J. Partridge,* 1684. 8°. T.C.II 87. O, OC.

       Abstract of the proceedings in Parliament. 1642. *See* England. Parliament.

142   An abstract of the proposals for the Bank. [*London,* 1695.] brs. L; LC, PU, Y.

       Abstract of the several acts. 1700. *See* England. Parliament.

143   An abstract of the several letters, and choice occurences, . . . brought . . . from Denmark. *For George Horton,* 1653. 4°.* LT.

144   An abstract of the title to the lands in Wapping-Marsh. [*n.p., after* 1677.] cap., fol.* L.

145   An abstract of the treaty of peace. *For Richard Baldwin,* 1697. brs. L.

145A   An abstract of the unfortunate and unparallel case of Eliz. . . . Foulkes. [*Dublin?* 1693]. brs. L.

146   An abstract of the unnatural rebellion. *Printed, to be sold by Richard Janeway,* 1689. 4°.* CT, DT; MH, NU, WF, Y.

       Abstract of those answers. *See* Williams, John, abp.

       Abstract of those laws. 1691. *See* England. Laws.

146A   An abstract of three letters from Belfast. colop: *For Tho. Parkhurst,* 1690. brs. C; PL, Y.

147   An abstract, or abbreviation of some few of the many . . . testimonys from . . . New-Jersey. *By Thomas Milbourn,* 1681. 4°.* L, EN; CH, RPJ, WF.

147A   An abstract or abridgment . . . concerning the payment of a tyth. [*London?* 1700.] cap., 4°.* L; WF.

148   An abstract or brief declaration of the present state. *For M. S.,* 1651. 4°. L, C, EC, DT; CN, LC, MH, NU, WF, Y.

148A   —[Anr. ed.] *For R. Baldwin,* 1692. 4°. CU, MB, MH, NN, Y.

149   An abstract, or short account of the duty laid upon paper imported. [*n.p.,* 1698?] brs. L.

       Abstract or the lawes of New England. 1641. *See* Cotton, John.

       Absurdity and falsness. 1685. *See* Field, John.

       Absurdity of that new. 1681. *See* Brydall, John.

150   **Abu Bakr Ibn A Tufail.** An account of the Oriental philosophy. [*London*], *printed,* 1674. 8°. L, OC, EN; CN, RPJ.

151   —The history of Hai Eb'n Yockdan. *For Richard Chiswell, and William Thorp, in Banbury,* 1686. 8°. T.C.II 166. L, O, C, BR, DT; CLC, CN, MIU, PL, HC.

152   —Philosophus autodidactus sive epistola. *Oxonii, exc. H. Hall,* 1671. 4°. MADAN 2877. L, O, C, EN, DT; MB, MBP, PL, Y.

153   — —Second edition. *Oxonii, e theatro Sheldoniano, excudebat Joannes Owens,* 1700. 4°. O, CJ, EN, E, AU; CH, CLC, MH, NC, Y.

154   **Abudacnus, Josephus.** Historia Jacobitarum. *Oxonii, e theatro Sheldoniano,* 1675. 4°.* MADAN 3041. L, O, C, DT, MR; IU, NC, NP, TSM, Y.

155   — —Second edition. *Oxonii, e theatro Sceldoniano* [sic], 1675. 12°. MADAN 3041.* O, DT; BN, IU, NP, WF.

156   —The history of the Cophtes. *For Eliphal Jaye, and published by R. Baldwin,* 1693. 4°.* L, O, C, ES; WF.

157   —The true history of the Jacobites, of Ægypt. *By Eliphal Jaye, and published by R. Baldwin,* 1692. 4°.* L, EN, ENC; CLC, MBP.

       Abul-Farajius, Gregorius. *See* Grighor, Abu al-Faraj.

       Abulfeda, Ismael. *See* Ismail Ibn 'Ali.

       Abuses discovered. [London, 1649.] *See* Gery, W.

       Abyssus mali. 1676. *See* Green, William.

157A   Academia Italica, the publick school of drawing. *By Peter Lillicrap, to be sold by Robert Walton,* [1666]. fol. LC, Y.

       Academiæ Edinburgenæ. *Edinburgi,* 1661. *See* Middleton, John, *earl of.*

       Academiæ Oxoniensis. *Oxoniæ,* 1665. *See* Fulman, William.

       Academy of complements. 1645. *See* Gough, John.

       Academy of eloquence. 1653. *See* Blount, Thomas.

       Academy of eloquence. 1664. *See* Blount, Thomas.

158   Entry cancelled.

       Academy of love. 1641. *See* Johnson, John.

159   Academy of pleasure. *For John Stafford & W. N. Gilbertson,* 1656. 12°. O.

160   —[Anr. ed.] *By R. Wood, for John Stafford,* 1665. 12°. CH.

       Academy of true wisdom. *Rotterdam,* 1694. *See* White, J.

Academy or colledge. 1671. *See* Chamberlayne, Edward.

161　**Accademia del cimento, Fiorenzi.** Essayes of natural experiments. *For Benjamin Alsop,* 1684. 4°. L, O, CT, LW, EN; CH, LC, MBP, NAE, MMO, HC.

Accedence commenc't. 1669. *See* Milton, John.

162　Accedit causa vetus conclamata. *Napoli sive Augustæ Trinobantûm.* [*London*], 1685. fol. L.

162A　Accentum Graecorum ratio in leges. *Impensis Hen. Mortlock; et vendes prostant apud Johan Meeks in Nottingham and Newark,* 1698. 8°. T.C.III 66. PL.

163　Accesserunt ad bibliothecam. [*Edinburgi, excudebat Iacobus Bryson,* 1641.] brs. ALDIS 982. O, HH, E; Y.

164–5　Entries cancelled.

Accomodation cordially desired. 1642. *See* Parker, Henry.

166　Accomodation discommended. [*London,* 1642.] cap., 4°.* L, O. C; MH.

167　—[Anr. ed.] *Printed, London,* 1643. 4°.* LT; CH, NU, WF.

Accomplish'd clerk. [1683?] *See* Ayres, John.

Accomplished commander. 1689. *See* C., R.

Accomplished courtier. 1658. *See* Du Refuge, Eustache.

Accomplished lady. 1684. *See* Norris, James.

Accomplished ladies' delight. 1675. *See* Wolley, Hannah.

Accomplished ladies rich closet. 1687. *See* Shirley, John.

Accomplisht physician. 1678. *See* Merret, Christopher.

167A　The accomplished sea-man's delight. *For Benj. Harris,* 1686. 18°. MSK.

Accomplish'd woman. 1656. *See* Du Bosc, Iacques.

Accompt. *See* Account.

168　Junii 30, 1645. According to an order from the ... Commons. [*n.p.,* 1645.] brs. LT.

Account at large, of the proceedings. [*n.p.,* 1681.] *See* England. Parliament.

169　The account audited, or the date. *For T. R. and E. M.,* 1649. 4°.* LT; MM, NU.

Account audited. 1658. *See* Cawdrey, Daniel.

170　Account concerning the fire and burning of Edenbourgh. *Dublin, printed,* 1700. brs. DT.

171　The account examined: or, a vindication of Dr. Arthvr Bvry. *Printed; to be sold by Randall Taylor,* 1690. 4°. T.C.II 350*. L, O, C, OC, DT; CH, MH, NU, WF, Y.

171A　An account from Flanders. colop: *For W. Downing,* 1693. cap., 4°.* MH.

172　An account from Lymrick [*sic*]. colop: *For A. Mason,* 1691. fol.* MH.

172A　—[Anr. ed.] *For Tho. Spratt,* 1691. brs. OC.

173　—[Anr. ed.] *Edinburgh, re-printed by the heir of Andrew Anderson,* 1691. brs. ALDIS 3121. L, EN.

174　An account from Paris of the articles of peace ... France and Spaine. [*n.p.,* 1659.] brs. LT, O, C; MH, Y.

174A　An account from Scotland and London-derry of the proceedings against ... Gordon. *By George Groom,* 1689. brs. EN; CH.

Account from the children. 1660. *See* Nayler, James.

Account from the city of Chester. 1700. *See* Rudd, Thomas.

Account given to a Catholick. Bruges, 1672. *See* Cane, John Vincent.

Account given to the parliament. 1647. *See* Cheynell, Francis.

175　An account how the Earl of Essex killed himself in the Tower. *By the assigns of John Bill, and by Henry Hills, and Thomas Newcomb,* 1683. fol.* L, O, C, HH, EN; CH, CN, MH, NP, Y.

176　—[Anr. ed.] colop: *Edinburgh, re-printed by the heir of Andrew Anderson,* 1683. fol.* EN.

177　An account of a bold desperate and notorious robbery. [*London*], *for J. Kingston,* [1700]. brs. L.

Account of a child. 1694. *See* V., G.

178　Entry cancelled.

179　An account of a dangerous combination and monopoly upon the collier-trade. [*London* ?1698.] cap., 4°.* MH, NC, Y.

180　An account of a fight between the French and Irish. colop: *For Richard Baldwin,* 1689. brs. L; CH, Y.

181　An account of a fight in the North. *August,* 1648. 4°. O.

181A　An account of a French mask in Paris. [*London?* 1700.] brs. L.

182　An account of a great & famous scolding-match. 1699. 4°. L.

183　Account of a horrid and barbarous murder on the body of a young person. *Croom,* 1684. brs. O, LG; Y.

184　An account of a late engagement at sea, near Rye. *For J. Smith,* 1691. brs. MH.

185　An account of a late horrid and bloody massacre. colop: *For T. Tiller,* 1688. brs. L, O, HH.

186　—[Anr. ed.] colop: [*Dublin?*], *printed,* 1689. cap., 4°.* L, C; MH, WF, Y.

186A　An account of a most barbarous murther ... by Mr. Parry. *Thomas White,* 1699. brs. CN.

187　An account of a most horrid and barbarous murther ... Captain Brown. colop: *Edinburgh, re-printed,* 1694. brs. L, O, EN.

188　An account of a most horrid conspiracy against ... his most sacred Majesty. [*n.p.,* 1696.] brs. L, MC; CN.

188A　—[Anr. ed.] *For J. C.,* 1699. brs. MIU, NN.

188B　An account of a most inhumane and barberous [*sic*] murder. colop: *Dublin: at the back of Dick's coffee-house* [1700]. brs. DI.

188C　An account of a most strange and barbarous action. colop: *By Tho. Moore,* 1685. brs. O.

189　An account of a new and strange discovery. *For the author,* 1700. brs. CN.

189A　An account of a paper, presented to the General Assembly. [*London?* 1691.] cap., 4°.* L; WF.

190　An account of a remarkable sea-fight. colop: *Printed April 11th, 1700, for Thomas Cockeril.* cap., fol.* L, C.

191　An account of a second victory obtained over the Turks. *By Edward Jones in the Savoy,* 1689. brs. O; CH, MH.

192　—[Anr. ed.] *Edinburgh, re-printed,* 1689. brs. L.

193　An account of a strange and prodigious storm of thunder, lightning & hail. *For N. I.,* 1680. 4°.* L, O, LG; CH, MH.

194　An account of a vindication of the English Catholicks. *For James Vade,* 1681. 4°.* O, OC, CT, OM; CH, MBA, MH, NU, WF, Y.

229   An account of the affairs in Ireland. *Printed at Dublin: and re-printed at London, for Nath. Brook,* 1659. brs. L, O, LG.

230   An account of the affairs of Scotland. *Printed, and are to be sold by Rich. Baldwin,* 1690. 4°.* T.C.II 314. L, O, LG, E, EN; CH, CU, MH, NU, PL, WF, Y.

231   An account of the apprehending, and taking of John Davis. *By J. W.,* 1700. brs. L.

232   An account of the apprehending & taking of Mr. John Robinson. colop: *For and sold by John Green,* 1699. brs. L.

233   An account of the apprehending of the treasonable designs. *Printed,* 1689. brs. L, C; CN.

234   An account of the apprehending two persons. [*London*], *by N. T.,* 1683. brs. O, HH, EN; MIU.

235   An account of the arbitrary exactions. [*London*], *printed,* 1647. 4°.* LT, O, OC, HH; CH, NC, WF.

236   An account of the arraignment, tryal, and condemnation of Jonathan Frost. *Printed,* 1675. 4°.* NU.
       Account of the arraignment, tryal, and condemnation of the dog. [1682.] *See* D., M.

237   An account of the arraignment, tryal & conviction of James Lord Preston. colop: *For T. Collins,* 1691. cap., 4°.* O.

237A   An account of the auction concerning the ladys. [*London,* 1691.] brs. HH; PL.

238   An account of the award of execution of death against Sr. Thomas Armstrong. colop: *By E. M.,* 1684. brs. MH.

239   An account of the barbarous attempt of the Jesuites upon Mr. De Luzancy. [*London,* 1675.] brs. L, O, LG, EN; MH, TSM.

240   Account of the barbarous usage. 1681. brs. EN.

241   An account of the behaviour, confession and last dying speech of Sir John Johnson. colop: *For Langley Curtiss,* 1690. brs. L, O, DC, MC, HH; CH, CLC.

242   —[Anr. ed.] *Re-printed,* 1691. cap., 4°.* O, E, EN; WF.

243   An account of the behaviour, confession, last dying words, and execution of Mr. Robert Charnock. colop: *For John Lee,* 1696. cap., fol.* SP.

244   An account of the behaviour, dying speeches, and execution of Mr. John Murphy. colop: *For T. Crownfield,* 1696. brs. L.

245   Entry cancelled.

246   An account of the behaviour of Henry Weller. [*London,* 1680.] cap., fol.* L; CH, MH.

247   Entry cancelled.

248   An account of the behaviour of Sir John Fenwick. *London, reprinted Edinburgh,* 1697. brs. ALDIS 3645. EN; CLC.

249   —[Anr. ed.] *Reprinted Glasgow,* 1697. brs. ALDIS 3646. EN.
       Account of the behaviour of the Jesuits. 1689. *See* W., W.

249A   An account of the besieging the castle of Edinburgh. colop: *By George Croom,* 1689. fol.* CH, MH.
       Account of the blessed end. [1696]. *See* Penn, William.

250   An accompt of the bloody massacre in Ireland. *For R. G.,* 1678. cap., 4°.* L, YM, EN; MH, TU.

251   —[Anr. ed.] —, 1679. cap., 4°.* L; MH, PL.

251A   An account of the bold and daring enterprize. *For R. Clavel,* 1689. brs. C.

252   An account of the bombarding of Granville. *By Edw. Jones in the Savoy,* 1695. brs. MC; MWA.

253   An account of the bombarding of St. Malo. *By Edw. Jones in the Savoy,* 1695. brs. L, HH, MC; MH, RPB.

254   —[Anr. ed.] *Edinburgh, re-printed by the heirs and successors of Andrew Anderson,* 1695. brs. ALDIS 3416. L.

255   An account of the book, entitled, Notitia monastica. [1694.] fol.* O.

256   An account of the burning and destroying five and thirty French ships. 1694. brs. L.

257   An account of the burning of Havre de Grace. *For Richard Baldwin,* 1694. brs. L; WF.

258   Account of the capitulation and surrender of Limerick. *By Edw. Jones in the Savoy,* 1691. brs. L, MC, OC; MWA.

258A   Account of the castle of Charlemont in Ireland. *Edinburgh,* 1689. fol.* ALDIS 2830. EN.

259   An account of the causes of some particular rebellious distempers. [*London* ?1670.] 8°.* L.

260   An account of the ceremonial at the coronation. *By Thomas Newcomb in the Savoy,* 1685. brs. L, O, LG, OP; CH, WF.

260A   [Same title] —, *By Edward Jones,* 1689. fol.* L, O.

261   An account of the ceremony of investing. *For R. Chiswell,* 1690. 4°. T.C.II 337. L, O, OM, MC, EN; CN, MBA, Y.

262   —[Anr. ed.] *London, reprinted Edinburgh,* 1690. 4°.* ALDIS 3000. L, EN; WF.

263   An account of the colledge of infants. 1686. 4°. O.

264   An account of the coming up of Tho. Earl of Danby. *For John Spicer,* 1682. fol.* L, O, LG, MR; CH, CN, MIU, Y.
       Account of the composing. ... [1672.] *See* Sherwin, William.

264A   An account of the condemnation ... Captain Francis Winter. *By J. B. for Randall Taylor,* 1693. brs. CN.

265   An account of the confession and execution of Captain Vratz. colop: *For S. T.,* 1682. brs. L; CH.
       Account of the constitution. 1683. *See* Murray, Robert.

266   An account of the conversation, behaviour and execution of William Anderton. *For John Wallis,* 1693. brs. L.

267   An account of the coronation of King James the Second. 1685. brs. MC.

268   An account of the Cossacks. *By T. N.,* 1672. 8°. ISC.
       Account of the court. 1700. *See* Colbatch, John.

268A   An account of the days of the ... carriers. colop: *By G. Conyers,* [169–]. cap., 8°.* CLC.

268B   An account of the death of the Earl of Essex. [*London?* 1686.] cap., 4°. OC, NLH; V.
       Account of the defeat of Count Teckely. 1683. *See* N., N.

269   An account of the defeat of the Irish Army. *For R. Baldwin,* 1689. brs. C, MC; MH.

270   An account of the defeat of the rebels. *London, by T. Newcomb, reprinted Edinburgh, by the heir of A. Anderson,* 1685. fol. ALDIS 2501. EN, BR; CLC.

271   —[Anr. ed.] *Reprinted,* 1689. brs. EN.

272   —[Anr. ed.] colop: *By Edw. Jones in the Savoy,* 1691. brs. L, OC, HH, MC.

273 —[Anr. ed.] *Reprinted Edinburgh, by the heir of A. Anderson*, 1691. brs. ALDIS 3123. EN.

274 An account of the deportment and last words of Mr. Richard Langhorne. *Printed*, 1679. fol.* L, C, EN; CH.

274A An account of the design of printing about 3000 Bibles in Irish. [*London?* 1690.] brs. OC.

275 An account of the design of the late narrative. [*London*], *by R. Janeway*, 1689. fol.* L; CH, MIU.

275A An account of the differences between the King of Denmark. *By Tho. Warren*, 1699. T.C.III 155. NC.

275B —[Anr. ed.] *By Tho. Warren for Tho. Bennet*, 1700. 4°.* L; MM.

276 An account of the digging up of the quarters of William Stayley. *For Robert Pawlet*, 1678. brs. L, O, C, LG, EN; CH, MH, TU, WF, Y.

277 An account of the discovery and siezing of Mr. Harrison. [*London*], 1692. brs. L; CH, CN, Y.

278 Account of the discovery of the new plot. colop: [*London*], *by W. Downing, for T. Benskin*, 1683. brs. O, EN; CH, MH, WF, Y.

Account of the dissection. 1700. *See* Hannes, Edward.

279 Entry cancelled.

280 An account of the doctrine and discipline of Mr. Richard Davis. *Printed*, 1700. 4°.* L, O, CT, LF, MR; MH, PH, PSC, Y.

281 An account of the Duke's bagnio. [*London*, 1683.] brs. DCH.

282 An account of the duty on tin. [*London?* 1698.] brs. L; MIU, Y.

283 An account of the East-India Companies war. [*London*, 1691.] brs. MIU.

284 An account of the elections of the convention of Scotland. *For John Flemming*, 1689. brs. L, O, OC, EN.

285 An account of the exact time of the birth of the present Christian princess. [*London?* 1698.] brs. PL.

286 An account of the examination of Captain Holland. *For R. Hayhurst*, 1689. brs. L, OC, MC; CH.

286A An account of the execution and last dying speeches. colop: *For Langley Curtis*, 1683. brs. WF.

287 An account of the execution of Brigadier Rookwood. colop: *For Richard Baldwin*, 1996. brs. L, O, CM, HH.

287A An account of the execution of the seaven [*sic*] notorious traytors. *For Langley Curtis*, 1683. brs. DCH.

288 Account of the execution of Tho. Watson. 1687. brs. O.

Account of the famous prince. 1692. *See* Hyde, Thomas.

289 An account of the fire at New-Prison. *For L. C.*, 1679. 4°.* O, LG, DT; CH, MH, WF.

290 An account of the flight, discovery and apprehending George Lord Geffries. [*London*, 1688.] brs. L, O; CH, Y.

291 —[Anr. ed.] *Reprinted Edinburgh*, 1688. brs. ALDIS 2732. EN; MH.

292 Account of the formalities of the citizens of the honourable city of London. *Printed and sold by J. W.*, 1697. brs. LS.

292A —[Anr. ed.] *For E. Whitlock*, 1697. brs. MH.

Account of the French usurpation. 1679. *See* Bethel, Slingsby.

292B An account of the full tryal . . . of Spence Cooper. *James Read*, 1699. brs. CN.

293 Account of the fund for the relief of the widows. 1673. brs. O.

Account of the gaines. 1660. *See* N., J.

294 An account of the general nursery. *By R. Roberts for E. Brewster*, 1686. 4°.* T.C.II 210. L, O, LG; CH, CN, NC, WF.

295 An account of the great and glorious actions of Mr. Walker. *For Langley Curtiss*, 1689. brs. MC; MH.

296 An account of the great defeat that Major General Kirk gave the Irish. *For J. C.*, 1689. brs. L, C; CH.

Account of the great divisions. 1692. *See* Keith, George.

297 An account of the great expressions of love. 1648. 4°. L.

298 An account of the great success and victory that the garison in Sligo. *For J. C.*, 1689. brs. MC; CH, MH.

299 An account of the grounds and reasons on which Protetant Dissenters desire their liberty. [*London*, 1680.] brs. L; MH.

Account of the growth of deism. 1696. *See* Stephens, William.

Account of the growth of knavery. 1678. *See* L'Estrange, *Sir* Roger.

Account of the growth of popery. *Amsterdam*, 1677. *See* Marvell, Andrew.

Account of the Jesuites. 1661. *See* Greene, Martin.

300 An account of the joyning of Major-General Kirk's forces. *For J. Green*, 1689. brs. L, C, MC; CH, Y.

Account of the King's. . . . 1647. *See* Prynne, William.

301 An account of the land-bank. [*London*, 1695.] brs. L, LG, HH; TU, Y.

302 An account of the last hours of Dr. Peter Du Moulin. *Oxford, by A. L. for R. Davis*, 1658. 8°.* MADAN 2381. L, O, C; NPT, WF, Y.

Account of the last houres of . . . Oliver. 1659. *See* Underwood.

Account of the last sickness. 1694. *See* Wagstaffe, Thomas.

303 Entry cancelled.

304 An account of the last Thursdays sea engagement. *Edinburgh, re-printed*, 1689. brs. L, EN.

305 An account of the late action and defeat, in Waterford-Bay. *For R. H.*, 1690. brs. CH, Y.

306 An account of the late actions at sea. *R. Hayhurst*, 1691. brs. CN.

306A An account of the late barbarous proceedings of the Earl of Tyrconnel. *For W. Downing*, 1689. brs. HH; CH.

307 An account of the late bloody engagement. 1681. brs. O.

307A An account of the late design of buying up the wooll. *Printed*, 1674. 4°.* L; NC.

307B An account of the late dreadful earthquake . . . Nevis. colop: *For A. Smith*, 1690. brs. RPJ.

307C An account of the late dreadful fire at Northampton. [*London*, 1675.] cap., 4°.* L.

308 Account of the late earthquake in Jamaica. *For Richard Baldwin*, 1693. 4°.* CT; MH.

309 An account of the late engagement at sea. [*London*, 1690.] 4°. MR; CH.

Account of the late establishment. 1692. *See* Sage, John.

309A —[Same title]. colop: *For J. Weekly*, 1691. brs. CH.

309B An account of the late great and famous victory . . . in the north of Scotland. *For. W. D.*, 1690. brs. CH.

309C An account of the late great and famous victory on the coast of Spain. 1690. CH.

310   An account of the late great victory, obtained at sea. *For John Rawlins*, 1692. 4°.* L, O, AU; CH, CN, LC, Y.

311   —[Anr. ed.] *London, Edinburgh reprinted, by the heir of Andrew Anderson*, 1692. 4°.* ALDIS 3210. L, E, EN; CH, CN, NN, WF.

312   An account of the late hardships . . . Quakers. *For Benjamin Clark*, 1682. 4°.* L, LF; MH, PH, PSC, Y.

      Account of the late horrid conspiracy. 1691. *See* Defoe, Daniel.

313   An account of the late most happy . . . victory. *For J. Sanders*, 1691. brs. OC.

314   An account of the late odious conspiracy. 1691. brs. MC.

314A —[Anr. ed.] colop: *Printed*, 1692. cap., fol.* L; PL.

315   An account of the late persecution of the Protestants in the vallys of Piemont. *Oxford, at the theatre for John Crosley*, 1688. 4°.* L, O, CK, EN, MC; CH, NU, PL, WF, Y.

      Account of the late proposals. [*London*, 1688.] *See* N., N.

      Account of the late revolution. [1689]. *See* Byfield, Nathaniel.

316   An account of the late terrible earthquake in Sicily. *For Richard Baldwin*, 1693. 4°.* O, LPO, OR, CT; CH, MH, MU, WF, Y.

317   —[Anr. ed.] *Boston, printed and sold by Benjamin Harris*, 1693. 4°.* NU.

318   An account of the late violence committed by some souldiers. *Printed*, 1653. 4°.* LT, YM.

      Account of the late visitation. [1688]. *See* Mews, Peter.

      Account of the life and death of Mr. Philip Henry. 1698. *See* Bates, William.

      Account of the life and death of the Blessed Virgin. 1687. *See* Fleetwood, William, *bp.*

318A An account of the life, conversation, birth. *For T. Hobs*, 1695. 12°.* PPRF.

319   The account of the life of Julian the Apostate vindicated. *For Langley Curtis*, 1682. 4°.* L, O, CT, EN, DT; CH, MH, NU, WF, Y.

319A An account of the magnificent publick entry . . . Hague. *For L. C.*, 1691. brs. CN.

319B —[Anr. ed.] *Edinburgh, by the heir of A. Anderson*, 1691. brs. ALDIS 3124. EN; CN.

319C An account of the main opinions . . . Presbyterians. 1680. 4°. O.

319D An account of the manner, behaviour . . . of Mary Aubry. colop: *By E. Mallet*, 1687. brs. O.

320   An account of the manner of executing a writ. *For Benj. Tooke*, 1684. fol.* L, O, OC, CS, BR; CH, CN, MH, WF, Y.

321   An account of the manner of taking the late Duke of Monmouth. colop: *By B. G. for Samuel Keble*, 1685. cap., fol.* L, O, SP; CH, CLC, CN, MH, Y.

322   —[Anr. ed.] *Edinburgh, by the heir of Andrew Anderson*, 1685. fol.* ALDIS 2502. EN.

323   —[Anr. ed.] *Dublin, by Benjamin Tooke; to be sold by Andrew Crook, and by Samuel Helsham*, [1685]. cap., fol.* L.

323A An account of the manner of taking the Lord Chancellor. [*London*, 1688.] brs. L, O; CH.

323B An account of the manner of the behaviour of the prisoners. colop: *By D. Mallet*, 1688. cap., fol.* O, EN; MIU.

323C An account of the many frauds and abuses. [*London*, 1700.] brs. L; CLC, Y.

      Account of the matrimonial alliances. 1662. *See* Howell, James.

324   An account of the men of war (not including privateers). [*London*, 1695.] fol.* HH, EN; CH, PL, Y.

324A An account of the methods and motives of the late union. [*London*], *printed*, 1691. 4°.* EN; WF, Y.

325   An account of the miserable . . . condition . . . France. *J. Wilkins*, 1694. brs. CN.

326   Accompt of the moneys paid. 1694. fol. DT.

327   An account of the most remarkable fights and skirmishes . . . in . . . Scotland. *For W. C.*, 1685. 4°.* L, O, HH.

328   An account of the most remarkable fights and skirmishes . . . in the West. *P. Brooksby*, [1685]. 4°. L, HH.

329   An account of the most remarkable occurrences relating to London-Derry. colop: *For Richard Baldwin*, 1689. brs. L, C, OC, MC.

330   An account of the most remarkable occurrences. *Corke*, 1651. 4°.* MIU.

331   An account of the movements of their Majesties royal fleet. *London, for J. C.*, 1691. brs. MC; CN.

      Account of the nature, causes. 1696. *See* Cockburn, William.

332   An account of the nature, situation, natural strength, and antient, and modern fortifications. *For W. Bonny, and R. Hayhurst*, 1690. 4°.* L, O, SP, LFEA; MH, Y.

      Account of the new sect. 1662. *See* P., S.

333   An account of the new sheriffs, holding their office. colop: *By Thomas Snowden*, 1680. fol.* L, O, LG, MC, LL; CH, CN, MH, WF, Y.

334   An account of the noble appearance. 1680. 4°. O.

335   An account of the noble reception of his Grace the D. of Monmouth. *For Roger Evans*, 1682. brs. O, EN; CH, Y.

335A An account of the office for transferring . . . land-bills. [*London*, 1696]. brs. L, LG.

335B An account of the opening of the Parliament of Ireland. colop: *In the Savoy, by Edw. Jones*, 1695. cap., brs. SP; Y.

      Account of the original, nature. [1700?] *See* B., J.

335C An account of the original of judging. [*London?* 1670.] brs. HH; MH.

      Account of the passages. 1690. *See* Netherlands. States general.

335D An account of the penitent behaviour . . . of Captain Charles Walsingham. *For J. C.*, 1689. brs. CH.

      Account of the persecutions. 1686. *See* Claude, Jean.

      Account of the Popes procession. 1689. *See* Reid, Robert.

336   An account of the present condition of the Protestants in the Palatinate. *By Richard Parker, sold by A. Baldwin*, 1699. 4°.* L, CS; CH, MB, NU.

337 An account of the present, miserable, state of affairs in Ireland. *For T. Wilkins*, 1689. brs. L, O, C, DT; CH.

Account of the present persecution. 1690. *See* Morer, Thomas.

338 An account of the present state of Ireland. *For R. Baldwin*, 1690. brs. MC.

339 Entry cancelled.

340 An account of the pretended Prince of Wales, and other grievanses. *Printed*, 1688. 4°.* L, O, CT, EN, AU; CH, CN, NC, WF, Y.

341 An account of the principal officers civil and military. *For Christopher Wilkinson*, 1684. brs. T.C.II 75. O, LG, HH; CH, PL.

342 —[Anr. ed.] *Dublin, reprinted by Andrew Crooke*, 1684. brs. L, O.

343 An account of the private league betwixt the late King James the Second, and the French King. *For Ric. Chiswell*, 1689. fol.* T.C.II 278. L, O, OC, AU, EN; CH, CLC, CN, WF, Y.

344 An account of the proceeding to judgment against Thomas Saxton. *By E. Mallet*, 1685. brs. O; CH.

345 An account of the proceeding to sentence against Miles Prance. *For A. M.*, 1686. brs. O, HH.

345A —[Anr. ed.] colop: *Dublin, by Andrew Crook and Samuel Helsham, assigns of Benajmin Tooke, and are to be sold by Andrew Crook and Samuel Helsham*, 1686. brs. Y.

346 An account of the proceedings against Capt. Edward Rigby. colop: *By F. Collins*, 1698. brs. L, O; Y.

347 An account of the proceedings against Francis Charleton. *By D. M.*, 1689. brs. CH.

348 An account of the proceedings against Nat. Thompson. colop: *For S. Gardiner*, 1682. brs. L, O, OC, LG; CH, NIC, Y.

349 An account of the proceedings against Nathaniel Thomson. colop: *For A. Banks*, 1684. brs. L, O, HH; CH.

350 An account of the proceedings against Richard Alborrow. *By E. Mallet*, 1686. brs. O, MC, EN.

351 An account of the proceedings against Samuel Johnson. colop: *For A. M.*, 1686. brs. L, O, EN; CH, CLC, MH, MIU, Y.

Account of the proceedings against the rebels. [1685.] *See* S., T.

352 An account of the proceedings against the rioters. colop: *By George Croom*, 1683. cap., fol.* DCH; CH, WF.

353 An account of the proceedings against Thomas Saxon. colop: *For S. Norris*, 1686. brs. O; CH, CN, WF.

354 An account of the proceedings and arguments of the counsel. colop: *For T. Davis*, 1681. brs. L, O, OC, EN; CH, MH, MIU, Y.

354A —[Anr. ed.] colop: *Dublin, for Samuel Helsham and Joseph Howe*, 1681. brs. DIX 191. DN.

354B An account of the proceedings and judgement against the charter. 1683. brs. DCH.

355 An account of the proceedings at Guild-hall, London, at the tolke-moot, ... 24th of June 1676. [*London*, 1676.] cap., 4°.* L, O; CH, MB, NU, WF, Y.

356 An account of the proceedings at Guild-hall on the 19th instant, 1682. colop: *For J. Heathcoate*, 1682. fol. L, O; CH.

356A An account of the proceedings at New-York, 1689. A declaration ... colop: *Boston* [*Mass.*], *by Samuel Green*, 1689. brs. LPR.

356B An account of the proceedings at the Guild-hall ... September 12, 1679. [*London*, 1679.] fol. L, OC; CH, MH, WF.

357 An account of the proceedings at the Guild-Hall ... September 13, 1679. [*London*, 1679.] fol.* L, O, C, HH, EN; CH, CN, MH, WF, Y.

358 An account of the proceedings at the Guild-hall, September the 29th, 1681. colop: *For Samuel Crouch*, 1681. brs. O, LG; CH, CN, MH, WF.

359 An account of the proceedings at the Kings-Bench Bar ... against the seven bishops. colop: *By George Croom*, 1688. brs. L, O; CH.

359A An account of the proceedings at the Session House. *For Langley Curtis*, 1681. brs. HH.

360 An account of the proceedings at the Sessions for the City of Westminster, against Thomas Whitfield. [*London*, 1680.] brs. L, O; CH, MH, TU, Y.

361 An account of the proceedings at the Sessions-house in the Old Bayly. colop: *For Roger Evans*, 1682. fol. LL; CH, WF.

362 An account of the proceedings at the Sessions of Oyer and Terminer, ... 10. of October 1683. colop: *For Langley Curtis*, 1683. cap., fol.* L, EN; WF.

363 An account of the proceedings at Westminster-Hall, on the 29th, and 30th of June, 1688. [1688.] brs. L, O, LG, OC; CH, MH, TU, WF, Y.

364 —[Anr. ed.] *Edinburgh, re-printed*, 1689. 4°.* ALDIS 2832. EN; MH, NC, NU, TU.

365 An account of the proceedings at White-hall. [*London*, ?1688.] brs. L, O, C, LG; CH, MH.

366 Entry cancelled.

Account of the proceedings in the House of Commons. [*London*, 1696.] *See* Wagstaff, Thomas.

367 An account of the proceedings of his Excellency, the Earl of Bellomont. *Printed and sold by William Bradford, of New-York*, 1698. fol.* EVANS 834. LPR; PL.

368 An account of the proceedings of His Majesties Army in Scotland. *Dublin, by Andrew Crook and Samuel Helsham*, 1685. 4°.* DIX 371. C.

Account of the proceedings of the corporation. 1700. *See* Cary, John.

369 An account of the proceedings of the French clergy. 1682. 4°. O.

370 An account of the proceedings of the new Parliament of Women. [*London*], *for J. Coniers*, [1683]. 4°.* CN.

Account of the proceedings of the right reverend ... Jonathan. Oxford, 1690. *See* Harrington, James.

371 An account of the proceedings of the two Houses. colop: *Dublin, by Joseph Ray, for John Bentley*, 1685. 4°.* DIX 213. C, DT.

372   Account of the proceedings on the crown side at the Lent assize. 1684. fol. LL.

373   An account of the proceedings to judgment against the charter. colop: *For Langley Curtis,* 1683. brs. L, O, C, HH; CH, CN, MH, WF, Y.

373A   An account of the proceedings upon His Majesties gracious pardon. *By E. Mallet, for the author,* 1685. brs. HH.

373B   An account of the proclaiming the King and Queen. *For W.D.,* 1689. brs. PL.

373C   An account of the produce of the glass-duty. [*London?* 1696.] brs. L, LG.

374   An account of the proportion of the forces. *Printed, and are to be sold by R. Taylor,* 1694. brs. O.
       Account of the province. 1682. *See* Wilson, Samuel.
       An account of the proposals of . . . Canterbury. 1688. *See* N., N.

375   An account of the publick affairs in Ireland. *Printed,* 1679. 4°.* L, O, C, DT; CH, MH, NU, Y.

376   —[Anr. ed.] *Dublin, reprinted,* [1679]. 4°.* DIX 175. OC, DK, DM, DT; CLC, NIC, WF, Y.

377   An account of the purging and planting of the congregation of Dalkeith. *Edinburgh, by George Mosman,* 1691. 4°.* ALDIS 3125. L, EN, ENC, FSF; NN, WF.

378   An account of the raising the siege of Esseck. *By Edward Jones in the Savoy,* 1690. brs. HH; CH, MH.

379   An account of the reasons of the nobility. *For Nathanael Ranew, and Jonathan Robinson,* 1688. fol.* T.C.II 257. L, O, CT, EN, LL; CN, LC, MH, NU, Y.
       Account of the reasons which. . . . 1689. *See* Maijole, J. B.

380   An account of the rejoycing at the Dyet at Ratisbonne. *By Edw. Jones,* 1688. brs. O, LG, CS.

381   Entry cancelled.
       Account of the secret services. Ratisbone, 1683. *See* L., S.

382   An account of the seducing of Ann, . . . Ketelbey, . . . to the Popish religion. colop: *Printed and sold by J. Nutt,* 1700. fol.* L, BAMB; CH.

383   An account of the seizing or apprehending. *John Wallis* [1693.] brs. CN.

384   An account of the sentence that passed upon William Ld. Russell. colop: *By J. Grantham,* 1683. brs. L, HH; CH, MH.

385   An account of the sentence which past upon Titus Oates. colop: *For A. Banks,* 1685. brs. HH; CH, MH, TSM.

386   —[Anr. ed.] *Edinburgh, heir of Andrew Anderson,* 1685. fol.* ALDIS 2503. EN; CH.

387   An account of the several plots, conspiracies, and hellish attempts. *For J. R. and W.A.,* 1679. 4°.* O, EN; NU.

388   An account of the siege of Mons. *Edinburgh, re-printed,* 1691. brs. ALDIS 3126. L, EN; CH, CN.

388A   —[Anr. ed.] colop: *By Edward Jones in the Savoy.* 1690. brs. Y.

389   An account of the siege of the famous city of Dunkirk. *For J. Johnson,* 1692. brs. MH.

389A   An account of the signal victory. colop: *Dublin, by Andrew Crook, assignes of Benjamin Tooke,* 1692. brs. DIX 377. DI.

389B   An account of the signing the general peace. [*London*], *by T. Snowden,* 1697. brs. HH.
       Account of the societies. 1699. *See* Woodward, Josiah.
       Account of the Socinian Trinity. 1695. *See* Leslie, Charles.

390   An account of the solemn funeral . . . Countess of Arran. *In the Savoy: by Tho. Newcombe,* 1668. 4°.* C.

391   An account of the solemn reception of Sir John Robinson. *For Joshua Coniers,* 1662. 4°.* CH.

392   An account of the sorts and numbers of ships. [*London?*], *printed,* 1695. fol.* L, O, LG; MH, Y.
       Account of the state of London-derry. 1689. *See* R., J.

393   An account of the state of the French fleet. colop: *For H. Jones,* 1689. brs. C; CH, CN.

394   An account of the state of the press in the Vniversity of Oxford. [*Oxford, Sheldonian,* 1680.] brs. MADAN 3272*. L.

395   An account of the succession. 1689. fol. O.

396   Account of the sufferings and dying words. *London, re-printed Edinburgh,* 1699. 8°. ALDIS 3816. EN.

397   An account of the surrender of Limerick. colop: *For R. G.,* 1690. brs. L.

397A   —[Same title]. *For A. Mason,* 1691. brs. Y.

398   An account of the surrender of the old charter of Northampton. [1682.] brs. L, O, OC; MBA, WF.

398A   An account of the taking Athlone. colop: *For John Smith,* 1691. brs. Y.

398B   An account of the taking by storme . . . Gallaway. *For W. Bonny,* 1691. brs. HH.

398C   An account of the taking John Penruddock. [*London?* 1654.] brs. OC.

399   An account of the taking of Captain Holland. *For S. Bowers,* 1689. brs. L; CH.

400   An account of the taking of Sligo. *By Edw. Jones in the Savoy,* 1691. brs. OC, MC.

401   An account of the taking of the fort of Ballymore. colop: *By Edw. Jones in the Savoy,* 1691. brs. C.

401A   —[Anr. ed.] *Edinburgh, reprinted, by the heir of A. Anderson,* 1691. brs. ALDIS 3127. E, EN.

401B   —[Anr. ed.] colop: *Dublin,* [1691]. brs. L.

402   An account of the taking of the new-fort in Kinsale. *For Y. S.,* 1690. brs. MC; CH, MH.

403   An account of the taking the Earl of Argyle. colop: *Printed,* 1685. brs. L.

404   An account of the taking the island of Martinego. *By W. Bonny,* 1693. brs. OC; MH.

405   An account of the taking the late Earl of Argyle. colop: *By Tho. Newcomb in the Savoy,* 1685. brs. L, O, LL, HH, EN; CH, MH, WF.

406   An account of the total defeat of the rebels in Scotland. [1680.] brs. L, EN; MH.

407   An account of the town and castle of Charlemont. *For Edward St. John,* 1689. brs. EN; CH, MH.

407A   —[Anr. ed.] *Re-printed at Edinburgh,* 1689. brs. ALDIS 2830. HH, EN.

408   An account of the trade between England and France. [*n.p.,* ?1690.] brs. CH, Y.

Account of the transactions in the North. 1692. *See* Michelborne, John.

409 An account of the transactions of the late King James in Ireland. *For Robert Clavell, Jonathan Robinson, and Joseph Watts*, 1690. 4°. T.C.II 339. L, O, C, DT, HH; CH, CU, MH, WF, Y.

Account of the translation. Oxford, 1659. *See* Chylinski, Samuel Boguslaus.

410 An account of the travels, sufferings ... of Barbara Blaugdone. [*London*], *printed, and sold by T.S.*, 1691. 8°. LF; PH, PSC.

411 An account of the treaty between His Excellency Benjamin Fletcher. *Printed and sold by William Bradford, New-York*, 1694. 4°.* L.

412 An account, of the tryal and conviction of Sir John Friend. colop: *For Edward Steel*, 1696. brs. L.

412A An account of the tryal and examination gf [*sic*] Count Conningsmarck. colop: *For H. Jones*, 1682. brs. CH, WF.

413 An account of the tryal and examination of Joan Buts. colop: *For S. Gardener*, 1682. brs. L, O, EN; CH.

414 An account of the tryal, confession and condemnation of Col James Turner. 1663. 4°. O.

415 An account of the tryal of Charles Bateman, chirugeon. *For E. Mallet*, 1685. fol.* L, O, CS, LWL, HH; CH, MH, NAM, NR, Y.

416 An account of the tryall of fourteen notorious prisoners. *For Alex. Reynolds*, 1694. brs. MC.

417 An account of the tryal of Mr Stephen College. [1681.] brs. L.

417A An account of the tryal of the Lord Mohun. 1692. brs. CN.

417B An account of the tryal of William Clamp. *R. Lyford*, 1693. brs. CN.

417C An account of the tryals of Captain J. Golden. [*London*], *J. Clare*, [1694]. brs. L.

418 An account of the tryals of several notorious malefactors. *For Langley Curtis*, 1682. fol.* O, HH; CH, IU.

419 —[Anr. ed.] *For Charles Leigh*, 1682. brs. O, DCH.

420 An account of the tryals of William Ld. Russell. colop: *By J. Grantham*, 1683. brs. O; CH, MH, WF.

Account of the unhappy affair. 1689. *See* Bury.

421 An account of the victory obtained by the King in Ireland. colop: *By Edw. Jones in the Savoy*, 1690. brs. L, C, OC, MC, DT; CH, MH, PL.

422 —[Anr. ed.] *Edinburgh, re-printed by the heir of Andrew Anderson*, 1690. brs. ALDIS 3001. L, EN; Y.

423 An account of the whole proceedings at the sessions, ... twelfth ... July. colop: *For Langley Curtis*, 1683. cap., fol.* L, O, C; CH, MH, WF, Y.

424 An account of the whole produce of the duties arising by glass-wares. [*London*, ?1696.] brs. L, LG.

424A An account of the wicked design. colop: [*London*], *printed*, 1688. cap., 4°.* L, DT.

424B An account of their Majesties fleet. *W. Haite*, 1691. brs. CN.

424C An account of their royal highnesses the Duke and Dutchess of York. [*London*, 1680.] brs. O.

424D —[Anr. ed.] *Edenborough*, 1680. brs. PU.

425 An account of, (together with) the writing it self. colop: *For Robert Pawlet*, 1679. cap., fol.* L, C, LG, OC, EN; CH, CN, LC, MH, NC, TU, Y.

426 An account of two late victories. *For E. Hawkins*, 1691. brs. L.

Account of tythes. [1678?] *See* Ellwood, Thomas.

426A An account of what captives hath been freed. colop: *E. Husband*, 1647. CSS.

426B An account of what duties were payable. [*London?* 1660.] brs. L.

427 An account of what English men-of-war. *Edward Jones*, 1695 [6.] 4°.* MR, LUS; CH, NN, WF.

428 An account of what has been done in Wales ... respecting Bibles. 1674. brs. MC.

429 Account of what has passed in the treaty. [1699.] 4°.* L, O; MH, NC.

430 An account of what hath been done in Wales. [*London?* 1680.] cap., fol.* L.

430A An account of what men of war. *Edward Jones*, 1695. fol.* CN.

431 An account of what pass'd at the execution of Sir John Fenwick. colop: *For R. Bentley, and A. Bosvile*, [1697]. brs. Y.

432 An account of what passed at the execution of Sir VVill. Parkyns. colop: *For Richard Baldwin*, 1696. brs. L, CCA, MC, EN; MH, NN.

433 An account of what passed at the execution of the late Duke of Monmouth. colop: *For Robert Horne, John Baker, and Benjamin Took*, 1685. cap., fol.* L, O, CM, MR, EN; CH, MH, NP, NU, WF, Y.

434 —[Anr. ed.] *London, reprinted Edinburgh, by the heir of A. Anderson*, 1685. fol. ALDIS 2504. EN; CH, CLC.

435 —[Anr. ed.] *Dublin, reprinted by Andrew Crook and Samuel Helsham: to be sold by Andrew Crook, and Samuel Helsham*, 1685. cap., fol.* L.

436 An account of what past on Monday the 28th of Oct. 1689. *For Matthew Granger*, 1690. 4°. L, CS, EN, DT; CH, CN, NC, WF, Y.

437 An account of what the subduing the rebellion of Ireland ... hath cost. [*London?* 1660.] brs. WF.

438 An account of what woven silks have been brought from Holland. 1692. brs. MC.

An accurate description of the United Netherlands. *See* Carr, William.

Accurate examination. 1692. *See* Nye, Stephen.

Accuser of our brethren. 1681. *See* Whitehead, George.

Acetaria. 1699. *See* Evelyn, John.

439 [**Achard, John**] Moon-shine: or, the restauration of jews-trumps and bagpipes. *For R. C.*, 1672. 4°.* L, O, CT, EN; CN, MH, NU, WF, Y.

440 — —[Anr. ed.] *For Walter Kettilby*, 1697. 8°. OC; CLC.

Atchievements of the Kings. 1682. *See* Fisher, Payne.

Achilles: or Iphegenia in Aulis. 1700. *See* Racine, Jean.

441 Ahitophel's policy defeated. *For W. Kettilby*, 1683. 4°.* T.C.II 38. L, O, C, EN; CH, MH, NU, WF, Y.

442 **Acontius, Jacob.** Darkness discovered. *By J. M., to be sold by William Ley*, 1651. 4°. LT, EN; MB.

443 —Satans stratagems. *By John Macock, to be sold by John Hancock*, 1648. 4°. LT, O, CT, LCL, EN; CH, CN, NPT, NU.

443A — —[Anr. ed.] *By John Macock, to be sold by G. Calvert*, 1648. 4°. O; CLC, LC, WF, Y.

444 —Stratagematvm Satanæ. *Oxoniæ, sumptibus Guil. Webb*, 1650. 8°. MADAN 2035. O, P; MH, Y.

445 Acrostick on Mary, Queen. *By J. S. for William Cox*, [1689–94?]. brs. O.

Act. *See also* Edinburgh. Town Council; England. Parliament; Ireland. Council; London. Lord Mayor; New York. General Assembly; Scotland. Commissioners of Excise, Estates General, Lords of Council and session, Privy Council; Venice.

446 The act against conventicles. *By W. G.*, 1670. 8°.* O; CH, CU.

Act of Parliament against religious meetings. 1670. *See* Sheldon, Gilbert.

447-8 Entries cancelled.

449 **Acton, George.** A letter in answer to certain quæries. *By William Godbid for Walter Kettleby*, 1670. 4°.* L, CS, LWL; CH, PL, WF.

450 —Physical reflections upon a letter written by J. Denis. *By T. R. for J. Martyn*, 1668. 4°.* L, O, LCP, LR, GK; CH, WF, HC.

451 **Acton, John.** Constiutiones Legatinæ. *Oxoniæ, excudebat H. Hall*, 1679. fol. MADAN 3221. DT; CN, MH, NP, Y.

452 **A[cton], Samuel.** Dying infants sav'd by grace. *For the author, and sold by M. Fabian*, 1699. 4°.* L, O; NHC, Y.

452A —A modest reply humbly offered to . . . S. Laurence. *For the author, and sold by M. Fabian*, 1692. 8°.* LW, OC.

453 **Acton, William.** A new journal of Italy. *For R. Baldwin*, 1691. 12°. T.C.II 381. L, O.

454 The actors' remonstrance, or complaint. *For Edw. Nickson, Januar.* 24, 1643. 4°.* LT, DT; MH, WF, Y.

Acts. *See also* Edinburgh. Town Council; England. Parliament; Ireland; Massachusetts Bay Colony; Scotland, Church of; Scotland. Estates.

Acts and life of . . . Robert Bruce. Edinburgh, 1670. *See* Barbour, John.

Acts and monuments of our late Parliament. 1659. *See* Butler, Samuel.

455 The acts and monuments of the late Rump. 1660. 4°.* O, C, HH; CU, MBA, MH, Y.

Acts and negociations. 1698. *See* Bernard, Jacques.

456 The acts of annuities reviewed and compared. [London, ?1700.] cap., 4°.* L, C, OC; MH, NC, Y.

456A The acts of great Athanasius. [London], *printed*, 1690. 4°.* O, C, EC, E, DT; CH, MH, NU, WF, Y.

457 Actes of the General Assembly of the clergy of France. *By J. R.*, 1682. 4°. CT, BAMB, P, MC; NC, NU.

458 Acts of the General Assembly of the French clergy. *Printed*, 1685. 4°.* L, O, MC, EN, DT; CH, MIU, NPT, WF, Y.

459 Actual justification rightly stated. *By B. Harris, and sold by J. Marshal*, 1696. 4°.* O; Y.

Acuña Christoval d'. Voyages and discoveries. 1698. *See* title.

Ad amplissimos simul. . . . [1700.] *See* Denniston, Walter.

Ad augustiss: majestatem. [1660.] *See* Windet, James.

Ad augustissimum invictissimvmque. [London? 1692.] *See* H., G.

460 Ad Carolum secundum, . . . protrepticon. [*Londini*], *excudebat*, 1649. 4°.* D, EN; MH.

Ad clerum . . . Oxford, 1670. *See* Sanderson, Robert.

461 Ad deliberationem Gaolæ Domini Regis de Newgate. *By Richard Cotes*, [1645]. brs. LT.

462 Ad epistolam synodi Warsawiensis. *Impensis Johannis Rothwell*, 1645. 4°.* O.

463 Ad Fairfaxum imperio. [London, 1651.] brs. LT.

463A Glouc. ss Ad generalem quarterial. [*London?*] *by A. Clark*, [1677]. brs. MH, WCL.

464 Midd. ss. Ad generalem sessionem. *For Walter Davies*, 1681. brs. L, O, OC; MH, WF.

464A Ad generalem quarterial sessionem, London. *By Andrew Clark*, 1677. brs. O, LG; MH.

464B —[Same title] [*London*, 1678]. brs. O.

464C —[Same title] [*London*, 1681]. brs. CH.

465 Ad general quarterial sessionem, Midd. ss. *By Thomas Hodgkin*, 1682. brs. L, O; WF. Y.

466 Bed. ss. Ad general session. *By T. H. and sold by Henry Bonwicke*, 1685. brs. O.

467 —[Anr. ed.] *By Tho. Braddyll*, 1691. brs. L; Y.

467A —[Anr. ed.] —, 1691/2. brs. OC.

467B —[Anr. ed.] —, 1692. brs. OC.

467C Midd. ss. Ad generalem sessionem. [*London*, 1692.] cap., fol.* L.

467D Ad general session. —apud Doncaster. *For Walter Davis*, 1683. brs. OC.

Ad grammaticen. 1648. *See* White, William.

Ad populum: or, a lecture. 1644. *See* Hausted, Peter.

468 Ad populum: or, a low-country lecture. *For G. B.*, 1653. 4°.* LT; WF.

469 Ad populum Phaleræ: or twin shams. [*London*, 1692?] 4°. in 2's.* L, O, EC; IU, MH, NN, Y.

Ad spectatissimum virum. 1649. *See* Harmer, John.

Ad testimonium. 1686. *See* Patrick, Symon.

Adagia Scotica. 1668. *See* B., R.

469A **Adair, John.** Queries in order. [*Edinburgh?* 1694.] brs. EN.

469B —The sea coast and islands of Scotland. *Edinburgh*, 1693. SA.

470 Adam armed: or, an essay. [1700.] cap., fol.* L, LG.

471 Adam Bell, Clim of the Clough. *By Richard Cotes, to be sold by Francis Grove*, 1648. 4°.* CN.

472 —[Anr. ed.] *By E. Cotes, to be sold by Francis Grove*, 1655. 4°.* CH, MBP, MH.

472A —[Anr. ed.] —, 1661. 4°.* O.

473 —[Anr. ed.] *By A. M. for W. Thackeray*, [1667?] 4°.* CM; CH, MBP, MH.

474 —[Anr. ed.] *By H. B for J. Wright, J. Clark, W. Thackery, and T. Passinger*, 1683. 4°.* O; MH.

475 [**Adames, Jones**] The order of keeping a courtleet. *For W. Lee and Daniel Parceman*, 1656. 4°. L.

475A   The Adamite, or the loves of Father Rock. *For Dorman Newman,* 1682. 12°. T.C.I 507. IU.

476   **Adams, Charles.** Catalogue of the library. 16 Nov. 1683. 4°.* L.

477   **Adams, Edward.** A brief relation of the surprizing several English merchants goods. *Printed,* 1664. 4°.* L.

478   —The young soldier's desire answered. *For John Evans, to be sold by William Jacob: and by the author,* 1678. 4°.* C.

      Adams, Jack. Perpetual almanack. 1662. *See Almanacs.*

479   **Adams, John,** *of Inner Temple.* Index villaris: or, ... *By A. Godbid and J. Playford, for the author,* 1680. fol. L, O, C, LL, DT; BN, CH, CN, LC, MH, Y.

480   [–] —[Anr. ed.] *For T. Sawbridge, and M. Gillyflower; also sold by T. Dring, S. Crouch and T. Horne,* 1690. fol. T.C.II 323. L, O, C, OM, LA; MBP, MH, WF, Y.

481   [–] —[Anr. ed.] *For S. and J. Sprint, J. Nicholson, and T. Newborough,* 1700. fol. T.C.III 177. L, C, ES, LGI, LS; CLC, MBA, TU.

482   —Proposals for the actual survey of all the counties. [*London, ?*1685.] brs. O, HH.

483   **Adams, John,** *Provost of King's College, Cambridge.* An essay concerning self-murther. *For Tho. Bennet,* 1700. 8°. L, O, C, EN, BQ; CH, LC, MH, NC, NU, Y.

484   —A sermon preached . . . 17th. of February, 1694/5. *By Benj. Motte,* 1695. 4°.* L, BR; WF.

485   —A sermon preach'd at White-hall . . . September 8, 1695. *For Thomas Bennet,* 1695. 4°.* L, C, OM, EC, EN; NU, TSM, WF, Y.

486   —A sermon preached . . . November the fifth, 1696. *By Sam. Bridge for Thomas Bennet,* 1696. 4°.* T.C.II 598. L, O, C, CT, EN; CH, CN, MBA, WF, Y.

487   —A sermon preached . . . the 29th of Septemb. 1700. *For D. Brown: and Peter Buck,* 1700. 4°.* L, O, EC, LF; CH, PH, WF, Y.

488   **Adams, Mary.** The Ranters monster. *For George Horton,* 1652. 4°.* LT.

489   —A warning to the inhabitants of England. *Printed,* 1676. 4°.* L, C, LF, BBN; IE, PH, PSC, RJP, Y.

490   **Adams, Richard,** *fellow of Brasenose College, Oxford.* Ὀικλα ἀπιγυθ. The earthly and heavenly building opened. *For John Weld,* 1699. 4°.* T.C.II 311. L, O, LW; CLC, NU, WF.

491   [**Adams, Richard,**] *merchant.* A true and terrible relation from Maletravis in Maligo. *Printed at London by E. P. for Francis Coles,* 1648. 8°.* L.

491A   **Adams, Simon.** Concerning the observation of the first day. [*London,*] 1663. 4°.* LF.

492   **Adams, Thomas,** U.U. God's anger. *By Tho. Maxey, for Samuel Man,* 1652. 4°. L, O, CT; MIU, NU, Y.

492A   ——[Anr. ed.] —, 1653. 4°. LT, O, LCL.

493   **Adams, Thomas,** M.A. The main principles of Christian religion. *Printed,* 1675. 8°. T.C.I 216. L, O, LCL, ENC; WF, Y.

494   ——Second edition. *By A. M. and R. R. for Tho. Parkhurst,* 1677. 12°. T.C.I 277. LCL, LW, CE, ENC; NPT, WF.

495   **Adams, Sir Thomas.** The humble petition of the worshipful. *For J. Norris, April 25,* 1648. 4°.* LT, O, OC, BR, HH; CLC, MH.

496   ——Second edition. —*April 25,* 1648. 4°.* LT, O, LG, C; BN, MIU, NU, WF, Y.

497   [–] Plain dealing or a fair warning. [*London*], *printed,* 1647. 4°.* LT, O, LW, OC; MH, NU, Y.

498   **Adams, William.** God's eye on the contrite. *Boston in New-England; by Richard Pierce for Samuel Sewall,* 1685. 4°.* EVANS 381. MH, MHS, MB, RPJ, Y.

499   —The necessity of the pouring out of the spirit. *Boston; by John Foster, for William Avery,* 1679. 4°.* EVANS 259. CH, MH, MWA, RPJ, Y.

499A   **Adamson, John.** Ioannis Adamsoni Carmen Εὐχαριστικον. [*Edinburgh*], 1651. brs. Y.

500   —The duty of daily frequenting the publick service. *By Ben Griffin for Sam. Keble,* 1698. 4°.* T.C.III 63. L, LW; CLC, WF.

501   **Adamson, William.** An answer to a book, titled, Quakers principles quaking. *For Giles Calvert,* 1656. 4°.* LT, LF, BBN; MH, PH.

502   Entry cancelled.

503   **Adamus, Johannes.** Ad celebres & eruditos academiæ. [1675?] brs. L.

504   —Londinum heroico carmine, the renovvned city of London surveyed. *By J. R. for the author,* 1670. 4°.* L, O, C, LGI, CK; CH, WF ,Y.

505   [**Adamus, Melchior.**] The life and death of Dr. Martin Lvther. *By: I: L: for Iohn Stafford,* 1641. 4°. LT, O, C, LW, MR; CH, CN, NU, WCL, Y.

506   ——[Anr. ed.] *By I.L. for Iohn Stafford,* 1643. 4°. O; CLC, TU, WF.

507   ——[Anr. ed.] 1644. 4°. E, DT.

508   ——[Anr. ed.] 1645. 4°. O, MR.

      Addenda & mutanda. 1686. *See Turner, John.*

509   **Adderley, Thomas.** The care of the peace. *By J. R. for John Williams,* 1679. 4°. T.C.I 356. O, CT; CH, NU, WF, Y.

510   **Addison, Joseph.** An ode on St. Cecilia's Day, November 22, 1699. [1699.] brs. MC.

511   —A poem to his Majesty. *For Jacob Tonson,* 1695. fol.* L, O, LCL, HH, OC; CH, CU, MH, TU, Y.

512   **Addison, Lancelot.** The Christians daily sacrifice. *For Robert Clavel,* 1698. 8°. T.C.III 89. OM, CT.

513   —The Christian's manual. *For W. Crooke,* 1691. 12°. T.C.II 341. O, C.

514   ——Fourth edition. *For W. Crooke,* 1693. 12°. T.C.II 469. O, OB, OC, SP; Y.

515   ——Fifth edition. *Printed, and are to be sold by Henry Bonwicke,* 1700. 12°. T.C.III 189. L, LW; CN, Y.

516   [–] Χριστος ἀυτο θεος, or an historical account. *By Tho. Hodgkin, for Robert Clavell,* 1696. 8°. L, O, LW, CT, EN; NC, NPT.

516A   [–] Devotional poems. *For Henry Bonwicke,* 1699. 8°, T.C.III 141. L, LLL; MH, WF.

517   —A discourse of Tangier. Second edition. *For W. C. and sold by Walter Davis,* 1685. 4°.* T.C.II 131. L.

518 [–] The first state of Mahumedism. *By J. C. for W. Crooke,* 1679. 8°. L, O, C, LAD, E; CU, MH, NU, TU, Y.

519 [–] [Anr. ed.] *For Will. Crook,* 1687. 8°. L, CM, P; CH, WF.

520 [–] The genuine use and necessity of the two sacraments. *For Robert Clavell,* 1697. 8°.* T.C.III 35. O, CT; CLC.

521 [–] An introduction to the sacrament. *For William Crook,* 1682. 8°. T.C.I 471. O; CLC.

522 ——[Anr. ed.] *For William Crooke,* 1686. 12°. T.C.II 171. L, O, OB; WF.

523 —The life and death of Mahumed. *For William Crooke,* 1679. 8°. L, CE, CT; NPT, WF, Y.

524 [–] A modest plea for the clergy. *For William Crook,* 1677. 8°. T.C.I 268. L, O, C, OB, DT; CLC, NU, WF.

525 [–] The Moores baffled. *For William Crooke,* 1681. 4°.* T.C.I 421. L, O, OC; CH, MH, RPJ, WF, Y.

526 —The present state of the Jews. *By J. C. for William Crooke, and to be sold by John Courtney in Sarum,* 1675. 8°. T.C.I 210. L, LW, OC, MR, E; CH, CLC, CN, MH, TU.

527 ——Second edition. *By J. C. for William Crooke,* 1676. 12°. T.C.I 223. L, O, OB, CS, EN; WF, Y.

528 ——Third edition. *For William Crook,* 1682. 12°. T.C.I 466. L, O, CS, AU, DT; UCLA, NN.

529 ——[Anr. ed.] 1684. 12°. CE.

530 —The primitive institution. *By J. C. for William Crook,* 1674. 12°. T.C.I 168. L, O, P, YM; NPT, NR, NU, PL.

531 ——Second edition. *For William Crook, and W. Baylie, in Litchfield,* 1690. 12°. T.C.II 325. L, O, OM; CLC.

532 —West Barbary. *Oxford, at the theater [by H. Hall] sold by John Wilmot,* 1671. 8°. T.C.I 79. MADAN 2878. L, O, C, E, DT; BN, CH, MH, NC, WF, Y.

532A An addition to the case of the paper-sellers. [*London,* 1690.] brs. L, LG.

Addition to the late proclamation. *Dublin,* 1644. *See* Ireland. Lord Lieutenant and Council.

Addition to the relation. 1643. *See* J., P.

Additional act. *See* England. Parliament; Scotland. Estates.

533 Additional annotations or, a collection of all the several additions to the third ... impression. *By Evan Tyler,* 1658. 8°. LT; NU, Y.

Additional article. 1653. *See* England. Parliament.

Additionall articles. [1643.] *See* England. Parliament.

Additional articles in Pope Pius's creed. 1688. *See* Altham, Michael.

Additional considerations. [1695.] *See* Cromarty, George Mackenzie, *earl of.*

Additionall directions. 1647. *See* England. Parliament.

Additional discovery. 1680. *See* W., B.

533A Additional heads proposed by the master-shipwrights. [*London?* 1694.] brs. L; Y.

534 Additional information for John Abernethie. [1695.] cap., fol.* L, EN.

Additional instruction. 1653. *See* England. Council of state.

Additional instructions. [1680.] *See* Scotland. Estates.

Additional ordinance. *See* England. Parliament.

535 Additional prayers to be used. colop: *By Charles Bill and Thomas Newcomb,* 1689. cap., 4°.* L, O, OC; NC.

Additional supplement. [1674.] *See* Sherwin, William.

Additional warrand [*sic*]. *Edinburgh,* 1689. *See* Scotland. Estates.

Additionals to the mystery. 1658. *See* Pascal, Blaise.

Additions answering. 1681. *See* Atwood, William.

Additions au traite. 1684. *See* Fitzgerald, Robert.

536 An address against the city bakers. *For E. Bradford,* 1694. brs. L, LG.

537 An address agreed upon at the Committee for the French War, ... April the 19th. 1689. *For Richard Janeway,* 1689. fol.* L, O, C, CCA; CH, CLC, MH, WF, Y.

538 —[Anr. ed.] colop: *Edinburgh, re-printed,* 1689. fol.* ALDIS 2853. L, EN.

539 An address from earth to heaven. *Printed,* 1681. 4°.* MH.

540 An address from Salamanca. colop: *For A. Banks,* 1682. brs. O, EN; CH, MH, WF, Y.

541 An address from the Justices of the Peace of the County of Middlesex. *By the assigns of John Bill, Thomas Newcomb, and Henry Hills,* 1681. fol.* L, O, CT, EN, DT; CH, NC, PU, WF, Y.

541A —[Anr. ed.] *Edinburgh, by the heir of A. Anderson,* 1681. fol.* ALDIS 2246. EN.

541B —[Anr. ed.] *Dublin, by Benjamin Tooke and John Crook; to be sold by Mary Crook and Andrew Crook,* 1681. fol.* DIX 186. DN, DT.

542 An address given in to the late King James. *For Ric. Baldwin,* 1690. 4°.* O, HH, EN; MH, PU, WF, Y.

543 The address of above twenty thousand of the loyal Protestant apprentices of London. colop: *For William Ingol the elder,* 1681. brs. L, LG; CH, MBA, MH, MIU.

543A The address of condolence to His Majesty. *Edinburgh,* 1695. brs. EN.

544 The address of divers tradesmen, ... to Sir John Chapman. [*London,* 1689.] brs. L, O, C, LG, EN; CH, MH, TU, Y.

544A The address of John Dryden. *Printed, and are to be sold by Randal Taylor,* 1689. fol.* L, O, DC, OC, HH; CH, MH, TU, WF, Y.

545 The addresse of some ministers of Christ. *By J. H. For J. Rothwell,* 1658. 4°.* L, C, LW; CH, CLC, NU.

546 An address of thanks. On behalf of the Church of England. colop: *By George Larkin,* 1687. brs. L, O, LG, OC, HH; CH, MM, TSM, Y.

546A Address of thanks to Father Peters. [*London?* 1688.] brs. MH.

547 An address of the dissenting ministers. colop: *For Jonathan Robinson,* 1689. 4°.* L, O, CS, LW, HH; CH, NU, MIU, WF, Y.

548 The address of the freeholders of the County of Middlesex. colop: *For Francis Smith,* 1680. brs. L, LG, HH; CH, MH, WF, Y.

549 The address of the Lieutenancy. 1688. 4°. O.

550 The address of the Nonconformist ministers. *For Thomas Cockerill,* 1689[/90]. brs. L, O, C, LUG, EN; CH, MIU, NHC, Y.

551 The address of the officers. 1660. brs. O.

552 The address of the Presbyterians to the King. 1687. 4°.* O.

553 The address of the representatives of their Majestyes Protestant subjects, in the Provinnce of Mary-Land. *St. Maryes*, 1689. brs. LPR; RPJ.

554 The address presented to His Majesty at Kensington the 11th day of June 1700. [1700.] brs. EN.

555 The address presented to the King at Belfast. *For R. Baldwin*, 1696. brs. Y.

556 An address presented to the King, August 7th, 1689. colop: *For R. Baldwin*, 1689. brs. L, O.

557 —[Anr. ed.] *Re-printed at Boston by Sam Green for Benjamin Harris*, 1690. brs. EVANS 543. MHS.

558 Entry cancelled.

559 An address presented to the reverend . . . ministers. colop: *For Randal Taylor*, 1688. 4° in 2's.* L, O, C, EN, DT; MH, MIU, NC, PL, WF.

560 —[Anr. ed.] colop: *Reprinted at Holy-Rood House*, 1688. cap., 4°. ALDIS 2747.* O.

561 An address sign'd by the greatest part of the members of the Parliament of Scotland. [1689.] 4°.* L, O, OC, EN; CH, MH, NU, PL, WF, Y.

Addresse to Gen: Monck. [1659?] *See* Peirce, *Sir* Edmond.

562 An address to his Grace the Lord Archbishop of Canterbury. *Printed and are to be sold by Randall Taylor*, 1688. 8 pp. 4°.* L, O, C, EN, DT; CH, MH, NU, WF, Y.

562A —[Anr. ed.] —1688. 11 pp. 4°.* L, O, OC; CH, NC, TU, WF, Y.

562B An address to His Majesty from several bishops. 1694. fol.* O.

563 An address to His Majesty, from the Common Council . . . of New Sarum. colop: *For Walter Davis*, 1681. brs. L, O, HH, EN; MH, MBA, WF.

564 An address to my Lord Mayor. *For Rowland Reynolds*, 1672. brs. L.

Address to Protestants. 1692. *See* Penn, William.

564A Address to the Anabaptists. 1690. O.

564B An address to the Church of England. [*London*, 1688]. cap., 4°.* L.

Address to the free-men. 1682. *See* Bohun, Edmund.

Address to the honourable city of London. 1681. *See* B., C.

565 An address to the hopeful young gentry of England. *By E. C. for G. Walbancke*, 1669. 12°. T.C.I 10. L, AN, M; CH, CLC, Y.

566 An address to the lyon in the Tower. *By G. L.*, 1689. brs. L; MH.

566A Address to the Lords . . . 23 Feb. 1692. *In the Savoy, by Edward Jones*, 1693. fol.* OC.

567 An address to the nobility, clergy and gentlemen of Scotland. [*London*, ? 1688.] 4°.* L, OC, E; CLC, WF, Y.

568 —[Anr. ed.] *Edinburgh*, 1689. 4°.* L, EN.

568A An address to the right hon. Sir John Fleet. *For Rand. Taylor*, 1693. brs. CT; CN.

Address to those of the Roman communion. 1700. *See* Willis, Richard.

569 The addresses importing an abhorrence of an association, . . . laid open. colop: *For R. Baldwyn*, 1682. cap., fol.* L, O, HH, MC, EN; CH, MH, MIU, TU, Y.

569A **Addy, William.** Stenographia. *Sold by D. Newman, and S. Crouch, and W. Marshall*, [1684?]. 8°. LLL.

570 — —[Anr. ed.] *Printed for ye author, sold by W. Marshall*, [1684?]. 12°.* T.C.II 87. LC.

571 — —[Anr. ed.] *For ye author: sold by Dorman Newman and Samuel Crouch, William Marshall, Tho: Cockerill, and I. Lawrence*, [1690?] 12°.* T.C.II 445. L, C, LG, CM, HH; NN, WF, Y.

572 — —[Anr. ed.] *For ye author: for John Lawrence*, 1695. 16°.* T.C.II 560. L, O, C, MC, EN; BN, NN.

573 **Adee, Nicholas.** A plot for a crovvn. *By R. W., to be sold by Walter Davis*, 1685. 4°.* L, O, C, CP; CH, MBA, MIU, NU.

574 The adept's case. [*London*, 1700.] brs. L.

575 [**Adis, Henry.**] A cup for the citie, and her adherents. [*London*], *printed*, 1648. 4°.* LT, OB, LG, DT; NHC.

576 —A declaration of a small society of baptized believers. *For the author*, 1659. brs. LT; CH, NHC, WF.

577 —A fannaticks addresse. *For the author*, 1661. 4°.* MIU, NHC, NU, WF, Y.

578 —A fannaticks alarm. *For the author*, 1661. 4°.* L, O, C; LC, NHC, NU.

578A — —Second edition. 1661. 4°. NHC.

579 —A fannaticks letter. *By S. Dover for the author*, 1660. 4°.* LT; CU, NHC.

580 —A fannatick's mite. *For the author*, 1660. 4°.* LT, O, LCL; CH, NHC, NU, WF.

581 — —Second edition. *By S. Dover, for the author*, 1660. 4°.* L, CS; NHC.

582 —A fannatick's primmer. *For Francis Smith*, [1660?]. 8°. L; LC, Y.

583 —A fannatick's testimony. *By S. Dover*, 1661. 4°.* LT, O; CH, NHC, NU, WF, Y.

584 —A letter sent from Syrranam. *Printed*, 1664. 4°.* GH; CH, NN, RPJ.

585 [–] A spie sent out of the Tower-chamber. [*London*,] *printed*, 1648. 4°.* LT; MB.

[**Adlington, John.**] England's faithful reprover. 1653. *See* Samwaies, Richard.

585A Admirable and glorious appearance. colop: 1684. * PHS.

586 Admirable and notable things of note. *For Francis Coules and Thomas Banks*, 1642. 4°. LT, EC.

Admirable curiosities. 1682. *See* Crouch, Nathaniel.

587 May the seventeenth, 1642. Admirable, good, true, and joyfull newes from Ireland. *Printed at London for Iohn Wright*, 1642. 4°.* LT, O, C, MR; CH, MIU, WF, Y.

587A An admirable new northern story. [*London*], *for William Thackeray and A. M.* [1680?] brs. L.

588 Admirable newes from Ireland. *Printed at London for Francis Coules*, 1641[2]. 4°.* LT; Y.

Admirable speech. 1654. *See* Frewen, Henry.

Admirable treatise of solid virtue. 1699. *See* Bourignon, Antoinette.

589 An admiration by way of answer to the petition. *For Thomas Homer*, 1642. 4°.* LT, C, LVF; CH, MH.

590 Entry cancelled.

591   The admonisher admonished. *For Thomas Malthus,* 1683. fol.* T.C.II 18. O, HH, EN; CH, MH, WF.

592   —Second edition. —, 1683. fol. O, EN; CH, TU.

593   Admonition a tous les grands de la terre. *Imprimé à Londres pour Giles Calvert,* 1655. 4°.* LT, O.

594   An admonition by way of quere, to all such as desire to be true to the King. [*London,* 1647.] brs. MH.

Admonition concerning a publick fast. 1691. *See* Stephens, Edward.

Admonition for the fifth of November. [1690?] *See* Grascombe, Samuel.

594A An admonition given unto Mr. Saltmarsh. *By John Dever & Robert Ibbitson, for Ralph Smith,* 1646. 4°. LT; CH, CN, NPT, NU, Y.

595   An admonition of the greatest concernment. [*London,* 1659.] brs. LT, O, LG; CH, MH.

Admonition to a deist. 1685. *See* Assheton, William.

596   An admonition to all lying brethren. *For J. P.,* 1642. 4°.* LT, O, OC, DT; CLC, LC, TU, Y.

597   Entry cancelled.

Admonition to all such. 1676. *See* Parker, Matthew.

Admonition to my Lord Protector. 1654. *See* Heath, James.

Admonition to the magistrates. [1689.] *See* Stephens, Edward.

Admonition to the reader. 1676. *See* Mainwaring, *Sir* Thomas.

598   Admonitions by the Supreame Councell. *At Waterford, by Thomas Bourke,* 26 Jan. 1643. 4°. O, C; CH.

599   An admonitory letter written by an old minister. *By J. G. for Richard Lowns,* 1658. 4°.* LT; Y.

Adoniram Byfield of the last edition. 1648. *See* S., H.

600   **Adrichomius, Christopher.** A briefe desription [*sic*] of Jerusalem. *York, by Stephen Bulkley,* 1666. 8°. L; MB.

600A [–] A description and explanation of 268. places in Jerusalem. *For R. I. and P. S. to be sold by Tho. Brewster* 1654. 4°. L, C, LCL; NHC, NU, WF, Y.

600B The advance of Sir Arthur Westlrog. *For George Hertorg.* [1659].4°.* MH.

601   The advantages of the Kingdome of England. [*London?* 1662.] cap., fol.* L; MH, NC.

Advantages of the present settlement. 1689. *See* Defoe, Daniel.

602   The advantages of the tobacco trade. [*London,* ?1685.] brs. L.

Advantages which will. 1668. *See* Culpeper, Thomas.

603   Advantagious proposals to the fortunate. [*London,* 1695.] cap., fol.* Y.

603A An adventure for a parcel of plate. [*Edinburgh,* 1700.] brs. EN.

Adventures of an English merchant. 1670. *See* S., T.

604   The adventures of Covent Garden. *By H. Hills for R. Standfast,* 1699. 8°. L; CLC.

Adventures of five hours. 1663. *See* Tuke, *Sir* Samuel.

Adventures of Telemachus. 1699. *See* Fenelon, François de Salignac de la Mothe.

605   The adventures of the Helvetian hero. *For R. Taylor,* 1694. 12°. T.C.II 492. L.

606   Advertisement [of a runaway servant, Matthew Jones, the property of Hannah Bosworth, of Hull]. [*Cambridge, Mass.,* 1684.] brs. MHS.

Advertisement, anent. Edinburgh, 1669. *See* Scotland. Privy council.

607   An advertisement as touching the fanaticks late conspiracy. *By H. Lloyd, and R. Vaughan,* 1661. 4°.* LT.

608   Advertisement be Agnes Campbell, relict. [*Edinburgh,* 1666.] brs. E.

Advertisement by A. M. [1695.] *See* Monro, A.

609   Advertisement by the Sheriff Deput of Aberdeen-shire. [*Aberdeen*], *Forbes,* 1696. fol. ALDIS 3534. AC.

609A Advertisement concerning East-New-Jersey. *Edinburgh, by John Reid,* 1685. brs. ALDIS 2529. EN; RPJ.

609B Advertisement concerning some mistakes ... Compleat history of England. [*London,* 1694.] brs. Y.

Advertisement concerning the province. Edinburgh, 1685. *See* Perth, James Drummond, *earl of.*

609C Advertisement concerning the right way ... of improving of bees. 1675. brs. OC.

610   An advertisement, concerning the royal fishery. *Printed,* 1695. brs. MH, NC.

610A Advertisement for the disposal of fine lace. [*London?* 1700.] brs. L.

Advertisement for the more easie. [1682?] *See* Murray, Robert.

611   Advertisement forasmuch as by His Majesty's gracious care. [*Boston,* 1686.] brs. MHS.

612   Advertisement from the charitable corporation for relief of industrious poor. [1700.] brs. OP.

612A An advertisement from the Company of tinn-plate-workers. [*London,* 1690.] brs. OC.

613   An advertisement from the garbling office. [1679.] brs. L.

614   An advertisement from the General Penny-Post-Office. [1685.] brs. O.

615   September, the 16th. 1681. An advertisement from the insurance-office for houses. [1681.] brs. L, LG.

615A An advertisement from the penny-post-office. [*London?* 1700.] brs. L; MH.

615B An advertisement from the Society of chymical physitians. *For John Starkey* [1665]. brs. L, HH.

615C An advertisement from Their Majesties general post-office. [*London?* 1690.] brs. L.

616   Advertisement, June, 1698, at Moncreff's Coffee-house, ... a monster. [1698.] brs. L.

Advertisement of two books. 1679. *See* Perrault, Nicolas.

617   An advertisement on the behalf of William Dockwra. [1699.] brs. O.

618   An advertisement, relating to lead sheathing. [1699.] brs. L.

Advertisement shewing that all former objection. 1696. *See* Hale, Charles.

619   Advertisement. The bank of credit. [*London,* 1682.] brs. L.

Advertisement. The projectors. [*London,* 1695.] *See* Briscoe, John.

620 Advertisement. There is now publish'd a treatise intit'led, Meditations. [*London? 1698.*] brs. CM.

621 An advertizement to all gent. souldiers. *For George Tomlinson, 1642.* brs. LT, EC; Y.

622 Advertisement to all who have occasion to make use of sheet-lead. *For T. H., 1690.* brs. L, O; Y.

Advertisement to booksellers. [1680.] *See* Baker, John.

Advertisement to the jury-men. 1653. *See* Filmer, Sir Robert.

Advertisement to the Parliament. 1644. *See* Field, John.

Advertisement to the subscribers. 1654. *See* Walton, Brian.

623 An advertisement to the whole kingdome. *By R. O. and G. D., 1642.* 4°.* LT, LG, DT; CH, CLC, MH, WF, Y.

624 Advertisement. Whereas at the instance and request. *Boston, 1691.* brs. MBS.

625 Advertisement. Whereas divers people are at great expence. *By Andrew Clark, 1675.* brs. L, O.

626 An advertisement, whereas the lands of Narrangansett. [*Cambridge, Mass., 1678.*] brs. LPR.

Advertisements from the delegates. [1663.] *See* Oxford University.

627 Advertisements from Yorke. *Printed, 1642.* 4°.* LT, O, CM, YM; WF, Y.

628 Advertisements partly for due order. 1564. *Reprinted,* [1700]. MR.

629 The advice. [*London, 1687?*] brs. L, O, C, OC, CT; CN, TU, WF, Y.

629A Advice about the new East-India stock. [*London, 1691.*] brs. LG; MH.

Advice and direction. 1642. *See* England. Parliament.

Advice before it be too late. [1688.] *See* Humfrey, John.

630 Advice, by way of Ostend, of the capitulation of . . . Namure. *For J. Read, 1695,* brs. MH.

Advice concerning bills. 1655. *See* Malynes, Gerard.

630A Advice concerning strict conformity. [*London, 1684.*] cap., 4°.* MIU.

630B An advice concerning the communication of trade. colop: *Edinburgh, by the heirs of Andrew Anderson, 1700.* fol.* NC.

Advice concerning the education. 1647. *See* Petty, Sir William.

631 Advice for chusing Common-Council men. [1689.] brs. C, MC; CN.

Advice for the poor. [1665.] *See* Dixon, Roger.

632 Advice from a Catholick to his Protestant friend. [*Douay?*] *printed, 1687.* 12°.* L; MH, Y.

633 Advice from a dissenter. *Printed, 1688.* 4°.* O, OC, HH; CH, CN, IU, MH, Y.

634 The advice of a father. 1664. 8°. T.C.I 65. L.

635 —[Anr. ed.] *By J. R. for Brabazon Aylmer, 1688.* 8°. T.C.II 304. L, O, C; CN, NU, WF, Y.

636 The advice of the Lords of Middleburrough. colop: *Reprinted at London, and sold by Walter Davis, 1684.* brs. O; CH, Y.

637 The advice of Tory to Whigg. colop: *For John Hobdy, 1682.* brs. O; CH.

Advice of W. P. 1648. *See* Petty, Sir William.

Advice sent in a letter. 1655. *See* Burt, Nathaniel.

Advice to a daughter. 1658. *See* Heydon, John.

—1699. *See* Halifax, George Savile, *marquis of.*

Advice to a friend. 1673. *See* Patrick, Symon, *bp.*

Advise to a friend discontented. 1660. *See* G., F.

Advice to a painter. [1666.] *See* Marvell, Andrew.

638 Advise to a painter; being a satyr. *For Randel Taylor, 1692.* 4°.* L, O, AU; CH, CN, MH, NP.

639 Advise to a painter on a poem to a friend. [*London.*] *for J. Darres, 1681.* 4°.* EN; CH, WF.

640 Entry cancelled.

Advice to a painter. Long since proposed. 1688. *See* P., J.

641 Advice to a parson. [*London*], *printed, 1691.* 8°.* L, O; CLC, IU, TU.

Advice to a physician. 1695. *See* Waldschmidt, J. J.

642 Advice to a souldier. *By John Shadd, for John Gay, 1680.* 4°.* DT; CU, MH, WF.

Advice to a son. Oxford, 1656. *See* Osborne, Francis.

643 Advice to a wavering friend. [*London, ?1680.*] brs. L; MH, Y.

Advice to a young lord. 1691. *See* Fairfax, Thomas. *4th baron.*

643A Advice to an apprentice. *By J. H. for Edw. Castle, 1698.* 12°. T.C.III 81. Y.

Advice to an only child. 1693. *See* Heywood, Oliver.

Advice to Balaam's ass. 1658. *See* Pecke, Thomas.

644 Advice to batchelors, or, a caution. [*London*], *for P. Brooksby*, [1685–88]. brs. L, O, HH; MH.

645 Advice to batchelours, or, the married mans lamentation. [*London*], *for J. Deacon*, [1685?]. brs. L; MH.

646 Advice to creditors. *For the author, to be sold by John Guillim, 1687.* 4°.* O, C, LUG.

646A Advice to electors. [*London? 1695.*] cap., 4°.* CH.

647 Advice to English Protestants, being a sermon. *By J. D. for Awnsham Churchill, 1689.* 4°.* L, O, CS, DT; CH, NU, PU, WF, Y.

647A Advice to freeholders. [1698?] O; CH.

Advice to freeholders. 1687. *See* Penn, William.

648 Advice to Gen. Monck. [*London, 1660.*] brs. LT.

648A Advice to high-sheriffs about taking the poll of clergymen. *Printed, 1690.* brs. L, C.

Advice to His Grace. [1681–2.] *See* Philips. Mrs. Joan.

Advice to lovers. 1680. *See* R., W.

648B Advice to Protestant dissenters. colop: *By and sold by Andrew Sowle, 1688.* 4°.* MH, MWA.

649 Advice to Protestants. *By Henry Hills, 1687.* 4°.* LIL, CS, A; CN, MH, TU, WF.

Advice to scattered flocks. 1684. *See* Hardy, Samuel.

649A Advice to the army. *For James Fothergill*, [1689]. brs. L; MH.

650 Advice to the citizens of London. colop: *For R. Baldwin, 1690.* brs. L, C; CH.

651 Advice to the city or the Wiggs loyalty. [*London*], *for C. Tebroc,* [*i.e.*, Corbet] [1682?] fol. O; CH, MH.

652 Entry cancelled.

Advice to the city: sung to the King. 1682. *See* D'Urfey, Thomas.

653   Advice to the confuter [Bp. Patrick] of Bellarmin. *By Henry Hills*, 1687. 4°.* L, OC, CCA, HH, DT; CH, MH, MIU, NU, WF.

Advice to the country. [1695.] *See* Ferguson, Robert.

654   Entry cancelled.

655   Advice to the English youth. colop: *By George Larkin*, 1688. 4°.* O, OC; WF, Y.

656   Advice to the freemen of England. colop: *For T. S.*, 1681. fol.* L, O, LG, OP, BR; CH, CN, MH, NP, TU, Y.

Advice to the ladies. [1686–88.] *See* D'Urfey, Thomas.

657   Advice to the livery-men. [1692.] brs. L, O, C, HH; NN, RPB.

657A   Advice to the maidens of London. [*London*], *for J. Blare* [1688]. brs. O.

658   Advice to the men of Monmouth concerning the present times. colop: *For T. Benskins*, [1681?]. brs. L, O; CH, CN, NN, Y.

659   Advice to the men of Shaftesbury. colop: *For John Smith*, 1681. cap., fol.* L, O, C, MR; CH, CN, MH, WF, Y.

659A   Advice to the merchants and traders of England. *E. Whitlock, February*, 1696. brs. L.

660   Advice to the nobility. [*London*, 1679.] cap., fol.* L, O, OC, MR, HH; CH, MH, NU, TU, WF, Y.

661   Advice to the painter, from a satyrical night-muse. *For Charles Leigh*, 1681. brs. L; MH, PU, Y.

662   Advice to the painter's adviser. [*London*, 1679?] cap., fol.* CN, MH, TU.

662A   Advice to the patrons of the test. [*London*, 1687.] brs. L; MH, TU, WF.

Advice to the readers. 1682. *See* Seymour, Thomas.

663   Advice to the Roman-Catholicks of England. *For Charles Brome*, 1700. 12°. T.C.III 195. OC; Y.

664   Advice to the women and maidens of London. *For Benjamin Billingsley*, 1678. 4°. T.C.I 303.* L, O.

665   Advice to this nation. 1679. fol. O.

665A   Advice to those who never received the sacrament. *For John Dunton*, 1697. 8°. O; RPB.

666   Advice to young gentlemen. *For J. Back*, [1685–88]. brs. L, O, HH; MH.

Advice touching chusing. [1697.] *See* A., J.

667   Advices brought by the mail from Holland. 1695. brs. MC.

668   Advices (by the Groyne Mart). *By Edw. Jones in the Savoy*, 1695. brs. MWA.

668A   Advis certain de la prise de Cork. *Kinsington*, [*sic*] *le 4/14 October*, 1690. brs. TU.

669   The advocate. *By William Du Gard*, 1651. fol.* L; MH, WF.

670   —[Anr. ed.] *By William Du-gard, to bee sold by Nicolas Bourn*, 1652. fol.* L, O, DT.

Advocate of conscience liberty. 1673. *See* Walsh, Peter.

671   The advocats complaint. [1688.] brs. EN.

672   **Advocates Library.** Catalogus librorum bibliothecæ juris utriusque. *Edinburgi, ex officina Georgii Mosman*, 1692. 4°. L, O, GU, EN; MHL, Y.

673   **Ady, Thomas.** A candle in the dark. *For Robert Ibbitson*, 1655. 4°. O, CK, GU.

674   —[Anr. ed.] *For R. I. to be sold by Tho. Newberry*, 1656. 4°. LT, O, CK, LLL, GU; CH, CN, LC, MH, NU.

675   Entry cancelled.

676   —A perfect discovery of witches. *For R. I to bee sold by H. Brome*, 1661. 4°. L, O, C, GU; CH, CLC, MH, NIC, NN.

677   [**Ælfric**]. A testimonie of antiquity. *Oxford, by Leonard Lichfield*, 1675. 4°.* MADAN 3042. L, O, C, OC; CLC, IU, NU.

678   [–] —[Anr. ed.] *For J. W. to be sold by Randal Taylor*, 1687. 4°.* O, CS, EN, DT, HH; MH, MIU, TU, WF, Y.

679   **Ælianus, Claudius.** His various history. *For Thomas Dring*, 1665. 8°. L, O, C, LL; CH, CN, MH, NC, Y.

680   — —[Anr. ed.] —, 1666. 8°. L, O; CH, PL, WF, Y.

681   — —[Anr. ed.] *T. Basset*, 1670. 8°. ES; MH, RPB.

682   Aen syne Koninghijcke majesteyt. *By H. Iones*, 1688. brs. MH.

Ænigmaticall characters. 1658. *See* Flecknoe, Richard.

683   **Æschines.** Αισχινου ο κατα Κτησιθωντος. Εκ θεατρου εν Οξονια, *excudebat Johan. Crooke*, [1696]. 8°. L, O, C, EN, DT; MH, PL, TU, WF, Y.

684   **Æschylus.** Αισχιλου . . . Tragœdiæ septem. *Typis Jacobi Flesher: prostant apud Cornelium Bee*, 1663. fol. L, O, C, EN, DT; CU, MH, NC, PL, Y.

685   — —[Anr. ed.] *Typis Jacobi Flesher, prostant apud Jonam Hart*, 1664. fol. L, O, CT, E, LM; CLC, MH, PL, WF, Y.

Æsop. Arranged chronologically by language.

686   —Æsop's fables. *By I. L. for Andrew Hebb*, 1646. 8°. L.

687   —The fables of Esop. *By F. B. for Andrew Hebb*, 1674. 8°. L; MH, NC, Y.

688   —Æsops fables, with their moralls. *Cambridge, by R. D. for Francis Eglesfield*, 1650. 12°. MH.

689   —The fables of Æsop paraphrased in verse. *By Thomas Warren for Andrew Crook*, 1651. 4°. LT, O, CT, E, OM; BN, CH, CN, MH, WF, Y.

690   —Æsops fables, with their moralls. *By R. D. for Francis Eglesfield*, 1651. 12°. L, C.

690A   — —[Anr. ed.] —, 1655. 12°. Y.

691   —Æsop's fables. English and Latine. *By W. Wilson*, 1657. 8°. MH.

692   —The fables of. *By J. Owsley and P. Lillicrap, for Abell Roper*, 1658. 12°. LT.

693   —The fables of . . . paraphras'd. *By Thomas Roycroft, for the author*, 1665–68. 2 pts., fol. L, O, CM, EN, DT; BN, CN, MH, TU.

694   Entry cancelled.

695   —Æsop's fables, with his life. *By R. Newcomb for Francis Barlow* [1666?]. fol. CH.

696   — —[Anr. ed.] *By William Godbid for Francis Barlow, and are to be sold by Anne Seile, and Edward Powell*, 1666. fol. L, O, C, DT; BN, CH, NN, WCL, WF.

697   —The fables of Æsop paraphras'd. Second edition. *By Thomas Roycroft*, 1668. fol. L, OC, BR, DT, LI; CH, CLC, MH, WF, Y.

698   —Æsopics: or, a second collection of fables. *By Thomas Roycroft, for the author*, 1668. fol. L, O; CH, IU, MH, WF.

699 — —Second edition. *By the author,* 1673. 8°. L, O, C;
CH, MIU, NP, PL, WF.

700 —The fables paraphrased. Third edition. *By the author at
his house,* 1673. 8°. T.C.I 158. O, C; LC, WF.

701 —The fables of . . . paraphrased. Second edition. *For T.
Basset, R. Clavel, and R. Chiswel,* 1675. 2v. 8°. CU.

702 —Third edition. *For T. Basset, R. Clavel, and R. Chiswel,
and to be sold by Samuel Keble,* 1675. 8°. L, O, DT; CH, Y.

702A —Æsop's fables, English and Latin. *By T. R. for the company of stationers,* 1676. 12°. T.C.I 261. Y.

702B —The fables of. *By S. and B. G. for G. Sawbridge and A.
Roper,* 1676. 12°. TU.

703 —Æsop's fables with his life. Second edition. *By H. Hills
jun. for Francis Barlow, and are to be sold by Chr. Wilkinson, Tho. Fox and Henry Faithorne,* 1687. fol. L, O, OC,
CT; CH, CN, LC, MH, WCL.·

704 —Æsop's fables, English and Latin. *By M. F. for the company of stationers,* 1689. 8°. C.

705 —Æsop's fables, with their morals. Twelfth edition. *For
Francis Eglesfield, to be sold by Randal Taylor,* 1691. 12°.
C.

706 —Fables of. *For R. Sare, T. Sawbridge, B. Took, M. Gillyflower, A. & J. Churchill, and J. Hindmarsh,* 1692. fol. L,
O, C, OB, CE; BN, CH, CU, LC, WF, Y.

707 — —Second edition. *For R. Sare, B. Took, M. Gillyflower
A. & J. Churchil, J. Hindmarsh, and G. Sawbridge,* 1694-
99. 2v., fol. L, OM, C, E, LW; BN, CU, NC, VC, WG, Y.

708 —Æsop's fables, with their morals. Fourteenth edition.
For J. Phillips, H. Rhodes, and J. Taylor, 1698. 12°. L.

708A —Fables and storyes moralized. *For R. Sare,* 1699. fol. O,
LW.

709 —Fables of. Third edition. *For R. Sare, B. Took, M. Gillyflower, A. & J. Churchil, G. Sawbridge, and H. Hindmarsh,* 1699. fol. L, O, C, E, LW; CH, LC, MB, WG, Y.

710 —Æsop's fables. *By R.E. for the company of stationers,*
1700. 8°. T.C.III 178. L.

711 —Æsopi Phrygis fabulae. *Edinburgh, J. Glen,* 1646. 8°. EN.

711A —Æsopi Phrigis fabulae. *Pro S. I. pro societatis stationarum,*
1648. V.

711B —[Anr. ed.] — 1649. CH.

711C — —[Anr. ed.] *Excudebat Rogerus Daniel pro societatis stationariorum,* 1653. 8°. CM; V.

712 — —[Anr. ed.] *Oxoniæ, typis L. Lichfield & H. Hall,*
1655. MADAN 2270. L, [t.p. only]; Y.

713 —Æsopi Phrygis fabulæ. *Cantabrigiæ: ex academiæ typographeo,* 1655. 8°. L, O.

714 — —[Anr. ed.] *Cantabrigiæ ex officina Joann. Field,* 1656.
8°. C.

715 —Fabulæ Æsopi. *Ex officina Rogeri Danielis,* 1657. 12°.
L, O, OC, C; MIU, NC, V, Y.

716 —Fabulæ. *Cantabrigiæ, ex officina Joann. Field,* 1658. 8°.
O, C.

716A — —[Anr. ed.] *Oxoniæ, excudebat A. Lichfield & H. Hall,*
1658. MB.

717 —Æsopi Phrygis fabulæ. *Cantabrigiæ, ex officina Joann.
Field,* 1662. 8°. L, C.

718 —Fabulæ. — 1663. 8°. DT.

718A —Æsopi Phrygis fabulæ. —, 1667. 8°. L.

719 —[Anr. ed.] *Excudebat S. Griffin, pro societate stationariorum,*
1668. 8°. O, CP, AU.

720 —Fabulæ. *Cantabrigiæ, ex officina Joann. Field,* 1668. 8°.
O, C.

720A — —[Anr. ed.] *Typis R. White pro societatis stationariorum,*
1670. 8°. BR.

721 —Æsopi Phrygis fabulæ. *Cantabrigiæ, ex officina Joann.
Hayes,* 1670. 8°. L, O; CLC, WF.

722 —Fabulæ Æsopi. *Ex officina Johannis Redmayne,* 1671. 12°.
L, C; NP, PU.

722A — —[Anr. ed.] *Oxonii, e theatro Sheldoniano,* 1673. 8°. MB.

723 — —[Anr. ed.] *Ex typographia societatis stationariorum,*
1675. 4°. L, LIL; Y.

724 — —[Anr. ed.] *Edinburgi, excudebat Thomas Brown,* 1676.
8°. ALDIS 2070. O, E, EN, SA; WF.

725 — —[Anr. ed.] *Cantabrigiæ, ex officina Joann. Hayes,*
1677. 8°. O.

726 — —[Anr. ed.] *Ex officina Johannis Redmayne,* 1697. sixes.
O, C; MIU, WF.

726A — —[Anr. ed.] *Ex typographia societatis stationariorum,*
1681. 8°. O; IU, MB.

727 —Æsopi fabulæ explicatæ. *Vnales* [sic] *prostant apud Tho.
Parkhurst,* 1682. 8°. L, O, CT, BAMB.

727A — —*Ex typographia societatis stationariorum,* 1688. 8°. IU.

728 —Æsopi Phrygis fabulæ. *Ex typographia societatis stationariorum,* 1691. 8°. L.

728A — —[Anr. ed.] *Impensis societatis stationarum,* 1695. 8°. NP.

728B — —[Anr. ed.] —, 1698, 8°. O; MB.

729 —Fabularum. *Oxoniæ, e theatro Sheldoniano,* 1698. *Excudebat Johan. Croke.* 8°. L, O, C, EN, MR; BN, CH, PL,
WCL, WF, Y.

729A —Fabulæ. *Excudebat Ben. Griffin, pro societatis typographorum,* 1700. 8°. WG.

729B —The frog. [*London?* 167-?] fol.* CH.

730 —Mythologia Æsopica. *Typis M. Clarke, impensis Sam.
Carr.* 1682. 12°. O, C, EC, RPL; MB, MH, MIU, WF, Y.

730A — —[Anr. ed.] *Typis J. H., impensis J. Slatter Etonensis &
prostant venales apud I. Newborough,* 1697. 12°. T.C.II 603.
EC; LC.

731 —Mythologia ethica: or, Three centuries. *For Thomas
Howkins,* 1689. 8°. L, O, CS; CH, MH, OCI.

732 —The Phrygian fabulist. *By W.D. for Nicolas Bourn,*
1650. 8°. LT; CH, LC, MH, TU, Y.

732A —Praecipuæ ac omnium elegantissimæ sexaginta . . .
fabulæ. *Typis Johannis Heptinstall,* 1684. CLC, NC, TU,
WCL.

733 —The swearers. *Printed,* 1681. 4°.* T.C.I 441. L, O; CH,
MH, WF.

Æsop. A comedy. 1697. *See* Vanbrugh, *Sir* John.

734 Æsop at Amsterdam. *Amsterdam, for Myn Heer Vanden
Flounder,* 1698. *Sold by the booksellers of London.* 8°.* O,
MR, DT; CH, MH, TU, WF, Y.

735 Æsop at Bathe. *For A. Baldwin,* 1698. 4°.* L, O, BR; MH,
WF, Y.

735A —Second edition. —, 1698. 4°.* CLC, OCI, TU.

736 Æsop at Epsom, by a cit. *Printed for, and sold by John Nut,* 1698. 8°.* O, MR; CLC, MH, TU, WF, Y.

737 —Second edition. 1698. 8°.* DT; MH, OCI.

738 Æsop at Richmond. *Printed,* 1698. 4°.* L, LVF; CH, OCI, WF.

739 Æsop at Tunbridge. *Printed, and are to be sold by E. Whitlock,* 1698. 8°. in 4's.* L, O, CS, MR, DT; CH, CN, MH, OCI, Y.

739A —[Anr. ed.] *Printed for, and are to be sold by the author,* 1698. 8°.* CLC, OCI, WF.

740 Æsop at Westminster. [n.p., ?1691.] cap., fol.* MH.

741 Æsop from Islington. [*London*], *printed,* 1699. 4°.* L, O, CT, DT; CU, IU, MH, Y.

742 Æsop improved. *For Tho. Parkhurst,* 1673. 8°. T.C.I 118. O, CT; CH, MH.

743 Æsop in select fables. Viz. I. At Tunbridge. *Printed and are to be sold by most booksellers in London and Westminster,* 1698. 8°. L, O; CLC, MH, PBM, WF, Y.

744 Æsop naturaliz'd. *Cambridge, by John Hayes, for Edward Hall,* 1697. 8°. T.C.III 40. L, C, CT, DT; CU, MBA, MH, WF, Y.

745 Æsop return'd from Tunbridge. *For J.F.,* [1698]. 8°.* L, O, OM, MR; CH, MH, NP, WF, Y.

746 Æsop's last will and testament. colop: *For the author,* 1698. brs. L; CH, CLC, MH.

747 Æternitati sacrum, or a monument. *By Peter Lillicrap, for H. Brome,* 1662. brs. L.

747A Afbeelding. *Amsterdam, by Marcus Willens Dournick.* [1665.] brs. O; WF.

Affairs of church. 1660. *See* Heylyn, Peter.

Affectuum decidua. Oxford, 1656. *See* Turner, Francis.

748 Affidavits in a cause between Sir Basil Firebrace. 1691. brs. MC.

Affirmations in defence. 1641. *See* W., J.

749 The afflicted Christian justified. *Printed [Larner's last press],* 18. May, 1646. 4°.* LT, DT.

Afflicted man's testimony. [1691.] *See* Edwards, Charles.

749A The afflictions of the afflicted. *Printed,* 1653. 4°.* LT; MH, Y.

Africa: being. 1670. *See* Dapper, Olfert.

After a pauze. [*London?* 1655.] *See* Gayton, Edmund.

750 An after game at Irish. [*Dublin*], *printed,* 1649. 4°.* Y.

751 After our hearty commendations; whereas by the Act of Parliament. 1679. brs. OP.

After-reckoning. 1646. *See* Ley, John.

Afternoon instructions. [1699.] *See* Gother, John.

752 **Ag., Ph.** The power and practice of courtleets. *For Samuel Speed,* 1666. WF.

Aga, Hadgi Giafer. *See* Ja'far Aghā, Hajā.

753 **Aga Mahomet, Dey.** A letter written by the governour of Algiers. *For Thomas Burrel,* 1679. fol.* L, LUG, HH; MH, Y.

754 Against marriage. [*London,* ?1690.] brs. L.

755 Against the coachmens bill. [n.p., ?1700.] brs. Y.

755A Against the observation of eden. [*London?* 1660]. cap., 4°.* WF.

756 Against universall libertie of conscience. *Printed at London, for Thomas Vnderhill,* 1644. 4°.* L, O, DT; MH, NHC, NU, WF, Y.

Ἀγάπαι. 1671. *See* Smythies, William.

757 **Agar, Benjamin.** Clericus mercati. 1641. 4°. LG; WF.

757A [–] The lost sheep is found. *Printed,* 1642. 4°.* WF.

758 **Agas, Benjamin.** Gospel conversation. *For Elizabeth Calvert,* 1667. 12°. NPT.

758A —The male of the flock. *By A: N. for Henry Eversden,* 1655. 4°.* LT.

Agathocles. 1683. *See* Hoy, Thomas.

758B The age of man. *For T. Passinger,* 1676. 8°. OP.

758C The age of riddles. [*London?* 1682.] brs. HH; CH.

759 The age of vvonders, or miracles are not ceased. *For Nehemiah Chamberlain,* 1660. 4°.* LT.

760 **Ager, Thomas.** A paraphrase on the Canticles *By A. Godbid and J. Playford, to be sold by Samuel Sprint,* 1680. 8°. T.C.I 401. L, O; MH, NPT, NU, Y.

Ages of mans life. 1653. *See* Cuffe, Henry.

761 Entry cancelled.

762 Aggravii Venetiani, &c. Or the Venetian and other grievances. *For Sam. Crouch, Abel Roper and Joseph Fox,* 1697. 4°.* L, O, OC, EN; CH, CU, MH, NC, WF, Y.

Agiatis. 1686. *See* Vaumorière, Pierre d'Ortigue de.

763 An agitator anotomiz'd. [sic] [*London*], *printed,* 1648. 4°.* LT, O, OC, CJ; CH, MH, MIU, WF, Y.

764 [**Aglionby, William.**] Painting illustrated. *By John Gain for the author, to be sold by Walter Kettilby,* 1685. 4°. L, O, LR, EN, DT; CH, CN, LC, NC, Y.

765 ——[Anr. ed.] *By John Gain, for the author, to be sold by Walter Kettilby, and Jacob Tonson;* 1686. 4°. T.C.II 159. L; Y.

766 —The present state of the United Provinces. *For John Starkey,* 1669. 12°. T.C.I 19. L, O, C, DC, E; CN, LC, MH, WF.

767 ——Second edition. —, 1671. 12°. T.C.I 61. L, O, C, OC; MH, NN, TU, Y.

Agnes de Castro. 1688. *See* Brilhac, J. B. de.

Agnes de Castro. 1696. *See* Cockburn, *Mrs.* Catherine (Trotter).

768 The agreement and resolution of severall associated ministers in . . . Corke. *Corke, by William Smith for Richard Plummer,* 1657. 4°.* L, C; NU, WF.

769 The agreement and resolvtion of the ministers of Christ associated within the city of Dublin. *Dublin, by W. Bladen,* 1659. 4°.* DIX 102. O, DT, DL; WF.

Agreement between the church. 1687. *See* Gother, John.

Agreement betwixt the present. 1689. *See* Fullwood, Francis.

770 The agreement for the surrender of the city of Exeter. *Imprinted at London for Matthew Walbancke,* 13 April, 1646. 4°.* LT, O, DT; CH, WF, Y.

771 The agreement in doctrine among the dissenting ministers. *For Thomas Cockerill, and John Dunton,* 1693. 4°.* L, LSC, EN; NU, PL.

772 —[Anr. ed.] *For H. Barnard,* 1693. 4°.* MH, Y.

773 The agreement of divers ministers of Christ . . . Worcester. *By R.W. for Nevil Simmons at Kidderminster, and are to be sold there by him, and at London by William Roybould,* 1656. 8°.* LT, O, OC, CS, EN; CLC, MH, NU.

774 —Second edition, —, 1656. 8°.* LW, EN; CU.

Agreement of the associated ministers and churches … Cumberland. 1656. *See* Gilpin, Richard.

775 The agreement of the associated ministers of … Essex. *For Edward Brewster,* 1658. 4°. L, O, LW, OC, YM; CLC, MH, NPT, NU.

776 —Second edition. —, 1658. 4°. LT.

777 —"Second" edition. *For Joseph Cranford,* 1658. 4°. L.

778 The agreement of the associated ministers in the county of Norfolk. *For Joseph Cranford and are to be sold [by him] in Norwich,* 1659. 4°. O; MH, NU, WF.

779 The agreement of the major, aldermen, and inhabitants of … Tenby. *Printed at Oxford by Leonard Lichfield,* 1643. brs. MADAN 1443, STEELE 2471. O.

780 An agreement of the people for a firme and present peace. *[London], printed,* 1647. 4°.* LT, O, OP; CH, CN, MH, NU, WF, Y.

781 An agreement of the people of England. *For John Partridge, Rapha Harford, Giles Calvert, and George Whittington,* 1649. brs. LT; CU, NC.

782 Agreement of the people proposed as a rule. 1648. 4°.* O.
Agreement of the Unitarians. 1697. *See* Nye, Stephen.

783 An agreement prepared for the people of England. *For John Partridge, R. Harford, G. Calvert and G. Whittington,* 1649. 4°.* HH, O, C, MC; BN, CH, CN, MH, NU, PL, WF.

784 **Agrippa, Henricus Cornelius.** Female pre-eminence. *By T. R. and M. D., to be sold by Henry Million,* 1670. 8°. T.C.I 57. L, O, C, EN, GU; CH, LC, MMO, WF, JF.

785 —Henricus Cornelius Agrippa his fourth book of occult philosophy. *By J. C. for John Harrison,* 1655. 4°. LT, C, LWL, GU; LC, TU, WF, Y.

785A — —[Anr. ed.] *Printed,* 1655. 4°. MH.

786 — —[Anr. ed.] *By J. C. for Tho. Rooks,* 1665. 4°. L; IU, NP.

786A — —[Anr. ed.] *By J. C. to be sold by Matthew Smelt,* 1665. 4°. Y.

787 —The glory of women; or, a looking-glasse. *By T. H. for F. Coles,* 1652. 12°.* L.

788 —The glory of women; or, a treatise. *For Robert Ibbitson,* 1652. 4°.* LT; Y.

789 —Three books of occult philosophy. *By R. W. for Gregory Moule,* 1651. 4°. LT, O, DC, EN, DT; CH, MH, MMO, NU, WF, Y.

790 —The vanity of arts and sciences. *By J. C. for Samuel Speed,* 1676. 8°. L, OME, C, LR, EN; CH, LC, MH, NU, Y.

791 — —[Anr. ed.] *By R. E. for R. B., to be sold by C. Blount,* 1684. 8°. T.C.II 49. L, O, C, GU, AU; CU, MIU, PBL, Y.

792 — —[Anr. ed.] *By R. Everingham for R. Bentley and Dan. Brown,* 1694. 8°. L, O, CT, GU, DT; MH, NR, TU, WF, Y.

793 **Agrippa, Marcus Vipsanius.** An oration of. *For Livewell Chapman,* 1657. 4°.* LT, C; CH, CSS, WF, Y.
Agrippa, King of Alba. 1675. *See* Quinault, Philippe.

794 Ah! cruel Damon, cease to teaze. *[London], T. Crosse,* [1700?] brs. L.
Ah, ha; tumulus. 1653. *See* Howell, James.

795 Ah lovely nymph I'm quite undone. *[London,* 1700?] brs. L.
Ahab's fall. 1644. *See* Herle, Charles.
Ahitophel. *See* Achitophel.

796 **Ahivah.** A petition to his Majesty. [1660.] brs. LT.

797 —A strange prophecy presented. *For R. Bannister,* 1660. 4°.* C.

798 **Aicken, Joseph.** An address to the magistrates. *Dublin, by Joseph Ray,* 1698. 4°.* DIX 306. DT.

799 —The English grammar. *For the author, sold by John Lawrence,* 1693. 8°. T.C.II 483. O, CT.

799A — —[Anr. ed.] *By M. B. for the author, sold at his school,* 1693. 8°. OC, LCS.

800 —Londerias, or, a narrative of the siege of London-Dery. *Dublin, by J. B. and S. P. for the author,* 1699. 4°. DIX 315. L; CH, MH, NN, WF.

801 —The mysteries of the counterfeiting of the coin. *By William Downing for the author,* 1696. 4°.* L, O, OC, ES; CU, LC, MH, NC, Y.

801A **[Ailesbury, Robert Bruce], earl of.** Bibliotheca illustrisi. *For T. Bentley and B. Walford,* 1687. 4°. L, O, OC, CA, HH; CH, MN, NG, WF, JF.

801B —Remainder of library. 1690. O; MH.

802 **[Ailesbury, Thomas.]** A treatise of the confession of sinne. *By J. G. for Andr. Crook,* 1657. 4°. L, O, C, P, SP; CLC, NU, WF.

803 **Ailmer, John.** Musæ sacræ: seu Jonas. *Oxoniæ, excudebat L. Lichfield & veneunt apud Ios. Godwin & Ric. Davis,* 1652. 8°. MADAN 2190. L, O, CM, LW, SC; CH, CN, MB, WF, Y.
Ailo, Thorny, *pseud.* *See* Taylor, John.

804 **A[ilward], J[ohn].** An historicall narration of the judgement of some most learned. *For Rebecca Nealand,* 1645. 4°. LT, HH, DT; CH, NU.

805 **Ainsworth, Henry.** A censure vpon a dialogue. *By W. Iones,* 1642. 4°. LT, O, C, CE, LCL; NPT, NU.

806 — —[Anr. ed.] —, 1643. 4°. HH.

807 —The communion of saints. *By T. B. for Iohn Bellamie and Ralph Smith,* 1641. 12°. L, DC, P, YM; CLC, IU, NHC, NU, Y.

808 — —[Anr. ed.] *Amsterdam,* 1642. 4°. CU.

809 —Covnterpoyson considerations. *[Amsterdam], printed,* 1642. 4°. LT, OCC, CT, P, DT; MB, MH, NU, Y.

810 —The old orthodox foundation of religion. *By E. Cotes, to be sold by Michael Spark,* 1653. 4°. L, O, CT, LCL, E; PH, WF.

811 —The orthodox foundation. *By R. C. for M. Sparke junior,* 1641[2]. 4°. LT, CT, BP, YM, EN; MH, NU, WF, Y.

812 —A seasonable discourse. *For Benjamin Allen,* 1644. 4°. LT, O, CT, LCL, LW; NHC, NU, PL, WF, Y.

813 — —[Anr. ed.] *By M. Simmons for Livewall Chapman,* 1651. 4°. O; CH, CLC, Y.

814 **[Ainsworth, Robert.]** The most natural and easie way of institution. *For Christopher Hussey,* 1698. 4°.* L, CS, M; CH, TU.

815 — —Second edition. —, 1699. 4°* T.C.III 66. L; NC.

816 **Ainsworth, Samuel.** A sermon preached … July 13 … 1642. *By Richard Cotes, for Stephen Bowtell,* 1645. 4°.* O; MH, MHS, MWA, TU.

817 —A sermon preached Decemb. 16. 1654. *For William Gilbertson, to be sold by Thomas Collins in Northampton,* 1655. 4°.* LT, O, LW, NNG, CS; WF.

818 **Ainsworth, William.** Medulla bibliorum. *For George Calvert*, 1652. 8°. L, CT, LCL, YM, E; CLC, CN, MH, NPT, WF, Y.

819 —Triplex memoriale. *York, by Tho. Broad*, 1650. 8°. L, LCL; Y.

820 **A[iray], C[hristopher].** Fasciculus praeceptorum logicorum. Fourth edition. *Oxoniæ, exc. H. H., per J. Godw.*, 1660. 4°. MADAN 2477. LL; MHS.

821 **Aitzema, Lieuwe van.** Notable revolutions. *By William Du-gard*, 1653. fol. L, C, CT, EN, DT; CH, CN, LC, PL, WF, Y.
 ʾΑκαματον πυρ, or . . . . 1667. *See* G., J.

822 **Akeroyde, Samuel.** The rays of dear Clarinda's eyes. *[London], Tho. Cross*, [1700?]. brs. L.
 Alais, Denis Vairasse d'. *See* Vairasse, Denis.

823 An alarme for London. *By G. B. and R. W.*, 1643. 4°.* LT, LG, CS, SP, DT,
 Allarum from heaven. 1649. *See* Wither, George.

824 An alarum from heaven: or a warning. *For Benjamin Harris*, 1677. 4°. CH.

824A An alarum from heaven to rash wishers. *For Joseph Blare*, 1683. 4°.* CM.

825 The alarum: or, an hue-and-cry. colop: *For M. Hooks*, 1683. brs. L, O EN; CH MH, PU, WF.
 Alarm sounded. 1661. *See* White, Dorothy.
 An alarum sounding forth. 1658. *See* Smith, Humphrey.
 Alarm to all flesh. 1660. *See* Burrough, Edward.

826 An alarum to arms. *For George Tomlinson, July 29*, 1642. 4°. LT, O, EC; CH, MH, TU, WF, Y.

826A An alarme to awake church-sleepers. *M. Symmons*, 1644. CH.

827 An alarum to corporations. *For Robert Page*, 1659. 4°.* CSS, AN; CN, MIU, NHC, WF, Y.
 Alarum to England. 1700. *See* C., W.

827A Alarm to England: or, a warning-piece to all Protestants. *For E. R. and J. R.*, 1688. fol.* O, LG; Y.

828 An alarme to England: or, a warning-piece to the inhabitants. colop: *For W. Ley*, 1657. cap., 4°.* LT, LG, DT; NU, Y.

829 An alarm to judgement. *[London?], anno* 1678. 8°. CH.

830 —[Anr. ed.] —, 1679. 12°. L.

831 Entry cancelled.
 An alarum to London. 1650. *See* Beech, William.
 Alarum to pamphleteers. 1659. *See* H., R. B.
 Alarum to poets. 1648. *See* Lane, John.

832 An alarum to the city and souldiery. *[London*, 1659.] brs. LT, O, LG; CLC, MH.

833 An allarme to the city of London, by the Scotch army. *[London], printed*, 1648. 4°.* LT, HH.
 Alarum to the counties. 1660. *See* Fuller, Thomas.

834 An alarum to the headquarters. *[London*, 1647.] cap., 4°.* LT, OC, CT; CH, CN, MH, WF, Y.
 Alarum to the House of Lords. *[London]*, 1646. *See* Overton, Richard.
 Alarum to the last. [1646.] *See* Smith, George.

835 An alarum to the officers and souldiers of the armies. *[London*, 1660.] 4°.* O, HH, LG, YM; MH, NPT.

835A An alarm to the present men in power. *[London], printed*, 1654. brs. LT.
 Alarm to the priests, 1660. *See* Ellwood, Thomas.

836 An alarm to the vvorld. *For Giles Calvert*, 1649. 4°.* LT.
 Alarm to trumpets. 1651. *See* Ford, Emanuel.
 Alarm to warre. 1642. *See* L., J.

837 Alas pore Parliament, how art thou betrai'd? *[London, by Nicholas Tew*, 1644.] brs. LT.
 Alas, poore scholler! [1641-68.] *See* Wild, Robert.

837A Alas poore trades-men what shall we do? *For Francis Grove* [1646?]. brs. MAU.

838 Alazono-Mastix: or the character of a cockney. *By R. I.*, 1652. 4°.* LT; WF.
 Alazonomastix Philalethes, *pseud.* *See* More, Henry.

839 **Albemarle, Christopher, *duke of*.** I Christopher Duke of Albemarle, &c. Chancellour . . . Orders and rules. *[Cambridge], June 27*, 1684. brs. O.

840 **Albemarle, George Monck, *duke of*.** A collection of several letters and declarations. *Printed*, 1660. 2 pts., 4°.* LT, O, C, YM, EN; CH, CN, MH, NU, WF, Y.

841 —The Commonwealth of England having used all . . . 4 May 1654. *Leith*, 1654. cap., brs. STEELE 3p 2116. O.

841A —A copie of a letter from. *Dublin, by William Bladen*, 1659. brs. DIX 103. HH.

842 —The declaration and speech of . . . to the right honourable the Lord Mayor. *For G. Horton*, [1660]. 4°.* L, LG; CH, CLC, MIU, WF, Y.

843 —A declaration of . . . touching the King of Scots. *For Nathaniel Bradley*, 1659. 4°.* L, O, CCA, HH; CH, MH, MIU.

844-5 Entries cancelled.

846 —General Monck's last letter. *For Francis Smith*, 1659. 4°.* L, O, C, HH; CH, CN, MH, WF, Y.

847 —A letter from . . . 11 of Feb. 1659. *By John Redmayn*, [1660]. 4°.* O, OC; CN, MIU.

848 —A letter from . . . from Dalkeith, 13 October 1659. *Printed*, 1659. 4°.* LT, O, CCA, HH, EN; CH, CN, MH, PL, WF, Y.

849 —A letter from . . . in Scotland. *Dublin*, [1659]. brs. DIX 103. L, O.

850 — —[Anr. ed.] *Printed at Dublin: and re-printed at London, for Nath. Brook*, [1659]. brs. STEELE 2p 606. LT, O.

851 —A letter from. 1660. brs. L; MH, WF.

852 —A letter from . . . November the 12th. *[London], printed*, 1659. 4°.* L, CCA; NU.

852A —A letter from . . . to King Charles. *Printed*, 1660. CN, MH, MIU.

853 —A letter from . . . to Major General Overton. *By James Cottrel*, 1660. 4°.* LT, LG; PL, Y.

854 —A letter from . . . to the Parliament; . . . Feb. 11th, 1659. *By John Macock*, 1660. 4°.* L, O, LG, E; CH, CN, MH, WF, Y.

855 —A letter from . . . to the Parliament . . . 11 Feb. 1659. *Edinburgh, reprinted by Christopher Higgins*, 1660. 4°. ALDIS 1653. L, EN; CH, WF, Y.

856 —A letter from. . . . *By John Macock*, 1669. [i.e., 1660.] 4°.* LT, HH; Y.

857   —A letter from . . . to the several and respective regiments. *By John Macock,* 1659. brs. STEELE 3155. LT, O, LS; CH.

858   —A letter of . . . Feb. 9, 1659[60]. *By John Macock,* 1659[60]. brs. STEELE 3151. LT, O, LG; MH, Y.

859   —A letter of November the 12th. [*London,* 1659.] brs. L; CN, MU.

860   — —[Anr. ed.] [*London*], *printed,* 1659. 4°.* L, O, LG, DT; CH, CN, MH, PL, Y.

861   —A letter of General George Monck's, dated at Leicester 23 Ian. *By John Redmayn,* 1660. 4°.* LT, O, HH, LG; CH, CN, MH, WF, Y.

862   —A letter sent by General Monck to Vice-Admirall Goodson. *By John Johnson,* [1659]. brs. LT, O, LS; MH.

863   —A letter sent from . . . Dec. 29, 1659. *By John Streater and John Macock,* 1659[60]. 4°.* LT, O, C; CH, CLC, MH, NU.

864   —Observations upon military and political affairs. *By A.C. for Henry Mortlocke and James Collins,* 1671. fol. L, O, C, EN, LUS; CH, CN, LC, MH, TU, Y.

865   —Several letters from the Lord Generall Monck. [*London*], *printed,* 1660. 4°.* O, LG, HH; CLC, MH, NU, WF, Y.

866   —A sober letter of. *Printed at London,* 1659. 4°.* L, EN; CH, MH, Y.

867   —The speech and declaration, . . . delivered at Whitehall . . . the 21. of February 1659. *By S. Griffin, for John Playford,* 1659[60]. 4°.* LT, O, C, EN, DT; CH, CN, MH, NU, WF, Y.

868   — —[Anr. ed.] *Edinburgh, Higgins,* 1660. 4°. ALDIS 1655. EN; Y.

869   —The Lord General Monck his speech delivered . . . Feb. 6. 1659. *By John Macock,* 1660. 4°.* LT, O, C, MR, E; CH, CN, MH, WF, Y.

870   — —[Anr. ed.] *Reprinted Edinburgh, by Christopher Higgins,* 1660. 4°.* ALDIS 1654. EN, FSF; OWC, Y.

871   —Three letters from. *Edinburgh, by Christopher Higgins,* 1659. 4°.* ALDIS 1611. LT, O, CS, EN, DT; CH, MH, MIU, PL, WF, Y.

871A   —To the reverend and honourable the Vice-Chancellor. [*Oxford?* 1660]. brs. MADAN 2509. O.

872   —To the right honourable Major General Sir Hardress Waller. [*London,* 1659.] brs. HH.

873   Entry cancelled.

874   —Two letters from the fleet at sea. 1653. 4°. LT; WF.

875   — —[Anr. ed.] *London, reprinted Leith,* 1653. 4°. ALDIS 1487. EN.

875A   Albert Durer revived. *By M. Simmons for T. Jenner,* 1652. fol. CH, PFL.

875B   —[Anr. ed.] *For John Garrett* [1660?] fol.* MB, Y.

875C   —[Anr. ed.] *By M. Simmons for T. Jenner,* 1666. 8°.* CH, PL.

875D   —[Anr. ed.] *For S. and B. Griffin for John Garrett* [1680]. T.C.I 371. fol.* LC.

875E   —[Anr. ed.] *By S. Griffin for J. Garrett,* 1679. fol.* LC.

875F   —[Anr. ed.] *By H. Hills, jun. for John Garrett,* 1685. T.C.II 131. fol.* LC.

875G   —[Anr. ed.] *By F. Collins, for John Garrett,* 1698. fol.* LC, Y.

875H   **Albertus Magnus.** The paradise of the soul. *By William Brooks,* 1682. 12°. L, DOWNSIDE; CH, CLC, CN, WF.

875I   —The secrets of. *By R. Cotes, to be sold by Fulke Clifton,* 1650. 8°. WSG.

875J   — —[Anr. ed.] *By M.H. and J.M. to be sold by J. Wright, J. Clarke, W. Thackeray and I. Passenger,* [1691?] 8°. WU.

876   —A treatise of adhering to God. *For Henry Herringman,* 1654. 12°. LT, O, C, LW, GK; MMO, NP, OCI, WF, Y.

877   —Unum necessarium; or. . . . *For R. Baldwin,* 1692. 12°. LW, P; CLC, LC.

878   Albertus the second: or, the curious justice. [*London?* 1700.] brs. L.

879   **Albin, Henry.** The dying pastor's farewell. *For J. Dunton,* 1697. 8°. LW, BR, EN; CLC.

    Albion and Albanus. 1687. *See* Dryden, John.

    Albion's congratulatory. Edinburgh, 1680. *See* Livingston, Michael.

    Albion's elegie. Edinburgh, 1680. *See* Livingston, Michael.

880   Albion's tears on the death of . . . Queen Mary. *For J. Place, sold by J. Whitlock,* 1695. fol.* L, O; CH, MH, TU, WF, Y.

881   [**Albizzi, Bartholomæus.**] The Alcoran of the Franciscans. *For L. Curtise,* 1679. 12°. T.C.I 361. O, C, CT, SP; CLC, NU, WF.

    Albumazar. 1668. *See* Tomkis, Thomas.

882   **Albumazar, Galbrion.** Mercurius phreneticus: shewing the effect of the terrible eclipse. *Printed,* 1652. 4°.* LT, CM; Y.

883   **Albyn, Benjamin.** An appeal to God and the king. *For the author,* 1679. 8°. L, O, LG, OC; CH, CN, WF, Y.

884   —Benjamin Albyn, merchant. Appellant. The apellant's case. [*London?* 1691.] brs. HH.

884A   Alcander and Philocrates: or, the pleasure. *For R. Parker, S. Briscoe, and S. Burrowes,* 1696. IU.

    Alcantara, Pedro de. *See* Peter [Garavito], *of Alcantara, Saint.*

    Alchemist. [1680.] *See* Jonson, Ben.

885   **Alchorne, William.** A sermon preached . . . December 24, 1673. *By William Godbid,* 1674. 4°.* L, O; Y.

886   **Alcinous.** Ἀλκίνου εἰς τά τοῦ Πλάτωνος Εἰσαγωγή. *Oxoniæ, typis Lichfieldianis,* 1667. 8°. MADAN 2762. L, O, C, EN, DT; CH, MH, PL, WF, Y.

887   [**Alcock, John.**] Plain trvths of divivinity [*sic*]. *For J.K.,* 1647. 8°. LT; CH.

888   **Alcoforado, Francisco.** An historical relation of . . . Madera [*sic*]. *For William Cademan,* 1675. 4°.* L, O, BAMB, E, EN; CH, CN, MH, RPJ, WF, Y.

889   [**Alcoforado, Marianna d'.**] Five-love-letters from a nun. *For Henry Brome,* 1678. 8°. T.C.I 302. L, O; CLC, MH.

890   — —[Anr. ed.] —, 1680. 12°. T.C.I 410. CT.

891   — —[Anr. ed.] *For R. Bentley, and are to be sold by S. Cownly,* 1686. 12°. T.C.II 281. L.

892   — —[Anr. ed.] *For R. Bentley,* 1693. 12°. L; CLC, NC, TSM, WF, Y.

893 —Seven Portuguese letters. *For H. Brome*, 1681. 8°. T.C.I 443. O.

894 —Seven love letters. *For C. Brome*, 1693. 4°. T.C.II 441. O.
     Alcoran of the Franciscans. 1679. *See* Albizzi, Bartholomæus.

894A **Alcos.** The certain predictions of. [*London?* 1681.] brs. MH.

894B **Aldam, Thomas.** A brief discovery of a threefold estate of Antichrist. *For Giles Calvert*, 1653. 4°. LT, LF, BBN; PH.

894BA [–] False prophets and their false teachers described. [*London*, 1652.] 4°.* LF, YM; PH.

894C —The searching out the deceit. [*London*], printed, 1655. 4°.* LF, OC; CSS, PH.

894D —A short testimony. *For Thomas Northcott*, 1690. 4°.* LF, BBN; CH, MH, PH, PSC, Y.

895 Entry cancelled.
     Aldred, Thomas. *See* Alured, Thomas.

896 [**Aldrich, Henry.**] Artis logicæ compendium. *Oxonii, e theatro Sheldoniano*, 1691. 8°. L, O, C, OC; MH, Y.

897 [–] —[Anr. ed.] —, 1692. 8°. L, O, CT, OC; CLC, MH, Y.

898 — —[Anr. ed.] —, *excudebat John Crooke*, 1696. 8°. O, C, EC, OC, CM; CH, IU, WF.

898A —Elementa geometriæ priora duo. 1674. 8°. OC.

899 [–] A reply to two discourses. Lately printed at Oxford. *Oxford, at the theater*, 1687. 4°. L, O, C, EN, DT; CH, MH, NU, TU, WF, Y.

900 —Dr. Aldrich his service in G. [*Oxford?* 1690?] fol.* L, OC.

901 [–] A vindication of the Oxford reply. [*Oxford*, 1688.] 4°. L, MC, DT; MIU.
     [**Aldworth, Charles.**] Impartial relation. 1688. *See* Fairfax, Henry.

901A **Aldworth, Richard.** The copie of a letter sent from the Maior of Bristol. *For A. N.*, 1643. 4°.* LT, BR; Y.

902 —A letter sent to the Right Worshipfull. William Lenthall . . . from the Major of Bristol. *For Edw. Husbands May 5*, 1643. 4°.* LT, LG, BR, DT; MH.

903 **Aleman, Mateo.** The rogue, or, the excellencie of history displayed. *By J. C. for the author; and are to be sold by Tho. Johnson and Stephen Chatfield*, 1655. 8°. LT, O; CH, CN, MB.

903A — — Fourth edition. *By W. B. for Phillip Chetwind*, 1656. fol. L, C; CN, TU, WF, Y.

904 — —Fifth edition. *By J. C. for Phillip Chetwind; and are to be sold by Jer: Hirons*, 1656. 4°. O; CLC, WF.

904A —The rogue or the second part. *By Henry Hills*, 1655. 4°. O; CLC, WF.

904B [–] The Spanish rogue. *For Andrew Thorncomb*, 1685. CLC.
     Alethocritus, Christianus, pseud. *See* Du Moulin Louis.

905 The ale-wives complaint. *For John Tomson*, 1675. 4°.* LVF; MH.

906 The alewives invitation. [*London*], *for P. Brooksby*, [1675–80]. brs. L, HH; MH.

907 **Alexander, of Aphrodisaias.** Ἀλεχανδρος Ἀφροδισεος προς τους αυτοκρατορας . . . de fato. *Typis Thomae Roycroft, impensis Jo. Martin, Jacobi Allestrye, & Tho. Dicas*, 1658. 8°. L, O, C, EN, DT; CLC, LC, PL, Y.

908 **Alexander VII, pope.** Ivdicivm theologicvm svper qvaestione. *Ecclesiopoli, at insigne pietatis*, 1648. 4°. L; NU.

909 **Alexander VIII, pope.** The bull of . . . colop: *Printed by Edw. Jones in the Savoy*, 1690. cap., fol.* L; MB, WF, Y.

909A —His Holyness the Pope of Rome's declaration. colop: *For J. M.*, 1689 [90]. brs. OC.

910 —The speech of this present Pope. colop: *For Tho. Salisbury*, 1689. brs. CH, WF.

911 [**Alexander,   .**] A copy of a letter concerning the traiterous conspiracy. *Printed*, 1641. 4°.* LT, C, MR; WF.

912 **Alexander, Alexander.** Philosophemata libera. *Aberdoniis, e typographæo Ioannis Forbesii Junioris*, 1669. 4°.* ALDIS 1970. O, AU, GU.

913 **Alexander, John of Berne.** Synopsis algebraica. *Impensis hospitii, typis Benj. Motte*, 1693. 8°. T.C.II 455. L, O, LCP, CT, AU; BN, CLC, MU, PL, WF, Y.

914 **Alexander, John, converted Jew.** God's covenant displayed. *For Walter Kettilby*, 1689. 4°.* T.C.II 268. L, O, C, OC, OM; CLC, MBA, MH, WF, Y.

915 **Alexander, John, of Leith.** Jesuitico-Quakerism examined. *For Dorman Newman*, 1680. 4°. T.C.I 401. L, O, LF, OM, GU; CLC, MH, NU, PH, WF.

916 **Alexander, John. Parliamentary man.** The last ioyfull intelligence from . . . Redding. *London, April 29. for Thomas Watson*, 1643. 4°.* LT.
     Alexander, Mary. *See* Stirling, Mary Alexander, countess of.

917 **A[lexander], William.** Medulla historiæ Scoticæ, being. *For Randal Taylor*, 1685. 12°. T.C.II 97. L, O, CT, E, DT; CH, CLC, PL, WF, Y.
     Alexander's feast. 1697. *See* Dryden, John.
     Alexipharmacon. 1700. *See* Chauncy, Isaac.

918 **Alexis, emperor of Russia.** A declaration of. [*London*], *printed*, 1650. 4°.* LT, CT.

919 **Aleyn, John.** Select cases. *For George Pawlet and are to be sold by Robert Vincent*. 1688. fol. O, LL, CT, EN; CH, LC, MH, MHL, NCL.

920 —. Select cases in B. R. *For Robert Pawlet*, 1681. fol. L, O, C, LL, DT; LC, MHL, MIU, PBL.

921 **Alford, Joseph.** The church triumphant. *By W. Bentley, for J. Williams*, 1649. 8°. O, P, SP; NU.

922 —The souls dispensatorie. *By W. B. for John Williams*, 1649. 12°. LT, LWL.

923 Algernoon Sidneys farewel. colop: *For W. Davis*, [1683]. brs. L, O, EN; CH, CN, MH, WF, Y.

924 The Algier slaves releasement. [*London*], *for J. Deacon*, [1685?]. brs. L, O, CM.

925 **Algood, major.** A sermon preached, at the funeral of . . . Mr. Georg Ritschel. *For Joseph Hall, Newcastle upon Tyne*, 1684. 4°.* T.C.II 92. O; NN, NPT, NU, Y.

926 Alidor and Calista. 1684. brs. O.

927 Entry cancelled.

Alimony arraign'd. 1696. *See* Ivie, Thomas.

928 **Alingham, William.** An epitome of geometry. *Printed,* 1700. 8°. L, C, CT; CLC.

929 —Geometry epitomized. *By J.M. and B.B. to be sold by Mister Mount,* 1695. 8°. LW, CK; WF.

930 [–] A short account, of the nature and use of maps. *Printed to be sold by Mr. Mount,* 1698. 12°. L, LPO; LC.

931 **Alipili.** Centrum naturæ concentratum; or, the salt. *For J. Harris,* 1696. 12°. T.C.II 569. L, GU; PU, WF.

Alius medicus, *pseud.*

All-conquering genius. 1685. *See* L., T. R. d'.

931A All corporations, and particular persons. [*London?* 1657.] brs. MH.

932 All for love, or, the happy match. [*London*], *for P. Brooksby,* [1672–95]. brs, L, O, HH.

932A All gentlemen, lovers of the noble society of archery. [*London,* 1673.] brs. OP.

933 All gentlemen merchants, and other persons, may please to take notice. [1653.] brs. LT, LG.

934 All gentlemen souldiers that will serve. [1645.] brs. LT.

935 All in an epistle, or, a letter. [*London*], *printed,* 1647. 4°.* LT, MR, DT; CH, CU.

All is not gould. 1648. *See* Jenkins, David.

935A All is not gold that glitters. *For G. Horton,* 1651. 4°.* L; WCL.

936 All is ours and our husbands. [*London*], *for P. Brooksby,* [1672–95]. brs. L, HH; MH.

All ordinances. 1646. *See* England. Parliament.

All persons. Dublin, 1662. *See* Ireland. Lord Lieutenant General.

937 All sorts of Bibles sold by Wm. and Ioseph Marshall. [*London*], [1680?] brs. OP.

938 All sorts of ye best shop books pocket books letter cases. [*London*], *sold by Ioseph Marshall,* [1680?] brs. OP.

939 All sorts of ye best shop books pockett books letter cases. *Sold by G: Rogers, London,* [1680?] brs. OP.

940 All sorts of well-affected persons, who desire a speedy end. [*n.p.,* 1643.] brs. LT; MH.

941 All such persons as have just cause to complaine. [1641.] brs. LT.

942 All that wish well to the safety of this kingdome. [1643.] brs. LT.

All the acts. [1652.] *See* England. Parliament.

All the chief points. 1697. *See* Marsin, M.

942A All the French psalm tunes with English words. [*London?* 1650.] 16°. L.

943 All the letters, memorials, and considerations, concerning the offered alliance. *For Robert Harford,* 1680. fol.* T.C.I 396. L, O, OC, EN; HR, CH, CLC, MH, WF, Y.

944 All the memorable & wonder-strikinge Parlamentary [sic] mercies. *Sould by Thomas Ienner,* [1642.] 4°.* LT; CH.

945 All the nine prophecies of the two famous prophets. *For Leonard Lane,* 1680. fol.* MH.

All the ordinances. 1642. *See* England. Parliament.

946 All the proceedings at the sessions of the peace holden at Westminster, on the 20. day of June, 1651. *By Thomas Harper,* 1651. 4°.* LT, LW; NU.

947 All the proceedings of His Excellency the Earl of Essex. *For Th. Tompson, October* 14, 1642. 4°.* LT; CN, IU, MH.

All the severall ordinances. 1644. *See* England. Parliament.

948 All the transactions between the noblemen and gentlemen now in arms. *Edinburgh, by Evan Tyler, and reprinted at London by John Field, Octob.* 17. 1648. 4°.* LT, CCA, HH; CLC, CU, WF, Y.

All things are dear. 1675. *See* W., L.

All these wel-affected creditors. [*London?* 1652.] *See* Chidley, Samuel.

949 All to Westminster. [*London*], *printed,* 1641. 4°.* LT, O, CT, MR; CU, MIU, NU.

950 All worthy commanders, officers, souldiers, ... of London. [1648.] brs. LT.

951 All worthy officers and soldiers, who are yet mindful. [1649.] brs. LT.

952 [**Allan,** .] A satyre upon F—s of D—r [Forbes of Disblair]. [1700.] brs. EN.

953 **Alle, Thomas.** A breif narration of the truth of some particulars. *By T. R. and E. M. for Ralph Smith,* 1646. 4°.* LT, GU, DT; CH, MB, NN, NU.

Allegations in behalf. 1690. *See* Morgan, Thomas.

Allegations made. [1687?] *See* Penn, William.

953A The allegations of the glass-makers examined. [*London?* 1694.] brs. L, LG.

954 The allegations of the Turkey company. 1681. fol.* L, O, OC, C; MBP, MH, MIU, NC, WF.

955 Allegiance and prerogative considered. [*Edinburgh? J. Reid*], 1689. 4°.* ALDIS 2857. L, EN; CLC, CN, NC, WF, Y.

956 —[Anr. ed.] *Edinburgh, printed,* 1689. *And reprinted at London, for Richard Janeway.* fol. T.C.II 255. L, C; CH, NN, NP, WF, Y.

957 Allegiance vindicated. *For Brabazon Aylmer,* 1690. 4°.* T.C.II 304. L, O, CT, EN, DT; CH, CLC, NU, WF, Y.

958 **Allein, Tobie.** Truthes manifest: or a full and faithful narrative. *For F. E.,* 1658. 8°.* O.

959 —Truths manifest revived. *By R. D. for Francis Eglesfield,* 1659. 8°. O, DT.

960 **Alleine, Joseph.** An alarme to unconverted sinners. 1671. 8°. LW.

961 ——[Anr. ed.] *By E. T. and R. H. and are to be sold by Nevil Simmons,* 1672. 8°. L, O, LCL, BR, YM; CLC, MH, NF, NU.

961A ——[Anr. ed.] *Printed, and are to be sold by Nevil Simmons,* 1672. 8°. O.

961B ——[Anr. ed.] —, 1673. 8°. L, CT.

962 ——[Anr. ed.] —, 1675. 8°. T.C.I 214. O, CP; CH, IU, WF.

963 ——[Anr. ed.] —, 1678. 8°. T.C.I 304. L; MH, WF, Y.

963A ——[Anr. ed.] *For T. Parkhurst,* 1691. 8°. LLL.

964 ——[Anr. ed.] *Edinburgh, by the heirs and successors of Andrew Anderson, to be sold by Matthew Duncan in Kilmarnock,* 1695. 12°. ALDIS 3438. L.

964A ——[Anr. ed.] *For T. Parkhurst,* 1696. 12°. BR.

965 [–] A call to Archippus. [London], printed, 1664. 4°.* L, O, LW, EN; CN, MH, NU, WF, Y.

966 [–] Christian letters. Printed for and sold by N. Simmons, 1673. 8°. L, O; CU, IU, TSM, Y.

967 —Mr Joseph Alleine's directions, for covenanting. For Nevil Simmons, 1674. brs. L.

968 —Divers practical cases of conscience satisfactorily resolved. For Nevill Simmons, 1672. 8°. L, O, LCL; CLC, MH, NU.

969 — —[Anr. ed.] —, 1673. 8°. EN.

970 — —[Anr. ed.] For Nevil Simmons, to be sold by Ralph Smith, 1675. 8°. O; CH, WF.

971 — —[Anr. ed.] Printed, and are to be sold by Nevil Simmons, 1678. 8°. L; MH.

972 — —[Anr. ed.] 1689. 8°. LCL.

973 —Hyfforddwr cyfarwydd i'r nefoedd. Printiedig yn Llundain gan Tho. Whitledge a W. Everingham, 1693. sixes. L, O, CPL, AN; CLC, MH.

974 —A most familiar explanation. For Edw. Brewster, 1672. 8°. L.

974A — —[Anr. ed.] —, 1674. 8°. L, O, C, BR; CH, NU, WF.

975 — —[Anr. ed.] 1682. 8°. T.C.II 345. L, O, LCL, BR; CLC.

975A — —[Anr. ed.] 1690. 8°. OC.

975B — —[Anr. ed.] Belfast, by Patrick Neill & company, 1700. 8°. L.

976 —Remaines. For Peter Parker, 1674. 8°. T.C.I 169. L, C, LW; CLC, MH, NU, WF, Y.

977 —A sure guide to Heaven. For Tho. Parkhurst, 1688. 12°. L.

978 — —[Anr. ed.] —, 1689. 12°. L, O, C, LCL; CLC, CU, NPT, NU.

979 — —[Anr. ed.] —, 1691. 12°. T.C.II 367. L, O; CLC, WF.

979A — —[Anr. ed.] —, 1696. 12°. O, BR.

980 — —[Anr. ed.] —, 1700. 12°. T.C.III 205. L.

981 —The true vvay to happiness. Printed, to be sold by Nevil Simmons, 1675. 8°. NU.

982 —The way to true happiness. Printed, and are to be sold by Nevil Simmons, 1678. 8°. O, LCL.

983 **A[lleine], R[ichard].** The best of remedies. 1667. 8°. O.

984 —Χειροθεσία του πρεσβυτερίου, or a letter. For J. S., 1661. 4°. L, O, C, BR, DT; CLC, MH, NU, TU, Y.

984A —A companion for prayer. For Thomas Cockerill, 1680. 8°.* CLC, Y.

985 —[Anr. ed.] By J. R. for T. C., 1684. 8°.* O, BR; NPT.

986 —Godly-fear. For Samuel Sprint and Brabazon Aylmer, 1674. 8°. T.C.I 185. L, O, LCL; MBC, NP, NU.

987 —The godly mans portion. 1662. 8°. LCL; MH, NF, NP.

988 — —[Anr. ed.] Printed, 1663. 8°. O, BR, EN, ENC, AU; CH, CU, MH, NU, WF.

989 — —[Anr. ed.] —, [1663]. 8°. L, O, LW, CT; CLC, CU, MH, NPT, WF, Y.

990 —Heaven opened. Printed, 1665. 8°. O, ON, LW, AN; CLC, MH, NU.

991 — —[Anr. ed.] —, 1666. 8°. L, O, LCL, DC, E; CH, CLC, CN, MH, NPT.

992 — —[Anr. ed.] For Peter Parker, 1671. 8°. ON; CLC, CU, MBC, NU, TU, Y.

993 — —[Anr. ed.] Boston: by B. Green & J. Allen, for Elkanah Pembrooke, 1699. 8°. EVANS 857. MB, MWA.

994 —Instructions about heart-work. For Jonathan Greenwood, 1681. 8°. T.C.I 451. O, LCL; CLC, NU, Y.

995 — —Second edition. By J. R. for Thomas Cockeril, 1684. 8°. L, O, LW, BR; CH, NPT, WF.

996 [–] A murderer punished and pardoned. 1668. 8°. L, O, LG, CT; CH, WF, Y.

996A — —Twelfth edition. —, 1669. 8°. L; CLC.

997 [–] —Thirteenth edition. 1671. 8°. L, O.

998 —Nature and necessity of godly fear. 1674. 8°. LW.

999 —A rebuke to backsliders. For J. Hancock, 1677. 8°. L, BR; CLC, MH, WF, Y.

1000 — —[Anr. ed.] By J. Astwood for John Hancock, 1684. 8°. T.C.II 54. L, O, LCL, EN; CU, MH, NU.

1001 — —[Anr. ed.] For H. Newman, 1694. 8°. T.C.II 518. LW; MH.

1002 —Vindiciæ pietatis. 1660. 4°. WSC.

1003 — —[Anr. ed.] Printed, 1663. 8°. L, O, AU; CH, NU.

1004 — —[Anr. ed.] —, 1664. 8°. L, O, CT, LW, EN; CLC, MH, NPT, NU, WF.

1005 — —[Anr. ed.] —, 1665. 8°. DT; Y.

1006 Entry cancelled.

1007 — —[Anr. ed.] For P. Parker, 1669. 8°. L, BR, ENC; CH, CLC, MHS, TSM.

1008 — —[Anr. ed.] For Peter Parker, 1676. 8°. L, LCL; CLC, CU, MH, NU, TU, WF.

1009 —The world conquered. Printed, 1668. 8°. L, O, LCL, DC, ENC; CH, MH, NU, WF, Y.

1010 — —[Anr. ed.] For Peter Parker, 1676. 8°. T.C.I 248. L, O, C; CU, NPT, NU, WF, Y.

1011 **[Alleine, Mrs. Theodosia.]** The life and death of Mr. Joseph Alleine. 1671. LW, DC; CLC, NPT.

1012 [–] The life and death of that excellent minister of Christ Mr. Joseph Alleine. [London], printed, 1672. 8°. L, LCL, LW, BR; NF, NU.

1013 [–] —[Anr. ed.] Lofdon [sic], for Nevil Simmon, 1672. 8°. T.C.I 123. O, CSS, N; CH, Y.

1013A [–] —[Anr. ed.] By J. Darby, for Nevil Simons; and by Dorman Newman, 1672. 8°. L, CS, BR; CLC, Y.

1014 [–] —[Anr. ed.] 1673. 8°. L, O, LIC; FSM.

1015 [–] —[Anr. ed.] For Nevil Simmons, and Thomas Sawbridge, 1677. 8°. T.C.I 297. L, O, LCL; MBP, NGT, WF.

1016 [–] —[Anr. ed.] By J. Darby, for N. Simons, 1693. 8°. CU.

1016A **Alleine, William.** Several discourses. Bristol, by Will. Bonny, for J. Alleine. 1697. 8°. O, BR; MBP, NPT, SN, WF.

1017 Αλληλοκρισια. A treatise concerning judging one another. For J. Wright, 1675. 8°. L, C; CH, WF, Y.

1018 **Allen, Benjamin.** The natural history of the chalybeat. Printed and sold by S. Smith and B. Walford, 1699. 8°. T.C.III 138. L, O, C, AM, DT; CLC, LC, NAM, WSG, HC.

1019 **[Allen, Charles.]** Curious observations in that difficult part. Dublyn, printed; and are to be sold in London, by William Whitwood, 1687. 4°. T.C.II 177. DIX 224. L, O, C, AM, DT; NAM.

1020 —The operator for the teeth. *York: by John White for the author,* 1685. 4°.* YM; PU.

1021 — [Anr. ed.] *Printed,* 1686. 4°. CT.

1022 — [Anr. ed.] *Dublin, Andrew Crook and Samuel Helsham, to be sold by Robert Thornton, and by the author.* [1686?] 4°. DIX 221. DT.

1023 **Allen, Daniel.** The moderate Trinitarian. *For Mary Fabian,* 1699. 4°.* L, LW, EC; CH, MH, NU, WF, Y.

1024 **Allen, Edward.** Vavasoris examen, & purgamen: or, . . . *For Thomas Brewster and Livewell Chapman,* 1654. 4°.* LT; MH, WF.

1025 **Allen, Hannah.** Satan his methods and malice baffled. *By John Wallis,* 1683. 8°. L, OB, LCL, LW; CLC, NPT, WF, Y.

1026 [**Allen, Isaac.**] Excommunicatio excommunicata. *By John Meacock, to be sold by Humphrey Moseley,* 1658. 4°. L, O, CT; NU.

[**Allen, J.**] Younger brother. *Oxford,* 1671. *See Ap-Robert, John.*

1027 **Allen, James.** Mans self-reflection. *Boston, by B. Green & J. Allen,* 1699. 8°.* EVANS 858. MBA, MH.

1027A —Neglect of supporting and maintaining the pure worship. *Boston, for Job How and John Allen, to be sold at Mr. Samuel Green's,* 1687. 4°.* EVANS 425. NN.

1028 —New-Englands choicest blessing. *Boston, by John Foster,* 1679. 4°.* EVANS 260. CH, MH, MHS, MWA, PRJ.

1029 [-] The principles of the Protestant religion maintained. *Boston, in New-England, by Richard Pierce,* 1690. 8°. EVANS 502. C; CH, MB, MH, NN, RPJ, Y.

1030 —Serious advice to delivered ones. *Boston, by John Foster,* 1679. 4°.* EVANS 261. MH, MHS, MWA, Y.

1031 — [Anr. ed.] *Boston, by John Foster, and sold by Edmund Ranger,* 1679. 4°.* EVANS 262. LW; MB, MHS, MU, PRJ.

1032 **Allen, John,** *bookseller.* Judicial astrologers totally routed. *For John Allen,* 1659. 8°.* LT, O, LWL; MH, Y.

1033 —Several cases of conscience, concerning astrologie. *Printed for, and to be sold by John Allen,* 1659. 8°.* LT.

1033A **Allen, John,** *ordinary of Newgate.* A full and true account of the behaviours, confessions, . . . of the condemn'd criminals. colop: *For E. Mallet,* [1700]. brs. L, O, HH; PL.

1034 **Allen, John,** *of Trinity College, Cambridge.* Of perjury, A sermon. *For Benj. Tooke, and George Atkinson, in Chester,* 1682. 4°.* T.C.I 482. L, O, C, DC, DT; CH, NU, V, WF, Y.

1035 **Allen, John,** *Reverend.* Animadversions upon the antisynodalia Americana. *Cambridge [Mass.]: by S. G. and M. J. for Hezekiah Usher of Boston,* 1664. 12°. EVANS 83. LC, MB, MHS, NN, V.

1036 —A defence of the answer. *By R. Cotes for Andrew Crooke,* 1648. 4°. L, C, CT, E, DT; LC, MH, NN, RPJ, Y.

1037 —The spouse of Christ. *Cambridge [Mass.]: by Samuel Green: and are to be sold by John Tappin of Boston,* 1672. 4°.* EVANS 165. CH, MH, MHS, MWA.

1038 —Their Majesties colony of Connecticut in New-England vindicated. *Boston, by Bartholomew Green,* 1694. 4°.* EVANS 686. CLC, MBA, MHS, MWA, RPJ.

1039 **Allen, Richard,** *Baptist.* A brief vindication of an essay. *For J. Harris, and Andrew Bell,* 1696. 8°. L, LLL.

1040 —An essay to prove singing of psalms. *By J. D. for John Harris,* 1696. 8°. L, O, OC; NPT, NR.

1041 —A gainful death. *For Andr. Bell, and M. Fabian,* 1700. 8°.* L, LW.

1042 **Allen, Richard,** *of Henfield, in Sussex.* A brief history of transubstantiation. *By J. Cotterel for the author, to be sold by Francis Kindon,* 1674. 4°.* L, C, CT; Y.

1043 —England's distempers, their cause and cure. *For the author, to be sold by Thomas Dring,* 1677. 4°.* L; CH, Y.

1044 —Insulæ fortunatæ. A discourse. *By J. C. for the author,* 1675. 4°.* O, SP, WCA; Y.

1045 **Allen, Richard,** *M.A.* An antidote against heresy. *By John Macock,* 1648. 8°. L, LCL.

1045A — [Anr. ed.] *By John Macock, to be sold by Nathaniel Brooks,* 1648. 8°. LT; Y.

1045B [**Allen, Robert.**] The cry of innocent blood. *[London], printed,* 1670. 4°.* L, O, C, LF, DT; CH, MH, NU, PSC, Y.

1045C —The cry of the oppressed for justice. *[London,* 1696.] brs. LG.

1046 **Allen, Thomas.** The glory of Christ. *By A. M. and R. R., for E. Giles in Norwich,* 1683. 8°. T.C.II 26. LCL; MB, NPT.

1047 —The way of the spirit. *Printed,* 1676. 8°. MB, MWA, NU.

1047A **Allen, Thomas,** *Minister.* A chain of scripture chronology. *By M. S. to be sold by John Allen,* 1658. 4°. MB.

1048 — [Anr. ed.] *By Tho. Roycroft, and are to be sold by Francis Tyton, and Nath. Ekins,* 1659. 4°. LT, O, C, LCL, YM; CLC, MH, WF, Y.

1049 — [Anr. ed.] *Printed, and are to be sold by John Allen,* 1668. 4°. L, O; MB, NP, Y.

1050 **Allen, Thomas,** *physician.* Χειρεξοκη. The excellency or handy-vvork. *By William Godbid for the author,* 1665. 4°.* L, O, LCP, LWL, GH; MH, WF.

1051 **Allen, William,** *Adjutant General.* The captive taken from the strong. *For Livewel Chapman,* 1658. 8°. L, O, LCL, LW; MB, NPT, Y.

1052 —A faithful memorial of that remarkable meeting. *For Livewel Chapman,* 1659. 4°.* LT, O, LG; MH, PL, WF.

1053 —A word to the army. *For Livewell Chapman,* 1660. 4°.* L, O, C, LVF; MH.

Allen, William, *pseud.* Killing no murder. *See Titus, Silas.*

1054 [**Allen, William**], *controversial writer.* Animadversions on that part of Robert Fergvson's book. *By T. R. for Walter Kettilby,* 1676. 8°. L, O, LCL, OC, OCC; MBA, NPT, NU, WF, Y.

1054A —An answer to Mr. J. G. his XL. queries. *For the author, and are to be sold by Hen Cripps, and L. Lloyd,* 1653. 4°. LT; NU.

1055 —Catholicism, or, Several enquiries. *By M. C. for Walter Kettilby,* 1683. 8°. T.C.II 1. L, O, C, AU, DT; CH, MBA, NU, PL, WF, Y.

1056 —Certain select discourses. *By S. H.,* 1699. fol. LW; NU, PU.

1057 —The Christians justification stated. *By A. C. for Walter Kettilby,* 1678. 8°. T.C.I 288. L, O, OC, CPE, BR; CH, MBA, NU, WF, Y.

1058 [–] The danger of enthusiasm discovered. *By J. D for Brabazon Aylmer,* 1674. 8°. T.C.I 162. L, O, CT, LF, DT; MH, NU, PH, WF, Y.

1059 —A discourse of divine assistance. *By M. C. for Walter Kettilby,* 1679. 8°. T.C.I 347. L, O, CT, LCL, ENC; CH, NC, NU, WF, Y.

1060 — —[Anr. ed.] *By Tho. Warren for Walter Kettilby,* 1693. 4°. L, O, LW; NPT, NU, PL.

1061 [–] A discourse of the nature, ends, and difference of the two covenants. *By J. Darby, for Richard Chiswell,* 1673. 8°. T.C.I 116. L, O, C, E, DT; CH, NC, NPT, NU, Y.

1062 —A discourse of the nature, series, and order of occurrences. *For Walter Kettilby,* 1689. 8°. T.C.II 284. L, O, CCA, LCL, LW; MBA, MH, NU, Y.

1063 —A doubt resolved. *By J. M. for H. Cripps, and L. Lloyd,* 1655. 4°.* L, AU, NMB; MH, MWA, NU.

1064 [–] A friendly call: or ... *For T. Basset and J. Leigh,* 1679. 4°. L, O, C, OC, DT; CH, IU, NU.

1065 —A glass of justification. *By G. Dawson, for Francis Smith,* 1658. 4°. LT, O, CT, LM, P; CLC, MH, NU, WF, Y.

1065A —The grand errour of the Quakers detected. *For Walter Kettilby,* 1680. 8°. T.C.I 380. L, LF; MH.

1065B —The last words and testimonies of. *Printed and sold by Benjamin Clark,* 1680. 8°.* LF.

1066 [–] The mystery of iniquity unfolded. *By J. M. for Walter Kettilby,* 1675. 8°. T.C.I 212, L, O, C, CT, E; CH, MH, NU, WF, Y.

1067 —Of the state of the church in future ages. *For Walter Kettilby,* 1684. 8°. T.C.II 67. L, O, C, CT, DT; CLC, MH, NU, WF, Y.

1068 —Persuasive to peace and unity. *For Brabazon Aylmer,* 1672. 8°. T.C.I 115. OCC, CT, AU, LW; MHS, NPT, NU, WF.

1069 — —Second edition. *For Walter Kettilby,* 1680. 8°. T.C.I 398. L, C, CT, LCL, DT; CN, MHS, NU, PL, VC.

1070 —A practical discourse of humility. *For Walter Kettilby,* 1681. 8°. T.C.I 457. L, C, CT, LCL, OC; CLC, NPT, NU, WF, Y.

1071 —A retraction of separation. *By M. S. for Henry Crips,* 1660. 4°. L, MAB, LG, LSC; NPT.

1072 —A serious and friendly address to the Non-Conformists. *By J. M. for Walter Kettilby,* 1676. 8°. T.C.I 234. L,˙O, C, OC; CH, NHC, NPT, NU, Y.

1073 — —Second edition. *By Tho. Warren for Walter Kettilby,* 1693. 8°. T.C.II 445. L, LW; NPT, NU, PL, VC.

1074 Entry cancelled.

1075 —Some baptismal abuses. *By J. M. for Henry Cripps, and Lodowick Lloyd,* 1653. 4°. LT, LCL, LW, EN; NHC, NU.

1076 [**Allen, William**], *Vicar of Bridgewater.* The mystery of the temple. *For B. Harris, to be sold at the Stationers Arms, and by T. Wall in Bristol,* 1677. 12°. L, O, C, P; IU, MH, WF.

1077 — —[Anr. ed.] —, 1679. 8°. L; MH, NU.

1078 —A practical improvement of the articles. *For J. Taylor, and J. Miller in Sherborne, and in Yeavill,* 1697. 4°.* T.C.III 35. L, CT, BR; WF, Y.

1079 —A sermon preacht ... February 27, 1680/1. *For G. S.,* 1681. 4°.* T.C.I 457. L; CH, WF, Y.

1080 **Allestree, Charles.** The desire of all men. *London, for Thomas Bennet, London, and Obediah Smith in Daventry,* 1694/5. 4°* T.C.II 547. L, O, C, OC, CT; CH, CN, MH, WF, Y.

1081 —A sermon preach'd ... 26th. of July 1685. *Oxford, for Henry Clements, and sold by Joseph Hindmarsh, London,* 1685. 4°. T.C.II 142. L, O, OC, BR; CH, MBA, WF, Y.

1081A — —[Anr. ed.] *By H. Hills, jun., for Joseph Hindmarsh,* 1685. 4°. OC; WF.

1081B [**Allestree, Richard.**] The works. *For B. Haite,* 1682. 12°. CT; NP.

1082 [–] The works. *Printed at the theater in Oxford, and in London, by Roger Norton, for George Pawlett,* 1684. 2 pts., fol. L, O, C, OC; CLC, LC, MH, NP, Y.

1083 [–] —Second edition. —, 1687. fol. O, C, BR, DC; CH, CU, MH, TU, WF, Y.

1084 [–] —Third edition. —, 1695. fol. O, C, BR, MR, DT; CLC, MBA, PPT, RBU.

1085 [–] The art of contentment. *At the theater in Oxford,* 1675. 8°. MADAN 3043. L, O, CT, E, DT; CH, CN, NU, WF, Y.

1086 [–] —Second edition. —, 1675. 8°. MADAN 3044. O, C, LW, OC; CH, MIU, V, Y.

1087 [–] —Third edition. —, 1675. 8°. MADAN 3045. L, O, C, LW; CH, CLC, TSM, Y.

1088 [–] —[Anr. ed.] *Glasgow, by Robert Sanders,* 1676. 8°. AU.

1089 [–] —Fourth edition. *At the theater in Oxford,* 1677. 8°. MADAN 3131. L, O, C, CK, DT; CH, CU, TU, WF, Y.

1090 [–] —Fifth edition. —, 1677. 8°. MADAN 3132. O; CH, V, WF, Y.

1091 [–] —[Anr. ed.] *Printed,* 1682. 12°. L, O; Y.

1092 [–] —[Anr. ed.] *At the theater in Oxford,* 1689. 8°. L, O; CLC, CN, PL, WF, Y.

1093 [–] —[Anr. ed.] —, 1694. 8°. L, O, CS; CLC, Y.

1094 [–] —[Anr. ed.] —, 1700. 8°. L, O, OC, EC, EN; CLC, TSM, Y.

1095 [–] The art of patience. *For W. Cademan,* 1684. 8°. T.C.II 58. L, O, P; CLC, WF, Y.

1096 [–] —Second edition. *By R. Smith for E. Mory,* 1694. 8°. T.C.II 551. L, O, C; CN.

1096A [–] The beauty of holiness. Fourth edition. *For Ben Crayle,* 1684. 8°. T.C.II 35. LSC; WF.

1097 [–] The causes of the decay. *By R. Norton for T. Garthwait,* 1667. 8°. L, O, C, DCH, EN; CLC, MH, TU, WF, Y.

1098 [–] —[Anr. ed.] —, 1668. 8°. L, O, C, E; CLC, NU, Y.

1099 [–] —[Anr. ed.] —, 1669. 8°. L, O, C, LCL, LW; CLC, TSM, Y.

1100 [–] —[Anr. ed.] *By R. Norton, for M. Garthwait,* 1671. 8°. L, DC, DT; CH, TU.

1101 [–] —[Anr. ed.] *By R. Norton for Robert Pawlett,* 1672. 8°. L, O, C, LG, LSC; CH, MH, NU, TU.

1102 [–] —[Anr. ed.] —, 1674. 8°. L, O, OC, BR; CSU.

1103 [–] —[Anr. ed.] —, 1675. 8°. L, O, CK, SP; CLC, NF, PL, WF, Y.

1104 [–] —[Anr. ed.] —, 1677. 8°. L, O, YM; CLC, CU, MH, V.

1105 [–] —[Anr. ed.] —, 1679. 8°. L, O, OB, CCA, EC; CLC, TU.
1106 [–] —[Anr. ed.] *Printed*, 1682. 12°. L, O, EN, DT; Y.
1107 [–] —[Anr. ed.] *By R. Norton for Robert Pawlett*, 1683. 8°. L, O, DT; CH, TU, WF, Y.
1108 [–] —[Anr. ed.] *By R. Norton for Edward Pawlett*, 1694. 8°. L, O, OC, CM, EC; CLC, CN, CU, TU, Y.
1109 [–] A discourse concerning the beauty of holiness. *By J. C. for Robert Sollers*, 1679. 8°. L, O, D; NU.
1109A [–] —Second edition. *For R. Sollers, to be sold by Stephen Foster*, 1680. 8°. T.C.I 376. CLC, Y.
1109B [–] —Third edition. *For Robert Sollers*, 1683. 8°. L.
1110 [–] A discourse concerning the period of humane life, *By H. C. for Enoch Wyer*, 1677. 8°. T.C.I 274. L, O, C, LCP, OC; CH, CLC, MH, WF.
1111 [–] —Second edition. *By J. R. for Enoch Wyer*, 1677. 8°. L, O, LW, CS, E; CH, MH, NPT, WSG, Y.
1111A [–] —Third edition. *To be sold by H. Bonwicke*, 1678. 8°. LSC.
1111B [–] A discourse, proving from scripture. *Printed, and are to be sold by H. Bonwicke*, 1680. 8°. T.C.I 397. C, SP.
1112 —The divine autority. *Oxford, at the theater*, 1673. 4°. T.C.I 147. MADAN 2965. L, O, C, CT, DT; CH, CN, MBA, NU, WF, Y.
1113 —Eighteen sermons. *By Tho. Roycroft, for James Allestry*, 1669. fol. T.C.I 17. L, O, CT, E, DT; CH, CU, MH, NU, WF, Y.
1114 —Forty sermons. *Printed at the theater in Oxford and in London, for R. Scott, G. Wells, T. Sawbridge, R. Bentley*, 1684. 2 pts., fol. T.C.II 89. L, O, C, E, DT; BN, CU, MU, NP, NU, Y.
1115 [–] The gentleman's calling. *For T. Garthwait*, 1660. 176 pp. 8°. LT, O, C, OC; CH, MH, NU, WF, Y.
1116 [–] —[Anr. ed.] —, 1660. 175 pp. 8°. L, O, OC, D; CH, CN, MU, TU, Y.
1117 [–] —Second edition. *By R. Norton for Timothy Garthwait*, 1662. 8°. C, BAMB, GK; CLC, CU, NC, WF, Y.
1118 [–] —[Anr. ed.] —, 1664. 8°. L, O; CLC, RPB, TU.
1119 [–] —[Anr. ed.] —, 1667. 8°. L, O, E; CLC, CU, WSC, Y.
1119A [–] —[Anr. ed.] *For R. Pawlett*, 1667. 8°. CU.
1120 [–] —[Anr. ed.] *By R. Norton, for T. Garthwait*, 1668. 8°. L, O, LW, E, LL; CLC, CN, NU, PBL, WF.
1121 [–] —[Anr. ed.] *By R. Norton, for M. Garthwait*, 1670. 8°. CH, TU.
1121A [–] —[Anr. ed.] *By R. Norton, for Robert Pawlet*, 1671. 8°. YM; Y.
1122 [–] —[Anr. ed.] —, 1672. 8°. O, C; CLC, NU, PU, TU, WF.
1123 [–] —[Anr. ed.] —, 1673. 8°. L, O, C, BR, ELY; CLC, CN, LC, MH, Y.
1124 [–] —[Anr. ed.] —, 1674. 8°. L, O, C, OC, EC; CLC, TU, Y.
1125 [–] —[Anr. ed.] —, 1676. 8°. L, O, C; CLC, VC, WF, Y.
1126 [–] —[Anr. ed.] —, 1677. 8°. O, CE, DT; CH, MH, NC, TU, Y.
1127 [–] —[Anr. ed.] —, 1679. 8°. L, O, CM, DT, GK; CH, NU, PL, TU, WF.
1128 [–] —[Anr. ed.] —, 1682. 8°. L, O, M; CH, CLC, LC, Y.
1129 [–] —[Anr. ed.] —, 1687. 8°. L, O, LVD; CLC, V.

1130 [–] —[Anr. ed.] *By Edward Jones, for Edward Pawlet*, 1696. 8°. L, O, OC, CS, EC; CSU, MH, PL, V, WF.
1131 [–] The government of the thoughts. *By R. Smith for R. Cumberland*, 1694. 8°. T.C.II 471. L, O, C, DC; CH, CLC, CN, WF, Y.
1132 [–] —Second edition. *For John Marshall*, 1700. 4°. CH, CLC, MH.
1133 [–] The government of the tongue. *At the theater in Oxford*, 1674. 4°. MADAN 3001. O, OC, CS, E; CH, NU, Y, JF.
1134 [–] —Second edition. —, 1674. 4°. MADAN 3002. L, O, C, BR; CLC, CN, WF, Y.
1135 [–] —Third edition. —, 1675. 8°. MADAN 3046. L, O, C, OB, DT; CH, CN, LC, NU, Y.
1136 [–] —Fourth edition. —, 1675. 8°. MADAN 3047. L, O, CS, EC, DT; CH, MH, PL, WF, Y.
1137 [–] —Fifth edition. —, 1667[1677]. 12°. MADAN 3133*. L, O, C, OC, GK; CH, CN, TU, Y.
1138 [–] —"Fifth" edition. —, 1667[1677]. 8°. MADAN 3133. L, O, D; CH, TU, Y.
1139 [–] —"Fifth" edition. —, 1693. 8°. T.C.II 471. L, O, OC, EN; CLC, NS, NU, Y.
1140 [–] Holl ddled-swydd dyn. *For R. Royston*, 1672. 8°. T.C.I 85. L, O, C, AN, E; MH.
1141 [–] The ladies calling. *Oxford, at the theater*, 1673. 8°. MADAN 2960–2. L, O, C, OC, E; CH, CU, MH, NP, WF, Y.
1142 [–] —Second edition. *At the theater in Oxford*, 1673. 8°. in 4's. MADAN 2963–4. L, O, C, DC, E; CLC, CN, MH, PL, WF, Y.
1143 [–] —Third edition. —, 1675. 8°. MADAN 3048. L, O, C, BR, DT; CLC, NC, TU, VC, Y.
1143A [–] —[Anr. ed.] *Edinburgh, J. Glen*, 1675. 12°. EN; NN.
1144 [–] —Fourth edition. *At the theater in Oxford*, 1676. 4°. MADAN 3094. O, C, DT, GK; CH, CLC, NC, TU, Y.
1145 [–] —Fifth edition. —, 1677. 8°. MADAN 3134. L, O, LSC, EC; CLC, CN, MH, WF, Y.
1146 [–] —"Fifth" edition. —, 1677. 4°. MADAN 3135. L, O; CH, NC, PL, Y.
1147 [–] —Sixth edition. —, 1693. 4°. L, O, CS, A; CH, CLC, TU, Y.
1148 [–] —Seventh edition. —, 1700. 2 pts., 8°. L, O, OC, EC; CLC, TU, WF, Y.
1149 [–] The lively oracles. *At the theater in Oxford*, 1678. 8°. T.C.I 329. MADAN 3169. L, O, CM, EN, DT; CH, CU, MH, NU, TU, WF, Y.
1150 [–] —Second edition. —, 1678. 8°. MADAN 3170. CS; CH, MH, PL, TSM, WWC, Y.
1151 [–] —"Second" edition. —, 1678. 8°. MADAN 3171. O; CLC, TSM, Y.
1152 [–] —Third edition. —, 1679. 8°. MADAN 3203. L, O, C, EN, DT; CLC, MB, TU, Y.
1153 [–] —[Anr. ed.] *[Oxford], printed*, 1682. 12°. O; Y.
1154 [–] —"Third" edition. *Printed at the theatre in Oxford, to be sold by George Monke, and William Ewrey*, 1688. 8°. O, C, EN.
1155 [–] —[Anr. ed.] *At the theater in Oxford*, 1696. 8°. O, OC; CLC, CN, TU, WF, Y.

—A new almanack. [1641]. *See* Almanacs.

1156 [–] Officium hominis. *Pro Roberto Pawlet,* 1680. 8°. L, O, LW, EN; CLC, CN, LC, MH, NPT, Y.

1157 [–] —[Anr. ed.] *Pro Edvardo Pawlet,* 1693. 8°. O, CM, BR; CH, CLC, NPT, WF, Y.

1158 [–] The practice of Christian graces. *By D. Maxwell for T. Garthwait,* 1658. 8°. O; CH, CLC.

1159 [–] —[Anr. ed.] *For T. Garthwait,* 1659. 8°. L, O, C; CH, CLC.

1160 [–] —[Anr. ed.] [1660.] 8°. O; WF.

1160A [–] La pratique des vertues chrétiens. *For R. Everingham,* 1686. 12°. CH, CLC, WF.

1161 [–] Private devotions for several occasions. *For T. Garthwait,* 1660. 8°. LT, O, CSE; CH, CLC, WF.

1161A [–] Scala sancta: or, the exaltation of the soul. *By T. Snowden, for Gab. Kunholt,* 1678. 8°. LLL; CLC, NU, WF.

1162 — —[Anr. ed.] *For Richard Wild,* 1692. 8°. O, LW; NPT.

1163 —A sermon preached . . . Jan. 6, 1660. *For Jo. Martin, Ja. Allestry, and Tho. Dicas,* 1660. 4°.* L, O, LL, CT, HH; CN, MH, NU, Y.

1164 —A sermon preached . . . 29th of May 1662. *By J. Flesher for John Martin, James Allestry, and Thomas Dicas,* 1662. 4°. L, O, CPE, EC; CLC, NU, MH, Y.

1165 —A sermon preached . . . October the 12th, 1662. *By Tho. Roycroft, for John Martin, and James Allestrey,* 1663. 4°.* L, O, CT, DC, LL; CH, CU, NU, TU, WF, Y.

1166 —A sermon preach'd before the King Decemb. 31, 1665. *Oxford, by W. Hall for J. Allestree [London], and R. Davis,* 1666. 4°.* MADAN 2736. L, O, CT, OC, YM; CLC, NU, WF, Y.

1166A — —[Anr. ed.] *Oxford, by W. Hall for John Martyn and James Allestry,* 1666. 4°.* EC; CH.

1167 —A sermon preached . . . Nov. 17, 1667. *By J. Flesher, for James Allestree,* 1667. 4°.* L, O, C, OC, LL; CH, CN, NU, WF, Y.

1168 [–] The vanity of the creature. *For J. Kidgell,* 1684. 8°. T.C.II 58. L, O, C; CLC, NP, WF, Y.

1168A [–] The whole duty of divine meditation. *For John Back,* 1694. 12°. IU, KU.

1169 [–] The whole dvty of man. *For Timothy Garthwait,* [1658]. 8°. LT, O, LSC; WF.

1170 [–] —[Anr. ed.] —, 1659. 8°. L, O, C; CLC.

1171 [–] —[Anr. ed.] —, 1661. 8°. C, CT.

1172 [–] —[Anr. ed.] —, 1663. 8°. O, CT.

1173 [–] —[Anr. ed.] *By R. Norton for T. Garthwait,* 1664. 12°. L, O.

1173A [–] —[Anr. ed.] —, 1667. 12°. PL.

1174 [–] —[Anr. ed.] —, 1668. 12°. L, O, OC.

1175 [–] —[Anr. ed.] —, 1669. 12°. L, LG.

1176 [–] —[Anr. ed.] *For M. Garthwait,* 1670. 12°. L.

1176A [–] —[Anr. ed.] —, 1671. 12°. O.

1176B [–] —[Anr. ed.] *By R. Norton for Robert Pawlett,* 1671. 12°. YM; Y.

1177 [–] —[Anr. ed.] —, 1673. 12°. O, OC, ELY; CLC, MH, Y.

1177A [–] —[Anr. ed.] —, 1674. 12°. L.

1178 [–] —[Anr. ed.] *For William Miller,* 1674. brs. L.

1179 [–] —[Anr. ed.] *By R. Norton, for Robert Pawlet,* 1675. 8°. C, LCL; CLC, WG.

1180 [–] —[Anr. ed.] —, 1676. 12°. C.

1181 [–] —[Anr. ed.] —, 1677. 8°. L, O, C, OC, DT; CH, NU, RPB, Y.

1182 [–] —[Anr. ed.] —, 1678. 8°. L, O; CH, CLC, CN.

1183 [–] —[Anr. ed.] *Edinburgh, J. Swintoun,* 1678. 12°. ALDIS 2144. I.

1184 [–] —[Anr. ed.] *Glasgow,* 1678. 12°. ALDIS 2145. O.

1184A [–] —[Anr. ed.] *By R. Norton for Robert Pawlet,* 1679. 8°. PU.

1185 [–] —[Anr. ed.] —, 1680. 12°. L, O, OB; WF.

1185A [–] —[Anr. ed.] —, 1681. 12°. CLC, WF.

1185B [–] —[Anr. ed.] —, 1682. 8°. EC; IU, MB, NGT, NU.

1185C [–] —[Anr. ed.] —, 1683. 8°. CSE.

1186 [–] —"Third" edition. *By R. Norton, for George Pawlet,* 1684. 8°. L, O, C, LL; CH, LC, MH.

1186A [–] —[Anr. ed.] —, 1685. 8°. L; Y.

1187 [–] —[Anr. ed.] —, 1687. fol. O, RPL; CLC, MH, TU, Y.

1188 [–] —[Anr. ed.] —, 1689. 12°. O.

1188A [–] —[Anr. ed.] —, 1690. 12°. L, LIC.

1189 [–] —[Anr. ed.] —, 1691. 12°. C.

1190 [–] —[Anr. ed.] —, 1692. 12°. O.

1191 [–] —[Anr. ed.] *By R. Norton for Edward Pawlet,* 1694. 12°. O, DT; LC.

1191A [–] —[Anr. ed.] —, 1695. 12°. NN, Y.

1192 [–] —[Anr. ed.] —, 1696. 12°. L, O, EN; CLC, NU, Y.

1192A [–] —[Anr. ed.] —, 1698. 8°. L; CLC.

1192B [–] —[Anr. ed.] *Dublin, by John Brocas,* 1699. 8°. DN; IU.

1193 [–] —[Anr. ed.] *By W. Norton for Edward Pawlet,* 1700. 8°. O, C, LW; PBL, Y.

1193A [–] The whole duty of man epitomized. *For John Laurence,* 1700. 12°. WF.

1194 [–] The whole duty of mourning. [*London*], *for J. Back,* [1695]. 12°. T.C.II 548. L, O, C; CH, MB, Y.

1194A [–] —Second edition. —, 1696. 12°. Y.

1195 [–] The whole duty of prayer. *For J. Back,* 1692. 12°. T.C.II 401. O.

1195A [–] —Second edition. —, 1693. 12°. Y.

1196 **Allestree, Thomas.** Epaphroditus's sickness. *For the author,* 1671. 8°. L, O, CT; CH, CU, MH, NU, WF, Y.

1197 —A funeral handkerchief. *For the author,* 1671. 2 pts., 8°. T.C.I 79. L, O, CT, EC, YM; CH, CU, MH, NU, WF, Y.

1198 — —[Anr. ed.] *For the author, and sold by Geo. Conyers,* 1692. 8°. T.C.II 392. C.

1199 **Alleyn, E.** A catalogue of the noblemen and peers. *For the author,* 1662. brs. O.

1200 **Alleyn, Thomas.** An elegie upon . . . Coll. Rainsborow. *Printed at London for Robert Ibbtison,* 1648. brs. LT; MH, Y.

1201 [**Alleyn, Thomas.**] The old Protestants letanie. [*London*], *printed,* 1647. 4°.* LT, O; CH, MH, Y.

1202 [**Allibond, John.**] Rustica academiæ Oxoniensis nuper Reformatæ descriptio. [*London?*], 1648. cap., fol.* MADAN 1993. O, OM; MM, Y.

1203 [–] —Second edition. [*London?*], 1648. brs. MADAN 1994. O; Y.

1204   ——[Anr. ed.] *Impensis G. Redmayne*, [1700?] 4°.* MADAN 1994. L, O, OC, CPE, GH; MH, NN, RPB, WF, Y.

Allin. See **Allen.**

1205   Entry cancelled.

1206   **A[llington], J[ohn].** A brief apologie for the sequestred clergie. *Printed*, 1649. 4°.* LT, O, CT, ENC, DT; CH, MH, NU, WF, Y.

1207   —A continuation of the grand conspiracy. [*London, for R. Royston*, 1660.] 12°. LT, C; CH, NPT, NU, WF.

1208   —The grand conspiracy of the members. *By J. G. for R. Royston*, 1653. 12°. LT, O; CLC, MIU, NU.

1209   ——"Tihrd" [sic] edition. *By E. C. for R. Royston*, 1654. 12°. L, O; CH, CN, NU, WF, Y.

1209A ——[Anr. ed.] *By J. G. for R. Royston*, 1654. 12°. C, CT.

1210   ——Fourth edition. *By E. C. for R. Royston*, 1655. 12°. EN; CLC.

1211   ——Fifth edition. *For R. Royston*, 1657. 12°. L, C, SC; NU, OWC.

1212   —The period. *By J. Grismond*, 1663. 12°. CT; Y.

1213   —The reform'd Samaritan. *By J. C. for Thomas Basset*, 1678. 2 pts., 4°. T.C.I 300. L, O, C, CT; MH, NU, PL, WF.

1214   —The regal proto-martyr. *By J. W. for W. Gilbert*, 1672. 4°.* T.C.I 95. L, O, LL, CT, EN; CH, CLC, MIU, WF, Y.

1215   **Allison, John.** Existentia Dei probatur. [1670.] brs. O.

1216   —Upon the late lamentable fire in London. *For H. Brome*, 1667. LG, EN; CH, CN, MH, Y.

1217   **Allison, Thomas.** An account of a voyage from Archangel in Russia in . . . 1697. *For D. Brown; and R. Parker*, 1699. 8°. T.C.III 138. L, O, EN, DT; CH, CN, MH, TU, WF, Y.

    [Allix, Pierre.] Account of the persecutions. 1686. See Claude, Jean.

1218   [–] Animadversions on Mr. Hill's book. *For Ri. Chiswell*, 1695. 4°. L, O, CS, EC, D; MH, NU, WF, Y.

1219   [–] A defence of the brief history of the Unitarians. *Printed*, 1691. 4°. L, O, C, OCC; CH, CN, MH, NU, WF, Y.

1220   [–] A discourse concerning penance. *For Richard Chiswell*, 1688. 4°.* T.C.II 271. L, O, C, EN, DT; CLC, MH, NU, TU, WF, Y.

1221   [–] A discourse concerning the merit of good works. *For Richard Chiswell*, 1688. 4°.* T.C.II 271. L, O, C, EN, DT; CLC, CU, MH, NU, TU, WF, Y.

    [–] Eclaircissements. 1687. See Jurieu, Pierre.

1222   [–] An examination of the scruples of those who refuse to take the oath. *For Richard Chiswell*, 1689. 4°.* L, O, C, EN, DT; CH, MH, NC, NU, WF, Y.

    [–] Fathers vindicated. 1697. See Deacon, J.

1223   [–] An historical discourse concerning the necessity of the ministers intention. *For Richard Chiswell*, 1688. 4°. L, O, C, E, DT; CLC, MH, NU, TU, WF, Y.

1224   [–] The judgment of the ancient Jewish church. *For Ri. Chiswell*, 1699. 8°. T.C.III 150. L, O, C, ENC, DT; BN, CH, MH, NU, WF, Y.

1225   [–] A letter to a friend concerning the behaviour of Christians. *For Rich. Chiswell*, 1693. 4°.* T.C.II 456. L, O, C, EN, DT; CN, MIU, NU, Y.

1226   —A preparation for the Lord's supper. *For Brab. Aylmer*, 1688. 8°. T.C.II 297. L, O, C, OM, NPL; CLC, MH, NU, WF, Y.

1227   —Reflexions upon the books of the Holy Scripture. *For Richard Chiswell*, 1688. 8°. L, O, C, EN, DT; CLC, LC, MH, NU, WF, Y.

1228   [–] Reflexions sur les cinq livres de Moyse. *Chés B. Griffin, pour Jean Cailloue*, 1687. 8°. L, O, CPE, ENC, DT; BN, CLC, NPT, WF.

1229   Entry cancelled.

1230   —Remarks upon the ecclesiastical history of the . . . Albigenses. *For Richard Chiswell*, 1692. 4°. T.C.II 378. L, O, C, AU, DT; BN, CH, MH, NU, WF, Y.

1231   —Some remarks upon the ecclesiastical history of the ancient churches of Piedmont. *For Richard Chiswell*, 1690. 4°. T.C.II 320. L, O, C, EN, DT; BN, CLC, MH, NU, WF, Y.

    Allwyd neu agoriad. *Luyck*, 1670. See Hughes, John.

    Almagesti botanici. 1700. See Plunkenet, Leonard.

ALMANACS

1231A **A. J.** A new prognostication for . . . 1667. *Edinburgh*, 1667. 8°. L.

1231B ——1668. —, 1668. 8°. L.

1231C ——1670. —, *James Glen*, 1670. 8°. L.

1232   **A., M.** Merlinus Anglicus, or, Englands Merlin: . . . 1650. *By Robert Wood*, 1650. 4°.* LT, O; CH, CLC, MH.

1232A **Abendano, Isaac.** An almanack for the year of Christ, 1692. *Oxford, at the theater*, 1692. 8°. OC.

1233   ——1693. —, [1693]. sixes. O, C, OC; Y.

1233A ——1694. —, [1694]. sixes. O, OC, CT.

1234   ——1695. —, 1695. sixes. O, CT, LG, DC; WF, Y.

1235   ——1696. —, 1696. sixes. O, CT.

1235A ——1697. —, [1697]. sixes. O, CT.

1236   ——1698. —, [1698]. sixes. O, CT; WF.

1237   —The Jewish kalendar. 1699.* O, C; CH, CLC, Y.

1238   Aberden's new almanack for the year of our Lord, 1682. *Iohn Forbes printer to Bon-Accord*, 1682. 8°.* ALDIS 2320. EN, ES.

1239   Aberdeen's true almanack. *Printed in Aberdeen, by Iohn Forbes*, [1685]. 8°.* ALDIS 2500. ES.

1240   **Adams, Jack.** Jack Adams, his perpetual almanack. *For the author*. 1662. 8°. O; WF.

1241   ——1663. 8°. CHRISTIE-MILLER.

1242   **Allestree, Richard.** Allestree, 1641. A new almanack . . . for . . . 1641. *Printed at London, by T. Cotes for the company of stationers*, [1641]. 8°.* O, DT.

1243   ——1642. *By R. Cotes for the company of Stationers*, [1642]. 8°.* O.

1244   ——1643. —, [1643]. 8°.* L, O.

1245   ——1651. —, 1651. 8°.* O.

1246   An almanack but for one day. *Glasgow, by Robert Sanders*, 1671. 8°.* ALDIS 1919. EN.

1246A —[Same title]. *For J. Clarke, W. Thackeray, and T. Passinger* [1686]. 8°.* L.

1246B An almanack for two days. *For J. Clarke, W. Thackeray, and T. Passinger* [c 1680]. 8°.* CM.

1247 An almanack. *Printed in Aberdene by John Forbes* [1666]. 4°.* L.

1247A An almanack for ... 1648. 1648. O.

   Almanack for ... 1650. Cambridge [Mass.], 1650. *See under* Almanacs, Oakes, Urian.

   Almanack for ... 1653. Oxford, 1653. *See under* Almanacs, Burton, W.

   An almanack, MDCLVI. Cambridge [Mass.], 1656. *See under* Almanacs, Shepherd Thomas.

   Almanack for ... 1660. Cambridge [Mass.], 1660. *See under* Almanacs, Cheever, Samuel.

   1669. An almanack. Cambridge [Mass.], 1669. *See under* Almanacs, Browne, Joseph.

   1670. An almanack. Cambridge [Mass.], 1670. *See under* Almanacs, Richardson, John.

   1671. An almanack. Cambridge [Mass.], 1671. *See under* Almanacs, Russell, Danniel.

1247B An almanack for ... 1673. 1673. brs. O.

   1674. An almanack. Cambridge [Mass.], 1674. *See under* Almanacs, Sherman, John.

   1678. An almanack. Cambridge [Mass.], 1678. *See under* Almanacs, Brattle, Thomas.

   1678. An almanack. Boston, 1678. *See under* Almanacs, Foster, John.

   An almanack ... for ... 1679. Cambridge [Mass.], 1679. *See under* Almanacs, Danforth, John.

1248 Almanack for ye year of our Lord, 1692. *For the company of stationers,* [1692]. 8°.* Y.

   1694. An almanack. Boston, 1694. *See under* Almanacs, Brattle, William.

1248A An almanack for the year of Christ, 1696. *Oxford, at the theatre,* 1696. 12°. LWL, OP.

1249 1680. An almanack of coelestial motions. *Printed for, and sold by Henry Phillips in Boston,* 1680. 4°.* MWA.

1249A —[Anr. ed.] *For John Usher of Boston,* 1680. 16°.* MHS.

1249B An almanack or, a new prognostication for 1695. *Edinburgh, Reid,* 1695. 8°.* EN.

1250 **Andrews, William.** Coelestes observationes: or An ephemeris, for ... 1669. *By Thomas Ratcliffe and Thomas Daniel for the company of stationers,* 1669. 8°.* L, O; CU, WF.

1251 — —1670. —, 1670. 8°.* O.

1252 — —1671. —, 1671. 8°.* O.

1253 —Andrewes. 1655. The caelestial [sic] observator. *By T. R. and E. M. for the company of stationers,* 1655. 8°.* O.

1254 — —1656. —, 1656. 8°.* O.

1255 —The coelestiall observator ... for ... 1657. *By S. Griffin for the company of stationers,* 1656. 8°.* O.

1256 —De rebus cælestibus, 1658, or an ephemeris. *By S. Griffin,* 1658. 8°.* O.

1257 —De rebus cœlestibus, or an ephemeris ... for ... 1659. *By Tho. Ratcliffe, for the company of stationers,* 1659. 8°.* O.

1258 — —1662. —, 1662. 8°.* L, O; WF.

1259 — —1663. —, 1663. 8°.* L, O, C; PAP.

1260 — —1664. —, 1664. 8°.* O; Y.

1261 —News from the stars, ... for ... 1660. *By Tho. Ratcliffe, for the company of stationers,* 1660. 8°.* O.

1262 — —1661. —, 1661. 8°.* O, C.

1263 — —1665. —, 1665. 8°.* O.

1264 — —1666. —, 1666. 8°.* L, O, C.

1265 — —1667. —, 1667. 8°.* L, O, C, LWL; MH.

1266 — —1668. —, 1668. 8°.* O; MH.

1267 — —1669. —, 1669. 8°.* C; PAP.

1267A — —1670. —, 1670. 8°. O.

1268 — —1672. *By Thomas Ratcliffe and Mary Daniel, for the company of stationers,* 1672. 8°.* L, O; PAP.

1269 — —1673. *By Thomas Ratcliffe and Nathaniel Thompson, for the company of stationers,* 1673. 8°.* O.

1270 — —1674. *By S. S. for the company of stationers,* 1674. 8°.* L, O, C; WF.

1271 — —1675. —, 1675. 8°.* O, LG; WF.

1272 — —1676. —, 1676. 8°.* L, O; WF, Y.

1273 — —1677. —, [1677]. 8°.* L, O; PAP.

1274 — —1678. *By J. Grover for the company of stationers,* [1678]. 8°.* L, O, EN; WF, HC.

1275 — —1679. —, [1679]. 8°.* O, C; MH, PAP, WF.

1276 — —1680. *By N. Thompson for the company of stationers,* [1680]. 8°.* L, O, C, LG; CH, CLC, WF, Y.

1277 — —1681. *By J. G. for the company of stationers,* 1681. 8°.* L, O, C, LWL; WF.

1278 — —1682. —, 1682. 8°.* O, C; PAP, WF.

1279 — —1683. *By A. G. for the company of stationers,* 1683. 8°.* O, C; CH, TU, WF, Y.

1280 — —1684. —, 1684. 8°.* L, O, C, LG; MB, MH, TU, WF, Y.

1281 — —1685. —, 1685. 8°.* O; MIU, WF.

1282 — —1686. —, 1686. 8°.* O, C; MH, WF.

1283 — —1687. —, 1686. 8°.* L, O, OP, CS; CN, WF, Y.

1284 — —1688. —, 1688. 8°.* T.C.II 238. O, C, LG, EO; HC, Y.

1285 — —1689. *By Eliz. Webster, for the company of stationers,* 1689. 8°.* L, O, C; CLC, MB, MH.

1286 — —1690. *By William Bonny for the company of stationers,* 1690. 8°.* L, O; MH, WF.

1287 — —1691. —, 1691. 8°.* L, O; Y.

1288 — —1692. *By W. and J. Wilde, for the company of stationers,* 1692. 8°.* L, O, C; CH, WF, Y.

1289 — —1693. —, 1693. 8°.* L, O, CH.

1290 — —1694. —, 1694. 8°.* L, O, C, LG, EN; CH, MH, PAP.

1291 — —1695. —, 1695. 8°.* L, O, C; CH, Y.

1292 — —1696. —, 1696. 8°.* L, O, C; CH, MH.

1293 — —1697. —, 1697. 8°.* L, O; CH, MH, PAP, WF.

1294 — —1698. —, 1698. 8°.* L, O, C; CH, MH, WF.

1295 — —1699. —, 1699. 8°.* L, O, C; CH, MH.

1296 — —1700. *By M. and J. Wilde, for the company of stationers,* 1700. 8°.* L, O, C; CH, MH, Y.

1297 —Physical observations for ... 1671. *By E. Crowch, for Thomas Vere,* 1671. 4°.* T.C.I 65. L, O, C.

1298   **Ashwell, Samuel.** Ashwell. 1641. A new almanacke ... for ... 1641. *Printed at London by Tho. Cotes, for the company of stationers,* [1641]. 8°.* L, O, DT.

1299   — —1642. *Printed at London by Rich. Cotes, for the company of stationers,* [1642]. 8°.* O; CLC.

1300   — —1643. —, [1643]. 8°.* L, O.

1301   —Entry cancelled.

1302   Astronomical observations and predictions for ... 1691. 1690. 4°. L.

1303   **Atkins, Samuel.** Kalendarium Pennsilvaniense; or, America's messinger. *Printed and sold by William Bradford in Philadelphia in Pennsilvania,* 1685. 8°.* PHS.

1304   — —*Printed and sold by William Bradford, sold also by the author and H. Murrey in Philadelphia, and Philip Richards in New York,* 1685. 8°. EVANS 382. PHS.

1305   **Atkinson, Charles.** Panterpe: or, ... *By T. Milbourn for the company of stationers,* 1670. 8°.* O.

1306   —Panterpe: id est. ... *For the company of stationers,* 1671. 8°.* O.

1307   —Panterpe: or, A pleasant almanack for ... 1672. *By Thomas Milbourn for the company of stationers,* 1672. 8°.* L, O. E.

1308   — —, 1673. —, 1673. 8°.* O.

1308A   — —, 1674. —, 1674. 8°.* O.

1309   **Atlee, Richard.** Εφημερις, sive almanack: or, A diurnall. *By John Dawson, for the company of stationers,* [1647]. 8°.* L, O.

1309A   **B., G.** Kalendarium Julianum. *Typis E. Cotes, venales prostant apud Sam. Thompson* [1666]. 8°. CCL, WCA.

1310   **Baston, James.** Mercurius hermeticus ... for ... 1657. *By T. C. for the company of stationers,* 1656. 8°.* O.

1311   —Mercurij hermetici ephemeris; or, An almanack, for ... 1659. *By Jane Bell, for the company of stationers,* 1659. 8°.* O.

1312   **Beridge, Ferdinando.** ό͑ι Δωδεκομζωοι: or, An almanack for 1654. *For the company of stationers,* 1654. 8°.* O.

1313   **Bird, Thomas.** Speculum anni, or a glasse of the year 1661. *By S. Griffin for the company of stationers,* 1661. 8°.* L, O, C.

1314   — —1662. *By E. Cotes, for the company of stationers,* [1662]. 8°.* L, O; WF.

1315   A black-almanack. *By J. Clowes,* 1651. 8°.* LT.

1316   The black Dutch almanack. *Print* [sic] *at Amsterdam, and reprinted at L* [sic] *by J. Clowes,* 1651. 8°.* LT.

1317   **Blagrave, Joseph.** Blagrave's ephemeris for 1659. *By J. C. for the company of stationers,* [1658]. 8°. LT, O; CU.

1318   — —1660. *For Nathanael Brook,* 1660. 8°.* L.

1319   — —1665. *By Thomas Milbourn, for the company of stationers,* [1665]. 8°.* O.

1319A   The bloody almanack. *For A. Vincent,* 1699. 4°. CT.

1320   The bloody almanack for ... 1666. [*London*], *William Roberts,* 1666. 4°.* L, HH; MIU.

1320A   The bloody almanack, or England's looking-glass, 1651. 4°.* LT.

1321   [**Blount, Thomas.**] Calendarium catholicum; or, an universall almanack, 1661. 1661. 12°.* O, LIL, CCL.

1322   [–] —1686. *Printed* 1686. 8°.* L, O, EC; PL.

1323   [–] —1689. *By Henry Hills,* 1689. 8°. L, O; MH, WF, Y.

1324   [–] A new almanack, after the old fashion, for 1663. 1663. 12°. O.

1325   **Blunt, Gabriel.** An almanack for ... 1656. *By Joh. Streater, for the company of stationers,* 1656. 8°.* O.

1326   — —1657. *For the company of stationers,* [1657]. 8°.* O.

1327   Bon-Accord's ephemeris, ... 1684. *Aberdeen, by Iohn Forbes,* [1684]. 8°.* ALDIS 2446. ES.

1328   **Booker, John.** Almanack et prognosticon. [*Londini*], *by F. K. for the company of stationers,* 1641. 8°.* L, DT.

1329   —M.D.C.XLII. —. —, [1642]. 8°.* L, O.

1330   —1643. —. —, [1643]. 8°.* L, O.

     —Bloody almanack. *See under* Almanacs, Napier, John.

1331   —A bloody Irish almanack. *Printed at London, for John Partridge,* 1646. 4°. LT, O, C, EC, DT; CLC, CN, LC, MH, Y.

1332   —Celestiall observations: ... 1651. *By F. K. for the company of stationers,* 1651. 8°.* O; CU.

1333   — —1652. *By R. Cotes, for the company of stationers,* 1652. 8°.* LT.

1334   — —1653. *By E. Cotes for the company of stationers,* 1653. 8°.* L, O, DT.

1334A   —Mercurius cœlicus, or a caveat. *By J. Raworth, for John Partridge,* 1644. 4°. L, O, HH; WF.

1335   —Mercurius cœlicus, sive almanack ... 1645. *By F. K. for the company of stationers,* [1645]. 8°.* O.

1336   — —1646. —, [1646]. 8°.* O; CH, WF.

1337   — —1647. [*London,* 1647.] 8°.* L, O.

1338   [–] The new bloody almanack for ... 1644. *By John Hammond,* 1643[4]. 4°.* LT, HH.

1339   [–] —1645. —, 1645. 4°.* LT, O, DT; WF.

1340   —An old almanack after a new fashion ... for 1658. *By E. Cotes, for the company of stationers,* 1658. 8°.* O, LG.

1341   —Ουρανοθεωρια. Cœlestiall observations. *By E. Cotes, for the company of stationers,* 1654. 8°.* O; MH.

1342   — — —, 1655. 8°.* O.

1343   — — —, 1656. 8°.* LT, O.

1344   — — —, 1657. 8°.* O.

1345   —Telescopium uranicum: or an ephemeris ... 1659. *By E. Cotes, for the company of stationers,* 1659. 8°.* O.

1346   — —Thirtieth edition. *For the company of stationers,* 1660. 8°.* O.

1347   — —Thirty first edition. —, 1661. 8°.* L, O, C.

1348   — —Thirty second edition. —, 1662. 8°.* L, O; WF.

1349   — —Thirty third edition. —, 1663. 8°.* L, O, C; PAP.

1350   — —Thirty fourth edition. —, 1664. 8°.* O, C; CH.

1351   — —[Anr. ed.] —, 1665. 8°.* O.

1352   — —[Anr. ed.] *By E. Cotes for the company of stationers,* [1666]. 8°.* L, O, C, DT; Y.

1353   — —Thirty seventh edition. —, [1667]. 8°.* L, O, C, LWL, CT; MH.

1354   —Uranoscopia or an almanack. *By F. K. for the company of stationers,* 1649. 8°.* O; CU.

1355   **Bourke, John.** Bourk's almanack ... 1685. *Dublin, Benjamin Took,* 1685. 8°. DIX 214. DI, DML.

1355A —Hiberniae Merlinus. *Dublin, by Benjamin Tooke and John Crooke, 1683.* 12°.* DIX 202. DN; Y.

1356 — —1684. —, *1684.* 8°. DIX 207. DML.

1357 **Bowker, James.** 1674. A new almanack. *For the companie of stationers, 1674.* 8°.* L, E; CU.

1358 —1675. — *By Andrew Clark, for the company of stationers, 1675.* 8°.* O, OP; WF.

1359 —1676. — —, *1676.* 8°.* O.

1360 —1677. — —, *1677.* 8°.* L, O, C, E; PAP.

1361 —1678. — *By W.L. and T.J. for the company of stationers, 1678.* 8°.* O, E, EN; WF, HC.

1362 —1679. *By Tho. James, for the company of stationers, 1679.* 8°.* O, C; MH, PAP, WF.

1363 —1680. — —, *1680.* 8°.* L, O, C, LG, E; CH, WF, Y.

1364 —1681. — —, *1681.* 8°.* L, O, C, LWL, E; WF.

1365 —1682. — —, *1682.* 8°.* O, C.

1366 —1683. — —, *1683.* 8°.* O, C, E; CH, CLC, TU, WF, Y.

1367 —1684. — —, *1684.* 8°.* L, O; Y.

1368 —Kalendarium astronomical. *By E. Cotes, for the company of stationers, 1668.* 8°.* L, O, C; MH, PL.

1369 — —, for . . . 1669. —, *1669.* 8°.* L, O, C, CT; PAP, WF.

1370 — —MDCLXX. *By E.C. and A.C. for the company of stationers, 1670.* 8°.* O; WF.

1371 — —1671. *By A.C. for the company of stationers, 1671.* 8°.* L, O; Y.

1372 — —MDCLXXII. *By Andrew Clark, for the company of stationers, 1672.* 8°.* L, O, LWL, E; PAP.

1373 — —MDCLXXIII. —, *1673.* 8°.* O.

1373 — —1674. —, *1674.* 8°.* L, O, C; WF.

1374A — —1675. —, *1675,* 8°. O.

1374B **B[radstreet], S[amuel].** An almanack for . . . 1657. *Cambridge, [Mass.] by Samuel Green, 1657.* 16°.* EVANS 44. MB, MWA.

1375 **Brakenbury, Samuel.** 1667. An almanack. *Cambridge, [Mass.] by Samuel Green, 1667.* 8°.* EVANS 113. MB, MWA.

1376 **B[rattle], T[homas].** 1678. An almanack. *Cambridge, [Mass.] by S. Green & S. Greene: 1678.* 8°.* EVANS 245. CHW.

1377 **[Brattle, William.]** 1694. An almanack of the cœlestiall motions. *Boston, by B. Green, for Samuel Phillips, 1694.* 8°.* EVANS 687. MHS, MWA.

1378 —Unius labor . . . an ephemeris . . . for . . . 1682. *Cambridge, [Mass.] by Samuel Green, 1682.* 8°.* EVANS 314. MHS, MWA, Y.

1379 **Brigden, Zechariah.** An almanack. *Cambridg, [Mass.] by Samuel Green, 1659.* 8°.* EVANS 54. LC.

1379A **Briscoe, John.** An almanack for the year, 1695/6. *London, 1696.* 8°.* Y.

1380 **B[rowne], J[oseph].** 1669. An almanack. *Cambridge: [Mass.] by S. G[reen] and M. J[ohnson], 1669.* 16°.* EVANS 135. MB, MU, MWA, Y.

1381 **Bucknall, John.** The shepherd's almanack . . . for . . . 1675. *By F.L. for the company of stationers, 1675.* 8°.* O, LG, E; WF.

1382 —Calendarium pastoris: or, The shepherd's almanack. *By J.C. for the company of stationers, 1677.* 8°.* L, O.

1383 — —1678. —, *1678.* 8°.* L, O, C; WF, Y.

1384 —[Hebrew] or, The shepherds almanack. *By F.L. for the company of stationers, 1676.* 8°.* L, O, E; WF, Y.

1385 **[?Burton, W.]** An almanack for . . . 1653. *Oxford, by L. Lichfield and H. Hall, 1653.* brs. MADAN 3295. O.

1386 — —1655. *Oxford, by H. Hall, 1655.* 8°.* MADAN 2271. O, OC.

1386A **C.,G.** An almanack . . . 1696. *Edinburgh, by the heirs of A. Anderson, 1696.* 12°.* ALDIS 3542. EN.

1386B — —1697. —, *1697.* 12°.* EN.

1386C — —1700. —, *1700.* 8°.* EN.

1386D **C., I.** A new prognostication for . . . 1675. *Edinburgh, 1675.* 8°. L.

1386E **Calendarium Catholicum.** *[London], printed, 1669.* 12°.* LW.

1387 **Calendarium Londinense** or Raven's almanack for . . . 1678. *For the company of stationers, [1678].* brs. O.

1387A —[Anr. ed.] 1686. brs. O.

1388 **The Catholick almanack** for 1687. *By Henry Hills, 1687.* 8°.* L, O; CN.

1389 **A Catholick & Protestant almanack** for . . . 1688. *By Henry Hills, 1688.* 12°.* O, E, EO.

1390 **Catlett, John.** A perpetual and universal almanack. *For L. Lloyd, 1656.* 8°. E.

1391 **Chamberlaine, Joseph.** Chamberlaine, 1647. A new almanacke. *By T.W. for the company of stationers, 1647.* 8°.* L, O; CU.

1391A —1648. — —, *1648.* 8°.* E; CU.

1392 —1649. — —, *1649.* 8°.* O, C.

1393 **The Chapmans and travellers almanack** for 1693. *By Tho. James for the company of stationers, 1693.* 8°.* L, O; CH.

1394 —1694. —, *1694.* 8°.* L, O, C, LG; CH, PAP.

1395 —1695. —, *1695.* 8°.* L, O, C; CH.

1395A —1697. —, *1697.* 8°.* PAP.

1396 **Chauncy, Israel.** MDCLXIII. An almanack. *Cambridge [Mass.]: by S. Green and M. Johnson 1663.* 8°.* EVANS 76. LC, MH, MU, MWA, NN.

1397 —An almanack of . . . 1664. *Cambridge [Mass.]: S. G. and M. J., 1664.* 8°.* EVANS 87. MWA.

1398 **Chauncy, Nathaniel.** An almanack for 1662. *Cambridg [Mass.]: Samuel Green, 1662.* 8°.* EVANS 69. LC, MWA.

1399 **C[heever], S[amuel].** An almanack for . . . 1660. *Cambridg, [Mass.] by Samuel Green, 1660.* 8°.* EVANS 57. LC, MWA, RPB.

1400 — —1661. *Cambridg, [Mass.] by S[aml] G[reen] and M[armaduke] J[ohnson], 1661.* 8°.* EVANS 66. LC, MWA, RPB.

1401 **Cherry, Thomas.** A new almanack. 1699. 8°. O, C.

1402 **Chesick, William.** A new almanack. 1661. 8°. O, C.

1403 **Childrey, Joshua.** 1653, Syzygiasticon. *By T. Mabb for the company of stationers, 1653.* 8°.* LT, O, DT; MB.

1403A **The city and country chapman's almanack** . . . 1685. *1684.* 8°. O; WF.

1404 —1686. *By Tho. James for the company of stationers, 1685.* 8°.* O, C; MH, MIU, WF.

1405 —1687. —, *1686.* 8°.* L, O, OP; CN, WF, Y.

[37]

1405A —1688. —, 1688. 8°.* CM.

1406 —1689. —, 1689. 8°.* T.C.I 11. L, O, C, EN; CLC, MH, WF, Y.

1407 —1690. —, 1690. 8°.* L, O.

1408 —1691. —, 1691. 8°.* T.C.II 238. O; Y.

1409 —1692. —, 1692. 8°.* L, O; CH, WF.

1410–12 Entries cancelled.

1413 **Clapp, John.** An almanack for ... 1697. *New York: by William Bradford,* 1697. 8°. EVANS 779. NN.

1414 Entry cancelled.

1415 **Clarke, William.** Synopsis anni: or, An almanack for ... 1668. *Cambridge, by John Field,* 1668. 8°.* O.

1416 **Clifford, Abraham.** Clifford 1642. An almanack and prognostication for ... 1642. *Printed at London by R. O. and G. D. for the company of stationers,* [1642]. 8°.* O.

1417 **Clough, Samuel.** The New-England almanack, for ... 1701. *Boston: by Bartholomew Green & John Allen,* 1700. 8°. EVANS 906. CH, LC, MB.

1418 **Coelson, Lancelot.** An almanack for the year ... 1671. *By E. Okes for the company of stationers,* 1671. 8°.* O; MIU.

1419 ——1672. —, 1672. 8°.* O.

1420 ——1673. —, 1673. 8°.* O.

1421 ——1674. *For the company of stationers,* 1674. 8°.* O; CU, WF.

1422 ——1675. —, 1675. 8°.* O; WF.

1423 ——1676. —, [1676]. 8°.* L, O; Y.

1424 ——1677. —, [1677]. 8°.* L, O.

1425 ——1678. *By J. Grover for the company of stationers,* [1678]. 8°.* L, O, C, LN; CH, WF, Y.

1426 ——1679. —, [1679]. 8°.* O.

1427 ——1680. —, [1680]. 8°.* O, LG; CH, WF.

1428 ——1681. —, [1681]. 8°.* L, O; WF.

1429 ——1682. Twefth [sic] impression. —, [1682]. 8°.* O, C; PAP, WF.

1430 ——1683. Thirteenth impression. *By A. Grover for the company of stationers,* [1683]. 8°.* O, C; CH, CLC, TU, WF, Y.

1431 ——1684. Fourteenth impression. —, [1684]. 8°.* L, O, LG; MB, MH, TU, Y.

1432 ——1685. Fifteenth impression. —, [1685]. 8°.* O, C; MIU, WF, Y.

1433 ——1686. Sixteenth impression. —, [1686]. 8°.* O, C; MH, WF.

1434 ——1687. Seventeenth impression. —, [1687]. 8°.* L, O; CN, WF, Y.

1434A ——1687. *By R. Holt for the company of stationers,* 1687. 8°.* OP.

1435 **Cole, Thomas.** Οὐρανολογια, being an ephemeris. *By B. M. for the company of stationers,* 1695. 8°.* L, O.

1435A **Coley, Henry.** Hemerologium. 1672. O.

1435B —— 1673. 1673. O.

1436 —Merlini Anglici ephemeris ... 1684. 1684. 12°. O, LCP; MB.

1436A ——1685. 8°. MIU.

1437 —Merlinus Anglicus junior: or, an ephemeris for ... 1686. *By J. Macock for the company of stationers,* 1686. 8°.* O, E; MH, WF.

1438 ——1687. —, 1687. 8°.* L, O, OP, E; WF, Y.

1439 ——1688. —, 1688. 8°.* T.C.II 238. O, C, LG, E; HC.

1440 ——1689. *By J. Macock for the company of stationers,* 1689. 8°.* L, O; WF, Y.

1441 ——1690. 1690. 8°.* O, E.

1442 ——1691. Twentieth edition. *By William Bonney, for the company of stationers,* 1691. 8°.* L, O; Y.

1443 ——1692. *By John Heptinstall, for the company of stationers,* 1692. Twenty first edition. 8°.* L, O, C, E; CH, WF, Y.

1444 ——1693. Two and twentieth edition. —, 1693. 8°.* L, O, E; CH.

1445 ——1694. Three and twentieth edition. —, 1694. 8°.* L, O, C, LG, EN; CH, MH, PAP.

1446 ——1695. Four and twentieth edition. —, 1695. 8°.* L, O, C; CH, Y.

1447 ——1696. Five and twentieth edition. —, 1696. 8°.* L, O, C, E; CH, MH.

1448 ——1697. Six and twentieth edition. —, 1697. 8°.* L, O, E; CH, MH, PAP, WF.

1449 ——1698. Seven and twentieth edition. —, 1698. 8°.* L, O, C, E; CH, MH, WF.

1450 ——1699. Eight and twentieth edition. —, 1699. 8°.* L, O, C, E; CH, MH.

1451 ——1700. Nine and twentieth edition. —, 1700. 8°.* L, O, C, E; CH, MH, Y.

1452 —Nuncius cœlestis: or, Urania's messenger ... 1674. *By S. S. for the company of stationers,* 1674. 8°.* O.

1452A ——1675. —, 1675. 8°.* O; MIU, WF.

1453 ——1676. —, 1676. 8°.* L, O, E; WF, Y.

1454 ——1677. —, 1677. 8°.* L, O, C; PAP.

1455 ——1678. *By J. Grover for the company of stationers,* [1678]. 8°.* L, O, E; CH, WF, Y.

1456 ——1679. —, [1679]. 8°.* O, C; MH, PAP, WF.

1457 —Nuncius cœlestis: or the starry messenger for ... 1680. *By J. Grover for the company of stationers.* [1680]. Ninth edition. 8°.* L, O, C, LG, E; CH, WF, Y.

1458 ——1681. Tenth edition. *By J. G. for the company of stationers,* 1681. 8°.* L, O, C, E; CH.

1459 ——1682. —, 1682. Eleventh edition. 1682. 8°. O, C; PAP, WF.

1460 ——1683. Twelfth edition. 1683. 8°. L, O, C, E; CH, TU, Y.

1461 ——1684. Thirteenth edition. *By A. G. for the company of stationers,* 1684. 8°.* L, O, C, LG, E; MB, MH, TU, WF, Y.

1462 —Nuncius uraneus 1685. Fourteenth edition. *By A. G. for the company of stationers,* 1685. 8°.* L, O, C; MIU, WF, Y.

1463 ——1686. Fifteenth edition. —, 1686. 8°.* O, C; MH, WF.

1464 ——1687. Sixteenth edition. —, 1687. 8°.* L, O; CN, MH, WF, Y.

1465 ——1688. Seventeenth edition. — 1688. 8°.* O, C, LG, EN, EO; Y, HC.

1466 — —1689. Eighteenth edition. *By E. W. for the company of stationers,* [1689]. 8°.* L, O, C, EN; CLC, MB, MH, WF, Y.

1467 — —1690. Nineteenth edition. *By William Bonny, for the company of stationers,* 1690. 8°.* L, O; MH, WF, Y.

1467A **Conyers, William.** Hemerologium astronomicum. *By J. Cottrell, for the company of stationers,* 1664. 8°. O.

1468 **Cookson, William.** Μηνολογιον; or an ephemeris . . . 1699. *By Tho. Ilive for the company of stationers,* 1699. 8°.* L, O, C; CH.

1469 — —1700. *By T. Ilive for the company of stationers,* 1700. 8°.* L, O, C; CH, MH, Y.

1469A **Cornelius, Gilbert.** Cornelius. 1647. A new almanack. *By T. R and E. M. for the company of stationers,* 1647. 8°. L, O.

1469B **Coronelli, Vincenzo Mario.** The royal almanack. *For E. Whitlock,* 1696. 4°.* EN; CH, CLC, NP, WF, Y.

1470 **Corss, James.** Mercurius cœlicus . . . 1662. *Glasgow, by Robert Sanders,* 1662. 8°,* L.

1470A — —1662. *Edinburgh, by a society of stationers,* 1662. 8°.* Y.

1471 — —1663. —, 1663. 8°.* L.

1472 —A new prognostication. *Glasgow, by Robert Sanders,* 1694. 8°.* ALDIS 3377. GU.

1473 [–] —1679. *Edinburgh,* 1679. 8°.* L.

1474–93 Entries cancelled.

1494 **Coulton, John.** Coulton. 1654. Prognostæ astralis diarium: or, an almanack for . . . 1654. *By R. & W. Leybourn, for the company of stationers,* 1654. 8°.* O.

1495 — —1655. *For the company of stationers,* 1655. 8°.* O.

1496 —Coulton. Theoria contingentium anni . . . 1653. *By R. & W. Leybourn, for the company of stationers,* [1653]. 8°.* O.

1496A The country almanac for 1675. *By F. L. for the company of stationers,* 1675. WF.

1496B —1676. —, 1676. WF.

1496C The country-man's kalendar for . . . 1692. [1691]. fol.* L.

1496D **Crabtree, Henry.** Merlinus rusticus 1685. *For the company of stationers,* 1685. 8°.* O; Y.

1497 **Crawford, Henry.** Vox uraniæ, or, astrological observations . . . for . . . 1676. 1676. 8°.* O; WF.

1498 — —1677. *By J. D. for the company of stationers,* 1677. 8°.* L, O, C, E.

1499 **Crooke, William.** Crooke, 1652. An almanack. *By S. I. for the company of stationers,* [1652[. 8°.* O; CU.

1500 — —1653. —, [1653]. 8°.* O.

1501 **Culpeper, Nathaniel.** Culpepper revived. *Cambridge, by John Hayes,* 1680. 8°.* O, C, LG; CH, WF.

1502 — — —, 1681. 8°.* L, O.

1503 — — —, 1682. 8°.* O, C.

1504 — — —, 1683. 8°.* O; CLC.

1505 — — —, 1684. 8°.* L, O; Y.

1506 — — —, 1685. 8°.* O.

1507 — — —, 1686. 8°.* O.

1508 — — —, 1687. 8°.* L, O, CS.

1509 — — —, 1688. 8°,* T.C.II 238. C, E; MH, HC.

1510 — — —, 1689. 8°.* L.

1511 — — —, 1690. 8°.* O.

1512 — — —, 1692. 8°.* L, O, C, E.

1513 — — —, 1693. 8°.* L.

1514 — — —, 1694. 8°.* L, O, LG.

1515 — — —, 1695. 8°.* L, O.

1516 — — —, 1696. 8°.* L, O, E; MH.

1517 — — —, 1697. 8°.* L; PAP.

1518 — — —, 1698. 8°.* L, O; WF.

1519 — — —, 1699. 8°.* O, C.

1520 — — —, 1700. 8°.* O.

1521 **Culpepper, Nicholas.** An ephemeris for . . . 1651. [*London*], *by Peter Cole,* 1651, 4°. LT.

1522 — —1652. *For T. Vere, and N. Brook,* 1652. 8°. LT; CU.

1523 — —1653. *By John Macock for the company of stationers,* 1653. 8°. LT, O, GU; MH.

1524 — —1654. —, 1654. 8°. O.

1525 — —1655. —, 1655. 8°. O.

1526 — —1656. —, 1656. 8°. O.

1526A **D., L.** A new prognostication for . . . 1673. *Glasgow, Robert Sanders,* 1673. 8°.* L.

1526B **Dade, William.** A compleat pocket almanack. *By T. H. for the company of stationers,* 1692. 12°. O.

1527 —Dade, 1684, or, the country-man's kalender. *By M. Haly, and J. Millet, for the company of stationers,* 1684. 8°.* L, O.

1528 — —1685. —, 1685. 8°.* O.

1529 — —1686. [*London*], *by J. Millet, for the company of stationers,* 1686. 8°.* O.

1530 — —1687. [*London*], —, 1687. 8°.* L, O; Y.

1531 — —1688. —, 1689. 8°.* T.C.II 238. CM, E.

1531A — —1689. —, 1689. 8°.* MH, WF.

1532 — —1690. —, 1690. 8°.* O.

1533 — —1692. —, 1692. 8°.* L, O.

1534 — —1693. —, 1693. 8°.* L.

1535 — —1694. [*London*], *by W. Onely, for the company of stationers,* 1694. 8°.* L, O, LG.

1536 — —1695. —, 1694. 8°.* L, O.

1537 — —1696. —, 1696. 8°.* MH.

1537A — —1697. —, 1697. 8°.* PAP.

1538 — —1698. —, 1698. 8°.* L, O; WF.

1539 — —1699. —, 1699. 8°.* O, C.

1540 — —1700. —, 1700. 8°.* O.

1541 —Dade, 1641. A new almanacke, . . . 1641. *By R. O. for the company of stationers,* [1641]. 8°.* L, O, DT.

1542 — —1642. *By R. O. & G. D. for the company of stationers,* [1642]. 8°.* O.

1543 — —1643. —, [1643]. 8°.* L, O.

1544 — —1647. *By Richard Bishop for the company of stationers,* [1647]. 8°.* L, O.

1545 — —1649. *For the company of stationers,* [1649]. 8°.* O, C.

1546 — —1651. —, [1651]. 8°.* O; PHS.

1547 — —1653. —, [1653]. 8°.* L, O, DT.

1547A — —1654. —, 1654. 8°.* L.

1548 — —1655. *By R. & W. Leybourn, for the company of stationers,* [1655]. 8°.* O.

1549 — —1657. —, 1657. 8°.* O.

1550 — —1658. —, 1658. 8°.* O.

1551 — —1659. —, 1659. 8°.* O; PHS.

1552 — —1660. —, 1660. 8°.* L; Y.

1553 — —1661. —, 1661. 8°.* O.

1554 — —1664. *By W. Wilson, for the company of stationers,* 1664. 8°.* O, E.

1555 — —1666. *For the company of stationers,* 1666. 8°.* O.

1556 — —1667. *By E. Okes, for the company of stationers,* 1667. 8°.* O.

1557 — —1669. *For the company of stationers,* 1669. 8°.* O.

1558 — —1670. *By Peter Lillicrap, for the company of stationers,* 1670. 8°.* O.

1558A — —1671. —, 1671. 8°.* O.

1559 — —1672. —, 1672. 8°.* O.

1560 — —1673. —, 1673. 8°.* O.

1561 — —1675. *By S. and B. G. for the company of stationers,* 1675. 8°.* O; WF.

1562 — —1676. *By A. P. for the company of stationers,* 1676. 8°.* O.

1563 — —1677. —, 1677. 8°.* L, O.

1564 — —1678. *By A.P. and I. H. for the company of stationers,* 1678. 8°.* L, O; WF, Y, HC.

1565 Entry cancelled.

1566 — —1679. *By A.P. and T.H. for the company of stationers,* 1679. 8°.* O.

1567 — —1680. —, 1680. 8°.* O, C, LG; CH, WF.

1568 — —1681. *By T.H. for the company of stationers,* 1681. 8°.* L, O.

1569 — —1682. —, 1682. 8°.* O, C.

1570 — —1683. —, 1683. 8°.* O.

1570A — Dade, 1678. A prognostication ... 1678. *By T. N. for the company of stationers,* 1678. 8°.* O; WF, HC.

1570B — —1683. — —, 1683. 8°.* CLC.

1571 — —1696. *T. J.,* [1695]. 8°.* MH.

1572 D[anforth], J[ohn]. An almanack ... for ... 1679. *Cambridge, [Mass.] by Samuel Green,* 1679. 8°.* EVANS 265. LC, MHS, MB, MWA, Y.

1573 [Danforth, Samuel.] MDCXLVI. An almanck for ... 1646. *Cambridge, [Mass.] Stephen Daye,* 1646. 8°.* EVANS 18. CH, MHS.

1574 — —1647. *Cambridge [Mass.], by Matthew Day, to be solde by Hez. Usher at Boston,* 1647. 8°.* EVANS 21. CH, MWA, NN, RPB.

1575 — —1648. *Printed at Cambridge, [Mass.] [Matthew Day],* 1648. 8°.* EVANS 23. CH, LC, MHS, MWA, NN.

1576 — —1649. *Printed at Cambridge, [Mass.] [by Samuel Green],* 1649. 16°.* EVANS 27. LC, NN.

1577 —The New-England almanack for—1685. *Cambridge, [Mass.]* 1685. 8°.* MWA.

1578 — —1686. —, 1685. 8°.* EVANS 403. LC, MHS, MWA, Y.

1579 — —1686. —, 1686. 8°.* EVANS 404. MHS.

1580 Daniel, Humphrey. Daniel, 1651. For London meridian an almanack. *By Gartrude Dawson, for the company of stationers,* [1651]. 8°.* O.

1581 — —1652. *By T. W. for the company of stationers,* 1652. 8°.* O; CU.

1582 — —1654. An almanack for ... 1654. —, 1654. 8°.* O; MH.

1583 — —1656. —, 1656. 8°.* O.

1584 Davis, William. Entry cancelled.

1585 —A compleat new almanack. *By R. R. for the company of stationers,* [1687]. 8°.* L, O.

1586 — —[1692]. 8°.* L, O.

1586A —A new ephemeris ... for ... 1689. *By R. R. for the company of stationers.* [1689]. 8°.* MH, WF.

1587 —News out of the West from the stars: or, a new ephemeris ... for ... 1688. *By R. R. for the company of stationers,* [1688]. 8°.* LG, EN; HC.

1588 Desmus, Raphael. Merlinus anonymus. An almanack, ... for ... 1653. *By F:N:* 1653. 8°.* LT; WF.

1589 — —1654. *By F. Neile:* 1654. 8°.* LT; CH.

1590 — —1655. —, 1655. 8°.* LT.

    Doubtful almanack. [1647.] *See under* Almanacs, Wither, George, *pseud.*

1591 Dove, Jonathan. Dove. An almanack. *Cambridge, R. Daniel,* [1641]. 8°.* O, DT.

1592 Dove. Speculum anni. *Cambridge,* 1642. 8°.* O, C.

1593 — —1643. *Printed at London by A. N. for the company of stationers,* 1643. 8°.* L, O.

1593A — —1644. *By R. Daniel, Cambridge,* 1644. 8°.* PHS.

1594 — —1645. *By I.N. for the company of stationers,* 1645. 8°.* C[FRAG.]; PHS.

1595 — —1647. *For the company of stationers,* 1647. 8°.* L O.

1596 — —1648. *Cambridge, by R. Daniel.* [1648]. 8°.* E.

1597 — —1649. *By T. W. for the company of stationers,* 1649. 8°.* O.

1598 — —1651. *Cambridge, by the printers to the universitie,* 1651. 8°.* O; PHS.

1599 — —1653. —, 1652. 8°.* L, O, DT.

1600 — —1654. —, 1654. 8°.* O; MH.

1601 — —1655. —, 1655. 8°.* O.

1602 — —1656. —, 1656. 8°.* O.

1603 — —1657. —, 1657. 8°.* O.

1604 — —1658. *Cambridge: by John Field,* 1658. 8°.* O, LG.

1605 — —1659. —, 1659. 8°.* O.

1606 — —1660. —, 1660. 8°.* O.

1607 — —1661. —, 1661. 8°.* L, O; WF.

1608 — —1662. —, 1662. 8°.* O.

1609 — —1663. —, 1663. 8°.* L, O, C; PAP, WF.

1610 — —1664. —, 1664. 8°.* L, O, C, E; CH.

1611 — —1665. —, 1665. 8°.* O.

1612 — —1666. —, 1666. 8°.* O, C, DT.

1613 — —1667. —, 1667. 8°.* L, O, C, LWL; MH.

1614 — —1668. *[Cambridge], by John Field,* 1668. 8°.* L, O, C; MH, PL.

1615 — —1669. —, 1669. 8°.* L, O, C; PAP, WF.

1616 — —1670. —, 1670. 8°.* L, O.

1617 — —1671. *Cambridge, by John Hayes,* 1671. 8°.* L, O.

1618 — —1672. *Cambridge, by John Field,* 1672. 8°.* O; PAP.

1618A — —1673. —, 1673. 8°.* O.

1619 —Dove. A new almanack for ... 1674. *Cambridge, by John Hayes,* 1674. 8°.* O, C; WF.

1620 —Dove. Speculum anni or an almanack for ... 1675. —, 1675. 8°.* L, O; WF.

1621 — —1676. —, 1676. 8°.* L, O; WF.

1622 — —1677. —, 1677. 8°.* L, O.

1623   — —1678. —, 1678. 8°.* O, E; CH, WF, HC.

1624   — —1679. —, 1679. 8°.* O, C; MH, WF.

1625   — —1680. —, 1680. 8°.* O, C, LG; CH, CLC, WF.

1626   — —1681. —, 1681. 8°.* L, O; WF.

1627   — —1682. —, 1682. 8°.* O, C.

1628   — —1683. —, 1683. 8°.* O; CLC.

1629   — —1684. —, 1684. 8°.* L. O; Y.

1630   — —1685. —, 1685. 8°.* O.

1631   — —1686. —, 1686. 8°.* O E.

1632   — —1687. —, 1687. 8°.* L, O; Y.

1633   — —1688. [Cambridge], by John Hayes, 1688. 8°.* C, LG, E; Y, HC.

1634   — —1689. Cambridge, by John Hayes, 1689. 8°.* T.C.II 238. L, O, C, EN; CLC, MB, MH, WF, Y.

1635   — —1690. —, 1690. 8°.* L, O, E; MH, WF, Y.

1636   — —1691. —, 1691. 8°.* L, E; Y.

1637   — —1692. —, 1692. 8°.* L, O, C, E; CH, WF.

1638   — —1693. —, 1693. 8°.* O; CH.

1639   — —1694. —, 1694. 8°.* L, O, LG, EN; CH, PAP.

1640   — —1695. —, 1695. 8°.* L, O, C; CH, CLC, Y.

1641   — —1696. —, 1696. 8°.* O, C; CH, MH.

1642   — —1697. —, 1697. 8°.* O; CH, PAP.

1643   — —1698. —, 1698. 8°.* L, O, E; CH, MH, WF.

1644   — —1699. —, 1699. 8°.* O, C; CH.

1645   — —1700. —, 1700. 8°.* O, C; CH.

1646   **Dudley, Joseph.** MDCLXVIII. An almanack . . . for . . . 1668. Cambridge [Mass.]: by Samuel Green, 1668. 8°.* EVANS 121. LC, MB, MWA, RPB.

1647   **Dunster, Thomas.** Δωδεκαμηνο-διετεο-γραφια. Or an almanack for two years, 1652, and 1653. By Will. Bentley, for Th. Dunster, 1652. brs. L, O.

1648   The Dutch bloudy almanack for . . . 1653. By John Clowse, 1653. 4°.* LT, LG.

1648A   **E., D.** A new prognostication for . . . 1670. Glasgow, Robert Sanders, 1670. 8°.* L.

1649   **Eland, William.** Hemerologium astronomicum: . . . 1656. By R. & W. L. for the company of stationers, 1656. 8°.* O.

1649A   Endymion, 1663. Or, the man-in-the-moon. Selenopolis, 1653. 12°. L, O.

1649B   England's almanack, shewing. For S. Bridge, 1700. brs. L.

1650   The English chapmans. 1692. 8°.* CH.

1650A   — —1693. 8°.* CH.

1650B   — —1694. 8°.* CH.

1650C   — —1695. 8°.* CH.

1651   The English chapmans and travellers almanack for . . . 1696. By Tho. James for the company of stationers, 1696. 8°.* L, O, C; MH.

1652   —1697. —, 1697. 8°.* L, O; CH, MH, WF.

1653   —1698. —, 1698. 8°.* L, O, C; CH, MH, WF.

1654   —1699. —, 1699. 8°.* L, O, C; CH, WF.

1655   —1700. —, 1699. 8°.* L, O; MH, Y.

        Ephemeris ad annum . . . 1688. 1688. See under Almanacs, Halley, Edmund.

1656   An everlasting prognostication. Aberdeen, by Iohn Forbes, 1686. 8°.* ALDIS 2640. ES.

1656A   **F., A.** A new prognostication for . . . 1674. Edinburgh, 1674. 8°.* ALDIS 2024. L, HH.

1657   **F., J.** A new prognostication for . . . 1685. Edinburgh, [heir of A. Anderson], 1685. 8°. ALDIS 2546. ES.

1657A   **F., M.** An almanack for . . . 1660. Cambridge, by John Field, [1659]. 8°.* O.

1657B   — —1661. —, 1661. 8°.* O.

1657C   — —1663. —, 1663. 8°.* O.

1657D   — —1664. —, 1664. 8°.* O.

1657E   — —1665. —, 1665. 8°.* O.

1657F   — —1674. —, 1674. 8°.* O.

1657G   — —1675. —, 1675. 8°.* O.

1657H   — —1694. —, 1694. 8°.* O.

1658   **Felgenhauer, Paul.** Postilion, or a new almanacke. By M. S. for H: Crips and Lodo: Lloyd, 1655. 4°. LT, O; CH, CLC, NC, WF.

1659   **Fitzsmith, Richard.** Syzygiasticon instauratum: or, an almanack . . . for . . . 1654. For the author, to be sold by Henry Eversden, 1654. 8°. LT, CT.

1660   **Flint, Josiah.** 1666. An almanack. Cambridge [Mass.], printed [by S. Green], 1666. 8°.* EVANS 107. MWA.

1660A   Fly, 1657. An almanack. For the company of stationers, 1657. 8°.* O.

1661   —1658. —, 1658. 8°.* O.

1662   —1659. —, 1659. 8°.* O.

1663   —1660. —, 1660. 8°.* L; Y.

1664   —1661. —, 1661. 8°.* O; CU.

1665   —1662. —, 1662. 8°.* O; PHS.

1666   —1664. —, 1664. 8°.* O, E.

1667   —1665. —, 1665. 8°.* O, E.

1668   —1666. —, 1666. 8°.* O. E,

1669   —1667. —, 1667. 8°.* O, E.

1670   —1668. S. G., [1668]. 8°.* O, CT, E; CLC.

1671   —1669. —, 1669. 8°.* O, E.

1672   —1670. By S. G. and B. G. for the company of stationers, 1670. 8°.* L, O, E.

1673   —1671. —, 1671. 8°.* O, E.

1674   —1672. —, 1672. 8°.* O, E.

1675   —1673. —, 1673. 8°.* O, E.

1676   —1674. —, 1674. 8°.* O, E.

1677   —1675. —, 1675. 8°.* L, O, E; WF.

1678   —1676. —, 1676. 8°.* O, E.

1679   —1677. —, 1677. 8°.* L, O, E.

1680   —1678. —, 1678. 8°.* O, EN; WF, Y, HC.

1681   —1679. —, 1679. 8°.* L, O, C; PAP.

1682   —1680. —, 1680. 8°.* O, C, LG; CH, WF.

1683   —1681. By B. Griffin for the company of stationers, 1681. 8°.* L, O.

1684   —1682. —, 1682. 8°.* O.

1685   —1683. —, 1683. 8°.* O; CLC.

1686   Fly: an almanack for . . . Cambridge, by John Hayes, 1684. 8°.* L, O; Y.

1687   —1685. —, 1685. 8°.* O.

1688   —1686. —, 1686. 8°.* O.

1689   —1687. —, 1687. 8°.* L, O, C.

1690   —1688. By J. Millet for the company of stationers, 1688. 8°.* C, E; Y.

1691 —1688. By B. Griffin, for the company of stationers, 1688. 8°.* Y, HC.

1692 —1689. By Ben. Griffin, for the company of stationers, 1689. 8°.* T.C.II 238. L, O, C, EN; MB, MH, WF, Y.

1693 —1690. Cambridge, by John Hayes, 1690. 8°.* O; WF.

1694 —1691. —, 1691. 8°.* O.

1695 —1692. —, 1692. 8°.* L, O.

1696 —1693. —, 1693. 8°.* L.

1697 —1694. —, 1694. 8°.* L, O, LG.

1698 —1695. —, 1695. 8°.* L, O.

1699 —1696. —, 1696. 8°.* O; MH.

1700 —1697. —, 1697. 8°.* O, E; PAP.

1701 —1698. —, 1698. 8°.* L, O, C; WF.

1702 —1699. —, 1699. 8°.* O, C, E; MH.

1703 —1700. —, 1700. 8°.* L, O, E; MH, Y.

1704 **Forbes, John.** The mariner's everlasting almanack. Aberdeen, by the author, 1683. 8°. ALDIS 2380. L, HH AU.

1705 — — — 1685. 4°. ALDIS 2548. L.

1706 **Foster, John.** 1675. An almanack. Cambridge [Mass.], by Samuel Green, 1675. 8°.* EVANS 198. MB, MWA.

1707 Entry cancelled.

1708 —1678. —. [Boston], by J. Foster, for John Usher of Boston, 1678. 8°.* EVANS 247. MWA.

1709 —1679. —. Boston: by John Foster, sold by Henry Phillips, 1679. 8°.* EVANS 268. CHW, MB, Y.

1710 —1680. —. [By John Foster] for John Vsher of Boston, 1680. 8°.* EVANS 283. CN, LC, MB, MHS.

1711 —1680 —. [By John Foster] for, and sold by Henry Phillips, 1680. 8°.* EVANS 284. MWA.

1712 —1681 —. Boston: by J[ohn] F[oster], 1681. 8°.* EVANS 300. CN, LC, MHS, MWA.

1713 —1681 —. Boston: by J.F for Samuel Phillips, 1681. 8°.* EVANS 301. MHS.

1714 **Foster, William.** An ephemeris of the celestial motions. By S.D. for the company of stationers, 1662. 8°.* O.

1715 **Fowle, Thomas.** Speculum uranicum; ... for ... 1680. For the company of stationers, 1680. 8°.* O, LG; CH, WF.

1716 — —1681. —, 1681. 8°.* L, O.

1717 — —1683. —, 1683. 8°.* O, C; CLC, WF, Y.

1718 — —1684. —, 1684. 8°.* L, O; Y.

1719 — —1685. —, 1685. 8°.* O.

1720 — —1686. —, 1686. 8°.* O.

1721 — —1687. By R.E. for the company of stationers, 1687. 8°.* L, O; Y.

1722 — —1688. —, 1688. 8°.* O.

1722A —An appendix to the precedent almanack. By M. C. for the company of stationers, 1688. CM.

1723 — —1689. —, 1689. 8°.* T.C.II 238. L; MH.

1724 — —1690. —, 1690. 8°.* O.

1725 — —1692. —, 1691. 8°.* L, O.

1726 — —1693. —, 1693. 8°.* L.

1727 — —1694. —, 1694. 8°.* L, O, LG.

1728 — —1695. —, 1695. 8°.* L, O.

1729 — —1696. By Robert and Richard Everingham, for the company of stationers, 1696. 8°.* MH.

1730 — —1697. —, 1697. 8°.* L; PAP.

1731 — —1698. —, 1698. 8°.* O; WF.

1732 — —1699. —, 1699. 8°.* O, C.

1733 — —1700. —, 1700. 8°.* O.

1734 **G., R.** MDCLXVI. Prognosticon ... 1666. 1666. brs. EN.

1735 **Gadbury, John.** Diarium astronomicum: or, a West-India almanack, for ... 1675. By Ja: Cotterel, for the company of stationers, 1675. 8°. L, O.

1736 —Ephemerides of the celestial motions for x. years: beginning anno 1672. ... 1681. By John Macock, for the company of stationers, 1672. 4°. T.C.I 104. L, O, C, LW, OC; BN, CH, CLC, MH, WF, Y.

1737 — —xx. years. By J. Macock, for the company of stationers, 1680. 21 pts., 4°. T.C.I 392. L, C, OC, E, DT; BN, CH, LC, MH, WF, Y.

1738 —Εφημερις: ... for ... 1659. By J. C. for the company of stationers, 1659. 8°.* O.

1739 — —1660. —, [1660]. 8°.* L, O.

1740 — —1661. By James Cottrel, for the company of stationers, 1661. 8°.* L, O, C.

1741 — —1662. By Ja: Cottrel, for the company of stationers, 1662. 8°.* L, O; WF.

1742 — —1663. By James Cottrel, for the company of stationers, [1663]. 8°.* L, O, C; PAP.

1743 — —1664. —, [1664]. 8°.* L, O, C, E; CH, Y.

1744 — —1665. By Ja. Cotterel, for the company of stationers, [1665]. 8°.* O, C.

1745 — —1666. —, [1666]. 8°.* L, O, C, DT.

1746 — —1667. By T. Milbourn for the company of stationers, [1667]. 8°.* L, O, C, LWL.

1747 — —1668. By Ja. Cotterel, for the company of stationers, [1668]. 8°.* L, O, C, DC; MH, PL.

1748 — —1669. For the company of stationers, [1669]. 8°.* L, O, C, DC; PAP, WF.

1749 — —1670. —, [1670]. 8°.* O; WF.

1750 — —1671. — [1671]. 8°.* L O.

1751 — —1672. — [1672]. 8°.* L O CT, E, DT; MIU.

1752 — —1673. —, [1673]. 8°.* O; MIU.

1753 — —1674. —, [1674]. 8°.* L, O, C, E; MIU, WF.

1754 — —1675. —, 1675. 8°.* L, O, LG, E; WF.

1755 — —1676. Westminster, by George Larken, for the assigns of John Seymore, 1676. 8°. O; MIU.

1756 — —1677. By J.D. for the company of stationers, 1677. 8°.* L, O, C, E; PAP.

1757 — —1678. —, 1678. 8°.* L, O, C, LVF, E; CH, WF, Y, HC.

1758 — —1679. —, 1679. 8°.* L, O, C; MH, PAP, WF.

1759 — —1680. —, 1680. 8°.* L, O, C, LG; CH, CLC, WF, Y.

1760 — —1681. —, 1681. 8°.* L, O, C, E; CH, WF.

1761 — —1682. —, 1682. 8°.* L, O, C, OP, E; PAP, WF.

1762 — —1683. —, 1683. 8°.* O, C, E; CH, TU, WF, Y.

1763 — —1684. —, 1684. 8°.* L, O, LG; CH, MH, TU, WF, Y.

1764 — —1685. —, 1685. 8°.* L, O, C, E; MIU, WF, Y.

1765 — —1686. —, 1686. 8°.* O, C, E; WF.

1766 — —1687. —, 1687. 8°.* L, O, OP, E; WF, Y.

1767 — —1688. —, 1688. 8°.* L, O, C, LG, E, EO; WF, HC.

1768 — —1689. —, 1689. 8°.* T.C.II 238. L, O, C, EN; CLC, MH, SW, WF, Y.

1769   ——1690. *By J. R. for the company of stationers*, 1690. 8°.* L, O, C, E; Y.

1770   ——1691. —, 1691. 8°.* L, O, E; Y.

1771   ——1692. —, 1692. 8°.* L, O, C; CH, WF, Y.

1772   ——1693. —, 1693. 8°.* L, O, E; CH.

1773   ——1694. —, 1694. 8°.* L, O, C, LG, EN; CH, CN, MH, PAP.

1774   ——1695. —, 1695. 8°.* L, O, C; CH, Y.

1775   ——1696. —, 1696. 8°.* L, O, C, E; CH, MH, WF.

1776   ——1697. —, 1697. 8°.* L, O, E; CH, MH, PAP, WF.

1777   ——1698. —, 1698. 8°.* L, O, C, E; CH, CN, MH, TU, WF.

1778   ——1699. —, 1699. 8°.* L, O, C, E; CH, CN, MBP, MH.

1779   ——1700. —, 1700. 8°.* L, O, C, E; CH, CN, MH, Y.

1780   —The Jamaica almanack ... for ... 1673. *By John Darby, for the company of stationers*, 1672. 8°. L, O.

1781   —Προγνοστκιον or an astrological prediction of ... 1658. *By W. Godbid for the company of stationers*, [1658]. 8°.* O.

1782   —Speculum astrologicum: or an astrological glasse. *By E. Brudenell, for the company of stationers*, 1656. 8°.* O.

1783   ——, 1657. 8°.* O.

1784   —The West-India or Jamaica almanack 1674. [*London*, 1673.] 8°. L, O.

1785   ——1675. 1675. 8°. O.

1785A **Gadbury, Timothy.** The young sea-mans guide. *For Francis Cossinet*, 1659. 8°. O, C.

1785B —[Anr. ed.] —, [1660]. 8°. LT.

1786   **Gallen, Thomas.** Gallen, 1642. An almanack. *By Rob. Young for the company of stationers* [1642]. 12°. O; CU.

1787   ——1643. *By James Young for the company of stationers*, [1643]. 12°. L.

1788   —Gallen, 1648. A new almanack. *By M. F. for the com-*

1788A ——1649. —, [1649]. 8°. L.

1789   —Gallen. 1658. A new almanack. *By J[ohn] F[ield] for the company of stationers*, [1658]. 8°. O, OP.

1789A ——1668. —, 1668. 12°. WF.

1790   ——1672. —, [1672]. 8°. O.

1790A ——1673. *By E. F. for the company of stationers*, 1673. 8°. L; MBP.

1790B ——1674. —, [1674]. 8°.* WF.

1791   ——1681. — *By M. F. for the company of stationers*, 1681. 12°. T.C.II 258. L.

1791A **Gallen, William.** Gallen, 1686. A complete pocket almanack for ... 1686. *By M. F. for the company of stationers*, 1686. 12°. OP.

1791B ——1688. —, 1688. 12°. CM.

1791C ——1689. *By F. F. for the company of stationers*, 1689. 12°.* Y.

1791D ——1694. —, 1694. 12°. LG.

1791E **Gardner, Robert.** Veteronarium meteorologist astrology. *By W. and J. Wilde for the company of stationers* 1697. 8°. O; PAP.

1791F **Gilbert, Samuel.** A sexennial diary. *For the company of stationers*, 1683. 8°.* O.

1792   **Gillam, Benjamin.** 1684. The Boston ephemeris. *Boston in New England, by Samuel Green for Samuel Phillips*, 1684. 8°.* EVANS 359. MHS, RPJ, Y.

1792A **Goldisborough, John.** An almanack for ... 1662. *For the company of stationers*, 1662. 8°. O.

1792B **Goldsmith, John.** Goldsmith. An almanack for 1663. *By R. White for the company of stationers*, 1663. 12°. WF.

1792C —1664. —, 1664. 12°. O.

1792CA —1665. —, 1665. 12°. WF.

1792D ———1671. Goldsmith, 1671. An almanack. *By R. White for the company of stationers*, 1671. 8°. Y.

1792E ——1671. *By T. Ratcliff for the company of stationers*, 1671. 8°. Y.

1793   ——1674. *By T. Ratcliffe, & N. Thompson, for the company of stationers*, 1674. 8°.* L.

1793A —1675. —, 1675. 8°.* Y.

1793B —1682. *By Mary Clarke for the company of stationers*, 1682. 8°. Y.

1794   —1685 — —, 1685. 8°.* L, C.

1795   —1686 — —, 1686. 8°.* C.

1796   —1687 — —, 1687. 8°.* T.C.II 238. C.

1796A —1688. — —, 1688. 24°. CM.

1797   —1692 — —, 1692. 12°.* L.

1797A —1693. — —, 1693. 24°. O, CT.

1798   —1694 — —, 1694. 8°.* C, LG; CLC.

1799   —1695 — —, 1695. 8°.* O.

1799A —1700. — —, 1700. 8°.* O.

1800   **Green, Christopher.** A new perpetual almanack beginning A: Do: 1691. *For the author*, [1691]. brs. L.

1801   **Greenwood, Nicholas.** Diarium planetarum: or, an ephemeris for ... 1690. *By R.E. for the company of stationers*, 1690. 8°.* L, O, E; Y.

1802–4 Entries cancelled.

1805   **[Halley, Edmond.]** Ephemeris ad annum ... 1686. *Typis J. Heptinstall, impensis Guilielmi Cooper*, 1686. 4°.* O.

1806   [–] —1687. —, 1687. 4°.* O.

1807   [–] —1688. —, 1688. 8°.* L, O.

1808   **Harflete, Henry.** Ἀρωνόφηγματα. An ephemeris for ... 1651. *By T. R. and E. M. for the company of stationers*, 1651. 8°.* O; CU.

1809   —Ουρανοδειξις. Cœlorum declaratio. An ephemeris for ... 1652. *By T. R. & E. M. for the company of stationers*, 1652. 8°.* O; CU.

1810   ——1653. —, 1653. 8°.* L, O, DT.

1811   ——1654. —, 1654. 8°.* O; MH.

1812   ——1656. —, 1656. 8°.* O.

1813   **[Harris, Benjamin.]** Boston almanack for ... 1692. *Boston, by Benjamin Harris, and John Allen*, 1692. 8°.* EVANS 595. MHS.

1814   **Harrisson, John.** Syderum secreta, or ... *By John Richardson for the company of stationers*, 1688. 8°.* CM.

1814A ——1689. 8°.* T.C.II 238. L, O, C, EN; MB, MH, WF, Y.

1815   **Healy, Richard.** Healy 1655. A new almanack. *By S. Griffin*, 1655. 8°.* O.

1816   —An ephemeris, ... for ... 1658. *By T. W. for the company of stationers*, 1658. 8°.* O.

1816A **Heathcott, William.** An almanack and prognostication for ... 1665. *By William Godbid, for the company of stationers*, 1665. 8°.* O.

1817 **Herbert, Thomas.** Herbert, 1651, speculum anni. *By Gartrude Dawson, for the company of stationers*, [1651]. 8°.* O; CU.

1818 — —1652. —, [1652]. 8°.* O.

1819 — —1653. —, [1653]. 8°.* L, DT.

1820 **Hewitt, Thomas.** Annus ab incarnatione Domini. Hewit, 1654. An almanack. *By Robert White*, 1654. 8°.* O.

1821 — —1655. —, 1655. 8°.* L, O.

1822 **Heyman, John.** An almanack for ... 1660. *By D. Maxwell for the company of stationers*, [1660]. 8°.* O.

1822A **Hill, Henry.** Αστρολογια or a starry lecture. *For the company of stationers*, 1684. 8°.* L, O; Y.

1823 **H[obart], N[ehemiah].** 1673. An almanack. *Cambridge [Mass.]: by Samuel Green*, 1673. 8°.* EVANS 175. MB, MWA.

1824 **Hobbs, Matthew.** An almanack for ... 1693. *By John Heptinstall, for the company of stationers*, 1693. 8°.* L, O; CH.

1825 —Chaldæus Anglicanus: being an almanack for ... 1695. *By John Heptinstall, for the company of stationers*, 1695. 8°.* L, O; CH.

1826 — —1696. —, 1696. 8°.* O; MH.

1827 **Holden, Mary.** The woman's almanack for ... 1688. *By J. Millet, for the company of stationers*, 1688. 8°. CM, E; PL.

1827A — —1689. —, 1689. 8°.* MH, WF.

1828 **Holmes, Walter.** An annual almanacke. *By Thomas Harper*, 1649. 8°.* LT, DT.

1829 **Hooker, Richard.** Cœlestis legatus: or, an astrological diarie, for ... 1668. *Cambridge, by John Field*, 1668. 8°.* O; MH.

1830 **Howell, Humphrey.** 1656. Duplus annua, or, a two-fold yeere. *For the company of stationers*, 1656. 8°.* O.

1831 —Duplex. ... *By T.C. for the company of stationers*, 1657. 8°.* O.

1832 **Jackson, Thomas.** Speculum perspicuum uranicum: or a glasse. *By E. Cotes, for the company of stationers*, 1653. 8°.* O.

1833 [–] — —, [1655]. 8°.* O.

1833A **Jessey, Henry.** A scripture almanack. *By M.B. for the company of stationers*, [1646]. brs. LW.

1833B — —Third edition. —, [1647]. 8°.* L.

1834 — —Fourth edition. [1648]. 8°.* L, O, E; CU.

1835 —A scripture calendar. Fifth edition. 1649. 8°.* O, C.

1835A — —Sixth edition. *By J.B. for the company of stationers*, [1650]. 8°.* LW.

1836 — —Seventh edition. —, 1651. 8°.* O.

1837 — —Eighth edition. —, 1652. 8°.* O.

1838 — —Ninth edition. —, [1653]. 8°.* L, O, DT.

1839 — —Tenth edition. —, [1654]. 8°.* O; MH.

1840 — —Eleventh edition. —, 1655. 8°.* O.

1841 — —Sixteenth edition. *By James Cottrel, for the company of stationers*, 1660. 8°.* L; Y.

1841A — —Seventeenth edition. 1661. 8°.* O.

1841B — —Nineteenth edition. *Printed*, 1668. 8°.* CHW.

1842 — —Twentieth edition. The Scripture kalendar revived. —, 1669. 8°.* L.

1843 **J[essop], H[enry].** A calculation for ... 1645. *By M. Bell for the company of stationers*, [1645]. 8°.* LT.

1844 **Jinner, Sarah.** An almanack or prognostication for ... 1658. *By J. Streater for the company of stationers*, [1658]. 8°.* O, LG.

1845 — —1659. *By J. S. for the company of stationers*, [1659]. 8°.* O; CH.

1846 — —1660. —, [1660]. 8°.* Y.

1847 — —1664. —, 1664. 8°.* E.

1848 —The woman's almanack. *For J.J.*, 1659. 8°.* LT.

1849 **Johnson, G.** 1659. An account astrologicall of ... *By J. G. for the company of stationers*, 1659. 8°.* O.

1850 — —1660. —, 1660. 8°.* O.

1851 **Johnson, R.** An almanack for ... 1683. *By R.E. for the company of stationers*, 1683. 8°.* O; CLC, WF, Y.

1852 **Jones, Thomas.** Almanack am y flwyddyn 1681. *Printiedig yn Llundain*, 1681. 8°.* AN.

1853 —Y lleiat o'r almanaccau ... am ... 1692. *Haerludd*, [1691]. 8°.* L.

1854 —Y mwyat o'r almanaccau. [1691.] 8°.* AN, CPL.

1855 **Kendal, Roger.** Ephemeris absoluta; or a compleat diary. *By B. Griffin for the company of stationers*, 1700. 8°.* L, O, C; CH, MH, Y.

1855A **Kirby, Richard.** A diurnal speculum. 1684. O.

1856 —An ephemeris for ... 1681. *For the company of stationers*, 1681. 8°. L, O, C; CH, Y.

1857 — —*By Evan Tyler and Ralph Holt*, 1682. 8°. O, C; WF.

1857A **L., T.** Englands almanack shewing how the East India trade. *For the author, by S.Bridge*, 1700. brs. L; NC, Y.

1858 **Langley, Thomas.** Langley, 1641. A new almanack ... for ... 1641. *By R.Bishop for the company of stationers*, [1641]. 8°.* L, O, DT; CU.

1859 — —1642. —, [1642]. 8°.* O.

1860 — —1643. —, [1643]. 8°.* L, O.

1861 — —1647. *For the company of stationers*, [1647]. 8°.* L, O.

1862 The last Protestant almanack. [*London*], *printed*, 1680. 4°.* L.

1862A A lasting almanack. *For Mad Tom*, [1660]. brs. L.

1863 **Lea, Philip.** London almanack for xxx years. [1680.] brs. O.

1864 **Leeds, Daniel.** An almanack for ... 1687. *Printed and sold by William Bradford, near Philadelphia in Pennsylvania*, 1687. brs. EVANS 408. L; MB, PHS, PL.

1865 —An almanack and ephemeris for ... 1693. [*Philadelphia*], *by William Bradford*, 1693. 8°. EVANS 646. CH, PHS.

1866 — —1694. *Printed and sold by William Bradford in New-York*, 1694. 8°.* EVANS 692. CH, NN, PHS.

1867 — —1695. —, 1694. 8°.* EVANS 716. CH, NN, Y.

1868 — —1696. —, 1696. 8°.* EVANS 744. CH, MWA, NN.

1869 — —1697. —, 1697. 8°.* EVANS 785. CH, NN.

1870 — —1698. —, 1698. 8°.* EVANS 821. LF; CH, MWA, NN.

1871 — —1699. —, 1699. 8°.* EVANS 865a. NN, PHS.

1872 — —1700. —, 1700. 8°.* EVANS 866. CH, NN.

1872A The levellers almanack for ... 1652. *For G. Horton,*
       1651. 4°.* L, OC.
1873   **Leybourn, William.** An almanack and prognostica-
       tion, for ... 1651. *For the company of stationers,* 1651.
       8°. O; CU.
1874   —Speculum anni, or a glasse. 1648. 8°.* E; CU.
1875   ——1649. *By S. I. for the company of stationers,* [1649].
       8°.* O, C.
1876   **Lilly, William.** Anglicus; or, an ephemeris for 1645.
       By T. B. for John Partridge and Humfrey Blunden, 1645.
       8°.* O.
1876A ——1646. —, 1646. 8°.* L, O, C; WF.
1877   —An English ephemeris ... for ... 1650. *Printed, to be
       sold by the stationers,* 1650. 8°.* LT.
1878   ——*Printed,* 1651. 8°.* L.
1879   —Merlini Anglici ephemeris 1647. *[London], by T. B.
       for John Partridge and Humphrey Blunden,* 1647. 8°.*
       LT, O, C; CLC.
1880   ——1648. —, 1648. 8°. LT, O, C.
1881   ——1649. *For J. Partridge and H. Blunden,* 1649. 8°. LT,
       O, C; CH, WF.
1882   ——1650. —, 1650. 8°. LT, O, C; BN.
1883   ——1651. *For the company of stationers, and H. Blunden,*
       1651. 8°. LT, O, LW.
1884   ——1652. —, 1652. 8°. LT, O; MH.
1885   ——1653. —, 1653. 8°. LT, O.
1886   ——1654. —, 1654. 8°. L, O; MH.
1887   ——1655. —, 1655. 8°. LT, O, LCL; BN, CH, Y.
1888   ——1656. *For the company of stationers,* 1656. 8°. LT, O,
       E; Y.
1889   ——1657. —, 1657. 8°. L, O.
1890   ——1658. —, 1658. 8°. L, O, LG; MH.
1891   ——1659. —, 1659. 8°. L, O; Y.
1892   ——1660. —, 1660. 8°. L, O, P; WF.
1893   ——1661. —, 1661. 8°. L, O, C.
1894   ——1662. —, 1662. 8°. L, O; WF.
1895   ——1663. —, 1663. 8°. L, O, C; PAP.
1896   ——1664. —, 1664. 8°. O, C, E; CH.
1897   ——1665. *By A. W. for the company of stationers,* 1665.
       8°. L, O, C.
1898   ——1666. *By I. N. for the company of stationers,* 1666.
       8°. L, O, C, DT; MH, Y.
1899   ——1666. *By F. W. for the company of stationers,* 1666.
       8°. O.
1900   ——1667. *By J. M. for the company of stationers,* 1667.
       8°. L, O, C, LWL; MH.
1901   ——1668. *By J. Macock, for the company of stationers,*
       1668. 8°. O, C; CH, MH, PL.
1902   ——1669. —, 1669. 8°. L, O, C; PAP, WF.
1903   ——1670. —, 1670. 8°. O; MIU, WF.
1904   ——1671. —, 1671. 8°. L, O; MH.
1905   ——1672. —, 1672. 8°. L, O, P, E; MH, PAP.
1906   ——1673. —, 1673. 8°. O; MH.
1907   ——1674. —, 1674. 8°. L, O, C; MH, WF.
1908   ——1675. —, 1675. 8°. L, O, LG, E.
1909   ——1676. —, 1676. 8°. L, O, E; WF, Y.
1910   ——1677. —, 1677. 8°. L, O, C, E; MBA, PAP, Y.

1911   ——1678. —, 1678. 8°. L, O, C, E, EN; CH, MIU, TU, Y,
       HC.
1912   ——1679. —, 1679. 8°. O, C; MB, MH, PAP, WF, Y.
1913   ——1680. —, 1680. 8°. L, O, C, LG, E; CH, CLC, WF, Y.
1914   ——1681. —, 1681. 8°. L, O, C, E; CH, MB, WF.
1915   ——1682. —, 1682. 8°. O, C, E; MH, PAP, WF.
1916   ——1683. —, 1683. 8°. O, C; CH, WF.
1917   ——1684. —, 1684. 8°. L, O, C, LG; MH, TU, WF, Y.
1918   ——1685. —, 1685. 8°. O, C; WF, Y.
1919   —Merlinus Anglicus junior. *By R. W. for T. V. and are to
       be sold by I. S.,* 1644. 8°.* LT, O, C, HH, DT; CH, CLC, CN,
       WF, Y.
1920   ———1644. Second edition. 8°.* L, O, C, HH; CN, MH.
1921   [**Livie, J.**] The bloody almanack, or monethly obser-
       vations ... 1654. *Imprinted at London, for G. Horton,*
       1654. 4°.* LT.
1922   [–] —*For G. Horton,* 1655. 4°.* LT.
1923   [–] ——1659. *For Iohn Reynor,* 1659. 4°.* LT.
1924   **Lodowick, Christian.** 1695. The New-England al-
       manack. *Boston, by B. Green for S. Phillips,* 1695. 8°.*
       EVANS 717. MWA.
1925   The London almanack for ... 1686. [1686]. brs. EC.
1925A —1690. *For the company of stationers,* [1689]. brs. L.
1926   The London almanack or, a compendium ... 1673. *By
       Thomas Ratcliffe and Nathaniel Thompson, for the com-
       pany of stationers,* 1673. 8°.* O.
1927   **Lord, John.** An almanack and prognostication for ...
       1678. *By J. D. for the company of stationers,* 1678. 8°.*
       L, O, C, LN; CH, WF, Y.
1928   **M., A.** The country almanack. *By F. L. for the company
       of stationers,* 1675. 8°.* O, LG; WF.
1929   [–] ——, 1676. 8°.* L, O; WF, Y.
1930   ——1677. *By A. M. and R. R. for the company of stationers,*
       1677. 8°.* L, O, C; PAP.
1931   The mad-merry Merlin: or, the black almanack. *For
       G. H.,* 1653. 4°.* LT.
1932   **Man, John.** Edinburghs true almanack; ... for ...
       1696. *Edinburgh, John Reid,* 1696. 8°.* ALDIS 3581. HH.
1933   ——1698. —, 1698. 8°.* ALDIS 3759. HH, EN.
1934   —Prognostication, for ... 1699. *Edinburgh,* 1699. 12°.
       ALDIS 3868. L.
1935   ——1700. *Edinburgh, Reid,* 1700. 8°.* HH[FRAG.], EN, AU.
1936   **Markham, George.** An almanack for ... 1656. *By
       Joh. Streater, for the company of stationers,* 1656. 8°. *O.
1937   ——1657. *For the company of stationers,* [1657]. 8°.* O.
1937A **Martin, Henry.** A bloody almanack ... for ... 1662.
       For Robert Mottibee, 1661. 4°.* O.
1938   **Mather, Cotton.** MDCLXXXIII. The Boston epheme-
       ris. *Boston in New-England, by S. G. for S. S[ewall],*
       1683. 8°.* EVANS 351. O; LC, MB, MHS, MU, MWA.
1939   **Mather, Nathanael.** 1685. The Boston ephemeris.
       Boston in New-England, by and for Samuel Green, 1685.
       8°.* HOLMES MM 19, EVANS 395. MB, MHS, NN, RPJ.
1940   —1686. —*New-England, Boston, printed and sold by
       Samuel Green,* 1686. 8°.* HOLMES MM 20, EVANS 418.
       MB, MHS, MWA, NN, RPJ.

1941 Mercurius civicus, or the London-almanack 1674. *By Thomas Ratcliffe and Nathaniel Thompson for the company of stationers*, 1674. 8°.* L, O, C, E; WF.

1942 Merlinus verax; or, an almanack for . . . 1687. *For the company of stationers*, 1687. 8°.* L, O, OP, E; CN, WF, Y.

1943 Merry Andrew, a prognostication for . . . 1699. *Edinburgh, James Watson*, 1699. 8°.* ALDIS 3872. HH, EN.

1944 **Metcalfe, Francis.** Hemerologeion ad annum . . . 1654. *For the company of stationers*, [1654]. 8°.* O; MH.

1945 **Missonne, François.** Merlinus Gallicus, or, a prediction for . . . 1660. *By T. J. for Fr. Cosinet*, 1660. 8°. LT, O; KT.

Montelion, 1660. [1659.] *See under* Almanacs, Phillips, John.

1946 **Moore, Francis.** Kalendarium ecclesiasticum: being a new two-fold kalendar for . . . 1699. *By E. Holt for the company of stationers*, 1699. 8°.* L, O, C, E; CH, MH.

1946A [**Morgan, Einon.**] Hysbys ruwdd. 1693. 8°.* AN.

1947 **Morton, Robert.** An ephemeris for . . . 1662. *By Simon Dover, for the company of stationers*, 1662. 8°.* O.

1947A **N., H.** 1678. A yea and nay almanack. *For the company of stationers*, 1678. 8°. L, O, LF, E; PH, WF, HC.

1947B — — 1679. 8°. L, O, C, LF; MH, PAP, PH, WF.

1947C — — 1680. 8°. L, O, C, LF, E; CH, PH, PSC, WF.

1948 [**Napier, John.**] The bloody almanack. *For Anthony Vincent*, 1643. 4°.* LT, O; CLC, TU.

1949 [–] — [London], 1644. 4°.* L.

1950 [–] — —, 1645. 4°.* L.

1951 [–] — —, *By John Clowes*, [1647]. 4°.* LT, O; MIU, TU, WF.

1952 [–] — —, 1648. 4°. LT, O.

1953 [–] — [London], *for Anthony Vincent*, 1649. 4°.* LT.

1954 [–] — *By J. C.*, 1651. 4°.* LT, DT; MH.

1955 [–] — [London], 1652. 4°.* L.

1956 [–] — —, 1654. 4°.* L; MH.

1957 **Neve, John.** A new almanacke, . . . for 1641. [1641]. 8°.* L, O, DT.

1958 — Neve, 1642. 1642. 8°.* O.

1959 — — 1643. *By R. H. for the company of stationers*, [1643]. 8°.* L, O.

1960 — — 1646. *By R. Bishop, for the company of stationers*, [1646]. 8°.* L.

1960A — — 1647. *For the company of stationers*, 1647. 8°.* L.

1961 — — 1648. 1648. 8°.* E; CU.

1962 — — 1649. Mercurius annalis. *By S. I. for the company of stationers*, [1649]. 8°.* O, C.

1963 — — 1653. A new almanack. —, [1653]. 8°.* L, O, DT.

1964 — — 1654. —, 1654. 8°.* O; MH.

1965 — — 1655. —, 1655. 8°.* O.

1966 — — 1656. —, 1656. 8°.* O.

1967 — — 1657. —, 1657. 8°.* O.

1968 — — 1658. —, 1658. 8°.* O.

1969 — — 1659. —, 1659. 8°.* O.

1970 — — 1660. —, [1660]. 8°.* Y.

1971 — — 1661. —, 1661. 8°.* O.

1972 **Neve, Richard**, Nox Britannica. 1661. 8°.* O.

1973 **Neve, Robert.** Neve, 1664. A new almanacke. 1664. 8°.* O, E.

1974 — — 1665. —, 1665. 8°.* O.

1975 — — 1666. —, 1666. 8°.* O.

1976 — — 1667. —, 1667. 8°.* O.

1977 — Merlinus verax, 1668. 1668. 8°.* O.

1978 — — 1669. *By Robert White, for the company of stationers*, 1669. 8°.* O.

1979 — — 1670. —, 1670. 8°.* O.

1980 — — 1671. —, 1671. 8°.* O.

1981 — — 1672. —, 1672. 8°.* O.

1982 A new almanack. *Printed in Aberdeen*, 1690. 8°.* ALDIS 3056. ES.

1983 — *Edinburgh, J. Reid*, 1690. 8°.* ALDIS 3057. EN, ES.

1984 A new and exact prognostication for this present year. *Printed in Aberdeen by Iohn Forbes*, 1681. 8°.* ES.

1984A A new perpetual almanack. [1691.] brs. L.

1984AA A new prognostication for . . . 1651. *Aberdeen, James Brown*, 1651. 8°.* ALDIS 1448. HH[FRAG.].

1984AB — 1658. —, [1658]. 8°.* ALDIS 1578. HH[FRAG.].

1984B — 1664. *Glasgow, Robert Sanders*, 1664. 8°. L.

1984C — 1665. —, 1665. 8°. L.

1984D — 1665. *Aberdene, John Forbes*, [1665]. 8°. L.

1984E — 1666. —, [1666]. 8°. L.

1984EA — 1674. —, 1674. 8°.* ALDIS 2024. HH[FRAG.].

1984F — 1677. —, *Glasgow, —*, 1677. 8°. L.

1984G — 1678. —, 1678. 8°. L.

1984H — 1679. —, 1679. 8°. L.

1984I — 1680. *Aberdeen, John Forbes*, 1680. 12°. ALDIS 2208. ES.

1984J — 1681. *Glasgow, by Robert Sanders*, 1681. ALDIS 2279. GU.

1984K — 1682. —, 1682. 8°.* ALDIS 2339. ES.

1984L — 1683. *Aberdeen, Iohn Forbes*, [1683]. 8°.* ALDIS 2396. ES, HH.

1984M — 1683. *Edinburgh, reprinted*, 1683. 8°.* ALDIS 2397. HH.

1984N — 1683. *Glasgow, by Robert Sanders*, 1683. 8°.* ALDIS 2395. GU.

1984O — 1684. *Aberdene*, 1684. 8°.* ALDIS 2463. ES.

1984P — 1684. *Glasgow, by Robert Sanders*, 1684. 8°.* ALDIS 2464. GU.

1984Q — 1685. —, 1685. 8°.* ALDIS 2562. GU.

1984R — 1686. *Edinburgh, by the heir of Andrew Anderson*, 1686. 8°.* ALDIS 2647. EN, ES.

1984S — 1686. *Aberdeen, by Iohn Forbes*, [1686.] 8°.* ALDIS 2649. ES.

1984T —, 1686. *Glasgow, by Robert Sanders*, 1686. 8°.* ALDIS 2648. GU.

1985 A new prognostication for the year . . . 1687. *Edinburgh, heir of A. Anderson*, 1687. 8°. ALDIS 2700. ES.

1985A — 1691. *Glasgow, by Robert Sanders*. 1691. 8°.* ALDIS 3164 EN.

1985B — 1692. —, 1692. 8°.* ALDIS 3234. GU.

1986 The new Protestant almanack. *By J. Darby, for the company of stationers*, 1677. 8°. L, O, E, EN; PAP, WF, Y.

1987 **Newman, Henry.** Non cessant anni, . . . Harvard's ephemeris . . . for . . . 1690. *Cambridge, [Mass.], by Samuel Green*, 1690. 8°.* EVANS 544. MHS, Y.

1988 — Ut fluctus fluctum, . . . an almanack. *Boston: by R. Pierce for Benjamin Harris*, 1691. 12°.* EVANS 574. LC, MB, MHS.

1989   **Nightingale, Robert.** Mercurius philastrogus or an almanack ... 1653. [*London*], *for the company of stationers*, [1653]. 8°.* L, O, DT.

1990   **Nowell, Alexander.** MDCLXV. An almanack. *Cambridge* [*Mass.*], *by Samuel Green*, 1665. 8°.* EVANS 104. LC, MH, MWA.

1991   **Nunns, Thomas.** An almanack ... for ... 1661. 1661. 8°.* O.

1992   — —1662. —, 1662. 8°.* O.

1993   — —1664. —, 1664. 8°.* O, E.

1994   — —1665. —, 1665. 8°.* O.

1995   — —1666. *By J. Dover, for the company of stationers*, 1666. 8°.* L, O.

1996   **Nye, Nathaniel.** Nye, 1642. A new almanacke. *By R. H. for the company of stationers*, [1642]. 8°.* O.

1997   — —1643. —, [1643]. 8°.* L, O.

1998   — —1645. *By M. Bell for the company of stationers*, [1645]. 8°.* LW; CH.

1999   — —1648. —, 1648. 8°.* E; CU.

2000   —Nye, 1643. A prognostication. *For the company of stationers*, 1643. 8°.* L.

2001   —A prognostication for the year, 1645. *By F. Neile for the company of stationers*, 1645. 8°.* LW.

2002   [**Oakes, Urian.**] MDCL. An almanack for ... 1650. *Printed at Cambridge*, [*Mass.*], [*Samuel Green*], 1650. 8°.* EVANS 32. CH.

      Oxford almanack. 1673. *See under* Almanacs, Wheeler, Maurice.

2003   **Parker, George.** A double ephemeris for ... 1700. *For the author, and sold by W. Hunt*, 1700. 8°.* O, C; CH.

2004   —An ephemeris ... for ... 1695. *For the author*, 1695. 8°.* CN.

2004A   — —1696. —, 1696. 8°.* T.C.II 605. O; CN, Y.

2004B   — —1697. —, 1697. 8°.* CN.

2004C   — —1699. —, [1699]. 8°.* L; CN.

2005   —Mercurius anglicanus, or the English mercury. ... for ... 1690. *By J. M. for the company of stationers*, 1690. 8°.* L, O, E; CH, MH, Y.

2006   — —1691. —, 1691. 8°.* T.C.II 340. L, O; CN, NP, Y.

2007   — —1692. —, 1692. 8°.* L, O, C, E; CH, CN, NP, WF, Y.

2008   — —*By Benj. Motte, for the company of stationers*, 1693. 8°.* L, O, E; CH, CN, NP, Y.

2009   — —1694. —, 1694. 8°.* L, O, C, LG, EN; CH, CN, NP, PAP, Y.

2010   — —*By M. C. for the company of stationers*, 1695. 8°.* T.C.II 538. O, C; CH, NP, Y.

2011   — —1696. —, 1696. 8°.* L, O, C, E; CH, MH, Y.

2012   — —1697. —, 1697. 8°.* L, O, E; CH, MH, WF.

2013   — —1698. —, 1698. 8°.* L, O, C; CH, CN, MH, WF.

2014   — —1699. —, 1699. *For the author, and to be sold at his house; and W. Hunt*, [1699]. 8°.* O; CH.

2015   **Parkhurst, Ferdinando.** An almanack ... for ... 1648. 1648. 8°.* E; CU.

2016   **Partridge, Dorothy.** The woman's almanack for ... 1694. *For J. S.* 1694. 12°. O.

2017   **Partridge, John.** Annus mirabilis; being an almanack for ... 1688. *By R. R. for the company of stationers*, [1688]. 4°.* LG, E, EO; HC.

2018   —Annus mirabilis or strange and wonderful predictions. *Printed, and are to be sold by Randal Taylor*, 1689. 4°.* L, O, C, EN, DT; CH, MBP, MH, WF, Y.

2019   —[Hebrew] Calendarium Judaicum: or, an almanack for ... 1678. *By J. D. for the company of stationers*, 1678. 8°.* O, E; WF, Y, HC.

2020   — —1679. —, 1679. 8°.* O.

2021   — —1680. —, 1680. 8°.* O.

2022   — —1681. —, 1681. 8°.* O.

2023   — —1682. —, 1683. 8°.* O.

2024   — —1683. —, 1683. 8°.* O.

2025   — —1684. —, 1684. 8°.* O.

2026   — —1685. —, 1685. 8°.* O.

2027   — —1686. —, 1686. 8°.* O.

2028   —'Εκκλησιαλογια; being an almanack for 1679. 1679. 8°.* O, C; PAP.

2029   — —1680. *By J. D. for the company of stationers*, 1680. 8°.* L, O, C, LG, E; CH, CLC, WF, Y.

2030   —Mercurius cœlestis. *By J. D. for the company of stationers*, 1681. 8°.* L, O, C, E; CH.

2031   — —1682. 8°.* O, C, E; PAP, WF.

2032   —Merlinus liberatus: being an almanack for ... 1690. *By R. R. for the company of stationers*, [1690]. 8°.* L, O, E; CU, MH, WF, Y.

2033   — —1691. —, [1691]. 8°.* L, O; Y.

2034   — —1692. —, [1692]. 8°.* L, O, C; CH, WF, Y.

2035   — —1693. *By R. Roberts for the company of stationers*, [1693]. 8°.* L, O, LG; CH, Y.

2036   — —1694. —, [1694]. 8°.* L, O, C, LG, EN; CH, MH, PAP.

2037   — —1695. —, [1695]. 8°.* L, O, C; CH, MH, Y.

2038   — —1696. —, [1696]. 8°.* L, O, C, E; CH, MH, Y.

2039   — —1697. —, [1697]. 8°.* L, O, E; CH, MH, PAP, WF.

2040   — —1698. —, [1698]. 8°.* L, O, C, E; CH, MH, WF, Y.

2041   — —1699. —, [1699]. 8°.* L, O, C, E; CH, MH, Y.

2042   — —1700. —, [1700]. 8°.* L, O, C, E; CH, MH, Y.

2043   —Merlinus redivivus: being an almanack for ... 1683. *By R. R. for the company of stationers*, [1683]. 8°.* L, O, C, E; CH, MIU, TU, WF, Y.

2044   — —1684. —, [1684]. 8°.* L, O, C, LG, E; MB, MH, TU, WF, Y.

2045   — —1685. —, [1685]. 8°.* L, O, C, E; CLC, WF, Y.

2046   — —1686. —, [1686]. 8°.* O, C, E; CLC, MH, WF.

2047   — —1687. —, [1687]. 8°.* L, O; CLC.

2048   **Partridge, Seth.** Partridge ... an almanack and prognostication for ... 1649. *For the company of stationers*, 1649. 8°.* O, C.

2049   — —1651. —, 1651. 8°.* O; CU.

2050   — —1652. —, 1652. 8°.* O.

2051   —A survey of the yeer 1653. *By Jane Bell for the company of stationers*, [1653]. 8°.* L, O, DT.

2052   — —1654. —, [1654]. 8°.* O.

2053   — —1655. —, [1655]. 8°.* O.

2054   —Synopsis anni 1656. 8°.* O.

2055   — —1657. —, 1657. 8°.* O.

2056 — —1658. —, 1658. 8°.* O.

2057 — —1659. —, 1659. 8°.* O.

2058 — —1660. —, 1660. 8°.* Y.

2059 **Paterson, James.** Edinburgh's true almanack. *Edinburgh, by John Colmer*, 1685. 8°.* ALDIS 2565. EN, ES.

2060 — —*Edinburgh, J. Reid*, 1686. 8°.* ALDIS 2651. ES.

2061 — —*Printed at Holy-Rood House [Watson]*, 1687. 8°.* ALDIS 2702. EN, ES.

2062 — — —, 1688. 8°.* ALDIS 2772. EN, ES.

2063 — —*Holy-Rood-House, by Mr. P.B.*, 1689. 8°.* ALDIS 2927. EN, ES.

2063A — —*Edinburgh, Anderson*, 1690. 8°.* EN.

2064 — —*Edinburgh, J. Reid*, 1691. 8°.* ALDIS 3166. EN, ES.

2065 — — —, 1692. 8°.* ALDIS 3237. O, EN, ES.

2066 —A new almanack ... 1693. *Edinburgh, J. Reid*, 1693. 8°.* ALDIS 3308. ES.

2067 —A new prognostication ... 1681. *Edinburgh*, 1681. 12°.* ALDIS 2282. ES.

2068 — —1683. *Edinburgh [by heir of A. Anderson]*, 1683. 8°.* ALDIS 2403. HH, EN, ES.

2069 — —1684. *Edinburgh, printed by David Lindsay and his partners*, 1684. 8°.* ALDIS 2466. EN, ES.

2070 **Perkins, Francis.** Perkins. A new almanack. 1655. 8°.* O.

2071 — —1656. —, 1656. 8°.* O.

2072 — —1657. —, 1657. 8°.* O.

2073 — —1658. —, 1658. 8°.* O.

2074 — —1659. —, 1659. 8°.* O.

2075 — —1660. —, 1660. 8°.* Y.

2076 — —1662. —, 1662. 8°.* O.

2077 — —1664. —, 1664. 8°.* O.

2078 — —1666. *By Robert White, for the company of stationers*, 1666. 8°.* O, CT.

2079 — —1667. —, 1667. 8°.* CT.

2080 — —1669. —, 1669. 8°.* O.

2081 — —1670. —, 1670. 8°.* O; WF.

2082 — —1674. —, 1674. 8°.* O.

2083 — —1675. *For the company of stationers*, 1675. 8°.* O; WF.

2084 — —1677. —, 1677. 8°.* L, O.

2085 — —1678. —, 1678. 8°.* L, O; WF, Y, HC.

2086 — —1679. —, 1679. 8°.* L, O.

2087 — —1680. —, 1680. 8°.* O, LG; CH, WF.

2088 — —1681. —, 1681. 8°.* L, O.

2089 — —1682. —, 1682. 8°.* O, C.

2089A — —1683. —, 1683. 8°.* CLC.

2090 — —1684. —, 1684. 8°.* L, O; Y.

2091 — —1687. —, 1687. 8°.* L, O; Y.

2092 — —1688. —, 1688. 8°.* T.C.II 238. Y.

2092A — —1689. —, 1689. 8°.* MH, WF.

2093 — —1692. —, 1692. 8°.* L, O.

2094 — —1693. —, 1693. 8°.* L.

2095 — —1694. —, 1694. 8°.* L, O, LG.

2096 — —1695. —, 1695. 8°.* L, O.

2097 — —1696. —, 1696. 8°.* MH.

2097A — —1697. —, 1697. 8°.* PAP.

2097B — —1698. —, 1698. 8°.* L.

2098 — —1699. —, 1699. 8°.* O, C.

2099 **Perkins, Samuel.** A new almanack ... for 1641. *By Iohn Dawson, for the company of stationers*, 1641. 8°.* L, O, DT.

2100 — —1642. —, 1642. 8°.* O.

2101 — —1643. —, [1643]. 8° L, O.

2101A A perpetual almanack. [*London*, 1670]. brs. LG.

2102 **Peter, John.** The astral gazette: or, an almanack for ... 1678. *By T.N. for the company of stationers*, [1678]. 8°.* L, O, C; CH, WF, Y.

2103 **Phillippes, Henry.** An almanack ... for ... 1654. *By T. Maxey, for the company of stationers*, [1654]. 8°.* O, MH, PHS.

2104 — —1655. *By A. Maxey, for the company of stationers*, [1655]. 8°.* O.

2105 — —1656. —, [1656]. 8°.* O.

2106 — —1657. —, [1657]. 8°.* O.

2107 — —1658. —, [1658]. 8°.* O, LG.

2108 —A constant kalender or an almanack for 300 years. *By R. and W. Leybourn, for Thomas Pierrepont*, 1656. 12°.* L, O; CH, CLC, MH, WF.

2108A — —1677. 12°. MH.

2109 **Phillips, John.** Montelion, 1660, or, the prophetical almanack. colop: [*London*], *sold by Henry Marsh*, [1659]. 8°.* L, O; CLC, WF.

2110 [–] —1661. *Sold by Henry Marsh*, [1661]. 8°.* LT, O, OC; CLC.

2111 — —1662. —, [1662]. 8°.* O.

2112 **Pierse, Matthew.** A new almanacke ... 1641. 1641. 8°. L, O, DT.

2113 **Pigot, Francis.** Pigot, 1660. An almanacke. *For the company of stationers*, 1660. 8°.* L; Y.

2114 — —1661. —, 1661. 8°.* O.

2115 — —1662. —, 1662. 8°.* O.

2116 —Speculum anni: a new almanack, ... for 1654. 1654. 8°.* O.

2117 — —1655. —, 1655. 8°.* O.

2118 — —1656. —, 1656. 8°.* O.

2119 — —1657. —, 1657. 8°.* O.

2120 — —1658. —, 1658. 8°.* O.

2121 — —1659. —, 1659. 8°.* O.

2122 — —1661. —, 1661. 8°.* O.

2123 — —1662. —, 1662. 8°.* O.

2124 **Plunkett, Patrick.** A new almanack for ... 1679. *Dublin, Benjamin Tooke*, 1679. 8°.* DIX 168. DN.

2125 — —1684. *Dublin, Benjamin Tooke & John Crooke*, 1684. 8°.* DIX 207. DML.

2126 **Pond, Benjamin.** A new almanack for ... 1689. *Oxford, at the theatre for Thomas Guy, London*, 1689. 8°.* O.

2127 **Pond, Edward.** Almanack for ... 1641. *Cambridge, R. Daniel*, 1641. 8°.* L, O, DT.

2128 —Pond's almanack for ... 1641. *By F. K. for the company of stationers*, [1641]. 8°.* PHS.

2128A — —1642. —, [1642]. 8°.* O.

2129 — —1643. *By R. Daniel, Cambridge*, 1643. 8°.* L.

2130 — —1644. *By F. K. for the company of stationers*, [1643]. 8°.* L, O.

2131 ——1647. *By R. Cotes, for the company of stationers,* 1647. 8°.* L, O.

2131A ——1647. *Cambridge, by Roger Daniel,* 1647. 8°.* PHS.

2132 ——1648. —, 1648. 8°.* E; CU, PHS.

2133 ——1649. —, 1649. 8°.* O.

2134 ——1652. *Cambridge: by the printers to the universitie,* 1652. 8°.* O; CU.

2135 —Pond an almanack ... 1653. *Cambridge, by the printers to the university,* 1652. 8°.* L, O, DT; PHS.

2135A ——1654. —, 1653. 8°.* O; MH.

2136 ——1655. —, 1655. 8°.* O; CU.

2137 ——1656. —, 1656. 8°.* O.

2138 ——1657. —, 1657. 8°.* O.

2139 ——1658. *Cambreids* [*sic*]: *printed by John Field,* 1658. 8°.* O, LG.

2140 ——1659. *Cambridge: by John Field,* 1659. 8°.* O.

2141 ——1660. —, 1660. 8°.* O.

2142 ——1661. —, 1661. 8°.* L O C.

2143 ——1662. —, 1662. 8°.* O.

2144 ——1663. —, 1663. 8°.* L, O, C, CT; PAP.

2145 —Pond. An almanack for ... 1664. *Cambridge; by John Field,* 1664. 8°.* L, O, C, E; CH.

2146 ——1665. —, 1665. 8°.* O, C.

2147 ——1666. —, 1666. 8°.* L, O, C, DT.

2147A ——1667. —, 1667. 8°.* O, LWL.

2148 ——1668. —, 1668. 8°.* L, O, C; MH, PL.

2149 ——1669. —, 1669. 8°.* L, O, C. [FRAG.]; PAP, PHS, WF.

2150 ——1670. —, 1670. 8°.* L, O.

2151 ——1671. *Cambridge, by John Hayes,* 1671. 8°.* L, O; PHS.

2152 ——1672. —, 1672. 8°.* L, O, E; PAP, PHS.

2153 ——1673. —, 1673. 8°.* O.

2154 ——1674. —, 1674. 8°.* L, O, E.

2155 ——1675. —, 1675. 8°.* O, LG, E; WF.

2156 —Pond. A new almanack for ... 1676. —, 1676. 8°.* O; WF.

2157 —Pond. An almanack for ... 1677. —, 1677. 8°.* L, O.

2158 ——1678. —, 1678. 8°.* L, O, C, LN; CH, WF, Y.

2159 ——1679. —, 1679. 8°.* O; MH, WF.

2160 ——1680. —, 1680. 8°.* O, C, LG; CH, WF.

2161 ——1681. —, 1681. 8°.* L, O; WF.

2162 ——1682. —, 1682. 8°.* C.

2163 ——1683. —, 1683. 8°.* O; CLC.

2164 ——1684. —, 1684. 8°.* L, O.

2165 ——1685. —, 1685. 8°.* O.

2166 ——1686. —, 1686. 8°.* O.

2167 ——1687. —, 1687. 8°.* L, O, C; Y.

2168 ——1688. —, 1688. 8°.* C, LG, E; Y, HC.

2169 ——1689. —, 1689. 8°.* T.C.II 238. L, O, C, EN; CLC, MH, WF, Y.

2170 ——1690. —, 1690. 8°.* L, O, E; CH, Y.

2171 ——1690. —, 1691. 8°.* O; Y.

2171A ——1691. —, 1691. 8°.* Y.

2172 ——1692. —, 1692. 8°.* L, O, C, E; CH, WF.

2173 ——1693. —, 1693. 8°.* L, O; CH.

2174 ——1694. —, 1694. 8°.* L, O, C, LG, EN; CH, MH, PAP.

2175 ——1695. —, 1695. 8°.* O; CH.

2176 ——1696. —, 1696. 8°.* O, C; CH, MH.

2177 ——1697. —, 1697. 8°.* O, CS; CH, PAP.

2178 ——1698. —, 1698. 8°.* L, O, E; CH, MH, WF.

2179 ——1699. —, 1699. 8°.* O, C; CH.

2180 ——1700. —, 1700. 8°.* O, C; CH.

2181 [**Pont, J.**] A register, or a generall almanack for every yeare. *By William Wilson,* 1646. 8°. LT, O; WF.

2182 **Poole, John.** Poole ... a new almanack ... for ... 1642. *By F.K. for the company of stationers,* [1642]. 8°.* O.

2182A ——1655. —, 1655. 8°.* O.

2182B ——1656. —, 1656. 8°.* L, O.

2182C ——1657. —, 1657. 8°.* O.

2183 Poor Robin, 1664. An almanack. *For the company of stationers,* [1664]. 8°.* L, O, E.

2184 ——1665. —, 1665. 8°.* O, CT.

2185 ——1666. —, 1666. 8°.* O, C, CT, DT.

2186 ——1667. —, 1667. 8°.* L, O, C; WF.

2187 ——1668. —, [1668]. 8°.* L, O, C, CT; PL, WF.

2188 ——1669. —, [1669]. 8°.* L, O; CU, PAP.

2189 ——1670. —, [1670]. 8°.* L, O; WF, Y.

2190 ——1671. —, [1671]. 8°.* L, O.

2191 ——1672. —, [1672]. 8°.* L, O, E; PAP, Y.

2192 ——1673. —, [1673]. 8°.* O; TU.

2193 ——1674. —, [1674]. 8°.* L, O, C, E; CU, WF.

2194 ——1675. —, [1675]. 8°.* L, O, LG; WF.

2195 ——1676. —, [1676]. 8°.* L, O; MB, WF, Y.

2196 ——1677. —, [1677]. 8°.* L, O, C, E; PAP.

2197 ——1678. —, [1678]. 8°.* L, O, C, LN; CH, WF, Y.

2198 ——1679. —, [1679]. 8°.* O, C; MB, MH, PAP, WF, Y.

2199 ——1680. —, [1680]. 8°.* L, O, C, LVF, E; CH, WF, Y.

2200 ——1681. —, [1681]. 8°.* L, O, C; CH, MB, WF, Y.

2201 ——1682. —, [1682]. 8°.* O, C; MB, PAP, WF, Y.

2202 ——1683. One and twentieth impression. —, 1683. 8°.* O, C; CH, TU, WF, Y.

2203 ——1684. Two and twentieth impression. —, 1684. 8°.* L, O, C, LG; MB, MH, TU, WF, Y.

2204 ——1685. Three and twentieth impression. —, 1685. 8°.* O, C; MIU, WF, Y.

2205 ——1686. Four and twentieth impression. —, 1686. 8°.* O, C; MH, WF, Y.

2206 ——1687. Five and twentieth impression. —, 1687. 8°.* L, O, OP, E; WF, Y.

2207 ——1688. Six and twentieth impression. —, 1688. 8°.* C, E, EO; MB, HC, Y.

2208 ——1689. Seven and twentieth impression. —, 1689. 8°.* T.C.II 238. L, O, C, LVF, EN; CLC, MB, MH, WF, Y.

2209 ——1690. Eight and twentieth impression. —, 1690. 8°.* L, O, E; MB, MH, WF, Y.

2210 ——1691. Nine and twentieth impression. —, [1691]. 8°.* L, O; Y.

2211 ——1692. Thirtieth impression. —, [1692]. 8°.* L, O, C, E; CH, MB, WF, Y.

2212 ——1693. One and thirtieth impression. —, 1693. 8°.* L, O; CH, MBA.

2213 ——1694. Two and twentieth impression. 8°.* L, O, C, LVF; CH, MH, PAP, WF.

2214 — —1695. Three and twentieth impression. —, 1695. 8°.* L, O, C; CH, Y.

2215 — —1696. Four and thirtieth impression. *By J.L. for the company of stationers,* 1696. 8°.* L, O, C, E; CH, MB, MBA, MH.

2216 — —1697. Thirty-fifth impression. *By J.Leake for the company of stationers,* 1697. 8°.* L, O, E; CH, MBA, MH, PAP, WF.

2217 — —, 1698. —, 1698. Thirty-sixth impression. 8°.* L, O, C, E; CH, MBA, MH, WF.

2218 — —1699. —, 1699. Thirty-seventh impression. 8°.* L, O, C, E; CH, MB, MBA, MH.

2219 — —1700. Thirty-eighth impression. —, 1700. 8°.* L, O, C, E; CH, MH, Y.

2220 Poor Robin. 1677. Or, a yea-and-nay almanack. *By George Larkin for the assigns of John Seymour.* 1677. 8°. LF.

2221 **Prince, Vincent.** The constables calendar. *By J. S. for the company of stationers,* 1660. 8°.* L, O; Y.

2222 The Protestant almanack. *For the company of stationers,* 1668. 8°.* O, OC, OM, CT; Y.

2223 —for . . . 1669. *Cambridge; printed,* 1669. 8°.* O, C, LL, OC; WF.

2224 —1680. *For the company of stationers,* 1680. 8°.* L, O, C, LG, E; CH, CLC, WF, Y.

2225 —1681. —, 1681. 8°.* L, O, C, E; CH, WF.

2226 —1682. —, 1682. 8°.* O, C.

2227 —1683. Fourth impression. —, 1683. 8°.* O, C, E; CH, WF, Y.

2228 —1684. Fifth impression. —, 1684. 8°.* L, O, C, LG, E; MB, MH, TU, WF, Y.

2229 —1685. Sixth impression. —, 1685. 8°.* O, C, E; MIU, Y.

2229A — —1689. —, 1689. 8°.* CLC.

2230 —1690. *By John Richardson for the company of stationers,* 1690. 8°.* L, O, E; CH, MH, WF, Y.

2231 —1691. —, 1691. 8°.* L, O; Y.

2232 —1692. —, 1692. 8°.* L, O, C, E; CH, WF, Y.

2233 —1693. —, 1693. 8°.* L, O, E; CH.

2234 —1694. —, 1694. 8°.* L, O, C, LG; CH, MH.

2235 —1695. —, 1695. 8°.* L, O, C; CH.

2236 —1696. —, 1696. 8°.* L, O, C, E; CH, MH.

2237 —1697. —, 1697. 8°.* L, O; CH, MH, WF.

2238 —1698. —, 1698. 8°.* L, O, C, E; CH, MH, WF.

2239 —1699. —, 1699. 8°.* L, O, C, E; CH, MH.

2240 —1700. —, 1700. 8°.* O, C; CH.

2241 **Ramsay, William.** Vox stellarum, or, . . . 1652. *For T. H. and Jo. Collins,* 1652. 8°.* LT, O, DC, A; MB, WF.

2242 **Readman, William.** An almanack and prognostication for . . . 1680. *By R. E. for the company of stationers,* 1680. 8°. O, LG; CH, WF, Y.

2243 **R[ichardson], J[ohn].** 1670. An almanack. *Cambridge* [*Mass.*]: *by S. G[reen] and M. J[ohnson],* 1670. 8°.* EVANS 154. MB, MWA.

2244 **Rider, Cardanus.** Riders: 1656. British Merlini. *By R. & W. Leybourn, for the company of stationers,* [1656]. 8°.* L.

2245 — —1658. —, [1658]. 8°.* L.

2246 — —1659. —, [1659]. 8°.* L.

2247 — —1660. —, [1660]. 12°.* O.

2248 — —1663. *By Will. Leybourn,* [1662]. 12°.* L; CLC.

2248A — —1664. —, [1663]. 12°.* CN.

2249 — —1668. —, [1668]. 12°.* O.

2250 — —1670. *By S. G. for the company of stationers,* [1670]. 8°.* L, O, EN.

2251 — —1672. —, 1672. 8°.* L, EN.

2252 — —1673. —, 1673. 8°.* C; CLC, CU.

2252A — —1674. *By T. N. for the company of stationers,* 1674. 12°. L.

2252B — —1675. —, 1675. 12°. O.

2253 — —1678. *By Tho. Newcomb, for the company of stationers,* 1678. 8°.* L; CH, Y.

2254 — —1679. —, 1679. 12°.* O, C.

2254A — —1680. —, 1680. 12°.* C; MBA.

2255 — —1681. —, 1681. 12°.* C, LG.

2256 — —1682. —, 1682. 12°.* L, O.

2256A — —1683. —, 1683. 12°.* Y.

2257 — —1684. —, 1684. 12°.* O.

2258 — —1686. —, 1686. 12°.* O.

2258A — —1687. —, 1687. 8°. OP.

2258B — —1688. —, 1688. 12°. CM.

2259 — —1689. *For the company of stationers,* 1689. 12°.* T.C.II 238. O.

2260 — —1690. —, 1690. 12°.* O.

2260A — —1692. —, 1692. 12°. LCS.

2261 — —1693. —, 1693. 12°.* O, LUG, RE; CH.

2262 — —1694. —, 1694. 12°.* O, LG.

2263 — —1696. —, 1696. 12°.* L, O, OP.

2263A — —1698. —, 1698. 12°.* O.

2263B — —1699. —, 1699. 12°.* Y.

2264 — —1700. —, 1700. 12°.* O.

2264A **Riders, T.** The black remembrancer. [1660.] brs. LT.

2265 **Rose, George.** Rose, 1656. A new almanack. 1656. 8°.* O.

2266 — —1657. —, 1657. 8°.* O.

2267 — —1659. —, 1659. 8°.* O.

2268 — —1660. *By S. Griffin for the company of stationers,* 1660. 8°.* L; Y.

2269 — —1661. —, 1661. 8°.* O.

2270 — —1662. —, 1662. 8°.* O.

2271 — —1664. —, 1664. 8°.* O.

2272 — —1665. —, 1665. 8°.* O.

2272 — —1666. —, 1666. 8°.* O.

2274 — —1667. —, 1667. 8°.* O.

2275 — —1668. —, 1668. 8°.* O.

2276 — —1669. —, 1669. 8°.* O.

2277 — —1670. —, 1670. 8°.* O.

2278 — —1671. —, 1671. 8°.* O.

2279 — —1672. —, 1672. 8°.* O.

2280 — —1673. —, 1673. 8°.* O.

2281 — —1674. —, 1674. 8°.* O.

2282 — —1675. *By Robert White for the company of stationers,* 1675. 8°.* O; WF.

2283 — —1676. —, 1676. 8°.* O.

2284 — —1677. *By E. H. and T. H. for the company of stationers,* 1677. 8°.* L, O.

2285 — —1678. *By Tho. Hodgkin, for the company of stationers,* 1678. 8°.* O; CLC, WF, Y, HC.

2286 — —1679. —, 1679. 8°.* L, O.

2287 — —1680. —, 1680. 8°.* O, LG; CH, WF.

2288 — —1681. —, 1681. 8°.* L, O.

2289 — —1682. —, 1682. 8°.* O, C.

2290 — —1683. —, 1683. 8°.* O; CLC.

2291 — —1684. —, 1684. 8°.* L, O; Y.

2292 — —1685. —, 1685. 8°.* O.

2293 — —1686. —, 1686. 8°.* O.

2294 — —1687. —, 1687. 8°.* L, O; Y.

2294A — —1688. —, 1688. 8°. CM.

2295 — —1689. —, 1689. 8°.* TC.II 238. L; MH.

2296 — —1690. —, 1690. 8°.* O; CH.

2297 — —1691. —, 1691. 8°.* O; Y.

2298 — —1692. —, 1692. 8°.* L, O.

2299 — —1693. —, 1693. 8°.* L.

2300 — —1694. —, 1694. 8°.* L, O, LG.

2301 — —1695. —, 1695. 8°.* L, O.

2302 — —1696. —, 1696. 8°.* MH.

2302A — —1697. —, 1697. 8°.* PAP.

2302B — —1698. —, 1698. 8°.* L.

2303 — —1699. —, 1699. 8°.* O, C.

2304 **Rowley, John.** Speculum perspicuum uranicum: or, a glass . . . 1651. *By S. I. for the company of stationers,* [1651]. 8°.* O; CU.

2305 —Κατοπλρον: sive, speculum . . . 1652. *By S. I. for the company of stationers,* [1652]. 8°.* O.

2305A The royall Merlin. *For George Horton,* 1655. 4°.* LT.

2306 **R[ussell], D[aniel].** 1671. An almanack. *Cambridge* [Mass.]: *by S. G. and M. J.,* 1671. 8°.* EVANS 164. LC, MB, MWA.

2306A **Russel, Dom.** A new almanack for . . . 1690. *Dublin, by Andrew Crook, the assign of Benjamin Tooke,* 1690. 12°.* DN.

2307 **Russell, John.** A cœlestiall prospect, . . . for . . . 1660. *By Thomas Mabb, for the company of stationers,* 1660. 8°.* Y.

2308 — —1661. —, 1661. 8°.* O.

2309 **Russell, Noadiah.** MDCLXXXIIII. Cambridge ephemeris. *Cambridge* [Mass.], *by Samuel Green,* 1684. 8°.* EVANS 376. MHS.

2309A **S., G.** A new prognostication for 1691. *Edinburgh, Anderson,* 1691. 8°.* EN.

2309B **S., H.** A new prognostication for 1693. *Glasgow, Sanders,* 1693. 8°.* GU.

2309C — —, 1696. —, 1696. 8°.* GU.

2310 **S., J.** A new prognostication for . . . 1692. *Edinburgh, heir of A. Anderson,* 1692. 8°. ALDIS 3264. EN, ES.

2311 — —1693. —, 1693. 8°. ALDIS 3339. EN, ES.

2312 **S., P.** A new prognostication for 1676. *Edinburgh,* 1676. 8°. L.

2313 **S., W.** A new prognostication for 1697. *Glasgow, Sanders,* 1697. 8°.* GU.

2313A — —1698. —, 1698. 8°.* GU.

2314 **Salmon, William.** Salmon's almanack for . . . 1684. *By T. Dawks, for the company of stationers,* 1684. 8°.* L, O; CH, Y.

2315 —The London almanck for . . . 1691. *By W. H. for the company of stationers,* 1691. 8°.* O; Y.

2316 — —1692. *By W. Horton for the compant of stationers,* 1692. 8°.* L, O, C; CH, WF, Y.

2317 — —1693. —, 1693. 8°.* L, O, E; CH.

2318 — —1694. —, 1694. 8°.* O, LG.

2319 — —1695. —, 1695. 8°.* L, O, C; CH, Y.

2320 — —1696. —, 1696. 8°.* L, O, C, E; CH, MH.

2321 — —1697. —, 1697. 8°.* L, O, E; CH, MH, PAP, WF.

2322 — —1698. —, 1698. 8°.* L, O, C, E; CH, MH, WF.

2323 — —1699. —, 1699. 8°.* L, O, C, E; CH, MH.

2324 — —1700. —, 1700. 8°.* L, O, C, E; CH, MH, Y.

2325 **Saunders, Richard.** 1654. Apollo Anglicanus. 1654. 8°.* O.

2326 —1656. —. 1656. 8°.* O.

2327 —1657. —. 1657. 8°.* O.

2328 —1658. —. 1658. 8°.* O, LG.

2329 —1659. —. 1659. 8°.* O; CU.

2330 —1660. —. 1660. 8°.* O.

2331 —1661. —. *By E. Cotes, for the company of stationers,* 1661. 8°.* L, O, C.

2332 —1662. —. —, 1662. 8°.* L, O; WF.

2333 —1663. —. —, 1663. 8°.* L, O, C; PAP.

2334 —1664. —. —, 1664. 8°.* L, O, C, E, DT; CH, Y.

2335 —1665. —. —, 1665. 8°.* L, O.

2336 —1666. —. —, 1666. 8°.* L, O, C, DT.

2337 —1667. —. —, 1667. 8°.* L, O, C, LWL; MH.

2338 —1668. —. —, 1668. 8°.* L, O, C; MH, PL.

2339 —1669. —. —, 1669. 8°.* L, O, C; CU, PAP, WF.

2340 —1670. —. *By E. C. & A. C. for the company of stationers,* 1670. 8°.* L, O; WF.

2341 —1671. —. *By A. C. for the company of stationers,* 1671. 8°.* L, O; CLC.

2342 —1672. —. *By Andrew Clark for the company of stationers,* 1672. 8°.* L, O, E; PAP.

2343 —1673. —. —, 1673. 8°.* O.

2344 —1674. —. —, 1674. 8°.* L, O, C, E; CU, WF.

2345 —1675. —. —, 1675. 8°.* L, O, LG, E; WF.

2346 —1676. —. —, 1676. 8°.* L, O, E; WF, Y.

2347 —1677. —. —, 1677. 8°.* L, O, C, E; CH, PAP, Y.

2348 —1678. —. —, 1678. 8°.* L, O, C, LN; CH, WF, Y.

2349 —1679. —. *By M. Clark for the company of stationers,* 1679. 8°.* O, C; MH, PAP, WF.

2350 —1680. —. —, 1680. 8°.* L, O, C, LG; CH, CLC, WF, Y.

2351 —1681. —. —, 1681. 8°.* L, O, C, E; CH, WF.

2352 —1682. —. —, 1682. 8°.* O, C, E; MB, PAP, WF.

2353 —1683. —. —, 1683. 8°.* O, C, E; CH, TU.

2354 —1684. —. —, 1684. 8°.* L, O, C, LG, E; MB, MH, TU, WF, Y.

2355 —1685. —. —, 1685. 8°.* O, C, E; MIU, WF, Y.

2356 —1686. —. —, 1686. 8°.* O, C, E; MH, WF.

2357 —1687. —. —, 1687. 8°.* L, O, OP, E; CLC, WF, Y.

2358 —1688. —. —, 1688. 8°.* C, LG, E, EO; Y, HC.

2359 —1689. —. —, 1689. 8°.* T.C.II 238. L, O, C, EN; CLC, MB, MH, WF, Y.

2360 —1690. —. —, 1690. 8°.* L, O, E; MH, WF, Y.

2361 —1691. —. —, 1691. 8°.* L, O, E; MB, Y.

2362 —1692. —. —, 1692. 8°.* L, O, C; CH, WF, Y.

2363 —1693. —. —, 1693. 8°.* L, O, E; CH.

2364 —1694. —. —, 1694. 8°.* L, O, C, LG, EN; CH, MH, PAP, Y.

2365 —1695. —. —, 1695. 8°.* L, O, C; CH, Y.

2366 —1696. —. —, 1696. 8°.* L, O, C, E; CH, MH.

2367 —1697. —. *By Mary Clark for the company of stationers,* 1697. 8°.* L, O; CH, MH, PAP, WF.

2368 —1698. —. *By M. Clark, for the company of stationers,* 1698. 8°.* L, O, C, E; CH, MH, WF.

2369 —1699. —. —, 1699. 8°.* L, O, C, E; CH, MH, Y.

2370 —1700. —. *By M. & J. Wilde, for the company of stationers,* 1700. 8°.* L, O, C; CH, MH, Y.

2371 **Seaman, Henry.** Kalendarium nauticum . . . for . . . 1675. *By T. N. for the company of stationers,* 1676. 8°.* O, LG, E; WF.

2372 — —1676. —, 1676. 8°.* L, O, E; Y.

2373 — —1677. —, 1677. 8°.* L, O, C, E; CU, PAP.

2374 A second edition of the nevv almanack for . . . 1656. *Printed,* 1656. 4°.* LT.

2375 **Seller, John.** An almanack for an age. [*London,* 1684.] 8°. L; CLC.

2376 —An almanck for the provinces of Virginia and Maryland. 1685. 12°. MBJ.

2377 —An almanack for xxx years. [*London,* 1682.] 12°. L.

2378 —Barbados almanack for xxx years. *Sold by the author in Wapping,* [1684]. 12°.* L.

2379 —Jamaica almanack . . . for xxx. yeares. *Sold by the author in Wapping, and by John Seller in London,* [1684]. 8°. L.

2380 —New-England almanack . . . for xxx years. *Sold by the author,* 1685. 8ll. MH.

2380A **Shakerley, Jeremy.** Synopsis compendiarae. *By T. R. and E. M. for the company of stationers,* 1651. 8°.* O.

2381 **Shepard, Jeremiah.** An ephemeris of . . . 1672. *Cambridge* [*Mass.*], *by Samuel Green,* 1672. 8°.* EVANS 172. MWA.

2381A The shepheard's kalender. 1656. fol. L.

2382 **S[herman], J[ohn].** 1674. An almanack. *Cambridge* [*Mass.*], *by Samuel Green,* 1674. 8°.* EVANS 196. CH, CN, MB, MHS.

2383 —1676. —*Cambridge* [*Mass.*], *by S. Green,* 1676. 8°.* EVANS 223. CN, MHS.

2384 —1677. —, 1677. 8°.* EVANS 241. CN, MHS.

2385 **Shinkin ap Shone.** Her prognostication for . . . 1654 *For the author,* [1654]. 4°.* LT, O.

2386 **Shon-ap-Lewis.** 1648. The Welch-mans new almanacke. *For Thomas Bates,* 1648. 8°.* L.

2387 **Silvester, John.** Astrological observations . . . for . . . 1681. 1681. 4°.* EN; WF.

2387A — —1682. *For the author,* 1682. 4°.* OC, SP.

2388 — —1691. —, 1690. 4°.* L, BR, EN.

2388A —Astrological and theological observations . . . for . . . 1700. *For the author, and are sold by W. Bonny, Bristol,* [1699]. 4°.* L.

2389 **Sliter, Robert.** A celestiall glasse, or ephemeris for . . . 1652. *For the company of stationers,* [1652]. 8°.* O.

2390 **Smith, John.** Hemerologium hermeticum or a mercuriall calendar . . . 1653. 1653. 8°.* O.

2391 — —1654. 1654. 8°.* O.

2392 — —1655. 1655. 8°.* O.

2393 — —1656. 1656. 8°.* O.

2394 —Smith . . . a new almanack . . . for . . . 1652. *For the company of stationers,* 1652. 8°.* O; CU.

2395 —Speculum anni . . . 1673. 1673. 8°.* O.

2396 — —1674. 1674. 8°.* O.

2397 — —1675. *By F. L. for the company of stationers,* 1675. 8°.* O; WF.

2398 **Sofford, Arthur.** Sofford. 1641. A new almanack . . . for . . . 1641. *By R. O. for the company of stationers,* [1641]. 8°.* L, O, DT.

2399 The States-man's almanack. [*n.p.,* 1683.] brs. OC, HH; MH.

2400 **Staynred, Philip.** Staynred. An almanack for . . . 1648. 1648. 8°.* E; CU.

2400A **Stevenson, Nicolas.** The royal almanacke. 1675. 12°. MH.

2400B — —1676. 8°. O.

2400C — —*By A. C. for the company of stationers,* 1677. 8°. O; MIU.

2401 **Stobo, John.** Mercurius Scotus, his almanack. *Edinburgh, heir of A. Anderson,* 1694. 8°. ALDIS 3408. EN, ES.

2402 **Streete, Thomas.** A compleat ephemeris for . . . 1682. *By Hen. Hills for the company of stationers,* 1682. 8°.* O, C, E; PAP, WF.

2403 — —1683. *By Th. Dawks, for the company of stationers,* 1683. 8°.* O, C; WF, Y.

2404 — —1684. *By J. Gain, for the company of stationers,* 1684. 8°.* L, O, C, LG, E; MB, MH, WF, Y.

2405 — —1685. —, 1685. 8°.* O, C, E; MIU, WF, Y.

2406 —A double ephemeris for . . . 1653. *By M. Simmons,* 1653. 8°.* LT, O.

2407 **Strut, Thomas.** The weaver's almanack for . . . 1688. 1688. 8°.* E.

2408 — —1690. *By Elizabeth Holt for the company of stationers,* 1690. 8°.* L, O, E; WF, Y.

2409 **Swallow, John.** Swallow. An almanack for 1641. 1641. 8°.* L, O, DT.

2410 — —1642. *Cambridge,* 1642. 8°.* O, C.

2411 — —1643. *By A. Norton for the company of stationers,* 1643. 8°.* L, O.

2412 — —1646. *By Iohn Dawson, for the company of stationers,* [1646]. 8°.* C.

2413 — —1647. —, [1647]. 8°.* L, O.

2414 — —1648. —, 1648. 8°.* E; CU.

2415 — —1649. —, 1649. 8°.* O, C.

2416 — —1651. *Cambridge, By the printers to the universitie,* [1651]. 8°.* O.

2417 — —1652. —, 1652. 8°.* L, O, DT.

2418 — —1653. —, 1653. 8°.* L, O.

2419 — —1654. —, 1653. 8°.* O; MH.

2420 — —1655. —, 1655. 8°.* O.

2421 — —1657. —, 1657. 8°.* O.

2422 — —1658. *Cambridge, by John Field*, 1658. 8°.* O, LG.
2423 — —1659. —, 1659. 8°.* O.
2424 — —1660. —, [1660]. 8°.* L, O; Y.
2425 — —1661. —, [1661]. 8°.* L, O.
2426 — —1662. —, 1662. 8°.* O.
2427 — —1663. —, 1663. 8°.* CHRISTIE-MILLER.
2428 — —1664. —, 1664. 8°.* O, E; Y.
2429 — —1665. —, 1665. 8°.* O.
2430 — —1666. —, 1666. 8°.* O.
2431 — —1667. —, 1667. 8°.* O.
2432 — —1668. —, 1668. 8°.* L, O, C; PL.
2433 — —1669. —, 1669. 8°.* O.
2434 — —1670. *Cambridge, by the printers to the university*, 1670. 8°.* O; WF.
2435 — —1671. —, 1671. 8°.* O.
2436 — —1672. —, 1672. 8°.* O.
2437 — —1673. —, 1673. 8°.* O.
2438 — —1674. —, 1674. 8°.* O.
2439 — —1675. —, 1675. 8°.* L, O; WF.
2440 — —1676. —, 1676. 8°.* O.
2441 — —1677. —, 1677. 8°.* L, O.
2442 — —1678. —, 1678. 8°.* O, E;, Y, HC.
2443 — —1679. —, 1679. 8°.* L, O, C; PAP.
2444 — —1680. —, 1680. 8°.* O, C, LG; CH, WF.
2445 — —1681. —, 1681. 8°.* L, O.
2446 — —1682. —, 1682. 8°.* O, C.
2447 — —1683. —, 1683. 8°.* O.
2448 — Swallow. A new almanack for . . . 1684. —, 1684. 8°.* L, O; Y.
2449 — —1685. —, 1685. 8°.* O.
2450 — —1686. —, 1686. 8°.* O.
2451 — —1687. —, 1687. 8°.* L, O; Y.
2452 — —1688. —, 1688. 8°.* E.
2453 — —1689. —, 1689. 8°.* T.C.II 238. L; MH.
2454 — —1690. —, 1690. 8°.* O; Y.
2455 — —1691. —, 1691. 8°.* O; Y.
2456 — —1692. —, 1692. 8°.* L, O, C; Y.
2457 — —1693. —, 1693. 8°.* L.
2458 — —1694. —, 1694. 8°.* L, O, C, LG; MH.
2459 — —1695. —, 1695. 8°.* L, O, C; Y.
2460 — —1696. —, 1696. 8°.* MH.
2461 — —1697. —, 1697. 8°.* L, O; MH, PAP, WF.
2462 — —1698. —, 1698. 8°.* L, O.
2463 — —1699. —, 1699. 8°.* O, C.
2464 — —1700. —, 1700. 8°.* O.
2465 **Swan, John.** An ephemeris, or almanack for . . . 1657. *Cambridge, by John Field*, 1657. 8°.* O.
2466 — —1658. —, 1658. 8°.* O; CU.
2467 — —1659. —, 1659. 8°.* O.
2468 — —1660. —, 1660. 8°.* Y.
2469 — —1661. —, 1661. 8°.* L, O, C.
2470 — —1662. —, 1662. 8°.* O; WF.
2471 — —1663. —, 1663. 8°.* L, O, C; PAP.
2472 — —1664. —, 1664. 8°.* O, E; Y.
2473 — —1665. —, 1665. 8°.* O.
2474 — —1666. *By John Field, Cambridge*, 1666. 8°.* L, O.
2475 — —1667. —, 1667. 8°.* L, O, C, LWL; MH.

2476 — —1668. —, 1667. 8°.* O; MH.
2477 — —1669. —, 1669. 8°.* L, O, C; CU, PAP, WF.
2478 — —1670. —, 1670. 8°.* O; WF.
2479 — —1671. —, 1671. 8°.* O.
2480 — —1672. —, 1672. 8°.* O, CT.
2481 — —1673. —, 1673. 8°.* O.
2482 — Swan. A new almanack for . . . 1674. *By John Hayes, Cambridge*, 1674. 8°.* O, E; CU, WF.
2483 — —1675. —, 1675. 8°.* L, O, C, LG, E; WF.
2484 — —1676. —, 1676. 8°.* O; WF.
2485 — —1677. —, 1677. 8°.* L, O.
2486 — —1678. —, 1678. 8°.* O, CS, E, EN; WF, HC.
2487 — —1679. —, 1679. 8°.* O.
2488 — —1680. —, 1680. 8°.* O, C, LG; CH, WF.
2489 — —1681. —, 1681. 8°.* L, O.
2490 — —1682. —, 1682. 8°.* O, C.
2490A — —1683. —, 1683. 8°. O; CLC.
2491 — —1684. —, 1684. 8°.* L, O; Y.
2492 **[Symson, Matthjas.]** The Caledonian almanack. *Edinburgh, printed,* 1700l 4°.* L, HH.
2493 **T., J.** Merlinus Scotus . . . for . . . 1698. *Edinburgh, James Watson,* 1698. 8°.* ALDIS 3805. HH.
2494 **Tanner, John.** Angelus Britannicus. *By John Streeter,* 1657. 8°.* O.
2495 — —1658. —, 1658. 8°.* O.
2496 — —1659. —, 1659. 8°.* O.
2497 — —1660. —, 1660. 8°.* O.
2498 — —1661. —, 1661. 8°.* O.
2499 — —1662. *By Thomas Mabb for the company of stationers,* 1662. 8°.* L, O; WF.
2500 — —1663. —, 1663. 8°.* O.
2501 — —1664. —, 1664. 8°.* L, O, C, E; CH, Y.
2502 — —1665. —, 1665. 8°.* O.
2503 — —1666. —, 1666. 8°.* L, O.
2504 — —1667. *By Peter Lillicrap, for the company of stationers,* 1667. 8°.* L, O, LWL.
2505 — —1668. *By Thomas Ratcliffe for the company of stationers,* 1668. 8°.* O; MH.
2506 — —1669. —, 1669. 8°.* O.
2507 — —1670. *By Thomas Ratcliffe and Thomas Daniel,* 1670. 8°.* L, O; WF.
2508 — —1671. *By Thomas Ratcliffe and Mary Daniel for the company of stationers,* 1671. 8°.* L, O.
2509 — —1672. —, 1672. 8°.* L, O, E; PAP.
2510 — —1673. —, 1673. 8°.* O.
2511 — —1674. *By Thomas Ratcliffe and Nath. Thompson, for the company of stationers,* 1674. 8°.* L, O, C, E; CU, MIU, WF.
2512 — —1675. —, 1675. 8°.* O, LG, E; WF.
2513 — —1676. —, 1676. 8°.* L, O, LVF, E; WF, Y.
2514 — —1677. *By E. Horton, for the company of stationers,* 1677. 8°.* L, O, C, E; PAP.
2515 — —1678. —, 1678. 8°.* L, O, LVF, E; WF, HC.
2516 — —1679. —, 1679. 8°.* O, C, LVF; MH, PAP, WF.
2517 — —1680. —, 1680. 8°.* L, O, C, LG, E; CH, CLC, WF, Y.
2518 — —1681. Twenty-fourth impression. —, 1681. 8°.* L, O, C, E; WF.

2519 ——1682. —, 1682. 8°.* O, C, E; PAP, WF.

2520 ——1683. Twenty-seventh impression. —, 1683. 8°.* O, C, E; CH, TU, WF, Y.

2521 ——1684. Twenty-eighth impression. —, 1684. 8°.* L, O, C, LG; MB, MH, TU, WF, Y.

2522 ——1685. Twenty-ninth impression. —, 1685. 8°.* O, C; Y.

2523 ——1686. Thirtieth impression. —, 1686. 8°.* O, C; MH, WF.

2524 ——1687. Thirty-first impression. —, 1687. 8°.* L, O, OP, E; CH, CN, WF, Y.

2525 ——1688. Thirty-second impression. —, 1688. 8°.* E; Y.

2526 ——1689. Three and thirtieth impression. *By W. H. for the company of stationers,* 1689. 8°.* T.C.II 238. L, O, C, EN; CLC, MB, MH, WF, Y.

2527 ——1690. Thirty-fourth impression. —, 1690. 8°.* L, O, E; MH, WF, Y.

2528 ——1691. Thirty-fifth impression. —, 1691. 8°.* L, O; Y.

2529 ——1692. Thirty-sixth impression. —, 1692. 8°.* L, O, C, E; CH, WF, Y.

2530 ——1693. Thirty-seventh impression. —, 1693. 8°.* L, O, E; CH.

2531 ——1694. Thirty-eighth impression. *By W. Horton for the company of stationers,* 1694. 8°.* L, O, C, LG, EN; CH, MH, PAP.

2532 ——1695. Thirty-ninth impression. —, 1695. 8°.* L, O, C; CH, Y.

2533 ——1696. Fortieth impression. —, 1696. 8°.* L, O, C, E; CH, MH.

2534 ——1697. One and fortieth impression. —, 1697. 8°.* L, O, E; MH, PAP, WF.

2535 ——1698. Forty-second impression. —, 1698. 8°.* L, O, C, E; CH, MH, WF.

2536——1699. Forty-third impression. —, 1699. 8°.* L, O, C, E; CH, MH.

2537 ——1700. Forty-fourth impression. —, 1700. 8°.* L, O, C, E; CH, MH, Y.

2537A **Tapp, John.** The seaman's kalender. *By T. Forcet, for G. Hurlock,* 1648. 4°. L.

2537B ——[Anr. ed.] *By W. G. for G. Hurlock,* 1669. 4°. L.

2537C ——[Anr. ed.] 1696. 4°. L.

2538 **Taylor, Jacob.** [An almanack.] *New York, William Bradford,* 1699. ROSENBACH.

2538A ——*Philadelphia, by Reynier Jansen,* 1669. PL. (I leaf.)

2539 **Taylor, John.** Εφημερις. Or, an almanack for . . . 1696. *By H. Clark for the company of stationers,* 1696. 8°.* L; MH.

2540 ——, 1697. —, 1697. 8°.* PAP.

2541 **Temple, Charles.** An almanack for . . . 1656. *For the company of stationers,* [1656]. 8°.* O.

2542 ——1657. —, [1657]. 8°.* O.

2543 **Trigge, Thomas.** Calendarium astrologicum . . . 1660. *By D. Maxwell, for the company of stationers* [1660]. 8°.* Y.

2544 ——1661. —, 1661. 8°.* O, C.

2545 ——1662. —, 1662. 8°.* O.

2546 ——1664. —, 1664. 8°.* O; Y.

2547 ——1665. —, 1665. 8°.* O.

2548 ——1666. —, 1666. 8°.* O.

2549 ——1667. *By A. Maxwell, for the company of stationers,* 1667. 8°.* L, O, C; MH.

2550 ——1668. —, 1668. 8°.* L, O, C; MH, PL.

2551 ——1669. —, 1669. 8°.* L, O, C; CU, PAP, WF.

2552 ——1670. —, 1670. 8°.* O; WF.

2553 ——1671. —, 1671. 8°.* L, O.

2554 ——1672. *By J. Winter for the company of stationers,* 1672. 8°.* L, O; PAP.

2555 ——1673. —, 1673. 8°.* O.

2556 ——1674. —, 1674. 8°.* O.

2557 ——1675. —, 1675. 8°.* L, O; WF.

2558 ——1676. —, 1676. 8°.* L, O; Y.

2559 ——1677. —, 1677. 8°.* L, O, C; PAP.

2560 —Kalandarium astrologicum. 1678. —, 1678. 8°.* O, C, LN; CH, WF, Y.

2561 ——1679. —, 1679. 8°.* L, O, C; MH, PAP.

2562 —Calendarium astrologicum. 1680. *Printed at London, by A. Godbid and J. Playford, for the company of stationers,* 1680. 8°.* L, O, C, LG; CH, WF, Y.

2563 ——1681. —, 1681. 8°.* L, O, C; CH, WF.

2564 ——1682. —, 1682. 8°.* O, C; PAP, WF.

2565 ——1683. —, 1683. 8°.* O, C; CH, TU.

2566 ——1684. *Printed at London, by J. Playford, for the company of stationers,* 1684. 8°.* L, O, C, LG; MB, MH, TU, WF, Y.

2567 ——1685. —, 1685. 8°.* O, C; MIU, WF.

2568 ——1686. *By B. Griffin for the company of stationers,* 1686. 8°.* O, C; MH, WF.

2569 ——1687. —, 1687. 8°.* L, O; WF, Y.

2570 ——1688. —, 1688. 8°. CM; Y.

2570A ——1689. —, 1689. 8°.* OP; MH, WF.

2571 ——1690. —, 1690. 8°.* O; MH.

2572 ——1691. —, 1691. 8°.* O; Y.

2573 ——1692. —, 1692. 8°.* L, O.

2574 ——1693. —, 1693. 8°.* L, O.

2575 ——1694. —, 1694. 8°.* L, O, LG.

2576 ——1695. —, 1695. 8°.* O.

2577 ——1696. —, 1696. 8°.* MH.

2577A ——1697. —, 1697. 8°.* PAP.

2578 ——1698. —, 1698. 8°.* L, O; NC.

2579 ——1699. —, 1699. 8°.* O, C.

2580 ——1700. —, 1600. 8°.* O.

2581 —Speculum astrologicum, for 1659. 1659. 8°.* O.

2582 **Tulley, John.** Tulley 1687. An almanack. *Boston, by S. Green for Benjamin Harris,* 1687. 8°.* EVANS 435. LC, MHS, MWA, PHS.

2583 ——1688. *Boston, by Samuel Green,* 1688. 8°.* EVANS 454. LC, MWA, PHS.

2584 ——1689. —, 8°.* EVANS 499. LC, MHS, MWA.

2585 ——1690. *Boston, printed and sold by Samuel Green,* 1690. 8°.* EVANS 548. LC, MB, MHS, MWA.

2586 ——1691. *Cambridge [Mass.]: by Samuel Green, and B. Green, and are · to be sold by Nicholas Buttolph, in Boston,* 1691. 8°.* EVANS 578. CH, LC, MB, MH, MWA.

2587   — —1692. *Cambridge [Mass.]: by Samuel Green, and Bartholomew Green, for Samuel Phillips, in Boston,* 1692. 8°.* EVANS 630. O; LC, MB, MH, MWA, PHS.

2588   — —1693. *Boston, by Benjamin Harris,* 1693. 8°.* EVANS 682. MB, MHS, MWA, PL.

2589   — —1693. *Boston, by Benjamin Harris for Samuel Phillips* 1693. 8°.* EVANS 683. CH, LC, CW, MH, PHS.

2590   — —1694. *Boston, printed and sold by Benj. Harris,* 1694. 8°.* MH.

2591   — —1695. *Boston, for John Usher, by Benjamin Harris,* 1695. 8°.* EVANS 740. MB, MHS, MWA.

2592   — —1696. *Boston, by Bartholomew Green, and John Allen, for John Usher,* 1696. 8°.* EVANS 776. LC, MHS, MWA.

2593   — —1697. —, 1697. 8°.* EVANS 815. LC, MHS, MWA.

2594   — —1698. —, 1698. 8°.* EVANS 854. CH, LC, MB, MH, MHS.

2595   — —1699. —, 1699. 8°.* EVANS 897. CH, LC, MHS, PHS.

2596   — —1700. —, 1700. 8°.* EVANS 955. CH, LC, MB, MH, MHS.

2597   **Turner, William.** An almanack for . . . 1687. *By J. Heptinstall, for the company of stationers,* 1687. 8°.* L, O; Y.

2598   — —1688. —, 1688. 8°.* E.

2598A   — —1689. —, 1689. 8°.* MH, WF.

2599   — —1690. —, 1690. 8°.* O.

2600   — —1691. —, 1691. 8°.* O; Y.

2601   — —1692. —, 1692. 8°.* L, O.

2602   — —1694. —, 1694. 8°.* L, O, LG.

2603   — —1695. —, 1695. 8°.* L, O.

2604   — —1696. —, 1696. 8°.* MH.

2604A   — —1697. —, 1697. 8°.* PAP.

2605   — —1698. —, 1698. 8°.* O.

2606   — —1699. —, 1699. 8°.* O, C.

2607   — —1700. —, 1700. 8°.* O.

2608   **Vaux, John.** Vaux, 1642. A new almanack. 1642. 8°.* O.

2609   — —1643. *By R. O. & G. D. for the company of stationers,* [1643]. 8°.* L, O.

2610   — —1649. —, 1649. 8°.* O.

2611   — —1652. —, 1652. 8°.* O; CU.

2612   —Vaux, 1653. Diarium. *By Gartrude Dawson, for the company of stationers,* [1653]. 8°.* L, O.

2613   —Vaux, 1654. A new almanack. —, 1654. 8°.* O.

2614   — —1655. —, 1655. 8°.* O.

2615   — —1656. —, 1656. 8°.* O.

2616   — —1657. —, 1657. 8°.* O.

2617   — —1658. —, 1658. 8°.* O.

2618   — —1659. —, 1659. 8°.* O.

2619   — —1660. —, [1660]. 8°.* Y.

2620   — —1661. —, 1661. 8°.* O.

2621   — —1662. —, 1662. 8°.* O.

2622   — —1664. —, 1664. 8°.* O.

2623   — —1665. —, 1665. 8°.* O.

2624   — —1666. —, 1666. 8°.* O.

2625   Vox uraniæ, or Aberdeen's true astral gazer, . . . 1687. *Printed in Aberdeen by John Forbes,* [1687]. 8°.* ALDIS 2731. ES.

2626   —1688. —, [1688]. 8°.* ES.

2627   —1689. —, [1689]. 8°.* ES.

2628   —1690. —, [1690]. 8°.* ALDIS 3108. ES.

2629   —1691. —, [1691]. 8°.* ES.

2630   —1692. —, [1692]. 8°.* ALDIS 3271. HH, ES.

2631   —1693. —, [1693]. 8°.* ES.

2632   —1694. —, [1694]. 8°.* ALDIS 3411. ES.

2633   **W., W.** An Episcopal almanack for . . . 1674. *By J. Macock for the company of stationers,* 1674. 8°.* L, O, C; CU, WF.

2634   — —1675. —, 1675. 8°.* L, O, LG; WF.

2635   — —1676. —, 1676. 8°.* L, O; WF, Y.

2636   — —1677. —, 1677. 8°.* L, O, C; PAP.

2637   — —1678. —, 1678. 8°.* L, O, C, LN; CH, WF, Y.

2638   **Waterman, Andrew.** Waterman: the sea-mans almanack. *By John Field, and sold by Thomas Vere and Nathaniel Brook,* 1656. 8°.* L.

2639   The Welsh-mans new almanack. *Printed,* 1643. 4°.* LT, AN; CLC, TU, WF.

2640   **Westley, James.** An ephemeris for . . . 1669. *By T. Milbourn for the company of stationers,* 1669. 8°. O; MIU.

2641   **Whalley, John.** Advice from the stars . . . for . . . 1697. [*Dublin*], 1697. 8°.* DIX 292. DML.

2641A   — —*Dublin, by Cornelius Colter for John Foster,* 1690. 8°. WF.

2642   — —*Dublin, printed at the authors' printing house,* 1700. 8°.* DIX 322. DML.

2643   —England's mercury. *By W. H. for the company of stationers,* 1690. 8°.* L, O; WF.

2644   — —1691. 8°.* O.

2645   —Mercurius Britannicus. —, 1691. 8°.* Y.

2646   —Mercurius Hibernicus . . . for . . . 1691. *Dublin, Andrew Crook, Assignee of B. Tooke,* 1691. 8°.* DIX 376. P. J. O'REILLY.

2647   — —1693. *Dublin, by Andrew Crook,* 1692. 8°.* DIX 253. DT.

2648   —Syderus nuncius . . . for . . . 1686. *Dublin, Benjamin Crook,* 1686. 8°.* DIX 220. DML.

2649   —Vox urani or an almanack. *Dublin, Andw. Crook,* 1685. 8°.* DIX 214. DML.

2650   **Wharton, *Sir* George.**—Wharton. 1645. An almanack. *Printed at Oxford, by Henry Hall,* 1645. 8°.* MADAN 2063. LT, O.

2651   —Calendarium Carolinum: or. . . . *By J. Grismond,* 1660. 8°. L.

2652   — —1661. *By J. G. for the company of stationers,* 1661. 8°. L, O, C; CLC, CU, MH, WF.

2653   — —1662. —, 1662. 8°.* L, O, R; WF.

2654   — —1663. —, 1663. 8°. L, O, C; CH, CLC, CU, MH, WF.

2655   — —1664. *By J. Grismond,* 1664. 8°. L, O, C, E; CH, WF, Y.

2656   — —1665. —, 1665. 8°. L, O, C, CT.

2657   — —1666. —, 1666. 8°. L, O, C, DT; CU, MBA, Y.

2657A   —Calendarium ecclesiasticum. *By John Grismond,* 1657. 8°. L, O; WF, Y.

2658   — —1658. —, 1658. 8°. L, O, C, LG.

2659   — —1659. —, 1659. 8°. L, O.

2660   — —1660. —, 1660. 8°. L, O; CLC.

2661 —Ephemeris: or, a diary ... for ... 1655. *For Tho. Vere, and Nath. Brook,* 1655. 4°. LT, O, E; WF.

2662 — —1655. *By M.J.,* 1655. 4°. L, O.

2663 —Hemerologium: or, a register ... for ... 1656. *By John Grismond,* 1656. 4°. LT, O; CH.

2664 —Hemeroscopeion, ... for ... 1649. [*London?*], *for the author,* 1649. 8°. LT, O.

2665 — —1650. —, 1650. 8°.* LT, O.

2666 — —1651. *By J. Grismond for the company of stationers,* 1651. 8°. O; CU.

2667 —Hemeroscopeion anni intercalaris 1652. *By J. Grismond the company of stationers,* 1652. 8°. LT, O; CU.

2668 —Hemeroscopeion anni æræ Christian. 1653. —, 1653 8°. LT, O; MH, WF.

2669 — —1654. *By J. G. for James Crumpe,* 1654. 8°. LT, O; CH, NN, Y.

2670 —Naworth 1641. A new almanack. *By J. N. for the company of stationers,* 1641. 8°.* L, O.

2671 — —1642. *By I. Dawson for the company of stationers,* [1642]. 8°.* O.

2672 — —1643. *By Iohn Dawson for the company of stationers,* [1643]. 8°.* L.

2673 — —1644. *Printed at Oxford by Henry Hall,* 1644. 8°.* 8°.* MADAN 2060. LT, O, OC.

2673A — —1645. —, 1645. 8°.* O.

2674 —No Merline, nor mercurie; but a new almanack ... for ... 1647. [*York?*], *printed,* 1647. 8°.* L, O; CH.

2675 — —1648. *For the author,* 1648. 8°. LT, O; CU.

2676 [**Wheeler, Maurice.**] The Oxford almanack for ... 1673. [*Oxford*], *at the theater,* 1673. 12°.* MADAN 2957. O; MH.

2677 [–] —1674. *Printed at the theater in Oxford,* [1673.] brs. MADAN 3297. L, O, EC.

2678 [–] —1675. —, [1675]. brs. O.

2679 [–] —1676. —, [1676]. brs. O, EC.

2680 [–] —1677. —, [1677]. brs. L, O, EC.

2681 [–] —1678. —, [1678]. brs. L, O, EC.

2682 [–] —1679. —, [1679]. brs. T.C.I 372. L, O, EC.

2683 [–] —1680. —, [1680]. brs. TC.I 418. L, O, EC.

2684 [–] —1681. —, [1681]. brs. L, O, EC.

2685 [–] —1682. —, [1682]. brs. L, O, EC.

2686 [–] —1683. —, [1683]. brs. L, O, EC.

2687 [–] —1684. —, [1683]. brs. L, O, EC.

2688 [–] —1685. —, [1684]. brs. L, O, EC.

2689 [–] —1686. —, [1686]. brs. L, O, EC.

2690 [–] —1687. —, [1687]. brs. O; WF.

2691 [–] —1688. —, [1688]. brs. L, O, EC; WF.

2692 [–] —1689. —, [1689]. brs. L, O; WF.

2693 [–] —1690. —, [1690]. brs. L, O, EC; WF.

2694 [–] —1691. —, [1691]. brs. O, EC.

2695 [–] —1692. —, [1692]. brs. T.C.II 403. L, O, WCA; PAP, Y.

2696 [–] —1693. —, [1692]. brs. L, O, EC.

2697 [–] —1694. —, [1694]. brs. O, CT.

2698 [–] —1695. —, [1695]. brs. O, CT, EC.

2699 [–] —1696. —, [1696]. brs. O, CT, EC.

2700 [–] —1697. —, [1696]. brs. L, O, CT, EC.

2701 [–] —1698. —, [1697]. brs. L, O, CT, EC.

2702 [–] —1698. —, [1698]. brs. O, CT.

2703 [–] —1699. —, [1699]. brs. O, EC.

2704 [–] —1700. —, [1700]. brs. O, EC.

2705 **White, Ambrose.** An almanack ... for ... 1665. *Dublin, by Nathaniel Thompson, for Robert Howes,* 1665. 8°.* DIX 127. DM, DT.

2706 **White, John.** White. 1677. The country-mans kalendar. *By T. D. for the assigns of John Seymour,* 1677. 8°.* L.

2707 —White. 1641. A new almanack ... 1641. 1641. 8°.* O, DT.

2708 — —1642. *By F. K. for the company of stationers,* 1642. 8°.* O.

2709 — —1643. —, [1643]. 8°.* L, O.

2710 — —1646. —, 1646. 8°.* O.

2711 — —1647. —, 1647. 8°.* L, O.

2712 — —1648. —, 1648. 8°.* E; CU.

2713 — —1649. —, 1649. 8°.* O, C.

2714 — —1651. —, 1651. 8°.* O; CU.

2715 — —1653. *By R. & W. Leybourn, for the company of stationers,* [1653]. 8°.* L, O, DT.

2715A **White, Thomas.** White, 1670. A new almanack. 1670. 8°.* L.

2716 — —1677. *By Robert White for the company of stationers,* 1677. 8°.* L, O.

2717 — —1678. —, 1678. 8°.* O, E; WF, Y.

2718 — —1679. —, 1679. 8°.* O.

2719 — —1680. *By Margaret White, for the company of stationers,* 1680. 8°.* O, LG; CH, WF.

2720 — —1681. —, 1681. 8°.* L, O.

2721 — —1682. —, 1682. 8°.* O, C.

2722 — —1683. —, 1683. 8°.* O; CLC.

2723 — —1684. *By Bernard White for the company of stationers,* 1684. 8°.* L, O; Y.

2724 — —1685. —, 1685. 8°.* O.

2725 — —1686. —, 1686. 8°.* O.

2726 — —1687. —, 1687. 8°.* L, O.

2727 — —1688. —, 1688. 8°.* E; Y.

2727A — —1689. —, 1689. 8°.* MH, WF.

2728 — —1690. —, 1690. 8°.* O.

2729 — —1691. —, 1691. 8°.* O; Y.

2730 — —1692. *By H. Clark, for the company of stationers,* 1692. 8°. L, O.

2731 — —1693. —, 1693. 8°.* L.

2732 — —1694. —, 1694. 8°.* L, O, LG.

2733 — —1695. —, 1695. 8°.* L, O; Y.

2734 — —1696. —, 1696. 8°.* MH.

2734A — —1697. —, 1697. 8°.* PAP.

2735 — —1698. —, 1698. 8°.* O.

2736 — —1699. —, 1699. 8°.* O, C.

2737 — —1700. —, 1700. 8°.* O.

2737A **White, William.** A briefe and easie almanack. [*London, 1650.*] brs. WF.

2738 —White. 1651. A new almanack. 1651. 8°.* CU.

2738A — —1652. —, 1652. 8°.* O.

2739 — —1653. —, 1653. 8°.* O.

2740 — —1654. *By R. & W. Leybourn for the company of stationers, 1654.* 8°.* O ; MH.

2741 — —1655. —, *1655.* 8°.* O.

2742 — —1656. —, *1656.* 8°.* O.

2743 — —1657. —, *1657.* 8°.* O.

2744 — —1658. —, *1658.* 8°.* O.

2745 — —1659. —, *1659.* 8°.* O.

2746 — —1660. *By Robert White, for the company of stationers,* 1660. 8°.* Y.

2747 — —1661. —, *1661.* 8°.* O.

2748 — —1662. —, *1662.* 8°.* O.

2749 — —1664. —, *1664.* 8°.* O.

2750 — —1665. —, *1665.* 8°.* O.

2751 — —1666. —, *1666.* 8°.* O.

2752 — —1667. —, *1667.* 8°.* O.

2753 — —1668. —, *1668.* 8°.* O.

2754 — —1669. —, *1669.* 8°.* O.

2755 — —1670. —, *1670.* 8°.* L, O.

2756 — —1671. —, *1671.* 8°.* O.

2757 — —1672. —, *1672.* 8°.* O.

2758 — —1673. —, *1673.* 8°.* O.

2759 — —1674. —, *1674.* 8°.* O.

2760 — —1675. —, *1675.* 8°.* O ; WF.

2761 — —1676. —, *1676.* 8°.* O.

2762 **Whiting, James.** An ephemeris for ... 1669. *By John Field, Cambridge,* 1669. 8°.* L, O, C, CT ; CU, PAP, WF.

2763 **Wilkinson, Thomas.** Apollo Northamptoniensis. [1659]. 8°.* O.

2764 —A kalender and prognostication for ... 1658. [1658]. 8°.* O.

2765 —Mercurius Northamptoniensis. Or. ... *By J. Bell for the company of stationers,* [1660]. 8°.* Y.

2766 —Wilkinson. 1643. A new almanack. *By F. K. for the company of stationers,* [1643]. 8°.* L.

2767 —Philosophia cœlestis: or an almanack ... for ... 1663. 1663. 8°.* CHRISTIE-MILLER.

2768 **Williams, William.** MDCLXXXV. Cambridge ephemeris an almanack. *Cambridge, [Mass.], by Samuel Green,* 1685. 16°.* EVANS 399. MHS, MWA.

2769 —1685. — Second edition. *Cambridge [Mass.], by Samuel Green for Samuel Phillips, in Boston,* 1685. 8°.* EVANS 400. Y.

2770 [-] 1687. — *Cambridge [Mass.], by S. G.,* 1687. 8°.* EVANS 436. MHS.

2771 **Wing, John.** Ολύμπια δώματα, or an almanack for ... 1680. *Cambridge, by John Hayes,* 1680. 8°.* O, C, LG, E ; CH, WF, Y.

2772 — —1681. —, *1681.* 8°.* L, O, C, E ; CH.

2773 — —1682. —, *1682.* 8°.* O.

2774 — —1683. —, *1683.* 8°.* O, C ; CLC.

2775 — —1684. —, *1684.* 8°.* L, O ; Y.

2776 — —1685. —, *1685.* 8°.* O ; Y.

2777 — —1686. —, *1686.* 8°.* O, C, E ; MH, WF.

2778 — —1687. —, *1687.* 8°.* L, O, C, OP, E ; CH, WF, Y.

2779 — —1688. —, *1688.* 8°.* C, LG, E ; HC.

2780 — —1689. —, *1689.* 8°.* L, O, C, EN ; CLC, MH, WF. Y.

2781 — —1690. —, *1690.* 8°.* L, O, E ; MH, Y.

2782 — —1691. —, *1691.* 8°.* L, O, C ; WF, Y.

2783 — —1692. —, *1692.* 8°.* L, O ; CH, WF.

2784 — —1693. —, *1693.* 8°.* L, O ; CH, WF.

2785 — —1694. —, *1694.* 8°.* L, O, LG, EN ; CH, PAP.

2786 — —1695. —, *1695.* 8°.* L, O ; CH, WF.

2787 — —1696. —, *1696.* 8°.* L, O, C, E ; CH, MH.

2788 — —1697. —, *1697.* 8°.* O ; CH, PAP.

2789 — —1698. —, *1698.* 8°.* L, O, E ; CH, MH, Y.

2790 — —1699. —, *1699.* 8°.* L, O, C, E ; CH, MH.

2790A — —1700. —, *1700.* 8°.* O.

2791 **Wing, Vincent.** An almanack ... for ... 1641. *By J. Norton for the company of stationers,* 1641. 8°.* L, O, DT.

2792 — —1642. *By A. N. for the company of stationers,* 1642. 8°.* O.

2793 — —1643. —, *1643.* 8°.* L, O.

2794 — —1647. *By L. Legatt and G. Millar for the company of stationers,* 1647. 8°.* L, O.

2795 — —1648. —, *1648.* 8°.* E.

2796 — —1667. —, *1667.* brs. O.

2797 — —1682. —, *1682.* brs. O.

2797A — —1684. *By Mary Clark, for the company of stationers,* 1684. brs. W.

2798 — —1692. —, *1692.* brs. O.

2799 — —1693. —, *1693.* brs. O.

2799A —An ephemerides of the coelestiall motions for vii years. *By Robert and William Leybourn, for the company of stationers.* 1652. 4°. L, O, C, LW, SC ; MH, WF, Y.

2800 —An ephemerides of the coelestial motions for xiii years. *By R. & W. Leybourn, for the company of stationers,* 1658. 4°. LT, O, OB, E, DT ; CLC, MH, Y.

2800A —Wing's ephemeris for thirty years. *By J. C. for Tho. Rooks.* 1669. 8°. T.C.I 13. L, O, C, LR, LW ; WF, W.

2801 —A new and exact prognostication for ... 1681. *Aberdeen, Forbes,* 1681. 12°. ALDIS 2319. ES.

2802 —'Ολύμπια δώματα ... 1653. *By J. L. for the company of stationers,* 1653. 8°.* L, O, DT ; WF.

2803 — —1654. —, *1654.* 8°.* O ; MH.

2804 — —1655. —, *1655.* 8°.* O.

2805 — —1656. —, *1656.* 8°.* O.

2806 — —1657. —, *1657.* 8°.* O ; PHS.

2807 — —1658. *By R. & W. Leybourn,* 1658. 8°.* L, O, LG ; Y.

2808 — —1659. —, *1659.* 8°.* O.

2809 — —1660. *By R. & W. Leybourn, for the company of stationers,* 1660. 8°.* L, O.

2810 — —1661. —, *1661.* 8°.* L, O, C.

2811 — —1662. *By William Leybourn for the company of stationers,* 1662. 8°.* L, O ; WF.

2812 — —1663. —, *1663.* 8°.* L, O, C ; PAP.

2813 — —1664. —, *[1664].* 8°.* L, O, C, E ; CH, Y.

2814 — —1665. —, *1665.* 8°.* O.

2815 — —1666. —, *[1666].* 8°.* L, O, C, CT, DT ; Y.

2816 — —1667. *By B. Wood, for the company of stationers,* [1667]. 8°.* L, O, C, LWL.

2816A —An appendix. *By E. T. for the company of stationers,* 1667. CT.

2817 — —1668. *By John Winter, for the company of stationers,* [1668]. 8°.* L, O, C ; MH, PL.

2818   ——1669. —, [1669]. 8°.* L, O, C; PAP, WF.

2819   ——1670. *By T. Milbourn for the company of stationers,* 1670. 8°.* L, O; WF.

2820   ——1671. *For the company of stationers,* 1671. 8°.* L, O.

2821   ——1672. *By Thomas Milbourn for the company of stationers,* 1672. 8°.* L, O, E; PAP.

2822   —'Ουρανιζομοι . . . 1651. *By J. L. for the company of stationers,* 1651. 8°.* O.

2823   ——1652. —, 1652. 8°.* O.

2824   —Speculum uranicum . . . 1649. *By J. L. for the company of stationers,* 1649. 8°.* O.

2825   **Winter, Frig.** Winter. 1646. An almanack. *By M. B. for the companie of stationers,* [1646]. 8°.* L.

2825A **Wither, George,** *pseud.* The doubtful almanack. [*London,* 1647]. 4°.* LT, LVF, OC, DT; CH, TU, Y.

2826   **W[ood], R[obert].** Novus annus luni-solaris. [*Londini,* 1680.] brs. L; WF.

2827   —A specimen of a new almanack. [*London,* 1680.] 4°. MR.

2828   **Woodhouse, John.** Woodhouse, 1641, a new almanack. 1641. 8°.* L, O.

2829   ——1642. *By Io. Dawson, for the company of stationers,* 1642. 8°.* L, O.

2830   ——1643. *By Io. Dawson for the companie of stationers,* [1643]. 8°.* L, O.

2831   ——1646. *By Iohn Dawson, for the company of stationers,* [1646]. 8°.* L; CU.

2832   ——1647. —, 1647. 8°.* L, O.

2833   ——1648. —, 1648. 8°.* E; CU.

2834   ——1649. —, 1649. 8°.* O, C.

2835   ——1653. *London* [sic] *by T. W. for the company of stationers,* 1653. 8°.* L, O.

2836   ——1654. —, 1654. 8°.* O.

2837   ——1655. —, 1655. 8°.* O.

2838   ——1657. —, 1657. 8°.* O.

2839   ——1658. —, 1658. 8°.* O.

2840   ——1659. —, 1659. 8°.* O.

2841   ——1660. *By A. W. for the company of stationers,* 1660. 8°.* L; Y.

2842   ——1662. —, 1662. 8°.* O.

2843   ——1664. —, 1664. 8°.* O, E.

2844   ——1665. —, 1665. 8°.* O.

2845   ——1666. —, 1666. 8°.* O.

2846   ——1667. —, 1667. 8°.* O.

2847   ——1669. —, 1669. 8°.* O.

2848   ——1670. *By Anne Maxwell, for the company of stationers,* 1670. 8°.* L, O.

2849   ——1671. —, 1671. 8°.* O.

2850   ——1672. —, 1672. 8°.* O.

2851   ——1673. —, 1673. 8°.* O.

2852   ——1674. —, 1674. 8°.* O.

2853   ——1675. *By J. C. for the company of stationers,* 1675. 8°.* O; WF.

2854   ——1676. —, 1676. 8°.* O.

2855   ——1677. *For the companie of stationers,* [1677]. 8°.* L, O.

2856   ——1678. *By J. C. for the company of stationers,* 1678. 8°.* L, O, E; WF, Y, HC.

2857   —Wood-House. 1678. A prognostication, for . . . 1678. *By J. Macock for the company of stationers,* 1678. 8°.* WF, HC.

2858   —Woodhouse, 1679. A new almanack. *By J. C. for the company of stationers,* 1679. 8°.* L, O.

2859   ——1680. *By R. E. for the company of stationers,* 1680. 8°.* O, C, LG; CH, WF.

2860   ——1681. —, 1681. 8°.* L, O.

2861   ——1682. —, 1682. 8°.* O, C.

2862   ——1683. —, 1683. 8°.* O; CLC.

2863   ——*By R. E. for the company of stationers,* 1684. 8°.* L, O; Y.

2864   ——1685. —, 1685. 8°.* O.

2865   ——1686. —, 1686. 8°.* O.

2866   ——1687. —, 1687. 8°.* L, O; Y.

2867   ——1688. —, 1688. 8°.* C, E; HC, Y.

2867A ——1689. —, 1689. 8°.* MH, WF.

2868   ——1690. —, 1690. 8°.* O.

2869   ——1691. —, 1691. 8°.* O; Y.

2870   ——1692. —, 1692. 8°.* L, O.

2871   ——1693. —, 1693. 8°.* L.

2872   ——1694. —, 1694. 8°.* L, O, LG.

2873   ——1695. —, 1695. 8°.* L, O.

2874   ——1696. *By Robert and Richard Everingham for the company of stationers,* 1696. 8°.* MH.

2874A ——1697. —, 1697. 8°.* PAP.

2875   ——1698. —, 1698. 8°.* L, O.

2876   ——1699. —, 1699. 8°.* O, C.

2877   ——1700. —, 1700. 8°.* O.

2878   **Woodward, Daniel.** Ephemeris absoluta. *By J. D. for the company of stationers,* 1689. 8°.* T.C.II 238. C; MH, WF, Y.

2879   ——1690. —, 1690. 8°.* L, O; MH, WF.

2880   ——1691. —, 1691. 8°.* O; Y.

2881   ——1692. —, [1692]. 8°.* L, O, C, E; CH, WF, Y.

2882   ——1693. —, 1693. 8°.* L, O, E; CH.

2883   ——1694. —, 1694. 8°.* L, O, C, LG, E; CH, PAP.

2884   ——1695. —, 1695. 8°.* O, C, E; CH, Y.

2885   ——1696. —, 1696. 8°.* L, O, C, E; CH, MH.

2886   ——1697. —, 1697. 8°.* L, O, E; PAP.

2887   ——1698. —, 1698. 8°.* L, O, E; CH, MH, WF.

2888   ——1700. *By B. Griffin, for the company of stationers,* 1700. 8°.* CH.

2889   —Vox uraniæ . . . 1682. *By J. D. for the company of stationers,* 1682. 8°.* O, C, E; PAP, WF.

2890   ——1683. —, 1683. 8°.* O, C; WF, Y.

2891   ——1684. —, 1684. 8°.* L, O; Y.

2892   ——1685. —, 1685. 8°.* O.

2893   ——1686. —, 1686. 8°.* O, C; MH, WF.

2894   ——1687. —, 1687. 8°.* L, O; CN, Y.

2895   ——1688. —, 1688. 8°.* LG, E, EO; Y, HC.

Al-man-sir. 1672. *See* Gaultier, Jacques.

2896   **Almanzor.** The following maxims were found. colop: [*London*], printed, 1693. brs. O, HH; LC, Y.

Almanazor and Almanzaida. 1678. *See* La Roche Guilhem, *Mlle.* de.

2897   **Almond, Robert.** The English horseman. *For Simon Miller.* 1673. 8°. T.C.I 127. L; Y.

      Almoni, Peloni, *pseud.*

2897A   Aloisa; or, the amours of Octavia. *For Jacob Tonson,* 1681. 8°. L; CN.

      An alphabet of elegiack groans. 1656. *See* Elys, Edmund.

2898   An alphabetical abridgement of the first Parliament. *Edinburgh, by the heirs and successors of Andrew Anderson,* 1698. 12°. ALDIS 3731. EN.

2898A   An alphabetical list of the fortunate adventurers. *For F. Collins,* 1699. brs. MH.

2899   An alphabetical list of the imprisoned and secluded members. [1648]. brs. LS.

2899A   An alphabetical list of the knights. *By Edward Jones in the Savoy, and sold by Jacob Tonson, and John Nutt,* 1699. L, OP; Y.

2899B   An alphabetical list of the subscribers. [London, 1688]. brs. Y.

2899C   An alphabetical table of the names of all those jury-men. [*London?* 1694]. brs. HH; PL.

2900   **Alphonso, *King of Portugal.*** Five treatises of the philosophers stone. *By Thomas Harper, to be sold by John Collins,* 1652. 4°. LT, LN, LWL, GU; CU, Y.

2900A   [—] The wise Christian's story. *Douay, M. Mairesse,* 1680. 12°. BUTE.

2901   **Alsop, George.** A character of the province of Maryland. *By T.J. for Peter Dring,* 1666. 8°. L, GH; CH, CU, LC, MH, RPJ.

2902   —An orthodox plea for the sanctuary of God. *For the author, and sold by R. Reynolds,* 1669. 8°. T.C.I 13. L, C, ENC; CH, NN, WF, Y.

2903   —A sermon preached at sea, ... Nov. 24th, 1678. *For L. Curtis,* 1679. 4°.* T.C.I 340. L, O; CH, PU, WF, Y.

2904   **Alsop, Nathaniel.** A sermon preached ... the twenty third day of March, 1681/2. *For S. Carr,* 1682. 4°.* T.C.I 492. L, O, C, EC, YM; CN, NU, V, WF, Y.

2905   [**Alsop, Vincent.**] Anti-sozzo. *For Nathanael Ponder,* 1675. 8°. L, O, CT, EN, LW; MH, NF, NP, NU, TSM.

2905A   — —[Anr. ed.] —, 1676. 8°. CH, MWA.

2906   —A confutation of some of the errors of Mr. Daniel Williams. *For John Marshal,* 1698. 4°.* T.C.III 92. L, O, CS, GU; NC, NU.

2907   —Decus & tutamen: or, practical godliness. *For John Barnes,* 1696. 8°. L, O, LCL, LW; MH, NU.

2908   —Duty and interest united. *For John Barnes,* 1695. 4°.* L, O, CS, EN.

2909   [–] An exercitation on that historical relation. *For Benj. Alsop,* 1680. 8°. O; NPT.

2910   [–] A faithful rebuke to a false report. *For John Lawrence,* 1697. 8°. T.C.III 34. L, O, LW, ENC, GU; INU.

2911   —God in the movnt. A sermon. *For J. Barnes,* 1696. 4°.* L, O, CS, LW, EN; INU, NU, WF.

2912   [–] The humble address of the Presbyterians. [London], *for J.W.,* 1687. 4°.* O, OC; CLC, MIU, NU, PL, WF, Y.

2913   [–] —[London], reprinted Edinburgh, heir of A. Anderson, 1687. brs. ALDIS 2692. EN; MH, NU.

2914   [–] Melius inquirendum, or a sober inquirie. [London], *printed,* 1678. 12°. L, O, LCL, CS, EN; CH, NPT, NU, WF.

2915   [–] —*Printed,* 1679. 8°. L, O, LCL, OC, CT; CU, LC, MH, NC, Y.

2916   [–] —Third edition. *For Benj. Alsop,* 1681. 8°. T.C.I 446. L, O, C, LCL; CH, CN, NP, NU, WF.

2917   [–] The mischief of impositions. *For Benj. Alsop,* 1680. 4°. L, O, CT, EN, DT; CH, MH, NU, WF, Y.

2918   [–] —Second edition. —, 1680. 4°. O, LCL, CS, HH, DT; CLC, NU, PL, TU, Y.

      [–] Notes upon the Lord Bishop. 1695. *See* Chorlton, John.

      [–] Of scandal; together. 1680. *See* Clark, Samuel.

      [–] Rector of Sutton. 1680. *See* Barret, John.

2919   [–] A reply to the reverend Dean of St. Paul's reflections. *By J. D. to be sold by Richard Janeway,* 1681. 4°. T.C.I 448. CT, SP; MH, NU.

2920   —A sermon preach'd. *For John Lawrence,* 1698. 8°. T.C.III 91. LW, EN, GU; MH, Y.

2921   —Mr. Alsop's speech to the king. [1687.] brs. L, O; CH, MH, PL, WF, Y.

2922   —Mr. Alsop's speech to King James II ... in April, 1687. [London, 1687.] 8°.* L, OM, CT, LG, LCL; CLC, MIU, Y.

2923   [–] A vindication of the faithful rebuke. *For John Lawrence,* 1698. 8°. LCL, ENC, GU; NU.

2924   **Alsted, Johann Heinrich.** The beloved city. *Printed,* 1643. 4°. LT, O, CT, ENC, DT; CH, CN, MH, NU, WF, Y.

2925   [–] Happy news to England sent from Oxford. [London], *printed,* 1642/[3]. 4°. MADAN 1241. LT, O, EC.

2925A   —The saint's reign on earth. 1643. 4°. SA.

2926   —Templvm mvsicvm: or the musical synopsis. *By Will. Godbid for Peter Dring,* 1664. 8°. L, C; CH, LC, MB, MH, Y.

2927   —The vvorlds proceeding vvoes. *Printed,* 1642[3]. 4°.* LT, O, CT, DT; MH, Y.

2928   **Alston, *Sir* Edward.** A paper delivered in by Dr. Alston, etc. for bathes and bath-stoves. *Printed,* 1648. 4°.* L, O, DT.

      Altar dispute. 1641. *See* Parker, Henry.

2929   Alter Amintor, or the case. *For J. Nutt,* [1700]. brs. MH.

      Alter Britanniæ. Oxford, 1645. *See* Walsingham, Edward.

      Alteration of the coyn. 1695. *See* Houghton, Thomas.

      Altham, Arthur. *See* Altham, Michael.

2930   **Altham, Edward.** The last speech and confession of. colop: *By George Croom,* 1688. cap., fol.* L, O; CLC.

2931   [**Altham, Michael.**] The additional articles in Pope Pius's creed. *By J.L. for Luke Meredith,* 1688. 4°. L, O, MC, EN, DT; CLC, MH, NU, TU, WF, Y.

2932   [–] The creed of Pope Pius the IV. *For L. Meredith,* 1687. 4°.* L, O, C, EN, DT; CLC, MH, NU, TU, Y.

2933   [–] A dialogue between a pastor. *By J.L. for L. Meredith,* 1684. 12°. T.C.II 91. Y.

2933A   [–] —Second edition. —, 1685. 12°. T.C.II 131. L, DT.

2933B [–] Popery unmasqu'd. 1686. CT.

2934 [–] Some queries to Protestants answered. *By J. H. for Luke Meredith*, 1686. 4°.* L, O, HH, EN, DT; CH, MU, NU, TU, Y.

2935 [–] —Second edition. —1687. 4°.* OC, CT, E, DT; MH, NPT.

2936 [–] A vindication of the Church of England from the foul aspersions. Part. I. *By J. H. for Luke Meredith*, 1687. 4°.* L, O, C, EN, DT; CH, MH, NU, TU, WF, Y.

2937 [–] —Part. II. *By J. H. for Luke Meredith*, 1687. 4°.* O, CT, HH, YM, DT; CH, CN, PHS, WF, Y.

2938 **Altham, Roger.** A true copy of Mr. Roger Altham's recantation. *Printed*, 1695. brs. O, OM, MC.

Although by proclamation. Dublin, 1641. *See* Ireland. Lord Justices.

Although the said council. Edinburgh, 1655. *See* Scotland. Council.

Although wee find. Kilkenny, 1648. *See* Ireland. Supreme Council.

2939 **Alton,** *capt.* A new plot discovered in Ireland. *For William Reynor*, 1642. 4°.* LT, EC; CH, MIU, Y.

2939A **Alured, Matthew.** The case of. *For L. Chapman*, 1659. 4°.* LT, O, LG, HH; CH, MH, NIC.

2940 [**Alured, Thomas.**] The coppie of a letter vvritten to the Dvke of Bvckingham. *Printed at London for George Tomlinson*, 1642. 4°.* LT, CS; CH, CLC, MIU, OWC, WF.

2940A —The humble advice of. *Printed*, 1643. 4°.* LT; CH, MH, WF, Y.

2941 **Alvarez, Emmanuel.** Grammatica, ... liber secundus. *Typis Henrici Hills: pro se & Matthæo Turner*, 1687. sixes. C; WG.

2942 —An introduction to the Latin tongue. *By Henry Hills for him, and Matthew Turner*, 1686. sixes. C; MH.

2943 —Prosodia. *Dublini, typis Regiis et impensis Mariæ Crooke*, 1671. 8°. DIX 142. DT.

2944 — —Second edition. *Dublini, typis Regiis*, 1677. 8°. DIX 159. DT.

2944A —Sunday's. *Typis Henry Hills*, [c1687]. sixes. WG.

2945 **Alvey, Thomas.** Dissertatiuncula epistolaris. *Excusum*, 1680. 4°.* L, LSC.

Amadeus. *See* Victor Amadeus, *King of Sardinia.*

Amanda. 1653. *See* Hookes, Nathaniel.

Amazement of future ages. 1684. *See* R., T.

2946 The embassadour of peace. colop: *Printed and sold by J. Bradford*, 1696. 8°.* L.

2947 —[Anr. ed.] *London, reprinted Edinburgh, by the heirs and successors of Andrew Anderson*, 1697. 8°.* ALDIS 3652. EN.

2948 —[Anr. ed.] *Glasgow, Sanders*, 1697. brs. ALDIS 3653. EN.

2949 The ambitious practices of France. *By Randal Taylor*, 1689. 4°. T.C.II 278. O, MR; CH, CLC, NC, NU, Y.

2950 Ambitious tyrany. [*London*], *printed*, 1659. 4°.* LT, O, OC, HH; CSS, MH, Y.

2951 **Ambresarius, F.** The art of physick made plain & easie. *By H. C. for Dorman Newman*, 1684. 12°. HC.

2952 **Ambrose, Isaac.** The compleat works of. *For Rowland Reynolds*, 1674. fol. T.C.I 180. L, C, LW, GU, DT; CU, MH, NU, WSC.

2953 — —[Anr. ed.] *By T. M. for R. Chiswel, B. Tooke, and T. Sawbridge*, 1682. fol. T.C.I 488. L, CS, EN; PU, WF.

2954 — —[Anr. ed.] *For R. Chiswel*, 1689. fol. T.C.II 261. CLC, NU.

2955 —The doctrine & directions. *By J. F. for Nathaniel Webb and William Grantham*, 1650. 8°.* L, DT; MH, WF, Y.

2956 —Looking unto Jesus. *By Edward Mottershed, for Nathanael Webb, and William Grantham*, 1658. 4°. L, C, AU, GU; CLC, CU, MU, WF.

2956A — —[Anr. ed.] *For Rowland Reynolds*, 1674, fol. MH.

2957 — —[Anr. ed.] *For Richard Chiswel, Benj. Tooke, and Thomas Sawbridge*, 1680, fol. L.

2958 —Media: the middle things. *By John Field for Nathanaell Webb and Wm. Grantham*, 1650. 4°. LT, GU; CN, MH, NP, WF.

2959 — —Second edition. *By T. R. and E. M. for Nathanael Webb and William Grantham*, 1652. 8°. L, CH, NNG.

2960 — —Third edition. —, 1657. 8°. L, E, AU, DT; Y.

2961 —Prima, media & ultima, the first, . . . things. *By J. F. for Nathanael Webb and William Grantham*, 1650. 8°. L, CS, GU, DT; CH, CLC, Y.

2962 — —[Anr. ed.] *By T. R. and E. M. for Nath. Webb and Will. Grantham*, 1654. 8°. L, C, LSC, SA, E; Y.

2963 — —[Anr. ed.] *By E. M. for I. A. to be sold by Nathanael Webb and William Grantham*, 1659. 8°. L, O, LCL, BPL, E; CN, WF.

2964 —Prima, the first things. *By J. F. for I. A. to be sold by Nathanael Webb and William Grantham*, 1650. 8°. L; CH, CLC, Y.

2965 — —[Anr. ed.] *By T. R. and E. M. for I. A. to be sold by Nathanael Webb and William Grantham*, 1654. 8°. L, AN.

2966 — —[Anr. ed.] *For Rowland Reynalds*, 1674. fol. L, O; MH.

2967 — —[Anr. ed.] *By T. M. for Rowland Reynolds*, 1674. fol. O; CH, NU, Y.

2968 —Redeeming the time. *By T. C. for Nath. Webb and William Grantham*, 1658. 4°.* LT, LCL, O, EC, DT; CLC, LC, MH, NU, TU, Y.

2969 — —[Anr. ed.] *For Rowland Reynalds*, 1674. fol.* L, C; MH, PU, WF, Y.

2970 —Ultima, the last things. *For J. A. to be sold by Nathanael Webb, and William Grantham*, 1650. 8°.* L, GU; CH, CLC, MH, Y.

2971 — —[Anr. ed.] *By T. R. and E. M. for I. A. to be sold by Nathanael Webb and William Grantham*, 1654. 8°. L, E, DT; CN, Y.

2972 — —[Anr. ed.] *By E. M. for Nathanael Webb, and William Grantham*, 1659. 8°. L, O, EC, AU; WF.

2972A —War with devils. *By S. and B. G. for Rowland Reynolds*, 1674. fol. CH, MH. ·

2973 — —[Anr. ed.] *For R. Chiswell, B. Tooke, T. Sawbridge*, 1682, fol. L.

2974   **Amelot de la Houssaye, Abraham Nicolas.** The history of the government of Venice. *By H. C. for John Starkey*, 1677. 8°. T.C.I 266. L, O, CM, ENC, DT; CH, CU, MBA, WF, Y.

Amend, amend. [1643.] *See* Douglas, *Lady* Eleanor.

2974A   Amendments humbly proposed to the bill, for setling the trade to Africa. [*London*, 1698]. brs. MH.

Amendments of Mr. Collier's. 1695. *See* Congreve, William.

America. 1655. *See* N., N.

America. 1671. *See* Ogilby, John.

2975   [**Ames, Richard.**] The Bacchanalian sessions. *For E. Hawkins*, 1693. 4°.* T.C.II 454. L, O, C, EN, DT; CH, MH, Y.

2975A   [–] Britannia victrix. *For Randal Taylor*, 1692. fol.* T.C.II 412. L, O, CT; MH, NN, Y.

2975AB   [–] The character of a bigotted prince. *For Richard Baldwin*, 1691. 4°.* T.C.II 384. L, O, CT, AU; CH, MH, NU, WF, Y.

2975AC   [–] Chuse which you will. *For H.N.*, 1692. 4°.* T.C.II 404. O, LVF.

2975AD   [–] —[Anr. ed.] *For R. Stafford*, 1692. 4°.* L, CT.

2975B   [–] A dialogue between claret. *For E. Richardson*, 1692. 4°.* L; CH, MH, TU, Y.

2976   [–] The double descent. *For John Dunton*, 1692. 4°.* CT, A, DT; Y.

2976A   [–] —[Anr. ed.] *For D. Kean*, 1692. 4°. in 2's.* L; CN, MH.

2977   [–] A farther search after claret. *For E. Hawkins*, 1691. 4°.* L, O, DT; CJC, MH, Y.

2978   [–] Fatal friendship; or, the drunkards misery. *For and sold by Randal Taylor*, 1693. 4°.* L, O, C, A; CH, CN, MH, Y.

2979   [–] The female fire-ships. *For E. Richardson*, 1691. 4°.* L, O, EN; TU, Y.

2980   [–] The folly of love; or, an essay. *For E. Hawkins*, 1691. 4°. L, O; CLC, NIC, Y.

2981   [–] —Second edition. —, 1693. 4°.* L, O, C; MH, Y.

2982   [–] —Fourth edition. —, 1700. 4°.* L.

2983   [–] Islington-wells. *For E. Richardson*, 1691. 4°.* L, O, C, LG, EN; CLC, CN, MH, WF.

2984   [–] The Jacobite conventicle. A poem. *For R. Stafford*, 1692. 4°.* L, O, C, EN, AU; MH, WF, Y.

2985   [–] The last search after claret in Southwark. *For E. Hawkins*, 1691. 4°.* L, LUG, DT; CJC, MH, Y.

2986   [–] Lawyerus bootatus & spurratus: or, the long vacation. *For E. Richardson*, 1691. 4°. in 2's* T.C.II 381. L, O, C, LL, EN; MH, PU, TU, Y.

2887   [–] The pleasures of love. *By H. N. and are to be sold by R. Baldwin*, 1691. 4°.* T.C.II 381. O, EN, DT; MH, WF.

2988   [–] The rake, or, the libertine's religion, a poem. *For R. Taylor*, 1693. 4°.* L, O, C, GK; CH, CN, MH, TU, Y.

2989   [–] The search after claret. *For E. Hawkins*, 1691. 4°.* T.C.II 381. L, O, DT; CJC, MH, TU, Y.

2990   [–] —. Second edition. —, 1691. 3°.* LG; CH, MH.

2991   [–] A search after wit. *For E. Hawkins*, 1691. 4°.* T.C.II 381. L, O, C; WF, Y.

2992   [–] The siege and surrender of Mons. *For Richard Baldwin*, 1691. 8°. T.C.II 381.* L, O, LG, OW, EN; CH, MB, WF, Y.

2992A   [–] Sylvia's complaint. *Printed, and are to be sold by Richard Baldwin*, 1692. 4°.* L, O, EN; CH, MH.

2992B   [–] —. Second edition. 1697. 4°.* O.

2992C   [–] —. Third edition. *For Robert Battersby*, 1698. 4°.* CN.

2992D   [–] Sylvia's revenge. *By Joseph Streater to be sold by John Southby*, 1688. 4°.* T.C.II 224. L, O, OC, EN; CLC, CN, MH, Y.

2992E   [–] —[Anr. ed.] *For Samuel Clement*, 1692. 4°.* CH, MH, Y.

2992F   [–] —. Second edition. *For Robert Battersby*, 1697. 4°.* L, O.

2992G   [–] —. Third edition. 1699. 4°.* A.

2993   **Ames, William.** The workes of. *For Iohn Rothwell*, 1643. 4°. LCL; MH, NPT, NU, Y.

2994   —An analytical exposition . . . Peter. *By E. G. for Iohn Rothwell*, 1641. 4°. C, LW, LCL, NPL, ENC; CH, CU, MH, NU, WF, Y.

2995   —Conscience, with the power. *By E. G. for I. Rothwell, T. Slater, L. Blacklock*, 1643. 4° L, CE, LW, LCL, EN; CH, MU, NU, WSC, Y.

2995A   ——[Anr. ed.] *By Edw. Griffin for John Rothwell*, 1643. 4°. LW, CT; CLC, MH, WF, Y.

2996   —Guilielmi Amesii, de conscientia. *Oxonii, typis Gulielmi Hall, sumptibus Joh. Adams*, 1659. 12°. MADAN 2431. L, O, OB, LCL, P; CH, WF.

2997   —Demonstratio logicæ. *Cantabrigiæ, ex officina Rogeri Danielis*, 1646. 12°. Y.

2998   —Disputatio theologica. *Cantabrigiæ, ex officina Rogeri Danielis*, 1646. 12°. DT; Y.

—English puritanisme. 1641. *See* Bradshaw, William.

2999   —Lectiones in omnes psalmos Davidis. *Excudebat J. D. impensis Andreae Kembe, & Johannis Hardesty*, 1647. 8°. L, C, EN, DT; CH, NU, WF, Y.

3000   —The marrow of sacred divinity. *By Edward Griffin for Henry Overton*, 1642. 12°. L, O, C, LW, ENC; CLC, CU, MH, NU, WF, Y.

3001   ——[Anr. ed.] *By Edward Griffin for John Rothwell*, [1643]. 4°. L, CCH, E; CU, MH, NU, WF, Y.

3002   —Philosphemata. Technometria. *Cantabrigiæ, ex officina Rogeri Danielis*, 1646. 12°. C, CK, DT; MB, MBA, WF, Y.

3003   —The svbstance of Christian religion. *By T. Mabb for Thomas Davies*, 1659. 8°. LT, LCL; CH, IU.

3004   —Vtriusque epistolæ . . . Petri. *Excudebat J. D. impensis Andrea Kembe*, 1647. 8°. L, C, LCL; Y.

3004A   **Ames, William. Quaker.** A declaration of the witness of God. [*London*], *printed*, 1656. 4°.* LF; PH, PL.

3005   — —Second edition, —, 1681. 8°.* L, LF; PHS, PSC.

3006   —Good counsell and advice. *For Thomas Simmons*, 1661. 4°.* L, O, LF, BBN; MH, PH, PL, WF, Y.

3007   —The light upon the candlestick. *For Robert Wilson*, 1663. 4°.* L, LF; CH, IE, MH, PH, WF, Y.

3008   [–] A sound out of Sion. *Printed and are to be sold by William Warwick*, 1663. 4°.* L, LF, BBN, BR; LC, MH, PH, PSC, Y.

3009 **Ames, William** *of Wrentham*. The saints security. *By M. Simmonds, for William Adderton*, 1652. 4°.* LT, O, CS, E, DT; CLC, MB, NU, WF, Y.

3010 —A sermon from I John ii 20. 1652. 4°.* MB.

Amesso, D'. *pseud. See* Fisher, Payne.

Amicable accomodation. 1686. *See* Gother, John.

3011 The amicable reconciliation of the dissenters. colop: *For R. Hayhurst*, 1689. brs. L, LG; CH, CN, WF, Y.

Amicable representation. 1686. *See* Lovell, John.

3012 Amintas and Claudia. *For W. Thackeray, T. Passenger, and W. Whitwood*, [1671]. brs. L, HH, GU; MH.

3012A —[Anr. ed.] *For W. Whitwood* [167-?]. brs. O.

3013 Amintas, or, the constant shepherds complaint. [*London*], *for P. Brooksby*, [1672–95]. brs. L, O, HH; MH.

3014 Amintor's answer to Parthenia's complaint. [*London*], *for P. Brooksby*, [1675?]. brs. L, O, HH; MH.

Amintor's lamentation. [1676.] *See* Duffet, Thomas.

3015 **Amiraut, Christopher.** Sacramental discourses. 1699. 12°. LCL.

3015A **Amman, Jan Conrad.** The talking deaf man. *For. Tho. Hawkins*, 1694. 12°. L; WSG.

3016 [**Ammonet, S.**] The key of knowledge. *Dublin*, 1696. 8°.* DIX 282. DI.

Amoret. 1682. *See* C., L.

Amoris effigies. [165-?]. *See* Waring, Robert.

Amorous abbess. 1684. *See* Bremond, Gabriel de.

3017 Amorous Betty's delight. [*London*] *for R. Burton* [1641–66] brs. L.

3018 Entry cancelled.

The amorous conquests of the great Alcander. 1685. *See* Courtilz, Gatsen de.

3019 The amorous convert. *By R.E. for R. Tonson*, 1679. 8°. T.C.I 330. O.

3020 An amorous dialogue between John and his Mistris. [*London*], *for P. Brooksby*, [1672–95]. brs. L, O, HH; MH.

Amorous fantasme. Hage, 1660. *See* Quinault, Philippe

3021 The amorous gallant. [*London*], *for F. Coles, T. Vere, and I. Wright*, [1655–65]. brs. L, O, HH; MH.

Amorous gallant. 1675. *See* Corneille, Thomas.

Amorous old-woman. 1674. *See* Duffet, Thomas.

Amorous Orontus. 1665. *See* Corneille, Thomas.

3021A The amorous travellers. *For Ambrose Isted, and J. Edwin*, 1671. 8°. T.C.I 89. O; CLC.

Amorous warre. 1648. *See* Mayne, Jasper.

Amours of Ann. 1689. *See* Le Noble, Eustache.

3021B The amours of Bonne Sforza. *By T. M. for R. Bentley*, 1684. 12°. T.C.II 70. L, O; CLC, MH.

Amours of Charles Duke of Mantua. 1685. *See* Leti, Gregorio.

Amours of Count Teckeli. 1686. *See* Préchac, Jean, *sieur* de.

Amours of Edward the IV. 1700. *See* Marana, Giovanni Paolo.

3022 The amours of Madame. *For B. C: obedience* [*i.e. R. Bentley and W. Cademan*], 1680. 12°. T.C.I 393. L.

3023 The amours of Messalina. *For John Lyford*, 1689. 4°.* L, O, OC, AU; CH, CU, MH, WF, Y.

Amours of Philander. 1693. *See* Behn, *Mrs.* Aphra.

3024 The amours of Philantus and Bellamond. *For F. Saunders*, 1690. 12°. T.C.II 313. L. [*t.p. only*]; CLC.

3025 The amours of Solon. *For Henry Herringman, and John Starkey*, 1673. 8°. T.C.I 141. CT; WF.

Amours of the Count de Dunois; 1675. *See* Desjardins, Marie Catherine Hortense, *Mme* de Villedieu.

3026 The amours of the Dauphin. *For R. Baldwin*, 1695. 12°. L; Y.

3027 Amours of the English gallantry. *For Simon Neale*, 1675. 8°. CHRISTIE-MILLER.

3028 The amours of the Sultana of Barbary. A novel. *To be sold by R. Baldwin*, 1689. 12°. T.C.II 299. L; MBP, MH.

3029 Amsterdam, and her other Hollander sisters put out to sea. *For Richard Harper*, 1652. 4°.* LT, O; CN.

Amsterdam: toleration. 1663. *See* O., J. V. C.

3030 **Amurath.** A provd and blasphemvs cahllenge [sic] given out. [1643] brs. LT, EC, HH.

3030A [**Amy, S.**] A memento for English Protestants. *For Jacob Sampson*, 1680. 4°. T.C.I 393. L, O, C, CT, SP; CH, NU, WF, Y.

3031 [–] A præfatory discourse to a late pamphlet, entituled, a memento. *By Tho. Dawks, for the author*, 1681. 4°.* T.C.I 422. L, O; Y.

3032 [–] —Second edition. —, 1681. 4°.* L, O, CS, SP; CH, CN, MH, WF, Y.

3032A [**Amyas, Richard**] An antidote against melancholy. *For the author*, 1659. 4°.* L.

3033 **Amydenus, Theodorus.** Pietas Romana et Parisiensis, or, a faithful relation. *Printed at Oxford*, 1687. 4°. OC, OM, BR, AU, DT; CLC, LC, NPT, PL, Y.

Amygdala. 1647. *See* Wither, George.

Amyntas, or the impossible dowry. 1688. *See* Randolph, Thomas.

Amyntor. 1699. *See* Toland, John.

3034 **Amyraut, Moses.** A discourse concerning the divine dreams. *By A. C. for Walter Kettilby*, 1676. 8°. T.C.I 234. L, O, C, LW, DT; CLC, LC, MH, NU, Y.

3035 Entry cancelled.

3036 —Evidence of things not seen. *For Tho. Cockerill*, [1700?] 8°. L, O, LW, P; MH, NPT, Y.

3037 —A treatise concerning religions. *By M. Simons, for Will. Nealand, in Cambridge*, 1660. 8°. LT, O, C, E, DT; CLC, CU, MH, NU, WF, Y.

3038 **Amyraut, Paul.** The triumph of a good conscience. *By Thomas Paine*, 1648. 4°.* LT.

Anabaptist preacher. 1672. *See* Rudyard, Thomas.

3038A An Anabaptist sermon. 1643. 4°.* L.

3039 The Anabaptists catechisme. [*London*], *for R. A.*, 1645. 8°.* LT; CH.

3040 The Anabaptists' faith and belief, open'd. *Printed*, 1659. brs. LT.

Anabaptists ground-work. 1644. *See* Etherington, John.

3041 The Anabaptists' late protestation. [*London*], *printed*, [1647.] 4°.* LT.

3041A The Anabaptists out of order. [*London*, 1646]. brs. MAU.

Anabaptists lying wonder. [London], 1672. *See* Rudyard Thomas.

Anabaptists' printed proposal. 1674. *See* Rudyard, Thomas.

3042 **Anacreon.** Anacreon. Bion. Moschus. [*London*], printed, 1651. 8°. LT, O, C, CT; CN, MH.

3043 —Odae. *Ex officina Rogeri Danielis*, 1657. 12°. C, CT, OC, OM.

3044 —Ανακρεοντος πηιου μελη. *Cantabrigiæ, ex officina Joan. Hayes, impensis Rich. Green, Cantabr.*, 1684. 12°.* L, C, CT, HH; NC, WF, Y.

3045 — —[Anr. ed.] *Apud Gualt. Kettilby*, 1695. 8°. L, O, C, MR, EN; BN, CH, CN, TU, WF, Y.

3046 —Anacreon done into English. *Oxford, by L. Lichfield, for Anthony Stephens*, 1683. 4°. L, O, C, CT, DT; CH, CU, MH, NC, WF, Y.

Analecta, or, . . . 1693. *See* Barker, Thomas.

3047 Analecta poetica Græca, Latina. [*Oxford*], by H. H. for the author, 1643. 8°.* MADAN 1567. O.

Analogia honorum: or, . . . 1677. *See* Logan, John.

Analogical discourse. 1693. *See* R., J. D.

Analysis libri. Oxoniæ, 1664. *See* Powell, Griffith.

3048 Ananias and Saphira discover'd. *By M. Clark, for Henry Brome*, 1679. 4°.,* L, O, C, OM, CT; CH, MH, NU, WF, Y.

Anapologesiates. 1646. *See* Goodwin, John.

Anarchia anglicana. 1648. *See* Walker, Clement.

Anarchy of a limited . . . 1648. *See* Filmer, *Sir* Robert.

3049–50 Entries cancelled.

Anarchie reviving. 1668. *See* Wright, Abraham.

3051 **Anastasius Sinaita.** Anastasii Sinaitae anagogicarum - contemplationum. *Typis M. Clark, impensis Roberti Littlebury*, 1682. 4°.* L, O, C, AU, DT; MIU, Y.

Anatomical account. 1682. *See* Mullen, Allan.

3052 The anatomy of a Jacobite, or, the Jacobites heart laid open. *Cambridge, printed*, 1692. 8°. L, AU; CN, NU, Y.

3053 The anatomy of a Jacobite-Tory. *For Richard Baldwin*, 1690. 4°.* T.C.II 315. L, O, C, EN, DT; CH, MH, NU, WF, Y.

Anatomy of a project. [1698?] *See* S., F.

3054 The anatomy of an arbitrary prince. *For R. Baldwin*, 1689. brs. L. O. C; CH.

Anatomy of an equivalent. [1688?] *See* Halifax, George Savile, *marquis.*

Anatomy of atheisme. 1693. *See* Dawes, *Sir* William.

3055 Anatomy of Dr. Gauden's idolized non-sence. *Printed* 1660. 4°.* LT, C, LW, HH, EN; CLC, MH, NPT, NU, Y.

Anatomy of et cætera. 1641. *See* Bray, Thomas.

Anatomy of humane bodies. 1682. *See* Gibson, Thomas.

Anatomy of independency. 1644. *See* Forbes, Alexander.

3056–7 Entries. cancelled.

Anatomy of legerdemain. 1683. *See* Hocus Pocus junior.

Anatomy of Lieut. John Lilbvrn's spirit. 1649. *See* Sydenham, Cuthbert.

Anatomy of melancholy. Oxford, 1651. *See* Burton, Robert.

Anatomy of play. 1651. *See* Denham, *Sir* John.

3058 The anatomy of popery. *By Tho. Milbourn, for Tho. Passenger*, 1673. 8°. T.C.I 141. L, O, CT, E; CLC, WF.

Anatomy of Simon Magus. *See* Brome, Charles.

3059 The anatomy of Simon Magus. *By W. Bowyer for Charles Brome*, 1700. 4°. O, OC, CT, OM; CLC, IU, Y.

Anatomie of the common prayer-book. 1661. *See* Bernard, John.

3060 The anatomie of the French and Spanish faction. *By Bernard Alsop*, 1644. 4°.* LT, OC; CH, MH, WF, Y.

Anatomy of the humane body. 1698. *See* Keill, John.

3060A The anatomie of the inward parts. colop: *For Peter Stent*, [c 1650]. fol. PL.

Anatomy of the separatists. 1642. *See* Taylor, John.

Anatomie of the service-book. [n.p., 1641.] *See* Bernard, John.

3061 The anatomy of transubstantiation. *For Richard Janeway*, 1680. 4°.* L, O, MC, DT; MH.

Anatomy of warre. [1642]. *See* Ward, Richard.

3062 The anatomy of Westminster Ivncto. [*London*, 1648.] cap., 4°.* LT; CH, MIU, WF.

3063–4 Entries cancelled.

3065 The ancient and modern practice of the two superior courts. 1674. 8°. EN.

Antient and modern stages. 1699. *See* Drake, James.

Antient and present state of Muscovy. 1698. *See* Crull, Jodocus.

3066 The ancient and present state of Poland. *For E. Whitlock*, 1697. 4°.* L, O; CH, LC, WCL.

3067 An ancient and true prophesie . . . Written in verse. *For R. Page*, 1659. 4°.* LT, OC; MH, WF.

Ancient bounds. 1645. *See* Rous, Francis.

Antient Christianity. 1688. *See* Pardoe, William.

3067A The ancient church catechism. [*London*? 1680]. cap., 8°. CH.

3067B The ancient honour of the famous city of London. *R. L.*, 1663. LG.

3067C The ancient hunting-notes of England. [*London*? 1656]. brs. L.

3068 The antient land-mark skreen or bank. *By T. W. for Daniel White*, 1659. 4°.* LT, C, LL; CH, MH, NC, TU, WF, Y.

3069 The ancient laws, customs and orders of the miners in . . . Mendipp. *For William Cooper*, 1687. 8°.* L, BR; TSM.

3070 Ancient legal course and fundamental constitution . . . Marshalsea. *For Robert Crofts*, 1663. 12°. L, O; MHL, YL.

3071 The antient manner of electing sheriffs of London. [*London*, 1695]. brs. L; MH, NN.

3071A The ancient manufacture of white salt-making. [*London*? 1655]. brs. MH.

Ancient of dayes. [London, 1657.] *See* G., J.

3072 The ancient practical laws of England compared. [*London*? 1700]. brs. L.

Ancient rites. 1672. *See* Davies, John.

The ancient sea-laws of Oleron. 1686. *See* Cleirac, Estienne.

3073 The ancient testimony and principle of the people called Quakers. [*London*, 1695/6.] brs. L, LF, LG, OC, BR; PSC.

3074 The antient testimony of the primitive Christians. *Printed*, 1680. 4°.* LF, OC; CH, MH, MU, PSC, Y.

3075 The ancient trades decayed repaired again. *By T. N. and are to be sold by Dorman Newman and T. Cockerel*, 1678. 4°. T.C.I 313. L, OC, CCA, BAMB; CH, CU, NC, PL, Y.

3076 Ancient truth revived. *Printed*, 1677. 4°. L; MB, WF, WSC.

Ancilla divinitatis, or, . . . 1659. *See* H., W.

Ancilla grammaticæ. 1663. *See* B., J.

And without proving. [1648?] *See* Douglas, *Lady* Eleanor.

3077 [**Anderdon, Christopher.**] A catechism for the use of His Royal Highness. *At Paris, to be sold at Thomas Moette*, 1692. 4°. O.

3078 **Anderdon, John.** Against Babylon and her merchants. *For Robert Wilson*, 1660. 4°.* O, C, LF, OC; CH, MH, PSC, WF, Y.

3079 — —[Anr. ed.] —,]1660?]. 4°.* L, O, LF, BR; CH, CLC, MH, PL, Y.

3080 —A call to all bishops. [*London*], *printed*, 1670. 4°.* L, O, C, LF, BBN; CH, MH, NU, PH, Y.

3081 —God's proclamation. *For Giles Calvert*, 1659. 4°.* CT, LF, BBN; PSC.

3082 —One blow at Babel. *Printed*, 1662. 4°.* L, O, LF, BBN, BR; PH.

3082A —Remarks upon a letter from a gentleman. *Printed*, 1699. 4°.* L, O, LF, BBN; MH, PH, PSC.

3083 —To those that sit in counsel. *For Thomas Simmons*, 1659. 4°.* LF; PH.

3084 —A visitation in love. *For Robert Wilson*, 1660. 4°.* L, O, LF, OC, BBN; NHC, PH, PL, PSC, Y.

3084A **Anderdon, Mary.** A word to the world. [*London*, 1662.] fol.* LF, BBN; CH.

3085 **Anderson, Sir Edmund.** Les reports . . . des mults pricipals cases. *By T. R. for Andrew Crook, Henry Twyford, Gabriel Bedell, Thomas Dring, and John Place*, 1664. fol. L, O, C, LL, LG; CH, LT, MB, MHL, NCL, NP.

3086 —La second part des reports. *By T. R. for Andrew Crook, Henry Twyford, Gabriel Bedell, Thomas Dring, and John Place*, 1665. fol. L, O, C, LG, LL; MB, MHL, NCL, NP, WF.

3087 **Anderson, Francis.** The copy of a letter from . . . to Sir Thomas Glemham the 20. Ianuary 1643. [*Oxford*], *by Leonard Lichfield*, 1643[4]. 4°.* MADAN 1528. O, OC, EC, EN; CLC, MBP, MH, NPT.

3088 — —[Anr. ed. "Ianuary 20."] [*Printed at Oxford*], *by Leonard Lichfield*, 1643 [4]. 4°.* MADAN 1529–30. LT, O, CT, EN, HH; BN, CH, CLC, MBP, WF, Y.

3089 — —[Anr. ed.] *Bristoll, by R. Barker and J. Bill*, 1643[4]. 4°.* O, HH.

3090 [**Anderson, George.**] The Scotch counsellor. *By R. Austine and A. Coe*, 1643. 4°.* LT, EN; CLC, MH, Y.

[**Anderson, Henry.**] Court convert. 1698. *See* Waring, Henry.

3091 —A loyal tear dropt. *For Luke Meredith*, 1685. 4°.* L, O, LSC, P; CH, MBA, MH, WF, Y.

3092 —Religion and loyalty maintained. *By J. M. for Will. Abington; and Will. Clark in Winchester*, 1684. 8°. T.C.II 83. L, LCL, LSC.

3093 —A sermon preached . . . xxix of May MDCLXXXI. *By J. M. for Joanna Brome*, 1681. 4°.* T.C.I 457. L, O; CH, Y.

3094 [**Anderson, Henry, M.P.**] A meanes to reconcile the present distempers. *Printed*, 1648. 4°.* LT, O, YM; MIU, NN, WF, Y.

3095 [–] The wonder, or, propositions for a safe and well-grovnded peace. *Printed*, 1648. 4°.* LT, O, EC, DT; MH, MIU.

3096 **Anderson, James.** Answers for. [*London?* 1688]. brs. L.

3097 —An historical essay. *Edinburgh*, 1700. 8°. ENC.

3098 **Anderson, P. J.** In obitum . . . Magistri Jacobi Kirtoni. [*Edinburgh?* 1699]. brs. ALDIS 3822. EN.

3099 **Anderson, Patrick.** The copie of a barons court. *Printed at Helicon, to be sold in Caledonia*, [1680]. 8°. ALDIS 2191. L, O, EN, ES, FSF; WF.

3100 —Grana Angelica: or, the rare and singular uses. [*London*], 1677. brs. O, EN.

3101 — —[Anr. ed.] [*London*], *printed*, 1681. brs. L, EN.

3102 **Anderson, Robert.** Dary's miscellanies examined. *For Philip Brooksby*, 1670. 8°.* O.

3102A —A friendly proposition. [*London*], 1675. brs. PL.

3103 —Gaging promoted. *By J. W. for Joshua Coniers*, 1669. 8°.* L, O, C; CLC, WF.

3104 —The genuine use and effects of the gunne. *By J. Darby, for William Berry, and Robert Morden*, 1674. 4°. T.C.I 169. L, O, C, LUS, E; CLC, CSU, MB, MU, PL, Y.

3105 —The making of rockets. In two parts. *For Robert Morden*, 1696. 8°. L, GU.

3106 —Stereometrical propositions. *By William Godbid for Joshuah Conniers*, 1668. 8°. T.C.I 5. L, O, C, E, DT; CLC, MIU, WF.

3107 —To cut the rigging. *For Robert Morden*, 1691. 4°.* L, O, LUS, CT, E; CLC.

3108 —To hit a mark. *For Robert Morden*, 1690. 4°. L, LUS, OC, E; CLC, MU, PL.

3109 [**Anderton, Lawrence.**] The English nunne. [*St. Omers, English college press*], 1642. 8°. L; CLC, Y.

3110 [**Anderton, Thomas.**] The history of the iconoclasts. *Anno* 1671. 8°. L, O, LCL; WF, Y.

3110A —A sovereign remedy against atheism. 1672. PL.

3111 **Anderton, William.** Bibliotheca Andertoniana. [*Oxford*, 1699.] fol.* L, OP.

3112 [–] Remarks upon the present confederacy. *Printed*, 1693. 4°.* L, O, C, MR, EN; CN, MM, TU, WF, Y.

3113 —A true copy of the paper delivered. *Printed*, 1693. brs. STEELE 2717. L, O, LG, HH, MC; MH, Y.

Andevers, Charles Howard. *See* Berkshire, Charles Howard, *earl*.

Andrade, Jacinto Freire de. *See* Freire de Andrade, Jacinto.

3113A **André, François.** Chymical disceptations. *For Tho. Dawks, and Benj. Allport,* 1689. 16°. T.C.II 252. L, LCS, GU; CLC, Y.

3114 **Andreae, Johann Valentin.** The hermetick romance. *[London], by A. Sowle,* 1690. 8°. T.C.II 324. L, MC, A, GU; CPB, LC, WF, Y.

3115 **Andres, Juan.** The confusion of Muhamed's sect. *For H. Blunden,* 1652. 8°. LT, O.

3116 **Andrew, George.** Four sermons. *Dublin, Andrew Crooke,* 1684. 4°. DIX 205. BELSHAW.

3116A **Andrews, Edward.** Gemelli pulmonales. The two greatest remedies extant. *[London? 1690].* brs. L.

3116B —Most welcome newes from York. *[London],* June 23. *For William Arding,* 1642. 4°.* L, EC.

3117 **Andrewes, Eusebius.** The last speech of. *By John Clovves,* 1650. 4°.* LT, CT; CH, MH, NU, TU, WF, Y.

3117A —The several arguments at law of. *For Daniel Pakeman,* 1660. 4°. WF.

3118 **Andrewes, John.** Andrewes caveat to win sinners. *For William Gilbertson,* 1655. 8°.* L.

3119 —The converted mans new birth. *By W. Wilson,* 1645. 8°.* CHRISTIE-MILLER.

3120 — —[Anr. ed.] —, 1648. 8°.* LT.

3120A — —[Anr. ed.] *[London] for T. Vere, and J. Wright* [1650]. 8°.* Y.

3121 —A gentle reflection on the modest account. *For Benj. Tooke, and Tho. Sawbridge,* 1682. fol.* L, O, C, LL, HH; CH, MH, NU, WF, Y.

3122 —Andrewes golden chaine. *For Iohn Wright,* 1645. 8°.* L.

3123 —A golden trumpet sounding. *For I. Wright,* 1641. 8°.* CN.

3123A — —Twenty-ninth edition. *For Edward Wright,* 1648. 8°.* L.

[–] Parallel, or, the new . . . . 1682. *See* Northleigh, John.

3124 —Andrewes repentance. *For Iohn Wright,* 1642. 8°.* L.

3125 **Andrewes, Lancelot, bp.** Αποσπασματια sacra: or a collection. *By R. Hodgkinsonne, for H. Moseley, A Crooke, D. Pakeman, L. Fawne, R. Royston, and N. Ekins,* 1657. fol. L, O, C, MR, DT; BN, CH, MH, NU, WF, Y.

3126 —The form of consecration of a church. *Sold by T. Garthwait,* 1659. 12°. LT, O; MH, WF, Y.

3127 — —[Anr. ed.] 1668. 12°. GU, DT; CN, WSM.

3128 — —[Anr. ed.] *[London, for R. Pawlet,* 1672.] 12°. YM; LC, PL.

3129 —Holy devotions. Fourth edition. *For Henry Seile,* 1655. 12°. L, YM; NGT, Y.

3129A — —Fifth edition. *For A. Seile,* 1663. 12°. OC, CM; MH.

3129B — —[Anr. ed.] *By Andrew Clark for Charles Harper,* 1675. 8°. CLC.

3130 — —Seventh edition. *For C. Harper and M. Clark, to be sold by W. Freeman,* 1684. 12°. T.C.II 89. L, O, OC, LSC; CLC, NU, WF.

3131 —A learned discourse of ceremonies. *For Charles Adams,* 1653. 12°. LT, O, C, CT, DT; CH, CU, NIC, NU, WF.

3132 —A manual of directions for the sick. *For Humphrey Moseley,* 1648. 8°. O, CT.

3133 — —[Anr. ed.] *By T. N. for Anne Mosley,* 1670. 8°. OB; MB, NU, PL, WF.

3134 — —[Anr. ed.] *For W. Freeman,* 1692. 8°. L; MBP.

3134A —A manvall of directions for the visitation of the sicke. *By R. Cotes for Samuel Cartwright,* 1642. 12°. CLC.

3135 A manual of the private devotions. *By W.D. for Humphrey Moseley,* 1648. 12°. L, OC, CT; CH, MH, NU.

3136 — —[Anr. ed.] *By T. N. for Anne Moseley,* 1670. 12°. T.C.I 52. L, O, OB, CPE, P; MB, NU, PL, WF.

3137 — —[Anr. ed.] *By T. Ratclif, & N. Thompson for Richard Bentley,* 1674. 12°. T.C.I 200. O, OC, CS; CLC, CN, MBP, MH.

3138 — —[Anr. ed.] *For A. Churchil,* 1682. 12° T.C.I 516. L, O, OB, OM; CH, PBM, WF, Y.

3139 — —[Anr. ed.] *For Will. Freeman,* 1692. 12°. T.C.II 396. L, O, EC; BN, CLC, MBP, NPT.

3140 —The morall law expovnded. *For Michael Sparke, Robert Milbourne, Richard Cotes, and Andrew Crooke,* 1642. fol. L, O, C, E; BN, CH, MH, NU, WF, Y.

3141 —Nineteen sermons. *Cambridge: by Roger Daniel,* 1641. 12°. L, C, CE, CT, NPL; BN, MIU, NU, WF.

3142 —XCVI sermons. Fourth edition. *By Richard Badger,* 1641. fol. L, O, OME, CT, DC; BN, CLC, CU, MH, NP, Y.

3142A — —Fifth edition. *For Gabriel Bedell & Thomas Collins,* 1661. fol. O, OM, CT; CU, MIU.

3142B — —"Fifth" edition. *For George Sawbridge,* 1661. fol. L, OC, CT, BR; CU, MIU, WF.

3143 —Of episcopacy. *[London], printed,* 1647. 4°. L, O, C, YM, DT; CH, MH, NU, WF.

3144 —Of the right of tithes. *For Andrew Hebb,* 1647. 4°.* L, O, C, MR; CH, CN, MH, MHL, NP.

3145 [–] A pattern of catechisticall doctrine. *For William Garret,* 1641. 12°. L, O, C, LW, DC; MH, NU, PL, Y.

3146 [–] —Second edition. *By R. B. for Wil. Garret,* 1641. 12°. L, C; CLC, MH.

3146A — —[Anr. ed.] *By R. D. for W. G. and are to be sold by Ben. Allen,* 1641. 12°. OC.

3147 — —"Second" edition. *By Roger Norton, to be sold by George Badger,* 1650. fol. L, O, C, MR, DT; CN, NU, PL, WF, Y.

3148 — —Third edition. *For M. G. and are to be sold by Geo. Swimmeck,* 1675. fol. T.C.I 224. L, O, C, ENC, DT; CLC, LC, NC, NU.

3149 —Rev. Patris Lanc. Andrews Episc. Winton. Preces privatæ. *Oxonii, e theatro Sheldoniano,* 1675. 12°. T.C.I 229. MADAN 3049. L, O, CT, EN, DT; BN, CH, NC, WF, Y.

3150 —The private devotions of. *For Humphrey Moseley,* 1647. 12°. LT, O; CH.

3151 —Sacrilege a snare. *By T.B. for Andrew Hebb,* 1646. 4°.* LT, O, C, CT, DC; CH, NU, WF.

3152 —A summarie view. *Oxford, by Leon Lichfield,* 1641. 4°.* MADAN 992. L, O, C, EN, DT; CH, MH, NU, PU, Y.

3153 —Three learned and seasonable discourses. *[London], printed,* 1647. NU.

3154 **Andrewes, R.** A perfect declaration of the barbarous and cruell practises. *Printed at London, for Fr. Couke,* 1642. 4°.* LT, O, HH; CH, MH, MU, WF.

3155 **Andrews, William.** Annus prodigiosus, or the wonderful year 1672. *By T. Ratcliffe, and N. Thompson,* 1672. 4°.* L; MH.

3156 —The astrological physitian. *For George Sawbridge,* 1656. 12°. LT, LWL; MH.

3157 —Choice discoveries. *For R. Reynolds,* 1677. 8°. T.C.I 294. CLC.

—Cœlestes observationes. 1669. *See* Almanacs.

—De rebus. 1658. *See* Almancas.

3158 —More news from Heaven. *By T. Ratcliffe, and N. Thompson,* 1672. 4°.* L.

—Newes from the stars. 1660. *See* Almanacs.

—Physical observations. 1671. *See* Almanacs.

3159 —The yearly intelligencer. *By E. Crowch, for T. Vere,* 1672. 4°.* MH.

3160 —[Anr. ed.] —, 1673. 4°.* O, C, OP, SP, GU; CH, CU, MH.

Andromache. 1675. *See* Racine, Jean Baptist.

Andromana. 1660. *See* Shirley, James.

Andronicus. 1661. *See* Fuller, Thomas.

Andronicus Comnenius. [1663.] *See* Wilson, John.

Andronicus Rhodius. Παραφρασις. Cambridge, 1679. *See* Aristotle.

3161 **Andros, Sir Edmund.** By His Excellency a proclamation . . . January 10, 1688. *Printed at Boston, in New-England by R. P.,* [1688]. brs. EVANS 449. MHS.

Anent the punishment. Edinburgh, 1688. *See* Scotland. Privy Council.

3162 **Angel, John.** Right government of thoughts. *For Nath. Ekins,* 1659. 8° L. O; CH, NPT.

3163 The angel Gabriel, his salvation. *For W. Thackeray, and T. Passenger,* [1680?] brs. MH.

3163A —[Anr. ed.] [*London*], *for F. Coles, T. Vere, I. Wright, and I. Clarke,* [1674–9]. brs. O.

3163B [**Angell, Philemon**] The way of peace. *For Henry Brome,* 1680. 4°.* T.C.I 394. L, O, C, OC; CH, IU, NU, WF, Y.

3163C [–] —[Anr. ed.] *For Charles Brome,* 1686. 4°.* L.

Angelographia. Boston [Mass.] 1696. *See* Mather, Increase.

Angelus, Francis, *brother. See* Mason, Richard Angelus.

Angelus, Johannes. *pseud.*

3163D **Angier, Francis.** The state of His Majesties revenue. *In the Savoy, by Tho. Newcomb,* 1673. fol. L, C, DT; CLC.

3164 **Angier, John.** An helpe to better hearts. *By A. M. for Christopher Meredith,* 1647. 12°. L, O, LCL, LW; CLC, NPT, TU.

3164A — —[Anr. ed.] *For Edward Brewster,* 1662. 12°. Y.

3165 [–] Lancashires valley of Achor. *For Luke Fawne,* 1643. 4°.* LT, O, OC, CT, DT; MH, Y.

3165A [**Angier, Samuel**] A short explanation of the shorter catechism. Second edition. *For J. Robinson,* 1695. 12°. LW.

Angler's vade mecum. 1681. *See* Chetham, James.

3166 **Anglesey, Arthur Annesley, earl.** Bibliotheca Angleseiana, sive catalogus. [*London*], 1686. 4°. L, O, C, OC, HH; CLC, CN, NPT, WF, JF.

3167 [–] England's confusion: or, a true . . . relation. *Printed,* 1659. 4°.* LT, O, C, HH, EN; HR, CH, CU, MH, WF, Y.

3168 [–] —Second edition. —, 1659. 4°. O, C, YM, HH, E; CH, CU, MH, NU, Y.

3168A [–] —Third edition. —, 1659. 4°.* VC.

3169 [–] The King's right of indulgence. *Printed, and sold by Randall Taylor,* 1688. 4°. T.C.II 209. L, O, CCA, MC, E; CH, CN, MH, NU, WF, Y.

3170 [–] A letter from a person of honour in the countrey. *For Nath. Ponder,* 1681. 8°. T.C.I 430. L, O, C, OC, P; CH, CN, MH, WF, Y.

3171 [–] —[Anr. ed.] *For R. Baldwin,* 1682. 4°. L, OC; CU, MU.

3172 —A letter from the right honourable Arthur. *For N. P.,* 1682. fol.* L, O, C, LL, DT; CH, TU, CN, WF, Y.

3173 —[Anr. ed.] *Published by R. Baldwin,* 1682. fol.* L, O, OC; NC.

3174 [–] A letter of remarks upon Jovian. *For H. Jones,* 1683. 4°.* L, O, OC; CH, CN, MH, NC, WF, Y.

3175 —Memoirs. *For John Dunton,* 1693. 8°. T.C.II 476. L, O, CS, EN, DT; BN, CH, CN, LC, MH, NU, Y.

3176 [–] Reflections on that discourse which a master of arts (once). *Printed,* 1676. 4°.* L, OC, CT, EN, DT; MH, MIU, NU, WF, Y.

—The Earl of Anglesey's state of the government. 1694. *See* Thompson, Sir John.

3177 Anglia grata, or, a hearty English-welcome to King William. *Printed and are to be sold by R. Baldwin,* 1695. 4°.* L, GU; LC, WF, Y.

3178 Anglia liberata, or, the rights of the people. *By T. Newcomb for R. Lowns,* 1651. 4°. LT, O, C, HH, DT; CH, CN, NN, TU, WF, Y.

Anglia redviva [sic]. 1647. *See* Sprigge, Joshua.

3179 Anglia rediviva: a poem. *By R. Hodgkinsonne for Charles Adams,* 1660. 4°.* LT, O; CH, MH, WF.

Anglia rediviva; being. . . . 1669. *See* Dunstar, Samuel.

3180 Anglia rediviva: or, England revived. 1658. 4°. L, BAMB, SP; CH.

Anglia sacra. 1691. *See* Wharton, Henry.

Anglia triumphans. 1700. *See* H., J.

3181 Angliæ decus & tutamen: or the glory and safety. *For R. Baldwin,* 1691. 4°. T.C.II 384. O; CU, LC, MH, NU, WF.

Angliæ notitia. 1668. *See* Chamberlayne, Edward.

Angliæ ruina; or, . . . 1647. *See* Ryves, Bruno.

Angliæ specvlvm: a glasse. 1678. *See* Patrick, Symon, bp.

Angliæ speculum morale. 1670. *See* Preston, Richard Graham, viscount.

Angliæ specvlvm, or Englands looking-glasse. [1646.] *See* Mercer, William.

3182 Angliæ tutatem, or, the safety. *For the author and are to be sold by John Whitlock,* 1695. 4°.* L, LG, A; MH, NC, PU, WF.

3183 Entry cancelled.

3184 Anglicani novi schismatis redargutio. *Oxonii, e theatro Sheldoniano,* 1691. 4°. O, OM, CT, MR; MIU, NU.

Anglicus, *pseud.*
Anglo-Judæus, or, . . . 1656. *See* Hughes, William.

3185   **Anglo-Saxon chronicle.** Chronicon Saxoni̇cum. *Oxonii, e theatro Sheldoniano,* 1692. 4°. L, O, C, EN, DT; CLC, LC, MH, NP, Y.

Anglo-tyrannus, or . . . 1650. *See* Walker, George.

Anglorum gesta; or, . . . 1675. *See* Meriton, George.

Anglorum singultus: or, . . . 1660. *See* Peirce, *Sir* Edmond.

Anglorum speculum, or . . . 1684. *See* Sandys, George.

3186   Entry cancelled. *See* Condé, Louis II de Bourbon, *prince de.*

Anima magica. 1650. *See* Vaughan, Thomas.

Anima mundi. Amsterdam, [1679]. *See* Blount, Charles.

Animadversion upon Generall Monck's. 1659. *See* Morice, *Sir* William.

3187   An animadversion upon the late Lord Protectors declaration. *Printed,* 1659. 4°.* LT; CN, CSS, MH, NU, WF, Y.

Animadversiones in libros. 1672. *See* Knatchbull, *Sir* Norton.

3188   Entry cancelled.
Animadversions and remarks. [London, 1684]. *See* Ward, S.

Animadversions animadverted. [1642.] *See* Parker, Henry.

Animadversions by way. 1687. *See* Reed, John.

3189   Animadversions on a discourse [by W. Lloyd] entituled, God's ways. *For W. Rayner,* 1691. 4°.* T.C.II 372. L, C, OC, LVF, DC; MB, MIU, NU, WF, Y.

3190   Animadversions on a discourse of God's ways. *For W. Rayner,* 1691. 4°.* CS; CLC, MN, MIU, NU, Y.

3191   Animadversions on a late book entituled The reasonableness of Christianity. *Oxford, by Leon. Lichfield for George West, and Anthony Piesley,* 1697. 4°. L, OC, OM, BR, MR; CLC, CU, MH, NU, WF, Y.

Animadversions on a late paper. 1687. *See* Care, Henry.

3191A   Animadversions on a paper, intituled A caution. colop: *Printed,* 1690. 4°.* O; Y.

Animadversions on a petition. 1653. *See* Flecknoe, Richard.

3192   Animadversions on a postscript to the defence of Dr. Sherlock. [*London?* 1695?] 4°.* L, O, OC, WCA, CJ; CH, MH, NU, WF, Y.

Animadversions on a pretended. 1694. *See* King, William.

Animadversions on a treatise. 1662. *See* Owen, John.

3193   Animadversions on Capt. Wilkinson's information. *For Walter Davis,* 1682. fol.* L, OC, CT, SP; CH, CN, LC, PL, Y.

Animadversions on Dr. Burnet's. 1682. *See* Comber, Thomas.

Animadversions on George Keith's Account. 1700. *See* A., J.

Animadversions on George Whitehead's. 1694. *See* Crisp, Thomas.

3194   Animadversions on King James, his letter to the Pope. *Printed and sold by the booksellers,* 1691. 4°. L, SP; CH, MH, NU, WF, Y.

3195   Animadversions on Mr. Congreve's late answer to Mr. Collier. *For John Nutt,* 1698. 8°. L, O, OC; CH, CN, MH, WF, Y.

Animadversions on Mr. Corbet's remains. 1685. *See* T., J.

Animadversions on Mr. Hill's. 1695. *See* Allix, Pierre.

Animadversions on Mr. Johnson's. 1691. *See* Hopkins, William.

Animadversions on that part. 1676. *See* Allen, William.

Animadversions on the apology. [1685]. *See* Penn, William.

Animadversions on the defence. 1697. *See* MacBride, John.

Animadversions on the eight. Oxford, 1687. *See* Smalridge, George, *bp.*

3196   Animadversions on the Lady Marquess. *For J. Jordan.* [1680?] brs. L.

Animadversions on the last speech and confession. [1683.] *See* Settle, Elkanah.

3197   Animadversions on the last speech of William Viscount Stafford. colop: *For R. Baldwin,* 1680. cap., fol.* L, CS, EN, MR; CH, LC, MH, WF, Y.

3198   —Second edition. 1681. fol. L.

Animadversions on the late vindication. [1681.] *See* W., W.

Animadversions on the medicinal. 1674. *See* B., T.

3199   Animadversions on the proposal for sending back the nobility . . . of Ireland. *For Tim. Goodwin,* 1690. 4°.* T.C.II 323. L, O, C, LVF, DT; CH, MH, NU, WF, Y.

Animadversions on the reflections. 1688. *See* Burnet, Gilbert, *bp.*

Animadversions on the Scotch. 1662. *See* L., J.

Animadversions on the speech. 1681. *See* P., W.

3200   Animadversions on two late books, one called Remarques. *By A. C. for William Hensman,* 1673. 8°. T.C.I 136. L, O, C; CLC, WF.

Animadversions on two pamphlets. 1696. *See* Hody, Humphrey.

Animadversions upon a book. 1673. *See* Clarendon, Edward Hyde, *earl of.*

3201   Animadversions upon a declaration of the proceedings against the xi members. *Cambridge, for Will. Armestrong,* 1647. 4°.* LT, YM; CH, MH.

Animadversions upon a late pamphlet. 1676. *See* Turner, Francis, b.p.

Animadversions upon a late treatise. 1683. *See* Thomas, Samuel.

Animadversions upon a letter. 1656. *See* Sedgwick, William.

Animadversions upon a paper. [1683]. *See* Settle, Elkanah.

Animadversions, upon a pretended. [1688?] *See* T., N.

3202 Animadversions upon a sheet of Mr. Baxters entituled An appeal. *Oxford, by H. Hall,* 1675. 4°.* MADAN 3080. O; NU.

3203 Animadversions upon Dr. Calamy's discourse. *Printed: to be sold by A. Baldwin,* 1700. 4°.* L, O, LW, EC, EN; CH, CN, NU.

Animadversions upon Dr. Sherlock's book. 1963. *See* South, Robert.

Animadversions upon John Lilburnes. 1646. *See* Sheppard, Simon.

3204 Animadversions upon Mijn Heer Fagels letter. *By G. Larkin,* 1688. 4°.* L, O, C, MR, HH; CLC, MB, MH, WF.

Animadversions vpon Sʳ Richard Baker's. Oxon. 1672. *See* Blount, Thomas.

Animadversions upon some passages. 1690. *See* Elys, Edmund.

3205 Animadversions upon that proclamation of September 13, 1693. [1693.] cap., fol.* O.

Animadversions upon the armies. 1648. *See* Walker, Clement.

3206 Animadversions upon the French King's declaration. *For John Smith,* 1681. 4°.* L, O, OC, DT; CH, CN, MH.

3207 Animadvertions upon the Kings answer, read . . . Ianu:. 13. 1642. [*London,* 1643.] 4°.* LT, O, CT, HH; CLC, LC, MH, TU, WF.

Aniamadversions upon the modern explanation. [1689.] *See* Collier, Jeremy.

Animadversions upon the remonstrants. 1641. *See* Milton, John.

Animadversions upon the responses. [1692.] *See* Collins, Hercules.

3208 Animadversions upon the speech of William (late) viscount Stafford. *For Richard Baldwin,* 1681. fol.* T.C.I 429. L, O, OC; CH, MH.

3208A —Second edition. —, 1681. fol.* CT, HH; CU, MIU, PL, Y.

3209 Animadversions vpon those notes. *For William Sheares,* 1642. 4°.* LT, O, C, EN, DT; CH, CU, MH, NU, WF, Y.

3210 —[Anr. ed.] colop: *For William Sheares,* 1642. cap., 4°.* O, CS; CH, MH, TU, Y.

3211 Anon., askew, intituled, I am a woman. [*London*], *for A. Milbourn, W. Onley, T. Thackeray,* [1670–89]. brs. L, HH, GU.

3212 —[Anr. ed.] *By and for A: M. and sold by the booksellers of London,* [1670–90]. fol.* L.

3213 —[Anr. ed.] [*London,* 1670–90]. brs. MH.

3214 —[Anr. ed.] *By and for W. O[nley],* [1680–90]. brs. HH.

Annæ dicata, or, . . . [1652?] *See* Tooke, George.

Annals of King James. 1681. *See* Frankland, Thomas.

Annals of love. 1672. *See* Desjardins, Marie Catherine Hortense.

3215 **Annand, William.** Catalogue of . . . books. *Edinburgh, society of stationers,* 1690. 4°. ALDIS 3027. HH, EN.

3216 —Doxologia. *By I. D. and are to be sold by George Sawbridge,* 1672. 8°. O, AU, GU.

3217 —Dualitas. *Edinburgh, by George Swintoun and James Glen; and are to be sold by Gideon Schaw,* 1674. 4°. ALDIS 2013. L, O, E, EN.

3218 —Fides Catholica. *By T. R. for Edward Brewster,* 1661. 4°. L, O, E, AU, DT; LC, NU.

3219 —A funeral elegie, upon the death of George Sonds, Esq. *By John Crowch,* 1655. brs. LT.

3220 —Mysterium pietatis. *For Robert Boulter,* 1671. 8°. O, LSC, E, EG, GU; NC, Y.

3220A — —[Anr. ed.] *Edinburgh, by Andrew Anderson,* 1671. 8°. NC.

3221 —Panem qvotidianvm: or, a short discourse. *For Edward Brewster,* 1661. 4°. LT, O, DT; NU.

3222 —[Anr. ed.] *For the author,* 1661. 4°. BP, EN; CH, NGT.

3223 —Pater-noster, our Father. *Edinburgh, by George Swintoun and James Glen,* 1670. 8°. ALDIS 1887. T.C.I 55. L, E, EN, GU, FSF; Y.

3224 **Anne, Queen of England.** The Princess Anne of Denmark's letter to the queen. [1688] brs. L, O, C, OC, EN; CH, CN, TU, WF, Y.

3225 [**Annesley, Samuel.**] Casuistical morning-exercises. The fourth volume. *By James Astwood for John Dunton,* 1690. 4°. T.C.II 472. L, O, C, E, DT; CH, MH, NPT, NU, PL.

3226 —Catalogue of library. 18 March 1697. 4°. L.

3227 —Communion vvith God. *By Evan Tyler; and are to be sold by Nathanael Web and William Grantham,* 1655. 4°. LT, O, LS, LCL; MH, NU, WF, Y.

3228 [–] A continuation of morning-exercise questions. *By J. A. for John Dunton,* 1683. 4°. T.C.II 12. L, HH, P, GU, E; MBA, MH, NPT, NU, WF.

3229 —The first dish at the Wil-shire feast. *By E. T. for Nathanael Webb and William Grantham,* 1655. 4°.* O, LCL, ENC; CH, NU.

3230 —The life and funeral sermon of the reverend Mr. Thomas Brand. *For John Dunton,* 1692. 4°. T.C.II 472. L, O, C, LCL, LW; BN, CH, WF.

3231 [–] The morning exercise at Cripplegate. *By A. Maxwell, and R. Roberts, for Tho. Cockerill,* 1661. 4v. 4°. O, LCL, P; CU, Y.

3232 [–] —[Anr. ed.] *For Joshua Kirton and Nathaniel Webb,* 1661. 4°. L, O, C, LG, DT; CLC, CU, LC, MH, NP.

3233 [–] —Second edition. *For Joshua Kirton,* 1664. 4°. L, LG, WCA, E.

3234 [–] —Third edition. *By T. Milbourn for J. Johnson, sold by Edward Brewster,* 1671. 4°. T.C.I 108. L, C, CT, RPL; IU, MH, NU, PH.

3235 [–] —Fourth edition. *By A. Maxwell, and R. Roberts, for Tho. Cockerill,* 1677. 4°. L, HH, E; MH, NF, NU, PL, WF.

3236 —A sermon preached . . . July 26. 1648. *By J. Macock, for Octavian Pullen,* 1648. 4°.* LT, O, C, LW, OCC; CH, CU, MH, NU.

3237 —A sermon preached at the funeral of . . . Will. Whitaker. *For Nevill Simmons,* 1673. 4°.* L, O, LW, OCC, CS; MB, MH, TU.

3238 — —[Anr. ed.] *For Tho. Parkhurst,* 1673. 8°.* L, O, LCL; MB.

3239 [–] A supplement to The morning-exercise at Cripplegate. *For Thomas Cockerill,* 1674. 4°. T.C.I 176. L, O, BP, HH, E; IU, MH, NPT, NU, WF.

3240 [–] —Second edition. —, 1676. fol. T.C.I 240. L, CT, LW, GU, E; BBE, MH, NPT, NU.

3240A The anniversary ode on His Majesties inauguration. *By Edward Jones*, 1686. 4°.* O.

3241 An anniversary ode upon the Kings birth-day. *Hague, for Samuel Browne*, 1654. 4°.* LT; MH, Y.

3242 —[Anr. ed. "2654"]. 4°.* MH, TU.

3243 An anniversary poem on the sixth of May. *For Jo. Hindmarsh*, [1683]. brs. L, O.

Anniversary to the kings. 1661. *See* Bold, Henry.

Anniversary upon the xxxth. 1660. *See* Crown, S.

Anno regni. *See* England. Parliament.

Annotationes in Vetus Testamentum. *Cantabrigiæ*, 1653. *See* Scattergood, A.

Annotations on Milton's. 1695. *See* Hume, Patrick.

Annotations on the book. 1669. *See* Reynolds, Edward, *bp*.

Annotations upon all the books. 1645. *See* Downame, John.

3244 Annotations upon certaine quæries. *For Abel Roper*, 1642. 4°.* LT, O, C, OC, HH; CH, MH, NU, WF, Y.

Annotations upon Religio. 1656. *See* Keck, Thomas.

3245 Annotations vpon the Earle of Straffords conclvsion. [*London*], *printed*, 1641. 4°.* L, O, LG, CT, YM; CH, MH, NP, WF, Y.

Annotations upon the Holy Bible. 1688. *See* Cooper, William.

Annotations upon the late. [1642.] *See* L., T.

Annotations upon the two. 1682. *See* More, Henry.

Annual miscellany. 1694. *See* Dryden, John.

3246 Annus MDCVL. Triumphalis annus. 1646. 4°. CM.

Annus luni-solaris novus. [*London?* 1680.] *See* W., R.

3247 Annus mirabilis, the year of prodigies. [*London*], 1661. 4°. MR, BAMB.

3248 Annus sophiæ jubilæus. The sophick constitution. *For A. Baldwin*, 1700. 8°. T.C.III 200. C, GU; Y.

Anonomus, Philanax, *pseud.*

Anonymous, *pseud.*

Anonymous, Basilius, *pseud.*

Anonymous, Eugenius, *pseud.*

Anonymous Persa. 1648. *See* Graves, John.

3249 Another ballad called The libertines lampoone. [1675?] brs. L.

3250 Another bloudy fight at Colchester. *For G. VV.*, 1648. 4°.* LT, DT.

3251 —[Anr. ed.] *Printed*, 1648. 4°.* LT.

3252 —[Anr. ed.] [*London*], *printed*, 1648. 4°.* LT; Y.

Another bloudy fight at sea. [June] 1652. *See* Cats.

—[July] 1652. *See* Pack.

3253 Another bloudy fight at sea upon the coast of Cornwal. *For George Horton*, 1652. 4°.* LT; WF.

3254 Another character of Poor Robin. *Printed*, 1680. brs. MH.

Another collection. 1665. *See* Renaudot, Eusèbe.

3255 Another cry of the innocent. *Printed*, 1664. 4°.* L, O, LF, OC, BBN; CH, LC, MH, PH, Y.

3256 —[Anr. ed.] [*London*], *printed*, 1665. 4°.* L, O, LF, BBN; CH, LC, MH, NC, PSC, Y.

Another declaration. 1641. *See* England. Parliament.

3257 Another declaration: wherein is rendred, a further account. *For T. Brewer*, 1653. 4°.* LT; WF.

3258 Another extract of more letters sent out of Ireland. [*London*, 1643.] cap., 4°. C.

3259 Another extract of severall letters from Ireland. *By George Miller*, 1643. 4°. LT, O, DC; MH, Y.

Another famous victorie. [1642.] *See* C., T.

3260 Another fight at Colchester. *For G. W.*, 1648. 4°.* LT; NU, Y.

3261 Another fight between the two armies of Scotch and English. [*London*], *printed*, 1648. 4°.* LT, DT.

3262 Another great and admirable victory obtained by … Monk. *By R. Wood*, 1654. 4°.* LT.

3263 Another great and bloudy fight in the North. *Printed*, 1648. 4°.* LT.

3264 Another great and blovdy fight in Ireland. *For G. W.*, *Aug.* 21. 1649. 4°.* LT, C, LFEA.

3265 Another great and bloody plot against His Highness the Lord Protector. *For G.Horton*, 1654[5]. 4°. LT, O; CH.

3266 Another great fight on Sunday morning. *Imprinted at Yondon*, [*sic*] *for R.VV.*, 1648. 4°.* LT.

3267 Another great victory obtained by the Lord Lambert. *For Edw.Horton*, 1659. 4°.* O; CH.

3268 Another great victorie obtained by Vice-Admiral Pen. *For G.Horton*, [1653]. 4°.* LT.

Another happy victorie. [1642.] *See* Balfour, William.

Another letter from Legorn. 1680. *See* B., J.

3269 Another message sent to the kings Majesty at Yorke. *For John Thomas*, 1642. 4°.* LT; MH.

3270 Another miraculous victorie obtained by the Lord Fairfax. *For Robert Wood*, 1643. 4°.* LT; YM, WF.

3271 Another New-Years-gift for arbitrary judges. colop: *Printed*, 1681. brs. L, O, HH, MC; CH, MH, PL, WF, Y.

3272 Entry cancelled.

Another order of. 1643. *See* England. Parliament. House of Commons.

3273 Another out-cry of the innocent. *Printed*, 1665. 4°.* LF, EN; CH, MH, PH, Y.

Another parcell. 1648. *See* Nethersole, Sir Francis.

3274 Another victory in Lancashire obtained against the Scots. *By B.A.*, 1651. 4°.* LT; CH, Y.

Another why not. [1649.] *See* Frese, James.

Another word. 1660. *See* C., C.

Ansloe, John. *See* Aynsloe, John.

Answer according. 1655. *See* Drayton, Thomas.

Answer and resolvtion. 1642. *See* Netherlands. Estates General.

3274A The answer and resolvtion of the Lord Fairefax, Sir Phillip Stapleton. *For I.Horton*, *June* 11, 1642. 4°.* BAMB; CH.

3275 An answer by an Anabaptist to the three considerations. *Printed*, 1688. 4°.* EN; NU, RPJ.

3276 —[Anr. ed.] *Printed and sold by Andrew Sowle*, 1688. 4°.* L, OC.

Answer by letter. 1644. *See* Maxwell, John, *bp.*

Answer for Mr. Calamie. 1663. *See* R., J.

3277 Answer for the African company. [*Edinburgh*, 1696.] brs. O.

Answer for the university. [*Aberdeen?* 1700]. *See* Campbell, George.

Answer from both houses. 1647. *See* England. Parliament.

Ansvvere from the committee. Edinburgh, 1650. *See* Scotland. Estates.

3278 An answer from the country, to a late letter to a dissenter. *For M. R.*, 1687. 4°. L, O, CS, MC, HH; CH, MB, MIU, TU, WF, Y.

3279 An answer in few words to Master Edwards. [c. 1646.] 4°.* E.

3280 An answer in just vindication of some . . . gentlemen of Pembrokeshire. 1646. 4°.* DT; CH.

Answer made by command. 1655. *See* Cotton, Sir Robert Bruce.

Answer of a citizen. [1681.] *See* P., N.

3281 The answer of a letter from a friend, concerning elections. [1688.] fol.* CLC, Y.

3282 An answer of a letter from a friend in the country. *By George Croom*, 1681. 4°.* L, O; MH, NU, WF, Y.

3283 An answer of a letter from an agitator. *Printed*, 1647. 4°.* L, LG; CH, CLC, CN, MH.

3283A An answer of a letter to a member. [*Edinburgh?* 1689]. cap., 4°.* CLC, IU.

Answer of a minister. 1687. *See* Cartwright, Thomas.

Answer of a person of quality. Dublin, 1662. *See* Orrery, Roger Boyle, *earl of.*

3284 The answer of a Protestant gentleman in Ireland, to a late letter from N. N. *For Ric. Chiswell*, 1689. 4°. L, O, C, EN, DT; CH, CN, MH, WF, Y.

Answer of both houses. 1642. *See* England. Parliament.

3285 The answer of Coleman's ghost. [*London*, 1679.] fol.* L, HH; CLC, CN, MH, TU, WF, Y.

3286 The answer of Mr. Wallers painter, to his many new advisers. *By Anne Maxwell*, 1667. 4°.* L, LG; CLC, WF, Y.

Answer of several ministers. Boston, 1695. *See* Mather, Increase.

3287 An ansvver of some if not all. [*London*, 1659.] cap., 4°.* CH, CN, MIU.

Answer of the assembly. 1645. *See* Westminster assembly of divines.

3287A The answer of the Bermuda company. [*London?* 1677]. brs. L.

3288 Answer of the burgesses . . . of Buckingham. [*London*, 1679.] fol.* CH, CU.

Answer of the chancellor. Oxford, 1649. *See* Langbaine, Gerard.

Ansvver of the city. Oxford, 1643. *See* Oxford.

Answer of the commission. Aberdene, 1651. *See* Church of Scotland.

Ansvver of the commissioners. 1647. *See* Scotland. Estates.

3289 The answer of the commissioners of the navie. [*London*], *by Will. Bentley*, 1646. 4°.* LT, O; CN, CU, MH, OWC.

Answer of the committee. [1683]. *See* East India Company.

3290 Answer of the company of royal adventurers. *Anno dom.* 1667. 4°.* L, EN, DT; MIU, NC, RPJ, WF.

Answer of the convention. Edinburgh, 1643. *See* Scotland. Estates.

Answer of the Corporation of moniers. 1653. *See* Violet, Thomas.

3291 Entry cancelled.

3292 The answer of the deputie lieutenants. 1641. 4°. EN.

3293 The answer of the deputie lieutenants of . . . Devon. *By R. Olton and G. Dexter, for Henry Overton*, 1642. 4°.* DT; CH, MH, Y.

3294 Answer of the divines attending. 1648. 4°. O, BAMB, DT; PL.

3295 —[Anr. ed.] 1660. 4°. O, YM.

Ansvver of the generall assembly. 1643. *See* Scotland. Estates.

3296 Answer of the elders and other messengers. *Cambridge, Mass., by S. Green*, 1662. 4°.* MHS.

Answer of the House of representatives. [1699]. *See* Massachusetts (colony).

3296A The answer of the master, workers . . . Trinity-house. [*London?* 1660]. 4°. CT.

3296B An answer of the most material objections. [*London?* 1699]. brs. MH.

3297 The answer of the new converts of France. *By Henry Hills*, 1686. 4°.* L, O, CT, EN, DT; CH, CN, MH, NU, WF, Y.

3298 The answer of the officers at Whitehall. *Edinburgh, by Christopher Higgins*, 1659. 4°.* ALDIS 1587. L, O, HH, E, EN; CH, MH, WF, Y.

3299 The answer of the people called Quakers. [*London*, 1687.] cap., fol.* HH.

3300 An answer of the purchasers of the lands, late of Sir John Starvel. *By Thomas Newcomb*, 1654. fol. LT, O, BR.

3301 The answer of the subscribers to the declaration. [*Boston*], 1680. brs. LPR.

3302 The answer of the sworn clerks in Chancery. [*London?* 1700]. brs. L.

3303 The answer of Wapping. [1694.] brs. L, LL.

Ansvver or necessary animadversions. 1642. *See* Burney, Richard.

3303A Answer out of the West. 1667. PL.

Answer returned. [1680.] *See* F., L.

Answer to a book called The Quaker's catechism. 1656. *See* Nayler, James.

Answer to a book entituled, An account. Paris, 1654. *See* T., R.

Answer to a book entitvled, An humble remonstrance. 1641. *See* Marshall, Stephen.

Answer to a book, entituled, Reason. 1687. *See* Bainbridge, Thomas.

3304   An answer to a book, intituled, The doctrine and discipline of divorce. *By G. M. for William Lee*, 1644. 4°.* LT, O, C, MR, E; CH, CN, MH, NU, WF, Y.

Answer to a book intituled, The state of the Protestants. 1692. *See* Leslie, Charles.

Answer to a book intituled, Tractatus. 1697. *See* Earbery, Matthias.

Answer to a book which Samuel. 1654. *See* Camm, John.

Answer to a book which will. [1693.] *See* King, William.

Answer to a catechism against Quakerism. 1693. *See* Field, John.

Answer to a certain writing. 1643. *See* Hollingworth, Richard.

Ansvver to a declaration of the commissioners. [*London*, 1648.] *See* Ward, Nathaniel.

Answer to a declaration of the Lords. 1646. *See* Nedham, Marchamont.

Answer to a discourse against. 1687. *See* Gother, John.

Answer to a discourse concerning. Oxford, 1688. *See* Tully, George.

Answer to a discourse intituled, Papists. 1686. *See* Sherlock, William.

Answer to a foolish pamphlet. 1641. *See* Walker, Henry.
Answer to a late book. 1699. *See* Whately, Solomon.
Answer to a late dialogue. 1687. *See* Sherlock, William.

3305   An answer to a late ill-natur'd libel, call'd, A trip to Holland. [*London*], *for J. Nutt*, 1699. fol. T.C.III 98. HR, MH, WF, Y.

3305A   An answer to a late pamphlet called A sober dialogue. *For Sam. Clark*, 1698/9. 4°.* C, CT, LF, SP; RPJ.

3306   An answer to a late pamphlet, called An essay concerning critical ... learning. *Printed and sold by E. Whitlock*, 1698. 8°.* L, C, MR; CH, TU, WF, Y.

3307   An answer to a late pamphlet; entituled, A character of a Popish successor. *By Nathaniel Thompson*, 1681. fol.* L, O, C, LG, HH; CH, CN, LC, MH, NU, Y.

3308   —[Anr. ed.] *Edinburgh, re-printed*, 1681. 4°. ALDIS 2247. EN; HR, LC, MB, PU, WF.

3308A   An answer to a late pamphlet, intituled A short abstract. [*London*, 1695] cap.,* LG, LUG.

3308B   An answer to a late pamphlet, intituled, A short scheme. [*London*, 1689.] cap., 4°.* L, HH; CH, Y.

Answer to a late pamphlet, intituled, Obedience. [1690.] *See* Wagstaffe, Thomas.

Answer to a late pamphlet intituled, Reasons. [1696.] *See* Briscoe, John.

3309   An answer to a late pamphlet, intituled, The judgment and doctrine. *For Ric. Chiswell*, 1687. 4°.* T.C.II 277. L, O, C, E, DT; CH, CN, MH, NU, TU, WF, Y.

Answer to a late printed paper. 1686. *See* Williams, John, *bp*.

3309A   An answer to a late printed paper, intituled The case of the creditors of Sir Robert Vyner. [*London?* 1690]. brs. L.

3310   An answer to a late scandalous libel. [*London*, 1689?] 4°.* L, SP; LC, Y.

Answer to a late scandalous pamphlet. 1677. *See* Sherlock, William.

Answer to a late scurrilous. 1642. *See* Norton, John.

3311   An answer to a late tract, entituled, An essay on the East-India trade. *For Tho. Cockerill*, 1697. 4°. T.C.III 8. L; CH, MH, NC, WF, Y.

Answer to a late treasonable. [1681.] *See* C., A.
Answer to a lawless pamphlet. 1641. *See* M., R.

3312   An answer to a letter concerning the Kings going from Holdenby. [*London*], *printed*, 1647. 4°.* LT, O, CS, HH; MH, MIU, TU.

Answer to a letter from a clergyman. [1688.] *See* Poulton.

3313   An answer to a letter from a freeholder of Buckingham-shire: to a friend in London. [*London?* 1679?] cap., fol.* L, O, C, HH, EN; CH, CN, MH, WF, Y.

3314   An answer to a letter from a gentleman in the country. *For G. Huddleston*, 1698. 4°.* L; CU, MH, NC, Y.

3315   —[Anr. ed.] *Dublin by Andrew Crook, and are to be sold by William Norman and Eliphet Dobson*, 1698. 4°.* DIX 299, L, C, DK, DT; NC, Y.

3316   —[Anr. ed.] *By John Darby, and sold by A. Baldwin*, 1699. 4°.* L, CS, EC, HH; CH, CN, MH, WF, Y.

3317   An answer to a letter from a minister. colop: *For John Blythe*, [1679]. fol.* L, O, C, HH; CH, MH, PU, WF, Y.

Answer to a letter of inquiry. 1671. *See* Bramhall, John, *abp*.

Answer to a letter sent from Mr. Coddington. 1678. *See* Williams, Roger.

3317A   An answer to a letter sent to the mayor of Salisbury. [*London?* 1690]. brs. LG.

3318   An answer to a letter to a bishop. 1690. 4°. O, OC, CS.

3319   An answer to a letter to a dissenter. *Printed*, 1687. 4°.* L, O, C, EN, DT; CLC, MH, NU, WF, Y.

Answer to a letter to a gentleman. [1684.] *See* S., H.

3319A   An answer to a letter to a member of the Convention. [*London?* 1688] cap., 4°.* TU.

Answer to a letter to Dr. Burnet. [1685.] *See* Burnet, Gilbert, *bp*.

Answer to a letter to Dr. Sherlock. 1692. *See* Wagstaffe, Thomas.

Answer to a letter vvritten at Oxford. 1647. *See* Steward, Richard.

3320   An answer to a letter written by a member of Parliament in the countrey. [*London*, 1679.] cap., fol.* L, O, MC, MR, HH; CH, MH, NC, TU, WF, Y.

Answer to a letter, written out. 1643. *See* E., R.

3320A   An answer to a lybel, called, A speech lately made. *Reprinted*, 1681. brs. MU, Y.

Answer to a libel entituled. 1696. *See* Chamberlen, Hugh.

Answer to a little book. 1682. *See* Con, Alexander.

3321 An answer to a lying pamphlet, entitled, The case of Thomas Price, Esq. [*London*, 1690]. brs. L.

3322 An answer to a most pernicious and factious petition. *Printed*, 1647. 4°.* LT, O, C, LFEA.

3323 An answer to a pamphlet called, The true Protestants appeal. colop: *For J.B.*, 1681. brs. L, O; MH, MU, NU.

Answer to a pamphlet, entitled, A declaration. 1648. *See* Clarendon, Edward Hyde, *earl of*.

Answer to a pamphlet intituled, A vindication. [1679.] *See* R., N.

3324 Answer to a pamphlet, entitled, The humble apologie of the English Catholicks. [*London*], 1667. 4°.* CH.

3325 An ansvver to a pamphlet intituled The Lord George Digby, his apologie. *For Thomas Iohnson*, 1643. 4°.* LT; CH, MM, WF, Y, HC.

3326 An answer to a paper, addressed to the ... Lords. [*London?* 1693]. brs. Y.

Answer to a paper; called, A petition. 1654. *See* Howgill, Francis.

3327 An answer to a paper, called, The case of the auditors. *By W. G.*, 1662. 4°.* L, O, SP; CH, MH, NC, PU, WF.

3328 An answer to a paper, entituled, a brief account of the designs of the Papists. colop: *For T. Davies*, 1681. cap., fol.* L, O, LL, HH, EN; CH, CU, MH, WF, Y.

3328A An answer to a paper, entituled, A letter to a friend. [*London?* 1690]. brs. CH.

3328B An answer to a paper, entituled, A new test. 1645. PL.

3329 An answer to a paper entituled A trve narrative of the cause and manner. *By T. N. for G. Calvert*, 1653. 4°.* LT, O, OC, HH; CH, MH, NU, WF, Y.

3329A An answer to a paper, intituled Considerations relating to the bill. [*London?* 1696]. brs. Y.

3330 An answer to a paper entituled Reasons against reducing. [*London*, 1694?] brs. L.

3331 An answer to a paper, entituled, Reflections on the Prince of Orange's declaration. [*London*, 1688.] cap., 4°.* O, HH, AU; CH, CN, PU, WF, Y.

Answer to a paper entituled The case. Dublin, 1696. *See* Pullen, Tobias.

3332 An answer to a paper, entituled, The grievances. *Printed*, 1689. fol.* L; MH, Y.

Answer to a paper importing. 1688. *See* Care, Henry.

Answer to a paper printed. [1687.] *See* Burnet, Gilbert, *bp*.

3333 An answer to a paper published. [*London*, 1698]. cap., fol.* L; MH.

3334 An answer to a paper set forth by the coffee-men. [*London*, 168–?] brs. CH.

Answer to a paper which. 1658. *See* Fox, George.

3335 An answer to a paper written by Count d'Avaux. *For Richard Baldwin*, 1694. 4°.* T.C.II 527. L, O, CT; MM.

Answer to a printed book. Oxford, 1642. *See* Digges, Dudley.

Answer to a printed letter. 1690. *See* Payne, William.

3336 An answer to a printed pamphlet called The case of the inhabitants of Croydon. [*London*, 1673.] cap., fol.* L; MH, WF.

3337 An answer to a printed paper called The Lord Craven's case. [*London*, 1659?] fol. L.

3338 An answer to a printed paper dispersed by Sir John Maynard. colop: *For Richard Baddeley*, 1653. 4°. L, O; CH.

3339 An answer to a printed paper entituled Articles. [*London*], *printed*, 1641. 4°.* LT, C; CN, WF, Y.

3339A An answer to a printed paper, entituled, The case of Mary Dutchess of Norfolk. [*London?* 1700]. brs. HH.

3340 An answer to a printed paper, intituled The state of the case of Mr. Henry Howard. [*London*, 1661.] brs. LU.

3341 An answer to a printed protestation. *For N. T.*, 1681. fol. L, O.

3342 An answer to a proposal for laying a duty upon hats. [*London?* 1696]. brs. L.

Answer to a proposition. 1659. *See* Prynne, William.

3343 An answer to a rash dialogue. *For the author*, 1698. 4°. NU.

Answer to a scandalous letter lately printed. 1662. *See* Orrery, Roger Boyle, *earl of*.

3344 An answer to a scandalous letter written by Hammond. *Printed*, 1648. 4°.* LT, HH; CH, MH, WF.

Answer to a scandalous lying pamphlet. [1642]. *See* H., G.

Answer to a scandalous pamphlet entituled, A letter. [1687.] *See* Payne, Henry.

3345 An answer to a scandalous paper, lately sent to ... the Lord Mayor. *For T. B.*, 1646. 4°.* LT, DT; MH.

Answer to a scandalous paper wherein. 1656. *See* Breck, Edward.

3346 Entry cancelled.

3347 An answer to a scoffing and lying lybell. colop: *For T. B.*, 1681. brs. L, O, LN, LWL; MH.

3348 An answer to a scurrilous pamphlet. 1642. 4°.* O.

Answer to a scurrilous pamphlet, lately printed. 1693. *See* Temple, *Sir* William.

3349 An answer to a seditious libel, called, A declaration from the people of God. *Printed*, 1670. brs. L.

3350 An answer to a seditious pamphlet, intituled, Plain English. [*Oxford, by L. Lichfield*], *printed*, 1642[/3]. 4°.* MADAN 1231. O, C, OC, OM, HH; MH, Y.

3351 —[Anr. ed.] [*London*], *printed*, 1643. 4°.* L, O, C, HH, EN; CH, CN, MH, NU, WF, Y.

Answer to a small treatise. 1693. *See* Hog, John.

Answer to a speech. [1646.] *See* Birkenhead, *Sir* John.

Answer to a treatise. 1691. *See* Bisbie, Nathaniel.

Answer to a worthy gentleman. Bristol, 1644. *See* Maxwell, John, *bp*.

Answer to all the excuses. 1697. *See* Synge, Edward.

3352 An answer to all the material objections. [*London*, 1689.] cap., fol.* LUG; MH, WF.

3353 An answer to an impertinent pamphlet lately set forth by Iohn Spencer. *By G. B. and R. W. for W. L.*, 1641. 4°.* LT, LW, HH; NU, Y.

Answer to an infamous. 1648. *See* Clarendon, Edward Hyde, *earl of*.

Answer to another letter. 1680. *See* J., P.

3354 An answer to Blundell the Jesuits letter. [*London*], *for F. F.*, 1679. brs. L, O, HH; CH, MH, PU, WF.

Ansvver to certaine observations. 1643. *See* Warmstry, Thomas.

An answer to certain scandalous papers. [*London*, 1681]. *See* Salisbury, Robert Cecil, *earl of.*

Answer to certain seditious. 1651. *See* Waring, Thomas.

Answer to Col: Nathaniel Fiennes. 1643. *See* Walker, Clement.

3355 An answer to Cold and raw. [*London*], *for J. Deacon, J. Blare.* [1686?] brs. L.

3356 An answer to Dagons fall. [*n.p.*, 1680.] cap., fol.* L, O; CH, CN, MH, TU, Y.

Answer to Doctor Burgess his book, 1659. *See* Fox, George.

3357 An answer to Doctor Chamberlaines scandalovs and faslse [sic] papers. *Printed*, 1649. 3°.* LT.

Answer to Doctor Fernes. 1643. *See* Herle, Charles.

Answer to Doctor Piercie's. 1663. *See* Simons, Joseph.

Answer to Dr. Scot's. 1700. *See* Collins, Anthony.

Answer to Dr. Sherlock's case. 1691. *See* Browne, Thomas.

Answer to Dr. Sherlock's examination. 1696. *See* Wallis, John.

Answer to Dr. Sherlock's preservative. 1688. *See* Sabran, Lewis.

Answer to Dr. Sherlock's vindication. 1692. *See* Wagstaffe, Thomas.

Answer to Dr. Stillingfleet's book. [1682]. *See* Humfrey, John.

Answer to Dr. Stillingfleet's Irenicum. 1680. *See* Rule, Gilbert.

Answer to Dr. Stillingfleet's mischief. 1680. *See* Howe, John.

Answer to Dr. Stillingfleet's sermon. 1680. *See* Humfrey, John.

Answer to Dr. Wallis's three letters. 1691. *See* Nye, Stephen.

Answer to five questions. Oxford, 1666. *See* Whitby, Daniel.

Answer to Francis Buggs. 1695. *See* Vaughton, John.

3358 An answer to Harvest home. [*London*], *for P. Brooksby, J. Dencon,* [sic] *J. Blare, and J. Back*, [1688–95]. brs. L, HH, GU.

3359 An answer to His Maiesties speech by the gentry of . . . Yorke. *For Richard Lowndes*, 1642. brs. LT, LG.

Answer to J. Lyons. 1659. *See* S., S.

Answer to John Gilpin's book. 1655. *See* Benson, Gervase.

Answer to lame Giles Calfines. 1642. *See* H., M.

3360 An answer to Love's the cause. [*London?* 1670]. brs. L.

3361 An answer to Malice defeated. 1680. fol. O; CH.

3362 An answer to Mercurius Aulicus. colop: [*London*], *for W. W.*, [1643]. cap., 4°.* LT; PHS.

Answer to mis-led Doctor Fearne. 1642. *See* Herle, Charles.

3363 An answer to Moggy's misfortune. [*London*], *for P. Brooksby, J. Deacon, J. Blare, J. Back*, [1685–92]. brs. L, HH; WCL.

3364 An answer to Monsieur de Meaux's book. *For T. Dring*, 1687. 4°. CSS, HH; MIU, Y.

Answer to Monsieur de Rodon's. Douay, 1681. *See* N., N.

3365 An answer to Monsieur Talon's plea. *Printed and sold by Randal Taylor*, 1688. 4°.* L, O, LIL, OC, HH; MIU, TU, NU, WF, Y.

3366 An answer to Mr. Cary's reply. [*London*, 1700?] brs. L; Y.

3367 An answer to Mr. Collier's defence. colop: *For R. Baldwin*, 1696. 4°.* L, O, CT, MR; CH, CN, MHL, NU, Y.

3367A An answer to Mr. Denn's Quaker no papist. [*London?* 1659]. 4°. CSS.

Answer to Mr. Fitz-gerald's state of the case. 1695. *See,* Walcot, William.

Answer to Mr. Ford's booke. 1641. *See* Roberts, *Sir* Walter.

Answer to Mr. George Walker's. 1642. *See* Gataker, Thomas.

Answer to Mr. Henry Payne's letter. [1689.] *See* Burnet, Gilbert, *bp.*

3367B An answer to Mr. Hewitson's petition. [*Dublin*, 1695]. brs. DI; CH.

Answer to Mr. Humphrey's. 1661. *See* Reynolds, John.

Answer to Mr. J. G. 1653. *See* A., W.

Answer to Mr. John Dury. 1644. *See* Robinson, Henry.

3368 An ansvver to Mr. Langhorn's speech. [*London*, 1679.] cap., fol.* L, O, C, BR, HH; MHL, NU, PL, TU, WF.

3369 An answer to Mr Lenthall's pretended case. [c. 1700.] brs. LL.

Answer to Mr. Lowth's. 1687. *See* Grove, Robert.

Answer to Mr. Molyneux. 1698. *See* Atwood, William.

3370 An answer to Mr. [Jos.] Read's case. *For the author*, 1682. 4°.* T.C.I 497. L, O, CS; CH, MH, NU, PU, TSM.

Answer to Mr. Spencer's book. 1660. *See* Ferne, Henry, *bp.*

3370A An answer to Mr. Stephen's sermon. *For the use of the Calves-head club.* [1700.] 4°.* MB, NN, NU.

Answer to Mr. Whitby's. 1664. *See* Sergeant, John.

Answer to Mr. William Prynn's. [1644.] *See* Robinson, Henry.

3370B An answer to Nanny O. [*London*], *for P. Brooksby*, [1685–88.] brs. L, O, HH.

3371 An answer to old Dr. Wild's new poem. [*London*, c. 1672.] fol.* L, O, LL, HH; CH, CN, TU, WF.

Answer to part of Dr. Stillingfleet's. 1674. *See* Cressy, Hugh Paulin.

3372 An answer to Pereat Papa. [*London*, ?1681.] fol.* L, OC, HH; CH, WF, Y.

3373 An ansvver to Prince Rvperts declaration. [*London*], *printed*, 1643. *February* 16. 4°.* LT, HH, BC; CH, MH, MIU, TU, WF, Y.

Answer to Richard Allen's essay. 1697. *See* Claridge, Richard.

3374 An answer to Sefautians farewell. [*London*], *for J. Deacon*, [1685–88] brs. L, O, HH, GU.

Answer to several late treatises. 1673. *See* Stillingfleet, Edward.

3375 An answer to several letters written by Scottish gentlemen. [1677.] fol. EN.

Answer to severall material passages. 1691. *See* Hogg, John.

Answer to several new laws. 1678. *See* Fox, George.

3376 An answer to several objections against the mine-adventurers. colop: *By Freeman Collins*, 1698. cap., fol.* L; MH.

3377 An answer to severall obiections made against some things in Mr. Thomas Chaloners speech. *By Francis Leach*, 1646. 4°.* LT, DT; CLC, MH, WF, Y.

Answer to several passages. 1694. *See* S., D.

3378 An answer to several reasons humbly offered ... Irish cattel. *By J.B.*, 1677. 4°.* L, C, OC, MR, DT; CU, MH, NC, WF, Y.

3379 An answer to several remarks upon Dr. Henry More his expositions. *By Miles Flesher, for Walter Kettilby*, 1684. 4°. T.C.II 82. O, C, LW, P, BAMB; CN, CU, MBA, NU, PL.

3380 An answer to Sir P. Leicester's addenda. 1673/4. 8°. L.

3381 An answer to Sr. Timothy Touchstone. [*London*, 1679]. brs. L; CH, WF.

Answer to six arguments. 1698. *See* Elys, Edmund.

Answer to sixteen queries, 1650. *See* Fisher, Edward.

Answer to some considerations. Oxford, 1687. *See* Atterbury, Francis, *bp*.

3382 An answer to some mistakes. [*London*, 1697.] brs. L; MH.

3383 An answer to some objections against returning and raising the exportation duty on tin. [1696.] brs. LL.

3384 An answer to some of the linnen-drapers objections. [*London?* 1698.] brs. L; NC, Y.

Answer to some papers. 1682. *See* Stillingfleet, Edward.

3384A An answer to some passages in Rushworth's dialogues. *For James Adamson*, 1687. 4°. OCC.

Answer to some queries, concerning. 1700. *See* Gandy, Henry.

Answer to some queries, propos'd. Oxford, 1694. *See* Hall, John.

Answer to some queries put out. 1656. *See* Nayler, James.

Answer to that common objection. [1660.] *See* Penington, Isaac.

3384B An answer to that seditious and lewd piece of poetry. [*London?* 1665] cap., 4°.* L.

Answer to the address. 1688. *See* Williams, John, *bp*.

Answer to the amicable. 1686. *See* Sherlock, William.

Answer to the animadversions. 1682. *See* Burnet, Gilbert, *bp*.

Answer to the animadversions on. 1696. *See* Collier, Jeremy.

3385 The answer to the appeal, expounded. [*London*], *printed*, 1680. 4°.* L, O; MM, NU, PL, WF, Y.

Answer to the appeal from the country. 1679. *See* L'Estrange, *Sir* Roger.

Answer to the arguments. [1661.] *See* Fox, George.

Answer to the articles. 1642. *See* Calamy, Edmund.

3385A The answer to the Assembly of Divines. 1648. NHC.

3386 An answer to the Athenian mercury, vol. 4, numb. 14. *For the author*, 1691. 4°.* MH, NHC, NPT.

Answer to the author of humble thanks. 1672. *See* Z., Y.

3387 An answer to the author of the letter. [*London*, 1689.] cap., 4°. L, O, C, BP, EN; MIU, Y.

3387A An answer to the baffl'd knight. [*London*], *for C. Bates*, [c 1693]. brs. CM.

Answer to the Bishop of Condom. 1686. *See* Gilbert, John.

Answer to the Bishop of Condom's book. Dublin, 1676. *See* La Bastide, Marc Antoine de.

3387B An answer to the Bishop of Exeter's case. [*London?* 1690*]*. brs. LG.

Answer to the Bishop of Oxford's reasons. 1688. *See* Lloyd, William, *bp*.

3388 An answer to the Bishop of Rochester's first letter. *For W. Haight in Bloomsberry*, 1689. 4°. L, O, CT, MR, EN; CH, MH, NU, WF, Y.

3389 An answer to the Bishop of Rochester's second letter. *Sold by J. Weld*, 1689. 4°. T.C.II 277. L, E, EN; MHL, Y.

3390 —[Anr. ed.] *For A. Smith*, 1689. 4°. OC, CT; CH, MH, NU, WF, Y.

3391 An answer to the bonny Scot. [*London*], *for P. Brooksby*, [1685–88]. brs. L, O, HH; MH.

3392 An answer to the booke called Observations of the old and new militia. *For W. G. Sept. 6*, 1642. 4°.* LT, O, HH, DT; CH, MH, NU, WF, Y.

Answer to the book written. [1690.] *See* Wilkinson, William.

3393 The answer to the buxome virgin. [*London*], *for J. Deacon*, [1684–95]. brs. L, O, CM, HH; CH, MH.

3394 The answer to The call to humiliation. *For Abel Roper* 1690. 4°.* MIU.

3394A —[Anr. ed.] *Ludlow, for E. Robinson*, 1691. 4°.* CN, NN, NU, WF.

3394B An answer to the case of the exporters of fish from Scotland. [*London?* 1700.] brs. MH.

3395 An answer to the case of the old East-India Company. *By K. Astwood, for the author*, 1700. 4°.* L, O, LG; CH, CU, MH, NC, WF, Y.

3396 An answer to the champion of the wooden-sword. *For the author*, 1698. 4°.* NU.

3396A An answer to the character of a Popish successor. [*London*, 1681]. cap., fol.* NU, Y.

3397 An answer to the character of an exchange-wench. *For Thomas Croskill*, 1675. 4°.* L, OC; CN, MH, Y.

3398 An answer to the chief, or materiall heads & passages in the late declaration. *For Robert White, Ian. 4*. 1648. 4°.* LT, O, C, EN, DT; CH, CN, MH, NU, TU, WF, Y.

3399 An ansvver to the cities representation set forth. *By Robert Ibbitson*, 1649. 4°.* LT, O, C, LG, CT; CU, MH, NC, NU, Y.

3399A An ansvver to the city-conformists letter. *By Mary Thompson*, [1688?] 4°. L, OC, CT; CLC, MIU, WF.

3400 An answer to the city ministers letter from his country friend. colop: [*Oxford?*], *printed*, 1688. fol.* L, OM, CT, MR, EN; CH, CN, MH, NU, Y.

3401 An answer to the coal-traders and consumptioners case. [*London*, 168–?]. brs. CH.

3402 An answer to the commoners of the manor of Epworth. [*London*, 169–?] brs. L.

Answer to the compiler. 1688. *See* Gee, Edward.

3403 An answer to the cook-maids tragedy. [*London*], *for J. Deacon*, [1685–95.] brs. L.

Answer to the declaration of the House. 1648. *See* Digby, *Sir Kenelm*.

3404 An answer to the declaration of the imaginary Parliament. *Rotterdam, by John Pieterson*, 1652. 4°.* LT, CT, HH, E, EN; CH, CU, MH, WF.

3405 An answer to the declaration of the pretended assembly at Dundee. [*Leith*], *by E. Tyler*, 1653. 4°. ALDIS 1470. L, EN, GU; WF.

3405A —[Anr. ed.] 1679. 8°. A.

Answer to the desertion. [1689.] *See* Bohun, Edmund.

Answer to the discussion. 1689. *See* Collier, Jeremy.

Answer to the Dissenters objections. 1683. *See* Clagett, William.

Answer to the Dissenters pleas. Cambridge, 1700. *See* Bennet, Thomas.

3406 An answer to The dragon and grasshopper. *Printed*, 1698. 8°.* L, O, LP; CH.

3407 An answer to the Earl of Danby's paper. [*London*, 1680?] brs. L, C, HH; CH, CN, MH, TU, WF.

Answer to the eighth chapter. 1687. *See* Taylor, James.

3408 An answer to the eleven queries. [*London?*] 1697]. brs. C; WF, Y.

Answer to the excellent. [*London*, 1679.] *See* B., H.

3409 An answer to The forc'd marrige. [*London*], *for E. Oliver*, [1676–85]. brs. O, HH; MH.

3410 An answer to the French declaration. *For the author*, 1665/6. brs. L, O; CU.

3411 An answer to the Geneva ballad. [*London*], *printed*, 1674. brs. L, HH; MH.

Answer to the gentleman's letter. 1680. *See* Womock, Laurence, *bp*.

Answer to the grounds. 1671. *See* Eachard, Laurence.

3412 An answer to the Hertford letter. colop: *For the author*, 1699. brs. L, HH.

3413 An answer to the late declaration of Scotland. *Printed at York by Stephen Bulkley*, 1643. 4°.* YM; Y.

Answer to the late exceptions. 1690. *See* Burnet, Thomas.

Answer to the late King James's declaration. 1689. *See* Wellwood, James.

Answer to the late K. James's last declaration. 1693. *See* Defoe, Daniel.

Answer to the late Lord Bishop. [c. 1700.] *See* Bury, Arthur.

3414 An answer to the late memorial. colop: [*London*], *for Thomas Malthus*, [1684]. brs. L, O.

3415 An answer to the letter directed. *Printed*, 1671. 8°.* EN; NN, WF, Y.

3416 An answer to the letter from Amsterdam. [*London*], 1678. 4°.* L, MR, HH; IU, MH.

Answer to the letter from Leghorn answered. 1681. *See* B., J.

Answer to the letter of the Roman. 1688. *See* Tenison, Thomas, *abp*.

3416A An answer to the Letter to a dissenter. *By Henry Hills*, 1687. 4°. CT, SP; CN, IU, MIU, WF, Y.

3416B —[Anr. ed.] 1689. 4°. MR.

3417 The answer to the letter written to a member of Parliament, upon the occasion of some votes. *Printed*, 1695. 4°. C; CH, MB, MIU, WF, Y.

3417A The answer to The London cuckold. [*London*], *for J. Deacon*, [1686–7]. brs. CM.

3418 The answer to The London lasses folly. [*London*], *for C. Dennisson*, [1685]. brs. L, O, CM, HH; MH.

3419 An answer to the London petition. [*London*, 1642.] cap., 4°.* LT, HH; CH, CU, MH, NU, WF, Y.

3420 An answer to the Lord Digbies speech in the . . . Commons. [*London*], *printed*, 1641. 4°.* LT, LG, WCA, EN; CH, CN, MH, NU, WF, Y.

3421 An answer to the Lord George Digbies apology. *For A. R.*, 1642. 4°. LT, O, OC, CT, MR; CH, MH, NU, WF, Y.

3422 An answer to The maidens frollick. [*London*], *for P. Brooksby, J. Deacon, J. Blare, J. Back*, [1688–92]. brs. L, CM, HH, GU; MH.

3423 An answer to The maiden's tragedy. [*London*], *for P. Brooksby, J. Deacon, J. Blare, and J. Back*, [1685–92]. brs. L, CM, HH, GU; MH.

3424 An answer to the Mantuan. colop: *Printed*, 1679. brs. L, O, HH; CN, MH, TU, Y.

3425 An answer to the merchants letter. [*London*, 1680.] brs. L, O, C, MR; CH, MH, MIU, WF, Y.

Answer to the most envious. 1641. *See* Herbert, Thomas.

3426 An answer to the most material objections. [*London*, 1699?] cap., fol.* L; MH, MIU, NC, Y.

Answer to the most materiall parts. 1654. *See* P., B.

3427 An answer to the nevv motions. *For Robert Bostock*, 1641. 4°.* LT, O, C, HH, EN; CH, CU, MH, NU, WF, Y.

Answer to the objection. [1700?] *See* Kirkwood, James.

3428 An answer to the objections against the Earl of Danby. [*London*, 1680.] cap., fol.* O, EC, HH; CH, CN, MH, WF, Y.

Answer to the order. [1682.] *See* Whitaker, Edward.

3429 An answer to the pamphlet called, The loyal feast. colop: *For J. Tacker*, 1682. brs. O, CT, HH, MC; CH, MH, WF.

Answer to the paper. 1690. *See* Fowler, Edward, *bp*.

3430 An answer to the petition sent from the Vniversitie of Oxford. *Printed*, 1641. 4°.* MADAN 985. LT, O, CT, HH; CH, CN, MH, WF, Y.

Answer to the poysonous. 1647. *See* Parker, Henry.

3431 Answer to the poor whore's complaint. [1685–92.] brs. CM.

3432 An answer to the Popes letter. [*London?* 1680.] cap., fol.* L, O, SP; CH, MBA, MH, NC, WF.

Answer to the postscript. [*London,* 1698?] *See* Bateman, Thomas.

3432A An answer to the preceding letter. *Printed,* 1645. 4°.* CLC.

3432B An answer to the pretended case. [*London?* 1670.] brs. L.

3433 An answer to the pretended letter, to a friend in the country; touching the present fears. [*London,* 1680]. brs. O, EN; MH.

3434 An answer to the pretended reasons of some drapers. *Printed,* 1675. brs. MR; MH, NC.

3435 An answer to the pretended refutation. *Edinburgh, by J. W. (for T. Carruthers),* 1699. 8°. ALDIS 3823. L, EN; WF, WSG.

3436 An answer to the pretended speech. *Printed,* 1694. 4°.* L, O, C, MR, EN; HR, CH, CN, NU, WF, Y.

3437 An answer to the protestation of the nineteen Lords. colop: *For Cave Pulleyn,* 1681. cap., fol.* L, O, MR, HH, EN; CH, LC, MH, WF, Y.

3438 —[Anr. ed.] *Edinburgh, by the heir of A. Anderson,* 1681. fol.* ALDIS 2248. MH.

Answer to the Provinciall letters. Paris, 1659. *See* Nouat, Jacques.

Answer to the query. [1687?] *See* C., J.

3439 An answer to the question why may not the English assist the Svvede. *Printed,* 1658. 4°.* O, OC.

The answer to the rattle-heads. *See* Taylor, John.

3439A An answer to the reasons against Leister's bill. [*London?* 1695.] brs. NN.

3439B An answer to the reasons against the wearing of . . . silke. [*London?* 1700]. cap., fol.* L; MH.

3439C An answer to the reasons for continuing the palace court. [*London?* 1700]. brs. L.

3440 An answer to the rector's libel. *Dublin, by Richard Wilde,* 1694. 4°.* DIX 263. O, C, CD, A.

3441 An answer to the reflections on the five Jesuits speeches. [*London,* ?1679.] cap., fol.* L, HH; CH.

Answer to the representer's. 1688. *See* Clagett, Nicholas.

Answer to the request. 1687. *See* Sherlock, William.

Answer to the satyr. [*London,* 1675?] *See* Pocock, Richard.

3442 An answer to the satyr upon the French King. *For E. Whitlock,* 1697. brs. O; MH.

3442A —[Anr. ed.] *John Harris,* 1697. brs. CN.

Answer to the Scotch Presbyterian. 1693. *See* Ridpath, George.

3443 An answer to the Scots declaration. Or, a survey. *Imprinted at London, by T.B.,* 1648. 4°.* LT, O, HH, E, EN; MH, MIU, NU, TU, WF.

Answer to the Scots Presbyterian. 1694. *See* Ridpath, George.

3444 An answer to the second letter from Legorn. [*London,* 1680.] cap., fol.* L, C, BR, HH; CH, CLC, PU, WF, Y.

Answer to the seditious. 1670. *See* Starling, *Sir* Samuel.

3445 An answer to the severall petitions of late exhibited. *For J. M. and J. A.,* 1652. 4°.* LT, LL; CN, MH, MIU, NC.

3446 —Second edition. *For J. M. and J. A.,* 1652. 4°.* L, C, HH; CH, CLC, MH, WF, Y.

3446A —[Anr. ed.] *For I. M.,* 1652. 4°.* LT; CLC, CN, MH, MIU, Y.

3447 An answer to The shepherd's happiness. [*London*], *for P. Brooksby, J. Deacon, J. Blare, and J. Back,* [1685–92]. brs. HH.

3448 An answer to the solemne league & covenant, presented. *For George Horton,* 1660. 4°.* LT, CT, SC.

3448A An answer to the speech of declaration of the Grand Turk. 1688. 4°. O.

3449 An answer to the sugar-bakers or sugar-refiners paper. colop: *Printed, to be sold by E. Whitlock,* 1695. cap., fol.* L, MC.

3450 An answer to The unconstant shepherd. [*London*], *for Charles Bates,* [1690–1702]. brs. L, CM, HH.

3451 An ansvver to the [sic] The unfortunate lady. [*London*], *for P. Brooksby, J. Deacon, J. Blare, and J. Back.* [1684?] brs. L, CM, HH.

Answer to the vindication of Dr. Hamond. 1650. *See* Ascham, Antony.

Answer to the vindication of the letter concerning. Oxford, 1690. *See* Wellwood, James.

Answer to the vindication of the letter from. 1690. *See* Jenkin, Robert.

3452 An answer to the weavers case. [c. 1699.] brs. L, LL.

3453 An answer to the Whiggish poem. colop: *For Allen Banks,* 1682. brs. L, O, EN; CH, MH, PU, WF, Y.

3454 An ansvver to this quodlibetical question. *For A. Seile,* 1661. 4°.* O, CT, SP; CH, MH, NU, TU, WF, Y.

Answer to Thomas Tillam's book. 1659. *See* Fox, George.

Answer to those questions. 1646. *See* Bakewell, Thomas.

Answer to three late pamphlets. 1687. *See* Sherlock, William.

Answer to three papers of Mr. Hobs. 1671. *See* Wallis, John.

Answer to three treatises. 1678. *See* Walsh, Peter.

3455 An answer to Timothy Touchstone. [*London,* 1679]. brs. L.

Answer to Tom-tell-troth. 1642. *See* Baltimore, George Calvert, *baron.*

Answer to twenty-eight queries. 1655. *See* Nayler, James.

3456 An answer to two Danish papers. *Daniel Pakeman,* 1658, CLC.

3457 An answer to two letters, concerning the East-India company. [*London*], *printed,* 1676. 4°.* L, LG, LUG; CU, MH, NC, WF, Y.

3457A An answer to two letters of T.B. *For H. Brome,* 1673. 8°. O, C, DC, CT; CH, CU, Y.

3457B An answer to two objections against a bill . . . for restraining East-India . . . silk. [*London?* 1695.] brs. NC, Y.

3458 An answer to two papers, called, A lords speech with-out-doors. *Printed*, 1689. 4°.* L, O, C, EN, DT; CH, MH, NU, TU, WF, Y.

3459 An answer to Unconstant William. [*London*], *for C Bates*, [c. 1680]. brs. L, O, CM, HH; MH.

Answer to Vox cleri. 1690. *See* Payne, William.

3459A An answer to W. P[enn] his key. *For R. Wilkin*, 1695. 8°. T.C. II 546. OC, CT; PHS.

3460 An answer to Wild. [166-]. brs. L, O; MH.

3461 An ansvver unto Mr. William Dell . . . his epistle. [*London*, 1646]. cap., 4°.* MH, NHC.

Answer unto thirty-two queries. 1656. *See* Rosewell, Thomas.

3462 An answerable remonstrance. *For J. Horton, May 31*, 1642. 4°. L, O; MIU, MM.

3462A The answers and case of Francis Wyvil. [*London?* 1690]. brs. L.

Answers commanded by His Majesty. *See* Charles II.

3463 Answers for Alexander Duff. [1689.] cap., fol.* L, EN.

3463A Answers for James Anderson and Agnes Campbell. [*London?* 1688.] brs. L.

3463B Answers for John Walkingshaw. [*Glasgow?* 1698.] cap., fol.* L.

3464 Answers for Mr William Vetch. colop: [*London*], *printed at the society of stationers printing-house*, 1690. cap., fol.* O.

3465 Answers for Sir John Hall. [169-.] cap., fol.* L, EN.

3465A Answers for the countess of Weymss [*sic*]. *Edinburgh*, 1693. fol.* O.

3466 Answers for the Duke of Gordon. [*Edinburgh*, 1689.] cap., fol.* O.

3467 Answers for the Earl of Lauderdale. *Edinburgh, by the heir of Andrew Anderson*, 1690. 4°. ALDIS 3022. EN.

3468 Answers for the Laird of Grant. [1689.] cap., fol.* L.

3468A Answers for the Presbytry of Dumfries. [1698.] brs. RPJ.

3468B Answers to several objections. [*London?* 1693]. brs. L.

3468C Answers to several reasons alledged. [*London?* 1692]. brs. L.

3469 Answers to the objections against a general insurance. [*London?* 1690.] brs. L.

3470 Answers to the objections against the college-bill. [169-.] brs. L, O.

3471 Answers to the reasons against passing the Earl of Clevelands bill. [*London*, 1664.] brs. L; MH.

3471A Answers to the reasons for reviving . . . the act for regulating printing. [*London?* 1693]. brs. MH.

3471B Answers to the reasons given against the bill for erecting courts of conscience. [*London?* 1675] brs. L.

Antapology. 1693. *See* Wetenhall, Edward.

Antelope's evidence. 1698. *See* Hale, Charles.

3472 An antheme sung at the consecration of the Archbishops of Ireland. [*Dublin*, 1661.] DIX 108. brs. LT.

3473 Anthems to be sung. [*Dublin*], *printed*, 1662. fol.* DIX 117. DT.

Antheologia, or . . . 1655. *See* Fuller, Thomas.

3474 Ανθολογια δευτερα. *Ex officina J. Redmayne*, 1667. 8°. L, OC.

3475 —[Anr. ed.] —, 1673. 8°. C, LW, DT; Y.

3475A —[Anr. ed.] *Ex officina Eliz. Redmayne*, 1684. 8°. O, DC; PL.

3475B —[Anr. ed.] —, 1696. 8°. CT.

3476 Ανθολογια seu selecta quædam poemata Italorum. *Impensis R. Green, & F. Hicks, Cantab.*, 1684. 12°. L, O, C, DC, EN; BN, CLC, NC, PL, TU, HC.

Ανθολογια. The life. 1651. *See* Garret, William.

3476A [**Anthonisz, Cornelis.**] The safeguard of sailors. *By W.G. for William Fisher and Benjamin Hurlock*, 1671. 4°. T.C.I 75. L; CN, Y.

Anthony, *King of Poland, pseud.*

3477 **Anthony, Charles.** Gods presence mans comfort. *By J. Y. for George Lathum*, 1646. 4°. LT, O, CT, YM, DT; NPT, NU, Y.

3478 [**Anthony, Edward.**] Practicall law, controlling. *Printed at Exeter*, 1648. 4°.* LT; MH.

3479 **Anthony, John.** The comfort of the soul. *For G. Dawson, to be sold by John Mountague*, 1654. 4°. LT, LSC, LW, CPE; CLC, NPT, NU, WF.

3480 [—] Lvcas redivivvs or the gospell-physitian. *For Henry Eversden*, 1655. 4°. L, LCL, AN, YM; NAM, NU, WF, Y.

3481 **Anthony, M.** Animæ humanæ non præexistunt. Jul. 4. 1681. [*Oxford?* 1681.] brs. MH.

3482 Anthony, and Mary Warde. *By G. Croom, on the ice, Febrewary* [*sic*] *1*. 1684. brs. OP. (Calling card.)

Ανθρωποκτονου ταφος, or . . . 1659. *See* B., J.

Ανθροπωλογια or . . . 1680. *See* Haworth, Samuel.

3483 Anthropologie abstracted: or the idea of humane nature reflected. *For Henry Herringman*, 1655. 8°. LT, C, CT, GH, GK; CLC, MU, WSG, Y.

Anthropometamorphosis. 1650. *See* Bulwer, John.

Anthroposophia. 1650. *See* Vaughan, Thomas.

Anti-Baal-Berith. 1661. *See* Gauden, John.

Anti-Boreale. [1662?] *See* Womock, Laurence.

3483A An anti-brekekekex-coax-coax. *Printed*, 1660. fol.* LW, OC; Y.

Antibrownistus Puritanomastix, *pseud.*

3484 Antichrist unhooded. *Printed*, 1664. 4°.* O.

Antichristi excidium. 1664. *See* Lee, Samuel.

3485 The Antichristian principle fully discovered. *Printed*, 1679. 4°.* L, O, CT, EN; CH, MH, NU, WF, Y.

Anti-Christian treachery. [c. 1686.] *See* Pearson, John.

Antichrists man of vvar. 1655. *See* Farnworth, Richard.

Antichrist's strongest hold. 1665. *See* Wigan, John.

3486 The Anti-confederacie, or, an extract of certain quæres. *Oxford, printed*, 1644. 4°.* MADAN 1592. LT, O, CT, EN, DT; CH, NU, WF.

3487 The anti-confederacy, or, a discovery. [*Oxford, by H. Hall*], *printed* 1644. 4°. MADAN 1694. O, LL, OC, CT, YM; CH, CU, NU, WF, Y.

Anti-Cotton. 1689. *See* Du Coignet, Pierre.

3488 Anti-Cotton answered. *For John Wright*, 1653. 4°.* L, C, OC; MH, Y.

3489 The anti-covenant, or a sad complaint. *Oxford, by Leonard Lychfield*, 1643. 4°. MADAN 1409. LT, O, C, DT; CH, CLC, MH, NU, Y.

3490 —[Anr. ed.] [*Oxford, by H. Hall*], printed, 1643. 4°.
MADAN 1410. L, O, LG, CT, HH; MH, WF, Y.

3490A The anti-curse. [*London?* 1690] brs. EN.

Antidote against a careless. 1694. *See* Pictet, Bénédict.

3491 An antidote against an infectious aire. [*London*], printed,
1647 [/8]. 4°.* LT, O, CT, MR, DT; CH, CU, MH, NU,
WF, Y.

Antidote against Antinomianisme. [1643]. *See* H., D.

Antidote against Arminianisme. 1641. *See* B., R.

3491A An antidote against bigotry. 1694. 4°. LCL; MM.

3492 An antidote against Dr. E. Stillingfleet's Unreasonableness. *For Richard Janeway*, 1681. 4°. CS; CH, NU, Y.

3493 An antidote against foure dangerous quæries. colop:
For Nathaniell Webb, 1645. 4°.* LT, O, C, LL, DT; CH,
CN, MH, NU, WF, Y.

Antidote against lay-preaching. 1642. *See* Bewick, John.

Antidote against melancholy. 1661. *See* D., N.

Antidote against Mr. Baxters.... 1670. *See* Bagshaw,
Edward.

Antidote against poison. [1683.] *See* Shower, Bartholomew.

3493A An antidote against pretended caution. *R. Baldwin*, 1690.
brs. L.

3494 An antidote against Romes infection. *For Robert Wood*,
1641. 4°.* LT, LG, HH, E; CH, NU, Y.

3494A An antidote against some principal errors. *For Richard
Cumberland*, 1696. 8°.* T.C.II 576. LW; NC.

Antidote against that poysonous.... 1676. *See* Haworth,
William.

Antidote against the common plague. 1657. *See* Gorton,
Samuel.

Antidote against the contagious air. 1644. *See* P., D. P.

Antidote against the errour. 1647. *See* Monson, *Sir*
John.

Antidote against the infection. [1696.] *See* D., M.

3495 An antidote against the infection of the times. *For T.
Brewster*, 1656. 4°. LT.

Antidote against the poyson. 1653. *See* Martindale,
Adam.

3496 An antidote against the present fears. *By R.E.*, 1679.
4°.* L, O, CT, MR, EN; CH, CN, NU, WF, Y.

Antidote against the throw-in opinion. 1647. *See* Skippon, Philip.

Antidote against the venome. 1697. *See* Whitehead,
George.

Antidote animadverted. [*London*, 1645.] *See* Prynne,
William.

3497 An antidote of rare physick. [*London*], *for J. Deacon*,
[1680?]. brs. L, O, CM; MH.

3498 The antidote proved a counterfeit. 1693. 4°. O, C.

Antidote to cure. 1664. *See* Womock, Laurence.

Antidote to prevent. 1693. *See* Shute, Giles.

3499 Antidotes against some infectious passages. *For Thomas
Underhill*, 1642. 4°.* LT, OCC, CE, EC, HH; MH, WF, Y.

Antidotum Britannicum: or, ... 1681. *See* W., W.

3500 Antidotum Culmerianum: or, animadversions. *Oxford,
by H. Hall*, 1644. 4°.* MADAN 1770. LT, O, CM, LG;
CH, CLC, NPT.

Antient. *See* Ancient.

Anti-fimbia, or an answer. 1679. *See* Warner, John.

Antigamus; or.... [1691.] *See* Sawyer, Thomas.

Anti-Goliath; or.... 1678. *See* Worsley, Edward.

Anti-Haman or.... 1679. *See* Warner, John.

3500A Αντικαιρος. Or, an answer. *Printed*, 1679. fol.* CH.

3501 The anti-leveller's antidote. colop: *By John Macock, to
be sold by Francis Tyton, and Nathaniel Brook*, 1652.
cap., 4°.* LT, LL, EC, HH; MB, NC, NU, WF.

Anti-Machiavelli. 1647. *See* Nedham, Marchamont.

3502 Αντιμοιχεια: or, the honest. [*London*, 1691]. brs. LG.

Antinomians and Familists. 1644. *See* Winthrop, John.

Antinomians Christ. 1644. *See* Bakewell, Thomas.

Anti-Paræus. York. 1642. *See* Owen, David.

3503 Antipharmacum saluberrimum; or, a serious & seasonable caveat. [*London*], printed, 1664. 4°.* LT, O, EC; WF.

Antipodes. Oxford, 1647. *See* H., I.

Αντιπροβαλη, or.... 1660. *See* Maudit, John.

3504 The anti-projector. [1646?] cap., 4°.* L, O.

3505 The anti-Protestant; or Miles against Prance. [*London*,
1682.] brs. L, O; CH, MBA, Y.

Antiquæ historiæ synopsis. Oxoniæ, 1660. *See* Robinson, Hugh.

3506 The anti-Quaker. *For R. Royston*, 1676. 4°.* T.C.I 220.
L, O, C, LF, EN; CH, MH, PH, PSC, Y.

3507 Anti-Quakerism; or, a character of the Quakers spirit.
For the author, 1659. brs. LT, O.

Antiquitates ecclesiæ orientalis. 1682. *See* Simon,
Richard.

Antiquities of Palmyra. 1696. *See* Seller, Abednego.

Antiquity & excellency. 1652. *See* Grant, W.

Antiquity and honours. [1690?] *See* D., P.

Antiquity and justice. 1694. *See* Atwood, William.

Antiquity of common-wealths. 1652. *See* Grotius,
Hugo.

3508 The antiquity of Englands superiority over Scotland.
By R. Ibbitson, 1652. 4°.* LT, CT.

3509 The antiquity of reformation. *By B. Alsop, and R. Harper*, 1647. 4°.* LT, DT; NU.

Antiquity of the Protestant. 1687. *See* Pelling, Edward.

3510 Antiquity reviv'd. *Printed*, 1693. 8°. L, O, CS; NN, WF, Y.

3511 An anti-remonstrance. [*London*], printed, 1641. 4°.* O,
DT; CLC, MH, NU, WF, Y.

3512 —Second edition. [*London*], printed, 1641. 4°.* L, O, HH;
CH, CSS, MH, NIC, WF.

Anti-romance. 1654. *See* Sorel, Charles.

3513 Anti scorbuticæ. Pills against that epidemic disease.
[1670?] brs. O.

Anti-sozzo. 1675. *See* Alsop, Vincent.

Antithelemite. 1685. *See* Maurice, Henry.

3514 Antitheta: or, political reasonings. *For Thomas Underhill*, 1657. 4°.* OC; CH, CU, MH, NN.

3515 Anti-toleration, or a modest defence. *By John Field for Ralph Smith,* 1646. 4°.* LT, O, CT, E, DT; CH, LC, MH, NU.

3516 The anti-weesils. A poem. *Printed, and are to be sold by Randal Taylor,* 1691. 4°.* L, O, C, OM, AU; CH, CN, LC, MH, TU, Y.

3517 [Antoine,   .] A vindication of the Roman Catholicks. *For John and Thomas Lane,* 688. 4°. L, SP; MH, NU, WF.

      Antoninus, Marcus Aurelius. *See* Aurelius Antoninus, Marcus.

3517A **Antonio, *de San Bernadino*.** Vita Minoritica. 1658. 8°. L, CT.

3518 **Antony, *prior of Crato*.** The royal penitent. *By R. D. for Iohn Dakins,* 1659. 12°. L, O.

3518A — —[Anr. ed.] *For M. Turner,* 1685. 12°. T.C.II 124. DT.

3519 —Royall psalmes. *For Humphrey Moseley,* 1659. 8°. LT, O.

3520 **Antrim, Randal Macdonnell, *marquis of*.** A continuation of the diurnall passages in Ireland. 1641. 4°. C, LLL.

3521 —A copie of a letter from the Lord Intrim. *For W. T.,* 1642. 4°.* LT, O, LFEA.

3521A — —[Anr. ed.] *For T. Powel,* 1642. 4°.* EC.

3522 **A[ntrobus], B[enjamin].** Buds and blossoms of piety. Second edition. *By H. Clark, for Thomas Northcott,* 1691. 8°. L, LF, BBN, EN; CLC, NC, PSC, WF.

3523 [–] Some buds and blossoms of piety. *Printed and sold by Andrew Sowle,* 1684. 8°. LF; LC, PH.

3524 **Antrobus, Richard.** Brevia selecta; or, choice writs. *By I. Streater, for Hen. Twyford,* 1663. 8°. O, LIL, DT; MHL, PUL, WF.

3525 Entry cancelled.

3526 **Apáfi, Michael, *prince of Transylvania*.** The declaration of the Hungarian war. *For Francis Smith,* 1682. fol.* L, O, MR, E, EN; CH, CN, MH, WF, Y.

3526A — —[Anr. ed.] colop: *By J. Grantham,* 1682. cap., 4°.* PL.

3527 The ape-gentle-vvoman, or the character of an ex-change-wench. *For Francis Pye,* 1675. 4°.* L, O, LG; CN, MH, Y.

3528 Aphorismi Vrbigerani, or certain rules. *For Henry Faithorne,* 1690. 4°. L, OC, CT, GU; CLC, MH, WF, Y.

      Aphorismes of the kingdome. [1642.] *See* Prynne, William.

      Aphorisms relating . . . 1689. *See* Coxe, *Sir* Richard.

3529 **Aphthonius.** Progymnasmata. *Excudebant T. P. & E. M. pro societate stationariorum,* 1650. 8°. L, DC; CU.

3530 —[Anr. ed.] — *Typis Du Gardianis,* 1655. 8°. MH.

3530A —[Anr. ed.] *Excudat. J. C. pro societate stationarum,* 1671. 8°. T.C.II 106. CM.

3531 —[Anr. ed.] — 1685. 8°. LL.

      Apiarium; or. . . . 1676. *See* Worlidge, John.

      Apobaterion vel. . . . 1655. *See* Fisher, Fitzpayne.

      Apocalypse unveyl'd. 1676. *See* Hayter, Richard.

      Apocalypsis Jesu. 1644. *See* Douglas, *Lady* Eleanor.

      Apocalyptical mysteries. 1667. *See* Knollys, Hanserd.

      Αποδειξις. 1643. *See* Barton, Thomas.

      Αποδοκιματιας. 1683. *See* Norris, John.

      Apollo mathematicus: or. 1695. *See* Eizat, *Sir* Edward.

3532 **Apollodorus.** . . . Γραμματικου. *Typis E. Redmayne,* 1686. 4°. T.C.II 168. L; CLC, MB, NC, WF, Y.

3533 **Apollonius.** Ars notoria: the notory art of Solomon. *By J. Cottrel, to be sold by Martha Harison,* 1657. 8°. LT, O, E; PU, WF, Y.

3534 **Apollonius, Pergæus.** Conica: methodo nova. *Excudebat Guil. Godbid, vaeneunt apud Robertum Scott,* 1675. 4°. L, C, OM, AU, DT; BN, MB, NC, NP, WF, Y.

3535 **Apollonius, Guilielmus.** Consideratio qvarvndam. *Typis G. M. sumptibus Georgij Tomason,* 1644. 8°. LT, O, C, AU, DT; MB, NU, Y.

3536 —A consideration of certaine controversies. *By G. M. for Tho. Vnderhill,* 1645. 8°. LT, C, LCL, LW; MH, NGT, NU, WF, Y.

      Apollo's banquet. 1691. *See* Playford, John.

3537 An apoligetick for the sequestred clergie. *Printed at New-Munster [London],* 1649. 4°.* LT, O, C, EN, DT; CH, CLC, MH, NN, WF, Y.

      Apologeticall account. 1647. *See* Smith, Robert.

3538 Apologeticall animadversions of certaine abuses. *Printed,* 1641. 4°.* LT, EN; CH, MH, NU, WF, Y.

3539 An apologeticall declaration of the conscientious Presbyterians . . . Ezek. 17. 15. 18.9. *Prented [sic],* 1649. 4°.* LT, O, HH, E, EN; CH, MH, NPT, NU.

3539A —[variant, Ezek. 17. 15. 18. 19] —, 1649. 4°. CSS, D; CN, MH, Y.

      Apologeticall relation. 1665. *See* Brown, John.

      Apologetical vindication. 1687. *See* Hickes, George.

      Apologia pro ministris. Eleutheropoli, 1664. *See* Hickman, Henry.

3540 Apologie pour les Protestans . . . An apology. 1681. 4° E.

      Apologist condemned. 1653. *See* Goodwin, John.

      Apology against a pamphlet. 1642. *See* Milton, John.

3540A An apology and advice from some of the clergy. *For A. E.,* 1674. 4°.* L; MIU, NU.

3541 An apolgie and vindication (from all false and malignant aspersions) for . . . Earle of Essex. *By Thomas Harper,* 1644. 4°. LT, O, CT, HH, SS; CN, WF, Y.

3542 Apologie and vindication of the major part of the members. *By Tho. Ratcliffe,* 1659. 4°.* LT, O, CCA, HH; CH, CU, MH, NU, WF, Y.

      Apology for a younger brother. Oxford, 1641. *See* Ap-Robert, John.

      Apology for, and an invitation. 1697. *See* Stephens, Edward.

      Apology for, and vindication. 1677. *See* Jamieson, Alexander.

      Apology for authorized. 1649. *See* Taylor, Jeremy.

3543 An apology for bishops or a plea. [*London*], *printed,* 1641. 4°.* LT, O, LG; MH, NU.

      Apology for congregational. 1698. *See* Young, Samuel.

      Apology for distressed innocence. 1663. *See* Hickersgill, Edmund.

3543A An apology for God's worship. *For the author*, 1683. 8°. LCL, LSC; MM, PPT.

Apology for His Majestie. 1642. *See* L., J.

3544 An apology for lovers ... by Erastophil. 1651. 12°. CH.

Apology for M. Antonia Bourignon. 1699. *See* Garden, George.

3545 An apologie for Mr. Iohn Goodwin. *For John Wright*, 1653. 4°.* LT, LW, P; NU.

Apology for Mr. R. Stafford. 1690. *See* Stephens, Edward.

Apologie for, or vindication. 1677. *See* Smith, Hugh.

Apologie for Paris. 1649. *See* Baron, Robert.

3546 An apologie for presbyterie. [*Edinburgh?*] printed, 1689. 4°.* ALDIS 2859. L, EN, AU, GU; MH, NC, NU, WF, Y.

Apology for private preaching. [1642.] *See* Taylor, John.

3547 An apology for purchases of lands late of bishops. [*London*, 1660.] cap., fol.* LT, O, OM; CH.

Apology for the ancient right. 1660. *See* Stephens, Jeremy.

Apology for the army, touching. 1647. *See* Jenkins, David.

Apology for the builder. 1685. *See* Barbon, Nicholas.

Apologie for the Church of England. 1685. *See* Bohun, Edmund.

Apologie for the Church of England, with. [1688.] *See* Burnet, Gilbert, *bp.*

Apology for the clergy. 1693. *See* Munro, Alexander.

Apology for the contemplations. 1687. *See* Cross, John, *alias* More.

Apology for the discourse. 1680. *See* Warren, Albertus.

Apology for the East-India Company. 1690. *See* Atwood, William.

3548 An apology for the English nation. [*London*, 1695?] cap., fol.* C; MH.

3549 An apology for the English Presbyterians. *Printed*, 1699. 8°. L, O, P; CH, IU, NPT.

3550 Apology for the failures. [*London*], printed, 1689. 4°.* L, C, LVF, HH, ES; CH, CN, MH, NU, WF, Y.

Apology for the ministers. 1694. *See* Lorimer, William.

Apology for the new separation. 1691. *See* Hickes. George.

3551 An apology for the organs. colop: *By B. Griffin*, 1692. brs. L; INU, MH.

3552 An apology for the Parliament, humbly representing to Mr. John Gailhard. *Printed*, 1697. 4°.* L, O, LW, OC, EC; CH, CLC, LC, Y.

Apology for the people. 1699. *See* Field, John.

3553 Apology for the perfections which should be in the professors. [*London*, 1697?] brs. L.

3554 An apology for the Protestants: being a full justification. L, O, C, LW, EN; CH, CN, MH, NP, WF, Y.

3555 An apology for the Protestants of France. *For S. Holt and E. Saunders*, 1683. 4°. T.C.II 18. L, O, C, EN, DT.

3555A —[Anr. ed.] *For John Holford*. 1683. 4°. L, O, CT, LW, SP; CLC, CN, MH, WF, Y.

3556 An apology for the Protestants of Ireland. *For Ric. Chiswell*, 1689. 4°.* T.C.II 277. L, O, C, EN, DT; CH, MH, NC, NU, Y.

Apology for the pulpits. 1688. *See* Williams, John, *bp.*

Apologie for the reformed churches. 1653. *See* Daillé, Jean.

Apology for the royal party. 1659. *See* Evelyn, John.

Apology for the service of love. 1656. *See* Niclas, Henry.

3557 An apologie for the six book-sellers. *By S. G. for Matthew Keinton*, 1655. 4°.* LT; CH, NU, WF.

Apology of Socrates Christianus. 1700. *See*, Stephens, Edward.

3557A An apology of some called Anabaptists. 1660. O.

Apology of the Church of England. 1685. *See* Whear, Degory.

Apology of the chvrches. 1643. *See* Mather, Richard.

3558 The apologie of the common souldiers of his excellencie Sir Tho. Fairfaxes army. *Printed, May 3*, 1647. 4°.* LT, O, OC, CT, HH; CH, CN, MH, WF, Y.

3559 An apollogie of the souldiers to all their commission officers. [1647.] cap., 4°.* LT.

Apology: or, the genuine memoires. 1679. *See* Bremond, Gabriel de.

3560 An apology vindicating the cavaleers. *Printed*, 1643. 4°.* LT, LVF, A.

3560A Apophthegmata aurea. *By William Du-gard for Francis Eglesfield*, 1649. 8°. LT, EN; CH, WF.

3560B The apophthegmes of the ancients. *For William Cademan*, 1683. 8°. T.C.II 19. L, LL, SP; Y.

3561 Apostacy punish'd, or, a new poem. colop: *by T. H. for the author*, 1682. brs. L, O; CH, PU.

Ἡ ἀποστασια. 1653. *See* Hall, Edmund.

Apostate conscience. 1699. *See* Docwra, Anne.

Apostate Protestant. 1682. *See* Pelling, Edward.

Apostles Paul and James reconciled. [*London*, 1670]. *See* Gataker, Charles.

3561A The apostolick decree of blood. [*London*], *printed*, 1673. 8°. NPT.

Apostolique institution. 1649. *See* Hall, Joseph.

Apostolical and true opinion. 1653. *See* Biddle, John.

Apostolicall institution. Oxford, 1644. *See* Chillingworth, William.

3562 An apostrophe from the loyal party. colop: *Printed*, 1681. fol.* L, O, C, LL; CH, CN, MH, WF, Y.

3563 —[Anr. ed.] colop: *Edinburgh re-printed by the heir of Andrew Anderson*, 1681. cap., fol.* ALDIS 2249. L, EN.

3563A The apothecarie's reply to the city's printed reasons. [*London*, 1697]. brs. L; RBU.

3564 The apothecaries vindication. [*London?* 1676]. brs. L.

3564A The apparent ruine of the glass-makers. [*London?* 1696]. brs. L; MH.

Appeal by the coming ... [169-?.] *See* B., T.

Appeal for judgement, 1664. *See* Crane, Richard.

Appeal from chancery. 1653. *See* Burt, Nathaniel.

Appeal from the country. 1679. *See* Blount, Charles.

3565 An appeale from the court to the country. [*London*], *printed*, 1656. 4°.* LT, O, OC, DT; CH, CN, TU, WF, Y.

Appeal from the twenty eight judges. [1692.] Keith, George.

Appeale in the case. 1660. *See* Peirce, *Sir* Edmond.

Appeal most humble. 1691. *See* Beverley, Thomas.

Appeal of murther. [1693.] *See* Grascome, Samuel.

3566 An appeale of the orthodox ministers of the Church of England. *Edenbvrgi*, 1641. 4°.* ALDIS 988. LT, C, OC, HH, EN; CH, MH, NU, TU, WF, Y.

3567 An appeal to all Protestant kings. *For Brabazon Aylmer*, 1700. 4°.* T.C.III 167. L, O, OC, MR, E; CH, CN, MH, NU, WF, Y.

Appeal to all true Englishmen. [1699.] *See* Grascome, Samuel.

Appeal to every impartiall. 1641. *See* Downing, Calybute.

Appeal to heaven. [1644.] *See* F., J. M.

Appeal to heaven and earth. 1691. *See* Stephens, Edward.

3568 An appeal to heaven: or, a prayer. *Printed*, 1649. 4°.* LT; CH, MH.

Appeal to the churches. 1656. *See* Woodward, Hezekiah.

Appeal to the conscience. 1684. *See* Lane, Bartholomew.

3568A An appeal to the men of New-England. colop: [*Boston*], *printed*, 1689. cap., 4°.* EVANS 455. LC, MH, NN.

Appeal to the Parliament. 1660. *See* Lamb, Thomas.

Appeal to the Scriptures. 1676. *See* W., J.

3569 An appeale to the world in these times. [*London*, 1642.] cap., 4°.* LT, O, CJ, EN, DT; CSS, CU, MH, NPT, WF, Y.

Appeal to thy conscience. [1643.] *See* Fisher, Edward.

Appellatio ad fratres. 1690. *See* Burgess, Daniel.

Appendix ad catalogam. Cantabrigiæ, 1663. *See* Ray John.

3570 Appendix librorum. *Oxford*, 28 Nov 1692. 4°. L.

3570A An appendix of books to be sold by auction on 2 June 1679. [*London*, 1679]. cap., 4°.* OP.

3571 An appendix of some books omitted in transcribing. [1677.] 4°.* O.

3572 An appendix of the lawes, articles, & ordinances. *Printed in the Hagh by Isaac Burchoorn*, 1643. fol. L; MBA, Y.

Appendix; or, a brief answer. [1692.] *See* Wennell, Thomas.

Appendix practica. Edinburgi, 1653. *See* Baillie, Robert.

Appendix sacra: or, . . . 1652. *See* Sparke, Edward.

Appendix to a discourse. [1700.] *See* Beverley, Thomas.

Appendix to A gentleman's religion. 1698. *See* Synge, Edward, *abp.*

3573 Appendix to Mercurius reformatus. *For R. Baldwin*, 1692. fol.* T.C.II 394. LUG; CH.

Appendix to Mr. Perkins. 1656. *See* Robinson, John.

Appendix to Solomon's. 1667. *See* Mead, Matthew.

Appendix to the agreement. 1648. *See* P., A.

Appendix to the answer. 1692. *See* Keach, Benjamin.

Appendix to the history of independency. 1648. *See* Walker, Clement.

Appendix to the history of the church. 1677. *See* Middleton, Thomas.

Appendix to the late answer. 1642. *See* Parker, Henry.

3574 Appendix to the late collection of books brought from France. [1699?] 4°. L.

Appendix to the life. 1697. *See* Wood, Thomas.

3575 An appendix to the proposal for raising the price of tin. [*London*, 1697?] 4°.* C, LUG.

3576 An appendix to the queries upon the 25th of Hen. VIII. Cap. 21. *For the author*, 1690. 4°.* L; MH.

Appendix to the third part. 1670. *See* Patrick, Symon, *bp.*

3577 An appendix to the translation of Tully's panegyrick. *W. Kettilby*, 1689. 4°. HH; NN, PU, WF.

3578 An appendix, wherein the hellish machinations. *T. Snowden*, 1681. 4°. HH, DT; MH.

3579 **Appianus.** The history of . . . , in two parts. *For John Amery*, 1679. fol. T.C.I 330. L, O, CS, EN; CH, CN, MH, NU, WF, Y.

3580 — —Second edition. *For John Amery*, 1690. fol. L, CS; LC, MH, NC, WSC, Y.

3580A — —"Second" edition. —, 1692. L, AN; LC, PL, Y.

3580B — —"Second" edition. —, 1696. 4°. NN.

3581 **Appleford, Robert.** Mechanica rerum explicatio. [*Cantabrigiæ*], 1676. brs. L.

3582 [**Appleton, Henry.**] A remonstrance of the fight in Legornroad. *By John Field*, 1653. fol.* LT, O, LUS; V, Y.

3582A The appointments of Edward Russell. [*London?* 1698]. brs. INU.

3583 The apprehending of Captayne Bvtler. *For F. C. and T. B.*, 1641. 4°.* LT, O, OC, EC; CH, WF, Y.

Apprentices advice. 1642. *See* Taylor, John.

3584 The prentices answer to The whores petition. *Printed*, 1668, brs. L, O.

Apprentices companion. 1681. *See* Crouch, Nathaniel.

3584A The apprentice's faithful monitor. [*London*, 1700]. fol.* L.

3585 The apprentices hue-and-cry after their petition. [*London*, 1660.] brs. LT, O.

Apprentices lamentation. [1642.] *See* W., P.

3585A Apprentices no slaves. *For J. Hawkins*, 1662. 4°. O, CT.

3586 The apprentices of Londons petition. *For John Greensmith*, 1641. 4°.* LT, O, LG, HH; CH, NC, NU, Y.

3587 The prentices prophecie. *Printed*, 1642. 4°.* LT; MH, NU.

3587A The prentices resolution. [1650?] brs. O.

3587B The 'prentices tragedy. *W. O.*, [1700?] 4°.* L.

3588 The approach and signal victory of K. Williams forces. colop: *For L. C.*, [1690]. brs. L, HH; MH.

3589 Approved and appointed collectors . . . of the several rates. [*London*], 1695. brs. O.

3590 An approved answer to the partiall and vnlikt of Lord Digbies speech. [*London*], *printed*, 1641. 4°.* LT, OC, HH, EN; CH, MH, NU, TU, WF, Y.

3590A An approved antidote or cordiall medicine. [*London?* 1650.] brs. L.

Approved, good, and happy newes. 1641. *See* Loftus, Edward.

3591 April horse race. *For J. Murrey,* [1680–90]. brs. HH.

3592 **A[p-Robert], J[ohn].** An apology for a younger brother. *Oxford, by Leonard Lichfield, for Edward Forrest,* 1641. 4°. MADAN 989. LT, CT; NU.

3593 [–] The younger brother his apologie. *Oxford, by Henry Hall, for E. Forrest, and I. Gilbert,* 1671. 4°.* MADAN 2879. L, O, C, LG, A; MH, NC, WF, Y.

3594 [**Apsley, Allen Algernon,** *viscount.*] Order and disorder. *By Margaret White for Henry Mortlock,* 1679. 4°. T.C.I 359. L; CH, MH, MU, WF.

Aqua salsa. 1683. *See* Fitzgerald, Robert.

3595 **Aranda, Emanuel d'.** The history of Algiers and it's slavery. *For John Starkey,* 1666. 8°. L, LG, OC, CM, MR; CN, MIU, TU, WF, Y.

3596 **Aratus.** Αρατου Σολεως φαινομενα. *Oxonii, e theatro Sheldoniano,* 1672. 8°. MADAN 2919. L, O, C, LVD, MR; CH, MH, PL, WF, Y.

3597–9 Entries cancelled. Arbitrary government. 1682. *See* May, Thomas.

3600 Arbitrium redivivum: or the law of arbitration. *By the assigns of Rich. and Edw. Atkins, for Isaac Cleeve,* 1694. 8°. L, LL; CLC, WF.

3601 **A[rbuthnot], J[ohn].** An examination of Dr. Woodward's account. *For C. Bateman,* 1697. 8°. L, O, CT, LNH, E; CN, MH, NN, HC.

3602 [–] Of the laws of chance. *By Benj. Motte, and sold by Randall Taylor,* 1692. 12°. L, O, DT; NIC.

3603 —Theses medicæ [*Edinburgh*], *ex officina Georgii Mosman,* 1696. 4°.* L, O, OC, AU; MMO.

3604 **Arbuthnott, Alexander.** Disputatio juridica. *Edinburgi, ex officina typographica haeredum Andreae Anderson,* 1697. 4°.* E.

Arcana aulica: or. . . 1652. *See* Du Refuge, Eustache.

Arcana dogmatum. 1659. *See* Womock, Laurence, *bp.*

Arcana microcosmi: or. 1652. *See* Ross, Alexander.

Arcana parliamentaria. 1685. *See* C., R.

Arcandam, *pseud. See* Roussat, Richard.

Archaeologiæ philosophicæ. 1692. *See* Burnet, Thomas.

3605 Αρχαιονομια, sive de priscis. *Cantabrigiæ, ex officina Rogeri Daniel; prostant Londini apud Cornelium Bee,* 1644. fol. L, O, CT, EN, DT; BN, CH, LC, MHL, NR, Y.

Αρχαιοσκοπια: 1677. *See* Hanmer, Jonathan.

Archbishop of Canterburie's dreame. 1641. *See* Milton, John.

Arch-cheate. 1644. *See* H., S.

3605A **Archdekin, Richard.** A treatise of miracles. *Lovanni, typis Andreae Bouvet,* 1667. 8°. L, C; WG.

3606 **Archer, Elias.** A true relation of the marchings. *For Edward Blackmore,* 1643. 4°.* L.

3607 Archer, Henry. A treatise of carefulness. *Fran. Coles,* 1641. 12°. LCL.

3608 **Archer, John,** *M.D.* Every man his own doctor. *By Peter Lillicrap for the author,* 1671. 8°. L, LCS, LWL.

3609 — —Second edition. *For the author,* 1673. 8°. T.C.I 130. L, O, C, LWL, GK; BN, CLC, MIU, NAM, WF, Y.

3609A — —[Anr. ed.] —, 1678. 8°. GK.

3610 —Secrets disclosed. *For the author,* 1684. 8°. L; WSG.

3611 — —[Anr. ed.] *For William Whitewood, and Anthony Feltham,* 1693. 8°. T.C.II 479. L, O, LWL.

[**Archer, John,** *preacher*]. Cheap-side crosse censured. 1641. *See* Abbot, George, *abp.*

3612 —Comfort for beleevers. *For Benjamin Allen,* 1645, 4°. LT, C; CH, NPT, NU, WF.

3612A — —[Anr. ed.] *For Livewell Chapman,* 1661. 12°. LSC; CLC.

3613 —Instructions about right beleeving. *For Benjamin Allen,* 1645. 4°. LT, YM; CH, NPT, NU.

3614 [–] The personall raigne of Christ upon earth. [*London*], *printed,* 1641. 4°. WCA; MWA, NU, Y.

3615 — —[Anr. ed. "By Henry Archer"] *Printed, to be sold by Benjamin Allen,* 1642. 4°. LT, O, OC, CCA, WCA; CH, CU, MH, TU, Y.

3616 — —[Anr. ed.] —, 1642. 4°. L, OC; CU, NU, Y.

3617 — —[Anr. ed.] —, 1642. 4°. L, C, CE, OC; CH, MIU, MWA, NU.

3618 — —Second edition. —, 1643. 4°. L, C, CM, ENC; NU.

3619 — —Fifth edition. *For Livewel Chapman,* 1661. 4°. O, LCL; NPT, NU, WF.

3620 —Sensible sinners. 1645. 4°.* LT; NU.

Archerie reviv'd. Edinburgh, 1677. *See* C., W.

3621 **Archimedes.** Archimedis opera. *Excudebat Guil. Godbid, voeneunt apud Rob. Scott,* 1675. 4°. T.C.I 206. L, O, C, EN, DT; CH, BN, MH, NC, WF, Y.

3622 —Αρχιμηδους . . . ψαμμιτης . . . Archimedis Syracusani arenarius, et dimensio circuli. *Oxonni, e theatro Sheldoniano, to be sold by Peter Parker,* 1676. 8°. MADAN 3095. L, O, C, CT, GH; CLC, LC, NC, PL, WF.

Arch-rebel found. 1696. *See* W., T.

Archy's dream. 1641. *See* Armstrong, Archibald.

3623 **Arderne, James,** *Dean of Chester.* Conjectura circa 'Επινομην. *Impensis Ben. Tooke,* 1683. 4°.* T.C.II 5. L, O, CS, P, DT; BN, TU, WF.

3624 —Directions concerning the matter and stile of sermons. *For Spencer Hickman,* 1671. 12°. T.C.I 78. L, O, CPE, LW; BN, MH.

3625 —A sermon preached at the visitation of . . . John, Lord Bishop of Chester. *For H. Brome,* 1677. 4°.* T.C.I 287. L, O, C, OC, OCC; NU, Y.

3625A —The Dean of Chester's speech. August the 27th. 1687. *For M. T.,* 1687. brs. O, CT.

3626 —[Anr. ed.] *London, reprinted Edinburgh by the heir of Andrew Anderson,* 1687. brs. ALDIS 2682. EN; MH, Y.

3627 **Arderne, James,** *Gent.* The kingdom of England. The best Commonwealth. *By J. H. for Matthew Keinton,* 1660. 4°.* L, CT; CN, PL, Y.

3628 **Ardron, Nicholas.** The ploughmans vindication. *By I. M. to be sold by M. Spark,* 1646. 4°. LT.

Ardua regni. [*London*], 1648. *See* Prynne, William.

Aretina. Edinburgh, 1660. *See* Mackenzie, *Sir* George.

Aretino, Peter, *pseud.*

3629 **Aretius, Benedictus.** A short history of Valentinus Gentilis. *Printed, and sold by E. Whitlock,* 1696. 8°. T.C.II 534. L, O, C, E, DT; CH, MH, NU, WSC, Y.

3630 [**Argences, d'.**] The countess of Salisbury. *For R. Bentley and S. Magnes,* 1683. 12°. T.C.I 507. L; CLC, CN, LC, MH, Y.

3630A — —[Anr. ed.] —, 1692. 12°. L.

3631 The argument against a standing army discuss'd. *Eliz. Whitlock,* 1698. 4°.* L, C, CT, LUS, AU; CN, LC, MH, WF, Y.

3632 An argument against a standing army rectified. *Printed,* 1697. 4°.* L, O, C, LUS, DT; CH, CN, NN, PL, WF, Y.

3632A The argument against the bill for regulating the stuffs. [*London?* 1662]. brs. L.

3632B The argument and reasons of the brethren of the Trinity House. [*London,* 1695]. brs. CN.

Argument concerning. [1699?] *See* Layton, Henry.

Argument for the bishops. 1682. *See* Hunt, Thomas.

Argument for toleration. 1681. *See* Whitaker, Edward.

Argument for union. 1683. *See* Tenison, Thomas, *abp.*

Argument in defence of the Hospitaller. 1689. *See* Turner, John.

Argument in defence of the right. 1653. *See* Nortcliffe, M.

An arvgment in justification of the five members. [1643.] *See* Bland, Peter.

3633 The argument of a learned counsel, upon an action. *For B. Aylmer,* 1696. 8°. L; CH, MBP, NPT, PL, WF.

Argument of the letter. Oxford, 1690. *See* Proast, Jonas.

Argument of the Lord Chief Justice. 1689. *See* Jeffreys, George.

Argument or, debate. 1642. *See* March, John.

3634 An argument, proving, that a small number of regulated forces. *For A. Baldwin,* 1698. 4°.* L, C, AU; CH, CLC, CN, WF, Y.

Argument proving, that according. 1700. *See* Asgill, John.

3634A An argument proving, that the reasons given. [*London?* 1695]. cap., fol.* MH, PL.

Argument, shewing that a standing army is. 1697. *See* Trenchard, John.

Argument, shewing, that a standing army, with. . . . 1698. *See* Defoe, Daniel.

Argument shewing that 'tis. 1699. *See* Berisford, John.

3635 An argument to prove that each subject. 1641. 4°. C, LVF.

3636 Arguments against all accomodation. [*London*], *printed,* 1648. 4°.* LT, LG, OC, DT; CLC, CN, MH, WF, Y.

Arguments against bovving. 1641. *See* Wickins, William.

3637 The arguments against the bill for regulating the stuffs in Norfolk. [1660–75]. brs. L.

3638 Arguments against the Common Councels engagement. [*London*], *printed,* 1648. 4°.* HH; NU.

Arguments and considerations. 1699. *See* Heylyn, Peter.

3639 Arguments and materials for a register. *For Samuel Lowndes,* 1698. 4°.* T.C.II 57. CCA, LUG; CLC, WF, YL.

3640 The arguments and reasons for and against engrafting upon the Bank of England. [*London?* 1697?] cap., 8°.* L, O, LG; MH, NC, WF, Y.

Arguments and reasons to prove the inconvenience. [London, 1650.] *See* Aucher, John.

3641 Arguments concerning the new-buildings in the parishes. [*London,* 1677/8.] brs. L, LUG.

3642 The arguments for a regulated company. [*London,* 169–?] brs. MH.

3643 Arguments for insuring houses from fire. [1680.] brs. CHRISTIE-MILLER.

3644 Arguments for toleration. *By Richard Cotes,* 1647. 4°.* LT, O, C, DT; CH, MH, MIU.

Arguments given in. 1641. *See* Scotland. Estates.

3645 Arguments, inviting all faithful marriners. *Printed,* 1649. brs. LT, LG; MH.

3646 Entry cancelled. *See* Somers, John Somers, *baron.*

3647 Arguments pro and con about the right of baptizing. *For Francis Smith,* 1675. brs. L; CLC, CN.

3648 Arguments, proving that we ought not to part with the militia. [*London,* 1646.] brs. LT, O, LG; MH.

Arguments proving, the iurisdiction. 1641. *See* H., W.

3649 Arguments upon the writ of habeas corpus. *By M. F. for W. Lee, M. Walbancke, D. Pakeman, and G. Bedell,* 1649. 4°. LT, O, CT, EN, DT; CH, CN, LC, MH, NU, Y.

Argumentum anti-Normannicum: or. 1682. *See* Coke, Edward.

3650 **Argyle, Archibald Campbell,** *marquis.* The Marquess of Argile his answer to his charge. [*London*], *printed,* 1661. 4°.* LT, O, C; TU.

3651 —A declaration of the Marquesse of Argyle. *Printed at Edenburgh by Evan Tyler, and reprinted at London for R. A.* 16 Octob. 1648. 4°.* LT, C, E; MH.

3652 —The Marques of Argyll his defences. [*Edinburgh?*], *Anno* 1661. 4°. L, O, HH, GM, ES; CH, MHL, NU, WF.

3653 ——[Anr. ed. "Marquis"] [*London*], *Anno* 1661. cap., 4°. CH, MH.

3654 —An honourable speech made . . . the thirtieth of September 1641. *By A. N. for I. M.,* 1641. 4°.* LT, O, EN; CLC, MH, NPT, WF, Y.

3655 ——[Anr. ed.] *By B. Alsop,* 1641. 4°.* LT.

3656 —Instructions to a son. *Printed at Edinborough, and reprinted at London, for D. Trench,* 1661. 12°. L, HH, E, ES; CH, CLC, CN, OCI, Y.

3657 ——[Anr. ed.] *For J. Latham,* 1661. 12°. MH.

3658 ——[Anr. ed.] *Printed and sold by Richard Baldwin,* 1689. 12°. L, OM, EN; CH, CN, PL, WF, Y.

3659 —A letter from. *Printed at York by Stephen Bulkley,* 1643. 4°.* O; NN.

3660 —A letter sent from . . . Apr. 9. 1652. *Imprinted at London, for George Horton,* 1652. 4°.* LT, HH; Y.

3661 —Letters from. *Oxford, by Henry Hall,* 1645. 4°.* MADAN 1767. LT, O, CT, EC, EN; CH, CN, MH.

3662 —A most noble speech spoken by the lord Cambel, of Lorne. *By B.Alsop*, 1641. 4°.* LT, O, C, HH, EN; CH, LC, MH, WF, Y.

3663 —Right honourable, the Lord hath this day. *For Robert Bostock, September* 18, 1645. cap., brs. LT; MIU.

3664 Entry cancelled.

3665 —The speech and plea of. *By H.Lloyd, and R.Vaughan, for Thomas Johnson*, 1661. 4°.* L, OC, HH, EN; CH, MH, Y.

3666 —A speech by the Marquesse of Argile . . . 25. June 1646. *For Iohn Wright*, 27 *June* 1646. 4°.* LT, O, C, HH; CH, MH, PU, WF, Y.

3667 —The Marqvesse of Argyle his speech concerning the king. *By Barnard Alsop*, 1648. 4°.* LT, EN, DT; CLC, MH, Y.

3668 —My Lord Marquis Argyle his speech upon the scaffold. [*Edinburgh*, 1661.] fol. ALDIS 1689. L; CH, MH, Y.

3669 —The speech of . . . May 27, 1661. *Printed at Edenburgh, and reprinted at London*, 1661. 4°.* L, O, C, HH, EN; CH, LC, MH, NU, TU, Y.

3670 — —[Anr. ed.] *By T.B.*, 1661. 4°.* MH, WF, Y.

3671 —The Lord Marques of Argyle's speech to a grand committee . . . the 25th of . . . June, 1646. *For Laurence Chapman, June* 27, 1646. 4°.* LT, O, C, EN, GU; CH, CN, LC, MH, NU, Y.

3672 —To the Kings most excellent majesty. *Printed*, 1661. brs. MH.

3673 —The true copy of a speech. *Printed*, 1641. 4°.* HH, OC; CH, MB, MH.

3674 **Argyle, Archibald Campbell, 9th earl.** A copy of the last speech. [*London*, 1685]. brs. Y.

3675 —The declaration of. *Reprinted Edinburgh*, 1680. brs. ALDIS 2184. EN.

3676 [–] The declaration and apology of the Protestant people. colop: *Printed at Campbell-toun, in Kintyre, in the shire of Argyle*, 1685. 4°.* ALDIS 2539. HH, EN.

3677 [–] — —[Anr. ed.] — *Reprinted*, [1685]. 4°.* O.

3678 —The speech of . . . at his trial on the 12th of December 1681. colop: *for Richard Janeway*, 1682. brs. LT, O, OC, HH, EN; CH, CN, MH, WF, Y.

3679 Argyles arraignment: or, treachery displayed. [*London*, 1660.] brs. LT.

Ariadne, *pseud.*
Ariana. 1641. *See* Desmarets de Saint Sorlin, Jean.

3679A **Arias Montanus, Benedict.** The practical rule of Christian piety. *Sold by J.Hindmarsh*, 1685. 12°. T.C.II III. O.

3680 **Aris, John.** The reconciler or, a sermon. 1651. 4°. OM.

3681 **Aristachus, Samius.** Ἀριστάρχου Σαμιου περι μεγε θων . . . De magnitudinibus. *Oxoniæ, e theatro Sheldoniano*, 1688. 8°. L, O, C, MR, E; BN, MH, V, Y.

3682 **Aristeas.** The ancient history of the septuagint. Second edition. *For W.Hensman, and Tho. Fox*, 1685. 12°. T.C.II 161. L, C, OB, EN, GK; MH, NPT, WF, Y.

3683 —Aristeae historia LXXII interpretum. *Oxonii, e theatro Sheldoniano*, 1692. 8°. T.C.II 394. L, O, C, DU, E; BN, CH, MH, NC, Y.

Aristippus, or the jovial philosopher. 1668. *See* Randolph, Thomas.

3684 **Aristophanes.** Κωμωδια δυο . . . Comodiæ duæ, Plutus Nubes. *Impensis Rob. Clavel*, 1695. 8°. T.C.II 550. L, O, C, MR, EN; BN, CH, CU, MH, NP, WF, Y.

3685 —Πλουτοφθαλμία πλουτογαμία. A pleasant comedie; entituled Hey for honesty. *Printed*, 1651. 4°. L, O, OW; CH, CU, LC, MH, WCL, Y.

3686 —The worlds idol. Plutus: a comedy. *By W.G. to be sold by Richard Skelton, Isaac Pridmore, and H.Marsh*, 1659. 4°. LT, O, LVF, DC; CH, CN, CU, MU, Y.

3687 **Aristotle.** Aristotelis artis rhetoricae compendium. *Typis Mariae Clarke*, 1683. 8°. O.

3688 —Ανδρονικου Ροδιου παράφρασις . . . Ethicorum Nichomacheorum. *Cantabrigiæ, excudebat Johannes Hayes, impensis Johannis Creed*, 1679. 8°. T.C.I 335. L, O, C, EN, DT; CLC, MH, MU, PL, WF, Y.

3688A —Aristotle's legacy. *For J.Blare*, [1699.] 4°.* TC.III 130. L; MWA.

3688AB —Logica seu introductio. *Dublini, typis et impensis William Bladen*, 1657. 12°. DIX 100. L.

3688B —Aristotles manuel of choice secrets. *For John Back*, 1699. 12°. IU.

3689 —Aristotles master-piece. *For J.How*, 1684. 12°. LCS, LG; HC.

3689A — —[Anr. ed.] *By F.L. for J.How*, 1690. 12°. T.C.II 341. LWL.

3689AA — —[Anr. ed.] *For W.B.*, 1694. 8°. L, O; MWA, WF.

3689BA — —[Anr. ed.] —, 1695. 8°. CLC.

3689C — —[Anr. ed.] 1698. 12°. GU; CH.

3690 —Αριστοτελους περι ποιητικης . . . De poetica liber. *Cantabrigiæ, apud Johannem Hayes, sumptibus Thomæ Dawson*, 1696. 8°. L, O, C, LL, EN; BN, CH, MH, WF, WSC, Y.

3691 —The problems of. *By T.N. for T.W.*, 1649. 8°. CHRISTIE-MILLER.

3692 — —[Anr. ed.] *By S.G. for W.K.*, 1666. 8°. O.

3692A — —[Anr. ed.] *For W.K.*, 1670. 8°. LWL; Y.

3692B — —[Anr. ed.] *For J.Wright, and R.Chiswell*, 1676. 8°. NAM.

3692C — —[Anr. ed.] —, 1680, 8°. L; MWA.

3692D — —[Anr. ed.] —, 1682. 8°. CLC.

3693 — —[Anr. ed.] *For J.Wright and R.Chiswel*, 1683. 8°. T.C.I 364. L; NAM, HC.

3694 — —[Anr. ed.] *For J.Wright and R.Chiswell, to be sold by John Smith*, 1684. 8°. L; CLM, PL, WF, WSG, HC.

3695 —Aristotle's rhetoric. *By T.B. for Randal Taylor*, 1686. 8°. L, O, C, E, DT; CH, CN, NP, PL, WF, Y.

3696 — —Second edition. *For S.Briscoe*, 1693, 8°. T.C.II 468. L, O; CU.

3696A —Rhetorices artis compendium, 1683. 8°. O.

3697 —Αριστοτελους τεχνης ρητορικης . . . de rhetorica. *Typis Ben. Griffini, impensis Edward Hall, Cantabr*, 1696. 4°. L, O, C, EN, DT; BN, CH, MH, NP, WF, Y.

Arithmetick in species. 1680. *See* Perkins,
Arithmetick symbolical. 1649. *See* B., R.
Arithmetick: vulgar. 1675. *See* Mayne, John.
Ark of the Covenant. 1677. *See* Gillespie, George.
Ark of the testament. 1661. *See* Gillespie, George.

3697A **Armand, William.** A funeral elegie upon the death of George Sonds. *For John Crowch*, 1655. brs. L.

Armante Gulielmo. [1692.] *See* Joyner, Edward.

3697B **Armenio, John.** Hereafter followeth the great ... vertue. 1658. brs. O.

3698 **A[rmin], R[obert].** The valiant Welshman. *For William Gilbertson*, 1663. 4°. L, O, C, LVD, EN; CH, CN, MH, WF, Y.

Arminian haltered. 1641. *See* S., T.

3699 The Arminian nvnnery. [*London*], *for Thomas Underhill*, 1641. 4°.* LT, CT; IU, MH, NGT, WF, Y.

3700 **Arminius, Jacobus.** The just man's defence. *For Henry, Eversden*, 1657. 8°. L, O, C, LW; CH, NPT, NU.

3701 **Armitage, Timothy.** Eight sermons. *Norwich*, [c. 1650]. LCL.

3702 —Sermons preached upon several occasions. *Printed*, 1678. 8°. L, O, CLC, MH, NPT.

3702A ——[Anr. ed.] *For E. Giles, Norwich*, 1682. 8°. T.C.I 483. TO.

3703 —The Son of God walking in the fire. *By J. Macock, for Henry Cripps*, 1656. 8°. LCL; MH.

3704 —A tryall of faith. *By M. S. for Henry Cripps*, 1661. 8°. LCL; MH, NPT.

3704A **A[rmour], J[ames].** A proposal to supply the defect of money. [*London*, 1700].*. LUG; NC, WF.

3705 [**Armstrong, Archibald**]. A banquet of jests new and old. *For R. Royston*, 1657. 12°. CH, IU, LC, WF.

3706 [–] A choice banquet of witty jests. *By T. J. to be sold by Peter Dring*, 1660. 8°. L; CH.

3707 [–] —Second edition. *For Peter Dring*, 1665. 8°. O; NN.

3708 [–] Archy's dream. [*London*], *printed*, 1641. 4°.* LT, O, CT, LVF, EN; MH, WF, Y.

3708A **A[rmstron], J[ohn].** Secret and family prayers. *Cambridge, by J. Hayes for the author*, 1677. 8°. C.

3708B —The soul's worth and danger. *Cambridge, for the author*, 1677. 8°. C.

Armuthaz, Bollicosgo, pseud.

Army-armed. 1653. *See* Hunton, Samuel.

3709 The army brought to the barre. [*London*], *printed*, 1647. 4°.* LT, O, LVF, LUS, HH; CH, MH, NU, TU, WF, Y.

3710 The army for a treaty. [*London*], *printed*, 1648. 4°.* LT, P; CH, CU, MH, WF, Y.

Armie for Ireland. 1642. *See* Leicester, Philip Sidney, earl.

Army, harmlesse. 1647. *See* Goodwin, John.

3711 The army mastered, or, Great Brittains joy. [*London*], *printed*, 1659. brs. LT, O, HH; MH.

3712 The army no usurpers. *For Giles Calvert*, 1653. 4°.* LT, HH; CN, MH, NU, Y.

Army's book of declarations. 1647. *See* Walker, Henry.

3712A The army's declaration; being. [*London*], *printed*, 1660. 4°.* LT, OC; CH, MH.

3713 The armies declaration examined. *Printed*, 1659. 4°.* LT, O, OC, CCA, HH; CH, MH, MIU, WF, Y.

Armies dutie. 1659. *See* M., H.

Armies last propositions ... June 28, 1647. *See* Smith, Thomas.

3714 The armies letanie. [*London*], *printed*, 1647. 4°.* LT, O, DT; MH, PL, WF, Y.

Army's martyr: or a faithful relation. 1647. *See* F., R.

3714A The army's martyr, or a more ful relation. *Printed*, 1649, 4°.* L, LG, EC; CH, MH, PT, WF.

3715 The armies petition: or a new engagement. [1648.] cap., 4°.* LT; CH, MH, WF.

3716 The army's plea for their present practice. *By Henry Hills*, 1659. 4°.* LT, O, CT, HH, EN; CH, CN, MH, NU, WF, Y.

3717 The armies proposalls to the Parliament. *Printed*, 1659. 4°.* L, O; CH, MBP, MH, WF, Y.

Armies remembrancer. 1649. *See* Rr.

3718 The armies vindication. [*London*], *for Peter Cole*, 1649. 4°. LT, CCA; CH, MH, Y.

3719 The armies vindication of this last change. *By T. M.*, 1659. 4°.* O, HH; CH, CU, MH, NC, WF, Y.

3720 [**Arnauld, Antoine.**] The King making doctrine of the Jesuites. *For W. Crooke, and I. Dring*, 1679. 4°. T.C.I 343. L, O, C, LCL, DT; CH, CN, MH, PL, WF, Y.

3721 [–] Logic: or, the art of thinking. *By T. B. for H. Sawbridge*, 1685. 8°. T.C.II 149. L, O, CK, RPL; CH, CU, NC, TU, Y.

3722 [–] —Second edition. *By T. B. for John Taylor*, 1693. 12°. T.C.II 445. L, O; CLC, CN, TSM, WF.

3723 [–] —Third edition. —, 1696. 12°. L, O; CLC, MB, NC.

3724 [–] Logica, sive ars cogitandi. *Typis Andr. Clark; impensis Joh. Martyn et Ed. Story, Cantabrigiensis*, 1674. 8°. L, O, OC, CM, E; CU, CN, IU, MB, WF.

3725 [–] —"Third" edition. —, 1677. 8°. T.C.I 260. CN, NP, PL.

3726 [–] —Second edition. *Impensis R. Littlebury, R. Scot, G. Scot, G. Wells, Londinensium, & J. Green Cantabiogiensis* [sic], 1682. 8°. L, ELY; NPT, TU.

3727 [–] —Third edition. *Impensis R. Littlebury, R. Scot, T. Sawbridge, & G. Wells*, 1687. 8°. OC, EC; PL, Y.

3728 [–] —"Third" edition. *Impensis Richardi Green*, 1687. 8°. O, CT; NIC, NP, WF, Y.

3729 [–] Μυστήριον της 'Ανομιας. That is, another part of the mystery of Jesuitism. *By James Flesher, for Richard Royston*, 1664. 8°. L, O, C, GK, DT; CH, NU, WF, Y.

3730 [–] The new heresie of the Jesuites. *Printed*, 1662. 4°.* L, O, LW, DT; WF, Y.

3731 **Arndt, Johann.** Mr. John Arndt (that famous German divine) his book of Scripture. *By Mat. Simmons for H. Blunden*, 1646. 8°. L, LSC; CH, NU, WF.

Αρνιοβοσκια: or. .... 1650. *See* D., W.

3732 **Arnold, Samuel.** David serving his generation. *Cambridge [Mass.], by Samuel Green*, 1674. 4°.* EVANS 185. CH, LC, MB, MH, MHS.

3733 **A[rnold], T[homas].** Ταπεινανος, humble praise. *For Luke Fawne,* 1660. 4°.* CH, NU.

3734 **A[rnway, John].** No peace 'till the king prosper. *Oxford, by Leonard Lichfield,* 1645. 8°.* MADAN 1805. LT, O; CH.

3735 —The tablet or conceptions of the affairs of England. 1664. 8°. CH.

3736 [–] The tablet or moderation. [*The Hague*], printed, 1649. 8°. O, OB, AU; NU.

3737 [–] —Second edition. —, 1649. 12°. L, DC, DT; WF.

3738 [–] —[Anr. ed.] *Hague,* printed, 1650. 12°. L.

3739 — —[Anr. ed.] *By A[lice] W[arren], to be sold by Henry Seile, and Richard Royston,* 1661. 8°. L, C, LW, ES; CLC, CN, TU, WF, Y.

Αροβατεριον, vel. 1655. *See* F., F.

Aron. *See* Aaron.

Aron-bimnucha: or. 1663. *See* Womock, Laurence.

3740 The arraignment and acquittal of Sr Edward Mosely. *By E. G. for W. L.,* 1647[8]. 4°.* LT, O, HH.

3741 The arraignment and condemnation of Cap. Bridges Bushell. *For Marmaduke Boat,* 1657. 4°.* LT; CH.

3742 The arraignment and condemnation of the late rebels in the West. colop: *By T. M. (for the author),* 1685. brs. L, O, HH; CH, CLC, LC.

3743 The arraignment and conviction of Mervin Lord Avdley. *For Tho: Thomas,* 1642[3]. 4°.* LT, O; CH, WF, Y.

3744 The arraignment and conviction of Sr Walter Rawleigh. *By William Wilson for Abel Roper,* 1648. 4°.* LT, O, CCA, OC, LVF; CH, CN, MHL, RPJ, WF.

3745 The araignment and impeachment of Major Generall Massie. [*London*], printed, 1647. 4°.* LT; MIU, WF.

3746 The arraignment and plea of Edw. Fitz-Harris. *For Fr. Tyton, and Tho. Basset,* 1681. fol. T.C.I 451. L, O, CT, MR, EN; CH, CN, MH, WF, Y.

3747 The arraignment & tryal of Algernon Sydney. *Dublin, Jo. Ray,* 1684. fol.* DIX 205. DCA.

3748 The arraignment and tryall with a declaration of the ranters. [*London*], *by B. A.,* 1650. 4°.* LT, HH; MH.

3748A The arraignment, confession, and condemnation of Alexander Knightley. *For Samuel Heyrick, and Isaac Cleave,* 1696. fol.* CT, WCA; MIU, WF, Y.

Arraignment, conviction, and condemnation. [*London*], 1649. *See* Prynne, William.

3749 The arraignment, conviction, and imprisoning of Christmas. *Printed,* 1646. 4°.* LT.

Arrainment of Christendom. 1664. *See* Philly, John.

Arraingment of co-ordinate power. 1683. *See* B. and Y.

Araignment of hypocrisie. 1652. *See* C., J.

Arrainnment of ignorance. 1659. *See* Gearing, William.

Arraingment of lewde, idle. 1645. *See* Swetnam, Joseph.

Araignment of Mr. Persecution. Europe, 1645. *See* Overton, Richard.

Arraignment of popery. 1667. *See* Fox, George.

3750 The arraignment of Sir Richard Grahame. [*London,* 1691.] fol. MR.

3751 The arraignment of svperstition. *For T. B. and F. C.,* 1641. 4°.* LT, O, LP; OCI, Y.

3752 The arraignment of the Anabaptists good old cause. *By John Morgan,* 1660. 4°.* LT, O, C.

3753 The arraignment of the divel. [*London,* 1659.] brs. LT, O; MH.

Arraignment of Thomas Howard. *See* Lacy, J.

3754 The arraignment, tryal & condemnation of Algernon Sidney. *For Benj. Tooke,* 1684. fol. T.C.II 60. L, O, CT, MR, EN; CH, LC, MH, NU, TU, Y.

3755 The arraignment, tryal, and condemnation of Ambrose Rookwood. *For Samuel Heyrick; and Isaac Cleave,* 1696. fol. L, OC, CT, WCA, HH; CH, LC, MH, PL, TU, Y.

3756 Arraignment, tryal, and condemnation of Frost the broker. [*London*], *Miller,* 1675. 4°. LG.

3757 The arraignment, tryal, and condemnation of Peter Cooke. *For Benjamin Tooke,* 1696. fol. L, OC, CT, HH, DT; CH, MH, NC, WF, Y.

3758 The arraignment, tryal and condemnation of Robert, Earl of Essex. *For Tho. Basset, Sam. Heyrick, and Matth. Gillyflower,* 1679. fol.* T.C.I 363. L, O, C, BR, MR; CH, LC, MH, WF, Y.

3759 The arraignment, tryal, and condemnation of Sir John Friend. *For Samuel Heyrick; and Isaac Cleve,* 1696. fol.* L, C, CT, WCA, HH; CH, MHL, NC, WF, Y.

3760 The arraignment, tryal and condemnation of Sir William Parkins. *For Samuel Heyrick, and Isaac Cleve,* 1696. fol. L, O, C, HH, DT; CH, MH, TU, Y.

3761 The arraignment, tryal and condemnation of Stephen Colledge. *For Thomas Basset, and John Fish,* 1681. fol. L, O, C, EN, DT; CH, MH, NU, WF, Y.

3762 —[Anr. ed.] *Dublin, Joseph Ray,* 1681. fol. DIX 185. C, DT, LW, DM, DW; LC.

3763 The arraignment, tryal, and condemnation of Thomas Harrison. [*London*], *for T. Vere, and W. Gilbertson,* 1660. 4°.* E; Y.

3763A The arraignment, tryal, and confession of Francis Deane. 1643. L.

3764 The arraignment, tryal and examination of Mary Moders. *For N. Brook,* 1663. 4°.* L, O; CH, NC, WF, Y.

3765 The arraignment, tryal, conviction and condemnation of Henry Harrison. *By Thomas Braddyll, and are to be sold by William Battersby, and R. Baldwin,* 1692. fol.* L, CT, P, E; CH, MHL, MMO, Y.

3765A The arraignment, tryal, conviction, and condemnation of John Ashton. *For Samuel Heyrick and Thomas Cockerill,* 1691. fol. PL.

3766 The arraignment, tryal, conviction, and confession of Francis Deane. *Printed at London for Richard Harper,* 1643. 4°.* LT, O, LG, EN; MHL, NU.

3767 The arraignment, trials, conviction and condemnation of Sir Rich. Grahme. *For Samuel Heyrick and Thomas Cockerill,* 1691. fol. L, O, OC, CT, LL; CH, CN, MH, PL, Y.

3768 The arraignments, tryals and condemnations of Charles Cranburne, and Robert Lowick. *For Samuel Heyrick, and Isaac Cleave*, 1696. fol. L, CT, OC, HH; CH, CLC, MH, MHL, Y.

Arrais, Edward Madeira. *See* Madeira Arrais, Duarte.

3769 **Arran, Richard Butler,** *earl.* A speech made by . . . eighth of January 1688. *For T.N.*, 1689. brs. L, O, C, HH; WF; Y.

3769A ——[Anr. ed.] *Edinburgh, by John Reid*, 1689. brs. ALDIS 2860. L, HH, EN.

Arrest of five unsober men. 1657. *See* Crofton, Zachary.

3770 An arrest of the court of Parliament. [*London*], *for Henry Seile Junior*, 1652. brs. LT.

Arrest on the East India privateer. [1681.] *See* K., H.

Arrian's vindication. [1691.] *See* Freke, William.

3771 The arrival and welcome of Mr. George Walker. *By H. Mills, jun. and sold by R. Taylor*, 1689. brs. MH.

Arrogancy of reason. 1655. *See* Baxter, Richard.

Arrow against profane. Boston, 1684. *See* Mather, Increase.

3772 **Arrowsmith, John.** Armilla catechetica. A chain of principles. *Cambridge: by John Field, and are to be sold . . . in London*, 1659. 4°. LT, O, C, E, DT; CH, MH, NU, WF, Y.

3773 —The Covenant-avenging sword brandished. *For Samuel Man*, 1643. 4°.* LT, O, C, EN, DT; BN, CH, MH, NU, TU, WF, Y.

3774 Entry cancelled.

3775 —Englands Eben-ezer. *By Robert Leyburn, for Samuel Man*, 1645. 4°.* LT, O, C, EN, DT; BN, CH, CN, MBP, MH, NU, Y.

3776 —A great wonder in Heaven. *By R.L. for Samuel Man*, 1647. 4°.* LT, O, C, HH, DT; CH, CN, MH, NU, WF, Y.

3777 —Tactica sacra. *Cantabrigiæ, excudebat Joannes Field, impensis Joannis Rothwell, Londini*, 1657. 4°. L, O, C, E, DT; BN, CH, MB, NU, Y.

3778 —Θεανθρωπος; or, God-man. *For Humphrey Moseley, and William Wilson*, 1660. 4°. LT, O, LW, CT, DT; BN, CH, MBC, MH, NU, WF, Y.

3779 **Arrowsmith, Joseph.** The loyal martyrs. [*London*, 1700?] brs. L.

3780 [–] The reformation. A comedy. *For William Cademan*, 1673. 4°. T.C.I 152. L, O, C, OW, EN; CH, CN, LC, MH, TU, Y.

3781 [–] —[Anr. ed.] —, 1683. 4°. L.

Ars clericalis: the art. 1690. *See* Gardiner, Robert.

Ars notoria: the notary art. 1657. *See* Apollonius.

Ars sciendi. 1681. *See* Gowan, Thomas.

3782 Arsy versy: or, the second martyrdom of the Rump. [*London*, 1660.] brs. LT, O; MH, WF, Y.

3783 The art and mystery of vinters. *For Will. Whitwood*, 1682. 12°. T.C.I 476. L, O, LG.

3784 L'art d'assassiner les rois. *Chez Thomas Fullher*, 1696. 12°. L, C, A; LC, WF, Y.

Art of angling. 1653. *See* Barker, Thomas.

3785 The art of assassinating kings. *Printed, and sold by E. Whitlock*, 1696. 12°. T.C.III 5. L, LG; CLC, CN, WF, Y.

3786 The art of catechising. *By J.L. for Henry Bonwicke*, 1691. 8°. T.C.II 355. L, O, OM; NU, TU, WF, Y.

3787 —Second edition. —, 1692. 12°. T.C.II 416. L, YM; CH, TSM.

3788 —Third edition. —, 1699. 12°. T.C.III 101. L, LW.

Art of complaisance. 1673. *See* Du Refuge, Eustache.

Art of contentment. Oxford. 1675. *See* Allestree, Richard.

3788A The art of courtship. *For John Stafford*, 1662. 8°. O.

3789 —[Anr. ed.] [*London*], *by I.M. for I.Back*, 1686. 8°.* L.

3789A —[Anr. ed.] —, 1687, 12°. CM.

3790 The art of cuckoldom. *Printed*, 1697. 8°. CH.

3790A The art of defence. *For John Marshall*, [1699].* T.C.III 163. NN, Y.

3791 The art of getting money. colop: 1691. 4°.* CH, CU.

Art of good husbandry. 1675. *See* T., R.

Art of heraldry. 1685. *See* Blome, Richard.

Art of living in London. 1642. *See* Peachum, Henry.

Art of love. 1700. *See* Hopkins, Charles.

Art of making devises. 1650. *See* Etienne, Henri.

3792 The art of making love. *By J. Cotterel, for Richard Tonson*, 1676. 12°. T.C.I 247. L, O, C, M; CH.

3793 The art of making love without speaking. *London, London* [sic], *for R.Bentley*, 1688. 12°. L; CLC.

Art of numbring. 1667. *See* Leybourn, William.

Art of painting. 1692. *See* Smith, Marshall.

Art of patience. 1684. *See* Allestree, Richard.

Art of practical gauging. 1669. *See* Newton, G.

Art of practical measuring. 1696. *See* Coggeshall, Henry.

3794 The art of preaching. [*n.p.*], *printed*, 1685. 8°. MH, NP.

Art of pruning. 1685. *See* Venette, Nicolas.

Art of ringing. 1676. *See* Stedman, Fabian.

Art of self-government. 1691. *See* B., G.

Art of speaking. 1676. *See* Lamy, Bernard.

3795 The art of thriving. [*London*], *for J. Coniers*, 1674. brs. L; MH.

3796 The art of water-drawing. *For Henry Brome*, 1660. 4°. LT, C, OC; CSU.

Art of wheedling. 1679. *See* Head, Richard.

3797 **Artaxerxes.** The folly and wisdom of the ancients. *For F. Smith*, 1661. 4°.* LT, YM; CH.

3798 **Artemidorus.** Gwir ddeonglida breuddwydion. *Shrewsbury*, 1698. 8°. AN.

3799 —The interpretation of dreames. Fourth edition. *By Bernard Alsop*, 1644. 8°. LT, CCH; MU.

3800 — —Fifth edition. *By Elizabeth Alsop*, 1656. 8°. L, O.

3801 — —Tenth edition. *By B.G. and S.K. and are to be sold by T.Bever*, 1690. 12°. T.C.II 327. MH.

Artemisa to Cloe. 1679. *See* Rochester, John Wilmot, *earl of.*

3802 **Arthur, John.** Catalogus librorum bibliothecae . . . Joannis Arthurii. [*London*, 1682/3.] 4°. L, O, OP, CS, HH; MH, NPT, JF.

3803 Articles against the Lord Mandevill. *For John Gr*, 1642. CS, EN; CH, CSS, WF.

Articles agreed on. Edinburgh, 1648. *See* Scotland. Estates.

3803A Articles agreed upon between Coll. Richard Thornton. 1645. 4°.* YM.

Articles agreed upon by the arch-bishops. [*London*], 1642. *See* Church of England.

3804 Articles agreed upon the 6. of May 1646. by Capt. Gannock. [*London*], *by T.B. for H. Tucke and F. Tyton*, 1646. brs. LT; MH.

Articles and acts. 1642. *See* England. Parliament.

3804A The articles and charge exhibited by the court-marshall ... Laughorn. *By B.A.*, 9 Ap. 1649. 4°.* CT.

3805 The articles and charge of impeachment against the German lady. *For G. Winnam*, 1663. 4°.* MH.

3806 The articles and charge of the armie against four-score of the Parliament men. [*London*], *for C.VV.*, 1648. 4°.* LT, CJ, HH, DT; CH, CN, MH.

3807 The articles and charge of the army, exhibited in Parliament. *For C.W.*, 1648. 4°.* LT; OWC.

3808 The articles and charge of the officers. October 18, 1648. [*London*], *printed Octob. 20*, 1648. 4°.* LT, O, HH; CN, WF, Y.

3809 The articles and charge proved in Parliament against Doctor Walton. *Printed*, 1641. 4°.* LT, O, HH; CLC, MBA, NN, Y.

3810 The articles and conditions of the perpetuall peace, concluded ... at Munster. *Printed at Rotterdam by Haest van Voortganck*, 1648. *Reprinted at London by Robert White*, 1648. 4°.* LT, O, MR; WF, Y.

Articles and orders. [1647.] *See* Company of adventurers.

Articles and ordinances. Edinburgh, 1643. *See* Scotland. Estates.

3811 Articles and rules for the better government of His Majesties forces. *Sold by M. Pitt, London*, 1673. 8°. T.C.I 154. L, O, OC; WF, Y.

3812 —[Anr. ed.] *Edinburgh, Andrew Anderson*, 1675. 4°. ALDIS 2041. EN.

3813 —[Anr. ed.] *Edinburgh, by the heir of Andrew Anderson*, 1678. 8°.* EN, FSF.

3813A —[Anr. ed.] —, 1691. 8°. WF.

3814 Articles concerning the svrrender of Newark. *For Edward Husband, May* 11. 1646. 4°.* LT, O, OC, DT.

3815 Articles concerning the svrrender of Oxford. *Oxford, by Leonard Lichfield*, 1646. 4°.* MADAN 1877. L, O, OC, CS, CT; CH, CN, WF, Y.

3815A Articles concerning the surrender of Wallingford. *Oxford, by Henry Hall*, 1676. 4°.* MADAN 1897. O, LSE.

3816 Articles concerning the svrrender of VVorcester. *Oxford, by Leonard Lichfield*, (*ca. July* 22) 1646. 4°.* MADAN 1896. OL.

3817 Articles concluded & agreed on for the surrender of Oxford. *For Edward Husband, Iune* 24. 1646. 4°.* MADAN 1880. LT, O, OC, CT, EN; CH, CN, MH, TU, Y.

3818 Articles concluded upon by the officers and souldiers ... 18, 20 Sept. *Edinburgh, by Evan Tyler*, 1648. 4°. ALDIS 1305. EN; WF, Y.

3819 Articles exhibited against Benjamin Spencer. [1642.] 4°.* CH, NU.

3820 Articles exhibited against Clonell [*sic*] Edward King. *Printed*, 1644. 4°.* DT.

3821 Articles exhibited against Sir Philipp Carteret. [*London*], *printed*, 1642. 4°.* LT, O; MHL, WF, Y.

3822 Articles exhibited against the King. *For John Gilbert*, 1648. 4°.* LT; LC, WF.

3823 Articles exhibited in the Parliament, against VVilliam Beale. [*London*], *printed*, 1641. 4°.* L, O, CT, E, DT; CN, MH, NU, WF, Y.

3824 Articles exhibited to the honourable House of Commons ... against the Lord Inchiquine. *For Hu. Tuckey*, 1647. 4°.* LT, LVF, OC; CH.

Articles for regulating. Edinburgh, 1670. *See* Scotland. Commissioners.

3825 Articles for the delivering up of Lichfield-Close. *For Edward Husband, July* 18, 1646. 4°.* LT, O, BC, SS, YM; WF, Y.

3826 Articles for the surrender of Colchester. [*London*], *for R.A.*, 1648. 4°.* LT, HH; NU.

3827 Februar. 1. 1645. Articles for the surrender of the city of Chester. *By Rich. Cotes*, 1645[6]. 4°.* LT; MH, NN, Y.

3828 Articles given by   and delivered to the church-wardens. *By Da. Maxwell*, 1662. 4°.* O, DT.

3829 —Anr. ed.] *For George Dawes*, 1664. 4°.* O.

3830 The articles in the treaty concluded concerning the succession. 1700. brs. O.

3831 Entry cancelled.

Articles of accusation. 1641. *See* England. Parliament, House of Commons.

3832 Articles of accusation and impeachment against VVilliam Pierce. *For George Thomlinson*, 1642. 4°.* LT, O, OC, BR, EN; MHL, Y.

3833 Articles of accusation exhibited against Sir Humphrey Davenport. 1641. 4°. O.

3833A Articles of agreement betwixt Prince Charles and the Parliament of Scotland. *For A.E.*, [1650]. brs. MAU.

3833B Articles of agreement, concluded, made, and agreed on ... Nicholas Dupin. [*London*, 1694] cap., 4°.* MH.

3834 The articles of agreement, for the surrender of Charles Fort. *By E.P.* 4 *June*, 1646, 1646. 4°.* MADAN 1869. LT, O, OC, DT; Y.

3835 The articles of agreement, for the surrender of the strong & invincible castle of Edinborough. *By R.W.*, 1651. 4°.* LT, EN, DT; Y.

3836 Articles of agreements, made, and concluded the 11th day of January, 1651 ... Barbadoes. *Prited* [*sic*] *for Francis Coles*, 1652. 4°. LT, GH; CH, RPJ.

3837 Entry cancelled.

Articles of Christian faith. 1689. *See* Cox, John.

3838 Entry cancelled.

Articles of Christian religion, approved. 1648. *See* Church of England.

3839 The articles of Exeter. *For John Williams*, 1647. 4°.* LT; UCLA.

3840 —[Anr. ed.] *Printed*, 1647. 4°.* MH, Y.

3841 The articles of Galway. *Dublin, Andrew Crook*, [1692]. 4°.* DIX 251. L, DCA, DI, DN.

3842 Articles of high crimes . . . against Lt. Col. Tho. Kelsey. *For Livewel Chapman*, 1659. 4°.* LT, O, LG, HH; CH, MIU, WF.

Articles of high misdemeanors humbly offered. [*London*, 1679/80.] *See* Oates, Titus.

3843 Articles of high-treason against Major General Harrison. *For Marm. Johnson*, 1660. 4°.* LT, YM; MH.

3844 Articles of high treason against William Petre. [c. 1684.] fol. O.

3845 Articles of high-treason and other high crimes and misdemeanours against the Dutchess of Portsmouth. [*London*, 1680.] brs. L; MH.

3846 —[Anr. ed. . . . misdemeanors . . . Dutches] [*London*, 1680.] brs. O; CH, MH, WF, Y.

3847 Articles of high treason, and other high misdemeanors, against the Lord Kymbolton. *By Robert Barker and the assignes of John Bull*, 1641 [2]. 4°.* LT, O, CJ, BR; CH, CU, MH, TU, WF, Y.

3848 —[Anr. ed.] [*London*], *for Iohn Hammond*, 1641 [2]. 4°.* MH.

3949 Articles of high-treason drawn up in the name of all the commoners of England against one hundred and fifty judges. *For George Horton*, 1652. 4°.* LT, OC.

3850 Articles of high-treason exhibited against the Fort-Royall. [*London*], *printed*, 1647. 4°.* LT, O; CH, CN, WF, Y.

3851 Articles of high treason, made and enacted. [*London*], *for Erasmus Thorowgood*, [1660]. 4°.* LT, CPL; CH, CLC, NU.

3852 Articles of impeachment against George Lord Digby. *For John Wright*, Feb. 28. 1642. 4°.* L, O, C, HH, EN; CH, CLC, NU, WF, Y.

3853 —[Anr. ed.] *For John Franke*, 1642. 4°.* LT, O, HH; WF, Y.

3854 Articles of impeachment against Sir John Gvrney. *July 12. For J. H. and T. Ryder*, 1642. 4°.* LT, O, C.

3854A Articles of impeachment against the Lord Maior of London. *Ryder*, 1642. 4°.* LG.

3855 Articles of impeachment, agreed upon by the army. *For George Whiting, June 19*. 1647. 4°.* LT, OC, CT.

3856 Articles of impeachment and accusation exhibited . . . against Colonell Nathaniel Fiennes. *Printed*, 1643. 4°.* LT, O, CT, BR, DT; CH, CN, MH, RPJ, Y.

3857 Articles of impeachment exhibited against Col. Robert Gibbons. *For G. Horton*, 1659. 4°.* LT; CH, MH.

Articles of impeachment of high treason. 1648. *See* Prynne, William.

3858 Articles of impeachment of high treason and other hgih [sic] crimes, . . . against Thomas Earl of Danby. [*London*, 1678.] cap., 4°.* L, O, MR, EN; CLC, CN, MH, WF, Y.

3859 Articles of impeachment of high treason, and other high crimes . . . against Thomas Lord Conningsby. 1693. brs. MC.

3860 Articles of impeachment of transcendent crimes . . . Philip Jones. *Printed*, 1659. 4°.* LT, O, C, AN; CH.

Articles of inquiry. *See* Church of England.

Articles of inquiry concerning. 1663. *See* Granville, Denis.

3860A Articles of enquirie for surveying the bishops-lands. *By R. Cotes, for John Bellamy*, 1697. 4°.* CLC, MIU.

3860B The articles of Limerick. [*London*, 1691.] cap., fol.* C, DRS.

3861 Articles of peace and union. 1654. fol. O, DT.

3862 Articles of peace concluded at Munster . . . 24 Oct. *Edinburgh, Evan Tyler*, 1648. 4°.* ALDIS 1306. OW, EN; Y.

3863 Articles of peace, made and concluded with the Irish rebels. *By Matthew Simmons*, 1649. 4°. LT, C, DT; CH, MH, WF, Y.

3864 Articles of peace, made, concluded. *Dublin, by William Bladen*, 1646. 4°.* L, C, HH; CN, WF.

3865 Articles of presentments, to be inquired of. *Dublin, by John Crook*, 1665. 4°.* C.

3866 Articles of regulation concerning the session. *Edinburgh, by the heirs and successors of Andrew Anderson*, 1695. fol. ALDIS 3440. L, EN; LC, WF.

3867–8 Entries cancelled.

Articles of religion. 1642. *See* Church of England.

3869 Articles of religion; or, the fourteen pillars. *For John Tompkins*, 1654. 4°.* LT; CH, MH.

3870 The articles of the charge of the VVardmore enquest. colop: *Printed at London by Richard Cotes*, [1649]. fol.* LT.

3870A —[Same title] [*London*] by   Clark, 1671. fol.* LG.

3871 The articles of the charge of Wardmore Inquest. *By Samuel Roycroft, London*, 1689, (torn). fol.* L.

3872 The articles of the faith of the church . . . at Gosport. *Printed*, 1697. Sixes. L, O; MH.

3873 The articles of the perpetual peace, concluded. *Faithfully translated out of the Dutch copie, printed there, and now reprinted at London May 2*. 1654. 4°.* LT, O, OC, CS; HR, CH, MH, NPT, WF, Y.

3874 The articles of the rendition of Edenburgh-Castle. *By E. Griffin*, 1650. 4°.* LT, O, CCL, EN, DT; CH, CN, MBP, WF, Y.

3875 The articles of the rendition of Elizabeth-Castle in the Isle of Jersey. *By Edw. Griffin*, 1651. 4°.* LT, O; CLC.

3876 The articles of the surrender of the city of Yorke. *For Mathew Walbancke, July 23*, 1644. 4°.* LT, E; NU, WF, Y.

3876A The articles of the treaty of peace. *By W. Onley, and are to be sold by R. Baldwin*, 1697. 4°. CH, WF.

3877 Articles of treason and high misdimeanours, committed by Iohn Pim. [*London*, 1649.] brs. LT.

3878 Articles of treason exhibited in Parliament, against Edward Earl of Clarendon. [1667.] brs. L, O, OP.

Articles of visitation. *See* Church of England.

3879–81 Entries cancelled.

3882 The articles or charge exhibited in Parliament, against Matthew Wren . . . [*London*], *printed*, 1641. 4°.* LT, O, CP, YM; NU.

3883 Articles presented against this Parliament. *Printed*, 1648. 4°.* MH, TU, WF.

3884   Articles published at Berlin. *Printed*, 1679. fol.* L; CLC, MH, Y.

3885   The articles, settlement and offices of the Free Society of Traders in Pennsylvania. *For Benjamin Clark,* 1682. fol.* L, O, LCP; CH, MH, PHS, RPJ, WCL.

3886   Articles stipulated and required from Old Nick. *Printed,* 1680. 4°.* CH, CLC, CN, WF, Y.

3886A   Articles to be diligently enquired of. [*London?* 1662.] brs. WF.

    Articles to be enquired of. *See* Church of England.

3887   Articles to be propounded and treated upon, touching the rendring of the garrison of Oxford. [*Oxford, by L. Lichfield*], 1646. cap., 4°.* MADAN 1863. O.

3888   Articles to unite the Catholicks and Evangelicks. *Printed,* 1661. 4°.* LT, O; MB.

3889   Articles whereupon it was agreed. *J. Bill & C. Barker* 1662. LIL.

3889A   Articulau neu byrgaiau. [1664].* AN.

3890   Articuli Lambethani. *Typis G. D. veneunt apud Rob. Beaumont.* 1651. 8°. L, O, CT, EN, DT; CLC, NU, WF.

3891   —[Anr. ed.] *Typis G. D.,* 1651. 12°. OC, CS; TSM.

3892   Articuli religionis xxxix. *Oxon,* 1691. 12°. C.

3893–4   Entries cancelled.

    Artificial clock-maker. 1696. *See* Derham, William.

    Artificiall embellishments. *Oxford,* 1663. *See* Jeamson, Thomas.

    Artificial versifying. 1689. *See* Pater, John.

    Artis logicæ. Oxonii, 1691. *See* Aldrich, Henry.

    Artis poeticæ. 1653. *See* Lloyd, Richard.

    Artis rationis. Oxonii, 1673. *See* Walker, Obadiah.

    Artless midnight thoughts. 1684. *See* Killigrew, *Sir* William.

3895   The arts and pernicious designs of Rome. *For Henry Brome,* 1680. 4°. T.C.I 396. O, CCL; CH, MIU.

    Arts master-piece. 1660. *See* Wecker, John Jeams.

    Art's master-piece, or. 1697. *See* K., C.

    Arts of grandeur. 1670. *See* Stubbe, Henry.

    Art's treasury. 1688. *See* White, John.

3896   **Arundell of Wardour, Henry Arundell, 3d lord.** Poems written by. colop: *Printed,* 1679. brs. L, O; CN, MH, Y.

3897   —[Anr. ed.]—colop: *Printed,* 1679. *By a copy under his own Hand.* brs. L, O; CH, MH.

3898   —Verses made by. [*London,* 1679?] brs. L; TU.

3899   **Arundell, Thomas.** The confession and conversion. *By J. Hayes, for the author, sold by S. Thomson,* 1662. 12°. L, O; CLL, NPT.

3899A   [–] The holy breathings of a devout soul. *For Joan Convers,* 1695. 12°. LW.

    Arundel, Thomas Howard, *earl*. *See* Norfolk, Thomas Howard, *duke of.*

3900   **Arwaker, Edmund, *elder*.** The ministration of publick baptism. *By J. Leake, for Edward Poole,* 1687. 4°.* L, O, CS, LCL, DT; CLC, NPT, NHC, NU, WF.

3901   —Thoughts well employ'd. *By Tho. Warren for Francis Saunders,* 1695. 8°. T.C.II 536. L, O, C, LSC; CSB.

3902   — —Second edition. —, 1697. 8°. L; CU, LC.

3903   **Arwaker, Edmund, *younger*.** The apparition. *For R. Bentley, and sold by R. Baldwin,* 1689. 4°.* C, CT.

3904   Entry cancelled.

3905   —An elegy on Her Grace Elizabeth Duches of Ormond. *In the Savoy, by Tho. Newcomb.* 1684. fol.* O, OC; CH, CLC, Y.

3906   —An elegy on His Excellency Lieutenant-General Tolmach. *For Francis Saunders, and sold by Randal Taylor,* 1694. fol.* L, O; TU.

3907   —An epistle to Monsieur Boileau. *By Tho. Warren for Francis Saunders,* 1694. fol.* L, O; CLC, CN, MH, TU, WF, Y.

3908   —Fons perennis. A poem. *For Henry Bonwicke,* 1686. 4°.* T.C.II 158. L, O, C, CT, DT; CH, CN, MH, WF, Y.

3909   —God's king the people's blessing. A sermon. *Dublin, Joseph Ray,* 1698. 4°.* DIX 307. L, DI.

3910   —A Pindaric ode upon our late soveraign lady of blessed memory, Queen Mary. *For Rich. Parker,* 1695. fol.* L, O, C, OC, AU; CH, CU, MH, TU, WF, Y.

3911   —A poem humbly dedicated to the Queen. *Randal Taylor,* 1688. fol.* O, HH, OC, AU; CLC, MB, MIU.

3912   —The second part of The vision. *By J. Playford for Henry Playford,* 1685. fol.* L, O, HH, SP; CH, CN, MH, PU, WF, Y.

3913   —The vision. *By J. Playford, for Henry Playford,* 1685. fol.* T.C.II 126. L, O, C, OB, HH; CH, CN, MH, TU, WF, Y.

3914   — —Second edition. *By J. Playford for H. Playford,* 1685. fol.* L, O, HH; CLC, MH, TU, WF, Y.

3915   —A votive table. *For W. Canning,* 1689. fol.* O, HH, OC, AU; CH, CLC, MH, PU, WF, Y.

    Arwaker, Edward. *See* Arwaker, Edmund.

3916   As it is not unknown. 1679. STEELE 3p 2461. cap. fol.* HAMILTON PALACE.

    As not unknowne. [1645.] *See* Douglas, *Lady* Eleanor.

3916A   As on the dearest Strephon's breast. [*London*] *for P. Brooksby,* [1687?] brs. L.

3917   As our declarations. 24 February 1640 [1]. cap., fol.* STEELE 1836. L, O, LS, HH.

    As you were. 1647. *See* Woodward, Hezekiah.

3917A   As you were, or, the new French exercise. [*London*], printed, 1674. 4°.* WF.

    Ascent to the mount. 1699. *See* Lead, Jane.

    Asceticks. 1696. *See* Stephens, Edward.

3918   **Ascham, Antony.** An answer to the vindication of Doctor Hamond. *For Francis Tyton,* 1650. 4°.* LT, O, CT; CH, WF, Y.

3918A   [–] The bounds & bonds of publique obedience. *For John Wright,* 1640. 4°. LT, O, ON, HH; CH, CN, NU, WF, Y.

3918B   [–] —Second edition. —, 1650. 4°. LT, LW, YM; CH, CU, NU, TC, Y.

3918C   [–] A combate between two seconds. *For John Wright,* 1649. 4°.* LT, O, ENC; MH, NU, WF.

3919   —A discourse: wherein is examined. *For Humphrey Moseley,* 1648. 8°. CT, OM, LW, LCL, E; NU.

3920   —[Anr. ed.] *Printed:* 1648. 8°. LT, O, C, LVF, YM; CH, CN, LC, MH, Y.

3921 [–] Γενεσις καὶ τελος ἐξουσιας, The original & end of civil power. *Printed*, 1649. 4°.* LT, O, C, MR, DT; CH, CU, NU, TU, WF, Y.

3922 —Of the confusions and revolutions of goverments [sic]. *By W. Wilson*, 1649. 8°. L, O, C, EN, DT; CH, CN, LC, MH, NU, Y.

3923 —A reply to a paper of Dr Sandersons. *By A. J., to be sold by T. R.*, 1650. 4°. LT, O, EC, HH, EN; CH, MH, MIU, WF, Y.

3924 [–] A seasonable discourse, wherein is examined what is lawful. *Printed, and are to be sold by Rich. Janeway*, 1689. 4°. T.C.II 255. L, O, C, MR, EN; CH, CN, LC, MH, NU, Y.

3925 [**Ascue, George.**] A letter sent to the Earl of Warwick. *For Edward Husband, July 8.* 1648. 4°.*LT, MR; CH, NN.

3926 [**Asgill, John.**] An argument proving, that according. [*London*] anno dom. 1700. 8°. L, O, CT, MR, EN; BN, CH, CU, LC, MH, NU, Y.

3927 —An essay on a registry. *Printed*, 1698. 4°.* L, O, LCP, LL; CLC, MB, NC, PU, YL.

3928 — —[Anr. ed.] *John Astwood*, 1698. 8°. L, CT; MH, MHL, Y.

3929 [–] Remarks on the proceedings of the commissioners. *London & Westminster, printed*, 1695. 8°.* L; LC, PU.

3930 [–] —[Anr. ed.] *Printed*, 1696. 8°.* L, O, LG; CH, LC, MH, NC, WF, Y.

3931 —The reply to some reflections on Mr. Asgill's essay. *John Attwood*, 1699. 12°.* L; NC.

3932 [–] Several assertions proved, in order to create another species of money. [*London*, 1696.] 8°. L, O, C; CH, LC, MH, NC, PU, Y.

3933 **Ash, St. George,** *bp.* A sermon preached . . . January the 9th, 1693[4]. *Dublin, by Joseph Ray for William Norman*, 1694. 4°.* DIX 259. L, O, C, DT, CD; NP, WF.

3934 **A[sh], T[homas].** Carolina; or a description. *for W. C. to be sold by Mrs. Grover*, 1682. 4°.* L, O, OC, AU, GH; CH, CN, LC, MH, RPJ, Y.

3935 **Ashburnham, John.** A letter written by . . . Novemb. 26, 1647. *For Richard Royston*, 1647. 4°.* LT, O, C; BN, CH, CLC, MH, Y.

3936 —The true copie of a letter from. [*London*], *printed*, 1648. 4°.* LT, O, LG, DT; CH, CU, MH, TU, WF, Y.

3937 **Ashby,** *Sir* **John.** The account given by . . . of the engagement at sea. *For Randal Taylor*, 1691. 4°.* L, O, C, MR; HR, CH, CN, RPJ, WF, Y.

3938 — —[Anr. ed.] — *Edinburgh*, 1691. 4°.* ALDIS 3122. EN; LC.

3939 **Ashby, Richard.** The defence of the people called Quakers. *Printed and sold by T. Sowle*, 1699. 4°. L, C, LF, BBN; IE, MH, PH, PSC, WF.

3940 —The folly of a libeller made manifest. *Printed and sold by T. Sowle*, 1699. 4°.* L, O, LF, BBN; CH, MH, PH, PSC, Y.

3940A —A remark upon the baths in . . . Bath. *Printed and sold by T. Sowle*, 1699. fol.* LF.

3941 —A salutation of love. *Printed and sold by T. Sowle*, 1699. 4°.* L, C, LF, BBN; IE, MH, PH, WF, Y.

3942 [–] Some general observations upon Dr. Stillingfleet's book. *Printed*, 1672. 4°. CS, MC; CN, NU, Y.

3943 [–] The true light owned and vindicated. *Printed and sold by T. Sowle*, 1699. 4°.* L, LF, BBN; MH, NU, PH, WF, Y.

3944 **Ashe, John.** An answer to divers scandals. *By Thomas Newcomb*, 1654. fol.* LT, O, BR; MH, NN.

3945 [–] A perfect relation of all the passages and proceedings of the Marquesse of Hartford. *For Joseph Hunscot, and I. Wright*, 12. Aug. 1642. 4°.* LT, O, C, EC, BR; MH, MIU, WF, Y.

3946 —A second letter sent from. *By A. N. for Ed. Husbands and I. Francke*, 1642. August 16. 4°.* LT, O, BR, HH, DT; CH, CN, LC, MH, Y.

3947-8 Entries cancelled.

3949 **Ashe, Simeon.** The best refvge for the most oppressed. *For Edward Brewster and Iohn Burroughs*, 1642. 4°.* LT, O, C, EN, DT; CH, MH, NU, WF, Y.

3950 —Christ the riches of the gospel. *By A. M. for G. Sawbridge*, 1654. 4°.* LT, O, LCL, LW; CH, MH, NU, WF, Y.

3951 —The church sinking. *By G. M. for Edward Brewster*, 1645. 4°.* LT, O, C, SS, EN; CH, MH, NU, WF, Y.

3952 —The doctrine of zeal explained. *By A. M. for George Saubridge*, 1655. 4°.* L, O, C, CK, SP; MB, MH, NU, WF.

3953 —The efficiency of Gods grace. *By A. M. for G. Sawbridge*, 1654. 4°.* L, O, C, LW, ENC; MB, MH, NNL, WF, Y.

3954 —The faithfull Christians gain by death. *By A. M. for George Sawbridge*, 1659. 4°.* LT, O, CS, ENC, DT; MH, MIU, NPT, WF, Y.

3955 —Gods incomparable goodnesse. *By W. Wilson for Edward Brewster*, 1647. 4°.* LT, O, C, SS, DT; CH, MH, NU, WF, Y.

3956 —Good covrage discovered. *By Iohn Dawson for Iohn Burroughs*, 1642. 4°.* LT, O, CS, BR, SS; CH, MH, NU, TU, WF.

3956A — —[Anr. ed.] *By John Dawson for Laurence Chapman*, 1642. 4°.* C, CT; MB, NU, TU.

3957 —The good mans death lamented. *By A. M. for George Sabwridge* [sic], 1655. 4°.* L, O, E, ENC; CH, MH, NU, WF, Y.

3958 [–] Gray hayres crowned . . . Redriff. *By A. M. for George Sawbridge*, 1655. 4°. LT; MH, NU, TU, WF, Y.

3959 — —[Anr. ed. . . . Redrith] —, 1655. 4°. L, O, C, E, EN; LLC, CN, NPT, WF, Y.

3960 Entry cancelled.

3961 —Living loves. *By T. M. for Ralph Smith*, 1654. 4°. LT, O, CSS, E, EN; CH, CN, NU, WF, Y.

3962 — —Second edition. *For Ralph Smith*, 1654. 4°. L, O, CK, ENC, DT; CH, CLC, CH, NPT, WF.

3963 — —Third edition. —, 1656. 4°. L, C, LG, E; CLC, MH, NU, WF, Y.

3964 —Reall thankfulnesse. *By G. Miller for Edward Brewster*, 1645. 4°.* O, LCL, LP, AN; CH, MB, MH, NPT, NU.

3965 —Religiovs covenanting directed. *By G. M. for Tho. Underhill*, 1646. 4°.* LT, O, C, SS, EN; CH, MH, NU, WF, Y.

3966 —Self-surrender unto God. *For E. Brewster*, [1648]. 4°.* LT, O, C, LSC, OCC; CH, MH, NU, WF, Y.

3967 —A svpport for the sinking heart. *By G. M. and are to be sold by Thomas Vnderhill,* 1642. 4°.* LT, O, LW, SS, DT; CU, MH, NPT, NU, WF, Y.

3968 —A trve relation, of the most chiefe occurrences. *By G. M. for Edward Brewster,* 1644. 4°.* LT, O, EC, HH; CLC, CN, MH, NU, WF, Y.

3696 **Ashe, Thomas.** A generall table. Third edition. *By I. Flesher, for W. Lee, D. Pakeman, and G. Bedel,* 1652. 8°. L, O, C; LC, MHL, WF.

3970 — —"Third" edition. —, 1653. 8°. L, CCA.

3971 — —Fourth edition. *By John Streater, Eliz. Flesher, and Henry Twyford, assigns of Richard Atkyns and Edward Atkyns. To be sold by George Sawbridge, John Place, John Bellinger, William Place, Tho. Basset, Robert Pawlet, Christopher Wilkinson, Tho. Dring, Will. Jacob, Allan Banks, Ch. Harper, John Amery, John Poole, John Leigh,* 1672. fol. L, LM, BAMB, DT; MH, WF.

3972 —The law of obligations and conditions. *For J. Walthoe,* 1693. 8°. T.C.II 439. L, O, C, EN, DT; MIU, NCL, PU, V, WF.

3973 **Ashenden, Thomas.** No penalty, no peace. *For John Smith,* 1682. 4°.* L, O; WF.

3973A [–] The Presbyterian Pater Noster. [*London?* 1680.] brs. L, O; CH, CN, MH, WF, Y.

3974 —Some reflections upon a late pamphlet. colop: [*London*], *for Joseph Hindmarsh,* 1681. brs. L, O; CH, CN, MH, WF.

3974A The ashes of the just smell sweet. [*London,* 1689.] brs. L, O, HH; CH, PL, Y.

3975 **Ashhurst, Sir Henry.** Some remarks upon the life of Nathaniel Heywood. *For Tho. Cockerill,* 1695. 8°. L, O, C, LW; NGT, WF.

3976 **Ashhurst, William.** Reasons against agreement with a late printed paper. *Printed,* 1648. 4°.* LT, O, C, OC, CT; BN, CH, CU, MH, NU, TU, WF, Y.

3977 — —[Anr. ed.] *For Tho. Underhill,* 1648. 4°.* L, OC, CT, HH; CH, CN, MH, NU, WF, Y.

3978 — —[Anr. ed.] *For Thomas Underhill,* 1648. *And now reprinted in* 1659. *At the charge of Sir Francis Nethersole.* 1659. 4°.* L, O, C; CLC, CN, MH, WF, Y.

3979 [**Ashley, Thomas.**] Prosperous proceedings in Ireland. *For Iohn Hancocke. October* 19, 1642. 4°.* LT, O, EC.

3980 —Speech to the House of Commons. 1673. fol.* O.

3981 **Ashmole, Elias.** Bibliotheca Ashmoliana. A catalogue of the library. 22 Feb. 1694. 4°. L, O, OP.

3982 —A catalogue of the peers. *For William Gilbertson,* 1661. brs. O.

[–] Fasciculus chemicus: or, 1650. *See* Dee, Arthur.

3983 —The institution, laws & ceremonies of the most noble order of the Garter. *By J. Macock, for Nathanael Brooke,* 1672. fol. T.C.I 110. L, O, C, EN, DT; BN, CH, CN, LC, MH, WF, Y.

3984 — —[Anr. ed.] *For Thomas Dring,* 1693. fol. T.C.II 459. L, O, CS, ES, DT; BN, MH.

3985 [–] Sol in ascendente: or, the glorious appearance of Charles the second. *For N. Brook,* 1660. 4°.* L, O; MH.

3986 [–] —[Anr. ed.] *Edinburgh, re-printed by Christopher Higgins,* 1660. 4°. ALDIS 1675. EN; MH, Y.

3987 —Theatrum chemicum Britannicum. *By J. Grismond, for Nath: Brooke,* 1652. 8°. LT, O, C, LPO, ES; BN, CH, CN, LC, MH, NC, Y.

3988 —The way to bliss. *By John Grismond for Nath. Brooke,* 1658. 4°. LT, O, LWL, GU; CLC, LC, MH, MMO, Y.

Ashrea, or, 1665. *See* Manning, Edward.

3989 **Ashton, Charles.** Aquæ baptismus. 1697. brs. O; WF.

3990 **Ashton, John.** A copy of Mr. Ashton's paper. [1691.] brs. L, O, OM, CS, EN; CH, CN, IU, WF.

3991 [–] De ventre inspiciendo: or, remarks. [*London*], April. [1691.] cap., fol.* L, LL, OC, CT, MR; TU.

3992 —A true copy of part of that paper which Mr. Ashton left. [*London,* 1691.] brs. OC, EC, OM, MR, EN; CN, Y.

3992A **Ashton, Ralph.** A great victory at Appleby. *For R. Smithurst,* 1648. 4°.* LT, LG; WF.

3992B **Ashton, Thomas.** Satan in Samuels mantle. *By T. R.,* 1659. 4°.* L, O.

3993 **Ashwell, George.** Catalogus librorum. Oxford, 5 May 1696. 4°. L, OC.

3994 —De ecclesia Romana dissertatio. *Oxoniæ, e theatro Sheldoniano,* 1688. 4°. O, C, OB, MC, DT; MH, NU, TU, WF, Y.

3995 —De socino et socinianismo dissertatio. *Oxoniæ, excudebat H: Hall, impensis Ric. Davis,* 1680. 8°. MADAN 3256. T.C.I 371, L, O, CT, NPT, DT; BN, NP, NU, Y.

3996 — —[Anr. ed.] *Oxoniæ impressi: prostant autem venales Londini apud J. Adamson,* 1693. 8°. T.C.II 425. O, LW.

3997 —Fides apostolica: or a discourse. *Oxford, by Leon. Lichfield, for Jo. Godwin and Ric. Davis,* 1653. 8°. MADAN 2222. LT, O, C, E, DT; CLC, MH, NU, WF, Y.

3998 —Gestvs evcharisticvs or a discourse. *Oxford, by W. H. for Joseph Godwin and Richard Davis,* 1663. 8°. MADAN 2630. L, O, CE, YM, EN; CH, MH, NU, Y.

Ashwell, Samuel. Ashwell, 1641. A new almanacke. [1641]. *See* Almanacs.

3999 **Ashwood, Bartholomew.** The best treasure. *For William Marshal,* 1681. 8°. T.C.I 414. L, O, LCL; MH, NPT, NU, WF, Y.

4000 —The heavenly trade. *For Samuel Lee,* 1678. 8°. CLC, CN, IU, NU, WF.

4000A — —[Anr. ed.] —, 1679. 8°. T.C.I 347. L, LCL, LW; CH, CN, NU, Y.

4001 — —Second edition. *For William Marshall,* 1688. 8°. T.C.II 234. L; NU.

4002 Asinus onustus. The asse overladen. *For John Williams,* 1642. 4°. L, O, CS, LG, DT; CH, CU, LC, MH, NU, Y.

Aslee, Richard. Εφημερις ... sive. [1647]. *See* Almanacs.

4003 **Aspin, William.** The envious man's character. *By B. W. for Ralph Smith,* 1684. 4°.* L, O, BP, DT; WF.

4003A **Aspinwall, William.** The abrogation of the Jewish sabbath. *By J. C. for Livewell Chapman,* 1657 .4°.* L; MH, MWA.

4004 —A brief description of the fifth monarchy. *By M. Simmons, to be sold by Livewell Chapman,* 1653. 4°.* LT, SP, DT; LC, MB, NN, NU.

4005 —Certaine queries touching the ordination of ministers. *By Mathew Simmons for Henry Overton, and are to be sold by J. Pounce,* 1647. 4°.* LT, O, C, E, DT; CH, MH, NU, RPJ, WF.

4006 —An explication and application of the seventh chapter of Daniel. *By R. I. for Livewell Chapman,* 1654. 4°.* LT, O, DC; NU.

4007 —The legislative povver is Christ's. *For Livewel Chapman,* 1656. 12°. LT, O, LCL; MH, NHC, NN, NU, RPJ, WF.

4008 —A premonition of sundry sad calamities. *For Livewell Chapman,* 1655, 4°.* LT, O, C; MB, NN, Y.

4009 —Thunder from Heaven against the back-sliders. *For Livewell Chapman,* 1655. 4°.* LT; MH.

4010 —The work of the age. *By R. I. for Livewell Chapman,* 1655. 4°. LT; NU, WF.

4011 **Aspley, John.** Speculum nauticum. A looking glasse for seamen. Fourth edition. *By Thomas Harper, to be sold by George Hurlock,* 1647. 4°. L.

4012 — —Fifth edition. *By Thomas Harper,* 1655. 4°. CT; CH.

4013 — —Sixth edition. *By. W. Leybourn, for George Hurlock,* 1662. 4°. L.

4014 — —[Anr. ed.] *By W. Godbid for George Hurlock,* 1668. 4°. O.

4015 — —Ninth edition. *By R. W. for William Fisher, R. Boulter and R. Smith,* 1678. 4°. T.C.I 337. OC; MH.

4016 **Assarino, Luca.** La stratonica: or the unfortunate queen. *By John Field,* 1651. 4°. LT, O, C; CLC, CN, MH, NC.

4016A — —[Anr. ed.] *By J. F. for H. Moseley,* 1651, 4°. CU.

4017 An assembly lecture or a sermon. [*London*], *printed,* 1674. 4°.* L, O, MR; CN, MIU, PU, Y.

Assembly-man. 1662/3. *See* Birkenhead, *Sir* John.

4018 The assembly of moderate divines. [1681.] brs. L, O.

4019 The assenters sayings. *For Henry Jones,* 1681. 4°.* T.C.I 475. L, O, BR, YM, SP; CH, NU, WF, Y.

4020 Assertio juris monarchici in regno Scotorum. 1653. 4°.* O, LL; WF.

Assertion for true . . . 1642. *See* Stoughton, William.

Assertion of the government. Edinburgh, 1641. *See* Gillespie, George.

Asses complaints. 1661. *See* Griffin, Lewis.

4021 An assessment upon the precinct of—. *Dublin, by William Bladen,* 1652. 4°.* DIX 350. DM.

4022 [**Assheton, William.**] An admonition to a deist. *By T. B. for Robert Clavel,* 1685. 4°.* T.C.II 112. L, O, C, CE, CT; CN, NU, PL, WF, Y.

4023 —The cases of scandal and persecution. *By J. D. for R. Royston & R. Chiswell,* 1674. 8°. T.C.I 164. L, O, CT, LW, DT; LC, WF.

4024 —A conference with an Anabaptist, part 1. *By R. R. for B. Aylmer,* 1695. 8°. T.C.II 517. O, C, CT, OC, EC; CLC, NPT, Y.

4025 [–] The country-parson's admonition. *Printed,* 1686. 8°.* T.C.II 245. CS, EC; Y.

4025A [–] —[Anr. ed.] *For R. Wilde,* 1688. 24°. T.C.II 229. OC.

4026 [–] The cry of royal innocent blood. *For Daniel Brown and T. Benskin,* 1653. 8°. T.C.II 4. L; CLC, WF, Y.

4027 —The danger of hypocrisie. *For Richard Royston,* 1673. 4°.* T.C.I 147. L, O, C, OC, CT; CLC, LC, NU, WF, Y.

4028 [–] A defence of the country parson's admonition. *Printed, and are to be sold by R. Taylor,* 1687. 8°.* OME, DT; Y.

4028A [–] —[Anr. ed.] *For R. Wilde,* 1688. 24°. OC.

4029 [–] A defence of the plain-man's reply. *By T. B. for R. Wild,* 1688. 4°.* OCC; Y.

4029A [–] —[Anr. ed.] *For R. Wilde,* 1688. 24°. OC.

4030 —A discourse against blasphemy. Third edition. *By T. B. to be sold by Richard Simpson,* 1694. 12°.* L, O.

4031 —A discourse against I. Drunkenness. *By Tho. Braddyll, to be sold by Richard Sympson,* 1692. 12°.* T.C.II 548. L, O, OC.

4031A [–] —[Anr. ed.] *For R. Wilde,* 1692. 24°. OC.

4032 —A discourse concerning a death-bed repentance. *For Brabazon Aylmer,* 1696. 12°. T.C.II 600. L, O; CLC.

4032A — —Second edition. —, 1700. 12°. NN.

4032B —Duwielder am ddydd yr arglwydd. [1698.] 8°. AN.

4033 [–] Evangelium armatum, a specimen. *For William Garret,* 1663. 4°. L, O, C, MR, HH; CH, CU, MH, NU, WF, Y.

4034 [–] Evangelium armatum: or, the Scripture abus'd. Second edition. *For W. Garret,* 1663. Re-printed 1682. *And sold by W. Davis,* 1682. 4°. L, O, CT, HH; CH, CN, MH, NU, WF, Y.

4035 —A method of daily devotion. *For B. Aylmer,* 1697. 12°.* T.C.III 37. L.

4035A [–] The parallel between, Doleman Bradshaw. colop: *By T. H. for R. Clavel, to be sold by R. Taylor,* 1684. brs. MH.

4036 [–] —[Anr. ed.] *For Ric. Chiswell.* 1687. 24°. OC.

4037 [–] —[Anr. ed.] *Printed,* 1688. 18°.* Y.

4038 [–] The royal apology. *By T. B. for Robert Clavel and are to be sold by Randolph Taylor,* 1684. 4°. L, O, C, P, EN; CH, MH, NU, WF, Y.

4039 — —Second edition. —, 1685. 4°. O; CH, CN, LC.

4040 —A seasonable apology for the honours. *For Richard Chiswell,* 1676. 8°. T.C.I 228. L, O, C, ENC, DT; CH, CU, NU, WF, Y.

4041 —A seasonable discourse against toleration. *For Richard Rumbold,* 1685. 4°. T.C.II 91. SP; CH.

4042 —A sermon preached . . . Dec. 5, 1699. *For B. Aylmer,* 1700. 8°. T.C.III 167. CT, OC, BAMB; MBA.

4043 —A sermon preached . . . November the 21th [sic], 1700. *For J. Back,* 1700. 4°.* T.C.III 208. L, O, C, OC; Y.

4044 —A short exposition (of the preliminary questions). *By Tho. Braddyll, to be sold by Richard Simpson,* 1694. 12°.* L, O.

4045 —The substance of a late conference with M. S. *For Richard Wild,* 1690. 8°. T.C.III 73. L, OM, CT, YM, DT; WF.

4046 —A theological discourse of last vvills. *For Brab. Aylmer,* 1696. 8°. L, O, CT, LW, EN; CH, WF, Y.

4047 [–] Toleration disapprov'd. *For Francis Oxlad sen. and are to be sold by John Williams,* 1670. 4°. MADAN 2849. T.C.I 60. L, O, C, EN, AU; CH, CU, LL, NU, WF, Y.

4048 [–] —[Anr. ed.] *Oxford by William Hall for Francis Ox-lad sen.,* 1670. 4°. MADAN 2848. L, O, C, LCL, CT; CLC, CN, MBP, NU, Y.

4049 — —"Second" edition. *Oxford, by William Hall for the author,* 1670. 4°. MADAN 2850. L, O, C, EN, DT; CH, MH, TU, WF, Y.

4050 — —Third edition. *Oxford, by W. Hall, for the author, and are to be sold by Richard Royston,* [London], 1671. 4°. MADAN 2880. T.C.I 82. L, O; MH.

Assigny, Marius d'. *See* D'Assigny, Marius.
Assize of bread. 1671. *See* Powell, John.

4051 The association. [*London*], *for J. Spoorn,* [1680–82]. brs. HH.

4052 The association, agreement and protestation of the covnties of Cornvvall, and Devon. Ianuary 5, 1643. *Printed at Oxford by Leonard Lichfield, Jan.* 18, 1643 [/4]. 4°.* MADAN 1515. O, C, HH, YM; MH, NU, Y.

4053 —[Anr. ed.] *Bristoll, by Robert Barker, and John Bili* [*sic*], 1643. 4°.* O.

4054 The association, agreement, and protestation, of the covnties of Somerset. *Printed at Oxford, by Leonard Lichfield,* 1644. 4°.* MADAN 1623. L, O, C, BR, EN; WF.

Association begun. Edinburgh, 1696. *See* Scotland. Privy Council.

4055 The association for joining with the Prince of Orange. 1688. brs. MC.

Association for K. William. [London, 1696.] *See* Humfrey, John.

4056 The association oath rolls of the city of London livery companies. 1696. 8°. LSG.

4057 The association. We, whose names. *For William Churchill,* 1688. brs. L, O, HH; PL, Y.

Association. Whereas. [1699.] *See* England. Parliament.
Associators cashier'd. 1683. *See* Womock, Laurence.
Assurance of the faithfull. 1670. *See* D'Assigny, Marius.

4058 [**Astell, Mary.**] An essay in defence of the female sex. *For A. Roper and E. Wilkinson, and R. Clavel,* 1696. 8°. T.C.II 580. L, O, C, OC, GK; CH, CN, TU, WF, Y.

4059 [–] —Second edition. *For A. Roper and E. Wilkinson,* 1696. 8°. L, O, CT, GK, M; CLC, CU, MH, WF, Y.

4060 [–] —Third edition. *For A. Roper, and R. Clavel,* 1679. L, O; CH, CN, LC, OCI, Y.

4061 [–] A farther essay relating to the female-sex. *For A. Roper and E. Wilkinson,* 1696. 8°. L, O, GK; CH, CN, CU, MH, WF.

4062 [–] A serious proposal to the ladies. *For R. Wilkin.* 1694. 12°. T.C.II 518. L; CLC, TU, WF, Y.

4063 [–] —Second edition. —, 1695. 12°. T.C.II 552. L; CH, MIU, NC, WF.

4064 [–] —Third edition. *By T. W. for R. Wilkin,* 1696. 12°. L, O; CH.

4065 [–] —"Second" edition. *For Richard Wilkin,* 1697. 12°. L, O, LW, AU; CJC, CN, MH, NU, TU, Y.

4065A [–] —Part II. —, 1697. 12°. T.C.III 10. L, O, OC; CH, CJC, OCI, TU, WF, Y.

4066 —Six familiar essays upon marriage. *For Tho. Bennet,* 1696. 8°. C; CLC, WF.

4067 —Some reflections upon marriage. *For John Nutt,* 1700. 8°. T.C.III 200. L, GU; CH, CLC, WF, Y.

4068 **Astell, Ralph.** Vota non bella. New-castle's heartie gratulation. *Gateshead, by Stephen Bulkley,* 1660. 4°.* L, O.

4068A Ο αστήρ του Χριστου Βασιλικος; or Nuncius. *For Dorman Newman,* 1681. 8°. L, LW; CH, NPT, Y, HC.

Asteria. 1677. *See* La Roche-Guilhem, *Mlle* de.

4069 **A[ston], R.,** *comp.* Placita Latinè rediviva: a book of entires. *For H. Twyford, T. Dring, and John Place;* 1660. 4°. LT.

4070 — —[Anr. ed.] —, 1661. 8°. LI, DC, EN; LC, MHL, WF, YL.

4071 [–] —Third edition. *For H. Twyford, John Place, and T. Basset,* 1673. 4°. T.C.I 159. L, LL, LGI, LIL; CU, MHL, NCL, NP.

4072 **Aston, Sir Thomas.** A collection of svndry petitions. [*London*], *for William Sheares,* 1642. 4°. LT, O, C, OC, BR; CN, CSS, NU, TU, WF, Y.

4073 [–] —[Anr. ed.] 1642. 4°. O, LL, CS; CH.

4074 [–] —[Anr. ed.] [*London*], 1642. 4°. O, LL, EN; WF.

4075 [–] —[Anr. ed.] *For Thomas Bankes,* 1642. 4°. LP, LG, CT, BP, EN; CN, CSS, NU, WF.

4075A [–] —[Anr. ed.] *By T. Mabb for William Shears,* 1660. 4°.* O; CLC, NN.

4076 [–] —[Anr. ed.] *Printed, and are to be sold by Walter Davis,* 1681. fol.* T.C.I 452. L, O, CS, AN, EN; CH, MH, PU, WF, Y.

4077 —A petition delivered in to the lords. [*London*], *for John Aston,* 1641. brs. STEELE 1840. LT, C, OC, LS; MH.

4078 —A remonstrance, against Presbitery. [*London*], *for Iohn Aston,* 1641. 4°. LT, O, C, EN, DT; CH, CN, MH, NU, WF, Y.

4079 —Two peititons. [*n.p.*], *printed,* 1641. 4°.* NPT, OWC, Y.

4080 **Aston, Thomas,** *capt.* July 22, 1642. A brief relation. *For Ralph Rounthwait,* [1642]. 4°.* LT, O, C, EC; CN, MH, WF.

4080A [–] April 2. Newes from the west of Ireland. *For William Wright,* 1642. 4°.* LT, O, MR, LFEA; MH.

4080B **Aston, Thomas, M.A.** A sermon preached ... 1st of July 1685. *By W. Wilde for Dan. Brown and Benjamin Crayle,* [1685]. 4°. IU, WF.

4081 —A sermon preached ... fifth of July 1685. *For Benjamin Crayle,* 1685. 4°. T.C.II 193. CS; CH.

4082 —A sermon preached ... March the 25th, 1691. *Printed,* 1691. 4°.* L, OM.

Astraea's tears. 1641. *See* Brathwaite, Richard.
Astrologer's bugg-beare. [1652.] *See* Price, Laurence.
'Αστρολογια. 1680. *See* Butler, John.
Astrological and theological. 1682. *See* Ness, Christopher.
Astrological institutions. 1658. *See* P., T.
Astrological observations. 1672. *See* H., C.
Astrological predictions for the year 1679. 1679. *See* Gadbury, John.

4083 Astrological predictions of Englands happy success. *For Robert Pawlet,* 1667. 4°.* HH; HR, MH.

Astrological predictions on the affairs. 1659. *See* Russel, John.

Αστρολογομανία: the madnesse. 1651. *See* Carleton, George, *bp.*

Astrology asserted. 1680. *See* Butler, John.

Astronomia crystallina. 1670. *See* H., J.

Astronomical description. Cambridge [Mass.], 1665. *See* Danforth, Samuel.

Astronomical observation. 1690. *See* Almanacs.

4084   Astronomy's advancement. *For Philip Lea.* 1684. 8°. T.C.II 84. L, CPE; HC.

Astroscopium: or, two hemispheres. 1673. *See* Lamb, Francis.

4085   **Astry, Thomas.** A true relation of a young man ... struck dumb. *For the author.* 1671. 4°.* L, GH; MH, TU.

4086   **Asty, Robert.** A treatise of rejoycing. *For E. Giles, in Norwich; sold in London,* 1683. 8°. T.C.II 26. L; NPT, Y.

4087   'Ασυστατα. The repugnancy and inconsistency. *London, printed,* 1659. 4°. LT, O; CH, CU, MH, NU, Y.

4087A   At a common-councel held in Guildhall ... Aprill 24, 1644. *By J. Flesher,* 1655. brs. Y.

4087AB At a common-hall. July 5 1695. [*London,* 1695]. brs. L.

4087B   At a council of the Royal Society. [*London,* 1691.] brs. L.

4088   At a councel of war held aboard, the 17 of October, 1654. [1654.] brs. LT.

4088A   At a court held at Stationers-Hall. [*London,* 1685.] brs. HH.

4088AA At a court held for ... Gloucester. [*London,* 1679.] brs. MH.

4088B   At a court holden Jan. 8, 1662. [*London,* 1662.] brs. L.

4088C   At a court of assistants. [*London,* 1686.] brs. LG.

4088D   At a court of the company of royal adventurers. [*London,* 1671.] cap., fol.* MH.

4088E   At a general and open quarter sessions ... holden at Rigate. [*London?* 1658.] brs. LG.

4089   Drapers-hall, London, December the 14th, 1695. At a general assembly of the subscribers of ... land-bank. [*London,* ?1695.] brs. MH.

4089A   At a general court martial held at the inns in Dublin. *Dublin,* 1689. brs. L.

4090   At a general court of the adventuers for the general joynt-stock to the East-Indies. [*London,* 1693.] brs. L; MH, WF.

4091   At a generall meeting of all the subscribers' to the stock of the Royal Company. [1671.] cap., fol.* RPJ.

4092   At a generall meeting of the Committee for Arrears, the 13th. of September. [1648.] brs. LT.

4092A   At a general meeting of the Lords. [*London,* 1677.] brs. L.

4093   At a generall meeting of the subcribers to the bank. [*London,* 1695.] brs. Y.

4094   At a grand committee, or court of assistants of the king and queen's corporation for the linen manufacture. [*London,* 1691.] brs. O, LG.

4094A   At a meeting of the commissioners and surveyors. [*London,* 1697.] brs. L.

4095   At a meeting of the Committee of Arrears the eleventh day of December, 1648. [*London,* 1648.] brs. LT.

4096   At Amsterdamnable-coffee-house on the 5th of Nov. next. [c. 1684.] brs. L, O, OC, EN; CH.

4097   At Grocers-Hall, Aug. 30. 1644. It is ordered by the committee. [*London,* 1644.] cap., brs. LT.

4098   At Mr. Croomes, at the signe of the shooe ... is to be seen the wonder of nature. [*London,* 1677.] brs. L.

4098A   At the brandy shop over against the Eagel and Child. [*London?* 1700]. brs. L.

4098B   At the committee appointed to consider the rates of wharfage. *Clarke,* [1674.] brs. LG.

4099   At the committee of the militia of London the 3d. of Iune, 1648. *By Richard Cotes,* [1648.] brs. LT.

4099A   At the committee of the militia ... by vertue of ... an act. [*London*], 1650. brs. LG.

4100   At the Queen's house in East Greenwich. 1693. brs. O.

4101   At the Rose in Wine Street this present day. [*London,* 1665?] brs. L.

4102   At the sign of the Elephant within a door or two of the Golden-Posts Tavern ... dwelleth a person that writes all the usual hands. [1680.] brs. O.

4103   At the Tovvn-Hall in Abingdon ... auction these following books. [1693.] brs. O.

4104   At the Town-House in Boston: April 18th. 1689 Sir, our selves as well. *Boston by Samuel Green,* 1689. brs. EVANS 458. MHS.

4105   At the two white posts. [*London,* 1691.] cap., 4°.* L.

Ataxiae obstaculum, being. 1677. *See* Vernon, George.

4106   **Atfield, Ambrose.** Catalogus variorum librorum. 1685. fol. L, O, OC; Y.

4107   **Athanasius.** The life of St. Antony. *For the author,* 1697. 8°. L, O, CM, OM, SP; CH, NGT, TSM, WF, Y.

Atheismus vapulans. 1654. *See* Towers, William.

Atheist silenced. 1672. *See* M., J.

4108   The atheist unmasked. *For Langley Curtiss,* 1685. 4°.* L, O; CH, CLC, MH.

4109   The atheisticall politition [*sic*]. [*London,* 1642.] cap., 4°.* LT; CH, CN, NU, WF, Y.

4110   The atheists help at a dead lift. [*London,* 1670?] brs. O; MH.

Athenæ Oxoniensis. 1691. *See* Wood, Anthony.

4111   **Athenagoras.** Του ... Αθεναγορου ... Opera. *Oxonii, e theatro Sheldoniano,* 1682. 12°. L, O, C, EN, DT; BN, CLC, MH, PL, WF, Y.

Athenian society unvail'd. 1692. *See* Wyeth, Joseph.

4112   **Atherton, Henry.** The Christian physician. *By T. James for William Leach,* 1683. 8°. T.C.II 25. C, LSC, LWL; CLC, WF.

4113   —Exploratio. 1673. brs. L, O.

4114   —The resurrection proved. colop: *By T. Dawks,* 1680. brs. MH.

4114A   **Atherton, John.** The pastor turn'd Pope. 1654. 8°.* NHC.

4115   **Athlone, Godert Ginkell, earl of.** His Majesty by ... 27 April 1691. *Dublin, A. Crooke,* [1691]. brs. STEELE 2p 1203. L, HH, DPR; PL.

4116   —The stealing of horses ... 12 May 1691. *Dublin, A. Crook,* [1691]. brs. STEELE 2p 1207. L, HH, DPR.

4117 —By . . . 4 February 1690 [1]. *Dublin, A. Crook,* [1691]. brs. STEELE 2p 1187. L, HH, DPR.

4118 —. . . Their Majesties forces. colop: *Dublin, by Andrew Crook, assignee of Benjamin Tooke,* 1690. cap., fol.* STEELE 2p 1166. L, HH, DPR.

4119 —Whereas directions . . . 25 November 1691. *Dublin, A. Crook,* [1691]. brs. STEELE 2p 1241. L, HH, DPR.

4120 —Whereas several considerable . . . 4 December 1691. *Dublin, A. Crook,* [1691]. brs. STEELE 2p 1242. L, HH, DPR.

4121 —Whereas the right honourable . . . [23 May 1691]. *Dublin, A.Crook,* [1691]. brs. STEELE 2p 1210. L, HH, DPR.

4122 — —[*Edenburgh,* 1696.] cap., fol.* EN; WF.

Athon, Joannes de. *See* Acton, John.

4123 **Atkin, Thomas.** By the mayor, whereas the slow comming in of the moneys. *For Edward Husband,* 1645. brs. LT.

4124 —Some reasons why the people called Quakers. *For Robert Wilson,* 1660. brs. LF; CH, MH.

Atkins, *Sir* Robert. *See* Atkyns, *Sir* Robert.

Atkins, Samuel. Kalendarium Pennsilvaniense. [New York], 1685. *See* Almanacs.

4124A **Atkins, *Sir* Thomas.** Hosanna: or, a song. [*London*], printed, 1649. 4°.* LT; CLC, CN, MIU.

4124B — —[Anr. ed.] [*London,* 1649.] fol. L, O; CH, WF.

4124C —Reverend alderman Atkins . . . his speech. [*London*], printed, 1648. 4°.* LT, LG; CH, Y.

4124D —A seasonable speech made by. [*London*], printed, 1660. 4°.* LT, O, C, MR, HH; CH, CN, MH, WF, Y.

4124E — —[Anr. ed.] [*London,* 1680.] cap., fol.* L, O, HH, EN; CLC, MH.

4125 **Atkins, William.** A discourse shewing the nature of the gout. *For Tho. Fabian,* 1694. 8°. L, LCS, LWL; BN, WSG.

Atkinson, Charles. Panterpe. 1670. *See* Almanacs.

4126 **Atkinson, Christopher.** Davids enemies discovered. *For Giles Calvert,* 1655. 4°.* LT, O, C, OC, LF; CH, MH, NU, PH, Y.

4126A —The discovery of a wolf in sheeps cloathing. *For W. Franckling, in Norwitch,* 1656. brs. CT.

4127 —Ishmael and his mother. *Londou* [sic], *for Giles Calvert,* 1655. 4°.* LT, O, C, LF, BBN; CH, PH, PSC, WF.

4128 —The standard of the Lord lifted up. *For Giles Calvert,* 1653. 4°.* LT, LF, OC, BBN; PH, PSC.

4129 —The svvord of the Lord drawn. *Printed, and are to be sold by Giles Calvert,* 1654. 4°.* LT, O, LF, OC, BBN; PH.

4129A **Atkinson, Elizabeth.** A breif and plain discovery of the labourers in mistery. [*London*], *P.L.,* 1669. 4°.* L, OC; MHS.

4129B —Weapons of the people called Quakers. 1669. 4°.* MHS.

4130 **Atkinson, Peter.** The spirits voice concerning himselfe. *By Thomas Lock for the author,* 1659. 4°.* L; WF.

4131 **Atkinson, Thomas.** The Christian's testimony against tythes. [*London*], printed, 1678. 4°.* L, CT, LF, BBN; MH, PH, PSC, Y.

4131A [–] —*Printed,* 1678. 4°.* LF; PH.

4132 —An exhortation to all people. [*London,* 1684.] 4°.* L, O, LF, BBN; PH.

4133 **[Atkyns, Richard.]** The king's grant of privilege. *By John Streater,* 1669. 4°.* L, CS.

4134 [–] The original and growth of printing. [*London, ?1660.*] brs. L, MC.

4135 — —[Anr. ed.] *By John Streater, for the author,* 1664. 4°.* L, O, C, ES, DT; CH, CJC, LC, PBL, Y.

4136 **Atkyns, *Sir* Robert.** A defence of the late Lord Russel's innocency. *For Timothy Goodwin,* 1689. fol.* T.C.II 252. L, O, C, EN, DT; BN, CH, CN, LC, MH, NU, Y.

4137 —An enquiry into the jurisdiction of the chancery. *Printed,* 1695. fol. L, C, HH; CH, MHL.

4138 —An enquiry into the power of dispensing with penal statutes. *For Timothy Goodwin,* 1689. fol. T.C.II 252. L, O, C, LL, AU; CH, MH, NU, WF, Y.

4139 — —Second edition. *For Timothy Goodwin,* 1689. fol. LI, EN, DT; LC, WF.

4140 —The Lord Russel's innocency further defended. *For Timothy Goodwin,* 1689. fol.* T.C.II 252. L, O, C, EN, DT; BN, CH, MBA, NU, WF, Y.

4141 —The power, jurisdiction, and privilege of Parliament. *For Timothy Goodwin,* 1689. fol. T.C.II 252. L, O, C, EN, DT; BN, CH, CN, LC, MHL, NU, Y.

4142 —The Lord Chief Baron Atkyns's speech to Sir William Ashhurst. *For R. Baldwin,* 1693. fol.* L, O, C, MR, DT; BN, MH, PL, TU, WF, Y.

4143 — —[Anr. ed.] colop: *Dublin, reprinted for M. Gunn,* 1694. fol.* O; MHL, NN.

4144 —A treatise of the true and ancient jurisdiction. *Printed,* 1699. fol.* L, HH, EN; CH, MHL.

Atlas chinensis. 1671. *See* Dapper, Olfert.

Atlas, or a geographicke description. Amsterdam, 1641. *See* Mercator, Gerard.

Atlee, Richard. Εφημερις. [1647]. *See* Almanacs.

4145 **The atachment, examination and confession of a Frenchman.** *For William Bowden,* 1641. 4°.* LT, O; WF, Y.

4145A **Attebion i'r holl was escusion.** 1698. 8°. AN.

Attempt for the explanation. 1661. *See* Hooke, Robert.

4146 **[Atterbury, Francis, *bp*.]** An answer to some considerations on the spirit of Martin Luther. *Oxford, at the theater,* 1687. fol. L, O, C, E, DT; CLC, CU, MH, NU, TU, WF, Y.

4147 —The Christian religion increas'd by miracle. *For Thomas Bennet,* 1694. 4°. T.C.II 519. L, O, OC, CT, EC; CH, CN, MH, NU, WF.

4148 —A discourse occasioned by the death of the . . . Lady Cutts. *For Tho. Bennet,* 1698. 4°.* L, O, C, OC; CH, MH, NU, TU, Y.

4149 — —Second edition. —, 1698. 4°.* L, O, C, CT; MH, WF.

4150 —The power of charity to cover sin. *By Tho. Warren, for Thomas Bennet,* 1694. 4°.* T.C.II 519. OC, CT, EC, DT; CH, NGT, NU, WF, Y.

4151   [–] The rights, powers, and priviledges of an English
       convocation. *For Tho. Bennet, 1700.* 8°. L, O, C, CT,
       DT; CU, NU, WF, Y.

4152   —The scorner incapable of true wisdom. *For Thomas
       Bennet, 1694.* 4°.* T.C.II 519. L, O, C, WCA, SC; CH, MH,
       NR, NU, WF.

4153   —A sermon before the queen at White-Hall. May 29,
       1692. *For Tho. Bennet, 1692.* 4°. T.C.II 418. L, O,
       C, OC, SC; MBA, NU, TU, WF, Y.

4154   **Atterbury, Lewis, elder.** Babylon's downfall. *Printed,
       and are to be sold by Randal Taylor, 1691.* 4°.* T.C.II 368.
       L, C, OC; WF.

4155   —A good subject. *For Robert Kettlewell, 1684.* 4°.
       T.C.II 81. L, O, OC, WCA; IU, TU, WF, Y.

4156   —The grand charter of Christian feasts. *For Christopher
       Wilkinson, 1686.* 4°.* T.C.II 165. L, O, OC, CT; CH,
       NU, TU, WF, Y.

4156A —A sermon preached . . . August the 4th, 1687. *By
       R.E. to be sold by Randal Taylor, 1687.* 4°.* C, OC,
       WCA; WF, Y.

4157   **Atterbury, Lewis, younger.** Ten sermons. *By J.H.
       for Henry Mortlock, 1699.* 8°. T.C.III 133. L, O, C, DT;
       CLC, MB, PL, WF, Y.

4158   An attest of the housholders within the parish of
       Buttolphs Aldgate London. *For James Nuthall, 1657.*
       4°.* LT, C, P; MH, MM, Y.

4159   The attestation of the ministers of . . . Norfolk. *By
       R. Cotes for Michael Sparke, 1648.* 4°.* LT, O, CS;
       NU, WF.

4160   The attestation of the ministers of . . . Somerset. *By
       Fr: Neile for Tho: Vnderhill, 1648.* 4°.* LT, CT, BR; NU.

4161   An attestation to the testimony of our reverend
       brethren. *By R. Cotes for Christopher Meredith, 1648.*
       4°. L, O, LW; NPT, NU, Y.

       Attourney of the court. 1642. *See* T., G.

       Atturneys gvide. 1656. *See* B., I.

4162   **Atwell, George.** An apologie, or, defence of . . .
       astrologie. *For Samuel Speed, 1660.* 8°. LT; CLC, WF.

4163   —The faithfull surveyor. *[Cambridge], for the author, at
       the charges of Nathanael Rowls, 1658.* 4°. C, CT, DCH;
       MU, WF.

4164   — —[Anr. ed.] *Cambridge, for William Nealand, 1662.*
       4°. L, O, C, CT, R; CLC.

4165   — —[Anr. ed.] 1665. 4°. LPO.

4166   **[Atwood, William.]** Additions answering the omis-
       sions. *For Edward Berry, 1681.* 8°.* EN; CH, MH,
       MHL, WF, Y.

4167   Entry cancelled.

       —Answer to Mr. Molyneux. 1698. *See* Cary, John.

4168   [–] The antiquity and justice of an oath of objuration.
       For Richard Baldwin, 1694. 4°. T.C.II 495. L, O, C,
       CT; LC, MH, WF, Y.

4169   [–] An apology for the East-India company. *For the
       author, 1690.* 8°.* L; MB, MH, NC, PU, WF.

       [–] Argumentum anti-Normannicum, or. 1682. *See*
       Coke, Edward.

4170   —A covert for the orthodox Christian. *For the author,
       1662.* 4°. O; NN.

4171   —The fundamental constitution of the English govern-
       ment. *By J.D. for the author, 1690.* fol. L, E, DT; CN,
       LC, MH, NC, WCL, Y.

4172   [–] The history, and reasons, of the dependency of Ire-
       land. *For Dan. Brown; and Ri. Smith, 1698.* 8°. L, O,
       C, EN, DT; CH, CN, MH, TU, Y.

4173   [–] —[Anr. ed.] *For Dan. Brown; and Tho. Leigh, 1698.*
       8°. T.C.III 77. L, C, OM, EN; CH, NU, WF.

4174   [–] Jani Anglorum. *For Thomas Basset, 1680.* 8°. T.C.I
       408. L, O, CS, LG, DT; CH, LC, MH, NC, Y.

4175   [–] Jus Anglorum ab antiquo: or, a confutation. *For
       Edward Berry, 1681.* 8°. L, O, C, LL, EN; BN, CH, CN,
       MH, WF, Y.

       [–] Letter of remarks. 1683. *See* Anglesey, Arthur
       Annesley, *earl of.*

4176   —The Lord Chief Justice Herbert's account examin'd.
       For J. Robinson, and Mat. Wotton, 1689. 4°. T.C.II
       251. L, O, C, MR, EN; CH, CN, MH, NCL, WF, Y.

4177   [–] A poetical essay towards an epitome of the Gospel.
       1678. 4°.* L, HH; WF.

4177A —Proposals for printing The fundamental constitution.
       [London, 1690.] fol.* L.

4178   [–] Reflections on Bishop Overall's convocation-book.
       Printed, 1690. fol.* L; LC, MH, WCL, Y.

4179   [–] Reflections upon a treasonable opinion. *Printed and
       sold by E. Whitlock, 1696.* 4°. L, O, C, CT, HH; CN,
       LC, MH, NU, WF, Y.

4180   [–] The rights and authority of the Commons. *Printed,
       1695.* fol.* L, LG, HH, EN; MH, WF, Y.

4181   [–] A safe and easy method for supplying the want of
       coin. colop: *For Roger Clavel, London, 1695.* cap.,
       fol.* L, O; MH, NC.

4182   —A seasonable vindication of the truly Catholic doc-
       trine. *For Jonathan Robinson, 1683.* 4°. T.C.II 27.
       L, O, CT, LW; CH, CN, MH, TU.

4183   [–] Three letters to Dr. Sherlock. *For Jonathan Robinson,
       1683.* 4°.* T.C.II 27. L, O, CT, LW, EN; CH, CN, MH, NU,
       WF, Y.

4183A [–] A true account of the unreasonableness of Mr.
       Fitton's pretences. *[London? 1685.]* fol.* L, O.

4184   **[Aubery du] Maurier, [Louis.]** The lives of all the
       princes of Orange. *For Thomas Bennet, 1693.* 8°.
       T.C.II 476. L, O, C, E, DT; CH, CN, LC, MH, TU, Y.

4185   **Aubignac, François Hédelin, abbé d'.** The whole art
       of the stage. *For the author, and sold by William Cade-
       man, Rich. Bentley, Sam Smith, & T. Fox, 1684.* 4°.
       T.C.II 50. L, O, C, OC; CH, CN, LC, MH, TU, Y.

4186   **[Aubigné, Théodore Agrippa d'.]** The Catholick
       confession. *For Job King, 1686.* 8°. L; CH, NU.

4187   [–] Hell illuminated. or, Sancy's Roman Catholic con-
       fession. *For L. Curtis, 1679.* 12°. T.C.I 361. L, CT, LIL,
       P, MAU; CH, MIU, WF.

4188   **Aubrey, John.** Miscellanies. *For Edward Castle, 1696.*
       8°. L, O, C, GK, EN; CH, LC, MH, NU, Y.

4189 —Proposals for printing Monumenta Britannica. [London, 1690?] brs. O.

4190 [**Aubri, John.**] The use of the horloge. *Deepe, by Pyter Acher.* 1680. 12°.* L.

4190A [**Aucher, John.**] Arguments and reasons to prove. [London, 1650.] 4°.* LT, O, C, OC, HH; CH, CN, MH, NU, TU, WF, Y.

4191 —The arraignment of rebellion. *By M. F. for William Abington,* 1684. 4°. L, O, C, DT; CH, CU, IU, WF, Y.

4192 Auctarium musaei Balfouriani. *Edinburgi, academiae typographus [heirs and successors of A. Anderson],* 1697. 8°. ALDIS 3655. E, EN; NS.

Auctio Davisiana. 1689. *See* Smalridge, George.

Auction; or. [1693.] *See* Johnston, Nathaniel.

4193 The audience. [1688.] brs. L, O, CT, HH, EN; CH, MH, TU, Y.

4194 [**Audiguier, Vital d'.**] A tragi-comicall history of our times, under the borrowed names of Lisander, and Calista. *For Rich. Lownes,* 1652. 8°. L, O; CU, LC, NNG.

4195 **Audland, Anne.** A true declaration of the suffering of the innocent. *Printed, and are to be sold by Giles Calvert,* 1655. 4°.* LT, O, LF, BBN, MR; CH, PH.

4196 **Audland, John.** The innocent delivered out of the snare. *For Giles Calvert,* 1655. 4°.* LT, O, C, LF, BBN; CH, MH, PH, PSC, Y.

4197 —The school-master disciplin'd. *For Giles Calvert,* 1655. 4°.* L, CT, LF, BBN; CH, CN, PH, PSC.

4198 —The suffering condition of the servants of the Lord. *Printed,* 1662. 4°.* L, O, LF, BBN, DT; CH, PH, PL, PSC, Y.

4199 —Two letters. *For Jonathan Edwin,* 1672. fol.* L, O, LF, OM; CH, CLC, MH, TU.

Audley, *Lady* **Eleanor.** *See* Douglas, *Lady* Eleanor.

[**Audley, Henry.**] Court convert. 1698. *See* Waring, Henry.

4200 **Audley, Hugh.** The way to be rich. *For E. Davis,* 1662. 4°.* L, EN; Y.

Audley, James. *See* Castlehaven, James Touchet, *earl of.*

4201 **Audley, John.** An account of a remarkable sea-fight. *For Randal Taylor,* 1690. brs. L; CH, MH.

4202 —Englands common-wealth. *By R. I; sold by Livewell Chapman,* 1652. 4°.* L, O, EN; CH.

4203 —Pædo-baptisme. *By Matthew Simmons,* 1647. 4°.* O; NPT, NU.

Audoeni, Joannis. *See* Owen, John.

4204 Augusta's restoration. 1683. brs. O.

4205 **Augustine,** *Saint.* Saint Austins care for the dead. Second edition. *Printed,* 1651. 12°. O, C; CN, MH, TU, WF, Y.

4206 —Saint Augustines confessions translated. *By T. R. & E. M. for Abel Roper,* 1650. 12°. L, O, LSC; BN, CH, CLC, MH, NP, Y.

4207 ——[Anr. ed.] *Printed,* 1679. 8°. L, O, OC; CH, NU, TU, WF, Y.

4208 [–] Digitus Dei, or God appearing. [1676?] 8°. L, O, EN; CLC, TU, WF, Y.

4209 [–] —[Anr. ed.] *For D. M.,* 1677. 8°. CHRISTIE-MILLER.

4210 —The judgment of the learned and pious St. *For James Collins,* 1670. 4°.* T.C.I 65. L, O, C, P; CLC, CN, MH, NU, WF, Y.

4211 —The life of S. Augustine. The first part, written by himself. *By J. C. for John Crook,* 1660. 8°. LT, O; CH, CLG, WC, WF.

4212 —The meditations, soliloqva. Second edition. *Printed at Paris, by Mrs. Blageart,* 1655. 12°. L, O; CLC, CN, NU, TU, WF, Y.

4212A ——[Anr. ed.] *For Matthew Turner,* 1686. 12°. L, FARM, WARES; CLC, CN, MBP, Y.

4213 —The profit of believing. *By Roger Daniel.* 1651. 12°. O, C, DC; CN, MH, TU, WF, Y.

4214 Augustissimo et optimo regi Carolo Secundo. *Typis Gulielmi Downing,* 1684. fol.* L, HH; CLC, MB.

4214A **Augustus, Caesar Octavianus.** Two speeches. *For J. B.,* 1675. 4°. O; CLC.

4215 Augustus Anglicus: a compendious view. *For Samuel Holford,* 1686. 12°. L, LG, EN; CH, CU, MH, TU, Y.

Aula lucis, or. 1652. *See* Vaughan, Thomas.

4216 Aulici cujusdam ad unum ex amicis Parlamentarium. [London, 1652.] 4°.* LT.

Aulicus coquinariae; or. 1650. *See* Sanderson, *Sir* William.

Aulicus his dream. 1644. *See* Cheynell, Francis.

Aulicus his hue. 1645. *See* Cheynell, Francis.

4217 The aulnage case. [London, c. 1693.] brs. LL, LS; MH.

4217A [**Aulnoy, Marie Catherine La Mothe, comtesse.**] The ingenious and diverting letters. *For Samuel Crouch,* 1691. 12°. T.C.II 379. CT; CLC, PT.

4217B [–] —Second edition. —, 1692. 12°. T.C.II 441. L, O, C, CT, E; NU, PL, Y.

4217C ——Fourth edition. —, 1697. 8°. T.C.III 30. L, O; CLC, CN, WF.

4218 —The memoirs of. *For Tho. Cockerill,* 1699. 8°. L; CLC, CN, MH, WF, Y.

4218A —Memoirs of the court of France. *For R. Bentley; and T. Benett,* 1692. T.C.II 402. 8°. L, O; CN, MIU, NP, WF, Y.

4219 ——[Anr. ed.] *For E. Whitlock,* 1697. 8°. L, CT; CLC, CN, PU, Y.

4220 [–] Memoirs of the court of Spain. *For T. Horn, F. Saunders, and T. Bennet,* 1692. 8°. L, O, CS; CH, TU, WF, Y.

4221 [–] The novels of Elizabeth queen of England. *For Marc Pardoe,* 1680. T.C.I 393. L, O; CLC, IU, WF.

4222 [–] —the last part. *By E. T. and R. H. for M. Pardow,* 1681. T.C.I 416. L; CLC, CN, WF.

4223 [–] The present court of Spain. *For H. Rhodes and J. Harris,* 1693. 12°. T.C.II 441. O; Y.

4223A [–] The second part of the ingenious . . . letters. *For Samuel Crouch,* 1692. 12°. T.C.II 379. O; PU, Y.

4223B [–] The third and last part of the ingenious . . . letters. *For Samuel Crouch,* 1692. 12°. T.C.II 393. O, CT; PU.

Aurea dicta. 1681. *See* Barksdale, Clement.

4224 **Aurelius Antoninus, Marcus.** Μαρκου Αντωνινου των εις εαυτον. . . . De seipso et ad seipsum. *Typis M. Flesher, sumptibus R. Mynne,* 1643. 8°. L, O, C, ENC, DT; CH, MBA, MH, WF, Y.

4225 —[Anr. ed.] De rebus suis. *Cantabrigiæ, excudebat Thomas Buck, veneunt per Antonium Nicolson,* 1652. 4°. LT, O, C, EN, DT; MH, NC, NP, TU, Y.

4226 —[Anr. ed.] *Oxoniæ, e theatro Sheldoniano* 1680. 12°. MADAN 3257. L, O, CS, LW, AU; MH, NC, PL, WF, Y.

4227 — —"Second" edition. *Impensis Edv. Millingtoni,* 1697. 4°. T.C.III 80. L, O, C, GH, DT; CH, MH, NC, NP, Y.

4228 —Meditations. Third edition. *By J. Flesher for F. Mynne,* 1663. 8°. C, CPE; IU, NC, Y.

4229 —M. Aurelius Antoninus, . . . his meditations. Fourth edition. *For Charles Harper,* 1673. 8°. T.C.I 138. L, O, C, EN, DT; CN, LC, NP, PL, Y.

4230 —The meditations of. Fifth edition. *For A. and John Churchill, and Sam. Smith and Tho. Bennet,* 1692. 8°. T.C.II 414. L, O, OC, CT; CH, LC, PL, TU, Y.

Aurelius Victor. *See* Victor, Sextus Aurelius.

4230A The auricular confession of Titus Oates. *Printed,* 1683. brs. L; MH.

Aurifontina chymica: or. 1680. *See* Houpreght, John Frederick.

4231 Aurigae flag. *For T. H.,* 1665. brs. LS.

4232 Aurora: or, a dawne. *Printed,* 1648. 4°.* LT, O, C, YM, DT; CH, CN, MIU, NU, WF, Y.

4233 **Austen, Ralph.** A dialogue, (or familiar discourse). *Oxford, by Hen. Hall for Thomas Bowman,* 1676. 8°. MADAN 3096. T.C.I 256. O, LPO; MH, NP, WF.

4234 —Observations upon some part of Sr Francis Bacon's natvrall history. *Oxford, by Hen. Hall for Thomas Robinson,* 1658. 4°. MADAN 2374. L, O, C, OC, R; BN, CH, MH, NC, WF, Y.

4235 —The spirituall use of an orchard. *[Oxford,* 1653.] 4°. MADAN 2224. LT, O, R, E; BN, LC, Y.

4236 — —Second edition. *Oxford, by Hen: Hall for Tho: Robinson,* 1657. 4°. MADAN 2328. LT, O, BR, NPL; MH, NPT, TU, WF.

4237 —The strong man armed. *For Peter Parker,* 1676. 8°. T.C.I 234. L, O, C, LF.

4238 —A treatise of frvit-trees. *Oxford, [by L. Lichfield] for Tho. Robinson,* 1653. 4°. MADAN 2223. LT, O, CT, R, E; BN, CH, CN, LC, MH, Y.

4239 [–] —Second edition. *Oxford, by Henry Hall for Thomas Robinson,* 1657. 4°. MADAN 2327. LT, O, C, YM, E; BN, CH, LC, MH, NC, Y.

4240 — —Third edition. *Oxford, by William Hall for Amos Curteyne,* 1665. 8°. MADAN 2692. L, O, C, MR, EN; CLC, MHO, WF, Y.

4241 **Austin, Benjamin.** The presvmptvovs mans mirrovr. *By G. M. for George Edwards,* 1641. 12°. L, O; NPT, Y.

4242 —Scripture manifestation. *For P. W. and John Wright,* 1650. 8°. LT, O, LCL, LW; IU, MH, NPT, Y.

4242A —A treatise of the holy family in unity. 1656. 12°. BAMB.

4242B **[Austin, John.]** The Catholiques plea. *For H. J.,* 1659. 8°. WARE; CLC.

4243 —The Christian moderator. *[London],* for *H. J.,* 1651. 4°.* LT, O, CT, MR, EN; CN, NHC, NU, WF, Y.

4244 [–] —Second edition. *By N. T. for H. J.,* 1652. 4°.* L, O, LW, MR, DT; CH, NU, WF.

4244A [–] —Third edition. *For H. J.,* 1652. 8°. CT.

4245 [–] —Fourth edition. —, 1652. 8°. LT, O, C, OC, EN; CLC, CN, MIU, WF.

4246 [–] —: the second part. *[London],* for *H. J.,* 1652. 4°.* LT, OC; NGT, NHC.

4247 [–] —[Anr. ed.] *By M.H. for W.C.,* 1652. 4°.* L, O, C, CS, MR; CH, CN, MBA, NU, WF, Y.

4248 [–] —Third part. *By J. G. for Richard Lowndes,* 1653. 4°.* LT, O, CT, MR, EN; CH, CN, NU, TU, WF.

4248A [–] Devotions in the ancient way of offices. *Paris,* 1668. 8°. L, C, CS, LW; CLC, CN, TU, WF, Y.

4249 [–] Devotions. first part. Second edition. *Roan;* 1672 [sic]. 12°. L, O, C, OC, DT; CN, MB, NU, WF, Y.

4250 [–] —Third edition. *Roan,* 1684. 8°. O, C, LSC; CN, NU, TU.

4250A [–] —Fourth edition. —, 1685. 8°. L, C, PC; CN, NPT.

4250B — —[Anr. ed.] *For W. Keblewhite, and J. Jones,* 1700. 12°. O, C, LLP.

4250C — —[Anr. ed.] *For J. Jones,* 1700. 12°. OC; CLC.

4251 [–] —, second part. *Printed* 1675. 8°. O, D, DT; CLC, CN, WF.

—Reflexions upon the oathe. 1661. *See* Sergeant, John.

4252 —A zealovs sermon, preached at Amsterdam by a Jew. *Printed at Amsterdam [London],* 1642. 4°.* LT, O, LG, CJ, CT.

4253 **Austin, Robert.** Allegiance not impeached. *Printed at London by Rich. Cotes, for Joh. Bellamy,* 1644. 4°. LT, O, C, CT, EN; CH, LC, MH, NU, TU, Y.

4254 —The Parliaments rules and directions. *By J. M. for John Bellamie,* 1647. 8°.* LT, OC, CM; CH, MBP, PL.

4255 **[Austin, Samuel.]** The character of a Quaker. *For T. Egglesfield,* 1671. 4°.* T.C.I 97. L, O, C, MR, DT; CH, CN, MH, NU, WF, Y.

4256 [–] —[Anr. ed.] *Printed,* 1672. 4°.* OC.

—Naps upon Parnassus. 1658. *See* Flatman, Thomas.

4257 —A panegyrick on his sacred Majesties royal person. *For William Miller,* 1661. 8°.* L; CH, TU.

4258 **Austin, Samuel,** *minister.* A practical catechisme. *For Tho. Underhill,* 1647. 8°.* LT.

4259 **Austin, William.** Atlas under Olympus; an heroick poem. *For the author,* 1664. 8°. L; CH, CN, MH, OCI, SW.

4259A — —, or the heroick poems of. *For Thomas Rooks,* 1664. 8°. SP; MH.

4260 —Επιλοιμια έπη. Or, the anatomy of the pestilence. *For Nath. Brooke,* 1666. 8°. L, O, LG; CH.

4261 —A joyous welcome to . . . Catherin. *[London,* 1662]. fol.* L; MH.

4262 —Triumphus hymenæus. A panegyrick. *By R. Daniel,* 1662. fol.* L; MH.

Aut Helmont. 1665. *See* S., G.

4263 Aut nvnc, aut nvnqvam, now or never. *Printed*, 1648. 4°.* LT, HH; MBP, MH, WF.

Autarchy. 1691. *See* Burghope, George.

4264 An authentical account of the formalities. *For Y.H.*, [1680]. 4°. O; MH, NC.

Authority abused. 1690. *See* Stephens, Edward.

Authority of the magistrate. 1672. *See* Humfrey, John.

Authority of the true. 1660. *See* Whitehead, George.

4265 The authors of the first case of salt-petre. [*London*, 1693.] brs. LL.

Autodidactice. 1657. *See* Goad, John.

Αυτοκατακριτοι, or, the Jesuits. 1679. *See* Greene, Martin.

Αυτοκατακριτος: or. 1662. *See* Boreman, Robert.

—1668. *See* Ford, Thomas.

Αυτομαχια: or. 1643. *See* DuMoulin, Louis.

Auvergne, Edward d'. *See* D'Auvergne, Edward.

4266 Avaritia coram tribunali: or, the miser arraign'd. *For Elizabeth Calvert*, 1666. 4°.* WF.

4266A **Avaux, Jean Antoine de Mesmes *comte d'*.** Discours de. *Dublin, by Jus. Ray for Will. Weston*, 1689. brs. DIX 237. CD.

4267 —An exact copy of a letter from. colop: *Hague: by Jacobus Sikeltus; reprinted London, for Randall Taylor*, 1684. cap., fol.* L, OC, MC; CH, MBA, NP, WF, Y.

4268 —A memorial delivered to the States-General. colop: *For Richard Morris*, 1684. brs. O, HH, LU; CH.

4269 —A memorial of. colop: *Reprinted in London for Walter Davis*, [1684]. brs. O, HH; CH, Y.

4270 ——[Anr. ed.] colop: *For T. Malthus*, [1684]. brs. L, O, LU, HH; CH, PU.

4270A —Memorials lately presented. [*Hague?* 1688]. brs. L, OC; CH.

4270B —The speech of. *Dublin, for William Weston*, 1689. brs. DIX 237. CD.

4271 **Averroes.** Averroeana being a transcript of several letters from. *Printed and sold by T. Sowle*, 1695. 8°. L, OR, GU, E; CH, CLC, NAM, WSG, JF.

4272 **Avery, Elizabeth.** Scripture-prophecies opened. *For Giles Calvert*, 1647. 4°. LT, C, LWL, CT, E; CH, CU, WF, Y.

4272A **Avery, Joseph.** Certaine letters and addresses. [*Hamburg?*] 1647. 4°. CT.

4273 —Two letters of great consequence, sent from Hamborovgh. [*London*], *for Edw. Husbands. Febr.* 14, 1643[4]. 4°.* LT, O; CLC, MH, MIU, WF, Y.

4274 **Avila, Juan *de*.** Certain selected spiritual epistles. *Rouen, John le Costurier*, 1631 [ie c 1650] 8°. O; CH, CN, MIU, WF, Y.

Avona; or. 1675. *See* S., R.

4275 **Avril, Philip.** Travels into divers parts of Europe and Asia. *For Tim. Goodwin*, 1693. 12°. T.C.II 452. L, O, C, ENC, DT; CLC, LC, MBA, PL, Y.

4275A Awake O England. *For Charles Prince*, 1660. 4°.* Y.

4275B Awake Sampson. *By S. Bridge, and sold by E. Whitlock*, 1696. 4°.* CLC, NC, WF.

4276 An awakening word in season. *For Arthor Jones*, 1684. 4°.* O.

4277 ——, Second edition. —, 1684. 4°.* T.C.II 120. O, OC, CT; CH, MIU, WF.

4277A An awakening word to the churches. 1664. 4°. O.

4278 Avvay vvith't quoth Washington. *For J. Phanatick*, 1660. brs. LT, O; CH.

4279 **Awdeley, Lewis.** July 8, 1648. A true relation sent. *For Edward Husband*, 1648. 4°.* LT, OC.

4279A The axe at the root. *Printed*, 1696. 4°.* L; WF.

Axe laid to the root. 1685. *See* Humfrey, John.

4280 **Axford, John.** An epitomy shewing. *For the author*, 1700. 8°.* CT, LF, BBN; NHC.

4280A —Hidden things brought to light. *Printed and sold by T. Sowle*, 1697. 12°.* LF.

4281 [-] Philosophical & astrological rare secrets. *By T. Sowle*, 1693. 8°.* L.

4282 **Aylesbury, Thomas.** Diatribæ de æterno Divini Beneplaciti. *Cantabrigiæ, excudebat Joann. Field*, 1659. 4°. LT, O, C, P, E; BN.

4283 ——[Anr. ed.] —, 1661. 4°.* GU.

4284 **A[ylett], R[obert].** Devotions, viz. 1 a good womans . . . prayer. *By T.M. for Abel Roper*, 8°.* LT; CH.

4285 —Divine, and moral speculations. *For Abel Roper*, 1654. 8°. LT, O, SP; CH, CN, MH, TU, WF.

4286 —A wife, not ready made. Second edition. *For A. R.*, 1653. 8°.* LT, O; CLC, CN, LC, MH, WC, Y.

4287 **Ayleway, William.** Epithalamia in nuptias lætissimas. *Typis Petri Lillicrap*, 1662. 4°.* L, O.

4288 —[Hebrew]. Ευασμος βασιλικος . . . Ovatio regalis. The royal solemnity. *By Peter Lillicrap for the author*, 1662. 4°. O.

4289 **Ayloffe, Thomas.** In querela. *Cambridge*, 1696. brs. O.

4290 **Ayloffe, William.** The government of the passions. *For J. Knapton*, 1700. 12°. T.C.III 175. CH, MIU, WF, Y.

4291 —Gulielmus pacificus: sive oratio de pace. *Cantabrigiæ, typis academicis*, [1697]. 4°.* L, O, C, OC, DT; NHS, NP, Y.

4292 **Aymé, Isaac.** Trichiasis admodum rara. *Typis H. Hills, Jun. impensis R. Bentley*, 1684. 8°.* T.C.II 115. O.

4292A **Aymes, John.** A rich store house. *By E. Crowch*, 1670. 12°.* L.

4292B ——Fourth edition. —, *to be sold by F. Coles*, 1676. 12°. L; WSG.

4293 **Aynsloe, John.** A besome of truth. *Printed*, 1664. 4°.* LF; Y.

4294 —An epistle written in the movings of God's holy Spirit. [*London*, 1664.] brs. LF.

4295 —A lamentation over Cambridge. [*London*], 1665. brs. LF.

4296 —Several things given forth. [*London*, 1683]. cap., 4°.* LF, CT; MH, PH, PS.

4297 —A short description of the true ministers and the false. [*London*], *printed*, 1672. 4°.* L, O, C, LF, BBN; NC, PH, PSC, WF, Y.

4297A **Ayray, James.** A sermon preached . . . December 12, 1686. *For William Grantham*, 1686. 4°.* L, O; CH, MH.

4297B —A sermon preached . . . April 10, 1687. *For John & Thomas Lane,* 1687. 4°.* L, O, WCA; MH, TU.

4297C **Ayres, John.** The a la mode secretary. [*London*, 1680]. 4°. CM.

4298 —The accomplish'd clerk. *Sould by γ^e author,* [1683?] fol.* T.C.II 30. L, CM; CN, MH, NC.

4299 —The accomplish'd clerk regraved. 1700. fol. L, O, CM; CN, PFL.

4300 —Arithmetick a treatise. *By J. R. for S. Crouch: and J. Blare,* 1693. 12°. O; WF, Y.

4301 — —Second edition. *For Sam. Crouch, and J. Blare,* 1695. 12°. L; NC.

4302 — —Third edition. —, 1698. 12°. T.C.III 83. L; MB, NP.

4303 — —Fourth edition. —, 1699. 12°. NC, TU.

4303A —The new a la mode secretary. *Sold by Hen. Hatley, Sam. Crouch, and Ben. Alsop,* 1682. 4°. L (t.p. only); CLC.

4303B — —[Anr. ed.] *By Sam. Crouch* [1686]. 8°. L.

4303C —The Paul's school round-hand. [*London*], *sold by γ^e author,* [1700]. NC.

4304 —The penmans daily practice. *Sold by γ^e author,* 1690. 4°. T.C.II 324. L, OP, CM.

4304A —The striking copy-book. [*London*], *sold by the author; and S. Crouch,* [1687.] 8°. T.C.II 209. NC.

4305 —The trades-mans copy-book. *Crouch,* 1688. *Sold by the author and Sa. Crouch.* fol.* T.C.II 224. MH.

4306 —A tutor to penmanship. *Sold by γ^e author, and by S. Crouch,* [*London,* 1698.] obl. fol. T.C.III 80. L, O, C, CM; CN, LG, NC, NN.

4307 **Ayres, Philip.** Cupids addresse to the ladies. 1683. *Sold by R. Bentley and S. Tidmarch.* 8°. C; CH, LC, NP, WCL.

4308 —Emblemata amatoria. Cupids addresse. *Sold by R. Bentley and S. Tidmarch,* 1683. 8°. L, O, C; CH, CN, LC, MH, TU, Y.

4309 —Emblems of love. Second edition. *For John Wren,* [1683]. 8°. L, O, C; CH, CN, LC, MH, WC, WCL, Y.

4310 — —[Anr. ed.] *Printed and sold by Hen. Overton,* [1683]. 12°. CH, WF.

4311 — —[Anr. ed.] *For J. Osborn,* [1687]. 12°. CH, MH, MIU, WF.

4312 —Lyric poems. *By J. M. for Jos. Knight and F. Saunders,* 1687. 8°. T.C.II 193. L, O, CT, LVD; CH, CN, MH, NC, WF, Y.

4313 —The revengeful mistress. *For R. Bentley, and R. Wellington,* 1696. 12°. T.C.II 588. L; Y.

4314 —Vox clamantis. *For John Playford, for Benjamin Tooke,* 1684. 8°. T.C.II 59. L, LG, CS; CN, MIU, Y.

4315 —The voyages and adventures of Capt. Barth. Sharp. *By B. W. for R. H. and S. T., and are to be sold by Walter Davis,* 1684. 8°. T.C.II 71. L, CS, CT, LWL, DT; CH, LC, MH, V, Y.

4315A **Ayscue, *Sir* George.** A letter from. *Robert Ibbitson,* 1649. brs. L.

4315B **Aytoun, John.** Unto his grace . . . petition. [*Edinburgh,* 1695.] brs. EN.

Azaria and Hushai. 1682. *See* Settle, Elkanah.

4316 **Azen, Solyman Mahomet.** A letter sent by the Grand Visier. colop: *Printed,* 1687. brs. O, SP.

B

1 **B.** The arraignment of co-ordinate power. [*London*], *for T. Hunt,* 1683. fol. L, O, CS, P, EN; CH, CN, MH, WF, Y.
—Dis-colliminium or. 1650. *See* Ward, Nathaniel.

2 —An elegy on the most accomplished virgin Madam Elizabeth Hurne. [*London*], *by N. T.,* 1983 [*i.e.,* 1683]. brs. L; MH.
—Excellent memorables. 1691. *See* Baxter, Richard.
—Memorables of the life. 1690. *See* Baxter, Richard.
B., A. Account of the late revolution. [1689.] *See* Byfield, Nathaniel.
—Answer of a minister. 1687. *See* Cartwright, Thomas.

3 —A brief relation of the beginning and ending of the troubles of the Barbadoes. *By Peter Cole,* 1653. 4°.* LT.
—Canterbury tale. 1641. *See* Brome, Alexander.
—Covent Garden drollery. 1672. *See* title.
—Demonstration how the Latine tongue. 1669. *See* Brett, Arthur.

4 —Dissertatio theoretico-practica de febribus. *Impensis Johannis Hepburn,* 1700. 8°. L, O.

5 —A dissuassive from Popery sent in a letter. *Dublin, by Benjamin Took & John Crook, to be sold by Mary Crook & Andrew Crook,* 1681. 8°.* DIX 190. C, DT.

6 —An epitaph, within this sacred vault. [1649.] brs. LT.
—Geographical and historical description. 1696. *See* Boyer, Abel.

7 —Gloria Britannica, or, the boast. *For Thomas Howkins,* 1689. 4°.* T.C.II 305. L, O, CM, LUS; WF, Y.

8 — —[Anr. ed.] *For Samuel Clark,* 1696. 4°.* O; CH.

8A —The horrible stratagems of the Jesuits. 1650. 4°.* MIU.
—Humane prudence. 1680. *See* Britaine, William de.

9 —Jacob at his journeys end. *For R. Lowndes,* 1665. 4°. O; CLC, NU.

10 —Learn to lye warm. *By H. Brugis for W. Gilbert,* 1672. 4°.* T.C.I 104. L, O, EN, DT; CH, WF.

11 —A letter from a friend in Abingdon. [*London,* 1679.] cap., fol.* L, O, MR, HH, EN; CH, WF, Y.

12 —A letter from a gentleman at Fez. colop: *By N. T.,* 1682. brs. O, OC; WF.

13 —A letter from a gentleman in Kent. *Printed*, 1648. LT, O, LG, HH; CH, MIU, WF, Y.

14 —A letter from a minister to a person of quality. [*London?* 1679.] fol.* L, O, C, EN; CH, MBA, MH, WF, Y.

15 —A letter of advice concerning marriage. *For William Miller*, 1676. 4°.* T.C.I 219. L, O; WF, Y.
—Letter of enquiry. 1689. *See* Taylor, James.

16 —A letter out of the country, to the clergy in and about the city of London. [*London*, 1692?] cap., 4°.* CS, BP, MR; CH, WF, Y.

17 —A letter to a friend: being an historical account of the affairs of Hungary. *For W. Davis*, [1684.] fol.* O, LG, HH; CH.
—Letter to a friend relating. 1690. *See* Prideaux, Humphrey.

18 —A letter to a friend: with remarks. *Printed*, 1700. 4°.* L, O, LW; CH, CLC, WF, Y.

19 —A letter to an honourable member of Parliament. *Printed for and sold by J. Nutt*, [1700.] fol.* O.
—Letter to Mr. Secretary Trenchard. [1694.] *See* Ferguson, Robert.

20 —A letter to the honourable Collonel Okey. *Printed*, 1659. 4°.* HH; Y.
—Lucky chance. 1687. *See* Behn, *Mrs.* Aphra.
—Merry tales of the mad-men. [London, 1690?] *See* Borde, Andrew.
—Model for a school. [1675.] *See* Lewis, Mark.

21 —Mutatus polemo. The horrible stratagems. *For Robert White*, 1650. 4°.* LT, O, C, EN, DT; CLC, LC, MBP, MH, Y.

22 —The mystery of phanaticism. *For T. Leigh and R. Knaplock*, 1698. 8°. T.C.III 74. L, O, CT, YM, DT; CLC, NU, TSM, WF, Y.

23 — —Second edition. *For D. Midwinter and T. Leigh*, 1698. 8°. T.C.III 100. O, DT.

23A — —"Second" edition. *For T. Leigh and R. Knaplock*, 1698. 8°. OC, OCC.

24 —News from Colchester. colop: *For Richard Janeway*, 1681. brs. L, O, LG, OC, CT; CH, WF, Y.

25 —An ode occasion'd by the death of the Queen. *By Tho. Warren for Francis Saunders*, 1695. fol.* O; CLC, MH, WF, Y.
—Pamphlet entituled, Speculum. 1688. *See* Wharton, Henry.
—Peccatum originale. Eleutheropoli, [1678.] *See* Beverland, Adriaan.

26 —The reasons for non-conformity examined and refuted. *For Walter Kettilby*, 1679. 4°.* T.C.I 367. L, O, C, EN, DT; CH, NU, WF, Y.
—Reflections on a late libel. 1680. *See* Hickeringill, Edmund.

27 —Rudiments of the Latine grammar. *For Dorman Newman*, 1678. 4°.* T.C.I 332. L, O, C, LL.

28 —The Sabbath truly sanctified. *Printed Jan*. 31, 1645. 4°.* LT, LSC, DT; CH, NU, Y.

29 —The saints freedom from tyranny vindicated. *Printed*, 1667. 4°.* L, O, C, CE; NU.
—Seasonable motives. [1689.] *See* Byfield, Nathaniel.
—Second vindication. 1697. *See* Locke, John.

30 —A serious admonition to those members of Parliament that sate alone. *For Thomas Parkhurst*, 1660. 4°.* L, O, P, HH, SP; Y.

31 —Some remarks upon government. [*London*, 1689.] cap., 4°.* L, O, C, BAMB; CH, CN, NC, WF, Y.

32 —Synopsis of vocal musick. *For Dorman Newman*, 1680. obl. 12°. T.C.I 432. L, O; LC.

33 Entry cancelled.

34 **B., A. J.** The honest citizen, or, faithful counsellor. [*London*, 1648.] cap., 4°.* LT, O, LG; CN, Y.

35 —VVhat kinde of Parliament will please the king. *Printed*, 1642. 4°.* LT, O, C, EN, DT; CH, MH, MIU, WF, Y.
B., B. Humble advice to Protestant. 1682. *See* Bird, B.

36 —A letter from St. Omers. colop: *For Langley Curtis*, [1681?] cap., fol.* L, O, C, OP; CH, CN, WF, Y.

37 —Remarks upon the two years raign of the Dauphin of France. [1690.] brs. O.

38 —The way to honour. *For Tho. Parkhurst*, 1678. 8°. L; MH, WF.

39 —The young gentleman's way to honour. *For Tho. Parkhurst*, 1678. 8°. T.C.I 322. O, C; CH.

40 **B., C.** An address to the honourable city of London. *For Allen Banks*, 1681. fol.* L, O, LG, HH, EN; CH, CN, LC, MH, TU, Y.

41 —A discovery of divine mysteries. *For Eben. Tracy*, 1700. 8°. T.C.III 208. DT; LC, MH, WF, Y.
—Disputation at Winchcombe. Oxford, [1653]. *See* Barksdale, Clement.
—Doctorum virorum elogia. 1671. *See* Barksdale, Clement.

42 —A letter sent from aboard His Highnesse the Prince of Wales. *For R. W.*, 1648. 4°.* LT, LG.
—Lusus amatorius. 1694. *See* Musæus.
—Memorials of Alderman Whitmore. 1681. *See* Barksdale, Clement.

43 Entry cancelled. —New quadrant. 1649. *See* Brookes, Christopher.
—No sacrilege. 1659. *See* Burgess, Cornelius.
—Nympha libethris: or the Cotswold muse. 1651. *See* Barksdale, Clement.

44 —The old gentleman's wish. *Cirencester*, 1685. fol. O.

45 —A paper of condemnation, past at York. [c. 1685.] 4°.* C, OCC, LF; PSC, Y.

46 —Religio militis. *By H. C. for John Taylor*, 1690. 4°.* T.C.II 289. L, O, C, LIL, DT; CH, NU, Y.
—Remembrancer of excellent men. 1670. *See* Barksdale, Clement.

47 —A short-method of physick. *By M. S. for Thomas Jenner*, 1659. 4°.* L, LWL, GH.
—Sion College, what it is. 1648. *See* Burgess, Cornelius.

48 —Vannus divinus; or a fanne. *For Francis Eglesfield*, 1670. 8°. T.C.I 64. O.
—Woollen shroud. 1679. *See* Barksdale, Clement.

48A **B., D.** In nuperam horrendam Montis Ætnæ eruptionem carmen. *Typis G. G., & impensis Mosis Pitt*, 1670. 4°.* Y.

—Insinuating bawd. [1699?] *See* Ward, Edward.

—Proposal of an inland exchange. [1695.] *See* Beeckman, Daniel.

—Two conferences between . . . 1650. *See* Brown, David.

48B —Two letters from two chief officers. *For H. Blunden,* 1642. 4°.* C, NL.

—Yet one warning more. 1660. *See* Baker, Daniel.

B., E. Alarm to all flesh. 1660. *See* Burrough, Edward.

—Apologie for the church of England. 1685. *See* Bohun, Edmund.

—Brief reflections on the Earl. 1682. *See* Borlase, Edmund.

—Brief relation of the persecutions. 1662. *See title.*

—Case of the people called Quakers. [1663.] *See* Burrough, Edward.

48C —Certain queries answered. *Printed,* 1667. 4°.* L; WF.

—Certaine queries concerning. 1647. *See* Buckler, Edward.

—Certaine sound. 1665. *See* Billing, Edward.

—Continuation of the history of the reformation. 1689. *See* Bohun, Edmund.

49 —Copy of a letter sent by. [*London,* 1679.] brs. L, O; CH, MH, MIU.

—Crying sinnes. 1656. *See* Burrough, Edward.

—Declaration of the sad. [1660]. *See* Burrough, Edward.

—Declaration to all the world. 1660. *See* Burrough, Edward.

—Description of an annuall vvorld. 1641. *See* Browne, Edward.

—Dialogue between the devil. [1649]. *See* Bradshaw, Ellis.

50 —Enchiridion medicina . . . or, a most noble panacea. *By A. Coe,* 1662. 4°.* CLM.

51 —An epistle to the beloved. 1660. 4°. O.

—Faithful testimony concerning. 1659. *See* Burrough, Edward.

—Faithful testimony for God. 1664. *See* Billing, Edward.

—General epistle to all the saints. 1660. *See* Burrough, Edward.

—A glance at the glories of sacred friendship. 1657. *See* Benlowes, Edward.

52 —The great benefit of the Christian education of children. *By R. H. for Dorman Newman,* [1663]. 4°.* MH, WF.

53 Entry cancelled.

—Hue and cry after the false prophets. 1661. *See* Burrough, Edward.

—Just and lawfull trial. 1657. *See* Burrough, Edward.

—Last conflicts and death of Mr. Thomas Peacock. 1646. *See* Bagshaw, Edward.

—Last visitation. 1660. *See* Bagshaw, Edward.

—Many strong reasons confounded. 1657. *See* Burrough, Edward.

—Message for instruction. 1658. *See* Burrough, Edward.

—Message proclaimed. [1658]. *See* Burrough, Edward.

—Midnights meditations of death. *See* Buckler, Edward.

—Mite of affection. 1659. *See* Billing, Edward.

—Principles of truth. 1665. *See title.*

54 Entry cancelled. —Proposal for the erecting. 1697. *See* Bohun, Edward.

—Returne to the ministers. 1660. *See* Burrough, Edward.

—Rules for kings. 1642. *See* Browne, Edward.

—Satan's designe. 1659. *See* Burrough, Edward.

—Some false principles. 1659. *See* Burrough, Edward.

—Something of truth made manifest. 1658. *See* Burrough, Edward.

55 —Strange and wonderful news of the birth. 1685. brs. O.

—Tender salutation of perfect love. 1661. *See* Burrough, Edward.

—Testimony against a great idolatry. 1658. *See* Burrough, Edward.

—Testimony of the Lord. 1657. *See* Burrough, Edward.

—Theophila, or. 1652. *See* Benlowes, Edward.

—To all dear friends. [*London,* 1662.] *See title.*

To the beloved and chosen. 1660. *See* Burrough, Edward.

—To the present assembly. [*London,* 1659.] *See* Burrough, Edward.

—True Christian religion. 1658. *See* Burrough, Edward.

—True faith. 1656. *See* Burrough, Edward.

—Vindication of the people. [1660]. *See* Burrough, Edward.

—Visitation of love, 1660. *See* Burrough, Edward.

—Visitation of the rebellious nation. 1656. *See* Burrough, Edward.

—Wofull cry. [1657]. *See* Burrough, Edward.

—VVord of reproof. 1659. *See* Billing, Edward.

56 **B., F.** The character of Sr. Arthur Haslerig. [*London,* 1661.] brs. LT.

57 —Clavis grammatica: or, the ready way. *For Robert Harford,* 1678. 8°. T.C.I 331. L.

—Collection of some passages. [1700.] *See* Pennyman, John.

58 —Considerations and proposals presented to . . . Oliver. 1659. 4°.* L.

59 —A free but modest censure. *For A. Baldwin,* 1698. 4°.* T.C.III 82. L, O, C, OC, LVD; CH, CN, NU, WF, Y.

—Innocency vindicated. [1684.] *See* Bugg, Francis.

60 —Judgments of God. 1668. 8°. LW.

61 [–] A letter from a gentleman in the country, to a member. *Dublin, reprinted for Patrick Campbell,* 1697. 4°.* DIX 290. DT.

62 — —[Anr. ed.] *Dublin, reprinted for Patk. Campbell,* 1698. 4°.* DIX 298. DT, DI.

62A —A letter to A. M. of the House of Commons. *George Huddleston,* 1698. 8°.* L; NC.

63 —The office of the good house-wife. *By T. Ratcliffe, and N. Thompson, for Richard Mills,* 1672. 8°. T.C.I 120. L, GU.

63A —On the coronation of King James II. *For B. Tooke,* [1685]. brs. O.

64 —To all that observe dayes. [*London,* 1660.] fol.* LF, BBN.

65 —Vercingetorixa: or, the Germane princess. *Printed,* 1663. 4°.* L, O, LG; CH, CN, MH.

B., G. Autarchy. 1691. *See* Burghope, G.

—Case of compulsion. 1688. *See* Burnet, Gilbert, *bp.*

—De linguarum orientalium. 1658. *See* Beveridge, William, *bp.*

—Declaration of almighty God. [1690.] *See* Burnet, Gilbert, *bp.*

—Engelland, wic stchts. 1688. *See* Burnet, Gilbert, *bp.*

66–7 Entries cancelled.

—Essay in morality. 1682. *See* Bright, George.

—More particular and exact relation. 1645. *See* Bishop, George.

68 —A panegyrick on His most excellent Majesty King William the IIId. *For Richard Baldwin,* 1697. fol.* L; TU.

69 Entry cancelled. —Rarities. 1665. *See* Bridges, Noah.

—Reflections on the relation of the English reformation. *Amsterdam,* 1688. *See* Burnet, Gilbert, *bp.*

—Relation of a conference. 1676. *See* Burnet, Gilbert, *bp.*

—To thee, Charls Stuart. [Bristol? 1660.] *See* Bishop, George.

70 —Two letters from the Hagve: of Prince Charles, his going into Scotland. *By B.A.,* 1649. 4°. LT, EN; Y.

—Voyce from Heaven, speaking. 1659. *See* Bownd, George.

71 —The way to be rich. *For E. Davis,* 1662. 4°.* L; MH, Y.

—Word to the wavering. 1689. *See* Burnet, Gilbert, *bp.*

72 **B., H.** An answer to the excellent and elegant speech made by Sir Thomas Player. [*London,* 1679.] cap., fol.* L, O, LG, HH; CN, MBA, MH, PU, Y.

—Boston almanack. Boston, 1692. *See under* Almanacs, Harris, Benjamin.

—Charity of church-men. 1649. *See* Brooke, Humphrey.

73 —The crafts-mens craft. *By J. and J.M. for W.L.,* 1649. 4°.* LT; CH.

—Critica juris. 1661. *See* Plowden, Edmund.

74 Entry cancelled.

—Divine examples of God's severe judgments. 1642. *See title.*

—Durable legacy. 1681. *See* Brooke, Humphrey.

—Englands old religion. Antwerp, 1658. *See* Beda, *venerable.*

—Jesu-worship confuted. 1641. *See* Burton, Henry.

—Landgartha. Dublin, 1641. *See* Burnell, Henry.

75 —The mantle thrown off. *For Richard Baldwin,* 1689. 4°.* L, O, C, LVF, EN; CH, MIU, WF, Y.

76 —Mephibosheth and Ziba: or, the appeal of the Protestants. *For R. Chiswell,* 1689. 4°. T.C.II 306. L, O, C, EN, DT; CH, NU, WF, Y.

Osculum pacis. 1641. *See* Byam, Henry.

—Peace-maker; or, solid reasons. 1646. *See* Burton, Henry.

77 —A reply to the excellent and elegant speech made by Sir Thomas Player. [*London,* 1679.] cap., fol.* O, LW, HH; CN, MH, WF.

78 —Schola urbanitatis. *Typis E.G., impensis G.Lee,* 1652. 8°.* L, M; WF.

79 —Solsitium Britannicum. [1660?] cap., 8°.* CH, WF.

80 —A true copy of a letter (intercepted) going for Holland. *For H.B. Feb. 10th,* 1680. fol.* L, O, HH; CH, MBA, WF, Y.

81 —A vindication of Sir Thomas Player. [*London,* 1679?] brs. L, O, C, LG, HH; CH, CN, MH, WF, Y.

—Wit a sporting. 1657. *See* Bold, Henry.

81A **B., H. G. C. L.** A discourse in defense of the Londoners last petition. *For Iohn Carter,* [1642]. 4°.* L, LG, DT; Y.

82 **B., I.** The attvrneys gvide. *By F.L. for Tho. Firby,* 1656. 8°. LT; MBA, MHL.

82A —The catechism of the church of England. *By E. Okes for R. Royston,* 1669. 8°. OC.

—Description of the province and bay. Edinburgh, 1699. *See* Blackwell, Isaac.

—Explanatory notes. 1698. *See* Butler, John.

—Groane at the funerall. [London], 1649. *See* King, Henry.

—Heavenly diurnall. 1644. *See* Blackwell, Jonathan.

—Herefordshire gardens. 1657. *See* Beale, John.

83 —Heroick edvcation, or choice maximes. *For William Hope and Henry Herringman,* 1657. 8°. LT, O, CS; CH, NC, WF, Y.

83A —An humble address to the livery-men of London. *For J.Bayly,* 1682. brs. L, O, LG.

—Innocency cleared. 1658. *See* Boweter, John.

84 —A letter from a gentleman in Colchester. [*London,* 1648.] brs. LT; MIU.

85 —A letter from an honourable gentleman in the court. [*London*], *printed,* 1647. 4°.* LT, C, HH; WF, Y.

—London's triumph. 1656. *See* Bulteel, John.

—Merchants remonstrance. 1644. *See* Battie, John.

86 —A nevv map of England. *Printed,* 1659. 4°.* LT, OC; CH, MIU, Y.

—Oxonian antippodes. 1644. *See* Brandon, John.

—Philocophus: or. . . . 1648. *See* Bulwer, John.

87 —Scripture motives for calendar reformation. 1650. 4°.* NHC.

88 —To the most honourable and high court of Parliament. The humble petition of the gentlemen . . . of Cornwall. [1642.] brs. STEELE 2062. LT, O, LL, LS, HH; CLC, MU.

B., J. Account of the French usurpation. 1679. *See* Bethel, Slingsby.

89 —An account of the original, nature, preparation, vertues, and use of the Vatican pill. [*London,* 1670?] cap., 4°.* L.

—Αγιαστρολογια. 1680. *See* Butler, John.

—1669. An almanack. Cambridge, [Mass.] 1669. *See under* Almanacs, Browne, Joseph.

90 —From aboard the Van-herring. Another letter from Legorn. colop: [*London*], *printed and are to be sold by Richard Janeway,* 1680. cap., fol. L, O, C, MR; CH, CN, MH, TU, WF, Y.

91 —From a-board the Van Herring. The answer to the letter from Leghorn answered. colop: *For T.Davies,* 1681. cap., fol.* L, O, LUG, LG; CH, MH, WF, Y.

92 —Ανθρωποκτονου ταφος, or, the bloody . . . fall. *For Robert Horne.* 1659. 4°. L.

—Anthropometamorphosis. 1650. *See* Bulwer, John.

—Argument shewing that 'tis. 1699. *See* Berisford, John.

—Assembly-man. 1681. *See* Birkenhead, *Sir* John.

—Astrology asserted. 1680. *See* Butler, John.

—Bellua marina: or. . . . 1690. *See* Butler, John.

93 —A bill and answer, betwixt Jack Catch, . . . and Slingsby Bethel. *By J.B. for Joseph Hindmarsh*, 1686. fol.* T.C.II 179. L, O; MH, WF, Y.
—Birinthea. 1664. *See Bulteel, John.*

94 —The blazing star. *For Sam. Speed*, 1665. 4°.* L, O; IU, MH, Y.
—Book for boys. 1686. *See Bunyan, John.*
—Breviate of saving. 1643. *See Brinsley, John.*
—Calendar-reformation. 1648. *See Brinsley, John, the younger.*

95 —Calumny condemned. *By J.C. for L. Chapman*, 1659. 4°.* EN; CH, CN, MH, WF, Y.
—Catholick schismatology. 1685. *See Browne, J.*

96 —Certain proposals humbly offered, for the preservation. [*London*], *printed*, 1674. 4°.* L, O, LG, OC; MH, NU, WF, Y.
—Chirologia: or . . . 1644. *See Bulwer, John.*
—Chironomia: or . . . 1644. *See Bulwer, John.*

97 —Christian queries to quaking-Christians. 1663. 8°. O.
—Compendious collection. 1675. *See Brydall, John.*

98 —A compleat and true narrative of the manner. *Printed and are to be sold by Henry Million*, 1679. fol.* L, O, CM, HH, EN; CH, CN, MBA, TU, WF, Y.

98A —Crumbs of comfort . . . A sermon. *For W. T., sold by J. Clarke*, [1680?] 8°. CM.

99 —The description and use of the carpenters-rule. *By W. G. for W. Lugger and W. Fisher*, 1656. 8°. O, LR.

99A — —[Anr. ed.] *By W. G. for William Fisher*, 1662. 12°. L, CM.

100 —Directions for the right receiving of the Lord's Supper. *For Tho. Parkhurst*, 1679. 8°. T.C.I 348. L, O, C.
—Discourse on the late funds. 1694. *See Briscoe, John.*
—Diurnal speculum. 1696. *See Bockett, John.*
—Divine and spiritual ambassadour. 1663. *See Bird, John.*
—Doctrine of the fathers. 1695. *See Braddocke, John.*
—English expositor. 1641. *See Bullokar, John.*
—Epitome of the art. 1669. *See Blagrave, Joseph.*

101 —A faire in Spittle fields. [*London*], *by J.C.*, 1652. 4°.* LT; CN, MH, WCL.
—Fifty queries. 1675. *See Brandon, John.*

102 —The filacers office. *For Tho. Firby*, [1657]. 8°. LT, DC; LC, MHL, WF, YL.
—A form of sound words. 1662. *See Brandon, John.*

103 —Glad tydings, Christ held forth in the seals. *By T. P.*, 1643. brs. LS, DT.

104 —Glad tydings of joy. [*London*], *printed*, 1643. 4°.* LT, C; MH.

105 —Good will towards men. 1675. 8°. LW, ENC.
—Groane fetch'd. 1649. *See King, Henry.*
—Harvest-home. 1674. *See Bryan, John.*
—Heart's ease. 1690. *See Bardwood, James.*
—Hereford orchards. 1657. *See Beale, John.*

106 —The Holy Scripture owned. [*London*], 1692. fol.° LF.
—Innocent usurper. 1694. *See Banks, John.*
—Journal or diary. 1656. *See Beadle, John.*
—Kedarminster-stuff. 1681. *See Browne, John.*

107 —The knight errant. *By E. C.*, 1652. 8°.* LT.

108 —The last will and testament of superstition. *By Iohn Hammond*, 1642. 4°.* LT, O.

109 —A letter from a citizen of Glasgow. [*Glasgow*], 1700. 4°.* EN.

110 —A letter from a gentleman of worth from Dublin. *For R. B. Jan. 7*, 1642[3]. 4°.* LT, O, C, LFEA.

111 —A letter from J. B. alias Oldcutt, to his friend Mr. Jenks. [*London*, 1679.] cap., fol.* LT, O, C, BR, EN; CH, CN, MBA, MH, TU, Y.

112 —A letter to a member of Parliament concerning the suppression of piracy. 1699/1700. fol. T.C.III 125. MB.
—Loyalties tears. 1649. *See Birkenhead, Sir John.*

112A —Lucerna scholastica. Or, the scholar's companion. *For Jonathon [sic] Robinson, sold by Robert Benson, Penreth*, 1680. 16°.* T.C.I. 374. L.

112AB —Ludus literarum. *For the author*, 1674. 4°. L, CS; WF.

113 —The morality of the seventh-day-sabbath. *By Francis Clark for L. Curtis*, 1683. 4°. O.

113A —A more particular and exact account of the totall defeat. [*London?*] *printed*, 1659. 4°.* CH, NN.
—Most sacred and divine science. 1680. *See Butler, John.*

114 —Mrs. Wardens observations upon her husbands reverend speech. [*London*, 1642.] cap., 4°.* LT, O, LG, C; MH, NU, Y.

115 —Muggleton's last will. 1679. 4°.* O; CH, MIU, NU.
—New additions. 1685. *See Blagrave, Joseph.*

116 —New observations dedicated to the King's most excellent Majestie. [*London*], *for George Tomlinson*, 1642. 4°.* LT, HH; CLC, MBP, MH, NU, Y.

117 —New poems. *Printed*, 1699. 8°. O.
—Pathomyotomia or. . . . 1649. *See Bulwer, John.*
—Pietatis in parentes. 1700. *See Brydall, John.*
—Poor mechanick's plea. 1699. *See Bockett, John.*
—Practical Christian. 1670. *See Bartlet, John.*

118 —A Presbyter of the Church of England. 1695. 4°. O.

119 —A proposal humbly offered to the Parliament, for suppressing of popery. [*London*], *printed, and are to be sold by R. Janeway*, 1680. cap., fol.* L, O, OM; CH, CN, Y.

120 —A Protestant letter to the Lords in the Tower. colop: *Printed*, 1680. brs. L, O; CH.
—Rarities of the world. 1651. *See Baildon, Joshua.*
—Relation of the troubles. 1645. *See Bulteel, John.*

121 —Royall and gracious priviledges. *H. Moseley*, 1645. 4°.* O; CH, Y.
—Saints' triumph. 1685. *See Blare, Joseph.*

122 —A seasonable word of advice. 1655. 4°. O.
—Serious item. 1666. *See Bangor, Josiah.*

123 —A sermon on Job xiv. lo; or, the survey of man. *Printed*, 1652. 4°.* O, SC, LW, WCA; WF.

123A —A sermon preached August 2, 1698. *For J. Roberts at Bridgewater and to be sold by him and by John Sprint* [*London*], 1698. T.C.III 90. LW, BR; WF.

124 —Several petitions presented to the honourable Houses of Parliament. *For Iohn Wright*, 1641. 4°.* LT, LL, HH, SP; CH, CLC, WF, Y.

125 —The shepherd's lasher lashd. [*London*], *printed*, 1665. brs. L.

—Short catechisme. 1646. *See* Ball, John.

126 Entry cancelled. —Sick-bed thoughts. 1667. *See* Batchiler, John.

—Sleepy spouse of Christ, 1667. *See* Bradshaw, James.

127 —Some reflections upon the Earl of Danby. [*London*, 1679.] cap., fol.* L, O, C, MR, EN; CH, CN, MH, TU, Y.

128 —Special newes from the army at Warwicke. *For Henry Overton*, Octob. 29. 1642. 4°.* LT, EC, HH.

—Sprightly comparison. 1695. *See* Banister, John.

129 Entry cancelled. —Tast of a catechisticall-preaching-exercise. 1667/8. *See* Batchiler, John.

—Testimony in that which separates. [1673.] *See* Bolton, John.

130 —Thanks upon thanks: or, the suburb's joy. colop: *Printed*, 1680. brs. L, O, C, MC; CH, MH, NC, PU, Y.

—Tradidi vobis: or. . . . 1662. *See* Belson, John.

—View of the people. 1654. *See* Bulwer, John.

—Vindication of the remarks on the Bishop of Derry's discourse, 1695. *See* Boyse, Joseph.

—Weighty reasons. 1679. *See* Briggs, Joseph.

131 —The young lovers guide. *Printed and are to be sold by the booksellers*, 1699. 8°. T.C.III 142. L, O, CS; CLC, CN, MH, WF.

131A **B., J. C.** Rebellious antedote. *By George Croom*, 1685. brs. L, O, HH; MH, WF.

132 **B., J. G.** Royall poems presented to . . . Charles the II. *For R. Wood*, 1660. 4°.* MH.

B., L. Claustrum animae. 1671. *See* Beaulieu, Luke de.

—Murther will out. [1692.] *See* Braddon, Laurence.

—New academy. 1671. *See* title.

—Reformed monastery. 1649. [i.e. 1699]. *See* Beaulieu, Luke de.

B., M. Church of Rome no guide. 1700. *See* Wake, William, abp.

133 —A description of a prerogative royal. *For T.B.*, 1642. 4°.* LT, HH; CH, CU, MH, NU, WF, Y.

—Elegiack essay humbly offered. 1699. *See* Browne, M.

134 —Good news for all parties. [*London*], *printed*, 1660. brs. MH.

135 —The ladies cabinet enlarged and opened. *By T. M. forr* [sic] *M. M., G. Bedell, and T. Collins*, 1654. 12°. LT; CH, LC, NC.

136 ——Second edition. *By T. M. for G. Bedell and T. Collins*, 1655. O; WF.

137 ——Fourth edition. *For G. Bedel, and T. Collins*, 1667. 12°. L, LWL; NN.

138 —Learne of a Turke. *Printed*, 1660. 4°.* LT, O, EN, DT; CH, CN, TU, WF, Y.

139 —A letter from a matron of rank quality in Windsor. colop: *For J. Shuter*, 1682. fol.* O, EN; MH, Y.

—Popery banished. Edinburgh, 1689. *See* title.

140–1 Entries cancelled.

—Roman-Catholick principles. 1680. *See* Corker, James.

B., M. C. Mercurius Cambro-Britannicus. 1652. *See* Griffith, Alexander.

142 **B., M. Z.** The battle of Nevvbvrne. Second edition. *Glasgow, by George Anderson*, 1643. 4°.* ALDIS 1071. EN, HG.

143 **B., N.** A copie of the oath taken by the papists. *For William Bladen*, 1642. 4°.* LT, O, LFEA; CH, MH, WF, Y.

—Discourse of trade. 1690. *See* Barbon, Nicholas.

144 —Elisha succeeding Elijah: or, a sermon. 1646. 4°. YM.

—Figure of foure. 1654. *See* Breton, Nicholas.

—History of the life and actions of St. Athanasius. 1664. *See* Bacon, Nathaniel.

145 —An inquiry into the design and nature. 1681. 4°. O, DT.

—Journal of meditations. 1669. *See* Bacon, Nathaniel.

—Κοσμοβρεφια, or. . . . 1658. *See* Billingsly, Nicholas.

—Lazarus redivivus. 1671. *See* Blake, Nicholas.

—Letter to a gentleman in the country, giving an account. 1684. *See* Barbon, Nicholas.

—Letter with a narrative, 1659. *See* Butter, Nathaniel.

—Modest and peaceable inquiry. 1681. *See* Humfrey, John.

—Proposal for raising the publick credit. [*London?* 1697]. *See* Barbon, Nicholas.

—Regenerate mans growth. 1646. *See* Barnett, Nehemiah.

—Resurrection founded. 1700. *See* Bear, Nicholas.

—Sermon, shewing the meanes. 1649. *See* Basely, N.

—Sir Philip Sydneys Ourania. 1653. *See* Baxter, Nathaniel.

—Stenographie. 1659. *See* Bridges, Noah.

146 —Two meditations. *Printed*, 1648. 4°. O.

147 **B., O.** A dialogue or, discourse betwixt two old acquaintance. *For R. K.*, 1647. 4°.* LT.

148 **B., O. F.** Tamisis triumphans, sive panegyris Jacobo II. *Anno* 1685. fol. O; MH, WF, Y.

B., P. Amours of bonne Sforza. 1684. *See* title.

—Court secret. 1689. *See* Bellon, Peter.

149 —A declaration against Prince Rupert. *Printed*, 1642[3]. 4°.* LT, DT; CH, MH, MIU, WF, Y.

—Defence of the lawfulnesse. 1645. *See* Barbon, Praisegod.

—Discourse tending to prove. 1642. *See* Barbon, Praisegod.

150 —A help to magistrates. *For N. Boddington*, 1700. 12°. T.C.III 175. CS, AU.

150A ——Second edition. —, 1700. 12°. T.C.III 204. LLL, O.

151 —Juvenilia sacra. *By Tho. Mabb, for John Playfere*, 1664. 8°. L, O.

152 —The means to free Europe from the French usurpation. *For R. Bently*, 1689. 8°. T.C.II 324. O, C, MR, SP; WF.

—Mock-duellist. 1675. *See* Bellon, Peter.

152A —A nosegay of divine truths. *For the author, sold by B. Crayle*, 1687. 12°. T.C.II 192. LSC.

153 —Pilulæ antipodendagriæ: or Venus's refuge. *For A. Brook*, 1669. 8°.* L.

154 —The priviledges of the House of Commons. *For J. R.*, 1642. 4°.* LT, O, CT, HH, DT; CH, MH, NU, WF, Y.

154A —Proposals humbly offered to the . . . Commons, for raising money. [*London?* 1700.] brs. L.

—Reply to the frivolous. 1643. *See* Barbon, Praisegod.

—Reviv'd fugitive. 1690. *See* title.

155 **B., R.** Adagia Scotica. *For Nath. Brooke,* 1668. 12°. O; CH.

—Admirable curiosities. 1682. *See* Crouch, Nathaniel.

156 —An antidote against Arminianisme. *For Sa. Gallibrand,* 1641. 12°. O, CM.

—Apologie for Paris. 1649. *See* Baron, Robert.

157 —Arithmetick symbolical. *For A. Crook,* 1649. 8°.* L, O.

—Αὐτοκατάκριτος: or. . . . 1662. *See* Boreman, Robert.

158 —A briefe account of some choice and famous medicines. *Oxford, L. Lichfield,* 1676. 4°.* MADAN 3097. LS; WSG.

159 —A briefe ansvver to R. H. *For Giles Calvert,* 1646. 4°.* LT, DT; CH, NHC.

160 —The Cambridge royallist imprisoned. [1643]. 4°.* LT, O; CH, MM.

—Capitall hereticks. 1659. *See* Brathwaite, Richard.

—Captive-captain. 1665. *See* Braithwaite, Richard.

—Catechism and confession. 1674. *See* Barclay, Robert.

161 —A caveat or warning. *For H. G.,* 1683. brs. O, CM.

—Christian virtuoso. 1690. *See* Boyle, Robert.

—Comment upon the two tales. 1665. *See* Brathwaite, Richard.

162 —The coppy of a letter from Paris. *For Edward Griffin,* 1648[9]. 4°.* LT; MH, WF.

163 —The coppie of a letter sent to a gentlevvoman, *Printed,* 1642. 4°.* MH.

164 —Coral and steel. *For the author, sold by S. Miller,* [1660?]. 12°. L; CH, LC.

—Country-mans catechisme. 1652. *See* Boreman, Robert.

—Covent Garden drollery. 1672. *See* title.

165 —Crums of comfort for the mournful babe of hope. [*London,* 1664.] 4°. LF; CH.

—De ipsa natura. 1687. *See* Boyle, Robert.

—Delightful fables. 1691. *See* Crouch, Nathaniel.

—Delights for the ingenious. 1684. *See* Crouch, Nathaniel.

—Disquisition about the final causes. 1688. *See* Boyle, Robert.

—Doctresse. 1656. *See* Bunworth, Richard.

166 —A door of salvation opened. *For Wil. Larner,* 1648. 8°. LT, CCH; MH, NPT.

—England's monarchs. 1685. *See* Crouch, Nathaniel.

—English acquisitions in Guinea. 1700. *See* Crouch, Nathaniel.

—English empire in America. 1685. *See* Crouch, Nathaniel.

—English heroe. 1687. *See* Crouch, Nathaniel.

—Epistle directed to all. 1642. *See* Bernard, Richard.

—Excellency of theology. 1679. *See* Boyle, Robert.

—Extraordinary adventures. 1683. *See* Crouch, Nathaniel.

—Female excellency. 1688. *See* Crouch, Nathaniel.

—Folly and envy. 1694. *See* Bridgman, Robert.

—Free enquiry into. 1685/6. *See* Boyle, Robert.

—Gagg for the Quakers. 1659. *See* Smith, Thomas.

—General history of earthquakes. 1692. *See* Crouch, Nathaniel.

—History of Oliver Cromwell. 1692. *See* Crouch, Nathaniel.

—History of the House of Orange. 1693. *See* Crouch, Nathaniel.

—History of the kingdom of Ireland. 1693. *See* Crouch, Nathaniel.

—History of the kingdoms of Scotland. 1685. *See* Crouch, Nathaniel.

—History of the nine worthies. 1687. *See* Crouch, Nathaniel.

—History of the principality. 1695. *See* Crouch, Nathaniel.

—History of the two late kings. 1693. *See* Crouch, Nathaniel.

—How the love of God. [1662?]. *See* Baker, Richard.

167-8 Entries cancelled.

—Isle of man. 1648. *See* Bernard, Richard.

—Kingdom of darkness. 1688. *See* Crouch, Nathaniel.

—Lachrymæ musarum. 1649. *See* Brome, Richard, *ed.*

—Life and death of the godly. 1676. *See* Bragge, Robert.

—Life of Dr. Thomas Morton. York, 1669. *See* Baddeley, Richard.

—Ministery of Christ asserted. 1658. *See* Brown, Robert.

—Miracles of art and nature. 1677. *See* Crouch, Nathaniel.

—Mirza: a tragedie. [1647]. *See* Baron, Robert.

—Monastichon Britanicum; or. . . . 1655. *See* Broughton, Richard.

—Monthly preparations. 1696. *See* Baxter, Richard.

—Mustur roll. 1655. *See* Brathwait, Richard.

—New birth. 1654. *See* Bartlet, Richard.

—Occasional reflections. 1669. *See* Boyle, Robert.

—Ὁμοτροπια naturæ. 1656. *See* Bunworth, Richard.

—Παιεια-Θριαμβος. The triumph. 1653. *See* Boreman, Robert.

—Parallel or briefe comparison. 1641. *See* Baillie, Robert.

—Paraphrase upon the Lord's prayer. 1641. *See* Brathwaite, Richard.

—Περιαμμα. 1659. *See* Walker, Obadiah.

—Πνευματου διακονια: or. . . . 1682. *See* Baxter, Richard.

—Pocula castalia. 1650. *See* Baron, Robert.

—A poem humbly presented. 1696. *See* Bovet, Richard.

—Proposal for sending back. 1690. *See* Buckley, Sir Richard.

—Proposals for printing [Hebrew] or, the Scripture treasury. [1690.] *See* Bentley, Richard.

169 —Proposals humbly offered to the honourable House of Commons, first, for a way. [*London,* 1696.] brs. LU.

—Questions propounded to George Whitehead. [1659]. *See* Blome, Richard.

170   —The revelation of God. *Printed*, 1665. 8°. L, O.

—Review of Doctor Bramble. Delf, 1649. *See* Baillie, Robert.

170A   —The royal plea. [*London*], *printed*, 1649. 4°.* WF.

—Satisfaction tendred. 1689. *See* Booker, Richard.

170B   —A school of divine meditations. *For Jonah Deacon*, [1683]. 8°. CM.

—Sea-men undeceived. 1648. *See* Badiley, Richard.

—Some motives. 1659. *See* Boyle, Robert.

—Strength and power of God. [1660?]. *See* Baker, Richard.

—Surprizing miracles. 1683. *See* Crouch, Nathaniel.

—Triumph of faith. 1654. *See* Boreman, Robert.

171   —A trve and fvll relation of the late sea fight. *For E. Golding, May* 10, 1647. 4°.* LT, MR.

—Unfortunate court favourites. 1695. *See* Crouch, Nathaniel.

—Unparalleled varieties. 1683. *See* Crouch, Nathaniel.

—Vanity of the life. 1688. *See* Crouch, Nathaniel.

171A   —The victorious proceedings of the Protestant army in Ireland. *By B. A.*, 1647. 4°.* LT, C, LV.

—View of the English acquisition. 1686. *See* Crouch, Nathaniel.

—Vinditiæ pædo-baptisme; or. . . . 1685. *See* Burthogge, Richard.

—Wonderful curiosities. 1682. *See* Crouch, Nathaniel.

—Wonderful prodigies. 1682. *See* Crouch, Nathaniel.

172   —A word in season; or, a letter from a reverend divine. *For R. G.*, 1679. 4°.* O; NR.

173   — —[Anr. ed.] *Edinburgh*, 1679. 4°.* ALDIS 2180. EN.

174   —A word of information & advice touching tythes. colop: *For Giles Calvert*, 1652. cap., 4°.* LT.

175   —The work of sin (in the flesh). *Printed*, 1663. 4°.* L, LF; CH, MH, PH, PSC.

—Youths divine pastime. 1691. *See* Crouch, Nathaniel.

B., S. An almanack for . . . 1657. Cambridge, 1657. *See under* Almanacs, Bradstreet, Samuel.

—Examination of Dr. Comber's. 1690. *See* Bolde, Samuel.

—Letter to the parishioners. 1700. *See* Brewster, Samuel.

176   —A letter wherein is shewed, first, what worship. *For William Churchill in Dorchester*, 1680. 4°. T.C.I 401. L, O, CT, HH, DT; MH, NGT, Y.

—Oppressed prisoners complaint. 1662. *See* Blackberry, Sarah.

—Second examination. 1691. *See* Bolde, Samuel.

—Small account. 1698. *See* Blandford, Susannah.

—Small treatise writ. 1700. *See* Blandford, Susannah.

177   —This coming to my hand, and reading it over, . . . how sin is strengthened. colop: *For Thomas Simmons*, 1657. cap., 4°.* LT, OC.

B., S. F. W. *See* Wortley, Sir Francis.

B., T. 1678. An almanack. Cambridge, [Mass.] 1678. *See under* Almanacs, Brattle, Thomas.

—Analecta: or. . . . 1693. *See* Barker, Thomas.

178   [–] Animadversions on the medicinal observations, of the Heidelberg, . . . Frederick Loss. *For William Willis*, 1674. 8°. L, O; WF, WSG.

—Animadversions upon Sᵣ Richard Baker's. Oxon, 1672. *See* Blount, Thomas.

179   —An appeal by the coming. [169–?] fol. O.

—Appeal most humble. 1691. *See* Beverley, Thomas.

—Brief view of the state. 1696. *See* Beverley, Thomas.

—Certification of two points. 1646. *See* Bakewell, Thomas.

—Charter granted. 1649. *See* Bayly, Thomas.

180   —A Christian admonition. *Printed*, [1641]. 4°.* O, CT; TU.

—Christianity the great mystery. 1696. *See* Beverly, Thomas.

—Countrie girle. 1647. *See* Brewer, Antony.

—Course of lectures. Oxford, 1696. *See* Bray, Thomas.

180A   —David and Saul: or His Majesty's case. *For the author, sold by John Clark*, 1696. 4°.* L, CT; MH.

180B   —The devil's an asse. *Printed*, 1660. 4°.* L; WF, Y.

181   —Directions about preparing. 1669. 8°. O.

—Discourse of miracles upon. 1699. *See* Beverley, Thomas.

—Discourse of the judgements. 1668. *See* Beverley, Thomas.

—Doctrinæ sphæricæ. Oxoniæ, 1662. *See* Brancker, Thomas.

—End to controversie. Doway, 1654. *See* Bayly, Thomas.

182   —The engagement vindicated. *By T. Mab and A. Coles for T. B.*, 1650. 4°.* LT, O, SP, DT; CN, MBP, MH, NU, TU.

—Epitome of sacred scriptvre. 1644. *See* Belke, Thomas.

183   —Extraordinary newes from the court of Spain. *For Richard Lowndes*, 1650. 4°.* LT, O; Y.

—Fragmenta antiquitatis. 1679. *See* Blount, Thomas.

—Fresh memorial. 1696. *See* Beverley, Thomas.

—Generall inefficacy. 1670. *See* Beverley, Thomas.

—Glossographia: or. . . . 1656. *See* Blount, Thomas.

—Great charter for. . . . 1696. *See* Beverley, Thomas.

—Grounds and occasions. 1670. *See* Eachard, John.

—Heresie detected. 1649. *See* Bakewell, Thomas.

—History of apparitions. 1658. *See* Bromhall, Thomas.

—Justification of two points. 1646. *See* Bakewell, Thomas.

184   —A letter from a gentleman in Manchester. *For John Whitlock*, 1694. 4°.* L.

185   —A letter written by a minister, for the satisfaction. *By Henry Hills*, 1686. 4°.* L, DT; NU.

185A   — —[Anr. ed.] —, 1688. 4°.* MH, Y.

—Line of time. 1696. *See* Beverley, Thomas.

186   —Λόγοι απολογητικοι. Foure apologicall tracts. [*London*], *printed*, 1649. 4°.* LT, O, OM, HH, DT; CH, CN, MH, WF, Y.

—Londons triumph. 1656. *See* Brewer, Thomas.

—Love will finde out. 1661. *See* Shirley, James.

187   —The loyalty of the last long Parliament. *For Francis Smith, senior*, 1681. 4°.* L, O, CT, MR, HH; CH, CN, MBA, NU, WF, Y.

188   —Marleborovves miseries. *Printed*, 1643. 4°.* LT, O, LCL.
     —Marrow of physicke. 1648. *See* Brugis, Thomas.

189   —A message from the Lord General Crumwel to the communalty of ... Scotland. *For J. J.*, 1650. 4°.* LT, EN.

190   —Minerva's check to the author. *For Rowland Reynolds*, 1680. brs. L, C; CH.
     —Mr. Hobb's state of nature. 1672. *See* Eachard, John.
     —Moderate ansvver to these. 1645. *See* Blake, Thomas.

191   —The muses congratulatory address to ... General Monck. [*London*, 1660.] brs. LT, O; CH, MH.

192   —Nevves from Rome. Or a relation of the Pope. [*London*], printed, 1641. 4°.* LT, O, CT; CH, MH, WF, Y.

193   —Nevves from Rome, or a trve relation. *Printed, and are to be sold by Henry Walker*, 1641. 4°.* LT, O, LVF; NU, Y.
     —Nuncius propheticus. 1642. *See* Le Wright, Raoul.

194   —Observations upon Prince Rupert's white dogge, called Boye. [*London*], printed, 1642. 4°.* L, O, LG, HH, EN; CN, MH, TU, WF, Y.

195   — —[Anr. ed.] *Printed*, 1643. 4°.* LT, O, CS, EN, DT.

196   Entry cancelled. —The original of kingly and ecclasiastical government. 1681. *See* Barlow, Thomas, *bp.*

197   —A perfect summary of the most remarkable passages. [*London*, 1648.] cap., 4°.* LT.
     —Philanax Anglicus: or, ... 1663. *See* Janson, *Sir* Henry.

198   —The presidente of presidents; or, an elegie on ... John Bradshaw. [1659.] brs. LT, O.

199   —The rebellion of Naples. *For J. G. & G. B.*, 1649. 8°. L, O, LVD, OW, EN; CH, CU, LC, MH, WF, Y.

200   — —[Anr. ed.] —, 1652. 8°. LT, O; WF, Y.
     —Resolution of the judges. 1670. *See* Blount, Thomas.
     —Royal charter granted. 1649. *See* Bayly, Thomas.

201–2   Entries cancelled.

203   —The saints inheritance. *By Richard Cotes, to be sold by John Sweeting*, 1643. 4°.* LT, CT, DT; CLC, NHC, WF.
     —Scripture enquiry. 1642. *See* Belke, T.
     —Several forms of instruments. 1674. *See* Blount, Thomas.
     —Several statutes concerning bankrupts. 1670. *See* Blount, Thomas.
     —Some observations upon the ansvver. 1671. *See* Eachard, John.
     —Some sacramentall instructions. 1649. *See* Bedford, Thomas.
     —Tidings of peace. [1692.] *See* Beverley, Thomas.
     —Treatise of specters. 1658. *See* Bromhall, Thomas.
     —Two faithful lovers. [1675.] *See* Bowne, Tobias.
     —Vindiciæ gratiæ. 1650. *See* Bedford, Thomas.
     —Waters of Marah. 1648. *See* Batt, Timothy.
     —World of errors. 1673. *See* Blount, Thomas.

204   —The young mans guide. Fourth edition. *For J. Coniers*, 1676. 8°.* L.

     B., T. R. T. Deliciæ Parnassi. *Dublinii*, 1700. *See* Rogers, Thomas.

     B., Th. Soveraign remedy. 1657. *See* Burroughs, Thomas.

205   **B., V.** A table of the 12 astrologicall houses. *For Simon Miller*, 1654. 8°. L, AU.

205A   **B., W.** An abridgment of the Life of S. Francis Xaverius. *S. Omers, for Thomas Geubels*, 1667. 8°. L.
     —Banishment for the testimony. 1664. *See* Borough, William.
     —Bonasus vapulans. 1672. *See* Hickman, Henry.
     —Century of select hymns. 1659. *See* Barton, William.
     —Christ and the covenant. 1667. *See* Bridge, William.

206   —A collection of so much of the statutes in force. *By Robert White*, 1661. 4°. LT, O, LL, DT; CH, NU, WF.
     —Corporal worship discuss'd. 1670. *See* Basset, William.

207   —Cupid's court of salutations. [*London*], *for J. Deacon, to be sold by R. Kell*: 1687. 8°.* O.

207A   —A declaration of the counsel of God's heavenly hosts. 1662. 4°. GU.

207B   —A dreaful account of a ... earthquake. *By W. Downing*. 1693. brs. MH.
     —Dreadful, and terrible day. [1665.] *See* Bayly, William.
     —Epistle general containing. [*London*], 1664. *See* Bayly, William.

207C   —An exact account of a late famous defeat. colop: *For R. Smith*, 1690. brs. Y.

208   —Exceeding good newes from Ireland. *For Richard Woodnoth*, 1646. 4°.* LT; Y.

209   —Exceeding good nevves from Ireland being a perfect relation. *January 7*, 1647. *For W. Smith*. 4°.* LT.

210   —Experiences and tears. *For M. S. & R. I.*, 1652. 4°. LT; Y.
     —Faithful warning once more. 1690. *See* Bingley, William.
     —For the king and Parliament. 1664. *See* Bayly, William.
     —Formulæ bene placitandi. 1671. *See* Brown, William.
     —Four centuries of select hymns. 1668. *See* Barton, William.

211   —A funeral sermon preached on the occasion of the right honourable the Earl of Sh—ys late interment. *By George Croom*, 1683. 4°.* O, HH.
     —General epistle to all Friends. [1662.] *See* Bayly, William.

212   —God fighting for vs in Ireland. [*London*], *for W. B. and are to be sold by Thomas Bates*, 1642. 4°.* LT, O, EC; MH, WF, Y.
     —Great and dreadful day. [1664.] *See* Bayly, William.
     —Hallelujah, or. ... 1651. *See* Barton, William.

213   —An impartial relation of the surrender and delivery of ... Dublin. colop: *For R. Hayhurst*, [1690]. cap., fol. CH.

214   —Ingenii fructus, or the Cambridge jests. *For William Spiller*, 1700. 12°. L.
     —Jacob is become a flame. 1662. *See* Bayly, William.

215   —The ladies milk-house. 1684. fol. O.

216   —A letter from. [*London*], *for I. H.*, 1683. brs. O, EN.
     —Life of Enoch. 1662. *See* Bayly, William.
     —Message sent forth. [*London*], 1662. *See* Bayly, William.

217   —Misopormist. *For G. L.*, 1667. 4°.* WF.

218 —The names, dignities, and places of all the collonells. *For Richard Thrale*, 1642. brs. STEELE 2078. LT, O, OC.

219 [–] —[Anr. ed.] —, 1642. brs. STEELE 2103. O, HH.

220 —A new history of the Roman conclave. *For Samuel Smith*, 1691. 4°.* T.C.II 380. L, O, OM, BR, EN; CH, MH, NU, WF, Y.

—Mystery of astronomy. 1655. *See* Bagwell, William.

—A new touch-stone for gold. 1679. *See* Badcock, William.

221 Entry cancelled.

—A new trial of the ladies. 1658. *See* Blake, William.

—Ode on the death. 1700. *See* Browne, William.

222 —The present condition of London-derry. colop: *For J. Morris*, 1689. brs. O, C, OC, MC.

—Pure encouragements. [*London*, 1664.] *See* Bayly, William.

223 —Regi sacrum. *For Tho: Dring*, 1660. 8°. LT, O, CT, BR, EN; WF, Y.

224 —Remarks and animadversions on Mr. Keith's two sermons. *For the author: and sold by the Booksellers of London and Westminster*, 1700. 8°. EN; WF.

225 —Sacred to the precious memory of Mris Mary Boyleston. *By John Macock*, 1657. 4°. LW; Y.

226 Entry cancelled.

—Sea-mans diall. 1648. *See* Batten, *Sir* William.

227 —A seasonable discourse: shewing how that the oaths. [*London*], *printed*, 1679. 4°.* O, OC, SC, EN, AU; CH, MH, NU, WF, Y.

228 —The sentinell's remonstrance. *Printed*, 1659. brs. LT, O.

—Serious letter sent by a private Christian. 1655. *See* Blake, William.

229 Entry cancelled.

—Short declaration of the purpose. [London], 1662. *See* Brend, William.

—Short relation or testimony. [1659.] *See* Bayly, William.

—Silent meeting a wonder. 1675. *See* Britten, William.

230 —Sir, in obedience to your commands, I here send you a short account of Dr. Hicks's book, . . . Linguarum veterum septentrionalium thesaurus. 1700. brs. OP.

—Sphynx Thebanus. [1664.] *See* Bagwell, William.

231 —Strange and wonderful news, from the Lords. colop: *For T.B.*, 1681. brs. L, O, HH; CH, MBA, WF.

—Testimony to the true light. 1668. *See* Bennitt, William.

—Touch-stone for gold. 1677. *See* Badcock, William.

232 —The Trappan trapt. *By Joseph Moxon*, 1657. 4°.* LT; MH.

—Treatise of fornication. 1690. *See* Barlow, William.

233 Entry cancelled.

—The triall of the ladies, Hide Park. 1656. *See* Blake, William.

234 —A true account of a letter sent from Vienna August the 23d. colop: *By Geogre* [*sic*] *Croom*, 1683. brs. L, O, EN; CH, Y.

235 —A true copy of a letter sent from Vienna, September the 2d 1683. colop: *For John Cox*, 1683. cap., fol. CH.

236 —A true relation of a great victory obtained by . . . Lord Willoughby. *For Thomas Johnson*, 1643. 4°.* LT, O, HH, DT.

236A —A true relation of a great victory obtained by the Parliament forces. *For Benjamin Allen, May 27*, 1643. 4°.* LT, CDC.

237 —A true relation of a great victory obtained by the Parliaments forces . . . neere Chester, [*London*], *by E. P. Novemb.* 27, 1643. 4°.* LT; MH, MIU.

238 —A true relation of the plot discovered in Ireland. *Lately printed in Dublin; reprinted and sold by B. W.*, London, [1641]. 4°.* LT, MR; WF.

239 —A true relation of the taking of Grafton House. *For John Wright*, 1643. 4°.* LT, O; Y.

—Two centuries of select hymns. 1670. *See* Barton, William.

—A view of many errors. 1655. *See* Barton, William.

—Vindication of the commands. [1663.] *See* Bayly, William.

—Vindiciæ Calvanisticæ. Dublin, 1688. *See* Boyse, Joseph.

—White rose. 1680. *See* Brydall, John.

—Wit's extraction. 1664. *See* Bagwell, William.

—Yellovv book: or a serious letter. 1656. *See* Blake, William.

240–2 Entries cancelled.

243 **B., W. D.** A letter to the right worshipful T. S. *Printed*, 1675. 4°.* L, O, C, HH, EN; CH, CN, NU, WF.

244 Babel and Bethel: or, the Pope in his colours. [*London*, 1680.] brs. MH.

Babell, written. 1692. *See* Pitcairne, Archibald.

Babel's builders. 1681. *See* Crisp, Thomas.

245 **Baber, John.** A poem upon the coronation. *By R. Everingham*, 1685. fol.* L, O; CH, CU, MH, WF, Y.

246 —To the king, upon the Queens being deliver'd. *By Mary Thompson*, 1688. fol.* L, O, HH, AU; CH, MH, PU, WF, Y.

246A The babes in the wood. [*London?* 1695]. brs. MH.

247 **Babington, Humfrey.** Mercy & judgment. *Cambridge, by John Hayes, for Henry Dickinson*, 1678. 4°.* L, C, CT, DC; CN, IU, MH, WF.

248 **Babington, Zachary.** Advice to grand jurors. *For John Amery*, 1677. 8°. T.C.I 268. L, O, C, LL; BN, CH, LC, MHL, NCL, WF.

249 — —[Anr. ed.] —, 1680. 8°. T.C.I 394. L, CJ, CM, EN; MHL, MIU.

250 — —"Second" edition. —, 1692. 8°. L; NPT.

251 Babylon blazon'd, or, the Jesuit jerk'd. *For William Leach*, 1681. fol.* O; CH, CN, MH, MIU, Y.

Babylon is fallen. 1651. *See* L., T.

Babylon is fallen. 1689. *See* P., T.

Babylonish Baptist. [1672.] *See* Whitehead, George.

Bacchanalia: or. . . . 1680. *See* Darby, Charles.

Bacchinalia coelestia: a poem. 1680. *See* Radcliffe, Alexander.

Bacchanalian sessions. 1693. *See* Ames, Richard.

251A Bacchus conculcatus, or, sober reflections. [*London*], *printed*, 1691. 4°.* LBR; IU.

252 Entry cancelled. Bacchus festival. [1660]. *See* Jordan, Thomas.

253 **Bache, Humphry.** A few words in true love. *For M. W.*, 1659. 4°.* L, O, LF; MH, PH, Y.

254 —The voice of thunder. *For Thomas Simmons*, 1659. 4°.* L, LF; CH, MH, PH, Y.

255–6 Entries cancelled. **Bacheler, John.** *See* Batchiler, John.

257 The batchellors answer to the maids complaint. *For J. Coniers*, 1675. 4°.* O; MH, WF, Y.

257A The batchelor's ballad; or, a remedy. [*London*], *for Philip Brooksby*, [1677]. brs. O.

257B The batchelers banquet. *By R.C. to be sold by Andrew Kembe*, 1651. 4°. L.

258 —[Anr. ed.] *By H.Bell, and are to be sold by Andrew Kembe*, 1660. Y.

259 —[Anr. ed.] *For E. Thomas*, 1677. T.C.I 297. L, CM.

259A The batchelor's choice. *For F. Coles, T. Vere and J. Wright*, [1674–9]. brs. O.

259B The batchelor's delight. *For F. G.*, [1641–61]. brs. L.

259C —[Anr. ed.] [*London?* 1680]. brs. O.

260 The batchelor's directory. *For Richard Cumberland; and Benjamin Bragg*, 1694. 12°. T.C.II 512. L, O, C, LWL.

261 —Second edition. *For Richard Cumberland*, 1696. 12°. L, LL; CH, Y.

261A The batchellors fore-cast. [*London*], *by P.L. for R.Burton*, [1667]. brs. GU.

262 The batchelour's guide. [*London*], *for P.Brooksby*, [1685–88]. brs. L, HH; MH.

262A The batchellors happiness. *For J. Clark*, [1675?] brs. O.

263 The batchelor's triumph. [*London*], *for P.Brooksby*, [1672–95]. brs. L, O, HH.

264 A back-blow to Major Huntington. [1648.] cap., 4°.* LT, LG; CSL, WF.

265 **Backhouse, Robert.** A true relation of a wicked plot. *For Ed. Husbands, May 7. 1644.* 4°.* LT, O, CCL, EN, DT; CH, MH, WF, Y.

265A **Backwell, Edward.** The proposal of. [*London?* 1677.] brs. Y.

266 **Backwell, John.** An abstract of the agreement. [*London, 1698?*] fol.* L.

266A **Bacon, Christopher.** A trumpet sounding an alarm. *Printed*, 1662. 4°.* LF, BBN; PH, PSC.

267 **Bacon, *Sir* Francis.** Sir Francis Bacon his apologie, in certain imputations. *Printed*, 1642. 4°.* LT, O, C, CE, MR; CH, CPB, MH, TU, WF, Y.

268 —The apology of. *By S.G. & B.G. for William Lee*, 1670. fol. L, O, LG; CH, CN, PL, TU, Y.

269 —Baconiana. *By I. D. for Richard Chiswell*, 1679. 8°. T.C.I 351. L, O, C, E, BQ; CH, CU, LC, MH, NN, Y.

270 ——Second edition. *For R. Chiswell, to be sold by John Southby*, 1684. 8°. T.C.II 88. L, O, EN, ES; CLC, CPB, MH, Y, JF.

271 —A breif discourse of the happy union. *For B. Griffin, to be sold by H.Newman*, 1700. 4°.* L, LCL, HH, EN; CLC, CN, MB, WF.

272 —Cases of treason. *By the assignes of John More, sold by Matthew Walbancke, and William Coke*, 1641. 4°.* LT, O, C, HH, DT; CH, CN, MH, TU, WF, YL.

273 Entry cancelled.

274 —Certain considerations. *Printed and are to be sold by Randal Taylor*, 1689. 4°.* T.C.II 298. L, O, C, EN, DT; CH, CPB, NU, WF, Y.

275 —Certain miscellany works of. *By T.J. for H.R to be sold by Wil. Lee*, 1670. fol. L, O, LG; CH, CN, PL, WF, Y.

276 —A charge given by. *For Robert Pawley*, 1662. 4°. O, C, WCA; CH, LC, MHL, TU, Y.

277 ——[Anr. ed.] *For Robert Pawlett*, 1676. 4°.* C, LG, YM; CN, MHL, NCL, Y.

278 —A collection of apophthegms, new and old. *For Andrew Crooke*, 1674. 12°. C, CT, DC; CPB, MH.

279 [–] A confession of faith, penned by an orthodox man. *For William Hope*, 1641. 4°.* L, C, OME, EN; CH, MH, NU, WF, Y.

279A ——[Anr. ed.] *By Rob Young, for Will. Hope*, 1641. 4°.* CPB, Y.

280 ——[Anr. ed.] *Printed*, 1641. 4°.* CS, CT, WCA, D, EN; CH, CN, MH, WF, Y.

281 —A discourse of the happy union. *By Tho. Milbourn, and sold by A.Baldwin*, 1700. 4°. CS; CH, CN, MH, WF, Y.

282 —An essay of a king. *Decemb. 2. For Richard Best*, 1642. 4°.* LT, O, LG, HH; CH, CSS, TU, Y.

283 —The essayes. *By Jo: Beale for Richard Royston*, 1642. 8°. CH, MH, WF.

284 ——[Anr. ed.] *By F. Redmayne, for Thomas Palmer*, 1663. 4°. L, C, CT; CPB, LC, PL, Y.

285 ——[Anr. ed.] *For H.R., and are to be sold by Thomas Palmer*, 1664. 12°. L, O, C, GK; CLC, CPB, MH, WF, Y.

286 ——[Anr. ed.] *By Thomas Ratcliffe and Tho. Daniel, for Humphrey Robinson*, 1668[9]. 12°. T.C.I 7. L, O, C; CLC, MH, MMO, WF, Y.

286A ——[Anr. ed.] —, 1669. 12°. CM.

287 ——[Anr. ed.] *By T. N. for John Martyn, S. Mearne, and H. Herringman*, 1673. 8°. T.C.I 156. L, C, LVF, LGI, GK; CH, MH, NP, WF, Y.

288 ——[Anr. ed.] *By M. Clark for Samuel Mearne, John Martyn, and Henry Herringman*, 1680. 8°. T.C.I 388. L, O, C, CT, ENC; CH, CN, MH, WF, Y.

288A ——[Anr. ed.] *By M.C. for Samuel Mearne*, 1680. 8°. Y.

289 ——[Anr. ed.] [*Philadelphia*], *printed*, 1688. 8°. EVANS 447. CH, NN, PHS.

290 ——[Anr. ed.] *For Abel Swalle, and Timothy Childe*, 1691. 8°. LT, CT, GK; CPB, PL, Y.

291 ——[Anr. ed.] *For A. Swall*, 1691. 8°. CPB, WF.

292 ——[Anr. ed.] *Sold by James Knapton*, 1691. 8°. T.C.II 373. CT; CLC, CSU, MH, NC, NU, Y.

293 ——[Anr. ed.] *For H. Herringman, R. Chiswell, T. Sawbridge, and R.Bentley*, 1691. 8°. T.C.II 387. CPB.

294 ——[Anr. ed.] *For George Sawbridge*, 1696. 8°. L, O, E; CPB.

295 ——[Anr. ed.] *Printed and sold by J. Newton*, 1696. 8°. CJ, CT, BR; CH, CPB, PL, V, Y.

295A ——[Anr. ed.] *By R. Roberts*, 1691. 8°. M.

295B — —[Anr. ed.] For A. Swalle and T. Childe, 1696. 8°. L; CLC, CPB, TU, Y.

295C — —[Anr. ed.] For Samuel Smith, and Benj. Welford, 1696. 8°. CPB, MU, Y.

296 — —[Anr. ed.] For H. Herringman, R. Scot, R. Chiswell, A. Swalle, and R. Bentley, 1696. 8°. L, O, C, EC, GK; CH, CPB, MH, PBM, WF.

297 —An extract by Mr. Bushell of his late abridgment. For Tho. Leach, 1660. 4°. L, C, LPO; CJC, MB, WCL, WF.

298 —The felicity of Queen Elizabeth. By T. Newcomb, for George Latham, 1651. 12°. LT, C, OC, CT; CH, CLC, MH, WF, Y.

299 —The historie of the reigne of King Henry the Seventh. Third edition. By R. Y. and R. H., and are sold by R. Meighen, 1641. fol. L, O, C, EN, DT; CH, CN, LC, MH, Y.

300 —The history of the reigns of Henry the Seventh. By W. G. for R. Scot, T. Basset, J. Wright, R. Chiswell, and J. Edwyn, 1676. fol. L, O, C, OC, DT; BN, CH, LC, MH, NP, Y.

301 —The learned reading of. For Mathew Walbancke, and Laurence Chapman, 1642. 4°. L, O, C, LGI, EN; CH, CU, LC, MHL, TU, Y.

302 —A letter of advice. For R. H. and H. B., 1661. 4°.* L, O, C, SC, YM; CH, MH, RPJ, WF, Y.

303 —The mirrour of state and eloquence. For Lawrence Chapman, 1656. 4°. LT, LGI, OC, EN; CLG, CPB, WF.

304 —Mr. Bushell's abridgement of the Lord Chancellor Bacon's philosophical theory. Printed, 1659. 4°. L, OC, E, ES; MH, PBL, Y.

305 —The naturall and experimentall history of winds, &c. For Humphrey Moseley, and Tho. Dring, 1653. 12°. LT, O, C, ES, DT; CH, LC, MH, WF, Y.

306 — —[Anr. ed.] For Anne Moseley, and Tho. Basset, 1671. fol. L, O, C; CH, CPB, CSU, MH, PL, Y.

307 —New Atlantis. [London, 1658?] 4°.* OC; LC, MH, MIU, Y.

308 — —[Anr. ed.] By Tho: Newcomb, 1659. 4°. L; Y.

309 — —[Anr. ed.] For John Crooke, 1660. 8°. LT, C, SP, GK; CH, MH, WCL, WF, Y.

310 —The novum organvm of. For Thomas Lee, 1676. fol.* L, O, HH, GK; CLC.

311 — —[Anr. ed.] For Thomas Lee, 1677. fol.* L; CN.

312 —Of the advancement and proficiencie of learning. For Thomas Williams, 1674. fol. T.C.I 181. L, O, C, AU, DT; GK; BN, CH, CU, LC, MH, NP, Y.

313 —The office of constables. [London], for Francis Cowley, 1641. 8°.* C, LL; WF.

314 —Opuscula varia posthuma. Excud. R. Daniel, impensis O. Pulleyn, 1658. 8°. L, O, C, CK, CT; LC, MH, PL, WF, Y.

315 Entry cancelled.

316 —Ordinances made by. For Mathew Walbanke, and Laurence Chapman, 1642. 4°.* L, O, C, EN, DT; CH, MHL, WCL, WF, Y.

317 —A preparatory to the history natural & experimental. By Sarah Griffing and Ben. Griffing for William Lee, 1670. fol.* L, O, LG; CH, CSU, PL, Y, JF.

318 —The remaines. By B. Alsop, for Lawrence Chapman, 1648. 4°. L, O, C, MR, DT; CH, CN, MH, TU, WF, Y.

319 —Resuscitatio. By Sarah Griffin for William Lee, 1657. fol. L, O, C, LM, EN; CH, CN, LC, MH, NC, TU, Y.

320 — —Second edition. By S. Griffin, for William Lee, 1661. fol. L, C, LL, E, DT; BN, CH, CU, MH, NU, WF, Y.

321 — —Third edition. By S. G. and B. G. for William Lee, 1671. fol. T.C.I 82. L, O, C, EN, DT; BN, CLC, MH, MBC, WF, Y.

322 —The second part of the resuscitatio. By S. G. & B. G. for William Lee, 1670. fol. T.C.I 45. L, O, CT, EN; CH, MH, PL, WF, Y.

323 —Entry cancelled.

324 [-] Several letters written by. By T. R. for William Lee, 1671. fol. L, O; CH, CN, LC, MH, Y.

325 —XVI Propositions concerning the raign and government of a king. For R. Wood, 1647[8]. 4°.* LT; CH.

326 —A speech delivered by. Printed, 1641. 4°.* LT, C, LCL, CT, EN; CH, CPB, LC, MH, WF, Y.

327 —Sylva sylvarvm. Sixth edition. By J. F. for William Lee, 1651. fol. L, O, C, EN, GM; CSU, LC, MH, WF, Y.

328 — —Seventh edition. For William Lee, and are to be sold by Thomas Williams and William Place, 1658. fol. L, O, C, E; CH, LC, MH, Y.

329 — —"Seventh" edition. By A. M. for William Lee, and are to be sold [by him] and by Thomas Johnson, 1658. fol. O, OC, CT; CLC, CPB, MH, TSM, Y.

330 — —Eighth edition. By J. F. and S. G. for William Lee, and are to be sold by Thomas Williams, 1664. fol. L, O, C, GK; CLC, MH, NC, TU, WF, Y.

331 — —Ninth edition. By J. R. for William Lee, and are to be sold by the booksellers, 1670. fol. T.C.I 32. L, C, LMS, R, DT; CLC, MH, NP, WF, Y.

331A — —"Ninth" edition. —, 1670. fol. CPB.

332 — —Tenth edition. By S. G. and B. Griffin for Thomas Lee, 1676. fol. L, O, C, CK, LR; BN, CPB, MH, WF, Y.

333 — —"Tenth" edition. —, 1677. fol. L, C, D; CPB, CH, LC, PBM, Y.

334 — —[Anr. ed.] For Bennet Griffin, 1683. fol. CLC, CPB, LC, PL, WF.

335 — —Eleventh edition. For B. Griffin, and are to be sold by Dan. Browne, and J. Sares, 1685. fol. T.C.II 34. O, C, DCH, DT, GK; PBL, WDA, KT, Y.

336 — —[Anr. ed.] By John Haviland for William Lee, sold by John Williams, 1685. fol. WF.

337 —Three speeches. By Richard Badger, for Samuel Brown, 4°. LT, O, C, EN, DT; CH, LC, MH, NU, TU, Y.

338 —A true and historical relation . . . Overbury. By T. M. & A. C. for John Benson and John Playford, 1651. 8°. C, OC, GU; CH, CN, WF, Y.

339 —True peace. For A. C., 1663. 4°.* O, SP; MH, Y.

340 —The union of the two kingdoms. Edinburgh, printed, 1670. 4°. ALDIS 1889. O, EN, ENC; CH, CPB, NP.

341 —The wisdome of the ancients. By S. G. for J. Kirton, 1658. 12°. L, CK; CH.

342 — —[Anr. ed.] Edinburgh, by John Swintoun, 1681. 12°. ALDIS 2250. EN; WF.

343 [–] A wise and moderate discourse. [*London*], *imprinted*, 1641. 4°.* LT, O, C, E, DT; CH, MH, NPT, NU, WF, Y.

343A **Bacon, Francis.** Catalogue of library. 1686. L.

344 **Bacon, James.** A plaine & profitable catechisme. *Oxford, by W. Hall for R. Davis*, 1660. 8°. MADAN 2478. LT, O, LSC; NU.

345 —The sinfulness of compliance. *Oxford, by W. Hall*, 1660. 8°. MADAN 2478. LT, O; NU.

346 [**Bacon, John.**] Scotlands thanksgiving for the return of their armie. *For T. Paine and M. Simmons*, 1642. 4°.* LT; CH, CSS, WF, Y.

347 —A true relation of severall overthrows. *Ioseph Hunscot, Sept. 26,* 1642. 4°.* LT, EC; CH, Y.

348 **Bacon, Nathaniel.** The continuation of An historicall discourse. *By Tho: Roycroft for Matthew Walbanck, and Henry Twyford*, 1651. 4°. LT, O, C, EN, DT; CLC, MH, NU, WF, Y.

348A —The fearful relations of Francis Spira. *Edinburgh*, 1693. 12°. ALDIS 3292. EN, GU; CLC.

—An historical and political discourse of the laws. 1689. *See* Selden, John.

349 [–] An historicall discourse of the uniformity. *For Mathew Walbancke*, 1647. 4°. L, O, C, EN, DT; BN, CH, CN, LC, MH, NU, Y.

350 —The history of Athanasius. *By D. Maxwell*, 1664. CE, P, WCA; NU, Y.

351 — —[Anr. ed.] History of the life and actions of. *By D. Maxwell for Christopher Ecclestone*, 1664. 8°. L, O, LG, LW, EN; CH, WF, Y.

352 —A journal of meditations. *Anno dom.*, 1669. 8°. L, C; CLC, CN, TU, WG.

353 — —Second edition. *Anno dom.*, 1674. 8°. L, O, OC; CN, TU, WF, Y.

354 — —Third edition. *By Henry Hills, for him and Matthew Turner*, 1687. 8°. L; CLC, CN, TU, WF.

355 —An ordinance presented to the honorable House of Commons, by. [*London*, 1646.] brs. LT; MH.

356 — —[Anr. ed.] *Printed*, 1646. 4°. LT, C, GU; NU, WF, Y.

357 —A relation of the fearfvl estate of Francis Spira. *By I. L. for Christoph. Meredith*, 1649. 12°. O, C, BPL; MH.

358 — —[Anr. ed.] *By J. L. for Christopher Meredith*, 1653. 12°. O.

358A — —[Anr. ed.] *By J. B. to be sold by Andrew Kemb*, 1657. 12°. O; NN, Y.

358B — —[Anr. ed.] —, 1662, 12°. CLC.

359 — —[Anr. ed.] *By R. I. for A. K. to bee sold by William Thackeray*, 1665. 12°. L; CN, WF.

359A — —[Anr. ed.] 1668. 12° P.

360 — —[Anr. ed.] *By T. Ratcliff and N. Thompson for Edward Thomas*, 1672. 12°. L, C; CH.

361 — —[Anr. ed.] *Edinburgh, by A. Anderson*, 1675. 12°. ALDIS 2042. LGI, EN.

362 — —[Anr. ed.] *By Thomas Dawks, for Edward Thomas*, 1678. 12°. T.C.I 297. L; CH, CPB, MH.

363 — —[Anr. ed.] *For Edward Thomas*, 1681. 18°. L, O; BN, CLC, NN, Y.

363A — —[Anr. ed.] *Boston, by Samuel Green*, 1682. 8°. EVANS 310. MHS.

364 — —[Anr. ed.] *For Benjamin Harris*, 1683. 12°. L, MC, ENC; CH.

364A — —[Anr. ed.] *For the widow Harris*, 1687. 12°. TU.

365 — —[Anr. ed.] —, 1688. 12°. L, O, CS, EN; MIU, WF.

366 — —[Anr. ed.] *Glasgow, Sanders*, 1695. 8°. ALDIS 3442. GM.

366A — —[Anr. ed.] *Printed and sold by Ben. Harris*, 1700. 8°. NC.

367 **Bacon, Sir Nicholas.** Argvments exhibited in Parliament. [*London*], *printed*, 1641. 4°.* LT, C, LG; CH, CSS, MH, WF, YL.

368 **Bacon, Robert.** Christ mighty in Himself. *By J. M. for Giles Calvert*, 1646. 12°. L; CLC.

369 —The labyrinth the kingdom's in. *Printed*, 1649. 4°.* LT, O, YM, DT; CH, CU, MH, WF, Y.

370 —The spirit of prelacie. *By R. L. for Giles Calvert*, 1646. 4°.* LT, O, LW, DT; CH, MH, NU, WF, Y.

371 —A taste of the spirit of God. *For Giles Calvert*, 1652. 4°.* LT, EN.

372 **Bacon, Roger.** The cure of old age. *For Tho. Flesher, and Edward Evets*, 1683. 8°. T.C.II 20. L, O, C, EN, DT; CH, CN, LC, MH, MMO, Y.

373 —Frier Bacon his discovery of the miracles of art. *For Simon Miller*, 1659. 12°. LT, O, LCS, LWL, GU; CH, MH, NAM, WF.

374 [**Bacon, William.**] A key to Helmont. *For John Starkey*, 1682. 4°.* T.C.I 472. L, O, LCP, LWL, DT; PL, WF, JF.

375 Bad English, yet not Scotch. *Printed*, 1648. 4°. DT.

Bad husband's experience. [1674.] *See* White, L.

376 The bad husbands folly. [*London*], *for J. Deacon* [1680?] brs. L, CM.

377 The bad husband's information. [*London*], *for P. Brooksby*, [1675–80]. brs. HH; MH.

378 —[Anr. ed.] 1676. brs. O.

379 The bad husbands reformation. [*London*], *for P. Brooksby*, [1685–88]. brs. L, HH; MH.

380 Bad money made good. [*London*, 1696.] brs. L.

Bad news from Ireland. 1642. *See* R., C.

381 **B[adcock], W[illiam].** A new touch-stone for gold. Second edition. *For J. Bellinger and T. Basset*, 1679. 8°. T.C.I 338. L, O, C, LL, OC; CH, MH, PL, WF, Y.

382 —A touch-stone for gold and silver wares. *For John Bellinger and Thomas Bassett*, 1677. 8°. T.C.I 256. L, O, C, LG, LPO; CH, MH, NC, WF, Y.

382A [–] —Second edition. —, 1678. 8°. LWL, CLC.

382B **B[addeley], R[ichard].** The life of Dr. Thomas Morton. *York: by Stephen Bulkley, to be sould by Francis Mawbarne*, 1669. 8°. L, O, OB, CS; CLC, CU, MH, Y.

383 [**Badger, John.**] The case between Dr. John Badger and the Colledge of Physicians London. [*London*, 1693.] cap., 4°.* L, O; WSG.

384 —An exact alphabetical catalogue of all that have taken the degree of Doctor of Physick. *Printed*, 1696. brs. L, O.

385 [–] A register of the doctors of physick in our two universities. *Printed*, 1695. 8°.* L, O; JF.

Badger in the fox-trap. [1680?] *See* Dean, J.

386 **Badiley, Richard.** Captain Baddeley's answer unto Capt. Appleton's remonstrance. *M. Simmons*, 1653. 4°. LT, CT.

387 Entry cancelled.

388 —Capt. Badiley's reply to certaine declarations. *By Matthew Simmons*, 1653. 4°.* LT, CT, HH; CLC, WF.

389 —The sea-men undeceived. *By Matthew Simmons*, 1648. 4°.* LT, C; CH.

390 **Badland, Thomas.** Eternity: or the weightiness. *For Sampson Evans, in Worcester, to be sold by N. Simmons*, 1676. 8°. O, LCL.

391 **Bagaley, Humphrey.** To the Parliament . . . The humble petition. [*London*, 1654.] brs. LT; MH.

392 **Bagg, William.** Calculi in humano corpore. [*Cambridge*, 1651.] brs. LT.

393 [**Bagshaw, Edward, *elder.*]** De monarchia absoluta. *Oxoniæ, excudebat Hen: Hall impensis Tho: Robinson*, 1659. 4°.* MADAN 2432. LT, O, CT, OC, P; CLC, CU, MH.

394 —Mr. Bagshavvs first speech. *Printed*, 1641. 4°.* LT; CN, MH, TU, WF.

395 —Mr. Edward Bagshaw, his first speech . . . seventh of Novemb. 1640. *For Francis Constable*, 1641. 4°.* CN, CSS, MIU, NU, Y.

395A — —[Anr. ed.] *For F. Grove*, 1641. 4°.* CT.

396 —A just vindication of the questioned part of the reading of. *Printed*, 1660. 4°.* LT, C, YM; MHL, NU, YL.

397 —The rights of the crown of England. *By A.M. for Simon Miller*, 1660. 4°. LT, O, C, LL, DC; CH, LC, MHL, NU, Y.

398 [–] A short censure of the book of W. P. [*London*], *printed* [*for Rich. Royston*], 1648. 4°.* MADAN 1962. O, OC, MR; MH, Y.

399 —Mr. Bagshaws speech in Parliament, February the ninth, 1640. *For Francis Constable*, 1641. 4°.* LT, O, C, HH, EN; CH, CN, MH, NU, TU, WF, Y.

400 —A speech made by . . ., concerning the triall of the twelve bishops. *For T. T.*, 1642. 4°.* LT, C, LVF, BR, EN; CH, MH, NU, TU, WF, Y.

401 —Two arguments in Parliament. *By George Miller*, 1641. 4°.* LT, O, C, LL, EN; BN, CH, CN, MH, NU, TU, WF, Y.

402 —Master Bagshaw his worthy speech. . . . Febr. 18. 1641. *By T. F. for J. Thomas*, 1641[2]. 4°.* LT, O, C, HH; CH, CN, MH, NU, WF, Y.

403 [**Bagshaw, Edward, *younger.*]** An antidote against Mr. Baxters palliated cure. [*London*], *printed*, 1670. 4°.* L, O, OC, YM; MBA, NU, PL, TU, WF.

404 —A brief enquiry into the grounds. *By A.M.*, 1662. 4°. L, O, CE, HH, DT; CU, MH, NU, WF.

405 —A brief treatise about the spiritual nature of God. *For C. G.*, 1662. 4°.* L, O, OC, HH; CH, PL, WF, Y.

406 —The case & usage of Mr. Edw. Bagshavv, drawn up by himself. *Printed*, 1664. 4°.* O; MBA, Y.

407 —A defence of the antidote. [*London*], *printed*, 1671. 8°.* L, O, OC, YM; CH, MBP, NU.

408 —A discourse about Christ. *For Simon Miller*, 1661. 4°. L, O, LCL, OC; CLC, NU, PL, WF, Y.

409 —Dissertationes duæ. *Excudebat Rogerus Daniel*, 1657. 12°. L, O, C, LW, DT; NPT.

410 —The doctrine of free grace. *By Abraham Miller, for the author*, 1662. 4°.* L, O, HH, OC; CH, WF.

411 —The doctrine of the kingdom. [*London*], *printed*, 1669. 4°.* L, O, LW, OC, BBN; MH, MIU, NU, Y.

412 —Exercitationes dvæ. *Excudit A. M. pro Simone Millero*, 1661. 4°. LT, O, CT, OM, LCL; MH, NPT, NU, WF.

413 [–] The great question concerning things indifferent. *Printed*, 1660. 4°.* L, O, LCL, BB, AU; CH, Y.

413A — —Second edition. —, 1660. 4°.* L, CCH, BIU; NU, PL, WF.

414 [–] —Third edition. —, 1660. 4°.* L, O, C, HH, EN; CLC, MH, NC, NPT.

414A —The last conflicts and death of Mr. Thomas Peacock. *By George Miller*, 1646. 12°. O, LCL, LW, CS.

414B —The last visitation. *For William Miller*, 1660. 12°. LT, C, LW; CLC.

414C —A letter to a person of quality. *Printed*, 1660. 4°.* MBA.

415 —A letter to Mr. Thomas Pierce. *By A.M.*, 1659. 4°.* O, OC; CLC, MH, TU, WF.

416 —A letter to the right honourable Edward Earl of Clarendon. *For J. S.*, 1662. 4°.* L, O, OC, OM; CH, CN, MH, NU, PL, Y.

417 [–] A letter unto a person of honour & quality. *Printed*, 1662. 4°.* L, O, C, HH, EN; CLC, MH, NPT, NU, PL, WF.

418 [–] The life and death of Mr. Vavasor Powell. [*London*], 1671. 8°. OB, AN; MH, NU.

418A —The marks of the Apocalyptical beast. *Printed*, 1667. 4°.* OC; WF.

419 —The necessity & use of heresies. *For S. M.*, 1662. 4°.* L, O, C, OC, HH; CLC, CU, MH, NU, TU, WF, Y.

420 —A practicall discourse. *Oxford, by Hen. Hall for Tho. Robinson*, 1659. 4°.* MADAN 2433. L, O, CT, OC, LCL; CH, NPT, NU, WF, Y.

421 —A review and conclusion of the antidote; against. . . . *Printed*, 1671. 4°.* L, O, OC, YM; CLC, MHS, NPT.

422 —Saintship no ground of soveraignty. *Oxford, by H: Hall for T. Robinson*, 1660. 8°. MADAN 2479. L, O, LCL, OC; CH, MHS, NPT, NU.

423 [–] A second letter unto a person of honour. 1662. 4°.* L, O, LW, OC, WCA; CH, MH, NU, WF, Y.

424 [–] The second part of the great question. *Printed*, 1661. 4°.* L, O, CCH, GU, HH; MH, NU, PL, WF, Y.

425 —Signes of the times. *For Simon Miller*, 1662. 4°.* L, O, LCL, OC; CH, CN, NU, WF, Y.

426 —A true and perfect narrative of the differences between Mr. Busby and. . . . *By A.M.*, 1659. 4°.* L, O, C, CT, MR.

427 [–] The xxiv cases concerning things indifferent. *Printed*, 1663. 4°. LW, CT, EN; CH, CU, NU, WWC.

428 **Bagshaw, Harrington.** A sermon preached . . . 3d of April. *For Sam. Keble*, 1698. 4°.* L; NU.

429 **Bagshaw, Henry.** Diatribae. *By T. H. for Ric. Chiswell*, 1680. 8°. L, LW, CT; NU, PL, WF, Y.

430   —The excellency of primitive government. *By W. Godbid,
       for Joseph Nevil, and Moses Pitt*, 1673. 4°.* T.C.I 125.
       L, O, WCA, OC; CLC, MBA, NU, WF, Y.

431   —A sermon preacht . . . July 4, 1666. *For G. Beadle
       and T. Collins*, 1667. 4°.* L, O, C, CE; OC; MBA, MH,
       WF, Y.

432   —A sermon preached before the king . . . January xxx.
       1675/6. *By William Godbid, to be sold by Moses Pitt*,
       1676. 4°.* L, O, C, EN, DT; CH, MIU, NU, TSM, Y.

432A   —A sermon preached . . . 3d of April. *For Sam. Keble*,
       1698. 4°.* NU.

433   **Bagshaw, William.** Living vvater. *By E. Cotes for
       Henry Seile*, 1653. 12°. O; CLC.

433A   —Principïis obsta. The readie way. *For Thomas Parkhurst*,
       1671. 8°. T.C.I 70. GU.

433AB —The riches of grace. *For Tho. Parkhurst*, 1674. 8°. T.C.I
       147. IU.

433B   —The riches of grace displayed in the great instances.
       For Ralph Shelmardine, 1685. 8°. NPT.

433C   —The riches of grace displayed in the instances. *For
       Ralph Shelmardine in Manchester*, 1685. 8°. LCL; NPT, Y.

433D   —A sermon of Christ's purchase. *For A. M. for Thomas
       Underhill*, 1653. 4°.* MM.

434   —Trading spiritualized. *For T. Parkhurst*, 1694. T.C.II 548.
       8°. LCL, AN, EN; LC.

435   **Bagwell, William.** An affectionate expostulation.
       [*London*, 1660?] brs. L.

436   —A concealment discovered for the publique advantage.
       By James Flesher, for Nicholas Bourne, 1652. brs. LT;
       HR, MH, Y.

437   —The distressed merchant. *For Richard Wodenothe*, 1645.
       4°. LT.

438   —A full discovery of a foul concealment. *Lodnon [sic],
       by James Flesher, for Nicholas Bourne*, 1652. fol.° LT.

439   —The merchant distressed. *By T. H. for F. E.*, 1644. 4°.
       C; CH, MH, Y.

440   —The mystery of astronomy. *By J. Cottrel, for Will:
       Larnar*, 1655. 8°. L, C, LPO, LWL; CH, MH, MU, WF, HC.

441   — —[Anr. ed.] *For Francis Smith*, 1673. 8°. L, O, CT; MH,
       WU.

442   —Sphynx Thebanus. *By J. C. for Dixy Page*, [1664]. 8°.
       O; MH.

443   —Wit's extraction. *Imprinted at London by Ja: Cottrel,
       for John Clark*, 1664. 8°. L, O; CN, MH.

444   **Bailey, Abraham.** The spightful sister. *For Thomas
       Dring the younger*, 1667. 4°. L, O, OW, LGI, EN; LC,
       TU, Y.

445   — —[Anr. ed.] *For Francis Kirkman*, 1667. 4°. L; CH,
       WF.

446   **Bailey, John.** Address to loving Christian friends in
       Limerick. *May 8*, 1684. 12°. LCL.

447   —Directions to glorify God. 1684. 12°. LCL.

448   —Man's chief end to glorifie God. *Boston by Samuel
       Green, and are to be sold by Richard Wilkins*, 1689.
       8°. EVANS 456. L; MB, MH, NN, RPJ.

449   —To my loving and most beloved Christian friends.
       [*Boston: by Samuel Green*, 1689.] 16°.* EVANS 457.
       L; MB, MHS, NN, RPJ.

450   **Bailey, Walter.** A briefe treatise touching the preserva-
       tion of the eye sight. *Oxford, by H. Hall for R. Davis*,
       1654. 8°. MADAN 2253. LT, CT.

451   — —[Anr. ed.] —, 1673. 8°.* MADAN 2966. L, CM, P, GH;
       HC.

451A   [**Baillet, Adrien.**] The life of Monsieur Des Cartes.
       For R. Simpson, 1693. 8°. T.C.II 464. L, O, C, LL, CK;
       CH, CN, LC, MH, WF, Y.

452   **Baillie, Robert.** Anabaptism the true fovntaine. *By
       M. F. for Samuel Gellibrand*, 1646. 4°. O, LB, HH; MB,
       NHC, NPT, Y.

452A   — —[Anr. ed.] —, 1647. 4°. LT, OC, DT; CH, CN, NU, RPJ,
       WF, Y.

453   —Anabaptism unsealed. *By M. F. for Samuel Gellibrand*,
       1647. 4°. LT, O, E, ENC, EN; CLC, CN, RPJ, V, WCL.

454   [–] Appendix practica ad . . . Buxtorfii. *Edinburgi,
       A. Anderson* 1654. 8°. ALDIS 1471. E, EN, FSF.

455   [–] Catechesis elenctica errorum. *Excudebat Thomas
       Maxey, impensis Sa. Gellibrand*, 1654. 12°. O, C, E,
       EN, AU; CLC, NU.

456   —A dissvasive from the errours of the time. *For Samuel
       Gellibrand*, 1645. 4°. LT, O, C, EN, DT; CH, CN, MH,
       NU, WCL, Y.

457   [–] —Second edition. —, 1646. 4°. L, O, OB, P, EN; LC,
       MH, NHC, NU, RPJ.

458   — —[Anr. ed.] *By Evan Tyler for Samuel Gellibrand*,
       1655. 4°. LT, O, EN, E, GU; CH, MH, NU, RPJ, WCL.

459   —Errours and induration. *By R. Raworth, for Samuel
       Gellibrand*, 1645. 4°. LT, O, C, EN, DT; CH, CU, MH, NU,
       WF, Y.

460   —An historicall vindication. *For Samuel Gellibrand*,
       1646. 4°.* LT, O, C, E, EN; CLC, MH, NPT, NU, WF, Y.

461   [–] Ladensivm. Αυτοκάτακρισις. The Canterbvrians self-
       conviction. Third edition. [*London*], *for Nathaniel
       Bvtter*, 1641. 4°. LT, O, C, EN; CLC, CU, MH, NU, Y.

462   [–] A large supplement of the Canterbvrian self-convic-
       tion. [*London*], *imprinted*, 1641. 4°. LT, O, P, EN; CH,
       MH, NU, Y.

463   —The life of William [Laud]. *For N. B.*, 1643. 4°. LT,
       O, P, YM, EN; MH, NN.

464   —A parallel of the liturgy. [*London*], *printed*, 1661. 4°.
       LT, LVF, LCL, E, EN; CLC, NU, WF.

465   —A parallel or briefe comparison of the ljtvrgje. *By
       Thomas Paine*, 1641. 4°. LT, O, C, EN, DT; CH, CN, MH,
       NU, WF, Y.

465A   [–] Prelacie is miserie. [*London*], *imprinted* 1641. 4°.* L, O,
       YM, E, DT; CH, NU, WF, Y.

466   —A review of Doctor Bramble [Bramhall]. *Printed at
       Delf, by Michiel Stael*, 1649. 4°. L, O, E, EN, DT; CH,
       NU, WF.

467   —A review of the seditious pamphlet. *Printed at Delph
       by Mich. Stait*, 1649. 4°. LT, O, OM, MR, EN; CLC, MH, NU,
       WF, Y.

468   —Satan the leader in chief. *For Samuel Gellibrand,* 1643[4]. 4°. LT, O, C, EN, DT; BN, CH, CN, MH, NU, WF, Y.

469   —A Scotch antidote. *For Samuel Gellibrand,* 1652. 12°. LT; NU, WF.

470   [–] The unlavvfvllnes and danger of limited Episcopacie. *For Thomas Vnderhill,* 1641. 4°. LT, O, E, EN, DT; CH, CN, NU, RPJ, WF, Y.

471   Entry cancelled.

Baily, Thomas. *See* Hall, Richard.

472   **Bainbridge, John.** Cl. v. Iohannis Bainbrigii, ... Canicvlaria. *Oxoniæ excudebat Henricus Hall, impensis Thomæ Robinson,* 1648. 8°. MADAN 2002. L, O, C, MR, DT; MH, NN, WF, Y.

473   [**Bainbrige, Thomas.**] An answer to a book, entituled, Reason and authority. *By J. H. for Brabazon Aylmer,* 1687. 4°. L, O, C, EN, DT; MH, NU, TU, WF, Y.

474   [–] Seasonable reflections, on a late pamphlet, entituled, A history of passive obedience. *For Robert Clavell,* 1689/90. 4°. T.C.II 305. L, O, C, AU, DT; CH, CN, MH, NU, WF, Y.

475   [**Bairdy, John.**] Balm from Gilead. *For Tho. Cockeril,* 1681. 8°. L, O, E, EN, AU; CH, NU, PU, WF, Y.

476   The baiting of the tyger. *Printed,* 1699. brs. MC.

Baitman. *See* Bateman.

477   The bak'd bully. *For P. Brooksby,* [1672–96]. brs. O.

478   **Baker, Col.** The blazing star. *For Theodorus Microcosmus,* 1660. 4°.* LT; CH.

479   **Baker, Aaron.** Achitophel befool'd: a sermon. *For Rich. Royston,* 1678. 4°.* T.C.I 327. L, O, CT, LG, BR; CLC, MH, NPT, NU, WF, Y.

[**Baker, Augustine.**] The holy practises of a devine lover. *See* More, Gertrude.

480   —Sancta Sophia. Or directions. *At Doway, by Iohn Patté, and Thomas Fievet,* 1657. 8°. L, O, C, LW, ELY; CH, MH, NU, WG, Y.

481   **Baker, Daniel,** *Quaker.* A certaine warning. [*London*], *for M. W.,* 1659. 4°.* L, LF, BBN; PH, WF.

482   [–] A clear voice of truth. [*London*], *printed,* 1662. 4°.* L, O, LF, BBN; LC, MH, NU, PH, WF, Y.

482A   —A copie of the several charges falsely sworn. [*London*], 1660. 4°.* LF; PH.

482B   —The guiltless cries and warnings of the innocent. *For Robert Wilson,* 1660. 4°.* LF, OC, BBN; PH, PSC.

482C   —Now heare this all yee persecuting rulers. [*London*], *for M. W.,* 1659. 4°.* LF, BBN; PH.

483   —Oh! the day, the dreadful. [*London,* 1660.] brs. L, LF; CH, MH, PH, PSC.

484   —The prophet approved. *By Thomas Hart, for Thomas Simmons,* 1659. 4°.* L, OC, LF; CH, MH, PH, PL, Y.

484A   — —[Anr. ed.] *For T. Simmons,* 1654. 4°.* CT.

485   —A single and general voice. *For Thomas Simmons,* 1659. 4°.* L, LF, OC, BBN; CH, PH, PL.

486   —A tender greeting and salutation. [*London,* 1663.] 4°.* L, O, LF, BBN; CH, IE, PH, PSC.

487   [–] This is a short relation of some of the cruel sufferings ... of Katherine Evans. *For Robert Wilson,* 1662. 4°. O; MH, RPJ, Y.

488   —A thundering voice out of Sion. *For Thomas Simmons,* 1658. 4°. LF, OC, BBN; CH.

488A   —To the bretheren in the travel ... greetings. [*London*], 1667. PH.

488B   —With the light is fifteen priests. *For Mary Westwood,* 1658. 4°. LF; PH.

489   —Yet one warning more. *For Robert Wilson,* 1660. 4°.* L, O, LF, OC, BBN; LC, MH, PH, RPJ, Y.

489A   **Baker, Daniel,** *rector of Fincham.* Poems upon several occasions. *For J. Jones, sold by Joseph Wilde,* 1697. 8°. T.C.III 55. L, O, CT, EN; CH, CN, LC, MH, NP, Y.

489B   **Baker, George.** Christ's last call. *Dublin, J. Crook,* 1665. 4°. C.

490   —Confession of. *For Randall Taylor,* 1685. brs. O, HH.

491   —Newes from the north: being a relation. *For J. Usher,* Decemb. 3, 1642. 4°.* LT.

492   **Baker, Humphrey.** Baker's arithmetick. *By E. C. & A. C. for Nathanael Brook,* 1670. 8°. T.C.I 60. L, O, C, OC, E; BN, CLC, WF.

493   — —[Anr. ed.] *By J. Richardson for William Thackery, and Matthew Walton, and George Conners,* 1687. 8°. MU, NC.

493A   —The well-spring of sciences. *By M. F. for Christopher Meredith,* 1646. 8°. L; MH, NIC, WF.

494   —[Anr. ed.] *By J. Flesher for Christopher Meredith,* 1650. 8°. L, LWL; CLC, MB, MU, Y.

495   — —[Anr. ed.] *By R. & W. L. to be sold by Andrew Kemb, and Edward Brewster,* 1655. 8°. L, LPO; RPB, V.

496A   — —[Anr. ed.] 1696. 8°. MH.

497   **Baker, John.** A short preparation. *Thomas Paine,* 1645. 8°. ENC.

498   **Baker, Joseph.** Advertisement to bookseller. [*London,* 1680.] brs. MADAN 3252. O.

499   **Baker, Sir Richard.** An abridgment of. *For John Kidgell, sold by Richard Janeway,* 1684. fol. L; CH, WF.

500   —An apologie for lay-mens writing in divinity. *By E. Griffin for F. Eglesfield,* 1641. 12°. L, CT, P; WF, Y.

501   —A chronicle of the kings of England. *For Daniel Frere,* 1643. fol. L, O, C, ELY, SC; BN, CH, MH, NN, WF, Y.

502   — —[Anr. ed.] *By R. C. & R. H. for Daniel Frere,* 1643. fol. WF.

503   — —Second edition. *By J. F. and E. C. and are sold by G. Bedell, and T. Williams,* 1653. fol. L, LW, CT, P, E; MH, WF.

503A   — —[Anr. ed.] *By J. Flesher and E. Cotes; and are to be sold by Laurence Sadler, and by Thomas Williams,* 1653. fol. L, OSA, CCH; CH, WF, WU, Y.

504   — —Third edition. *By E. Cotes, and sold by G. Saubridge, and T. Williams,* 1660. fol. L, O, CSI, HH, AU; BN, CH, CU, MH, WF, Y.

505   — —Fourth edition. *By E. Cotes for G. Saubridge, and T. Williams,* 1665. fol. L, O, OB, BR, DT; CH, MBC, MH, PBL, WF.

505A   ——[Anr. ed.] *For Nathaniel Ranew, and Jonathan Robinson, 1665.* fol. CJ.

506   ——Fifth edition. *For George Sawbridge, and Thomas Williams, 1670.* fol. T.C.I 44. L, OC, OM, EC, LVF; CH, KT, LC, WF.

507   ——Sixth edition. —, *1674.* fol. T.C.I 190. L, O, C, NPL, DT; CH, MH, NU, WF, Y.

508   ——Seventh edition. *For George Sawbridge, and the assigns of Thomas Williams, 1679.* fol. T.C.I 344. L, O, CPE, E, DT; CH, NPT, WF, WG, Y.

509   ——Eighth edition. *For H. Sawbridge, B. Tooke, and T. Sawbridge, 1684.* fol. T.C.II 76. L, O, LG, CS, EN; BN, CH, CU, MH, NU, WF, Y.

510   ——Ninth edition. *For Ben. Tooke; A. and J. Churchill; and G. Sawbridge, 1696.* fol. T.C.III 8. L, O, CT, DCH; CH, LC, MH, NC, Y.

510A   —Meditations and disquisitions upon the creed. *By John Dawson, for Francis Eglesfield, 1676.* 12°. LSC, OC.

511   —Meditations and motives for prayer. *For R. Royston and Francis Eglesfield, 1642.* 12°. L, O; CLC.

512   —A soliloquy of the soule. *By T. Paine, for Francis Eglesfield, 1641.* 12°. P; CN, WF, Y.

512A   ——[Anr. ed.] *For T. Eglesfield, 1641.* 12°. LSC.

513   —Theatrum redivivum. *By T. R. for Francis Eglesfield, 1662.* 8°. LT; CLC, CN, LC, MH, WF.

514   —Theatrum triumphans; or. . . . *By S. G. and B. G. for Francis Eglesfield, 1670.* 8°. L, O, C, LW, ES; CH, CU, LC, WF.

514A   **Baker, Richard,** *Quaker,* Concerning the judgements of God. *[London, 166–?]* 4°.* LF; CH, CU.

514B   —How the love of God is the true ground. *[London, 166–?]* 4°.* L, LF; CH, MH, PH, PSC, Y.

514C   —The strength and power of God. *[London, 1660?]* 4°.* L, LF; CH.

514D   —A testimony to the power of God. *Printed and sold by T. Sowle, 1699.* 8°. L, LF, BBN; MH, PH, PSC, Y.

514E   **[Baker, Richard, Merchant].** The merchants humble petition. *By Joseph Moxon, 1659.* fol.* L, O; MH, MIU, PU.

515   **Baker, Robert.** Cursus osteologicus; being a compleat doctrine of the bones. *By I. Dawks, for D. Browne, and R. Clavell, 1697.* 8°. T.C.III 6. L, LSC, LWL, GH; NAM.

516   ——Second edition. *Printed and sold by T. Leigh and D. Midwinter, 1699.* 8°. T.C.II 83. LCS, E; WSG, WU.

516A   —The description and uses of a most acurate [*sic*] planisphere. *By H. C. for P. Lea, 1686.* 4°. T.C.II 157. O, HH; CLC.

516B   **Baker, Thomas.** A catalogue of the mathematical works of. *[London, 1683?]* 4°.* L, O, C.

517   —Clavis geometrica catholica. *Typis J. Playford & prostant venales apud R. Clavel, 1684.* 4°. T.C.II 73. L, O, C, E, DT; CLC, LC, MU, NC, HC.
    —Geometrical key. 1684. See his Clavis.

518   [–] The head of Nile. *Printed, and are to be sold by Walter Davis, 1681.* 4°.* T.C.II 7. L, O, C, LCL, EN; CH, CN, NU, WF, Y.

518A   [–] ——[Anr. ed.] *For R. Taylor, 1687.* 4°.* T.C.II 184. O; CN.

---

519   [–] Reflections upon learning. *For A. Bosville, 1699.* 8°.* T.C.III 135. L, O, CS; NP, PL, Y, HC.

520   [–] —Second edition. —, *1700.* 8°. L, O, C, LW, DT; CLC, MIU, NU, PL, TU, WF.

521   [–] —Third edition. —, *1700.* 8°. L, O, LWL, CT, MC; CLC, CN, NHS, WF, Y.

522   —The spirituall nursery deciphered. *For John Crooke, and John Baker, 1651.* 4°.* O, OC, CS.

523   —The unspotted high-court of justice erected. *For the author, 1657.* 12°. O.

524   —The wicked mans plot defeated. *[London], for the author, 1656.* 12°. L.

525   The bakers and brewers warning-piece. *For G. Freeman, 1662.* 4°.* LG; WF.

    [Bakewell, P.] Discourse tending to prove. 1642. *See* Barebon, Praisegod.

526   **Bakewell, Thomas.** An answer, or confutation of, divers errors. *For Henry Shepheard and William Ley, 1646.* 4°. LT, O, CS, YM, DT; NHC, NPT, NU.

526A   [–] An answer to those questions. *For William Ley, 1646.* 4°.* LT, O, C, EN, DT; CLC, MBP, MH, NU, WF, Y.

527   [–] The Antinomians Christ confovnded. *For Thomas Bankes, 1644.* 4°. LT, O, C, LCL, GU; CH, NU, WF.

528   [–] A brief ansvver to obiections of all sorts. *By Francis Leach, 1650.* 4°.* LT, E, EN; CLC, NU.

529   —A certification of two points now in controversie. *For Henry Sheperd, and for William Ley, 1646.* 4°.* LT.

530   [–] A confutation of the Anabaptists. *By M. O. for T. Bankes, 1644.* 4°. LT, LCL, CT; CN, NHC, NU, WF.

531   —The dippers plunged. *For John Dallam, 1650.* 4°.* LT, DT.

532   —Doctor Chamberlain visited. *For John Dallam, 1650.* 4°.* LT, O, DC, DT.

533   —A faithfull messenger sent. *By M. Okes, for T. Bankes, 1644.* 4°.* LT, O, LCL, SC, GU; CH, CLC, MH, NU, RPJ.

533A   —Heresie detected. *For William Ley, 1649.* 4°. NU.

534   —A justification of two points. *For Henry Sheperd and William Ley, 1646.* 4°.* LT, O, DT; CLC, IU, NC, NHC.

535   [–] The ordinance of excommunication rightly stated. colop: *For Henry Shepheard, and William Ley, 1646.* cap., 4°.* LT, LG, ENC; CH, MIU, NU.

536   —A plea for Mr. Strong's church members. *For Iohn Dallom, 1650.* 4°.* LT, SP.

537   [–] A short view of the Antinomian errovrs. *By T. B. for Ed. Blakmore and Tho. Bankes, 1643.* 4°.* L, O, LCL, HH, E; CH, MH, NU, RPJ, Y.

538   Balaams asse, or the city-fast for cursing the King. *[London], printed, 1649.* 4°.* LT, C, OC, HH; CH, MM, TU.
    Balaams reply. 1661. *See* H., W.

538A   Balaam's wish; a sermon. *By T. Leach for John Sims, 1670.* 8°. NPT.

539   **Balam, Richard.** Algebra; or. . . . *By J. G. for R. Boydell, 1653.* 12°. LT, O, OC, CS; PL.

540   The ballance adjusted. *[1688?]* 4°.* L, O, CT, LL; CH, MM, TU, WF, Y.

541   The ballance pvt into the hand. *[London], printed, 1646[7].* 4°.* LT, O, OC; CH, MH, PL, WF, Y.

542 [**Balbani, Niccolò.**] The Italian convert. Fourth edition. *For Edward Archer*, 1655. 8°. L, O, CS; CH, CN, MH, WF, Y.

543 [–] —[Anr. ed.] *By T. R. for Abel Roper*, 1662. 8°. L, O; NN.

544 [–] —[Anr. ed.] *By T. Ratcliffe and T. Daniel for A. Roper*, 1668. 8°. CLC, MH, TU, Y.

544A [–] —[Anr. ed.] *For Abel Roper*, 1677. 8°. L, SP; CLC, MH, NPT, WF, Y.

545 [–] —[Anr. ed.] —, 1689. 12°. T.C.II 241. L, P; CLC, TU, Y.

546 **Baldwin, D.** Ireland cured of all distempers. *By J. Millet for the author.* 1690. brs. Y.

547 **Baldwin, William.** A marvellous history intituled Beware the cat. *For Jane Bell*, 1652. L[frag].

548 —A treatise of morall philosphie. Sixth edition. *By Richard Bishop*, 1651. 12°. L, O; CLC, IU, MU, NC, WF.

549 **Bales, Peter.** Infirmity inducing to conformity. *Printed*, 1650. 4°.* O; MM.

550 —Oratio Dominica; or. . . . *For F.E.*, 1643. 4°.* LT, CS, HH, DT; CH, CU, NU, WF, Y.

551 **Balfour, Andrew.** Bibliotheca Balfourniana. *Edinburgi, ab hæredibus ac successoribus Andreæ Anderson*, 1659. 4°. ALDIS 3444. O, EN; MH, HC.

552 **Balfour, Sir Andrew.** Letters write [sic] to a friend. *Edinburgh, printed*, 1700. 4°. L, LAD, CT, E, ENC; CLC, TU, WF.

553 —Letters writen [sic] to a friend. *Edinburgh, printed* 1700. 8°. O, EN, ES, FSF; CLC, CN, MMO, NPT, Y.

554 **Balfour, Sir James.** A catalogue of curious manuscripts. *Edinburgh, by the heirs and successors of Andrew Anderson*, 1698. 8°.* ALDIS 3738. L, O, EN; MH.

555 —Catalogus . . . librorum. *Edinburgi*, 12 June 1699. *successores Andreas Anderson.* 8°. ALDIS 3835. L, O, EN.

556 [**Balfour, William.**] Another happy victorie obtained by . . . Essex. [*London*], Decem. 23. *for Henry Liech*, [1642]. 4°.* LT.

557 **Balfour, Sir William.** Sir William Balfores letter . . . to the Earl of Essex. *For Laurence Blaiklock*, 1644. 4°.* LT; CLC, MH, MIU, WF, Y.

558 **Ball, John.** An answer to two treatises. *By R.B. and are to be sold by John Burroughes*, 1642. 4°. L, O, C, NPL, E; CLC, CN, MH, NU, WF, Y.

559 —A declaration from the city of Bristoll. *For Joseph Matthews, and John Nicolls*, Decemb. 23, 1642. 4°.* LT, BR.

560 —Mr. Balls grounds & arguments. 1647. EN.
[–] A letter of many ministers in old England. 1643. *See title.*

561 —The power of godlines. *By Abraham Miller, for George Sawbridge*, 1657. fol. L, O, C, LW, E; CH, CU, MH, NU, WF, Y.

562 —A short catechisme: composed. *By E. P. for Abel Roper*, 1646. 8°.* LT.

562A — —[Anr. ed.] *By W. W. for Abel Roper*, 1646. 12°.* L.

563 [–] A short catechisme containing. Nineteenth edition. *By T.B. for John Wright*, 1642. 8°.* O; Y.

564 [–] —Twentieth edition. *For Edward Brewster*, 1642. 8°.* O.

565 [–] —Three and twentieth edition. —, 1645. 8°. CH.

566 [–] —Thirty-first edition. *For John Wright*, 1650. 8°.* L, O.

567 [–] —Thirty-second edition. *For E: Brewster*, 1651. 8°.* O.

568 [–] —Thirty-fourth edition. —, 1653. 8°.* L.

568A [–] —Thirty-third edition. *By E. Crowch for J. Wright*, 1673. 8°. OC.

568B [–] —Fifty-first edition. —, 1671. 8°. LW.

569 [–] —Fifty-sixth edition. *By A.P. and T.H. to be sold by J. VVright*, 1678. 8°.* O.

569A [–] —Fifty-fourth edition. *By R.R. for Edw. Brewster*, 1688. 8°. NU.

569B [–] —Forty-eighth edition. *For John Wright*, 1689. 8°.* MH.

570 [–] A short catechisme to prepare young ignorant people. *Oxford, by L.L. for 'Edward' Thorne*, 1657. brs. MADAN 2331. O.

570A —Short questions and answers. Second edition. *By E. G. for H.O. to be sold by Iohn Long at Dorchester*, 1641. 8°. OC; PL.

570B [–] A short treatise containing all the principall grounds. Twelfth edition. *For John Wright*, 1646. 8°. CLC.

571 — —Thirteenth edition. —, 1647. 8°. C.

571A [–] —Thirteenth edition. *For Edward Brewster*, 1650. 8°. L, O, LSC; NU.

572 [–] —Fourteenth edition. *By John Wright*, 1654. 8°. C, LCL; MH, NPT, NU.

572A [–] —[Anr. ed.] *For E. Brewster and George Sawbridge*, 1654. 8°. LW, P; MH, NN, NPT.

573 [–] —Fifteenth edition. *Imprinted at London, for E. Brewster & George Sawbridge*, 1656. 12°. LCL, E; MB, NPT, NU.

574 [–] —"Fourteenth" edition. *By E. C. for E. Brewster, and J. Wright*, 1670. 8°. T.C.I 39. L; CLC, NU.

575 [–] —[Anr. ed. in Arabic]. [*Oxford*, 1660?] 8°. MADAN 2480. O.

576 —A treatise of divine meditation. *For H. Mortlock*, 1660. 8°. LT, LCL, P; NPT.

577 —A treatise of faith. 1654. 4°. E.

578 — —Third edition. *For Edward Brewster*, 1657. 4°. C, LCL, AU; NP, NU.

579 —A treatise of the covenant of grace. *By G. Miller for Edward Brewster*, 1645. 4°. L, O, C, LCL, E; MBC, NU, RPJ, WF, Y.

580 Entry cancelled.
—A tryall of the new-chvrch way. 1644. *See title.*

581 **Ball, Nathaniel.** Spiritual bondage. *For Jonathan Robinson*, 1683. 8°. O, LCL; MH, NPT, NU.

582 **Ball, Richard.** An astrolo-physical compendium. *For H. Nelme*, 1697. 12°. L, LWL; Y.

583 —The true Christian-man's duty. *By A.G. and J.P. for John Playford*, 1682. 4°.* T.C.I 499. O, C, LL, BAMB; CH, PL, V, Y.

584 **Ball, Thomas.** Ποιμηνοπυργος. Pastorum. *By S. G. for John Wright*, 1656. 4°. LT, LW, O, C, LCL; CH, MBA, NU, WF, Y.

585 —Two books of elegies: in imitation. *For Richard Cumberland*, 1697. 8°. T.C.III 27. L, CS; CLC, CN, NN.

585A [-] Verses upon several occasions. 1697. 8°. IU.

586 **Ball, William.** A briefe treatise concerning the regulation of printing. *Printed*, 1651. 8°.* LT.

587 —A caveat for subjects, moderating. *Printed at London*, 1642. 4°.* LT, O, C, EN, DT; CH, CN, MH, NU, TU, WF, Y.

588 —Constitutio liberi populi, or, the rule of a free-born people. [*London*], *printed*, 1646. 4°.* LT, O, LCL, CT, HH; CH, CN, CU, MH, WF, Y.

588A —A digest of government. *For Thomas Johnson*, 1659. 4°.* NP, Y.

589 —Europa lachrymans. *Apud Thoman Harperum*, 1650. 4°.* L; MH.

590 —An illegall way to get another mans estate. *Printed*, 1653. 4°. EN; MM.

591 —Law and state proposals. *For the author*, 1659. 4°.* L.

592 —A narrative. [*London*, 1656.] brs. L.

593 —Power juridicent. [*London*], *by H. T.*, 1650. 4°.* LT; WF, Y.

594 —The power of kings discussed. *For John Harris*, 1649. 4°.* LT, O, LW, OC, AN; CH, CN, MH, NU, WF, Y.

595 —State-maxims. *By G. Dawson for T. Brewster*, 1655. 4°.* LT, O; CH, CU, MM, NP, NU.

596 —To the honourable the ... Parliament, the humble propositions of. *By Barnard Alsop for Thomas Bayle*, 1641. 4°.* LT, C, HH, EN, GU; CH, CSS, WF, Y.

597 —Tractatvs de jure regnandi. [*London*], *printed*, 1645. 4°.* LT, O, C, HH, ES; CLC, CU, MH, NU, WF, Y.

597A —A true narrative of the undue ... proceedings of Edward Bullock. *Printed*, 1652. 4°.* CLC, WF.

598 —Ball, his vindication against Bullock. [*London*], *printed*, 1652. 4°.* LT.

599 A ballad. [*First line:* I sing the praise of a worthy wight.] [c. 1673-4.] brs. L, O, HH; MH, MIU.

600 The ballad, Assist me. [*London*, 1681.] brs. L; MH.

601 A ballad, called The libertine's lampoone. *For F. K. and Edward Thomas*, 1674. brs. MC.

602 A ballad intituled, The old mans complaint. [1670?]. brs. L, O.

602A —[Anr. ed.] *Printed for, and sold by W. Thackeray, J. M and A. M.*, [1690.] brs. L, CM, HH, GU.

603 The ballad of the cloak. [*London*], *for P. Brooksby*, [1660?] brs. L, O, HH, EN; MH.

604 —[Anr. ed.] *Reprinted by the author*, [1681-2]. brs. L, O, OC, HH, GU; CH, MBA, MH, PU, TU.

604A —[Anr. ed.] [*London*], *for A. M., W. O., and T. Thackeray*, [c. 1700]. brs. HUTH.

604AA Ballad of the plotting head. [*London*, 1681.] brs. L.

604B A ballad of the strange and wonderful storm of hail. [*London*], *for F. Coles, T. Vere, J. Wright, J. Clarke, W. Thackeray, and T. Passinger*, [1680]. brs. CM.

Ballad on the gyants. [1662.] *See* Gayton, Edmund.

604C A ballad on the most renowned Shuff of Newberry. [*London*, 1684.] brs. L.

Ballad. The third part, to the same tune. [*London*, 1680?] *See* Powys, *Lady* Elizabeth.

605 Ballad. To the tune of Couragio. [1688.] brs. O, C, HH; MH, MIU, TU.

Ballad upon the popish plot. [1679.] *See* Powis, *Lady* Elizabeth.

606 **Ballamie, Richard.** The leper clensed. *Printed, to be sold by Francis Eglesfield*, 1657. 4°.* L; NU.

Balm from Gilead. 1681. *See* Bairdy, John.

Balm presented. [1680.] *See* Oates, Titus.

607 **Balmerino, John Elphinstone,** *baron.* The Lord Balmerino's speech ... Novemb. 4, 1641. *Printed at London, for T. B.*, 1641. 4°.* LT, C, EC, HH; CLC, CN, MBP, MH, Y.

608 **Balmford, Samuel.** Habakkuks prayer. *By E. M. for Adoniram Byfield*, 1659. 8°. LT.

609 **Balmford, William.** The seaman's spiritual companion. *For Benj. Harris*, 1678. 8°. T.C.I 300. L, LCL; Y.

610 **Baltharpe, John.** The straights voyage, or St. Davids poem. *By E. C. for T. Vere*, 1671. 12°. T.C.I 81. L, O; CH, Y.

611 **Baltimore, George Calvert,** *baron.* The answer to Tom-tell-troth. *Printed*, 1642[3]. 4°.* LT, O, C, CT, OC; CH, CN, MH, WF, Y.

612 **Balzac, Jean Louis Guez,** *sieur de.* Aristippus, or, Mon^sr de Balsac's masterpiece. *By Tho. Newcomb, for Nat. Eakins, and Tho. Johnson*, 1659. 12°. LT, O, OC, CM, P; CH, CU, MH, WF, Y.

613 —The choyce letters of. *For Thomas Dring*, 1658. 8°. L, O, CT; CLC, CN, MH, WF, Y.

614 —The letters of. *For John Williams and Francis Eaglesfield*, 1654. 4°. LT, C, LL, CT, DT; CH, CN, LC, NC, Y.

615 —The prince, vvritten in French by. *For M. Meighen, and G. Bedell*, 1648. 12°. L, O, C, CE; CH, CN, PL, WF, Y.

616 —Balzac's remaines. *For Thomas Dring*, 1658. 8°. LT, P; CH, CN, CU, MH, WF.

617 —The Roman conversation. *By T. N. for J. Holden*, 1652. 12°. DC, SP; MH.

618 Entry cancelled.

Bamfiild, Joseph. *See* Bampfield, Joseph.

619 **Bamfield, Francis.** [Hebrew] Παγγνωσια παντεχια πανσοφια. All in one. The first part [*London*], *printed*, 1677. fol. L, O, C, LCL, E; CLC, NPT, NU, WF, Y.

620 [-] A continuation of a former Just appeal. [*London*, 1684.] cap., fol.* L.

621 [-] [Hebrew] The Holy Scripture the Scripture of truth. *For John Lawrence*, 1684. fol.* L.

622 [-] [Hebrew] The house of wisdom. *For the author, to be sold by John Lawrence*, 1681. fol.* L, O, LWL; TU, WF, Y.

623 —The judgement of. *By W. Godbid, for Joseph Nevill*, 1672. 8°. T.C.I 97. L, O, C; IU, NPT, NU, Y.

624 —The judgment of Mr. Francis Bampfield, with Mr. Ben's sober answer. *By W. Godbid for Sarah Nevill*, 1677. 8°. T.C.I 269. LCL; CH.

625 [-] A just appeal from lower courts. colop: *For the authour*, 1683. cap., fol.* L.

626 [-] The Lords free prisoner. colop: *For W. T. and sold by L. Curtiss*, 1683. cap., fol.* L, O; CH, MBA, PU, WF.

627 [-] [Hebrew] A name, an after-one. *For John Lawrence,* 1681. fol.* L, O, LWL; WF.

628 —[Hebrew] Σαββατικη 'ημερα. . . . The second part. [*London*], *printed,* 1677. fol. L, O, LWL, HH, EN; CH, CLC, WF, Y.

628A **Bampfield, Joseph.** Colonell Joseph Bamfeild's apologie. [*The Hague?*] *anno* 1685. 4°. L, O, BR; CH, WF.

629 **Bampfield, Thomas.** An enquiry whether the Lord Jesus Christ made the world. *For the author, to be sold by Tho. Fabian,* 1692. 4°. T.C.II 401. L, BB, EN; CH, NU, WF, Y.

630 —A reply to Doctor Wallis. *For Thomas Fabian,* 1693. 4°. T.C.II 471. L, O, C, LW, OM; CH, MH, NU, Y.

631 **Banaster, Thomas.** An alarm to the world. *Giles Calvert,* 1649. 4°.* LT, DT.

632 [**Banckes, Matthew.**] The several ways of resolving faith. *York, by Stephen Bulkley, to be sold by Richard Lambart,* 1677. 8°. T.C.I 272. L, O, CT, OC, YM; NU, TU.

633 [-] —Second edition. *For H. Faithorne, and J. Kersey,* 1682. 8°. T.C.I 467. O, C, CS, P, SP.

634 [**Bancroft, John.**] Henry the Second, King of England. *For Jacob Tonson,* 1693. 4°. L, O, OM, EN; BN, CH, CN, MH, NC, TU, WF, Y.

635 [-] King Edward the third. *For J. Hindmarsh, R. Bently, A. Roper, and Randall Taylor,* 1691. 4°. T.C.II 347. L, O, C, EN, DT; CH, CN, LC, MH, TU, Y.

636 —The tragedy of Sertorius. *For R. Bentley and M. Magnes,* 1679. 4°. T.C.I 350. L, O, OW, CS, EN; CH, CN, LC, MH, NC, TU, Y.

637 **Bancroft, Richard,** *abp.* Dangerous positions. 1641. 4°. DT; CN.

638 [-] A survey of the pretended holy discipline. *By Richard Hodgkinsonne,* 1663. 4°. L, O, OB, LCL, BR; CH, MH, NU, WF, Y.

639 [-] —[Anr. ed.] *By R. Hodgkinson, to be sold by Nathaniel Brooks,* 1663. 4°. P; Y.

639A — —[Anr. ed.] *By R. Hodgkinson, sold by Gab. Bedell,* 1663. 4°. OC, CM.

640 **Bancroft, Thomas.** The heroical lover or Antheon & Fidelta. *By W. G. and are to be sold by Isaac Pridmore,* 1658. 8°. L, O.

641 —[Anr. ed.] *By William Godbid,* 1658. 8°. CH.

642 —Times's out of tune. *By W. Godbid,* 1658. 8°. MH.
Banders disbanded. 1681. *See* MacWard, Robert.

643 The bane to the Devonshire cant. *T. Rawe,* 1681. brs. L.

643A **Banes, William.** A few words. *Printed,* 1659. 4°.* MH.

644 **B[angor], J[osiah].** A serious item to secure sinners. *Printed,* 1666. 8°. LCL, OM; CLC, NPT, NU, WF.

645 The banish'd duke: or, the tragedy of Infortunatus. *For R. Baldwin,* 1690. 4°. T.C.II 336. L, O, OW; CH, CN, MH, WF, Y.

645A The banishment of poverty. [*London?* 1695]. brs. MH.

646 **B[anister], J[ohn].** The sprightly companion. *By F. Heptinstall, for H. Playford,* 1695.* L.

647 Bank-credit: or. *By John Gain,* 1683. 8°.* L, O, LG, EN, DT; LC, MBA, MH, NC, Y.

648 A bank dialogue between Dr. H. C. and a country gentleman. [*London,* 1695]. cap., fol.* L, LG; MH.

649 Bank of credit upon land security. [*Edinburgh,* 1696] cap., fol.* MC; Y.
Bank of England. 1697. *See* N., P.

650 Banker's and creditor's case. 1675. 8°. LL.

651 **Banks, John,** *Minister.* The blessed effects of true and saving faith. *Printed,* 1684. 4°.* L, O, LF, BR, BBN; CH, MH, NU, PH, WF, Y.

652 —An epistle to Friends. *Printed and sold by T. Sowle,* 1692. 4°.* LF, BBN; CLC, MH, PH, PSC, Y.

652A — —Second edition. —, 1693. 4°.* LF; CH, PSC.

653 — —Third edition. —, 1696. 4°.* L, LF; MH, WF, Y.

654 —An exhortation to Friends. *Printed, and sold, by Andrew Sowle,* 1687. 4°.* L, O, C, LF, BBN; CH, MH, PH, PSC, Y.

655 [-] A general epistle to the flock of God. [*London,* 1698.] cap., 4°.* L, LF, BBN; PH, PL, PSC, Y.

656 **Banks, John,** *playwright.* Cyrus the great. *For Richard Bentley,* 1696. 4°. L, O, C, LVD, EN; CH, CN, LC, MH, NC, TU, Y.

657 —The destruction of Troy. *By A. G. and J. P. and are to be sold by Charles Blount,* 1679. 4°. T.C.I 350. L, O, LVD, OW; BN, CH, CN, LC, MH, NC, TU, WCL, Y.

658 —The innocent usurper. *For R. Bentley,* 1694. 4°. T.C.II 511. L, O, OW, LVF, EN; CH, CN, LC, MH, NC, Y.

659 —The island queens. *For R. Bentley,* 1684. 4°. L, O, LVF, OW, ES; CH, CN, LC, MH, NC, TU, Y.

660 [-] Oh! take him gently from the pile. [*London*], *T. Cross,* [1697]. brs. L.

661 —Prologue to a new play, called Anna Bullen. colop: *For Allen Banks,* 1682. brs. O, MC, EN; CH, MH, WF.

662 —The rival kings. *For Langley Curtis,* 1677. 4°. T.C.I 291. L, O, LVD, LVF, OW; BN, CN, MH, NC, WF, Y.

662A — —[Anr. ed.] *For L. C.,* 1677. 4°. L, O, LG; CH, CN, MH, TU, WF.

662B — —[Anr. ed.] *For W. Cademan,* 1677. 4°. LC, MH, Y.

663 —The unhappy favourite. *For Richard Bentley and Mary Magnes,* 1682. 4°. T.C.I 462. L, O, C, LVD, EN; CH, CN, LC, MH, TU, Y.

664 — —[Anr. ed.] —, 1685. 4°. T.C.II 118. L, O, LVD; CH, NC, TU, WF, Y.

665 — —[Anr. ed.] *For Richard Bentley,* 1693. 4°. O, OW, LGI, HH; MH, MU, NC, WF, Y.

666 — —[Anr. ed.] *For Richard Wellington, and Edmund Romball, sold by Bernard Lintot,* [1699]. 4°. T.C.III 128. L, O; CU, MU, Y.

667 —Vertue betray'd. *For R. Bentley and M. Magnes,* 1682. 4°. L, O, C, LVF, EN; BN, CH, CN, LC, MH, NC, TU, Y.

668 — —Second edition. *For R. Bentley,* 1692. 4°. T.C.II 590. L, O, LVD, OW; CLC, CN, MH, NF, WF, Y.

668A — —[Anr. ed.] —, 1696. 4°. MB.

668B **Banks, Jonathan.** Janua clavis, or, Lilly's syntax. *For the author to be sold by Benjamin Clarke,* 1679. 8°. L. O.

669 —The life of the right reverend Father in God, Edw. Rainbow. *By Samuel Roycroft, for Robert Clavell,* 1688. 8°. T.C.II 259. L, O, CT, LW, OB; CH, CN, NPT, WF, Y.

670   **Banks, Noah.** Gods prerogative. *By R.B.*, 1650. 4°.*
LT; CLC, MH, NU.

671   [**Banks, Richard.**] Religion and reason adjusted. *For
the author*, 1688. 8°. T.C.II 225. L, O, CS, YM, DT; MH,
MIU, NPT, WF, Y.

672   [–] —Second edition. *By J. Rawlins, to be sold at Furnivals
Inn gate, and by Randal Taylor*, 1696. 8°. O.

672A   —A sermon preached . . . September 20, 1699. *A. & J.
Churchill*, 1700. 8°. LW, BAMB.

The banner of justification. 1659. *See* Goodwin, John.

673   The banner of truth displayed. [*London*, 1656.] 4°. LT.

674   The banners of grace and love. *By W. Godbid for Edw.
Farnham*, 1657. 4°. O, ENC; MH.

Banners of love. 1654. *See* Tillam, Thomas.

Banquet of jests. 1657. *See* Armstrong, Archibald.

Banquet of musick. 1688. *See* Playford, Henry.

674A   The banqueting room's ornament. *For the author and sold
by William Marshal and John Marshal*, 1696. 8°. MIU.

Baptism, before. 1669. *See* Fisher, Samuel.

675   Baptism, infant-baptism, and Quakerism. *Printed*, 1674.
8°. L, O; NPT.

Baptismal bonds. 1687. *See* Heywood, Oliver.

Βαπτισμῶν διδαχη, or. 1648. *See* Dell, William.

Baptisms in their verity. 1648. *See* E., J.

Baptismus redivivus, or. . . . 1678. *See* St. Nicholas,
John.

675A   **Baptist, Mr.** An ode to the King. *For R. Bentley*, 1684.
4°.* Y.

Baptist not Babylonish. 1672. *See* Grigg, Henry.

Baptista, *Mantuan*. *See* Spagnouli, Baptista.

Baptists answer. 1675. *See* Knollys, Hanserd.

676   Bara i blant. *Gan John Astwood*, 1695. 8°.* AN.

677   **Baratti, Giacomo.** The late travels into the countries
of the Abissins. *For Benjamin Billingsley*, 1670. 8°.
T.C.I 56. L, O, C, CT, E; BN, CLC, CN, MU, LC, Y.

678   **Barba, Alvaro Alonso.** The art of metals. *For S.
Mearne*, 1674. 8°. T.C.I 177. L, O, LWL, GU, AU; CLC,
LC, MH, WF, Y.

679   —The first book of the art of mettals. *For S. Mearne*,
1670. 8°. L, LR, LM, CT, GU; CLC, LC, RPJ, Y.

680   — —[Anr. ed.] *For S. Mearne*, 1674. 8°. L, O, C, ES, DT;
BN, MB, PAP, RPJ, Y.

681   —The second book of the art of mettals. *For S. Mearne*,
1670. 8°. L, O, LR; RPJ, Y.

682   — —[Anr. ed.] *For S. Mearne*, 1674. 8°. L, O; CLC, IU, LC,
RPJ, Y.

682A   **Barbadoes.** Acts and statutes of. *By Will Bentley*, [1654].
8°. L; MB, MHL, PL.

682B   —The laws of. *For William Rawlin*, 1699. fol L; MHL,.
PAP, RPJ, TU.

683   Barbara Allen's cruelty. [*London*], *for P. Brooksby, J.
Deacon, J. Blare, J. Back*, [1685–92]. brs. L, O, HH; MH.

683A   **Barbaro, Francesco.** Directions for love and marriage.
For John Leigh and Tho. Burrell, 1677. 8°. L; CLC, MH,
WF, Y.

684   The barbarous and bloody inn-keeper. *For P. Brooksby*,
1675. 4°.* L.

685   Barbarous and bloody newes from the parish of St.
Giles's. colop: [*London*], *for W. Hethcock*, 1690. CH, CN.

686   Barbarous and cruell passages. 1642. 4°. O.

687   Barbarous & inhumane proceedings against the professors. *By M. S. for Tho: Jenner*, 1655. 4°. L; CLC, CH,
NS, WF.

688   A barbarous murther . . . Henry Jones. 1672. 4°. DT.

689   The barbarous murther of James late Lord Arch Bishop
of St. Andrews. [*Edinburgh*], *reprinted*, 1679. brs. ALDIS
2155. L.

689A   [**Barbe, Simon.**] The French perfumer. *For Sam.
Buckley*, 1696. 12°. T.C.II 591. CT, GU; CH, WF.

689B   [–] —Second edition. —, 1697. 8°. T.C.III 17. LWL.

689C   — —Third edition. —, 1700. 8°. T.C.III 191. GU.

690   **Barber, Abraham.** The psalme tunes. In four parts.
York, by John White for Abraham Barber, 1700. 12°. L.

691   **Barber, Edward.** An answer to the eight quaeries.
[*London*, 1648]. cap., 4°.* LCL; Y.

692   —An answer to the Essex watchmens watch-word.
[*London*, 1649]. 4°.* L, O, DT; NC.

692A   [–] Certain queries, propounded to the church. [*London?
1650*.] 4°.* WF.

693   —A declaration and vindication of the cariage of Edward
Barber. [*London*, 1648]. 4°.* LT, O, C; NHC.

694   —A small treatise of baptisme, or, dipping. [*London*],
printed, 1641. 4°.* LT, O, DT; MIU, NHC, NU.

695   —The storming. *Printed*, 1651. 4°. CT.

696   —To the kings most excellent Maiesty . . . the humble
petition. [*London*], *printed*, 1641. brs. LT.

697   —A true discovery of the ministry of the gospell.
Printed, 1645. 4°. CT, DT.

[**Barber, Nicholas.**] Discourse of trade. 1690. *See*
Barbon, Nicholas.

697A   **Barber, William.** De Welchmans sermon. *Vor Evan
Harry-Watkin, ant are to be sold by Griffin Clyder ap
Shinkin*, 1660. 4°.* Y.

697B   **Barberini, Antonio, cardinal.** At the auction-house
for pictures. [*London? 1680*]. brs. L.

697C   **Barbet, J.** A book of architecture. *To be sold by Robert
Pricke*, 1670. fol.* T.C.I 30. L; LC.

697D   **Barbette, Paul.** A compleat treatise of chirurgery.
Second edition. *By W. G. and are to be sold by Moses
Pitt*, 1674. 8°. T.C.I 191. O.

698   —The practice of. *By T. R. for Henry Brome*, 1675. 8°.
T.C.I 204. L, O, C, LCS, LM; CLC, MH, MMO, WF, WSG.

699   —Thesaurus chirurgiæ. The chirurgical and anatomical
works of. *By J. Darby, and sold by Moses Pitt*, 1672.
8°. T.C.I 103. L, LWL, E, GH; WSG, HC.

700   — —Third edition. *Printed, and to be sold by M. Pitt*,
1676. 8°. T.C.I 231. O, C, LCS, LM, LWL; CH, LC, NAM,
PU, WF, WSG.

701   — —Fourth edition. *For Henry Rhodes*, 1687. 8°. T.C.II
182. L, C, LM, LWL; NAM, WSG.

Barbier, John. The famous game of chesse-play. 1672.
See Saul, Arthur.

702   [**Barbieri, Giovanni Francisco.**] A booke of portraiture. *By Godfrey Richards*, 1655. 12°. CH, WWC.

703 **Barbon, John.** Λειτουργια Θειοτερα εργια: or, liturgie a most divine service. *Oxford, by A. & L. Lichfield,* 1662. 4°. MADAN 2584. L, O, CT, SP; NHC, NPT, NU, Y.

703A **Barbon, Nicholas.** An advertisement being a proposal. colop: *By S. Darker and D. Newman, to be had gratis and at Ric. Southbys,* 1694. brs. MH, Y.

704 —An apology for the builder. *For Cave Pullen,* 1685. 37pp. 4°.* L, O, EN; CH, MBA, MH.

704A [–] —[Anr. ed.] —, 1685. 26 pp. 4°.° L, C, LPO, EN.

705 — —[Anr. ed.] *Printed,* 1689. 4°.* LG; CH, MBA, MH, NC, RPJ, WF.

706 —A discourse concerning coining the new money lighter. *For Richard Chiswell,* 1696. 8°. T.C.II 591. L, O, CT, EN, ES; BN, LC, MH, NC, WCL, Y.

707 —A discourse of trade. *By Tho. Milbourn for the author,* 1690. 8°. LO, OM; MH, NC, PU, Y.

707A —A letter to a gentleman in the country, giving an account. colop: *By Tho. Milbourn,* 1685. cap., fol.* L, LG.

708 —A proposal for raising the publick credit. *[London, 1697].* brs. L, LUG.

709 **[Barbour, John.]** The acts and life of . . . Robert Bruce. *Edinburgh, by Andrew Anderson,* 1670. 12°. ALDIS 1890. L, C, EN, GU, DT; MH, WF.

710 [–] —[Anr. ed.] *Glasgow, by Robert Sanders,* 1672. 12°. ALDIS 1937. EN, FSF; Y.

711 —Ancilla grammaticae: or, an epitome. *For Tho. Pierpoint,* 1663. 8°. O.

711A —An epitome of grammar. *Oxford, by Henry Hall,* 1668. 8°. WF.

712 —The life and acts. "Second" edition. *Edinburgh: by Gedeon Lithgow,* 1648. 8°. ALDIS 1307. E, EN; CH.

713 **[Barclay, Alexander.]** The shepheards kalender. *By Robert Ibbitson, and are to be sold by Francis Grove,* 1656. fol. L, R; CH, CN, MB.

714 **Barclay, John.** Jo. Barclaii Argenis. *Cantabrigiæ, ex officina Joann. Hayes,* 1673. *Impensis Joann Creed.* 8°. T.C.I 165. L, O, C, CT, AU; CLC, CN, MH, PL, WF, Y.

715 —John Barclay his defence. *By Mary Thompson; and sold by Matthew Turner; and John Lane,* 1688. 4°.* L, O, OM, CT, BAMB; MH, TU.

716 —John Barclay his vindication. *[London], by Mary Thompson: and sold by Matthew Turner; and John Lane,* 1688. 4°.* L, AU.

717 **Barclay, John, minister.** A description of the Roman Catholick church. *[Aberdeen], printed,* 1689. 4°. ALDIS 2862. L, HH, EN, E, AU; CH, TU, WF.

718 **Barclay, Robert.** The anarchy of the ranters. *[London], printed,* 1676. 4°. L, C, LF, HH, AU; CH, MH, MU, NU, PH.

719 Entry cancelled.

720 —An apology for the true Christian divinity. *[Aberdeen, John Forbes], printed,* 1678. 4°. L, O, C, LF, GU; LC, MH, NU, PH, RPJ, Y.

721 — —Second edition. *[London?], printed,* 1678. 4°. L, O, LF; CH, LC, NU, PH, Y.

722 —A [sic] apology. Third edition. *[London?], printed,* 1678. 4°. LF; Y.

723 —Robert Barclay's apology. *Printed,* 1679. 4°. AU; RPJ.

724 —Robert Barclay's apology . . . vindicated. *Printed,* 1679. *And are to be sold by Benjamin Clark, at London.* 4°. L, LF, AU, GU; MH, NU, PSC, RPJ, Y.

724A —Baptism and the Lord's supper. *Printed, and sold by T. Sowle,* 1696. 4°. LF, CT; CH, NG, NU, PH, Y.

725 —A catechism and confession of faith. *[London, 1673.]* 8°. L, LF, LLP; CH, PU.

726 — —[Anr. ed.] *[London], printed,* 1674. 8°. LF, CT, E; BN, PSC.

727 — —Second edition. *[London], printed,* 1676. 8°. LF; CH, PH.

728 — —[Anr. ed.] *For Benjamin Clark,* 1682. 8°. LF.

729 — —Third edition. *For A. Sowle,* 1690. 8°. C, LF; NGT, PSC.

—The concurrence & unanimity of the . . . Quakers. 1694. *See title.*

730 —An epistle of love. *Printed for, and sold by Benjamin Clark,* 1679. 8°.* L, LF, BBN; PH, PSC, WF.

731 —The necessity and possibility of inward. 1676. 4°. LCL.

732 —The possibility and necessity of the inward revelation. *[London],* 1676. 4°.* LCL; PH.

732A — —[Anr. ed.] —, 1685. 4°.* PH.

732B — —[Anr. ed.] —, 1686. 4°.* LF, BBN, EN; NU, PH, PHS.

733 —Quakerism confirmed. *[Aberdeen], printed, [Forbes?],* 1676. 4°. ALDIS 2071. L, O, LF, BBN, EN; LC, MH, PHS, WU, Y.

734 —A seasonable warning. *[Aberdeen, 1672.]* 4°.* HH, AU, BBN; MH, PSC.

735 —Some things of weighty concernment. *[London, 1670.]* 4°.* HH; CH.

736 —Theologiæ verè Christianæ apologia. *Apud Benjamin Clark, Roterodami, apud Isaacum Næranum, Francofurti, apud Henricum Betkium,* 1676. 4°. LF, D; CH, MH, PH, RPJ, WF, Y.

736A — —[Anr. ed.] *Typis excusa,* 1676. *Pro Jacob Claus, veneunt præterea Londini, apud Benjamin Clark. Roterodami, apud Isaacum Næranium, Francofurti, apud Henricum Berkium.* 4°. MH, PL.

737 —Theses theologicæ. *[London, 1675.]* 16°.* L, O, AU, BBN; MU.

738 —Truth cleared of calumnies. *[Aberdeen], printed,* 1670. 4°. ALDIS 1891. L, LF, HH, EN, AU; MH, NU, PH, WF, Y.

739 — —[Anr. ed.] *For Thomas Northcott,* 1691. fol. LW; PH, PL.

740 —Truth triumphant. *For Thomas Northcott,* 1692. fol. L, O, C, LF, EN; CH, NU, PH, WF, Y.

741 —Universal love considered. *[Holland?], printed,* 1677. 4°.* L, O, C, LF, AU; MH, NU, PH, PL, Y.

742 —William Michel unmasqued. *[Aberdeen], printed,* 1672. 4°. ALDIS 1938. L, O, CT, EN, AU; CLC, MH, PH, WF, Y.

743 **Barclay, William.** Callirhoe. *As it was printed by Andro Hart, [Edin.], 1615. And now reprinted at Aberdene by Iohn Forbes younger, 1670.* 8°.* ALDIS 1892. L, HH, E, EN.

744 —Octupla; hoc est. *Edinburgi, excudebant heredes & successores Andreæ Anderson, 1696.* 8°. ALDIS 3586. L, O, C, E. EN.

745 **Bard, W.** A speech to the lord general Monck at Skinners-Hall. *For John Towers, 1660.* brs. LT.

746 **Bardon, George.** Traite contenant une nouvelle méthode, . . . longitudes. *A Londres, par C.Lucas, 1700.* 4°.* L, O.

747 **B[ardwood], J[ames].** Heart's ease in heart trouble. *For J.Robinson, 1690.* 12°. T.C.II 331. LCL.

747A [–] —Second edition. —, *1691.* 12°. L, O, LCL; CLC.

748 [–] —"Second" edition. —, *1694.* 12°. L.

Barebon, Nicholas. *See* Barbon, Nicholas.

749 **B[arebon], [Praisegod].** A defence of the lawfvlnesse of baptizing infants. *By M.Bell for Benjamin Allen, 1645.* 4°. LT, LW; MH, MWA, NHC, WF.

750 —A discourse tending to prove the baptisme. *By R.Oulton & G.Dexter, and are to be sold by Benj.Allen, 1642.* 4°.* LT, O, CT, SP; NHC, NPT, NU, WF, Y.

750A — —[Anr. ed.] *For B.Allen, 1643.* 4°.* CLC.

751 —Good things to come. *Printed, 1675.* 4°. LCL; MWA, PL.

752 —Mr. Praise-God Barbone his petition. *By R.W., 1660.* brs. MH, Y.

753 —The petition of. *Printed, 1659[60].* brs. L, O; MHS.

754 —A petition presented by. [*London, 1660.*] brs. OP; MH.

755 —A reply to the frivolous and impertinent ansvver of R.B. *Printed, 1643.* 4°. LT, O; NU, WF, Y.

756 —To the right honorable, the High Court of Parliament, . . . the illegal and immodest petition of. *By Hen.Mason, 1660.* brs. LT, LG; MH.

757 **[Barecroft, Charles.]** A letter to a lady, furnishing her with Scripture testimonies. *For John Taylor, 1688.* 4°. T.C.II 243. L, O, C, EN, DT; CH, TU, MH, MIU, WF, Y.

758 [–] The reformed Christian's New-Year-Gift. *For R.Baldwin, 1690.* 4°. T.C.II 298. L, O, C.

759 The bare-faced Tories. *H.Jones, 1682.* brs. L, O.

760 **Barford, John.** Paraphastical meditations. *By W.D. and are to be sold by Tho.Euster, 1649.* 8°. L, CE.

761 —His petition to God. [*1645.*] brs. LT.

762 The bargain which the Duke of Luxembourg made. *Reprinted London, 1692.* brs. L, EN.

763 —[Anr. ed.] [*Edinburgh?*], *reprinted for S.Daniel, 1692.* brs. L, HH.

764 **Bargishai, Eleazar.** A brief compendium. *Printed, 1652.* 4°.* LT; NU.

765 **Barham, Mr.** Catalogue of library. 7 June 1692. L.

766 **Barker, Edmund.** A sermon preached at the funerall of the right honourable . . . Lady Elizabeth Capell. *By I.R. for Iohn Williams, 1661.* 4°. LT, O, C, CT; CH, MH, TU, WF, Y.

767 —Votum pro Cæsare. *For John Williams, 1660.* 4°.* L, CT, SP, DT; CN, NU, TU, WF, Y.

768 **Barker, George.** Sermons upon several texts. *York: by John White, for Francis Hildyard, Richard Mancklin, and Thomas Baxter, 1697.* 8°. T.C.III 23. L, YM; WF.

769 **Barker, James.** The royal robe. *By E.M. for Robert Gibbs, 1661.* 8°. LT, O, LCL, CPE; NPT, WSC.

770 **Barker, Mrs. Jane.** Poetical recreations. *For Benjamin Crayle, 1688.* 8°. T.C.II 207. L, O, C, CT, LVD; CH, CN, MH, NC, WF, Y.

771 **Barker, John.** Extraordinary newes from Colonel Iohn Barkeer. *By E.G. for John Rothwell, 1643.* brs. LT.

771A —The measurer's guide. *For T.Salusbury, 1692.* T.C.II 410. CCA; CLC.

771B **Barker, Matthew.** An account of the state of the differences. *1692.* PL.

772 —A Christian standing. *By M.S. for R.Harford, 1648.* 4°. LT, O, C, EN, DT; CH, MU, NU, WF.

773 —The faithful and vvise servant. *By J.Macock, for Luke Fawne, 1657.* 4°. O, LSC; NU, RPB, WF.

774 —Flores intellectuales: or. . . . *By J.Astwood, for John Dunton, 1691.* 8°. L, LCL, SP; CLC, CU, WF, Y.

775 — —, the second part. *By Tho.Sbowden, for John Dunton, 1692.* 12°. L, LCL; MIU, Y.

776 —Jesus Christ the great vvonder. *By R.W. for Rapha Harford, 1651.* 4°. LP, LSC, C, CM, LW; NU.

777 —Natural theology. *For Nathaniel Ranew, 1674.* 8°. T.C.I 147. L, O, CT, LW, EN; CLC, MWA, NU, Y.

777A [–] Reformed religion. *By J.A. for John Dunton, 1689.* 12°. T.C.II 268. LW; CLC, WF.

777A **Barker, Ralph.** A sermon preached . . . May xxxi, 1691. *For James Adamson, 1691.* 4°.* T.C.II 366. L, O, C, CT, DT; CH, MH, NU, WF, Y.

778 **Barker, Sir Richard.** Consilium anti-pestilentiale: or, seasonable advice. *For the author, 1665.* 4°.* L, O.

778A [–] The excellency and usefulnesse of the true spirit of salt. *For Nathanael Webb, 1663.* 4°.* L; Y.

779 [–] The great preservative of mankinde. *By R.D., 1662.* 4°.* L; WF, HC.

780 [–] Sudorificum regale: or, the royal sudorifick, *1676.* 8°.* L.

781 **B[arker], T[homas], gent.** Analecta: or, a collection. *For Richard Cumberland, 1693.* 8°. T.C.II 482. L, O, LPO; CLC, NC, WF, Y.

782 Entry cancelled.

783 **Barker, Thomas, of Bracemeale, Salop.** The art of angling. Second edition. *Printed, 1653.* 4°.* L, O, OR; CH, CN, MH, WF, Y.

784 [–] The country-mans recreation. *By T.Mabb, for William Shears, 1654.* 4°. LT, O, C; BN, CH, MH, WF, Y.

785 —Barker's delight: or, the art of angling. *By J.G. for Richard Marriot, 1657.* 8°. LT; NN, NP.

786 — —Second edition. *For Humphrey Moseley, 1659.* 8°. LT, O, C; CH, MH, TU, Y.

787 **Barker, Thomas, poet.** Nassau: a poem. *For Will.Rogers, and F.Hicks, in Cambridge, 1698.* fol.* T.C.III 55. L, O, LVF; CH, CLC, MH, Y.

788 —A poem, dedicated to the memory of Dr Joseph Beaumont. *Cambridge, by John Hayes, for Edward Hall,* 1700. 4°. T.C.III 173. L, CS, E; MH, Y.

789 **Barksdale, Clement.** Apanthismata. Memorials ... two new decads. *Oxford, A. and L. Lichfield, for E. Thorn,* 1664. LCL, LW, H; CN.

790 ——[Anr. ed.] *Oxford, A. and L. Lichfield, sold by S. Thomson,* 1664. 8°. CT.

[–] Avrea dicta. 1681. *See* Charles II.

791 —Behold the husbandman. 1677. 8°. O.

792 —Characters, and historical memorials. *For J.W.,* 1662. 12°. L, O.

793 —The disputation at Winchcombe. *Oxford, by L.L. to be sold by Edmund Thorne,* [1653]. 8°.* MADAN 2225. L, O.

793A [–] —[Anr. ed.] *Oxford, by L.L. to be sold at Winchcombe, by Nathaniel Hyet,* [1653]. 8°.* WF.

794 [–] —[Anr. ed.] *For William Lee,* 1654. 8°. L, SP; MH, NPT, NU.

794A ——"Second" edition. *By T.W. to be sold at Oxford by Edmund Thorn, and at Winchcomb by Nathaniel Hyat,* 1654. 8°. MH, NPT.

795 —The king's return. *For R. Royston,* 1660. 4°.* LT, O; WF, Y.

796 [–] The lives of ten excellent men. *For Mark Pardoe,* 1677. 8°. O; WF.

796A —The magistrates authority. 1655. 8°. LCL.

797 [–] Memorials. Examples of memorable men. *For John Barksdale,* 1675. 8°. MH.

798 —Memorials of Alderman Whitmore. *By J. Redmayne for John Barksdale, in Cirencester,* 1681. 8°.* L, O.

799 ——[Anr. ed.] *By J. Redmayne for Sam. Lee,* 1681. 8°.* MH.

800 —Memorials of worthy persons: two decads. *By I.R.,* 1661. 12°. L, O, C, CT, HH; CH, CN, MH, WF, Y.

801 —Memorials of worthy persons. The third decad. *Oxford, by A. & L. Liechfield,* 1662. 8°. MADAN 2585. L, O, CT, HH, E; CH, MH, MIU, Y.

802 —Memorials of worthy persons. The fourth decad. *Oxford, by A. and L. Lichfield,* 1663. 8°. MADAN 2631. L, O, CT; CH, MH, Y.

803 [–] Noctes Hibernæ. *By Tho. Warren, for Edmund Thorn at Oxford,* 1653. 8°.* MADAN 2226. O; Y.

804 [–] Nympha libethris: or the Cotswold muse. *For F. A. at Worcester,* 1651. 8°. L, O; CH, CLC, MH.

804A [–] An Oxford conference. *[Oxford], printed,* 1660. 8°.* MADAN 2422. O; MH.

805 [–] Parerga. I. Suffolk and Glocestershire. *[London], printed,* 1660. 8°.* MH.

806 [–] A remembrancer of excellent men. *For John Martyn,* 1670. 8°. L, O, C, LCL, HH; CH, CU, MH, NU, WF, Y.

807 —The sacrifice. A short sermon ... Sept. 3 1637. *By T.W. for W. Lee,* 1655. 4°. MH, MWA, NU.

808 —A sermon preached vpon the fifth of November, 1679. *Oxford for John Barksdale, in Cirencester,* 1680. 4°.* MADAN 3258. O.

809 [–] Three ministers communicating their collections. *For Samuel Keble,* 1675. 8°. T.C.I 210. O, HH.

809A [–] The Whincomb-papers reviewed. *For Richard Royston,* 1657. 12°.* MH.

810 —The Winchcomb-papers revived. *For John Barksdale,* 1675. 8°. L; MH.

811 —A woollen shroud. *For John Barksdale,* 1679. 4°.* T.C.I 329. O, C.

811A **Barkstead, John.** The case and apology of. *Printed,* 1662. brs. KU.

812 [–] The first and second parts of invisible John made visible. *Printed at London,* 1659. 4°.* LT, O, LVF, OC, LW; HR, MH, MU, NU, TU, Y.

813 —May 27, 1651. Forasmuch as the inhabitants of Pauls churchyard. [1651]. brs. LT.

813A —Invisible John made visible. *Printed,* 1659. 4°.* C, OC, SP; CH, MBP, Y.

814 —A letter from Colonel Barkestead. *Printed,* 1662. 4°.* L, O, C, CCH; CH, CLC, CN, WF.

815 [–] The new Lord's winding-sheet. *[London], printed,* 1659. 4°.* LT, O, C; HR, CH, NU, Y.

816 —The speeches and prayers of. *For Nathaniel Brook, and Edward Thomas,* 1662. 4°.* L, O, OC, EN; CH, MH, NU, WF, Y.

817 —The speeches, discourses, and prayers of. *[London], printed,* 1662. 4°. L, O, C, HH, EN; CH, CN, MH, NU, WF, Y.

817A [–] White-hall fayre. *[London], for A.P.,* 1648. 4°.* LT, LV; MH, Y.

818 **Barlee, William.** A necessary vindication. *For George Sawbridge,* 1658. 4°. LW, OC, CJ, E, DT.

819 —Prædestination, as before privately. *By W.H. for George Sawbridge,* 1656. 4°. LT, LCL, CJ; MH, NPT, WF.

819A **Barlow, Francis.** A booke containing such beasts. *Sould by G. Barker,* [1667]. 4°.* MELLON.

820 —Illustrissimo heroi Richardo Domine Maitland . . . Lauderdale. *[London,* 1700?] obl., fol.* L.

821 —Multæ et diversæ avium species. *[Londini,* 1671.] 4°.* L; WF

822 —Several wayes of hunting. *Sould by John Overton,* 1671. obl. 4°. T.C.I 88. C; CH, CLC, MH, Y.

823 **Barlow, James.** Sermon before House of Lords. 1695. 4°. LCL.

824 **Barlow, Thomas, bp.** Αυτοσχεδιασματα, de studio theologiæ. *Oxford, by Leon. Lichfield,* 1699. 4°. T.C.III 158. L, O, C, LG, DT; CH, CN, LC, MH, NU, Y.

825 ——Second edition. *Oxford,* 1700. 4°. O, YM, E, DT.

826 —Brutum fulmen: or, the bull of Pope Pius V. *By S. Roycroft for Robert Clavell,* 1681. 4°. L, O, C, EN, DT; CLC, CN, LC, MIU.

827 ——Second edition. *By S. Roycroft for Robert Clavel,* 1681. 4°. T.C.I 467. L, O, ENC, DT; CH, MH, NU, WF, Y.

828 [–] A discourse concerning the laws ecclesiastical. *For Thomas Basset,* 1682. 4°. T.C.I 465. L, O, CT, LIL, DT; CH, CN, MH, NU, WF, Y.

829 [–] A discourse of the peerage & jurisdiction of the lords spiritual. *Printed,* 1679. fol.* L, O, C, LVF, MR; CH, MH, NP, WF, Y.

830   —Exercitationes aliquot metaphysicæ. *Second edition.* *Oxoniæ, excudebat A. Lichfield, impensis Jos. Godwin & Tho. Robinson,* 1658. 4°. MADAN 2375. LT, O, C, E, DT; BN, CU, NPT, NU, WF, Y.

831   [–] A few plain reasons why a Protestant. *For R. Clavel,* 1688. 4°. L, O, C, EN, DT; CLC, MH, NU, TU, WF, Y.

832   —The genuine remains. *For John Dunton,* 1693. 8°. T.C.II 483. L, O, C, EN, DT; CH, CN, MH, NU, WF, Y.

833   [–] The gunpowder-treason. *By Tho. Newcomb and H. Hills, to be sold by Walter Kettilby,* 1679. 8°. T.C.I 349. L, O, C, LG, EN; CH, CN, LC, NU, Y.

834   —A letter concerning invocation of saints. *By John Macock for John Martyn,* 1679. 4°.* T.C.I 366. L, O, C, LL, DT; CH, MH, NU, WF, Y.

835   —My reverend brother, whereas. [1686.] brs. L.

835A   —The original of kingly . . . government. [*London*], *for R. Clavell, and W. Hensman,* 1681. 12°. T.C.I 419. O, CS, OB; CLC, WF, Y.

836   —Papismus regiæ. *Veneunt apud bibliopolas,* 1681. 8°. T.C.I 432. O.

837   ——[Anr. ed.] *Apud Jacobum Collins et Samuelem Lowndes,* 1682. 8°. L, CT, SC, EC, E, GK; BN, WF.

838   [–] Pegasus, or the flying horse. [*London*], *printed at Mongomery, heretofore called Oxford,* [1648]. 4°.* MADAN 1988. LT, O, C, OC, HH; CH, MH, WF, Y.

839   [–] Popery. *In the Savoy: by T. Newcomb, and sold by James Collins,* 1679. 4°. T.C.I 354. L, O, C, EN, D; CLC, MH, NU, WF, Y.

840   ——[Anr. ed.] *In the Savoy: By Tho. Newcomb, for James Collins,* 1679. 4°. L, O, C, EC, DT; CH, MBA, NC, TU, WF.

841   ——[Anr. ed.] *By J. C. and Fr. Collins, for James Collins,* 1679. 8°. L, C, OC, EN, DT; CLC, MB, WF.

841A   ——[Anr. ed.] *For J. C. to be sold by Langley Curtis,* 1683. 8°. LSC; CLC, PL.

842   [–] Les principes et la doctrine de Rome. *Londres, chez Benjamin Tooke,* 1679. 8°. L; BN, WF.

         [–] Rights of the bishops. 1680. *See* Hunt, Thomas.

843   —Several miscellaneous and weighty cases of conscience. *Printed, and sold by Mrs. Davis,* 1692. 8°. L, O, C, EN, DT; CH, MH, NU, WF, Y.

844–5 Entries cancelled.

846   [–] The triall of a black-pudding. *By F: N. and are to be sold by John Hancock,* 1652. 4°.* LT, O; NU, WF.

847   **Barlow, William,** *bp.* The summe and substance. *By A. Warren, to be sold by Joshua Kirton,* 1661. 12°. OC; NN, WF.

848   **Barlow, William,** *of Chalgrove, Oxford.* A treatise of fornication. *For John Dunton,* 1690. 8°. T.C.II 330. L, O, OB; WF.

849   **Barnabas, Saint.** Barnabæ et Hermæ epistola. *Oxoniæ, e theatro Sheldoniano,* 1685. 12°. L, O, CS, LW, DT; BN, MH, NPT, TU, WF, Y.

850   Barnabies summons. [*London,* 1652.] brs. LT.

         Barnard, *Dr. See* Bernard, Nicholas.

851   [**Barnard, J.**] A full relation of the murder. *For R. A.,* 1648. 4°.* LT.

852   [**Barnard, John.**] Censvra cleri, or, a plea. *For Giles Calvert,* 1660. 4°.* LT, O, LCL, P, SP; CLC.

853   —The first book of selected church musick. *By Edward Griffin,* 1641. fol. L, OC.

854   —Theologo-historicvs, or the true life of . . . Peter Heylyn. *For J. S. and are to be sold by Ed. Eckelston,* 1683. 8°. L, O, C, EN, DT; CH, CN, MU, NU, Y.

854A   ——[Anr. ed.] *For Daniel Brown,* 1683. T.C.II 6. WCA; MH, WF.

855   [**Barnardiston, Giles.**] A testimony against Jeffery Bullock. [*London*], *printed,* 1676. 4°.* L, LF, BBN; MH, PH, PSC, Y.

856   **Barne, Miles.** The authority of church-guides. *Second edition. For Richard Green in Cambridge,* 1685. 4°.* L, OC, CT, EC; CH, LC, NU, Y.

857   —A discourse concerning the nature of Christ's kingdom. *Cambridge, by J. Hayes, for R. Green,* 1682. 4°. L, O, C, CP, CT; CH, MH, NU, WF, Y.

858   ——Second edition. —, 1682. 4°. L, CT, E.

859   —A sermon preached . . . October 17, 1675. *By T. Milbourn for W. Cademan,* 1675. 4°.* T.C.I 225. L, O, C, DC, DT; CH, MBA, NU, WF, Y.

860   —A sermon preached before the king at Newmarket April 24. 1670. *Cambridge; by John Hayes and to be sold by Edm. Story in Cambridge,* 1670. 4°.* L, O, C, CP, CT; CLC, IU, NU, WF, Y.

861   —A sermon preach'd . . . the 9th of September. *Cambridge, by J. Hayes; for R. Green,* 1683. 4°.* L, O, C, EN, DT; CH, MH, NU, WF, Y.

862   ——[Anr. ed.] *For R. Royston,* 1683. 4°.* T.C.II 41. OB, CT, HH, WCA; CLC, MBA, MIU, NPT, WF, Y.

863   ——Fourth edition. *For R. Royston,* 1683. 4°.* L, O, C, CK; CH, TU.

864   —A sermon preached . . . July 10th. 1684. *Cambridge, by J. Hayes: for R. Green,* 1684. *To be sold by Walt. Davis in London.* 4°.* T.C.II 95. L, O, C, CP, CT; CH, IU, WF, Y.

865   **Barnes, John.** Catholico-Romanus pacificus. *Oxoniæ, e theatro Sheldoniano,* 1680. 8°. MADAN 3259. L, O, C, CT, AU; BN, WSC, Y.

865A   —The great robbery in the West. 1678. 12°.* O; MHL.

866   —Select discourses. *By R. I.,* 1661. 8°. O, C; CH, NU, RPB.

866A   **Barnes, Joshua.** Apology for the orphans of Christ's hospital. 1679. 4°. O.

867   —The apotheosis of . . . Charls the II. [*London*], *Anno Domini,* 1685. fol.* O; CN, MH.

868   —Αὐλικοκατοπτρον; sive, Estherae historia. *Typis M. C. impensis authoris, et protsant venales apud Benj. Tooke,* 1679. 8°. T.C.I 343. L, O, C, LVD, EN; BN, CLC, CN, MH, NC, WF, Y.

868A   ——[Anr. ed.] *Vaeneunt apud B. Tooke; Cantabrigiae apud H. Dickenson,* 1679. 8°. CPE.

869   —An elegy on the death of the Reverend Doctor John Goad. *Printed,* 1689. brs. O; MH.

870   —Gerania: a new discovery. *By W. G. for Obadiah Blagrave,* 1675. 8°. T.C.I 218. L, O, C, MR, DT; BN, CH, CN, MH, NC, WF, Y.

871 —The history of . . . Edward III^d. *Cambridge, by John Hayes for the author*, 1688. fol. L, O, C, EN, DT; BN, CH, CN, LC, MH, WSC, Y.

872 —A Pindarick congratulatory poem. *Printed, and are to be sold by Walter Davis*, 1685. fol.* L, O, CT, HH; CLC, CN, IU, MH, Y.

873 **Barnes, Thomas.** Preparatory-grace. *For Ann Baldwin*, 1699. 8°. CT.

874 **Barnet, Nehemiah.** Gods lift-up hand. *By W. Wilson, for John Williams*, 1646. 8°. LT; WF.

875 —The regenerate mans growth. *By John Dawson, for John Williams*, 1646. 8°. LT; WF.

875A [**Barnett, Andrew**]. The helmet of hope. *Printed for, and are to be sold by Obed. Smith at Daventry*, 1694. MH.

875B —A just lamentation. *For Tho. Parkhurst*, 1695. 4°.* T.C.II 548. LW, CM; CLC, MH, NP, Y.

876 [**Barnewal, Robert.**] Syntomataxia del' second part du Roy Henry VI. Second edition. *By George Sawbridge, William Rawlins, and Samuel Roycroft, assigns of Richard and Edward Atkins. To be sold by H. Twyford, F. Tyton, J. Bellinger, T. Basset, R. Pawlet, S. Heyrick, C. Wilkinson, T. Dring, W. Jacob, C. Harper, J. Leigh, J. Amery, J. Place and J. Poole*, 1679. fol. L, O, CJ; YL. Barnstable agreed. 1646. *See* T., T.

877 **Baron, George.** No-body his complaint. *By B. Alsop*, 1652. 8°.* LT.

878 **Baron, James.** Quæstiones theologicæ. *Oxonii, excudebat W. H. per J. Forrest*, 1657. brs. MADAN 2320. O.

879 **Baron, John.** A sermon preached June 1, 1699. *Oxford, by Leon. Lichfield, sold by Henry Clements*, 1699. 4°.* L, O, C, CS, OCC; CH, MA, NU, Y.

880 **Baron, Robert** *of Aberdeen.* Ad Georgii Turnebulli. *Excudebat R. N. pro Jos. Kirton*, 1657. 12°. L, OC, CS, P, DT; BN, CLC, MH, PL.

881 —Disputatio theologica. *Oxonii, typis Gulielmi Hall, impensis Rob. Blagrave*, 1658. 12°. MADAN 2376. O, SC, E, ENC, DT; Y.

881A ——[Anr. ed.] *Excudebat pro Jos. Kirton*, 1658. 12°. OC; CLC.

882 —Rob. Baronii . . . Metaphysica generalis. *Ex officina J. Redmayne*, [1657?]. 12°. L, O, ENC, SC; CH, CLC, CU, MH.

883 ——[Anr. ed.] *Ex officina R. Danielis, & væneunt apud Th. Robinson & Ri Davis . . . Oxonienses*, 1658. 12°. L, O, OC, CM, AU; MBA, WF, Y.

884 ——[Anr. ed.] —. *Oxon*, [1669?]. 12°. C, OC; NU.

885 ——[Anr. ed.] *Cantabrigiæ, ex officina Johan. Hayes. Impensis H. Sawbridge*, 1685. 12°. T.C.II 147. L, O, C, EN, DT; CH, IU, PL, JF.

886 —Philosophia theologiæ ancillans. *Oxoniæ, excudit Leonardus Lichfield, impensis Guliel: Davis & Tho: Robinson*, 1641. 8°. MADAN 990. O, C, LW, EN, DT; CLC, NU.

887 ——[Anr. ed.] [*Oxford*], *impensis T. Robinson & R. Davis*, 1658. 12°. L, O, C, OM, DT; CN, PAP, WF, Y.

888 **Baron, Robert,** *of Gray's Inn.* An apologie for Paris. *For Th. Dring*, 1649. 8°. L, O, C, SP; CH, CLC, CN, MH, WF.

889 —Ἐρωτοπαιγνιον or, the Cyprian academy. [*London*], *by W. W. and are to be sold by J. Hardesty, T. Huntington, and T. Jackson*, 1647. 8°. L, O, EN; CH, IU, MH, TU, WF.

890 ——[Anr. ed.] —, 1648. 8°. LT, O, C; CH, CN, MH, WF, Y.

891 —Mirza. A tragedie. *For Humphrey Moseley and are to be sold at his shop: and for T. Dring*, [1647]. 8°. LT, O, C, CT, EN; CH, CN, MH, NC, WF, Y.

892 Entry cancelled.

893 —Pocula castalia. The authors motto. *By W. H. for Thomas Dring*, 1650. 8°. LT, O; CH, CN, LC, MH, NC, WCL, Y.

894 **Baron, William.** Demetrius and the craftsmen. *For William Cademan*, 1683. 4°.* T.C.II 40. OC, CS, WCA, DT; NN, NU.

895 [–] The Dutch way of toleration. *For the author*, 1698. 4°.* L, O, C, OC; CLC, MM, NU, PBL, Y.

896 [–] ——Second edition. *Printed*, 1699. 4°.* L, O, CT, AU; CLC, NPT, WF, Y.

897 [–] A just defence of the royal martyr K. Charles I. *For A. Roper, and R. Basset, and for W. Turner*, 1699. 8°. L, O, C, MR, EN; CH, CN, NU, WF, Y.

898 [–] Regicides no saints nor martyrs. *For W. Keblewhite*, 1700. 8°. T.C.III 186. L, O, GU; CH, CU, NU, WF, Y.

899 Baron and feme. A treatise. *By the assigns of Richard and Edward Atkyns, for John Walthoe*, 1700. 8°. T.C.III 198. L, O, LIL, OC; CU, LC, MHL, MIU, WF.

900 Baron Tomlinson's learned speech. *Printed*, 1659. 4°.* L, O, HH, LG, OC; CN, MIU.

901 **Barozzi, Giacomo.** The regular architect. *For William Sherwin, and Rowland Reynolds*, 1669. fol. T.C.I 18. CCC, LIB, DCH; CLC, WF, Y.

902 ——[Anr. ed.] *For John Marshall*, [1700?] fol. T.C.III 163. L.

903 —Vignola, or the compleat architect. *By J. Moxon*, 1655. 8°. L, O, C, LR; CH, TU, WF.

904 ——Second edition. *By W. Leybourn, for Joseph Moxon*, 1665. 8°. L, LPO; CLC.

905 ——Third edition. *Lonon* [*sic*], *by Joseph Moxon*, 1673. 8°. T.C.I 138. O, CE, CS; CLC, PL.

905A ——[Anr. ed.] —, 1692. 8°. CT.

906 ——Fourth edition. *Printed and sold by J. Moxon*, 1694. 8°. L; Y.

906A **Barret, John.** Analecta; or fragments offered. 1672. 4°. O.

907 —The Christian temper. *For Jonathan Robinson, and Samuel Richards in Nottingham*, 1678. 8°. T.C.I 309. L, LCL, LW; CLC, MH, NPT, Y.

908 —God's love to man. *For S. R. and are to be sold by J. Robinson*, 1678. 8°. T.C.I 319. LCL, LW; NPT.

909 [–] Good will towards men. *For Sam. Richards in Nottingham, and Tho. Guy*, 1675. 8°. T.C.I 185. LCL, LW; NPT, NU, Y.

910 [–] The rector of Sutton committed. *By J. D. to be sold by Richard Janeway*, 1680. 4°. T.C.I 413. L, O, CS, MR, DT; CH, MH, NU, WF, Y.

910A [–] ——[Anr. ed.] *By J. D. to be sold by S. Richards in Nottingham*, 1680. 4°. BR.

910B   [–] A reply to the reverend dean. *By J. D. to be sold by Richard Janeway*, 1681. 4°. O, LW, SP; CH, MH.

910C   —A sermon preach'd . . . November 24, 1698. *By T. Snowden and sold by J. Richards*, 1699. 8°. T.C.III 121. LCL, LW.

911   —A short account of the life of . . . William Reynolds. *For Tho. Parkhurst*, 1698. 8°. L, LCL, LW.

912   **Barret, Joseph.** The remains of. *For Tho. Parkhurst, and are to be sold by him and John Richards at Nottingham*, 1700. 8°. L, LW, ENC; MH, NC.

913   **Barret, Robert.** A companion for midwives. *For Tho. Ax*, 1699. 8°. L, LM, LWL, GH.

914   —The perfect and experienced farrier. *By T. Fawcet, for Fr. Coles*, 1660. 4°. LT.

   [**Barrett, William.**] Bonasus vapulans. 1672. *See* Hickman, Henry.

915   [–] The Nonconformists vindicated. *For Thomas Parkhurst*, 1679. 8°. T.C.I 415. L, O, CS, P, LW; NPT, NU, PL.

916   **Barri, Giacomo.** The painter's voyage of Italy. *For Tho. Flesher*, 1679. 8°. T.C.I 349. L, O, C, EN, DT; BN, CH, CU, LC, MH, Y.

917   **Barriffe, William.** Military discipline. Third edition. *By John Dawson, and are to be sold by Andrew Crooke*, 1643. 4°. L, LUS, EN; BN, CN, MH, RPB.

918   — —Fourth edition. *By Iohn Dawson*, 1643. 4°. L, O, OC, LL; CH, LC, NN, Y.

918A   — —"Fourth" edition. *By M.C., M.M., C.G., sold by Peter Cole*, 1643. 4°. C, E; MIU, WF.

919   — —Fifth edition. *By John Dawson*, 1647. 4°. CCA; CLC, MH.

919A   — —"Fifth" edition. *For John Walker*, 1648. 4°. CN.

920   — —Sixth edition. *By Gartrude Dawson*, 1661. 4°. L, LAI, LG; BN, CN, MBA, MH, WF, Y.

921   **Barrough, Philip.** The method of physick. *By Abraham Miller, to be sold by John Blague and Samuel Howes*, 1652. 8°. L, C, LCP; CLC; GK; WSG.

922   **Barrow, Henry.** The pollution of vniversitie-learning. *Printed*, 1642. 4°.* MADAN 1281. L, O, EC, E; MH, Y.

923   **Barrow, Humphrey.** The relief of the poore. *Dublin, by William Bladen*, 1656. 4°.* DIX 353. C.

924   — —[Anr. ed.] *Reprinted, to be sold by William Larner*, 1656. 4°.* L.

924A   — —[Anr. ed.] *By R.W.*, 1656. 4°.* NC.

925   **Barrow, Isaac.** The works of. *By M. Flesher, for Brabazon Aylmer*, 1683–87. 4 vols. fol. T.C.II 24. L, C, OM, ENC, DT; BN, MH, NP, NU, PL, V.

926   — —Second edition. *By Miles Flesher, for Brabazon Aylmer*, 1687–86. 4 vols. fol. T.C.II 173. O, C, LL, E, DT; CLC, CN, MH, WF.

927   — —Third edition. *For Brabazon Aylmer*, 1700. 3v. fol. T.C.III 188. L, O, C, DC, DT; CH, MB, NU, TU, Y.

928   —A brief exposition of the Lord's prayer. *By M. Flesher, for Brabazon Aylmer*, 1681. 8°. T.C.I 470. L, C, OC, CP, DC; CH, NU, WF, WSC, Y.

929   —A brief exposition on the creed. *By J. H. for Brabazon Aylmer*, 1697. 8°. T.C.III 1. L, O, C, LL, DT; CLC, NPT, NU, WF, Y.

930   —A brief state of the Socinian controversy. *For Brabazon Aylmer*, 1698. 12°.* T.C.III 72. L.

931   —A defence of the B. trinity. *For Brabazon Aylmer*, 1697. 8°. T.C.III 11. L, C, OM, EC; CH, MBA, NU, PL, WF, Y.

932   —A discourse concerning the unity of the church. *For Brabazon Aylmer*, 1680. 8°. T.C.I 401. L, O, CT, EC; LC, NU, WF, Y.

933   —The duty and reward of bounty. *By Andrew Clark, for Brabazon Aylmer*, 1671. 8°. T.C.I 78. L, O, C, CT, AU; CH, NU, TU, WF, Y.

934   — —Second edition. *By J.D. for Brabazon Aylmer*, 1677. 8°. T.C.I 279. L, O, OC, CP; CH, CN, MU, Y.

935   — —Third edition. *By M.F. for Brabazon Aylmer*, 1680. 8°. L, DC; CLC, LC, NU, TU, Y.

936   —Lectio reverendi. *Typis J. Redmayne, prostant apud F. Williams & J. Dunmore*, 1687. 8°.* O, C, CT, LG, EC; CH, MU, NU, WF, Y.

937   —Lectiones aliquot geometricæ. *William Godbid*, 1672. 4°. LI, CP, CT, DT.

938   —Lectiones xviii. *Typis Gulielmi Godbid, & prostant venales apud Johannem Dunmore, & Octavianum Pulleyn Juniorem*, 1669. 4°. T.C.I 26. L, O, C, E, DT; PL, WF, Y.

939   — —[Anr. ed.] *Typis Gulielmi Godbid, & prostant venales apud Gualterum Kettilby*, 1672. 4°. T.C.I 105. CT, OC, P, ENC, DT.

940   —Lectiones geometricæ. *Typis Gulielmi Godbid & prostant venales apud Johannem Dunmore & Octavianum Pulleyn, juniorum*, 1670. 4°. T.C.I 49. L, O, SC, CT, E; BN, MH, PL, WF.

941   —Lectiones habitæ. *Typis J. Playford, pro Georgio Wells*, 1683. 12°. T.C.II 48. O, CT, E, DT; CSU, NC.

942   — —[Anr. ed.] 1684. 8°. L, O, CPE, LR, E; CSU, NC, WF.

943   —Lectiones mathematicæ. 1684. 12°. LR, LSL, BAMB, EO; NC, WF.

944   — —[Anr. ed.] *Typis J. Playford, pro Georgio Wells*, 1685. 8°. L, O, C, LI, DT; BN, NC, TU, WF, JF.

945   —Lectiones opticæ. *Typis Gulielmi Godbid, & prostant venales apud Robertum Scott*, 1674. 4°. L, O, C, EN, DT; BN, MU, NC, WF, Y.

946   —Of contentment. *By M. Flesher, for Brabazon Aylmer*, 1685. 8°. T.C.II 135. L, O, C; CH, CN, MIU, TU, WF, Y.

946A   — —[Anr. ed.] *For Brabazon Aylmer*, 1685. 8°. L; CN, LC, MH, MIU, WF, Y.

946B   — —[Anr. ed.] —, *to be sold by T. Salusbury, and J. Salusbury*, 1685. 8°. T.C.II 135. NU, WF, Y.

947   —Of industry. *By J. H. for Brab. Aylmer*, 1693. 8°. T.C.II 422. L, O, CT, DU; CH, CN, MH, NC, WF, Y.

948   — —[Anr. ed.] *By W.B. for Brab. Aylmer*, 1700. 8°. T.C.III 210. L, O, C, CP; CLC, TSM, WF.

949   —Of the love of God. *By Miles Flesher, for Brabazon Aylmer*, 1680. 8°. T.C.I 401. CP, CT, OC; BN, CH, WF, Y.

950   Entry cancelled.

951   —Practical discourses. *By J. H. for Brabazon Aylmer*, 1694. 8°. T.C.II 517. L, O, C, EN; CLC, CU, Y.

952   —Proposals for the first volume of the works. 1682. brs. O.

953 —A sermon preached on the fifth of November, MDCLXXIII. *By J.D. for Brabazon Aylmer*, 1679. 4°.* T.C.I 376. L, O, CT; NU, TSM.

954 —A sermon upon the passion of our blessed Saviour ... 13th day of April, 1677. *For Brabazon Aylmer*, 1677. 4°.* T.C.I 271. L, O, C, LG, EN; CH, CN, MBA, NU, WF, Y.

955 — —[Anr. ed.] —, 1678. 12°. L, O, DC, EN; CLC, MU, Y.

956 — —[Anr. ed.] *By M. Flesher, for Brabazon Aylmer*, 1682. 8°. L, O, C, CP; CH, LC, TU.

957 —Sermons preached upon several occasions. *By E. Flesher for Brabazon Aylmer*, 1678. 8°. L, O, CP, LCP, AU; BN, CH, CU, TU, WF, Y.

958 — —Second edition. *For Brabazon Aylmer*, 1679. 8°. T.C.I 345. L, CT, OC, LL; NGT, NU.

959 —Several sermons. *For Brabazon Aylmer*, 1678. 8°. T.C.I 318. L, O, C, LW, CP; CH, CU, NP, NU, WF, Y.

960 —Spiritus sanctus est persona distincta. [*Cambridge*], *July* 4, 1670. brs. L, O.

961 —A treatise of the Pope's supremacy. *By Miles Flesher, for Brabazon Aylmer*, 1680. 4°. T.C.I 367. L, O, C, LL, DC; CH, LC, MH, NU, Y.

962 — —Second edition. —, 1683. 4°. L, OB, OM, CSS, EC; MB, NU, TSM, V.

962A — —Third edition. —, 1687. 4°. CLC.

963 — —Fourth edition. *For Brabazon Aylmer*, 1700. fol. CS; CH, MB, Y.

964 **Barrow, J.** Membrorum principalium apostasia, or, a short view. [*London?* 1670?] 4°. L[frag.].

965 **Barrow, James.** The Lord's arm stretched ovt. *Printed*, 1664. 4°.* L, O; MH, PL.

966 **Barrow, John.** A sermon preached ... Sept. 6. 1683. *By Ralph Holt, for John Gellibrand*, 1683. 4°.* T.C.II 40. L, O, C, OC, WCA, BAMB; CH, MH, NU, WF, Y.

967 **Barrow, Robert.** A briefe answer to a discourse lately written by one P. B. *Printed*, 1642. 4°.* NU, WF.

967A —The testimony of. [*London*, 1691.] brs. MH, PHS.

968 **Barry, James.** A brief and plain discovery of the falseness. *For the author*, 1699. 4°. NPT, NU.

968A —The case of tenures. *Dublin, by the society of stationers*, 1673. 4°. DT; MBP, PUL.

969 — —[Anr. ed.] *Dublin, by Benjamin Took & John Crooke*, 1682. 4°. DIX 196. DW.

969A —The doctrine of particular ... election asserted. *For the author*, 1700. 12°. LF; MH, NPT.

970 —The only refuge of a troubled soul. *For the author*, 1700. 12°. LW, BBN; WF.

971 [–] A reviving cordial. *For the author*, 1699. 8°. L; MH.

972 [**Barry, John.**] The most blessed and truest newes, that ever came from Ireland. *For J. Harton, May* 27, 1642. 4°.* C; MH, Y.

973 — —[Anr. ed.] *For T.W. & G.H.*, 1642. 4°.* L, C, EC, MR.

973A [**Barry, Paul de**] Pious remarks upon the life of St. Joseph. *By T.F.*, 1700. 16°. BN, WF.

974 **Bartholin, Caspar.** Specimen philosophiæ naturalis. *Oxoniæ, typis Leon. Lichfield, impensis Henr. Clements*, 1698. 8°. L, O, DCH, P, EN; NAE, WF, HC.

975 **Bartholin, Thomas.** The anatomical history of. *By Francis Leach for Octavian Pulleyn*, 1653. 12°. LT, LCS, LM; CLM, MBA, MU, WSG.

976 —Anatomy. *By Peter Cole*, 1663. fol. GK; CJC, MIU, HC.

977 — —[Anr. ed.] *By John Streater*, 1668. fol. L, LCS, LWL, CCC, LSC; NAM, TU, WF, WSG, HC.

978 —De lacteis thoracicis. *Impensis Octaviani Pulleyn, typis Johannis Grismond*, 1652. 12°. LT, C, LCS, CT, GH; BN, MH.

979 **Bartholmew, William.** The strong man ejected. *By W. Godbid, for Richard Thrale*, 1660. 4°.* LT, O; CLC, MWA, Y.

980 Bartholomew faire, or variety of fancies. *For Richard Harper*, 1641. 4°.* LT, O, LN, A; CSS, CU, MH, VC, WCL, WF.

981 A Bartholomevv fairing, new, new, new. *Printed*, 1649. 4°.* LT, LG; CH.

982 **B[artlet], J[ohn].** The practical Christian. *By T.M. for Thomas Parkhurst*, 1670. 12°. LCL, LW; CLC, NPT, NU, Y.

983 — —[Anr. ed.] *For T. Parkhurst, and are to be sold by M. Hide*, 1670. 12°. LW.

984 **B[artlet], R[ichard].** The new birth. *By W.H. for L. Blaiklock, to be sould at Temple Bar, and by John Hancock*, 1654. 8°. LT, LCL.

984A —The new creature. 1655. 8°. O.

985 **Bartlet, William.** Eye salve to anoint the eyes. 1649. 4°. LCL.

986 —'Ιχνογραφια. Or a model. *By W. E. for H. Overton*, 1674. 4°. LT, O, LCL, DT; CLC, LC, MH, NPT, NU, Y.

987 —[Hebrew], or soveraigne balsome. *Imprinted at London by G. Dawson, for Elizabeth Overton*, 1649. 4°. LT, O, O, LCL, EN, DT; CH, NU, Y.

988 **Bartoli, Daniello.** The learned man defended. *By R. and W. Leybourn, sold by Thomas Dring*, 1660. 8°. LT, O, LL, CT, P; CH, CN, LC, MH, NC, Y.

989 **Barton, David.** Mercy in the midst of judgment. *For James Allestry*, 1670. 4°. T.C.I 48. L, O, CSS, WCA, DT; MH, NC, NU, WF, Y.

989A **Barton, Nathaniel.** The representation or defence. [*London*, 1654.] cap., 4°.* CH, MH.

990 **Barton, Samuel.** A sermon preached ... 20th. of January, 1688/9. *For Thomas Cockerill*, 1689. 4°.* L, OCC; NPT, WF, Y.

991 —A sermon preached ... 16th. of July. *For Brabazon Aylmer*, 1690. 4°.* L, O, C, LG, OP; CLC, NU, WF, Y.

992 —A sermon preached ... Octob. 27th. 1692. *By J. Richardson, for Brabazon Aylmer*, 1692. 4°.* T.C.II 422. L, O, OCC, OM; CLC, LC, NU, WF, Y.

993 —A sermon preach'd ... 16th of April, 1696. *For Tho. Cockerill, senr and junr*, 1696. 4°.* L, O, C, CT, OCC; CH, MH, NU, PL, WF, Y.

994 —A sermon preached ... Octob. 2, 1699. *For Matthew Wotton*, 1700. 8°.* T.C.III 169. L, LG, EC; LC, WF.

995   —A sermon preach'd before the right honourable the lord mayor. *For Brabazon Aylmer,* 1698. 4°.* T.C.III 89. L, LG, OCC; CLC, NU, Y.

996   **Barton, Thomas.** Ἀντιτειχισμα, or, a counter-scarfe. *By R. C. for Andrew Crooke,* 1643. 4°. LT, O; NPT.

997   [–] Ἀποδειξιστοῦ ἀντιτειχίσματος; or, a tryall. *By Thomas Purslow, for Andrew Crooke,* 1643. 4°. LT, LSC, DT.

998   —King David's church-prayer. [*London*], *printed,* 1649. 4°.* LT, O, CS, LW, YM; CLC, MM, NU, WF.

999   —Λόγος ἀγωνιος; or, a sermon. [*Oxford*], *by L.L.,* 1643. 4°.* MADAN 1378. LT, OC, OM, DT; NU, WF.

1000 **B[arton], W[illiam].** A century of select hymns. *By T. R. for Francis Eglesfield and Thomas Underhill, and Francis Tyton,* 1659. 12°. LT.

1000A —The choice and flower of the old Psalms. *By G. Miller; sold by S. Gellibrand, I. Kitson, Tho. Underhill, and Stephen Bowtell,* 1645. 12°. L.

1001 —Four centuries of select hymns. *For Tho. Parkhurst,* 1668. 12°. T.C.I 4. L, O, EN.

1002 —Hallelujah, or, certain hymns. *By J. Macock,* 1651. 8°. LT.

1002A —Man's monitor. *By W. D. for Tho. Underhill,* 1655. 8°. EC.

1003 —Psalms and hymns composed. *By William DuGard, October 21.* 1651. 8°.* O, AU.

1004 —Six centuries of select hymns. Fourth edition. *By J. Heptinstall, for William Cooper,* 1688. 12° T.C.II 210. L, O, LCL, EN; CLC, MH, MIU, NPT, NU.

1005 —Two centuries of select hymns. *For the author by W. Godbid, to be sold by Fran. Tyton: and by Wil. Cooper,* 1670. 8°. T.C.I 32. O; MH, NPT.

1006 ——[Anr. ed.] *By W. Godbid, for Francis Tyton and Will. Cooper,* 1672. 8°. T.C.I 106. O.

1007 —A view of many errors. *By W. D. and are to be sold by F. Eglesfield and Thomas Underhill, and F. Tyton,* 1655. 4°.* LT, O, EN; MH, NN, NPT.

1007A **Barwick, Grace.** To all present rulers. colop: *For M. W.,* 1659. cap., 4°.* PH, PL.

      [**Barwick, John**]. Certain disquisitions and considerations representing to the conscience. Oxford, 1644. See title.

1008 —Ἱερονικης, or the fight. *For R. Royston,* 1660. 4°. L, O, C, EN, DT; MBP, MH, VC, WF, Y.

1009 [–] Querela Cantabrigiensis: or, a remonstrance. *Oxoniæ,* 1646. 8°. MADAN 1889. LT, O, C, CK, P; CH, CU, LC, MH, NU, Y.

1010 [–] —[Anr. ed.] [*n.p.*], 1647. 8°.* L, O, C, OB, OC; CN, NP, WF, Y.

1011 **Barzia y Zambrana, Joseph de.** A discourse of the excellency of the soul. *For Matthew Turner,* 1685. 4°.* T.C.II 124. L, O, CS; CLC, MBA, NPT, TU, WF.

1012 **B[asely], N.** A sermon, shewing the meanes. *For Rich: Royston,* 1649. 4°.* LT, O, C.

1013 The bashful batchelor. [*London*], *for J. Deacon,* [1688–92]. brs. L, CM, GU, HH; MH.

1014 The bashful virgin. *For W. Thackery, T. Passenger, and W. Whitwood,* [1670–77]. brs. L, CM, HH; MH.

1014A **Basil, the great, abp.** Of solitude. 1675. CCH.

1014B —Ὁμιλια. Oxonii, 1694. 8°. CCA.

1015 **Basil Valentine.** His last will and testament. *Printed,* 1657. 8°. L, CK, CT; CLC, MMO, HC.

1016 ——[Anr. ed.] 1658. 8°. LPO, GU.

1017 —Basilius Valentinus his last testament. *By S. G. & B. G. for Edward Brewster,* 1670. 12°. T.C.I 68. L, LM, GU; MBA, NU, HC.

1018 —The last vvill. *By S. G and B. G. for Edward Brewster,* 1671. 8°. L, O, LCS, OC, SC; CLC, CJC, MH, WF, Y.

1019 —Basilius Valentinus . . . Of natural & supernatural things. *Printed and are to be sold by Moses Pitt,* 1670. 8°. T.C.I 57. O, CT, OR, GU; CLC, LC, MH, PL, WF.

1020 ——[Anr. ed.] —, 1671. 8°. T.C.I 58. L; NIC, PL, WU, Y.

1021 —The triumphant chariot of antimony. [*Oxford, by A. Lichfield*], *for Thomas Bruster of London,* 1660. 8°. MADAN 2534. O, GU; CJC, PL, HC.

1022 ——[Anr. ed.] *For W. S. to be sold by Samuel Thomson,* 1661. 8°. LT, OR; LC, WSG.

1023 —[Anr. ed.] *For Dorman Newman,* 1678. 8°. T.C.I 310. L, O, CT, LCP, GU; CH, LC, MH, Y, HC.

1024 Entry cancelled.

      Βασιλικον συγγραμμα. A panegyrick. 1685. See Basset, William.

      Basilius Anonymous, pseud.

1025 **Basill, William.** A declaration of the Irish armie in Ulster. *By William Du-Gard,* 1650. 4°.* LT, O, C, HH; CH, WF, Y.

1026 [–] A letter from the atturney of Ireland . . . 11 of October. *For Robert Ibbitson, Octob.* 4 [sic]. 1649. 4°.* LT, O, C, LFEA; CH.

1027 —A letter from William Basill. *By Edward Husband and John Field,* 1650. 4°.* LT, O, C, LVF; CN, MH, Y.

1028 —Two letters from. *By John Field for Edward Husband,* 1649. 4°.* LT, C, LVF, OC, HH; CH, MH, Y.

      Basiphilaus, pseud.

1029 **Basire, Isaac.** The ancient liberty of the Britannick church. *For John Mileson, to bee sold by Elisha Wallis,* 1661. 8°. L, O, C, LW, DT; BN, CH, CLC, MH, NU.

1030 Entry cancelled.

1031 —The dead mans real speech. *By E. T. & R. H. for James Collins,* 1673. 8°. T.C.I 148. L, O, C, CT; CN, MIU, NU, TU, WF.

1032 —Deo et ecclesiae sacrum. Sacriledge arraigned. *Oxford, by Leonard Lichfield,* 1646. 4°. MADAN 1865. L, O, CT, OC, DT; CH, CLC, NU, WF, Y.

1033 ——Second edition. *By W. G. for W. Wells and R. Scot,* 1668. 8°. L, O, C, E, DT; CH, CLC, TU, WF, Y.

      [–] History of the English & Scotch. Villa Franca, [*London*], 1659. See Du Moulin, Pierre.

1034 —Sacrilege arraigned. 1646. 4°. LCL, LI, YM.

1035 ——Second edition. *W. Wells and R. Scot,* 1668. 8°. LSC, EC, YM, SA; BN.

1036 **Basire, John.** An excellent letter to his son. *In the Savoy, by Tho. Newcomb,* 1670. 12°.* L, OC; WF.

1037-9 Entries cancelled.
    Bassa, Calvin, *pseud.*
1040 **Basset, *capt.*** A true relation of certaine passages. *By R.O. and G.D. for Iohn Bull,* 1642. 4°.* LT, O, C, EC, HH.
1041 **Basset, John.** Hermæologium, or an essay. 1650. 8°. O.
1042 [**Basset, Joshua.**] Reason and authority. *By Henry Hills,* 1687. 4°. L, O, C, MC, DT; CH, MH, NU, WF, Y.
1042A **Basset, Thomas.** Catalogue of books printed for. *By R. Battersby for Thos. Bassett,* 1672. 8°. DC.
1043 —A catalogue of the common and statute law-books. [*London*], *sold at the George,* 1671. 8°. T.C.I 58. O, LL; LC, MHL, NP, WF.
1044 ——[Anr. ed.] [*London*], *to be sold by Thomas Bassett,* 1682. 12°. T.C.I 507. L, O, LIL, OC, CCA; CH, LC, PU, YL.
1045 ——Third edition. 1694. 8°. O, LGI, CE, EN; MHL, NCL, WF, YL.
1046 —An exact catalogue of the common & statute law books. [*London*], 1673. brs. L, O; MHL.
1047 ——[Anr. ed.] *By Thomas Basset,* 1684. brs. T.C.II 89. O, LG.
1048 **Basset, William.** An answer to the brief history of the Unitarians. *Printed, and sold by Randal Taylor,* 1693. 8°. L, OM, LW; NU.
1049 ——[Anr. ed.] *For John Everingham,* 1693. 8°. L, O, OC, CT, ENC; NU, WF, Y.
1049A [–] Βασιλικου συγγραμμα. A panegyrick. *For Walter Davis,* 1685. fol.* L, O; CH, CLC, MH, PU, WF.
1050 —Catalogue of library. 4 Feb. 1697. 4°.* L; MH.
1051 —Corporal worship discuss'd. *For Tho. Basset,* 1670. 4°.* T.C.I 35. L, O, CT; CLC, NGS, PL, WF.
1052 —A discourse on my lord arch-bishop of Canterbvry's … letters. *For Tho. Basset,* 1684. 4°.* T.C.II 69. L, O, OM, CS, LP; CH, MH, NU, WF, Y.
1053 —A sermon at the Warwick-shire meeting. November 25, 1679. *For T. Basset,* 1679. 4°.* T.C.I 403. L, C, CT; CLC, WF.
1054 —Unity stated. *For Walter Davis,* 1683. 4°.* L, O, OCC, CS, WCA; CH, NPT, NU.
1055 —A vindication of the two letters. *For Richard Baldwin,* 1690. 4°. CT.
    Bastard. 1652. *See* Manuche, Cosmo.
    Baston, James. Mercurius Hermeticus. 1656. *See* Almanacs.
1056 **Baston, Samuel.** A dialogue between a modern courtier. colop: *Printed,* 1696. 4°.* L, O; INU, WF.
1056A ——[Anr. ed.] —, 1697. 4°.* L; CH, NN, WF.
1057 Baston's case vinciated. *Printed,* 1695. L, O, C; NN, WSG, Y.
1058 **Bastwick, John.** The church of England a true church. *For A. Crooke and I. Rothwell,* 1645. 4°. LT, O, CS, YM, DT; MH, NU.
1059 —The confession of the faithfull witnesse of Christ. *Printed, and are to bee sold by H.W.,* 1641. 4°.* LT, O, LG, BR; CN, MH, NU, WF, Y.
1060 —[Anr. ed.] [1645.] cap., 4°.* LL.
1061 —A declaration demonstrating and infallibly proving. *Printed,* 1643. 4°. LT, O, C, CT, DT; MH, NAM, NU, WF, Y.

1062 —Flagellum pontificis et episcoporum Latialium. *Typis Edward Griffini, sumptibus Michaelis Sparkes,* 1641. 12°. L, O, CS, EN, AU; MH, MU, NU, PL.
1063 —Independency not Gods ordinance. *By John Macock, for Michael Spark junior,* 1645. 4°. LT, LCL, CS, DT; CU, MH, NHC, NU, Y.
1064 —The independents catechisme. *By John Macock,* 1645. 8°.* LT, O; CH.
1065 [–] A ivst defence of. *Printed at London by F. Leech, for Michaell Sparke junior,* 1645. 4°.* LT, O, CT, HH, DT; CH, CN, MH, NU, WF, Y.
1066 —A learned, vsefull and seasonable discourse concerning the church of England. *For John Wright,* 1643. 4°.* LT, O, C; NU, WF, Y.
1067-8 Entries cancelled.
    —Lombard Street lectures. 1692. *See title.*
1069 —The second part of that book call'd Independency. *By John Macock, for Michael Spark junior,* 1645. 4°. LT, C, CS, DT; MH, NHC, NU, Y.
1070 Entry cancelled.
    —The severall humble petitions of. [*London*], 1641. *See title.*
1071 —The storming of the Anabaptists garrisons. *By T.W. for Joshua Kirton,* 1647. 4°. LT, O, CS, E, DT; NHC, NPT, NU, WF.
1072 —The utter routing of the whole army. *By John Macock, and are to be sold by Michael Spark,* 1646. 4°. L, O, YM, EN, DT; CH, CN, MH, NU, WF, Y.
1072A ——[Anr. ed.] *By E.C.,* 1653. 4°. PT.
1073 **Bastwick, Susannah.** To the high court of Parliament. [*London,* 1654.] brs. LT; MH.
    Batavia: or. 1672. *See* Feltham, Owen.
1073A **Batchiler, John.** Χρυσαμμος. Golden sands. *Giles Calvert,* 1647. 8°. O; PS.
1073B —A letter to goe along with the book. [*London,* 1668.] cap., fol.* WCA.
1074 —London's New Years gift. 1669. 12°. LG, OC.
1075 —Sick bed thoughts. [*London*], *printed,* 1667. 12°. LCL, LW, DC.
1076 [–] A tast of a catechisticall-preaching-exercise. *Printed,* 1667/8. 4°. O, LW.
1077 —The virgins pattern. *For Simon Dover,* 1661. 8°. L, O, LCL, LW; CH, CLC, NC, NPT.
1078 [**Bate, George.**] A compendious narrative of the late troubles in England. *Printed,* 1652. 12°. L, O, CT; NU, CH, CN, NU, WF, Y.
1079 —Elenchus motuum nuperorum in Anglia. *Edimburgi, sumptibus Theodorici Veridici,* 1650. 12°. ALDIS 1412. L, O, C; CLC, IU, LC, Y.
1080 ——[Anr. ed.] *Typis J. Flesher & prostant apud R. Royston,* 1661. 8°. LT, O, C, CE, MR; BN, CH, NU, WF, Y.
1081 ——[Anr. ed.] *Typis J. Flesher, prostat veneles apud R. Royston,* 1663. 8°. L, O, C, ENC, DT; NAM, NP, TU, WF, Y.
1082 ——[Anr. ed.] *Typis R.W. pro R. Royston, prostat apud J. Martyn, R. Chiswell, et B. Tooke,* 1676. 8°. T.C.I 260. L, O, C, LCL, EN; BN, CLC, MH, NP, WF, Y.

1083 — —[Anr. ed.] *For Abel Swalle*, 1685. 8°. L, O, C, MR, EN; CH, CN, LC, MH, NU, WSC, Y.

1084 —The lives, actions, and executions of the prime actors. *For Tho. Vere*, 1661. 12°. L, O, LVF; CH, NP, Y.

1085 —Pharmacopœia Bateana. In qua. *Impensis Sam. Smith*, 1688. 8°. T.C.II 208. L, O, OME, C, LSP; BN, MH, PL, WSG.

1086 — —Second edition. *Impensis S. Smith*, 1691. 12°. T.C.II 386. L, O, C, LCS, E; BN, CH, CLC, PL, WSG, HC.

1087 — —Third edition. *Apud Sam. Smith et Benj. Walford*, 1700. 12°. T.C.III 216. L, C, OC, LM, LCS; CLM, WSG, HC.

1088 —Pharmacopœia Bateana; or Bate's dispensary, *Apud S. Smith et B. Walford*, 1694. 8°. T.C.II 478. L, O, C, LWL, GU; BN, CJC, CLC, NC, WF, HC.

1089 — —Second edition. *For S. Smith and B. Walford*, 1700. 12°. T.C.III 161. L, C, OC, E, GH; BN, CJC, WSK, HC.

1090 [–] The regall apology. [*London*], *printed*, 1648. 4°. LT, O, C, MR, EN; CH, CN, MH, NU, TU, WF, JF.

      [–] Royal apologie. *Paris*, 1648. *See* Digby, *Sir* Kenelm.

1091 **Bate, Henry.** Prince Charles sailing. *Printed*, 1648. 4°.* LT, O; MH, Y.

1092 **Bate, John.** The mysteries of nature and art. Third edition. *By R. Bishop for Andrew Crook*, 1654. 4°. L, CCH, LNL, LWL, GU; CH, LC, MH, NPT, Y.

1092A **Bateman, Sir Anthony.** By the mayor. [*London*, 1664.] brs. L.

1093 **Bateman, Christopher.** Sale of stock of books. 24th [Dec?], 1696. 4°. L.

1094 **Bateman, George.** An answer to (vindicate the cause). [*London*, 1653.] 4°.* L, LF; NU.

1095 —The arrow of the Almighty. *By R. I. for William Hutcheson in Durham*, 1653. 4°. LT, O.

1096 —A brief narration of the examination of Geo. Bateman, *Printed*, 1654. 4°.* LT.

1096A **Bateman, Robert.** A gentle dose. [*London*, 1680?] brs. L.

1096B —Batemans hue-and-cry. [*London*, 1680?] brs. L.

1096C —The true spirit of scurvey-grass. [*London*, 1680?] brs. L.

1096D —The true spirits of scurvey-grass. [*London*, 1680?] brs. L.

1097 [**Bateman, Susanna.**] I matter not how I appear to man. [1657.] cap., 4°.* LT; PH, WF.

1098 [**Bateman, Thomas.**] An answer to the postscript of a paper published by Sir H. M. [*London*, 1698.] cap., fol.*, L; MH.

1099 **Bates.** A tract on the fourth commandment. *For Tho. Parkhurst, and for Joh. Robinson*, 1692. 4°. L.

1099A **Bates, Thomas.** The covenant sealed. 1655. 4°. YM.

1099B —Mr. Humphrey's second vindication. 1656. 4°. YM.

1100 **Bates, William.** The works of. *For B. Aylmer. And J. Robinson*, 1700. fol. L, O, C, E, DT; CH, CU, MH, NU, WF, Y.

1100A [–] An account of the life and death of Mr. Philip Henry. *For T. Parkhurst and J. Lawrence*, 1698. 12°. T.C.III 38. LCL; CLC, MH, WF.

1100B [–] — —Second edition. *For T. Parkhurst*, 1699. 8°. T.C.III 121. O; CH, Y.

1101 —Considerations of the existence of God. *By J. D. for Brabazon Aylmer*, 1676. 8°. T.C.I 251. L, O, LG, E; CLC, Y, PJB.

1102 — —Second edition. —, 1677. 8°. T.C.I 278. L, LCL, OC, DT; MBA, MH, NC, NU, WF.

1103 —The danger of prosperity. *For Brabazon Aylmer*, 1685. 8°. T.C.II 143. L, C, LCL, OC, ENC; CH, WF.

1104 —The divinity of the Christian religion. *By J. D. for Brabazon Aylmer*, 1677. 8°. T.C.I 272. O, LW, OC; CLC, MBA, NU, WF, Y.

1105 —The four last things. *For Brabazon Aylmer*, 1691. 8°. T.C.II 346. L, CE, LCL, OC; CH, NF, WF, Y.

1106 — —Second edition. —, 1691. 12°. T.C.II 374. L, O, C, BAMB; CH, CLC, NNG, NU, Y.

1107 —A funeral-sermon for ... Mr. Richard Baxter. *For Brab. Aylmer*, 1692. 16°. T.C.II 390. L, O, C, CE, LG; CH, CN, NPT, NU, WF, Y.

1108 — —Second edition. —, 1692. 8°. L, O, OC, SP, GK; CLC, MH, WF, Y.

1109 —A funeral sermon, preached upon ... Mr. Thomas Manton. *By J. D. for Brabazon Aylmer*, 1678. 59 pp. 4°. T.C.I 287. L, O, C, LG, EN; CH, NU, TU, WF, Y.

1110 — —[Anr. ed.] —, 1678. 115 pp. 8°. T.C.I 306. O, LG; CLC, WF.

1111 —The great duty of resignation. *By J. D. for Brabazon Aylmer*, 1684. 8°. T.C.II 93. L, O, C, LCL; CH, NU, TU, WF, Y.

1112 — —Second edition. *By R. R. for Brabazon Aylmer*, 1698. 8°. T.C.III 83. L, C.

1113 —The harmony of the divine attributes. *By J. Darby, for Nathaniel Ranew, and Jonathan Robinson; and Brabazon Aylmer*, 1674. 4°. T.C.I 161. L, O, CE, LG, E; NU, PL, SW, WF, Y.

1114 — —Second edition. *By J. M. for Nathanael Ranew, Jonathan Robinson, and Brabazon Aylmer*, 1675. 4°. T.C.I 214. L, O, CP, EN, DT; BN, CH, CN, MH, NU, Y.

1115 — —Third edition. *For N. Ranew, J. Robinson, and B. Aylmer*, 1688. 8°. T.C.II 240. LG, CM, ENC; CLC, NGT, VC.

1116 — —Fourth edition. *For J. Robinson; A. and J. Churchill; J. Taylor; and J. Wyat*, 1697. 8°. T.C.III 30. L, CPE, BR; CLC, IU, MB, V.

1117 —The peace-maker. [*London*], *printed*, 1662. 4°.* O, YM; MB.

1118 —A sermon preached upon the ... death of ... Queen Mary. *For Brabazon Aylmer*, 1695. 8°.* T.C.II 548. L, CT, LW, WCA; CH, MH, NC, WF, Y.

1119 — —Second edition. —, 1695. 4°.* L, O, C, CCA, WCA; CH, CLC, NU, TU.

1120 — —Third edition. —, 1695. 4°.* L, O, C, LCL, EN; CH, CN, MH, WF.

1121 — —Fourth edition. —, 1695. 4°.* L, LG, LW; LC, MH, NU, TU, Y.

1122 —Sermons preach'd on several occasions. *By J. D. for Jonathan Robinson*, 1693. 8°. L, O, CT, LCL; CLC, MBA, PU.

1123 —Sermons upon death. *By J. D. for Brabazon Aylmer*, 1683. 8°. T.C.II 24. L, O, CT, LCL, EN; CLC, NGT, Y.

1124 —Sermons upon Psalm cxxx. ver. 4. *By J.D. for Brabazon Aylmer,* 1696. 8°. L, LCL; CH, CLC, MU, WF.

1125 —A short description of the blessed place. *By J.D. for J. Robinson,* 1687. 8°. T.C.II 175. L, CE, LG, LCL, AU; CLC, NGT, NU, WF, Y.

1126 —The soveraign and final happiness of man. *By J.D. for Brabazon Aylmer,* 1680. 8°. T.C.I 368. L, LG, OC, AU; CLC, CN, WF, Y.

1127 —The speedy coming of Christ. *For J. Robinson,* 1687. 8°. T.C.II 205. L, O, C, LG, AU; CLC.

1128 —Spritual perfection, unfolded. *For Jonathan Robinson; and Brabazon Aylmer,* 1699. 8°. T.C.III 122. L, LCL, E, ENC, DT; MB, MIU, NU, VC, WF.

1129 —The sure trial of uprightness. *For Jonathan Robinson,* 1689. 8°. T.C.II 272. L, O, C, LG, LCL; CH, CN, NU, WF, Y.

1129A —The upright Christian discovered. 1693. 8°.* L, O.

1130 [–] Vitæ selectorum. *Typis A.G. & J.P. & prostant venales apud Georgium Wells,* 1681. 4°. T.C.I 432. L, O, C, EN, DT; BN, CH, CU, NU, WF, Y.

1131 —The way to the highest honour. *For J. Robinson,* 1687. 8°. T.C.II 205. L, O, LG, LCL; CLC, NU, WF, Y.

1132 **Bath, Henry Bourchier,** *earl of.* A declaration made by. *For John Wright, Septemb.* 29. [1642]. 4°.* LT, LVF, EC, D; CH, CN, MH, TU, Y.

1132A **Bathe, Henry de.** The charter of Romney Marsh. *By Tho. Cotes, for John Parker,* 1647. 8°. Y.

1133 — —[Anr. ed.] *By S. R. for S. Keble,* 1686. 8°. T.C.II 160. L, O, CM, LGI, OC; CLC, LC, MBP, MHL, WF.
Bathonia rediviva. 1660. *See* Prynne, William.
Bathoniensum. 1676. *See* Pugh, Robert.

1133A **Bathurst, Charles.** The doting Athenians. *For Thomas Northcott,* 1692. fol.* LF.

1134 —A serious exhortation to the people. [*London?*], *printed,* 1669. 4°.* L, LF, BBN; IE, LC, MH, PH, Y.

1135 **Bathurst, Edward.** Motus. 1676. brs. O.

1135A [**Bathurst, Elizabeth.**] An expostulatory appeal to the professors. [*London,* 1680?] 4°.* LF, BBN; PH, Y.

1135B —The sayings of women. [*London*], *printed and sold by Andrew Sowle,* 1683. 8°.* LF, BBN.

1135C —Truth vindicated. [*London*], *for T. Sowle,* 1691. 8°. LF.

1136 —[Anr. ed.] *Printed and sold by T. Sowle,* 1965 [i.e., 1695]. 12°. LF, O, CT, RPL; CLC, MH, PH, PL, WF, Y.

1137 —Truth's vindication. [*London*], *printed,* 1679. 4°. L, O, LF; MH, NG, PH, PSC, Y.

1138 [–] —[Anr. ed.] *Printed and sold by Andrew Sowle,* 1683. 8°. L, LF, LG; BN, NU, PL, PSC, WF.

1139 [–] —[Anr. ed.] *Printed, sold by W. S., and J. B.,* 1983 [i.e., 1683]. 8°. NU.

1140 Entry cancelled.

1141 **Baston, Edmund.** A funeral sermon on the death of Mrs Paicc. *By Samuel Bridge,* 1700. 8°. L, C, LW.

1142 **Batt, Antony.** A hidden treasvre of holie prayers. *Printed at Paris by Wil: Bavdry,* 1641. Sixes. L, O, LSC.

1143 [**Batt, Gil.**] Some particular animadversions. 1646. 4°. CT; CH.

1144 **Batt, Jasper.** A true and reall manifestation. [*London*], *printed,* 1661. 4°.* LF; NS, WF.

1144A —Truth & innocency triumphing. *For John Bringhurst,* 1681. 4°.* LF, BBN; MH.

1145 **Batt, Michael.** A sermon preached . . . May 5th. 1668 [sic]. *For William Oliver in Norwich; to be sold by B. Aylmer in London,* 1686. 4°.* L, O, C, CE, BAMB; CH, NNG, NPT, WF, Y.

1146 **Batt, Timothy.** Christs gratious message. *Printed,* 1644. CLC, NU.

1147 —A treatise concerning the free grace of God. *By T. P. & M. S. for Ed. Blackmore,* 1643. 12°. L, C.

1148 —The waters of Marah sweetned. *For Francis Eglesfield, to be sold by George Treagle in Taunton,* 1648. 4°.* LT, O; RPB.
Batt upon Batt. 1680. *See* Speed, John.

1148A **Battell, Ralph.** The civil magistrates coercive power. *By R.E. for Walter Kettilby,* 1684. 4°.* T.C.II 95. CHW, WF, Y.

1149 —The lawfulness and expediency of church-musick. *By J. Heptinstall. for John Carr,* 1694. 4°.* L, O, C, CP, BAMB; CLC, LC, NU, PU.
[–] Περιαμμα επιδημιον; or. . . . 1659. *See* Walker, Obadiah.

1150 [–] Vulgar errors in divinity removed. *For Benj. Tooke and Joanna Brome,* 1683. 8°. T.C.II I. L, O, C, NPL, DT; CH, CU, MIU, NU, WF, HC.

1151 **Battley, John.** A sermon preach'd . . . May vi. 1694. *By Tho. Warren, for Walter Kettilby,* 1694. 4°.* T.C.II 509. L, O, C, OM, EN; CH, CLC, NU, WF, Y.

1152 **Batten, Sir William.** A declaration of. *At London, printed,* 1684. 4°.* LT, O, CE, HH, MR; CH, MIU, NN, WF, Y.

1153 —The sea-mans diall. [*London*], *printed,* 1648. 4°.* LT.

1154 —The true relation of. *By Matthew Simmons,* 1647. 4°.* LT, O, BR; CH, MH, NN, Y.

1155 [–] A true relation of what past betweene the fleet. 1648[9]. 4°.* LT.

1156 Battering rams against Rome's gates. [*London?* 1680.] brs. O; CH, Y.

1157 **B[attie], J[ohn].** The merchants remonstrance. *By R. H. February 12.* 1644. 4°* LT, O; MH, NC, NR, Y.

1158 — —[Anr. ed.] *By Ric. Cotes, for William Hope,* 1648. 4°.* L, O, OM, MR; CU, MBA, NC, Y.

1159 **Battie, William.** A sermon preached at Sudbury. *For Sam. Carr,* 1680. 4°.* T.C.I 381. L, O, C, CT, LCL; CH, CN, NU, WF, Y.

1160 —A sermon preached . . . November 18, 1677. *By E; Flesher for R. Royston,* 1678. 4°.* L, O, C, LG, BAMB; CH, MBA, NN, WF, Y.

1160A The battell at Namptwich. 1643. 4°.* LT.

1160B The battel at sea. *Printed and sold by T. Moore,* 1694. brs. MH.

1160C The battle at Torperley. 1643. 4°.* LT.

1161 A battaile fought betvveen a Presbyterian cock. *Printed,* 1647. 4°.* LT, O, OC; MH, Y.

1161A The battle of Glenlivot. A ballad. *Printed,* 1681. 12°.* CM.

Battle of Nevvbvrne. Glasgow, 1643. *See B., M. Z.*

1162 The battaile on Hopton-heath. *[Oxford], by H. Hall,
1643.* 4°.* MADAN 1294. LT, O, CJ, OC, DT; Y.

1163 **Bauderon, Brice.** The expert physician. *Printed at
London by R. I. for John Hancock, 1657.* 8°. LT, O, C,
LCS, LWL; LC, WSG.

1164 **Baudier, Michel.** The history of the administration
of Cardinal Ximenes. *For John Wilkins, 1671.* 8°.
T.C.I 56. L, O, C, CE, LIL; BN, CH, LC, MH, NU, Y.

1164A — —[Anr. ed.] *By Peter Parker, 1679.* 8°. MBA.

1165 [–] The history of the court of the king of China. *By
H. B. for Christopher Hussey, 1682.* 12°. T.C.I 461. L,
CCH, RPL, SP; CN, MH, WF, Y.

1166 The bawds tryal and execution. *For L. C., 1679.* fol.*
L, O; MH, Y.

1167 The bawdy-house tragedy. *Printed and sold by J. Read,
1698.* brs. L.

1168 **Bauthumley, Jacob.** A brief historical relation of the
most material passages. *1676.* 8°. L, O.

1169 —The light and dark sides of God. *For William Learner,
[1650].* 8°. LT, O, OB, OC.

Baxter. Benjamin, *pseud.*

1170 **Baxter, Benjamin.** Mr. Baxter baptiz'd in bloud.
Printed, 1673. 4°.* L, O, LG; MB, NN, RPJ.

1170A —The doctrine of self-posing. *For Peter Parker, 1666.*
8°. LW; MM.

1171 —Non-conformity, without controversie. *By A. M.
for Tho. Parkhurst, 1670.* 12°. L, O, LCL; MHS, NPT, NU,
Y.

1172 —A posing question. *For George Sawbridge, [166–?]* 8°.
O; MB, NPT, WF.

1172A — —[Anr. ed.] —, *1662.* 8°. IU, WF, Y.

1173 — —[Anr. ed.] *For John Jones, in Worcester, 1662.* 8°.
L, LCL, ENC; NU, Y.

1173A **Baxter, Isaac.** The ancient liberty of the Britannick
church. *1661.* 12°. CCA.

1174 **Baxter, Nathaniel.** Sir Philip Sydneys Ourania.
Printed, 1653. 4°. L; CH, MH, Y.

1175 — —[Anr. ed.] *For Jane Bell, 1655.* 4°. CN, LC.

1176 **[Baxter, Richard.]** An accompt of all the proceedings
of the commissioners. *For R. H., 1661.* 2 pts. 4°.
LT, O, C, LL, HH; CH, MH, PL, WF, Y.

1177 [–] —[Anr. ed.] *Printed, 1661.* 2 pts. 4°. L, O, LLL, OC,
DT; CH, MH, NC, NU, WCL.

1178 —Richard Baxter's account of his present thoughts.
For Tho. Vnderhill and F. Tyton, 1657. 4°.* LT, O, CS,
EN, DT; BN, CLC, MH, NU, WF, Y.

1179 —Richard Baxter his account to his dearly beloved,
. . . of Kidderminster. *Printed, 1662.* 4°. L, O, MR,
EN, GU; CLC, NU.

1180 —Additional notes on the life and death of Sir Matthew
Hale. *For Richard Janeway, 1682.* 8°.* L, O, C, LW,
OM; CH, CN, MH, NC, WF, Y.

1180A —Additions to the Poetical fragments. *For B. Simmons,
1683.* 8°. T.C.II 17. L, EN; CLC, MH.

1181 —Rich. Baxter's admonition to Mr. William Eyre. *By
A. M. for Thomas Vnderhill, and Francis Tyton, 1654.*
4°. LT, O, C, LCL, EN; CH, CLC, NU, WF, Y.

1182 —Against the revolt to a foreign jurisdiction. *For Tho.
Parkhurst, 1691.* 8°. T.C.II 358. L, O, C, LCL, LW; CH,
LC, MH, NPT, NU, Y.

1183 —Richard Baxter's answer to Dr. Stillingfleet's charge.
For Nevil Simmons, and Thomas Simmons, 1680. 4°.
T.C.I 408. L, O, CS, EN, DT; BN, CU, MH, NU, WF, Y.

1184 —An answer to Mr. Dodwell. *For Thomas Parkhurst,
1682.* 4°. T.C.I 483. L, O, LCL, LW, CS; BN, CU, MH, NU, Y.

1185 —Aphorismes of justification. *For Francis Tyton, 1649.*
12°. L, O, CE, LW, ENC; CLC, CU, MH, NPT, NU, Y.

1186 — —[Anr. ed.] *Hague, by Abraham Brown, 1655.* 12°.
L, O, C, LCL, E; CLC, CU, PL, WF, Y.

1187 —Rich. Baxters apology against the modest exceptions
of Mr. T. Blake, *For T. Vnderhill and F. Tyton, and
are to be sold by Jos. Nevil and Jos. Barbar, 1654.* 4 pts.
4°. LT, O, P, E, DT; BN, CH, CU, MH, NU, WF, Y.

1188 — —[Anr. ed.] *By A. M. for Thomas Vnderhill, and
Francis Tyton, 1654.* 4°. L, OC, CP; NNG, NP, NU.

1189 —An apology for the Nonconformists ministry. *For
T. Parkhurst and D. Newman, 1681.* 4°. T.C.I 437. O, C,
LCL, LW; BN, CLC, CU, NP, NU.

1189A — —[Anr. ed.] *For Thomas Parkhurst, 1681.* 4°. OC; Y.

1190 —An appeal to the light. *For Nevil Simmons, 1674.* 4°.*
L, O; NU, WF, Y.

1191 Entry cancelled.

1192 [–] The arrogancy of reason. *By T. N. for Tho. Underhil, 1655.* 8°. LT, O, OC, ENC; CH, IU, NU, WF, Y.

1193 —A breviate of the doctrine of justification. *For Tho.
Parkhurst, 1696.* 8°. CLC, MH, NGS.

1194 [–] A breviate of the life of Margaret . . . Charlton.
For B. Simmons, 1681. 4°. T.C.I 462. L, O, CM, LW; CH,
CU, MH, NU, WF, Y.

1195 —Cain and Abel malignity. *For Tho. Parkhurst, 1689.*
8°. T.C.II 311. L, O, LCL; CLC, CU, MH, NU, WF, Y.

1196 —A call to the unconverted. *By R. W. for Nevil Simmons
in Kederminster, to be sold by him there, and by Nathaniel
Ekins, 1658.* 12°. L, LG; CLC.

1196A — —Fifth edition. —, *1652.* 12°. MH, Y.

1196B — —Eighth edition. *By R. W. for Nevil Simmons at Kederminster, to be sold by Mr. Wright, 1660.* 12°. LCL, LW,
DC, NPL; IU.

1197 — —Ninth edition. —, *1660.* 12°. LCL, LW.

1198 — —Tenth edition. *By R. W. for N. Simmons at Kederminster, to be sold by John Daniel, 1663.* 12°. L.

1198A — —Eleventh edition. —, *1665.* 8°. SP.

1198B — —"Eleventh" edition. —, *sold by Henry Mortlock,
1665.* 8°. PL.

1199 — —Thirteenth edition. *By R. W. for N. Simmons,
1669.* 8°. O, CT; NPT, NU.

1200 — —Fifteenth edition. *For Nevil Simmons, 1671.* 8°.
T.C.I 90. DC.

1201 — —Eighteenth edition. —, *1675.* 12°. T.C.I 192. LCL;
PH.

1202 — —Twentieth edition. —, *1678.* 12°. LCL; WF.

1202A — —Twenty-first edition. *For B. Simmons,* 1682. 12°. CU.

1203 — —Twenty-third edition. —, 1685. 12°. CT; BN.

1203A — —[Anr. ed.] *For Ben. Cox,* 1687. 12°. V.

1204 — —"Twenty-second" edition. *For Richard Wilde and Richard Baldwin,* 1692. 12°. LCL; WF.

1205 —The catechizing of families. *For T. Parkhurst, and B. Simmons,* 1683. 8°. T.C.I 505. L, O, C, OB, LCL; BN, CH, CN, MH, NU, WF, Y.

1206 —Catholick communion defended against both extreams. *For Tho. Parkhurst,* 1684. 5 pts. 4°. T.C.I 68. L, O, LVF, LCL, BAMB; BN, CH, MH, NU, WF, Y.

1207 — —, in two parts. [Anr. ed.] —, 1684. 4°.* L, O, CS, LW; NU.

1208 —Catholick communion doubly defended: by Dr. Owens vindicator and R. Baxter. *For Thomas Parkhurst,* 1684. 4°. T.C.II 93. L, O, CS, P, YM; BN, NU.

1209 —Richard Baxter's Catholick theologie. *By Robert White for Nevill Simmons,* 1675. 5 pts. fol. T.C.I 203. L, O, C, LW, E; BN, CH, MH, NU, WF, Y.

1210 —Catholick unity. *By R. W. for Thomas Underhill and Francis Tyton,* 1660. 8°. LT, O, C, LW, E; BN, CLC, CU, NPT, OCC, Y.

1211 —Certain disputations. *By William Du-Gard for Thomas Johnson,* 1657. 4°. LT, O, LG, CM, E; CH, CU, NU, WF ,Y.

1211A —[Anr. ed.] *By William Du-Gard for Nevil Simmons in Kederminster,* 1657. 4°. LW.

1212 — —Second edition. *By R. W. for Nevil Simons in Kederminster, to be sold by him there; and by Nathaniel Ekins,* 1658. 4°. L, O, CS, ENC, DT; MB, MH.

1213 —The certainty of Christiantiy. *For Nevil Simmons,* 1672. 8°. T.C.I 115. O, LW, CT, P, AU; BN, CU, NPT, NU, WF, Y.

1214 —The/certainty/of the/worlds of spirits./ *For T. Parkhurst, and J. Salisbury,* 1691. 8°. LW, GU; CN, CSU, MH, PT, WF.

1215 —The certainty of the/worlds of spirits./ *For T. Parkhurst, and J. Salusbury,* 1691. 8°. T.C.II 378. L, O, C, E, DT; CH, CN, NU, TU, WF, Y.

1216 — —Third edition. —, 1691. 8°. LW.

1217 —The character of a sound confirmed Christian. *By R. White for Nevil Simmons,* 1669. O, LW; CH, MH, NP, TSM, WF.

1218 —Christian concord. *By A. M. for Thomas Underhill and Francis Tyton,* 1653. LT, O, C, OC, DT; CU, MH, NU, WF, Y.

1219 —A Christian directory. *By Robert White for Nevill Simmons,* 1673. fol. T.C.I 132. L, O, C, EN, GU; CLC, MH, NU, WG, Y.

1220 — —Second edition. *By Robert White, for Nevil Simmons,* 1678. fol. T.C.I 304. L, O, LW, DC, ENC; BN, MH, NU, WF, WSC, Y.

1221 —The Christian religion. *Printed,* 1660. 8°. O, SP; NU, WF.

1222 —The Christian's converse with God. *For John Salusbury,* 1693. 12°. T.C.II 419. L, O, C, LCL, AN; NPT.

1223 —Church concord. *For Tho. Parkhurst,* 1691. 4°. T.C.II 358. L, O, C, LCL, LW; MH, NPT, NU, Y.

1224 —Church-history of the government of bishops. *By B. Griffin, and are to be sold by Thomas Simmons, and John Kidgell,* 1680. 4°. T.C.I 402. L, O, C, LW, E; CU, MBC, NPT, NU, Y.

1224A — —[Anr. ed.] *Printed, and are to be sold by John Kidgell,* 1680. 4°. CCA, BR, AN; CU, IU, MH.

1225 — —[Anr. ed.] *For Thomas Simmons,* 1681. 4°. LW, CT, P, EN; BN, CH, CU, NP, NU, WF.

1226 —The church told of Mr. Ed. Bagshaw's scandals. *Printed,* 1672. 4°.* T.C.I 95. O, C, CT, LW, OC; CH, CU, LC, NU, Y.

1227 —Chwychw: daddu cyn ôl ec Sampl-Abraham. [*Tros Edward Brewster*], 1659. 12°. L.

1228 —Compassionate counsell to all young-men. *By T. S. to be sold by B. Simmons, and Jonath. Greenwood,* 1681. 12°. T.C.I 457. L, O, C, LCL; BN, CLC, NU, WF, Y.

1229 — —[Anr. ed.] —, 1682. 8°. T.C.I 509. L.

1230 — —"Second" edition. *By H. Clark for George Conyers,* 1691. 12°. T.C.II 342. L, O, LG.

1231 —Rich: Baxter's confesssion [sic]. *By R.W. for Thos. Vnderhil and Fra. Tyton,* 1655. 4°. LT, O, C, E, DT; BN, CH, CU, MH, NU, WF, Y.

1232 —Confirmation and restauration. *By A. M. for Nevil Simmons in Kederminster, and are to be sold by Joseph Cranford,* 1658. 8°. LT, O, C, NPL, E; BN, CH, CU, MH, NU, WF, Y.

1232A — —[Anr. ed.] *By A. M. for Nevil Simmons sold by him and N. Ekins,* 1658. 8°. TU, WF.

1233 —The crucifying of the world. *By R. W. for Nevill Simmons in Kederminster, and are to be sold by him there, and by Nathaniel Ekins,* 1658. 4°. LT, O, C, LCL, ENC; BN, CH, CU, MH, NU, WF, Y.

1233A — —[Anr. ed.] *For Joseph Cranford, to be sold by Richard Scott in Carlisle,* 1658. 4°. OC.

1234 —The cure of church-divisions. *For Nevil Symmons,* 1670. 8°. L, O, C, LW, ENC; BN, CH, CU, LC, MH, NU, Y.

1235 — —Second edition. —, 1670. L, O, CS, MC, E; CLC, LC, NU, WF.

1236 — —Third edition. —, 1670. 8°. L, O, CCA, LCL, LW; CLC, CU, NP, WF, Y.

1237 —The dangerous schismatick clearly detected. *For Thomas Parkhurst,* 1683. 4°. O, LCL, LW; CH.

1237A —Dattodiad y qwestiwn mawr. *Liundain gan Tho. Whitledge a W.Everingham,* 1693. Sixes. AN; Y.

1237B —A defence of Christ. *By Tho. Parkhurst,* 1690. 8°. CLC, MH, NGS.

1238 —The defence of the Nonconformists plea for peace. *For Benjamin Alsop,* 1680. 8°. T.C.I 401. O, C, LCL, LW, CE; BN, WF.

1239 —A defence of the principles of love. *For Nevil Simmons,* 1671. 2 pts. 8°. T.C.I 64. L, O, C, LCL, E; BN, CH, CU, MH, NU, WF, Y.

1240 —The description, reasons & reward. *For Francis Tyton, and Nevil Simmons in Kederminster,* 1664. 4°. MH, NGS.

1241 —A determination of this question. *By R.W. for Thomas Underhill, and for F. Tyton,* 1655. 8°. LT, O, C, ENC; CH, NIC, NU, WF, Y.

1242 —The difference between the power of magistrates. *For Nevil Simmons*, 1671. 4°. T.C.I 81. L, O, C, CE, ENC; BN, CH, MH, NU, WF, Y.

1243 —Directions and perswasions. *By A. M. for Nevil Simmons in Kederminster, and are to be sold by him ... and by N. Ekins*, 1658. 8°. O, C, E; Y.

1244 ——[Anr. ed.] *By A. M. for Nevil Simmons in Kederminster, to be sold by Joseph Cranford*, 1658. 8°. LT, CE; IU.

1245 ——Second edition. *By R. W. for Nevil Simmons*, 1659. 12°. LCL; WF.

1245A ——[Anr. ed.] 1662. 12°. NPT.

1246 ——"Second" edition. *For W. Whitwood*, 1667. 8°. OC; CH.

1247 ——"Second" edition. *By R. W. to be sold by John Lutton*, 1670. 8°. L, LW; CU, Y.

1248 ——Third edition. *By R. W. for Nevill Simmons*, 1673. 8°. T.C.I 156. O, LW; BN, NU, OCI.

1249 —Directions for weak distempered Christians. *By R. White for Nevil Simmons*, 1669. 8°. T.C.I 12. L, O, LCL, E, ENC; BN, CU, MH, NP, NU, Y.

1250 —Directions to justices of peace. 1654. brs. E.

1251 —[Anr. ed.] *By Robert White for Nevil Simmons*, 1657. brs. L, O; BN, MH.

1252 Entry cancelled.

1253 —The divine appointment of the Lords Day proved. *For Nevil Simmons*, 1671. 8°. T.C.I 70. L, O, C, LCL, E; BN, CH, CU, MH, NU, WF, Y.

1254 —The divine life. *For Francis Tyton, and Nevil Simmons, in Kederminster*, 1664. 4°. L, O, LCL, HH, ENC; BN, CH, CU, LC, MH, NU, Y.

1255 —The duty of heavenly meditation. *For Nevil Simmons*, 1671. 4°.* T.C.I 65. L, O, C, LW, YM; BN, CH, LC, MH, WF, Y.

1256 —Richard Baxter's dying thoughts upon Phil. I 23. *By Tho. Snowden, for B. Simmons*, 1683. 8°. T.C.II 24. L, O, LCL, LG, CE; CH, MH, CU, WF, Y.

1257 ——Second edition. *By H. Clark for Benjamin Cox*, 1688. 8°. T.C.II 281. L, C, LCL, LW, GU; CLC, CN, IU, NF, NU.

1258 —An end of doctrinal controversies. *For John Salusbury*, 1691. 8°. T.C.II 367. L, O, C, LW, ENC; NF, NP, NU, WF, Y.

1258A —Englands warning-piece. *[London], for J. Conyers*, 1678. 8°.* CLC.

1259 —The English Nonconformity. *For Tho. Parkhurst*, 1689. 4°. T.C.II 247. L, O, CPE, LW, LCL; CH, CN, MH, NU, WF, Y.

1260 ——Second edition. *For Tho. Parkhurst*, 1690. 4°. T.C.II 316. L, C, LCL, LW, ENC; CH, CU, NF, NP, NU.

1261 —Excellent memorables for all mourners. *For Tho. Parkhurst*, 1691. brs. L.

1262 Entry cancelled.

1263 [–] Fair warning: or, xxv. reasons. *For S. U. N. T. F. S.*, 1663. 4°. L, O, C, EN, DT; CH, MH, NU, WF, Y.

1264 Entry cancelled.

1265 —Faithful souls shall be with Christ. *For Nevil Simmons*, 1681. 4°. T.C.I. 437. L, O, C, LW, OC; BN, CU, LC, MH, NU, TU, Y.

1266 —Richard Baxter's farewel sermon. *For B. Simmons* 1683. 4°.* T.C.II 38. O, LCL, LW; CH, NU, PL, WF, Y.

1267 —Five disputations. *By R. W. for Nevil Simmons, and are to be sold by him in Kederminster and by Thomas Johnson*, 1659. 4°. LT, O, C, LL, E; BN, CH, CU, MH, NU, WF, Y.

1268 ——[Anr. ed.] *By R. W. for Nevil Simmons in Kederminster, and are to be sold by him there, and by N. Ekins, and by J. Baker*, 1659. 4°. LCL, LW, CT, ENC, DT; NU, YD.

1269 [–] For prevention of the unpardonable sin. *Printed*, 1655. 8°. LT, O, ENC; CH, IU, NU, WF, Y.

1270 —Full and easie satisfaction. *For Nev. Simmons*, 1674. 8°. T.C.I 146. L, O, C, LVF, E; BN, CH, LC, MH, NU, Y.

1271 ——[Anr. ed.] *Glasgow, by Robert Sanders*, 1674. 12°. ALDIS 2015. L, GU, I; WF.

1272 —Galwad ir annychweledig. *Tros. Edward Brewster*, 1659. 12°. L, AN.

1273 ——[Anr. ed.] *Thomas Dawks tros E. Brewster*, 1677. 12°. AN; CN.

1274 —Gildas Salvianus. *By Robert White for Nevil Simmons at Kederminster*, 1656. 8°. L, O, AN; CU, MH, WF.

1275 ——[Anr. ed.] *By Robert White for Nevil Simmons, and are to be sold by William Roybould*, 1656. 8°. LT, O, C, E, DT; BN, CH, MH, NU, WSC, Y.

1276 ——"Second" edition. *By Robert White, for Nevil Simmons, to be sold by Joseph Nevill*, 1657. 8°. L, O, C, GU, AU; CH, CN, NU, WF, Y.

1277 —The glorious kingdom of Christ. *By T. Snowden, for Thomas Parkhurst*, 1691. 4°. T.C.II 346. L, O, C, LCL, EN; CH, CU, MBA, NU, WF, Y.

1278 —God's goodness, vindicated. *For N. Simmons*, 1671. 12°. T.C.I 71. L, O, CPE, OC; BN, NPT, NU, WF, Y.

1278A [–] The grand debate between the most reverend the bishops. *Printed*, 1661. 4°. L, O, CS, E, DT; CH, MH, NU, WF, Y.

1279 —The grand question resolved. *For Tho. Parkhurst*, 1692. 12°.* T.C.II 509. L; WF.

1280 —The Grotian religion discovered. *By R. W. for Nevill Simmons in Kederminster, and are to be sold by him there and by Tho. Brewster, and by John Starkey*, 1658. 8°. LT, O, C, E, DT; BN, CU, NPT, NU, WF, Y.

1281 —A holy commonwealth. *For Thomas Underhill, and Francis Tyton*, 1659. 8°. LT, O, C, EN, DT; BN, CH, CU, LC, MH, NU, Y.

1281A ——[Anr. ed.] *Printed, and are to be sold by Nevil Simmins in Kederminster*, 1659. 8°. LW, AN.

1282 —How far holinesse is the design of Christianity. *For Nevill Simmons*, 1671. 4°.* T.C.I 85. O, C, LCL, P, DT; NU, PH, WF.

1283 —How to do good to many. *For Rob. Gibs*, 1682. 4°. T.C.II 2. LT, O, C, CT; CLC, CN, NU, WF, Y.

1284 —Humble advice. *For Thomas Vnderhill and Francis Tyton*, 1655. 4°.* LT, O, LCL, LG, E; BN, CH, MH, NPT, NU, Y.

1285 [-] The humble petition of many thousands, gentlemen . . . of the county of *Worcester*. *By Robert White for Francis Tyton and Thomas Underhill*, 1652. 4°.* LT, O, C, LW, EN; CH, MIU, NU, WF, Y.

1286 —Imputative righteousness. *By J. D. to be sold by Jonathan Robinson, and William Abington*, 1679. 12°. LCL, LG; NPT, NU.

1287 [-] The invaluable price of an immortal soul. [*London*], *for J. Clark*, 1681.* LW; NU.

1288 —The judgment and advice of the Assembly. *For T. Vnderhill, and F. Tyton*, 1658. 4°.* L, O; CH, CU, MH, NU.

1289 —Mr. Baxter's judgment and reasons. [*London*], *printed*, 1684. 4°.* L, O; MHS, NU.

1290 —The judgment of Mr. Baxter concerning ceremonies. *For R. Jenaway*, [sic] 1667. 8°.* L, O, C, BPL, MR; CH, NN.

1291 — —[Anr. ed.] *Edinburgh*, 1689. 4°. ALDIS 2863. EN; NN.

1292 [-] The judgment of Non-conformists about the difference. [*London*], *printed*, 1678. 4°. O, LW, SP, EN; MB, MH.

1293 [-] The judgment of Non-conformists, of the interest. *Printed*, 1676. 4°.* L, O, C, CT, EN; CH, CU, MIU, NU.

1294 —A key for Catholicks. *By R. W. for Nevil Simmons, and are to be sold by him there, and by Thomas Johnson.* 1659. 2 pts. 4°. LT, O, C, E, DT; CH, CU, MH, NU, WF, Y.

1295 — —Second edition. *For Nev. Simmons*, 1674. 2 pts. 8°. T.C.I 166. LCL, LW, LIL; BN, CLC, MH.

1296 —Last legacy. *Robert White*, 1696. 4°. CT.

1297 — —[Anr. ed.] *Printed and are to be sold by E. Whitlock*, 1697. 4°. O, OC, CT; Y.

1298 —The last work of a believer. *By B. Griffin, for B. Simmons*, 1682. 4°. T.C.I 466. L, O, LW; CLC, MH, NPT, NU, WF.

1299 —The life of faith, as it is. *By R. W. and A. M. for Francis Tyton and Jane Underhill, and are to be sold at . . . and by Nevil Simmons*, 1660. LT, O, C, EN, DT; CU, MH, NU, WF, Y.

1300 — —[Anr. ed.] *By R. W., for Francis Tyton, and are to be sold [in London]: and by Nevil Simmons at Kederminster*, 1660. 4°. LW; CH, MH, NPT, NU, Y.

1301 —The life of faith. In three parts. *By R. W. for Nevill Simmons*, 1670. 4°. T.C.I 29. L, O, C, DC, E; BN, CH, CU, NU, WF, Y.

1302 [-] London's mortality. [*London*], *G. Horton*, [1665]. 4°.* HH.

1303 —Making light of Christ. *By R. White, for Nevil Simmons in Kederminster*, 1655. 8°. LT, O, C, LW; BN, CLC, Y.

1304 — —[Anr. ed.] —, 1656. 8° LT, O, CM; CLC, WF.

1305 — —[Anr. ed.] *By R. White for Nevil Simmons*, 1658. 8°. C; NU.

1306 — —"Second" edition. *For Nevil Simmons*, 1691. 4°. L, O, LW.

1307 —Memorables of the life of faith. *For Tho. Parkhurst*, 1690. brs. L.

1308 —Methodus theologiæ Christianæ. *Typis M. White & T. Snowden & prostant venales apud Nevil Simmons*, 1681. fol. T.C.I 444. L, O, C, E, DT; BN, CH, MH, NU, WF, Y.

1308A — —[Anr. ed.] *Prostant apud Abel Swalle*, 1682. fol. MIU.

1309 —The mischiefs of self-ignorance. *By R. White for F. Tyton*, 1662. 8°. L, O, LCL, LW; BN, CH, CU, NU, WF, Y.

[-] Model for the maintaining. 1648. *See* Poole, Matthew.

1310 —Monthly preparations. *For Tho. Parkhurst*, 1696. 12°. L; NF, NPT, NU.

1311 —A moral prognostication. *For Thomas Simmons*, 1680. 4°. T.C.I 402. L, O, LCL, OM, ENC; BN, CU, MH, NU, TU, WF, Y.

1312 —More proofs of infant church-membership. *For N. Simmons and J. Robinson*, 1675. 8°. T.C.I 195. L, O, C, LCL, LW; CLC, CU, MH, NU, WF, Y.

1313 —More reasons for the Christian religion. *For Nevil Simmons*, 1672. 12°. L, O, C, OC, E; BN, CLC, CU, MH, Y.

1314 —Much in a little: or, an abstract of Mr. Baxter's plain scripture-proof. *For Tho. Parkhurst*, 1678. 8°. T.C.I 318. L, O, LW; NHC.

1315 —Naked popery. *For N. Simmons*, 1677. 4°. T.C.I 265. L, O, C, LCL, E; BN, CH, MH, NU, WF, Y.

1316 —The nature and immortality of the soul. 1682. 12°. O, LCL; MWA.

1317 [-] The Nonconformists advocate. *For Thomas Simmons*, 1680. 4°. L, O; CH, IU, MH, NU, Y.

1318 —The Nonconformists plea for peace. *For Benj. Alsop*, 1679. 8°. L, O, C, LW, ENC; CH, MH, NU, WF, Y.

1319 —Nonconformity without controversie. *By A. M. for T. Parkhurk [sic] to be sold by Sampson Evans, in Worcester*, 1670. 16°. L; MHS, Y.

1320 —Now or never. *Printed*, 1662. 8°. O; CU, NU.

1320A — —[Anr. ed.] *By R. W. for F. Tyton*, 1662. 12°. L, LSC, O, CS; Y.

1321 — —[Anr. ed.] *By R. W. for F. Tyton, and Nevill Simmons*, 1669. 12°. O; WF, Y.

1322 — —[Anr. ed.] —, 1671. 12°. T.C.I 90. C, LW; NPT, Y.

1323 — —[Anr. ed.] *Edinburgh, by Andrew Anderson*, 1672. 12°. ALDIS 1939. MH, NPT.

1324 — —[Anr. ed.] *Glasgow, by Robert Sanders*, 1672. 8°. GU.

1324A — —Ninteenth edition. *For T. Passinger*, 1676. 8°. OP.

1325 — —[Anr. ed.] *By R. E. for N. Simmons*, 1677. 12°. T.C.I 296. O, LCL; BN, CH.

1326 — —[Anr. ed.] *By B. Griffin for N. Simmons in Sheffeild*, 1689. 12°. T.C.II 264. L, O, P, CPL; NPT.

1327 —Obedient patience in general. *For Robert Gibs*, 1683. 12°. T.C.II 2. LCL, CPL; NPT.

1328 —Of justification. *By R. W. for Nevil Simmons, in Kederminster, and are to be sold by him . . . and by Nathaniel Ekins*, 1658. 4°. L, O, DC, ENC, DT; BN, CH, CU, MH, NU, WF, Y.

1329 —Of national churches. *By T. Snowden, for Thomas Parkhurst*, 1691. 4°. T.C.II 358. L, O, LCL, BAMB; CH, CLC, CU, NU, WF.

1330 —Of saving faith. *By R. W. for Nevill Simmons, and are to be sold by him in Kederminster and by Nathaniel Ekins,* 1658. 4°. LT, O, OC, DT; BN, CH, CU, MH, NU, WF.

1330A ——[Anr. ed.] *By R. W. for Nevil Simmons, to be sold by John Starkey,* 1658. 4°. OC, LW.

1331 —Of the immortality of mans soul. *For B. Simmons,* 1682. 12°. T.C.I 492. L, O, C, LW, GU; MH, MU, NF, NP, Y.

1332 —Of the imputation of Christ's righteousness. *For Nevil Simons and Jonathan Robinson,* 1675. 8°. C, ENC; CH, MH, NU, Y.

1333 —Of the nature of spirits. *For B. Simmons,* 1682, 8°. O, C; MH, NPT, NU.

1334 —One sheet against the Quakers. *By Robert White for Nevil Simmons,* 1657. 8°.* L, O, C, BBN, DT; BN, CH, CLC, MH, NU, PH, Y.

1335 —One sheet for the ministry. *By Robert White for Nevil Simmons,* 1657. 8°.* L, O, C, CT, DT; BN, CH, CU, MH, NU, Y.

1336 —The one thing necessary. *For J. Salusbury,* 1685. 12°. LCL, LW, EN.

1337 [–] The papers that passed between the commissioners. *[London,* 1661.] cap., 4°. LL, LIL; CN, MB, MBA.

1338 —A paraphrase on the New Testament. *For B. Simmons,* 1685. 4°. L, O, LW; CLC, CU, MBA, NU, Y.

1339 ——Second edition. *For T. Parkhurst; S. Sprint; J. Taylor; and J. Wyat,* 1695. 8°. T.C.II 553. L, O, LW, CS, BR; NU, WF, Y.

1340 Entry cancelled.

1341 —Richard Baxter's penitent confession. *For Tho. Parkhurst,* 1691. 4°. T.C.II 366. L, O, C, CT, LCL; CU, MH, NU, Y.

1342 [–] A petition for peace. *Printed,* 1661. 95 pp. 4°. LT, O, CJ, EN; CLC, CU, MH, NU, WF, Y.

1343 [–] ——[Anr. ed.] —, 1661. 101 pp. 4°. LT, O, CT, EN, DT; CH, CN, MH, NU, WF, Y.

1344 —Plain scripture proof. *For Robert White,* 1651. 4°. L, O, C, ENC, DT; CH, MH, NPT, NU, Y.

1345 ——Third edition. —, 1653. 4°. L, O, CM, E, AU; CLC, CU, MH, NU, Y.

1346 ——Fourth edition. *For T. V. F. T. and are to be sold by John Wright,* 1656. 4°. LT, O, C, RB, EN; BN, CU, MH, NU, WF, Y.

1347 [–] A plea for Congregationall government. *For Tho: Vnderhill,* 1646. 4°.* LT, CJ, EC, E, DT; CH, CN, NU, Y.

1348 —Πνεύματου διαχονία: or, gospel-churches. *By T. M. for Tho. Parkhurst,* 1682. 4°. T.C.I 483. L, O, E; NU, Y.

1349 —Poetical fragments. *By T. Snowden for B. Simmons,* 1681. 8°. T.C.I 462. L, O, C, LCL, EN; BN, CH, MH, NU, WC, Y.

1350 ——Second edition. *For J. Dunton,* 1689. 12°. T.C.II 294. L, LW, EN; CH, MH, MU, NPT, WF.

1351 ——Third edition. *For Tho. Parkhurst,* 1699. 12°. T.C.III 166. L, O, LW; CH, CU, MH, NU, WF, Y.

1352 —The poor man's family book. *By R. W. for Nevill Simmons,* 1674. 8°. T.C.I 167. L, O, LW; CU, NPT, NU, WF, Y.

1353 ——Second edition, —, 1675. 8°. L, LW; CH, CLC, CU, MH, Y.

1354 ——Third edition. *By Robert White, for Nevill Simmons,* 1677. 8°. T.C.I 285. L, LW; MH, MU, TSM.

1355 ——Fourth edition. *For T. Simmons,* 1680. 8°. T.C.I 409. LCL, LSC; CLC.

1356 ——Fifth edition. *For Benjamin Simmons,* 1684. 12°. T.C.II 104. L, O, LW; BN, NPT.

1357 ——Sixth edition. *By R. Everingham,* 1697. 12°. L, YM; CH, MH, MU, NU.

1358 —The poor man's help to devotion. *[London], for P. Brooksby,* 1681. 8°.* Y.

1358A —Preparation for suffering. *For Josiah Blare,* 1687. 8°.* LW.

1359 —The Protestant religion truely stated. *For John Salusbury,* 1692. 12°. T.C.II 407. L, O, C, LCL, LW; CLC, MH, NPT, NU, WF, Y.

1360 [–] Qu. Whether the King. colop: *Printed, and are to be sold by Richard Janeway,* 1689. brs. Y.

1360A [–] ——[Anr. ed.] colop: *Edinburgh, re-printed,* 1689. 4°. Y.

1361 —The Quakers catechism. 1651. 4°. EN.

1362 ——[Anr. ed.] *By A. M. for Thomas Underhill and Francis Tyton,* 1655. 4°. LT, O, C, LCL, EN; BN, CU, MH, NU, PH, PSC, Y.

1363 —The Quakers catechism [sic]. —, 1655. 4°. O, OC, EN; MH, PSC.

1364 ——[Anr. ed.] *By A. M. for Thomas Underhill, and Francis Tyton,* 1656. 4°. LT, C, SP, ENC; CH, MH.

1365 ——[Anr. ed.] —, 1657. 4°. L, CT, LF, ENC; MH, PH, WF.

1366 —The ready way of confuting Mr. Baxter. colop: *For R. Janeway,* 1682. cap., 4°. O, CT; CH, CU, NU, TU, Y.

1367 —The reasons of the Christian religion. *By R. White for Fran. Titon,* 1667. 4°. L, O, C, E, DT; BN, CH, CU, MH, NU, WF, Y.

1368–9 Entries cancelled.

1370 —Reliquiæ Baxterianæ. *For T. Parkhurst, J. Robinson, J. Lawrence and J. Dunton,* 1696. fol. T.C.II 601. L, O, C, MR, EN; BN, CH, CU, LC, MH, NP, Y.

1371 —A reply to Mr. Tho. Beverley's answer. *For Tho. Parkhurst,* 1691. 4°.* LT, O, LCL, P; CH, CU, MBA, NU, WF, Y.

1372 —Richard Baxter's review of the state of Christians infants. *For Nevil Simons,* 1676. 8°. T.C.I 233. O, C.

1373 ——Second edition. *For Tho. Parkhurst,* 1700. 8°. T.C.III 166. O; Y.

1373A —The right method for a settled peace. *For T. Vnderhill, F. Tyton, and W. Raybould,* 1653. 12°. L, O, OCC, CT, LW; CH, MH, NPT, NU.

1374 ——Second edition, —. 1653. 8°. LT, O, OC, CS, E; CH, CU, NF, NU, WF.

1375 ——Third edition. *For Tho. Underhill, and Fra. Tyton,* 1657. 8°. L, O, CS, LCL, EN; BN, IU, MH, MIU, Y.

1376 ——Fourth edition. *By R. W. for Francis Tyton,* 1669. 8°. O, CP; CLC, MHS, NU.

1377 —Right rejoycing. *By R. W. and A. M. for Francis Tyton and Jane Underhil,* 1660. 4°. LT, O, C, LCL, HH; BN, CH, CU, LC, MH, NU, Y.

1378 [–] Roman tradition examined. 1676. 4°. L, O, C, OC, MC, YM; BN, CH, CLC, MBA, NPT, WF.

1379 —Mr. Baxter's rules & directions. *By H. Brugis for J. Conyers*, 1681. brs. L.

1380 [–] Sacrilegious desertion. [*London*], *printed*, 1672. 8°. T.C.I 109. L, O, LCL, LW, OC; BN, CLC, CU, MH, NU, Y.

1381 —The safe religion. *By Abraham Miller, for Thomas Underhill and Francis Tyton*, 1657. 8°. L, O, C, LCL, ENC; CH, CU, MH, NU, WF, Y.

1382 —A saint or a brute. *By R. W. for Francis Tyton, and Nevil Simmons*, 1662. 2 pts. 4°. L, O, C, LSC, E; BN, CH, CU, MH, NU, WF, Y.

1383 —The saints everlasting rest. *By Rob. Wilson, for Thomas Vnderhil and Francis Tyton*, 1649. 4°. LCL.

1383A ——[Anr. ed.] —, 1650, 4°. L, O, CT, LCL, GU; CH, CU, MH, NU, TU, Y.

1384 ——Second edition. *For Thomas Underhill and Francis Tyton*, 1651. 4°. L, O, LCL, AU; CLC, MH, NU, OCI, Y.

1385 ——Third edition. —, 1652. 4°. L, O, YM; CLC, NU, PL, WSC, Y.

1386 ——Fourth edition. —, 1653. 4°. LT, O, C, LCL, AU; IU, MBA, NPT, V, Y.

1387 ——Fifth edition. *For Thomas Vnderhill, and Francis Tyton*, 1654. 4°. L, O, LCL, CP, OC; MBA, NU, Y.

1388 ——Sixth edition. *For Thomas Underhill and Francis Tyton*, 1656. 4°. L, O, CP, LW, AU; MH.

1389 ——Seventh edition. —, 1658. 4°. L, O, C, LW, ENC; CH, CU, LC, NU, Y.

1390 ——Eighth edition. —, 1659. 4°. L, O, LW, CCA, CSS; CU, NN, Y.

1391 ——Ninth edition. *For Francis Tyton and Jane Vnderhill*, 1662. 4°. L, O, CS, GU, E; CH, MH, NU, WF, Y.

1392 ——Tenth edition. *By R. W. for Francis Tyton*, 1669. 4°. L, O, OC, ENC; CLC, NHC, NU.

1392A ——"Tenth" edition. *For Francis Tyton and Jane Underhill*, 1669. 4°. LW, CCT, D; CLC, MB, TU.

1393 ——Eleventh edition. *By R. W. for Francis Tyton and Robert Boulter*, 1671. 4°. L, O.

1394 ——"Eleventh" edition. *For Francis Tyton: and Robert Boulter*, 1677. 4°. T.C.I 284. O, LCL, LVD, BR; CLC, NPT, Y.

1395 ——Twelfth edition. *For Thomas Parkhurst; Ric. Chiswell; and Dorman Newman*, 1688. 4°. T.C.II 266. L, O, LW, EN; CLC, MH, NF, RPT.

1396 [–] Schism detected in both extreams. *For Tho. Parkhurst*, 1684. O, LW; MM.

1397 —The scripture gospel defended. *For. Tho. Parkhurst*, 1690. 8°. T.C.II 311. L, O, LCL, LW; CLC, CU, MH, NU, WF.

1398 Entry cancelled.

1399 —A search for the English schismatick. *For Nevil Simmons*, 1681. 4°.* T.C.I 427. L, O, CT, LCL, ENC; BN, LC, MH, NPT, NU, Y.

1400 —A second admonition to Mr. Edward Bagshaw. *For Nevill Simmons*, 1671. 8°. T.C.I 88. L, O, LCL, LW, E; BN, CLC, MH, NPT, NU, WF.

1401 [–] The second part against schism. *For Tho. Parkhurst*, 1684. 4°.* O; CH, MH, NU, Y.

1402 —The second part of The Nonconformists plea for peace. *For John Hancock*, 1680. 4°. T.C.I 398. O, C, LCL, LW, SP; CLC, CU, MH, NU, WF.

1403 —The second sheet for poor families. *By Robert White, for Francis Tyton; and for Nevill Simmons in Kederminster*, 1665. 8°.* L, O; Y.

1404 —A second sheet for the ministry. *By R. White for Nevil Simmons*, 1657. 8°.* L, O, C, CT, DT; BN, CU, MH, NU, PH, Y.

1405 —A second true defence. *For Nevil Simons*, 1681. 4°. T.C.I 438. L, O, CP, LW, BR; BN, CLC, CU, MH, NU, WF, Y.

1406 —Select arguments and reasons against popery. *Printed*, 1675. 4°.* O, LW; WF.

1407 —Richard Baxter's sence of the subscribed articles. colop: *For Ben. Cox*, 1689. 4°.* L, O, LCL, LW; CH, IU, NU, Y.

1408 —A sermon of judgment. *By R. W. for Nevil Simmons in Kederminster*, 1655. 12°. L, C, CT.

1409 ——[Anr. ed.] *By R. W. for Nevill Simmons in Kidderminster*, 1656. 8°. LT, O, LG, CM; CLC, WF.

1410 ——[Anr. ed.] *By R. W. for Nevil Simmons*, 1658. 8°. C; NPT.

1410A ——[Anr. ed.] 1662. 12°. GU.

1411 ——[Anr. ed.] *W. Whitwood*, 1668. 12°. BN.

1412 ——[Anr. ed.] *For Nevil Simmons*, 1672. 8°. O; CU, NU.

1413 [–] A sermon of repentance. *By R. W. and A. M. for Francis Tyton and Jane Underhil*, 1660. 4°. L, LCL; CH, CU, MBA, TU, WCL.

1414 ——[Anr. ed.] —, 1660. 4°. LT, O, CT, LW, DT; BN, CH, MH, NU, Y.

1415 ——[Anr. ed.] *By R. W. for Francis Tyton*, 1662. 4°. O, LW, D; NU, WF.

1416 —A sermon preached at the funeral of . . . John Corbet. *For Thomas Parkhurst*, [1680]. 4°.* L, O, LG, LW, E; BN, CH, CU, LC, MH, NU, Y.

1417 —Short instructions for the sick. [*n.p.*], *reprinted*, 1673. brs. L.

1417A —The substance of Mr. Cartwright's exceptions. *For Nevil Simmons and Jonath. Robinson*, 1675. 8°. O, CT, LCL, ENC; CH, MH, NU, Y.

1418 —The successive visibility of the church. *By R. W. for Nevil Simmons, and are to be sold by Francis Tyton*, 1660. 8°. L, O, CS, LW; BN, CU, MH, NU, WF, Y.

1419 —A third defence of the cause of peace. *For Jacob Sampson*, 1681. 8°. T.C.I 426. LCL, LW, CS; BN, CU, MH.

1420 —Three treatises tending to awaken secure sinners. [*London*], *to be sold by John Rothwell*, 1656. 8°. O, C, P; CLC, WF.

1421 ——[Anr. ed.] *By R. W. to be sold by Nevil Simmons, and by Nathaniel Ekins*, 1658. DC; NU.

1422 —To my dearly beloved the inhabitants of . . . Kederminster. [*n.p.*], 1662. cap., 4°. EN.

1422A —To the King's most excellent majesty. The due account. 1661. 4°.* ENC.

1423 —A treatise of conversion. *By R. W. for Nevil Simmons in Kederminster, and are to be sold by Joseph Nevil, 1657.* 4°. LT, O, C, LCL, AU; CH, MH, TU.

1424 — —[Anr. ed.] *By R. W. for Nevill Simmons in Kederminster and by Nathaniel Ekins, 1658.* 4°. LT, O, CS, LW; BN, CH, CU, MH, NF, NU, WF, Y.

1425 —A treatise of death. *By R. W. for Nev. Simmons in Kederminster, to be sold by him there, and by Tho. Johnson, 1660.* 12°. L, O, LW; MH, Y.

1425A — —[Anr. ed.] *— to be sold by Robert Boulter, 1666.* 12°. OC.

1426 — —[Anr. ed.] *For Nevil Simmons, 1672.* 12°. L, O; BN, CU, NC, NU.

1427 —A treatise of episcopacy. *For Nevil Simmons and Thomas Simmons, 1681.* 2 pts. 4°. T.C.I 414. L, O, C, E, DT; BN, CH, CU, MH, NU, WF, Y.

1428 —A treatise of justifying righteousness. *For Nevil Simmons and Jonath. Robinson, 1676.* 8°. T.C.I 215. L, O, C, E, DT; CH, CU, MH, NU, WF, Y.

1429 —A treatise of knowledge. *For Tho. Parkhurst, 1689.* 4°. T.C.II 311. L, O, LCL, LW, ENC; CH, CU, LC, MBA, NU, Y.

1430 —A treatise of self-denyall. *By Robert White, for Nevil Simmons in Kederminster, and are to be sold by him . . . and by William Gilbertson, and by Joseph Nevil, 1660.* 4°. LT, O, C, LCL, E; CH, CU, NU, WF, Y.

1431 — —Second edition. *By Robert White, for Nevil Simmons, 1675.* 8°. T.C.I 200. L, O, LW; BN, NPT, WF.

1432 —The true and only way of concord. *For John Hancock, 1680.* 8°. T.C.I 378. L, O, CS, LCL, ENC; BN, CLC, MH, NU, WF, Y.

1433 —A true believers choice and pleasure. *By R.E., 1680.* 4°. T.C.I 378. L, O, LW; TU.

1434 — —[Anr. ed.] *For John Hancock, 1680.* 12°. L, LCL; BN, CU, NPT, TU.

1435 —The true Catholick. *By A. M. for T. Underhill and F. Tyton, 1660.* 12°. LT, O, LCL, E, AU; BN, CLC, CU, IU, NU, Y.

1436 —True Christianity. *For Nevill Simmons in Kidderminster, and are to be sold by William Roybould, 1655.* 12°. LT, O, C, LCL, DC; BN, CH, NPT, Y.

1437 — —[Anr. ed.] *For Nevil Simmons in Kidderminster, 1656.* 8°. LT, O, CM; CLC, WF.

1438 —The true history of councils. *For Tho. Parkhurst, 1682.* 4°. T.C.I 506. L, O, LCL, LW, ENC; BN, CU, MH, NU, WF, Y.

1439 —Two disputations of original sin. *For Robert Gibbs, 1675.* 8°. T.C.I 204. L, O, C, LCL, E; BN, CU, MH, NU, TU.

1440 [–] Two papers of proposals concerning the discipline and ceremonies of the Church of England. *Printed, 1661.* 4°. L, O, CM, EN, DT; CH, MH, NU, TU, WF, Y.

1441 —Two sheets for poor families. *By Robert White for Francis Tyton: and for Nevill Simmons, in Kederminster, 1665.* 8°.* L, O; Y.

1442 —Two treatises: the first of death. *For Nevil Simmons, 1672.* 16°. T.C.I 106. L, O, LCL; CLC, CU, NU, WF.

1443 —Two treatises tending to awaken secure sinners. *For Jonas Luntley, 1696.* 12°. L, SP; NPT.

1444 —Universal concord. The first part. *By R. W. for Nevil Simmons, 1660.* 8°. L, O, SP; BN, CU, NPT, NU, WF, Y.

1445 —Universal redemption. *For John Salusbury, 1694.* 8°. T.C.II 509. L, O, C, LCL, ENC; CH, MH, NF, NU, Y.

1446 —The vnreasonableness of infidelity. *By R. W. for Thomas Underhill, and for F. Tyton, 1655.* 4 pts. 8°. LT, O, C, E, DT; BN, CH, CU, MH, NU, WF, Y.

1447 Entry cancelled.

1448 —The vain religion of the formal hypocrite. *By R. W. for F. Tyton, and Nevel Simmons, 1660.* 12°. L, O, LCL; BN, CU, MH, NPT, WF.

1449 Mr. Baxter's vindication of the Church of England. *For Walter Kettilby, 1682.* 4°.* L, O, C, CT, LW; CH, MH, NU, WF, Y.

1450 —Wehkomaonganoo asquam peantogig. *Cambridge [Mass.] Samuel Green kah Marmaduke Johnson, 1664.* 16°. EVANS 84. CH.

1451 — —Second edition. *Cambridge [Mass.]: by S. G. for the Corporation in London, 1688.* 16°. EVANS 440. MB, MHS, MWA, Y.

1452 —Whether parish congregations be true Christian churches. *For Thomas Parkhurst, 1684.* 4°. L, O, C, LCL, EN; CLC, MH, NU, WF, Y.

1453 —Which is the true church? *Printed, and are to be sold by Richard Janeway, 1679.* 4°. T.C.I 357. L, O, C, LCL, CT; BN, NU, WF.

1454 —A vvinding-sheet for popery. *By Robert White, for Nevil Simmons in Kederminster, 1657.* 8°. LT, O, C, LF, DT; BN, CH, MH, NU, Y.

1455 [–] The Worcester-shire petition to the Parliament. *For Tho. Vnderhill: and Francis Tyton, 1653.* 4°. LT, O, CS, EN, DT; BN, CLC, MH, NU, WF, Y.

1456 [**Baxter, Simon.**] Reasons, humbly offered to the honourable House of Commons, for bringing in a bill. *[London, 1700?]* brs. L; MH.

1457 **Baxter, William.** De analogia. *Typis R. Everingham, ac impensis T. Simmons, 1679.* 8°. T.C.I 335. L, O, C, EC, BAMB; BN, MH, WF, Y.

1458 **Bayard, Nicholas.** A journal of the late actions of the French at Canada. *For Richard Baldwin, 1693.* 4°.* L, O; CH, MH, NN, RPJ, WCL.

1459–61 Entries cancelled.

1462 —A narrative of an attempt made by the French of Canada. *colop: [New York], printed and sold by William Bradford, 1693.* fol.* EVANS 632. LPR.

1463 **Bayfield, Robert.** Enchiridion medicum: containing the causes. *By E. Tyler for Joseph Cranford, 1655.* 8°. LT, LCP, LWL, GK; WSG, HC.

1464 —Excercitationes anatomicæ. *Typis Anno Dom., 1666.* 12°. O, LM.

1465 — —[Anr. ed.] *Anno Dom., 1668,* 12°. L, O, C, LCP, LM; BN, WSG, HC.

1466 — —Second edition. *Sumptibus Dorman Newman, 1677.* 12°. T.C.I 262. O, P, EN, AU, GH; BN, WF, HC.

1467 —Της ʼιατρικης καπτος; or a treatise. *By D. Maxwel, to be sold by Richard Tomlins, 1663.* 8°. L, O, P, E, GK; BN, CLC, WSG, JF.

1468 [–] 'Ομοτροπια naturæ. 1656. *See* Bunworth, Richard.

1468 —Η' πρόβολη τῆς αληθειας. Or the bul-warke of truth. *By T. R. for Edw. Dod*, 1657. 8°. LT, LCL; CLC, NPT, JF.

1469 —Tractatus de tumoribus. *For Richard Tomlins*, 1662. 12°. L, O, C, LM, E; CLC, JF.

1469A — [Anr. ed.] *P. Parker*, 1679. 12°. LWL.

1469B [**Bayle, Pierre.**] Commentaire philosophique sur ces paroles. *A Cantorbery, chez Thomas Litwel*, 1686. 12°. DM; BN, VC, WF, Y.

1470 **Bayle, Thomas.** A relation of a man's return. [*London*, c. 1677.] 4°.* L, LF, BBN; CLC, IE, PH, PSC.

1471 —A testimony to the free and universal love of God. *Printed*, 1675. 4°.* L, C, LF, BBN; CH, MH, NC, PH, PSC.

Baylie, Robert. *See* Baillie, Robert.

1472 **Bayly, Charles.** The causes of God's wrath. *Printed*, 1665. 4°.* O, LF, BBN, EN.

1473 —Concerning the puer meek spirit of the Lamb. [*London*], *for W. M.*, [1670?]. brs. L, LF, BBN.

1473A —A seasonable warning and word of advice. *Printed*, 1663. 4°. LF, BBN; PH.

1473B —A seasonable warning to such. *Printed*, 1663. 4°. LF, BBN; CH.

1473BA —A seasonable word of advice. 1648. 4°. O.

1473C —A true and faithful warning sounded forth. *Printed*, 1663. 4°. LF, BBN; CH, PH, Y.

1474 **Bayly, Francis.** An antidote against immoderate sorrow. *By W. Godbid, for Richard Thrale*, 1660. 4°.* LT, EN, DT; MH, MWA, NU, WF.

1475 **Bayly, Lewis, *bp*.** Manitowompae pomantamoonk. *Cambridge* [*Mass.*]: *printed* [*by S. Green*], 1665. 8°. EVANS 95. O, WCA; MHS, MWA, Y.

1476 — —Second edition. *Cambridge* [*Mass.*], *for the right honerable Corperation* [*sic*] *in London*, 1685. 8°. EVANS 383. L, CS; LC, MB, MH, NN.

1477 —The practise of pietie. Thirty-first edition. *Printed at Amsterdam, by Iohn Handson*, 1642. 16°. L, C, CE, CT.

1477A — —Thirty-fourth edition. *Edinburgh, by Robert Young and Evan Tyler*, 1642. 12°. CLC.

1477B — —Thirty-fourth edition. *For Andrew Crook*, 1643. 16°. CSU, NPT.

1478 — —Thirty-first edition. *Printed*, 1648. 16°. O.

1479 —[Anr. ed.] *Printed at Delff, by Michael Stael*, 1648. 8°. NU.

1480 — —[Anr. ed.] *Edenburgh, for Andrew Wilson*, 1649. 12°. ALDIS 1376. O, EN.

1481 — —[Anr. ed.] *Amsterdam, by J. Stafford*, 1649. 32°. CT, MC; CLC, WF.

1482 — —Thirty-third edition. *For Philip Chetwin*, 1653. 12°. L; CLC.

1483 — —"Thirteenth" edition. *For Philip Chetwinde*, 1654. 12°. L.

1484 — —"Thirty-third" edition. *By S. G. for Philip Chetwind*, 1656. 12°. L; CLC, MH, NGT.

1485 — —"Thirty-fifth" edition. *Delf, by Abraham Iacobs*, [1660?]. 12°. L; CH, CU.

1486 — —Thirty-fourth edition. *For Philip Chetwinde*, 1661. 1661. 12°. L; WF.

1486A — —[Anr. ed.] —, 1663, 12°. NF.

1486B — —[Anr. ed.] *For P. Chetwind*, 1665. 12°. CLC.

1487 — —Thirty-fifth edition. *For Philip Chetwinde*, 1669. 12°. L, OG, CT, LW; CLC, CN, NU.

1488 [–] —[Anr. ed.] *Glasgow, by Robert Sanders*, 1670, 12°. ALDIS 1907. I.

1489 — —[Anr. ed.] *For Philip Chetwinde*, 1672. 8°. O, C; NU.

1490 — —"Thirty-third" edition. 1672. 8°. O, C.

1490A — —Thirty-fourth edition. *Edinburgh, R. Young and E. Tyler*, 1672. 12°. EN.

1491 — —"Thirteenth" edition. *For Philip Chetwinde*, 1675. 16°. L, LLP.

1491A — —[Anr. ed.] *Rotterdam, for Gerard van der Viuyn*, 1675. 12°. CLC.

1492 — —[Anr. ed.] 1678. 12°. RPL.

1492A — —[Anr. ed.] *For Philip Chetwind*, 1679. 12°. CLC, IU.

1493 — —"Thirty-second" edition. –1680. 12°. L, CT.

1494 — —Thirty-fifth edition. *Amsterdam, for Mercy Browninge*, 1680. 12°. L.

1495 — —Forty-fifth edition. *For Philip Chetwinde*, 1680. 12°. CT, ENC, DT.

1495A — —Thirty-fifth edition. *For the widdow Chitwin, sold by Samuel Lee*, 1683. 12°. L.

1496 — —[Anr. ed.] *Sold by E. Brewster*, 1684. 24°. T.C.II 89. DC.

1497 [–] —[Anr. ed.] *For Edward Brewster*, 1685. 8°. L, O, LSC; NU, WF.

1498 [–] —Fortieth edition. —, 1687. 12°. O.

1499 — —[Anr. ed.] *For Edward Brewster*, 1689. 12°. L, O.

1500 — —"Thirty-fifth" edition. *Printed*, 1690. 12°. IU.

1501 — —"Forty-first" edition. 1692. W. FREELOVE.

1502 — —Forty-second edition. *For Edward Brewster*, 1695. 12°. L, AN; WF.

1503 — —[Anr. ed.] —, 1699. 12°. LW.

1504 —Yr Ymarter o dduwioldeb. *Gan Sarah Griffin tros Philip Chetwind*, 1656. 12°. AN.

1505 — —[Anr. ed.] *Printiedieg yn Llundin gan Tho. Dawks, dros Ph. Chetwin*, 1675. 8°. L, AN, CPL.

Bayly, Robert. *See* Baillie, Robert.

1506 **Bayly, Thomas.** Certamen religiosum: or, a conference. [*London*], *by H. Hils, to be sold by George Whittington, John Williams and Edw. Blackmore*, 1649. 8°. LT, O, C, E, DT; BN, CH, LC, NU, TU, Y.

1507 [–] —[Anr. ed.] *For W. Lee, and R. Royston*, 1651. 4°. L, O, CE, E, ENC; BN, CH, CN, NU, WF, Y.

1508 [–] —[Anr. ed.] —, 1652. 4°. L, O, CP, LW, DT; LC, NPT, NU, WSC, Y.

1509 [–] —[Anr. ed.] [*London*], *by H. Hills for John Williams and E. Blackworth*, 1662. 12°. GK.

1510 —An end to controversie. *Printed at Doway*, 1654. 4°. L, O, CT, DC, GU; CH, NU, TU, WF, Y.

1511 —Herba parietis: or, the wall-flower. *By J. G. to be sold by John Holden*, 1650. fol. LT, O, AN, CT, YM; CH, CN, PL, WF, Y.

1512   [–] A legacie left to Protestants. *Dowa[Douai], printed,* 1654. 4°. LT, CT; Y.

1513   —The life & death of . . . John Fisher. *Printed,* 1655. 8°. LT, O, C, LL, LVF; BN, CH, CN, MH, NU, Y.

1514   —The royal charter granted unto kings, by God himself. *Printed,* 1649. 8°. LT, O, C, AN, E; BN, CH, CU, MH, NU, WF, Y.

1514A   — [Anr. ed.] —, 1656. 8°. L, CT, YM, AN; CLC.

1514B   — [Anr. ed.] *For Robert Crofts,* 1660. 8°. WC.

1515   — [Anr. ed.] *For W.Leach,* 1682. 4°. T.C.I 482. L, O, CT, LL, SA; CH, MH, NC, PU, Y.

1516   —The wall-flower. As it grew. *By I.G., and are to be sold by Peter Parker,* 1679. fol. CLC, MH, NU.

1517   **Bayly, William.** A collection of the several wrightings [*sic*] of. [*London*], *printed,* 1676. 4°. L, O, C, LF, E; BN, CH, NU, PH, Y.

1518   —An arrovv shot against Babylon. *Printed,* 1663. 4°.* L, LF, BBN; MH, PH, PSC, WF, Y.

1519   —The blood of righteous Abel. *For M.W.,* [1659]. 4°.* L, LF, BBN; PH.

1520   [–] A brief declaration to all the world. [*London*], *for W.M.,* 1662. 4°.* L, LF.

1521   —A call and visitation from the Lord God. [*London*], *printed,* 1673. 4°.* L, O, C, LF, BBN; MH, PH, PL, WF, Y.

1522   —Deep calleth unto deep. *Printed,* 1663. 4°. L, LF, BBN, BP; MH, PH, PSC, Y.

1523   —The dreadful, and terrible, day. [*n.p.,* 1665?] 4°.* L, LF, BBN; PH, PSC.

1524   —An epistle general containing wholsome exhortations. [*London*], *printed,* 1664. 4°.* L, O, OC, LF, BBN; CH, MH, NU, PH, Y.

1524A   — [Anr. ed.] —, 1676. 4°.* WF.

1525   —A faithful testimony and warning. [*London*], *printed,* 1672. 4°.* L, O, C, LF, BBN; CLC, NC, PH, WF, Y.

1525A   —A few seasonable words. [*London*], *for M.W.,* 1663. brs. LF, BBN.

1526   —For the king and Parliament, and his Covncel and teachers. [*n.p.*], *printed,* 1664. 4°.* L, LF, BBN; IE, NU, PH, Y.

1527   —A general epistle to all Friends. colop: [*n.p.*], *for W.M.,* [1662]. cap., 4°.* L, LF, BBN; MH, PH, PL, Y.

1528   —The great & dreadful day. [*London,* 1664.] cap., 4°.* L, O, LF, MIU, PSC.

1529   —A grievous lamentation. *Printed,* 1663. 4°.* L, O, LF, BBN, BP; CH, MH, NU, PH, Y.

1530   —Iacob is become a flame. [*London,* 1662?] cap., 4°.* L, LF, BBN; MH, PH, PSC, Y.

1531   —The lambs government. *Printed,* 1663. 4°.* L, LF, BBN; MH, NU, PH, PSC, Y.

1532   —The life of Enoch again revived. *For Thomas Simmons,* 1662. 4°.* L, O, LF, BBN, EN; CLC, MH, PH, WF, Y.

1533   —A message sent forth from the risen seed of God. colop: [*London*], *for W.M.,* 1662. 4°.* L, LF; MH, PH, PSC, Y.

1534   —Pure encouragements from the spirit of the Lord. [*London,* 1664.] 4°.* L, LF, BBN; CLC, IE, MH, PH, Y.

1535   [–] Seven thunders vttering their voices. [*London,* 1665]. cap., 4°.* L, O, LF, BBN; CH, MBP, PH, PSC, Y.

1536   —A short discovery of the state of man. *For Mary Westwood,* 1659. 4°.* L, LF.

1537   —A short relation or testimony. *For Mary Westwood,* 1659. 4°.* LT, O, LF; PSC.

1538   [–] Some words given forth. colop: [*n.p.*], *for W.M.,* [1662]. cap., 4°.* L, LF, BBN; PL, PSC, Y.

1539   —A testimony against drunkenness. [*London*], *printed,* 1675. 4°.* LF; PH, PSC.

1540   [–] A testimony of truth against all the sowers. *Printed,* 1667. 4°.* L, O, LF, BBN; CH, MH, NU, PH, Y.

1541   —To the camp of Israel. *Printed,* 1663. 4°.* L, OC, BBN; MH, PL, Y.

1542   —The true Christ ovvned. *Printed,* 1667. 4°.* L, O, LF, BBN; MH, PH, Y.

1543   —A vindication of the commands and doctrine of Christ Jesus. colop: [*London*], *for W.M.,* [1663]. 4°.* L, LF, BBN; MH, PSC.

1543A   —A warning from the Lord. colop: *For Mary Westwood,* 1659. 4°.* LF; MH.

1544   —A warning from the spirit of truth. *Printed,* 1658. 4°. C, LF, OC, BBN; CLC, PH, PSC.

1545   —A word from the Lord. [*London,* 1659.] cap., 4°.* L, C, LF, BBN, EN; MH, PH, PSC.

1545A   **Bayne, James.** Unto His Majesties high commissioner. The petition of. [*Edinburgh,* 1695.] brs. EN.

1545B   **Bayne, Rudolph.** In proverbia Salomonis. 1660. fol. O.

1545C   **Baynes, Paul.** A commentarie upon the first chapter of the Epistle . . . to the Ephesians. *Printed,* 1643. fol. GU; NU, Y.

1546   —A commentary upon the whole Epistle . . . to the Ephesians. Fifth edition. *For S. Miller, Tho. Davies, & H. Mortlock,* 1658. L, LW, LLL, ENC; LC, MWA, V.

1547   —The diocesans trial. [*London*], *printed,* 1641. 4°. L, CE, LCL, BR; CLC, MH, NU, WF.

1548   — [Anr. ed.] *For John Bellamie,* 1644. 4°. L, O, C, E; MH, NU, TU.

1549   —An entire commentary vpon the vvhole Epistle of the Apostle Pavl to the Ephesians. *By M.F. for R. Milbourne, and I. Bartlet,* 1643, fol. L, CT, DCH, ENC; CH, MH, NU, WF.

1550   — —[Anr. ed.] *By M. Flesher for I. B. to be sold by Samuel Gellibrand,* 1647. fol. L, O, CCA, P, E; MU.

1551   **Baynton, Sir Edward.** A letter to the Earle of Pembroke. *For Thomas Creake,* 1642. 4°.* LT.

1552   — — [Anr. ed.] —, 1643. 4°.* L, BR; Y.

     Be it enacted. [1650.] *See* England. Parliament.

1552A   Be it kend to all men. [*Edinburgh?* 1700]. brs. HH.

1553   Be it knowne and declared to all the world, that these ministers. [*n.p.,* 1649.] LT, OP.

1554   Be it knowne and declared to all the world, that these ministers, . . . since the former publishing. [*n.p.,* 1649.] brs. LT.

1554A   Be it known unto all men. [*Dublin?* 1655]. brs. L.

     Be it ordained. 1644. *See* England. Parliament.

1555 Be merry and wise. *Printed March* 13, 1660. 4°.* LT, O, HH; CH, MIU, NU, WF.

1555A Be valiant still . . . A new song. [*London*, 1670?] brs. L, EN.

Be ye also ready. 1694. *See* Wetenhall, Edward, *bp.*

1556 [**Beacher, Lyonell.**] Wonders if not miracles. *Printed*, 1665. 4°.* O, EN; CLC.

Beacon flameing. 1652. *See* Cheynell, Francis.

Beacon set on fire. 1652. *See* Fawne, Luke.

Beacons quenched. 1652. *See* Pride, Thomas.

1557 **B[eadle], J[ohn].** The journal or diary of a thankful Christian. *By E. Cotes, for Tho. Parkhurst*, 1656. 8°. LT, O, CT, LCL; IU, MHS, NPT, NU, WF.

1558 **B[eale], J[ohn].** The Herefordshire orchards. *By R. Daniel*, 1657. 8°. L, O, OB; MH, MHO, WDA.

1558A —Letters about improvements. 1677. 4°. O; WU.

1559 **Beale, Thomas.** A bloudy plot, brought to life. [*London*], *printed*, 1641. 4°.* L; CH.

1559A ——[Anr. ed.] A true discovery of a bloody plott. *For the author, to be sold by Henry Walker*, 1641. 4°.* L, O, EC; CLC, WF.

1560 [**Bealing, Benjamin.**] An epistle from the meeting for sufferings. [*London*, 1696.] cap., 8°.* L, LF; CH, MH, MU.

1560A [–] The epistle to the monthly and quarterly meetings. [*London*, 1692.] fol.* Y.

1560B ——[Same title.] [1693.] fol.* OC; MH.

1560C ——[Same title.] [1695.] fol.* Y.

1560D Beams of divine light. *Sold by William Marshall*, 1700. 12°. T.C.II 209. LW; NP.

1560E Beams of divine love. [*London*, 1660.] cap., fol.* OP.

Beames of eternal brightness. 1661. *See* Perrot, John.

Beames of former light. 1660. *See* Nye, Philip.

1561 [**Beane, Richard.**] A discourse concerning Popish perjurers. *For H. Brome*, 1681. 4°.* T.C.I 443. L, O; CH, NIC, WF, Y.

1562 ——[Anr. ed.] *Dublin, reprinted*, 1681. 4°.* DIX 184. C, DT, CD.

1563 **Beare, Nicolas.** Metamorphosis Christiana. *For James Collins*, 1679. 4°.* O; MM.

1564 —The resurrection founded on justice. *For Thomas Helder*, 1700. 8°. T.C.III 167. L, O, DC, DT; Y.

1565 **Beard, Thomas.** The theatre of Gods judgements. Fourth edition. *By S.I. & M.H. and are to be sold by Thomas Whitaker*, 1648. fol. L, CE, CK, ENC, ES; CH, MH, NU, TU, WF, Y.

Beast that was. 1659. *See* Howet, Henoch.

Beaten oyle. 1641. *See* Womock, Laurence, *bp.*

1566 Beatis manibus invictissimi herois Olivarii Cromwelli. *Excudebat J.B. impensis Edvardi Brewster*, 1659. fol.* LT; MM.

1567 **Beaton, John.** Synonyma: sive, copia. *Excudebat J.Y. impensis Gulielmi Adderton*, 1647. 12°. L, C, DCH, AN; NN, Y.

1568 **Beaton, Nehemiah.** No treason to say, kings are Gods subjects. *For S. Gellibrand*, 1661. 4°. LCL, OM; NU.

Beau defeated. [1700.] *See* Pix, *Mrs.* Mary.

Beavfrons. 1681. *See* Jenner, David.

1569 **Beaulieu, Jean de.** Sale of stock of books. [*n.p.*, 1699?] 4°. L.

1570 **B[eaulieu], L[uke de].** Claustrum animæ. 1671. 8°. O; CLC.

1571 ——[Anr. ed.] *For Henry Brome*, 1677–1676. 2 pts 12°. T.C.I 251. L, O, C, OM, E; CH, MH, NU, WF, Y.

1572 [–] A discourse shewing that Protestants are on the safer side. *For Richard Chiswell*, 1687. 4°.* L, O, C, EN, DT; CH, MH, NU, TU, WF, Y.

1573 [–] The history of the Romish inquisition. *For William Whitewood*, 1700. 8°. Y.

1574 [–] The holy inquisition. *For Joanna Brome*, 1681. 8°. T.C.I 461. L, O, CS, OM, P; CLC, CN, NU, TU, WF.

1575 —The reformed monastery. Second edition. *For Henry Brome*, 1678. 12°. T.C.I 336. L, CT, LSC; CLC, NNG, WF, Y.

1575A ——Third edition. *For Charles Brome*, 1688. 12°. LIC.

1576 ——Fourth edition. —, 1649. [i.e., 1699] 12°. T.C.III 162. L, LW, EN; CLC, NU.

1577 —A sermon preach'd . . . December the 27th 1685. *By T. Moore, for Charles Brome*, 1686. 4°.* T.C.II 156. L, O, CS, OM, BAMB; CLC, MBA, NU, Y.

1578 —Take heed of both extremes. *For Henry Brome*, 1675. 8°. T.C.I 205. L, O, EN.

1579 —The terms of peace. *For Charles Brome*, 1684. 4°.* L, O, CS, WCA, BAMB; NU.

1580 [**Beaumont,   .**] The emblem of ingratitude. A true relation. *For William Hope*, 1672. 8°. T.C.I 114. L, OC; WF, Y.

1581 **Beaumont, Francis.** Comedies and tragedies. *For Humphrey Robinson, and for Humphrey Mosely*, 1647. fol. L, O, C, LVD, E; CH, CN, MH, TU, WF, Y.

1582 —Fifty comedies and tragedies. *By I. Macock, for Iohn Martyn, Henry Herringman, Richard Marriot*, 1679. fol. T.C.I 344. L, O, C, E, DT; BN, CH, CN, LC, MH, NP, TU, Y.

1583 —The beggars bush. *For Humphrey Robinson and Anne Mosely*, 1661. 4°.* L, O, LVD; CH, CN, MH, WF, Y.

1584 —Bonduca. *For Richard Bentley*, 1696. 4°. T.C.II 590. L, O, AN; CH, CN, MH, TU, WF, Y.

1585 —The elder brother. Second edition. *For Humphrey Moseley*, 1650. 4°. O, CT; Y.

1586 —"Second" edition. *For Humphrey Moseley*, 1651. 4°. L, O, CT, LVD; CH, CN, LC, MH, TU, Y.

1587 ——[Anr. ed.] *Printed*, 1661. 4°. L, O; CH, LC, MH, TU, Y.

1588 ——[Anr. ed.] *By T.N. for D.N. and T.C. to be sold by George Marriott*, 1678. 4°. T.C.I 296. L, OW, CPE; CH, MB, MH, WF, Y.

—Humorous lieutenant. 1697. *See* Fletcher, John.

1589 —A king and no king. Fifth edition. *For William Leak*, 1655. 4°. L, O, OC; CH, MB, TU, WF, Y.

1590 ——"Fourth" edition. *Printed*, 1661. 4°. L, O, LVD; CH, MH, V, WF, Y.

1591 ——[Anr. ed.] *By Andr. Clark, for William and John Leake*, 1676. 4°. T.C.I 240. L, O, OW; CU, MH, NN, TU, WF, Y.

1592   ——[Anr. ed.] *For R. Bentley*, 1693. 4°. O, OW, EN;
        CH, MH, TU, WF, Y.

1593   —The loyal subject. *For H. N. to be sold by W. Keble,*
        [1700?] 4°. L, OW; MB, MH, WF, Y.

1594   —The maids tragedie. Fifth edition. *By E. P. for William*
        Leake, 1641. 4°. L, O, LVF, EN; BN, CH, CU, MH, WF, Y.

1595   ——Sixth edition. *For William Leake*, 1650. 4°. L, O;
        CH, CN, LC, MH, WF, Y.

1596   ——"Sixth" edition. *Printed*, 1661. 4°. L, O, LVD;
        LC, MH, V, WF, Y.

1597   ——[Anr. ed.] *For R. Bentley and S. Magnes*, 1686.
        4°. T.C.II 190. L, O, OW, CK; CU, MB, MH, WF, Y.

1598   —Philaster. Fifth edition. *For William Leake*, 1652. 4°.
        L, O, CK, LVD, OW; CH, MB, MH, WF, Y.

1599   ——Sixth edition. *For William Leake*, [1661]. 4°.
        L, O, CS; CH, CU, LC, MH, WF, Y.

1600   ——[Anr. ed.] *For Richard Bentley, and S. Magnes*, 1687.
        4°. T.C.II 190. L, O; CLC, CU, MH, TU, WF, Y.

1601   [–] ——[Anr. ed.] *For R. Bentley*, 1695. 4°. L, O, LG, LVD,
        EN; CH, CN, LC, MH, NC, Y.

1602   —Poems. Second edition. *For Lawrence Blaiklock*, 1653.
        8°. LT; CH, CN, CU, MH, Y.

1603   ——"Second" edition. *For William Hope*, 1653. 8°. LT,
        O, OW; CLC, MH, NP, WF.

1604   ——"Second" edition. —, 1660. O; CN, NN, WF, Y.

1605   —The prophetess. *For Jacob Tonson*, 1690. 4°. L, O, CT,
        EN, DT; CH, CN, MH, NP, TU, WF, Y.

1606   —Rule a wife. *For Sam. Briscoe and sold by Richard*
        Willington, 1697. 4°. L, OW; CH, MB, OCI, WF, Y.

1607   Entry cancelled.

1608   —The scornfull lady. "Sixth" edition, [Applause] *For*
        Humphrey Moseley, 1651. 4°. O, CT, LVD, EN; CH,
        CN, MB, WF, Y.

1609   ——"Sixth" edition. [Scornfvll . . . applause.] —, 1651.
        4°. L, O; CH, MH, WF, Y.

1610   ——Seventh edition. *By A. Maxwell and R. Roberts, for*
        D. N. and T. C. to be sold by Langley Curtis, 1677.
        4°. L; MB, MH, WF, Y.

1611   ——"Seventh" edition. *By A. Maxwell and R. Roberts,*
        for D. N. and T. C. to be sold by Simon Neale, 1677.
        4°. T.C.I 285. L, CT, OW; MB, MH, WF.

1612   ——Eighth edition. *For Dorman Newman*, 1691. 4°.
        T.C.II 405. L, O, OW, CS; CU, MH, NC, PU, WF, Y.

1613   ——Tenth edition. *For J. T. to be sold by G. Harris and*
        J. Graves, J. Barnes, D. Newman, J. Harding, W. Lewis,
        and ·T. Archer, B. Lintot and E. Sanger, J. Knapton, R.
        Smith and G. Strahan, [1695?]. 4°. L, O, C, OW; CN,
        CU, MB, WF.

1614   Entry cancelled.

1615   —A song on the tragedy of Bonduca. [*London*, 1690.]
        brs. L; MH.
        —Thierry and Theodoret. 1649. *See* Fletcher, John.
        —The tragedy of Thierry. 1649. *See* Fletcher, John.

1616   —The wild-goose chase. A comedie. *For Humpherey*
        Moseley, 1652. fol. L, O, C, LVD, EN; CH, MH, TU, WF, Y.

1617   —Wit without money. Second edition. *For Andrew*
        Crooke, 1661. 4°. L, O, CK, LVD, EN; CH, MB, MH, WF, Y.

1618   [–] The woman hater. *For Humphrey Moseley*, 1648.
        4°.* L, O, C, OW, LVD; CH, CU, MH, WF, Y.

1619   ——[Anr. ed.] —, 1649. 4°.* L, O, CT, OC; CLC, CU, MH,
        TU, WF, Y.

Beaumont, Henry. *See* Harcourt, Henry.

1620   **Beaumont, John.** Considerations on a book. *For the*
        author, 1693. 4°. L, O, C, LW, DT; CJC, CLC, MU, HC.

1621   [–] ——[Anr. ed.] *For the author, to be sold by Randal*
        Taylor, 1693. 4°. L, O, LPO, CS, EC; CH, CLC, NC, WF.

1622   —A postscript to a book. colop: *To be sold by Randal*
        Taylor, 1694. 4°.* L, O.

1623   —The present state of the universe. *Sold by Randal*
        Taylor, 1694. 4°. T.C.II 509. L, O, CT; CH, CN, NP, Y.

1623A   ——[Anr. ed.] *William Whitwood*, 1696. 12°. LC.

1623B   ——Second edition. *By B. M. to be sold by W. Whit-*
        wood, 1697. 12°. T.C.III 4. L, OC; WF, Y.

1624   [**Beaumont, John**] *Lieut.-colonel.* A letter to the
        honourable Major Slingsby. [*London?* 1688.] brs. L,
        O, C, HH, EN; CH, MH, NP, PL, Y.

1625   **Beaumont, Joseph.** Psyche. *By John Dawson for*
        George Boddington, 1648. fol. L, O, C, LVD, EN; CH,
        CU, MH, WF, Y.

1626   ——[Anr. ed.] *For George Boddington*, 1651. fol. L, O,
        C, DT; CLC, MH, PH.

1627   —Remarks on Dr. Henry More's expositions. *By T. M.*
        for the author, 1690. 4°. LW.

1628   —Some observations upon the apologie of H. More.
        Cambridge, by John Field, 1665. 4°. L, O, C, D, DT;
        CH, CN, NU, OCI, WF.

1629   **Beaumont, Robert.** Loves missives to virtue. *By*
        William Godbid, 1660. 8°. L, O, CT; CH, CN, MH, WF, Y.

1630   **Beaumont, Thomas.** A speech delivered in the Com-
        mons House . . . 6. of November, 1644. *For John*
        Thomas, Novemb. 9. 1644. 4°.* LT, O, LECL; CLC, MH.

        Beau's academy. 1699. *See* Phillips, Edward.

1631   Beauteous Jenny. [*London*], *for P. Brooksby*, [1688–92].
        brs. HH.

        Beauty's cruelty. [*n.p.*, 1685–88.] *See* D'Urfey, Thomas.

1632   Beautys overthrow. [*London*], *for J. Clarke*, [1680?].
        brs. L.

1633   Beauties triumph. [*London*], *for P. Brooksby*, [1672–95].
        brs. L, HH; MH.

1634   Beauties warningpiece. [*London*], *for. J. Wright, J. Clark,*
        W. Thakery, and T. Passenger, [1650?]. brs. L.

1635   The beautiful garden of golden roses. [*London*], *by J.*
        M. for J. Deacon, [c. 1690]. CHRISTIE-MILLER.

1636   Beautiful Moggy. [*London*], *for P. Brooksby, J. Deacon,*
        J. Blare, and J. Back, [1695?]. brs. L, HH.

1637   Beautifull Nancy. [*London*], *for P. Brooksby, J. Deacon,*
        J. Blare, J. Back, [1685–92]. brs. HH.

1638   The beautiful shepherdess. *For A. M. W. O. and T.*
        Thackeray, [1685]. brs. L, O, HH.

1639   The beautiful shepherdesse of Arcadia. *For William*
        Gilbertson, [1660?]. brs. L.

1640   The beavty of godly government. [*London*], *printed*,
        1641[2]. 4°.* LT, O, C, MR, DT; MH, NU, PL, TU, WF.
        Beauty of holiness. 1683. *See* Allestree, Richard.

1640A **Beauvais, Charles de.** De disciplinis et scientiis in genere. 1648. 8°. O.

1640B —Excercitations concerning the pure and true. *By J. R. for Francis Eglesfield,* 1665. 8°. L, O; MHS.

1640C —Lettres sur la mort. *Per Tho. Newcomb, pour Tho. Whitaker,* 1649. 8°. L.

1640D —Tractatus brevis. *Typis J. Flesher, & prostant apud R. Royston,* 1662. 8°.* L, O; WF.

1640E **Beaven, Thomas.** John Plimpton's ten charges . . . answered. *Bristol: by Will. Bonny for the author,* 1696. 8°.* LF.

1641 [**Beccadelli, Lodovico.**] Vita Reginaldi Poli. *Impensis Jacobi Adamson,* 1690. 8°. T.C.II 337. L, O, CT, EN, DT; CH, CN, TU, WF, Y.

1641A [–] —[Anr. ed.] *Impensis Tho. Bennet,* 1696. 8°. OC.

1642 **Becher, Johann Joachim.** De nova temporis dimetiendi ratione. *Typis T. N. & venales prostant apud Marcum Pardoe,* 1680. 4°.* T.C.I 385. L, O, C, LR; BN, CU, PU, WF.

1643 —Magnalia naturae: or, the philosophers-stone. *By Tho. Dawks. Sold also by La. Curtiss,* 1680. 4°.* L, O, CT, GU, EO; MBA, MH, NN, WF, WU, HC.

1644 [–] —[Anr. ed.] *By Tho. Dawks,* 1686. 4°. LCP.

1645 —Minera arenaria perpetua. *Typis T. N. & venales prostant apud Marcum Pardoe,* 1680. 4°. T.C.I 385. L, GU; WF, WU.

1646 **Beck, Cave.** Le charactere universel. *Imprimé à Londres, chez A. Maxey, pour Guillaume Weekly, en Ipswich,* 1657. 8°. L, O, CS, E; CLC, WF.

1647 —The universal character. *By Tho. Maxey, for William Weekley, and and [sic] . . . in Ipswich,* 1657. 8°. LT, O, C, MR, EN; CH, CU, MB, SW, WF, Y.

Beck, John. Certain and true relation. [London], 1680. *See title.*

1648 **Beck, Margaret.** The reward of oppression. *Printed,* 1655. 4°.* LT, O; CSS.

1649 — —[Anr. ed.] *Printed,* 1656. 4°.* O; MH, MHL.

1650 **Beck, William.** The whole duty of man. *For J. Bradford,* 1700. 8°.* L.

1651 **Becket, Thomas.** The prophecie of. *For G. Freeman,* 1666. 4°. MADAN 2725. O, CT; WF, Y.

1652 **Beckham, Edward.** A brief discovery of some of the blasphemous and seditious principles. *For John Harris,* 1699. 4°.* L, O, C, LF, BBN; CH, CN, MH, NU, WF, Y.

1653 —The principles of the Quakers further shewn. *For Brabazon Aylmer,* 1700. 4°. L, O, C, LF, CT; MH, NU PH, PSC, Y.

1654 [–] The Quakers' challenge. *By H. Hills, for Edward Poole,* 1699. 4°. L, O, C, LF, BAMB; MH, MIU, PH.

—Some few of the Quakers many horrid blasphemies. 1699. *See title.*

1655 **Beckher, Daniel.** Medicus microcosmus. *Prostant apud Jo. Martin, Ja. Allestry & Tho. Dicas,* 1660. 12°. LT, O, LL, LM, E; BN, MU, WSG, WU.

1655A **Beckman, M.** A description of the royal fireworks. [London, 1688]. brs. EN.

1655B **Beckwith, Marmaduke.** A true relation of the life & death of Sarah Beckwith. [London], *printed,* 1692. 8°.* LF.

1656 **Beconsall, Thomas.** The doctrine of a general resurrection. *Oxford; by Leon Lichfield, for George West,* 1697. 4°.* L, O, C, LCL, BAMB; CLC, MBA, NU, WF, Y.

1657 —The grounds and foundation of natural religion, discover'd. *By W.O. for A. Roper, A. Bosvile; and G. West in Oxford,* 1698. 8°. L, O, CS, E, GU; CN, NU, WF, Y.

1657A Bed. ss. Ad general session. *By T. H. and sold by Henry Bonwicke,* 1685. brs. HH.

1658 **Beda, venerabilis.** Bedæ Venerabilis opera. *Typis S. Roycroft, impensis Roberti Clavell,* 1693. 4°. L, O, CT, NPL, EN; BN, CLC, NC, TU, WF, Y.

1659 —Englands old religion. *At Antwerp,* 1658. 8°. L, O, CS, LCL; CLC, CN, NU, WF.

1660 —Venerabilis Bedæ epistolæ duæ. *Dublini: Typis John Crook, sumptibus Sam. Dancer et sociorum,* 1664. 8°. DIX 124. L, O, EN, DM, DT; BN, Y.

1661 —Historiæ ecclesiasticæ. *Cantabrigiæ, excudebat Rogerus Daniel,* 1643. fol. L, O, C, EN, DT; CH, NPT, PAP, PL, Y.

1662 — —[Anr. ed.] *Cantabrigiæ, ex officina Rogeri Daniel, prostant Cornelium Bee, Londini,* 1644. fol. L, O, C, EN, DT; BN, CH, CU, MH, WF, Y.

1663 [**Beddevole, Dominique.**] Essayes of anatomy. *Edinburgh, by George Mosman,* 1691. 8°. ALDIS 3143. L, O, C, E, GH; CU, NIC, WF, WSG.

1664 — —Second edition. *For Walter Kettilby,* 1696. 8°. T.C.III 5. L, C, LCS, LWL; CH, CLC, WSG.

1665 **Bedford, James.** The perusal of an old statute. *By J. M. for Francis Tyton,* 1657. 4°. LT, O, C, LW, ENC; CLC, MH, MWA, TU, Y.

1666 [**Bedford, Samuel.**] A brief relation of the taking of Bridgewater. *For Edw. Husband, July 25,* 1645. 4°.* LT, O, BR; CH, MH, WF, Y.

1667 **Bedford, Thomas.** An examination of the chief points of Antinomianism. 1646. 4°. DT.

1668 — —[Anr. ed.] *By John Field for Philemon Stephens,* 1647. 4°. LT, O, CT, E, DT; LC, MIU, NU, Y.

1668A —The respondent Thomas Bedford's case. [London? 1678]. brs. Y.

1669 —Some sacramentall instructions. *By R. C. for William Hope,* 1649. 12°. LT, LW, DT.

1670 —Vindiciæ gratiæ sacramentalis, duobus. *Typis Guil. Du-Gard,* 1650. 8°. O, CSSX, LW, E, DT; CLC, IU, NU, WF.

1670A **Bedford, William.** Concio ad clerum. *Typis R. R., impensis Gulielmi Rogers,* 1698. 4°.* T.C.III 79–80. LG, EC, BAMB.

1671 —Two sermons preach'd. *For S. Manship,* 1698. 4°. T.C.III 79. L, C.

1672 **Bedford, William Russell, earl of.** A letter written from. *For Hugh Perry, Septemb.* 15. 1642. 4°.* LT, O, C, BR, AN; CH, CLC, MH.

1673 —A relation of the actions of the Parliaments forces. *For E. Husbands and J. Franck, Sept.* 13. [1642]. 4°.* LT, BR; MH.

1674 The Bedford-shire widow. [*London*], *for P.Brooksby, J. Deacon, J.Blare, and J.Back*. [1689–92]. brs. L, CM, HH; MH.

1674A Bedlam broke loose. *Printed*, 1677. 4°.* L.

1675 **Bedle, Joseph.** A sermon preached . . . on the fifth of November . . . 1678. *By R.Everingham for W. Kettilby*, 1679. 4°.* L, O, E; CH, MBA, WF, Y.

1676 **Bedloe, William.** The excommunicated prince. *For Tho. Parkhurst, D.Newman, Tho. Cockerill, and Tho. Simmons*, 1679. fol. L, O, C, BR, HH; CH, CN, LC, MH, TU, Y.

1677 —A narrative and impartial discovery of the horrid popish plot. *For Robert Boulter, John Hancock, Ralph Smith, and Benjamin Harris*, 1679. fol.* T.C.I 358. L, O, C, LL, EN; BN, CN, CH, LC, MH, NU, Y.

1678 **Bee, Cornelius.** Mr. Bee's answer to Mr. Poole's second vindication. [*n.p.*, 1668.] cap., fol.* O.

1679 **Beech, William.** An alarum to London: or, the famous London's blowing up. *By Matthew Simmons*, 1650. 4°.* LT, LG, HH; CN, NU.

1680 —More sulphur for basing. *For Iohn Wright*, 1645. 4°.* LT, YM, DT; CH, NU, TU.

1681 [–] A nevv light-house at Milford. [*n.p.*, *for the author*, 1650. 4°.* L.

1682 [–] A plot from Edom. *For Iohn Walker*, 1649. 8°. LT.

1683 [–] A view of Englands present distempers. *For William Raybould*, 1650. 8°. L.

1684 **Beecher, E.** The Christian school. *By T.D. for the author, sold by Hen. Broom*, 1676. 8°. L, LSC; CH.

1685 **Beecher, Henry.** Two petitions from the kingdome of Ireland. *For J. Reynor*, 1641. 4°.* L, O, HH; CH, CLC, IU, WF, Y.

1686 [**Beeck, J.**] The triumph-royal: containing. *For Hen. Rhodes and John Harris*, 1692. 8°. T.C.II 410. L, O, LG, EN; CLC, WF, Y.

1686A **B[eeckman], D[aniel].** A proposal of an inland exchange. [*London*, 1696]. brs. LUG.

1687 —To the honourable the Commons . . . Proposals humbly offered to lay down a method. [*London*, 1695.] 4°.* L.

1688 —To the honourable the Commons. . . . Proposals humbly offered to raise five hundred thousand pounds. [*London*, 1695?] cap., 4°.* L, O, GH; CH, CU, MH, WF, Y.

1689 **Beedome, Thomas.** Poems, divine, and hvmane. *By E.P. for Iohn Sweeting*, 1641. 8°. L, O; CH, MB, MH, Y.
      Beekham, Edward. *See* Beckham, Edward.

1689A **Beeland, Humphrey.** Gods eternal decree. *By Thomas Symmons*, 1659. 4°. OC.

1690 **Beere, Serj. Maj.** An exact relation of the defeat given to a party. [*n.p.*], *for Andrew Coe*, 1644. 4°.* LT.

1690A **Beerman, William.** Sorrow upon sorrow. *For F. Smith*, 1674. 4°.* LW.

1691 **Beesley, Henry.** Ψυχομαχια, or, the soules conflict. *For P. Brown*, 1656. 8°. O; NU.

1692 ——[Anr. ed.] *For Henry Brome*, 1657. 8°. LT; MH, NPT.

1692A ——[Anr. ed.] *For the use and benefit of Thomas Gibbes*, 1660. 8°. YM; CLC.

1693 ——[Anr. ed.] [*n.p.*] *For T.G.*, 1661. LSC, CE.

1694 **Beeston, Henry.** A poem to his most excellent majesty, Charles the Second. *By Edward Husbands, and Thomas Newcomb*, 1660. fol.* LT, O; TU, Y.

1695 **Beeston, Sir William.** [Proclamations] by the honourable. colop: *Re-printed at Edinburgh*, 1699. fol.* ALDIS 3895. EN; RPJ.

1696 **Beevan, John.** A loving salutation. colop: *For Thomas Simmons*, 1660. 4°.* L, LF, OC, BBN; CH, NU, PH, PSC, Y.
      Before the Lords second coming. [*n.p.*], 1650. *See* Douglas, *Lady* Eleanor.

1696A **Begg, Alexander.** A new years gift. [*London*], *printed*, 1686. brs. O.
      Beggars chorus. [*n.p.*, 1670?] *See* Brome, Richard.

1697 The beggars delight. [*London*], *for P.Brooksby*, [1680?]. brs. L, HH; MH.

1698 —[Anr. ed.] *For J. Dean;* 1684. brs. O; CLC.

1699 The beggars wedding. *For R. C.*, 1676. brs. L; MH.
      Beginning and progress. 1691. *See* Stephens, Edward.

1700 The beginning of civil-warres in England. *For J. Tompson, July 9.* 1642. 4°.* O, CCL; CH, MH, MIU, Y.
      Beginning, progresse, and conclusion. 1649. *See* C., F.

1701 The beginning, progress and end of man. *By B. Alsop*, 1650. brs. LT, O; MH.

1702 The beginning; progresse, and increase of the sect. *By Francis Leach*, 1646. 4°.* LT, DT; CH, CLC, NU.

1703 **Béguin, Jean.** Tyrocinium chymicum: or, chymical essays. *For Thomas Passenger*, 1669. 8°. T.C.I 9. L, O, C, LCS, GU; CH, LC, MH, WU, Y.

1704 The behaviour and execution of Robert Green. *For L. C.*, 1678/9. 4°.* L; CH, WF.

1705 The behaviour, confession, and execution of four prisoners. 1685. fol. O.

1706 The behaviour, confession, & execution of the several prisoners. *Printed*, 1679. 4°.* LG; NN, NU, WF.

1707 The behaviour, confession, and execution of the twelve prisoners. [*London*], *for C.L.*, 1678/9. 4°.* LG; MH, NN, NU.
      Behaviour, last dying words, . . . of John Hutchins. [*n.p.*, 1684]. *See* Smith, Samuel.

1708 The behaviour, last speeches, confessions, and execution of the prisoners. *For L. C.*, 1678/9. 4°.* MH, NU.

1708A The behaviour, last words, and execution of the five grand Jesuits. [*London*, 1679]. cap., fol.* OC; CH, CLC, WF, Y.

1708B The behaviours, last words, no-confession . . . Richard Langhorne. [*London*, 1679]. cap., fol.* C; CH.

1709 The behaviour of Mr. Will. Staley in Newgate. *For R. G.*, 1678. 4°.* L, CT; MH, MIU, Y.

1710 The behaviour, confessions, last speeches, and execution of seven notorious malefactors. colop: *For Langley Curtis*, 1683. fol.* O, HH; MH, WF.
      Beheaded Dr. John Hewytts ghost. 1659. *See* Prynne, William.

Behemoth. 1680. *See* Hobbes, Thomas.

Behmen, Jacob. *See* Böhme, Jakob.

1711 **Behn, *Mrs.* Aphra.** The histories and novels of. *For S. Briscoe,* 1696. 8°. T.C.II 578. L, O, EN; CH, CLC, MH, Y.

1711A —Histories, novels, and translations. Second volume. *By W.O. for S. B. and sold by M. Brown,* 1700. 8°. CH, IU, LC, Y.

1712 —All the histories and novels. Third edition. *For Samuel Briscoe,* 1698. 8°. T.C.III 38. O, A; CH, CU, MIU, NP, Y.

1713 — —Fourth edition. *For R. Wellington, to be sold by R. Tuckyr,* 1699. 8°. PU, TU.

1714 —The histories and novels of. Fourth edition. *For R. Wellington, and are to be sold by R. Tuckyr,* 1700. 8°. CLC, CN, NNC, WF.

1715 —Abdelazar. *For J. Magnes and R. Bentley,* 1677. 4°. L, O, OW, EN; CH, CN, MH, TU, WF, Y.

1716 — —[Anr. ed.] *For Thomas Chapman,* 1693. 4°. L, O, HH; CLC, MH, TU, WF, Y.

—Agnes de Castro. 1688. *See* Brilhac, J. B. de.

1717 —The amorous prince. *By J. M. for Thomas Dring,* 1671. 4°. T.C.I 80. L, O, CCA, LG, EN; CH, CN, MH, TU, WF, Y.

1718 [–] The amours of Philander and Silvia. *Printed,* 1687. 12°. CH, IU, LC, MB, Y.

1719 —The city-heiress. *For D. Brown, and T. Benskin, and H. Rhodes,* 1682. 4°. T.C.I 495. L, O, OW, EN; CH, CN, LC, MH, WCL, WF, Y.

1719A — —[Anr. ed.] *For Richard Wellington,* 1698. 4°. T.C.III 102. L, O; MH, NC.

1720 — —[Anr. ed.] *For Richard Wellington, sold by Percival Gilborne and Bernard Lintott,* 1698. 4°. CLC, MH, NP, WF, Y.

1721 —A congratulatory poem to her . . . Majesty. *For Will. Canning,* 1688. 4°.* L, O; CH, MH, TU, Y.

1722 — —[Anr. ed.] *Edinburgh, by the heir of Andrew Anderson,* 1688. 4°.* ALDIS 2748. C, AU; CN, Y.

1723 —A congratulatory poem to . . . Queen Mary. *By R. E. for R. Bentley, and W. Canning,* 1689. fol.* L, O, OP, AU; CH, CN, MH, TU, WF, Y.

1724 —A congratulatory poem to the king's . . . on the happy birth of the Prince of Wales. colop: *For W. Canning,* 1688. brs. L, O; MH, TU, Y.

1725 Entry cancelled.

—The counterfeit bridegroom. 1677. *See* Middleton, Thomas.

—Debauchee. 1677. *See* Brome, Richard.

1726 —The Dutch lover. *For Thomas Dring,* 1673. 4°. T.C.I 151. L, O, OW, EN; CH, CN, LC, MH, NC, TU, WCL, Y.

1727 —The emperor of the moon. *By R. Holt for Joseph Knight and Francis Saunders,* 1687. 4°. T.C.II 200. L, O, OW; CH, MH, NN, WF, Y.

1728 — —Second edition. —, 1688. 4°. T.C.II 217. L, O, LG, LVF, EN; CH, LC, MH, TU, WF, Y.

1729 —The fair jilt. *By R. Holt, for Will. Canning,* 1688. 4°. L, O; CH, LC, MH, Y.

1730 —The false count. *By M. Flesher for Jacob Tonson,* 1682. 4°. L, O, OW; CH, CN, LC, MH, WCL, Y.

1731 — —[Anr. ed.] *For Jacob Tonson,* 1697. 4°. L, O, EN; MH, WF.

1732 —A farce call'd The false count. *By M. Flesher for Jacob Tonson,* 1682. 4°. MH.

1733 —The feign'd curtizans. *For Jacob Tonson,* 1679. 4°. T.C.I 350. L, O, OW, EN; BN, CH, CN, LC, MH, TU, WCL, Y.

1734 —The forc'd marriage. *By H.L. and R.B. for James Magnus,* 1671. 4°. T.C.I 66. L, O, CCA, OW, EN; CH, LC MH, WF, Y.

1735 — —Second edition. *For James Knapton,* 1688. 4°. T.C.II 223. O; CH, CN, MH, TU, WF, Y.

1736 — —[Anr. ed.] —, 1690. 4°. L, O, OW.

1737 —The history of the nun. *For A. Baskerville,* 1689. 12°. L; Y.

1738 —The lady's looking-glass. *By W. Onley, for S. Briscoe,* 1697. 8°.* L; CU.

1739 [–] The lives of sundry notorious villains. *For the author, and sold by Sam. Crouch,* 1678. 12° T.C.I 289. L, O; CLC, Y.

1740 [–] Love letters between a noble-man and his sister. *Printed, and are to be sold by Randal Taylor,* 1684. 12°. T.C.II 49. O; LC, TU, Y.

1741 — —[Anr. ed.] *For J. Hindmarsh and J. Tonson,* 1693. 3V. 12°. T.C.II 503. L, O; CH, WF, Y.

1742 — —[Anr. ed.] *For J. H., J. T., sold by T. Bennett,* 1694. 8°. PU.

1743 [–] Love letters between Polydorus the Gothick king. *Paris, J. Lyford,* 1689. 8°. O; MH, Y.

1743A [–] Love letters from a nobleman . . . second part. *For Jacob Tonson, and Joseph Hindmarsh,* 1693. 12°. T.C.II 529. DT; CH, Y.

1744 —The luckey chance. *By R. H. for W. Canning,* 1687. 4°. T.C.II 187. L, O, C, OW, EN; CH, CU, LC, MH, NP, WCL, Y.

1745 —The lucky mistake. *For R. Bentley,* 1689. 12° T.C.II 251. L; CLC, MH.

[–] Lycidus. 1688. *See* Tallemant, Paul.

1746 —Memoirs on the court of the King at Bantam. *For Samuel Briscoe,* 1697.* NP.

[–] Miscellany, being a collection of poems. 1685. *See* title.

[–] La montre. 1686. *See* Bonnecorse, Balthazar de.

1747 [–] A new song sung in Abdelazar. [*London?* 1695]. brs. L.

1748 Entry cancelled.

1749 —Oroonoko. *For Will. Canning,* 1688. 8°. L, O, HH; CH, PBL, TU, WF, Y.

[–] Perplex'd prince. [1682.] *See* S., T.

1750 —A pindarick on the death of our late sovereign. *By J. Playford, for Henry Playford,* 1685. fol.* T.C.II 126. L, O, OC, HH; CH, CU, MH, TU, WF, Y.

1751 — —Second edition. —, 1685. fol.* L, O, CS, OP; CU, MH, TU, WF, Y.

1752 ——[Anr. ed.] *Dublin, reprinted by Andrew Crook and Samuel Helsham,* [1685?] 4°.* DIX 211. O, DT; CU, MH, WF, Y.

1753 —A pindarick poem on the happy coronation. *By J. Playford for Henry Playford,* 1685. fol.* L, O, OB, HH; CH, CN, MH, NC, TU, WF, Y.

1754 —A pindaric poem to the reverend Doctor Burnet. *For R. Bentley, and are to be sold by Richard Baldwin,* 1689. 4°.* L, O; CN, MH, WF.

1755 —A poem humbly dedicated to the great patern of piety . . . Catherine. *By J. Playford for Henry Playford,* 1685. fol.* T.C.II 126. L, O, OC, OP; CH, MH, NP, TU, WF, Y.

1756 —A poem to Sir Roger L'Estrange. *For Randal Taylor,* 1688. 4°.* L, O; CLC, MH, TU.

1757 —Poems upon several occasions. *For R. Tonson and J. Tonson,* 1684. 8°. T.C.II 73. L, O, LVD, DT; CH, CN, MH, TU, WF, Y.

1758 ——Second edition. *For Francis Saunders,* 1697. 8°. L, LVD, A.

1759 —A prologue by . . . to her new play, called Like father. colop: *For J.V.,* 1682. brs. MC, EN; CH, MH.

1759A —Prologue spoken by Mrs. Cook. colop: *For Charles Tebroc,* [1684]. brs. L; CLC.

1760 —Prologue to Romulus. colop: *By Nath. Thompson,* 1682. brs. L, O, EN; CH, MH, WF, Y.

1761 —The Roundheads. *For D. Brown, and T. Benskin, and H. Rhodes,* 1682. 4°. T.C.I 473. L, O, OW, EN; CH, CN, LC, MH, WCL, WF, Y.

1762 ——[Anr. ed.] *For Richard Wellington, and sold by Percival Gilborne and Bernard Lintott,* 1698. 4°. L, O, CS; CN, MH, NIC, WF, Y.

1763 [–] The rover. *For John Amery,* 1677. 4°. T.C.I 291. L, O, OW, LVF, EN; CH, CN, LC, MH, TU, WF, Y.

1764 ——Second edition. *By J. Orme, for R. Wellington,* 1697. 4°. T.C.III 15. L, O, OW; BN, CN, MH, WF, Y.

1765 —The second part of The rover. *For Jacob Tonson,* 1681. 4°. T.C.I 451. L, O, LVF, OW, EN; CH, CN, LC, MH, NC, TU, Y.

1766 —Sir Patient Fancy. *By E. Flesher for Richard Tonson and Jacob Tonson,* 1678. 4°. T.C.I 303. L, O, OW, EN; BN, CH, CN, LC, MH, NC, TU, WCL, Y.

1766A —Three histories. *For W. Canning,* 1688. 8°. T.C.II 230. O; MH.

1767 [–] To poet Bavius. *For the author,* 1688. 4°.* L, O, C, OC; CH, MH, Y.

1768 —To the most illustrious Prince Christopher. *For John Newton,* 1687. 4°.* L, O, LVF; MH, Y.

1769 —The town-fopp. *By T. N. for James Magnes and Rich. Bentley,* 1677. 4°. T.C.I 267. L, O, OW, EN; CH, CN, LC, MH, TU, Y.

1770 ——[Anr. ed.] *For R. Wellington, B. Lintott; and E. Rumbold,* 1699. 4°. L, O, OW; PU, WF.

1770A [–] The town raves. A song. [*London?* 1696.] brs. CH.

1771 —Two congratulatory poems. Second edition. *For Will. Canning,* 1688. 4°.* T.C.II 231. L, O, OC, CS; CN, LC, MH, WF, Y.

1772 —The unfortunate bride. *For S. Briscoe,* 1698. 8°.* CLC, CN, IU, NP.

1773 ——[Anr. ed.] *For S.B.,* 1700. 8°.* CH.

1773A —The wandring beauty. *For Sam. Briscoe,* 1698. 8°.* CN, IU, NP, Y.

1773B ——[Anr. ed.] —, 1700. 8°.* CLC.

1774 —The widdow ranter. *For James Knapton,* 1690. 4°. T.C.II 301 L, O, EN; BN, CH, CN, LC, MH, TU, Y.

1775 [–] Young Jemmy. [*London*], *for P. Brooksby,* [c. 1681]. brs. L, HH; MH.

1776 —The young king. *For D. Brown, T. Benskin and H. Rhodes,* 1683. 4°. T.C.I 509. L, O, OB, OW, EN; CH, CU, LC, MH, TU, Y.

1777 ——[Anr. ed.] *For Richard Wellington,* 1698. 4°. L, O, EN; CLC, NP, TU, WF.

1778 —The younger brother. *For J. Harris and sold by R. Baldwin,* 1696. 4°. T.C.III 15. L, O, OW, LVD, EN; CH, CN, LC, MH, WCL, Y.

1778A Behold a cry! 1662. 4°.* L.

1778B Behold, here is a word. *Sold by Mrs. Edwards,* 1649. 4°. CT.

1779 Behold, the summe of all the blood, treasures. [*n.p.,* 1648.] brs. LT.

Behold you rulers. 1658. See Nayler, James.

1780 **Behr, Hans.** The declaration of. [*n.p.,* 1644.] brs. LT; CH.

1780A **Beilby, John.** Several useful and necessary tables. *By J. H. for L. Meredith,* 1694. 12°. L, O.

1781 **Bekker, Balthasar.** The world bewitch'd. Vol. I. [*London*], *for R. Baldwin,* 1695. 12°. T.C.II 527. L, C, LWL, EN, AU; CH, LC, MBA, MH, V.

1781A —The world turn'd upside down. *For Eliz. Harris,* 1700. NIC, PU.

1781B **Belasyse, John.** *baron.* Articles of peace. *By Tho. Newcomb,* 1666. fol.* L.

1781C ——[Anr. ed.] *Re-printed at Edinburgh,* 1666. 4°.* ALDIS 1807. EN; CH.

1782 [**Belcamp, John V.**] Consilium & votum. *By T. Mabb and Coles, for the authors use,* 1651. fol.* LT, DT; CH, MH, NN, WF.

1783 **Belcher, Joseph.** The worst enemy conquered. *Boston, by Bartholomew Green, and John Allen,* 1698. 4°.* EVANS 816. CHS, LC, MHS, RPJ, V.

1784 The Belgick boar. [*London*], *printed in the year one thousand six hundred ninety five.* brs. L, O, HH; MH.

Belgick lyon. 1665. See R., N.

Belgick, or Netherlandish Hesperides. 1681. See Commelin, Johannes.

1785 Belgii foederati collectio. 1695. 8°. LW.

1786 [**Belhaven, John Hamilton, baron.**] The contreymans rudiments. *Edinburgh, by the heirs and successors of Andrew Anderson,* 1699. 4°. ALDIS 3837. LUG, EN, A; NC.

Belides, or. . . . 1647. See Tooke, George.

1787 The belief of praying for the dead. *Printed and sold by Matthew Turner,* 1688. 4°. O, C, OC; NU, TU, WF.

1788 The belief of the Athanasian creed. [*n.p.,* 1693.] cap., 4°.* L, C, LW, WCA; CH, CN, NU, WF, Y.

Believer's duty. 1665. *See* Hickman, Henry.

1789 Belinda's pretty, pleasing form. [*London*], *T. Cross*, [*1700?*]. brs. L.

1790 [**Beling, *Sir* Richard.**] The eighth day. Second edition. *By Iohn Redmayne*, 1661. 4°. L; CH.

1790A **Belke, Michael.** Directions at large. *For the author*, 1667. 4°.* L.

1791 **B[elke], T[homas].** An epitome of sacred scriptvre. *For William Larnar*, 1644. 4°.* L, O, C; Y.

1792 [–] A paire of gold-weights. (*n.p.*, 1646.] cap., 4°.* LT; MM.

1793 —A scripture inquirie or helpe. *By G. M. for Chr. Meredith*, 1642. 8°. O.

1794 —To the honourable committee of Kent. [*n.p.*, 1645.] cap., 4°.* MH.

1795 **Bell, Andrew.** January 15, 1696/7. There is now in the press, . . . The present state of England. *For Andrew Bell*, 1697. 8°.* MH.

1796 [**Bell, Henry.**] Lutheri posthuma. *By William Du-Gard*, 1650. 4°.* L; WF.

1797 —A true relation of the abominable injustice. [*n.p.*], *printed*, 1646. 4°.* LT, DT; WF.

1798 [**Bell, James.**] To the king, and kingdom, of writing books. [*n.p.*, 1697.] cap., 4°.* Y.

1799 [–] To the kings most excellent Majesty, representing God. [*n.p.*, 1697.] cap., 4°.* Y.

1799A **Bell, James, *priest.*** The confession, obstancy, and ignorance, of Father Bell. *For Thomas Bates*, 1643. 4°.* LT, HH; Y.

1800 **Bell, John.** London's remembrancer: or, a true accompt. *Printed and are to be sold by E. Cotes*, 1665. 4°.* L, LG, CM, LWL, MR; BN.

1801 [–] Witchcraft proven. *Glasgow, by Robert Sanders*, 1697. 18°.* ALDIS 3719. GU.

1802 **Bell, Susanna.** The legacy of a dying mother. *Printed and are to be sold by John Hancock senior and junior*, 1673. 8°. T.C.I 146. O, C; MB.

1803 [**Bell, Thomas.**] Grapes in the wilderness. *Printed*, 1680. 8°. LW, EN; MBP, WF, Y.

1804 —Nehemiah the Tirshatha. *Edinburgh, by George Mosman*, 1692. 8°. ALDIS 3214. L, O, E, EN, ENC; CLC, MH, NPT, NU, Y.

1805 —Roma restituta. *Glasguæ, excudebat Robertus Sanders*, 1672. 8°. ALDIS 1940. L, O, CJ, EN, GU; CLC, CN, NU, WF, Y.

1806 — —[Anr. ed.] —, 1673. 8°. ALDIS 1972. EN; WF.

1807 — —[Anr. ed.] *Glasguæ*, 1674. 8°. ENC.

1808 — —[Anr. ed.] *Excusum pro Roberto Boulter*, 1677. 12°. T.C.I 282. L; CLC, MH, WF.

1809 **Bell, William.** City security stated. *For John Baker*, 1661. 4°.* L, O, CT; MH, MWA, NU.

1809A —The excellency, necessity. *For Nevil Simmons*, 1674. 8°. T.C.I 185. O; NPT.

1810 —Joshua's resolution. *By Ben. Griffin for Rich. Tomlins*, 1672. 4°.* T.C.I 106. L, O, C, LG, LL; WF, Y.

1811 —A sermon preached . . . 15th. of November, 1678. *By Mary Clark, sold by Benj. Tooke*, 1679. 4°.* T.C.I 348. L, O, CT, WCA; WF.

1812 —Well-doing. *By F. N. for T. Underhill*, 1650. 4°. CT, MAU, YM.

1813 **Bell, William, *of Highton.*** Incomparable company-keeping. *By M. S. for George Eversden*, 1657. 8°. LT; TU.

Bella Scot-Anglia. [*n.p.*], 1648. *See* Howell, James.

1814 **Bellamie, John.** A ivstification of the city remonstrance. *By Richard Cotes*, 1646. 4°. LT, O, HH, P, DT; CH, CN, MH, NU, WF, Y.

1815 —Lysimachus enervatus, Bellamius reparatus: or, a reply. *By G. Miller*, 1645. 8°. LT, O, LG, P; CH, MH.

1816 —A plea for the commonalty of London. *By George Miller*, 1645. 8°.* LT, O, C, LG; MH, NPT, WF, Y.

1817 — —Second edition. *By George Miller*, 1645. 8°.* L, O, LG; MH, Y.

1818 —A vindication of the humble remonstrance and petition of the Lord Major. *Printed at London for Richard Cotes*, 1646. 4°.* LT, LG, P, HH, DT; CH, CN, MH, NU, WF, Y.

1819 Bellamivs enervatvs: or, a full answer. *By Richard Cotes*, 1645. 4°.* LT, CT, OC, A, DT; CLC, NU, WF.

Bellamy, Thomas, *pseud.* *See* Janson, *Sir* Henry.

1820–1 Entries cancelled.

1822 **Bellarmino, Roberto.** Christian doctrine. [*n.p.*], *for A. L.*, 1676. 12°. O.

1823 Entry cancelled.

1824 —The use and great moment. *By Nathaniel Thompson*, 1687. 4°.* L, O, OC, OME, CPE; CLC, WF.

1825 Bellarminus junior enervatus. [*London?*], 1684. 4°.* L; MHS.

1826 **Bellers, Fulk.** Abrahams interment. *By R. I. for Tho. Newberry*, 1656. 4°. L, O, LG, LW; CH, CU, MH, NPT.

1827 —Jesus Christ the mysticall or gospell-sun. *By T. Maxey for John Rothwell*, 1652. 4°.* LT, LP, LW; CH, MH, NPT, NU, Y.

1827A **Bellers, John.** An epistle to Friends. *Printed and sold by T. Sowle*, 1697. 4°.* LF, LUG, BBN, IE.

1828 —Essays about the poor. *Printed and sold by T. Sowle*, 1699. 4°.* T.C.III 170. L, O, C, LF, BBN; CLC, CU, MH, NC, Y.

1829 [–] Proposals for raising a colledge of industry. *Printed and sold by T. Sowle*, 1695. 4°.* L, EN; PH, VC, Y.

1830 — —[Anr. ed.] —, 1696. 4°.* L, O, CT, LPO, ES; CH, MH, NC, WF, Y.

1831 —To the children of light. [*London*, 1695.] 4°.* LF.

1832 [–] To the Lords and Commons in Parliament assembled. A supplement to the proposal. [*London*, 1696?] cap., 4°.* L, LF; CH, MH, PH, WF, Y.

1833–4 Entries cancelled.

1835 **Bellomont, Richard Coote, *earl of.*** By His Excellency . . . a proclamation . . . second day of April, 1698. *By William Bradford, of New-York*, 1698. brs. EVANS 838. LPR; NS.

1836   —By His Excellency . . . a proclamation . . . April 7, 1698. *By William Bradford, of New-York, 1698.* brs. EVANS 840. LPR; NS.

1837   —By His Excellency . . . a proclamation . . . May 9, 1698. *Printed and sold by William Bradford, of New-York, 1698.* brs. EVANS 842. LPR.

1838   —By His Excellency . . . a proclamation . . . October 6, 1698. *Printed and sold by William Bradford, of New-York,* [1698]. brs. EVANS 843. LPR; NN.

1839   —By His Excellency . . . a proclamation . . . twenty-third day of November, 1698. *By William Bradford, of New-York, 1698.* brs. EVANS 844. NS.

1840   —By His Excellency . . . a proclamation whereas His Majesty by his letters patent. *By William Bradford, of New-York, 1698.* brs. EVANS 837. LPR.

1840A —By His Excellency . . . a proclamation whereas His most excellent Majesty. *By W. Bradford in New York, 1699.* brs. EVANS 885. PHS.

1841   —By His Excellency . . . a proclamation whereas I have received information . . . 16th day of March. 1699. *By William Bradford, of New-York, 1699.* brs. EVANS 884. NS.

1842   —By His Excellency . . . a proclamation whereas it is of absolute necessity. *By William Bradford, of New-York, 1698.* brs. EVANS 839. LPR; NS.

1843   —By His Excellency . . . a proclamation whereas in the moneth of November . . . July 26, 1700. *By W. Bradford, in New-York, 1700.* brs. EVANS 942. LPR.

1844   —His Excellency . . . speech to the honorable the Council . . . 29. of May. 1700. [*Boston: by Bartholomew Green, and John Allen, 1700.*] brs. EVANS 907. MHS.

1845   —Province of the Massachusetts-Bay . . . By His Excellency . . . a proclamation. *Boston, by Bartholomew Green, and John Allen, 1699.* brs. EVANS 870. MHS.

1845A —His Excellency the Earl of Bellomont his speech to the representatives. colop: *Printed and sold by William Bradford of New York, 1698.* brs. EVANS 845. PL.

1845B — —[Same title] —, 1699. cap., fol.* EVANS 888. PHS.

1846   —His Excellency, the Earl of Bellomont's speech. [*Boston, by Bartholomew Green and John Allen, 1669.*] brs. LPR.

1847   — —[Anr. ed.] [*Boston, by B. Green and J. Allen, 1700.*] brs. EVANS 943. MHS.

1848   —To the kings most excellent Majesty, the humble address of. [*New York, by Wm Bradford, 1698.*] brs. EVANS 847. LPR, HH.

1849   Entry cancelled.

1850   [**Bellon, Peter.**] The court secret: a novel. *By R. E. for R. Baldwin, 1689.* 12°. CLC, CN, LC, MH, Y.

1851   [–] —[Anr. ed.] *For R. Bentley and S. Magnes, 1689.* 12°. T.C.II 251. L; CLC.

1852   —The Irish spaw. *Dublin, by J. R. for M. Gunne, and Nat. Tarrant, 1684.* 12°. DIX 205. L, O, C, LCS, DWL.

1853   Entry cancelled.

1854   —The mock-duellist. *By J. C. for William Crooke, 1675.* 4°. T.C.I 219. L, O; CH, CN, LC, MH, NC, Y.

1855   —The pilgrim. The second part. *For R. Bentley and M. Magnes, 1681.* 12°. T.C.I 461. CN, Y.

1856–8 Entries cancelled.

1859   The bellowings of a vvild-bull. [*London, 1680.*] cap., fol.* L, O; CH, MBA, MH, WF, Y.

Bells founder confounded. [*London, 1656*]. *See* Chidley, Samuel.

Bellua marina. 1690. *See* Butler, John.

1860   Bellum Belgicum secundum, or a poem attempting something. *Cambridge, by J. Field and are to be sold by Robert Nicholson, 1665,* 4°.* L, CS; CH, MH.

Bellum grammaticale. Edinburgh, 1658. *See* Guarna, Andreas.

1860A Bellum medicinale: or, the papers. [*Edinburgh*], 1699. 8°. ALDIS 3828. EN.

Belphegor. 1691. *See* Wilson, John.

1860B **Belson, John.** Remedies against the infection of the plague. [*London? 1665.*] brs. LG, HH.

1861   —Tradidi vobis: or the traditionary conveyance of faith. *Printed, 1662.* 12°. L, C; CLC, CN, NU, TU, WG.

1862   **Belts, John.** Catalogue of library. [*n.p.*], 3 June 1695. 4°. L.

1863   **Belwood, Roger.** Bibliotheca Belwoodiana. [*London, 4 Feb., 1694.*] 4°. L, C; MH.

1864   **Belwood, Thomas.** A remonstrance of all the proceedings. *By John Thomas, Sept. 13, 1642.* 4°.* LT, YM.

Bembridge. *See* Bainbridge.

Bemoaning letter. 1700. *See* Mucklow, William.

1865   **Benbrigge, John.** Christ above all exalted. *For John Stafford, 1645.* 4°.* LT, O, CS, GU, DT; CH, CLC, NU, WF, Y.

1866   —Gods fury, Englands fire. *By John Dawson for Edward Blackmore, 1646.* 4°. LT, O, EN, DT; CH, NU.

1867   —Vsvra accommodata, or a ready vvay. *By M. S. for Nathaniel Brookes, 1646.* 4°.* LT, CT, EN, DT; CH, PU, RBU.

1867A **Bendish, Sir Thomas.** The vindication of. [c. 1650.] 4°.* CT.

Bendlowes, Edward. *See* Benlowes, Edward.

Bendloes, William. *See* Benloe, William.

Bendo, Alexander, *pseud. See* Rochester, John Wilmot, *earl of.*

Benediction. [*n.p.*], 1651. *See* Douglas, *Lady* Eleanor.

Benefice. 1689. *See* Wild, Robert.

Benefit of the ballot, [*n.p., 1680?*] *See* Harrington, James.

Benefits of our Saviour. Oxford, 1680. *See* Walker, Obadiah.

1867B **Benese, Richard.** The hidden treasure discovered. *By T. B., 1651.* 8°. SP; WF.

Benet, Sir Richard. *See* Benese, Richard.

Benjamin, *pseud.*

1868   The Benjamin's lamentation. [*London*], for F. Coles, T. Vere, J. Wright, and J. Clarke, [1655–80]. brs. L, O, HH.

1869   —[Anr. ed.] [*London*], for J. Wright, J. Clarke, W. Thackeray, and T. Passinger. [1676–84.] brs. L, O.

1870 **Benloe, William.** Les reports de . . . des divers pleadings. *By the assigns of R. and E. Atkins, for Samuel Keble, Daniel Brown, Isaac Cleave, and William Rogers,* 1689. fol. T.C.II 300. L, O, C, LL, EN; KT, LC, MHL, NCL, YL.

1871 —Les reports de . . . des divers resolutions. *For Timothy Twyford,* 1661. fol. L, O, LG, LL, LMT; LC, MHL, NCL.

1872 **Benlowes, Edward.** A glance at the glories. *By R. D. for Humphrey Moseley,* 1657. brs. LT.

1873 [–] Magia coelestis. colop: *Oxoniæ, exc. Lichfield,* 1673. obl., fol.* MADAN 2967. O.

1873A —On St. Pauls Cathedrall. [*London*], *sold by John Overton,* [1658]. brs. O, EC; MH, WF.

1874 [–] Oxonia elogia. [*Oxford, at the theatre,* 1673.] brs. MADAN 2968. O.

1875 [–] Oxonii encomium. colop: *Oxonii, exc. H. Hall,* 1672. fol.* MADAN 2915. L, O, OC; Y.

1876 —Papa perstrictus, (Echo) ictus. *Typis Jacobis junii,* 1645. brs. LT.

1877 —A poetick descant. [*n.p.,* 1649.] brs. LT.

1878 —The summary of wisedome. *For Humphrey Mosely,* 1657. 4°.* L, O; CH.

1879 —Theophila, or loves sacrifice. *By R. N. Sold by Henry Seile, and Humphrey Moseley,* 1652. fol. L, O, C, LVD, DC; CH, CN, MH, NC, WC, WCL, Y.

1880 **Benn, William.** Soul-prosperity. *For Awnsham Churchil, and William Churchil in Dorchester,* 1683. 8°. T.C.I 505. O, LCL, LW; CLC, MH, MHS, NU.

1881 **Bennet, Rev. Dr.** Catalogue of library. [*London*], 18 May, 1694. 4°. L.

1882 **Bennet, Christopher.** Tabidorum theatrum: sive pthisios. *Typis Tho. Newcomb, impensis Sam. Thompson,* 1656. 8°. L, O, CT, LCP, E; BN, PL, RBU, WF, HC.

1883 —Theatri tabidorum vestibulum. *Typis Tho. Newcomb, impensis Sam. Thomson,* 1654. 8°. LT, O, CS, P, GH; MBA, MH, PL, HC.

1883A **Bennet, Dorcas.** Good and seasonable counsel. *Printed,* 1670. 12°. LW; MH.

1883B **Bennet, Isaac.** Good and true intelligence from Reading. *For Ph. Smith,* 1643. 4°.* LT; CH, MH, MIU.

1884 [**Bennet, John.**] Constantius the apostate. *For Walter Kettilby,* 1683. 8°. T.C.I 511. L, O, C, CT, LCL; CH, MH, PU, WF, Y.

1885 —Of the eternity of God's election. *By I. C. for Livewel Chapman,* 1655. 8°. NU.

1885A [**Bennet, Joseph**]. A true and impartial account of the most material passages. *For John Avery,* 1689. 4°.* L, O, C, LW, OC; CH, MH, PL, WF, Y.

1885B **Bennett, Philip.** Answers to several queries. 1654. 4°. O.

1886 **Bennet, Robert.** King Charle's [sic] triall iustified. *For R. A.* 1649. 4°.* LT, O, HH, EN; CH, CN, MIU, Y.

1887 —A theological concordance. *By J. Streater, to be sold by G. Sawbridge,* 1657. 8°. LT, O, C, LCL; CH, MH, RBU, Y.

1888 [**Bennet, Thomas.**] An answer to the dissenters pleas. *Cambridge, at the university press for A. Bosvile,* 1700. 8°. L, O, C, CT, NPL; SCU.

1889 [–] —Second edition. *Cambridge, at the university press for Alexander Bosvile,* 1700. 8°. L, O, C, OM, CSS; CH, CN, NU, WF, Y.

1889A —Discourses on schisme. 1700. 8°. L.

1889B [**Benningfield, W.**] Dublin, 9 May, 1642. An exceeding true relation of a renowned victory. *For John Reynor,* 1642. 4°.* LT, EC; MH.

1890 **Bennion, John.** Moses's charge. *Printed at Oxford, to be sold by Francis Dollif,* 1681. 4°.* T.C.II 2. L, O, C; CH, Y.

1890A **Bennison, Robert.** The last speech and confession of. *By R. Smith for G. Croom,* 1692. brs. HH.

1891 **Bennit, William.** A collection of certain epsitles. *Printed and sold by Andrew Sowle,* 1685. 4°. L, O, LF, OC; CH, LC, MH, NU, PH, Y.

1892 —God only exalted in his own work. [*London*], *printed,* 1664. 4°.* L, CT, LF, BBN; MH, PH, PHS, WF, Y.

1892A —A loving exhortation. [*London,* 1675.] brs. LF, BBN.

1893 —Some prison meditations. [*London*], *printed,* 1666. 4°.* L, O, C, LF, BBN; PH, PSC, Y.

1894 —A tender and unfeigned salutation of love. [*London*], *printed,* 1664. 4°.* L, LF.

1895 —A testimony of the true light. [*London*], *printed,* 1668. 4°.* L, C, LF; PH, PL, PSC.

1896 —The work and mercy of God. [*London?*], *printed,* 1669. 4°.* L, C, LF; PH, PSC.

1897 — —[Anr. ed.] [*London*], *reprinted,* 1677. 4°.* L, C, LF; NU, Y.

1898 [**Benoit, Elie.**] The history of the famous edict of Nantes. *For John Dunton,* 1694. 2 v. 4°. L, O, LIL, ENC, DT; CH, CN, MH, NU, PL, WF, Y.

[**Benson, —.**] Man of sin. 1677. *See* Hughes, William.

1899 [**Benson, Gervase.**] An answer to John Gilpin's book. *For Giles Calvert,* 1655. 4°. L, LF, OC, MR, BBN; PH.

1900 [–] The cry of the oppressed. *For Giles Calvert,* 1656. 4°. L, O, LF; CH, IE, MH, PH, PSC, Y.

1901 —A second testimony. [*London*], *printed,* 1675. 4°.* L, O, LF, BBN; MH, PH, PSC, Y.

1901A — —[Anr. ed.] —, 1679. 4°.* PSC.

1902 —A true testimony concerning oaths. *Printed,* 1669. 4°.* L, O, C, BBN; MH, NU, PH, WF, Y.

1903 —A true tryall of the ministers. colop: *For Giles Calvert,* 1655. cap., 4°.* LT, LF, OC; PH.

1904 — —[Anr. ed.] *For Giles Calvert,* 1656. 4°.* L, CT, OC, LF; CH, PH.

1905 Entry cancelled.

1906 [**Bent, James.**] An impartial history of the life and death of George Lord Jeffreys. *For John Dunton,* 1689. 4°. L; MB, MHL, NU, Y.

1907 **Bentall, Edward.** Βασιλεὺς Βασιλέων, or the regality of Jesus Christ. *Oxford, by A. Lichfield,* 1660. 8°.* MADAN 2481. O, LCL; WF.

1908 **Bentham, Joseph.** Χοροθεολογν, or two briefe. By Tho. Roycroft, for Philemon Stephens, 1657. 4°. LT, O, LW, OC; MM, NU, Y.

1909 —A disswasive from error. Printed, and are to be sold by William Thompson, in Harborow, 1669. 4°. O, CS, LW.

1909A —The right of Kings by Scripture. By E. C. for William Thompson in Harborough, 1661. 4°. L.

1910 **Bentivoglio, Guido.** The compleat history of the warrs of Flanders. For Humphrey Moseley, 1654. fol. L, O, C, E, AU; BN, CH, CN, MH, NN, TU, Y.

1911 —Historicall relations of the United Provinces. For Humphrey Moseley, 1652. fol. L, O, C, LI, OME; CH, CN, NC, WF, Y.

1912 —The history of the warrs of Flanders. For D. Newman, T. Cockerill, S. Heyrick, C. Smith, and J. Edwin, 1678. fol. T.C.I 316. L, O, C, LL, EN; CH, LC, MH, NU, WF, Y.

1912A — —[Anr. ed.] For Dorman Newman, 1678. fol. OC.
Bentivolio and Urania. 1660. See Ingelo, Nathaniel.

1913 Bentivolyo, or good will to all . . . unconformists. [n.p.], printed, 1667. 4°.* O.

1914 **Bentley, John.** A list of vvoods, under woods, timber. [London], printed, 1648. 4°.* LT, LG, DT; MH, WF, Y.

1915 **Bentley, Richard.** A confutation of atheism from the origin. Part I. For Henry Mortlock, 1692. 4°.* T.C.II 408. L, O, C, LL, EN; CH, CN, PL, TU, WF, Y.

1916 — —Second edition. By J. H. for Henry Mortlock, 1694. 4°.* C, CT, CE, CC, E; MH, MIU, TU, WF.

1917 — — —Part II. For H. Mortlock, 1693. 4°.* T.C.I 408. L, C, LL, OB, OM; CH, CN, MH, TU, WF, Y.

1918 — —Third and last part. —, 1693. 4°.* T.C.II 418. L, O, C, LL, EN; CH, CN, MH, TU, WF, Y.

1919 —A confutation of atheism from the structure. Part I. For Tho. Parkhurst and H. Mortlock, 1692. 4°.* L, C, OC, EN, DT; CH, CN, MH, PL, TU, WF, Y.

1920 — —Second edition. For H. Mortlock, 1693. 4°.* L, C, OB, E, DT; WF, Y.

1921 — —Third edition. By J. H. for H. Mortlock, 1693. 4°.* L, C, E; MH, MIU, TU, WF.

1922 — —Part II. For Tho. Parkhurst and H. Mortlock, 1692. 4°.* L, C, LL, OM, DT; CH, MBA, PL, TU, WF, Y.

1923 — —Second edition. By J. H. for Henry Mortlock, 1693. 4°.* L, C, OB, OC, E; CSU, MH, MIU, TU, WF.

1924 — —Third edition. —, 1693. 4°.* L, C, E.

1925 — —The third and last part. For Henry Mortlock, 1692. 4°.* T.C.II 418. L, O, C, LL, OM; CH, NPT, PL, TU, WF, Y.

1926 — —Second edition. —, 1692. 4°.* L, O, OC, CS, E; CSU, WF, Y.

1927 — —Third edition. —, 1694. 8. 4°.* L, C, OM, E, DT; MH, TU, WF.

1928 —A dissertation upon the epistles of Phalaris. By J. Leake, for Peter Buck, 1697. 8°. L, O, CE, ENC, DT; CH, CN, MBP, NP, HC.

1929 — —[Anr. ed.] By J. H. for Henry Mortlock and John Hartley, 1699. 8°. T.C.III 110. L, O, CT, E, DT; BN, CH, CN, MH, NU, WF, Y.

1930 —The folly and unreasonableness of atheism. By J. H. for H. Mortlock, 1693. 4°. T.C.II 449. L, O, C, E, DT; CU, MH, NU, TU, WF, Y.

1931 — —Fourth edition. —, 1699. 4°. T.C.III 84. L, C, CT, P, DT; CH, MH, NU, WF, JF.

1932 —The folly of atheism. For Tho. Parkhurst and H. Mortlock, 1692. 4°.* T.C.II 408. L, O, C, LW, OP; CH, CN, NPT, PL, TU, Y.

1933 — —Second edition. —, 1692. 4°.* L, LL, OC, CT, DT; NU, WF.

1934 — —Third edition. For Henry Mortlock, 1692. 4°.* C, CT, EN; CU, Y.

1935 — —Fourth edition. By J. H. for H. Mortlock, 1693. 4°.* L, O, C, OC; MBA, MH, TU, WF, Y.

1935A — —"Fourth" edition. —, 1699. 4°.* CT.

1936 —Matter and motion cannot think,. For Tho. Parkhurst and Henry Mortlock, 1692. 4°.* T.C.II 408. L, C, LW, OP, SP; CH, CN, NU, TU, WF, Y.

1937 — —Second edition. —, 1692. 4°.* L, O, C, EN, DT; NPT.

1938 — —"Second" edition. For Henry Mortlock, 1693. 4°.* C, CT, LL; NGT, Y.

1939 — —Third edition. By J. H. for H. Mortlock, 1693. 4°.* L, O, C, OC, E; MIU.

1940 — —"Third" edition. —, 1694. 4°.* O, CE; CLC, MBA, MH, WF.

1941 —Miracula. [n.p.], 1696. brs. O

1942 —Of revelation and the Messias. By J. H. for Henry Mortlock, 1696. 4°.* L, O, C, NPL, DT; CH, MBA, NU, WF, Y.

1943 [–] A proposal for building a royal library. [London, 1697.] brs. L; CH.

1943A —Proposals for printing [Hebrew] or, the Scripture treasury. [London? 1690.] cap., fol.* CH.

1944 **Bentley, William.** The case of. [n.p., 1656.] brs. LT.
Berachah. 1646. See P., R.

1945 **Berachoth.** [Hebrew] Masseceth Beracoth, titulus Talmudicus. Oxoniæ, excudebat H. Hall, 1667. 4°.* MADAN 2763. O, CT; Y.

1946 Beraldus, prince of Savoy. For W. Grantham and J. Crump, 1675. 12°. T.C.I 204. L, O; CLC, CN.

1947 **Bérault, Pierre.** Bouquet ou un amas de plusieurs veritez. Pour l'autheur par T. M., 1684. 8°. YM; WF, Y.

1947A — —[Anr. ed.] —, 1685. 12°. L, O; CH, CN, MIU, Y.

1948 —The Church of England. By T. Hodgkin, for the author, 1682. 12°. O, OB, CT, OC; CLC, NPT, Y.

1948A — —[Anr. ed.] —, 1683. 12°. L, O.

1949 —The church of Rome evidently proved heretick. By Tho. Hodgkin for the author, 1681. 12°. L, O, OB, OM, CE; CLC, NU, WF, Y.

1949A — —[Anr. ed.] —, 1682. 12°. CT; CH, NPT.

1949B — —[Anr. ed.] Boston, by S. Green for James Cowse, 1685. 16°. EVANS 384. MB, MBC, MWA.

1950 —A discourse. I. of the Trinity. By William Redmayne for the author, 1700. 12°. L, O; CLC, CN, CU, WF, Y.

1951 —Lettre a son altesse royale. brs. HH.

1952 —Logick. By Thomas Hodgkin, 1690. 12°. L, RPL, GU; WF.

1953 —A new, plain, short . . . grammar. *By Tho. Hodgkin, for the author,* 1681. 12°. CLC.

1953A — —[Anr. ed.] —, 1688. 8°. T.C.II 232. C, CS; CLC.

1953B — —Second edition. *For Richard Baldwin,* 1691. 8°. T.C.II 385. LUC.

1954 — —Third edition. *By T. Hodgkin, for Robert Clavel,* 1693. 8°. T.C.II 468. O, C, DT; MU.

1955 — —Fourth edition. *By T. Hodgkin for John Nutt,* 1700. 8°. T.C.III 291. CT.

1956 —Rome tyrannous. *By W. Redmayne for the author, to be sold by Richard Parker,* 1698. Sixes. L; CLC, WF.

1957 —Le veritable & assuré chemin du ciel. *Pour l'autheur, par Tho. Hodgkin,* 1681. 12°. T.C.I 493. L, O, C, OM; CH.

1957A **Berchet, Toussaint.** Στοιχειωσις. Elementaria traditio. *Impensis J. D. sumptibus R. Whitakeri,* 1648. 8°. CT.

1958 **Berd, Robert.** To the Parliament of the Commonwealth of England, . . . a representation of the outrages. *For Thomas Simmons,* 1659. 4°.* L, LF; PH.

1958A **Berengario, Jacopo.** A brief and practical anatome. *By R. J., for Livewell Chapman,* 1660. 12°. LSC, CPE.

1959 —Μικροκοσμογραφια: or, a description of the body of man. *For Livewell Chapman,* 1664. 8°. L, O, LWL, GH; MH, NAM, WSG, HC.

1959A **Berford, Ignatius.** Illustrissimo hero. [*London,* 1687.] cap., fol.* WF.

1959B **Bergice, Dan.** A lecture held forth. *For C. G.,* 1692. CH.

1959C **Bergius, Johannes.** Noma pacis ecclesiasticae. A treatise. *Thomason,* 1646. 4°. P.

1960 —The pearl of peace & concord. *By T. G. for John Rothwell, and John Wright,* 1655. 8°. LT, O, LW, SC; NU, WF.

Beridge, Ferdinando. Οἱ Δωδέκομζωοι. 1654. *See* Almanacs.

Berinthia. 1664. *See* Bulteel, John.

1961 [**Berisford, John.**] An argument shewing that 'tis impossible for the nation. *Printed, and sold by C. D. in T.,* 1699. 4°.* L.

1962 — —[Anr. ed.] *For Richard Standfast,* 1699. 4°.* L, O, LL; CLC, MHL, WF, Y.

Berith anti-Baal. 1661. *See* Crofton, Zachary.

1963 [**Berkeley, George Berkeley, earl of.**] Historical applications. *By J. Flesher for R. Royston,* 1666. 12°. L; CH, MH.

1964 [–] [Anr. ed.] *By J. Macock, for R. Royston,* 1670. 8°. T.C.I 57. L, O; CLC, CN, CPB, WF, Y.

1965 [–] —Third edition. *By M. Flesher for R. Royston,* 1680. 8°. T.C.I 396. L, O, C, CE, ES; CLC, CU, LC, WF, Y.

1966 [–] —Fourth edition. *For L. Meredith,* 1698. 8°. T.C.III 43. L, LVF; CN, IU, MU, Y.

1967 —A speech made . . . to the Levant Company. *For R. Royston,* 1681. 4°.* O, BR; CH.

1968 —The Earl of Berkeley's speech to the Corporation of the Trinity House. *For R. Royston,* 1681. 8°.* L, O.

1969 —The Earl of Berkeley's speech to the Corporation. *For R. Royston,* 1683. 8°.* O, P.

1970 **Berkeley, George, Rev.** A sermon preached at the assizes . . . July xxii MDCLXXXVI. *By J. Macock, for R. Royston,* 1686. 4°.* LT, O, CT; MH, Y.

1970A **Berkeley, Sir John, baron.** By the Lord Lieutenant and council. [*Dublin,* 1670.] cap., fol.* PL.

1971 —Memoirs of. *By J. Darby, for A. Baldwin,* 1699, 8°. L, O, CE, LCL, LL; BN, CH, CN, NC, WF, Y.

1972 **Berkeley, Sir Robert.** Judge Barkely his penitentiall complaint. [*London*], *printed,* 1641. brs. LT, O, CT, HH.

1973 [–] The judges resolution. *For G. Usher, Oct. 21,* 1642. 4°.* LT, O, EC; WF, Y.

1974 **Berkeley, William.** Diatribae. Discourses. *For Sam. Keble,* 1697. 8°. L, OM, BP.

1975 **Berkeley, Sir William.** A discourse and views of Virginia. [1663.] cap., 4°.* L, OC, DT; CH, NP.

1976 —The speech to the burgesses. *Hagh, by Samuel Brown,* 1651. 4°.* SC, DT.

1977 Entry cancelled.

1978 **Berkshire, Charles Howard, earl of.** A true copy of the Lord Andevers two speeches. *For Francis Constable,* 1641. 4°.* LT, C, EC, HH; MBP, NU, WF, Y.

1979 —The Lord Andevers two speeches. [*London*], *printed,* 1641. 4°.* L, O, C; CH, CN, MHL, WF, Y.

1980 **Berlu, John Jacob.** The treasury of drugs unlock'd. *For John Harris, and Tho. Howkins,* 1690. 12°. T.C.II 300. L, O, C, LCS, E; CLC, MH, NAM, WF, HC.

Bermudas preacher. 1683. *See* Estlacke, Francis.

1980A **Bernard, Saint.** A looking-glass for all new-converts. *Printed,* 1685. 4°. L.

1981 —A mirror that flatters not. *For Moses Pitt,* 1677. 4°. T.C.I 280. O, DT; Y.

1982 — —[Anr. ed.] *Printed,* 1677. 4°. O, P; CH, WF, Y.

1982A —S. Bernard's pious meditations. *For N. Boddington,* 1700. 12°. O.

1982B —Saint Bernards vision. [*London*], *for I. Wright* [1683?] brs. L.

1983 [**Bernard, Catherine.**] The Count of Amboise. Part I. *For R. Bentley and M. Magnes,* 1689. 8°. T.C.II 287. L; CLC, CN, MH, Y.

1984 [–] The female prince. *For H. Rodes,* 1682. 8°. T.C.I 472. L; MH.

1985 **Bernard, Edward.** Bibliotheca Bernardina: . . . (25) die Octobris 1697. 1697. fol.* L, O, CS, OP; WF.

1986 [–] Catalogi librorum manuscriptorum. *Oxoniæ, e theatro Seldoniano,* 1697. fol. O, CM, OME, E; CH, CN, W, Y.

1987 —Edvardi Bernardi de mensuris et ponderibus. *Oxoniæ, e theatro Seldoniano,* 1688. 8°. L, O, C, EN, DT; BN, CH, CN, MH, NC, WF, Y.

1988 —Librorum manuscriptorum academiarum Oxoniensis. [*n.p.*], 1694. brs. O.

1989 —Orbis eruditi literaturam a charactere Samaritico. *Oxoniæ, apud theatrum,* 1689. brs. L, O, CM, OM, EN; NNC.

1990 — —[Anr. ed.] —, 1700. brs. CN, MBA, MH.

1991 [–] Private devotion and a brief explication. *Oxon, at the theater for Henry Clements,* 1689. 8°. O, C.

1992　**Bernard, Francis, *M.D.*** A catalogue of the library of. [*London*], *Octob.* 4 1698. 8°. L, O, C, MR, EN; WF, WSG, HC.

1993　**Bernard Francis, *Francisian.*** Entry cancelled. *See* Eyston, Bernard Francis.

1994　[**Bernard, Jacques.**] The acts and negotiations, ... concluded at Ryswick. *For Robert Clavell, and Tim Childe,* 1698. 8°. T.C.III 53. L, O, CT, P, E; CH, CN, MB, MIU, NNC, Y.

1995　[**Bernard, James.**] A poem upon his sacred Majesties distresses. *For R. Marriot,* 1660. 4°.* MH, WF.

1996　[**Bernard, John.**] The anatomie of the common prayer-book. [*n.p.*], *printed,* 1661. 4°. L, CT; NU, TSM, Y.

1997　[–] The anatomie of the service book. [*n.p.*], *printed,* [1641]. 4°. LT, O, CJ, P, MR; CH, CLC, NPT, NU, WF.

1998　[–] —[Anr. ed., anatomy.] —, [1641]. 4°. LT, O, CS, SP, D; CH, CU, NU, TU, Y.

1999　[–] —[Anr. ed., anatomie.], [*London*], *printed,* 1642. 4°. L, O, CT, EN, DT; CU, MB.

2000　[–] —[Anr. ed., anatomy.] —, [1643?]. CT; CU.

2001　Entry cancelled.
　　　—A short view of the prelatical Church of England. *See* Bernard, Richard.

2002　—Truths triumph over treacherous dealing. [*n.p.*, 1657.] cap., 4°.* O.

2003　**Bernard, John. *A.M.*** The lives of the Roman emperors. *For Charles Harper,* 1698. 8°. T.C.III 77. L, OC, AU, DT; CN, MIU, NR, Y.

2004　**Bernard, John, *Capt.*** To his Highness the Lord Protector of England, ... the humble petition of. [*London*, 1657.] brs. LT.

2005　—A true confutation of a fals and scandalous pamphlet. *By Will. Du-Gard,* 1650. 4°.* LT, HH; CN, NN, WF.

2006　**Bernard, Nathaniel.** Εσοπτρον της αντιμαχιας, or a looking-glasse for rebellion. *Oxford, by Leonard Lichfield,* 1644. 4°.* MADAN 1661. LT, O, OM, DT; CH, WF.

2007　**Bernard, Nicholas.** Clavi trabales, or, nailes fastned. *By Richard Hodgkinson, and are to be sold by R. Marriot,* 1661. 4°. L, O, CS, LCL, DT; CN, NP, NU, WF, Y.

2008　[–] Devotions of the ancient church. *For R. Royston,* 1660. 8°. LT, O, C, LW, DT; CLC, CN, CU.

2009　—The fare-well sermons. *By Robert Ibbitson,* 1651. 8°. L.

2010　—A letter of Dr. Barnards to a friend at court. [1660?] cap., 4°.* CH.

2011　—A letter sent from. *For Nathanael Butter,* 1641. 4°.* LT, C, EC; CU, MH.

2012　—The life & death of ... D^r. James Usher. *By E. Tyler, and are to be sold by J. Crook,* 1656. 8°. LT, O, C, E, DT; BN, CH, CN, MH, NU, WF, Y.

2013　——[Anr. ed.] *Dublin, by William Bladen,* 1656. 8°. DIX 99. L, C.

2014　—The penitent death of ... John Atherton. *Dvblin, by the society of stationers,* 1641. 4°.* DIX 74. LT, O, C, A, DI; LC, NC, WF.

2015　——Second edition. *By G. M. for W. Bladen, and are to be sold by R. Royston,* 1642. 12°. L, O, C, E, DT; CH, CLC, NU, TU, Y.

2016　——Third edition. *By R. Ibbitson; sold by A. Williamson,* 1651. 8°. L, C, OC; CH, MH, MIU, WF.

2017　—A sermon preached at the bvriall ... December the fifth, 1640. *Printed at Dublin,* 1641. 4°.* DIX 74. LT, O, DI; NC, WF.

2018　[–] The still-borne nativitie. *Printed,* 1648. 4°.* LT, LSC; CH, MM, NU, WF.

2019　—A true and perfect relation of all the severall skirmishes. *For Iohn Wright,* 1641. 4°.* L, O, C, MR, EN; MH.

2020　—The whole proceedings of the siege of Drogheda. *By A. N. for William Bladen,* 1642. 4°. LT, O, C, LVF, CE; CH, LC, MH, OWC.

2021　——[Anr. ed.] —, 1648. 4°. HH.

2022　**Bernard, Richard.** The article of Christ's descension into Hell. *By Jo: Beale for Thomas Underhill,* 1641. 4°.* L, O, C, EC, P; CN, NC, NGT, NU, WF.

2023　—The Bibles abstract and epitomie. *Imprinted at London by G. M. for Andrew Crooke,* 1642. fol. L, O, CS, LCL, NPL; CH, MH, NU, TU, Y.

2024　—Certaine positions seriously to bee considered of. *For Giles Clavert,* 1644. 4°. CT, E.

2025　—An epistle directed to all iustices of peace. *For M. S.,* 1641[2]. 4°.* LT, HH; CH, MH, WF.

2026　—The isle of man. Twelfth edition. *By J.D. for E. Blackmore,* 1648. 12°. L, C.

2026A　——Thirteenth edition. *By R.I. for Edward Blackmore,* 1658. 12°. RPL; LC, MH, NPT.

2027　——"Thirteenth edition." *For Nathanael Ranew,* 1659. 12°. L; NC.

2028　——Fourteenth edition. *By T. Milbourn, for T. S. to be sold by John Wright,* 1668. 12°. L, O, BR; CH, CLC, Y.

2029　——Fifteenth edition. *Glasgow, R. Sanders,* 1674. 12°. C, EN.

2030　——"Fifteenth" edition. *By R.E. for J. Wright,* 1677. 12°. P, BR; CN, CU, MH.

2030A　——"Fifteenth" edition. *For William Bromwich,* 1677. 12°. MH, NBL.

2031　——Sixteenth edition. *By T.M.,* 1683. 12°. T.C.II 55. L, BR; MBP, NN.

2031A　—The ready way to good works. *By F. Kingston,* 1683. 12°. LSC.

2032　[–] A short view of the praelaticall Church of England. [*London*], *printed,* 1641. 39 pp. 4°.* O, C, BR, E, DT; CH, CSS, CU, MIU, Y.

2033　[–] —[Anr. ed.] [*London*], *printed,* 1641. 43 pp. 4°.* LT, O, C, EN, DT; CH, CN, NU, WF, Y.

2034　[–] —[Anr. ed.] [*London*], *printed,* 1661. 4°.* L, O, CT, GU, DT;.IU, MH, NU, TSM, Y.

2035　—Thesaurus biblicus. *Imprinted at London by Felix Kingston,* 1644. fol. L, O, C, E, DT; BN, CH, CU, MH, NU, WF, Y.

2036 ——Second edition. *Imprinted at London, for Andrew Crook, Luke Fawne, and John Williams, 1661.* fol. L, O, C, LCL; PAP, Y.

2037 —A threefold treatise of the Sabbath. *By Richard Bishop for Edward Blackmore, 1641.* 4°. L, O, CT, EN, DT; CH, MH, NPT, NU, Y.

2038 **Bernard, Samuel.** Ezekiel's prophesie parallel'd. *For Andrew Crook, 1652.* 4°.* O, LCL; Y.

2039–41 Entries cancelled.

2042 **Bernier, Francois.** A continuation of the memoires. Tome iii. and iv. *Printed, and are to be sold by Moses Pitt, 1672.* 8°. T.C.I 86. L, O, C, CT, AU; CH, MB, PL, TU, Y.

2043 —The history of the late revolution of the empire of the Great Mogol. *Printed, and sold by Moses Pitt, Simon Miller, and John Starkey, 1671.* 8°. T.C.I 66. L, O, C, E, DT; CH, NC, NP, PL, WF, Y.

2044 ——Second edition. *Printed, and sold by M. Pitt, and S. Miller; and J. Starkey, 1676.* 8°. T.C.I 23. L, C, OC, AU, DT; LC, MB, NN, PL, TU.

2045 [**Berniers Louvigny, Jean de.**] The interiour Christian. *Antwerp, printed, 1684.* 8°. L, O, LW; CH, NU, TU, WF, Y.

2046 **Berry, Richard.** A sermon upon the Epiphany. *Dublin, by Benjamin Tooke, to be sold by Joseph Wilde, 1672.* 4°.* DIX 146. L, O, C, DT; MBA, WF.

Bertie, Robert. See Lindsey, Robert Bertie, earl of.

2047 Entry cancelled.

2048 [**Bertius, Pierre.**] The life and death of James Arminius. *By Tho. Ratcliff and Nath. Thompson, for Francis Smith, 1672.* 8°. T.C.I 96. L, O, CT, BP, BR; CH, MH, NPT, Y.

2049 **Bertramus, presbyter.** The book of Bertram. *For Thomas Boomer, 1686.* 12°. T.C.II 164. L, O, OM, LIL, LCL; CLC, CN, MB, WSC, Y.

2049A ——[Anr. ed.] *For William Taylor, 1686.* 12°. L, O, C, E, DT; NU, Y.

2049B ——[Anr. ed.] *By B. Griffin, 1686.* 12°. L, O; MB, TU.

2049BA ——[Anr. ed.] —, *sold by S. Keble, 1686.* 12°. TU.

2049C ——[Anr. ed.] *For Ch. Shortgrave, and sold by Sam. Smith, 1686.* 12°. CK, D; MIU, TU.

2049D ——[Anr. ed.] *For Ch. Shortgrave, 1686.* 8°. SP; TU, Y.

2050 ——[Anr. ed.] *By B. Griffin, to be sold by Sam. Keble, 1687.* 12°. T.C.II 156. L, O, DC; MH, TSM.

2051 —Bertram or Ratram. "Second" edition. *By H. Clark for Thomas Boomer, 1688.* 8°. L, O, C, LIL, MC; CLC, CN, MM, NU, WF.

Berwick's beauty. 1650. See Denton, Robert.

2052 [**Besongne, Nicolas.**] Galliæ notitia: or, the present state of France. *Printed, and are to be sold by John Taylor, 1691.* 12°. T.C.II 333. L, O, DT; CLC, NC, Y.

2052A [–] The present state of France. *For John Starkey, 1671.* 12°. L, O, OC; MBA, WF.

2052B —[Anr. ed.] *For Gilbert Cownley, 1687.* 12°. T.C.II 199. LL, DT; CH, CN, WF, Y.

Bespotted Iesuite. 1641. See Crashaw, William.

2053 **Best, Paul.** Mysteries discovered. [*London*], *printed, 1647.* 4°.* L, O, CT, LCI, HH; CLC, MH, NU.

2054 —To certaine noble and honorable persons. [*London, 1646.*] brs. LT.

2055 The best and happiest tydings from Ireland. *Imprinted at London, for H. Bluron, 1642.* 4°.* LT, LFEA.

2055A The best and plainest English spelling book. The first part. [*London, 1700.*] cap., 8°.* MH.

Best exercise. 1671. See Horne, John.

2056 The best fence against popery. *For J. Robinson, and S. Crouch, [1670?].* 4°. L, LL, OC; MH, NC, NP, NU, TU.

2057 —[Anr. ed.] *For J. Johnson, 1686.* 4°. L, O, HH, SP, DT; CLC, CN, MH.

2057A The best means to defeat, *Printed, 1696.* brs. MH.

2058 The best newes from York. *Printed at London by J. H. for T. Powel, 1642.* 4°.* LT, EC.

2059 The best nevves that ever was printed. *For I. A., 1643.* 4°.* LT, DT; CH, MH, WF, Y.

Best of remedies. 1667. See Alleine, Richard.

Best portion. Exon, 1699. See Winnell, Thomas.

Best schoole. 1642. See M., R.

Best way of disposing. [n.p.], 1696/7. See Neale, Thomas.

2059A **Betham, John.** A sermon of the epiphany. *For Matthew Turner, 1687.* 4°.* WF, Y.

2060 —A sermon preach'd ... March 25, 1686. *By Henry Hills, sold by Matthew Turner, 1686.* 4°.* L, O, CT, EN, DT; CH, MH, NU, TU, WF, Y.

2061 **Bethel, Hugh.** Col: Bethels letter to his excellence the Lord Fairfax. *For J. Playford, Decemb. 25, 1648.* 4°.* LT, O, CCL, YM; WF.

2062 [**Bethel, Slingsby.**] An account of the French usurpation upon the trade of England. *Printed, 1679.* 4°.* L, O, CT, MR, EN; CH, CU, MH, WF, Y.

2062A [–] A discourse of trade. *Printed 1675.* 4°.* L, LUG.

2063 —Slingsby, Bethell, esq.; his enquiry after William Baly. colop: *By J. Grantham, 1683.* brs. L; MH, PL.

2063A [–] Et a Dracone: or. *Printed, 1668.* 4°.* O, C, OC, CT; CN, CU, MH, TU, WF, Y.

2064 [–] The interest of princes and states. *For John Wickins, 1680.* 8°. T.C.I 395. L, O, MR; CH, CN, MH, NC, WF, Y.

2065 ——Second edition. *By J. M. for J. Wickins, 1681.* 8°. T.C.I 433. L, C, WCA, ENC; CH, CU, MH, WF, Y.

2066 ——Third edition. *For George Grafton, 1689.* 8°. O; CLC, MIU.

2067 ——Fourth edition. *For M. Wotton, 1694.* 8°. L, O.

2068 [–] Ludlow no lyar. *Amsterdam, printed, 1692.* 4°. L, O, C, EN, DT; CH, CN, NU, WF, Y.

2069–71 Entries cancelled.

2072 [–] The present interest of England stated. *For D. B., 1671.* 4°.* L, O, C, EN, DT; CH, CU, MH, NC, WF, Y.

2073 [–] —Second edition. *1681.* 4°.* EN.

2074 [–] The providences of God. *For R. Baldwin, 1691.* 4°. EN; CH, MBA, NU, WF, Y.

2075 ——[Anr. ed.] *1694.* 12°. L, LCL.

2076 ——Second edition. *By J. D. for Andrew Bell, 1697.* 8°. T.C.III 32. L, LCL, CT, ES; CLC, MIU, NPT.

2076A —To the right honourable the Lords ... the humble petition of. [*London, 1681*]. brs. MBA.

2077   [–] A true and impartial narrative of the most material debates. *For Thomas Brewster,* 1659. 4°.* LT, LG; HR, CH, MB, NU, WF.

2078   [–] The vindication of. *Francis Smith,* 1681. fol.* L, O, LG, MR, DT; CH, CN, LC, WF, Y.

2079   [–] The world's mistake. *Printed,* 1668. 4°.* L, O, CT, LG, EN; CH, CU, LC, MH, NU, Y.

2080   Bethel and Smith; or a sober answer. *For S. F.,* [1681.] brs. L, O; CH, CN, IU, MH, WF.

     Bethlehem signifying. [n.p.], 1652. *See* Douglas, *Lady Eleanor.*

2081   Bethlehems beauty. *For Thomas Sear,* 1676. brs. L.

2082   **Bethune, David.** Disputatio juridica. *Edinburg, heirs of A. Anderson,* 1695. 4°. ALDIS 3443. EN.

2083   Better late than never. [n.p., 1689?] cap., 4°.* LL, CT; CH, CN, MM.

     [Betterby, W.] Brief examination of the present. 1689. *See* Gardiner, Samuel.

2084   **[Betterton, Thomas.]** The revenge. *For W. Cademan,* 1680. 4°. T.C.I 418. L, O, OW; CH, CN, MH, TU, WF, Y.

2085   **[Bettris, Jeane.]** A lamentation for the deceived people of the world. colop: *For Thomas Simmons,* 1657. cap., 4°.* LT; PH.

2086   —Spiritual discoveries. Second edition. [n.p.], 1657. 4°.* LF.

2087   **Betts, John.** De ortu et natura sanguinis. *Ex officina E. T., vaeneuntque apud Gulielmum Grantham,* 1669. 8°. T.C.I 6. L, O, CCA, E, GH; BN, CJC, PL, WF, Y.

2088   **Betts, Robert.** A body of divinity. *By Richard Cotes, for Io. Bellamie,* 1646. 8°.* LT, O, OC; WF.

2089   **Beuningen, Coenraad van.** The French King's dream. *For R. B. to be sold by Richard Baldwin,* 1689. 4°.* T.C.II 292. L, O, EN.

2089A   **Bevan, Thomas.** [Hebrew] the prayer of prayers. *For P. Parker,* 1673. 8°. O, AN; MH, WF.

2090   **Beveridge, William, *bp.*** Codex canonum ecclesiæ primitivæ vindicatus. *Typis S. Roycroft, prostant apud Robertum Scott,* 1678. 4°. L, O, C, EN, DT; BN, CH, MHL, NU, WF, Y.

2091   —Concio ad synodum. *Excudebat S. Roycroft, sumptibus Roberti Clavell,* 1689. 4°.* T.C.II 288. L, O, LW, EN, DT; CH, MH, WF, Y.

2091A   — —Second edition. —, 1689. 4°.* L, C, LW; NU.

2092   —De linguarum orientalium. *Excudebat Thomas Roycroft,* 1658. 8°.* L, O, CT, EN, DT; BN, CH, CU, MH, NU, WF, Y.

2092A   — —Second edition. —, 1664. 8°.* CSS; MH.

2093   —[Syriac] Id est, grammatica linguæ Domini nostri. *Excudebat Thomas Roycroft, & venales prostant apud Octavianum Pulleyn,* 1658. 8°. L, O, C, EN, DT; BN, CH, CU, MH, NU, WF, Y.

2094   — —[Anr. ed.] *Excudebat Thomas Roycroft, & venales prostant apud Humphredum Robinson,* 1664. 8°. EN; BN, MH.

2095   —Institutionum chronologicarum libri II. *Typis Tho. Roycroft & prostant apud Gualterium Kettilby,* 1669. 4°. T.C.I 6. L, O, C, EN, DT; BN, CN, NC, WF, WSC.

2096   — —[Anr. ed.] *Excudebat Tho. Roycroft, & prostant venales apud Sam. Gellibrand,* 1669. 4°. OC, CM, CT; CLC, Y.

2097   —Of the happiness of the saints. Second edition. *For Thomas Speed,* 1695. 4°.* T.C.II 551. L, BR; CH, TSM, Y.

2098   — —Third edition. —, 1698. 4°.* T.C.III 46. L.

2099   — —Fourth edition. —, 1700. 4°.* T.C.III 177. L, O, CS, EC; CLC, LC, NU, WF, Y.

2099A   —Pregeth ynghylch Godiddugrwydd. [*London*], *J, R. acarworth gan S. Manship,* 1693. AN, CPL.

2100   —A sermon concerning the excellency and usefulness of the common prayer . . . Nov. 27, 1681. *By T. James for Richard Northcott,* 1682. 4°.* L, O, C, LL, YM; NC, PU.

2101   — —Second edition. —, 1682. 4°.* L, O, OC, CJ, HH; CLC, MBA, MH, TU, Y.

2102   — —Third edition. —, 1682. 4°.* T.C.I 490. L, C, WCA, YM; CN, MH, NU, WF, Y.

2103   — —Fourth edition. —, 1682. 4°.* OC, CPL; CH, MH, PU, WF, Y.

2104   — —Fifth edition. —, 1683. 4°.* L, OM, C, EN; CH, MH, WF, Y.

2105   — —Seventh edition. *By T. James, for Richard Northcott,* 1684. 4°.* L, C, LP, EN, DT; TU.

2106   — —Eighth edition. *By A. Grover for Richard Northcott,* 1687. 4°.* L, C, HH, DT; LC, MIU, NC, Y.

2107   — —Tenth edition. *For S. Manship,* 1695. 4°.* CPE; Y.

2108   — —Eleventh edition. *For S. Manship,* 1696. 4°.* O, DT; CLC.

2109   — —Twelfth edition. *Dublin, by Andrew Crook, for Jacob Milner,* 1698. 4°. DIX 303. DT; WF.

2109A   — —"Thirteenth edition." *For S. Manship,* 1700. 12°. TU.

2110   — —Thirteenth edition. *Dublin, by J.B. & S.P. for Jacob Milner,* 1700. 8°. DIX 321. C, DI, Y.

2111   — —[Anr. ed.] *Edinburgh, printed,* 1700. 4°. L, EN; CH.

2112   —A sermon preach'd . . . Nov. 18, 1689. *For N.R. and J. Bullord,* 1689. 4°. T.C.II 298. L, O, CT, EC, E; WF.

2113   — —Second edition. —, 1689. 4°.* EN; NU, WF, Y.

2114   —A sermon preached . . . October 12, 1690. *For Richard Northcott,* 1690. 4°.* T.C.II 329. L, O, C, EN, DT; CLC, MB, NC, WF, Y.

2115   —Συνοδικον sive pandectae. *Oxonii, e theatro Sheldoniano, sumptibus Guilielmi Wells & Roberti Scott, Lond,* 1672. fol. T.C.I 112. MADAN 2916. L, O, CS, EN, DT; MH, NP, NU, Y.

2116   **Beverland, Adriaan** . . . De fornicatione. *Apud Christoph. Bateman,* 1697. 8°. L, O, MR, GU, DT; BN, CH, LC, WF, Y.

2117   —Peccatum originale κατ᾽ ἐξοχην. *Eleutheropoli* [*London*], [1678]. 8°. L, O, LVD, EN, GH; BN, CLC, MB, TU, WF.

2118   **Beverley, John.** Unio reformantium. *Excudebat J.H. pro S. Thomson,* 1659. 8°. LT, O, CT, LW; MB, MH, Y.

2119   — —[Anr. ed.] *By Ja. C. for John Allen,* 1659. 8°. LT.

2119A   **Beverley, Matthew.** Meditatio mortis. *For the author,* 1695. 4°.* Y.

2120 **Beverley, Thomas.** An apology for the hope. *Printed for and sold by Will. Marshall and John Marshal,* 1697. 4°.* O, LCL, OC.

2121 —An appeal most humble. 1691. *For John Salusbury.* 4°.* C, LCL, LSC; LC.

2122 — —[Anr. ed.] [*n.p.,* 1696.] fol.* O.

2123 [–] An appendix, to a discourse of indictions. colop: *For W. and J. Marshall,* 1700. 4°.* L, O.

2124 —The blessing of Moses. *By J. A. for John Harris,* 1693. 4°.* L, C, LCL; CLC, NU, WF, Y.

2125 —A brief view of the state of mankind. [*London,* 1690.] 4°. EN.

2126 —The catechism of the kingdom. *For the author,* 1690. 4°.* L, O; TU.

2127 — —Second edition. *Printed for and sold by William Marshal,* 1696. 4°.* T.C.II 585. L, C; NU, Y.

2128 [–] A Catholick catechism. *For Tho. Parkhurst and Will. Miller,* 1683. 4°. O; NU.

2129 [–] A chain of principles. [*n.p.,* 1692.] cap., 4°.* O, LW, GU.

2130 [–] —[Anr. ed.] [*n.p.,* 1969.] 4°.* O.

2131 —Christianity the great mystery. *Dondon* [*sic*], *for W. Marshal: and John Marshall.* 1696. 8°. T.C.II 588. L, O, LCL; MH, NU, TU, WF, Y.

2132 [–] The command of God to his people. [*London*], *printed,* 1688. 4°.* L, C, OC, P, EN; CH, NU, PL, WF, Y.

2133 —A compendious assertion. *For William Marshall,* 1694. 4°.* T.C.II 585. L, O, CT, LSC; NPT, NU, Y.

2134 —A conciliatory discourse. *For William Marshall,* 1692. 4°.* T.C.II 922. L, O, C, GU, DT; NU, WF, Y.

2135 —A conciliatoy [*sic*] judgment. *Printed and sold by William Marshall,* 1690. 4°.* T.C.II 311. L, O, GU; NU, WF.

2135A —A demonstrative scripture proof. *Printed,* 1692. 4°.* WF.

2136 —A discourse, being the substance of several sermons. *Printed for and sold by William Marshall, and also by John Marshal,* 1696. 4°. T.C.II 585. L, LCL; MH, NU, TU.

2137 —A discourse of the judgements of God. *By J. M. for Henry Herringham,* 1668. 8°. O, C, LSC, LW; CLC, NU.

2138 —A discourse upon the powers. *For the author, and are to be sold by William Marshall,* 1694. 4°. T.C.II 507. L, O, C, LCL, LWL; MIU, NPT, NU, WF, Y.

2139 [–] A disquisition upon our Saviour's sanction of tithes. *By Th. Dawks,* 1685. 4°.* T.C.II 124. L, O, SP; NU.

2140 —Evangelical repentance. *By R. Smith, for W. Miller,* 1693. 8°. T.C.II 419. L, O, LCL, LW, ENC; NPT, NU, TU, WF, Y.

2141 —An exposition of the divine standard. *For John Salusbury,* 1692. 4°. L, O; LC, NU, Y.

2142 — —Second edition. *For William Marshal, and John Salusbury,* 1693. 4°. C, LCL; TU, Y.

2143 —An exposition of the divinely prophetick Song of Songs. *For the author,* 1687. 4°. L, O, OC, GU; CH, IU, MIU, WF, Y.

2144 Entry cancelled.

2145 —The first part of the Scripture line of time. [*London*], *for the author,* 1687. 4°. L, LSC, P, WCA; MWA, Y.

2146 —A fresh memorial. *For William Marshall and John Salusbury,* 1693. 4°.* T.C.II 449. L, O, CT, AU, ES; MBA, WF, Y.

2147 —The general inefficacy and insincerity. *By John Redmayne for W. Grantham,* 1670. 4°. T.C.I 25. L, OC, OM, CT, LCL; CH, NPT, WF, Y.

2148 — —[Anr. ed.] *By R. Smith, for William Miller,* 1692. L, O, LW; NPT, NU, WF, Y.

2149 —God all in all. *For Will. Marshall, and John Marshal,* 1698. 4°. T.C.III 75. L, C, CS, CT, LCL; NPT, NU, Y.

2150 —The good hope through grace. *For William Marshall, and John Marshal,* [1700]. 4°. L, O.

2151 [–] The grand apocalyptical vision. [*London*], *for John Salusbury,* [1690?]. 4°.* L, O, C; CLC, MWA, NU, WF.

2152 —The great charter. *For the author,* 1694. 8°. LSC.

2153 [–] The great gospel-grace of faith. *For W. Marshal,* 1695. 8°.* T.C.II 536. L, O, C, LCL; NPT, NU, WF, Y.

2154 —The great soul of man. *For William Grantham,* 1675. 8°. CU, LC.

2154A — —[Anr. ed.] —, 1676. 8°. T.C.I 216. O, E, GU; CN, NU.

2154B — —[Anr. ed.] *For William Miller,* 1676. 8°. CN, LC.

2155 — —[Anr. ed.] —, 1677. 8°. L, LCL, LW; NPT.

2156 [–] An humble remonstrance concerning some additional confirmations. [*London,* 1690?] cap., 4°.* L.

2157 —Indictions, or accounting by fifteens. *For W. Marshal and J. Marshal,* 1699. 4°.* T.C.III 136. L, O; CLC.

2158 —Jehovah-jireh. *For the author,* 1695. 4°.* T.C.II 555. L, O, CT, LCL, EN; WF.

2159 —The kingdom of Jesus Christ. [*London*], *printed,* 1689. 4°. T.C.II 272. L, O, C, DT; LC, WF.

2160 —The late great revolution. [*London*], *for John Salusbury,* 1689. 4°.* L, O, CT, OC; CH, TU.

2161 —The loss of the soul. *For W. Marshall,* 1694. 4°.* L, O, C, LCL, SP; NU, TU, WF, Y.

2162 —A memorial of the kingdom of Our Lord. [*London,* 1696.] cap., 4°.* L, O, LW.

2163 [–] A model of the gospel-sanctification. [*n.p.,* 1693.] 4°.* GU.

2164 [–] A most humble representation in a further review. colop: [*London*], *printed for and sold by William Marshall,* 1698. 4°.* O.

2165 —The parable of the ten virgins. *Printed for, and sold by Will. Marshal, and John Marshal,* 1697. 4°. T.C.III 19. L, O, LCL, GU; NU.

2166 —The patriarchal line of time. [*London*], *for the author,* 1688. 4°. L, C, DT.

2167 —The pattern of the divine temple, sanstuary [*sic*]. [*London*], *printed, and are to be sold by John Salusbury,* [1690]. 4°.* L, O, C, E; LC, MWA, TU.

2168 [–] Positions containing a full account. [*London,* 1688]. cap., 4°.* PL.

2169 —The prophetical history of the Reformation. [*London*], *printed,* 1689. 4°. L, O, C, E, DT; CLC, MWA, NU, WF, Y.

2170 [–] Reflections upon the theory of the earth. *For Walter Kettilby*, 1699. 4°. T.C.III 111. L, O, OC, CS, DT; LC, NU, WF, Y.

2171 —A review of what God hath been pleased to do. *For William Marshal and John Marshal*, 1698. 4°.* L, O.

2172 [–] A scheme of prophesy. [*London*, 1696.] 4°.* C, MC, E, EN; CLC, LC, NU.

2173 —A scripture-line of time. [*London*], *printed*, 1684. 4°. L, C, LCL; CH, MBC, MU, NU, WF.

2174 ——[Anr. ed.] *Printed*, 1692. 4°.* L, O, C, LW; CLC, PL, WF, Y.

2175 —A sermon of the true, spiritual transubstantiation. [*London*], *for the author*, 1687. 4°. L, O, CSS, OB, BAMB; TU, WF.

2176 —A sermon upon Revel. 11. 11. *For John Salisbury*, 1692. 4°.* L, C, SP; LC, Y.

2177 —A solemn perswasion. *For and sold by W. Marshall, and J. Marshall jun.*, 1695. 4°.* T.C.II 547. L, O, LCL, LW; CH, MH, NU, WF, Y.

2178 ——[Anr. ed.] *For W. Marshall*, 1695. 4°.* CT; CH, NPT, NU.

2179 [–] A summary of arguments. [*n.p.*, 1692.] 4°.* GU.

2179A —The testimony of. [*London*, 1691.] brs. LW.

2180 —The thousand years kingdom of Christ. 1690. 4°.* O.

2181 ——[Anr. ed.] *Printed*, 1691. 4°.* L, O, LW; MWA.

2182 —Tidings of peace. [*Utrecht*, 1692.] 4°. C.

2183 —To the high court of Parliament. [*London*, 1691.] brs. L.

2184 [–] True religion the interest of nations. [*London*, 1683.] 4°. NU.

2185 —The true state of gospel truth. *For William Marshall*, 1693. 4°. T.C.II 450. L, O, C, GU, DT; LC, MH, NU, WF, Y.

2186 —The universal Christian doctrine. *Printed*, 1691. 4°.* L, O, C; LC, MWA, WF.

2187 [–] The wonderful confirmation of the succession of the kingdom of Christ at 1697. [*London*, 1690?] cap., 4°.* L; CSB.

2188 **Beverley, Thomas, *of Lilley*.** The principles of Protestant truth. *For Tho. Parkhurst and Will. Miller*, 1683. 8°. T.C.II 13. L, O, LSC, SP, WCA; NU.

2188A [–] The woe of scandal. *For Tho. Parkhurst*, 1682. 4°. T.C.I 505. O, SP; NU.

2188B **Bew, Thomas.** [Promise to provide horses]. [*Oxford*], 1678. brs. MADAN 3171*. OA.

2189 Beware of false prophets. *By John Hammond*, [1644.] 4°.* LT; TU.

2190 Beware the bearc, the strange, but pleasing history of Balbulo and Rosina. *For Edward Crowch*, 1650. 8°.* LT.

2191 **Bewick, John.** An answer to a Quakers seventeen heads of queries. *By T. R. for Andrew Crook*, 1660. 4°. LT, O, LF; MHS, MU.

2192 [–] An antidote against lay-preaching. *For Andrew Crook*, 1642. 4°.* LT, O, CT, LLP, OC; CH, CLC, NU, WF, Y.

2193 —Confiding England vnder conflicts. *By I. D. for Andrew Crooke*, 1644. 4°. LT, O, E, EN, DT; CU, NU.

2194 **Bewick, William.** A sermon preached . . . 26th of June, 1696. *Printed and are to be sold by E. Whitlock*, 1696. 4°.* T.C.II 599. CH.

2195 **Bèze, Théodore de.** Theodori Bezæ . . . epitaphia selecta. *Pro Jo. Barksdale, Cirencestriensi*, 1680. 12°.* O; CH.

2196 —A learned treatise of the plague. *By T. Radcliffe, to be sold by E. Thomas*, 1665. L, LWL, HH, P.

2197 Entry cancelled.

BIBLES

BIBLE. ANGLO-SAXON. OLD TESTAMENT.

2198 Heptateuchus, liber Job. *Oxoniæ, e theatro Sheldoniano, typis Jvnianis*, 1698. 4°. L, O, C, EN, DT; CH, CN, LC, MH, NC, Y.

2199 —*Oxoniæ*, 1699. 4°. E.

BIBLE. ENGLISH.

2200 The Holy Bible. *Printed at London by Robert Barker, and by the assignes of John Bill*, 1641. 8°. L, LBS; CH, CN, LC.

2201 ——, 1642. 8°. L, CPE.

2201A ——, 1642. 12°. L, O, LBS; MH.

2202 —*Amsterdam by Joost Broerss*, 1642. fol. L, O, LBS, CCA.

2203 —*Printed at London by Robert Barker: and by the assignes of Iohn Bill*, 1643. 8°. L, O, LBS.

2204 ——, 1643. 12°. L.

2205 ——, 1644. 12°. L, O, LBS.

2206 —*Amsterdam, by Thomas Stafford*, 1644. fol. L, CT, D; CH, MBP, SW.

2207 —*Amsterdam, for C. P.*, 1644. 16°. L, O, LBS, CT.

2207A —*By the assignes of Robert Barker*, 1645. 12°. MBP.

2208 —*Cambridge, by Roger Daniel*, [1645]. 8°. L.

2209 ——, 1645. 12°. L, CT, LBS.

2210 —[*Amsterdam?*], *according to the copie, printed by Roger Daniel, Cambridge*, 1645. 4°. L, LBS, CT.

2211 —*Amsterdam, for C.P.*, 1645. 12°. C, LBS.

2212 —*By William Bentley*, 1646. 8°. L, O, C, LBS, MR.

2213 —*Printed*, 1646. 8°. LBS [frag.]

2214 —*Printed at London by Robert Barker: and by the assignes of John Bill*, 1646. 12°. L, C, LBS; TU.

2215 —*By the assignes of Robert Barker*, 1646. 12°. L.

2216 —*By the company of stationers*, 1647. 8°. L, O, LBS, GK.

2217 —*By the assignes of John Bill and Christopher Barker*, 1647. 8°. LBS; CH.

2218 —colop: *By Robert White and Thomas Brudenell*, 1647. 12°. L.

2219 —*Printed at London, by Robert Barker; and by the assignes of John Bill*, 1647. 12°. L, O, LBS, MR; WF.

2220 —*Cambridge, R. Daniel; London, R. Barker*, 1647. 12°. LBS.

2220A —*Amsterdam, John Canne*, 1647. 8°. LLL.

2221 —*For the company of stationers*, 1648. 4°. L, O, C, LBS, BR.

2222 —*By the company of stationers*, 1648. 8°. L, O, C, LBS; CH, WF.

2223 —*By the companie of stationers*, 1648. 12°. L, O, LBS.

2224 —*By William Bentley*, 1648. 8°. L, O, LBS, OC; CH.

2225 —*By John Field*, 1648. 4°. L, O, LBS, CCA; CLC.

2226 —*By Roger Dainel [sic], Cambridge*, 1648. 12°. L, O, C, LBS, CT; CH, OCI, PL, WF, Y.

2227 Entry cancelled.

2228 —*By the company of stationers*, 1649. 4°. L, O, CT, LBS, GK; BBE.

2229 — —, 1649. 12°. LBS, GK.

2230 —*Edinburgh, by Evan Tyler*, 1649. 12°. ALDIS 1357. L, LBS, EN.

2231 —*By the company of stationers*, 1650. 8°. L, O, LBS, P; CLC, MH.

2232 —*By the companie of stationers*, 1651. 8°. L, O, LBS; NN.

2233 — —, 1651. 12°. L, O, LBS.

2234 — —, 1652. 12°. L, O, LBS, LG; CLC.

2235 —*By John Field*, 1652. 12°. L, LBS; Y.

2236 —*For Giles Calvert*, 1653. 12°. C, LBS.

2237 —*By Evan Tyler for a society of stationers*, 1653. 12°. L, C.

2238 —*By Iohn Field*, 1653. 12°. L, LBS, LG, OC; CH, MBA, MBP, MH TU.

2239 — —, 1653. 12°. L, O, LBS, OC, DT; MH, NU, PL, WCL, Y.

2240 —*By John Field*, 1653. 12°. L; MH, WCL.

2241 —*By Roger Daniel*, 1654. 4°. L, O, LBS, CM, EN.

2242 —*Imprinted at London by Evan Tyler, for a society of stationers*, 1654. 12°. L, O, LBS, YM; CLC.

2243 —*By Evan Tyler for a society of stationers*, 1655. 12°. L, LBS.

2244 —*By E. T. for a society of stationers*, 1655. 4°. L, O, LBS; CLC.

2245 — —, 1655. 8°. L, O, LBS, CK; CH.

2246 —*By Iohn Field*, 1655. 12°. L, O, LBS.

2247 — —, 1656. 12°. LBS.

2248 — —, 1657. 12°. L, O, LBS; TU.

2249 —*By R. Daniel*, 1657. 8°. L, LBS.

2250 —*By Henry Hills and John Field*, 1657. 12°. L, LBS.

2251 —*By Iames Flesher*, 1657. 12°. L, C; Y.

2252 —*Cambridge, by John Field*, 1657. 8°. L, O, C, LBS, DT; CN, MH.

2253 —*By Iohn Field*, 1658. 12°. L, O, C, LBS, MR; MBP, MH, TU, WF, Y.

2254 —*By Henry Hills, and John Field*, 1658. 12°. L.

2255 —*Cambridge, John Field*, 1659–60. 2 v. fol. L, O, CT, LBS, DT; CH, MBA, TU, WCL.

2256 —*By Henry Hills and John Field*, 1660. 8°. L, O, C, LBS, DT; MH, NGT, NP, WF.

2256A —*By Henry Hills*, 1660. 8°. L; MH.

2257 —*By Iohn Feild, [sic]* 1660. 12°. L, O, LBS.

2258 —*Cambridge, by John Field*, 1660. fol. L, O, C, E, DT; CH, MB, NU, PL, Y.

2259 —*C. Barker, H. Hills*, 1661. 4°. L, LBS.

2260 —*By Christopher Barker*, 1661. 8°. L.

2261 —*C. Barker, J. Field*, 1661. 12°. LBS.

2262 —*By Christopher Barker*, 1661. 12°. L, C.

2263 —*By J. Field*, 1661. 12°. LBS; CH.

2264 —*By John Bill and Christopher Barker*, 1661. 12°. L, EC; CH, V, WF.

2265 —*Cambridge, by John Field*, 1661. 8°. L, O, C, LBS, DT; CH, CN, WF.

2266 —*[Amsterdam?] printed*, 1662. 12°. L, LW.

2267 —*By Iohn Bill and Christopher Barker*, 1663. 8°. L, LBS; PL, WWC.

2268 —*Cambridge, by John Field*, 1663. 4°. L, O, C, LBS, CT.

2269 — —, 1663. 8°. L, C, CCA, LBS.

2270 —*By John Bill, and Christopher Barker*, 1664. 12°. L, LBS.

2271 —*[Amsterdam?], printed*, 1664. 12°. L, LBS; Y.

2272 —*Cambridge, by John Field*, 1664. 12°. LBS.

2273 —*By John Bill and Christopher Barker*, 1665. 12°. L, LBS.

2274 — —, 1666. 12°. L, O, LBS.

2275 —*Cambridge, by John Field*, 1666–8. 4°. L, O, CCH, E, DT; CH, WF, Y.

2276 —*By John Bill and Christopher Barker*, 1668. 12°. LBS.

2277 —*Cambridge, by John Field*, 1668. 4°. L, O, C, LBS, ENC; CH, CU, V, Y.

2278 —*By John Bill and Christopher Barker*, 1669. 8°. L, O, C, LBS; MB, WCL.

2279 — —, 1669. 12°. L, LBS, CCH.

2279A — —, 1670. 8°. Y.

2280 —*By the assigns of John Bill and Christopher Barker*, 1670. 12°. L, O.

2281 —*Cambridge, by John Hayes*, 1670. 4°. L, O, C, LBS; CH.

2282 —*By John Bill and Christopher Barker*, 1671. 8°. L, O, C, LBS, EN.

2283 —*By the assigns of John Bill and Christopher Barker*, 1671. 12°. L, O, LBS, DT.

2284 —*Amsterdam, Stephen Swart*, 1672. fol. C.

2285 —*[Amsterdam], printed*, 1672. fol. L, O, LBS, YM.

2286 —*By the assigns of J. Bill & Chr: Barker*, 1672. 12°. L, O, LBS; CH.

2287 —*Imprinted at London by Robert Barker, and by the assigns of John Bill*, 1673. 12°. L, O, LBS.

2288 —*By the assigns of John Bill and Christopher Barker*, 1673. 12°. L, O, LBS; MB.

2289 —*Cambridge, by John Hayes*, 1673. 4°. L, O, C, LBS, MR; WF, Y.

2290 —*By the assigns of J. Bill & Chr: Barker*, 1674. 24°. L, C, LBS.

2291 —*Cambridge by John Hayes*, 1674. fol. T.C.I 175. L, O, C, LBS, OC; CLC.

2292 —*By the assigns of John Bill and Christopher Barker*, 1675. 8°. LBS.

2293 — —, 1675. 12°. L, LBS.

2294 —*Cambridge by John Hayes*, 1675. 4°. L, O, C, LBS; MBP.

2295 —*Oxford, at the theater*, 1675. 8°. MADAN 3084. L, O, C, LBS; NP, Y.

2296 —*C. Barker*, 1676. 4°. LBS.

2297 —*By John Bill and Christopher Barker*, 1676. 8°. L, O, LBS; CH.

2298 —*By the assigns of J. Bill and Chr Barker*, 1676. 12°. L, LBS.

2299 —*By the assigns of John Bill and Christopher Barker*, 1676. 24°. LBS, BR.

2300 —*Edinburgh, by Andrew Anderson*, 1676. 8°. ALDIS 2072. L, LBS, EN, GU.

2301 —*By Christopher Barker*, 1677. 4°. L, LBS.

2302   —*By the assigns of John Bill and Christopher Barker, 1677.* 12°. L.

2303   —*Cambridge, by John Hayes, 1677.* 4°. L, O, C, LBS, D; CH, MIU, WWC.

2304   —*By John Bill, Christopher Barker, Thomas Newcomb, and Henry Hills, 1678.* 8°. L, O, LBS, OC, BR; BBE.

2305   —*By John Bill, Christopher Barker, Tho. Newcomb, and Henry Hills, 1678.* 8°. L; WCL.

2306   —*Edinburgh, heir of A. Anderson, 1678.* 4°. ALDIS 2115. L, EN, GU.

2306A — —, *1679.* fol. DC, ENC.

2307   —*By Jo. Bill Tho. Newcomb, and H. Hills, 1679.* 8°. L, O, LBS, DC, MR; WF.

2308   — —, *1679.* 12°. LBS.

2309   —*At the theater in Oxford, 1679.* 8°. MADAN 3243. L, O, LBS; MB, Y.

2310   —*[Amsterdam?], printed, 1679.* fol. L, O, EN; CH, NU.

2311   —*Amsterdam, for Stephen Swart, 1679.* fol. L, C, LBS, E; CN, NC.

2312   —*By John Bill and Christopher Barker, 1680.* 12°. L, O, LBS.

2313   —*By Jo. Bill, Tho. Newcomb, and H. Hills, 1680.* 12°. LBS.

2314   —*Oxford at the theater, 1680.* colop: *Printed at the theater in Oxford, and to be sold by Moses Pitt, Peter Parker, William Leake and Thomas Guy, London, 1680.* fol. MADAN 3284. L, O, C, LBS, EN; CH, MBA, MHS.

2315   —*At the theater in Oxford, 1680.* 8°. MADAN 3285. L, O, LBS; Y.

2316   —*By the assigns of J. Bill, T. Newcomb, and Hen. Hills, 1681.* 12°. L, O, LBS.

2317   —*By the assigns of John Bill, Thomas Newcomb, and Henry Hills, 1681.* 12°. L, LBS.

2318   —*Oxford, at the theatre, for T. Guy, London, 1681.* 12°. LBS; Y.

2318A —*Printed at the theatre in Oxford, to be sold by Moses Pitt, Peter Parker, William Leake, Thomas Guy, London, 1681.* fol. L; Y.

2319   —*[Amsterdam], printed, 1682.* 12°. L, O, C, HH, MR; NHC, V, WF.

2320   —*By the assigns of John Bill, and by Henry Hills, and Thomas Newcomb, 1682.* 8°. L, O, C, LBS, OC; MB, MBA, Y.

2321   — —, *1682.* 12°. L, LBS.

2322   — —, *1682.* 12°. L, LBS, LCL.

2323   —*Cambridge, by John Hayes, 1682.* 4°. LBS, LG, CS, DCH, YM; CH.

2324   —*Oxford, at the theater, to be sold by Ann Leake, London, 1682.* fol. T.C.I 513. L, O, LBS.

2325   —*Oxford, at the theater, to be sold by Peter Parker, London, 1682,* fol. L, LW, CSE, DT; CH, Y.

2326   —*Printed at yᵉ theater in Oxford, sold by P. Parker, [London, 1682].* 12°. O.

2327   —*Printed at yᵉ theatre in Oxford, sold by M. Pitt, [1682].* 4°. L; WWC.

2328   —*Oxford, at the theatre for T. Guy, London, 1682.* 8°. LBS.

2329   Entry cancelled.

2330   —*[Amsterdam], printed, 1683.* fol. L, O, LBS, MR, DT.

2331   —*By C. Bill, H. Hills, and Tho. Newcomb, 1683.* 12°. L, LBS.

2332   —*By the assigns of John Bill, and Henry Hills, and Thomas Newcomb, 1683.* 12°. LBS.

2333   —*Cambridge by John Hayes, 1683.* 4°. L, O, C, LBS, CT; MH, MIU, PL.

2334   —*Oxford, at the theater, 1683.* 4°. L, O, LBS, MR, EN.

2335   —*By the assings [sic] of J. Bill, Thomas Newcomb, and Henry Hills, 1684.* 12°. L, O, LBS, DT; CH, MH.

2336   —*By the assigns of J. Bill, and H. Hills, and T. Newcomb, 1684.* 12°. L, LBS.

2337   —*By the assigns of J. Bill, T. Newcomb, and Hen. hills [sic], 1684.* 24°. LBS, EC; MB.

2338   —*Oxford, at the theater, sold by Thomas Guy, London, 1684.* fol. L, LBS.

2339   —*By the assigns of John Bill: and by Henry Hills, and Thomas Newcomb, 1685.* 8°. L, O, LBS; TU.

2340   — —, *1685.* 12°. LBS.

2341   —*Oxford, printed at the theater, 1685.* fol. L, LBS, OC; PL, WWC.

2342   —*Printed at the theater in Oxford, to be sold by Thomas Guy, London, 1685.* 12°. L, O, C, LBS.

2343   —*By Charles Bill, Henry Hills, and Thomas Newcomb, 1686.* 12°. L, LBS; CH.

2344   —*Oxford, at the theatre, for P. Parker, London, 1686.* 4°. O, LBS.

2345   —*Oxford, at the theatre, for T. Guy in London, 1686.* 12°. LBS.

2346   —*By Charles Bill, Henry Hills, and Thomas Newcomb, 1687.* 12°. L, DT.

2347   —*Oxford, at the theatre, for T. Guy, London, 1687.* 4°. LBS, EN.

2348   — —, *1687.* 12°. LBS.

2349   —*By Charles Bill, Henry Hills, and Thomas Newcomb, 1688.* 12°. L, LBS.

2350   —*Oxford, at the theater, to be sold by Thomas Guy, London, 1688.* fol. L, O, LBS.

2351   —*Printed at the theater in Oxford, to be sold by Thomas Guy, London, 1688.* 12°. O, LBS.

2352   —*By the assigns of J. Bill, T. Newcomb and Henry Hills, 1689.* 12°. L, O.

2353   —*Oxford, at the theater to be sold by Thomas Guy, London, 1689.* 8°. L, O, LBS.

2354   —*By J. Rawlins, for Richard Chiswell and Jonathan Robinson; and Brabazon Aylmer, 1690.* fol. L, O, C, LBS, DT; CU, PL, WCL.

2355   —*By C. Bill and T. Newcomb, 1690.* 8°. L, LBS.

2356   —*By C. Bill, and the executrix of T. Newcomb, 1691.* 12°. LBS.

2357   —*Printed at the theater in Oxford, to be sold by Thomas Guy, London, 1691.* 12°. L, O, LBS; NR.

2358   Entry cancelled.

2359   —*By Charles Bill and the executrix of Thomas Newcomb, 1692.* 8°. O, LBS.

2360   — —, *1693.* 8°. L.

2361   — —, *1693.* 12°. L, LBS.

2362   — —, *1694.* 12°. L, O, LBS; Y.

2363 —*Edinburgh, by the heir of Andrew Anderson, 1694. 4°.* LBS, EN.

2364 —*By Charles Bill, and the executrix of Thomas Newcomb, 1695. 8°.* L, LBS.

2365 — —*, 1695. 12°.* LBS.

2366 —*Oxford, by the university-printers, 1695. 12°.* L, O, LBS, OC; CH, Y.

2367 —*By Charles Bill, and the executrix of Thomas Newcomb, 1696. fol.* L, O, LG; CLC.

2368 —*1696. 12°.* ENC.

2369 —*Oxford: by the university-printers, 1696. 12°.* L, O, C, LBS; Y.

2370 —*Edinburgh, by the heirs and successors of Andrew Anderson, 1696. 12°.* ALDIS 3540. L, EN.

2371 —*By Charles Bill, and the executrix of Thomas Newcomb, 1697. 4°.* L, HH.

2371A — —*, 1697. 12°.* L, O.

2372 —*Oxford: by the university-printers, 1697. 4°.* L, O, LBS, OC, EC; Y.

2373 —*By Charles Bill, and the executrix of Thomas Newcomb, 1698. 12°.* L, O, C, LBS, ENC; CLC, MBP, NU, V, Y.

2374 —*Edinburgh, by the heirs and successors of Andrew Anderson, 1698. 12°.* ALDIS 3733. O, LBS, EN; NGT.

2375 —*By Charles Bill and the executrix of Thomas Newcomb, 1699. 8°.* L, O, LBS, LCS.

2376 —*Oxford: by the university-printers, 1699. 12°.* L, O, LBS.

2377 —*By Charles Bill and the executrix of Thomas Newcomb, 1700. 8°.* L, O, LBS, EN, DT; CLC.

2378 — —*, 1700. 12°.* O, LBS; V.

2378A —*Edinburgh, by the heirs and successors of A. Anderson, 1700. 4°.* L, EN.

BIBLE. ENGLISH. OLD TESTAMENT

2379 The Old Testament: with annotations. *By J. Rawlins for Brabazon Aylmer, 1690. fol.* L; WF.

BIBLE. ENGLISH. OLD TESTAMENT. SELECTIONS.

2380 The third part of the Bible. *Edinburgh, E. Tyler, 1642. 16°.* ALDIS 1030. L, LBS.

BIBLE. ENGLISH. PSALMS.

2381 The whole book of psalmes. *By G. M. for the companie of stationers, 1641. 4°.* L, O, E, DT; CH, LC, Y.

2382 —*By E. G. for the company of stationers, 1641. 4°.* L; CH.

2383 —*For the company of stationers, 1641. 4°.* L.

2384 — —*, 1641. 8°.* L, O, YM; MB, MH, OCI, WF.

2385 —*By M. F. for the company of stationers, 1641. 12°.* L, O.

2386 —*By I. Okes, for the company of stationers, 1641. 4°.* L.

2386A — —*By the printer to the University of Cambridge, 1641. 12°.* CCC.

2387 The psalmes of David, in metre. *Edinburgh, by Robert Bryson, 1641. 8°.* ALDIS 1015. L.

2388 The psalmes of David, in prose and metre. *Edinburgh, by Robert Bryson, 1641. 16°.* ALDIS 1016. EN.

2389 The whole book of psalmes. *For the company of stationers, 1642. 12°.* L, O.

2390 —*By G. M. for the companie of stationers, 1642. 12°.* L, CT; MIU.

2391 —*By M. F. for the company of stationers, 1642. 12°.* L.

2391A —*By I. L. for the company of stationers, 1642. 8°.* L, OC.

2391B —*By R. Y. for the company of stationers, 1642. 12°.* Y.

2391C The psalter, or psalms. *For the societie of stationers, 1642. 8°.* OC.

2392 The cl. psalmes of David in meeter. *Edinburgh by James Bryson, 1642. 12°.* L.

2393 The psalmes of David in meeter. *Edinburgh, by Robert Bryson, 1642. 12°.* ALDIS 1052. L, EN.

2393A The booke of psalmes in English metre. *1642. 16°.* MB.

2394 The whole booke of psalmes. *By I. L. for the company of stationers, 1643. 8°.* L, O; Y.

2394A —*By G. M. for the company of stationers, 1643. 8°.* L.

2395 —*By R. C. for the company of stationers, 1643. 8°.* L, O, LP; CH, MB.

2396 The psalmes of David in English meeter. *By James Young, for Philip Nevill, 1643. 8°.* AU.

2397 — —*, 1643. 24°.* L.

2398 The CL. psalmes of David. *Edinburgh, by Evan Tyler, 1643. 4°.* ALDIS 1101. L, O, EN, ENC; NN.

2399 The psalmes of David, in prose and meeter. *Edinburgh, by Robert Bryson, 1643. 16°.* ALDIS 1100. C, EN; Y.

2400 The whole booke of psalmes. *By G. M. for the companie of stationers, 1644. 12°.* L, DC.

2400A —*By Robert Barker, and the assignes of John Bill, 1644. 12°.* L.

2400B —*By R. Bishop for the company of stationers, 1644. 12°.* L.

2401 The book of psalms in metre. *By Matthew Simmons, for the companie of stationers, 1644. 12°.* L, O, LW, AU, GU, PPT.

2402 The psalter of David. *Oxford, by Leonard Lichfield, 1644. 8°.* MADAN 1626. L, O; MB, Y.

2403 The psalmes of David in meeter and prose. *Edinburgh, by Evan Tyler, 1644. 16°.* ALDIS 1152. L, EN; CH.

2404 The psalter. *Dublin, 1644. 8°.* O.

2405 The booke of psalmes. *Amsterdam, by Thomas Stafford, 1644. 8°.* L, O, C, YM, EN; MBP, NPT, WWC, Y.

2405A The whole book of psalmes. *Amsterdam, for C. P., 1644. 12°.* CT; MBA.

2406 The whole book of psalmes. *1645. 8°.* O.

2407 The book of psalmes in metre. *For G. M. sold by S. Gellibrand, J. Kirton, T. Vnderhill, S. Bowtell, 1645. 12°.* L, O, CT; CH.

2408 The psalter or psalms. *1645. 8°.* O.

2409 The whole book of psalmes. *Cambridge, by Roger Daniel, 1645. 4°.* L, O.

2410 — —*, 1645. 12°.* L.

2410A —*Amsterdam, for C. P., 1645.* MBA.

2410B —*[Amsterdam], according to the copie, printed by R. Daniel, Cambridge, 1645. 4°.* CT.

2411 —*For the companie of stationers, 1646. 8°.* L, O, MR; TU.

2412 —*[London], by I. L. for the company of stationers, [1646]. 8°.* L.

2413 —*By A. M. for the companie of stationers*, 1646. 8°. L, AU.

2414 —*By E. G. for the company of stationers*, 1646. 8°. L.

2415 —*By G. M. for the company of stationers*, 1646. 8°. L, CT, BR; Y.

2416 —*By G. M. for the companie of stationers*, 1646. 12°. L; CH, MBP.

2417 —[*n.p.*], *by I. L. for the companie of stationers*, 1646. 8°. L.

2418 The psalms of David in English meeter. *By Miles Flesher, for the company of stationers*, 1646. 12°. L, O, C, LCL, AU; CLC, MH, Y.

2419 The psalter of David. Second edition. *For R. Royston*, 1646. 8°. MADAN 1626. LT, O; CH, Y.

2420 The whole booke of psalmes. *Printed by the printers to the university of Cambridge*, 1646. 12°. L.

2421 The psalmes of David, ... Zachary Boyd. Third edition. *Printed at Glasgow by George Anderson*, 1646. 4°. ALDIS 1216. EN.

2422 The whole book of psalms. *By A. M. for the companie of stationers*, 1647. 8°. L, O, BR; CH, MBA, Y.

2422A —*By M. B. for the company of stationers*, 1647. 8°. C; PPT.

2423 —*By E. G. for the company of stationers*, 1647. 8°. CH.

2424 —[*n.p.*], *by I. L. for the company of stationers*, 1647. 8°. L.

2425 The whole book of psalms. *By R. Bishop for the companie of stationers*, 1647. 8°. L.

2426 The psalter of David. Third edition. 1647. 8°. O; CLC, WF.

2427 The whole book of psalmes. Second edition. [*Cambridge, Mass. by Stephen Daye*], imprinted, 1647. EVANS 20. L; RPJ.

2428 A paraphrase upon the divine poems, ... George Sandys. *For O.D.*, 1648. 8°. L, O, AU; NPT.

2428A The psalter or psalmes of David. *Imprinted at London for the societe of stationers*, 1648. 8°. NN.

2429 The whole book of psalms. *By the companie of stationers*, 1648. 12°. L.

2430 —*By M. F. for the company of stationers*, 1648. 4°. L, O, CCA; CLC.

2431 —*By A. M. for the companie of stationers*, 1648. 8°. L, O, D; CH, WF.

2431A ——1648. 12°. L.

2432 —*By Roger Daniel, Cambridge*, 1648. 18°. L, O, CT; OCI, Y.

2433 The psalms of David in meeter. *Amsterdam, Joach. Mosche*, 1648. 16°. O.

2434 The psalmes of David, ... Zachary Boyd. *Printed at Glasgow, by the heires of George Anderson*, 1648. 12°. ALDIS 1311. L, AU, EN, GM, GU; CLC, NN.

2435 The whole book of psalmes. *By Richard Cotes, for the company of stationers*, 1649. 4°. CT.

2436 —*For the company of stationers*, 1649. 8°. L, BR; CLC, MB, MH, NU.

2436A ——*By A. M. for the companie of stationers*, 1649. 8°. DT; Y.

2437 —*By M. F. for the company of stationers*, 1649. 8°. L; CH.

2438 —*By William Bentley*, 1649. 8°. L, O, OC; Y.

2439 The psalter of David. Fourth edition. *By J. F. for R. Royston*, 1650. 12°. MADAN 1626. L, O.

2440 The whole book of psalms, paraphrased: ... by George Abbot. *By William Bentley*, 1650. 12°. L, CT.

2441 The psalms of David in meeter. *Edinburgh, by Evan Tyler*, 1650. 4°. ALDIS 1418. O, EN.

2442 The psalmes of David in meeter.—, 1650. 8°. ALDIS 1419. O, E, EN; MH (t. p. only), Y.

2443 The psalmes of David in meeter. —, 1650. 18°. ALDIS 1421. L, C, OCC, EN, AU; CH, MH, NN.

2444 —*Edinburgh, by Gedeon Lithgow*, 1650. 24°. ALDIS 1423. L, AU.

2445 The whole book of psalmes. *By A. M. for the companie of stationers*, 1651. 12°. L, O, OC, CT; WF.

2446 The psalmes of David, from the new translation of the Bible, turned into meter. *By Ed. Griffin, to be sold by Humphrey Moseley*, 1651. 12°. LT, O, LW, EN; CH, LC, WCL, Y.

2447 The psalms hymns and spiritual songs. Third edition. *By Samuel Green at Cambridge in New-England*, 1651. 8°. EVANS 33. NN.

2447A —Psalms of David in meter. *Edinburgh, Lithgow*, 1651. 4°. ALDIS 1450. EN.

2448 The whole book of psalms. *By A. M. for the company of stationers*, 1652. 12°. L, BR.

2448A —*J. Field*, 1652. 12°. BR.

2449 —*By the companie of stationers*, 1653. 12°. L; Y.

2450 —*By A. M. for the companie of stationers*, 1653. 8°. L; CLC, MH.

2451 —*By John Field*, 1653. 12°. L, CT.

2452 —*By Gartrude Dawson for the company of stationers*, 1653. 8°. L, O.

2453 —*By Roger Daniel*, 1653. 4°. L; CH.

2453A The psalms of David in meeter. *Edinburgh, by Gedeon Lithgow*, 1653. 12°. L; PBM.

2454 —1654. 8°. O.

2455 —*By John Field*, 1654. 12°. L, O; MBP.

2456 Book of psalms in metre, ... William Barton. *By Roger Daniel and William Du-Gard, sold by Francis Eglesfield, and Thomas Underhill*, 1654. 12°. L, O, C; CH, NPT.

2457 The psalmes of David, from the new translation. *By S. G. to be sold by Humphrey Moseley*, 1654. 12°. L, C, LCL, AU, GK; LC, TU, WF, Y.

2458 The vvhole book of psalms. *Lonodn [sic]: for the company of stationers*, 1655. 4°. L, O, CK; MH.

2459 The whole book of psalms. *By A. M. for the companie of stationers*, 1655. 12° L, O, CM, HH, AU; CH, NU.

2460 Davids psalms in metre. *By S. Griffin for J. Rothwel, sold by William Churchil*, 1655. 12°. LT, AU; CH, PL.

2461 The psalter of David. Fifth edition. *By J. F. for R. Royston*, 1655. 12°. MADAN 1626. L, O, CT; MH.

2462 Select psalmes of a nevv translation, to be sung. [*London*, 1655.] 4°. CH.

2463 The psalms of David in meeter. *Edinburgh, Lithgow*, 1655. 4°. ALDIS 1524. L, O; NN.

2464 The whole book of psalms. *By the companie of stationers*, 1656. 12°. L, CT; CH.

2465 —*By John Field*, 1656. 12°. L.

2466 The psalms of David in meeter. *Edinburgh, Lithgow,* 1656. 8°. ALDIS 1555. L; NN.

2467 The whole book of psalms. *Cambridge, by John Field,* 1657. 8°. L, BR, DT; MH.

2468 Entry cancelled.

2469 The psalms of David and the New Testament. *Printed,* 1658. 8°. L, O.

2470 The whole book of psalms. *By Iohn Field,* 1658. 12°. L, O; MBP, MH, Y.

2470A The whole book of psalms. *By R. W. for the company of stationers,* 1658. 8°. WWC.

2470B —The psalms, hymns, and spiritual songs. *Cambridge* [*Mass.*], *for Hezekiah Usher of Bostoo* [*sic*], [*c.* 1658.] EVANS 49. MWA, NN.

2471 Psalms of David in meeter. colop: *Edinburgh, Gedeon Lithgovv,* 1659. 8°. AU.

2472 The whole book of psalms. *For the company of stationers,* 1660. 8°. L.

2473 ——1661. 8°. L, OC, AU; CN, MB, NGT.

2473A Samuelis primitiæ or, an essay . . . psalms. *By Thomas Milbourne,* 1661. 8°. LLP; MB.

2474 The psalter of David. *By J. F. for R. Royston,* 1661. 12°. O, OC, AU.

2475 The whole booke of psalmes. *By S. G. for the company of stationers,* 1661. fol. L, OC, CSE; MB.

2476 —*Cambridge, by John Field,* 1661. 8°. L, O, CT, OC, EC; CLC.

2477 The psalms of David in meeter. *Edinburgh, by Evan Tyler,* 1661. 4°. ALDIS 1716. L, O, EN, AU; CLC, V.

2477A The whole book of psalms. *Dublin, by John Crook,* 1661. 4°. DIX 112. L.

2478 The psalter or psalms of David. *By the printers to the kings most excellent majesty,* 1662. fol. L; WWC.

2478A —*By T. N. for the company of stationers,* 1662. fol. OC.

2479 The psalms of King David. 1662. 8°. O.

2480 The whole book of psalms. *Cambridge, by John Field,* 1662. 8°. L, O, CT; WF.

2481 —*For the company of stationers,* 1663. 4°. L; CH.

2481A ——1663. 8°. L, OC; WWC.

2482 —*For the company of stationers,* 1663. 12°. L, O; CH.

2483 —*By John Field, Cambridge,* 1663. 8°. L, O, C, CT, DCH.

2484 —[*n.p.*], *printed,* 1664. 12°. L, O.

2485 The psalms of King David. 1664. 8°. O.

2486 The whole book of psalms. *For the company of stationers,* 1664. 12°. L; CH, LC.

2486A —The psalms paraphrased. *By Thomas Garthwait,* 1664. 8°. LLP.

2486B —*By John Field, Cambridge,* 1664. 12°. OC.

2486C The psalter or psalmes. *Dublin by John Crook, to be sold by Samuel Dancer,* 1664. 4°. DIX 126. L, DN, DT; NN.

2487 The psalms, hymns, and spiritual songs. *Cambridge* [*Mass.*], *for Hezekiah Usher, of Boston* [*c.* 1664]. 12°. CH, MB, MWA, NN.

2488 —Fifth edition. *Cambridge:* [*Mass.*], *for Hezekiah Usher of Bostoo* [*sic*], [1665]. 12°. EVANS 96. CH, MWA, NN.

2488A The whole book of psalms. *For the company of stationers,* 1665. 12°. NU.

2489 The whole book of psalms. *For the company of stationers,* 1666. 8°. L, DC; NPT.

2490 —*By John Field, Cambridge,* 1666. 4°. L, O, CT, E, DT; CH, NGT, V.

2491 A paraphrase upon the psalms of David, by Sam Woodford. *By R. White, for Octavian Pullein,* 1667. 4°. L, O, C, EN, AU; CH, CU, LC, MH, NU, Y.

2492 —*By R. W. for Jo. Dunmore and Octavian Pulleyn,* 1667. 4°. CH.

2493 The whole book of psalms. *By J. M. for the company of stationers,* 1668. 8°. L.

2494 The psalms of King David paraphrased . . . by Miles Smyth. *For T. Garthwait,* 1668. 8°. L, O, CS, EN, DT; CH, MB, NU, Y.

2495 The psalter of David. Seventh edition. *By B. Tyler for R. Royston,* 1668. 12°. T.C.I 3. L.

2496 The whole book of psalms. *By T. N. for the company of stationers,* 1669. fol. L.

2497 —*By T. R. for the company of stationers,* 1669. 8°. L, O; MB, NU, WCL, WWC.

2498 —*By G. M. for the companie of stationers,* 1669. 12°. L, CT; NU, Y.

2499 The psalmes of David in meeter. *Edinburgh, by Andrevv Anderson,* 1669. 4°.* ALDIS 1878. L, O, EN, AU; Y.

2500 —*Edinburgh, by Andrevv Anderson,* 1669. 8°. ALDIS 1879. L; NN.

2501 The whole book of psalms. *By J. M. for the company of stationers,* 1670. 12°. L, O.

2502 A paraphrase upon the psalms of David. *Dunmore,* 1670. 4°. CN.

2503 The vvhole book of psalms. *By John Hayes, of Cambridge,* 1670. 8°. L, O, SC; CH, NU.

2503A Psalms of David in meeter. *Edinburgh, by A. Anderson for A. Heslop,* 1670. 4°. ALDIS 1911. EN.

2504 —*By Tho. Newcomb, for the company of stationers,* 1671. 8°. L, O, EC, DT; MB.

2505 —*By J. M. for the company of stationers,* 1671. 12°. L.

2505A The psalms, hymns, and spiritual songs. Fifth edition. *By A. C. for Ric. Chiswel,* 1671. 12°. L; NN.

2506 The psalms of David. Second edition. *By S. and B. Griffin, sold by John Playford,* 1671. 8°. L, C, LCL; CH, NU, Y.

2507 The psalms of David in meeter. *Edinburgh, by Andrew Anderson for J. Miller,* 1671. 4°. ALDIS 1929. O; NN.

2508 —*Edinburgh, by George Swinton and Thomas Brown, and are to be sold by James Glen and David Trench,* 1671. 12°. ALDIS 1931. LW, AU; MH, Y.

2509 The psalter of David. Eighth edition. 1672. 12°. O, YM.

2510 The whole book of psalms. *For the company of stationers,* 1672. 12°. L.

2511 —*By J. M. for the company of stationers,* 1673. 12°. L, O, CS, BR; MB.

2511A The whole book of psalms. *By Robert Barker and by the assigns of John Bill,* 1673. WF.

2511B The psalms of David in meeter. *For the company of stationers, to be sold by Thomas Parkhurst, and Dorman Newman,* 1673. 12°. SP; MB.

2512   Psalms in metre. [*Cambridge*], 1673. 4°. MR.

2513   The whole book of psalms. *By John Hayes, Cambridge,* 1673. 8°. L, O, CS; WF, Y.

2514   —[*London*], *for the company of stationers,* 1674. 24°. L, O.

2515   Entry cancelled.

2516   The whole book of psalms. *By J.M. for the company of stationers,* 1675. 12°. L.

2517   —*By John Hayes, Cambridge,* 1675. 4°. L, O, CS; MBP.

2518   —*At the theater in Oxford,* 1675. MADAN 3091. 4°. L, O, EC; Y.

2519   The psalms of David in meeter. *Edinburgh, by George Swintoun,* 1675. 8°. ALDIS 2060. O, EN; NN.

2519A —*Edinburgh, by Thomas Brown,* 1675. 12°. ALDIS 2061. EN.

2520   The whole book of psalms. *By J.C. for the company of stationers,* 1676. 8°. L, LW, CSE; CH, MH, NU, WF.

2520A —*By J.M. for the company of stationers.* 1676. 12°. L, BR.

2521   A paraphrase upon the psalms of David. *By William Godbid, for George Sawbridge,* 1676. 8°. CLC, LC, V.

2521A —*By W. Godbid, for Abel Roper,* 1676. 8°. L, OC; CH, MBP, NPT, WF.

2522   A paraphrase upon the divine poems. Fourth edition. *By J.M. for Abel Roper,* 1676. 8°. T.C.I 261. L, OM, LCL, LV, E; CH, CN, LC, MH, NU, Y.

2522A —[*Anr. ed.*] *By J.M. for G. Sawbridge,* 1676. 8°. CT.

2523   The whole book of psalms. [*Cambridge*], *by John Hayes,* 1676. 4°. L, O.

2524   The psalms of David in meeter. *Edinburgh, by Andrew Anderson,* 1676. 4°. ALDIS 2085. L, C, D, EN; MBA, NN.

2525   —*Edinburgh, by Andrew Anderson,* 1676. 8°. ALDIS 2086. L, O, EN; NN.

2525A The whole book of psalms. [*London*] *for the company of stationers,* 1677. 12°. L.

2526   The whole book of psalms. *By A.C. for the company of stationers,* 1677. 12°. L, CJ, HH; MB, RPJ, Y.

2527   —*By W. Godbid for the company of stationers, and are sold by John Playford,* 1677. 8°. L, O, CM; CLC, MH, NPT.

2527A —*By W. Godbid and A. Clark for the company of stationers,* 1677. fol. CT.

2527B —*For the company of stationers,* 1678. 4°. L, OC, BR.

2528   —*By J.M. for the company of stationers,* 1678. 12°. L, O; WCL.

2529   A paraphrase upon the psalms. Second edition. *By J.M. for John Martyn, John Baker; and Henry Brome,* 1678. 8°. T.C.I 315. L, O, CT, LCL, AU; MIU, NU, WF, Y.

2530   The psalms of David in meeter. *Edinburgh, by T.Brown,* 1678. 8°. ALDIS 2141. O.

2531   The whole book of psalms. *For the company of stationers,* 1679. fol. L, O, DC, MR; MB.

2531A —*By E.T. and R.H. for the company of stationers,* 1679. 8°. MB, WF.

2532   —*By J.C. for the company of stationers,* 1679. 12°. L, O.

2533   —*Oxford, at the theater,* 1679. 8°. MADAN 3251. L, O; MB, Y.

2534   —[*Cambridge*], *by John Hayes,* 1679. 4°. L, CS, CT, YM; Y.

2535   The psalms. *Edinburgh, by the heir of Andrew Anderson,* 1679. 18°. ALDIS 2174. C, E, EN; NN.

2535A —*Edinburgh, by Evan Tyler,* 1679. fol.* PPT.

2536   A century of select psalms. *By F.M. for Richard Royston,* 1679. 8°. T.C.I 370. L, OC, YM; MH, NPT, PPT.

2537   The whole book of psalms. *For the company of stationers,* 1680. 8°. L, E, DT; MB, Y.

2538   The book of psalms paraphras'd. *By M. Flesher for R. Royston,* 1680. 8°. L, O, C, DC, EC; PPT, TU, Y.

2538A The psalms, hymns, and spiritual songs. Fifth edition. *For Richard Chiswell,* 1680. 12°. L, GU; MB, NN.

2538B The whole book of psalms. *Dublin, by Benjamin Took and John Crook, sold by Mary Crook,* 1680. 4°. DIX 179. C, DT.

2539   The psalms of David in metre. *Dublin, by J.Brent and S.Powell,* [1680?]. 12°. L; CH.

2539A The loyal man's Psalter. [*London?* 1680.] cap., 4°.* CH, MH.

2540   The whole book of psalms. *By J.M. for the company of stationers,* 1681. 12°. L, OC.

2541   —[*n.p.*], *for the company of stationers,* 1682. 12°. L; WWC.

2542   —*For the company of stationers,* 1682. 8°. L, O, BR, MR, AU; WF.

2543   —*By the assings* [*sic*] *of John Bill, Thomas Newcomb and Henry Hills,* 1682. 12°. L, O.

2544   —*By the assigns of John Bill, Thomas Newcomb and Henry Hills,* 1682. 12°. L.

2545   —*By W.R. for the company of stationers,* 1682. 12°. L; NU.

2546   —*By H.Hills, for the company of stationers,* 1682. 8°. L, LG, DT; NGT.

2546A —*By J.Macock, for the company of stationers,* 1682. 12° L; PL.

2546B The book of psalms in metre. *For the company of stationers,* 1682. 12°. L, O; MB, NPT, Y.

2547   —*Printed at the theater in Oxford, and are to be sold by Moses Pitt, Peter Parker, William Leake, Thomas Guy, London,* 1682. fol. L, O; CH, WWC, Y.

2548   —*Printed at the theater in Oxford, to be sold by Moses Pitt, Peter Parker, Ann Leake, Thomas Guy, London,* 1682. 4°. L.

2549   —*Oxford, at the theater, to be sold by Peter Parker, London,* 1682. 8°. L.

2550   The psalms of David in meeter. *Edinburgh, by Evan Tyler,* 1682. 12°. ALDIS 2357. L, O, AU, GE, FSF; CH, NN.

2551   —*Edinburgh, by Thomas Brown and James Glen,* 1682. 12°. AU.

2551A The psalter for children. *Cambridge* [*Mass.*], *by S. Green, for John Usher of Boston,* 1682. 12°. EVANS 311. MB.

2551B The whole book of psalms. *For the company of stationers,* 1683. 12°. OC; MB.

2552   The psalter of David. Tenth edition. *By J.Macock for Rich. Royston,* 1683. 12°. L, O.

2552A The whole book of psalms. [*Cambridge*], *by John Hayes,* 1683. 4°. L, CS, EC.

2552B —*For the company of stationers,* 1684. 8°. L; MB.

2553   A century of select psalms. Second edition. *By M.F. for R. Royston,* 1684. 8°. T.C.II 55. L, O, LSC; CN.

2554   The paslter or psalms. Second edition. *Oxford by L. Litchfield, for Jo. Crosley,* 1684. 8°. T.C.II 126. O, OC, EN, AU.

2555   The whole book of psalms. *By J. Macock, for the company of stationers,* 1685. 12°. L.

2556   The psalter or psalms. Third edition. *Oxford,* 1685. 8°. O.

2557   The whole book of psalms. *Oxford, at the theatre, to be sold by Thomas Guy,* 1685. 12°. O; MB, Y.

2558   A century of select psalms. Third edition. *By M. F. for R. Royston,* 1686. 8°. O.

2559   The whole book of psalms. *By J. Macock, for the company of stationers,* 1686. 12°. L; CH.

2560   The psalms of David in meeter. *Edinburgh, by the heir of Andrew Anderson,* 1686. 12°. FSF.

2561   The whole book of psalms. *By J. M. for the company of stationers,* 1687. fol. L, O, OC.

2562   —*By J. Macock, for the company of stationers,* 1687. 12°. L, O.

2563   —*By R. Holt, for the company of stationers,* 1687. 12°. NU.

2564   The psalmes of David in meeter. *Glasgow, by Robert Sanders,* 1687. 12°. ALDIS 2718. L.

2565   The whole book of psalms. *By R. Everingham for the company of stationers,* 1688. 12°. L, CCL, CK.

2565A The whole book of psalms. *By R. Everingham, for the company of stationers, to be sold by E. Brewster, and S. Keble,* 1688. 12°. L, SP.

2566   —*By T. Hodgkin and M. Flesher, for the company of stationers,* 1688. fol. L, O, CM.

2567   —*By H. Hills jun. for the company of stationers,* 1688. 8°. L, O, LIC; Y.

2568   —*By J. Macock, for the company of stationers,* 1688. 12°. L, O.

2568A Psalms, or psalm-hymns in metre. *By J. Heptinstall,* 1688. 12°. LLP.

2568B A century of select psalms. Fourth edition. *For Luke Meredith,* 1688. 8°. L.

2569   A new version of the psalms. *By J. H. for Brabazon Aylmer,* 1688. 12°. L, O, EN, AU; MB, Y.

2569A The book of psalms. *By Samuel Smith,* 1688. 12°. L; Y.

2570   The whole book of psalms. *By J. Macock, for the company of stationers,* 1689. 12°. L.

2570A The psalter or psalms. *By J. M. for the company of stationers,* 1689. WF.

2571   The psalms of David in meeter. *Edinburgh, by John Reid,* 1689. 12°. AU.

2571A The whole book of psalms. *By J. Macock, for the company of stationers,* 1690. 12°. L.

2572   The psalms of David in metre. *Edinburgh, by the heir of Andrew Anderson,* 1690. 12°. ALDIS 3087. O, AU.

2573   —*Edinburgh, society of stationers,* 1690. 12°. ALDIS 3088. FSF; NN.

2574   The whole book of psalms. *By J. Macock, for the company of stationers,* 1691. 12°. L.

2575   The book of psalms in metre. *By F. Collins, for the company of stationers,* 1691. 12°. T.C.II 362. L, O, LW; CN.

2576   A century of select psalms. Fifth edition. *By J. H. for L. Meredith,* 1691. 12°. T.C.II 386. L, OC, BR; CH, NU.

2577   The book of psalms paraphras'd, ... Symon Patrick. Second edition. *By J. H. for L. Meredith,* 1691. 8°. T.C.373. L, O, C, E; CLC, PL, TU, VC, WF.

2578   The psalter of David. Eleventh edition. *By R. N. for Luke Meredith,* 1691. 12°. L, O.

2579   The whole book of psalms. *Amsterdam, for the widow of Steven Swart,* 1691. 12°. L.

2580   Mr. Richard Baxter's paraphrase on the psalms. *For Thomas Parkhurst; and Jonathan Robinson,* 1692. 12°. L, O, C, LCL, LW; MH, NU.

2581   The whole book of psalms. *Oxford, for the university printers,* 1692. 12°. L; NU.

2581A A century of select psalms. *Hamburg, by Thomas Wiering,* 1692. 8°. L, O, AU; NPT.

2582   The psalms of David in meeter. *Edinburgh, heir of A. Anderson,* 1692. 4°. ALDIS 3259. EN; NN.

2582A The psalter or psalms of David. *Dublin, Andrew Crook,* 1692. 8°. DIX 255. CD.

2583   The whole book of psalms. *For the company of stationers,* 1693. 8°. L.

2584   —*By H. Hills, for the company of stationers,* 1693. 8°. O, AU.

2585   The psalms. *By John Leake,* 1693. 4°. LLP.

2585A The psalms of David in meeter. *For the company of stationers, to be sold by Thomas Parkhurst and Dorman Newman,* 1693. 12°. L.

2585B —*Edinburgh, by George Mosman,* 1693. 4°. ALDIS 3333. E, AU, FSF; TU.

2586   —colop: *Edinburgh by George Mosman,* 1693. 8°. ALDIS 3334. O, HH, AU; CH.

2587   —*Edinburgh, by George Mosman,* 1693. 12°. ALDIS 3335. L.

2588   The whole book of psalms. *For the company of stationers,* 1694. 12°. L, O.

2589   The psalms of David in meeter. *For A. & J. Churchill and L. Meredith,* 1694. 12°. L, O, C, LCL, CT; PPT.

2590   —*Edinburgh, by George Mosman,* 1694. 8°. ALDIS 3407. LCL, FSF; NN.

2590A The psalms hymns and spiritual songs. *For R. Chiswell,* 1694. 12°. LSC.

2591   An essay of a new version ... Tate and Brady. *For the company of stationers,* 1695. 8°. L, O, GK; CH, MH, TU.

2592   The whole book of psalms. *For the company of stationers,* 1695. 8°. L.

2593   —Second edition. *In the Savoy, by Edw. Jones, for the company of stationers, to be sold by Henry Playford,* 1695. 8°. L, O, C, CK.

2594   The psalms hymns and spiritual songs. Eighth edition. *Boston, by John Allen and Vavasour Harris, for Samuel Phillips,* 1695. EVANS 714. 16°. MHS, RPJ.

2595   The book of psalms in metre. *By Tho. Snowden, for the company of stationers,* 1696. 12°. L, O; MBA, NPT.

2596   The whole book of psalms. *For the company of stationers,* 1696. 12°. L, O.

2597   —*By W. and J. Wilde, for the company of stationers,* 1696. 8°. L, O.

2598   A new version of the psalms of David . . . Tate and . . . Brady. *By M. Clark for the company of stationers,* 1696. 8°. T.C.I 598. L, O, CS, MR, DT; CH, CN, MH, NU, WF, Y.

2599   The whole book of psalms. *Oxford: by the university-printers,* 1696. 12°. O.

2600   —*Cambridge, by John Hayes,* 1696. fol. L, EC; Y.

2601   The psalms of David in metre. *Edinburgh, by the heirs and successors of Andrew Anderson,* 1696. 4°. ALDIS 3624. L.

2602   — —, 1696, 24°. ALDIS 3625. L.

2602A   A new version of some select psalms. *Dublin, by and for Jospeh Ray and are to be sold by John North,* 1696. 8°. DIX 284. DN.

2602B   The psalms, hymns, and spiritual songs. *By S. W, for the use of His Majesty's colony in New-England.* 1697. 12°. MBC, MH.

2603   The whole book of psalms. *By J. Richardson, and T. Hodgkin, for the company of stationers,* 1697. fol. L, O, BR.

2603A   —*By W. Horton, for the company of stationers,* 1697. 4°. * L.

2604   —Third edition. *By J. Heptinstall, for the company of stationers: to be sold by Samuel Sprint; and Henry Playford,* 1697. 8°. L, C, AU; CN, NPT.

2604A   Select psalms and hymns. *By J. Heptinstall for the company of stationers,* 1697. 12°. L, O, C, CT.

2604B   The book of psalms in metre. *Dublin, by Joseph Ray, for Eliphal Dobson, and Matthew Gunn,* 1697. 12°. DIX 289. L, O.

2604C   Some select psalms of David. *Dublin, for Matthew Gunn,* 1697. 4°. DT.

2605   —*For the company of stationers,* 1698. 8°. L, O.

2606   A new version . . . Tate and Brady. *By T. Hodgkin, for the company of stationers,* 1698. 8°. T.C.III 68. L, O, C, BAMB, DT; CH, LC, NPT, Y.

2607   —*By M. Clark, for the company of stationers,* 1698. 12°. L, O; MB, NPT, WF.

2608   The psalms of David in meter. *For A. and J. Churchill and L. Meredith,* 1698. 8°. L, O; MB, Y.

2609   The psalms of David, in English metre . . . Luke Milbourne. *For W. Rogers, R. Clavill, and B. Tooker, J. Lawrence, and J. Taylor,* 1698. 12°. L, O, C, EN, LCL; CH, MB, MH, NPT, NU.

2609A   —*For W. Rogers and B. Tooke,* 1698. 12°. CH.

2610   The whole book of psalms. Fourth edition. *By J. Heptinstall, for the company of stationers; to be sold by Samuel Sprint; and Henry Playford,* 1698. 8°. T.C.III 99. L, C; CLC, CN, MB, Y.

2610A   Davideos, or a specimen. *For W. Keblewhite,* 1798 [i.e. 1698]. 8°. LLP, CS.

2611   Some of the psalms in metre. *Cambridge, for J. Hayes,* 1698. 8°. C, CT; WF.

2612   The psalms, hymns, and spiritual songs. Ninth edition. *Boston, by B. Green, and J. Allen, for Michael Perry,* 1698. EVANS 817. 16°. MHS, V.

2613   The psalms of David in metre. *Edinburgh, by the heirs and successors of Andrew Anderson,* 1698. 24°. O, FSF; NN.

2614   —*Edinburgh, by the heirs and successors of Andrew Anderson,* 1698. 12°. ALDIS 3796. FSF.

2615   The psalms of David in meeter. *Edinburgh, by Evan Tyler,* 1698. 12°. ALDIS 3797. L, O, AU; NN.

2616   — —, 1698. 18°. ALDIS 3799. L, O, AU; WCL.

2616A   —*Dublin, by J. Brent and S. Powell, to be sold by Peter Lawrence* [1698]. 12°. L.

2617   The whole book of psalms. Fifth edition. *By J. Heptinstall, for the company of stationers,* 1699. 8°. L; CLC, CN, MB, TSM.

2617A   —*By G. Groom, for the company of stationers,* 1699. 8°. L.

2618   —*By W. and J. Wilde, for the company of stationers,* 1699. 8°. L, O.

2618A   A new version of the psalms. *By T. Hodgkin, for the company of stationers,* 1699. 12°. L; WF.

2619   Some of the psalms of David. *Cambridge,* 1699. 8°. O; NP.

2620   The psalms of David in meeter. *Edinburgh, the heirs and successors of A. A.,* 1699. 4°. ALDIS 3899. L, EN; NN, WCL.

2620A   —*Belfast, by Patrick Neill & Company,* 1699. 12°. BLH.

2621   The psalmes of David, translated. *[Paris],* 1700. 12°. L, LCL, AU; CH, TU, WF, Y.

2622   A new version of the psalms. *[n.p.], printed,* 1700. 8°. AU.

2623   The whole book of psalms. Sixth edition. *By J. Heptinstall, for the company of stationers: to be sold by Samuel and John Sprint; and Henry Playford,* 1700. 8°. L; CH, CLC, PPT.

2623A   —*By John Macock, for the company of stationers,* 1700. 4°. L.

2624   Supplement to the new version. *By J. Heptinstall, sold by D. Brown and J. Wilde,* 1700. 8°. O, BR; CLC.

2625   The book of psalms paraphras'd . . . Symon Patrick. *By J. H. for L. Meredith,* 1700, 8°. L, O, DT; CH, PPT, Y.

2625A   The psalms, newly translated. *By Thomas Parkhurst,* 1700. 12°. LLP.

2626   The whole book of psalms. *Oxford: by the university-printers,* 1700. 12°. L.

2626A   The psalms of David meeter. *Edinburgh, for Mr. Henry Knox, John Vallange, and Alexander Henderson,* 1700. WF.

2627   The psalms of David in meeter. *Belfast, by Patrick Neill and Company,* 1700. 12°. BF.

2628   The psalmes of David, translated from the Vulgat. *[St. Germains],* 1700. 12°. L, E, AU; CLC, CN, NU, TU, WG, Y.

2629   The whole book of psalmes. *Dublin, Andr. Crook and E. Dobson,* 1700. 4°. DIX 321. DT.

OLD TESTAMENT, APART FROM PSALMS

2629A A paraphrase vpon the song of Solomon. *By Iohn Legatt,* 1641. 4°.* L, O, CK, OC, EC; CSS, NU, TU, V̇, Y.

2629B —[Anr. ed.] *For H. S. and W. L.* 1642. 4°.* LT, O, OME; CLC, V.

2629C Solomons song of songs in English metre. *[Amsterdam, Richt Right Press],* 1642. 4°. CM.

2629D The song of Solomon in meeter. *By T. R. & E. M. for Ralph Smith,* 1655. 8°.* LT.

2629E The song of Solomon rendered. *By J. H. for J. Rothwell,* 1659. 8°.* O; Y.

2630 The canticles, or song of Solomon, reduced into a decasyllable . . . by R. K. *[London],* 1662. 8°. CH.

2630A Solomons proverbs. 1666. 8°. LBS.

2631 The song of Solomon. *Edinburgh, by Andrew Anderson,* 1669. 4°.* EN.

2631A Solomons proverbs. *By J. R. for Nathan Brookes,* 1674. 8°. NC.

2631B —*By J. R. for William Redmayne,* 1676. 8°. T.C.I 181. L; NHC.

2632 The book of the song of Solomon in meeter . . . by T. S. *For Francis Smith,* 1676. 4°. T.C.I 236. O; CH.

2632A A paraphrase upon the canticles . . . Samuel Woodford. *By J. D. for John Baker, and Henry Brome,* 1679. 8°. T.C.I 328. L, O, LCL, LW, EN; CH, CN, NU, TU, WF, Y.

2633 [Hebrew] or, Solomon's song paraphras'd. *By H. Hills, for Henry Faithorne and John Kersey,* 1681. 4°. L, CS, DT; CH, MH, Y.

2634 —[Anr. ed.] —, 1682. 4°. L, O, C, OM; MH, NU, Y.

2635 The proverbs of Solomon paraphrased. *By M. Flesher, for R. Royston,* 1683. 8°. T.C.I 502. L, O, C, E, EC; CH, CPB, NU, Y.

2636 Solomon's proverbs. *For Hen. Mortlock,* 1689. 12°. T.C.II 281. L.

2637 The proverbs of Solomon. *By J. H. for Luke Meredith,* 1694. 8°. T.C.II 533. L, O, CJ, LL, DT; WF.

2637A Solomon's proverbs. *Sold by Henry Mortlock,* 1699. 12°. T.C.III 102. L.

2637B A version of Solomon's song. *For Dan Brown and Andr. Bell,* 1700. 12°. O; NHC.

2637C The song of Solomon. *Edinburgh, printed,* 1700. L, EN.

2638 Patientia victrix: . . . Job. [Arthur Brett.] *For Richard Gammon,* 1661. 8°. L; MH, Y.

2639 The book of Job paraphras'd, . . . Symon Patrick. *For R. Royston,* 1679. 8°. T.C.I 368. L, O, CM, E, DT; TU, Y.

2639A —Second edition. *By J. Macock for R. Royston,* 1685. 8°. OC, CM; CH, PL.

2640 The book of Job paraphrased. *By J. Heptinstall for L. Meredith,* 1697. 8°. L, O, BR; NU, WF.

2640A The book of Job in meeter. *Tho. Parkhurst,* 1700. 12°. L.

2641 A paraphrase on the book of Job, . . . Sir Richard Blackmore. *For Awnsham and John Churchill,* 1700. fol. L, O, LCP, E, ES; CH, CN, MH, NU, WF, Y.

2642 A paraphrase upon the books of Ecclesiastes, . . . Symon Patrick. *For Rich. Royston,* 1685. 8°. T.C.II 91. L, OC, EC, DC, E; CH, NU, PL, WF, Y.

2643 —*By W. H. for Luke Meredith,* 1700. 8°. L, O, LL, DT; CH.

BIBLE. ENGLISH. NEW TESTAMENT.

2644 The New Testament. *Imprinted at London by Robert Barker: and by the assignes of John Bill,* 1641. 8°. L, LBS.

2645 ——, 1641. 12°. L, LBS.

2645A —*Edinburgh, R. Bryson,* 1641. 24°. ALDIS 990. EN.

2645B —[Anr. ed.] *By Robert Barker, and by the assignes of John Bill,* 1642. 8°. RPJ.

2646 —*Edinburgh, by Iames Bryson,* 1642. 12°. ALDIS 1032. L, LBS.

2647 —*Imprinted at London by Robert Barker: and by the assignes of Iohn Bill,* 1643. 12°. L.

2648 —*Edinburgh, by Evan Tyler,* 1643. 8°. ALDIS 1070. L, O, C.

2649 —*Amsterdam, by Joost Broersz,* 1643. fol. L.

2650 —*Imprinted at London by Robert Barker: and by the assignes of Iohn Bill,* 1644. 12°. LBS, C.

2651 —*Amsterdam, for C. P.,* 1644. 12°. L; PL.

2652 —*By the company of stationers,* 1647. 12°. O, C.

2653 —*By the assignes of J. Bill and Christopher Barker,* 1647. 12°. LBS.

2654 —*Edinburgh: by Evan Tyler,* 1647. 8°. ALDIS 1262. L, WCA.

2655 —*By John Field,* 1648. 4°. L; CLC, WWC.

2656 —*By the company of stationers,* 1650. 12°. MR, WCA.

2657 —*R. Daniel,* 1653. 8°. L, O, LBS.

2658 ——, 1655. 8°. LBS, P.

2659 —*John Streater,* 1656. 8°. LBS.

2660 —*By Iohn Field,* 1658. 8°. O; Y.

2661 Entry cancelled.

2662 —*Cambridge: by John Field,* 1659. fol. L; CLC, NU, WWC, Y.

2663 —1660. 8°. O; V.

2664 —*By Henry Hills,* 1661. 4°. L.

2664A —*Cambridge, J. Field,* 1661. 8°. EVANS 64. MWA.

2665 —*Cambridge, by John Field,* 1662. 8°. L, O, C; CLC.

2666 —*Printed,* 1664. 8°. L, O.

2667 —*Cambridge, by John Field,* 1666. 4°. L, C; CLC, MH, V, WCL.

2668 —colop: *Glasgow, by Robert Sanders,* 1666. 12°. ALDIS 1808. GU.

2669 —*In the Savoy, by the assignes of J. Bill and C. Barker,* 1667. 8°. CT.

2669A —*Cambridge, by John Hayes,* 1670. 8°. UCLA.

2670 —*Glasgow, by Robert Sanders,* 1670. 12°. ALDIS 1893. GU.

2671 —*Cambridge, by John Hayes,* 1673. 4°. L, O, CS; WWC.

2672 ——, 1675. 4°. O, CS.

2673 —*Oxford, at the theater,* 1675. 8°. L.

2674 —*Edinburgh, by Andrew Anderson, and his partners,* 1675. 12°. ALDIS 2043. LBS.

2675 —*By Christopher Barker,* 1676. 4°. L.

2676 —*By the assigns of John Bill and Christopher Barker,* 1676. 8°. LBS, HH.

2677 —*Cambridge, by John Hayes,* 1677. 4°. L.

2678 —By John Bill, Christopher Barker, Thomas Newcomb, and Henry Hills, 1678. 8°. L.

2679 —Edinburgh, by the heir of Andrew Anderson, 1678. 8°. L.

2680 —By John Bill, Thomas Newcomb, and Henry Hills, 1679. 8°. L, BR; Y.

2681 — —, 1679. 12°. L.

2682 —Printed at the theater in Oxford, to be sold by Moses Pitt, Peter Parker, Thomas Guy, and William Leake, London, 1679. 8°. L, O; MB.

2683 —[Glasgow], printed, 1679. fol. ALDIS 2146. L, GU.

2684 —Cambridge, by John Hayes, 1680. 4°. L.

2685 —By the assigns of John Bill, Thomas Newcomb, and Henry Hills, 1681. 8°. LBS; PL.

2685A —Printed, 1682. 12°. V.

2686 —Oxford, at the theater, to be sold by Moses Pitt, Peter Parker, William Leake, Thomas Guy, London, 1682. fol. L.

2687 —[London], printed, 1683. fol. L, DT.

2688 —For Tho. Simmons, 1683. 4°. L, O, GU; CH.

2689 —By the assigns of John Bill: and by Henry Hills, and Thomas Newcomb, 1683. 8°. L.

2690 —Cambridge, by John Hayes, 1683. 4°. L, EC.

2691 —By the assigns of J.Bill, Thomas Newcombe, and Henry Hills, 1684. 12°. O; MH.

2692 —Amsterdam, widow of Steven Swart, 1684. 12°. O, LBS; WF.

2693 —By the assigns of John Bill: and by Henry Hills, and Thomas Newcomb, 1685. 8°. L; TU.

2694 —By John Bill, Henry Hills, and Thomas Newcomb, 1686. 8°. LBS.

2695 —By J. Heptinstall for Brabazon Aylmer, 1690. fol. L.

2696 —By Charles Bill and Thomas Newcomb, 1691. 8°. L.

2697 —Glasgow, by Robert Sanders, 1691. 12°. ALDIS 3132. L, LBS, GU.

2698 —Oxford, by the university-printers, 1694. 8°. LBS.

2699 —Edinburgh, by the heirs and successors of Andrew Anderson, 1694. 12°. ALDIS 3358. L.

2700 —By Charles Bill, and the executrix of Thomas Newcomb, 1696. fol. L; CLC.

2701 — —1696. 8°. L.

2702 —Oxford, by the university-printers, 1696. 12°. O.

2703 —Oxford: —, 1697. 8°. L.

2704 —Oxford, —, 1699. 8°. L, O.

2705 —Oxford: —, 1699. 12°. L.

2706 —By Charles Bill, and the executrix of Thomas Newcomb, 1700. 8°. L, LBS; V.

2707 —Amsterdam, by the widow of Steven Swart, 1700. 12°. L, LBS; WF.

BIBLE. FRENCH.

2707A La Bible. Par R.Everingham, & se vend chez R.Benteley, et chez J.Hindmarsh, 1687. 12°. L, CT; CH, CN, LC, MH, Y.

2707B La Sainte Bible. Par B.Griffin & R.Everingham, 1688. 4°. PL.

2707C —Daniel Duchemin, 1693, fol. L.

2708 Les pseaumes de David. Par R. Everingham, & se vend chez R. Bentley, et chez J. Hindmarsh, 1686. 12°. L; CH, CLC, CN, MH.

2709 —Par R.Everingham, 1688. 8°. L.

2709A Le nouveau testament. R. Everingham, R. Bentley, J. Hindmarsh, 1686/7. 12°. DT.

2710 —Chez Daniel Du Chemin, 1693. 8°. L.

BIBLE. GAELIC.

2711 Leabhuir na seintiomna. The books of the Old Testament. 1685-81. 2v. 4°. T.C.II 155. L, O, C, EN, DT; CH, CN, MH, NC.

2712 An Biobla naomhtha. Arna chur a glcó re R. Ebheringtham, 1690. 12°. L, O, C, MR, ENC; CH, CN, MB, NU, Y.

2713 An ceud chaogad do Shalmaibh Dhaibhidh. A Nglasgo, le Aindra Ainderson, 1659. 12°. ALDIS 1613. L, EN, GUF; Y.

2714 Psalma Dhaibhidh. N Dun-Edin le M. Sémus Kniblo, Iosua van Solingen agus Seón Colmar, 1684. 12°. ALDIS 2487. L, E, EN, ENC, AU; NN.

2715 Tiomna nuadh. Robert Everingham, 1681. 4°. T.C.I 482. L, O, C, EN, GU; CH, CLC, CN, MH, NU.

2716 —1685. 4°. C.

2717 —Arna chur a glcó re R. Ebheringthaim, 1690. 12°. O, SA, EN; CN, MH.

BIBLE. GREEK.

2178 Ἡ Παλαιὰ Διαθήκη κατὰ τους ἑβδομήχοντα. Vetus Testamentum. Excudebat Rogerus Daniel, prostat autem venale apud Joannem Martin & Jacobum Allestrye, 1653. 8°. L, O, C, E, DT; CH, CN, LC, MH, NP, Y.

2719 —Cantabrigiæ, excusum per Joannem Field, 1665. 12°. L, O, C, EN, DT; CH, CU, MH, NU, Y.

2719A Ψαλτεριον του Δαβιδ. [London], ex officina Rogeri Danielis, 1652. 12°. L, CT, EC.

2719B —Ex officina R. Danielis, [1652]. 12°. L, CT.

2720 —Κανταβριγια, 1664. 8°. O, CK, CM, CT, EC.

2721 Paraphrasis poetica psalmorum. Excudebat R. Daniel & venalis prostant apud S. Thomson, 1657. Y.

2722 Ψαλτεριον του Δαβιδ. Ex officina R. Danielis, 1658. 12°. OC.

2723 —Κανταβριγια, excudebat Johannes Field, 1665. 8°. C, CCL, OC; PL, Y.

2724 Entry cancelled.

2725 Ψαλτήριον psalterium. Oxoniæ, e theatro Sheldoniano, 1678. 8°. MADAN 3201. L, O, C, MR, DT; LC, MB, MH, Y.

2726 Δαβιδης εμμετρος. Impentis [sic] Richardi Chiswell, 1684. AU.

2727 Musæ sacræ: seu Jonas, Jeremias . . . reddite carmine. Oxoniæ, L.Lichfield, & veneunt apud Jos. Godwin & Ric. Davis, 1652. CH.

2728 Novum Testamentum. Cantabrigiae, ex officina Rogeri Danielis. 1642. Londini venales prostant. fol. MB, MBA, MH, Y.

2729 —*Excudebat M. F. prostant apud Danielem Frere, 1648.* 12°. CM, CT.

2730 Της καινης Διαθηκης Απαντα. *Novi Testamenti. Ex officina Rogeri Danielis, 1652.* 12°. L, C, CT, DC, ENC.

2731 — —, 1653. 8°. L, O, C, CT, DT; CLC, MH, Y.

2731A —*Typis Rogeri Danielis, impensis Josuæ Kirton & Samuelis Thomson, 1653.* 8°. CM, RIPON.

2731B —*Excudebat R. Nortonus pro. J. Kyrton, 1653.* 12°. CT; CH.

2732 —*Excudebat R: Nortonus pro Josh. Kyrton; 1664.* 12°. L, O, C; PU.

2733 —Κανταβριγία, [1665]. 12°. L, O, C, MR, DT; CLC, CU, MIU, WWC.

2734 —*Excudebat S. G. pro G. K. & prostant apud Nath. Ranew, 1672.* 12°. T.C.I 100. O, CS; NU.

2735 —*Excudebat Andr. Clark pro Sam. Mearne, Joan Martyn, et Henr. Herringman, 1674.* 12°. T.C.I 174. L, C, CPE, CT, BR; CN, NU.

2736 —[*Oxoniæ*], *e theatro Sheldoniano, 1675. Sixes.* MADAN 3087. L, O, C, OC, EC; CU, MH, NR, Y.

2737 —*Oxonii, e theatro Sheldoniano, 1675. Sixes.* MADAN 3088. L, O, CT, ENC, DT; CLC, CN, NU, PL, Y.

2738 —*Apud Sam. Smith, 1688.* 12°. LBS.

2739 —[*London*], *1700.* 12°. C.

2740 [–] Κανταβριγια, [1700]. 8°. L, O, C, MR, DT.

BIBLE. HEBREW.

2741 [Hebrew] Moses fasciatus. 1664. 4°. EN.

2742 [Hebrew] Sepher Tehillim. *For the author, to be sold by H. Robinson, A. Crook, L. Fawn and S. Thomson, and by G. Sawbridge, 1656.* 8°. L, O, C, E, EN; MB, NC, PL, TSM.

2743 —*Cantabrigiæ, typis Johen Hayes, prostant, vero, venales Londini, 1685.* 12°. L, C, OC, CT, DT; CLC, MH, NPT, PL, Y.

2744 —[Hebrew] The book of psalmes. *By Samuel Smith, 1688.* 12°. L, C; CH, CN, RPJ, V.

2744A —*Printed at Utrecht, by John van de Water, 1688.* 12°. MB, Y.

2745 —[Hebrew] Liber psalmorum. *Sumptibus Samuelis Smith, 1688.* 12°. MB, RPJ, Y.

2746 [Hebrew] Lex Dei summi nova. *Typis Thomas Roycroft, 1661.* 8°. L, O, C, CT, P; MH.

BIBLE. INDIAN.

2747 The Holy Bible. *Cambridge [Mass.]: by Samuel Green and Marmaduke Johnson, 1662.* 4°. CH.

2748 The Holy Bible: . . . translated into the Indian language. *Cambridge [Mass.]: by Samuel Green and Marmaduke Johnson, 1663.* 4°. EVANS 72. CJ; CN, NNM, MWA, Y.

2749 — —, 1663. 4°. EVANS 72. NU, RPJ, NNM, MZ.

2750 — —, 1663. 4°. EVANS 72. L, O, DT; BN, LC, MH, NN, WCL.

2751 — —, 1663. 4°. EVANS 72. NN.

2752 — —, 1663. 4°. EVANS 72. MH.

2753 — —, 1663. 4°. EVANS 72. MWA.

2754 — —, 1663. 4°. EVANS 72. RPJ.

2755 Mamusse Wunneetupanatamwe. *Cambridge [Mass.]: nashpe Samuel Green kah Marmaduke Johnson, 1663.* EVANS 73. L, OC, GU, MR, DT; CH, CN, MH, NN, PL, RPJ.

2756 —*Cambridge [Mass.], nashpe Samuel Green, 1685.* EVANS 385. L, O, CT, MR, EN; BN, CH, CN, LC, MH, NN, Y.

2757 The New Testament. *Cambridg [Mass.]: by Samuel Green and Marmaduke Johnson, 1661.* 4°. EVANS 64. L, LBS, E, GU, DT; CH, CN, LC, MH, NN, RPJ.

2758 Wusku wuttestamentum. *Cambridge [Mass.]: by Samuel Green and Marmaduke Johnson, 1661.* 4°. EVANS 65. O, OC; CN, MH, MWA, NU, RPJ.

2759 —*Cambridg [Mass.], for the right honourable Corporation in London, 1680.* 4°. EVANS 279. MH, MHS, MWA.

BIBLE. IRISH. *See* BIBLE. GAELIC.

BIBLE. ITALIAN.

2760 Salmi di David. *M. F. per Rodolfo Rounthwaite, 1644.* 12°. L.

BIBLE. LATIN.

2761 Biblia sacra. *E: T: et A: M: sumpt: societ: 1656.* 12°. L, O, CCC, CT, YM; CH, MH, NR, NU, WCL.

2762 —*Typis E. Tyler, 1661.* 12°. L, O, DC, MAU, EN; MBA, TU.

2763 —*Exc. R. Nortouus [sic] prostat venales apud Nathanielem Ponder, 1680.* 12°. T.C.I 385. L, BAMB, YM; MH, NR, VC.

2763A Vetus testamentum. *Excudebat Rog. Daniel, 1653.* 8°. GU.

2764 Septuaginta. *Juxta exemplar Vaticanum Romæ. 1653.* 8°. LW, EC.

2764A [Hebrew] Targum Hierosolymitanum. *Typis T. Harperi, impensis L. Sadleri, 1649.* 4°. L, O, CT, P, DT; CLC, NU, WF. Y.

2765 Psalmorum Davidis. *Apud Edvv. Griffinum, 1648.* 12°. L; CLC, MB, PPT.

2766 —*Apud Sarah Griffinum, 1648.* 12°. AU.

2767 Paraphrasis Psalmorum. *Typis S. G. sumptibus Thomas Malthus, 1653.* 12°. L.

2768 Psalmorum Davids. *Apud Sarah Griffinum, 1660.* 12°. L, O, FSF; CLC, TU, WF, Y.

2769 Psalmi aliquot Davidici in metrum Latinum traducti. *Oxoniæ, excudebat W. Hall, prostant venales apud Rich. Davis, 1660.* 8°.* MADAN 2468. L, O, CS, CT; Y.

2769A —*E. Tyler, 1661.* 12. CT.

2770 Liber psalmorum Davidis. *Dublinæ, excudebat Gul. Bladen, 1661.* 8°. DIX III. L, O, C.

2770A Psalmi aliquot Davidici. *Oxoniæ, excudebat H. H. prostant R. Davis, 1670.* 16°.* MADAN 2846. Y.

2770B Paraphrasis Psalmorum. *Abredoniæ, excudebat Ioannes Forbesius junior, prostat apud Jacobum Miller, & Joannem Masson, 1672,* 8°. ALDIS 1941. HH, FSF.

2770C Psalmorum Davidis. *Typis S. G., sumptibus Thomas Malthus, 1683.* 12°. T.C.II 10. L; MBC.

2771 Paraphrasis psalmorum Davidis poetica, . . . George Buchanan. *Glasguæ, excudebat Robertus Sanders*, 1684. 12°. GM, FSF.

2772 Ecphrasis paraphraseos. *Edinburgi, typis J. W. & impensis Joannis Vallange*, 1699. 8°. ALDIS 3831. L, O, CT, EN, AU; NPT.

2773 Cato divinus. *Prostant venales apud Thomam Cockerill*, 1699. 8°. T.C.III 100. L, C, OC, LVD, EN; MB, Y.

2774 Cantici canticorum. *Edinburgi, Higgins*, 1660. 4°. ALDIS 1626. EN.

2775 Solomonis cantici canticorum. *Typis Fr. Collinii, pro authore*, 1699. 8°. L, C, OC; WF.

2776 Targum prius et posterius in Estheram. *Typis M.S. impensis H. Eversden*, 1655. 4°. LT, LW, P, DT; CLC, WF.

2776A Novum testamentum. *Cantabrigiæ, ex officina Rogeri Danielis*, 1641. 12°. PL.

2777 —1648. 12°. C.

2777A —*Typis T. M. et A. C. væneunt apud J. Blaiklock*, 1651. 24°. CP.

2778 —*Ex officina Rogeri Danielis*, 1652. 12°. C.

2779 —*R. Nortonus pro Josh. Kyrton*, 1653. 12°. LW.

2780 —*Typis Milonis Flesher et Rob. Young*, 1656. 12°. O, P, RPL.

2781 —1657. 8°. C.

2782 —1659. fol. C.

2783 —*Ex officina E. Tyler*, 1659. 12°. L, C, LBS.

2784 —1661. 8°. C.

2785 —1662. 8°. C.

2786 —1666. 4°. C.

2787 —1670. 4°. C.

2788 —*Cantabrigæ ex officina Ioannis Field*, 1676. 12°. L, C.

2789 —*Cantabrigiæ, ex officina Jo. Hayes*, 1677. 24°. C.

2789A —*Oxonii, e theatro Sheldoniano*, 1679. sixes. T.C.I 345. MADAN 3248. L; WF, Y.

2790 Novum Jesu Christi testamentum. *Apud Sam: Mearne*, 1682. 12°. T.C.I 466. L, CK, CT; CH, CLC, TU, WF.

2791 Novum testamentum. *Cantabrigiæ*, 1683. 12°. C.

2792 —*Cantabrigiæ*, 1686. 8°. O, C.

2793 Novum Jesu Christi testamentum. *Ex typographeo M. Clark, prostant apud J. Nicholson, and T. Newborough*, 1696. 12°. T.C.II 603, L, C; MB.

2794 Jesu Christi . . . Novum testamentum. *Excudebat W. H. pro societate stationariorum*, 1699. 12°. T.C.III 142. L.

BIBLE. LITHUANIAN.

2795 [Holy Bible] [*Edinburgh, Tyler*, 1661-8.] 8°. ALDIS 1840. L.

BIBLE. MALAYAN.

2796 Jang ampat evangelia. *Oxford, by H. Hall*, 1677. 4°.* MADAN 3164. O, C, OC, EN, DT; CN, Y.

BIBLE. PERSIAN.

2796A Quatuor evangeliorum. *Typis Jacobi Flesher*, 1657. fol. L, LSC, OC, CK, CT.

BIBLE. POLYGLOT.

2797 Biblia sacra polyglotta . . . Bryan Walton. *Imprimebat Thomas Roycroft*, 1657. 6 v. fol. L, O, C, MR, EN; CH, CN, MH, NP, NU, RPJ, Y.

2797A Specimens of a polyglot of the Old Testament. [*London*, 1655?] cap. fol.* L.

2798 The psalmes of David in 4 languages . . . W. Slatyer. [*London*], *by Tho. Harper for George Thomason & Octavian Pullen*, 1643. 12°. LT, O, CT, LLP, LW; CH, MB, MH.

2799 —*By P. Stent*, 1652. 12°. L, O; CH, CLC.

2800 [Job.] *Cantabrigiæ, apud Thomas Buck, veneunt per Gulielmum Graves*, 1653. 8°. L, CT.

2801 [New Testament.] *R. Daniel, Cantabrigiæ*, 1642. fol. L, C, EC, LL, E; CH, CU, MBP, NU, Y.

2801A —*Prostant apud S. Smith & B. Walford*, 1698. fol. CPE, CT.

BIBLE. SHORTHAND.

2802 The Bible in shorthand. *For the author, and Peter Story, and sold by Tho. Fabian, Dorman Newman, Sam: Crouch, Wm. Marshall, Thomas Cockerill, I. Lawrence*, [1687]. 8°. T.C.II 198. L, O, C, LBS, EN; CH, NN, WF, Y.

2803 The whole book of psalms. [*London*], *sold by the author, Iohn Clarke, and Danl. White*, [1659]. 8°. L, LW; CH.

2804 —[*London*], *sold by Iohn Clarke*, [1660?]. 64°. in eights. CH, NN.

2805 —*Printed and are sold by Samuel Botley*, [1669?]. 8°. L, HH; MH.

2806 —[*London*], *sold by Tho: Cockerill*, [1679?] 16°. L, O, LBS; Y.

2807 The whole book of psalms, . . . Jeremiah Rich. *For the author*, [1660]. 64°. L, O, MRL, EN; NN.

2808 The book of the New Testament . . . Ieremiah Rich. *Printed and are sold by Samuel Bottley*, 1659. 64°. L, O, C; NN.

2809 —*For the author*, [1660]. 64°. L, O, LBS, HH; NN, Y.

2810 —[*n.p.*, 1668?] 64°. L.

2811 —*Printed and are sold by Samuel Botley*, [1673?]. 64°. L, EN; CH, NN, WF, Y.

2812 —*For Wm. Marshall, & Jnº Marshall*, [1697?]. 64°. T.C.III 9 L, LBS, MRL; MH, NN, WF.

BIBLE. TURKISH.

2813 Domini Nostri Iesv Christi Testamentum Novvm. Turcice redditvm. *Oxoniæ, exc. H. Hall*, 1666. 4°. MADAN 2727. O, C, OC, CT, DT; Y.

BIBLE. WELSH.

2813A Y Bibl cyss-egr-lan. *Gan James Flesher & Thomas Brewster*, 1654. 8°. L, AN, CPL.

2814 —*Printiedig yn Llundain gan John Bill, Christopher Barker, Tho. Newcomb, a Henry Hills i ac a werthir gan John Hancock*, 1667. 8°. L, O, AN, CPL, DT.

2815 — —, 1678. 8°. LW.

2815A —*Gan Charles Bill a Thomas Newcomb,* 1689. 8°. L, CCC, RPL, AN; RPB.

2816 —*Rydychain, yn y theatr,* 1690. fol. L, O, C, AN, DT; NP, NPT.

2816A [Psalms] Llytr y psalmau. *Printio,* 1648. 12°. AN.

2816B Testament Newydd. *Gan Matthew Symmons,* 1646. 12°. AN.

2816C ——, 1647. 12°. L, CM, AN.

2817 [New Testament.] [*n.p.*], *M. S. for J. Allen,* 1654. 8°. CT.

2818 [Psalms and New Testament.] Leytr y Psalmau, ynghd a Thestament Newydd. *E. Tyler a R. Holt, ac a werthir gan Samuel Gellibrand, a chan Peter Bodvil, a John Hughes,* 1672. 8°. T.C.I 102. L, AN; CH, PL.

2819 Bibliotheca Anglicana: or, a collection . . . 5th of May, 1686. [*London,* 1686.] 4°.* L, HH.

2820 Bibliotheca curiosa, or, a choice collection of books. [*London,* 1697.] 4°. L, C.

2821 Bibliotheca curiosa, or, a collection. [*n.p,*], 1692. 4°. L.

2822 Bibliotheca curiosa, sive catalogus. [*n.p.*], 1689. 4°.* O, LM.

2823 Bibliotheca curiosa. sive catalogus librorum. [*London*], 1690. 4°.* O; JF.

2824 Bibliotheca excellentissima: composed. [*n.p.*], 1694. 4°. L, OP.

2825 Bibliotheca eximia: the library. [*n.p.*], 1695. 4°. L.

2826 Bibliotheca fanatica; or, the phanatique library. [*London*], printed, 1660. 4°.* LT, O, C, HH; MH, MIU, NHC, WF.

2827 Bibliotheca Gallica, Italica, Hispanica, continens libros. 1685. 4°.* L, O, OC, HH.

2828 Bibliotheca generalis ex bibliothecis duorum doctissimorum. [*London*], 1690. 4°. L, O; JF.

2829 Bibliotheca Graeco-Latina. 23 May 1699. 8°. L, O, OP.

2830 Bibliotheca illustris medii templi societatis. 1700. 8°. L, C, LMT, LL, EN; CH, WF.

2831 Entry cancelled.

2832 Bibliotheca insignis: or, a catalogue. [*n.p.*], 12 June, 1693. 4°. L.

2833 Entry cancelled.
Bibliotheca instructissima ex bibliothecis duorum. 1691/2. *See* Lauderdale, John Maitland, *duke of.*

2834 Bibliotheca instructissima: or, a catalogue. [*n.p.*], 13 Dec. 1694. 4°. L.

2835 Bibliotheca latino-anglica. [*London*], 1687. 4°. L, O, HH.

2836 Bibliotheca lectissima: or, a catalogue. [*n.p.*], 30 May, 1692. 4°. L.

2837 Bibliotheca librorum rarissimorum. [*Oxford,* 1700.] 8°. O.

2838 Bibliotheca locupletissima ex bibliothecis duorum virorum. [*London*], 1690. 4°.* L, OP; JF.

2839 Bibliotheca luculenta, sive, catalogue. [*n.p.*], 31 Jan 1694. 4°. L, OP.

2840 Bibliotheca medica, et mathematica . . . 30 die Aug., 1686. [*London,* 1686.] 4°. L, O.

2841 Bibliotheca militum: or the souldiers publick library. *Printed,* 1659. 5°.* LT, O, C, LG, LP; CH, CN, MH, NC, NU, Y.

2842–3 Entries cancelled.
Bibliotheca Norfolciana. 1681. *See* Norfolk, Henry Howard, *6th duke of.*

2844 Bibliotheca novissima: or a catalogue. *To be sold by Randal Taylor,* June 1693. 8°.* O.

2845 Bibliotheca ornatissima: or, a catalogue. 1692. fol. L, OP.
Bibliotheca Parliamenti. 1653. *See* Birkenhead, *Sir* John.
Bibliotheca parochialis. 1697. *See* Bray, Thomas.
Bibliotheca politica. 1691/2. *See* Tyrell, *Sir* James.
Bibliotheca regia. 1679. *See* Heylyn, Peter.

2846–9 Entries cancelled.

2850 Bibliotheca selecta, a catalogue of Greek. [*n.p.*], 8 Mar. 1694. 4°. L, OP.

2851 Bibliotheca selecta seu catalogus librorum. [*London*], 1690. 4°.* L; JF.

2852 Bibliotheca selecta: sive catalogue variorum librorum . . . 21 die Maii, 1688. [*London*], 1688. 4°. O; JF.

2853 Entry cancelled.
Bibliotheca selectissima diversorum. 1687. *See* Lauderdale, John Maitland, *duke of.*

2854 Bibliotheca selectissima librorum omnigenorum. 9 Nov. 1691. 4°. L.

2855 Bibliotheca selectissima: or, a catalogue. [*n.p.*], 9 Feb. 1692. 4°. L.

2856 Bibliotheca selectissima seu catalogus. [*n.p.*], 8 May 1689. 4°.* O, LM.

2857 Bibliotheca Sturbitchiana. *Cambridge,* 8 Sept. 1684. 4°. L, O, CS.

2858 Bibliotheca Sturbrigiensis. 8 Sept. 1685. 4°. L, OP, CS, HH.

2859 Bibliotheca theologico-miscellanea: sive catalogue variorum. [*London*], 1689. 4°.* JF.

2860 Bibliotheca trilinguis: or, a catalogue. [*n.p.*], 2 May 1694. 4°. L.

2861 Entry cancelled.
Bibliotheca universalis. Edinburgh, 1688. *See* Le Clerc, Jean.

2862 Bibliothecæ nobilissimæ: . . . pars prior. 1694/5. fol. L, O, CS.

2863 Bibliothecæ nobilissimæ pars tertia & ultima. 1695. fol.* L, OC, CS.

2864 La bibliotheque d'Oxfort . . . sixième dialogue. *Chez Abraham Scott,* 1690. sixes. Y.

2864A **Bicaise, Honoré.** Manuale medicorum. *John Martyn, James Allestree, and Thomas Dicas,* 1659. 8°. O; WSG.

2864B **Bidbanck, William.** A present for children. *By J. D. for R. Robinson,* 1685. 12°. EN.

2864C **Biddle, Hester.** Oh! wo, wo, from the Lord. colop: *For Thomas Simmons,* 1659. 4°.* PL.

2864D —To the inhabitants of the town of Dartmouth. 1659. PL.

2864E —The trumpet of the Lord God. *Printed,* 1662. 4°. LF, BBN; PH, PSC.

2865 —The trumpet of the Lord sounded. *Printed*, 1662. 4°.* L, O, LF; MB, MU, PSC, WF, Y.

2866 —A warning from the Lord God of life. *For Robert Wilson*, 1660. 4°.* L, O, LF, BBN, YM; PH, PSC, WF.

2866A —Wo to the towne of Cambridge. [*London*, 166–?]. brs. LF, CT.

2867 —Wo to thee city of Oxford. [*London*, 1655.] brs. MADAN 2268. LT, LF.

2868 **[Biddle, John.]** The apostolical and true opinion. *Printed*, 1653. 8°. LT, O, C, LCL, OC; MH, NU, Y.

2869 [–] —[Anr. ed.] *For Richard Moone*, 1653. 8°. OC.

2870 [–] Brevis disquisitio: or, a brief enquiry. *For Richard Moone*, 1653. 8°. LT, O, C, OC, OCC; NU.

[–] Brief history of the Unitarians. 1687. *See* Nye, Stephen.

2871 Entry cancelled.

2872 —A confession of faith. 1647. 12°. LCL.

2873 [–] —[Anr. ed.] *Printed . . . Year*, 1648. 4°. LT, O, CT; CH, NU, WF, Y.

2874 [–] —[Anr. ed.] *Printed . . . yeer*, 1648. [1653]. 8°. L, O, CCL, OC, EC; MH, NU, Y.

2875 —Duæ catecheses. [*London*, 1664.] 8°. L, O, C, EC, P; MH, NU, PPT.

2876 [–] The faith of one God. *Printed*, 1691. 4°. L, C, OC, ENC, DT; CH, CN, MH, NU, WF, Y.

2877 [–] The testimonies of Irenaeus. *Printed at London*, [1653]. 8°. LT, O, C, OC, EC; MH, NU, Y.

2878 [–] A testimony of the ministers in the province of Essex. *By A. M. for Tho. Vnderhill*, 1648. 4°.* LT, O; CLC, MIU, MM, NPT, NU.

2879 —Twelve arguments. [*London*], *printed*, 1647. 4°.* LT, O, CT, HH, DT; MB, NU, WF.

2880 —XII. arguments. [*n.p.*], *printed*, 1657. 4°.* CCL; MH, NU, PH, Y.

2881 —Two letters of. *Printed*, 1655. 4°.* LT, HH, PL.

2882 —A twofold catechism. *By J. Cottrel, for Ri. Moone*, 1654. 8°. LT, O, C, LCL, ENC; CLC, MWA, NU, WF, Y.

2883 **Biddle, Thomas.** Gods glory vindicated. *For William Ley*, 1647. 4°.* LT, O; CH.

2884 Biddle dispossest. *For Francis Tyton*, 1654. 8°. CLC, NU.

2885 **Bidpai.** The fables of Pilpay. *For D. Brown, C. Connigsby* [*sic*], *D. Midwinter and T. Leigh*, 1699. 12°. T.C.III 96. L, CT; Y.

2886 **Bidwell, Robert.** The copy of the covenant of grace. *By E. T. for Tho. Johnson*, 1657. 8°. LT.

2887 Bifrons Janus. *Printed* 1673/4. brs. L,

2888 **Biggs, Noah.** Matæotechnia medicinæ praxews. The vanity. *For Giles Calvert*, 1651. 4°. LT, O, CT, LCS, E; CLC, CLM, WF.

2888A — —[Anr. ed.] *For Edward Blackmore*, 1651. 4°. L, LWL; CJC, NAM, HC.

2889 **Bilberg, Johan.** A voyage of the late king of Sweden. *For Edward Castle*, 1698. 8°. L, O, OM, CS, LR; CJC, CLC, LC, MH, PL, Y.

2890 **[Bill, Edward.]** Certain propositions sent by the states of Holland. *By Robert Wood*, 1651. 4°.* LT.

Bill and answer. 1686. *See* B., J.

2891 The bill for regulating abuses in elections. 1679. fol.* OP; Y.

2892 Entry cancelled.

2893 A bill of ease to all Protestants. 1680. fol. O.

2894 The bill of indictment exhibited against John Giles. [*n.p.*, 1680].] cap., fol. O, C; CH, Y.

2896 Bill of lading. [*Cambridge, Mass.*, 1683] brs. MBS.

2896 —[Anr. ed.] [*Boston*, 1694.] brs. MB.

2896A A bill of sale. In Westminster. [*London*], *printed*, 1689. brs. L, LG, HH; MH.

2897 A bill read to compel the creditors. [*London*, 1689] brs. CH.

Billa vera: 1682. *See* Womock, Laurence, *bp.*

2898 **Billers, J.** Potentia irresistibilis. [*n.p.*, 1675.] brs. O.

2899 **[Billing, Edward.]** A certaine sound; or, an alarm. *Printed*, 1665. 4°.* L, LF, BBN; MH, MU, NU, WF, Y.

2899A —Dear friends, the Lord God of heaven and earth forever praised. [*London*, 1681.] brs. PHS.

2900 —A faithful testimony for God & my country. *For the author*, 1664. 4°.* L, O, C, LF, EN; CH, MH, NU, RPJ, WF, Y.

2901 —For every individual superior. *For the author*, 1662. brs. L, LF; CH, MH, PSC.

2902 —A mite of affection. *For Giles Calvert*, 1659. 4°.* LT, O, C, LF, BBN; CH, MH, PH, WF, Y.

2903 —A vvord of reproof, and advice. *For Thomas Simmons*, 1659. 4°. L, O, LF, OC, BBN; MU, PL.

2904 —Words in the word. [*London*, 1661.] cap., 4°.* L, O, CT, BBN, DT; CH, MH, PH, WF, Y.

2094A **[Billing, R.]** A letter from on board. Major-general Kirke. colop: *For J. Wilson*, 1689. brs. O, C, OC, MC; Y.

2905 **Billinghurst, George.** Arcana clericalia. *For H. Twyford*, 1674. 8°. T.C.I 173. L, O, CT, LL, E; CH, CN, MHL, NCL, WF, Y.

2906 —The judges resolutions. *For H. Twyford*, 1676. 8°. T.C.I 263. L, O, LL, LI, EN; CH, MHL, NCL.

2907 **Billingsley, John.** The believer's daily exercise. *For Tho. Parkhurst*, 1690. 8°. T.C.II 311. O, LW.

2908 —A sermon preach'd . . . January the 10th. 1699/1700. *For A. and J. Churchil: and Thomas Ryles, in Hull*, 1700. 8°. L, LW.

2909 —Strong comforts for weak Christians. *For John Wright*, 1656. 4°.* O.

2909A **Billingsley, Martin.** The pen's excellency. [*London*], *to be sold by William Humble*, 1641. 8°. O; PL.

2910 **Billingsley, Nicholas.** Brachy-martyrologia. *By J. Cottrel for Tho. Johnson*, 1657. 8°. L, A; CH, CLC, CN, WF.

2911 — —[Anr. ed.] *By J. C. for Austin Rice*, 1657. 8°. LT, O, ES; CLC, CN, MH.

2912 —Κοσμοβρεφεα, or, the infancy of the world. *For Robert Crofts*, 1658. 8°. LT, O; CH, CLC, CN, MH.

2913 [–] θερχυρο-φυλακιον, or, a treasury. *For the author*, 1667. 8°. L, O, CCN; CH, MH, Y.

—A treasury of divine raptures. *By T. J. for Thomas Parkhurst*, 1667. 8°. L, O, CCH; CH, MH, Y.

2913A **B[illingsley], R[obert].** An idea of arithmetick. *By J. Flescher, to be sold by W. Morden, in Cambridge*, 1655. 8°.* L, O, CS, CT, SCK.

2914 **Bils, Lodewyk.** The coppy of a certain large act [obligatory]. 1659. 8°.* L, O, LCP.

2914A **Binckes, Joseph.** Light breaking forth. *By R. A. for William Larnar*, 1653. 4°.* CH.

2915 **[Binet, Etienne.]** Purgatory survey'd. *Printed at Paris*, 1663. 12°. L, C, LSC; CLC, CN, NU, TU, WF.

[Bingham, Joseph.] Doctrine of the fathers. 1695. See Braddocke, John.

2916 **Bingley, William.** An epistle of love. *[London], by Andrew Sowle*, 1689. 4°.* L, LF, BBN; CLC, IE, MH, MU, PH, PSC.

2917 —An epistle of tender love to all. *Printed and sold by Andrew Sowle*, 1683. 4°.* L, LF, BBN; IE, MU, PH, PSC.

2918 —An epistle of tender love, to Friends in Ireland. *[London], printed, and sold by T. S.*, 1692. 4°.* L, LF; MH, PSC, WF, Y.

2919 —A faithful warning once more. *[n.p.], printed and sold by Andrew Sowle*, 1690. 4°.* L, LF, OC, BBN; IE, MU, PH, WF, Y.

2920 —A lamentation over England. *Printed and sold by Andrew Sowle*, 1682. 4°.* L, LF; CLC, MH, MU, PH.

2921 — —[Anr. ed.] —, 1683. 4°.* L, C, LF; MH, PH, PSC, WF, Y.

2922 — —[Anr. ed.] *Printed, sold by Benjamin Clark*, 1683. 4°.* LF, LSC; PSC, Y.

2923 —Tender counsel and advice. *Printed and sold by T. Sowle*, 1697. 8°. LF, BBN; PH, PHS, PSC.

2924 **Binning, Hugh.** The common principles of Christian religion. *Glasgow, by Andrew Anderson*, 1659. 12°. ALDIS 1588. L.

2924A — —Second edition. *Printed*, 1660. 8°. LW.

2925 — —Second edition. *Glasgow, society of stationers*, 1660. 12°. E, EN.

2925A — —Second edition. *Edinburgh by a society of stationers*, 1660. 12°. ALDIS 1625. I.

2926 — —Fourth edition. *Glasgow, by R. S.*, 1663. 12°. MURRAY.

2927 — —Fifth edition. —, 1666. 12°. ALDIS 1809. L, ENC, GM.

2928 — —"Fifth" edition. *Glasgow, R. Sanders*, 1667. 12°. L.

2929 — —Sixth edition. *Edinburgh, Swintoun, Glen, and Brown*, 1671. 12°. ALDIS 1921. EN, FSF.

2930 —Fellowship with God. *Edinburgh, by George Swintoun and James Glen, to be sold by them, and by David Trench and Thomas Brown*, 1671. 8°. ALDIS 1920. LW, AN, EN, SA; NU, Y.

2931 —Heart-humiliation. *By T. Brown*, 1676. 12°, LW.

2932 — —[Anr. ed.] *Edinburgh, J. Glen*, 1676. 12°. LW, AU, EN, GU.

2933 —The sinner's sanctuary. *Edinburgh, by George Swintoun and James Glen*, 1670. 4°. ALDIS 1895. T.C.I 54. L, EN, GU, FSF; CLC, MH.

2934 —An useful case of conscience. *[Edinburgh?], printed*, 1693. 4°. L, O, C, LCL, EN; CH, NU, WF.

2934A **[Binning, John.]** Honoured Sir, it cannot but be pleasant. *[London? 1695]*. cap., 4°.* Y.

2934B **Binning, Thomas.** A light to the art of gunnery. *By John Darby for the author*, 1676. 4°. L; LC, MBA, NN, Y.

2934C — —. *By J. S. for W. Fisher and R. Mount*, 1677. 4°. T.C.I 268. DCH; CLC, CN, MH, MIU, MU.

2934D — —[Anr. ed.] *By J. D. for the author, to be sold by W. Fisher, J. Thorton, and J. Atkinson*, 1677. 4°. CN, MIU.

2934E — —[Anr. ed.] *By J. D. for W. Fisher and R. Mount*, 1689. 4°. MH, NN.

Biochimo. See Greco, Gioachino.

2935 **Biondi, Giovanni Francesco.** Il Coralbo. A new romance. *For Humphrey Moseley*, 1655. fol. L, O, CT; CH, CN, CU, MH, NP, Y.

2936 —An history of the civill vvarres. *Imprinted by T. H. and I. D. for John Benson*, 1641. fol. L, O, C, EN, DT; CH, CU, LC, NC, WSC, Y.

2936A —The second part of the history. *By E. G. for Richard Whitaker*, 1646. fol. L, EN; LC, MB, Y.

2936B **Biondi, Giuseppe.** The penitent banditto. 1663. 12°. L, O; BN, CN, WF, Y.

2937 **Birch, Peter.** A funeral sermon preach'd on the decease of Grace Lady Gethin. *By D. Edwards*, 1700. 4°.* L, O, DT; CH, Y.

2938 —A sermon preached before the . . . House of Commons, November 5, 1689. *In the Savoy: by E. Jones; and are to be sold by W. Nott, and R. Taylor*, 1689. 4°.* L, O, OB, C, CT; CH, CN, MH, NU, WF, Y.

2938A — —[Anr. ed.] *In the Savoy: by Edward Jones for William Nott*, 1689. 4°. L, OC.

2939 —A sermon preached before the . . . House of Commons, . . . Janvary 30. 1694. *For Tho. Nott, to be sold by Randal Taylor*, 1694. 4°.* L, O, C, LVF, MR; CH, MH, NU, WF, Y.

2940 **Birchall, John.** The non-pareil. *York: by Tho. Broad*, 1644. 4°.* L, O, YM; NU.

Birchedus, Henricus. See Birkhead, Henry.

2941 A birchen rod for Dr. Birch. *[London], printed*, 1694. 4°.* L, O, C, EN, DTC; CH, MH, NU, WF, Y.

2942 **Birchensha, John.** The eagle prophesie. *By T. C. to be sold by Jeremy Hierons*, 1656. 4°. LT.

2943 —The history of divine verities. *By T. C. for John Wright*, 1655. 4°. LT, O, C; CH, MH, NR.

2943A —The history of the Scriptures. *For W. Rands*, 1660. 4°. AN.

Birchley, William, *pseud.* See Austin, John.

2944 **Birckbeck, Simon.** A cordiall for a heart-qualme. *For Richard Best*, 1647. 12°. O.

2945 —The Protestants evidence. Second edition. *By John Streater*, 1657. fol. L, O, C, CT, DT; BN, CH, MBP, MH, MIU, NPT, WF.

2946 —A treatise of the four last things. *By A. M. for Edward Brewster*, 1655. 8°. LT, LSC, LW; WF.

2947 **Bird, Benjamin.** The catechism of the church of England. *By Andrew Clark, for the company of stationers*, 1674. 8°.* T.C.I 168. O, OC.

2948   —Humble advice to Protestant dissenters. *For Jonathan Robinson*, 1682. 4°.* T.C.II 11. L; NPT.

2949   —The Jacobites catechism. *Edinburgh*, 1691. 8°.* ALDIS 3133. C, EN; MIU.

2949A — —[Anr. ed.] *For T. Wesley*, 1691. 4°.* MIU, NN.

2950   — —[Anr. ed.] *For T. Wesly and re-printed at Boston, for Benjamin Harris*, 1692. 4°.* EVANS 587. MWA.

2950A —The Williamites catechism. *For T. Wesley*, 1691. 8°.* WCA.

2951   — —[Anr. ed.] *Edinburgh*, 1691. 8°. ALDIS 3134. C.

2952   **Bird, John, *at Cheddinton*.** The divine and spiritual ambassadour described. *By Sarah Griffin, for Robert Pawlet*, 1663. 4°.* L, O, CPE, SC; CH, MIU, Y.

2953   **Bird, John, *schoolmaster*.** Grovnds of grammer penned. *Oxford, by Leonard Lichfield, for Humphrey Mosley*, 1641. 8°. MADAN 991. L, O; MH, Y.

2954   **Bird, John, *of Sion College*.** Ostenta Carolina: or the late calamities. *For Fra. Sowle, to be sold by Robert Harrison*, 1661. 4°. L, O, LSC, P, AU; CH, WF, WSG.

       Bird, Thomas. Speculum anni. 1661. *See Almanacs.*

2955   **Bird, William.** The magazine of honour. *[London], for William Sheares*, 1642. 8°. L, O, C, EN, E; CH, CN, LC, MH, NC, TU, Y.

2956   [–] A treatise of the nobilitie of the realme. *By A. N. for Matthew Walbanke and Richard Best*, 1642. L, O, CS, LL, MC; BN, CH, CU, LC, NCL, TU, Y.

2956A The birds harmony. *[London] for M. Coles, T. Vere, J. Wright, J. Clark, W. Thackeray, and T. Passinger*, [c 1676]. brs. O, CM.

2957   The birds lamentation. *[London], for P. Brooksby*, [1676]. brs. CM, HH.

       Bird noats. 1655. *See* H., C.

2958   **Birgitta, Saint.** The most devout prayers of. *Printed at Antwerp*, 1659. 12°. L, O, OCC; WF.

2958A — —[Anr. ed.] *Doway, Balthazar Bellere*, 1663. 8°. O.

2959   — —[Anr. ed.] *Printed at Antworp for T. D.*, 1686. 8°.* L, O.

2959A —The prayers of. *[London], printed*, 1686. 8°.* Y.

       Birinthea. 1664. *See* Bulteel, John.

2960   **[Birkenhead, *Sir* John.]** An ansvver to a speech without doores. *[London*, 1646.] 4°.* LT, O, CCA, LVF, DT; CLC, CU, MH, NU, WF, Y.

2961   [–] The assembly-man. *For Richard Marriot*, 1662/3. 4°.* L, O, C, EN, DT; CH, CU, LC, NU, TU, Y.

2962   — —[Anr. ed.] *For Walter Davis*, 1681. 4°.* O, C, CT, MR; MH, WF, Y.

2963   — —[Anr. ed.] *For W. Davis*, 1681/82. 4°.* O, C, EN, DT; CH, CN, NU, WF, Y.

       [–] Aulicus his hue. 1645. *See* Cheynell, Francis.

2964   [–] Bibliotheca Parliamenti, libri, theologici. *Printed at London*, 1653. 4°.* LT, O, CT, MR, ES; CH, LC, MH, PL, Y.

2964A [–] —Classis secunda. *[London]* 1653. 8°.* CH, CLC, PL, Y.

2965   [–] Cabala, or an impartial account. Second edition. *Printed*, 1663. 4°.* L, O, C, CCL, EN; CH, NHC, NU, WF.

2965A [–] The foure legg'd elder. *[London*, 1647.] brs. LT, CJ, HH; MH.

2965B [–] —[Anr. ed.] *[London], printed*, 1647. *Reprinted for D. Mallet.* brs. L, HH; MH, WF.

2966   —Loyalties tears flowing. *[London?]*, 1649. 8°.* LT, O, CE; TU, WF.

2967   [–] —[Anr. ed.] *[n.p.*, 1649.] cap., 4°.* LT, O.

       [–] Mercurius menippeus. The loyal satyrist. 1682. *See* Butler, Samuel.

2967A —The necessity of Christian subjection. *Oxford, printed* 1644. 4°.* MADAN 1691n. DC.

2967B —The necessity of Christian subjection. *Oxford, printed*, 1644. 4°.* DC.

2967C [–] A new ballad of a famous German prince. *By James Cotterel*, 1666. brs. L, O.

2967D [–] —[Anr. ed.] *Printed and reprinted, Edinburgh*, 1666. brs. MH.

2968   [–] Nevves from Pembroke & Mongomery. *Printed at Mongomery [i.e. Oxford] [but really at London]*, 1648. 4°.* MADAN 1982. LT, O, C, CT, AN; MH, MIU, WF, Y.

2969   [–] Newes from Smith the Oxford jaylor [*sic*]. *For J. B.*, 1645. 4°.* LT; MH, WF, Y.

2970   [–] Pavl's chvrch-yard. Libri theologici. *[n.p.*, 1651/2.] cap., 4°.* LT, O, C, LG, LP; MH, NC, NPT, NU, Y.

2971   —A sermon preached . . . on the 3. of Novemb. 1644. *Oxford, printed*, 1644. 4°.* MADAN 1691. LT, O, CJ, DT; CH, NU, WF, Y.

2972   [–] The speech without doores defended without reason. colop: *[London], printed*, 1646. cap., 4°.* LT, CJ, DT; CH, NU, WF, Y.

2973   [–] Two centvries of Pauls Church-yard. *[London*, 1653] 4°. L, O, LP, OW, MR; CH, CN, MH, WF, Y.

2974   **Birket, Cuthbert.** A pleasant new song between a seaman and his love. *[London*, 1670?] brs. L.

2975   **Birket, John.** The godfather's advice to his son. Second edition. *For J. Knapton*, 1700. 12°. T.C.III 178. C; NU, WF.

2976   **Birkhead, Henry.** Otium literatum. *Oxoniæ, exc. H. Hall pro E. Forrest*, [1658?]. 8°. MADAN 2377. O, C, OC, CT, MAU; Y.

2977   [–] Poematia. *[Oxford]*, 1645. 4°.* MADAN 1841. O.

2978   [–] Poematia in elegiaca, iambica. *Oxonii, typis L. Lichfield, impensis E. Forrest*, 1656. 8°. MADAN 2295. LT, O, CT, EN, DT; CH, MH, WF, Y.

2978A **[Birnie, *Sir* Andrew.]** A compend or a breviot of the . . . rights. *Edinburgh, by the heirs and successors of Andrew Anderson*, 1700. 8°. EN; WF, Y.

       Birshensha, John. *See* Birchensha, John.

       The birth and burning of the image. 1681. *See* Sherman, Edmund.

2978B The birth, life and death of John Frank. *By J. M. for J. Deacon, and C. Dennisson* [c 1680] 12°. O, CM.

2979   The birth, life, death, vvil, and epitaph, of Iack Pvffe. *For T. P.*, 1642. 4°.* LT; CH, MM.

       Birth of mankind. 1654. *See* Roesslin, Eucharius.

2980   **[Bisbie, Nathaniel.]** An ansvver to a treatise out of ecclesiastical history. *Printed and are to be sold by J. Wells*, 1691. 4°.* LT, O, MR, EN, DT; CH, MH, NU, WF, Y.

2981 —The bishop visiting. *For Walter Kettilby,* 1686. 4°.* T.C.II 165. L, O, C, OB, CE; CLC, CN, MBA, NU, WF.

2982 —The modern pharisees. *For Walter Kettilby,* 1683. 4°.* T.C.I 504. L, O, C, CT, DT; CH, MIU, NU, WF, Y.

[–] Modest and peaceable inquiry. 1681. *See* Humfrey, John.

2983 —Prosecution no persecution. *For Walter Kettilby,* 1682. 4°.* T.C.I 493. L, O, C, CT, E; CH, NU, V, WF, Y.

2984 —Two sermons. *For Walter Kettilby,* 1684. 4°. T.C.II 37. L, C, OCC, EC, YM; CH, NU, WF.

2985 [–] Unity of priesthood necessary. *Printed,* 1692. 4°. L, O, C, MR, EN; CH, NP, NU, WF, Y.

2986 **Bisco, John.** The glorious mystery of Gods mercy. *By Richard Bishop,* 1647. 8°. L, O, LCL, LW; CLC, NPT, NU, WF, Y.

2987 —The grand triall of trve conversion. *By M. S. for G. Eversden,* 1655. 8°. LT, O, LCL, LW; CLC, MH, NPT, NU, WF, Y.

2988 **Bishop, George.** A book of warnings. *For Robert Wilson,* 1661. 4°.* L, O, C, LF, BBN; CH, MH, NU, PSC, WF, Y.

2989 —The burden of Babylon. *For Robert Wilson,* 1661. 4°.* L, O, LF, BBN; CH, MH, NU, PH, WF, Y.

2990 —The cry of blood and Herod. *For Giles Calvert,* 1656. 4°. LT, O, CT, BBN, MR; CH, PH, PSC, WF, Y.

2991 —The dominion of the seed of God. *Printed,* 1667. 4°.* L, O, LF, BBN; MH, NU, PH, PSC, Y.

2992 —An epistle of love to all the saints. *For Robert Wilson,* 1661. 4°.* L, O, LF, BBN, BR; MH, MU, NGC, PH, WF.

2993 —A few words in season. *For Rob. Wilson,* 1660. 4°.* L, O, CT, LF, BBN; CH, MH, NU, PH, WF, Y.

2994 —An illumination to open the eyes. *Printed,* 1661. 4°. L, LF, LW; CH, PH, VC, Y.

2994A ——[Anr. ed.] —, 1662, 4°. LF.

2995 —Jesus Christ the same today, as yesterday. *For Giles Calvert,* 1655. 4°.* LT, O, C, LF, CT; CH, MU, PH, PSC, Y,

2996 —The last trump. *Printed,* 1662. 4°.* L, LF, OC, BBN, BR; CH, MU, NU, PH, PSC.

2997 —A little treatise concerning things. [*London*], *printed,* 1663. 4°.* L, C, LF, OC, BR; CH, IE, MU, PH, Y.

2997A —A little treatise concerning sufferings. *Printed,* 1664. 8°. LF; MH, PH, PSC, WF, Y.

2998 —A looking-glass for the times. *Printed,* 1668. fol. L, O, C, LF, E; BN, MH, NU, PH, RPJ, WF, Y.

2999 —A manifesto, declaring. *Printed,* 1665. 4°. LF; CH, MU, PH, PSC.

3000 —Mene tekel. *Printed, and are to be sold by Tho. Brewster,* 1659. 4°.* LT, O, CT, LF, BBN; CH, MH, NU, PH, PSC, Y.

3001–2 Entries cancelled.

3003 —New England judged. *For Robert Wilson,* 1661. 4°. L, O, CT, LF, BBN; CH, LC, MH, NN, PSC, Y.

3004 ——The second part. *Printed,* 1667. 4°. L, O, OC, LF, BBN; CH, MH, NN, PH, WF, Y.

3004A —A rejoinder consisting of two parts. *For Thomas Simmons,* 1658. 4°. L, LF; MIU, MU, PSC.

3005 —A salutation of love. *For Robert Wilson,* 1661. 4°. L, O, LF, OC, BBN; CH, NHC, PH, PL, WF.

3006 —The stumbling-stone and rock of offence. *For Robert Wilson,* 1662. 4°. C, LF, OC, BR, BBN; CH, MU, PH, PL, PSC.

3007 —A tender visitation of love. *Printed for Robert Wilson, and are to be sold at his shop . . . and also by Richard Moon, in Bristol,* 1660. 4°.* MADAN 2469. LT, O, C, BBN, MR; MH, MU, NU, PH, WF, Y.

3008 —The throne of truth exalted. *For Giles Calvert,* 1657. 4°. LT, LF, BBN; CH, MU, PH, PSC, Y.

3008A —To the King, and both houses. [*London,* 1664.] brs. LF; Y.

3009 —To the King and his both houses. 1662. cap., fol. LF, EN; PH.

3010 —To thee, Charls Stuart, king. [*Bristol?* c 1660.] 4°. L, O, C, LG, BR; IE, MH, NU, PH, Y.

3011 ——[Anr. ed.] [*Bristol?* 1660.] 4°. L, LF; CH.

3011A —A treatise concerning election. [*London*], *printed,* 1663. 8°. O, LF; IE, MH, PH, PSC.

3012 —A treatise concerning the resurrection. [*London*], *printed,* 1662. 4°. L, O, LF, CT, BBN; CH, MU, MH, PH, Y.

3013 —Two treatises. *For R. Wilson,* 1663. 8°. L, CT, LF; MU.

3014 —A vindication of the principles. [*London?*], *printed,* 1665. 4°. L, O, LF, BBN, BR; BN, CH, LC, MH, NU, PH, Y.

3015 —The warnings of the Lord to the King. *Printed,* 1667. 4°. L, O, LF, BBN, BR; CH, IE, MH, PH, Y.

3016 —The warnings of the Lord to the men. *By M. Inman. to be sold at the Three Bibles, and by Richard Moon in Bristol,* 1660. 4°.* LT, LF, BBN; CH, LC, MU, PH. Y.

3017 Entry cancelled.

3018 ——[Anr. ed.] *Printed,* 1667. 4°.* O.

3019 —Yet one warning more. *For Robert Wilson,* 1661. 4°.* L, O, LF, BBN; MH, MU, NU, PH, PSC, Y.

3019A **Bishop, George,** *capt.* A modest check to part of a scandalous libell. [*n.p., c.* 1650.] cap., 4°.* O.

3019B —A more particvlar and exact relation of the victory. *By Richard Cotes,* 1645. 4°.* LT, O; CH, MH.

3019C **Bishop, John.** An appendix to the marrow. *By J. Streater,* 1688. 4°. PL.

3020 —The marrow of astrology. The second part. *For Joseph Streater,* 1687. 4°. L, O, MC.

3021 ——[Anr. ed.] *For J. Streater,* 1688. 4°. O, LWL, BR; CU, HC.

3021A ——Second edition. *For William Fisher and Richard Mount,* 1688. 4°. L, OC; MB, MH, WF, Y.

Bishop of Armaghes direction. 1642. *See* Udall, Ephraim.

3022 The Bishop of Canterbury his confession. *Printed,* 1644. 4°.* LT, O; CN, MIU, WF.

3023 The Bishop of London, the Welsh curate. *Printed at London,* 1652. 4°.* AN.

3024 The Bishop of St. Davids case. [*n.p.,* 1699.] brs. LL, CS.

Bishop of Waterford's case. Dublin, 1760. *See* Stanhope, Arthur.

Bishop's appeale. Newcastle, 1661. *See* Hooke, Richard.

Bishops are not to be judges. [*n.p.*], 1679. *See* Holles, Denzil.

Bishops courts. 1681. *See* Whitaker, Edward.

Bishops downefall. [n.p.], 1642. See Elys, Edmund.

3025　Bishops-gate lamentation. For L. C., 1678. brs. L; MH.

3026　Bishops, judges, monopolists. [London, 1641.] 4°. LT.

3027　The bishops last good-night. Printed, 1642. brs. LT, EC; CH.

3028　The bishops last vote in Parliament. For Iohn Thomas, 1641[2]. 4°.* LT, HH; CH, MH, Y.

Bishops looking-glasse. 1641. See P., R.

3029　The bishops manifest. For W. R., 1641. 4°.* LT, O, BR, YM, EN; CH, CSS, CU, NU, Y.

3030　The bishops mittimvs to goe to Bedlam. For I. W., 1641. 4°.* L, LG, CT; CH, CN, NU, WF, Y.

3031　Entry cancelled.

3032　The bishops potion. [London], printed, 1641. 4°.* LT, O, LSE, LVF; MH, NIC, PHS, WF.

3033　The bishops' right to vote. [n.p.], 1680. 12°. LIC, LSC.

3034　[Bispham, Thomas.] Iter Australe, a reginensibus Oxon. [Oxoniæ, 1660.] 4°.* MADAN 2364. L, O, CSS, BR, MR; CH, MH, WF, Y.

3034A　A bitt by the by. [London], for E. Oliver, [1690?] brs. O.

Bitte to stay the stomacks. [n.p.], 1647. See H., A.

3035　The biter bitten. [London], for J. Blare, [1685–88]. brs. L, CM, HH, GU.

3035A　Bix, Angelus. Sermon on the passion. For S. G., 1688. 4°. DOWNSIDE; IU.

3036　Bl., Ro. A letter from a Christian friend. [London, 1655]. cap., 4°.* O, OC, HH; CH, TU.

3037　Black, William. Illustrissimo ac per honorifico domino D. Alexandro Seton. Aberdeis: excudebat Joannes Forbesius, 1690. fol.* AU.

3038　—Theses, problemata & paradoxa philosophica. Abredeis, excudebat Ioannes Forbesius, 14 Iunii. 1686. 4°.* ALDIS 2672. HH.

Black almanack. 1651. See Almanacs.

3039　The black and terrible vvarning piece. For George Horton, 1653. 4°.* LT.

3040　Entry cancelled.

Black book of Newgate. 1677. See W., W.

3041　The black book opened. For Theodorus Microcosmus, 1660. brs. LT, OC; MH, Y.

3042　The black box of Roome opened. [London], printed, 1641. 4°.* LT, O; CH, MH, WF, Y.

3043　The black box of Rome or, a true and short discourse. [n.p.], printed, 1641. 4°.* L; MH, NU, TU.

Black Dutch almanack. Amsterdam, 1651. See Almanacs.

3043A　A black list of the names, or reputed names. Printed, 1698. brs. MH.

3044　Black Munday: or, a full and exact description of . . . eclipse . . . 29. day of March 1652. For William Ley, 1651. 4°.* LT, LG; CH, MH, Y.

3044A　—[Anr. ed.] 1652. 4°.* L; MH.

3045　Black Munday turned white. For G. Whiting, 1652. 4°.* LT, O; CLC, Y.

Black nonconformist. 1682. See Hickeringill, Edmund.

3046　Blacke Tom, his speech. [London, 1647.] brs. LT.

3047　Blackall, Offspring, bp. No reason to desire new revelations. By J. Leake, for Walter Kettilby, 1700. 4°.* T.C.III 209. L, O, C, OC, WCA; CLC, CN, NU, PL, WF, Y.

3048　—Mr. Blackall's reasons for not replying. For Walter Kettilby, 1699. 8°.* T.C.III 135. L, O, LCL, EC; CH, CU, NU, WF, Y.

3049　— —Second edition. 1699. 4°.* O, C, LVD, CM, BAMB.

3050　—St. Paul and St. James reconcil'd. Cambridge, at the university press, for Edmund Jeffery, in Cambridge, 1700. 4°.* T.C.III 209. L, O, C, CT, DT; CH, MBA, NU, TU, WF, Y.

3051　—A sermon preach'd . . . October the 7th, 1693. For Will. Rogers, 1694. 4°.* L, O, C, OM, CT; MH.

3052　— —Second edition. —, 1699. 4°.* T.C.III 115. L, CS, EC; IU, TSM, WF, Y.

3053　—A sermon preached . . . January 30th. 1698/9. By J. Leake, for Walter Kettilby, 1699. 4°.* T.C.III 107. L, O, C, EC, YM; CH, MBA, NU, WF, Y.

3054　—The sufficiency of a standing revelation. By J. Leake for Walter Kettilby, 1700. 4°.* L, O, C, OC; CU, NU, PL, WF, Y.

3055　— —In eight sermons. By J. Leake, for Walter Kettilby, 1700. 4°. T.C.III 212. L, O, C, LCL, DT; CH, MBC, MH, PL, WF.

3056　Entry cancelled.

3057　—The sufficiency of the Scripture-revelation, as to the matter of it. By J. Leake, for Walter Kettilby, 1700. 4°.* T.C.III 182. L, O, C, OC, WCA; CLC, MH, NU, TU, Y.

3058　—The sufficiency of the Scripture-revelation, as to the proof of it. Part I. By J. Leake, for Walter Kettilby, 1700. 4°.* T.C.III 182. L, O, OC; CLC, MH, NU, PL, TU, WF, Y.

3059　— —Part II. Two sermons. —, 1700. 4°.* T.C.III 196. L, O, C, OC; CLC, MH, PL, TU, WF, Y.

3060　— —Part III. —, 1700. 4°.* L, O, C, OC; CLC, MH, PL, TU, WF, Y.

3061　Blackborrow, Peter. The longitude not found. For Robert Harford, 1678. 4°. T.C.I 311. L, O, E.

3061A　— —Second edition. 1679. L (t.p. only), P, SP.

3062　—Navigation rectified. By John Playford, to be sold by Joseph Hindmarsh, 1684. 8°. T.C.II 98. C, LI; CLC, WF.

3063　[Blackborrow, Sarah.] Herein is held forth the gift and good-will of God. For Thomas Simmons, 1659. 4°. L, LF; LC, PH, PSC.

3064　—The just and equal ballance discovered. For M. W., 1660. 4°.* L, LF, BBN; CH, PH.

3064A　—The oppressed prisoners complaint. [London? 1662]. brs. WF.

3065　—A visit to the spirit in prison. For Thomas Simmons, 1658. 4°.* LT, LF, BBN; CH, IE, MH, PH, Y.

3066　Blackburn, Richard. Clitie, a novel. For Ric. Bentley and S. Magnes, 1688. 12°. T.C.II 216. CLC, MH.

3067　Blackburne, Lancelot, abp. The love of God manifested. By Tho. Warren for Thomas Bennet, 1697. 4°.* T.C.III 2. L, O, C, OC; MH, NGT, NU, TSM, Y.

3068　—The vnreasonableness of anger. By Tho. Warren for Thomas Bennet. 1694 4°.* T.C.II 519. L, O, C, OC, YM; CLC, NU, Y.

3069   **Blackerby, Samuel,** *barrister.* An historical account of making the penal laws. *For William Churchill and John Weld,* 1689. fol. T.C.II 273. L, O, C, HH, AU; CH, MBP, MH, WF, YL.

3070   **Blackerby, Samuel,** *minister.* Sermons preached on several occasions. *For Nevil Simmons,* 1674. 8°. T.C.I 162. O, C.

3071   —The substance of Mr. Blackerby's speech . . . 9th of March, 1695. *R. Baldwin,* 1696. fol.* HH.

3072   **Blackhall, G.** Rules for assizing of bread. *Dublin, Joseph Ray,* 1699. 4°.* DIX 313. L, DI, DM.

3073   **Blacklach, John.** Conviction for the Jewes. *By M. S. for Henry Cripps,* 1656. 4°. O, CT; MM.

3074   **Blackleach, John.** Endevors aiming at the glory of God. *By John Macock for the author,* 1650. 4°. LT, DT; MH, WF.

3075   [**Blackley, James.**] A lying wonder discovered. *For Thos. Simmons,* 1659. 4°.* L, C, LF; CH.

3075A [**Blackmore, Sir Richard.**] Discommendation verses. *Printed,* 1700. fol.* L, O, HH; CH, MH, TU, WF, Y.

3076   —Homer and Virgil not to be compared with the two Arthurs. *By W.B. for Luke Meredith,* 1700. 12°. T.C.III 200. O, LVD, OC, CS; MH, TU, WF.

3077   —King Arthur. *For Awnsham and John Churchil, and Jacob Tonson,* 1697. fol. T.C.III 27. L, O, C, E, DT; BN, CH, CU, MH, NP, TU, WF, Y.

3078   —Liber primus principis Arcturi. *Anno Dom.,* 1700. 4°. L, O, C, LVD, AU; CLC, Y.

3079   Entry cancelled.
       —A paraphrase on the Book of Job. *See* Bible. English. O.T. Job.

3080   —Prince Arthur. *For Awnsham and John Churchil,* 1695. fol. T.C.II 539. L, O, C, EN, DT; CH, CN, MH, WF, Y.

3081   — —Second edition. *For Awnsham and John Churchil,* 1695. fol. L, O, C, DT; CU, LC, MH, OCI, PL, Y.

3082   — —Third edition. —, 1696. fol. T.C.II 572. L, O, C, E, DT; CLC, MH, NC, WF, WSC.

3083   — —"Third" edition. 1697. fol. LW.

3084   [–] A satyr against wit. *For Samuel Crouch,* 1700. fol.* L, O, CS, EN, DT; CH, CU, MH, TU, WF, Y.

3085   [–] —Second edition. —, 1700. fol.* L; CH, CN.

3086   [–] —Third edition. —, 1700. fol.* L, O, LCP; MH, TU.

3087   — —[Anr. ed.] *Dublin,* [*John Whalley*], 1700. 4°.* DIX 323. DI, DML; CU, MU, WF, Y.

3088   [–] A short history of the last Parliament. *For Jacob Tonson,* 1699. 4°. L, O, CT, DT; CH, MH, NU, WF, Y.

3089   **Blackwell, Edward.** The proposal of. [*n.p.,* 1682.] fol. EN.

3090   **Blackwell, Elidad.** A caveat for magistrates. *By Robert Leyburn for Richard Wodenothe,* 1645. 4°. LT, O, CS, GU, DT; CH, NPT, NU, RPB, WF.

3091   **B[lackwell], I[saac].** A description of the province and bay of Darien. *Edinburgh, by the heirs and successors of Andrew Anderson,* 1699. 4°.* ALDIS 3829. O, EN; LC, MIU, RPJ, WF.

3091A **Blackwell, James.** The nativity of Mr. Will. Lilly. *By Tho. Johnson,* 1660. WF.

3092   **Blackwell, John,** *capt.* A more exact relation of the great defeat. *Londn* [*sic*], *for Henry Overton,* 1645. 4°.* LT, O; MH.

3093   **Blackwell, John,** *merchant.* An essay towards carrying on the present war against France. *For the author,* 1695. 8°.* L, O, LUG; BN, CH, LC, MH, NC, Y.

3094   **B[lackwell], I[onathan].** A heavenly diurnall. *Printed,* 1644. 4°.* LT, LI, CM; Y.

3095   The Blackwell-Hall factors case against a proviso to prohibit. [*London,* 1696?] brs. L; MH.

3095A [Same title] against a proviso to the bill. [*London,* 1696]. brs. L; MH.

3096   **Blackwood, Christopher.** Apostolicall baptisme. *Printed,* 1645. 4°. LT, C, E, GU; CH, MBA, NHC, NU, WF.

3097   Entry cancelled.

3098   —Expositions and sermons. *By Henry Hills, for Francis Tyton,* 1659. 4°. LT, O, LCL, LW; NU, Y.

3099   —Four treatises. *By T.M. for Giles Calvert,* 1653. 4°. LCL, E; MBA, NHC, NPT, NU.

3100   —Some pious treatises. *For Giles Calvert,* 1654. 4°. LT, O, E; MBA, NHC, NPT, NU.

3101   —A soul-searching catechism. Second edition. *By J.C. for Giles Calvert,* 1653. 4°. LW, E, DT; CLC, MBA, NHC, NU.

3102   — —Third edition. *For Giles Calvert,* 1658. 4°. L, LCL; NPT.

3103   —The storming of Antichrist. [*London*], *printed,* 1644. 4°. LT, C, E, DT; CH, MBA, NPT, NU, WF.

3104   —A treatise concerning deniall of Christ. *For Edward Blackmore,* 1648. 4°. LT, O, C, E, DT; CH, MBA, NPT, NU.

3105   —A treatise concerning repentance. *By J.C. for Giles Calvert,* 1653. 4°. C, E; MBA, NHC, NPT, NU.

3106   [**Bladen, William.**] Irelands trve divrnall. *For Wm. Bladen, to be sold by Richard Royston,* 1641[2]. 4°.* LT, O, MR; CH, TU, Y.

3107   [–] A true and exact relation of the chiefe passages in Ireland. *By T. H. for Rich. Royston,* 1642. 4°.* C, CT, SP; CH, CN, MH.

3108   **Blaeu, Willem Janszoon.** Guilielmi Blaeu institutio astronomica. *Oxoniæ, excudebat W. Hall impensis J. Forrest,* 1663. 8°. MADAN 2632. L [frag]; BN, WF.

3108A — —[Anr. ed.] —, 1665. MADAN 2694. 8°. L; Y.

3108B —The sea-beacon. *Amsterdam, by John Williamson Blaeu,* 1643–44. 3 pts. fol. L.

3109   —A tutor to astronomy. *For Joseph Moxon,* 1654. DC; CH.

3109A **Blagrave, Charles.** Blagrave's advertisement of his spirits. [*London?* 1680]. brs. L.

3109B —Directions for the golden purging spirit. [*London?* 1680]. brs. L.

3109C —Doctor Blagrave's excellent and highly approved spirits. *By Tho. James,* [1685?] brs. L.

3110   **Blagrave, Jonathan.** The nature and mischief of envy. *For John Southby, and sold by R. R. Taylor,* 1693. 4°.* O, C; NU, Y.

3111 —A sermon preach'd . . . August 23, 1691. *By G. C. for John Southby, and T. Jones,* 1691. 4°.* L, O, OP, CT, WCA; CLC, WF.

3112 **Blagrave, Joseph.** Blagraves astrological practice ot physick. Discovering. *By S. G. and B. G. for Obad. Blagrave,* 1671. 8°. T.C.I 79. L, O, C, LWL, GU; CLC, MH, NAM, WF, Y.

3113 ——[Anr. ed.] —, 1672. 8°. CH.

3114 ——[Anr. ed.] *For Obadiah Blagrave,* 1689. 8°. T.C.II 265. L; MH, MIU, WSG, HC.

—Ephemeris. [1658.] *See* Almanacs.

3115 —The epitome of the art of husbandry. *For Ben. Billingsley and Obadiah Blagrave,* 1669. 8°. T.C.I 9. L, O; MH, MIU.

3116 ——Second edition. *For Benjamin Billingsley,* 1670. 8°. T.C.I 32, L, GK; WU.

3117 ——Third edition. —, 1675. 8°. T.C.I 200. L, C, OC, LWL, R; MH, MHO, VC, WDA.

3118 ——Fourth edition. *Sold by B. Billingsley,* 1685. 8°. T.C.II 173. L, LPO, EC, R; CH, CU, MH, NC, Y.

3119 —Blagrave's introduction to astrology. *By E. Tyler and R. Holt, for Obadiah Blagrave,* 1682. 8°. T.C.I 474. L, O, LWL, GU; CH, MH, NN, WF, Y.

3119A [–] New additions to the art of husbandry. *For Benjamin Billingsley,* 1670. 8°. PL.

3120 —[Anr. ed.] —, 1675. 8°. L, OC, LWL, EN; MH, MHO, MIU.

3120A ——, 1685. 8°. CJC, MB, PL, WF, Y.

3121 —Blagrave's supplement. *For Obadiah Blagrave,* 1674. 8°. T.C.I 150. L, O, C, LWL, AU; CLM, LC, MB, WSG.

3122 ——Second edition. —, 1677. 8°. T.C.I 284. LSC, GU; NAM, HC.

3123 **Blagrave, Obadiah.** A catalogue of books in quires. 1691. 8°.* L.

3124 [**Blague. Thomas.**] A great fight at Market-Harborough. *For Nathaniel Ginnings,* 1646. 4°.* ŁT, DT; WF.

Blaikie, Nicholas. *See* Blake, Nicholas.

3125 **Blair, Bryce.** The vision of Theodorus Verax. *For William Leake.* 1671. 8°. T.C.I 66. L, O; CLC, CN, MH, WF, Y.

3126 **Blair, Hugh.** Gods soveraignity. *Glasgow, by Robert Sanders,* 1661. 4°.* ALDIS 1691. L, C, EN, AU.

3127 **Blair, William.** Theses hasce philosophicas. *Glasguæ, ex typographeo Roberti Sanders,* 1671. brs. GU.

3128 [**Blaise de Vigenère.**] A discovrse of fire and salt. *By Richard Cotes,* 1649. 4°. L, O, LPO, P, GU; WF, WV, Y.

3129 **Blaithwaite, Mary.** The complaint of. [*London,* 1654.] cap., 4°,* ŁT; CSS.

3130 Entry cancelled.

B[lake], C[harles]. Lusus amatorius. 1694. *See* Musæus.

3131 **Blake, James.** Applausus in honorem . . . Jacobi II. *Typis Nat. Thompson,* 1685. 4°.* O; MH, Y.

3132 —A sermon of the Blessed Sacrament . . . June 3rd, 1686. *By Henry Hills,* 1686. 4°.* L, MC, WCA, DT; CH, NU, TU, WF, Y.

3133 **Blake, Martin.** An earnest plea for peace. *For Francis Eglesfield,* 1661. 4°.* MR, SC, DT; NU, Y.

3134 —The great qvestion. *For the author, to be sold by Charles Green,* 1645. 4°. ŁT, O, C, LW, E; MH, MBA, RPJ, Y.

3135 **Blake, Nicholas.** Baruch's work finished. *For Dorman Newman,* 1681. 4°.* T.C.I 437. L, LW, E; CH, CLC, NU, WF, Y.

3136 [–] Lazarus redivivus. *Printed,* 1671. 8°. L, GU; MH.

3137 **Blake, Sir Richard.** Sir Richard Blake his speech in the . . . Commons, . . . June xxviii, 1641. *Printed,* 1641. 4°.* ŁT, O, CT, EN, DT; CH, CN, LC, MH, Y.

3138 **Blake, Robert.** A true relation of the late great sea fight. *By Henry Hills, to be sold at his house, and by Thomas Brewster,* 1653. 4°.* ŁT, CT, BR; MH.

3139 **Blake, Stephen.** The compleat gardener's practice. *For Thomas Pierrepoint,* 1664. 4°. L, O, C, OC; LC, MB, MH, WU.

3140 **Blake, Thomas, *of London,*** Eben-Ezer, or, profitable truths. *Printed,* 1666. 8°. L, O, DC.

3141 **Blake, Thomas, *Puritan divine.*** Mr. Blakes answer, to Mr Tombes his letter. *By R. L. for Abel Roper,* 1646. 4°. ŁT, O, CK, YM, DT; NHC, NPT, NU, WF.

3142 —The birth-privilege. *By G. M. for Tho. Vnderhill,* 1644. 4°.* 14 pp. O, C, LW, BB, MF; CN, MH, NHC, NPT, WF.

3143 ——[Anr. ed.] —, 1644. 4°.* 33 pp. ŁT, O, CS, CT; CH, MH, NU, WF, Y.

3144 —The covenant sealed. *For Abel Roper,* 1655. 4°. ŁT, O, CE, E; CH, MH, NU, WF, Y.

3145 Entry cancelled.

3146 —Infants baptisme. *By R. W. for Thomas Vnderhill,* 1645. 4°. ŁT, O, CS, YM, DT; CH, LC, NU, WF, Y.

3146A —Living truths in dying times. *Printed,* 1665. 8°. CLC, NPT.

3147 —Mr Humphrey's second vindication. *By A. M. for Abel Roper,* 1656. 4°.* ŁT, O, YM; CLC, NU, WF.

3148 —A moderate ansvver to these two qvestions. *By I. N. for Abel Roper,* 1645. 4°.* ŁT, O, CT, DT; CH, CU, NU, WF, Y.

3149 —Vindiciae foederis. *For Abel Roper,* 1653, 4°. ŁT, O, CS, E, DT; CH, MH, NU, WF, Y.

3150 ——Second edition. —, 1658. 4°. O, LW; NPT, NR, NU.

3151 **Blake, William.** An embassage from the Kings. [*London*], *printed,* 1654. 4°. O; CH, MH.

3151A **Blake, William, *house-keeper.*** Charity martyr'd. [*London?* 1685] cap. LG.

3151B —The farmers catechism. *Printed and are to be sold by R. Butler,* 1657. 8°. L, NN.

3152 —The ladies charity school-house roll of Highgate . . . Silver Drops. [*London,* 1670.] 8°. L, LG, OP, YM, EN; CH, CLC, CN, WF, Y.

3153 —A new trial of the ladies. *By T. Butler & T. Brewster,* May 1, 1658. 4°. ŁT, O; Y.

3153A —A serious letter sent by a private Christian. *Printed, and are to be sold by Mr. Butler,* 1655. 4°.* ŁT, OC; WF.

3153B —The triall of the ladies, Hide Park. *Printed and are to be sold by Mr. Butler,* May the first, 1656. 4°.* ŁT, C, LG; Y.

3153C ——Second edition. —, 1657. 4°.* L.

3153D —The yellow book. *Printed and are to be sold by Mr. Butler*, 1656. 4°.* LT; WF.

3153E ——*Printed, and are to be sold by Tho. Butler, and by Tho. Brewster*, 1658. 4°.* LT; Y.

3153F ——[Anr. ed.] —, 1659. 4°.* O.

3154 **Blake, William, *prisoner*.** The condemned mans reprieve. *By Richard Bishop*, 1653. 4°.* LT.

3154A **Blake, William, *Scot*.** Theses. *Aberdeen, Forbes*, 1686. 4°. ALDIS 2672. HH.

[Blakey, Nathanael.] Lazarus redivivus. 1671. *See* Blake, Nicholas.

3154B **[Blanch, John.]** An abstract of the grievances of trade. *Printed*, 1694. 4°.* I, C, S; CU, MH, NC, WF, Y.

3154C **[–]** The interest of England considered. *For Walter Kettleby*, 1694. 8°. T.C.II 482. O, CJ; CU, MBA, MU, NC, Y.

3154D **[–]** The naked truth in an essay. *Printed*, 1696. 4°.* L, EN; CN, MH, NC, WF, Y.

Blanckaert. *See* Blankaart.

Blancourt. *See* Haudicquier de Blancourt, Jean.

3155 **Bland, Edward.** The discovery of Nevv Brittaine. *By Thomas Harper for John Stephenson*, 1651. 4°.* L, CT; CH, LC, NHS, RPJ, Y.

3156 **Bland, Francis.** The souldiers march to salvation. *Printed at York*, 1647. 4°. L, O; CH.

3157 **Bland, John.** To the kings most excellent Majesty, the humble remonstrance of. [*London?* 1661.] fol.* L.

3158 **[–]** Trade revived, or a way. *For Thomas Holmwood*, 1659. 4°. CH, MH, MHS, PU.

3159 **[–]** ——[Anr. ed.] *By T. Leach, for Tho. Holmwood*, 1660. [*pasted over* 1659] 4°. L, EN; NC.

3160 **Bland, Peter.** An answer to the late scandalous . . . pamphlet. *For John Field*, 1643. 4°.* LT, CT, LG, HH, EN; CH, CU, MH, NU, WF, Y.

3161 —An argvment in ivstification of the five members. *For John Field*, [1643]. 4°.* LT, O, CT, LCL, DT; CH, CN, MH, NU, WF, Y.

3162 —Resolved vpon the question. [*London*], *for Matthew Walbancke*, 1642. 4°.* LT, O, C, ENC, DT, CH, CN, MH, WF, Y.

3162A —Souldiers march to salvation. 1647. YM.

3162B —Souldiers search for salvation. 1647. YM.

3163 —A royall position. *For John Field*, 1642. 4°.* LT, O, C, MR, DT; CH, CN, LC, MH, NC, NU, Y.

3163A **Blandford, Susannah.** A small account given forth. [*London*], *printed*, 1698. 8°. C, LF; PSC.

3163B —A small treatise writ by one of the true Christian faith. *Printed*, 1700. 8°. LF.

3164 **Blankaart, Stephen.** A physical dictionary. *For S. Crouch and J. Gellibrand*, 1684. 8°. L, LM, CE, OM, OR; Y.

3164A ——[Anr. ed.] *By J. D. and sold by John Gellibrand*, 1684. 8°. L, LCS, LWL; MIU, WF, WU.

3164B ——[Anr. ed.] *By J. D. to be sold by Samuel Crouch*, 1684. 8°. CLC, MIU, WF, WSG, HC.

3165 ——Second edition. *For S. Crouch*, 1693. 8°. T.C.II 445. L, O, C, LM, LWL; CLC, WSG.

3166 ——Third edition. —, 1697. 8°. T.C.III 30. LCP, LWL; NAM, WU, HC.

3167 Blanket-fair. [*London*], *for Charles Corbet*, 1684. brs. L, O, LG, HH; CLC, MH, Y.

3167A The blasphemer. *For J.B.*, 1676. fol.* OC.

Βλασφημοκτονια the blasphemer. [1653.] *See* Poole, Matthew.

Blasphemous and treasonable paper. Edinburgh, 1681. *See* Ker, Walter.

Blasphemous charge. [n.p.], *See* Douglas, *Lady* Eleanor.

Blast blown. 1680. *See* Robinson, Richard.

Blatant beast. [n.p.], 1691. *See* N., N.

3168 **Blau, Robert.** Fraus elusa. *Edinburgi, heir of A. Anderson*, 1686. 8°. ALDIS 2631. E.

3169 Entry cancelled.

3170 —Index poeticus. *Edinburgi, excudebat hæres Andreæ Anderson*, 1688. 8°.* ALDIS 2750. AU, E.

3171 —Praxis oratoria. *Edinburgh, by George Mosman*, 1696. 8°.* AU.

3172 —Syntaxis vernacula. *Edinburgi, heir of A. Anderson*, 1686. 8°. ALDIS 2632. E.

3173 ——Second edition. *Edinburgh, by the heir of Andrew Anderson, July 1*, 1691. 8°. EN.

3174 ——[Anr. ed.] *Printed at Edinburgh*, 1691. 8°. FSF.

3175 ——Third edition. *Edinburgi, haeres et successores A. Anderson*, 1696. 4°. ALDIS 3541. EN.

3175A —Vocabularium duplex. *Edinburgh, by the heirs and successors of Andrew Anderson*, 1698. 8°. ALDIS 3735. L, E, AU.

3176 **Blaxland, Stephen.** Speculum Culmerianum; wherein. 1657. 8°. O.

3177 **[Blaxton, John.]** A remonstrance against the non-residents of great Brittaine. *By T. Badger, for Rich. Royston*, 1642. 4°. LT, O, CT, OC, E; CH, CN, NU, WF, Y.

3178 **Blay, John.** Loyal constancy. [*London*], *for P. Brooksby*, [1672–95]. brs. L, O, CM, HH.

[Blaykling, John.] Anti-Christian treachery. [n.p., *c.* 1686.] *See* Pearson, John.

3178A **Blayney, Allan.** The blessed birthday of Jesus. *By T. M. for Stephen Chatfield*, 1658. P; NC.

3179 **[–]** Festorvm metropolis. *By Matthew Simmons*, 1652. 4°. LT, O, C, OC, CT; CH, MH, NGT.

Simmons, 1652. 4°. LT, O, C, OC, CT; CH, MH, NGT.

3180 ——Second edition. *By T. M. for Steven Chatfield*, 1654. 8°. LT, O; WF.

3180A **[–]** The metropolitan feast. Third edition. *By T. M. for Robert Horn*, 1662. 8°. L; Y.

3181 The blazing-star. *For Francis Fox*, 1664. 4°.* L.

Blazing star. 1665. *See* B., J.

3182 A blazing starre seene in the West. *For Jonas Wright, and I. H.*, 1642. 4°.* LT; CH, Y.

3183 **[Blechynden, Richard.]** Two useful cases resolved. *For Henry Bonwicke*, 1685. 4°.* T.C.II 123. L, O, C, OC, CT; CH, LC, NU, TU, Y.

3184 ——[Anr. ed.] —, 1698. 4°.* T.C.III 63. O, CT, EN; CN.

Bleeding Iphegenia. [n.p., 1675.] *See* French, Nicholas.

Bleeding lover. [n.p., 1676–80.] *See* Duffett, Thomas.

3185 The bleeding lovers lamentation. [*London*], *for P. Brooksby, J. Deacon, J. Blare, and J. Back*, [1688–92]. brs. L, O, CM, HH; MH.

3186 **Blégny, Nicolas de.** New and curious observations on . . . venereal disease. *For Tho. Dring; and Tho. Burrel*, 1676. 8°. T.C.I 246. O, CCA, DT; NAM, WSG.

3187 —A true history of a child anatomized. *By Tho. James for Samuel Lee*, 1680. 12°. T.C.I 383. L, EN, DT.

3187A **[Bleming, Jone.]** The new prayers for K. William. colop: *J. Bond*, 1693. cap., fol.* CH.

Blemish of government. 1655. *See* Younge, Richard.

3187B **Blennerhasset, John.** Proposals for encouraging a linnen manufactory. [*London?* 1700]. brs. L.

Blessed are the epace-makers. [*sic*]. Oxford, 1642. *See* A w[h]isper in the eare.

3188 Blessed is he that considereth the poore. [*n.p.*, 1658.] brs. LT.

Blessed openings. [*n.p.*, 1661.] *See* Perrot, John.

3189 **Blewit, Martin.** Catalogue of library. [*n.p.*, 1693.] 4°. L.

3190 **[Blight, Francis.]** A true and impartial account of the dark and hellish power of witchcraft. *Exeter, by Sam. Darker and Sam. Farley*, 1700. fol.* L.

3191 The blind eats many a flye. [*London*], *for P. Brooksby*, [1672–95]. brs. L, HH.

Blind man's folly. 1666. *See* R., S.

Blind obedience. [*n.p.*], 1698. *See* Jenks, Silvester.

3192 **[Blinman, Richard]** An essay tending to issue the controversie about infant baptism. *For Rich. Chiswel*, 1674. 12°. T.C.I 203. O, LCL, LW; CLC, NHC, NPT.

3192A —A rejoinder to Mr. Henry Danvers. *For Thomas Wall*, 1675. 12°.* L.

3193 **Blith, Walter.** The English improover. *For I. Wright*, 1649. 4°. L, O, CCL, E, DT; CH, MH, WDA, WF, Y.

3194 ——Second edition. —, 1649. 4°. LT, LWL, R; MH, NNC, NR, WU, Y.

3195 —The English improver improved. Third edition. *For John Wright*, 1652. 4°. LT, O, C, R, E; BN, CH, CN, LC, MH, NC, WDA, Y.

3196 ——"Third" edition. —, 1653. 4°. L, O, C, LWL, R; CLC, LC, MH, NR, PL.

3197 **Blithe, Nathaniel.** A plain and brief explanation. Second edition. *For Edw. Millington*, 1674. 8°. T.C.I 182. O, OCC; Y.

3198 **Blochwitz, Martin.** Anatomia sambuci, quae non solùm. *Typis Johannis Field sumptibus Octaviani Pulleyn*, 1650. 12°. L, C, OB, LCP, E; CH, JF.

3199 —Anatomia sambuci: or, the anatomie of the elder. *For Tho. Heath*, 1655. 12°. LT, C, E, EN, GU; CLC, PL, WU, Y.

3200 ——[Anr. ed.] *For Tho. Sawbridge, to be sold by H. Brome*, 1670. 12°. T.C.I 51. L, LCP, LWL, CS, AU; CJC, WF, WSG.

3201 ——[Anr. ed.] *For H. Brome and Tho. Sawbridge*, 1677. 12°. T.C.I 285. L, CE, LWL; CH, MH, NAM, WF, WU, HC.

3202 **Blois, Louis de.** Enchiridion parvulorum. 1655. 12°. LW.

3203 —A mirrour for monkes. *Printed at Paris*, 1676. 12°. L, WARE; CN, NU, TU, WF, WCL.

3204 —Seven exercises. *For M. Turner*, 1686. 12°. L, CT.

3205 **[Blome, Richard.]** The art of heraldry. *For Hannah Sawbridg*, 1685. 8°. T.C.II 149. L, LG; GLC, MWA, Y.

3206 [–] —Second edition. *For S. Briscoe*, 1693. 8°. T.C.II 468. L, O, MC; MH, WF, Y.

3207 —Britannia: or, a geographical description. *By Tho. Roycroft for the undertaker, Richard Blome*, 1673. fol. T.C.I 166. L, O, C, EN, DT; BN, CH, CN, LC, MH, NC, TU, Y.

3208 ——[Anr. ed.] *For John Wright*, 1677. fol. NL.

3209 —A description of the island of Jamaica. *By T. Milbourn, and sold by S. Williams junior*, 1672 .8°. L, O, OC, GU, DT; CH, CN, LC, MH, RPJ, Y.

3210 ——[Anr. ed.] *By J.B. for Dorman Newman*, 1678. 8°. T.C.I 336. L, O, OC, CPE, E; BN, CH, CN, LC, PH, RPJ, Y.

3211 [–] An essay to heraldry. *By T.B. for Rich. Blome*, 1684. 8°. L, O, MC; CH, CLC, LC, Y.

3212 [–] The fanatick history. *For J. Sims*, 1660. 8°. LT, O, CPE, LCL, LF; CLC, CU, NPT, NU, PHS.

3213 [–] The gentlemans recreation. *By S. Roycroft, for Richard Blome*, 1686. fol. L, O, C, CT; CH, CN, MH, NN, WF, Y.

3214 —A geographical description of the four parts of the world. *By T.N. for R.Blome, and are also sold by Nath. Brooks, Edw. Brewster, and Tho. Basset*, 1670. fol. L, O, C, MR, E; BN, LC, MH, MHS, NC, Y.

3215 [–] The present state of His Majesties isles and territories in America. *By H. Clark, for Dorman Newman*, 1687. 8°. T.C.II 176. L, O, C, MR; BN, CH, CN, LC, MH, RPJ, Y.

3216 —Proposals for printing a geographical description. [*Oxford*], 1671. fol. O.

3217 —Proposals for printing of [fifth edition] Gvillim's heraldry. [*London*, 1674.] brs. O.

3218 —Propositions concerning the printing of a book which is to contain these arts and sciences. [*n.p.*, 166–?] brs. OP.

3219 —Questions propounded to George Whitehead. [*London*, 1659]. cap., 4°.* LT, O, CT, LF; CH, MH, MIU, PH, Y.

3219A **Blondeau, Pierre.** A most humble remonstrance of. [*London*, 1653.] cap., 8°.* L.

3220 **Blondel, David.** A treatise of the sibyls. *By T.R. for the authour, to be sold by Thomas Dring*, 1661. fol. L, O, C, DC, EN; CH, CU, LC, MH, NC, Y.

3221 **Blondel, François.** The comparison of Pindar and Horace. *For T.Bennet*, 1696. 8°. T.C.II 571. L, O, C, EC; CLC, CU, NC, WF, Y.

3222-3 Entries cancelled.

Blood for blood, Oxford, 1661. *See* Reynolds, John.

3224 Blood washed away. 1657. 4°. LT.

3224A Blood will out. *Philadelphia, printed and sold by William Bradford*, 1692. 4°.* EVANS 588. NN, RPB.

Bloody almanack. 1643. *See under* Almanacs: Napier, John.

—1654. *See under* Almanacs: Livie, J.

Bloody and barbarous murther. 1677. *See* R., E.

3225 Bloody and barbarous news from Bishopsgate-street. *For L. C.*, 1678. 4°.* NU.

3226 A bloody and cruel plot. *For H. R.*, 1643. 4°.* LT; CH, MH, Y.

3226A The bloody and treacherous design of the French King. *For W. D.*, 1688. brs. Y.

Bloody assizes. 1689. *See* Tutchin, John.

Bloody Babylon. 1689. *See* Gaujac, Pierre Gally de.

3227 Bloody Babylon discovered. [*London*], *printed*, 1659. 8°. LT, LG; NU.

Bloudy battel at Preston. [n.p.], 1648. *See* Walton, J.

3227A A bloudy battaile betwixt the Weymarish. 1646. 4°. O.

3228 A bloody battell or the rebels overthrow. *For John Greensmith*, 1641. 4°.* LT, O; CSU, WF, Y.

3229 The bloody bed-roll. *Printed at Oxford by L. Lichfield: and re-printed at London* [1660]. brs. MADAN 2482. O.

3230–1 Entries cancelled.

3232 The bloody diurnall from Ireland. *Printed at Kilkenny, reprinted at London*, 1647. 4°.* LT, O, C; CH, MH, Y.

3233 The bloody duke. *For W. Bonny*, 1690. 4°. T.C.II 313. L, O, EC, BR, AU; CH, CN, LC, MH, NC, Y.

3234 The bloudy field. *Imprinted at London for George Horton*, 1654. 4°.* LT, DT; Y.

3235 A bloody fight at Balrvd-Derry. *Printed at London by Robert Ibbitson*, 1647. 4°.* LT, C, EN; CH, MH, Y.

3236 A bloody fight at Black-water in Ireland. *By Iane Coe, Iune the 15.* 1646. 4°.* LT, O, C, AN, EN; CH, MIU.

3237 A blovdy fight at Dvblin. *For R. Williamson*, 1649. 4°.* LT, C, LFEA; MH.

3238 A blovdy fight at Pontefract Castle. [*London*], *printed*, 1648. 4°.* LT.

3239 A bloudy fight at sea. *For G. W.*, 1650. 4°.* O, BR.

3240 A bloudy fight at sea disputed. [*London*], *for R. Emerson*, 1648. 4°.* LT, NN.

3241 A bloudy fight between the Parliaments forces. *For G. Horton*, 1659. 4°.* LT; CN, Y.

3242 A bloudy fight in Essex. *For R. W.*, 1648. 4°.* LT; CH.

3243 A bloudy fight in France. *For S. Holden*, 1651[2]. 4°.* LT.

3244 A bloudy fight in France, between the Kings army. *For Richard Hare*, 1652. 4°.* LT.

3245 A blovdy fight in Hartford-shire. *For R. W.*, 1649. 4°.* LT; MH.

3246 A bloudy fight in Ireland: and a great victory. *By R. I.*, 1649. 4°.* LT, C, LFEA.

3247 A bloudy fight in Ireland between the Lord Deputies forces. *By R. W. for George Horton*, 1651. 4°.* LT.

3248 A bloudy fight in Ireland, . . . between the Parliaments forces. *For G. Norton*, 1652. 4°.* LT; Y.

Bloody fight in Scotland. 1648. *See* Margetts, Thomas.

3249 A bloudy fight in Scotland, between the English, Irish, and Scots. *Imprinted at London for R. W. 26. March*, 1649. 4°.* LT.

3250 A bloudy fight in Scotland, between the Parliaments forces. *Imprinted at London, for G. Laurenson, Aprill 9*, 1649. 4°.* LT, HH, E, DT.

3251 A bloody fight in the North on Munday last July 17. 1648. *For H. Becke*, 1648. 4°.* LT, DT; CH, MH.

3252 A bloudy fight neer Newark. *For G. S.*, 1648. 4°.* LT.

3253 The bloody game at cards. [*London*, 1643]. 4°.* LT, LVF, OC; CH, MH, WF, Y.

3254 The bloody husband, and crvell neighbovr. Two mvrthers. *By Tho. Warren*, 1653. 4°.* LT, LG, CM; CLC, WF, Y.

3255 A bloody independent plot discovered. [*London*], *printed*, 1647. 4°.* LT, O, CT, HH; CH, MH, NU, Y.

3256 The bloody innkeeper. *Printed*, 1657. 4°.* L.

Bloody Irish almanack. 1646. *See* Almanacs.

3257 The bloody lover. [*London*], *for P. Brooksby*, 1673. 4°.* L, LG.

3258 A bloody masacre [*sic*] plotted by the Papists. *For M. R.*, 1641. 4°.* LT, O, C, LG; WF, Y.

3259 The bloody murtherer. *By H. Lloyd for Jonathan Edwin*, 1672. 8°. T.C.I 104. L; WF.

3260 The bloody murther in Gloucester-shire. *For John Hose*, [1668]. 4°. MORETON.

3261 The bloody murderer discovered. [n.p.], *for Henry Johnson*, 1674. 4°.* L; NU.

3261A The bloody murtherers executed. *William Powel*, 1675. 4°.* L.

3261B Bloody news from Angel-alley. *For D. M.*, 1678. 4°.* O.

3262 Bloudy nevves from Bedford-shire. *Printed at London*, 1648. 4°.* LT, AN.

3263 Bloody news from Chelmsford. *Oxford, printed*, 1663. brs. MADAN 2636. L, O, HH.

3264 Bloody news from Clerken-well. *For J. Jones*, 1661. 4°.* CH.

3264A —[Same title] [*London*], *P. B.*, [1670?] 4°.* L.

3265 Bloudy nevves from Colchester. *For R. W.*, 1648. 4°.* LT, HH.

3265A Bloody news from Covent Garden. *For T. O.*, 1683. brs. L, LG, DCH.

3266 Bloody news from Devonshire. 1694. 4°. O.

3267 Bloody newes from Dover. [*London*], *printed, Feb. 13.* 1647. 4°.* LT; MB.

3268 Bloudy nevves from Enfield. *For George Horton*, [1659]. 4°.* L.

3269 Bloudy news from Germany. [n.p.], *for Philip Brooksby*, fol.* L.

3270 Bloudy newes from Holland. *For E. Cotton*, 1652. 4°.* LT; Y.

3271 Blovdy nevves from Ireland. *For Marke Rookes*, 1641. 4°.* LT, O, C; CLC.

3272 Entry cancelled.

3273 Bloudy nevves from Kent. *For R. W.*, 1648. 4°.* LT, O, DT; CN, MIU, Y.

3274 Bloody newes from Norwich. *For Iohn Greensmith*, 1641. 4°.* LT, CT, MR.

3274A Bloody news from Paris. colop: *For R. Baldwin*, 1689. brs. L, C, HH; CN.

3275 Bloody newes from St. Albans. *For John Johnson*, 1661. 4°.* C; MIU.

3276 Bloudy nevves from Scotland declaring. [n.p.], for C. W., 1648. 4°.* LT.

3277 Bloudy nevves from sea: a perfect narrative. By B.A., 1652. 4°.* LT; Y.

3278 Bloudy newes from sea: being a perfect narrative. For G. Horton, 1652. 4°.* LT, O.

3279 Bloody news from Shrewsbury. [London], for R.Burton, and P.Brooksby, 1673. 4°.* L.

3279A Bloody news from Southwark. For D.M., 1676. 4°.* Y.

3279B Bloody news from Stanes. By P.Lillicrap for J.Cock, 1674. 4°.* Y.

3280 Bloudy newes from the Barbadaes [sic]. For G. Horton, 1652. 4°.* LT; RPJ.

3281 Bloudy newes from the East-Indies. For George Horton, 1651. 4°.* LT.

3282 Bloudy nevves from the Isle of Wight. For Nathaniel Gibson, 1648. 4°.* LT.

Bloudy newes from the Lord Byron. 1648. See Wilkinson, Thomas.

Bloudy newes from the North, and. 1650. See Tilbury, Samuel.

3283 Bloudy nevves from the North declaring the engagement. [London], September 8. for G.VV., 1648. 4°.* LT.

Bloudy newes from the North, declaring the particulars. 1648. See Smith, R.

3284 Bloody nevves rom [sic] the Scottish army. Printed, 1648. 4°.* LT, O; MH, WF.

3285 Bloody nevves from Wales. [n.p.], September 5. for R. VV., 1648. 4°.* LT, AN; CH.

3285A Bloody news from York-shire. For R.Roffe, 1674. 4°.* L, DT; Y.

3286 The bloody papist. colop: By George Larkin, 1683. brs. O, EN; MH, Y.

3287 The bloody Parliament, in the raigne of an unhappy prince. Printed, 1643. 4°.* LT, HH, EC; CLC.

3287A The bloody persecution of the Protestants in France. For Richard Melvin, 1641. 4°.* EC; CH.

3288 A bloody plot discovered against the Independents. For G.E. January 21, 1647. 4°.* LT, DT; Y.

3289 A bloody plot discovered to surprize the Tower. Printed at London by Robert Ibbitson, 1647. 4°.* LT, O; CH, CN, MH, Y.

3290 Entry cancelled.

3291 Bloody plots against the Parliament. For E.P. Iune 4. 1646. 4°.* LT, HH, DT; CH, NU, WF.

Bloody prince. 1643. See W., I.

Bloody proiect. [n.p.], 1648. See Walwyn, William.

3291A The bloody siege of Vienna; a song. For J.Dean [1688]. brs. CLC, MH.

3292 A bloody slaughter at Pembrooke-Castle. Printed at London by Robert Ibbitson, 1648. 4°.* LT, AN.

3292A The bloody sons warning-piece. [London], for Thomas Johnson, 1676. 4°.* Y.

Blovdy tenent. [n.p.], 1644. See Williams, Roger.

3293 A bloudy tenent confuted. For H.S. and W.L., 1646. 4°.* LT; MH, Y.

3294 The bloody treatie; or, proceedings. For J.C., 1645. 4°.* LT, O; CH, CN.

3295 Entry cancelled.

3295A Bloome, Hans. A description of the five orders. W. Fisher and Overton, 1668. fol.* L; BN.

Blosius, Lewis. See Blois, Louis de.

3296 Blount, Charles. The miscellaneous works of. [London], printed, 1695. 12°. L, O, C, EN, DT; BN, CH, CN, MH, NU, TU, WF, Y.

3297 [–] Anima mundi. Amsterdam, anno mundi 00000 [London? 1679?]. 4°. L, LW; CN, MH, Y.

3298 — —[Anr. ed.] Sold by Will. Cademan, 1679. 8°. T.C.I 373. L, O, C, OM, BQ; BN, CLC, NP, NU, WF, Y.

3299 — —[Anr. ed.] Printed, 1679. 12°. L, O, CT, LI, OC; CU, LC, MH, PL, VC, Y.

3300 [–] An appeal from the country to the city, for the preservation of His Majesties person. Printed, 1679. fol.* L, O, C, EN; CH, CN, MH, NU, TU, WF, Y.

3300A [–] —[Anr. ed.] [London, 1679]. cap., fol.* C, CCA.

3300B [–] —[Anr. ed.] Printed, 1679. 4°.* L, O, C, OC, DT; CLC, MH, PBL, TU, WF, Y.

3301 [–] —[Anr. ed.] —, 1680. 4°.* L.

3302 [–] —[Anr. ed.] —, 1695. 4°.* O, OC, BAMB; CU, NU, PL, TU, Y.

3303 [–] Great is Diana of the Ephesians. Printed, 1680. 8°. L, CT; BN, CLC, CU, MH, VC, WF.

3304 [–] —[Anr.ed.] —, 1695. 8°. L, O, OC; NP, NU, PL, VC, Y.

3305 [–] —[Anr. ed.] Cosmopoli [London, 1700?]. 4°. L, LW, HH; CH, CU.

3306 —Janua scientiarum. [London], by Nath. Thompson, 1684. 8°. L, O, C, OC; CH, CU, MIU, WF, Y.

3307 [–] A just vindication of learning. Printed, 1679. 4°.* L, O, CT, M; CLC, CU, LC, NC, Y.

3308 [–] —[Anr. ed.] —, 1695. 4°. O, OC, BAMB; CLC, CN, MH, NU, PL.

3309 [–] King William and Queen Mary conquerors. For Richard Baldwin, 1693. 4°. L, C, LVF, MR, AU; BN, HR, CH, CN, NU, WF, Y.

3310 [–] Miracles, no violations of the lavvs of nature. For Robert Sollers, 1683. 4°.* T.C.I 511. L, O, C, OC, DT; CH, MH, NU, WF, Y.

3311 [–] Mr. Dreyden vindicated. For T.D., 1673. 4°.* T.C.I 135. L, O, LVD; CH, MH, NP, Y.

3312 —The oracles of reason. Printed, 1693. 12°. L, O, C, E, DT; CH, CU, MH, NU, WF, Y.

3313 [–] Reasons humbly offered for the liberty of unlicens'd printing. Printed, 1693. 4°.* L, O, C, CT; CH, CN, MH, NC, WF, Y.

3314 [–] Religio laici. For R.Bentley and S.Magnes, 1683. 12°. T.C.II 50. L, O, C, OC, CT; CLC, MH, MMO, WF, Y.

3315 [–] The sale of Esau's birth-right. [n.p., 1679.] brs. L, O, LW, HH; CH, CN, TU, Y.

3316 Blount, Sir Henry. A voyage into the Levant. Fourth edition. By R.C. for Andrew Crooke, 1650. 12°. L, O, CT, EN; CLC, CN, LC, MH, NIC.

3317 [–] —Fifth edition. By T.M. for Andrew Crook, 1664. 12°. L, C, LR, E; CLC, NC, NN.

3318 — —[Anr. ed.] *For William Crook,* 1669. 12°. T.C.I 23. L, O, LWL, OR, AU; CLC, MH, Y.

3319 — —Eighth edition. *By J. C. for William Crook,* 1671. 12°. T.C.I 91. L, O, OC; CH, LC, MH.

3320 Entry cancelled.

3321 **Blount, Thomas.** The academic of eloquence. *By T. N. for Humphrey Moseley,* 1654. 12°. LT, O; CU, MU, NIC, Y.

3322 — —Second edition. —, 1656. 12°. L, GU; CH, LC, MH, WF.

3323 — —Third edition. *By H. L. for Anne Moseley,* 1663. 12°. C; WF.

3324 — —"Third" edition. *For Anne Moseley, to be sold by Thomas Clark,* 1664. 12°. L.

3325 — —Fourth edition. *By Tho. Johnson for Peter Parker,* 1670. 12°. T.C.I 58. L, AU, ES; CLC, CN, CU, LC, MH.

3326 — —Fifth edition. *For Chr. Wilkinson, and Cha. Harper,* 1683. 12°. T.C.II 21. L, C; IU, Y.

3327 —Animadversions upon Sʳ Richard Baker's chronicle. *Oxon., by H. H. for Ric. Davis,* 1672. 8°. T.C.I 97. MADAN 2920. L, O, C, EN, DT; BN, CH, CU, MH, TU, WF, Y.

3328 [–] Boscobel: or the compleat history. *For A. Seile,* 1662. 8°. L, O; CH, MH, NU, WF.

3329 [–] Boscobel: or, the history of His Sacred Majesties most miraculous preservation. *For Henry Seile,* 1660. 8°. L, O, CT, MR, GU; CH, CN, MH, WF.

3330 [–] —Second edition. *For Henry Seile,* 1660. 8°. L, LVF; CH, CN, MH, Y.

3331 [–] —Third edition. *By M. Clark and are to be sold by H. Brome and C. Harper,* 1680. 8°. T.C.I 447. L, O, OM, CM, BR; CH, CN, MH, WF, Y.

3332 Entry cancelled.
[–] Calendarium catholicum. [n.p.], 1661. *See* Almanacs.

3333 —Fragmenta antiquitatis. *By the assigns of Richard and Edward Atkins, for Abel Roper, Tho. Basset and Christopher Wilkinson,* 1679. 8°. T.C.I 342. L, O, C, EN, DT; BN, CH, CN, LC, MH, NCL, Y.

3334 —Glossographia: or a dictionary. *By Tho. Newcomb, to be sold by Humphrey Moseley and George Sawbridge,* 1656. 8°. LT, O, CJ, LPO, DC; CH, CN, LC, NP, TU, Y.

3334A — —[Anr. ed.] *By Tho. Newcomb, sold by Humphrey Moseley and George Sawbridge,* 1659. 8°. AN.

3335 — —Second edition. *By Tho. Newcomb for George Sawbridge,* 1661. 8°. L, C, CT, EN; CH, CU, TU, WF, Y.

3336 — —Third edition. *By Tho. Newcomb, to be sold by John Martyn,* 1670. 8°. T.C.I 24. L, O, C, BR, EN; BN, CSU, LC, MH, TU, Y.

3337 — —Fourth edition. *In the Savoy, by Tho. Newcomb, to be sold by Robert Boulter,* 1674. 8°. T.C.I 191. L, C, OB, LLL, ES; CLC, MH, NP, TU, Y.

3338 — —Fifth edition. *By Tho. Newcomb, to be sold by Tho. Flesher,* 1681. 8°. T.C.I 433. L, O, C, CT, E; CLC, CU, NN, TU, WF, Y.

3339 Entry cancelled.
[–] New almanack. 1663. *See* Almanacs.

3340 —Νομο-λεξικον: a law-dictionary. *In the Savoy: by Tho. Newcomb, for John Martin and Henry Herringman,* 1670. fol. T.C.I 58. L, C, OME, EN, DT; BN, CLC, CN, LC, MHL, TU, YL.

3341 — —Second edition. *For H. Herringman, T. Newcomb, R. Chiswel, and R. Bentley; and sold by Tho. Salusbury,* 1691. fol. T.C.II 351. L, O, CS, ENC, DT; LC, MHL, WF, Y.

3342 —The resolutions of the jvdges. *For T. Twyford and are to be sold by Hen. Twyford,* 1670. 8°. T.C.I 35. L, O, C; CH, MHL.

3343-4 Entries cancelled.

3345 —A world of errors. *In the Savoy: by T. N. for Abel Roper, John Martin, and Henry Herringman,* 1673. fol. T.C.I 120. O, LG, CS; CN, IU, NR, Y.

3345A **Blount, Sir Thomas Pope.** An advertisement to all learned gentlemen. [*London,* 1690]. brs. OC.

3346 —Censura celebriorum authorum. *Impensis Richard Chiswel,* 1690. fol. L, O, C, EN, DT; BN, CH, CU, LC, MH, NU, TU.

3347 —De re poetica. *By Ric. Everingham, for R. Bently,* 1694. 4°. T.C.II 513. L, O, C, EN, DT; BN, CH, CN, LC, MH, NP, TU, WSC, Y.

3348 —Essays on several subjects. *For Richard Bently,* 1691. 8°. L, O, C, CT, BR; CLC, CU, NP, TU, WF, Y.

3349 — —Second edition. —, 1692. 8°. L, LW, AU, M; CH, CU, MH, WF, Y.

3350 — —Third edition. —, 1697. 8°. L, LVF, OC, EN, DT; CH, CU, MH, NPT, WF.

3351 —A natural history. *For R. Bentley,* 1693. 8°. T.C.II 513. L, O, C, EN, DT; CH, CN, LC, MH, Y.

3352 [**Blount, Sir Walter Kirkham.**] The spirit of Christianity. *By Henry Hills,* 1686. 12°. L, O, CT, EC; CH, NU, TU, WF, Y.

3353 **Blow, John.** Amphion Anglicus, a vvork of many compositions. *By William Pearson, for the author; to be sold at his house, and by Henry Playford,* 1700. fol. L, O, C, F, DT; CH, CN, LC, MH, NP, WCL, Y.

3354 —A choice collection of ayres. *Sold by John Young,* 1700. obl., 4°. T.C.III 198. L.

3355 —A second musical entertainment. *By John Playford, and are to be sold by Iohn Carr,* 1685. 4°. L; CLC, CN, MH, NN, WF, Y.

3356 —Three elegies upon the . . . loss of . . . Queen Mary. *By J. Heptinstall for Henry Playford,* 1695. fol.* L, OC; CLC, CN, LC, MH, WF.

3357 —Twelve new songs, *By, and for William Pearson; and sold by Mr. Playford; Mr. Scott; Mr. J. Hair; Mr. Hudgebutt,* 1699. fol. T.C.III 109. LCM; LC.

Blow at modern Sadducism. 1668. *See* Glanvill, Joseph.

3358 A blow at the root. *For John Wright,* 1650. 4°. LT, O, C, SP; IU, MH, NU, WF, Y.

3359 Blew cap for me. *Printed at London for Thomas Lambert,* [1641?]. brs. L.

3360 [**Blumerel, Johannes.**] Elegantiæ poeticæ. Seventh edition. *Typis E. Cotes pro A. Crook & J. Baker,* 1667. 12°. EN; Y.

3361   ——[Anr. ed.] *Oxonii, e, theatro Sheldoniano,* 1679. 12°. MADAN 3204. O, C, CT; PL, WF, Y.

3361A   **Blundell,** *Sir* **George.** Remarks upon a tract. *For Jacob Tonson,* 1683. 8°. L, O, CQ.

3362   **Blundell, Nicholas.** Blundel the Jesuit's letter of intelligence. [*London*], printed, 1679. brs. L, O, HH, MR, EN; CH, MH, NU, TU, WF, Y.

3362A   **Blundell, William.** A letter vvrit to a friend. *By B. G.,* 1688. brs. MIU.

3363   **Blunden, William.** The faithful lovers of the West. [*London*], *for P. Brooksby,* [1680–85]. brs. L, O, HH; MH, Y.

      Blunt, Gabriel. Almanack. 1656. *See* Almanacs.

3364   **Blunt, Leonard.** Asse upon asse. *For the author,* 1661. 8°.* O; CH.

3365   ——[Anr. ed.] [1661.] 8°.* L.

3366   **Boaistuau, Pierre.** The theatre of the world. *For Sam Ferris,* 1663. 8°. L; CH.

3366A   ——[Anr. ed.] *For R. Bentley and M. Magnes,* 1679. 12°. LSC, CPE; MH.

3367   Boanerges, or the Parliament of thunder. *Printed,* 1643. 4°.* LT, HH; CLC, NU, WF, Y.

3367A   ——[Anr. ed.] *For R. Bentley and M. Magnes,* 1679. 12°. MH.

3368   **Boate, Arnold.** Animadversiones sacræ. *Typis Richardi Bishopii & Jacobi Junii, impensis Laurentii Sadleri,* 1644. 4°. LT, O, C, E, DT; CU, NPT, NU, Y.

3369   [–] The character of a trvlie vervovs and piovs vvoman, . . . Mistris Margaret Dvngan. *Paris, by Ste. Mavcroy for the authour,* 1651. Sixes. L, O, CPE, CS, OB; PL.

3370   —Observations medicae. *Excudebat Tho. Newcomb pro Tho. Whitaker,* 1649, 12°. L, O, CPE, LCP, AU; PL, WSG.

3371   —A remonstrance. *By R. Badger, for Richard Lovvnds,* 1642. 4°.* LT, O, LVF, OC, EC; CH, CN, MH, WF.

3372   **Boate, Gerard.** Irelands naturall history. *Imprinted at London for John Wright,* 1652. 8°. L, O, C, ES, DT; CN, MA, MH, PL, Y.

3373   ——[Anr. ed.] *For John Wright,* 1657. 8°. L, LCS; CH, CJC, MH.

3374   —Philosophia naturalis reformata. *Dublinj, ex officina typographica societatis bibliopolarum,* 1641. 4°. DIX 74. L, O, C, AU, DT.

3375   The boatswains call. [*London*], *for P. Brooksby, J. Deacon, J. Blare, and J. Back,* [1688–92]. brs. L, O, CM, HH; MH.

3376   [**Bobart, Jakob.**] Catalogus plantarum. [*Oxoniæ*], *excudebat Henricus Hall, Oxon.,* 1648. 8°. MADAN 2003. O, OR, LW, SC, DT; BN, CLC, MH, PL, Y.

3377   Bobbin lo: or, the longing lass. [*London*] *for J. Coniers,* 1662. brs. O.

      Bocalini jun., *pseud.*

3378   **Boccaccio, Giovanni.** The novels and tales. Fifth edition. *For Awnsham Churchill,* 1648. fol. T.C.II 106. L, O, CT, LL, E; CN, LC, MBP, MH, Y.

3379   —Boccace's tales. Fourth edition. *By E. Cotes, and are to be sold by Joseph Cranford,* 1657. 12°. L, O; CN, V, WF, Y.

3380   **Boccalini, Trajano.** I ragguagli di Parnasso: or advertisements. *For Humphrey Moseley, and Thomas Heath,* 1656. fol. L, O, CT, DC, EN; BN, CH, CN, LC, MH, Y.

3381   ——[Anr. ed.] —, 1657. fol. C, BAMB; CLC, CU.

3382   ——Second edition. *For T. Dring, J. Starkey, and T. Basset,* 1669. fol. T.C.I 3. L, O, C, E, EN; CH, CN, MH, NP, WF, Y.

3383   ——Third edition. *Printed; and are to be sold by Tho. Guy,* 1674. fol. T.C.I 173. L, OM, CK, LL, DT; CN, MH, NU, TU.

3384   ——"Third" edition. *Printed; and are to be sold by Peter Parker,* 1674. fol. L, LG, CS; CH, TU, Y.

3385   **Boccone, Paolo.** Icones et descriptiones. [*Oxford*], *e theatro Sheldoniano, prostant apud Robertum Scott,* 1674. 4°. T.C.I 180. MADAN 3003. L, O, C, E, DT; BN, CLC, MH, MHO, WDA, Y.

3386   **Bochart, Samuel.** Hierozoicon sive bipertitum. *Excudebat Tho. Roycroft, impensis Jo. Martyn, & Jac. Allestry,* 1663. fol. L, O, C, E, DT; BN, CN, NP, WF.

      Bochim. Sighs. [n.p., 1667.] *See* T., J.

3387   **B[ockett], J[ohn].** A diurnal speculum. *Printed and sold by T. Sowle, and also sold by J. Peacock,* 1696. 12°. L, O, LF; CLC, PSC.

3388   —The poor mechanick's plea. *Printed and sold by T. Sowle,* 1699. 8°.* LF; MH, PH, PHS.

3389   ——Second edition. —, 1700. 8°.* L, O, LF; MH, PH, PSC.

      Bode, Robert. *See* Boyd, Robert.

3390   **Boden, Joseph.** An alarme beat vp in Sion. *By I. L. for Christopher Meredith,* 1644. 4°.* LT, O, LW, SP; CH, IU, NU, Y.

      Bodenham, John. Politeuphuia. *See* Ling, Nicholas.

3391   **Bodington, John.** The mystical Solomons coronation. 1662. 8°. O; MH, MWA.

      Bodio, John. *See* Boyd, John.

      Bodleius [*n.p.,* 1677.] *See* Wroughton, Charles.

3392   **Bodley,** *Sir* **Thomas.** The life of . . . vvritten by himselfe. *Oxford, by Henry Hall,* 1647. 4°.* MADAN 1925. LT, O, OC, EN; BN, CH, CN, MMO, V, Y.

3393   **Bodwell, John.** Carolus secundus . . . Johanni Bodvell . . . teste. [*London,* 1661/2]. brs. Y.

      Boece, Hector. *See* Boethius, Hector.

3394   **Boecthott, Jo.** Memoria crucis. 1651. 12°. LW.

3395   **Böhme, Jacob.** An apologie concerning perfection. *By M. S. for Giles Calvert,* 1661. 4°. L, O, C, OC, E; CH, CU, NP, NU, Y.

3396   —An apology or defence for the requisite refuting. *By M. S. for Giles Calvert,* 1661. 4°. L, O, C, OC, E; CH, CU, NP, NU, Y.

3397   —Aurora, that is, the day-spring. *By John Streater, for Giles Calvert,* 1656. 4°. LT, O, NPL, BR, E; CH, CU, MBA, NU, WF.

3398   —Concerning the election of grace. *By John Streater, for Giles Calvert, and John Allen,* 1655. 4°. LT, O, C, OC, BR; CH, CN, MH, NC, WF, Y.

3399   ——[Anr. ed.] *By J. Streater, for Giles Calvert,* 1656. NPL, E; CU.

3400 —A consideration upon the book of Esaias Stiefel. *By John Macock,* 1653. 8°. L, GU; CN, VC.

3401 —Considerations vpon Esaiah Stiefel. *By M. S. for Giles Calvert,* 1661. 4°.* L, O, C, OC, E; CH, CU, NP, NU, Y.

3402 —A consolatory treatise of the four complexions. *By T. W. for H. Blunden,* 1654. 12°. L, C, EN; CH.

3403 —A description of the three principles of the divine essence. *By M. S. for H. Blunden,* 1648. 4°. L, O, CE; CLC, PBL.

3404 —The epistles of. *By M. Simmons for Gyles Calvert,* 1649. 12°. L, C, LCL, LUS, E; CLC, CN, MH, NU, WF, Y.

3404A — —[Anr. ed.]. *By Matthew Simmons,* 1649. 4°. L, EC; MH, WCL.

3405 —The fifth book of the authour, in 3 parts. *Printed by J. M. for Lodowick Lloyd,* 1659. LT, CPE, E, BR; CH, CU, IU, MH, Y.

3406 —The first apologie to Balthazar Tylcken. *By M. S. for Giles Calvert,* 1661. 4°. L, O, C, OC, E; CH, CN, NP, NU, Y.

3407 —Forty questions. *[London], for L. Lloyd,* 1665. 8°. L, O, LLL, LW; NU, WF.

3408 —XL, qvestions concerning the soule. *By Matth. Simmons,* 1647. 4°. L, O, C, OB, BQ; CH, CN, MH, WF, Y.

3408A — —[Anr. ed.] *By M. S. for H. Blunden,* 1647. 4°. CM; PL.

3409 —Mercurius Teutonicus. *By M. Simmons, for H. Blunden,* 1649. 4°. LT, O, C, E, DT; CH, CU, NN, WF, Y.

3410 — —[Anr. ed.] *Printed and are to be sold by Lodowick Lloyd,* 1656. 4°. LT; WU.

3411 —Mysterium magnum. Or an exposition. *By M. Simmons for H. Blunden,* 1654. fol. L, O, LG, E; CN, CU, MH, NP, WF.

3411A — —[Anr. ed.] *Printed, and are to be sould by Lodowicke Lloyd,* 1656. fol. IU, MB.

3412 —Of Christs testaments. *By M. Simmons, to be sold . . . Golden Lion or by H. Blunden,* 1652. 4°. LT, O, CK, E, DT; CH, CN, NU, WF, Y.

3413 — —[Anr. ed.] *Printed and are to be sould by Lodowick Lloyd,* 1656. 4°. LT, C.

3414 —Of the four complexions. *By M. S. for Giles Calvert,* 1661. 4°.* L, O, C, OC, E; CH, CU, LC, NP, NU, Y.

3415 —The remainder of books. *By M. S. for Giles Calvert,* 1662. 4°. L, O, C, OC, E; CH, CN, MH, NU, WF, Y.

3416 —The second apologie to Balthazar Tylcken. *By M. S. for Giles Calvert,* 1661. 4°. L, O, C, OC, E; CH, CU, NP, NU, Y.

3417 —The second booke. *By M. S. for H. Blunden,* 1648. 4°. L, O, C, OC, E; CH, MU, NU, WF, Y.

3418 —Several treatises. *For L. Lloyd,* 1661. 4°. L, LW, NPL, BR, E; CN, IU, WF, WU, Y.

3419 —Signatura rerum. *By John Macock, for Gyles Calvert,* 1651. 4°. LT, O, CPE, NPL, E; CH, CN, NU, WF, Y.

3420 —Theosophick letters. *By M. S. for Giles Calvert,* 1661. 4°. L, O, C, OC, E; CH, CU, NP, NU, Y.

3421 —Jacob Behmen's theosophick philosophy unfolded. *For Tho. Salusbury,* 1691. 4°. T.C.II 383. L, O, LCL, LG, E; CH, CN, MBA, NPT, Y.

3422 —The third booke of the authour. *By M. S. for H. Blunden,* 1650. 4°. L, O, CPE, LWL, E; CH, CN, MH, NU, WF, Y.

3422A — —[Anr. ed]. *Printed and are to be sold by Lodowick Lloyd,* 1656. 4°. MH.

3423 —The tree of Christian faith. 1644. 4°. L, C; NN.

3424 — —[Anr. ed.] *By John Macock,* 1654. 4°. LT; NN.

3425 —Two theosophicall epistles. *By M. S. for B. Allen,* 1645. 12°. LT, O, CC.

3426 —The way to Christ discovered. *By M. S. for H. Blunden,* 1648. 12°. LT, O. CE, P, E; BN, CN, MH, NU, Y.

3426A — —[Anr. ed.] *For H. Blunden,* 1654. 12°. CH.

3427 — —[Anr. ed.] *Printed and are to be sold by Lodowick Lloyd,* 1656. 12°. L, C.

3427A —Yr Ymroddiad neu bapuryn. *[London] printiwyd,* 1657. 12°. L, AN, CPL.

3427B **Boekell, Martin.** A remonstrance of some fallacies. *By Tho. Newcomb,* 1659. 4°.* LG; CN, MH, NC.

3428 **Boethius, Anicius Manlius Torquatus Severinus.** The consolation of philosophy. *By James Flesher for the author,* 1664. 8°. L, OB, SP; NC, Y.

3429 —An Manl. Sever. Boethii consolontionis. *Oxoniæ, e theatro Sheldoniano,* 1698. 8°. L, O, CT, MR, GH; CLC, CN, LC, MH, TU, Y.

3430 —Anicii Manlii Torquati Severini Boethii de consolatione philosophiae libri v. *Oxonii, typis Will. Hall,* 1663. 8°. MADAN 2633. L, O, RPL, DT; NC, TU, Y.

3431 —Boethius de consolatione, Anglo-Latinæ, expressus. *Excusum,* 1654. 4°. L, O, CS; CH, MH.

3432 —Anicii Manlii Torquati Severnini Boethii de consolatione philosophiae. *Excusum,* 1655. 4°. O; CH, MH, Y.

3433 —Anticius Manlius Severinus Boetius of the consolation of philosophy. *By J. D. for Awnsham and John Churchill and Francis Hildyard, and in York,* 1695. 8°. T.C.II 540. L, C, OM, EN, DT; CLC, CN, LC, MBP, MH, NP, Y.

3434 —Summum bonum, or an explication. *Oxford, by H. Hall, for Ric. Davis,* 1674. 8°. MADAN 3004. T.C.I 184. L, O, C; CH, CU, MH, NU, WF, Y.

3435 **Boethius, Hector.** A true account of the life and death of all the kings of Scotland. *Edinburgh, by the heir of Andrew Anderson,* 1687. 4°.* ALDIS 2730. ES.

3436 The bogg-trotters march. *[London], for C. Bates,* [1690]. brs. HH.

3437 Bogg-witicisms. *[London], for Evidansh Swear-all,* [1700?] sixes. L, CS; CLC, WF, Y.

3438 **Bogan, Zachary.** Clavis. *Oxford, Henry Hall,* 1643. 8°. CT.

3439 —A help to prayer. *Oxford, by W. H. for Thomas Robinson,* 1660. 12°. MADAN 2483. LT, O.

3440 —Homerus Ἑβραΐζων: sive, comparatio. *Oxoniæ, excudebat H. Hall, impensis T. Robinson,* 1658. 8°. MADAN 2378. LT, O, C, MR, GH; CH, MH, NP, WF, Y.

3441 —Meditations of the mirth of a Christian life. *Oxford, By H. Hall for R. Davis*, 1653. 8°. MADAN 2227. LT, O, C, LCL, EN; MH, NU, TU, WF, Y.

3442 —A view of the threats. *Oxford, by H. Hall for R. David*, 1653. 8°. MADAN 2228. LT, O, C, LCL, ENC; CH, MH, NU, WF, Y.

3443 **Bohemus, Mauritius.** A Christian delight. *By Tho. Maxey for John Rothwell*, 1654. 8°. LT, LCL, LW; NPT.

3444 Entry cancelled.

3445 [**Bohun, Edmund.**] An address to the free-men and free-holders. *For George Wells*, 1682. 4°. T.C.I 496. L, O, C, EN, DT; CH, CN, LC, MH, NU, Y.

3445A — —Second edition. —, 1683. 4°. L, SP, WCA; LC, MHL, Y.

3446 [–] Answer to the desertion discuss'd. colop: *Printed, and sold by Rich. Janeway*, 1689. cap., 4°.* L, O, OC, DT; CH, MBA.

3447 —An apologie for the Church of England. *For W. Kettilby*, 1685. 4°.* T.C.II 128. L, O, C, LF, MC; CH, MBA, NU, WF, Y.

3448 —The character of Queen Elizabeth. *For Ric. Chiswell*, 1693. 8°. T.C.II 440. L, O, C, EN, DT; BN, CH, CU, MH, NU, WF.

3449 —A continuation of the history of the Reformation. *Printed*, 1689. fol. NU, PPT.

3450 [–] A defence of Sir Robert Filmer. *For W. Kettilby*, 1684. fol.* T.C.II 62. L, O, CT, HH; CH, CN, MH, NCL, WF, Y.

3451 [–] The doctrine of non-resistance or passive obedience. *For Richard Chiswell*, 1689. 4°.* L, O, CS, MR, EN; CH, CN, NU, WF, Y.

3452 —A geographical dictionary. *For Charles Brome*, 1688. 8°. T.C.II 224. L, C, LW, LI, NPL; CH, CN, LC, NU, Y.

3453 — —Second edition. —, 1691. 8°. T.C.II 372. L, O, C, OC; CLC, CN, RPJ, Y.

3454 — —Third edition, —, 1693. fol. T.C.II 442. L, O, C, EN, DT; CLC, CN, MH, NU, WF.

3455 — —Fourth edition. —, 1695. fol. T.C.II 528. O, OC; CJC, LC, PL, Y.

3456 [–] The history of the desertion. *For Ric. Chiswell*, 1689. 4°. T.C.II 255. L, O, C, EN, DT; CH, CU, LC, MH, NU, Y.

3457 [–] —Second edition. —, 1689. 4°. L, O, C, EN, DT; CH, CN, LC, MH, Y.

3457A —The justice of peace his calling. *For George Wells*, 1684. 8°. T.C.II 87. C, DT; CLC, LC, MHL, MIU, YL.

3458 —[Anr. ed.] *For T. Salusbury*, 1693. 8°. T.C.II 442, L, O, LI; PUL, WF.

3458A —A proposal for the erecting of county registers. *For Richard Cumberland and sold by Elizabeth Whitlock*, 1697. 4°.* T.C.II 604. L, LUG, EN; CH, MH, NC.

3458B [–] The proposal for the raising of the silver coin. *For Richard Cumberland*, 1696. 4°.* L, CT, LUG; CH, LC, MH, NC.

3459 [–] Reflections on a pamphlet, stiled A just and modest vindication. *By M. Clark, for George Wells*, 1683. 4°. L, O, CT, EN, DT; CH, MIU, NU, WF, Y.

3460 [–] The second part of The address to the free-men. *By A. Godbid and J. Playford for George Wells*, 1682. 4°. L, O, CS, P, EN; CH, MH, NU, WF, Y.

3461 [–] The third and last part of The address to the free-men. *For George Wells*, 1683. 4°. L, O, CS, P, EN; CH, CN, MH, NU, WF, Y.

3462 —Three charges delivered. *For Robert Clavell*, 1693. 4°.* T.C.II 442. L, O, C, MR, YM; MHL, WF.

3463 **Bohun, Ralph.** A discourse concerning the origine and properties of wind. *Oxford: by W. Hall for Tho. Bowman*, 1671. 8°. MADAN 2881. T.C.I 112. L, O, CM, E, DT; BN, CH, LC, MMO, PL, Y.

[**Boileau, Jacques.**] Discourse shewing that Protestants. *London*, 1687. *See* Beaulieu, Luke.

3463A [–] A just and seasonable reprehension of naked breasts. *Sold by Jonathan Edwin*, 1678. 8°. T.C.I 293. L, O; CH, LC, NU, TU, Y.

3464 **Boileau-Despréaux, Nicolas.** The art of poetry. *For R. Bentley and S. Magnes*, 1683. 8°. T.C.II 47. L, O, C, EN, DT; CH, CN, MH, TU, WF, Y.

3464A —The internal observation. *Sold by B. Tooke, W. Davis and Mr. Beaulieu*, 1684. 8°. T.C.II 62. P.

3465 —Le lutrin: an heroick poem. *By J. A. for Benjamin Alsop*, 1682. 4°.* L, O, C, OC, DT; CH, CN, MH, WF, Y.

3466 —Ode de . . . sur la prise de Namur. *Chez R. Bentley, R. Parker*, [1695]. 8°.* L, OM.

3466A —Ode pindarique . . . sur la prise, *R. Baldwin*, 1695. fol.* MH, MU.

3467 —The second, fourth, and seventh satyrs of . . . imitated. *For R. Sare; and H. Hindmarsh*, 1696. 8°. O; CH, CLC, WF.

Boisius, Johann. *See* Boys, John.

3468 **Bois-Robert, François le Matel de.** The Indian history. *By S. G. for J. Kirton*, 1657. 8°. L, O, CK; Y.

3469 [**Bold, Henry.**] Anniversary to the kings most excellent majesty Charles the II. colop: *For Henry Brome*, 1661. cap., fol.* CH, Y.

3470 —Elegy on the death of Her Highness Mary . . . of Aurange. *For Edward Husbands*, 1660. brs. LT; MH.

3471 —Latine songs, with their English. *For John Eglesfield*, 1685. 8°. T.C.II 114. L, O, OB; CH, CU, MH, WF, Y.

3472 —On the thunder, happening after the solemnity of the coronation. *For R. Crofts*, 1661. brs. LT, C.

3473 —Poems lyrique macaronique heroique, &c. *For Henry Brome*, 1664. 8°. L, O; CH, LC, MH, WF.

3474 —St. George's Day. *For R. Crofts*, 1661. fol.* LT, C, SP; MH, Y.

3475 —Satyr on the adulterate coyn. *Printed*, 1661. brs. L; MH.

3476 —VVit a sporting. *For W. Burden, and are to be sold at his shop and by S. L.*, 1657. 8°. L; MH.

3477 [**Bolde, Samuel.**] A brief account of the first rise of the name Protestant. *Printed*, 1688. 4°.* L, O, C, EN, DT; CH, CN, NU, WF, Y.

3477A [–] The Christian belief. *By W. Onley for Alex. Bosvile*, 1696. 8°. T.C.II 599. L, OC, CT, E, DT; CH, NU, WF.

3477B [–] —Second edition. 1697. 8°. LCL, P.

3478 —Christ's importunity. *For Awnsham Churchill, to be sold by William Churchill in Dorchester, 1687.* 12°. T.C.II 215. CT, LW; MH. WF, Y.

3479 —An examination of Dr. Comber's Scholastical history. *For Richard Janeway, 1690.* 4°. L, ON, CS, E, DT; CH, MH, NU, WF, Y.

3480 —An exhortation to charity. *For Awnsham Churchill, 1689.* 4°.* T.C.II 284. L, O, CT, EN, DT; CH, CLC, CN, WF.

3480A —The holy life. *For Henry Brome, 1675.* 4°. T.C.I 210. OC.

3481 —Man's great duty. *By R. Smith, to be sold by R. Baldwin, 1693.* 8°. T.C.II 463. O, CS, LW, RPL.

3482 —Meditations concerning death. *For A. & J. Churchill, 1696.* 12°. T.C.II 568. L.

3483 —Observations on the animadversions (lately printed). *For A. and J. Churchill, 1698.* 8°. T.C.III 50. O, OM, CS, EC; MH, MBP, NU, Y.

3484 —A plea for moderation towards dissenters. *For R. Janeway, 1682.* 4°.* T.C.I 505. L, O, P, MR; CH, MH, NU, WF, Y.

3485 — —[Anr. ed.] *For Awnsham Churchill, 1683.* 4°.* L, O, CT, EN; CLC, MH, MIU, PU.

3485A — —Second edition. *For R. Janeway, 1683.* 4°.* WCA.

3486 —A reply to Mr. Edwards's brief reflections. *For A. and J. Churchill, 1697.* 8°. O, LIC; MH, NGT, NU, Y.

3487 —A second examination of Doctor Comber's Scholastical history. *For Richard Janeway, 1691.* 4°. L, O, CT, E, DT; MBA, MH, MIU, NU, Y.

3488 —A sermon against persecution. *Printed 1682, and published by Richard Janeway.* 4°.* T.C.I 494 L, O, CT, OC; CN, NU, VC, WF, Y.

3489 — —Second edition. *Printed, 1682, and published by R. Janeway.* 4°.* L, O, CT, WCA, ENC; CH, WF.

3490 — —Third edition. *Printed, 1682. And published by Richard Janeway.* 4°.* O, SP; MH, NU, WF, Y.

3491 — —Fourth edition. *1682.* 4°.* E, EN.

3492 — —[Anr. ed.] *Printed, 1683, and published by Richard Janeway.* 4°.* L, O.

3493 —A short discourse of the true knowledge of Christ Jesus. *For A. and J. Churchil, 1697.* 8°. T.C.III 1. O, OC, EC, BAMB; MB, NU, Y.

3494 —Some considerations on the principal objections. *For A. and J. Churchill, 1699.* 8°. O, CT, EC, EN; CLC, CU, MH, NU, Y.

3495 —Some passages in The reasonableness of Christianity. *For A. and J. Churchil, 1697.* 8°. O, LIC, OC, EC, BAMB; CU, MH, Y.

Bold challenge. [n.p.], 1652. *See* Griffith, George, bp.

3496 **Bolde, Thomas.** Rhetorick restrained. *For Tho. Parkhurst, 1660.* 4°.* LT, O, C, EN, DT; CLC, CN, NPT, NU, WF.

3497 **Bolnest, Edward.** Aurora chymica: or, a rational way. *By Tho. Ratcliffe & Nat. Thompson, for John Starkey, 1672.* 8°. T.C.I 111. L, O, C, LWL, GU; CLC, LC, MH, NAM, HC.

3498 —Medicina instaurata, or: a brief account. *For John Starkey, 1665.* 12°. L, O, LWL, GU; WSG, WU.

3499 **Bolron, Robert.** An abstract of the accusation of. *For C. R., 1680.* fol.* L, O, DT; CLC, WF.

3500 —Animadvertions on the Papists . . . oath. colop: *For J. B., 1681.* brs. L, O, HH; CH, MBA, MU, NU, Y.

3501 —The narrative of. *For Thomas Simmons, and Jacob Sampson, 1680.* fol.* T.C.I 383. L, O, C, EN, DT; CH, CN, MH, NU, WF, Y.

3502 [-] The Papists bloody oath of secrecy. *For Randal Taylor, 1680.* fol.* L, O, C, EN, DT; CH, MH, NU, WF, Y.

3503 — —[Anr. ed.] *Dublin, Joseph Ray, 1681.* 4°.* DIX 184. C, DT, DM, CD; MC, NU, PU.

3504 —The Papists oath of secrecy. *To be sold by Randal Taylor, 1680.* brs. L, O, HH; CH, MH, NU, Y.

3505 [**Bolton, Edmund.**] The cities great concern. *By William Godbid, 1674.* 8°. L, O, LG; CH, LC, MH, WF, Y.

3506 [**Bolton, John.**] Judas his thirty pieces not received. *[n.p., c. 1660.]* cap., 4°.* L, LF, BBN; MH, PH, PSC.

3507 —Judas his treachery still continued. *Printed, 1670.* 4°.* L, LF, BBN; PH, Y.

3508 —A justification of the righteous judgement of God on Nathaniel Smith. *[London], printed, 1669.* 4°.* L, LF, BBN; NU, PH, PSC.

3509 [-] A short account of the latter end and dying words of Francis Howgil. *[n.p.], printed and published 1671, for friends.* 4°.* L, LF, CT, BBN; CH, MH, NR, PH, PSC.

3510 —A testimony in that which separates between the pretious and the vile. *[London, 1673.]* cap., 4°.* L, LF, BBN; MH, PH, WF, Y.

3511 **Bolton, *Sir* Richard.** A justice of the peace for Ireland. Second edition. *Dublin, by Benjamin Tooke and John Crooke, 1683.* fol. T.C.II 117. DIX 198. O, EN, DT, DM, DML; LC, MHL, MIU, NCL.

3511A —Rules for a grand-juror. *Dublin, for William Winter, to be sold by the booksellers of Dublin, 1681.* 4°.* DIX 181. DN.

3512 **Bolton, Robert.** The vvorkes of. *By George Miller, 1641.* 4°. L, O, C, LW, E; BN, CH, NU, WF, Y.

3513 —A cordiall for a fainting Christian. *By T. Paine for Mathew Walbanck, 1644.* 4°.* LT, O, CT, DT; CH, MH, NU, WF, Y.

3514-5 Entries cancelled.

3516 **Bolton, Samuel.** Ἁμαρτωλος Ἁμαρτια: or, the sinfulnes of sin. *By G. M. for Andrew Kemb, 1646.* 4°.* LT, O, C, LCL, DT; CH, MH, NU, WF, Y.

3517 —The arraignment of errour. *By G. Miller for Andrew Kembe, 1646.* 4°. LT, O, LCL, LW; CH, CU, MH, NU, WF, Y.

3518 —The dead saint speaking. *By Robert Ibbitson, for Thomas Parkhurst, 1657.* fol. L, C, LCL, E; CU, MH, NPT, NU, WF, Y.

3519 —Deliverance in the birth. *Cambridge by Roger Daniel, to be sold by Andrew Kembe in [London], 1647.* 4°.* LT, O, C, CT, DT; CH, MH, NU, WF, Y.

3520 —The guard of the tree of life. *By M. Simmons for A. Kembe, 1644.* 8°. L; CLC.

3521 — —[Anr. ed.] *1645.* 12°. O, LCL.

3522 ——[Anr. ed.] *By A. Miller for A. Kembe,* 1647. 8°. LW, CT; NNG, NPT, NU, WF.

3522A ——[Anr. ed.] *For A. Kemb,* 1650. 8°. MB.

3523 ——[Anr. ed.] *By R. & W. Leybourn, for A. Kemb, Southwark,* 1654. 8°. CCH.

3523A ——[Anr. ed.] —, 1656. 8°. L, C, LCL; Y.

3524 ——[Anr. ed.] 1661. 12°. LCL, DC.

3525–6 Entries cancelled.

3527 —A tossed ship making to safe harbor. *By L.N. for Philemon Stephens,* 1644. 8°. L, LCL, CCH, LSC; CH, MIU, NPT, NU, WF.

3528–31 Entries cancelled.

3532 —The trve bovnds of Christian freedome. *By J.L. for Philemon Stephens,* 1645. 8°. LT, O, CE, LW, ENC; MH, NPT, NU, WF.

3533 ——[Anr. ed.] *For P.S. to be sold by Austin Rice,* 1656. 8°. LT, O, C, MC; MH.

3534 Entry cancelled.

5335 **Bolton, William.** Core redivivus. *For James Norris,* 1684. 4°.* T.C.II 41. L, O, CS, CT; CH, CLC, IU, NU, Y.

3536 —Joseph's entertainment of his brethren. *By Miles Flesher, for Charles Harper,* 1684. 4°.* L, O, CT; CH, IU, WF.

3537 [–] A poem upon a laurel-leaf. colop: *For W. Crooke,* 1690. 4°.* T.C.II 336. L, O, LWL; HC.

3538 **Bombast von Hohenheim, Philipp Aurel Theophrast.** Archidoxis. *For W.S. to be sold by T. Brewster,* 1660. 24°. LPO, GU; CLC, MH, HC.

3539 ——[Anr. ed.] *For W.S. to be sold by Samuel Thomson,* 1661. 8°. LT, LSC, GU; WU.

3539A ——[Anr. ed.] *For Lodowick Lloyd,* 1663. 8°. L.

3540 —Aurora. *For Giles Calvert,* 1659. 12°. LT, O, C, DC, E; CH, MH, MMO, PL, WF, HC.

3541 —Dispensatory. *By T.M. for Philip Chetwind,* 1656. 12°. LT, GU.

3542 —Medicina diastatica, or sympatheticall mumie. *By T. Newcomb for T. Heath,* 1653. 8°. L, OR, GU; CLC, MB, MMO, Y.

3543 —Of the chymical transmutation . . . of metals. *For Rich: Moon, and Hen: Fletcher,* 1657. 8°. LT, CT, LCS, GU, E;, CLC, CPB, MB, MH, HC.

3544 —Of the supreme mysteries. *By J.C. for N.Brook and J.Harison,* 1656. 8°. LT, LCS, LPO, GU, E; LC, MMO, WU.

3544A —Three books of philosophy. 1697. 8°. O.

Bon Accord's ephemeris. Aberdeen, [1684]. *See* Almanacs.

3545 **Bona, Giovanni,** *cardinal.* A guide to eternity. Second edition. *For Hen. Brome,* 1680. 12°. T.C.I 399. L, O, CT, OC; NU, Y.

3546 ——Third edition. *For J.Knapton,* 1688. 12°. T.C.II 212, O; CLC, CN, MBA, PL, WF.

3547 ——Fourth edition. *For R.Bentley; J.Hindmarsh; and J. Tonson,* 1693. 12°. O, ELY; MIU.

3548 ——"Fourth" edition. *For R.B., J.H., J. T. and sold by Tho. Bennet,* 1694. 12°. L, CM; BN.

3549 A guide to heaven. [*London?*], printed, 1672. 12°. O, LSC; BN, CLC, LC.

3550 ——[Anr. ed.] *Printed at Roan:* 1673. 12°. L, O; CLC, CN, NU, WF, Y.

3551 —Manuductio ad coelum. *By A.C. for Henry Brome,* 1672. 8°. T.C.I 109. L, O, C, LW, OC; CLC, CU, NU, WF.

3552 ——[Anr. ed.] *For R.Bentley and M.Magnes,* 1681. 4°.* L, SP; CH, IU, MH, Y.

3553 —Precepts and practical rules. *By M.Clark, for H. Brome,* 1678. 12°. T.C.I 299. L, O, C; CH, CLC, NU, WF, Y.

3554 **Bonarelli della Rovere, Guido Ubaldo de.** Filli di Sciro, or Phillis of Scyros. *By J.M. for Andrew Crook,* 1655. 4°. L, O, LVD, EN; BN, CH, CU, MH, WF.

Bonasus vapulans. 1672. *See* Hickman, Henry.

3554A **Bonatti, Guido.** Anima astrologiæ: or a guide. *For B. Harris,* 1676. 8°. L, O; MH.

3554B ——[Anr. ed.] —, 1683. 8°. MB. 12°. L, O, AN; CH, CLC, MB, TU, Y.

3555 **Bonaventura, Saint.** The soliloquies of. *For H. Twyford and R. Wingate,* 1655. 12°. L, O, BR.

3556 —Stimulus divini amoris: that is, the goade of divine love. *At Doway, by the widow of Mark Wyon,* [1642]. 12°. L, O, AN; CH, CN, MB, TU, WF, Y.

3557 [**Bond, Cimelgus.**] Scutum regale, the royal buckler. 1660. 8°. L, O, C, CT, P; CH, CN, MH, NU, WF, Y.

3558 [**Bond, Edward.**] Oneale and Colonell Brunslow. *For Andrew Coe and Marmaduke Boat,* 1642. 4°.* LT, C, LVF; CN, Y.

3559 **Bond, Henry.** The art of apparelling and fitting of any ship. Second edition. *For the widow Seyle,* 1663. 4°.* CM, ES.

3560 —The boateswaines art. *Printed at London by Richard Cotes, for William Lugger,* 1642. 4°.* L, O; MHS.

3560A ——[Anr. ed.] *By William Godbid for William Fisher,* 1664. 4°.* CM.

3561 ——[Anr. ed.] —, 1670. 4°.* L; BN.

3562 ——[Anr. ed.] *By W.Godbid, for William Fisher; and Eliz. Hurlock,* 1677. 4°.* L; CLC, MIU.

3563 ——[Anr. ed.] *For Richard Mount,* 1699. 4°.* L.

3564 —The longitude found. *By W.Godbid, to be sold by the author Henry Bond; Robert Greene; Godfrey Richards; John Thornton,* 1676. 4°. L, O, OC, CM, SC; IU, NAE, PAP, PL.

3565 [–] A plain and easie rule to rigge any ship. *For William Fisher,* 1664. 4°.* L, CM.

3566 [–] ——[Anr. ed.] *By W.Godbid, for William Fisher; and Eliz. Hurlock,* 1676. 4°.* L; CLC.

—The seamans kalendar. 1648. *See* Tapp, John.

3567 **Bond, John,** *of Grey's Inn.* A complete guide for justices of peace. *By T.B. for Hannah Sawbridge,* 1685. 8°. T.C.II 145. O, OC, LMT; CH, LC, MHL.

3567A ——[Anr. ed.] *Printed and are to be sold by W. Freeman,* 1687. 8°. L; MHL, WF, WU.

3568 ——Second edition. *By the assigns of Richard and Edward Atkins, for Matthew Gilliflower, Isaac Cleave, and William Freeman,* 1696. 8°. T.C.II 594. L, CT, NPL; LC, MHL, NCL.

3569 **Bond, John,** *Master of the Savoy.* A doore of hope. *By G. M. for John Bartlet,* 1641. 4°. L, O, LCL, YM, DT; NPT, RPB, WF, Y.

3570 —Eschol, or grapes (among) thorns. *By M. F. for Samuel Gellibrand,* 1648. 4°.* LT, O, C, LW, DT; CLC, MH, NU, WF, Y.

3571 —Exon. Aprill 8. 1643. Having lately seene a pamphlet. [*Exeter?* 1643.] brs. LT.

3572 —Occasus occidentalis: or, Job in the VVest. *By J. D. for Fran. Eglesfield,* 1645. 4°. LT, O, C, BR, DT; NU, WF.

3573 —Ortus occidentalis: or, a dawning in the VVest. *By J. D. for Fr. Eglesfield,* 1645. 4°. LT, C, BR, ENC, DT; CH, MH, WF.

3574 —Salvation in a mystery. *By L. N. for Francis Eglesfeild,* 1644. 4°. LT, O, C, E, EN; CH, MH, NU, WF, Y.

3575 —The state's stability. 1693. 4°. OC, CS, DT; WF.

3576 **Bond, John,** *of St. John's, Cambridge.* The downfal of old common-covnsel-men. *For T. H.,* 1641. 4°.* 4 ll. LT, HH; MH, NU, WF, Y.

3577 ——[Anr. ed.] —, 1641. 4°.* 5 pp. LT, O, LG; NU.

3578 —Englands rejoycing for the Parliaments returne. *By F. L. for T. Bates,* 1641. 4°.* LT; CLC, NC, WF.

3579 —King Charles his welcome home. *By F. L. for T. Bates and F. Coules,* [1641]. 4°.* LT, O, CS, EN, ES; CH, WF.

3580 —The Parliaments and Londons preparation. *For Iohn Tompson,* 1641. 4°.* LT, LG; MH, Y.

3581 ——[Anr. ed.] *For R. A.,* 1641. 4°.* Y.

3582 —Poet's knavery. *For T. H.,* [1642]. 4°.* LT, O, EC; MH, MIU, TU, WF.

3583 —The poets recantation. *For T. A. and Ioseph Wren,* 1942 [i.e. 1642]. 4°.* LT, O; CH, NU.

3584 **Bond, Sampson.** Arme, arme; or, the souldiers alarmum for Ireland: a sermon. 1650. 4°. MR.

3585 —A publick tryal of the Quakers in Barmudas. *Boston in New England, by Samuel Green, upon assignment of Samuel Sewall,* 1682. 12°. EVANS 313. OC; CH, LC, MH, MHS, RPJ.

3586 —A sermon preached . . . 20th of May 1646. *By John Macock, to be sold by Iames Nuthall,* 1646. 4°. LT, O, EN, DT; CLC, NU, WF, Y.

3587 —The sincere milk of the word. colop: *Boston, by B. Green & J. Allen,* 1699. cap., 4°. RPJ.

3588 **Bond, William.** To the honourable the House of Commons, for raising of monies. [*London?* 1698/9.] brs. LUG.

3589 A bond. [*Cambridge, Mass.,* 1685.] brs. MBS.

3590 A bond given to the captain of every ship by the seamen. [*n.p.*], 1692–3. brs. MC.

Bonduca. 1696. *See* Beaumont, Francis.

3591 **Bonet, Théophile.** A guide to the practical physician. *For Thomas Flesher,* 1684. fol. T.C.II 97. L, LCS, OC, CK, E; CU, MH, NAM, PL, WF, Y.

3592 **Bonham, Josias.** The churches glory. *For the author,* 1674. 16°. CLC.

3593 **Bonhome, Joshua.** The arraignment and conviction of atheism. *By Tho. James, for Dorman Newman,* 1679. 8°. T.C.I 329. L, O, C, OC, P; NPT.

3594 —A new constellation. *By W. G. to be sold by Moses Pitt,* 1675. 4°.* T.C.I 203. L, O, OC, CT, DT; CLC, NU, WF.

Boni omnis votum: a good omen. [1656]. *See* Wither, George.

3594A **Bonifield, Abraham.** An expedient for peace. [*London,* 1692.] 4°. LF; PH.

3595 ——[Anr. ed.] *Reading,* 1693. 4°. L.

3595A —Hidden things revealed. *Printed,* 1694. 4°.* LF.

3595B —The treacherous taken in his treachery. [*London*], 1692. 4°.* LF.

3595C **Bonille, Juana.** A short treatise of the quiet of the soul. [*London*], 1700. 8°.* C.N.

3596 [**Bonnecorse, Balthazar de.**] La montre. *By R. H. for W. Canning,* 1686. 8°. T.C.II 188. L, O; CH, CN, MH, TU, WF, Y.

3597 [**Bonnefons, Nicolas de.**] The French gardiner. *By J. C. for John Crooke,* 1658. 12°. KEYNES, EVELYN, 5. O, GK; MH.

3598 [–] —[Anr. ed.] —, 1658. 12°. KEYNES 6. CH.

3599 [–] —[Anr. ed.] *For John Crooke,* 1658. 12°. KEYNES 7. LT, C, GK; CH, MH, WF.

3600 [–] —Second edition. *By J. M. for John Crooke,* 1669. 8°. T.C.I 11. KEYNES 8. L, O, OC, GK; CH, LC, MH, PL, TU, WDA, Y.

3601 [–] —Third edition. *By S. S. for Benj. Tooke,* 1672. KEYNES 9. L, CS, GK; CLC, CN, MH, Y.

3602 [–] —"Third" edition. *By T. R. & N. T. for B. Tooke,* 1675. 8°. KEYNES 10. L, O, C, OC, GK; MH, MHO, PRM, WF, Y.

3603 [–] —Fourth edition [i.e. fifth]. *By T. B. for B. Took,* 1691. 8°. KEYNES 11. L, O, OC, GK; CH, MH, WF.

3603A The bonny black-smith's delight. [*London*] *for F. Coles T. Vere, J. Wright, and J. Clarke* [1674–9]. brs. O.

Bonny Dundee. n.p., [1685–88.] *See* D'Urfey, Thomas.

3603B The bonnie lassie to its own pleasant new tune. [*n.p.,* 1695.] brs. MH.

3604 The bonny Scot. [*London, for E. Brooksby,* 1670?] brs. L, OP.

3605 The bonny Scottish lad. [*London*], *for J. Conyers,* [1682–91]. brs. L, CM, HH; MH, WCL.

3605A The bonny Scottish lovers. [*London*], *for F. Coles, T. Vere, J. Wright, and J. Clarke,* [1674–9]. brs. O.

3606 [**Bononcini, Giovanni Battista.**] The Italian song call'd Pastorella. [*London,* 1699.] fol.* L; WF.

3607 **Bononcini, Giovanni Maria.** Bononcini's ayres in 3 parts. *I. Walsh and I. Hare,* [1700?]. obl., fol. L.

3608 Bons advis svr plvsievrs mavvais advis. [*n.p.,* 1650.] 4°.* LT.

3609 A book and map of all Europe. *By James Moxon for Thomas Jenner,* 1650. 8°.* LT.

3610 A book containing the several rates for wharfage. *By Andrew Clark,* 1676. 4°.* L, O; NC, PU, WF.

Book for boys. 1686. *See* Bunyan, John.

3611   Entry cancelled.
3612   The book of common prayer. *By Robert Barker, and by
          the assignes of John Bill,* 1641. 4°. L, O, CS, BAMB, YM;
          MB, TU.
3613   — —, 1642. 8°. L, O, OC; CH, MBA, WF, Y.
3614   —1645. 12°. O, RPL.
3615   —*Imprinted at London,* 1660. fol. L, HH, DT; WWC.
3616   —*By Christopher Barker,* 1660. fol. L, OC; MB.
3617   —*By John Bill and Christopher Barker,* 1660. 4°. L, OC;
          NGT.
3618   —1660. 8°. L, O, LCL; CH, CN, MB, TU.
3618A   —1660. 12°. OC.
3619   —*[Cambridge],* 1660. fol. L, LMT, OC, DT; CH, CLC, NN, Y.
3620   —*For John Bill,* 1661. fol. L, O, OC.
3621   —*By Christopher Barker,* 1661. 8°. L.
3622   —*By His Ma:ties printers,* 1662. fol. L, O, CS, LP, DUC;
          CH, MH, NU, RPJ, Y.
3623   —*By John Bill and Christopher Barker,* 1662. fol. L, OB, OC,
          CSSX, MR; CH, WF.
3624   — —, 1662. 12°. L, OC; CH.
3625   —*Cambridge, by John Field,* 1662. 8°. L, O, CS, ENC, DT;
          CH, MB, Y, WWC.
3626   —*By John Bill and Christopher Barker,* 1663. 8°. O; MN.
3626A   — —, 1663. 12°. L.
3627   —*Cambridge, by John Field,* 1663. 4°. L, O.
3628   —*By John Bill and Christopher Barker,* 1664. 8°. L, O, OC,
          BR, YM.
3629   —*Llyfr gweddi gyffredin. A brintiwyd yn Llundain, gan S.
          Dover, tros Edward Ffowks a Phetr Bodvel,* 1664. fol. L,
          LSC, YM, AN; CH.
3630   —*By John Bill and Christopher Barker,* 1665. 8°. L, O; MB,
          NGT, WCL.
3631   — —, 1665. 12°. L, OC.
3632   —Βιβλος της δημοσιας ευχης. κανταβριγια, Ιοανος
          Φιελδος, 1665. 12°. L, LMT, OC, CT; CH, MB, PL, WWC,
          Y.
3632A   —*Dublin, by John Crook,* 1665. 4°. DIX 168. DT.
3633   —*By John Field, Cambridge,* 1666. 4°. L, O, CT, OC, EC;
          CH, MB, MIU, NGT.
3633A   —*Dublin, by John Crooke, to be sold by Samuel Dancer,*
          1666. 4°. DIX 132. L, DN.
3633B   —*In the Savoy, by the assigns of John Bill and Christopher
          Barker,* 1668. 12°. L.
3634   —*Dublin: by John Crook,* 1668. 4°. DIX 136. L.
3635   —*By His Maties printers,* 1669. fol. L, O, MR, DT; MB, NN,
          NR, TU, V.
3636   —*In the Savoy, by the assigns of John Bill and Christopher
          Barker,* 1670. 12°. L, O.
3637   —*Cambridge, by John Hayes,* 1670. 4°. L, O, SC; UCLA.
3638   —*In the Savoy; by the assigns of John Bill, and Christopher
          Barker,* 1671. 8°. L, O, OC, EC, MR; CH; JU, NN, UC, IA.
3639   —*By the assigns of John Bill and Christopher Barker,* 1673.
          12°. L, O, OC; MB.
3640   —*Cambridge, by John Hayes,* 1673. 4°. L, O, CS, MR; NN,
          TU, WWC, Y.
3641   —*By the assigns of John Bill, & Ch:Barker,* 1674. 12°. L;
          CLC, RPJ.

3641A   —[Arabic] Litvrgiae ecclesiae Anglicanae. *Oxoniæ, typis
          et impensis per Academiam,* 1674. 4°. MADAN 3000. OC,
          CS, DT; MW, Y.
3642   —*By the assigns of John Bill and Christopher Barker,* 1675.
          12°. L.
3643   —*Cambridge, by John Hayes,* 1675. 4°. L, CS.
3644   —*Oxford, at the theater,* 1675. 4°. MADAN 3090. L, O, OC,
          EC; NN, V, Y.
3645   —*By the assigns of John Bill and Christopher Barker,* 1676.
          fol. L, HH.
3646   — —, 1676. 8°. L; RPJ.
3647   — —, 1676. 12°. L.
3648   —*Cambridge, by John Hayes,* 1676. 4°. L, O, CS; PU.
3649   —*By the assigns of John Bill and Ch.Barker,* 1677. 12°. L,
          O, OC; NN, WF.
3650   —*By John Bill, Christopher Barker, Thomas Newcomb, and
          Henry Hills,* 1678. 4°. L, O, OC, BR; BBE.
3651   — —, 1678. 12°. L; GLC, MB, TU, WCL.
3652   —*Llyfr gweddi gyffredin. Printiedig yn Llundaingan John
          Bill, Christopher Barker, Thomas Newcomb, a Henry
          Hills: ac a werthir gan John Hancock,* 1678. 8°. L.
3653   —*By John Bill and Christopher Barker,* 1679. fol. L, O;
          CLC, MU, NN.
3654   —*By John Bill, Christopher Barker, Thomas Newcomb,
          and Henry Hills,* 1679. 8°. L, O; WF.
3655   — —, 1679. 12°. L, O.
3656   —*Cambridge, by John Hayes,* 1679. 4°. L, CT, LP, YM; Y.
3657   —*Oxford, at the theater,* 1679. 4°. MADAN 3249. L, O; MB,
          NM, Y.
3658   —*By John Bill, Thomas Newcomb, and Henry Hills,* 1680.
          fol. L, CK, MR, HH, YM; CH, NNG.
3659   — —, 1680. 4°. L, O; MB.
3660   —*At the theater in Oxford,* 1680. 8°. MADAN 3286. O, LG;
          CLC.
3661   —*Printed at the theater in Oxford, for M. Pitt, P. Parker,
          W. Leake, and T. Guy,* 1680. 12°. MADAN 3287. O.
3662   —*Dublin, by Benjamin Tooke and John Crooke, and sold by
          Mary Crooke,* 1680. 4°. DIX 178. C, DT.
3662A   —*By the assigns of John Bill, Thomas Newcomb and Henry
          Hill,* 1681. 12°. OC.
3663   —1681. fol. E.
3663A   —*Oxford, at the theater, to be sold by Moses Pitt,* 1681. fol.
          L, OC; NN, Y.
3663B   —*Oxford, at the theater, to be sold by Peter Parker, London,*
          1681. fol. CM, CSE.
3664   —*At the theater in Oxford, to be sold by Moses Pitt, Peter
          Parker, William Leak, Thomas Guy, London,* 1681. 8°.
          T.C.I 437 L, O, RPL, D, DT; Y.
3665   —*By the assigns of John Bill, Thomas Newcomb, and Henry
          Hills,* 1682. 12°. L; PL, TU.
3666   —*Oxford, sold by M. Pitt, London,* [1682?]. 4°. L.
3667   —*Oxford, at the theater, to be sold by Ann Leake, London,*
          1682. fol. L, O, DT; Y.
3668   —*Printed at the theater in Oxford, to be sold by Peter Parker,
          London,* 1682. fol. L; CH, Y.
3668A   —*Printed at Oxford for Thomas Guy,* 1682. 24°. MB, WP.

3669   —*By the assigns of John Bill: and by Henry Hills, and Thomas Newcomb*, 1683. fol. L, O, E.

3670   —*Cambridge, John Hayes*, 1683. 4°. L, O, CT, EC, YM; MBA, NNM.

3671   —*Oxford, for Moses Pitt*, [1683?]. fol. L, CM, HH.

3672   —*Oxford, at the theater, sold by Thomas Guy, London*, 1683. fol. L, O, HH, DT; CLC, NN, NPT, WF.

3673   —*By the assigns of John Bill: and by Henry Hills, and Thomas Newcomb*, 1684. 8°. L, O, OC; CLC, MB.

3674   —*Printed at the theatre in Oxford, to be sold by Thomas Guy, London*, 1684. 12°. L.

3675   —*By the assigns of John Bill, and by Henry Hills and Thomas Newcomb*, 1685. 8°. O, CS.

3676   —*Printed at the theater in Oxford, to be sold by Thomas Guy, London*, 1685. 12°. O.

3677   —*Printed at the theatre in Oxford, to be sold by Peter Parker, London*, 1686. 12°. L, O.

3678   —*Oxford, at the theater, to be sold by Thomas Guy, London*, 1686. 8°. O; MB, NU.

3679   —*By Charles Bill, Henry Hills, and Thomas Newcomb*, 1687. fol. L, O, LP, E, DT; MB, MG, Y.

3680   — —, 1687. 12°. L, O.

3681   —*Printed at the theater in Oxford, to be sold by Peter Parker, London*, 1687. 12°. L, O.

3682   —*By Charles Bill, Henry Hills, and Thomas Newcomb*, 1688. 8°. O; MB, MH, NS.

3683   —*Oxford, at the theater, to be sold by Thomas Guy, London*, 1688. fol. L.

3683A   — —*to be sold by Peter Parker, London*, 1688. 8°. Y.

3683B   —*By Charles Bill and the executrix of Thomas Newcomb*, 1691. 8°. L; NN.

3684   —*Printed at the theater in Oxford, to be sold by Peter Parker, London*, 1691. 12°. L, O.

3685   —*By Charles Bill, and the executrix of Thomas Newcomb*, 1692. 4°. L, O.

3686   — —, 1692. 8°. L; MU, RPB.

3687   — —, 1693. fol. L, O.

3688   — —, 1693. 4°. L; CH; NN.

3688A   —*By T. Hodgkin and M. Flesher for the company of stationers*, 1693. fol. CM.

3689   —*Oxford, by the university-printers*, 1693. fol. L, O; CLC.

3690   —*By Charles Bill, and the executrix of Thomas Newcomb*, 1694. 8°. L; CLC.

3691   — —, 1695. 8°. L; CLC.

3691A   —*Oxford, by the university-printers*, 1695. 12°. OC.

3692   — —. 1696. fol. L, O, LG.

3693   —*Cambridge, by John Hayes*, 1696. fol. L, LW, OC, EC; Y.

3694   —*Oxford*, 1696. 8°. O.

3695   —*By Charles Bill, and the executrix of Thomas Newcomb*, 1697. 12°. L.

3696   —*Oxford*, 1697. 12°. O.

3697   —*By Charles Bill, and the executrix of Thomas Newcomb*, 1698. fol. L; CLC.

3698   —*Oxford: by the university-printers*, 1698. 8°. L, OC.

3699   —*By Charles Bill, and the executrix of Thomas Newcomb*, 1699. 8°. L, O.

3700   —1699. 12°. O.

3701   —*Oxford, by the university printers*, 1699. 12°. L, O; CLC, NN.

3702   —*By Charles Bill and the executrix of Thomas Newcomb*, 1700. fol. LW, CCL, BR, EN; CH, CLC, MU, Y.

3703   —*Oxford: by the university-printers*, 1700. 8°. L, O; CLC.

3704   —*Dublin, by and for Andrew Crook*, 1700. 4°. O, DT, LFEA.

3704A   The book of common prayer . . . vindicated. *For John Thomas*, 1641. 4°.* L, O, E; CLC, KN, TU, NU.

3705   A book of cookery. *By Jeane Bell*, 1650. 8°. LT.

3705A   A book of directions and cures. [*London?* 1685]. cap., 4°.* L.

Book of drawing. 1652. *See* Jenner, Thomas.

3705B   A book of entries. *For John Newton*, 1694. 8°. LC, PL.

3706   A booke of flowers fruicts beastes birds. [*London*], *to bee sold by P. Stent*, [1661]. fol.* L.

3707   The book of fortune. *By J. Heptinstall for Brabazon Aylmer*, 1698. fol. CLC, Y.

3708   A book of fruits & flowers, shewing. *By M. S. for Tho: Jenner*, 1653. 4°. LT; NN, PL.

3709   —[Anr. ed.] —, 1656. 4°. L; MH, WU.

3710   The booke of merry riddles. *For John Stafford & W. G.*, 1660. 8°. L.

3711   —[Anr. ed.] *By E. C. for J. Wright*, 1672. 8°.* CH.

3712   —[Anr. ed.] [*London*] *For W. T. and sold by John Back*, 1685. 8°.* CM.

Book of new epigrams. 1695. *See* Killigrew, Henry.

Book of oaths. 1649. *See* Garnet, Richard.

Book of palmestry. 1691. *See* Indagine, Joannes, *ab*.

Book of portraiture. [1665?] *See* Barbieri, G. B.

3713   A boke of presidentes. *By the assignes of I. More*, 1641. 8°. L, LW, DT; CH.

3714   The book of pretty conceits. *For P. Brooksby*, 1685. 8°.* O.

3715   The book of subscriptions, for insuring of houses. *By S. Roycroft*, [1681?]. brs. L, O.

Book of the cathedral. 1672. *See* King, Daniel.

3716   A book of the continuation of forreign passages. *By M. S. for Thomas Jenner*, 1657. 4°. LT; CH, LC, MH, NN, RPJ, WF.

Book of the general laws and liberties. Cambridge [Mass.], 1648. *See* Massachusetts Bay Colony.

Book of the general laws for the people. Cambridge [Mass.], 1673. *See* Connecticut Colony.

Book of the general laws of the inhabitants. Boston, 1685. *See* Plymouth Colony.

3717   A book of the names of all parishes. *By M. S. for Tho. Jenner*, 1657. 4°. L, LL, OC, CT; CN, MIU.

3717A   —[Anr. ed.] —, 1662. 4°. L, O; MH, WF.

3718   —[Anr. ed.] —, 1668. 4°. L, O, LG, EN; MBA, PL, WF.

3719   —*By S. S. for John Garret*, 1667. T.C.I 253. L; CH, CLC, PL, Y.

Book of the Revelation. 1693. *See* Waple, Edward.

3720   A book of the valuations of all the ecclesiasticall preferments. [*London?*], *printed*, 1680. 12°. L, O, C, OC, YM; CH, CU, MH, NU, PL, Y.

3721   —[Anr. ed.] 1695. 8°: O.

3722   A book without a title. [n.p.], 1649. cap., 4°.* LT; CN.

3722A The bookbinders case unfolded. [*London*, 1684–95]. brs.
       CM.

Booker, John. Almanack. [*n.p.*], 1641. *See* Almanacs.

3723 —25 Novemb. 1646. Lievtenant Colonell John Booker
      being sent out. [*London?* 1646.] cap., brs. L; NU.
      —Bloody almanack. 1643. *See* Almanacs.
      —Bloody Irish almanack. 1646. *See* Almanacs.

3724 —A brief judgment astrological. *Printed*, 1649. cap., 4°.*
      LT, OC; NN, Y.
      —Celestial observations. 1651. *See* Almanacs.

3725 —The Dutch fortune-teller. *By Ja. Cottrel, for Edw.
      Blackmore*, 1650. fol. L.

3726 — —[Anr. ed.] *Printed*, [*n.d.*], fol. CH, CLC, WF

3727 — —[Anr. ed.] [1690.] fol. LN.

3728 — —[Anr. ed.] *By I. M. for W. Thackeray; I. Deacon;
      Matt. Wotton; and Geo. Conyers.* [1693]. fol. T.C.II 487.
      OP; CH.
      [–] Mercurius coelicus. 1644. *See* Wharton, *Sir* George.
      —Mercurius coelicus. [1645.] *See* Almanacs.
      —New bloody almanack. 1643. *See* Almanacs.

3729 —No mercurius aquaticus. [*London*], *for G. B.*, 1644. 4°.*
      LT, LVD, HH, MR; CH, MH.
      —Old almanack. 1658. *See* Almanacs.
      —Ουρανοθηωρια coelestiall observations. 1654. *See*
      Almanacs.

3730 [–] A rope for a parret. *For John Partridge*, 1643/4. 4°.*
      LT, O, C; NHC, WF.

3731 [–] A rope treble-twisted, for John Tayler. *For G.
      Bishop, Septemb.* 27. 1644. 4°.* LT; CH. MH.
      —Telescopium uranicum. 1659. *See* Almanacs.

3732 —Tractatus paschalis, or, a discourse . . . of Easter. *For
      the author*, [1664?]. 8°.* O.

3733 — —[Anr. ed.] *By J. Brudenell, for the author*, 1664. 8°.*
      WF.
      —Uranoscopia. 1649. *See* Almanacs.

3734 **B[ooker], R[ichard].** Satisfaction tendred. colop:
      Printed, and sold by Rich. Janeway, 1689. 4°.* O, LI;
      CH, MBA, NC, WF, Y.

3735 Booker rebuk'd. *For R. Crofts*, 1665. 4°.* O.

3736 August 1660. Books lately printed. [*n.p.*], *for J. Rothwel*,
      1660. brs. LT.

[Boon, A.] Examen legum. 1656. *See* Booth, A.

3737 The boon companion. *For C. Barnet*, 1696. brs. HH.

Boot, Arnold. *See* Boate, Arnold.

3738 **[Booth, A.]** Examen legum Angliae. *By J. Cottrel*, 1656.
      4°. L, O, C, LL, EN; CH, MH, NCL, WF, YL.

Booth, George. *See* Delamere, George Booth, *baron.*

Booth, Henry. *See* Delamere, Henry Booth, *earl of.*

3738A **[Booth, William.]** The compleat solicitor. *By John
       Streater, James Flesher, and Henry Twyford.* 1666. 8°.
       L; PU, Y.

3738B [–] —[Anr. ed.] —, 1660. 8°. MM, WG.

3738C [–] —[Anr. ed.] *By Ja. Cotterell*, 1668. 8°. C, CCA, LJL;
       CH, LC, MHL.

3738D [–] —Fourth edition —, 1672. 8°. T.C.I 93. L, LIL; CLC,
       LC, WF.

3738E [–] —[Anr. ed.] *By the assigns at Richard and Edward
       Atkyns, the James Cotterell and Freeman Collins*, 1683.
       8°. T.C.I 45. O; MHL, NCL, PL, WF, YL.

3739 [–] An exact and faithful account of the late bloody
      engagement. *For E. L. by John Gain*, 1681. brs. O, LG;
      CH, LC, WF.

3740 —The humble petition of. *York: by Robert Barker, and
      by the assigns of John Bill*, 1642. 4°.* L, C; CH, MH.

3741 — —[Anr. ed.] *By Robert Barker, and by the assignes of
      John Bill*, 1642. 4°.* LT, O, CS, GH, DT; CH, MH, NU,
      TU, WF, Y.

3742 **Boothby, Mrs. Frances.** Marcelia. *For Will. Cademan,
      and Giles Widdowes*, 1670. 4°. T.C.I 20. L, O, CS, LVD,
      EN; CH, CN, LC, MH, TU, Y.

3743 **Boothby, Richard.** A breife discovery or description
      of . . . Madagascar. *By E. G. for John Hardesty*, 1646.
      4°. LT, O, C, EC, DT; CH, MH, RPJ, WF, Y.

3744 [–] —Second edition. *For Iohn Hardesty*, 1647. 4°. GH; CH,
      LC, MH.

3744A —An excellent encouragement for setling . . . Madagas-
       car. 1645. 4°. P.

3745 —A true declaration of the intollerable wrongs done to.
      [*London*], June 10, 1644. 4°. L; NC, WF.

3746 **Boothhouse, Samuel.** A brief remonstrance of several
      national injuries. *By William Bentley*, 1653. 4°. LT; CH.

3747 Bo-Peep or the jerking parson. [*London*], *printed for the
      belman of Algate*, [1661]. brs. LT.

3748 **Boraston, George.** The royal law. *For Walter Kettilby*,
      1684. 4°.* T.C.II 58. L, CS; CH, WF, Y.

3749 **[Borde, Andrew.]** The merry tales of the mad-men of
      Gotam. [*London*], *by J. R. for G. Conters & J. Dacon*,
      [1690?] brs. L.

3750 —Scogin's jests; full of witty mirth. *For W. Thackeray
      and J. Deacon*, [1680]. 4°.* L, CM, CT; CH, LC, WF.

3751 **Border, Daniel.** Πολυφαρμακος και χυμιστης. Or,
      the English unparalell'd physitian. *By B. Alsop*, 1651.
      4°. L, O, LCS, LM, E; CLM, NAM, WF.

Borealis, *pseud.*

3752 **[Boreel, Willem, baron.]** The propositions of their
      Excellencies the Ambassadovrs of . . . the Netherlands.
      By T. Badger, 1644. 4°.* LT, O, OC; CH, MH, MIU, WF, Y.

3753 **Borel, Pierre.** A new treatise, proving a multiplicity
      of worlds. *By John Streater*, 1658. 12°. LT, O, CE, P,
      GU; CLC, MB, NN, WF, JF.

3754 —A summary or compendium of the life of . . . Des-
      cartes. *By E. Okes for George Palmer*, 1670. 8°. L, C, OM,
      LPO, E; CLC, IU, WF, Y.

3755 **Boreman, Robert.** An antidote against swearing. *For
      R. Royston*, 1662. 8°. O, CS, LSC, P; CN, MH, NU, WF, Y.

3756 —Αυτοκατακριτος: or hypocrisie vnvail'd. *For R.
      Royston*, 1662. 4°.* L, O, LLI, CS, OC; CH, MH, NU, TU,
      WF, Y.

3757 —The country-mans catechisme. *For R. Royston*, 1652.
      4°.* LT, O, C, LG, DT; CH, MH, NU, WF, Y.

3758 [–] A mirrour of Christianity. *By E. C. for R. Royston,
      and for J. Collins*, 1669. 4°. L, O, C, LCL, CT; CH, CLC,
      NU, WF, Y.

3759 [–] A mirrovr of mercy and judgement. *For Thomas Dring*, 1655. 4°.* L, O, CSS, EN; CH, CLC, WF, Y.

3760 —Παιδεια-Θριαμβος. The triumph of learning. *For R. Royston*, 1653. 4°.* LT, O, C, CT, MR; CLC, NU, TU, WF, Y.

3761 —The pattern of Christianity. *For R. Royston*, 1663. 4°.* L, O, CT, LL; WF.

3762 —The triumph of faith over death. *By J. G. for R. Royston*, 1654. 4°.* L, O, C, CT, BP; CH, MWA, NPT, WF, Y.

3763 [**Borfet, Abiel.**] The minister of Richmond's reasons. colop: *For John Harris*, 1696. cap., 4°.* T.C.III 7. O, OC, CT; MIU, NN.

3764 [–] The minister of Richmonds sermon. *Printed*, 1696. 4°.* T.C.II 585. O, OC.

3765 —Postliminia Caroli II. The palingenesy. *For M. Wright*, 1660. 4°.* LT, O; CH, MH, WF, Y.

Borialis, pseud.

3766 B[orlase], E[dmund]. Brief reflections on the Earl of Castlehaven's memoirs. *For George West*, 1682. 8°. T.C.I 476. L, O, C, OM, DT; CH, MB.

3767 [–] The history of the execrable Irish rebellion. *For Henry Brome, Robert Clavel, and Richard Chiswell*, 1680. fol. T.C.I 368. L, O, C, EN, DT; BN, CH, CN, LC, MH, NU, Y.

3768 [–] —Anr. ed.] *For Robert Clavel*, 1680. fol. T.C.II 263. L, LG, CM; CN, LC, PL, WF, Y.

3769 [–] Latham spaw in Lancashire. *For Rob. Clavel*, 1670. 8°. T.C.I 29. L, O, C, EN, DT; CH, WF.

3770 [–] —[Anr. ed.] *For Robert Clavel*, 1672. 8°. T.C.I 111. O, MC; CH, HC.

3771 [–] The reduction of Ireland to the crown of England. *By Andr. Clarke, for Robert Clavel*, 1675. 8°. T.C.I 187. L, O, CT, EN, DT; CH, CN, LC, MH, NC, Y.

3771A **Borovius, Georgius.** Vox rugientis leonis. *Excudebat anno*, 1679. 4°.* L, CT, P, EN; IU, MH, MM, WF, Y.

3772 Borrough of Ivelchester in Com. Sommerset. The case of Sir Edward Wyndham. [*n.p.*, 1688/9.] brs. LL.

3773 **Bos, Lambert van den.** Florus Anglicus; or an exact history. *For Simon Miller*, 1657. 8°. LT, O, C, LVF, EN; CH, CN, MBP, WF, Y.

3774 — —Third edition. —, 1658. 8°. L, EN, ES, LC

3775 — —, 1660. 8°. LCL, ES.

3776 — —Fourth edition. 1662. 8°. O.

3777 —The life and raigne of King Charles. *For Simon Miller*, 1659. 8°. LT, O, CCA; CH, CLC, MIU, Y.

3778 **Bosboom, Simon.** A brief and plain description of the five orders of columns. *For Robert Pricke*, 1676. fol. T.C.I 246 LIB; NC, Y.

Boscobel. 1660. *See* Blount, Thomas.

3779 **Bosevile, Thomas.** To the supreme authority of this nation . . . the humble petition of. [*London*, 1650.] brs. LT.

3779A [**Bosse, Abraham**] Mr. De Sargves universal way of dyaling. *By Tho. Leach, to be sold by Isaac Pridmore*, 1659. 4°. L, C, LG, OC, DT; MH, NC, WF, WU.

3780 **Bossuet, Jacques Bénigne, bp.** A conference with Mr. Claude. *For Matthew Turner*, 1687. 4°. L, O, C, EN, DT; CH, MIU, NU, WF, Y.

3781 —A discourse on the history of the whole world. *For Matthew Turner*, 1686. 8°. L, O, C, LL, DT; CH, CLC, PL, WF, Y.

3782 —An exposition of the doctrine of the Catholic church. *Paris, by Vincent du Moutier*, 1672. 12°. L, O, HH; BN, CLC, CN, TU, WF, Y.

3783 — —[Anr. ed.] *Printed*, 1685. 4°. L, O, C, ENC, DT; CH, MH, NU, WF, Y.

3784 — —"Second" edition. *By Henry Hills*, 1686. 12°. L, O, C, EN, DT; CLC, CU, MH, NU, WF, Y.

3784A — —"Second" edition. *Printed*, CLC, MBA. 1686. 12°. L, OC, CSSX; CLC, MBA.

3784B — —[Anr. ed.] *For Rihcard Chiswel*, 1686. 4°. CM; NN.

3785 — —Third edition. [*London?*], 1687. L, O, E.

3786 —Maxims and reflections upon plays. *For R. Sare*, 1699. 8°. L, O, LL, OC, RPL; CN, LC, MH, TU, WF, Y.

3787 —A pastoral letter from. *By Henry Hills*, 1686. 4°.* L, O, CT, EN, DT; CH, MH, NU, WF, Y.

3788 —[Anr. ed.] *Printed*, 1686. 4°.* EN; CH, NU, WF.

3789 —Quakerism a-la-mode. *For J. Harris and A. Bell*, 1698. 8°. L, CS, E; MH, Y.

3790 —A relation of the famous conference. *By H. C. for Thomas Malthus*, 1684. fol.* T.C.II 69. L, O, LG, OC, HH; CH, CN, NU, WF, Y.

3791 —A sermon preached . . . Sept. 1. 1683. *Printed at Paris, reprinted at London, by J. C. and F. C. for H. H. and sold by Samuel Crouch*, 1684. 4°.* T.C.II 42. L, O, C, CS, MC; CH, MH, NU, WF, Y.

3791A —A sermon preached at the funeral of a person of the highest quality. *Printed at Paris, to be sold by I. V.*, 1686. 4°.* T.C.II 163. WCA; RPB, Y.

3792 —A treatise of communion under both species. *Printed at Paris, by Sebastian Mabre Cramoisy*, 1685. 12°. L, O.

3793 — —[Anr. ed.] *For Matthew Turner*, 1687. 4°. L, C, OME, EN, DT; CLC, CN, MH, NU, WF, Y.

3794 [**Bostock, Robin.**] Herod and Pilate reconciled; a new dialogue. [1647.] cap., 4°.* LT, OC, HH; TU, WF.

3795 [–] Herod and Pilate reconciled: or, a late dialogue. [*London*, 1647?] cap., 4°.* LT; CH, IU, MH, TU, Y.

3795A [–] Herod and Pilate reconciled: or the concord of Papists. *For Laur. Chapman*, 1663. 4°.* CCA.

3796 [–] The Scots constancy. [*London*, 1647.] 4°.* LT; WF, Y.

Boston almanack. Boston, 1692. *See under* Almanacs: Harris, Benjamin.

Boston ephemeris. Boston, 1683. *See under* Almanacs: Mather, Cotton.

3797 **Boswell, James.** Disputatio juridica, de postulando. *Edinburgh, heirs of A. Anderson*, 1698. 4°. ALDIS 3736. EN.

3798 [**Bosworth, Benjamin.**] Signs of apostasy lamented. [*Boston*, 1693.] cap., fol.* EVANS 633. L; MH, RPJ.

3799 **Bosworth, William.** The chast and lost lovers. *By F. L. for Laurence Blaiklock*, 1651. 8°. LT; CH, MH, WF.

3800 — —Second edition. *For William Shears*, 1653. 8°. CH.

Boteler. *See also* Butler.

3801 **Boteler, Edward.** Gods goodnesse. *For G. Bedel and T. Collins*, 1662. 8°. L, O, P; CLC.

3802 —Jus poli et fori or, God and the king. *For G. Bedell, and T. Collins*, 1661. 8°. LT, O; CLC.

3803 —No home but heaven. *For G. Bedel, and T. Collins*, 1664. 8°. O, LW.

3803A —The servants audit. *For G. Bedell & T. Collins*, 1662. 8°. CLC.

3803B —Urbs deplorata. A sermon. *By J. C. for Octavian Pulleyn*, 1669. 8°. CT; WF.

3804 —The worthy of Ephratah. *By T. N. for G. Bedell and T. Collins*, 1659. 8°. LT, O, C, LW; CLC, WF.

3805 Boteler's case, being an impartial narrative. [*London*], *for J. Clarke, and P. Brooksby*, [1678]. 8°. T.C.I 313. L, O; WF.

3806 **Botley, Samuel.** Maximum in minimo or Mr Jeremiah Rich pens dexterity compleated. *Printed and sould by Samuel Botley*, [1674?] 8°. L, O, C, HH, EN; LC, MHL, NN.

3807 — —[Anr. ed.] *For Robert Clavell*, 1674. 8°. NN.

3808 — —[Anr. ed.] *For John Man*, [169–?]. 16°. LLL, C, CM; NN.

3809 — —[Anr. ed.] *For Nat^h Sackett*, [169–?]. 8°. L, LG, LLL, MRL, EN; CH, CN, NN, WF, Y.

3810 [**Botrie, J.**] Religio jurisconsulti. *For Henry Hood*, 1649. 8° LT; CH, MMO.

3811 A bottle of holy tears. *Yorke by Tho. Broade*, 1695. 4°.* O.

3812 **Boughen, Edward.** An account of the church Catho- lick. *By E. Cotes, for Richard Royston*, 1653. 4°. LT, O, CT, E, DT; CH, CLC, NU, WF, Y.

3813 —Mr. Gerees case of conscience sifted. *Printed*, 1648. 4°. LT, O, C, CE, HH; CH, NU, WF, Y.

3814 — —[Anr. ed.] *Printed*, 1650. 4°. L, O, LCL, DC.

3815 [–] Observations upon the ordinance of the Lords and Commons. *Oxford, by Leonard Lichfield*, 1645. 4°.* MADAN 1842. O, CT, OC, EN, DT;CH, MH, NU.

3815A [–] —[Anr. ed.] *Oxford* [*London?*], *by Leonard Lichfield*, [1645?] 4°.* MADAN 1843. L, O, CJ, CS, EN; MH, MIU, Y.

3816 —The principles of religion. *Oxford, by Leonard Lichfield*, 1646. 8°. MADAN 1885. O, CT; CH.

3816A —A short exposition of the catechism. 662 8°. P.

3817 —[Anr. ed.] *For T. Garthwait*, 1663. 8°. O, CS, P; WF.

3818 — —[Anr. ed.] *By A. M. for Tim Garthwait*, 1668. 8°. L.

3819 — —[Anr. ed.] *For Christopher Wilkinson*, 1671. 8° T.C.I 70. L.

3820 — —[Anr. ed.] *By R. Battersby for Christopher Wilkinson*, 1673. 8°. T.C.I. 123. O, C, CE, OC; CLC.

3821 — —[Anr. ed.] *For Christopher Wilkinson*, 1675. 8°. T.C.I 208. C.

3822 — —[Anr. ed.] —, 1679. 8°. T.C.I 376. NU.

3822A — —[Anr. ed.] *By W. R. for H. Mortlock*, 1700. 8°. T.C.III 179. Y.

3823 [**Bouhours, Dominique.**] Christian thoughts. [*n.p.*], 1680. 24°. BN.

3823A — [Anr. ed.] *For George Powell*, 1686. 12°. T.C.II 143. OC.

3824 [–] —[Anr. ed.] *For Edw. Pawlet*, 1692. 12°. L, OC; CH.

3824A [–] —[Anr. ed.] —, 1698. 12°. L; NPT.

3825 —The life of St. Francis Xavier. *For Jacob Tonson*, 1688. 8°. L, O, C, EN, MC; CH, MH, TU, WF, Y.

3826 —The life of St Ignatius. *By Henry Hills*, 1686. 8°. L, O, C, OC, CT; CH, CU, MH, NU, TU, WF, Y.

3827 [–] The life of the renowned Peter d'Aubusson. *For Geo. Wells, and Sam. Carr*, 1679. 8°. T.C.I 330. L, O, OC, CS, EN; CH, CLC, NC, WF, Y.

3827A **Boulbie, Judith.** A few words to the rulers of the nation. [*London*, 1673.] fol.* LF.

3828 — A testimony for truth against all hireling priests. [*London*, 1665.] 4°.* L; LF, BBN; PH, PSC, Y.

3828A —To all justices of peace, or other magistrates. [*London*, 1667.] 4°.* LF, BBN; PSC.

3828B —A warning and lamentation over England. [*London*], 1679. fol.* LF.

3828C **Boules, Dr.** The Queens royal closet newly opened. *For Francis Cole, T. Vere, I. Wright and J. Clark*, 1675, 8°., WU.

3829 **Boulton, Richard.** An examination of Mr. John Colbatch his books. *For A. and J. Churchill*, 1698. 8°. O.

3830 — —[Anr. ed.] *For T. Bennet*, 1699. 8°. T.C.III 109. O, OC, CCA, OM; CLC, WSG.

3831 —A letter to Dr. Charles Goodall. *For A. Baldwin*, 1699. 4°.* L, LCP, OC; PL.

3832 —A treatise concerning the heat of the blood. *For A. and J. Churchill*, 1698. 12°. T.C.III 109. L, LCP, OC, CCA, GH.

3833 —A treatise of the reason of muscular motion. *By A. and J. Churchill*, 1697. 12°. T.C.III 5. L, C, LCP, OC, GH; CLC, WSG, HC.

3833A **Boulton, Samuel.** Medicina magica. *By T. C. for Nath. Brook*, 1656. 8°. LT, LWL, GU; CH, CLC, LC, HC.

3833B — —[Anr. ed.] —, 1665. 8°. LPO, LWL; WF.

3833C **Bouncher, Samuel.** The enemies overthrow. *For John Littleton*, 1692. 4°.* Y.

3833D —[Anr. ed.] *For the author*, 1695. 4°.* CS.

3834 **Bound, William.** Amdiffyniad y bedyddwyr. *Argraphwyd*, 1658. 8°. AN.

Bounds and bonds. 1649. *See* Ascham, Anthony.

3834A The bounds set to France. *For Richard Baldwin*, 1694. 12°. T.C.II 527. L; CLC, WF, Y.

3835 **Boune, Abraham.** The clergie in their colors. *For T. M. to bee sold by T. Brewster and G. Mould*, 1651. 8°. LT, EN.

3836 —The pride and avarice of the clergie. *For T. M.*, 1650. 12°. L, LCL.

3837 The bountiful brewers. [*n.p.*, 1688–1702.] brs. HH.

3838 **Bourchier, Sir John.** Die lune 6 Junii, 1642. The copy of a letter sent from. *For Joseph Hunscott, June 7, 1642.* fol. STEELE 2170. L, O, ES; Y.

3839 [–] A letter sent by a Yorkshire gentleman to a friend in London. [*London*, 1642.] cap., 4°.* LT, O, CJ, EC, SP; CH, CN, WF, Y.

3840 [**Bourignon, Antionette.**] An admirable treatise of solid virtue. *At Amsterdam, by Henry Wetstein*, 1693. 1698. 12°. L, LW; NU.

3841 ——[Anr. ed.] *Printed*, 1699. 8°. T.C.III 89. L, O, LW, EN, ENC, GU; NU, PH, Y.

3842 —The light of the world. *Printed*, 1696. 8°. L, OM, LW, EN; CN, NN, PH, Y.

3842A —The second part of The light of the world. *Printed*, 1696. 8°. L; CN, Y.

3843 **Bourk, Hubert.** The information of. *For Randolph Taylor*, [1680]. fol.* L, O, C, LCL, EN; CH, CN, MBC, WF, Y.

Bourke, John. Almanack. Dublin, 1685. *See* Almanacs. — Hiberniæ Merlinus. Dublin, 1683. *See* Almanacs.

3844 **Bourne, Benjamin.** The description and confvtation of mysticall anti-Christ. *By Matthew Symons for B. B.*, 1646. 4°. LT, GU, DT; WF, Y.

3845 **Bourne, Edward.** An answer to Doctor Good. [*n.p.*], *printed*, 1675. 4°.* L, LF, OC, BBN; MB, MH, PH, PSC.

3845A —Certain queries answered. [*London*], *printed*, 1667. 4°. LF, BBN.

3846 —An epistle to Friends. *By J. Bringhurst*, [1682]. fol.* LF, BBN.

3846A —A few words to those who look for another dispensation. [*London*, 1679.] brs. LF.

3846B —For the inhabitants of Worcester. colop: *Printed and sold by Andrew Sowle*, 1682. 4°.* LF, BBN.

3847 —A looking-glass, discovering. [*London*], *printed*, 1671. 4°.* L, LF, BBN; MH, PH, PHS, PSC, Y.

3848 —The truth of God cleared. *For Thomas Simmons*, 1657. 4°.* L, LF, BBN; CH, MH, PH.

3849 —A warning from the Lord God out of Sion. *For Robert Wilson*, 1660. 4°.* L, LF; IE, LC, PH, PSC, Y.

3850 —A warning from the Lord God to the inhabitants . . . of Warwick. [*n.p.*], 1661. brs. L, LF, BBN.

3851 **Bourne, Immanuel.** A defence and justification of ministers maintenance by tythes. *For John Allen*, 1659. 8°. LT, O, C, LG, SP; CLC, MH, NU.

3852 —A defence of the Scriptures. *For John Wright*, 1656. 4°. O, LF, BP, SP; CH, CLC, NU.

3853 —A gold chain of directions. *By J. Streater, for George Sawbridge*, 1669. 12°. O, C.

3854 —A light from Christ. *For John Wright*, 1645. 8°.* LT; CH, NPT, Y.

3855 ——[Anr. ed.] 1646. 8°. L, O, LCL, GU; CH, NU, WF.

3856 ——Second edition. 1647. 8°. LLP.

3857 [**Bourne, Nehemiah.**] The copy of a letter from the reare-admiral. *By G. D. for William Hope*, 1652. 4°.* LT, LL, OC; NN.

3858 **Bourne, Reuben.** The contented cuckold. *Printed, and sold by Randal Taylor*, 1692. 4°. L, O, LVD, EN; CH, CN, MH, MU, WF.

3859 **Bourne, William.** The arte of shooting in great ordinance. *Printed*, 1643. 4°. L, O, OC, EN, AU; MH, MU, WU, Y.

3859A [**Boursalt, Edmé.**] Deceptio visus: or seeing. *For Iohn Starkey*, 1671. 8°. T.C.I 79. L, O; CLC, CN, LC, MH, Y.

3860 —The prince of Conde. *For H. Herringman*, 1675. 12°. T.C.I 226. L; CLC, CN, CU, RPB, Y.

3860A [**Boutauld, Michel.**] The counsels of wisdom. *By J. Shadd, for N. Turner*, 1680. 12°. L, O; CH, LC, Y.

3860B [–]—[Anr. ed.] *Amsterdam, for Stephen Swart*, 1683. 12°. T.C.II 32. L; CU, WF.

3860C [–]—[Anr. ed.] *For S. Smith*, 1683. 12°. CU, WF.

3860D —A method of conversing with God. *By Mary Thompson*, 1688. 8°. L; WF.

3860E [–]—Second edition. *By Tho. Hales*, 1692. 8°. L; CN, WG.

3861 **Bouvet, Joachim.** The history of Cang-Hy. *For F. Coggan*, 1699. 8°. L, C; CH, NN, MH, WF, Y.

3862 —The present condition of the Muscovite empire. *For F. Coggan*, 1699. 8°. L, OM, CS, CT, EN; CH, CLC, MH, WF, Y.

3863 [**Bovet, Richard.**] A congratulatory poem, to the honourable Admiral Russel. colop: *Printed and sold by T. Moore*, 1693. cap., 4°.* Y.

3864 —Pandæmonium, or the devil's cloyster. *For J. Walthoe*, 1684. 8°. T.C.II 102. L, O, EN, GU; BN, CH, MH, WCL, WF, Y.

3864A ——[Anr. ed.] *For Tho. Mathew*, 1684. 8°. PU.

3865 —A poem humbly presented to His most Excellent Majesty. *By J. Dover, for Richard Baldwin*, 1696. fol.* HH; MH, NP, Y.

3866 **Bowber, Thomas.** A sermon preached . . . March 10th 1694/5. *For William Rogers*, 1695. 4°. L, O, C, WCA; CH, IU, MH, NP, Y.

3867 **Bowchier, Richard.** A sermon preach'd . . . Novemb. 13. 1692. *For Walter Kettilby*, 1692. 4°.* T.C.II 437. L, O, LG, CT, DT; CLC, MBA, WF, Y.

3868 [**Bowen, William.**] A perfect and trve relation of the great and bloudy skirmish. *For John Thomas*, 1642. 4°.* LT; CLC.

3869 **Bower, Edmund.** Doctor Lamb revived. *By T. W. for Richard Best, and John Place*, 1653. 4°.* LT, O, LN, LWL, GU; CH, CN, MH, WF, Y.

3869A **Bower, Richard.** To the Kings most excellent majesty. [*London*, 1661]. brs. MH.

3870 **Boweter, John.** Innocency cleared from iyes. *For Thomas Simmons*, 1658. 4°.* L, LF, BBN; NU, PSC.

3870A —A salutation of love from a prisoner. [*London*, 1679.] brs. LF, BBN.

3870B —Something concerning the proceedings of Thomas Willmott. [*London*, 1681.] 4°.* LF; PH.

3870C ——Second edition. —, [1681.] 4°.* PH.

Bowker, James. Kalendarium astronomical. 1668. *See* Almanacs.

Bowker, John. New almanack. 1674. *See* Almanacs.

Bowlbie, Judith. *See* Boulbie, Judith.

3871　**Bowles, Edward.** The dutie and danger of swearing. *Printed and sold in York by Tho. Broad,* 1655. 4°.* L, YM; WF.

3872　—Good counsell for evil times. *By F: Neile for Samuel Gellibrand,* 1648. 4°.* L, O, CS, LP, DT; CH, NU, TU, Y.

3873　[–] Manifest truth. *By M.S. for Henry Overton, and Giles Calvert,* 1646. 4°. L; CH, CN, PL, WF, Y.

3874　[–] Manifest truths. *By M.S. for Henry Overton, and Giles Calvert,* 1646. 4°. LT, CT, HH, EN, DT; CH, CN, MH, NU, WF.

3875　[–] The mysterie of iniquitie. *Printed at London by A. B.,* 1643. 4°. L, O, C, LVF, CT.

3876　[–] —[Anr. ed.] *Printed at London by A.B.,* [1643]. 4°. LT, AU, D; MH, Y.

3877　[–] —[Anr. ed.] *For Samvel Gellibrand,* 1643. 4°. L, O, C, EN, DT; CH, CU, MH, NU, WF, Y.

3878　[–] Plaine English; or, a discourse. [*London*], *printed,* 1643. 4°.* LT, O, C, EN, DT; CH, CU, MH, NU, WF, Y.

3879　Entry cancelled.

3880　**Bowles, Oliver.** De pastore evangelico tractatus. *Apud Samuelem Gellibrand,* 1649. 4°. LT, O, C, LW, AU; CH, IU, NC, WF, Y.

3881　— —[Anr. ed.] 1653. 4°. E.

3882　— —[Anr. ed.] *Apud Sa. Gellibrand,* 1655. 8°. L, CT, ENC, GU, DT; MB, NPT.

3883　— —[Anr. ed.] 1659. 8°. LW; NU.

3884　—Zeale for Gods house qvickned. *By Richard Bishop for Samuel Gellibrand,* 1643. 4°. LT, O, C, EN, DT; CH, MH, NU, TU, WF, Y.

3885　**Bowman, Henry.** Songs, for one, two & three voices. [1677]. fol. L, OCC.

3886　— —[Anr. ed.] *Oxford,* [*by L.Lichfield*] *for T.Bowman,* 1678. fol. MADAN 3172. O; LC, Y.

3887　— —"Second" edition. *Oxford, for Ric. Davis,* 1679. fol. MADAN 3205. T.C.I 345. LCM, GU; CLC, WF.

3888　[**Bownd**], G[eorge]. A voyce from heaven, speaking. *By S. Griffin, for J. Kirton,* 1659. 4°. LT, LG, LW; NU, WF.

3889　**Bowne, Martin.** Tithes re-mounted. *For Thomas Bates,* 1646. 4°.* LT, LCL, LSC, DT; CH, WF, Y.

3890　[**Bowne, Tobias.**] Doubtful Robin. [*London*], *by P. Brooksby,* [1676–85]. brs. L, O, HH.

3891　—The doubting virgin. [*London*], *for P.Brooksby,* [1672–85]. brs. L, CM, HH; MH.

3892　—A fairing for young-men and maids. [*London*], *for P. Brooksby,* [1680?]; 8°. brs. L, O; MH.

3893　[–] The hasty wedding. [*London*], *for P.Brooksby,* [1672–95]. brs. L, HH, GU.

3894　[–] Kind William, or, constant Betty. [*London*], *for J. Deacon,* [1684]. brs. L, O, CM, HH.

3895　[I] Shall I? shall I? No, no. [*London*], *for P.Brooksby,* [1684]. brs. L, O, HH.

3896　—Tobias advice. [*London*], *for P.Brooksby,* [1672–95]. brs. L, CM, HH; MH.

3897　—Tobias observation. [*London*], *for P.Brooksby,* [1685–88]. brs. L, CM, HH; MH.

3897A　[–] Tobies experience explain'd. [*London*] *for P.Brooksby,* [1670–90]. brs. L, CM.

3897B　—Tom and Roger's contract. [*London*], *by Philip Brooksby* [1670–90]. brs. O, CM.

3898　—The two faithful lovers. [*London*], *for J.Wright, J. Clark, W.Thackeray, and T.Passinger,* [c. 1686]. brs. L, O, CM, HH.

3899　[–] —[Anr. ed.] *For A.M. W.O. and T.Thackeray,* [1670–80]. brs. L, O, HH, GU; WCL.

3900　[–] —[Anr. ed.] *For F.Coles, T.Vere, J.Wright, and J. Clark,* [1690?]. brs. L, O.

3901　[–] The west-country maids advice. [*London*], *for P. Brooksby,* [1672–95]. brs. L, HH; MH.

　　　Box of spikenard. [1659.] *See* Malpas, Thomas.

3901A　**Boyce, Thomas.** An answer to the Quakers pretended charity. 1676. 4°. O.

3902　—The Quakers cruelty. *Printed,* 1675. 4°. L, LF, YM; CH, PH, PL.

3902A　—To the most powerful in authority, to unloose the bonds. [*London*], 1694. 4°.* LF.

3903　**Boyd, John.** Theses philosophicæ. *Glasguæ, R. Sanders,* 1693. 4°.* ALDIS 3343. EN.

3904　**Boyd, Robert.** R. Bodii . . . in Epistolam Pauli . . . ad Ephesios. *Impensis societatis stationiorum,* 1652. fol. L, O, CT, EN, AU; CLC, NR.

3905　**Boyd, Zacherie.** I. Crosses, 2. Comforts. *Printed at Glasgow by George Anderson,* 1643. 8°. ALDIS 1072. EN.

3906　—The garden of Zion. *Glasgow, by George Anderson,* 1644. 8°. ALDIS 1132. E, EN; NN.

3907–9　Entries cancelled.

3910　—The songs of the Old and New Testament. *Glasgow, by the heires of George Anderson,* 1648. 12°. ALDIS 1310. L, GM.

3911　—The sword of the Lord. *Glasgow, by George Anderson,* 1643. 8°. ALDIS 1073. EN.

　　　Boyer, Abel. Achilles: or, Iphigenia in Aulis. 1700. *See* Racine, Jean.

3912　—Characters of the virtues & vices. *For Abel Roper, E.Wilkinson, and Roger Clavell,* 1695. 8°. L, O; CH, CU, TU, WF, Y.

3913　The compleat French-master. *For Tho. Salusbury,* 1694. 8°. T.C.II 494. L, E; CH, CLC, WF.

3914　— —Second edition. *For R.Sare, and John Nicholson,* 1699. 8°. L, O, CS; Y.

3914A　—A description historical and geographical of Flanders. *D.Browne and Tho.Axe,* 1698. 8°. MBA.

3915　[–] A geographical and historical description. *Printed and are to be sold by D. Browne, and T. Axe,* 1696. 8°. LW, SP.

3916　The martial field of Europe. *For Tho. Salusbury,* 1694. 8°. AN, E, WF.

3917　—The royal dictionary. *For R.Clavel, H.Mortlock, S. Lowndes, J.Robinson, D.Brown, W.Hensman, S. Crouch, E.Evets, J.Laurence, R.Sare, A.Churchill, S. Smith, L.Meredith, J.Taylor, F.Saunders, T.Bennet, J. Knapton, J.Wyat, E.Castle, D.Midwinter,* 1699. 4°. T.C.III 125. L, O, C, DT; CH, PL, TU, WF, Y.

3917A　— —[Anr. ed.] —, 1700. 4°. L, CPE, BP; CH, IU, WU.

3918 —The wise and ingenious companion. *By G. C. for Tho. Newborough, and J. Nicholson*, 1700. 8°. T.C.III 160. L, O; CN, WF, Y. .

3919 **Boyer, Pierre.** The history of the Vaudois. *For Edward Mory*, 1692. 8°. T.C.II 380. OC; LC, NU, WF, Y.

3919A — —Second edition. —, 1692. 8°. T.C.II 405. L, O, C, BR, ENC; CN, WF, Y.

3919B —The negotiations of the Embassadors. *For R. Bentley*, 1691. 8°. T.C.II 380. L, O; NPT, VC.

3920 **Boyer, Thomas.** Επιδιορθωσις or a modest enquiry. *By R. W. for Nathaniel Ekins, and for Stephen Lincoln in Leicester*, 1659. 12°. LT.

Boyle, Charles. *See* Orrery, Charles Boyle, earl of.

3920A **Boyle, Michael.** Rules and orders for the court and chancery of Ireland. *Dublin*, 1685. 12°. DIX 213. L; WF.

Boyle, Richard. *See* Cork, Richard Boyle, earl of.

3921 **Boyle, Robert.** The works of. *For J. Phillips, and J. Taylor*, 1699–1700. 3v. 8°. T.C.III 142. FULTON 243. L, C, LPO, GK, E; CH, LC, NAM, WF, JF, vol. I.

3922 —Works, vol. 4. *To be sold by Thomas Bennet and John Wyat*, 1700. 8°. FULTON 243. L, C, LPO, E, GK; CH, PL, WF, Y.

3923 —An advertisement of Mr. Boyle, about the loss of many of his writings. [*London*, 1688.] brs. L, O.

3924 —Advertisements about the Experiments and notes. [*London*, 1675.] 8°. O, OC.

3925 —The aerial noctiluca. *By Tho. Snowden, and are to be sold by Nath. Ranew*, 1680. 8°. FULTON 138. L, O, CT, GU, DT; BN, CH, CJC, MH, WF, JF.

3926 —Animadversions upon Mr. Hobbes's Problemata. *By William Godbid, to be sold by Moses Pitt*, 1674. 8°. L, O, C, OC, SC; MM, PL, WF, Y.

3927 —Apparatus ad historian naturalem sanguinis humani. Pars I. *Impensis Samuelis Smith*, 1684. 8°. T.C.II 63. FULTON 147n. O, C, LCS, GK; CLC, PL, JF.

3928 —A catalogue of the philosophical books and tracts written by the Hon. Robert Boyle, Esq. *By Edward Jones*, 1689. 8°.* L.

3928A — —[Anr. ed.] *For Sam. Smith*, 1690. 8°.* L, O, E, GU, BR; CLC, MIU, NP, PL, WSG.

3928B —Catalogus librorum tractatuumq. *Excudit Edovardus Jones*, 1688. 8°.* L.

3929 —Certain physiological essays. *For Henry Herringman*, 1661. 4°. FULTON 25. L, O, C, EN, DT; BN, CLC, NP, WF, Y, JF.

3930 — —Second edition. —, 1669. 4°. FULTON 26. L, O, C, E, DT; CH, MH, MMO, PL, WF, JF.

3930A —A chymical treatise concerning colours. *Printed*, 1676. 12°, CU.

3931 —The Christian virtuoso. The first part. *In the Savoy: by Edw. Jones for John Taylor, and John Wyat*, 1690. 8°. T.C.II 398. FULTON 191. L, O, C, LR, E; CH, CN, NU, WF, JF.

3931A — —[Anr. ed.] *In the Savoy, by Edw. Jones for John Taylor*, 1690. 8°. L, O, OC, CS; CN, PU, JF.

3932 —Chymista scepticus. *Excudebat J. C. veniuntque apud Johannem Crooke*, 1662. 8°. FULTON 36. C, E, GU; MBA, HC.

3933 —Roberti Boyle . . . cogitationes de S. Scripturæ stylo. *Oxoniæ, typis W. H. impensis Ric. Davis*, 1665. 12°. MADAN 2695. FULTON 47. L, O, OC, GK; CLC, WG, JF.

3934 —A continvation of nevv experiments. *Oxford, by Henry Hall, for Richard Davis*, 1669. 4°. T.C.I 5. MADAN 2820. FULTON 16. L, O, C, E, DT; BN, CH, MH, NC, WF, Y, JF.

3935 — —, the second part. *By Miles Flesher, for Richard Davis, in Oxford*, 1682. 4°. FULTON 18. L, O, C, LM, DT; CJC, MMO, NAM, NC, Y, JF.

3936 —De hypothesis mechanicæ excellentia et fundamentis considerationes. *Typis T. N. impensis Henrici Herringman*, 1674. 12°. FULTON 117. L, O.

3937 [–] De ipsa natura *Typis H. Clark, Impensis J. Taylor*, 1687. 12°. T.C.II 179. GK; BN, MH, JF.

3938 — —[Anr. ed.] *Typis H. Clark, impensis Johannis Taylor*, 1688. 12°. FULTON 171. O, E.

3939 —De specificorum remediorum. *Impensis Sam. Smith*, 1686. 12°. FULTON 167. E; BN, NAM, PL, WU, JF.

3940 [–] Debita Deo ab humano intellectu. *Impensis Richardi Davis*, 1684. 12°. FULTON 155. L, E.

3941 —A defence of the doctrine touching the spring . . . of the air. *By J. G. for Thomas Robinson*, 1662. 8°. FULTON 14. L, O, CE, LR, EN; CH, Y.

3942 — —Third edition. *By M. Flesher for Richard Davis*, 1682. 4°. FULTON 15. L, OR, CK, BAMB, DT; NC, JF.

3943 —Defensio doctrinæ de elatere & gravitate aëris. *Excudebat J. Redmayne impensis Johannis [?]*, 1663. 8°. FULTON 21. O, GK; BN, CLL, PU, JF.

3944 [–] A discourse of things above reason. *By E. T. and R. H. for Jonathan Robinson*, 1681. 8°. L, O, C, CT, AU; CN, NU, PL, WF, HC.

3945 — —[Anr. ed.] *By E. T. and R. H. for Jonathan Robinson*, 1681. FULTON 144. O, OC, OH, GK, DT; CLC, JF.

3946 —A disquisition about the final causes. *By H. C. for John Taylor*, 1688. 8°. FULTON 186. CLC, PL, PU, WU, JF.

3946A — —Second edition. —, 1688. 8°. FULTON 186A. L, O, C, EN, DT; CH, CJC, MH, NU, WF, HC.

3947 —An essay about the origine & virtves of gems. *By William Godbid, and are to be sold by Moses Pitt*, 1672. 8°. FULTON 96. L, O, C, EN, DT; CH, CJC, MH, WF, Y.

3948 [–] An essay of the great effects of even languid and unheeded motion. *By M. Flesher, for Richard Davis*, 1685. 8°. FULTON 163. L, OC, LR, EN; MH, JF.

3949 — —Second edition. — —, 1685. 8°. FULTON 164. L, C, OQ, LR, GK; CLC, MH, WU, JF.

3950 — —[Anr. ed.] *Sold by Sam. Smith*, 1690. 8°. T.C.II 314. FULTON 165. L, O, C, EN, DT; CH, MH, PL, WF, JF.

3951 —Essays of the strange subtilty of effluviums. *By W. G. for M. Pitt*, 1673. 8°. T.C.I 153. FULTON 105-6. L, O, C, EN, DT; CLC, LC, MH, NAE, NP, Y, JF.

3952 — —Third edition. *By W. G. for M. Pitt*, 1673. 4°. FULTON 107. O, LWL, GK; MH, HC, JF.

3953-4 Entry cancelled.

3955 —The excellency of theology. *By T.N. for Henry Herringham*, 1674. 8°. T.C.I 179. FULTON 116. L, O, LR, EN, DT; CH, MH, NU, TU, WF, JF.

3956 —Exercitatio de origine & viribus gemmarum. *Typis Guilielmi Godbid, & venales prostant apud Mosem Pitt*, 1673. 12°. T.C.I 121. FULTON 97. L, LCS, P; BN, MU, WGS, WF, JF.

3957 —Exercitationes de atmosphæris. *Typis Guil. Godbid; impensis Mosis Pitt*, 1673. 12°. T.C.I 172. FULTON 108. GH, GU; BN, CLC, WF, JF.

3958 —Experimenta et considerationes de coloribus. *Impensis Henrici Herringman*, 1665. 12°. FULTON 59. LWL, GK; MU, WF, JF.

3959 —Experimenta & observationes physicæ. *For John Taylor, and John Wyat*, 1691. 8°. FULTON 193. L, O, C, E, DT; CH, MH, WF, Y, JF.

3960 —Experimenta nova atque observata. *Typis R.E. pro B. Tooke*, 1682. 12°. O; BN, JF.

3961 —Experimenta nova circa. *M. Pitt*, 1676. 12°.* BN.

3962 —Experimenta, observationes, &c. *Impensis Samuelis Smith*, 1692. 8°. FULTON 125. O; MW, PU.

3963 [–] An experimental discourse of some unheeded causes. *By M. Flesher, for Richard Davis, Oxford*, 1685. 8°, MH, JF.

3964 Entry cancelled.

3965 —Experimentorum novorum. *Excudebat Milo Flesher, pro Richardo Davis, Oxoniensi;* 1680. 8°. MADAN 3205. FULTON 17. O, CCL, LR, OB, DT; BN, MBA, Y, JF.

3966 —Experiments and considerations about the porosity of bodies. *For Sam. Smith*, 1684. 8°. T.C.II 101. FULTON 149. L, O, C, EN, DT; BN, CLC, MH, WF, Y, JF.

3967 —Experiments and considerations touching colours. *For Henry Herringham*, 1664. 8°. FULTON 57. L, O, C, EN, BQ; CH, CJC, MH, WF, Y, JF.

3968 — —[Anr. ed.] —, 1670. 8°. T.C.I 24. FULTON 58. L, O, CT, OJ, GK; CU, MH, MMO, Y, JF.

3969 —Experiments and notes about . . . corrosiveness. *By E. Flesher, for R. Davis in Oxford*, 1675. 8°. L, O, C, OC, CK; CJC, MBP, MH, JF.

3970 Entry cancelled.

3971 —Experiments and notes about . . . magnetism. *By E. Flesher, for R. Davis in Oxford*, 1676. 8°.* L, O, C, CT, GU; CJC, MBP, MH, JF.

3972 [–] Experiments and notes. About . . . producibleness. *Oxford, by H. Hall for R. Davis*, 1680. 8°. MADAN 3260. L, O, C, E, DT; CH, LC, MH, WF, Y, JF.

3973 —Experiments, and notes, about . . . volatility. *By E. Flesher, for R. Davis in Oxford*, 1675. 8°. L, O, OC, CK; CJC, MBP, MH, JF.

3974 —Experiments, and observations, about . . . odours. *By E. Flesher, for R. Davis in Oxford*, 1675. 8°. L, O, C, OC, CK; CJC, MBP, MH, NC, JF.

3975 —Experiments, and observations, about . . . tasts. *By E. Flesher, for R. Davis in Oxford*, 1675. 8°.* L, O, C, OC, CK; CJC, MBP, MH, NC, Y, JF.

3976 —Experiments, notes, &c. about the mechanical origine. *By E. Flesher, for R. Davis, in Oxford*, 1675. 8°.* MADAN 3051. FULTON 123. L, O, C, LPO, LR, DT; CJC, CLC, MBP, NAE, NC, Y, JF.

3977 — —[Anr. ed.] *By E. Flesher, for R. Davis, in Oxford*, 1676. 8°.* T.C.I 255. MADAN 3098. FULTON 124. L, O, CT, OJ, AU; CH, CJC, MH, NP, WF, JF.

3977A — —[Anr. ed.] *Printed and sold by Sam. Smith*, 1690. 8°. EC, P.

3978 —A free discourse against customary swearing. *By R. R. for Thomas Cockerill, sen^r and jun^r*, 1695. 8°. FULTON 197. L, O, C, EN, DT; CH, CU, MH, WF, Y, JF.

3979 —A free enquiry into the vulgarly receiv'd notion of nature. *By H. Clark, for John Taylor*, 1685/6. 8°. T.C.II 170. FULTON 170, L, O, C, EN, DT; CH, CN, LC, MH, NU, Y, JF.

3980 —General heads for the natural history of a country. *For John Taylor, and S. Holford*, 1692. 12°. T.C.II 428. FULTON 195. L, O, C, LCP, DT; BN, CH, CN, LC, MH, JF.

3981 —The general history of the air. *For Awnsham and John Churchill*, 1692. 4°. T.C.II 467. FULTON 194. L, O, C, LL, DT; BN, CLC, MH, MMO, Y, JF.

3981A —A general idea of the epitomy of the works of. *Printed* 1700. 8°. PL.

3982 [–] Good and solid reasons why a Protestant. *By H. C. for John Taylor*, 1688. 8°.* FULTON 177A. L, O, OC, MC, GK; CH, TU, Y, JF.

3983 [–] Greatness of mind, . . . the first part. *By Edward Jones, for John Taylor*, 1691. 9°. L, O, CK, CM, AU; CH, CN, NU, WF.

3984 [–] [An historical account?] of a degradation of gold. *By T. N. for Henry Herringham*, [1678]. 4°.* FULTON 136. L, LWL; Y.

3985 —Hydrostatical paradoxes. *Oxford, by William Hall, for Richard Davis*, 1666. 8°. MADAN 2738. FULTON 72. L, O, C, EN, DT; BN, CH, CJC, MH, WF, JF.

3986 [–] The martyrdom of Theodora. *By H. Clark, for John Taylor, and Christopher Skegnes*, 1687. 8°. T.C.II 193. FULTON 173. L, O, C, CT, DT; CH, CU, WF, HC, JF.

3987 — —[Anr. ed.] *By H. Clark, for John Taylor*, 1617. 8°. FULTON 173A. WU.

3988 —Medicina hydrostatica. *For Samuel Smith*, 1690. 8°. T.C.II 346. FULTON 189. L, O, C, E, DT; CH, MMO, NAM, WF, HC, JF.

3989 —Medicinal experiments. *For Sam. Smith*, 1692. sixes. T.C.II 403. FULTON 179. L, O, CE, LCP, LR; CH, CJC, MH, PL, WF, JF.

3990 — —Second edition. —, 1693. 3v. 12°. T.C.II 467. FULTON 180. L, O, C vol. 3, RCS 2 v., OJ v. 2; MMO 2 v., MMO 2 v., NAM, WF, JF v. 3.

3991 — —Third edition. *For Samuel Smith, and B. Walford*, 1696. 2v. 12°. FULTON 181. O, C, LR, CT, AU; CH, MH, NAM, WF, JF.

3992 — —, third and last volume. *For J. Taylor*, 1694. 12°. T.C.II 493. L, LCS, OC, CCA, GK; CH, MH, PL, HC.

3992A — —[Anr. ed.] —, 1698. 12°. T.C.III 43 FULTON 182. O, CT, GK; LC, JF.

3993 —Memoirs for the natural history of humane blood. *For Samuel Smith*, 1683/4. 8°. FULTON 146. L, O, C, LM, LCP; CH, MH, MMO, PL, JF.

3994 — [Anr. ed.] —, 1684. 8°. T.C.II 63. C, LCS, LM, EN, DT; BN, BBE, CLM, NAM, WF, JF.

3995 —New experiments, and observations, made upon the icy noctiluca. *By R.E. for B. Tooke*, 1681/2. 8°. T.C.I 486. FULTON 139. L, O, CK, GU, DT; BN, CH, LC, MH, PL, Y, JF.

3996 —New experiments and observations touching cold. *For John Crook*, 1665. 8°. FULTON 70. L, O, C, LCP, E; BN, CH, MH, PL, Y, JF.

3997 — —Second edition. *For Richard Davis*, 1683. 4°. FULTON 71. L, O, C, E, DT; CH, CU, MH, WF, Y, JF.

3998 —New experiments physico-mechanicall. *Oxford: by H. Hall, for Tho: Robinson*, 1660. 8°. MADAN 2484. FULTON 13. LT, O, CT, E, DT; CH, MH, PL, Y, HC, JF.

3999 — —Second edition. *Oxford, by H. Hall, for Tho: Robinson*, 1662. 4°. MADAN 2586. FULTON 14. L, O, CT, LPO, EN; CH, MH, WF, Y, JF.

4000 — —Third edition. *By Miles Flesher for Richard Davis*, 1682. 4°. T.C.II 7. FULTON 15. L, O, CCA, GK, DT; MMO, NC, PL, Y, JF.

4000A —New experiments to make the parts of fire and flame. *By William Godbid for Moses Pitt*, 1673. 8°. CCA, BAMB, BR; MH.

4001 —Noctiluca aeria. *Typis R.E. pro B. Tooke*, 1682. 12°. sixes. T.C.II 16. FULTON 140. O, GK; BN, TU, JF.

4002 —Notæ, etc. de atmosphaeris. *M. Pitt*, 1673. 12°.* BN.

4003 —Nova experimenta. *Oxoniæ, excudebat H. Hall, impensis Tho: Robinson*, 1661. 8°. MADAN 2547. FULTON 19. O, LCP, LR, CP, E; CH, MH, WF, JF.

4004 —Observationes de generatione. *M. Pitt*, 1676. 12°.* BN.

4005 [–] Occasional reflections. *By W. Wilson for H. Herringman*, 1665. 4°. FULTON 64. L, O, CM, GK, DT; CH, CN, MH, NU, WF, Y, JF.

4006 — —Second edition. *For Henry Herringman*, 1669. 8°. FULTON 65. L, O, C, GK, E; CLC, MH, PL, WF, JF.

4007 [–] Of a degradation of gold. *By T.N. for Henry Herringman*, 1678. 4°.* FULTON 136. L; WU, JF.

4008 —Of the cause of attraction by suction. *By William Godbid, to be sold by Moses Pitt*, 1674. 8°. L, O, C, OC, GK; MM, PL.

4009 [–] Of the high veneration man's intellect owes to God. *By M.F. for Richard Davis, in Oxford*, 1685. 8°. FULTON 152. L, O, C, GU, GK; BN, CH, MH, NU, WF, HC.

4010 —Of the imperfection of the chymist's doctrine. *By E. Flesher, for R. Davis in Oxford*, 1675. 8°. L, O, OC, CK; CJC, MBP, MH, JF.

4011 —Of the mechanical causes of chymical precipitation. *By E. Flesher, for R. Davis in Oxford*, 1675. 8°. L, O, C, OB, OC; CJC, MBP, MH, JF.

4012 —Of the mechanical origine of heat. *By E. Flesher, for R. Davis in Oxford*, 1675. 8°. L, O, C, CK, BR; CJC, MBP, MH, JF.

4013 —Of the reconcileableness of specifick medicines. *For Sam. Smith*, 1685. 8°. T.C.II 199. FULTON 166. L, O, C, E, DT; CH, CJC, MH, MMO, WF, JF.

4014 —The origine of formes and qualities. *Oxford, by H. Hall, for Ric: Davis*, 1666. 8°. MADAN 2739. FULTON 77. L, O, C, GK, EN; CH, PL, WF, Y, HC, JF.

4015 — —Second edition. —, 1667. 8°. MADAN 2765. FULTON 78. L, O, C, E, DT; BN, CH, CJC, MH, WF, Y, JF.

4016 —Origo formarum et qualitatum. *Oxoniæ, excudebat A. & L. Lichfield, impensis Ric. Davis*, 1660. 12°. FULTON 80. YM, GU; BN, PL, WU.

4017 —Paradoxa hydrostatica. *Oxonii, typis Henrici Hall, impensis Ri: Davis*, 1669. 12°. T.C.I 15. MADAN 2821. FULTON 73. L, OJ, C, P, GK; CJC, NC, WU, JF.

4018 [–] Reasons why a Protestant should not turn Papist. *By H. Clark, for John Taylor*, 1687. 4°.* FULTON 175. L, O, C, EN, DT; CH, MH, NU, WF, Y, JF.

4018A — —Third edition. —, 1688. 8°.* FULTON 177. OC; JF.

4019 [–] Reflections upon a theological distinction. *In the Savoy; by Edw. Jones, for John Taylor*, 1690. 8°.* L, O, C, CK; CH, CN, NU, WF, JF.

4020 —Reflections upon the hypothesis of alcali. *By E. Flesher, for R. Davis in Oxford*, 1675. 8°.* L, O, C, OC, CK; CJC, MBP, MH, JF.

4021 —The sceptical chymist. *By J. Cadwell for J. Crooke*, 1661. 8°. FULTON 33. L, O, CP, E, DT; CH, MH, NAE, Y, JF.

4022 [–] —[Anr. ed.] *Oxford, by Henry Hall for Ric. Davis, and B. Took*, 1680. 8°. T.C.I 387. MADAN 3261. FULTON 34. L, O, C, E, DT; CH, LC, MH, Y, JF.

4023 —Short memoirs for the natural experimental history of mineral waters. *For Samuel Smith*, 1684/5. 8°. T.C.II 124. FULTON 159. L, O, C, EN, DT; BN, CLC, LC, MH, MMO, WF, JF.

4024 [–] Some considerations about the reconcilableness of reason and religion. *By T.N. for H. Herringman*, 1675. 8°. T.C.I 197. L, O, CT, EN, GK; MH, NU, WF, HC, JF.

4025 —Some considerations touching the style of the H. Scriptures. *For Henry Herringman*, 1661. 8°. FULTON 41. LT, O, C, EN, DT; BN, CH, MH, NU, HC, JF.

4026 — —Second edition. —, 1663. 4°. FULTON 42. L, O, C, OB, DT; BN, CLC, CU, MH, WF, Y.

4027 — —Third edition. —, 1668. 8°. FULTON 43. O, CS, ELY, EN, GK; BN, MH, PL, WF.

4028 — —Fourth edition. —, 1675. 8°. FULTON 44. L, O, C, EN, DT; MH, MMO, NU, PL, WF, JF.

4029 [–] Some considerations touching the vsefvlnesse. *Oxford, by Hen. Hall, for Ric. Davis*, 1663. 4°. MADAN 2634. FULTON 50. L, O, LM, CP, GK; CH, LC, MMO, WF, HC, JF.

4030 — —Second edition. *Oxford, by Hen: Hall, for Ri: Davis*, 1664. 4°. MADAN 2655. FULTON 51. L, O, C, E, DT; CH, CN, LC, MH, NP, Y, JF.

4031 ——Second tome. *Oxford, by Henry Hall, for Ric. Davis*, 1671. 4°.* MADAN 2882. FULTON 53. L, O, C, GK, DT; CH, CN, MH, NP, JF.

4032 —Some motives and incentives to the love of God. *For Henry Herringman*, 1659. 8°. FULTON 1. L, O, OC, LWL, GK; CH, LC, MH, NU, WF, Y, JF.

4033 ——Second edition. —, 1661. 8°. FULTON 2. LT, O, C, CT, NPL; CLC, CN, NP, PL, WF, JF.

4034 ——Third edition. —, 1663. 8°. FULTON 3. L, O, C, CT, GK; CU, MH, TU, WF, JF.

4035 ——Fourth edition. —, 166*5*. 8°. FULTON 4. L, O, C, CM, GK; BN, MH, NAM, NP, PL, JF.

4036 ——Fifth edition. *Edinburgh, by George Swintoun & James Glen*, 1667. 8°. ALDIS 1830. D, E, EN, GK; JF.

4037 ——Fifth [English] edition. *For Henry Herringman*, 1670. 8°. FULTON 5. O, OC, CPE, ENC, GK; MHS, Y, JF.

4038 ——Sixth edition. *In the Savoy, by T. N. for Henry Herringman*, 1678. 8°. FULTON 6. L, O, C, EN, GK; MBA, PL, WF, JF.

4039 ——Seventh edition. *In the Savoy, by Edw. Jones, for Henry Herringman, and sold by Francis Saunders*, 1692. 8°. FULTON 7. L, O, OJ, GK; TU, Y, JF.

4040 ——"Seventh" edition. *In the Savoy: by Edw. Jones, for Henry Herringman, and sold by Thomas Bennet*, 1692. 8°. FULTON 7A. L, GK; MH, NC, WU, Y.

4040A ——"Seventh" edition. *In the Savoy, by Edw. Jones, for Henry Herringman, and sold by John Taylor*, 1692. 8°. FULTON 7B. O; WU, Y.

4040B ——"Seventh" edition. *In the Savoy, by Edw. Jones, for Henry Herringman, and sold by Thomas Horn*, 1692. 8°. FULTON 7C. O; WU, Y.

4041 ——Eighth edition. *In the Savoy: by Edw. Jones, for Henry Herringman; and sold by Thomas Bennet*, 1700. 8°. T.C.III 179. FULTON 8. L, C, OQ, GK; CH, PL, WF, Y, JF.

4042 —Some physico-theological considerations. *By T. N. for H. Herringman*, 1675. 8°.* L, O, C, OB, D; NPT, NU.

4043 [–] Some receipts of medicines. 1688. 12°.* L.

4044 [–] Specimen unum atque alterum. *Impensis H. Herringman*, 1661. 4°. O, OC.

4045 —Tentamen porologicum. *Impensis Samuelis Smith*, 1684. 8°. FULTON 150. L, LWL; WU.

4046 —Tentamina quædam physiologica. *Impensis H. Herringman*, 1661. 4°. FULTON 27. L, OC, CM, P, GK; BN, VH.

4047 ——Second edition. —, 1667. 4°. FULTON 28. GK; BN, JF.

4048 ——Third edition. —, 1668. 4°. FULTON 30. GK; CLC, MH, MMO.

4049 —Three tracts written by. *Oxford, by W. H. for Ric. Davis*, 1671. 8°. O, C, CCA; CH, WF.

4050 —Tractatus de qualitatibus rerum. *Impensis Ric. Davis*, 1672. 12°. FULTON 88. P, YM, GK; BN, PL, TU, JF.

4051 —Tractatus. In quibus continentur, I. suspiciones. *Typis Gulielmi Godbid, impensis Mosis Pitt*, 1676. 12°. T.C.I 291. FULTON 120. LCHS, YM, GK; BN, CJC, PL, TU, WF, JF.

4052 —Tractatus scriptia … ubi I. Mira æris. *Impensis Henrici Herringman*, 1670. 12°. FULTON 91. LWL; WSG.

4052A ——[Anr. ed.] —, 1671. 12°. FULTON 92. L, O, GK; BN, CLC, NAE, JF.

4053 —Tracts consisting of observations about the saltness of the sea. *By E. Flesher for R. Davis*, 1674. 8°. T.C.I 154. MADAN 3005. FULTON 113. L, O, C, EN, DT; BN, CH, CJC, MH, PL, WF, JF.

4053A ——Second edition. *Sold by S. Smith*, 1690. 8°. EC; PU, JF.

4054 —Tracts: containing I. Suspicions about some hidden qualities of the air. *By W. G. and are to be sold by M. Pitt*, 1674. 8°. T.C.I 198. FULTON 119. L, O, C, E, DT; BN, CH, LC, MH, PL, Y, JF.

4054A ——[Anr. ed.] —, 1675. 8°. FULTON 119A. O, LR; MH.

4055 ——Second edition. —, 1690. 8°. C.

4056 —Tracts, written by. *Oxford, by W. H. for Ric. Davis*, 1670. 8°. T.C.I 58. L, O, OB, OC; MH, Y, JF.

4057 ——[Anr. ed.] —, 1671. 8°. MADAN 2851. FULTON 83. O, C, AU, EN, DT; BN, CH, CN, LC, WF, HC, JF.

4058 ——"Second" edition. —, 1671. 8°. FULTON 84. O, OJ, GK; JF.

4059 —Tracts written by … of a discovery. *By T. N. for Henry Herringman*, 1671. 4°.* MADAN 2883. FULTON 94. L, O, C, LR, DT; CH, MH, RPJ, JF.

4060 Tracts written by … , containing new experiments. *For Richard Davis*, 1672. 8°. MADAN 2920.* FULTON 101. L, O, C, LCS, DT; BN, CH, MH, NP, TMO, Y, JF.

4061 ——[Anr. ed.] *For Richard Davis, in Oxon*, 1673. 8°. T.C.I 135. L, LCS, LR, OC; MH, NN, PL.

4062 Entry cancelled.

Boyle, Roger. *See also* Orrery, Roger Boyle, *earl of.*

4063 **Boyle, Roger,** *bp.* Inquisitio in fidem Christianorum hujus sæculi. *Dublini, typis Johan. Crook, & veneunt apud Samuel Dancer*, 1665. 8°. DIX 127. L, O, C, LW, DT; MH, WF, JF.

4064 —Summa theologiae Christianae. *Dublin, typis regiis*, 1681. 4°. DIX 183. O, C, DI, DM, DT; WF.

4065 **Boys, Edward.** Sixteen sermons. *By Richard Hodgkinson, for William Oliver, in Norwich*, 1672. 4°. T.C.I 115. L, C, CE, NPL; CH, CLC, WF.

4065A ——[Anr. ed.] *By B. W.*, 1687. 4°. LSC.

4065B **Boys, John.** Remains. *For Humphrey Robinson*, 1662. 4°. PL.

4066 —Veteris interpretis cum Beza. *Typis T. Roycroft, impensis R. Beaumont*, 1655. 8°. L, C, OC, E, DT; BN, CH, CLC, Y.

4066A ——[Anr. ed.] *Typis T. Roycroft, impensis R. Littlebury*, 1655. 8°. CPE.

4067 **Boys, William.** The narrative of. *For Dorman Newman*, 1680. fol.* T.C.I 404. L, O, C, ES; CH, CN, NU, WF, Y.

4068 The boys whipt home. colop: *For Lu. Smith*, 1681. brs. L, O; CH, MH, TU, WF, Y.

Boys-Robert. *See* Boisrobert.

4069 [**Boyse, Joseph.**] The case of the dissenting Protestants of Ireland. [*Dublin*, 1695]. fol.* DIX 267. O, DML, DT.

4070 [–] The case of the Protestant dissenters in Ireland. *Dublin*, 1695. fol.* DIX 267. O, DT.

4071 —Great news from the camp before Limrick [sic]. *For Tho. Parkhurst, to be sold by Rich. Baldwin*, 1690. brs. L, MC.

4072 —Remarks on a late discourse. *For J. Lawrence, and J. Dunton*, 1694. 8°. T.C.II 508. L, O, C, OB, EN; CLC, NU, Y.

4073 — —[Anr. ed.] [*Dublin, for Eliphal Dobson, Matthew Gun, & Patrick Campbell*], 1694. DIX 262. EN, GU, DI, DM, DT; WF.

4074 —Sacramental hymns. *Dublin, for Matthew Gunn*, 1693. 8°. DIX 257. L, O, DW.

4075 — —[Anr. ed.] *Dublin, and reprinted at London by Thomas Parkhurst*, 1693. 8°. T.C.II 463. L, O, C, LCL, OB; CN, NU.

4076 —A sermon preach't . . . Jan. 6, 1697/8. *Dublin, by J. B. & S. P.*, 1698. 4°.* DIX 303. C, DI, DT.

4077 —The sin and danger of quenching the spirit. *For Thomas Parkhurst* 1691. 4°.* T.C.II 345. L, O, C, LW, DT; MH, NU, WF.

4078 [–] Some impartial reflections on D. Manby's considerations. *Dublin, by Andrew Crook and Samuel Helsham*, 1697. 4°. DIX 225. O, CD, DI, DT; WF.

4078A —Some remarkable passages in the holy life . . . of . . . E. French. *For T. Parkhurst; and J. Robinson*, 1693. 8°. T.C.II 462. L, O,P; CH, Y.

4079 —Two sermons preach't. *Dublin, for William Norman, Eliphal Dobson, and Patrick Campbell*, 1695. 4°. DIX 268. L, O, C, DI, DT; CH, MH.

4080 [–] A vindication of the remarks on the Bishop of Derry's discourse. *For John Lawrence*, 1695. 8°. T.C.II 554. L, O, CS, LW; NU.

4081 [–] —[Anr. ed.] *Dublin*, 1695. 4°. DIX 268. O, DI, DM, DT.

4082 —A vindication of the reverend Mr. Alexander Osborn. *For Tho. Parkhurst, Tho. Cockerill, John Lawrence, and John Dunton*, 1690. 4°.* T.C.II 303. L, O, C, LVF, EN; MH, NC, PL, WF, Y.

4083 —Vindiciæ Calvanisticæ. *Dublin, A. Crook & S. Helsham*, 1688. 4°. DIX 231. LLP, LW, OE, BAMB, DM.

4084 [–] Vox populi: or, the sense of the sober lay-men. *For Randall Taylor*, 1690. 4°. T.C.II 303. L, LVF, LM, HH, DT; CH, CN, MH, NU, WF, Y.

4085 **Br, D.** Epitaph de Charles Second. *A Londres chez I. de Beaulieu*, 1685. brs. MH.

4086 —P. M. S. Heneagii, Nottinghamiæ comitis . . . epitaphium. [*London*, 1682.] brs. L, O, OC; CH.

Br., J. Jesuite counter mind. 1679. *See* Bradshaw, John.

4087 **Brabourne, Theophilus.** An answer to Mr. Cawdry's two books *For M. Franklin, Sold Norwich*. 1654. 12°. LW.

4088 — —[Anr. ed.] *Printed*, 1659. 8° LW, OC.

4089 —A confutation of the Dutch-Arminian tenent. *By Will. Bentley*, 1651. 12°. O, LCL; NPT.

4090 —A defence of the kings authority. *For the author, to be sold by William Nowell, in Norwich*, 1660. 4°.* O, HH.

4091 — —Second edition. —, 1660. 4°.* O; MH, NU, Y.

4092 —God save the king, and prosper him. *For the author, to be sold in London and by Wm. Nowell, in Norwich*, 1660. 4°.* LT, O.

4093 —The humble petition of. [*London*], *for the author*, 1661. 4°.* LT, SP; CLC, MH, MIU.

4094 —Of the lawfulness [sic] of the oath of allegiance. [*London*], *for the author*, 1661. 4°.* LT, O, LF.

4094A —Of the Sabbath day. 1660. 8°. LW.

4095 —A reply to Mr. Collings Provocator provocatus. *For the author*, 1654. 8°. O, CE.

4096 —The second part of the change of church-discipline. *For the author*, 1654. 4°. LT, O, CT, EN.

4097 [–] Svndry particulars concerning bishops. [*London*], *for the author, to be sold by William Nowell in Norwich*, 1661. 4°.* O, LCL, MH, WF.

4098 **Brachet de la Militière, Théophile.** The victory of truth. *Printed at the Hague*, 1653. 8°. L, O, C, OC, DC; CH, CN, NU, CU. Y.

4099 — —Second edition. —, 1654. 8°. L, O, CK, P, SC; NU, TU, WF.

4100 **B[raddocke], J[ohn].** The doctrine of the fathers and schools consider'd. Pt. 1. *For W. Rogers*, 1695. 4°. T.C.II 556. L, O, C, MR, EN; MBA, NU, WF, Y.

4101 **Braddon, Lawrence.** Essex's innocency and honour vindicated. *For the author*, 1690. 4°. L, O, C, EN, DT; CH, CN, LC, MH, NU, Y.

4102 —Murther will out. [*London*, 1692.] cap., fol.* L, LL, EC, SP; CN, NC, PL, WF, Y.

4103 **Bradford, John.** Catalogus . . . librorum. [*London*, 1686.] 4°.* L O, CS, HH; MH.

4104 —A fruitfull treatise full of heavenly consolation. *Edinburgh*, 1641. 8°. ALDIS 991. EN.

4105 —The godly exhortation of. *For T. Passinger*, 1683. 8°.* O.

4106 —The good old way. *Oxford, by L. Lichfield*, 1652. 8°. MADAN 2191. O; IAU, MH.

4107 **Bradford, Samuel, *bp*.** Apostate men. *For Tho. Parkhurst*, 1699. 4°.* L, O, C, CT, CE; CH, CN, NU, WF, Y.

4108 —The credibility of the Christian revelation. *For Tho. Parkhurst*, 1700. 4°. T.C.III 197. L, O, CS, GU, DT; CH, CU, MH, NU, WF.

4109 —The description and the benefits of a regular education. *By William Redmayne*, 1700. 4°.* L, EC, E; WF.

4110 —The excellency of the Christian revelation, . . . September the 4th, 1699. *For Tho. Parkhurst*, 1699. 4°.* L, O, C, CT, EC; CH, CLC, CN, TU, WF, Y.

4111 —The excellency of the Christian revelation, . . . November the 6th. 1699. *For Tho. Parkhurst*, 1699. 4°.* L, O, C, CT, EC; CH, CN, TU, WF, Y.

4112 —The excellency of the Christian revelation, as it prosposeth . . . October the 2d. 1699. *By Tho. Snowden, for Tho. Parkhurst*, 1699. 4°.* L, O, C, CT, EC; CH, CN, TU, WF, Y.

4113 —The excellency of the Christian revelation, as it removes . . . April the 3rd, 1699. *For Tho. Parkhurst*, 1699. 4°.* L, O, C, CT, EC; CH, CN, NU, WF, Y.

4114 —The excellency of the Christian revelation, as it teacheth . . . May the 1st, 1699. *For Tho. Parkhurst,* 1699. 4°.* L, O, C, OC, CT; CH, CN, NC, WF, Y.

4115 —The imperfect promulgation. *For Tho. Parkhurst,* 1700. 4°.* L, O, C, OCC, EC; CH, TU, NU, WF, Y.

4116 —The nature of that salvation. *For Tho. Parkhurst,* 1699. 4°.* L, O, C, CT, EC; CH, CN, NU, WF, Y.

4117 —A perswasive to peace and vnity. *For Brab. Aylmer,* 1698. 4°.* L, OC, CS, EC; CH, CN, MBA, NU, WF.

4118 —The qualifications requisite. *For Tho. Parkhurst,* 1699. 4°.* L, O, C, CS, EC; CH, CN, MH, NU, WF, Y.

4119 —A sermon preach'd . . . November 5. 1696. *For B. Aylmer,* 1697. 4°.* T.C.II 600. L, O, LSC, CSSX, EC; CH, CN, MBA, WF, Y.

4120 —A sermon preach'd . . . Octob. 4. 1697. *For B. Aylmer,* 1697. 8°. T.C.III 37. L, OC, CM, LW, EC; CH, CLC, MH, NU.

4121 —A sermon preached before the king . . . January 30th 1698/9. *By J. L. for Matt. Wotton,* 1699. 4°.* T.C.III 106. L, O, CS, CT, EC; CH, CN, NU, WF, Y.

4122 —A sermon preach'd . . . September the 28th, 1700. *For Matt. Wotton,* 1700. 4°. T.C.III 211. L, O, CT, EC; CN, WF.

4123 **Bradford, William.** Proposals for the printing of a large Bible. [*Philadelphia: by William Bradford,* 1688.] brs. EVANS 441. PHS.

4123A **Bradley, Christopher.** The dignitie and dutie of the ministers. *York, by Stephen Bulkley, for Francis Mawbarne,* 1667. 4°. WCA.

4124 —The eye of faith. *York, by Stephen Bulkley, to be sold by Francis Mawbarne,* 1666. 4°.* L; Y.

4125 **Bradley, John.** An impartial view of the truth of Christianity. *By W. Downing, for Michael Johnson: to be sold by R. Clavel, S. Smith, and B. Walford, T. Leigh, and D. Midwinter, and J. Back,* 1699. 8°. T.C.III 123. L, O, C, EN, DT; LC, NU, WF, Y.

[**Bradley, Richard.**] Concerning the judgements. [*n.p.,* 166–?] *See* Baker, Richard.

[–] How the love of God. [*n.p.,* 166–?] *See* Baker, Richard.

[–] Strength and power of God. [*n.p.,* 1660?] *See* Baker, Richard.

4125A —This is foɪ all you the inhabitants of Whitwell to consider. [*London,* 1660] 4°.* LF, BBN; PH.

4125B **Bradley, Samuel.** The afflicted and retired mans meditations. [*London*], *for the author,* 1663. 4°. LSC; Y.

4126 —The cause of the innocent pleaded. *For the author,* 1664. 4°. L.

4127 **Bradley, Thomas.** Appello Cæsarem, or, an appeal. *York, by Alice Broad,* 1661. 8°.* L.

4128 —At the metropoliticall visitation. A sermon. *Yorke: by Alice Broade,* 1663. 4°.* HAILSTONE.

4129 —Cesar's due. *Yorke: by Alice Broade, to be sold by Richard Lambert,* 1663. 4°.* L, C, YM; WF, Y.

4130 —Comfort from the cradle. *Oxford, by Henry Hall,* 1650[1]. 4°. MADAN 2033. LT, O, OME, DT; CH, PU, WF, Y.

4131 —Elijah's epitaph. *York, by Stephen Bulkley, to be sold by Francis Mawbarne,* 1670. 4°. L, O, LW.

4132 —Elijah's nunc dimittis. *York, by Stephen Bulkley,* 1669. 4°. L, O, YM; Y.

4133 ——[Anr. ed.] *York: by Stephen Bulkley, to be sold by Francis Mawbarne,* 1670. 8°. YM.

4134 —Nosce te ipsum. *York: by Stephen Bulkley, to be sold by Richard Lambert,* 1668. 4°. L, O, YM, SP; Y.

4135 —A præsent [sic] for Caesar. *For the author, to be sold by Stephen and Thomas Lewis,* [1658]. 8°. L, O.

4135A ——[Anr. ed.] *F.L.,* [1657?] 8°. MH.

4136 —The second Adam. *York: by Stephen Bulkley, to be sold by Francis Mawbarne,* 1663. 4°.* L, WCA, YM; NU.

4137 —A sermon ad clerum. *Yorke: by Stephen Bulkley, to be sold by Francis Mawbarne,* 1663. 4°.* L, YM; NU.

4137A —A sermon preach't . . . 23 of Aprill last. *Yorke, by Alice Broade,* 1661. 4°.* YM; Y.

4138 —A sermon preached . . . thirtieth day of March, 1663. *Yorke: by Alice Broade,* 1663. 4°. L, O, YM; NU.

4139 **Bradmore, Mrs. Sarah.** Prophecy of the wonders. *By S. J.,* 1686. fol. O.

4139A **Bradshaw, Ellis.** A compendious answer to a book called A brief survey. *By H. Hills, to be sold by T. Brewster,* 1652. 4°.* MRL; IU.

4140 —The conviction of James Naylor. *By M. S. for Lodowicke Lloyd,* 1656. 4°. O, CT, LF, SC; PSC.

4141 —A cordial-mediator. *Printed, and are to be sold by Lodowick Lloyd, also by Henry Crips, and by Thomas Brewster,* 1658. 4°.* O, OM; MH.

4142 —A dialogue between the devil & Prince Rupert. *For T. B.,* [1649]. 4°.* LT; MH, WF.

4143 —Downfal of tythes no sacriledge. *For H. Cripps, and L. Lloyd,* 1653. 4°.* LT.

4144 —An husbandmans harrow. *For the author,* 1649. 4°. L, DT; CH, NU.

4145 ——[Anr. ed.] *For E. B. to be sold by Giles Calvert,* 1649. 4°. LT.

4146 —A new and cleer discovery. *By Gartrude Dawson for Thomas Brewster,* 1649. 4°.* LT, O, CT.

4147 —The Quakers quaking principles examined. *For Lodowicke Lloyd,* 1656. 4°.* LT, O, LF; NU.

4148 —The Quakers' vvhitest divell unvailed. [*n.p.*], *printed,* 1654. 4°.* LF; CLC, NU, PH, PSC.

4149 —A true relation of the strange apparitions seen in the air. *For Tho. Brewster, and Gregory Moule,* 1650. 4°.* LT, LF; CH, MH.

4150 —A vveek-daies lecture. *By Gar: Dawson for Tho: Brewster and Gr: Moule,* 1649. 4°.* LT, DT; CH.

4151 **Bradshaw, James.** A sleepy spouse of Christ awaked. *For Samuel Crouch,* 1667. 8°. CLC, MH.

4151A ——[Anr. ed.]—1667. 8°. T.C.I 265. LW, E; CH.

4151B **Bradshaw, John.** Anastasis Britannica & Hibernica, Great Britain. *For John Rothwell,* 1660. 4°.* L; MWA, Y.

4152 —Death disarmed. *By Richard Constable, for Henry Shepheard,* 1650. 4°.* LT, LW, DT; MU, MWA, NU.

4152A —Discourse of the nature and obligation of oaths. 1662. 4°. O.

4152B —The Jesuite countermind. *Printed*, 1679. 4°.* T.C.I 361. O, LIL, CS; CH, MH, NU, PL, Y.

4153 —The last will and testament of. *Printed*, 1659. 4°.* O, CE; CH, WF, Y.

4154 —A moderate short discourse concerning ... conscience. *By John Best for Andrew Crook*, [1663]. 4°.* L, O, CE, OC; V, WF.

4155 —A true relation of the proceedings, examination, tryal and horrid murder of Col. Eusebius Andrewe. *For Daniel Pakeman*, 1660. 4°. L, O; CH, Y.

4156 **Bradshaw, William.** A discourse of the sinne against the Holy Ghost. *By R. H. for Iohn Rothwell*, 1649. 12°. LSC; NU.

4157 —Dissertatio de justificationis doctrina. *Oxonii, typis Gulielmi Hall, impensis Rob. Blagrave*, 1658. 12°. MADAN 2379, L, O, OC, P SC; CLC.

4158 [–] English Puritanisme. [*London*], *printed*, 1641. 4°.* LT, O, C, LW, EN; MB, MIU, PL, WF.

4159 —A preparation. Eleventh edition. *By Iohn Beale*, 1643. 12°. LSC, P, D.

4160 [–] A protestation of the kings supreamacie. *For R. Royston*, 1647. 4°.* LT, O, C, LSC, MR; CH, CLC, MU, NU.

4161 —Several treatises of worship. [*London*], *printed for Cambridge and Oxford, to be sold* [*London*], 1660. 4°. LT, O, C, EN, DT; CH, MH, NU, WF, Y.

4162 ——[Anr. ed.] *Printed*, 1660. 4°. O, EN; MH, NPT, NU, WF.

4162A —A treatise of justification. *By W. H. for E. Brewster and G. Sawbridge*, 1652. 12°. LCL, CM, CSSX; CH, CLC.

4163 Bradshaw's ghost; a poem: ... 1660. [*London*, 1660.] cap., fol.* L, C, LG, HH; CH, MBA, MH, NU, TU, Y.

4164 Bradshaw's ghost: being a dialogue. [*London*], *printed*, 1659. 4°.* L, O, C, OC, HH; CH, CN, MH, MIU, Y.

4165 —Third edition. —, 1659. 4°.* CH, CN, MH, MIU, NN. Bradshaw's ultimum vale. *Oxon*, 1660. *See* O., J.

4166 **Bradstreet, Anne Dudley.** Several poems. Second edition. *Boston, by John Foster*, 1678. 8°. EVANS 244. L; CH, MH, MHS, MWA, RPJ, Y.

4167 [–] The truth muse lately sprung up. *For Stephen Bowtell*, 1650. 8°. LT, CT; CH, LC, MB, NN, RPJ, Y.

4168 **Bradwill, J.** The young-man's warning piece. [*London*], *for P. Brooksby*, 1682. brs. L.

4169 **Brady, Nicholas.** Church-musick vindicated. *For Joseph Wilde*, 1697. 4°.* T.C.III 37. L, O, C, EN, DT; CH, LC, NPT, WF, Y.

4170 [–] The rape: or the innocent imposters. *For F. Saunders*, 1692. 4°. T.C.II 411. L, O; CH, WF, Y.

4171 [–] —[Anr. ed.] *For R. Bentley*, 1692. 4°. O, LVF, OW, EN, DT; CH, CN, LC, NC, WF, Y.

4172 [–] —[Anr. ed.] *For Samuel Crouch*, 1692. 4°. O; LC, WF, Y.

4173 [–] —[Anr. ed.] *For F. Bennet*, 1692. 4°. NP, PU, WF, Y.

4174 —A sermon preached ... 26th of November, 1691. *For Samuel Crouch*, 1692. 4°.* T.C.II 392. L, O, CCA, LFEA; TU, WF.

4175 —A sermon preached before the king ... 23d day of October, 1692. *For S. Crouch*, 1693. 4°.* L, O, C; CH, NU, WF, Y.

4176 —A sermon preached ... November 24. 1692. *For James Knapton*, 1693. 4°.* T.C.II 462. L, O, C, LVD; NP, TU.

4177 —A sermon preached ... June 30th, 1694. *For Rich. Parker*, 1694. 4°.* L, O, C; CH, CN, MM, WF, Y.

4178 —A sermon preached ... March 3. 1694/5. *For Richard Parker*, 1695. 4°.* L, O, CCA, LG, EC; CH, MH, NU, WF, Y.

4179 —A sermon preach'd ... Sept. 12. 1695. *For Richard Parker*, 1695. 4°.* L, O, CT, LG.

4180 —A sermon preached ... 1st of March, 1695/6. *For Richard Parker*, 1696. 8°.* C, CCA, CT, EC; CH, WF, Y.

4181 —A sermon preached ... 29th of June, 1696. *For Rich. Parker*, 1696. 4°.* L, O, CS, LG; CH.

4182 —A sermon preach'd ... April the 5. 1699. *For Joseph Wild*, 1699. 4°.* L; CH, WF.

4183 —A song for new-yeares-day. [*London*], *for R. Baldwin*, 1692. brs. L, LG.

4184 —A thanksgiving-sermon ... Decemb. the 2d. 1697. *By J. B. for Joseph Wilde*, 1697. 4°.* L, O, C, CT, DT; CH, CLC, NU, WF.

4185 [–] 'Tis nature's voice. [*London*], *Tho: Cross*, [1693?]. brs. L.

4186 **Brady, Robert.** A complete history of England. *In the Savoy: by Tho. Newcomb for Samuel Lowndes*, 1685. fol. T.C.II 144. L, O, C, EN, DT; CH, CN, LC, MH, TU, Y.

4187 —A continuation of the complete history of England. *In the Savoy, by Edward Jones for Sam. Lowndes, and John Churchill*, 1700. fol. T.C.III 153. L, O, CT, EN, DT; CH, CN, LC, MBP, MH, Y.

4187A ——[Anr. ed.] —, *and Awnsham and John Churchill*, 1700. fol. OC, CM, CS; MIU, PL.

4188 [–] A full and clear answer to a book, written by William Petit esquire, entituled, The rights of the commons asserted. *In the Savoy, by T. N. for S. Lowndes*, 1681. 16°. L, O, P, EN, DT; CH, MH, MIU, NN, Y.

4189 [–] A full and clear answer to a book, written by William Petit esq; *printed. For Samuel Lowndes*, 1681. 8°. L, O, C, OC, CT; CH, CN, MH, NU, TU, WF.

4190 [–] A full answer to all the particulars. *In the Savoy, by T. N. for S. Lowndes*, 1684. fol. LWL; CH, LC, NC, NN.

4191 [–] The great point of succession discussed. *For H. Rodes*, 1681. fol.* T.C.I 440. L, C, LVF, HH, EN; CH, CN, LC, TU, WF, Y.

4192 —An historical treatise of cities, and burghs. *For Samuel Lowndes*, 1690. fol. L, O, CK, CS, DT; LC, MHL, RPJ, WF, Y.

4193 [–] An inquiry into the remarkable instances of history. [*London*, 1690?] cap., 4°.* L, CT, MR, AU, EN; CH, MH, MIU, WF, Y.

4194 —An introduction to the old English history. *By Tho. Newcomb for Samuel Lowndes*, 1684. fol. T.C.II 83. L, O, C, EN, DT; CH, LC, MH, NC, WSC, Y.

4195 [–] A true and exact history of the succession of the crown. *For Cave Pulleyn*, 1681. fol.* T.C.I 450. L, O, CS, LL, HH; CH, CN, MH, WF, Y.

4196 Entry cancelled.

4197 The braggadocia souldier. [*London*], *for J.L.*, 1647. brs. LT.

4198 The bragadocio; or, the bawd turn'd Puritan. *For Richard Baldwin*, 1691. 4°. T.C.II 347. L, O, CS, EN; CH, CN, MH, TU, WF, Y.

4199 **Bragge, Francis.** A minister's counsel. *For R. Wellington*, 1699. 8°. T.C.III 120. L, O, CS, BP, RPL; CLC, NC, WF.

4200 —The passion of Our Saviour. *Sold by John Stuart*, [1694?] 8°. L; MH, WF.

4201 —Practical discourses. *For S. Manship*, 1694. 8°. T.C.II 500. L, C, ENC; CLC, NN, WF.

4202 **Bragge, Robert.** A cry for labourers in God's harvest. *Printed, and are to be sold by John Hancock senior and junior*, 1674. 4°.* T.C.I 168. L, O; CH, CN, MH, NU, WF, Y.

4203 —The life and death of the godly man . . . Thomas Wadsworth. *For Joseph Collier*, 1676. 4°.* L, O, LG, LW; CLC, MB, WF, Y.

4204 — —[Anr. ed.] *For Dorman Newman*, 1677. 8°.* L, LM, WCP, OCC; NU.

4205 [**Brague, Thomas.**] An end of one wonder. *Printed* 1651. 4°.* Y.

      [**Braidley, Margaret.**] Certain papers. [*London*, 1655.] *See* Taylor, Christopher.

4206 **Braithwait, John.** The ministers of England. *For Robert Wilson*, 1660. 4°. L, O, CT, LF, BBN; IE, PH, PSC.

4207 — —A serious meditation upon the dealings of God, [*London*, 1660]. cap., 4°.* L, O, LF, BBN; IE, MH, PH, WF, Y.

4208 —To all those that observe dayes. *For Robert Wilson*, 1660. brs. LF, BBN; CH, MH, PH, PSC.

      Brakenbury, Samuel. 1667. An almanack. Cambridge [Mass.], 1667. *See* Almanacs.

4209 **Bralesford, Humphrey.** The poor man's help. *For R. Clavell*, 1689. 8°. L, O, CT; WF.

      Bramble berry. 1643. *See* L., W.

4210 **Bramhall, John, abp.** The works. *Dublin, at His Majesty's printing-house*, 1676. fol. T.C.I 248. DIX 157. L, O, C, E, DT; MH, NU, PBL, WF, Y.

4211 — —Second edition. *Dublin, by Benjamin Tooke*, 1677. fol. DIX 159. L, O, C, EN, DM; CH, CLC, CN, MH, NC.

4212 —An answer to a letter of inquiry. *For Nath. Ranew, and J. Robinson*, 1671. 8°. L, O, C, LL, EN; CLC, CN, MH, TU, WF, Y.

4213 —An answer to Monsieur de La Militiere. *Hague, printed*, 1653. 12°. LT, O, C, LW, YM; CH, CN, NU, TU, WF, Y.

      [–] Answer to two letters. 1673. *See* Eachard, John.

4214 —Castigations of Mr. Hobbes. *By E. T. for J. Crook*, 1657. 8°. O, C, OC, DT; MH, NU.

4215 — —[Anr. ed.] —, 1658. 8°. LT, O, C, YM, EN; CH, CN, MH, NU, WF, Y.

4216 —The consecration and succession, of Protestant bishops. *Gravenhagh, by John Ramzey*, 1658. 8°. L, O; CH, MH, NU, WF, Y.

4217 — —[Anr. ed.] *For John Crook*, 1664. 8°. LW, CPE, CS, DT; CLC, WF.

4218 —A defence of true liberty. *For John Crook*, 1655. 8°. LT, O, C, EN, DT; CH, CU, MH, NU, Y.

4219 —Bramhall and Hobbes's discourses on liberty. 1656. 4°. LW.

4220 —A fair warning for England to take heed. [*London?* 1661.] 4°.* L, O, CCA, CT, HH; NN, Y.

4221 [–] Fair warning, or, the burnt child dreads the fire. [*n.p.*, 1649?] cap., fol.* L, O, C, MR, EN; CH, CN, TU, WF, Y.

4222 [–] A fair warning, to take heed. [*London*], *printed*, 1649. 32pp. 4°.* LT, O, CS, CT, DT; CH, MH, NN, NU, Y.

4223 — —[Anr. ed.] —, 1649. 36 pp. 4°.* LT, O, CE, MR, EN; CH, MH, NU, WF, Y.

4224 [–] [Anr. ed.] *Hague*, 1659. 8°. O.

4225 [–] —[Anr. ed.] [*London*] *sold by Thomas Parkhurst*, 1674. 4°. O, C, CT; CN, MM.

      [–] History of the English & Scotch. *Villa Franca*, 1659. *See* DuMoulin, Pierre.

4226 —A just vindication of the Church of England. *For John Crook*, 1654. 8°. L, O, C, E, ENC; CH, MH, NU, WF, Y.

4227 — —[Anr. ed.] *By J. C. for John Crooke*, 1661. 8°. O, LW, SC, SP; NU.

4228 —A replication to the bishop of Chalcedon. *By R. H. for John Crook*, 1656. 8°. L, O, CT, EN, DT; MH, NGT, NU, WF, Y.

4228A —The right way to safety. *Dublin, by John Crook: to be sold by John North*, 1661. 4°.* O, CS; WF.

4229 —Ρομφαια διστομος 'οξεια, or, the Church of England defended. *Printed at the Hague, and published at London*, 1658. 8°. L, OC, YM; WF.

4230 — —[Anr. ed.] —, 1659. 8°. L, O, C, DC, DT; NU, WF, Y.

4231 Entry cancelled.

4232 —Schisme guarded. *Gravenhagh, by John Ramzey*, 1658. 8°. L, O, SC, YM; CLC, CN, MH, NU, WF, Y.

4233 [–] A sermon preached . . . June 30. 1643. *Printed at York by Stephen Bulkley*, 1643. 4°.* L, YM; MH.

4234 —A sermon, preached . . . January, 28. 1643. *Printed at York by Stephen Bulkley*, 1643[4]. 4°.* L, O, CJ.

4235 —A sermon preached at Dublin upon the 23 of Aprill, 1661. *Dublin, by William Bladen*, 1661. 4°. DIX 111. C, LW, DT.

4236 [–] The serpent salve. [*n.p.*], *printed*, 1643. 4°. O, C, YM; CLC, NU, WF.

4236A — —[Anr. ed.] *York, Stephen Bulkley*, 1643. 4°. YM.

4236B —Three treatises. *Hagh, by S. Brown*, 1661. 4°. LW.

4237 —Bishop Bramhall's vindication of himself. *By A. C. for James Collins*, 1672. 8°. L, O, C, AU, DT; CLC, MH, NU, WF, Y.

4238 **Bramhall, William.** The loyal prophet. *York*, 1668. 8°. CT, YM.

4239 **Bramley, David.** Christs result of his Fathers pleasure. [*London*], *printed*, 1647. 4°.* LT, DT; CH.

4240 —The preacher's plea. [*London*], *printed*, 1647. 4°.* LT, CS, HH, DT; NHC.

4241 **Bramstone, John.** Fifteen loyal queries. *By G. Horton,* 1660. 4°.* LT, O; CH, MIU.

4242 **Bramston, William.** The necessity of a present repentance. *By John Leake, for William Keblewhite,* 1695. 4°.* T.C.II 546. C; NU, Y.

4243 —A sermon, preached at the opening of the lecture. *For R. Clavell,* 1647. 4°.* T.C.III 35. L, O, C, CT, DT; CH, CLC, NU.

Branch of Quakerism. 1676. *See* Cheney; John.

4244 **B[rancker], T[homas].** Doctrinæ sphæricæ adumbratio. *Oxoniæ, excudebat H: Hall, impensis J. Adams,* 1662. brs. MADAN 2587. O.

4245 Entry cancelled.

4246 **Brand, Adam.** A journal of an embassy . . . into China. *For D. Brown; and T. Goodwin,* 1698. 8°. L, O, LW, LWL; CN, CSU, NC, WF, Y.

Brandenburg, elector. *See* Frederick III.

4247 [**Brandon, John, Gent.**] The nevv army regulated. *By John Hammond,* 1645. 4°.* LT, O, DT; PL.

4248 —The Oxonian Antippodes. *For Richard Lounds,* 1644. 4°.* MADAN 1531. LT, O, CT, BAMB, DT; CH, CN, NU, WF, Y.

4249 [–] The reformed army. *For J. B.,* 1645. 4°.* LT, DT.

4249A [**Brandon, John.**] Fifty queries. *For Nevil Simmons, and Jonathan Robinson,* 1675. 8°.* T.C.I 220. LW; WF.

4249B —A form of sound words. *For Jonathan Robinson,* 1682. 8°. T.C.I. 470. CT; MH.

4250 —Happiness at hand. 1687. 4°. L, AU.

4251 —Τὸ πῦρ τὸ αἰώνιον: or, everlasting fire. *For Henry Brome,* 1678. 4°. T.C.I 287. L, O, C, YM, E; CH, NHC, NPT, NU, WF.

4252 **Brandon, Richard.** The confession of. [*London*], *printed,* 1649. 4°.* LT; CH, MH, WF.

4253 —A dialogue; or a dispute between the late hangman and death. [*London,* 1649.] brs. LT.

4254 —The last will and testament of. [*London*], 1649. 4°.* LT, O; WF, Y.

Brandy-wine. [n.p.], 1652. *See* W., J.

4255 **Brasse, Samuel.** A ship of arms. *Printed,* 1653. 8°. MH.

4256 [**Brathwaite, Richard.**] Astraea's teares. An elegie. *By T. H. for Philip Nevil,* 1641. 8°. L, O, LU, YM; CH, MH, WCL, WF, Y.

4257 —Capitall hereticks. *For William Shears,* 1659. 8°. O; NU.

4258 [–] The captive-captain. *By J. Grismond,* 1665. 8°. L.

4259 [–] The chimneys scuffle. *Printed,* 1662. 4°.* L, O, OC, EN; CH, CU, MH, TU, WF, Y.

4260 [–] A comment upon the two tales of . . . Chaucer. *By W. Godbid and are to be sold by Robert Crofts,* 1665. 8°. L, O, CT, LG, OB; CH, CN, LC, MH, WCL, Y.

4260A [–] —[Anr. ed.] *By W. Godbid, and are to be sold by Robert Clavell,* 1665. 8°. O; LC, MH.

4260B [–] —[Anr. ed.] *By W. Godbid, and are to be sold by Peter Dring,* 1655, 8°. CPE, CS; MH, PL.

4261 [–] The devills white boyes. *For R. S. Octob. 26.* 1644. 4°.* LT; CLC, TU, Y.

4262 —The English gentleman and the English gentlevvoman. Third edition. *By John Dawson,* 1641. fol. L, O, C, LVF, EN; CH, CN, LC, MH, NC, TU, Y.

4263 Entry cancelled.

4264 —The history of moderation. *For Tho. Parkhurst,* 1669. 8°. T.C.I 20. L, O, CT, SP; CLC, CN, MH, PL.

4265 —History surveyed in a brief epitome. *For J. E. and are to be sold by Nathanael Webb and William Grantham,* 1651. 4°. L; MH, NP.

4266 — —[Anr. ed.] *By J. E. for Nathaniel Webb and William Grantham,* 1652. 4°. L.

4267 [–] The honest ghost. *By Ric. Hodgkinsonne,* 1658. 8°. L, O, LU, LVD; CH, CU, MH, WC, WF, Y.

4268 —Lignum vitæ. Libellvs. *Excudebat Joh: Grismond,* 1658. 8°. LT, O, P; CH, IU, MH, WCL.

4269 [–] Mercurivs Britannicus judicialis. [*London,* 1641?] 4°.* LT, C, WCA; CH, MH, WF, Y.

4269A — —Second edition. [–1641] 4°.* CN, PU, WF.

4270 [–] Mercurius Britanicus, or the English intelligencer. A tragic-comedy. [*London*], *printed in the yeare,* 1641. 4°.* LT, O, C, LVD, OW; CH, CN, MH, TU, WF, Y.

4271 Entry cancelled.

4272 —A mustur roll of the evill angels. *For William Sheers,* 1655. 12°. LT, DC; CH, NU.

4273 [–] Panthalia: or the royal romance. *By J. G. and are to be sold by Anthony Williamson,* 1659. 8°. LT, O; CH, CN, MH, WF, Y.

4274 —A paraphrase upon the Lords Prayer. *Printed,* 1641. brs. HH; MH.

4275 [–] The penitent pilgrim. *By Iohn Dawson, and are to be sold by Iohn Williams,* 1641. 12°. L, DC; CH, MH, WF, Y.

[–] Preparative to studie. 1641. *See* Heywood, Thomas.

4275A —Regicidium sanguinis scrutinium. Tragi-comoedia. *Typis J. Grismond,* 1665. 8°. Y.

4276 —Times treasury. *For Nath. Brooke,* 1652. fol. L, O; CH, CN, LC, MH, WF.

4277 —To His Majesty upon his happy arrivall. *For Henry Brome,* 1660. 4°.* LT; CH, MH, Y.

4278 —Tragi-comoedia. *Typis J. G. & prostat venalis in officina Theodori Sadleri,* 1665. 8°. L, O, P; CH, CN, MH, PU, Y.

4278A [–] The trimmer; or, the life and death of moderation. *For D. Newman,* 1683. 8°. T.C.II 48. L; Y.

B[rattle], T[homas]. 1678. An almanack. Cambridge [*Mass.*], 1678. *See* Almanacs.

Brattle, William. Unius labor. Cambridge [*Mass.*], 1682. *See* Almanacs.

4279 The brave boys of Bristol. [*For J. Deen, c.* 1661–85?] brs. O.

4280 The brave English souldiers resolution. 1666. brs. HH.

Brave newes from Ireland. 1641. *See* Hursey, Roger.

4281   Brave newes of the taking of the city of Chitchester [sic]. *For T.Underhill, Decemb.* 30. 1642. 4°.* LT, O, YM; Y.

4281A   The brave resolution of Edward Peto. *For Jo. Hansot* [sic], 1642. brs. EC.

4282   **Bray, Thomas.** The acts of Dr. Bray's visitation. *By William Downing,* 1700. fol.* L, OC, LSC, BAMB; MH, NN, V, Y.

4283   ——[Anr. ed.] *By W.Downing,* 1700. fol.* L, O, EN; CH, LC, NN, RPJ.

4284   [–] The anatomy of et cætera. 1641. 4°.* LT, CT; MH, MIU, NU, WF, Y.

4285   —Apostolick charity. *By W.Downing, for William Hawes,* 1698. 4°.* WCA, DT; CH, LC, NN, RPJ, Y.

4285A   ——[Anr. ed.] —, 1699. 4°.* L, O; MBA, NIC.

4286   ——Second edition. *For William Hawes,* 1699. 4°.* L, O; CH, MBA, MU, PHS, RPJ.

4287   ——Third edition. *By E. Holt for William Hawes,* 1700. 4°.* L, LG, CT, EC, BAMB; CH, LC, MH, NN, RPJ, Y.

4288   —An appendix to the discourse upon the doctrine. *For Will. Hawes,* 1698. 8°. D; NU.

4288A   ——[Anr. ed.] —1699. 8°. L; NGT, WF.

4289   —Bibliotheca catechetica. *For William Hawes,* 1699. 4°. LC, MBA, WF.

4290   —Bibliotheca parochialis . . . Part I. *By E. H. for Robert Clavel,* 1697. 4°. T.C.III 2. L, O, CS, EC, ENC; CH, CU, LC, MB, RPJ, Y.

4291   —Letter I. A circular letter. [n.p., 1700.] cap., fol.* L, O, OC; CH, MH, NN, RPJ, Y.

4291A   —Country dances. *For and sold by James Young,* 1699. 4°. T.C.III 156. SHARP.

4291B   ——[Anr. ed.] *By William Pearson,* 1700. 4°. L.

4292   —A course of lectures. v. I. *Oxford, by Leonard Lichfield for the author,* 1696. fol. L, O, CT, OC, DT; PL, Y.

4292A   ——Second edition. —, 1697. fol. L, C, CPE; MBA, NPT, PL.

4293   —An essay towards promoting all necessary and useful knowledge. *By E. Holt for Robert Clavel,* 1697. 4°.* T.C.III 16. L, O, C, LG, DT; LC, MBA, NU, PBL, RPJ.

4293A   —A letter from. [London, 1700]. cap., fol.* EVANS 903. L, LSC; CH, MH, RPJ, Y.

4294   —A memorial, representing the present state of religion. *By William Downing, for the author,* 1700. fol.* L, O, C, LF, EN; CH, MH, NN, RPJ, Y.

4295   —The necessity of an early religion. *Annapolis, by Tho: Reading, for Evan Jones,* 1700. 4°.* EVANS 904. MNS, NN, RPJ.

4295A   [–] A new sect of religion descryed. [London], printed, 1641. 4°.* O, WCA; MH.

4296   [–] Proposals for the encouragement and promoting of religion. [London, c. 1695.] cap., fol.* OC; MHS, RPJ.

4296A   ——[Anr. ed.] [London, 1696/7]. cap., fol.* L; CH, RPJ.

4296B   ——[Anr. ed.] [August 1697] cap., fol.* LSC; CH, RPJ.

4296C   ——[Anr. ed.] [London, 1699] cap., fol.* OC.

4296D   —Proposals to their clergy. *For William Hawes,* 1698. fol. OC.

4296E   [–] A short account of the several kinds of societies. colop: *For J. Brudenel,* 1700. cap., fol.* L O; MH, Y.

4297   —A short discourse upon the doctrine of our baptismal covenant. *By E. Holt, for Rob. Clavel,* 1697. 8°. T.C.III 35. L, O, C, CE; CLC, CU, NPT, PL, RPJ, Y.

4298   ——Second edition. *For W. Hawes,* 1698. 8°. T.C.III 101. C, D; CU, MB, MH, NU, Y.

4299   ——Third edition. *By E. Holt for Will. Hawes,* 1699. 8°. L; MBP, NPT, WF.

4299A   ——"Second" edition. —, 1700. 8°. RPL; PL, Y.

4299B   —Supplement to the bibliotheca parochialis. *For Robert Clavel,* 1697. 4°. OC.

4300   **Bray, William, Capt.** The afflicted prisoner's appeale. *G. Calvert,* 1651. 4°.* HH.

4301   —An appeal in the humble claim of justice. *Printed,* 1649. 4°.* LG; Y.

4302   —God magnified, man dethroned. 1647. 4°. CH.

4303   —Heaven and earth. *Imprinted at London,* 1649. 4°.* LT; CLC, CU, NU, WF.

4304   —Innocency and the blood. 1649. 4°.* LT, LSC, HH; CH, MH, NN, WF, Y.

4305   —A letter to His Excellencie Sir Thomas Fairfax. *By Francis Leach,* 1647. 4°.* LT, O, DT; MBP, MH, WF, Y.

4306   —A plea for the peoples fundamental liberties. *By John Clowes for the author,* 1659. 4°.* O; CH, CSS, IU, MH, NN.

4307   —A plea for the peoples good old cavse. *By J. C. to be sold by Francis Smith,* 1659. 4°.* LT, O, OC, CCA; CH, MHL, MIU.

4308   —A representation to the nation. [London], 1648. 4°.* LT; WF.

4309   —To the General His Excellency Thomas Lord Fairfax. [London], 1649. 4°.* LT.

4310   —To the Parliament of the common-wealth of England. The petition. [London, 1659.] 4°.* HH.

4311   —To the right honourable the Commons . . . the humble petition of. [London, 1659?] brs. L.

4312   —To the right honourable the supreme authority . . . an appeal. 1649. 4°.* LT, O, HH, E, EN; BN, CH, CU, NU, WF, Y.

4313   [–] To the right honorable the svpreme, avthority . . . A second appeale. 1649. 4°.* LT, LG; CH, MH, NU, Y.

4314   —To the supreme authority, the Parliament. *Imprinted at London,* 1652. 4°.* MH, RPJ.

4315   —True excellency of God [n.p., 1649] cap., 4°.* LT, HH, DT; CU, WF.

4316   **Bray, William, D. D.** A sermon of the blessed sacrament. *By T. and R. C. for Henry Seile,* 1641. 4°. LT, O, C, E, DT; CLC, CU, MH, NU, WF, Y.

4317   **Brayne, John.** Astrologie proved to be . . . of demons. *By M. S. for John Hancock,* 1653. 4°.* L, O, AU, EN; Y.

4318   —The authority of God. *For Rich. Moone,* 1653. 4°.* LT, O.

4319   —Babels fall. *For T.B.,* 1649. 4°.* LT, C, LSC, DT; NU.

4320   —The churches going in. *For George Whittington,* 1649. 4°.* L; NU.

4321   —The churches resurrection. *For George Whittington,* 1649. 4°. L; NU.

4322 [–] The divinity of the Trinity cleared. *By J.C., to be sold by Edw.Blackmore*, 1654. 4°.* LT.

4323 —Doctrine of baptismes handled. *Printed*, 1652. 4°. CT.,

4324 —An exposition upon the Canticles. *By Robert Austin* 1651. 4°.* O.

4325 —Gospel advice to godly builders. 1648. 4°.* LT, DT; CH.

4326 —The gospel-pattern. *For George Whittington*, 1649. 4°.* L; NU.

4327 —Heavens witnesse. *Printed*, 1652. 4°. CT.

4328 —Mr. John Biddle's Strange and new trinity. *Edward Blackmore*, 1654. 4°. L, CSSX, D.

4329 —The mysterie of the true ministry unvailed. 1649. 4°.* L, O; CN.

4330 —The new earth. *For Richard Moon*, 1653. 4°. LT, O, C.

4331 —The rules of dispute. *For Richard Moon*, 1653. 4°.* LT, O.

4332 —The smoak of the temple cleared. *For Thomas Vere*, 1648. 4°. LT, LCL, DT; CH, MM.

4333 —A treatise of the high rebellion of man. *For Richard Moon*, 1653. 4°.* LT, O.

4334 —The unknown being of the spirit. *For Richard Moon*, 1654. 4°. O, EC; NU.

Brazen serpent. 1655. *See* Farnworth, Richard.

4335 Breach of covenant a ruinating sin. 1648. 4°. O.

4336 The breaches and contraventions. *For R.Bentley and S.Magnes*, 1684. 8°. O, SP; Y.

4337 Bread for the poor. *For D.M.*, 1678. 4°.* L, MR; CH, NC.

—Exeter, 1698. *See* Dunning, Richard.

4338 The break-neck of presumptuousnesse in sinning. *Oxford, by Leonard Lichfield*, 1644. 4°.* MADAN 1746. L, CT, YM, DT; CH, CU, MH.

Breathings of the devout soul. 1648. *See* Hall, Joseph, *bp.*

Breathings of true love. [*n.p.*, 1660.] *See* Fox, George.

4339 **Breck, Edward.** An answer to a scandalous paper. *For Giles Calvert*, 1656. 4°.* LT; LC, MH, MU, RPJ, V.

[–] Declaration of the sad. [1660.] *See* Burrough, Edward.

4340 The breech wash'd. *Oxford, for Carolus Gustavus*, [1660.] brs. MADAN 2434. LT, O; MH.

4341 [**Breedon, Zacheus.**] The humble advice and earnest desires of certain well-affected ministers. *For Iames Boler*, 1649. 4°.* LT, O, C, E, DT; CH, MM, NU, WF, Y.

4341A — [Anr. ed.] *Reprinted*, 1660. 4°. OC.

4342 **Brégy, Charlotte de Flécelles, comtesse.** The royal standard of King Charles the II. *For G. Horton*, 1660. 4°.* LT.

4343 [**Brémond, Gabriel de.**] The amorous abbess. *For R.Bentley*, 1684. 12°. L; CLC.

4344 [–] The apology: or, the genuine memoires of Madam Maria Manchini, constabless of Colonna. *For J.Magnes and R.Bentley*, 1679. 8°. T.C.I 330. L, O, CT; CH, CN, WF, Y.

4345 [–] The cheating gallant. *For James Magnes and Richard Bentley*, 1677. 12°. T.C.I 267. L, O; CLC.

4345A [–] The circle. *Printed*, 1675. 8°. CN, Y.

4345B [–] —[Anr. ed.] *For the author, to be sold by John Carre, Richard Hunt, George Miller*, 1676. 8°. T.C.I 237. L.

4346 —Le double cocu. *Imprimé à Paris pour J.Magnes et R.Bentley*, 1678. 12°. L; Y.

4346A [–] —[Anr. ed.]—, 1679. 12° CN, WU.

4347 —Gallant memoirs. *For R.Bentley and M.Magnes*, 1681. 12°. T.C.I 461. L; CLC, Y.

4348 [–] The happy slave. *For J.Magnes, and R.Bentley*, 1677. 12°. T.C.I 253. L, O; WF.

4348A — —By T.R. & N.T. for James Magnes and Richard Bentley, 1678. 12°. Y.

4349 [–] —Second edition. *For Gilbert Cownley*, 1685. 12°. T.C.II 139. L; CLC, MH.

4349A [–] —[Anr. ed.]—, 1686. 12°. MH.

4349B [–] —[Anr. ed.] *For R.Wellington and E. Rumbal*, 1699. 12°. CLC.

4349C [–] —Second part. *For J.Magnes, and R.Bentley*, 1677. 12°. T.C.I 268. O; Y.

4349D [–] —The third and last part. —, 1678, 12°. T.C.I 291. O; Y.

4350 —Hattige: or the amours of the king. *For R.Bentley*, 1676. 12°. CT.

4351 [–] —[Anr. ed.] *Amsterdam [London], for Simon the African [R.Bentley?]*, 1680. 12°. L; CN, CU, MH.

4352 [–] —[Anr. ed.] —, 1683. 12°. L, HH; CLC, CN, Y.

4352A —L'heureux esclave. *Cologne, et se vend à Londres, chez Mrs Jacques Magnes & Richard Bentley*, 1677. 12°. CJ.

4353 —The pilgrim. *For R.Bentley and M.Magnes*, 1680. 12°. T.C.I 393. L; Y.

4353A — —For R.Bentley, 1684. 12°. CLC, CN, WF.

4354 — —[Anr. ed.] *For R. Wellington and E. Rumball*, 1700. 8°. L; CU, Y.

4354A [–] The politick and heroick vertues of love. *Printed*, 1686. 8°. CN.

4355 [–] The princess of Montferrat. *For R.Bentley, and M.Magnes*, 1680. 12°. T.C.I 428. L; CLC, MH, WF.

4356 [–] —Part II. *For R.Bentley and M.Magnes*, 1681. 12°. L; CLC.

4357 —The triumph of love over fortune. *For J.Magnes and R.Bentley*, 1678. 12°. T.C.I 320. L; CLC, CN.

4358 [–] The viceroy of Catalonia. *By J.B. for J.Magnes and R.Bentley*, 1678. 12°. T.C.I 320. L, O, C; CN, Y.

4359 [**Brend, William.**] A loving salutation to all friends. [*n.p.*, 1662.] cap., 4°.* L, LF, BBN; CH, MH, PH, PSC, Y.

4359A —O ye magistrates. [*London*, 1664.] brs. LF.

4359B —A seasonable warning. [*London*, 1664.] brs. LF.

4360 —A short declaration of the purpose and decree. [*London*], 1662. 4°.* L, O, LF, EN, BBN; IE, MH, PH, WF, Y.

4361 —Some addition to a former paper. *For R.Wilson*, 1663. 4°.* L, LF, BBN; CH, PH.

4362 [–] A tender visitation and friendly exhortation. [*London*, 1664.] cap., 4°.* L, C, LF, OC, BBN; MH, PH, PSC, WF, Y.

4363 **Brent, William.** A discourse upon the nature of eternitie. *For Richard Moon*, 1655. 8°. LT, O, CT; CLC, MH, MIU.

4364 — —Second edition. *By J.C. for the author,* 1674. 4°.* T.C.I 174. L, O, EC, P, EN; CH, CLC, NU, WF, Y.

4365 — —Third edition. *For the author; to be sold by Tho. Basset,* 1689. 8°. T.C.II 265. L.

4366 **B[r]ereton, William.** Catalogue of library. [*London*], 8 *June* 1697. 4°.* L; CN, MH.

4367 —A copy of the summons from. *For Matthew Walbancke,* 31 *March,* 1646. 4°.* LT.

4368 —Sir William Breretons letter concerning the surrender. *For Edward Husband, February* 6. 1645. 4°.* LT, O, CT, A, DT; CH, IU, MH, MU.

4368A —A letter from . . . of a victory . . . Middlewich. 1643. 4°.* LT.

4369 —Sir William Breretons letter sent to the honoble William Lenthal. *For Edw. Husband, March* 5. 1645. 4°.* LT, O, CT, EN, DT; CH, MH, Y.

4370 —Letters from. *For Iohn Wright, Septemb.* 24. 1644. 4°.* LT, O, CCL, LVF, AN; CH, MH, WF, Y.

4371 [–] Shrewsbury taken. *By Robert Austin,* 1645. 4°.* LT, O, AN; CH, CN, MH, WF, Y.

4372 —The successes of our Cheshire forces. *For Thomas Underhill,* 1644. 4°.* LT, CT.

4373 —Two intercepted letters from. [*Oxford*], *printed verbatim by Leonard Lichfield,* 1643. 4°.* MADAN 1406. L, O, OL; WF.

4374 **Brerewood, Edward.** Elementa logicæ. *Apud Ed. Griffin, pro Tho. Whitaker,* 1649. 12°. O, OM, CT, AU; WF, WG.

4375 — —[Anr. ed.] *Oxoniæ, excudebat Hen: Hall impensis Ric. Davis,* 1657. 12°. MADAN 2329. OBR; MH.

4376 — —[Anr. ed.] *Oxoniæ, excudebat H. Hall, impensis Ric. Davis,* 1668. 12°. MADAN III, p. 233. L, O, OM, YM.

4377 — —[Anr. ed.] *Excudebat Milo Flesher, impensis Ric. Davis, Oxeniensis,* 1684. 12°. L, O, EC; CU, WF, Y.

4378 —Enquiries touching the diversity of languages. *For Samuel Mearne, John Martyn, and Henry Herringman,* 1674. 8°. T.C.I 166. L, O, C, LCP, EN; CH, LC, MBP, MH, Y.

4379 — —[Anr. ed.] *For S.M., J.M, and H.H. to be sold by Walter Kettilby,* 1674. 8°, CK, CM, CP, EC; CLC, PL, TU, WWC, WF.

4380 —Tractatus quidam logici de prædicabilibus. *Oxoniæ, exc. H. Hall per J. Adams,* 1659. 8°. MADAN 2435. L, O, C, OC, EN.

4381 **Brès, Guy de.** The rise, spring and foundation of the Anabaptists. *Cambridge* [*Mass.*]: *printed, and to be sold by Marmaduke Johnson,* 1668. 4°. EVANS 119. LW; CH, LC, MH, MHS, MWA, V, Y.

4382 Brethren in iniquity. *Printed, to be sold by Randal Taylor,* 1690. 4°. T.C.II 323. L, O, C, LIL, EN; CH, NC, NU, WF, Y.

4383 The brethren's answer in London. *For H. Jones,* 1683. brs. O, OC, EN.

Breton, Nicholas. The court of honor. [*London*], 1679. *See title.*

4384 [–] Englands selected characters. *For T.S.,* 1643. 4°.* LT, O, LG, HH; CN, MH, WF, Y.

4385 —The figure of foure. The last part. *For W. Gilbertson,* 1653. 8°. CH.

4386 — —[Anr. ed.] —, 1654. 8°. L.

4387 [–] A poste with a packet of mad letters. *For John Marriot,* [1650?] 4°. L, O.

4387A [–] —[Anr. ed.] *For Richard Tomlins,* 1660. 4°. Y.

4388 [–] [Anr. ed.] *By E. Okes, for R.T. to be sold by Robert Boulter,* 1669. 4°. CH.

4388A [–] —[Anr. ed] 1674. 4°. P.

4389 [–] —[Anr. ed.] *By J.C. for T. Fabian,* 1678. 4°. T.C.I 337. WF.

4390 [–] —[Anr. ed.] *For Thomas Fabian,* 1685. 4°. LC, WF.

4391 Entry cancelled.

4392 —The souls harmony. Eleventh edition. [*London*], *for F. Coles, T. Vere, J. Wright, and J. Clarke,* 1676. 8°.* L.

4393 [–] Wits private wealth. *By Thomas Fawcet, for George Hvrlock,* 1642. 4°.* L.

4394 — —Seventh edition. *For Benjamin Hurlock,* 1670. 4°. L; CH.

4395 **B[rett], A[rthur].** A demonstration how the Latine tongue may be learn't. *For J.S.,* 1669. 4°.* L, O.

4396 Entry cancelled.

4397 —The restauration. *By J.H. for Samuel Thomson,* 1660. 4°.* LT, O, OB, CS; CH, MH, NP, WF.

4398 —Threnodia. *Oxford, by H: Hall for Ric: Davis,* 1660. 4°.* MADAN 2485. LT, O, OC; CH, CN, MH, WF, Y.

4399 **Brett, Henry.** The history of the birth, life, sufferings, and death of . . . Jesus Christ. *By T.J. for H.E.,* 1679. 8°.* T.C.I 358. L.

4400 **Brett, Samuel.** A narrative of the proceedings of a great council of Jews. *For Richard Moon,* 1655. 4°.* LT, O; CU, MB, MIU, WF.

Bretz. *See* Brès.

4400A **Bréval, François Durant de.** Caroli Secundi Magnæ Britanniæ regis, epitaphium. [*London*], *excudebat Thomas Newcombe,* 1685. brs. L, OP; CH, MH, Y.

4401 —, La couronne de vie. *Par Tho. Newcomb pour Will. Nott,* 1670. 4°.* L, O, OM, CT; CLC.

4402 —Faith in the just victorious. *For Will. Nott,* 1670. 4°.* T.C.I 35. O, OM, WCA; CH, CLC, NU.

4403 —La foy victorieuse. *Par T.N. pour Will. Nott,* 1670. 4°.* O, OM, CPE, HH; CH, Y.

4404 —Harangue à son altesse. *Par T. Nieucomb, pour W. Noot,* 1670. 8°.* HH.

4405 —Le Juif baptisé. Sermon. *Par Thomas Niewcomb, & se vend chez Hen. Herringman, & chez Wil. Nott,* 1671. 4°.* CH, NPT, NU, TU.

4406 —Play is the plot. *For J. Tonson,* 1678. 4°. WF.

4407 —A speech made to His Highnesse the Prince of Orange. *Printed,* 1671. 4°.* O; Y.

Breviarium chronologicum. 1699. *See* Sault, Richard.

Breviary of alchemy. 1678. *See* Starkey, George.

Breviary of the history. 1650. *See* May, Thomas.

4408 A breviate for the bishops, in vindication of the proceedings. colop: *For Joseph Bowers,* 1688/9. cap., 4°.* L, O, BP, DT; CH, CR, Y.

4408A A breviate for the defendants. [*London?* 1682.] brs. TU.

4409 A breviate for the members of the convention. [London, 1689?] cap., fol. CN.

4410 The breviate of a sentence given against Jerome Alexander. 1644. fol. LT.

Breviate of saving. 1643. *See* Brinsley, John.

4411 A breviate of the case of Exeter. [*London*], 1660. cap., 4°.* Y.

4411A A breviate of the case of the convex-light. [*London*, 1694.] brs. LG.

4412 A breviate of the cause depending, and proofes made. [*n.p.*, 1655?] 4°.* LT.

4413 A breviate of the establishment of the friendly society. [*London?* 1684.] brs. L, O; Y.

Breviate of the life. 1681. *See* Baxter, Richard.

4414 A breviate of the proceedings of France. *Printed at Cologne, and reprinted at London, to be sold by Walter Davies,* 1684. 8°. T.C.II 70. L, O, OC, CS, BAMB; CLC, LC, WF.

4415 A breviate of the state of Scotland in its government. *For Ric. Chiswell,* 1689. fol.* T.C.II 255. L, O, C, WCA, EN; CH, MH, MHL, WF, Y.

4416 A breviate of the weavers business. [*n.p.*, 1648.] cap., 4°.* LT.

4417 **Brevint, Daniel.** The Christian sacrament. *At the theater in Oxford,* 1673. 12°. T.C.I 133. MADAN 2969. L, O, C, CT, MC; MH, WF, Y.

4418 ——Second edition. —, 1673. 12°. MADAN 2070. O, CSSX, CT, OC; CH.

4419 ——Third edition. —, 1679. 8°. MADAN 3206. O, LW; NU, Y.

4419A ——Epitaphe de Charles second. *Chez J. de Beaulieu,* 1685. brs. MH.

4419B ——P. M. S. Heneagii Nottinghamiæ. . . epitaphium. [*London?* 1682.] brs. L, O, OC; CH.

4420 ——Missale Romanum, or the depth and mystery of Roman mass. *At the theater in Oxford,* 1672. 8°. T.C.I 115. MADAN 2921. L, O, C, E, DT; CN, MH, NU, WF, Y.

4421 ——Second edition. *Oxford, at the theater,* 1673. 12°. MADAN 2971. L, O, CT, AU, DT; CLC, CU, MH, TU.

4421A ——Third edition. —, 1673. 12°. OC, OCC, CT, EN; NHS, Y.

4421B ——[Anr. ed.] —, 1684. 12°. CLC, OC.

4422 ——[Anr. ed.] *For E. Taylor,* 1686. 12°. DT.

4423 ——Saul and Samuel at Endor. *Oxford, at the theater,* 1674. 8°. T.C.I 186. MADAN 3006. L, O, C, MC, EN; CH, LC, MH, NU, WF, Y.

4424 Brevis demonstratio: the truth and excellency. *For W. Crook,* 1674. 12°. T.C.I 161, L, CK, E; CLC, TU.

Brevis disquisitio. 1653. *See* Biddle, John.

Brevissima instituto. Dublin, 1671. *See* Lily, William.

Brevissimum metaphysicæ. Oxonii, 1690. *See* Willis, John.

4424A **Breviter, Richard.** The mighty Christ the saints help. *By M. S. for Henry Cripps,* 1662, 8°. L; CLC, MH.

4425 **Brewer, Anthony.** The covntrie girle. *For A. R.,* 1647. 4°. L, O, LVD, OW; CH, CN, MH, NC, WF, Y.

[–] Lingua; or, the combat. 1657. *See* Tomkis, Thomas.

4426 ——The love-sick king. *For Rob. Pollard, and John Sweeting,* 1655. 4°. L, O, LVD, OW, EN; CH, CU, LC, WF, Y.

4427 **Brewer, Thomas, Gent.** To the Parlament of the common-wealth. . . . The humble petition of. [*London,* 1654.] brs. LT; MH.

4428 ——To the right honourable the knights, citizens, . . . The humble petition of. [*London,* 1659?] brs. L.

4429 **Brewer, Thomas, late a prisoner.** Gospel publique worship. *By W. Godbid, for Henry Eversden,* 1656. 8°. LT, O; NU, Y.

4430 [**Brewer, Thomas, Poet.**] A knot of fooles. *For Francis Grove,* 1658. 4°.* LT; CH, NN, WF.

4430A ——Londons triumph. *For N. Brook,* 1656. 8°.* L; CH.

4431 ——The merry jests of Smug the smith. *For F. Coles,* 1657. 4°. MH.

4432 The brevvers plea. *For I. C.,* 1647. 4°.* LT; LC, NC.

4433 [**Brewster, Sir Francis.**] A discourse concerning Ireland. *For Tho. Nott, and are to be sold by E. Whitlock,* 1697/8. 4°. L, C, HH, SP; MH, NC, WF, WU, Y.

4434 ——Essays on trade. First part. *For Tho. Cockerill,* 1695. 8°. T.C.II 540. L, C, OC, E; CH, CU, LC, MH, NC, Y.

4435 [**Brewster, Humphrey.**] To the mayor, aldermen . . . of London, . . . for you to receive. [*London,* c. 1662.] cap., 4°.* L, LF, BBN; MH, PH, PSC, Y.

4436 B[**rewster**], **Samuel.** A letter to the parishioners of St. B. A. *For Geo. Strahan,* 1700. 12°.* L, C.

Brez. *See* Brès.

4437 **Brian, Thomas.** The pisse-prophet. *By S. G. for R. Thrale,* 1655. 12°. C, LWL, CCA; CLC, CU, NAM.

4438 ——[Anr. ed.] *By S. and B. Griffin, to be sold by Ben. Thrale,* 1679. 12°. T.C.I 344. L, O, C, LG.

4439 **Briber, Francis.** The declaration of. colop: *For Randal Taylor,* 1688. 4°.* L, O, C, EN, DT; CH, CN, NU, WF, Y.

4440 [**Brice, Germain**]. A new description of Paris. *For Henry Bonwicke,* 1687. 12°. T.C.II 176. L, O, CT, LWL, OC; CLC, MMO, NC, WF, Y.

4440A ——Second edition. *For H. Bonwicke,* 1688. 12°. T.C.III 69. CH.

4441 The brick-makers lamentation from New-gate. *For Philip Brooksby,* [1685?]. brs. L.

4442 The bride's burial. [*London*], *by and for A. M.* [1670–97]. brs. L, O, HH, GU.

4443 ——[Anr. ed.] *For W. T. and T. Passinger,* [1680?]. brs. L.

4444 **Bridge, Francis.** A sermon preached . . . fifth of November 1684. *For Walter Kettilby,* 1685. 4°.* T.C.II 95. L, O, C, OM, CT; CH, MBA, NU, WF, Y.

4445 **Bridge, William.** The works of. The first volume. *For Peter Cole,* 1649. 4°. LT, O, CE, NPL, AU; CH, MBA, NU, PL, WF.

4446 ——The second volumn [sic]. *By Peter Cole,* 1649. 4°. LT, O, LCL, BR, AU; CH, CU, PL, WF, Y.

4447 ——The third volumn. —, 1649. 4°. L, O, DC, BR, AU; CH, CU, MBA, WF, Y.

4448 ——Babylons downfall. A sermon. *By I. N. for Iohn Rothwell,* 1641. 4°.* LT, O, CM, LW; CH, CN, MH, NU, WF, Y.

4449   —Christ and the covenant. *For Thomas Parkhurst*, 1667. 8°. LW; CLC, NU.

4450   Entry cancelled.

4451   —Christs coming opened. *For Peter Cole*, 1648. 4°.* LT, O, C, AN, DT; CLC, MH, NU, TU, WF, Y.

4452   —England saved with a notwithstanding. *For R. Dawlman*, 1648. 4°.* LT, O, C, CM, DT; CLC, MH, NU, WF, Y.

4453   —The false apostle. 1656. 4°. LCL.

4454   —The freeness of the grace and love of God. *For Nath. Crouch*, 1671. 8°. T.C.I 84. L, O, C, LCL; CH, IU, MH, NU, WF.

4455   —Grace and love beyond gifts. *By Peter Cole*, 1649. 4°.* LT, OC, DT; CH, MH, NU.

4456–7 Entries cancelled.

4458   —The loyall convert. *For Edward Husbands*, 1644. 4°.* LT, O, C, LCL, EN; CH, NU, TU, WF, Y.

4459   —Bridge's remains. *Printed, and are to be sold by John Hancock senior and junior*, 1673. 8°. T.C.I 126. L, O, C, LCL, LW; MH, NU, WF.

4460   —The righteous man's habitation. *For T. J.*, 1665. 4°.* L, O, HH; CLC, Y.

4461   —The saints hiding-place. *For Peter Cole*, 1647. 4°.* LT, O, C, LCL, BR; CH, MH, NU, TU, WF, Y.

4462   —Scripture light, the most sure light. *By Peter Cole*, 1656. 4°. L, LCL, E; CLC, MH, NPT, NU, Y.

4463   —Seasonable truths in evil-times. *For Nath. Crouch*, 1668. 8°. T.C.II. L, LSC; LC, MH.

4464   —A sermon containing some comfortable directions. *For Beniamin Allen*, 1642. 4°.* LT, O, CT; CU, MH, NU, WF, Y.

4465   —A sermon preached . . . Novemb. 29. 1643. *For R. Dawlman*, 1643. 4°.* LT, O, C, EN, DT; CH, MH, NC, TU, WF, Y.

4466   —A sermon preached unto the voluntiers. *By J. F. for Ben. Allen*, 1642[3]. 4°.* LT, C, HH, DT; CH, MH, NU, WF, Y.

4466A —The sinfulnesse of sinne. *Printed*, 1667. 8°. LCL; MH, WF.

4467   —The truth of the times vindicated. *By T. P. and M. S. for Ben: Allen*, 1643. 4°. LT, O, CS, HH, DT; CH, MH, NU, WF, Y.

4468   —Twelve several books of. *By Peter Cole*, 1654. 12°. LSC, AN; NN, NU, WF, Y.

4469   —Twenty one several books of. *By Peter Cole*, 1657. 4°. L, O, CE, LW; WF, Y.

4470   —Two sermons. *For Benjamin Allen*, 1642. 4°.* LT, O, LW; CH, NPT, NU, RPJ, Y.

4471   —[Same title.] *By Peter Cole*, 1656. 4°.* L, LCL, CE; CH, NGT, NU, WF, Y.

4472   —A vindication of ordinances. *By Peter Cole*, 1650. 4°. LT, OC, ENC, DT; CH, MIU, MH, NU, TU.

4473   — —Second edition. —, 1650. 4°. NU.

4474   — —[Anr. ed.] —, 1653. 4°. L, O, BR; CH, CLC, MH, NU, WF, Y.

4475   —Word to the aged. *Boston: by John Foster for John Griffin*, 1679. 12°.* EVANS 264. LC, V.

4476   —The wovnded conscience cured. *For Benjamin Allen*, 1642. 4°. LT, C, LCL, CT, DT; CH, MH, NC, NU, WF, Y.

4477   — —Second edition. —, 1642. 4°. LW; WF, Y.

4478   **Bridges, John.** A letter from. *By R.B. for Humphrey Tuckey, April 24.* 1645. 4°.* LT; Y.

4479   [–] A perfect narrative of the grounds & reasons. *By Tho. Newcomb*, 1660. 4°.* LT, O, WCN, LFEA, SP; CH, MH, WF, Y.

4480   **Bridges, Noah.** Lux mercatoris. Arithmetick natural and decimal. *By R. I. for Thomas Johnson*, 1661. 8°. LT, C; CH, MIU.

4481   — —[Anr. ed.] *P. Parker*, 1665. 8°. OC; BN.

4481A [–] Rarities: or. *By J. G. for Nath. Brook*, 1665. 8°.* O, C, LLL, MC; WG.

4482   —Stenographie and crytographie [sic]. *By J. G., for the author*, 1659. 8°. L, O, C, CM, HH; LC, NN, Y.

4483   —Vulgar arithmetique. *[London], for the author, to be sold by A. Crook, and H. Tucky*, [1653]. 8°. L, OC, CT, CU, E; MB, NC.

4483A **Bridges, Walter.** A catechism for communicants. *Crooke*, 1645. 8°. O.

4484   [–] Division divided. *For Andrew Crooke*, 1646. 4°. O, LCL, WCA; CU, NC, NPT, NU, Y.

4484A **Bridges, Walter.** Ioabs covnsell. *By R. Cotes, for Andrew Crooke*, 1643. 4°.* LT, O, C, LW, DT; CH, MPB, MH, NC, TU, Y.

4484B **Bridges, William.** Christianity no enthusiasm. 1678. 8°. YM.

       Bridget, *Saint. See* Birgitta, *Saint.*

4485   **Bridgewater, Benjamin.** A poem upon the death of . . . Queen Mary. *For Richard Baldwin*, 1695. fol* O, HH, E; CH, CLC, MH, TC, WF, Y.

4486   —Religio bibliopolæ. *For P. Smart*, 1691. 8°. T.C.II 370. L, O, CT, GK; BN, CLC, CN, MH, MMO, WF, Y.

4487   **Bridgman, Sir John.** Reports of. *By Tho. Roycroft, for H. Twyford, Tho. Dring, and Jo. Place*, 1659. fol. L, O, CT, EN, DT; CH, KT, MHL, NCL, WF, YL.

4488   **Bridgman, Sir Orlando.** Sir Orlando Bridgmans conveyances. *By the assigns of Ri. Atkyns and Ed. Atkyns, for William Battersby, and Thomas Basset*, 1682. fol. T.C.I 507. O, LL, LIL, LMT; MHL, MIU, PL, WF.

4489   — —Second edition. *By the assigns of Richard and Edward Atkins, for William Battersby, T. Basset; sold by T. Sawbridge, M. Gillyflower, and W. Hensman*, 1689. 2 v. fol. T.C.II 300. L, O, C; WCA; LC, MH, PUL.

4489A — —"Second" edition. —, 1690. 2 v. fol. MHL.

4490   — —Third edition. *By the assigns of Richard and Edward Atkins, for William Battersby. To be sold by J. Cleave, J. Walthoe, and R. Vincent*, 1699. fol. LL, LIL; CH, CU, MHL.

4491   —The judgment of. *[London, 1690]* brs. L. O; CH, MIU, PL, Y.

4492   **Bridgman, Robert.** An account of the Quakers politicks. *By W. Redmayne, for B. Alner*, 1700. 4°. C.

4493   —Folly and envy detected. *Printed and sold by T. Sowle*, 1694. 8°.* LF, BBN; PH.

4494 —Some reasons why Robert Bridgman, and his wife . . . have left the society of the people called Quakers. *For Brab. Aylmer, and Char. Brome,* 1700. 4°.* T.C.III 195. L, O, C, LF, OC; CH, MH, PH, Y.

4494A A bridle for the tongue. 1700. 8°. O.

4495 **Bridoul, Toussaint.** The school of the Eucharist established. *For Randal Taylor,* 1687. 4°. L, O, C, NPL, E; CH, MH, NU, TU, WF, Y.

4496 — —, Second edition. —, 1687. 8°. L, O, CJ, EC, EN; CLC, MB.

4497 A brief abstract of the great oppressions . . . of the East-India company. [*London,* 1698.] cap., fol.* O, LUG; CH.

Briefe abstract of the Kings letters to the Queene. 1648. *See* E., S.

Brief account, and seasonable improvement. [*n.p.,* 1675/6.] *See* N., N.

Brief account concerning. 1691. *See* Mather, Increase.

4498 A brief account from several places, of a signal victory. *Edinburgh, by the heir of A.Anderson,* 1683. fol.* ALDIS 2369. HH.

4499 A brief account of a great engagement which hapned between the English . . . and the whole French fleet. *By W.Davis,* 1689. brs. O, MC; CH.

A Brief account of ancient. 1662. *See* Woodhead, Abraham.

4500 A brief account of Captain William Govan. [*Edinburgh,* 1685?] 4°.* L.

4501 A brief account of Charleroy. colop: *Printed and sold by J.Wallis,* 1693. brs. MH.

4502 A brief account of His Sacred Majestie's descent. *Edinburgh, by the heirs of Andrew Anderson,* 1681. fol.* ALDIS 2252. L, MC, EN; WF.

4503 A brief account of many memorable passages of the life . . . of the Earle of Shaftsbury. *For J.Coniers,* [1683]. cap., 4°. L, O, EN; CH, CLC, Y.

Brief account of some choice. Oxford. 1676. *See* B., R.

Brief account of some expressions. Oxford, 1663. *See* Towerson, Gabriel.

Brief account of some of the late and present. 1680. *See* Whitehead, George.

Brief account of some of the late incroachments. [*n.p.,* 1695.] *See* Ferguson, Robert.

Brief account of some reasons. [*n.p.,* 1665] *See* Penington, Isaac.

4503A A brief account of the behaviour of Major-General Harrison. [*London*], 1660. cap., 4°.* CN.

4503B A briefe account of the commitment of the Earl of Sh. colop: *For H.R.,* 1681. brs. WF.

4504 A brief account of the designs which the Papists have had. colop: [*London*], *for R.Baldwin,* 1681. cap., fol.* O, HH, CT, BR, DT; CH, CU, LC, MH, NU, TU, Y.

4505 A brief account of the dispensary. [*n.p.,* c. 1700.] fol O, LG.

4506 A brief account of the evidence given on behalf of Edmund Warner. [*n.p.*], 1693. brs. MC; MH, NC.

Brief account of the first rise. 1688. *See* Bolde, Samuel.

4506A A brief account of the great oppressions. [*London?* 1695]. cap., fol.* MH, MIU, NC.

4507 A brief account of the indictment tryal, conviction, . . . of Mr. Robert Bailzie. colop: *For W.Davies,* 1684. brs. L, O, HH, EN; CH, CLC, MH, PL, WF.

Brief account of the intended. 1694. *See* Paterson, William.

4508 A brief account of the late and present sufferings. 1680. 4°. O.

4508A A brief account of the late depredations of the Dutch. 1695. 4°. O.

4509 A brief accompt of the maintenances. [*London,* 1671?] fol.* L, LG; MH, WF.

4510 A brief account of the meeting, proceedings, and exit of the Committee of Safety. *For Thomas Williamson,* 1659. 4°.* LT, O, C, HH, EN; CH, CU, MH, NU, WF.

4511 Entry cancelled.

Brief account of the most remarkable prodigies. 1696. *See* L., W.

Brief account of the nature. Edinburgh, 1700. *See* Cullen, *Sir* Francis Grant.

Brief account of the new sect. 1662. *See* Patrick, Symon.

4512 A brief account of the nullity of King James's title. *For Richard Chiswell,* 1689. 4°.* O, CT, OB; CLC, MH, NU, WF, Y.

4513 A brief account of the Pope's pretences. *Oxford, by Leon Lichfield for Richard Davis, to be sold by Moses Pitt, Henry Mortlock,* 1679. brs. O, HH.

4514 A brief account of the present declining state. *For John Harris,* 1695. 4°.* L; NN, TU.

4515 A brief account of the priviledges and immunities. *For Anthrop Isted,* 1671. 4°.* L, O; MIU, NC.

Brief account of the proceedings against. [*n.p.,* 1680.] *See* Lumsden, Alexander.

4516 A brief account of the proceedings of the French clergy. *For Tho. Simmons,* 1682. 4°. L, O, C, E, EN; CH, MH.

4517 A brief account of the province of East-Jersey in America. *For Benjamin Clarke,* 1682. 4°.* L, LF; CH, LC, RPJ.

4518 A brief account of the province of East: New-Jarsey in America. *Edinburgh, by John Reid,* 1683. 4°.* ALDIS 2370. L, E, AU; CH, CN, NN, RPJ, Y.

Brief account of the province of Pennsilvania. 1682. *See* Penn, William.

4519 A brief account of the reasons for which. *Printed,* 1695. 4°.* EN; MH.

4519A A brief account of the reformation from Popery. *For W. Whitwood, and Mrs. Feltham,* 1689. 12°.* CLC.

Brief account of the royal. 1662. *See* Howell, James.

4520 A brief account of the several plots, conspiracies, and hellish attempts of the bloody-minded Papists. *For J. R. and W. A.,* 1679. 4°.* L, O, SP, WCA; CH, MH, NU, WF, Y.

Brief account of the Socinian. 1695. *See* Leslie, Charles.

4521 A brief account of the state of the differences. *Oondon* [sic], *for T. Cockerill*, 1692. 4°. T.C.II 421. L, O, C; NU, PL, WF.

4522 A brief account of the tryal of Peter Cooke. colop: *For R. Greene*, [1696]. brs. L.

4523 A brief accompt of the Turks late expedition. *By Richard Hodgkinson, and Thomas Mab*, 1663. 4°. L, O, HH, WCA; CH, MH, NNG, WF, Y.

Brief account of the virtues. 1688. *See* Lower, Richard.

Brief account of what passed. [*n.p.*, 1681.] *See* London. Council.

Brief admonition of some. 1659. *See* Howell, James.

Brief advertisement. 1672. *See* Carter, William.

Brief advertisement, concerning East-New-Jersey. [*Edinburgh*, 1685.] *See* Scot, George.

4524 A brief anatomie of women: being an invective. *By E. Alsop*, 1653. 4°.* LT.

4525 A briefe and compendious narrative of the renowned Robert, Earle of Essex. *By Jane Coe*, 1646. 4°.* LT, O, AN; CH, CLC, MIU, WF.

Brief and easie explanation. 1648. *See* W., J.

4526 Entry cancelled.

4527 A briefe and exact treatise declaring how the sheriffs . . . elected. *For T.I.*, 1642. 4°.* LT, MR; CH, CN, LC, MH, Y.

4528 A brief and full account of Mr. Tate's and Mr. Brady's new version. *For Joseph Wild*, 1698. 8°.* T.C.III 95. L, O, C; NPT.

Brief and impartial account. 1682. *See* Owen, John.

Brief and methodical catechism. 1664. *See* Cawdrey, Zachery.

Brief and methodicall view. 1647. *See* Freeman, William.

Brief & modest reply. Dublin, 1699. *See* Wetenhall, Edward, *bp.*

4529 A brief and modest representation of the present state condition of Ireland. colop: *For W. Nott*, 1688. brs. CH, PL, Y.

Brief and perfect journal. 1655. *See* S., I.

Briefe and perfect relation. 1647. *See* R., S.

Briefe and perspicuous manuductio. 1670. *See* C., B.

4530 A brief and plain discourse upon the decrees of God. *By T. S. for Edw. Giles in Norwich*, 1692. 4°.* O.

4531 A brief and plain discvssion of that question. *For John Wright*, 1652. 4°.* LT, LSG, CT; WF.

Brief and serious warning. [n.p., 1678.] *See* Rigge, Ambrose.

4531A A brief and seasonable word. [*London*, 1675.] cap., 4°.* Y.

4532 A brief and summary narrative of the many mischiefs. [*London*, 1690?] brs. L; MH.

4532A A brief and true account of the notorious principles . . . of . . . Lodowick Muggleton. *For B. H.*, [1676?] CN.

4532B Brief and true account of the persecutions. 1690. 4°.* O.

4533 A brief and true account of the sufferings of the Church of Scotland. *Printed*, 1690. 4°.* L, O, CT, HH, EN; CH, MH, NU, PL, WF, Y.

4534 A brief and true narration of the late wars risen in New-England. *For J. S.*, 1675. 4°.* L, WCA, GH; CH, MH, NN, PHS, RPJ.

4535 A briefe and true relation of the great disorders and riot. *By I. C. to be sold by Henry Overton*, [1647]. 4°.* LT, LG; MH, WF, Y.

4536 A briefe and true relation of the siege and surrendering of Kings Lyn. colop: [*London*], *by G. Bishop and R. White*, [1643]. cap., 4°.* LT, O, SP; CU, MH, WF, Y.

4537 A brief and true remonstrance of the illegal proceedings of Roger Osburn. [*n.p.*, 1654.] brs. O.

4538 A brief and witty discourse or dialogue, between a Yorkshire man. *By R. W. for D. B.*, 1650. 4°.* LT.

4539 A briefe ansvver to a booke called The declaration of the kingdomes of England and Scotland. *Oxford, by H. Hall*, 1644. 4°.* MADAN 1627. LT, O, CT, DC, DT; CH, CLC, MBP, MH, WF, Y.

4540 A briefe answer to a book intituled, His Majesties letter. *Printed*, 1642 [3]. 4°.* LT, LG, HH; CH, MBP, MH, WF, Y.

Brief answer to a false. [n.p.], 1678. *See* Penn, William.

Brief answer to a late. [n.p., 1691.] *See* Grascome, Samuel.

Brief answer to a late scandalous pamphlet. [*London*], 1647. *See* Talbot, William.

4540A A brief answer to a pamphlet intitled, A short review. [*London.*] 1677, cap., 4°.* MH.

4541 A brief answer to a scandalous pamphlet called, Ill news from New-England. [*n.p.*, 1653.] cap., 4°. LT; MB, PL.

4542 A brief ansvver to a scandalous pamphlet, entituled A speech. *For Francis Nicolson*, 1643. 4°.* LT, O, LG; CLC, NU, WF, Y.

4543 A brief answer to Mr. L'Estrange his appeal. colop: *For T. Davis*, 1680. cap., fol.* O; CH, MH, WF.

Brief answer to Mr. Marlow's. 1700. *See* Winnel, Thomas.

Brief answer to obiections. 1650. *See* Bakewell, Thomas.

Briefe answer to R. H. 1646. *See* B., R.

4544 A brief answer to several popular objections. *For Randal Tayler*, 1694. 4°.* O, CT, SP, EN; CLC, MIU, Y.

Brief answer to some. 1656. *See* Collier, Thomas.

4545 Entry cancelled.

4546 A briefe-answere to the late-resolves. *Printed*, 1649. 4°.* LT, DT; CH, MH, NU, WF.

Brief answer to the many. 1672. *See* Walton, John.

Brief answer to three books. [1674]. *See* Lawrence, Thomas.

4547 A brief answer to three very great and concerning questions. [*London*, 1685?] 4°.* L; WF.

Brief answer to two papers. [n.p., 1692.] *See* Budd, Thomas.

Brief answer unto the Cambridge. 1658. *See* M., E.

Brief apology for all. 1649. *See* Prynne, William.

4548 A brief apologic for the pious and painfull ministers. *For John Wright*, 1653. 4°.* LT, LW, SP; CN, MH, NU, TU, WF, Y.

Brief apologie for the sequestred. [n.p.], 1649. *See* Allington, John.

Brief but full vindication. 1688. *See* Steward, Richard.

4549 A brief but most true relation of the late . . . plot . . . Barbadoes. *George Croom*, 1693. brs. CN.

Brief, but weighty, appendix. [n.p., 1672.] *See* Sherwin, William.

4550 A brief character of Ireland. *Sold by R. Taylor*, 1692. 8°. T.C.II 384. L, O, DT.

Brief character of the antient. 1695. *See* Mather, William.

Brief character of the Low-countries. 1652. *See* Feltham. Owen.

4551 A brief character of the Protector. *Sold by R. Taylor*, 1692. 4°. T.C.II 429. CT; HR.

Brief chronicle of all the chief. 1662. *See* Heath, James.

Brief chronicle of the late. 1663. *See* Heath, James.

4552 A brief chronicle of the Turkish War. *By Tho. Mabb, for Henry Brome*, 1664. 8°. O, GH; WF, Y.

4553 A brief cronology of Great Britain. *By T. C. to be sold by T. Crosse*, 1656. brs. LT, O.

4554 A brief chronology of the most remarkable passages. *By T. N. for Edmund Thomas*, 1658. brs. L, CM; Y.

4555 A briefe, cleere, and methodicall view. [*London*], 1647. 4°.* LT, OC, HH; CH, MH.

Brief collection of some forgotten votes, 1647. *See* England. Parliament. House of Commons.

4555A A brief collection of some memorandums. 1689. cap., 4°.* L; MH, MWA, Y.

4556 A brief collection out of the records of the city, touching elections of the sheriffs. colop: [*London*], *by S. Roycroft*, 1682. cap., fol.* L, O, C, LL, HH; CH, MH, PL, WF, Y.

4556A —[Anr. ed.] [*London*], 1684. fol. EN.

4557 Briefe collections out of Magna Charta. *For George Lindsey*, 1643. 4°.* LT, LG, LSC, DT; CH, CN, MH, NU, WF, Y.

Brief commentary. 1649. *See* Sterne, Richard.

4558 A brief compendium of the birth, education, . . . Thomas Earl of Ossory. [*n.p.*, 1680.] cap., fol.* L; CH, MH, TU, WF.

4559 A brief confession or declaration of faith; set forth by . . . Ana-Baptists. *By G. D. for Francis Smith*, 1660. 4°.* LT, CCA, SP; NHC, NU, Y.

4560 —[Anr. ed.] *For Francis Smith*, 1660. brs. LT.

4561 —[Anr. ed.] *Reprinted*, 1691. brs. L.

4562 Briefve declaration du royaume d'Escosse. *Edinburgh, Tyler*, 1644. 4°. ALDIS 1134. L, OP.

4563 A briefe declaration of all the civill warres. *Printed*, 1643. 4°.* LT, A, DT; MH, MIU, Y.

Briefe declaration of all the penall statuts. 1643. *See* England. Laws.

Brief declaration of the barbarous. 1641. *See* S., G.

Brief declaration of the Lord's Supper. 1688. *See* Wharton, Henry.

4564 A briefe declaration of the reasons that moved King James. *By E. P. for Nicholas Bourne*, 1645[6]. 4°.* LT, LG.

Brief declaration of the several passages in the Treaty. 1647. *See* Bushell, Thomas.

4564A A brief declaration of the state of .·. St. Paul. [*London*, 1685]. brs. WF.

4564B A brief declaration of the treaty. 1647. 4°.* LT.

4565 London. Anno Dom. 1647. A brief declaration of those that have accepted the trust. 1647. 4°.* MADAN 1919. LT, O, LG, HH; Y.

Brief declaration to all. 1662. *See* Bayly, William.

4566 A brief deduction of the case between George Carew. [*n.p.*, 1676.] cap., fol.* L.

Brief description by way. [1655.] *See* Cotton, *Mrs.* Priscilla.

4567 A brief description of an edition of the Bible, in the original Hebr. Samar. and Greek. colop: *By R. Norton for Timothy Garthwait*, 1652. fol.* L.

4567A —[Anr. ed.] —, 1653. fol.* LT.

4568 A brief description of the excellent vertues of . . . coffee. *For Paul Greenwood*, 1674. brs. L.

4569 A brief description of the first ten persecutions. *Glasgow, Andro Anderson*, 1660. GRAY.

4570 A brief description of the future history of Europe. [*London*], 1650. 4°. LT, O, C, LWL, EN; CLC, CU, MH, MIU, NU, WF, Y.

Brief description of the nature. [n.p., 1680?] *See* Salgado, James.

4571 A brief description of the province of Carolina. *For Robert Horne*, 1666. 4°.* L, O; CH, CN, LC, NN, NHS, RPJ.

4572 A briefe description of the two revolted nations Holland and England. [1650]. 4°.* LT; NC.

4573 A breife description or character of the religion and manners . . . phanatiques. *Printed*, 1660. 8°. LT, CT; Y.

4574 A brief dialogue between creditor & prisoner. *By Tho. Newcomb*, 1653. 4°.* LT; MHL.

4575 A brief dialogue between Zelotopit. *For John Biard*, [1642]. 4°.* LT, HH; CN, NGT, TU, WF, Y.

Briefe directer for these. [London, 1642]. *See* Taylor, John.

Brief directions for our. 1693. *See* Cornwallis, Henry.

4576 Brief directions how to tanne leather. 1680. brs. L.

Brief directions shewing. 1659. *See* Harrington, James.

4577 A brief discourse betwen [*sic*] a sober Tory and a moderate Whig. colop: *For J. Adams*, [1682]. fol. L, LG, LUG; CH, TU.

4578 A brief discourse concerning printing and printers. 1663. 4°. L; NC.

Brief discourse concerning singing. 1690. *See* Marlow, Isaac.

Brief discourse concerning the different wits. 1669. *See* Charleton, Walter.

Brief discourse concerning the lawfulness. 1693. *See* Williams, John, *bp.*

Brief discourse concerning the notes. 1687. *See* Sherlock, William.

Brief discourse concerning the power. 1640[1]. *See* Cotton, Sir Robert Bruce.

Brief discourse concerning the spirituality. 1667. *See* T., R.

Brief discourse concerning the unlawfulness. [*n.p.*, 1686.] *See* Mather, Increase.

4579 Entry cancelled.

4580 A brief discovrse, declaring the impiety and unlawfulnesse of the new covenant. [*Oxford, by H. Hall*], 1643. 4°. MADAN 1478. LT, O, CSS, SP; CH, CLC, CU, NN, WF.

4581 A briefe discourse examining from the authority of Scriptures. *For Giles Calvert*, 1648. 4°.* LT, O, E, DT; CH, MH, NU, WF, Y.

4582 A brief discourse of changing ministers tithes. *By S. G. for W. Lee*, 1654. 4°.* L, O, C, OC, HH; CH, CN, NU, WF, Y.

Brief discourse of right worship. 1684. *See* Warner, John.

4582A A brief discourse of the most assured ways. *By J. H. for B. Aylmer*, 1687. 8°. T.C.II 180. O; CLC, Y.

4583 A brief discovrse of the present miseries of the kingdome. [*London*], 1648. 4°.* LT, O, C, HH, YM; CH, CN, MH, NU, WF, Y.

Brief discourse of the present power. 1649. *See* R., L.

Brief discourse of the real presence. 1686. *See* More, Henry.

Brief discourse of the trovbles. 1642. *See* Whittingham, William.

4584 A briefe discourse vpon tyrants. [*London*, 1642.] cap., 4°.* LT, C, LG, EC; CH, MH, NU, WF, Y.

4585 A brief discovery of a threefold estate. *For Giles Calvert*, 1653. 4°.* L, CT.

Brief discovery of the blasphemous. 1643. *See* Etherington, John.

Brief discovery of the corruption. 1647. *See* Collier, Thomas.

4586 A brief discovery of the estate of the Church. *By Matthew Simmons*, 1644. 8°. CH.

Brief discovery of the kingdom of Antichrist. [*London*, 1653]. *See* Farnworth, Richard.

Brief discovery of the threefold estate of Antichrist. 1653. *See* Buttirent, Samuel.

Briefe discovery, or description. 1647. *See* Boothby, Richard.

4587 A brief display of the French counsels. *Sold by Randal Taylor*, 1694. 8°. T.C.II 513. L, O, CT; CLC, NU.

Brief disquisition of the law. 1692. *See* Tyrrell, James.

4588 A brief dolorous remonstrance. [*London*, 1648.] brs. LT; MH.

Brief English tract. [*n.p.*], 1677. *See* Good, Thomas.

Brief essay concerning. [*n.p.*, 1692.] *See* Collier, Jeremy.

4589 A brief essay of discourse. *By Rich. Smith, for Will. Miller*, 1693. 4°.* T.C.II 428. MH.

4590 A brief examination and consideration of the unsound principles. *For Humphery Tuckey*, 1660. 4°.* MH, NU.

4591 A briefe examination; of a certaine pamphlet [by R. Baillie] lately printed in Scotland. [*n.p.*], 1644. 4°. cap., 4°. LT.

Brief examination of some. [1700.] *See* Milner, John.

Brief examination of the present. 1689. *See* Gardiner, Samuel.

Brief exhortation to all. [Philadelphia, 1691]. *See* Wilsford, John.

Brief explanation of the life. Inverary, 1686. *See* C., C.

4591A A briefe explanation of the xx. chapter of the Revelation of Saint John. *By R. Oulton for John Wright, the younger*, 1641. 4°. CCA; CLC.

Brief explication. Douay, 1652. *See* W., E.

4592 Brief explications of truth & error. [*n.p.*], 1689. 12°.* MCL; MH.

4592A A brief exposition of Our Lord's Prayer. [*London?* 1700.] cap., 4°.* L.

Brief exposition of the church. 1689. *See* Williams, John.

4593 Entry cancelled.

Briefe exposition of thd xi. xii. and xiii. chapters of the Revelation. 1651. *See* L., Y.

4593A A brief exposition of the first six chapters of Ezekiel. *For Nath. Ponder*, 1676. 12°. NPT.

4594 A breiffe for a fire at Lancaster. *In the Savoy, by Edward Jones for William Fall*, 1698. brs. MC.

4595 Brief for charity sermons in aid of the parish church of Towyn. [*n.p.*], 1694. brs. MC.

4596 A brief historical account of several. *For John Wells*, 1699. 8°.* O.

4597 A brief historical account of the behaviour of the Jesuites. *For James Adamson*, 1689. 4°. T.C.II 250. L, O, CT, LIL, OB; CH, MH, NU, TU, WF, Y.

Brief historical relation. 1654. *See* F., J.

4598 A brief history of Presbytery and independency. *For Edward Faulkner*, 1691. 4°. T.C.II 359. L, OC, CS, CT; CH, CN, NPT, NU, Y.

Brief history of the life of Mary Queen of Scots. 1681. *See* D., M.

Brief history of the pious. 1695. *See* S., J.

4599 A brief history of the rise, growth, reign, supports, ... of Popery. [*London*], 1690. 4°.* L, O, LIL, OC, CT; CH, MH, NU, WF, Y.

4600 —[*Anr. ed.*] *For the author*, 1690. 4°.* CN.

Brief history of the several plots contrived. London, 1692. *See* Wake, William, *abp.*

Brief history of the succession. [*n.p.*, 1681.] *See* Somers, John Somers, *baron.*

Brief history of the times. 1687-8. *See* L'Estrange, *Sir* Roger.

Brief history of the Unitarians. [*n.p.*], 1687. *See* Nye, Stephen.

Brief history of transubstantiation. 1674. *See* Allen, Richard.

Brief enquiry into leagues; 1682. *See* M., *Sir* P.

Brief enquiry into the ancient. 1695. *See* Tyrrell, James.

Brief enquiry into the true nature. 1690. *See* Henry, Matthew.

Brief enquiry touching. 1653. *See* Stegman, Joachim.

4601 A brief instruction in the principles of Christian religion. 1695. 12°. L.

Brief instruction in the worship. [n.p.], 1667. *See* Owen, John.

4602 Briefe instructions for church wardens. [*London*, 1650]. cap., 4°.* CT.

Brief instructions for making. 1696. *See* Woodward, John.

Brief instructions for the exercising. 1661. *See* Barriffe, John.

Brief introduction. 1654. *See* Playford, John.

Brief jvstification. 1647. *See* Prynne, William.

Brief justification. 1689. *See* Ferguson, Robert.

Brief letter. 1697. *See* Wallis, John.

Brief manifestation. 1664. *See* Davenport, Thomas.

Brief memorial of the Bible. 1688. *See* Chorley, Joseph.

4603 A brief memorial of what hath been done. [*n.p.*, 1674.] brs. O; Y.

4604 A brief memorial, wherein the present case of the ancient leases. 1674. 4°. O, LG.

Brief method of catechizing. 1644. *See* Egerton, Stephen.

4605 Entry cancelled.

Brief method of the law. 1680. *See* Brewster, Samuel.

4606 A briefe narration of some arbitrary proceedings of the committee of Kent. *Printed*, 1648. 4°.* LT, LG; CH, MIU, NU, WF, Y.

Brief narration of some church courses. 1644. *See* Rathband, William.

4607 A briefe narration of the carriage and successe of the English affaires. colop: *For Samuel Gellibrand*, 1643. cap., 4°.* O, MR, DT; MH, MIU, WF.

4608 A brief narration of the imprisonment of Mr. Francis Bampfield. [*n.p.*], *printed*, 1662. 4°.* O.

Brief narration of the plotting. 1650. *See* Waring, Thomas.

Brief narration of the practices. 1645. *See* Welde, Thomas.

Brief narration of the sufferings. [*n.p.*, 1700.] *See* Gould, Daniel.

Brief narration of the tryall of Captain Clement Nedham. 1653. *See* N., T.

Brief narrative and deduction. 1679. *See* Graves, Edward.

4609 A brief narrative how things were carried. [*London*], *printed*, 1660. 4°. L, C, MR, DT.

4610 A brief narrative of a strange and wonderful old woman that hath a pair of horns. *By T. J.*, 1676. 4°.* L; WF.

4611 Brief narrative of that stupendous tragedie. *For Charles Adams*, 1662. 4°. L, O,CT, EN; CH, LC, NU, Y.

4612 —[Anr. ed.] *Printed*, 1663. 4°. O, LG; MIU, NU.

4613 A brief narrative of the great victorie, which it hath pleased God. *By William Du-gard*, 1650. 4°.* LT, O; CN, WF, Y.

4613A A brief narrative of the harbor of . . . Rye [*London? 1677.*] cap., 4°.* WF.

4614 A brief narrative of the late treacherous and horrid designe. *For Edward Husbands, June 15.* 1643. 4°.* LT, O, HH, CT, DT; CH, MH, NU, TU, WF, Y.

4615 —[Anr. ed.] *For Edward Husbands, July 12.* 1643. 4°.* L, O; CN, MH, NU, Y.

Brief narrative of the manner. 1660. *See* Prynne, William.

Brief narrative of the proceedings. [n.p.], 1677. *See* Rawbone, Joseph.

4615A A brief narrative of the renowned Robert Earle of Essex. *By Jane Coe*, 1646. 4°.* LT.

Brief narrative of the second meeting. [n.p.], 1674. *See* Mead, William.

4616 A brief narrative of the several Popish treasons. *For P. B.* [1678]. 4°.* O; CH, MH.

Brief narrative of the state of the Protestants. 1677. *See* H, J.

Brief natural history. 1669. *See* Vaughan, Thomas.

Brief notes. 1660. *See* Milton, John.

4616A Brief notes on the creed. [1694?] 4°. OC; IU, WF, Y.

Brief observations concerning. 1668. *See* Child, *Sir* Josiah.

Brief observations of J. C. [n.p.], 1668. *See* R., H.

4616B Brief observations upon the vindication of the Trinity. [*London?* 1690.] cap., 4°.* LW, DT; MIU, NPT.

Brief of an act. [n.p., 1642.] *See* England. Parliament.

4617 A brief of the case of the officers belonging to the court of wards. [*n.p.*, 1654.] brs. LT.

4618 A brief of the papers touching a market . . . in Clements Inne Fields. [*n.p.*, 1654.] brs. LT.

Brief of two treatises. [n.p., 1687?] *See* Fitzgerald, R.

Brief, pithy discourse. 1661. *See* Prynne, William.

4619 Brief reasons humbly offered against convex-light. *Printed*, 1692. brs. Y.

Brief receipt. 1658. *See* Humfrey, John.

Brief recitall. 1641. *See* W., T.

Brief reflections for our more devout. 1693. *See* C., H.

Brief reflections on the Earl. 1682. *See* Borlase, Edmund.

4620 Brief reflections upon the inconveniences. *M. Pardoe*, 1684. fol.* L, O, HH.

4621 A brief rehersal of the belief. *For Giles Calvert*, 1656. 4°.* NU.

4622 A briefe relation, abstracted out of severall letters. *By Richard Bishop, for Lawrence Blaiklock*, 1642/3. 4°.* LT, BR; CH, MH, WF, Y.

A brief relation containing an abreviation of the argvments. 1658. *See* Cromwell, Oliver.

4623 A brief relation of a victory, obtained by the forces under . . . Doyley. *Edinburgh, by Christopher Higgins*, 1659. 4°.* ALDIS 1589. EN.

Brief relation of a wonderful. [n.p.], 1679. *See* C., I.

4624 A brief relation of several passages of the life and death of William Barton. *For John Allen*, 1664. 12°. L, O, LW; TU.

Brief relation of Sir Walter Ralegh's. 1669. *See* Raleigh, Carew.

Brief relation of some part. [n.p.], 1672. *See* Holme, Thomas.

Brief relation of that which. 1641. *See* Dury, John.

Brief relation of the beginning. 1653. *See* B., A.

Brief relation of the death. Oxford, 1644. *See* Heylyn, Peter.

Brief relation of the dismal disaster. Guernsey, 1692. *See* H., W.

Briefe relation of the gleanings. [n.p.], 1646. *See* Taylor, John.

4624A   A brief relation of the inhumane cruelties of the Turks. 1657. 4°.* LT.

Brief relation of the irreligion. 1653. *See* Higgenson, Francis.

A brief relation of the life & death of Elizabeth Braythwaite. [n.p., 1684.] *See* C., T.

Brief relation of the life ... Vincent Wing. 1670. *See* Gadbury, John.

4625   A brief relation of the march of the imperial army. colop: *For H. Hills, and are sold by Ran. Taylor, 1685.* brs. O, HH, AU; CH.

4625A   —[Anr. ed.] *Edinburgh, re-printed by the heir of Andrew Anderson, 1685.* brs. ALDIS 2530. HH.

4626   A briefe relation of the most remarkable feates. *Waterford, by Thomas Bourke, 1644.* 4°. L.

4627   A brief relation of the order and institute of the English religious women at Liege. [*Liège*, 1652.] 8°. O.

4628   A brief relation of the persecution and sufferings of the Reformed churches of France. *By A. Maxwell, 1668.* 4°.* L, O, CT, EN; CH, CN, NU, WF, Y.

4629   A brief relation of the persecutions and cruelties ... Quakers. *Printed, 1662.* 4°.* L, LP; CH, MH, PHS, VC, Y.

4629A   A brief relation of the present state of Tangiers. *T. Mabb, 1664.* 4°.* L, O, SC; NN, WF, Y.

4630   A briefe relation of the present troubles in England. *Oxford, by Henry Hall, 1645.* 4°. MADAN 1813. LT, O, CT, HH; CH, MH.

4631   A brief relation of the proceedings before His Highness Councel concerning the petitioners of the Isle of Ely. [n.p., 1654.] cap., 4°.* LT.

4632   A brief relation of the proceedings in the kingdom of Scotland. *For R.B., 1648.* 4°.* LT, HH.

4633   A briefe relation of the proceedings of our army in Ireland. *By R. Oulton, and G. Dexter for Benjamin Allen, 1642.* 4°.* LT, EC, SP, MR; CH, MH.

Brief relation of the remarkeable. [n.p.], 1642. *See* Heylyn, Peter.

4634   A briefe relation of the siege at Newark. *For Peter Cole, March 26. 1644.* 4°.* LT, CCL; CH, IU, MH, Y.

4635   A brief relation of the siege of Vienna. [*London*], 1683. brs. HH, EN.

Brief relation of the state of man. 1659. *See* Woodrove, Thomas.

Brief relation of the state of New England. 1689. *See* Mather, Increase.

4636   Entry cancelled.

Brief relation of the strange and unnatural practices of Wessel Goodwin. *See* Vernon, Samuel, 1654.

Brief relation of the surprise. 1644. *See* Ince, Peter.

Brief relation of the taking. 1645. *See* Bedford, Samuel.

4637   A brief relation or remonstrance of the injurious proceedings ... of the Turks. [n.p., 1657.] cap., 4°.* LT.

4638   A brief remembrance when the report. [*London*, 1653.] fol.* LT.

4639   Entry cancelled.

4640   A brief remonstrance of the laws. [*London*, 1654.] 4°. L.

4641   A brief remonstrance touching the pre-emption of tyn. [n.p., 1654.] cap. 4°.* LT.

Brief reply to a late answer. 1672. *See* More, Henry.

Brief reply to some part. 1653. *See* Higgenson, Francis.

Brief reply to that part of Spira's despair. 1695. *See* Wells, John.

Brief reply to the history. 1698. *See* Defoe, Daniel.

Brief reply to the narration. [n.p., 1653.] *See* Clarke, Frances.

Brief representation and discovery. 1649. *See* J., T.

4642   A brief representation of the Protestant cause in Germany. 1658. 4°.* L, O, OC; NU, WF.

Brief representation of the Quakers, [n.p., 1694]. *See* Ecclestone, Theodore.

4643   A briefe representation of the sad and lamentable condition of ... Marleborovgh. [n.p., 1653.] brs. LT.

4644   A briefe resolution of that grand case of conscience. *Printed, 1650.* L, O, CM; CH, MBP, WF, Y.

4645   A brief resolution of the present case ... Scotland. [*London*], *printed, 1661.* 4°.* EN; WF, Y.

Brief return. 1674. *See* Shewen, William.

4646   A brief review of the most material Parliamentary proceedings. *By M. S. for Tho: Jenner, 1652.* 4°. LT, O, OB, HH; CN, MH, Y.

A brief rule to guide the common-people of New-England. Boston, 1677. *See* Thacher, Thomas.

4647   A brief state of the account of all monies received and paid. [*London*, 1696.] brs. LG.

4648   A brief state of the case and tryal. colop: *For Isaac Cleave, 1694.* fol.* CH.

4649   A brief survey (historical and political) of the life and reign of Henry the III. *Printed, 1680.* 4°.* L, SP; TU, WF, Y.

4650   —[Anr. ed.] *For James Vade, 1680,* [pasted over preceding imprint.] 4°.* T.C.I 393. L; CH, CLC, NU, WF.

4651   Entry cancelled.

4652   A brief survey of our losses by the exportation of wool. [*London*, 1695?] cap., 4°.* L; NC, NN, Y.

Brief survey of the English laws. 1653. *See* W., J.

4653   A brief survey of the growth of usury in England. *Printed, 1671.* 4°.* O; NC.

Brief survey of the Lord of Derry. Paris, 1655. *See* Smith, Richard, *bp.*

4653A   A brief survey of the loss our nation sustains ... wool. [*London?* 1700]. brs. L.

4653B   A brief survey of the old religion. [*Douay?*] 1672. 8°. L, LCL; CLC, Y.

4654   A brief survey or inquiry. 1653. 4°. L, LCL.

Brief testimony. 1695. *See* Tomkins, John.

Brief tract. 1692. *See* Chafie, Thomas.

Brief treatise of the use of the globe. 1647. *See* T., R.

4655 A brief view and defence of the reformation of the Church of England. *For Simon Miller*, 1654. 8°. LT, HH.

Brief view of Mr. Coleman. 1645. *See* Byfield, Adoniram.

Brief view of the state. 1696. *See* Beverley, Thomas.

Brief vindication of the Non-conformists. 1680. *See* Owen, John.

4656 A brief vindication of the Parliamentary proceedings against the late King James IId. *Printed and sold by Randall Taylor*, 1689. 4°. T.C.II 291. C, MR, HH, YM; CH, MH, NU, WF, Y.

4656A A brief vindication of the Royal Society. *For John Martin*, 1670. 4°.* DT.

4657 A brief warning concerning the just judgement of God. [*London*] 1469. 4°.* L; WF.

4658 **Brierley, Roger.** A bundle of soul-convincing, directing and comforting truths. *Edinburgh, for James Brown, in Glasgow*, 1670. 8°. L, EN; MH.

4658A ——[Anr. ed.] *Glasgow, J. Brown*, 1676. 8°. EN.

4659 ——[Anr. ed.] *By J. R. for Samuel Sprint*, 1677. 12°. L, YM, E; CLC, NPT, WF.

Brigden, Zechariah. Almanack. Cambridg [Mass.], 1659. *See* Almanacs.

4660 **Briggins, Joseph.** The living words of a dying child. [*London?*], *printed*, 1675. 8°.* L, LF, OC; IE, PSC, Y.

4661 ——Second edition. —, 1677. 16°.* L, LF; Y.

4662 **Briggs, Joseph.** Catechetical exercises. *Cambridge, by Joh. Hayes, for Edw. Hall. To be sold by Luke Meredith, London*, 1696. 8°. T.C.II 599. L, C, CT, YM; Y.

4663 —Sound considerations for tender consciences. 1675. 8°. LCL.

4664 —Weighty reasons for tender conscientious Protestants. *For O. Blagrave*, 1679. 8°. T.C.I 339. L, O, C, CT, P.

4665 **Briggs, Thomas.** An account of some of the travels and sufferings. [*London*], *printed*, 1685. 4°.* LF, D; CH, MH, PH, PSC, Y.

4666 —Primæva communitas. [*Cambridge*], 1660. brs. L.

4667 **Briggs, William.** Nova visionis theoria. *Typis J. P., impensis Sam. Simpson, Cantab. & prostant venales apud Sam. Smith, Londini*, 1685. 12°. L, CT, LCS, MAU, BBE; CJC, PL, WSG, HC.

4668 —Ophthalmo-graphia. *Cantabrigiæ, excudebat Joann Hayes, impensis Jon. Hart*, 1676. 12°. L, O, C, GH, DT; CLC, PU, WF, WSG, Y.

4668A ——[Anr. ed.] *Typis J. P., impensis Sam. Simpson, Cantabrig. & prostant venales apud Sam. Smith, London*, 1685. 8°. T.C.II 131. C, LCS, OR, GH, DT; BN, CU, MH, PL, WSG.

4669 —[Anr. ed.] *Typis M. C., impensis R. Green, Cantabrigiæ*, 1687. 12°. LI, LCP, CT, MAU, GH; NAM, WSG, HC.

4670 **Bright, George.** Autarchy. *For Dorman Newman*, 1691. 8°. CT.

4671 —Christian prudence. *For Matt. Wotton, and G. Conyers*, 1699. 8°. L.

4672 —An essay in morality. *For John Wright*, 1682. 12°. T.C.I 458. O, OCC, P; CH, CU, Y.

4673 —] The faith by which we are justified. *For W. Marshal*, 1695. 4°. T.C.II 555. L, O, LCL; NPT.

4674 —Religionis, seu legis Christianæ tabulæ. *Imprimebat, Joh. Darby, impensis authori*, [*sic*] 1687. fol. T.C.II 201. L, C, OC, OM.

4675 —Six sermons. *By J. H. for Walter Kettilby*, 1695. 8°. T.C.II 547. L, C, OM, CE, LW; CLC, NU.

4676 —Tabulæ mosaicæ duæ. *Impensis Johannis Wright*, 1680. fol. T.C.I 412. L, OC.

4677 —A treatise of prayer. *For John Wright*, 1678. 8°. T.C.I 287. L, O, C, LW, AU; CLC, MBA, NPT, NU, WF.

Bright shining light. 1680. *See* Pennyman, John.

4678 Brightest nymph and fairest creature. [*London*], T. Cross, [1700?]. brs. L.

4679 **Brightman, Thomas.** The workes of. *By John Field for Samuel Cartwright*, 1644. 4°. L, CT, LCL, DC, ENC; CU, MH, NPT, NU, Y.

4680 ——[Anr. ed.] *By John Field for T. Slater*, 1644. 4°. LW.

4681 —The art of self-deniall. *By T. F. for I. Rothwell*, 1646. 12°. LT, C, CE.

4682 —Reverend M. Brightmans judgement or prophecies. *For R. H.*, [1641]. 4°.* LT, HH, MR.

4683 ——[Anr. ed.] *For R. Harford*, 1642. 4l. 4°.* CT; MIU, WF, Y.

4684 ——[Anr. ed.] —, 1642. 1pl., 6pp. 4°.* CJ, LWL, EN; NU, WF, Y.

4685 ——[Anr. ed.] [*London*], *printed*, 1643. 4°.* CT; CLC, MH.

4686 ——[Anr. ed.] [*London*], *for R. Harford*, 1643. 4°.* O, OC, HH; CLC, CU, IU, MH, NU.

4687 ——[Anr. ed.] *For R. Harford*, 1643. 4°.* L; NU, Y.

4688 ——[Anr. ed.] *For Richard Harper*, 1644. 4°.* Y.

4688A ——[Anr. ed.] *Edinburgh, by J. L. for John Threipland*, 1644. 8°.* AU.

4689 ——[Anr. ed.] *By Thomas Harper, for Richard Harper*, 1650. 8°.* LT, LW, DC; NU, WG.

4690 —Brightmans predictions and prophesies. [*London*], *printed*, 1641. 4°.* LT, O, CT, LCL, EN; CSS, IU, MH, NU, WF, Y.

4691 —Brightman redivivus. *By T. F. for John Rothwell, and Hannah Allen*, 1647. 4°. LT, O, CS, ENC, DT; CH, CN, NU, Y.

4692 —The revelation of Saint John. *Amsterdam, by Thomas Stafford*, 1644. 4°. L, O, C, LW, SC; NC, NPT, NU, WF, Y.

4693 ——Fourth edition. *Imprinted at London for Samuel Cartwright*, 1644. 4°. LSC, OW; MIU, NU, Y.

Brigitta, Saint. *See* Birgitta, saint.

4693A [**Brilhac, J. B. de.**] Agnes de Castro. *For William Canning*, 1688. 4°. O; CN, MH, NP, WF, Y.

4693B [—] The fatal beauty. *For R. Bentley*, 1688. 12°. T.C.II 238. L; CLC, MH.

4694 The Brimigham ballad. *For Nath. Thompson*, 1682. brs. L, O, HH.

Brimpahir, George, *pseud.*

4695 **Bringhurst, Isaac.** The easiness and difficulty of the Christian religion. *For Jonathan Robinson*, 1689. 4°.* T.C.II 272. L, O, WCA; CH, NU, TU, WF, Y.

4696   **Brinkelow, Henry.** The true coppy of the complaint of. [London], printed, [1642]. brs. LT, LS.

4697   [**Brinley, John.**] A discourse proving by Scripture . . . that there are witches. By J. M. and sold by John Weld, 1686. 8°. T.C.II 159. L, C; CH.

4698   —A discovery of the impostures of witches. For John Wright, and sold by Edward Milward, in Leitchfield, 1680. 8°. L, EN, GU; CH, CN, NIC, WF, Y.

4699   **B[rinsley], J[ohn], elder.** The posing of the parts. Tenth edition. By M. F. and J. Y. for Andrew Hebb, 1647. 4°. L.

4700   — —"Tenth" edition. [1648] 4°. WF.

4701   [–] —Eleventh edition. By M. F. and J. L. for Henry Hood, 1653. 4°. MB, Y.

4702   [–] —The "last" edition. By John Field, 1665. 4°. O.

4703   [–] —Twelfth edition. Printed, 1669. 4°. L; WF.

4703A   [–] —Thirteenth edition. For A. Roper, G. Sawbridge, T. Basset, J. Wright, R. Chiswell, W. Leake, 1677. 8°. T.C.I 297. CH, IU.

4703B   — —Fourteenth edition. For H. Herringman, T. Basset, N. Ranew, J. Wright, R. Chiswell, J. Robinson, and H. Sawbridge, 1682. 8°. T.C.I 488. MHS, NU.

4703C   — Fifteenth edition. [–] [1685?] 8°. LLL, LSC; WF.

4704   [–] —Fifteenth edition. For H. Herringman, T. Basset, N. Raven, M. Wotton, R. Chiswell, J. Robinson, H. Sawbridge, G. Conyers, 1687. 8°. L, AN.

4705   **Brinsley, John, younger.** An antidote against the poysonous weeds. By T. R. & E. M. for Ralph Smith, 1650, 4°. LT, O, LCL, EN, DT; CLC, NPT, NU, WF.

4706   —Aqua cœlestis: or, a soveraigne cordial. For George Sawbridge, 1663. 8°. L, LCL, E, AU.

4706A   — —[Anr. ed.] For John Tuthill in Great Yarmouth, 1663. 8°. CLC, NPT.

4707   —The araignment of the present schism. By John Field for Ralph Smith, 1646. 4°. LT, O, CT, EN, DT; CH, CU, LC, NU, Y.

4708   —A breviate of saving knowledge. By G. M. for Iohn Burroughes, 1643. 8°.* L, CQ.

4709   —Calendar-reformation. By Francis Neile, 1648. 4°.* LT, O, OP, CM; CH, MH, NU, WF, Y.

4710   —The Christians cabala. For George Sawbridge, 1662. 8°. LCL; MH, NU, PH.

4710A   — —[Anr. ed.] For John Tuthill in Great Yarmouth, 1662. 8°. NPT.

4711   —Church reformation. By G. M. for John Burroughes, 1643. 4°. LT, O, CS, EN, DT; Y.

4712   —The doctrine and practice of pædobaptisme. For Charles Greene, 1645. 4°. LT, O, CT, E, DT; NHC, NPT, NR, NU, Y.

4713   —The drinking of the bitter cup. By E. C. for Joseph Cranford, 1660. 8°. LT, LW, P; CH, MH, NPT, NU.

4714   —The false teacher tried and cast. By J. T. for Thomas Newberry, 1658. 8°. LT, LCL, E, AU; Y.

4714A   —Glosso-chalinosis; or, a bridle for the tongue. By A. Maxwell for John Tuthill in Great Yarmouth, 1664. 8°. NPT.

4715   —Gospel-marrow. By S. Griffin for Richard Tomlins, 1659. 8°. LT, LCL, E, AU; LC, NPT, NU, WF, Y.

4716   —The healing of Israels breaches. For John Bartlet, 1642. 4°. LT, O, LSC, E, DT; CU, MH, NU, WF, Y.

4717   —A looking-glasse for good vvomen. By John Field for Ralph Smith, 1645. 4°. LT, O, CT, OC, DT; CH, CN, NU, PL, WF, Y.

4718   —Μεσιτης: or, the one and onely mediatour. By Tho. Maxcy for Ralph Smith, 1651. 8°. LCL, CE, AU; CH, MH, NU, Y.

4719   —The mystical brasen serpent. By Thomas Maxcy for Ralph Smith, 1653. 8°. LT, LCL, LW, P, EN; CU, MH, NU.

4720   —Mystical implantation. 1651. 8°. LW.

4721   — —[Anr. ed.] By T. Maxcy for Ralph Smith, 1652. 8°. LT, LCL; CH, MBP, MH, NU, Y.

4722   —A parlie with the sword. By G. M. for John Burroughes, 1643. 4°.* L, O, LCL, LSC, P; CH, MH, NPT, NU, WF, Y.

4723   —Περιφερεια: the spirituall vertigo. 1655. 8°. LCL, E; NPT, NU.

4724   —Prayer and praise. For John Tuthill, in Yarmouth, 1661. 4°.* O.

4725   —The sacred and soveraigne church-remedie. By Moses Bell for Edward Brewster, 1645. 4°. LT, O, CT, LSC, DT; CH, CU, NU, WF, Y.

4726   —The sacred ordinance. By Rob. Ibbitson, for Tho. Newberry, 1656. 8°. LT, LCL, OC, CM, AU; CLC, NPT, NU, WF.

4727   Entry cancelled.

4728   —The saints solemne covenant. By Andrew Coe, 1644. 4°.* LT, O, CS, LCL, LSC; CH, CN, NU, WF.

4729   —Stand still. For William Frankling, 1647. 4°. O, LSC, DT.

4730   — —[Anr. ed.] For Richard Tomlins and Nathaniel Brook, 1647. 4°. LT, LCL, CT, E, EN; MH, NPT, NU.

4731   — —[Anr. ed.] For Richard Tomlins, 1652. 4°. LT, EN.

4731A   —Tears for Jerusalem. By J. L. for Tho. Newberry, 1656. 8°. LW; NU, Y.

4732   —Three sacred emblems. By J. L. for Tho. Newberry, 1656. 8°. LW; Y.

4733   —The true watch. For Humphrey Robinson, 1648. 12°. DC.

4734   —Two treatises. I. A groan for Israel. For Tho. Newberry, 1655. 8°. LT, LW, P; CLC, MB, NPT, NU, WF.

4735   —Two treatises: I. The saints communion. For Tho. Newberry, 1654. 12°. LT, CT; CLC, NPT.

4736   —Two treatises. I. Three sacred emblems. By J. L. for Tho. Newberry, 1656. 8°. L, LCL, P, E; CLC, MH, NU, WF, Y.

4737   —Two treatises: the one, handling. By T. Maxcy for Ralph Smith, 1651. 8°. LT, P, E, EN; CH, MBP, MU, NU, Y.

4737A   [**Briord, Gabriel.**] The French ambassador's speech. colop: Dublin, re-printed by C. Carter, 1700. brs. DIX 322. DI.

4738   **B[riscoe], J[ohn.]** An abstract of the discourse on the late funds. Printed, 1694. 4°.* LT, LUG, ES; MH, NC, WF, Y.

4739   —An account of the national land-bank. colop: By John Darby, [1695?]. brs. L; NC, RPB, Y.

4740 —Advertisement. I have been desired. [*London*, 1695]. brs. LG; Y.

4741 [–] Advertisement. The projectors. [*London*, 1695.] brs. Y.

4742 [–] An answer to a late pamphlet, intituled, Reasons offer'd. [*London*, 1696.] cap., fol.* L; MH, NC.

4743 —Mr. J. Briscoe, a director in the National Land-Bank, his defence. *Printed and sold by T. Sowle*, 1696. brs. L, LG, LUG, HH; MH.

4744 [–] A discourse of money. *For Sam. Briscoe*, 1696. 8°. L, O, CM, E, EN; CU, LC, MH, NC, Y.

4745 [–] A discourse on the late funds of the million-act. *Printed*, 1694. 4°. L, C, ES; CN, LC, MH.

4746 —[Anr. ed.] *By J. D. and sold by R. Baldwin*, 1694. 8°. L, LUG, LCL; LC, MH, NC, NU.

4747 — —Second edition. —, 1694. 4°. L, LG, LUG, OC, EN; CH, LC, MH, NC, Y.

4748 — —Third edition. *By J. D. for Andrew Bell*, 1696. 8°. L, LG, LUG, ES; CH, LC, MH, NC, Y.

4749 —An explanatory dialogue of . . . A discourse on the late funds. *Printed*, 1694. 4°.* L, LG, LU, ES; CH, LC, MH, NC, Y.

4750 [–] The following proposals for, and accounts of, a national land-bank. *Edinburgh, by George Mosman, by order of Joseph Blake*, 1695. cap., fol.* L.

4751 —The freehold estates of England. *By John Darby*, [1695]. brs. L, LG, OC; NC.

4751A [–] Historical and political essays or discourses. *For. W. Chandeler, and T. Scott*, 1698. 8°. CU, PL.

4751B [–] The humble offer of the national land-bank. [*London*, 1696]. brs. LG; MH.

4752 —A list of names of the subscribers. [*London*, 1695]. brs. LG, EN; Y.

4752A [–] Mr. John Asgill his plagiarism detected. *For Andrew Bill*, 1696. 8°.* L, LUG, CS; MH, NC.

4752B [–] The names of 51 persons. [*London*, 1695]. brs. L, LG.

4753 —Proposals for raising money for the national land-bank. *By John Darby*, [1695?] brs. L, LG; CH, PU, Y.

4754 —Reasons humbly offered for the establishment of the national land-bank. [*London?* 1695]. brs. LG, LUG; MH, Y.

4755 —Mr. Briscoe's reply to a pamphlet. [*London*, 1695?] brs. L, LG, HH; MH, NC.

4755A —Mr. B-coe's reply to the almanack. [*London*, 1696]. fol.* LUG.

4756 —To the honourable the knights . . . 2 Dec. 1695. [*London*, 1695.] brs. L, LUG; MH, NC, Y.

4756A — —[Anr. ed.] [*London*, 1695.] brs. L, C; MH, NC.

4757 —To the knights, citizens and burgesses. . . . A short scheme. [*London?*, 1695.] brs. L, LG, LUG; NC.

4758 —To the Lords spiritual and temporal. [*London*, 1696.] cap., fol.* L; MH, NC, Y.

4759 **Briscoe, William.** Love and charity. *Printed Decemb. 24th.* 1668. brs. L.

4760 —Verses presented to his masters. *Printed Decemb. the 24th.* 1667. brs. L.

4761 **Bristol, George Digby**, *earl of*. The Lord George Digbies apologie. [*Oxford*], *printed*, 1642 [3]. 4°.*. MADAN 1161. L, O, C, LG, LVF; CLC, CN, MH, NU, WF, Y.

4762 — —[Anr. ed.] *Oxford* [*i.e., London*], 1642. 4°.* MADAN 1162. LT, O, CT, EN, DT; CH, CN, MH, WF, Y.

4763 —The Lord George Digby's cabinet. *For Edward Husband, March 16.* 1646. 4°. LT, O, CT, OC, HH; CH, CN, MH, WF, Y.

4763A — —[Anr. ed.] *March 26*, 1671. 4°. LT, OC, NR; CH, LC, MIU, NU, Y.

4764 [–] Elvira. *By E. Cotes for Henry Broom*, 1667. 4°. T.C.II 291. L, O, LVD, OW; CH, CN, LC, TU, Y.

4765 [–] —[Anr. ed.] *By A. C. for Henry Brome*, 1677. 4°. T.C.I 291. CH, CLC, CU.

4766 —The Irish papers. *By F. Leech*, 1646. 4°.* LT, O; CH, MH, MIU, WF, Y.

4767 —The Lord Digby his last speech. [*London?*], *printed* 1641. 4°.* LT, O, C, OC, EN; CH, CN, MH, NC, WF, Y.

4768 —Letters between the Ld . . . and Sr Kenelm Digby Kt. concerning religion. *For Humphrey Moseley*, 1651. 8°. LT, O, CT, LW, EN; CH, CN, MH, MMO, MU, WF, Y. (Two issues: 1 dated Sherburn, March 39, 1639; 1 dated Sherborn, March 30, 1639.)

4769 —A printed paper cald the Lord Digbies speech to the Bill of Attainder. *By William Iones*, 1641. 4°.* LT, O, CT, GU; CH, MHL, Y.

4770 Entry cancelled.

4771 —The Lord Digbies speech in the House of Commons . . . 21 April 1641. [*London*], *printed* 1641. 4°.* L, O, C, LL, DT; BN, CH, MH (3 eds.), NU, TU, WF, Y.

4772 —The Earl of Bristol his speech in the House of Lords, the xx day of July 1660. *Printed*, 1660. 4°.* L, O, LG, DT; CH, MH, Y.

4773 — —[Anr. ed. "Earle"] *Printed*, 1660. 4°.* LT, O, LL, P; CLC, CN, MH, WF, Y.

4774 —The speeches of. [*London*], *for Thomas Walkely*, 1641. 4°.* LT, O, C, LL, HH; CH, CN, LC, MH, TU, Y.

4775 —The third speech of. [*n.p.*], *for Tho: Walkley*, 1640 [1]. 4°.* LT, O, LL, CT, EC; CH, CN, MH, NC, WF, Y.

4776 — —[Anr. ed.] [*n.p.*], *for Thomas Walkley*, 1641. 4°.* L; CLC, CU, MH, WF, Y.

4777 [–] A trve and impartiall relation of the battaile betwixt, His Majesties army and that of the rebells. [*Oxford, by L. Lichfield*], 1643. 4°.* MADAN 1453. O, C, SC; MH, Y.

4778 [–] —[Anr. ed.] *Printed at Oxford by L. Lichfield*, 1643. 4°.* MADAN 1454. LT, O; CH, WF, Y.

4779 —Two letters of note. *Printed*, 1642. 4°.* LT, O, LG, HH, EN; CLC, CN, MH, WF, Y.

4779A — —[Anr. ed.] *For John Tompson*, 1642. 4°.* OC.

4780 —Two letters of the Lord Digby. *For Edward Husband, Decem. 4.* 1647. 4°.* LT, O, C, LVF, HH; MH, NN.

4781 —Two letters, the one from. *By A. N. for Richard Lownds*, 1642. 4°.* L, O, C; OWC.

4782 —Two letters, the one from. *For George Lindsey*, 1642. 4°. O, BR.

4783 —August 5. Two letters, the one from. *By R. O. and G. D. for John Bartlet*, 1642. 4°.* LT, O, HH, CJ, EC; CH, CN, MH, NU, WF, Y.

4784 —August 6. Two letters the one from. *For Iohn Wright*, 1642. 4°.* L, O, SP; MH.

4785 —Two remarkable letters concerning the Kings correspondence. *By F. Neile*, 1645. MADAN 1810. 4°.* LT, O, C, LVF, EN, OT; CH, MH, Y.

4786 —Two speeches of. *Printed*, 1674. 4°.* L, O, C, MR, EN; CH, MH, NU, TU, WF, Y.

4787 **Bristol, John Digby, *earl of*.** An apologie of. *Caen*, 1647. fol. BN.

4788 — —[Anr. ed.] *Caen, printed 1647, and reprinted in London*, 1656. 4°. LT, O; CH, MBP.

4789 — —[Anr. ed.] [*Caen*], *printed*, 1657. 4°. L, CT, HH; CH, MH, NU, WF, Y.

4790 — —[Anr. ed.] *First printed at Caen, and now reprinted at London*, 1660. 4°. CT; CH, NU, OWC.

4791 —Articles drawn up by. *Printed at London for I. A.*, 1642. 4°.* LT; CH, WF, Y.

4792–3 Entires cancelled.

4794 —A speech made by ... May 20. 1642. *For Richard Marriot*, 1642. 4°.* LT, O, C, EN, DT; CH, CN, MH, NU, WF, Y.

4795 — —[Anr. ed.] *For Nath. Butter*, 1642. 4°.* CJ, EC, HH; MIU, WF.

4796 — —[Anr. ed.] *For W. G.*, 1642. 4°.* L, O; CH, CU, MH, TU, WF, Y.

4797 — —[Anr. ed.] *For I. Smith and A. Coe*, 1642. 4°.* LT, O, CS, HH; CH, MH, PU, WF.

4798 —Two speeches spoken at the Councill-table at Oxford. *Printed at Oxford by Leonard Lichfield, and now reprinted at London for Iohn Hanson*, 1642. 4°.* MADAN 1136. LT, O, LVF, HH, DT; CH, CU, MH, NU, Y.

4799 The Bristol address. To the right worshipful Sir Richard Hart. colop: *For Henry Brome*, 1681. brs. L, O, C, BR, EN; CH, MBA, MH, WF, Y.

Bristol drollery. 1674. *See* Crutwell, N.

4800 The Bristol garland. In four parts. [*London?* 1700?] brs. L; MH.

4801 Bristols second address. colop: *For Henry Broom*, 1681. brs. O, LG, HH, BR; CH, CLC, Y.

4802 **Bristow, Richard.** Motives indvcing to the Catholike faith. Third edition. [*St. Omer's, English college press*], *permissu superiorum*, 1641. 12°. L.

4803 Britain reviv'd in a panegyrick to William and Mary. colop: *For N. Cox in Oxon*. [1689.] brs. MH.

4803A —[Anr. ed.] colop: *For R. Baldwin*, 1689. brs. OC; CH, Y.

4804 **Britaine, William de.** The Dutch usurption. *For Jonathan Edwin*, 1672. 4°.* T.C.I 110. L, O, C, LL, EN; HR, CH, NC, NU, WF, Y.

4805 —Humane prudence. *For Robert Harford*, 1680. 12°. T.C.I 396. O, CS; CN.

4805A [–]—Second edition. *For John Lawrence*, 1682. 12°. T.C.I 486. LLL; CLC, MU, Y.

4805B [–] —Third edition. *By J. Rawlins, for Richard Sare*, 1686. 12°. T.C.II 171. L; CLC, TU.

4805C [–]—Fifth edition. —, 1689. 12°. T.C.II 326. OC, CT; CU, WF, Y.

4806 [–] —Sixth edition. *By J. Rawlins, for R. Sare*, 1693. 12°. T.C.II 459. L, O, C, AN; CH, CN, NR, PL.

4807 [–]—Seventh edition. *For Richard Sare*, 1697. 12°. T.C.III 82. CH, CN, NN, TU.

4807A [–]—Eighth edition. —, 1700. 12°. MH, RPB.

4808 [–] The interest of England in the present war with Holland. *For Jonathan Edwin*, 1672. 4°.* L, O, C, OC, BP; CH, LC, NC, RPJ, Y.

4809 [–] A sober inquiry, whether it be lawful. *For A. Banks*, 1684. fol.* L, O, HH; CH, WF, Y.

4809A Britain's alarum. [*London?* 1700.] brs. L.

4810 Britains glory: being a relation. *For Edw. Farnham*, 1660. 4°.* LT; WF.

4811 Britain's honour, in the two valiant Welchmen, who fought against fifteen. [*n.d.*] brs. O.

Britains jubilee. 1689. *See* Fleming, Robert.

4811A Britain's King revived. 1660. 4°. OC; WF.

4812 Britains sorrowful lamentation, for the loss of ... Queen Mary. *Printed at London, and reprinted at Edinburgh, by John Reid*, 1695. brs. ALDIS 3445. L, ES.

Britains triumph. 1660. *See* S., G.

4813 Britains triumphs, or a brief history. *For Edward Farnham*, 1656. 8°. L, C, CT; CH, LC, MH, RPJ, Y.

Britannia iterum. 1662. *See* W., W.

Britannia languens. 1680. *See* Petyt, William.

4814 Britania nova illustrata. Being. *For E. Whitlock*, 1698. 4°.* T.C.III 67. L, CT.

4815 Britannia nova: or a seasonable discourse. *For Matthew Gilliflower and Hugh Newman*, 1698. 4°. LUG.

Britannia, or. .... 1673. *See* Blome, Richard.

4816 Britannia passionately and historically rembring her misery. colop: [*London*], *by G. B. and R. W.*, [1643/4]. 4°.* LT, HH; CH, NN.

4816A Britannia reflorescens, in a prospect. *Hussey*, 1684. 12°. LG.

4817 Britannia triumphalis; a brief history of the warres. *For Samuel Howes*, 1654. 8°. LT, O, SP, EN; CH, CU, MH, MIU, WF.

4818 Britannia's triumph. *E. Witlock*, 1697. brs. CN.

4819 Britanniae speculum or, a short view of ... Great Britain. The first part. *By Thomas Milbourn, for Christopher Hussey*, 1683. 12°. T.C.II 3. L, O, CT, LG, DT; CH, CLC, CN, PL, WF.

Britannian magazine. 1694. *See* Y-Worth, William.

4820 Entry cancelled.

Britannicæ virtutis. Oxford, 1644. *See* Walsingham, Edward.

4821 Britannicus his blessing. colop: *Cambridge, by Roger Daniel*, 1646. 4°.* LT, O, C; WF.

4822 Britannicus his pill to cvre malignancy. *For Robert White*, 1644. 4°.* LT, HH; CH, CU, MH, NU, WF, Y.

4822A Britanicvs vapulans: or the whipping of poore British Mercury. [*London*, 1643.] 4°. HH, DT; CH.

Britannophilus, Alethophilus Basilophilus, *pseud.*

4823   The British bell-man. [*London*], *printed*, 1648. 4°.*
    LT, O; CH, MH, MIU, WF, Y.

    British lightning. [*n.p.*], 1643. *See* V., G. L.

4824   [**Britten, William.**] Concerning the kingdoms of God
    and men. [*London?*, 1660?] cap., 4°.* L, LF, BBN, BR;
    PH, PSC, WF, Y.

4824A —The moderate Baptist. *For J. Collins,* 1654. 8°. OC;
    NHC.

4824B —The power of God. *For the author,* 1660. 8°. LF, BR;
    PH.

4825   —Silent meeting. *For Robert Wilson,* 1660. 4°.* L, C,
    CT, LF, BBN; CH, IE, NU, PH, WF, Y.

4826   [–] —[Anr. ed.] [*London*], *printed,* 1671. 4°.* LF, OC,
    CT, EN; CH, MH, NR, PH, Y.

4827   [–] —[Anr. ed.] —, 1675. 4°.* L, LF; CH, MH, NC, Y.

4828   **Britton, Thomas.** The library of. [1694.] 4°.* L, O,
    HH; MH.

4829–30 Entries cancelled.

4831   A broad-side against marriage. [*London*], *printed,* 1675.
    brs. L.

4832   A broadside for the Dutch. *By J. C. for Samuel Speed,*
    1672. brs. L.

4832A A broad-side more for the Dutch. *Printed, and Edin-*
    burgh, reprinted, 1666. brs. MH.

4833   **Brocardo, Francisco.** Francis Broccard (Secretary to
    Pope Clement the Eighth) his alarm. *By T. S. for*
    William Rogers, 1679. 4°.* T.C.II 285. L, O, C, EN, DT;
    CH, CN, MH, NU, WF, Y.

4834   **Brock,**   . Datâ indicatione forti. [*n.p.*] *Jul. 4.* 1653.
    brs. O.

4834A **Brocke, Joseph.** The case of the appellant. [*London?*
    1693.] brs. L.

4834B **Brodie, Alexander.** Penn's practice. [*Edinburgh,* 1696.]
    CH.

4835   **Brodie, James.** Answers for Sir John Hall. [*n.p.*, 1689.]
    fol. L, EN.

4836   —To His Grace, His Majesties High Commissioner.
    [*n.p.*, 1690.] fol.* L.

4837   **Brodrick,** *Sir* **Saint John.** Sʳ St. John Brodrick's
    vindication of himself. [*London*], *for the author,* 1690.
    4°.* T.C.II 323. L, C, LVF, AU; CH, MIU, NC, WF, Y.

4838   Entry cancelled.

    [**Broe, Samuel de.**] History of the triumvirates. 1686.
    See Citri de La Guette, 5.

4839   Entry cancelled.

4840   **Broekhuizsen, Benjamin, van.** Catalogus librorum.
    1684. fol. L, OC, HH; MH.

4841   **Brograve, Robert.** A sermon preach'd . . . May the
    12th. 1689. *For William Rogers,* 1689. 4°.* T.C.II 268.
    L, C, OC, EC, BAMB; CLC, CN, MBA, MH, WF, Y.

4842   **Brokeman, J.** The tradesmans lamentation. *For the*
    author, 1663. brs. L.

4843   The broken merchants complaint. *By Nat. T.,* 1683.
    4°.* L, O; NC, NN, Y.

    Broken title. 1642. *See* Burgess, Cornelius.

4844   [**Brokesby, Francis.**] A perswasive to reformation.
    For Walter Kettilby, 1680. 4°.* L, O, OC, LW, EN; CH,
    NGT, NU, SW, TU.

4845   **Brokett, John.** Gods statute. *By I. L. for Richard*
    Thraule, 1642. 4°.* LT, O; MBP, NPT, WCL, WF, Y.

4846   **Brokett, William.** Good newes from Ireland. *For I.*
    Thomas, Octob. 6. 1642. 4°.* LT, EC; MH.

4846A [**Brome, Alexander.**] Bumm-foder or, waste-paper.
    [*London,* 1660.] brs. L; MH, Y.

4847   — A Canterbury tale. [*London*], *printed* 1641. 4°.* LT;
    CH, MH, WF.

4848   —Caroli τον μαηαειτω. 1649. 8°. L.

4848A —The clown's complaint. [1647.] brs. L.

4849   —A congratulatory poem, on the miraculous, . . . re-
    turn of . . . King Charls the II. *For Henry Brome,* 1660.
    4°.* LT, O; CH, MH, TU, WF, Y.

4849A [–] A copie of verses. [*London,* 1648], brs. LT.

4850   —The cunning lovers. A comedy. *For Will. Sheares,*
    1654. 4°. L, O, LVD, DC, EN; CH, CN, LC, MH, NC, Y.

4850A [–] A record in rithme. [*London,* 1670?] cap., 4°.* L,
    O; MH.

4850B — The rump or a collection of songs. *For H. Brome and*
    H. Marsh, 1660. 4°. LT, O, LG, A; CH, MH, OCI, WF.

4851   [–] Rump: or an exact collection of the choycest poems
    and songs. *For Henry Brome, and Henry Marsh,* 1662.
    8°. L, O, C, GH, DT; CH, LC, MH, TU, Y.

4852   —Songs and other poems. *For Henry Brome,* 1661. 8°.
    L, O, C; CH, CN, MH, TU, WF, Y.

4853   — —Second edition. —, 1664. 8°. L, CT; BN, CH, CU,
    MH, NC, WF, Y.

4854   — —Third edition. —, 1668. 8°. L, O, LVD, EN, DT;
    CH, CU, MBP, MH, Y.

4855   [**Brome, Charles.**] To the memory of Mr. Dryden. *For*
    Charles Brome, 1700. fol.* T.C.III 199. L; CH, CLC, MIU.

4856   **Brome, James.** The famine of the word. *By M. Clark,*
    for Richard Chiswel, 1679. 4°. T.C.I 356. L, BR; MH,
    WF, Y.

4857   —An historical account of Mr Roger's three years
    travels. [*n.p.*], *printed and sold by J. Moxon & B.*
    Beardwell, 1694. 8°. L, C, LW; CLC, Y.

4858   — —Second edition. *For A. Roper and R. Clavel,* 1697.
    8°. C, CT; CN, WF.

4858A —An historical account of Mr. Brome's travels. *For*
    Abel Roper, Rich. Basset, and Will. Turner, 1700. 8°. L,
    O, LG, CCN, EN; BN, CH, CN, PL, TU, WF, Y.

4859   —The original of plotts. *For Samuel Lee,* 1684. 4°.* O;
    CLC, MH, Y.

4860   —A sermon preached . . . June the first, 1694. *For*
    Eben Tracy, 1694. 4°.* L, O; WF.

4861   Entry cancelled.

4862   [**Brome, Richard.**] The beggars chorus in The Jovial
    crew. [*London,* 1670?] brs. L.

4863   [–] —[Anr. ed.] [1683.] brs. O.

4863A [–] —[Anr. ed.] [*London*], *for P. Brooksby,* [1672–95.]
    brs. L.

4864   [–] —[Anr. ed.] [*London*], *for J. Walter,* [1695–1700].
    brs. L, C, HH.

4865 [–] —[Anr. ed.] [London, 1700?] brs. L.

4866 [–] The city wit. By T.R. for Richard Marriot, and Thomas Dring, 1653. 8°. L; CU, MH, NF, NP, Y.

4867 —The court beggar. For Richard Marriot, and Tho. Dring, 1653. 8°. L; MBP, MH, NF, WF.

[–] Covent Garden drolery. 1672. See title.

4868 [–] The damoiselle. By T.R. for Richard Marriot and Thomas Dring, 1653. 8°. L; CU, MH, NF, NIC, Y.

4869 [–] The debauchee. For John Amery, 1677. 4°. T.C.I 263. L, O, CS, OW, EN; CH, LC, MH, NC, Y.

4869A —The English Moor. Printed, 1659. 8°. LT, O, LVD, OW, EN; CH, CN, LC, MH, Y.

4870 —Five new playes. For Humphrey Moseley, Richard Marriot, and Thomas Dring, 1653. 8°. LT, O, LVD, DC, EN; BN, CH, CU, TU, WF, Y.

4871 ——[Anr. ed.] By J.F. to be sold by J.Sweeting, 1654. 8°. L, O; MH, WF, Y.

4872 ——[Same title.] For A. Crook, and for H.Brome, 1659. 8°. LT, O, LVD, OW, EN; CH, CN, MH, WF, Y.

[–] Joviall crew. 1651. See Sheppard, Samuel.

4873 —A joviall crew. By J.Y. for E.D and N.E., 1652. 4°. L, O, LVD, EN; CH, CU, LC, MH, TU, WCL, Y.

4874 ——[Anr. ed.] For Henry Brome, 1661. 4°. L, O, LG, OW, CM; CN, MBP, MH, WF, Y.

4875 ——[Anr. ed.] For Joseph Hindmarsh, 1684. 4°. T.C.II 61. L, O, C, OC, DT; CH, CN, MH, WF, Y.

4876 —Lachrymæ musarum; the tears of the muses. By Tho. Newcomb, 1649. 8°. L, O; CH, Y.

4877 ——[Anr. ed.] By T.N. to be sold by John Holden, 1650. 8°. LT, CT, LVD, LVF; CH, MH, TU, WCL, Y.

4877A —The love-sick court. 1658. 8°. O.

4878 —The northern lasse. Second edition. For A. Moseley, 1663. 4°. L, O, OW, LVD; CH, IU, MB, Y.

4879 ——[Anr. ed.] For D.Newman, 1684. 4°. T.C.II 73. L, O, EN; CH, MH, NP, TU, WF, Y.

4880 —The novella. For R.Marriot and T.Dring. 1653. 8°. L; CU, MBP, NF.

4881 Entry cancelled.

4882 —The queenes exchange. For Henry Brome, 1657. 4°. L, O, LVD, OW; CH, CN, MH, TU, WF, Y.

4883 —The royal exchange. A comedy. For Henry Brome, 1661. 4°.* LT; CH, Y.

4884 —The weeding of the Covent-Garden. For Andrew Crook, and Henry Brome, 1658. 8°. LT, O; CH, MH, TU, Y.

4884A Bromfield, M. As there is hardly anything. [London, 1680.] brs. L.

4884B —A brief account of some wonderful cures. [London? 1680.] brs. L.

4884C —A brief account of the chief causes. 1679. 4°.* L.

4884D —A brief but most useful account of scurvy. [London, 1681/2.] brs. DCH.

4884E —A brief discovery of the chief causes of ... scurvy. Printed, 1679. 4°.* L.

4884F ——[Anr. ed.] 1685. 4°.* L, LWL.

4884G ——[Anr. ed.] 1694. 8°.* MH.

4884H —A brief discovery of the true causes. Printed, 1672. 8°.* NAM, WS

4885 B[romhall], T[homas]. A history of apparitions, oracles, prophecies. By John Streater, 1659. fol. CH.

4886 —A treatise of specters. By John Streater, 1658. fol. L, O, P, EN, GU; CH, CN, MH, WF, Y.

4887 Bromley, Richard. The case of Richard Bromley. [London, 1700?] cap., fol.* L.

4888 Bromley, Thomas. A catalogue of Mr. T. Bromley's library. 1691. cap., 4°.* L.

4888A —The way to the sabbath of rest. By John Streater, for Giles Calvert, 1655. 4°. LT, O, LW; Y.

4888B ——[Anr. ed.] Printed and are to be sold by Randal Taylor, 1692. 4°. CH, WF.

4889 [Bromley, William.] Remarks in the grande tour. By E.H. for Tho. Bassett, 1692. 8°. T.C.II 424. L; CLC, CN, NP, WF, Y.

4890 [–] Remarks made in travels. For Thomas Basset, 1693. 8°. L, O, C, DCH; CH, CLC, NP, WF.

4891 Brommerton, William. Confidence dismounted. Printed, April 5. 1652. 4°.* LT.

Bromwell. See Bramhall.

4892 Bromwich, Isaac. The spoiles of the Forrest of Deane asserted. Printed, 1650. 4°.* L, O; WF.

Brontius, Adolphus, pseud.

4893-4 Entries cancelled.

4895 Brook, Chidley. To their excellencys. [New York, William Bradford], 1696. fol.* MU, NHS, RPJ.

4896 Brook, Sir Robert. The reading of ... Magna Carta, chap. 16. By M.Flesher, and R.Young, and are sold by Laurence Chapman and William Coke, 1641. 4°.* L, O, CT, LL, DT; CH, LC, MH, TU, WF, YL.

4897 —The reading of ... upon the statue of limitations. For Hen. Twyford, 1647. 8°. L, O, LL, EN; CH, LC, MHL, NCL.

4898 —Some new cases ... Hen. 8, Edw. 6 and Qu. Mary. Sixth edition. By T.N. for Richard Best, & John Place, 1651. 8°. L, LI, LL, LIL, LM; LC, MHL, WF.

Brooke, Fulke Greville, baron. First fourteen years. 1651. See Wilson, Arthur.

—Five years. 1643. See Wilson, Arthur.

4899 —The life of the renowned Sr Philip Sidney. For Henry Seile, 1652. 8°. LT, O, C, OB, DT; CH, CN, MH, TU, WF, Y.

4900 —The remains of. By T.N. for Henry Herringman, 1670. 8°. L, O, C, LVD, OC; CH, MH, NP, WF, Y.

4901 [–] The tragedy of that famous Roman oratovr Marcus Tullius Cicero. By Richard Cotes, for John Sweeting, 1650. 4°.* L, O.

4902 [–] —[Anr. ed.] —, 1651. 4°.* LT, O, LVD, EN; CH, CN, CU, Y.

4903 Brooke, Humphrey. Cautionary rules for preventing the sickness. By James Flesher, 1665. 4°.* L, LG.

4903A —The charity of church-men. By H.Hills, to be sold by W.Larnar, 1649. 4°.* LT, O, LG; CH, CU, MIU, NU.

4904 —The durable legacy. By M.White, 1681. 8°. L, O, OME; NAM, NPT.

4905 —Υγιεινη. Or a conservatory of health. *By R. W. for G. Whittington*, 1650. 12°. LT, LCP, LCS, LM, LWL; NAM, WF, WSG, HC.

4906 **Brooke, John.** A sermon at the funeral of . . . John Symonds. *For Tho. Parkhurst*, 1693. 4°.* L; CH, MH, Y.

4907 [**Brooke, Nathaniel.**] Englands glory, or, an exact catalogue. *For Nath. Brooke, and Hen. Eversden*, 1660. 8°. L, O, CM, MR, SC; CH, CN, MH, WF, Y.

4908 **Brooke, Richard.** The resolution and remonstrance of the navie. *For George Roberts*, 1649. 4°.* LT; CH.

4909 Entry cancelled.

4910 [**Brooke, Robert Greville, baron.**] Catalogus librorum ex bibliotheca nobilis. [*n.p.*], 2 Dec., 1678. 4°. L, O, CS, HH; Y.

4911 —A discourse opening the natvre of that episcopacie. *By R. C. for Samuel Cartwright*, 1641. 4°. LT, O, CT, EN, DT; CH, CN, MH, TU, WF, Y.

4912 — —Second edition. —, 1642. 4°. L, O, CT, LSC, E; CU, NU, TU, WF, Y.

4912A — —[Anr. ed.] *Printed*, 1681. 4°. OCC, SP; CLC.

4913 —The nature of truth. *By R. Bishop, for Samuel Cartwright*, 1641. 12°. L, O, LSC, DT; CH, MH, NU, OCI, Y.

4914 —Three speeches spoken in Gvild-Hall. *By J. F. for Peter Cole*, 1642. 4°.* LT, O, C, LCL, EN; CH, CLC, CN, LC, MH, TU, Y.

4915 —A worthy speech. *February the 26. printed at London for Iohn Vnderwood*, 1643. 4°.* LT, CCL, CT, BC, A; MH, Y.

4916 **Brooke, Samuel.** Catalogus librorum. [*London*, 1680/1.] 4°.* L, OC, CS, OP, HH; CN.

4917 **Brooke, William.** Exceeding happy newes from Ireland, being a true relation. *By T. F. for J. R., June 16.*, 1642. 4°.* L, MR.

4917A **B[rookes], C[ristopher].** A new quadrant. *Printed*, 1649. 8°.* L, O.

4917B **Brookes, Matthew.** The perfect work of patience. *Printed*, 1655. 8°. MWA, Y.

4918 —The sacred and most mysterious history of man's redemption. *By William Wilson, for the author*, 1657. fol. L, LI, OC, ENC; CH, LC, NPT, NU.

4919 **Brookes, Thomas.** Τον ανεξιχνιαστον πλουτον. The unsearchable riches. *By Mary Simmons, for John Hancock*, 1655. 4°. LT; MH, MWA, Y.

4920 — —[Anr. ed.] *By M. S. for John Hancock*, 1657. 4°. L; NPT, NU, Y.

4921 — —Third edition. —, 1661. 4°. L, LCL; CH, NGT, NU, TSM, WF.

4922 — —Fourth edition. *For John Hancock*, 1671. 8°. T.C.I 70. L, LW; MIU, NU, PPT, Y.

4923 —Apples of gold. Second edition. *By R. I. for John Hancock*, 1657. 8°. O, LSC.

4923A — —Third edition. —, 1659. 8°. MH, MHS.

4924 — —"Third" edition. —, 1660. 8°. LT; NPT, WF.

4925 — —Fourth edition. —, 1662. 8°. C; CLC.

4925A — —Fifth edition. —, 1664. 8°. PH.

4926 — —Sixth edition. —, 1665. 8°. LW; NU.

4926A — —[Anr. ed.] —, 1667. 8°. CN, NPT.

4926B — —Eighth edition. —, 1661. 8°. CLC.

4927 — —[Anr. ed.] 1669. 12°. LCL.

4928 — —[Anr. ed.] 1672. 12°. LW.

4928A — —Twelfth edition. 1676. 8°. CLC.

4928B — —[Anr. ed.] 1679. 12°. T.C.I. 336. IAU.

4928C — —Sixteenth edition. *By J. A. for John Hancock*, 1690. 12°. T.C.II 341. WF.

4928D — —Seventeenth edition. *For John Hancock*, 1693. 12°. T.C.II 532. MH, NPT.

4929 —An arke for all Gods Noahs. *By M. S. for Henry Cripps*, 1662. 8°. O, LCL, OB; CU, MH, MWA, NPT, NU.

4930 — —[Anr. ed.] —, 1666. 8°. NPT, NU.

4930A — —[Anr. ed.] *By M. S. for J. Hancock*, 1666. 8°. CLC, IAU.

4931 — —[Anr. ed.] *By R. I. for Henry Cripps*, 1666. 8°. L; WF.

4932 —A beleevers last day. *For T. Underhill*, 1653. 4°.* O; LC, NU, WF.

4933 — —[Anr. ed.] *Printed, to be sold by John Hancock*, 1657. 8°.* L, LCL, P; CH, CLC, Y.

4934 — —[Anr. ed.] *For John Hancock*, 1660. 8°.* L, LW; CLC.

4935 — —[Anr. ed.] *Printed, and are to be sold by John Hancock*, 1665. 8°. L, O; Y.

4936 — —[Anr. ed.] *For J. Hancock, senior & junior.*, 1673. 8°.* NU.

4937 —A cabinet of choice jevvels. *Printed, to be sold by John Hancock*, 1669. 4°. T.C.I 12. L, O, C, LW; CH, MH, NU, WF, Y.

4938 —Cases considered and resolved. *By M. Simmons, for John Hancock*, 1653. 4°.* LT, O, C, EN; CH, NU, WF, Y.

4939 —The crovvn & glory of Christianity. *For H. Crips, J. Sims, and H. Mortlock*, 1662. 4°. L, O, LCL, LW; CLC, MH, NPT, NU WF, Y.

4939A —The dying ministers last sermon. *For J. Conyers*, [1680]. 8°.* CM.

4940 —The glorious day of the saints appearance. *By M. S. for Ralph Harford and Matthew Simmons*, 1648. 4°.* LT, O, C, LCL, NPT, NU, WF, Y.

4941 —Gods delight. *By M. S. for R. Harford, and Thomas Brewster*, 1649. 4°. LT, O, C, OCC, DT; MH, NU, WF.

4942 —A golden key. *For Dorman Newman*, 1675. 4°. T.C.I 194. L, O, C, LCL, LW; CH, MH, NU, WF, Y.

4943 —Heaven on earth. *By R. I. for John Hancock*, 1654. 8°. LT, BR; CLC, IU, NPT, NU, WF.

4944 — —Second edition. *By M. S. for John Hancock*, 1657. 8°. L, LCL; CH, CLC, IU, NU.

4945 — —Third edition. —, 1660. 8°. L, LSC, CCH, LW; MH, MHS, Y.

4946 — —Fourth edition. —, 1664. 8°. L, O; CH.

4947 — —Fifth edition. *For John Hancock, senior and junior*, 1673. 8°. T.C.I 156. CCH; NU.

4948 —A heavenly cordial. *Printed for, and are to be sold by John Hancock*, 1666. 8°. O; CLC, MH, WF.

4949 —The hypocrite detected. *By Fr: Neile for Hanna Allen*, 1650. 4°.* LT, O, DT; CH.

4950 —London's lamentations. *For John Hancock and Na-thaniel Ponder*, 1670. 4°. T.C.I 18. L, O, C, LG, LCL; CH, MH, NU, TU, WF, Y.

4951 —The mute Christian. *For John Hancock*, 1669. 12°. T.C.I 11. O; NPT.

4951A — —[Anr. ed.] —, 1671. 8°. T.C.I 75. CLC.

4951B — —Sixth edition. *For John Hancock, sen. & jun.* 1675. 12° T.C.I 191. MH.

4951C — —Seventh edition. —, 1679. 12°. IAU.

4951D — —Eighth edition. —, 1684. 12°. T.C.II 121. MWA, Y.

4952 — —Ninth edition. *For John Hancock*, 1698. 12°. L, LG, LSC; MH.

4953 —Paradice opened. *For Dorman Newman*, 1675. 4°. T.C.I 225. L, LCL, LSG; MII, NPT, NU, WF.

4953A —Precious remedies. *By Matthew Simmons for John Hancock*, 1652. 8°. CLC, NGT, NPT.

4954 — —Second edition. *By M. Simmons, for John Hancock*, 1653. 8°. LT, LSC; CLC, NPT, NU, PH.

4955 — —Third edition. —, 1656. 8°. LCL; CH, NU, WF, Y.

4956 — —Fourth edition. —, 1658. 8°. O, AU; CLC, MH.

4957 — —[Anr. ed.] [*London*], *by M. Simmons, for John Hancock*, 1661. 8°. LSC; NC, NPT, NU.

4958 — —[Anr. ed.] *By H. Lloyd, for John Hancock*, 1669. 8°. T.C.I 11. L, O, C, LCL, AN; CLC, NPT.

4959 — —Seventh edition. *By R. White, for John Hancock*, 1671. 8°. T.C.I 92. L, LW.

4960 — —Eighth edition. *For John Hancock*, 1676. 8°. T.C.I 230. L.

4960A — —Nineth edition. —, 1683. 12°. T.C.II 8. NPT.

4961 —The privie key of Heaven. *Printed for, and are to be sold by John Hancock*, 1665. 8°. L, O, C, LCL; CLC, CU, MIU, NPT, NU, PJB.

4961A — —Second edition. —, 1681. 12°. T.C.I 466. EN.

4962 —The silent sovl. *By R. I. for John Hancock*, 1659. 8°. O; CLC, MH, NPT.

4962A — —[Anr. ed.] —, 1660. 8°. LT, LCL; CH, MH, NPT, NU, WF.

4963 —A string of pearles. *By R. I. for John Hancock*, 1657. 8°. LT, O, ENC; CLC, NPT, NU, WF, Y.

4964 — —Second edition. —, 1660. 8°. LT; CLC, MH.

4965 — —[Anr. ed.] *By R. T. for John Hancock*, 1662. 8°. DC; NU.

4966 — —[Anr. ed.] *Printed*, 1667. 12°. L.

4967 — —[Anr. ed.] *For John Hancock*, 1668. 12°. O.

4967A — —[Anr. ed.] —, 1671. 12°. T.C.I 74. Y.

4968 — —Eighth edition —, 1674. 12°. T.C.I 191, LCL; CLC.

4969 — —Tenth edition. *For John Hancock*, 1684. 12°. T.C.II 121. CH.

4970 —A word in season. *For Dorman Newman*, [1675]. 4°. LCL; NU, WF.

4971 [**Brookhaven, John.**] A letter sent to Mr. Speaker, from the commissioners in the county of Essex. *For Joseph Hunscott*, 1642. 4°.* LT, O, CM, HH, DT; CH, CSS, WF, Y.

4972 **Brookhouse, Thomas.** The temple opened. *By George Larkin, jun. to be sold at his house, and by J. Whitlock*, 1696. 4°. L, O, LW; CLC, WF.

4973 **Brooks, Francis.** Barbarian cruelty. *For I. Salusbury, and H. Newman*, 1693. 12°. T.C.II 453. L, O, CT; CLC, MH, NN.

4973A — —[Anr. ed.] *Boston: reprinted for S. Phillips*, 1700. 16°. EVANS 905. MHS.

4974 **Brooksbank John [*i.e.*, Joseph.]** The compleat school-master in two books. *For Edward Brewster*, 1660. 8°. LT, O; WF.

4975 —An English monosyllabary. *Printed at London*, 1651. 8°.* LT, O, LG; PL.

4975A —The inestimable profit. [*London?* 1654.] brs. MH.

4975B —The organs fvnerall. *G. Kirby*, [1642?] 4°.* LC.

4976 —Plain, brief, and pertinent rules for . . . syllabication. *For the author*, 1654. 8°.* LT, O.

4976A —Rebels tried and cast. 1661. 12°. O.

4976B —The saints imperfection. *Printed* 1646. 12°.* CLC.

4977 —[Anr. ed.] —, 1648. 8°.* LT.

4978 — —[Anr. ed.] *For VV: L.* 1656. 8°.* L.

4979 —Two books more exact. *For the author*, 1654. 8°.* L.

4980 —Vitis salutaris: or, the vine. *By W. D. to bee sold by John Marshal*, 1650. 8°. LT.

4981 — —[Anr. ed.] *For W. L.;* 1656. 8°. L.

4982 —The well-tuned organ. *Printed*, 1660. 4°. L, O, CPE, CT; IU, LC, NPT, WF.

4983 **Brooksop, Joan.** An invitation of love. *For Robert Wilson*, [1662]. 4°.* L, LF, BBN; CH, MH, NN, PH, RPJ.

4983A **Brossard Diary.** The country-mens new art of plenty. *By Jane Bell, to be sold by John Wright.* 1651. 4°. O, C, LPO, YM; WF.

4983B [-] —[Anr. ed.], *By Jane Bell*, 1652. 4°. L, EN; MH.

4983C [-] —[Anr. ed.], —, 1656. L.

Brotherly and friendly censure. 1645. *See* Walker, George.

Brotherly exhortation. Edinburgh, 1649. *See* Ker, A.

4984 The brotherly meeting of the masters and workmen-printers. [*n.p.*, 1680.] brs. L; MH.

4985 The brothers of the blade. [*London*], *for Thomas Bankes and Iohn Thomas*, 1641. 4°.* LT; CH, NU.

4986 The brothers of the separation. *Printed at London, by Tho: Harper*, 1641. 4°.* LT, CT; WF, Y.

4987 **Brough, William.** The holy feasts. *By J. G. for John Clark*, 1657. 12°. LT, O, C, DC, EN; CH, NC, NU, WF.

4988 [-] A preservative against the plague of schisme. 1650. 12°. L.

4989 [-] —[Anr. ed.] *For I. Clarke*, 1652. 12°. L, C, LW, CS; CLC, NU, Y.

4990 —Prifannau sanct aidd. *Caerludd, gan Sara Griffin tros Philip Chetwinde*, 1658. 8°. L, AN; EN.

4991 [-] Sacred principles, services, and soliloquies. *By J. G. for John Clark*, 1650. 12°. LT.

4992 [-] —Second edition. —, 1652. 12°. L, O, YM; CH, CLC.

4992A [-] —Third edition. —, 1656. 12°. L; CH, CLC, NPT.

4993 [-] —Fourth edition. —, 1659. 12°. L, O; NU.

4994 — —Fifth edition. *By W. R. for P. Parker*, 1671. 12°. T.C.I 92. L; NPT.

4994A — —'Fifth' edition. —, 1672. 12°. EN; CLC.

4995 — —"Fifth" edition. *For P. Parker*, 1679. 12°. T.C.I 345. C, CS.

4996 [**Brougham, Henry.**] Reflections to a late book, en-tituled, The genuine remains of Dr. Tho. Barlow. *For Robert Clavell*, 1694. 4°.* T.C.II 519. L, O, C, LII, EC; CN, NN, WF, Y.

4997 **Broughton, Hugh.** The vvorks of. *For Nath.Ekins*, 1662. fol. L, O, C, LCL, ENC; CLC, MH, MU, NU, Y.

4998 —An advertisement to the reader . . . a schedule of the works of. [*n.p.*, 1650.] brs. LT, O.

4999 **Broughton, John.** Aliquid est. [*n.p.*], 1698. brs. O.

5000 B[roughton], R[ichard]. Monastichon [sic] Britanicum; or, a historical narration. *For Henry Herringman*, 1655. 8°. LT, O, C, ES, DT; NNG, TSM, Y.

5001 —A true memorial of the ancient, . . . state of Great Britain. [*London*], *permissu superiorum*, 1650. 8°. L, O, C, ES, DT; BN, CH, MH, NU, TU, WF, Y.

5002 **Broughton, Robert.** To His Excellencie the Lord General Monck: the humble gratulation and acknowledgement of. [*London*, 1660.] brs. LT, LS; CH, MH.

5003 **Brousson, Claude.** The support of the faithful. *By Tho: Snowden, for Tho. Parkhurst*, 1699. 4°. T.C.III 121. L, O, C, CT, EN; CLC, CU, MH, WF, Y.

5004 **Browene, Richard.** The Parliament's endeavors. *By John Hammond*, 1642. 4°.* LSE; CH.

Brown. *See also* Browne.

5005 **Brown, Andrew.** Bellum medicinale. *Edinburgh*, 1699. 8°. ALDIS 3828. EN.

5006 —De febribus continuis. *Edinburgi, imprimebat Jacobus Watson*, 1695. 4°. ALDIS 3446. EN, ES, AU; WF.

5007 —The epilogue to the five papers. *Edinburgh, by John Reid*, 1699. 12°.* ALDIS 3830. L, EN; TU, WF, WSG.

5008 [–] In speculo teipsum contemplare Dr. Black. *Edinburgh, by the heir of Andrew Anderson*, 1692. 8°. ALDIS 3228. L, EN; TU.

5009 [–] A letter written to a friend in the countrey. [*Edinburgh, by the heir of Andrew Anderson*, 1692.] 4°.* ALDIS 3231. EN, ECP; TU.

5010 —A third letter. [*Edinburgh, Anderson*, 1692.] 4°.* EN.

5011 —A vindication of Dr. Sydenham's new method. *For John Hepburn*, 1700. 8°. O, GH.

5012 —A vindicatory schedule concerning . . . fevers. *Edinburgh, by John Reid*, 1691. To be sold be [sic] *John Mackie*. 12°. ALDIS 3135. L, O, LCP, EN, AU; CH, CLC, WF, HC.

5013 Entry cancelled.

5014 [**Brown, David.**] The naked vvoman, or a rare epistle *For E.Blackmore*, 1652. 4°.* LT; CN, MH.

5015 —To the supream authority of England, the Parliament. *By John Field*, 1652. 4°.* LT; WF.

5016 —Two conferences between some of those that are called Separatists. *By John Clowes*, 1650. 4°.* LT, LSC, NU.

Brown, Edward. Fascicules rerum expetendarum. 1690. *See* Gratius, Ortwinus.

5016A —A sermon preach'd . . . Novemb. 16. 1699. *For J. Back*, 1699. 4°.* L, C, YM; CH, WF, Y.

5017 [**Brown, G.**] A perfect narrative of the phanatick wonders. *For Charles Gustavus*, 1660. 4°.* LT, OC, HH.

5018 **Brown, George.** An account of the apprehending, trial, . . . of . . . idleness. *For the author, and sold by M. Fabian*, 1700. 8°.* L; WF.

5019 —An account of the rotula arithmetica. *Edinburgh, for the author*, 1700. 8°. C, EN, ENC, ES; CLC, WF.

5020 **Brown, Humfrey.** The ox muzzled. *By W. D. for John Stephenson*, 1649[50]. 4°.* MADAN 2020. LT, O, OC, EN; CH, CLC, MH, NU, Y.

[**Brown, Ignatius.**] Pax vobis. [*n.p.*], 1679. *See* Griffith, Evan.

5021 [–] An unerrable church or none. [*Douai*], 1678. 8°. L, O.

5022 [–] The vneering and vnerrable chvrch. [*Douai*], *anno*, 1675. 8°. L, O, CS, DT; CLC, CN, MH, TU, Y.

5023 **Brown, James.** Scripture redemption freed. 1673. 4°. O.

5024 **Brown, John,** *of Cork.* A true and exact relation of two great victories. [*London*], *printed*, 1647. 4°.* LT, LFEA.

5024A **Brown, John,** *of London.* A brief narrative of the case. [*London?* 1682]. cap., fol.* TU.

5025 —A brief remonstrance of the grand grievances. *Printed*, 1680. fol.* L, C, HH, EN; MH.

5026 **Brown, John,** *of Wamphray.* An apologeticall relation, of the particular sufferings. [*n.p.*], *printed*, 1665. 8°. L, O, CT, EN, AU; CH, CN, MH, NU, WF, Y.

5027 —Christ in believers the hope of glory. *Edinburgh, J. Reid*, 1694. 12°. ALDIS 3359. C.

5028 —Christ the way. *Rotterdam, by H. G.*, 1677. 12°. LCL, E, EN; MH, NU, Y.

5028A — —[*Amr. ed.*] —*for John Bruns in Edinburgh*, 1677. 12°. MH.

5028B — —Second edition. *Glasgow R. Sanders*, 1678. 12°. EN.

5029 [–] The history of the indulgence. [*Edinburgh?*], *printed*, 1678. 4°. L, E, EN; CN, MH, NPT, NU, Y.

5030 —The life of faith. [*n.p.*], *for the author*, 1679. 12°. AU; NU.

5031 —The life of justification opened. [*Holland*], *printed*, 1695. 4°. L, O, LCL, NPL, EN; MH, NU, WF, Y.

5032 Entry cancelled.

5033 —Quakerisme the pathway to paganisme. [*Flushing*] *for John Cairns, and other booksellers in Edinburgh*, 1678. 4°. ALDIS 2116. L, C, LF, EN, GU; CH, MH, NU, PH, WF, Y.

5034 —The swan-song. [*n.p.*], *printed*, 1680. 12°. NU.

5035 **Brown, John,** *Philomath.* The carpenters joynt-rule. *For J. and T.Browne*, 1684. 12°. MU.

5036 —A collection of centers. [*London*, 1670.] cap., 12°.* L.

5037 —A delineation of a mathematical instrument. 1671. brs. MC.

5038 —The description and use of a joynt-rule. *By T. J. for J.Brown, and H. Sutton*, 1661. 12°. L, E.

5039 —The description and use of an ordinary joynt-rule. *For William Fisher*, 1669. 4°.* L, DT.

5039A — —[*Anr. ed.*] *Printed* 1675. 4°* NC.

5039B — —[*Anr. ed.*] *Printed* 1686. 4°.* GU; NC, Y.

5039C —The description and use of the carpenters rule. *By W. G. for William Fisher*, 1666. 12°. NN.

5040 —[Anr. ed.] *For W. Fisher and R. Mount*, 1688. 12°. L, C; LC.

5041 —The description and use of the triangular quadrant. *By John Darby for John Wingfield, to be sold at his house; and by John Brown; and by John Sellers*, 1671. 8°. T.C.I 80. L, O, DCH, DT, LWL; CH, LC, MU, PL, WF.

5042 —Horologiographia: or, the art of dyalling. *By John Darby, for John Wingfield, sold at his house, and by John Brown, and by John Sellers*, 1671. 8°. T.C.I 80. L, C, LWL, DCH, EN; CH, CLC, PL, WF, Y.

5042A —The practical gauger. *For J. Brown and R. Morden*, 1678. 8°. T.C.I 300. O.

5042B —A supplement to the Line of proportion. *Printed*, 1676. 12°. L; NC.

5043 —The triangular quadrant. [London], *to be sold at his house, or at Hen. Sutton's*, 1662. 12°.* L, E.

5044 **Brown, Joseph.** Panegyrick upon His Majestie's glorious. *For A. Bosvile to be sold by E. Whitlock*, 1697. fol.* LVF, NAM; LLC, NP.

5045 —A psalm of Thanksgiving, to be sung by the children of Christ's-hospital. *Miles Flesher*, 1688. brs. L.

5046 —A Scotch song. [London, 1700?] brs. L.

5046A **Brown, Richard.** A Psalm of thanksgiving. *Miles Flesher*, 1685. brs. L.

5046B —A Scotch song. [London? 1700.] brs. L.

5046C **Brown, Robert.** An advertisement. [Edinburgh, 1680]. brs. ALDIS 2183. L, E.

5047 [–] Jerubbaal: or, a vindication. *Printed*, 1668. 4°. LCL, LW, MF; CLC, MB, MH, NHC, NU, WF.

5047A —The ministry of Christ asserted. *S. Calvert and D. White*, 1656. LW.

5048 —Rudimentorum rhetoricorum. *Aberdoniæ, excudebat Ioannes Forbesius*, 1666. 8°. ALDIS 1810. EN, GU.

5049 ——[Anr. ed.] *Edinburgi, impensis Davidis Trencii*, 1667. 8°. ALDIS 1831. EN, GU.

5050 [–] The subjects sorrovv. *Printed*, 1649. 4°.* L, O, C, LVF, DT; BN, CH, CU, NU, TU, WF, Y.

5051 **Brown, Thomas.** Amusements serious and comical. *For John Nutt*, 1700. 8°. T.C.III 176. L, O, C, LG, LWL; CH, CN, MH, TU, WF, Y.

[–] Clarret drinker's song. [n.p., 1680.] *See* Oldham, John.

5052 —A collection of miscellany poems. *For John Sparks*, 1699. 8°. L, DT; CLC, MH, NP, WCL, WF.

5053 ——Second edition. *For Abel Roper*, 1699. 8°. Y.

5054 ——"Second" edition. *For J. Nutt*, 1700. 8°. L.

5055 —A congratulatory poem on His Majesty's happy return from Holland. *For Thomas Jones*, 1691. fol.* L; CH, MH, PU, Y.

5056 [–] A description of Mr. D[ryde]n's funeral. A poem. *For A. Baldwin*, 1700. fol.* L, HH; CH, CLC, MH, TU, WF, Y.

5057 [–] — Second edition. —, 1700. fol.* L; MH, WF.

5058 [–] — Third edition. —, 1700. fol.* L, CS; CH.

5059 [–] Heraclitus ridens redivivus. [London, 1688.] cap., 4°.* L, OC, CT, HH; CU, MH, NU, WF, Y.

5060 [–] — Second edition. colop: *Oxford; printed*, 1688. 4°.* L, O, C, CT, EN; CH, CU, MH, NU, WF, Y.

5061 [–] The late converts exposed. *For Thomas Bennet*, 1690. 4°. T.C.II 303. L, O, LVD, EN, DT; CH, CN, MH, TU, WF, Y.

5062 Entry cancelled.

5063 [–] The moralist: or, a satyr. *Printed*, 1691. 4°.* T.C.II 347. L, O, AU; CH, CN, LC, MH, NU, TU, Y.

5064 [–] Mr. Haynes his recantation-prologue. colop: *For Richard Baldwin*, 1689. brs. O; CLC, CN, MH, WF.

5065 —Nature's cabinet unlock'd. *For Edw. Farnham*, 1657. 12°. LT, NCL, AU, GU, GK; MMO, NAM, WF, HC.

5066 [–] Novus reformatus vapulans. *For the assigns of Will. Pryn*, 1691. 4°.* T.C.II 349. L, O, C, EN, DT; CLC, CN, NU, Y.

5067 [–] —[Anr. ed., "reformator."] —, 1691. 4°.* L, LG, OC, CS, EN; CH, MH, TU, WF, Y.

5068 —Physick lies a bleeding. *For E. Whitlock*, 1697. 4°.* L, O, LCP; CH, CU, LC, TU, WCL, HC.

5069 [–] The reasons of Mr. Bays. *For S. T.*, 1688. 4°.* L, O, CT, MR, EN; BN, CH, CN, MH, NU, TU, WF, Y.

5070 [–] — Second edition. *For T. Bennet and A. Roper*, 1691. 4°.* T.C.II 364. L, O, SP; CH, CU, NU, WF, Y.

5071 [–] The reasons of Mr. Joseph Hains. *For Richard Baldwin*, 1690. 4°.* L, OC, CS; CH, CN, MH, NU, TU, WF, Y.

5072 [–] — [Anr. ed.] *For T. Bennet and A. Roper*, 1691. 4°.* L, O; CLC, MH, NN, Y.

5073 [–] The reasons of the new convert's taking the oaths. *Printed*, 1691. 4°.* T.C.II 349. L, O, CT, EN, DT; CLC, CN, MH, NU, WF, Y.

5074 —Tho. Brown's recantation of his satyr. *Printed*, 1697. brs. HH.

5075 [–] The Salamanca wedding. [1643.] 4°.* L.

[–] Satyr against wooing. 1698. *See* Gould, Robert.

[–] A satyrical epistle to the female author of a poem, call'd Sylvia's revenge. 1691. *See* Gould, Robert.

5076 [–] The weesil trap'd: a poem. *For Abel Roper, and Joseph Fox*, 1691. 4°.* T.C.II 347. L, O, CT, OC, A; CH, CN, MH, WCL, Y.

5077 [–] The weesils. A satyrical fable. *Printed*, 1691. 4°.* T.C.II 347. L, O, C, LL, E; CH, CN, MH, NU, TU, WF, Y.

[–] Wit for money. 1691. *See* Fidge, George.

Brown, Tobias. *See* Bowne, Tobias.

5078 **Brown, William.** Astraæ abdicatæ restauratio. Or advice to justices. [London], *for H. Newman, A. Roper, and R. Parker*, 1695. 12°. L, CT, LGI; CH, LC, MHL, Y.

5079 [–] The clerk's tutor in chancery. *For Henry Mortlock*, 1688. 8°. T.C.II 206. O, C, LL, DT; CH, MHL, PU, YL.

5080 [–] — Second edition. *By the assigns of Rich. and Ed. Atkins, for Henry Mortlock*, 1694. 8°. T.C.II 514. L, O, C, LIL; LC, MHL.

5080A [–] — "Second" edition. — *and sold by J. Raven*, 1695. 8°. LC.

5081 [–] A compendious and accurate treatise of recoveries. *By G. Sawbridge, W. Rawlins, and S. Roycroft, assigns of Edward and Richard Atkins, and are to be sold by Langley Curtis*, 1678. 8°. T.C.I 303. O, C, CP; LC, MHL, MIU, NCL.

5082 —— Second edition. *By the assigns of Edward and Richard Atkins for L. C. and are to be sold by J. Place*, 1684. 8°. MHI, YL.

5083 —— Third edition. *By the assigns of Rich. and Edw. Atkins, for J. Walthoe*, 1693. 8°. T.C.II 432. LM; LC, MHL, NCL.

5083A —— "Third" edition. *By the assigns of Rich. and Edw. Atkins, for Isaac Cleave*, 1693. 8°. WF.

5084 [–] A compendium of the several branches . . . exchequer. *By the assigns of R. and E. Atkins, for H. Mortlocke*, 1688. 8°. T.C.II 231. O, C, EN; CH, LC, MHL, NCL, Y.

5084A —The duty and office of high constables. *By G. Sawbridge, T. Roycroft, and W. Rawlins, the assigns of R. Atkins and E. Atkins*. 12°. MHL.

5085 —The entring clerk's vade mecum. *By G. Sawbridge, W. Rawlins, and S. Roycroft; assigns of Richard and Edward Atkins; for W. Jacob, and C. Smith*, 1678. 8°. T.C.I 303. L, O, C; LC, MHL, MIU, NCL, WF.

5086 —— Second edition. *By the assigns of Richard and Edward Atkins, for Nathaniel Ponder*, 1695. 8°. L, LIL; MHL, NR.

5087 —Formulæ bene placitandi. A book of entries. *By E. Flesher, J. Streater, H. Twyford, assigns of Richard Atkyns and Edward Atkyns, for J. Place, W. Place, and Tho. Basset*, 1671. fol. T.C.I 89. L, O, CS, LL, LGI; LC, MB, MHL, NCL, WF, Y.

5088 —— Second edition. *For W. Place, Tho. Basset, and J. Place*, 1675. fol. T.C.I 155. L, O, CP, LL, LIL; CU, LC, MHL, MIU, NCL.

5089 —— Pars secunda. *By E. Flesher, J. Streater, H. Twyford, assigns of Richard Atkyns and Edward Atkyns, for J. Place, W. Place, and Tho. Basset*, 1674. fol. L, LM, CS; MHL, YL.

5090 [–] Methodus novissima . . . or, a new, . . . method. *By the assigns of Richard and Edward Atkins, for D. Brown, T. Leigh, and D. Midwinter, and F. Coggan*, 1699. 8°. T.C.III 137. L, O, LI, DT; LC, MHL, NCL, WF.

5091 —Modus intrandi placita generalia: the entring clerk's introduction. *For George Dawes*, 1674. 8°. T.C.I 165. LL, LM, CCA; LC, MHL, WF.

5091A —— Second edition, *By the assigns of R. and Edw. Atkins. For T. Basset, J. Walthoe, and W. Hensman*, 1687. 8°. T.C.II 202. L; MHL, NCL, YL.

5092 —Modus transferendi status per recorda: a compleat collection. *By the assigns of Richard and Edward Atkins, for M. Gillyflower, W. Freeman, A. Roper, and T. Leigh*, 1698. 8°. T.C.III 76. L, O, LM, EN; LC, MHL, YL.

5092A —— [Anr. ed.] *By the assigns of R. and E. Atkins, for A. R. and sold by W. Turner*, 1700. 8°. LC.

5093 [–] The practice of His Majestie's court of exchequer. Second edition. *For H. Mortlock*, 1699. 8°. T.C.III 145. L, LM; MHL.

5094 —The practice of the courts of Kings-Bench. *For Abel Roper, and Elizabeth Wilkinson and R. Clavel*, 1696. 8°. L, LL, OC; WF.

5095 — —Second edition. *By the assigns of Rich. and Edw. Atkins for Richard Basset*, 1700. 8°. T.C. II 179. O.

5096 [–] Praxis almæ curiæ cancellariæ: a collection. *For A. Roper and E. Wilkinson*, 1694–5. 2v. 8°. T.C.II 501. L, O, LL, EN; LC, MHL, V, WF.

Brown dozen of drunkards. 1648. *See* Taylor, John.

5096A **Brownd, George.** A voyce from heaven. 1659. 4°. ENC.

5096B **Browne, Alexander.** An appendix to the Art of painting. 1675. fol. O.

5097 —Ars pictoria: or an academy. *By J. Redmayne, for the author, to be sold by him, and Richard Tompson, and Arthur Tooker*, 1669. fol. T.C.I 14. L, O, LWL, DT; LC, MU, NP, UCLA, WF.

5098 —— Second edition. *For Arthur Tooker; and William Battersby*, 1675. fol. T.C.I 207. L, C, OP, DCH; CH, CN, MH, NP, Y.

5099 —A compendious drawing-book. [London], *for Austin Oldisworth*, [1677?]. fol. L, CCA; Y.

5100 **Browne, Arthur.** Arthur Browne, a seminary priest, his confession. *August 25. Printed at London, for George Tomlinson*, 1642. 4°.* LT, EC; CH, CLC, OWC.

5101 **Browne, Edward, clerk.** A compendiovs and patheticall retractation. *Printed*, 1643. 4°. C; Y.

5102 —A description of an annuall vvorld. *By E. G. for William Ley*, 1641. 8°. L, O, C, LSC, P; CH, MH, NU, WCL, X.

5103 [–] A paradox usefull for the times. [London, 1642.] cap., 4°.* LT, O, C; CH, CU, MH, NU, WF, Y.

5104 [–] A potent vindication for book-making. [London, 1642.] cap., 4°.* LT, O, C; MH, NU, Y.

5105 —A rare paterne of iustice and mercy. *Printed at London, for William Ley*, 1642. 8°. LT, O; WF.

5106 [–] Sacred poems. *By E. Griffin*, 1641. 8°. L, O, C, LSC; CH, CN, NU, WF, Y.

5107 [–] Sir James Cambels clarks disaster. *Printed*, 1642. 4°.* LT, C, HH, DT; TSM, Y.

5107A —Time well spent. *For Iohn Clerke, VVilliam Hope, VVilliam Lee, and John Browne*, [1643.] 4°.* DT; Y.

5108 **Browne, Edward, compiler.** Rules for kings, and good counsell for subjects. *For T. Paibody, and E. Dobson*, 1642. 4°.* LT, O, C, DT; CH, CN, MH, NU, WF, Y.

5109 **Browne, Edward, M.D.** An account of several travels through a great part of Germany. *For Benj. Tooke*, 1677. 4°. T.C.I 253. L, O, C, E, DT; CH, MH, NC, WF, Y.

5110 —A brief account of some travels. *By T. R. for Benj. Tooke*, 1673. 4°. T.C.I 134. L, O, C, MR, EN; CN, LC, MH, MMO, NC, Y.

5111 —— Second edition. *For Benj. Tooke*, 1685. fol. T.C.II 143. L, O, C, EN, DT; CH, CN, LC, MH, MMO, Y.

5112 —— "Second" edition. *For Benj. Tooke, and are to be sold by Tho. Sawbridge*, 1687. fol. T.C.II 213. L, C, LW, DT, GK; LC, MIU, MMO.

5113 —Judicium de somniis est medico utile. [Cambridge], 1663. brs. L.

5114 **Browne, George.** A modell of the fire-workes. *For George Lindsey*, 1647. brs. LT; MH.

5115 **Browne, Humphry.** A map of the microcosme. *By T. Harper, for John Williams*, 1642. 12°. L, O, LWL, GK; CN, IU, NNG, WF.

5116   **B[rowne], J.** Catholick schismatology. *For Anthony Steevens in Oxon.*, 1685. 8°. O, CT; WF.

5117   **Browne, John,** *captain.* A brief survey of the prophetical and evangelical events. *By Gartrude Dawson,* 1655. 4°. LT, O; NU.

5118   **Browne, John,** *Jesuit.* The confession of. [*London*], *by Barnard Alsop,* 1641. 4°.* LT, O, DT; WF.

5119   —A discovery of the notorious proceedings of William Laud . . . in bringing innovations into the Church. *Printed, and are to be sold by Henry Walker,* 1641. 4°.* LT, LG, LSC, HH; CH, MH, NU, WF, Y.

5120   **Browne, John,** *M.P.* A worthie speech. *For H. Homer,* 1642. 4°.* LT, C, LVF; CH, LC, MH, NU, Y.

5120A   **Browne, John,** *Quaker.* In the eleaventh month, on the nineth day of the moneth, as I was waiting. [*London*], *printed.* 1678. brs. LF.

5121   —Kedarminster-stuff. *For Randal Taylor,* 1681. 4°. T.C.I 444.* L, O, CT, LVF, DT; CH, LLC, PU.

5122   **Browne, John,** *surgeon.* Adenochoiradelogia. *By Tho. Newcomb for Sam. Lowndes,* 1684. 8°. T.C.II 46. L, O, LCP, ES, BQ; CH, MH, MMO, NAM, WF, HC.

5123   Entry cancelled.

5124   —A compleat discourse of wounds. *By E. Flesher, for William Jacob,* 1678. 4°. T.C.I 319. L, O, C, LCS, GK; BN, WSG, JF.

5125   —A compleat treatise of preternatural tumours. *By S. R. for R. Clavel, and George Rose,* 1678. 4°. L, O, C, LM, GH; BN, MU, NAM, WF, JF.

5126   —A compleat treatise of the muscles. *In the Savoy, by Tho. Newcombe for the author,* 1681. fol. L, O, C, CK, LCS; CLM, LC, MH, NAM, HC.

5126A   — — [Anr. ed.] *For Dorman Newman,* 1683. fol. LCP, LW, GK; NAM, WSG.

5127   —Myographia nova sive musculorum. *Excudebat Joannes Redmayne,* 1684. fol. L, O, CM, GH, GK; BN, CJC, MMO, NAM, WF, HG.

5128   —Myographia nova: or, a graphical description. Third edition. *By Tho. Milbourn for the author,* 1697. fol. L, O, CM, LCS, DC; CH, CLM, NAM, WF, WSG.

5129   — — Fourth edition. *By Tho. Milbourn, for the author,* 1698. fol. L, O, C, GH, DT; BN, CU, MIU, WSG, JF.

5129A   —Proposals by way of contribution for writing a natural history of Yorkshire. [*London,* 1697.] brs. C.

5130   —Proposals for printing a treatise of muscular dissection. [*n.p.*], 1680. brs. OP.

     B[rowne], J[oseph]. 1669. An almanack, Cambridge [*Mass.*], 1669. *See Almanacs.*

5131   Entry cancelled.

5132   [**Browne, M.**] An elegiack essay humbly offered. *For John Marshall,* 1699. T.C.III 157. fol.* MH, Y.

5133   **Browne, Mathias.** The opinions of divers philosophers. *For Tim: Smart,* 1656. 8°. LT, P.

5133A   —το' αγαδον ανερωπινον. A tract of mans chiefest good. *By Thomas Harper,* 1652. 8°. LSC, LWL; CLC, CU, NN, WF.

5134   **Browne, Peter,** *bp.* A letter in answer to a book. *Dublin, by Joseph Ray, for John North,* 1697. 8°. DIX 290. L, C, DT, BAMB, EN; CH, WF.

5135   — — [Anr. ed.] *For Robert Clavell,* 1697. 8°. T.C.III 35. L, O, CS, CT, EC; CH, LC, NH, NU.

5136   —Letters on Christianity. *Dublin,* 1697. DIX 290. DUGAN.

5137   —A sermon preached . . . April, 17, 1698. *Dublin, Joseph Ray,* 1698. 12°.* DIX 302. DI, DT.

5138   **Browne, Philip,** of Halstead. The observation of holy days justified. *For Walter Kettilby,* 1684. 4°.* T.C.II 111. L, O, CSSX, LSC, BAMB; CH, CLC, WF, Y.

5139   —The sovereign's authority. *By M. Flesher, for Walter Kettilby,* 1682. 4°.* L, O, C, BAMB, E; CLC, NGT, NPT, WF, Y.

     Browne, Richard. General history of earthquakes. 1692. *See Crouch, Nathaniel.*

5140   **Browne, Richard,** apothecary. Περί αρχων liber. *Impensis authoris, & venales prostat apud Thomam Passinger,* 1678. 8°. T.C.II 312. L, O, C; MH.

5141   —Prosodia pharmacopoeorum: or. *For Benj. Billighsley,* 1685. 8°. T.C.II 97. L, O, C, LCS, AU; CLC, NAM, WF, WSG, WU.

5141A   **Browne, Sir Richard,** lord mayor. By the mayor . . . 26th Feb. [*London*], *by James Flesher* [1661]. bis. L.

5141B   —[Same title 19 Oct.] —[1661]. brs. L.

5141C   [–] The speech of . . . the Lord Mayor of London. *For Tho. Rooks,* 1661. 4°.* LT, EN; NP.

5142   **Browne, Sir Richard,** major-general. The declaration of. [*London*], *for C. VV.,* 1648. 4°.* LT; WF, Y.

5143   [–] The intentions of the armie concerning the King's Majestie. [*n.p.*], *printed,* 1647. 4°.* LT, DT.

5144   —A letter sent from Major-generall Brown. *For Iohn Thomas,* 1644[5]. 4°.* LT, O, LCL; CU, MU, NU, TU, WF, Y.

5145   —The Lord Digbies designe to betray Abingdon. *For Laurence Blaiklock,* 1644[5]. 4°.* MADAN 1727. LT, O, C, DT; CH, CU, TU, WF, Y.

5146   Entry cancelled.

5147   **Browne, Richard,** of Rugby. The English examiner. *By Edw. Jones, for Tho. Basset,* 1692. 8°. T.C.II 429. L, O, C.

5148   —The English school reformed. *For A. and J. Churchill, and E. Castle,* 1700. 8°. L, O.

5149   **Browne, Samuel.** An account and testimony of. [*London*], 1693. 12°. LF; PSC.

5150   **Browne, Sir Thomas.** The works of the learned. *For Tho. Basset, Ric. Chiswell, Tho. Sawbridge, Charles Mearn, and Charles Brome,* 1686. fol. T.C.II 173. KEYNES 201. L, O, C, EN, DT; BN, CH, CN, MH, NP, WF, Y.

5151   —Certain miscellany tracts. *For Charles Mearn,* 1683. 8°. KEYNES 127. O, OB, CK, NCL, GK; MMO, NU, MH, WSG, HC.

5152   — — [Anr. ed.] *For Charles Mearne, and are to be sold by Henry Bonwick,* 1684. 8°. T.C.II 62. KEYNES 128. L, O, C, LCS, GH; CH, CN, MH, TU, WF, Y.

5153   Entry cancelled.

5154 —Hydriotaphia, urne-buriall. *For Hen. Brome,* 1658. 8°. KEYNES 93. LT, O, CT, EN, DT; BN, CH, CN, MH, MMO, NC, WF, Y.

5155 — — [Anr. ed.] *For Henry Brome,* 1669. 4°. KEYNES 96. L, C, CP; CH, CN, NP, HC, V.

5156-7 Entries cancelled.

5158 —A letter to a friend. *For Charles Brome,* 1690. fol.* KEYNES 135. L, O, LLL, NCL, GK; CLC, MH, TU, V, Y.

5159 —Pseudodoxia epidemica. *By T. H. for Edward Dod,* 1646. fol. KEYNES 73. L, O, C, E, DT; BN, CH, CU, MH, MMO, NP, TU, WF, Y.

5159A — —[Anr. ed.] *By Tho. Harper for Edvvard Dod,* 1646. 4°. KEYNES 73A. OW.

5160 — — Second edition. *By A. Miller, for Edw. Dod and Nath. Ekins,* 1650. fol. KEYNES 74. L, O, C, EN, DT; CLC, CU, MH, MMO, NP, NU, WF, Y.

5161 — — Third edition. *By R. W. for Nath. Ekins,* 1658. fol. KEYNES 75. L, O, C, CE, GK; BN, CLC, LC, MH, MMO, JF.

5162 — — Fourth edition. *For Edward Dod, and are to be sould by Andrew Crook,* 1658. 4°. KEYNES 76. LT, O, C, NCL, DT; CLC, CN, LC, MH, MMO, NC, Y.

5163 — — The "last" edition. *For Nath. Ekins,* 1659. fol. KEYNES 77. L, O, CK, NCL, GK; MBA, MMO, NP, Y.

5164 — — Fifth edition. *For the assigns of Edward Dod,* 1669. 4°. KEYNES 78. L, O, C, GK, E; CH, MH, MMO, WF, Y.

5165 — — Sixth edition. *By J. R. for Nath. Ekins,* 1672. 4°. KEYNES 79. L, O, C, ENC, DT; CLC, LC, MH, NP, NU, WF, JF.

5166 —Religio medici. *[London], for Andrew Crooke,* 1642. 190pp. 8°. KEYNES I. L, O, C, NCL, DT; CH, MH, LC, MMO, Y.

5167 — — [Anr. ed.] —, 1642. 159pp. 8°. KEYNES 2. L, O, C, NCL, DT; CH, LC, MH, MMO, NAM, Y.

5168 Entry cancelled.

5169 —A true and full coppy of . . . Religio medici. —, 1643. 8°. 183pp. KEYNES 3. L, O, C, NCL, DT, GK; CH, CN, MH, WF, Y.

5170 — —[Anr. ed.] —, 1645. 8°. KEYNES 4. L, O, CT, NCL, DT; CLC, MH, MMO, WF, Y.

5171 — — Second auth. ed. reset. —, 1645. KEYNES 5. L, O, GK; CLC, MH, MMO, WSG, Y, JF.

5172 — — Fourth edition. *By E. Cotes for Andrew Crook,* 1656. 8°. KEYNES 6. L, O, CM, E, GK; CLC, MH, NP, WF, Y.

5173 — — [Anr. ed.] *[London], printed,* [1659?] KEYNES 7. fol. MMO.

5174 — — Fifth edition. *By Tho. Milbourn for Andrew Crook,* 1659. 8°. KEYNES 8. L, O, CM, NCL, E; CH, MH, NAM, WF, Y.

5175 — — Sixth edition. *By Ja. Cotterel, for Andrew Crook,* 1669. 8°. T.C.I 15. KEYNES 9. L, O, NCL, MR, GK; CLC, CU, MH, MMO, NU, Y, JF.

5176 [-] — Seventh edition. *For Andrew Crook,* 1672. 4°. KEYNES 10. L, O, CP, ENC, DT; CH, CLC, MH, MMO, NU.

5177 [-] — "Seventh" edition. *For R. Scot, T. Basset, J. Wright, R. Chiswell,* 1678. T.C.I 245. KEYNES 11. L, O, C, ENC, DT; MH, MMO, NP, Y, JF.

5178 — — Eighth edition. *For R. Scot, T. Basset, J. Wright, R. Chiswell,* 1682. 8°. KEYNES 12. L, O, CS, NCL, EN; MH, MMO, WF, Y, JF.

5179 [-] Some reflections on a late pamphlet. *Printed,* 1691. 4°.* O, C; CH, CN, NU, Y.

5180 Entry cancelled.

5181 **Browne, Thomas.** Animæ brutorum. [*n.p.*], 1680. brs. O.

5181A **Browne, Thomas, *canon of Windsor.*** A key to the King's cabinet. *Oxford, by Leonard Lichfield,* 1645. 4°. MADAN 1803. LT, O, CT, EN, DT; CH, CN, MH, WF, Y.

5182 **Browne, Thomas, *fellow of St. John's.*** An answer to Dr. Sherlock's case of allegiance. *Printed,* 1691. 4°. L, O, C, AU, DT; CH, CU, NU, TU, WF, Y.

5183 [-] The case of allegiance to a king in possession. [*London*], *printed,* 1690. 4°. L, O, C, MR, AU; CH, CU, MHL, NU, WF, Y.

5184 —Concio ad clerum. *Cantabrigiæ, ex officina Joan. Hayes, impenis H. Dickinson, Cantab. & Sam. Smith, Lond.,* 1688. 4°. T.C.II 217. L, O, C, E, EN; BN, CH, MH, NU, TU, WF, Y.

5184A [-] Miracles work's above . . . nature. *For Samuel Smith,* 1683. 4°. T.C.II 32. L, O, C, DC, DT; HR, CH, MH, NU, Y.

5185 **Browne, Thomas, *Gent.*** Vox veritatis or a brief abstract. [*Westminster*], *printed,* 1683. 4°. L.

5185A **Browne, Thomas. *of London.*** The absolute accomptant. *By W. Godbid, and are to be sold by Nath. Brooke and John Hancock,* 1673. fol.* T.C.I 150. MH.

5185AB —The accurate accountant. 1669. fol. SC.

5185B —[Anr. ed.] *By William Godbid for John Hancock,* 1670. fol. L.

5186 **Browne, Thomas, *of Ruberdown.*** A true relation of the prosperous successe. *For Philip Smith,* 1643. 4°.* LT; OWC.

Browne, William. History of Polexander. 1647. *See* Gomberville, Marin Le Roy, *sieur de.*

5187 —An ode on the death of William Duke of Gloucester. *Printed, and sold by J. Nutt,* 1700. fol.* O; CLC, MH, WF, Y.

5187A **Browning, Mrs. Mary.** A catalogue of theological . . . books. *Amsterdam,* [1680]. 8°. L.

5188 **Browning, Thomas.** Prison thoughts, written by. *Printed, to be sold by the author,* 1682. 4°. L, O, LG.

5189 The Brownist hæresies confvted. [*London*], *printed,* 1641. 4°.* L, O; CN, NU, TU, WF, Y.

Brownists conventicle. [n.p.], 1641. *See* Taylor, John.

5190 The Brownists faith and beliefe opened. *For T. W.,* 1641. brs. LT, OC; WF, Y.

5191 Brownists synagogue. [*n.p.*], *printed,* 1641. 4°.*LT, O, C; CH, LC, OWC, Y.

5191A **Brownlow, Richard.** The works of. *By T. R. for Henry Twyford,* 1654. 4°. L, CS.

5192 —Brevia judicialia: or, an exact collection. *For Ch. Adams, John Starkey, and Tho. Basset,* 1662. fol. O, LI, LMT, LL, LGI; CU, LC, MHL, NCL, WF.

5193　—Declarations and pleadings in English. *By Thomas Roy-croft for Henry Twyford*, 1652. 4°. L, LL, LMT, LGI; LC, MHL, NP, Y.

5194　— — Second edition. *By Tho. Roycroft, for Henry Twyford*, 1653. 4°. O, LI, EN; CU, LC, MHL, WF, Y.

5195　— —Third editions. —, 1659. 4°. LT, O; LC, MIU, PUI.

5196　—Declarations counts and pleadings in English: the second part. *For Matthew Walbancke, and John Place*, 1654. 4°. LT; MIU, NC, WF, Y.

5197　—Brownlow Latinè redivivus: a book of entries. *By the assigns of Richard and Edward Atkyns, to be sold by S. Heyrick, T. and G. Sawbridge and M. Gilliflower*, 1693. fol. L, CS, LL, LGI, LIC; LC, MHL, NCL, WF, YL.

5198　—Reports, of diverse choice cases. *By Tho. Roycroft, for Matthew Walbancke, and Henry Twyford*, 1651. 4°. L, O, CT, LMT, DT; MIU.

5199　— —Second edition. *By F. L. for Matthew Walbancke, and Henry Twyford*, 1654. 4°. L, LL, LGI; MH, NCL, YL.

5200　— -- Third edition. *For Henry Twyford; and Samuel Heyrick*, 1675. 4°. T.C.I 242. L, O, C, EN, DT; CH, MH, NCL, WF, Y.

5201　—Reports: (a second part). *By Tho. Roycroft, for Matthew Walbancke*, 1652. 4°. LT, O, CT, DT; TU.

5202　— — Second edition. *For Henry Twyford*, 1675. 4°. L, CJ, LL, EN, DT; MHL, WF.

5203　—Writs judiciall. *By Tho. Roycroft, for Henry Twyford*, 1653. 4°. LT, O, LGI, LI, DC; LC, MHL, NCL, WF.

5204　**Brownrig, Ralph, bp.** Fourty sermons. *By Tho: Roycroft, for John Martyn, James Allestry, and Thomas Dicas*, 1661. fol. L, O, C, AU; CH, MB, NU, WF, Y.

5205　— —[Anr. ed.] 1664. fol. O, NPL; CU.

5206　— —First volume. *By E. Cotes, for John Martyn, and James Allestry, to be sold by Peter Parker*, 1665. fol. L, E; CU, PPT, Y.

5206A　— —[Anr. ed.] *to be sold by Dorman Newman*, 1665. fol. OC.

5207　— —[Anr. ed.] *By R. E. for R. Chiswell, T. Sawbridge, G. Wells, and R. Bentley*, 1685. fol. T.C.II 139. L, C, CCL, WCA; WF.

5208　—Repentance and prayer. *For T. Robert*, 1660. 12°. LW.

5209　—A sermon on the 5th of November. *For Robert [sic] Crofts*, 1660. 12°. LT, O.

5210　—A sermon preached . . . March 7, 1644. *For John Williams*, 1661. 4°.* NU, WF.

5211　—Sixty five sermons by . . . in two volumes. *By Tho. Roycroft, for John Martyn, and are to be sold by Robert Boulter*, 1674. fol. T.C.I 173. L, O, CCO, AU, DT; BN, MH, NPT, WF.

5212　—Twenty five sermons. *By Tho. Roycroft, for John Martyn, and James Allestry*, 1664. fol. L, C, OC, AU, E; CH, MH, NU, Y.

5213　—Twenty five sermons . . . second volume. *By John Macock, for John Martyn*, 1674. fol. L, LL, AU, DT; MH.

5214　— —[Anr. ed.] *By R. Everingham*, 1685. fol. L, O, C; CH, CU.

5214A　**Brownsword, William.** Englands grounds of joy. *By Matthew Inman*, 1660. 4°.* WCA.

5215　—The Quaker-Jesuite. *By J. M. are to be sold by Miles Harrison, in Kendal*, 1660. 4°.* LT, LF; PSC.

5216　—Romes conviction. *By J. M. for Luke Fawn*, 1654. 8°. LT, O, C, LCL, DC; NU.

5217　**Broxolme, Charles.** The good old way: or, Perkins' improved. *For John Rothwel and Thomas Maxey*, 1653. 8°. LT, O, C, LSC; CLC.

5218　— —[Anr. ed.] *For John Rothwel*, 1657. 8°. O, LCL, SP, E; CH.

5219　**Bruce, Lord.** The Lord Bruce and Lady Elizabeth his wife desire a bill. *[London? 1680]*. brs. L.

5220　**Bruce, Michael.** The rattling of the dry bones. *[n.p.]*, 1672. 4°. EN, ENC.

5220A　—A sermon preached. *[London? 1668]*. 4°.* EN.

5221　**Bruce, Titus.** Monarchy maintained. *By J. R. for Fincham Gardiner*, 1682. 4°.* T.C.II 2. O, CT; CH, WF.

5221A　**Bruele, Gualtherus.** Praxis medicinæ. Third edition. *By R. Cotes for William Sheares*, 1648. 4°. L; CJC, MH, MIU, WF, WSG.

5222　**Brugis, Thomas.** The discovery of a proiector. *By R. H. and are to be sold by Lawrence Chapman, and William Cooke*, 1641. 4°.* L, O, CS, LCL; CH, PL, MH, WF.

5223　—The marrow of physicke. *By T. H. and M. H. sold by Thomas Whittaker*, 1648. 4°. C; NAM, WSG.

5224　— —[Anr. ed.] *For Peter Parker*, 1669. 4°. L; CLC.

5225　—Vade mecum: or, a companion for a chyrurgion. *By T. H. for Thomas Williams*, 1652. 8°. LT, LWL, GU, E; CH, NAM.

5226　— Second edition. *By T. H. for Tho. Williams*, 1653. 8°. O, CP, LM; CH, MHS, WSG, HC.

5227　— —Third edition. —, 1657. 12°. LCP, OR.

5227A　— —Fourth edition. *By E. C. for Th. Williams*, 1665 12°. LWL; WSG.

5227B　— —Fifth edition. —, 1670. 12°. LWL.

5228　— —Sixth edition. *For T. Flesher*, 1679. 12°. T.C.I 353. LCS, LM, LWL.

5228A　—Seventh edition. *For Thomas Flesher*, 1681. 12°. LCP; WF, WSG.

5229　— —"Seventh edition." *For B. T. and T. S. and sold by Fr. Hubbert*, 1689. 12°. T.C.II 262. L, C, GH, GU; MIU, WSG.

5229A　— —"Seventh" edition. *For T. Sawbridge*, 1689. 12°. PL.

5229B　**Brun, A.** A conference between a Presbyterian minister. 1651. 8°. O.

5230　**[Brunel, Antoine de.]** A journey into Spain. *For Henry Herringman*, 1670. 8°. T.C.I 43. L, O, CS, LW, EN; CH, CN, PL, WF, Y.

5231　**Bruning, Benjamin.** Βλάστημα ’ἐξ “υψους or, the best wisdome. *By D. Maxwell, for W. Weekly of Ipswich, to be sold by John Rothwell*, 1660. 4°. O, C, LW, BAMB; CH.

5232　**Brunning, Samuel.** Non datur talis causarum. *[n.p., 1661.]* brs. O.

5233　**Brunsell, Samuel.** Solomons blessed land. *By E. C. for Henry Seile*, 1660. 4°.* LT, O; MH, NU.

5234　**Brunskel, Percival.** An abstract of Mr. Brunskel's case. *[London, 1694]*. brs. L; MHL.

5234A —A brief vindication of. *Printed*, 1695. 4°.* L, O, LUG, CS; CH, CLC, WF, Y.

5235 —Mr. Brunskel's case. [*London*, 1694.] fol.* L, LL.

5236 —Mr. Brunskell's case and proposals. [*London*, 1690.] fol.* LL.

5236A —To the honourable the Knights . . . in Parliament assembled, the humble petition of. [*London?* 1693.] brs. O, CS; CH, MH, Y.

5237 [–] A vindication of the case relating to the green-wax-fines. *Printed*, 1683. 4°. L, O, LL; PU, Y.

5238 [–] — [Anr. ed.] —, 1684. 8°. L, O, C; NC.

5239 **Brush, Edward.** The invisible power of God. *Printed and sold by T. Sowle*, 1695. 4°.* L, LF; PH.

5240 —A vindication of the Christian Quakers. [*London*, 1694.] brs. L, LF, BBN; PH.

5241 **Brusoni, Girolamo.** Arnaldo, or, the injur'd lover. *For Thomas Dring*, 1660. 8°. LT; CU, LC, MH, Y.

Brutum fulmen. 1681. *See* Barlow, Thomas, *bp.*

Brutus, Stephanus Junius, *pseud.*

5241A [**Bruzeau, Paul.**] The faith of the Catholick church. *Printed at Holy-rood-house*, 1687. 8°. ALDIS 2688. EN, AU, GU; BN, WCL, Y.

5242 **Bryan, John.** A discovery of the probable sin. *For Richard Best*: 1647. 4°.* LT, O, C, BC, CC; CH, NU, WF, Y.

5243 —Dwelling with God. *By T. M. for James Allestry*, 1670. 8°. T.C.I 25. L, CT, LCL, LW, SA; WF, Y.

5244 —Harvest-home. *For the author*, 1674. 4°. L, LCL, LW, DT; CH.

5245 —A publick disputation sundry dayes at Killingworth. *For W. Larnar*, 1655. 4°. LT, O.

5246 **Bryan, Matthew.** The certainty of the future judgment. *For Walter Kettilby*, 1685. 4°.* T.C.II III. L, O, CT, OCC, LG; CLC, NU, WF.

5247 —A perswasive to the stricter observation. *For S. Keble, and D. Brown*, 1686. 4°.* T.C.II 165. L, O, C, OCC, EN; CH, MIU, NU, WF.

5248 —St. Paul's triumph. *For the author*, 1692. 4°.* L, O, CT, MR; CLC, NU, NC, WF, Y.

5249 [**Bryan, Robert**]. A prophetick demonstration of many remarkable passages. *By J. S. for R. B.*, 1680. 4°. CH, WF.

5249A **Brayanston, John.** The mutations of the seas. *By George Larkin*, 1683. 4°.* L, O; NLC, NN, Y.

5250 **Brydall, John.** An abridgment of the lawes of England. *For J. Bellinger, and T. Dring*, 1679. 8°. T.C.I 334. LL, EN.

5251 [–] The absurdity of that new devised state-principle. *For T. D. and are to be sold by Randal Taylor*, 1681. 4°.* L, O, LL, SP; CH, CU, PU, Y.

[–] Appeal to the conscience. 1684. *See* Lane, Bartholomew.

5252 —Ars transferendi dominium: or, a sure law-guide. *By the assigns of R. and E. Atkyns; for Samuel Heyrick, and Isaac Cleave*, 1697. 8°. L, LL, LM; LC, MHL, PUL.

5253 —Camera regis. *For William Crooke*, 1676. 8°. T.C.I 222. L, O, C, LP, ES; CH, CU, MH, NC, WF, Y.

5254 [–] —[Anr. ed.] *For W. Crooke*, 1678. 8. L, O, LL; NP.

5255 [–] The clergy vindicated. *By E. T. and R. H.*, 1679. fol.* T.C.I 372. L, O, CT, MR, EN; CH, CN, MH, NU, WF, Y.

5256 —A compendious collection of the laws. *For John Bellinger and Tho. Dring*, 1675. 8°. L; BN, LC, MIU, NCL.

5257 ——[Anr. ed.] 1676. 8°. O, LL.

5258 ——[Anr. ed.] 1679. 8°. O.

5259 —Decus & tutamen: or a prospect. *By G. Sawbridge, W. Rawlins, and S. Roycroft, assigns of Ed. Atkins; to be sold by Geo. Dawes*, 1679. 12°. T.C.I 342. L, O, LIL, EN; CH, CU, LC, MHL, NCL, WF.

5260 [–] Jura coronæ. His Majesties royal rights. *For George Dawes*, 1680. 8°. T.C.I 384. L, O, C, LL, DT; CN, LC, MHL, NU, WF.

5261 —Jus imaginis apud Anglos; or, the law of England. *For John Billinger, and Geo Dawes*, 1675. 8°. T.C.I 199. L, O, C, LL, EN; BN, CH, CN, LC, MHL, TU, YL.

5262 [–] Jus primogeniti: or the dignity. colop: *For R. Battersby*, 1699. cap., 4°.* T.C.III 175. L, O, CCO, LL, EN; CH.

5263 [–] Jus sigilli: or, the law of England. *By E. Flesher for Thomas Dring and John Leigh*, 1673. 12°. T.C.I 144. L, O, CS, LL, LG; BN, CU, LC, MHL, WF, Y.

5263A —A letter to a friend. 1679. fol. CT.

5264 [–] A New-Years-gift for the anti-prerogative-men. *By H. H. for John Fish*, 1682. 4°.* L, O, HH, BP, MR; CH, MH, MM, NU, WF, Y.

5265 —Non compos mentis: or, the law relating to natural fools. *By the assigns of Richard and Edward Atkins; for Isaac Cleave*, 1700. 8°. L, C, LL, LGI, LI; CU, MHL, PL, WF, YL.

5266 —Pietatis in parentes disquisitio: or the duty of children. *For R. Battersby*, 1700. 4°.* LL.

5267 —Speculum juris Anglicani, or, a view. *By John Streater, Eliz. Flesher, and H. Twyford, assignes of Rich. Atkyns and Edward Atkyns, to be sold by G. Sawbridge, J. Place, J. Bellinger, Wil. Place, T. Basset, Rob. Pawlet, Christ. Wilkinson, Tho. Dring, Wil. Jacob, Ch. Harper, J. Leigh, J. Amery, J. Poole*, 1673. 8°. T.C.I 130. L, O, CT, LG, EN; LC, MHL, MIU, NCL.

5268 [–] The white rose. *Printed*, 1680. fol.* L, O, LL, BP, EN; CH, MBA, NC, WF, Y.

Buc, *Sir* George. *See* Buck, *Sir* George.

5269 **Bucanus, Gulielmus.** A body of divinity. *For Daniel Pakeman, Abel Roper, and Richard Tomlins*, 1659. 4°. LT, C, LSC.

5270 **Bucer, Martin.** The ivdgement of. *By Matthew Simmons*, 1644. 4°.* LT, O, C, LW, DT; CH, CN, LC, MH, NU, TU, Y.

5270A **Buchan, John.** Memorial showing the advantages. [*n.p.*], 1700. MH.

5271 —Theses philosophicæ. *Abredoniæ, excudebat Ioannis Forbes*, 1681. 4°.* ALDIS 2311. E.

5271A —Unto his grace . . . the humble petition. [*Edinburgh*, 1698.] brs. EN.

5272 [**Buchanan, David.**] An explanation of some truths. *Printed*, 1645[6]. 4°. LT.

5273   [–] A short and true relation of some main passages. *By R. Raworth, for R. Bostock,* 1645. 8°. LT.

5274   [–] Truth its manifest, or a short and true relation. *Printed,* 1645. 8°. LT, O, CT, HH, EN; BN, CH, MB, NU, PL, WF, Y.

5275   **Buchanan, George.** De jure regni apud Scotos. [*n.p.*], *printed,* 1680. 12°. L, O, C, E, EN; CLC, MHL, NU, PL, WF, Y.

5276   ——[Anr. ed.] *For Richard Baldwin,* 1689. 4°. T.C.II 257. L, O, C, EN, DT; CH, CN, MH, NU, TU, Y.

5277   —De prosodia libellus. *Edinburgi, ex officina societatis stationariorum,* 1660. 8°.* MH.

5278   ——[Anr. ed.] *Glasguæ, excudebat Robertus Sanders,* 1667. 12°. ALDIS 1832. EN, AU.

5278A   ——[Anr. ed.] *Edinburgh, excudebat Thomas Brown,* 1678. 12°. ALDIS 2117. Y.

5279   ——[Anr. ed.] *Glasgow,* 1684. 12°. ALDIS 2450. L, GM.

5280   ——[Anr. ed.] *Edinburgi,* 1694. 12°. AU.

5281   —A detection of the actions of Mary Queen of Scots. [*London?*], *printed,* 1651. 12°. LT, O, C, CE, OB; BN, CLC, CN, Y.

5282   ——[Anr. ed.] *Printed, and are to be sold by Richard Janeway,* 1689. 4°. L, CT, HH, EN, DT; CH, LC, MH, NU, TU.

5283   —The history of Scotland. *By Edw. Jones, for Awnsham Churchil,* 1690. fol. T.C.II 312. L, O, C, E, DT; BN, CH, LC, NU, WF, Y.

5284   —Octupla; hoc est. *Edinburgi, excudebant hæredes & successores Andreæ Anderson,* 1696. Et vænales prostant ex officinâ M. Hen. Knox., 4°. ALDIS 3586. L, O, C, AU, FSF.

5285   —Paraphrasis psalmorum . . . Jephthes. *Edinburgh, Mosman,* 1694. 12°. ALDIS 3360. EN.

5286–9   Entries cancelled.

5290   —Poemata postrema. *Edinburgh, prostant apud J. Cairns,* 1677. 12°. ALDIS 2094. L, O.

5291   —Poëmata quæ supersunt omnia. *Edinburgh, prostant apud Joannem Cairns,* 1677. 12°. ALDIS 2095. L, AU, EN.

5292   ——[Anr. ed.] *B. Griffin prostant,* 1686. 12°. T.C.II 173. L, C, OM, AU, DT; CH, CN, MH, NC, WG, Y.

5293–5   Entries cancelled.

5296   —Rerum Scoticarum historia. *Edinburgi, ad exemplar A. Arbuthneti editum,* 1643. 12°. L, E, EN, GM; BN, LC, MHL, PU, TU, Y.

5297   ——[Anr. ed.] *Edimbvrgi, es typographæo Georgii Mosman,* 1700. 12°. L, O, AU, EN; CH, CU, NU, WF.

5298   [–] Tyrannicall-government anatomized. *For John Field,* 1642[3]. 4°.* LT, O, LVD, EN; CH, CLC, CN, MH, NC, WF, Y.

5299   **Buchius, Paulus.** The divine being. *Printed, and are to be sold by Randal Taylor,* 1693. 8°. L, O, C, OC, DT; CLC, LC, MIU, NPT, Y.

5299A   ——[Anr. ed.] *For the author,* 1693. 8°. NPT; WF.

5300   **Buchler, Johann.** Sacrarum profanarumque phrasivm poeticarvm thesaurus. Thirteenth edition. *In officina E. G. sumptibus Joannis Rothwelli,* 1642. 12°. L, DC, SA; CH, IU, MH, NBL, PAP, RPJ.

5301   ——Fourteenth edition. *In officina T. R. & E. M. sumptibus Joannis Rothwelli,* 1652. 12°. L, DC, MIU.

5302   ——Fifteenth edition. *Impensis Joannis Rothwell,* 1658. 12°. L, DC.

5302A   ——Sixteenth edition. *Typis T. N. prostatque venalis per Gulielmum Raybould & Josephum Nevil,* 1664. 12°. MB.

5303   ——Seventeenth edition. *Typis T. N. venalis per Georgium Sawbridge,* 1669. 12°. T.C.I 40. CLC, NPT, WF.

5304   ——[Anr. ed.] *Typis T. Newcomb,* 1679. 12°. PL.

5305   ——Eighteenth edition. *Typis Thomæ Newcombe,* 1679. 12°. L, C, EN; MB, MH, NPT, PL, WF.

5306   **Buck, *Sir* George.** The history of the life and reigne of Richard the Third. *By W. Wilson and are to be sold by W. L. H. M. and D. P.,* 1646. fol. L, O, C, E, DT; BN, CH, CU, LC, MH, NP, WCL, Y.

5307   ——Second edition. —, 1647. fol. L, C, LG, MR, E; BN, CH, IU, MH, NR, WF.

5308   **Buck, James.** St. Pauls thanksgiving. *By J. G. for John Playford,* 1660. 4°.* LT, O, LL, LW, WCA; TU, NU, WF, Y.

5308A   **Buck, John.** A sermon preached at the funeral of . . . Nich. Thorowgood. *For Tho. Cockerill,* 1692. 4°.* L; Y.

    Buckingham, George Villiers, *duke of*. The chances. 1682. *See* Fletcher, John.

5309   —Chorus poetarum. *For Benjamin Bragg,* 1674 [i.e. 1694]. 8°. L; CH, CN, MH, WF, Y.

5309A   ——[Anr. ed.] —, 1694. 8°. L; MH.

5310   —The declaration of. *Printed,* 1648. 4°.* LT, O, C, HH, YM; CH, MH, TU, WF, Y.

5311   [–] An epitaph upon Thomas late Lord Fairfax. [*London?* 1680?] brs. L, O, CT, OP; CH, CN, TU, WF, Y.

5312   [–] A letter to Sir Thomas Osborn. *For Henry Brome,* 1672. 16pp. 4°.* L, OC, CT, HH, DT; CLC, CN, MH, NC, WF, Y.

5313   [–]——[Anr. ed.] —, 1672. 19pp. 4°.* L, OC, CT, WCA, EB; CH, MH, MIU, NP, Y.

5314   —The Duke of Buckingham His Grace's letter, to the unknown author of a paper, entituled, A short answer. colop: *By J. L. for Luke Meredith,* 1685. cap., fol.* T.C.II 129. L, O, C, CT, OC; CH, MBA, NU, TU, WF, Y.

5315   Entry cancelled.

5316   —Poems on affairs of state. [*London*], *printed,* 1697. 8°. L, O, C, LVF; MBP, MH, WF, Y.

5317   ——Second edition. [*London*], *printed,* 1699. 8°. O; Y.

5318   —Poems, on several occasions. *Printed, and are to be sold by Dan. Browne and Tho. Axe,* 1696. 8°. T.C.II 590. MH.

5319   [–] Poetical reflections on . . . Absalom. *For Richard Janeway,* 1681. fol.* L, O, LVD; CH, CLC, NP, Y.

5320   [–]——[Anr. ed.] —, 1682. fol.* L, CT; CH, CU, MH, MU, TU, WF.

5321   —The poetical remains of. *Printed, and are to be sold by Thomas Minton,* 1698. 8°. L, CK.

5322   —A prophetick lampoon. [*London, c.* 1689.] brs. L, HH; MH, Y.

5323   [–] The rehearsal. *For Thomas Dring,* 1672. 4°. T.C.I 111. L, O, OC, OW; CH, CN, MH, WF, Y.

5324   [–] ——Second edition. *By T. Dring,* 1673. 4°. O, OW; CLC, LC, MH, WF, Y.

5325   [–] ——Third edition. *For Thomas Dring,* 1675. 4°. T.C.I 199. L, EN; CH, CU, MH, WF, Y.

5326 [–]—Fourth edition. *For R. Bentley and S. Magnes*, 1683. 4°. T.C.II 52. L, O, C, OB, CT; CH, CU, MH, NP, WF, Y.

5327 [–]—Fifth edition. *For Thomas Dring, and sold by John Newton*, 1687. 4°. L, O, C, LVD, LGI; CH, NP, TU, WF, Y.

5328 — —Sixth edition. *For T. Dring, and sold by Jacob Tonson*, 1692. 4°. L, O, C, EC; CLC, MH, NP, WF, Y.

5328A — —[Anr. ed.] *For R. Bentley and S. Magnes*, 1693. 4°. CH.

5329 —A short discourse upon the reasonableness. *By John Leake, for Luke Meredith*, 1685. 4°.* T.C.II 129. L, O, C, DC, MR; CH, CN, MH, TU, WF, Y.

5329A — —Second edition. —, 1685. 4°.* L, O, C, BP, EC; OCI, RPJ, WG, Y.

5330 — —Third edition. —, 1685. 4°.* L, O, C, E, EN; CH, CLC, WF.

5331 —His Grace the Duke of Buckingham's speech for liberty. *J. Curtis*, 1689. CH.

5332 —The Duke of Buckingham's speech in a late conference. *For M.I.*, 1668. 4°.* L, O, C, MR; CH, MH, TU, WF, Y.

5333 —The Duke of Buckingham's speech spoken in the House of Lords, Feb. 15th, 1678. *Amsterdam*, 1677. 4°.* O, HH; CH.

5334 —The Duke of Buckingham his speech to the king . . . Aprill 4. 1628. *Printed*, 1641. 4°.* LT; CH, MH, NN, WF, Y.

5335 Entry cancelled.

5336 [Buckingham, John Sheffield, *duke of*.] The character of Charles II. *Printed, to be sold by Richard Baldwin*, 1696. 8°.* L, LVF, CT, HH; CH, CN, NC, NLC, WF.

5337 —An essay on poetry. Second edition. *For Jo. Hindmarsh*, 1691. fol.* L, O, C, E; CLC, CN, MH, TU, WF, Y.

5338 — —[Anr. ed.] *For F. Saunders*, 1697. fol.* L, CLC, MH, WF, Y.

5339 [–] An essay upon poetry. *For Joseph Hindmarsh*, 1682. 4°.* T.C.I 508. L, O, C, CT; CH, CU, MH, NP, TU, WC, WF, Y.

5340 [–] —[Anr. ed.] *Dublin, Joseph Ray*, 1683. 4°.* DIX 199. DIX.

5341 [–] —"Second" edition. *For Jo. Hindmarsh*, 1685. 4°.* O, C, EC; CH, WF.

5342 [–] An ode in memory of . . . Queen Mary. [*London*, 1695.] fol. E.

5343 —Poemata quaedam. 1695. 4°.* L.

5344 —The Earl of Mulgrave's speech. [*London*, 1693?] fol.* O, HH.

5345 —To Dr. Tillotson. [*London*, 1689.] cap., fol.* L, OC, EN; Y.

5346 —A true copy of a letter from. colop: *Printed, and are to be sold by Randal Taylor*, 1689. cap., fol.* L, O, C, HH, E; CH, MH, TU, WF, Y.

5347 B[uckler], E[dward]. Certaine queries concerning the lawfullnes. *For Rich. Royston*, 1647. 4°.* LT, O, CT, EN, DT; MH, WF, Y.

5347A — —[Anr. ed.] —*to be sold by John Long in Dorchester*, 1647. 4°.* OC.

5348 [–] Death dis-sected. [*London*], *for the use of the author*, [1649]. 8°. LG, LVD; CH, MH, WCL.

5348A —The door open for sinners. 1695. 8°.* MHS.

5349 —God all in all. *For Luke Fawne*, 1655. 8°. LT, O, C; CH, CN, MH, NPT, Y.

5350 [–] Midnights meditations of death. *By John Macock*, 1646. 8°. LT; CH, MH, Y.

5351 —Salus populi or a nations happinesse. *For Iohn Rothwel*, [1658]. 4°.* O, LSC, DT.

5351A —The sin and folly of drunkenness. 1682. 12°. MHS.

Buckler of state. 1667. *See* Lisola, François Paul de.

5352 **Buckley, Francis.** A true relation of the proceedings, examination, tryal and horrid murder of Col. Eusebius Andrewe. *For Daniel Pakeman*, 1660. 4°. LT; CH, WF, Y.

[**Buckley, John.**] Short catechisme. 1646. *See* Ball, John.

5353 Entry cancelled.

5354 **Buckley, *Sir* Richard.** The proposal for sending back the nobility and gentry of Ireland. *For Samuel Holford, and sold by R. Baldwin*, 1690. 4°.* L, O, C, AU; CH, CN, Y.

5354A **Buckley, Samuel.** Catalogus liborum. 1695. 8°. OP.

Bucknall, John. Shepherd's almanack. 1673. *See* Almanacs.

Bucksome. *See* Buxom.

5354B **Buckworth, Edmund.** Directions for taking the . . . lozanges. [*London.* 1666.] brs. L.

5354C **Buckworth, Theophilus.** The approved success . . . lozanges. [*London?* 1660]. brs. L.

5354D —Serenæ veritatis gratia. [*London?* 1664.] brs. MH.

5355 [**Budd, Thomas**]. A brief answer to two papers. colop: *Philadelphia by William Bradford*, 1692. cap., 4°.* EVANS 589. LF; CH, LC, NN, PHS, RPJ.

5356 Entry cancelled.

5357 [–] An expostulation with Thomas Lloyd. [*Philadelphia, by William Bradford*, 1692.] 4°.* EVANS 593. CH, LC.

5358 —Good order established in Pennsilvania. [*Philadelphia, by William Bradford*] *printed*, 1685. 4°.* EVANS 386. L, O, LF; CH, CN, LC, NN, PHS, RPJ.

5358A [–] The great doctrines of the gospel of Christ. *For Nath. Crouch*, 1694. 12°. T.C.II 518. LF; CLC, PH, WF.

5359 —A just rebuke to several calumnies. [*Philadelphia: by Wm. Bradford*, 1692.] 4°.* EVANS 590. LF; CH, MU, NN, PHS, RPJ.

5360 [–] A testimony and caution. [*Philadelphia*, 1692.] 4°.* EVANS 437. LF; CH, LC, NN, PHS.

5360A —A true and perfect account of the disposal of the one hundred shares. 1685. brs. PHS.

5361 [–] A true copy of three judgments . . . against George Keith. [*Philadelphia, by William Bradford*, 1692.] 4°.* EVANS 608. LF; CH, LC, PHS, RPJ.

5361A **Buddle, George.** The doctrine of evangelical fasts 1969. 4°. O.

5362 **Budgell, Gilbert.** A discourse of prayer. *For W. Crook*, 1690. 4°.* T.C.II 297. L, O, C, OC; CH, CLC, LC, WF, Y.

Buds and blossoms. 1691. *See* Antrobus, Benjamin.

5362A **Buenting, Heinrich.** Itinerarium totius Sacræ Scripturæ. A description. *By S.I.*, 1652. 4°. NCH.

5362B **Buenting, Heinrich.** Itinerarium totius Sacræ Scripturæ, or the travels. *By J. Harefinch for T. Basset,* 1682. 4°. T.C.II 20. CSS, CT, LSC; CLC, MBA, NU, WF, Y.

5363 **Buerdsell, James.** Discourses and essays. *Oxford, by Leon: Lichfield,* 1699. 8°. CLC.

5363A ——[Anr. ed.] —, 1700. 8°. L, O, CT, OM, E; CLC, NU.

5364 [**Bufford, Samuel**] A discourse against unequal marriages. *For Dan. Browne, and T. Axe,* 1696. 12°. T.C.II 592. L.

5365 —An essay against unequal marriages. Second edition. *For T. Salusbury,* 1693. 12°. T.C.II 442. EN.

5365A **Bugg, Francis.** An apologetical introduction to the history. [1695.] 4°. OC.

5366 —Battering rams against new Rome. *For Joh. Gwillim,* Jan. 12. 1690/1. 4°. L, C, LF, OC, BAMB; CH, IE, PH, WF, Y.

5367 —A brief history of the rise, growth, and progress of Quakerism. *Printed,* 1697. 8°. LF, CM, OC, BAMB; MH, NU, PSC, RPJ, WF, Y.

5368 —A brief reply to George Whitehead's book. *By R. Janeway, jun. and sold by J. Robinson, and C. Brome,* 1700. 8°.* L, O, C, LF, OC; CH, MH, PH, WF, Y.

5368A —A brief reply to two papers. 1696. brs. OC.

5369 —The Christian ministry of the Church of England vindicated. *For the author, and are to be sold by J. Robinson and H. Rhodes,* 1699. 8°.* L, O, C, CE, OC; MH, PH, PSC, WF, Y.

5370 —De Christiana libertate, or, liberty of conscience. *For the author, and are to be sold by Enoch Prosser,* 1682. 8°. L, C, LF, OC, P; CLC, MH, MU, PH, PHS.

5371 —Innocency vindicated. [*London,* 1684.] 4°.* L, C, LF, BBN, OC; MH, PSC, WF.

5372 —Jezebel withstood. [*London,* 1699]. cap., 8°.* L, O, C, LF, OM; MH, PH, PSC, Y.

5372A —A just rebuke to the Quakers' insolent behaviour. *For the author by Rich. Janeway, Jun.,* 1700. brs. LF, OC.

5373 [–] A letter to the arch-bishops, bishops. [*London,* 1697.] fol.* LL.

5374 [–] A letter to the Quakers. *For the author, Aug. 30.* 1690. brs. L, LF, BAMB, BBN; CH, CN.

5374A [–] —[Anr. ed.] *For S. Norris, Aug. 30.* 1690. brs. CM; CH.

5374B —A looking-glass for the Quakers. *Printed* 1689. 4°. LF, OC; PH.

5375 —A modest defence of my book. *By R. Janeway, jun. for the author, and sold by J. Robinson, H. Rhodes, Ch. Brome, and J. Marshall,* 1700. 8°. L, O, C, LCL, LF; CH, MH, PH, WF, Y.

5376 —New Rome arraigned. *For the author, and are to be sold by J. Dunton, R. Baldwin, and J. Gwillim,* 1693. 4°. L, C, LF, CK; CLC, LC, MH, PH, PSC.

5377 ——Second edition. *Reprinted for the author, and are to be sold by J. Gwillim,* 1694. 4°. L, O, C, LF, GU; LC, MH, NU, PH, WF, Y.

5378 —New Rome unmask'd. *For the author,* 1692, *and are to be sold by John Gwillim, and John Dunton, and Sam. Manship,* 4°. L, O, C, LF, OC; NPT, PH, PSC, WF, Y.

5379 —One blow more at new Rome. *For Joh. Gwillim,* 1691. 4°.* L, C, LF, OC, BAMB; CLC, IE, PH, PSC, WF.

5380 —The painted-harlot both stript and whipt. *By J. Gain, for the author,* 1683, *and are to be sold by F. Smith.* 4°. L, C, LF, OC, BAMB; CLC, PH, PSC, VC, WF, Y.

5381 —The picture of Quakerism. *Printed for, and are to be sold by W. Kettleby, and W. Rogers,* 1697. 8°. T.C.III 13. L, O, C, LF, CE; CH, CN, MH, NU, PH, WF, Y.

5382 —The pilgrim's progress, from Quakerism. *Printed for, and are to be sold by W. Kettleby,* 1698. 4°. L, O, C, LF, CT; CH, CN, MH, NU, PH, WF, Y.

5383 ——Second edition. *By R. Janeway, jun., for the author; and sold by J. Robinson; and Ch. Brome,* 1700. 8°. T.C.III 190. L, O, C, LF, AU; CH, MH, NU, PH, WF, Y.

5384 [–] Quakerism anatomized. [*London,* 1694.] cap., 4°.* L, O, C, LF, GU; CH, MH, NU, PH, WF, Y.

5385 —Quakerism expos'd. *For the author, and are to be sold by J. Robinson, and H. Rhodes,* 1699. 8°. L, O, C, LCL, OM; CH, MH, PH, RPJ, WF, Y.

5386 —Quakerism withering. *For the author, and sold by J. Dunton, and J. Guillam,* 1694. 8°. L, O, C, LF, OM; MH, NU, PH, PSC, Y.

5387 —The Quakers detected. *For the author, and are to be sold by Edward Gyles in Norwich, and Ralph Watson in St. Edmunds-Bury,* 1686. 4°.* L, C, LF, OC, BBN; CH, MH, PH, WF, Y.

5388 —The Quakers set in their true light. *For the author, and are to be sold by C. Brome,* 1696. 4°. T.C.II 577. L, O, C, LF; CH, MH, NU, PH, Y.

5389 ——[Anr. ed.] *For the author, to be sold by C. Brome, and J. Guillim,* 1696. 4°. OC; MH, NPT, PSC, WF, Y.

5390 ——[Anr. ed.] 1697. 4°. PSC.

5391 —The Quaker's yearly meeting [sic]. colop: *For the author, and are to be sold by John Gwillam,* 1695. 4°.* L, O, C, LF, BBN; IE, LC, MH, NU, PH, PSC, Y.

5392 [–] A second summons to the city. colop: *For the author, and are to be sold by John Gwillam,* 1695. 4°.* L, O, C, LF, BBN; MH, NU, PH, WF, Y.

5393 [–] Seventy queries to seventy Quakers. colop: *Sept. 1698, and sold by W. Kettleby, London.* cap., 4°.* L, O, C, LF, CT; IE, NU, PH, PSC, Y.

5394 —A sober expostulation. *For C. Brome,* [1697/8]. 8°.* T.C.III 49. L, O, C, LF, CT; LC, PH, PSC, WF, Y.

[–] Some few of the Quakers many horrid blasphemies. 1699. See title.

5395 [–] Some of the Quakers principles. *For John Gwillim,* 1693. 4°.* L, O, C, GU, DT; NN, PH, PSC, WF.

5396 —Some reasons humbly proposed to the Lords. *For the author by Rich. Janeway, Jun. and sold by J. Robinson,* 1699. brs. LF; NU.

5396A ——Second edition. *For Rich. Janeway and E. Harris, and sold by J. Robinson and W. Kettilby,* 1699. brs. OC.

5397 [–] Something in answer to the allegations of the Quakers. [*London,* 1693.] cap., 4°. L, O, LF, OC, BAMB; MH, NU, PH.

5398 —To the most reverend the arch-bishops. [*London,* 1699.] brs. L, OC.

5399 —William Penn, the pretended Quaker. [*London,* 1700.] cap., 8°.* L, O, C, LF, OC; CN, MH, PH, RPJ, Y.

5399A   ——[Anr. ed.] *For J. Guillim*, 1700. 8°.* L, SP; PSC, WF, Y.

5400   The bugle-bovv. [*London*], *for F. Coles, T. Vere, J. Wright, and J. Clarke*, [1665-70]. brs. L, CM, HH; MH.

5401   **Bulkeley, Gershom.** The people's right to election. *Philadelphia, by assignes of William Bradford*, 1689. 4°.* EVANS 459. 4°. L; CH, MBA, MHS, NN.

5401A   [–] Some seasonable considerations for the good people of Connecticut. colop: *New York [by William Bradford]*, 1694. 4°. EVANS 688. BAMB; MH, MU.

5402   **Bulkeley, John J.** Short & plain directions. *Dublin, Jos. Ray*, 1697. DIX 288. LLP.

5403   **Bulkley, Peter.** The gospel covenant. *By M. S. for Benjamin Allen*, 1646. 4°. LT, C, LCL, RPL, YM; CLC, CN, LC, NU, Y.

5404   ——"Second" edition. *By Matthew Simmons, to be sold by T. Kembe and A. Kembe*, 1651. 4°. L, O, CT, LW, OC; CH, LC, MH, NU, WCL.

5404A   ——"Second" edition. —, 1653. 4°. Y.

5405   —The gospel covenant opened. [*London*], *sold by Tho. Parkhurst*, 1674. 4°. L; CLC.

5406   **Bulkley, Richard.** A sermon preached . . . May the 29th 1684. *For William Crook*, 1685. 4°.* O, WCA; CH, LC, WF.

5407   **Bulkley, Thomas.** An appeal unto Cæsar. *For the author*, 1696. fol.* L.

5407A   —The monstrous injustice . . . Nicholas Trott. *Printed*, 1698. 4°.* NN.

5408   —To the Right Honourable William, Earl of Craven. [1694]. 4°.* RPJ.

5409   **Bull, Digby.** The church's request. *For the author; to be sold by J. Whitlock*, 1695. 4°.* O, OC, CSS; TSM, WF.

5410   —The contrariety of Popery. *For the author; to be sold by J. Whitlock*, 1695. 4°. L, O, CM, LW, OC; CH, CU, MBA, WF, Y.

5411   —An exhortation to trust in God. *For the author; to be sold by John Whitlock*, 1695. 4°.* O, OC, CSSX; CH, MBA, WF.

5412   —A letter of a Protestant clergy-man. *For the author*, 1695. 4°. L, O, CT, OC, WCA; MBA, NU, PU, WF, Y.

5413   —The vvatch-man's voice. *For the author; to be sold by J. Whitlock*, 1695. 4°.* T.C.II 557. L, OC, LCL, LW; CH, NU, TSM, WF, Y.

5414   **Bull, George, bp.** Defensio fidei Nicænæ. *Oxonii, e theatro Sheldoniano*, 1685. 4°. L, O, C, AU, DT; BN, CH, WF, Y.

5415   ——Second edition. —, 1688. 4°. O, CJ, CM, MR, AU; BN, MH, NP, NU, Y.

5416   —Examen censvræ. *Typis Eliz. Flesher, prostant apud Richardum Davis, Oxon*, 1676. 4°. T.C.I 248. MADAN 3099. L, O, C, E, DT; BN, MBA, NPT, NU, WF, Y.

5417   —Harmonia apostolica. *Sumptibus Guliel. Wells & Rob. Scott*, 1670. 4°. T.C.I 21. L, O, C, E, AU, DT; BN, CH, NU, PL, WF, Y.

5418   —Judicium ecclesiæ Catholicæ. *Oxonii, e theatro Sheldoniano, impensis Georg. West*, 1694. 8°. T.C.II 533. L, O, C, AU, DT; IU, MBA, MH, NU, WF, Y.

5419   **Bull, Jonathan.** A relation of Captain Bull. [*Boston: by Samuel Green*, 1689.] brs. EVANS 460. MHS.

5420   Bull-feather hall. *Printed*, 1664. 4°.* L; Y.

5421   A bull from Rome. *Printed, to be sold by Henry Walker*, 1641. 4°.* LT.

5422   A bull sent by Pope Pius. *For D. M.*, 1678. brs. L; CH, MH.

5423   [**Buller, John.**] July 19, 1642. An exact relation of two victorious battels. *By L. N. and I. F. for E. Husbands and I. Franck*, [1642]. 4°.* LT, C, LFEA; WF.

5424   **Bullingham, Nicolas.** A parænesis to the dissenting clergy. *Printed*, 1665. 4°.* L, E.

5424A   **Bullock, Jeffrey.** Antichrist's transformations. [*London*, 1678?] 4°.* LF.

5425   [–] One blow more against Antichrist's ministers. colop: *For Francis Smith*, 1678. 4°.* L, LF.

5426   —Several testimonies given forth by. [*n.p.*, 1686.] 4°.* L, LF, BBN; IE, PH, PSC, Y.

5426A   —A testimony against the Quakers false-doctrine. *For the author, to be sold by Francis Smith*, 1677. 4°. LSC, OC.

5427   [–] A testimony against the 66 judges call'd Quakers. [*London?* 1680?] 4°.* L, LF, OC, CM, CT; PH, PSC.

5428   **Bullock, William.** Virginia impartially examined. *By Iohn Hammond*, 1649. 4°. LT, O, C, E, GH; CH, CN, LC, NN, RPJ, Y.

5429   **B[ullokar], J[ohn].** An English expositor. Third edition. *By John Legatt, to be sold by Andrew Crooke*, 1641. 8°. L, O, DC; CLC, CU, MH, WF, Y.

5429A   ——[Anr. ed.] *By J. L. sold by Edward Brewster*, 1654. 8°. AN.

5430   ——Fourth edition. *By J. L. to be sold by Simon Waterson*, 1656. 8°. L, O, CT, AN; CH, IU, MB, NS.

5430A   ——"Third" edition. *By J. Field, to be sold by Thomas Williams*, 1663. 8°. O, CK, AN; CN.

5431   ——"Fourth" edition. *Cambridge, by John Field*, 1667. 12°. L, C, CS; CU, LC, MH, V.

5431A   ——"Fourth" edition. *Cambridge, by John Hayes, sold by G. Sawbridge*, 1671. 12°. T.C.I 75. O, C; MH, WF.

5432   [–]—Fifth edition. *Cambridge, by John Hayes, to be sold by G. Sawbridge, London*, 1676. 12°. L, C, OC, CT; CLC, CU, MH, WSG, Y.

5433   ——Sixth edition. —, 1680. 12°. O; IU, LC, PL, TU.

5434   ——Seventh edition. *Cambridge, for John Hayes, to be sold by H. Sawbridge*, 1684. 8°. T.C.II 107. L, C, AN, E, DT; CLC, MH, MU, Y.

5435   ——Eighth edition. —, 1688. 12°. C; CN, MH, MM.

5435A   ——Ninth edition. *For Awnsham & John Churchil*, 1695. 12°. L, O; CLC, IU, MHS, NP, WF.

5436   [–]—"Ninth" edition. —, 1698. 12°. L; CU, TU.

5437   The bulls feather. [*London*], *for F. Coles, T. Vere, J. Wright, and J. Clarke*, [1655-80]. brs. L, O, CM, HH, GU; MH.

5438   The bully Whig, or, the poor whores lamentation for . . . Sir Thomas Armstrong. [*London*], 1684. brs. L, O; CH, CLC, MH.

5439   **Bulmer, John.** A note of such arts and mysteries. [*n.p.*, 1649.] brs. LT.

5440   —The proposition of Captaine . . . (20 March 1647). [*London*, 1648.] brs. LT; Y.

5441 —The propositions of. [*London*, 1643.] brs. LT, LG.

5442 —To the right honourable the Lords, . . . the humble petition of. *For John Harrison*, 1641[2]. brs. LT, LS.

5443 **Bulstrode, Edward.** A golden-chain. [*London*], *by F. L. for W. Lee, D. Pakeman, and G. Bedel*, 1657. 8°. LT; NPT, NU.

5444 —The reports of . . . divers resolutions. *For W. Lee, D. Pakeman, and G. Bedell*, 1657. fol. L, O, C, LL, DT; CH, LC, MH, MHL, NCL.

5445 — —Second edition. *By W. Rawlins, S. Roycroft, and M. Flesher, assigns of Rich. and Edw. Atkyns; for H. Twyford, T. Bassett, T. Dring, B. Griffin, C. Harper, M. Pitt, T. Sawbridge, S. Keble, D. Brown, J. Place, G. Collins, M. Wotton*, 1688. fol. L, O, C, LL, EN; BN, CH, LC, MBP, NCL, YL.

5446 —The second part of The reports. *For W. Lee, D. Pakeman, and G. Bedell*, 1658. fol. L, O, CS, CT; CH, MHL, NCL, WF.

5447 — —Second edition. *By the assigns of Richard and Edward Atkins*, 1688. fol. L, O; CH, NCL.

5448 —The third part of The reports. *For W. Lee, D. Pakeman, and G. Bedell*, 1659. fol. L, O, CM; CH, MHL, NCL.

5449 — —Second edition. *By the assigns of Richard and Edward Atkins*, 1688. fol. L, O; CH, MHL, NCL.

5450 [**Bulstrode, Whitelocke.**] Μετεμψυχωσις or an essay of transmigration. *By E. H. for Tho. Basset*, 1692. 8°. T.C.II 404. L, CT, E, EN, DT; BN, CH, NU, PL, WF, Y.

5451 — —[Anr. ed.] —, 1693. 8°. L, O, C; CU.

5452 **Bulteel, John, elder.** A relation of the troubles of the three forraign churches in Kent. *Imprinted at London for Sam. Enderbie*, 1645. 4°. LT, O, LG, LW, DT; CH, CN, NU, Y.

5453 —Sermon fait . . . 29 d'aoust, 1652. *Chez Humphrey Robinson*, 1653. 8°. O, DT.

5453A —A sermon preached . . . 29 day of August, 1652. *By T. M. for Edward Archer*, 1654. 4°.* WF.

Bulteel, John, younger. Amorous gallant. 1675. *See* Corneille, Thomas.

—Amorous Orontus. 1665. *See* Corneille, Thomas.

5454 —Birinthea, a romance. *By Tho. Mabb for John Playfere*, 1664. 8°. L, O; CN, CU, MH, NC, Y.

5454A [–] A collection of apothegmes. *For William Whitwood*, 1686. 8°. L; CH, NP, WF.

5455 [–] Londons triumph: or, the solemn . . . reception . . . Robert Tichborn. *For N. Brook*, 1656. 4°.* LT; CH.

5456 [–] Melpomene: or, the muses delight. *For H. Rogers*, 1678. 8°. O; CH.

5456A A new collection of new songs and poems. *By J. C. for William Crooke*, 1674. 8°. HARDING.

5457 —A new collection of poems. *By J. C. for William Crook*, 1674. 8°. T.C.I 163. L, O, C; CH, CN, CU, MH.

5458 [–] —[Anr. ed.] —, 1674, 8. O; SCU, MH, WF.

5459 **Bulwarke, William.** A true copie of an intercepted letter sent from Mr. [*London*], *for Francis Wright*, 1642. brs. LT, EC; CN.

5460 **B[ulwer], J[ohn].** Anthropometamorphosis. *For J. Hardesty*, 1650. 8°. L, LWL; CLC, LC, MB, V, Y.

5461 — —Second edition. *By William Hunt*, 1653. 4°. LT, O, C, ES, GH; BN, CH, CN, LC, MH, Y.

5462 —Chirologia. *By Tho. Harper, and are to be sold by Henry Twyford*, 1644. 8°. L, O, C, CT, ES; CLC, CN, LC, WCL, Y.

5462A — —[Anr. ed.] *By Tho. Harper, to be sold by R. Whitaker*, 1644. 8°. LCS, OC, CM, GK; CLC, IU, LC, TU, HC.

5463 — —[Anr. ed.] *Printed by Tho. Harper for R. Whitaker, and are to be sold by Henry Twyford*, 1644. 8°. LT, LW, MR, E, EN; BN, CH, CJC, LC, NP.

5464 — —[Anr. ed.] *By T. H. and Tho. Harper*, 1648. 8°. MMO, WSG, Y.

5465 —Chironomia. *By T. H. and Tho. Harper*, 1644. 8°. LW; BN, MMO.

5466 — —[Anr. ed.] *By Tho. Harper, to be sold by Henry Twyford*, 1644. 8°. L, LWL; CN, WCL, WF, Y.

5467 — —[Anr. ed.] *By Tho. Harper, to be sold by Richard Whitaker*, 1644. 8°. LT, O, OC, LCS; CH, CLC.

5468 —Pathomyotomia or a dissection. *By W. W. for Humphrey Moseley*, 1649. 12°. L, O, CK, E, GH; CLC, MH, MMO, NAM, WSG, HC.

5469 —Philocophus: or, the deafe and dumb mans friend. *For Humphrey Moseley*, 1648. 12°. L, O, MR, E, ES; BN, CH, MH, MMO, WF, Y.

5470 —A view of the people of the vvhole vvorld. *By William Hunt*, 1654. 4°.* L; CH, NC, WSG, Y.

5470A — —[Anr. ed.] *For the use and benefit of Thomas Gibbs*, 1658. 4°. IU.

5471 Bumm-foder or, waste-paper. [1660.] *See* Browne, Alexander.

5472 **Bunce, James.** Alderman Bunce his speech. *By T. S. for O. H.*, 1660. 4°.* LT, E; CH, NU, TU, WF, Y.

Bunch of grapes. [n.p., 1654–55.] *See* Farnworth, Richard.

Bundle of myrrhe. 1653. *See* Prime, H.

5473 **Bundy, John.** Great Britain's glory. *By W. Onley, for Nicholas Boddington*, 1696. 12°. T.C.II 591. L, CT, AU.

Bunting, Henry. *See* Buenting, Heinrich.

5473A **Bunworth, Richard.** Cosmographia physica. *Impensis autoris*, 1650. WF.

5474 [–] The doctresse: a plain and easic method. *By J. F. for Nicolas Bourne*, 1656. 12°. LT, LSC.

5475 [–] Man in paradise. *Printed at London by James Cottrel*, [1656]. 8°. L; JF.

5476 —A new discovery of the French disease. Second edition. *For Henry Marsh*, 1662. 8°. L, LCS, CPE.

5477 — —"Second" edition. 1666. 12°. LCP.

5478 —Ὁμοτροπια naturæ. A physical discourse. *By J. C. to be sold by Jer. Hirons*, 1656. 12°. 8°. L, O, LCP, LWL, P; CH, WU, JF.

5478A —Two excellent discourses. *For S. Waterson*, 1657. 12°. CPE.

5479 **Bunyan, John.** The works. The first volume. *Printed, and are to be sold by William Marshall*, 1692. fol. T.C.II 506. L, O, C, LG, BPL; CLC, CN, NU, TU, WF, Y.

5480 —The acceptable sacrifice. *Printed for, and are to be sold by George Larkin*, 1689. 12°. L, O; CH, MH, NC, WF.

5481 — —Second edition. *For Eliz. Smith*, 1691. 12°. L, O; CLC.

5482   ——Third edition. *By Rich. Janeway, jun. for John Gwillim*, 1698. 12°. L, BPL; CH, MBJ, CN, Y.

5483   —The advocateship of Jesus Christ. *For Dorman Newman*, 1688. 12°. L, BPL, MR, YM.

5484   —The barren fig-tree. *For Jonathan Robinson*, 1673. 12°. CN.

5485   ——Second edition. *For J. Robinson*, 1688. 12°. T.C.II 238. L, O, MR; CH, CLC, MB, MH, WF.

5486   ——Third edition. —, 1692. 8°. T.C.II 387. L, O, C, BPL; CLC.

5487   ——Fourth edition. *For Andrew Bell.*, 1695. 12°. L, O.

5487A   ——Fifth edition. *Glasgow, Sanders*, 1697. 16°. ALDIS 3656. PRF.

5488   ——Fifth edition. *By R. Joneway, for Jonathan Robinson*, 1698. YM.

5489   —A book for boys and girls. *For N.P.*, 1686. 8°. L; MH.

5490   —A case of conscience resolved. *For Benj: Alsop*, 1683. 4°. L, O.

5491   —A caution to stir up to watch against sin. *For N. Ponder*, [1684]. brs. L, O.

5492   —Christian behaviour. *For F. Smith*, [1663]. 12°. L; CH.

5493   ——Second edition. —, [1680]. 12°. O; CH.

5494   ——Third edition. —, [1690?] 12°. L, O.

5495   —Come & welcome, to Jesus Christ. *For B. Harris*, 1678. 8°. L, O; CH, CLC.

5496   ——Second edition. *For Benj. Harris*, 1684. 12°. L; Y.

5497   ——Third edition. *By Benj. Harris for Jo. Harris*, 1685. 12°. BPL, Y.

5498   ——"Third" edition. *For B.H. to be sold by J. Harris*, 1686. 12°. L.

5499   ——Fourth edition. *By J.A. for John Harris*, 1688. 12°. L, WF, Y.

5500   ——Fifth edition. *By G.L. for John Harris*, 1690. 12°. BPL; TU.

5501   ——Sixth edition. *For John Harris*, 1691. 12°. L, BPL, BML, BR; CLC.

5502   ——Seventh edition. —, 1694. 12°. BPL; MIU.

5503   ——Eighth edition. —, 1697. 12°. BPL.

5504   ——"Eighth" edition. *By T. Mead for Eliz. Harris*, 1700. 12°. O, BPL.

5505   ——Ninth edition. *Printed and sold by Benj. Harris*, 1700. 12°. L, O, BPL, DM; Y.

5506   [–] A confession of my faith. *For Francis Smith*, 1672. L, MRL; NU.

5507   —A defence of the doctrine of iustification. *For Francis Smith*, 1672. 4°. L, O, OC, BPL; CH, CLC, MH, PRF, Y.

5508   ——[Anr. ed.] —, 1673. 4°. L; CLC, PRF.

5509   —Differences in judgment about water-baptism. *For John Wilkins*, 1673. 8°. L, O, LW, MR, GU; CH, NU, TU, WCL, WF.

5510   —A discourse of the building. *Printed, to be sold by George Larkin*, 1688. 8°. L, O.

5511   Entry cancelled.

5512   —A discourse upon the Pharisee. *For Joh. Harris*, 1685. 12°. L, O, MR; CH, MH, TU, WF, Y.

5513   —The doctrine of the lavv and grace unfolded. *For M. Wright*, 1659. 8°. LT.

5514   ——[Anr. ed.] *For Matthias Cowley in Newport-Pannell*, 1659. 8°. HARMSWORTH.

5515   ——"Second" edition. *For Nath. Ponder*, 1685. 12°. L, O, BPL; PRF, WF.

5516   —A few sighs from Hell. *By Ralph Wood, for M. Wright*, 1658. 8°. LT, BPL.

5517   ——Third edition. [*n.p.*, 1672?] 8°. HARMSWORTH.

5518   ——Fourth edition. [*n.p.*], 1674. 8°. T.C.I 182. HARMSWORTH.

5519   ——Fifth edition. [*n.p.*], 1675. 8°. O, LSC.

5520   ——Ninth edition. [*n.p.*], 1692. 8°. HARMSWORTH.

5521   ——Tenth edition. —, 1700. 8°. T.C.III 146. BPL.

5522   —Good news for the vilest of men. *Printed, and are to be sold by George Larkin*, 1688. 12°. L.

5523   —Grace abounding to the chief of sinners. *By George Larkin*, 1666. 8°. L; CH.

5524   ——Third edition. *For F. Smith*, [1679]. 12°. T.C.I 363. NNM.

5525   ——Fifth edition. *For Nath. Ponder*, 1680. 8°. BPL; PRF, WF.

5526   ——Sixth edition. —, 1688. 12°. L, BPL, LCL, BR, MR; PRF.

5527   ——Seventh edition. —, 1692. 12°. L, O, BPL; MH, NN.

5528   ——Eighth edition. *For N. Ponder*, [1693?]. 12°. L, O, MR, MRL; Y.

5529   ——"Sixth" edition. *Glasgow, by Robert Sanders*, 1697. sixes. LW, EN.

5529A   ——Seventh edition. *For Robert Parker*, 1695. 12°. WF.

5530   —The greatness of the soul. *For Ben. Alsop*, 1683. 12°. T.C.I 504. L, LG; CH, WF.

5531   ——[Anr. ed.] *For Richard Wilde*, 1691. 12°. L, O,

[–] Heart's ease. 1690. *See* Bardwood, James.

5532   —The heavenly foot-man. *For Charles Doe*, 1698. 8°. T.C.III 75. L, O; CH, CLC.

5533   ——Second edition. *For John Marshall*, 1700. 12°. T.C.III 189. O; MR, NN.

5534   —The holy city. *Printed*, 1665. 8°. L, O.

5535   ——[Anr. ed.] *By J. Dover*, [1665]. 8°. L, BPL; CH, CLC, Y.

5536   ——"Second" edition. *For Francis Smith*, 1669. 8°. T.C.I 12. L, O, LW; PRF, Y.

5537   —A holy life. *By B.W. for Benj. Alsop*, 1684. 12°. T.C.II 41. L, O, LCL; CLC, TU, Y.

5538   —The holy war, made. *For Dorman Newman; and Benjamin Alsop*, 1682. 8°. T.C.I 469. L, O, LCL, BPL, ES; CH, MH, NN, TU, WF.

5538A   ——Second edition. *For Dorman Newman*, 1684. 12°. BBE, MH.

5539   —The holy war, betwixt. *For D. Newman; and B. Alsop*, 1684. Second edition. 12°. T.C.II 78. L, O, BPL; CLC, MWA.

5540   ——Third edition. *By the assigns of B.A. and sold by Nah. Ponder*, 1696. 8°. L, O; WF.

5541   —I will pray with the spirit. Second edition. *For the author*, 1663. 12°. L; NNM.

5542   ——Third edition. —, [1685?]. 12°. L.

5543   ——Fourth edition. 1692. 12°. CLC.

5544   —Instruction for the ignorant. *For Francis Smith*, 1675. 8°. O.

5545 —The Jerusalem-sinner saved. Second edition. *Printed, to be sold by George Larkin,* 1689. 12°. L, O; CH, CLC, CU.

5546 ——Third edition. [*n.p.*], 1691. 12°. O, HARMSWORTH.

5547 ——"Third" edition. *For John Gwillim,* 1697. 12°. L, O, YM, CPL.

5548 ——"Third" edition. —, 1700. 12°. L, O, IC; Y.

5548A —The labours of. [*London,* 1690?] brs. L.

5549 —Mr. John Bunyan's last sermon. *By George Larkin,* 1689. 8°.* NNM.

5550 —The life and death of Mr. Badman. *By J. A. for Nath. Ponder,* 1680. 12°. T.C.I 382. L, O, OC; CH, MH, NN, WCL, Y.

5551 ——Second edition. ———, 1685. 12°. HARMSWORTH.

5552 ——"Second" edition. 1688. 12° L.

5553 ——Third edition. *For W. P., sold by N. Ponder,* 1696. 12°. L, BPL, YM; Y.

5554 —Light for them that sit in darkness. *For Francis Smith,* 1675. 8°. L, O, LG.

5554A —A map shewing the order. *Printed and sold by William Marshall,* 1691. brs. MH, NN.

5555 —One thing is needful. Second edition. *For Francis Smith,* [167–?] 12°. CLC.

5555A ——Third edition. *For Nath. Ponder,* 1683. 12°. L.

5556 ——Fourth edition. *Printed,* [1700?] 12°. L; BJH, WCL.

5557 —The pilgrim's progress. *For Nath. Ponder,* 1678. 12°. T.C.I 299. L, MR; CH, IU, LC, NN, PRF, Y.

5558 ——Second edition. *For N. Ponder,* 1678. 8°. L, O, C; NN, Y.

5559 ——Third edition. —, 1679. 12°. L, O; CH, CLC, NN, Y.

5560 ——Fourth edition. *Dondon* [*sic*]*, for Nath. Ponder,* 1680. 12°. T.C.II 382. L; CN, NN, Y.

5561 ——"Fourth" edition. *For Nath. Ponder,* 1680. 12°. BPL, CPL; CH, NN.

5562 ——Fifth edition. —, 1680. L, LLL, GU; BN, CH, MWA, NN, WCL.

5563 ——"Fifth" edition. *Edinburgh, for Iohn Cairns,* 1680. 12°. L.

5564 ——Sixth edition. *For Nath. Ponder,* 1681. 12°. L; CH, LC, NN, WCL.

5565 ——Seventh edition. *For Nathaniel Ponder,* 1681. 12°. L; NN.

5566 ——[Anr. ed.] *Boston in New England, by Samuel Green upon assignment of Samuel Sewall and are to be sold by John Vsher of Boston,* 1681. 8°. EVANS 299. CH, LC, MB, MWA, NN.

5567 ——"Fifth" edition. *For Nath. Ponder,* 1682. 12°. L; BN, CLC, NN, Y.

5568 ——Eighth edition. *For Nathaniel Ponder,* 1682. 12°. L, LSC, BPL; CLC, CN, NN, PRF, Y.

5569 ——Ninth edition. *For Nathaniel Ponder,* 1683. 12°. L, MR, BPL; CH, NN, WCL, Y.

5569A ——"Sixth" edition. *Edinburgh, John Reid,* 1683. 12°. L.

5570 ——"Ninth" edition. *For Nathaniel Ponder,* 1684. 12°. L, O; NN, WCL.

5571 ——Tenth edition. *For Nathaniel Ponder,* 1685. 12°. T.C.II 132. L, BPL; CH, CN, MH, NN, PRF.

5572 ——Eleventh edition. —, 1688. 12°. L, BPL; CH, NN.

5573 ——Twelfth edition. *For Robert Parker,* 1689. 8°. CH.

5573A ——"Twelfth" edition. *For R. Ponder,* 1689. 12°. NN.

5574 ——Thirteenth edition. *For Robert Ponder, and are to be sold by Nich. Boddington,* 1693. 12°. L; MH, NN, PRF.

5575 ——Fourteenth edition. *For W. P.,* 1695. 12°. L, O; CLC, NN, Y.

5575A ——"Sixth" edition. *Edinburgh, by the heirs and successors of Andrew Anderson,* 1696. PRF.

5576 ——Second part. *For Nathaniel Ponder,* 1684. 12°. L, MR; CH, LC, NN, WCL.

5577 ——[Anr. ed.] 1685. 12°. NNM.

5578 ——Second edition. *For Nathaniel Ponder,* 1686. 12°. L.

5579 ——"Second" edition. [*n.p.*] —, 1687. 12°. L; NN, PRF.

5580 ——Third edition. *For Robert Ponder,* 1690. 12°. L; CH.

5581 ——Sixth edition. *For Robert Ponder, and sold by Nicholas Boddington,* 1693. 12°. L, O; CH, CN, NN.

5582 ——Seventh edition. *For W. P.,* 1696. 12°. L, O.

5583 ——The third part. *By E. Millet, for J. Deacon, J. Back, and J. Blare,* 1693. 12°. L, O; CH, CN, NN.

5584 ——Second edition. *By W. O. for J. Back, and J. Blare,* 1695. 12°. L, C.

5585 ——Fourth edition. [*n.p.*]*, W. Onley for J. Back,* 1700. 12°. T.C.III 191. L.

5586 —Profitable meditations. *For Francis Smith,* [1661]. 4°.* L.

5587 —Questions about the nature and perpetuity. *For Nath. Ponder,* 1685. 12°. T.C.II 95. L, O, CT; CH, WCL, WF, Y.

5588 —Reprobation asserted. *For G. L.,* [1674?]. 4°.* L, O; PRF.

5589 ——Second edition. *By George Larkin jun. for William Marshal, also sold by John Marshal,* 1696. 4°.* L, O, LCL, GU; WF.

5590 —The resurrection of the dead. *For Francis Smith,* [1665]. 8°. L, O.

[–] Saints' triumph. 1685. *See* Blare, Joseph.

5591 —Scriptural poems. *By J. Blare,* 1700. 8°. L; CH.

5592 —Seasonable counsel. *For Benjamin Alsop,* 1684. 12° L, O, BPL; CH, CLC, WCL, WF, Y.

5593 —Sighs from Hell. Second edition. *For F. Smith,* [1666?] 8°. L.

5593A ——Fifth edition. —, 1675. 8°. O.

5593B ——Seventh edition. *For F. Smith,* [1680?] 8°. LSC.

5593C ——Eighth edition. *For Awnsham Churchill,* 1686. 12°. EN; WF.

5594 ——Tenth edition. *Belfast, by Patrick Neill and company,* 1700. 12°. L.

5595 —Solomon's temple spiritualiz'd. *Printed for, and sold by George Larkin,* 1688. 12°. L, O, BPL, MR, YM; CH, CLC, PRF, RBU, Y.

5596 ——Second edition. *Eliz. Smith,* 1691. 12°. L, CT, BPL; CLC, Y.

5597 ——Third edition. *For John Gwillim,* 1698. 12°. L, BML, BR, BPL; WF, Y.

5598 —Some gospel-truths opened. *For J. Wright the younger,* 1656. 12°. L, BPL, CM.

5599 ——[Anr. ed.] *For J. W. and are to be sold by Mathias Cowley,* 1656. 12°. MR.

5600 —The strait gate. *For Francis Smith*, 1676. 8°. T.C.I 216.
O, C.

5601 —Taith y peverin. *[London], gan J. Richardson*, 1688. 12°.
AN, CPL; MH, V.

5602 ——[Anr. ed.] *Mythig, gan Thomas Jones*, 1699. 12°. L,
AN; CU.

5603 —A treatise of the fear of God. *For N. Ponder*, 1679. 12°.
T.C.II 381. L, O, EN; CLC, NNM, Y.

5604 [-] A true and impartial narrative of some illegal . . .
proceedings. *[London]*, 1670. 4°.* L, E; CH, LC, Y.

5605 —A vindication of the book called Some gospel-truths
opened. *For John Wright*, 1657. 4°. CT, LF.

5606 ——[Anr. ed] *For Matthias Cowley, in Newport*, 1657.
4°. CT, LF.

5607 —The water of life. *For Nathanael Ponder*, 1688. 8°. L, O,
BPL; CH, MB, MH, WF.

5608 —The work of Jesus Christ. *For Dorman Newman*, 1688.
12°. L, O, LW, EN, GU; CLC, CN, NU, WF, Y.

5609-10 Entries cancelled.

5611 **Burbury, John.** A relation of a journey of . . . my Lord
Henry Howard from London to Vienna. *For T.
Collins, I. Ford and S. Hickman*, 1671. 12°. T.C.I 72.
L, O, CT, E, GH; BN, CH, CN, MH, WF, Y.

5612 **Burch, Dorothy.** A catechism of the several heads. *By
Matthew Simmons for John Hancock*, 1646. 8°.* LT; CH.

5613 **Burches, George.** Mans inbred malady. *By W. Wilson,
to be sold by Thomas Johnson*, 1655. 12°. LT, O.

5614 —The marrow of divinity. *For Marmaduke Boat*, 1649.
4°. LT.

5615 —A sermon preached at Owbvrne . . . on the twenty-
seaventh of Iuly. *Oxford, by Leon. Lichfield*, 1641. 4°.*
MADAN 993. O; WF.

5616 **Burd, Richard.** A sermon preached . . . May 29, 1684.
For Samuel Keble, 1684. 4°. T.C.II 81. L, O, C, LP, OC;
CLC, NN, WF, Y.

5617 The burden of a loaden conscience. Entry cancelled.

5618 The burden of England, Scotland, & Ireland. *For
Gifford Galton*, 1646. 4°. LT, LCL, CT, DT; CH, CU, MBP,
MH.

5618A —[Anr. ed.] *Th. Slater*, 1646. 4°. L.
Burthen of Issachar. [n.p.], 1646. See Maxwell, John abp.

5619 [**Burdet, John.**] The resolution of the Prince of Wales,
concerning the landing. *Printed*, 1648. 4°.* LT, O, DT;
CH, MH.

5620 [**Burdet, W.**] A wonder of wonders. *By John Clowes*,
1651. 4°.* MADAN 2151. LT.
[**Burdett, Thomas.**] Declaration from the Isle of
Wyght. 1648. See Hewat, John.

5621 **Burdwood, James.** Helps for faith. *For J. Robinson*,
1693. 8°. T.C.II 474. L, O.

5622-23 Entries cancelled.

5624 [**Burfoit, T.**] New papers from the armie. *For Thomas
Reynolds, June 13*, 1647. 4°.* LT, O, DC; WF.

5625 **Burgersdijck, Franco.** Collegium physicum. Third
edition. *Ex officina Rogeri Danielis, Cantabrigiensis*,
1650. 12°. C, CT, LWL, EN, AU; CLC, MW, WF.

5626 ——Fourth edition. *Oxoniæ, typis W. Hall, impensis
Joseph Godwin*, 1664. 12°. MADAN 2656. O, CCL; WF.

5627 —Idea philosophiæ tum moralis. *Oxonii, excudebat Leon:
Lichfield, impensis Henrici Curteyne*, 1641. 12°. MADAN
994. O, P, E; Y.

5628 ——[Anr. ed.] *Oxonii, excudebat Rob. Blagrave*, 1654. 12°.
MADAN 2254. O, CCH, CP, CS, OC; CLC, IU, NPT, WF, Y.

5629 ——[Anr. ed.] *Oxonii, excudebat W.H., impensis Jos.
Godwin & Ric. Davis*, 1667. 12°. MADAN 2766. O, OC,
CPE; CLC, CSB, MH, NN, Y.

5630 —Fr. Burgersdicii Institutionum logicarum. *Cantebrigiæ
[sic], ex officina Rogeri Daniel*, 1644. 12°. C, LW, CCL,
DC, E; MH.

5631 ——[Anr. ed.] *Cantabrigiæ, ex officina Rogeri Daniel*,
1647. 8°. L, C, YM, EN, DT; MH, Y.

5632 ——[Anr. ed.] *Ex officina Rogeri Danielis*, 1651. 8°. L, O,
C, BQ, D; LC, MB, NP, WF, Y.

5633 ——[Anr. ed.] *Cantabrigiæ, apud Joann. Field*, 1660. 8°.
O, C, YM; MH, MWA, NR.

5634 ——[Anr. ed.] ——, 1666. 8°. L, O, C; CH, CU, MBA, WF,
Y.

5635 ——[Anr. ed.] —, 1668. 8°. L, O, C, LL, CT; CLC, MH, NP,
WG.

5636 ——[Anr. ed.] *Cantabrigiæ, apud Joann. Hayes*, 1680.
Prostant venales apud Guil. Graves jun. 8°. L, O, C, DC,
AU; CH, CU, MH, PL, WF, Y.

5637 —Institutionum metaphysicarum. 1651. 12°. LSC.

5638 ——Third edition. *Typis R. N. prostant apud J. Crook,
& J. Baker*, 1653. 12°. L, O, CM, CT, E; CU, MB, VC.

5639 ——[Anr. ed.] *[Oxon], typis H. Hall, impensis Ric. Davis*,
1675. 12°. MADAN 3052. L, O, OC, EC; CLC, MH, WF, Y.

5640 —Monitio logica: or, an abstract. *For Ric. Cumberland*,
1697. 8°. T.C.II 604. LL; CU, MH, PL, Y.

5641 [**Burgess,   .**] To the honourable the knights, citizens,
and burgesses of the Commons . . . the humble peti-
tion of sundry ministers. *For John Bellamie and Ralph
Smith*, 1641. brs. LT, LS, CJ, CT; MH, Y.

5642 **Burgess, Anthony.** A demonstration of the day of
judgment. *For T. Underhill*, 1657. 12°. LT.

5643 —The difficulty of, and the encouragements to a reformation. *By R. Bishop for Thomas Vnderhill*, 1643. 4°.*
LT, O, C, EN, DT; CH, CU, MH, NU, WF, Y.

5644 —Doctrine of justification. 1655. 4°. O, LW, SA.

5645 —The doctrine of original sin. *By Abraham Miller for
Thomas Underhill*, 1658. fol. O, LCL, OB; CH, CU, MBA,
WF.

5646 ——[Anr. ed.] —, 1659. fol. L, LW, CS, RB, ENC; CH, MH,
NPT, NU, Y.

5647 —An expository comment, doctrinal, controversal. *By
A. M. for Abel Roper*, 1661. fol. O, C, LCL, LW, GU; NU.
PPT.

5648 —The godly mans choice. *By Abraham Miller for Thomas
Underhill*, 1659. fol. O, C, LCL, OB, AU; CLC, NPT, NU, Y.

5649 —Ivdgements removed. *By M. Simmons for Thomas
Underhill*, 1644. 4°.* LT, O, CS, BC, DT; CH, CU, MH, NU,
WF, Y.

5650 —The magistrates commision. *By George Miller for Thomas Vnderhill*, 1644. 4°.* LT, O, CS, BC, DT; CH, CU, MH, NU, WF, Y.

5651 —CXLV. expository sermons. *By Abraham Miller for Thomas Underhill*, 1656. fol. L, O, C, LCL, E; CU, MH, NU, WF, Y.

5652 —Paul's last farewel. *For Abel Roper*, 1658. 4°.* LT, O, LW; NPT, NR, NU, WF, Y.

5653 —Publick affections, pressed in a sermon. *By J. Y. for Thomas Vnderhill*, 1646. 4°.* LT, O, C, EN, DT; CH, CU, MH, NU, Y.

5654 —The reformation of the church. *By G. M. for T. Vnderhill*, 1645. 4°.* LT, O, C, BC, EN; CH, CU, MH, NU, WF, Y.

5655 —Romes cruelty. *By George Miller for Tho. Vnderhill*, 1645. 4°.* LT, O, C, EN, DT; CH, CU, MH, NU, WF, Y.

5656 —The Scripture directory. *By Abraham Miller for T. U. to be sold by Thomas Underhill, George Calvert and Henry Fletcher*, 1659. fol. L, O, C, ENC; CLC, CU, MH, NU, Y.

5657 —Spiritual refining. *By A. Miller for Thomas Underhill*, 1652. fol. L, O, C, LCL, E; BN, CU, MH, NU, WF, Y.

5657A — —Part II. —, 1654. 4°. L, CP; TSM.

5658 — —[Anr. ed.] *By A. M. to be sold by Thomas Newberry*, 1654. 4°. L, LCL, CE, EN, DT; NU, PPT, Y.

5658A — —[Anr. ed.] *For T. U. and are to be sold by T. Newberry*, 1654. fol. LC, PJB.

5659 —Spiritual refinings. Second edition. *By J. Streater, for T. U., to be sold by Tho. Johnson*, 1658. 2 pts. fol. L, CS, RPL, ENC, GU; CLC, CU, MH, NU, Y.

5660 Entry cancelled.

5661 —A treatise of self-judging. *By J. H. for T. Underhill, and M. Keinton*, 1658. 12°. LT, O, AN.

5662 —The true doctrine of ivstification asserted. *By Robert White, for Thomas Vnderhil*, 1648. 4°. LT, C, BC, ENC, DT; CH, NHC, NU, WCL, WF.

5663 — —Second edition. *By A. Miller for Tho. Underhil*, 1651. 4°. L, CT, DC, E, DT; CH, CU, MH, WF, Y.

5664 — —[Anr. ed.] *For Thomas Vnderhill*, 1654. 4°. LT, CT, DC, E, ENC; CLC, NPT, NU, WF, Y.

5665 — —Third edition. *By A. M. for Tho. Vnderhill*, 1655. 4°. LW, CS, BR, ENC; CLC, CU, NPT, NU.

5666 —Vindiciæ legis: or, a vindication. *By James Young, for Thomas Underhill*, 1646. 4°. LT, O, CT, EN, DT; CH, CU, MH, NU, WF, Y.

5667 — —Second edition. *By James Young, for Thomas Underhill*, 1647. 4°. L, C, LCL, LW, E; CH, MH, NP, NU.

5667A — —Weighty cases of conscience. *Printed and sold by R. Janeway*, 1688. 8°.* Y.

5668 **Burgess, Cornelius.** Another sermon preached . . . November the fifth, 1641. *By R. B. for P. Stephens and C. Meridith*, 1641, 4°. O, C, YM, E, DT; CH, CU, MH, NU, WF, Y.

5669 [–] The broken title of episcopal inheritance. *For John Bellamie, and Ralph Smith*, 1642. 4°.* LT, O, C, HH, DT; CH, MH, NU, WF, Y.

5670 [–] A case concerning the buying of bishops lands. *Printed*, 1659. 4°. L, OB, C, MR, DT; CH, MH, NU, WF.

5671 —The first sermon. *By I. L. for Philemon Stephens and Christopher Meredith*, 1641. 4°. LT, O, C, CE, LP; CLC, NU, TU, WF, Y.

5672 [–] An humble examination of a printed abstract of the answers to nine reasons. *For P. Stephens and C. Meredith*, 1641. 4°. LT, O, C, E, EN; CH, CU, MH, NU, WF, Y.

5673 —The necessity of agreement with God. *By G. Miller for Philemon Stephens*, 1645. 4°. LT, O, C, EN, AU; CH, MH, NU, TU, WF, Y.

5674 —No sacrilege nor sinne to alienate or purchase cathedral lands. *By J. C. and sold by Ed. Brewster*, 1659. 8°. O, CT.

5675 — —Second edition. *By J. C. and sold by Ed. Brewster*, 1659. 8°. L, C, LCL, CM, EN; CH, MIU, NGT, NU, WF.

5676 — —Third edition. *By James Cottrel*, 1660. 4°. LT, O, C, EN, DT; CH, CU, NPT, WF, Y.

5677 —Prudent silence. *Printed at London, by James Cottrel*, [1660]. 8°.* C; NU.

5678 [–] Reasons shewing the necessity of reformation. *By Ja: Cottrel*, 1660. 4°. LT, O, C, EN, DT; CH, CU, MH, NU, WF, Y.

5679 [–] —Second edition. —, 1660. 4°. L, O, C, HH, DT; CH, MBA, NU, WF, Y.

5680 —The second sermon, preached . . . April 30. 1645. *By J. R. for Philem. Stephens*, 1645. 4°. LT; MH, NU, WF, Y.

5681 — —[Anr. ed.] *By J. R. for Christoph. Meredith*, 1645. 4°. O, C, OCC, EN; MH, MWA, NU.

5681A — —[Anr. ed.] *Printed* 1645. 4°. Y.

5682 —A sermon preached . . . Novem. 17. 1640. *By Iohn Legatt, for P. Stephens, and C. Meredith*, 1641. 4°. O, C, LW, EN, DT; CH, CU, MH, TU, WF, Y.

5683 — —[Anr. ed.] *By T. Badger, for P. Stephens, and C. Meredith*, 1641. 4°. CM, OC, LW, BR; CH, CU, MH, TU, WF, Y.

5684 — —Third edition. *By John Legatt, for P. Stephens and C. Meredith*, 1641. 4°. O, C, BR, EN; CU, MH, TU, WF, Y.

5685 —Sion College what it is. *For Ralph Smith*, 1648. 4°.* LT, C, E, DT; CH, MH, NU, WF.

5686 [–] Some of the differences and alterations in the present Common-Prayer-book. [n.p., 1660.] cap. 4°.* O, OC, CM, CS; WCA, WF, WWC.

5687 —Tvvo sermons. *By T. B. and I. O. for S. Man, P. Stephens, and C. Meredith*, 1641. 4°. EN, DT; CH, MH, NU, WSC, Y.

5688 — —[Same title.] *By J. R. for Phil. Stephens*, 1645. 4°. L, O, C, EN, DT; BBE, MH, NU, WF, Y.

5689 — —[Anr. ed.] *By J. R. for Cristopher Meredith*, 1645. 4°. LT, O, BR, AU; NGT, NU, Y.

5690 [–] A vindication of the ministers of the gospel. *By A. M. for Th. Vnderhill*, 1648. 4°.* LT, O, C, HH, EN; CH, CN, NU, TU, WF, Y.

5691 [–] —[Anr. ed.] —, 1649. 4°.* EN; NU.

5691A — —[Anr. ed.] *Printed at London and reprinted at Edinburgh*, 1649. 4°.* ALDIS 1393. HH, EN, ENC; IU.

5692 [–] A vindication of the nine reasons of the House of Commons. *For P. Stephens, and C. Meredith*, 1641. 4°. MADAN 999. O, C, EN; CH, NU, PL, WF.

5692A **Burgess, Daniel.** Advice to parents and children. *By J. R. for Tho. Parkhurst, and J. Lawrence,* 1690. 12°. T.C.II 311. CLC, NU.

5693 —, 'Αποκαραδοκια κ'ευχη η χριστιανικη. Christians earnest expectation. *[London?] for O. C.,* 1675. 8°. T.C.I 217. L, O; CLC, NU.

5694 [–] Appellatio ad fratres exteros. [*n.p.*], *typis S. N. impensis L. S.,* 1690. 4°.* O, LW, P; NP, NU, WF, Y.

5695 —A call to sinners. *For Tho. Parkhurst, and Robert Gibbs,* 1689. 12°. T.C.II 248. LCL, LW; CLC, NU.

5696 [–] Causa Dei: or, counsel. *For Joseph Fox,* 1697. 8°. L; NU.

5697 —Characters of a godly man. *For Tho. Parkhurst,* 1691. 8°. T.C.II 358. L, O, C, LCL, EN; NU, WF, Y.

5698 —Christian commemoration. *For Tho. Parkhurst,* 1691. 8°. T.C.II 332. L, LCL; CLC.

5699 —The Christian temper. *For T. Parkhurst, and R. Gibbs,* 1688. 8°. T.C.II 248. LCL, LW; CLC, NU.

5700 —The church's triumph. *By J. D. for Tho. Parkhurst, and Andr. Bell and J. Luntley,* 1694. 12°. T.C.II 520. L, O, LCL, GU; MH, NGT, NU.

5701 —Counsel to the rich. 1697. 12°. LCL.

5702 —The death and rest, . . . of the saints. *For John Lawrence,* 1692. 12°. T.C.II 407. L, O, LCL, LW, BR.

5703 —Directions for daily holy living. *For Tho. Parkhurst,* 1690. brs. L.

5704 —Eighteen directions for saving conversion . . . God. By. *For Tho. Parkhurst,* 1691. 8°.* T.C.II 346. O.

5705 —Eighteen directions for saving conversion . . . God. With. *For Tho. Parkhurst,* 1691. 8°.* O.

5706 —Foolish talking and jesting. *For Andrew Bell and Jonas Luntley,* 1694. 8°. L; CLC, MB, NU, PPT, Y.

5706A —Forty aphorisms concerning riches. *For Tho. Parkhurst,* 1696. 8°.* MHS, MIU, MU.

5706B —A funeral sermon preach'd upon . . . Mrs. Sarah Bull. *Printed and sold by A. Bell and J. Lonsley,* 1694. 8°. LW.

5707 —The golden snuffers. *By J. Darby, for T. Parkhurst,* 1697. 8°. T.C.III 24. L, O, CM, LCL, EN; MH, MIU, NPT.

5707A —Hastiness to anger. *For Jonathan Robinson,* 1695. 8°. MH, NU.

5708 —Holy union, and holy contention. *For Andrew Bell,* 1695. 8°. LCL, EN; MH.

5709 —Mans whole duty. *By J. Richardson for Tho. Parkhurst; and John Lawrence,* 1690. 12°. O; CLC, NU.

5710 —The most difficult duty. 1694. 12°. LCL.

5711 —Proofs of God's being. *For T. Parkhurst,* 1697. 8°.* L; WF.

5712 ——Second edition. *For Tho. Parkhurst,* 1698. 8°.* L.

5713 —Rules and motives to holy prayer. *For T. Parkhurst,* 1696. 8°.* T.C.III 24. EN.

5714 —Rules for hearing the word of God. *For Andrew Bell and Jonas Luntly,* 1693. Second edition. 8°. C, AN, EN.

5715 —A seasonable question plainly resolved. *For Tho. Parkhurst, and R. Gibbs,* 1689. 8°. T.C.II 247. LCL, LW; CLC, NU.

5716 ——[Anr. ed.]. *Edinburgh, Mosman,* 1694. 8°. ALDIS 3361. EN.

5717 Entry cancelled.

5718 —The sure way to wealth. *For Andrew Bell and Jonas Luntley,* 1693. 8°. O, EN; Y.

5718A —Three questions resolved. *For Tho. Parkhurst and Robert Gibbs,* 1688. 8°. T.C.II 248. LW; CLC, NU.

5719 —The way to peace. *By J. D. for Jonathan Robinson and Brab. Ailmer,* 1695. 8°. L, LW.

5720 **Burgess, John.** A sermon preached . . . 19. of Iuly, 1604. *By Thomas Brudenell,* 1642. 4°.* LT, O; RPB.

5720A —A sermon preached . . . 29 Oct. 1645. 1645. 4°. YM.

5721 **Burgess, Paul.** The three worthy butchers. [*London*], *for P. Brooksby,* [1678?]. brs. L, HH; MH.

5722 ——[Anr. ed.] [*London,* 1680?] brs. L, HH.

5723 [–] The youth's guide. [*London*], *for P. Brooksby,* [1672–95]. brs. L, HH.

5724 The burgess ticket of Buckhaven given to A. Bryson. [*n.p.,* 1698.] brs. EN.

5725 **Burghall, Edward.** The great benefit of Christian education. [*n.p.*]. *By R. H. for D. Newman,* 1663. 4°.* LCL, LW.

5725A —The perfect way to die in peace. *For Francis Eglesfield,* 1659. 8°. NPT.

5726–8 Entries cancelled.

5729 **Burghley, William Cecil,** *baron.* The copie of a letter sent out of England. *By George Miller,* 1641[2]. 4°.* LT, O; MH, PL.

—Scrinia Ceciliana, mysteries. 1663. *See title.*

5730 **B[urghope], G[eorge].** Autarchy, or the art of self government. *For D. Newman,* 1691. 8°. T.C.II 384. L, OB, LW, M; CH, CLC, CN, NC, WF.

5731 — A discourse of religious assemblies. *For Tho. Bennet,* 1697. 8°. T.C.III 12. L, O, OB, OM, BR; CH.

5732 —An essay to revive the necessity. *For Walter Kettilby,* 1695. 8°. T.C.II 547. O, OC, OM, CK; CLC, WF, Y.

5733 [**Burgine, Darby.**] Victorious newes from Ireland. *July 8. for Marmaduke Boat,* [1642]. 4°. * LT, EC.

5734 **Burkhead, Henry.** A tragedy of Cola's fury. *To be sold in Kilkenny,* 1646. 4°. L.

5735 **Burkitt, William.** An argumentative and practical discourse of infant-baptism. *By T. S. for Tho. Parkhurst,* 1692. 8°. CLC, NU.

5735A ——Second edition. *By T. M. for Tho. Parkhurst,* 1695. 8°. O.

5736 —Expository notes, with practical observations on the four holy evangelists. *By R. J. for T. Parkhurst; J. Robinson, and J. Wyat,* 1700. fol. T.C.III 228. L, O, C, GU.

5737 —The people's zeal provok't. *By M. W. for Ralph Smith,* 1680. 4°.* L, O, CS, LW, CT; LC, WF.

5738 —The poor man's help. Second edition. *For Tho. Parkhurst,* 1694. 8°. T.C.II 521. L.

5738A ——Third edition. —, 1697. 8°. T.C.III 30. L.

5739 **Burlacey, Miles.** The King of France his message. *Decemb. 9. for T. Wright,* 1642. 4°.* LT; Y.

5740 **Burles, Edward.** Grammatica Burlesa: or a new English grammar. *By T. N. for Humphrey Moseley,* 1652. 12°. LT, O; CH, NC.

Burlesque news. [Edinburgh, 1661.] *See* Sydserfe, *Sir Thomas.*

Burlesque upon burlesque. 1675. *See* Cotton, Charles.

5740A **Burling, Elias.** A call to back-sliding Israel. *Printed and are sold by William Bradford in New York*, 1694. 4°.* C.

5741 **Burnaby, Anthony.** An essay upon the excising of malt. *For the author*, 1696. 8°. L, O, LUG; MH, NC, NN, WF, Y.

5742 —Two proposals. *Printed*, 1696. 4°.* L, LUG, EN; CH, MH, NC, WF, Y.

5743 [**Burnaby, William.**] Corinna with a gracefull air. [*London*, 1700.] brs. L.

5744 [–] Fond woman with mistaken art. [*London*, 1700.] brs. L.

5745 [–] The reform'd wife. *For Thomas Bennet*, 1700. 4°. L, O, C, OW, DT; CH, CN, LC, MH, TU, WCL, Y.

5746 [–] —Second edition. —, 1700. 4°. T.C.III 186. L, O, OC; CH, CN, NC, WF, Y.

5747 [–] —Third edition. —, 1700. 4°. CN.

5748 **Burnam, Robert.** A remonstrance. *By Thomas Paine*, 1645. 4°.* LT, DT.

5749 [**Burne, Nicol.**] A delectable new ballad, intituled, Leader-Haughs. [*London?* 1690?] brs. L.

5750 [–] —[Anr. ed.] [*Edinburgh?* 1700?] brs. L.

5751 **B[urnell], H[enry].** Landgartha. A tragie-comedy. *Printed at Dublin*, 1641. 4°. DIX 74. L, O; CH, MB, MH.

5752 **Burnet, Alexander,** *abp.* The blessedness of the dead. *Glasgow, by Robert Sanders*, 1673. 4°.* ALDIS 1975. EN, GU.

5752A **Burnet, Andrew.** Anatomy spiritualised. *For John Marshal*, 1696. 12°. T.C.II 594. NU, WF.

5753 —Spiritual anatomy of man. *By T. S. for John Lawrence*, 1693. 8°. L, LW; NPT, NU.

5754 **Burnet, Gilbert,** *bp.* The abridgment of the History of the Reformation. *By J. D. for Richard Chiswell*, 1682. 8°. L, O, C, AU; CH, MBP, NC, NU, Y.

5755 — —[Anr. ed.] *For R. C., and to be sold by John Lawrence*, 1682. 8°. T.C.I 484. L, O, C, E, GU; CN, MBP, MIU, KIRK.

5756 — —Second edition. *By J. D. for Richard Chiswell*, 1683. 8°. T.C.II 20. L, O, C, CT, ENC; BN, CH, CU, NU, WF, MIU, Y.

5756A — —[Anr. ed.] 1696. 12°. O.

5757 [–] Animadversions on the Reflections upon Dr. B's Travels. [*Amsterdam?*] *printed*, 1688. 12°. L, OC, CS; CLC, CN, NU, Y.

5758 [–] An answer to a letter to Dr. Burnet. colop: *For Richard Baldwin*, 1685. 4°.* L, O, C, EN, DT; CH, CN, MH, NU, TU, WF, Y.

5759 [–] An answer to a paper printed with allowance. [*London*, 1687.] cap., 4°.* L, OC, EN, AU, DT; CH, MH, NU, WF, Y.

5760 [–] An answer to Mr. Henry Payne's letter. [*n.p.*, 1687.] cap., 4°.* L, C, LIL, EN; CH, MH, NU, WF, Y.

5761 —An answer to the Animadversions. *For Richard Chiswell*, 1682. 4°.* T.C.I 509. L, O, C, EN, DT; CH, CN, MH, NU, WF, Y.

5762 [–] An apology for the Church of England, with. [*Amsterdam*, 1688.] cap., 4°.* L, O, LL, EN, DT; CH, CN, MH, NU, WF, Y.

5763 — —[Anr. ed.] [*n.p.*], 1689. 4°.* ENC.

5764 Entry cancelled.

5765 —The case of compulsion in matters of religion stated. *By T. S.*, 1688. 8°.* L, C, LCL, OC, EN; CLC, IU, NU.

5765A — —[Anr. ed.] *By J. Bradford*, [1689?] 8°.* LW.

5766 —Charitable reproof. *For Ri. Chiswell*, 1700. 4°.* T.C.III 251. L, O, C, OC, CT; CH, CU, MH, NU, WF, Y.

5767 —The citation of. [*The Hague?* 1687.] 4°.* L, O, LCL, CT, EN; CH, MH, MIU, WF, Y.

5768 —A collection of eighteen papers. *Reprinted at London for John Starkey and Richard Chiswell*, 1689. 4°. T.C.II 254. L, O, C, MR, EN; BN, CH, CN, LC, MH, NU, Y.

5769 —A collection of papers against popery. *Printed at Amsterdam, and sold by J. Robinson in London*, 1689. 4°.* NU.

5769A [–] A collection of records. *By J. D. for Richard Chiswell*, 1680. 4°. IU.

5770 —A collection of several tracts and dsicourses [*sic*]. *For Ric. Chiswell*, 1685. 4°. C, LG, MR, ES, DT; CH, NU, WWC.

5770A — —[Anr. ed.] —, 1689. 4°. CLC, MU.

5771 —A continuation of Reflections on Mr. Varilla's History of heresies. *Amsterdam, for J. S.*, 1687. 12°. L, O, C, MR, EN; CH, CU, NU, WF, Y.

5771A [–] A continuation of the second part of the Inquiry. [*London*, 1688.] cap., 4°.* IU, WF.

5772 [–] The conversion & persecutions of Eve Cohan. *By J. D. for Richard Chiswell*, 1680. 4°.* T.C.I 416. L, O, C, EN, DT; CH, CN, IU, NU, WF, Y.

5773 —The declaration of Almighty God. [*London*, 1690.] brs. HH, MR, EN.

5774 —A defence of the Reflections. *Amsterdam, for J. S.*, 1687. 12°. L, O, C, LIL, EN; BN, CH, CU, NP, NU, WF, Y.

5775 [–] A discourse concerning transubstantiation. *Printed*, 1688. 4°.* L, O, C, EN, DT; CN, MH, NU, WF, Y.

5775A [–] —[Anr. ed.] *For J. Watts*, 1688. 4°.* CPE.

5776 —A discourse of the pastoral care. *By R. R. for Ric. Chiswell*, 1692. 4°. T.C.II 423. L, O, C, E, DT; CH, MH, NU, WF, Y.

5777 — —Second edition. —, 1692. 8°. L, LCL, P; CU, CLC, TU, Y.

5778 [–] A discourse on the memory of . . . Sir Robert Fletcher. *Edinburgh, by a society of stationers*, 1665. 8°. ALDIS 1789. L, O, E, EN, AU.

5779 —A discourse wherein is held forth the opposition. *For J. Watts*, 1688. 4°. L, O, C, EN, DT; CH, CU, MH, NU, WF, Y.

5780 — —Second edition. —, 1688. 4°. T.C.II 263. L, O, C, EN, DT; CN, NA, MH, MU, Y.

5781 [–] The Earle of Melfort's letter. [*n.p.*, 1689.] cap., 4°.* CH, NPT, NU, WF, Y.

5781A [–] An edict in the Roman law. [*London*], 1688. cap., 4°.* L, CT, OC; CH, MIU, WF, Y.

5782 —Engelland wie stehts. *Londen*, 1689. 4°. L, AU; MH, NP.

5783 —An essay on the memory of the late Queen. *For Ric. Chiswell*, 1695. 8°. T.C.II 550. L, C, LCL, ENC, DT; BN, CH, CN, LC, MH, NP, TU, Y.

5784 ——[Anr. ed.] *Edinburgh, re-printed by George Mosman*, 1695. 8°. ALDIS 3447. E, EN, ES, GU, FSF; KYU.

5785 ——[Anr. ed.] *Dublin, Jos. Ray*, 1695. 4°.* DIX 271. O, DK, DT, CD; MB, Y.

5786 ——"Second" edition. *For Ric. Chiswell*, 1696. 8°. L, O, CT, ES; CLC, CU, NU, TU, WG, Y.

5787 —An exhortation to peace and union. *For Richard Chiswell*, 1681. 4°.* T.C.I 457. L, O, C, EN, DT; CH, CN, NU, TU, WF, Y.

5788 —An exhortation to peace and unity. *For Richard Chiswell*, 1689. 4°.* T.C.II 295. L, O, C, CT, EN; CH, CN, NU, WF, Y.

5789 ——"Second" edition. —, 1690. 12°. T.C.II 299. L, O, CS, DT; MH.

5790 [–] The expedition of His Highness the Prince of Orange. colop: [*London*], *for T. W.*, 1688. 4°.* L, O, HH, AU, EN; CH, CN, NU, WF, Y.

5790A [–]—[*London*], *printed*, 1688. 4°.* LW; CH, CLC, LC, Y.

5791 —An exposition of the thirty-nine articles. *By R. Roberts, for Ri. Chiswell*, 1699. fol. T.C.III 150. L, O, C, EN, DT; CH, NP, NU, PL, WF.

5792 ——Second edition. *By R. Roberts for Ri. Chiswell*, 1700. fol. L, O, CT, NPL, AU; BN, CH, MH, NP, WF, Y.

5793 —Four discourses. *For Richard Chiswell*, 1694. 8°. T.C.II 499. L, O, C, EN, DT; BN, CH, NP, NU, WF, Y.

5794 —Fourteen papers Viz. *Printed and are to be sold by Richard Baldwin*, 1689. 4°. L, O, C, CT, EN; CH, CN, MH, NU, WF, Y.

5795 —Histoire de la Réformation. *Chez Richard Chiswell, & Moise Pitt*, 1683–85. 2v. 4°. C, OC; BN, CLC, MB.

5796 [–] The history of the persecution of the valleys of Piedmont. *For Tho. Newborough*, 1688. 4°. T.C.II 273. L, LIL, OC, EN; CH, CU, NBA, NU, WF, Y.

5797 —The history of the Reformation. *By T. H. for Richard Chiswell*, 1679. fol. T.C.I 357. L, O, C, EN, DT; MBC, MH, PL, TU, Y.

5798 ——Second edition. —, 1681. fol. T.C.I 428. L, O, C, EN, DT; CLC, MH, NU, WF, Y.

5798A ——Second part. —, 1681. fol. BR; PL.

5799 ——"Second" edition. Part two. —, 1683. fol. NPL, CS, BR, EN; CLC, MH, NR, Y.

5800 —The history of the rights of princes. *R. Chiswell*, 1681. 8°. O, C, NPL, ENC, ES; BN, CLC, CN.

5801 ——[Anr. ed.] *By J. D. for Richard Chiswell*, 1682. 8°. T.C.I 472. L, O, CT, EN, DT; CH, CU, MH, NU, WF, Y.

5802 [–] The ill effects of animosities. [*London?*], *printed*, 1688. 4°.* L, O, C, MR, EN; CH, CU, LC, MH, NU, WF, Y.

5803 [–] An impartial collection. *For Richard Chiswell*, 1679. 4°.* AU.

5804 [–] An impartial survey and comparison of the Protestant religion. *For Richard Chiswell*, 1685. 8°. T.C.II 134. L, O, OC, CT, EU; CLC, Y.

5805 —The infallibility of the church of Rome examined and confuted. *By M. Clark, and are to be sold by H. Brome and B. Tooke*, 1680. 4°. T.C.I 410. L, C, CSSX, SC, DT; WF.

5806 —Injunctions for the archdeacons of the diocese of Sarum. colop: *For Ric. Chiswell*, 1690. 4°.* L, O, C, EC, DT; CLC, NC, NU.

5807 —An enquiry into the measures of submission. [*n.p.*], 1687. 4°.* LIL, OC.

5808 [–]—[Anr. ed.] [*London*, 1688.] cap., 4°.* L, O, C, E, DT; CH, CN, LC, MH, NU, TU, Y.

5809 [–]—[Anr. ed.] *Printed*, 1688. cap., 4°.* L, O, LCL, E, AU; CLC, LC, MH, NP, Y.

5809A [–]—[Anr. ed.] *Edinburgh, printed*, 1688. 4°.* ALDIS 2759. L, EN.

5809B [–]—[Anr. ed.] [*London*], *printed*, 1689. 4°.* WF.

5810 ——[Anr. ed.] *For Ric. Chiswell*, 1693. 4°.* L, O, C, LCL, HH; BN, CH, NPT, NU, WF, Y.

5811 [–] An enquiry into the present state of affairs. *For John Starkey; and Ric. Chiswell*, 1689. 4°.* T.C.II 255. L, O, C, EN, DT; CH, CU, LC, MH, NU, TU, Y.

5812 [–] —[Anr. ed.] colop: *Edinburgh, re-printed* [*heir of A. Anderson?*], 1689. 4°.* ALDIS 2883. L, EN; MH, WF, Y.

5813 [–] An enquiry into the reasons for abrogating the test. [*London*, 1688.] cap., 4°.* L, O, C, AU, DT; CH, CN, NU, WF, Y.

5814 —The last confession, prayers and meditations of Lieuten. John Stern. *For Richard Chiswell*, 1682. fol.* L, O, C, MR, AU; CH, MH, NP, TU, WF, Y.

5815 [–] A letter containing some reflections on His Majesties declaration. [*London?* 1689.] cap., 4°.* L, O, C, OC, CS; CH, MH, NU, WF, Y.

5816 [–] A letter, containing some remarks on the two papers. [*London*, 1686.] cap., 4°.* L, O, CS, EN, AU; CH, MH, NU, WF, Y.

5817 [–] —[Anr. ed.] [*London*, 1689.] cap., 4°.* NU.

5818 —A letter from . . . to Mr. Simon Lowth. colop: *For Richard Baldwin*, 1685. cap., 4°.* L, O, C, EN, DT; CH, MH, NU, TU, WF, Y.

5819 —A letter occasioned by the second letter to Dr. Burnet. colop: *For Richard Baldwyn*, 1685. 4°.* L, O, C, ENC, DT; CH, MH, NU, TU, Y.

5820 —A letter to a lord. colop: [*n.p.*], *printed*, 1688. cap., 4°.* L, O, CT; VC, WF, Y.

5821 Entry cancelled.

5822 —Dr. Burnet's letter to his friend in London. colop: *By G. C. for A. Gad*, 1683. brs. L, O, OP, EN; CH, WF.

5822A ——[Anr. ed.] colop: 1688. CH.

5823 —A letter to Mr. Thevenot. *For John Starkey and Richard Chiswell*, 1689. 4°. T.C.II 254. L, O, C, MR, EN; BN, CH, CN, MH, NU, WF, Y.

5824 —A letter writ . . . to the Lord Bishop of Cov. *For Ric. Chiswell*, 1693. 4°.* L, O, C, HH, EN; BN, CH, CN, NU, WF, Y.

5825 [–] A letter, written upon the discovery. *For H. Brome and R. Chiswel*, 1678. 4°.* T.C.I 331. L, O, C, AU, DT; CH, CN, MH, NC, WF, Y.

5826 —The libertine overthrown. *Printed and sold by J. Brad-ford*, [1690?]. 4°.* L.

5827 —The life and death of Sir Matthew Hale. *For William Shrowsbery*, 1681. 8°. T.C.I 461. L, O, CCA, E, EN; CU, LC, MHL.

5828 ——Second edition. —, 1682. 8°. L, O, C, BPL, ENC; BN, CH, CN, MH, NU, TU, WF, Y.

5828A ——[Anr. ed.] *For William Taylor*, 1682. 12°. MH, TU.

5828B —[Anr. ed.] For William Shrowsbury, 1696. CSB, MH, PU.

5829 ——[Anr. ed.] *For William Shrowsbury*, 1700. 8°. O; CH, MH, NN, NP.

5830 [–] The life of William Bedell. *For John Southby*, 1685. 8°. L, O, C, EN, DT; BN, CH, CN, MH, NU, WF, Y.

5831 ——Second edition. *For Richard Chiswell*, 1692. 8°. T.C.II 423. L, O, C, LCL, OB; CLC, CSU, MBP, TU.

5832 —The memoires of the lives and actions of . . . Dukes of Hamilton. *By J. Grover, for R. Royston*, 1677. fol. T.C.I 312. L, O, C, EN, DT; BN, CH, CU, LC, MH, NU, Y.

5833 [–] A modest and free conference betwixt a Conformist. *[Edinburgh?]*, 1669. 8°. ALDIS 1868. L, C, E, GM.

5834 [–] —Second edition. *[Edinburgh?]*, 1669. 8°. ALDIS 1869. C.

5835 [–] A modest survey of the most considerable things. *For Moses Pitt*, 1676. 4°.* T.C.I 246. L, O, C, EN, AU; CH, CN, MH, NU, TU, WF, Y.

5836 [–] —Second edition. —, 1676. 4°.* T.C.I 261. L, O, C, EN, DT; BN, NPT, TU, WF, Y.

5837 —The mystery of iniquity unvailed. *[Glasgow]*, *printed*, 1672. 8°. EN, GU, HG, CLC, NP.

5838 ——[Anr. ed.] *By W. Godbid, and are to be sold by M. Pitt*, 1673. 8°. T.C.I 154, L, O, C, LCL, EN; CLC, MU, NU, PBL, WF, Y.

5839 [–] News from France: in a letter. *For Richard Chiswel*, 1682. 4°.* T.C.I 497. L, O, C, EN, DT; CH, MH, NU, WF, Y.

5840 [–] Observations on the first and second of the canons. *Glasgow, by Robert Sanders*, 1673. 8°. ALDIS 1976. C, LCL, EN, GM, DT; CH, MHL, NCL, NU, Y.

5841 —Of charity to the household of faith. *For Ri. Chiswell*, 1698. 4°.* T.C.III 62. L, C, OM, CT, DT; CH, CN, NU, WF, Y.

5842 —A pastoral letter writ by. *For J. Starkey; and Ric. Chiswell*, 1689. 4°.* L, O, C, EN, DT; BN, HR, CH, CN, LC, MH, NU, TU, Y.

5843 ——[Anr. ed.] colop: *Edinburgh, re-printed*, 1689. cap., fol.* ALDIS 2864. L, EN.

5844 Entry cancelled.

5845 [–] The Protestant's companion. *For Richard Chiswell*, 1685. 4°. L, O, C, EN, DT; CLC, CN, MH, NU, WF.

5846 —A rational method. *For Richard Royston*, 1675. 8°. T.C.I 203. L, O, C, EN, DT; CU, IU, WWC, Y.

5847 [–] Reasons against the repealing the acts. *[n.p.]*, *printed*, 1687. 4°.* L, O, CS, DT; CH, CN, MH, NU, WF, Y.

5848 —Reflections on a book entituled, The rights, powers. *For Ri. Chiswell*, 1700. 4°.* T.C.III 251. L, O, C, LCL, AU; CH, CLC, LC, NU, Y.

5849 [–] Reflections on a late pamphlet, entitled, Parliamentum pacificum. colop: *Amsterdam, for P. Savouret*, 1688[9]. cap., 4°.* L, O, C, HH, EU; CH, MH, NU, WF, Y.

5850 [–] Reflections on a paper, intituled. His Majesty's reasons. *For John Starkey; and Ric. Chiswell*, 1689. 4°.* L, O, C, EN, DT; CH, CN, LC, MH, NU, TU, Y.

5851 [–] Reflections on His Majesties proclamation. *[n.p.]*, 1687. 4°. MC, A.

5852 —Reflections on Mr. Varillas's history. *Amsterdam, for P. Savouret*, 1686. 12°. L, O, C, LW, EN; CH, CN, NU, WF, Y.

5852A ——[Anr. ed.] *Amsterdam, printed*, 1686. 12°. LW, OC, SP; CLC, NC, NU, TU.

5852B ——[Anr. ed.]

5853 ——[Anr. ed.] *Printed*, 1689. 12°. L, C, LW, EN, AU; CLC, LC, NP, WF.

5854 [–] Reflections on the relation of the English Reformation. Part I. *Amsterdam, for J. S.*, 1688. 96pp. 4°. L, C, OB, MR, EN; CH, CN, MH, NU, TU, Y.

5855 [–] —[Anr. ed.] *Amsterdam: for J. S.*, 1688. 56pp. 4°. O, C, OME, DT; Y.

5856 [–] —[Anr. ed.] —, 1688. 64pp. 4°. L, CS, MC, EN, AU; CLC, NC, NU, TU, WF.

5857 [–] —*Amsterdam, for P. Bleau*, 1688. 4°. L, CS, CT; CLC, MH, PL, WF, Y.

5858 [–] —[Anr. ed.] *[London?]*, 1688. 4°. L.

5859 [–] —[Anr. ed.] *For J. S.*, 1689. 4°. L, EN; CN.

5859A [–] —[Anr. ed.] *For Ric. Chiswell*, 1689. 4°. TU.

5860 —Reflections upon a pamphlet. *For Ri. Chiswell*, 1696. 8°. L, O, C, LIL, EN; CH, NU, WF, Y.

—Reflections upon Mr. Varillas his history. *[n.p.]*, 1688. *See* Hannes, Edward.

5861 —A relation of a conference. *Printed and are to be sold by Moses Pitt*, 1676. 8°. L, O, C, EN, DT; CH, CU, MH, NU, WF, Y.

5862 ——[Anr. ed.] 1679. 8°. E.

5863 [–] —[Anr. ed.] *Printed, to be sold by Randal Taylor*, 1687. 4°. L, O, C, E, DT; CH, CN, NU, TU, WF, Y.

5863A —A relation of the death of the primitive persecution. *Amsterdam, for J. S.*, 1687. 12°. GK.

5864 —Remarks on the two papers. *Hague*, 1687. 4°. MC.

5865 —Remarques sur les actes. 1673. 12°. EN.

5866 ——[Anr. ed.] *R. Bentley*, 1683. 12°. DT; BN.

[–] Representation of the threatning dangers. [n.p.], 1689. *See* Ferguson, Robert.

5867 —Rights of princes. 1682. 8°. LW; MHL.

5868 [–] Romes glory. *Printed, and are to be sold by Moses Pitt*, 1673. 8°. T.C.I 141. L, O, CS, LIL; CH, CLC, WF, WU.

5869 —The royal martyr and the dutiful subject. *For R. Royston*, 1675. 4°.* T.C.I 208. L, O, C, LCL, E; CH, IU, MBA, TU, Y.

5870 —The royal martyr lamented. *For Luke Meredith*, 1689. 4°.* T.C.II 266. L, O, C, OM, DT; CLC, CN, NU, WF, Y.

5871 —A sermon preached . . . 18th of July 1678. *By Mary Clark*, 1678. V°.* L, O, LW; MH, WF, Y.

5872 —A sermon preached . . . September 2, 1680. *For Richard Chiswel*, 1680. 4°.* T.C.I 413. L, O, C, OM, AU; CH, MBA, NU, WF, Y.

5873 ——Second edition. *For Richard Chiswel*, 1681. 4°.* L, O, C, EN, DT; CH, CN, NC, NU, Y.

5874 —A sermon preached . . . Decemb. 22. 1680. *By J. D. for Richard Chiswell*, 1681. 4°.* T.C.I 435. L, O, C, MR, EN; CH, CN, MH, NU, WF, Y.

5875 —A sermon preached . . . Jan. 30. 1680/1. *For Richard Chiswel*, 1681. 4°.* T.C.I 435. L, O, C, E, DT; CH, MBA, NU, WF, Y.

5876 ——Second edition. —, 1681. 4°.* L, C, CT, SC; CLC, MH, MIU, TU, WF, Y.

5877 —A sermon preached . . . 29th of September, 1681. *For Richard Chiswell*. 1681. 4°.* L, OP, MR, BAMB, AU; CH, MBA.

5878 —A sermon preached . . . June 28, 1682. *For Richard Chiswel*, 1682. 4°.* T.C.I 502. L, O, C, EN, DT; CH, CN, MBA, NU, WF, Y.

5879 —A sermon preached . . . the fifth of November, 1684. *For the author, and are to be sold by R. Baldwin*, 1684. 4°.* L, O, C, EN, DT; CH, CN, MH, NU, WF, Y.

5880 ——[Anr. ed.] *For R. Baldwin*, 1684. 4°.* L, C, CT; CLC, Y.

5881 —A sermon preached . . . the 23rd of December, 1688. *For Richard Chiswell*, 1689. 4°.* T.C.II 254. L, O, C, EN, DT; BN, HR, CH, LC, MH, NC, NU, Y.

5882 ——[Anr. ed.] *Edinburgh, J. Reid*, 1689. 4°.* ALDIS 2865. FSF.

5883 ——[Anr. ed.] *Edinburgh, re-printed*, 1689. 4°.* ALDIS 2866. L, AU, EN; MH, NP, WF, Y.

5884 ——"Second" edition. *For Richard Chiswell*, 1689. 4°.* L, C, OC, EC, DT; CN, MH, PL, TU.

5885 —A sermon preached . . . 31st January, 1688. *london* [sic]; *for John Starkey; and Ric. Chiswell*, 1689. 4°.* T.C.II 248. L, O, C, EN, DT; BN, CH, CN, LC, MH, NC, NU, Y.

5886 ——[Anr. ed.] *Boston in New-England, by S. Green, and sold by Samuel Phillips*, 1689. 4°.* EVANS 461. CH, MH, MHS, NN, Y.

5887 Entry cancelled.

5888 —A sermon preached . . . April 11. 1689. *For J. Starkey; and Ric. Chiswell*, 1689. 4°.* T.C.II 248. L, C, OM, EN, DT; BN, CH, CN, LC, MH, NU, Y.

5888A ——[Anr. ed.] *Edinburgh, re-printed*, 1689. 4°.* ALDIS 2867. EN; WF.

5889 —A sermon preached . . . 5th of November 1689. *For Ric. Chiswel*, 1689. 4°.* T.C.II 299. L, O, C, EN, DT; BN, CH, CN, NU, WF, Y.

5890 —A sermon preached . . . on Christmas-Day, 1689. *For Richard Chiswell*, MDCLXC [sic, i.e. 1690]. 4°.* T.C.II 299. L, O, C, CT, DT; CH, CN, MH, NU, WF, Y.

5891 —A sermon preached . . . on March 12. 1689/90. *For Richard Chiswell*, 1690. 4°.* T.C.II 319. L, C, CT, EN, DT; CH, CN, LC, NU, WF, Y.

5892 —A sermon preached . . . 16th day of July, 1690. *For Ric. Chiswell*, 1690. 4°.* T.C.II 333. L, C, CT, EN, DT; CH, CN, NC, NU, WF, Y.

5893 —A sermon preached . . . 19th day of October, 1690. *For Ric. Chiswell*, 1690. 4°.* T.C.II 332. L, C, CT, EN, DT; CH, CN, LC, NU, Y.

5894 ——Second edition. —, 1690. 4°.* L, O, C, CS, EN; CLC, MH, NU, TU, Y.

5895 —A sermon preached . . . the 19th day of February, 1690/1. *For Ric. Chiswell*, 1691. 4°.* T.C.II 357. L, O, C, CT, DT; CH, CN, MBA, WF, Y.

5896 —A sermon preached . . . 29th of April, 1691. *For Ric. Chiswell*, 1691. 4°.* T.C.II 357. L, O, C, EN, DT; BN, CH, CN, NU, WF, Y.

5897 —A sermon preached . . . 26th of Novemb. 1691. *For Ric. Chiswell*, 1691. 4°.* T.C.II 378. L, O, C, EN, AU; CH, CN, NU, TU, WF, Y.

5898 ——[Anr. ed. "November."] *For Richard Chiswell*, 1691. 4°.* L; CN, TU.

5899 —A sermon preached . . . January 7, 1691/2 at the funeral of . . . Robert Boyle: Jan 7, 1691/2. *For Ric. Chiswell, and John Taylor*, 1692. 4°.* T.C.II 401. L, O, C, CT, EN; CH, CN, MH, NU, WF, Y.

5900 —A sermon preach'd . . . 11th of March, 1693/4. *For Ric. Chiswell*, 1694. 4°.* T.C.II 499. L, O, C, CT, EN; CH, CN, MH, NU, WF, Y.

5901 —A sermon preached . . . 29th of May, 1694. *For Ri. Chisell*, 1694. 4°.* T.C.II 506. L, O, C, CT, EN; CLC, CN, NPT, NU, WF, Y.

5902 —A sermon preached at the funeral of . . . John . . . Archbishop of Canterbury . . . [30th of November]. *For Ri. Chiswell*, 1694. 4°.* T.C.II 517. L, O, C, EN, DT; CH, CN, MH, NU, TU, WF, Y.

5902A ——[Anr. ed.] *Edinburgh, by the heirs and successors of Andrew Anderson*, 1694. 4°.* ALDIS 3362. E; IU.

5903 —A sermon preached. *Dublin, for Jacob Milner*, 1694. 4°.* DIX 262. L, C, DI, DT, CD; WF, Y.

5904 —A sermon preach'd . . . 10th. of February 1694/5. *For Ri. Chiswell*, 1695. 4°.* T.C.II 546. L, O, C, EN, DT; CH, CN, NR, NU, Y.

5905 —A sermon preached . . . on Christmas-Day, 1696. *For Ri. Chiswell*, 1697. 4°.* T.C.III 1. L, O, C, WCA, DT; CH, CN, NU, WF, Y.

5906 —A sermon preach'd . . . 7th day of March 1696/7. *For Ri. Chiswell*, 1697. 4°.* T.C.III 19. O, C, OC, EC, CT; CH, CN, NU, WF, Y.

5907 —A sermon preached . . . second of December, 1697. *For Ri. Chiswell*, 1698. 4°.* T.C.III 37. L, O, C, EN, DT; CH, MH, NU, WF, Y.

5908 ——[Anr. ed.] *Printed at London and re-printed at Edinburgh, by the heirs and successors of Andrew Anderson*, 1697. 4°.* ALDIS 3657. L, EN, FSF; MH, NC, NU, TU.

5909 ——"Second" edition. *For Ri. Chiswell*, 1698. 4°.* T.C.III 68. L, CT; CU, CN, MBA, TU.

5910 Entry cancelled.

5911 —Sermon prononcé devant la Chambre des Communes le trente unième de Jan. 1688/9. *Pour R.E. pour E. Chiswel,* 1689. 4°.* T.C.II 254. L, O; WF.

5912 —Six papers. [*Holland*], *printed,* 1687. 4°. L, O, C, EN, DT; CN, MH, NU, TU, Y.

5913 ——[Anr. ed.] *Printed,* 1689. 4°. L, O, C, OM, EN; CH, MIU, NU, WF, Y.

5913A [–] Some extracts, out of Mr. James Stewart's letters. [*London,* 1689.] cap., 4°.* L, OC; CH, MB, MIU, WF, Y.

5914 —Some letters. *At Amsterdam, printed,* 1686. 12°. L, C, CK, RPL; CU, NC, NU, TU, Y.

5915 ——[Anr. ed.] *At Rotterdam, by Abraham Acher,* 1686. 8°. L, O, C, E, EN; BN, CH, CN, MH, NP, WF, Y.

5916 ——[Anr. ed.] 1686. 12°. O, ENC, ES; CH, CLC, MIU, TU.

5917 ——[Anr. ed.] [*n.p.*], *printed,* 1687. 12°. L, O, C; CH, CU, NP, TU, Y.

5918 ——"Second" edition. *Rotterdam, for Abraham Acher,* 1687. 8°. L, O, C, MR, ENC; CH, CLC, CU, PL, Y.

5919 ——Third edition. —, 1687. 12°. L, O, CS, LCP, AN; CH.

5920 ——"Third" edition. *Amsterdam, for the widow Swart,* 1688. 12°. L.

5921 ——[Anr. ed.] *Printed and are to be sold by J. Robinson, and Awnsham Churchil,* 1689. 12°. L, CT, EN; CH, NP, PL, TU, Y.

5921A ——[Anr. ed.] *Rotterdam, by J. S. and are to be sold by J. Robinson,* 1698. 12°. NP.

5922 —Some passages of the life and death of . . . Rochester. *For Richard Chiswel,* 1680. 8°. T.C.I 417. L, O, C, E, DT; BN, CH, CN, LC, MH, NC, TU, Y.

5923 ——[Anr. ed.] *Dublin, Joseph Ray, for William Winter,* 1681. 8°. DIX 182. CK, DI, DT, CD; MBA.

5924 ——[Anr. ed.] *For Richard Chiswell,* 1692. 8°. LCL, CS, EC, EN, AU; BBE, Y.

5924A ——[Anr. ed.] —*and sold by John Salusbury,* 1693. 8°. CK; CLC, NGT, Y.

5925 ——Fifth edition. *For Rich. Chiswell,* 1700. 8°. L, LCL, C, CT, EN; CLC, IU, PU, Y.

5926 [–] Some reflections on His Majesty's proclamation. [*n.p.,* 1687.] cap., 4°.* L, O, OC, CS, CT; CH, MH, NPT, WF, Y.

5927 —The story of Jetzer. *Printed, and are to be sold by Randal Taylor,* 1689. 4°.* LIL, HH, YM; CH, PL, WF, Y.

5928 —Subjection for conscience-sake. *For R. Royston,* 1675. 4°.* T.C.I 194. L, O, C, EN, AU; CH, MH, NU, TU, Y.

5929 ——[Anr. ed.] *For Luke Meredith,* 1689. 4°.* L, OC, OCC, OM, DT; CLC, CN, NU, WF, Y.

5930 [–] Their highnesses the Prince and Princess of Orange's opinion. *Printed and are to be sold by Richard Janeway,* 1689. 4°.* L, O, C, CS, DT; CH, CN, MBA, WF, Y.

5931 [–] Three letters concerning the present state of Italy. [*London,*] *printed,* 1688. 8°. L, O, CT, EN, DT; CH, CN, NU, WF, Y.

5932 ——[Anr. ed.] —, 1688. 12°. L, O, C, AU, DT; CH, CU, NC, PL, WF, Y.

5933 —Dr. G. Burnet's tracts. *For J. Robinson; and A. Churchil,* 1689. 12°. T.C.II 259. L, O, OC, EN, DT; CH, CN, PL, WF, Y.

5934 —Dr. Burnet's travels. *Amsterdam, for Peter Savouret and W. Fenner,* 1687. 12°. L, O, C, GU, GK; CH, MB, MH, WF, Y.

5935 [–] The unreasonableness and impiety of Popery. *For R. Chiswell,* 1678. 4°.* T.C.I 332. L, O, C, AU, DT; CH, CN, MH, NU, WF, Y.

5936 —Dr. Burnet's vindication of himself. [*Amsterdam?*], 1688. 4°.* L, OC, EN; IU, MH, WCL, WF, Y.

5937 —[Anr. ed.] 1696. 4°. LW.

5938 —A vindication of the authority. *Glasgow, by Robert Sanders,* 1673. 8°. ALDIS 1976. L, O, C, EN, DT; CH, MH, NU, WF, Y.

5939 —A vindication of the ordinations. *By E.H. and T.H. for R. Chiswel,* 1677. 8°. T.C.I 274. L, O, CS, EN, DT; CH, CN, NU, WF, Y.

5940 [–] —Second edition. *For Ric. Chiswell,* 1688. 4°. T.C.II 280. L, O, C, EN, DT; CH, MH, NU, TU, Y.

5941 Entry cancelled.

5942 [**Burnet, Thomas, at Charter house.**] An answer to the late exceptions made by Mr Erasmus Warren. *By R. Norton, for Walter Kettilby,* 1690. fol. T.C.II 314. L, O, C, OM, AU; CH, CU, MH, NU, WF, Y.

5943 [–] Archaeologiae philosophicae. *Typis R.N. impensis Gualt. Kettilby,* 1692. 4°. T.C.II 425. L, O, C, E, DT; BN, CH, OCI, WF, WSC, Y.

5943A [–] Reflections upon the theory. *For Walter Kettilby,* 1699. 4°. T.C.III 111. L, O, OC, CT, DT; CH, LC, NU, WF, Y.

5944 [–] Remarks upon an Essay concerning humane understanding. *For M. Wotton,* 1697. 4°.* L, CS, OC, EC, GK; MH, NU, WF, Y.

5945 [–] A review of The theory of the earth. *By R. Norton, for Walter Kettilby,* 1690. fol. L, O, C; CH, CSU, MH, NU, WF.

5946 [–] Second remarks upon An essay. *For M. Wotton,* 1686. 4°.* MH, NU.

5946A [–] —[Anr. ed.] —, 1697. 4°.* L, O, CS, EC, GK; MH, NU, WF, Y.

5947 [–] A short consideration of Mr Erasmus Warren's Defence. *By R. Norton, for Walter Kettilby,* 1691. fol.* T.C.II 370. L, O, C, LWL, CM; CH, MH, NU, WF, Y.

5948 [–] Telluris theoria sacra. Libri duo priores. *Typis R.N. impensis Gualt. Kettilby,* 1681. 4°. T.C.I 432. L, O, C, E, DT; BN, CLC, MH, NU, TU, WF, Y.

5948A ——Second edition. —, 1689. 4°. LWL, OC; CN, MH, NP, OCI.

5949 ——Libri duo posteriores. —, 1689. 4°. T.C.II 239. L, O, C, EN, DT; CH, MH, PL, WF, Y.

5950 [–] The theory of the earth. The two first books. *By R. Norton, for Walter Kettilby,* 1684. fol. T.C.II 74. L, O, C, AU, DT; BN, CH, CU, LC, MH, Y.

5951 [–] —[Anr. ed.] —, 1690. fol. T.C.II 302. L, LWL, OC, CCO, EN; CLC, CSU, MH, NU, WF.

5952 [–] —Second edition. —, 1691. fol. T.C.II 362. L, O, C, EN, NPL; CH, MH, NP, NU, WF.

5953 ——Third edition. *By R.N. for Walter Kettilby,* 1697. fol. T.C.III 8. L, C, LVF, OR, EN; CH, CU, MH, MU, WF, Y.

5954 [–] —The two last books. *By R. Norton, for Walter Kettilby*, 1690. fol. L, O, CCO, ENC, DT; CH, CN, MH, NP, TU, WF, Y.

5955 [–] Third remarks upon an Essay. *For M. Wotton*, 1699. 4°.* T.C.III 142. L, OC, CS, EC, GK; MH, NU, WF, Y.

5956–58 Entries cancelled.

5959 **Burnet, Thomas, M.D.** Thesaurus medicinæ practicæ. *Excudebat G. R. pro R. Boulter, & prostant apud R. Brown, J. Carnes, & J. Mason*, 1673. 4°. T.C.I 120. O, C, LCS, E, GU; CN, MIU, WF.

5959A ——[Anr. ed.] *Excudebat G. R. pro Roberto Boulter*, 1673. 4°. OC, CCA, CT.

5960 **Burnet, Thomas, of Marischal college.** Theses philosophicæ. *Abredoniæ, excudebat Ioannes Forbes*, 1686. 4°.* ALDIS 2673. L, EG, AU.

5961 **Burnet, William.** The capital principles of the people called Quakers. *Printed*, 1668. 4°. L, O, C, LW, LF; MHS.

5962 **Burnett, Andrew.** A sermon preach'd at Barbican. *For Rich. Baldwin*, 1696. 4°.* L, LG, EN; CU, WF, Y.

5963 [**Burney, Richard.**] An ansvver or necessary animadversions upon some late impostumate observations. *For T. Paibody*, 1642. 4°.* LT, O, C, OC, DT; CH, CN, MH, NU, WF, Y.

5964 —Κερδιστον δωρον. King Charles the Second. *By I. Redmayne, for the authour*, [1660]. 4°. LT, O; CH, MH, NGT, WF.

Burning bush. Edinburgh, 1679. *See Hart, John.*

5965 The burning of the whore of Babylon. *Printed and are to be sold by R. C.*, 1673. 4°. L, LG, CT, YM; CH, MH, Y.

5965A The burning shame. [*London?* 1700.] brs. MH.

Burnt child. 1675. *See Denton, William.*

5965B **Burnyeat, John.** An epistle from. colop: *Printed and sold by William Bradford near Philadelphia*, 1686. 4°.* EVANS 401. LF; PH, PHS, PL.

5966 —The holy truth and its professors defended. *Printed*, 1688. 4°. O, LF; PH.

5966A ——[*Dublin?* 1688.] 4°. DIX 229. MBP.

5967 [–] The innocency of the Christian Quakers manifested. [*Dublin*], *printed*, 1688. 4°.* DIX 229. LF, DT; PH, PSC, Y.

5968 —The truth exalted. *For Thomas Northcott*, 1691. 4°. L, O, C, LF, OC; CH, CU, LC, MH, NU, PH, Y.

5969 **Burrell, Andrewes.** A briefe relation. Discovering plainely. *For Francis Constable*, 1642. 4°.* LT, O, CS; WF.

5970 [–] A cordjall for the calentvre. *Printed*, 1648[9]. 4°.* LT, C, HH, DT; Y.

5971 —Exceptions against Sir Cornelius Virmudens Discourse. *Printed at London by T. H. to be sold by Robert Constable*, 1642. 4°.* LT, O, C; MH, NU, WF.

5972 —An explanation of the drayning workes. [*London*], *printed*, 1641. 4°.* O, C.

5973 —To the right honourable, the High Court of Parliament. [*London*, 1646]. cap., 4°.* LT, C; NN, WF, Y.

5974 **Burrell, John.** The divine right of kings. *Cambridge, by John Hayes, for Sam. Simpson*, 1683. 4°.* L, CS; NPT, WF, Y.

5975 **Burridge, Ezekiel.** Historia nuperæ rerum mutationis in Anglia. *Typis J. H. impensis autem A. & J. Churchill*, 1697. 8°. T.C.III 6. L, O, C, EN, DT; BN, CH, CN, MH, MIU, Y.

5975A ——[Anr. ed.] *Sumptibus Sam. Buckley*, 1697. 8°. O, C; MIU, TU.

5975B [–] —[Anr. ed.] *Prostant venales apud Edw. Castle, & Sam. Buckley*, 1697. 8°. WF.

5976 **Burridge, Richard.** The apostate prince. *Printed*, 1700. fol.* L, LVD, HH; Y.

5977 —The consolation of death. *For William Pinnocke*, 1700. 8°.* L.

5977A [–] Hell in an uproar. *For S. Cook*, 1700. fol.* L; W.

5978 [–] The shoe-maker beyond his last. *For S. Cook*, 1700. fol.* L; CLC, MH, TU.

5979 **Burrington, John.** The case of Sir Bouchier Wrey. [*n.p.*, 1697/8.] brs. L, LL.

5980 **Burrough, Edward.** The memorable works of. [*London*], *printed and published*, 1672. fol. L, O, C, LF, BPL; CH, LC, MH, NU, PH, Y.

5981 —An alarm to all flesh. *For Robert Wilson*, 1660. 4°.* L, O, CT, LF, OC; CU, MH, NU, PH, Y.

5982 —An answer to a book, called Choice experiences. [*London*], *printed*, 1654. 4°.* LF; PH.

5983 —An answer to a declaration put forth. *For Thomas Simmons*. 1659. 4°.* LF, BBN; PH, PSC.

5983A —Answer to Baxter's sheet, 1657. PSC.

5984 —Ansvvers to several queries. *For Giles Calvert*, 1654. 4°.* LT, LF, BBN; PH, Y.

5985 —Antichrist's government justly detected. *For Robert Wilson*, 1661. 4°. L, O, LF, BBN, BPL; CH, LC, MU, NU, PH, Y.

5986 —The case of free liberty of conscience. *For Thomas Simmons*, 1661. 4°.* L, C, LF, BBN, DT; CH, CN, MH, NU, PH, WF, Y.

5987 [–] The case of the people called Quakers (once more) stated. *For Robert Wilson*, [1661]. 4°. L, O, LF, BBN; CH, MH, MU, PH, WF, Y.

5988 —The crying sinnes reproved. *For Thomas Simmons*, 1656. 4°.* L, O, C, LF, BBN; CH, PH, PSC, Y.

5989 [–] A declaration from the people called Quakers. *Printed*, 1659. 4°.* L, LF, CT, OC; CH, MH, NU, PH, Y.

5990 [–] —[Anr. ed.] *For Thomas Simmons*, 1659. 4°. L, CS, LF, BBN; PH, PL.

5991 Entry cancelled.

5992 [–] —[Anr. ed.] 1689. 4°. O.

5993 [–] A declaration of the present sufferings. *For Tho. Simmons*, 1659. 4°.* LT, O, CT, BBN, AN; CN, MH, NU, WF, Y.

5994 —A declaration of the sad and great persecution . . . of . . . the Quakers. *For Robert Wilson*, [1660 i.e., 1661]. 4°.* LT, C, LF, BBN; CH, LC, MB, PH, WCL, Y.

5995 —A declaration to all the world of our faith. *For Thomas Simmons*, 1657. 4°.* L, C, LF, BBN; MU, PH, WF.

5995A ——[Anr. ed.] colop: —, 1658. 4°.* OC, CT; WF.

5996 [–] —[Anr. ed.] —, 1659. 4°.* LT, O, C, LF, OC; PSC.

5997 [–] —[Anr. ed.] —, 1660. 4°.* CT; CH, MH, NU, PH, Y.

5997A [–] —[Anr. ed.] *For Robert Wilson*, [1660]. 4°.* PL.

5998 —A description of the state and condition of all man-kinde. *For Giles Calvert*, [1657]. 4°.* LT, O, LF, OC; CN, LC, PH, PSC.

5999 —A discovery of divine mysteries. *For Robert Wilson*, 1661. 4°.* L, O, LF, BBN, GU; CLC, MH, PH, WF, Y.

5999A —A discovery of some part of the war. *For Robert Wilson*, 1659. 4°. LF, BBN; MH, PH, PL.

6000 —An epistle to friends of truth. *Printed*, 1667. 4°. L, O, LF, BBN; CH, PH, PHS, WF, Y.

6001 —The everlasting gospel of repentance. *For Robert Wilson*, [1660?]. 4°.* L, O, C, CT, LF; CH, LC, MH, NU, PH, Y.

6002 —A faithful testimony concerning the true worship of God. *For Thomas Simmons*, 1659. 4°. LF, LG, BBN; MH, MU.

6003 —For the souldiers and all the officers. [*London*, 1654.] brs. LT, LF.

6004 [–] A generall epistle, and greeting. *For Thomas Simmons*, 1657. 4°.* L, O, LF, BBN; CH, MH, MU, PH, PSC, Y.

6005 —A general epistle to all the saints. *For Robert Wilson*, 1660. [i.e., 1661]. 4°.* L, O, C, LF, CT; CH, MH, NU, PH, WF, Y.

6006 [–] Good counsel and advice. *For Thomas Simmons*, 1659. 4°. L, LF, BBN, EN; CH, MH, NP, PH, Y.

6007 —A hue and cry after the false prophets. colop: *For Robert Wilson*, 1661. 4°. L, O; C, CT, LF; MH, PH, PSC, WF, Y.

6008 —A just and lawful triall of the teachers. *For Thomas Simmons*, 1657. 4°.* LT, O, LF, OC; MU, NNG, PH, Y.

6009 — —[Anr. ed.] —, 1659. 4°.* L, C, LF; Y.

6010 — —[Anr. ed.] —, 1660. 4°.* L, O, CT, LF, WCA; CH, MH, NU, PH, WF, Y.

6011 —A just and righteous plea. colop: *For Robert Wilson*, 1661. 4°.* L, O, C, LF; CH, MH, NU, PH, WF, Y.

6011A —Many strong reasons confounded. *For Thomas Simmons*. 1657. 4°.* L, LF, BBN; CH, MU, PH, PSC, Y.

6012 —A measure of the times. *For Thomas Simmons*, 1657. 4°.* LT, O, LF, BBN; CH, MH, NU, PH, WF, Y.

6013 —A message for instruction . . . how far the magistrates power reacheth. *For Thomas Simmons*, 1658. 4°.* L, C, CT, LF, BBN; CH, MU, NU, PH, Y.

6013A —A message proclaimed. By divine authority. *For Thomas Simmons*, [1658] 4°.* L, LF, OC, CT; MH, MU, PH, WF, Y.

6014 [–] A message to all kings and rulers. [*London*, 1659.] cap., 4°.* L, C, LF, BBN; MH, PH, PL, PSC, Y.

6015 —A message to the present rulers of England. *For Giles Calvert*, 1659. 4°.* L, O, LF, BBN; CH, MH, PH, PL, Y.

    [–] Mite of affection. 1659. *See* Billing, Edward.

6016 [–] Persecution impeached. *For R. W.*, 1661. 4°.* L, C, LF, BBN, BP; MH, NU, PH, WF, Y.

6017 —A presentation of wholesome informations. *Printed at London; and are to be sold by Richard Moon, in Bristol*, 1660. 4°.* LT, O, C, LF, BBN; CH, IE, MH, NU, PH, PSC, Y.

6018 —The principles of truth. [*London?* 1660.] 8°. L, C, OC; CH, NU, Y.

6019 [–] —[Anr. ed.] 1665. 12°. BN.

6019A [–] —[Anr. ed.] [*London*], *printed* 1668. 8°. WF.

6019B [–] —[Anr. ed.] *Printed*, 1671. 8°. CLC.

6020 —The reign of the whore discovered. *For Thomas Simmons*, 1659. 4°.* E; MH.

6021 —A returne to the ministers of London. *For Robert Wilson*, 1660. 4°.* L, O, C, EN, DT; CH, MH, PH, PSC, WF.

6022 —Satan's designe defeated. *For Thomas Simmons*, 1659. 4°.* L, O, LF; CH, PH, PL.

6023 —A seasonable word of advice unto all that . . . back-slide from the truth. [1658?] brs. L, LF; CH.

6023A —Some false principles. *For Thomas Simmons*. 1659. 4°.* LF, BBN; PH, PL.

6024 —Some of the principles of the Quakers. *Printed*, 1658. 4°. C, LF, BBN; PH, PSC.

6025 —Something in answer to a book. [*London*], *printed*, 1654. 4°.* LT; PH.

6026 —Something of truth. *For Thomas Simmons*, 1658. 4°. L, CT, LF, BBN; CH, MH, PH, PSC, Y.

6027 —The son of perdition revealed. *For Thomas Simmons*, 1661. 4°. O, LF, BBN; PH, PSC, WF.

6028 —Stablishing against Quaking thrown down. *For Giles Calvert*, 1656. 4°.* LT, O, LF, BBN; CH, MH, PH, PSC.

6029 —A standard lifted up. *For Giles Calvert*, 1657. 4°.* LT, BBN; MH, PH, PL.

6030 — —[Anr. ed.] —, 1658. 4°. L, O, C, LF, EN; CH, CN, PH, WF, Y.

6031 —A tender salutation of perfect love. *For the author*, 1661. 4°.* L, LF, BBN; IE, MH, PH, PSC, WF.

6032 —A testimony against a great idolatry. *For Thomas Simmons*, 1658. 4°.* L, LF, BBN; MH, MU, PH, WF, Y.

6033 —The testimony of the Lord concerning London. *For Giles Calvert*, 1657. 4°.* LT, LF; PH, WF.

6034 —To Charles Fleetwood Steward. [*London*], 1658. 4°.* PH.

6035 —[Anr. ed.] *For Thomas Simmons*, 1659. 4°. L, O, C, LF, BBN; CH, PL.

6036 [–] To the beloved and chosen of God. colop: *For Thomas Simmons*, 1660. cap., 4°.* L, C, CT, LF, BPL; CH, MH, PH, WF, Y.

6037 Entry cancelled.

6038 —To the Parliament of the Commonwealth. [*London*, 1659.] brs. L, O, LF; MU.

6038A —To the Parliament of the Commonwealth . . . a pre-sentation. *For Thomas Simmons*, 1659. brs. PL.

6039 —To the Parliament of the Common-wealth of Eng-land, . . . councel and advice. [*London*, 1659.] cap., 4°.* O, L, LF; MH, PH, PL, Y.

6040 [–] To the present Assembly, . . . the consideration of a servant of the Lord. [*London*], 1659. brs. L, LF; PL.

6040A —To the rulers. *For Thomas Simmons*, 1659. 4°.* L, LF, BBN; MH, PH, WF.

6041 —To the whole English army. *For Giles Calvert*, 1659. brs. L, LF; PL.

6042 —To you that are called Anabaptists. [*London*], *printed*, 1657. 4°.* LF.

6043 [–] The true Christian religion againe discovered. *By Roger Norton, junior, for Giles Calvert,* 1658. 4°.* LT, O, LF, OC; MU, NPT, PH, WF, Y.

6044 [–] —[Anr. ed.] *For Thomas Simmons,* 1658. 4°.* LF, CT, BBN; CH, MH, MU, PSC, Y.

6045 —A true description of my manner of life. *For Robert Wilson,* 1663. 4°.* L, LF, BBN; CH, MH, PH, WF, Y.

6046 —The true faith of the gospel. *For Giles Calvert,* 1656. 8°.* LT, LF, BBN, BPL; CH, NPT, PH, Y.

6047 —The true state of Christianity. *For Thomas Simmons,* 1658. 4°.* LF; CH, MH, MU, PH.

6048 —A trumpet of the Lord sounded out of Sion: which gives. *For Giles Calvert,* 1656. 4°.* C, LF, OC; CH, MH, PH, WF.

6048A — —which sounds. — 1656. 4°.* LT, O, CT, LF, DT; CH, PH, PSC, WF, Y.

6049 —Truth defended: or, certain accusations answered. [*London,* 1654.] 4°.* LT, LF; MH, Y.

6050 — —[Anr. ed.] *For Thomas Simmons,* 1656. 4°.* LF; CH, PH, PSC, WF.

6051 —Truth (the strongest of all). *For Giles Calvert,* 1657. 4°. LT, O, CT, LF, DT; PH.

6052 —Two general epistles. *For R. Wilson,* 1663. 4°.* L, O, C, LF, BBN; CH, MH, NU, PH, Y.

6053 —A vindication of the people of God, called Quakers. *For Robert Wilson,* [1660]. 4°. L, O, C, LF, BBN; CH, IE, LC, MH, PH, YU, Y.

6054 —A visitation and presentation of love unto the king. *Printed and are to be sold by Robert Wilson,* 1660. 4°.* O, LF, CCA, YM; CH, LC, MBA, MH, TU, Y.

6055 —A visitation & vvarning proclaimed. *For Thomas Simmons,* 1659. 4°.* L, O, LF BBN; KT LC MH NU PH Y.

6056 [–] A visitation of love unto the king. *Printed and are to be sold by Robert Wilson,* 1660. 4°. LT, O, C, BBN, EN; CH, MH, NU, PH, TU, WF, Y.

6056A —The walls of Iericho razed down. *For Giles Calvert* [1654.] 4°.* LF, OC, BBN; PH.

6057 —A warning from the Lord to the inhabitants of Underbarrow. *For Giles Calvert,* 1654. 4°.* LT, LF, BBN; PH, Y.

6057A —We the servants. [*London,* 1655.] brs. LF.

6058 —The wofull cry of unjust persecutions. *For Giles Calvert,* [1657]. 4°.* LT, O, LF, OC, BBN; CH, PH, WF, Y.

6058A —A word of reproof. 1659. PL.

6058B **Burrough, William.** An account of the blessed Trinity. *For Richard Baldwin* 1694. 4°. O CS, CT, LW, EC; CLC, NP, WF.

6059 **Burroughes, Jeremiah.** A briefe answer to Doctor Fernes booke. [*London,* 1643.] cap., 4°.* L, O, OC, EN; CU, MH, NC, NU, WF.

6060 —Christ inviting sinners. *By Peter Cole,* 1659. 4°. MH, NGT, NU.

6061 —The difference between the spots of the godly and of the wicked. *Printed,* 1668. 8°. L, LCL, LW; MH, NU, Y.

6062 — —[Anr. ed.] *For Tho. Parkhurst,* 1687. 8°. T.C.II 212. CLC.

6063 —The eighth book of . . . .Being a treatise of the evil of evils. *By Peter Cole,* 1654. 4°. LT, O, C, LCL, BR; CH, MH, NU, WF, Y.

6064 —The excellency of a gracious spirit. *By G. Dawson for Francis Eglesfield,* 1649. 8°. L, O, CM, LCL, LW; CH, CU, NU, WF, Y.

6065 — —[Anr. ed.] *By A. Weile for Francis Eglesfield.* 1657. 8°. L, O; NN, NPT.

6066 —The excellency of holy courage. *By Peter Cole, and Edward Cole,* 1661. 4°. L, LCL; CU, MIU, NR, NU.

6067 — —[Anr. ed.] —, 662. 4°. LW; MH, NU.

6068 —An exposition of the prophesie of Hosea. *By W.E. and J.G. for R. Dawlman,* 1643. 4°. LT, O, C, LCL, E; MH, MIU, NU, Y.

6069 — —Second edition. *For R. Dawlman,* 1652. 4°. LCL, CS, P, AN; NPT, NU, WF, Y.

6070 —An exposition with practical observations continued upon the fourth . . . seventh chapters of . . . Hosea. *For Peter Cole,* 1650. 4°. LT, OC, CS, P, ENC; MH, NGT, NU, Y.

6070A —An exposition . . . upon the eighth . . . thirteenth chapters of Hosea. *By Peter Cole,* 1654. 4°. L; NGT.

6070B —An exposition with practical observations continued upon the eighth, . . . tenth chapters of . . . Hosea. *By Peter Cole,* 1650. 4°. OC, CS, P, BR; MH, Y.

6071 —An exposition with practical observations continued upon the eleventh . . . thirteenth chapters of . . . Hosea. *By Peter Cole,* 1651. 4°. L, CS, LCL, BR; MH, NPT, NU, WF, Y.

6072 —Four books on the eleventh of Matthew. *By Peter Cole,* 1659. 4°. LT, O, C, E; CU, MH, NU, WG, Y.

6073 —Four useful discourses. *For Thomas Parkhurst,* 1675. 4°. L, O, C, LCL; MH, NU, Y.

[–] Glimpse of Sions glory. 1641. *See* Knollys, Hanserd.

6074 [–] The glorious name of God. *For R. Dawlman,* 1643. 4°. L, O, CT, P, ENC; MH, NN, RPB, WF.

6075 — —[Anr. ed.] —, 1643. 4°. L, O, C, EN, DT; CH, CU, MH, NU, WF, Y.

6076 —Gospel-conversation. *For Peter Cole,* 1648. 4°. LT, O, GU; LU, MIU, NU, WF, Y.

6076A — —[Anr. ed.] —, 1650. 4°. LW; CH, NGT, Y.

6077 — —[Anr. ed.] *By Peter Cole,* 1653. 4°. L, LW, RPL; CLC, MH, NU, VC, Y.

6078 — —[Anr. ed.] 1656. 4°. LCL.

6079 —Gospel-fear. *By J. D. for B. Aylmer,* 1674. 8°. T.C.I 168. O, LCL; CLC, LC, MB, MH, NPT, NU.

6080 —Gospel-reconciliation. *By Peter Cole,* 1657. 4°. L, O, C, LW, E; CLC, NPT, NU, WF, Y.

6081 —Gospel remission. *For Dor. Newman,* 1668. 8°. L, O, GU; CLC, CU, LC, MH, NU, Y.

6082 — —Second edition. —, 1674. 4°. T.C.I 173. O, C, LCL, ENC; MH, WF, Y.

6083 —Gospel-revelation. *For Nath. Brook, and Thomas Parkhurst,* 1660. 4°. LT, O, LCL, LG, EN; CU, MH, NU, WF, Y.

6084 —Gospel-worship. *For Peter Cole and R. W.,* 1648. 4°. LT, O, LW, OM, AU; CH, CU, MH, NU, WF, Y.

6084A ——[Anr. ed.] *For Peter Cole, to be sold by John Walker,* 1648. 4°. TSM, TU, Y.

6084B ——[Anr. ed.] *For Peter Cole,* 1650. 4°. LSC; IU, MH, NGT, TU, Y.

6085 ——[Anr. ed.] *By Peter Cole,* 1653. 4°. L, LCL; CLC, Y.

6086 ——[Anr. ed.] —, 1658. 4°. L, C; IU, PPT, WSC, Y.

6087 Entry cancelled.

6088 —Irenicvm, to the lovers of truth. *For Robert Davvlman,* 1646. 4°. LT, O, C, ENC, DT; CH, CU, MH, NU, WF, Y.

6089 ——Second edition. —, 1653. 4°. L, O, CS, E, GU; IU, MH, NF, NU, Y.

6090 —Jacob's seed. *By Roger Daniel, Cambridge,* 1643. 12°. LT.

6091 —Jerusalems glory. *[London], for Giles Calvert,* 1675. 12°. L, O, ENC; CLC, IU, MH, NF, NU.

6092 [–]—[Anr. ed.] *By J.A.,* 1684. 12°. LCL, P; CLC, NU, WF, Y.

6093 ——[Anr. ed.] *By J. H. to be sold by J. Sprint,* 1697. 8°. T.C.III 9. L; NU.

6094 —Moses his choice. *By M. F. and R. D. and are to be sold by H. Overton, and T. Nichols,* 1641. 4°. L, O, C, LCL, ENC; CU, MH, NU, WF, Y.

6095 ——[Anr. ed.] *By John Field, to be sold by Thomas Eglesfield,* 1650. 4°. L, O, LW, ENC; CH, CU, IU, NU, Y.

6096 ——[Anr. ed.] *By Tho. Ratcliffe for Robert Doleman,* 1659. 4°. L; NU, PPT.

6096A ——[Anr. ed.] —*to be sold by Thomas Vere,* 1660. 4°. OC; WF.

6097 —Moses his self-denyall. *By T. Paine, and are to be sold by H. Overton and T. Nichols,* 1641. 8°. L, O, LCL; CH, MH, NGT, NU, Y.

6098 ——[Anr. ed.] *By J. Dawson for Francis Eglesfeild [sic],* 1649. 8°. L, C, LSC, LW, D; CLC, MH, MIU, V, WF.

6099 ——[Anr. ed.] *By G. Dawson for Francis Eglesfield,* 1657. 8°. O; IU, MH, NU, NPT.

6100 —The ninth, tenth, and eleventh books of. *By Peter Cole,* 1655. 4°. LT; CU, MH, NU, WF, Y.

6101 ——[Anr. ed.] *T. Goodwyn,* 1655. 4°. O; CU, MH.

6102 —The rare jevvel of Christian contentment. *For Peter Cole,* 1648. LT, O, C, LCL, DT; NU.

6103 ——[Anr. ed.] —, 1649. 4°. L, O, GU; CN, CU, MH, NU, MIU.

6104 ——[Anr. ed.] —, 1650. L, LW, DC; MH, NU.

6105 ——[Anr. ed.] *By W. Bentley, for L. Sadler and R. Beaumont,* 1651. 4°. L, O, C, OCC; IU, NU, WF, Y.

6105A ——[Anr. ed.] *By W. Bentley, for L. S. and R. B.,* 1651. 4°. L; TU.

6106 ——[Anr. ed.] *By Peter Cole,* 1652. 4°. O, OB, BR, RPL; CH, CLC, LC, Y.

6107 ——[Anr. ed.] —, 1655. 4°. L, CPE; CLC, IU, MH, WF.

6107A ——[Anr. ed.] —, 1659. 4°. NPT.

6107B ——[Anr. ed.] *For Ben. Billingsley,* 1666. 4°. SP; LCL, LC, MB, Y.

6108 ——[Anr. ed.] *By John Streater, to be sold by Richard Chiswel,* 1670. 4°. T.C.I 27. L, LSC; CH.

6109 ——[Anr. ed.] *By S. Streater for George Sawbridge,* 1677. 4°. T.C.I 304. L, LW; V, WF.

6110 ——[Anr. ed.] *By W. W. for H. Sawbridge,* 1685. 4°. T.C.II 152. LCL, OW; NU, PFL.

6111 —The saints duty. *For Peter Cole,* 1648. 4°. LT, C, LCL, LG, DT; NGT, NU.

6112 —The saints happinesse. *By M. S. for Nathaniel Brook, and for Thomas Parkhurst,* 1660. 4°. LT, O, LG, LW, EN; CLC, CU, LC, MH, NU, WF, Y.

6113 —The saints inheritance. *For Francis Eglesfield,* 1657. 4°. IU, NPT, NU, Y.

6113A ——[Anr. ed.] *For Iohn Allen,* 1658. 4°. NPT.

6114 —The saints treasury. *By T. C. for John Wright,* 1654. 4°. L, O, CM, LCL, E; CU, MH, NU, WF, Y.

6115 ——[Anr. ed.] —, 1656. 4°. L, O; CH, CLC, IU, NU.

6115A ——[Anr. ed.] *For J. Wright,* 1660. 4°. LSC.

6116 —The second (third and fourth) book on Matth. 11. 29. *By Peter Cole,* 1659. 4°. LT; CLC, NGT, NU, Y.

6117 —A sermon preached . . . 26. of Novemb. 1645. *For R. Dawlman,* 1646. 4°. LT, O, C, LCL, EN; CH, NPT, NU, WF, Y.

6118 —A sermon preached . . . August 26. 1646. *By Matthew Simmons, for Hanna Allen,* 1646. 4°.* LT, O, C, OCC, DT; CH, CU, NU, WF, Y.

6119 —Sions joy. *By T. P. and M. S. for R. Dawlman, to be sold by Ben. Alline,* 1641. 4°. LT, O, C, DC, DT; CH, CN, MH, NU, WF, Y.

6120–1 Entries cancelled.

—Three treatises of. *For Peter Cole, and Richard Westbrook,* 1648. 4°. MH, Y.

6122 ——[Anr. ed.] 1655. 4°. LW.

6122A —A treatise of the excellency of holy courage. *By Pet. Cole,* 1661. 4°. LSC.

6123 —The treatises of. *By Peter Cole, for A. D. and J. C.,* 1656. 4°. LCL; NU, WF.

6124 —Two sermons. 1643. 4°. NPL; RBU.

6125 —Two treatises of. *For Peter Cole,* 1649. 4°. LT, O; MH, MIU, NU, Y.

6125A ——[Anr. ed.] —, 1652. 4°. LCL; CH, MH, NN, V.

6125B ——[Anr. ed.] *By Peter Cole for A. D. and J. C.,* 1656. 4°. LCL, OC; CLC, MIU, NU, WF.

6126 —A vindication of Mr Bvrrovghes against Mr Edwards. *For H. Overton,* 1646. 4°.* LT, O, C, LCL, DT; CH, MH, NU, WF, Y.

6127 **Burroughs, Cornelius.** Rich news from Jamaica. *By M. Simmons,* 1659. 8°.* NN, RPJ.

6128 **Burroughs, J.** A narrative of the conversion of Thomas Mackernesse. *For John Dunton,* 1694. 4°.* L.

6128A **Burroughs, Sir John.** Burrhi impetus juveniles. *Oxoniæ, excudebat Leonardus Lichfield,* 1643. 12°. L, O, OC, CS; Y.

6129 —The soveraignty of the British seas. *H. Moseley,* 1651. 12°. L, O, C, E, DT; BN, CH, LC, MH, NC, Y.

6129A ——[Anr. ed.] *By I. Redmayne for Richard Chiswell,* 1686. fol.* LL, LMT, BAMB; IU, MB, NC, PL, V.

6130 **Burroughs, Thomas.** Christ the sts advantage. *By T. R. and E. M. for John Bellamy,* 1646. 12°. LT.

6131 —A soveraign remedy for all kinds of grief. *By S. G. for John Baker,* 1657. 4°.* LT, O, LW, OC; Y.

6132 ——Second edition. *By T. R. for John Baker*, 1662. 4°.* L, OC, LW; CH, CLC, TU, WF.

6133 ——Third edition. *For John Baker*, 1675. 12°. T.C.I 207. L, O, LCL, LW; CLC, NPT.

6134 ——[Anr. ed.] *Printed and sold by Dan. Brown*, 1697. 12°. T.C.II 608. L.

6135 **Burrowes, Samuel.** Good instrvctions for all young-men. *Printed at London for T. B.*, 1642. 4°.* LT, O; IU, WF.

6136 **Burscough, Robert.** A discourse of schism. *For Tho. Bennet and Charles Yeo in Exeter*, 1699. 8°. T.C.III 134. L, O, CT, LW, EN; CH, NPT, NU, Y.

6137 —A treatise of church-government. *For Samuel Smith*, 1692. 8°. T.C.II 420. L, O, C, EN, DT; CLC, MH, NPT, NU, WF, Y.

6138 **Burston, Daniel.** Christ's last call. *Dublin, by John Crook, and sold by Samuel Dancer*, [1665]. 4°. DIX 358. C.

6139 —Εὐαγγελιστὴς ἔτι εὐαγγελιζόμενος The evangelist yet evangelising. *Dublin, by John Crook*, 1662. 4°. DIX 116. L, O, DT; NPT.

6140 [**Burt, Nathaniel.**] Advice, sent in a letter from an elder brother. *For the author*, 1655. 4°.* LT.

6141 [–] An appeal from Chancery. *Printed at London*, 1653, *to be sold by Will: Larnar*. 4°.* LT, O, HH, DT; MHL, NN.

6142 [–] For every individuall member of the honourable House of Commons. [*London*, 1649.] cap., 4°.* LT; CSS, Y.

6143 [–] An individual letter to every man that calls himself a minister. *Printed*, 1651. 4°.* LT, AN.

6144 —Militarie instructions or the souldier tried. [*London*, 1644.] brs. LT.

6145 [–] A Nevv-yeers-gift for England. *Printed at London, to be sold by Will: Larnar*, 1653. 4°.* LT; CH, CU, NU.

6146 **Burt, William.** Concio Oxoniæ. *Oxoniæ, excudebat Hen: Hall, impensis Thomæ Robinson*, 1659. 12°. MADAN 2436. LT, O, CT, LSC; WF, Y.

6147 **Burthall, Raunce,** *pseud?* An old bridle for a wilde asse-colt. *For Stephen Dagnall, at Alsbury*, [1650]. 4°.* LT; MH, NN, NU.

6148 **Burthogge, Richard.** An argument for infants bap-risme. *For Jonathan Greenwood*, 1684. 8°. T.C.II 40. O, LCL, LW; NPT, Y.

6149 —Cavsa Dei, or an apology for God. *For Lewis Pun-chard in Totnes in Devon, and are to be sold by F. Tyton* [*London*], 1675. 8°. T.C.I 185. L, O, C, LW; MWB, NU, Y.

6150 —An essay upon reason. *For John Dunton*, 1694. 8°. L, O, C, E, DT; BN, CH, CN, LC, MH, NU, Y.

6151 [–] The nature of church-government. [1690.] 4°. L; NU.

6152 [–] —[Anr. ed.] *For S. G.*, 1691. 4°. L, C, P; MBA, NGT, WF.

6153 [–] Of the soul of the world. *For Daniel Brown*, 1699. 4°.* T.C.III 143. L, C, LCL, WCB, E; CH, MH, NC, WF, Y.

6154 —Organum vetus et novum. *For Sam. Crouch*, 1678. 8°. T.C.I 302. L, O, C, EC; CH, MBA, MH, NU, WF.

6155 [–] Prudential reasons for repealing. *For Matthew Turner*, 1687. 4°.* L, O, OC, CT; CH, MHL, MIU, NP, WF.

6156 —Ταγαθον; or, divine goodness. *By S. and B. Griffin, for J. Collins*, 1671. 8°. T.C.I 102. O; CU, MH, NC.

6157 —[Anr. ed.] *By S. and B. Griffin, for James Collins*, 1672. 8°. L, O, C, CSS, SC; MH.

6157A —Vinditiæ pædobaptismii; or, a confirmation. *For Tho. Simmons*, 1685. 8°. CT; NPT, NU.

6158 **Burton,** . Scepticorum. [*n.p.*, 1655.] brs. O.

6159 **Burton, Edward.** The fathers legacy. *By John Clowes, for Mathew Walbancke*, 1649. 12°. L, LSC.

[**Burton, Henry.**] Answer to Mr. William Prynn's. [*n.p.*, 1644.] *See* Robinson, Henry.

6160 —Conformitie's deformjty. *For Giles Calvert*, 1646. 4°.* LT, O, CT, MR, DT; CH, IC, NU, Y.

6161 [–] A divine tragedie lately acted. *Printed*, 1641. colop: *Printed for John Wright junior and for Tho. Bates*, 1641. 4°.* LT, O, CT, HH, YM; CN, MH, NU, WF, Y.

6162 —Englands bondage. *Printed*, 1641. 4°.* LT, O, C, LP, DT; CN, MH, NU, WF, Y.

6162A [–] A full and satisfactorie ansvvere. *By Jane Coe*, 1645. 4°.* LT, O, C, OC, EN; CH, CN, MH, NU, Y.

6163 —The grand impostor vnmasked. *For Giles Calvert*, [1644/5.] 4°.* LT, O, C, EN, DT; CH, CU, MH, NU, WF, Y.

6164 —The humble petitions of. [*London*], printed, 1641. 4°.* LL, OC, HH; MH, NN, Y.

6165 —Jesv-worship confvted. *T. Bates*, 1641. 4°. I, CS, LP, YM, WF, Y.

6166 ——[Anr. ed.] *For H. C.*, 1660. 4°.* L, O, LW; CH, CLC, MH, MIU, PL, Y.

6167 —Meditations upon I Sam. xxvi. 19. *For Giles Calvert*, 1647. 4°.* LT; LC.

6168 —A most godly sermon: preached . . . 10 Oct. 1641. *By B. Alsop*, 1641. 4°.* LT, O, LG; LLC, MIU, NU, TU, Y.

6169 —A narration of the life of Mr. Henry Burton. *Printed*, 1643. 4°. LT, O, CT, LP, HH; BN, CN, NU, WF, Y.

6169A ——[Anr. ed.] *For John Rothwell*, 1643. 4°. LT, LW; WF.

6170 —The peace-maker: or, solid reasons. *For Giles Calvert*, 1646. 4°.* LT, O, C, HH, DT; CH, MH, NU, Y.

6171 [–] The protestation protested. [*London?*], printed, 1641. 4°.* [imprint in roman.] LT, O, C, EN, DT; BN, CH, CU, MH, NU, TU, WF, Y.

6171A [–] —[Anr. ed.] —, 1641, 4°.*. (imprint in italic.) C, OC, HH; MH, MIU, NU.

6172 —The sovnding of the two last trvmpets. *For Samuel Gellibrand*, 1641. 4°. LT, LCL, CT, YM, EN; CU, NU, WF.

6173 —Truth shut out of doores. *For Giles Calvert*, 1645. 4°.* LT, CT, LG, LP, DT; LC, MIU, NU, Y.

6174 —Truth, still truth. *For Giles Calvert*, 1645. 4°.* LT, CT, LP, EN, DT; MH, MIU, NU, WF, Y.

6175 —A vindication of churches commonly called Indepen-dent. *For Henry Overton*, 1644. 4°. LT, O, C, LCL, DT; CH, CU, MH, NU, Y.

6176 ——Second edition. —, 1644. 4°. O, CJ, LP, YM, EN; CLC, MB, NU, WF, Y.

6176A ——Third edition. —, 1644. 4°. CCA; MH, NN.

6177 —Vindiciæ veritatis. *By M. S. for Gyles Calvert*, 1645. 4°.* LT, O, CT, LP, YM; CH, LC, MB, NU, Y.

6178 **Burton, Hezekiah.** A second volume of discourses. *For Richard Chiswell, and sold by John Salusbury*, 1685. 8°. T.C.II 122. L, O, LW, RPL, D; MH, PL, WF, Y.

6179 —Several discourses. *For Richard Chiswell, and sold by John Lawrence, 1684.* 8°. T.C.II 80. L, O, C, ENC, DT; CLC, NPT, NU, PL, WF, Y.

6180 **Burton, John.** The history of Eriander. The first part. *By R. Davenport for John Williams, 1661.* 8°. LT, C.

Burton, Richard, *pseud. See* Crouch, Nathaniel.

6181 [**Burton, Robert.**] The anatomy of melancholy. Sixth edition. *Oxford, for Henry Cripps, 1651.* colop: *By R. W. for Henry Cripps, to be sold by Andrew Crook, and by Henry Cripps and Lodowick Lloyd, 1651.* fol. MADAN 2164. L, O, CT, DT, GK; CH, MH, NP, WCL, Y.

6182 [–] —"Sixth" edition. *Printed and are to be sould by Hen: Crips & Lodo Lloyd, 1652.* fol. MADAN 2165. L, O, CK, CT, GK; BN, CLC, MH, MMO, WF, Y.

6183 [–] —Seventh edition. *For H. Cripps, and are to be sold [by him] and by E. Wallis, 1660.* fol. L, O, CT, EC, LVD; CH, CN, MH, MMO, WF, Y.

6184 ——Eighth edition. *For Peter Parker, 1676.* fol. T.C.I 230. L, O, CT, MR, GH; MH, NC, MMO, WF, Y.

[**Burton, W.**] Almanack. *Oxford, 1653. See* Almanacs.

6185 **Burton, William.** A commentary on Antoninus his Itinerary. *By Tho. Roycroft, and are to be sold by Henry Twyford, and T. Twyford, 1658.* fol. L, O, C, EN, DT; BN, CH, CN, LC, MH, TU, WF, Y.

6186 —Graecæ linguæ historia. *Nunc demum typis excusa Londinii, Augustæ Trinobantum. Apud Thomam Roycroft, prostat autem venales apud Jo. Martin, & Ja. Allestrye, 1657.* 8°. MADAN 2321. L, O, C, CT, EN; BN, CH, PL, WF, Y.

6187 —Nobilissimi herois, Dn. Caroli Howardi ἀποθέωσις. *[London, 1643.]* brs. LT.

Burwood, James. *See* Burdwood, James.

6188 Entry cancelled.

6189 **Bury, Arthur.** The bow: or the lamentation of David. *For Henry Brome, 1662.* 4°. L, O, CJ, LL; CH, MB, NPT, NU, WF.

6190 [–] The case of Exeter-colledge, in the University of Oxford. Related and vindicated. *Printed, and are to be sold by Randal Tayler, 1691.* 4°. T.C.II 350. L, O, C, MR, DT; CH, CN, MH, WF, Y.

6191 —The constant communicant. *Oxford, by Leon. Lichfield, for Stephen Bolton, 1681.* 8°. L, O, C, LW, OB; CLC, MHS, Y.

6192 ——Second edition. *Oxford, by L. Lichfield to be sold by Henry Bonwick, 1683.* 8°. T.C.II 21. O, P; NU.

6193 —The danger of delaying repentance. *For Nathanael Ranew, 1692.* 4°.* T.C.II 402. L, O; LLC, NU, PL, WF, Y.

6194 [–] A defence of the doctrines of the Holy Trinity. *[London, 1694.]* cap., 4°. O, WCA.

6195 [–] The doctrine of the Holy Trinity. *Printed, 1694.* 4°. T.C.II 475. L, OC, CS, WCA, OCC; NU, WF, Y.

6196 [–] The judgment of a disinterested person. *Printed and are to be sold by E. Whitlock, 1696.* 4°. T.C.II 600. O, CS, WCB, EC, BAMB; LLC, CN, NU, WF, Y.

6197 [–] Latitudinarius orthodoxus. *Impensis Sam. Buckley, 1697.* 8°. T.C.III 14. L, O, C, LW, OC, OM; BN, CLC.

6198 —The mystery of iniquity, discovered. *For Francis Eglesfield, 1660.* 4°.* O; NU, WF.

6199 [–] The naked gospel. Part I. *[London], printed, 1690.* 4°. L, O, C, LIL, EN; CH, CN, MH, WF, Y.

6200 [–] —[Anr. ed.] *[London, 1691.]* 4°. CT, DT.

6201 [–] —[Anr. ed.] *C. Poyner, 1691.* 4°. L.

6202 ——[Anr. ed.] *For Nathanael Ranew, 1691.* 4°. T.C.II 356. L, O, OC, LW; CLC, IU, MH, OM.

6203 —Not fear, but love. *Oxford, by L. Lichfield, 1683.* 8°. C, CT; NU.

6203A —To avoid the intolerable drudgery. *[Oxford, 1689/90.]* brs. O.

6204 **Bury, Edward.** Death improv'd. *For Tho. Parkhurst, 1673.* 8°. CLC.

6204A ——[Anr. ed.] —, *1693.* 8°. T.C.I 217. L, CK, LSC.

6205 —England's bane. *For Tho. Parkhurst, 1677.* 8°. T.C.I 271. L, O, C.

6206 —A help to holy walking. *By F.L. for Nevil Simmons, 1675.* 8°. T.C.I 186. L, O, C, LCL; CLC.

6207 —The husbandman's companion. *For Tho. Parkhurst, 1677.* 8°. T.C.I 271. L, O, C, LCI; CLC, CU, NPT, TU, WF, Y.

6208 —Immoderate sorrow for deceased friends reproved. *1693.* 8°. LCL.

6209 [–] A looking-glass for the unmarried. *For Tho. Parkhurst, 1697.* 8°. TU.

6210 —A short catechism. *By R. W. for Nevil Simmons, 1660.* 8°.* O.

6210A —The souls looking-glass. *By Robert White for Nevil Simmons, 1660.* 8°. CLC.

6211 —A sovereign antidote against the fear of death. *By J. A. for Thomas Parkhurst, 1681.* 8°. T.C.I 449. LW, CCH; CLC, NPT.

6212 **Bury, Jacob.** Advice to the Commons. *By Henry Hills, jun. for Richard Northcott, 1685.* 4°. L, O, CS, EN; CH, CN, WF, Y.

6213 ——[Anr. ed.] *For Richard Northcott, 1688.* 4°. EN; CH.

6214 **Bury, John.** The discovery of. *[London], printed, 1679.* 4°.* O; CLC, CN, MIU.

6215 [–] A true narrative of the late design of the Papists. *For Dorman Newman, 1679.* fol.* T.C.I 349. L, O, C, HH, EN; CH, CN, NU, PL, WF, Y.

6216 [–] —[Anr. ed.] *Reprinted at Dublin, 1679.* 4°.* DIX 168. C, DK, DT, CDL.

6217 **Busbeq, Ogier Ghislain de.** Aug. Gislenii Busbequii quæ extant omnia. *Ex officina R. Danielis, 1660.* 12°. L, O, C, CT, AU; CH, NC, PL, Y.

6218 —A. Gislenii Busbequii omnia quæ extant. *Oxoniæ, exc. udebat W. H. impensis Tho. Robinson & Sa. Pocock, 1660.* 12°. MADAN 2486. O, CT, LCP, AU, DT; BN, CPB, MH, PL, WF, Y.

6219 —The four epistles of . . ., concerning his embassy into Turkey. *For J. Taylor, and J. Wyat, 1694.* 8°. T.C.II 510, L, O, C, ES, DT; CH, MH, NF, WF, Y.

6219A [**Busby, Richard.**] Graecæ grammaticæ institutio compendaria. *Impensis A. Swalle & T. Childe, 1694.* CS.

6220 —Graecæ grammatices rudimenta. *Cantabrigiæ ex officina Rogeri Daniel, 1647.* 8°. O, OC; NC.

6221 [-] —[Anr. ed.] —, 1651. 8°. C, CCH, YM; PL.

6222 [-] —[Anr. ed.] *Ex officina Johannis Redmayne*, 1663. 8°. O, C, OC; MH, RPB, Y.

6222A [-] —[Anr. ed.] —, 1671. 8°. T.C.I 92. OC, CCH, EC; CLC, PL, Y.

6223 [-] —[Anr. ed.] *Ex officina Eliz. Redmayne*, 1683. 8°. T.C.II 77. L, O, C, CJ, LCP; BN, CLC, LC, MB, PL, Y.

6223A [-] —[Anr. ed.] —, 1689. 8°. OP; WU, Y.

6224 [-] —[Anr. ed.] —, 1693. 8°. L, O; PL, WF, Y.

6224A [-] —[Anr. ed.] *For A. and J. Churchill and T. Child*, 1700. 8°. RPL.

6225 —Grammatica. *Ex officina Eliz. Redmayne*, 1696. 8°. OC, DT; CLC.

6226 [-] Rudimentum Anglo-Latinum grammaticae. *Ex. Officina Eliz. Redmayne*, 1688. 8°. O, OC, CK, DCH, EC; CN, MH.

6227 [-] —[Anr. ed.] 1689. 8°. O.

6227A [-] Rudimentum grammaticæ Græco-Latinæ metricum. *Ex officina Eliz. Redmayne*, 1689. 8°. OC.

6228 [-] Rudimentum grammaticæ Latinæ. —, 1688. 8°. C, OC.

6229 **Buscher, Antonius.** Ethicæ ciceronionæ. *Typis G. Du-Gard, veneunt apud T. Matthews*, 1652. 12°. CPE.

6229A [-] A short institution of grammar. *Cambridge*, 1647. 8°. O.

6230 **Busenello, Giovanni Francesco.** A prospective of the naval triumph of the Venetians. *For Henry Herring-man*, 1658. 8°. LT, OW, EN; CH, LC, MH, TU, Y.

6231 **Bush, John.** The necessity and reward of a willing mind. *For Mich. Hyde in Exon*, 1693. 4°.* L; WF.

6231A **Bush, Rice.** The poor man's friend. *By A. M. for Tho. Vnderhill*, 1649 [50]. 4°.* LG; IU, NN, Y.

6232 **Bush, William.** The celestial race. *For John Dunton*, 1642. [i.e. 1692]. 8°. T.C.II 390. L, C.

6233 —The frailty and uncertainty of the life of man. *For John Dunton*, 1693. 8°. O; LC.

6234 **Bushell, Edward.** The case of Edward Bushil. [*London*], 1670. brs. LL.

6235 **Bushell, John.** A true and perfect narrative of the late dreadful fire. *By Peter Lillicrap*, [1668]. 4°.* L; MU, NN.

6236 **Bushell, Seth.** The believer's groan for Heaven. *For Tho. Sawbridge, and Philip Burton, at Preston, Lancs.*, 1678. 4°.* T.C.I 308. L; CH, WF.

6237 —Cosmos-meros. The worldy portion. *For Will. Thackery*, 1682. 12°. T.C.I 503. MH, Y.

6238 —A warning-piece for the unruly. *For Will. Cademan: and Tho. Passinger*, 1673. 4°. T.C.I 132. L, O, C, WCA, CU, MIU.

Bushell, Thomas. Mr. Bushell's abridgment of . . . Bacon's philosophical theory. 1659. *See* Bacon, *Sir* Francis.

6239 —The apologie of. *Antwerp, printed*, 1650. 4°.* L.

6240 [-] A brief declaration of the severall passages in the treaty . . . Lvndy. *Printed*, 1647. 25pp. 4°.* LT, HH, EN; CH, CJC, MH, WF.

6241 ——[Anr. ed.] *Printed*, 1647. 20pp. 4°.* LT, O, EN; CH.

6242 —The case of. *Printed*, 1649. 4°.* L, DT; NC, Y.

6243 ——[Anr. ed.] [*London*, 1659?] brs. L.

—An extract by Mr. Bushel of his late abridgment. 1660. *See* Bacon, *Sir* Francis.

6244 Entry cancelled.

6245 —A just and true remonstrance of His majesties mines-royall. *Printed at London by E. G.*, 1641. 4°.* L, AN; Y.

6246 ——[Anr. ed.] —, 1642. 4°. L, AN, DT; CH, WL, MH, WF.

6247 ——[Anr. ed.] *Shrewsbury, by Robert Barker: and by the assignes of John Bill*, 1642. 4°.* L.

6248 —Mr. Bushell's quæres. [*Antwerp*, 1665?] brs. L.

6249 —A table setting forth the manner. [*London*, 1659.] cap., 4°.* MH, Y.

6250 —To the right honourable Lords assembled in Parlia-ment. The humble petition of. [*London*, 1659?] brs. L.

6251 **Busher, Leonard.** Religions peace. *For John Sweeting*, 1646. 4°.* LT, O, LW, E, DT; CLC, MIU, NU, WF.

6251A —Wholesome severity. 1645. 4°. O.

6252 **Bushnell, Edmund.** The compleat ship-wright. *By W. Leybourn for George Hurlock*, 1664. 4°. O, CM.

6252A ——Second edition. *For George Hurlock*, 1669. 4°. OC.

6253 ——Third edition. —, 1669. 4°. O; PL.

6254 ——Fourth edition. *By R. W. for William Fisher, T. Passinger, R. Boulter, and R. Smith*, 1678. 4°. T.C.I 337. L, LUS.

6255 ——Fifth edition. *By R. H. for William Fisher, T. Passinger, and E. Smith*. 1688 4°. L.

6255A ——Sixth edition. *For Richard Mount*, 1699. 4°. PL.

6256 **Bushnell, Walter.** A narrative of the proceedings of the commissioners. . . for ejecting scandalous . . . ministers. [*London*], *for R. Clavell*, 1660. 8°. LT, O, C, LCL, OB; CH, CN, WF.

6257 **Busschof, Hermann.** Two treatises, the one medical of the gout. *By W. C. and sold by Moses Pitt*, 1676. 8°. T.C.I 236. L, O, C, E, DT; BN, CH, WF, WSG.

6258 [**Bussières, Jean de.**] Flosculi historici delibati nunc delibatiores redditi. Fifth edition. *Oxoniæ, exc. udebat W. Hall impensis Ioseph Godwin*, 1663. 8°. MADAN 2634*. L, O, OC, CM, CS; CH, CN, MH, WF, Y.

6259 ——Sixth edition. —, 1668. 12°. MADAN 2796. L, O, AU.

6259A **Bussy, Roger de Rabutin,** *comte de.* Loves empire. *For Dorman Newman*, 1682. 8°. T.C.I 462. CH, MH.

Bussy, d'Ambrose, 1641. *See* Chapman, George.

6260 **Busteed, Michael.** Orationes duae funebres. [*Canta-brigiæ*], *ex officina Joh. Hayes*, 1696. *Impensis Edm. Jeffery, Cantab.* 12°. L, C.

6261 **Butcher, Richard.** The survey and antiquitie of the towne of Stamford. *By Tho: Forcet*, 1646. 4°. LT, O, C, CM, CT; LC, MB, WF, Y.

Butchers blessing. 1642. *See* Goodwin, John.

Butler, Prince, pseud.

6262 **Butler, Charles.** Monarchia foeminina. *Typis A. C., impensis authoris*, 1673. 8°. T.C.I 121. L, O, C, EN, DT; BN, WF.

6263 —Monarchia fœminarum. *Oxon, typis Lichfieldianis*, 1682. 8°. O; MB.

6264 —Rhetoricæ libri duo. *Excudebat R. H.*, 1642. 8°. L, LW; MH, MWA, PU.

6265 ——[Anr. ed.] *Cantabrigiæ, ex officina R. Danielis,* 1642. 12°. DC; MH, WF.

6266 ——[Anr. ed.] *Ex officina Gulielmi Bentley, pro Johanne Williams,* 1649. 12°. L; Y.

6267 ——[Anr. ed.] *Ex officina Gulielmi Bentley, pro Andr. Crook,* 1655. 12°. L, DC, DT.

6267A ——[Anr. ed.] 1667. 8°. ELY, YM.

6267B ——[Anr. ed.] *Ex officina J. W. pro Andræa Crook,* 1671. 8°. CLC, WF.

6267C ——[Anr. ed.] *Sumptibus R. Scot, T. Basset, J. Wright, & R. Chiswell,* 1684. 12°. T.C.II 104. C; MH.

6268 **B[utler], J[ohn].** *B.D.* Ἁγιαστρολογία *Or, the most sacred . . . astrology. For the author; to be sold by William Bromwich,* 1680. 8°. T.C.I 385. L, O, LW, CS; CH, CU, MH, WF, Y.

6269 —*Bellua marina: or the monstrous beast. By George Croom, to be sold by Richard Baldwin,* 1690. 4°. L, C, LSC; CLC, WF, Y.

6270 —Χριστολογία. *or a brief (but true) account. By Joseph Moxon, and sold by him, and by Hen. Broom,* 1671. 8°. T.C.I 65. L, O, C, EC, E; CH, LC, MH, NU, Y.

6271 —*Explanatory notes upon a mendacious libel. For the author,* 1698. 8°.* L, O; Y.

6272 [–] *God made man. For the author,* 1675. 8°. L; NU, WF, Y.

6273 —*God's judgments upon regicides. By T. Moore and J. Ashburne for Awnsham Churchill,* 1683. 4°.* L, O, OC, DT.

6274 [–] *A letter sent to the honorable William Lenthal . . . December 24,* 1659. *J. Streater,* 1659. 4°.* L, HH; CH, MBP.

6274A —*A sermon preached on the 30th of January,* 1684. *For R. Taylor,* 1684. 4°. T.C.II 59. O, WCA.

6275 —*The true state of the case of. For the authot* [sic], 1617 [i.e., 1697]. 4°.* L, O, C, CT; CH.

6276 ——[Anr. ed.] —, 1697. 8°.* L, OC, CSS; CLC, WF, Y.

6277 **Butler, John,** *canon.* Christian liberty asserted. *By M. C. for Walter Kettilby,* 1678. 4°.* T.C.I 339. L, O, C, E, DT; CH, CN, NU, TU, WF, Y.

6278 **Butler, John,** *oculist.* In the Strand near the Middle Exchange in Salisbury Street. [*London,* 1682.] brs. O.

6278A **Butler, Lilly.** A sermon preached . . . 16th of September. *For R. Baldwin,* 1691. 4°.* L, OC; WF, Y.

6279 —*A sermon preached . . . March 27,* 1694. *For Brabazon Aylmer,* 1694. 4°.* L, O, LG; CLC, MHS, Y.

6280 —*A sermon preached . . . 26th of June. For B. Aylmer,* 1696. 4°.* T.C.II 587. L, O, C, LG, CS; CLC, NU, Y.

6281 —*A sermon preached before the . . . Lord Mayor . . . Feast of St. Michael.* 1696. *For Brab. Aylmer,* 1696. 4°.* T.C.II 600. L, O, C, OC; CLC, NU, WF.

6282 —*A sermon preach'd . . . to the Societies for reformation of manners, April 5.* 1697. *For B. Aylmer,* 1697. 8°. T.C.III 11. L, O, OC, CM, EC; MH, Y.

6283 —*A sermon preached . . . 28th of April. For Brabazon Aylmer,* 1697. 4°.* T.C.III 51. L, O; CLC, NU.

6284 —*A sermon preached . . . Jan. 31,* 1697/8. *By J. H. for Brabazon Aylmer,* 1698. 4°.* T.C.III 51. C, OC; CH, MH.

6285 **Butler, Nathaniel,** *of Alton.* Blood washed away. *By W. G. for Isaac Pridmore, and Henry Marsh,* 1657. 4°.* LT.

6286 [–] A serious advice to the citizens of London. [*London,* 1657.] 8°. L, O.

6287 **Butler, Nathaniel,** *Captain.* Colloquia maritima: or sea-dialogues. *Printed and sold by William Fisher and Richard Mount,* 1688. 8°. CH, WF, Y.

6288 —*Six dialogues about sea-services. For Moses Pitt,* 1685. 8°. L, CM, CT; BN, CLC, MH, NN, WF, Y.

6288A —*War practically perform'd. By Edward Thomas,* 1664. MH.

6288B ——[Anr. ed.] *By J. C. for Hen. Fletcher,* 1663. MH, WF.

6289 **Butler, Peter.** Oratio in inauguratione D. Petri Butler. *Dublin, ex typographia I. Windsor,* 1667. 4°.* DIX 135. DT.

6290 **[Butler, Samuel.]** The acts and monuments of our late Parliament. *Printed,* 1659. 4°.* LT, O, LG, MR, E; CH, CN, MH, WF, Y.

[–] Chimneys scuffle. 1662. *See* Brathwait, Richard.

6291 —A continuation of the acts and monuments. *Printed,* 1659. 4°. LT, O, HH; MH, WF, Y.

6291A [–] The Geneva ballad, *London, printed,* 1674. brs. L, O.

6291B [–] —[Anr. ed.] *For R. Cutler,* 1674. brs. L, MC, HH.

6291C [–] —[Anr. ed.] *For Henry Brome,* 1674. brs. T.C.I 193. L; CH, CLC.

6292 —[Anr. ed.] —, 1678. O, HH; CH, MH, WF, Y.

6293–95 Entries cancelled.

HUDIBRAS

6296 [–] Hudibras. The first part. (First unauthorized edition) *Printed,* 1663. (t.p.: crowned rose and thistle; errata on H8ʳ.) 8°. CHEW A. THORSON F. L; CH, INU, WF, Y.

6297 [–] —(Second unauthorized edition.) —, 1663. (t.p.: as in 6296: no errata.) 8°. CHEW B. THORSON G. O; CH, CLC, PT, Y.

6298 [–] —(Third unauthorized edition.) —, 1663. (t.p.: type ornaments in inverted pyramid, 14 in top row.) 8°. CHEW C. THORSON H. L, O; CH, MH, IU, NN.

6299 [–] —(Fourth unauthorized edition.) —, 1663. (t.p.: type ornaments, fleurs de lys, in inverted pyramid, 13 in top row.) 8°. CHEW C+. THORSON I. C, CM; CH, CLC.

6300 [–] —(First authorized edition.) *By J. G. for Richard Marriot,* 1663. 8°. CHEW D. THORSON A. L, O, CP, MR, GK; CH, CU, MH, NIC, NP, Y.

6301 [–] —(Second authorized edition.) —, 1663. 8°. CHEW E. THORSON B. L, O; CH, CLC, LC, MH, TU, Y.

6301A [–] —[Anr. ed.] —, 1663. 8°. THORSON C. CH, NP.

6302 [–] —(Third authorized edition.) —, 1663. 12°. CHEW F. THORSON D. L, O, C, CT, GK; CH, MH, NN, WC, Y.

6302A [–] —[Anr. ed.] —, 1663. 12°. THORSON E. IU.

6303 [–] —[Anr. ed.] *By T. N. for Henry Herringman, and are to be sold by T. Basset,* 1684. 8°. I, O, OC, CT; MH, WC, Y, KIRK.

6304 [–] —[Anr. ed.] *For Henry Herringman, and are to be sold by Tho Sawbridge,* 1689. 8°. L, O, CM; CH, WF, Y.

6304A [–] —[Anr. ed.] *By T. Warren for Henry Herringman, and are to be sold by R. Bentley, J. Tonson, F. Saunders, and T. Bennet, 1694.* 8°. O, OC, GK; CH, CN, MH, WG, Y.

6305 [–] —[Anr. ed.] *By Tho. Warren, for Henry Herringman, to be sold by Jacob Tonson, and Thomas Bennet, 1700.* 8°. L, O, C, EC, BAMB; CN, KT.

6306 [–] —The second part. (First spurious edition.) *Printed, 1663.* 8°. CHEW G. THORSON J. L, O, CT; CH, CN, MH, WF, Y.

6306A ——[Anr. ed.] *For R. Chiswell, T. Sawbridge, R. Wellington, G. Wells, 1700.* 8°. CN.

6307 [–] —(Second spurious edition.) —, 1663. 8°. CHEW H. O; CH, IU.

6308 [–] —Last edition corrected (third spurious edition). —, 1663. 8°. CHEW H. THORSON L. L; CH, TU.

6308A [–] —[Anr. ed.] —, 1663. 8°. THORSON M. Y.

6309 [–] —The second part. (First authorized edition.) *By T. R. for John Martyn, and James Allestry, 1664.* 8°. CHEW I. THORSON N. L, O, C, CT, MR; CH, CU, MH, WF, Y.

6310 [–] —(Second authorized edition.) —, 1664. 8°. CHEW K. THORSON O. L, O; CH, LC, MH, NN, Y.

6311 [–] —The first and second parts. *By T.N. for John Martyn and Henry Herringman, 1674.* 8°. T.C.I 191. THORSON P. L, O, CT, EN, DT; CH, CU, MH, NU, TU, WF, Y.

6311A [–] —[Anr. ed.] —, 1675. 8°. WF.

6312 [–] —[Anr. ed.] —, 1678. 8°. THORSON Q. L, O, CPE, BR, GK; CU, LC, MH, NP, Y.

6313 [–] —The third and last part. *For Simon Miller, 1678.* (Verso of t.p. blank.) 8°. CHEW L. THORSON R. L, O, CS, EN, DT; BN, CH, CN, LC, MH, Y.

6314 [–] —Second edition —, 1678. (Verso of t.p.: Licensed and entred . . .) 8°. CHEW M. THORSON S. L, O, OC, CT, EC; CH, CU, MH, NN, WF, Y.

6315 [–] —[Anr. ed.] *For Robert Horne, 1679.* 8°. T.C.I 377. THORSON T. L, O, C, OC, BR; CH, CU, MH, NP, WF, Y.

6316 [–] —[Anr. ed.] —, 1680. 8°. THORSON U. O, AN, D; MH, NIC, TU.

6317 [–] —[Anr. ed.] *For Robert Horne, to be sold by Tho. Basset, 1684.* 8°. L, O, OC, CT; MH, TU, Y, KIRK.

6317A [–] —[Anr. ed.] *For Thomas Horne, 1689.* 8°. L, CM; MBP, BCN.

6318 [–] —[Anr. ed.] —, 1694. 8°. L, O; CH, CN, MH, WG.

6319 [–] —In three parts. *Printed, and are to be sold by W. Rogers, 1684.* 8°. T.C.II 89. L, O, C, D; MIU, NC, Y, KIRK.

6320 [–] —*Printed, and are to be sold by Richard Parker, 1689.* 8°. L, OC, CM, CS; CH, MH, TU, WF, Y.

6321 [–] —*Printed, and are to be sold by Nathaniel Sackett, 1694.* 8°. L, O, C, OME, DT; CLC, IU, MU, V, WU, JF.

6322 [–] —*By Tho. Warren, for Henry Herringman, to be sold by Jacob Tonson and Thomas Bennet, 1700.* 8°. L, O, BAMB; CLC, CN, TSM, Y.

6322A —Hudibras compleat. *Printed and sold by Thomas Horne, 1700.* °. NP, WF, Y.

6323 [–] A letter from Mercurius Civicus to Mercurius Rusticus. [*Oxford*], *printed, 1643.* 4°.* MADAN 1441. LT, O, C, OC, AN; CLC, CN, CU, MH, NU, Y.

6324 [–] A letter from Mercvrivs Civicvs. [Anr. ed.] [*London*] *printed, 1643.* 4°.* MADAN 1441n. O, CLC, CN, MH, WF, Y.

6325 [–] Mercurius Menippeus. The loyal satyrist. *For Jos. Hindmarsh, 1682.* 4°.* T.C.I 475. L, O, C, LG, EN; CLC, CN, MH, NU, TU, WF, Y.

6325A [–] Mola asinaria. *Printed at London, 1659.* 4°.* LT, O, C, LL, MR; CH, CN, MH, NU, WF, Y.

6326 [–] A new ballad of King Edward and Jane Shore. *Printed, 1671.* brs. L.

6327 [–] The plagiary exposed. *For Tho. Bennet, 1691.* 4°.* T.C.II 384. L, O, C, LVF, MR; CLC, CN, MH, NP, NU, WF, Y.

6328 [–] The priviledge of our saints. colop: *For Benj. Tooke, 1681.* brs. L, O, CT, MC; CH, MH, TU, WF, Y.

6329 [–] A proposal humbly offered for the farming of liberty of conscience. [*London?*], *printed, 1662[3].* fol.* L, O, CT, P, HH; MH, MIU.

6330 [–] —[Anr. ed.] [*London*], *printed, 1663.* fol.* L, C, CM, CT, MR; CH, MB, MIU, WF.

6331–5 Entries cancelled.

6336 [–] To the memory of the most renowned Du-Vall: a pindarick ode. *For H. Brome, 1671.* 4°.* L, O; CH, MH.

6337–8 Entries cancelled.

6339 **Butler, Thomas.** The little Bible of the man. *For Giles Calvert, 1649.* 12°. LT, DC; MH, NPT, Y.

Butler's ghost. 1682. See D'Urfey, Thomas.

6339A **B[utter], N[athaniel.]** A letter with a narrative. *For Nath. Butter, 1659.* brs. LG.

6340 **[Butterent, Samuel.]** A brief discovery of a threefold estate of Antichrist. *For Giles Calvert, 1653.* 4°.* L, C, CT; NNM, PH, PSC.

6341 **Buttock, Roger.** Catalogus librorum bibliothecis. [*London*], 24 Oct., 1681. 4°. L, O, OP, HH; CN.

6341A The button-makers case. [*London? 1692.*] brs. LG.

Buxom Joan. [1692–5.] See Congreve, William.

6342 The bucksome lass of Westminster. [*London*], *for P. Brooksby, J. Deacon, J. Blare, and J. Back,* [1688–92]. brs. L, HH; MH.

6343 **Buxtorf, Johann.** Epitome grammaticæ hebrææ, *Cantabrigiæ, ex officina R. Daniel, 1646.* 8°. C, CT, DC, EC, NPL; NU.

6344 ——[Anr. ed.] *Ex officina Rogeri Daniel, 1653.* 8°. L, C, CT, P, AU; CH, MB, MH, PL, WF.

6345 ——Ninth edition. *Ex officina Johannis Redmayne, prostant venales apud Henricum Eversden, 1666.* 8°. L, O, CT; CLC, MBC, NU, PL.

6346 ——Tenth edition. —, 1669. 8°. OB, CPE, CS, DU; MHS.

6347 —The Jewish synagogue. *By T. Roycroft for H. R. and Thomas Young, 1657.* 4°. C, EN.

6348 —Lexicon Hebraicum. *Typis Jacobi Junii & Mosis Bell, sumptibus Richardi Whitakeri & Samuelis Cartwright, 1646.* 8°. L, O, C, DT; CH, MH, NU, WF, Y.

6348A —Masora. A collection. *For Matthias Thurston, 1665.* 8°. MB.

6349 —A short introduction to the Hebrew tongue. *By Roger Daniel, for Humphrey Moseley, 1656.* 8°. LT, O, C, LW, CT; IU, MIU, WF.

6349A **Buy, John.** A stop to the false characterizer's hue-and-cry. [*London*], *by Andrew Soule*, 1685. 4°.* LF, BBN; PH, PSC.

By authority of the Parliament. 1651. *See* England. Parliament.

6349B By consent. Characters of some young women. [*London*, 1691.] brs. CN.

By His Excellency the Lord Fairfax and the Council of State. 1653. *See* England. Council.

By His Highnes Council. Edinburgh, 1658. *See* Scotland. Council.

6350 By His Majestys authority. At the [blank] is to be seen two monsters. [*n.p.*, 1696.] brs. L.

6351 By His Majesty's authority, at the sign of Charing-Cross, . . . there is to be seen a strange and monstrous child. [*London*, 1699.] brs. L.

By His Majesties commissioners. [n.p., 1666.] *See* Ireland.

6352 By His Majesties commissioners, for examining and enquiring. [*Cambridge, Mass.*, 1683.] brs. EVANS 348. MHS.

6353 The by-law to be read at the administring of the freemans oath. [*n.p.*, c. 1670.] brs. OP.

6354–5 Entries cancelled.

6356 By reason of the distraction that is in the Romane Empire. [*n.p.*], *printed*, 1648. 4°.* LT, O; NU.

6357 By the appointment of the committee of the Lords and Commons for the safety of the kingdom. [*n.p.*, 1642.] brs. LS.

6357A By the commissioners appointed for the repairing the highwayes. [*London*] *For J. G.*, 1652. brs. L.

6358 By the commissioners for charitable uses, whereas. *By Thomas Newcomb*, 1655. brs. LT, LG; MH.

6359 By the commissioners for charitable uses, whereas there is a special commission. [*n.p.*, 1656.] brs. LT.

6360 By the commissioners for executing the office of Lord High Admiral. [*London*, 1697?] fol. LG, HH; Y.

6360A —[Same title.] [*London*, 1695.] brs. L.

6360B By the commissioners for settling & sewring . . . Ulster. *Dublin*, 1653. brs. L.

6360C By the commissioners for the removing obstruction. 1654. brs. OP.

By the committee for the affairs. [n.p., 1658.] *See* Trevor, John.

6360D By the commissioners of the county of [blank]. [*London*, 1692.] brs. OP.

6361 Vicessimo nono Julij, 1645. By the committee of Grocers-Hall. [*London*, 1645.] brs. LT.

6361A By the company of the Royal fishery of England. [*London?* 1681.] cap., 4°.* OC; MU.

6362 By the company of vvoodmongers whereas. [*London*, 1657.] brs. LT.

6363 By the covncil . . . (Dec. 16. 1653). *By Henry Hills*, 1653. brs. NU, Y.

6363A By the ecclesiastical congregation of the clergy of Ireland, for avoyding. [*Kilkenny*, 1646.] brs. DI.

6363B By the farmers of excise for . . . York. *In the Savoy, by Tho. Newcomb*, 1671. brs. NC.

By the Generall Assemblie of the confederate. Kilkenny, 1647. *See* Kearnie, P.

6363BA By the governour of Edinburgh, Leith and Barwick, Whereas. *Printed, at Leith, by Evan Tyler*, 1651. brs. Y.

6363C London, September 24th, 1694. By the governour . . . of the company of copper-miners. [*London*, 1694.] brs. MH.

6363D By the King of Kings his prophets; a proclamation. *By A. Coe*, 1644. brs. LT.

6364 By the Kings Majestie, were accused with seven articles of high treason. *For Iohn Thomas*, 1641[2]. 4°. LT, O, OC, SP; Y.

6365 —[Anr. ed.] *For F. C. & J. W.*, 1641. 4°.* CT.

6366–8 Entries cancelled.

6369 By the master and wardens of the company of stationers. [*London*, 1645.] brs. LT.

6370 By the master, wardens and assistants of the company of free-fishermen . . . a deputation. *By J. How.*, 1697. 8°.* L, LG.

6371 By the providence of God Biship of London: to our well-beloved in Christ [blank]. [*London*, 166-?] brs. O.

6371A By the supreme councell of the Confederat Catholicks. *Waterford, by Thomas Bourke*, 1644. brs. DI.

6371B By the wardens and commonalty of the . . . mercers. colop: *By R. Roberts*, 1698. cap., fol.* PL.

6372 By vertue of a commission granted by the right honourable Edward, Earl of Manchester, . . . day of April 1643. [*n.p.*], 1643. brs. OP.

6373 No. [blank] exchequer. [blank] 1697. By vertue of an act of Parliament passed in the VIII year. [*n.p.*, 1697] brs. OP.

6374 By vertue of severall ordinances of Parliament, authorizing. [*n.p.*, 1648.] brs. LT.

6374A **B[yam], H[enry].** Osculum pacis. Concio. *Par J. Raworth pro N. Butter*, 1641. 4°. MH.

6375 —XIII sermons. *By T. R. for Robert Clavell*, 1675. 8°. T.C.I 184. L, O, C, SC, EN; CH, CN, NU, Y.

6376 **[Byam, William.]** An exact relation of the most execrable attempts of John Allin. *For Richard Lowndes*, 1665. 4°.* L, O, CM; CH, LC, MH, PL, Y.

6377 —Surinam justice. *For the authour*, 1662. 4°. L, O; PL.

6378 **[Byfield, Adoniram.]** A brief view of Mr. Coleman his new-modell of church government. *By John Field for Ralph Smith*, 1645. 4°.* LT, O, OC, CJ, HH; CH, MH, MIU, NU.

6379 **Byfield, Nathaniel.** An account of the late revolution in New England. *For Ric. Chiswell*, 1689. 4°.* L, O, OM, EN, GH; HR, CH, CN, LC, MH, NN, Y.

6380 ——[Anr. ed.] colop: *Edinburgh, re-printed*, 1689. 4°.* ALDIS 2868. EN; CH, NN, RPJ, WCL, Y.

6381 [–] —[Anr. ed.] [*Boston: by Benjamin Harris*, 1689.] 4°.* EVANS 462. RPJ.

6382 [–] Seasonable motives. [*Philadelphia, by Will. Bradford*], 1689. brs. EVANS 463. MHS, MU.

6383 **Byfield, Nicholas.** Directions for the private reading of the Scriptures. Fourth edition. *By M. F. for P. Stephens*, 1648. 12°. L, O, LCL, LSC; CU, NPT, NU, WF.

6384 —An exposition upon the Epistle to the Colossians. Fourth edition. *By Miles Flesher, sold by Ralph Smith,* 1649. fol. L, OB, CCH, YM; CU, IU, MBA, MH, NNG.

6385 —The marrow of the oracles of God. Twelfth edition. 1647. 12°. LCL, AN; CLC, CU, NPT.

6386 ——Thirteenth edition. *By John Field, to be sold by Peter Dring,* 1660. 12°. L, LCL, LW; CLC, Y.

6387 Entry cancelled.

6388 —The mystery of reconciliation. 1659. 12°. LCL.

6389 —The principles, or the patterne of wholesome words. Seventh edition. *By E. T. for Peter Dring,* 1665. 12°. L, LSC; CLC, Y.

6390 **Byfield, Richard.** The gospel's glory. *By E. M. for Adoniram Byfield,* 1659. 8°. LT, LW, AU; NPT.

6391 [-] A message sent from the kingdom of Scotland to His Highnesse the Prince of VVales. *For R. W.,* 1648. 4°.* LT; Y.

6392 —The power of the Christ of God. *By R. Cotes for Jo. Bellamie, and Ralph Smith,* 1641. 4°. LT, O, ENC, DT; CLC, IU, MBA, NU, Y.

6393 —A short treatise describing the true church of Christ. *For Ralph Smith,* 1653. 4°.* L, O, E, EN; NU, Y.

6394 —Temple-defilers defiled. *By John Field for Ralph Smith,* 1645. 4°.* LT, O, CS, E, DT; CH, MH, NU, WF, Y.

6395 —Zion's answer. *By John Field for Ralph Smith,* 1645. 4°.* LT, O, C, EN, DT; CH, LC, MH, NU, Y.

6396 **Byfield, Timothy.** The artificial spaw. *By James Rawlins, for the author,* 1684. 12° L, C; LC, WSG.

6396A —A discourse of consumptions. *For Randall Taylor,* 1685. 4°. LCP; PL.

6397 —Horæ subsecivæ: or, some long-vacation hours. *J. Whitlock,* 1695. 4°.* LG, E; CLC, LC, MIU.

6398 —A short and plain account of . . . wells at Hoxdon. *Printed, to be sold by Christopher Wilkinson, Thomas Fox, and John Harris,* 1687. 12°. T.C.II 187. L, O, C, LG, LPO; WF, HC.

6399 —A short description and vindication of the true sal volatile oleosum. *For R. Cumberland,* 1699. 8°. T.C.III 94. LCP, OC, CM.

6400 —A short discourse of the rise . . . of the small-pox. *For John Harris,* 1695. 4°.* C, LWL, E; WSG.

6401 —Two discourses: one of consumptions. *For Dorman Newman,* 1685. 4°.* T.C.II 171. L, O, C, LCS, D; MH, PL.

6402 **Byne, Magnus.** The scornfull Quakers answered. *By William Bentley for Andrew Crook,* 1656. 4°. L, O, CT; PSC.

6403 **Bynns, Richard.** A sermon preached . . . January 30. 1692. *In the Savoy, by Edw. Jones, for William Crooke,* 1693. 4°.* L, O, C, CT, SC; CH, CN, NU, WF, Y.

6403A **Byrd, William.** Parthenia. *For John Clarke,* 1651. fol.* L.

6403B ——[Anr. ed.] —, 1655. fol.* L, GU; NN.

6403C ——[Anr. ed.] —, 1659. fol.* L; CH.

6404 **Byrdall, Thomas.** A glimpse of God. *By A. Maxwel for Thomas Parkhurst,* 1665. 8°. C, LW; NU.

6405 —The parable of the barren fig-tree. 1666. 12°. LCL.

6406 —The profit of godliness. *For Nevil Simmons in Kederminster,* 1666. 8°. O, LCL; NPT, Y.

6406A ——[Anr. ed.] *Printed,* 1666. 8°. WF.

6407 [**Byrne, Gerrald.**] Several instances of the wrongs and oppressions by Q's and R's, suffered by the sailers. colop: *By G. Croom,* 1699. fol* CH, PL.

6408 **Byrom, John.** The necessity of subjection. *For Benj. Tooke,* 1681. 4°.* L; CH, Y.

6409 **Byron, John,** *baron.* The Lord Byrons first articles. *By Iohn Field, Feb. 10.* 1645[6]. 4°.* LT, CCL, AN; WF.

6409A —Sir John Byrons relation to the secretary. *York, Stephen Bulkley,* 1643. 4°.* L.

6409B —Two letters. *York, by Stephen Bulkley,* 1643. L; CH.

6410 **Byshop, Henry.** An advertisement from. [*London,* 1660?] brs. L; MH.

6411 **Bysshe,** *Sir* **Edward.** Bibliotheca Bissaeana: sive catalogus librorum. [*London,* 1679.] 4°. L, C, HH; CN.

6412 **Bythner, Victorinus.** Clavis linguæ sanctæ. *Cantabrigiæ, ex officina Rogeri Daniel,* 1648. 8°. L, O, C, LW, ENC; BN, CH, MB, NPT, NU, WF, Y.

6413 —[Hebrew] lingua eruditorum. *Cantabrigiæ, impensis authoris,* 1645. 8°. O, C, CT.

6414 ——[Anr. ed.] *Ex officina Jacobi Flesher,* 1650. 12°. LT, O, C, LW, EN; CH, NC, NU, PL, Y.

6415 ——[Anr. ed.] *Typis Jacobi Flesher, & venalis prostat apud Jonam Hart,* 1664. 12°. L, OC, OME, CPE; CN, IU, MH, Y.

6416 ——[Anr. ed.] —, 1675. 12°. L, O, C, E, DT; TU, WF.

6416A ——[Anr. ed.] *Typis Elizabethe Flesher,* 1679. 4°.* MBA, TSM, TU.

6417 —Lyra prophetica. 1644. 4°. NPL; CU.

6418 ——[Anr. ed.] *Typis Jacobi Flesher,* 1650. 4°. L, O, C, OM, E; CH, NPT, PL, WF, Y.

6418A ——[Anr. ed.] *Impensis W. Wasse, prostant apud J. Sherley, & T. Garthwait,* 1650. 4°. CCA, CCO, CSS.

6419 ——[Anr. ed.] *Typis Jacobi Flesher: prostat apud Cornelium Bee,* 1653. 4°. L, O, C, LIL, E; MBC, MH, NU, Y.

6420 ——[Anr. ed.] —, 1654. 4°. LT.

6421 ——[Anr. ed.] *Typis Jacobi Flesher: prostat vero apud Edm. Beechinoe, Cantabrigiæ,* 1664. 4°. L, O, C, E, DT; CH, CN, MH, TU, Y.

6422 ——[Anr. ed.] *Typis Jacobi Flesher: prostat vero venalis apud Gul. Morden, Cantabrigiæ,* 1664. 4°. L, CT, P, WCA; MB, NPT.

6423 ——[Anr. ed.] *Typis E. Flesher, apud G. Morden, Cantabrigiæ,* 1679. 4°. L, C. RPL, ENC, DT; BN, MH, NC, NP, WF, Y.

6423A ——[Anr. ed.] —, 1689. 4°. TU.

—Present state of Russia. 1671. *See* Collins, Samuel.

C

1   **C.** The deposition and farther discovery of the late horrid plot. *For F. F.* [1679.] 4°.* O; MH.

1A   —A friendly conference concerning the new oath of allegiance. *For Samuel Smith*, 1689. 4°.* T.C.II 258. L, O, C, CT, MR; CLC, CN, MH, NU, WF, Y.

2   —The true law of free monarchy. *Printed, to be sold by T. P.*, 1642. 4°.* LT, LL, HH, EN, DT; WF.

3   —Upon the death of that incomparable princess, Q. Mary. *Edinburgh, by the heirs and successors of Andrew Anderson*, 1695. brs. ALDIS 3515. L, ES.

    C., A. Ad populum: or, a lecture. [n.p.], 1644. *See* Hausted, Peter.

4   —An answer to a late treasonable pamphlet, entituled, Treason in grain. colop: *By N. T.*, 1681. brs. L, O, OM; CH, MH, MIU, WF, Y.

    —Daily exercise, Amsterdam, 1657. *See* Crowther, Arthur Anselm.

    —De loco parallelo. Edinburgi, 1656. *See* Colvill, Alexander.

    —Divine teachings. 1649. *See* Coppe, Abiezer.

5   —Emmanuel manifested. *Printed at London for William Larnar*, 1655. 8°. LT.

6   —The English oracle. *For W. M.*, 1679. 4°.* L; MBA, MH.

    —Essay concerning church government. [n.p.], 1689. *See* Cunningham, Alexander.

    —Glimpse of eternity. 1667. *See* Caley, Abraham.

    —Jesus, Maria, Joseph. Amsterdam, 1657. *See* Crowther, Arthur Anselm.

7   —A letter to a freind [*sic*]. Shewing, the illegall proceedings. *Printed*, 1645. 4°.* MADAN 1784. L, O, CJ, EN; CH, TU, Y.

8   —A mite from three mourners: in memorial of Thomas Glass. [*n.p.*, 1666.] brs. L.

9   Entry cancelled.

    —Satyre against Seperatists. 1642. *See* Hausted, Peter.

    —Στραταλογια. 1662. *See* Cooper, Andrew.

10   —The tyrannical usurpation. *For Gideon Andrews*, 1663. brs. L.

11   —A vindication of Lieut. Gen. Cromwell. *For Laurence Chapman*, 1647[8]. 4°.* LT, HH; CH, OWC, TU, WF, Y.

12   **C., A. B.** Dumbritons Castle dolefull commendations. [*n.p.*, 1643.] brs. LT.

13   —A trve coppy of a bold and most peremptory letter. *By B. Alsop*, 1641. 4°.* LT, EC; MBP, OWC, WF, Y.

13A   **C., B.** A brief and perspicuous manuduction. *By S. R. for Henry Eversden*, 1670. 8°.* LW.

    —Letter to his worthy friend. [n.p., 1696.] *See* Connor, Bernard.

14   —A letter touching a colledge of maids. [*London*], 1675. 8°. O, C.

    —Quakers cleared. 1696. *See* Coole, Benjamin.

15   —The souldiers alarum bell. [*n.p.*], *printed*, 1659. 4°. O, C; WF.

16   **C., C.** Another word to purpose. *For Thomas Dring*, 1660. 4°.* LT; CH, NC, NU, Y.

16A   —A brief explanation of the life . . . of Argyle, *Imprinted at Inverlochie, to be sold at Inverary, by D. F.*, 1656. 4°.* EN; NN.

    —Compleat gamester. 1674. *See* Cotton, Charles.

17   —Sad and serious thoughts. [*London*, 1653.] cap., 4°.* LT, O, HH; WF.

    —Scoffer scoffed. 1684. *See* Cotton, Charles.

18   —Sylla's ghost. *By John Harefinch, to be sold by R. Reynolds and J. Norris*, 1683. fol.* CH, TU, Y.

18A   ——[Anr. ed.] —, 1683/4. fol.* L, O, OC, HH; CH, CLC, MH, WF, Y.

19   —Treason's master-piece. *For Daniel Major*, 1680. 8°. T.C.I 393. L, O, OC, EN, DT; CH, CU, MH, NU, PL, WF.

20   **C., D.** An essay towards the deciding of the so much, . . . controverted case of usury. *For John Rothwell*, 1661. 4°.* L, O, OC, CS, HH; NC, NR.

    —Inconsistencie of the independent way. 1651. *See* Cawdrey, Daniel.

    —Lenten litany. 1698. *See* Coward, William.

20A   —A letter from Holland. [*London?* 1673.] brs. HH.

21   —Sathan discovered. *For John Wright*, 1657. 4°.* O; NU, Y.

    —Superstitio superstes. 1641. *See* Cawdrey, Daniel.

    —Vindiciæ spei. 1641. *See* Cawdrey, Daniel.

    —Vindiciæ vindicarum. 1651. *See* Cawdrey, Daniel.

    C., D. D. Institutiones logicæ. Dublin, 1697. *See* Marsh, Narcissus, *abp.*

    C., E. Answer to the articles. 1642. *See* Calamy, Edmund, *elder.*

    —Englands fortresse. 1648. *See* Calver, Edward.

22   —A faithful account of the present state of affairs, in England. *For Tho. Bever*, 1690. 12°. T.C.II 299. L, O, C, SP; LC, WF.

    —Here is something of concernment. [*London?* 1660.] *See* Cooke, Edward.

23   —A full and final proof of the plot. *For Thomas Simmons and Jacob Sampson*, 1680. fol.* L, O, C, EN, DT; CH, MH, NC, TU, WF, Y.

24   —A new catechisme commanded. *By B. Alsop*, 1647. 8°.* LT; CH.

25   Entry cancelled.

    —On the recovery. 1664. *See* Cooper, Edmund.

26   —The poor doubting Christian drawn to Christ. Fourth edition. *For John Wright*, 1669. 8°.* L.

26A   ——Sixth edition. *By J. Raworth for Luke Fawne*, 1641. 12°. NL.

26B   ——Ninth edition. *By H. B. for J. Wright, J. Clark, W. Thackeray, and T. Passinger*, 1683. 12°.* CM.

27   —The Scots remonstrance or declaration. *For G. H.*, 1650. 4°.* LT, O, HH, EN, DT; WF, Y.

28   Entry cancelled. Timothy's lesson. 1699. *See* Graile, Edmund.
— True and perfect narrative of the inhumane positions. 1680. *See* Cooke, Edward.
29   — The Wiltshire-petition for tythes explained. *For William Larnar*, 1653. 4°.* LT; MH, WF.
C., El. The ladies answer, 1670. *See* Letters of Elizabeth.
30   **C., F.** The beginning, progresse, and conclusion of the late troubles in France. *Printed*, 1649. 4°.* LT, O, HH; Y.
— New treatise of three languages. 1689. *See* Colsoni, François.
31   — Two letters: the one from a Dutch-man. [*London*], *printed*, 1673. 4°.* L, O, C, OC, DT; MH, NU, TU, WF, Y.
— Wealth discovered. 1661. *See* Cradocke, Francis.
C., G. Almanack . . . for . . . 1696. Edinburgh, 1696. *See* Almanacs.
— Αστρολογομανία the madnesse. 1651. *See* Carleton, George, *bp.*
31A — Discourse in defence of infants-baptism. 1651. 12°. NHC.
32   — Envy and folly detected. *For Sarah Howkins*, 1695. 4°.* LF; NU.
— Fraud & oppression. [*n.p.*], 1676. *See* Carew, George.
33   — Gloria Deo. Finis coronat opus. On the crowing-cock. [*n.p.*, 1695.] brs. L.
— Liberty of conscience. 1689. *See* Care, George.
— Reply to the answer of the man. 1685. *See* Care, George.
— Several considerations offered. [*n.p.*, 1675.] *See* Carew, George.
— Severall grounds. [1660]. *See* Carew, George.
34   **C., G. B.** Plots, conspiracies and attempts of domestick and forraigne enemies. *For Ralph Rounthwait*, 19 *Sept.*, 1642. 4°.* LT, HH, YM, EN, GU; CH, CN, MH, NU, WF, Y.
35   — — Second edition. *By G. M. for Ralph Rounthwait*, 1642. 4°.* L, BR, EN; CH, CN, MH, WF.
C., H. Animadversions on a late paper. 1687. *See* Care, Henry.
— Animadversions upon the responses. [1692]. *See* Collins, Hercules.
— Art of practical measuring. 1690. *See* Coggeshall, Henry.
— Bank dialogue. [*n.p.*, 1696.] *See title.*
— Brief directions for our. 1693. *See* Cornwallis, Henry.
36   Entry cancelled.
37   — The character of an honest lawyer. *For Jonathan Edwin*, 1676. fol.* L, SP; TU, Y.
— Compendium of the laws. 1699. *See* Curson, Henry.
— Country-curate's advice. 1693. *See* Cornwallis, Henry.
38   — Cupid's love-lessons. [*London*], *for J. Clarke, senior*, 1683. 8°.* CM.
— Darkness of atheisme. 1683. *See* Care, Henry.
— Downfall of pride. [1656]. *See* Crouch, Humphrey.
— Draconica. 1687. *See* Care, Henry.
— Elegie sacred to the memory of Sir Edmund-bury Godfrey. 1678. *See* Care, Henry.
— England's jests refin'd and improv'd. 1687. *See* Crouch, Humphrey.
— English dictionary. 1642. *See* Cockeram, Henry.
39   — An epitome of history. *By M, Simmons*, 1661. 8°. SP.

40   — An extract out of a letter from a gentleman of quality. [*n.p.*], 1659. brs. L, O; CH.
41   — A fairing for young-men. [*n.p.*, 1656] brs. L.
— Galliæ speculum. 1673. *See* Care, Henry.
42   Entry cancelled.
— Liberty of conscience. 1687. *See* Care, Henry.
— Lisarda. 1670. *See* Cox, H.
— More cheap riches. 1660. *See* Church, Nathaniel.
43   — News from Dublin, relating. *For J. Wright*, 1647. 4°.* LT, O, LVF, HH; CN, WF.
44   Entry cancelled.
45   — The plain Englishman's historian. *For Langley Curtis*, 1679. 8°. T.C.I 330. O, LG, OC; CLC, WF, Y.
— Practice of the spiritual. 1685. *See* Consett, Henry.
46   — Remarks on the giving vomits. *Edinburgh*, 1700. 8°. LPO, EN.
— Set on the great pot. A sermon. 1694. *See* Cornwallis, Henry.
— Some reasons for separation. 1682. *See* Collins, Hercules.
— Some remarks upon a late nameless. [*n.p.*, 1696.] *See* Chamberlen, Hugh.
46A — The taming of the shrew. [*London.*] *for F. Coles* [1670?] brs. O; WF.
— Trials of love. 1691. *See* Cox, H.
— Treatise of measures. 1682. *See* Coggeshall, Henry.
— Word in season. 1679. *See* Care, Henry.
47   **C., I.** A brief relation of a wonderful accident, a dissolution. [*London*], *sold by Nath. Ponder*, 1679. 4°.* L; CH, MH, WF.
— Christs impressions. [*n.p.*], 1700. *See* Clark, James.
— De moribus. Oxoniæ, 1665. *See* Casa, Giovanni della.
— Ecclesia enucleata. 1684. *See* Chauncy, Isaac.
48   — An elegie offered up to the memory of . . . Mr. Jeremiah Burroughs. *By B. A.*, 1646. brs. LT, LVF; MH.
— Essay upon the inscription. Edinburgh, 1678. *See* Cunningham, James.
49   — The gyant whipt by his godmother. [1681.] brs. L, O, C, DCH; CH, NU, WF.
— Miracula mundi. To the king. Edinburgh, 1683. *See* Cunningham, James.
50   — The mystery of godlines. *For Philemon Stephens*, [1654.] 8°. L, O.
— New prognostication. Edinburgh, 1675. *See* Almanacs.
— Peters patern. 1659. *See* Caryl, Joseph.
— Plea for the antient gospel. 1697. *See* Chauncy, Isaac.
— Wits interpreter. 1655. *See* Cotgrave, John.
C., J. Antient and present state of Muscovy. 1698. *See* Crull, Jodocus.
— Answer to the animadversions. [*n.p.*], 1696. *See* Collier, Jeremy.
51   — An answer to the query of a deist. [*n.p.*, 1687?] cap., 4°.* NU, Y.
— Apology for the contemplations. 1687. *See* Cross, John, *alias* More.
52   — The araignment of hypocrisie. *Printed at London by John Crowch and T. W.*, 1652. 8°.* LT.
— Articles of Christian faith. [*n.p.*], 1689. *See* Cox, John.

—A branch of Quakerism cut off. 1676. *See* Cheney, John.

—Brief memorial of the Bible. 1688. *See* Chorley, Joseph.

—Brief observations concerning. 1668. *See* Child, *Sir* Josiah.

—Castramentation. 1642. *See* Cruso, John.

—Character of a country. 1649. *See* Cleveland, John.

—Character of a diurnal-maker. 1654. *See* Cleveland, John.

—Character of a moderate. [n.p., 1647.] *See* Cleveland, John.

52A —Christ's voice to England. Fifth edition. *By H. B. for J. Wright, J. Clark, W. Thackeray and T. Passinger,* 1683. 12°. CM.

—Conforming non-conformist. 1680. *See* Cheney, John.

—Contemplations on the life. Paris, 1685. *See* Cross, John.

—Copy of a printed letter. [n.p., 1672.] *See* Cressick, James.

—Defence of the absolution. [n.p., 1696.] *See* Collier, Jeremy.

—Defence of the true church. 1659. *See* Crook, John.

—Defensative armour. 1680. *See* Collinges, John.

—Denmark vindicated. 1694. *See* Crull, Jodocus.

52B —Discourse against transubstantiation. 1675. 8°. O.

—Divine services. 1663. *See* Clifford, James, *comp.*

52C —An elegy upon . . . Henry Gorge. *Printed,* 1674. brs. MH.

53 —An elegie upon the death of the most incomparable, M^ris. Katharine Philips. [1664]. brs. L; MH.

—Elegie, upon the death of the right honourable Anne. 1657. *See* Crouch, John.

—Englands troubles. 1644. *See* Cockayne, John.

54 Entry cancelled.

55 —An epithalamium upon the auspicious nuptials. [n.p.], 1658. 4°. O.

—Excellent woman discoursed. 1669. *See* Collinges, John.

—Full answer to that question. 1680. *See* Cheney, John.

—Great honour. 1697. *See* Child, *Sir* Josiah.

56 —A guide to the true religion. *For D. Newman,* 1668. 8°. NU.

57 ——[Anr. ed.] *Edinburgh, by Andrew Anderson,* 1669. 8°. ALDIS 1855. O, OC, EN, I; CLC, WF.

58 —The Independants catechism. Second edition. *Printed,* 1654. 4°.* LT.

58A —The informer; or, a treatise to shew. [*London*], printed, 1641. 8°.* CT; Y.

—Enquiry into the nature. 1696. *See* Cockburn, John.

—Intercourses of divine love. 1676. *See* Collinges, John.

—Interest of England in the matter. 1660. *See* Corbet, John.

59 —A lesson for all true Christians. *By and for A. M.,* [1670?]. brs. L, O, CM.

59A ——[Anr. ed.] *For F. Coles, J. Wright and J. Clarke,* [1674–79.] brs. O.

60 —A letter to the author of Milton's life. *By J. H.,* 1699. 4°.* O; MB, Y.

—Letter with animadversions. 1661. *See* Collop, John.

61 —The magistrates ministery. *Cambridge,* 1655. 8°. O.

62 —Magna Charta: containing. *For Francis Smith,* 1659. brs. LT.

—Medici Catholicon. 1656. *See* Collop, John.

63 Entry cancelled.

—Memoirs of Denmark. 1700. *See* Crull, Jodocus.

64 —The merry bell-man's out-cryes, or the city's o-yes. [n.p.], *printed,* 1655. 4°.* MH.

—Mixt poem. 1660. *See* Crouch, John.

—Modest plea for the Lord's day. 1669. *See* Collinges, John.

—Muses mistresse. 1660. *See* Cotgrave, John.

65 —A narration of the grievous visitation, and dreadfull desertion of M^r. Peacock. *By R. H. for Robert Milbourn,* 1641. 12°. L, CT.

66 —Naufragia publicanorum esse. *Typis Gulielmi Godbid, impensis Edovardi Dod,* 1657. 4°. L, C, SC.

—New fiction. 1661. *See* Croxton, James.

67 —A New-Years gift: being an help. *For Tho. Parkhurst,* 1690. brs. L, O.

68 —The Nonconformists plea for the conformists. *For James Cheak, and sold by Benj. Harris,* 1683. 4°. CT, BR; CH.

—Obedience to magistrats. 1683. *See* Clapham, Jonathan.

69 —The obligation which lyes upon ministers. *Printed,* 1679. 4°.* L, O, C, LW, D; CH, Y.

—Observations concerning trade. 1668. *See* Child, *Sir* Josiah.

—One sheet against. 1677. *See* Cheyney, John.

—Par nobile: two treatises. 1669. *See* Collinges, John.

—Philadelphia. 1669. *See* Crosbie, J.

70 —A pleasant comedy, called, The two merry milkmaids. Second edition. *By Tho. Johnson, to be sold by Nath. Brook, Francis Kirkman, Tho. Johnson, and Henry Marsh,* `1661. 4°. L, O, C, LG, EN; CH, CN, MH, WF, Y.

—Poems. [London], 1651. *See* Cleveland, John.

—Principles of the most ancient. 1692. *See* Conway, Anne, *viscountess.*

71 —Proposals for regulating the silver coyne. [*London,* 1695.] brs. L, LUG.

—Q. F. F. Q. S. A new fiction. 1661. *See* Croxton, James.

—Quakerism proved. 1677. *See* Cheyney, John.

—Quakerism subverted. 1677. *See* Cheyney, John.

72 —Quercus regia in agro Staffordiensi. [*London,* 1660?] brs. L.

72A —Reasons for passing the bill for relieving. [*London,* 1700]. brs. L, LUG.

—Reply to the absolution. [n.p.], 1696. *See* Collier, Jeremy.

—Rustick rampant. 1658. *See* Cleveland, John.

—Second part of the interest. 1660. *See* Corbet, John.

—Sermon preached at the kirk. Edinburgh, 1690. *See* Clerk, James.

72B —A short discourse against transubstantiation. 1675. 8°. O; MBA.

—Shibboleth of Quakerism. 1676. *See* Cheyney, John.

73 —A short treatise of the epidemical diseases. *Printed and are to be sold by R. Vaughan,* [1662?]. 8°.* L, CCA; MB, NC.

—Skirmish made. 1676. *See* Cheyney, John.

——Some arguments to prove. 1682. *See* Cheyney, John.

74 —The state of the Papist and Protestant proprieties in the kingdom of Ireland. *For Richard Baldwin*, 1689. 4°.* O, CT, LVF, HH, DT; CH, CN, MH, WF, Y.

—Strength in weakness. A sermon. 1676. *See* Collinges, John.

75 —Thesaurus brevium. *For C. Adams, J. Starkey, and T. Basset*, 1661. fol. L, LGI; WF.

76 ——Second edition. *By W. Rawlins, S. Roycroft, and M. Flesher, assigns of Richard and Edward Atkins, for T. Basset, R. Clavell, T. Dring, J. Robinson, A. Churchill, and S. Leigh*, 1687. fol. T.C.II 206. L, O, CJ, EN, DT; BBE, LC, MHL, NCL.

—To the King and both houses. 1664. *See* Coale, Joseph.

—Topicks in the laws. 1646. *See* Clayton, John.

—Touch-stone: whereby. 1660. *See* Collens, John.

—True discovery of the ignorance. 1654. *See* Camm, John.

—True information. [n.p.], 1664. *See* Crook, John.

—Twenty cases of conscience. [166-?] *See* Crook, John.

—Upon the death of that aged. [n.p., 1687.] *See* Cotton, John.

—Vindication of oaths. 1680. *See* Cheyney, John.

77 —A warning for swearers. *For W. Thackeray, T. Passenger, and W. VVhitwood*, [1677]. brs. L.

—Weavers pocket-book. 1675. *See* Collinges, John.

—Word in season. 1660. *See* Collens, John.

78 —The word of the Lord to awaken. *For the author*, 1658. 4°.* LF.

79 ——[Anr. ed.] [London, 1658.] 4°.* LF.

79A C., J. B. A Venice looking-glasse. [London], printed 1675. 4°.* LT, O, DT, GK; CH, CN, NU, WF, Y.

C., J. V. Epistle to the authour. [n.p.], 1663. *See* Canes, John Vincent.

—Fiat lux. [n.p.], 1661. *See* Canes, John Vincent.

—Τω καθολικω Stillingfleeton. Bruges, 1672. *See* Canes, John Vincent.

—Something in answer. 1667. *See* Canes, John Vincent.

—Three letters declaring. [n.p.], 1671. *See* Canes, John Vincent.

C., K. Good counsell, to the petitioners. [n.p., 1645.] *See* Chidley, Katherine.

—Ode in imitation of Pindar. 1681. *See* Chetwood, Knightly.

80 C., L. Amoret, or, policy defeated. *For Daniel Brown*, 1682. 4°.* T.C.I 476. L, O, CT; CH, CN, IU, MH.

—Fundamenta chymica. 1658. *See* Combach, Ludovicus.

—Generall charge. 1647. *See* Clarkson, Lawrence.

81 —A key to the Epsom love-letter. [n.p., 1675?] brs. OP.

82 Entry cancelled.

—Single eye. [n.p., 1650.] *See* Clarkson, Laurence.

83 —Some animadversions upon a case inserted in a book. *For the author*, 1682. fol.* L.

C., M. Discourse of the terrestrial paradise, 1666. *See* Carver, Marmaduke.

84 —A letter written by a Iesvite to the Qveens Majestie. *For Iohn Watkins*, [1642]. 4°.* LT, EC, SP; CH, CSS, WF, Y.

—Most true and exact relation. [n.p.], 1650. *See* Carter, Matthew.

85 —A treatise of the distempers. 1698. 8°. O.

86 —A word of remembrance. [London, 1663.] brs. O.

86A C., N. An account of the chief points in controversie. 1696. 8°. O

—Bristol drollery. 1674. *See* Crutwell, N.

87 —Carmen elegiacum, Englands elegie. [London, 1643.] 4°.* LT.

88 —The great necessity and advantage of preserving our own manufactures. *For T. Newborough*, 1697. 8°.* L, LUG, DT; MH, MIU, NC, WF.

—Modest and true account of the chief. Antwerp, 1696. *See* Colson, Nicholas.

89 —A rule for ministers and people. *For Giles Calvert*, 1654. 4°.* LT; Y.

—Sermon preached at the ordination. 1681. *See* Coxe, Nehemiah.

89A —The weavers case stated. *For E. Whitlock*, 1697. 8°.* CCA.

90 C., O. The conduct and character of Count Nicholas Serini. *For Sam. Speed*, 1664. 12°. L, O, C, P; CH, MH, WF, Y.

C., P. A brief description by way. 1655. *See* Cotton, Mrs. Priscilla.

91 —A collection of many wonderful prophecies. *For Rich. Baldwin*, 1691. 4°. T.C.II 349. L, O, C, P, CT; WF, Y.

—Complementum fortunatarum. 1662. *See* Cardonnel, Pierre de.

92 —An exact collection of many wonderful prophesies. *For Thomas Salusbury*, 1689. 4°.* L, LWL, EN; CH, MH, TU, WF, Y.

93 Entry cancelled.

94 —The inquisition of a sermon . . . by Robert Daborne. Waterford, by Thomas Bourke, 1644. 4°. DM.

—Introductio ad chronologiam. Oxoniæ, 1691. *See* Holder, William.

95 —Mutatus polemo revised. *For Robert White*, 1650. 4°. LT, O, OB, OC; CLC, MIU, NU, Y.

—Short and impartial view. [n.p.], 1699. *See* Fletcher, Andrew.

—Tunbrigalia. 1684. *See* Causton, Peter.

—Visitation of love unto all. 1661. *See* Cotton, Mrs. Priscilla.

96 C., R. The accomplished commander. *For J. Taylor, and S. Holford*, 1689. 12°. T.C.II 276. L, O; CH.

—Answer to Richard Allen's essay. 1697. *See* Claridge, Richard.

97 —Arcana Parliamentaria. *For M. Gilliflower*, 1685. 12°. T.C.II 138. L, O, CCA, LL, GU; CH, CN, MH, NC, WF, YL.

—Avona. 1675. *See* Cooke, Roger.

—Brief survey of the Lord of Derry. Paris, 1658. *See* Smith, Richard, bp.

—Carmen Deo nostro. Paris, 1652. *See* Crashaw, Richard.

—Certain prayers and graces. 1687. *See* Crowley, Robert.

98-100 Entries cancelled.

101 —The Conformists charity to Dissenters. *By J. R. for John Salusbury*, 1689. 4°. T.C.II 283. L, O, C, DT; CN, MH, NU, WF, Y.

102 —The Conformists sayings. *For the author*, 1690. 4°. T.C.II 332. L, CT; CH, MH, Y.
—Cry of Newgate. 1662. *See* Crane, Richard.
—Diana, Dutchess of Mantva. 1679. *See* Carleton, Rowland.
—Discovrse concerning the trve nation. 1642. *See* Cudworth, Ralph.

103 —Divine hymns, and other extempory poems. *For the author*, 1695. 8°.* L.
—Downfal of Anti-Christ. 1644. *See* Carpenter, Richard.

104 —Eight very serious and considerable queries. *Printed*, 1646. 4°.* LT, CS, SP, EN; CLC, NU.

104A —An elegie on the death of . . . Robert Blake. *For Tho. Vere and W. Gilbertson*, 1657, brs. L; MH.
—God's holy name magnified. [n.p.], 1665. *See* Crane, Richard.

105 —The harmony of the muses. *By T. W. for William Gilbertson*, 1654. 8°. CH, MH.
—His Majesties propriety. 1665. *See* Clavell, Robert.
—Lamentation over thee. 1665. *See* Crane, Richard.

106 —A letter to a friend concerning usury. *Printed*, 1690. 8°.* L, HH; LC.
—Lithobolia. 1698. *See* Chamberlayne, Richard.

107 —The Long Parliament is not revived. *For N. W.*, 1660. 4°.* LT, O, LL, OC, HH; CH, CN, MH, NU, WF, Y.

108 —Minerva, or, the art of weaving. *For Joseph Moxon, and sold at his shop; and by James Moxon*, 1677. 4°. T.C.I 273. L, LVD; CH, NC, Y.

109 —Μυθολογια, sive quarundam tabularum explicatio. *For C. Coningsby*, 1693. 8°. T.C.II 455. O.
—Notion of schism. 1676. *See* Conold, Robert.

110 Entry cancelled.
—Poetica stromata. [n.p.], 1648. *See* Corbet, Richard, *bp*.

111 —The present condition of Dublin in Ireland. *For Henry Crips, and Lodowick Lloyd*, 1649. 4°.* LT, C; CH.

112 —The prodigals pilgrimage; a poem. *For J. Nutt*, 1698. 4°.* L; MH.

112A —The Protestant's plain confession. 1645. 8°. YM.

113 —Quæries propounded to George Fox. *For Anna Brewster*, 1669. 4°. L.

113A —Salvation laid on its right foundation. *Printed, & sold by R. Baldwin*, 1698. 4°.* T.C.III 52. L.

114 —A scholasticall discourse, demonstrating. *By J. G. for R. Royston*, 1663. 4°.* L, O, OC, CS, OM; MIU, NU, WF.
—Serious considerations. [n.p.], 1641. *See* Cotton, *Sir* Robert Bruce.

115 —Several choice prophecyes. 1666. 4°. O; WF.
—Something spoken. [1660.] *See* Crane, Richard.
—Treatise concerning the regulation. 1696. *See* Coke, Roger.

116 —The triumphant weaver. [*London*], *for J. Deacon*, 1682. 4°. T.C.I 509. L; MH.

117 —Trve newes from Hull. *For Fr. Wright*, [1642]. 4°.* LT; Y.

118 —A trve report of the late good svccesse in Ireland. *By Matthew Simmons*, 1642. 4°.* LT.
—Union of Christ. 1642. *See* Cudworth, Ralph.

—Vermiculars destroyed. 1690. *See* Clark, R.
—Warming stone. [1670.] *See* Carew, *Sir* Richard.
—Way to happiness. 1641. *See* Crofts, Robert.

C., S. Almanack for . . . 1660. Cambridg [Mass.], 1660. *See under* Almanacs. Cheever, Samuel.
—Anniversary upon the xxxth. 1660. *See* Crown, S.

119–20 Entries cancelled.
—Chief principles. 1668. *See* Cradock, Samuel.
—Christ alone. 1693. *See* Crisp, Samuel.
—Christian plea. [1642.] *See* Chidley, Samuel.
—Collection of several treatises in answer. [n.p.], 1672. *See* Cressy, Hugh Paulin.
—Englands covenant. 1643. *See* Clarke, Samuel.
—Epistle apologetical. [n.p.], 1674. *See* Cressy, Hugh Paulin.

121 —The famous and delectable history of Cleocriton. *By J. B. for Charls Tyus*, [166–?]. 4°. L; CH.
—Fanaticism fanatically imputed. [n.p.], 1672. *See* Cressy, Hugh Paulin.
—First question. 1686. *See* Cressy, Hugh Paulin.
—Grand impostor detected. Edinburgh, 1673. *See* Colville, Samuel.
—Historian's guide. 1676. *See* Clarke, Samuel.

122 —A horrible and bloody plot to murder Sir Thomas Fairfax. *By B. Alsop, for E. Griffin*, 1646. 4°.* LT, SP; CH, WF.

123 Entry cancelled.

123A —A new and true description of the world. *For the author, S. C.*, 1673. WF.
—Non est inventus returned. [n.p.], 1662. *See* Cressy, Hugh Paulin.
—I. Question. Why are you. 1686. *See* Cressy, Hugh Paulin.
—Reports of sevral [*sic*] cases. 1688. *See* Carter, Samuel,
—Roman-Catholick doctrines. [n.p.], 1663. *See* Cressy. Hugh Paulin.
—Scotch Hudibras. 1692. *See* Colville, Samuel.

124 Entry cancelled.
—The sinfulness and cure. 1676. *See* Charnock, Stephen.

125 —The XXXth of January. Or, an anniversary. *Printed at Paris*, 1652. 4°.* TU.

126 —The truth and excellence of the Christian religion. *For John Gellibrand*, 1685. 8°. L, C, LW, CK, SP; CH, Y.
—Whiggs supplication. Edinburgh, 1687. *See* Colville, Samuel.

C., T. Advantages which will. 1668. *See* Culpeper, Thomas.
—Animadversions on George Whitehead's. 1694. *See* Crisp, Thomas.

127 —Another famous victorie obtained by His Excellencie the Earle of Essex. *Decemb. 6. for Ioseph Neale*, [1642]. 4°.* MADAN 1104. LT, O; CLC.
—Babel's builders. 1681. *See* Crisp, Thomas.
—Brief discovery of the corruption. 1647. *See* Collier, Thomas.

128 —A brief relation of the life and death of Elizabeth Braytwjaite [*sic*]. [*London*, 1684]. cap., 8°.* CH.

128A —A brief remembrancer. *By E. T. and R. H. for William Miller,* 1672. brs. L.

—Brief tract. 1692. *See* Chafie, Thomas.

129 —The Christian's crown of glory. *For Tho. Passenger,* 1670/1. 8°. T.C.I 64. O.

—Church-catechism. 1681. *See* Comber, Thomas.

130 Entry cancelled.

—Discourse of duels. 1687. *See* Comber, Thomas.

—Discovery of the accursed thing. [n.p., 1695.] *See* Crisp, Thomas.

131 Entry cancelled.

—Examiner examined: being. 1691. *See* Comber, Thomas.

132 —A glasse for the times. *By Robert Ibbitson,* 1648. 4°.* LT, LCL; MM, NU, WF.

—Glory of Christ. 1647. *See* Collier, Thomas.

133 —Great news from Dublin: in a letter. *Sold by Richard Janeway,* 1690. brs. O; Y.

134 —Great news from Falmouth. colop: *For Timothy Iohnson,* 1690. cap. 4°.* CH.

—Greek English lexicon. 1658. *See* Caryl, Joseph.

—Huls pillar of providence. 1644. *See* Coleman, Thomas.

135 —An impartial examination and refutation of . . . Thomas Moor. *For Tho. Parkhurst,* 1698. 4°.* T.C.III 86. L; Y.

—Isagoge ad Dei providentiam. 1672. *See* Crane, Thomas.

—Labyrinthvs Cantvariensis. *Paris,* 1658. *See* Carwell, Thomas.

—Morall discourses. 1655. *See* Culpeper, *Sir* Thomas.

136 —A more full and exact relation from Reading. *By R. Oulton, and G. Dexter. Aprill 21,* 1643. 4°.* L, O; MH.

137 —A more true and an exacter relation of the battaile. *[London], for Edward Blackmore, Novem.* 26. 1642. 4°.* LT; Y.

138 —Myn Heer. T. Van C's answer. *[n.p.,* 1690.] cap., 4°.* O, CT; WF.

139 —The new atlas: or, travels and voyages. *For J. Cleave, and A. Roper,* 1698. 8°. T.C.III 138. L, LA, OM; CH, CM, PL, RPJ, WF, Y.

140 ——[Anr. ed.] *For J. Cleave, and A. Roper,* 1699. 8°. RPJ.

—Period of humane life. 1688. *See* Cruso, Timothy.

—Prospect of divine providence. 1672. *See* Crane, Thomas.

—Red ribbond; news. 1647. *See* Coxcombe, T.

141 —The schismaticke sifted. *By R. A. for S. W.,* 1646. 4°.* LT, O, HH, DT; MH, NU.

—The sixth part of Babel's-builders. *[London?* 168–]. *See* Crisp, Thomas.

142 —Strange newes from the north. *By J. Clowes, June* 11, 1650. 4°.* LT.

142A —A true and exact relation of the proceedings of . . . army in Cheshire. *For M. Batt, Octob.* 5. 1642. 4°.* LT, EC; CN, MH.

143 —Vindiciæ pharmacopolæ; or, an answer. *[London,* 1675?] brs. L.

—Vox & votum populi. 1669. *See* Cooper, Thomas.

C., W. Account of the nature, causes. 1696. *See* Cockburn, William.

144 Entry cancelled.

—An alarum to England. 1700. *See* Carter, William.

145 —Archerie reviv'd. *Edinburgh, by the heir of Andrew Anderson,* 1677. 4°.* ALDIS 2096. HH, EN.

—Bespotted Iesuite. 1641. *See* Crashaw, William.

145A —The character of a Church of England man. 1688. 8°. OC.

—Character of a trimmer. 1688. *See* Halifax, George Savile, *marquis of.*

—Christian rules. [n.p.], 1659. *See* Clifford, William.

146 —Clavis calendria. *For John Nutt,* 1700. 8°. L, O, LW, CS, YM; CLC, WF, Y.

147 Entry cancelled.

148 —Colonell [Ralph] Weldens taking of Inch-house. *For Matthew Walbancke,* 30 *March,* 1646. 4°.* LT; WF.

—Decimarum & oblationum tabula. 1658. *See* Crashaw, William.

149 —A description of love. 1653. 4°. DC.

150 —A discourse (by way of essay) humbly offer'd. *For the authour,* 1695/6. 4°.* L, LUG; MH, NC, WF, Y.

151 —A discourse for a king and Parliament. *For G. Bedell and T. Collins,* 1660. 4°.* LT, O, CS, HH; CH, CN, MH, NU, WF, Y.

—Englands interest by trade. 1671. *See* Carter, William.

—An exposition on the fourth chapter. 1693. *See* Cross, Walter.

152 —The first [second] part of the renowned historie of Fragosa. Second edition. *By Bernard Alsop,* 1646. 2v. 4°. L; MB, NC.

—Gesta grayorum. 1688. *See* Canning, William.

153 —The great designs of parliaments. *[London,* 1695?] brs. L; MH.

154 —The history of the Commons warre of England. *For Joshua Coniers,* 1662. 8°. L, O, CT, YM; CN, LC, OWC, WF.

155 —The history of the most renowned Fragosa. Second edition. *By E. Alsop, and Robert Wood, by the assignes of Thomas Cook, to be sold by Charles Tynson,* 1663. 4°. CH.

156 —The intentions of the army discovered. *Printed,* 1647. 4°.* LT, DT; Y.

157 —A letter from His Excellencies qvarters, of a discovery. *By Barnard Alsop, August* 27, 1646. 4°.* LT, O, AN; WF.

—Letter written to Dr. Burnet. 1685. *See* Coventry, *Sir* William.

—Little manval. *Paris,* 1669. *See* Clifford, William.

158 —A manvall of prayers, collected, for the use of Sir Ralph Duttons regiment. *Oxford, by Henry Hall for the author,* 1462 [i.e. 1642/3]. 8°. MADAN 1260. O.

—Moderate enquirer. 1659. *See* Caton, William.

159 —A more full relation of the continved svccesses of . . . Fairfax. *For Francis Coles,* 1645[6]. 4°.* LT, O, AN; Y.

160 —Mr. George Keith, at Turner's Hall . . . contradicting Mr. George Keith at the Tolbooth. *Printed and sold by E. Whitlock,* 1696. 4°.* L; Y.

161 —Mr. Keith no Presbyterian nor Quaker. *Printed, and sold by E. Whitlock,* 1696. 4°.* L; MH, RPJ.

161A —The new light. 1664. 4°. LF.

—Particular account of this last siege. 1676. *See* Carr, William.

—Petition of. [n.p.], 1641. *See* Castell, William.

—Philosophical epitaph of. 1673. *See* Cooper, William.

162 —Poems on several occasions. *For the author, and published by R. Taylor,* 1684. 8°. T.C.II 85. L, LVD; CLC, MH.

163 —The Prince of Wales his coming to Yarmouth. *By Robert Austin, July 27.* 1647. 4°.* LT, DT.

164 —A proclamation to all of all sorts. [n.p.], *printed,* 1643. 4°.* LT, O; CLC, MIU, NU.

—Purpura Anglicana, being. 1689. *See* Cole, William.

165 —Reflections on a libel, intituled, A plea for the apothecaries. *For Richard Chiswell,* 1671. 4°.* L, O, C; CH, NAM.

166 —The renowned history of Fragosa. *By E. Alsop,* 1656. 4°. L, O.

—The reply of. [1677.] *See* Carter, William.

167 —A schoole of nurture. *For Simon Miller,* 1656. 8°. O.

168 —A sermon on the 2nd of February 1674. *For T. Cockerill,* 1674. 4°.* LW.

168A —A short discourse of the year. 1664. 8°. O.

169 —The siege of Vienna; a poem. *For H. Hills jun.,* 1685. 4°.* L, CJ; CH, MH, Y.

170 —Some observations on Thomas Curtis. *By J. Bradford,* 1697. 4°. O, LF.

—Summ of two sermons. 1692. *See* Cross, Walter.

—Summary of certain papers. 1685. *See* Carter, William.

171 —Trades destruction is England's ruine. *Printed,* 1659. 4°.* LT; NC, Y.

172 —The treatie for the surrendring of Exeter. *For Matthew Walbancke, April 9,* 1646. 4°.* LT, O, DT.

173 —Trepidantium malleus. *Printed, and sold by E. Whitlock,* 1696. 4°.* O; Y.

—Turning table, 1662. *See* Carleton, William.

—Usurpations of France. 1695. *See* Carter, William.

173A —A vindication of the true Episcopal religion. *For W. Chandler,* 1681. 4°.* NU, Y.

C., Z. Discourse of patronage. 1675. *See* Cawdrey, Zachary.

—Fraterna correptio. 1655. *See* Crofton, Zachary.

174 —Marriage-musick. [London, 1670?] brs. L.

—People's need. 1657. *See* Crofton, Zachary.

—Pursuit of peace. 1660. *See* Crofton, Zachary.

175 The C—'s petition to the parliament of women. *For A. Chamberlain,* 1684. brs. MC.

176 C. C. the Covenanter vindicated from perjurie. *By T. Paine,* 1644. 4°. LT, O, C, CE, HH; CH, NU, WCL, WF, Y.

177 C. R. in a cloud. [n.p.], *printed,* 1647. brs. LT; CH.

178 **Ca, W.** A sad and serious discovrse upon a terrible letter. *For Giles Calvert,* 1648[9]. 4°.* LT, O, OC, HH; CH, MH, Y.

179 The cabal. Now the reformer. [London, 1679/80.] brs. L, O, HH; CH, MH, NN, WF, Y.

180 The cabal of Romish ghosts. *For Norman Nelson,* 1680. fol.* L, O, C, HH; CH, NU, WF, Y.

181 The cabal of several notorious priests and Jesuits. [London], *printed,* 1679. fol.* T.C.I 361. L, O, C, BR, HH; CH, MH, NU, WF, Y.

182 The cabal: or, a voice of the politicks. [London], *for J. W. J. C. W. T. and T. P.,* [1680?]. brs. L, HH.

183 Cabala, mysteries of state. *For M. M. G. Bedell, and T. Collins,* 1654. 4°. LT, CT, NPL, YM, EN, GK; CH, CN, MHL, TU, WF, Y.

Cabala, or. 1663. *See* Birkenhead, *Sir* John.

184 Cabala, sive scrinia sacra: mysteries of state. *For G. Bedel, and T. Collins,* 1654. 4°. L, O, C, EN, DT; CLC, MH, NU, WF, Y.

185 —[Anr. ed.] *For G. Bedell and T. Collins,* 1663. fol. L, O, C, CT, EN; CH, MH, NU, WF, Y.

186 —Third edition. *For Tho. Sawbridge, Mat. Gillyflower, Ric. Bentley, Mat. Wooton, and Geo. Conniers,* 1691. fol. L, O, C, EN, DT; CH, CN, LC, MH, Y.

Cabbalistical dialogue. 1682. *See* Helmont, F. M. van.

187 A cabinet of choice jewels. [London], *by J. M. for J. Deacon,* 1688. 12°.* O.

187A —[Anr. ed.] *By J. W. for B. Deacon* [c. 1690]. 8°. CHRISTIE-MILLER.

188 A cabinet of grief. *For J. Blare,* 1688. 8°.* O.

Cabinet of Hell. 1696. *See* Nicholetts, C.

189 The cabinet of the Jesuits secrets opened. *For Jonathan Robinson, and George Wells,* 1679. 4°.* T.C.I 351. L, O, C, LIL, ENC; CH, LC, MH, NU, Y.

190 Entry cancelled.

191 **Caddy, William.** To the supream authority, the Parliament. . . . The humble petition of. [London, 1654.] brs. LT.

192 **Cade, Anthony.** Conscience it's [sic] nature and corruption. *For John Williams.* 1661. 4°. L, O, CSSX, GU; MB, WF.

193 **Cade, John, Capt.** The last speeches and confession of. *Imprinted at London, by Iane Coe,* 1645. 4°.* LT, O.

193A **Cade, John, Quaker.** The true light owned. *Printed and sold by T. Sowle,* 1699. 4°.* L, LF; PSC, Y.

194 **Cade, William.** The foundation of Popery shaken. *By T. M. for Robert Clavel,* 1678. 4°.* T.C.I 329. L, O, CT, MC, EN; CH, CN, NU, WF, Y.

195 **Cademan, Thomas.** The distiller of London. *For Tho. Huntington and Wil. Nealand,* 1652. 8°. L, O, DC.

196 —The Earle of Bedfords passage to the highest court. *For Hugh Perry,* 1641. 4°.* LT, O; MH, WF.

197 Entry cancelled.

198 **Cæsar, Caius Julius.** C. Julii Cæsaris quæ exstant. *Impensis Abelis Swall,* 1693. 8°. L, O, C; MB, NC, WF.

199 —Commentaries. *By R. Daniel, to be sold by Henry Twyford, Nathaniel Ekins and Iohn Place,* 1655. fol. L, O, C, LUS, E; CH, IU, MH, WF, Y.

200 ——[Anr. ed.] *In the Savoy, by Tho. Newcomb, for Jonathan Edwin,* 1677. fol. T.C.I 260. L, O, CT, LG, AU; CH, CN, PL, TU, Y.

201 ——[Anr. ed.] *In the Savoy, by Edward Jones, for Matthew Gillyflower; and Richard Bently,* 1695. fol. L, O, C, LUS, RPL; CLC, MBA, NC, PL, WF, Y.

202 —The compleat captain: or, an abridgement. *For S. Briscoe,* 1694. 8°. O, C, OC, EC; MIU, Y.

202A Entry cancelled. *See* Somner, William.

203   **[Caesar, Charles.]** Numerus infaustus. A short view. *For Ric. Chiswell*, 1689. 8°. O, LW; CH, CN, WF.

204   **Caesar, Peter.** The speech and confession of. *For Charles . . . [sic] Gustavus*, 1664. 4°.* O.

205   Cæsarem & fortunam vehis, paraphras'd. colop: *For G. Wallup*, 1690. brs. L; TU, Y.

        Caesarion. 1685. *See* Saint-Réal, Cæsar Vischard de.

        Cæsar's due. [n.p.], 1679. *See* Fox, George.

        Cæsar's penny. [n.p., 1655?] *See* Farnworth, Richard.

206   **Caffyn, Matthew.** The deceived, and deceiving Quakers discovered. *By R. I. for Francis Smith*, 1656. 4°. LT, CT, LF; WF.

206A   —Envy's bitterness corrected. 1674. 4°.* O.

207   —Faith in Gods promises. [n.p.], 1660. 4°. LF; NHC.

207A   —A raging wave foming. 1675. 4°.* O.

207B   **Caillières, Jacques de.** The courtier's calling. *By I. C. to Richard Tonsen*, 1675. 12°. T.C.I 198. L, O, CK, BP; CH, CN, LC, MW, Y.

208   **Cailloüé, Jean.** Traité du jubilé romain. 1700. 12°. MR; CH.

208A   Caines bloudy race. *For Thomas Simmons.* 1657. 4°. L, O; RPJ.

209   Cains off-spring demonstrated. colop: *For Thomas Simmons*, 1659. cap., 4°. L, LF; PH.

209A   **Calamy, Benjamin.** The case of compelling men to the sacrament. 1684. 4°. SA.

210   —Conseil évangélique aux consciences. *Imprimé chez George Wells*, 1683. 8°. OC, CS; WF.

210A   ——[Anr. ed.] —, 1684. 8°. T.C.II 60. BN.

211   —A discourse about a scrupulous conscience. *For Rowland Reynolds*, 1683. 4°.* T.C.II 12. L, O, C; CSU, MH, NU, WF, Y.

212   ——Second edition. —, 1683. 4°. L, C, CS; CH, NIC, TU, Y.

213   [–] ——[Anr. ed.] *For T. Basset, and B. Tooke*, 1684. 4°.* L, O, C, OC, ON; CH, MH, NU, WF, Y.

214   —A sermon preached before the . . . Lord Mayor . . . 13th of July, 1673. *For Nathaniel Brooke*, 1673. 4°.* T.C.I 146. L, O, C, LG, CT; CH, NU, PL, WF, Y.

215   —A sermon preached . . . 29th of May 1682. *By J. M. for Walter Kettilby*, 1682. 4°.* T.C.I 493. L, O, C, DT; CH, NPT, NU, PU, WF, Y.

216   ——Second edition. —, 1682. 4°.* L, C, LG; CH, MH, NU, PU, V, WF, Y.

217   —A sermon preached . . . 9th of September, being the day of thanksgiving. *By R. E. for W. Kettilby*, 1683. 4°.* T.C.II 38. L, O, C, LG; CH, MH, NU, WF, Y.

218   —A sermon preached . . . 30th of September, 1683. *For W. Kettilby*, 1683. 4°.* L, O, C, CT, DT; CH, CN, MH, NU, WF, Y.

219   —A sermon preached . . . September the second, 1684. *For Walter Kettilby*, 1685. 4°.* T.C.II III. L, O, C, LG, CT; CH, CU, MBA, NU, WF, Y.

220   —A sermon preached . . . December 2, 1684. *For John Baker*, 1685. 4°.* T.C.II 112. L, O, C, LG, CT; CH, CLC, WF, Y.

221   —Sermons preached upon several occasions. *By M. Flesher, for Henry Dickenson and Richard Green, in Cambridge, to be sold by Walter Davis*, 1687. L, O, C, LL, DC; CH, CN, LC, NGT, WF.

222   ——Second edition. *By M. Clark, for Henry Dickenson and Richard Green, in Cambridge, to be sold by Walter Davis*, 1690. 8°. L, O, CPE, E, DT; CLC, CU, MIU, Y.

223   ——Third edition. *By John Darby*, 1700. 8°. L, C, OME, LW, EC; CH, IU, NN, NU, WF.

224   [–] Some considerations about the case of scandal. *By H. Hills jun. for T. Basset; B. Tooke; and F. Gardiner*, 1683. 4°. L, O, CT, GU, DT; CH, CN, MH, NU, WF, Y.

225   [–] ——[Anr. ed.] *For T. Basset, and B. Took*, 1685. 4°. L, C, OCC; CH, WF, Y.

        [Calamy, Edmund, *elder*.] Answer to a book entitvled, An humble remonstrance. 1641. *See* Marshall, Stephen.

226   [–] An answer to the articles against Master Calamy. *For William Bond*, 1642. 4°.* LT, O, C, HH; CH, MH, NU, WF, Y.

227   —The art of divine meditation. *For Tho. Parkhurst, to be sold at his shop, and by J. Collier*, 1680. 8°. T.C.I 415. L, C, LCL, ENC, E; CH, MH, NU, WSC, Y.

228   —The city remembrancer. *By S. G. for John Rothwell*, 1657. 8°. LT, LP; CN, NU.

229   —The doctrine of the bodies fragility. *For Joseph Moore*, 1655. 4°.* LT, O; MH, NPT, WF.

230   [–] The door of trvth opened. *For Christopher Meredith*, 1645. 4°.* LT, O, LG, CS, DT; CH, MH, NU, WF, Y.

231   —Eli trembling for fear of the ark. *Oxford, printed*, 1662. 4°.* NU, Y.

232   ——[Anr. ed.] —, 1663. 4°.* L, O, C, LL; CH, CLC, NU, WF.

233   —Englands antidote. *By I. L. for Christopher Meredith*, 1645. 4°.* L, O, C, EN, DT; CH, CN, MH, NU, TU, WF, Y.

234   ——[Anr. ed.] *By A. Miller for Christopher Meredith*, 1652. 4°. LW, CPE; CH, MB, NPT, TU, WF, Y.

235   —Englands looking-glasse. *By I. Raworth, for Chr. Meredith*, 1641. 4°. LT; CN, MM, WF.

236   ——[Anr. ed.] —, 1642. 4°.* O, C, LCL, DC, EN; MH, NC, PBL, WF, Y.

237   ——[Anr. ed.] —, 1642. 4°. LT, O, OC, DT; CH, MH, NU, WF, Y.

238   [–] ——[Anr. ed.] *For Cadwallader Greene*, 1642. 4°.* L, O, CJ, OC; CN, CU, MB, MIU, TU.

239   ——Fourth edition. —, 1642. 4°.* L, O, EN; IU, LC, MH, TU, Y.

240   —Evidence for Heaven. *For Simon Miller*, 1657. 4°. NU.

241   —An exact collection of farewel sermons. [n.p.], *printed*, 1662. 8°. L; MH, Y.

242   —The farewell sermons of the late London Ministers, . . . August 17th 1662. *Printed*, 1662. 8°. LW, CS, CT; CU, MH, NU, VC, WF.

243   —Farewel sermons preached by. *Printed*, 1663. 4°. O, C, LG, LW; CH, CU, MIU, NU, WF.

244   —The fixed saint. *Printed*, 1662. 4°.* O, WCA, DT; NU, WF.

245   —Old Mr. Edmund Calamy's former and latter sayings. *For W. B.*, 1674. brs. L.

246   Entry cancelled.

247 —The godly mans ark. *For John Hancock, (brother to the late deceased Eliz. Moore). And for Tho. Parkhurst,* 1657. 8°. LT, LCL, LW, EN; CH, MH, NU, WF.

248 ——Second edition. —, 1658. 8°. L, O, CPE, LCL; CN, Y.

248A ——Third edition. *For John Hancock and for Thomas Parkhurst,* 1661. 8°. CT; CU, IU.

249 ——Fifth edition. —, 1667. 8°. L, DC.

250 ——Sixth edition. —, 1669. 8°. L, AU; CLC, NU.

250A ——Seventh edition. —, 1672. 8°. LSC; NPT.

251 ——Eighth edition. *For John Hancock, (brother . . .) and for Thomas Parkhurst,* 1678. 12°. T.C.I 336. L; WF.

251A ——[Anr. ed.] *For John Hancock,* 1687. 12°. T.C.II 9, PU.

252 ——Seventeenth edition. *For Thomas Parkhurst, and for John Hancock,* 1693. 12°. L; IU, MH.

253 —Gods free mercy to England. *For Christopher Meredith,* 1642. 4°. LT, O, C, EN, DT; CH, CU, MH, NU, WF, Y.

254 —The great danger of covenant-refusing. *By M.F. for Christopher Meredith,* 1646. 4°.* LT, O, LCL, EN, DT; CH, LC, MH, NU, Y.

255 —The happinesse of those who sleep in Jesus. *By J.H. for Nathanael Webb,* 1662. 4°.* L, O, LW; MHS, NU, WF, Y.

256 —An indictment against England. *By I.L. for Christopher Meredith,* 1645. 4°. LT, O, C, ENC, DT; CH, MH, NU, WF, Y.

257 —A just and necessary apology. *For Christopher Meredith,* 1646. 4°.* LT, O, P, HH, DT; CH, NPT, NU, WF, Y.

258 —Master Edmund Calamies leading case. *Printed,* 1663. 4°.* L, O, HH, CCA, LSC.

259 —The monster of sinful self-seeking. *By J.G. for Nath: Webb, and Will: Grantham,* 1655. 4°.* O, C, LP, LW; CH, NU, RPB, WF, Y.

260 [–] The noble-mans patterne. *[London], by G.M. for Christopher Meredith,* 1643. 60pp. 4°. O, LCL.

261 ——[Anr. ed.] *By G.M. for Christopher Meredith,* 1643. 59pp. 4°. LT, O, C, LCL, DT; CH, MH, NU, WF, Y.

262 —A patterne for all. *For Edward Brewster,* 1658. 4°.* LT, O, LW, ENC, DT; CH, NP, NU, WF, Y.

262A —The righteous mans death lamented. *Printed,* 1662. 8°.* WCA; CLC.

263 —Saints memorials. *Printed,* 1674. 8°. L, O; NU, WF.

264 —The saint's rest. *By A. M.,* 1651. 4°.* LT, O, LSC, LW; CLC, MB, NNG, NU, OWC.

264A ——[Anr. ed.] *By A. Miller,* 1656. 4°.* CH.

265 —The saints transfiguration. *For Joseph Cranford,* 1655. 4°.* L, O, C, OC, ENC; CH, MH, NU, WF, Y.

266 —A sermon preached . . . Aug. 24. 1651. *For G. Horton,* [1651]. 4°.* L; NU.

267 —A sermon preached at Aldermanberry-Church, Dec. 28. 1662. *Oxford, printed,* 1663. 4°.* MADAN 2635. L, C, OC, LW, MR; CH, CU, MH, NU, WF, Y.

268 [–] Two solemne covenants made between God and man. *For Thomas Banks,* 1647. 4°.* LT, O, CS, LW, BR; NU.

269 [**Calamy, Edmund, younger.**] A discourse concerning the rise and antiquity of cathedral worship. *Printed, and are to be sold by A.Baldwin,* 1699. 4°.* T.C.III 135. L, O, CS, LCL, EN; CU, MH, NU, WF, Y.

270 Entry cancelled.

271 —A funeral sermon, preach'd at the interment of Mr. Samuel Stephens. *For Abraham Chandler,* 1694. 4°.* T.C.II 490. L, O, C, LW, E; CLC, WF.

272 —A funeral sermon, preached upon occasion of the decease of Mrs. Elizabeth Williams. *For J.Lawrence,* 1698. 8°. T.C.III 90. L, LW, E; MH, MWA, NP, RPB.

273 —A practical discourse concerning vows. 1692. 8°. L, LCL; MH.

274 ——[Anr. ed.] *By Geo. Larkin jun. to be sold by John Lawrence,* 1697. 8°. T.C.III 19. L, O, CT, P, E; CLC, NPT, NU, PL, WF, Y.

275 —A sermon preach'd . . . Feb. 20, 1698/9. *For John Lawrence,* 1699. 8°. T.C.III 120. L, LG, EC, E, DT; CH, MBC, MH.

276 A calculate of tobacco. [*London,* 1694?] brs. L.

Calculation for . . . 1645. [1645.] *See under* Almanacs. Jessop, Henry.

277 [**Calder, Robert.**] A letter to a Non-conformist minister. *For B. Tooke,* 1677. 12°. T.C.I 287. L, O, CS, OCC; MH.

[–] Scotch Presbyterian eloquence. 1692. *See* Crockat, Gilbert.

278 [**Calderwood, David.**] The pastor and the prelate. Second edition. *Edinburgh, for Alexander Henderson,* 1692. 4°.* ALDIS 3236. L, O, EN, GU; CH, MH, NPT, NU, RPJ.

279 —The true history of the church of Scotland. [*Edinburgh?*], *printed,* 1678. fol. L, O, CT, EN, AU; CH, CN, MH, NU, WF, Y.

280 ——[Anr. ed.] —, 1680. fol. L, LW, CT, MR, DT; MBC, MH, PU, TSM, Y.

280A ——[Anr. ed.] *Sold by R. Baldwin,* 1681. fol. T.C.I 418. LW.

281 ——[Anr. ed.] [*Holland?*], *printed,* 1704 [1678]. fol. HH; MH.

Caleb's inheritance. 1656. *See* Warren, Edward.

282 Caledonia; or, the pedler turn'd merchant. *Printed and sold by the booksellers of London and Westminster,* 1700. 4°.* T.C.III 173. L, O, EN, DT; CH, CN, LC, MH, NN, Y.

283-4 Entries cancelled.

285 Caledonia triumphans: a panegyrick. *Edinburgh, by the heirs and successors of Andrew Anderson,* 1699. brs. ALDIS 3833. EN; RPJ.

286 —[Anr. ed.] [*Edinburgh,* 1699.] brs. EN; RPJ.

Caledonian almanack. Edinburgh, 1700. *See* Almanacs. Symson, M.

Caledonias covenant. [n.p.], 1641. *See* Lauder, George.

287 Caledonia's farewell. *Edinburgh, by the heir of Andrew Anderson,* 1685. brs. ALDIS 2533. EN.

Caledons complaint. [n.p., 1641.] *See* Moore, *Sir* William.

288 **Calef, Robert.** More wonders of the invisible world. *For Nath. Hillar and Joseph Collyer,* 1700. 4°. T.C.III 217. L, O, C, LCL, GU; CH, CU, LC, RPJ, WCL, Y.

289 A calendar of prophetick time. *For the author,* 1684. 4°. O, CS; Y.

Calendar-reformation. 1648. *See* Brinsley, John.

Calendarium Carolinum. 1663. *See* Almanacs.

Calendarium catholicum. 1661. *See* Almanacs. Blount, Thomas.

Calendarium Londinense. [1678.] *See* Almanacs.

Calendarium lunæ. Glasguæ, 1699. *See* Law, John.

290 **C[aley], A[braham].** A glimpse of eternity. 1667. 8°. LGI, P.

290A ———Second edition. *For Thomas Parkhurst and by G.B.* 1679. 12°. NPT, NU, Y.

291 ———Third edition. —, 1683. 12°. T.C.II 659. L, LCL, LW, LSC; WF.

292 **Calfine, Giles.** An answer, in defence of A messe of pottage. *Printed*, 1642. 4°.* LT, OC; NU, Y.

293 —The Book of common prayer confirmed. *By T. M. for William Potter*, 1660. 4°.* L, O; CLC, WF, Y.

294 [–] A fresh bit of mutton. [*London*], *for T. P.*, 1462 [i.e., 1642]. 4°.* LT; CH, MH, NU, WF, Y.

295 —A messe of pottage. *Printed*, 1642. 4°.* LT, O, CJ, OC; CLC, MH, NU, WF, Y.

Call from God. 1662. *See* White, Dorothy.

296 A call from Heaven to God's Elisha's. *Printed*, 1667. 4°.* LW; NU, WF.

296A A Call from Heaven to the unconverted. *J. Williams* [1698?]. 8°.* LW.

Call in the universal spirit. 1692. *See* Parke, James.

Call out of Egypt. 1656. *See* Parker, Alexander.

Call to all bishops. 1670. *See* Anderdon, John.

Call to all the shepherds. [1681.] *See* N., S.

Cal to all the souldiers. 1647. *See* Wildman, Sir John.

Call to Archippus. 1664. *See* Alleine, Joseph.

Call to back-sliders. 1680. *See* Stoddon, Samuel.

297 A call to Charon. [*London*], *for C. Dennisson*, [1685–88]. brs. L, O, CM, HH.

Call to prayer. 1677. *See* Cheyney, John.

298 A call to Scotland. *Edinburgh, printed*, 1698. 8°.* C.

298A A call to seriousness in religion. *For T. Parkhurst*, 1693. 12°.* LW.

298B A call to sinners to sin no more. *For Francis Smith*, 1675. brs. MH.

Call to the officers. 1658. *See* R., S.

Call to the races. [1685–88.] *See* D'Urfey, Thomas.

Call to the universal seed. 1665. *See* Fell, Margaret.

Call unto the seed. [1688.] *See* Fell, Margaret.

298C **Callander, John.** Unto His Majesties high commissioner. [*Edinburgh*, 1695.] cap., fol.* EN.

299 **Calle, Caleb.** On His Royal Highnes's miraculous delivery. colop: *For Edward Vize*, 1682. brs. L, O; CH, MH, TU, Y.

300 —A pindarique ode on the birth of the young Prince of Wales. *For Randal Taylor*, 1688. fol.* O; CU.

300A **Callières, François.** The lovers' logick. *For George Palmer*, 1670. 8°. C; CN, WF.

301–2 Entries cancelled.

Callincohus, *pseud.*

303 **Callis, Robert.** The case and argument against Sir Ignoramvs. *For Matthew Walbancke*, 1648. 4°.* LT, O, C, EN, DT; CH, CU, MHL, WF, Y.

304 —The reading of. *For William Leak*, 1647. 4°. L, O, C, LL, DC; CH, CN, LC, MHL, NCL, YL.

305 ———Second edition. *By M. Flesher, for Thomas Basset*, 1685. fol. L, O, CS, LGI, EN; LC, MHL, MW, NCL, YL.

306 ———"Second" edition. *For Tho. Basset, to be sold by William Canning*, 1686. 4°. T.C.II 160. L, CJ, LL, LM, LWL; LC, MHL.

Calm and sober enquiry. 1694. *See* Howe, John.

Calm answer to a bitter. 1683. *See* Cawdrey, Zachary.

Calm answer to a violent. 1677. *See* Du Moulin, Peter.

307 A calme consolatory view. [*London*], *printed*, 1647. 4°. LT, O, C, DT; CH, CN, MH, TU, Y.

308 **Calthrop, *Sir* Henry.** The liberties usages, and customes of the city of London. *By B. Alsop for Nicholas Uavasour*, 1642. 4°.* LT, O, C, LG, EN; CH, MH, NC, WF, Y.

309 [–] —[Anr. ed.] *Printed*, 1674. 4°.* L, O, LG, LL, HH; MH, NU, WF, Y.

310 —Reports of speciall cases. *For Abel Roper*, 1655. 8°. LT, O, LI, LG; CH, MBP, MH, MHL, NCL.

311 ———[Anr. ed.] —, 1670. 8°. T.C.I 63. L, O, CT, LG, LIL; BN, CH, CN, MHL, NCL, WF, YL.

312 **Calthrope, *Sir* Charles.** The relation between the Lord of a manor. Second edition. 1650. 4°. L, LL, LGI, LM, R; MBP, MHL, WF.

Calumny condemned. 1659. *See* B., J.

312A **Calver, Edward.** Bayes for our dayes. *By Richard Cotes for Fra. Grove*, 1642. 4°. OC.

313 —Divine passions. *By T. H. for Richard Harper*, 1643. 4°. L; MH, WC.

314 —Englands fortresse. *Printed*, 1648[9]. 8°. LT.

315 [–] Englands sad postvre. *By Bernard Alsop, and are to be sold by Richard Harper*, 1644. 8°.* LT; CH, CLC, MH.

316 [–] Passion and discretion in yovth and age. *By T. & R. Cotes for Francis Grove*, 1641. 4°. L, O, YM; CH, IU, NC.

317 —Calver's royall vision. [*London*, 1648.] 4°.* LT; Y.

318 [–] Zions thankful ecchoes from the clifts of Ireland. [*London*], *for Richard Harper*, 1649. 4°.* LT; CH, TU.

319 **Calvert, James.** Naphtali: seu colluctationes. *Typis Andreæ Clark, impensis Ric. Lambert, Eboraci, & apud Jo. Martyn, Londini*, 1672. 4°. T.C.I 89. O, C, LCL, EN, DT; BN, LC, MB.

320 **Calvert, Philip.** A letter from the chancellour of Maryland. colop: *For A. Banks*, 1682. brs. L, O; MBH, RPJ.

321 **Calvert, Thomas.** The blessed Jew. *Printed at York by Tho. Broad*, 1648. 4°. LT, O, LCL, DC, AU; CH, CLC, WF, Y.

322 Entry cancelled.

323 —Heart-salve. *Printed at York by Tho: Broad, to be sold by Nathaniel Brookes*, 1647. 8°. LT.

324 ———Second edition. *For T. Passinger*, 1675. 12°. T.C.I 217. LSC, YM.

325 —Mel coeli, medulla evangelii or, Isaiah's prophecie. *For Tho. Pierrepont*, 1658. 4°. L, LCL, P; MH.

326 —Mel cœli, medulla evangelii: or, the prophet Isaiah's crucifix. *For Tho. Pierrepont*, 1656. 4°. L; CLC, MH.

326A ——[Anr. ed.] —, 1657. 4°. O, LW, YM; CH, CSU, Y.

327 —The wise merchant. *By H. Bell, for Charles Tyus*, 1660. 8°. L; CLC, MHS.

327A ——[Anr. ed.] *For Charles Passinger*, 1674. 8°.* Y.

328 **Calvin, Jean.** The catechisme. *Edinburgh, by Evan Tyler,* 1645. 8°. ALDIS 1185. L; Y.

329 —Compendium Christianae religionis. *Oxoniæ: impensis L: Lichfield,* 1655. MADAN 2272. NU.

329A —The true forme of the government of the church of Geneva. *For L. Chapman,* 1659. 4°. Y.

330 The Calvinist's cabinet unlock'd. *For R. Royston,* 1659. 12°. LW, LSC, ELY.

Calvinus redivivus; or. 1673. *See* Long, Thomas.

331 The Cambridge case. *Printed, to be sold by Randal Taylor,* 1689. fol.* L, O, C, CT; CH, MHL, NU, WF, Y.

Cambridge ephemeris. Cambridge [Mass.], 1689. *See* Almanacs. Williams, William.

332 Cambridge jests. *For Samuel Lowndes,* 1674. 12°. T.C.I 152. L, O; LC, Y.

Cambridge royallist imprisoned. [n.p., 1643.] *See* B., R.

332A **Cambridge University.** Academiæ Cantabrigiensis affectus decendente Carolo II. *Cantabrigiæ,* 1684/5. 4°. LLL.

333 —Academiæ Cantabrigiensis Σωστρα. *Cantabrigia, excudebat Joannes Field,* 1660. 4°. LT, O, C, CT, YM; CH, CN, MH, TU, WF, Y.

333A —Cogitatio non competit materiæ. [*Cambridge*], 1697/700. brs. O.

334 —Epicedia Cantabrigiensia in obitum . . . Annæ. *Cantabrigiæ, ex officina Joann. Hayes,* 1671. 4°. L, O, C, CT, OM; CN, MH, TU, WF, Y.

335 —Epithalamia Cantabrigiensia. *Cantabrigiæ, ex officina Joannis Field,* 1662. 4°. L, O, C, CT; CH, CN, MH, WF, Y.

336 —Epithalamium in desideratissimis nuptiis. *Cantabrigiae, ex officina Joann. Hayes,* 1677. 4°. L, O, C, CT, OB; CN, MH, TU, Y.

337 —Gratulatio academiæ Cantabrigiensis de reditu. *Cantabrigiæ, typis academicis,* [1697]. fol. L, O, C, MR, EN; CN, MBA, MH, WF, Y.

338 —Hymenæus Cantabrigiensis. *Cantabrigiæ, ex officina Johannis Hayes,* 1683. 4°. T.C.II 47. L, O, C, MR, EN; CH, CN, MH, TU, WF, Y.

339 —Illustrissimi principis Ducis Cornubiae. *Cantabrigiae, ex officina Joan. Hayes,* 1688. 4°. T.C.II 234. L, O, C, CT, E; CH, CN, MH, NP, WF, Y.

340 —Irenodia Cantabrigiensis. [*Cambridge*], *ex officina Rogeri Daniel,* 1641. 4°. LT, O, C, CT, OB; CH, CN, MH, TU, WF, Y.

341 —Lacrymæ Cantabrigienses in obitum . . . Henriettæ. *Cantabrigiæ, ex officina Joann. Hayes,* 1670. 4°. L, O, C, CT, OB; CH, CN, MH, TU, WF, Y.

342 —Lacrymæ Cantabrigienses in obitum . . . Mariæ. *Cantabrigiæ, ex officina Johan. Hayes,* 1694/5. 4°. L, O, C, CT, EN; CH, CN, MH, TU, WF, Y.

343 —Mœstissimæ ac laetissimæ academiæ. *Cantabrigiæ, ex officina Joan. Hayes,* 1684/5. 4°. L, O, C, CT, E; CH, CU, MH, NC, TU, WF, Y.

344 —Musæ Cantabrigienses. *Cantabrigiæ, ex officina Joan. Hayes,* 1689. 4°. L, O, C, MR, EN; CH, CN, MH, WF, Y.

345 —Musarum Cantabrigiensium luctus & gratulatio. *Cantabrigiæ: excudebat Joannes Field,* 1658. *Londini prostant.* 4°. L, O, C, CT, MR; CH, MH, MIU, NU, Y.

346 — —*Cantabrigiæ: apud Joannem Field,* 1658. 4°. O, CCL; CH, CN, MH, PL, Y.

347 —Musarum Cantabrigiensium threnodia. *Cantabrigiæ, ex officina Joann. Hayes,* 1670. 4°. L, O, C, OB, DT; CH, CN, MH, TU, WF, Y.

348 —Oliva pacis. *Cantabrigiæ: ex academiæ typographeo.* 1654. 4°. LT, O, C, CT, MU; CH, CN, LC, NU, TU, Y.

349 —The petition of the gentlemen and students of the universitie of Cambridge. *For Iohn Greensmith,* 1642. 4°.* LT, C, CPE, HH; CLC, CN, Y.

350 —Petition of the University of Cambridge. [*n.p.*], 1643. brs. O.

351 —Selectae aliquot legum, atque ordinationum. [*Cambridge*], *Novemb. 24.* 1663. brs. O.

352 —Statuta legenda. [*Cantabrigiæ,* 1695.] brs. L.

353 —Statuta quaedam. *Cantabrigiæ, ex officina Joan. Hayes.* 1684. 8°. T.C.II 100. 8°.* L, O, CT, YM; MH, MWA, Y.

354 —Threni Cantabrigienses in funere duorum principum, *Cantabrigiæ: excudebat Joannes Field,* 1661. 4°. LT, C, CK, CT, DT; CH, CN, MH, WF, Y.

355 —Threni Cantabrigiensis in exequiâs. *Cantabrigiæ, ex officina typographica academiae,* 1669. 4°. L, O, C, CK, CT; CH, CN, MH, WF, Y.

356 —Threnodia in obitum. *Cantabrigiæ J. Hayes.* 1670. 4°. CT.

357 —Threnodia academiæ Cantabrigiensis. *Cantabrigiæ, typis academicis,* 1700. 12°. L, O, C, MR, EN; CH, IU, MH, WF, Y.

357A —Threnodia in immaturum obitum . . . Glocestriensi. *Cantabrigiæ, typis Academis,* 1700. CT.

358 —To the honourable the Lords and Commons . . . the humble petition of the University of Cambridge. [*n.p.,* 1643.] brs. LT, O.

358A **Cambridge University. Trinity College.** Singuli in dies singulas. [*Cambridge?* 1662.] 8°.* CT.

359 **Camden, William.** Camden's Britannia. *By F. Collins, for A. Swalle, and A. and J. Churchil,* 1695. fol. L, O, C, AU, DT; BN, CLC, CN, LC, MH, TU, WSC, Y.

360 —V. Cl. G. Cambdeni elogia Anglorum. *Excudebat T. W. pro Gulil. Lee,* 1653. 8°.* L, O, LW; CN.

360A — —[Anr. ed.] *Excudebat T. Warren, pro Edmundo Thom. Oxoniensi,* 1653. 4°. O.

361 —V. Cl. Gulielmi Camdeni, et illustrium virorum ad G. Camdenum epistolæ. *Impensis Richardi Chiswelli,* 1691. 4°. T.C.II 382. L, O, C, MR, E; BN, CH, CN, LC, MH, NC, Y.

362 —The history of the most renowned and victorious princess Elizabeth. Third edition. *By E. Flesher, for C. Harper, and J. Amery,* 1675. fol. T.C.I 200. L, O, C, CK, DT; CSU, LC, MH, NC, YL.

363 — —Fourth edition. *By M. Flesher, for J. Tonson,* 1688. fol. T.C.II 240. L, O, C, HH, ENC; CN, LC, MBC, WF, Y.

363A — —"Fourth edition." *By M. Flesher, for R. Bentley,* 1688. fol. L; CH, CN, MH, VC, WF.

364 [–] Institutio compendaria grammatices Græcæ. *Typis Mil. Flesher & Jde, Young, per assigned from R. Norton, Vincent apud PWL News,* 1673. 8°. O.

365 [–] —[Anr. ed.] 1693. 8°. OME.

366 [–] —[Anr. ed.] *Miles Flesher,* 1647. 8°. CT.

367 [–] —[Anr. ed.] 1650. 12°. C, CS.

367A [–] —*Typis & impensis Rogeri Norton,* 1656. 8°. EC; MB.

367B [–] —[Anr. ed.] —, 1658. 8°. L.

368 [–] —[Anr. ed.] *Excudit Rogerus Nortonus,* 1662. 12°. L, C, CLC, TU.

368A [–] —[Anr. ed.] —, 1665. 8°. IU, PL.

368B [–] —[Anr. ed.] *Excudit Rogeri Nortonus,* 1667. 8°. L, O, OC, CS; IU, MH, WF.

368C [–] —[Anr. ed.] —, 1670. 8°. IU, WF.

369 [–] —[Anr. ed.] —, 1673. 8°. C.

370 [–] —[Anr. ed.] —, 1676. 8°. O; NC.

370A [–] —[Anr. ed.] —, 1681. 16°. Y.

371 [–] —[Anr. ed.] —, 1682. 8°. O; WF.

371A — —[Anr. ed.] —, 1684. 8°. MB.

371B [–] —[Anr. ed.] 1685. 8°. I.

372 [–] —[Anr. ed.] 1692. 12°. L, LS; IU.

372A — —[Anr. ed.] —, 1694. 8°. TU.

372B [–] —[Anr. ed. —, 1695. 8°. L, LG; MH.

372C [–] —[Anr. ed.] —, 1697. 8°. IU.

372D [–] —[Anr. ed.] —, 1699. 8°. L; Y.

373 —New proposals to print, by subscription, Cambden's Britannia. [*n.p.*], 1693. fol. O.

374 —Remaines. Sixth edition. *For Simon Miller and Robert Clavell,* 1657. 4°. L, O, C, NPL, MAU; CU, MH, NU, WF.

374A — —"Sixth" edition, *For Simon Waterson and Robert Clavell,* 1657. 4°. L, O, CS, BR, EN; MH, PL, TU, WF, Y.

374B — —"Sixth" edition. *By Thomas Warren for Isabella Waterson,* 1657. 4°. CT; CH, MB.

374C — —"Sixth" edition. *For Simon Miller,* 1657. 4°. L, EC; CPB, IU, LC, MH, Y.

375 — —Seventh edition. *For Charles Harper, and John Amery,* 1674. 8°. T.C.I 158. L, O, CP, DC, DT; BN, CH, CU, MH, NP, WF, Y.

376 —A second edition of Camden's description of Scotland. *Edinburgh, by the heirs and successors of Andrew Anderson,* M.D.XCV [sic] 1695. 8°. ALDIS 3448. L, O, EN, ES, GU; CLC, NC, Y.

Camera regis. 1675. *See* Brydall, John.

377 **Camfield, Benjamin.** The commination prescribed. *For H. Brome, and R. Chiswell,* 1680. 4°.* T.C.I 391. I, C, OCC, SC, E; CH, MH, NU, WF, Y.

378 [–] A consolatory discourse for the support of distressed widows. *For John Newton,* 1690. 4°.* L.

379 Entry cancelled.

380 —An examination of the independents' catechism. 1669. 8°. LCL, ELY.

381 —Of Episcopal confirmation. *For R. Chiswel,* 1682. 8°. T.C.I 470. O, C, CT, YM, DT; CH, CLC, WF, Y.

382 —Of God Almighty's providence. *For R. Chiswell,* 1684. 4°.* T.C.II 59. L, O, CT, WCA, OC; CH, CSU, TU, WF, Y.

382A —A practical discourse on the rule of righteousness. 1671. 8°. LW.

382B —A profitable enquiry. *For William Leach,* 1679. 8°. T.C.I 336. NPT.

382C —Quod tibi, hoc alteri: . . . A profitable enquiry. *By A.C. for H.Eversden,* 1671. 8°. T.C.I 84. LW, DCH; MH, WF.

383 [–] A serious examination. *By J. Redmayne, for the author: to be sold by Henry Eversden,* 1668. 8°. O, OB, CE, LW, CT; CLC, NU, Y.

384 — —[Anr. ed.] 1669. 8°. OC, OM, E.

385 —A sermon preached . . . November the xii^{th}. 1678. *By J. Macock for Henry Brome,* 1678. 4°. T.C.I 340. L, O, C, CT; CH, CLC, NU, TSM, WF, Y.

386 —A sermon preach'd upon the first Sunday after . . . February the 10th. 1684/5. *For Charles Brome,* 1685. 4°.* L, O, C; CH, NU, WF, Y.

387 — —Second edition. —, 1687. 4°.* O, WCA.

388 —A theological discourse of angels. colop: *By R.E. for Hen. Brome,* 1678. 8°. T.C.I 318. L, O, C, CE, E; CH, CN, MH, NU, WF, Y.

388A Camiltons discoverie. *By T.Favvcet,* 1641. 4°.* LT, O, CT, P, EN; CH, CN, MH, WF, Y.

389 [**Camm, John.**] An answer to a book which Samuel Eaton put up to the Parliament. *For Giles Calvert,* 1654. 4°. LT, LF; PSC, WF.

390 —The memory of the righteous revived. *Printed and sold by Andrew Sowle,* 1689. 8°. L, O, LF, LW, OC; CH, MH, NU, PSC, WF, Y.

391 [–] Some particulars concerning the law, sent to Oliver Cromwell. *Printed,* 1654. 4°.* LT, O, LF.

391A — —[Anr. ed.] *Printed,* 1655. 4°.* L, LF, OC; PH, PSC.

392 —This was the Word of the Lord. *Printed,* 1654. 4°.* LT, LF, BBN; PH, PSC.

393 —A true discovery of the ignorance, blindness. *For G. Calvert,* 1654. 4°.* LT, LF, BBN; CH, PH.

394 **Camm, Thomas.** The admirable and glorious appearance. *By John Bringhurst,* 1684. 4°. CT, LF; CLC, PH, PL.

395 —The line of truth. *By John Bringhurst,* 1684. 4°.* L, LF, BBN; IE, NU, PH, PSC.

396 —An old apostate justly exposed. *Printed and sold by T. Sowle,* 1698. 8°. L, LF, O, BBN; CH, MH, PH.

396A —A testimony to the fulfilling the promise of God. [*London*], *by Andrew Soule,* 1689. 4°. LF, BBN; CLC, IE, PH, PSC, Y.

397 **Camoes, Luiz de.** The Lusiad. *For Humphrey Moseley,* 1655. fol. L, O, CT, LW, E; CH, CN, LC, MH, NC, TU, Y.

397A — —[Anr. ed.] *For A. Mosely,* 1664. fol. IU.

Camp at Gilgal. Oxford, 1643. *See* Ferne, Henry.

Camp discipline. 1642. *See* Newark, David Leslie, *baron.*

398 The camp of Christ. [*n.p.,* 1642.] cap., 4°.* LT, CCL, LW, HH; CH, MH, NU, WF.

399 The camp on Hounslow-Heath. *By George Croom,* 1686. brs. O.

399A The campaign, 1692. [*London,* 1692]. cap., 4°.* MH.

399B The campagne of the French King. *For T. Dring,* 1679. 8°. T.C.I 332. CLC, MIU, WF.

Campaneologe, or, 1677. *See* Stecman, Febian.

400 **Campanella, Tommaso.** Thomas Campanella, an Italian friar . . . His advice to the King of Spain. *For Philemon Stephens,* [1660]. 4°. LT, C, LL, EN, ES; CN, MH, RPJ, WF, Y.

401 —A discourse touching the Spanish monarchy. *For Philemon Stephens,* 1654. 4°. LT, O, C, EN, DT; CH, MH, NC, PL, WF, Y.

Campanella revived. 1670. *See* Stubbe, Henry.

Campbell, Archibald, *See* Argyle, Archibald Campbell marquis of.

401A **Campbell, David.** Sacramental visitations. *Falkirk, Patrick Marr,* 1602. 12°. MH.

401B **Campbell, George.** Answer to the university. [*Aberdeen,* 1700.] cap., 4°.* EN.

401C —To his grace His Majesties high commissioner. [*Edinburgh,* 1700.] brs. HH.

Campbell, John. *See* Loudoun, John Campbell, earl of.

402 **Campbell, Robert.** Prayer for a gracious king. *For A. Bell.* 1696. 12°. LW.

403 **Campbell,** *Sir* **William.** [To his grace.] [*n.p.,* 1688.] brs. EN.

404 —Theses philosophicæ. *Edinburgh,* 1657. 4°. EN.

405 **Campion, Abraham.** The inheritance of the saints in light. *By J. Leake, for Walter Kettilby,* 1700. 4°.* L, O, CS, CT, EC; CH, MBA, NU, WF, Y.

406 —A sermon concerning national providence. *For Anthony Piesley in Oxford,* 1694. 4°.* L, O, C, OC, EN; CLC, NPT, NU, WF, Y.

407 **Campion, Edmund.** Reasons of a challenge. *For Mat. Turner,* 1687. 4°.* L, C; MH, MIU, NU, WF, Y.

408 **Campion, Robert.** The case between the right honourable city of London, and . . . [*London,* 1659.] brs. LT.

408A ——[Anr. ed.] *For W. T.* 1681. brs. L, LG, OP; Y.

408B ——[Anr. ed.] colop: *Printed,* 1681. brs. WF.

409 [**Campion, Thomas.**] A friends advice, in an excellent ditty. *By E. C. for F. Coles, T. Vere, and J. Wright,* [1658–60]. brs. L, O, CM, HH; MH.

410–11 Entry cancelled.

[**Campion, William.**] *See* Wigmore, William.

Camus, Hieronymo. *See* Simon, Richard.

412 **Camus, Jean Pierre,** *bp.* Diotrephe . . . or, an history of valentines. *By Th. Harper,* 1641. 12°. L, O, ELY; WF.

413 [–] Elise or innocencie guilty. *By T. Newcomb for Humphrey Moseley,* 1655. fol. L, LVD, CT; CH, CN, MH, WF, Y.

414 —Forced marriage. Second edition. *For W. Jacob,* 1678. 8°. T.C.I 305. L.

415 —The loving enemie. *By J. G. and are to be sold by John Dakins,* 1650. 8°. LT, O, DT; CH, CN, LC, MH, WF, Y.

416 ——Second edition. *For Thomas Rooks,* 1667. 12°. L.

417 —Nature's paradox. *By J. G. for Edw. Dod and Nath. Ekins,* 1652. 4°. L, O, C, CT; CH, CN, MH, NC, WF, Y.

418 Entry cancelled.

419 —A true tragical history of two illustrious Italian families. *For William Jacob,* 1677. 8°. T.C.I 253. L, O, P; CH, CN, MH, WF, Y.

Canaan's calamitie. 1677. *See* Dekker, Thomas.

420 **Canaries, James.** A discourse representing the sufficient manifestation. *Edinburgh, by the heir of Andrew Anderson,* 1684. 8°. ALDIS 2447. O, E, ENC, I, EN; CH, MH, NPT, Y.

421 —Rome's additions to Christianity. *Edinburgh, printed,* 1686. 4°.* ALDIS 2634. L, O, CE, EN, LG; CLC, WF, Y.

421A ——[Anr. ed.] *For Robert Sampson,* 1686. 4°.* CT; Y.

422 —A sermon preacht at Selkirk . . . 29th of May, 1685. *Edinburgh, heirs of A. Anderson,* [1685]. 4°. L, O, E, ENC.

423 —A sermon preached . . . 30th of January, 1689. *Edinburgh, printed,* 1689. 4°. ALDIS 2869. L, O, EN.

423A Cancer; comoedia. *By R. G. for Andrew Grove.* 1648. 8°. O; LC, MH.

424 A candle for the blinde citizens of London, to see by. [*London*], *printed in the yeer of blindnes, the month of stupidnes, the day of dulnes, and the hour of unnaturalnes,* 1648. 4°.* LT, HH.

Candle in the dark. [1656.] *See* Ady, Thomas.

Candle to see. [1647.] *See* Goodwin, John.

425 **Cane, Andrew.** The stage-players complaint. *For Tho: Bates,* 1641. 4°.* LT; CU.

425A **Cane, Thomas.** Three hymns. *For C. Brome,* 1700. 8°.* EN.

425B **Canepari, Pietro Maria.** De atramentis. *Excudebat J. M., impensis Jo. Martin, Ja. Alestry, Tho. Dicas,* 1660. 4°. LT, O, C, LW, EN; BN, CH, CN, LC, NC, TU, Y.

426 Entry cancelled.

427 [**Canes, John Vincent.**] Diaphanta: or, three attendants on Fiat lux. [*Douay*], 1665. 8°. L, O, GK; CH, CN, NU, TU, Y.

428 —An epistle to the authour of the Animadversions upon Fiat lux. [*Douay?*], 1663. 8°. L, O, C, DT; CH, MBA, NC, NU, TU.

429 —Fiat lux, or a general conduct. [*Douay?*], 1661. 12°. LT, O. CS, LW, EN; BN, CLC, CN, MH, NU, VC.

430 ——Second edition. [*London*], 1662. 8°. L, O, C, DC, DT; BN, CH, MBC, NU, WF, Y.

431 [–] —[Anr. ed.] [*Douay?*], 1664. 8°. L.

432 ——Third edition. [*n.p.*], *printed,* 1665. 8°. L, O, CJ; CLC, PH, WF.

432A —Infallibility. [*London,* 1662.] 8°.* C.

433 —Τω καθολικω Stillingfleeton. Or an account. *Bruges, by Luke Kerchove,* 1672. 8°. L, O, CS, CT, GK; CLC, CN, NU, TU, WG, Y.

434 —The Pope's posie. 1663. 4°. DT.

435 [–] The reclaimed Papist. [*London*], 1655. 8°. LT, O, C, OC; CH, CN, NU, TU, WF, Y.

436 —Three letters declaring. [*Douay?*], 1671. 8°. L, C, UBL; CN, MIU, NP, TU.

Canidia. 1680. *See* Dixon, Robert.

Canne, Abednest, *pseud.*

Canne, John, *pseud. See also* Butler, Samuel.

437 **Canne, John.** The discoverer, Being an answer . . . Second part. *By Matthew Simmons,* 1649. 4°. LT; CH, CN, NU, WF, Y.

438 ——VVherein is set forth . . . First part. *By Matthew Simmons,* 1649. 4°. LT, HH, DT; CH, CN, NU, WF, Y.

439 —Emanuel, or God with us. *By Matthew Simmons*, 1650. 4°. LT, C, E, EN; CH, MH, NHC, NU, WF.

440 —The golden rule. *For Peter Cole*, 1649. 4°.* LT, O, CT, E, DT; CH, MH, NU, WF, Y.

441 —The improvement of mercy. *By M. Simmons*, 1649. 4°.* LT, O, C, LVF, E; MH, NU, WF.

442 —A seasonable word to the Parliament-men. *By J. C. for L. Chapman*, 1659. 4°.* LT, O, LCL, EN; CH, MH, NU, WF, Y.

442A —A second voyce from the Temple. *By M. Simmons*, 1653. 4°.* LT, O, LW, SP; NHC, NU, WF, Y.

442B —The snare is broken. *For M. Simmons*, 1649. 4°. LT, LW, DT; CH, CN, MH, NU, WF.

442C [–] Shows prerogative, royal. *Printed at Amsterdam*, 1641. 8°. L, O, CT, DT; JF.

442D —The time of finding: shewing. *For Livewel Chapman*, 1658. 8°. LCL, LSC; MH.

443 —The time of the end. *For Livewel Chapman*, 1657. 8°. L, O, C, LCL, YM, CLC, MH; MIU, NHC, NU.

443A —Truth with time. *By J. C. for Livewel Chapman*, 1656. 4°. L, O, LCL; NU, PL.

443AB —A two-fold shaking of the earth. *For L. Chapman*, 1659. 8°. WF.

443B —A voice from the Temple. *By Matthew Simmons*, 1653. 4°.* LT, O, LCL, LW, YM; CLC, NHC, NU, WF, Y.

444 **[Canning, W.]** Gesta grayorum. *For W. Cunning*, 1688. 4°. T.C.II 230. L, O, LVD, LGI, EN; CH, CN, MH, WF, Y.

444A —A proposal to the honourable the knights. [*London*, 1696?] brs. MH.

444B Canon of the squares and cubes of all numbers under 1000. [*London?* 1660] 8°. CCA.

444C Canones sinuum. Entry cancelled. *See* Ocghtred, William.

445 The canonical states-man's grand argument discuss'd. *For the assigns of General Ludlow*, 1693. 4°.* O; CLC, CN, LC, MH, Y.

446 The canons and decrees of the Council of Trent. *For T. Y.*, 1687. 4°. L, LIL, CM, MC; BBE, NU, WF, Y.

Canons and institutions. 1669. *See* Fox, George.

446A **Cant, Andrew.** Ευχη Βασιλικη votum pro rege. *Edinburgi, excudebat*, 1661. brs. Y.

447 —A letter from the protesters. [*Edinburgh, Andrew Anderson*], 1653. 4°. ALDIS 1479. E, EN; CH.

448 [–] Oratio de concordia theologorum. *Edinburgi, excudebat Thomas Brown*, 1676. 4°.* ALDIS 2078. E, EN, AU; WF.

449 —A sermon preached . . . the 13. day of June 1638. [*n.p.*], 1682. 4°.* E, EN.

450 ——[Anr. ed.] *Edinburgh, for Alexander Henderson*, 1699. 4°.* ALDIS 3834. L, O, EN, AU; NPT.

451 —Theses et problemata. *Abredoniis, e typographeo Jacobi Brouni*, 1654. 4°. ALDIS 1500. O, EN.

452 —Theses philosophicæ. *Aberdoniis, e typographæo Jacobi Broun*, 1658. 4°. ALDIS 1586. O, HH, E, AU.

Canterburians self-conviction. [*n.p.*], 1641. *See* Baillie, Robert.

453 Canterbvry Christmas. *For Humphrey Harward*, 1648. 4°.* LT, O, EN; CH, PRF.

454 Entry cancelled.

455 Canterbvrie march beaten up on the day of King Charles his inavgvration. [*London*], printed, 1648. 4°.* LT; CH, MH.

Canterbury tale. 1641. *See* Brome, Alexander.

455A Canterbury tales: composed. *For J. Back*, 1687. 8°. CM.

456 Canterbvries amazement. [*London*], *for F. Coules*, 1641. 4°.* L, O; MB, MH, NU, TU.

457 Canterburies conscience convicted. [*n.p.*], 1641. brs. L, O.

458 Canterbvries dreame. [*London*], printed, 1641. 4°.* LT, O, CT, LVF, YM; MH, MIU, TU, WF, Y.

459 Canterbvries pilgrimage. *For H. Walker*, 1641. 4°.* LT, O, LVF, OC; CSS, CU, MH, NNG, Y.

460 Canterbvries potion. [*n.p.*], printed, 1641. 4°.* LP; WF.

Canterburies tooles. [1642.] *See* Prynne, William.

461 Canterbury's will. [*London*], printed, 1641. 4°.* LT, O, LVF; LC, WF.

462 The canter's confession. [*London*], *for P. Brooksby*, [1680–85]. brs. L, CM, HH.

Canting academy. 1673. *See* Head, Richard.

462A Cantique de rejouissance sur la prise de Namur. *Chez Richard Baldwin*, 1697. 4°.* WF.

462B Cantique de triomphe. *J. Delage*, 1692. 4°.* L.

Cantium catholicum. 1675. *See* Pope, Walter.

463 A canto on the new miracle wrought by the D. of M. [*n.p.*, 1680/1.] brs. L, HH.

463A A canto to a canter. [*London?* 1682.] brs. CN, MH, TU, WF, Y.

Cantus, songs. Aberdene, 1662. *See* Davidson, Thomas.

464 **Caoursin, William.** The history of the Turkish war. *For Will Whitwood*, 1683. 8°. T.C.II 44. L, LSC; CN, Y.

Capel, Arthur. *See also* Essex, Arthur Capel, *earl of.*

465 **[Capel, Arthur Capel, baron.]** Certain letters written to severall persons. [*London*], *anno Dom.*, 1654. 4°.* LT, O, C; CH, CU, MIU, TU, WF, Y.

466 [–] —[Anr. ed.] —, 1655. 12°. O; CU, WF.

467 [–] Daily observations or meditations. [*London*], *anno Dom.*, 1654. 4°. LT, O, C, OB; CH, MIU, NP, TU, Y.

468 [–] —[Anr. ed.] —, 1655. 12°. L, O; CLC, CU, NC.

468A ——[Anr. ed.] *For J. Williams*, 1679. 12°. T.C.I 376. L.

469 —Excellent contemplations. *For Nath. Crouch*, 1683. 12°. T.C.II 42. L, O, CF, BR, EN; CH, CN, MH, NU, WF, Y.

470 —Arthur lord Capell, lieutenant generall . . . to all commanders. *Imprinted at Shrewsbury, by Robert Barker; and by the assignes of John Bill*. 1643. brs. LT.

470A **Capel, Henry, lord.** . . . his speech. *Dublin, by Andrew Crook*, 1649. fol.* DIX 273. DI.

471 **Capel, Richard.** Capel's remains. *By T. R. for John Bartlet*, 1658. 8°. L, O, CS, LCL, OC; MH, MIU, NC, NU, WF, Y.

472 —Tentations. Fourth edition. *By T. B. for Iohn Bartlet*, 1650. L, O, LSC; LLC, NU, WF, Y.

473 ——Fifth edition. *By E. B. for John Bartlet*, 1655. 8°. O, C, DT; CN, CU, LC, NC, NU, Y.

474 ——Sixth edition. *By Tho. Ratcliffe, for John Bartlet*, 1658. 8°. L, LW, OC, RPL; NPT.

475 ——"Sixth" edition. —, 1659. 8°. L, O, C, LCL, CE; CH, MH, NC, NU.

476 ——The fourth part. *By T. R. & E. M. for John Bartlet*, 1655. 8°. L; LC, NC, TSM, Y, PJB.

477 ——Second edition. *By Tho. Ratcliffe, for John Bartlet*, 1659. 8°. L, E; MH, NC, NF, NU.

478 The caping trade. A new song to an excellent tune. [*London?* 1700?] brs. L; MH.

Capitall hereticks. 1659. *See* Brathwaite, Richard.

479 The capitall lawes of New-England. *Printed first in New-England, and re-printed in London for Ben. Allen*, 1643. brs. LT.

480 Entry cancelled.

481 **Capoa, Leonardo di.** The uncertainty of the art of physick. *By Fr. Clark for Thomas Malthus*, 1684. 8°. T.C.II 49. L, O, OM, LCS, P; CLC, MIU, WF, HC.

482 **Cappel, Louis.** The hinge of faith. [*London*], *for Thomas Dring*, 1660. 8°. LT, LCL, OCC; NPT, WF.

483 **Capriata, Pietro Giovanni.** The history of the wars of Italy. *By J. Macock, to be sold by Tho. Dring*, 1663. fol. O,·C, OM, EN, DT; CH, CN, CU, NC, Y.

483A ——[Anr. ed.] *By J. Macock, and are to be sold by Luke Fawne*, 1663. fol. L.

483AB ——[Anr. ed.] *By J. Macock to be sold by Francis Tyton*, 1663. fol. WF.

483AC ——[Anr. ed.] *By J. Macock to be sold by R. Royston*, 1663. 1663. fol. MIU.

483B The captain beguiled the lady. [*London?* 1670]. brs. L.

484 Captain Burley his speech. *Printed at London by Robert Ibbetson*, 1648. 4°.* LT, LG; CH, MH, Y.

485 Capt. [John] Johnsons last farewel. [*London*], *for Charles Bates*, [1690]. brs. L, HH; CH.

486 Captain Kid's farewel to the seas. [*n.p.*, 1700.] brs. HH.

487 Capt. Vrat's ghost. colop: *For J. V.*, 1682. brs. O; CH, MH.

487A The captain's ghost. colop: *For H. Jones*, 1682. brs. DCH, MH, Y.

Captive-captain. 1665. *See* Brathwaite, Richard.
Captivity improved. *See* Cressy, Edmund.
Capuchin; or, the pharisaisme. 1675. *See* Du Moulin, Pierre.

488 **Caradoc, of Lancarvan.** The history of Wales. *By M. Clark, for the author; sold by R. Clavell*, 1697, 8°. T.C.III 38. L, O, C, MR, DT, BN, CH, CN, MH, TU, WF, Y.

489 The card of courtship. *By J. C. for Humphrey Moseley*, 1653. 8°. LT.

490 **Cardano, Girolamo.** Cardan his three books of consolation English'd. *For B. Aylmer and S. Croutch*, 1683. 8°. T.C.II 7. L, CK, CP, CT, EN; CH, CLC, MH, WF, JF.

491 **Cardell, John.** God's soveraign power over nations. *By John Field for Henry Overton*, 1648. 4°. LT, O, LCL, LW, WCA; MM, NU.

492 —God's vvisdom justified. *By John Field for Henry Cripps*, 1649. 4°.* LT, O, OCC, LW, DT; WF, Y.

493 —The magistrates support & burden. *By Peter Cole*, 1650. 4°. LSC; CH.

494 —Morbus epidemicus: or, the danger of self-seeking. *By John Field*, 1650. 4°.* LT, LW, DT; WF.

495 —The necessity of divine instructions. *By John Field for Henry Overton*, 1648. 4°. DT; CH.

495A **Cardenas, Alonso de.** The address of. *Edinburgh, E. Tyler*, 1650. 4°.* EN.

496 —A speech, or complaint, lately made by the Spanish embassadour. *For Nathaniel Butter, Jan 17, 1643*. 4°.* MADAN 1191. LT, O, CT, DT; LC, MH, MIU, RPJ.

497 Cardinal Mazarine and Cromwell's design. 1666. 12°. LW.

Cardinalismo di Santa Chiesa. 1670. *See* Leti, Gregorio.

498 **C[ardonnel], P[hilip] de.** Complementum fortunatarum insularum. *By W. G.*, 1662. 8°. L; CH, CN, LC, TU, Y.

499 ——[Anr. ed.] *For the author*, 1662. 8°. SP; CH, MH.

500 [–] Proposals for increase of wealth. *For Nathanael Brooke*, 1675. 4°.* L, O, LG, MR; Y.

501 [–] Proposals for subscriptions or money. *For Nan. Brooke*, 1674. 4°.* L, O, LL, HH; CH, LC, MH, Y.

502 —Tagus, sive epithalamium Caroli II. *Typis Guil. Godbid*, 1662. 8°. L; CH, MH.

503 **C[are], G[eorge].** Liberty of conscience asserted and vindicated. *For Jonathan Robinson*, 1689. 4°.* T.C.II 260. L, O, C, EN, AU; CH, CLC, MH, NU, Y.

504 —A reply to the Answer of the man of no name. *By John Leake, for Luke Meredith*, 1685. 4°.* T.C.II 129. L, O, C, P, A; MH, MIU, NC, WF, Y.

505 **C[are], H[enry].** Animadversions on a late paper, en-tituled, A letter to a Dissenter. *Printed for J. Harris*, 1687. 4°.* L, O, C, MC, DT; CH, CN, LC, MH, NU, Y.

506 [–] An answer to a paper importing a petition of the Archbishop of Canterbury. *By Henry Hills*, 1688. 31 pp. 4°.* L, O, CT, LG, EN; CLC, MH, NU, WF, Y.

507 [–] ——[Anr. ed.] —, 1688. 24 pp. 4°.* L, OCC, CSSX, HH; CN, PL, TU, WF, Y.

508 [–] The character of a turbulent, pragmatical Jesuit. *For Langley Curtis*, 1678. 4°.* L, O, LL; CH, MH, NU, WF, Y.

509 —The darkness of atheisme expelled. *For D. Brown, and T. Benskin*, 1683. 8°. T.C.I 510. O; WF.

510 —Draconica; or, an abstract. *By George Larkin*, 1687. fol.* L, O, OC, HH, EN; CH, CN, LC, MH, Y.

511 ——Second edition. —, 1688. 4°.* L, O, CT, MC, EN; CH, MHL, MIU, WF, YL.

512 ——Third edition. —, 1688, 4°.* L, O, CT, OC, BR; LC, MH, PL, WF.

513 —An elegie sacred to the memory of Sir Edmund-bury Godfrey. *For L. C.*, 1678. brs. L, O, HH; CH. LC, MH, TU.

514 ——[Anr. ed.] *For Langley Curtis*, 1678. brs. L.

515 [–] English liberties. *By G. Larkin, for Benjamin Harris*, [1680?]. 8°. L, O, LCL; BN, CH, IC, MHL, NU, Y.

516 [–] ——[Anr. ed.] *By G. Larkin, for John How*, [1680?]. 12°. L, LW, CJ; CH, NC, PL, WF.

517 [–] ——[Anr. ed.] *By George Larkin*, 1682. 12°. L; BN, CLC, MHL, MIU, NN.

518 [–] ——[Anr. ed.] *For Sarah Harris*, 1691. 12°. T.C.II 416. L, LG; CN, MBP, NU, Y.

518A ——[Anr. ed.] *Printed and sold by Benjamin Harris*, 1700. 12°. L; CLC, MH, NC, WF.

519 —The female secretary. *By Thomas Ratcliffe and Mary Daniel for Henry Million*, 1671. 8°. T.C.I 88. CT; CH, CN.

520 —Galliæ speculum, or, a new survey. *By W. Downing, for F. Eglesfield*, 1673. 8°. L, DC, O, CT, OM; CH, CU, MBA, WF, Y.

520A [–] The grandeur and glory of France. *For Francis Eglesfield*, 1673. 8°. T.C.I 133. L; Y.

[–] Heraclitus ridens redivivus. [*n.p.*, 1688.] *See* Brown, Thomas.

521 Entry cancelled.

522 [–] The history of the damnable Popish plot. *For B. R. L. W. H. C. to be sold by Langley Curtiss*, 1680. 8°. T.C.I 382. L, O, C, BR, EN; CH, CN, NU, TU, WF, Y.

523 [–] —Second edition. *For B. R. to be sold by L. Curtiss*, 1681. 8°. T.C.I 446. L, O, CT; CN, CU, LC, MBP.

524 —The Jewish calendar explained. *For T. Passinger*, 1674. 8°.* L; Y.

525 —The last legacy of. *For Tho. Cockerill*, 1688. 8°. T.C.II 242. O.

526 —Harry Care's last will and testament. [*n.p.*, 1688.] brs. MC.

527 [–] The legality of the court. *Printed, and are to be sold by Richard Janeway*, 1688. 4°.* L, O, C, EN, DT; CH, LC, MH, NU, Y.

528 —Liberty of conscience asserted. *Printed and sold by R. Janeway*, 1687. 4°. LIL, OC, EN; NU.

529 [–] A modest enquiry whether St. Peter were ever at Rome. *For Randall Taylor*, 1687. 4°. L, O, C, EN, DT; CH, CU, MH, NU, WF, Y.

529A [–] A most safe and effectual cure for the rickets. [*London*, 1676?] brs. L.

530 [–] Observations on a paper intituled The declaration of the Lord Petre. colop: *By George Larkin*, 1684. cap., fol.* L, O, CT, HH; BN, CH, CU, MH, WF, Y.

531 [–] A perfect guide for Protestant Dissenters. *For R. Baldwin*, 1682. fol.* T.C.I 487. L, O, HH; CH, CN, MIU, WF, Y.

532 [–] Towser the second a bull-dog, or a short reply to Absalon and Achitophel. [*London, for T. J.*, 1681.] brs. L, O; CH, CN, MH, WF, Y.

533 —The tutor to true English. *By George Larkin*, 1687. 8°. L, O, CT, AU.

534 ——[Anr. ed.] —, 1688, 8°. DC; NC.

534A ——[Anr. ed.] —, 1690. 8°. CLC, NC.

534B ——Second edition. *For E. Mory*, 1699. 8°. L; CLC.

535 —Utrum horum: or, the nine and thirty articles. *For R. Janeway*, 1682. 8°. T.C.I 493. L, O, C, OM, E; CLC, MH, NC, WF.

536 [–] A vindication of the proceedings of His Majesties ecclesiastical commissioners. *By Tho. Milbourn, and published by Richard Janeway*, 1688. 4°. L, O, CT, EN, DT; CH, CN, MH, NU, TU, WF, Y.

537 —A word in season: being. *For Francis Smith*, 1679. 4°. T.C.I 361. L, O, C, LW, ENC; LC.

538 **Care, John.** Primitive religion. *Printed*, 1680. 4°. CLC, NU.

539 The carefull wife's good counsel. [*London*], *for P. Brooksby, J. Deacon, J. Blare, J. Back*, [1685–92]. brs. L, O, CM, HH.

Careless, Franck, *pseud.* *See* Head, Richard.

540 The careless curate. [1662.] brs. O.

Careless gallant. [*n.p.*, 1675–80.] *See* Jordan, Thomas.

Careless shepherdess. 1656. *See* Goffe, Thomas.

540A **[Carew, Abel.]** To the high court of Parlement, a vindication. [*London?* 1690]. cap., fol.* MH.

541 —To the honourable the Commons . . . . The second humble petition of. [*London*, 1695?] brs. CH.

542 [–] A vindication of King William. [*London*, 1695.] cap., fol.* L.

543 **Carew, *Sir* Alexander.** A speech or confession of. *For Tho. Bates, and J. W. J.*, 1644. 4°.* LT, LG; CLC, MH, WF, Y.

544 **Carew, George.** An appeal from the supream court of judicature of Holland. [*Middelburgh?*], *printed*, 1674. 4°.* L.

545 —A briefe deduction of the case. [*Amsterdam*, 1679.] cap., fol.* L, LUG; MH.

546 —Fraud and oppression detected and arraigned. [*London*], *printed*, 1676. fol.* L, O, CM, LGI, LUG; MH, WF, Y.

547 —Fraud and violence discovered and detected. *By William Godbid*, 1662. fol. L, O, DC.

548 —The insinuation and protest of. [*London*, 1675?] cap., fol.* L, LUG.

549 [–] Lex talionis: or the law of marque. *Printed*, 1682. fol.* L, LUG; MHL, Y.

550 —A retrospect into the kings certain revenue. *Printed*, 1661. fol.* L, O, C, LGI; WF, Y.

551 —Severall considerations offered to the Parliament. [*London*, 1675.] cap., 4°.* L.

552 [–] Several grounds, reasons . . . and propositions offered. [*London*, 1660.] brs. L.

553 —The title and interest of Jeremy Elwes. *Printed*, 1659. fol.* L.

554 —To the honnorable [*sic*]: the knights, . . . The humble petition of . . . Courten. [*Middleburg?* 1675.] cap., 4°.* L, LUG; MH.

554A —To the honourable the Knights, . . . The humble petition of . . . Pyndar. [*Middleburg?* 1675.] cap., 4°.* L.

555 **Carew, *Sir* George.** Reports or causes in chancery. *By E. G. for W. Lee, D. Pakeman and G. Bedell*, 1650. L, O, LI, LL, LM; CH, MHL, NCL.

556 ——[Anr. ed.] *By A. Maxwell for William Lee, M. Pakeman, and G. Bedell*, 1665. L, OC, CT, DC, EN; CH, MHL, NCL, WF, YL.

557 —A vindication of the severall actions at law. *Printed at Middelburgh, by Thomas Berry*, 1675. 4°. L.

558 **Carew, *Sir* Richard.** Excellent helps really found out. *For John Bartlet*, 1652. 4°.* LT, LG.

559 ——Third edition. —, 1660. 4°.* L; WF.

560 —The warming stone. *For Thomas Rooks*, [1670?]. 8°.* L, O.

561–2 Entries cancelled.

563 **Carew, Thomas, *Gent.*** Hinc illæ lacrymæ; or, an epitome. *Printed*, 1681. fol.* L, LG, P, HH, DT; CH.

564 **Carew, Thomas, *Poet.*** Poems. Second edition. *By I. D. for Thomas Walkley*, 1642. 8°. L, O, CM, LVD, GK; CH, CN, MH, WF, Y.

565 ——Third edition. *For H. M., and are to be sold by J: Martin*, 1651. 8°. L, O, C, DC, GK; CH, CLC, CN, WF, Y.

566 — —Fourth edition. *For Henry Herringman, 1670.* 8°. T.C.I 62. L, O, OC, OW, LVD; BN, CH, CLC, MH, WF, Y.

567 — —"Fourth" edition. *For H. Herringman, and are to be sold by Hobart Kemp, 1671.* 8°. L; CH, MH, TU, WF, Y.

Carey, Sir George. *See* Carew, *Sir* George.

Carey, Henry. *See* Monmouth, Henry Carey, *earl of.*

[**Carey, W.**] Englands wants. 1667. *See* Chamberlayne, Edward.

568 **Cargill, Donald.** A lecture and sermon. [*Edinburgh, 1681?*] 4°.* L, D, EN; NPT, NU, Y.

569 —A letter from. [*Glasgow? 1681.*] 8°.* EN, A.

570 Entry cancelled.

571 The cargo's of seven East-India ships. [*n.p., 1664.*] brs. L.

572 **Carier, Benjamin.** A missive to His Majesty of Great Britain, King James. *First, printed at Liege, and novv reprinted at Paris: 1649.* 12°. L, O, CM, OC, SP; CH, CLC, TU, WF, Y.

573 — —"Last edition." *For Matthew Turner, 1687.* 12°. L; MH, MIU, NU, TU.

574 [**Carisbrick, Edward.**] The life of the Lady Warner of Parham. *By Tho: Hales, 1691.* 8°. L.

575 [–] —Second edition. —, *1692.* 8°. L; CH, CN, NF, TU, WG, Y.

576 [–] —Third edition. *By Thomas Hales, 1696.* 8°. L, O.

577 [**Carkesse, James.**] Lucida intervalla. *Printed, 1679.* 4°. L, C; CH, LC, MH, WCL, Y.

578 **Carlell, Lodowick.** The deserving favorite. *For Humphrey Moseley, 1659.* 8°. L, O, C; CH, CN, LC, MH, WF, Y.

579 —The famous tragedy of Osmond the great Turk. *For Humphrey Moseley, 1657.* 8°. L, C; CH, MH, NC, Y.

580 —The fool would be a favourit. *For Humphrey Moseley, 1657.* 8°. L, C; CH, MH, NC, PU, Y.

—Heraclitus. 1664. *See* Corneille, Pierre.

581 —The passionate lovers. *For Humphrey Moseley, 1655.* 8°. L, O, LVD, EC; CH, CU, MH, TU, WF, Y.

581A — —[Anr. ed.] —, *1655.* 8°. LT, O, C, LVD, CT; CH, CN, LC, MH, TU, Y.

582 —Two new playes. *For Humphrey Moseley, 1657.* 8°. L, O, C, LVD, EN; CH, CN, LC, MH, TU, WF, Y.

583 **Carles, Thomas.** A sermon preached at the Cathedral Church in Gloucester. *By T. R. for Peter Dring, 1661.* 4°.* L; NU.

584 **C[arleton], G[eorge], bp.** Ἀστρολογομανία: the madnesse of astrologers. *By R. C. for John Hammond, 1651.* 8°. LT, C, CT, LWL, DC; CLC, CU, MH, WF, Y.

585 —Bp. Carleton's testimonie. *For Nath: Butter, 1642.* 4°.* LT, O, CSS, CT; HR, NU, Y.

585A **Carleton, John.** The replication. *By the authors appointment, 1663.* 4°.* EN; CN, MH.

586 —The ultimum vale of. *For J. Jones, 1663.* 4°. L, O, EN, ES; MH.

586A **Carleton, Mary.** The case of. *For Sam: Speed and Hen: Marsh, 1663.* 12°. CLC, CN, MH, MM.

587 —The memoires of. 1673. *See* G., J.

C[arleton], R[owland]. Diana, dutchess of Mantva. *By T. H. and are to be sold by Henry Brome, 1679.* 8°. T.C.I 349. L; CH, CU, MH.

588 —The Italian princess. *Printed and are to be sold by H. Bonwicke, 1681.* 8°. T.C.I 450. MH.

588A **Carleton, Thomas.** The captives complaint. [*London*], *printed, 1668.* 8°. L; PSC.

588B —The confider in falsehood confounded. *1684.* 4°.* PH.

589 —A general epistle. [*n.p., 1676.*] cap. 4°.* L, LF, O, BBN, BP; CH, CLC, MH, PH.

589A —The memory of that faithful servant. [*London*], *printed, 1694.* 8°. LF.

590 **Carlile, James.** The fortune-hunters. *For James Knapton, 1689.* 4°. T.C.II 275. L, O, C, OW, EN; CH, CN, MH, NC, TU, WCL, WF, Y.

591 **Carlingford, Francis Taaffe, earle of.** The case of Francis, Earl of Carlingford. [*London, 1697.*] brs. L, LL.

592 —Count Taaffe's letters. *For T. B. to be sold by William Abbington, 1684.* 4°.* T.C.II 75. L, O, CS, SP, E; CH, MH, MIU, WF.

[**Carlisle, Charles Howard, earl of.**] A relation of three embassies . . . performed by. 1669. *See* Miege, Guy.

592A **Carlos II.** His most catholick Majesty's answer. colop: *For Randal Taylor, 1692.* brs. Y.

593 —The last will and codicil of Charles II. King of Spain. *For H. Rhodes; A. Bell; and E. Castle, 1700.* 4°. L, O, CS, BAMB, E; CH, CN, MH, WF, Y.

593A —A letter from. colop: [*London*] *for Richard Baldwin, 1690.* brs. CH, Y.

593B —The true will of. *Printed, 1700.* 4°.* L, O; CN, LC, NC, PU, Y.

593C —The late King of Spain's will. *Dublin, re-printed, 1700.* 4°.* DIX 320. DI, DN; Y.

594 **Carlyle, James Hay, earl of.** A declaration by. [*London, 1648.*] brs. LT.

595 The car-man's poem. [*London, 1680?*] brs. L, O; MH, PU, Y.

Carmen Deo nostro. Paris, 1652. *See* Crashaw, Richard.

Carmen elegiacum. [*n.p., 1643.*] *See* C., N.

Carmen encomiasticum. [*n.p., 1674.*] *See* Settle, Elkanah.

596 Carmen gratulatio Edwardo Hide. [*n.p.*], *1660.* brs. O.

Carmen in serenissimæ. [*1681.*] *See* Selyedo, James.

597 Carmen memoriale or a memoriall to keep unspotted to posterity . . . Colonel Thomas Rainsborough. *Novemb. 14, 1648.* brs. L.

597A Carmen natalium. To his highness the Duke of Glocester. *For A. Baldwin, 1700.* fol.* MH.

Carmen pastorale. 1700. *See* Fowler, John.

598 Entry cancelled.

Carmen sœwlare. 1700. *See* Prior, Matthew.

599 **Carmeni, Francesco.** Nissena; an excellent new romance. *For Humphrey Moseley, 1653.* 8°. LT, O; CN, MH, NN, WF.

Carmens remonstrance. 1649. *See* Spratt, Stephen.

600 **Carmichael, Alexander.** Believers mortification of sin. *For Dorman Newman, 1677.* 8°. L, LCL, CT, GU; MH, WF.

601 **Carmichael, G.** Theses philosophicæ. *Glasgow, Sanders, 1699.* 4°. ALDIS 3913. EN.

601A **Carmichael, William.** Disputatio juridica. *Edinburgi, ab hæredibus ac sucssoribus [sic] A. Anderson, 1695.* 4°.* EN.

[273]

602 Carmina colloquia: or, a demonaicall and damnable dialogue. [n.p.], printed, 1649. 4°.* LT, E; MH, Y.

603 Carmina vestalia. Being three epistles. Printed and sold by J. Nutt, 1700. fol.* L; NN.

Carminum proverbalium. 1654. See I., S. A.

604 Carnal prudence display'd. For B. Shirley, 1682. fol.* O, CM; CH, WF, Y.

Carnal reason. 1669. See Younge, Richard.

604A **Carney, D.** On His Majesties birth-day. By William Weston, 1694. brs. TU.

Caro-carita. A treatise. 1658. See W., L.

605 **Carolan, Neal.** Motives of conversions. Dvblin, by Jos. Ray, for William Norman, and Eliphal Dobson, 1688. 4°. DIX 228. T.C.II 237. L, C, OE, DT, DM; CH, NU, WF.

Caroli secundi, magnæ. [n.p.] 1685. See Breval, François Durant de.

Caroli τοῦ μακαριτου. 1649. See Pierce, Thomas.

606 Carolina described more fully. Dublin, printed, 1684. 4°. CH, NN, RPJ, WCL.

Carolina, or. 1682. See Ash, Thomas.

Carolo II regi votum. [n.p.], 1669. See Newport, Maurice.

Caroloiades, or. 1689. See Howard, Edward.

Carolus I Britanniarum rex. Dvblini, 1652. See Morisot, Claude Barthélemy.

607 **Caron, Frans.** A true description of the mighty kingdoms of Japan and Siam. By Samuel Broun and John de l'Ecluse, 1663. 8°. L, O, OCC, EN; CN, MH.

608 ——[Anr. ed.] For Robert Boulter, 1671. 8°. T.C.I 86. L, C, LW, CT; CH, CN, LC, MIU.

609 **Caron, Raymond.** Loyalty asserted. By T. Mabb, 1662. 4°. L, O, C, CPE, DT; TU, WF.

610 —Remonstrantia Hibernorum. [London?], 1665. fol. L, O, C, E, DT; BN, CH, WF.

611 [–] A vindication of the Roman Catholicks. Printed, 1660. 4°.* LT, OC, SP; CH, CU, MH, NU, Y.

612 [**Carpender, William.**] Jura cleri: or an apology. Oxford, by A. and L. Lichfield, for Tho. Robinson, 1661. 4°. MADAN 2548. L, O, CCH, EN, DT; CH, MH, NU, TU, WF, Y.

613 **Carpenter, Agricola.** Pseuchographia anthropomagica. For John Browne, 1652. 4°.* LT, O, C, GU; CH, CLC, MH, WF, Y.

614 **Carpenter, Henry.** The deputy divinity. For N. Webb, & W. Grantham, 1657. 12°. LT, LCL, DC, P.

614A —A sermon preached . . . July 23, 1653. By John Macock for Octavian Pullen, 1653. 4°.* WCA; MH, MWA, WF.

615 **Carpenter, John.** Epicedium in obitum . . . Gulielmi Glocestriæ ducis. [London, 1700]. cap., fol.* L.

616 **Carpenter, Nathaniel.** Philosophia libera. Oxoniæ, exc. H. Hall per R. Davis, 1675. 8°. T.C.I 200. MADAN 3053. OC, OM; Y.

617 **Carpenter, Richard.** The Anabaptist washt and washt, and shrunk. By W: H., to be sold by George Badger, 1653. 12°. LCL, LB; CLC, NU.

618 ——[Anr. ed.] By William Hunt, [1653]. 8°. LT, O, CK; NPT, WF, Y.

619 —Astrology proved harmless. By Ja: Cottrel, for John Allen, and Joseph Barber, 1657. 4°.* LT, O, LW, CCL; CLC, NPT, NU, WF.

620 —The downfal of Anti-christ. Printed at London for Iohn Stafford, 1644. 4°. L, LW; NPT, NU.

620A ——[Anr. ed.] 1677. 8°. LW, ENC.

620B —Experience, historie, and divinitie. By I.N. for John Stafford, 1641. 8°. A; CN, NU.

621 —[Anr. ed.] By R. C. for Andrew Crook, 1642. 8°. L, O, C, E, EN; CH, MH, NU, WF, Y.

622 —The Iesuit, and the monk. By Francis Leach, 1656. 4°.* LT, O, LCL, DT.

623 —The last and highest appeal. For the author, 1656. 8°. LT.

624 —A new play call'd The pragmatical Jesuit new-leven'd. For N. R., [166–?]. 4°. L, O, CK; CH, CN, MH, WCL, WF, Y.

625 —The perfect-law of God. By F.L., 1652. 8°. LT, LCL; CLC, NPT, NU, WF.

626 —Rome in her fruits. By T. Ratcliffe for H. R., 1663. 4°.* L, O, LIL, CK; CH, CLC, NU, WF.

627 **Carr, Alan.** A peaceable moderator. By G. Miller for William Crooke, 1665. 4°. L, CT, LCL, CP; CH, NU, WF.

628 **Carr, Richard.** Epistolæ medicinales. Impensis Stafford Anson, 1691. 8°. T.C.II 382. L, O, C, LCS, AU; BN, CH, MMO, NAM, WF, HC.

629 **Carr, Robert.** An antidote against lust. By J. Astwood for John Dunton, 1690. 12°. T.C.II 311. P; NP, Y.

630 **Carr, Robert.** The delightful companion. Second edition. For J. Playford, 1686. obl., 4°. L.

631 **Carr, William.** An accurate description. For Timothy Childe, 1691. 8°. T.C.II 359. L, O, CT, E; CH, WF, Y.

632 —Carrs case being a brief relation. Amsterdam, printed, 1670. 4°.* L, LL; CH, CU, PL, WF, Y.

632A [–] Coffo philo or the coffy house dialogue. [Ratisbon] printed London, 1672. 8°. L.

633 [–] A particular account of the present siege of Mastricht, [London, 1676]. cap., 8°.* CH.

634 —A particular account of this last siege of Mastricht. For G. Kunholt, and Moses Pitt, 1676. 4°.* T.C.I 253. L, O, CS, CT, MR; HR, CH, LC, MIU, WF, Y.

635 [–] Pluto furens & vinctus; or, the raging devil bound. Amstelodami, in usum Theatrii Amstelredemonsis, 1669. 4°.* L, O; CH, MH, WF, Y.

636 —Remarks of the government of severall parts of Germanie. Printed in Amsterdam, 1688. 12°. T.C.II 339. L, O, CT, LUG, CLC, MIU, Y.

637 —The travellours guide. [London], for Eben Tracy, 1695. 12°. T.C.II 549. L, O, EN; CN.

638 **Carré, Ezekiel.** The charitable Samaritan. Boston, by Samuel Green, 1689. 4°.* EVANS 464. LC, NN.

639 —Echantillon. Imprimé à Boston par Samuel Green, 1690. 4°.* EVANS 504. MWA.

639A —La morte des justes, ou sermon. Par C. Lucas, 1697. 4°.* WF.

640 **Carre, James.** A letter by the Lord Generals direction, from Collonel Carre. For Matthevv Walbancke, 1644. 4°.* LT, CCL, LFEA; MH, WF.

Carre, Thomas. See Pinkney, Miles.

640A **Carre, Thomas.** A treatise of subiection. *For Andrew Kember*, 1651. 4°. L, O, CJ.

641 **Carrey, Edward.** A serious meditation for sinners. [*London*], *for J. Blare*, [1688?]. 8°.* L.

642 [**Carrington, John.**] The Lancashire Levite rebuk'd: or, a vindication. *By Rich. Janeway, jun. and sold by Richard Baldwin*, 1698. 4°.* T.C.III 51. L, O, CS, CT, OC; CLC, MH, NU, WF, Y.

643 **Carrington, S.** The history of the life and death of . . . Oliver. *For Nath. Brook*, 1659. 8°. LT, LCL, CS, CT, EN; CH, MH, NU, TU.

644 **Carrol, James.** A narrative of the Popish plot in Ireland. *For Richard Janeway*, 1681. fol.* L, O, C, HH; CH, CN, PL, WF, Y.

645 —A new discovery of the sham-Presbyterian plot. colop: *For Richard Janeway*, 1681. brs. L, O, LG, HH; CH, MH, MIU, Y.

646 —To the kings most excellent majesty. A true and exact relation. [*n.p.*, 1681?] cap., 4°. C.

Carroll, Susannah. *See* Centlivre, *Mrs.* Susannah.

Carrouse to the emperor. [*n.p.*, 1683.] *See* D'Urfey, Thomas.

647 **Carstairs, John.** A song for this sad times. *Edinburgh, by John Reid*, 1691. 8°. EN.

647A **Carstairs, William.** The deposition of. colop: *Edinburgh, by the heir of Andrew Anderson*, 1684. fol.* ALDIS 2448. EN; CH, NN, NU, PU.

648 ——[Anr. ed.] colop: *Edinburgh, by the heir of Andrew Anderson; and reprinted at London by Tho. Newcomb, for Susanna Forester*, 1684. fol.* O, CS, MC, EN; CH, NU, WF, Y.

649 **Carswell, Francis.** England's restoration parallel'd in Judah's. *For Awnsham Churchill*, 1689. 4°.* T.C.II 284. L, O, C, CT, SP; CH, NC, NU, WF, Y.

650 ——Second edition. —, 1689. 4°.* L, O, SP, WCA, DT; MBA, NNG.

651 —The state-reformer inquired into. *By J. Macock for Awnsham Churchil*, 1684. 4°.* L, OCC.

651A **Carte, John.** The frontispiece of the cosmographical clock. [*London*, 1700.] brs. Y.

651B —A geographical clock. [*London*, 1695.] brs. Y.

651C **Carte, Samuel.** A dissuasive from murmuring. *For Richard Baldwin*, 1694. 4°.* O; WF, Y.

652 **Carter, Edward.** Bibliotheca Carteriana, sive catalogus. [*London*], 1689. 4°.* OC; JF.

653 —A remonstrance of. [*n.p.*, 1660.] 4°.* NN, Y.

654 **Carter, John.** The nail & the vvheel. *By J. Macock for M. Spark*, [1647]; 4°. LT, LCL, LSC; CH, MB, MIU, WF, Y.

655 ——[Anr. ed.] — *and are to be sold by William Franklin in Norwich*, 1647. 4°. L, O, LCL; CH, MH.

656 [–] The tomb-stone, and a rare sight. *By Tho: Roycroft, for E.D. and N.E. to be sold by John Sprat, in Norwich*, 1653. 8°. L, O, LCL, SP; BN, MH.

656A ——[Anr. ed.] *By Tho. Roycroft, for Edm Dod and Natn. Ekins*, 1653. 8°. L; MH, NPT, Y.

657 —Vindiciae decimarum. Of tithes. 1641. 4°. MHS.

658 **Carter, Matthew.** Honor rediviuus or an analysis. *By E. Cotes*, 1655. Sould by Thomas Heath and Henry Herringman. 4°. LT, C, OC, MR; CH, MH, NC, WF, Y.

659 ——Second edition. *For Henry Herringman*, 1660. 8°. LT, O, CT, LG, EN; BN, CH, MBP, WF, Y.

660 [–] —Third edition. *For Henry Herringman*, 1673. 8°. T.C.I 143. L, O, C, AU, EN; CH, CN, LC, MH, Y.

661 ——Fourth edition. *For Richard Bentley, Jacob Tonson, Francis Saunders, and Tho. Bennet*, 1692. 8°. NHL, E.

662 —A most trve and exact relation of that . . . expedition of Kent. [*London*] *printed*, 1650. 12°. L, O, C, MR, EN; CH, CN, MH, WF, Y.

663 [**Carter, R.**] Life & death offered. *Printed*, 1662. 4°. NU.

663A **Carter, Richard.** A beneficial proposal. *For W. Marshal*, 1695. WF.

663B —A proposal humbly offered to the . . . Commons. [*London*, 1694?] cap., 4°.* MH, NC, Y.

664 —The schismatick stigmatized. *By J. Okes, for Francis Coles*, 1641. 4°.* LT, C, HH; CLC, MH, NU, OCI, WF.

665 **Carter, Samuel.** Lex custumaria: or, a treatise. *By the assigns of Richard and Edward Atkins, for John Walthoe*, 1696. 12°. L, LL, LGI, LIL, CS; CH, CN, MHL, NCL, WF.

666 —Reports of sevral [sic] special cases. *By W. Rawlins, S. Roycroft, and M. Flesher, assigns of Rich. and Edw. Atkyns; for Thomas Bassett, Charles Harper, and Samuel Keble*, 1688. fol. T.C.II 223. L, O, C, LL, EN; LC, MHL, NCL, NP.

667 [**Carter, Thomas.**] Non-conformists no schismaticks. [*London*], *printed*, 1670. 4°.* L, O, OC, EC, HH; NU.

668 —Prayers prevalencie for Israels safety. *By Richard Cotes, and are to be sold by John Bellamie and Ralph Smith*, 1643. 4°.* LT, O, C, EN, DT; CH, MH, NU, TU, WF, Y.

669 **Carter, William,** *clothier.* An abstract of the proceedings of. *For the author*, 1694. 4°.* L; CH, CN, NC.

670 —An abstract of the proceedings to prevent exportation of wooll. *By J. Streater, for the author*, 1688. 4°.* L, C; MH.

670A ——[Anr. ed.] —, 1689. 4°.* O.

671 [–] An account of some proceedings lately made for an effectual prohibition of the exportation of wooll. [*London*, 1685?] cap., 4°.* L; NC.

671A —An alarum to England. *By K. Astwood for Mary Fabian*, 1700. 8°.* L; WF.

672 [–] A brief advertisement to the merchant and clothier. *For the authour*, 1672. 4°.* L; NC, WF.

673 [–] Englands glory. By the benefit of wool. colop. *By T. M.*, 1662. cap., 4°.* CH, MH, MIU, WF, Y.

674 [–] England's interest asserted. *For Francis Smith, and Henry Mortlock*, 1669. 4°.* L, C, OC; CH, MH, MIU, NC, NN.

675 —Englands interest by trade. Second edition. —, 1671. 4°. L, C, OC, CCA, EN; CH, CU, MH, NC, WF, Y.

675A ——[Anr. ed.] *By Joseph Streater, for the author*, 1689. 4°.* LUG; LC, NC, PU.

676 —A narrative of William Carter's proceedings. [*n.p.*, 1685.] 4°.* L.

676A —The proceedings of. [*London*, 1694.] 4°.* NC.

676B [–] The proverb crossed. [*London*], *for the authour.* 1677. 4°.* L, LUG; SCH, MH, NC.

676C [–] —Second edition. —, 1677. 4°.* L; MH, Y.

676D [–] The renewing of a caveat. [*London, for the author by E. Holt*, 1691.] cap., 4°.* MH, NC, Y.

676E —The reply of W. C. [*London*, 1677.] cap., 4°.* MH, NC.

677 —A summary of certain papers about wooll. *For the author*, 1685. 4°. L, LUG, EN; MH, PU.

677A —To the merchants and clothiers. [*London*, 1685.] cap., 4°.* NC.

678 —The usurpations of France. *For Richard Baldwin*, 1695. 4°.* L, LUG, SP; CH, CU, MH, NC, WF, Y.

679 **Carter, William,** *minister.* The covenant of God with Abraham, opened. *By T. C. for John Rothwell*, 1654. 4°. LT, O, LCL; MB, NHC, NPT, NU, WF, Y.

679A —Israels peace with God. *For Giles Calvert, to be sold by Christopher Meredith*, 1642. 4°.* LT, O, C, LCL, DT; CH, MH, NU, WF, Y.

680 —Light in darknesse. *By M. Simmons, for Giles Calvert*, 1648. 4°.* LT, O, CT, LCL, DT; BBE, MH, NU, WF, Y.

680A [**Cartigny, Jean de**] The conviction of world-vanity. *By G. L. for John Harris*, 1687. 12°. T.C.II 186. L, LCL; CN.

681 —The voyage of the wandering knight. *By Richard Bishop, and are to be sold by William Gilbertson*, 1650. 4°. O, C; CN, Y.

681A ——[Anr. ed.] *By John Cadwell for Andrew Crooke*, 1661. 4°. L; NP.

682 ——[Anr. ed.] *By E. Crowch, for Andrew Crooke*, 1670. EN; LC, MRS, Y.

683 **Cartwright, Christopher.** A brief and plain exposition of the creed. *Printed at York by T. Broad*, 1649. 8°. LT, O.

684–5 Entries cancelled. *See* Bayly, Thomas.

686 —The doctrine of faith. *By R. A. for Richard Lovvndes*, 1649. 8°. LT.

687 ——[Anr. ed.] —, 1650. 8°. O, CT, CE, LW, DT; CLC, MH, NPT, NU, Y.

688 —Electa thargumico-rabbinica . . . in Genesin. *Typis Guil. Dugard, impensis Sam. Thomson*, 1648. 8°. L, O, C, LW, DT; BN, MH, NC, NU, WF, Y.

689 —Electa thargumico-rabbinica . . . in Exodum. *Typis Thomae Mabb: prostant apud Sam. Thomson*, 1653. 8°. O, C, OM, P, DT; BN, NU, PL, Y.

690 ——[Anr. ed.] *Typis T. M. prostant apud Matt. Keinton*, 1658. 8°. LT, CM, CS, CT; MH, NPT.

691 —Exceptions against a vvriting of Mr. R. Baxters. *For Nevil Simmons and Jonath. Robinson*, 1675. 8°. O, C, LCL, YM, ENC; CH, MH, NU, WF, Y.

692 —The magistrate's authority. *For Tho. Underhill*, 1647. 4°.* LT, O, C, CP, DT; CLC, NU.

693 —A practical and polemical commentary or exposition on the whole fifteenth Psalm. [*London*], *for Nath. Brook*, 1658. 4°. O, LCL, YM, AU; IU, MH, NPT, WF.

694 **Cartwright, George.** The heroick-lover. *By R. W. for John Symmes*, 1661. 8°. L, O, LVD; CLC, LC, MH, WF, Y.

694A —Upon the just judgment. [*London*, 1660]. brs. MH.

695 [**Cartwright, Joanna.**] The petition of the Jewes. *For George Roberts*, 1649. 4°.* LT; CH, CSS, WF.

696 [**Cartwright, Thomas,** *bp.*] An answer of a minister of the Church of England. *For J. L.*, 1687. 4°. L, O, CT, DC, EN; CH, MH, NU, WF, Y.

697 —The danger of riches. *By R. Davenport for John Baker*, 1662. 4°.* L, O, D; MH, MWA, WF.

—A directory of church government. 1644. *See* Travers, Walter.

698 —God's arraignments of Adam. *For John Baker*, 1659. 4°.* LT, O, C, LP, YM.

699 —The good man's epitaph. *By D. Maxwel, for John Baker*, 1659. 4°.* LT, O, OC; MH, MWA.

700 —Helpes for discovery of the truth. *For Thomas Banks*, 1648. 4°.* LT, LSC, YM, DT; NU, WF, Y.

701 —The judgment of M. Cartwright and M. Baxter concerning separation. *Printed*, 1673. 4°. T.C.I 133. O, CS, YM, E, DT; CH, NU, WF.

701A [–] A letter from a clergy-man in the country. *In the Savoy, by Edw. Jones, and published by Randal Taylor*, 1688. 4°.* OC; CLC, MH, MIU, WF, Y.

702 —A sermon preached . . . January the 9th, 1675/6. *In the Savoy: by Tho. Newcomb, to be sold by Jonathan Edwyn*, 1675/6. 4°.* T.C.I 233. L, O, C, LL, DT; CH, CLC, WF, Y.

702A ——[Anr. ed.] *By Thomas Newcomb*, 1675/6. 4°.* WCA, OC; PL.

703 —A sermon preached July 17. 1676. *In the Savoy: by Tho. Newcomb; to be sold by Jonathan Edwyn*, 1676. 4°.* T.C.I 272. L, O, C, CT, EN; CH, MH, NU, WF, Y.

703A ——[Anr. ed.] *By Tho. Newcomb, to be sold by R. Lambert in York*, 1676. 4°.* CT, BR; MH, MWA, PL, WF, Y.

704 —A sermon preacht . . . 30 January, 1681/2. *Edinburgh, by David Lindsay*, 1682. 4°.* ALDIS 2330. CT, YM, EN; IU, NU, V, Y.

704A ——[Anr. ed.] — *and reprinted at London, sold by Walter Davis*, 1682. 4°.* L, O, CT, LL, EN; CH, NP, NU, V, WF.

705 —A sermon preached . . . 24th of June, 1684. *For Tho. Flesher*, 1684. 4°.* T.C.II 94. L, O, C, WCA, YM; CH, MH, NU, WF, Y.

706 —A sermon preached upon the anniversary solemnity of the happy inauguration of . . . King James II, . . . February the 6th. 1685/6. *By J. Leake, to be sold by Walter Davis*, 1686. 4°.* L, O, C, OM, EN; CH, CN, MH, NU, WF, Y.

707 ——Second edition. —, 1686. 4°. LVF, C, CS, WCA; MBA, TU, WF, Y.

708 ——[Anr. ed.] *Edinburgh*, 1686. 4°. ALDIS 2635. EN, FSF; NPT.

709 **Cartwright, William,** *playwright.* Comedies, tragi-comedies, with other poems. *For Humphrey Moseley*, 1651. 8°. LT, O, C, LVF, EN; BN, CH, CN, LC, MH, NC, TU, Y.

710 —The lady-errant. *For Humphrey Moseley*, 1651. 8°. CH, CLC, WF, Y.

711 [–] November. [*n.p.*, 1671.] brs. LT, O, HH.

712 —Of the signal days of the month. November. *In the Savoy, by T. N. for Henry Herringman*, 1671. 4°.* L, O; CH.

713 —An off-spring of mercy. *By A. M. to be sold by Iohn Brown*, 1652. 8°.* LT, O, E; CH.

714 —The ordinary, a comedy. *For Humphrey Moseley*, 1651. 8°. LT, LG; CH, CLC, WF, Y.

715 —To the right honourable Philip Earle of Pembroke . . . vpon his . . . election. [*London*], *for T. W.*: 1641. brs. MADAN 966. LT; MH.

716 ——[Anr. ed.] *Printed*, 1641. brs. L, O, CT.

716A [–] Verses made upon the several festivals of November. *Printed* 1685. cap., fol.* O; CH, CLC, IU, MH.

717 **Cartwright, William, *stenographer*.** Semography: or, short and swift writing. *Printed*, 1642. 8°.* L.

717A ——[Anr. ed.] *By E. P. for N. Gamage*, 1644. 8°. CT.

718 **C[arver], M[armaduke].** A discourse of the terrestrial paradise. *By James Flesher, and are to be sold by Samuel Thomson*, 1666. 8°. L, O, CS, OC; BBE, IU, LC.

719 ——[Anr. ed.] —, 1666. 8°. L, O, CS, P; CN, PL, WF, Y.

719A —Jerusalem restored. 1661. 8°. YM.

720 **Carwardine, Daniel.** A brief discourse touching a broken heart. 1652. 12°. LCL.

721 **C[arwell], T[homas].** Labyrinthvs cantvariensis: or Doctor Lawd's labyrinth. *Paris, by Iohn Billaine*, 1658. fol. L, O, CT, LM, ES; CH, CU, NU, WG, Y.

722 **[Cary, Edward.]** The catechist catechiz'd. [*n.p.*], *printed*, 1681. 8°. CS; CLC, CN, NU, TU, WF.

Cary, *Sir* George. See Carew, *Sir* George.

723 **Cary, Henry.** The law of England. *For the author*, [1666]. 12°. O; MHL, NC, WF, YL.

Cary, Henry. See Falkland, Henry Cary, *viscount*.

724 **[Cary, John.]** An account of the proceedings of the corporation of Bristol. *By F. Collins, and are to be sold by John Nutt*, 1700. 8°.* L, O, OC, EC, EN; CH, CN, MH, NC, WF, Y.

725 [–] An answer to Mr. Molyneux his case. *For Rich. Parker*, 1698. 8°. L, O, C, DT; CH, CN, LC, MH, NU, Y.

726 —A discourse concerning the East-India trade. *For E. Baldwin*, 1699. 4°.* L, LUG, BR; LC, MH, Y.

727 —A discourse concerning the trade of Ireland and Scotland. *Bristol printed*, 1695; *London reprinted*, 1696. 4°. L, CS, BR, EN, ES; CH, MH, NC, WF, Y.

728 —An essay, on the coyn. *Bristol, by Will. Bonny*, 1696. 12°.* O; BN, CN, CU, MH, VC.

729 ——[Anr. ed.] *Bristol; by Will. Bonny, and sold London*, 1696. 8°.* L, O, BR; MH, TU, WF, Y.

730 —An essay on the state of England. *Bristoll: by W. Bonny, for the author, and are to be sold in London by Sam Crouch and Tim Goodwin, also by Tho. Wall and Rich. Gravett, in Bristol*, 1695. 8°. L, O, CT, LPO, EN; BN, CH, CN, MH, NC, PL, WF, Y.

731 —An essay towards the setlement of a national credit. *By Freeman Collins, to be sold by S. Crouch and E. Whitlock*, 1696. 8°.* L, O, CK, OC, BR; CH, CU, MH, WF, Y.

732 [–] A proposal offered to the committee of the House of Commons. *Printed*, 1690. 8°.* OC.

732A ——[Anr. ed.] [*London*, 1700?] cap., 8°.* L, O, LUG, OC; PU, Y.

733 [–] A reply to a paper delivered. [*London*, 1700?] cap., fol.* L; MIU, NC, Y.

733A [–] To the free holders . . . Bristol. [*Bristol?* 1698.] cap., 8°.* LUG.

734 —A vindication of the Parliament. *By Freeman Collins, and are to be sold by Sam. Crouch and Eliz. Whitlock*, 1698. 8°. L, O, LL; CN, MH, NU, TU, Y.

735 ——[Anr. ed.] —, 1700. 8°. L, ES; CH.

Cary, Lucius. See Falkland, Lucius Cary, *viscount*.

736 **Cary, Mary.** The little horns doom. *For the author*, 1651. 12°. LT, O, LW; CH, CLC, NHC, NU.

737 —The resurrection of the witnesses. *By D. M. for Giles Calvert*, 1648. 12°. L; CLC.

738 ——Second edition. *By H. Hills for R. C. to be sold by T. Brewster, and L. Chapman*, 1653. 4°. LT, LCL; NHC.

739 —A vvord in season. *By R. W. for Giles Calvert*, 1647. 4°.* LT, LCL, HH, DT; CH, NHC, Y.

[Cary, Nicholas.] Some considerations upon the question. 1676. See Holles, Denzil Holles, *baron*.

740 **Cary, Philip.** A disputation. *By B. W. for the author, to be sold by R. Baldwin*, 1684. 12°. L, O; MIU, NU.

741 —A just reply to Mr. John Flavell's arguments. *For J. Harris*, 1690. 12°. T.C.II 339. L; NHC, NU.

742 —A solemn call. *For John Harris*, 1690. 8°. L, LCL, LW; NGT, NHC, NPT, NU.

743 **Cary, Robert.** Palæologia chronica. A chronological account. *By J. Darby, for Richard Chiswell*, 1677. fol. T.C.I 252. L, O, C, EN, DT; BN, CH, LC, MH, NC, Y.

743A **Cary, Thomas.** A sermon preached . . . 15th of July 1691. *By F. C. for T. Wall in Bristol*, 1691. 4°. O, BR.

743B ——[Anr. ed.] *By F. C. for T. Guy*, 1691. 4°. CT.

743C **Cary, William.** A vindication of the Parliament. 1698. 8°. CCA.

744 **[Caryl, John.]** The English princess. *For Thomas Dring*, 1667. 4°. T.C.I 289. L, O, CM, LVD, A; CH, CN, LC, MH, TU, Y.

744A [–] ——[Anr. ed.] *By R. B. for Thomas Basset, and are to be sold by William Cademan*, 1673. 4°. O; CLC, PU, TU.

745 [–] ——[Anr. ed.] —, 1674. 8°. T.C.I 152. C, EN; CU, NC, WF, Y.

745A [–] Naboth's vineyard. *For C. R.*, 1679. fol.* L, O, LV, CT, OC; CLC, CN, TU, WF, Y.

745B [–] ——[Anr. ed.] —, 1679. 4°.* L, O, OC; CH, MH, TU, WF, Y.

746 [–] Sir Salomon. *For H. Herringman*, 1671. 4°. T.C.I 72. L, O, LVF, OW, EN; CH, CN, LC, MH, NC, TU, WF, Y.

747 [–] ——[Anr. ed.] —, 1691. 4°. LVD, EN; NP.

748 ——[Anr. ed.] *For H. Herringman, sold by Jacob Tonson*, 1691. 4°. L, O, C; LC, MH, NC, WF, Y.

749 **Caryl, Joseph.** The arraignment of unbelief. *By G. Miller for Giles Calvert*, 1645. 4°. LT, O, C, EN, ENC; CH, CN, MH, NU, WF, Y.

750 —Davids prayer for Solomon. *By G. M. for Giles Calvert, to be sold by Christopher Meredith*, 1643. 4°.* LT, O, C, LG, DT; CH, MH, NU, TU, WF, Y.

751 —England's plus ultra. *By T. F. for John Rothwell*, 1646. 4°.* LT, C, LW, DT; CH, CN, MBA, NU, V, WF.

752 ——[Anr. ed.] *By G. M. for John Rothwell, and Giles Calvert*, 1646. 4°.* LT, O, HH, E; CH, MH, OWC, Y.

753 —An English-Greek lexicon of the New Testament. 1661. 8°. L, LCL, CS; CH, CLC, WF, Y.

754 —An exposition with practicall observations vpon the three first chapters of . . . Iob. By G. Miller, for Henry Overton, and Luke Fawne, and Iohn Rothwell, 1643. 4°. L, OB, NPL, SP, GU; CLC, MH, TU, Y.

755 ——[Anr. ed.] —, 1644. 4°. LT, O, CP, LBS, AU; MH, NU, WF.

755A ——[Anr. ed.] —, 1647. 4°. P, RPL; CU, IU, NPT, TU, WWC.

755B ——[Anr. ed.] For Luke Fawne, and H. Cripps and L. Lloyd, 1651. 4°. O, LW, BR; IU, MH, NP, WCL.

756 ——[Anr. ed.] By S. Simmons; to be sold by N. Ranew & J. Robinson, 1664. 4°. L.

757 ——[Anr. ed.] By M. Simmons, to be sold by Francis Haley, 1669. 4°. NU, VC, PJB, PPT.

758 ——[Anr. ed.] By Samuel Simmons, 1676. fol. T.C.I 230. O, C, LCL, LL, E; CU, NPT, NU, PL, PPT.

759 ——fourth . . . seventh chapters. By G. Miller, for H. Overton, L. Fawne, I. Rothwell, and G. Calvert, 1645. 4°. L, CP, LBS; CH, MB, MH, PJB, WF.

760 ——[Anr. ed.] By J. Macock for H. Overton, L. Fawne, J. Rothwel, and G. Calvert, 1648. 4°. O, CS, LCL, P, E; MH, NU, WCL, Y.

760A ——[Anr. ed.] For L. Fawne, L. Lloyd, and M. Simmons, 1656. 4°. L; Y.

760B ——[Anr. ed.] By M. Simmons, 1671. 4°. TU.

761 ——eighth . . . tenth chapters. By A. Miller, for Henry Overton, and Luke Fawne, and John Rothwell, 1647. 4°. AN; MH, Y.

762 ——[Anr. ed.] By E. Griffin, for Luke Fawne, and J. Rothwell, and Giles Calvert, 1649. 4°. L, O, CS, P, E; NU, PL, WCL, WF, Y.

762A ——[Anr. ed.] By M. Simmons, to be sold by George Calvert, Edward Thomas, and Samuel Sprint, 1669. 4°. T.C.I 24. L, SP, AN; MH, MWA, TU, Y.

762B ——eleventh . . . fourteenth chapters. By A. Miller for L. Fawn, J. Rothwell, and G. Calvert, 1649. 4°. L, LG, P; WCL, Y.

763 ——[Anr. ed.] By J. Macock, for Luke Fawne, 1652. 4°. L, CS, BR; Y.

764 ——[Anr. ed.] For Thomas Sawbridge, 1670. 4°. L, SP, ENC; MH, NBL, NU, TU, WF.

765 ——fifteenth . . . seventeenth chapters. By Matthew Simmons, to be sould by Thomas Eglesfeild, 1650. 4°. L, CS, P, BR; CLC, MH, WCL, WWC, PJB, Y.

765A ——[Anr. ed.] By Matthew Simmons; to be sould by Edward Dod & Nathanael Ekins, 1653. 4°. L; TU.

766 ——[Anr. ed.] By S. Simmons, 1671. 4°. SP, ENC; NU, WF.

767 ——eighteenth . . . twenty-one chapters. By Matthew Simmons, to be sold by Giles Calvert, 1653. CS, P, BR; TU, WCL, Y.

768 ——[Anr. ed.] By M. Simmons, to be sould by Joseph Cranford, 1658. 4°. L, O, LCL, SP; NU, WF, WWC.

769 ——twenty-second . . . twenty-sixth chapters. By M. Simmons, to be sould by John Allen, and Joseph Barber, 1655. 4°. LT, O, LCL; MBA, TU, WWC, Y.

770 ——[Anr. ed.] By M. Simmons, 1659. 4°. L, O, LCL, BR; MH, NBL, NU, V, WF.

771 ——twenty-seventh . . . twenty-ninth chapters. By M. S. for Elisha Wallis, 1657. 4°. LT, O, LCL; CH, CSU, TU, WCL, WWC, Y.

772 ——[Anr. ed.] By M. Simmons, to be sold by William Birch, 1670. 4°. L, BR, SP; NU, Y.

773 ——thirtieth and thirty first chapters. By M. Simmons, for Elisha Wallis, 1659. 4°. LT, O, LCL, BR, SP; MH, NU, WCL, WWC, Y.

774 ——thirty second . . . thirty fourth chapters. For M. Simmons, to be sold by Thomas Parkhurst, 1661. 4°. L, SP, AN; TU, WCL, WF.

775 ——[Anr. ed.] By M. Simmons, for Giles Widdowes, 1669. 4°. L, BR, ENC; BN, NU, WWC.

776 ——thirty-fifth . . . thirty-seventh chapters. By M. Simmons, 1664. 4°. L, O, DC, SP, ENC; MH, NU, WCL, WWC, Y.

777 ——thirty-eighth . . . forty-second (being the five last) chapters. By M. and S. Simmons, to be sold by Robert Boulter, 1666. 4°. L, O, C, SP, ENC; NU, TU, WCL, WWC, Y.

778 —Gospel-love. By John Hancock, senior and junior, 1675. 8°. T.C.I 185. MH.

779 —Heaven and earth embracing. By G. M. for George Hurlock, and Giles Calvert, 1646. 4°.* LT, O, C, OCC, AU; CH, MH, NU, WF, Y.

780 —Ioy out-joyed. By G. M. for John Rothwel, and Giles Calvert, 1646. 4°.* LT, C, P, E, DT; CH, MBA, NU, V, WF, Y.

780A [-] Memorable Joyes and workes of God. For J. Bartlett, 1646. 4°.* LT, O; CH, CLC, MH.

780B [-] The moderator. For John Bellamy, 1652. 4°. LT, OC, CT, BR, EN; CU, LC, MH, NU.

781 —The nature and principles of love. Printed, to be sold by John Hancock, senior and junior, 1673. 8°. T.C.I 146. L, C, LCL, E; MH, NU, WF.

782 —The nature, solemnity, grounds, property. By E. G. for John Rothwell and Giles Calvert, 1643. 4°.* LT, O, C, EN, DT; CH, MH, NU, TU, WF, Y.

783 —The opressor destroyed. By J. G., [1651]. 4°.* LT, O, LP, SP; CH, NU.

784 —Peters patern. Printed, 1659. 4°.* LT, OC, EN; CH, CN, MH, MIU.

785 ——[Anr. ed.] —, 1680. 4°.* L, O, OC; CH, MH, MIU, WF, Y.

786 —The present duty and endeavour of the saints. By T. Forcet for George Hurlock, 1646. 4°.* LT, O, CS, LP, LW; MBA, MH, NU, WF.

787 —The saints thankfull acclamation. By G. M. for Giles Calvert, 1644. 4°. LT, O, C, EN, DT; CH, CN, MH, NU, WF. Y.

788 —A sermon pressing to, and directing in, that great duty. By M. Simmons, to be sould by John Hancock, 1657. 4°.* LT, O, LW, HH; CH, MH, NU, WF, Y.

789 —The white robe. [n.p.], printed, 1662. 4°.* O, LW.

790 —The workes of Ephesus explained. [London], printed for Iohn Bartlet and William Bladen, 1642. 4°. LT, O, C, EN, DT; CH, MH, NU, WF, Y.

791 **Casa, Giovanni della, abp.** The arts of grandeur and submission. By A. M. for William Lee. First printed in English May Day, 1665. 8°. O, OC, CT, EN.

792   ——[Anr. ed.] *By T. J. for William Lee*, 1670. 12°. L, O, C, P; CH, MH, MMO, NU, WF, Y.

793   —I. C. de moribus et enchiridion. *Oxoniæ, excudebat W. H. impensis J. Forrest*, 1665. 12°. MADAN 2697. O; WF.

794   [–] The refin'd courtier. *By J. G. for R. Royston*, 1663. 12°. L, O, LG, SP; CLC, CN, WF, Y.

795   [–] —[Anr. ed.] *For R. Royston, to be sold by Matth. Gilly-flower and Will. Hensman*, 1679. 12°. L, C, LW, M; CH, CN, MH, PL, Y.

796   ——[Anr. ed.] *For Matth. Gillyflower*, 1686. 16°. L, OC; CN, MH, MIU.

797   **Casas, Bartholome de las.** An account of the first voyages. *By J. Darby for D. Brown, J. Harris, and Andr. Bell*, 1699. 8°. T.C.III 184. L, O, LA, E, DT; CH, CN, LC, MH, NN, Y.

798   —Popery truly display'd. *For R. Hewson*, 1689. 4°. T.C.II 273. O, LIL, EC; CH, CN, RPJ, WF, Y.

798A —A relation of the first voyages. *For Daniel Brown, and Andrew Bell*, 1699. 8°. CCC; CLC, MB, PL, Y.

799   —The tears of the Indians. *By J. C. for Nath. Brook*, 1656. 8°. LT, O; CH, CN, LC, MH, NN, Y.

800   **Casaubon, Méric.** De nupera Homeri. *Typic Tho. Roycroft, impensis J. Shirley*, 1659. 8°. L, O, C, CT, OB; BN.

801   —Merici Casauboni, de quatuor linguis. *Typis J. Flesher, sumptibus Ric. Mynne*, 1650. 8°. L, O, C, EN, DT; BN, CH, CN, MH, TU, WF, Y.

802   —Merici Casauboni, de verborum usu. *Typis M. Flesher, sumptibus R. Mynne*, 1647. 12°. L, O, C, LW, CT; BN, BBE, CLC, IU, MH, Y.

803   —A discourse concerning Christ. *By M. F. for R. Mynne*, 1646. 4°. LT, O, C, OM, DT; CH, CU, MH, NU, WF.

804   —A king and his subjects unhappily fallen out. *Printed*, 1660. 4°.* L, CS.

805   —A letter of. *Cambridge, for William Morden*, 1669. 4°.* L, O, C, MAU, EN; CH, CN, MH, WF, JF.

806   —Of credulity and incredulity; in things divine. *By T. N. for Samuel Lownds*, 1670. 8°. T.C.I 31. L, O, C, E, DT; BN, CH, MH, NC, MMO, WF, Y.

807   —Of credulity and incredulity, in things natural. *For T. Garthwait*, 1668. 8°. T.C.I 6. L, O, C, LW, DT; CH, CN, NU, WF, Y.

808   —Of the necessity of reformation. *By A. Maxwel for Timothy Garthwait*, 1664. 4°. L, O, OB, EN, DT; CH, NU, PL, WF, Y.

809   —The originall cavse of temporall evils. *By M. F. and are to be sold by Richard Minne*, 1645. 4°. LT, O, C, LCL, DT; CH, CU, NU, WF, Y.

810   —The question, to whom. *For Timothy Garthwait*, 1663. 4°.* L, O, C, LCL, DT; CH, IU, MH, NU, HC.

811   —To J. S. (the author of Sure-footing) his letter, lately published. *For Timothy Garthwait*, 1665. 4°.* L, CS.

812   —A treatise concerning enthvsiasme. *By R. D. and are to be sold by Tho. Johnson*, 1655. 8°. LT, O, C, ES, DT; BN, CH, CN, LC, MH, NU, JF.

813   ——Second edition. *By Roger Daniel and are to be sold by Thomas Iohnson*, 1656. 8°. L, O, C, EN, DT; CH, MH, NU, WF, Y.

814   —A treatise proving spirits, witches. *For Robert Pawlet*, 1672. 8°. L, C, E, EN; MH, KT.

815   ——[Anr. ed.] *For Brabazon Aylmer*, 1672. 8°. T.C.I 97. L, LWL, OC, EC, EN; CH, OCI, PL, WF, HC.

816   [–] The use of daily pvblick prayers. *For Iohn Maynard*, 1641. 4°.* LT, O, DC, E, DT; CH, MH, NU, WF.

816A [–] —[Anr. ed.] —, 1643. 4°.* CH.

817   —A vindication of the Lord's prayer. *By T. R. for Thomas Johnson*, 1660. 8°. LT, O, C, LCL, LW; NU.

    Casaus. See Casas.

818   **Case, John.** The angelical guide. *By I. Dawks*, 1697. 8°. T.C.III 67. L, O, GU; CH, WF.

819   —Compendium anatomicum. *Impensis authoris, typis J. Moxon & B. Beardwell*, 1695. 12°. T.C.II 525. L, O, CCA, AU, GH.

819A ——[Anr. ed.] *Typis J. Moxon & R. Beardwell, & prostant venebs apud Nathaneelen Rolls*, 1695. 12°. LSM.

819B —Εξηγητης Ιατρικοσ; or, one medical expositor. *S. Dawks*, 1698. T.C.II 65. MC; NSG.

819C —J. Case, who succeeds in the room of Mr. Tho. Satfold. [*London*, 1692.] brs. L.

819D —John Case an approved English . . . physician. [*London?* 1695.] brs. L.

819E —A most infallible and sure . . . cure. [*London?* 1695.] brs. L.

820   —A prophecy on the conjunction of Saturn. *For J. Smith*, 1682. 4°.* O, EN; WF.

821   —The wards of the key to Helmont. *For the author; and are to be sold by John Smith*, 1682. 4°.* L, O; CLC, WSG, Y.

822   **Case, Thomas.** Ἁγιω-μιμεσις. The imitation of the saints. *By A. M.*, 1666. 8°. L, LW.

823   —Ἀσαρκοκαυκημα, or the vanity of vaine-glory. *By T. R. and E. M. for Robert Gibbs*, 1655. 12°. L, O, LW; CH, CLC, MH, Y.

824   —Correction, instruction. *By J. M. for Luke Favvn*, 1652. 12°. LT, O, E; NPT, Y.

825   ——Second edition. —, 1653. 12°. L; CLC, NU, WF.

825A ——[Anr. ed.] *For Luke Fawne*, 1653. 12°. Y.

826   ——[Anr. ed.] *By T. R. and M. D. for Jonathan Robinson*, 1671. 12°. T.C.I 91. LW, E; CH, MH, NPT, NU, Y.

827   —Deliverance-obstruction. *By Ruth Raworth, for Luke Fawne*, 1646. 4°.* LT, O, C, EN, DT; CH, MH, NU, WF, Y.

828   —Eliah's abatement. *By E. T. for Luke Fawn*, 1658. 8°. LT, C, LCL, LW; CLC, AU, Y.

829   —The excellent woman. *For Robert Gibs*, 1659. 4°. LCL, LW; CH, NPT.

830   —Gods rising, his enemies scattering. *By J. R. for Luke Fawne*, 1644. 4°. LT, O, LCL, OM, DT; CH, CN, MH, NU, WF, Y.

831   —Gods vvaiting to be graciovs vnto his people. *By Felix Kingston for Luke Fawne*, 1642. 4°. LT, O, LCL, EN; CH, MH, NPT, NU, Y.

831A ——[Anr. ed.] *For Thomas Smith*, 1642. 4°. WF.

832   —Jehosaphats caveat to his judges. *By Felix Kingston, for Luke Fawn*, 1644. 4°.* LT, O, LW, EN, DT; MH, NPT, NU, Y.

833 —A model of true spiritual thankfulnesse. *By Ruth Raworth, for Luke Fawne*, 1646. 4°.* LT, O, C, CM, CS; CH, MH, NU, WF, Y.

834 —The morning-exercise. *By T. R. and E. M. for Robert Gibbs*, 1655. 12°. LT, LCL, P; CLC.

835 [–] The morning exercise methodized. *By E. M. for Ralph Smith*, 1660. 4°. LT, O, C, E; CLC, MH, NU, WF, Y.

836 [–] —[Anr. ed.] *By R. W. for Ralph Smith*, 1676. 4°. T.C.I 239. L, C, LW, HH, DT; BBE, MH, NPT, PL.

837 —Movnt Pisgah. *By Thomas Milbourne, for Dorman Newman*, 1670. 4°. T.C.I 54. L, O, C, LCL, ENC; MH, NU, WCL, WF, Y.

838 —The quarrel of the covenant. *For Luke Fawne*, 1644. 4°. LT, O, CS, LCL, DT; CH, MH, NPT, NU, WF.

839 —The root of apostacy. *By J. R., for Luke Fawne*, 1644. 4°.* LT, O, C, LIL, DT; CH, CN, MH, NU, TU, WF, Y.

840 —The saints, Gods precious treasure. *For Robert Gibs*, 1659. 12°. LT, LW, YM.

841 —Sensuality dissected. *By T. N. for R. Gibbs*, 1657. 12°. LT, O, LW; CLC.

842 —A sermon preached . . . August 22. 1645. *By Ruth Raworth, for Luke Fawne*, 1645. 4°.* LT, O, C, EN, DT; CH, MH, NU, WF, Y.

843 —Spirituall vvhordome discovered. *By J. Macock, for Luke Favvne*, 1647. 4°.* LT, O, C, CS, OC; CH, MH, NU, TU, WF, Y.

844 —A treatise of affections. 1671. 12°. LCL, LW.

844A — —Second edition. *For L. F.*, 1653. 12°. LSC.

845 —Two sermons lately preached. *By I. Raworth for Luke Fawne*, 1641. 4°. LT, O, CM, CT, DT; CH, CLC, NP, NU, WF.

846 — —Second edition. —, 1642. 4°. L, O, C, LCL, DT; CU, MH, NPT, NU, TU, Y.

847 The case and circumstances of paper-making in England. [*n.p.*, 1690.] brs. L, LG, LL.

847A The case and complaint of the lace men. [*London?* 1697.] brs. L.

847B The case and condition of the corporals. [*London*, 1698.] brs. L.

848 The case and cure of persons excommunicated. *For J. R. sold by Richard Janeway*, 1682. 4°.* T.C.I 496. L, O, CT, P, EN; CH, LC, NU, WF, Y.

848A The case and memorial of John Knapp. [*London*, 1695.] brs. L.

849 The case and proceedings of at least sixty gentlemen. *Printed*, 1656. fol.* O; WF.

850 The case and proposals of the free-journeymen-printers. [*n.p.*, 1666.] brs. L.

851–2 Entries cancelled.

853 The case between Sir Jerome Alexander and Sir William Ashton. [*n.p.*, 1661.] fol. L, C.

854–5 Entries cancelled.

856 The case between the farmers of the excise and the merchants, . . . brandy. [*London*, 1668?] brs. L.

857 The case between the Lᵈ. Mayor & Commons of London concerning the election of sheriffs. colop: *For R. Read*, 1682. cap., fol.* L, O, LG; CN, PU, Y.

858 The case between the merchants and the farmers of the excise . . . brandy. [*London*, 1668?] cap., fol. brs. L.

859 The case betwixt Mr. Pool and Mr. C. Bee. [*n.p.*, 1667?] 4°.* L, OC; MBA.

860 The case betwixt Thornton Cage, esq., and his wife. [*London*, 1684?] brs. L.

860A The case briefly stated, between the East-India company. [*London?* 1680.] cap., fol.* L.

861 The case concerning Monmouth election. 1680. brs. MH.

Case concerning the buying. 1659. *See* Burgess, Cornelius.

862 The case concerning the election of Barnstaple, Devon. 1680. brs. MH.

862A The case concerning the election of burgesses . . . for Eye in Suffolk, 1680. brs. MH.

863 The case concerning the election of Sir Christopher Calthrop. [1680.] brs. O.

864 The case concerning the office of clerk of the Treasury. [*London*, 168–?] brs. CH.

864A The case concerning the palace of Westminster. [*London?* 1652.] cap., fol.* L.

864B The case concerning Westbury election. 1680. brs. MH.

864C The case concerning wools. [*London?* 1700.] brs. L.

865 A case decided upon examination. [*n.p.*], 1653. 4°. DT.

865A The case fairly stated between the alderman. [*London?* 1695.] brs. L.

865B The case for making the rivers Aire . . . navigable. [*London*, 1699.] brs. L.

866 A case for Nol Cromwells nose. [*London*], *printed*, 1648. 4°.* LT; CH, MH, Y.

867 A case for the city-spectacles. [*London*] *printed*, 1648. 4°.* LT, O, CT, LVF, LG; CN, MH, TU, WF, Y.

868 The case in general of the horse, foot, and dragoons. [*n.p.*, 1695.] brs LL.

869 The case is altred [sic]: both thy case, and my case. [*London*], *printed*, 1649. 4°.* LT.

870 The case is alter'd now. colop: *For J. P.*, 1683. brs. L, O; CH, MH, NP, WF, Y.

870A The case is altered, or, a discourse. *For John Andrew*, 1660. 4°.* Y.

871 The case is altered, or, dreadful news from Hell. *For John Andrews*, [1660]. 8°.* LT.

871A The case is altered; or, Sir Reverence the Rumps last farewel. *For John Andrews*. [1660?] brs. L.

872 The case of a murther in Hertfordshire. colop: *Printed*, 1669. brs. L, HH.

873 The case of a standing army. *Printed*, 1698. 4°.* L, O, MR, EN; CH, CLC, LC, WF, Y.

874 The case of Abjohn Stokes. [*n.p.*, 1698.] brs. LL.

875 The case of Alexander MacDonnel. [*n.p.*, 1677.] cap., fol.* O.

875A The case of all crucifixes, images. [*London*], *printed*, 1643. 4°. LCL, OC; MH.

876 The case of all persons comprized in the articles or capitulations of the city of Waterford. [*n.p.*, 1691/2.] brs. L, LL.

877 The case of all the goldsmiths. [*n.p.*, 1697.] brs. LL.

878   The case of all the non-commissio 'd [*sic*] officers. [*n.p.*, 1695.] 4°. L, LL; CH.

878A   The case of all the weavers of England. [*London?* 1695.] brs. Y.

Case of allegiance in. 1689. *See* Masters, Samuel.

Case of allegiance to. [n.p.], 1690. *See* Browne, Thomas.

Case of an oath. 1693. *See* Stillingfleet, Edward.

879   The case of Andrew Clifford. [*London*, 1649]. cap., fol.* LL; Y.

880   The case of Andrew Fountaine. [*London*, 1695?] brs. L, LG.

881   The case of Ann, wife to the late Baron Slane. [*n.p.*, 1698.] brs. LL.

882   The case of Angela Margarita Cottington. [*London*, 1680.] brs. LUG.

883   The case of Anthony, Earl of Shaftsbury. *By K. P. for C. R.*, 1679. fol.* L, DC, C, OC, EN; CH, MH, PL, WF, Y.

884   The case of Anthony Ettrick. [*London*, 1698?] brs. L.

884A   The case of Anthony Gomezsera. [*London*, 1689–94.] cap., fol.* Y.

885   The case of Arrabella Lady Howard. [*London*, 1690?] brs. L, LL.

886   The case of assurances as they now stand. [*London*, c. 1699–1700.] brs. L, LL.

887   Entry cancelled.

888   The case of Capt. John Hutchinson. [*n.p.*, 1699–1700.] brs. L, LL; WF.

889   The case of Captain John Key. [*n.p.*, 1694.] brs. L, LL.

890   The case of Charles, Duke of Southampton. [*London*, 1693?] brs. L.

891   Case of Charles Earl of Banbury. [*London*, 1698.] brs. L, O, LU.

892   The case of Charles Howard, Esq. [*London*, 1685?] brs. L.

893   The case of Charles Price, merchant, and others. [*London*, 1689?] brs. CH, MIU.

Case of clandestine marriages. 1691. *See* Prideaux, Humphrey.

893A   The case of Colonel Adam Murray. [*London*, 1694.] brs. DC.

894   The case of Colonel John Lambert. *For S. S.*, 1661. brs. O; MH.

895   Entry cancelled.

896   The case of Col. Samuel Venner. [*n.p.*, 1699–1700.] brs. L, LL.

897   The case of compelling men to the Holy Sacrament. *For Abel Swalle, and Fincham Gardiner*, 1684. 4°. T.C.II 69. L, O, C, DT; CH, MH, NU, WF, Y.

Case of compulsion. 1688. *See* Burnet, Gilbert, *bp.*

898   The case of Conrad Greibe. [*London?* 1696.] brs. L.

Case of conscience concerning eating. [n.p., 1697.] *See* Mather, Increase.

Case of conscience concerning flying. 1643. *See* Torshell, Samuel.

Case of conscience resolved concerning. 1649. *See* Dury, John.

Case of conscience resolved, viz. Oxon, 1660. *See* Parry, John, *bp.*

Case of conscience. Whether. 1669. *See* Humfrey, John.

899   The case of contractors for making and vending copper halfpence and farthings. [*London*, 1695?] brs. L.

900   The case of Cornelius Bee and his partners. [*n.p.*, 1666?] brs. O.

901   The case of corporations. [*London*, 1690?] brs. L.

901A   The case of creditors. [*London?* 1694.] brs. LG.

901B   Case of Dame Margaret Areskine. *Edinburgh*, 1690. 4°. ALDIS 3025. EN.

902   The case of disbanding the army. [*London*], *by John Nutt*, 1698. 4°.* L, EN; CH, MH, TU, WF, Y.

903   The case of divers creditors of King Charles I. [*London*, 1699.] brs. LUG; MH, Y.

904   The case of divers noblemen and gentlemen of the county of York. [*n.p.*, 1642.] brs. L.

904A   The case of divers persons. [*London?* 1698.] brs. L.

905   The case of divers Roman-Catholicks. *For Anne Seile*, 1662. brs. L, OP.

905A   The case of divers tradesmen. [*London?* 1692.] brs. L.

Case of divorce. 1673. *See* Wolseley, *Sir* Charles.

905B   The case of Dowgate, and Aldersgate wards. [*London?* 1690.] LG.

905C   The case of Edmond Griffin. [*London?* 1695.] brs. L.

906   The case of Edmond Prideaux. [*London?* 1680.] brs. MH.

907   The case of Edmund Warner. [*London*, 1700?] brs. L.

908   The case of Edward Clavill. [*London*, 1698.] brs. L, LL.

908A   The case of Edward Douglas. [*London*, 1699.] cap., fol.* CH.

909   The case of Edward Lloyd. [*London*, 1678.] brs. L.

909A   The case of Edward Strode. [*London?* 1686.] brs. L.

910   The case of Edward Williams. [*n.p.*, 1695.] brs. LL.

911   The case of Elisabeth and Margaret Cholmley. [*London*, 1673.] brs. LU.

911A   The case of Elizabeth, dutchess of Albemarle. [*London?* 1695.] brs. L.

912   The case of Elizabeth, the wife of Charles Stuteville. [*n.p.*, 1699–1700.] brs. L, LL.

912A   The case of Ellin Brown. [*London?* 1700.] brs. OP.

912B   The case of England, and the Protestant interest. [*London?* 1692.] cap., 4°.* WF, Y.

Case of Exeter-Colledge. 1691. *See* Bury, Arthur.

912C   The case of forfeitures in Ireland. *Printed*, 1700. 4°. NU.

Case of founders kinsmen. [1700.] *See* Cawley, John.

913   The case of Francis Blake. [*London?* 1671.] brs. OP.

914   The case of Francis Stratford. [*n.p.*, 1698–99.] brs. LL.

915   The case of George Booth. [*n.p.*, 1689.] brs. LL.

Case of great and present use. 1677. *See* Nye, Phillip.

916   The case of great numbers of silk weavers. [*n.p.*, 1695.] brs. LL.

916A   The case of Griffith Wynn. [*London?* 1667.] cap., fol.* L.

917   The case of Henry Million. [*n.p.*, 1680.] brs. MH.

918   The case of Henry Powle. [*n.p.*, 1689.] brs. LL.

919   The case of Her Grace the Dutchess of Cleaveland. [*London*, 1690?] brs. L.

919A   The case of His Majesties sugar plantations. [*London?* 1670.] cap., fol.* L; MB.

919B   The case of Ignatius Gould, merchant. 1691. brs. OP.

Case of indifferent things. 1682/3. *See* Williams, John, *bp.*

919C The case of indifferent things . . . examined. *For Joseph Collier*, 1683. 4°. SP; CH.

Case of infant-baptism. 1683. *See* Hickes, George.

Case of interest. 1673. *See* Seymour, Thomas.

920 The case of J. Howe touching the election of Cirencester. [*n.p.*, 1690.] brs. LL.

921 The case of J. Swinton. [*n.p.*], 1690. 4°. EN.

922 The case of James Fitzgerald, Esq. [*London*, 1697.] brs. L.

922A The case of James Lennox. [*Dublin*, 1697.] brs. DI.

923 The case of James Percy, claymant to the earldom of Northumberland. *Printed*, 1685. fol.* O, P; CH.

924 The case of James Percy, the true heir-male and claimant. [*London*, 1680?] cap., fol.* CH, MH.

925 The case of John Baker, a minor. [1695?] brs. L.

926 The case of John Burke. [*n.p.*, 1692?] brs. L, LL.

927 The case of John Coombes. [*n.p.*, 1676.] brs. L, O.

927A The case of John Danvers. [*London?* 1691.] cap., fol.* L.

928 The case of John Degrave. [*n.p.*, 1700.] brs. L, LL.

929 The case of John Ellis. [*London*, 1700.] brs. L.

930 The case of John Farrington, Gent. [*London*, 1690?] brs. L.

930A The case of John Foster. [*London?* 1690.] brs. L.

931 The case of John Goudet. [*n.p.*, 1698.] brs. LL.

932 The case of John Hinde. *Printed*, 1685. 4°.* L.

932A The case of John James. [*London?* 1680.] brs. L.

933 The case of John Lemott Honywood. [*n.p.*, 1692/3.] brs. LL.

934 The case of John Paschal. [*n.p.*], 1694. brs. MC.

934A The case of John Peachey, [*London?* 1679.] brs. MH.

935 The case of John Prideaux. [*London*, 1698–99] brs. L, LL.

935A The case of John St. Leger. [*London?* 1685.] brs. L.

935B The case of John Van den Bende. [*London?* 1692.] cap., fol.* MH.

936 The case of John, Viscount Grandison. [*n.p.*, 1699–1700.] brs. LL.

937 The case of Joseph Gardner. [*n.p.*, 1699.] brs. LL.

938 The case of Katherine Harris. [*n.p.*, 1695.] brs. LL.

Case of kneeling. 1683. *See* Evans, John.

Case of lay-communion. 1683. *See* Williams, John, *bp.*

939 The case of Mainwaring, Hawes, Payne and others. [*London*], *printed*, 1646. 4°.* LT, C, DT; CH, CN, MH, NU, WF.

940 The case of many coachmen in London. [*n.p.*, 1670.] brs. L, O.

941 The case of many hundreds of poor English-captives, in Algier. [*London*, 1680] cap., fol.* L, O; CH, MH, WF, Y.

942 The case of many inhabitants of the town of Chattham. [*n.p.*, 1699.] brs. LL.

943 The case of many inhabitants of the town of Deptford. [*n.p.*, 1699.] brs. L, LL.

944 The case of many of the inhabitants. 1655. fol. O.

945 The case of many Protestant freeholders. [*n.p.*], 1680. fol. O.

946 The case of many Protestants in the county of Cambridge. [1681.] brs. L, CS; MH.

947 The case of many thousands of His Majesty's subjects. [*London*, 1699/1700.] brs. LUG.

948 The case of Marmaduke Darell, Esq. [*London*, 1673.] brs. L.

949 The case of Mary, Duchess of Norfolk. [*London*, 1700.] cap., fol.* L, LL; LC, TU.

950 The case of Mary Walwyn. [*n.p.*, 1691.] brs. LL.

951 The case of Michael Crake. [*London*, 1669?] brs. L.

Case of ministring. 1683. *See* A., T.

Case of mixt communion. 1683. *See* Freeman, Samuel.

952 The case of mixt-communion . . . friendly discourses. *Printed, and are to be sold by A. Baldwin*, 1700. 4°.* T.C.III 228. L, EC, EN, DT; CLC, MH, NU, WF.

953 The case of Mr. Benjamin Leech brick-layer. colop: *For A. Green*, [1682.] fol.* O, C, LG, MC; CH, MH, WF, Y.

954 The case of Mr. Daniel Gwyn. [*n.p.*, 1699.] brs. LL.

955 The case of Mr. Francis Jenkes. *Amsterdam*, 1677. 4°. O, LUG.

956 The case of Mr James Trefusis. [*n.p.*, 1693.] brs. LL.

957 The case of Mr. John Griffith. 1683. brs. LL.

The Case of Mr. Jones Proast. [*Oxford*, 1685.] *See* Finch, L. W.

957A The case of Mr. Joseph Hussey. colop: *For Will. Marshall*, 1699. cap., fol.* T.C.III 142. CS; PL.

957B The case of Mr. Phillip Nisbett. [*London?* 1698.] cap., fol.* PL.

958 The case of Mr. Robinson and Mr. Thompson. [*n.p.*, 1698.] brs. L, LL.

959 The case of Mr. William Cook. [*London?* 1675.] brs. L.

959A The case of Mr. Wyndham. [*London?* 1700.] brs. L.

960 The case of Mrs Arabella Thompson. [*London*, 1680?] brs. LL.

961 The case of Mrs Mary Stout. [*London*, 1699?] cap., fol.* L; WF, YL.

962 —[Anr. ed.] [*London*, 1700?] cap., fol.* L, LUG.

963 The case of Nathaniel Herne. [*n.p.*, Feb. 15, 1672/3.] brs. LL.

Case of our affaires. [*n.p.*], 1643. *See* Spelman, *Sir* John.

964 The case of peoples duty. *For Sam. Tidmarsh*, 1684. 4°.* L, O, CCH, SP, D; CH, MH, NU, WF, Y.

Case of persecution. 1689. *See* Long, Thomas.

965 The case of Peter Blackborow. 1677. brs. OP.

966 The case of pluralities. *For Richard Baldwin*, 1694. 8°. L, O, OB, OC, EC; NU, Y.

967 The case of present distresses on Non-conformists, examined. colop: *For Richard Oswell*, 1682. cap., fol.* L, O, CT; MIU, NHC, NU, PU.

Case of Protestant dissenters. 1680. *See* Rudyard, Thomas.

Case of Protestants. 1681. *See* Clarkson, David.

967A The case of Reginald Tucker. [*London*, 1695.] brs. Y.

967B The case of Richard and Ann Ashfield. [*London?* 1698.] brs. HH.

968 The case of R[ichard] Gee. [*n.p.*, 1694/5.] brs. LL.

969 The case of Richard Dashwood. [*London*, 1690?] brs. L.

970 The case of Richard Hutchinson. [*n.p.*, 1693/4.] brs. LL.

970A The case of Richard Radley. [1680.] brs. MH.

971 The case of Richard Stafford. [*n.p.*, 1689.] brs. O; CN.

972 The case of Richard Thompson. *Printed*, 1677. 4°.* L, LUG, MR, EN; LC, MH, NC, WF, Y.

972A ——Second edition. —, 1678. 4°.* L; CH, MH.

973 The case of Robert Balch. [*n.p.*, 1691/2.] brs. LL.

974   The case of Robert Blackburne. [n.p., 1700.] brs. LL.

975   The case of Robert Edgworth. [London, 1700?] fol. L.

976   The case of Robert Hastings. [London, 168–?] brs. CH.

976A The case of Robert Husey. [London, 168–.] brs. OC.

977   The case of Robert Walley. [London, 1670?] brs. L.

978   The case of Robert Weston. [n.p.], 1688–89. brs. LL.

979   The case of Roger Price. [n.p., 1680.] brs. LL.

980   The case of Rupert Browne, Gent. [London, 1695.] brs. L.

980A The case of Saint Edmunds-Bury. 1680. brs. MH.

981   The case of salt-petre. [n.p., 1693.] brs. L, LL.

982   The case of Samuel White. [London, 168–?] fol. CH.

983   The case of several English Catholicks. [London? 1680.] brs. L.

983A The case of several hackney coachmen. [London, 169–], brs. CH.

983B The case of several innocent persons in Ireland. [London, 169–?] brs. L.

984   The case of several Italian merchants. [n.p., 1693.] brs. LL.

984A The case of several merchants and others. [London? 1696.] brs. MH.

984B The case of several merchants trading to . . . America. [London, 1698.] cap., fol.* L; MH.

984C The case of several merchants trading to Ireland. [London, 169–.] brs. L.

984D The case of several of His Majesties loyal subjects. [London, 169–.] brs. OC.

985   The case of several of His Majesties subjects in Ireland. [London, 1698.] cap., 4°.* L, O, HH; NU, Y.

986   The case of several of the band of gentlemen pensioners. [n.p., 1694.] brs. LL.

986A The case of several of the four hundred ancient hackney-coachmen. [London? 1695.] brs. L, LUG.

      Case of several of their Majesties subjects. [169–?] See Johnson, Thomas.

987   The case of several thousands concerned and employed . . . iron wire. [n.p., 1689.] brs. LL.

988   The case of several thousands of His Majesty's subjects. [London, 1699/1700.] brs. L, LL, LUG; MH, NC, Y.

989   The case of several tradesmen. [London, 1696?] brs. L; MH.

990   The case of Sir Charles Holt. [n.p., 1693/4.] brs. LL.

991   The case of Sir Charles Porter. [n.p., 1690.] brs. LL.

992   The case of Sir Christopher Wren. [n.p., 1690.] brs. LL.

993   The case of Sir Edward Hales. For J. Watts, 1689. fol.* T.C.II 251. L, C, LL, HH, EN; CH, MHL, NC, WF, Y.

993A The case of Sir Edward Turner. [London? 1690.] brs. L.

993B The case of Sir Francis Fane. [London? 1685.] brs. L.

993C The case of Sir James Jefferyes. [Dublin, 1697.] brs. DI.

994   The case of Sir John Edwards. [London, 1680.] cap., fol. O.

995   The case of Sir John Lenthall. Printed, 1653. 4°. O; WF.

996   The case of Sir Nathaniel Napper, baronet. [London, 1689?] CH.

996A The case of Sir Oliver Boteler. [London? 168–.] brs. MH.

997   The case of Sir Paul Whichcot. [London, 1674?] brs. L.

998   The case of Sir Richard Temple. [n.p., 1689.] brs. LL.

999   The case of Sir Robert Atkyns. Printed, 1695. fol.* L, C, LLP, EN; CH, MHL, WF.

999A The case of Sir Robert Cleark. [London? 1685.] brs. L.

1000 The case of Sir Robert Killigrew. [London, 1665?] brs. L.

1001 The case of Sʳ T. Cullum. Printed, 1680. 4°.* L; CH, Y.

1001A The case of Sir Thomas Longueville. [London, 1659.] brs. OP.

1001B The case of Sir Thomas Pilkington. colop: Printed, 1689. cap., fol.* LG; CH, PL.

1002 The case of Sir William Bassett. [London, 1674.] brs. CH.

1002A The case of Sir William Drake. 1680. brs. MH.

1003 The case of Sir William Glynne. [n.p., 1685.] brs. L, O.

1004 The case of Sir William Portman. [n.p., 1688/9.] brs. LL.

1004A The case of some of the adventures . . . great level. [London? 1664.] cap., 4°.* RPJ.

1005 The case of Spencer Cowper. [London? 1700.] cap., fol.* LUG.

1006 The case of subjects in arms. [London], 1660. brs. L.

      Case of succession. [n.p.], 1679. See G., W.

1007 The case of Susanna Smith. [n.p., 1689.] brs. L; Y.

      Case of tenures. [n.p., 1698.] See Santry, James Barry, baron.

      Case of the accomodation. [n.p.], 1671. See MacWard, Robert.

1008 The case of the administrators of the goods . . . of Sir William Godolphin. [London? 1697.] brs. L.

1008A The case of the adventurers in the East and West Fenns. [London? 1665.] brs. L.

1009 The case of the adventurers in the million lottery. [n.p., 1697.] brs. L.

      Case of the afflicted clergy. [n.p., 1691.] See M., G.

1010 The case of the ancient burrough of Knaresborough. [n.p., 1688/9.] brs. LL.

1010A The case of the ancient free carmen of London. [London? 1690.] brs. L; MH, Y.

1011 The case of the antient hackney-coachmen. [London, 1676.] brs. L.

1012 The case of the auncient tenants. [n.p., Nov. 4. 1650.] brs. LT.

1013 The case of the army soberly discussed. Printed July, 1647. 4°.* LT, HH, SP; CLC, CU, MH, WF, Y.

      Case of the armie truly. 1647. See Wildman, John.

1014 The case of the artificers. [n.p., 1690?] brs. Y.

1015 The case of the assignees of the goldsmiths. 1689. brs. L, MC; CH, MH.

1015A The case of the auditors. [London, 1662.] cap., 4°.* PU, WF.

1016 The case of the bayliffs and burgesses of . . . Droytwich. [London, 168–?] brs. CH.

      Case of the bankers. [n.p.], 1674. See Turner, Thomas.

1017 The case of the booksellers and printers stated. [n.p., 1666.] brs. L.

1017A The case of the booksellers trading beyond sea. [London? 1700.] brs. L; MH, MIU.

1018 The case of the brewers. [n.p., 1700.] brs. L, LG, LL, LUG; MH.

1019 The case of the brine-pits truly stated. [London, 1695?] brs. L.

1020　The case of the burgesses of Nottingham. colop: *For Brabazon Aylmer*, [1682]. cap., fol.* L, O, LG, MR, EN; MH, NC.

1021　The case of the burrough of Buckingham. [*London*, 1689?]. brs. CH.

1022　The case of the burrough of Dunwich in Suffolk. [*n.p.*, 1689.] brs. L, LL.

1022A　The case of the borough of Hertford. [*London?* 1700.] brs. Y.

1022B　The case of the borough of Marlborough. [*London*, 1679.] cap., fol. MH.

1023　The case of the burrough of New-Windsor. [*London*, 1680?] fol.* L, O, LUG, HH; CH, MH, WF, Y.

1023A　The case of the borough of Southwark. [*London?* 1645.] brs. L.

1024　The case of the cane-chair makers. [*n.p.*], 1689. brs. C, LL.

1024A　The case of the captains of His Majesty's fleet. [*London*, 1699.] brs. L.

1025　Entry cancelled.

1026　The case of the charter of London stated. *For John Kidgell*, 1683. fol.* T.C.II 29. L, O, C, LG, HH; CH, CN, LC, MH, WF, Y.

1027　The case of the children of Coll. John Burke. [*n.p.*, 1700?] brs. L, O, LL.

　　　Case of the Church of England, briefly. 1681. *See* Parker, Samuel.

　　　Case of the Church of England by law. [n.p., 1700.] *See* Stephens, Edward.

1027A　The case of the church-wardens . . . Southwark. [*London?* 1696.] brs. WF.

1027B　The case of the citizens and shop-keepers of London. *To be sold by Mrs. Billingsley*, 1691. brs. Y.

1027C　The case of the city of London against the bill. [*London?* 1700.] brs. L, LG.

1028　The case of the city of London in reference to the debt. *By Samuel Roycroft*, 1691. brs. L, LG; MH, Y.

1029　—[Anr. ed.] —, 1692. brs. LG, LL.

1030　—[Anr. ed.] —, 1693. brs. L.

1031　The case of the city of London, in reference to their debts. [*London*], *by Samuel Roycroft*, 1689. brs. O, LL; CH, MH.

1032　The case of the city of Londonderry. [*London*, 1695?] brs. L, O; Y.

1033　—[Anr. ed.] [*n.p.*, c. 1698.] fol.* L, LL.

1034　The case of the city of Oxford. [*n.p.*], 1687. fol. O; CH.
　　　—[Same title] [n.p., 1690.] *See* Wright, William.

1035　The case of the clothiers. [*n.p.*, 1698.] brs. LL, LU.

1036–7　Entries cancelled.

1038　The case of the clothiers of Glocestershire. [*n.p.*, 1688.] fol.* LL; MH, NC.

1039　The case of the clothiers, weavers, hosiers. [*n.p.*, 1693.] brs. L, LG, LL, HH; MH, NC.

1040　The case of the coachmen. [*n.p.*, 1695.] brs. LL.

1041　The case of the coal-meters. [*London*, 1689.] cap., brs. LL; CH, Y.

　　　Case of the coin. [n.p., 1697.] *See* M., C.

1042　The case of the college of physicians. [*London*, 1688?] cap., fol.* L, LG.

1043　The case of the commission of array stated. [*n.p., Oct. 20.* 1642.] cap., 4°.* LT, O, CCL, CS; CH, CLC, MH, WF, Y.

1043A　The case of the commissioners for hackney-coaches. [*London?* 1693.] brs. LG.

1044　The case of the common brewers. [*London*, 1700.] brs. LL; CH.

1045　The case of the commoners of the mannor of Epworth. [*London*, 169–?] brs. L, O.

1046　The case of the company of cutlers in Hallamshire. [*London?* 1680.] brs. NC.

1047　Entry cancelled.

1048　The case of the company of glass-sellers. [*London*, 1697?] brs. L, LG.

　　　Case of the company of grocers. 1682. *See* Ravenhill, William.

1049　The case of the company of masons. [*London*, 1700?] brs. L.

1050　The case of the company of merchant-adventurers. [*London*, 1697?] brs. L; Y.

1051　The case of the company of vintners. [*London?* 1690.] brs. L.

1052　The case of the company of white paper makers. [*London*, 1689.] fol.* L, O, LL; CH, Y.

1052A　The case of the contractors, for making . . . copper half-pence. [*London*, 169–?] brs. L, LUG; MH, Y.

1053　The case of the contractors with the Czar of Moscovy. [*London*, 1695?] brs. L, LL, LU; Y.

1054　The case of the corporation of the great level of the fenns. [*London?* 1665.] brs. L.

1055　The case of the corporations of England. [*London*, 1692?] fol.* LG, HH.

1056　The case of the country common brewers. [*London*, 168–?] brs. CH.

1057　The case of the cow-keepers. [*London*, 1700?] brs. L, LL; Y.

1058　The case of the creditors of Joseph and Nathaniel Hornby. [*n.p.*, 1699–1700.] brs. LL.

1059　The case of the creditors of Sir Robert Vyner. [*London?* 1695.] brs. WF.

1059A　The case of the creditors of the company of grocers. [*London?* 1671.] brs. L, LG.

1059B　The case of the creditors of the merchant-adventurers. [*London?* 1680.] brs. L; MH.

　　　Case of the cross. 1684. *See* Resbury, Nathaniel.

1060　The case of the daughters of the late Earl of Rochester. [*n.p.*, 1692.] brs. LL.

　　　Case of the Dissenters. Dublin, 1695. *See* Dopping, Anthony, *bp.*

　　　Case of the dissenting Protestants. *See* Boyse, Joseph.

1061　The case of the distillers in and about London. [*n.p.*, 1689.] brs. LL.

1061A　The case of the distillers of malted corn. [*London?* 1700.] brs. Y.

1062　The case of the distressed orphans. [*n.p.*], 1691. fol.* L, LL.

1063   —[Anr. ed.] [*n.p.*, 1692?] brs. LL; NC.

1064   The case of the Dutchess of Albemarle. 1694. fol. L, C.

1064A   The case of the Dutchess of Richmond. [*London?* 1682.] brs. LG; Y.

1065   The case of the Duke of Norfolk. [*London*, 1685?] brs. L, O.

1065A   The case of the Duttch [*sic*] and French Protestant churches in England. [*London?* 1692.] brs. OP.

1065B   The case of the duty on molasses. [*London?* 1695.] brs. L; MH.

1066   The case of the Earl of Argyle. [*n.p.*], *printed*, 1683. fol. L, HH, E, EN; CH, WF.

1066A   The case of the Earl of Macclesfield. [*London?* 1685.] cap., fol.* L.

1067   The case of the East India company. [*n.p.*, 1694.] brs. L, O.

1067A   The case of the election for the city of Bristol. [1680.] brs. MH.

1068   The case of the English company. [*n.p.*, 1698.] cap., fol.* L, O, LUG; MH, NC, Y.

1068A   The case of the English paper-makers. [*London?* 1700.] brs. Y.

1069   The case of the English weavers. [*London*, 1670.] brs. MH, NC.

1070   The case of the executors, creditors, and legatees of the late Countess of Portland. [*London*, 1700?] brs. L, LUG.

1071   The case of the exported coales. [*London*, 1680?] brs. O.

1072   The case of the fann-makers. [*n.p.*, 1695?] brs. O, LL; MIU.

1072A   The case of the farmer. [*London?* 1691.] brs. MH.

1072B   The case of the first undertakers. [*London*, 1653.] cap., fol.* L.

1072C   The case of the fishermen. [*London?* 1699.] brs. L.

1072D   The case of the fishermen in Kent. [*London?* 1694.] brs. L.

1072E   The case of the fishmongers. [*London*, 1699.] fol.* L; NC.

1073   The case of the forfeitures in Ireland. *Printed*, 1700. 4°. L, O, CS, LL, LUG; CH, WF, Y.

1074   —Second edition. 1700. 8°. L, LG, OC, DT; CH, CN, IU, WF, Y.

1075   The case of the four hundred coach men. [*London*, 169–?] cap., fol.* LG; CH, MH.

1076   The case of the free butchers. [*n.p.*, 1695?] brs. LL.

1077   The case of the free distillers. [*London*, 1698?] brs. L, LL.

1077A   The case of the free fishmongers. [*London*, 1699.] brs. L.

1077B   The case of the free-men and free-holders of the city of Bristol. 1680. brs. MH.

1078   The case of the freemen and freeholders of the town of Newark upon Trent. [*London*, 1675.] brs. LUG.

1078A   The case of the freemen pavyors. [*London?* 1669.] brs. LG.

1079   The case of the free-shipwrights of England. [*London*, 167–?] brs. LG, LS; Y.

1080   The case of the French Protestant ministers. [*London*, 168–?] brs. CH.

1080A   The case of the French Protestants refugees. [*London*, 1690.] brs. MH, NC, Y.

1080B   The case of the garbler for the city of London. [*London*, 169–?] brs. L, LG; MH.

1080C   The case of the gentlemen freeholders. [*London?* 1681.] brs. L.

1081   The case of the glass-trade. [*London?* 1695.] brs. MH.

1081A   The case of the goldsmiths of the city. [1680.] brs. MH.

1082   The case of the governour and company. [*London*, 1698.] fol. L, LUG; MH, MIU, WF, Y.

1083   The case of the governour and garrison. [*London*, 1700?] brs. L.

1084   The case of the governor, officers. [*London*, 1695?] brs. L.

1085   The case of the gun-makers. [*London*, 1680?] brs. L.

1086   The case of the hackney coachmen. [*n.p.*, 1695?] brs. L, LL.

1087   The case of the hamlet of Wapping. [*n.p.*, 1694.] cap., fol.* L, LG, LL.

1088   The case of the honourable Fytton Gerard. [*n.p.*, 1693/4.] brs. LL.

1089   The case of the Hudsons-Bay-company. [*London?* 1696.] brs. LG.

Case of the impeached lords. [*n.p.*], 1648. *See* Prynne, William.

1089B   The case of the inhabitants for fifty . . . miles round London. [*London?* 1700.] brs. MH.

1090   The case of the inhabitants of the hamblet of Wapping. [*n.p.*, 1693/4.] brs. LL.

1091   The case of the inhabitants of the liberty of Westminster. [*London?* 1700.] brs. LG.

1091A   The case of the inhabitants of the parish. [*London?* 1675.] brs. LG.

1092   The case of the inhabitants of the town and parish of Croydon. [*London*, 1673.] cap., fol.* L, O, C, LG; MH.

1093   The case of the inhabitants of the town of Bradford. [*n.p.*, 1689?] brs. LL.

1093A   The case of the innholders of . . . Westminster. [*London?* 1700.] brs. L.

Case of the Irish Protestants. 1691. *See* Wetenhall, Edward, *bp.*

1094   The case of the Jevves stated. *By Robert Ibbitson*, 1656. 4°. SP.

1095   The case of the joyners company. [*London*, 1700?] brs. L.

1096   The case of the journeymen potmakers. [*London*, 1698?] brs. L; MH.

1096A   The case of the Kerry quit-rent. [*Dublin?* 1681.] cap., fol.* L, DN.

1097   The case of the Kersey-clothiers. [*n.p.*, 1700?] fol.* LL.

1097A   The case of the King and publick. [*London?* 1696.] cap., fol.* C.

1098   The case of the King and Queen dowager. [*n.p.*, 1684.] brs. O.

1099   The case of the King stated. [*London*], *printed*, 1647. 4°.* LT, O, C, CE, YM; CH, CU, WF, Y.

Case of the kingdom. 1647. *See* Nedham, Marchamont.

1100   The case of the King's mannour of Crowland. [*London*, 1661.] brs. LU.

1101   The case of the ladies Margaret, Catherine and Elizabeth McCarty. [*n.p.*, 1700?] brs. L, LL.

1102   The case of the Lady Henrietta Maria Wentworth. [*London*, 1677.] brs. LUG.

1102A The case of the Lady Wandesford. [*London?* 1660.] brs. WF.

1103 The case of the landlords, of St. George's parish, in the burrough of Southwark in Surry. [*n.p.*, 1699.] brs. L, LL.

1104 The case of the landlords of St. George's parish, in the burrough of Southwark, in the county of Surrey. [*n.p.*, 1699.] brs. L, LL.

1104A The case of the late African company. [*London?* 1694.] cap., fol.* MH.

1104B The case of the lenders of 650000 pounds. [*London?* 1694.] brs. MH.

1105 The case of the lieutenants of the late Second Marine Regiment. [*n.p.*, 1699.] brs. LL.

1105A The case of the Lord Jeffereys. [*London?* 1690.] brs. L.

1106 The case of the Lord Mayor and aldermen of London. colop: *For John Harris*, 1690. brs. L, OC, DC, MC, E; CH, CN, MH, PL, RPJ, WF, Y.

1107 The case of the Lord Viscount Gormanston. [*London*, 1698.] brs. L.

1108 The case of the lords, owners, and commoners of 22. townes in the Soake of Bullingbrooke. [*London*, 1661.] brs. LU.

1109 The case of the makers of quilts for beds only. [*n.p.*, 1696?] brs. LL.

1110 The case of the makers of vinegar. [*n.p.*, 1690?] brs. LL.

1111 The case of the malsters [sic]. [*n.p.*, 1698?] brs. LL.

1112 The case of the mannor of Epworth. [*London*, 169–?] brs. L; CN.

1113 The case of the manufacturers of grograin yarn. [*London?* 1700.] brs. L.

1114 The case of the manufacturers of iron in England. [*London?* 1690.] brs. C.

1114A The case of the Marquess of Hertford touching. [*London*, 1642.] brs. WF.

1114B The case of the marriners. [*London*, 1690.] brs. L; NC.

1114C The case of the master and fellows of Jesus College. [*London*, 1690.] brs. LUG.

1115 The case of the master taylors residing within . . . London. [*London*, 1700?] brs. CH, Y.

1115A The case of the merchants & clothiers. [*London?* 1693.] brs. L.

1115B The case of the merchants, importers of wines. [*London?* 1700.] brs. MH.

1116 The case of the merchants of London. *Printed*, 1662. 4°.* NC.

1116A The case of the merchants-sufferers. [*London?* 1700.] brs. MH.

1117 The case of the miserable orphans. [*n.p.*, 1692?] brs. LL.

1117A The case of the non-commission officers. [*London?* 1696.] brs. L.

Case of the oath of abjuration. 1693. *See* Stillingfleet, Edward, *bp.*

Case of the oaths. 1689. *See* Wynne, Robert.

1118 The case of the officers, ministers and attendants of His Majesty's late descent. [*n.p.*, 1693?] brs. LL.

1119 The case of the officers of the customs. [*London*, 1693?] brs. L.

1119A The case of the old governors of the free grammar school in Birmingham. [*London?* 1689.] brs. C.

Case of the old secured. [n.p., 1660.] *See* Prynne, William.

1120 The case of the orphans and creditors. [*London*, 1688.] fol.* HH; WF.

1121 The case of the orphans of the city of London. [*n.p.*, 1690?] brs. LL; MH.

1121A The case of the owners and masters of ships trading for coles. [*London?* 1687.] brs. MH.

1122 The case of the owners and masters of the transport ships. [*n.p.*, 1699.] brs. LL.

1123 Entry cancelled.

1124 The case of the owners of ships . . . coal trade. [*London*, 1695.] cap., fol.* L; Y.

1125 The case of the owners of the ship Averilla. [*London*, 1696?] brs. L.

1125A The case of the owners of the ship Redbridge. [*London*, 1694.] brs. CN, WF.

1126 The case of the paper-traders. [*London*, 1696/7.] brs. L, LUG; MH.

1126A The case of the parish of Alhallows. [*London*, 1696.] brs. L.

1127 The case of the participants purchasers. [*London*, 1661.] brs. LU.

1128 The case of the patentees. [*n.p.*, 1681?] cap., brs. MH, Y.

1129 The case of the people, call'd Quakers, as it concerns an affirmation. [*London*, 1698?] brs. CH.

Case of the people called Quakers (once more.] [n.p., 1661.] *See* Burrough, Edward.

1130 The case of the people called Quakers, relating to oathes. [*London*], *printed*, 1673. 8°.* L, LF, OC, BBN, EN; IE, MH, NU, PH, PSC.

1130A The case of the people called Quakers. With some reasons. [*London*, 1696?] brs. L.

1131 The case of the people commonly called Quakers. [*London*, 1696?] brs. L, OC; CH, CN, PH, Y.

1132 The case of the people of England. *Printed, and are to be sold by Randall Taylor*, 1689. 4°.* T.C.II 255. L, O, C, EN, DT; CH, MH, MIU, WF, Y.

Case of the persecuted and oppressed Protestants. 1674/5. *See* Oxenstrevra, Benedict.

1133 The case of the petitioners complaining. [*London?* 1700.] brs. L.

1134 The case of the petitioners, William Strode and John Speke. [*n.p.*, 1688/9.] brs. LL.

1135 The case of the petitioners for making the River Dunmore navigable. [*n.p.*, 1697?] brs. LL.

1136 The case of the petitioners touching. [*London?* 1683.] brs. L.

1137 The case of the pewterers. [*n.p.*, 1690?] brs. L, LL; MH.

1138 The case of the planters and traders. [*n.p.*, 1690?] brs. LL.

1138A The case of the poor ancient creditors of the Navy. [*London?* 1695.] brs. L.

1139 The case of the poor brewer. [*n.p.*, 1700?] brs. LL.

1140   The case of the poor fishermen. [*London*, 1699.] brs. L.

1141   The case of the poor French refugees. [*London*, 1697?] fol.* L, O; Y.

1142   The case of the poor orphans of London. [*London?* 1700.] brs. HH.

1142A   The case of the poor prisoners for debt. [*London?* 1700.] brs. L.

1142B   The case of the poor sailors. [*London?* 169–.] cap., fol.* LG; MH, Y.

1143   The case of the poor widows. [*n.p.*, 1685.] fol. O.

1144   The case of the poor work-men glass-makers. [*n.p.*, 1695?] brs. L, LG, LL.

1145   The case of the port of Rye. [*n.p.*, 1689/90.] brs. LL.

        Case of the present. 1690. *See* Sage, John.

1145A   The case of the present distresses on Nonconformists. 1682. fol. L.

1145B   The case of the present merchants. [*London?* 1696.] brs. MH.

1146   The case of the prisoners in the King's Bench prison. [*London?* 1700.] brs. OP.

1147   The case of the proprietors . . . of stage coaches. [*London?* 169–?] brs. MH.

1148   The case of the proprietors of the Bristol water-works. [*n.p.*, 1699–1700.] brs. LL.

        Case of the Protestant dissenters in Ireland. Dublin, 1695. *See* Boyse, Joseph.

        Case of the Protestant dissenters of Ireland. Dublin, 1695. *See* Pullen, Tobias, *bp.*

        Case of the Protestant dissenters represented. [*n.p.*, 1689.] *See* Howe, John.

1149   Entry cancelled.

1150   The case of the purchasers of publick lands. *For L. H.*, 1660. 4°.* LT, LVF; CLC, IU, MH, WF.

1150A   The case of the purchasers under the Earl of Athlone. [*London?* 1700.] brs. L.

        Case of the Quakers. 1674. *See* S., J.

        Case of the Quakers concerning. [*n.p.*], 1674. *See* Whitehead, George.

1151   The case of the Quakers relating. *For C. Brome*, 1696. 4°. T.C.II 580. O, C.

1152   The case of the quo warranto. *For George Grafton*, 1690. fol. L, MC; MIU, WF.

1153   The case of the refiners. [*n.p.*, 1698?] brs. LL.

1154   The case of the refiners of rock-salt. [*London*, 1695?] brs. L.

1155   The case of the refiners of sugar. [*London?* 1695.] brs. L, LG; MH, NC.

        Case of the regale. [*n.p.*], 1700. *See* Leslie, Charles.

1156   The case of the registred seamen. [*n.p.*, 1697?] brs. L, LL; Y.

1157   The case of the respective artificers. [*n.p.*, 1694?] brs. LL.

1158   The case of the right honourable Thomas Earl Rivers. [*London?* 1688.] brs. L.

1159   The case of the right honourable William Harbourd. [*n.p.*, 1689/90.] brs. L, LL.

1160   The case of the rock salt. [*London*, 1695?] brs. L.

1160A   The case of the rope-makers of London. [*London?* 1700.] brs. L; MIU, NC.

1161   Entry cancelled.

1162   The case of the salt-refiners. [*n.p.*, 1695.] brs. LL.

1162A   The case of the sea-captains. [*London?* 1700.] brs. L.

1163   The case of the several landlords. [1700?] brs. L.

1164   The case of the sheriffs for the year 1682. *For Thomas Parkhurst*, 1682. 4°.* L, O, CS, MR, DT; CH, CN, MH, NU, WF, Y.

1165   The case of the ship-wrights. [*n.p.*, 1700?] brs. Y.

1166   The case of the sitting members that serve for . . . Southwark. [*London*, 1689?] brs. CH.

1166A   The case of the six clerks of chancery. [*London?* 1700.] brs. L.

1167   The case of the stannaries stated. [*London*, 1650?] 4°. L.

1167A   The case of the stationers. [*London*, 1698?] brs. L.

        Case of the suffering people. 1664. *See* Whitehead, George.

1168   The case of the suspended bishops considered. *For W. Rayner*, 1691. 4°. T.C.II 349. O, CT, A, DT.

1168A   The case of the sworn attorneys. [*London?* 1680.] brs. L.

        The case of the tenants of the manor or Epworth. [1651.] *See* Lilburne, John.

1168B   The case of the tobacco-pipe-makers of England. [*London?* 1695.] brs. LG.

1169   The case of the towns of great Yarmouth. [*n.p.*, 1698–99.] brs. L, LL.

1169A   The case of the transport ships. [*London?* 1692.] brs. L.

1169B   The case of the Turkey, West-India and other merchants. [*London*, 1680?] brs. L; MH.

        Case of the two absolvers. 1696. *See* Collier, Jeremy.

1170   The case of the undertakers and promoters of the bill. [*London*, 1685?] brs. LL; NC, Y.

1171   The case of the undertakers for the draining of Deeping-fenns. [*London?* 1685.] brs. L.

1172   Entry cancelled.

1173   The case of the vniversity of Oxford. [*London, for Rich. Royston*], printed, 1648. 4°. MADAN 1992. LT, O, OC, CJ; CLC, CN, MH, MIU, Y.

1174   —[Same title.] *Oxford, at the theater*, 1690. 4°. OC; CN, NU, WF, Y.

1175   —[Anr. ed.] [*Oxford*, 1690?] cap., fol. O, OC, MR; CH.

1175A   The case of the upholsters. [*sic*] [*London?* 1680.] brs. L; Y.

1175B   The case of the waggoners. [*London?* 1700.] brs. L; WF.

1176   The case of the weavers. [*n.p.*, 1700?] brs. Y.

1177   The case of the weavers, who are petioners [*sic*]. [*London*, 1695/6.] brs. L, LUG.

1178   The case of the wholesale and retale dealers in coffee. [*n.p.*, 1690?] brs. LL.

1178A   The case of the widdow . . . of John Sayer. [*London?* 1690.] brs. L.

1178B   The case of the wooll-combers. [*London*, 1693]. brs. MH.

1179   The case of the woollen-drapers. [*n.p.*, 1698?] brs. L, LL.

1179A   The case of the workers of iron. [*London?* 166–] brs. LUG; MH.

1179B   The case of Their Majesties antient . . . office of assurance. [*London?* 1690.] brs. L.

1179C The case of Their Majesties subjects in . . . Wales. *Printed*, 1689. brs. WF, Y.

1179D The case of Their Majesties sugar plantations. [*London?* 1689.] brs. L; MH.

1180 The case of Theodore Barthurst, esq. [*London*, 1689.] cap., fol.* CH.

1181 The case of Tho. Dangerfield. *For the author*, 1680. fol.* L, O, C, BR, HH; CH, CN, LC, MH, NU, Y.

1182 The case of Thomas Bulkley. [*London*, 169-?] brs. CH.

1183 The case of Thomas Bushell. *Printed*, 1649. 4°.* L; Y.

1184 The case of Thomas Christy. [*n.p.*, 1690.] brs. LL.

1184A The case of Thomas Earl of Limerick. [*London?* 1699.] cap., fol.* L.

1185 The case of Thomas Earl of Pembroke. [*London?* 1700.] brs. L.

1186 The case of Thomas Eyre. [*n.p.*, 1684.] brs. O.

1187 The case of Thomas Goodwin. [*London*], 1700. fol. L.

1188 The case of Thomas Hawles. [*n.p.*, 1662?] fol. O.

1188A The case of Thomas Rowney. [*London?* 1680.] brs. L.

1189 The case of Thomas Samson. [*London*, 1698.] 4°. L, O; MIU.

1190 The case of Thomas Sherley. [*n.p.*, 1678.] fol. O.

1190A The case of Thomas Wise. [*London*, 1680.] brs. OP.

1190B The case of those persons that. [*London?* 1698.] brs. L.

1190C The case of those persons who. [*London?* 1660.] brs. L.

1191 The case of Ursula Cartwright, widow. [*London*, 1680?] brs. L.

1191A The case of using or forbearing the establish'd liturgie. *Printed*, 1672. 8°. EC.

1192 The case of usury further debated. *By J. D. for Jonathan Robinson*, 1684. 4°.* T.C.II 102. L, O; CU, MH, NC.

1192A The case of William Adderley. [*London?* 1688.] brs. L.

1193 The case of William Coryton. [*n.p.*, 1689.] brs. LL.

1194 The case of William Eyre, esq. concerning his right to the half-baron of Shelelah. [*London*, 1670?] cap., fol.* L.

1195 The case of William Eyre, Gent. bayliffe of Southwark. [*London*, 1675?] brs. LL; CH.

1195A The case of William Gutteridge. [*London?* 1680.] brs. CH.

1196 The case of William Lenthall. [*n.p.*, 1700?] brs. LL; WF.

1196A The case of William Love. [*London?* 1672.] brs. HH.

1197 The case of William now Earl of Derby. [*London?* 1688.] brs. L.

1198 The case of William Warner. [*n.p.*, 1700.] brs. L, O, LL.

1199 The case, or petition of the corporation of pin-makers. [*London*, 1690.] brs. L.

1200 The case, or present state of the refiners of sugar. [*n.p.*, 1690?] brs. LL.

Case put. 1679. *See* L'Estrange, *Sir* Roger.

Case put & decided. [*New York*, 1698.] *See* Leeds, Daniel.

1201 The case relating to the bill for preventing . . . vexatious suits. [*London*, 1700?] brs. L, O; WF.

1202 A case relating to the making navigable the River Dee. [*n.p.*, 1699.] brs. LL.

1203 The case setting forth His Majestie's right. [*London*, 1670?] brs. L.

1204 The case stated between England and the United Provinces. *By Tho. Newcomb, to be sold by Anthony Williamson*, 1652. 8°. L, LUS, HH, EN; HR, CH, CN, MH, RPJ, WF, Y.

Case stated between the Church of England. 1700. *See* S., E.

1204A The case stated concerning the doctors. *For B. Tooke*, 1682. brs. DCH.

Case stated concerning the judicature. [*n.p.*], 1675. *See* Holles, Denzil Holles, *baron*.

Case stated of the jurisdiction. 1676. *See* Holles, Denzil Holles, *baron*.

1205 The case stated touching the soveraigns prerogative. *For Charles King*, 1660. 4°.* LT; MH, NU, WF, Y.

1206 The case truly stated. [*n.p.*, 1700?] cap., fol.* Y.

1207 The case truly stated betwixt the Dean and chapter of Christs Church in Oxford. [*Oxford?* 1667.] brs. MADAN 2777. O, LU.

1208 The case upon the writ of error between Richard Brown and A. Waite. [*London*, 1691.] brs. L.

1209 **Caseley, Samuel.** The holy rebell. *Printed at York by Stephen Bulkley*, 1642. brs. L.

1210–11 Entries cancelled.

Cases argued. 1697. *See* Keck, *Sir* Anthony.

Cases in Parliament. 1698. *See* Shower, *Sir* Bartholomew.

Cases of conscience. 1673. *See* Norman, John.

1212 Cases of conscience about things indifferent. 1661. 12°. LW.

1213 **Casimir, Mathias.** Lyricorum libri IV. *Cantabrigiæ; apud Ricardum Green*, 1684. 12°. L, O, C, OC, CT; CN, MB, PL, RBU, WF.

1214 —The odes of Casimire. *By T. W. for H[umphrey] Moseley*, 1646. 12°. LT, C, LL, LW; CH, CN, MH, WF, Y.

Casimir, king of Poland. 1681. *See* Rousseau de la Valette, Michel.

1215 **[Cassagnes, Jacques.]** A moral treatise upon valour. *For the author*, 1694. 12°. L.

1215A [–] —[Anr. ed.] *For Benj. Bragg*, 1695. 12°. WF.

Cassandra. 1652. *See* La Calprenède, Gaultier de Coste, *seigneur de*.

1215B [–] —[Anr. ed.] *For the author*, 1696. 12°. CLC.

1216 **Cassin, Conly.** Willisius male vindicatus. *Dublin*, 1667. 8°. DIX 134. L, O.

1217 **Cassini, Giovanni Domenico.** A prognostication concerning the frost. colop: *Printed, to be sold by E. Whitlock*, 1697. cap., 4°.* L.

1217A **Castaing, John.** An interest book. *For the author*, 1700. 12°. O.

Castallio, Sebastian. *See* Châteillon.

Castanaeus, Henricus Ludovicus. *See* Chasteignier de la Rochepozay, Henri Louis.

Castaniza, Juan. *See* Scupoli, Lorenzo.

1218–20 Entries cancelled.

1221 **Castel Moncayo, Baltaser** *marquis de.* An ansvver to the late memorial of the Count D'Avaux. [*London*], *sold by D. Newman and Thomas Malthus: printed for Thomas Malthus.* [1684]. brs. LU, HH; INU, Y.

1222 **Castell, Benedict.** The mensuration of running waters. 1661. fol. E, AU.

1223 **Castell, Edmund.** Bibliotheca Castelliana. 1686. 4°.* L, O, CS, LSC.

1224 —Lexicon heptaglotton. *Imprimebat Thomas Roycroft, prostant apud Gulielmum VVells et Robertum Scott.* 1669. 2v. fol. I, O, C, EN, DT; BN, LC, MH, NC, NU, Y.

1225 ——[Anr. ed.] *Imprimebat Thomas Roycroft,* 1669. fol. CT, OC; CN, PL.

1226 ——[Anr. ed.] —, *sumptibus R. Scott,* 1686. 2v. fol. L, C, CCH, E; BN, CH, IU, PL.

1227 —Oratio in scholis theologicis. *Typis Thomae Roycroft, & prostant apud Sam. Thomson,* 1667. 4°.* L, O, C, OC, CT; CH, CU, PL, Y.

1227A —Serenissimo & potentissimo principi . . . Carolo . . . Secundo. [*London,* 1660.] 4.* MBA, MH.

1228 —Sol Angliæ oriens. *Typis Tho. Roycroft; impensis Jo. Martin, Ja. Allestry, & Tho. Dicas,* 1660. 4°.* LT, O, CS, DT; BN, CH, CLC, MH, Y.

1229 **Castell, William.** The Iesvits undermining. *By E.G. for Joseph Hunscot,* 1642. 4°.* LT, O, LG, OC, DT; BN, CH, CN, NC, WF, Y.

1230 —A petition of W.C. [*London*], *printed,* 1641. 4°.* LT, O, HH, EN, GU; CH, CN, LC, MH, NN, Y.

1231 —A short discoverie of the coasts . . . of America. *Printed,* 1644. 4°. L, O, CT, LA, GH; CH, CN, LC, MH, NN, Y.

1231A Castigatio temporum: or a short view. *Printed,* 1660. 4°.* CH, MHL, WF.

Castiglione, Sebastiano. *See* Châteillon, Sébastien.

1232 [**Castillo Solóranzo, Alonso de.**] The life of Donna Rosina. *Printed and sold by B. Harris* [1700?] 12°. LC, MH, NP, WF.

1232A —La picara; or, the triumphs of female subtilty. *By W. W. for J. Starkey,* 1665. 8°. L, O; CH, CN, WF, Y.

1233 **Castle, George.** The chymical Galenist: a treatise. *By Sarah Griffin for Henry Twyford, and Timothy Twyford,* 1667. 8°. L, O, C, OC, P; CLC, MMO, WF, HC.

Castle, William. *See* Castell, William.

1234 **Castlehaven, James Touchet,** *earl of.* The memoirs of . . . his engagement. *For Henry Brome,* 1680. 8°. T.C.I 404. L, O, C, LVF, LW; CH, CLC, CN, MH, WF.

1235 ——[Anr. ed.] *For Joanna Brome,* 1681. 8°. T.C.I 428. L, O, C, OC; CLC, WF, Y.

1236 —A remonstrance of the right honovrable Iames Earle of Castlehaven. *Printed at VVaterford by Thomas Bourke,* 1643. 4°.* LT.

1237 —The Earl of Castlehaven's review. *For Charles Brome,* 1684. 8°. L, C, CT, P, DT; CLC, CN, MH, WF, Y.

1238 **Castlemaine, Roger Palmer,** *earl of.* An account of the present war. *By J. M. for H. Herringman,* 1666. 8°. L, O, C, LW, CT; CH, CN, MH, WF, Y.

1239 —Advertisement. There is invented. *Sold by T. Moxon,* [1679]. brs. Y.

1240 [–] The Catholique apology. Third edition. [*London?*] *printed,* 1674. 8°. L, O, CS, MC, DT; CH, CN, MH, NU, WG, Y.

1241 [–] The compendium: or, a short view of the late tryals, in relation to the present plot. *Printed,* 1679. 4°. L, O, C, EN, DT; CH, CN, MHL, NU, WF, Y.

1242 —The English globe. *For Joseph Moxon,* 1679. 4°. L, O, LPO, OB, OC; CH, MIU, WF, Y.

1243 ——Second edition. —, 1696. 4°. LC.

1244 —A full answer and confutation of a scandalous pamphlet. [*Antwerp*], 1673. 4°.* L, O, C, MR, EN; CLC, NGT, WF, Y.

1245 —The Earl of Castlemain's manifesto. [*London?*], *printed,* 1681. 8°. L, C, CS, SC, ES; CH, CN, MH, NU, WF, Y.

1246 [–] A reply to the ansvver of the Catholiqve apology. [*London?*], 1668. 8°. L, O, C, CS, OC; CH, NU, TU, WF, Y.

1247 —A short and true account of the material passages. *In the Savoy, for H. Herringman,* 1671. 8°. T.C.I 66. L, C, OC; MH, RPJ, WF, Y.

1248 ——Second edition. —, 1672. 8°. T.C.I 113. L, O, C; BN, CN, Y.

1249 [–] To all the Royallists that suffered. [*London*], 1666. 4°.* OC; CH, TU, WF, Y.

1250 Castor and Pollux. 1666. brs. O.

Castramentation. 1642. *See* Cruso, John.

1251 A casual discourse about banks. [*London,* 1695.] cap., fol.* L, LG; Y.

Casuistical morning-exercises. 1690. *See* Annesley, Samuel.

1251A **Caswell, George.** The confession of. *For L. Curtis,* 1691. brs. OP.

1252 **Caswell, John.** A brief (but full) account of the doctrine of trigonometry. *By John Playford, for Richard Davis, in Oxford,* 1685. fol.* L, O, C, AU, DT; BN, CH, MU, NU, WF, Y.

Cat may look. 1652. *See* Weldon, Sir Anthony.

Cata-baptism. 1655. *See* Goodwin, John.

1253 Catalogi librorum manuscriptorum Angliæ et Hiberniæ in unum collecti. *Oxoniæ, e theatro Sheldoniano,* 1697. 2v. fol. T.C.III 95. L, O, C, MR, GH; BN, CH, CU, LC, MH, Y.

1254 Catalogi, librorum theologicorum, historicorum. Pars prior. 1691/2. 8°.* L.

1255 A catalogue containing variety of ancient, and modern English books . . . 30th day of November, 1685. [*London*], 1685. fol. L, O, HH.

1256 A catalogue containing variety of books, of the common & statute law. [*London*], *18 Feb.* 1685/6. 4°.* L, O; JF.

1257 A catalogue containing variety of English books in divinity. [*London*], *20 Dec.* 1686. 4°. L, OC; CN, JF.

1258 Catalogue de livres latins, françois. [*London*], *12 March,* 1695. 4°. L.

1259 Catalogue des livres françois anciens & modernes. *Exeter Exchange, Strand, 13 Mar.,* 1693. 4°.* L.

1260   Catalogue des livres françois et italiens. [*London*], *26 Oct.,*
        1693. 4°. L.

1261   Catalogue des livres françois, italiens. [*London*], *15 May,*
        1693. 4°. L.

1262   Catalogue des nouveaux livres françois. [*London*], *27*
        Nov., *1693.* 4°. L.

1263   —[–] [*London*], *14 Nov., 1694.* 4°. L.

1264   A catalogue of a remainder of several sorts of Bibles.
        [*London*], *December 10. 1685.* brs. L.

        Catalogue of all graduats. Oxford, 1689. *See* Peers,
        Richard.

        Catalogue of all the books. 1673. *See* Clavel, Robert.

        Catalogue of all the chiefest rarities. Leiden, 1683. *See*
        Schuyl, Frans.

1265–7 Entries cancelled.

1268   A catalogue of all the colledges in . . . Cambridge. *For*
        J. Blyth, sold by J. Playford, 1678. brs. T.C.I 311. L, O, EN.

        Catalogue of all the discourses. 1689. *See* Gee, Edward,
        younger.

1269   A catalogue of all the musick books. [*London*, 1670].
        4°. L; NN.

1270   A catalogue of all the names of the prisoners taken . . .
        at Nampwitch. [*London*], *for Edward Husbands. Febr. 1.*
        1643[4]. brs. LT, LG.

        Catalogue of all the peers. 1661. *See* Ashmole, Elias.

1271   A catalogue of all the stitch'd books . . . to Jan. 1679/80.
        1680. 4°. O.

1272   A catalogue of all the stitch'd books . . . to June 25. 1680.
        1680. 4°. O.

1273   A catalogue of ancient and modern books . . . tenth of
        July, 1693. [*Norwich*], 1693. 4°.* O.

1273A   A catalogue of ancient and modern books . . . 26 of
        March, 1694. [*London*], 1694. fol.* CLC.

1274   A catalogue of antient and modern books. [*n.p.*], *14*
        Nov., 1699. 4°. L.

1275   A catalogue of ancient and modern books . . . Decemb.
        2d. 1700. [*Norwich*], 1700. 4°.* O.

1276   A catalogue of ancient and modern books. *Southwark,*
        24 Sept., 1694. 4°. L.

1277   A catalogue of ancient and modern English books.
        Ninth day of May 1692. [*n.p.*], *9 May,* 1692. 4°.* L, O.

1278   A catalogue of ancient and modern musick books. 1691.
        8°.* L.

        Catalogue of approved divinity-books. [*n.p.*], 1657. *See*
        Rothwell, John.

1279   A catalogue of batchelors. [*London*, 1691.] brs. CN.

1280   A catalogue of books consisting of divinity. *7 Mar.,*
        1691/2. cap., 4°.* L.

1281   A catalogue of books (for the most part very scarce).
        [*London*, 1690.] brs. JF.

1282   A catalogue of books in divinity. [*n.p.*], *8 Feb., 1697.*
        4°. L.

1283   A catalogue of books in folio. [*n.p.*], *31 July, 1691.* 4°. L.

1284   A catalogue of books in Latin and English. [*n.p.*], *25*
        Feb., 1695. 4°. L.

1285   A catalogue of books in quires. [*London*], *15 March,*
        1688/9. brs. LM; JF.

1285A   A catalogue of books in several faculties. [*Dublin*, 1698.]
        cap., 4°.* DT.

1286   A catalogue of books of the newest fashion. [*London*,
        1690?] 4°.* L, CT, MR, EN; CH, MH, Y.

1287   A catalogue of books of two eminent mathematicians.
        21 May, 1691. 4°.* L.

1288   Entry cancelled.

        Catalogue of books printed in England. 1696. *See* Clavel,
        Robert.

1289   A catalogue of books to be sold by auction. [*London*],
        1690. cap., 4°.* JF.

1290   —[*n.p.*], *1 August, 1692.* L.

1291   —[*n.p.*], *14 Oct., 1692.* L.

1292   A catalogue of books viz divinity, history, philology.
        [*London*], 1687/8. 4°.* O, OC; JF.

1293   A catalogue of books viz. in divinity, history. [*London*,
        1696?] 4°.* HH.

1294   A catalogue of choice and valuable books: consisting.
        1 Oct., 1691. 4°.* L.

1295   A catalogue of choice and valuable books English and
        Latin . . . *30th of April, 1688.* [*n.p.*], *1688.* 4°. O.

1296   A catalogue of choice and valuable books in Greek.
        [*n.p.*], *20 August, 1694.* 4°. L.

1297   A catalogue of choice and valuable books, Latin and
        English. *Printed,* 1689. 4°.* JF.

        Catalogue of choice books. [*n.p.*, 1686.] *See* Whitwood,
        William.

1298   A catalogue of choice books (chiefly civil law). [*n.p.*],
        25th of February, 1685. brs. L.

1299   A catalogue of choice books in divinity. [*n.p.*], *9 May,*
        1687. 4°. L, O.

1300   A catalogue of choice books in several languages. [*n.p.*],
        11 March, 1688/9. 4°.* LM.

1301   A catalogue of choice books, paintings and prints.
        [*London*, n. d.] 4°.* JF.

1302   A catalogue of choice English books, consisting of di-
        vinity. [*London*], *10 Jan., 1686/7.* 4°.* L, O; JF.

1303   A catalogue of choice English books. [*n.p.*], *6th August,*
        1688. 4°.* O, LM.

1304   A catalogue of choice Latin and English books. [*n.p.*],
        28 Nov., 1694. 4°. L.

1305   A catalogue of considerable books, Latin and English.
        [*London*], 1689. 4°.* JF.

1306   The catalogue of contented cuckolds. [*London*, 1670?]
        brs. L.

1307   —[*Anr. ed.*] *For J. Conyers,* [1685?] brs. L, CM; MH.

1308   May the 8th 1686. A catalogue of divers excellent Italian
        pictures . . . 11th . . . May. [*n.p.*, 1686.] cap., fol.* O.

1309   A catalogue of divines approved of by the . . . Commons.
        1642. fol.* CPE.

1310   A catalogue of divinity, history, physick. *7 Oct., 1691.*
        4°.* L.

1311   A catalogue of dukes, marquesses, earls. *For Thomas*
        Walkley, 1652. 8°.* LT.

1312   A catalogue of English & Latin books. [*n.p.*], *22 January,*
        1688/9. 4°.* O, LM.

1313 A catalogue of English and Latin books in quires. [London, 1690?] 4°.* JF.

1314 —[Anr. ed.] [London], 1690. 4°. JF.

1315 —[Anr. ed.] [London], 1691. cap., 4°.* JF.

1316 A catalogue of English & Latin books, viz. divinity. [London], 16 March, 1690/1. 4°. L; JF.

1317 A catalogue of English and Latin books. [n.p.], 15 March, 1694. 4°. L.

1318 A catalogue of English books, both ancient. [n.p.], 6 June, 1692. 4°. L.

1319 A catalogue of English books, consisting of the bound stock of a book-seller lately deceased. [London], 1690. 4°.* JF.

1320 A catalogue of English books in divinity. [n.p.], 3 Dec., 1696. 4°. L.

1321 A catalogue of English books, viz. divinity. 9 April, 1696. fol.* L.

1322 A catalogue of English, French, Italian, Dutch and Spanish books. [London], 1689. 4°.* LR; JF.

1323 A catalogue of English, Greek, and Latin books. [n.p.], 13 Oct., 1697. 4°. L.

1324 Catalogue of excellent and rare books. Edinburgh, 1688. 4°.* HH.

1325 A catalogue of excellent and rare books . . . of Mr. W. Annand. Edinburgh, by a society of stationers, 1690. 4°.* ALDIS 3027. HH, EN.

1326 A catalogue of excellent books, in Greek. [n.p.], 15 Oct., 1694. 4°. L.

1327 A catalogue of excellent English books. [n.p.], 1 Feb., 1691. 4°. L.

1328 —29 June, 1691. 4°.* L.

1329 —[n.p.], 27 June, 1693. 4°. L.

1330 A catalogue of excellent Greek, Latine and English books. 13 Oct., 1691. 4°. L.

1331 A catalogue of extraordinary Greek and Latin books. [n.p.], 1 June, 1692. 4°. L.

1332 A catalogue of fees established. colop: Printed and sold by William Bradford, in New-York, 1693. cap., fol.* EVANS 673. LPR; CH, NN, NS, PHS.

1333 A catalogue of Greek, Latine, and English books. 13 July, [1691]. 4°.* L.

1334 —21 Dec., 1691. 4°.* L.

1335 —29 Feb., 1691/2. 4°.* L.

1336 —[n.p.], 4 April, 1692. 4°.* L.

1337 —[n.p.], 26 April, 1693. 4°.* L.

1338 —[n.p.], 28 Nov., 1694. 4°.* L.

1339 —[n.p.], 1699?] 4°.* L.

1340 A catalogue of jilts. R. W., 1691. brs. CN.

1341 A catalogue of late books: by . . . Mr. Thomas Beverly. [Printed for, and sold by William Marshall, and John Marshall, 1695.] 4°.* GU.

1342 A catalogue of Latin and English books. [n.p.], 2 Jan., 1695. 4°. L.

1343 —[n.p.], 12 July, 1697. 4°. L.

1344 A catalogue of Latin and English books . . . common and statute law. [London], 1689/90. 4°.* JF.

1345 A catalogue of Latin and English books in quires. Printed 7 Sept., 1691. 4°.* L, CS.

1346 A catalogue of Latin and English books of divinity. [n.p.], 1687/8. 4°. O.

1347 A catalogue of Latin and English books, to be sold by auction. 29 May, 1691. cap., 4°.* L.

1348 A catalogue of Latin and English books, viz. divinity. 11 May, 1691. 4°.* L.

1349 A catalogue of Latin and English physick-books. [n.p.], 30 July, 1694. 4°. L.

1350 A catalogue of Latin and French books. Smithfield, 29 May, 1691. 4°. L.

1351 A catalogue of Latin and French books. [n.p.], 1 Oct., 1694. 4°. L.

1352 A catalogue of Latin, French, and English books. [London], 17 Oct., 1687. 4°. L, O; JF.

1353 —[n.p.], 30th April, 1688. 4°.* O, LM, LR.

1353A —[n.p.], 2 May, 1692. 4°. OP.

1354 —[n.p.], 22 August, 1692. 4°. L.

1355 —[n.p.], 13 Sept., 1692. 4°. L.

1356 A catalogue of Latine Greek & English books. 15 June, 1691. 4°.* L.

1357 A catalogue of Latine, Greek and English books. 17 Aug., 1691. 4°.* L, EC.

1358 —6 Oct., 1691. 4°.* L.

1359 A catalogue of Latin, Greek and English books. [n.p.], 5 Sept., 1692. 4°. L.

1360 —[n.p.], 2 Nov., 1692. 4°. L.

1361 —[n.p.], 12 Dec., 1692. 4°. L.

1362 —[n.p.], 13 Feb., 1693. 4°. L.

Catalogue of new books. 1660. See London, William.

Catalogue of our English writers. 1668. See Crowe, William.

Catalogue of part of those rarities. [n.p.], 166–? See Hubert, Robert.

A catalogue of printed books written by VVilliam Prynne. 1643. See Sparke, Michael.

1363 A catalogue of prints and drawings . . . 9th . . . March, 1690/1 [n.p.], 1691. 4°.* L.

1364 A catalogue of prints and paintings. [London], 2 August, 1689. 4°. L.

1365 A catalogue of remarkable mercies conferred upon the seven associated counties. By Roger Daniel, Cambridge, 1643[4]. 4°.* LT, O, CM, CS; MH, MIU, WF.

1365A —[Anr. ed.] [n.p.] Anno Dom., 1644. 4°.* L, O, CT.

Catalogue of several sorts. 1685. See Pitt, Moses.

1366 Catalogue of succession, of all the kings. By George Croom. brs. L. [date trimmed].

Catalogue of such books. 1664. See T., G.

Catalogue of such testimonies. [n.p.], 1641. See Prynne, William.

1367 A catalogue of sundrie knights, aldermen, doctors . . . are in custody in Gresham Colledge. [London], for Iohn Iackson, G. Green, and F. Smith, 1642. Novemb. 7, brs. LT, O, LG; MH.

1368 A catalogue of the baronets of this kingdom. By E. Cotes for A. Seile, 1667. 4°. L; CH, WF, Y.

1368A A catalogue of the bowes of the town. [*London*, 1691.] brs. CN.

1369 A catalogue of the choicest, and most valuable books. [*n.p.*], *14 Feb.*, *1687*. 4°. L.

1370 A catalogue of the colleges and halls in . . . Oxford. *By J. M. for J. Blyth, and are to be sold at Mr. Playford's shop*, 1678. brs. MADAN 3166. L, O, EN; CH.

1371 A catalogue of the damages for which the English demand reparation. *For Henry Brome*, 1664. 4°. L, O, C, CT, HH; HR, CH, CN, MH, NC, WF, Y.

1372 A catalogue of the divines approved of. *For T. P.*, 1642. brs. L, O, LS, EC; CH, MH, Y.

Catalogue of the dvkes. 1642. *See* Walkley, Thomas.

1373 A catalogue of the earles, lords, knights. *For John Hancock*, 1647. brs. LT.

1374 Entry cancelled.

1375 The catalogue of the Fellows and other members of the Royal College of Physicians. *Printed*, 1696. brs. L, O.

1376 A catalogue of the Fellows of the College of Physicians. [*London*], 1694. brs. L, O.

1377 —[*London*], 1695. brs. L, O.

1378 A catalogue of the gentlemen of worth. *For John Hancock*, 1647. brs. LT.

Catalogue of the Hebrew saints. Newcastle, 1659. *See* Shaw, John.

A catalogue of the libraries of two eminent persons, consisting. [*Tunbridge Wells*], 1684. *See* Gellibrand, John.

1379 A catalogue of the libraries of two eminent persons deceased. [*London*], 1684. fol. L, HH.

1380 A catalogue of the library of a person of honour. [1700.] 4°.* L; Y.

1381 A catalogue of the library of an eminent person, deceased. [*n.p.*], *12 Dec.*, *1700*. 4°. L.

1382 A catalogue of the lords, earles. *T. F., June 8*, 1642. 4°. BR, HH, DT.

Catalogue of the lords, knights. 1655. *See* Dring, Thomas.

1383 A catalogue of the lords, knights and gentlemen (of the Catholick religion). [*n.p.*, 1658–60.] brs. O; CH.

1384 A catalogve of the lords spiritvall and temporall. *By I. D. for Tho. Walkley*, 1640[1]. 8°. LT; CH.

1385 A catalogue of the moneys, men, and horse, already subscribed unto by several counties. *First printed at Yorke, and now reprinted at London, for John Thomas*, 1642. brs. LT, LS; Y.

1385A A catalogue of the most approved divinity books. *For John Rothwell*, 1655. 12°.* CM.

1386 A catalogue of the most considerable books in the . . . law. [*n.p.*], *18th February*, *1689*. 4°.* LM.

1387 A catalogue of the most valuable, and useful books in . . . law. [*n.p.*], *14th of May*, *1688*. 4°. LM.

Catalogue of the most vendible. 1657. *See* London, William.

Catalogue of the names of all His Majesties justices. 1680. *See* N., S.

1387A A catalogue of the names of all such who were summon'd to any Parliament. *For Robert Pawley*, 1661. 8°. L, LG, CT; CH, CLC, CN, WF, Y.

1388 A catalogue of the names of so many of those commissioners. [*London*, *1660*.] cap., 4°.* LT, O, OC, CS, HH; CH, MH, MIU, WF, Y.

1389 A catologue [*sic*] of the names of such persons. [*London*, 1649?] fol. L, OC, HH; CN.

1390 A catalogue of the names of such persons as are, . . . of the Romish religion. *Printed*, 1680. brs. O; CH, MH, WF, Y.

1391 A catalogve of the names of the divines approved of. *By T. Fawcet, for Thomas Bankes*, 1642. 4°.* LT, DT; CH, NN.

1392 A cattalogue of the names of the dukes, marqvesses, earles. *For Iohn Thomas*, 1642. brs. LT, LS, OC, SP; MH.

1393 —[*Anr. ed.*] [*London*], *printed*, 1642. 4°.* LT, O, CT, HH, SP; CH, CLC, CN, WF, Y.

1394 A catalogue of the names of the knights, citizens, and burgesses, that have served in the last four Parlaments [*sic*]. *By Tho. Newcomb*, 1656. 8°. MADAN 2293. LT, O; WF.

1395 A catalogve of the names of the knights for the counties. *For Tho: Walkley*, 1640[1]. 8°.* LT, C, BR; CH.

1396 —[*Anr. ed.*] —, 1691. 8°.* C, CT.

1396A A catalogue of the names of the lords spiritual. *For Robert Pauley*, 1661. 4°.* MIU, PL.

1397 A catalogue of the names of the lordes that subscribed. *For Richard Lownes*, 1642. brs. STEELE 2198. LT, O, LS, EC; CH, MIU, Y.

1398 A catalogue of the names of the lords that subscribed. [*n.p.*], 1642. brs. LT, LS; CH.

1399 A catalogue of the names of the members of the last Parliament. *By A. M.*, 1654. brs. MADAN 2249. LT.

1400 A catalogve of the names of the new lords created by the king. *For John Field, Nov. 10*, 1645. 4°.* LT, DT; CLC, MH.

1401 A catalogue of the names of the new representatives. [*n.p.*, 1653.] brs. LT.

1402 A catalogue of the names of the orthodox divines. *By T. Fawcet for Thomas Bankes*, 1642. 4°. C, E; WF.

1403 A catalogue of the names of this present Parliament. *By D. Maxwell*, 1659. brs. LT; CH, MH.

1404 A catalogue of the names of those holy martyrs. *Printed*, 1679. brs. T.C.I 405. L, O, HH; CH, CU, MH, WF, Y.

1405 A catalogue of the names of those honourable persons, who are now members . . . Lords. [*n.p.*, 1658.] brs. LT; MH.

Catalogue of the nobility. 1661. *See* Walkley, Thomas.

1406 Entry cancelled.

1407 A catalogue of the nobility and principal gentry (said to be) in arms. [*n.p.*, 1688.] brs. L, C, EC, HH; CH, CN, WU, Y.

1408 A catalogue of the peers of the Kingdom of England. *By D. Maxwel*, 1660. brs. LT, O; MH.

1408A A catalogue of the petitions, ordered. [*London?* 1645.] cap., 4°.* WF.

1409   A catalogue of the prelates and clergie of . . . Canterbury. *For Nath. Brooke,* 1661. brs. L, O.

1410   A catalogue of the present convention of estates. *For J. Partridge, M. Gilliflower, S. Heyrick, and sold by R. Taylor,* 1689. brs. L, O; CH, INU.

1410A   A catalogue of the right honorable and noble Lords, Earles. *By T. F.,* 1642. *June 8.* 4°.* L, LSE, EC, YM, DT; Y.

1410B   A catalogue of the sermons printed. 1644. 4°.* LT.

1410C   A catalogue of the several members of the Society of apothecaries. [*London,* 1693.] brs. L.

1411   A catalogue of the severall sects and opinions. [*London*], *by R.A.,* 1647. brs. LT.

1411A   A catalogue of the succession of all the kings. *G. Croom,* 1685. brs. L.

1412   A catalogue of two choice and considerable libraries . . . 22d day of . . . November, 1680. [*n.p.,* 1680.] 4°. L, O, CS, OP.

1413   A catalogue of valuable and choice books. [*n.p.,* 1699?] 4°. L.

1414   A catalogue of valuable and scarce books English and Latin in folio. [*n.p.,* *10 June,* 1689. 4°.* LM.

1415   A catalogue of valuable and useful books. [*London*], *24 May,* 1688. 4°.* LM, OC; JF.

1416   A catalogue of valuable books, viz. in divinity, humanity. [*London*], 1689. fol.* L; JF.

1417   A catalogue of valuable books, viz divinity. [*n.p.*], *20 March, 1693.* 4°. L.

1418   —[*n.p.*], *18 Oct., 1693.* 4°. L.

1419   A catalogue of variety of books in quires. [*n.p.*], *12 Jan., 1687.* 4°. L.

1420   A catalogue of variety of books Latin & English. [*London*], 1689/90. 4°.* L; JF.

1421   A catalogue of variety of English books. [*n.p.*], *29th April, 1689.* 4°.* LM.

1422   —[*London*], *7 May, 1691.* 4°.* L; JF.

1423   A catalogue of vendible and useful English and Latin books. [*London*], *18 March, 1688/9.* 4°.* O, LM, HH; JF.

1424   A catalogue of vendible and useful Latin and English books. [*London*], *12 Aug., 1689.* 4°.* L; JF.

1425   A catalogue of very good English and Latin books. [*London*], *9 Sept., 1689.* 4°.* L; JF.

1426   A catalogue of very good Greek, Latin, and English books. [*London*], 1690. 4°.* JF.

1427   A catalogue of very good Latin, French, and English books. *20 April, 1691.* 4°.* L.

Catalogus impressorum. Oxonii, 1674. *See* Oxford, University.

1428   Catalogus insignum rarissimorumque. [*n.p.*], *29 Nov., 1692.* 4°. L.

1429   Catalogus libris exquisitissimis. *Oxford, 20 June, 1700.* 4°. L; WF.

1430   Entry cancelled.

1431   Catalogus librorum . . . 29 Martii 1680. [*London*], *per Edvardum Millington,* 1680. 4°. O, HH.

1432   Entry cancelled.

1433   Catalogus librorum bibliothecæ viri cujusdam literati . . . 6 Junii, 1681. [*London,* 1681.] 4°.* O, OC, HH.

1434   —, Feb. 14, 1686/7. [*London,* 1687.] 4°. L, O, CS, LR, HH; NG.

1435   Catalogus librorum domi. *Sam. Smith & Benj. Walford,* 1695. 12°. OC, OP.

Catalogus librorum ex bibliotheca nobilis cujusdam Angli. 1678. *See* Brooke, Robert Greville, *baron.*

1436–8   Entries cancelled.

1439   Catalogus librorum in omni facultate . . . insignium. [*Oxford?* 1687.] 4°. L, OC, OP.

1440   —[*London*], *9 Oct.,* 1690. 4°.* L; JF.

1441   Entry cancelled.

1442   Catalogus librorum in omni genere insignium. 1657. 4°. L, O.

Catalogus librorum instructissimæ bibliothecæ. 1688. *See* Lauderdale, John Maitland, *duke of.*

1443   Catalogus librorum Italiae. 1647. 4°. DT.

Catalogus librorum manuscriptorum. Oxoniae, 1697. *See* Bernard, Edward.

1444   Catalogus librorum medicorum . . . 13 Julii, 1686. [*London,* 1686.] 4°.* L, O, HH.

1445   Catalogus librorum modernorum & antiquorum. 12 Oct., 1691. 4°.* L.

1446   Catalogus librorum, quibus bibliothecam Academiae Jacobi regis Edinburgenæ. *Edinburgi, excudebat Thomas Brown,* 1678. 4°. ALDIS 2119. LCS, EN, AU; WF.

1447   Catalogus librorum quos de nundinis Francofurtensibus. *E. Richard Whittaker.* [1645.] 4°. O, OP, DT.

1448   Catalogus librorum tam antiquorum quam recentium. *Oxford, Feb. 28, 1686/7.* 4°. L, O, OC.

1449   —, Novemb. 9. 1692. *Oxford,* 1692. fol. L, OP.

—, Maij 5. 1696. [*Oxford,* 1696.] *See* Ashwell, George.

1450   Catalogus librorum theologicorum. [*n.p.*], *5 Feb., 1692.* 4°. L.

1450A   Catalogus medicamentorum. *Apud Guliel. Miller,* 1685. 12°. L.

Catalogus plantarum. Oxon, 1648. *See* Bobart, Jacobus.

Catalogus plantarum. Cantabrigiae, 1660. *See* Ray, John.

1451   Catalogus selectissimorum. *Edinburgi, heirs of A. Anderson,* 1699. 12°. ALDIS 3835. EN.

Catalogus universalis librorum in omni facultate. 1699. *See* Hartley, John.

Catalogus universalis librorum omnium. 1650. *See* Spencer, J.

1452   Entry cancelled.

1453   Catalogus variorum & insignium librorum. *19 Oct., 1691.* 4°. L.

1454   Catalogus variorum & insignium tam antiquorum quam recentium librorum. [*London*], 1690/1. 4°. OC, CS; JF.

1455   Catalogus variorum in plurimis facultatibus variisq. [*London*], 1687/8. 4°. JF.

Catalogus variorum librorum. [*n.p.*], 1685. *See* Parkhurst, Thomas.

1456   Catalogus variorum librorum antiquorum & recentiorum . . . (15) die Martii 1698/9. *Oxford,* 1699. fol. L.

1457 Catalogus variorum librorum apud theatrum Sheldon-ianum . . . 24 die Februarii, 1678/9. [*Londini*, 1679.] 4°.* MADAN 3202.* L, O, OP.

1458 Entry cancelled.

1459 Catalogus variorum librorum in omnigena literatura. [*n.p.*], *20 Nov.*, *1693*. 4°. L.

1460 Entry cancelled.

Catalogus variorum librorum theologicorum juridi-corumque. [1683.] *See* Wilson, Samuel.

1461 Catalogus variorum librorum theologicorum. [*n.p.*], *21 Jan.*, *1695*. 4°. L.

1462 Catalogus variorum, tam recentium, quam antiquorum, rei medicæ. [*Londini*], *6 June*, *1689*. 4°.* L, LM.

Cataplus. 1672. *See* A., M.

Catastrophe mundi. 1683. *See* Lilly, William.

Catcall, Critic, *pseud.*

Catch that catch can. 1667. *See* Playford, John.

1463 Κατηχήσεις τῆς χριστιανικῆς πιστεως. *Cantabrigiæ; ex officina Rogeri Daniel*, 1648. 12°. C, DC; PL, Y.

1463A —[Anr. ed.] *Excudebat R. Daniel, venales apud Samuelen Thomson*, 1651. 12°. CPE, DC.

1464 [Hebrew] Catechesis brevior religionis Christianæ. *Sam. Roycroft*, 1689. 8°.* L, CT, LW, E.

1465 Catechesis ecclesiarum quae in regno Poloniae. *Racoviae* [*London*], 1651. 12°. LT, O.

Catachesis elenctica. 1654. *See* Baillie, Robert.

1466 Catechesis religionis. *Edinburgi, excudebat, Gideon Lithgo*; 1657. 8°.* ALDIS 1565a. L.

1467 —[Anr. ed.] 1660. 8°.* C, E.

1468 —[Anr. ed.] *Glasguæ, excudebat Robertus Sanders*, [1671]. 4°.* ECS.

Catechism and confession. [*n.p.*], 1674. *See* Barclay, Robert.

1468A Y catechism a osod wyd allan yr llytr. *Oxford*, 1682. 8°. AN.

1468B A catechism containing the substance. *By J. Grover to be sold by S. Crouch*, 1676. 8°. T.C.I 265. LW.

1469 —[Anr. ed.] *By A. Grover, to be sold by S. Crouch, and B. Ailmer*, 1683. 8°.* L, EC, DT.

1469A —[Anr. ed.] *By A. Grover, to be sold by B. Ailmer*, 1683. 8°.* OC.

1470 —[Anr. ed.] *By J. D. to be sold by Jonathan Robinson, and Samuel Crouch*, 1693. 8°.* O, CT.

Catechism for children. 1657. *See* Fox, George.

Catechism for children in years. 1644. *See* Stalham, John.

1471 A catechism for souldiers. *By T. M. for Edward Thomas*, 1659. 8°.* LT.

1472 The catechism for the curats. *By Henry Hills, for him and Matthew Turner*, 1687. 8°. L, O, C, LIL, MC; CH, CN, NU, TU, WG, Y.

Catechisme for the times. 1645. *See* K., J.

Catechism for the use. Paris, 1692. *See* Anderdon, Christopher.

1473 A catechisme for young children. [*Edinburgh?*], *printed*, 1641. brs. L, O.

1474 Catechism made practical. *For Jonathan Robinson*, 1688. 8°. T.C.II 237. L, O, C; NU.

1475 A catechisme of Christian religion. *At Amsterdam, by John Frederick Stam*, 1652. 12°. L; Y.

Catechism of penance. 1685. *See* Roucourt, Jean.

1475A The catechism of the Book of Common-Prayer explained. Third edition. *By T. R. and N. T. for Richard Thrale*, 1672. 8°. EC.

Catechisme of the Church of England. 1668. *See* B., I.

Catechism of the Church of England. 1678. *See* Wetenhall, Edward.

1475B The catechism of the Church of England briefly paraphrased. *For John Taylor*, 1688. 8°.* L; NU.

1476 (The catechism of the Church of England, translated into Arabic.) [*Oxford*, 1671.] 8°.* MADAN 2885. O.

Catechism of the church: with proofs. 1694. *See* Isham, Zachary.

Catechism of the Council. 1687. *See* Bromley, John.

1477 The catechism or, brief instruction. *For the use of the Church*, 1700. 8°.* O.

1478 The catechism or, Christian doctrine. [*London*, 1683?] sixes* Y.

Catechisme, or institution. 1647. *See* Nowell, Alexander.

Catechism set forth. Oxford, 1679. *See* Marshall, Thomas.

Catechisme shorter. 1649. *See* L., S.

1479 A catechisme to be learned for the training up of youth. *By Robert Ibbitson*, 1653. 8°.* LT.

Catechism truly representing. 1686. *See* Williams, John, bp.

1479A A catechism wherein the learner. *For Sam. Richards in Nottingham*, 1674. 12°. CLC.

1479B Catechism yn cynwys. *Alice Grover*, 1682. 12°. AN.

1479C Catechismus, cum ordine. *Prostant apud Sam. Carr; & B. Tooke*, 1685. 8°. T.C.II 148. Y.

Catechismus pro parvulis. 1660. *See* Fox, George.

Catechist catechiz'd. [*n.p.*], 1681. *See* Cary, Edward.

Catechistical discourses. Paris, 1654. *See* Errington, Anthony.

1480 A catechistical guide to sinners. *By J. D. to be sold by Fr. Smith, and W. Crook*, 1680. 8°. L, LCL, OC; NU, WF.

1481 The catechumen, or an account given. *For W. Crooke*, 1690. 12°. T.C.II 297. LC, Y.

1481A —Second edition. —, 1690. 12°. T.C.II 325. L, O, OC; TU.

1482 **Cateline, Jeremy.** The rvles and directions of the ordinances of Parliament. *By A. M. for Christopher Meredith*, 1647. 8°.* LT.

1483 ——[Anr. ed.] —, 1648. 8°.* L, O.

Catena. 1647. *See* King, R.

1484 **Cater, Samuel.** A general epistle to all friends. *By Andrew Sowle*, 1680. 4°.* LF, BBN; IE, PH, Y.

1485 —The innocent cleared. [*London*], *printed*, 1676. 4°.* L, LF, OC, CS, BBN; CH, MH, NG, PH, Y.

1486 [–] The liberty of an apostate conscience discovered. *By John Bringhurst*, 1683. 8°. L, LF, OC.

1487 —The life of Christ magnified. *For John Bringhurst*, 1681. 8°. L; PH, PL.

1488 [–] A relation of some of the most material matters. [*n.p.*, 1676.] cap., 4°.* L, LF; MH, PH, PSC.

1489 —A salutation in the love of God. [*London*], *printed, 1672.* 4°.* L, CT, LF, BBN; CH, LC, MH, PH, Y.

1490 The catterpillars of this nation anatomized. *For M. H.,* 1659. 4°.* L, O; CH, CLC, WCL.

Cathedral and conventuall churches. [n.p.], 1656. *See* King, Daniel.

1491 **Catherall, Samuel.** A sermon preach'd . . . last day of February, 1691/2. *For Robert Clavell, 1692.* 4°.* T.C.II 408. L, O; WF, Y.

Catholick almanack. 1687. *See* Almanacs.

Catholick & Protestant almanack. 1688. *See* Almanacs.

Catholick answer. 1687. *See* N., N.

Catholique apology. [n.p.], 1668. *See* Castlemaine, Roger Palmer, *earl of.*

Catholick ballad. [n.p., 1674.] *See* Pope, Walter.

Catholic ballance. 1687. *See* Hill, Samuel.

Catholick catechism. 1683. *See* Beverley, Thomas.

Catholick-cause. 1678. *See* Sixtus V, *pope.*

Catholick confession. 1686. *See* Aubigné, Théodore Agrippa d'.

Catholick doctrine of transubstantiation. *Paris,* 1657. *See* Campion, William, *alias* Wigmore.

1492 The Catholick gamesters, or a dubble match of bowleing. [*London*] *sold by William Marshall,* [1680?] brs. T.C.I 406. L, O; MH.

1493 —[Anr. ed.] [*Edinburgh*], *printed, February 14, 1680.* brs. MH.

Catholick hierarchie. 1681. *See* Chauncy, Isaac.

1494 Catholick hymn, on the birth of the Prince of Wales. 1688. brs. CH.

Catholick letter. 1688. *See* N., N.

Catholick medicine. 1684. *See* Maynwaringe, Everard.

1494A The Catholick mirrour. *Printed at Paris,* 1662. 8°. HEYTHROP; CN, TU.

Catholick naked truth. 1676. *See* Hubert, William, *alias* Berry.

1494B Catholick news from Purgatory. *For E. E.,* 1679. 4°.* MBA.

1495 A Catholick pill to purge Popery. *For J. Coles, and Will. Miller,* 1677. 8°. T.C.I 283. L, O, CT; CLC, MIU, WF, Y.

Catholick representer. 1687. *See* Gother, John.

Catholick schismatology. 1685. *See* Browne, J.

Catholike scriptvrist. *Gant,* 1662. *See* Mumford, James.

Catholick theses. [n.p., 1689.] *See* Woodhead, Abraham.

1496 The Catholike yonger brother. [n.p.], 1642. 8°. DUC.

Catholicism. 1683. *See* Allen, William.

1497 Entry cancelled.

1498 Catholicon: the expediency. *Printed,* 1674. 4°. T.C.I 155. O, C, OC, SC, SP; CLC, NC, NU, Y.

Catholicks defence. *Oxford,* 1687. *See* Woodhead, Abraham.

Catholicks no idolaters. [n.p.], 1672. *See* Godden, Thomas.

1499 The Catholikes petition to Prince Rupert. [n.p.], *for G. B. August 1, 1644.* 4°.* LT, YM; CH, CLC, MIU, Y.

Catholiques plea. 1659. *See* Austin, John.

1500 A Catholicks resolution. *Printed,* 1668. 4°.* O, CCA, YM; MH, NU, Y.

Catiline his conspiracy. 1669. *See* Jonson, Ben.

Catlett, John. Perpetual and universal almanack. 1656. *See* Almanacs.

1501 **Cato, Dionysius.** Catonis disticha de moribvs. *Typis M. F. impensis Societatis stationariorum,* 1641. 8°. WF.

1502 ——[Anr. ed.] *Typis W. Wilson, impensis societatis stationariorum,* 1646. 8°. C.

1503 ——[Anr. ed.] 1651. 8°. E.

1504 ——[Anr. ed.] *Oxoniæ, escudebat L. L. & H. H.,* 1652. 8°. C.

1504A ——[Anr. ed.] *Oxoniæ, excudebat Hen. Hall,* 1652. 8°. Y.

1505 ——[Anr. ed.] *By W. Wilson for the company of stationers,* 1659. 8°. L, AU.

1506 ——[Anr. ed.] *By R. W. for the company of stationers,* 1670. 8°. O; CU.

1506A ——[Anr. ed.] *Typis E. Hodgkinson & T. Hodgkin, impensis societatis stationariorum,* 1676. 8°. C; IU.

1506B ——[Anr. ed.] *Cantabrigiæ, ex officina Joann Hayes,* 1676. 8°. Y.

1506C ——[Anr. ed.] *By T. M. for the company of stationers.* 1678. 8°. NC.

1507 ——[Anr. ed.] *Cantabrigiæ, ex officina Joan. Hayes,* 1679. 8°. O; Y.

1508 ——[Anr. ed.] *By B. G. for the company of stationers,* 1688. 8°. L.

1509 ——[Anr. ed.] —, 1693. 8°. CT.

1510 ——[Anr. ed.] *Glasguæ, ex typis Roberti Sanders,* 1693. 8°.* GU.

1511 ——[Anr. ed.] *Edinburgi,* 1700. 8°. AU.

1512 —His four books of moral precepts. *Edinburgh, printed,* 1700. 8°.* L, EN.

Caton, William. An abridgement or a compendious commemoration. 1661. *See* Eusebius, *Pamphili,* bp.

1513 —An epistle to King Charles the II. *For Thomas Simmons,* 1660. 4°. L, O, C, LF, BBN; CH, IE, PH, PSC, WF.

1514 —A journal of the life of. *For Thomas Northcott,* 1689. 4°. L, LF, BBN; CH, NU, PH, WF, Y.

1515 —The moderate enquirer. [n.p.], 1658. LSC, CT.

1515A —The moderate enquirer resolved. *Printed, and are to be sold by Lodowick Lloyd,* 1659. 8°. LF; MH, MU.

1516 ——[n.p.], *printed,* 1671. 4°.* L, O, CT, LF; CH, MU, PH, PSC, Y.

1517 —Moderatus inquisitor resolutus. *Pro Roberto Wilson,* 1660. 8°. L, O, OC, LF.

1518 —William Caton's salutation and advice. *For Thomas Simmons,* 1660. brs. LT, LF, BBN; PH.

1519 —The sea-men's invitation. *For Thomas Simmons,* 1659. 4°.* LT, O, C, LF, BBN; IE, PH, PSC, Y.

1520 —The testimony of a cloud of witnesses. [*London*], *printed,* 1662. 4°. L, LF, BBN; CH, MH, MU, PH, PSC, Y.

1521–2 Entries cancelled.

1523 —Truths caracter of professors. *For Thomas Simmons,* 1660. 4°. L, O, CT, LF, BBN; CH, CN, MH, NU, PH, WF, Y.

1524 **Cats, Jacob.** Self-conflict. *For Robert Sollers,* 1680. 8°. T.C.I 404. CH, MH, TU, WCL, WF.

1525   [–] Triumphant chastity. *For Benjamin Crayle, 1684.* 8°.
        L, C, LG; CN, MH, NP, WF, Y.

1526   **Catullus.** Caius Valerius Catullus, et in eum Isaaci
        Vossii. *[Leyden], apud Isaacum Littleburii, Londinensem,*
        1684. 4°. L, O, C, LL, AU; BN, CU, MH, OCI, WF. Y.

1527   **Caus, Isaac de.** New and rare inventions of water-
        works. *By Joseph Moxon, 1659.* fol.* L, C, LPO, E, DT;
        CH, LC, MH, WF, Y.

1528   —Novvelle invention. *Imprime a Londre, 1644.* fol.*
        I, DT; BN, CLC, NN.

1529   ——[Anr. ed.] *Pour Thomas Davies, 1657.* fol.* MH,
        MU, NC.

1530   —Wilton garden. *[London], are to bee sould by Thomas*
        Rowlett, [1645?]. obl., 4°. L; MU, NC, WDA.
        Causa Dei. 1697. *See* Burgess, Daniel.

1531   Causæ veteris epitaphii. *Neapoli sive Augustæ Trino-*
        bantus: prostant in officina B. Tooke, 1685. fol.* T.C.II
        127. L, O, C, CS, CT; CH, NP, WF, Y.

1532   Causæ veteris epitaphium. colop: *Paganapoli, Guilielmi*
        Abington [London, 1682]. cap., fol.* L, O, OC, HH, EN;
        CH, MH, TU, WF, Y.

1533   The cause of God, and of these nations. *Printed, 1659.*
        4°.* LT, LG, HH; MB, MH, NU, PL, WF, Y.
        Cause of our divisions. 1657. *See* J., W.

1534   The cause of the long afflicted . . . Humphrey Smith.
        [London], printed, [1662.] 4°.* Y.
        Cause of the widows. *[n.p., 1665?] See* Rudyard,
        Thomas.
        Causeless ground. *[n.p., 1694.] See* Keith, George.
        Causes & cure. 1665. *See* Rosewell, Thomas.

1535   The causes and cures of an unwilling warre. *[London],*
        printed, 1645. 4°.* L; MH.

1536   The causes and manner of deposing a Popish king in
        Swedeland. *For R. Baldwin, 1688.* brs. L, O, HH, EN;
        TU, WF.

1537   The causes and remedy of the distempers of the times.
        For Jonathan Edwin, 1675. 8°. T.C.I 219. O, P, E; CLC.

1538   The causes of Scotland's miseries. A poem. *Edinburgh,*
        by James Watson, 1700. 4°.* L, O, E, EN; CLC, WF.
        Causes of the decay. 1667. *See* Allestree, Richard.

1539   The causes of the fast, appointed . . . last Wednesday of
        March. *Edinburgh, 1645.* brs. E.
        Causes of the Lord's vvrath. *[n.p.], 1653. See* Warriston,
        Archibald Johnston, *lord.*

1540   Entry cancelled.

1541   **Caussin, Nicolas.** The angel of peace. *[London], printed,*
        1650. 12°. LT, O; CLC, CN, NC, NL.

1542   —The Christian diary. *[Cambridge], printed 1648.* 12°.
        LT, O, C, AN; CLC, CU.

1542A   ——[Anr. ed.] —, 1649. 12°. CCA.

1542B   ——[Anr. ed.] *By R. Daniel for J. Williams, 1656.* 12°.
        CLC.

1543   ——[Anr. ed.] *For John Williams, 1652.* 12°. O, CE; WF.

1544   ——[Anr. ed.] —, 1662. 12°. MH.

1544A   —The Christian diurnal. Third edition. *[London], printed,*
        1686. 12°. C; CN, TU.

1544B   [–] Entertainments for Lent. *For I. W. to be sold by*
        Philip Stephens, 1661. 12°. L; CN.

1545   ——[Anr. ed.] *For John Williams to be sold by Matth.*
        Turner, 1607 [i.e., 1670?]. 8°. C.

1545A   [–] —*For John Dakins, 1661.* 12°. L, O, M.

1546   ——[Anr. ed.] *For John Williams, 1672.* 12°. L; CH, WF.

1546A   ——[Anr. ed.] *For John Williams, to be sold by R. Moore,*
        1682. 12°. WF.

1456B   ——[Anr. ed.] *For J. Williams, 1687.* 12°. TU.

1456C   ——[Anr. ed.] —, *to be sold by Math. Turner, 1687.* 12°.
        L; WG.

1547   —The holy court. *By William Bentley, to be sold by John*
        Williams, 1650. fol. L, O, C, LL, NPL; CH, MH, NU, WF, Y.

1548   ——Second edition. *For John Williams, 1663.* fol. RPL,
        SA; BBE, LC, NN, V, Y.

1548A   —Third edition. —, 1663. fol. CT, AU; CN.

1549   ——Third edition. *For J. W. to be sold by Thomas*
        Rookes, 1664. fol. L, C, P, E; TU.

1550   ——Fourth edition. *For John Williams, 1678.* fol. T.C.I
        304. L, O, CS, BR, EN; CLC, CU, MB, TU, Y.

1551   —The holy history. *For W. Crook and Jo. Baker, 1653.*
        4°. P, DT.

1551A   —A short treatise of the church militant. *[Paris], anno,*
        1661. 12°. O, CT; CLC.

1551B   —The unfortunate politique. *For William Sheares, 1653.*
        8°. L; CN.

1551C   [–] A voice from the dead. *Printed, and sold by Richard*
        Janeway, 1681. 4°.* L, O, YM, EN; CH, CN, MBA, NC, WF,
        Y.

1552   **Causton, Peter.** Carmina tria. *Typis J. Richardson, pro-*
        stant venalis apud Thomam Mercer, 1689. 4°.* L, O, LG;
        CLC, MH.

1552A   —Tunbrigalia, 1684. 8°.* L.

1553   ——[Anr. ed.]— *Typis J. Richardson, 1686.* 8°.* L, CSSX;
        LC, MH, Y.

1553A   ——[Anr. ed.] *Aug. 23, 1686.* brs. OC.

1554   ——[Anr. ed.] *For Richard Baldwin, 1688.* 4°.* NN.
        Caution against inconsistency. *[n.p., 1690.] See* Collier,
        Jeremy.
        Caution against sacriledge. 1659. *See* Clarke, Samuel.
        Caution against suretiship. 1688. *See* A., R.

1555   A caution against tumultuous petitions. *[n.p.], 1679.* brs.
        MC.

1556   —[Anr. ed.] colop: *For W. C., 1680.* brs. L, LG, HH; CH,
        CN, MH, WF, Y.

1557   A caution for scolds. *[London], for P. Brooksby, [1685–88].*
        brs. L, HH; MH.
        Caution humbly offer'd. *[n.p., 1698?] See* Penn, William.

1558   A caution to all true English Protestants. *For Richard Jane-*
        way, 1681. fol.* T.C.I 421. L, O, CT, MR, EN; CH, MH,
        MIU, WF, Y.

1559   A caution to Christians. *[London], for W. Thackeray, J.*
        Millet, and A. Milbourn, [1690?]. brs. L.

1560   A cavtion to keepe money. *For G. Lindsey, and are to be*
        sold by F. Coules, I. Wright, and T. Bates, 1642. 4°.* LT,
        OC, DT; LC, Y.

1561 A caution to married couples. *For D. M.*, 1677. 4°.*
      L; Y.

1562 A caution to Protestants not to forsake. [*n.p.*], 1697. 12°.
      L, OC, MC; WF.

1563 Caution to the good people of England. colop: *Printed*,
      1690. brs. L, C, OP, HH; PL, WF.

      Caution to the Parliament. 1653. *See* Ufflet, John.

1563A Cautionary advice to the livery-men of London. [*London*, 1695.] brs. L, LG; RPB.

1564 Cautionary rules for preventing the sickness. *J. Flesher*,
      1665. 4°.* HH.

1564A Cautions humbly offer'd about passing the bill. [*London*,
      1698.] cap., 4°.* L.

1565 The Cavalliers advice to His Maiesty. *Printed at London
      for Thomas Banks*, 1642. 4°.* MADAN 1039. LT, O, EC,
      AN; MH.

1566 The Cavaliers Bible, or a squadron. [*London*], *by Jane Coe*,
      1644. 4°.* LT, O; CN, MH, Y.

1567 The Cavaliers catechisme. *For Thomas Watson*, 1643.
      4°.* LT, A; WF.

1568 —[Anr. ed.] *For Richard Burton*, 1647. 8°.* LT, O, C, HH;
      CH, CLC, MIU.

1569 The Cavalier's complaint. *Printed*, 1660. brs. MC.

1570 —[Anr. ed.] *For N. Butter*, 1660. brs. L, O.

1571 —[Anr. ed.] *For Robert Crofts*, 1661. brs. LT, O; MH.

1572 The Cavaliers diurnall. [*n.p.*, 1647.] cap., 4°.* LT, OC,
      HH; MIU, Y.

1573 The Cavalier's genius. [*London*, 1663?] brs. L, O.

1574 The Cavaliers jubilee. *For William Ley*, 1652. 4°.* LT;
      NN.

1575 The Cavaliers letanie. [*London*], *printed*, 1648. 4°.* LT, O;
      TU, WF, Y.

1576 —[Same title.] *For Robert Crofts*, 1661. brs. LT, MC.

1577 —[Same title.] *For Charles Brome*, 1682. brs. L, O, MC,
      HH, EN; CH, MH, NU, TU, Y.

1578 The Cavaliers new common-prayer booke vnclasp't.
      Printed at York, by Stephen Buckley, 1644. *And re-
      printed at London by G.B.*, 1644. 4°.* MADAN 1678.
      LT; MB, MH, NGT, Y.

      Cavaliers thanks-giving. 1661. *See* H., T.

1579 [**Cavalli, Stefano.**] A short account of the life and death
      of Pope Alexander the VII. *For Moses Pitt*, 1667. 4°.*
      L, O, CT, HH, EN; CLC, CN, RPJ, TU, WF.

1580 **Cave, John.** Christian tranquility. *For R. Chiswell*, 1685.
      4°.* T.C.II 134. C, LCL, OCC, CT; MH, Y.

1581 —Daphnis. A pastoral elegy. *Oxford, by Leonard Lichfield,
      for the author*, 1685. brs. O.

1582 —The duty and benefit of submission. *For Richard Chis-
      well*, 1682. 4°.* L, O; CLC, MHL, WF.

1583 —The gospel preached to the Romans. *By J. D. for Rich.
      Chiswell*, 1681. 8°. L, O, CS, LSC; CLC, NPT.

1584 —King David's deliverance. *For Richard Chiswell*, 1683.
      4°. T.C.II 41. L, O; CLC, MHL, WF.

1585 [–] A sermon preached in a country-audience . . .
      January 30. *For Richard Chiswell*, 1679. 4°.* T.C.I 368.
      L, O, CS, WCA, OC; CH, TSM, WF, Y.

1586 —A sermon preached . . . July 31. 1679. *By M. Clark,
      for Richard Chiswel*, 1679. 4°.* T.C.I 368. NU, WF.

1586A **Cave, William.** Antiquitates apostolicæ. *By R. Norton
      for R. Royston*, 1675. fol. HH; CLC, OC, MH, NN.

1587 —[Anr. ed.] *For R. Royston*, 1676. fol. T.C.I 224. L, OC,
      CK, OME, EN; CH, TSM.

1587A —[Anr. ed.] *By R. Norton for R. Royston*, 1676. fol.
      CS, CT; CLC, CU, NGT, TU.

1588 —Third edition. —, 1677. fol. T.C.I 314. L, OC, CCO,
      CE, ES; CLC, IU, NPT, WF.

1588A —Fourth edition. —, 1678. fol. NU.

1589 —Fifth edition. *By M. Flesher, for R. Royston*, 1684.
      fol. L, O, CPE, OM, DT; BN, CSU, MH, NU, WF, Y.

1590 —Apostolici: or, the history. *By A. C. for Richard Chis-
      wel*, 1677. fol. T.C.I 252. L, O, C, E, DT; CH, MH, NU,
      WF, Y.

1591 —Second edition. *By J. R. for Richard Chiswell*, 1682.
      2v. fol. T.C.I 513. L, CCA, CCH, CM, BR; BN, CLC, NC, NU,
      WSC, Y.

1592 —Third edition. *By B. W. for Richard Chiswell*, 1687.
      fol. T.C.II 184. L, OB, NPL, E, DT; CLC, CU, MH, NU, WF, Y.

1593 —Chartophylax ecclesiasticus. *Impensis Richard Chiswell*,
      1685. 8°. L, O, C, EN, DT; CH, CN, NU, WF, Y.

1594 [–] A discourse concerning the unity of the Catholick
      church. *For B. Tooke, and F. Gardner*, 1684. 4°. T.C.II
      67. L, O, C, EN, DT; BN, CH, MH, NU, TU, WF, Y.

1595 —A dissertation concerning the government of the
      ancient church. *For R. Chiswel*, 1683. 8°. T.C.I 506.
      L, C, OM, ENC, DT; CH, CU, NU, WF, Y.

5196 —Ecclesiastici. *By J. R. for Richard Chiswel*, 1683. fol.
      T.C.I 506. L, O, CT, LL, DT; CH, CN, MH, NU, PL, Y.

1597 —Wilhelm: Cave . . . Epistola apologetica. *Impensis Sam.
      Smith et Benj. Walford*, 1700. 8°. T.C.III 199. L, O, C, CT,
      DT; BN, NC.

1598 —Primitive Christianity. *By J. M. for Richard Chiswell*,
      1673. 8°. T.C.I 116. L, O, CT, ENC, DT; CH, CU, MBC,
      NU, Y.

1599 — —Second edition. —, 1675. 8°. T.C.I 191. L, O, CPE,
      BR, E; CLC, MH, WF, Y.

1600 — —Third edition. *For Richard Chiswell*, 1676. 8°. T.C.I
      261. L, O, CS, EC, EN, DT; BN, CLC, MB, MH, TU, Y.

1601 — —Fourth edition. *By J. H. for R. Chiswel*, 1682. 8°.
      T.C.I 513. L, O, C, OM, ENC; CLC, CN, NPT, PBI, TU, Y.

1601A — —Fifth edition. *For R. Chiswell*, 1698. 8°. T.C.III 45.
      CLC.

1602 —Scriptorum ecclesiasticorum historia literaria. *Typis
      T. H., impensis Richardi Chiswell*, 1688-98. 2v. fol.
      T.C.II 254. L, O, C, E, DT; BN, CU, MH, PL, WF, Y.

1603 [–] A serious exhortation with some important advices.
      By T. Moore, & J. Ashburne, for Fincham Gardiner,
      1683. 4°.* T.C.II 26. L, O, C, GU, DT; CH, CN, MH, NU,
      WF, Y.

1604 [–] —[Anr. ed.] *For T. Basset; B. Tooke; and F. Gardiner*,
      1684. 4°.* C, OC; MH, NU, TU, Y.

1605 —A sermon preached before the king . . . January xxiij.
      1675/6. *By W. Godbid for Richard Chiswell*, 1676. 4°.*
      T.C.I 226. L, O, C, DT; CLC, MH, NU, PL, WF, Y.

1606 —A sermon preached before . . . the lord mayor . . . fifth of November 1680. *By M. White, for R. Chiswel*, 1680. 4°.* T.C.I 413. L, O, C, CS, BAMB; CH, MH, NU, WF, Y.

1607 —A sermon preached . . . January 18th. 1684/5. *For Richard Chiswel*, 1685. 4°.* T.C.II 110. L, O, C, LCL, DT; CH, CN, NU, WF, Y.

1608 —Tabulæ ecclesiasticæ. colop: *Typis J. D. impensis Richardi Chiswell*, 1674. fol.* T.C.I 155. L, O, EN.
Caveat against drunkenness. 1676. *See* Phelpes, Charles.
Caveat against flattery. 1689. *See* Stephens, Edward.

1608A A caveat against generall indemenity. [*London*, 1659.] brs. MH.
Caveat against sedvcers. 1664. *See* Standfast. Richard.

1609 A caveat enter'd by divers eminent citizens. 1682. fol. DT.

1610 A caveat for cut-purses. [*London*], *for W. Gilbertson*, [1663?]. brs. L.

1611 A caveat for knaves. [*London*], *printed*, 1648. 4°.* LT; CH, CN, Y.

1612 A caveat, for my countreymen in generall. [*n.p.*, 1659.] brs. LS; MH.

1613 A caveate for sherriffs. *Printed*, 1655. 4°.* LT; NC.

1614 A caveat for sinners. 1683. brs. O.
Caveat for the Protestant clergy. [*n.p.*], 1671. *See* E., Y.

1614A A caveat from a treacherous pattern. [*London?* 1674.] brs. HH.
Caveat or warning. 1683. *See* B., R.
Caveat to conventiclers. 1670. *See* P., J.

1614B A caveat to Protestants. *For R. Bentley*, 1689. 8°. T.C.II 256. CLC.
Caveat to the Cavaliers. 1661. *See* L'Estrange, *Sir* Roger.

1615 A caveat to the city of London. colop: *Printed*, 1689. brs. L, O, LG; CH, PL, WF, Y.

1616 A caveat to the three kingdomes. 1696. 4°. O.

1617 A caveat to those that shall resolve, whether right or wrong, to destroy J[ohn] L[ilburne]. [*n.p.*, 1653.] cap., 4°.* LT, CT.

1618 [**Cavendish, George.**] The life and death of Thomas Woolsey. *For Dorman Newman*, 1667. 8°. L, O, CCA, EC, EN; CH, CN, MH, TU, HC.

1619 [–] The negotiations of Thomas Woolsey. *For William Sheeres*, 1641. 4°. LT, O, CT, MR, EN; BN, CH, MH, TU, WCL, Y.

1619A [–] —[Anr. ed.] *For the good of the common-wealth*, [1650.] 4°. L, MH, NU, WF.
Cavendish, Margaret. *See* Newcastle, Margaret Cavendish, *duchess of*.
Cavendish, William. *See* Newcastle, William Cavendish, *duke of*.

1620 Caveto cavetate: being an answer. [*London*, 1695.] brs. LC.

1621 **C[awdrey], D[aniel].** The account audited. *By Ralph Wood, for M. Wright*, 1658. 8°. LT, OC, E; CSB, MM, NU.

1622 Entry cancelled.

1623 —Bovving towards the altar. *For J. Rothwel*, 1661. 4°.* L, O, C, CP, HH; CU, NU, PL, TU, WF.

1624 —Church-reformation promoted. *By W. Wilson, for John Wright*, 1657. 8°. L, LCL, CP, E, AU; NU.

1625 [–] The depths of Satan discovered. *For John Wright*, 1649. 8°.* LT, O, LCL; CH, CN, IU, LC.

1626 —Diatribe triplex: or a threefold exercitation. *For John Wright*, 1654. 8°. L, O, C, CP, ENC; CH, MH, NU, WF, Y.

1627 —Family reformation promoted. *By T. C. for John Wright*, 1656. 8°. O; CLC, NU.

1628 —The good man a publick good. *By Tho. Harper, for Charles Greene, and P. W.*, 1643 [4]. 4°.* LT, O, C, E, DT; CH, MH, NU, TU, WF, Y.

1629 —The inconsistencie of the independent way. *By A. Miller for Christopher Meredth* [*sic*], 1651. 4°. LT, O, LCL, E, DT; MH, NPT, NU, RPJ, WF, Y.

1630 —Independencie a great schism. *By J. S. for John Wright*, 1657. 8°. L, O, C, CP, E; CH, NPT, NU, WF, Y.

1631 —Independency further proved to be a schism. *For John Wright*, 1658. 8°. L, O, C, ENC; NU, WF, Y.

1632 —A late great shipwrack of faith. *For Joseph Cranford*, 1655. 4°.* LSC, LW, OC; NU.

1633 —Sabbatum redivivum. 1642. 4°. LW.
1633A — —[Anr. ed.] 1643. 4°. NPT.
1634 — —[Anr. ed.] *By Robert White for Thomas Vnderhill*, 1645-58. 4°. LT, O, C, ENC, DT; CH, MH, NU, WF, Y.

1635 — —Second part. *By Thomas Maxey, for Samuel Gellibrand, and Thomas Underhill*, 1652. 4°. LT, C, LCL, NPL, E; CH, MH, NU, WCL, Y.

1635A —Selfe-examination required. *By J. Y. for Thomas Walkley*, 1646. 8°. OC.

1635B — —Second edition. *For Thomas Walkley*, 1648. 8°. CLC.

1636 —A sober answer, to a serious question. *For Christopher Meredith*, 1652. 4°.* LT, O, CT, E, GU; CH, MH, NPT, NU, WF, Y.

1637 —Superstitio svperstes: or, the reliques of superstition. *For P. W.*, 1641. 4°. LT, O, C, EN, DT; CN, MH, NU, WF, Y.

1637A — —[Anr. ed.] *For Peter Whalley of Northampton*, 1641. 4°. OC.

1637B [–] —[Anr. ed.] *By A. M. for I. M.*, 1644. 4°. CN.

1638 —Three sermons. *By R. Y. for Phil. Nevill*, 1641. 4°. O, C, LCL, LW, OC; NU, Y.

1639 — —[Anr. ed.] *By R. Y. for Ph. Nevill, and are to be sold by Peter Whaley*, 1641. 4°. OC; NU.

1640 [–] Vindiciæ clavivm: or, a vindication of the keyes. *By T. H. for Peter Whaley*, 1645. 4°. LT, O, CM, E, DT; CH, MH, NU, WF, Y.

1641 —Vindiciæ vindicarum, or a further manifestation. *By A. M. for Christopher Meredith*, 1651. 4°.* SA; NU, WF.

1642 — —[Anr. ed.] [*n.p.*], 1657. 4°.* LCL.

1643 [**Cawdrey, Zachary.**] A brief and methodical catechism. *For the author*, 1664. 12°. ECS.

1644 [–] A calm answer to a bitter invective. *For Joseph Pool*, 1683. 4°.* CLC, NU.

1645 —The certainty of salvation. *For Peter Gillworth in Newcastle in Staffs. and James Thurston, in Nantwich*, 1684. 4°.* L, O, HH; CH, MH, WF, Y.

1645A —The Christians prize. *For J. Leigh*, 1680. 4°. P.

1646 —A discourse of patronage. *For John Leigh, and Thomas Cockerel*, 1675. 4°.* L, O, CE, LL, EN; CH, CN, NC, WF, Y.

1647 — —[Anr. ed. "by Z.C."] —, 1675. 4°.* T.C.I 206. L, O; NU.

1647A — —[Anr. ed.] *For John Leigh*, 1675. 4°.* OC.

1648 [–] A preparation for martyrdom. *For Tho. Parkhurst*, 1681. 4°.* T.C.I 484. L, O, CT, LW, OC; CH, NU, Y.

1649 [**Cawley, John.**] The case of founders kinsmen. *For J. Whitlock*, [1695?]. 4°.* T.C.II 540. L, O, CS, WCA, MR; CH, CLC, WF. Y.

1650 —The nature and kinds of simony discussed. *For R. Baldwin*, 1689. 4°.* L, O, C, WCA, EN; CH, MH, NU, WF, Y.

1651 **Cawley, William.** The laws of Q. Elizabeth. *For J. Wright, and R. Chiswell*, 1680. fol. T.C.I 405. L, O, C, LL, MC; BN, CH, CU, LC, MHL, NCL, YL.

1652 **Cawton, Thomas.** Balaam's wish: a sermon. 1670. 12°. LCL.

1653 [–] The life and death of that holy and reverend man of God, Mr. Thomas Cawton. *For Tho. Basset and R. Hall*, 1662. 8°. L, O, LCL, LG; CH, NC, NPT, NU, Y.

1653A **Cebes.** The tablet of. *Cambridge, for John Pindar*, 1699. 12°. L, C, CS; CLC, MH, MU.

1654 Cedrus Britanica [sic] et laurus regia . . . A poetical hexameron. *Printed*, 1660. 4°.* WF.

Celeusma, seu clamor. 1679. *See* Jenkyn, William.

1654A Celia's answer to Amintor's lamentation. [*London*], *for Philip Brooksby* [1670]. brs. O.

1655 Celias answer to the lover's complaint. [*London*], *for Charles Barnet*, [c. 1694]. brs. L, HH.

1656 Celia's complaint. [*London*], *for Charles Passenger*, [1670–82]. brs. L, HH; MH.

1656A Celia's kind answer. [*London*], *for F. Coles, T. Vere, J. Wright, J. Clarke, W. Thackeray, & T. Passenger*, [1680?] brs. MH.

1657 Celia's triumph. [*London*], *for P. Brooksby*, [1678]. brs. L, HH; MH.

1658 Celinda's last gasp. [*London*], *for J. Deacon*, [1680]. brs. L, HH; MH.

1659 **Cellier, Elizabeth.** Maddam Celliers answer to the Popes letter. colop: *By D. Mallet*, 1680. cap., fol.* O, LG; MH, NU, WF.

1660 —The ladies answer to that busiebody. *Printed*, 1670. brs. MH.

1660A —Mistriss Celliers lamentation. colop: *For S. J.*, 1681. fol.* L; CH, MH, WF, Y.

1661 —Malice defeated. *For Elizabeth Cellier*, 1680. fol.* L, O, C, MR, DT; CH, CN, MH, NU, WF, Y.

1662 —The matchless rogue. *For Elizabeth Cellier*, 1680. fol.* O, LCL, LG, LC, NU, WF, Y.

1663 [–] To Dr. — an answer to his queries. [*London*, 1688.] cap., 4°.* L, O, LCS, LG; MM, NU, PU, WF.

1663A [–] A true copy of a letter of consolation. colop: *For W. Johnson*, 1681. brs. O; CH, MH, Y.

1663B **Celsus, Julius.** De vita et rebus gestis. *Apud Sam. Smith & Benj. Walford*, 1697. 8°. O, OC, CCA, CSSX.

1664 **Censorinus.** De die natali. *Cantabrigiæ, ex officina Joh. Hayes, impensis Tho. Dawson, jun.*, 1695. 8°. L, O, C, EN, DT; BN, CH, CN, MH, TU, WF, Y.

Censvra cleri. 1660. *See* Barnard, John.

1665 Censvra symboli apostolorvm. [n.p., 1643.] cap., 4°.* LT.

1666 The censure and declaration of the General Assembly of the clergy of France. *Printed and sold by J. Nutt*, 1700. fol.* MH, Y.

1667 Entry cancelled.

Censvre of the rota. On Mr. Driden's Conquest of Granada. Oxford, 1673. *See* Leigh, Richard.

Censure of the rota, upon Mr. Milton's book. 1660. *See* Harrington, James.

1668 Entry cancelled.

A censure of three scandalous pamphlets. *See* Young, Samuel., 1699.

Censure upon certaine passages. Oxford, 1670. *See* Stubbe, Henry.

Censure upon Lilly's grammar. 1684. *See* G., R.

1669 The censures of the church reviewed. *For George Eversden*, 1659. 4°. LT, CT, LCL, E; NGT, NU.

1670 **Cent, Nehemiah.** A word to London's provinciall assembly. *For the author*, 1650. 4°. LT, C, LG, DT; MH, NC, NPT, NU.

1671 [**Centlivre, Mrs. Susannah.**] The perjur'd husband. *For Bennet Banbury*, 1700. 4°.* L, O, LVD, LVF, EN; CH, CN, LC, MH, TU, WCL, Y.

Century of observations. 1686. *See* Guidott, Thomas.

1672 A century of sacred disticks. Oxford, 1685. 8°. O.

Century of select hymns. 1659. *See* Barton, William.

Century of the names. 1663. *See* Worcester, Edward Somerset, *marquis*.

Cerbyd jechydwriaeth. 1657. *See* Powell, Thomas.

1672A [**Cerdan, Jean Paul de., comte.**] The Emperour and the empire betray'd. *For R. Bentley and M. Magnes*, 1681. 12.° T.C.I 430. O, EN; CN, CU.

1672B [–] —[Anr. ed.] *For B. M.*, 1681. 12.° L, OC, WCA; CH, CM, MIU, PU, WF.

1672C [–] —[Anr. ed.] —, 1682. 12.° L, CT, SP; CLC, Y.

1673 —Europe a slave. *For W. D.*, 1681. 12.° T.C.I 444. L, O, CS, ĠU, GK; CH, CLC, WF, Y.

1673A [–] —Second edition. —, 1681. 12.° OC.

1674 [–] —Second edition. *For R. Reynolds*, 1683. 8°. L; CLC.

1675 The ceremonies us'd, for the healing of them that be diseased with the kings evil. *By Henry Hills*, 1686, 8°.* L, O, CT, LWL, YM; CH, NIC, TU, WF, Y.

1676 The ceremonies, form of prayer, and services used in Westminster-Abby at the coronation of King James the First. *Printed and are to be sold by Randal Taylor*, 1685. fol.* T.C.II 129. L, O, OP; CH, CN, MB, MIU, WF, Y.

1677 Entry cancelled.

1678 [**Ceriziers, René de**] Innocency acknowledg'd. *At Garnt: by Iohn van den Kerchoue*, 1645. 8°. L; CN.

1679 —The innocent lady. *By T. Mabb for W. Lee*, 1654. 8°. O; CLC, Y.

1680 — —Second edition. *For William Lee*, 1674. 8°. T.C.I 165. L, CE; CLC, IU, MH, Y.

1681' —The innocent lord. *By S. G. for Charles Adams, 1655.* 8°. LT, C; CH, MH.

1682 —The triumphant lady. *For Ga. Bedell and Thos. Collins, 1656.* 8°. LT, O; CH, CN, MH, WCL, WF.

1683 Certain acts and declarations made by the Ecclesiasticall Congregation . . . at Clonmacnoise. *Printed at Cork the 25 of February 1649, and reprinted at Dublin by W. B.* 4°.* DIX 84, LC, Y.

1683A —[Anr. ed.] *Kilkinney, printed 1649. Reprinted at London by Robert Ibbitson.* 4°.* LT, C, LFEA.

1684 Certaine additionall reasons . . . by the ministers of London. *For Giles Calvert, 1645.* 4°.* LT, O, OC, HH, DT; CH, CN, MH, NU, WF, Y.

Certaine affirmations. 1641. *See* W., I.

1685 Certaine and true news from Somerst-shire. *Printed at London for I. Vnderwood, 1642. October 15.* 4°.* LT, EC, BR; MH.

1686 A certaine and true relation of a great and glorious victory. *For Nicholas Iones,* [1642]. 4°.* LT, LFEA.

1686A A certain and true relation of the heavenly enjoyment. [*London*], *printed 1680.* 4°.* LF; MH, PH.

1687 Certain annotations upon some texts of scripture. *By R. N., 1647.* brs. LT, O.

Certain assayes propounded. 1652. *See* D., S.

Certain briefe observations. [*n.p.*], 1644. *See* Robinson, Henry.

1687A Certain briefe treatises. *Oxford, by Leonard Lichfield, 1641.* 4°. MADAN 992. L, O, C, E, DT; CH, CN, NU, WF, Y.

Certain cases of conscience. 1683. *See* Scott, John.

1688 Certain considerable and most materiall cases of conscience. [*Oxford, by L. Lichfield*], 1645. cap., 4°.* MADAN 1729. LT, O, EC, P; CH, CN, Y.

1689 Certain considerations and cautions agreed upon by the ministers. *For Luke Fawne, 1646.* 4°.* CLC, NU.

1690 —[Anr. ed.] *By T. R. and E. M. for Ralph Smith, 1646.* 4°.* LT, O, CM, LW, HH; CH, MH, NU, WF, Y.

1690A —[Anr. ed.] *Underhill, 1646.* 4°.* LG.

1691 Certain considerations: being the legitimate issue. *Printed, 1660.* 4°.* LT, O; CH, MH, NN, Y.

1692 Certain considerations proposed. [*n.p.*, 1659.] brs. O; MH.

1693 Certain considerations relating to the Royal African company. [*London*], *printed, 1680.* 4°.* L, O, LUG; CLC, CN, MH, NC, WF, Y.

1694 Certaine considerations shewing the imminent danger of this city. [*n.p.*, 1645.] cap., 4°.* LT, O, CS; CN, MH.

1695 Certain considerations tending to promote peace . . . amongst Protestants. *For Thomas Parkhurst, 1674.* 4°.* T.C.I 171. L, O, C, P, DT; CH, NU, TU, WF, Y.

1696 —[Anr. ed.] *For Tho. Parkhurst, 1679.* 4°.* L, O, CS, CT; MH, NU.

1696A Certaine considerations to dis-swade. *For Ralph Smith,* [1643.]. 4°.* LT, O, HH, YM, D; CH, MH, NU, TU, WF, Y.

1697 Certaine considerations touching the present factions. *Printed, 1648.* 4°.* LT, O, C, HH, YM; MH, NU, WF, Y.

Certain considerations vpon the dvties. Oxford, 1642. *See* Spelman, *Sir* John.

1698 Certaine considerations wherein the prelates doe acknowledge that they stand by . . . King and Parliament. [*London, 1642?*] cap., 4°.* LT, O, OC; CH, MH, MIU.

1699 Certain desires for the settlement and improving of ministers meanes. *For G. E., 1646.* 4°.* LT, LW, DT; CH, NU, WF, Y.

1700 Certain directions for the sowing, planting and transplanting of tabaco. [*n.p.*, 165–?] 4°.* R.

Certain disputations. 1658. *See* Baxter, Richard.

1700A Certain disquisitions and considerations representing to the conscience. *Oxford, by Leonard Lichfield, 1644.* 4°. MADAN 1608. LT, O, C, CT, DC; CH, MH, NU, WF, Y.

1700B Certain elegies upon the death of Peter Whalley. 1657. 8°.* LT; WF.

Certaine grievances. [*n.p.*], 1641. *See* Hughes, Lewis.

1701 Certaine inducements to well minded people. [*London, 1643?*] 4°.* L; CU, RPJ.

Certain information from Devon. [*London*], 1642. *See* M., T.

Certaine intelligence from Yorke. 1642. *See* Ford, Philip.

1702 Certain letters, evidencing the Kings stedfastness. *By Thomas Newcomb for Gabriel Bedell, and Thomas Collins, 1660.* 4°.* LT, O, CT, EN, DT; CH, MH, NU, WF, Y.

Certain letters written. [*n.p.*], 1654. *See* Capel, Arthur, *of Hedham, baron.*

Certain material and useful considerations. 1680. *See* Mathew, John.

1703 Certain materiall considerations touching the differences of the present times. *Printed, 1642*[3]. 4°.* LT, OC, CT, HH, DT; CH, CN, MH, NU, WF, Y.

1704 Certain meditations upon justification. *For Elizabeth Andrews,* [1664?] brs. L.

1704A —[Anr. ed.] *By J. Astwood, 1683.* brs. MH.

1705 —[Anr. ed.] —, *1684.* brs. L.

1706 Certaine modest observations and considerations of the true Protestants. *For Iohn Thomas, 1641.* 4°.* LT, O, HH, E; CH, CLC, MH, NU, Y.

1707 Certaine motives, provocations and reasons to encite. [*n.p.*, 1643.] brs. LT.

1708 Certain necessary directions, as well for the cure of the plague. *By John Bill and Christopher Barker, 1665.* 4°.* L, O, C, MR, E; CH, MH, NAM, NC, JF.

1709 —[Anr. ed.] [*Oxford*], *reprinted by W. Hall for R. Davis, 1665.* 4°.* MADAN 2714. O, LCP, LL, GH; TU.

1710 Certain necessary resolutions of . . . the intended obedience. *For W. M., 1649.* 4°.* O, HH; CH.

1711 Certain news of Lambert's being taken. 1660. brs. L.

Certain observations concerning the office. 1651. *See* Brackley, Thomas Egerton, *viscount.*

1712 Certaine observations on that letter written to the two Houses from the army. [*London*], *printed, 1647.* 4°.* LT, O, SP; BN, CH, MH, NU, Y.

1713 Certaine observations tovching the two great offices of the . . . High-Stewardship. *For L. Chapman; Octob. 17, 1642.* 4°.* LT, LG, OC, CT, EN; CH, MBP, MHL, WF, Y.

Certaine observations upon some texts. [*n.p.*], 1648. *See* M., T.

1714   Certain observations vpon the New League. *Bristoll, for Richard Harsell,* 1643[4]. 4°. L, O, CT, HH, YM; CH, MH, NN, WF, Y.

1715   Certaine observations upon the tryall of Lieut. Col. John Lilbvrne. [*n.p.,* 1649.] cap., 4°.* MH, NU, WF.

1716   Certaine observations upon the two contrary covenants. *Oxford, by Leonard Lichfield,* 1643. 4°.* MADAN 1426. L, O, EC, E; CH, CU, MH, NU, WF.

1717   Certaine orders meete to be observed. *By R. C. for Michael Sparke, senior,* 1642. 4°.* LT; CH, MIU, NN, Y.

1718   Certain orders thought meet to be put in execution . . . plague. *Imprinted at London, by Robert Barker and by the assigns of John Bill,* 1641. brs. STEELE 1890. LT, O, LPR; WSG, Y.

1719   —[Anr. ed.] *By Richard Cotes,* 1646. brs. STEELE 1891. LT, O.

1720   Certaine papers concerning the Earl of Lindsey his fennes. [*London,* 1649.] cap., 4°.* L; CN, MH.

1721   Certain papers from Scotland, or the last proceedings. *For Laurence Chapman, March 1, 1647*[8]. 4°.* LT, O, LFEA; CH, MH, WF, Y.

     Certain papers which is the word of the Lord. [*n.p.,* 1655.] *See* Tayler, Christopher.

1722   Certain particvlars, further tending to satisfie the tender consciences. *By Robert White,* 1651. 4°.* LT; CLC.

1723   Certaine petitions presented by the lord maior, and commonalty of the citie of London. *For George Badger,* 1641. 4°.* LT, LG, OC, CCL, EC; CN, CSS, WF, Y.

     Certaine plaine and easie demonstrations. 1657. *See* Shaw, John.

1724   Certain positions concerning the fundamentals of Christianity. *For Richard Woodnothe,* 1657. 4°.* HH, YM; NU, WF, Y.

     Certain prayers and graces. 1687. *See* Crowley, Robert.

1725   Entry cancelled.

1726   Certaine prophesies presented before the Kings Maiesty by the scholers of Trinity Colledge, in . . . Cambridge. *Printed at London for T. B.,* 1642. 4°.* LT, C.

     Certaine proposals for regulating. [*n.p.,* 1652.] *See* Shepard, John.

     Certain proposals humbly offered. [*n.p.*], 1674. *See* B., J.

1727   Certain proposals humbly offered by the bayliff of . . . Cricklade. *For Robert Clavell,* 1680. brs. Y.

     Certain-proposals humbly presented. 1653. *See* Vilvain, Robert.

1728   Certain proposals of divers attorneys of the court of common-pleas. *By W. Lee and D. Pateman,* 1650. 4°.* LT, O, C, LL, DT; CLC, CU, MHL, NCL, TU, WF.

1729   Certain proposals of divers clerks and attorneys of the court of common pleas. *For J. Starkey,* 1661. 4°.* LL, SP; MHL, YL.

     Certain propositions, by which. 1694. *See* Fowler, Edward.

1730   Certaine propositions offered to the consideration of the honourable Houses of Parliament. [*Oxford*], *printed,* 1642. 4°.* MADAN 1125. LT, O, CT, HH, DT; CH, WF, Y.

1731   —[Anr. ed.] *Printed,* 1642. 4°.* MADAN 1125*. O; MH, NN, WF.

1732   Certain propositions relating to the Scots plantation. colop: *Glasgow, printed,* 1700. fol. brs. O, HH, EN; MIU, RPJ.

     Certain propositions sent. 1651. *See* Bill, Edward.

1733   Certain propositions tending to the reformation of the parish-congregations. *For William Frankling, in Norwich,* 1655. 4°.* LT, O, OC, EN; NC, NU, WF.

1734   Certaine propositions, whereby the distressed Protestants of Ireland. *For Joseph Hunscott, April 19, 1642.* 4°.* LT, O, CT, HH, DT; CH, LC, MH, Y.

1734A   Certain quæries and anti-quæries, concerning the Quakers. *Printed,* 1653. 4°.* MH, PH.

1735   Certain qveres, and the resolutions of the trayned-bonds [sic] . . . of London. [*Oxford,* 1643.] brs. MADAN 1449n. LT, LG, CH, WF.

     Certain queries answered. 1667. *See* B., E.

1736   Certaine qveres concerning the Booke of common prayer. *Printed,* 1643. *April the 1.* 4°.* LT, E; CH, NU, Y.

     Certaine queres concerning the lawfulness. 1647. *See* Buckler, Edward.

1737   Certain quaeres for the publike good. *For Francis Leach,* 1647. 4°.* LT; MH, MIU, WF.

1738   Certain qvaeres humbly presented in way of petition. *For Giles Calvert,* 1648[9]. 4°.* LT; CLC, Y.

     Certain queries humbly proposed. 1658. *See* N., S.

1739   Certain queries lovingly propounded to Mr. William Prynne. [*London*], *printed,* 1647. 4°.* LT, O, CCA, LL; CH, MH, NU, WF, Y.

1740   Certain queres, not vnfitting to be read. *Oxford, by Leonard Lichfield,* 1643. 4°.* MADAN 1449. LT, O; CH, CN, MH, WF, Y.

1741   Certaine queries of some tender conscienced Christians. [*London*], *printed,* 1641. 4°.* LT, O, C, LL, HH; CH, CN, MH, NU, WF, Y.

1742   Certain quaeries offered to the consideration of all serious . . . men. [*n.p.,* 1675.] cap., 8°.* O.

     Certain qveries, or. 1651. *See* T., D.

1743   Certaine quaeres propounded, and sent by the divines of Oxford. *Oxford, by Leonard Lichfield,* 1643. brs. MADAN 1425. O, CJ, OC, EC; CH.

     Certain queries, propounded to the churches. [1650.] *See* Barber, Edward.

1744   Certaine queries propounded to the standing English army. [*n.p.,* 1647.] brs. L, O.

     Certain queries touching. 1647. *See* Aspinwall, William.

1745   Certain queries upon Dr. Pierces sermon. *Printed,* 1663. 4°.* CJ, SP; CH, MH, TU.

1746   Certain qveries vpon the disolving of the late Parliament. *Printed,* 1659. 4°.* LT, OC, HH; CH, CU, MH, NU.

1747   Certain quaeres, which are desired may bee speedily answered. [*n.p.,* 1648.] brs. LT, O; MH.

1748   Certain queries, worthy mature consideration. *Printed,* 1659. 4°.* L, OC; CSS, MH, Y.

     Certain questions propounded. 1646. *See* Richardson, Samuel.

1749   Certaine reasons (by way of reply to some objections
       . . .). [*n.p.*, 1650?] 4°.* O.

1750   Certaine reasons presented to the Kings . . . Majesty
       Feb. 24, 1641[2]. *By R. Olton and G. Dexter for John
       Wright*, 1642. 4°.* LT, O, EC, HH; CH, MH, WF, Y.

1751   Certaine reasons tending to prove the vnlawfulnesse . . .
       of all diocesan episcopacy. [*London*], *printed*, 1641. 4°.*
       L, O, C, E, EN; CH, CN, NU, WF, Y.

1752   —[Anr. ed.] [*Edinburgh, J. Bryson*], 1641. 4°.* ALDIS 994.
       E; CH.
       Certain reasons why tanned leather. 1641. *See* W.,J.
       Certaine reasons why the booke. 1641. *See* W., I.
       Certaine relation of the Earle. 1642. *See* L., W.

1753   A certain rule to find out how many. 1688. brs. O.
       Certain scripture-prophecies. 1650. *See* Penington, Isaac.
       Certaine scrvples and doubts. [*n.p.*, 1645.] *See* Gauden,
       John *bp*.
       Certaine scuples from the army. 1647. *See* P., J.

1754   Certain seasonable considerations. [*n.p.*, 1654.] 4°.* AN;
       CH, CLC.

1755   Certaine seasonable qværies propounded for divers
       parties. *Printed*, 1647. 4°.* LT, MR; CH, MH, TU, WF.

1756   Certain seasonable reflections upon the bill for raising
       the penalty of 500 £. [*London*, 168–?] fol. CH.
       Certaine serious thoughts. 1647. *See* Wyvill, *Sir* Christo-
       pher.
       Certaine sermons or homilies. 1673. *See* Church of
       England.
       Certaine sound. 1665. *See* Billing, Edward.
       Certain things. [*n.p.*], 1665. *See* Raunce, John.

1757–61 Entries cancelled.

1762   Certain uncertain proposals from free-born subjects.
       [*n.p.*, 1647.] cap., 4°.* LT, O; CLC, MH.
       Certain useful tables. 1660. *See* Cuslon, Phinehas.
       Certain verses. 1653. *See* Denham, *Sir* John.

1763   A certain way to prevent Popery in England. *For R. W.*,
       1681. fol.* T.C.I 442. L, O, CT, SP; CH, MH, WF, Y.

1764   The certain way to save England. *For Richard Baldwin*,
       1681. fol.* T.C.I 429. L, O, CCA, LL, HH; CH, MH, TU,
       WF, Y.
       Certainty and causes. 1698. *See* Sheere, *Sir* Henry.

1765   Certamen Brittanicum, Gallico Hispanicum. A true
       relation of a conference holden between Charles
       Stuart. *Printed*, 1659. 4°.* LT, O, C, E, EN; CH, CU, MIU,
       WF, Y.
       Certamen religiosum. [*n.p.*], 1649. *See* Bayly, Thomas.

1766   A certificate from Northampton-shire. *For William
       Sheares*, 1641. 4°.* LT, O, CT, E, DT; CH, MH, NU, WF, Y.

1767   The certificate of the deputy lieutenants for [sic] county
       of Warwick. *By Luke Norton and Iohn Field, for Edward
       Husbands and Iohn Franck: July 11, 1642. 4°.* CJ, BC;
       CH.

1768   Certificate of what hath been done upon the poll-money.
       *Imprinted at London, by Robert Barker and by the assignes
       of John Bill*, 1641. brs. STEELE 1900. LT, LPR, DT.

1769   The certificates of several captains. colop: [*n.p.*], *by John
       Harefinch*, 1685. brs. L.

       Certification of two points. 1646. *See* Bakewell, Thomas.

1770   **Cervantes, Miguel de.** Delight in severall shapes. *For
       William Sheares*, 1654. fol. L; CLC, CN, MH, Y.

1771   —The delightful history of Don Quixot. *For Benj.
       Crayle*, 1689. 12°. T.C.II 287. L.

1772   —The famous history of Don Quixote. *For G. Conyers*,
       1686. 8°. O.

1773   [–] The history of the ever-renowned Knight Don
       Quixote. *By and for W. O. sold by H. Green*, [1695?].
       4°.* L; LC.

1773A [–] The history of the most ingenious Knight Don
       Quixote. *For R. Chiswell, R. Battersby, A. and F.
       Churchill, S. Smith and B. Walford, M. Wotton, and G.
       Conyers*, 1700. 2v. 8°. T.C.III 154. L; CN, LC, MH.

1774   [–] The history of the most renowned Don Quixote. *By
       Thomas Hodgkin and sold by William Whitwood*, 1687.
       fol. T.C.II 198. L, O, C, MC, EN; BN, CN, CSU, LL, MH, Y.

1774A ——[Anr. ed.] *By Tho. Hodgkin, and sold by John New-
       ton*, 1687. fol. T.C.II 234. L, O; CH, CPB, MB, MIU, WF.

1775   —The history of the renown'd Don Quixote. *For Sam.
       Buckley*, 1700. 12°. T.C.III 155. L, O; CH, LC, MH, NN, WF.

1776   [–] The history of the valorous and vvitty-knight-
       errant, Don Quixote. *By Richard Hodgkinsonne, for
       Andrew Crooke*, 1652. fol. L, O, C, LCP, EN; CH, CN, LC,
       WF, Y.

1777   ——[Anr. ed.] *For R. Scot, R. Basset, J. Wright, R. Chis-
       well*, 1675. fol. L, C, OC, OM, OME; CH, MH, PL, WF, Y.

1778   —The much-esteemed history of the ever-famous
       knight Don Quixote. *For N. Boddington*, 1699. 12°.
       T.C.III 171. L; MBP, MH.

1779   —Select novels. *For Charles Brome and Thomas Horne*,
       1694. 8°. T.C.II 510. L; CLC, CN.

1780   Entry cancelled.

1781   —The troublesome and hard adventures in love. *By B.
       Alsop*, 1652. 4°. LT; CH, CN, MH, WF, Y.

1782   **Cespedes y Meneses, Gonsalo de.** The famous history
       of Auristella. *For J. Hindmarsh*, 1683. 12°. T.C.II 43.
       L; CN.

1783   —Gerardo the vnfortunate Spaniard. *By William Bentley,
       and are to be sold by William Shears*, 1653. 8°. LT, O, A;
       CN, CU.

1784   Cethegus's apology for non-appearance upon his con-
       jurer's summons. *For the assigns of Jack Thumb, and
       L. C.*, [1682?] brs. O, EN; CH, MH, Y.

1784A [**Chabbert, John.**] The most humble remonstrances.
       [*London?* 1696.] cap., 4°. CH, WF.

1785   **Chace, Richard.** Catalogus librorum bibliothecarum
       . . . Martii 24. 1683/4. [*London*, 1683/4.] 4°. L, O, OC,
       HH, WCA.

1786   **Chadlicot, Thomas.** A speeche spoken by. *For Tho.
       Banks, August 26.* 1642. 4°.* LT, CT; CLC, CN, MBP, MH,
       Y.

1787   **Chadwell, William.** The marrow of the Scriptures.
       *By G. Dawson, for the author and may be had at her house
       and at Fran. Smiths*, 1659. 8°. NPT.

1788   —A profitable and well grounded concordance. *By G.
       Dawson, for Francis Smith*, 1660. 8°. LT.

1788A ——Second edition. *By S. Dover, and John Price, and by the author*, 1663. 8° LCL; NA.

1788B **Chadwick, Daniel.** A sermon preached . . . to the Society for reformation of manners. *For John Richards in Nottingham*, 1698. 8°. T.C.III 121, L, LW, GU.

1789 **C[hafie], T[homas].** A brief tract on the Fourth Commandment. *For Tho. Parkhurst, and for Jon. Robinson*, 1692. 4°. T.C.II 420. L, O, CT, E, EN; NGT, NU, WF, Y.

1790 ——The seventh-day Sabbath. 1651. 4°. E.

1791 ——[Anr. ed.] *By T. R. and E. M. to be sold by J. B.*, 1652. 4°. LT, O, LW, EN.

1792 ——[Anr. ed.] *By T. R. and E. M. to be sold by John Brown*, 1652. 4°. EN, ENC; CH, NF, NU, Y.
Chain of principles. [*n.p.*, 1692.] *See* Beverley, Thomas.
Chaldaeus anglicanus. 1696. *See* Almanacs: Hobbs, Matthew.

1793 **Chalfont, Richard.** A sermon preached . . . the tenth day of May 1644. *Oxford, by Henry Hall for H. Curteyne*, 1644. 4°.* MADAN 1677. LT, O, LCL, OM, DT; CH, MH, NU, WF, Y.

1794 **Chalkhill, John.** Thealma and Clearchus . . . . friend of Edward Spencer. *For Benj. Tooke*, 1683. 8° CH, CLC, LC, MH, Y.

1795 ——[Anr. ed. "Edmund Spencer"] —, 1683. 8°. T.C.II 29. L, O, LVD, DT, GK; CH, CU, LC, MH, NN, TU, Y.

1796 The challenge sent by a young lady. *Printed and sold by E. Whitlock*, 1697. 12°. L, O, C, LG, LWL; CH, MB, OCI, WF, Y.

1797 A chaleng sent from Prince Rupert. *For Thomas Greene*, 1643. 4°.* LT, O; CH, Y.
Challenge sent to Master E. B. 1641. *See* Wilcock, James.

1798 A challenge to Caleb Pusey. [*New York, William Bradford*, 1693.] cap., 4°.* MWA.

1798A **Challes, Robert.** A new voyage to the East-Indies. *For Daniel Dring*, 1696. 8°. MIU.

1799 **Chalmers, John.** English orthography. *For Joseph Hindmarsh*, 1687. 8°. T.C.II 181. L, AU; Y.

1800 **Chaloner, Richard.** Mr. Challenor his confession and speech. *By Peter Cole*, 1643. 4°.* LT, LG, OC, CT, DT; CH, MH, NU, TU, WF, Y.

1801 **Chaloner, Thomas.** An answer to the Scotch papers. *By Francis Leach*, 1646. 8pp. 4°.* L, C, HH, E, EN; CH, CU, MH, WF.

1802 ——[Anr. ed.] —, 1646. 15pp. 4°.* LT, O, C, EN, DT; LC, MH, NU, WF, Y.

1803 Entry cancelled.

1804 ——A speech made in the House of Commons the 26th . . . October, 1646. [*London*, 1646.] 4°.* OC, HH; CH, Y.

1805 [–] A true and exact relation of the strange finding out of Moses his tombe. *By J. G. for Richard Lowndes*, 1657. 8°.* LT, O, OC, GU, EN; CH, MH.

1806 [–] XII resolves concerning the disposall of the person of the king. *By Iane Coe*, 1646. 4°.* LT, EN, DT; MH, NU, WF, Y.

1807 **Chaloner, William.** The defects of the present constitution of the mint. [*London*, 1693?] brs. L; MH.

1808 ——To the honourable, the knights, citizens, and burgesses, . . . proposals. [*n.p.*, 1695.] fol.* L, LUG; NC, Y.

1809 ——To the honourable the knights, citizens, and burgesses, reasons humbly offered against an act. [*London*, 1695.] brs. L, LUG; NC.
Chamberlain, Hugh. *See* Chamberlen, Hugh.
Chamberlain, Peter. *See* Chamberlen, Peter.

1810 **Chamberlain, Robert,** *accomptant.* The accomptants guide. *For J. Clarke*, 1679. 4°. T.C.I 333. L, O, C; BN.

1811 ——Second edition. —, 1686. 4°. MBA, PU.

1812 ——Chamberlain's arithmetick. *For John Clark*, 1679. 12°. L, O; WF.

1813 ——[Anr. ed.] *For Richard Mount*, 1696. CLC.

1814 **Chamberlain, Robert,** *poet.* Balaams ass cudgeld. *For the author.* 1661. brs. L.

1815 ——Nocturnall lucubrations. Second edition. *By T. F. for the use and benefit of Andrew Pennycuicke*, 1652. 8°. CH.

1815A The chamberlain's tragedy. [*London,* c. 1695.] brs. L.

1815B **Chamberlaine, George.** The remonstrance and declaration of. [*London*, 1653.] cap., fol.* EN.

1816 **Chamberlaine, James,** *Rev.* Catalogus variorum librorum. [*n.p.*], *to be sold at Sturbridge*, 1686. 4°.* L, CS.

1817 **Chamberlaine, Sir James.** A sacred poem. Wherein the birth, miracles, . . . of the most holy Jesus are delineated. *By R. E. for R. Bentley, and M. Magnes*, 1680. 8°. T.C.I 394. L, O, C, LVD, AU; CH, CN, MH, NC, WF, Y.

1817A ——[Anr. ed.] *Printed and sold by Arthur Bettesworth*, 1699. 8°. T.C.III 124. Y.
Chamberlaine, Joseph. A new almanacke. 1647. *See* Almanacs.

1817B **Chamberlaine, T.** A full supply of such . . . secrets. *For Nathaniel Brooks*, 1659. 8°. HC.

1817C **Chamberlayne, Thomas.** The compleat midwifes practice. *For Nathaniel Brooks*, 1656. 8°. LT.

1817D ——Second edition. —, 1659. 8°. LT.

1817E ——Third edition. —, 1663. 8°. L; WSG, HC.

1817F ——Fourth edition. *For Obadiah Blagreve*, 1680. 8°. T.C.I 64. LWL; WF.

1817G ——Fifth edition. *For H. Rhodes, I. Philips, J. Taylor and R. Bentley*, 1698. 8°. L; MIU, WSG, HC.

1817H ——Dr. Chamberlayne's midwives practice. *T. Rooks*, 1665. 12°. GHS; WSG.

1818 [**Chamberlayne, Edward.**] An academy or colledge: wherein young ladies and gentlewomen may . . . be duly instructed. *In the Savoy, by Tho. Newcomb*, 1671. 4°.* L, O; WF, Y.

1819 ——Anglia notitia. *In the Savoy, by T. N. for John Martyn*, 1669. 12°. L, O, C, LG, OC; MH, NC, Y.

1820 ——Second edition. —, 1669. 12°. T.C.I 11. L, O, CM, EN, DT; CH, MBP, NC, Y.

1821 ——Third edition. —, 1669. 12°. T.C.I 23. L, O, C, LG, ES; MH, NC, PBM, Y.

1822 ——Fourth edition. —, 1670. 12°. T.C.I 33. L, O, C, OM, AU; CH, MBP, NC, Y.

1823 ——Fifth edition. —, 1671. 12°. T.C.I 76. L, O, C, LG, CE; CH, CN, MBP, NC, Y.

1824   ——Sixth edition. *In the Savoy, by T. N. for J. Martyn,*
       1672. 12°. L, O, C, LG, CE; CH, MBP, MH, NC, Y.

1825   ——Seventh edition. —, *1673.* 12°. T.C.I 138. L, O, C,
       YM, E; BN, MBP, MH, NC, WF, Y.

1826   ——Eighth edition. —, *1674.* 12°. T.C.I 191. L, O, C, BR,
       ES; CH, LC, MH, NC, Y.

1827   ——Ninth edition. —, *1676.* 12°. T.C.I 240. L, O, C, CK,
       GU; CH, CN, MH, NC, Y.

1828   ——Tenth edition. —, *1677.* 12°. T.C.I 306. L, O, C, ENC,
       ES; CH, CN, CU, NC, Y.

1829   ——Twelfth edition. —, *1679.* 12°. T.C.I 376. L, O, LG,
       LM, BR; CH, CN, MH, NC, Y.

1830   ——Fourteenth edition. *By T. Newcomb for R. Littlebury,*
       R. Scott, and G. Wells, to be sold by S. Tidmarsh, 1682.
       12°. T.C.I 516. L, O, C, LG, DT; CH, CN, LC, MH, NC, Y.

1831   ——Fifteenth edition. *By J. Playford, to be sold by R.*
       Bentley, 1684. 12°. T.C.II 89. L, O, C, LG, EN; BN, CH, CN,
       MH, NC, Y.

1832   ——Fifteenth edition. *For T. Sawbridge, and G. Wells,*
       1684. 12°. CS, OC, EN; CLC, CU, MH, NC, Y.

1833   ——Sixteenth edition. *For R. Chiswel, T. Sawbridge, G.*
       Wells, and R. Bentley; and sold by Matthew Gilliflower,
       and James Partridge, 1687. 12°. T.C.II 203. L, O, C, LG,
       CT; BN, CH, CN, MH, WF, Y.

1834   ——Seventeenth edition. *By T. Hodgkin for R. Scot, and*
       T. Sawbridge, R. Chiswell; to be sold by them and by
       Mat. Gilliflower, James Partridge, and S. Smith, 1692.
       12°. T.C.II 385. L, O, C, LG, DT; CH, CN, LC, MH, Y.

1835   ——Eighteenth edition. *By T. Hodgkin, for R. Scot, R.*
       Chiswell, M. Gillyflower, and G. Sawbridge, 1694. 8°.
       L, O, C, ES, DT; CH, CN, MBP, MH, TU, Y.

1836   ——Nineteenth edition. *By T. Hodgkin, for R. Chiswell,*
       M. Gillyflower, S. Smith and B. Walford, M. Wotton, G.
       Sawbridge, and B. Tooke, 1700. 8°. T.C.III 161. L, O, C,
       EN, AU; CH, CN, MH, NC, Y.

1837   [–] Angliæ notitia, sive. *Oxonii, typis Leon. Lichfield, im-*
       pensis Henric. Clements, 1686. 12°. in sixes. L, O, C, DT;
       CH, MH, NU, WF, Y.

1838   [–] The converted Presbyterian. *For R. Needham, 1668.*
       4°.* O; CH, NU, WF.

1839   [–] Englands wants. *For Jo. Martyn, 1667.* 4°.* L, O, C,
       OC, OM; CN, MH, NP, WF, Y.

1840   [–] —Second edition. —, *1668,* 4°.* L, O, CT, MR, EN;
       CH, LC, MH, WF, Y.

1841   ——[Anr. ed.] *Printed for, and sold by Randal Taylor,*
       1685. 4°.* L, O, C, LIL, YM; CU, LC, MH, NC, WF.

1842   ——[Anr. ed.] *[London], for R. Baldwin, 1689.* 4°.* T.C.II
       338. L, OC; LSS, LC, WF.

1843   —The late warre parallel'd. *For John Starkey, 1660.* 4°.*
       LT, O; CLC, MH, TU, WF, Y.

1844   [–] The present state of England. Part III. and Part IV.
       For William Whitwood, 1683. 12°. T.C.II 30. L, O, CK;
       CN, WF, Y.

1845   [–] The present vvarre parallel'd. *[London], printed, 1647.*
       33pp. 4°.* LT, O, LL, HH, DT; CH, CN, MH, TU, WF, Y.

1846   [–] —[Anr. ed.] *[London], printed, 1647.* 22pp. 4°.* L, SP;
       CH, MH, NU, TU.

1847   —The second part of the present state of England. *In the*
       Savoy, by T. N. for John Martyn, 1671. T.C.I 66. 12°.
       L, O, DT; BN, CH, NC.

1848   ——Second edition. —, *1671.* 12°. L; MBA, NC, NU, Y.

1849   ——Third edition. *In the Savoy, by T. N. for J. Martyn,*
       1671. 12°. L, O; CH, MBP, MH, NP, Y.

1850   ——Fourth edition. —, *1673.* 12°. O; MBP, MH, NC.

1851   ——Fifth edition. —, *1674.* 12°. L, O, BR, ES; CH, LC,
       MH, NC, Y.

1852   ——Sixth edition. —, *1676.* 12°. L, O, CK, CS; CH, CN,
       MH, NC, Y.

1853   ——Seventh edition. —, *1677.* 12°. L, O, ENC, ES; CH,
       CN, MH, NC, Y.

1854   ——Ninth edition. —, *1679.* 12°. L, O, OC, BR; CH, CN,
       MH, NC, Y.

1855   ——Eleventh edition. *By T. N. for R. Littlebury, R.*
       Scott, and G. Wells. To be sold by Sam. Tidmarsh, 1682.
       12°. L, O, CS, DT; CH, CN, LC, MH, NC, Y.

1856   ——Twelfth edition. *For T. Sawbridge, and G. Wells,*
       1684. 12°. L, O, LL, EN; BN, CH, CN, MBP, MH, NC.

1857   ——Thirteenth edition. *By Thomas Hodgkin, 1687.* 12°.
       L, BR; CH, CN, MH, NC, WF, Y.

1858   ——Seventeenth edition. *By Tho. Hodgkin, 1691.* 12°.
       L, O, OC; CH, CN, LC, NC, Y.

1859   [**Chamberlayne, John.**] The natural history of coffee,
       chocolate, thee. *For Christopher Wilkinson, 1682.* 4°.*
       T.C.I 495. L, O, C, EN, DT; CH, MH, RPJ, WF, Y.

1860   **Chamberlayne, Peregrine Clifford.** Compendium
       geographicum: or, a more exact, . . . introduction.
       For William Crook, 1682. 8°. CPE; CH.

1861   ——Second edition. —, *1685.* 12°. T.C.II 104. L, O, SP;
       CH, CLC, NIC, WF, Y.

1862   **C[hamberlayne], R[ichard].** Lithobolia. *Printed, and*
       are to be sold by E. Whitlock, 1698. 4°.* L, O; CH, LC,
       MH, RPJ.

       Chamberlayne, Thomas. The compleat midwifes
       practice. 1656. *See* Chamberlen, Peter.

1863   [**Chamberlayne, William.**] Englands jubile. colop:
       For Robert Clavell, 1660. cap., 4°.* L.

1864   [–] Eromena: or, the noble stranger. A novel. *For James*
       Norris, 1683. 8°. T.C.II 3. L; CLC, MH, WF.

1865   —Love's victory. *By E. Cotes, and are to be sold by Robert*
       Clavell, 1658. 4°. L, O, LVD, OW, A; CH, CN, LC, TU, Y.

1866   —Pharonnida: a heroick poem. *For Robert Clavell, 1659.*
       8°. T.C.I 291. LT, LVD, CT, EN; CH, LC, MH, NP, Y.

1867   [–] Wits led by the nose. *For William Crook, 1678.* 4°.
       T.C.I 291. L, O, OW; CH, CN, MB, WF, Y.

1868   [–] —[Anr. ed.] *For Langly Curtis, 1678.* 4°. L, O; CH, PU,
       WCL, WF, Y.

1868A [**Chamberlen, Hugh.**] An answer to a libel. colop:
       Printed and sold by T. Sowle, 1696. cap., 4°.* L, LG;
       MH, NC, Y.

1868B [–] A bank-dialogue. colop: *For T. Sowle, 1695.* cap.,
       fol.* L, HH; NC, Y.

1869   —A brief narrative of the nature, & advantages of the
       Land-bank. colop: *By T. Sowle, [1695].* brs. L, LUG,
       HH; NC, Y.

1870 —A collection of some papers writ. *For Benj. Tooke,* 1696. 4°.* L, CT, LUG; MH, NC, PU, WF, Y.

1871 —The constitution of the office of land-credit. colop: *Printed, and are to be sold by T. Sowle,* 1696. cap., fol.* L, LUG; CH, MH, NC, WF, Y.

1871A [–] A description of the office of credit. *For Thomas Rooks,* 1665. 4°.* L, O, C, LG; CLC, LC, MH, NC, Y.

1872 —A few proposals. *Edinburgh, printed,* 1700. 4°.* I, LUG, EN, ES; CH, CU, MH, NC, WF.

1873 —A few queries relating to the practice of physick. *T. Sowle,* 1694. 12°. L, AU; NAM, WSG.

1874 [–] A fund for supplying and preserving our coin. [*n.p.,* 1696?] 4°. L, GH; CH, MH, NC, WF.

1875 —An humble proposal to the honourable the House of Commons. [*London,* 1695.] brs. MC, HH; BN.

1876 —Manuale medicum, or a small treatise. *By J. Gain, for the author,* 1685. 8°. L, O, LPO, LWL.

1877 —Papers, relating to a bank of credit. *Edinburgh, by the heir of Andrew Anderson,* 1693. fol.* ALDIS 3293. EN; CLC, MH, NC, Y.

1878 — —[Anr. ed.] [*Edinburgh,* 1693.] cap., 4°.* L, LG, LUG, ES; MH, WF.

1879 —Dr. Chamberlen's petition. [*London,* 1693.] cap., brs. L, LG, LUG, HH; MH, Y.

1879A [–] Positions supported by their reasons. [*London,* 1696.] cap., fol.* L; CH, MH, NC.

1879B —A proposal and considerations relating. *Printed and sold by T. Sowle,* 1697. 4°.* LUG; MH, NC.

1880 —A proposal by. colop: *By T. Sowle,* 1695. cap., fol.* L, OC, HH; BN, MH, NC, WF.

1881 —Proposal, by. [*Edinburgh,* 1700?] cap., brs. EN; Y.

1882 —The proposal for a general fishery. [*London,* 1694?] fol.* MH, Y.

1883 [–] A proposal for encouraging of persons to subscribe. [*London,* 1691?] fol.* L, LG, HH; CH, NC, Y.

1884 [–] A proposal for erecting a general bank. *By E. Whitlock,* 1695. brs. L, LUG; BN, MH.

1885 [–] A proposal for the better securing of health. [*n.p.,* 1689.] cap., fol.* L.

1885A [–] The proposal for the fishery-stock.   *Sowle,* 1692. brs. LG.

1886 —Dr. Hugh Chamberlen's proposal to make England rich and happy. [*London,* 1690.] cap., brs. MC; NC, Y.

1886A [–] A reply to a pamphlet, called, Observations. *By John Whitlock,* 1694. cap., 4°.* LG.

1887 —A rod for the fool's-back. *John Whitlock,* 1694.4°.* L.

1888 [–] The several articles or parts of the proposal . . . explained. colop: *By T. Sowle,* 1695. cap., fol.* L, OC, HH; MH, NC, WF.

1889 [–] Several matters, relating to the improvement of the trade. [*Edinburgh?* 1700.] 4°.* LUG; MH, NC.

1890 [–] Several objections sometimes made. [*London,* 1682?] cap., 4°.* L, O, LG, EN; CH, MH, NC, WF, Y.

1890A [–] Several particulars of the highest concern. *Edinburgh by the heirs and successors of Andrew Anderson,* 1700. fol.* EN.

1890B —A short abstract of. [*London,* 1696.] brs. LG, OC, HH.

1891 —Some few considerations. *Printed,* 1693. brs. L.

1892 —Some remarks upon a late nameless and scurrilous libel. colop: *Printed and sold by T. Sowle,* 1696. cap., fol.* L, HH, SP; MH.

1892A [–] Some useful reflections. *By T. S.: and are to be sold by Randal Taylor,* 1694. 4°.* L, CM, LUG; MH, WF.

1892B [–] —Second edition. *By T. S.,* 1694. 4°.* LG; NC, Y.

1893 [–] A supplement to the proposal for a general fishery. [*London,* 1695?] brs. L, HH; CH, Y.

1893A —To His Grace William Duke of Hamilton. [*London,* 1693.] fol.* EN; NC.

1893B **Chamberlen, Paul.** Some proposals humbly offer'd. [*London?* 1696.] brs. HH.

1894 [**Chamberlen, Peter.**] The declaration and proclamation of the army of God. *By J. C. for the author,* 1659. 4°.* CH, CN, CSS.

1894A [–] —Second edition. *By J. Clowes for the authour,* 1659. 4°.* LT, C.

1895 —England's choice. *For H. Jones,* 1682. cap., fol.* EN; CH.

1896 —Legislative povver in problemes. *By John Clowes,* 1659. fol.* LT, O, YM; NHC, PL.

1897 [–] A letter to Mr. Braine. [*n.p.,* 1650.] cap., 4°.* O.

1898 —Master Bakewells sea of absurdities. *By J. C. to be sold by Giles Calvert,* 1650. 4°.* L, SP.

1899 —A paper delivered in by Dr. Alston . . . together with an answer. *Printed,* 1648. 4°.* L, O, LW, DT.

1900 —Plus vltra to the Parliament. [*London,*] *10. April, 1651.* brs. LT; CU.

1901 [–] The poore mans advocate. *For Giles Calvert,* [1649]. 4°. LT, O, LW, DT; CH, MH, NC, NU, Y.

1902 Entry cancelled.

1903 [–] A scourge for a denn of thieves. *By J. C. for the author,* 1659. 4°.* LT, O, HH; MIU, WF.

1904 —The sober man's vindication. *By Jane Clowes,* 1662. brs. L.

1904A —A solemn scriptured cell. [*London*] *For William Marshall and John Marshall,* 1696. brs. INU.

1905 —The sons of the East. 1682. brs. EN.

1906 [–] A speech visibly spoken in the presence. *For the author,* [1662]. 4°.* C; CH, NU, TU, WF, Y.

1906A —To all arch-bishops. [*London*], *May 29, 1682.* brs. MH.

1907 —To my beloved friends. [*London,* 1650.] brs. LT.

1908 —To the Honourable House of Commons . . . the humble petition of. [*London,* 1649?] brs. L.

1908A —To the two lights of England; the two universities. [*London*], 1682. brs. MH.

1909 —A vindication of publick artificiall baths. *Printed,* 1648. 4°.* L, O, LM, LW, DT; WSG, WU.

1910 —A voice in Rhama. *By William Bentley: for John Marshall,* 1647. 8°.* LT, LW.

1911 **Chamberlin, Absalom.** The Quaker's prophesie. colop: *For the author,* 1682. brs. L, EN; CH, MH.

1912 **Chambers, Humfry.** Animadversions on Mr. William Dells book. *By R. N. for Sa. Gellibrand,* 1653. 4°. LT, O, OCC, LCL; NU, WF, Y.

1913 —An answer of. *For Thomas Johnson,* 1660. 4°.* LT, O.

1914   —An apology for the ministers. *For Ralph Smith, 1654.* 4°.* LT; CH, MH, NU.

1915   —A divine ballance. *By M.F. for Samuel Man, 1643.* 4°.* LT, O, C, EN, DT; CH, MH, NU, WF, Y.

1916   —A motive to peace and love. *For John Wright, 1649.* 4°.* LT, O, LP, LW, DT; CH, MIU, NU, WF.

1917   Entry cancelled.

1918   [**Chambers, Peter.**] They must needs go, that the devil drives: or, a whip. *For G. Horton, 1652.* 4°.* LT.

1919   **Chambers, Richard.** To the Parliament of the Commonwealth . . . the . . . remonstrance and . . . petition of [*London, 1654.*] brs. L.

1920   —To the right honourable the Lords; . . . the humble petition of. [*London, 1646.*] fol.* LT.

1920A —To the supreem authority of the nation, the Parliament . . . the humble petition of. [*London? 1652.*] brs. LG.

1921   **Chambers, Thomas.** A catalogue of the library of. [*n.p.*], *29 May, 1689.* 4°.* LM.

1922   **Chambray, Roland Fréart, sieur de.** An idea of the perfection of painting. *In the Savoy: for Henry Herringman, 1668.* 8°. T.C.I 3. L, O, C, LVF, EN; CH, CU, MH, TU, WF, Y.

1923   —A parallel of the antient architecture. *By Tho. Roycroft, for John Place, 1664.* fol. L, O, C, E, GK; CH, LC, NC, TU, WF.

1924   —The whole body of antient and modern architecture. *For J.P. sold by C. Wilkinson, T. Dring, C. Harper, R. Tonson, and J. Tonson, 1680.* fol. L, CT, GK; RPJ, WF, Y.

Chambrun, Jacques. *See* Pineton de Chambrun, Jacques.

Chamfield, master, pseud.

1924A **Chamilly, Noel Bouton, marquis de.** Five love-letters. *For R. Wellington and E. Rumbold, 1700.* CN.

1924B **Champant, Sir John.** The case of. [*London? 1690.*] brs. WF.

1924C [**Champs, Etienne Agne de.**] The secret policy of the Iansentsts. *Troyes, by Christian Roman, 1667.* 8°. L; CN.

1925   The chancellor turned tarpaulin; or Jefferies case. [*London, 1689?*] brs. CH, MH, Y.

1925A The chancellors examination. [*London*], *for W. Cademan,* [1689]. brs. C, LG; LC, MH.

Chances. 1682. *See* Fletcher, John.

Chancy, Charles. *See* Chauncy, Charles.

1926   **Chandler, Henry.** An effort against biggotry. *For John Lawrence, 1699.* 4°.* T.C.III 120. L, LW, WCA; PL, WF, Y.

1927   —A sermon preached for the funeral of . . . Nathanael Smith. *For Thomas Cockerill, 1691.* 4°.* O, ENC.

1927A **Chandler, Jacob.** A tender salutation. [*London*], *printed, 1664.* 4°. LF, P, BBN; CLC, PSC.

1927B **Chandler, John.** A narrative plainly shewing that the priests. *For the author, 1659.* 4°.* LF; PH.

1928   —A seasonable word and call. *For the author, 1659.* 4°.* LF; NU, PH.

1929   —A true relation of the unjust proceedings . . . against . . . Quakers. [*London*], *printed, 1662.* 4°.* L, LF, BBN; CH, MH, PH, PSC, WF.

1930   **Chandler, Samuel.** The country's concurrence. *For John Dunton, and John Salusbury, 1691.* 8°. T.C.II 407. L, O, LW.

1931   —A dialogue between a Pædo-Baptist, and an anti-Pædo-Baptist. *For A. Chandler, and sold by A. Baldwin,* 4°.* L; NHC.

1932   —An impartial account of the Portsmouth disputation. *Exon: by Sam. Darker and Sam. Farley, for Philip Bishop, 1699.* 4°. EN; NU.

1933   ——[Anr. ed.] *For John Lawrence, and Abraham Chandler; to be sold by A. Baldwin, 1699.* 8°. C, LW, EN; NHC, NP, NPT, NU, Y.

1933A ——Second edition. *For A. Chandler, 1699.* 8°. CT; WF.

1934   **Chandler, William.** A brief apology. *For Thomas Northcott, 1693.* 4°. L, LF; PSC, WF.

1934A ——Second edition. *By Thomas Northcott, and are to be sold by William Longford, Warminster, 1694.* 8°. L, O, LF; PSC.

1935   ——Third edition. *For Thomas Northcott,* [1700.] 8°. LF; PH.

1935A —Further vindication of the Church of England. *For the author, 1682.* CLC.

Changeable covenant. 1650. *See* May, Thomas.

Changeling. 1668. *See* Middleton, Thomas.

Changling no company. 1660. *See* H., W.

1936   **Channel, Elinor.** A message from God. [*London*], *printed, 1653. Or, as the vulgar think, 1654.* 8°.* LT, OC.

1937   Chaos. Ante mare & terras—as the wanton poet sings. colop: *For Livewel Chapman, 1659.* cap., 4°.* LT; CSS, MH.

1938   Chaos; or, a discourse. *For Livewel Chapman, 1659.* 4°. LT, O; CH, CU, MH, PBL.

1939   Chap. I. Of Magistracy. colop: *For L.C., 1688.* cap., fol.* L, HH; MIU, MM.

1939A —[Anr. ed.] [*London, 1688.*] cap., fol.* CH, PL, Y.

1940   The chaplains petition to the honourable House for redress. colop: *For the use of the petitioners; and sold by Tho. Ranew, 1693.* 4°.* Y.

1940A **Chapman, George.** Comedies, tragi-comedies, & tragædies. *Printed, 1652.* 4°. CH.

1941   —Bussy d'Ambois. Second edition. *By A.N. for Robert Lunne, 1641.* 4°. L, O, CT, LVD, EN; CH, CN, MH, NP, TU, WF, Y.

1942   [–] —[Anr. ed.] *By A.N. for Robert Lunne, and are to be sold . . . ., 1641.* 4°. CH.

1943   [–] —[Anr. ed.] *By T.W. for Robert Lunne, 1646.* 4°. L; CH, MH, WF.

1944   ——[Anr. ed.] *For Joshua Kirton, 1657.* 4°. L, LVD.

1945   [–] —[Anr. ed.] *For R. Bentley, Jo. Hindmarsh, and Abel Roper, 1691.* 4°. T.C.II 360. L, O, C, LVF, EN; CH, CN, MH, NC, TU, WF, Y.

1946   —Caesar and Pompey. Second edition. *Printed, 1652.* 4°. MH, TU.

1947   ——[Anr. ed.] —, *1653.* 4°. LT, LVD, CT.

1948   —Revenge for honour. *Printed, 1654.* 4°. L, O, LG, LVD, EN; CN, MH, WF, Y.

1949 ——[Anr. ed.] *For Richard Marriot,* 1654. 4°. LT, O, EN; CH, MH, WF, Y.

1950 Entry cancelled.

1951 ——Third edition. *For Humphrey Moseley,* 1659. 4°. L, O, LVD, EN; CH, MB, WF.

1952 —The tragedy of Alphonsus emperour of Germany. *For Humphrey Moseley,* 1654. 4°. L, O, LVD, EN; CH, LC, MH, WC, WCL, Y.

1952A ——[Anr. ed.] *Printed,* 1657. 4°. CT; TU.

1953 **Chapman, Henry.** Thermæ redivivæ: the city of Bath described. *For the author, to be sold by Jonathan Edwin,* 1673. 4°.* L, O, C, BR, DT; CH, MH, NAM, WSG.

1954 **Chapman, John.** A sermon preached . . . Sept. 9, 1683. *By H. Hills jun. for Charles Harper,* 1684. 4°.* T.C.II 59. O, WCA; CH, NGT, NU, WF, Y.

      The chapmans and travellers. 1693. *See* Almanacs.

1955 **Chappel, Samuel.** A diamond or rich jewel. *For John Clowes,* 1650[1]. 4°.* LT, ES; CLC, NC, WF, Y.

1956 [**Chappell, William, bp.**] Methodus concionandi. *Ex typographia M. F. sumptibus Timoth. Garthwaite,* 1648. 12°. L, O, CT, E, DT.

1957 —The preacher. *For Edw. Farnham,* 1656. 12°. LT, C, CM, EC; CLC, NU, Y.

1958 —The use of Holy Scripture. *By E. C. for Andrew Crook,* 1653. 8°. O, CE, LW, P, AU.

1959 [**Chappuzeau, Samuel.**] The history of jewels. *By T. N. for Hobart Kemp,* 1671. 8°. T.C.I 81. L, DCH, GU, E; CLC, CN, PL, RPJ, WF.

1960 The character. [*London?* 1680.] brs. L, O, C; CN, MH, TU, Y.

1961 The character and qualifications of an honest loyal merchant. *By Robert Roberts,* 1686. 4°.* L, O, E; CN, MH, WF, Y.

1962 The character of a bad woman. [*London,* 1697]. brs. MH.

1963 The character of a believing Christian. *For Richard Wodenothe,* 1645. 4°.* LT, E; CH.

      Character of a bigotted prince, 1691. *See* Ames, Richard.

1964 The character of a cavaliere. *For W. H.,* 1647. 4°.* LT, O, DT; CH, MIU, Y.

      Character of a Church of England man. 1688. *See* C., W.

1965 The character of a church-papist. colop: *For John Kidgell,* 1681. brs. L, O, LVF; CH, MH, Y.

1966 The character of a church-trimmer. colop: *For W.A.,* 1683. brs. L, O, OC, HH, EN; CH, CN, MH, WF, Y.

1967 The character of a coffee-house. [*London*], printed, 1665. 4°.* L, O.

1968 —[Anr. ed.] *For Jonathan Edwin,* 1673. fol.* L, LL, LVF, CS; CH, MH, TU, WF, Y.

      Character of a compleat physician. [*n.p.,* 1680?] *See* Mee, Dr.

      Character of a country. 1643. *See* Cleveland, John.

1969 The character of a disbanded courtier. colop: *For N. Thompson,* 1681. brs. L, O, EN; CH, CN, MH, TU, Y.

1970 —[Anr. ed.] colop: *For R. J.,* 1682. cap., fol.* L, O, CM, LG; CH, MH, PU, WF, Y.

      Character of a diurnal-maker. 1654. *See* Cleveland, John.

1971 The character of a phanatique. *For Henry Marsh,* 1660. brs. LT. O, LS; CH, MH.

1972 The character of a fanatick. *Printed,* 1675. 4°.* L, O, SC; IU, MH, MIU.

1973 The character of a fanatick in general. colop: *For N. T.,* 1681. cap., fol.* L, O, HH, EN; CH, CN, MH, Y.

      Character of a female cockney. 1656. *See* T., R.

1974 The character of a good man, neither Whig nor Tory. colop: *For Jonathan Robinson,* 1681. brs. L, O, LG, OC, MC; CH, CN, MH, NC, WF, Y.

1974A The character of a good woman. colop: *For R. Baldwin* [1697]. brs. MH.

1975 The character of a Grumbletonian. *Printed and are to be sold by Richard Janeway,* 1689. brs. O, LG, E.

1976 The character of a Jacobite. *For the author,* 1690. 4°.* L, O, C, MR, DT; CH, MH, NU, WF, Y.

1977 The character of a Jesuit. colop: *For J. Newton,* 1681. brs. L, O, LVF; CH, MH, WF.

1978 The character of a leading petitioner. colop: *For W. Davis,* 1681. brs. L, O, LVF; CH, MH.

      Character of a London diurnal. [*n.p.*], 1644. *See* Cleveland, John.

1979 The character of a London scrivener. 1667. 4°.* L; CH, CN.

1979A A character of a loyal statesman . . . Shaftesbury. *W. Downing,* 1678/9. brs. OP.

      Character of a moderate intelligencer. [*n.p.,* 1647.] *See* Cleveland, John.

1980 The character of a modern sham-plotter. colop: *For R. Janeway,* [1681?]. brs. L, LVF; CH, MH, Y.

1981 The character of a modern Whig. colop: *For John Smith,* 1681. brs. L, O, LG, LVF; CH, CN, CU, MH, Y.

1982 The character of a Papist. *Printed,* 1673. 4°.* L, O, OC, CT, DT, TSM.

1983 The character of a pilfering taylor. *Printed,* 1675. 4°.* L, O; MH, WF, Y.

      Character of a Popish successour. 1681. *See* Settle, Elkanah.

      Character of a Popish successor. Part the second. 1681. *See* Phillips, John.

1983A The character of a presbyter. *For John Calvin,* 1660. 4°.* LT, O, HH, E; CH, MH, MIU, NU, Y.

1984 The character of a prince. *Printed, and are to be sold by Randall Taylor,* 1689. 4°.* L, O, EN; CH, CN, MH, Y.

1985 —[Anr. ed.] colop: *Edinburgh, re-printed,* 1689. cap., 4°.* ALDIS 2871. EN; OCN, MH, TU.

1986 The character of a Protestant Jesuite. colop: *For W. Davis,* 1682. brs. L, O; CH, CN, MH.

1987 The character of a Puritan. [*London*], printed, 1643. 4°.* LT, O; CH.

      Character of a quack-astrologer. 1673. *See* S., J.

1988 The character of a quack-doctor. *For Thomas Jones,* 1676. fol.* L, O, LL; MH, WF.

      Character of a quaker. 1671. *See* Austin, Samuel.

      Character of a rebellion. 1681. *See* Nalson.

      Character of a right malignant. [*n.p.,* 1645.] *See* May, Thomas.

1988A The character of a rigid Presbyterian. *Assignes of J. Colwin*, 1661. 4°.* O.

Character of a sham-plotter. [n.p., 1681.] *See* Hickering-ill, Edmund.

1989 The character of a soliciter. *For K. C. I. F.*, 1675. 4°.* L; CN, MH, MM, Y.

Character of a tavern. 1675. *See* Earle, John.

1990 The character of a through-pac'd Tory. *For Joseph Collier*, 1682. 4°.* L, O; CH, NPT, WF, Y.

Character of a time-serving saint. [n.p., 1652.] *See* Lockier, Lionel.

1991 The character of a Tory. colop: *For Thomas Burrel*, 1680. 4°.* NC, TU.

The character of a Tory. 1681. *See* Buckingham, John Sheffield, duke of.

1992 The character of a town-gallant. *For W.L.*, 1675. 4°.* L, O; CLC, MH, TU, WF, Y.

1993 —[Anr. ed.] colop: *For Rowland Reynolds*, 1680. fol.* L, O, DT; CH, CN, MH, Y.

1994 The character of a town-misse. *For W.L.*, 1675. 4°.* L, O, OC; CN, MH, SW, WF, Y.

1995 —[Anr. ed.] colop: *For Rowland Reynolds*, 1680. cap., fol.* L, O, EN; CH, CN, MH, WF.

1995A The character of a trimmer. *For Jo. Hindmarsh*, 1683. brs. L, O, HH; CH, MH, Y.

Character of a trimmer. His opinion. [n.p., 1682.] *See* Halifax, George Savile, marquis of.

1995B The character of a trimmer, neither Whigg nor Tory. colop: *For T. S.*, 1682. brs. O; MH, Y.

1996 The character of a true and false shepherd. [*London*], printed, 1670. 4°.* MH.

1997 The character of a true English Protestant souldier. colop: *By E. W. for J. Gibbs*, 1689. 4°.* L, O; CN.

1998 The character of a true English souldier. *For D. M.*, 1678. 4°.* O, CT; Y.

1999 The character of a true Protestant. colop: *For T. S.*, 1682. brs. O, EN; CH, MIU, Y.

2000 The character of a true-Protestant ghostly father. colop: *For Richard Waite*, 1683. brs. L, O, LL, MC; MBA, Y.

Character of a trvlie vertvous. Paris, 1651. *See* Boate, Arnold.

Character of a turbulent. 1678. *See* Care, Henry.

Character of a weaned Christian. 1675. *See* Smith, Samuel.

2001 The character of a Whig. *Printed*, 1700. 8°. L, C, AU; CH, CN, MH, TU, WF, Y.

2002 The character of a Williamite. *For Richard Baldwin*, 1690. 4°.* T.C.II 339. L, O, C, EN, AU; CH, MH, NU, WF, Y.

2003 The character of an agitator. [*London*], printed, 1647. 4°.* LT, O, OC; CH, TU, WF, Y.

2004 The character of an Anabaptist. *By J. Clowes, for P. C.*, 1660[1]. brs. LT, LS.

2005 A character of an antimalignant. *By F. N. for Robert Bostock*, 1645. 4°.* LT, O, C, EN, DT; CH, MH, MIU, NR, WF.

2006 The character of an Englishman. 1680. fol. L.

2007 —[Anr. ed.][*London*, 1681?] brs. L, O, HH; CH, CN, MH, TU.

2008 The character of an honest and worthy Parliament-man. [1688?] brs. C, HH; CH.

Character of an honest lawyer. 1676. *See* C., H.

Character of an honest man. 1683. *See* A., P.

2009 The character of an ignoramus doctor. colop: *By M. T.*, 1681. brs. L, O, C, LVF, EN; CN, MH, WF, Y.

2010 The character of an ill-court-favourite. [*London*], for T. Davis, 1681. fol.* T.C.I 443. L, O, C, HH, EN; CH, CN, MH, WF, Y.

2011 The character of an informer. *For T. P.*, 1675. 4°.* L, O, SP; CH, CN, Y.

2012 The character of an Irish-man. colop: [*n.p.*], printed, 1689. cap., 4°.* O, C; CH, MH.

2013 The character of an old English Protestant. [*n.p.*, 1670.] brs. O; CH, MH.

2014 The character of an Oxford-incendiary. colop: *For Robert White*, [1645.] cap., 4°.* MADAN 1771. LT, O, C, CJ; CH, CN, MH, WF, Y.

2015 The character of an vnjust judge. colop: *For T, VV.*, 1681. brs. L, O, LG; CH, MH, Y.

Character of Charles II, King of England. 1696. *See* Buckingham, John Sheffield, *duke of*.

Character of Charles the Second, written. 1660. *See* Tuke, *Sir* Samuel.

Character of coffee and coffee-houses. 1661. *See* P., M.

Character of England. 1659. *See* Evelyn, John.

2016 A character of France. *For Nath: Brooke*, 1659. 12°. L, O, OC, GK; CH, CLC, MH, WF.

2017 A character of His most sacred Maiesty, King Charles the II. *For D. Maxwell*, 1660. 8°.* LT; CH, MH.

Character of His Royal Highness William Henry Prince of Orange. 1689. *See* Terry, Edward.

Character of Holland. 1672. *See* Marvell, Andrew.

2018 The character of Italy. *For Nath. Brooke*, 1660. 12°. LT, O, GK; CH, MH, MIU, Y.

2019 A character of London-village. colop: *For J. Allen*, 1684. brs. L, O; CLC, MH.

2020 The character of love, guided. *For R. Bentley*, 1686. 12°. T.C.II 156. L; CLC, WF.

2020A —[Anr. ed.] —, 1692. 12°. L.

2021 The character of Mercurius Politicus. [*n.p.*, 1650.] cap., 4°.* LT, C, CM; CH.

2021A A character of Mr. Blow's book entituled Suadela victrix. [*Edinburgh?* 1696] cap., 4°.* MH.

2022 The character of Popery. [*n.p.*, 1688.] brs. L, OC, HH, EN; CH, CU, MH, TU, Y.

2023 A character of Popery and arbitrary government. [*London*, 1681.] fol.* L, O, C, LG, HH; CN, MH, NU, TU, WF, Y.

Character of Sir Arthur Haslerig. [n.p., 1661.] *See* B., F.

2024 The character of Spain. *For Nath. Brooke*, 1660. 12° LT, O, GK; CLC, MH.

Character of that glorious. 1660. *See* P., W.

2025 The character of the beaux. *Printed*, 1696. 8°.* L; WF.

Character of the late Dr. Samuel Annesley. 1697. *See* Defoe, Daniel.

2025A The character of the late upstart House of Lords. *Printed*, 1659. 4°. OC, BAMB; CLC.

2025B The character of the Lord Baron Gruckle. *Gedruckt veer de copy van Londen, ins Gravenhage, by Jan Adberts,* 1671. 4°.* L; HR, NN.

2026 A character of the nevv Oxford libeller. *By M. S. for H. B.,* 1645. 4°.* MADAN 1728. LT, O, OC; WF.

Character of the Oliverians. 1660. *See* Spelman, Clement.

Character of the Protestants. 1689. *See* Halifax, George Savile, *marquis of.*

2027 The character of the Rump. *Printed,* 1660. 4°.* LT, HH, EN; CH, CU, MH, MIU, WF, Y.

2028 A character of the true blue Protestant poet. colop: *For A. Banks,* 1682. cap., fol.* L, O; CH, MH, MIU, WF, Y.

2029 The character of those two Protestants in masquerade. colop: *For E. Ryddal,* 1681. brs. L, LVF; CLC, MBA, MH, Y.

Character of warre. 1643. *See* Ward, Richard.

2030 The character of William, Prince of Orange. *Tot de Hague, geduckt, door Hans Verdraught,* 1688. brs. LG, MR; CH, TU.

2031 The character of wit's squint-ey'd maid. colop: *For W. Davis,* 1681. brs. L, O; CH, CN, MH, MIU, TU, WF, Y.

2032 The character or ear-mark of Mr. William Prinne. *Printed,* 1659. 4°.* LT, O, LG; MH, MIU, TU, WF, Y.

2033 —Second edition. *Printed,* 1659. 4°.* O, HH; CN, Y.

2034 Character. Sir, in answer to your last. *Tot de Hague, gedruckt dor Hans Verdraght,* 1688. brs. L, O, OC, HH; MH, Y.

Carracters in blood. 1671. *See* Ottee, Robert.

Characters or pourtraicts. 1668. *See* Montpensier, Anne Marie Louise d'Orleans, *duchesse de.*

2035 Entry cancelled.

Characters: or, wit. 1663. *See* Lenton, Francis.

2036 [**Charant, Antoine**]. A letter, in answer to divers curious questions. *By B. G. to be sold by Moses Pitt,* 1671. 8°. L, O, SP; CLC, CN, MIU, WF, Y.

2037 **Charas, Moise.** New experiments upon vipers. *By T. N. for J. Martyn,* 1670. 8°. T.C.I 143. L, O, CE, OC, CK; CH, CLC, LC, Y, HC.

2038 ——[Anr. ed.] *For J. Martyn,* 1673. 8°. L, LCP, LWL, LCS; PAP, MMO, WF, HC.

2039 ——[Anr. ed.] *For Mark Pardoe,* 1677. 8°. L, C.

2040 —The royal pharmacopœa. *For John Starkey and Moses Pitt,* 1678. fol. L, O, C, LCP, AU; MMO, NAM, WF, HC.

2041 **Chardin, Jean.** Journal du voyage du Chevalier Chardin en Perse. Première partie. *Chez Moses Pitt,* 1686. fol. L, OC, CT, DCH; CH, LC, MIU, VC, Y.

2042 —Preface. [*London,* 1686.] brs. OC.

2043 —The travels of . . . into Persia. *For Moses Pitt,* 1686. fol. T.C.II 230. L, O, C, GH, DT; CH, CJC, CN, LC, MH, NC, Y.

2044 ——[Anr. ed.] *For M. P. to be sold by George Monke, and William Ewrey,* 1689. fol. O, EN.

2045 ——[Anr. ed.] *For Christopher Bateman,* 1691. fol. C, LA, LWL, WCA; CLC, MBP, MH, NC, Y.

2046 The charge against the King discharged. [*n.p.*], *printed,* [1649]. 4°.* LT, OC, EN; CH, WF.

2047 The charge and articles of high-treason exhibited against the Earl of Derby. *For George Wharton,* 1651. 4°.* LT.

2048 A charge and impeachment of high-treason against Sir John Geyer. *For Len. Norton,* 1647. 4°.* L, LG, HH; CN, Y.

Charge at the general quarter sessions. 1689. *See* Dayrell, *Sir* Marmaduke.

2049 A charge consisting of severall heads . . . Earl of Lincoln . . . impeached. [*London*], 1647. 4°.* OC, HH; CH, INU, WF.

2050 A charge delivered in the name of the army. *For Laurence Chapman, Iune 18,* 1647. 4°.* LT, O, CT, LL, MR; CH, CN, MH, NU, WF, Y.

2051 The charge given to the committee of . . . Essex. *For Richard Best, October 6,* 1642. 4°.* CH, MH, WF.

2052 The charge of a Tory plot maintain'd. *For N. L. to be sold by Richard Janeway,* 1682. 4°.* L, O, C, CS, HH; CH, CN, MH, NU, WF, Y.

2052A The charge of companies of merchants. [*London?* 169–?] cap., fol.* MH.

2053 The charge of high-treason: delivered . . . against Cap. Rolph. *Printed,* 1648. 4°.* LT, CCA; CH, MU, TU, WF, Y.

2054 A charge of high-treason drawn up by the citizens of Paris. *For G. Horton,* 1652. 4°.* HH; HR.

2055 A charge of high treason exhibited against Oliver Cromwell. [*London,* 1653.] brs. LT, O.

2056 The charge of high treason, murders, oppressions, . . . against the marquess of Argyle. *For Richard Lowndes,* 1661. 4°.* LT, O, C, CT, EN; CH, MH, WF, Y.

2057 A charge of high-treason, prepared by the London-apprentices. *For C. Gustavs,* [1660]. 4°.* LT.

Charge of scandal. 1683. *See* Hesketh, Henry.

Charge of schism continued. 1691. *See* Norris, John.

Charge of schism renewed. 1680. *See* Thomas, Samuel.

Charge of Socinianism. Edenburgh, 1695. *See* Leslie, Charles.

2058 The charge of subduing the Irish-rebellion in 1641. *For R. Clavel and Ch. Brome,* 1689. brs. O; CH, Y.

2059 The charge of the admirals of England. *For Tho. Batcheler,* 1693. brs. MH.

2060 The charge of the army, and covnsel of war, against the king. [*n.p.*], *printed,* 1648. 4°.* LT; CSS.

2061 The charge of the govenours of St. Thomas's Hospital. [*London?* 1700.] brs. L.

2062 Entry cancelled.

2063 The charge voted against Bishop Wren. [*London*], *printed,* 1641. 4°.* CP, CT, HH; MB, MH, WF, Y.

Χαρις και ειρήνη: or. 1662. *See* Gauden, John, *bp.*

Charitable Christian. 1658. *See* Hart, John.

2064 A charitable chvrch warden. *For John Thomas,* 1641. 4°.* LT, O.

2065–6 Entries cancelled.

2067 The charitable Samaritan. *Printed,* 1698. 4°.* L, WCA; MH, PL.

Charity and integrity. 1696. *See* Gregory, Thomas.

2068 The charity and loyalty of some of our clergy. *For Richard Janeway,* 1689. 4°.* L, O, C, LW, CSSX; LC, MIU, NU, Y.

Charity of church-men. 1649. *See* Brooke, Humphrey.

Charity of church-men. 1649. *See* Brooke, Henry.

Charity triumphant. 1655. *See* Gayton, Edmund.

2069   **Charke, Ezekiel.** A pretended voice from Heaven. *For Andrew Kembe,* 1659. 4°. LT, LCL; NU.

CHARLES I.

2070   Reliquiæ sacræ Carolinæ. The vvorkes of that great monarch. *Hague, by Sam: Browne,* [1648]. 8°. ALMACK 19. L, O, C, MR, ENC; CLC, MBC, PBL, WF.

2071   —[Anr. ed.] —, [1649]. 8°. L, DC, D; CH, MB, MBP.

2072   —[Anr. ed.] *Hagve, by Samuell Browne,* 1650. 8°. ALMACK 31. L, O, C, EC, BR; CH, CN, LC, MH, NU, Y.

2073   —[Anr. ed.] *Hague, by Samuell Browne,* 1651. 8°. ALMACK 22. LT, O, C, EN, ENC; CH, MB, TU, WF, Y.

2073A   —[Anr. ed.] —, 1651. ALMACK 49. PL.

2074   —[Anr. ed.] *Hague, by Samuel Browne,* 1657. 24°. AL-MACK 40n. L, C, OC, ELY; MBP, MH, NN, PAP.

2075   Βασιλικη. The works of. *By James Flesher for R. Royston,* 1662. fol. ALMACK 61. L, O, C, EN, DT; BN, CH, CU, MH, WF, Y.

2076   —Second edition. *For Ric. Chiswell,* 1687. fol. ALMACK 64. L, O, C, E, DT; CH, CN, LC, MH, NP.

2076A   The accvsation given by His Maiestie against the Lord VVilmot. *By Francis Leach, August 30,* 1644. 4°.* LT, HH; CH, MH, WF, Y.

2077   An act which His Maiesty hath promised. *R. Ibbitson,* [1648]. STEELE 2797. LT, LG, O; MIU.

2078   The additional propositions of . . . and his Majesties commissioners in Ireland. *For Peter Cole, and W. R., Sept. 22,* 1645. 4°.* LT, O, SP; CH, MH.

2079   An agreement betwixt His Majesty and the inhabitants of the county of Oxford. *Printed at Oxford by Leonard Lichfield.* 1642. 4°.* MADAN 1134. L, O, CJ, CT; CH.

2080   —[Anr. ed.] *At Oxford, Decemb. 21. by Leonard Lichfield,* 1642. 4°.* LT; MIU.

2081   The agreements made between His Maiesty and the gentlemen . . . of Glocester. *Printed at Oxford by Leonard Lichfield, Dec. 29,* 1643. 4°.* MADAN 1505. OCC, OL.

2081A   —[Anr. ed.] *Bristoll, by Robert Barker, and John Bill,* 1643. 4°.* WF.

2082   The agreements made between His Maiesty and the knights, . . . of Berks. *Printed at Oxford by Leonard Lichfield, Oct. 19,* 1643. 4°.* MADAN 1476. O.

2083   The agreements made between His Maiesty and the knights, . . . of Oxford. *Printed at Oxford by Leonard Lichfield, Sept. 30,* 1643. 4°.* MADAN 1458. L, O; CLC, MH, Y.

2084   The agreements made between His Maiesty and the knights, . . . of Southampton. *Printed at Oxford by Leonard Lichfield, March 20,* 1643[/4]. 4°.* MADAN 1559. O.

2085   The agreements made between His Maiesty and the knights, . . . of Wilts. *Printed at Oxford by Leonard Lichfield,* 1643. 4°.* MADAN 1496. O.

2086   The kings Majesties alarum for open war. [*London*], *for Tho. Richards, August 25,* 1642. 4°.* LT, C, CCC, HH; CH, MH, Y.

2087   Entry cancelled.

2088   Another gracious message from. *By J. C. Novemb. 27,* 1647. 4°.* LT, O, DC, HH, DT; CLC, MH, Y.

2089   His Majesties answer, by vvay of declaration to a printed paper. *Printed, May 23,* 1642. 4°. L, O, LCS, SP; CN, MH.

2090   —[Anr. ed.] *By Robert Barker; and by the assignes of John Bill,* 1642. 4°.* LT, O, C, EN, DT; CH, CN, MH, NU, TU, WF, Y.

2090A   —[Anr. ed.] *York,* —, 1642. 4°.* L, CF; MH, WF.

2091   The King's Majesties answer or, foure propositions. *For T. Ryder, Iuly 25,* 1642. 4°.* LT, O; MH, Y.

2092   His Majesties answer to a book, entituled, The declaration, or remonstrance. *By Robert Barker and the assignes of John Bill,* 1642. 4°.* LT, O, CT, MR, DT; CH, CN, MH, TU, WF, Y.

2093   —[Anr. ed.] *York: By Robert Barker, and by the assignes of John Bill,* 1642. 4°. L, CF, CJ, CT, YM; CH, MH.

2094   —[Anr. ed.] *Printed at Yorke, and reprinted at London, for W. G. and N. A.,* 1642. 4°.* L; CSS, MH, TU, WF, Y.

2095   —[Anr. ed.] *Imprinted at Yorke and reprinted at London, for R. Lownes, & H. Tuckey,* 1642. 4°.* L, O, C, LCL, EN; CLC, MH, NC, NU, TU.

2096   —[Anr. ed.] *Cambridge, R. Daniel,* 1642. 4°.* CT.

2097   His Majesties answer to a late petition . . . 16 March 1643. *Oxford, L Lichfield,* 1642[3]. 4°.* STEELE 3, 1785. LT.

2098   —*Edinburgh, by Robert Bryson,* 1643. 4°.* ALDIS 1074. STEELE 3p 1786. L, CT, HH, EN, GU; CH, CLC, MH, NU, Y.

2099   His Majesties answer to a late petition presented. [*London,* 1646?] 4°.* HH.

2100   His Majesties answer to a message sent . . . by the House. *Imprinted at London, by Robert Barker & by the assignes of John Bill,* 1641[2]. brs. STEELE 2055. L, O, C, EC, YM; MH, Y.

2101   —[Anr. ed.] *For John Thomas,* 1641[2]. 4°.* LT; C; CH, CLC, WF, Y.

2102   His Majesties answer to a petition presented . . . at York April 18, 1642. *For R. A.,* 1642. 4°.* O, HH; MH.

2102A   —[Anr. ed.] *For I. T.,* 1642. 4°.* MH.

2103   His Majesties answer to a printed book, entituled, A remonstrance. *By Robert Barker and the assignes of John Bill,* 1642. 4°.* LT, O, C, LL, HH; CH, CN, MH, TU, WF, Y.

2104   —[Anr. ed.] *Printed at York and reprinted at London, John Harrison,* 1642. 4°.* O, LVF, LCL, EN; MBP.

2105   —[Anr. ed.] *Printed at York and reprinted at London for William Ley,* 1642. 4°.* L, O, HH; CLC, MBP, TU, Y.

2106   —[Anr. ed.] *Imprinted at Yorke and reprinted at London, for R. Lownes,* 1642. 4°.* L, O, CS, DC, HH; CN, MH.

2107   —[Anr. ed.] *Printed at Cambridge, by Roger Daniel,* 1642. 4°.* CS, CT, YM; NN, TU.

2108   —[Anr. ed.] *Oxford, by Leonard Lichfield,* 1642. 4°.* MADAN 1006. O, OC, CM, DT; CLC, CSS, NU.

2109   His Majesties answer to a printed paper, intituled, A new declaration. *York: by Robert Barker, and by the assignes of John Bill,* 1642. 4°.* O, C, CF, CT, YM; MH, WF.

2110   His Majesties answer to the bills and propositions. *For John Wright, Jan. 3,* 1647[8]. 4°.* LT, CS, CT, E, DT; CH, MH, NPT, Y.

2111   The Kings ansvver to the Commissioners concerning His Majesties coming from Newcastle. *By J. Coe,* 1647. 4°.* LT, DT; Y.

2112   His Maiesties answer to the declaration and votes of both Houses concerning Hull; sent 4 May, 1642. *For S. E.,* 1642. 4°.* L, O, CT, P, EN; CH, MBP, MH, WF, Y.

2113   His Maiesties answer to the declaration of both Houses . . . concerning the commission of array. of the first of July, 1642. *York, by Robert Barker and by the assignes of John Bill,* 1642. 4°.* L, O, CCL, YM, DT; CH, TU, WF.

2114   —[Anr. ed.] *Printed at York by Robert Barker, and now reprinted at London,* 1642. 4°.* LT, O, C, LCL, HH; CH, CN, MH, WF, Y.

2115   —[Anr. ed.] *Printed at York and reprinted at Oxford,* 1642. 4°.* MADAN 1013. L, O, DT; MH, Y.

2116   —[Anr. ed.] *Cambridge, by Roger Daniel,* 1642. 4°.* LT, O, C, LL, CT; CH, CSS, MH, Y.

2117   The Kings Majesties answer to the declaration of the Lords and Commons . . . With a gracious answer. [London], *Roger Garthwaite,* 1641[/2]. 4°.* HH; MH, Y.

2118   His Maiesties ansvver to the humble petition of the gentlemen, . . . of Chester. *For John Sweeting,* 1642. brs. STEELE 2117. LT, O, LS, HH, YM; MH.

2119   His Maiesties answer to the last message . . . 2 March 1641[2]. *For J. Wright,* [1642]. brs. STEELE 2006. L, O, OC; CN, MH, Y.

2120   Entry cancelled.

2121   His Maiesties ansvver to the XIX propositions. *Oxford, by Leonard Lichfield,* 1642. 4°.* MADAN 1007. O, C, DT; NU, Y.

2122   —[Anr. ed.] *By Robert Barker and the assignes of John Bill,* 1642. 30pp. 4°.* LT, O, C, LVF, DT; CH, CN, MH, TU, WF, Y.

2123   —[Anr. ed.] —, 1642. 14pp. 4°.* O, HH, EN; CLC, MH, Y.

2123A   —[Anr. ed.] *For Math. Walbanke and Lau. Chapman,* 1642. 4°. C, OC.

2124   —[Anr. ed.] *For L. W. and R. C.,* 1642. 4°.* CS, HH; MH, MIU, Y.

2124A   —[Anr. ed.] *Cambridge, by Roger Daniel,* 1642. 4°.* MH, WF.

2125   The Kings Majesties answer to the paper delivered in by the reverend divines. *By E. Griffin, for T. Hewer,* 12 *October,* 1648. LT, O, C, HH, EN; CH, CN, MH, NU, WF. Y.

2126   —[Anr. ed.] *By E. G. for T. H.* 12 *October 1648. Reprinted,* 1660. 4°.* LT, O, OC, HH; CLC, CN, MH, NU, WF, Y.

2127   The King's Majesties answer to the Parlinment's [sic] replication. *For H. Blunon, August 9,* 1642. 4°.* LT, YM; CH, WF, Y.

2128   His Majesties answer to the petition and three votes. *By Robert Barker and the assignes of John Bill,* 1642. 4°.* LT, O, CT, LL, HH; CH, CN, MH, TU, WF, Y.

2129   Entry cancelled.

2130   His Maiesties ansvver to the petition; concerning the disbanding of his gavrd [sic]. *Printed the first of Iune for W. Gaye,* 1642. 4°.* L, O, CJ, HH, DT; CLC, MH, NU, TU, WF, Y.

2131   His Majesties answer to the petition of both Houses . . . 23rd of May, 1642. *First printed at York, and now reprinted at London,* [1642]. 4°.* O, C, HH; MIU, WF, Y.

2131A   —[Anr. ed.] *York, printed, London, reprinted for Charles Greene,* 1642. 4°.* CM, HH; MH, WF.

2131B   —[Anr. ed.] *For S. E.,* 1642. 4°.* EC; MH, PT, WF.

2132   The Kings Maiesties answer to the petition of the House of Commons. *For Iohn Burroughes,* 1642. brs. STEELE 1966. LT, O, LG; MH, WF, Y.

2132A   —[Anr. ed.] *Iohn Thomas,* 1641[2]. 4°.* L.

2133   —[Anr. ed.] *For T. Bates,* 1642. brs. STEELE 1967. L.

2134   —[Anr. ed.] [1642.] brs. STEELE 1968. HH.

2135   —[Anr. ed.] *Printed at London, for F. C. I. W.,* 1642. brs. STEELE 1969. L, O.

2136   His Majesties answer to the petition of the Lords and Commons. *York: by Robert Barker, and by the assignes of John Bill,* 1642. 4°.* CCA, YM, YS.

2137   —[Anr. ed.] *By Robert Barker and by the assignes of John Bill,* 1642. 4°.* LT, O, C, HH, DT; CH, CN, MH, TU, WF, Y.

2137A   —[Anr. ed.] *By B. A. for Robert Wood,* 1642. 4°.* CLC, MH.

2137B   —[Anr. ed.] *Printed,* 1642. 4°.* CT; MH, TU.

2138   His Majesties answer to the petition which accompanied the declaration. *By Robert Barker, and by the assignes of John Bill,* 1641. 4°.* LT, O, CT, LG, DT; CH, MH, NU, TU, WF, Y.

2139   —[Anr. ed.] [1641], *reprinted Edinburgh.* 4°.* ALDIS 995. L, E, EN, CW.

2140   His Majesty's answer to the proposition of the 13th instant. [*n.p.,* 1648.] brs. LS.

2141   The kings answer to the propositions for peace. *By R. A. and I. C.,* 1645. 4°.* LT, O, DT; MH, Y.

2142   His Maiesties answer to the propositions of. *Oxford, by Leonard Lichfield: and now reprinted at London,* 1643. 4°.* MADAN 1299. O; CLC, MH, NU, WF.

2143   The Kings Majesties answer to the propositions presented. *By E. Griffin,* 1647. 4°.* LT, OC, HH; CH, MH, WF, Y.

2144   The Kings Majesties answer to the propositions, propounded concerning. *For B. A. Feb. 12,* 1647. 4°.* LT, MR, DT; NU, Y.

Apophthegmata aurea. 1649. *See title.*

2145   —Arcane impressr, or the casquet-royall. *Printed,* 1660. 16°. CLC.

2146   Articles of agreement already concluded upon, betwixt the Kings Majesty. [*London*], *for G. W.,* 1647. 4°.* LT, O, YM, EN; CU, MH, PT.

2147   Articles of peace and commerce, between . . . Charles . . . and John . . . of Portugal. *By Robert Barker: and assignes of John Bill,* 1642. 4°.* LT, O, OC, DT; CH, CN, MH, TU, WF, Y.

2147A —Articles of peace between Charles . . . John. *For J. Harrison*, 1642. 4°.* MH.

2147B —[Anr. ed.] *By the assignes of John Bill and Christopher Barker*, 1667. 4°.* OC.

2147C ——[Anr. ed.] *By and for H. Seile*, 1642. 4°.* C.

2148 —Articles of the large treaty, concerning the establishing of the peace. [*London*], *for Henry Seile*, 1641. 4°. L, O, C, HH, EN, DT; CH, MH, NU, WF, Y.

2149 Articles or demands made by . . . to the gentry and commonalty of the county of Salop. *For Henry Hvtton, Octob. 12*, 1642. 4°.* LT, OC; MH, Y.

2150 At the court at York. 28 Martii 1642. *York, Barker & assigns of Bill*, 1642. cap., brs. STEELE 2063. L, O.

2150A Aurea dicta: the gracious words of. *Oxford*, 1682. 4°. ALMACK 76. O.

2151 Bibliotheca regia, or, the royal library. *For Henry Seile*, 1659. 8°. ALMACK 76. LT, C, LVF, MR, ENC; CLC, CN, LC, MH, NU, Y.

2152 A briefe abstract of the Kings letters to the Queene. *For Hannah Allen*, 1648. 4°.* LTC; CH, MIU, TU, WF, Y.

2153 By the Kings Maiestie, were accused with seven articles of high treason . . . Ian. 3. 1641. *For Iohn Thomas*, 1641. 4°.* C, CT; CH, CLC, MH, NU, Y.

2153A —[Anr. ed.] *For F. C. & J. W.*, 1641. 4°.* MH, WF.

2153B Carolus Dei gratia Angliæ . . . Hen. com. Huntington. *For John Wright*, 1642. brs. LT, O, EC, HH; Y.

2154 Certaine papers which passed betwixt his Maiestie. *Haghe*, 1649. 4°. SC, E, EN.

2155 Certaine qveries, proposed by. *For John Giles, Aprill 27. 1647.* 4°.* LT, O, DT; CSS, MH, WF.

Certamen religiosum: or, a conference between his late Majestie. 1651. *See* Bayly, Thomas.

2156 The Kings Majesties charge sent to all the judges of England. *For Laurence Blaiklock, July 26*, 1642. 4°.* LT, O, CT, LG, HH; CH, MBP, MH, TU, Y.

2157 A collection of declarations, treaties. *By James Flesher for R. Royston*, 1662. fol. CCC, CJ; LC.

2158 A collection of His Maiesties most gracious messages for peace. *Oxford, by Leonard Lichfield*, 1645[/6]. 4°.* MADAN 1835. L, O, HH; MH, WF.

2159 A collection of severall speeches, messages, and answers. *By Richard Badger, for E. H. and I. B.*, 1642. 4°. LT, O, CT; CLC, MH, TU, WF, Y.

2160 His Majestie's commission granted to Mr. George Le Strange, for the betraying Lyn to the enemy. *For R. Mason*, 1644. 4°.* LT, O; CH, Y.

2161 Entry cancelled.

2162 His Majesties concessions to the bill of abolition of archbishops. [*London*], *printed*, 1648. 4°.* LT, C, LVF, HH, DT; CH, CN, NU, TSM, Y.

2163 The copies of the kings letter, and generall order. *For F. L., June 19*, 1646. 4°.* LT, DT.

2163A A copy of a letter that His Majesty left. *In's Gravenshage, by Samuel Broun*, 1647. 4°.* WF.

2164 The copy of a warrant from. *For Ralph Rounthwait, June 5*, 1642. brs. STEELE 2205. LT, O, CT, LS, OP.

2165 A copy of an intercepted letter from His Majesty, to the Lords. [*n.p.*, 1648.] brs. LT, LS; MH, Y.

2166 A copie of certaine letters, which manifest. [*London*], *printed*, 1643[4]. 4°.* LT, C, HH; Y.

2167 A copy of His Maiestys most graciovs letter to the lord maior . . . 26 December 1643. [*London*, 1647.] brs. STEELE 2520. L.

2168 A copy of the commission of array: . . . to the Marquesse of Hertford. *August 24. 1642. By L. N. and I. F. for E. Husbands and J. Franck*, 4°.* LT, O, CPE, HH, DT; CH, CN, MH, WF, Y.

2168A —[Anr. ed.] *For E. Husbands and I. Franck, August 24, 1642.* 4°.* L, CJ, YM, BR; CH, CLC, MH, TU, WF.

2169 A copie of the commission sent from. *For Richard Best*, 1643. 4°.* LT, O, LG; CLC, MH, MHL, WF, Y.

2170 A copie of the Kings commission granted to Sir Nicholas Crispe. *For R. Austin*, 1645. 4°. LT, SP, EN; MH, WF, Y.

2171 A copie of the Kings message sent by the Duke of Lenox. *By Iane Coe*, 1644. 4°.* MADAN 1688. LT, O, BR; MH, Y.

2172 Entry cancelled.

A copie of verses, said to be composed by His Majestie. [1648.] *See* Browne, Alexander.

2173 Regiæ Majestatis declaratio de causa Palatina. *Ex typographio regio*, 1641. 4°.* C.

2174 —[Anr. ed.] *Edinburgi, R. & J. Bryson*, 1641. 4°.*. ALDIS 998. EN, FSF.

2175 Declaratio serenissimi potentissimique . . . ultra-marinis Protestantium ecclesiis transmissa. *Oxoniæ, excudebat Leonardus Lichfield*, 1644. 8°.* MADAN 1672. LT, O, CM, GU, DT; CH.

2176 His Majesties declaration and command. [*London*], *J. Norton, July 6*, 1642. 4°.* O, HH.

2177 His Maiesties declaration and finall resolution. *Printed at Oxford by Leonard Lichfield*, 1643. 4°.* MADAN 1176. LT, O, CT, HH; CH, MH, Y.

2178 His Majesties declaration and manifestation to all his souldiers. *For William Gay*, 1642. 4°.* LT, O, LL, OC; CH, MH, WF, Y.

2178A —[Anr. ed.] [*London*], *for W. Gay*, 1642. 4°.* MH.

2179 —[Anr. ed.] [*Oxford, L. Lichfield*], 1642. 4°.* MADAN 1060. O, OC.

2180 His Majesties declaration and message, to the Marquis of Ormond. *Printed*, 1648. 4°.* LT, C; MH.

2181 The Kings Majesties declaration and profession. *Cambridge: for Nathaniel Smith*, 1647. 4°.* LT, C; MH.

2182 His Majesties declaration and propositions propounded . . . Decemb. 19. 1642. *Decemb. 22 for I. H. and William Anderton*, 1642. 4°.* LT; CSS, WF, Y.

2183 His Majesties declaration and propositions: to the major, . . . of Coventry. *For T. West, Octob. 22*, 1642. 4°.* LT; Y.

2184 His Majesties declaration and remonstrance. *For W. Fielding*, 1648. 4°.* LT; CH, CLC, MH.

2185 His Majesties declaration and speech concerning his comming from VVindsor to VVhite-hall. *For W. Fielding*, 1648. 4°. LT, SP, DT; MH.

2186 His Majesties declaration and speech to the Parliaments Commissioners. *For R. Smith*, 1648. 4°. LT, DT; MH.

2187 The Kings declaration, and the Princes honour. *For J. Harrison, June 4, 1642.* 4°.* LL, OC, YM, SP; MH, WF.

2188 The Kings declaration at Newcastle. *For Nathaniel Smith*, 1647. 4°.* LT, O, HH, DT; MH, WF.

2189 A declaration by . . . Novemb. 11, 1647. *By Robert Ibbitson, 1647.* 4°.* O, C, HH; CLC, PT, WF.

2190 His Majestie's declaration concerning leavies. *By Robert Barker and by the assignes of John Bill, 1642.* 13pp. 4°.* LT, O, C, AN, DT; CH, MH, TU, WF, Y.

2191 —[Anr. ed.] —, 1642. 6pp. 4°.* O, CT, LVF, HH; CSS, MIU, WF.

2192 —[Anr. ed.] *For M. Walbancke and L. Chapman*, 1642. 4°.* O, CT, HH; CH.

2193 —[Anr. ed.] *Reprinted at Oxford, by Leonard Lichfield, 1642.* 4°. MADAN 1012. L, O; CLC, NU, Y.

      His Majesty's declaration concerning the charge of the army, 1649. *See* Willis, John.

2194 The Kings Majesties declaration concerning the high and honourable court of Parliament. *For R. Wood*, 1647. 4°.* LT, YM; MH, TU.

2195 His Majesties declaration concerning the proclamation of the army. *[n.p.], for John Gilbert*, 1648. 4°.* LT; CH, NU.

2196 His Majesties declaration concerning the treaty. *Printed*, 1648. 5pp. 4°.* LT, O, CJ, ENC, DT; CH, CN, MH, TU, WF, Y.

2197 —[Anr. ed.] *[n.p.]*, printed, 1648. 7pp. 4°.* LT, CT, SP; CH, CN.

2198 His Maiesties declaration delivered at Newport. *For H. Becke*, 1648. 4°.* LT; MH, Y.

2199 His Majesties declaration, directed to all persons of what degree. *By Jane Coe*, 1644. 4°.* LT, BR, SP, AN; WF.

2200 The Kings declaration for a pacification. *For R. R., Nov. 5, 1642.* 4°.* HH; CSS, MH, Y.

2201 A declaration for peace from the Kings most Excellent Majesty. *Imprinted at London, for R Smith*, 1648. 4°.* LT; CH.

2202 The Kings Majesties declaration for peace, to all his subjects. *Septemb. 28. for Joseph Hunter*, 1648. 4°.* LT, HH; MH.

2203 His Majesties declaration, for the relief of . . . Derby. *York, Robert Barker and the assigns of John Bill, 1642.* brs. STEELE 2248. LS.

2204 His Majesties declaration from Carisbrooke Castle. *Printed at Edenburgh by Evan Tyler, re-printed at London for Robert Wood*, 1648. 4°.* LT, E; CH, MH, Y.

2205 —[Anr. ed.] *Imprinted at London for G. VVharton*, 1648. 4°.* LT, CT, DT; MH, Y.

2206 His Majesties declaration in answer to a declaration. *York, Robert Barker and the assignes of John Bill, 1642.* 4°.* CJ, HH.

2207 —[Anr. ed.] *Printed at Oxford by Leonard Lichfield*, 1642. 4°.* MADAN 1022. O, HH, DT; CSS, Y.

2208 —[Anr. ed.] *Cambridge, by Roger Daniel*, 1642. 4°.* LT, O, C, LL, DT; CH, CN, MH, TU, WF.

2208A —[Anr. ed.] *[London]*, printed, 1642. 4°.* SP; MH, NN.

2209 His Maiesties declaration in defence of the true Protestant religion. *First printed at Oxford by Leonard Lichfield, and since re-printed at London, June 16. 1643.* 4°.* MADAN 1384. LT, O, OC, DT; NU, WF, Y.

2210 His Majesties declaration in the Isle of Wight. *[London]*, 1648. 4°.* LT, AN; MH.

2210A A declaration made by . . . concerning His Majesties going away. *By Robert Ibbitson*, 1647. 4°.* MH.

2211 His Majesties declaration, made the 13. of June, 1642. *Printed at York, and re-printed at London by Robert Young; [1642].* 4°.* LT, O, CJ, E, DT; CH, MH, TU, WF, Y.

2212 His Majesties declaration Novemb. 17. from the Isle of Wight. *For M W.*, 1648. 4°.* LT, DT; WF.

2213 A declaration of His Maiesties royall pleasvre, expressed. *First printed at Oxford, by Leonard Lichfield and now reprinted at London for John Rivers, [1642].* 4°.* MADAN 1139. LT, O, CT, SP; CH, MA, WF, Y.

2214 A declaration of the Kings Majesties most gracious messages for peace. *Oxford, by Leonard Lichfield, 1645. Reprinted at London, for Matthew Wallbank, February 2, 1645[/6].* 4°.* MADAN 1835n. LT, O, CJ, LG, DT; CH, MH, TU, WF, Y.

2215 A declaration of the Kings most Excellent Majestie. Wherein is manifested. *[London]*, printed, 1648. 4°.* LT, DT; CN, MH, WF, Y.

2216 A declaration of the Kings resolution. *Printed at London for Iohn Ashton*, 1642. 4°.* LT, LG.

2217 His Majesties declaration on Wednesday last. Delivered to the commissioners. *For Robert Wilkinson*, 1648. 4°.* LT; WF.

2218 His Majesties declaration sent to Lieuteuant [sic] Generall Cromwel. *For G. Calvin*, 1648. 4°.* LT; Y.

2219 The Kings Maiesties declaration sent to the Speaker of the House of Peeres. *For Iohn Giles*, 1647. 4°.* L, DT; CH.

2220–1 Entries cancelled.

2222 His Maiesties declaration to all his loving subjects, after his late victory. *Printed at Oxford by Leonard Lichfield*, 1642. 4°.* MADAN 1057. L, O, CT, BR, DT; CN, MH.

2223 —[Anr. ed.] *Printed at Oxford, by Leonard Lichfield, 1642. And now reprinted at London*, 4°.* MADAN 1058. LT, O, OC, HH, EN; CSS, WF.

2224 —[Anr. ed.] *Oxford [London]*, 1642. 4°.* MADAN 1059. O, EC; Y.

2225 His Majesties declaration to all his loving subjects, after his victories. *At Oxford, July 30, by Leonard Lichfield, 1643.* 4°.* MADAN 1429. L, O, C, CT, BR; CH, CLC, MH, TU, WF.

2226 —[Anr. ed.] *Printed at Oxford, July 30. And reprinted at York by Stephen Bulkley*, 1643. 4°.* O, YM.

2227 —[Anr. ed.] *Shrewsbury, by Robert Barker: and by the assignes of John Bill*, 1643. 4°.* C; PT, WF.

2228 A declaration to all His Majesties loving subjects . . . concerning a king. *Imprinted at York by Tho: Broad, and reprinted at London*, 1648. 4°.* Y.

2229   His Majesties declaration to all his loving subjects, con-
        cerning his gracious inclination. [London], printed,
        August 27, 1647. 4°.* LT, O, OC, EC, HH; CLC, MH, WF, Y.

2229A   His Majesties declaration to all his loving subjects con-
        cerning the proceedings. Cambridge by Roger Daniel,
        1642. WF.

2230   His Maiesties declaration to all his loving subjects, con-
        cerning the remonstrance of the army. For Richard
        Brysons, 1648. 4°. LT, O, SP, DT; MH.

2231   His Maiesties declaration to all his loving subjects, in
        answer to a declaration . . . 3. Iune. 1643. Shrewsbury,
        by Robert Barker: and by the assignes of John Bill, 1643.
        4°. C.

2232   —[Anr. ed.] Printed at Oxford, by Leonard Lichfield, 1643.
        48pp. 4°. MADAN 1374. LT, O, DT; CH, MH, NU, WF, Y.

2233   —[Anr. ed.] —, 1643. 30pp. 4°.* MADAN 1375. L, O, CT,
        EC, P; CH, MH, WF, Y.

2233A   —[Anr. ed.] York, Bulkley, 1643. 4°.* LSE.

2234   His Majesties declaration to all his loving subjects, in
        answer to the petition. For R.B., 1643. 4°.* CLC, MH, Y.

2234A   His Majesties declaration to all his loving subjects in his
        kingdom. Hage, by Samuel Broun, 1649. 4°.* ALMACK
        72. LT; CH.

2235   His Majesties declaration to all his loving subjects; in his
        three kingdomes . . . Octob. 3. 1648. For R. Rishton,
        1648. 4°.* LT; NU.

2236   His Maiesties declaration to all his loving subiects in . . .
        Cornwall. Printed at Oxford by Leonard Lichfield, 1643.
        brs. MADAN 1446. STEELE 2476. LT, O, CJ, P; CH, WF.

2237   His Majestie's declaration to all his loving subjects,
        occasioned by a false and scandalous imputation. By
        Robert Barker and the assignes of John Bill, 1642. 4°.* LT,
        O, C, EN, DT; CH, MH, NU, TU, WF, Y.

2238   —[Anr. ed.] York, by Robert Barker and the assignes of Iohn
        Bill, 1642. 4°.* C, YM; CH, Y.

2238A   —[Anr. ed.] Cambridge, by Roger Daniel, 1642. 4°.* L,
        CT; Y.

2239   —[Anr. ed.] T.Bach, 1642. 4°.* O, C, HH; MH.

2240   —[Anr. ed.] For N. Allen, 1642. 4°.* LG; CSS, MIU.

2241   His Majesties declaration to all his loving subjects, of
        August 12, 1642. Printed at Cambridge, by Roger Daniel,
        1642. 4°.* LT, O, C, LVF, DT; CH, CU, MH, NU, TU, WF, Y.

2242   —[Anr. ed.] Cambridge, by N.N., 1642. 4°.* L, O, CK,
        HH, EN; CH, CN, LC, TU, WF.

2243   —[Anr. ed.] [Cambridge], by N.N., 1642. 4°.* LC, MH.

2244   The King's Majesties declaration to all his loving sub-
        jects of . . . Scotland. With an act. Shrewsbury, by
        Robert Barker: and by the assigns of John Bill, 1643. 4°.*
        C.

2245   —[Anr. ed.] Edinburgh, by Evan Tyler, 1643. 4°. ALDIS
        1075. LT, CT, HH, E, EN; WF, Y.

2245A   —[Anr. ed.] Oxford, by Leonard Lichfield, 1643. 4°.*
        MADAN 1376. CLC, MH.

2246   His Majesties declaration to all his loving subjects, of his
        true intentions. Oxford by Leonard Lichfield, 1642. 4°.*
        MADAN 1082. LT, O, CT, E, DT; CH, MH, TU, WF, Y.

2247   —[Anr. ed.] Robert Barker and by the assignes of John Bill,
        1642. 4°.* HH.

2248   His Majesties declaration to all his loving subjects, of the
        12 of August. 1642. York: by Robert Barker. and by the
        assigns of John Bill, 1642. 4°. C. CT. YM, D; CH, CSS, TU,
        WF.

2249   —[Anr. ed.] Printed at Yorke and reprinted at Oxford, 1642.
        4°. MADAN 1025. L, O, C, EC, DT; CN.

2249A   —His Majesties declaration to all his loving subjects. Pub-
        lished. Printed, 1641. 4°.* L, CF, CCH, CT, SP; CH, MH,
        TU, WF, Y.

2249B   —[Anr. ed.] Cambridge, R. Daniel, 1642. 4°.* CT.

2250   —[Anr. ed.] By Robert Barker, and the assignes of J. Bill,
        1641 [2]. 6 pp. 4°.* L, O, HH; CH, NC.

2251   —[Anr. ed.] By Robert Barker, and by the assignes of John
        Bill, 1641[2] 25pp. 4°.* LT, O, C, LL, HH; CH, NU, TU,
        WF, Y.

2252   —[Anr. ed.] Edinburgh, 1641. 4°.* E.

2253   —[Anr. ed.] Edinburgh, [R.Bryson], 1642. 4°.* ALDIS
        1035. EN.

2254   His Majesties declaration to all his loving subjects; shew-
        ing his true intentions. By Robert Barker; and by the
        assignes of John Bill, 1642. 4°.* LT, O; CH, MH, NU, TU,
        WF, Y.

2255   His Maiesties declaration to all his loving subjects, upon
        occasion of a late printed paper. Oxford by Leonard
        Lichfield, 1642. 4°.* MADAN 1065. LT, O, CT, HH, DT;
        CH, LC, MH, TU, WF, Y.

2256   —Second edition. —, 1642. 4°.* MADAN 1066. LT, O, CM,
        LG, HH; CH, MH, WF.

2256A   —Third edition. —, 1642. 4°.* MADAN 1067. MH, WF.

2257   His Maiesties declaration to all his loving subjects, upon
        occasion of his late messages. Oxford, by Leonard Lich-
        field, 1642. 4°.* MADAN 1045. LT, OC, BR; CH, MH, NU,
        TU, Y.

2257A   —[Anr. ed.] By His Majesties special command, 1642.
        4°.* CH.

2258   —[Anr. ed.] For Iohn Benson, and Iohn Vavasor, 1642.
        4°.* AN; CLC, MH.

2259   —[Anr. ed.] Oxford by Leonard Lichfield, 1642. 4°.*
        MADAN 1046. LT, O, CT, EN, DT; CH, CN, MH, WF, Y.

2260   His Majesties declaration to all his loving subjects upon
        occasion of the aforesaid ordinance. [London? 1642.]
        cap., 4°.* HH, AN; MH.

2261   His Majesties declaration to all his loving subjects upon
        occasion of the late ordinance and declaration. Printed
        at Oxford by Leonard Lichfield, Decemb. 8, 1642. 4°.*
        MADAN 1108. O, OW, BR, DT; CSS, CU, MH, TU, WF, Y.

2262   His Majesties declaration to all his loving subjects, upon
        occasion of the ordinance and declaration. Printed at
        Oxford, December 8. by Leonard Lichfield, 1642. 4°.*
        MADAN 1110. L, OC, HH, EN; MH, TU, Y.

2263   His Maiesties declaration to all his subjects of his king-
        dom of Scotland. Printed at Oxford, by Leonard Lichfield,
        Jan. 9, 1643. 4°.* MADAN 1509. STEELE 3p, 1815. LT, O,
        CT, EN, DT; CH, CU, MH, WF, Y.

2264   The kings declaration: to all his subjects, of whatsoever nation. [*London*], *printed*, 1648. 4°.* LT, O, C, LG, HH; CH, MH, TU, WF, Y.

2264A   —[Anr. ed.] [*London*], *for Richard Royston*, 1648. 4°.* CLC, MH, MM.

2265   His Majesties declaration to all his subjects, the reasons of his proceedings. *By Robert Ibbitson*, 1647. 4°.* LT; TU, WF.

2266   His Majesties declaration to both Houses . . . *Martii* 21, 1641 [2]. *York, by Robert Barker and by the assignes of John Bill*, 1642. 4°.* CF, HH; MH, WF.

2267   His Majesties declaration to both Houses of Parliament (which he likewise recommends). *York: by Robert Barker, and by the assignes of John Bill*, 1642. 20pp. 4°.* L, O, C; Y.

2268   —[Anr. ed.] *By Robert Barker, and by the assignes of John Bill*, 1641[2]. 18pp. 4°.* LT, O, C, EN, DT; CH, CN, MH, TU, WF.

2269   —[Anr. ed.] —, 1641[2]. 6pp. 4°.* O, SP; CN, CSS, MH, TU, Y.

2270   —[Anr. ed.] *For John Smith*, 1641[2]. 4°.* OC; CH, TU, WF.

2270A   —[Anr. ed.] *For I. T.*, 1642. 4°.* C; MH.

2271   —[Anr. ed.] *For I. T. and John Smith*, 1642. 4°.* O; NU.

2272   —[Anr. ed.] [*London*], *printed, and divulged by Thomas Powell*, 1642. 4°.* CSS, MH, WF.

2272A   —[Anr. ed.] *For Thomas Bankes*, 1642. 4°.* C; MH, MIU.

2273   —[Anr. ed.] *Printed at Edinburgh, [R. Bryson]*, 1642. 4°.* ALDIS 1036. C, E, EN; Y.

2274   His Majesties declaration to his loving subjects . . . 21 *April* 1643. *Edinburgh, E Tyler*, 1643. 4°.* STEELE 3p, 1788. LT, E.

2275   His Majesties declaration to the city and kingdom, concerning. *For R Rishton*, 1648. 4°.* LT; Y.

2276   Entry cancelled.

2277   The King of Great-Brittaines declaration to the high & mighty Lords the States Generall. [*n.p.*], *printed*, 1643. 4°.* O; HR.

2278   His Majesties declaration [*sic*] to the honourable House Commons, . . . *October the* 11. *For Richard West*, 1642. 4°.* O, OC; MH, NC, Y.

2279   His Majesties declaration to the Marquesse of Ormond, concerning. *For William Orton*, 1646. 4°.* LT, O; MH, WF.

2279A   His Majesties declaration to the ministers. *York: By Robert Barker; and by the assignes of John Bill*, 1642. 4°.* L, OC, CP, YM; WF.

2280   —[Anr. ed.] *Printed at York by Robert Barker, reprinted at London for Alice Norton*, 1642. 4°.* LT, CM, HH; CH.

2281   —[Anr. ed.] *First printed at Yorke and now reprinted for Charles Greene*, 1642. 4°.* CJ, SP, DT, HH.

2282   —[Anr. ed.] *York: by Robert Barker; and by the assignes of John Bill; and reprinted at London, for John Sweeting*, 1642. brs. STEELE 2160. LT, OP, HH, EC.

2283   —[Anr. ed.] *For E. Husbands*, 1642. brs. STEELE 2161. O.

2284   —[Anr. ed.] *For E. Husbands. 6 June*, 1642. brs. STEELE 2162. O, CJ, LS, OC.

2285   —[Anr. ed.] [*London*], *for R. Lownes*, [1642]. brs. STEELE 2163. LG.

2286   —[Anr. ed.] *By T. P. and M. S. for W. Gay, June 7, 1642.* 4°.* O, CT, HH; CSS, TU.

2287   —[Anr. ed.] *By E. Griffin for R. Best*, 1642. 4°.* L, CT; CH, CN, WF, Y.

2287A   His Majesties declaration, touching his proceedings. *Printed*, 1642. 4°.* LT, CSSX; CLC, MH, WF, Y.

2288   His Majesties declaration upon his departure from the Isle of Wyght. *For Giles Cotton*, 1648. 4°. LT, O, EN; MH.

2289   By the king. His Majesties declaration whereby to repeale . . . licenses. *Printed at Oxford by Leonard Lichfield*, 1643. brs. MADAN 1500. STEELE 2515. LT, LG; CH.

2290   His Majesties declarations to all his loving subjects, I. upon occasion. *Printed at Cambridge, by Roger Daniel*, 1642. 4°.* CJ, CT, CC, HH; WF, Y.

2290A   —[Anr. ed.] *Printed at Oxford by Leonard Lichfield*, 1642. 4°.* CH.

2291   King Charles his defence against some trayterous observations. [*n.p.*, 1642.] cap., 4°.* LT, EC; CH, CSS, WF, Y.

2291A   —King Charles the 1st's defence of the Church of England. *Hague, by S. and G. Browne* [1649?] 12°. CN.

2292   The Kings Majesties demand of the House of Commons . . . *Jan. 4.* 1641. *For Iohn Thomas*, 1641. 4°.* LT, C; CH, MH, NU, WF, Y.

2293   The Kings Maiesties demands and propositions propounded. *For Hen. Rydiar, Septemb. 23.* 1642. 4°.* LT, SS.

2294   —[Anr. ed.] *For Thomas Rider Sept. 29.* 1642. 4°.* LT, C.

2295   His Maiesties demands to the gentry of York-shire. *For Richard Lowndes*, 1642. brs. LT, O, OP; Y.

2296   His Majesties demands to the . . . honourable House of Parliament. *For Iohn Ionson, July 28,* 1642. 4°.* LT, O, EC, HH; CH, Y.

2296A   —[Anr. ed.] *Printed*, 1642. 4°.* BR.

2297   His Majesties desires and command to all the trayned bands. [*London*], *July 6. for Iohn Norton*, 1642. 4°.* LT.

2298   His Majesties desires and propositions to all his subjects in Scotland. *First printed at Edinburgh in Scotland by Rob. Bryson, and now reprinted at London, for Joseph Scot*, 1642. 4°.* LT; MM.

2299   The Kings Majesties desires to . . . Sir Thomas Fairfax. *For G. Wilkinson, Iune 17,* 1647. 4°.* LT, OC, SP, HH; WF.

2300   —[Anr. ed.] *For R. Williamson, July 13,* 1647. 4°.* LT, YM; CLC, MH, Y.

2301   Entry cancelled.
        Divine penitential meditations and vowes. 1649. *See title.*

2302   Effata regalia. Aphorismes. *For Robert Horn*, 1661. 12°. LT, O, C, ES; CH, CU, MH, WF.

2303   His Majesties enlargement of concessions in his last answer. *For Richard Lowndes*, 1648. brs. STEELE 2803. LT, O, LS, HH.
        King Charles his farewell. 1649. *See title.*

2304   Entry cancelled.

2305 His Maiesties farewel speech. [*London*, 1648.] brs. STEELE 2805. LT, O, CJ; WF.

2306 His Majesties finall ansvver concerning Episcopacie. *For Richard Best*, 1648. 4°.* LT, O, C, EN, DT; CH, CN, MH, NU, WF, Y.

2307 —[Anr. ed.] *For R.B.*, 1648. *And reprinted*, 1660. L, O, OC, HH; CLC, CN, MH, NU, WF, Y.

2308 His Majesties finall remonstrance and gracious message. *For G. Wharton*, 1648. 4°.* LT, O, HH.

2309 —[Anr. ed.] *For R Rishton*, 1648. 4°.* LT; MH, Y.

2309A His Majesties finall remonstrance and ultimate answers. *For G. Wharton*, 1648. 4°.* LT, CT; MH.

2310 Five severall papers, delivered by. *By Robert Ibbitson*, [1648]. 4°.* EN; MH, OWC, TU.

2311 For a finall answer to your proposition of . . . 17 October 1648. [*London*], *for R Royston*, 1648. brs. STEELE 2800. LT.

2312 —[Anr. ed.] [*n.p.*], 1648. brs. STEELE 2801. HH.

2313 From Scotland. Tvvo coppies of letters. [*London*], *for Tho. Bates*, 1641. 4°.* LT, O, HH, EN; MH, NU, OWC, TU, WF.

2314 His Majesties fuller condescentions to all the propositions. *For Adam Marsh*, 1648. 4°.* MH, Y.

2315 His Majesties gallant resolution to come to Holmby House. *For D W. January* 26, [1647]. 4°.* LT.
The golden apophthegmes of. 1660. *See title.*

2316 His Majesties gracious and last message . . . to both Houses . . . from Nottingham, 25 August 1642. [*London*] *for Fr. Coles, this* 30 *Aug.* [1642.] 4°.* OC, HH; MH, WF, Y.

2317 His Majesties gratious answer, and royall resolvtion. [*n.p.*], *January* 3, *for I. H. and T. Rogers*, 1642[3]. 4°.* LT, O.

2318 A gracious ansvver from the King for a treaty with the Parliament. *By B. A.*, 1648. 4°.* LT, DT; MH.

2319 His Maiesties gracious ansvver to the different opinions. *First printed at Oxford by Leonard Lichfield, and now re-printed at London for John Rivers*, [1642]. 4°.* MADAN 1137. LT, O, DT; MH.

2320 His Majesties gracious ansvver to the message . . . from London. *Printed at London for Thomas Massam*, 1643. 4°.* LT, O, LG, HH, DT; CH, MH, Y.

2321 His Majesties gracious ansvver to the proposition of . . . Parliament for Ireland. *For J. T.*, 1641[2]. 4°.* L; CH, Y.

2322 His Majesties gracious assent to the petition. *For J. Harrison, June* 10, 1641. 4°.* LT, O, HH; WF, Y.

2323 His Majesties gracious message and propositions . . . Novemb. 19, 1647. *By Robert Ibbitson*, 1647. 4°.* LT, HH; CH, CN, MH, NU, WF.

2324 His Maiesties gratiovs message and summons to . . . Glocester Aug. 10. 1643. *Printed at Oxford by Leonard Lichfield*, 1643. brs. MADAN 1439. STEELE 2467. O.

2325 His Majesties gracious message for peace, December, 5th. *Oxford, by Leonard Lichfield*, 1645. 4°.* MADAN 1828. O, HH.

2326 His Majesties gracious message of the fifth of this instant May. *Printed at Oxford by Leonard Lichfield*, 1643. 4°.* MADAN 1344. LT, O, C, OC, CM; CH, MH, TU, WF, Y.

2326A His Majesties gracious message sent to both his Houses . . . February 20. *Oxford, L. Lichfield*, 1642. brs. CT.

2327 His Maiesties gracious message sent to his Commons . . . Decemb. 19. 1642. [*n.p.*], *Decemb.* 21. *for J. Franks*, 1642. 4°.* LT, LG; CSS, MBP, MH, TU.

2328 His Maiesties gracious message to both his Houses . . . February the 20th. [*Oxford*, 1642/3.] brs. STEELE 2371. LT; CH.

2329 —[Anr. ed.] [*London*, 1643.] brs. STEELE 2372. LT, HH, EC.

2329A His Maiesties gracious message, to both Houses . . . the 14 of Febr. 1641. *For Iohn Wright*, 1641[/2]. 4°.* L, O, HH; NU, WF.

2330 —[Anr. ed.] *For F. Coules, & T. Bancks*, 1641 [2]. 4°.* OC, BP; CN, MH, TU, WF, Y.

2331 —[Anr. ed.] *For Iohn Wright*, 1642. 4°.* L, C, CM, CT, SP; MH, SP, CH, WF.

2332 His Majesties gracious message to both Houses . . . from Nottingham the 25. of August 1642. *Imprinted at York by Robert Barker: and by the assignes of John Bill*, 1642. brs. STEELE 2251. LT, O, LG, EC.

2333 —[Anr. ed.] *By Robert Barker: and by the assignes of John Bill*, 1642. 4pp. 4°.* LT, O, C, HH; CH, CU, MH, TU, WF, Y.

2334 —[Anr. ed.] *By Robert Barker; and by the assignes of John Bill*, 1642. 14pp. 4°.* LT, O, LL, MR, EN; CH, CN, MH, NU, TU, WF.

2335 —[Anr. ed.] *For I. Wright, Septemb.* 17, 1642. 4°.* MH, Y.

2336 His Majesties gracious message to both Houses of Parliament: Feb. 20. Forasmuch. [*n.p.*, 1643.] brs. LT, O, HH; MH, MHS.

2337 His Maiesties gracious message to both Houses of Parliament . . . on Munday Novemb. 27 *For G. Wharton*, 1648. 4°.* LT; WF.

2338 His Majesties gracious message to His Highness, the Prince of Wales. *Imprinted at London*, 1648. 4°.* LT; MIU, Y.
His Majesties gracious message to the citizens of London. 1648. *See Ruswel, W.*

2339 His Majesties gracious messages for peace. *Oxford, by Leonard Lichfield*, 1645. 4°.* MADAN 1836. O, CT; MH, WF.

2340 By the king. His Majesties gratious offer of pardon. *Printed at Oxford by Leonard Lichfield*, 1643. brs. MADAN 1323. STEELE 2409. O.

2341 —[Anr. ed.] *Oxford* [*London*], *by Leonard Lychfield*, 1643. brs. MADAN 1324. STEELE 2410. LT, O, OW; Y.

2342 By the king. His Majesties gratious proclamation to the cittyes of London. [*Oxford, L. Lichfield*], 1642. fol.* MADAN 1044. STEELE 2284. O, OC, BP, BR.

2343 —[Anr. ed.] *Imprinted at London by Robert Barker and by the assignes of John Bill*, 1642. fol.* STEELE 2285. LT, HH; Y.

2344 —[Anr. ed.] [*n.p.*, 1642.] fol.* STEELE 2286. LT, LPC, LS.

2345 His Majesties gracious speech at Newport. *Printed*, 1648. 4°.* LT; MH.

2346 His Majesties grievances sent by a message. *By Robert Ibbitson*, 1647. 4°.* LT, O, C, LG, HH; CH, MH, MIU, WF, Y.

2347 Having taken speciall notice . . . fifth day of November, . . . 1644. *Printed at Oxford by Leonard Lichfield*, [1644]. brs. MADAN 1689. STEELE 2590. O.

2348 Iniunctions concerning the garrison of Oxford. *Oxford, by Leonard Lichfield*, 1645. 4°.* MADAN 1827. O.

2349 His Majesties instructions to his commissioners of array. *York: by Robert Barker: and by the assignes of John Bill*, 1642. 4°.* L, O, C, CJ, HH; CN, MH, NU, TU.

2350 —[Anr. ed.] *Yorke, by Robert Barker* [London], *reprinted for R. Best, September 16, 1642*. 4°.* LT, O, CM, HH, D; CH, CN, MH, WF, Y.

2351 The Kings Majesties instructions vnto the Earle of Northampton. *For A. Norton*, 1642. 4°.* LT, CCC, EC, DT; LC, MH, Y.

2352 The Kings Majesties intention concerning the setting up of his standard. *For H. Blunon, August 6, 1642*. 4°.* LT, EC, HH; CN, WF, Y.

2353 Entry cancelled.

2354 The Kings Majesties joyfull letter to the city of London. *For R W.*, 1648. 4°.* LT, AN; MH.

2355 A joyfull message from the Kings most Excellent Majesty. *For R. Rbshton* [sic], 1648. 4°.* LT; MH, Y.

2356 A joyfull message sent from. [*n.p.*], *for Richard Seymour, August 4, 1642*. 4°.* LT, O, YM.

2357 Entry cancelled.
      The Kingly myrrour. 1649. *See title*.

2358 The Kings cabinet opened. *For Robert Bostock*, 1645. 4°. MADAN 1790. LT, O, C, EN, DT; CH, CN, LC, MH, TU, Y.

2359 The King's packet of letters. *For R. Austin, and J. Coe, Octob. 13, 1645*. 4°. LT, O, C, LVF, OC; CH, MH.

2360 The King's possessions. *Newcastle: by Stephen Bulkley*, 1647. 4°.* LT, O, CT, NP, HH.

2361 His Majesties last answer to the papers. [*London*, 1649.] brs. STEELE 3p 2017. LT.

2362 His Majesties last answer to the Parliament . . . August 29, 1648. *By Robert Ibbitson*, 1648. brs. L, LS; WF.

2363 His Majesties last declaration, and finall resolution. *First printed at Oxford by Leonard Lichfield, and now re-printed at London for Adam Bell*, [1642]. 4°.* MADAN 1133. LT, O, HH, DT; CH, MIU, WF, Y.

2364 His Majesties last declaration to all his loving subjects. *For Iohn Wilson, Jan. 19, 1643*. 4°.* LT, O, LG, DT; MH, WF, Y.

2365 The Kings Majesties last declaration to the Lord Mountague. *For R. Rishton, Iuly 3. 1647*. 4°.* LT, OC, DT; MBP, TU, Y.

2366 His Majesties last generall pardon. *For Henry Watson, Feb. 7, 1642*. 4°.* LT, O, HH, DT; MH, Y.

2367 His Maiesties last graciovs message. *Printed*, 1643. brs. NU.

2368 The King's majesties last gracious message for peace. *For Matthew Walbank, Feb. 10, 1645*[/6]. 4°.* LT, C, HH, CLC; CH, CLC, CN, MH.

2369 The Kings Majesties last message and declaration to . . . Fairfax. *By J. C. for G. Horton*, 1647. 4°.* LT, O; CH, WF.

2370 His Maiesties last message, September 11. 1642. [*London*], *for Edw. Husbands and John Franck, Septem. 17, 1642*. 4°.* LT, O, C; CLC, CN, MH, WF, Y.

2371 His Maiesties last message, Septemb. 12. 1642. *For J. Wright. 14. Septemb., 1642*. 4°.* O, C, OC, CJ; MH, WF.

2372 His Majesties last message to the Parliament. *For R. Smithurst*, 1648. 4°.* LT, DT; CH, MH, MIU, WF, Y.

2373 His Majesties last most gracious message of Decemb. 20, 1646. [*London*], *printed*, 1646. 4°.* LT, C, OC, CJ, HH; CLC, MH, TU, WF, Y.

2374 The King's Majesties last most gracious message . . . 20 of January 1645[/6.] [*London*], *printed*, 1646. 4°.* O, C, OC, HH, DT; Y.

2375 The last papers betwixt His Maiesty, and the commissioners . . . concerning church-government. *For Richard Lownes*, 1648. 4°.* LT, P, HH; CH, CN, MBP, Y.

2376 Last proposals to the officers of the armie, . . . Dec. 27, 1648. [*n.p.*, 1648.] 4°.* LT, DT.

2377 His Majesties last propositions to the commissioners. *For R. Rishton*, 1648. 4°.* LT, O, LCL, DT; MIU.

2378 His Maiesties last remonstrance to the whole kingdome. *Printed at Oxford by Leonard Lichfield, Jan. 23*, [1642/3]. 4°.* MADAN 1205. LT, O, CT, EN, DT; CH, MH, NU, WF, Y.

2379 His Maiesties last speech, and protestation. *Oxford for W. Web, and since reprinted at London for R. Sutton*, [1642/3]. 4°.* MADAN 1240. LT, O, HH, DT; CN, MH.

2380 The Kings Maiesties last speech in the Isle of Weight [sic]. *By J. C. for R. G.*, 1648. 4°.* LT; MH.

2381 His Maiesties last speech, to the Lords. *First printed at Oxford by Leonard Lichfield, and now re-printed at London for Iohn Rogers*, [1642/3]. 4°.* MADAN 1154. LT, O, HH, DT; CLC, MH, NU, WF, Y.

2382 His Maiesties late commission of array. [*Oxford, by H. Hall*], *printed*, 1643. 4°.* MADAN 1399. OCC; CN, WF, Y.

2383 His Majesties late gratious message . . . to the city of Gloucester. *Printed at Oxford by Leonard Litchfield*, 1643. brs. MADAN 1439.* O; CH.

2384 His Majesties late protestation before his receiving of the Sacrament. [*London*], *printed*, 1643. brs. MADAN 1408. STEELE 2451. LT, O, EC; BBE, CH, Y.

2385 His Majesties letter and declaration to the sherifs. *Printed at Oxford Ianuary 18. by Leonard Lichfield*, 1642[/3]. 4°.* MADAN 1193. LT, O, C, EN, DT; CH, CN, MH, TU, WF, Y.

2386 The Kings Majesties letter direct to the Lords. [*Edinburgh*], *E. Tyler*, 1642. brs. ALDIS 1037. STEELE 3, 1774. L, ER.

2387 His Majesties letter, directed to the Lords and Commons . . . March 9, 1643. *For Iohn Wright, March. 13*, 1643[/4]. 4°.* LT, O, C, LVF, E; CN, CSS, MH, NU, TU, WF, Y.

2388 His Majesties letter for the Speaker. *For M. Walbancke*, 1647. brs. STEELE 2733. O.

2389 His Majesties letter Ianvary the 24th. *For Henry Twyford*, [1642]. brs. STEELE 1955. LT, O, LS, OC; MH, Y.

2390 —[Anr. ed.] *For T.Bates*, 1641[2]. brs. STEELE 1956. L; CLC.

2391 —[Anr. ed.] *For John Thomas*, 1641. 4°.* L, CT; MH, NU, WF.

2392 His Majesties letter of instruction. *Printed at Oxford by Leonard Lichfield, Feb. 7, 1642.* 4°.* MADAN 1224. O, HH, DT; MH, WF, Y.

2393 A letter sent from His Majesty to the high sheriffes of . . . Yorke. *For I. T.*, 1642. brs. STEELE 2110. LT, O, CJ.

2394 A letter sent from His Maiesty to the Lord Maior. *For T. Powell, 18 June, 1642.* brs. STEELE 2179. CCA, HH; CU.

2395 The Kings Maiesties letter; sent from Holmby. *Printed, 1647.* 4°.* LT, HH; MH.

2396 A letter sent from the Kings Majestie to the Lords. *By Robert Young,* [1642]. brs. STEELE 1757. LT, LG, EC, CJ, ES.

2396A —[Anr. ed.] *[Edinburgh by Evan Tyler, 1672.]* brs. STEELE 3p 1756. ALDIS 1038. Y.

2397 The Kings Maiesties letter, sent to the House of Commons. *Printed at London for Iohn Wright, 1643.* 4°.* LT, SP; MH, NU, WF, Y.

2398 20. Ianuarii 1641. His Majesties letter to both Houses. *For F. C. and T. B.*, 1641[2]. brs. LT, O, C, LG, CT; Y.

2399 —[Anr. ed.] *For John Thomas*, 1641[/2]. 4°.* C, HH.

2400 His Majesties letter to both Houses . . . concerning the manifold distractions. *For George Williams and Richard Wilson, 1642. August 22.* 4°.* O; CSS, MH.

2401 His Majesties letter to both Houses of Parliament, dated at New-Castle, the 10th of June, 1646. *Oxford by Leonard Lichfield, 1646.* 4°.* MADAN 1873. O; Y.

2401A His Majesties letter to his right trusty . . . subjects. *For R. Rishton, 1648.* 4°.* LT; MH.

2402 His Majesties letter to the gentry of Yorkshire. *By A. N. for Humphrey Tuckey, 1642.* brs. STEELE 2138. L, LG, EC; Y.

2402A —[Anr. ed.] *For I. Tonson and A. Coe, 1642.* 4°.* OC.

2403 King Charles his letter to the Great Turk. *For H. Blunon, August 11, 1642.* 4°.* LT; Y.

2404 His Majesties letter to the high-sheriffe and justices of the peace of . . . Glocester. *Printed at Oxford by Leonard Lichfield, Feb. 14, 1642[/3].* 4°.* MADAN 1234. O, OC, CT, HH, DT.

2404A His Majesties letter to the high sherife of . . . Yorke. *Printed at York, by Robert Barker, and reprinted in London* [1641]. brs. L, OC, OP, CCA; Y.

2405 His Majesties letter to the Lord Keeper of the Great Seale . . . Mar. 9. 1641. *For Iohn Wright by Iohn Francke, 1641[/2].* brs. STEELE 2012. LT, O, CT, LS, EC; MH, Y.

2406 His Majesties letter to the Lord Keeper together with his message . . . Feb. 28. 1641[2]. *For John Francke, 1642.* 4°.* LT, O, CT, EC, HH; CH, LC, MH, NPT, Y.

2407 —[Anr. ed.] *For J. Wright and J. Francke*, 1641[2]. 4°.* O; CH, TU, WF.

2407A His Maiesties letter to the . . . lord major, aldermen, . . . London. *By Richard Cotes, 1646.* 4°.* LG; MH.

2408 His Maiesties letter, to the lord maior and aldermen of . . . London. *For Tho. Hewer and W. Moulton, 1642.* 4°.* L, O, C, LG, DT; CH, CU, MH, TU, WF, Y.

2409 The Kings Majesties letter to the Lord Willoughby . . . eighth of June 1642. *For A. N.*, [1642]. 4°.* O, C, HH, CM, SP; CH, CSS, MH, WF, Y.

2410 Letter to the Lords and Commons, concerning a treaty. 1643. 4°.* O, DT.

2411 His Maiesties letter to the Lords of his Privy Councell. *For Nathaniel Allen, June 8, 1642.* 4°.* L, O, DT; CSS, MH.

2412 His Maiesties letter to the Major, aldermen . . . of Bristoll. *[Oxford, by L. Lichfield]*, 1643. brs. MADAN 1367. STEELE 2428. O.

2413 His Maiesties letter to the maior of Bristol. *Oxford [London], by Leonard Lichfield, 1642[3].* 4°.* MADAN 1156. LT, O, C, BR, DT; MH, WF, Y.

2414 His Maiesties letter to the maior of Kingston upon Hull, 25. of Aprill. 1642. *Printed at Yorke, and now re-imprinted in London, for Thomas Bankes,* [1642]. brs. STEELE 2086. LT, O, CCA, EC, HH; CH, MH, MHS, Y.

2415 The kings letter to the Marquesse of Ormond. *By I. C. Iune 8, 1646.* 4°.* LT, C, LG, HH; CH, CN, LC, MH, NU, TU, Y.

2416 —[Anr. ed.] *Dublin, Wm. Bladen, 1646.* brs. DIXP 80. O.

2417 His Maiesties letter to the Parliament. *For R. Robinson, 1648.* 4°.* LT, HH.

2418 The Kings Maiesties letter to the Queen; concerning. *For G. Oreton, 1648.* 4°.* LT, O, EN; MH.

2419 His Maiesties letter to the right honovrable the lord major. *By Richard Cotes, 1646.* 4°.* LT, C, CT, DT; CLC, CN, TU, WF, Y.

2420 The letters from His Maiesty, and from the officers of His Majesties army. *Oxford, by Leonard Lichfield, 1644.* 4°.* MADAN 1675. LT, O, CJ, EN, DT; CLC, WF, Y.

2421 Majesty in misery. [1660?] brs. L, LS.

2422 —[Anr. ed.] colop: 1681. brs. L, O; MH, TU, Y.

2423 His Maiesties manifest, touching the Palatine cavse. *Edinburgh, By Robert and James Brysons, [sic] 1641.* 4°. ALDIS 996. L, EN, D, I; CN, MBP, TU, WF.

2424 Entry cancelled.

2425 —[Anr. ed.] *By Robert Barker and the assignes of John Bill,* 1641. 4°.* LT, O, C, HH; CH, CN, MH, TU, WF, Y.

2426 His Maiesties manifestations. *[London?], printed,* 1641. 4°.* LT, O, CT, HH; CLC, MBP, MH, WF, Y.

2427 The Kings Maiesties manifesto to the kingdome of Ireland. *[London], by I. G.,* 1647. 4°.* LT, O, OC, HH, DT; CH, MH, Y.

2428 The Kings Majesties message and demands to Lieut. Gen. Cromwell. *For R. W.,* 1648. 4°.* LT.

2429 The Kings Majesties message brought by Captain Titus . . . October 2. *By Robert Ibbitson, 1648.* 4°.* LT, C, DT; CH.

2430 His Majesties message concerning licences. *By Robert Barker and the assignes of John Bill,* 1641[2]. 4°.* LT, O, C, CM, HH; CH, CSS, MB, NC, TU, WF, Y.

2431 —[Anr. ed.] *Printed at London,* 1641. 4°. L, C, MR, HH, DT; MBP, MH, TU, Y.

2432   A message from His Majesty to the House of Peeres on Friday the 11 of Feb. 1641[2]. *For J. Wright, 1642.* brs. STEELE 1985. L.

2433   A message from His Majestie to the Speaker. *Newcastle, by Stephen Bulkley, 1646.* 4°.* L.

2434   Message from the royall prisoner at Windsor to the Kingdome of Scotland. *For W. Fielding, 1648.* 4°.* LT, DT; MH, OWC.

2435   His Majesties message sent by the Lord Chamberlain . . . the 28. of December. 1641. *Imprinted at London, by Robert Barker and by the assigns of John Bill, 1641.* brs. STEELE 1912. LT, CT, LS, DT.

2436   His Majesties message sent from Beverley. *York: by Robert Barker; and by the assignes of John Bill, 1642.* 4°.* L, CF, YM; CH, MH, TU, WF, Y.

2437   A message sent from the Kings Majesty, with certaine propositions. *Printed at London for Tho. Banks and Will. Ley, 1642.* 4°.* LT, O, CM, OC, EC; MH, Y.

2438   His Maiesties message, sent the twentieth of May, MDCXLIII. *Oxford, by Leonard Lichfield, 1643.* brs. MADAN 1363. STEELE 2427. LT, O, LG, LS; MH, Y.

2439   His Majesties message sent to both Houses of Parliament, January 20, 1641. *Imprinted at York by Robert Barker, and by the assignes of John Bill, 1642.* brs. STEELE 1948. L, CF; MH.

2440   —[Anr. ed.] *For F. C. and T. B., 1641[2].* brs. STEELE 1949. LT, O.

2441   —[Anr. ed.] *By Robert Barker and by the assigns of John Bill, 1641[2].* brs. STEELE 1946. L, O, LPR.

2442   —[Anr. ed.] *For J. Hunsott, 1641[2].* brs. STEELE 1951. L, LVF.

2443   —[Anr. ed.] *For J. Wright, [1642].* brs. STEELE 1953. L, HH.

2444   His Majesties message sent to the high court of Parliament 8 April, 1642. *York, by Robert Barker and the assignes of John Bill, 1642.* 4°.* L, HH, YM; WF.

2445   —[Anr. ed.] *For J. Smith, 1642.* 4°.* HH.

2446   —[Anr. ed.] *For J. Wright, 1642.* 4°.* HH; CH, MH, WF.

2447   His Majesties message sent to the Parliament, April 8. 1642. concerning . . . Ireland. *By Robert Barker: and by the assigns of John Bill, 1642.* 4°.* LT, O, C, LG; CH, CN, MH, TU, WF, Y.

2448   —[Anr. ed.] *I. T., 1642.* 4°.* L, O, C, LCL, EN; CLC, WF, Y.

2448A   —[Anr. ed.] *For D. I., 1642.* 4°.* CLC, MB, MH.

2448B   —[Anr. ed.] *For John Wright, 1642.* 4°.* L, C, OC; WF.

2449   The Kings message to both Houses. January 12. 1641. *Imprinted at London by Robert Barker and by the assignes of John Bill, 1641[2].* brs. STEELE 1934. LT, CCA, CT; MH, Y.

2450   His Majesties message to both Houses . . . January 20. *By Robert Barker: and by the assignes of John Bill, 1641.* 4°.* LT, O, C, DT; CH, CN, MH, NU, TU, WF, Y.

2451   His Majesties message to both Houses . . . Febr. 14. 1641. *By Robert Barker: and by the assignes of John Bill, 1641[2].* 4°.* STEELE 1988. LT, O, C, LL, LS; CH, MBP, TU, WF, Y.

2451A   —[Anr. ed.] —, 1641[2]. brs. LT; Y.

2452   His Majesties message to both Houses . . . Mar. 15. 1641[2]. *By Robert Barker, and by the assignes of John Bill, 1641[2].* brs. O, LG, OP, CJ; CH, CLC.

2453   His Majesties message to both Houses . . . April 28, 1642, . . . concerning his refusall. *By Robert Barker, and by the assignes of John Bill, 1642.* 4°.* LT, O, C, LL, DT; CH, CN, CSS, MH, TU, WF, Y.

2453A   —[Anr. ed.] *Imprinted at London for H. Bluron [sic], 1642.* 4°.* C.

2454   His Majesties message to both Houses . . . , 28 April, 1642, declaring. *York: by Robert Barker, and by the assignes of John Bill, 1642.* 4°.* C, YM; CH, NC.

2455   His Maiesties message to both Houses . . . eleventh of Iuly. 1642. *Printed at Yorke, and re-printed at London by A. N. for Richard Best, 1642.* 4°.* OC, CT, HH, DT; NU.

2456   —[Anr. ed.] *By Robert Barker and by the assignes of John Bill, 1642.* 4°.* LT, O, CCA, HH, EN; CH, CN, MH, TU, WF, Y.

2457   —[Anr. ed.] *By E. G. for I. W., 1642.* 4°.* L, O; CH, CN, MH, TU, WF.

2458   His Majesties message to both Houses April 12. 1643 concerning disbanding. *Printed at Oxford by Leonard Lichfield, 1643.* 4°.* MADAN 1359. O, C; TU.

2459   His Majesties message to both Houses . . . May 5. 1643. *Printed at Oxford by Leonard Lichfield, 1643.* 4°.* MADAN 1343. O, OCC, OL; Y.

2460   His Majesties message to both Houses . . . 23 Martii, 1645. *Printed at Oxford by Leonard Lichfield, 1645[/6].* brs. MADAN 1840. STEELE 2648. L.

2461   His Majesties message to both Houses, concerning disbanding of both armies. *Printed at Oxford by Leonard Lichfield, 1643.* 4°.* MADAN 1318. O; LLC, MH, TU.

2462   —[Anr. ed.] *By His Majesties command at Oxford, 1643.* brs. MADAN 1319. STEELE 2407. LT, C; CH.

2463   His Majesties message to both Houses . . . concerning His Majesties going to Hull. *July 8. By Robert Barker, and by the assignes of John Bill, 1642.* 4°.* CH, WF.

2464   His Majesties message to both Houses, concerning the militia. *February 22. For Joseph Hunscott, [1642].* brs. STEELE 1991. LT, O, EC, HH; MH, WF, Y.

2465   His Majesties message to both Houses . . . from the Isle of Wight, Novemb. 17. 1647. *By Robert Austin, 1647.* 4°.* LT, O, CT, MR, HH; CH, MH, NU, TU, WF, Y.

2466   His Maiesties message to both Houses . . . from the Isle of Wight . . . fourteenth of August 1648. *[London], printed, 1648.* 4°.* LT, O, C, EN, DT; CH, CN, MH, NPT, TU.

2467   His Majesties message to both Houses . . . upon his removall to the citie of York. *Imprinted at London by Robert Barker and by the assignes of John Bill, 1641[2].* brs. STEELE 2029. LT, O, CT, LG, EC; Y.

2468   —[Anr. ed.] *For Francis Coules and Thomas Banks, [1642]* brs. STEELE 2033. HH; MH, WF.

2469   —[Anr. ed.] *For F. C. and T. B., 1641[2].* brs. STEELE 2034. L.

2470   —[Anr. ed.] *For John Franke, 1641[2].* brs. STEELE 2035. LT.

2471   —[Anr. ed.] *For Robert Fowler, [1642].* brs. LS.

2472 His Maiesties message to Colonell Goring. *August 8, for for I. H. and T. Rider,* [1642]. 4°.* LT, O; CH.

2473 His Majesties message to the House of Commons. February 7. 1641[2]. *Imprinted at London, by Robert Barker, and by the assigns of John Bill,* 1641[2]. brs. STEELE 1977. LT, O, LS, HH; MH.

2474 —[Anr. ed.] *Printed* 1641[2]. brs. STEELE 1978. L; WF, Y.

2475 —[Anr. ed.] *For Iohn Franke,* 1641[2]. 4°.* C, CM, LG, EC, HH; CSS, CU, MH, NU, TU, WF, Y.

2476 His Majesties message to the House of Commons . . . 13 August 1642. *Imprinted at York, by Robert Barker: and by the assignes of John Bill,* 1642. brs. STEELE 2246. LT, CCA, YM.

2477 His Majesties message to the House of Commons, concerning an order. *For Edward Husbands and John Franck, September 6, 1642.* 4°.* HH, DT; CH, MH, MIU, WF.

2478 —[Anr. ed.] *By Luke Norton and John Field, for E. Husband and J. Franck, September 5, 1642.* 4°.* LT, O, C, OC; CH, MH, TU, WF, Y.

2479 —[Anr. ed.] *For John Wright, September 6, 1642.* 4°.* L, C, OC, EC, HH; CSS, CU, MH, WF, Y.

2480 His Maieties [sic] message to the Hovse of Commons from the court at Yorke. *Oxford, by Henry Hall,* 1642. 4°.* MADAN 1027. L, O, DT; Y.

2481 His Majesties message to the House of Peers. April 22, 1642. *Imprinted at London, by Robert Barker, & by the assignes of John Bill,* 1642. brs. STEELE 2081. LT, O, CCA, LS, HH; MH, WF, Y.

2481A —[Anr. ed.] *Imprinted at York, by Robert Barker and by the assignes of John Bill,* 1642. brs. STEELE 2080. LT, OP.

2482 —[Anr. ed.] 1642. brs. STEELE 2083. O.

2483 —[Anr. ed.] *By T. Fawcet for J H.,* 1642. brs. STEELE 2084. O; MH.

2484 The Kings Majesties message to the inhabitants of the city of Winchester . . . Decemb. 13. *[London], for J. H. Decemb. 19, 1642.* 4°.* HH, DT; MH, Y.

2485 His Maiesties message to the kingdome of Scotland. *For L. Chapman, 26 May, 1646.* 4°.* LT, O, CT, EN, DT; CH, MH, NU, TU, WF, Y.

2486 His Majesties message to the Lord Generall Fairfax; and his act. *For Nathaniel Richardson,* 1648. 4°.* LT.

2487 His Majesties message to the Lord Generall Fairfax, and the councell . . . 30 Novemb. 1648. *Imprinted at London, for Thomas Mason,* 1648. 4°.* LT.

2488 His Majesties message to the Lords and Commons, . . . Sept. 5. September 6. 1642. *London, by L. N. and J. F. for E. Husbands and J. Franck.* 4°.* OC; CH, MH, OWC, TU, WF.

2489 —[Anr. ed.] —, *September 7, 1642.* 4°.* LT, O, C, HH; CSS, MH, TU, WF, Y.

2490 —[Anr. ed.] *For Edw. Husbands and John Franck, Septem. 7. 1642.* 4°.* L, C, OC, DT; MH, TU.

2491 —[Anr. ed.] *Hugh Perry, September the 8th, 1642.* 4°.* HH, BR; CLC, MH, WF.

2492 Message to the Parliament, April 8, 1642, concerning his resolution. 1642. 4°. DT; WF.

2493 A message with a letter sent by. *[n.p.], for I. Vnderwood,* 1643. 4°.* LT, O, C, A; WF.

2494 Military orders and articles established by His Maiesty. *Printed at Oxford by Leonard Lichfield,* 1643. 4°.* MADAN 1210. O, OL, OP, DT.

2495 —[Anr. ed.] *Reprinted at Oxford by Leonard Lichfield,* 1642[/3]. 4°.* MADAN 1211. L, C, LUS, LW, HH, BR.

2496 —[Anr. ed.] *Re-printed at Oxford by Leonard Lichfield,* [1643]. 4°.* MADAN 1212**. LT, O, CPE, CT, DT; CH, MH, WF, Y.

2497 —[Anr. ed.] *Bristoll, by Robert Barker, and John Bill,* 1643. 4°.* Y.

2498 His Maiesties most earnest and sincere desire for peace. *Oxford, by Leonard Lichfield,* 1644. 4°.* MADAN 1680. O, EN, DT; MH, TU, Y.

2499 His Majesties most gratious ansvver at the delivery of the propositions for peace. *[London], printed,* 1647. 4°.* LT, O.

2500 His Majesties most graciovs answer to the bils & propositions . . . Decemb. 24, 1647. *For Richard Royston,* 1648. 4°.* LT, O, CJ, YM, HH; CH, CN, MH, TU, WF, Y.

2501 His Maiesties most graciovs answer to the proposition . . . twenty fourth of February 1642. *[n.p., 1642.]* brs. STEELE 1998. LT.

2502 —[Anr. ed.] *J. Franke,* 1642. brs. STEELE 1999. L, O.

2503 His Majesties most gracious answer to the votes. *Printed August 15, 1648.* 4°.* LT, CT, LL, YM; CH, CN, MH, WF, Y.

2503A —[Anr. ed.] *Printed August 15, 1642.* 4°.* OC, CM.

2504 His Majesties most gracious concessions concerning church-government. *For Richard Royston, Nov. 27, 1648.* 4°.* LT, O, C, EN, DT; CH, CLC, MH, NU, Y.

2505 The kings most gracious concessions delivered. *For R. Royston,* 1648. 4°.* LT, OC, CJ, CT; CLC, MH, WF, Y.

2506 His Majesties most gracious declaration from the Isle of Wyght. *By Robert Ibbitson,* 1647. 4°.* LT, C, HH; CH, CLC, MH, Y.

2507 His Majesties most gracious declaration, left by him . . . 11. Novemb. *For Richard Royston [by L. Lichfield at Oxford],* 1647. 4°.* MADAN 1959. LT, O, C, DC, DT; CH, MH, TU, WF, Y.

2508 The Kings Majesties most gratious letter to his sonne, . . . James. *By Moses Bell,* 1647. 4°.* LT, OC, DT; MH, WF, Y.

2509 —[Anr. ed.] *By Moses Bell and Robert Ibbitson,* 1647. 4°.* LT, DC, HH; BN, CH, CLC, WF.

2510 The Kings Majesties most gratious message in foure letters. *By Robert Ibbitson,* 1647. 4°.* LT, HH, EN; CH, MH, TU, WF.

2511 His Majesties most gracious message, May 12th. *For Richard Royston,* 1647. 4°.* LT, C, LL, DT; CLC, CN, MH, NU, TU, WF, Y.

2512 His Majesties most gratious message, read . . . Sept. 14, 1647. *By Robert Ibbitson,* 1647. 4°.* LT, EN; CH, TU, Y.

2513 His Majesties most gracious message: sent to both Houses . . . by Captain Henry Heron, . . . thirteenth . . . April. *Oxford, by Leonard Lichfield,* 1643. brs. MADAN 1320. STEELE 2408. LT, O, LS; WF, Y.

2514 The Kings Majesties most gracious message sent to His Excellency Sir Thomas Fairfax. *Imprinted at London for Lawrence Gibson, 1647.* 4°.* LT, OC; WF.

2515 His Maiesties most gracious message to both Houses . . . October 11. 1648. *For Robert White, 1648.* 4°.* LT, O, HH, SP, E; CN, MH, NU, WF.

2516 His Majesties most gracious message to his great councell of Scotland. *Imprinted at Edinburgh by Robert Bryson, re printed at London, 1648.* 4°.* LT, LW, EN, DT; MH, Y.

2517 His Majesties most gracious message to his two Houses . . . Decemb. 6, 1647. *By John Bill, 1647.* 4°.* LT, CJ, CT, LG, HH; CH, MH, TU, WF, Y.

2518 Entry cancelled.
      The Kings Majesties most gracious message to his Parliament, 1647. *See Sharpe, W.*
      His Majesties most gracious message to the Speaker. 1647. *See Tracey, H.*

2519 His Majesties most gracious message to the two Houses. *Oxford, by Leonard Lichfield, 1645.* 4°.* MADAN 1837. O, EN; MH, Y.

2520 The Kings most gracious messages for peace. [*London*], *printed, 1648.* 4°. LT, O, C, HH, EN; CH, CN, MH, NU, WF, Y.
      The Kings Maiesties most gracjovs speech, declaring. 1648. *See title.*

2521 The King His Maiesties most gracious speech, made to the lord maior, . . . November the 25, 1641. *For W. R., 1641.* 4°.* LG, EC, YM, EN; CSS, MH, TU, Y.

2522 The Kings Maisties [sic] most gratiovs speech to both Houses . . . second of December. 1641. *For Iohn Thomas, 1641.* 4°.* LT; MH, Y.

2523 —[Anr. ed.] [*London*], *for S. S., 1641.* 4°.* HH; CH, WF, Y.

2524 Carisbrooke, Septemb. 7. 1648. My lord, and M. Speaker, I have received your letter of the 2d of this . . . 5 September 1648. [*n.p., 1648.*] brs. STEELE 2791. LT; MH, Y.

2525 Nevv matters of high and great consequence. *Printed at London for Francis Coules and Thomas Bankes. 1642.* 4°.* SP; CLC, CSS, MH, Y.

2526 Newes from Scotland. His Majesties manifest. *First printed at Edinburgh in Scotland by Robert and Iames Brysons. And now printed at London by T. Favvcet for T. Bates, 1641.* 4°.* LT, O, CT, HH, EN; CH, NU, TU, WF, Y.

2526A Not Popery, but the Protestant religion. colop: *For L. C.* [1672]. cap., fol.* L, O, LG, MC; CH, MH, TU, WF, Y.

2527 By the king. His Majesties offer of pardon. [*London, 1642.*] brs. STEELE 2280. O, CJ, CT.

2528 —[Anr. ed.] [*Oxford, L. Lichfield*], *1642.* brs. MADAN 1043. STEELE 2277. O.

2529 —[Anr. ed.] *Imprinted at London by Robert Barker: and by the assignes of John Bell, 1642.* brs. STEELE 2278. LT, HH.

2530 Orders and institvtions of vvar. [*London*], *for J. Johnson, 1642.* 4°.* LT, CM, EC; CH, MH, WF, Y.

2531 Orders, by the king. To our trusty & wellbeloved our Colonells. *Printed at Oxford by Leonard Lichfield,* [1643]. brs. LS.

2532 By the King. Our will and pleasure is, that the ministers. *York. Barrer & the assigns of John Bill, 1642.* brs. STEELE 2158. YM.

2533 His Majesties paper containing severall questions. *By Moses Bell, 9 Octob. 1648.* 4°.* LT, C, OME, EN, DT; CH, CU, LC, MH, NU, Y.

2534 Entry cancelled.

2535 The papers which passed at Nevv-Castle betwixt His Sacred Majestie and . . . Henderson. *For R: Royston, 1649.* 8°. LT, O, C, LVF, E; CH, CU, LC, MH, NU, Y.

2536 A part of the late king's answer to the humble petition. [*London*], *printed, 1659.* 4°.* EC, SP, DT; CLC, Y.

2537 A perfect true copie of His Majesties answer to the propositions. *For L. F., 1646.* 4°.* LT, O, LL, HH; CLC, CU, MH, NU, TU, Y.

2537A The pious politician, or remains. *By T. James for B. Harris, 1684.* 12°. P; CLC, MH, NN, Y.

2538 His Majesty pittying the distressed condition. *Oxford, L. Lichfield, 1643.* brs. MADAN 1457. STEELE 2486. O; MBA.

2539 His Majesties prayers. *Printed at London, 1649.* 8°.* LT, LL.
      Princely pelican. Royall resolves. [*London*], *1649.* *See title.*

      NOTE: Proclamations usually begin with the form "By the King."

2540 His Majesties proclamation against a traiterous band. *Printed at Edinburgh by Evan Tyler, 1646.* brs. ALDIS 1219. STEELE 3p 1904. LT, AU, ER; WF.

2541 A proclamation against the forcible seizing. *Imprinted first at Yorke and reprinted at London by F. L. for Mary Thomas, 1642. July the ninth.* 4°.* STEELE 2208. LT.

2542 A proclamation against the oppression of the clergy. [*Printed at Oxford by Leonard Lichfield, May 16, 1643.*] brs. MADAN 1351. STEELE 2422. O.

2543 —[Anr. ed.] *Prinred [sic] at Oxford by Leonard Lichfield, 1643.* brs. MADAN 1352. STEELE 2423. LT, O, CJ, LS, HH; MH.

2544 A proclamation against the spoyling and loosing of armes. *Printed at Oxford by Leonard Lichfield, 1642.* brs. MADAN 1279. STEELE 2386. O.

2545 —[Anr. ed.] [*London, Barker, 1643.*] brs. STEELE 2387. LT.

2546 A proclamation against wast. *Printed at Oxford by Leonard Lichfield, 1643.* brs. MADAN 1377. STEELE 2435. O; CH.

2547 His Majesties proclamation and declaration concerning a clause. *Printed at Oxford by Leonard Lichfield, 1643.* brs. MADAN 1346. STEELE 2421. LT, O.

2548 His Maiesties proclamation and declaration to all his loving subjects. *Oxford, by Leonard Lichfield, 1642.* 4°.* MADAN 1008. L, O, LG, OC, YM; CSS, MBP, MH, WF, Y.

2549 The Kings proclamation and determination concerning the Earle of Essex. [*London*], *for T. Thomson, 1642. August 16.* 4°.* LT, O, HH; Y.

2550 The Kings most excellent Majesties proclamation and the estates of Parliament in Scotland. *First printed at Edinburgh by Robert Brison. And now printed at London, by B. Alsop for Thomas Bates,* 1641. 4°.* LT, CCA, CT, HH; MH, NU, WF, Y.

2550A A proclamation about the weight of dollars. *Edinburgh, by Evan Tyler,* 1642. brs. L.

2550B A proclamation by His Majestie, requiring the aid. *Imprinted at York, by Robert Barker, and by the assignes of John Bill,* 1642. brs. STEELE 2244. LT, O, CCA, LVF, HH.

2550C —[Anr. ed.] —, 1642. fol.* STEELE 2245. LVF; CH, MH.

2550D —[Anr. ed.] *Cambridge, R. Daniel,* 1642. 4°.* OP.

2551 A proclamation commanding all debts, rents, and mony. *Printed at Oxford by Leonard Lichfield,* 1643. brs. MADAN 1501. STEELE 2516. O, LPC, LVF.

2552 A proclamation commanding all His Majesties subjects and servants . . . 22 March 1643[4]. *Printed at Oxford by Leonard Lichfield,* 1643[/4]. brs. MADAN 1565. STEELE 2546. L, O, LVF.

2553 A proclamation commanding Henry Percy. *Imprinted at London, by Robert Barker: and by the assigns of John Bill,* 1641. brs. STEELE 1855. L, O, LG, LS; Y.

2554 A proclamation commanding the due execution. *Printed at Oxford by Leonard Lichfield,* 1644. brs. MADAN 1633. STEELE 2562. O.

2555 A proclamation commanding the due observation of the desires. *Printed at Oxford by Leonard Lichfield,* 1643[/4]. brs. MADAN 1537. STEELE 2530. O; WF.

2556 A proclamation commanding the muster Master Generall. *[Oxford,* 1643.] brs. MADAN 1487. STEELE 2507. L, O (frag.)

2557 A proclamation commanding the use of the Book of common-prayer. *Printed at Oxford by Leonard Lichfield,* 1645. brs. MADAN 1825. STEELE 2637. LT, O, CJ, LVF, EN; WF.

2558 —[Anr. ed.] *[Oxford],* 1645. fol.* MADAN 825*. fol.* O, CJ, HH; Y.

2559 A proclamation concerning a cessation of armes. *Dublin, by William Bladen,* 1643. 4°.* LT, E.

2560 —[Anr. ed.] *Dublin, by William Bladden, reprinted at London for Edw. Husbands, October 21,* 1643. 4°.* LT, C; CH, MIU, PL, WF, Y.

2561 A proclamation concerning His Majesties navy. *Printed at Oxford by Leonard Lichfield,* 1642[/3]. brs. MADAN 1263. STEELE 2382. O, LPC.

2562 A proclamation concerning some illegal warrants. *Printed at Oxford by Leonard Lichfield,* 1643. brs. MADAN 1373. STEELE 2432. O.

2563 His Majesties proclamation, concerning the Book of common-prayer. *Oxford, by Leonard Lichfield; and reprinted at London, by R. Austin,* 1645. 4°.* MADAN 1826. LT, C, BAMB, EC, DT; CH, MH, NU, TU, WF.

2564 A proclamation concerning the brewing of beere. *Printed at Oxford by Leonard Lichfield,* 1643. brs. MADAN 1381. STEELE 2437. O, OA.

2565 His Majesties proclamation concerning the bringing in of armes. *[Oxford, by L. Lichfield],* 1642. brs. MADAN 1122. STEELE 2322. O.

2566 A proclamation concerning the covenant and league. *By Andrew Coe,* 1644. brs. LT.

2567 A proclamation concerning the due and orderly proceedings. *Printed at Oxford by Leonard Lichfield,* 1643. brs. MADAN 1488. STEELE 2508. LT, O.

2568 A proclamation concerning the fortifications. *Printed at Oxford by Leonard Lichfield,* 1643. brs. MADAN 1415. STEELE 2463. O.

2569 A proclamation concerning the true payment of tonnage. *By Robert Barker and by the assigns of John Bill,* 1641. fol.* STEELE 1881. LS; MH.

2570 A proclamation containing and declaring. *Dublin, society of stationers,* 1641. fol.* STEELE 2338. DPR.

2571 A proclamation by the King, dated at the court at York, the fifth day of May, 1642. *Imprinted at Yorke by Robert Barker, and reprinted at London for J. B.,* 1642. brs. L.

2572 A proclamation by the King, dated at the court at York the 14th day of May, 1642. *Imprinted at York by Robert Barker, and by the assignes of John Bill,* 1642. brs. L.

2573 A proclamation declaring certain monies. *Printed at Oxford by Leonard Lichfield,* 1643. brs. MADAN 1472. STEELE 2501. L frag., O.

2574 His Maiesties proclamation, declaring his expresse command. *Reprinted at Oxford by Leonard Lichfield,* 1642. 4°.* MADAN 1023. O, HH; CSS, Y.

2574A —[Anr. ed.] *Cambridge, R. Daniel,* 1642. 4°.* CCA, CJ, CT.

2575 A proclamation declaring His Majesties expresse command. *Imprinted at London, by Robert Barker, and by the assignes of John Bill,* 1642. brs. STEELE 2243. LT, O, CJ, LG, LS; MH.

2575A —[Anr. ed.] *York, by Robert Barker and by the assignes of Robert Bill,* 1642. fol.* CJ.

2576 A proclamation declaring His Majesties grace to the mariners. *Printed at Oxford by Leonard Lichfield,* 1643. fol.* MADAN 1411. STEELE 2452. O.

2577 A proclamation declaring His Majesties resolution. *Reprinted at Oxford by Leonard Lichfield,* 1644. brs. MADAN 1683. STEELE 2587. L, O, LVF.

2578 A proclamation declaring our purpose. *By Robert Barker and by the assignes of John Bill,* 1642. 4°.* STEELE 2216. LT.

2579 —[Anr. ed.] *Imprinted at York by Robert Barker: and by the assignes of John Bill,* 1642. fol.* O.

2580 —[Anr. ed.] *Printed at York, and now reimprinted at London,* 1642. 4°.* YM, SP; WF.

2581 A proclamation direction the manner of paying. *Printed at Oxford by Leonard Lichfield,* 1644. brs. MADAN 1635. STEELE 2565. OA.

2582 A proclamation for a generall fast. *By Robert Barker and by the assignes of John Bill,* 1641[2]. brs. STEELE 1925. L, O, LPC, LVF, LS; Y.

2583 A proclamation for a generall fast. *Printed at Oxford by Leonard Lichfield, 1643.* brs. MADAN 1466. STEELE 2492. LT, O, LPC.

2584 —[Anr. ed.] *Oxford, by Leonard Lichfield, 1643.* brs. MADAN 1467. STEELE 2493. LT, LG, CJ; CH.

2585 A proclamation for a solemne fast . . . fifth of February. *Printed at Oxford by Leonard Lichfield, 1644[/5].* brs. MADAN 1702. STEELE 2596. LT, O, CJ; CH.

2586 A proclamation for making of severall pieces of foreigne coyne. *Printed at Oxford by Leonard Lichfield, 1643[/4].* brs. MADAN 1551. STEELE 2536. L, O.

2587 A proclamation for obedience to be given. *Imprinted at London, by Robert: Barker: and by the assigns of John Bill,* brs. STEELE 1865. LT, LPC, LS; MH.

2588 A proclamation for obedience to the lawes. *Imprinted at London, by Robert Barker and the assignes of John Bill, 1641.* brs. STEELE 1903. LT, O, LS, CT, DT; MH, Y.

2589 A proclamation for preventing of disorders. *Printed at Oxford by Leonard Lichfield, 1645[/6].* brs. MADAN 1838. STEELE 2641. O.

2590 A proclamation for preventing the plundring. *Printed at Oxford by L. Lichfield, 1642[/3].* brs. MADAN 1274. STEELE 2390. L, O, LVF.

2591 A proclamation for prevention of abuses of informers, clerkes. *[London, 1642].* fol.* CH.

2592 A proclamation for putting the lawes against Jesuites. *By Robert Barker and by the assigns of John Bill, 1640[1].* fol.* STEELE 1839. L, LS, HH; WF.

2593 A proclamation for putting the laws against Popish recusants. *Imprinted at London, by Robert Barker: and by the assignes of John Bill, 1641[2].* brs. STEELE 2039. LT, O, CS, LG, EC; MH, Y.

2594 A proclamation for repealing and making voyd. *Printed at Oxford by Leonard Lichfield, 1644.* brs. MADAN 1699. STEELE 2593. LT; CH.

2595 A proclamation for taking of prizes at sea. *Printed at Oxford by Leonard Lichfield, 1644.* brs. MADAN 1634. STEELE 2563. LT, O; CH.

2596 His Majesties proclamation for the adjournment of . . . Michaelmasse term. *Imprinted at London, by Robert Barker: and by the assignes of John Bill, 1642.* brs. STEELE 2271. LT, O, LPC, LS, HH; MH.

2597 —[Anr. ed.] *Printed at Oxford by Leonard Lichfield, 1643.* brs. MADAN 1462. STEELE 2490. O; CH.

2598 A proclamation for the apprehending. *Printed at Oxford by Leonard Lichfield, 1643.* brs. MADAN 1497. STEELE 2513. L, O, LPC.

2599 A proclamation for the assembling the members of both houses. *Printed at Oxford for Leonard Lichfield, 1643.* brs. MADAN 1504. STEELE 2517. O, LPC; CH.

2600 A proclamation for the attendance of the members. *Imprinted at London, by Robert Barker: and by the assigns of John Bill, 1641.* brs. STEELE 1905. L, LS, DT; MH, Y.

2601 A proclamation for the authorizing an vniformitie of the Booke of common prayer. *Printed at London, 1642[3].* brs. LT, O, LG.

2602 A proclamation for the better defence of the Kings royall person . . . 28 April 1644. *Printed at Oxford, by Leonard Lichfield, 1644.* brs. MADAN 1617. STEELE 2560. L, O, LPC.

2603 —[Anr. ed.] *Printed at Oxford by Leonard Lichfield, 1644.* brs. MADAN 1646. STEELE 2568. LPC, LVF.

2604 A proclamation for the better government of . . . Glocester. *Printed at Oxford by Leonard Lichfield, 1642[/3].* brs. MADAN 1270. STEELE 2379. O.

2605 A proclamation for the better government of His Majesties army. *[Oxford, by L. Lichfield, 1642.]* fol.* MADAN 1088. STEELE 2309. O, LG; WF.

2606 —[Anr. ed.] *[London, 1642.]* brs. STEELE 2310. LT, O, CT, LPC, HH; CH, MH, MIU, Y.

2607 A proclamation for the better government of . . . Worcester. *Printed at Oxford by Leonard Lichfield, 1642[/3].* brs. MADAN 1280. STEELE 2391. O, OC.

2608 A proclamation for the better meanes of making provision. *[Oxford, by L. Lichfield], 1642/3.* brs. MADAN 1236. O.

2609 A proclamation for the better preserving of the corne. *Printed at Oxford by Leonard Lichfield, 1643.* brs. MADAN 1300. STEELE 2399. O, LPC.

2609A A proclamation for the discovery of rebells. *Oxford, by Leonard Lichfield, 1643.* brs. O.

2610 A proclamation for the ease of the citty of Oxford, and suburbs, and . . . Jan. 20. *[Oxford, by L. Lichfield], 1642/3.* brs. MADAN 1192. STEELE 2352a. O.

2611 —[Anr. ed. ". . . suburbs of . . ."] *[Oxford i.e. London by L. Lichfield], 1642/3.* brs. MADAN 1192n. STEELE 2352. LT, O, LS, HH; Y.

2612 A proclamation for the free and safe passage of all clothes . . . 1 November. *[Oxford, by L. Lichfield], 1642.* brs. MADAN 1112. STEELE 2318a. L, O.

2613 A proclamation for the free and safe passage of all clothes . . . 8 December. *[London, Alice Norton, 1642.]* brs. STEELE 2318. LT, O, LG, OC, EC.

2614 A proclamation for the free and safe passage of all persons. *[Oxford, by L. Lichfield,] 1642.* brs. MADAN 1061. STEELE 2287. L, O, LPC, BR.

2615 A proclamation for the free and safe resort to the markets of . . . Cyrencester. *[Oxford, by L. Lichfield], 1642/3.* brs. MADAN 1228. STEELE 2365. O, LPC.

2616 A proclamation for the further restraint of prophane swearing. *Printed at Oxford by Leonard Lichfield, 1644.* brs. MADAN 1602. STEELE 2554. O.

2617 —[Anr. ed.] —, *1644.* brs. MADAN 1615. STEELE 2555. LT, O, LG, HH; CH.

2618 His Majesties proclamation for the more free passage. *By A. N. for R. Lownds, 1642.* 4°.* STEELE 2189. LT, O; MH.

2619 A proclamation for the payment of His Majesties rents. *[Oxford, by L. Lichfield], 1642/3.* brs. MADAN 1232. STEELE 2363. O.

2620 A proclamation for the prizing of wines. *Imprinted at London, by Robert Barker: and by the assignes of John Bill, 1641[2].* fol.* STEELE 1954. L.

2621 A proclamation for the redresse of certaine grievances. *Printed at Oxford by Leonard Lichfield,* 1643. brs. MADAN 1370. STEELE 2429. O.

2622 A proclamation for the regulating of His Majesties souldiers. *Printed at Oxford by Leonard Lichfield,* [1644/5]. brs. MADAN 1732. STEELE 2602. LPC.

2623 A proclamation for the reliefe of His Majesties army . . . in Ireland . . . 28 February. *Printed at Oxford by Leonard Lichfield,* 1643[/4]. brs. MADAN 1539. STEELE 2533. O.

2624 —17 March 1643. —, 1643[/4]. brs. MADAN 1555. STEELE 2544. O.

2625 A proclamation for the removing of the courts of Kingsbench. *Printed at Oxford by Leonard Lichfield,* 1643. fol.* MADAN 1507. STEELE 2522. O, LVF.

2626 A proclamation for the safety of His Majesties navy. [*Oxford, by L. Lichfield*], 1642/3. brs. MADAN 1247. O, LVF.

2627 A proclamation for the securing of the peace. *Imprinted at London, by Robert Barker: and by the assigns of John Bill,* 1641. fol.* STEELE 1896. L, OQ; MH.

2628 A proclamation for the security and protection . . . in . . . Southampton. *Printed at Oxford by Leonard Lichfield,* 1643[/4]. brs. MADAN 1557. STEELE 2541. O.

2629 A proclamation for the security and protection . . . in . . . Wilts. *Printed at Oxford by Leonard Lichfield,* 1643[/4]. brs. MADAN 1553. STEELE 2539. L, O, LVF.

2630 A proclamation for the speedy calling in. *Printed at Oxford by Leonard Lichfield,* 1644. brs. MADAN 1586. STEELE 2547. O.

2631 A proclamation for the speedy clearing of lodgings. *Printed at Oxford by Leonard Lichfield,* 1643[/4]. brs. MADAN 1514. STEELE 2524. O.

2632 A proclamation for the speedy payment of all such summes. [*Oxford, by L. Lichfield*], 1642/3. brs. MADAN 1252. STEELE 2376. L, O.

2633 —[Anr. ed.] [*London,* 1643.] brs. STEELE 2377. LT, O, LG, LS, EN; WF, Y.

2634 A proclamation for the speedy payment of the monies. *By Robert Barker and by the assignes of John Bill,* 1641. brs. STEELE 1866. L, OQ, CT, LPC, LS; CH, MH, MHS, Y.

2635 A proclamation for the strict observance. [*Oxford, by L. Lichfield*], 1642[/3]. brs. MADAN 1246. STEELE 2366. O; Y.

2636 A proclamation for the suppressing of the present rebellion. *Imprinted at York by Robert Barker: and by the assignes of John Bill,* 1642. fol.* STEELE 2242. O.

2637 His Maiesties proclamation, for the suppressing of the present rebellion. *Reprinted at Oxford by Leonard Lichfield,* 1642. 4°.* MADAN 1020. STEELE 2242. O, DT; CSS, WF, Y.

2638 A proclamation for the vent of cloth. *Printed at Oxford by Leonard Lichfield,* 1644. brs. MADAN 1603. STEELE 2557. L.

2639 A proclamation for the venting and transporting. *Printed at Oxford by Leonard Lichfield,* [1643]. brs. MADAN 1492. STEELE 2510. L, O, LPC.

2640 A proclamation forbidding all assessing. *Printed at Oxford by Leonard Lichfield,* 1642[3]. brs. MADAN 1269. STEELE 2384. L, O, LPC, LVF; NC.

2641 —[Anr. ed.] [*London, by Robert Barker and by the assigns of John Bill,* 1642[3].] brs. STEELE 2385. LT, OC; MH.

2642 His Majesties proclamation forbidding all his loving subjects . . . of Glocester. [*Oxford, by L. Lichfield*], 1642. brs. MADAN 1147. O, CJ.

2643 His Majesties proclamation forbidding all his loving subjects of the counties of Kent, Surry. [*Oxford, by L. Lichfield*], 1642/3. brs. MADAN 1248. STEELE 2369. O.

2644 —[Anr. ed.] [*London*], 1642/3. brs. MADAN 1248n. LG, OW; MH.

2645 —[Anr. ed.] —, 1643. brs. MADAN 1248n. STEELE 2370. LT, O, LG, LPC, LS; WF, Y.

2646 A proclamation forbidding all His Majesties subjects belonging. *York, by Robert Barker and by the assigns of John Bill,* 1642. brs. STEELE 2150. L, LCP, CF.

2647 —[Anr. ed.] *London,* 1642. brs. STEELE 2151. HH; MH.

2648 —[Anr. ed.] *Imprinted first at York, and now re-printed at London, for Edward Husbands, May 31,* 1642. brs. STEELE 2152. LT, O, CJ, LG, LS; Y.

2649 —[Anr. ed.] *Imprinted first at York and now re-printed at London, 9 June,* 1642. brs. STEELE 2153. L, O.

2650 —[Anr. ed.] [*n.p.,* 1642.] brs. STEELE 2154. L, O.

2650A A proclamation forbidding all levies of forces. *York: by Robert Barker, and by the assigns of John Bill,* 1642. 4°. STEELE 2186. L, O, LPC, EN, DT.

2651 —[Anr. ed.] colop: *Imprinted at London, by Robert Barker: and by the assignes of John Bill,* 1642. fol.* STEELE 2187. LT, O, CJ, LPR, EC; CH, MH, MHS.

2652 —[Anr. ed.] colop: *First printed at Yorke, reprinted at London, by E. G. for L. C.,* 1642. 4°.* STEELE 2188. L, LG, LCL, CM, HH; CH, MH, TU, WF, Y.

2653 —[Anr. ed.] colop: *Reprinted for Thomas Winter and Thomas Hewer,* 1642. 4°.* HH; CH, MH.

2653A —[Anr. ed.] *T. Winter and W. Moulton,* 1642. 4°.* HH.

2653B —[Anr. ed.] *Cambridge, R. Daniel,* 1642. brs. CT.

2654 A proclamation forbidding all the tenants or debtors. *Printed at Oxford by Leonard Lichfield,* 1643. brs. MADAN 1455. STEELE 2481. LT O; CH, WF.

2655 —[Anr. ed.] *Printed at Oxford by Leonard Lychfield,* 1643. brs. MADAN 1456. STEELE 2482. L, O, LVF; MH.

2656 A proclamation forbidding any of His Majesties subjects to assist the rebells. *Printed at Oxford by Leonard Lichfield,* 1643. brs. MADAN 1417. STEELE 2457. L, O, LVF.

2657 His Majesties proclamation forbidding the tendering or taking of a late covenant . . . 9 October. *Printed at Oxford by Leonard Lichfield,* 1643. brs. MADAN 1481. STEELE 2496. O, LPC.

2658 —[Anr. ed.] *Oxford, by Leonard Lichfield,* 1643. brs. MADAN 1482. STEELE 2497. LT; CH.

2659 His Majesties proclamation forbidding the tendring or taking . . . 21 June. *Printed at Oxford by Leonard Lichfield,* 1643. brs. MADAN 1394. STEELE 2442. LT, O, LVF, LPR; CH, NU.

2660 —[Anr. ed.] [Oxford, by L. Lichfield], 1643. brs. MADAN 1395. STEELE 2443. L, O, LPC, HH; MH, WF.

2661 —[Anr. ed.] For Will. Sheares, 1660. brs. STEELE 2444. L, HH.

2662 A proclamation inhibiting the assembly of any divines. [Oxford, by L. Lichfield], 1643. brs. MADAN 1392. STEELE 2445. O, ES.

2663 A proclamation of grace and pardon to all such as . . . seek His Majesties mercy. Printed at Oxford by Leonard Lichfield, 1645. brs. MADAN 1768. STEELE 2609. LT, O, CJ, LPC; CH.

2663A A proclamation of His Majesties grace . . . Berks. [Oxford, L. Lichfield], 1642. brs. BR.

2663B A proclamation of His Majesties grace . . . Bristoll. Oxford, [L. Lichfield], 1642. brs. BR.

2664 A proclamation of His Majesties grace, . . . Buckingham. [Oxford, by L. Lichfield], 1642. brs. MADAN 1138. O.

2665 A proclamation of His Majesties grace, . . . Chester. [Oxford, by L. Lichfield], 1642. brs. MADAN 1114. O.

2666 A proclamation of His Majesties grace, . . . Devon. [Oxford, by L. Lichfield], 1642. brs. MADAN 1073. STEELE 2299. L, LPC, CT, OC, BR.

2667 A proclamation of His Majesties grace, . . . Dorsett. [Oxford, by L. Lichfield], 1642. brs. MADAN 1077. STEELE 2307. LPC, BR.

2668 A proclamation of His Majesties grace, . . . Essex. [Oxford, by L. Lichfield], 1642/3. brs. MADAN 1175. O.

2669 A proclamation of His Majesties grace, . . . Exceter. [Oxford, by L. Lichfield], 1642. brs. MADAN 1071. STEELE 2300. LT, BR.

2669A A proclamation of His Majesties grace . . . Glocester. Oxford, [L. Lichfield], 1642. brs. BR.

2670 A proclamation of His Majesties grace, . . . Hertford. [Oxford, by L. Lichfield], 1642/3. brs. MADAN 1169. O.

2671 A proclamation of His Majesties grace, . . . Kent. [Oxford, by L. Lichfield], 1642. brs. MADAN 1069. STEELE 2298. LT, LPC.

2672 A proclamation of His Majesties grace, . . . Lancaster. [Oxford, by L. Lichfield], 1642. brs. MADAN 1115. O.

2673 A proclamation of His Majesties grace, . . . Lincolne. [Oxford, by L. Lichfield], 1642/3. brs. MADAN 1184. STEELE 2348. O.

2674 A proclamation of His Majesties grace, . . . Oxon. Oxford, 1642. brs. MADAN 1053. STEELE 2290. LT, O, LPC, BR.

2675 A proclamation of His Majesties grace, . . . Somersett. [Oxford, by L. Lichfield], 1642. brs. MADAN 1072. STEELE 2301. LT, LPC, BR.

2676 A proclamation of His Majesties grace, . . . Southampton. [Oxford, by Leonard Lichfield], 1642. brs. MADAN 1089. STEELE 2314. LG, BR.

2677 A proclamation of His Majesties grace, . . . Stafford and Derby. [London, Barker, 1643.] brs. STEELE 2395. LT.

2678 —[Anr. ed.] Printed at Oxford by Leonard Lichfield, 1642[3]. brs. MADAN 1296. STEELE 2394. LT, LS.

2679 A proclamation of His Majesties grace, . . . Sussex. [Oxford, by L. Lichfield], 1642. brs. MADAN 1068. STEELE 2296. LT, BR.

2680 A proclamation of His Majesties grace, . . . Willts. Oxford, 1642. brs. MADAN 1051. STEELE 2288. LT, BR.

2681 A proclamation of His Majesties grace, . . . to all seamen. [Oxford, by L. Lichfield], 1642. brs. MADAN 1074. STEELE 2302. LT, LPC, BR.

2682 A proclamation of His Majesties gracious resolution. Printed at Oxford by Leonard Lichfield, 1643. brs. MADAN 1339. STEELE 2416. O.

2683 His Majesties proclamation on the behalfe of Sir Ralph Hopton. Printed at Oxford by Leonard Lichfield, 1642[/3]. brs. MADAN 1273. STEELE 2388. L, O, LG, LPO, LVF.

2683A A proclamation proclaimed in London the ninth of June. [London], 1642. brs. L, LG; MH, Y.

2684 A proclamation proclaimed throughout the kingdome of Scotland. August 24th 1643. First printed at Edinborurgh [sic] reprinted at London, for P. Cole, 1643. 4°.* L, HH, DT; TU, WF, Y.

2685 A proclamation prohibiting all persons within . . . Oxford. [Oxford, by L. Lichfield], 1642/3. brs. MADAN 1167. STEELE 2344. O.

2686 A proclamation prohibiting free-quarter. Printed at Oxford, by Leonard Lichfield, 1643. brs. MADAN 1498. STEELE 2514. L, LPC.

2687 A proclamation prohibiting from henceforth all entercourse of trade. Printed at Oxford by Leonard Lichfield, 1643. brs. MADAN 1414. STEELE 2455. L, O, LG, LVF; CH, MH.

2688 —[Anr. ed.] [London, 1643.] brs. STEELE 2456. LS.

2689 A proclamation prohibiting the assessing . . . weekly taxes. Printed at Oxford by Leonard Lichfield, 1643. brs. MADAN 1311. STEELE 2404. O.

2690 —[Anr. ed.] —, 1643. brs. MADAN 1312. STEELE 2405. O; MH.

2691 A proclamation prohibiting the buying or disposing . . . lading . . . Sancta Clara. [Oxford, by L. Lfchield, 1642/3.] brs. MADAN 1158. STEELE 2338a. LT, O, LS, EC; MH, Y.

2692 A proclamation prohibiting the payment and receipt . . . of customes. [Oxford, by L. Lichfield], 1642. brs. MADAN 1129. STEELE 2326. O, LVF, EN; Y.

2693 —[Anr. ed.] [London, 1642.] brs. STEELE 2327. LT, O, LG, LPC, OC; MH, Y.

2694 A proclamation prohibiting the payment and receipt of tonnage. [Oxford, by L. Lichfield], 1642. brs. MADAN 1130. STEELE 2325a. O.

2695 A proclamation requiring all His Majesties tenants. [Oxford, by L. Linchfield], 1642/3. brs. MADAN 1182. STEELE 2347. O.

2696 Entry cancelled.

2697 A proclamation, requiring the aid and assistance. Reprinted at Oxford by Leonard Lichfield, 1642. 4°.* MADAN 1024. L, O, DT; CH, CLC, CSS, Y.

2698 —[Anr. ed.] Cambridge, R. Daniel, 1642. 4°.* OP.

2699 His Majesties proclamation to all the inhabitants of his counties of Oxford. [*Oxford, by L. Lichfield*], 1642. brs. MADAN 1116. STEELE 2319. O, BR.

2700 A proclamation to declare, the procez of green waxe. *Printed at Oxford by Leonard Lichfield*, 1643. brs. MADAN 1471. STEELE 2500. O, LPC; MH.

2701 A proclamation to give assurance unto all His Majesties subjects in the islands and continent of America. [*Oxford, by L. Lichfield*], 1643. brs. MADAN 1493. STEELE 2512. O.

2702 A proclamation to informe all our loving subjects *York, by Robert Barker and by the assigns of John Bill*, 1642. fol.* STEELE 2194. LPC.

2703 —[Anr. ed.] *Imprinted first at York, and now reprinted at London*, 1642. brs. STEELE 2195. LT, O, LPC, LG, OC; MH.

2704 —[Anr. ed.] *By A. W. for R. Lownds*, 1642. 4°.* STEELE 2196. LT, O.

2705 A proclamation to prorogue the Assembly. *Bristol, by R Barker and J. Bill*, 1644. brs. STEELE 2585. O.

2706 —[Anr. ed.] *Printed at Oxford by Leonard Lichfield*, 1644. brs. MADAN 1681. STEELE 2586. L, LPC, LVF.

2707 A proclamation to restrain all trade or commerce with . . . London. *Printed at Oxford by Leonard Lichfield*, 1643. fol.* MADAN 1480. STEELE 2502. LT, O, LG; CH.

2708 A proclamation touching the adjourning of part of Hilary terme. [*Oxford*], 1642. fol.* MADAN 1140. STEELE 2336. LT, O; Y.

2709 —[Anr. ed.] [*London*, 1642.] brs. MADAN 1140n. STEELE 2337. L, O, CJ, CT, LS; MH, Y.

2710 A proclamation touching the adjournment . . . Easter terme. *Printed at Oxford by Leonard Lichfield*, 1643. brs. MADAN 1303. STEELE 2400. O, LS, LVF.

2711 A proclamation touching the adjournement . . . Trinity terme. *Printed at Oxford by Leonard Lichfield*, 1643. brs. MADAN 1357. STEELE 2426. O, CT.

2712 A proclamation touching the counterfeit Great Seale. *Printed at Oxford by Leonard Lichfield*, 1643. brs. MADAN 1494. STEELE 2511. O, LVF.

2713 A proclamation touching the excise layd. *Printed at Oxford by Leonard Lichfield*, 1644. brs. MADAN 1616. STEELE 2559. O, OQ, LVF.

2714 A proclamation touching the lodgers in the vniversity. *Printed at Oxford, by Leonard Lichfield*, 1643. brs. MADAN 1461. STEELE 2491. LPC.

2715 A proclamation touching the new Seale. *Printed at Oxford by Leonard Lichfield*, 1643[/4]. fol.* MADAN 1513. STEELE 2523. L, O, OCC.

2716 A proclamation warning all His Majesties good subjects. *Printed at Oxford by Leonard Lichfield*, 1643. fol.* MADAN 1387. STEELE 2440. LT, O, LVF; MH.

2717 —[Anr. ed.] [*London*, 1643.] brs. MADAN 1388. STEELE 2441. L, LPC, LS.

2718 His Majesties profession and addition. *By Robert Barker and by the assigns of John Bill*, 1641[2]. brs. STEELE 1940. LT.

2719 His Majesties proposition sent to the two Houses. *Oxford, by Leonard Lichfield*, 1645. 4°.* MADAN 1829. LT, C, CT; WF, Y.

2720 —[Anr. ed.] —, 1645. 4°.* MADAN 1831. LT, O; MH.

2721 His Majesties propositions, (for coming to London). *For R. Smithurst*, 1648. 4°.* OC, YM.

2722 His Maiesties propositions for peace, and the cessation. *Oxford, by L. L.*, 1642. 4°.* MADAN 1102. LT, O, HH; CSS, MH, Y.

2723 Propositions for peace, propovnded by the kings. [*London*], June 28. *for William Arding*, 1642. 4°.* LT, O, HH; WF.

2724 —[Anr. ed.] *By T. F. for N. R. June 28*, 1642. 4°.* CT, EC, HH; MIU, Y.

2725 —[Anr. ed.] *For Henry Seymour, Septem. 27*, 1642. 4°.* LT; MH.

2726 Propositions from the Kings Majesty . . . Novem. 26, and Novem. 27. 1647. *By Robert Ibbitson*, 1647. 4°.* LT, O, HH; CLC, MH, TU, WF, Y.

2727 Propositions from the Kings Most Excellent Majesty. *For Henry Fowles*, 1642. 4°.* LT.

2728 His Majesties propositions sent yesterday. [*London*], *by Robert Ibbitson*, 1648. 4°.* LT, HH, DT; CH, MH.

2729 His Majesties propositions to his loyall and faithfull subjects. *December 28. 1646. London, for William Reynor*, 1646. 4°.* LT, DT.

2730 His Majesties propositions to Sir John Hotham. *July 15. London for Edward Iohnson*, [1642]. 4°.* LT, O, YM; MH, Y.

2731 The Kings Majesties propositions to the Earle of Pembroke. *For Edward Horton*, 1647. 4°.* LT, DT; WF, Y.

2732 The Kings Maiesties propositions to the gentry and commonalty of Nottingham. *Septemb. 9. for I. Rider*, 1642. 4°.* LT; Y.

2733 The Kings Majesties propositions to the Lords and Commons, concerning. [*London*], *Febr. 22. printed*, 1647. 4°.* LT, DT; NU.

2734 The Kings Majesties propositions to the states of Scotland. *For John Horton*, 1647. 4°.* LT, DT.

2735 Psalterium Carolinum. Entry cancelled. *See* Stanley Thomas.

2736 His Majesties qvaeres to the Scots commissioners. *For Edward Husband, January 23. 1646[7]*. 4°.* LT, C; CH, MH, NU, TU, WF, Y.

2737 His Majesties queries upon the remonstrance. *For H. B.*, 1648. 4°.* LT, C, CT, OC, EN; WF.

2738 His Maiesties reason vvhy he cannot . . . consent to abolish the Episcopall government. *By William Wilson*, 1648. 4°.* LT, O, CT, EN, DT; CH, CU, MH, NU, WF, Y.

2739 —[Anr. ed.] *For Abel Roper*, 1660[1]. 4°.* LT, O, C, OC, HH; CLC, CU, MH, NU, WF, Y.

2740 His Majesties reasons against the pretended jurisdiction of the High Court of Justice. [*London*], *printed*, 1648[9]. brs. STEELE 2822. LT, O, LS, HH; MIU, WF.

2741 The Kings Majesties remonstrance to his subjects of England. *By J. C. for G. Horton*, 1647. 4°.* LT; CLC, CN, MH.

2742 His Majesties reply, to the answer of both Houses. *For J. Wright, Septemb. 9, 1642.* 4°.* O.

2743 His Majesties resolvtion, and instructions to his commissioners of array. *York: by Robert Barker; and now reprinted at London for T.S. Septemb. 16, 1642.* 4°.* L, CCA; CH, CSS, MH, WF, Y.

2743A The Kings Maiesties resolution and intention concerning his loyal subjects. *[London], 1648.* 4°.* LT; MH, Y.

2744 The Kings Majesties resolution and the Parliaments determination. *By B, Alsop, sold by Henry Walker, 1641.* 4°.* L, O, C, CCA, HH; CH, MH, TU, WF, Y.

2744A —[Anr. ed.] *By B. Alsop, 1641.* 4°.* CT; MH.

2744B The Kings resolution concerning his coming from Banbury. *For Tho. Watson and J. Greene, Octob. 25, 1642.* 4°.* LT, YM; CSS, MH.

2745 The Kings Maiesties resolvtion concerning his marching. *By T. Fawcet, for R. C., Nov. 1, 1642.* 4°. MADAN 1050. LT, O.

2746 The Kings Maiesties resolution concerning Hvll. *For J. Horton, 1642. June 4.* 4°.* O, OL, YM, EN, DT.

2746A —[Anr. ed.] *By T. F. for F. S., 1642.* 4°.* OC.

2747 The King's resolvtion, concerning Portsmouth. *For T. Rider, Aug. 13, 1642.* 4°.* LT, BR.

2748 The Kings Maiesties resolvtion concerning Robert Earle of Warwick. *[n.p.], for J. Smith. July 12, 1642.* 4°.* LT, O, SC; CSS, MIU.

2748A —[Anr. ed.] *—, July 11, 1642.* 4°.* OC.

2749 His Maiesties resolution, concerning some great and weighty affairs. *For John Webb, 1642.* 4°.* LT, YM; MH, WF, Y.

2750 His Maiesties resolution, concerning the city of London. *For I. H. and T. R. Iuly 2, 1642.* 4°.* LT, O, CT, LG, EC.

2751 May the 16. 1642. His Majesties resolution concerning the establishment. *[London], for I. Tomson and A. Coe, 1642.* 4°.* OC, YM, HH; NU, WF.

2752 May the 17, 1642. His Majesties resolution concerning the establishment. *Yorke, London reprinted, I. Tomson and A. Coe, 1642.* 4°.* HH.

2752A —[Anr. ed.] *Dublin, reprinted 1642.* 4°.* L.

2753 King Charles his resolution concerning the government. *Printed at London, 1641.* 4°.* LT, O, LVF, MR; CH, MBP, NU, WF, Y.

2754 The Kings Majesties resolution concerning the lord major of London. *For I. Smith. July 28, [1642].* 4°.* O, LG, HH.

2754A His Majesties resolution concerning the magazine in the Tower. *[London], for J. Smith, July 14, 1642.* 4°.* LT, BR; CLC, MH, WF, Y.

2755 The King's Majesties resolution concerning the Parliaments last petition. *For John Rider, 1642.* 4°.* C, SP; MH.

2756 His Majesties resolution concerning the setting up his standard at Nottingham. *For J. Hanscott, August 18, 1642.* 4°.* LT, HH; WF, Y.

2757 —[Anr. ed.] *[n.p.], for Iohn Iackson. August 18, 1642.* 4°.* LT, HH, YM.

2758 —[Anr. ed.] *[n.p.], for I. Thompson and A. Coe, June 18, 1642.* 4°.* LT, O, OC, HH; MH, WF.

2759 His Maiesties resolution concerning the setting up of his standard neere Newcastle. *For I. H. and T. Rider, Iuly 7, 1642.* 4°.* LT.

2760 The Kings Maiesties resolution concerning York-shire. *For J. Horton, 1642. May 26.* 4°.* O, EC, YM.

2761 Right trusty and entirely beloved cousin . . . third day of April, 1646. *Imprinted at Dublin, by VVilliam Bladen, 1646.* brs. O.

2762 His Maiesties royall and last declaration. *Oxford, by Leonard Lichfield, 1642.* 4°.* MADAN 1282. O, C; CH, NU, TU, WF, Y.

2763 His Maiesties royall declaration and protestation to all his loving subjects. *Oxford, Leonard Lichfield, [1642?].* 4°.* C, HH; CSS, TU, WF, Y.

2764 The royall legacies . . . paraphrase upon His Majesties . . . speech. *[London], printed, 1649.* 4°.* LT, O, C, EN, CH, CU, MH, NU, WF, Y.

2765 A royall message. *For John Greensmith, 1641.* 4°.* LT, EC; WF.

2765A The royall missive to the Prince of Wales. *Caen, by Clavde Le Blanc, 1660.* 4°.* CH.

2766 A royall protestation. *By T. F. for I. Horton. Iuly 28, 1642.* 4°.* LT, CT, YM; MH.

2767 His Maiesties royall protestations. *For William Gay, 1642.* 4°.* LT, O, HH, EN, DT; CN, MH, NU.

2768 His Majesties second message sent. *York, by Robert Barker, and by the assigns of John Bill, 1642.* brs. STEELE 2095. YM, HH; WF.

2769 —[Anr. ed.] *Imprinted at London, by Robert Barker and by the assignes of John Bill, 1642.* brs. STEELE 2096. L, O, CT, LG, LS; Y.

2770 —[Anr. ed.] *Printed at Yorke by Robert Barker and by the assigns of John Bill. And now printed at London for I. F., 1642.* brs. STEELE 2098. L, LL, LS, OP, CT.

2771 The severall copies of the Kings letters. *For Jane Coe, 1646.* 4°.* LT, O, C, OC, HH; CH, MH, NN, WF, Y.

2772 His Maiesties speciall command . . . To suppresse . . . assemblies. *For John Thomas, 1641.* 4°.* LT, O, LG; CH, MH, NU.

2773 Charles R. The Kings Majesties speciall direction. *Printed at Oxford by Leonard Lichfield, 1643.* brs. MADAN 1372. STEELE 2433. O; WF.

2774 The Kings Majesties speech . . . 17 August 1641. *Edinburgh, R & J Bryson, [1641?].* brs. ALDIS 997. STEELE 3 p. 1730. ES, FSF.

2775 His Majesties speech and protestation . . . 19th of September, 1642. *Shrewsbury, by R. Barker and the assigns of J. Bill, 1642.* brs. STEELE 2263. O, HH.

2776 —[Anr. ed.] *Imprinted at London: by Robert Barker and by the assigns of John Bill, 1642.* 4°. STEELE 2264. LT, O, C, SS, EN; CH, CSS, TU, WF, Y.

2776A —[Anr. ed.] *—, 1642.* brs. L.

2777 His Ma.ties speech, & the Queenes speech, concerning. *[n.p.], printed, 1641.* brs. STEELE 1870. L; MH.

2778 The Kings Maiesties speech, as it was delivered the second of November. *First printed at Oxford, and now reprinted at London, 1642. Novemb. 9. 4°.* MADAN 1056. LT, O, LL, CJ, HH; CH, MH, NU, TU, WF, Y.

2779 The Kings Majesties speech at Carisbrook Castle concerning the Prince of Wales. *For G. Wharton, 1648. 4°.* LT, AN, DT.

2780 His Majesties speech at Leicester. *Imprinted at Yorke, and re-printed at London, by Alice Norton, 1642.* brs. STEELE 2228. LT, LS, OC, EC; CH, Y.

2781 —[Anr. ed.] —, *1642.* brs. STEELE 2229. L, O, LG; MH.

2782 His Majesties speech at Shrewsbury. *For H. S., 1642.* brs. STEELE 2269. LT, LG, LS, OC, EC; CH.

2783 A speech delivered by . . . in the Convocation House at Oxford. *Printed at Oxford by Leonard Lichfield, 1643. 4°.* MADAN 1170. LT, O, OC, SP, EN; CH, CLC, WF.

2784 His Majesties speech delivered the twenty second of Ianuary, 1643. *Printed at Oxford, by Leonard Lichfield, 1643[4]. 4°.* MADAN 1519. LT, O, C, EN, DT; CH, CN, MH, TU, WF, Y.

2785 —[Anr. ed.] *Bristoll, by Robert Barker, and John Bill, 1643[/4]. 4°.* MADAN 1522. O.

2786 His Majesties speech delivered to both Houses . . . 14th of December 1641. *By Robert Barker and the assignes of John Bill, 1641. 4°.* LT, O, HH, EN, DT; CH, MH, TU, WF, Y.

2787 The Kings Majesties speech delivered to the commissioners . . . 20 Sept. 1648. *For R. Smithurst, 1648. 4°.* LT, EN; MH.

2788 His Majesties speech in the House of Commons 4 Ianuarii 1641. *By Robert Barker: and by the assignes of John Bill, 1641[2]. 4°.* LT, O, C, HH; CH, MH, NU, TU, WF, Y.

2788A — —[Anr. ed.] *By Robert Barker, 1642. 4°.* C, HH, D; MH.

2789 The Kings Maiesties speech in the House of Lords . . . 14 day of Decemb. 1641. *For John Greensmith, 1641. 4°.* LT, O, EC; CH, CN, MH, WF, Y.

2790 The Kings Maiesties speech, made in the House of Peers . . . May the 1. 1641. *Printed, 1649.* brs. STEELE 1843. LT, LPR, HH.

2791 The King his Maiesties speech made . . . November the 25, 1641. *For W. R., 1641. 4°.* L, O, HH; CLC.

2791A His Majesties speech made to the gentlemen . . . of Sommerset. *Bristoll, by Robert Barker & John Bill, 1644. 4°.* L, LG.

2792 King Charls his speech made upon the scaffold. *For Peter Cole, 1649. 4°.* LT, O, C, EN, DT; CH, CU, MH, NU, WF, Y.

2792A The speech of our most gracious soveraigne. *[London], for Thomas Bankes, 1641. 4°.* L; CLC, MH.

2792B His Majesties speech on the scaffold. *For R. W. [1649.] 4°.* CLC, MH, WF.

2793 The Kings Maiesties speech on the 2. day of December, 1641. *For John Greensmith, 1641. 4°.* LT, C, SP, YM; MB, WF, Y.

2794 His Majesties speech read in the Commons . . . December the 8th 1641. *By Robert Barker; and by the assigns of John Bill, 1641. 4°.* CH, TU.

2795 His royall Maiesties speech: spoken in the High Court of Parliament . . . December the 2. 1641 *[London], by B. Alsop, 1641. 4°.* LT; MH.

2796 His Majesties speech spoken to the mayor, aldermen . . . of Oxford. *Printed at Oxford by Leonard Lichfield, 1643. 4°.* MADAN 1181. LT, O, CM, CT; CH, MH, WF, Y.

2797 His Majesties speech to both Houses . . . June 22, 1641. *[London, 1641?] 4°.* CH, MBP.

2797A His Majesties speech to both Houses, . . . July the 5th 1641. *Printed, 1641. 4°.* MH, WF, Y.

2798 His Majesties speech, to both Houses . . . December the second. 1641. *By Robert Barker and the assignes of John Bill, 1641. 4°.* LT, O, OC, HH; CH, CN, TU, WF, Y.

2799 The Kings Maiesties speech to the commissioners at Nottingham . . . 13 of February. *For E. H., February 19, 1647. 4°.* LT, DT; WF, Y.

2800 His Maiesties speech, to the committee the 9th March 1641. *For John Wright and I. Franke, 1641[/2]. 4°.* O, C, CCA, HH; CH, TU, Y.

2801 —[Anr. ed.] *Imprinted at London, by Robert Barker and by the assignes of John Bill, 1641[2].* brs. STEELE 2017. L, O, CT, HH; MH, Y.

2801A His Majesties speech to the gentlemen clergy of . . . Oxon. *[London? 1742.]* brs. CT.

2802 His Majesties speech to the gentlemen of Yorkshire. *York: by Robert Barker: and by the assignes of John Bill, 1642. 4°.* O, C, CF, HH, YM; CH, MH, Y.

2803 —[Anr. ed.] *Printed at York by Robert Barker and reprinted at London by A. Norton, August 8, 1642. 4°.* L, LL, HH, DT; BN, CLC, MH, NN, TU, WF.

2804 —[Anr. ed.] *Printed at Yorke by Robert Barker, and reprinted at London for Tho. Banks. and Will. Ley, 1642. 4°.* LT, O, CCC, OP; CH, CSS, MH, WF, Y.

2805 His Majesties speech to the gentry of the county of York . . . 12 of May 1642. *York, by Robert Barker, and by the assignes of John Bill, 1642.* brs. STEELE 2120. CF, YM.

2805A —[Anr. ed.] *Printed at Yorke, and now reprinted at London by Alice Norton, for Humphrey Tuckey, 1642.* brs. STEELE 2121. LT, LS, LCL, LSC, OP; CH, MBP, Y.

2806 —[Anr. ed.] *16 May, 1642.* brs. STEELE 2122. L, LS, CCA, HH.

2807 —[Anr. ed.] *For John Sweeting, 1642.* brs. STEELE 2124. L.

2808 —[Anr. ed.] *For Edward Blackmore, 1642. 4°.* LT, O, CJ, HH; BN, CH, LC, MH, TU, Y.

2808A —[Anr. ed.] *For John Richman, 1642. 4°.* L; MH.

2809 The Kings Maiesties speech to the Hon. House of Parliament. *For John Greensmith, 1641. 4°.* LT, C.

2810 His Majesties speech to the inhabitants of Denbigh . . . 27 Septemb. 1642. *For R. L., 1642. 4°.* LT, O, C, EN, DT; BN, CH, MH, TU, WF, Y.

2811 His Maiesties speech to the knights, gentlemen, and freeholders of . . . Lincoln. *Imprinted at York by Robert Barker: and by the assignes of John Bill, 1642.* brs. O, OP.

2812 His Majesties speech to the Lords & Commons . . . Aprill 16. 1644. *Printed at Oxford, by Leonard Lichfield, 1644. 4°.* MADAN 1612. LT, O, LCL, HH; CH, LC, TU, Y.

2813　—[Anr. ed.] "April 26" —, 1644. 4°.* MADAN 1613. L, O, CJ, EC; CH, CLC, TU, WF.

2814　His Majesties speech to the Lords for the raising of forces . . . June 29. *For I. H. and T. R., July 5, 1642.* 4°.* L, O, HH, DT; MH, Y.

2815　His Majesties speech to the members . . . the seventh of February, 1643. [*Bristol, printed by John Barker and John Bill*], Feb., 1643/4. 4°.* MADAN 1535. O.

2816　His Majesties speech to the peers of Scotland. *For Thomas Burdet,* 1644. 4°.* LT, C, OC, DT; Y.

2817　The Kings Majesties speech to the sixe heads. [*London*], *Printed 20 July,* 1641. brs. STEELE 1869. L, CT; MH, MHS, Y.

2818　His Majesties speech: with Mr. Speakers speech . . . 22 June 1641. [*London,* 1641.] brs. STEELE 1864. L, O.

2819　The Kings Maiesties speeches in this great and happy Parliament . . . Novemb. 3 1640. [*London*], *printed,* 1641. 4°.* L, O, CT; CH, MH, TU, WF, Y.

2820　The speeches of the Kings most excellent Majesty in this great court of Parliament. [*London*], *printed,* 1641. 4°.* CSS, MH, WF, Y.

2820A　Suspiria regia, or, verses. [*London?* 1682.] brs. CH.

2821　His Majestie taking into his princely consideration. *Imprinted at London, by Robert Barker: and by the assigns of John Bill,* 1641. brs. STEELE 1911. LT, OQ.

2822　—[Anr. ed.] *Oxford, by Leonard Lichfield,* 1643. cap., brs. MADAN 1345. STEELE 2418. O.

2823　That the mouthes of all schismaticall and seditious persons may be stopped, . . . His Maiesties late protestation. [*London*], *printed,* 1648. brs. MADAN 1995. LT.

2824　Three proclamations by. *Imprinted first at Yorke, and now re-printed at London by F. L. for Mary Thomas.* 1642. *July, the ninteh* [*sic*]. 4°.* LT, O, CM, LG, EC; CH, MH, TU, WF, Y.

2825　Three speeches made by. *For Rich. Johnson,* [1642]. 4°.* LT, O, C, OC, HH; BN, CH, MH, WF, Y.

2826　Charles by the grace of God . . . to our lovits [blank] messengers. [*Edinburgh,* 1643.] brs. LT, CT, FSF; WF, Y.

2827　Charles, by the grace of God, . . . to our lovits [blank] our lion king at arms. [*n.p.,* 1646.] brs. LT.

2828　By the king. To our trusty and welbeloved high shiriffe of . . . York. *Imprinted at Yorke by Robert Barker, and now reprinted at London, to be sold by G. B.,* 1642. brs. LT, O, EC, HH.

2829　—[Anr. ed.] *Imprinted at Yorke by Robert Barker, and now reprinted at London and are to be sold by T. P.,* 1642. brs. O.

2829A　—[Anr. ed.] *Yorke, by Robert Barker, and now reprinted at London for J. W. I.,* 1642. brs. CT.

2830　By the king. To our trusty and welbeloved our colonells. [*Oxford, by L. Lichfield*], 1642/3. brs. MADAN 1186. STEELE 2349. O, CT.

2831　—[Anr. ed.] *Printed at Oxford by Leonard Lichfield,* 1642[/3]. brs. MADAN 1199. STEELE 2350. LT, O, LG, HH; Y.

2832　Charles R. To our trustie and welbeloved, the lord major . . . of London. *Imprinted at London, by Robert Barker: and by the assigns of John Bill,* 1642. brs. STEELE 2175. LT, O, LPR, EC, HH; CH, MH, MIU, Y.

2833　—[Anr. ed.] *For T. A.,* 1642. brs. STEELE 2177. HH.

2834　—[Anr. ed.] [*n.p.*], 1642. brs. STEELE 2178. L, O, CJ.

2835　To the inhabitants of the county of Cornwall, a letter of thanks . . . Sept. 10. 1643. [*London,* 165–?] brs. CH.

2836　The trve copie of His Maiesties gracious pardon. *First printed at Oxford, and now re-printed at London,* 1642[/3]. 4°.* MADAN 1227. LT, O, LCL, DT; MH, Y.

2837　A true copy of His Majesties letter to the late-sitting Generall Assembly. *By L. Norton and J. Field for C. A. August 30, 1642.* 4°.* LT, O, CCA, EC, HH; CH, MH, NU, WF, Y.

2838　A true copy of His Maiesties message sent. [*London,* 1647.] brs. STEELE 2692. LT; MH.

2839　A true copie of the commission under the Great Seal. *For F. C.,* [1643]. MADAN 1379. O, LG, E, EN; NN.

2840　Munday 29th January, 1648. A true relation of the king's speech to the Lady Elizabeth. [*London,* 1649.] brs. LT, LS, CT; WF.

2841　Trusty and wel-beloved . . . 23 January 1642[3]. *Shrewsbury,* 1642[3]. cap., brs. STEELE 2353. O, LPC.

2842　—*Yorke, by Robert Barker and by the assigns of John Bill,* 1642. brs. STEELE 2105. O; MH.

2843　—*For J. B.,* 1642. brs. STEELE 2106. L.

2844　—*Sold by T. P.,* 1642. brs. STEELE 2107. O.

2845　—*Sold by G. B.,* 1642. brs. STEELE 2108. LT, O, LS, HH.

2846　—[1642.] brs. STEELE 2109. L.

2847　—14. day of February, 1643. [*London,* 1643/4.] brs. O.

2848　Charles R. Trusty and well-beloved We greet you well . . . eighteenth day of May. 1643. [*London,* 1643.] brs. MADAN 1356. STEELE 2425. O, OP.

2849　Trusty. Whereas the members of both Houses. [*Oxford, L. Lichfield,* 1644.] brs. STEELE 2529. O, LPR.

2849A　His Majesties two declarations, one to the knights. *Yorke,* 1642. 4°.* CT.

2850　Two declarations. The first, from. *For R. Rishton,* 1647. 4°.* LT, DT; MIU, TU, WF.

2851　Two letters of His Sacred Maiesty, one in vindication. *Oxford, by Leonard Lichfield,* 1645. 4°.* MADAN 1808. LT, C, OC, EC; CH, Y.

2852　Two letters of . . . left upon the table. [*London*], *for Mathew Walbancke,* 1647. 4°.* C, CT, MR; BN, CH, MH, TU, WF, Y.

2853　His Majesties two letters one to the vice-chancellour . . . of Oxford. *For Richard Lownds, August 3, 1642.* 4°.* MADAN 1016. LT, O, CJ, EC, HH; CH, MH, TU, WF, Y.

2854　Two messages from His Maiesty to both Howses . . . 28 of April 1642. *For John Wright,* 1642. 4°.* L, O, LCL, YM; CN, MH, WF.

2855　Two messages from the Kings Majestie. *Oxford, by Leonard Lichfield,* 1642[/3]. 4°.* MADAN 1271. L, O, C, OC, HH; CH, MH, TU, WF, Y.

2856 His Maiesties two messages to both Houses of Parliament, concerning his chaplains. [*London*, 1647.] cap., 4°.* LT, C, DT; MH, Y.

2857 Two proclamations by the king. His Majesties proclamation. *Printed at York and re-printed at London, by A. N. for Richard Lownds*, 1642. 4°.* LT, OC, CT, EC, HH; CH, MH, TU, WF, Y.

2858 Two proclamations by the king. The first declaring. *Printed at Yorke, reprinted* [*London*], *for Iohn Thomas*, 1642. 4°.* LT, OC, EC, YM, HH; MH, MIU, WF, Y.

2859 Two proclamations from. *First printed by His Majesties printers, and new* [*sic*] *reprinted at London for William Gay, August 30, 1642.* 4°.* EC; CSS, MIU, WF.

2860 His Maiesties two proclamations to the counties of Southampton and Dorset. *Oxford, printed*, 1642. 4°.* MADAN 1105. LT, O, CT, EN, DT; CH, CLC, MH, WF, Y.

2861 Tvvo severall copies: the one being His Majestie's declaration. *Printed at London, for G. B. Aug. 14, 1644.* 4°.* LT, O, C, CT, DT; CLC, MH, NU, WF, Y.

2862 Two speeches delivered by His Maiesty. *Oxford, by Leonard Lichfield*, 1643[/4]. 4°.* MADAN 1534. O, C; MH, TU, Y.

2863 Two speeches delivered by the Kings most excellent Majestie at Oxford. *First printed at Oxford by Leonard Lichfield, and reprinted at London for Iohn Turner*, [1642]. 4°. MADAN 1126. LT, O, C, OC, DT; CH, MH, VC, WF, Y.

2864 —[Anr. ed.] *Printed at York by Stephen Bulkley*, 1642. 4°.* MADAN 1126n. CF, YM.

2865 His Majesties two speeches: one to the knights . . . of Nottingham. 1641. 4°. EN.

2866 —[Anr. ed.] *By Robert Barker and by the assignes of John Bill*, 1642. 4°.* O, LG, LL, HH, DT; BN, CH, CSS, MBP, MH, TU.

2867 —[Anr. ed.] *For F. N. and L. J.*, 1642. 4°.* L, O, HH; MH, WF, Y.

2868 —[Anr. ed.] *For John Wright, Iuly 18, 1642.* 4°.* CH, CSS, MH.

2869 —[Anr. ed.] *For Thomas Bankes*, 1642. 4°.* L, O, CJ, OC; CSS, LC, MH, Y.

2870 Two speeches spoken by. [*London*], *by B. A., Feb. 11,* [*1647*]. 4°.* LT, CS, HH; MH.

2871 Two speeches, the first. *January 2,* [*London*], *for I. H. and W. Whightfield*, 1643. 4°.* MADAN 1157. LT, O, DT; CLC, WF.

2872 —[Anr. ed.] *For F. I. Iune the 9, 1647.* 4°.* LT, CDC, DT.

2873 His Maiesties vltimate ansvvers to the papers. *For Richard Lowndes*, 1648. 4°.* LT, O, C, HH, E; CH, CLC, MH, WF, Y.

2874 We are so highly sensible of the extra. *Printed at Oxford, by Leonard Lichfield*, 1643. brs. STEELE 2474. L; WF.

2875 We take into our princely consideration, that. *Reprinted by F. L. for M Thomas, 9 July, 1642.* cap., 4°. STEELE 2210. LT.

2876 Whereas divers lewd and wicked persons. *Imprinted at London, by Robert Barker: and by the assignes of John Bill*, 1641[2]. brs. STEELE 1915. LT, O, CT, LG, LS; Y.

2877 Octob. 16. 1642. Whereas the Kings most Excellent Majesty was graciously pleased. *Printed at Oxford by Leonard Lichfield*, [1643?]. brs. MADAN 1506. STEELE 2666. O; Y.

2878 By the King. Whereas this country. [*Oxford, by Leonard Lichfield*], 1642. brs. MADAN 1090. STEELE 2311. O; MIU.

2879 —[Anr. ed.] [*London*, 1642.] brs. STEELE 2312. LT, O, HH, LG, EC; WF.

2880 By the King, whereas, upon summons from vs, divers. *Imprinted at York, by Robert Barker and by the assigns of John Bill*, 1642. brs. STEELE 2134. L, LPR, YM.

2881 —[Anr. ed.] *Imprinted at York, and reprinted at London, for Edward Blackmore*, 1642. brs. STEELE 2135. LT; WF.

2882 —[Anr. ed.] *Yorke, by Robert Barker, and by the asignes of John Bill*, 1642. *London, by A. N. for I. T.* brs. STEELE 2136. L, LS; MH, Y.

2883 Charles . . . Whereas we have taken into our . . . 9 September . . . *Dublin, W. Bladen*, 1642. cap., fol.* STEELE 2p 372. DIXP 76. DPR.

2884 Whosoever will serve the king as. [*Oxford, by Leonard Lichfield*, 1642.] brs. MADAN 1101. STEELE 2316. L.

CHARLES II.

2885 An abstract of a charter granted by His Majesty . . . July 1, 1678. *J. Playford*, 1683. fol.* LL; MH.

2885A —[Anr. ed.] *For Arthur Tooke* [1683]. brs. LL, OC.

2886 An abstract of the patents granted by His Majesty. *Delivered gratis by Henry Brome, London*, [1678]. brs. OC.

2887 An account of what His Majesty said. *Printed by the assigns of John Bill deceased: and by Henry Hills, and Thomas Newcomb*, 1684. brs. SP; CLC, MH.

2888 An additional proclamation concerning coffee-houses. *By the assigns of John Bill and Christopher Barker*, 1675/6. brs. STEELE 3625. L, O, C, MC, DT; CH, MH.

2889 His Highnesse the Prince of Wales his answer to the Earle of Warwicks summons. [*London*], *printed*, 1648. cap., 4°.* LT, O, DT; CH, MH, Y.

2890 The answers commanded by. colop: *By the assigns of John Bill, Thomas Newcomb, and Henry Hills*, 1681. cap., fol.* L, O, C, CT, EN; CH, CN, MH, NC, WF, Y.

2890A —[Anr. ed.] *Edinburgh, re-printed by the heir of Andrew Anderson*, 1681. fol.* PU.

2890B —[Anr. ed.] colop: *Dublin, re-printed by Benjamin Took and John Crook, to be sold by Mary Crook and Andrew Crook*, 1681. cap., fol.* DIX 187. DN.

2890C —[Anr. ed.] [*London*] *reprinted for the use of the managers of the Bank of England* [1700?] brs. L.

2890D The answeres of His Highness the Prince of Wales to a loose paper. [*n.p.*, 1648]. 4°.* DT.

2891 His Majestie's approval of the judges' report. 1678/9. brs. LL.

2892 Articles of alliance and commerce, between . . . Charles II . . . and . . . Christian V. *In the Savoy, by the assigns of John Bill, and Christopher Barker*, 1671/2. 4°.* L, O, LL; MIU, MM.

2893 The articles of alliance, between England & Spain. *Printed*, 1680. fol.* LT, HH; CH, MH, WF, Y.

2893A Articles of peace & alliance between . . . Charles II . . . and King of Sweden. *By John Bill and Christopher Barker*, 1662. 4°.* WF, Y.

2894 Articles of peace and alliance between . . . Charles II, . . . and . . . Frederick III. *By the assigns of John Bill and Christopher Barker*, 1667. 4°.* O, CT, OC, LL, DT; CH, CLC, MBA, V, Y.

2894A —[Anr. ed.] *Edinburgh*, 1667. 4°.* ALDIS 1829. EN.

2895 Articles of peace and alliance between . . . Charles II, . . . and . . . Lewis XIV. *By the assigns of John Bill and Christopher Barker*, 1667. 4°.* O, CT, OC, LL, DT; CH, LC, MH, WF, Y.

2896 Articles of peace & alliance between . . . Charles II, . . . and the . . . States General. *By John Bill and Christopher Barker*, 1662. 4°.* L, SC; HR, CH, NCL, RPJ, WF, Y.

2896A —[Anr. ed.] *Edinburgh, reprinted by E. Tyler*, 1663. 4°.* CT.

2897 Articles of peace & alliance, between . . . Charles II . . . States General . . . 21/31 day of July 1667. *In the Savoy, by the assigns of John Bill and Christopher Barker*, 1667. 80 pp. 4°. L, O, CT, OC, HH; HR, CH, LC, MH, RPJ, Y.

2898 —[Anr. ed.] —, 1667. 31 pp. 4°.* L, LL, DT; CH, CLC, WCL, WF.

2899 —[Anr. ed.] *Edinburgh, re-printed by Evan Tyler*, 1667. 4°.* ALDIS 1829. C, EN; CLC, MH, NU.

2900 Articles of peace and commerce between . . . Charles II, and . . . the Bashaw. *In the Savoy, by the assigns of John Bill, & Christopher Barker*, 1671/2. 4°.* O, DT; CH, MIU, WF.

2901 Articles of peace & commerce between . . . Charles II . . . , Halil Bashaw, . . . of Tripoli. *By the assigns of John Bill and Christopher Barker*, 1676. 4°.* L, CT; CH, Y.

2902 Articles of peace & commerce between . . . Charles II . . . , the Bashaw, . . . of Algiers. *By the assigns of John Bill and Christopher Barker*, 1677. 23 pp. 4°.* L, C, P; WF, Y.

2903 Articles of peace & commerce between . . . Charles II . . . , the Bashaw, . . . of Tripoli. *By the assigns of John Bill and Christopher Barker*, 1677. 12 pp. 4°.* L, P; CH, Y.

2904 Articles of peace & commerce between . . . Charles II . . . , the Bashaw, . . . of Algiers. *By the assigns of John Bill: and by Henry Hills, and Thomas Newcomb*, 1682. 4°.* L, C; CH, MH, NCL, WF, Y.

2904A —[Anr. ed.] *Edinburgh, re-printed* 1682. 4°.* ALDIS 2327. L.

2905 Articles of peace, between . . . Charles II . . . Netherlands. *By the assigns of John Bill and Christopher Barker*, 1673/4. 4°.* L, O, C, EN, DT; CH, MB, PL, WF, Y.

2906 Articles of peace, between . . . Charles II . . . States General. *Edinburgh, His Majesties printers*, 1674. fol.* ALDIS 2014. L, EN; CH, Y.

2907 Articles of peace between . . . , Charles the II . . . and the city and kingdom of Algiers. *By Thomas Mabb*, 1664. 4°.* L, O, CT, SC; MH, WF, Y.

2908 —[Anr. ed.] *Edinburgh, re-printed*, 1664. 4°.* EN.

2909 Articles of peace between . . . Charles II . . . and several Indian kings. *By John Bill, Christopher Barker, Thomas Newcomb and Henry Hills*, 1677. 4°.* L; CH, LC, PL, RPJ, WCL.

2909A Articles of peace between . . . Charles II . . . Tunis. *By the assigns of John Bill and Christopher Barker*, 1677. 4°.* L, P; Y.

2910 Articles of peace, commerce & alliance, between . . . Great Britain and Spain. *In the Savoy, by the assigns of John Bill and Christopher Barker*, 1667. 32 pp. 4°.* L, O, C, OC, DT; CH, WF, Y.

2911 —[Anr. ed.] —, 1667. 47 pp. 4°.* L, LL, OC, CS; HR, CH, MH.

2912 —[Anr. ed.] *Edinburgh, Tyler*, 1667. 4°.* ALDIS 1828. EN.

2913 Articles of peace . . . between England and France . . . 3 Nov. *Edinburgh, by Christopher Higgins*, 1655. 4°.* ALDIS 1504. EN; Y.

2914 Articles of peace concluded between . . . Algiers. *By John Bill and Christopher Barker*, 1662. 4°.* Y.

2915 Articuli confœderationis & commercii inter . . . Carolum II . . . et . . . Christianum V. *Excusum per assignatos Johannis Bill & Christophori Barker*, 1671/2. 4°.* L; CH.

2916 Articuli pacis & amicitiæ, inter . . . Carolum II . . . et . . . Ordines Generales. *Excudebant assignati Johannis Bill & Christophori Barker*, 1673/4. 4°.* L, O; CH.

2917 Articuli pacis & confœderationis . . . Carolum II . . . Fridericum III. 1661. 4°.* MIU.

2918 Articuli pacis & confœderationis inter . . . Carolum II . . . et . . . Ordines Generales. *Excusum per Johannem Bill & Christophorum Barker*, 1662. 4°.* L; HR, CH, MH, MIU, RPJ, Y.

2919 Articuli pacis & confœderationis inter . . . Carolum II . . . et . . . Ordines Generales. *Excusum per assignatos Johannis Bill & Christophori Barker*, 1667. 4°. L, O, CJ, CT; CH.

2920 At the court at Hampton Court, the thirteenth of June 1683. colop: *By the assigns of John Bill, and by Henry Hills and Thomas Newcomb*, 1683. brs. L, C; CH.

2921 At the court at Oxford, the sixt of October 1665. *Oxford, by L. Lichfield*, 1665. brs. MADAN 2685. STEELE 3441. O.

2922-4 Entries cancelled.

2925 —, January 2. 1671/2. —, 1671/2. 4°.* C; CH, CN.

2926 Entry cancelled.

2927 —, the eleventh of December, 1672. —, 1672. cap., fol.* CH.

2928 Entry cancelled.

2929 Aurea dicta. The king's gracious words. *By J. Grantham, for Walter Davis, and are to be sold by John Barksdale, in Cirencester*, 1681. 4°.* L, O, C, CS, HH; CH, MH, NU, WF, Y.

2930 The capitulations and articles of peace between the King of England and the Sultan of the Ottoman Empire. *Constantinople, Abraham Gabai chat nahat*, 1663. 4°. L, O, MR; CH.

2931 —[Anr. ed.] *For J. S.* 1679. 4°.* L, O; CH, LC, WF, Y.

2932   His Majesties charge to all the justices of the peace of the county of Middlesex . . . 25th day of February. [n.p., 1681.] brs. L, CS, CT; CH, MH, NC, Y.

2933   Charles . . . 21 July. [Thirsk.] By W. G. for assigns of J Bodington, [1661]. brs. STEELE 3314. L.

2934   Charles . . . observed the great plenty of fish, . . . 22 August. [Royal fishing.] By John Bill & Christopher Barker, 1661. brs. STEELE 3323. L, O, OQ, LPR.

2935   Charles the second, by the grace of God . . . 12 July [Lithuania]. By John Bill & Christopher Barker, 1661. brs. STEELE 3312. L.

2936   Charles the second, by the grace of God . . . 14 June. [Alrewas.] J. Playford, 1684. brs. STEELE 3759. L.

2937   A collection of His Majestie's gracious letters. By John Bill, 1660. 4°. LT, O, C, LCL, CT; CH, CN, MH, WF, Y.

2938   His Majesties commission concerning the reparation of . . . St. Paul. By John Bill and Christopher Barker, 1663. fol.* L, O, C, LG, HH.

2939   His Majesties commission for the rebuilding of the cathedral church of S. Paul. By the assigns of John Bill and Christopher Barker, 1674. fol.* L, LL, CS, HH, P; CH, TU, WF.

2940   A commission to . . . Richard lord viscount Ranelagh. [London] by Thomas Newcomb, 1673. CLC, WF.

2941   A conference between King Charles and the Marquis of Worcester. 1651. 4°. LW.

2942   Copies of two papers. [London, 1685.] brs. L, OC, CS, EC, MR; CH, MBP, MH, WF, Y.

2943   Copies of two papers written by. By Henry Hills, 1686. 11 pp. fol.* L, CS, MC, E, DT; CH, CN, MH, TU, WF, Y.

2944   —[Anr. ed.] By H. Hills, 1686. 14 pp. 4°.* O, C, OC, OCC, EN; CLC, MH, NC, WF, Y.

2945   —[Anr. ed.] Dublin, re-printed for Robert Thornton, 1686. 4°.* C; NU.

2946   —[Anr. ed.] Dvblin, reprinted by Jos. Ray, for Rob Thornton, 1686. 4°.* MBP, NU.

2946A —[Anr. ed.] By Henry Hills, 1687. brs. HH.

2947   The copy of a letter from His Highnesse . . . to the Speaker. [London, 1648.] brs. LT, O, CJ, LG, OC; MH, WF, Y.

2948   A copy of His Highnesse Prince Charles letter. By Robert Ibbitson, 1648. 4°.* LT, AN, DT; MH, WF, Y.

2949   A coppy of the kings letter. [Edinburgh], 1676. fol.* ALDIS 2074. EN, ES.

2950   His Majesties declaration . . . 22 February 1664[5]. By John Bill & Christopher Barker, 1664[5]. brs. STEELE 3408. L, LG, OQ.

2951   His Majesties declaration . . . 5 September 1666. In the Savoy, by the assigns of John Bill & Christopher Barker, 1667. brs. STEELE 3472. L, C, OQ, LG, LPC.

2952   His Majestie's declaration against the French. By John Bill and Christopher C. Barker, 1666. fol.* STEELE 3455. L, O, C, LG, LL; CH, CLC, WF, Y.

2952A —[Anr. ed.] Edinburgh, re-printed by E. Tyler, 1666. fol.* L.

2953   His Majesties declaration against the States Generall. In the Savoy, by the assigns of John Bill and Christopher Barker, 1671/2. fol. L, O, C, LL, HH; HR, CH, CN, MH, TU, WF, Y.

2954   —[Anr. ed.] Edinburgh, reprinted by Evan Tyler, 1672. 4°.* ALDIS 1942. CT, EN; NU.

2955   —[Anr. ed.] Reprinted at Dublin, by Benjamin Tooke, to be sold by Joseph Wilde, 1672. brs. STEELE 2, 822. DIX 143. DK, DPR.

2956   The declaration and resolution of His Highnesse the Prince of Wales, upon the death of his royall father. Edinburgh, by Evan Tyler, 1649. 4°.* ALDIS 1361 b. EN; CH, MH.

2957   The declaration and resolution of the King of Scotland to all his loving subjects. Imprinted at London, for R. W. May 7, 1649. 4°.* LT, DT; CN, MH, NU.

2958   A declaration by. Edinburgh, by Evan Tyler, 1650. 6 pp. 4°.* ALDIS 1399. O, HH, P, EN; CH, CN, NU, WF, Y.

2959   —[Anr. ed.] Edinburgh, by Evan Tyler, 1650. 14 pp. 4°.* ALDIS 1400. STEELE 2051. HH, E, EN.

2960   —[Anr. ed.] Edinburgh?], printed, 1650. [i.e. 1660). 4°.* ALDIS 1401. LT, OC, HH, EN; MH, MIU, NM, Y.

2960A —[Anr. ed.] According to the copie printed, 1651. 4°.* PL, WF.

2961   Prince Charles his declaration, commended to the publique. [n.p.], anno, 1648. 4°.* LT, O, SP; CH.

2962   Prince Charles his declaration concerning the citizens of London. For R. Wells, 1648. 4°.* LT, HH; CLC, MIU.

2963   His Majesties declaration concerning the province of East-New-Jersey. Edinburgh reprinted by the heir of Andrew Anderson, 1683. brs. ALDIS 2372. EN.

2964   His Majesties declaration for encouragement of seamen. By John Bill and Christopher Barker, 1664. brs. STEELE 3402. O, LPR, LS; CH, Y.

2965   His Majestie's declaration for enforcing a late order. By the assigns of John Bill and Christopher Barker, 1674/5. fol.* L, C, LL, HH; CH, CLC, MIU, WF, Y.

2965A —[Anr. ed.] Reprinted at Dublin by Benjamin Tooke, to be sold by Joseph Wilde, 1694. fol.* DIX 153. DK.

2966   Prince Charles his declaration for satisfaction . . . July 31, 1648. [London], printed, 1648. 4°.* LT, O, HH; CH, CN, MH, TU, Y.

2967   His Majestie's declaration for the dissolution of his late Privy-Council. By John Bill, Thomas Newcomb, and Henry Hills, 1679. fol.* L, C, LL, MR, HH; CH, MH, NP, TU, WF, Y.

2968   —[Anr. ed.] Reprinted Edinburgh, by the heir of Andrew Anderson, 1679. 4°.* ALDIS 2147. OP, EN; TU.

2969   —[Anr. ed.] Dublin, reprinted by Benjamin Tooke, and John Crook, to sold [sic] by Mary Crook, 1679. 4°.* C.

2970   A declaration from . . . concerning the illegall proceeding of the Commons. Printed, 1648[9]. 4°.* LT, HH, YM; CH, MH, MIU, WF, Y.

2971   A declaration from His Majestie the King of Scots, vvherein is declared how the army. Printed, 1659. 4°. CU, MBP, MIU, PL.

2972　The declaration of his Highnesse Prince Charles concerning his present engagement upon the fleet. *Printed*, 1648. 4°.* LT, O, CT, AU, E; CH, CN.

2972A　The declaration of His Highnesse Prince Charles, to all His Majesties loving subjects. *Printed*, 1648. 4°.* O, CM, D; CH, MH, MIU, WF, Y.

2973　The declaration of His Highnesse the Prince of Wales, to Sir Marmaduke Langdale. [*London*], *or* [*sic*] *G. H.*, 1648. 4°.* LT.

2974　The declaration of His Highnesse the Prince of Wales, to the severall princes. [*London*], *printed*, 1648. 4°.* LT.

2975　The declaration of the King of Scotland concerning the Parliament. *Edinburgh, by Evan Tyler*, 1649. 4°.* ALDIS 1361a. LT; MH.

2976　A declaration of the King of Scots concerning the Presbyterians: . . . 12th of December, 1651. *Printed at Paris, by H. de la More; and re-printed at London, for G. Horton*, 1651. 4°.* C, HH; WF, Y.

2977　The declaration of the King of Scots, to the king and councel of France. *Imprinted at London, for George Horton*, 1651. 4°.* LT, HH; CH, Y.

2978　The declaration of the Prince of Wales to the commissioners. *For G. H. May, 22, 1649*. 4°.* LT; WF.

2979　The King of Scots' declaration to all his loving subjects. *Printed at Edinburgh, and reprinted at London; June 20, 1649*. 4°.* LT, CU, Y.

2980　His Majesties declaration to all his loving subjects . . . the 31. day of October 1649. *Hage, by Samuel Broun*, 1649. 4°.* LT, C, CJ, DT; CH, WF.

2981　His Maiesties declaration to all his loving sbviects . . 5 of August, [*n.p.*, 1651.] 1651. brs. STEELE 2940. LT.

2982　Charles rex, His Majestys declaration to all his loving subjects. *Aberdene, James Brown*, 1651. brs. STEELE 299. ALDIS 1437. L.

2983　The kings declaration to all his loving subjects . . . 30 March 1660. *For Richard Parker*, 1660. fol.* STEELE 3173. LT, O.

2984　King Charls II. His declaration to all his loving subjects . . . the 4/14 of Aprill 1660. *By W. Godbid for John Playford*, 1660. 4°.* LT, O, C, OC, HH; CN, NU, PL, Y.

2984A　—[Anr. ed.] *For John Playford*, 1668. fol.* Y.

2985　—[Anr. ed.] *Reprinted Edinburgh, C. Higgins*, 1660. brs. ALDIS 1627. STEELE 3177a. EN.

2986　King Charles II., his declaration to all his loving subjects . . . May 1. *Edinburgh, C Higgins*, 1660. brs. ALDIS 1628. STEELE 3p 2168. EN, FSF; WF.

2987　His Majesties declaration to all his loving subjects. *Dublin, William Bladen*, 1660. fol.* DIX 107. DK, DT.

2988　His Majesties declaration to all his loving subjects, December 26, 1662. *By John Bill and Christopher Barker*, 1662. fol.* L, O, C, LL, HH; CH, MH, NU, TU, WF, Y.

2988A　—[Anr. ed.] *Edinburgh, by Evan Tyler*, 1663. brs. ALDIS 1751a. L; MH.

2988B　—[Anr. ed.—— —, 1663. 4°.* ALDIS 1751. L, CT.

2988C　—[Anr. ed.] *Dublin, by John Crook for Samuel Dancer*, 1662. fol.* DIX 116. DK, DT.

2989　His Majesties declaration to all his loving subjects . . . 18th day of June 1667. *In the Savoy, by the assigns of John Bill and Christopher Barker*, 1667. brs. STEELE 3493. L, O, C, LG, LPR; CH, MH, NC, Y.

2990　His Majesties declaration to all his loving subjects, March 15 1671/2. *In the Savoy, by the assigns of John Bill and Christopher Barker*, 1671/2. fol.* L, O, C, LL; CH, MH, TU, WF, Y.

2991　His Majesties declaration to all his loving subjects, . . . 14 March. *Edinburgh, reprinted by Evan Tyler*, 1672. brs. STEELE 3p 2353. REG; Y.

2992　Declaration to all his loving subjects, March 15th. *Dublin, Benjamin Tooke*, 1672. 4°.* DIX 363. DM.

2993　His Majesties declaration to all his loving subjects, . . . April 20th. *Dublin, Benjamin Tooke & John Crook*, 1679. 4°.* DIX 170. CD, DT.

2994　His Majesties declaration to all his loving subjects, June the second, 1680. *By John Bill, Thomas Newcomb, and Henry Hills*, 1680. fol.* L, C, OC, MR, EN; CH, MH, NC, TU, WF, Y.

2995-6　Entries cancelled.

2997　His Majestie's declaration to all his loving subjects . . . concerning ecclesiastical affairs. *By John Bill and Christopher Barker*, 1660. fol.* LT, O, C, LL, HH; CH, MH, NU, TU, WF, Y.

2998　His Majesties declaration to all his loving subjects, concerning the treasonable conspiracy. *By the assigns of John Bill; and by Henry Hills and Thomas Newcomb*, 1683. 4°.* L, C, LL, OP, MR; CH, CN, MH, NU, TU, WF, Y.

2998A　—[Anr. ed.] *Edinburgh, reprinted by the heir of Andrew Anderson*, 1683. 4°.* ALDIS 2372. MBA.

2999　—[Anr. ed.] *Dublin, reprinted by Benjamin Tooke & John Crooke, to be sold by Mary Crooke and Andrew Crooke*, 1683. 4°.* DIX 199. L, C, EC, DM, DT.

3000　His Majesties declaration to all his loving subjects, . . . touching. *By the assigns of John Bill, Thomas Newcomb, and Henry Hills*, 1681. fol.* L, C, MR, HH, EN; CLC, CN, LC, MH, NC, TU, Y.

3001　—[Anr. ed.] *Edinburgh, re-printed by the heir of Andrew Anderson*, 1681. fol.* ALDIS 2254. L, FSF; Y.

3001A　—[Anr. ed.] *Dublin, by Benjamin Tooke & John Crook, to be sold by Mary Crook and Andrew Crook*, 1681. 4°.* DIX 181. C, DC, DI, DT; WF.

3002　A declaration to all His Majesties loving subiects . . . 13 February 1659[60]. *Antwerp*, 1659. STEELE 3150. L, LG, LS, OC.

3003　A declaration to all His Majesties loving subjects, for the setling. *By R. Wood*, 1660. 4°. OC.

3004　His Majesties declaration to all his subjects of . . . twenty third of October 1649. [*London*, 1649.] brs. STEELE 2878. LT, O, LG, LS.

3005　His Majestie's declaration to his city of London, . . . fire. *By John Bill and Christopher Barker*, 1666. fol.* L, O, C, LL, HH; MH, WF, Y.

3006　Prince Charles his declaration to the Kings Majesties loyall subjects. *For George Laurenson*, 1647. 4°. LT, EN.

3007 His Majesties declaration touching his proceedings. *By John Bill and Christopher Barker,* 1664[/5]. fol.* L, O, C, HH; CH, MH, WF.

3007A —[Anr. ed.] *Edinburgh, reprinted by E. Tyler,* 1665. fol.* L.

3007B The demands of his gracious Maiesty. *For G. Horton,* 1661. 4°.* NN, WF.

3008 A fountain of loyal tears, poured forth by a sorrowful son. *Paris,* 1649. 8°.* CH.

3009 His Majesties gracious answer to the Earle of Manchesters speech. *By John Macock, and Francis Tyton,* 1660. 4°.* O, HH, OC, SP; CLC, MH, NU, Y.

3010 His Majesties gracious commission to search into . . . purchases of the honours. *For Rich. Marriot, and John Playford,* 1660. fol.* LT, O, SP; CH, MH, WF.

3011 His Majesties gracious declaration for the encouraging the subjects of the United Provinces. *In the Savoy, by the assigns of John Bill and Christopher Barker,* 1672. fol.* L, O, OC, HH; CH, LC, MH, WF, Y.

3012 —[Anr. ed.] *Reprinted Edinburgh,* [*A. Anderson*], 1672. brs. STEELE 3p 2361. HH, EN; MH.

3013 His Majestie's gracious declaration for the settlement of . . . Ireland. *By John Bill,* 1660. fol.* LT, O, C, LL, HH; CH, MH, MIU, TU, WF, Y.

3014 —[Anr. ed.] *Dublin,* 1660. fol.* DIX 109. LI.

3015 His Majesties gracious letter and declaration. *By John Macock, and Francis Tyton,* 1660. 4°.* LT, C, OC, MR, HH; HR, CLC, MH, NU, TU, WF, Y.

3016 —[Anr. ed.] *Dublin, William Bladen,* 1660. 4°.* DIX 109. DIX.

3017 His Majesties gracious letter, directed to the Presbytery . . . Aug. 10. *Edinburgh, C Higgins,* 1660. brs. ALDIS 1631. STEELE 3p 2181. EN, ES; WF.

3018 —[Anr. ed.] *Edinburgh, a society of stationers,* 1660. brs. ALDIS 1632. STEELE 3p 2182. HH.

3019 —[Anr. ed.] *Printed at Edinburgh, and reprinted for George Calvert,* 1660. brs. STEELE 3p 2183. LT, O, LG, OP; CH, MH.

3020 His Majesties gracious letter to his Parliament of Scotland, June 4, 1663. *Edinburgh, by Evan Tyler, and re-printed at London,* 1663. fol.* L; CH, WF.

3021 His Majesties gracious letter to his Parliament of Scotland: December 9. 1669. *In the Savoy by Tho. Newcomb,* 1669. fol.* L, O, HH; CH, TU, Y.

3022 His Majestie's gracious letter to his Parliament of Scotland, May 23rd, 1672. *In the Savoy, by T. Newcomb,* 1672, fol.* L, LL, OC, CT, HH; CLC, MA, NC, WF, Y.

3023 —[Anr. ed.] *Reprinted Edinburgh, by Andrew Anderson,* 1672. fol.* ALDIS 1943. EN.

3024 The Kings Majesties gracious letter to his Parliament, . . . twelfth of November, 1673. *Edinburgh, by Andrew Anderson,* 1673. fol.* ALDIS 1979. EN, FSF; MB, MH.

3025 His Majesties gracious letter to his Parliament of Scotland: . . . 28th day of July, 1681. *In the Savoy: by Thomas Newcomb,* 1681. fol.* L, C, LL, OC, HH; CH, CN, LC, MH, Y.

3026 —[Anr. ed.] colop: *For John Smith,* 1681. brs. LL, EN; CH, CN, WF, Y.

3027 —[Anr. ed.] *Edinburgh, by the heirs of Andrew Anderson,* 1681. fol.* ALDIS 2255. L, EN; MIU, Y.

3028 —[Anr. ed.] *Dublin, reprinted by Benjamin Took & John Crook, to be sold by Mary Crook & Andrew Crook,* 1681. 4°.* DIX 190. C, DW.

3029 His Majesties gracious letter to the convention . . . 13th of June, 1678. *In the Savoy, by T. N. for Andrew Forrester,* 1678. fol.* L, O, C, HH, EN; CLC, CN, MH, NC, TU, WF, Y.

3030 —[Anr. ed.] *Edinburgh, re-printed by the heir of Andrew Anderson,* 1678. fol.* ALDIS 2120. L, EN; MH.

3031 —[Anr. ed.] *Dublin, re-printed by Benjamin Tooke;* 1678. 4°.* DIX 164. C, DT; Y.

3032 His Majesties gracious letter to the House of Commons to pass the bill for confirming the Act of Oblivion . . . June 22. 1661. *By John Bill and Christopher Barker,* 1661. fol.* O, C, LL, OC, HH; CH, CLC, Y.

3032A His Majesties gracious letter to the Lord Maior. [*London,* 1660]. brs. L.

3033 His Majesties gracious letter to the Parliament of Scotland. *By Thomas Newcomb in the Savoy; and reprinted at Edinburgh, by the heir of Andrew Anderson:* 1685. fol.* L, EN.

3034 His Majestie's gracious message to all. *For Charls Prince,* 1660. 4°. LT, O, OC.

3035 C. R. His Majesties gracious message to General Monk. *Printed at Paris,* 1659. brs. STEELE 3135. LT, O; MH, Y.

3036 His Majesties gracious message to the Commons . . . January the fourth, 1680/81. *By the assigns of John Bill, Thomas Newcomb, and Henry Hills,* 1680/81. fol.* L, C, OC, MR, HH; CH, MBP, MH, NC, WF, Y.

3037 —[Anr. ed.] *Reprinted Edinburgh, by the heir of Andrew Anderson,* 1680/81. fol. ALDIS 2256. EN; MH.

3038 His Majesties gracious message to the House of Commons. *By John Bill and Christopher Barker,* 1660. fol.* LT, O, C, HH, EN; CH, CLC, MH, TU, Y.

3038A His Majesties gracious order at Council Board. [*London,* 1665?] cap., 4°.* L.

3039 His Majesties gracious patent to the goldsmiths. *By John Bill, Christopher Barker, Thomas Newcomb, and Henry Hills,* 1677. fol.* L, O, LG, LUG, HH; CH, MH, TU, WF, Y.

3040 His Majesties gracious proclamation concerning the government of . . . Scotland. *Edinburgh, by a society of stationers,* 1660. brs. WF, Y.

3041 Prince Charles his gracious resolution. *First printed at Oxford by Leonard Lichfield, and now re-printed at London for John Rivers,* [1642]. 4°.* MADAN 1145. LT; CLC, NU.

3042 His Majestie's gracious speech to both Houses . . . on the 29th day of August, 1660. *By John Bill and Christopher Barker,* 1660. 4°.* LT, O, C, LL, EN; CH, CN, MH, NU, TU, WF, Y.

3042A —[Anr. ed.] *Edinburgh, re-printed by Christopher Higgins,* 1660. 4°.* ALDIS 1633. CT, EN; Y.

3043 His Majestie's gracious speech to both Houses . . . July 8, 1661. *By John Bill and Christopher Barker,* 1661. fol.* L, O, C, CT, EN; CH, NC, TU, WF, Y.

3044 His Majestie's gracious speech to both Houses . . . July 30, 1661. By John Bill and Christopher Barker, 1661. fol.* L, O, C, LL, HH; CH, MH, NC, WF, Y.

3044A —[Anr. ed.] London, reprinted Edinburgh, 1661. 4°.* CT.

3045 His Majesties gracious speech to both Houses . . . November 20th 1661. By John Bill and Christopher Barker, 1661. fol.* L, O, C, OC, HH; CLC, MH, NC, TU, WF, Y.

3046 —[Anr. ed.] By Roger Norton, 1661. 4°.* LL; NU.

3047 —[Anr. ed.] Printed at London, and re-printed at Edinburgh, 1661. 4°.* ALDIS 1695. FSF.

3048 His Majestie's gracious speech to both Houses . . . February the 18th, 1662[3]. By John Bill and Christopher Barker, 1662[3]. fol.* L, O, C, LL, HH; CH, MH, NC, TU, Y.

3049 His Majesties gracious speech to both Houses . . . April 5, 1664. By John Bill and Christopher Barker, 1664. fol.* L, O, C, EC, HH; CH, MH, NC, WF, Y.

3050 His Majesties gracious speech to both Houses . . . May 17, 1664. By John Bill and Christopher Barker, 1664. fol.* L, O, CS, LL, HH; CH, CLC, NC, WF, Y.

3050A —[Anr. ed.] Edinburgh, re-printed by E. Tyler, 1664. 4°.* CT.

3051 His Majesties gracious speech to both Houses . . . November 24, 1664. By John Bill and Christopher Barker, 1664. fol.* L, O, C, LL, OC, HH; CLC, NC, TU, WF, Y.

3052 His Majesties gracious speech to both Houses . . . 10th of October 1665. Oxford, by Leonard Lichfield, for John Bill and Christopher Barker [London], 1665. 19 pp. fol.* MADAN 2678. L, O, LG, OC, HH; CH, Y.

3053 —[Anr. ed.] By John Bill, and Christopher Barker, 1665. 11 pp. fol.* C, LL, HH; MA.

3053A —[Anr. ed.] Reprinted at York, by Stephen Bulkley, 1665. fol.* NC.

3054 —[Anr. ed.] Reprinted Edinburgh, Tyler, 1665. fol.* ALDIS 1786. EN; WF.

3055 His Majesties gracious speech to both Houses . . . at their prorogation, November 4. 1673. By the assigns of John Bill and Christopher Barker, 1673. fol.* L, C, LL, AN; CLC, LC, NC, WF, Y.

3056 His Majesties gracious speech to both Houses . . . January 14/24, 1673/4. By the assigns of John Bill and Christopher Barker, 1673/4. fol.* L, O, C, LL, E; CLC, LC, MH, NC, TU, Y.

3057 —[Anr. ed.] Reprinted Edinburgh, by Andrew Anderson, 1674. fol.* ALDIS 2019. EN, FSF; CH.

3058 His Majesties gracious speech to both Houses . . . 9th of June, 1675. By the assigns of John Bill and Christopher Barker, 1675. fol.* L, HH; CH, CLC, NC, WF, Y.

3059 —[Anr. ed.] Edinburgh, re-printed by Andrew Anderson, 1675. fol.* ALDIS 2046. L, EN; MH.

3059A —[Anr. ed.] Dublin, reprinted by Benjamin Tooke, 1675. fol.* DIX 156. DK; NC.

3060 His Majesties gracious speech . . . 28th of January, 1677/8. By John Bill, Christopher Barker, Thomas Newcomb, and Henry Hills, 1677/8. fol.* L, C, LL, HH; CH, LC, MH, NC, RPJ, Y.

3061 —[Anr. ed.] Reprinted Edinburgh, by the heir of Andrew Anderson, 1678. fol.* ALDIS 2121. L, EN; MH.

3062 —[Anr. ed.] Edinburgh, T. Brown, 1677/8. 4°.* ALDIS 2122. EN.

3063 —[Anr. ed.] Dublin, by Benjamin Tooke, to be sold by Joseph Wild, 1678. 4°.* DIX 167. L; MBA.

3064 His Majesties gracious speech to both Houses . . . 26th of January 1679/80. By John Bill, Thomas Newcomb, and Henry Hills, 1679/80. fol.* L, C, CT, HH; CH, CLC, TU, WF, Y.

3065 —[Anr. ed.] Reprinted Edinburgh, by the heirs of Andrew Anderson, 1680. fol. ALDIS 2186. EN.

3065A —[Anr. ed.] Dublin, reprinted by Benjamin Took and John Brook, 1679/80. fol.* NC.

3066 His Majesties gracious speech to both Houses . . . 21st of October, 1680. By the assigns of John Bill, Thomas Newcomb, and Henry Hills, 1680. fol.* L, O, C, LL, EN; CH, LC, MH, NC, TU, Y.

3067 —[Anr. ed.] Edinburgh, reprinted by the heir of Andrew Anderson, 1680. fol.* ALDIS 2187. EN.

3068 —[Anr. ed.] Edinburgh, reprinted by John Swintoun, 1680. fol.* ALDIS 2188. L, EN.

3069 His Majesties gracious speech to the honorable House of Commons, . . . March 1st, 1661[/2]. By John Bill and Christopher Barker, 1661[/2]. fol.* L, O, CD, SP, LL; CLC, MH, NC, TU, Y.

3070 His Majestie's gracious speech to the House of Peers, the 27th of July, 1660. By Christopher Barker and John Bill, 1660. fol.* LT, O, C, LL, EN; CLC, LC, MH, NC, Y.

3071 His Majesties gracious speech to the Lords & Commons, together . . . 8th day of May, 1661. By John Bill and Christopher Barker, 1661. fol.* L, O, C, CT, EN; CLC, MH, NC, TU, WF, Y.

3072 —[Anr. ed.] Edinburgh, 1661. 4°.* ALDIS 1694. CT, EN.

3073 His Majestie's gracious speech, together with the Lord Chancellor's, . . . 13 of September, 1660. By John Bill and Christopher Barker, 1660. fol.* O, CT, LL, HH; RPJ, Y.

3074 His Majestie's gracious speech, together with the Lord Chancellor's, . . . 29th day of December, 1660. By John Bill, 1660[1]. fol.* LT, O, C, LL, CT; CH, MH, NC, WF, Y.

3074A —[Anr. ed.] Edinburgh, society of stationers, 1661. 4°.* CT.

3075 His Majestie's gracious speech together with the Lord Keepers, . . . January 7. 1673/4. By the assigns of John Bill and Christopher Barker, 1673/4. fol.* L, O, C, LL, HH; LC, MH, NC, Y.

3076 —[Anr. ed.] Reprinted Edinburgh, by His Majesties printers, 1674. fol.* ALDIS 2018. L, EN; CH.

3077 —[Anr. ed.] Dublin, Benjamin Tooke, 1673. 4°.* DIX 150. DK.

3078 His Majesties gracious speech together . . . April 13. 1675. By the assigns of John Bill and Christopher Barker, 1675. fol.* L, O, C, LL, HH; CH, LC, MH, NC, TU, Y.

3079 —[Anr. ed.] Reprinted Edinburgh, by His Majesties printers, 1675. fol.* ALDIS 2045. L, EN, FSF; MH.

3080 —[Anr. ed.] Reprinted at Dublin by Benjamin Tooke, to be sold by Joseph Wilde, 1675. 4°.* DIX 156. DK; NU.

3081 His Majesties gracious speech together . . . 13th of October, 1675. *By the assigns of John Bill and Christopher Barker*, 1675. 4 pp. fol.* L, O, CT; LC, MH, NC, TU, Y.

3082 —[Anr. ed.] —, 1675. 12 pp. fol.* L, C, LL, OC; CLC, MH, WF.

3083 —[Anr. ed.] *Edinburgh, re-printed by Andrew Anderson*, 1675. fol.* ALDIS 2047. L, EN, FSF.

3084 His Majesties gracious speech, together . . . 15th of February, 1676/7. *By the assigns of John Bill and Christopher Barker*, 1676/7. fol.* L, O, C, LL; CLC, MH, NC, TU, WF, Y.

3084A —[Anr. ed.] *Edinburgh, by the heir of Andrew Anderson*, 1676/7. 4°.* ALDIS 2097. EN; MH.

3084B —[Anr. ed.] *Reprinted at Dublin by Benjamin Tooke, to be sold by Joseph Wilde*, 1676. 4°.* DIX 366. C, DK.

3085 His Majesties gracious speech, together . . . 23d of May, 1678. *By John Bill, Christopher Barker, Thomas Newcomb and Henry Hills*, 1678. fol.* L, O, C, LL, EN; CH, MH, NC, TU, WF, Y.

3086 —[Anr. ed.] *Reprinted Edinburgh, by the heir of Andrew Anderson*, 1678. 4°.* ALDIS 2123. EN, FSF.

3087 —[Anr. ed.] *Dublin, Benjamin Tooke*, 1678. 4°.* DIX 164. CD, DI, DT.

3087A —A great fight between the Kings forces. *Imprinted at Yondon [sic] for R. VV.* 1648. 4°.* LT; MH, WF.

3088 Charles R. His Majesty in his princely compassion . . . fifth day of September 1666. *By John Bill and Christopher Barker*, [1666]. brs. STEELE 3470. O, C, LPR, OQ; MH.

3089 —[Anr. ed.] *York, Stephen Bulkley*, [1666]. cap., brs. STEELE 3471. LPR.

3090 His Majesties last answer to the papers . . . 19/29 May 1649. *[London], printed*, 1649. brs. STEELE 3p 2017. LT, O, EN.

3091 A league of union agreed on betwixt His Majesty, and the Estates General. *In the Savoy, by the assigns of John Bill and Christopher Barker*, 1668. 4°.* L, O, CT, OC; HR, CH, CN, MH, WF.

3092 —[Anr. ed.] *Edinburgh, by Evan Tyler*, 1668. 4°.* ALDIS 1844. EN; NU.

3093 —[Anr. ed.] *Dublin, John Crooke*, 1668. 4°.* DIX 136. DK, DT.

3094 Prince Charles, his letter and declaration [sic] to his trusty and wel-beloved the bailiffes, . . . of Yarmouth. *Imprinted at London, for R. W.*, 1648. 4°.* LT, O; CGS, MH.

3095 Prince Charles his letter brought to His Excellency . . . Fairfax. *For H. Becke*, 1648. 4°.* LT, AN.

3096 A letter from His Majesty. To the Speaker of the Commons. *By Edward Husbands and Tho. Newcomb*, 1660. fol.* L, O, CS, EC, EN; PL, TU, Y.

3097 —[Anr. ed.] *Edinburgh, reprinted by Christopher Higgins*, 1660. brs. ALDIS 1629. STEELE 3p 2169. L, EN, FSF.

3097A A letter from K. Charls the Second, . . . to Mr. Cawton. *By William Wilson for Richard Lownds*, 1660. 4°.* L, O, CM; CH, NU, WF, Y.

3098 A letter from the King of Scots, to the Pope of Rome. *Imprinted at London for G. Horton*, 1651. 4°.* SP; Y.

3099 A letter from the king to F. M. Bruxels, 10 April, 1660. *[London, 1660.]* brs. STEELE 3177. LT, O, LG, LL, HH; MH.

3100 Charles P. A letter sent from His Highness the Prince of Wales. *[London], for G. Lawrenson, Octob. 6*, 1648. 4°.* LT, LG; MH, Y.

3101 His Maiesties letter to His Excellency the Lord General Monck. *By John Macock*, 1660. 4°.* LT, O, C, HH, GH; CN, MH, NU, TU, Y.

3102 —[Anr. ed.] *Dublin, by William Bladen*, 1660. brs. DIX 109. STEELE 2p 617, L.

3103 —[Anr. ed.] *Reprinted Edinburgh, Christopher Higgins*, 1660. brs. ALDIS 1630. STEELE 3p 2173. EN; CH, Y.

3104 His Majesties letter to his Parliament in Scotland . . . October 19th 1669. *In the Savoy, by Tho. Newcomb*. 1669. fol.* L, O, OC, HH; CH, MH, TU, WF, Y.

3105 —[Anr. ed.] *Edinburgh, Tyler*, 1663. fol. ALDIS 1752. L, EN.

3106 —[Anr. ed.] *Reprinted Edinburgh, by Andrew Anderson*, 1669. fol.* ALDIS 1856. EN.

3107 The Kings Majesties letter to his Parliament of Scotland . . . 28 of July, 1670. *In the Savoy, by Tho: Newcomb*, 1670. fol.* L, O, HH; WF, Y.

3108 A letter from His Maty King Charls II^d to his Peers. *[London], for Charls Gustavus*, 1660. brs. STEELE 3172. LT, O.

3109 A letter from the king of Scots to Major Generall Massey. *For Robert Ibbitson*, 1651. 4°.* LT, HH, AN; Y.

3110 The King of Scots letter to Major Generall Massey. *By R. Wood*, 1651. 4°.* LT.

3111 Entry cancelled.

3112 A letter of the Kings . . . Majesty to . . . William [Juxon] Lord Archbishop of Canterbury. *Dublin, for S. Dancer*, 1662. 4°.* DIX 117. DK.

3113 His Majestie's letter to the artillery company. colop: *For V. T.*, 1681. brs. L, DT; CH, MH, WF.

3114 His Majesties letter to the generals of the navy at sea. *By S. Griffin for John Playford*, 1660. 4°.* L, O, HH, MR; TU, WF, Y.

3115 Prince Charles his letter to the Lady Marie. *For William Reynor*, 1642. 4°.* LT, SP; HR, CLC, MH, WF, Y.

3116 The Kings Majesties letter to the Lord Mayor, and court of aldermen. *For William Garret*, 1661. brs. L, O, LG, HH.

3117 The King of Scots letter to the states of Holland. *For George Horton*, 1652. 4°.* LT; CH, Y.

3118 Letters patents granted by. *Printed*, 1669. fol. L; MH, WF.

3119 —[Anr. ed.] *In the Savoy, by Tho. Newcomb*, 1672. fol. C; CLC, CU, MH, WF.

3120 His Majesties letters to the Bishop of London. colop: *By S. Roycroft*, 1681. brs. C, HH, EN; CH, CN, MH, WF.

3121 Prince Charles, his letany. *[n.p.], printed*, 1648. 12°.* C; CH.

3122 The King of Scots his message and remonstrance. *For G. Laurenson*, 1649. 4°.* LT, EN, DT.

3123 A message from His Highness the Prince of Wales to His Majesty. *For G. Lawrenson, Octob. 6*, 1648. 4°.* CH.

3123A —[Anr. ed.] *Printed at Corck*, 1648. 4°.* C.

3124 Prince Charles his message; sent from his court at St. Germans. *For Iohn Clowes*, 1648. 4°.* LT, EN; CH, MH, MIU, WF, Y.

3125 A message sent from His Highnesse the Prince of Wales, to the citizens of London. *Novemb. 24. imprinted at London for H. Wels*, 1648. 4°.* LT, O, SP, DT; Y.

3126 —[Anr. ed.] *For W. Fielding*, 1648. 4°.* LT; CH, MIU.
Message sent from His Highnesse the Prince of Wales. [*n.p.*], 1648. *See* Green, Robert.

3127 A message sent from the King of Scots, to the . . . King of Spain. *For Augustus Prince*, 1660. 4°.* OC; MBP, MIU, WF, Y.

3128 A message sent from the King of Scots, . . . to the Lord Douglas. *Printed at Aberdeen, by David Strangham*, [1659]. 4°.* ALDIS 1610. L, O, E, EN; CH, MIU, NP, Y.

3129 His Majestie's message to the Commons . . . 9th day of November, 1680. *For Richard Taylor*, 1680. fol.* L, O, C, OC, HH; CH, MBP, MH, WF, Y.

3130 Prince Charles his message to the Levellers in the West. *For G. Laurenson, September 13*, 1649. 4°.* LT; MH.

3131 Prince Charles his message to the Parliament. [*n.p.*], *published*, [1648]. 4°.* LT.

3132 Prince Charles his message to the Parliament of Scotland. *For R. Williamson*, 1649. 4°.* LT; MH.

3133 His Majesties most gracious and royal commission. *For M. D., to be sold by Nathaniel Webb*, 1664. 4°.* L, O, LL, SP; CH, CN, MH, WF, Y.

3134 The Kings Majesties most gracious letter and declaration. *For John Jones*, 1660. brs. STEELE 3237. LT, LG, HH, MR; MBP, MH, Y.

3135 —[Anr. ed.] *J Clowes*, 1660. brs. STEELE 3238. DT; CLC.

3136 His Majesties most gracious speech, to both Houses . . . seven and twentieth of July, 1663. *By John Bill and Christopher Barker*, 1663. fol.* L, O, C, LL, HH; CH, NC, TU, WF, Y.

3137 His Majesties most gracious speech to both Houses . . . the one and twentieth day of March, 1663/4. *By John Bill and Christopher Barker*, 1663/4. fol.* L, O, LL, HH; CH, MH, NC, TU, WF, Y.

3138 —[Anr. ed.] *Reprinted Edinburgh, Tyler*, 1664. fol.* ALDIS 1767. EN.

3139 His Majesties most gracious speech to both Houses . . . one and twentieth day of September, 1666. *By John Bill and Christopher Barker*, 1666. fol.* L, O, C, LL, HH; CLC, MH, NC, WF, Y.

3140 His Majestie's most gracious speech to both Houses . . . eighteenth day of January, 1666[/7]. *In the Savoy, by the assigns of John Bill, and Christopher Barker*, 1666[/7]. fol.* O, C, LL, OC, HH; CLC, LC, MH, NC, Y.

3141 —[Anr. ed.] *Dublin, John Crooke*, 1666. 4°.* DIX 133. DK.

3142 His Majestie's most gracious speech to both Houses . . . 8th of February, 1666[/7]. *In the Savoy, by the assigns of John Bill and Christopher Barker*, 1666[/7]. fol.* L, O, C, LL, HH; CLC, MH, NC, WF, Y.

3143 —[Anr. ed.] *Edinburgh, by E. Tyler*, 1667. 4°.* ALDIS 1834. EN.

3144 —[Anr. ed.] *Dublin, John Crooke*, 1666[7]. 4°.* DIX 131. DIX.

3145 His Majesties most gracious speech to both Houses . . . October 10. 1667. *In the Savoy, by the assigns of John Bill and Christopher Barker*, 1667. fol.* O, C, LL, OC, HH; CH, LC, MH, NC, Y.

3146 —[Anr. ed.] *Reprinted Edinburgh, Tyler*, 1667. fol.* ALDIS 1835. EN.

3147 His Majesties most gracious speech to both Houses . . . 10th of February, 1667[/8]. *In the Savoy, by the assigns of John Bill and Christopher Barker*, 1667[/8]. fol.* L, O, LL, OC, HH; CLC, MM, NC, WF, Y.

3148 His Majesties most gracious speech to both Houses . . . October 19, 1669. *In the Savoy, by the assigns of John Bill and Christopher Barker*, 1669. fol.* L, O, C, LG, HH; CLC, MH, TU, WF, Y.

3149 —[Anr. ed.] *Edinburgh, by Andrew Anderson*, 1669. 4°.* ALDIS 1857. EN; NU.

3150 —[Anr. ed.] *Dublin, Benjamin Tooke*, 1669. 4°.* DIX 139. DK.

3151 His Majesties most gracious speech to both Houses . . . February 14, 1669/70. *In the Savoy, by the assigns of John Bill and Christopher Barker*, 1669/70. fol.* L, O, LG, LL, HH; CLC, MH, NC, WF, Y.

3152 —[Anr. ed.] *Reprinted Edinburgh, Tyler*, 1670. 4°.* ALDIS 1897. EN, FSF.

3153 —[Anr. ed.] *Dublin, Benjamin Tooke*, 1670. 4°.* DIX 141. DK; CN.

3153A His Majesties most gracious speech to both Houses . . . March 8. *By the assigns of John Bill and Christopher Barker*, 1672/3. fol.* L, C, SP; CH, CLC, NC, WF, Y.

3153AB —[Anr. ed.] *Reprinted at Dublin, by Benjamin Tooke, to be sold by Joseph Wilde*, 1672. 4°.* DIX 148. DK.

3153B His Majesties most gracious speech . . . November 4, 1673. *By the assigns of John Bill and Christopher Barker*, 1673. fol.* O, HH; WF.

3154 —[Anr. ed.] *Dublin, Benjamin Tooke*, 1674. 4°.* DIX 152. DK.

3155 His Majesties most gracious speech to both Houses . . . Feb. 15. *Edinburgh, by the heir of Andrew Anderson*, 1677. 4°.* ALDIS 2097. EN, FSF.

3156 His Majestie's most gracious speech to both Houses . . . 9th of November, 1678. *By John Bill, Christopher Barker, Thomas Newcomb, and Henry Hills*, 1678. fol.* L, O, C, LL, EN; CLC, MH, NC, TU, Y.

3157 —[Anr. ed.] *Dublin, Benjamin Tooke*, 1678. 4°.* DIX 166. CD.

3158 His Majesties most gracious speech to both Houses . . . 26th of January 1679/80. *By John Bill, Thomas Newcomb, and Henry Hills*, 1680. fol.* O, MR, DT; CLC.

3159 His Majesties most gracious speech to both Houses . . . 15th of December, 1680. *By the assigns of John Bill, Thomas Newcomb, and Henry Hills*, 1680. fol.* L, O, C, HH, MR; CLC, CN, LC, NC, TU, Y.

3160 —[Anr. ed.] *Edinburgh, heir of A Anderson*, 1680. fol.* ALDIS 2189. L, EN.

3161 —[Anr. ed.] *Dublin, Benjamin Took & John Crook,* 1680. 4°.* DIX 177. NC.

3162 His Majesties most gracious speech to both Houses . . . 21st of March, 1680/1. colop: *By the assigns of John Bill, Thomas Newcomb, and Henry Hills,* 1680/1. cap., fol.* L, O, CT, MR, EN; CLC, CN, LC, MH, NC, TU, Y.

3163 —[Anr. ed.] *Oxford, at the theatre,* [1681]. fol.* L, OC, CCA, CS; CH, MB, NC, PU, TU.

3164 —[Anr. ed.] *Edinburgh, re-printed by the heir of Andrew Anderson,* 1681. fol.* ALDIS 2257. L, EN; Y.

3165 —[Anr. ed.] *Dublin, Benjamin Took & John Crook,* 1681. 4°.* DIX 186. DIX.

3166–7 Entries cancelled.

3168 His Majesties most gracious speech to both Houses . . . 9th of November, 1685. *By the assigns of John Bill, and by Henry Hills and Thomas Newcomb,* 1685. fol.* EN; CLC, NC, TU, Y.

3169 His Majesties most gracious speech, together . . . 13 of September, 1660. *By John Bill and Christopher Barker,* 1660. fol.* LT, C, OC, OP; CH, CN, MH, NC, TU, WF, Y.

3169A —[Anr. ed.] *Edinburgh, re-printed by Christopher Higgins,* 1660. 4°.* ALDIS 1634. EN; WF, Y.

3170 His Majesties most gracious speech, together . . . nineteenth of May, 1662. *By John Bill and Christopher Barker,* 1662. fol.* L, O, C, LL, HH; CH, LC, MH, NC, TU, Y.

3171 —[Anr. ed.] *London, reprinted Edinburgh, Tyler,* 1662. 4°.* ALDIS 1734. EN.

3172 His Majesties most gracious speech, together . . . February 4 . . . 1672/3. *By the assigns of John Bill and Christopher Barker,* 1672/3. fol.* L, O, C, LL, EN; CH, MH, NC, TU, WF, Y.

3173 —[Anr. ed.] *Edinburgh, by His Majesties printers,* 1673. fol.* ALDIS 1980. EN; MH.

3174 —[Anr. ed.] *Dublin, Benjamin Tooke,* 1672. 4°.* DIX 148. L, DK.

3175 His Majesties most gracious speech together . . . March 8, 1672/3. *By the assigns of John Bill and Christopher Baker,* 1672/3. fol.* L, LG, LL, HH; CLC, WF.

3176 —[Anr. ed.] *Dublin, Benjamin Tooke,* 1672. 4°.* DIX 148. DK.

3177 His Majesties most gracious speech, together . . . October 27. 1673. *By the assigns of John Bill and Christopher Barker,* 1673. fol.* L, O, C, LL; CH, MH, NC, WF, Y.

3178 —[Anr. ed.] *Reprinted Edinburgh, by His Majesties printers,* 1673. fol.* ALDIS 1981. EN, FSF.

3179 —[Anr. ed.] *Dublin, Benjamin Tooke,* 1673. 4°.* DIX 151. DK.

3180 His Majesties most gracious speech, together . . . 9 June, 1675. *Dublin, Benjamin Tooke,* 1675. fol.* DIX 156. DK.

3181 His Majesties most gracious speech, together . . . 13th of October, 1675. *Dublin, Benjamin Tooke,* 1675. 4°.* DIX 365. DM.

3182 His Majesties most gracious speech, together with the Lord Chancellors, . . . 21th [*sic*] of October, 1678. *By John Bill, Christopher Barker, Thomas Newcomb, and Henry Hills,* 1678. fol.* L, O, C, LL; CH, LC, MH, NC, TU, Y.

3183 —[Anr. ed.] *Reprinted Edinburgh, by the heir of Andrew Anderson,* 1678. fol.* ALDIS 2124. L, EN; MH.

3184 —[Anr. ed.] *Dublin, by Benjamin Tooke, to be sold by Mary Crooke,* 1678. 4°.* DIX 165. C, CD, DT.

3184A His Majesties most gracious speech, together . . . 6th of March 1678/9. *By John Bill, Christopher Barker, Thomas Newcomb, and Henry Hills,* 1678/9. fol.* L, O, C, LL, EN; CH, LC, MH, NC, TU, Y.

3185 His Majesties most gracious speech, together . . . 6th March, 1678/9. *Edinburgh, by the heir of A. Anderson,* 1679. fol.* HH, EN.

3185A —[Anr. ed.] *Re-printed at Dublin by Benjamin Tooke,* 1679. fol.* DIX 170. CD, DN, DT; PU.

3186 His Majesties most gracious speech, together . . . 30th of April, 1679. *By John Bill, Thomas Newcomb, and Henry Hills,* 1679. fol.* L, O, C, LL, EN; CH, LC, NC, TU, Y.

3187 —[Anr. ed.] *Edinburgh, re-printed by the heir of Andrew Anderson,* 1679. 4°.* L, FSF; WF.

3187A —[Anr. ed.] *Dublin, reprinted by Benjamin Tooke, to be sold by Mary Crook,* 1679. 4°.* DIX 170. DT.

3188 Most reverend father in God, our right trusty . . . 2 February 1683[4]. *Assigns of Bill,* 1683[4]. brs. STEELE 3756. L, C, LG.

3189 Most reverend father in God, we greet you well. [*n.p.,* 1660.] brs. LT.

3190 —, colop: 1674. brs. CH, WCL.

3190A —14 November 1684. *By the assigns of John Bill,* 1684. brs. STEELE 3762. L, LG.

3191 Murder will out. [*London*], *printed,* 1663. 4°.* C, BIU; CSU, MH, Y.

3191A —[Anr. ed.] 1689. 4°.* L.

3192 New propositions sent from. *Imprinted at London, for R. VV.,* 1648. 4°.* LT, LVF.

3193 —[Same title]. *For E. Colton, Aug. 17,* 1649. 4°.* L.

3194 Ordered by His Highnesse in Councell . . . 27 July 1648 [i.e. 17th]. [*n.p.*], *printed,* 1648. brs. STEELE 2780. LT.

3194A Orders and rules to be observed within His Majesties palace. [*London,* 1666.] brs. STEELE 3484. HH.

3195 Orders by His Highnesse the Prince of Wales, in Council. [*n.p.,* 1648.] brs. LS.

3196 A perpetual league of mutual defence and allyance between His Majesty, and the Estates General. *In the Savoy, by the assignes of John Bill and Christopher Barker,* 1668. 4°.* L, O, CT; HR, CH, CN, MH, WF, Y.

3197 —[Anr. ed.] *Reprinted Edinburgh, by Evan Tyler,* 1668. 4°. ALDIS 1848. EN, FSF.

3198 —[Anr. ed.] *Dublin, reprinted by John Crooke, sold by J. Dancer,* 1668. 4°. DIX 136. CT, DK.

Note: Most proclamations begin with the form "By the King."

3199 A proclamation . . . 2 October 1659. *Antwerp,* [1659]. brs. STEELE 3131. L, LG, CCA; Y.

3200 A proclamation . . . 25 January 1659[60]. *Anwerpe* [*sic*], *printed,* 1659[60]. brs. STEELE 3148. L; Y.

3201 A proclamation . . . twenty sixth day of April 1665. *By John Bill and Christopher Barker,* 1665. fol.* STEELE 3416. L, C, OQ, LPR, DT; CH.

3202 A proclamation . . . 7 December 1670. *In the Savoye, by the assigns of Jo. Bill and Chris. Barker*, 1670. brs. STEELE 3541. L, C, OQ, LPR, DT; CH.

3203 A proclamation . . . 13 March. *By the assigns of John Bill and Christopher Barker*, 1672/3. fol.* STEELE 3579. L, O, LPR, DT; CH.

3204 A proclamation . . . against jesuits, . . . 13 March. *Edinburgh*, 1673. brs. ALDIS 1992. STEELE 3p 2367. REG.

3205 A proclamation . . . 13 January 1674[5]. *By the assigns of John Bill and Christopher Barker*, 1674[5]. brs. STEELE 3606. L, O, C, LPR, DT; CH, MH.

3206 A proclamation . . . 5 February 1674/5. *By the assigns of John Bill and Christopher Barker*, 1674/5. brs. STEELE 3609. L, O, C, LPR, DT; CH, WF.

3207 A proclamation . . . 26 May 1676. *By the assigns of John Bill and Christopher Barker*, 1676. fol.* STEELE 3631. L, C, OQ, LG, DT; CH, MH.

3208 A proclamation . . . 29 June 1679. *Edinburgh, by the heir of Andrew Anderson*, 1679. brs. STEELE 3p 2466. ALDIS 2167. EN, HH, ES.

3209 —[Anr. ed.] *Edinburgh, by the heir of Andrew Anderson*, 1679. *Re-printed at London.* brs. STEELE 3p 2468. L, O, LG; CH, TSM, WF.

3210 A proclamation about dissolving . . . Parliament. *By John Bill, Christopher Barker, Thomas Newcomb, and Henry Hills*, 1678/9. brs. STEELE 3679. L, O, LPR, LG, DT; CH, MH, WF, Y.

3211 —[Anr. ed.] *Edinburgh, reprinted, heir of A Anderson*, 1679. brs. STEELE 3p 2449. EN.

3211A A proclamation adjourning the Parliament. *Edinburgh, reprinted at London by G. Crown*, 1683. brs. STEELE 2555. OP.

3212 Proclamation against all meetings of Quakers, . . . 22 Jan. [*Edinburgh, Tyler*, 1661]. brs. ALDIS 1709. EN; MH.

3212A —[Anr. ed.] *Edinburgh, printed; London reprinted for R. Thrale*, 1661. brs. LT.

3213 A proclamation against duels. *By John Bill, Thomas Newcomb, and Henry Hills*, 1679/80. brs. STEELE 3710. L, O, C, LG, DT; CH, MH.

3214 A proclamation, against exportation. colop: *By John Bill and Christopher Barker*, 1661. fol.* STEELE 3309. L, O, C, LG, DT; CH, MH, NC, Y.

3215 A proclamation against fighting of duells. *By John Bill and Christopher Barker*, 1660. brs. STEELE 3245. LT, O, C, EN, DT; CH, MH, WF, Y.

3215A —[Anr. ed.] *Edinburgh, by Andrew Anderson*, 1677. brs. L.

3216 A proclamation against new buildings. *In the Savoy, by the assigns of John Bill and Christopher Barker*, 1671. brs. STEELE 3549. L, O, C, LPR, MC; CH, Y.

3217 A proclamation against numerous conventicles. *In the Savoy, by the assigns of John Bill and Christopher Barker*, 1669. brs. STEELE 3529. L, O, C, MC, DT; CH.

3218–19 Entries cancelled.

3220 A proclamation against the deceitful winding . . . of woolls. *By John Bill and Christopher Barker*, 1663[4]. brs. STEELE 3392. L, C, OQ, LPR, LS; MH.

3221 A proclamation against the rebels in Ireland. *By Christopher Barker and John Bill*, 1660. brs. STEELE 3220. L, O, C, MC, DT; MH, Y.

3222 —[Anr. ed.] *Reprinted Edinburgh, C Higgins*, 1660. brs. ALDIS 1659. STEELE 3p 2177. EN, ES; WF.

3223 —[Anr. ed.] *By Christopher Barker and John Bill*, 1660. *And reprinted at Dublin by William Bladen*, 1660. brs. STEELE 2p 620. C, DPR.

3224 A proclamation against the resetting of tenents . . . Feb. 11. *Edinburgh, by the heir of Andrew Anderson*, 1678 [9.] brs. ALDIS 2137. STEELE 3p 2137. EN; CH, Y.

3225 A proclamation against the resset of the rebels. *Edenburghe, by the heirs of Andrew Anderson*, 1679. *reprinted London.* brs. ALDIS 2168. STEELE 2464. L, O; CH, MH, Y.

3226 A proclamation against tumultuous petitions. *By John Bill, Thomas Newcomb, and Henry Hills*, 1679. brs. STEELE 3703. L, O, C, LG, DT; CH, MH, WF.

3227 A proclamation against vicious, debauch'd and prophane persons . . . thirieth day of May. *By Christopher Barker and John Bill*, 1660. LT, O, C, MC, DT; CH, MH, WF, Y.

3228 —[Anr. ed.] *Reprinted Edinburgh, C Higgins*, 1660. brs. ALDIS 1658. STEELE 3p 2176. L, EN; Y.

3229 —[Anr. ed.] *Dublin, W Bladen*, 1660. brs. STEELE 2p 619. DPR.

3229A A proclamation anent pedagogues. *Edinburgh, by the heir of Andrew Anderson. Reprinted [London], by George Croom*, 1683. brs. L, O; CH, MH.

3230 A proclamation anent persons denunced [*sic*] fugitives . . . 5 May. *Edinburgh, by the heir of Andrew Anderson*, 1684. fol.* ALDIS 2477. L, HH, EN; CH.

3230A A proclamation anent the sumptuary act. *Edinburgh, by the heir of Andrew Anderson*, 1684. brs. CH.

3231 A proclamation appointing some forraigne species. *Edinburgh, by the heir of Andrew Anderson*, 1677. brs. ALDIS 2106. L, EN; NC.

3232 A proclamation appointing the general fast. *By John Bill and Christopher Barker*, 1665. brs. STEELE 3437. L, C, LPR, LPC, HH.

3233 —[Anr. ed.] *Oxford, for J.Bill and C.Barker*, 1665. brs. MADAN 2683. STEELE 3438. O, LPR, OQ.

3234 A proclamation commanding all cashiered officers. *By John Bill*, 1660. brs. STEELE 3270. LT, O, C, MC, DT; MH.

3235 A proclamation commanding all Jesuites . . . to depart. *By John Bill and Christopher Barker*, 1663. fol.* STEELE 3381. L, O, C, EN, DT; MH, WG, Y.

3236 —[Anr. ed.] *Edinburgh, E Tyler*, 1663. fol.* ALDIS 1758. STEELE 3p 2245. EN.

3237 A proclamation commanding all masters . . . of ships. *In the Savoy, by the assigns of John Bill and Christopher Barker*, 1671. brs. STEELE 3551. L, O, LPC, LPR, LS; CH.

3238 —[Anr. ed.] *By the assigns of John Bill, Thomas Newcomb, and Henry Hills*, 1681. brs. STEELE 3729. L, O, C, LG, LPR; CH, MH, WF, Y.

3239 A proclamation commanding all Papists, . . . 4 May 1679. *By John Bill, Thomas Newcomb, and Henry Hills*, 1679. brs. STEELE 3686. L, O, C, LG, LPR; CH, MH, WG, Y.

3240 A proclamation commanding all Papists, . . . 3 December 1679. *By John Bill, Thomas Newcomb and Henry Hills,* 1679. brs. STEELE 3701. L, O, C, LG, DT; CH, MH, WG, Y.

3241 A proclamation commanding all Papists, . . . 4 October 1680. *By John Bill,* 1680. brs. STEELE 3718. L, C, OQ, LPR, LS, DT; CH, WG.

3242 A proclamation commanding all persons being Popish recusants. *By John Bill, Christopher Barker, Thomas Newcomb, and Henry Hills,* 1678. fol.* STEELE 3660. L, O, C, LPR, MC; CH, MH, NU, WG.

3243 —[Anr. ed.] *Reprinted Edinburgh, by the heir of Andrew Anderson,* 1678. brs. ALDIS 2139. STEELE 3p 2445. EN; Y.

3244 —[Anr. ed.] *Dublin, B. Took,* 1678. brs. STEELE 2p 890. ORM.

3245 A proclamation, commanding all seamen and mariners to return. *Oxford, by L. Lichfield, for John Bill and Christopher Barker,* 1665[/6]. brs. MADAN 2730. STEELE 3449. L, O, LPR, OQ.

3246 A proclamation commanding all seamen to repair to the ships. *By the assigns of John Bill and Christopher Barker,* 1673. brs. STEELE 3580. L, O, C, LPR, DT; CH, MH, WF.

3247 A proclamation commanding the immediate return. *By the assigns of John Bill and Christopher Barker,* 1675. brs. STEELE 3612. L, O, C, LPR; CH, MH, WF.

3248 —[Anr. ed.] *Dublin, B Tooke,* 1675. brs. STEELE 2p 858. DPR.

3249 —*By John Bill, Christopher Barker, Thomas Newcomb, and Henry Hills,* 1678[9]. fol.* STEELE 3675. L, O, C, MC, DT; CH, MH, Y.

3250 A proclamation concerning building, in and about London. colop: *By John Bill and Christopher Barker,* 1661. fol.* STEELE 3322. L, O, C, EN, DT; CH, MH, WF, Y.

3251 The King's Majesties proclamation concerning church affairs . . . 10 June. *Edinburgh, by Evan Tyler,* 1661. brs. ALDIS 1713. STEELE 3p 2207. AC; Y.

3252 A proclamation, concerning His Majesties coronation pardon. colop: *By John Bill,* 1661. fol.* LT, O, C, EN, DT; CH, MH, Y.

3253 —[Anr. ed.] *Edinburgh,* 1661. brs. ALDIS 1712. STEELE 3p 2205. L, ES.

3254 A proclamation concerning His Majesties gracious pardon. *By John Bill and Christopher Barker,* 1660. fol.* STEELE 3229. LT, O, C, EN, DT; MH, MIU, TSM, WF, Y.

3255 A proclamation concerning passes and sea-briefs. *By the assigns of John Bill and Christopher Barker,* 1675/6. brs. STEELE 3628. L, O, C, LPR, DT; CH, MH, WF.

3256 A proclamation concerning passes for ships. *By the assigns of John Bill and Christopher Barker,* 1676. brs. STEELE 3629. L, O, C, LPR, DT; CH, WF.

3257 A proclamation concerning the act for the revenue. *By John Bill and Christopher Barker,* 1662. brs. STEELE 3358. L, O, C, EN, DT; MH, NC.

3258 A proclamation concerning the acts of navigation. *By John Bill and Christopher Barker,* 1663. fol.* STEELE 3387. L, O, C, LPR, DT; CLC, MH, NC.

3259 A proclamation concerning the adjournment of Hilary Term. *By John Bill and Christopher Barker,* 1665[6]. fol.* STEELE 3450. L, C, LG, LPR, DT.

3260 —[Anr. ed.] *Oxford, by A. & L. Lichfield for J. Bill & C. Barker, London,* 1665[/6]. fol.* MADAN 2731. STEELE 3451. OQ, LPC, LPR.

3261 A proclamation concerning the adjournment of Michaelmas Term. *By John Bill and Christopher Barker,* 1665. fol.* STEELE 3439. L, OQ, C, LPR, LS.

3262 —[Anr. ed.] *Oxford, by L. Lichfield for J. Bill & C. Barker of London,* 1665. fol.* MADAN 2684. STEELE 3440. L, OQ, LG, LPC, LPR.

3263 A proclamation, concerning the advocats . . . 12 Dec. *Edinburgh, by Andrew Anderson,* 1674. brs. ALDIS 2033. STEELE 3p 2395. L, O.

3264 The Kings Majesties proclamation, concerning the carriage. *Edinburgh, by Evan Tyler,* 1660. brs. STEELE 3p 2191a. L, EH, REG; Y.

3265 A proclamation concerning the collecting . . . of revenue. *By the assigns of John Bill and Christopher Barker,* 1674. brs. STEELE 3598. L, O, C, LPC, LPR; CH, MH.

3266 —*By John Bill,* 1679. fol.* STEELE 3697. L, O, C, LG, DT; CH, MH.

3267 —*By the assigns of John Bill; and by Henry Hills, and Thomas Newcomb,* 1684. fol.* STEELE 3761. L, O, C, LG, LPR; CH, MH.

3268 A proclamation concerning the granting of licences. *By John Bill and Christopher Barker,* 1661. fol.* STEELE 3327. L, O, C, MC, DT; MH.

3269 A proclamation concerning the payment of the watch-money . . . 1 Sept. *Edinburgh by the heirs of Andrew Anderson,* 1682. brs. ALDIS 2353. L, EH, ES.

3270 A proclamation concering the President and Council of Wales. *By John Bill and Christopher Barker,* 1661. fol.* STEELE 3329. L, OQ, C, AN, EN; CH, MH.

3271 A proclamation concerning the prorogation of the Parliament. *By John Bill and Christopher Barker,* 1665. brs. MADAN 2680. STEELE 3433. L, OQ, C, LPR, HH.

3272 —[Anr. ed.] *Oxford, by Leonard Lichfield,* 1665. brs. MADAN 2681. STEELE 3434. LPR.

3273 A proclamation concerning the sale of fee-farm rents. *In the Savoy, by the assigns of John Bill and Christopher Barker,* 1670. brs. STEELE 3540. L, OQ, LPR, LS, DT; CH.

3274 A proclamation concerning the times of holding this summer assizes. *By John Bill and Christopher Barker,* 1660. brs. STEELE 3234. LT, O, C, EN, DT; CH, MH, WF, Y.

3275 A proclamation concerning wine-licences. *By John Bill and Christopher Barker,* 1661. fol.* STEELE 3351. L, OQ, C, LPR, DT.

3275A — —, 1662. fol.* STEELE 3355. L, C; MH.

3276 — —, 1663. fol.* STEELE 3385. L, OQ, C, LPR, DT; MH.

3277 A proclamation, containing His Majesties gracious pardon . . . 27 July. *Edinburgh, by the heir of Andrew Anderson,* 1679. brs. ALDIS 2168. STEELE 3p 2470. O, HH, REG, ES; WF.

3278 —[Anr. ed.] *Reprinted,* [1679]. brs. STEELE 3p 2473. L, O; MH.

3279 —[Anr. ed.] *Reprinted, for A. Forrester*, [1679]. brs. STEELE 3p 2474. O, LG.

3280 A proclamation declaring a former proclamation . . . void. *By John Bill and Christopher Barker*, 1663. fol.* STEELE 3380. L, OQ, C, LPR, LS; MH.

3281 A A [sic] proclamation declaring and enjoying observance of . . . peace. *In the Savoy, by the assigns of John Bill and Christopher Barker*, 1667[8]. brs. STEELE 3513. L, O, C, MC, DT; CH, MH.

3282 A proclamation declaring His Majesties grace. *By John Bill and Christopher Barker*, 1662. fol.* STEELE 3365. L, OC, LPR, DT; MH, WF.

3283 A proclamation, declaring His Majesties pleasure to settle . . . Tangier. *By John Bill*, 1660[1]. fol.* LT, O, C, EN, DPR.

3284 —*By John Bill and Christopher Barker*, 1662. fol.* STEELE 3369. L, O, C, EN, DT; CH, MH.

3284A A proclamation declaring His Majesties pleasure touching his royal coronation. *By John Bill*, 1660. brs. STEELE 3289. L, C, LG, OP, CT; CH, MH, WF, Y.

3285 A proclamation declaring Iames Marqves of Ormond. *Printed at Kilkenny*, 1649. brs. STEELE 2p 458. O.

3286 A proclamation declaring Mr. Richard Cameron, and others, rebels. *Reprinted for Andrew Forrester*, 1680. brs. STEELE 3p 2489. L, O; CH.

3287 A proclamation declaring the cessation of hostility, . . . Spain. *By John Bill and Christopher Barker*, 1660. fol.* STEELE 3254. L, O, C, EN, DT; CH, MH, WF, Y.

3288 A proclamation declaring the confirmation of the treaties. *By John Bill and Christopher Barker*, 1660. brs. STEELE 3263. L, O, C, EN, DT; CH, MH, MIU, Y.

3289 A proclamation declaring the letters of mart. *By John Bill, Thomas Newcomb, and Henry Hills*, 1680. brs. STEELE 3716. I, O, C, LG, DT; CH, WF.

3290 A proclamation declaring the Parliament shall be prorogued. *By John Bill, Christopher Barker, Thomas Newcomb, and Henry Hills*, 1678. brs. STEELE 3654. L, O, LG, LPR, DT; CH, MH, WF, Y.

3291 —*By John Bill, Thomas Newcomb, and Henry Hills*, 1679. brs. STEELE 3696. L, O, C, LPR, DT; CH, MH.

3292 A proclamation declaring the Parliament shall sit. *By John Bill, Thomas Newcomb, and Henry Hills*, 1680. brs. STEELE 3717. L, O, C, LG, DT; CH, MH, WF, Y.

3293 A proclamation declaring the rates at which gold. *By John Bill and Christopher Barker*, 1661. fol.* STEELE 3324. L, O, C, EN, DT; CH, MH, Y.

3294 Entry cancelled.

3295 A proclamation enjoying the observance of the peace. *By the assigns of John Bill and Christopher Barker*, 1674. fol.* STEELE 3603. L, O, C, LPR, DT; CH, WF.

3296 —[Anr. ed.] *Edinburgh, by Andrew Anderson*, 1674. brs. ALDIS 2032. STEELE 3p 2392. EN.

3297 A proclamation enjoyning the prosecution. *By the assigns of John Bill and Christopher Barker*, 1674. brs. STEELE 3605. L, O, LG, LPC, LPR; CH, MH.

3298 A proclamation, for a general fast. *By John Bill and Christopher Barker*, 1661. brs. STEELE 3307. L, O, C, MC, DT; CH, MH, Y.

3299 —, 8th day of January [1661/2]. —, 1661 [2]. brs. STEELE 3349. L, O, C, EN, DT; CH, MH, WF, Y.

3300 —, sixth day of March. —, 1664[5]. fol.* STEELE 3410. L, OQ, C, LPR, DT.

3301 —, sixth day of July. —, 1665. fol.* STEELE 3426. L, O, C, LPC, LPR.

3301A —[Anr. ed.] *York, by Stephen Bulkely*, 1665. 4°.* RIPON.

3302 —, 28 May 1666. —, 1666. brs. STEELE 3463. L, OQ, LPC, LPR, HH.

3303 —, thirteenth day of September. —, 1666. brs. STEELE 3474. L, O, C, LPR, DT.

3304 —, tenth of October. —, 1666. fol.* O.

3305 —, 22 March 1671/2. *In the Savoy, by the assigns of John Bill and Christopher Barker*, 1971/2 [i.e. 1671/2]. brs. STEELE 3558. L, O, C, MC, DT; CH.

3306 —, Sixteenth day of January 1673/4. colop: *By the assigns of John Bill and Christopher Barker*, 1673/4. fol.* STEELE 3587. L, O, C, MC, DT; CH, MH, WF.

3307 —, thirtieth day of March 1678. *By John Bill, Christopher Barker, Thomas Newcomb, and Henry Hills*, 1678. brs. STEELE 3649. L, O, C, LG, DT; CH, MH, WF.

3308 —, 25 October 1678. —, 1678. brs. STEELE 3659. L, O, C, LG, DT; CH, WF.

3309 —, twenty eighth day of March 1679. *By John Bill, Thomas Newcomb, and Henry Hills*, 1679. brs. STEELE 3683. L, O, C, MC, DT; CH, MH.

3310 —, second day of December 1680. *By the assigns of John Bill, Thomas Newcomb, and Henry Hills*, 1680. fol.* STEELE 3722. L, O, C, MC, DT; CH, MH, MM, WF, k Y.

3311 A proclamation for a publick general fast . . . 28 June 1666. *Edinburgh, E Tyler*, 1666. brs. STEELE 3p 2297. LPR, REG.

3312 A proclamation for a thanksgiving. *By John Bill and Christopher Barker*, 1665. fol.* STEELE 3421. L, O, C, LPR, LS.

3313 ——, 1666. brs. STEELE 3467. L, OQ, LPR, LPC, LS; CH, MH.

3314 By His Highnesse the Prince of Great Britain, . . . a proclamation, for all persons within our quarters. *Imprinted at Exeter by Robert Barker and John Bill*, 1645. brs. STEELE 2639. LT.

3315 A proclamation for appointing commissioners. *By John Bill and Christopher Barker*, 1663/4. fol.* STEELE 3394. L, OQ, C, LPR, DT; MH.

3315A A proclamation for apprehending of robbers. *By the assigns of J. Bill*, 1681. brs. L.

3316 A proclamation for apprehension of Edward Whalley and William Goffe. *By Christopher Barker and John Bill*, 1660. fol.* STEELE 3257. LT, O, C, EN, DT; CH, MH, WCL, WF, Y.

3316A A proclamation for authorizing an uniformity. *W. Sheares*, 1660 [61]. brs. L.

3317 A proclamation for banishing all Popish priests . . . 10 Nov. *In the Savoy, by the assigns of John Bill and Christopher Barker,* 1666. fol.* STEELE 3479. L, O, C, MC, DT; CH, MH, WG, Y.

3318 A proclamation for better cleansing of the streets. *In the Savoy, by the assigns of John Bill and Christopher Barker,* 1672. fol.* STEELE 3561. L, O, OQ, LPR, HH; CH.

3319 A proclamation for calling a convention of estates . . . 25 Oct. *Edinburgh, E Tyler,* 1665. brs. ALDIS 1821. STEELE 3p 2280. AU.

3320 —, 23 May. *Edinburgh, by the heir of Andrew Anderson,* 1678. brs. ALDIS 2138. STEELE 3p 2441. L; Y.

3321 A proclamation for calling home. *In the Savoy, by the assigns of John Bill and Christopher Barker,* 1672. brs. STEELE 3565. L, OQ, C, LPC, LPR; CH, MH.

3322 A proclamation for calling in, and suppressing of two books written by John Milton. *By John Bill and Christopher Barker,* 1660. fol.* STEELE 3239. LT, O, LVF, LG, LPR; CH, CLC, MH, Y.

3323 —[Anr. ed.] *By John Bill,* 1660. fol.* STEELE 3240. L, OQ, C, EN, DT; MHS, WCL.

3324 The Kings Majesties proclamation for calling of his Parliament . . . 10 Oct. *Edinburgh, E. Tyler,* 1660. fol.* ALDIS 1666. STEELE 3p 2191. AU, REG.

3325 A proclamation for commanding the magistrates, and officers. *By the assigns of John Bill, and by Henry Hills, and Thomas Newcomb,* 1683. brs. STEELE 3740. L, O, C, LG, DT; CH, MH, WF.

3326 A proclamation for continuing the officers of the excise. *By John Bill,* 1660. brs. STEELE 3276. LT, O, C, EN, DT; MH, Y.

3327 A proclamation for disarming . . . Popish recusants. *By John Bill, Christopher Barker, Thomas Newcomb, and Henry Hills,* 1678. brs. STEELE 3672. L, O, LG, LPC, LPR; CH, MH, WG, Y.

3328 A proclamation for discovering and preventing. colop: *By John Bill and Christopher Barker,* 1661. fol.* STEELE 3319. L, O, C, EN, DT; MH, NC, WF.

3329 A proclamation for discovery and apprehension of several. *By John Bill and Christopher Barker,* 1664. fol.* STEELE 3401. L, OQ, C, LPR, DT; CH, MH.

3330 A proclamation for discovery of robberies. *By John Bill and Christopher Barker,* 1661. fol.* STEELE 3348. L, C, OQ, EN, DPR; MH, Y.

3331 A proclamation for dissolving the Parliament . . . 19 May 1677 [i.e. 1674]. *Edinburgh, by Andrew Anderson,* 1674. brs. ALDIS 2028a. STEELE 3p 2386. EN; Y.

3332 —, 19 May 1674. *Edinburgh, A Anderson,* 1674. brs. ALDIS 2028. STEELE 3p 2387. HH.

3332A A proclamation for dissolving the present parliament. 1679. brs. STEELE 3679. OP.

3333 A proclamation for dissolving this present Parliament. *By John Bill, Thomas Newcomb, and Henry Hills,* 1679. brs. STEELE 3691. L, O, C, LG, DT; CH, MH, Y.

3334 —*By the assigns of John Bill, Thomas Newcomb, and Henry Hills,* 1680[1]. brs. STEELE 3724. L, O, C, EN, DT; CH, MH, WF, Y.

3335 —*Dublin, by Benjamin Tooke and John Crook,* [1680/1]. brs. STEELE 2p 919. L, O, ORM.

3336 A proclamation for due execution. *In the Savoy, by the assigns of John Bill and Christopher Barker,* 1667. brs. STEELE 3507. L, OQ, C, LPR, DT; CH, MH.

3337 A proclamation for incouragement of the further discovery. *By John Bill, Thomas Newcomb, and Henry Hills,* 1680. brs. STEELE 3720. L, O, C, MC, DT; CH, MH, WG, Y.

3338 A proclamation for enforcing the due execution. *In the Savoy, by the assigns of John Bill and Christopher Barker,* 1669. fol.* STEELE 3527. L, OQ, C, LPC, LPR; CH.

3339 —*By the assigns of John Bill, Henry Hills, and Thomas Newcomb,* 1683. fol.* STEELE 3753. L, O, C, LG, DT; CH, MH.

3340 A proclamation for inforcing the laws. *In the Savoy, by the assigns of John Bill and Christopher Barker,* 1667/8. brs. STEELE 3514. L, O, C, LPR, MC; CH, MH, WG, Y.

3341 A proclamation for further proroguing the Parliament. *By John Bill and Christopher Barker,* 1664. brs. STEELE 3399. L, OQ, C, LPR, LS; MH.

3342 —, twenty fourth day of May 1665. —, 1665. brs. STEELE 3419. L, O, C, LPC, LPR.

3343 —, ninth day of July. —, 1665. brs. STEELE 3427. L, OQ, C, LPR, HH.

3344 —*Oxford: by A. & Leonard Lichfield for John Bill and Christopher Barker,* [London], 1665[/6]. brs. MADAN 2733. STEELE 3453. L, O, C, LPR, DT.

3345 —*In the Savoy, by the assigns of John Bill and Christopher Barker,* 1671. brs. STEELE 3552. L, O, LPC, LPR; CH.

3346 —, 17 September 1672. —, brs. STEELE 3574. L, O, C, LPC, LPR; CH.

3347 —, 25 September 1678. *By John Bill, Christopher Barker, Thomas Newcomb, and Henry Hills,* 1678. brs. STEELE 3655. L, O, C, LG, LS; CH, MH, WF, Y.

3348 A proclamation for making currant His Majesties farthings. *In the Savoy, by the assigns of John Bill and Christopher Barker,* 1672. fol.* STEELE 3573. L, O, C, LPR, MC; CH, MH.

3349 A proclamation for observation of the thirtieth day of January as a day of fast. colop: *By John Bill,* 1660 [/1]. fol.* STEELE 3283. LT, O, C, EN, DT; CH, MH, WF, Y.

3350 —*By the assigns of John Bill and Christopher Barker,* 1674. brs. STEELE 3285. L, O, LS, MC; CH.

3351 — —, 1675/6. fol.* STEELE 3286. O, LPC, LPR, HH.

3352 A proclamation for payment of the duty of excise. colop: *By John Bill and Christopher Barker,* 1660. fol.* STEELE 3260. LT, O, C, EN, DT; MH, NC, Y.

3353 A proclamation for preventing frauds. *By John Bill and Christopher Barker,* 1662. fol.* STEELE 3370. L, OQ, C, EN, DT; MH, WF.

3354 A proclamation for preventing the fears. *By the assigns of John Bill and Christopher Barker,* 1673/4. fol.* STEELE 3586. L, O, C, MC, DT; CH, MH, WG.

3355 A proclamation for preventing the importation of foreign corn. colop: *In the Savoy, by the assigns of John Bill and Christopher Barker*, 1669. brs. STEELE 3525. L, OQ, C, LPR, DT; CH, MH.

3356 A proclamation for prevention of disorders. *By the assigns of John Bill and Christopher Barker*, 1672. fol.* STEELE 3576. L, O, C, LPR, MC; CH, MH.

3357 A proclamation for prizing of wines . . . Feb. 4, 1661[2]. *By John Bill and Christopher Barker*, 1661[2]. fol.* STEELE 3352. L, O, C, EN, DT; MH, NC.

3358 —, 27th day of January 1663/4. —, 1663/4. fol.* STEELE 3391. L, O, C, LPR, DT; MH.

3359 —, eighth day of February 1664[5]. —, 1664[5]. fol.* STEELE 3407. L, OQ, C, LPR, DT; MH.

3360 —, twentieth day of January. *Oxford: by A. & Leonard Lichfeild for John Bill and Christopher Barker, London*, 1665[/6]. fol.* MADAN 2734. STEELE 3454. O, C, OQ, LPC, LPR.

3361 —, 19th day of January. colop: *In the Savoy, by the assigns of John Bill and Christopher Barker*, 1666/7. fol.* STEELE 3485. L, O, C, LL, LPR; MH.

3362 —, 31th day of January. —, 1667[8]. fol.* STEELE 3511. L, OQ, C, LPR, DT; CH, MH.

3363 —, 22 January. —, 1668[9]. fol.* STEELE 3524. L, OQ, LPR, DT; CH.

3364 —, twenty fourth day of January, 1669/70. —, 1669/70. fol.* STEELE 3532. L, OQ, C, LPR, DT; CH, MH.

3365 —, 23 March 1670/1. —, 1670/1. fol.* STEELE 3546. O, C, OQ, LPC, LPR; CH.

3366 —, 10 January 1671/2. —, 1671/2. fol.* STEELE 3556. L, O, LPR, LS, DT; CH.

3367 —, 11 January 1672/3. *By the assigns of John Bill and Christopher Barker*, 1672/3. fol.* STEELE 3578. L, O, LG, LPR, DT; CH.

3368 —, 6 February 1673/4. —, 1673/4. fol.* STEELE 3589. O, OQ, LPR, LS, HH; CH, MH.

3369 —, 13 January 1674[5]. —, 1674[5]. fol.* STEELE 3607. L, O, OQ, LG, LS; CH, MH.

3370 —, 22 January 1675/6. —, 1675/6. fol.* STEELE 3627. L, O, C, OQ, LG; CH, MH, WF.

3371 —, 17 January 1676/7. —, 1676/7. fol.* STEELE 3639. L, O, C, OQ, DT; CH, MH, WF.

3372 —, 12 January 1677/8. *By John Bill, Christopher Barker, Thomas Newcomb, and Henry Hills*, 1677. fol.* STEELE 3646. L, O, C, LG, DT; CH, MH, WF.

3373 —, 24 January 1678/9. —, 1678/9. fol.* STEELE 3678. L, O, C, LG; CH, MH, WF.

3374 —, 23 January 1679[80]. —, 1679/80. fol.* STEELE 3708. L, OQ, LG, LPR, LS; CH, MH.

3375 A proclamation for prohibiting dirt-boats. *In the Savoy, by the assigns of John Bill and Christopher Barker*, 1671. brs. STEELE 3547. L, OQ, LG, LPR, MC; CH.

3376 A proclamation for prohibiting the imbezlement. *By the assigns of John Bill and Christopher Barker*, 1661. brs. STEELE 3333. L, O, C, LPR, EN; MH.

3377 A proclamation for prohibiting the exportation of iron ordnance. *By the assigns of John Bill*, 1681. brs. STEELE 3730. L, O, C, LG, LS; CH, MH.

3378 A proclamation for prohibiting the importation of commodities. *By the assigns of John Bill and Christopher Barker*, 1675. fol.* STEELE 3619. L, O, C, OQ, DT; CH, MH, MIU.

3379 A proclamation for prohibiting the importation or retailing. *By John Bill and Christopher Barker*, 1664/5. brs. STEELE 3413. L, OQ, C, LPR, DT; CH, MH, MIU.

3380 A proclamation for prohibiting the transportation. *By the assigns of John Bill and Christopher Barker*, 1665[6]. fol.* STEELE 3452. L frag., OQ, LPR, HH.

3381 —*In the Savoy, by the assigns of John Bill and Christopher Barker*, 1668. fol.* STEELE 3521. L, OQ, LG, LPR, HH.

3382 A proclamation for proroguing the Parliament. *In the Savoy, by the assigns of John Bill and Christopher Barker*, 1668. brs. STEELE 3520. L, O, C, LPR, DT; CH.

3383 —*By the assigns of John Bill and Christopher Barker*, 1674. brs. STEELE 3601. L, O, C, LPR, LS; CH.

3384 —*By John Bill, Thomas Newcomb, and Henry Hills*, 1679. brs. STEELE 3702. L, O, C, LPR, DT; CH, MH.

3385 A proclamation for publishing a former proclamation. *By John Bill and Christopher Barker*, 1660. brs. STEELE 3242. LT, O, C, EN, DT; CH, MH, WF, Y.

3386 A proclamation for publishing the peace . . . Denmark. *In the Savoy, by the assigns of John Bill and Christopher Barker*, 1667. brs. STEELE 3501. L, O, C, MC, DT; CH, MH.

3387 —*Dublin, J. Crook*, 1667. brs. STEELE 2p 787. DPR.

3388 A proclamation for publishing the peace . . . French king. *In the Savoy, by the assigns of John Bill and Christopher Barker*, 1667. brs. STEELE 3500. L, O, C, MC, DT; CH, MH.

3389 —*Dublin, J. Crooke*, 1667. brs. STEELE 2p 786. DPR.

3390 A proclamation for publishing the peace . . . Netherlands. *In the Savoy, by the assigns of John Bill and Christopher Barker*, 1667. brs. STEELE 3502. L, O, C, MC, DT; CH, MH.

3391 —*Edinburgh, E Tyler*, 1667. brs. STEELE 3p 2311. REG.

3391A —. *Dublin, J. Crook*, 1667. brs. STEELE 2p 788. DPR.

3392 —*By the assigns of John Bill and Christopher Barker*, 1673/4. brs. STEELE 3590. L, O, C, MC, DT; CH.

3393 —, 27 Feb. *Edinburgh, by His Majesties printers*, 1674. brs. ALDIS 2026. STEELE 3, 2379. L, HH.

3394 —*Dublin, B Tooke*, 1673[4]. brs. STEELE 2, 848. DPR, ORM.

3395 A proclamation for putting off the Fair. *By John Bill and Christopher Barker*, 1666. brs. STEELE 3476. L, OQ, C, LPR, LS.

3396 A proclamation for quieting possessions. *By John Bill and Christopher Barker*, 1660. brs. STEELE 3217. L, OQ, C, EN, DT; MH, WF.

3397 —*By Christopher Barker and John Bill*, 1660. brs. STEELE 3218. LT, O, C, MC, DT; CH, MH.

3398 A proclamation for quieting the Post-master-general. *By John Bill*, 1660[/1]. fol.* STEELE 3280. LT, O, C, EN, DT; MH, Y.

3399 —*In the Savoy, by the assigns of John Bill and Christopher Barker*, 1667. fol.* STEELE 3496. L, OQ, C, LPR.

3400 —*By the assigns of John Bill and Christopher Barker*, [1673]. STEELE 3497. L, C, LG.

3401 A proclamation for reassembling the Parliament. *In the Savoy, by the assigns of John Bill and Christopher Barker*, 1667. brs. STEELE 3495. L, O, C, LPR, MC; CH.

3402 A proclamation for recalling and prohibiting seamen. colop: *By John Bill*, 1661. fol.* STEELE 3298. LT, OQ, C, EN, DT; CH, MH, Y.

3403 —*By John Bill and Christopher Barker*, 1662. fol.* STEELE 3361. L, O, C, EN, DT; CH, CLC, MH, WF.

3404 —*By John Bill and Christopher Barker*, 1664. fol.* STEELE 3398. L, OQ, C, LPR, LS; CH, MH, WF.

3405 —, *7 June. Edinburgh reprinted E Tyler*, 1664. brs. ALDIS 1779. STEELE 3p 2265. HH, AU.

3406 —*In the Savoy, by the assigns of John Bill and Christopher Barker*, 1671/2. fol.* STEELE 3557. L, O, C, LPR, LS; CH, MH.

3407 —*By John Bill, Christopher Barker, Thomas Newcomb, and Henry Hills*, 1677/8. fol.* STEELE 3648. L, O, C, LPR, DT; CH, MH, WF.

3408 A proclamation for recalling dispensations. *In the Savoy, by the assigns of John Bill and Christopher Barker*, 1667. brs. STEELE 3499. L, O, C, MC, DT; CH, LC, MH, WF.

3409 —*By the assigns of John Bill and Christopher Barker*, 1673/4. brs. STEELE 3593. L, O, C, LPR, DT; CH, MH.

3410 A proclamation for recalling of commissions at sea. *By John Bill and Christopher Barker*, 1660. brs. STEELE 3228. LT, O, C, EN, DT; CH, CLC, MH, WF, Y.

3411 A proclamation for recalling private commissions. *Oxford: by Leonard Lichfield for John Bill and Christopher Barker of London*, 1665[/6]. brs. MADAN 2729. STEELE 3448. OQ, C, LPC, LPR, HH.

3412 A proclamation for recalling proclamations. *In the Savoy, by the assigns of John Bill and Christopher Barker*, 1667. brs. STEELE 3508. L, OQ, C, LPR, DT; CH, MH.

3413 A proclamation for registring knights. *By the assigns of John Bill and Christopher Barker*, 1673. brs. STEELE 3582. L, OQ, C, LG, LPR; CH.

3414 A proclamation for regulating the colours. *By the assigns of John Bill and Christopher Barker*, 1674. fol.* STEELE 3599. L, O, LPR, LS; CH, MH.

3415 —*By the assigns of John Bill, and by Henry Hills and Thomas Newcomb*, 1683. fol.* STEELE 3600. C, LG, HH; MH.

3416 A proclamation for removing the receipt. *By John Bill and Christopher Barker*, 1665. brs. STEELE 3428. L, OQ, C, LG, LPR.

3417 A proclamation, for removing the receipt of His Majesties exchequer. *Oxford: by Leonard Lichfield for John Bill and Christopher Barker of London*, 1665[/6]. brs. MADAN 2728. STEELE 3447. OQ, C, LPR, HH.

3418 A proclamation for restoring and discovering His Majesties goods. *By John Bill and Christopher Barker*, 1660. brs. STEELE 3248. LT, O, C, EN, DT; CH, MH, Y.

3419 A proclamation for restoring goods. *By John Bill and Christopher Barker*, 1666. fol.* STEELE 3475. L, O, C, LG, LPR.

3420 A proclamation for restraining the payment. *By John Bill and Christopher Barker*, 1661[2]. brs. STEELE 3351. L, OQ, C, EN, DT; MH, NC, Y.

3421 A proclamation for restraint of killing, . . . flesh in Lent. colop: *by John Bill*, 1660[1]. fol.* STEELE 3287. LT, O, C, EN, DT; MH, WF, Y.

3422 —*By John Bill and Christopher Barker*, 1661. fol.* STEELE 3330. L, OQ, C, EN, DT; MH.

3423 —*R. Norton*, 1661. fol.* STEELE 3332. O, LG, LS.

3424 —, *seventeenth day of January* 1662[3]. *By John Bill and Christopher Barker*, 1662[3]. fol.* STEELE 3376. L, OQ, C, LPR, LS; MH.

3425 —, *25 January* 1663/4. —, 1663/4. fol.* STEELE 3390. L, O, C, LPR, LS; MH.

3426 A proclamation for setting apart a day . . . 5 June 1660. *By Christopher Barker and John Bill*, 1660. fol.* STEELE 3222. LT, O, C, EN, DT; CH, MH, WF, Y.

3427 A proclamation for speeding the payment of the arrears. *By John Bill and Christopher Barker*, 1660. brs. STEELE 3259. LT, O, C, EN, DT; MH, WF, Y.

3428 A proclamation for suppressing the printing and publishing unlicensed news-books. *By John Bill, Thomas Newcomb, and Henry Hills*, 1680. brs. STEELE 3715. L, O, C, MC, DT; CH, MH.

3429 A proclamation for suppression of Popery. *By the assigns of John Bill and Christopher Barker*, 1673. brs. STEELE 3584. L, O, C, LPR, MC; CH, MH, WG, Y.

3430 —*Dublin, B Tooke*, 1673. brs. STEELE 2p 846. DIX 150. DK, DPR.

3431 A proclamation for suspending the execution. *By John Bill and Christopher Barker*, 1666. fol.* STEELE 3469. OQ, LPC, LPR, LS.

3432 A proclamation for suspending the prosecution. *By John Bill and Christopher Barker*, 1662. brs. STEELE 3368. L, O, C, EN, DT; MH.

3433 A proclamation for taking away any restraint. *By John Bill and Christopher Barker*, 1665. fol.* STEELE 3417. L, O, C, LPR, DT; MH.

3434 A proclamation for taking off the late restraint. *In the Savoy, by the assigns of John Bill and Christopher Barker*, 1672. brs. STEELE 3569. L, O, LG, LPR, LS; CH, MH, WF, Y.

3435 A proclamation for the apprehending certain offenders. *By John Bill, Christopher Barker, Thomas Newcomb, and Henry Hills*, 1678. fol.* STEELE 3663. L, O, C, LG, DT; CH, MH, WG.

3436 A proclamation for the apprehending certain persons. *By John Bill, Christopher Barker, Thomas Newcomb, and Henry Hills*, 1678/9. brs. STEELE 3676. L, O, C, LG, MC; CH, MH.

3436A A proclamation, for the apprehending James Duke of Bucclough . . . 4 July, 1683. *Edinburgh, by the heir of Andrew Anderson*, 1683. brs. STEELE 3p 2548. WF.

3436B —[Anr. ed.] —, *reprinted at London by G. Croom*, 1683. brs. BR.

3437 A proclamation for the apprehending of Aron Smith. *By John Bill, Christopher Barker, Thomas Newcomb, and Henry Hills*, 1677. brs. STEELE 3641. L, O, C, LG, DT; CH, MH, WF.

3438 A proclamation for the apprehending of certain persons. *By John Bill, Thomas Newcomb, and Henry Hills*, 1679, 1679. brs. STEELE 3694. L, O, C, LG, DT; CH, MU, WF.

3439 A proclamation for the apprehending of Colonel John Rumsey. *By the assigns of John Bill, and by Henry Hills and Thomas Newcomb*, 1683. brs. STEELE 3744. L, O, C, LG, DT; CH, MH, WF.

3440 A proclamation for the apprehending of James Duke of Monmouth. *By the assigns of John Bill, and by Henry Hills, and Thomas Newcomb*, 1683. brs. STEELE 3748. L, O, C, MC, DT; CH, MH, WF.

3441 —*Edinburgh, heir of Andrew Anderson*, 1683. brs. ALDIS 2413. STEELE 3p 2544. MC, EN, REG; WF.

3442 A proclamation for the apprehending of robbers. *By John Bill*, 1677. brs. STEELE 3642. L, O, C, LG, DT; CH, MH.

3443 — —, 1679/80. brs. STEELE 3709. L, O, C, LG, DT; CH.

3444 —*By the assigns of John Bill, Thomas Newcomb, and Henry Hills*, 1681. brs. STEELE 3728. L, OQ, C, LPR, DT; CH, MH.

3445 —*By the assigns of John Bill and by Henry Hills and Thomas Newcomb*, 1682/3. brs. STEELE 3738. L, C, LPC, LPR, HH; CH.

3446 A proclamation for the apprehension of certain notorious robbers. *In the Savoy, by the assigns of John Bill and Christopher Barker*, 1668. fol.* STEELE 3522. L, OQ, C, LPC, LPR; CH, MH.

3447 A proclamation for the apprehension of Edmund Ludlow. *By John Bill and Christopher Barker*, 1660. fol.* STEELE 3251. LT, O, C, EN, DPR; CH, MH, Y.

2448 Entry cancelled.

3449 A proclamation for the apprehension of notorious robbers. *In the Savoy, by the assigns of John Bill and Christopher Barker*, 1669. fol.* STEELE 3530. L, OQ, C, LPR, LS; CH.

3450 A proclamation, for the better collecting. *By the assigns of John Bill and Christopher Barker*, 1675. brs. STEELE 3614. L, LG; NC.

3451 A proclamation for the better discovery of seditious libellers. *By the assigns of John Bill and Christopher Barker*, 1675[6]. brs. STEELE 3624. L, O, C, MC, DT; CH, MH, Y.

3452 A proclamation for the better ordering. *By John Bill and Christopher Barker*, 1662. fol.* STEELE 3364. L, O, C, EN, DT; CH, MH.

3453 — —, 1665. fol.* STEELE 3418. L, OQ, C, LPR, DT; MH.

3454 —*By the assigns of John Bill, and by Henry Hills, and Thomas Newcomb*, 1683. fol.* STEELE 3742. L, O, C, LG, DT; CH, MH.

3455 A proclamation for the better putting in execution. *By John Bill, Thomas Newcomb, and Henry Hills*, 1679/80. fol.* STEELE 3706. L, O, C, LG, DT; CH, MH, NC.

3456 A proclamation for the better quieting the Post-Master-General. *By John Bill and Christopher Barker*, 1663. fol.* STEELE 3382. L, OQ, C, LG, LPR; MH.

3457 A proclamation for the better regulating His . . . proceedings. *By John Bill*, 1661. brs. STEELE 3297. LT, OQ, C, EN, DT; CH, MH, Y.

3458 A proclamation for the better regulating of lotteries. *By John Bill and Christopher Barker*, 1665. fol.* STEELE 3423. L, OQ, C, LPR, LS.

3459 A proclamation for the calling in all moneys. *By John Bill and Christopher Barker*, 1661. fol.* STEELE 3326. L, O, C, EN, DT; CH, MH, NC, WF, Y.

3460 A proclamation for the careful custody. *In the Savoy, by the assigns of John Bill and Christopher Barker*, 1669. brs. STEELE 3528. L, OQ, C, LPC, LPR; CH.

3461 A proclamation for the confinement of Popish recusants. *By John Bill, Christopher Barker, Thomas Newcomb, and Henry Hills*, 1678. fol.* STEELE 3662. L, O, C, MC, DT; CH, MH, WG, Y.

3462 Proclamation for the convention of estates. *Edinburgh, E. Tyler*, 1666. brs. ALDIS 1821. STEELE 3p 2301. AU.

3463 A proclamation for the discovery and apprehending all Popish priests. *By John Bill, Christopher Barker, Thomas Newcomb and Henry Hills*, 1678. brs. STEELE 3666. L, O, C, LG, LS; CH, WG.

3464 —*Dublin, B Took*, 1678. brs. STEELE 2p 894. ORM.

3465 A proclamation for the discovery and apprehending of several persons. *By John Bill*, 1679. brs. STEELE 3688. L, O, C, LG, DT; CH.

3466 A proclamation for the discovery and apprehension of a French Jesuite. *By the assigns of John Bill and Christopher Barker*, 1675. fol.* STEELE 3618. L, O, C, MC, DT; CH, MH, WF, WG.

3467 A proclamation for the discovery and apprehension of Captain Don Philip Hellen. *By the assigns of John Bill and Christopher Barker*, 1675. fol.* STEELE 3617. L, O, C, MC, DT; CH.

3468 A proclamation for the discovery and apprehension of George Duke of Buckingham. *In the Savoy, by the assigns of John Bill and Christopher Barker*, 1666/7. brs. STEELE 3486. L, O, C, LPR, DT; CH, WF, Y.

3469 A proclamation for the discovery and apprehension of Jesuites. *By the assigns of John Bill and Christopher Barker*, 1674. fol.* STEELE 3597. L, O, C, MC, DT; CH, MH, WG, Y.

3470 A proclamation for the discovery and apprehension of John Lockier. *In the Savoy, by the assigns of John Bill and Christopher Barker*, 1667. brs. STEELE 3498. L, OQ, C, LPR, DT; CH.

3471 A proclamation for the discovery and apprehension of several . . . conspirators. *By John Bill and Christopher Barker*, 1663. fol.* STEELE 3389. L, O, C, LPR, LS; CH, MH, Y.

3472 A proclamation for the discovery and apprehension of the Earl of Bristol. *By John Bill and Christopher Barker*, 1663.* fol. STEELE 3386. L, O, C, LPR, DT; CH, MH, WF, Y.

3473 A proclamation for the discovery of the death of John Powell. *By John Bill, Christopher Barker, Thomas Newcomb, and Henry Hills*, 1678. brs. STEELE 3668. L, O, C, LG, LS; CH, CN, MH, WF, Y.

3473A A proclamation for the discovery of the late horrid design. *By John Bill, Christopher Barker, Thomas Newcomb, and Henry Hills,* 1678. brs. STEELE 3670. MH.

3474 A proclamation for the discovery of the murtherers of Sir Edmund-Bury Godfrey. *By Johh Bill, Christopher Barker, Thomas Newcomb, and Henry Hills,* 1678. brs. STEELE 3656. L, O, C, LPR, DT; CH.

3475 A proclamation for the due observance. *By John Bill and Christopher Barker,* 1665. fol.* STEELE 3420. L, OQ, C, LPC, LPR; MH.

3476 A proclamation, for the due observation of certain statutes. *By John Bill and Christopher Barker,* 1661. fol.* L, O, C, EN, DT; MH, WF, Y.

3477 A proclamation for the due payment of the subsidy. *By John Bill and Christopher Barker,* 1660. fol.* STEELE 3262. LT, O, C, EN, DT; MH, NC, WF, Y.

3478 A proclamation for the effectual prosecution. *By John Bill and Christopher Barker,* 1666. fol.* STEELE 3464. L, OQ, LPR, LS; MH.

3479 A proclamation for the encouraging of planters. *By John Bill and Christopher Barker,* 1661. fol.* STEELE 3346. L, O, C, EN, DT; CH, MH, RPJ.

3480 A proclamation, for the entring and putting in of claims in Ireland. colop: *By John Bill and Christopher Barker,* 1661. fol.* STEELE 3311. L, OQ, C, EN, DT; MH, Y.

3481 —*Dublin, W Bladen,* 1661. brs. STEELE 2p 649. DPR.

3482 A proclamation for the free exportation of leather. *By John Bill and Christopher Barker,* 1666. brs. STEELE 3460. L, O, OQ, LPR, DT.

3483 A proclamation for the free exportation of woollen manufactures. *By John Bill and Christopher Barker,* 1662. brs. STEELE 3354. L, O, C, EN, DT; MH, NC, Y.

3484 —, 1666. brs. STEELE 3458. C, OQ, LPC, LPR.

3485 —*In the Savoy, by the assigns of John Bill and Christopher Barker,* 1667. brs. STEELE 3489. L, OQ, C, LG, LPR; MH, NC.

3486 A proclamation for the further adjourning . . . 3 July 1668. *In the Savoy, by the assigns of John Bill and Christopher Barker,* 1668. brs. STEELE 3515. L, OQ, C, LG, LPR; CH.

3487 A proclamation for the further adjournment . . . 19 September 1668. *In the Savoy, by the assigns of John Bill and Christopher Barker,* 1668. brs. STEELE 3517. L, O, C, OQ, LPR; CH.

3488 —, 26 October 1677. *By John Bill, Christopher Barker, Thomas Newcomb, and Henry Hills,* 1677. brs. STEELE 3643. L, O, C, LG, DT; CH, MH, WF.

3489 A proclamation for the further discovery. *By John Bill, Christopher Barker, Thomas Newcomb, and Henry Hills,* 1678. brs. STEELE 3669. L, O, C, LG, LS; CH, MH, WG, Y.

3490 A proclamation for the further proroguing the Parliament. *By John Bill and Christopher Barker,* 1666. brs. STEELE 3457. L, O, C, LPR, LS; MH.

3491 A proclamation for the keeping of markets. *By John Bill and Christopher Barker,* 1666. brs. STEELE 3473. L, O, C, LPR, LS; CH, MH.

3492 A proclamation for the more effectual and speedy discovery . . . of the Popish plot. *By John Bill, Thomas Newcomb, and Henry Hills,* 1679. brs. STEELE 3698. L, O, C, MC, DT; CH, MH, WG, Y.

3493 A proclamation for the more effectual discovery of Jesuits. *By John Bill, Thomas Newcomb, and Henry Hills,* 1679. brs. STEELE 3700. L, O, LG, LPR, DT; CH, MH, WG.

3494 A proclamation for the more effectual suppressing of Popery. *By John Bill, Thomas Newcomb, and Henry Crofts,* 1679. fol.* STEELE 3705. L, O, C, MC, DT; CH, WG.

3495 A proclamation for the more exact and punctual collecting. *In the Savoy, by the assigns of John Bill and Christopher Barker,* 1666. fol.* STEELE 3483. L, O, C, LPR; MH, NC, Y.

3496 A proclamation for the more speedy bringing in of seamen. *In the Savoy, by the assigns of John Bill and Christopher Barker,* 1672. fol.* STEELE 3566. L, O, OQ, LPR, HH; CH, Y.

3497 A proclamation for the observation of the Lords Day. *By John Bill and Christopher Barker,* 1663. fol.* STEELE 3383. L, O, C, LPR, MC; CH, CLC, MH.

3498 A proclamation, for the observation of the nine and twentieth day of May. *By John Bill and Christopher Barker,* 1661. fol.* STEELE 3305. L, O, C, EN, DT; MH, Y.

3499 A proclamation for the preservation of the . . . fens. *By John Bill and Christopher Barker,* 1662. fol.* STEELE 3357. L, OQ, LPR, LS, HH; CH, MH.

3500 A proclamation for the preventing of the exportation of wools. *By John Bill and Christopher Barker,* 1660. fol.* STEELE 3256. LT, O, C, EN, DT; MH, MIU, WF.

3501 A proclamation for the prevention of frauds. *By John Bill and Christopher Barker,* 1662. fol.* STEELE 3372. L, OQ, C, LPR, LS; MH.

3502 — —, 1665. fol.* STEELE 3443. L, OQ, C, LPR, HH; MH.

3503 —*Oxford, by L. Lichfield, for John Bill and Christopher Barker of London,* 1665. fol.* MADAN 2687. STEELE 3444. OQ, LPC, LPR.

3504 —*In the Savoy, by the assigns of John Bill and Christopher Barker,* 1671. fol.* STEELE 3445. L, LG.

3505 A proclamation for the prizes of victuals. colop: *By John Bill and Christopher Barker,* 1662. fol.* STEELE 3353. L, O, C, EN, DT; MH, NC, Y.

3506 A proclamation for the prohibiting the importation of blue paper. *By John Bill and Christopher Barker,* 1666. fol.* STEELE 3466. OQ, LPC, LPR, LS, HH.

3507 A proclamation for the prohibiting the importation of glass-plates. *By John Bill and Christopher Barker,* 1664. fol.* STEELE 3400. L, OQ, C, LPR, LS; MH.

3508 A proclamation for the publishing of an act. *By John Bill,* 1660[1]. fol.* STEELE 3290. LT, O, C, EN, DT; MH, NC.

3509 A proclamation for the putting in execution of the several laws. *By the assigns of John Bill, and by Henry Hills, and Thomas Newcomb,* 1683. fol.* STEELE 3743. L, C, OQ, LG, DT; CH, MH, NC.

3510   A proclamation for the re-printing. *By John Bill and Christopher Barker*, 1662. brs. STEELE 3371. L, OQ, C, LPR, EN; CH, MH.

3511   A proclamation for the restraining all His Majesties subjects. colop: *By the assigns of John Bill, Thomas Newcomb, and Henry Hills*, 1681. cap., fol.* STEELE 3731. L, O, C, LG, LS; CH, MH, NC, Y.

3512   A proclamation for the speedy putting in execution. *By John Bill and Christopher Barker*, 1664/5. fol.* STEELE 3411. L, OQ, C, LPR, DT; MH.

3513   A proclamation for the suppressing of disorderly and unseasonable meetings. *By John Bill and Christopher Barker*, 1660. fol.* STEELE 3261. LT, O, C, EN, DT; CH, MH, Y.

3514   A proclamation for the suppressing of seditious . . . books. *By John Bill, Thomas Newcomb, and Henry Hills*, 1679. fol.* STEELE 3699. L, O, C, LG, DT; CH, MH, Y.

3515   A proclamation for the suppression of coffee-houses. *By the assigns of John Bill and Christopher Barker*, 1675. fol.* STEELE 3622. L, O, C, MC, DT; CH, MH.

3516   A proclamation for the suppression of riots. *By the assigns of John Bill and Christopher Barker*, 1675. brs. STEELE 3615. L, O, C, MC, DT; CH, WF.

3517   A proclamation for the well-ordering the making of white-starch. colop: *By John Bill and Christopher Barker*, 1661. cap., fol.* STEELE 3317. L, O, C, EN, DT; MH, NC, WF, Y.

3518   A proclamation forbidding foreign trade. *By John Bill and Christopher Barker*, 1664/5. brs. STEELE 3409. L, O, C, LPR, DT; MH, MIU.

3519   A proclamation, forbidding His Majesties subjects. *By the assigns of John Bill and Christopher Barker*, 1675. brs. STEELE 3613. L, O, C, LPR, DT; CH, MH, WF.

3520   A proclamation, indicting a Parliament, . . . 28 July. *Edinburgh, by the heir of Andrew Anderson*, 1681. brs. ALDIS 2296. STEELE 3p 2504. L, MC, EN, ES; WF.

3520A   A proclamation indicating a solemn and publick thanksgiving. *Reprinted by G. Croom*, 1683. brs. CT.

3521   Entry cancelled.

3522   A proclamation of general pardon to all seamen. *By the assigns of John Bill and Christopher Barker*, 1672. brs. STEELE 3577. L, O, OQ, LPR, HH; CH, WF.

3523   A proclamation of grace, for the inlargement. *By John Bill and Christopher Barker*, 1661. fol.* STEELE 3301. L, O, MC, EN, DT; CH, TSM, WF.

3524   The proclamation of the King of Scots at Paris in France. *For G. Horton*, 1651. 4°.* LT.

3525   A proclamation proclaiming Charles . . . 1 February, [1649]. [*n.p.*, 1649.] brs. STEELE 2824. LT.

3525A   A proclamation prohibiting all ecclesiastical meetings. *Reprinted for R. Thrale*, 1662[3]. 4°.* CT.

3526   A proclamation prohibiting all unlawful and seditious meetings. colop: *By John Bill*, 1660[/1]. fol.* STEELE 3278. LT, O, C, EN, DT; CH, MH.

3527   A proclamation prohibiting His Majesties subjects to go. *By the assigns of John Bill and Christopher Barker*, 1674. brs. STEELE 3594. L, O, C, LPR, DT; CH, MH.

3528   A proclamation prohibiting His Majesties subjects to take. *By the assigns of John Bill and Christopher Barker*, 1676. brs. STEELE 3630. L, O, C, LG, LS; CH, MH, WF.

3529   A proclamation prohibiting the exportation of saltpeter. *By John Bill and Christopher Barker*, 1663[4]. brs. STEELE 3395. L, OQ, C, LPR, DT; MH, WF.

3530   A proclamation prohibiting the importation of all sorts of manufactures. *In the Savoy, by the assigns of John Bill and Christopher Barker*, 1666. fol.* STEELE 3481. L, O, C, MC, DT; CH, MH, MIU, NC, Y.

3531   A proclamation prohibiting the importation of all wines. *In the Savoy, by the assigns of John Bill and Christopher Barker*, 1666. fol.* STEELE 3482. L, O, C, LPR, DT; MH, MIU, Y.

3532   A proclamation prohibiting the importation of allome. *In the Savoy, by the assigns of John Bill and Christopher Barker*, 1667. brs. STEELE 3490. L, OQ, C, LPC, LPR; CH.

3533   A proclamation prohibiting the importation of cordage. *By the assigns of John Bill and Christopher Barker*, 1674/5. brs. STEELE 3611. L, O, C, OQ, DT; CH, NC.

3534   A proclamation prohibiting the importation of divers foreign wares. colop: *By John Bill and Christopher Barker*, 1661. fol.* STEELE 3335. L, OQ, LPR, EN, DT; MH, Y.

3535   —. *By R. Norton*, 1661. fol.* STEELE 3336. L, O, C; MH.

3536   A proclamation prohibiting the importation of earthen ware. *By the assigns of John Bill and Christopher Barker*, 1675. brs. STEELE 3636. L, O, C, LG, DT; CH, MH.

3537   A proclamation prohibiting the importation of foreign needles. *In the Savoy, by the assigns of John Bill and Christopher Barker*, 1669. fol.* STEELE 3526. L, OQ, C, LPR, HH; CH, MH.

3538   A proclamation prohibiting the importation of foreign playing-cards. *By the assigns of John Bill: and by Henry Hills. and Thomas Newcomb*, 1684. brs. STEELE 3760. L, O, C, MC, DT; CH, MH.

3539   A proclamation prohibiting the importation of painted earthen wares. *In the Savoy, by the assigns of John Bill and Christopher Barker*, 1672. brs. STEELE 3571. L, O, LPC, LPR, LS; CH, MH.

3540   —*By the assigns of John Bill and Christopher Barker*, 1675. brs. STEELE 3572. LG, OQ.

3541   A proclamation prohibiting the keeping of Barnwell-Fair. *By John Bill and Christopher Barker*, 1665. brs. STEELE 3422. L, OQ, C, LPC, LPR.

3542   — —, 1666. brs. STEELE 3462. LPC, LPR, LS, OQ, HH.

3543   A proclamation prohibiting the keeping of Bartholomew Fair. *By John Bill and Christopher Barker*, 1665. fol.* STEELE 3429. L, O, C, LPR, MC.

3544   — —, 1666. fol.* STEELE 3468. LPC, LPR, LS, OQ.

3545   A proclamation prohibiting the keeping of St. James Fair. *By John Bill and Christopher Barker*, 1665. brs. STEELE 3424. L, OQ, C, LPC, LPR.

3546   A proclamation, prohibiting the keeping of the fair at Bristol. *Oxford: by Leonard Lichfield, for John Bill and Christopher Barker, of London*, 1665. brs. MADAN 2688. STEELE 3446. C, LPC, LPR, OQ, HH.

3547 A proclamation prohibiting the keeping the Fair of Holden. *By John Bill and Christopher Barker*, 1665. fol.* STEELE 3430. L, OQ, C, LPR, HH.

3548 A proclamation prohibiting the keeping of the Fair of Wanting. *By John Bill and Christopher Barker*, 1665. brs. STEELE 3435. L, OQ, C, LPR, HH.

3549 —*Oxford, by L. Lichfield*, 1665. brs. MADAN 2682. STEELE 3436. O, OQ, LPR.

3550 A proclamation prohibiting the keeping of the mart at Boston. *Oxford, by Leonard Lichfield, for John Bill and Christopher Barker of London*, 1665. brs. MADAN 2686. STEELE 3442. C, OQ, LPC, LPR, HH.

3551 Proclamation prohibiting the nobility, . . . third day of January, 1678. *Edinburgh, by the heir of Andrew Anderson*, 1678. brs. FSF; Y.

3552 A proclamation, prohibiting the planting, . . . tobacco. *By John Bill*, 1661. fol.* STEELE 3293. LT, OQ, C, EN, DT; CH, MH, NN.

3553 A proclamation prohibiting the seizing of any persons. *By John Bill*, 1660[/1]. fol.* STEELE 3281. LT, O, C, EN, DT; CH, MH, WF, Y.

3554 A proclamation recalling former proclamations. *In the Savoy, by the assigns of John Bill and Christopher Barker*, 1667. brs. STEELE 3505. L, OQ, C, LG, LPR; CH, MH.

3554A A proclamation regulating the prices of ale. *Edinburgh, by the heir of Andrew Anderson*, 1679. fol.* Y.

3555 A proclamation relating to the articles. *By the assigns of John Bill and Christopher Barker*, 1675. fol.* STEELE 3620. L, O, C, LG, DT; CH, MH, WF, Y.

3556 A proclamation, requiring all cashiered officers. *By John Bill*, 1661. brs. STEELE 3296. LT, O, C, EN, DT; MH, Y.

3557 A proclamation requiring all officers. *By John Bill and Christopher Barker*, 1661. fol.* STEELE 3339. L, OQ, C, EN, DT; CH, MH, Y.

3558 —. *By Robert Norton*, 1661. brs. STEELE 3340. L, O, CT, LG; MH.

3559 —*By John Bill and Christopher Barker*, 1662. fol.* STEELE 3362. L, O, C, EN, DT; MH, Y.

3560 — —, 1663/4. fol.* STEELE 3397. L, OQ, C, LPR, DT; MH.

3561 —, 3 November 1664. —, 1664. fol.* STEELE 3403. L, LPR, LS; MH.

3562 —, eighteenth day of November 1664. —, 1664. fol.* STEELE 3404. L, OQ, C, LPR, HH.

3563 —, twenty eighth day of June 1665. —, 1665. fol.* STEELE 3425. L, OQ, C, LG, LPR.

3564 —, 10 June 1670. *In the Savoy, by the assigns of John Bill and Christopher Barker*, 1670. brs. STEELE 3533. L, O, C, LPR, DT; CH.

3565 A proclamation requiring all seamen. *In the Savoy, by the assigns of John Bill and Christopher Barker*, 1672. brs. STEELE 3563. L, O, C, OQ, LPR; CH.

3566 A proclamation requiring some of His Majesties subjects . . . to return. *By John Bill and Christopher Barker*, 1666. fol.* STEELE 3459. L, O, C, LPR, LS.

3567 A proclamation requiring the immediate tenants. *In the Savoy, by the assigns of John Bill and Christopher Barker*, 1670. brs. STEELE 3535. L, O, C, LPR, DT; CH, MH.

3568 A proclamation requiring the members of both Houses. [Dec. 23.] *In the Savoy, by the assigns of John Bill and Christopher Barker*, 1669. brs. STEELE 3531. L, O, C, LPR, DT; CH.

3569 —, Aug. 21. —, 1670. brs. STEELE 3539. L, OQ, LG, LPR, DT; CH.

3570 —, Dec. 10. *By the assigns of John Bill and Christopher Barker*, 1673. brs. STEELE 3585. L, O, C, MC, DT; CH, MH.

3571 —, Dec. 20. —, 1676. brs. STEELE 3638. L, O, C, LS, DT; CH, WF.

3572 —, 2 May. —, 1677. brs. STEELE 3640. L, O, C, LG, DT; CH, MH, WF, Y.

3573 —, 7 December. *By John Bill*, 1677. brs. STEELE 3645. L, O, C, LG, LS; CH, MH.

3574 —, 2 August. —, 1678. brs. STEELE 3653. L, O, C, LG, LS; CH, MH, WF.

3575 A proclamation requiring the putting in execution. *By John Bill*, 1678. brs. STEELE 3651. O, OQ, LPC, LPR, HH; CH.

3576 A proclamation that the moneys lately called in. *By John Bill and Christopher Barker*, 1661. brs. STEELE 3342. L, O, C, EN, DT; MH, NC.

3577 —*By Roger Norton*, 1661. brs. STEELE 3344. L.

3578 A proclamation to prevent the exacting of excessive prices. *By the assigns of John Bill and Christopher Barker*, 1674. fol.* STEELE 3596. L, O, C, LG, LPR; CH, MH, NC.

3579 A proclamation to restrain the abuses of hackney coaches. *By John Bill and Christopher Barker*, 1660. fol.* STEELE 3267. LT, O, C, EN, DT; MH, Y.

3580 A proclamation to restrain the excessive carriages in wagons. *By John Bill and Christopher Barker*, 1661. fol.* STEELE 3321. L, O, C, EN, DT; MH.

3581 A proclamation to restrain the spreading of false news. colop: *In the Savoy, by the assigns of John Bill and Christopher Barker*, 1672. fol.* STEELE 3570. L, O, CT, LG, DT; CH, Y.

3582 —[Anr. ed.] *Reprinted Edinburgh*, 1672. brs. ALDIS 1958. STEELE 3p 2359. HH, EN.

3583 —*By the assigns of John Bill and Christopher Barker*, 1674. fol.* STEELE 3595. L, O, C, MC, DT; CH, MIU, Y.

3584 Proclamation to summon the persons therein named. *By John Bill and Christopher Barker*, 1660. brs. STEELE 3224. LT, O, C, EN, DT; CH, MH, Y.

3585 —, 6 June. *Reprinted Edinburgh, C Higgins*, 1660. brs. ALDIS 1660. STEELE 3p 2178. EN.

3586 A proclamation touching mariners. *By John Bill and Christopher Barker*, 1664. fol.* STEELE 3405. L, OQ, C, LPR, DT; MH, WF.

3587 A proclamation touching passes. *By the assigns of John Bill and Christopher Barker*, 1675. fol.* STEELE 3621. L, O, C, OQ, DT; CH, CLC.

3588 A proclamation touching the articles of peace . . . Argiers. *By John Bill and Christopher Barker*, 1662[3]. fol.* STEELE 3377. L, OQ, C, LPR, LS; MH.

3589   A proclamation touching the charitable collections. *In the Savoy, by the assigns of John Bill and Christopher Barker*, 1668. brs. STEELE 3519. L, OQ, C, LPR, DT; CH.

3590   A proclamation touching the election. *For M. B.*, 1660. brs. LT; MH.

3591   A proclamation touching the free importation of nutmegs. *By John Bill and Christopher Barker*, 1662. fol.* STEELE 3374. L, OQ, C, LPR, LS; MH.

3592   —*In the Savoy, by the assigns of John Bill and Christopher Barker*, 1667. fol.* STEELE 3375. L, DT.

3593   A proclamation touching the planters. *In the Savoy, by the assigns of John Bill and Christopher Barker*, 1671. brs. STEELE 3555. L, O, OQ, LPR, DT; CH.

3594   A proclamation, touching the speedy calling. *By John Bill*, 1660[1]. fol.* STEELE 3292. LT, O, C, EN, DT; MH, Y.

3595   A proclamation touching the transportation of corn. *In the Savoy, by the assigns of John Bill and Christopher Barker*, 1667. fol.* STEELE 3503. L, O, C, LG, LPR; CH, MH, NC, Y.

3596   A proclamation. Whereas by the death . . . May the 14, 1660. *Dublin, by William Bladen*, 1660. brs. STEELE 3545. L, C.

3596A   A proclamation. Whereas it is found by experience. *By the assigns of J. Bill and C. Barker*, 1674. brs. MH.

3596B   A proclamation. Whereas our loyal subjects. *By the assigns of John Bill and Christopher Barker*, 1672/3. brs. STEELE 3599. L, LG; MH, Y.

3597   A proclamation. Whereas the safeguard. *In the Savoy, by the assigns of John Bill and Christopher Barker*, 1667. brs. STEELE 3512. L, OQ, LPR, LPC, LS; CH.

3597A   —, 12 March 1683/4. —, 1683/4. fol.* STEELE 3757. L, O, LPR, LG, DT; CH.

3598   A proclamation. Whereas upon Tuesday. *In the Savoy, by the assigns of Jo: Bill, and Chris. Barker*, 1670. brs. C, LG; CH.

3598A   A remonstrance of His Highnesse the Prince of Wales. *Printed*, 1648. 4°.* LT, O; CH, MH.

3599   Prince Charles his resolution. *Imprinted at London, for R. W.*, Aprill 25, 1649. 4°.* LT, DT; MH.

3600   The resolution of His Highnesse, the Prince of Wales, concerning his coming. 1648. 4°.* LT; WF.

3601   The resolution of Prince Charles, being generall. [*London*], August 11. for H. W. and H. T., 1642. 4°.* LT, HH; CH.

3602   The resolution of the Prince of Wales, concerning Lieutenant General Cromwell. *Printed*, 1648. 4°.* LT; MH.

3603   Right trusty and well-beloved, we greet you . . . 23 July. *For Jane Bourne*, [1660]. brs. STEELE 3235. LT; MH, WF.

3604   —*By John Bill and Christopher Barker*, 1661. cap. STEELE 3236. L, O; WF.

3604A   Several treaties of peace and commerce concluded. *By the assigns of John Bill, deceased, and by Henry Hills and Thomas Newcomb*, 1685. 4°. WCA, CJ; CH, CN, MH, RPJ, WF, Y.

3605   —. *By His Majesties printers, and sold by Edward Poole*, 1686. 4°. L, C, CS, OC, P; CH, NC, WCL, WF, Y.

3606   King Charles II's speech against the tackers. colop: *For Ben. Bragg*, 1675. cap., 4°.* CS; Y.

3607   A speech or declaration of the declared King of Scots upon the death of Montrosse. *For J. C.*, 1650. 4°.* LT, HH; WF.

3608   King Charles his speech to the six eminent persons . . . 18/8 March. *Anwerp* [*sic*], *printed*, 1660. brs. STEELE 3164. LT, O.

3609   Prince Charles his summons. *For R. Smithurst*, 1648. 4°*. LT, DT; MH, WF.

3610   Three intercepted letters. The one from Charles Stuart. *By M. Simmons*, 1649. 4°.* LT, O, C, LVF, DT; CH, MH, Y.

3611   To all our loving subjects unto whom these presents . . . 15 day of February 1681/2. [*n.p.*, 1682.] brs. O.

3612   To our trusty and well-beloved General Monck. *Dublin, by William Bladen*, 1660. brs. STEELE 2p 610. L.

3612A   To the most reverend father in God accepted. colop: *Edinburgh, reprinted*, 1662. cap., 4°.* CLC.

3613   To the most reverend father in God William . . . Canterbury. *By John Bill and Christopher Barker*, 1662. cap., fol.* L, O, OC, CS, HH; CH, CN, NU, TU, Y.

3613A   Tractatus de componendis controversiis. *Excusum assignatos J. Bill & C. Barker*, [1670.] 4°.* L; Y.

3614   Tractatus marinus inter . . . Carolum II . . . et . . . Ludovicum XIV. *Excuderunt assignati Johannis Bill & Christophori Barker*, 1677. 4°.* L, LLI; MH, Y.

3615   Tractatus marinus inter . . . Carolum II . . . et . . . Ordines Generales. *Excuderunt assignati Johannis Bill & Christophori Barker*, 1674. 4°.* L; CH, Y.

3616   Tractatus pacis & amicitiæ inter coronæ Magnæ Britanniæ et Hispaniæ. *Excusum per assignatos Johannis Bill & Christophori Barker*, 1667. 4°.* L, O; CH.

3616A   A treaty for the composing of differences, . . . Spain. *In the Savoy, by the assigns of John Bill and Christopher Barker*, 1670. 4°.* L; CH, CN, RPJ.

3616B   —[Same title.] *By Charles Bill and the executrix of Thomas Newcomb*, 1698. 4°.* WF.

3617   A treaty marine between the most serene . . . Charles II, . . . and . . . Lewis XIV. *By the assigns of John Bill and Christopher Barker*, 1677. 4°.* L, O, CT, LL, HH; CH, MIU, WF, Y.

3618   —*Edinburgh re-printed by the heir of Andrew Anderson*, 1677. 8°.* FSF.

3619   A treaty marine between the most serene . . . Charles II . . . and . . . the States General. *By the assigns of John Bill and Christopher Barker*, 1674. 4°.* L, O, LVF; CH, MH, WF, Y.

3619A   —[Anr. ed.] *Dublin, reprinted by Benjamin Tooke, to be sold by Joseph Wilde*, 1674. 4°.* DIX 153. CD, DK, DN; CH.

3620   A treaty of friendship, and commerce, between His Majesty . . . and . . . the Duke of Savoy. *By the assigns of John Bill, and Christopher Barker*, 1673. 4°.* L; CH, WF, Y.

3621 Treatie of marine between . . . Charles the Second . . . and the . . . States General. *In the Savoy, by the assigns of Iohn Bill and Christopher Barker*, 1675. 4°.* CH.

3622 The two charters granted by King Charles IId. to . . . Carolina. *Printed, to be sold by Richard Parker*, [1698]. 4°. L, LG, LW, GH; CH, MH, NN, PL, RPJ, WCL.

3623 His Majesties two gracious letters, . . . April 1660. *Edinburgh, C Higgins*, 1660. brs. ALDIS 1635. STEELE 3p, 2167. E, EN, ES, FSF; Y.

3624 Two letters from. *By Edward Husbands and Tho. Newcomb*, 1660. fol.* LT, O, C, EN, DT; CH, MH, NU, TU, WF, Y.

3624A —[Anr. ed.] *Edinburgh, re-printed by a society of stationers*, 1660. 4°.* CT.

3625 Charles . . . Whereas a great number of our good . . . 10 August. *T Milbourn*, 1670. brs. STEELE 3537. L.

3626 Charles . . . Whereas commissions have been . . . 31 January. [*n.p.*, 1662/3.] brs. STEELE 3378. LPR.

3627 Whereas complaint hath been made unto us, . . . 23 July 1670. *In the Savoy, by the assigns of John Bill and Christopher Barker*, 1670. brs. STEELE 3536. OQ.

3628 Whereas complaint hath often been made . . . 2 February. *By the assigns of John Bill and Christopher Barker*, 1673[4]. brs. STEELE 3588. L, C, LG, OP, HH.

3629 Whereas divers scandalous untruths. [*n.p.*, 1660.] brs. STEELE 3258. LT.

3630 Whereas His Majesties servants the kings heralds . . . 6 December. [*n.p.*, 1671.] brs. STEELE 3554. O, LPR.

3631 Whereas His Majesty hath received information. *By John Bill, Christopher Barker, Thomas Newcomb, and Henry Hills*, 1678. brs. STEELE 3658. L, C, LG, LUG; CH, MH, WF.

3632 Whereas His Majesty, in consideration of the . . . 2 April 1681. *Assigns of Bill*, 1681. brs. STEELE 3727. L; CH, PL.

3633 By the King. Whereas it is found . . . 30 November. *By the assigns of John Bill and Christopher Barker*, 1674. fol.* STEELE 3604. L, O, LG, LPR, LS; CH, MIU.

3634 Whereas Joshua Kirton and Nathaniel Webb . . . 21 November, 1661. [*London*, 1661.] brs. STEELE 3337. LPR.

3635 Charles. . . . Whereas our late dear and . . . 5 September. *By W.C. for the assigns of J. Redman*, [1661]. brs. STEELE 3325. LPR.

3636 By the King. Whereas our loyal subjects . . . 23 March 1670/1. *In the Savoye: by the assigns of Jo: Bill and Chris. Barker*, 1670/1. fol.* STEELE 3545. L, O, LPR, DT; CH.

3637 Charles. . . . Whereas several of our . . . 9 January. *T Milbourn*, [1667/8]. brs. STEELE 3510. LPR.

3638 Charles. . . . Whereas the Lord hath been pleased . . . 27 July 1650. [*Edinburgh, E Tyler*, 1650.] brs. ALDIS 1417. STEELE 3p 2048. L, O, REG.

3639 Charles. . . . whereas the cathedral church of St. Pauls . . . 26 February. *W. Godbid*, 1678. brs. STEELE 3647. L, O, CS, DM.

3640 Whereas upon the nineteenth day of May . . . 15 October. *John Macock*, 1666. brs. STEELE 3478. HH.

3641 Entry cancelled.

3642 Charles. . . . Whereas we are credibly given to . . . 15 October. *By W. G. for the assigns of J. Bodington*, [1660]. brs. STEELE 3266. HH.

3643 Entry cancelled.

3644 —, 26 November. *In the Savoy, T Newcomb*, 1667. brs. STEELE 3509. HH.

3645 —[Same title, 14 August.] *W. Godbid*, 1676. brs. STEELE 3632. O.

3646 —[Same title, 15 February.] [*n.p.*, 1682/3.] brs. STEELE 3739. L.

3647 Charles. . . . Whereas we are credibly informed that on . . . 8 September 1660. *By W. G. for the assigns of J. Bodington*, [1660]. brs. STEELE 3253. HH.

3648 Charles. . . . Whereas we have been given to . . . 22 March 1670/71. [*n.p.*, 1671.] brs. STEELE 3543. L.

3649 Carolus. . . . Whereas we have been lately informed . . . 19 June. [1662.] fol.* STEELE 3360. LPR.

Charles II, *king of Spain*. *See* Carlos II, *king of Spain*.

3650 **Charles V**, *duke of Lorraine.* Political and military observations. *For J. Jones and W. Hawes*, 1699. 8°. T.C.III 98. L; CH, CLC, MIU, Y.

3651 **Charles V**, *emperor.* The advice of. *For H. Mortlock*, 1670. 12°. T.C.I 44. L, OC, CCA, CCH; CH, Y.

3652 Entry cancelled.

3653 **Charles X, Gustavus.** The last will and testament of. [*n.p.*], *for William Leadson*, 1660. 4°.* LT, O.

3654 —A message sent from. *For G Mharton* [*i.e.*, Wharton], 1654. 4°.* LT.

3655 —The most heavenly and Christian speech of. *For Tho. Vere*, 1660. 4°.* LT, O; WF.

3656 —A remonstrance of. *By R. Wood for D. Pakeman*, 1659. 4°. Y.

3657 **Charles XI, of Sweden.** His Majes t [sic] the king of Swedens letter to the States Generall. [*n.p.*], *printed*, 1675. 4°.* L, O; CH, WF, Y.

3658 **Charles Louis, elector Palatine.** A declaration of the Prince Paltsgrave. [*London*], *for J. Greene, October 1*, 1642. 4°.* LT, HH; CH, MIU.

3659 —A manifesto of. *For Richard Lownds*, 1657. 4°.* LT, SP.

3660 Entry cancelled.

3661 Charles, King, James, Duke, Katharine, Queen, Mary Dutchess. *By G. Croom on the Ice, January 31, 1684*. brs. OP.

Charles, King of England. 1660. *See* Mason, Martin.

3662 **Charles Peregrine.** *Printed on the river of Thames being frozen, 5 Feb 1684*[5]. brs. OP.

3663 Charles R. For a finall answer to your proposition. [*London*], *for Richard Royston*, 1648. brs. LT.

3664 [**Charleton, Walter.**] A character of His Most Sacred Majesty Charles the Second. *For Henry Herringman*, 1661. 4°.* L, LG, EN, GK; MH, NP, Y.

3665 —Chorea gigantum. *For Henry Herringman*, 1663. 4°. L, O, C, MR, EN; BN, CH, MH, MMO, NP, TU, WF, Y.

3666 [–] The Cimmerian matron. [*London*], *for H. Herringman*, 1668. 4°. L, O; CU, MH, NC, Y.

3667 —[Anr. ed.] *For H. Herringman, and are to be sold by J. Knight and F. Saunders,* 1684. 8°. T.C.II 71. CN.

3668 —The darkness of atheism dispelled. *By J. F. for William Lee,* 1652. 4°. L, O, C, LCS, E; BN, CLC, CU, MH, NU, WF, JF.

3669 —De scorbuto liber singularis. *Typis E. Tyler, & R. Holt, prostant apud Guliel. Wells & Rob. Scot,* 1672. 8°. T.C.I 89. L, O, C, LCS, EN; BN, CLC, MMO, NAM, PL, WF, HC.

3670 [–] The Ephesian and Cimmerian matrons. *[London], for Henry Herringman,* 1668. 8°. T.C.I 3. L, O, CT; CH, CN, MH, NC, WF, Y.

3671 [–] The Ephesian matron. *For Henry Herringman,* 1659. 12°. LT, O, DC.

3672 —Gualteri Charletoni exercitationes de differentiis & nominibus animalium. Second edition. *Oxoniae, e theatre Sheldoniano,* 1677. fol. MADAN 3137. L, O, C, E, DT; BN, CH, CJC, LC, MH, MMO, Y.

3673 —Exercitationes pathologicae. *Typis Tho. Newcomb, prostant venales apud Joh. Martin, Jac. Allestree & Tho. Dicas,* 1661. 4°. LT, O, C, LCS, E; BN, CLC, CLM, NAM, PL, WF, JF.

3674 [–] The harmony of natural and positive divine laws. *For Walter Kettilby,* 1682. 8°. T.C.I 493. L, O, C, CT, LW; CH, CLC, MH.

3675 [–] The immortality of the human soul. *By William Wilson for Henry Herringman,* 1657. 4°. LT, O, CT, EN, DT; CLC, CN, NU, WF, Y.

3676 ——[Anr. ed.] *For Richard Wellington and Edmund Rumbold,* 1699. 4°. T.C.III 128. L.

3677 [–] An imperfect pourtraicture of His Sacred Majesty Charls the II. *For Henry Herringman,* 1661. 4°.* LT, O, C, CT; CH, CU, LC, MIU, MMO.

3678 —Enquiries into human nature. *By M. White, for Robert Boulter,* 1680. 4°. T.C.I 370. L, O, C, EN, DT; CLC, MH, MMO, NAM, WF, HC.

3679 ——[Anr. ed.] *For J. Conyers,* 1697. 4°. LW; CH.

3680 —G. Charletoni inquisitio physica. *Impensis Gualt. Kettilby,* 1685. 8°. T.C.II 127. L, O, CS, P, GH; BN, CLC, PL.

3681 —Inquisitiones II. anatomico-physicæ. *Typis Societatis regali, impensis Octaviani Pulleyn junioris,* 1665. 8° L, O, CT, GH, DT; NAM.

3682 [–] Matrona Ephesia. *Impensis authoris,* 1665. 12°. L, CM, CT, LCP; BN, CLC, MH, WF, Y.

3683 ——[Anr. ed.] 1665. 12°. L, O, CT; CH.

3684 —Natural history of nutrition. *For Henry Herringman,* 1659. 4°. L, O, CPE, LCS, GH; CJC, CLC, NAM, WF, HC.

3684A —Natural history of the passions. *In the Savoy, by T. N. for J. Magnes,* 1674. 8°. T.C.I 171. L, O, LCP, E, DT; CLC, CN, LC, NC, Y.

3685 —Oeconomia animalis, novis. *Typis R. Danielis, & J. Redmanni,* 1659. 12°. L, O, C, LCS, E.

3686 ——Third edition. *Roger Daniel,* 1666. 12°. C, CT, OR, LR, GK; WSG, HC.

3687 ——Fourth edition. *Ex officina Johannis Redmayne, prostant venales apud Johannem Creed, Cantab.,* 1669. 12°. L, O, C, LM, LCS; CLC, NAM, PL, WF, WSG.

3688 —Onomasticon zoicon. *Apud Jacobum Allestry,* 1668. 4°. T.C.I 6. L, O, CCA, MR, EN; BN, CH, CU, MH, NAM, WF, Y.

3689 —Ονομαστικὸν ζωικὸν, continens. *Apud Jacobum Allestry,* 1671. 4°. L, LNH, LCS, DCH, E; BN, IU, MH, MMO.

3690 —Oratio anniversaria habita. *Sumptibus Joannis Baker,* 1680. 4°.* T.C.I 418. L, O, CS, LCP, EN; MIU, MMO, HC.

3691 —Physiologia Epicuro-Gassendo-Charltoniana. *By Tho. Newcomb for Thomas Heath,* 1654. fol. L, CT, LCS, NPL, E; CH, CU, MMO, NAM, HC.

3692 —Συνθεω. Consilium. [1661.] cap., 4°.* L, O; Y.

3693 —Three anatomie lectures. *For Walter Kettilby,* 1683. 4°. T.C.II 46. L, O, LCS, LG, GH; BN, LC, MMO, NAM.

3694 [–] Two discourses. I. Concerning the different wits. *By R. W. for William Whitwood,* 1669. 8°. T.C.I 14. L, O, CS, E, GK; CU, MH, TU, WF, JF.

3695 ——Second edition. *By F. L. for William Whitwood,* 1675. 8°. T.C.I 199. L, O, C, LCS, DT; MH, NAM, WDA, WF, JF.

3696 ——"Second" edition. —, 1676. 8°. BN.

3697 ——Third edition. *For Will. Whitwood,* 1692. 12°. T.C.II 432. L, O, GU; CLC, HC.

3697A [–] The routiers mystery display'd. *For T. Weaver* [1700?]. 12°. L; CCJ, MH.

3698 **Charlton, *Sir Job.*** Speech to the king. 1672/3. fol. O, OM, P.

3699 A charme for Canterburian spirits. *[London], for J. C. February the 14,* 1645. 4°.* LT; MIU, NU.

3700 Charming Amintas. *[London], for P Brooksby,* [1685–88]. brs. L, HH.

Charming bride. *[n.p.,* 1690?] *See* Southern, Thomas.

3701–2 Entries cancelled.

3703 **Charnock, Stephen.** The works of. Vol. I. *For Ben. Griffin, and Tho. Cockeril,* 1684. fol. T.C.II 42. L, O, CK, LCL, GU; MH, NP, NU, WF, Y.

3704 ——Third edition. *For Ben. Griffin; John Lawrence; Eliz. Harris, and John Nicholson; and Tho. Cockerill,* 1699. fol. T.C.III 127. L, C, LW, AU, DT; MBA, MH, NP, NR, Y.

3705 ——Vol. II. *By A. Maxwell, and R. Roberts, for Tho, Cockerill,* 1684. fol. T.C.II 42. L, O, LCL, CK, GU; MH, NP, NU, WF, Y.

3706 ——Second edition. *For Ben. Griffin; John Lawrence; Eliz. Harris; and John Nicholson, and Thomas Cockerill,* 1699. fol. T.C.III 127. L, C, LW, AU, DT; CU, MH, NP, Y.

3707 —Bibliotheca Charnockiana. *[London],* 1680. 4°.* L; MH, NG, Y.

3708 —A discourse of divine providence. *By R. Roberts for Thomas Cockerill,* 1684. 8°. T.C.II 151. LW; MHS, TU, WF.

3709 —The sayings of. *For R. J.,* 1680. brs. L, O, LS.

3710 —A sermon preached by. *By Thomas Milbourn, for J. K. to be sold by Langley Curtis,* 1680. 4°.* T.C.I 416. O, C, LW; IU.

3711 —Several discourses upon the existence . . . of God. *For D. Newman, T. Cockerill, Benj. Griffin, T. Simmons, and Benj. Alsop,* 1682. fol. L, O, CS, E, DT; MH, NPT, NU, WSC, Y.

3711A —The sinfulness and cure of thoughts. 1674. 4°. O.

3711B ——[Anr. ed.] 1676. 4°. L.

3711C —A supplement to the several discourses. *For Thomas Cockerill,* 1683. fol. DT; MBC, NU, Y.

3712 —A treatise of divine providence. *For Tho. Cockeril,* 1680. 8°. L, LCL, LW, OC, P; CLC, HH, PL, PPT, Y.

3713 —Two discourses: the first, of man's enmity. *For Tho. Cockeril,* 1699. 8°. L, LCL, GU; NP, WF, Y.

3714 **[Charpentier, François.]** A treatise touching the East-Indian trade. *By Thomas Mabb for Henry Brome,* 1664. 4°. L, O, EN, DT; CN, MH, NC, NP, Y.

3715 [–] —[Anr. ed.] *For H.B. and are to be sold by Robert Boulter,* 1676. 4°.* L, LG, LUG; CH, CN, MH, NC, WF, Y.

3716 [–] —[Anr. ed.] *Edinburgh, re-printed by the heirs and successors of Andrew Anderson,* 1695. 4°. ALDIS 3512. D, EN; CH, LC, MB, NC, RPJ.

3717 **Charron, Pierre.** Of wisdome. Sixth edition. *For Luke Fawne,* 1651. 4°. L, C, CCA, DC, DT; CH, CLC, MH, PL, V.

3718 ——[Anr. ed.] —, 1658. 4°. L, O, CCH, SA, DT; CU, MBC, MH, TU, Y.

3719 ——[Anr. ed.] *For Nathaniel Ranew and Ionathan Robinson,* 1670. 4°. T.C.I 60. L, C, LWL; CU, LC, MH, NU, Y.

3720 ——[Anr. ed.] *for M. Gillyflower, M. Bentley, H. Bonwick, J. Tonson, W. Freeman, M. Wotton, J. Walthoe, S. Manship and R. Parker,* 1697. 8°. L, CS, AN; CN, NP, PL, WF, WSC, Y.

3721 —The right of kings. *S. Miller,* [1684?]. 4°.* O, HH; CN, Y.

Chartæ scriptæ. [n.p.], 1645. See Gayton, Edmund.

3722 The charter; a comical satyr. *For Alex. Banks,* 1682. 4°.* L, OC, HH; CH, CU, MH, NC, WF, Y.

Charter granted. 1649. See Bayly, Thomas.

—Boston, 1692. See Massachusetts Bay Province.

3723 A charter granted to the apothecaries of London. *By F. Leach,* 1695. 4°.* L, O, OC, CCH; NU, WF.

3724 The charter of Londons answer. colop: *For Langley Curtis,* 1683. brs. L, O, C, LG, EN; IU, MH, TU.

3725 The charter of the company of clothworkers. 1648. 4°.* L; MH.

3726 The charter of the Royal Lustring company. [n.p., 1697.] fol.* LL.

3727 **Charters, Alexander.** The declaration of. *Edinburgh, by Evan Tyler,* 1650. 4°.* ALDIS 1402. O, HH, E, EN, FSF.

3728 **[Chassepol, François de.]** The history of the grand visiers. *For H. Brome,* 1677. 8°. T.C.I 266. L, O, C, LVF, ENC; CH, CN, MH, PL, WF, Y.

Chaste seraglian. 1685. See Préchac, sieur de.

3729 **Chasteigner de la Roche-Pozay, Henri Louis.** Celebriorum distinctionum philosophicarum synopsis. *Oxoniæ, excudebat Hen. Hall, per Jos. Godwin & Edw. Forrest,* 1657. 8°. MADAN 2330. L, O, C, OC, DT; PL, WF, Y.

3730 Chastities conquest. [London], *for P. Brooksby,* [1685–88]. brs. L, O, CM, HH, GU; MH, Y.

3731 **Chateillon, Sebastien.** A conference of faith. *By J. R. for John Barksdale,* 1679. 12°. T.C.I 327. O.

3732 —Dialogorum sacrorum. *Cantabrigiæ: ex academiæ celeberrimæ typographeo,* 1651. 8°. C, OC, ELY; CLC.

3732A ——[Anr. ed.] *Excudebat Guil. Wilsonus,* 1657. 8°. WF.

3732B ——[Anr. ed.] *Excudebat Anne Maxwel, sumptibus stationariorum,* 1667. 8°. EC.

3732C ——[Anr. ed.] *Edinburgi, excudebat Jacobi Alen,* 1669. 8°. L; Y.

3732D ——[Anr. ed.] *Edinburgh: excudebat Georgius Swintoun,* 1676. 8°. D.

3733 ——[Anr. ed.] *Glasguæ, excudebat Robertus Sanders,* 1685. 8°. ALDIS 2534. BAIN.

3734 ——[Anr. ed.] *Edinburgi, ex officina Societatis bibliopolarum,* 1689. 12°. FSF; CH, CLC.

3734A ——[Anr. ed.] *B. Griffin,* 1690. 8° TSM.

3734B ——[Anr. ed.] *Excudebat F. Collins, sumptibus stationariorum,* 1700. 8°. L.

3734C —[Anr. ed.] *Edinburgi, ex typographæo Georgii Mosman,* 1700. 12°. L; MH.

3735 **Chatfield, John.** The trigonal sector. *By Robert Leybourn, to be sold by James Nuthall,* 1650. 8°.* LT, OC; NC.

3736 **Chaucer, Geoffrey.** The works of. *Printed,* 1687. fol. T.C.II 195. L, O, C, E, DT; CH, CN, MH, NC, WCL, WF, Y.

—Canterbury tale. [London], 1641. See Brome, Alexander.

3737 **Chaucer, junior, pseud.** Canterbury tales: composed for the entertainment. [London], *for J. Back,* 1687. fol. CM.

Chaucer's ghoast. 1672. See Ovid.

3737A **Chaumont, Alexandre de.** A new letter concerning the Jevves. *By A. Maxwell for Robert Boulter,* 1666. 4°.* L, O, EN; MH.

3737B ——[Anr. ed.] *Reprinted Edinburgh by a society of stationers,* 1666. 4°.* ALDIS 1819. EN.

3737C —A relation of the late embassy of. *For Henry Mortlock,* 1687. 12°. T.C.II 176. L, O, LWL; NIC, PL, WF, Y.

3737D **Chauncy, Charles.** Anti-synodalre scripte. [London, 1652.] cap., 4°.* MHS, RPJ, VY

3737E —The doctrine of the sacrament. *By G. M. for Thomas Underhill,* 1642. 8°. O; PL.

3738 —Gods mercy. *Cambridge in New-England, by Samuel Green,* 1655. 8°. EVANS 40. L; CH, NN, PHS.

3739 —[Hebrew] or the plain doctrine of the justification. *By R. I. for Adoniram Byfield,* 1659. 4°. LT, C, CT, LCL; MH, NPT, NU, RPJ, Y.

3740 —The retractation of. *Printed,* 1641. 4°.* LT, C, CT, DT; CH, MH, NU, RPJ, Y.

3741 **Chauncy, Sir Henry.** The historical antiquities of Hertfordshire. *For Ben. Griffin, Sam. Keble, Dan. Browne, Dan. Midwinter and Tho. Leigh,* 1700. fol. T.C.III 212. L, O, C, MR; BN, CH, MH, TU, WF, Y.

3742 —Proposals for printing the history. [London, 1700.] cap., fol. O.

3743 **Chauncy, Ichabod.** Innocence vindicated. *By George Larkin,* 1684. 4°. L, LW, BR; PL, WF, Y.

3744 **Chauncy, Isaac.** Alexipharmacon: or, a fresh antidote. *Printed for, and sold by W. Marshall,* 1700. 4°. T.C.III 196. L, LCL, LW, GU; CN, LC, MH, NU, RPJ, Y.

3745 [–] The Catholick hierarchie. *For the author, to be sold by Sam. Crouch; and Tho. Fox,* 1681. 4°. T.C.I 427. L, C; CH, MHS, MWA, NU, Y.

3746 —Christ's ascension *For Nath. Hillar*, 1699. 8°. L; MB.

3747 —A discourse concerning unction. *For Nath. Hiller*, 1697. 12°.* L, LG; MH, NU, Y.

3748 —The divine institution. *For Nathanael Hiller*, 1697. 12°. L, O, LCL, LG; CH, MH, NU, RPJ, WF, Y.

3749 —The doctrine which is according to godliness. *For the author by H. Hills, to be sold by Will. Marshal, T. Fabin, and H. Barnard*, [1694?]. 12°. T.C.III 74. L, LG, LW; MB, MH, NU, RPJ, Y.

3750 —Ecclesia enucleata: the temple opened. *By George Larkin*, 1684. 8°. C, LW; MB, NPT, Y.

3751 [–] Ecclesiasticvm: or a plain. *By T. S. for the publisher, to be sold by W. Marshall*, 1690. 8°. T.C.II 345. LCL; MB, MIU, NU, Y.

3752 —An essay to the interpretation. *For Nath. Hiller*, 1699. 8°. L, LCL; CLC, MH, WF, Y.

3753 [–] Examen confectionis pacificæ: or, a friendly examination. *Printed, and are to be sold by Richard Baldwin*, 1692. 4°.* L, O, LCL, LW; CLC, LC, MB, MH, NU, Y.

3753A —The interest of churches. *For the author*, 1690. 4°.* O, CT, LCL, LW; MHS, MWA.

3754 —Neonomianism unmask'd. *For J. Harris*, 1692. 4°. T.C.II 437. L, O, C, LCL, LW; CH, MB, NU, RPJ, WF, Y.

3754A —, second part. *For H. Barnard*, 1693. 4°. L, CS, LW, GU; CLC, MH, PL, WF, Y.

3755 ——Part three. *For H. Barnard*, 1693. 4°. L, LCL, AU; MB, NU, RPJ, WF, Y.

3756 —A plea for the antient gospel. *Printed and sold by W. Marshall, and J. Marshall*, 1697. 4°. T.C.III 20. LCL, GU; CLC, NU.

3757 —A rejoynder to Dr. Daniel Williams, his reply. *For H. Barnard*, 1693. 4°.* L, LCL, GU; MB, MH, NU, WF, Y.

3757A [–] A theological dialogue. *For the author*, 1684. 4°. LL, LSC, LW, BR; MM.

3757B —The unreasonableness of compelling men. 1684. 4°. O; LW.

Chauncy, Israel. Almanack. Cambridge [Mass.], 1663. *See* Almanacs.

3757C **Chavron, Pierre.** De naturali religione liber. *Roterdam, apud Petrum van der Steart, sumptibus Semialis Oliveri, Novvicensis*, 1693. 8°. L; CN, NPT, PL.

3757D **Chavigny, sieur.** The gallant hermaphrodite. *For Samuel Manship*, 1687. 12°. T.C.II 206. CN.

3758 ——[Anr. ed.] —, 1688. 8°. L.

3759 [–] The inconstant-lover. *For T. Dring*, 1671. 8°. T.C.I 81. L; CLC.

Cheap and good husbandry. 1648. *See* Markham, Gervase.

Cheap-side crosse censured. 1641. *See* Abbot, George, *abp.*

3760 Entry cancelled.

3761 [**Cheare, Abraham.**] Sighs for Sion. *For Livewell Chapman*, 1656. 4°.* LT, O; CLC.

3762 [–] —[Anr. ed.] *For Livewel Chapman*. 1657. 4°.* L; Y.

3763 —Words in season: from. *For Nathan Brookes*, 1668. 8°. L, O, C, LCL; MH, NHC, NPT, WF.

3764 A cheat in all trads. [*n.p.*, 1640–50.] brs. HH.

3765 Cheat upon cheat. [*London*], *for, I. Blare*, [1684–90]. brs. HH; MH.

Cheaters speculum. [*n.p.*, 1700.] *See* Fuller, William.

3766 The cheating age. *By E. M.* [1700?] brs. MH.

Cheating gallant. 1672. *See* Brémond, Gabriel de.

3767 The cheating soliciter cheated . . . life and death of Richard Farr. *For T. J.*, 1665. 4°. L, LG; CH, CLC, Y.

Cheats. 1664. *See* Wilson, John.

Cheaumont. *See* Chaumont.

3768 Entry cancelled.

Check: or, inquiry. 1662. *See* Holden, Henry.

Checke to Brittanicus. 1644. *See* Prynne, William.

Check to debauchery. 1692. *See* D., L.

Check to the checker. 1644. *See* Nedham, Marchamont.

Check to the loftie. 1655. *See* Mason, Martin.

3769 The chearful husband. *For J. Blare*, [1689–90]. brs. L, HH.

3770 Entry cancelled.

3771 **Cheesman, Ab.** The dove, with an olive-braunch. *For the author*, 1663. 4°.* O, LW, GU; CLC, WF.

3772 **Cheesman, Christopher.** Berkshire's agent's humble address. *By J. C. for the author*, 1651. 4°.* LT; CLC.

3773 —An epistle to Charles the second. [*Reading*, 1661.] cap., 4°.* L, O, LF, OC, BBN; CH, IE, MH, PH, PSC, Y.

3773A —The lamb contending with the lion. [*London*], *printed* 1649. 4°.* LT; CH, CU, MH, Y.

3773B —The oppressed man's out-cry for justice. [*London*, 1649.] cap., 4°.* MWA.

3773C —The oppressed man's record outcry. 1652. CSS.

3774 **Cheesman, Thomas.** Death compared to a sleep. *For Thomas Parkhurst*, 1695. 4°.* L, LW; WF.

3775 —Peace triumphant. *For Tho. Parkhurst*, 1697. brs. MC; MH.

3775A —The saints jewel. *For G. Griffith*, 1663. 4°. C.

3775B —To the Kings most excellent majesty, giving thanks. *For Richard Janeway*, 1688. brs. L; Y.

3776 —Via lactea. The saints only way. *For the vindication of the author*, 1663. 4°.* O.

Cheever, Samuel. Almanack. Cambridg [Mass.], 1660. *See* Almanacs.

3776A **Cheevers, Sarah.** To all people upon the face of the earth; a sweet salutation. [*London*], 1663. 8°.* PH.

Cheiragogia. 1659. *See* Thor, George.

Χειρεξοκη. The excellency. 1665. *See* Allen, Thomas.

3777 Το Χειφυς τωγ ωαρτυρωγ. Or, a bract narration. *By Samuel Brovvn, at the Hague*, 1651. 4°. LT, O, CS, SP, MR; CH, CN, MH, NU, WF, Y.

Χειροθεσια ον. 1649. *See* Hall, Joseph, *bp.*

Χειροθεσια τοὺ πρεσβυτεριόυ. 1661. *See* Alleine, Richard.

3778 **Cheke, Sir John.** The trve subject to the rebell. *Oxford, by Leonard Lichfield*, 1641. 4°. MADAN 995. L, O, C, MR, EN; CH, CN, LC, NU, Y.

Chymical dictionary. 1650. *See* French, John.

3779 Chymical, medicinal, and chyrurgical addresses: made to . . . Hartlib. *By G. Dawson, for Giles Calvert*, 1655. 8°. LT, O, LCP, LWL; CN, PU, WSG, Y, HC.

3779A La chemin abregé. Or, a compendious method. *For Humphrey Moseley,* 1654. 12°. L, O, LWL, SP; CLC, WF, Y.

3779B **Cheneau, François.** Francis Cheneau's French grammar. [*London*] *by N. T. for Charles Mearne,* 1685. 8°. CLC, MB, MH, WF.

Cheney. *See* Cheyney.

Chernocke, Robert. *See* Charnock, Robert.

Cherry, Thomas. New almanack. [*n.p.*], 1699. *See* Almanacs.

3780 **Cheshire, Thomas.** A sermon preached . . . tenth of October, 1641. *Printed at London,* 1641. 4°.* LT, OC, LW, YM, DT; MH, WF.

3781 —A sermon preached at Saint Peters. *Printed at London, for the author.* 1642. 4°.* LT, O, CJ, YM, DT; MH, NU, Y.

3782 —A true copy of that sermon . . . tenth day of October last. *Printed at London,* 1641. 4°.* LT, O, CT, EN; CH, MH, NU, WF, Y.

3783 The Cheshire petition for establishing of the Common-prayer-booke. *For Iohn Aston,* 1642. LT, O, LS, OC; MH.

3784 Cheshires successe. *For Thomas Underhill,* 1643. 4°.* LT, O, CCL, HH, DT; CH, CLC, MH.

Chesick, William. New almanack. [*n.p.*], 1661. *See* Almanacs.

3784A **Chester, Stephen.** A funeral elegy upon . . . John Winthrop. [*Cambridge, Mass.,* 1676]. brs. MHS.

3784B **Chesterfield, Philip Stanhope,** *earl of.* To the . . . Lords . . . the humble petition of. *Printed,* 1646. 4°.* OC.

3785 [**Chestlin,**   .] Persecutio vndecima. The chvrches eleventh persecution. [*London*], *printed,* 1648. 4°. LT, O, C, YM, EN; CH, CN, MH, NU, WF.

3786 [–] —[Anr. ed.] Re-printed, 1681. *To be sold by Walter Davis.* 4°.* T.C.I 452. L, O, C, OM, DT; CH, NC, NU, PU, Y.

3787 [–] —[Anr. ed.] *Printed,* 1648. *And now reprinted* 1682, *by H. Brugis, to be had at his house, or Mr. Hammonds.* 4°. L, C, DT; MH, NU, TU.

3788 [**Chetham, James.**] The angler's vade mecum. *For Tho. Bassett,* 1681. 8°. T.C.I 444. CH, CN, Y.

3789 [–] —[Anr. ed.] *For Mordecai Moxon,* 1681. 8°. CLC, LC, MH, NN.

3790 [–] —Second edition. *For T. Bassett,* 1689. 12°. T.C.II 265. L; LC, MH, NN, Y.

3791 [–] —Third edition. *For William Battersby, and William Brown,* 1700. 12°. L, O; CH, LC, MH, NN, Y.

3792 **Chetwind, Charles.** A narrative of the depositions of Robert Jenison. *For Henry Hills, Thomas Parkhurst, John Starkey, Dorman Newman, Thomas Cockeril, Thomas Simmons, and Jacob Tonson,* 1679. fol.* L, O, C, LL, EN; CH, CN, MH, NU, WF, Y.

3793 **Chetwind, John.** Anthologia historica. *By J. R. for P. C.,* 1674. 8°. T.C.I 169. L, O, BR; CH, CN, NIC, WF, Y.

3794 —Collections, historical, political, theological. Second edition. *For William Miller,* 1691. 8°. T.C.II 363. O; PBM.

3795 —The dead speaking. *By T. W. for John Place,* 1653[4]. 4°. LT, O, C, LCL, BR; WF, Y.

3796 —Eben-ezer, a thankful memorial. *Printed, and are to be sold by Tho. Wall, at Bristol,* 1682. 4°.* T.C.I 484. L, WCA, DT; CH, V, WF, Y.

3796A ——[Anr. ed.] *For Tho. Parkhurst,* 1682. 4°.* BR; NC.

3797 —A memorial for magistrates. *For Thomas Parkhurst,* 1682. 4°.* T.C.I 484. L, C, WCA; WF, Y.

3798 —The watch charged. *By Roger Daniel, to be sold by Edward Brewster,* 1659. 8°. LT, O, LCL, LW, BR; MH, NPT.

3799 **Chetwind, Philip.** To the supreme authority of England . . . the humble petition of. [*London,* 1650.] brs. LT; Y.

3799A **C[hetwood] K[nightly].** An ode in imitation of Pindar on . . . Ossory. *For Samuel Carr,* 1681. fol.* L, O, C; CLC, CN, MH, WF, Y.

3800 [**Chevalier, Pierre.**] A discourse of the original, countrey, manners, . . . of the Cossacks. *By T. N. for Hobart Kemp,* 1672. 8°. T.C.I 102. L, O, CT, EN, DT, GK; CH, LC, MH, NC, PL, Y.

3801 [**Chevreau, Urbain.**] The great Scanderbeg. *For R. Bentley,* 1690. 12°. T.C.II 320. L; CLC, MH.

3802 —The mirror of fortune. *T. N., sold by Sam. Lowndes,* 1676. 8°. T.C.I 228. L, O, CS; CLC, CN, WF.

3803 [–] A relation of the life of Christina Queen of Sweden. *By J. C. for Henry Fletcher; and Nath. Heathcoate,* 1656. 4°.* LT, O, CT, E; CH, RPJ, WF.

3803A [**Chevremont, Jean Baptiste de**] The knowledge of the world. *For John Dunton,* [1694]. 4°. L, CT; CH, CN.

3804 **Chewney, Nicholas.** Anti-Socinianism. *By J. M. for H. Twyford, and T. Dring,* 1656. 4°. LT, O, C, LCL, DT; CH, MH, NU, WF, Y.

3805 —Hell, with the everlasting torments. *By J. M. for Tho. Dring,* 1660. 8°. LT.

3805A ——[Anr. ed.] *E. Smith* [1700]. 8°. LW.

3806 [**Cheynell, Francis..**] An account given to the Parliament by the ministers. *By M. F. for Samuel Gellibrand,* 1647. 4°. MADAN 1917. LT, O, C, EN, DT; CH, CU, NU, TU, WF, Y.

3806A [–] —[Anr. ed.] *By F. K. for Samuel Gellibrand,* 1647. 4. MADAN 1917.* OC; Y.

3807 [–] Aulicus his dream. [*London*], *printed,* 1644. 4°.* LT, LCL; CH, CU, MH, TU, WF, Y.

3807A ——[Anr. ed.] *Printed,* 1644. 4°.* LT.

3808 [–] Aulicus his hue and cry. *Printed,* 1645. 4°.* LT, O, OC, HH, DT; CH, MH, Y.

3809 [–] The beacon flameing. *By Abraham Miller,* 1652. 4°.* LT, O, CE, EN, DT; CH, CN, MH, NU, WF, Y.

3810 —Chillingworthi novissima, or, the sicknesse, heresy, death . . . of William Chillingworth. *For Samuel Gellibrand,* 1644. 4°. LT, O, C, EN, DT; BN, CH, CN, MH, NU, WF, Y.

3811 —The divine trinunity of the Father. *By T. R. and E. M. for Samuel Gellibrand,* 1650. 8°. L, O, C, LCL, AU; MH, MU, NPT, NU, WF, Y.

3812 —The man of honour. *By J. R. for Samuel Gellibrand,* 1645. 4°. LT, O, C, EN, DT; CH, CN, MH, NU, TU, WF, Y.

3813   Entry cancelled.

3814   —A plot for the good of posterity. *For Samuel Gelli-brand, 1646.* 4°. LT, O, C, LCL, DT; CH, MH, NU, TU, WF, Y.

3815   —The rise, growth, and danger of Socinianisme. *For Samuel Gellibrand, 1643.* 4°. LT, C, OME, E, DT; CH, CU, MH, NU, WF, Y.

3816   —Sions memento. *For Samuel Gellibrand, 1643.* 4°. LT, C, OM, EN, DT; CH, MH, NU, TU, WF, Y.

3817   [–] The svvorne confederacy. *Printed, 1647. June the 5th.* 4°.* MADAN 1924. LT, O, C, LG; CH, MH, NU, WF, Y.

3818   [–] Truth triumphing over errour and heresie. *For E. B. and S. G., 1646[/6].* 4°.* MADAN 1909. LT, O, DT; MIU, NHC, Y.

3818A   **Cheyney, John.** A branch of Quakerism cut off. *For Richard Butler, 1676.* 4°.* SP; CH, MH.

3819   [–] A call to prayer, in two sermons. *Printed, 1677.* 8°. L, C, LF, LW.

3820   —The conforming Non-conformist. *For J. Robinson, 1680.* 8°. T.C.I 381. O, LCL, CE, CPE; NPT.

3821   A full answer to that question. *By J. M. for J. Robinson, 1680.* 8°. T.C.I 413. O, LCL, LSC, CPE, CT.

3822   —One sheet against the Quakers. *For Richard Butler, 1677.* 4°.* L, LF, SP; CH, PH, WF.

3823   —Quakerism proved to be gross blasphemy. *For Richard Butler, 1677.* 4°.* L, O, C, LF, SP; CH.

3824   — —Second edition. *For Richard Butler, 1678.* 4°.* T.C. 1340. L.

3825   —Quakerism subverted. *Printed, 1677.* 4°. L, O, C, LF, D.

3826   [–] The Shibboleth of Quakerism. *For Richard Butler, 1676.* 4°.* LF; CH, PH.

3827   —A skirmish made upon Quakerism. *For Richard Butler, 1676.* 4°. O, LF, WCA, SP; CH.

3828   [–] Some arguments to prove. *For J. Robinson, 1680.* 8°. T.C.I 391. L; CLC, NPT.

3829   —Two sermons of hypocrisie. *By R. Butler, 1677.* 8°. T.C.I 272. L, P; PSC, WF.

3829A   —A vindication of oaths and swearing. *For R. Butler, 1677.* 4°.* T.C.I 332. O, DT; CH, PH.

3829B   — —Second edition. *For R. Butler, 1680.* 4°.* L, LW.

3830   —A warning to souls to beware of Quakerism. *Loudon [sic], for Dorman Newman, 1677.* MC, D; MWA.

3831   **C[hidley], K[atherine].** Good counsell, to the petition-ers. *[London, 1645.]* brs. LT; MH, MHS.

3832   —The ivstification of the independant chvrches of Christ. *For William Larnar, 1641.* 4°. LT, O, CT, MR, DT; CSB, MIU, NPT, NU, Y.

3833   —A New-Yeares-gift, or a brief exhortation. *[London], printed, 1645.* 4°.* LT, O, CT, DT; Y.

3834   **Chidley, Samuel.** An additionall remonstrance. *For the author, 1653.* 4°.* LT, O, HH; CH, MH, MIU, WF, Y.

3834A   [–] All those wel-affected creditors. *[London? 1653.]* brs. MH.

3834B   [–] Bells founder confounded. *[London? 1658.]* cap., 4°.* WF.

3834C   [–] A Christian plea against Christmas. *For the author, 1656.* CSS.

3835   —A Christian plea for Christians baptisme. *[1642.]* 8°.* DT.

3836   — —[Anr. ed.] *By T. P. and M. S. to be sold by Ben. Allen, 1643[4].* 4°.* LT, O, LCL; CU, MH, NU, WF.

3836A   —A Christian plea for infants baptism. —, *1643[4].* 4°. LT, LCL, LW, CK, CS; MPT, FPT.

3837   — —[Anr. ed.] *Printed and are to be sold by H. Allen, 1647.* L; NU.

3838   [–] [Hebrew], a cry against a crying sinne. *Printed at London, for Samuel Chidley, 1652.* 4°.* LT, O; CH, CN, MHL, WF, Y.

3839   —The dissembling Scot. *[London], printed, 1652.* 4°.* LT, O; MB, MH, MIU.

3839A   [–] An epistle directed to the parliament. *[London, 1652.]* cap., 4°.* L.

3840   —A remonstrance to the creditors. *[London, 1653.]* brs. LT; NC.

3841   —A remonstrance to the valiant. *For the author, 1653.* 4°.* LT, O, LCL; CLC, MH, WF.

3842   —The Separatist's answer. *By J. C., 1651.* 4°.* LT.

3843   [–] [Hebrew] Thunder from the throne of God. *[London, 1653.]* cap., 4°.* LT, EN; CLC, MH, NU, PH.

3844   [–] To His Highness the Lord Protector. &c. and to the Parliament of England. Valiant swordmen. *[London, 1656.]* cap., 4°.* LT; MHL, Y.

3845   —To the honourable committee for petitions: the humble petition of. *[London, 1652.]* brs. LT.

3846   [–] To the Parliament of the Commonwealth of England. Sirs, you know. *[London, 1657.]* cap., 4°.* LT; Y.

Cheif [sic] affairs. 1651. *See* Parker, Henry.

3846A   The chief principles of Popery confuted. *For William Gilbert, 1673.* 4°.* Y.

Chief principles of the Christian faith. 1668. *See* Crad-ock, Samuel.

3847   **Chilcot, William.** A practical treatise concerning evil thoughts. *Exon, by Samuel Darker, for Charles Yeo, John Pearce, and Philip Bishop, 1698.* 8°. L, O, C, OB; CH, CLC, WF.

3847A   —A sermon preached . . . April 4, 1697. *By Freeman Collins for Philip Bishop, in Exon, 1697.* 4°.* Y.

3848   **Child, James.** To the right honourable the knights, . . . the great grievances and oppressions of. *[London, 1689?]* brs. L.

3849   **Child, John.** Mr. John Child's book, entituled, A second argument . . . republished. *How, 1684.* 4°.* CP, EN; CN.

3850   —A moderate message to Quakers. *[London], printed, 1676.* 8°. LF; MH, Y.

3851   —New-Englands Jonas cast up. *For T. R. and E. M., 1647.* 4°.* LT, O, OC, BAMB, DT; CH, CU, LC, MH, NN, RPJ, WCL.

3852   **C[hild], *Sir* J[osiah].** Brief observations concerning trade, and interest of money. *For Elizabeth Calvert, and Henry Mortlock, 1668.* 4°.* L, O, CCA, OM, DT; CH, CU, LC, MH, NC, Y.

3853   [–] A discourse about trade. *[London], by A Sowle, 1690.* 8°. T.C.II 371. O, C, LI, E, EN; CU, LC, MH, PHS, Y.

3854 [–] A discourse concerning trade. colop: *Printed and sold by Andrew Sowle*, 1689. 4°.* I, LUG; MIU, NC, Y.

3855 [–] A discourse of the nature, use, and advantages of trade. *Printed, to be sold by Randal Taylor*, 1694. 4°.* L, CT; CU, MH, NC, Y.

3856 [–] An essay on wool. *For Henry Bonwicke*, 1693. 4°.* T.C.II 441. L, O, C; MH, NC, WF, Y.

3857 —The great honour and advantage of the East-India trade. *For Thomas Speed*, 1697. 4°.* T.C.II 605. L, LUG; CU, MH, NC, Y.

3858 —A method concerning the relief and employment of the poor. *Printed*, 1699. 8°.* L, OC; CH, MH, NC.

3859 Entry cancelled.

3860 —A new discourse of trade. *Printed and sold by John Everingham*, 1693. 8°. L, CT, YM; MH, NC, NP, RPJ, Y.

3861 ——Second edition. *Printed, and sold by Sam. Crouch, Tho. Horne, and Jos. Hindmarch*, 1694. 8°. T.C.II 485. L, O, C, OM, EN; BN, CH, LC, MH, VC, Y.

3862 ——[Anr. ed.] *Printed and sold by T. Sowle*, 1698. 8°. T.C.III 175. L, AU, DT; CH, CU, MH, RPJ, TU, Y.

3862A ——Fourth edition. *F. Hodges*, 1700. 4°. OP.

3863 —Sir Josiah Child's proposals for the relief of the poor. [*London*, 1670?] 4°.* L, O, LUG; NC.

3864 [–] A short addition to the observations concerning trade. *For Henry Mortlock*, 1668. 4°.* L, DT; CH, MH, NC, WF.

3865 [–] A supplement, 1689. To a former treatise. [*London*, 1689.] cap., 4°.* L, O, LG, LUG; CH, CN, NC, WF, Y.

3866 [–] A treatise wherein is demonstrated, I. That the East-India trade. *By T. J. for Robert Boulter*, 1681. 4°.* T.C.I 430. L, OC, EN, ES, DT; CH, CN, MH, MU, NC, WF, Y.

3866A [–] —[Anr. ed.] *By J. R. for the East India company*, 1681. 4°.* LG; CH, LC, MH, NP,

3867 **Child, William.** Choise musick to the Psalmes. *For John Playford*, 1656. 12°. L.

3867A —The sealed book opened. *By T. R. & E. M. for Anthony Williamson*, 1656. 4°. LT.

3868 The children in the wood. [*n.p.*], 1665. brs. MC.
Children of Abraham's faith. 1663. *See* Watkins, Morgan.
Children of Beliall. [*n.p.*], 1647. *See* Scott, Thomas.

3869 The children's example. [*London*, 1700?] brs. L.

3869A The children's petition. *For Richard Chiswell*, 1669. 12°. T.C.I 27. L, O, M; WF.

3870 **Childrey, Joshua.** Britannia Baconica. *For the author, and are to be sold by H. E.*, 1660. 8°. L.

3871 ——[Anr. ed.] —, 1661. 8°. L, O, C, EN, DT; CH, CN, LC, MH, Y.

3872 ——[Anr. ed.] —, 1662. 8°. L, CM, DCH, OR, AU; CH, MH, MIU, WF, Y.

3873 —Indago astrologia: or, a brief and modest enquiry. *For Edward Husband*, 1652. 4°.* LT, O, LWL; NIC.
—1653. Syzygiasticon. 1653. *See* Almanacs.

3874 The child's Bible. *For the author*, 1677. 8°. Y.

3875 The childes catechism. *Paris*, 1678. 8°. O.
Child's de-light. [*n.p.*, c. 1695.] *See* Lye, Thomas.
Child's instructor. 1679. *See* Keach, Benjamin.

3875A The child's recreation. colop: *By Will. Bonny, for Tho. Howkins*, 1692. 8°. NC.

3876 **Chillenden, Edmund.** The inhumanity of the kings prison-keeper at Oxford. *By G. D. for John Bull*, 1643. 4°.* MADAN 1431. LT, O, CT, HH, DT; CH, MH, MIU, WF, Y.

3877 —Nathans parable. *Printed at London*, 1653. 4°.* LT.

3878 —A pitifvll relation of the kings prison keeper at Oxford. *Printed at London, by G. D. for Iohn Bull*, 1643. 4°.* O, E; Y.

3879 —Preaching vvithout ordjnatjon. *Imprinted at London, for George Whittington*, 1647. 4°.* LT, O, LCL, HH, DT; CH, CU, MH, NU, WF, Y.

3880 [–] A true relation of the state of the case between . . . Parliament. *By J. C.*, 1659. 4°.* LT, O, C, OC, CCA; CH, CN, MIU, NU, WF, Y.

3881–2 Entries cancelled.

3883 **Chillingworth, William.** Additional discourses of. *For Richard Chiswell*, 1687. 4°. L, O, C, EC, D; CH, CN, NU, PL, WF, Y.

3884 [–] The apostolicall institvtion of Episcopacy. *Oxford, by H. Hall*, 1644. 4°.* MADAN 1597. LT, O, OC, EC; CH, NU, WF.

3884A —[Anr. ed.] *By E. Cotes*, 1664. 4°.* MH, TSM.

3885 —Mr. Chillingworth's book called The religion of Protestants. *For R. Chiswell, C. Harper, W. Crook, and J. Adamson*, 1687. 4°. L, O, C, ES, DT; CH, CU, NU, PL, WF, Y.

3886 —Mr. Chillingvvorth's judgment of the religion of Protestants. *For Francis Smith*, 1680. fol.* L, O, HH; CN, MH, PU, WF, WU.

3887 ——[Anr. ed.] colop: *For Fr. Smith*, 1689. cap., 4°.* L, O, C, OC, E; CH, NU, WF, Y.

3887A ——[Anr. ed.] [*London*, 1692.] cap., 4°.* C, OC; CH, LC, MH, NU, TU, Y.

3888 —Mr. Chillingworths letter touching infallibility. *By D. Maxwell, for Timothy Garthwait*, 1661. 4°.* WF.

3888A ——[Anr. ed.] —, 1662. 4°.* L, CPE, YM, DT; CU, MH, NU.

3888B [**Chillingworth,   .**] The petition of the most svbstantiall inhabitants of the citie of London. *Printed at Oxford by Leonard Lichfield*, 1642[/3]. 4°.* MADAN 1165. LT, O, C, LL, DT; CSS, MIU, TU, WF, Y.

3888C [–] —[Anr. ed.] *Edward Husband*, 1642[3]. 4°.* L, OC, HH; CH, CLC, CSS.

3888D [–] —[Anr. ed.] *Printed at York by Stephen Bulkley*, 1642. 4°.* YM.

3889 —Reasons against Popery. Second edition. *For Robert Pawlet*, 1673. 4°.* L, CE, YM; WF, Y.

3890 —The religion of Protestants. Third edition. *By E. Cotes, for J. Clark, to be sold by Thomas Thornicroft*, 1664. fol. L, O, C, AU, DT; CU, LC, MH, NPT, Y.

3891 ——Fourth edition. *By Andrew Clark, for Richard Chiswell*, 1674. fol. T.C.I 190. L, O, C, ENC, DT; CSU, MH, TSM, WF, Y.

3892 ——Fifth edition. *By M. C. to be sold by William Crook and Charles Harper*, 1684. fol. T.C.II 64. L, C, OC, ENC; BN, CH, IU, TSM, Y.

3893 Entry cancelled.

3894   —A sermon preached at the publike fast. *Oxford, by Henry Hall*, 1644. 4°.* MADAN 1655. LT, O, C, CT, BP; CH, MM, NN.

3895   —A sermon preached before His Majesty at Reading. *Oxford, by H. Hall for N. Davis*, 1644. 4°.* MADAN 1654. L, O, CT, OM, DC; MH, MM, NU, WF.

3896   **Chilton, Thomas.** The way of deliverance from bondage. *For Thomas Simmons*, 1659. 8°.* L, LF, BBN; MU.

3897   Chimney-sweepers sad complaint. *Johnson*, 1663. 4°. LG.
       Chimneys scuffle. 1662. *See* Brathwaite, Richard.
       China and France. 1676. *See* Grueber, Johann.

3898   Chipps of the old block. *Printed at the Hague, for S. Browne*, 1659. brs. LT, O; MH, WF, Y.
       Chirologia. 1644. *See* Bulwer, John.
       Chironomia. 1644. *See* Bulwer, John.

3899   **Chisenhale, Edward.** Catholike history. *By J. C. for Nath. Brooks*, 1653. 8°. LT, O, C, OC, HH; CH, NU, WF, WSC, Y.

3900   **Chishull, Edmund.** Gulielmo tertio. *Oxonii, e theatro Sheldoniano. Prostant apud Joh. Crosley*, 1692. 4°.* T.C.II 426. L, O; CH, MH, Y.

3901   —A sermon preached . . . January 16. . . . 1697/8. *For S. Manship*, 1698. 4°.* T.C.III 52. L, O, C, OCC, DT; CH, WF, Y.

3902   **Chishull, John.** A brief explication of the Ten Commandments. *For the authour*, 166–? brs. L.

3903   —The danger of being almost a Christian. *By A. Neile for Francis Eglesfield*, 1657. 12°. LT, LW; CH, CLC, MH.

3903A —Second edition. *By J. Twyn for Francis Eglesfield*, 1658. 12°. LCL; CLC, MH, NU, WF.

3904   —Two treatises. The first, the young-mans memento. *By A. N. to be sold by F. Eglesfield*, 1657. 12°. LT, O; Y.

3905   ——[Anr. ed.] *By W. B. to be sold by F. Eglesfield*, 1658. 12°. L; CLC, V.

3906   —A word to Israel. *For Francis Eglesfield*, 1668. sixes. O, C; NPT.

      Chisman. *See* Cheesman.

3907   **Chiverton, Sir Richard.** Chiverton, mayor, Tuesday, the eighth day of December, 1657. An order. *By James Flesher*, [1657.] brs. L, LG.

3908   Entry cancelled.
       Choice. 1700. *See* Pomfret, John.
       Choice ayres. 1679. *See* Playford, John.
       Choice banquet. 1660. *See* Armstrong, Archibald.

3909   Choice cases in chancery. [*London*], 1672. 12°. LL, LIL.

3910   A choice collection of books in divinity. [*London*], 14 *March*, 1694. 4°.* L.

3911   A choice collection of Greek, Latin, and English books. 17 *Feb.*, [1691/2.] 4°.* L.
       Choice collection of 120. 1684. *See* Thompson, Nathaniel.
       Choice collection of 180. 1685. *See* Thompson, Nathaniel.

3912   A choice collection of valuable Latin and English books. [*London*], 2 *Jan.*, 1691. 4°.* L.

3913   A choice collection of valuable paintings . . . 10th . . . November, 1691. [*London*], 1691. 4°.* L.

3914   A choice collection of valuable paintings . . . 17th . . . November, 1691. [*London*], 1691. 4°.* L.

3915   A choice collection of wonderful miracles. colop: *For Benjamin Harris, and sold by Langley Curtis*, 1681. cap., fol.* L, O, LG, LWL; CLC, MBA, MH, MU, Y.
       Choice compendium. 1681. *See* H., J.

3916   Choyce drollery. *By J. G. for Robert Pollard, and John Sweeting*, 1656. 8°. O; CH, MH.
       Choice manual, or rare one scored secrets. 1667. *See* W., J.
       Choice narrative of Count Gondamer's transactions. 1659. *See* Scott, Thomas.
       Choice new songs. [*n.p.*], 1684. *See* D'Urfey, Thomas.

3917   Choice novels, and amarous tales. *By T. N. for Humphrey Moseley*, 1652. 8°. O, EN; CH, MH, Y.

3917A The choice of a recorder consider'd. [*London*, 1692.] brs. LG, HH.

3918   Choyce poems. *For Henry Brome*, 1661. 4°.* L, C; MH.
       Choice proverbial dialogues. 1660. *See* P., P.

3919   Choice remarks on the most observable actions. *For Richard Janeway*, 1681. fol.* T.C.I 450. L, O; LC, MH, NC, Y.

3920   Choice songs and ayres for one voyce . . . First book. *By W. G. to be sold by John Playford, and John Ford*, 1673. fol. L, A, GU; WF.

3920A Choice texts of Holy Scripture. *Printed*, 1663. 4°.* WF.

3920B **Choke, John.** The famous and virtuous necklaces. [*London, c.* 1680?] brs. L.

3920C —The great traveller. [*London*, 1685.] brs. L.

3921   A choak-peare for the Parliament. *Printed at Colechester*, 1648. 4°.* LT, O; CH.

3922   **Cholgius.** shah. Astronomica quædam. *Typis Jacobi Flesher*, 1650. 4°. O, C, P, EO, DT.

3923   ——[Anr. ed.] *Typis Jacobi Flesher: prostant apud Cornelium Bee*, 1652. 4°. L, O, C, EN, DT; MU, NN, WF, Y.

3924   **Cholmley, Sir Hugh, elder.** Tvvo letters the one being intercepted. [*London*], *for Edw. Husbands*. Iuly 12, 1643. 4°.* L, O, CCL.

3925   [**Cholmley, Sir Hugh, younger.**] A short account of the progress of the Mile at Tangier. [*London*, 1680?] cap., fol.* L; CH, Y.

3925A —Two letters the one being intercepted. [*London*], *for Edward Husbands*, *July* 12, 1643. 4°.* LT, O, CCL, YM.
       Chuse which you will, 1692. *See* Ames, Richards.

3926   **C[horley], J[osiah].** A brief memorial of the Bible. 1688. 8°. EN.

3927   **Chorlton, John.** The glorious reward of faithful ministers declared. *For T. P. to be sold by Zachary Whitworth in Manchester*, 1696. 4°.* L, CS, LW; CLC, MC, LC, NU, WF, Y.

3928   [–] Notes upon the Lord Bishop of Salisbury's four late discourses. *In usum Sarum*, 1695. 4°.* L, OC, CT, EN, DT; MIU, NU, WF, Y.
       Chorographia. Newcastle, 1649. *See* Gray, William.

3929   **Choune, Edward.** A whip for the lecturers of Lewis. *For the author, to be sold at Mr. Richard Dudson's at Lewes*, 1657. 4°.* DT; NHS, WF.

3929A **Choute, George.** Discourse in defense of infant baptism. *By R. C. to be sold by Richard Thraile*, 1651. 8°. NPT.

Christ alone. 1693. *See* Crips, Samuel.

3930 Christ and anti-Christ. [*London*], *printed*, 1662. 4°. L, CCA; PL, TU.

Christ and not the Pope, 1675. *See* Baxter, Richard.

Christ and the covenant. 1667. *See* Bridge, William.

3931 Christ confessed. [*London*], *printed*, 1665. 4°. L, O, CT, LW, DT; CLC, MB, MH, WF, Y.

Christ exalted, and. 1698. *See* Crisp, Samuel.

Christ exalted into. [*n.p.*, 1655.] *See* Parnell, James.

3931A Christ in the clouds. *By T. H. for J. Wright, J. Clarke, W. Thackeray, and T. Passenger*, 1683. 12°. CM.

3931B Christ is the bread of life. [*London*, c. 1645.] 4°. CM.

Christ knocking at the door. 1698. *See* W., J.

Christ made sin. 1691. *See* Crisp, Samuel.

Christ mysticall. 1647. *See* Hall, Joseph, *bp.*

Christ under the law. 1664. *See* Sadler, John.

3932 A christal for the clergie. *For R. P.*, 1641[2]. 4°.* LT, O, C, E; CH, NU, WF, Y.

3933 Christendom; or, the nature of Christ's kingdom. 1687. 4°. EN.

Christendom's call. 1661. *See* Smith, William.

Christenings make not. 1645. *See* Williams, Roger.

3934 Christi servus etiam. *For M. S.*, 1653. brs. LT, CM; CH, MH, WF.

3934A —[Anr. ed.] *For Edward Thomas*, 1659. brs. TU.

3935 **Christian IV,** *king of Denmark.* The king of Denmarks resolvtion concerning Charles. *July 5.* [*London*], *for J Tompson, and A. Coe*, 1642. 4°.* LT; CH.

3936 —Two manifesto's or declarations. [*London*, 1644.] cap., 4°.* LT, O, HH; CH, CN, MBP, WF.

3936A **Christian V,** *King of Denmark.* His Majesty the King of Denmarks letter to . . . Duke of Holstein. [*London*], *printed* 1677. 4°.* EN; MH.

3936B **Christian, Edward.** The earl of Danby vindicated. colop: *For Freeman Collins*, 1679. cap., fol.* OC, EN.

3937 —Reflections upon a paper intituled, Some reflections. colop: *For Freeman Collins*, 1679. cap., fol.* L, O, C, OC, HH; CLC, MH, NC, TU, WF, Y.

Christian a Quaker. 1674. *See* Loddington, William.

Christian admonition. [*n.p.*, 1641.] *See* B., T.

Christian advice both to old and young. 1671. *See* Mockett, Thomas.

3938 A Christian and brotherly exhortation to peace. *For Richard Wodenothe*, [1653]. 4°.* LT.

Christian and conjugall counsell. 1661. *See* Thomas, William.

3939 A Christian hnd [sic] sober wish. *Printed*, 1662. 4°.* O, SP; NU, WF, Y.

3940 A Christian beleefe, concerning bishops. [*London*], *printed*, 1641. brs. L, EC; MH.

3941 Entry cancelled.

Christian caveat. 1684. *See* P., A.

—1650. *See* Fisher, Edward.

Christian champion. [*n.p.*], 1689. *See* Walker, George.

Christian charity. 1699. *See* A., P.

3942 The Christian conquest. [*London*], *for J. Wright, J. Clark, W. Thackery, and T. Passinger*, [1683]. brs. L.

3943 Christian consolations. *For Rich. Royston*, 1671. 12°. T.C.I 71. O, CK, CT, LL.

Christian covenanting confession. [*n.p.*, 1680?] *See* Eliot, John.

3944 The Christian conventicle: or, the private-meetings of God's people. [*n.p.*], 1670. 8°. L, EN.

3945 Christian devotion. *For W. Thackery; T. Passinger and C. Passinger*, 1679. 12°. T.C.I 329. L, O.

Christian directions. 1674. *See* Gouge, Thomas.

Christian divrnall. 1650. *See* M., A.

Christian doctrine. Dublin, 1652. *See* Perkins, William.

—1678. *See* S., J.

—1693. *See* Whitehead, George.

Christian education. 1678. *See* Varet, Alexander.

Christian faith. Philadelphia, 1692. *See* Keith, George.

3945A A Christian indeed: or, Heaven's assurance. *By A. P. and T. H. for J. Wright*, 1677. 12°.* CM.

Christian information. 1664. *See* Ellington, Francis.

Christian letters. 1673. *See* Alleine, Joseph.

Christian liberty. [*n.p.*], 1674/5. *See* Penn, William.

3946 The Christian life and death, of Mistris . . . Brettargh. *By Felix Kingston, for Iohn Wright, the elder*, 1641. 4°.* NN, Y.

Christian life manifested. [*n.p.*, 1661.] *See* Smith, William.

Christian man. 1650. *See* Senault, Jean F.

Christian mans triall. 1641. *See* Lilburne, John.

Christian moderator. [*n.p.*], 1651. *See* Austin, John.

Christian monitor. 1686. *See* Rawlet, John.

Christian physician. 1683. *See* Atherton, H.

Christian pilgrim. Paris, 1652. *See* Scupalo, Lorenzo.

Christian plea. [1642.] *See* Chidley, Samuel.

3947 The Christian principle and peaceable conversation. [*London*], *printed*, 1685. 4°.* L, O, LF, LG; IE, MH, PH, PSC, Y.

Christian prudence. 1691. *See* Kettlewell, John.

Christian queries. 1663. *See* B., J.

Christian reader. [*n.p.*, 1645.] *See* Hunt, James.

Christian religious meetings. [*n.p.*], 1664. *See* Farnworth, Richard.

Christian reprehension. [*n.p.*], 1690. *See* Whitehead, George.

Christian rules. [*n.p.*], 1659. *See* Clifford, William.

Christian sacrifice. 1671. *See* Patrick, Symon, *bp.*

3948 The Christian scholar. *For Richard Sare, to be sold by Henry White and William Shepey*, 1700. 4°. O, BAMB.

3948A Christian seasonable considerations. *Printed and sold by J. Nutt*, 1699. 8°. CT.

Christian sodality [*n.p.*], 1652. *See* Gage, John.

Christian souldier. 1642. *See* Jordan, Thomas.

3949 The Christian souldiers magazine. *Printed at London, by G. Bishop*, 1644. 8°.* LT.

3949A The Christian soldier's penny Bible. *By R. Smith, for Samuel Wade*, 1693. 8°.* L.

Christian supports. 1691. *See* Cooke, Shadrach.

3949B Christian testimony against sinfull complyance. *For the author,* 1664. 4°. PL.

Christian-testimony born. [n.p.], 1679. *See* Gibson, William.

Christian-testimony born. 1681. *See* Field, John.

Christian testimony of some. [n.p., 1696.] *See* Sandilands, Robert.

Christian thoughts. [n.p.], 1680. *See* Bouhours, Dominique.

Christian tolleration. [*London*], 1664. *See* Farnworth, Richard.

3950 Christian unity exhorted to. [*London*], printed, 1678. 4°.* L, LF; CH, NU, PH, PSC.

3951 Christian valor encouraged: or, the Turk's downfal. *By John Leake, sold by Randal Taylor,* 1684. 4°.* L, O.

Christian virtuoso. [n.p.], 1690. *See* Boyle, Robert.

Christian warfare. 1680. *See* L., J.

Christiane OOnoowae sampoowaonk. A Christian covenanting confession. [n.p., 1670?] *See* Eliot, John.

Χριστιανισμου στοιχειωσιζ 1670. *See* Nowell, Alexander.

Christianissimus. 1678. *See* Nedham, Marchamont.

Christianity, a doctrine. 1691. *See* Kettlewell, John.

Christianity abused. 1679. *See* Williams, John, *bp.*

Christianity no enthusiasm. 1678. *See* Comber, Thomas.

Christianity not mysterious. 1696. *See* Toland, John.

3952 Entry cancelled.

Christianity the great mystery. 1696. *See* Beverly, Thomas.

Christians best exercise. 1689. *See* Comber, Thomas.

Christians best garment. 1661. *See* Hart, John.

3953 The Christian's birth right. 1690. 8°. O.

Christian's blessed choice. 1668. *See* Hart, John.

Christians combat. 1664. *See* Love, Christopher.

3954 The Christians comfort. *For W. Thackeray,* 1673. 8°.* Y.

Christians crown. 1671. *See* C., T.

Christians dayly solace. 1659. *See* Head, Richard.

Christians daily walk. [1660.] *See* Oasland, Henry.

3955 The Christians guide. *Hen. Rodes,* 1683. 8°. T.C.II 13. LSC, P; WF.

3956 A Christian's journal. Or brief directions. *For the author and sold by R. Bentley,* 1684. 12°. L, P; CH, CLC, Y.

Christians justification. 1678. *See* Allen, William.

Christians liberty. 1645. *See* Graunt, John.

Christians' new victory. [1685.] *See* S., J.

3957 The Christian's New-Years-gift. *For W. B.,* 1688. brs. O; MH.

3958 A Christian's nightly care. [*London,* 1650?] brs. L.

Christians pattern. 1657. *See* Thomas à Kempis.

3959 The Christian's spiritual conflict. [*London,* 1657.] brs. LT.

3960 A Christian's sure anchor. *For S. Keble,* 1693. 4°.* L, O, C, CS, CT; WF.

Christians testimony against tythes. [*London*], 1678. *See* Atkinson, Thomas.

3961 The Christians triumph over temptation. *For Jonah Deacon,* [1687.] 12°. CM.

Christians victory. [n.p.], 1670. *See* Ward, Seth.

3962 The Christians way to Heaven. *Printed,* 1700. 8°.* O, EC, BAMB.

Christianus, Socrates, *pseud. See* Stephens, Edward.

Christianus Londinatus, *pseud.*

3963 **Christina,** *queen of Sweden.* A declaration of. *Imprinted at London, for R. W. 17 Aprill,* 1649. 4°.* LT; CH, LC.

3964 — —[Anr. ed.] *For George Horton,* 1652. 4°.* LT.

3965 —A letter sent from. *For G: Horton,* 1652. 4°.* LT.

3965A Christmas carols. 1674. O.

Christmas-contemplations. 1688. *See* T., T.

Christ-mas day. 1656. *See* Woodward, Hezekiah.

Christmas ordinary. 1682. *See* Richards, William.

Χριστολογια, ον. 1671. *See* Coles, Elisha.

Χριστοζ 'αυτοθεοζ, ον. 1696. *See* Addison, Lancelot.

3965B Χριστοζ ικαιοσυνη, or Jesus Christ, given. *For Thomas Passenger,* 1667. 4°.* NPT.

3966 Christs banner of love. *For John Wright,* 1648. 4°.* LT; CH, NU.

Christs birth misse-timed. 1649. *See* Skinner, Robert.

3967 Christ's birth not mis-timed. *For Richard Royston,* 1649. 4°.* LT, O, CT, OC, EN.

Christs first sermon. 1656. *See* Hart, John.

Christ's hundred commandments. 1682. *See* Clark, Benjamin.

Christs impressions. [n.p.], 1700. *See* Clark, James.

Christs kingdome. 1645. *See* Hayne, Thomas.

Christ's lambs. 1691. *See* Whitehead, George.

Christ's last sermon. 1679. *See* Hart, John.

Christ's light spring. [n.p., 1660.] *See* Fisher, Samuel.

Christs light the only. [n.p.], 1662. *See* Fox, George.

3968 Christs order, and the disciples practice. [*London,* 1644.] cap., 4°.* LT, CM; MBA, MH, NU, WF, Y.

Christ's passion. 1687. *See* Grotius, Hugo.

3968A Christs personal reign on earth. *By T. Lock for Wil. Burden,* 1654. 4°.* MH.

3969 Christ's satisfaction. [n.p.], 1669. 4°. CE.

Christ's submission. 1644. *See* Estwick, Nicholas.

3969A Christs teares over Jerusalem. *For I. Coles, T. Vere, J. Wright, and J. Clarke* [1675]. brs. O, CM.

Christ's voice to England. 1683. *See* C., J.

Christ's voice to sinners. 1680. *See* O., T.

Christ's yoke. 1675. *See* Taylor, Jeremy.

Christus Dei, or. Oxford, 1642. *See* Jones, John.

Christus Dei, the Lords annointed. Oxford, 1643. *See* Morton, Thomas.

3970 Christus natus est, Christ is born. *By T. H. for VV. Thackeray,* [1680?]. brs. L; MH.

3971 Christus redivivus: or, the history of. *By A. P. and T. H. for P. Brooksby,* [1680?]. brs. L.

Chronica iuridicialis. 1685. *See* Cooke, Edward.

Chronicle of the late intestine war. 1676. *See* Phillips, John.

Chronicon Saxonicum. Oxonii, 1692. *See* Anglo-Saxon chronicle.

Chronographicall history. 1641. *See* Heywood, Thomas.

Chronological account. [*n.p.*], 1694. *See* Keith, George.

Chronological revise. 1647. *See* Tooke, George.

3972 Chronological table of events. 1651. brs. O.

3973 A chronological table of the pedigree and lineall descent. *Cork, William Smith,* [1690?] DMC.

Chronological tables. [1689.] *See* Parsons, William.

3974 Chronologicvm epitaphium . . . Roberti Devereux. [*n.p.*, 1646.] brs. L; MH.

3975 The chronology. [1653.] 4°. MR.

3976 Chronology of the growth and rise of Popery. *Printed,* 1680. 4°.* L, SP, EN; CH, NU, WF.

Chronometra aliquot. *Cantabrigiæ,* 1645. *See* Sictor, John.

Chronosticon [1662]. *See* Fisher, Payne.

3977 Chronostichon decollationis Caroli regis. [*n.p.*, 1649.] brs. LT; CH, MH.

Chronosticon. [*n.p.*, 1661.] *See* F., P.

Chrysaspis. 1660. *See* White, Thomas.

3977A **Chrysostom, Saint John.** De sacris precibus oratio prima. *Typis Henr. Hills,* [1695?] SIXES. WF.

3978 —The golden book of. *By D. M. for G. Bedel and T. Collins,* 1659. 12°. KEYNES, EVELYN 12. LT, O, OC, AM, GK; CH, CN, WF.

3979 —[Anr. ed.] —, 1659. 12°. KEYNES, EVELYN, 13. CK, CS, SP, GK, M; CLC, MH.

3980 —His paraenesis, or admonition. *For Thomas Dring,* 1654. 12°. LT, O.

3981 **Chudleigh, *Sir* George.** A declaration published in the county of Devon. *By L. N. for Richard Clutterbuck,* 1644. 4°.* LT, EN; CH, MH, WF, Y.

3982 —A letter from Exceter. *For C. M.,* 1642. 4°.* LT, BR.

3983 **Chudleigh, James.** Serjeant Major Iames Chudleigh his declaration. [*Oxford, by L. Lichfield*], *printed,* 1643. 4°.* MADAN 1398. O, C, DT; MH, Y.

3984 [**Chudleigh, *Lady* Mary.**] The female advocate. *For Andrew Bell,* 1700. 8°. O, OC; WF.

3984A [–] The female preacher. [1699.] 8°.* NN, Y.

3985 **Church, Andrew.** To the right honourable the knights, . . . the humble petition of. [*London,* 1641.] brs. LT, LG.

3986 **Church, Henry.** Church-incense. *For J. Rothwell,* 1655. 12°. LT; CLC.

3986A **Church, John.** A compendious enchiridion. *For the author,* 1682. 8°. LWL.

3986B **Church, Josiah.** The Christian's daily monitor. *For T. Parkhurst,* 1669. 12°. LSC.

3987 —The divine warrant of infant-baptism. *By John Macock, for George Calvert,* 1648. 4°. LT, O, LCL, CS, DT; CH, NPT, NU, WF, Y.

3988 — —[Anr. ed.] *For George Calvert,* 1652. 4°. C; CH, NHC, NU.

3989 **Church, Nathaniel.** Cheap riches. *For John Perry,* 1654. 12°. LT; CN.

3990 — —[Anr. ed.] *By S. G.,* 1657. 12°. L; NPT.

3990A — —[Anr. ed.] *For William Gilbertson,* 1657. 12°. Y.

3991 —More cheap riches. *By D. M. for J. Rothwell,* 1660. 12°. L.

3992 **Church, Thomas.** To the right honourable the Lord Major, . . . the remonstrance and petition of. [*London,* 1644.] 4°.* LT.

3993 The church & crown's felicity consumated. colop: *For T. Tillier,* 1689. brs. CH, CN.

Church catechism. 1666. *See* Comber, Thomas.

Church catechism enlarged. 1697. *See* M., R.

3994 The church catechism explained. *Dublin, by and for Joseph Ray,* 1699. 4°. DIX 312. DT.

Church-covenant. 1656. *See* Woodward, Hezekiah.

3994A The church defended. *Printed,* 1699. 4°. O; WF.

Church-government and. 1643. *See* Mather, Richard.

Church-government part V. *Oxford,* 1687. *See* Woodhead, Abraham.

Church-lands. [n.p.], 1648. *See* Warner, John, *bp.*

3995 Church-levellers. *By A. M. for Tho. Vnderhill,* 1649. 4°.* LT, HH, EN, DT; CH, CU, NU, WF.

3996 The church-lurcher unkennelled. *For the autor* [*sic*]. 1660. 4°.* P; NU.

3997 The church-man and the Quaker dialoguing. *Printed, and sold by the booksellers,* 1699. 8°.* LF; PSC, RPJ.

Church-members. 1648. *See* Woodbridge, Benjamin.

Church of Christ in Bristol. 1657. *See* Purnell, Robert.

CHURCH OF ENGLAND

3998 Articles agreed vpon by the arch-bishops and bishops. [*London*], *printed,* 1642. 4°.* L, OC, CK, CT, BR; CLC, MH, WF, Y.

3999 —[Anr. ed.] *By Robert Barker: and by the assignes of John Bill,* 1642. 4°.* L, O, C, MR, DT; CSS, NU, WF, Y.

3999A —[Anr. ed.] *Theophilus Brown,* 1642. 4°.* L.

4000 —[Anr. ed.] *By John Bill and Christopher Barker,* 1662. 4°.* L, O, C, LL, HH; CH, MH, NU, TU, Y.

4000A —[Anr. ed.] —, 1669. 4°.* L, O, OC, CT; MB, MIU, Y.

4000B —[Anr. ed.] —, 1673. 4°.* C.

4000C —[Anr. ed.] —, 1674. 4°.* O.

4001 —[Anr. ed.] *By the assigns of John Bill and Christopher Barker,* 1675. 4°.* L, O, C, WCA, OB; PL, WF, Y.

4002 —[Anr. ed.] *By John Bill, Christopher Barker, Thomas Newcomb, and Henry Hills,* 1677. 4°.* L, LW; CH, MBA, MH, NU, Y.

4003 —[Anr. ed.] *By John Bill, Thomas Newcomb, and Henry Hills,* 1679. 4°.* L, O, CT; MB, MH, NU.

4004 —[Anr. ed.] *By the assigns of John Bill, Thomas Newcomb, and Henry Hills,* 1681. 4°.* L, O.

4004A —[Anr. ed.] —, 1683. 4°.* WF.

4005 —"Fourth" edition. *By the assigns of John Bill: and by Henry Hills, and Thomas Newcomb,* 1684. 4°.* L, O, C, OB, OC; CH, MH.

4006 —[Anr. ed.] *By Charles Bill, Henry Hills, and Thomas Newcomb,* 1686. 4°.* L, O, OC, EC; CH, WF.

4007 —[Anr. ed.] [*Boston*], *printed,* 1688. 4°.* EVANS 448. L; CH, MB, MBA, MWA, V.

4007A —[Anr. ed.] *C. Bill,* 1690. 4°.* L, O.

4008 —[Anr. ed.] *By Charles Bill, and the executrix of Thomas Newcomb,* 1693. 4°.* L, O, OC.

4009 —[Anr. ed.] —, 1696. 4°.* L, BAMB; CLC, WF, Y.

4009A Articles of Christian religion. *For Edward Husband, June 27, 1648.* 4°.* O, CT; MH, MHL, NU, WF, Y.

4009B Articles of religion agreed upon. *For Theopholus Brown, 1642.* 4°. LC, CT; NU.

4009C —[Anr. ed.] [London.] *printed 1681.* 4°.* O, EC, A; MB, MH, PU, Y.

4010 Articles to be enquired of, and answered. *Cambridge: by John Field, 1667.* 4°.* O.

4011 Articles to be enquired of by the churchwardens. *Dublin, Benjamin Tooke & John Crooke, 1679.* 4°.* DIX 171. L.

4012 —[Anr. ed.] *Dublin, by Benjamin Tooke and John Crooke; and are to be sold by Mary Crooke and Andrew Crooke, 1682.* 4°.* DIX 195. Y.

4013 Articles to be enquired of in the metropolitical visitation of . . . William Arch-bishop of Canterbury. *For Richard Royston, 1663.* 4°.* L, OC, CS; NU, WF.

4014 Articles to be enquired of in the visitation. *York: by John White, 1692.* 4°.* YM.

4014A Articles of visitation . . . **Bath and Wells.** *By J. G. for William Ellis, 1662.* 4°.* L, O, DT.

4014B Articles of visitation . . . Bath and Wells. *Cambridge, by John Field, 1662.* 4°.* OC.

4015 Articles of visitation . . . Bath and Wells. *Oxford, by L. Lichfield, 1676.* 4°.* MADAN 3113. O, CSE.

4015A Articles of visitation . . . Bath and Wells. [*London*], *printed 1679.* 4°.* O.

4015B Articles of visitation . . . Bath and Wells. 1692. 4°.* CSE.

4015C Articles of enquiry . . . **Bedford.** *Cambridge, 1669.* 4°.* CJ.

4016 Articles of enquiry . . . Bedford. *Cambridge, printed, 1670.* 4°.* CCL, CS, CSS; Y.

4017 Articles to be enquired of . . . Bedford. *Cambridge, printed, 1667.* 4°.* O.

4017A Articles of visitation . . . **Berks.** *Oxford, by William Hall,* [1667.] 4°.* OC.

4018 Articles to be ministered, enquired of, and answered . . . **Bristol.** *For H. Brome, 1662.* 4°.* L, O, C, YM, DT; MH.

4019 Articles of enquiry exhibited . . . Bristol. *For Henry Brome, 1673.* 4°.* NU.

4020 Articles of enquiry . . . within the jurisdiction of . . . William, ... Bishop of Bristol. *For William Crook, 168[2?].* 4°.* L, CT.

4020A Articles of enquiry . . . Jonathan . . . Bishop of Bristol. *For C. Brome, 1686.* 4°.* BR.

4021 Articles of visitation and enquiry . . . within the diocese of **Canterbury.** *In the Savoy, by Tho. Newcomb, 1682.* 4°.* O; NU.

4022 —[*London*], *printed, 1695.* 4°.* L; NU.

4022A Articles recommended . . . Canterbury. 1668. 4°. CCA.

4022B Articles to be enquired of . . . Canterbury. *For R. Royston, 1663.* 4°. CT.

4022C Articles to be of enquired of . . . **Carlisle.** *For Timothy Garthwait, 1663.* 4°.* CPE, DT.

4023 —, 1666. 4°. L, CT.

4024 —1678. 4°. L.

4024A Articles to be enquired of . . . **Chester.** *Yorr [sic] by Stephen Bulkley, 1660.* 4°.* OC.

4025 *For Joh. Williams junior, 1674.* 4°.* L, O, OC.

4025A —Chester, *printed, 1691.* 4°.* OC.

4026 Articles of visitation and enquiry . . . within the diocess of **Chichester.** *For Henry Herringman, 1662.* 4°.* L, O, C, CS, YM; Y.

4027 —*A. Maxwell, 1670.* 4°.* L, CS.

4028 —*For W. Crooke, 1678.* 4°.* L.

4029 Articles of enquiry, exhibited . . . Chichester. *For Obadiah Blagrave, 1679.* 4°.* L, CT; NU.

4030 Articles to be enquired of and answered. *For Richard Chiswell, 1690.* 4°.* L, BR; CLC, WF.

4031 Articles to be enquired of . . . within the archdeaconry of **Colchester.** *For Timothy Garthwait, 1662.* 4°.* L, YM.

4031A Articles to be considered . . . **Derby.** [*London, by Tho. and Rich. Cotes, 1641.*] 4°.* EC.

4032 Articles to be ministred, enquired of, and answered, . . . **Dorset.** *For Obadiah Blagrave, 1683.* 4°.* O.

4033 Articles of inquiry, concerning matters ecclesiastical, . . . **Durham.** *By T. Garthwait, 1662.* 4°.* L, O, EN, CS, YM; NGT.

4033A ——, 1663. 4°.* CPE, EN, DT.

4033B ——*J. Collins, 1676.* 4.* L, EN.

4033C ——*York, by John Bulkley, 1683.* 4°.* L.

4033D —*York, by John Bulkley, 1684.* 4.* DD.

4034 Articles of enquiry, (with some directions intermingled) for . . . **Ely.** *For Timothy Garthwait, 1662.* 4°.* L, O, C, YM, DT; NU, Y.

4035 Articles of enquiry . . . Ely. *For Timothy Garthwait, 1665.* 4°.* CS, WCA; TU.

4035A Articles of visitation . . . Ely. *Cambridge, John Field, 1668.* 4°.* CJ.

4036 Articles for visitation . . . Ely. *Cambridge, by John Hayes, 1671.* 4°.* C, CJ, CS.

4037 Articles of visitation and enquiry within the diocese of Ely. *By S. Roycroft, 1679.* 4°.* L, O, C, YM.

4037A Articles of visitation . . . Ely. *Cambridge, 1682.* 4°. L.

4037B Articles of visitation . . . Ely. *J. Hayes, 1686.* 4°. CT; WF.

4037C Articles to be enquired of . . . Ely. *For R. Chiswell, 1692.* 4°. CT.

4037D Articles to be enquired of . . . Ely. *Cambridge, 169[2].* 4°. CT.

4038 Articles to be enquired of within the archdeaconry of **Essex.** *By Richard Hodgkinson, 1662.* 4°.* L, O, YM, DT.

4038A Articles to be enquired of within the commissarating at Essex. *For Timothy Garthwait, 1662.* 4°.* L, DT.

4039 Articles to be enquired of, and answered unto . . . in . . . Essex. *By E. Tyler and R. Holt, 1672,* 4°.* L, O.

4040 Articles to be enquired of . . . in Essex. *Anno Dom., 1680.* 1680. 4°.* L.

4040A Articles to be enquired of . . . Essex. *Oxford, 1683.* 4°.* LCL.

4041 Articles of visitation & enquiry . . . Seth . . . bishop of **Exeter.** *For T. Garthwait, 1662.* 4°.* L, O, CPE, YM, DT; Y.

4042   Articles of visitation and enquiry . . . Anthony, . . . bishop of Exeter. 1674. 4°.* L.

4043   Articles of visitation and enquiry, . . . Exeter. *For James Collins,* 1677. 4°.* O.

4043A   Articles of visitation and enquiry . . . Exeter. *Printed,* 1689. 4°. CLC.

4044   Articles of visitation and enquiry . . . **Gloucester.** *For William Leake,* [1661]. 4°.* L, O, OC.

4045   Articles of visitation and enquiry . . . Gloucester. *For William Leak,* 1663. 4°.* O.

4046   Articles of visitation and enquiry . . . arch-deaconry of Gloucester. *For George Dawes,* 1664. 4°.* L.

4047   —*Printed,* 1665. 4°.* O; Y.

4047A   —*Oxford,* 1687. 4°.* LSC.

4047B   Articles of enquiry . . . Gloucester. *Oxford, by Leonard Lichfield,* 1697. 4°.* L.

4048   Articles of visitation and enquiry . . . **Hereford.** *For G. Bedell, and T. Collins,* 1662. 4°.* L, O, CPE, YM, DT.

4049   Articles to be enquired of within the diocess of Hereford. *Oxford, printed,* 1692. 4°.* O.

4050   Articles of enquiry . . . **Huntington.** *By James Cotterel.* 1670. 4°.* O.

4051   Articles of visitation & enquiry . . . **Landaffe.** *For T. Garthwait,* 1662. 4°.* L, O, CPE.

4051A   Articles to be enquired of . . . **Langford.** *Oxford, printed,* 1663. 4°.* OC, CPE, CS; Y.

4052   Articles of inquiry . . . **Lichfield and Coventry.** *For John Place,* 1662. 4°.* L, O, YM.

4052A   —*For George Dawes,* 1664. 4°.* O.

4052AB   —*For John Place,* 1665. 4°.* EC.

4052B   — —, 1668. 4°.* L.

4053   Articles to be enquired of within the diocese of **Lincoln.** *By M. F.,* 1641. 4°.* LT, O, C, CT, YM; CH, MH, WF.

4054   Articles of visitation and enquiry conerning matters ecclesiastical: . . . Lincoln. *For A. Seile,* 1662. 4°.* L, O, CJ, MR, YM; WF.

4055   Articles to be enquired of by the ministers, . . . of Lincolne. *For Timothy Garthwait,* 1662. 4°.* L, YM, DT; NU.

4056   Articles exhibited . . . Lincoln. 1663. 4°.* L, O.

4057   Articles of visitation & enquiry . . . Lincolne. *For T. Garthwait,* 1664. 4°.* O, OC; TU, WF.

4058   —*For A. Seile,* 1666. 4°.* O.

4058A   Entry cancelled.

4059   Articles to be enquired of within the diocese of Lincolne. *In the Savoy, by Tho. Newcomb,* 1668. 4°.* O, OC.

4060   — —, 1671. 4°.* L, O.

4060A   Articles of visitation . . . Lincoln. 1673. 4°. L.

4061   Articles of enquiry . . . Lincolne. *For N. Brooke,* 1674. 4°.* O, OC.

4062   Articles of visitation & enquiry . . . Lincoln. *Printed,* 1679. 4°.* L, O.

4063   —*In the Savoy, by Tho: Newcomb,* 1686. 4°.* L, O, CS, CT.

4064   —*For Robert Clavel,* 1690. 4°.* O, CS, MR.

4064A   —1693. 4°.* L, O, MR.

4064B   Articles concerning matters ecclesiastical . . . Lincoln. *For John Everingham,* 1697. 4°.* OC.

4065   Articles of visitation and enquiry concerning matters ecclesiastical: . . . **London.** *For A. Seile,* 1662. 4°.* NU.

4066   Articles to be enquired of by the ministers, . . . of London. *For Timothy Garthwait,* 1662. 4°.* L, O, OC, CPE, YM.

4067   Articles of enquiry concerning matters ecclesiastical . . . London. *For T. Garthwait,* 1664. 4°.* L, O, OC; NU.

4067A   Articles of visitation . . . London. 1677. 4°.* L.

4067B   Articles of enquiry . . . London. 1693. 4°.* L.

4067C   Articles of visitation . . . London. *By Benj. Motte,* 1697. 4°.* OC.

4068   Articles to be enquired of vvithin the archdeaconrie of **Middlesex.** *For Richard Royston,* 166[blank]. 4°.* L, OC.

4069   —*For T. Garthwait,* 1662. 4°.* L, O, CS, YM, DT; NU, WF, Y.

4069A   Articles of enquiry . . . Middlesex. *For Henry Brome,* 1676. 4°.* CLC.

4069B   —1671. 4°.* L.

4070   Articles to be inquired of within the archdeaconry of **Northampton.** *By J. G. for Richard Royston,* 1662. 4°.* L, O, YM; MH.

4070A   —*For J. Williams,* 1663. 4°.* OC.

4070B   Articles to be enquired of . . . Northampton. 1666. 4°. CT.

4070C   Articles to be enquired of . . . Northumberland. *For Timothy Garthwait,* 1662. 4°. L, CJ, CPE, DT.

4071   Articles to be enquired of within the dioces of **Norwich.** 1657. 4°.* E.

4072   Articles to be enquired of in the diocesse of Norvvich. *By T. R. for G. T.,* 1662. 4°.* L, O, OC, CJ, YM; MH, NU.

4072A   — —, 1663. 4°.* OC.

4072B   —*By J. Grismond,* 1663. 4.* OC.

4072C   Articles to be enquired of . . . within the archdeaconry of Norwich. *Printed,* 1666. 4°.* MH.

4072D   Articles collected . . . Norwich. *For William Crook,* 1673. 4°.* OC.

4072E   Articles of visitation . . . Norwich. *For Robert Pawlet,* 1677. 4°.* L.

4072F   Articles collected out of the rubrick. *For W. Croke,* 1678. 4°. SP.

4072G   Articles to be enquired of . . . Norwich. *W. Rogers,* 1692. 4°.* L.

4073   Articles of visitation and enquiry concerning matters ecclesiasticall: . . . **Oxon.** *Oxford, by W. Hall,* 1662. 4°.* MADAN 2612. O, CS.

4074   —*Oxford, by William Hall,* 1666. 4°.* MADAN 2737. O; NU.

4075   Articles of visitation & enquiry . . . Oxford. *For Nathanael Hooke,* 1672. 4°.* O.

4076   Articles of visitation. *Oxford, by L. Lichfield,* 1674. 4°.* L, O.

4076A   —*Oxford, at the theater,* 1679. 4.* OC.

4076B   — —, 1682. 4°.* OC.

4077   Articles of visitation and enquiry . . . **Peterborough.** *For A. Seile,* 1662. 4°.* O, CT, YM, HH, DT; Y.

4077A   Articles of visitation . . . Peterborough. *For T. Garthwait,* 1664. 4°. CT.

4077B —*For Henry Brome*, 1673. 4°.* OC.

4078 Articles of visitation and enquiry concerning matters ecclesiasticall: . . . Peterborough. *For Henry Brome*, 1680. 4°.* O, CS.

4079 —*For William Hendsman*, 1683. 4°.* O.

4079A —*Printed*, 1689. 4°.* OC.

4079B —*For Robert Clavel*, 1692. WF.

4079C Articles of visitation . . . **Rochester.** *By J. G. for Richard Royston*, 1662. 4°.* OC.

4079D —*By Andrew Coe*, 1666. 4°.* WF.

4079E —*Printed*, 1677. 4°.* WF.

4080 Articles to be enquired of within the archdeaconry of **Saint Albans.** *For Timothy Garthwait*, 1662. 4°.* L, O, CJ, YM, DT.

4081 Articles of visitation & enquiry . . . **Saint Asaph.** *For T. Garthwait*, 1662. 4°.* L, O, CPE, YM.

4081A —*For Joseph Clark*, 1671. 4°.* O.

4081B —*By J. D. for Brabazon Aylmer*, 1678. 4°.* OC.

4082 Articles of visitation & enquiry . . . **Saint-David.** *For T. Garthwait*, 1662. 4°.* O, OC, CPE, YM, DT; NU.

4083 —*For N. Brooke*, 1671. 4°.* O.

4084 Articles to be enquired of in the diocese of **Salisbury.** *For Timothy Garthwait*, 1662. 4°.* L, O, C, CPE, CS.

4084A —*For T. Garthwait*, 1664. 4°.* OC.

4084B —*Thomas Newcomb*, 1671. 4°.* L.

4084C —*J. Collins*, 1674. 4°.* L.

4084D Articles to be enquired of . . . Sarum. *Oxford, by H. Hall*, 1675. 4°.* MADAN 3072. O.

4084E —*For Joanna Brome*, 1683. 4°.* OC.

4084F —. *Oxford, printed* 168[8?] 4°.* L.

4084G Articles of visitation. *For Ric. Chiswell*, 1689. 4°. OC, EN.

4085 Articles to be enquired of by the ministers, . . . of **Sudbury.** *Cambridge*, 1663. 4°.* CHRISTIE-MILLER.

4085A Articles of visitation . . . Sudbury. *Cambridge, John Hayes*, 1672. 4°.* CJ.

4085B —*Printed and sold by R. Baldwin*, 1700. WF.

4086 Articles to be enquired of within the commissariship of **Westminster.** *For Timothy Garthwait*, 1662. 4°.* O, CPE, YM, DT.

4087 Articles of visitation & enquiry . . . **Winchester.** *For T. Garthwait*, 1662. 4°.* L, O, OC, CS, YM; CU, WF.

4087A ——, 1665. 4°.* OC.

4088 —*By S. and B. G. for James Collins*, 1674. 4°.* O, LL; WF, Y.

4089 Articles of visitation and enquiry concerning matters ecclesiastical, . . . Winchester. *Printed*, 1685. 4°.* O.

4089A ——, 1686. 4°.* OC.

4090 Articles of visitation and enquiry . . . **Worcester.** *By J. G. for Richard Royston*, 1662. 4°.* L, O, CPE, YM; WF.

4090A —*T. Ratcliffe*, 1664. 4°.* L.

4091 Articles of visitation and enquiry, concerning matters ecclesiastical, . . . Worcester. *By Thomas Ratcliff*, [1666]. 4°.* L, O.

4091A ——, 1668. 4°.* L.

4091B —*Oxford, L. Lichfield*, 1674. 4°.* L.

4091C —*Printed*, 1690. 4°.* L, OC.

4091D —*For Henry Mortlock*, 1693. 4°.* Y.

4091E Articles of visitation . . . York. *York, by Alice Brooke*, 1662. 4°.* MR; WF.

4091F Articles to be enquired of . . . **York.** *York, by John White*, 1698. 4°.* BAMB, YM; CN.

4091G Certain acts and declarations made by the ecclesiastical congregation . . . at Clonmacnoise. *Kilkenny printed*, 1649. *And reprinted at London by Robert Ibbitson*. 4°.* LT, C; MH.

4091H —[Anr. ed.] *Printed at Cork the 25 of February 1649, and reprinted at Dublin by W. B.*, [1650?] 4°.* DIX 84. DK.

4091I Certain prayers fitted to severall occasions. *Exeter, by Robert Barker and John Bill*, 1645. 4°.* LT, SC.

4091J —[Anr. ed.] *Printed*, 1648. 8°.* LT, O, CM, DT; CH, LC, MH.

4091K Certain sermons or homilies. *By T. R. for Andrew Crooke, Samuel Mearne, and Robert Pawlet*, 1673. fol. T.C.I 133. L, CM, LW, EN, DT; CH, LC, MH, NU.

4091L —[Anr. ed.] *By T. R. for Samuel Mearne, and for Robert Pawlet*, 1676. fol. L, O, DT; MBA, MBC, MH, MIU, Y.

4091M —[Anr. ed.] *For Ann Mearn, and Blanch Pawlet*, 1683. fol. L, C, CT, D; NR, NU.

4091N —[Anr. ed.] *Oxford, at the theatre, and are to be sold by Thomas Guy, London*, 1683. 12°. O, CT, OC, LW, DT; NN, PL, TU, UCLA, Y.

4091O —[Anr. ed.] —*to be sold by Moses Pitt*, 1683. fol. L; MHS, NP, TSM, WF.

4091P —[Anr. ed.] —*to be sold by P. Parker*, 1683. fol. L, CCC.

4091Q —[Anr. ed.] *For George Wells, Abel Swall, and George Pawlett*, 1687. 12°. L, OC, BR, YM; CH, CN, PL, WF, Y.

4091R A collect to be used. *Dublin, by Andrew Crook*, 1691. 4°.* MB.

4092 —A collection of prayers and thanksgivings. *Printed at Oxford by Leonard Lichfield*, 1643. 4°.* MADAN 1450. L, CT, HH, YM, DT; NU, WF, Y.

4093 ——[Anr. ed.] [*Oxford*, 1643.] 4°.* MADAN 1451. O; Y.

4094 ——[Anr. ed.] *Printed at Oxford by Leonard Lichfield*, 1643. 4°.* MADAN 1452. LT, O; CH, MH.

4095 Constitutions and canons ecclesiastical. *For John Williams*. 1660. 4°. L.

4096 —1662. 4°. L, O, OC, CK, CT; CH, CLC, WF.

4096A —*Dublin, by John Crooke, to be sold by Samuel Dancer*, 1664. 4°. DIX 125. L, DI.

4097 —1665. 4°. O, OB, WCA; CLC, CU, PH.

4098 —*Dublin, by Benjamin Tooke, to be sold by Samuel Dancer*, 1669. 4°. DIX 138. CD, EC, DT, DWL.

4099 —*For A. Crook, S. Mearn, and R. Pawlett*, 1673. 4°. O, OB, OC, CS, HH; CLC, NU, WF, Y.

4100 —*By the assigns of John Bill and Christopher Barker*, 1676. 4°. L, O, EC, HH, DT; CN, MBA, MH, NP.

4101 —*For Samuel Mearne, and Robert Pawlet*, 1678. 69 pp. 4°. L, O, CT, EN, DT; CLC, NC, NPT, NU, WF, Y.

4102 ——, 1678. 64 pp. 4°. O, LG, CT; NC, NU.

4103 —*By the assigns of John Bill, and by Henry Hills, and Thomas Newcomb*, 1683. 4°. L, O, CT, OC, HH; TU, Y.

4103A —*Oxford, at the theater*, 1683. fol. CT.

4103B —*Dublin, by Andrew Crook and Samuel Helsham, to be sold by Samuel Helsham*, [1687.] 4°. DIX 224. L, CD, DN; MIU, PFL, WF.

4103C —A copy of the proceedings of some worthy . . . divines. *Printed at London,* 1641. 4°.* L, E; MH, NU, TU, WSC, Y.

4103D ——[Anr. ed: "A/copie/of/] *Printed,* 1641. 4°.* LT, O, CM, CT, HH; MH, NU, TU.

4103E ——[Anr. ed. "A/Copie of/] —, 1641. 4°.* O, OC, CCA, CJ; CH, CN, NU, WF, Y.

4103F ——[Anr. ed.] *By A. W.,* 1660. 4°.* LT, OC; CH, MIU, NU.

4104 ——[Anr. ed.] *Printed,* 1641, *and now re-princed [sic].* 1660. 4°.* O; NU.

4105 The form and manner of making & consecrating bishops. *By Robert Barker and John Bill,* [1660]. 4°.* LT, OC, CS, HH; MB, NN, WF, Y.

4106 —*By John Bill,* 1661. 8°. O.

4107 —*B. Norton and J. Bill,* 1629. *Reprinted,* [c. 1700]. 8°. MR.

4108 A form of common prayer, for Gods blessing . . . to be used . . . April the tenth. *By John Bill, Christopher Barker, Thomas Newcomb, and Henry Hills,* 1678. 4°. L, O, LL, CS, EC; CH, MH, PL, WF.

4109 A forme of common prayer. *York, Stephen Bulkeley,* 1643. 4°. CT.

4110 A forme of common-prayer to be used . . . second Friday in every month. *Bristoll, by Robert Barker, and John Bill,* 1643. 4°. OC; Y.

4111 A forme of common-prayer, to be used upon the solemne fast. *Printed at Oxford by Leonard Lichfield,* 1643. 4°. MADAN 1469. LT, O, OCC, BAMB, DT; CH, MH, WF, Y.

4112 —*Oxford, by Leonard Lichfield,* 1644[/5]. 4°.* MADAN 1703. LT, O, OCC, EN; CH, MH, Y.

4113 A form of common prayer, to be used upon the thirtieth of January. *By John Bill,* 1661. 4°. LT, O, OC, MR, YM; CH, MH.

4114 —[Anr. ed.] *By John Bill and Christopher Barker,* 1661. 4°.* L, CCH, CJ, CS; CH, MB, NU, Y.

4115 A form of common prayer to be used . . . 5th of April. *By John Bill and Christopher Barker,* 1665. 4°. L, O, LL, CS, YM; CH, MB, WF.

4116 A form of common prayer, to be used . . . tenth day of October. *By John Bill and Christopher Barker,* 1666. 4°. L, O, LL, CS, EC; LC, MB, MH, MIU, WF.

4117 A form of common prayer to be used . . . the 27th of March, 1672. *In the Savoy by the assigns of John Bill and Christopher Barker,* 1672. 4°. L, O, LL, CS, EC, DT; CH, MB, NU.

4118 A form of common prayer, to be used . . . 4th of February, 1673/4. *By the assigns of John Bill and Christopher Barker,* 1673/4. 4°. L, O, LL, CS, EC; CH, CLC, MB.

4119 A form of common prayer, together with an order of fasting. *By John Bill and Christopher Barker,* 1665. 4°. L, O, LL, LWL, CJ; MB, MIU, PL.

4119A —[Anr. ed.] *Re-printed at Oxford for Ric. Davis,* 1665. 4°. L, OC; MH, PL.

4119B A form of common prayer with fasting. *Dublin, by Benjamin Tooke,* 1685. 4°.* DIX 209. O, DM.

4120 A form of common prayer, with thanksgiving . . . the 20th of June. *By John Bill and Christopher Barker,* 1665. 4°. L, O, LL, CS, EC; CH, MB, MU, MH, NNG.

4121 A form of common prayer, with thanksgiving . . . 14th of August. *By John Bill and Christopher Barker,* 1666. 4°. L, O, LL, CJ, EC; CH, MB, MH, MU.

4121A A form of common prayer . . . 20th Nov. *In the Savoy, by the assigns of John Bill and Christopher Barker,* 1666. 4°. L, OC, LWL; MH, WSG.

4121B A form of common prayer and humiliation. 1690. 4°. Y.

4122 A form of prayer and solemn thanksgiving . . . the 26th of this July. *By the assigns of John Bill; and by Henry Hills, and Thomas Newcomb,* 1685. 4°.* L, O, OC, CS, OP; CH, MH, NU, WF, Y.

4123 Entry cancelled.

4124 A form of prayer and thanksgiving. *By Charles Bill, Henry Hills, and Thomas Newcomb,* 1686. 4°.* L, O, CS; CH, CN, MH, WF.

4125 A form of prayer and thanksgiving to Almighty God, . . . 31 of January. *In the Savoy: by Edw. Jones,* 1688. 4°.* L, O, OC, CS, EC; CH, CN, MH, NC, WF, Y.

4125A —*By Charles Bill and Thomas Newcomb,* 1690. 4°.* L, O, OC, EC, CS; CH, MH, Y.

4125B A form of prayer and thanksgiving . . . sixteenth November. *Dublin by Andrew Crook, assigne of Benjamin Tooke,* 1690. 4°.* DIX 242. CD, DM.

4126 A form of prayer and thanksgiving . . . sixth and twentieth of November. *By Charles Bill and the executrix of Thomas Newcomb,* 1691. 4°.* L, O, OC, CS, OP, WCA; CH, MH, NU, WF, Y.

4126A —[Anr. ed.] *Dublin, by Andrew Crook, assignee of Benjamin Tooke,* 1691. 4°.* DIX 246. CD, DM.

4127 A form of prayer and thanksgiving, to be used . . . 27th day of . . . October. *By Charles Bill and the executrix of Thomas Newcomb,* 1692. 4 pp. 4°.* L, O, OP; MH, Y.

4128 —[Anr. ed.] —, 1692. 10 ll. 4°.* L, O, OC, OCC; MH, NU, Y.

4128A —tenth . . . November. *Dublin, by Andrew Crook, assignee of Ben. Tooke,* 1692. 4°.* DIX 254. O, DM.

4129 A form of prayer and thanksgiving . . . 12 day of November. *By Charles Bill, and the executrix of Thomas Newcomb,* 1693. 4°.* L, O, OC, OCC, OP; CH, MH, NU, WF, Y.

4130 A form of prayer and thanksgiving. *Dublin, by Andrew Crook,* 1693. 4°.* DIX 258. O, DM.

4131 A form of prayer and thanksgiving . . . second day of December. *By Charles Bill, and the executrix of Thomas Newcomb,* 1694. 4°.* L, O, OC, OP, WCA; MH, NU, WF.

4132 A form of prayer and thanksgiving . . . sixteenth of April. *By Charles Bill, and the executrix of Thomas Newcomb,* 1695. 18 ll. 4°.* O, OC, CS, EC; MH, NU, WF.

4133 —eighth day of . . . September, 1695. 10 ll. 4°.* L, O, OC, OP; MH, NU, WF, Y.

4133A —*By Charles Bill, and the executrix of Thomas Newcomb,* 1695. 4°.* L.

4134 ——, 1696. 4°.* L, O.

4134A —*Dublin, by Andrew Crook,* 1696. 4°.* DIX 285. DK, DM.

4135 ——, 1697. 4°.* L, O, OC, CS, OP, MB; MH, WF, Y.

4136 A form of prayer for married persons. *Exeter, by S. Dawkes, for Charles Yeo and John Padree,* 1698. 8°.* DT.

4137 A form of prayer: to be used for both the days of publique thanksgiving. [*n.p.*], printed, 1629 [i.e. 1649]. 4°.*
LT; CH, WF, Y.

4137A A form of prayer to be used in all churches . . . every day.
By C. Bill and T. Newcomb, 1691. 4°.* Y.

4138 A form of prayer to be used next after. *By Charles Bill
and the executrix of Thomas Newcomb*, 1691. 4°.* O.

4139 —[Anr. ed.] —, 1692. 4°.* L, O, OC, CS, OP; MH, WF.

4140 —[Anr. ed.] —, 1693. 4°.* L, O, OC; MH.

4141 —[Anr. ed.] —, 1696. 4°.* L, O, OC; MH.

4141A —[Anr. ed.] —, 1697. 4°.* L, OC; MH.

4142 A form of prayer, to be used upon the fifteenth of January. *By John Bill snd Christopher Barker*, 1661. 4°. L, O,
LL, OC, CJ, MR; CH, MIU.

4143 A form of prayer, to be used upon the twelfth of June.
By John Bill and Christopher Barker, 1661. 4°. L, O, LL,
OC, CJ, P; CH, MB, NU, WF.

4144 A form of prayer . . . 29th of May. 1662. 4°.* C, YM, E;
MB.

4145 A form of prayer, to be used . . . November the thirteenth. *By John Bill, Christopher Barker, Thomas Newcomb, and Henry Hills*, 1678. 4°.* L, O, C, OC, LL; CH,
CN, MH, PL, WF, Y.

4146 A form of prayer, to be used . . . the eleventh of April.
By John Bill, Thomas Newcomb, and Henry Hills, 1679.
4°.* L, O, OC, OP, LL; CH, MH, WF, Y.

4147 A form of prayer, to be used May 29. *Dublin, by Benjamin Took, and John Crook, to be sold by Mary Crook*,
1679. 4°. L, O, DK, DT.

4148 A form of prayer, to be used^d . . . 22^d of December. *By
the assigns of John Bill, Thomas Newcomb, and Henry
Hills*, 1680. 4°.* L, O, OC, OP, LL; CH, MB, MH, PL, WF.

4149 Entry cancelled.

4150 A form of prayer to be used . . . the twelfth day of March.
By Charles Bill and Thomas Newcomb, 1689. 4°.* L, O,
OC, EC; CH, MH, NU, Y.

4151 A form of prayer to be used on . . . 5th day of June. *By
Charles Bill, and Thomas Newcomb*, 1689. 4°.* L, O, CT,
LVF, OP; CH, CN, MH, NU, WF, Y.

4152 A form of prayer to be used on . . . twelfth day of March.
By Charles Bill and Thomas Newcomb, 1690. 4°.* O,
OCC; CH, WF.

4152A —15th of August. *Dublin, by Edward Jones*, 1690. 4°.*
DIX 239. L, O, DM; MB.

4153 A form of prayer to be used . . . the twenty ninth day of
this present April. *By Charles Bill, and the executrix of
Thomas Newcomb*, 1691. 4°.* L, O, CJ, BR, DT; CH, MH,
NU, Y.

4153A —third day of July. *Dublin, by Andrew Crook, assignee of
Benjamin Tooke*, 1691. 4°.* DIX 246. CD, DM, DT.

4154 A form of prayer to be used . . . eighth day of April. *By
Charles Bill, and the exectrix of Thomas Newcomb*, 1692.
4°.* L, O, OC, CJ, OP; CH, MH, WF.

4155 The form of prayer to be used . . . twentieth of . . . July.
Dublin, by Andrew Crook, assignee of Benjamin Tooke,
1692. 4°.* DIX 254. O, DM.

4156 A form of prayer to be used . . . the tenth day of May.
By Charles Bill, and executrix of Thomas Newcomb, 1693.
4°.* L, O, C, OC, DT; MH, NU, Y.

4156A —[Anr. ed.] *Dublin, by Andrew Crook, assignee of Benjamin Tooke*, 1693. 4°.* DIX 257. DM.

4157 A form of prayer to be used . . . the three and twentieth
day of . . . May. *By Charles Bill, and the executrix of
Thomas Newcomb*, 1694. 4°.* L, O, OC, OP; MH, NU.

4157A —twelfth day of July. *Dublin, by Andrew Crook*, 1695.
4°.* DIX 273. DM.

4158 A form of prayer to be used . . . nineteenth day of June.
By Charles Bill, and the executrix of Thomas Newcomb,
1695. 4°.* L, O, OC, OP; MH, NU, WF, Y.

4159 A form of prayer to be used . . . eleventh day of . . .
December. *By Charles Bill and the executrix of Thomas
Newcomb*, 1695. 4°.* L, O, OC, CS, OP; CH, CLC, MH, WF.

4160 A form of prayer to be used . . . twenty sixth day of June.
By Charles Bill, and the executrix of Thomas Newcomb,
1696. 4°.* L, O, OC, OP; CU, MH, NU, WF, Y.

4161 A form of prayer to be used yearly on the second of
September. *By Charles Bill, and the executrix of Thomas
Newcomb*, 1696. 4°.* L, O, LG; WF.

4162 A form of prayer to be used . . . twenty eighth day of
April. *By Charles Bill and the executrix of Thomas Newcomb*, 1697. 4°.* L, O, OC, CS, DT; CH, CLC, MH, NU, WF.

4163 A form of prayer to be used . . . fifth day of April. *By
Charles Bill, and the executrix of Thomas Newcomb*,
1699. 4°.* L, O, OC, CS, EC; CH, MH, NU, WF.

4164 A form of prayer, to be used . . . fourth day of April. *By
Charles Bill, and the executrix of Thomas Newcomb*, 1700.
4°.* L, O, OC, EC, WCA; CH, CLC, MH, NU, Y.

4165 A forme of prayer used at Newport . . . 15 of September.
For Richard Royston, 1648. 8°.* LT, O; CH, MB, MH, WF.

4165A A forme of prayer, used in the King's Chappel. [*Paris*],
1649. 4°.* L, OC.

4166 —[Anr. ed.] *Hage: by Samuell Broun*, 1650. 4°.* LT, O; CH.

4167 A form of prayer with fasting . . . the 30th of January.
*By the assigns of John Bill: and by Henry Hills and
Thomas Newcomb*, 1685. 4°.* L, O, OC, CS, EC; CH, CN,.
MH, NU, WF, Y.

4167A —[Anr. ed.] *Dublin, re-printed by Benj. Tooke: to be sold
by Andrew Crook, and by Samuel Helsham*, 1685. 4°.*
DIX 209. O, DM.

4168 A form of prayer with thanksgiving for the safe delivery
of the Queen. *By Charles Bill, Henry Hills, and Thomas
Newcomb*, 1688. 4°.* O, LVF, CS, EC, AU; CH, MH, TSM,
WF, Y.

4169 —[Anr. ed.] *Holy-Rood-House, by Mr. P.B.*, 1688. 4°.*
ALDIS, 2761. EN, FSF; WF.

4169A —[Anr. ed.] *Dublin, by Andrew Crook and Samuel Helsham, assigns of Benj. Tooke: to be sold by A. Crook and
S. Helsham*, 1688. 4°.* DIX 231. DM.

4170 A form of prayer, with thanksgiving, to be used . . .
28th. of June, 1660. *By John Bill and Christopher
Barker*, 1660. 4°.* LT, O, LL, CS, EC; CH, MB, NGT, Y.

4171   A form of prayer, with thanksgiving, to be used . . . the
        29th of May yearly. *By John Bill and Christopher Barker,
        1661.* 4°.* L, O, LL, OC, CS; CH, MH, WF, Y.

4171A   A form of prayer, with thanksgiving . . . 29th of May.
        By John Bill and Christopher Barker, 1662. 4°.* WCA.

4172   A form of prayer with thanksgiving . . . September the
        9th. *By the assigns of John Bill: and by Henry Hills, and
        Thomas Newcomb, 1683.* 8°.* L, O, C, LL, OC; CH, CU,
        MH, NU, WF, Y.

4172A   —[Anr. ed.] *Dublin, by Benjamin Took and John Crook,
        to be sold by Mary Crook and Andrew Crook aud [sic] by
        Joseph Wilde, 1683.* 4°.* DIX 204. L, O, EC, DM, DN; MB,
        NU.

4173   A form of prayer, with thanksgiving to Almighty God.
        *By the assigns of John Bill; and by Henry Hills, and
        Thomas Newcomb, 1685.* 4°.* L, O, OC, CS, EC; CH, MH,
        NU, RPJ, WF, Y.

4174   —Sixth day of February. —, *1685.* 4°.* OC.

4175   —[Anr. ed.] *Dublin, by Benjamin Tooke; to be sold by
        Andrew Crook, and by Samuel Helsham, 1685.* 4°.* DIX
        209. O, EC, DM.

4176   A form of prayer, with thanksgiving. [Sept. 12]. *By
        Charles Bill, Henry Hills, and Thomas Newcomb, 1686.*
        4°.* L, LSC; CH, CN.

4177   —first . . . July. —, *1688.* 4°.* L; MH, WF, Y.

4178   —fifth day of November. *By Charles Bill and Thomas
        Newcomb, 1690.* 4°.* L, O, LSC, CS, EC; MH, WF, Y.

4179   The form of prayers and services used in Westminster
        Abbey at the coronation. *For Randal Taylor, 1689.*
        fol.* L, O, OC, OP, HH; CH, NGT.

4180   A form of thanksgiving to be used in all churches. *By
        Charles Bill and the executrix of Thomas Newcomb, 1691.*
        4°.* L, OC; Y.

4181   — —, *1693.* 4°.* L.

4181A   A forme of thanksgiving for the late defeat. *Oxford, by
        Leonard Lichfield, 1644.* brs. MADAN 1596. L.

4181B   A form of thanksgiving to be used thorowout . . . Lin-
        coln. *1641.* 4°.* LT; MH.

4182   A form of thanksgiving to be used . . . London. *By
        Charles Bill and Thomas Newcomb, 1691.* 4°.* L; Y.

4183   A form, or order of thanksgiving . . . 15th of January.
        *By Charles Bill, Henry Hills, and Thomas Newcomb,
        1687.* 4°.* L, OC, CS, AU, EN; CH, CN, MH, TU, WF, Y.

4184   Forma precum in untrâque domo convocationis. *Typis
        Car. Bill & Tho. Newcomb, 1689.* 4°.* L, O, OC, EC,
        LSC; CH, Y.

4185   Forme precum sive descriptio. *Typis Car. Bell &
        executrreis Tho. Newcomb, 1700.* 8°.* L, C, OC; CLC, WF.

4186   Formes of prayer used in the court of Her Highness, the
        Princesse royall: at the solemne fast for the preserva-
        tion of the king. *[London], 1649.* 8°.* LP; MB, WF.

4187   Il libro delle preghiere publiche. *Appresso Moise Pitt,
        1685.* 12°. T.C.II 168. LL; PL, WF, Y.

4188   Liturgia, seu liber precum. *Excudit Rogerus Nortonus,
        Væneuntque apud Sam. Mearne, 1670.* 8°. T.C.I 42. L,
        OB, CS, HH, DT; CLC, MB, MBP, NC, NU, WF.

4188A   —Second edition. —, *1670.* 8°.* C; NU.

4188B   —[Anr. ed.] *Apud Sam. Mearne, 1681.* 12°. L, OC; MIU.

4188C   —[Anr. ed.] *Apud Car. Mearne, 1685.* 8°. L, CM; CLC, NU.

4188CA —[Anr. ed.] *Apud Henricum Bonwick, 1687.* 12°. T.C.II
        189. L; TSM, UCLA, WF, Y.

4188CB —[Anr. ed.] —, *1690.* 12°. L; MB.

4188D   —[Anr. ed.] *Excudebat E. Jones, impensis A. Swall & T.
        Childe, & prostant apud Jacobum Knapton, 1696.* 12°.
        T.C.II 570. L, YM, ENC; CH, PHS, PL, TU.

4188E   The order in which divine service. *[London], 1694.* 4°.*
        OC.

4188F   —A prayer for the King. colop: *By Charles Bill and
        Thomas Newcomb, 1690.* cap., 4°.* O, OC, CS, EC, OM;
        MH, NU.

4188G   — —[Anr. ed.] *Edinburgh, by the heir of A. Anderson, 1690.*
        brs. ALDIS 3059. EN.

4188GA — —[Anr. ed.] *By Charles Bill, and the executrix of
        Thomas Newcomb, 1691.* 4°.* L.

4188H   — —[Anr. ed.] *By Charles Bill, and the executrix of
        Thomas Newcomb, 1695.* 4°.* L; MB.

4188HA —A prayer for the present expedition. *[London, 1688.]*
        brs. ᐟOC.

4188I   —A prayer for the Prince of Orange. *In the Savoy, by
        Edw. Jones, and for James Partridge, Matthew Gylly-
        flower, and Samuel Heyrick, 1688.* 4°.* L, OC, CS, EC;
        CH, MH, Y.

4188IA —A prayer to be used on Wednesday, November 13.
        [London, 1678.] brs. L.

4188IB — —December 2, 1697. *[London, 1697.]* cap., 4°.* L; Y.

4188IBA —Prayers for the King. colop: *By the assigns of John Bill,
        and by Henry Hills, and Thomas Newcomb, Febr. 6, 1684.*
        4°.* L, O, OC; CH, CN, MH, WF.

4188IC —Prayers for the Parliament. *By the assigns of John Bill
        deceased, and by Henry Hills and Thomas Newcomb,
        1685.* fol. L.

4188ID Prayers to be used during the Queens sickness. *By Charles
        Bill and the executrix of the Thomas Newcomb, 1699.*
        4°.* L.

4188J   —Prayers to be used during this time. colop: *By Ch.
        Bill, H. Hills, and T. Newcomb, 1688.* cap., 4°.* L, O,
        CS; CH, MH, MIU, WCL, WF.

4188JA Prayers to be used in all. *By Ch. Bill, H. Hills, and T.
        Newcomb, 1688.* 4°.* L.

4188K   — —[Anr. ed.] *Holy-rood-house, by Mr. P.B., 1688.* 4°.*
        ALDIS 2779. EN; WCL.

4188L   — —[Anr. ed.] *Dublin, by Andrew Crook, and Samuel
        Helsham, assigns of Benj. Took, [1688].* 4°.* DIX 232.
        DM.

4189   A remonstrance, by way of address from the Church of
        England. . . . 29th. May, 1685. *[London, 1685.]* cap.,
        fol.* L, O, OP, HH; CH, CLC, NGT, WF, Y.

4190   The remonstrance of the Church of England to the
        House of Commons. *[London], 1643.* 4°. C.

4190A   The seasonable address of. *1677.* 4°.* O, CS.

4190B   A second remonstrance. *[London, 1686.]* cap., fol.* L, C,
        OC, LW, HH; CLC, WF, Y.

4190C —To the Kings most excellent majesty, . . . the humble petition and protestation of all the bishops. [*London*, 1641.] brs. DT; NU, Y.

4190D ——[Anr. ed.] *By Joseph Hunscott*, 1642. brs. STEELE p 1913. LT, LS, DT; CH.

4190E ——[Anr. ed.] *By Joseph Hunscott*, 1642. brs. LS, DT; MH.

4190F ——[Anr. ed.] *Printed*, 1641; *reprinted by Philemon Stephens junior*, 1661. 4°.* BR; MH, WF.

Church of England, and the continuation. *See* M., P.

4191 The Church of England as by law established. colop: *For Sam. Tomason*, 1685. fol.* O, C; MM, Y.

Church of England free. 1683. *See* Hooper, George, *bp.*

4192 The Church of England truly represented. *For the author, and sold by Matthew Turner*, 1686. 4°.* L, OC, CT, EN, DT; CH, CN, MH, NU, Y.

Church of England vindicated. 1680. *See* M., J.

4193 The Church of England's complaint in vindication of her loyalty. [*London*, 1688.] cap., 4°.* L, OC; CH, MH, MIU, V, Y.

4194 The Church of England's glory. *For R. W.*, 1688. brs. MC; MH, Y.

4195 The Church of Englands mans private devotions. *For S. Keble*, 1698. 8°. T.C.III 75. LEWIS.

Church of Rome no guide. 1700. *See* Wake, William, *abp.*

Church of Rome not sufficiently. York. 1663. *See* Sammuels, Peter.

4196 The Church of Rome unmask'd. *For Isaac Cleave*, 1679. 4°. T.C.I 329. L, DT; CH, NU.

CHURCH OF SCOTLAND

4196A An abridgment of the reverend Assemblies shorter catechism. [c. 1662]. 8°.* OP.

4196B Act and overture of the General Assembly [*Edinburgh*], *printed*, 1651. 4°.* L, EN; Y.

4196C Act concerning the receiving of engagers. *Edinburgh, by Evan Tyler*, 1649. 4°.* ALDIS 3561. L, NU, D, GM; NU, WF, Y.

4196CA Act of the General Assembly anent a solemn national fest. colop: *Edinburgh, by the ex. of Andrew Anderson*, 1690. 4°.* ALDIS 3003. L, O, EN; CN.

4196D Act of the General Assembly, enact and solemn test. [*Edinburgh*], 1691. cap., 4°.* CN.

4196E Act of the Generall Assembly, at Edinburgh. [*Edinburgh, by the heirs of G. Anderson*, 1652.] cap., 4°.* ALDIS 1459. HH; Y.

4196F Act of the synod of Lothian and Tweeddale. *Edinburgh, by the heirs & successors of Andrew Anderson*, 1698. brs. ALDIS 3726. EN, ES.

4196G An act published by the General Assembly of Scotland. *Edinburgh, by R. W.; London, reprinted by B. Alsop, to be sold by Henry Walker*, 1641. 4°.* L, LL, EC, EN; MH, V, Y.

4197 The acts of the General Assemblies . . . 1638. to . . . 1649. [*Edinburgh*], *sold by George Mosman*, 1691. 8°. ALDIS 3128. L, C, EN; CH, CN, MH, WF, Y.

4198 The acts of the General Assemblies of the Church of Scotland. [*n.p.*], *printed*, 1682. 8°. L, LL, LW, P, GU; CH, NPT, NR, NU, Y.

4199 The answer of the commission of the Generall Assemblie. *Aberdene, by James Brown*, 1651. 4°. ALDIS 1436. L, HH, EN, AU, FSF; CH, MH, NU, WF, Y.

4199A The answer of the commissioners. *For Robert Bostock*, 1677. 4°.* LT, O, CT, HH, DT; CH, CU, MH, NU, WF, Y.

4200 The answer of the commissioners . . . (17 Dec.). *Edinburgh, E. Tyler*, 1647. 4°.* ALDIS 1261. HH, E, EN, AU; Y.

4201 The answer of the commissioners of the General Assembly . . . August 15, 1648. *Edinbvrgh, by Evan Tyler*, 1648. 4°.* ALDIS 1302. OW, EN, AU, GM; CH, MH, NPT, NU, Y.

4201A The answer of the General Assembly. *By G. Dewer for Henry Walker*, 1643. 4°.* L; MIU, NN.

4201B Causes of a publicke fast. —, 1647. brs. ALDIS 1265. LT, EN; Y.

4201C —*Aberdene, by James Brown*, 1650. 4°.* ALDIS 1398. HH, EN, ENC, AU, GU.

4201CA Causes of a publicke thanksgiving. *Printed at Edinburgh by Evan Tyler*, 1647. brs. Y.

4201D The causes of a solemne fast. *Printed at Edinburgh by Evan Tyler*, 1646. brs. ALDIS 1218. LT; MH.

4201E The causes of a solemn national fast . . . 4. of June. *Edinburgh*, 1696. brs. ALDIS 3543. EN, ES; RPJ.

4201F —*3d of Dec. Edinburgh, by the heirs & successors of Andrew Anderson*, 1696. brs. ALDIS 3544. STEELE 3p 3113. EN, ES.

4201G *Edinburgh, Aug. 6, 1649. Causes of a solemn public humiliation.* [*Edinburgh*], 1649. brs. NU.

4201H Causes of an humiliation. [*Edinburgh*, 1653] brs. EN; MH.

4201I The causes of the fast, appointed . . . last Wednesday of March. *Edinburgh*, 1645. brs. E.

4201J The charge of the Scottish commissioners. [*London*], *printed* 1641. 4°.* L, O, CT, HH, EN; MH, NPT, NU, WF, Y.

4201K —[Anr. ed.] *For Nath. Bolton*, 1641. 4°. L, O, C, EN, DT; CH, NU, TU, WF, Y.

4202 *Perth. Decemb. 14. 1650. The commission of the Generall Assembly considering.* [*n.p.*, 1650.] brs. LT, EN.

4202A The Kirk of Scotlands conclusion. *Edinburgh*, 1646. CN.

4202AB —[Anr. ed.] *Printed at Edinburgh, and reprinted at London. For R. A.*, 1646. 4°.* CN, Y.

4202B Teh [*sic*] confession of faith. *By Thomas Paine*, 1641. 4°.* CJ, CT, HH, EN; CSS, MH, Y.

4202C —[Anr. ed.] *Printed*, 1641. brs. LT, LG, HH; MH.

4202CA The confession of the Church of Scotland. *Printed*, 1647. 4°.* Y.

4202D The copie of a letter sent from the commissioners of the Church of Scotland. *Londod*[*sic*], *for Ralph Smith*, 1648. 4°.* LT, O, HH, EN; MH, MIU, NU, WF, Y.

4203 The copie of the letter, sent from the commissioners, colop: *For George Anderson in Glasgow*, [1645]. 4°.* GM, EN.

4203A Declaretio deputatorum a Comitis regnt Scotrice. *Edinburg: escudit E. Tyler*, 1650. 8°.* Y.

4203B A declaration against the crosse petitition. *Edinburgh, by Evan Tyler, 1673.* 4°.* ALDIS 1078. L, CT, E, EN, GM; CN, NU, WF, Y.

4204 A declaration and brotherly exhortation of the Generall Assembly. *For Rob. Bostock, 1647.* 4°.* LT, E, EN, GU; CH, CU, MH, NU, WF, Y.

4205 —[Anr. ed.] *Edinburgh, Evan Tyler, 1647.* 4°.* ALDIS 1267. O, EN, AU; CH, CLC, MH, Y.

4206 A declaration and exhortation of the General Assembly of the Church of Scotland. *For Ralph Smith, 1648.* 4°.* LT, O, EN; CH, MH, NU, WF, Y.

4207 A declaration and warning to all the members of this kirk. *Edinburgh, by Evan Tyler, 1649.* 4°.* ALDIS 1363. L, HH, EN, GM; CH, MH, MM, NU, WF.

4208 —[Anr. ed.] *Edinburgh, by Evan Tyler, 1649; and re-printed at London for Robert Bostock, May the 22, 1649.* 4°.* LT, HH; MH, NU, Y.

4209 —*Edinburgh, by Evan Tyler, 1650.* 4°.* ALDIS 1405. L, EN, GM; CH, MH, NU, WF, Y.

4210 Declaration from the commission of the Generall Assembly . . . stumbling blocks. *Edinburgh, E. Tyler, 1646.* 4°.* ALDIS 1222. L, EC, EN, AU, GU; CN.

4211 —[Anr. ed.] *For Robert Bostock, 1646.* 4°.* LT, O, CJ, CT; CH, MH, NU, WF, Y.

4212 A declaration from the commissioners of the Generall Assemblie. *Imprinted at Edenburg by Evan Tyler; re-printed at London, 1648.* 4°.* LT, O, EN, DT; MH, NN, PU, Y.

4213 A declaration from the Generall Assemblie of the king-dome of Scotland in answer to a declaration. *For R. W., 1648.* 4°.* LT, DT; MIU, WF, Y.

4214 A declaration of the commission . . . to the whole kirk . . . if . . . I March 1648. *Edinburgh, by Evan Tyler, 1648.* 4°.* ALDIS 1316. STEELE 3, 1948. EN, REG; Y.

4215 A declaration of the commission of the Generall Assembly. *[Edinburgh?, Tyler, 1648].* cap. 4°.* ALDIS 1317. STEELE 3, 1949. HH, EN, AU, GM, REG; NU, WF, Y.

4216 —*For R. Smith, 1648.* 4°. HH, DT.

4217 A declaration of the commissioners of the Generall Assembly. *Printed at Edinburgh by Evan Tyler, 1648.* 4°.* ALDIS 1316. LT, AU, EN, GM, GU; NU, Y.

4218 A declaration of the commissioners of the General Assembly, to the whole kirk and kingdome of Scotland. *Printed at Edinburgh, by Evan Tyler, and re-printed at London for Robert Bostock, 1648.* 4°.* L, O, EN; CH, CN, MH, WF, Y.

4219 —[Anr. ed.] *Printed at Edinburgh for Evan Tyler, and re-printed at London for H. H., 1648.* 4°.* L, EN; CLC, CN, MH, NGT.

4220 A declaration of the Generall Assembly of the Kirk of Scotland. *Edinburgh, by Evan Tyler, 1650.* 4°.* ALDIS 1411. EN, GM; CLC, MIU, NU, WF, Y.

4221 A declaration of the Kirk of Scotland . . . 5 of March, 1647. *Printed at London by Robert Ibbitson, 1648.* 4°.* LT, HH, E; MH, NU.

4221A A declaration of the reasons for assisting the Parliament of England. *For John Bellamy and Ralph Smith, 1643.* 4°.* L, CT, D, EN; HR, CLC, CN, MH, NU, WF, Y.

4221B A declaration of the representations. *Printed at Edenburgh by Evan Tyler. Re-printed at London, 1647.* 4°.* LT, O, EN; CH, MH, NU, Y.

4221C A declaration or remonstrance from the kingdom of Scotland. *For G. Horton, 1647.* 4°.* LT, DT; CN, NU, TU, WF, Y.

4221D A declaration sent to the Lord Clifford. *November 28 by T. F. for L. W., 1672.* 4°.* LT, EC, HH; CH, WF, Y.

4222 Directions of the Generall Assembly concerning secret . . . worship. *Printed at Edinburgh, by Evan Tyler, 1647.* 4°.* ALDIS 1272. LT, O, HH, EN, AU; MH, PU, WF, Y.

4223 —[Anr. ed.] *Printed at Edenburgh by Evan Tyler, 1647. And reprinted for Robert Bostock, 1647.* 4°.* LT, OC, HH, MR, EN; CH, CLC, MH, NU.

4224 The doctrine and discipline of the Kirke of Scotland. *[London], by Rob. Young, to be sold by John Sweeting, 1641.* 4°. LT, O, P, HH, EN; CH, MH, NU, TU, WF, Y.

4224A Eight propositions of the desires. *Printed at London by Robert Ibbitson, 1648.* 4°.* LT, LW, HH, EN; MH, MIU, NU, Y.

4224B The explanation of a former act. *Edinburgh, by Evan Tyler, 1648.* 4°.* ALDIS 1323. EC, AU, E, EN; MH, WF, Y.

4224C The first and second booke of discipline. *Printed, 1641.* 4°. L, CT; CLC, CU, NN, NU, Y.

4225 Generall demands, concerning the late covenant. *Aberdene, reprinted by John Forbes, 1662.* 4°. ALDIS 1736. L, O, EN, AU, SA; CH, NU, Y.

4226 The generall demands, of the reverend doctors of divinitie. *Aberdene, by John Forbes, 1663.* 4°. ALDIS 1753. L, O, C, EN, AU; NU, WF.

4227 Generall demands . . . concerning the late covenant. *Edinburgh, [Forbes], 1683.* 4°. ALDIS 2382. EN.

4227A Good counsell come from Scotland. *Edinburgh, by Evan Tyler, 1676.* 4°.* ALDIS 1224. LT, O, OC, EN, DT; CH, MH, NU, WF, Y.

4227B The great sin and direct guiltiness of Scotland. *[Edinburgh], printed 1654.* 4°.* L, HH, D, E; NU, WF.

4227C —[Anr. ed.] *Edinburgh, by A. A., 1655.* 4°.* ALDIS 1518. EN, GM; NPT, NU, Y.

4227D Heads and conclusions of the policie of the kirk. *[Edinburgh], reprinted 1680.* 8°.* L, O, EN; MH, NU, WF, Y.

4228 The humble petition of the commissioners. *Edinburgh, by Evan Tyler, 1643.* 4°.* ALDIS 1084. L, O, CT, EN; NN, WF, Y.

4229 The humble remonstrances of the commission. *Aberdene, by James Brown, 1651.* 4°.* ALDIS 1446. L, EN, ER, EU, AU; LC.

4229A The humble remonstrance of the commissioners. *By Evan Tyler, 1647.* 4°.* ALDIS 1102. EN, Y.

4229B —[Anr. ed.] *Edinburgh, by Evan Tyler, 1647. London, reprinted by Robert Ibbitson, 1647.* 4°.* L, OC; MH, Y.

4229C   The humble remonstrace of the commission of the General Assembly. *Aberdene, by J. Brown,* 1656. 4°.* LC.

4229D   Edn. 28 April, 1673. The humble representation. *For John Dallon,* 1648. 4°.* CLC, LC, MH, MIU, Y.

4229E   Edinb. 6. Junii, 1648. The humble vindication of the commissioners. [*Edinburgh,* 1648.] cap., 4°.* ALDIS 1330. OW, EN, AU, GM; MH, WF, Y.

4229F   In the national assembly. *Edinburgh, by Robert Bryson* [1641.] brs. L, E; MH.

4230   A letter from the commission of the General Assembly. *Edinburgh, by George Mosman,* 1699. 4°.* ALDIS 3863. L, A, EN; CN, NN, RPJ, WF, Y.

4231   —*Glasgow, by Robert Sanders,* 1699. 4°.* ALDIS 3864. L, EN; MH, NU, RPJ.

4231A   A letter from the General Assembly. 1645. 4°.* CN.

4231B   —[Anr. ed.] *By Richard Cotes,* 1646. 4°.* LT, OC, EN; CN, MH, NU, WF, Y.

4231BA   Memorial for the members to be chosen. [*Edinburgh?* 1699.] cap., 4°.* ALDIS 3871. L.

4231BB   The nationall assembly of Scotland. *By T. Favvcet,* 1641. 4°.* LT, O, CCA, HH, EN; CA, MH, NU, TU, WF, Y.

4231C   The national covenant. *Edinburgh, by a society of stationers.* 1660. 8°.* LW, E, GU; MH.

4231D   —[Anr. ed.] *Printed,* 1678. 8°. A; MHL, NU.

4232   —[Anr. ed.] [*Edinburgh*], *printed,* [1689.] 4°. ALDIS 2922. L, E, EN; NU, WF.

4232A   Papers from Scotland. *Edinburgh, for Evan Tyler,* 1677. 4°.* ALDIS 1281. LT, EN; MH, NN, TU, Y.

4232B   A petition delivered to the Parliament of Scotland. *By Robert Ibbitson,* 1648. 4°.* LT, HH, EN, DT; MH, MIU, NU, WF, Y.

4233   The principal acts of foure Generall Assemblies. *Edinburgh: by Evan Tyler,* 1642. 4°. ALDIS 1025. L, E, EN; CN, NPT, NU, WF.

4234   The principall acts of the General Assembly. *Edinburgh, by Evan Tyler,* 1643. 4°. ALDIS 1067. L, OP; CH, CN, NPT, NU, WF, Y.

4235   —*Printed at Edinburgh by Evan Tyler, and re-printed at London, for Humphrey Tuckey,* 1643. 4°.* LT, CCA, EN; CH, MH, NU, TU, Y.

4236   —*Edinburgh, by Evan Tyler,* 1644. 4°.* ALDIS 1129. L, EN; CH, CN, NPT, NU, WF.

4237   —*For Evan Tyler,* 1644. 4°.* ALDIS 1130. LT, CCA; CH, CLC, MH, PL.

4238   —*For Evan Tyler of Scotland,* [1644]. 4°.* CH, NU.

4239   —*Edinburgh: by Evan Tyler,* 1645. 4°.* ALDIS 1183. L, EN; CH, CN, NPT, NU, WF.

4240   — —, 1646. 4°.* ALDIS 1212. L, EN; CH, CN, NPT, NU, WF.

4241   — —, 1647. 4°.* ALDIS 1260. L; CH, CN, NPT, NU, WF.

4242   —*Edinvrgh, by Evan Tyler,* 1648. 4°. ALDIS 1300. L, EN; CH, CN, NPT, NU, WF.

4243   —*Edinburg, by Evan Tyler,* 1649. 4°.* ALDIS 1355. L, EN, ES; CH, CN, NPT, NU.

4244   —[*n.p.,* 1690.] 4°.* D; NR, NU.

4245   —*Edinvrgh, by George Mosman,* 1691. fol.* ALDIS 3129. LGI, ES, EN; CH, CN, NR, NU, PBL, WF, Y.

4246   —*Edinbvrgh, by George Mosman.* 1691. *And re-printed at London for Nathanael Ranew,* 1692. 4°.* T.C.II 404. L, OC, CJ, CT, EN; NN, NU, WF.

4247   —*Edinbvrgh, by George Mosman,* 1694. fol.* EN; CN, MH, NU, PBL, WF, Y.

4247A   — —, 1695. fol.* ALDIS 3434. EN; MH, NPT.

4248   — —, 1696. 4°.* ALDIS 3532. EN; NPT, NU, PBL, WF, Y.

4248A   — —, 1697. fol.* ALDIS 3651. EN; CN, NPT, PBL, WF, Y.

4249   — —, 1698. fol.* ALDIS 3729. EN; CN, NPT, NU, PBL, WF, Y.

4250   —*Edinburgh, by George Mosman,* 1699. fol. ALDIS 3821. L, EN; CN, NPT, PBL, WF, Y.

4251   — —, 1700. fol.* L, EN, ES; CN, NPT, PBL, WF, Y.

4251A   The proceedings of the commissioners. *Edinburgh, by Evan Tyler,* 1649. 4°.* ALDIS 1377. LT, EN, AU; NPT, NU, WF.

4251B   —[Anr. ed.] —, *re-printed for Robert Bostock,* 1649. 4°.* L, CCA, GU; MH, WF, Y.

4251C   The protestation given in by the dissenting brethren. *Printed at Leith by Evan Tyler,* 1652. 4°.* ALDIS 1464. L, HH, EN; NU, WF, Y.

4251D   Reasons of a fast. [*Aberdeen, by James Brown,* 1650.] cap., 4°.* ALDIS 1424. HH, EN; Y.

4251E   The reformation of the discipline and service. *For Mathew Welbanck and Laurence Chapman,* 1673. 4°. LT, O, LSC; CH, CN, MH.

4252   A remonstrance and declaration of the Generall Assembly. *Edinburgh, by Evan Tyler,* 1649. *And re-printed at London for Robert Bostock,* 1649. 4°.* LT, C, CT, EN; CH, MH, NU, WF, Y.

4253   The remonstrance of the commissioners of the General Assembly. *Edinburgh, by Evan Tyler,* 1643. 4°.* ALDIS 1102. L, O, CT, HH, E; CH, NU, Y.

4254   —*First printed at Edinburgh by Evan Tyler, and now re-printed at London by Thomas Paine and Matthew Simmons, July 13,* 1643. 4°.* LT, HH, MR; MH, NU, WF, Y.

4254A   [Same title.] *Aberdeen, Jas. Brown,* 1651. 4°.* STEELE 3,2061. ALDIS 1451. HH, EN, AU; Y.

4255   The remonstrance of the Generall Assembly. *Imprinted at London by M. B. for Robert Bostock,* 5. July 1645. 4°.* LT, O, CT, HH, EN; CH, MH, NU, WF, Y.

4256   —*For R. B.,* 1647. 4°.* LT; MH, MIU, NU.

4257   *Imprinted at London,* 1652. 4°.* LT, C, EN; CH, MH, NU, WF, Y.

4257A   The remonstrace or representation. *For Robert Bostock,* 1645. 4°.* CLC.

4258   —[Anr. ed.] —, *And now reprinted for Giles Calvert,* 1648. 4°.* LT, O, OC, CCA, HH; CH, MH, NU, WF, Y.

4258A   A seasonable and necessary warning. *Edinburgh, by Evan Tyler,* 1650. 4°.* ALDIS 1428. L, HH, EN; NU, WF.

4258B   A short declaration of the Assembly of Divines. *By Iohn Field for Ralph Smith, July 25, 1645.* 4°.* LT, DT; CH, NU, Y.

4259   A short declaration to the whole Kirk. *Edinburgh, by Evan Tyler,* 1648. 4°. ALDIS 1340. HH, E, EN, GU, ENC; NU, WF, Y.

4259A   A short exhortation and warning. [*Aberdeen, by James Brown,* 1651.] 4°.* ALDIS 1452. L, HH, EN, AU; NU, WF.

4259B A short information. [Edinburgh], printed 1648. 4°.*
ALDIS 1341. L, HH, EN, AU, GM; CN, NU, WF, Y.

4259C —Printed Edenburgh, reprinted London, for Joseph Hunscot,
1648. 4°.* L, EN; CH, MH, Y.

4259D A short warning and exhortation. Aberdeen, by Iames
Brown, the 22. of August, 1651. brs. EU.

4259E A solemn acknowledgement of publick sins. Edinburgh,
by Evan Tyler, 1648. 4°.* ALDIS 1342. L, HH, E, EN, GH;
MH, NU, WF, Y.

4259F —[Anr. ed.] Edinburgh, by Evan Tyler, and reprinted at
London for Robert Bostock, Novem. 22, 1648. 4°.* LT, O,
C, HH, EN; CLC, MIU, NN, Y.

4259G A solemn and seasonable warning. Edinburgh: by Evan
Tyler, 1645. 4°.* ALDIS 1201. STEELE 3p 1860. HH, E,
EN, AU, GM; CLC, NU.

4259H —[Anr. ed.] By J. Raworth, 1645. 4°.* LT, C, HH, EN;
CH, NN, WF, Y.

4259I —[Anr. ed.] Edinburgh, by Evan Tyler, 1646. 4°.* ALDIS
1236. LT, LW, EC, EN; CH, NU.

4260 A solemn league and covenant, for reformation. Aberdene, by Edw. Raban, 1643. 8 pp. 4°.* AU.

4261 —Aberdene by Edw Raban, 1643. 14 pp. 4°.* AU.

4262 —For Edward Husbands, Sept. 22, 1643. 4°.* CH, Y.

4263 — —, 1643. brs. LT; CH.

4264 —By Thomas Ienner, [1643]. 4°.* CH.

4265 —Edinburgh, by Evan Tyler, 1643. 4°.* ALDIS 1108. O, CT,
EN, GH; NU, Y.

4266 — —, 1648. 4°.* ALDIS 1343. E, EN, AU, GH, FSF; NP, Y.

4267 A solemne publike fast appointed by the Generall Assembly of the Church of Scotland . . . last Wednesday
of March 1645. For Iohn Wright, 1645. 4°.* LT, EN, DT;
WF.

4268 A solemn testimony against toleration. Edinburgh, by
Evan Tyler, 1649. 4°.* ALDIS 1390. OW, EN, AU, ENC,
GU; CH, MH, NU, WF, Y.

4269 A solemn warning to all the members of this Kirk.
Aberdene, by James Brown, 1651. 4°.* ALDIS 1454. L, HH,
E, EN, AU; CH, MH, Y.

4269A A thanksgiving unto God. Printed at Edinburgh by Thomas
Bassandyne, 1575, London, for Frances Constable, 1641.
brs. L; CLC.

4269B Three acts of the Generall Assembly. [Leith?], printed,
1652. 4°.* ALDIS 1460. L, EN; CH, MH, NU, WF, Y.

4269C To our reverend and well-beloved brethren. For Ralph
Smith, 1647. 4°.* LT, O, EN, DT; CH, CN, MH, NU, WF, Y.

4270 To the Kings most excellent Maiestie. The humble petition of the commissioners of the Generall Assembly
of the Kirke of Scotland. For Henry Overton, 1642[3].
4°.* MADAN 1250. LT, O, CJ, CT, MR; CSS, MH, NGT, WF,
Y.

4271 —Printed at Oxford March 20 by Leonard Lichfield, 1642[3].
4°.* MADAN 1275. LT, O, OC, CJ; CH, MH, NU, WF, Y.

4271A To the right honourable the committee of Estates: the
humble remonstrance. Edinburgh: by Evan Tyler, 1647.
4°.* ALDIS 1289. OC, EN, AU, GM; CH, MH, NU, WF, Y.

4271B —[Anr. ed.] Edinburgh, by Evan Tyler, London reprinted
for Robert Bostock, 1647. 4°.* O; MH, Y.

4271C —[Anr. ed.] Edinburgh, by Evan Tyler, London, re-printed
by Tho. Walkley, 1647. 4°.* CH, MH, MIU, WF, Y.

4271D A true copy of the humble desires. For Robert Bostock,
1648. 4°.* LT, O, CCA, HH, EN, DT; CH, CN, MH, NU,
WF, Y.

4272 A true copy of the whole printed acts. [Edinburgh?],
printed, 1682. 8°. L, P, E, EN; CN, MH, NU, WF, Y.

4272A A warning and declaration from the generall assembly
. . . Aberdene by James Brown, 1651. 4°.* ALDIS 1455. E.

Church-pageantry. 1700. See Owen, John.

Church papist. 1680. See Underwood, John.

4272B The church renewed covenant [Boston, by John Foster,
1680]. 8°.* EVANS 281. MWA, NN.

Church wounded. [n.p.], 1681. See Fleming, Robert.

4273 The churches complaint against sacriledge. Printed, 1643.
4°.* DT; CH.

Churches publick order. 1643. See G., J.

Chvrches pvrity. [n.p.], 1641. See Walker, Henry.

Churches security. 1694. See White, Richard.

Churches thank-offering. 1642. See Woodward, Hezekiah.

4274 The churches victory. For M. F. [1641–61] brs. MH.

4274 **Churchill, John.** See Marlborough, John Churchill,
duke of.

4275 **Churchill, Sir Winston.** Divi Britannici: being. By
Tho. Roycroft, to be sold by Francis Eglesfield, 1675. fol.
L, O, C, EN, DT; CH, CN, LC, MH, Y.

4275A **Churchman, William** pseud. The devout souldier.
For the author, 1661. 12°. CLC.

Churchman, Theophilus. See Heylyn, Peter.

4276 The church-vvardens repentance. [n.p.], printed, 1641.
4°.* LT, O, LCL, EC, SP.

4277 **Chute, Chaloner.** Mr. Chute's case upon the Lady
Dacres appeal. [n.p., 1685.] brs. O; MH.

4278 —Mr. Chute's case upon the matter. [London, 1681?].
brs. O; MH.

4279 —Mr. Chute's petition of appeal. [n.p., 1685.] brs. O.

4280 [**Chylinski, Samuel Boguslaus.**] An account of the
translation of the Bible into the Lithuanian tongue.
Oxford, by Hen. Hall, 1659. 4°.* MADAN 2423. L, O, CM,
SP; CSS, WF.

4280A Chymia curiose variis . . . Impensis H. Gellords & C.
Wellich, 1687. 8°.* L, LWL; HC.

Chymical. See Chemical.

4281 **Cibber, Colley.** Love's last shift For H. Rhodes, R.
Parker, and S. Briscoe, 1696. 4°. T.C.II 570. L, O, C, ES,
DT; BN, CH, CN, LC, MH, TU, Y.

4282 —A poem on the death of our late soveraign lady, Queen
Mary. For John Whitlock, 1695. 4°.* T.C.II 559. L, O,
C; CH, CU, MH, WF, Y.

4282A [–] A song in The lady in fashion [London? 1698]. brs. L.

4283 —Woman's wit. For John Sturton, 1697. 4°. L, O, C, CS,
DT; CH, CU, MH, NP, WF, Y.

4284 —Xerxes. By J. Nutt for Richard Basset, 1699. 4°. C, DT;

4284A — —[Anr. ed.] For Richard Basset, 1699. 4°. O; CH, MB.

4285 — —[Anr. ed.] Printed and are to be sold by John Nutt,
1699. 4°. C, LVF, EN, DT; CH, CN, MH, TU, WF.

4286 **Cicero.** Opera quae extant omnia. *Impensis J. Dunmore, T. Dring, B. Tooke, T. Sawbridge, and C. Mearne,* 1681. 4v. fol. T.C.I 444. L, O, C, EN, DT; BN, LC, MH, PL, WF, Y.

4287 —Cicero against Catiline. *By T. N. for Samuel Lowndes,* 1671. 8°. T.C.I 73. L, O, C, DC, LL; CH, CLC, TSM, WF, Y.

4288 —Cato major: or, the book of old age. *For William Leake,* 1648. 12°. L, O, CCH, DC, EN; CLC, NC, Y.

4289 — —Second edition. —, 1671. 12°. L; CH, NP, PL, WF.

4290 —De officiis. Libri III. *Typis G. Wilson, sumptibus stationariorum,* 1648. 8°. L.

2490A — —[Anr. ed.] —, 1651. 8°. L.

4291 — —[Anr. ed.] *Cantabrigiæ, apud Joannem Field,* 1660. 8°. O, Y.

4292 — —[Anr. ed.] 1667. 8°. MB, NP.

4292A — —[Anr. ed.], 1668. 8°. PL.

4293 — —[Anr. ed.] *Excudebat A. Maxwell, pro Societate Stationariorum,* 1669. 8°. DC.

4293A — —[Anr. ed.] *Excudebat J. M. pro Societate Stationariorum,* 1674. 8°. C; IC, MH, NC, YU.

4294 — —[Anr. ed.] *Cantabrigiæ, apud Joannem Hayes,* 1674. 8°. L, CS; MH, NC, TU, WCL.

4295 — —[Anr. ed.] 1683. 8°. O, DCH; CH, MBC.

4296 — —[Anr. ed.] *Richard Bentley,* 1688. 12°. CT.

4297 — —[Anr. ed.] *Oxoniæ, e theatro Sheldoniano,* 1695. 4°. T.C.II 559. L, O, C, CT, EC; NC, PU, WF.

4298 —M. Tullius Cicero de oratore. *Oxoniæ, e theatro Sheldoniano,* 1696. 8°. L, O, C, RPL, DT; CLC, CU, NC, WF, Y.

4299 —Epistolæ selectæ. *Excudebat Rogerus Daniel,* 1657. 12°. C, CS; CH, MB, Y.

4299A — —[Anr. ed.] *Ex officina Eli. Redmayne,* 1689. 12°. NC.

4299B —M. Tulli Ciceronis epistolarum libri IV. *Excudebat Guil. Du-Gard, pro Societate stationariorum,* 1656. 8°. WF.

4300 —[Anr. ed.] *Abredoniæ, excudebat Joannes Forbesius,* 1665. 8° ALDIS 1787. HH.

4301 — —[Anr. ed.] *S. G. & B. G. pro Societate stationarum,* 1669. 8°. L; NR.

4302 — —[Anr. ed.] *Cantabrigiæ: ex officina Joann. Hayes,* 1670. 8°. C.

4303 — —[Anr. ed.] *Glasguæ, ex typographéo Roberti Sanders,* 1674. 8°. HG.

4304 — —[Anr. ed.] 1685. 8°. DC.

4304A — —[Anr. ed.] *Excudebat M. Flesher, pro societate stationariorum,* 1685. 8°. TU.

4304B — —[Anr. ed.] *Edinburgh, apud A. Anderson,* 1694. 8°. EN.

4304C — —[Anr. ed.] *Excudebat J. Roberts pro Societate Stationariorum,* 1700. 8°. DC.

4305 —Epistolarum selectarum. *Pro societate stationariorum. Venales prostant apud Obadiam Blagrave,* 1689. 8°. O, C, CM, CT.

4305A — —Ethicæ Ciceronianæ. *Typis Guil. Du-Gardi. Veneunt apud Thomam Matthews,* 1652. 12°. GU; MB.

4306 —Familiar epistles. 1671. 12°. LW.

4307 —The five days debate at Cicero's house. *For Abel Swalle,* 1683. 8°. T.C.II 6. L, O, C; CH, Y.

4307A — —[Anr. ed.] *For Tho. Simons,* 1683. 8°. EN; CLC, CN, NPT, PL, WF, Y.

4308 —Cicero's Lælius. A discourse. *For William Crooke,* 1691. 8°. T.C.II 362. L, O, C, CK, AM; CLC, CN, LC, Y.

4309 —Tully's offices. *For Henry Brome,* 1680. 8°. T.C.I 397. L, OC, CS; CH, CLC, NP, OCI, Y.

4310 — —Second edition. —, 1681. 8°. T.C.I 447. L, C; CH, CLC, MH, PL.

4311 — —Third edition. *For Charles Brome,* 1684. 8°. T.C.II 107. L, O, CQ, LL; IU, MH, NP, TU, Y.

4312 — —Fourth edition. *For R. Bently, J. Hindmarsh and J. Tonson,* 1688. 12°. L, O, C, AM, EN; CH, CU, TU, WF, Y.

4313 — —Fifth edition. *By M. B. for J. Tonson, R. Knaplock, and H. Hindmarsh,* 1699. 8°. L, C, LW, DT; MBA, MH, NC, TU, Y.

4314 —The oration of Cicero for M. Marcellus. *For Walter Kettilby,* 1689. 4°.* T.C.II 258. L, O, C, CT, DT; CN, MH, NC, V, WF, Y.

4315 —M. T. Ciceronis orationes quaedam selectae. *Cantabrigiae, ex officina Johann. Hayes,* 1692. *Impensis Hen. Dickinson.* 8°. T.C.II 403. C, LVD, OC, EC, BAMB; IU.

4316 — —*Cantabrigiæ, ex officina Johan. Hayes, impensis R. Clavell, S. and J. Spring, S. Smith and B. Walford,* 1699. 8°. T.C.II 125. CCA, CPE, AU; MH, PL, TU.

4316A —Orationum selectarum liber. *Typis E. Cotes, pro Johanne Pierrepont,* 1667. 12°. L; IU, Y.

4316B —[Anr. ed.] *Typis Andr. Clark, pro R. Scot, T. Basset, J. Wright, et Ri. Chiswell; sold by Rob. Clavell,* 1675. 12°. T.C.I 222. C, YM; IU, NPT.

4317 — —*Typis T. H. pro R. Scot, T. Basset, J. Wright & R. Chiswel,* 1679. 8°. AU, DT; Y.

4318 —M. Tulii Ciceronis orationum selectarum liber. *Typis T. Hodgkin, pro R. Scot, T. Basset, R. Chiswel, M. Wotton, & G. Conyers,* 1686. 12°. T.C.II 171. L, DC; IU, WF.

4318A —[Anr. ed.] —, 1694. 12°. L.

4319 —[Anr. ed.] *Impensis R. Chiswell, A. & J. Churchill, S. Smith, B. Walford, M. Wotton, & G. Conyers,* 1700. 12°. CT, AU; MBC, MH, Y.

4320 —Cicero's prince, the reasons and counsels. *For S Mearne,* 1668. 8°. T.C.I 5. L, O; CH, CN, LC, MH, MIU.

4321 —Sententiæ. *Ex typographeo societate stationariorum,* 1648. 8°. DT; MB.

4322 —Tully's three books of offices, in English. *For Sam. Buckley,* 1699. 12°. L, O, C, CM; CH, CLC, CN, NIC, Y.

4323 —Cicero's three books touching the nature of the gods. *For Joseph Hindmarsh,* 1683. 12°. T.C.I 509. L, O, C, DC, ENC; CH, CN, PL, MBP, WF, Y.

4324 **Cillard,** *alderman.* A continvation of the Irish rebels proceedings. *Printed at London for Geo. Lindsey,* 1642. 4°.* LT, O, C, LF, EA; CH, MH.

Cimmerian matron. [*n.p.*], 1668. *See* Charleton, Walter.

Circle. 1676. *See* Brémond, Gabriel de.

4325 A circular letter from the master. [*n.p.*], 1675/6. brs. O; CH, CLC.

Circular letter to the clergy of Essex. 1690. *See* L., H.

The circumstances before and after the speech of William late Viscount Stafford. 1680. *See* Rous, John.

4326 Entry cancelled.

4327 The cities corporations poore. [*London,* 1652.] brs. LT.

4328 The cities farewell to the Parliament. colop: *Printed at London, for M.P.*, [1642?] fol.* HH; TU.

Cities great concern. 1674. *See* Bolton, Edmund.

4329 The cities just vindication. [*London*, 1682?] cap., fol.* L, O, C, LG, HH; CH, CN, MH, WF, Y.

4330 The cities loyalty display'd. *Printed*, 1661. 4°.* LT, O, YM; CH, Y.

4331 The cities loyaltie to their King. [*London*, 1647.] brs. LT, O, HH; CH, MH.

Cities new poet's mock-show. [*n.p.*, 1659.] *See* T., M.

4332 The cities propositions, and the Parliaments ansvver. *Printed at London, by Richard Cotes*, 1642[3]. 4°.* LT, LG, SP, DT; CH, CN, MBP, WF, Y.

4333 The city's remonstrance and addresse. *By R.D. for Tho. Rooks*, 1661. 4°.* LT, GK; MBA, Y.

4333A —[Anr. ed.] *Printed at London and reprinted at Edinburgh*, 1661. 4°.* CLC.

4334 The cities X commandements, commanded. [*London*, 1648.] brs. LT; MH.

4335 The cities thanks to Southwarke. [*London*, 1647.] brs. LT.

4336 The cities warning-peece. [*London*], *printed*, [1643]. 4°.* LT, O, HH; MH, Y.

4337 The cities welcome to Colonell Rich. [*London*], *printed*, 1648. brs. LT.

4338 The citizens companion. *By J.C. for Barber Tooth*, 1673. 8°. T.C.I 153. O, LG; CN, MH, NC, WCL, WF.

Citizens complaint. 1663. *See* M., G.

4339 The citizens joy for the rebuilding of London. *By P. Lillicrap for Richard Head*, 1667. brs. L.

4340 The citizens lamentation for the Lord Chancellor's loss of the purse. *For S.M.*, 1688. brs. L, C; CH.

4341 The citizens loss, when the charter of London is forfeited. colop: *For Francis Smith senior*, 1683. cap., fol.* L, O, C, LG; CH, CN, MH, TU, WF, Y.

4341A The citizens of London by their charter. [*London?* 1680.] brs. MH.

4342 The citizens of London their petition. *John Johnson*, 1642. brs. L.

4343 The citizens of London's humble petition to the right honourable the knights, citizens, and burgesses of the Commons. *Printed at London, for T.B.*, 1641. 4°.* LT, O, CT, HH, DT; CSS, MH, TU, WF, Y.

4344 The citizens reply to the whores petition. *Printed*, 1668. brs. L; MH.

Citizens sacred entertainment. 1666. *See* Fydge, Thomas.

4344A The citizen's vindication. [*London, for P. Brooksby, c.* 1672–80] brs. O.

4345 [**Citri de La Guette, Samuel.**] The history of the trivmvirates. *For Charles Brome*, 1686. 8°. T.C.II 157. L, O, C, MP, DT; CH, CN, LC, NC, TU, WCL, Y.

4345A [–] —Second edition, —, 1690. 8°. T.C.II 443. OC; WF.

Citt and bumpkin. 1680. *See* L'Estrange, Sir Roger.

4346 The city alarvm. *For Ioshua Kirton*, 1645. 4°.* LT, O, C, EN, DT; CH, CU, MH, NU, TU, WF, Y.

4347 The city and country's loyalty. [*London*], *for C. Bates*, [1690]. brs. L, CM, HH; MH, Y.

City and country chapmans almanack. 1686. *See* Almanacs.

4348 The city and country garland. [*London*], *for P. Brooksby, J. Deacon, J. Blare, J. Back*, [c. 1690]. 8°.* CHRISTIE-MILLER.

City and country purchaser. [1667.] *See* Primate, Stephen.

City bride. 1696. *See* Harris, Joseph.

4349 The city caper. [*London*], *for P. Brooksby*, [1672–95]. brs. L, O, HH; MH.

4350 The city-dames petition. [*London*], *printed*, 1647. 4°.* LT, O, OC; MH, TU, Y.

4351 A citie-dog in a saints doublet. [*London*], *printed*, 1648. 4°.* LT; MH, WF, Y.

4352 The city. Draw neere. *Oxford, for VVilliam VVeb.* 1643. brs. MADAN 1317. LT, HH.

4352A City justice, or, true equity exposed. [*London*, 1690] fol. PL.

4353 The city-law, or, the course. *By B. Alsop, for L. Chapman, and L. Blaiklocke*, 1647. 4°. LT, O, LG, LL, DT; CH, MH, NU, WF, Y.

4354 The city law, shewing. *By T.R. for Timothy Twyford*, 1658. 8°. L, O, LG, LL; WF, Y, YL.

4355 The citie letany. [*London*], *printed*, 1648. 4°.* L, LG; CN, MH, TU.

City match. *Oxford*, 1659. *See* Mayne, Jasper.

4356 The citie matrons. [*London*], *printed*, 1654. 4°.* LT.

City-ministers. 1649. *See* Dell, William.

4357 The city of God, or kingdom of Christ. *Printed*, 1672. 12°. NU.

Citie of London reprov'd. [1660.] *See* Fell, Margaret.

4358 The city of Londons loyal plea. *For Randal Taylor*, 1682. fol.* T.C.I 495. L, LG, O, OC; CH, CN, MH, WF, Y.

4359 The city of Londons new letany. [*London*], *for L:C.*, 1659. brs. L; CH, Y.

4360 The city of London's plea. *Printed*, 1682. *And published by Randal Taylor*. fol.* L, O, C, LG, EN; CH, CN, MH, WF, Y.

4361 The city of Londons rejoinder. *Printed and are to be sold by L. Curtiss*, 1682. fol.* L, O, C, LVF, DT; CH, LC, MH, WF, Y.

4362 The city of Londons resolution. [*London*], *for I. Tompson and A Coe*, 1642. 4°.* LT, O, LG, HH; WF, Y.

City-remonstrance. 1646. *See* Price, John.

City revels, 1690. *See* C., T.

4362A The city-wifes petition, against coffee. colop: *For A.W.:* 1700. cap., 4°.* MH.

City wit. 1653. *See* Brome, Richard.

4362B The civil and military articles of Limerick. [*London?* 1691.] cap., 4°.* C.

4363 The civil articles of Lymerick. *Dublin, by Robert Thornton*, 1692. 4°.* DIX 278. C, LVF, CD, DK, DT; CU, WF.

4363A —[Anr. ed.] [*London?* 1692.] cap., 4°.* L.

4364 A civil correction of a sawcy impudent pamphlet. colop: *For A.B.*, 1681. cap., fol.* L, O, HH, EN; CH, CU, MBA, PU, WF, Y.

4364A —[Anr. ed.] colop: *Edinburgh, re-printed by the heirs of Andrew Anderson,* 1681. fol.* ALDIS 2258. L, EN.

4365 The civil orange. [*n.p.*], 1689. brs. O.

Civil right. 1650. *See* Elderfield, Christopher.

4366 Entry cancelled.

4366A The civil wars of Bantam. *By H. C. for Tho. Malthus,* 1683. fol.* T.C.II 28. L, O, CS, HH, P; CH, MBA, Y.

Civill wars of England. 1649. *See* Ricraft, Josiah.

Civil wars of France. 1655. *See* London, William.

Civil warres of Great Britain. 1661. *See* Davies, John.

4366B The civill warrs of the citie. *For Francis Coles,* 1645. 8°.* OW.

4367 Civitas Bristoll. To the right worshipful the mayor. *Bristol: W. Bonny,* 1696. brs. L.

4368 **Clagett, Nicholas.** The abuse of Gods grace. *Oxford, by A. Lichfield, for Thomas Robinson and Samuel Pocock,* 1659. 4°. MADAN 2437. LT, O, LCL, E; NPT, NU, Y.

4369 Entry cancelled.

4370 [–] A perswasive to an ingenuous tryal of opinions in religion. *For Tho. Basset,* 1685. 4°. T.C.II 93. L, O, C, MC, DT; CH, MH, NU, TU, WF, Y.

4371 —A persuasive to peaceableness. *For John Marston, to be sold by W. Kettilby,* 1683. 4°. C, CS, CT, EC, DT; CH, MBA, NC, NU, WF.

[–] Sermon preached at the ordination. 1681. *See* Coxe, Nehemiah.

4372 —A sermon preached . . . May 4. 1686. *By J. R. for John Weld,* 1686. 4°.* T.C.II 165. L, O, LW, OC, ENC; NGT, NPT.

4373 [**Clagett, William.**] An answer to the Dissenters objections. *For T. Basset, B. Took, and F. Gardiner,* 1683. 4°.* T.C.II 15. L, O, C, LCL, EN; CH, CN, NU, WF, Y.

4374 [–] —[Anr. ed.] —, 1684. 4°.* L, O, CT, EN, DT; CH, CU, MH, NC, NU.

4374A — —[Anr. ed.] 1687. 4°.* YM.

4375 [–] —[Anr. ed.] *For Thomas Basset, and Benjamin Took,* 1688. 4°.* L, BP; Y.

4376 [–] An answer to the Representer's reflections. *For Ric. Chiswell,* 1688. 4°. T.C.II 271. L, O, C, MC; DT; CH, MH, NU, TU, WF, Y.

4377 [–] The difference of the case, between the separation of Protestants. *For Thomas Basset, and Fincham Gardiner,* 1683. 4°. T.C.II 25. L, O, C, E, DT; CH, MH, NU, TU, Y.

4378 [–] —[Anr. ed.] *By F. Collins, for Thomas Basset,* 1686. 4°. LCL, LIL, HH, EN; MBP, MH, NPT, NU, WF.

4379 [–] A discourse concerning the operations of the Holy Spirit. *By J. C. for Hen. Brome,* 1678. 8°. T.C.I 287. L, C, OC, EC; CH, CLC, CU, PL.

4380 — —Second edition. *For Henry Brome,* 1680. 8°. T.C.I 402. L, O, C, E, DT; BN, CLC, NU, PL, WF, Y.

4381 — —Second part. —, 1680. 8°. L, C, LCL, E, ENC; CLC, NL, PL, WF, Y.

4382 — —Second edition. *Sold by T. Sawbridge,* 1690. 8°. T.C.II 295. LW.

4383 [–] A discourse concerning the pretended sacrament of extreme unction. *For Richard Chiswell,* 1687. 4°. T.C.II 271. L, O, C, EN, DT; CLC, CU, MH, NU, TU, WF, Y.

4384 [–] A discourse concerning the worship of the Blessed Virgin. *For T. Basset, and T. Newborough,* 1686. 4°.* T.C.II 165. L. C, MC, EN, DT; CH, MH, NU, TU, WF, Y.

4385 —Eleven sermons. The second volume. *For William Rogers,* 1693. 8°. T.C.II 471. L, O, C, ENC, DT; CH, NGT, WF.

4386 — —Second edition. —, 1699. 8°. T.C.III 98. L, OME; NU.

4387 —Of the humanity and charity of Christians. *By J. D. for J. Robinson, and Thomas Newborough,* 1687. 4°.* T.C.II 192. L, OC, CT; CH, MH, NU, Y.

4388 [–] A paraphrase with notes, and a preface, upon the sixth chapter of St. John. *By J. D. for J. Robinson, and T. Newborough,* 1686. 4°. L, O, C, EN, DT; CH, MH, NU, TU, WF, Y.

4389 — —Second edition. *For J. Robinson, and T. Newborough,* 1693. 8°. T.C.II 474. L, O, CT, EC, DT; LG.

4390 [–] The present state of the controversie. *For Tho. Basset, James Adamson, and Tho. Newborough,* 1687. 4°.* L, O, C, MC, DT; CH, LC, MH, NU, TU, Y.

4391 [–] The queries offered by T. W. . . . answered. *By H. Clark, for James Adamson,* 1688. 4°.* L, O, C, E, DT; CH, MH, NU, TU, WF, Y.

4392 —The religion of an oath. *For Will. Rogers,* 1700. 8°.* T.C.III 183. L, O, C, CS; NR, Y.

4393 [–] A reply to a pamphlet called The mischief of impositions. *For Walter Kettilby,* 1681. 4°. T.C.I 435. L, O, C, CT, EN; CH, LC, MH, NU, Y.

4394 Entry cancelled.

4395 A second letter from the author of the Discourse on unction. *For Ric. Chiswell,* 1688. 4°.* L, O, C, E, DT; CLC, MBA, MIU, TU, WF, Y.

4396 —Seventeen sermons. *For W. Rogers,* 1689. 8°. T.C.II 268. L, O, C, LGI, ENC; CH, CLC, WF, Y.

4397 — —Second edition. —, 1694. 8°. T.C.II 495. LW, EC, D, DT; CH, WF.

4398 — —Third edition. —, 1699. 8°. T.C.III 98. L, OME, RPL; MHS.

4399 —Several captious queries. *By H. Clark for James Adamson,* 1688. 4°.* L, O, CT, EN, DT; CLC, CN, MH, NU, WF, Y.

4400 [–] The state of the Church of Rome. *For William Rogers, and Samuel Smith,* 1688. 4°.* T.C.II 246. L, OB, C, EN, DT; CH, MH, NU, TU, WF, Y.

4401 —The summ of a conference. *For William Rogers,* 1689. 8°.* L, O, C, OME, D; CH, TU, Y.

4401A —Second edition. —, 1694. 8°.* D.

4402 [–] A view of the whole controversy. *For William Rogers,* 1687. 4°. T.C.II 285. L, O, C, LIL, EN; CH, CU, MH, NU, TU, WF, Y.

4403 Clamor sanguinis martyrum, or the bloody inquisition of Spain. *By A. M. for Fr. Tyton,* 1656. 12°. LT, O, LW, EN; CH, CN, MH, MM, WF.

4404 Clamor sanguinis: or, the cry of blood. colop: *For R. Janeway,* 1680. cap., fol.* L; CH, WF, Y.

Clancie's cheats. 1687. *See* Settle, Elkanah.

4405 **Clannie, Hugh.** Inquisitio nova, or a just and true narrative. 1698. 4°. L, LCL, EN; WF.

4406 **Clanricarde, Ulrick de Burgh, marquis of.** A declaration of the resolutions of His Majesties forces. *For A. H.*, 1648. 4°.* LT, C, OC; CH, MH, MIU, Y.

Clap, John. Almanack. New York, 1697. *See* Almanacs.

4407 **Clapham, Jonathan.** A full discovery and confutation of the wicked . . . doctrines of the Quakers. *By T. R. & E. M. for Adoniram Byfield*, 1656. 4°. LT, O, C, CT, LF; CLC, NU, PH, PSC.

4408 —Obedience to magistrates recommended. *By T. S. for Edward Giles, in Norwich*, 1683. 4°.* T.C.II 41. L, O; WF.

4409 ——[Anr. ed.] 1684. 4°.* T.C.II 68. O, WCA, EN.

4410 —A short and full vindication of that sweet and comfortable ordinance. *Printed*, 1656. 4°.* LT, O, C, LF, BBN; CLC, PH, WF.

4411 —The stone smiting the image on the feet. *By by[sic] Wm Du-Gard: to bee sold by Stephen Boutel*, 1651. 4°.* LT.

Claramont. *See* Clermont.

4412 [**Clare, R.**] A declaration to the English nation. *Printed*, 1649. 4°. LT, O; CH, WF, Y.

4413 [**Clare, William.**] A compleat system of grammar, English and Latin. *For H. Walwyn*, 1699. 4°. T.C.III 97. L, O, OC, EC; MH, Y.

4413A —Via naturalis: the natural way. *Sold by R. Wild*, 1688. 8°. T.C.II 233. O.

4414 [**Clarendon, Edward, Hyde, earl of.**] Animadversions upon a book, intituled, Fanaticism. *For R. Royston*, 1673. 8°. L, O, C, MR, DT; CH, MIU, NU, PL, TU, Y.

4415 [–]—Second edition. —, 1674. 8°. T.C.I 164. L, C, MC, EN; DT; NU, TSM, WF, WSC, Y.

4416 [–]—Third edition. —, 1685. 8°. LIL; CH, NU.

4417 [–] An answer to a pamphlet, entit'led A declaration of the Commons of England. [*London*], printed, 1648. 4°.* LT, O, C, HH, DT; CH, CN, MH, WF, Y, HC.

4418 Entry cancelled.

4419 —Mr: Hides argvment before the Lords. [*London*], printed, 1641. 4°.* LT, O, CT, LL, MR; CH, CN, MH, NC, TU, WF, Y.

4420 —A brief view and survey. [*Oxford*], at the theater, 1676. 4°. MADAN 3110. L, O, C, MR, EN; CLC, CN, LC, MH, NU, TU, Y.

4421 ——Second edition. *Oxon: printed at the theater*, 1676. 4°. MADAN 3111. L, O, C, LL, CK; BN, CH, LC, MH, Y.

4422 Entry cancelled.

4423 [–] A full answer to an infamous and trayterous pamphlet, entituled, A declaration of the Commons. [*London*], for R. Royston, 1648. 4°. LT, O, C, CT, HH; BN, CH, CN, MBP, NU, WF, Y.

4424 [–] A letter from a true and lawfull member of Parliament. [*Holland?*], printed, 1656. 4°. LT, O, CT, HH, MR; CH, CN, MH, NU, WF, Y.

4424A [–] Plenvm Responsvm. [*London*], impressum pro R. Royston, 1648. 8°. SC; NU, Y.

4425 [–] Second thoughts. [*London*, 1660?] cap., 4°.* L, O, C, CT, YM; CLC, CN, MIU, NU, WF, Y.

4426 —Mr. Edvvard Hyde's speech at a conference . . . the 6th. of July, 1641. *Printed at London for Abel Roper*, 1641. 4°.* LT, O, CT, EN, DT; CSS, MH, NU, TU, WF, Y.

4427 —To the right honourable, the Lords . . . the hvmble petition and address of. [*London*, 1667?] brs. MH, Y.

4428 [–] Transcendent and mvltiplied rebellion. [*Oxford, by L. Lichfield*], 1645. 4°.* MADAN 1823. LT, O, CT, EN, DT; CH, CU, WF, Y.

4429 —Two letters written by. [*London*, 1680?] cap., fol.* L, O, C, OC, HH; CH, NC, TU, WF, Y.

Clarret drinker's song. [*n.p.*, 1680.] *See* Oldham, John.

4429A [**Clarges, Sir Thomas.**] Hypo[c]notes [sic] unmasked. *For Goodman Constant*, 1659. 4°.* LT, O; CH, MIU, PL, Y.

4430 **Claridge, John.** The shepheards' legacy. *Printed and are to be sold by John Hancock junior*, 1670. 8°.* L; CH.

4431 **C[laridge], R[ichard].** An answer to Richard Allen's essay. *Printed*, 1697. 8°. L, O, LF; RPJ.

4432 [–] A defence of the present government under King William. *For R. Baldwin*, 1689. 4°.* T.C.II 305. L, C, CT, MR, AU; CH, MB, RPJ, WF, Y.

4433 —A looking-glass for religious princes. *For the author, and are to be sold by William Marshall*, 1691. 4°.* T.C.II 422. L, O, C; MH, MWA.

4434 —Mercy covering the judgment seat. *Printed and sold by T. Sowle*, 1700. 4°.* L, O, LF, BBN; MH, NU, PH, WF, Y.

4435 —A second defence of the present government. *For John Mountford in Worcester, and sold by Richard Baldwin*, 1689. 4°. L, MR, EN; MWA, Y.

Clarior e tenebris. 1683. *See* Garbrand, John.

4436 [**Clark, Benjamin.**] Christ's hundred commandments. *For Benjamin Clark*, 1682. 8°. O, CT, LF.

4436A **Clarke, Sir Edward.** By the Mayor. *By Samuel Roycroft*, 1697. brs. L.

4437 **Clark, Edward.** The Protestant school-master. *By T. B. to be sold by John How*, 1680. 12°. O; Y.

4438 ——[Anr. ed.] *By T. James for J. How*, 1682. 12°. L; NP.

4439 [**Clark, Frances.**] A briefe reply to the narration of Don Pantaleon Sa. [*London*, 1653.] cap., 4°.* LT, OME.

4440 **Clarke, Francis.** Praxis Francisci Clarke. *Dvblinii, per Nathanielem Thompson*, 1666, & prostat venalis apud Johannem Leach. 4°. DIX 130. L, O, C, DK, DT; LC, MIU.

4441 ——[Anr. ed.] *Impensis Guliel. Crooke*, 1667. 8°.* L, O, CS, LL, DT; BN, CLC, LC, PL.

4442 ——[Anr. ed.] *Impensis Guliel. Crooke*, 1679. 12°. T.C.I 336. O, C, EN; LC, MWA, PL.

4443 ——"Second" edition. *Excudebat T. B. impensis Hannah Sawbridge*, 1684. 4°. T.C.II 65. L, O, C, EN, DT; BN, CH, LC, MHL, NCL, YL.

4443A ——[Anr. ed.] 1686. 4°. YM.

4444 —Proposals for printing by subscription Clarke's Praxis. [*n.p.*, 1667?] 8°. O.

4444A **Clarke, George.** The case of our English wool. [*London*, 1685?] cap., 4°.* L; MH, NC, Y.

4444B [–] A treatise of wool and cattel. *By J. C. for Will. Crook*, 1677. 4°.* T.C.I 275. L, LUG, R, A; CU, LC, MH, NC, Y.

4445   [–] —[Anr. ed.] *By J. C. for William Crook*, 1685. 4°.* T.C.II 116. L, O, BR; CH, MH, NC, WF, Y.

4446   **Clark, Gilbert.** Astronomica specimina. *Typis Milonis Flesher, veneunt apud Ric. Davis, Oxoniensen*, 1682. 8°.* O, OC, EO, DT; CLC, PL, WF.

4447   —De plenitudine mundi. *Apud Jo. Martin, Ja. Allestry, & Th. Dicas*, 1660. 8°. LT, O, CS, CSS; BN, V, WF.

4448   —Oughtredus explicatus. *Typis Milonis Flesher; veneunt apud Ric. Davis, Oxoniensen*, 1682. 8°. T.C.II 5. O, CT, LPO, EN, DT; BN, MH, MU, NC, PL, WF, Y.

4449   —The spot dial. *By J. M. for Walter Kettilby*, 1687. 4°.* T.C.II 178. L, O, C, LG, P; WPO.

4450   —Tractatus de restitutione corporum. *Excudebat J. H. pros S. Thomson*, 1662. 8°. L, CCH; BN, MH.

4451   —Tractatus tres. [*London*], *anno Domini*, 1695. 8°. L, OC, CS, P, DT; CLC, WF.

4452   **Clark, Henry.** A clovd of witnesses. *For Giles Calvert*, 1656. 4°.* LT, CT, OC, LF; MH, PH.

4453   —A description of the prophets. *For Giles Calvert*, 1655. 4°.* LT, O, C, LF, BBN; IE, PH, PSC, Y.

4454   —Englands lessons. *For Giles Calvert*, 1656. 4°.* LT, LF, OC, BBN, DT; CH, MH, PH.

4454A   —Here is the swearers. *For the author*, 1661. 4°.* LF, BBN; PH, WF, Y.

4455   —Here is true magistracy described. *For Robert Wilson*, 1660. 4°. O, LF, OC, BBN; IE, PH.

4456   [–] His Grace the Duke of Monmouth honoured in his progress. colop: *For Benjamin Harris*, 1680. brs. L, O, LN, BR; CH.

4457   —A rod discover'd. *For the author, the sixth month*, 1657. 4°. LT, CT, LF, IW; PH, PSC.

4458   ——Second edition. *For Thomas Simmons*, 1659. 4°. L, O, LF; CH, IE, NU, PH, Y.

4459   —The wise taken in their own craftiness. *For Giles Calvert*, 1656. 4°.* LT, O, C, LF, BBN; PH, Y.

4459A   **Clark, J.** Seder olam; or the order of ages. 1694. 8°. O.

4460   [**Clark, J. W.**] Mr. John Mackenzyes narrative of the siege of London-derry a false libel. *For R. Simpson*, 1690. 4°.* L, OC, CT, OP, DT; CN, WF, Y.

4461   C[lark], I[ames]. Christs impressions strong. [*n.p.*], 1700. 8°. EN.

4462   [–] Master Clark defended. [*n.p.*, 1691.] 4°.* ON; WF.

4463   ——[Anr. ed.] [*Edinburgh*], *J. Wardlaw*, 1691. 4°. ALDIS 3137. EN.

4464   [–] Memento mori, or a word. *Edinburgh, by the heirs and successors of Andrew Anderson*, 1699. 8°. ALDIS 3870. EN.

4465   [–] Plain truth or, a seasonable discourse of the duties of people. *Edinburgh, by J: Reid*, 1693. *To be sold by James Wardlaw*, 4°.* L, FSF; Y.

4466   —A sermon preached at the kirk of auld Hamstocks, . . . September the 28, 1690. *Edinburgh, by John Reid*, 1690. 4°.* ALDIS 3024. EN; CH, MH, NU, WF.

4467   **Clark, John.** A brief and pithy treatise about comfort. *By E. T. and R H. for William Miller*, 1670. 12°. T.C.I 35. O, LW.

4467A   —Dux grammaticus. Fourth edition. *Imprimebat I. L. sumptibus C. M.*, 1650. 12°. OC; IU.

4468   ——[Anr. ed.] *Typis R. I. & prostant venales apud Andreum Kembe*, 1664. 12°. O.

4468A   ——Seventh edition. *Sumptibus Edvardi Thomasii*, 1677. 12°. L; CLC, Y.

4468B   [–] Formulae oratoriæ . . . Sixth edition. *Impensis W. B. & H. I.*, 1647. 12°. IU, MWA.

4468C   [–] —Seventh edition. *Impensis Fran. Eglesfeild*, [*sic*] 1653. 12°. CM.

4468D   [–] —Eighth edition. *Impensis Fran. Eglesfeild*, 1659. 12°. CLC, CU; MH, PL.

4468E   ——Ninth edition. *Impensis F. Eglesfeild*, 1664. 12°. EN; MWA.

4469   [–] —, Tenth edition. *Impensis. Fran Eglesfeild*, 1670. 12°. T.C.I 27. L, O; CU, WF.

4470   ——Eleventh edition. 1673. 12°. T.C.I 143. LW.

4471   —Ill newes from New-England. *By Henry Hills*, 1652. 4°. LT, O, CT, E, EN; CH, CN, LC, NN, RPJ, Y.

4472   —Leaven, corrupting the childrens bread, *By John Macock, for Luke Fawne*, 1646. 4°. LT, O, CT, EN, DT; Y.

4473   [–] Phraseologia puerilis Anglo-Latina. Second edition. *By William Du-gard for Francis Eglesfield*, 1650. 8°. L; IU.

4474   ——Third edition. *By R. D. for Francis Eglesfield*, 1655. 8°. C, CT, EN.

4474A   ——Fourth edition. *By J. R. for Francis Eglesfield*, 1670. 8°. T.C.I 62. CP; MWA.

4475   —The plotters unmasked. *Printed*, 1661. 4°. LT, C; Y.

4476   —Repressaliæ sunt licitæ. [*Cambridge*], 1663. brs. L.

4477   —A sermon preached at the funeral of Mr. Nathaniel Aske. *For George Swinnock*, 1676. 4°.* L, C, LW; CH, NU, WF.

4478   —A sermon preached . . . on the 29th. of May, 1684. *For George Downes*, 1684. 4°.* L, WCA; IU, NU, WF.

4479   **Clark, Joshua.** A sermon preached . . . 5th of July, 1691. *For William Rogers*, 1691. 4°.* T.C.II 376. L, O, C, CT, BR; CH, MH, NU, WF, Y.

4480   —A sermon preached . . . July 12. 1697. *For John Everingham*, 1698. 4°.* L, C, CS, CSS, YM; CLC.

4481   —Two sermons preached. *Cambridge, by the printers to the universitie*, 1655. *Sold by William Morden*. 8°. L, O, OC, CM, CT.

4482   **Clark, Margaret.** The true confession of Margret [*sic*] Clark. *Printed, to be sold by Joseph Collier*, 1680. 4°.* L, O, LG; CH, MBA, WF, Y.

4483   —Warning for servants. *For Tho. Parkhurst, by Joseph Collier*, 1680. 4°.* T.C.I 421. L, C, EN; CH, MH, NU, TU, WF, Y.

4483A   **Clark, Mary.** The great and wonderful success. [*London, c 1685.*] brs. L.

4484   C[lark], R. Vermiculars destroyed. *By R. Wilkins, for the author*, 1690. 4°.* L, LWL, AU.

4485   ——[Anr. ed.] *By J. Wilkins, for the author*, [1691?]. 4°.* L; CH, PL, WSG.

4485A   ——Fifth edition. —, 1694. 4°.* PL.

4486   —Sixth edition. —, 1693. 4°.* L, GH.

4487   **Clark, Robert.** A letter concerning Colonel Monks surprizing . . . Carrickfergus. *For Edward Husband, September* 30, 1648. brs. LT; MH.

4488   —The lying-vvonders. *Printed,* 1660. 4°.* LT; CLC, MH.

4488A   **Clarke, Samuel,** *younger.* Aurea legenda. *For N. Ranew,* 1682. 12°. T.C.I 465. LCL; CN, WF.

4489   —A brief concordance to the Holy Bible. *For Thomas Parkhurst, Jonathan Robinson, Thomas Cockerill, Sen. & Jun., Brabazon Aylmer, John Lawrence, and John Taylor,* 1696. 12°. L, O, LCL, LW; CH, LC, MH, TU, WF, Y.

4489A   —A discourse concerning the testimony. 1699. 8°. O.

4490   —The divine authority. *For Jonathan Robinson,* 1699. 8°. T.C.III 106. O, CM, LW, E, DT; MH, PL.

4491   —An exercitation concerning the original. *Printed* 1698. 8°. L, O; NN, PL.

4492   —The holy history in brief: or, an abridgement of the historical parts of the Bible. *For Johnathan Robinson,* 1690. 12°. T.C.II 312. L, O, LCL, LW; WF.

4493   —A Lent-sermon, preached . . . March 3. 1699/700. *By T. M. for Benj. Tooke,* 1700. 4°.* T.C.III 181. CS; CH, NU, Y.

4494   —Ministers dues. *By A. M. for William Miller,* 1661. 4°. LT, O, OC, CPE, EN; CH, MM, NU.

4494A   —Neck and all. A sermon. *For Samuel Marsh,* 1691. 4°.* CT; Y.

4495   [-] Of scandal; together. *For Benj. Aslop,* 1680. 12°. O, LCL, LW; KT, NPT, WF, Y.

4495A   —Proposals for Mr. Clarks Supplement to his Annotations. [*London?* 1699]. 4°.* LW.

4496   —Scripture-justification. *By S. Bridge, for Tho. Parkhurst,* 1698. 8°. L, LCL, CS, HH, ENC; MIU, NU.

4497   —A sermon preached . . . eleventh of November. *For W. Crooke. And sold by R. Taylor,* 1693. 4°.* T.C.II 448. L, C, WCA; Y.

4498   [-] Some reflections on that part of a book called Amyntor. *For James Knapton,* 1699. 8°.* T.C.III 120. O, C, CT, LVD, DB; CH, CN, MH, NP, WF, Y.

4499   —A survey of the Bible. *By J. D. for J. Robinson.* 1693. 4°. T.C.II 474. L, C, LCL, LW, ES; BN, CLC, LC, MBC, PPT.

4500   Entry cancelled.

4501   **Clarke, Samuel,** *of St. Bennet Fink.* An antidote against immoderate mourning. *By E. M. for George Calvert,* 1659[60]. 4°. LT, O, C, LW; CH, MBA, MIU, NU, WF.

4502   —The blessed life and meritorious death of our Lord. *For William Miller,* 1664. 4°. L, O, C, LL, EN; NU, WF, Y.

4502A   — —Second edition. —, 1665. 4°. IU.

4503   —A briefe and yet exact, and accurate description of . . . Germany. *By A. M. for William Miller,* 1665. 4°. L, O; WF.

4504   —A caution against sacriledge. *By Abraham Miller for Thomas Vnderhill,* 1659. 4°.* LT, OC, HH, WCA; CH, CLC, MIU, NU, WF.

4505   —Christian good-fellowship. *For Thomas Underhill,* 1655. 4°.* O, C, CM, EN; NU, WF.

4506   —A collection of the lives of ten eminent divines. *For William Miller,* 1662. 4°. L, O, LW, OC, A; CN, MH, NU, RPJ, WF, Y.

4507   —A description of the seaventeen provinces . . . Low-countries. *For William Birch,* 1672. 8°. T.C.I 120. L, O, C, LCL; MH, V.

4508   —Englands covenant proved lavvfull. *For Henry Overton,* 1643. 4°.* LT, C, LSC, YM; CH, MH, NU, RPJ, TU, Y.

4509   — —Second edition. —, 1643. 4°.* NU.

4510   —England's remembrancer. [*London*], *printed by J. G. for John Rothwell,* 1657. 12°. L, AN; CN, Y.

4511   [-] —[Anr. ed.] *For John Hancock,* 1676. 8°. T.C.I 260. O; MH.

4511A   — —[Anr. ed.] *For W. Crooke,* 1676. 8°. OC.

4512   — —[Anr. ed.] *For J. Hancock,* 1677. 8°. LCL, LG; LC, NU, Y.

4512A   — —Fourth edition. —, 1679. 8°. T.C.I 345. L; CH.

4513   —A generall martyrologie. *By A. M. for T. Underhill and J. Rothwell,* 1651. fol. L, OC, CS, AU; CH, CU, MBP, MH, NU, Y.

4513A   Entry cancelled.

4514   — —Second edition. *By Tho. Ratcliffe, for Thomas Underhill and John Rothwell,* 1660. fol. O, LG, DT; CN.

4515   — —Third edition. *For William Birch,* 1677. fol. T.C.I 269. L, C, OB, LW, E; CN, NU, WF, WSC, Y.

4516   —A geographicall description of all the countries. *By R. I. for Thomas Newberry,* 1657. fol. O, C, LCL, OC; LC, MH, MU, RPJ, Y.

4517   — —[Anr. ed.] *By Tho. Milbourn for Robert Clavel, Tho. Passinger, William Cadman, William Whitwood, Tho. Sawbridge, and William Birch,* 1671. fol. LUS; CH, CN, LC, NU, TU, Y.

4518   —Golden apples. *By Tho. Ratcliffe, for Tho. Underhill,* 1659. 8°. LT, O, LCI, LW, E; CH, MB, NPT, NU, WF, Y.

4519-22   Entries cancelled.

4523   —The history of the glorious life, reign, and death of . . . Elizabeth. *For Henry Rodes,* 1682. 12°. T.C.I 462. L, LW, CE, EN; CH, CN.

4524   — —Second edition. —, 1683. 12°. T.C.II 8. L, EN; CSU, WF, Y.

4525   [-] An item against sacriledge. *By Abraham Miller for Thomas Underhill,* 1653. 4°.* LT, O, C, OC, CT; CU, MH, NU, WF, Y.

4526   —The life and death of Alexander the Great. *For William Miller,* 1665. 4°. L, O; CN, LC, WF.

4527   —The life and death of Charles the Great. *For William Miller,* 1665. 4°. L.

4528   —The life and death of Hannibal. *For William Miller,* 1665. 4°. L, O; CH, CN.

4529   —The life and death of Julius Caesar. *For William Miller,* 1665. 4°. L, O; CLC, IU, Y.

4530   —The life & death of Nebuchaadnezzer the Great. *For William Miller,* 1664. 4°. O; CN, WF.

4530A   — —[Anr. ed.— —, 1665. 4°. CLC, IU.

4531   —The life & death of Pompey. *For William Miller,* 1665. 4°. O; CLC, Y.

4532 —The life and death of the thrice noble . . . Edward. *For William Birch*, 1673. 4°.* T.C.I 127. L, CT, LW; IU, WF.

4533 —The life and death of the valiant . . . Sir Francis Drake. *For Simon Miller*, 1671. 4°. T.C.I 66. L, O, CT, P; CH, CN, MH, RPJ, Y.

4534 —The life & death of William, surnamed the Conqueror. *For Simon Miller*, 1671. 4°.* L, O, LW; CLC, MH, NU, TU, WF, Y.

4535 [–] The life of Tamerlane the Great. *By T. R. and E. M. for Tho: Underhill*, 1653. 4°. LT, O, SP, EN; CU, WF.

4535A [–] —[Anr. ed.] 1662. 4°. YM.

4535B [–] —[Anr. ed.] *By J. H. for Simon Miller*, 1664. 4°. BP; CN, Y.

4536 —The lives and deaths of such worthies. *By A. M. for Will. Miller*, 1665. 4°. LCL; CLC.

4537 —The lives and deaths of most of those eminent persons. Second edition. 1675. fol. GU; NPT, PPT.

4538 —The lives of sundry eminent persons. *For Thomas Simmons*, 1683. fol. T.C.II 3. L, O, C, LL, ENC; CH, CN, MH, NU, WF, Y.

4539 —The lives of the thirty two English divines. Third edition. *For William Birch*, 1667. fol. L, OC, CT, CPE, ES; NC, NGT.

4540 —The lives of two and twenty English divines. *By A. M. for Thomas Underhill and John Rothwell*, 1660. fol. L, O; WF.

4540A —A looking glass for good women. *W. Miller*, 1677. 12°. LW.

4541 —A looking-glass for persecutors. *For William Miller*, 1674. 12°. T.C.I 176. L; CH, LC, OWC.

4542 — —Second edition. —, 1675. 8°. T.C.I 207. L, O, C, LCL; MH.

4543 —The marrow of ecclesiastical historie. *By William Du-Gard*, 1650. 4°. LT, O, CE, LCL, ENC; CH, CN, NPT, NU, RPJ.

4544 — —Second edition. *For T. V. to be sold by William Roybould*, 1654. 4°. L, OC, CK, LCL, AU; CH, WF, WSC, Y.

4544A — —"Second" edition. *By Robert White for William Roybould*, 6154. 4°. CN, WF.

4545 — —Third edition. *For W. B. and are to be sold by Tho. Sawbridge, and by William Birch*, 1675. 2 pts. fol. T.C.I 222. L, O, C, LG, EN; CU, MH, NU, WF, Y.

4546 —A martyrologie. *By T. Ratcliffe and E. Mottershed, to be sold by John Browne*, 1652. fol. L, O, LCL, CS, OC; CH, CU, MH, NU, WF, Y.

4546A — —Third edition. 1677. fol. L.

4547 —Medvlla theologiæ. *By Thomas Ratcliffe, for Thomas Vnderhill*, 1659. fol. L, LCL, LG, CS, E; CU, MH, NU, WF, Y.

4548 —A mirrovr or looking-glasse. *By Ric. Cotes, for John Bellamie*, 1646. 8° LT, O, LCL, LW, ENC; MB, MIU.

4549 — —Second edition. *For Tho. Newberry*, 1654. 8°. L, CPE, CS, GU; CSB, CN, MH, NU, WF.

4550 — —[Anr. ed.] *R. Gaywood*, 1656. fol. WSC.

4551 — —Third edition. *By T. R. and E. M. for Tho. Newberry*, 1657. fol. L, C, LCL, OC, GU; LC, MH, NU, Y.

4552 — —Fourth edition. *By Tho. Milbourn, for Robert Clavel, Tho. Passinger, William Cadman, William Whitwood, Tho. Sawbridge, and William Birch*, 1671. 2v. fol. T.C.I 70. L, O, C, LUS, ES; LC, MH, NU, RPJ, TU, Y.

4553 —Narrative of those two deliverances. 1657. 12°. LUS.

4554 —A new description of the world. *For Hen. Rhodes*, 1689. 12°. L, LCL, GU; MB, MIU, MU, RPJ.

4554A — —Second edition. —, 1696. 12°. CT; CLC, RPJ.

4554B [–] The reign of Gustavvs. *By A. Maxey, to be sold by J. Rothwel*, 1658. 4°. OC, SP; MH, MIU, Y.

4555 —The saints nose-gay. *By I. D. for Henry Overton*, 1642. 12°. L, C, CPE, CT; NU.

4556 —The second part of the Marrow. Book I. *For Robert White, and William Wilson*, 1650. 4°. LT, CS, OC, SC; CH, CN, NP, RPJ, WF.

4556A — —Book II. *By Robert White*, 1650. LT, OC, CS, D; CH, CN, RPJ.

4556B —A sermon preached . . . eleventh of November. *By W. Crooke, sold by A. Taylor*, 1693. 4°.* L, WCA; CLC, Y.

4556C —The thrice noble and illustrious life and death of Edward. *By William Birch*, 1673. 4°.* L.

4557 —To the kings majesty. The humble and grateful acknowledgement of many ministers in . . . London. *For Joh. Rothwel*, 1660. brs. L; CH, Y.

4558 —A true and faithful account of the four chiefest plantations. *For Robert Clavel, Thomas Passinger, William Cadman, William Whitwood, Thomas Sawbridge, and William Birch*, 1670. fol. CH, CN, LC, MH, NU, Y.

4559 —A true and full narrative. *For J. Hancock*, 1671. 8°. T.C.I 57. L; CH, MIU, WF.

4560 —The wicked life, and wofull death of Herod. *For William Miller*, 1664. 4°. L, O, MR, SP, EN; MIU, NPT, NU, WF, Y.

4561 **Clarke, Samuel, *of St. James, Westminster*.** Three practical essays. *For James Knapton*, 1699. 8°. T.C.III 120. L, O, C, OM, DT; WF.

4561A **Clark, Simon.** The case of. 1661. 4°.* L.

4562 **[Clarke, Thomas].** Meditations in my confinement. *By W. G. for the use of the authour*, 1666. 4°.* L.

4562A —A warning to the inhabitants of Barbadoes. *For Robert Wilson*, 1661. 4°.* LF, BBN.

4562B — —[Anr. ed.] *For Thomas Simmons*, 1661. 4°.* PL.

4563 **Clarke, William, *advocate*.** Marciano, or the discovery; a tragicomedy. *Edinburgh, printed*, 1663. 8°. ALDIS 1756. L, O, LVD, OW, EN; CH, LC.

4564 **Clarke, William, *fellow of Oriel*.** The natural history of nitre. *By E. Okes for Nathaniel Brook*, 1670. 8° T.C.I 48. L, O, C, LG, DT; CH, CLC, WF, WU, Y.

4565 **Clarke, William, *of Hennington, Northamptonshire*.** The rest-less ghost. *For John Millet*, [1675]. 4°.* L.

—Synopsis anni. Cambridge, 1668. *See* Almanacs.

4566 **Clarke, William, *of North Crawley, Bucks*.** Αγαπαι ασπιλοι, or the innocent love-feast. *For William Lee*, 1656. 4°.* LT, O, LW, OCC, DT; IU, MH, NU.

[–] Decimarum & oblationum tabula. 1658. *See* Crashaw, William.

4567　Entry cancelled.

4568　**Clarke, William,** *of Pembroke, Camb.* The grand tryal . . . Book of Job. *Edinburgh, by the heir of Andrew Anderson,* 1685. fol. ALDIS 2535. L, EN, FSF; CH, MH, MU.

4568A　**Clarke, William,** *Quaker.* One blow more at the Sadducees. colop: *By J. Bradford,* 1697. cap., 4°.* MH.

4569　**[Clarkson, David].** The case of Protestants in England under a Popish prince. *For Richard Janeway,* 1681. 4°.* L, O, CT, EN, DT; CH, CN, MH, NU, WF, Y.

4570　——[Anr. ed.]. *Printed, to be sold by Richard Janeway,* 1689. 4°.* T.C.II 257. L, O; CH, NPT.

4571　[–] Diocesan churches not yet discovered. *For Thomas Parkhurst,* 1682. 4°. O, CT, LCL, EN, AU; NPT, NU, WF, Y.

4572　—A discourse concerning liturgies. *For Tho. Parkhurst, Jonathan Robinson, and Tho. Cockeril,* 1689. 8°. T.C.II 244. L, O, C, ENC, DT; BN, CH, MH, NU, WF, Y.

4573　—A discourse of the saving grace. *By J. Astwood, for Tho. Parkhurst,* 1688. 8°. T.C.II 229. L, LCL, LW, E, AU; CH, NP, NU, WF.

4574　[–] No evidence for diocesan churches. *For Thomas Parkhurst,* 1681. 4°. T.C.I 449. L, O, CT, LW, ENC; BN, CH, CLC, NU, WF, Y.

4575　[–] The practical divinity of the Papists. *For Tho. Parkhurst and Nath. Ponder,* 1676. 4°. T.C.I 226. L, O, C, E, DT; CH, NU, PL, WF, Y.

4576　—Primitive episcopacy. *For Nath. Ponder,* 1688. 8°. L, O, CT, LCL, ENC; CH, MH, NPT, NU, WF.

4577　——[Anr. ed.]. *For N. P. to be sold by Jonathan Robinson,* 1689. 4°. T.C.II 243. L, LCL, CT, AU; NPT, Y.

4578　—Sermons and discourses. *For Thomas Parkhurst,* 1696. fol. T.C.III 23. L, O, LCL, LW, ENC; NPT, NU, WF, Y.

4578A　**Clarkson, Lawrence.** A generall charge or, impeachment. *Printed,* 1647. 4°.* LT, OC; MH.

4579　—Look about you, for the Devil. *For the author, to be sold by William Learner,* 1659. 8°. L.

4580　—The lost sheep found. *For the author,* 1660. 4°. L, A; LC.

4581　—A paradisical dialogue. *For the author,* 1660. C, LLP; LC, PH.

4582　—The Quakers downfal. *For the authour, and are to be sold by Will. Learner,* 1659. 4°. LF, C, LLP; LC, MH, MU, PH.

4583　—The right devil discovered. *For the author, and are to be sold by Francis Cossinet,* 1659. 8°. L.

4584　—A single eye all light. *Imprinted at London by Giles Calvert,* [*Oct. 4, 1650*]. 4°.* LT, A.

4585　—Truth released from prison. *By Jane Coe, for John Pounset,* 1646. 8°.* LT.

　　　Claro Vado, Edward de, *pseud.*

　　　Claromont, C. *See* Clermont, C.

4585A　**Clarton, F.** Some considerations concerning the French protestant refugees. *E. Whitlock,* 1698. brs. L.

4586　**Claude, Isaac.** The Count d'Soissons. *By J.B. for R. Bentley and S. Magnes,* 1688. 12°. T.C.II 216. L; CLC, CN, MH.

4587　—A sermon upon the death of the Queen of England. *For John Dunton, to be sold by Edm. Richardson,* 1695. 4°.* L, O, LW; CH, MH, WF, Y.

4588　**[Claude, Jean.]** An account of the persecutions and oppressions. [*London*], *printed,* 1686. 4°. L, O, CT, EN, DT; CLC, CN, NU, PL, WF, Y.

4589　[–]—[Anr. ed.]. *For J. Norris,* 1686. 4°. L, O, C, HH, ENC; CH, MH, WF, Y.

4590　[–]—[Anr. ed.]. *Dublin, Reprinted for Joseph Howes,* 1686. 4°.* DIX 218. C, E, CD, DT; MBA.

4591　—Mr. Claude's answer to Monsieur de Meaux's book. *For T. Dring,* 1687. 4°. L, O, C, EN, DT; CH, MH, MIU, NU, Y.

4592　—The Catholick doctrine of the eucharist. *For R. Royston,* 1684. fol. T.C.II 37. L, O, C, CLC, ENC; NU, WF, Y.

4592A　—M. Claude's conference with M. de Condon. *Tho. Dring,* 1688. CH.

4593　—An historical defence of the Reformation. *By G.L. for John Hancock; and Benj. Alsop,* 1683. 4°. T.C.I 506. L, O, C, ENC, DT; CH, MH, NU, WF, Y.

4593A　——[Anr. ed.] *By G. Larkin, to be sold by T. Malthus,* 1683. 4°. LC.

4594　Entry cancelled.
　　　— A relation of the famous conference held about religion at Paris. 1684. *See* Bossuet, Jacques Bénigne, *bp.*

4595　—The second part of Mr. Claud's answer to Monsieur de Meaux's book. *For T. Dring,* 1688. 4°. L, O, CSS, EN, DT; CH, CN, MH, TU, Y.

4596　—Sermon sur le vers. 14 du chapit. vii de l'Ecclésiaste. *B. Griffin,* 1686. 8°.* OC; BN, LC.

4597　—A treatise of self-examination. *For Samuel Smith,* 1683. 8°. T.C.I 503. L, CT, P, GU.

4597A　——[Anr. ed.] *Edinburgh, by the heir of A. Anderson,* 1685. 12°. ALDIS 2536. EN.

4597B　A clause humbly offered to the consideration of the . . . Commons. [*London?* 1700.] brs. L.

4597C　The clauses chiefly objected against. [*London,* 1685.] brs. OC.

　　　Claustrum animæ. 1671. *See* Beaulieu, Luke de.
　　　Claustrum regale. 1667. *See* Wyndham, Anne.

4598　**Clavell, Robert.** A catalogue of all the books printed in England . . . 1666, to . . . 1672. *By S. Simmons for R. Clavel,* 1673. fol. O, OB, OC, WCA; CH, MN, WF.

4599　[–] A catalogue of books . . . 1666, to 1695. Fourth edition. *For R. Clavel, and B. Tooke,* 1696. fol. T.C.II 570. L, O, CT, EN, DT; BN, CH, CN, LC, WF, Y.

4600　—The general catalogue of books . . . to 1674. Second edition. *By Andrew Clark for Robert Clavel,* 1675. fol. T.C.I 192. L, O, CT, MR, ES; CH, CN, LC, MH, WCL, Y.

4601　——to 1680. Third edition. *By S. Roycroft for R. Clavell,* 1680. fol. L, O, C, OC, EN; BN, CH, CN, MBP, MH, WF.

4602　—His Majesties propriety. *By T. Mabb, for Andrew Kembe, and Edward Thomas; and Robert Clavel,* 1665. 8°. L, O, OC, E, EN; BN, CH, CN, LC, MHL, NC, RPJ, Y.

4603　——[Anr. ed.]. *For Edward Thomas,* 1672. 8°. L, OC; CH, LC, Y.

4604　**Clavell, Roger.** Tabulæ fœneratoriæ, or tables. *By J. Flesher for Nicholas Bourn,* 1653. 12°. LT; CLC.

4604A　——Second edition. *For R. Royston,* 1669. 4°. T.C.I 22. YM; Y.

4604B ——"Second" edition. *By John Macock for John Spicer*, 1669. 4°. OC; WF.

4605 ——Third edition. *For R. Horne, to be sold by Matthew Gillyflower and Henry Rogers*, 1683. 4°. T.C.II 34. L, O, C, LWL; Y.

Clavem, Gulielmum Liberam. *See* Freke, William.

4606 Clavis ad aperiendum carceris ostia. Or, the high point. *By James Cottrel, to be sold by him and by Richard Moone*, 1654. 4°. LT, O, LL; CH, MHL, WF.

Clavis apocalyptica ad incudem. [1653]. *See* Strong, William.

4607 Clavis apocalyptica: or, a prophetical key. *By William Du Gard for Thomas Matthewes, to bee sold by Giles Calvert*, 1651. 12°. LT, O, C, LW; NU.

4608 Clavis Apocalyptica: or, the Revelation. Second edition. *By W. D. for Tho. Matthews*, 1651. 8°. O, P.

Clavis calendaria. 1700. *See* C., W.

Clavis grammatica. 1678. *See* B., F.

Clavis Homerica. 1647. *See* Roberti, Antonius.

4608A Clavis Terentiana. *By G. Croom, to be had at H. Bonwicks, H. Hindmarsh*, [167–?] 8°. CS; MH.

Claxton, Laurence. *See* Clarkson, Laurence.

4609 **Clayton, Anne.** A letter to the King. [*London*, 1660.] brs. LF.

4610 **Clayton, John.** Reports and pleas of Assises at Yorke. *By Ja. Flesher, for W. Lee, D. Pakeman, and G. Bedell*, 1651. 8°. L, O, CT, LL, LIC; CH, MHL, NCL, WF, YL.

4611 —A sermon preached . . . February the 23d, 1700. *Dublin; by Joseph Ray*, [1700]. 4°.* L, OC, CS; TU.

4612 —Topicks in the laws of England. *By R. L. for William Leake*, 1646. 8°. L, O, C, LL, EN; CH, MHL, NCL, WF, YL.

4613 ——[Anr. ed.]. —, 1647. 8°. CP; BN, MHL.

4614 **Clayton, Prudence.** John Clayton, executor of Dame Mary Clayton, . . . Prudence Clayton, respondent. [*London*, 1699]. brs. L.

4614A **Clayton, *Sir* Robert.** By the mayor . . . 29 Nov. *By Samuel Roycroft*, 1679. brs. L.

4614B —By the mayor . . . Mar. 23. [*London*, 1680.] brs. L.

4614C —By the mayor. To the alderman's son. *By Samuel Roycroft*, 1680. brs. L, LG.

4615 —The speech of. colop: *For Tho. Collins*, 1679. cap., fol.* L, O, C, LG, HH; CH, CN, MH, WF, Y.

[–] Truth vindicated. 1681. *See* Treby, George.

4616 —By the mayor. Whereas it appears. *By Samuel Roycroft, London*, [1680]. brs. L.

Cleare and evident way. 1650. *See* Keymor, John.

4617 A cleere and full vindication of the late proceedings of the armie. *For William Larnar*, 1647. 4°.* LT, OC, SP, YM; CLC, CN, MH, WF, Y.

4618 A cleare answer to the armies late remonstrance. [*London*], printed, 1648. 4°.* LT, C, YM; CH, MH, TU, WF, Y.

Cleere antithesis. 1644. *See* Downing, Calybute.

Clear, attractive, warning beam. *Aberdeen*, 1657. *See* Guthrie, William.

Clear discovery of the errors. 1700. *See* T., L.

Clear discovery. [*n.p.*], 1662. *See* Fox, George.

4619 A clear discovery of the malicious falshoods. *Edinburgh, by the heir of Andrew Anderson*, 1679. fol.* ALDIS 2149. EN; MH.

Clear explanation upon all the chief points. 1697. *See* Marsin, M.

Clear looking-glas. Roane, 1657. *See* Eyston, Bernard Francis.

4620 A clear proof of the certainty and usefulness of the Protestant rule of faith. *By Henry Hills*, 1688. 4°.* LIL, OC, CT, EN, DT; NU, TU, WF.

4621 The cleere sense: or, a just vindication. *By M. Simmons*, 1645. 4°.* LT, LSC, YM; CH, CLC, MH, NU, WF.

Clear vindication. [*n.p.*], 1659. *See* Davenport, Francis.

Clear voice of truth. [*n.p.*], 1662. *See* Baker, Daniel.

4622 The clearing of Master Cranford's text. *By Tho. Paine, for John Sweeting*, [1646]. brs. LT, LUG; MH.

4623 **Cleaver, John.** The subjects duty. *For Rich. Chiswell*, 1676. 4°. T.C.I 245. CT, WCA; Y.

4623A ——[Anr. ed.] *For William Oliver in Norwich*, 1676. 4°. WF.

4624 Entry cancelled.

4625 [**Cleeve, C.**] The songs of Moses and Deborah paraphras'd. *For Luke Meredith*, 1685. 8°. T.C.II 98. L, P; CU, MH, WF, Y.

4625A **Cleevelye, William.** The deceitful spirit discovered. [*London*, 1667.] 4°.* LF, BBN; PH.

4626 **Clegate, Edward.** Clegates travails, from Terra Incognita. *By H. H. for G. C.*, 1650. 8°. LT.

4626A [**Cleirac, Etienne**]. The ancient sea-laws of Oleron. *By J. Redmayne, for T. Basset and Eliz. Smith*, 1686. fol.* LL, BAMB; LC, MB, MHL, NC, PL.

Χλεἰζ ευαγγελίου. 1672. *See* Sherwin, William.

4626B **Cleland, Thomas.** The Christians encouragement. *By D. M.*, 1660. 4°. LSC.

4627 **Cleland, William.** A collection of several poems and verses. [*n.p.*], *printed in* 1697. 8°.* L, A, E, AU, EN; CH, MH, Y.

Clelia. 1655. *See* Scudéry, Madeleine de.

4628 **Clemens, Titus Flavius, Alexandria.** Κλημεντοζ . . . Λογοζ Liber. *Oxoniæ, e theatro Sheldoniano*, 1683. 12°. L, O, CT, EN, DT; CH, WF, Y.

4629 **Clemens I, Romanus, pope.** Clement, the blessed Pavl's fellow-labourer . . . his first epistle. *By J. Y. for J. P. and O. P.*, 1647. 4°. LT, O, C, EN, DT; CH, NU, WF, Y.

4630 —The first epistle of. *For Andrew Crook*, 1652. 4°. L, O, C, LW, E.

4631 —Κλήμεντοζ πρὸζ Κοριηθίουζ ἐπιστολή. Ad Corinthios. *Oxoniæ, exc. A. & L. Lichfield*, 1669. 12°. MADAN 2822. L, O, C, CT, E; CLC, CU, IU, WF, Y.

4632 —Τού ἐν ἀγίοζ αδιοις . . . S. Patris Clementis ad Corinthios epistola. *Oxoniæ, e theatro Sheldoniano*, 1677. 12°. MADAN 3138. L, O, C, EN, DT; CLC, NC, OCI, WF, Y.

4633 —S. Clementis epistolæ duæ. *Impensis Jacobi Adamson*, 1687. 8°. T.C.II 179. L, O, C, YM, DT; MH, NR, TU.

4634 ——[Anr. ed.] —, 1694. 8°. T.C.II 534. L, CK, CT, LW, DT; MBA.

4635 — —[Anr. ed.] *Impensis Jaoobi* [*sic*] *Adamson.* 1695. 8°.
O, C, DT; CH.

4636 **Clement IX, *pope*.** A letter. *Printed,* 1674. 4°. L, CT.

4637 [**Clement, Simon.**] A dialogue between a countrey gentleman and a merchant. *By James Astwood for Samuel Crouch,* 1696. 4°.* L, CT, E; CH, CU, MH, WF, Y.

4638 [–] A discourse of the general notions of money. *Printed,* 1695. 4°.* L, O, C, EN, GH; CH, CU, MH, WF, Y.

4638A [–] The interest of England as it stands. *By John Attwood,* 1698. 4°.* L, LUG; CH, CN, MH, WF, Y.

4638B [–] —[Anr. ed.] *Dublin,* 1698. 4°.* DIX 303. DK.

4639 [**Clenche, John.**] Tour in France and Italy, made by an English gentleman . . . 1675. *For the author,* 1676. 4°. L, HH; WF, Y.

4640 [**Clenche, William.**] St. Peter's supremacy faithfully discuss'd, . . . first book. *By Henry Hills,* 1686. *to be sold by Matthew Turner,* 4°. L, O, LIL, OME, MC; CH, NPT, NU, WF, Y.

4641 **Clendon, Thomas.** Justification justified. *By Robert Ibbitson,* 1653. 4°.* LT, O, LG, LSC, CM; NU, WF.

4641A —A serious and brief discourse touching the Sabbath. *By A. M. for Edward Brewster,* 1674. 4°.* T.C.I 176. SP, EN; CH, NGT, Y.

Cleombrotus, *pseud.*
Cleopatra, 1652. *See* La Calprenède, Gautier de Coste de.
Cleophilus. [*n.p.*], 1700. *See* Waterhouse, David.

4642 **Clerambault, Philippe de.** The conversations. *Henry Herringman,* 1672. 8°. T.C.I 119. O, CT; CN, Y.

4643 — —[Anr. ed.] *By J. C. for Henry Brome,* 1677. 12°. T.C.I 281. L, O, C, P, M; CN.

4644 The clergyes bill of complaint, or submissive suite. *At Oxford* [*London*], *for Leonard Lichfield,* 1643. 4°.* MADAN 1180. LT, O, CT, LG, YM; CH, CLC, NU, WF, Y.

4645 —[Anr. ed.] *Richard Badger,* 1643. 4°. CT.

4646 Entry cancelled.

4647 The clergy's late carriage to the king. *colop: For H. L. and I. K. 2 July,* [1688]. brs. L, O, C, CT; CH, TU, Y.

Clergie in their colors. 1651. *See* Boun, Abraham.
Clergy vindicated. 1679. *See* Brydall, John.
Clergy-man of the Church. 1688. *See* Elys, Edmund.
Clericus. *See* Clarke, Samuel.
Clericus, Johannes. *See* LeClerc, Jean.

4648 **Clerk, Robert.** The speech of . . . to the mayor-elect. *colop: For Rob. Chown,* 1684. fol.* O; CH, CN.
Clerk of assize. 1660. *See* W., T.

4649 The clerk of the rope-yard's weekly return. [*n.p.*], 1688. brs. MC.

Clerke. *See* Clarke.
Clerks assistant. 1683. *See* F., G.
Clerk's grammer. 1683. *See* F., G.

4650 The clerk's manual. *By George Sawbridge, William Raw-lins, and Samuel Roycroft, assigns of Edward Atkins* 1678, *and are to be sold by J. Harrison, and J. Hill.* 8°. T.C.I 290. L, O, LL; LC, MHL, NCL.
Clarks tutor for arithmetick. [*n.p.*, 1667.] *See* Cocker, Edward.

Clerks tutor in Chancery. 1688. *See* Brown, William, *clerk.*

4651 The clerks vade mecum. *By T. M. for W. Lee, D. Pake-man, and G. Bedell,* 1655. 8°. L; MHL, WF.

4652 **Clermont, Charles.** De aëre, locis, & aquis. *Typis Thomae Roycroft, & impensis Johannis Martyn,* 1672. 12°. T.C.I 98. L, O, C, EN, AU; BN, CH, NAM, WF, HC.

4653 [**Cleveland, Barbara Palmer, *countess of*.**] The graci-ous answer of. [*London,* 1668.] brs. L.

4654 **Cleveland, John.** The works of. *By R. Holt, for Oba-diah Blagrave,* 1687. 8°. T.C.II 211. L, O, C, EN, DT; BN, CH, CN, MH, NC, TU, WF, Y.

4655 — —[Anr. ed.] *For O. B. and are to be sold by J. Sprint,* 1699. 8°. T.C.III 127. L, O, CT, LVF, ENC; CH, CU, MBP, MH, Y.

4656 [–] The character of a country committee-man. *Printed,* 1649. 4°.* LT, O, SP, DT; BN, CH, CN, MH, NU, WF.

4657 —A character of a diurnal-maker. *Printed . . . year,* 1654. 4°.* LT, O, LL; CH, LC, WC, Y.

4658 — —[Anr. ed.] *Printed . . . yeare,* 1654. 4°.* L; CN.

4659 [–] The character of a London diurnall. [*Oxford, by L. Lichfield*], *printed,* 1644[/5]. 4°.* MADAN 1708. LT, O, C, CJ; CH, CN, MH, Y.

4660 [–] —Second edition. —, 1644[/5]. 4°.* MADAN 1709. L, O; CH, Y.

4661 [–] —Third edition. [*n.p.*], *printed in the yeare,* 1644. 4°.* O; CH, NHS, W.

4662 [–] —Third edition, 17 poems. [*n.p.*], *printed,* 1647. 4°. LT, O, C, LL, DC; CH, CU, MH, WF, Y.

4663 [–] —Third edition, 18 poems. [*n.p.*], *printed,* 1647. 4°. OC, CM, CSS; CH, CLC, MH, WF, Y.

4663A [–] —Third edition, 20 poems. [*n.p.*], *printed,* 1647. 4°. L; CH, MH.

4664 [–] —Fourth edition. —, 1647. 4°. L, OW, AN; CH, MH.

4665 Entry cancelled.

4666 [–] —"Fourth" [i.e., sixth] edition. 22 poems. —, 1647. 4°. L, CCH, DM; CH, MH, TU, WF.

4667 [–] —"Fifth" [i.e., seventh] edition, 23 poems. —, 1647. 4°. O, EN; CH, MH, MU, WF, Y.

4668 —The character of a moderate intelligencer. [*London,* 1647.] 4°.* LT, O, CJ, HH; CH, WF.

4669 —Clievelandi vindiciæ. *For Nath. Brooke,* 1677. 8°. O, OM, CCH, CM, CS; CH, CN, MH, NP, WF, Y.

4670 — —Second issue. *For Obadiah Blagave,* 1677. 8°. T.C.I 284. L, CT, LVD, OC, EN; CH, CU, MH, TU, WF, Y.

4671 — —Third issue. *For Robert Harford,* 1677. 4°. LG, DM; CH, MH, NU, TU, Y.

4671A [–] The hue and cry after Sir John Presbyter [*London* 1649.] brs. LT, O.

4672 [–] The idol of the clownes, . . . with his fellow kings. *Printed in the year,* 1654. 8°. LT, O, C, MR, EN; CH, CU, LC, MH, TU, WC, Y.

4673 [–] The idol of the clownes, . . . with his priests. *Printed,* 1654. 8°. OC, CS, CT; CH, MH, NU, WF, Y.

4674 —J. Cleaveland revived: poems, orations. *For Nathaniel Brook,* 1659. 8°. L, O, CS; CH, CN, MH, WF, Y.

4675 — —Second edition. *For Nathaniel Brooke*, 1660. 8°. LT, O, CS, DC, GU; CH, CN, MH, NU, Y.

4676 — —Third edition. *For Nathaniel Brook*, 1662. 8°. L, O, C, EN; CH, LC, MH, TU, Y.

4677 — —Fourth edition. *For Nathaniel Brooks*, 1668. 8°. L, O, OB, CS; CH, CU, MH, TU, WF, Y.

4678 [-] The kings disguise. [*London*, 1646.] cap., 4°.* LT, O, OC; CH, MH, Y.

4679 [-] Majestas intemerata. Or, the immortality of the king. [*London*], printed, 1649. 12°. LT, O, C, EN, DT; BN, CH, CU, LC, MH, NU, Y.

4680 [-] —[Anr. ed.] —, 1689. 4°. O, OC, OM, CT, MR; CLC, TU, WF, Y.

[-] Midsummer-moone. [*n.p.*], 1648. *See* Winyard, Thomas.

4681 [-] Monumentum regale or a tombe. [*London*], printed, 1649. 8°.* LT, O, OC, YM, E; CH, CN, MH, TU, WF, Y.

4682 [-] News from Newcastle. *Printed*, 1651. *By William Ellis*, 4°.* LT, O.

4683 —Cleaveland's petition to His Highnesse the Lord Protector. [*London*], *for William Sheares*, [1657.]. brs. LT, O, CS, HH; CH, CLC, NIC.

4684 [-] Poems. [*n.p.*], printed, 1651. 50ll. C, CK; CH, CU, MH.

4685 — — —, 1651. 56ll. L, OC, CCH; CH, CN.

4686 — —[Anr. ed.] [*n.p.*], 1651. 40ll. L; CH, CLC, MH, NN, WF.

4687 — —Sixth edition, 28 poems. [*London*], printed . . . year, 1651. 8°. O, OW, CS; NIC.

4687A — —Seventh edition, 32 poems. . . . *yeare*, 1651. 8°. C, OC; CH.

4688 — —Eighth edition, 33 poems. —, 1653. 8°. O, CS, CT, P; BN, CH, CN, MH, WF, Y.

4689 — —Ninth edition, 38 poems. [*n.p.*], printed . . . year, 1653. 8°. L, EN; CH, CLC, CU, MB, WF.

4689A — —Tenth edition. — 1654. 8°. L, O, C; CLC, CN, MH, NIC, WF.

4690 [-] —Eleventh edition. [*London*], printed . . . year, 1654. 8°. O, C, EC; CH, LC, MH, TU, WC, Y.

4691 [-] —Twelfth edition. [*London*], printed . . . yeare, 1656. 8°. L, LVF, OC, DT; CH, MH, WF, Y.

4692 — —Thirteenth edition. [*n.p.*], printed . . . year, 1657. 8°. L, O, CS; CH, CU, MH, TU.

4692A — —[Anr. ed.] —, 1658. 12°. CQ, DT.

4693 — —[Anr. ed.] *Printed*, 1658. 12°. L, CT; MH.

4694 — —Fourteenth edition. [*London*], *for W. Shears*, 1659. 8°. L, O, OW, LG, CS; BN, CH, CU, MH, TU, Y.

4695 — —Fifteenth edition. *For John Williams*, 1661. 8°. L, O, CE, CT, LVF; CH, CN, MH, WF, Y.

4696 — —Sixteenth edition. *For W. Shears*, 1662. 8°. L, O, C, LVF, EN; CH, MBP, NN, TU, Y.

4697 — —Seventeenth edition. *By S. G. for John Williams*, 1665. 8°. L, CCH, CS, GK; CH, MH, WF, Y.

4698 — —Nineteenth edition. *By J. R. for John Williams*, 1669. 8°. L, O, OB, OC; CH, CU, LC, MH, TU, Y.

4698A [-] The rebellion of the rude multitude. *Printed and sold by J. R.*, 1680. 4°. MH.

4699 —The rustick rampant. Third edition. *For F. C.*, 1658. 8°. LT, O, CT, A; CH, CN, MH, WF, Y.

4699A [-] The Scots apostasy. [*London*, 1647.] brs. LT; FU, MH.

4699B [-] —[Anr. ed.] [*London*, 1648.] 4°.* LT, O, HH, DT; CH, MH.

4699C **Clieland, William.** To his Grace, His Majesties Commissioner. [*London?* 1690.] cap., fol.* L.

4700 **Cliffe, E.** An abreviate of Hollands deliverance. *Printed*, 1665. 4°. L, CT; CH, RPJ, WF, Y.

Clifford, Abraham. Almanack. [1642.] *See* Almanacs.

[-] Discourse of the nature, ends. 1673. *See* Allen, William.

4701 —Methodus evangelica. *By J. M. for Brabazon Aylmer*, 1676. 12°. T.C.I 234. L, O, C, LCL, ENC; NPT, NU, Y.

Clifford, Henry. *See* Cumberland, Henry Clifford, earl of.

4702 **Clifford, James.** A catechism containing the principles of Christian religion. *For J. Deacon*, 1694. 8°. T.C.II 508. O, C.

4702A — —[Anr. ed.] *By J. Wilde, for S. Deacon*, 1695. 8°. CT.

4703 —The divine services and anthems. *By W. G. to be sold by Henry Brome*, 1663. 8°. O, C; CLC, Y.

4704 — —Second edition. *By W. G. to be sold by Nathaniel Brooke: and Henry Brome*, 1664. 12°. L, O, CT, YM; LC, MH, WF, WWC.

4705 **Clifford, John.** Sound words. *By W. Pearson, for John Lawrence*, 1699. 12°. T.C.III 120. LW.

4706 **Clifford, Martin.** Notes upon Mr. Dryden's poems. *Printed*, 1687. 4°.* L, O, C, CT, LVD; BN, CH, CN, MH, MU, NP, TU, WF, Y.

4707 [-] A treatise of humane reason. *For Hen. Brome*, 1674. 12°. L, LW, CT, EC, P; CSU, NU, PL, WF, HC.

4708 [-] —[Anr. ed.] —, 1675. 12°. L, O, C, LCL, CT; BN, CLC, CU, MH, NU, WF, Y.

4709 — —"Second" edition. *For Charles Brome*, 1691. 8°. T.C.II 353. L, O, AU; OCI, Y.

4709A **Clifford, Thomas.** A true copy of the Lord High Treasurer's letter. [*London*, 1672.] cap., 4°.* L.

4710 **C[lifford], W[illiam].** Christian rules proposed. [*Paris*], printed, 1659. 12°. L, OC; BN, TU.

4711 — —Third edition. —, 1665. 8°. L, O, C; NU, TU, WF, Y.

4712 —The little manvel of the poore mans dayly devotion. *Printed at Paris by Vincent dv Movtier*, 1669. 12°. L; NU.

4713 — —Second edition. —, 1670. 12°. L, OC; BN.

4714 — —Third edition. —, 1682. 12°. O; YM.

4715 —The power of kings. *By Samuel Roycroft, for Robert Clavell, to be sold by Francis Bentley in Hallifax*, 1682. 4°.* T.C.I 483. L, O, C, YM; CH, MH, NU, PU, WF, Y.

4715A **[Clift, Samuel].** A true relation of the persecution of. [*London*, 1657.] 4°.* L, LF, BBN; MH, PH.

Climsall, Richard, *pseud.*

4716 The clippers execution: or, treason justly rewarded. [*n.d.*] brs. O.

4716A **Clipsham, Margery.** The spirit that works abomination. [*London*, 1685.] brs. LF; PH, Y.

4716B — —[Anr. ed.] [*London*], printed, 1685. 4°.* L, LF, BBN; PH, PSC.

4717 **Clipsham, Robert.** The grand expedient. *For William Freeman,* 1685. 8°. T.C.II 100. L, O, C, CT, EN; MH, NU, WF.

Clito: a poem. 1700. *See* Toland, John.

4718 A cloak for knavery. [*n.p.,* 1642?] brs. LS.

4719 The cloak in its colours. *Printed,* 1679. 4°.* LT, O, LL, LVF, WCA; CH, CU, WF, Y.

4719A —[Anr. ed.] *By N. T.,* 1679. 4°.* OC.

4720 **Cloake, Hugh.** A call from sin to holiness of life. *Printed,* 1685. 4°.* LF, BBN; CH.

4721 The cloak's knavery. [*London,* 1660?] brs. L.

4722 **Clobery, Christopher.** Divine glimpses of a maiden muse. *By James Cottrel,* 1659. 8°. L; CH.

4722A The clock makers reasons. [*London,* 1698.] brs. MH.

Clod, Barnaby, *pseud.*

4722B **Clodius, Joannes.** Brevis dissertatio de ratione status. 1658. 8°. O, C.

4723 **Clodoveus,** *king.* A sweet prosopopeia of the speech of. [*n.p.,* 1643.] brs. LT, MC.

Clod-pate's ghost. [*n.p.,* 1679.] *See* Smith, Francis.

4724 **Clogie, Alexander.** Vox corvi: or, the voice of a raven. *By W. B. to be sold by R. Baldwin,* 1694. 12°. T.C.II 474. L, O, C, LCL, CT; MH, NPT, WF.

4725 Cloria and Narcissus. *By S. G., and are to be sold by Anth. Williamson,* 1653. 8°. L, LW, HH; CH, CU, MH, NC, Y.

4725A —[Anr. ed.] —, 1658. 8°. CU, CLC, Y.

4726 Cloria and Narcissus continued. *By S. G. to be sold by Anth. Williamson,* 1654. 8°. LT, LW, DC, HH; CH, CN, MH, NC, Y.

4726A Cloria the mortle grave. [*London?* 1690]. brs. L.

Close hypocrite discovered. 1654. *See* N., G.

4727 Closet-devotions. *For Henry Mortlock,* 1692. 12°. T.C.II 378. L, O.

4727A A closet for ladies. *By Richard Hodgkinson,* 1641. 12°. VC.

4727B —[Anr. ed.] *For Charles Green,* 1644. 12°. CLC.

4728 —[Anr. ed.] *By R. H. for Charles Greene,* 1647. 12°. L; ICT, WF.

4729 —[Anr. ed.] *By R. H.,* 1651. 12°. L, LWL.

4730 —[Anr. ed.] —, 1654. 12°. L, CT; LC.

4731 —[Anr. ed.] —, 1656. 12°. L; NN.

4732 The cloath-worker caught in a trap. *For W. Thackeray, T. Passenger, and W. Whitwood,* [1670]. brs. L, O, CM, HH.

4732A The cloathiers answers. [*London?* 1700.] brs. MH.

4733 The clothiers case truly stated. [*n.p.,* 1693?] brs. C, LL.

4734 The clothiers complaint. *For Randal Taylor,* 1692. 4°.* T.C.II 427. L, O, C, EN; MH, NC, Y.

4734A The clothier's delight. [*London*], *for F. Coles, T. Vere, J. Wright and J. Clarke,* [1682.] brs. L.

4735 The clothiers petition to His Majestie. *For Peter Cole,* 1642. brs. STEELE 1982. LT, LG, EC.

4735A The clothiers reasons for establishing the Company of merchant adventurers. [*London,* 169-?] brs. MH, NC.

4735B The clothiers reply to the Dutch interloper. [*London,* 169-?] brs. MH, NC.

4736 Cloathing for the naked woman. *Printed, and to be sold by Giles Calvert,* 1652. 4°.* LT.

Cloud of witnesses. 1665. *See* Mall, Thomas.

—[*n.p.,* 1700?] *See* Mather, Cotton.

4737 The cloud opened. *Printed A. D.,* 1670. L, O, EN; CH, MM.

Cloudie clergie. 1650. *See* Price, John.

4738 [**Clouet, François.**] The converted Capuchin. *By E. G. and are to be sold by Richard Harper,* 1641. 4°.* LT, O, LSC; NU, WF.

4739 **Clough, James.** A true copy of the paper delivered by. colop: [*London*], *T. Paine,* [1680?]. brs. L.

Clough, Samuel. New-England almanack. Boston, [1700]. *See* Almanacs.

Club, Roger. *See* Crab, Roger.

4740 **Clüver, Philip.** An introduction into geography. *Oxford, by L. Lichfield for R. Blagrave,* 1657. 8°. MADAN 2333. L, O; MH, WF.

4741 —Philippi Cluverii introductionis in vniversam geographiam. *Oxoniæ, per R. Blagrave,* 1657. 12°. MADAN 2332. O, CM, P; RPJ.

4741A ——[Anr. ed.] *Prostant apud Sam. Smith & Benj. Walford,* 1697. 12°. WF.

Cluster of coxcombes. 1642. *See* Taylor, John.

Cluster of sweetest grapes. 1664. *See* Jelinger, Christopher.

Cluster of Worcestershire fruit. 1675. *See* P., J.

4742 **Clutterbuck, John.** A plain and rational vindication of the liturgy. *By J. L. for William Keblewhite,* 1694. 8°. T.C.II 519. L, O, C, CT, BAMB; NU.

4743 ——Second edition. *For William Keblewhite,* 1699. 8°. T.C.III 114. NU, WF.

4744 **Clutterbuck, Thomas.** A spittle-sermon. *For Walter Kettilby,* 1687. 4°. T.C.II 192. L, O, C, BAMB; NPT, NU, WF, Y.

Cluverius, P. *See* Clüver, Philip.

Clypeus septemplex. [*n.p.*], 1677. *See* Sergeant, John.

4745 Entry cancelled.

4746 **Coachman, Robert.** The cry of a stone. *By R. Oulton, and G. Dexter,* 1642. 4°. LT, O, C, CT, LCL; CLC, Y.

4747 Entry cancelled.

4748 The coal traders and consumers case. [*n.p.,* 1692?] brs. LL; CH.

4748A **Coale, Benjamin.** A short testimony. [*London,* 1694.] 4°.* LF.

4749 **Coale, Joseph.** A testimony of the Father's love. *For Robert Wilson,* 1661. 4°.* L, O, LF, BBN; IE, PH, PSC, Y.

4750 —To all that desire. *Printed,* 1667. 4°.* L, O, LF, BBN, BP; CH, MH, PH, WF, Y.

4750A —To all you ministers. [*London*], 1666. brs. LF.

4751 **Coale, Josiah.** The books and divers epistles. [*London*], printed, 1671. 4°. L, O, LG, OC, CT; CH, CN, MH, NU, WF, Y.

4752 —England's sad estate lamented. [*London*], printed, 1665. 4°.* L, O, LF, BBN; CH, MH, PH, PSC, WF.

4753 —An epistle to the flock of God. [*London*], printed, 1665. 4°. L, O, LF, BBN; PH, PSC.

4754 —An invitation of love. *For Thomas Simmons,* 1660. 4°.* L, O, CT, BBN; CH, MH, PH, PSC, Y.

4755 —A salutation to the suffering-seed. *For William War-wick*, 1663. 4°.* L, O, LF, BBN; CH, MH, PH, WF, Y.

4756 —A song of the judgments and mercies. [*London*], *printed*, 1662. 8°.* LF.

4756A — —[Anr. ed.] —, 1663. 4°.* L, LF, BBN; CLC, PH, PHS, PSC.

4757 — —[Anr. ed.] —, 1669. 4°.* L, O, C, LF; CH, PH, RPJ, TU, WF, Y.

4758 —To all the babes in Christ. [*London*], *printed*, 1664. 4°.* L, O, LF, BBN; CH, MH, PH, PSC, Y.

4759 —To the King and both houses. [*London*], 1664. brs. LF, BBN; MH, PSC, PW.

4760 —The whore unvailed. [*London*], *printed*, 1665. 4°. L, LF, LW, BBN; PSC, Y.

4760A — —[Anr. ed.] —, 1667. 4°.* MH, PHS.

4761 [**Coale, Leonard.**] To the bishops and their ministers, or any of them. [*London*], *printed*, 1671. 4°.* L, C, LF, EN; CH, MH, NR, PH, PSC, Y.

4762 **Coales, John.** A glasse of truth. *Imprinted at London*, 1649. 4°.* O; CN.

4763 The coat of arms of N.T. J.F. & R.L. An answer to Thomson's ballad call'd The loyal feast. colop: *Dublin, for A. Banks*, [1682?], brs. L; CH, MH, Y.

4764 The coat of armes of Sir John Presbyter. [*London*], *printed*, 1658. brs. LT, O.

4765 —[Anr. ed.] [*London*], *by R. Eeles*, 1661. brs. L.

4766–7 Entries cancelled.

4768 —[Anr. ed.] *Printed*, 1678. brs. CH.
       Coat of divers colovrs. [*n.p.*], 1656. *See* W., Jos.

4769 **Cob, Christopher.** The sect every where. *By J. Macock for Giles Calvert*, 1651. 8°. LT, O, C, LCL; MH, MIU, NU, WF.

4770 **Cobb, Samuel.** Bersaba: or, the love of David. *Printed and are to be sold by J. Whitlock*, 1695. 4°.* L, CT, DT.

4771 —Pax redux: a Pindarick ode. *For E. Whitlock*, 1697. fol.* L; MH.

4772 —A pindarick ode: humbly offer'd to the ever-blessed memory of our late gracious sovereign. *For John Whitlock*, 1694. fol.* L, O, CT; CH, CN, MH, WF, Y.

4772A — —Second edition, —, 1694. fol.* L, LG; CLC, MH, TU, WF, Y.

4773 [–] Poetae Britannici. A poem. *For A. Roper, and R, Basset, sold by Mr. Jeffries in Cambridge*, 1700. fol.* L. O, CS, HH; TU, WF.

4774 **Cobbet, Ralph, Col.** A letter sent by . . . Oct. 27, 1659. *Printed*, 1659. 4°. L, DT; CH, MH, MU, PL, WF, Y.

4775 **Cobbet, Robert.** A word to the upright. *Printed*, 1668. 4°.* O; MBA.

4776 **Cobbet, Thomas.** The civil magistrates power. *By W. Wilson for Philemon Stephens*, 1653. 4°. LT, O, LCL, LW, ENC; CH, CN, MH, NU, RPJ, Y.

4777 —A fruitfull and usefull discourse. *By S. G. for John Rothwell*, 1656. 8°. L, O, CT, LCL, LW; CH, CN, MH, RPJ, HC.

4778 —A jvst vindication of the Covenant. *By R. Cotes for Andrew Crooke*, 1648. 4°. O, C, LCL, EN, DT; NPT, NU, RPJ, WF, Y.

4779 —A practical discourse of prayer. *By T. M. for Ralph Smith*, 1654. 8°. LT, C; MB, MH, NU, Y.

4780 — —[Anr. ed.] *By T. M. for Joseph Cranford*, 1654. 8°. L; CN, MH, NPT, RPJ, WF, Y.

4781 — —[Anr. ed.] *By R. I. for Thomas Newberry*, 1657. 8°. L, O, LCL, LW, CE; CH, MH, NU, RPJ, Y.

4782 The cobler turned courtier. *For F. Haley*, 1680. 4°.* L, O; CN, MH, Y.

4783 Entry cancelled.
       Coblers end, 1641. *See* Vincent, Humphrey.

4784 The cobler's golden prize. *For J. Shooter*, [1697–99]. brs. HH.

4785 The cobler's last will and testament. [*London*, 1660?] brs. L, O; MH.

4786 **Cobham, Joshua.** Joshua Cobham's testimony. *Printed and sold by T. Sowle*, 1693. 8°.* LF, BBN; PH, PSC.
       Cochleia whose sur, 1676. *See* Mollenbrock, Valentia Andres.

4787–8 Entries cancelled.

4789 **Cock, Charles George.** English-law: or, a summary survey. *By Robert White for T. G. and Francis Tyton*, 6151. fol. L, O, C, CT, LM; MHL, NCL, NPT, WF, Y.

4790 **Cock, Thomas.** Advice for the poor by way of cure. [*n.p.*, 1665.] cap., 4°.* O, LG, LWL, HH; MH.

4791 —Ὑγιεινη; or, a plain and practical discourse. *By E. C. for Philem. Stephens, sen, Stephens jun., Peter Dring, Joseph Leigh*, 1665. 4°.* L, O, LWL, HH; CH, NAM, HC.

4791A [–] Kitchin-physick. *For J. B.* [1675?] 8°.* WF, WSG.

4792 [–]— —[Anr. ed.] *For the author, to be sold by T. Basset*, 1676. 8°. T.C.I 226. L, LW, LWL, LCS; CH, WSG, HC.

4792A [–]— —[Anr. ed.] *For Dorman Newman*, 1676. 8°. LWL.

4792B [–]— —[Anr. ed.] *For J. B.*, [c. 1686.] 8°. CH, WF, WU, HC.

4793 [–] Miscelanea medica: or, a supplement to kitchin-physick. *Printed*, 1675. 8°. L, LW, LWL; CH, WF, WSG, WU, HC.

4793A **Cock, William.** Doctrinæ substantiarum. *Edinburgi, Thomas Brown & Joannes Swintoun*, 1679. 8°. ALDIS 2150. L, GU.

4794 —Meteorologiæ, or, the true way of fore-seeing . . . the weather. *By J. C. for Jo. Conyers*, 1671. sixes T.C.I 55. O.

4794A —Revelatio revelata. *Edinburgi, typis Gideonis Shaw*, 1678. 12°. ALDIS 2125. EN, GU; Y.

4795 The cock crowing. [*n.p.*, 1659.] brs. O.

4796 The cock-pit combat. colop: *Printed*, 1699. brs. L, O, MC; CN, MH, NC, Y.

4796 **Cockain, Sir Aston.** *See* Cokayne, Sir Aston.

4796A C[ockarne], T[homas]. A Greek-English lexicon. *Printed and are to be sold by Warwick Lloyd*, 1650. 8°. LT; WF.

4797 **Cockburn, Alexander.** Illustrissimo . . . domino D. Gulielmo Marchioni de Quensberry. *Edinbrugi, hæres A Anderson*, 1684. brs. ALDIS 2495. E.

4798 —Nobilissimis . . . viris D. Magno Prince. *Edinburgi, hæres A Anderson*, 1688. brs. ALDIS 2824. E.

4799 —Theses philosophicæ. *Edinburgi, excudebat Andreas Andersonus*, 1675. 4°.* ALDIS 2068. E, SA, HG.

4800 — —*Edinburgi, excudebant Thomas Brown, & Ioannes Swintoun*, 1679. 4°.* ALDIS 2178. E, SA.

4801   [**Cockburn**, *Mrs.* **Catherine (Trotter**).] Agnes de Castro. *For H. Rhodes, R. Parker, and S. Briscoe*, 1696. 4°. T.C.II 570. L, O, OW, EN; CH, CN, LC, MH, NC, Y.

4802   [–] Fatal friendship; a tragedy. *For Francis Saunders*, 1698. 4°. L, O, CT, LGI, EN; CH, CN, LC, MH, NC, TU, Y.

4803   **Cockburn, John.** An account of the Presbyterian-government. *For Jos. Hindmarsh*, 1693. 4°. EN.

4804   —Bourignianism detected. Narrative I. (–II). *For W. Keblewhite, and H. Hindmarsh*, 1698. 4°. T.C.III 34. L, O, C, EN; CH, MIU.

4805   — —[Anr. ed.] *For C. Brome, W. Keblewhite, and H. Hindmarsh*, 1698. 4°. CT; MIU, WF.

4806   [–] A continuation of The historical relation. *By B. Griffin, for Samuel Keble*, 1691. 4°. T.C.II 385. L, O, CT, EN, AU; CH, CN, NU, PL, WF, Y.

4807   —Eight sermons. *Edinburgh, by John Reid; and are to sold [sic] at Andrew Chalmer's and Mrs. Ogstons shops and at John Vallange's shop*, 1691. 8°. ALDIS 3138. EN, NPT.

4808   —Fifteen sermons. *By J. L. for William Keblewhite*, 1697. 8°. T.C.III 21. L, LW, CT, ENC, EU; CLC, WF, Y.

4809   [–] An historical relation of the late General Assembly. *For J. Hindmarsh*, 1691. 4°. T.C.II 358. L, O, C, EN, AU; CH, CN, NU, PL, WF, Y.

4809A   [–] An historical relation of the late Presbyterian General Assembly. *For J. Hindmarsh*, 1691. 4°. CT, LW, HH, E; NU, TU.

4810   —An enquiry into the nature, necessity. Part I. *For William Keblewhite*, 1696. 8°. T.C.II 576. L, O, C, MR, DT; CLC, PL.

4811   — —Second edition. —, 1699–7. 8°. T.C.III 114. O, LW, OB, CS, DT; NU, PL, WF, Y.

4812   —Jacobs vow. *Edinburgh, by J. Reid for Alexander Ogston*, 1686. 8°. ALDIS 2636. L, E, EN, GU; NPT, WF.

4813   — —[Anr. ed.] *Edinburgh, for Alexander Ogston; to be sold by William Keblewhite*, 1696. 8°. T.C.II 598. EN; CLC.

4814   —A letter from. *For William Keblewhite; and Hannah Hindmarsh*, 1698. 4°.* T.C.III 63. L, O, C, BP, EN; MH, WU.

4815   **C[ockburn], W[illiam].** An account of the nature, causes, symptoms . . . distempers . . . incident to sea-faring people. *For Hugh Newman*, 1696. 12°. L, C, LCS, LR, OM; BN, HC.

4816   —A continuation of the account of the nature. *For Hugh Newman*, 1697. 12°. L, LR, LWL, EN; MIU.

4817   —Œconomia corporis animalis. *Excudebat F. Leach, impensis Hugonis Newman*, 1695. 8°. T.C.II 559. O, C, LCP, GH; BN, CLC, MH, WSG.

4818   **Cocker, Edward.** Cocker's accomplish'd schoolmaster. *For J. Back*, 1696. 8°. T.C.II 604. Y.

4818A   —Arithmetick. *E. Midwinter*, 1677. 8°. OP.

4819   — —*For T. Passenger and T. Lacy, and sold by C. Passinger*, 1678. 12°. T.C.I 290. L; CH, LC, WCL.

4819A   — —Second edition. *By T. Passenger for R. Sollers, C. Passenger and S. Foster*, 1678. 12°. T.C.I 376. LG.

4820   — —Third edition. —, 1680. 12°. L; MH, NC.

4821   — —Fourth edition. —, 1681. 12°. T.C.I 480. L, LG.

4822   — —[Anr. ed.] *[London], for Thomas Passinger*, 1685. 8°. LI, CCL; CSU.

4823   — —[Anr. ed.] *By R. Holt, for T. Passinger, to be sold by T. Lacy, Southwark*, 1688. 12°. T.C.II 213. O, C; MU, Y.

4824   — —[Anr. ed.] *For T. P. to be sold by John Back*, 1691. 12°. T.C.I 372. L; MU, Y.

4825   — —[Anr. ed.] *By J. R. for T. P. and are to be sold by John Back*, 1694. 12°. T.C.II 484. L, CT, EN; CLC.

4826   — —[Anr. ed.] *By J. R. for E. Tracey*, 1696. 12°. NC, WCL, WF, Y.

4827   — —Twenty-second edition. *By J. R. for Eben Tracey*, 1697. 12°. T.C.III 31. L, O, CS, LWL, D; CH.

4828   — —[Anr. ed.] *By J. R. for Eben Tracey*, 1698. 12°. T.CIII 68. L; CLC.

4829   — —"Twentieth" edition. —, 1700. 12°. T.C.III 203. L.

4830   —Arts glory. *[London], sold by Peter Stent, and William Fisher*, 1657. 8°. O.

4830A   — —Second edition. —, 1659. 8°. CM; CN.

4831   — —[Anr. ed.] *For, and are to be sold by Iohn Overton*, 1669. obl., fol. C.

4831A   — —[Anr. ed.] —, 1674. 8°. CN.

4832   — —[Anr. ed.] —, 1685. obl., 4°. L.

4832A   [–] The clarks tutor for arithmetick. [1667.] 8°. CN.

4832B   —The compleat writing master. *Sold by E. Pawlet*, [1670?] 4°.* CN.

4833   —Cocker's decimal arithmetick. *By J. Richardson, for Tho. Passinger, and Tho. Lacy*, 1685–4. 8°. T.C.II 109. L, O, EO; CH, CU, LC, MU, PL.

4833A   — —[Anr. ed.] *By J. Richardson, for Tho. Passinger and Tho. Sawbridge*, 1685. 8°. L, C; Y.

4834   — —Second edition. *For George Sawbridge: and Richard Wellington*, 1695. 8°. L, O, CPE; BN, CH, CLC, Y.

4835   —England's pen-man. *Printed, and sold by Henry Overton, and J. Hoole, London*, [1665?]. obl., 4°. L, LV; CN, NN.

4835A   — —[Anr. ed.] —, 1668. 4°. OP; CN.

4835B   — —[Anr. ed.] *For N. Brooke*, 1671. obl., 4°. T.C.I 81. OP.

4836   — —[Anr. ed.] 1677. obl., 4°. C.

4837   — —[Anr. ed.] *For Obadiah Blagrave*, 1678. obl., 16°. T.C.I 364. C; MH.

4838   —The guide to penmanship. *Sold by Robert Snow and by William Rumbold*, 1664. fol. L, O, CM; CH, CN.

4838A   — —Second edition. *For John Ruddiard*, 1673. fol. CN.

4839   —The London writing master. *[n.p.], sold by Robert Pask, and by T. L. Southwark*, 1672. obl. 4°.* T.C.I 120. L, CM.

4840   — —[Anr. ed.] *[London], sold by Robert Pask*, [1677]. obl., 4°. L; MH, NC.

4841   —Magnum in parvo or the pens perfection. *By J. Redmayne, to be sold by Tho. Rooks*, 1672. obl., 4°. T.C.I 114. L, LV; CN, Y.

4842   — —[Anr. ed.] *[London], sold by John Garrett*, [1675]. obl., 4°. L, O, EN; CN.

4843   —Cocker's morals. *By W. D. for T. D., and T. L.*, 1675. 4°. T.C.I 219. L; MH, TU.

4843A   — —[Anr. ed.] *For Thomas Drant*, 1675. 4°. MH.

4844   — —[Anr. ed.] *For Thomas Lacy*, 1694. 4°. L, O, DT; CN, NC, WF.

4845 —Multum in parvo. *To be sold by William Place and by Thomas Rookes, 1660.* obl., 4°. LG.

4846 ——[Anr. ed.] —, 1661. obl., 4°. L, CM; CN.

4847 ——[Anr. ed.] *[London], for Geo. Sawbridge,* [1680?] obl., 4°. T.C.I 386. L.

4847A ——[Anr. ed.] *[London], to be sold by Tho. Sawbridge,* 1683. 4°. T.C.II 65. L.

4848 ——[Anr. ed.] *For Samuel Manship,* 1687. 8°. WF.

4849 —Penna volans. *[London], for J. Ruddiard,* 1661. obl., 4°. O, LV, OP, CM; BN, CN.

4849A —The pen's celerity. *Robert Walton,* 1673. 8°. CN.

4850 —The pens transcendency. *[London], by Robert Walton,* [1660.] obl., fol. L; CH, CN.

4851 —The pen's triumph. *Sold by Samuel Ayre, London,* 1658. obl., 4°. L, O; CN.

4851A ——[Anr. ed.] *To be sold by John Dowse.* 1659. 4°. L; CN, Y.

4851B ——[Anr. ed.] *To be sold by Robert Walton,* 1660. 8°. WCL.

4852 —The rules of arithmetic. *[London,* 1660?] obl., fol.L.

4853 ——[Anr. ed.] *[London?* 1670?] obl., fol. L.

4854 —The tutor to writing. *Sold by Tho. Rooks, London,* 1664. obl., 4°. L; CLC.

4855 —Cocker's Urania. *By I.R. for Tho. Rooks,* [1670.] 4°. L.

4856 ——[Anr. ed.] *By W.G. and sold by William Rumbold.* [*n.d*] 4°. L [t.p. only].

4856A —The young clerks tutor. *For Robert Crofts,* 1662. 8°. L.

4856B ——[Anr. ed.] —, 1663. 8°. O.

4857 ——[Third edition. —, 1664. 8°. L, LPO, EN; MHL.

4857A ——[Anr. ed.] *By John Streater, James Flesher, and Henry Twyford, assigns of Richard Atkyns and Edward Atkyns,* 1668. 8°. WF.

4858 —The young clerks tutor enlarged. Fourth edition. *For R.C.,* 1668. 8°. BBE; CH, LC, MHL.

4859 ——Sixth edition. *For, and sold by Thomas Basset, and Robert Pawlet,* 1670. 8°. T.C.I 68. L; CN, LC, MHL.

4859A ——Eighth edition. —, 1675. 8°. T.C.I 201. MHL, Y.

4860 ——Ninth edition. *For Tho. Basset and Robert Pawlet,* 1680. 12°. T.C.I 389. L; BBE, CH, MHL, NC.

4861 ——Tenth edition. *Printed for, and are to be sold by Thomas Basset, and Robert Pawlet,* 1682. 8°. T.C.I 516. L, O; CN, MHL, NCL.

4862 ——Eleventh edition. —, 1685. 8°. L, LG, EN; MHL, NC.

4862A ——Twelfth edition. *For T.Basset, and G.Pawlet,* 1689. 8°. T.C.II 294. L; MHL, NCL.

4862B ——Thirteenth edition. *To be sold by Thomas Basset and Edward Pawlet,* 1693. 8°. CN, MHL, NCL.

4862C ——Fourteenth edition. *For, and are to be sold by William Battersby and Edward Pawlet,* 1700. 8°. CN, MHL, NC.

4863 —The young lawyer's vvriting master. *[London], printed and are to be sold by Robert Walton,* [c. 1685]. 4°.* O; CLC.

4863A —The youth's direction. *[London] sold by J. Overton,* 1652. 8°. CN.

4864 C[ockeram], H[enry]. The English dictionarie. Seventh edition. *By G.M. for T.W. to be sold by Andrewe / Crooke,* 1642. 8°. L, O, CT; CLC, CU, MH.

4865 ——Eighth edition. *By A.M. for TW to be sold by Andrew Crooke,* 1647. 8°. CLC, IU, LC, PBM.

4866 ——Ninth edition. *By A. Miller, to be sold by Andrew Crooke,* 1650. 8°. L, LLL, DT; CU, MBA, TU, Y.

4867 Entry cancelled.

4868 ——Tenth edition. —, 1651. 8°. L, LLL; LC.

4869 ——"Tenth," revised. *By A.M. and are to be sold by Andrew Crooke,* 1655. 8°. L, LG; CH, MBP, WF.

4870 ——Eleventh edition. —, 1658. 8°. L, O, AN, GU; CLC, CU, MH, MM.

4871 ——Twelfth edition. *For W. Miller,* 1670. 12°. T.C.I 62. L, O, LSC, AU; CLC, CU, PU, TU, Y.

4872 Cockers farewel to brandy. *For R.P.,* 1675. brs. L.

4873 **Cockin, Francis.** Divine blossoms. *By W.G. for E. Farnham,* 1657. 8°. LT, LSC; MH.

4873A **Cockman, Thomas.** Proposals for printing . . . all Cicero. *[Oxford, c.* 1700.] 8°.* L.

4873B [Cocks, John.] Reasons humbly offered to the honourable House of Commons for a bill. *[London?* 1691.] brs. LG.

4874 **Cocks, Roger.** An ansvver to a book set forth by Sir Edward Peyton. *For Nath. Butter,* 1642. 4°.* LT, O, CJ, LSC, EN; NU, WF.

4875 **Coddington, William.** A demonstration of true love. *[London], printed,* 1674. 4°.* L, LF, BBN; CH, MH, NN, PH, RPJ.

4876 **Codrington, Robert.** A collection of many select, and excellent proverbs. *By S. and B. Griffin, for William Lee,* 1672. 8°. L, C, BR, EN.

[-] His Majesties propriety. 1665. See Clavell, Robert.

4877 —The life and death, of the illvstriovs Robert Earle of Essex. *By F. Leach for L. Chapman,* 1646. 4°. LT, O, CT, EN, DT; CH, CN, MH, WF, Y.

4878 [-] The second part of Youths behaviour. *For W. Lee,* 1664. 8°. L, O, M; CH, LC, MH, NC, Y.

4879 [-] —Second edition. *By S, and B, Griffin, for W. Lee,* 1672. 8°. T.C.I 113. L, CT; MIU.

4879A **Codrington, Thomas.** A sermon preach'd . . . Nov. 28, 1686. *Nathaniel Thompson,* 1687. 4°. NU, TU.

4880 —A sermon preached . . . February the 6th. 1686/7. *By William Grantham,* 1687. 4°.* L, O, C, MC; CN, MH, NU, TU.

4881 **Coe, Richard.** An exact dyarie or a breife relation. *For Humphrey Tuckey, July 19,* 1644. 4°.* LT, O; CH, CN, Y.

Coelestis academia. 1655. See Rous, Francis.

Cœlestis legatus. 1668. See Almanacs: Hooker, Richard.

4882 **Coell, Francisco.** Fides hosti data est servanda. *[n.p.,* 1671.] brs. O.

4883 **Coelson, Lancelot.** Philosophia maturata: an exact piece. *For G. Sawbridge,* 1668. 12°. L, O, C, LWL, GU; MBP, WF, WU, Y.

4884 —The poor-mans physician. *By A.M. for Simon Miller,* 1656. 8°. LT, C, LCS, LWL, GU; BN.

—Speculum perspicuum. 1674. *See* Almanacs.

Coffee-house dialogue. [*n.p.*, 1679?] *See* Yarranton, Andrew.

4885 The coffee-house dialogue examined. [*London*, 1680?] fol.* L, O, C, CT; MBA.

Coffee-house jests. 1677. *See* Hickes, William.

4886 The coffee house: or news mongers hall. *By E. Crowch, for T. Vere*, 1672. brs. L; MBA.

4887 Coffee-houses vindicated in ansvver to the late published Character of a coffee-house. *By J. Lock for J. Clarke*, 1673. fol.* CH.

4887A The coffee-mans granado. *For J. Johnson*, 1663. 4°.* L; MH.

Coffee scuffle. 1662. *See* Woolnoth.

4888 A coffin for King Charles. [*London*, 1649.] brs. LT; MB, MH.

4889 A coffin for the good old cause. colop: *For the author*, 1660. cap., 4°.* LT, O, C, LG, HH; CH, CN, MH, NU, TU, Y.

Coffin opened. 1660. *See* P., H.

Coffo philo or. [*n.p.*], 1672. *See* Carr, William.

4890 **Coga, Nathaniel.** Bibliotheca Cogiana. Catalogue of library. *Cambridge, 27 Nov.*, 1694. 4°. L, OP.

4890A **C[oggeshall], H[enry].** The art of practical measuring. *For Thomas Basset*, 1690. 12°. T.C.II 335. EN; IU.

4891 —Timber-measure by a line. *For the author, to be sold by Robert Pricke*, 1677. 8°.* T.C.I 290. L; CLC, WF.

4892 —A treatise of measures. *By A. G. and J. P. to be sold by Henry Wynn*, 1682. sixes. L, C, LR.

Cogitations upon death. Aberdeen, 1681. *See* Dunbar, William.

4892A **Cogneau, Paul.** A sure guide to the French toungue. Second edition. *For R. Whitaker*, 1645. 8°. CCH.

4892B ——[Anr. ed.] *For Ioshua Kirton*, 1651. 8°. OC.

4893 ——[Anr. ed.] *By S. G. for Joshua Kirton*, 1658. 8°. LT.

4894 **Cokaine, Sir Aston.** A chain of golden poems. *By W. G., sold by Isaac Pridmore*, 1658. 8°. O, EN; CH, MH, WF, Y.

4895 —Choice poems of several sorts. *For Francis Kirkman*, 1669. 8°. L, O, EC; CH, CN, LC, MH.

4896 —The obstinate lady. *By W. Godbid for Isaac Pridmore*, 1657. 4°. L, O, LVD, EN; CH, CU, LC, MH, WCL, Y.

4897 —Poems. *For Phil. Stephens, junior*, 1662. 8°. L, LVD; CH, WF, Y.

4897A ——[Anr. ed.] *For Francis Kirkman*, 1662. 8°. L.

4898 —Small poems of divers sorts. *By Wil. Godbid*, 1658. 8°. L, O, OW; CH, MB, TU, WF, Y.

4899 —The tragedy of Ovid. *For Phil. Stephens junior*, 1662. 8°. WF, Y.

4900 ——[Anr. ed.] *For Francis Kirkman*, 1669. 8°. L, O; CH, LC, Y.

4901 **Cokayn, George.** Divine astrologie. *By Robert White for Thomas Brewster*, 1658. 4°.* L, O, HH, SP, YM; MH, WF.

4902 —Flesh expiring. *For Giles Calvert*, 1648. 4°.* LT, O, LCL, LW, DT; CH, MH, NU, TU, WF.

4903 [**Cokayne, John.**] Englands trovbles anatomized. *For Richard Tomlins*, 1644. 4°. LT, O, LVF, DT; CH, CN, MH, NU, WF, Y.

4904 **Cokayne, William.** The fovndations of freedome, vindicated. *For John Harris*, 1649. 4°.* LT, O, LCL, OC, DT; BN, CH, CU, MH, NU, WF, Y.

4905 **Coke,——.** A true narrative of the great solemnity of the circumcision. *By J. C. for W. Crook*, 1676. fol.* L, O, OC, HH; BN, CN.

4906 **Coke, Sir Edward.** An abridgement of the Lord Coke's commentary on Littleton. Second edition. *For W. Lee, D. Pakeman, and G. Bedell*, 1651. 8°. L, O, CJ, CP, AN; NC.

4906A ——[Anr. ed.] *By the assigns of Richard Atkyns and Edward Atkyns*, 1685. 12°. L, C; CH, LM; MHL, WF, YL.

4907 [–] Argumentum anti-Normannicum: or an argument. *By J. D. for Mat Keinton, Jonath. Robinson, Sam. Sprint*, 1682. 8°. T.C.I 496. L, O, C, LL, DT; BN, CH, CN, LC, NU, Y.

4907A [–] ——[Anr. ed.] *By John Darby*, 1682. 8°. LG, OC, CS, WCA; CN, PL, TU, WF, WU.

4908 —A book of entries. *By John Streater, James Flesher and Henry Twyford, assigns of Richard Atkins and Edward Atkins*, 1671. fol. T.C.I 77. L, OC, CT, EN, DT; CU, LC, MB, MHL, NCL, YL.

4908A ——Second edition. *By John Streater and are to be sold by George Sawbridge*, 1671. fol. L.

4909 —Certain select cases in law. *By Tho. Roycroft, for J. Sherley, H. Twyford, and Tho. Dring*, 1659. fol. L, O, CJ, LL; CH, LC, MIU.

4910 ——Second edition. *By the assigns of R. and E. Atkins, for H. Twyford, T. Basset, and B. Sherley*, 1677. fol. L, O, C, EN, DT; CH, MB, WF.

4911 —Le cinquiesme part des Reports del. *By the assigns of Rich. and Edw. Atkins; for Samuel Keble, and John Walthoe*, 1697. fol. L, O, C, LIL, DT.

4912 —The complete copyholder. *By T. Cotes for W. Cooke*, 1641. 4°. L, C, LL, CE, CT; CH, LC, MH, MHL, NCL.

4913 ——[Anr. ed.] *For Matthew Walbanck, and Richard Best*, 1644. 4°. L, LIL, CS, CT, DC; MHL, NCL, WF.

4914 ——[Anr. ed.] *For W. Lee and D. Pakeman*, 1650. 4°. L, C, LL, LM, LGI; MBP, MHL, NCL, NS, WF.

4915 ——[Anr. ed.] *By J. Streater, J Flesher, and H Twyford, assignes of R. Atkyns and E. Atkyns*, 1668. 8°. L, O, C, LGI, EN; LC, MHL, NCL.

4916 ——[Anr. ed.] *By E. Flesher, John Streater, and Henry Twyford, assignes of Richard Atkyns, and Edward Atkyns*, 1673. 8°. T.C.I 159. L, C, LI, LL, EN; LC, MHL, NCL, PL, WF.

4917 —The declarations and other pleadings. *For W. Lee, D. Pakeman, and G. Bedell*, 1659. fol. L, C, CJ, CP; MB, MHL, MIU.

4918 —La dixme part des Reports de. *By the assigns of Rich. and Edw. Atkins; for Samuel Keble, and John Walthoe*, 1697. fol. L, O. C. LIL, DT.

4919   —An exact abridgment in English of the . . . Reports. *By M. Simmons, for Matthew Walbancke, and H. Twyford*, 1650. 8°. L, O, C, CT, DC, P; LC, MIU, WF.

4920   ——Second edition. *For Matthew Walbancke, and John Place*, 1651. 12°. LL; LC, CN, NCL.

4920A ——Third edition. *By F. Leach, for Matthew Walbancke and H. Twyford*, 1656. 8°. NCL.

4921   ——"Third" edition. *By F. Leach, for Matthew Walbancke*, 1657. 8°. L, O, C, OC, CCA; LC, NCL.

4921A ——"Third" edition. *For G. Dawes*, 1666. 8°. OP.

4922   —An exact abridgment of the two last volumes of Reports. *Imprinted at London; to be sold by Henry Twyford and Timothy Twyford*, 1670. 8°. T.C.I 35. L, C, LM; NCL, WF, YL.

4923   —Un exact alphabetical table de tout. *For W. Lee; and H. Twyford*, 1664. 8°. L, O, C, LM, AN; CH, NCL, WF.

4924   —The first part of the Institutes. Fifth edition. *For the company of stationers*, 1656. fol. L, O, C, LCP, DT; LC, MH, NCL.

4925   ——Sixth edition. —, 1664. fol. L, CCA, CJ, DT; CN, LC, MHL, MIU.

4926   ——Seventh edition. *By John Streater, James Flesher, and Henry Twyford, assigns of Richard Atkins and Edward Atkins, and are to be sold by George Sawbridge, John Place, John Bellinger, William Place, Thomas Basset, Robert Pawlet, Christopher Wilkinson, Thomas Dring, William Jacob, Ch. Harper, John Amery, John Poole, John Leigh*, 1670. fol. T.C.I 53. L, O, C, EN, DT; BN, CN, LC, MHL, NCL, PL.

4927   ——Eighth edition. *For the society of stationers*, 1670. fol. L, OC, CK, CS; LC, MHL.

4928   ——Ninth edition. *By William Rawlins, Samuel Roycroft, and H. Sawbridge, assigns of Richard Atkins and Edward Atkins. Sold by Christopher Wilkinson, Richard Tonson, and Jacob Tonson*, 1684. fol. L, LSC, LL, WCA; LC, MHL, NCL, NR, YL.

4929   —The fourth part of the Institutes. *By M. Flesher, for W. Lee, and D. Pakeman*, 1644. fol. L, O, C, LIL, LUS; BN, CH, LC, MHL, NCL, YL.

4930   ——Second edition. —, 1648. fol. L, O, C, LL, DT; LC, MHL, NL.

4931   ——Fourth edition. *For A. Crooke, W. Leake, A. Roper, F. Tyton, T. Dring, T. Collins, J. Place, W. Place, J. Starkey, T. Basset, R. Pawlet, S. Heyricke, and G. Dawes* 1669. fol. L, O, CJ, LL, DT; CH, LC, MHL, NP, YL.

4932   ——Fifth edition. *By John Streater, Henry Twyford, Elizabeth Flesher, assigns of Richard Atkyns and Edward Atkyns*, 1671. fol. L, O, CK, CT, DT; BN, LC, MHL, NL.

4933   ——Sixth edition. *By W. Rawlins, for Thomas Basset*, 1681. fol. L, LIL, EC, WCA, EN; CN, LC, MHL, NP, PL, YL.

4934–6 Entries cancelled. *See* Ashe, Thomas.

4937   —La huictme part des Reports de. *By the assigns of Rich. and Edw. Atkyns; for Samuel Keble; and John Walthoe*, 1697. fol. L, O, C, LIL, DT.

4938   —Judges judged out of their own mouthes. *By W. Bently, to be sold by E. Dod & N. Ekins*, 1650. 12°. LT, C, LG, DC, CPE; CU, MHL, NU, WF.

4939   —[Anr. ed.] *By W. Bentley, to be sold by John Williams*, 1650. 12°. LG.

4940   —La neufme part des Reports del. *By the assigns of Rich. and Edw. Atkins; for Samuel Keble, and John Walthoe*, 1697. fol. L, O, C, LIL, DT.

4941   —A perfect abridgement of the eleven bookes of Reports. *By I. G. for W. Lee, D. Pakeman, and G. Bedell*, 1651. 12°. LT, O; LC, MH, MHL, MIU, YL.

4942   —Le quart part des Reports de. *By the assigns of Rich. and Edw. Atkyns; for Samuel Keble; and John Walthoe*, 1697. fol. L, O, C, LIL, DT.

4943   —Le reading del MonSeignior Coke, sur lestatute de 27 E. I. *Excudebat T. R. sumptibus G. Lee, D. Pakeman & Gabr. Bedell*, 1662. 4°.* L, C, LGI, LL, EN; LK, MHL, MIU, YL.

4944   —The reports of. *For W. Lee, M. Walbanck, D. Pakeman, and G. Bedell*, 1658. fol. L, O, C, LM, CE; LC, MB, MHL, PBM.

4945   —Les reports de. *By John Streater, Eliz. Flesher and Henry Twyford, assignes of Richard Atkyns and Edward Atkyns. To be sold by George Sawbridge, John Place, John Bellinger, William Place, Tho. Basset, Robert Pawlet, Christopher Wilkinson, Tho. Dring, Will. Jacob, Ch. Harper, J. Leigh, J. Amery, J. Poole*, 1672. fol. L, OC, CJ, EC, EN.

4946   ——Second edition. *For H. Twyford, T. Collins, T. Basset, J. Wright, S. Heyrick, T. Sawbridge, M. Pitt, C. Harper, and J. Place*, 1680. fol. T.C.I 424. L, C, LIL, EN; CH, NCL, WF.

4947   ——[Anr. ed.] *By the assigns of Rich. and Edw. Atkyns; for Samuel Keble; and John Walthoe*, 1697. fol. T.C.III 113. L, O, C, LIL, DT; MHL.

4948   —The second part of the Institutes. *By M. Flesher, and R. Young, for E. D., R. M., W. L. and D. P.*, 1642.fol. L, O, C, E, DT; BN, CH, CU, LC, MHL, NC, YL.

4949   ——Second edition. *By J. Flesher, for W. L., D. P., and G. B.*, 1662. fol. O, CCA, CT; LC, MHL, WF.

4950   ——Third edition. *For A. Crooke*, 1669. fol. T.C.I 3. L, CJ, LGI, LL, DT; LC, MHL, NCL, NR, YL.

4951   ——Fourth edition. *By J. Streater, H. Twyford, Elizabeth Flesher, assigns of R. Atkyns, and E. Atkyns*, 1671. fol. O, C, CK, CS, DT; BN, CN, LC, MHL, NCL, NP.

4952   ——Fifth edition. *By John Streater, Henry Twyford, Elizabeth Flesher, assigns of Richard Atkyns, and Edward Atkyns*, 1671. fol. O, OME; NC.

4952A ——"Fifth" edition. *For A. Crooke, W. Leake, A. Roper, F. Tyton, T. Dring, T. Collins, J. Place, W. Place, J. Starkey, T. Basset, R. Pawlett, S. Heyrick, and G. Dawes*, 1671. fol. CT; LC, MH, PU.

4953   ——Sixth edition. *By W. Rawlins for Thomas Basset*, 1681. fol. T.C.I 467. L, CSS, LIL, EN, ES; LC, MB, MHL, NCL, YL.

4954   —Le second part des Reports del. *By the assigns of Rich. and Edw. Atkins; for Samuel Keble, and John Walthoe*, 1697. fol. L, O, C, LIL, DT.

4955 —Le sept part des Reports de. *By the assigns of Rich. and Edw. Atkins, for Samuel Keble; and John Walthoe,* 1697. fol. L, O, C, LIL, DT.

4956 —Le size part des Reports del. *By the assigns of Rich. and Edw. Atkins; for Samuel Keble, and John Walthoe,* 1697. fol. L, O, C, LIL, DT.

4957 [–] A supplement by way of additions to. *By E. Flesher, John Streater, and Henry Twyford, assignes of Richard Atkyns, and Edward Atkyns,* 1673. 8°. L, OC; NC.

4958 —Synopsis. *By E. G. for M. Walbancke and H. Twyford,* 1652. 8°. C, LIL, OM, LL, DT; CH, LC, MHL, NC, YL.

4959 Entry cancelled.

4960 —The third part of the Institutes. *By M. Flesher, for W. Lee, and D. Pakeman,* 1644. fol. L, O, C, LI, LGI; CH, LC, MHL, NCL, YL.

4961 —The third and fourth parts of the Institutes. *By M. Flesher, for W. Lee and D. Pakeman,* 1648. fol. L, O, C, LGI, OM; BN, CH, LC, MHL, NCL.

4962 —The third part. Third edition. *By J. Flesher for W. Lee, and D. Pakeman,* 1660. fol. CCA, CT, LW, DT; LC, MBP, MHL, WF, YL.

4963 ——Fourth edition. *For A. Crooke, W. Leake, A. Roper, F. Tyton, T. Dring, T. Collins, J. Place, W. Place, J. Starkey, T. Basset, R. Pawlet, S. Heyrick, and G. Dawes,* 1669. fol. L, CJ, DT; CH, LC, MHL, WG, YL.

4964 —"Fourth" edition. *By J. Streater, J. Flesher and H. Twyford,* 1670. fol. L, CK, CS, DT; BN, LC, MHL, NP.

4965 —Fifth edition. *For A. Crooke, W. Leake, A. Roper, F. Tyton, T. Dring, T. Collins, H. Place, W. Place, J. Starkey, T. Basset, R. Pawlett, S. Heyrick, and G. Dawes,* 1671. fol. OME, CT; CLC, MHL, NC.

4966 ——Sixth edition. *By W. Rawlins, for Thomas Basset,* 1680. fol. L, CSS, LIL, EN, ES; CN, LC, MHL, NCL, YL.

4967 Entry cancelled.

4968 —Le tierce part des Reportes del. *By the assigns of Rich. and Edw. Atkyns; for Samuel Keble; and John Walthoe,* 1697. fol. L, O, C, LIL, DT; WF.

4969 —The twelfth part of the reports of. *By T. R. for Henry Twyford and Thomas Dring,* 1656. fol. LL, CJ, EN, DT; CN, PL, WF.

4970 ——[Anr. ed.] *For Hehry Twyford and Thomas Dring,* 1658. fol. OC, OME; CH.

4971 ——"Second" edition. *By the assigns of Richard and Edward Atkins, for Hen. Twyford and Tho. Basset,* 1677. fol. T.C.I 297. L, O, CM, EN, DT; CH, LC, MB.

4972 —La unzime part des Reports de. *By the assigns of Rich. and Edw. Atkins; for Samuel Keble, and John Walthoe,* 1697. fol. L, O, C, LIL, DT.

4973 **Coke, Roger.** A detection of the court and state of England. *Printed,* 1694. 2 v. 8°. L, C, OM, LVF, DT; CH, CN, MIU, PL, Y.

4974 ——Second edition. —, 1696. 2 v. 8°. L, C, MR, BAMB, E; BN, CH, MH, MU, NC, Y.

4975 ——Third edition. *For Andr. Bell,* 1697. 2 v. 8°. T.C.III 32. L, O, C, EN, DT; BN, MH, TU, WF, Y.

4976 —A discourse of trade. *For H. Brome: and R. Horne,* 1670. 4°. T.C.I 31. L, O, CT, EN, DT; CH, MH, NC, WF, Y.

4977 ——Second edition. 1671. 4°. EN.

4978 —England's improvements. *By J. C. for Henry Brome,* 1675. 4°. T.C.I 227. L, O, CS, EN, DT; BN, CH, CN, MH, NC, WF, Y.

4979 —Justice vindicated. *By Tho. Newcomb, for G Bedell and T. Collins,* 1660. fol. L, C, LL, CT, EN; CH, CU, MH, MHL, WF.

4980 —Reflections upon the East-Indy and Royal African companies. *Printed,* 1695. 4°.* L, LG; LC, MH, NC, WF.

4980A [–] A reply to an Answer from a friend, to the Apology. *Printed,* 1692. 4°. L; HR, MH, NC.

4981 —Supplement to the first edition of The detection. *For Andrew Bell,* 1696. 8°. EN; CH, WF, Y.

4982 —A survey of the politicks of Mr. Thomas White. *For G. Bedell and T. Collins,* 1662. fol. L, CJ.

4983 —A treatise concerning the regulation of the coyn of England. *For Roger Clavel,* 1696. 4°.* L, CS, CT, ES; CU, MH, NC, WF, Y.

4984 —A treatise wherein is demonstrated. *By J. C. for Henry Brome; and Robert Horn,* 1671. 4°. L, O, CT, EN, DT; CH, CN, LC, MH, NC, Y.

4985 —Treatises of the nature of man. *By J. Cotterel, and F. Collins for the author,* 1685. fol.* T.C.II 129. HH; PL, WF.

4986 **Coke, Zachary.** The art of logick. *By Robert White, for George Calvert,* 1654. 8°. LT, C, LCL, OC, E; CH, CU, MH, WF, Y.

4987 ——Second edition. [n.p.], 1657. 8°. LGI; CLC, IU, NC.

4988 **Coker, Matthew.** A prophetical revelation. *By James Cottrel,* 1654. 4°.* LT.

4989 —A short and plain narrative of. *By James Cottrel,* 1654. 4°.* LT, LG.

4990 —A whip of small cords. *By James Cottrel,* 1654. 4°.* LT, LCI; NN, NU.

Colasterion. [n.p.], 1645. *See* Milton, John.

4991 [**Colbatch, John.**] An account of the court of Portugal. *For Thomas Bennet,* 1700. 8°. T.C.III 170. L, O, C, EN, DT; CH, CN, MH, PL, WF, Y.

4992 —A collection of tracts chirurgical. *For Dan. Brown,* 1699. 8°. T.C.III 108. LM, LWL; BN.

4993 ——[Anr. ed. —, 1700. 8°. L, O, C, CT; BBE, CLC, NC, WF.

4994 —The doctrine of acids. *For Dan. Brown; and Abel Roper,* 1689. 8°. L, O; CLC, MIU, WSG.

4995 ——[Anr. ed.] —, 1698. 8°. T.C.III 54. O, LM, LCS, LW; NAM, WF, HC.

4996 —The doctrin of acids further. Second edition. —, 1699. 8°. LCS, GH; WF.

4997 —Four treatises. Second edition. *For D. Brown,* 1698. 8°. T.C.III 54. L, C, LW, LWL; TU.

[–] Memoirs of Denmark. 1700. *See* Crull, Jodocrus.

4998 —Novum lumen chirurgicum: or, a new light of chirurgery. *For D. Brown,* 1695. 8°. T.C.II 552. L, O, C, E; CJC, CLM, WF, HC.

4999 ——Third edition. *By J. D. for D. Brown,* 1698. 8°. LCS; CLC, RPJ.

5000 ——Fourth edition. —, 1699. 8°. LCS, GH; MH, WF, WSG, HC.

5001 —Novum lumen chirurgicum vindicatum: or, the new light. *For D. Brown*, 1695. 8°. L, C, OC, CE; MIU, HC.

5002 ——Third edition. 1698. 8°. C, LCS; WF.

5003 —A physico-medical essay. *For Dan. Browne*, 1696. 8°. T.C.II 569. L, C, CE, LCP, LWL; MIU, WF, HC.

5004 ——Second edition. *For D. Brown*, 1698. 4°. L, ELY.

5005 ——Third edition. 1698. 8°. LCS; CLC.

5006 ——Fourth edition. 1699. 8°. C, LCS, GH.

5007 —A relation of a very sudden and extraordinary cure of a person bitten by a viper. *For Dan. Brown; Abel Roper, and Tho. Leigh*, 1698. 8°. T.C.III 77. L, O, C, LCS, LM; CH.

5008 ——Second edition. 1699. 8°. C, LCS, GH; WF.

5009 —Some farther considerations concerning alkaly. *For Fr. Mills and W. Turner*, 1696. 8°. T.C.II 589. L, C; CH, HC.

5010 ——[Anr. ed.] *For Dan. Brown*, 1696. 8°. OC; MIU, WF, HC.

5011 ——Third edition. 1698. 8°. LCS.

5012 ——Fourth edition. 1699. 8°. LCS, GH.

5013 —A treatise of the gout. *For Daniel Brown, and Roger Clavel*, 1697. 8°. T.C.III 6. L, O, CCA, LW, AU; NC, Y.

5014 ——Second edition. 1698. 8°. LCS.

5015 ——Third edition. 1699. 8°. C, LCS, GH; WF.

5015A **Colbert, Jean Baptiste.** An oration made. *Sold by Richard Baldwin*, 1694. 4°.* WCL.

5016 Entry cancelled.

5017 Colchester surrendered to the Lord Generall. [*London*], *by Robert Ibbitson*, 1648. 4°.* LT, HH.

5018 Colchester's teares. *For John Bellamy*, 1648. 4°.* LT, O, HH, DT; MH.

5019 **Coldwell, C.** Regulæ morum ostensivæ. [*Cambridge*, 1651.] brs. LT, O.

5020 **Cole, Charles.** Triumphant Augustus. A congratulate poem. *Printed*, 1695. 4°.* L.

5021 **Cole, E.** The young schollar's best companion. *For John Harris*, [1690?]. 12° T.C.II 290. L.

5022 Entry cancelled.

5023 **Cole, John.** A full and more particular account of the late fire. *For John Smith*, 1683. brs. L, O, C; CH, Y.

5024 [**Cole, Robert.**] The last trve intelligence from Ireland. *For H. Blunden*, 1642. 4°.* L, O, C, LVF, MR; MH.

5025 —More good and true news. *For F. Coules*, 1642. 4°.* LT, O.

5026 —Newes from Ireland. VVherein. *For F. Coles*, 1641[/2]. 4°.* EC, MR; MH, Y.

5027 [–] The trve coppies of two letters sent from Ireland. *For J. B. and R. Smith*, 1643. 4°.* LT, O, C; CN, WF, Y.

5028 [–] Trve intelligence from Ireland, dated. *For H Blunden*, 1642. 4°.* LT, O, C, EC; MIU.

5029 **Cole, Thomas.** A discourse of Christian religion. *By R. R. for Thomas Cockerill*, 1692. 8°. L, LCL; MH, NU, WF, Y.

5029A —A discourse of faith. *For Thomas Cockerill*, 1689. 8°. MH.

5030 —A discourse of regeneration. *For Thomas Cockerill*, 1689. 8°. T.C.II 246. L, LCL, LW, ENC; MH, NF, NU.

5031 —The incomprehensibleness of imputed righteousness. *For Tho. Cockerill*, 1692. 12°. L, GU; NPT, NU.

5032 —The old apostolical way of preaching. *For Thomas Cockeril*, 1676. 4°.* L, O, CS, WCA; MB, WF.

——Ουρανολογια. 1695. *See* Almanacs.

5033 **Cole, Sir William.** The answere and vindication of. [*London*, 1645.] 4°.* LT, C; CH.

5034 **Cole William, *of Gray's Inn*.** Legal and other reasons (with all . . .) presented to . . . Charles II. *Printed*, 1675. 4°.* L, O; MH, MHL.

5035 ——[Anr. ed.] —, 1680. 4°.* L; CJC, WF.

5036 **Cole, William, *a lover of his country*.** The Irish cabinet: or His Majesties secret papers. *For Edw. Husband*, *Ian. 20*, 1645[6]. 4°.* LT, O, C, MR, DT; CH, CSU, CU, NU, WF, Y.

5037 —Noah's dove. *By James Cottrel, for Nathanael Webb*, 1661. 4°.* O.

5038 —Prospective for the discovery. 1656. 12°. OR.

5039 —A rod for the lawyers. *Printed*, 1659. 4°.* LT, O, E; MHL, WF.

5039A ——[Anr. ed.] *For Giles Calvert*, 1659. 4°.* HR, CH, MH.

5040 —Severall proposals humbly tendered. *Printed*, 1659. 4°.* O, HH, OC; CH, MH, NC.

5041 **Cole, William. M.D.** De secretione animali cogitata. *Oxon, e theatro Sheldoniano*, 1674. 12°. MADAN 3007. T.C.I 189. L, O, C, GH, DT; CH, CJC, NP, WF, Y.

5042 —Novæ hypotheseos. *Impensid D. Browne, & S. Smith*, 1693. 8°. T.C.II 465. L, O, C, LM, AU; BN, WF, HC.

5043 —A physico-medical essay. *Oxford, at the theater*, 1689. 8°. L, O, C, LM, AU; MMO, NAM, PL, WF, HC.

5044 —Purpura Anglicana, being a discovery. *By Joseph Streater*, 1689. 4°.* L, O, GU; WF.

5045 [**Cole, William,**] *of Newcastle*. The perfect Pharisee. *Gateside, by S. B. to be sould by Will: London, in Newcastle*, 1653. NSA, EN; MH.

5045A [–] —[Anr. ed.] *For Richard Tomlins*, 1654. 4°. LT, O, CT, NM, YM; CH, MH, NU, PH, WF, Y.

5046 **Coleman, Edward.** Mr. Coleman's two letters to Monsieur l'Chaise. [*London*], *printed*, 1678. 4°.* L, O, C, MR, EN; CH, MH, NU, WF, Y.

5047 **Coleman, Nathaniel.** An epistle to be read in the assemblies. [*London*, 1682.] 4°.* LF; PSC.

Coleman, Thomas. A brief view of Mr. Coleman his new-modell. 1645. *See* Byfield, Adoniram.

5048 —A brotherly examination re-examined. *For John Clark*, 1645. 4°.* L, NU.

5049 ——[Anr. ed.] —, 1646. 4°.* L, O, C, EC, ENC; CH, CU, MH, WF, Y.

5050 —The Christians covrse and complaint. *By I.L. for Christopher Meredith*, 1643. 4°. LT, O, C, LCL, EN; CH, MH, NU, WF, Y.

5051 —Gods unusuall answer. *For Christopher Meredith*, 1644. 4°.* LT, O, C, EN, DT; CH, CN, MH, NU, WF, Y.

5052 —The hearts engagement. *For Christopher Meredith*, 1643. 4°.* LT, O, C, EN, DT; CH, MH, NU, WF, Y.

5053 —Hopes deferred and dashed. *For Christopher Meredith*, 1645. 4°.* LT, O, C, EN, DT; CH, CN, MH, NU, WF, Y.

5054 ——Second edition. —, 1645. 4°.* C; NU, WF, Y.

5055 —Huls pillar of providence erected. *For Ralph Rounth-wait*, 1644. 4°.* LT, HH, YM; MH, Y.

5056 —Male dicis, maledicis: or, a brief reply. *For John Clark*, 1646. 4°.* LT, O, CM, P, DT; CH, MH, NU, WF, Y.

5057 Colendissimo viro Guilielmo Scroggs. *Typis J. C. pro Tho. Norman*, 1680. brs. L, O; MH, PU.

5058 **Colepeper, John, baron.** Sir Iohn Cvlpeper his speech in Parliament. [*London*], *printed*, 1641. 4°.* LT, O, C, LVF, E; CLC, CN, LC, MH, NU, Y.

5059 **Colepepyr, Robert.** A new method . . . for speedy preservation. [*London*, 1700?] fol. L.

5060 —A proposal to prevent further decay. [*London*, 1698?] brs. L.

5061 —To the Hon. the Commons . . . a proposal. [*London*, 1689?] brs. L.

5062 **Coler, Richard.** Christian-experiences. *For Tho. Brewster*, 1652. 8°. LT; WF.

5063 [**Coleraine, Henry Hare, baron.**] La scala santa: or, a scale. *By A. Godbid and J. Playford*, 1681. fol. L, E, AU; CH, NPT, NU, WF, Y.

5064 [–] The situation of Paradise found out. *By J. C. and F. C. for S. Lowndes, and H. Faithorne, and J. Kersey*, 1683..8° T.C.II 13. L, O, CS, CT, DT; CN, MH, TU, WF, Y.

5064A [**Coles, Elisha, elder.**] A practical discourse of God's sovereignty. *By Ben. Griffin for E. C.*, 1673. 4°. L, O, C, LW, OC; CH, MH, NU, WF, Y.

5065 [–] —Third edition. *By Ben. Griffin for E. C. to be sold by Tho. Parkhurst, Rob. Boulter, and Nath. Ponder*, 1678. 8°. L, LCL; INU, NU.

5065A ——Fourth edition. *For Nath. Ponder*, 1685. 8°. T.C.III 132. WF.

5066 ——Fifth edition. *For T. Cockerill*, 1699. 8°. T.C.III 100. E.

5067 [**Coles, Elisha, younger.**] Χριστολογια. Or a metrical paraphrase. *For Peter Parker*, 1671. 8°. T.C.I 87. L, EN; CN, IU, MH.

5067A —The compleat English school-master. *For Peter Ponder*, 1674. 8°. T.C.II 152. O.

5067B ——[Anr. ed.] —, 1692. 8°. TU, Y.

5068 —A dictionary, English-Latin. *By John Richardson for Peter Parker and John Guy*, 1677. 4°. T.C.I 293. O, C, OC, E; CSU, IU, LC, MBP.

5069 ——Second edition. *By John Richardson, for Peter Parker: and Thomas Guy*, 1679. 4°. L, O, LVD, EC; BN, MIU, NN, Y.

5069A ——"Second" edition. *By John Richardson for G. Sawbridge, T. Basset, S. Wright, R. Chiswell*, 1679. 8°. CT.

5069B ——[Anr. ed.] *By John Richardson, for Peter Parker, Thomas Guy, Henry Mortlock, Moses Pitt and William Leak*, 1679. 8°. MIU.

5069C ——Third edition. *By R. E. for Tho. Guy*, 1692. 8°. TU.

5069D ——Fourth edition. *By R. E. for P. Parker*, 1699. 8°. CT.

5070 —An English dictionary. *For Samuel Crouch*, 1676. 8°. T.C.I 255. L, O; CH, MIU, WF, Y.

5071 ——[Anr. ed.] *For Peter Parker*, 1677. 4°. L, O, C, OC, AN; CH, NP, OCI, TU, Y.

5072 ——[Anr. ed.] —, 1684. 8°. CT; BN, CU.

5073 ——[Anr. ed.] —, 1685. 4°. L, O, C, AN; CLC, CN, MH, PL, Y.

5074 ——[Anr. ed.] —, 1692. 4°. T.C.II 415. L, O; CLC, CU, IU, TU, Y.

5075 ——[Anr. ed.] —, 1696. 4°. L, LSC, CS, EN; CU, MH, NC, TU, Y.

5076 —The harmony of the four evangelists. *For Peter Parker*, 1679. 8°. T.C.I 340. O, LCL; CLC, MH, WF.

5077 —The history of the life and death of . . . Jesus Christ. *For Peter Parker*, 1680. 8°. L; MH, Y.

5078 —The newest, plainest, and shortest short-hand. *For Peter Parker*, 1674. 16°.* T.C.I 172. O, C, CM, HH; LC, NN, Y.

5079 —Nolens volens. *By Andrew Clark for T. Basset*, 1675. 8°. T.C.I 212. L, O; NN, WF, Y.

5080 ——Second edition. *By T. D. for T. Basset and H. Brome*, 1677. 8°. T.C.I 284. L, O; MIU, NC, Y.

5080A ——Third edition. *By J. R. for T. Basset, and J. Brome* 1682. 8°. T.C.I 516. L; CH.

5081 —Syncrisis, or, the most natural . . . method of learning Latin. *By H. L. for Tho. Drant, and Tho. Lacey*, 1675. 8°. T.C.I 219. L; CU, WF.

5082 [–] —[Anr. ed.] *For Robert Sollers*, 1677. 8°. O; BN.

5083 **Coles, Gilbert.** A dialogue between a Protestant and a Papist. *Oxford, at the theater, for M. Pitt, P. Parker, W. Leak & T. Guy, of London*, 1679. 4°. MADAN 3207. O; NN, NU, Y.

5084 [–] Four conferences concerning I. reading the Holy Scriptures. *Oxford, at the theatre, to be sold by Randal Taylor*, 1688. 4°. MADAN 3207n. L, CS, LIL, HH; CH, NU, TU, WF, Y.

5085 —Theophilus and Philodoxus. *At the theater in Oxford*, 1674. 4°. MADAN 3008. L, O, CT, MC, EN; NU, WF, Y.

5086 **Coles, Joseph.** England to be wall'd with gold. *For the author*, 1700. 4°.* L.

5087 **Coles, William.** Adam in Eden. *By J. Streater, for Nathaniel Brooke*, 1657. fol. L, O, C, LCS, EN; CH, MH, PL, WF, Y.

5088 ——[Anr. ed.] —, [1657]. fol. L, LCS.

5089 —The art of simpling. *By J. G. for Nath: Brook*, 1656. 12°. LT, O, C, OM, GU; BN, WF.

5089A ——[Anr. ed.] —, 1657. 12°. CH, Y.

5090 **Colet, Claude.** The famous, pleasant and delightful history of Palladine of England. *By T. J. for Andrew Kembe and Charls Tyus*, 1664. 4°. A; CH, NP, WCL, WF.

5090A ——Second edition. *By J. F. and sold by John Marshall* [1700?] 4°. L; CN.

5090B **Colet, John.** Daily devotions. *By E. G. for John Benson*, 1641. 12°. OCC.

5091 ——[Anr. ed.] *For Giles Widdowes; and Charles Smith*, 1673. 12°. T.C.I 157. LG, LLP.

5092 ——[Anr. ed.] *By H. B. for Giles Widdowes*, 1674. 12°. C, LP, OC.

5093 ——Nineteenth edition. *For Nath. Ponder, and Edw. Evets*, 1684. 12°. T.C.II 104. L, LW, OC; CLC.

5094 — —Twentieth edition. *By J. H. for Edw. Evets*, 1693/5. 12°. LSC; Y.

5095 — —Twenty-first edition. —, 1700. 12°. MP; WF.

5096 —A sermon of conforming. *Cambridge, by J. Field for William Morden*, 1661. 8°. L, O, C, LG, EN; WF.

5097 **Cole-Venman, John.** A true alarm in weakness. [*London*, 1654.] brs. LT.

5098 **Coley, Henry.** Clavis astrologiæ: or, a key. *For Jos. Coniers*, 1669. 8°. T.C.I 5. L, O, A, EN; CH, CLC, Y.

5099 —Clavis astrologiæ elimata: or a key. Second edition. *For Benjamin Tooke, and Tho. Sawbridge*, 1676. 8°. T.C.I 241. L, O, C, E; CH, MBP, PL, WF, HC.

5100 —Genethlialogia or, the genethliacal part of astrology. *By J. W. for Josuah Coniers*, 1668. 8°. O; WF.

5101 —Hemerologium astronomicum. or, a brief description. *By John Darby, for the company of stationers*, 1672. 8°.* L, O, E; MIU.

Coley, Henry. Merlini Anglici ephemeris. 1684. *See* Almanacs.

—Nuncius cœlestis, or. 1676. *See* Almanacs.

—Nuncius syderus: or. 1687. *See* Almanacs.

5101A **Colgar, John.** The lives of the glorious Saint David. *Printed at Waterford by Peter de Prenne, to be sold in Kilkenny*, 1647. 12°.* DL.

5101B Colin and Phoebe. A pastoral. [*London?* 1665.] brs. L.

5102 **Colinson, Robert.** Idea rationaria: or, the perfect accountant. *Edinburgh, by David Lindsay, James Kniblo, Joshua van Solingen, & John Colmar*, 1683. fol. ALDIS 2373. L, E, EN; MH, NC, RBU, WF.

5102A **Collard, Thomas.** Animadversions on a fatal period. *For T. Basset*, 1678. 8°. T.C.I 322. O.

5102B A collect to be used in the morning service. *Dublin, Crook*, 1651. fol.* MB.

5103 Collectanea chymica; a collection. *For W. Cooper*, 1684. 8°. T.C.II 46. L, OR, LW, AU, GU; LC, MH, MU, NPT; Y.

5104 Collectio multifaria diversorum. [*London*], 6 Feb., 1695. 4°. L, OP.

Collection of acts of Parliament. [*n.p.*], 1660. *See* Merrett, Christopher.

5105 Collection of acts relating to the clergy. *For Jos. Hindmarsh*, 1693. 4°. L, CT; WF.

5105A A collection of addresses. 1681. fol. O.

5106 A collection of advertisements, advices, and directions relating to the royal fishery. *Fo H. M. to be sold by J. Whitlock*, 1695. 4°. L, C; CLC, CN, MH, NC, WF, Y.

5107 A collection of all the acts, memorials, & letters, that passed . . . Nimeguen. *By H. Hills and to be sold by Walter Kettilby*, 1679. 8°. L, OL; CLC, CU, MHL, PL.

5108 A collection of all the papers which passed upon the late treaty. *Dublin, Wᵐ Bladen*, 1643. DIX 77. DI.

5109 —[Anr. ed.] *Dublin, Wᵐ Bladen*, 1646. DIX 80. OCC.

5110 The collection of all the particular papers that passed between His Majesty, . . . concerning the cessation. *Printed at Oxford by Leonard Lichfield*, 1643. 4°. MADAN 1329. L, O, C, HH, EN; CH, LC, MBP, MH, Y.

5111 The collection of all the particular papers that passed between His Majesty, . . . concerning the late treaty. *Printed at Oxford by Leonard Lichfield*, 1643. 48 pp. 4°.* MADAN 1336. O, CM, CT; Y.

5112 —[Anr. ed. "Maiestie"] —, 1643. 37 pp. 4°. MADAN 1337. LT, O, CT, LVF, DT; CH, NU, TU, WF, Y.

5113 —[Anr. ed.] *Shrewsbury, by Robert Barker: and by the assignes of John Bill*, 1643. 4°. C.

Collection of apothegms. 1686. *See* Bulteel, John.

Collection of articles, injunctions. 1661. *See* Church of England; Sparrow, Anthony, *bp.*

5114 A collection of cases, and other discourses to recover dissenters. In two volumes. *For T. Basset, and B. Tooke*, 1685. 4°. T.C.II 110. L, O, CT, DT; CN, MBP, TU, Y.

5115 —The second volume. —, 1685. 4°. T.C.II 110. L, O, OC, BAMB, DT; CN, MBA, TU, Y.

5116 —Second edition. *For Thomas Basset, and Benj. Tooke, R. Chiswell, Walter Kettilby, B. Aylmer, Will. Rogers, and C. Brome*, 1694. fol. T.C.II 47. L, O, C, DC, DT; CLC, MH, PL, WWC.

5117 —Third edition. *For Benjamin Took, and William Battersby*, 1698. fol. T.C.III 98. L, CT, BR, RPL, DT; MB, NU, WF, Y.

5118 A collection of certain horrid murthers in several counties of Ireland. *For Henry Brome*, 1679. 4°.* T.C.I 349. L, O, C, MR, DT; CH, MH, WF, Y.

5119 A collection of choice books in divinity, history. [*London*], 1685/6. 4°.* L, O; JF.

5120 A collection of curious original paintings, . . . 8th of July, 1690. [*n.p.*], 1690. 4°.* L.

5121 A collection of curious paintings, . . . 27th . . . October, 1691. [*n.p.*], 1691. fol.* L.

5122 —, sixth . . . November, 1691. [*n.p.*], 1691. 4°., L.

5123 —[*London*, 1699.] 4°.* L, HH.

5124 A collection of curious pictures, viz. paintings & limnings . . . 20th . . . February, 1689/90. [*n.p.*], 1690. 4°.* L.

5125 —, 19th, . . . March, 1689/90. [*n.p.*], 1690. 4°.* L.

5126 —, 30th [April] 1690. [*n.p.*], 1690. 4°.* L.

5127 —, 20th . . . May, 1690. [*n.p.*], 1690. 4°.* L.

5128 —, 25th, . . . June, 1690. [*n.p.*], 1690. 4°.* L.

5129 —, 4th . . . August, 1690. [*n.p.*], 1690. 4°.* L.

5130 —, 15th . . . September 1690. [*n.p.*], 1690. 4°.* L.

5131 —, 8th . . . October 1690. [*n.p.*], 1690. 4°.* L.

5132 —, 7th . . . November 1690. [*n.p.*], 1690. 4°.* L.

5133 —, 20th, . . . November 1690. [*n.p.*], 1690. 4°.* L.

5134 —, 15th, . . . December 1690. [*n.p.*], 1690. 4°.* L.

5135 —, 15th, . . . January, 1691. [*n.p.*], 1691. 4°.* L.

5136 —, 27th . . . January, [*n.p.*, 1691.] 4°.* L.

5137 —, 28th . . . January, 1691. [*n.p.*], 1691. 4°.* L.

5138 —, 27th. [Feb. 1691]. [*n.p.*, 1691.] 4°.* L.

5139 A collection of curious prints, paintings, and limnings, . . . 13th . . . August, 1689. [*n.p.*], 1689. 4°.* L.

5140 Collection of curious travels. *For Sam. Smith and Benj. Walford*, 1693. 8°. T.C.II 464. CT.

5141   A collection of discourses lately written. *Edinburgh re-printed by John Reid, for Thomas Brown, Gideon Schaw, Alexander Ogston, and George Mosman,* 1687. 8°. ALDIS 2684. EN, D, GU, FSF; MH, NP, NU, WF.

5142   Entry cancelled.

5143   A collection of divers orders & rules. *For Laurence Blaiklock,* 1650. 4°.* LT; CH, NU.

5144   A collection of divers papers presented unto the Houses of Parliament . . . since May last, 1645. *By Moses Bell,* 1645. 4°.* LT, CT, MR, HH, DT; MBP, NU, WF, Y.

   Collection of eighteen papers. 1689. *See* Burnet, Gilbert, *bp.*

   Collection of 86 loyal poems. [*London*], 1685. *See* Thompson, Nathaniel.

   Collection of English proverbs. *Cambridge,* 1670. *See* Ray, John.

   Collection of entries. [*n.p.*], 1670. *See* Rastell, William.

5145   A collection of excellent English books. [*London*], 23 *May,* 1693. 4°.* L.

5145A A collection of farewel-sermons. [*London*], *printed,* 1662. 8°. CLC, Y.

   Collection of letters and other writings. 1681. *See* Treby, *Sir* George.

5146   A collection of letters and poems: written . . . to the late Duke and Duchess of Newcastle. *For Langly Curtis,* 1678. fol. T.C.I 312. L, O, LVD, SP; MH, NP, Y.

   Collection of many wonderful prophecies. [*n.p.*], 1689. *See* C., P.

5147   A collection of modern English books. [*London*], 31 *October,* 1693. 4°.* L.

   Collection of modern relations. 1693. *See* Hale, *Sir* Matthew.

   Collection of narrative. 1655. *See* Stouppe, I. B.

5148   A collection of new songs. *By I. Heptinstall, for Henry Playford,* 1698. fol.* T.C.III 94. L; CH.

5148A —[Same title.] *Sold by J. Walsh and J. Hare,* [1696]. 8°.* T.C.III 139. L.

5149   A collection of novels. *For R. Wellington, and E. Rumball,* 1699. 8°. T.C.III 143. LW; CLC, CN, WF, Y.

   Collection of offices. 1658. *See* Taylor, Jeremy.

   Collection of one hundred and eighty. 1694. *See* Thompson, Nathaniel.

5150-1 Entries cancelled.

5152   A collection of original drawings and prints . . . fourth of . . . May, 1689. [*n.p.*], 1689. 4°.* L.

5153   A collection of paintings . . . 25th. of Septemb. 1689. [*n.p.*], 1689. 4°.* L.

5154   —, 6th. of Novemb. 1689. [*n.p.*], 1689. 4°.* L.

5155   —, 16th . . . Decemb. 1689. [*n.p.*], 1689. 4°.* L.

5156   —, 26th. of February 1689/90. [*n.p.*], 1690. 4°.* L.

5157   —, 3d. of April. [*n.p.*], 1690.] 4°.* L.

5158   —, 15th . . . April. [*n.p.*], 1690.] 4°.* L.

5159   —, 29th. of April. [*n.p.*], 1690.] 4°.* L.

5160   —, 12th . . . May 1690. [*n.p.*], 1690. 4°.* L.

5161   —, 27th. May, 1690. [*n.p.*], 1690. 4°.* L.

5162   —, 20th . . . October 1690. [*n.p.*], 1690. 4°.* L.

5163   —, 25th . . . November, 1690. [*n.p.*], 1690. 4°.* L.

5164   A collection of paintings and limnings, . . . 1st of November, 1689. [*n.p.*], 1689. 4°.* L.

5165   —, 6th . . . December, 1689. [*n.p.*], 4°.* L.

5166   —, 29th, . . . January, 1689/90. [*n.p.*], 1690. 4°.* L.

5167   —, 7th, . . . February 1689/90. [*n.p.*], 1690. 4°.* L.

5168   A collection of paintings, drawings, and prints, . . . 28th . . . June, 1689. [*n.p.*], 1689. 4°.* L.

5168A Entry cancelled.

5168B A collection of papers relating to Parliaments. [*London*], *printed.* 1689. 4°.* CH, NU.

5169   A collection of papers relating to the calling and holding the Convention of Estates. *Edinburgh,* 1689. 4°.* ALDIS 2873. E, EN, AU, FSF; CLC, CN, MH, WF.

5169A A collection of papers relating to the present juncture of affairs. [*London*], *printed,* 1688. 4°.* L, O, C, EN, DT; CH, MH, NU, WF, Y.

5169B —Third edition. *Printed, and are to be sold by Richard Janeway,* 1689. 4°.* L, OC, CT, HH, DT; CH, CLC, MH, RPJ, Y.

5170   A collection of passages, concerning His Excellency and officers. *Printed at London by Robert Ibbitson,* 1648. 4°.* LT; NU, TU, Y.

5171   A collection of philological . . . books. [*n.p.,* 1699?] 4°.* L, BR.

5172   A collection of pictures, . . . ninth [March 1691]. [*n.p.,* 1691.] 4°.* L.

5173   A collection of pictures with several fine prints, . . . sixteenth of August. [*n.p.,* 1690.] 4°.* L.

5173A A collection of pleasant modern novels. Vol. II. *For J. Tonson, R. Wellington, E. Rumbole, and J. Wild,* 1700. 8°. WF.

5174   A collection of poems by several hands. *By T. Warren, for Francis Saunders,* 1693. 8°. L, O, CK, CT; CH, CU, MH, NP, WF, Y.

5175   Entry cancelled.

5176   A collection of poems on affairs of State. *Printed,* 1689. 4°. L, O, C, P, GK; CH, CN, MH, TU, WF, Y.

5177   A collection of poems, written upon several occasions by several persons. *For Hobart Kemp,* 1672. 8°. T.C.I 141. L, CK, CM; CH, CLC, NP, TU, Y.

5178   —[Anr. ed.] *For Tho. Collins and John Ford, and Will. Cademan,* 1673. 8°. L, O; CH, CN, MH, NC, Y.

5179-81 Entries cancelled.

5182   A collection of precedents. 1685. 8°. O.

5183   A collection of prints and paintings, . . . 2d . . . July, 1689. [*n.p.*], 1689. 4°.* L.

5184   —, 5th . . . July, 1689. [*n.p.*], 1689. 4°.* L.

5185   —, 12th . . . July, 1689. [*n.p.*], 1689. 4°.* L.

5186   —, 19th . . . July, 1689. [*n.p.*], 1689. 4°.* L.

5187   —, 26th . . . July, 1689. [*n.p.*], 1689. 4°.* L.

5188   —, 2d . . . August, 1689. [*n.p.*], 1689. 4°.* L.

   Collection of private devotions. 1655. *See* Cosin, John, *bp.*

5189   A collection of private forms of prayer. *For Sam. Keble, and Dan. Brown,* 1690. 12°. T.C.II 330. O; CLC.

   Collection of rewards, 1680. *See* Burnet, Gilbert. *bp.*

5190 A collection of records of the great misfortunes. *For Henry Iackeson*, 1642. 4°.* LT; MIU, Y.

5190A A collection of Scotch proverbs. *By R. D.*, 1663. 12°. L, O.

5191 A collection of select discourses out of the most eminent wits of France and Italy. *By S. R. for Henry Brome*, 1678. 8°. T.C.I 313. L, O, CM, CT; CH, CN, NP, Y.

Collection of seven and fifty. 1665. *See* J., W.

5192 A collection of several ingenious poems. 1660. 8°. O; CU.

Collection of several passages. 1659. *See* Walker, Henry.

5192A A collection of several symphonies. [*London*], *William Nott*, 1688. 4°. L.

Collection of several tracts. 1685. *See* Burnet, Gilbert, *bp*.

5192B A collection of several treatises concerning the . . . penal laws. *For Richard Royston*, 1675. 4°. T.C.I 205. L, O, C, EN, DT; CH, MH, NCL, PBL, WF.

5192C —[Anr. ed.] *For R. Royston*, 1677. 4°. CCC, CT.

5193 —Second edition. *Printed, and sold by Randal Taylor*, 1688. 4°. T.C.II 266. L, C, LIL, EN, DT; CH, MBA, NU, WF, Y.

Collection of several treatises in answer. [*n.p.*], 1672. *See* Cressy, Hugh Paulin.

Collection of so much. 1661. *See* B., W.

Collection of some of the murthers. 1662. *See* S., R.

Collection of some passages. [*n.p.*, 1700.] *See* Pennyman, John.

5194 A collection of speciall passages and certaine informations . . . from Munday Octob. 17. *For Francis Coles, Novemb. 2*, 1642. cap., 4°.* LT, O.

5195 A collection of such of the orders heretofore used in Chancery. *By John Macock for Francis Tyton*, 1649. 8°. LT, CCA, DT; WF, YL.

5196 —[Anr. ed.] *By Robert White, for Francis Tyton*, 1652. 12°. DC, OC; CH, MHL.

5197 —[Anr. ed.] 1660. 12°. LL; YL.

5198 —[Anr. ed.] *For Henry Chase, to be sold at his shop, and by Humphery [sic] Tuckey*, 1661. 12°. L, LGI, LL; LC, MHL, WF.

5199 —[Anr. ed.] *Dublin, John Crooke*, [1667?]. 8°. DIX 135. DIX.

5200 —[Anr. ed.] *R. Pawlet*, 1669. 12°. T.C.I 53. LL; MHL.

5200A —[Anr. ed.] *Dublin, Benjamin Tooke*, 1673. DIX 149. DK.

5200B —[Anr. ed.] 1676. 8°. O; MHL, NCL.

Collection of such statutes. 1685. *See* England, Laws; H., T.

Collection of svndry petitions. [*n.p.*], 1642. *See* Aston, Sir Thomas.

Collection of texts. 1686. *See* Drelincourt, Charles.

Collection of the brave exploits. 1686. *See* Assigny, Samuel d'.

5201 A collection of the choyest [sic] and newest songs. Second book. *For and sold by Iohn Crouch*, [1687]. 4°.* L.

Collection of the church-history. 1688. *See* Milner, John.

5202 A collection of the dying speeches, letters of those . . . Protestants who suffered . . . under . . . Lord Jeffreys. [*London*], *sold by J. Dunton*, 1689. 4°. T.C.II 258. L, YM.

5203 A collection of the funeral orations, . . . upon the death of . . . Mary II. *For John Dunton, to be sold by Edmund Richardson*, 1695. 4°. L, C, OB; CH, CN, LC, Y.

5204 A collection of the names of the merchants living in . . . London. *For Sam. Lee, to be sold at his shop; and Dan. Major*, 1677. 16°. T.C.I 294. L, O, LG, MRL; CH, MH.

5204A A collection of the newest and choicest songs. *For C. Corbett*, 1684. fol.* CLC.

5205 A collection of the newest and most ingenious poems, . . . Popery. *Printed*, 1689. 4°.* L, O, C, MR, EN; CLC, CU, MH, NU, WF, Y.

5206 —[Anr. ed.] *Printed*, 1689. 4°.* L; CU, MIU, TU.

5207 A collection of the rights and priviledges of Parliament. *For Lawrence Chapman*, 1642. 4°.* LT, O, C, EN, DT; CH, CN, MH, WF, Y.

5208 A collection of the several addresses in the late King James's time. [*London*, 1700.] fol.* L, LG, OC, CS, HH; CH, TU, WF, Y.

5209 A collection of the several late petitions, &c. to the honourable House. *Printed*, 1693. 4°.* L, MH, Y.

Collection of the several papers. [*n.p.*], 1655. *See* Stouppe, Jean Baptiste.

Collection of the statues. 1667. *See* England: Laws.

Collection of the substance of several speeches. 1681. *See* England, Parliament, House of Commons.

Collection of tracts. 1692. *See* Monro, Alexander.

5210–11 Entries cancelled.

5212 Collection of treatises on the penal laws. 1677. 4°. LW.

5213 Collection of twenty-four songs. *By F. Leach for Charles Corbet, and published by W. Davis*, 1685. 4°.* CH.

Collection or narative [sic]. 1655. *See* Stouppe, J. B.

Collection out of the best approved authors. 1657. *See* Gaule, John.

5214 Entry cancelled.

5215 A collection out of the book called Liber regalis. *By R. D. for Charls Adams*, 1661. 4°.* LT, O, C, LL, CT; CN, MH, WF, Y.

Collections of acute diseases. 1687. *See* Pechey, John.

5216 Collections of letters from severall parts. *Printed at London for Robert Ibbitson*, 1649. 4°.* LT, C, LFEA; CH, Y.

5217 Collections of notes taken at the kings tryall . . . on Saturday last, Janua. 20. 1648. *By Robert Ibbitson*, 1648[9], 4°.* LT, HH, SP; CH, MIU, WF.

5218 —, on Munday last, Janua. 22. 1648. —, 1648[9]. 4°.* LT, SP.

5219 —, on Tuesday last, Janua. 23. 1648. —, 1648[9]. 4°.* LT, O; MIU.

5220 —, on Saturday last, Janua. 27, 1648. colop: —, 1649. cap., 4°.* LT, HH, SP; CH, WF.

Collections of scripture. 1695. *See* M., G.

5221 Collections out of Magna Charts. 1643. 4°. DT.

Collections out of the late Lord Chief Justice Hale's. 1689. *See* Nepos, Cornelius.

5222 The collectors of the old clothes. [*London*], 1672. brs. CH.

5223 **College, Stephen.** The last speech and confession of. colop: *For A. Banks*, 1681. brs. L, O, C, LL; CH, CN, MH, NP, Y.

5224 —A letter from. colop: [London], for Francis Smith, 1681. brs. L, OM, HH; CH, MH, WCL, Y.

5225 —A letter written from Oxford by. colop: By N. T., 1681. brs. L, O; CH, MH, Y.

5226 —A letter written from the Tower by. colop: For R.J., 1681. brs. L, O; CH, MBA, Y.

5226A —Ra-ree show. For A.B., 1681. brs. L, MC; CH, MH, PU, WF, Y.

5227 [–] A satyr against in-justice. [n.p., 1682–85.] brs. L, C, CT, HH; CH, CN, MH, TU, Y.

5228 —The speech and carriage of Stephen Colledge. colop: For Edith Colledge, 1681. cap., fol. LG; CN, WF, Y.

5229 ——[Anr. ed.] For Thomas Basset, and John Fish, 1681. fol.* L, O, CM, MR, DT; CH, MH, PL, TU, Y.

5230 ——[Anr. ed.] colop: For T. Basset and John Fish, 1681. brs. L, C, LL, OM, HH; CH, MBP, MH, NU, WF.

5231 —A true copy of the dying words of. colop: For Edith Colledge, 1681. brs. L, O, CM, EN, DT; CH, MH, NU, TU, WCL, WF.

5231A Collegii Medicorum Londinensium fundatores. [London, 1662.] fol. L.

[Collens, John.] Defence of the true church. 1659. See Crook, John.

5232 —A lamentation taken up. [n.p., 1658.] 4°.* LF.

5233 —A message from the spirit. colop: By M.I. for Robert Wilson, 1660. 4°.* L, LF, OC, BBN; MH, PH.

5233A —Something written after the manner of a discourse. For J.C., 1662. 8°.* LF.

5234 —A touch-stone: whereby. For Robert Wilson, 1660. 4°.* L, O, C, LF, BBN; MH, NU, PSC, WF, Y.

5235 —A word in season to all in authority. For Robert Wilson, 1660. 4°.* L, O, C, LF, BBN; CH, MH, PH, WF, Y.

5236 **Collet, William.** Whereas there has been unjust and malicious reflections . . . the depositions of. [n.p., 1700.] brs. L.

5237 **Collier, Giles.** An answer to fifteen questions. For Edward Brewster, 1656. 4°. LT.

5238 —The taking away of righteous & merciful persons. Oxford, by W. Hall, 1661. 4°.* MADAN 2550. L; MH, WF.

5239 —Vindiciæ thesium de Sabbato. For Christopher Meredith, 1653. 4°. LW; MH, NU, Y.

5240 ——[Anr. ed.] For Edward Brewster, 1656. 4°.* LT.

5241 [**Collier, Jeremy.**] Animadversions upon the modern explication of II Hen. 7. Cap. I. [London, 1689.] cap., 4°.* L, C, OM, MR, EN; CU, MH, NP, WF, Y.

5241A [–]—[Anr. ed.] [London, 1689.] brs. OC, MR, HH.

5242 —An answer to the animadversions on two pamphlets. [London, 1696.] cap., 4°.* O, CT, MR, AU, EN; CH, MH, NC, WF, Y.

5243 Entry cancelled.

5244 [–] A brief essay concerning the independency of church power. [London, 1692.] cap., 8°.* O, CS, CT, LL, DT; MBA, MIU.

5245 [–] The case of the two absolvers. 1696. 4°. O, MR.

5246 [–] A caution against inconsistency. [London, 1690.] cap., 4°.* O, C, MR, AU, EN; CH, NC, TU, WF, Y.

5246A —Χρισιζ τελειωτικη. A discourse of confirmation. For R. Royston, 1664. 8°. CT.

5246B —Dagon is fallen! For Barnaby C . . . R., [1696.] 8°. CT.

5247 —A defence of the absolution given to Sr. William Perkins. [London, 1696.] 4°.* L, O, CT, EN, AU; CH, MH, NC, WF, Y.

5248 —A defence of the Short view. For S. Keble, R. Sare, and H. Hindmarsh, 1699. 8°. L, O, CE, LVD, ES; BN, CH, CN, LC, MH, NU, TU, Y.

5249 [–] The desertion discuss'd. [London, 1689.] cap., 4°.* L, O, C, EN, DT; CH, CN, NU, TU, WF, Y.

5250 [–]—[Anr. ed.] 1689. 8°.* O; CJC.

5251 —The difference between the present and future state. For Sam. Smith, 1686. 4°.* T.C.II 164. L, O, CS, EC, YM; MH, NP, WF, Y.

5252 [–] Dr. Sherlock's case of allegiance considered. Printed, 1691. 4°. L, O, C, AU, DT; CH, CN, MB, NU, WF, Y.

5253 —Essays upon several moral subjects. Second edition. For R. Sare and H. Hindmarsh, 1697. 8°. T.C.III 29. O, C, LI, EC, DT; BN, CN, LC, PU, Y.

5254 ——Third edition. —, 1698. 8°. T.C.III 82. L, O, CJ, BR, ENC; CH, CU, MBC, PL, Y.

5255 ——Fourth edition. For Richard Sare, and H. Hindmarsh, 1700. 8°. L, O, CPE; BN, NU, OCI, TU, Y.

5255A [–] Great questions in the case of the absolution. [London, 1696.] cap., 4°.* CH.

5256 —Miscellanies: in five essays. For Sam. Keeble, and Jo. Hindmarsh, 1694. 8°. T.C.II 526. O, C, LCL, OC, GK; CH, CU, MH, NU, WF, Y.

5257 —Miscellanies upon moral subjects. The second part. For Sam. Keeble, and Jo. Hindmarsh, 1695. 8°. T.C.II 551. OC, RPL; CH, MH, NU, TU, WF.

5258 [–] The office of a chaplain enquir'd into. Cambridge, by John Hayes; for Henry Dickinson. And are to be sold by Sam. Smith, London, 1688. 4°.* L, O, C, MR, E; CN, MH, NC, WF, Y.

5259 [–] A perswasive to consideration. Printed, 1693. 4°.* O, C, MR; CH, MM.

5260 [–]—Second edition. —, 1695. 4°.* L, O, CT, DC, AU; CH, CN, NU, WF, Y.

5261 —A reply to The absolution of a penitent. [London, 1696]. cap., 4°.* L, OC, CT, MR, EN; CH, CLC, MH, NC Y.

5262 —A second defence. For S. Keble, R. Sare and G. Strahan, 1700. 8°. L, O, C, ENC, DT; BN, CH, CN, LC, MH, NC, TU, Y.

5263 —A short view of the . . . English stage. For S. Keble, R. Sare, and H. Hindmarsh, 1698. 8°. T.C.III 66. L, O, C, E, DT; BN, CH, CN, LC, MH, NC, TU, Y.

5264 ——Second edition. —, 1698. 8°. L, O, C, LG, CT; BN, CN, MH, NC, TU, WF, Y.

5265 ——Third edition. —, 1698. 8°. L, D; CH, MH, NC, TU, WF, Y.

5266 ——Fourth edition. For S. Keble, and R. Sare, 1699. 8°. L, O, CS, LG, EN; BN, CLC, CN, MH, NU, TU, WF, Y.

5267 [–] Vindiciæ juris regii: or, remarques. Printed, 1689. 4°. L, O, C, LL, MR; CH, MH, NU, WF, Y.

5267A **Collier, Thomas.** The works of. *By Robert White for Giles Calvert,* 1652. 8°. MH, NHC, Y.

5267B —An answer to An epistle. [*London,* 1657.] cap., 4°.* LC.

5268 —The body of divinity. *For Nath. Crouch,* 1674. 8°. T.C.I 167. L, O, C, LCL; NHC.

5269 [–] A brief answer to some of the objections. *By Henry Hills, to be sold by Thomas Brewster,* 1656. 4°.* LT, LCL; CSS, NPT.

5270 —A brief discovery of the corruption of the ministry. *Printed,* 1647. 8°.* LT, C, YM, DT; NN.

5271 ——[Anr. ed.] *For Giles Calvert,* [1647]. 4°.* YM; NU, TSM.

5272 ——[Anr. ed.] *For Giles Calvert,* [1649?]. 4°.* NGT, NU.

5273 —Certaine queries. [*London*], *printed,* 1645. 8°.* LT; NHC.

5274 —A compendious discourse about . . . Christian faith. *By H. H. for Tho. Fabian,* 1682. 8°. O.

5275 —A confession of faith. *For Francis Smith,* 1678. 8°. L.

5276 —The decision & clearing of the great point. *For G. C.,* 1659. 4°.* L, O, CS, BB, YM; NHC.

5276A —A dialogue between a minister. *Thomas Brewster,* 1656. LF.

5277 —A discourse of the true gospel blessedness. *By H. Hills, for the author, to be sold by Giles Calvert, and Thomas Brewster,* 1659. 8°. L; NHC, NU.

5278 —A discovery of the new creation. *For Giles Calvert,* 1647. 8°.* LT, C, CT; NU.

5279 ——[Anr. ed.] —, 1649. 4°.* YM; NU, WF.

5280 —A doctrinal discourse of self-denial. *For Thomas Fabian,* 1691. 8°. T.C.II 331. O, C.

5281 —The exaltation of Christ. *By R. L. for Giles Calvert,* 1646. 8°. LT, C; CLC, NU.

5282 ——Second edition. —, 1647. 4°. LW; NGT, NU.

5283 ——Third edition. *By G. D. for Giles Calvert,* 1647. 4°. L, YM; NU.

5284 ——Fourth edition. *For Giles Calvert,* 1651. 8°.O.

5285 —The font-guard routed. *For the author, to be sold by Giles Calvert,* 1652. 4°. O, CT, LW; NHC.

5286 —A general epistle. *For Giles Calvert,* 1648. 8°. C; CU, NU.

5287 ——[Anr. ed.] —, 1649. 4°. YM; CU, NGT, NU, WF.

5288 —The glory of Christ. *Printed,* 1647–49. 2 v. 8°. L, C, YM; NHC, NU.

5289 —The interest of Christ. 1659. 4°. LCL.

5290 [–] A looking-glasse for the Quakers. *For Thomas Brewster,* 1657. 4°.* LT, O, CS, LF; NHC, NU, WF.

5291 —The marrow of Christianity. *For Giles Calvert,* 1647. 8°. LT; NHC, NU.

5292 ——[Anr. ed.] *By Charles Sumptner for Giles Calvert,* 1650. 4°. YM; NU.

5293 ——[Anr. ed.] [*n.p.*], 1651. 4°. YM.

5294 —Pulpit-guard and font-guard routed. 1652. O, LB, LW, BB, MBC.

5295 —The pulpit-guard routed. *For the author, to be sold by Giles Calvert,* 1651. 4°. LT, LD, YM, DT; MBA, MH, NHC, NU, WF.

5295A ——Second edition. —, 1652. 4°. LW, BR; WF.

5296 —The right constitution. *By Henry Hills,* 1654. 8°. LT; MHS.

5297 —A second generall epistle. *For Giles Calvert,* 1649. 8°. C; CH, NGT, NU, WF.

5298 —The second volume of the works. *For Giles Calvert,* 1649. 16°. L, YM; NU, WF.

5299 —A third generall epistle. *For Giles Calvert,* 1649. 4°. CU, NGT, NU, WF.

5299A —Three great queries. 1645. 8°.* NHC.

5300 —The titles of the severall pieces. *For Giles Calvert,* 1647. 4°. NU.

5300A —To all the churches of Jesus Christ. *For Thomas Brewster,* 1657. brs. MH.

5301 —A vindication of the army-remonstrance. *For Giles Calvert,* [1648]. 4°.* LT, O, C; CH, NHC, NPT, PL, WF.

5302 —A word in season. *By Henry Hills,* 1655. 4°.* BBN; NU, Y.

5303 **Collinges, John.** The vvorks of. First volume. *For Richard Tomlins,* 1655. 4°. L.

5304 —A caveat for old and new profaneness. [*n.p.*], 1651. 4°. LCL, CJ.

5304A —Certamina. *For Rich. Tomlins,* 1655. 4°. CLC.

5305 —A cordial for a fainting soule. *For Richard Tomlins,* 1649. 4°. C, LCL, LW, AU; CH, LC, MB, WF.

5306 ——Second edition. *For Richard Tomlins,* 1652. 4°. LT, O, DC, ENC; MH, NU, Y.

5307 ——Third edition. *For Rich. Tomlins,* 1657. 4°. L; MH, PJB, TU.

5308 ——[Anr. ed.] *For Richard Tomlins,* 1659. 4°. NU.

5309 ——Part II, being the sum. —, 1650. 4°. O, LCL, LW, AU, DT; MH, NU, WF, Y.

5310 ——[Anr. ed.] —, 1659. 4°. L; MH, TU, WF.

5311 ——Part III. —, 1652. 4°. LT, O, LW, DC, AU; MH, NU, TU, WF, Y.

5312 —Defensative armour. *For Benjamin Alsop, and Edward [sic] Giles in Norwich,* 1680. 8°. T.C.I 438. L, C, LCL; CH, MH, NPT, NU, Y.

5313 —Elisha's lamentation for Elijah. *By J. Streater, for Richard Tomlins,* 1657. 4°. LT, O, OC, ENC; CH, NU, WF.

5313A ——[Anr. ed.] *By J. Streater, for W. Frankling in Norwich,* 1657. 4°. YM; Y.

5314 —Τὸ ἐναρκη. An exercitation. [*n.p.*], *Printed,* 1675. 4°. LCL; PL.

5315 —English Presbytery. 1680. 4°. LCL; CH.

5316 —The excellent woman discoursed. 1669. 8°. L, YM; NPT.

5316A —Faith & experience. *For Richard Tomlins,* 1649. 8°. MH.

5317 —Five lessons for a Christian to learne. *For Rich: Tomlins,* 1650. 8°. O, C, LCL, LW; NPT, NU, WF, Y.

5318 —The happiness of brethrens. *By T. S. for Edward Giles. in Norwich,* 1689. 4°.* L, O, LCL; MH, NU.

5319 [–] The history of conformity. *By A. Maxwell, and R. Roberts,* 1681. 4°.* T.C.I 452. L, O, SP; CH, MBA, NU, WF, Y.

5320 [–] —[Anr. ed.] *By R. Roberts,* 1689. 4°.* T.C.II 258. L, C, LW, WCA, BR; CH, MB, MM, NU.

5321 —The improvableness of water-baptism. *By A. Maxwell and R. Roberts,* 1681. 4°.* L, O, CK, LW, EN; MBA, NHC, NC, NU.

5322 —Indoctus doctor edoctus: or a short ansvver. *By H: Hills for R. Tomlins*, 1654[5]. 4°. LT, O, YM, EN; NPT, NU.

5323 —The intercourses of divine love. *By A. Maxwell for Tho. Parkhurst*, 1676. 4°. T.C.I 215. L, O, CCH, RPL, GU; MH, NHC, NPT, NU.

5324 — —[Anr. ed.] *By T. Snowden, for Edward Giles in Norwich*, 1683. 4°. T.C.II 26. L, CCH, LW, RPL, GU; LC, NHC, NPT, NU.

5325 —A lesson of self-deniall. *For Rich: Tomlins*, 1649. 4°. MH, NU, WF, Y.

5325A —Light in darkness. 1669. 8°. LSC, YM.

5325B —The lost sheep brought home. 1649. OW.

5326 —A memorial for posteritie. *For William Franklin, in Norwich*, 1647. 4°. MH, MWA, NPT.

5327 —A modest plea for the Lord's Day. *Printed*, 1669. 8°. O; NU.

5328 —A new lesson for the indoctus doctor. *By J. G. for Joseph Cranford*, 1654. 4°.* LT, O, CJ, YM; MH.

5329 [–] Par nobile. Two treatises. *Printed*, 1669. 8°. L, O, LCL, LW, SA; CU, MH, NU, WF, Y.

5329A —Provocator provocatus. *For William Francklyns in Norwich*, 1654. 4°. CJ; MBA.

5330 [–] A reasonable account, why some pious, nonconforming ministers. [*n.p.*], 1679. 8°. L, O, CT, LCL, OB; CH, MH, NU, WF, Y.

5331 —Responsoria ad erratica pastoris. *For R. Tomlins*, 1652. 4°. LT, O, E, EN, DT; CH, NPT, NU, WF, Y.

5332 —Responsoria ad erratica piscatoris. Or, a caveat. *For Richard Tomlins*, 1653. 4°. LT, O, CT, E, EN; MBA, NPT, NU, Y.

5333 —Responsoria bipartita. *By H. Hills for Richard Tomlins*, [1655]. 4°. LT, O, LCL, LW, EN; MB, NPT, NU.

5334 Entry cancelled.

5335 —Several discourses. *For Tho. Parkhurst, sold by E. Giles in Norwich*, 1678. 4°. T.C.I 328. L, C, LCI, E, ENC; MH, NF, NPT, NU, Y.

5336 [–] Short animadversions upon a sermon lately preached. *Printed*, 1680. 4°.* L, O, CS, EC, DT; CH, NU, WF, Y.

5337–8 Entries cancelled.

5339 —The spouse under the apple-tree. *For Rich: Tomlins*, 1649. 4°. LSC; MH, NPT, NU, WF.

5340 Entry cancelled.

5341 —The spouses hidden glory. *For Richard Tomlins*, 1647. 4°. LT, O, LCL, YM, DT; NU, WF.

5342 —Strength in weakness. A sermon. *For John Hancock*, 1676. 4°.* T.C.I 251. L, LW; MH, MHS, NU, WF.

5343 [–] A supplement to a little book, entituled, A reasonable account. *Printed*, 1680. 8°. O, CT, LW; MH, NU, WF, Y.

5344 —Thirteen sermons. *By T. S. for Edward Giles in Norwich*, 1684. 8°. T.C.II 68. O, LCL, ENC; MH, NU, Y.

5345 [–] The vindication of liturgies. *For Benjamin Alsop*, 1681. 8°. T.C.I 458. L, LCL, LW, P, GU; CLC, Y.

5346 —Vindiciæ ministerii evangelici; a vindication. *For Rich. Tomlins*, 1651. 4°. O, CS, LCL, EN, DT; NHC, NPT, NU, WF, Y.

5347 — —Second edition. —, 1651. 4°. LT, LCL; CH, NU.

5348 —Vindiciæ ministerii evangelici revindicatæ: or. . . . *By S. G. for Richard Tomlins*, 1658. 4°. LT, O, LW, E, ENC; MBA, NHC, NU, Y.

5349 —The weavers pocket-book. *By A. Maxwell for Tho. Parkhurst*, 1675. 8°. T.C.I 210. L, O, LCL, E; MH, NC.

5350 — —[Anr. ed.] *Edinburgh*, [1675?] 8°. O.

5351 — —[Anr. ed.] [*n.p.*], *printed*, 1695. 8°. L; NU.

5352 **Collings, Richard.** Men, women, or children, Feb. 10. 1688. [*n.p.*, 1688.] brs. L.

5353 —October the 6th. 1690. Ruptures or broken bellies cured. [*n.p.*, 1690.] brs. L.

5354 **Collinne, William.** The spirit of the phanatiqves dissected. [*London*], *for F. Wallis*, 1660. 4°.* LT, HH; CH, MH, MIU.

5355 **Collins, Anne.** Divine songs and meditacions. *By R. Bishop*, 1653. 8°. CH.

5356 [**Collins, Anthony.**] An answer to Dr. Scot's cases against Dissenters. *For A. Baldwin*, 1700. 4°. T.C.III 228. L, O, EC, EN, DT; CH, MM,V, WF.

5357 Entry cancelled.

5358 **Collins, Grenville.** Great Britain's coasting-pilot. *By Freeman Collins, and are to be sold by Ric. Mount*, 1693. fol. L, O, LG, DCH, EN; CH, CLC, WF, Y.

5358A [**Collins, Hercules.**] Animadversions upon the responses of the Athenian Mercury. [*London*, 1692.] fol.* L.

5358B —An answer to an epistle written. [*London*, 1660.] LC.

5359 —An antidote to prevent the prevalency of Anabaptism. *For W. Marshall*, 1693. 4°. L, O, ENC; CH.

5360 —Believers-baptism from Heaven. *For the author, and sold by J. Hancock*, 1691. 8°. L, LCL, LW; NHC.

5361 —Counsel for the living. *By George Larkin for the author*, 1684. 4°.* L, O, LW, MBC; LC, NHC, VC.

5362 —The marrow of gospel-history. *For the author*, 1696. 12°. L, O; NHC, NPT.

5363 —Mountains of brass. *For John Harris*, 1690. 4°.* L, O, LCL.

5364 —An orthodox catechism. *Printed*, 1680. 12°. L.

5365 —A poem of the . . . life . . . of our Lord Jesus Christ. [*n.p.*], 1696. 4°.* LCL.

5366 —The sandy foundation of infant-baptism shaken. *For the author, and are to be sold by Will. Marshall, and John Marshall*, 1695. LF.

5367 —Some reasons for separation. *For John How*, 1682. 4°.* L, O, SP, DT; Y.

5368 —Three books: viz. I. The scribe. *Printed, and sold by the author at Wapping, and R. Mount*, 1696. 12°. L, LCL; MH, NHC.

5369 —A voice from the prison. *By George Larkin, for the author*, 1684. 4°.* L, O; NHC.

5370 **Collins, John.** A curious collection of law-books, . . . 2d day of July, 1683. [*London*], *2 July, 1683.* 4°. L, O, OC; PL.

5371 —The description and uses of a general quadrant. *Printed*, 1658. 4°. L, O, C, LR, OC; CLC, MB, PL, RPJ.

5372 —The doctrine of decimal arithmetick. *By R. Holt for Nath. Ponder*, 1685. T.C.II 138. L, C, LR, DT; WF.

5372A [–] Exchanges ready computed. [*London?* 1655]. cap., fol.* WF.

5373 —Geometricall dyalling. *By Thomas Johnson for Francis Cossinet; also to be sold by Henry Sutton,* 1659. 4°. L, C, LPO, CT, E; NC, WF, Y.

5374 —An introduction to merchants accounts. *By James Flesher for Nicholas Bourn,* 1653. fol. NC, PL, WF.

5375 ——Second edition. *By James Flesher,* 1664. fol. LR, SC.

5376 —[Anr. ed.] *By William Godbid for Robert Horne,* 1674. fol. T.C.I 170. O, C; CU, PL, Y.

5377 Entry cancelled.

5378 —The mariner's plain scale. *By T.J. for Fr. Cossinet,* 1659. 4°. LT, O, C, LR, E; BN, MH, MU, PL, WF, Y.

5379 —A plea for the bringing in of Irish cattel. *By A. Godbid and J. Playford, and sold by Langley Curtis,* 1680. 4°. L, O, C, OC, EN; CH, CU, LC, MH, NC, Y.

5380 —Salt and fishery. *By A. Godbid and J. Playford, and are to be sold by Mr. Robrrt Horne,* 1682. 4°. L, O, C, LPO, E; CH, CU, MH, NC, WF, Y.

5380A ——[Anr. ed.] *By A. Godbid and J. Playford,* 1682. 4°. OC.

5380B ——[Anr. ed.] *—to be sold by Robert Horne, John Kensey, Henry Faithorn, William Bury,* 1682. 4°. OC, LWL, CM; MIU, WF.

5381 —The sector on a quadrant. *By J. Macock,* 1658. 4°. LT, O, LG, LPO, OC; MU, PL, WF, Y.

5382 ——[Anr. ed.] *By J. M. for George Hurlock, Thomas Pierrepont; William Fisher; and Henry Sutton,* 1659. 4°. O, C, LR, OC, E; MB, MH, Y.

5383 **Collins, Richard,** *supervisor.* The country gaugers vade mecum. *By W. Godbid, to be sold by M. Pitt, and by Anthony Owen of Bristol,* 1677. 8°. L, BR.

5383A ——Fifth edition. *By W. Horton, for W. Shrowsbery,* 1688. 8°. LC.

5384 [**Collins, Richard,** *victim.*] The cause of England's misery. *Printed,* 1698. 4°. L, O, LL; CLC, WF, Y.

5384A **Collins, Samuel, M.A.** Prudenter, piè, prosperè. A sermon. *By F. Collins for Tho. Guy,* 1698. 4°.* T.C.III 52. L, O, CT; CN.

5385 C[ollins, Samuel, *M.D.*] The present state of Russia. *By John Winter, for Dorman Newman,* 1671. 8°. T.C.I 72. L, O, C, CT, E; CH, CN, MH, PL, WF, Y.

5386 Entry cancelled.

5387 —A systeme of anatomy. *In the Savoy, by Thomas Newcomb,* 1685. 2 v. fol. L, O, C, LCP, E; BN, CH, CU, NAM, WF, Y.

5388 **Collins, Thomas.** Choice and rare experiments in physick. *By J. T. for Francis Eglesfield,* 1658. 12°. LT; HC.

5389 [**Collins, William.**] Missa triumphans. *Printed at Louain,* 1675. 8°. L, O, C, E, DT; CH, MB, NU, TU, WF.

Collin's walk. 1690. *See* D'Urfey, Thomas.

5390 [**Collop, John.**] Charity commended. *Printed,* 1658. 4°. NU.

5390A ——[Anr. ed.] *By M. S.,* 1660. 4°. LG.

5391 ——[Same title.] *—,* 1667. 4°. L.

5392 —Itur [sic] satyricum: in loyall stanzas. *By T. M. for William Shears,* 1660. 4°.* L, O, EN; CN.

5393 —A letter with animadversions upon the animadverter. *For M. B.,* 1661. 4°.* O, C, LW, OC, CJ; CH, MH, NC, NU, Y.

5394 —Medici Catholicon, or a Catholick medicine. *For Humphrey Moseley,* 1656. 8°. LT, O, C, CP; NU, Y.

5395 —Poesis rediviva: or, poesie reviv'd. *For Humphrey Moseley,* 1656. 8°. LT, O, C, CP, GK; CH, CN, LC, MH, Y.

Colloquium Davidis. 1679. *See* Petty, Sir William.

5395A **Colly, Anthony.** A more full discovery. 1671. 4°. O.

5395B —Natures champion. *For the author,* 1670. L, LG.

5396 **Collyn, Nicholas.** A briefe summary of the lawes. *By R. Constable, for Math. Walbanck, and H. Twyford,* 1650. 12°. L, O, CCA, ES; MHL.

5397 ——[Anr. ed.] *By T. L. for Mathew Walbancke,* 1655. 12°. LL, CE, CT; LC, MHL, YL.

5398 ——Fourth edition. *By T. M. for Elizabeth Walbanck, and Samuel Heyrick,* 1663. 12°. L; LC, MHL, WF, YL.

5399 [**Colman, Benjamin.**] Gospel order revived. [*New York*], *Printed,* 1700. 4°. C, LC, MH, NN, Y.

5400 [**Colmenero de Ledesma, Antonio.**] Chocolate: or, an Indian drinke. *By J. G. for Iohn Dakins,* 1652. 8°. LT, O, CS, GH; MHS.

5401 **Colom, Jacob Aertsz.** The fierie sea-colomne. *Amsterdam,* 1644. 43. fol. E.

5402 —The lightning-colom. *Amsterdam,* 1660. fol. LAD.

5403 [–]—[Anr. ed.] *—,* 1662. fol. LAD, E.

5403A [–]—[Anr. ed.] *—, by Peter Goos,* 1669. fol. LAD; RPJ.

5403B [–]—[Anr. ed.] *—,* 1678. fol. MB.

5403AB [–]—[Anr. ed.] *By Jacob and Casparus Louts-man,* 1670. fol. LUG.

5403AC [–]—[Anr. ed.] *—,* 1674. fol. LUG.

5403C [–]—[Anr. ed.] *—,* 1680. fol. Y.

5403D [–]—[Anr. ed.] *Amsterdam, C. Loots-man,* 1689. fol. LC.

5403E [–]—[Anr. ed.] *—,* 1692. fol. LC.

5403F [–] The new enlarged lightning sea column. *At Amsterdam, by Jacob Robyn,* 168-. fol. Y.

5403G —The new fierie sea-columne. *Amsterdam, J. Colom,* 1649. fol. L, LAD; Y.

Colemesius, P. *See* Colomiès, Paul.

5404 **Colomiès, Paul.** Ad Gulielmi Cave . . . chartophylacem. *Impensis Richardi Chiswell,* 1686. 8°. L, O, C, AU, EN; CH, NGT, PL, WF, Y.

5405 ——Second edition. *—,* 1687. 8°. O, C, CS; PL.

5406 —Observationes sacræ. *Impensis J. Adamson,* 1688. 8°. T.C.II 254. L, O, C, OM, Y.

5406A ——Second edition. *—,* 1688. 8°. OC, CS, CSS; WU.

5407 ——"Second" edition. *—,* 1695. 8°. O.

5408 Collonel Grey's portmanteau opened. *By William Dugard,* 1650. 4°.* LT, O, CT, LVF, E; CH, MIU, NC, WF, Y.

5409 Colonel Huson's (or the cobler's) confession. [*London, printed,* 1659.] 4°.* L, O, OC, HH; MH, MIU, WF.

5409A Colonel John Okie's lamentation. *Printed,* 1660. brs. LT, O; MH, WF.

5410 Collonel Morgans letter concerning his taking the strong garrison of Kildrummie. *By F: Neile,* 1654. 4°.* LT.

5411 Colonell Poyers forces in Wales totally routed. *By B. A.,* 1648. 4°.* LT, O, AN; MH.

5412 Colonell Rainsborowes ghost. colop: *Printed at London*, 1648. fol.* LT.

5412A Coll. Sidney's lamentation. *For J. Dean*, 1683. brs. CLC, WF.

5413 Collonel Sidney's overthrow. [*London*], *for J. Deacon*, [1683]. brs. L.

Colonel Weldens taking. 1646. *See* C., W.

5414 [Colquitt, Anthony.] Modern reports. *For T. Basset, J. Wright, R. Chiswell, and S. Heyrick*, 1682. 5 v. fol. T.C.I 495. L, O, LL, WCA, DT; CH, MHL, NCL, NR, WF.

5415 [–] —[Anr. ed.] *For W. Battersby, Samuel Heyrick, Rich. Chiswel, Samuel Keble, A. and J. Churchill, and Matthew Wolton*, 1700. fol. L, O, CJ; WF.

5416 [–] —The second part. *By the assigns of Richard Edw. Atkins, for Charles Harper*, 1698. fol. CJ; WF.

5416A [–] —The third part. —, 1700. fol. CJ; WF.

5417–8 Entries cancelled.

Colson, Lancelot. *See* Coelson, Lancelot.

5419 Colson, Nathaniel. The mariner's kalendar. 1676. 4°. AU.

5420 —The mariners new kalendar. *By J. Darby for William Fisher; Robert Boulter, and Ralph Smith*, 1677. 4°. T.C.I 211. L.

5420A ——Third edition. —, 1679. 4°. OC.

5421 ——[Anr. ed.] *For R. Mount*, 1696. 4°. BN.

5421A ——[Anr. ed.] *By J. P. for Richard Mount*, 1697. 4°. NN.

5421B ——Sixth edition, 1699. 4°. CLC.

5422 C[olson], N[icholas]. A modest and true account of the chief points in controversie. *Antwerp: Printed*, 1696. 8°. L, O; AU, WF.

5422A Colson, Francesco Casparo. Elegiacus ultramarinæ palladis planctus. [*n.p.,*] 1648. brs. L.

5422B —The new trismagister. *For B. Griffin & R. Wilde*, 1688. 8°. T.C.II 305. C, LL, LW; WF.

Colthrop, *Sir* Henry. *See* Calthrop, *Sir* Henry.

5422C Colton, *Dr.* The artist's vade mecum. *For E. Tracy*, 1698. 8°. T.C.III 66. C.

Coluino, Ludiomæo. *See* DuMoulin, Louis.

5423 C[olvill], A[lexander]. De loco parallelo. *Edinburgi, Anderson, pro G. Suintoun*, 1656. 4°. ALDIS 1534. E, EN.

5424 Colvill, James. Disputatio juridica, de interdictis. *Edinburgi, Mosman*, 1696. 4°. ALDIS 3546. EN.

5425 Colvill, Samuel. The grand impostor discovered. *Edinburgh, by His Majesties printers, for the author*, 1673. 4°. ALDIS 1982. L, LIL, E, EN, FSF; CH, MH, NU, WG, Y.

5426 [–] Mock poem, or, Whiggs supplication. *Printed*, 1681. 8°. L, CM, E, EN, GU; CH, CN, CU.

5427 [–] The Scotch Hudibras. *By T. B., sold by Randal Taylor*, 1692. 8°. L, BAMB; CH, CN, MH, WF, Y.

5428 —Whiggs supplication. A mock poem. *Edinburgh, by J. Reid, for A. Ogston*, 1687. 8°. ALDIS 2685. L, EN; CLC, MH, Y.

5429 —Whiggs supplication: or a mock poem. *Edinburgh*, 1695. 8°. ALDIS 3450. L, LW, EN, FSF; CH, CN, MH, WF.

5430 Colvill, William. Philosophia moralis Christiana. *Edinbvrgi, excudebant Georgius Swintoun, & Jacobus Glen*, 1670. 8°. ALDIS 1898. L, O, EN, AU, FSF; CH, CU, NU, WF, Y.

5431 —Refreshing streams. *By A. M. for Joseph Cranford*, 1655. 4°. LT, LCL, E, ENC, GU; MH, NPT, NU, WF, Y.

5432 —The righteous branch growing. *Edinburgh, by George Swintoun, James Glen, and Thomas Brown*, 1673. 4°. ALDIS 1983. L, E, GU, I; NPT, NU, WF.

5433 ——[Anr. ed.] *Sold by Moses Pitt*, 1673. 8°. T.C.I 168. ENC.

Colvin, Ludiomæus. *See* DuMoulin, Louis.

5434 Coma Berenices; or, the hairy comet. *For Jonathan Robinson, and John Hancock*, 1676. 8°.* T.C.I 180. O.

5435 Combach, Joannes. Metaphysicorum libri duo. *Oxonii, excudebat W. Hall, per R. Davis*, 1662. 12°. MADAN 2588. O.

5436 ——[Anr. ed.]. —, 1663. 12°. MADAN 2588n. OC, OCC.

5436A —Fundamenta chymica: or a sure guide. *By William Godbid, for William Barlow*, 1658. 8°. GU.

5437 A combate between Satan tempting. [*London*], *printed*, 1648. brs. LT.

5438 —[Anr. ed.] [*London*, 1648.] brs. MH.

5439 Entry cancelled.

5440 [Comber, Thomas]. Animadversions on Dr. Burnet's History of the rights of princes. *Printed*, 1682. 4°.* L, O, C, EN, DT; CH, NU.

5441 [–] Christianity no enthusiasm. *By T. D. for Henry Brome*, 1678. 8°. T.C.I 299. L, C, OB, LF, DT; MBA, NU, PH, WF, Y.

5442 [–] The Christian's best exercise. *For Randal Taylor*, 1689. 4°. O, OC, AN; CH, NU, WF, Y.

5443 [–] The church-catechism resolved. 1666. 8°. O.

5444 ——[Anr. ed.] *For T. Parkhurst*, 1681. 8°. T.C.I 449. O.

5444A ——[Anr. ed.] *By M. C. for Henry Brome and Robert Clavel*, 1681. 8°.* C, OC; WF, Y.

5444B ——[Anr. ed.] *For the company of stationers*, 1682. 8°. T.C.I 482. BAMB.

5445 ——[Anr. ed.] *By M. C. for Joanna Brome and Robert Clavel*, 1683. 8°.* O; NU, Y.

5445A ——[Anr. ed.] *For the company of stationers*, 1685. 8°. T.C.II 111. OC, EC; Y.

5445B ——[Anr. ed.] *Charles Brome*, 1685. 8°. MBA.

5446 ——[Anr. ed.] *By M. C., for Robert Clavell & C. Brome*, 1686. 8°.* T.C.II 171. L, CT; NU.

5446A ——[Anr. ed.] *For Robert Clavel and Charles Bloom*, 1700. 8°.* L, WF.

5447 —The church history clear'd. *By Samuel Roycroft, for Robert Clavell*, 1695. 4°. T.C.II 557. L, O, CT, LCL, DT; MBA, NU, WF.

5448–9 Entries cancelled.

5450 —A companion to the altar. *By J. Macock, for John Martyn, and Richard Lambert, at York*, 1675. 8°. T.C.I 194. L, O, EC, EN; MIU, NU, Y.

5450A ——Second edition. —, 1678. 8°. T.C.I 305. L, OC, CSS, D; WF, Y.

5450B ——Third edition. *By J. Macock, for Robert Littlebury and Robert Scott, George Wells and Richard Lambert, at York,* 1681. 8°. L, OC; CH, TSM.

5451 ——Fourth edition. *By M. Clark, for R. Lambert, R. Chiswel, T. Sawbridge, R. Bentley, and G. Wells,* 1685. 8°. L, C; CH, NC, NU, PL, WF.

5452 [–] A companion to the temple and closet. *By T. R. for Hen. Brome, and Robert Clavell,* 1672. 8°. T.C.I 109. L, C, CT, DC, YM; MH, Y.

5453 ——Second edition. *By Andrew Clark, for Henry Brome,* 1676. 8°. T.C.I 248. L, CT, LCL, YM, E; NN, NU, TU, WF.

5454 ——Third edition. *By M. Clark, for Henry Brome,* 1679. 8°. OC, ELY, YM, D; CH, CN, MBP, NU, Y.

5455 ——[Anr. ed.] *By S. Roycroft, for Joan. Brom, R. Littlebury, R. Scot, R. Clavell, G. Wells, and R. Lambert,* 1684. fol. L, O, C, CT, ENC; BN, WF, Y.

5455A ——[Anr. ed.] *By Samuel Roycroft for Joanna Brome & Abel Swalle,* 1684. fol. OC, CT, EC; TU, WWC.

5456 ——"Third" edition. *By Miles Flesher, for Charles Brome,* 1688. fol. L, O, C, OB, DT; PL, TU, Y.

5457 —A companion to the temple. Part II. *For Henry Brome,* 1676. 8°. T.C.I 233. L, OC, CT, EC, E; CN.

5458 ——Second edition. *By S. R. for Henry Brome,* 1679. 8°. OC, NPL; NU, PL, WF, Y.

5459 —A discourse concerning excommunication. *For Robert Clavell,* [1684]. 4°. L, O, C, CS, E; CH, CN, NU, TU, WF.

5460 —A discourse concerning the daily frequenting the common prayer. *For Charles Brome,* 1687. 8°.* T.C.II 227. L, O, CT, E; CN, Y.

5461 [–] A discourse concerning the second Council of Nice. *For Walter Kettilby,* 1688. 4°. L, O, C, EN, DT; CH, MH, NU, TU, WF, Y.

5462 —A discourse of duels. *By Samuel Roycroft, for Robert Clavell,* 1687. 4°. T.C.II 194. L, O, OC, CS, DT; CH, CU, MH, NU, WF, Y.

5463 —A discourse on the offices. *By Samuel Roycroft, for Robert Clavell,* 1696. 8°. L, O, C, CT, ELY; CH, NC, NU, WF, Y.

5464 —A discourse upon the form. *By Samuel Roycroft. for Robert Clavell,* 1699. 8°. T.C.III 89. L, O, C, EN, DT; CH, MIU, NU, WF, Y.

5465 —The examiner examined: being. *For Robert Clavell,* 1691. 4°. T.C.II 367. L, O, CT, LCL, YM; CH, MH, NU, WF, Y.

5466 —Frequent and fervent prayer. *For R. Clavell,* 1687. 8°.* L, O, C, CT, EC; CH, WF.

5467 —Friendly and seasonable advice to the Roman Catholicks. *For Henry Brome,* 1674. 8°. O, CT, LIL, P; CLC.

5467A [–] —Second edition. —, 1675. 12°. L; CLC.

5468 [–] —Third edition —, 1677. 8°. L, O, OB, OC, CT; MH, NU.

5468A [–] —"Third" edition. —, 1680. 12°. CSSX; CLC, TU.

5469 [–] —Fourth edition. *For Charles Brome,* 1685. 12°. L, C, OC, YM, DT; CH, CLC, MIU, SW.

5470 [–] —"Fourth edition" —, 1686. 12°. T.C.II 161. O, C, LG, DC, YM; CN, SW, TU, V, WF.

5471 [–] —Fifth edition. *For Charles Brome,* 1685, *reprinted at Edinburgh,* 1686. 12°. L, EN, ENC; MH.

5472 —An historical vindication of the divine right of tithes. *By S. Roycroft, for Robert Clavel,* 1682. 4°. T.C.I 459. L, OM, CT, LF, LL; CH, CU, MHL, NC, WF, Y.

5473 ——Second edition, Part I. —, 1685. 4°. T.C.II 142. L, O, NPL, EN, DT; CH, CN, MHL, NU, TU, WF.

5474 ——Part II. —, 1685. 4°. L, O, C, LCL, OC; CH, CN, MHL, NU, WF.

5475 [–] A letter to a bishop. [*Edinburgh*], 1689. 4°.* ALDIS 2912. FSF; CH, CLC, NN.

5476 [–] —[Anr. ed.] *For Robert Clavel,* 1689. 4°.* T.C.II 276. L, O, CT, MR, DT; CH, CN, MH, NU, WF, Y.

5477 [–] —Second edition. —, 1689. 4°.* L, O, CT, HH, DT; CLC, MH, NU, WF, Y.

5478 [–] —Third edition. —, 1689. 4°. L, C, LG, CS, MR; NC, WF, Y.

5479 —The nature and usefulness of solemn judicial swearing. *By S. Roycroft, for Robert Clavell, to be sold by Richard Lambert,* 1682. 4°.* T.C.I 482. L, O, C, LL, DT; CH, CLC, MHL, NU, Y.

5480 —The occasional offices of matrimony. *By M. C. for Henry Brome, and Robert Clavel,* 1679. 8°. T.C.I. 347. L, C, NPL, OC, EC; CH, NN, PL, WF, Y.

5481 [–] The plausible arguments of a Romish priest answered. *For R. Clavell,* 1686. 8°. T.C.II 165. L, O, CT, MC, EN; CH, MH, NPT, Y.

5482 [–] —[Anr. ed.] *For R. Clavell, to be sold by John Crosly in Oxford,* 1687. 8°. L, O, OC, CT, EC; CH, MBA, NU.

5482A [–] —[Anr. ed.] *For Robert Clavell,* 1687. 8°. OC, OCC; CH, CLC, WF.

5482B [–] —[Anr. ed.] —, *sold by F. Hildyard, York,* 1687. 8°. CT.

5483 [–] —[Anr. ed.] *For Robert Clavell,* 1688. L, LIL, OC; NU, WF.

5483 [–] Pretences of the French invasion. 1692. *See* Lloyd, William, *bp.*

5484 [–] The Protestant mask taken off. *By William Wilde, for Robert Clavel,* 1692/3. 4°. T.C.II 428. L, O, C, EN, DT; CH, MBA, NU, WF, Y.

5485 —The reasons of praying. *For Robert Clavel,* 1694. 4°.* T.C.II 519. L, O, C, EN, DT; CH, CLC, NU, WF, Y.

5486 [–] Religion and loyalty. *For Robert Clavel,* 1681. 4°. T.C.I 465. L, O, C, EN, DT; CH, CN, LC, MH, NP, NU, Y.

5487 [–] —Second edition. —, 1683. 4°. T.C.II 34. I, O, CT, EN, DT; CH, MIU.

5488 [–] The right of tythes asserted. *For E. Croft,* 1677. 8°. T.C.I 294. OC, LF, CS, YM, EN; CJC, MH, NU, PH, WF.

5489 [–] The right of tithes re-asserted. *For H. Brome, and R. Clavel,* 1680. 8°. L, OC, CT, LF, DT; CH, MHL, TU, WF, Y.

5490 —Roman forgeries. *By Samuel Roycroft, for Robert Clavell,* 1689. 4°. T.C.II 282. L, O, C, EN, DT; CH, MH, NU, TU, WF, Y.

5491 ——[Anr. ed.] —, 1695. 4°. L, LIL, CE.

5492 —A scholastical history. *By S. Roycroft, for Robert Clavell,* 1690. 8°. T.C.II 312. L, O, C, ENC, DT; CH, MH, NU, WF, Y.

5493 —A sermon preached . . . on the second of December. *By Samuel Roycroft, for Robert Clavell,* 1697. 4°. L, O, C, EN, DT; CLC, NU, WF.

5493A [–] The several kinds of inspirations. *For C. Brome*, 1698. 8°. T.C.III 49. LF; NIA.

5494 —Short discourses. *By Samuel Roycroft, for Robert Clavell*, 1684. 8°. T.C.II 82. L, O, CT, LCL, YM; CH, LC, NU, Y.

5495 ——Second edition. —, 1688. 8°. L, CT, YM; CLC, PL, TU, WF.

5496 [–] Three considerations proposed to Mr. William Pen. [*London*, 1688.] cap., 4°.* L, C, LF, OC, EN; CH, CN, LC, MH, NU, PH, Y.

5497 **Comberladge, John.** Putredo. [*Cantabrigiæ*], 1673. brs. L, O.

5498 The combers whistle. [*London*], *for F. Coles, T. Vere, J. Wright, and J. Clarke*, [1670–80]. brs. L, O, CM, HH.

Combes, Sieur, *pseud. See* Morellet, Laurent.

5498A Come all that wish well. 1700. brs. L.

5499 Come, come all you that are with Rome offended, . . . The lineage of locusts. [*n.p.*, 1641.] brs. LT.

5500 Come to it at last. [*London*], *for J. Wright, J. Clark, W. Thackery, and T. Passinger*, [1680–82]. brs. L, HH; MH.

5501 Come turn to mee. *For W. Thackeray, T. Passenger, and VV. VVhitwood.* [1660?]. brs. L.

5502 —[Anr. ed.] *For Charles Tyus*, [c. 1663]. brs. L, CM, HH; MH, Y.

5503 Come worldling see what paines. *For Henry Gossan*, [1650?]. brs. L.

Comedy called the marriage broker. 1662. *See* W., M.

5504 **Comenius, Johann Amos.** Ars ornatoria. *Ex officina Rogeri Danielis*, 1664. 8°. L, C, CCA; Y.

5504A ——[Anr. ed.] *Ex officina Johannes Redmayne*, 1671. 8°. WF.

5505 —Ars sensualium pictus: . . . visible world. *For J. Kirton*, 1664. 8°. L, LW.

5505A ——[Anr. ed.] *Ex officina Johannes Redmayne*, 1671. 8°. WF.

5506 —A continuation of. [*London*], *for R. L.*, [1648]. 4°.* LT, LUG, O; CH.

5507 —An exhortation of the churches. *For Thomas Parkhurst*, 1661. 4°. L, O, CCL, CS, EN; CN, MIU, NU, Y.

5507A [–] A generall table of Europe. [*London*], 1669. 8°. LLL, CT; MWA, MPB.

5507B [–] —[Anr. ed.] —, *for Benjamin Billingsley*, 1670. 4°. L; CLC, PU.

5508 [–] The history of the Bohemian persecution. *By B. A. for Iohn Walker*, 1650. 8°. LT, O, CT, OM, EN; CH, CN, NU, PL, HC.

5508A —Janua lingarum cum versione Anglicana. *Ex officina Rogeri Danielis*, 1665. 8°. CH, NC.

5509 ——[Anr. ed.] *By John Redmayne*, 1670. 8°. T.C.I 27. L, O, OM, C; CLC, CN, NC, PL.

5510 —Janua linguarum novissime. Fourth edition. *Ex officina Joannis Baker*, 1674. 8°. C.

5511 —Janua linguarum reserata: . . . the entry doore. Fifth edition. *By R. Young, and are to be sold by T. Slater*, 1641. 8°. CH.

5512 —Janua linguarum reserata: . . . the gate. Sixth edition. *By James Young, and are to be sold by Thomas Slater*, 1643. 8°. L, LWL, OC, DC; CLC, NN, TU.

5512A ——[Anr. ed.] 1645. 8°. L; MBP.

5513 ——[Anr. ed.] *By James Young for Thomas Slater*, 1647. 8°. C, OC, LU, EC; MBP.

5514 ——[Anr. ed.] *By W. Du-gard for T. Slater*, 1650. 8°. L, O, LWL, DC; MH, Y.

5515 ——[Anr. ed.] *By Edw. Griffin and Wil. Hunt for Thomas Slater*, 1652. 8°. LL, LPO, DT; CU, LC, NC, PL.

5516 ——[Anr. ed.] *By E. Cotes, for the company of stationers*, 1659. 8°. CLC, MH.

5516A ——[Anr. ed.] —, 1667. 8°. L; LC, MH, WF.

5517 ——[Anr. ed.] *For John Baker*, 1673. 8°. L; CU, LC, WF, Y.

5517A ——[Anr. ed.] *By T. R. and N. T. For the company of stationers*, 1673. 8°. L; CN, LC, MH, Y.

5518 —Janua linguarum trilinguis. *Ex officina Rogeri Danielis*, 1662. 8°. L, O, C, OC, E; NC, PL, TU, WF, Y.

5518A Entry cancelled.

5519 ——[Anr. ed.] *Typis J. Redmayne*, 1670. 8°. T.C.I 27. I, O, C, CM, EN; CH, MH, NP, WF, HC.

5519A ——[Anr. ed.] — *et veneunt apud J. Williams*, 1670. 8°. CS.

5520 ——[Anr. ed.] *Ex officina Eliazabethæ Redmayne*, 1685. 8°. T.C.II 139. LW, AU; CU, MB, MH, PL.

5521 —Latinæ linguæ janua reserata . . . the gate of the Latine tongue unlocked. *By Wm. Du-Gard; to be sold by John Clark*, 1656. 8°. LT, C, DC, GU; BN, CH, CU, MH, WF, Y.

5522 —Naturall philosophie. *By Robert and William Leybourn, for Thomas Pierrepont*, 1651. 8°. LT, O, C, ES; BN, CN, MH, NU, HC.

5523 —J. A. Commenii Orbis sensualium pictus. Visible world. *For J. Kirton*, 1659. 8°. LT, LW.

5523A ——[Anr. ed.] —, 1664. 8°. L.

5524 ——[Anr. ed.] *By T. R. for S. Mearne*, 1672. 8°. T.C.I 121. LG, O, OP, EC; CLC, NC, Y.

5525 ——[Anr. ed.] *For Charles Mearne*, 1685. 8°. CN, WCL, WF, Y.

5525A ——[Anr. ed.] *By J. R. for Abel Swall*, 1689. 8°. L; UCLA.

5526 ——[Anr. ed.] *For, and sold by John Sprint*, 1700. 8°. T.C.III 221. NN, WF.

5526A [–] Panegyricus carolo Gustavo. *Veneunt apud Richardum Wodenothy*, 1656. 4°.* LT; CSS, WF.

5527 —A patterne of universall knowledge. *By T H to be sold by Thomas Collins in Notthampton* [sic], 1651. 8°. LT, O, C.

5528 ——[Anr. ed.] *For T. H. and Jo. Collins*, 1651. 8°. CS; CN, LC, Y.

5529 —A reformation of schooles. *For Michael Sparke senior*, 1642. 4°. L, C, LCL, EN; CH, CN, NU, WF, Y.

5530 —Schola-ludus. *Impensis T. Parkhurst*, 1664. L, P, E; CU, MH, WF.

5531 —Vestibulum . . . last porch. *By R. Hodgkinsonne*, 1647. 8°. L; Y.

5531A ——[Anr. ed.] 1658. 8°. L.

5532 ——[Anr. ed.] 1659. 8°. DC.

5533 —Vestibuli linguarum auctarium. *Typis Joannis Redmayne*, 1666. 8°.* C, CT.

5533A —Vestibulum novissimum linguæ Latinæ. 1657. 8°. L.

5533B —Vestibulum technicum. *For Thomas Parkhurst*, 1682. 8°. T.C.I 489. NOT; TO.

5533C ——[Anr. ed.] —, 1684. 8°. T.C.II 108. Y.

5534 Comes amoris; or the companion of love. The first book. *By Nat. Thompson for John Carr and Sam. Scott, to be sold by John Carr*, 1687. fol.* L, O; CH, LC.

5535 —, second book. *By Tho. Moore, for John Carr, and Sam. Scott*, 1688. fol.* L; CH, LC, MH.

5536 —, third book. *By T. Moore and J. Heptinstall, for John Carr and Sam. Scott*, 1689. fol.* L, CK; CH, LC, WF.

5537 —, fourth book. *By J. Heptinstall for John Carr and Samuel Scott*, 1693. fol.* L, GU; CH, LC.

5538 —, fifth book. *By J. Heptinstall for John Carr*, 1694. fol.* L, GU; CH, LC.

Comes facundus in via. The fellow-traveller. 1658. *See* Edmundson, Henry.

Cometomantia. A discourse. 1684. *See* Edwards, John.

Comfort in affliction. 1682. *See* O., J.

Comfortable newes. 1660. *See* L., T.

5538A A comforting farewel word. 1664. 8°. O.

Comforts of divine love. 1700. *See* Gilpin, Richard.

5538B The comforts of whoreing. Second edition. 1694. 12°.* L.

5538C The comical and tragical history of Fortunatus. *For C. Brown*, [c. 1700.] WF.

5538D A comical dialogue between the Williamites. 1697. 8°. LLL.

5538E The comical dream. *H. Bruges*, 1674. 4°.* L.

5539 A comical elegy on the death of Evan Morgan. *By J. W.*, 1700. brs. L.

Comical history. [n.p.], 1655. *See* Sorel, Charles.

5540 Comical remarks on the publick reports. colop: *Printed and are to be sold by Randal Taylor*, 1690. brs. L, O, CT.

Comical revenge. 1664. *See* Etherege, *Sir* George.

5541 **Comines, Philippe de.** The history of. Third edition. *By S. G. for Joshua Kirton*, 1665. fol. L, O, MC; CU, Y.

5542 ——Fourth edition. *For Samuel Mearne, John Martyn, and Henry Herringman*, 1674. fol. T.C.I 190. L, O, OC, CT, ES; CH, CN, MH, NC, WG, Y.

5543 —The memoirs of. *For John Starkey*, 1674. 8°. T.C.I 196. L, O, C, OM, EN; CN, MBC, NU, WF, Y.

5543A Comments for the exercise of foot. [London, 1690?] cap., 8°.* L.

Command of God. [n.p.], 1688. *See* Beverly, Thomas.

5544 **Commelyn, Jan.** The Belgick, or Netherlandish Hesperides. *For J. Holford, to be sold by Langly Curtis*, 1683. 8°. T.C.II 18. L, O, CT, OC, EN; CH, CN, MH, WF, Y.

5545 Commemoration of the thirtieth day of January, 1648. colop: *For Thomas Benskin*, 1681. fol. CH.

Commemoration, or.. . . 1654. *See* Turner, John.

5545A A commemoration sermon. *By T. D. for Henry Brome*, 1678. 8°.* T.C.I 287. L.

5546 The commencement of the treaty between the Kings Majesty and the commissioners of Parliament at Newport. A prayer, drawne by His Majesties speciall direction and dictates, for a blessing on the treaty at Newport. *Newport, Septemb. 6, 1648.* brs. LT, O, LS; MH.

5547 Commendatory verses, on the author of the two Arthurs. *Printed*, 1700. fol.* L, O, CS, EN, DT; CH, CU, MH, TU, WF, Y.

Comment on Ruth. 1654. *See* Fuller, Thomas.

Comment upon the two tales. 1665. *See* Brathwaite, Richard.

Commentariorum. 1686. *See* Manley, *Sir* Roger.

5548 Entry cancelled.

Commentarie, or exposition. 1652. *See* Marbury, Edward.

Commentary upon the present. [n.p.], 1677. *See* Penn, William.

5549 A commentation on the late wonderful discovery. *For T. Addams*, 1680. brs. L, O; MH.

Commercial resolutions of the Irish Parliament. 1685 [i.e., 1785].

Commercium epistolicum. *Oxonii*, 1658. *See* Wallis, John.

5550 A commission and instructions to Charles Fleetwood, Esq. *For Giles Calvert, Thomas Brewster, and by and for Hen. Hills*, 1653. fol.* LT, O, C; Y.

5550A The commission for discoveries. *By Tho. Newcomb*, 1656. 4°.* L, OC; CH, MH, WF.

5551 The commission for taking subscriptions. [London, 1694.] fol.* O, LUG; MH.

5551A —[Same title.] 1696. * EN.

5552 The commission of array arraigned. *Septem. 19. by T. F. for H. H.*, 1642. 4°.* LT, CCL, EC, EN, DT; CH, CN, MH, WF, Y.

5553 A commission of excise for setting up rates upon wares. [Oxford, by L. Lichfield, 1644.] 4°.* MADAN 1638. O.

5554 Commission of justiciary for securing the peace. *Edinburgh, by the heirs and successors of Andrew Anderson*, 1697. fol. ALDIS 3658. EN.

5555 The commission opened. *Printed*, 1648. 4°.* DT; CSS, MH, NU, Y.

5556 A commission or, position: wherein all English subjects. [London], *printed*, 1648. 4°.* LT, O, HH; MH, NU, WF.

5557 The commissioners for administration of justice to the people in Scotland considering . . . 8 January 1653. *Leith*, 1653. brs. STEELE 3, 2098. EN.

5557A The commissioners for receiving the duties on pipes. [London? 1697.] brs. L; MH.

5558 The commissioners for the Association now sitting at Cambridge. [n.p.], 1643. brs. CDC.

5559 The commissioners having proposed questions to Sir Edmund Jennings. [London, 1688?] brs. L, OC, HH; CH.

5560 The commissioners last desires to the King. [London], *printed*, [1648]. 4°.* LT, HH; MH.

5561 The commissioners' proposals to His Royal Highness . . . Orange. colop: *For R. Bentley*, 1688. brs. L, O, C, MC, BR; CH, CLC, CN, MH, WF, Y.

The committee: a comedy. 1665. *See* Howard, *Sir* Robert.

5562 The committee appointed by a General Court the 23d April 1697. [London, 1697.] fol.* HH.

5563 Committee for the Navy and Customs. Die Martis 18 Martii, 1644[5]. Whereas the Lords and Commons. [*London*, 1645.] brs. LT.

Committee-man curried. 1647. *See* Sheppard, Samuel.

5564 The committee-mans complaint. [*London*, 1647.] brs. LT, O.

5565 The committee-mans last will and testament. [*London*], *printed*, 1647. brs. LT, LVF.

Committee of citizens adventurers. [*London*, 1645.] *See* Watkins, David.

5566 The committee of the militia London, and the liberties thereof earnestly. [*London*, 1648.] brs. LT.

5567 The committee of the militia of London, and the liberties thereof, taking. [*London*, 1648.] brs. LT; MH.

5568 The committie of warre within the shyrefdom of Aberdene. At *Aberdene*, *13 June*, 1646. brs. AU, FSF.

The committee: or, popery. 1680. *See* L'Estrange, Sir Roger.

Common good. 1652. *See* Tayler, Sylvanus.

5568A The common hunt. [1679.] brs. CLC, CN, TU.

5569 The common interest of King & kingdom. colop: *By T. M.*, 1688. cap., 4°.* L; CH, CN, MH.

5570 Entry cancelled.

5571 A common observation upon these times [*London*], *printed*, 1645. brs. LT, LVF.

Common-place-book out of. 1673. *See* Marvell, Andrew.

Common-place book to the Holy Bible. 1697. *See* Locke, John.

5572 Common-prayer-book devotions. [*n.p.*], *printed*, 1666. 4°. L, CT, LW, DC, DT; MBA, NPT, NU, PL.

Common-prayer book the best. Oxford, 1687. *See* Howell, William.

5573 The common prayer book unmasked by divers ministers of Gods word. [*London*], *reprinted*, 1660. 4°. LT, OC, LW, P, DT; CN, NU, PL, WF, Y.

Common writing. [*n.p.*], 1647. *See* Lodowyck, Francis.

Commoner's complaint. [*n.p.*], 1647. *See* Overton, Richard.

Commoners liberty. [*n.p.*], 1648. *See* Twysden, Sir Roger.

5574 The Commons dis-deceiver. [*London*], *printed*, 1648. 4°.* LT, O, CPE; CLC, MIU, NPT.

Commons petition of long. 1642. *See* I., C.

Commons war. 1646. *See* Heath, James.

5575 A commonvvealth, and commonvvealths-men, asserted. *For Henry Fletcher*, 1659. 4°.* LT, O, HH; CSS, CU, MH, NU, WF, Y.

Common-wealth of Israel. 1659. *See* Stubbe, Henry.

Common-wealth of Oceana. 1656. *See* Harrington, James.

Common-wealth of women. 1686. *See* Fletcher, John.

5576 A common-vvealth or nothing. *For Livewell Chapman*, 1659. 4°.* LT, OC, HH; CH, MH, WF.

5577 The common-wealths great ship commonly called the Soveraigne of the seas. *By M. Simmons, for Tho: Jenner*, 1653. 4°.* L, LG, HH; CH, CN, MH, NN, RPJ, WF.

Commonwealths-man unmasqu'd. 1694. *See* Rogers, Thomas.

Common-wealthsh's [*sic*] remembrancer. 1659. *See* Hubberthorn, Richard.

5578 The communicant instructed. *Printed, and are to be sold by R. Pawlett, and Edward Pawlett in Grantham*, 1668. 12°. O; WF.

5579 Entry cancelled.

Communicant's guide. 1683. *See* Warmstry, Thomas.

5580 The communicant's instructor. *For Tho. Parkhurst*, 1692. 8°. T.C.II 419. L, O.

Communion of the saints. Amsterdam, 1642. *See* Ainsworth, Henry.

5580A Companies in joynt-stock unnecessary. [*London*, 1691.] fol.* LUG; MH, MIU, NC, Y.

5581 A companion for debtors. *Printed and sold by A. Baldwin*, 1699. 8°. O, LUG; CH, MH.

Companion for the persecuted. [*n.p.*], 1693. *See* Kettlewell, John.

Companion to the temple. 1672. *See* Comber, Thomas.

5582 The companions of good consciences. *For Giles Calvert*, 1653. 4°.* LT.

5583 **Company of adventurers for the plantation of the islands of Eleutheria.** Articles and orders, made and agreed upon the 9th day of July, 1647. [*London*, 1647.] brs. L.

5584 **Company of Scotland trading to Africa and the Indies.** At a council-general of the Company of Scotland. [*Edinburgh*, 1699.] brs. MH, RPJ.

5585 —At a court of directors of the Company of Scotland. [*Edinburgh*, 1699.] brs. ALDIS 3282. RPJ.

5586 —Edinburgh, April 3rd, 1696. At a general meeting of the Company of Scotland. [*Edinburgh*, 1696.] brs. ALDIS 3555. O, EN; CN, RPJ.

5587 —Edinburgh the 17th. day of April, 1696. —[*Edinburgh*, 1696.] brs. ALDIS 3556. O, EN; CN, RPJ.

5588 —Edinburgh the 12th of May 1696. —[*Edinburgh*, 1696.] fol.* ALDIS 3557. RPJ, WF.

5588A —Edinburgh, 20th of May, 1696. —[*Edinburgh*], 1696. brs. ALDIS 3558. HH.

5589 —At a meeting of the committee. [*Edinburgh*, 1696.] brs. SPENCER.

5590 —At a meeting of the Council-General of the Company of Scotland. [*Edinburgh*, 1699.] brs. ALDIS 3824. LUG.

5591 —Edinburgh, March 24th, 1696. At a meeting of the subscribers. [*Edinburgh*, 1696.] brs. ALDIS 3554. EN; CN, RPJ.

5592 —At Edinburgh, the 15 of June, 1696. The Council-General. [*Edinburgh*, 1696.] brs. ALDIS 3538. EN; RPJ.

5593 —At Edinburgh the 9th day of July, 1696. Whereas. [*Edinburgh*, 1696.] brs. ALDIS 3539. RPJ.

5594 —Constitutions of the Company of Scotland. [*Edinburgh, G. Mosman?* 1696]. fol.* ALDIS 3548. O, LUG, EN; MIU, NC, RPJ.

5594A —Copy of an act presented to the Parliament. [*Edinburgh*, 1695.] cap., fol.* MIU.

5595 —The Council-general of the Indian and African Company's petition. [*Edinburgh*, 1699]. brs. ALDIS 3836. O, EN; CN, NN, RPJ.

5596 —The declaration of the council constituted. colop: *Boston, printed May, 15th, 1699.* 4°.* MWA, NN, RPJ.

5597 —The Company of Scotland . . . do hereby give notice. [*London?* 1696.] brs. MIU.

5597A ——*Boston printed and re-printed at Glasgow by Robert Sanders, 1699.* brs. ALDIS 3839. EN.

5597B —An exact history of all the men. *Edinburgh, by George Mosman, 1699.* brs. ALDIS 3847. L, O; CN, MIU.

5597C —A full and exact collection of all the considerate addresses. [*Edinburgh*], *printed, 1700.* 8°. L, O, E, ES, GM; CN, MH, NC, WF, Y.

5598 —A list of the subscribers to the Company of Scotland, . . . April 21. [*Edinburgh*, 1696]. fol.* ALDIS 3580. EN; MH, RPJ, WF, Y.

5598A —Literate patentes sev concessus. *Edinburgh, excudebat hærdes Andrew Anderson, 1695.* 8°.* ALDIS 3467. RPJ, WF.

5598B —The original papers and letters. [*Edinburgh*], *printed, 1700.* 8°. L, O, LUG, EN; CH, MH, NN, PBL, Y.

5599 —A perfect list of the several persons residenters. *Edinburgh, printed and sold by the heirs and successors of Andrew Anderson, 1696.* fol.* ALDIS 3588. L, O; CN, RPJ.

5599A —The representation and petition of the Council-general. *Edinburgh, printed, 1700.* 8°.* EN; MH, NC, NN, RPJ, Y.

5599B —Scotland's right to Caledonia. [*Edinburgh*], *printed, 1700.* 8°.* O, EN; MH, NC, NN, RPJ, WF.

5599C —A short proposal for. [*Edinburgh?* 1700.] cap., 4°.* MH.

5599D —A supplement of original papers. [*Edinburgh?*] 1700. 8°.* L, LUG, EN; NC, WF.

5599E —The three following memorials. [*Edinburgh?* 1700.] cap., 4°.* MH.

5600 —To His Grace His Majesties High Commissioner . . . The humble petition of the council-general. [*Edinburgh*, 1698]. brs. ALDIS 3808. O, LUG, EN; MIU, RPJ.

5601 —To His Grace, His Majesty's High Commissioner . . . The humble representation. [*Edinburgh*, 1700]. brs. O, LUG; CN, RPJ.

5602 ——[Anr. ed.] [*Edinburgh*, 1700]. fol.* EN; RPJ.

5603 Comparatis comparandis: the second part. [*London*], *printed, 1647.* 4°.* MADAN 1958. L, HH, SP; CH, CU, MH, NC, WF.

Comparative theology. [*n.p.*], 1700. *See* Garden, James.

Comparison between the eloquence. Oxford, 1672. *See* Rapin, René.

Comparison of Plato. 1673. *See* Rapin, René.

Compassion to all. [*n.p.*, 1665.] *See* Crook, John.

Compassion to the captives. 1656. *See* Fox, George.

5604–6 Entries cancelled.

A compend or a breviat of the most important . . . rights. *Edinburgh*, 1700. *See* Birnie, *Sir* Andrew.

Compendious abridgment. [*n.p.*], 1661. *See* D., M.

Compendious and accurate treatise. 1678. *See* Brown, William.

Compendious catechisme. 1645. *See* F., J.

Compendious collection. 1675. *See* Brydall, John.

Compendious discourse on. Oxford, 1688. *See* Woodhead, Abraham.

5607 A compendious discourse proving Episcopacy. *By E. G. for Richard Whitaker, 1641.* 4°.* LT, O, C, ENC, DT; CH, CLC, NPT, NU, Y.

Compendious history of the most. 1680. *See* L'Estrange, *Sir* Roger.

5607A A compendious history of the royal family of York. *Printed, and are to be sold by J. Taylor, 1688.* 12°. T.C.II 249. Y.

5608 A compendious history of the taxes of France. *By J. M. and B. B. for Richard Baldwin, 1694.* 4°.* T.C.II 476. L, O, CT, LG; CH, CJC, MH, NC, WF, Y.

5608A A compendious narration of . . . Countess of Shrewsbury. [*London*], *printed, 1677.* 8°. WF.

Compendious narrative. [*n.p.*], 1652. *See* Bate, George.

Compendious prologue. [*n.p.*, 1645?] *See* T., J.

5609 The compendious school-master. *For Samuel Lowndes, 1688.* 8°. L.

5609A A compendium, containing exact rules . . . muster. *For William Gilbert, 1673.* T.C.I 151. brs. MH.

Compendious view. 1685. *See* Wright, James.

Compendium linguae. 1679. *See* Matern, John.

5610 Entry cancelled.

Compendium of the laws. 1699. *See* Curson, Henry.

Compendium of the several branches. 1688. *See* Brown, William, clerk.

Compendium: or. 1679. *See* Castlemaine, Roger Palmer, *earl of*.

Compendium politicum. 1680. *See* Yalden, John.

5610A The complaining shepherdess. [*London*], *for T. Wright, J. Clarke, W. Thackeray and T. Passenger*, [1682.] brs. L, CM.

5611 The complaining testimony of some meeting at Abingdon. *For Livewell Chapman, 1656.* 4°.* CT; CSS, MH.

5612 A complaint and petition of the whole kingdome of England. [*Oxford, by H. Hall*], *for W. Webb, 1643.* 4°.* MADAN 1330. O, LW; Y.

Complaint of liberty. 1681. *See* Nalson, John.

5612A The complaint of divers liege-master-weavers. [*London?* 1692.] brs. LG.

5613 The complaint of Mrs. Celiers, and the Jesuits in Newgate. colop: *For T. Benskin*, [1680?] fol. CH, CLC, MB, MH, WF.

5613A The complaint of Mis. Page. [*London*], *for F. Coles, T. Vere, and I. Wright* [1680?] brs. MH.

5614 The complaint of the bovtefev scorched in his own kindlings. *By Matthew Simmons, 1649.* 4°.* LT, O, LVF, LFEA; MH.

5615 The complaint of the county of Brecon. [*n.p.*, 1654.] 4°.* AN.

5616 The complaint of the kingdome against the evill members of both Houses. [*London*, 1643?] cap., 4°.* L, C; Y.

5617 The complaint of the poor. [*n.p.*], *printed, 1700.* 8°.* CH.

5618 The complaint of Ulallia. [*London*], *by and for Alex Milbourn*, [1670–80]. brs. HH.

5619 —[Anr. ed.] [*London*], *by and for W.O. and sold by B. Deacon*, [1685]. brs. HH.

5620 A complaint to the House of Commons, and resolution taken up. *Oxford*, [*London*], *by Leonard Lichfield*, 1642. 4°.* MADAN 1148. LT, O, C, OC, HH; CH, CN, NU, TU, WF, Y.

5621 —[Anr. ed.] —, 1642. 4°.* MADAN 1150. LT, O, LG, OC, EC; CLC, MBP, MH, WF, Y.

5622 —[Anr. ed.] *Printed at Oxford, by Leonard Lichfield*, 1642. 4°.* MADAN 1152. L, O, C, HH, DT; CLC, MH, NU, Y.

5623 —[Anr. ed.] *Oxford, by Leonard Lichfield*, 1642[/3]. 4°.* MADAN 1179. LT; WF, Y.

5624 Complainte de l'Eglise Francoise de Londres. [*Londres*], *imprimé* 1645[6]. 4°.* LT.

Complaints and queries. 1659. *See* D., E.

5625 Complaints concerning corruptions. [*London*], *printed*, 1641. 4°.* C, CT, OC; CH, CSS, MH, TU, WF, Y.

5626 —[Anr. ed.] —, 1660. 4°.* LT, O, OC, CT, EN; CLC, MH, MIU, Y.

5627 The complaisant companion, or new jests. *By H.B.*, 1674. 8°. T.C.I 180. CH, WF.

Complementum fortunatarum. 1662. *See* Cardonnel, Pierre de.

5627A The compleat academy. Second edition. *By R.Battersby for John Ruddiard*, 1672. fol.* CLC, HC.

5627B —[Anr. ed.] *For T.Passenger and W.Whitwood*, 1676. T.C.I 259. TAYLOR.

5627C Compleat ambassador. *By T.Newcomb, for G.Bedell & T.Collins*, 1655. fol. CT.

Compleat & perfect concordance. *Oxford*, 1655. *See* Wickens, Robert.

Compleat and true narrative. 1679. *See* B., J.

Compleat angler. 1655. *See* Walton, Izaak.

Compleat arithmetician. 1691. *See* Newton, John.

5628 Complete attorney. [*n.p.*], 1654. 12°. CU.

5628A —[Anr. ed.] 1676. 12°. LIL.

5629 The compleat book of knowledge. 1698. 12°. L; CN.

5630 A compleat catalogue of all the stitch'd books. [*London*], *printed*, 1680. 4°.* T.C.I 386. L, O, OC, MR; CN, MH, NU, ISM, WF.

5631 The compleat character of Sr John Fenwick. *J.Bradford*, 1697. 4°.* HH.

Compleat Christian. [*n.p.*], 1643. *See* Slatyer, William.

5632 The compleat citt. [*London*], *for P.Brooksby*, 1683. brs. L, O, HH.

Compleat clerk. 1677. *See* H., I.

5633 The compleat clark, and scriveners guide. *By T.R. for H.Twyford, N.Brookes, J.Place, and R.Wingate*, 1655. 4°. LT, OC, CS; CH, LC, MHL, NCL, PL.

5634 The compleat clark, containing. *By J.S. for H.Twyford, N.Brook, and J.Place*, 1664. 8°. LL; LC, MHL, NCL, WF.

5635 —Second edition. *By T.R. for J.Place*, 1671. 8°. L, C; LC, YL.

5636 —Third edition. —, 1671. 8°. T.C.I 77. L, C, EN; MHL, NCL.

5636A —Fourth edition. *By T.Sawbridge, T.Roycroft, and W.Rawlins, assigns of Richard & Edward Atkyns, for H.Twyford*, 1677. 4°. LC, MIU, PU, Y.

5636B —Fifth edition. 1683. 4°. CCA; LC, MIU, PL.

5637 A complete collection of books and pamphlets. [*n.p. c.* 1685?] 8°. L, O.

5638 A compleat collection of farewel sermons. *Printed*, 1663. 4°. L, O, CT, LW, E; CH, CN, NU, WF, Y.

5638A A compleat collection of papers, in twelve parts. *By J.D. for R.Clavel, Henry Mortlock, and Jonathan Robinson*, 1689. 4°. T.C.II 276. L, O, CM, AU, EN; LC, NU, RPJ, WF, Y.

Compleat collection of the lives. 1661. *See* S., W.

Compleat constable, 1700. *See* Gardner, Robert.

Compleat cook. 1655. *See* M., W.

5638B The compleat English and French cook. Second edition. *For William Miller*, 1620. 12°. T.C.II 316. WF.

Compleat English schoolmaster. 1673. *See* Coles, Elisha.

5639 Compleat entering clerk. [*n.p.*], 1683. 12°. LIL.

5639A Compleat excise man. 1671. 8°. NCL.

Compleat fencing-master. 1692. *See* Hope, William.

Compleat form of liturgy. [1700?] *See* Stephens, Edward.

Compleat gamester. 1674. *See* Cotton, Charles.

Compleat gardeners practice, 1664. *See* Blake, Stephen.

Complete guide to the English tongue. [1699?] *See* Miège, Guy.

Compleat gunner. 1672. *See* T., W.

Compleat history of Europe. 1698. *See* Jones, David.

Compleat history of independency. [*n.p.*], 1648. *See* Walker, Clement.

Complete history of the late revolution. 1691. *See* Miege, Guy.

5640 A compleat history of the pretended Prince of Wales. *Printed*, 1696. 8°. T.C.III 5. L, LG, EN; MH, MIU, Y.

Compleat history of the warrs. [*n.p.*], 1660. *See* Wishart, George.

5641 The compleat husband-man. *A.Brewster*, 1659, 52. L.

5641A A compleat index to the Act of Settlement. *Dublin, by John Crook, and are to be sold by Sam. Danar*, 1666. fol.* DIX 132. O, C, DI, DK, DN; CH, WF.

5641B The compleat instructor to the flute. *Printed, and sold by I: Young*, 1700. 4°.* Y.

5642 The complete jockey. 1680, 4°.* Y.

5642A ——[Anr. ed.] [*London*], *printed* 1695. 4°.* CH, CLC, WF.

5643 Complete justice; a compendium. [*n.p.*], 1642. 12°. LIL.

5643A The compleat justice. Being an exact. *By James Flesher, for William Lee and Daniel Pakeman*, 1656. 12°. CH, LC, MH.

5644 —Seventh edition. *By James Flesher for William Lee and Daniel Pakeman*, 1661. 12°. L; CH, LC, MHL.

5645 —[Anr. ed.] *By John Streater, James Flesher, and Henry Twyford, assigns of Richard Atkyns, and Edward Atkyns*, 1667. 12°. L, O, LL, RPL; CN, LC, MHL, WF.

5645A —[Anr. ed.] *By the assigns of Richard Atkins and Sir Edward Atkins, and sold by Henry Twyford*, 1681. 8°. L, O, CJ, LI, LM; CH, MHL, PL, WF, YL.

5646 A compleat list of the knights, citizens and burgesses. *Printed, and are to be sold by Eliz. Whitlock*, 1698. brs. L.

5646A A compleat list of the royal navy of England. *Sold by E. Whitlock*, 1697/8. brs. L.

Compleat memoirs. 1694. *See* Settle, Elkanah.

Compleat mendicant. 1699. *See* Defoe, Daniel.

Compleat midwifes practice. 1656. *See* Chamberlaine, Thomas.

5647 Compleat narrative of the tryal of Elizabeth Lillyman. *Brooksby*, 1675. 4°.* LG.

5648 The compleat office of the Holy Week. *For Matthew Turner*, 1687. 8°. L, O, OB; CLC, CN, TU.

5649 The compleat planter and cyderist. *For Tho. Basset*, 1685. 8°. T.C.II 103. LPO, NPL; CH, MH, MIU, WF.

5650 —[Anr. ed.] —, 1690. 8°. T.C.II 338. CLC.

5651 The compleat politician. *For Edward Brewster*, 1656. 12°. OC, P; MH.

Compleat scholler. 1666. *See* Vernon, John.

Compleat schoole of warre. 1642. *See* M., R.

Compleat school-master. 1700. *See* T., T.

The compleat servant-maid. 1680. *See* Wolley, Hannah.

5652 Entry cancelled.

5653 The compleat sheriff. *By the assigns of R. and E. Atkyns of J. Walthoe*, 1696. 8°. L, C, LIL, LGI, LL; CLC, NCL, PL, WF.

Complete ship-wright. 1678. *See* Bushnell, Edmund.

5653A The compleat soldier. *By A. G. and J. P. for Thomas Sawbridge*, 1681. 8°. T.C.I 452. RPL; CLC, Y.

5654 The compleat solemnity of St. Georges Day. *By W. M. and sold by Walter Davis*, 1685. fol.* O; CH, TSM, WF, Y.

The compleat sollicitor. 1666. *See* Booth, William.

5655–7 Entries cancelled.

5658 The compleat statesman. *For Benjamin Alsop, and Thomas Malthus*, 1683. 8°. T.C.II 3. L, C, RPL, EN, DT; CH, CN, MH, TU, WF, Y.

5659 The compleat swearing-master. *For Allen Banks*, 1682. brs. O; CH, MH, Y.

Compleat system of grammar. 1699. *See* Clare, William.

Compleat tradesman. 1684. *See* H., N.

Compleat troller. 1682. *See* Nobbes, Robert.

5660 The compleat violist. *Printed for & sould by I: Hare: also sould by B.: Norman*, [ca. 1700].* T.C.III 124. IU, LC.

5661 **Complin, Nicholas.** The faithfvlnesse of the upright. colop: *For M. W.*, 1663. 4°. L, C, LF, BBN; CH, PH.

Comprehension promoted. [n.p., 1673?] *See* Humfrey, John.

Comprehension with indulgence. [n.p., 1680?] *See* Humfrey, John.

5662 A comprehensive, tho' compendious character of the late royal martyr King Charles I. [*London*, 1670?] brs. L.

5663 **Compton, Henry, bp.** The Bishop of London's charge to the clergy. *By Benj. Motte*, 1696. 4°.* L, O, LG, OC, EC; NU, PL.

5664 Entry cancelled.

5665 —Th Bishop of London's eighth letter to his clergy. *By Benj. Motte*, 1692. 4°. O, OC, WCA, ENC; IU.

5666 —Episcopalia. *For Timothy Westly, in Lothbury*, 1686. 12°. L, O, C, EN, DT; CH, NU, PL, WF, Y.

5666A —The Bishop of London's fourth letter. *For W. Abington*, 1683. brs. OC.

5666B —Good brother, be pleased to give notice. [*London?* 1684/5.] brs. EC.

5667 —Incestuous marriages. *For Robert Pawlet*, 1677/8. brs. HUTH.

5668 Entry cancelled.

5669 —The Bishop of London his letter to the clergy. *For H. Brome*, [1679]. brs. L, O, OC, EN; CH.

5670 —A list of the præbendaries of St. Paul's church. *For W. Kettilby*, 1686. brs. CH.

5671 —The Bishop of London's ninth conference. *By Benj. Motte*, 1699. 4°.* L, O, LG, OC, EC.

5671A —Prayers appointed by. *By M. Flesher*, 1686. 4°.* MIU.

5672 —The Bishop of London's second letter. *For H. Brome*, [1680]. 8°. T.C.I 415. L, O, LG, OC; MH, Y.

5673 —The Bishop of London's seventh letter. *By Benj. Motte*, 1690. 4°.* L, O, OC, EC, EN; MBA.

5674 —Sir, you may remember. *For Henry Brome*, [1679]. brs. L.

5674A [–] You perceive by His Majesty's letters patents. [*London*, 1678.] cap., fol.* L; WCL.

Compulsion of conscience. 1683. *See* H., T.

Compunction, or pricking. 1648. *See* J., R.

5675 Computatio universalis, seu logica rerum. Being an essay. *Printed and sold by J. Moxon*, 1697. 8°. L; CN, WF.

5676 A computation, shewing, that the two several proposals. [*London*, 1696?] cap., fol.* L, LG; Y.

5677 A computation of what a tax laid only on shooes, boots, . . . may amount unto. [*London*, 1694.] brs. L, LG, LUG.

5678 Computus: university revenue. [n.p., 1700.] fol. O.

5679 **Comyne, Eustas.** A good pook. [*sic*] colop: *For the author*, 1682. cap., fol.* L, O, MC; Y.

5680 —The information of. *For Thomas Fox*, 1680. fol.* L, O, C, DT; CH, MBC, MH, WF, Y.

5681 [**Con, Alexander.**] An answer to a little book call'd Protestancy. [n.p.], 1682. 12°. ON.

5682 [–] —[Anr. ed.] [*Aberdeen?*], 1686. 12°. ALDIS 2629. E, EN, ES, AB; TU.

5683 Entry cancelled.

5684 **Conant, John.** Sermons preach'd on several occasions. *For Richard Chiswell, and Tho. Cockerill*, 1693. 8°. T.C.II 451. L, O, C, LW, CT; CH, MBA, PL, PPT.

5685 — —Second edition. —, 1699. 8°. T.C.III 127. CPE, LSC, O, E, EN.

5686 —Sermons preach'd on several occasions. Second volume. *For Ri. Chiswell, and Tho. Cockerill*, 1697. 8°. T.C.III 20. L, LW, OC, CT; MBA.

5687 — —Second edition. —, 1699. 8°. O, LSC, E, EN.

5688 —Sermons preach'd on several occasions. The third volume. *For Thomas Cockerill; and H. Walwyn*, 1698. 8°. T.C.III 62. L, OC, CPE, CT, EN.

5689 —The vvoe and vveale of Gods people. *By G. M. for Christopher Meredith*, 1643. 4°. L, O, C, LCL, EN; CH, MH, NU, WF, Y.

5690 **Conant, Malachi.** Urim and Thummim. *Oxford, by H. Hall for J. Collins, London,* 1669. 4°.* MADAN 2824. O.

5691 ——[Anr. ed., "Vrim."] *For James Collins,* 1669. 4°.* L, O, C, CT, LL; CH, NU, PL, WF.

5692 Concavum cappo-cloacorum; or, a view in little of the great wit. *For Benj. Tooke,* 1682. 4°. T.C.I 511. L, O, C, CT, P; CH, CN, NU, WF, Y.

5693 Concealed murther reveil'd [sic]. *For William Aldredge,* [1699]. brs. L.

5694 A concealment discovered. *By James Flesher, for Nicholas Bourne,* 1652. brs. O; HR, Y.

5695 The conceited lover. [1690?] brs. O.

5695A Concerning Christ and his blood. Second edition. *Sold by B. Aylmer,* 1700. brs. CM.

Concerning Christ the spiritual. [n.p.], 1677. *See* Fox, George.

Concerning good-morrow. 1657. *See* Fox, George.

Concerning images. *Oxford,* 1689. *See* Woodhead, Abraham.

Concerning marriage. [n.p., 1661.] *See* Fox, George.

Concerning marriage. A letter. [n.p.], 1663. *See* Lawrence, Thomas.

Concerning meeting. [n.p., 1683.] *See* Fox, George.

5695B Concerning penal laws. *For Thomas Cockeril,* 1680. fol.* MH.

Concerning sons. [n.p., 1660?] *See* Fox, George.

Concerning the antiquity. 1689. *See* Fox, George.

Concerning the apostate. 1688. *See* Fox, George.

Concerning the case. [n.p., 1689.] *See* Dodwell, Henry.

5695C Concerning the congregation of Iesuits. [*Douai?* 1679.] cap., 4°.* L.

5696 Concerning the constitution of an aire infected. *Oxford, by Leonard Lichfield,* 1644. 4°.* MADAN 1682. O.

5696A Concerning the government of the present Parliament. colop: *Anno,* 1651. cap., 4°.* HR.

Concerning the judgements. [n.p., 166-?] *See* Baker, Richard.

Concerning the kingdoms. [n.p., 1660?] *See* Britten, William.

Concerning the new library. 1677. *See* North, J.

5697 Concerning the prices of vvine, &c. Die Mercurii. Maii 26. 1641. [n.p., 1641.] brs. STEELE 1857. L, O, LG.

5698 Concerning the priviledge of the under clarks. 1649. 4°. O.

Concerning the sum. [n.p., 1666.] *See* Penington, Isaac, jr.

Concerning the workhouse. [1688]. *See* Fox, George.

5699 Entry cancelled.

Concerning the worship. [n.p., 1661.] *See* Penington, Isaac, jr.

Concerning this present Cain. 1648. *See* Guifthaile, Henry.

5700 Concilium apud Fernham . . . the censure of. [n.p., 1644.] brs. STEELE 2564. LT.

Concio ad clerum. Cantabridgia, 1688. *See* Browne, Thomas.

Conciones et orationes. Oxonii, 1660. *See* Perion, Joachim.

5701–13 Entries cancelled.

Conclave of physicians. 1684. *See* Harvey, Gideon.

Concordance to the Holy Scriptures. Cambridge, 1662. *See* Newman, Samuel.

Concordia discors. 1659. *See* Prynne, William.

Concordia rara. 1653. *See* D., I.

5714 Concubinage and poligamy disprov'd. *For R. Baldwin,* 1698. 8°. T.C.III 73. L, O, CT, OC; CH, CLC, NC, WF, Y.

5715 The concurrence & unanimity of the people called Quakers. *For Nath. Crouch,* 1694. 8°. L, O, C, LCL; CH, MH, RPJ, WF.

5716 A concurrent declaration of . . . Westminster. [n.p., 1660?] brs. L, O, LG.

5717 The concurrent testimony of the ministers in . . . VViltes. *By R. Cotes for Stephen Bowtell,* June 26, 1648. 4°.* LT; CH, CLC, MH, NU, WF.

5718 **Conde, Louis II de Bourbon, prince de.** Articles agreed by the Duke of Angvyn. *By E. E.,* 1676 [*i.e.* 1646]. 4°.* CT, AN; MH, WF, Y.

5719 The condemnation, behaviour, last dying words and execution of Algernon Sidney. [*London*], *printed for L.,* 1683. fol.* CH.

Condemnation of Monsieur DuPin. 1696. *See* Harlay-Chanvallon, François de, *abp.*

5720 The condemnation of Oliver Plunket. colop: *For Langley Curtis,* [1681]. brs. O; CH, MH, WF, Y.

5720A ——[Anr. ed.] [*Dublin,* 1681.] cap., fol.* DN.

5721 The condemnation of the cheating Popish priest. *For L. C.,* 1679. 4°.* HH, MR; Y.

5722 The condemnation of the two notorious traytors, Oliver Plunket. colop: *By D. Mallet,* 1681. brs. L, O; MH, WF.

5723 The condemnation of Whig and Tory. *For R. W.,* 1681. brs. L, O; CH, MH, PU.

5723A The conditions for new planters. [*Cambridge, Mass.,* 1665]. brs. EVANS 98. MHS.

5724 Conditions upon which the most Christian king [Louis XIV] consents. colop: *By J. C. and F. Collins,* 1683. brs. O, HH; CH, WF, Y.

5724A The conditions upon which the patentees. *By John Harefinch,* 1684. brs. L.

Conduct and character of . . . Serini. 1664. *See* C., O.

Conduct and conveyance. [n.p.], 1690. *See* Houschone, William.

Conduct of France. 1684. *See* Courtilz de Sandras, G. de.

Conference abovt the next. [n.p.], 1681. *See* Parsons, Robert.

5725 A conference between a Bensalian bishop and an English doctor. *For Tho. Parkhurst and Joseph Collier,* 1681. fol.* T.C.I 421. L, O, CS, CT, HH; CH, CN, MH, WF, Y.

5725A A conference between a Papist and Protestant. *By W. D.,* 1689. fol.* C; Y.

5725B Conference between a rich alderman. 1670. 12°. ELY.

5725C A conference between the ghost of the Rump. [*London,* 1660.] cap., 4°.* L.

5725D A conference between an Inniskillingman. colop: *By James Beale*, 1689. brs. Y.

5726 A conference between the Lady Jane Grey. [*n.p.*, 1688.] brs. L.

5727 A conference betweene the Pope, the Emperour, and the King of Spaine. *For A. Coe, and T. A. Iuly* 14, 1642. 4°.* LT; NU.

5728 A conference betweene the two great monarchs of France and Spaine. [*London*], printed, 1641. 4°.* LT, O, MR; CH, CLC, WF, Y.

Conference between two Protestants. [*n.p.*], 1673. *See* Lloyd, William, *bp*.

5729 A conference between two soldiers. The first part. *Printed at Newcastle*, 1659. 4°.* L, NE, EN; CH, WF, Y.

Conference betwixt a modern atheist. 1693. *See* Sault, Richard.

Conference betwixt a Papist. 1678. *See* Mayo, Richard.

Conference betwixt a Protestant. 1678. *See* Mayo, Richard.

Conference betwixt the kings. 1647. *See* Nichols, T.

5730 A conference concerning this question. 1655. 8°. O.

5731 A conference held between the old Lord Protector. 1660. 4°.* LT, OC, HH; CH, MIU, WF.

5732 A conference held in the Tower of London. *Printed*, 1660. 4°.* LT; TU, Y.

Conference of some Christians. 1656. *See* Woodward, Hezekiah.

5733-6 Entries cancelled.

Conference with the souldiers. 1653. *See* Lilburne, John.

Conferences on the public debts. 1695. *See* Paterson, William.

5737 Confessio fidei in conventu. *Cantabrigiæ: excudebat Johannes Field*, 1656. 8°. L, C, CT, LW, EN; NPT, NU, TU, WF, Y.

5738 —[Anr. ed.] —, 1659. 8°. LT, C, CS, CT, EN; MB, MIU, NPT, NU.

5739 —[Anr. ed.] *Glasguæ, excudebat Andreas Anderson*, 1660. 12°. ALDIS 1636. L, EN, GM, HG, FSF; Y.

5739A —[Anr. ed.] —, *impensis societatis stationariorum*, 1660. 12°. Y.

5739B —[Anr. ed.] *Edinburgh, excudebat Gideon Lithgo*, 1660. 12°. ALDIS 1637. EN, AU, GU; CH.

5740 —[Anr. ed.] *Edinburgi, excudebat ex officina societatis stationariorum*, 1670. 12°. ALDIS 1899. EN, ENC, GU.

5741 —[Anr. ed.] *Glasguæ, excudebat Robertus Sanders*, 1670. sixes ALDIS 1900. EN, GM.

5742 —[Anr. ed.] *Edinburgi: excudebat ex officina societatis stationariorum*, 1671. 12°. ALDIS 1922. L, EN.

5743 —[Anr. ed.] *Edinburgi, excudebat hæres Andreæ Anderson*, 1680. 12°. ALDIS 2190. L, EN, ENC, GU; WF.

5743A —[Anr. ed.] *Edinburgh, society of stationers*, 1689. 12°. ALDIS 2874. EN, ENC.

5743B —[Anr. ed.] *Edinburgi, apud Andreæ Anderson hæredes & successores*, 1694. sixes, ALDIS 3363. LW, EN, ENC, FSF; WF.

5744 —[Anr. ed.] *Edinburgi, ex officina typographica Georgii Mosman*, 1694. sixes ALDIS 3364. C, LW, EN, ENC, FSF.

5744A The confession and execution as well of the several prisoners. *For D. M.*, 1678. 4°.* CH.

5744B The confession and execution of Mr. Barney. *By E. M.*, 1684. brs. WF.

5745 The confession and execution of Mr. Rich. Langhorn. [*London*, 1679.] cap., fol.* L, O, HH; CH, CN, WF, Y.

5746 The confession and execution of the eight prisoners. *D. M.*, 1676. 4°. LG, MR.

5747 The confession and execution of the five prisoners. *For D. M.*, 1677. 4°.* L; CH, NU.

5748 —[Anr. ed.] *For L. C.*, 1678. 4°.* MH, NU.

5749 —[Anr. ed.] [*London*, 1680.] fol.* HH; MH.

5750 The confession and execution of the nine prisoners . . . 28th April, 1680. [*London*, 1680.] fol.* HH; MH.

5751 The confession and execution of the prisoners . . . 17th . . . May, 1676. *For D. M.*, [1676.] 4°.* LG, MR; MH, NU.

5752 The confession and execution of the prisoners at Tyburn, 5th July 1676. 1676. 4°. MR.

5752A —[Same title.] 9th of . . . May, 1679. *For D. M.*, 1679. 4°.* L.

5753 —[Same title.] 11th of . . . June, 1679. —, 1679. 4°.* MH, NU.

5754 The confession and execution of the seven prisoners. *For D. M.*, 1677. 4°.* NU.

5755 —[Anr. ed.] —, 1678. 4°.* NU.

5756 The confession and execution of the six prisoners. 1676. 4°. MR.

5756A The confession and execution of the three prisoners. *For D. M.*, 1677. 4°.* CH.

5757 The confession and execution of the two prisoners. *For R. G.*, 1678. 4°.* NU.

5757A The confession and manner of the execution. 1682. fol.* DCH.

5757B The confession and repentance of George Sanders. [*London*], *for F. Coles, T. Vere, J. Wright, and J. Clarke*, [1680?] brs. L, O, CM.

5758 The confession of a Papish priest, vvho was hanged. [*n.p.*, 1641.] brs. LT, HH; MH.

5758A Entry cancelled.

5759 A confession of faith, according to the best-reformed churches. *For T. B.*, 1647. 4°.* LT, LIL, DT; MH.

5760 The confession of faith and catechisms. *For Robert Bostock*, [1649]. 12°. LT, O.

5760A The confession of faith, and the larger and shorter catechism. *Amsterdam, by Luice Elsever for Andrew Wilson*

5760B —[Anr. ed.] *Edinburgh, by E. Tyler*, 1649. 12°. CU.

5761 —[Anr. ed.] *Edinburgh, Lithgow*, 1650. 12°. ALDIS 1403. L, C, ENC.

5762 —[Anr. ed.] *First printed at Edenburgh, reprinted at London, for the company of stationers*, 1651. 12°. L, O, CE, CT, ENC; CN, NU, WCL, WF.

5763 —[Anr. ed.] *Edinburgh, by the heirs of George Anderson*, 1652. 24°. ALDIS 1461. L, ENC.

5764 —[Anr. ed.] *First printed at Edenburgh, and now reprinted at London for the company of stationers*, 1652. 8°. OC, CE, EN; NPT, NU.

5765 —Fourth edition. *Leith*, 1653. 4°. ALDIS 1473. EN.

5766 —[Anr. ed.] [London], printed, 1655. 12°. L, DC; NU.

5766A —[Anr. ed.] Edinburgh, by G. Lithgow, 1656. 12°. NN.

5767 —[Anr. ed.] First printed at Edinburgh, and now reprinted at London for the company of stationers, 1656. 8°. GU; NU.

5768 —"Second" edition. By E. M. for the company of stationers and to be sold by John Rothwell, 1658. 4°. L, O, CPE, DC, ENC; NC, TU, V, WF.

5768A —[Anr. ed.] Edinburgh, Lithgow, 1659. 12°. ALDIS 1590. EN.

5768B —[Anr. ed.] Edinburgh, by Evan Tyler, 1660. 12°. OC.

5768C —[Anr. ed.] First published at Edinburgh, and now reprinted at London for the company of stationers, 1660. 12°. L; Y.

5768D —[Anr. ed.] Glasgow, by Robert Sanders, 1669. 12°. ALDIS 1858. LL, ENC.

5769 —[Anr. ed.] Edinbourg, by George Swintoun and Thomas Brown, to be sold by James Glen and David Trench, 1671. 12°. ALDIS 1923. L, ENC, DT, FSF; NN, NU.

5770 —Fourth edition. Printed at London, for the company of stationers, 1658. Re-printed at Glasgow by Robert Sanders, 1675. 4°. ENC; WF.

5770A —[Anr. ed.] Edinburgh, by the heir of Andrew Anderson, 1679. 18°. ALDIS 2151. EN.

5770B —[Anr. ed.] Edinburgh, by G. Swintoun and T. Brown, to be sold by T. Malthus, 1683. 12°. LSC.

5771 —[Anr. ed.] Edinburgh, by the heir of Andrew Anderson, 1685. 12°. ALDIS 2537. ENC, FSF.

5772 —[Anr. ed.] Glasgow, by, Robert Sanders, 1687. 12°. ALDIS 2686. L.

5772A —Third edition. For the company of stationers, to be sold by T. Parkhurst, and D. Newman, 1688. 12°. CT.

5773 —[Anr. ed.] [Edinburgh], printed, 1688. 12°. EC, ENC; WF.

5774 —[Anr. ed.] Edinburgh, by John Reid, 1689. 12°. ALDIS 2875. ENC, AU, FSF; NN, PL.

5775 —[Anr. ed.] Glasgow, by Robert Sanders, 1690. 12°. OC, GU.

5776 —[Anr. ed.] —, 1693. 12°. ALDIS 3295. EN, ENC, GU, FSF.

5776A —[Anr. ed.] [London], printed, 1694. 16°. OC, ENC.

5776B —[Anr. ed.] Edinburgh, by the heirs and successors of Andrew Anderson, 1697. 12°. ALDIS 3659. EN; MB.

5777 —[Anr. ed.] Printed, 1700. 12°. OC; WF.

5778 A confession of faith, composed. 1668. 4°. BPL.

5779 A confession of faith, in the most necessary things. Second edition. Printed and sold by William Bradford in Philadelphia, 1693. 4°.* EVANS 635. PHS.

5780 A confession of faith of seven congregations. Second edition. By Matth. Simmons, and are to be sold by John Hancock, 1646. 4°.* LT, O, C, LG, DT; MH, MIU, NU, WF, Y.

5781 —Third edition. For the company of stationers, 1651. 12°.* CE, CT; Y.

5782–3 Entries cancelled.

5784 The confession of faith, of the Reformed churches. Amsterdam, by the widow of Steven Swart, 1689. 12°. L; NU, WF, Y.

5785 A confession of faith of the Roman Catholicks in Ireland. By Richard Janeway, 1689. brs. C, HH; CH, MIU.

5786 A confession of faith, of the several congregations. Third edition. By M. S. to be sold by F. Tyton, and L. Chapman, 1651. 4°.* L, CCL, SP; MH, NU, Y.

5787 —Fourth edition. By Henry Hills, 1652. 4°.* O; NHC, WF.

5787A —"Fourth" edition. By M. S., 1652. 4°.* NHC.

5788 —"Fourth" edition. 1653. 4°. L, EN.

5789 The confession of faith of those churches which are . . . called Anabaptists. Printed, 1644. 4°.* LT, C, OC, CM, P; CLC, NHC, Y.

5790 —[Anr. ed.] By Matthew Simmons, 1644. 4°.* O, C, LW, OC, DT; NU.

5791 The confession of faith of those called Arminians. For S. Walsall, 1684. 8°. T.C.II 81. L, C, DT.

5792 A confession of faith owned and consented unto. Boston, by John Foster, 1680. 8°. EVANS 280. O; CH, MH, MWA, RPJ, Y.

5793 —[Anr. ed.] Boston. Re-printed by Bartholomew Green and John Allen, 1699. 8°. EVANS 860. L, O; MB, MH, NN, RPJ, Y.

Confession of faith, penned. 1641. See Bacon, Sir Francis.

5794 A confession of faith, put forth by the elders. [n.p.], printed, 1677. 16°. LSC, BB; NHC, NU.

5794A —[Anr. ed.] For Benjamin Harris, 1679. 8°. L; CH.

5795 —[Anr. ed.] For John Harris, 1688. 12°. T.C.II 237. O, CS, YM; MH, NHC, WF.

5795A —Third edition. By S. Bridge, for Eben. Tracy, Will. Marshall, and John Marshall, 1699. 12°. T.C.III 202. L; NHC, NPT, WF, Y.

5796 The confession of faith, together with the larger and lesser catechismes. Second edition. By E. M. for the company of stationers, to be sold by John Rothwel, 1658. 4°. LT, OC, CM, E, DT; CH, CN, NU, TU, Y.

5797 —Fourth edition. Printed at London, for the company of stationers, 1658. And reprinted at Glasgow, by Robert Sanders, 1675. 4°. ALDIS 2049. L, O, E, GU, FSF; NPT, NU.

5798 —Third edition. Sold by T. Parkhurst, and D. Newman, 1688. 12°. T.C.II 237. L, C, LIL, LW, ENC; NPT.

Confession of faith touching. 1648. See Biddle, John.

Confession of my faith. 1672. See Bunyan, John.

5799 Confession of the Christian faith. [London, 1680?] brs. MR.

5800 The confession of the faith and doctrine. Edinburgh, re-printed by the heir of Andrew Anderson, 1681. fol.* ALDIS 2261. O, EN, FSF; NU, WF.

5801 A confession of the faith of several churches of Christ, in . . . Somerset. By Henry Hills, to be sold by Thomas Brewster, 1656. 4°. LT, O.

Confession of the new-married. 1683. See Marsh, A.

Confession or declaration. 1676. See Taylor, Thomas.

5802 The confession, profession and conversion of . . . young gentlewoman. For B. Aylmer, 1684. 8°. EN.

Confessions and proofes. Oxford, 1644. See Morton, Thomas, bp.

5802A The confessions, behaviour and dying speeches. colop: For E. Mallet, [1700.] brs. L.

5803 The confessions of the faith of all the Christian and reformed churches. *For Anstin Rice*, 1656. 8°. EN; CH,
BBE, MB, WF.

5803A Confidence corrected, error detected. 1692. 4°. L; NHC.
Confident questionist. 1658. *See* E., N.

5804 The confined lover. [*London*], *for J. Deacon*, [1680?]. brs. L.
Confinement. 1679. *See* Cotton, Charles.

5804A The confinement of the seven bishops. [*London*, 1689.]
brs. L, OC; CH, MB.
Confirmation of a late epistle. 1700. *See* Young, Samuel.
Conflagratio Londinensis. 1667. *See* Ford, Simon.
Conflagration. 1667. *See* Ford, Simon.
Conflict in conscience. Glasgow, 1685. *See* Livingstone,
William.
Conforming Non-conformist. 1680. *See* Cheney, John.
Conformists charity. 1689. *See* C., R.
Conformist's fourth plea. 1683. *See* Pearse, Edward.
Conformists plea. 1681. *See* Pearse, Edward.

5805 The Conformists reasons. [*n.p.*, 1691.] cap., 4°.* L, O, LW;
CH, CN, NU, TU, WF, Y.
Conformists sayings. 1690. *See* C., R.
Conformist's second plea. 1682. *See* Pearse, Edward.
Conformist's third plea. 1682. *See* Pearse, Edward.
Conformity among modern. 1667. *See* Mussard, Pierre.
Conformity re-asserted. 1664. *See* Womock, Laurence.

5806 **Confucius.** The morals of. *For Ronald Taylor*, 1691. 8°.
L, O, C, OC, EN; CH, CU, LC, NU, TU, Y.

5807 Confused characters of conceited coxcombs. *By T. M.
for Typographus*, 1661. 8°. L, O, OC.

5808 Confusion confounded: or. Entry cancelled, 1654. *See*
Hall, John.

5809 The confusion of Babel: a poem. *For W. Davis*, [1683?]
4°.* T.C.II 29. L; CH, MH, Y.
Confutation of a late pamphlet. 1698. *See* Johnson,
Samuel.
Confutation of a late paper. [*n.p.*, 1681.] *See* I., W.

5810 Confutation of a letter ballancing. 1698. 4°. LUS, BAMB.

5811 A confvtation of M. Lewes Hewes his dialogve. *For
I. M.*, 1641. 4°. LT, O, C, CM; CLC, MH, NU.

5811A A confutation of some pretended reasons for His Majesty's . . . pardon. *For R. Chiswell*, 1689. C.

5812 A confutation of sundry errors in Dr. Sherlock's book.
[*London*, 1691]. 4°.* LG, CT, HH; CH, NU, Y.
Confutation of the Anabaptists. 1644. *See* Bakewell,
Thomas.

5813 A confvtation of the Earle of Newcastles reasons. *For
Henry Overton*, 1643. 4°.* LT, HH, YM, DT; CH, MH,
WF, Y.
Confutation of the solemne league. 1648. *See* L., R.

5813A A congratulation for His Sacred Majesty, Charles. *Edinburgh, June 13*, 1660. brs. ALDIS 1638. EN.

5814 A congratulation of the Protestant-joyner to Anthony,
King of Poland. colop: *For N. Thompson*, 1683. cap.,
fol.* O, HH, EN; CH, CU, MH, WF, Y.

5815 A congratulation on the happy discovery of the hellish
fanatick plot. 1682. brs. O.

5815A —[Anr. ed.] [*London*, 1681.] brs. CS; CH, MH, WF, Y.

Congratulation to His Sacred Majesty. 1661. *See* Pestell,
William.
Congratulation to our newly restored. 1659. *See* H,,
W.

5816 A congratulatory address of the House of Representatives. colop: *Boston, by Bartholomew Green, and John
Allen*, 1699. brs. LPR.

5816A A congratulatory address to the right hon. Sir William
Ashurst. *For R. Hayhurst*, 1693. brs. CT; CN.

5817 A congratulatory encomium upon the happy conjunction of . . . Mr. Robert Buckle. *Amsterdam, by Steven
Swart*, 1671. brs. L.

5817A A congratulatory epithalamium. *Printed*, 1673. fol.* WF,
Y.

5818 A congratulatory letter of thanks from the corporation
of North Allerton. [*n.p.*, 1681.] brs. L, O.

5819 A congratulatory ode to Admiral Russel. [*London*], *by
Edward Jones*, 1692. fol.* MC; MH.
Congratulatory Pindarick. [*n.p.*, 1683.] *See* P., C.

5820 A congratulatory poem dedicated to his excellency the
ambassador from the Emperor of Fez and Morocco.
colop: *For W. Davis*, 1682. brs. O; CH.

5821 A congratulatory poem dedicated to His Majesty. colop:
Printed, 1687. brs. L, O; CLC, Y.
Congratulatory poem on His Highness. 1689. *See* Shad-
well, Thomas.

5821A A congratulatory poem on His Highness the Prince of
Orange. colop: *For W.P.*, 1688. brs. C; Y.

5821B A congratulatory poem on His Majesties happy return.
colop: *By H. Hills*, 1690. brs. MH.

5822 A congratulatory poem on His R[oyal] H[ighness]'s entertainment. *For Joanna Brome*, 1682. brs. O, EN; CH.

5823 A congratulatory poem on His royal Highness James
Duke of York. colop: *For J. Johnson*, [1682.] fol.*
CH, MH.

5824 A congratulatory poem on His Royal Highnesses restauration. *By E. Mallet*, 1684. brs. L; Y.

5824A A congratulatory poem on King William's victories in
Ireland. *For James Blackwell*, 1696. brs. MH.

5825 A congratulatory poem on occasion of His Highness the
Prince of Orange his marriage. *By T. D. for Henry
Brome*, 1678. brs. L.

5825A A congratulatory poem on the arrival of His Sacred
Majesty. [*Dublin? 1687.*] brs. L.

5826 A congratulatory poem on the meeting together of the
Parliament. colop: *For Langley Curtis*, 1680. cap., fol.*
O; CH, CN, MH, WF, Y.

5827 A congratulatory poem on the most illustrious William
Henry, Prince of Orange. colop: *For Joseph Raven*,
1689. brs. O; CH, Y.
Congratulatory poem on the right honourable Heneage
Lord Finch. 1680. *See* W., W.

5828 A congratulatory poem on the right honourable Sr.
Orlando Bridgman. [*London*], *for William Cadman*,
[1667?]. brs. L, O; WF.
Congratulatory poem on the right honourable Sir
Patience Ward. 1680. *See* W., W.

5829 A congratulatory poem on the safe arrival of King William. *For A. H.*, 1699. brs. MH.

5829A A congratulatory poem on the safe arrival of . . . Monmouth. *By Nat. Thompson*, 1679. brs. L, O, HH; MH, Y.

Congratulatory poem on the safe arrival of the Scots. [*Edinburgh?* 1699.] *See* A., R.

5830 A congratulatory poem on the Whigg's entertainment. *For E. Smith*, 1682. brs. L, O, MC, EN, DT; CH, CN, MH, WF, Y.

5831 A congratulatory poem on the wonderful atchievments of Sir John Mandevil. [*London*], *for Fr. Smith sen.*, 1683. brs. L; CLC, MH.

5832 A congratulatory poem presented to the right honourable Sr. Joseph Sheldon. [*n.p.*], *printed*, 1675. brs. L.

5833 Entry cancelled.

Congratulatory poem to Her Royal Highness, 1682. *See* B., C.

5834 A congratulatory poem to His Highness the Prince of Orange. [*n.p.*, 1689.] brs. L.

5835 A congratulatory poem, to His illustrious Highness Prince Rupert. *By Edward Crowch*, 1673. fol.* L, HH; CN.

5835A A congratulatory poem to His Royal Highness the Prince of Orange. [*London*, 1688.] brs. OC.

5835B —[Same title.] *For Anthony Baskervile*, 1689. 4°.* Y.

5836 A congratulatory poem to Sir John Moor. colop: *For W. Davis*, 1681. brs. L, O, LG; CH, MH, Y.

5837 Entry cancelled.

5838 A congratulatory poem, to the high and mighty Czar. *Printed and sold by J. Bradford*, 1698. brs. L, O.

Congratulatory poem, to the honourable Admiral Russel. [*n.p.*, 1693.] *See* Bovet, Richard.

Congratulatory poem to the ministers sons. 1687. *See* Dunwin, John.

5839 Entry cancelled.

5840 A congratulatory poem to the right honourable Sir William Pritchard. [*London*], *for P. Brooksby*, 1682. brs. L, LG, MC; CH, PU.

5841 A congratulatory poem upon the arrival of His Electoral Highness. *For Langley Curtiss*, 1680. brs. L; CH, MH.

5842 A congratulatory poem upon the happy arrival of . . . James Duke of York. colop: *By N. Thompson*, 1682. fol.* O, MC, EN; CH, PU, WF.

Congratulatory poem written by. 1685. *See* S., J.

5843 The Congress at the Hague. *For Ric. Baldwin*, 1691. 8°. T.C.II 379. L; MH.

5844 **Congreve, William.** Amendments of Mr. Collier's false. *For J. Tonson*, 1698. 8°. L, O, C, EN, DT; CH, CN, LC, MH, NC, TU, WF, Y.

5845 —The birth of the muse. *For Jacob Tonson*, 1698. fol.* L, O, CS, HH, DT; CH, MH, TU, WF, Y.

5846 [–] Buxom Joan of Lymas's love. *For P. Brooksby*, [1693–95]. brs. L, HH.

5847 —The double-dealer. *For Jacob Tonson*, 1694. 4°. L, O, C, CT, EN; CH, CN, LC, MH, NP, TU, Y.

5848 [–] Incognita. *For Peter Buck*, 1692. 8°. T.C.II 440. L, O; CH.

5849 [–] —[Anr. ed.] *For R. Wellington*, 1700. 8°. L; CU, WF.

5850 —The judgment of Paris. *For Jacob Tonson*, 1700. 4°. HUTH.

5851 —Love for love. *For Jacob Tonson*, 1695. 92 pp. 4°. L, C, OC, OW, EN; CH, LC, MH, TU, Y.

5852 ——Second edition. —, 85 pp. 1695. 4°. L, O, CK, CT; CH, CU, MH, TU, WF, Y.

5853 ——[Anr. ed.] —, 1695. 64 pp. 4°. L, C; CH, CN, MH, TU, WF, Y.

5854 ——Third edition. —, 1697. 4°. L, CT, BR, DT; BN, CU, MH, NP, WF, Y.

5855 —Love's but the frailty. [*London*], *T. Cross*, [1700]. brs. L.

5856 —The mourning bride. *For Jacob Tonson*, 1697. 4°. L, O, CT, OW, EN; CH, CN, LC, MH, TU, Y.

5857 ——Second edition. —, 1679[1697]. 4°. L, O, C, EN, DT; CH, CU, MH, TU, WF, Y.

5858 ——"Second" edition. —, 1697. 4°. L, O, C, OW, EN; CU, MH, NP, WF, Y.

5859 —The mourning muse of Alexis. *For Jacob Tonson*, 1695. fol.* L, O, CT, OC, HH; CH, CN, MH, TU, WF, Y.

5860 ——Second edition. —, 1695. fol.* L, O, C, EC, GK; MH, WF, Y.

5861 ——Third edition. —, 1695. fol.* L, O, CS, E, DT; CLC, MH, TU, Y.

5862 ——"Third" edition. *Dublin, for William Norman, and Jacob Milner*, 1695. fol.* L.

5863 —The old batchelour. *For Peter Buck*, 1693. 4°. L, O, CK, OW, DT; CH, CN, LC, MH, TU, Y.

5864 ——Second edition. *For Peter Buck*, 1693. 4°. L, OC, EN, DT; CSU, MH, WF, Y.

5865 ——Third edition. —, 1693. 4°. MH, PBL, TU, WF, Y.

5866 ——Fourth edition. —, 1693. 4°. L, LG, O; CN, MH, TU, WF, Y.

5867 ——[Anr. ed.] 1693. 4°. CH.

5868 ——Fifth edition. *For P. Buck, to be sold by James Knapton*, 1694. 4°. L, O, EN; CH, CU, MH, TU, WF, Y.

5869 ——[Anr. ed.] *For James Knapton*, 1694. 4°. OC, CT, EN; MH, WF.

5870 ——Sixth edition. *For Peter Buck*, 1697. 4°. L, O, C, EN, DT; BN, MH, NC, TU, WF, Y.

5871 —A pindarique ode humbly offer'd to the king. *For Jacob Tonson*, 1695. fol.* L, O, C, HH, GK; CH, CN, TU, WF, Y.

5872 [–] A soldier and a sailor . . . Love for love. [*London*, 1696.] brs. L.

5873 [–] —[Anr. ed. "soidier"] 1700. brs. CH.

5874 [–] A song in Love for love. [*London*], 1695. brs. MC.

5875 [–] A song in ye comedy call'd The old batcheler. [*London*], 1693. brs. MC.

5875A —A song in the comedy call The way of the world. [*London?* 1700.] fol.* L.

5876 [–] A song sung by Mr. Doggett in . . . Love for love. [*London*, 1695.] brs. L, MC.

5877   [–] Two songs from The double dealer. colop: *By J. Heptinstall, for John Hudgebutt. And are to be sold by Mr. Jo. Money.* [1694]. fol.* MH.

5878   —The way of the world. *For Jacob Tonson,* 1700. 4°. L, O, C, LVF, EN; CH, LC, MH, TU, WCL, Y.

5878A   **Coningsby, Robert.** Μυθολογια, sive. 1693. 8°. O.

5878B   [**Coningsby, Thomas**]. The many sufferings of an undone gentleman. [*London?* 1648.] cap., 4°.* MH, MIU.

5879   —26. of August. 1647. To all the world . . . to judge of. *Printed,* 1647. 4°.* LT; MIU.

     Conjugall counsell. 1653. *See* Hilder, Thomas.

     Conjugium conjurgium. 1684. *See* Ramsay, William.

5880   Conjugium languens: or, the natural, civil, and religious mischiefs. *By R. Roberts,* 1700. 4°.* L, O, OC, E; CN, NU, PL, WF, Y.

5880A   Conjuratio Jesuitica. [*London*], *Anno Dom.,* 1680. fol.* L, O; Y.

5881   **Connecticut Colony.** The book of the general laws for the people within the jvrisdiction of Connecticut. *Cambridge* [*Mass.*]: *by Samuel Green,* 1673. 4°. EVANS 173. MB, MHL, MHS, PHS, Y.

5882   The connexion: being choice collections. *For W. Crook,* 1681. 8°. T.C.I 440. L, OC, E, EN, GU; CH, CN, MH, WF, Y.

5883   Entry cancelled.

     Conningsmarck. *See* Königsmark.

5884   **Connor, Bernard.** A copy of a letter sent His Grace * * *. colop: *For Sam. Briscoe,* 1696. brs. L.

5885   —Dissertationes medico-physicæ. *Oxonii, e theatro Sheldoniano, sumptibus Henrici Clement,* 1695. 8°. L, O, C, LM, E; BN, CLC, NAM, WF, HC.

5886   —Evangelium medici. *Sumptibus Richardi Wellinton,* 1697. 8°. L, OM, C, LCP, E; BN, MH, MMO, NPT, WSG.

5887   ——Second edition. *Sumptibus Samuelis Briscoe,* 1697. 8°. LM, CS, DT; CH, CLC, WF.

5888   —The history of Poland. Vol. I. *By J. D. for Dan. Brown, and A. Roper,* 1698. 8°. T.C.III 52. L, O, C, EN, DT; BN, CH, LC, MH, WF, Y.

5889   ——Vol. II. *For Dan. Brown, and A. Roper and T. Leigh,* 1698. 8°. L, O, C, EN, DT; BN, CH, LC, MH, WF, Y.

5890   —A letter to his worthy friend, D. B. M. colop: *For Sam. Briscoe,* 1696. brs. L.

5891   **Conold, Robert.** The notion of schism stated according to the antients. *By R. W. for William Oliver and George Rose, to be sold by them and Nath. Brooks and R. Chiswell,* 1676. 8°. T.C.I 257. O, OB, CS, OM, NPL; CH, NU, WF.

5892   ——Second edition. *For W. Oliver in Norwich, sold by Richard Chiswell,* 1677. 8°. T.C.I 278. O, CSSX, CT, LCL, YM; CLC, NPT.

5893   —A sermon preached . . . January 31. 1674/5. *For George Rose in Norwich, to be sold by him there, and by Nath. Brook,* 1675. 4°.* T.C.I 204. L; CN, WF, Y.

     Conoway. *See* Conway.

5894   The conquering virgin. [*London*], *for P. Brooksby,* [1690?] brs. L, HH.

5895   The conquest of France. [*London*], *by A. M. for Charles Bates,* [1680?]. 4°.* L, O; CLC, WCL.

5896   La conquête d'Irlande: dialogue en vers. *Chez R. Baldwin,* 1691. 4°. L, O, EN.

5897   **Conring, Hermann.** In nomine Jesu Christi. Vindiciæ pacificationis Osnabruccensis. 1653. 4°. L, DT.

5898   Conscience caution'd. [*London*], *printed,* 1646. 4°.* LT, C, HH; CH, CN, NU, WF, Y.

5898A   Conscience complaint. *Printed,* 1686. brs. HH.

5899   Conscience puzzel'd. [*London*], *printed,* 1650. 4°.* LT, O, C, DT; MH, MIU, NU, WF, Y.

     Conscientious cause. 1664. *See* Whitehead, George.

5900   A conscionable couple. *For F. Coles, T. Vere, J. Wright, and J. Clark,* [1660–70]. brs. L, O, HH.

5900A   The consecration of Marcellus. An ode. *For H. Playford; A. Roper; and are to be sold by John Nutt,* 1700. fol.* OP; CLC, IU, MH.

5900B   Conseil spirituel, ou avis d'un pere. *Chez la veuve Marret & Henri Ribbotteau,* 1698. 12°. OC.

5900C   The consequences of tolerating gold and silver to be exported. [*London?* 1692.] cap., fol.* L; NC.

5901   **C[onset], H[enry].** The practice of the spiritual or ecclesiastical courts. *For T. Basset, to be sold by Will. Hensman,* 1685. 8°. T.C.II 98. L, O, C, LIL, EN; CH, MHL, NCL, NU, WF.

5902   ——Second edition. *For W. Battersby; sold by J. Deere,* 1700. 8°. T.C.III 176. LCL, AN; CU, MHL, Y.

5902A   **Conset, John.** The olive branch. *By T. R. for the author,* 1660. 4°. O, EC, YM.

5903   —The rod of recompense. *By T. R. for the author,* 1660. 4°.* EC; MH.

5904   Die Martis, viz: primo die Junii, Ann: Domi 1647. Considente domo longe frequentissima. [*Oxford,* 1648]. 4°.* MADAN 1976. O; Y.

     Considerable considerations. [*n.p.*], 1654. *See* L., S.

     Consideration and a resolution. 1641. *See* Dering, *Sir* Edward.

5905   Entry cancelled.

5906   Considerations about subscription. *Printed,* 1690. 4°.* T.C.II 303. L, O, OC, CS, EC; CH, CN, MH, NU, WF, Y.

5907   Considerations about the currancy of guineas. [1696?] fol.* L, CT, LUG.

5907A   Considerations about the transportation of wool. [*London?* 1698.] brs. L; MH.

     Considerations against the dissolving. 1653. *See* Philipps, Fabian.

5908   Considerations and cautions agreed upon by the ministers at London. 1646. 4°. DT.

     Considerations and exhortations. 1700. *See* A., P.

     Considerations and proposals. 1659. *See* B., F.

     Considerations concerning common fields. 1654. *See* Lee, Joseph.

     Considerations concerning free-schools. Oxford, 1678. *See* Wase, Christopher.

5908A   Considerations concerning Ireland. [*London?* 1690.] cap., fol.* L, C.

5908B Considerations concerning the African-companies petition. [*London*, 1698.] brs. NC.

Considerations concerning the present. 1649. *See* Durie, John.

Considerations concerning the Trinitie. 1698. *See* Gastrell, Francis.

Considerations for competitors. [*n.p.*, 1690.] *See* Stephens, Edward.

5909 Considerations for the Commons. [*London*, 1642.] cap., 4°.* LT, CJ, CT, HH; CH, MH, NU, WF, Y.

Considerations humbly offered for taking the oath. 1689. *See* Whitby, Daniel.

5909A Considerations humbly offered in relation to the East-India trade. [*London?* 1697.] brs. LUG; MH.

5909B Considerations humbly offered to the Great Councel. [*London?* 1699.] brs. MH.

5909C Considerations humbly offered to the honourable House of Commons. [*London*, 1697.] brs. L; MH, WF.

5909D Considerations humbly offered to the Lords spiritual. [*London*, 1694.] brs. L.

Considerations humbly proposed. 1658. *See* L., T.

5909E Considerations humbly proposed for preventing. [*London*], 1693/4. brs. Y.

Considerations humbly recommended. 1673. *See* S., T.

5910 Considerations in relation to the bill for the more effective prohibiting the importation. [*London*, 1694.] brs. LL.

Considerations in the behalf. [*n.p.*, 1662.] *See* Herbert, William.

5910A Considerations most humbly proposed. [*London?* 1695.] brs. MH.

Considerations moving. 1685. *See* Penn, William.

Considerations of importance. [*n.p.*, 1698/9.] *See* Leslie, Charles.

Considerations of present concernment. 1675. *See* Dodwell, Henry.

Consjderatjons of present use. [*Oxford*], 1644. *See* Hammond, Henry.

5911 Entry cancelled.

5912 Considerations offered to all the corporations of England. *For William Cademan*, 1681. fol.* O, C, HH, SP; CH, MH, WF, Y.

Considerations on a book. 1693. *See* Beaumont, John.

Considerations on Mr. Harrington's. 1657. *See* Wren, Matthew.

Considerations on the Council. [*n.p.*], 1671. *See* Woodhead, Abraham.

Considerations on the explications. [*n.p.*], 1693. *See* Nye, Stephen.

5912A Considerations on the nature of Parliaments. [*London*, 1698.] 4°.* L, C; CH, MB.

Considerations on the trade. [*n.p.*, 1698.] *See* T., D.

5912B Considerations proposed to the electors of the . . . Convention. [*London*, 1689.] brs. C; MH.

5913 Considerations relating to the African bill. [*London?* 1698.] cap., fol.* L; MH, Y.

5913A Considerations relating to the bill for regulating. [*London?* 1697.] brs. Y.

5913B Considerations relating to the bill for restraining. [*London?* 1700.] brs. C; MH, Y.

5914 Considerations relating to the intended duties on paper. [*London*, 1698?] brs. L; Y.

5915 Considerations relating to the settling of the government. 1689. 4°. DT.

5916 Considerations requiring greater care for trade in England. *For S. Crouch*, 1695. 4°.* L; CH, LC, MH, NC, Y.

Considerations tending. [*n.p.*, 1647.] *See* Hartlib, Samuel.

5917 Considerations touching His Majesties revenue. [*London?* 1663.] 4°.* LUG; MH.

Considerations touching that question. 1687. *See* Briggs, Henry.

5917B Considerations touching the bill for settling. [*London*, 1698.] cap., fol.* L.

5918 Considerations touching the dissolving or taking away the court of chancery. *By F. L. for Thomas Heath*, 1653. 4°. L, C, CCA, LL, LW; CH, CLC, MH, MHL, WF.

5919 Considerations touching the excise of native . . . commodities. [*London*, 1644?] cap., fol. L; WF.

5920 Considerations touching the late treaty for a peace. *Printed at Oxford by Leonard Lichfield*, 1645. 4°.* MADAN 1773. L, C, HH, EN, DT; CH, NPT, TU, WF, Y.

5920A —[Anr. ed.] —, 1645. 4°.* MADAN 1774. LT, O, C, OC; CH, CN, MH, Y.

Considerations touching the likeliest. 1659. *See* Milton, John.

Considerations touching the true way. 1677. *See* Lloyd, William, *bp*.

5921 Considerations tovching trade. [*London*], *printed*, 1641[2]. 4°.* LT, CT; CSS, NC, NR, WF, Y.

Considerations upon a printed sheet. 1683. *See* L'Estrange, *Sir* Roger.

5922 Considerations upon the act of Parliament. for reversing the judgment. [*London*, 1690?] 4°. L, LG, LL.

Considerations upon the bill. [*n.p.*, 1700?] *See* Penn, William.

5922A Considerations upon the bill for the better discovery of clippers. [*London*, 1694.] * LG.

5923 Considerations upon the choice of a speaker . . . Commons. [*London*], *printed*, 1698. 4°.* L, CS, MR; CH, CN, MH, TU, WF, Y.

5924 Considerations upon the late transactions and proceedings of the army. *For Isaac Pridmore*, [1659]. brs. LT; MH, Y.

5925 Considerations upon the management of the Bank of England. [*London*, 1697.] cap., fol.* LUG.

5925A Considerations upon the present state of the United Netherlands. 1672. fol.* L.

5926 Considerations upon the proclamation for the thanksgiving. [*London*, 1692?] cap., 4°.* O, CS, LL, EN; NP, Y.

Considerations upon the question. 1676. *See* Holles, Denzil Holles, *baron*.

Considerations upon the reputation. 1680. *See* Hobbes, Thomas.

5927   Considerations upon the resignation. 1654. 4°. LCL.

Considerations upon the second canon. 1693. *See* Grascome, Samuel.

Consilium de reformanda. 1642. *See* Du Moulin, Louis.

Consilium & votum. 1651. *See* Belcamp, John V.

Consolation of philosophy. 1664. *See* Boethius.

Consolatory discourse. 1665. *See* Patrick, Symon.

Consolatory discourse for the support. 1690. *See* Camfield, Benjamin.

5928   A consolatory epistle to D. T[itus] O[ates]. *For Walter Davis*, [1685?]. fol.* L, O, CT, HH; CH, WF.

5929   —[Anr. ed.] *Dublin*, 1685. 4°.* DIX 214. DN.

5930   Consolatory letter. *For Thomas Bennet*, 1698. 4°.* CT; Y.

5930A The consolidating advertisement. [*London?* 1695.] brs. LG.

5931   The conspiracy. [*London*], printed 1683. brs. O; CLC, MH.

5931A Conspiracy by the Papists in the Kingdome of Ireland. *For John Thomas*, 1461. [*i.e.*, 1641.] 4°.* MH.

5932   A conspiracie discovered: or . . . the report. [*London*], printed, 1641. 4°.* LT, O, C, LG, HH; CH, CN, MH, NU, WF, Y.

5933   The conspiracy of Aeneas & Antenor. *For John Spicer*, 1682. 4°.* L, O, C, LVD; CH, MH, MU, NU, WF, Y.

Conspiracy of guts. [*n.p.*, 1693.] *See* Rogers, Thomas.

Conspiracy of the Spaniards. 1675. *See* Saint-Réal, César Vichard de.

5934   A conspiracre [*sic*] of the twelve bishops in the Tovver. *For W. Bond*, 1641. 4°.* LT, CT; NU, OWC, Y.

5935   **Constable, Robert.** God and the king. *For W.L.*, 1680. 4°.* T.C.I 395. O, CT, DT; CH, CN, Y.

5936   Constance and Anthony. [1700?] brs. L; MH, WCL.

5937   Constance of Cleveland. [*London*], *for F. Coles, T. Vere, J. Wright, and J. Clarke*, [1655–80]. brs. L, CM, HH.

5937A The constancy of the people called Quakers. [*London*], colop: *Printed, and sold by Andrew Sowle*, [1689.] fol.* LF, OC, CT; PSC.

5938   A constant and a kinde maid. [*London*], *for F. Coules*, [1650?]. brs. L.

5939   A constant and kind maid. [*London*, 1690?] brs. L.

5940   Constant Cloris. [*London*], *for P. Brooksby*, [1690?]. brs. L, HH.

5941   Constant Coridon. [*London*], *for P. Brooksby, J. Deacon, J. Blare, J. Back*, [1688–92]. brs. L, CM, HH.

5942   The constant country maid. *For W. Whitwood*, [1670?]. brs. L.

5943   The constant country-man. [*London*], *for P. Brooksby, J. Deacon, J. Blare, and J. Back*, [1688–92]. brs. L, CM, HH.

Constant kalender. 1656. *See* Philippes, Henry.

5943A The constant lady and false-hearted squire. *For R.B.*, [1686?] brs. CM.

Constant lover. [*n.p.*, 1685–88.] *See* D'Urfey, Thomas.

5944   The constant lovers mortal mistake. *For F. Coles, T. Vere, J. Wright, J. Clark, W. Thackeray, and T. Passenger*, [1655–65]. brs. L, HH; MH.

Constant maid. 1667. *See* Shirley, James.

5945   The constant maidens resolution. [*London*], *by J.L. for J.C.*, [1674?]. brs. L, O.

Constant man's character. 1650. *See* W., S.

5946   The constant nymph: or, the rambling shepheard. *For Langley Curtis*, 1678. 4°. T.C.I 291. O, C, LVD, EN, DT; CH, CN, MH, NC, WF, Y.

5947   A constant wife, and a kind wife. [*London*], *for F. Coles, T. Vere, J. Wright, and J. Clarke*, [1675?]. brs. CM, HH, GU; MH.

Constantia. Edinburgh, 1655 [*i.e.*, 1755].

5947A **Constantine, Henry.** A sermon preached . . . July the 23d, 1683. By J. Grantham, for Isaac Cleare, 1683. 4°.* O, CT; Y.

5948   [**Constantine, William.**] The interests of England, how it consists in vnity. *By E. Griffin, for Lawrence Blaicklocke*, 1642. 4°.* LT, O, CT, LCL, DT; CH, MH, NU, WF, Y.

5949   [–] The second part of the interest of England considered. *By Richard Bishop for Lawrence Blaiklock*, 1645. 4°. LT, O, CT, EN, AU; CH, CN, MU, NU, WF, Y.

5950   [**Constantini, Angelo.**] A pleasant and comical history of the life of Scaramouche. *For Robert Gifford*, 1696. 12°. L.

Constantius the apostate. 1683. *See* Bennet, John.

Constitution of Parliament. 1680. *See* Pettus, *Sir* John.

Constitutions and canons ecclesiastical. 1660. *See* Church of England.

Consultation about religion. 1693. *See* Lessius, Lernare.

5951   A consultation between the Pope and a Jesuit. *For N. M.*, 1679. brs. L.

Contemned Quaker. 1692. *See* Whitehead, George.

Contemplation of heaven. Paris, 1654. *See* White, Thomas.

Contemplation on Bassets down-hill. [*n.p.*, 1658.] *See* Kemp, *Mrs.* Anne.

Contemplations moral. 1676. *See* Hale, *Sir* Matthew.

Contempations of a statesman. 1687. *See* Nuremberg, Juan Eusebio.

Contemplations on the life. Paris, 1685. *See* Cross, John.

5952   Contemplations on the love of God. *For Sam. Keble*, 1699. 4°. O.

Contemplations upon these times. 1646. *See* Lewis, John.

Contented cuckold. [*n.p.*, 1660–70.] *See* R., T.

5953   The contented pilgrim. [*London*], *for P. Brooksby*, [1672–85]. brs. L, CM, HH; MH.

5953A The contented subjects. [*London*], *for P. Brooksby*, [1682.] brs. L, CT.

5954   Content's a treasure. [*London*], *for J. Blare*, [1684?]. brs. L.

5955   [**Conti, Louise Marguerite, princesse de**], Intrigues of Love. *For R. G. and sold by B. Crayle*, 1689. 12°. T.C.II 250. CLC, WF.

5956   The continuance of the high court of chancery vindicated. *For Lawrence Chapman*, 1654. 4°.* LT; CH.

5957   Continuatio epicediorvm super octo senatores Londinenses. *Cantabrigiæ, ex officina Rogeri Danielis*, 1641. 4°.* O; Y.

Continuation and vindication. 1682. *See* Long, Thomas.

5957A A continuation of a discourse lately printed and entitled A brief accompt of the Turks. *By Richard Hodgkinson and Thomas Mab*, 1663. 4°. NC.

Continuation of a former. [*n.p.*, 1684.] *See* Bampfield, Francis.

Continuation of morning-exercise. 1683. *See* Annesley, Samuel, *ed.*

5958 A continuation of news from . . . His Majesties fleet. colop: *For John Dunton*, 1689. brs. CH, MH.

5959 The continuation of our forraine occurrences. *N. Butter*, 1642. 4°.* CN.

5960 A continvation of our weekly intelligence from His Majesties army. [*London*], *printed, September 16*, 1642. 4°.* LT.

Continuation of Sir Philip Sydney's Arcadia. 1651. *See* Weamys, Anne.

Continuation of the Answer. 1693. *See* Ridpath, George.

Continuation of the coffee-house dialogue. [*n.p.*, 1680.] *See* Yarranton, Andrew.

Continuation of the collection. 1641. *See* Trussel, John.

5960A A continuation of the compleat catalogue of stitch'd books. *Printed*, 1680. 4°.* L, O, OC; CN, MH, TSM.

5961 A continuation of the curious collection of paintings . . . 14th of January. [*n.p.*, 1692.] brs. L.

5962 —4th . . . February. [*n.p.*, 1692.] brs. L.

5963 A continuation of the Dialogue between two young ladies. Part the second. *Printed*, 1696. 8°.* L; CH, LC, Y.

5964 A continvation of the divrnal occvrrences and proceedings . . . in Ireland. *For I. T.*, 1642. 4°.* LT, O, EC; MH, Y.

Continuation of the friendly debate. 1669. *See* Patrick, Symon, *bp.*

Continuation of the grand conspiracy. [*n.p.*, 1660.] *See* Allington, John.

Continuation of the historical relation. 1691. *See* Cockburn, John.

5965 A continuation of the histories of forreine martyrs. *By Ric. Hearne, for the company of stationers*, 1641. fol. WCA; IU, MH, TSM, WF.

Continuation of the history of passive obedience. Amsterdam, 1690. *See* Seller, Abednego.

Continuation of the history of the Reformation. 1689. *See* Bohun, Edmund.

5966 A continuation of the inquest after blood, and goaldelivery of Newgate, April 13, 1670. colop: *By Tho. Newcomb*, 1670. fol. CH.

5967 A continvation of the late proceedings of His Majesties army at Shrewsbury. *For M. Batt. October 12*, 1642. 4°. LT, EC; WF.

5968 Entry cancelled.

Continuation of The present state. 1688. *See* Wake, William, *abp.*

5969 A continuation of the proceedings of the Scots army before Hereford. *By M. B. for Robert Bostock, 15 Aug.*, 1645. 4°.* LT, O, AN; CH, WF, Y.

Continuation of the second part of the Enquiry. [1688.] *See* Burnet, Gilbert, *bp.*

5970 A continuation of The secret history of Whitehall. *R. Baldwin*, 1697. 8°. L, HH.

5971 A continuation of the state of New-England. *By T. M. for Dorman Newman*, 1676. fol.* O, LG, WCA; CH, CN, LC, MH, NN, RPJ, Y.

Continuation of the svbiect. 1567 [sic]. *See* May, Thomas.

5972 Aprill the first, 1642. A continuation of the tryumphant and couragious proceedings. *For John Wright*, 1642. 4°.* LT, O, LVF, MR; WF, Y.

5973 A continuation of the trve narration of the most observable passages. *By I. D., for Francis Eglesfield, May 10*, 1644. 4°.* LT, HH, DT; CH, MH, WF.

Continuation of this session. 1659. *See* Streater, John.

5974 A continuation, or second part, of the most pleasant and delightful history of Reynard the Fox. *By A. M. for Edward Brewster*, 1672. 4°. T.C.I 103. DT; CH.

Continued cry. [*n.p.*], 1675. *See* Penn, William.

Contract answer. 1698. *See* M., J.

5975 The contractors for sale of the lands and possessions of the late king. [*n.p.*, 1650.] brs. STEELE 2890. LT.

Contra-replicant. [*n.p.*, 1642.] *See* Parker, Henry.

Contrite and humble heart. [*n.p.*], 1693. *See* Jenks, Silvester.

Contrivances of the fanatical. 1685. *See* Smith, William.

5976 The contriving lover. [*London*], *for R. Kell*, 1690. brs. L, CM, HH.

Controversial discourses. Doway, 1697. *See* Wilmot, John.

Controversial letters. 1673. *See* Walsh, Peter.

5977 The controversie between Robin and Doll's housekeeping. [1690?] 4°. brs. O.

5977A Controversy between the East-India Company. [*London?* 169–] brs. MH.

5977B A controversy between the Quakers and bishops. *Printed*, 1663. 4°. BBN; PH.

Controversy ended. 1673. *See* Hedworth, Henry.

Controversy-logicke. Roan, 1674. *See* White, Thomas.

Controversy of the Lord. [*n.p.*], 1676. *See* Lynam, John.

Controversy which hath been. [*n.p.*, 1666.] *See* Fox, George.

5978 **Contzen, Adam.** Looke about you. [*London*], *imprinted*, 1641. 4°.* L, O, CT; CLC, MIU, PL, Y.

5979 Conventicula fanaticorum dissipata. colop: *For Walter Davis*, 1685. brs. L, O, MC; CH, WF.

5980 Entry cancelled.

Conversion & persecutions. 1680. *See* Burnet, Gilbert, *bp.*

5981 Conversion exemplified. *Printed*, 1669. 8°. O, C; CLC.

5982 The convert Scot, and apostate English. colop: *For A. B.*, 1681. fol.* L, O, CS; CH, CN, MH, TU, WF, Y.

Converted Capuchin. 1641. *See* Clouet, François.

5983 The converted Cavaliers confession. *By Bern: Alsop*, 1644. 4°.* CH, NU, WF, Y.

Converted fryar. 1673. *See* P., W.

5984 The converted Jacobite. 1690. 4°. L.

Converted Presbyterian. 1668. *See* Chamberlayne, Edward.

Converted twins. 1667. *See* Medbourne, Matthew.

5985 The converts. [*London*, 1686?] brs. L, C, OC, HH; CH, CN, MH, TU, Y.

5986 The converts letter. [1643?] 4°. DT.
Converts letter to his old friends. 1645. *See* R., W.

5987 The converts; or the folly of priest-craft. *For Richard Baldwin*, 1690. 4°. CH, WF.
Conviction of worldly vanity. 1687. *See* Cartigny, Jean de.

5988 The convinc'd petitioner. *Printed, Jan.* 13, 1643. 4°.*
MADAN 1163. LT, O, C, HH, EN; NC, NU, WF, Y.

5989 [**Conway, Anne Finch**] *viscountess.* The principles of the most ancient and modern philosophy. *Amsterdam, by M. Brown*, 1690. *And reprinted at London*, 1692. 8°.
T.C.III 37. L, O, CT, LW; MH, PL, WF, Y.

5990 Entry cancelled.

5991 Conovvay [Conway] taken by storme. *By I. C.*, 1646. 4°.* LT, AN, DT; PT.

5991A **Cony, Thomas.** A true copy of a Popish VVill. [*London*, 1680.] cap., fol.* L, EN; CH, MH, PU, WF.

5992 The cony-catching bride. *Printed at London by T. F.*, 1643. 4°.* CH, Y.

5993 **Conyer,** . A true copy of a dispute lately held at Rome. colop: *For John Bringhurst*, 1681. brs. L, MC; MH, WF.

5993A **Conyers, Tobias.** A good conscience. [*London*], printed, 1663. 4°. SP: MBA.

5994 —A pattern of mercy . . . a sermon. *By M. I.*, 1660. 4°.*
LT, O, CP, LW, YM; MB, NU, WF, Y.
[–] Plotters doom. 1680. *See* Palmer, Samuel.

5995 —Popery and hypocrisy detected. *For Richard Janeway*, 1680. 4°.* LW; MH, NU, WF, Y.
Conyers, William. Heremologium. 1664. *See* Almanacs.
Cook. *See also* Cooke.

5996 **Cook, Aurelian.** Titus Britannicus; an essay. *For James Partridg*, 1685. 8°. L, O, LCL, EN; CH, CLC, CN, MH, Y.
Cooke. *See also* Cook.

5997 **Cooke, Edward,** *colonel.* Certain passages which happened at Newport. *For Richard Chiswell*, 1690. 4°.*
T.C.II 306. L, O, C, LVF, AU; CH, CN, MH, WF, Y.

5998 [**Cooke, Edward,** *of Inner Temple.*] Memorabilia. *For Nevil Simmons, Tho. Simmons, and Sam. Lee*, 1681. fol.
T.C.I 442. O, C, WCA, HH, E; CH, CN, LC, MHL, Y.

5999 **Cooke, Edward,** *of Middle Temple.* Chronica juridicialia. *For H. Sawbridge, and T. Simmons*, 1685. 12°.
L, O, C, NPL, DT; CH, LC, MH, WF, YL.

5999A [–] Here is something of concernment. [*London*, 1660]. cap., 4°.* L.

6000 [–] The history of the successions. *For Thomas Simmons, and John Kidgel*, 1682. fol. L, O, OC, MC, EN; CN, MH, MIU, WF.

6001 [–] A seasonable treatise, wherein is proved. *For J. Robinson*, 1689. 8°. T.C.II 260. L, C, EN; CN.

6001A [–] A short historical account of the Kings of England. *For Tho. Simmons*, 1684. fol. T.C.II 84. L, O, OC, CS, MC; LC, TSM, WF.

6002 —A true and perfect narrative of the inhumane practices. *For Samuel Day*, 1680. fol.* L, O; CH, CN, MIU, TU, WF, Y.

6003 —A true narrative of the inhumane positions. *For Samuel Tidmarsh*, 1680. fol.* T.C.I 404. L, OC, MR, WCA, EN; CH, WF, Y.

6004 **Cooke, Edward,** *poet.* Love's triumph. *By Thomas James, to be sold by him and by William Leach*, 1678. 4°.
T.C.I 310. L, O, OW; CH, CN, LC, MH, NC, TU, Y.

6005 [**Cooke, Edward,** *Quaker.*] A second account in short, of the substance. [*London*, 1658.] cap., 4°.* L, BBN.

6006 [–] A short accovnt of the vniust proceedings. colop: *For Thomas Simmons*, 1658. cap., 4°.* L, O, C, BBN; CH, MH, NU, PH, WF.

6007 —Some considerations. [*London?*], printed, 1670. 4°. L, O, C, LF, BBN; CH, MH, NU, PH, Y.

6008 **Cooke, Frances.** *Mris.* Cooke's meditations. *Corke printed, and reprinted at London by C. S. to be sold by Thomas Brewster and Gregory Mould*, [1650]. 4°.* LT; MIU.

6009 **Cooke, Francis.** The old proverbe, as good. colop: *By Thomas Paine*, 1645[/6]. cap., 4°.* LT, O, C, OC, HH; CSS, MH, MIU, WF.

6010 —The true Protestant's prayer. [*London*, 1642.] brs. LT

6011 **Cooke, Henry.** Catalogue of the library of. [*London*, 1699?] 4°. L.

6011A —A little manuel of counsels. *For the author*, 1662. 8°. SP.

6012 **Cooke, James.** Mellificium chirurgiæ. Or the marrow. *Printed at London for Samuel Cartwright*, 1648. 12°. C, LCP, LCS, OM, CT; CLM, MIU, NAM, WSG, HC.

6013 ——[Anr. ed.] *By T. R. for John Sherley*, 1662. 12°. L, LCS, LWL, GU; MIU, WF, JF.

6014 ——[Anr. ed.] *By J. D. for Benj. Shirley*, 1676. 8°. T.C.I 230. L, O, LWL, LCS, LR; NAM.

6015 ——Fourth edition. *By T. Hodgkin, for William Marshall*, 1685. 4°. T.C.II 104. C, LCP, LCS, OME, GH; CH, MH, PAP, WF.

6016 ——"Fourth" edition. *For W. Marshall*, 1693. 4°. T.C.II 486. C, LCS, LWL; CLC, WSG, WG, HC.

6016A ——"Fourth" edition. *J. Phillips*, 1700. 4°. LWL.

6017 —Supplementum chirurgiæ or the supplement to The marrow of chyrurgerie. *For John Sherley*, 1655. 12°. LT, OM, CCA, LCS, RPL; NAM, WF, JF.

6018 **Cooke, John,** *of Cuckstone, Kent.* A sermon preached Decemb. 19th 1675. *By H. Cruttenden, to be sold by Moses Pitt*, 1676. 4°. T.C.I 233. L, O, CS, CT; WF, Y.

6019 **Cook, John,** *of Ireland.* Monarchy no creature of Gods making. *Printed at Waterford in Ireland, by Peter de Pienne*, 1651. 8°. L, C, CT, DN.

6020 —[Anr. ed.] —, 1652. 8°. L, C, OW, LCL.

6021 —[Anr. ed.] *Printed at Waterford in Ireland, by Peter de Pienne, and are to be sold in London, by Thomas Brewster*, 1652. 8°. LT, O, C, CT; CH, CLC, NU.

6022 —A true relation of Mr. Iohn Cook's passage by sea. *Printed at Cork, and re-printed at London, to be sold by T. Brewster and G. Moule*, 1650. 4°.* LT, O, CE; WF, Y.

6023 — —Second edition. *Printed and are to be sold by T.B.,* [1652?]. 4°.* L, C, LW; CH, MH, Y.

6024 **Cooke, John,** *of Mersham, Kent.* A sermon preached May 13. 1683. *For Moses Pitt,* 1683. 4°.* L, O, CS, WCA, CT; Y.

6025 **Cooke, John,** *solicitor general.* King Charls his case. *By Peter Cole, for Giles Calvert,* 1649. 4°.* LT, O, OM, MR, DT; CH, CN, MH, NU, WCL, WF, Y.

6026 —Redintegratio amoris, or a union of hearts. *For Giles Calvert,* [1647]. 4°. LT, O, C, E, DT; CH, MH, NU, PL, Y.

6027 —Unum necessarium: or, the poore man's case. *For Matthew Walbancke,* 1648. 4°. LT, O, LW, ES; CH, MH, NC, WF, Y.

6028 —The vindication of the law. *For Matthew Walbancke,* 1652. 12°. LT, CCA; MHL.

6029 —The vindication of the professors. *Printed at London, for Matthew Walbancke,* 1646. 4°. LT, O, C, EN, DT; CH, CN, MHL, NCL, Y.

6030 — —[Anr. ed.] —, 1652. 4°. L, EN.

6031 —What the independents would have. *By R.L. for Giles Calvert,* 1647. 4°.* LT, O, C, E, DT; CH, MH, WF, NU, Y.

6032 **Cooke, Moses.** The manner of raising, ordering, and improving forrest-trees. *For Peter Parker,* 1676. 4°. T.C.I 238. L, O, CT, R; CH, MH, MHO, MIU, WF.

6033 —The manner of raising, ordering and improving forest and fruit-trees. *For Peter Parker,* 1679. 4°. L, CT, LAS, R, ES; CH, MH, PL, WF, Y.

6034 Entry cancelled.

6034A **Cooke, Robert.** A memorial of a few significant proposals. [*London?* 1690.] brs. LG.

Cooke, Roger. Treatise concerning the regulation. 1696. *See* Coke, Roger.

6035 [**Cooke, Shadrach.**] Christian supports under the terrors of death. *By Bennet Griffin, for Sam. Keble,* 1691. 4°.* T.C.II 378. L, O, CT; Y.

6036 — —[Anr. ed.] *For E. Whitlock,* 1696. 4°.* L, O.

6037 —An exhortation to firmness. *By J. Redmayne,* 1689. 4°.* L, O, CS; CH.

6038 —A sermon preached . . . 26th day of July, 1685. *By R. N. for Walter Kettilby,* 1685. 4°.* T.C.II 141. L, O, C, CCH, BAMB; WF, Y.

6038A —Newgate, Octob. 22, 1693. Whereas it was witnessed. [*London,* 1693.] brs. L, HH.

6039 **Cooke, Thomas.** Episcopacie asserted. *By Tho. Favvcet, for Nath. Bvtter,* 1641. 4°.* LT, O, C, EN, DT; CH, CN, MH, NU, WF, Y.

6040 **Cooke, William.** A dose for Chamberlain. [*London,* 1661.] brs. L.

6041 —The font uncover'd. [*London*], 1649. 4°. LCL.

6042 — —[Anr. ed.] *By A. Miller for Tho. Vnderhill,* 1651. 4°. O, LM, SS, EN; CH, MH, NU, WF, Y.

6043 —A learned and full answer to a treatise. *By I.L. for Christopher Meredith,* 1644. 4°. LT, O, CT, EN; CH, MH, NU, WF, Y.

6044 [–] The true character of a noble generall: . . . Essex. *By Iohn Hammond,* 1644. 4°.* LT; WF, Y.

Cookson, William. Μηνολογιον. 1699. *See* Almanacs.

6044A A coole conference between the cleared reformation. [*London?* 1643.] cap., 4°.* CH, MH, NN, WF, Y.

6045 A coole conference between the Scottish commissioners . . . 1644. [*London,* 1686?] cap., 4°.* LT, OB; CH, NPT, NU, WF, Y.

6046 **Coole, Benjamin.** Honesty the truest policy. [*London*], *for the author,* 1700. 8°. L, O, LF, BR; CH, PH, RPJ, WF, Y.

6047 —The Quakers cleared from being apostates. *Printed and sold by T. Sowle,* 1696. 8°. L, LF, BBN; MH, PH, PSC, RPJ, WF.

6047A [–] Religion and reason united. *Printed and are to be sold by T. Sowle,* 1699. 8°. LF; PH.

6047B —Sophistry detected. *Bristol, Printed and sold by W. Bonny,* 1699. 4°. L, O, LF; PH, PSC.

6048 [**Cooper, Andrew.**] A speedy post; vvith more news from Hvll. *For Iohn Thomas,* 1642. 4°.* LT, EC.

6049 —Στρατολογια; or, the history of the English civil warrs. *For Joseph Cranford,* 1660. 8°. L, EN; MH, WF.

6050 — —[Anr. ed.] —, 1662. 8°. L, O; CH, CN, Y.

Cooper, Anthony Ashley. *See* Shaftesbury, Anthony Ashley Cooper, *earl of.*

6051 **Cooper, Christopher.** The English teacher. *By John Richardson, for the author, to be sold by Walter Kettleby,* 1687. 8°. T.C.II 209. O, C.

6051A —[Anr. ed.] *By John Richardson for George Coniers,* 1688. 8°. T.C.III 103. MH.

6052 —Grammatica linguæ Anglicanæ tripartita. *Typis J. Richardson, impensis Benj. Tooke,* 1685. 8°. T.C.II 100. L, O, C, OM, DT; BN, NU, WF, Y.

6053 **Cooper, Edmund.** The asse beaten for bawling. *By J. Brudenell,* 1661. brs. L.

6054 —On the recovery of our most gracious Queen Katharine. *Printed,* 1664. 4°.* O.

6055 **Cooper, Joseph,** *cook.* The art of cookery refin'd. *By J. G. for R. Lowndes,* 1654. 12°. L.

6056 **Cooper, Joseph,** *Hebraist.* The dead witnesse. 1663. 8° O, LCL; NPT.

6057 —[Hebrew]. Hoc est, domus Mosaicæ clavis. *Typis T. R. impensis Nath. Ponder,* 1673. 8°. T.C.I 121. L, O, C, AU, DT; BN, NPT, WF, Y.

6058 —Μισθοσκοπια. A prospect. *By W. Redmayne and to be sold by John Cooper, and Joseph Cooper,* 1700. 8°. L, LCL, LW; NPT, NU, Y.

[**Cooper, Robert.**] Propositions concerning optic-glasses. Oxford, 1679. *See* Walker, Obadiah.

6059 C[ooper], T[homas]. Vox & votum populi Anglicani, shewing how deeply. *Printed,* 1660. 4°.* LT, O, C, MR; CH, CN, MH, NU, PL, Y.

6060 — —[Anr. ed.] *For Henry Seile,* 1660. 4°.* O, C, HH; WF.

6061 **Cooper, William,** *bookseller.* A catalogue of chymicall books. *Printed,* 1675. 8°. L, O, C, MR, E; LC, MH, PL, WF, Y.

6062 —The philosophical epitaph of. *By T. R. and N. T. for William Cooper,* 1673. 8°. L, O, C, LPO, GU; MH, WF, Y, HC.

6063 **Cooper, William,** *of St. Olave's, London.* The good man perished. *Printed,* 1677. 4°.* L, LW, E.

6064 —[Hebrew.] Ierusalem fatall. *By J. C. for the author,* 1649. 4°.* LT, O, LCL, LW, DT; NU.

Cooper of Norfolk. [1670–97.] *See* Parker, Martin.

Coopers hill. 1642. *See* Denham, *Sir* John.

6065 **Coore, Richard.** Christ set forth. 1683. 8°. LCL.

6065A —The practical expositor. *For Randolph Taylor,* 1683. 8°. T.C.II 25. L.

Coote, Charles. *See* Mountrath, *Sir* Charles Coote.

6066 **Coote, Chidley.** Irelands lamentation. *By R. C. for H. S.,* 1644. 4°.* LT, C, LVF; CH, MH, WF, Y.

6067 **Coote, Edmund.** The English schoole-master. Nine-teenth edition. *By B. A. and T. F. for the company of stationers,* 1641. 4°. O.

6068 — —Twenty-ninth edition. *R. & W. Leybourne, for the company of stationers,* 1658. 4°. CN.

6069 — —Thirty-first edition. *By William Leybourn, for the company of stationers,* 1662. 4°. L.

6070 — —Thirty-second edition. —, 1663. 4°. CP.

6071 — —Thirty-third edition. —, 1665. 4°. L; MH.

6072 — —Thirty-fifth edition. [*London*], *by E. Tyler, for the company of stationers,* 1669. 4°. O.

6073 — —Thirty-sixth edition. *By A. Maxwell, for the company of stationers,* 1670. 4°. WF.

6074 — —Thirty-seventh edition. —, 1673. 4°. L.

6074A — —Thirty-eighth edition. —, 1675. 4°. GU.

6075 — —40th edition. *By A. M. and R. R. for the company of stationers,* 1680. 4°. WF.

6076 — —42th [sic] edition. *Dublin, Andrew Crooke,* 1684. 4°. DIX 207. L.

6076A — —44th edition. *By A. Maxwell and R. Roberts for the company of stationers,* 1684. 4°. Y.

6076B — —Forty-sixth edition. *By R. Roberts, for the company of stationers,* 1687. 4°. IU.

6076C — —[Anr. ed.] *By R. Roberts for the company of stationers,* 1691. L, O; NS.

6077 — —47th edition. *By I. Millet, for the company of stationers,* 1692. 4°. L; CLC, NC.

6078 — —48th ed. [*London*], *by R. Roberts for the company of stationers,* 1696. 4°. L.

6078A — —49th edition. —, 1700. 4°. NC.

6079 The copies of all letters, papers. *For Edward Husband, August 14, 1648.* 4°. LT, O, HH, EN, DT; CH, MH, NU, WF, Y.

Copies of papers from the armies. 1654. *See* Corbet, Roger.

Copies of several letters. 1660. *See* Fox, George.

6079A Copies of several of the papers. [*London?* 1657.] cap., 4°. CH, MH.

6080 The copies of several papers that passed between the king. *For R. Smithurst,* 1648. 4°.* LT.

6080A Copies of some few of the papers given into. [*London,* 1657.] cap., 4°.* MH.

6081 The copies of such bills as were presented. *For Edward Husbands, July 19, 1643.* 4°. MADAN 1412. LT, O, OC, E, DT; CH, MH, NU, WF, Y.

6081A The copies of the forementioned affadavits. [*London?* 1651.] brs. HH.

Copies of the informations. 1685. *See* Sprat, Thomas, *bp.*

6082 The copies of two petitions from the officers and soul-diers of Col. Charles Fleetwoods regiment. *By John Clowes,* 1648. 4°.* LT; CH, MH, WF.

6083 **Copleston, John.** Moses next to God. *By W. Godbid for Richard Thrale,* 1661. 4°.* L, O; Y.

6084 **Copley, Joseph.** The case of the Jews is altered. *The author,* 1656. 8°. LG.

6085 **[Copley, Lionel.]** A letter sent from a gentleman to Mr. Henry Martin. *By L. Norton, for E. Husbands and Iohn Frank,* 1642. 4°.* L, O, C, EC; CH, CLC, WF, Y.

6086 **Coppe, Abiezar.** A character of a true Christian. *By T. D: sold by La: Curtiss,* 1680. brs. L; MH.

6087 —A fiery flying roll. *Imprinted at London,* 1649[50]. 4°.* LT, C, DC.

6088 Entry cancelled.

6089 —A remonstrance or the sincere and zealous protesta-tion. *By James Cottrel,* 1651. 4°.* LT; NU.

6090 —Copp's return to the wayes of truth. *By Tho. New-comb,* 1651. 4°.* LT, O, EN; WF, Y.

6091 [–] A second fiery flying roule. [*London*], *printed,* 1642 [1649]. 4°.* LT.

6092 [–] —[Anr. ed.] —, 1649[50]. 4°.* LT, DC.

6093 [–] Some sweet sips. *For Giles Calvert,* 1649. 8°. O; CH, NPT.

6094 **Coppin, Richard.** A blow at the serpent. *By Philip Wattleworth, and sold by William Larner,* 1656. 4°. O, OC.

6095 —Crux Christi, and iudgement executed. *For VVilliam Larner,* 1657. 4°. L, O, C.

6096 —Divine teachings. *For Giles Calvert,* 1649. 4°. LT; CH, Y.

6097 — —Second edition. *Printed, to be sold by William Larner, and by Richard Moon,* 1653. 4°. O, CT; NU.

6098 —The exaltation of all things in Christ. Third part. *For Giles Calvert,* 1649. 4°. LT, O; CH, Y.

6099 —The gloriovs mysterie of divine teachings. *Printed,* 1653. 4°.* O; NU.

6100 —A hint of the glorious mystery. *For Giles Calvert,* 1649. 4°.* LT; MH.

6101 —A man-child born. *Printed, to be sold by William Larnar, and by Richard Moon,* 1654. 4°.* LT, O; NU.

6102 —Man's righteousness examined. *Printed, to be sold by William Larnar,* 1652. 4°.* L, O; NU.

6103 —Michael opposing the dragon. *Printed,* 1659. 4°. L; NPT, NU.

6104 —Savl smitten. *Printed, to be sold by William Larnar, and by Richard Moon,* 1653. 4°.* LT, O; NU.

6105 —Truths testimony. *Printed,* 1655. 4°. LT, O; NU, PL.

6106 —The twenty-five articles. [*London,* 1656?] 4°. MR.

6107 **Copping, Jeremiah.** A catalogue of the libraries of. 21 March 1686/7. [*London,* 1687.] 4°. L, HH.

6108 **Coppinger, Matthew.** Poems, songs and love-verses. *For R. Bentley, and M. Magnes,* 1682. 8°. T.C.I 485. L, O; CH, CN, MH, WF, Y.

6109 **Coppinger, Sir Nathaniel.** A seasonable speech by. *By B. A. for T. Bates,* 1641. 4°.* LT, C, LG, LVF, CT; CH, CN, LC, MH, NU, Y.

6110 The copy of a barbarous and bloody declaration by the Irish rebels. *For N.E.*, 1646. 4°.* LT, C; CH, MH, WF, Y.

Copy of a brief treatise. 1693. *See* Dean, Richard.

6111 A copy of a commission under the Great Seale of Ireland. *For E. Husbands and J. Franck, October 6*, 1642. 4°.* LT, C, EC, MR; MH.

Copy of a letter addressed. 1643. *See* Maynard, John.

6112 A copie of a letter against the engagement. [*London*], *printed*, 1650[1]. 4°.* LT, CCL, CS; WF.

6113 A copy of a letter concerning the election of a Lord Protector. *By Tho. Newcomb*, 1654. 4°.* LT, O, C; CH, CN, MH, NU, WF, Y.

Copy of a letter concerning the traiterous conspiracy. 1641. *See* Alexander, *of Kells*.

Coppy of a letter found. [*n.p.*], 1641. *See* Suckling, *Sir* John.

6114 The copie of a letter from a commander in the fleet. [*London*], *printed*, 1648. 4°.* LT, MR; MH, WF.

6115 The copy of a letter from a gentleman in Dort. [*London*, 1692.] CJ, CS, CT, MR; CH, CN.

6115A The copie of a letter from a gentleman in London, to his friend in Dublin. [*Kilkenny*, 1648.] 4°.* DIX.

6116 The copy of a letter from a Lincolnshire gentleman. [*London*], *printed*, 1660. 4°.* LT; NU, WF.

6117 A copie of a letter from a principall person in Paris. [*London*], *imprinted*, 1647. 4°.* LT, HH; MBP, MH, TU, WF, Y.

Copy of a letter from Alisbury. 1643. *See* Wittewrong, John.

6118 The copy of a letter from an eminent commander. *For Francis Coles*, 1645. 4°.* MADAN 1782. LT.

Copy of a letter from an officer. [*n.p.*, 1656.] *See* Milton, John.

Copy of a letter from an officer under. 1659. *See* S., S.

Coppie of a letter from Major Generall Poines. 1645. *See* Hopkinson, James.

Copy of a letter from Min Heer T. V. L. [*Amsterdam*, 1689.] *See* L., T. V.

Copy of a letter from Newcastle. 1646. *See* N., E.

6119 The copie of a letter from Paris, the 24 Jun. 4 July 1642. *Printed at London, for J. B.*, 1642. 4°.* LT, O, C, HH; CLC, MIU.

Coppy of a letter from Paris, 1648. *See* B., R.

6120 The copy of a letter from Scotland to His Grace the Lord Archbishop of Canterbury. colop: *For S. Gardner*, 1682. brs. L, O, LL, HH; CH, MH, PU.

6121 The coppie of a letter from Sir Thomas Fairfax his quarters. [*London*], *by Barnard Alsop, and Iane Coe*, [1645]. 4°.* LT.

Copie of a letter from the commission. Edinburgh, 1647. *See* Douglas, Robert.

6122 The copie of a letter from the commissioners about the propositions. *By Iane Coe*, 1646. 4°.* LT, HH, DT; MH.

6123 The copie of a letter from the commissioners with the King. *For R. Simpson*, 1647. 4°.* LT; CH, MIU, WF.

6124 A copy of a letter from the committee of Lincoln. *For J. Horton*, 1642. brs. CT.

Copy of a letter from the generals excellency. 1647. *See* Smart, Roger.

6125 The copie of a letter from the Lord Generall [Fairfax] his quarters. *By Jane Coe*, 1644. 4°.* LT, YM.

6126–8 Entries cancelled.

6129 A copy of a letter from the Speakers of both Houses . . . dated Iuly 4. 1643. *Printed at Oxford by Leonard Lichfield, Novemb. 18*, 1643. 4°.* MADAN 1490. LT, O, CT, HH; CH, MH, WF, Y.

6129A —[Anr. ed.] —, *Oct. 19*, 1643. 4°.* MADAN 1489. O.

6130 Copie of a letter of speciall consequence from Rotetrdam [*sic*]. 1642. 4°. DT.

6131 A copie of a letter of the taking of Leicester. *By Tho: Forcet*, 1645. 4°.* LT, O; WF.

6132 The copy of a letter presented by a member of the Commons. *By L. N. and I. F. for Edward Husbands and John Franck, August 19*, 1642. 4°.* LT, O, EC, SP, DT; CH, CLC, MH.

6133 The copy of a letter printed at New-Castle, July the 6, 1647. *For Tho. Vere*, [1647]. 4°.* LT, DT; MH.

Copy of a letter sent by E. B. [*n.p.*, 1679.] *See* B., E.

Copy of a letter sent by Mr. D. T. 1644. *See* T., D.

6134 A copy of a letter sent by the agents of severall regiments. [*n.p.*, 1647.] cap., 4°.* LT; WF.

6135 A coppy of a letter sent by the burga-masters and councel of Amsterdam. colop: *Printed at Rotterdam, Feb. 19. 1684. New Stile, by Peter Martin, and reprinted in London by J. Millet.* brs. L, O, OC, HH; CH, Y.

6136 The coppy of a letter sent by the last post. [*n.p.*, 1648.] brs. LT.

6137 The coppy of a letter sent by the rebells in Ireland. *For Io. Thomas*, 1641. 4°.* LT, O, C, MR; MIU, Y.

6138 A copy of a letter sent from a gentleman in Carisbrooke-Castle. *Printed at London*, 1648. 4°.* LT, O; CH, MH.

6139 A copie of a letter sent from a gentleman in His Majesties army. [*London*], *printed*, 1642. 4°.* C, CJ; CSS, WF.

Copy of a letter sent from a gentleman of quality. 1642. *See* Norwood, Thomas.

Copy of a letter sent from a person. [*n.p.*], 1648. *See* I., C.

Copy of a letter sent from a person that was present. 1683. *See* M., E.

6140 August 3 1642. The copie of a letter sent from a speciall friend in Coventry. [*London*], *for H. Overton*, 1642. brs. LT, LG, EC; CH.

6141 The copy of a letter, sent from a well affected gentleman of . . . Surrey. [*London*], *printed*, 1648. 4°.* LT, LG; CH, CN, MIU, Y.

Copy of a letter sent from an unknown land. 1648. *See* P., P.

Copy of a letter sent from Bristoll. [*n.p.*], 1643. *See* W., T.

6142 The copie of a letter sent from divers knights and gentlemen . . . Nottingham. *York: by Robert Barker, and by the assignes of John Bill*, 1642. 4°.* O, OME, YM; CSS.

6143 The coppy of a letter sent from Dvblin, dated. *For G. L.*, 1642. 4°.* LT, C, EC; CH, MH.

Copy of a letter sent from E. M. 1683. *See* M., E.

Copy of a letter sent from Exeter. 1643. *See* S., I.

6144　A coppie of a letter, sent from one of the agitators. *Printed*, 1647. 4°.* LT, O, C, MR, DT; CH, CU, MH, WF, Y.

6144A　The coppie of a letter sent from one of the Qveenes servants. *For I. T.* 1642. 4°.* EC; MH, Y.

6145　The copy of a letter sent from Shirbourne. *For Thomas Warren*, 1642. brs. LT.

6146　A copie of a letter sent from the agitators of . . . Sir Thomas Fairfax's armie. *For R. A.*, 1647. 4°.* LT, O; CH, CN, MH, WF.

Copie of a letter sent from the commander. 1643. *See* Wardlace, James.

6147　Entry cancelled.

6148　A copy of a letter sent from the committee at Lincoln. *For J. Horton*, 1642. June 6. 4°.* LT, CM.

6149　The copy of a letter sent from the committee at Lincoln to the House of Commons. *June 6. For Joseph Hunscott*, 1642. brs. STEELE 2167. LT, O, OC, EC, HH; CH, MH.

Copy of a letter sent from the Kings army. [*n.p.*, 1644.] *See* Crofts, John.

6150　The copie of a letter sent from the Lord Chiefe jvstices. *Printed*, 1641. 4°.* LT, O, C; CH, MH, MHL, WF, Y.

6151　A copie of a letter sent from the Lords Justices. *Imprinted at York, by Robert Barker and by the assigns of John Bill*, 1642. brs. STEELE 2085. L, OP, YM, ES.

6152　Entry cancelled.

Copy of a letter from the maior of Bristoll. 1643. *See* Akworth, Richard.

6153　The copie of a letter sent from the roaring boyes in Elizium. [*London*], 1641. 4°.* LT, LG, EC; CH, CU, MH, TU, WF.

6154　The copy of a letter, sent from two thousand youthfull citizens. *March 4. London, by John Raworth*, 1641[2]. brs. LT.

Copie of a letter sent out of England. 1641. *See* Burghley, William Cecil, *baron*.

6155　The copy of a letter sent out of Wiltshire. *For Livewell Chapman*, 1654. 4°.* LT, O, HH.

Coppie of a letter sent to a gentlevvoman. 1642. *See* B., R.

6155A　The copy of a letter sent to Dr. Sherlock. [*London?* 1691.] brs. HH.

6156　A coppie of a letter sent to Lieutenant Generall Crumvvell. [*London*], *printed*, 1647. 4°.* L, C, LG, OC, HH; CLC, MH, WF, Y.

6157　A copy of a letter sent to the Commissioners of accounts. [*London*, 1693?] cap., 4°.* CT, WCA, MR; INU, Y.

6158　A copie of a letter sent to the most illustrious and high borne Prince Rupert. *By Moses Bell, 12 Aug.* 1644. 4°.* LT; CLC, MH, MIU, WF, Y.

6159　A copy of a letter. Sir, having lately proposed the establishing of . . . the China company. [*London*], *Novemb.*, 1695. brs. L; MIU, Y.

6160　The copy of a letter to a countrey collonel, or, a serious dissuasive. [*London*, 1659]. 4°.* CH, MH, NN, RPB.

6161　A copy of a letter to an officer of the army. 1656. 4°. L.

6162　A coppie of a letter, to be sent to Lieutenant Generall Crumvvel from the well-affected partie in the city. [*n.p.*], *printed*, 1647. 4°.* LT, O; CSS, CU, NU, WF, Y.

6163　The coppy of a letter to Generall Monck. *Printed*, 1660. 4°.* LT, YM; MBP, MH, MIU, Y.

6164　The copy of a letter to His Excellency Sir Thomas Fairfax. *Printed at London, by Robert Ibbitson*, 1647. 4°.* LT, HH, SP; CH, CLC, Y.

6165　A copie of a letter to the Lord Marquesse of Hartford. *Novemb. 22. London for John Cave*, 1642. 4°.* LT, SP.

6166　A copy of a letter vvhich Master Speaker is ordered by the Commons . . . to send. *Printed at London by T. P. for T. B.*, [1642]. brs. STEELE 2074. LT.

6167　A copy of a letter, with its answer, concerning a conflict at VVorcester. [*n.p.*, 1656.] cap., 4°.* LT.

6168　A copie of a letter write from the agitators. 1647. 4°. O.

Copy of a letter written by a friend. [*Edinburgh*, 1692.] *See* S., M. T.

Copy of a letter written by a friend to one. 1657. *See* C., R.

6169　A copy of a letter written by a Jesuit. [*London*, 1679?] brs. L, OP; Y.

6170　The copie of a letter written by Mercvrivs Britanicvs. [*n.p.*, 1644.] brs. LT, O.

Copy of a letter written from His Excellency. 1642. *See* Essex, Robert Devereux, *earl of*.

6171　A copie of a letter vvritten from His Holinesse court at Rome. *Printed*, 1642. 4°.* LT; MIU, WF.

6172　A copy of a letter written from His Majesties camp at Gerpines. *For J. Smith*, 1691. brs. L, HH.

6172A　The copy of a letter written from Northampton. *For Ralph Smith*, 1646. 4°.* LT, DT; CLC, MH, Y.

6173　A copy of a letter written to a private friend. *By R. B. for I. O. and are to be sold by I. S.*, 1643. 4°.* LT, CM; NU, WF.

6173A　A copy of a letter written to an officer. *By Tho. Newcombe*, 1656. 4°.* LT, O, V, HH; CH, MH, ML, NU, WF, Y.

6174　A copy of a letter written to His Excellencie the Marquesse of Newcastle. *Printed at York by Stephen Bulkley*, 1643. 4°.* YM.

6175　A copy of a letter vvritten to Master Stephen Marshall. 1643. 4°.* LT, CJ, SP, EN; CH, NU, WF, Y.

Copy of a letter vvritten to Mr. Alexander Henderson, 1643. *See* Dury, John.

6176　The copy of a letter written to one of the members. 1659. 4°. O.

Coppie of a letter vvritten to the Dvke of Bvckingham. 1642. *See* Alured, Thomas.

6176A　The coppy of a letter written to the lower House. *By John Dawson for Thomas Warnley*, 1641. 4°. LT, O, CT, HH; CH, CU, MH, NU, WF, Y.

Copy of a letter written unto. 1641. *See* Pym, John.

6177　A copy of a list of all the cavalliers and brave commanders. *For Francis Wright*, 1642. brs. LT, O, LS, OC, EC; Y.

6177A　A copy of a marriage-certificate of the . . . Quakers. [*London*, 1685.] fol.* LF, CM.

6178 The copy of a most pithy and pious letter. *By Robert White*, [1645]. 4°.* LT, LW; MH, MIU, OWC, WF, Y.

6179 The copy of a narrative prepared for His Majesty. [*n.p.*, 1674.] 4°.* LL.

6180 A copy of a paper by His Majesties commissioners. 1686. brs. O.

6181 A copy of a paper, concerning three propositions . . . Octob. 13. 1648. *By Robert Ibbitson*, 1648. 4°.* LT, HH; MH, WF.

6182 A copy of a paper distributed. [*n.p.*, 1692.] 4°. O.

6183 Copy of a paper . . . entituled, Considerations. *Edinburgh, by the heir of Andrew Anderson*, 1691. 4°. ALDIS 3139. EN.

6183A The copy of a paper found on the Speakers chair. [*London*, 1689.] brs. O, C; MH.

6183B Copy of a paper presented . . . in the year, 1681, to the then Duke of York. *Edinburgh, by the heir of Andrew Anderson*, 1691. 4°.* LUG; INU, MH.

6184 The copy of a paper presented to the Kings . . . Majesty. [*London*, 1661.] brs. L, O.

6185 The copie of a paper presented to the Parliament. *By A. W. for Giles Calvert*, 1659. 4°.* LT, LG, HH, BBN; HR, CH, CU, MH, NU, WF, Y.

6186 A copy of a petition, commended to the peace-making association in the West. *Exeter, imprinted*, 1645. 4°.* LT.

6187 Copy of a petition from the governor and company of the Sommer Islands [Bermuda]. *For Edward Husband*, 1651. 4°. L, LVD; CN, MH, RPJ.

Copy of a printed letter. [*n.p.*, 1672.] *See* Cressett, James.

6188 Entry cancelled.

6189 A copy of a remonstrance lately delivered. *Printed*, 1645. 4°.* O, CJ, CM; MBA, MH, V, WF, Y.

6190 A copy of a remonstrance setting forth the sad condition of the army. *For M. W. and H. A.*, 1647. 4°.* LT; MH, Y.

6190A Copy of a treasonable and bloody paper. 1680. fol.* O.

6191 The copy of an act for the abolishing and taking away of all arch-bishops. *Printed at London, Jan. 26*, 1643[/4]. brs. LT, LS; Y.

6191A A copy of an adress to the King. [*London*], *printed* 1689. fol.* O, BR, HH; IU, MH, MIU, Y.

6192 A copy of an award referring to the publick markets of . . . London. *Printed*, 1697. brs. L.

6193 A copie of certaine letters, which manifest the design. [*London*], *printed*, 1643. 4°.* LT, O, DT; CH, MH, NU, WF, Y.

6194 A copy of divers intercepted letters. [*n.p.*], 1648. fol. O.

6195 A coppie of divers letters sent. [*n.p.*], 1641. 4°. O.

6196 A coppy of I. The letter sent by. *Printed at London*, 1641. 4°.* LT, O, HH, BR, DT; CSS, LC, MH, NU, TU, Y.

6197 A copie of quæries, or, a comment. colop: *Printed in Utopia*, 1659. cap., 4°.* LT, OC; CSS, MH, MIU.

6198 A copy of several letters which were delivered to the King. 1660. 4°. L.

6198A A copy of some papers lately passed between the Lord Fairfax. *Printed*, 1648. 4°.* CJ; MIU.

Copy of some papers past. 1647. *See* Hammond, Henry.

6199 A copie of that letter mentioned in a letter printed July 12 . . . out of Lancashire. [*n.p.*], *printed*, 1647. 4°.* LT, DT.

6200 A copy of that letter which was sent in the name of the army. [*n.p.*], 1647. 4°. DC.

6201 Coppy of the addres; of a great number of the members. *Edinburgh, re-printed by John Reid*, 1700. brs. EN; CN, RPJ, WF, Y.

6202 A copy of the address of the free-men of Portsoaken-ward. *Adamson*, [1696.] brs. LG.

6203 A copie of the articles agreed upon at the surrender of the city of Bristol. *For Henry Overton*, [1643]. 4°.* LT, O, BR; CH, MH, WF, Y.

6203A A copy of the articles for the surrender of . . . Worcester. *For F. Coles*, 1646. 4°.* L.

6204 A copy of the articles for the svrender of . . . Yorke. *By G. B. for Robert Bostock, and Samuell Gellibrand*, 1644. 4°.* L, OC; NU.

6205 The copy of the association signed at Exeter by the lords and gentlemen. [*London*, 1688?] brs. L, O, C, EC, BR; CH, MH, Y.

6206 Entry cancelled.

6207 A copy of the captives petition. [*London*, 1661?] brs. L.

6208 Copy of the charter granted. [*n.p.*, 1661.] 4°. EN.

6209 A copy of the church-covenants. *Boston, by J. G.*, 1680. 4°.* EVANS 295. MWA.

6210 A copie of the covenant, both as it was first formed. [*Oxford, by L. Lichfield*], *printed*, 1644. 4°.* MADAN 1649. O, C, OC, CJ, LSC.

6211 A copy of the foure reasons to diswade. [*n.p.*], *printed*, 1641. brs. STEELE 1876. L, O, LPR, OQ.

6212 The copie of the major and baylifs of the towne of Weixford their letter. [*Kilkenny*, 1648.] 4°.* DIX.

Copie of the oath. 1642. *See* B., N.

6213 Copy of the orders for repealing of several acts . . . 22d day of August 1695. colop: *Boston, by Bartholomew Green, and John Allen*, 1697. fol.* EVANS 781. MWA, NN.

6214 A copy of the orders of sessions made of Middlesex. 1687. fol. O.

6215 A copy of the petition delivered on behalf of the prisoners. [*London?* 1690.] cap., 4°.* CT.

6216 A copy of the petition delivered to the King at Newark. *For John Franke*, 1641[2]. brs. STEELE 2050. LT, LS, EC; MH.

6217 A copy of the petition presented to the King's Majestie by the High Sheriff . . . of Rutland. *For Joseph Hunscott, March 22*, 1641[2]. brs. STEELE 2045. L, LS; MH.

6218 —[Anr. ed.] *For Richard Harper*, 1642[3]. brs. STEELE 2046. LT, O, LG, LS, EC.

6219 A copy of the presentment and indictment, found and exhibited by the Grand-Jury of Middlesex, . . . 1659. Against Collonel Matthew Alured. *For Edward Thomas*, 1660. brs. STEELE 3151a. L, O, LL, LS, MC; CH, Y.

6220   A copy of the pretended letter, whereupon the indite-
       ment against Henry Navile-paine is founded. [1692].
       brs. RPJ.

6221   A coppy of the prisoner's jvdgment. By Thomas Paine,
       1641. 4°.* LT, LG; CH, WF.

       A copy of the proceedings of some worthy and learned
       divines. See Church of England.

6222–27 Entries cancelled.

6228   A copy of the propositions sent from the army. For G. R.
       May 24, [1647.] 4°. OC, DT; BBE.

6228A A copy of the report of the Committee of Common
       Council. [London, 1696.] brs. L.

6229   A copy of the resolution of the States Provincial of
       Freezland. colop: Printed at Rotterdam, Feb. 19. 1684.
       New stile, by Peter Martin, and reprinted in London for
       Walter Davis. brs. L, O; CH.

6230   The copie of the summons sent to Ludlow. 1646. 4°. O.

6231   A copy of the test which is to be taken by all such per-
       sons . . . in Scotland. colop: For E. Ryddal, 1681. brs.
       L, O; WF, Y.

6232   The copie of three petitions. For William Larnar, 1647.
       4°.* LT, O, HH, MR; CH, NU, WF.

6233   A copie of two letters, sent from divers officers. [Lon-
       don, 1648.] brs. LT, LG; CH, MH.

       Copie of tvvo letters; vvritten. 1643. See Taylor, Jeremy.

6234   A copy of two remonstrances, brought over the River
       Stix. Printed, 1643. 4°.* LT; Y.

6235   A copie of two writings sent to the Parliament [Amster-
       dam], printed, 1641. 4°.* LT, EN.

6236   A copy of verses, containing, a catalogue. [London], for
       P. Brooksby, J. Deacon, J. Blare, J. Back, [1680?] brs. L,
       CM, HH.

6237   A copy of verses delivered to a minister. By J. Redmayne,
       for William Battersby, 1683. brs. O, EN; CLC, MH, Y.

6238   A copy of verses presented to His royal Highness. Colop:
       By G. Croom, for the author, 1684. brs. O; CLC.

       Copy of verses said to be composed. [London, 1648]. See
       Brome, Alexander.

6239   A copy-book of the newest and most usefull hands. For
       John Hancock, [1674]. 4°.* T.C.I 191. CH.

6240   The copy-holders' plea. By Peter Cole, 1653. 4°.* LT, EN.

       Coral and steel. [1650?] See B., R.

6241   **Corbet, Edward.** Gods providence. By Tho: Badger,
       for Robert Bostock, 1642[3]. 4°.* LT, O, C, ENC, DT; CH,
       MH, NU, TU, WF, Y.

6242   — —[Anr. ed.] By F: Neile, for Robert Bostock, 1647. 4°.*
       O, CM, OCC; MH, NU.

6243   [**Corbet, Jeffery.**] Englands warning-piece: or, the un-
       kenneling. Printed, 1654. 4°.* LT; NU, WF.

6244   —Eye-salve for English-men. 1654. 4°. LG.

6245   —The lawyers looking glass. For J. Corbett, 1655. 4°. EN.

6246   —The Protestant's warning piece. [London, 1656.] brs.
       LT.

6247   **Corbet, John. 1603–41.** The epistle congratulatory of
       Lysimachus Nicanor. Oxford, by Leon Lichfield, and
       are to be sold by Tho. Fickus, 1684. 4°. T.C.II 65. L, O,
       CT, ENC, DT; CH, MH, WF, Y.

6248   —An historicall relation of the military government of
       Gloucester. By M. B. for Robert Bostock, 1645. 4°. LT,
       O, CS, LCL, EN; BN, CH, CN, MH, WF, Y.

6249   [–] A true and impartiall history of the military govern-
       ment of the citie of Gloucester. Second edition. For
       Robert Bostock, 1647. 4°. LT, A, DT; MH, WF.

6250   —A vindication of the magistrates . . . of Gloucester.
       For Robert Bostock, 1646. 4°.* LT, O, CT, EN; CH, WF.

6251   **Corbet, John, 1620–80.** An account given of the prin-
       ciples & practises. For Tho. Parkhurst, 1682. 4°.*
       T.C.I 484. L, O, C, LCL, EN; CH, CU, MH, NU, WF, Y.

6252   [–] A discourse of the religion of England. Printed, 1667.
       4°. L, O, C, EN, DT; CH, CN, LC, MH, NU, Y.

6252A [–] Dolvs an virtvs? Or, an answer. For Henry Brome,
       1668. 4°.* L, O, C, OC, HH; CH, MH, NU, WF, Y.

6253   —A humble endeavour of some plain and brief explica-
       tion. For Tho. Parkhurst, 1683. 4°. T.C.II 13. L, O, CS, OC,
       EN; CH, MH, NU, WF, Y.

6254   —An enquiry into the oath. For Tho. Parkhurst, 1682.
       4°.* T.C.I 505. L, O, CS, HH, EN; CH, MBA, NPT, NU, WF.

6255   —The interest of England in the matter of religion. By
       J. M. for G. T., 1660. 8°. LT, O, C, CT, LCL; CLC, CU,
       MH, NU, WF, Y.

6256   — —Second edition. For George Thomason, 1661. 8°.
       L, CS, LW, E, DT; CH, CLC, NPT, Y.

6257   — —[Anr. ed.] —, 1662. 8°. L.

6258   —The kingdom of God among men. For Thomas Park-
       hurst, 1679. 12°. T.C.I 415. L, C, LW, CT, EN; CLC, CN,
       MH, NF, NU.

6259   —The Nonconformist's plea. For Thomas Parkhurst, 1683.
       4°.* T.C.II 13. L, O, LCL, EN, DT; CH, MIU, NU, WF, Y.

6260   [–] The point of church-unity. 1679. 8°. L.

6261   —Entry cancelled.

6262   —The remains of. For Thomas Parkhurst, 1684. 4°. T.C.II
       68. L, O, CS, LW, E; CH, CN, NU, WF, Y.

6263   [–] A second discourse of the religion of England.
       Printed, 1668. 4°.* L, O, C, LCL, E; CH, MH, NU, WF, Y.

6264   —The second part of the interest of England, in the
       matter. For G. T., 1660. 12°. LT, SP, E; NNG, NU, WF, Y.

6265   —Self-imployment in secret. For Thomas Parkhurst,
       1681. 12°. T.C.I 449. L, LW.

6265A — —Second edition. —, 1681. 12°. CH, MU, WF.

6266   — —Third edition. Boston in New-England, by Richard
       Pierce for Joseph Brunning, 1684. 4°. EVANS 357. MHS,
       MWA, RPJ.

6266A — —"Third" edition. For Thomas Parkhurst, 1691, 12°.*
       LLL; Y.

6267   — —[Anr. ed.] Edinburgh, by George Mosman. [1700?].
       8°.* L, EN, D; Y.

6268   **Corbet, Miles.** A most learned and eloquent speech.
       [London, 1647.] cap., 4°.* LT, O, LSC, HH; CH, CN, MH,
       NC, Y.

6269   — —[Anr. ed.] [London, 1680?] fol. L, O, CM; NC.

6270   **Corbet, Richard, bp.** Certain elegant poems. By R.
       Cotes for Andrew Crooke, 1647. 8°. LT, O, CE; BN, CH,
       CN, MH, TU, WF, Y.

6271 —Poems. Third edition. *By J.C. for William Crook,* 1672. 12°. T.C.I 99. L, O, C, LVD, EN; BN, CH, CN, MH, WF, Y.

6272 —Poëtica stromata. [*Holland*], *Anno,* 1648. 8°. L, O, CT, LVD, ES; CH, CN, MH, TU, WF, Y.

6273 **[Corbet, Roger.]** The copies of papers from the armies. *For R. Simpson.* 1657 [*i.e.,* 1647.] L; CH, WF.

6274 [–] A letter from His Majetties [sic] covrt at Holmbie. *By B. A. May 21* 1647. 4°.* LT, EN; MBP, MH.

6275 [–] Papers of the desires of the souldiers of the army. *For A.B.,* 1647. 4°.* LT, O, CT, DT; CLC, IU, MH, WF.

6276 [–] A treatie between the commissioners. *For B.A.,* 1647. 4°.* L, O, OC; CN, WF.

6276A **Corbet, Thomas.** Gospel-incense. 1653. 12°. GU.

6277 —A just vindication of the covenant. 1648. 4°. E, GU.

6278 **Corbin, William.** Ευχαριστια. *Richard Baldwin,* 1695. 4°.* L, CT; WF, Y.

6278A **Corbyn, Samuel.** Advice to sinners. 1669. 8°. O.

6279 —An awakening call. 1672. 24°. LCL.

6280 ——[Anr. ed.] *Sold by John Hancock,* 1677. 12°. T.C.I 277. O, LCL; MB.

Corda Angliæ; or. [*n.p.*], 1641. *See* Walker, Henry.

6281 **Cordemoy, Louis Géraud de.** [Des Fourneillis, *pseud.*] A discourse written to a learned frier. *Printed, to be sold by Moses Pitt,* 1670. 8°. T.C.I 57. L, O, CS, GH, YM; CH, CU, NP, NU, WF.

6282 [–] A philosophicall discourse concerning speech. *In the Savoy, for John Martin,* 1668. 12°. T.C.I 57. L, O, E; CLC, CU, LC, MH, Y.

6283 Cordiall covncell, in a pateticall [sic] epistle. *By Tho. Paine, to be sold by James Crump,* 1645. 4°.* LT, CT, DT; CH.

6284 A cordial elegie & epitaph upon . . . Henry Duke of Glocester. *For George Horton,* 1660. 4°.* LT, O.

Cordial for Christians. Edinburgh, 1696. *See* Hamilton, Alexander.

Cordjall for the calentvre. 1648. *See* Burrell, Andrewes.

6284A A cordial for England. [*London,* 1678]. brs. LW.

6284B **Cordier, Mathurin.** Colloquia scholastica. *Excudebat T.R. & E.M. pro societate stationiorum,* 1653. 8°. Y.

6284C ——[Anr. ed.] *Excudebat S.G. pro societate stationariorum,* 1667. 8°. CP; Y.

6285 ——[Anr. ed.] *Excusa pro societate stationariorum,* 1694. 8°. MHS, NP, Y.

6285A —Colloquiorum scholasticorum. *Imprimibat T. Newcomb pro societate bibliopolarum,* 1651. 8°. Y.

6286 ——[Anr. ed.] *Cantabrigiæ: apud Joann. Field,* 1657. 8°. C; NC.

6287 ——[Anr. ed.] *Typis T.R. pro societate stationariorum,* 1669. 8°. MH.

6288 ——[Anr. ed.] *Glasguæ, excudebat Robert Sanders,* 1675. 8°. ALDIS 2050. HG, EN.

6288A ——[Anr. ed.] *Cantabrigiæ, ex officina John Hayes,* 1678. 8°. C; CLC.

6289 ——[Anr. ed.] *Typis M. F. & J. G. pro societate stationariorum,* 1679. 8°. L.

6290 ——[Anr. ed.] *Cantabrigiæ, ex officina Joann. Hayes,* 1681. 8°. C.

6290A ——[Anr. ed.] *Excudebat Johannes Richardson,* 1689. 8°. WF, Y.

6290B ——[Anr. ed.] *Cantabrigiæ, ex officina Joann. Hayes,* 1698. 8°. PL.

6290C ——[Anr. ed.] *Excudebat Ben. Griffin, pro societate typographorum,* 1700. 8°. L; CLC.

6291 —Corderius dialogues. *For William Leake,* 1653. 8°. L, CS, SP.

6292 —Mathurin Corderius's school-colloquies. *By Sarah Griffin, for the company of stationers,* 1657. 8°. L; CH.

6292A ——[Anr. ed.] *By T. Ratcliffe for the company of stationers,* 1663. 8°. IU, WF.

6292B ——[Anr. ed.] *By S. Griffin, for the company of stationers,* 1667. 8°. LSC.

6293 ——[Anr. ed.] *For the company of stationers,* 1676. 8°. L.

6293A ——[Anr. ed.] —, 1688. 8°. AN.

6293B **Corelli, Archangelo.** Parte prima sonate. [*London*], *sold by Iohn Walsh,* [1700.] L; CLC.

6293C —Twelve new sonatas. *For J. Walsh,* 1700. fol. T.C.III 214. L.

6294 **Corey, John.** The generous enemies. *By H. Lloyd for James Magnus,* 1672. 4°. T.C.I 103. L, O, OW, EC, A; CH, CN, LC, MH, NC, TU, Y.

6294A **Corey, Philip.** A solemn call. 1690. 8°. L.

6294B **Corey, Thomas.** The course and practise of the court of common pleas. *By John Streater, Henry Twyford, and E. Flesher, assigns of Richard Atkins, and Edward Atkins,* 1672. 4°. O, CT; MHL, TU, WF.

6295 Coridon and Parthenia. [*London*], *for P. Brooksby,* [1675?]. brs. L, O, HH; MH.

6296 —[Anr. ed.] [*London*], *for F. Coles, T. Vere, J. Wright, J. Clarke, W. Thackery and T. Passinger,* [1670–80]. brs. L, O, MC, GU; MH, Y.

6297 Corinna: or, humane frailty. *By J. W. and sold by J. Nutt,* 1699. 4°.* LVF, A; MH.

6298 **Cork, Richard Boyle,** *1st earl of.* A letter of. *For Edward Blackmore, May the ninth,* 1642. 4°.* LT, O, LG, LVF, DT.

6299 **Cork, Richard Boyle,** *2d earl of.* A trve relation of thee miseralble [sic] estate that Ireland now standeth in. *By Iohn Hammond. February 9,* 1642. 4°.* C, EC, MR.

6300 **Corker, James.** A rational account given by a young gentleman. [c. 1680.] 4°.* OC.

6301 [–] A remonstrance of piety and innocence. *Printed,* 1682. 12°. O, C; MH, PPT.

6301A [–] [Anr. ed.] *Printed,* 1683. 12°. O, LSC; CLC, CN, MIU, TU.

6302 [–] Roman-Catholick principles. *Printed,* 1680. 4°.* O; CLC, CN, INU.

6303 [–] —Third edition. [*London*], *printed,* 1680. 4°.* L, O; CH, Y.

6304 [–] —[Anr. ed.] [*n.p.,* 1680?] brs. L, MC, DT; WF.

6305 [–] —[Anr. ed.] [*n.p.,* 1687?] cap., 4°.* OC, BAMB; CN, MIU, NU, TU, Y.

6306 [–] Stafford's memoires. *Printed,* 1681. fol. L, O, C, CT, DT; CH, NU, PU, WF, Y.

6307 [–] —[Anr. ed.] —, 1682. 12°. L, O, CS; CLC, CN, TU, WF, WU.

6308 **Corker, Samuel.** The great necessity. *Dublin: by Joseph Ray*, 1695. fol. DIX 272. L, C, EN, OM, DW.

6309 **Corneille, Pierre.** The Cid. Second edition. *By W. Wilson for Humphrey Moseley*, 1650. 12°. L, O, LVD, EN; BN, CH, CN, LC, MH, Y.

6310 —Heraclius. *For Iohn Starkey*, 1664. 4°. L, O, OW, EC; CH, CN, LC, MH, NC, TU, Y.

6311 —Horace, a French tragedy. *For Henry Brome*, 1671. 4°. T.C.I 72. L, O, OM, OW; CH, CN, TU, WF, Y.

6312 [–] —[Anr. ed.] *By A. C. for Henry Brome*, 1677. 4°. T.C.I 291. C; MH.

6313 [–] Horatius. *For G. Bedell and T. Collins*, 1656. 4°. L, O, LVD, OW; CH, CU, LC, NC, Y.

6314 [–] The mistaken beauty. *For Simon Neale*, 1685. 4°. T.C.II 99. L, O, C, OW; CH, CU, LC, NC, Y.

6315 —Nicomede. *For Francis Kirkman*, 1671. 4°. T.C.I 80. L, O, C, LVD, EN; BN, CH, LC, MH, NC, TU, Y.

6315A — —[Anr. ed.] *For John Dancer*, 1674. 4°. L.

6316 [–] Polyeuctes. *By Tho. Roycroft for G. Bedell and T. Collins*, 1655. 4°. L, O, OW, LVD, EN; CH, CN, LC, MH, NC, Y.

6317 [–] Pompey. A tragedy. *For John Crooke*, 1663. 4°. L, O, C, LVD; CH, MH, WF, Y.

6318 [–] —[Anr. ed.] *Dublin, by John Crooke, for Samuel Dancer*, 1663. 4°. DIX 114. O, C, OW; MU, TU, WF, Y.

6319 [–] Pompey the great. *For Henry Herringman*, 1664. 4°. L, O, CM; CH, CN, LC, MH, TU, Y.

6320 Entry cancelled.

6321 [**Corneille, Thomas.**] The amorous gallant. *By J. C. for William Crook*, 1675. 4°. T.C.I 211. L, O, OW, EN; CH, CN, LC, MH, NP, Y.

6322 [–] Amorous Orontus. *By G. M. for John Playfere*, 1665. 4°. L, O; CH, CN, NIC, NC, Y.

6323 —The extravagant sheepherd. *By J. G. for Tho: Heath*, 1654. 4°. L, O, LVD, OW; CH, CN, MH, WF, Y.

6324 [–] The feign'd astrologer. *For Thomas Thornycroft*, 1668. 4°. L, O, OW; CH, CN, LC, MB, MU, Y.

Cornelius, Peter, *pseud.* See Peters, Hugh.

6325 **Cornish, Henry.** A true account of the behaviour and manner of the execution of Elizabeth Gaunt. 1685. fol.* L.

6326–7 Entries cancelled.

Cornish comedy. 1096. See Powell, George.

Cornucopia; a miscellanium. [*n.p.*, 1652?] See Hartlib, Samuel.

6328 Cornu-copia. or, roome for a ram-head. *For John Reynolds*, 1642. 4°.* LT, HH; CH, MH, WF.

6328A **Cornwall, H.** Biblioteca Cornwalliana. *Cantabrig.* 22 *April*, 1700. 4°.* OC; Y.

6329 **Cornwallis,** *Sir* **Charles.** A discourse of the most illustrious prince, Henry. *For Iohn Benson*, 1641. 4°.* LT, O, CT, MR, GK; BN, CH, CN, MH, WF, Y.

6330 —The life and death of our late most incomparable and heroique prince, Henry. *For Iohn Dawson, for Nathanael Butter*, 1641. 12°. L, O, CS, E, EN; BN, CH, MH, Y.

6330A —The short life . . . of Henry. [*London*], *printed*, 1664. 8°. WF.

6331 **C[ornwallis], H[enry].** Brief directions for our more devout behaviour. *For J. Robinson*, 1693. Second edition. 8°.* T.C.II 451. L, O, C.

6332 —[Anr. ed.] *Dublin, reprinted*, 1700. 8°.* DIX 324. DI.

6333 —The country-curate's advice. *By T. W. for J. Robinson*, 1693. 8°. T.C.II 450. L, O.

6334 —Set on the great pot. *Printed for the sons of the prophets*, 1694. 8°.* T.C.II 537. L, CT.

6335 **Cornwell, Francis.** A conference Mr. John Cotton held at Boston. *By J. Dawson, to be sold by Fr. Eglesfield*, 1646. 8°. LT, O, LCL, OC; MB, MH, NPT, V, WCL.

6336 —A description of the spirituall temple. *By John Dawson*, 1646. 8°. LT, LCL, OC, WCA; CH, LC, NPT, V, WCL, Y.

6337 —Gospel repentance. *By John Dawson*, 1645. 8°. LT, C; MB, NHC.

6338 [–] Two qveries worthy of serious consideration. [*London*, 1645/6]. cap., 4°.* LT, HH, EC; WF, Y.

6339 —The vindication of the royall commission. [*London*], *printed*, 1644. 4°.* LT, O, MR, GU, DT; CH, LC, NHC, NU.

6340 Coronæ jura, or. [*n.p.*], 1680. 8°. LI.

6341 The coronation of Charles the second. *Aberdeen*, 1651. 4°. ENC.

Coronation of Queen Elizabeth. 1680. See D., J.

6342 **Coronelli, Vincenzo Maria.** An historical and geographical account of the Morea. *For Matth. Gillyflower and W. Canning*, 1687. 12°. T.C.II 198. L, O, C, OC, EN; CH, MBA, NC, PL, WF, Y.

—Royal almanack. 1696. See Almanacs.

Corporal worship discuss'd. 1670. See Basset, William.

Corporation-credit. 1682. See Murray, Robert.

6343 The corporations of weavers at London. 1689. brs. O.

6344 Corpus disciplinæ: or the discipline. *By John Field for Ralph Smith*, 1645. 4°. LT, CT, E, EN, DT; HR, CH, MH, NU, WF, Y.

Corpus sine capita. [*n.p.*], 1642. See M., I.

6344A [**Corraro, Angelo.**] A new relation of Rome. *By T. Mabb, for John Starkey*, 1664. 8°. L, O, C, CT; CLC, NU, PL, WF.

6345 [–] Rome exactly describ'd. *By T. Mabb, for Mich. Young, J. Starkey, and J. Playfere*, 1664. 8°. O, C, BR, EN; CH, CN, NU, WF, Y.

6346 — —[Anr. ed.] *For T. Palmer*, 1668. 8°. L, C; CU, NC, NU.

6346A A correct copy of some letters. *For H. Chauklin in Taunton*, 1698. L.

Correct copy of some notes. 1655. See Pierce, Thomas.

Correct tide table. 1684. See F., J.

Corrector corrected. 1672. See Ives, Jeremiah.

Corrector of the answerer. *Edinburgh*, 1646. See Marten, Henry.

Corruption of man's nature. 1676. See Given, William.

Corss, James. Mercurius coelicus. *Glasgow*, 1662. See Almanacs.

—A new prognostication. *Aberdeen*, 1651. See Almanacs.

6347 —Ουρανοσχοπια, or the contemplation of the heavens. *Edinburgh, a society of stationers,* 1662. 8°. ALDIS 1735. L, EN; NN.

6347A —Practical geometry. *Edinburgh,* 1666. ALDIS 1813. EN.

6347B **Corss, John.** Unto his grace the Duke of Argile . . . the petition of. [*Edinburgh?* 1650.] brs. EN.

6348 Corydon and Cloris. *For W. Thackeray, T. Passinger, and W. Whitwood,* [1677?] brs. L, O.

Corye, *See* Corey.

6349 Cosens revived, or the French academy. *Sold by R. Walton,* 1686. T.C.II 169. L. [*t.p. only*].

6350 **Cosin, John, *bp.*** An answer to certain printed reasons. [*London,* 1665?] brs. L.

6351 —Bishop Cozens's argument. [*London,* 1700.] L, O, LL, HH, EN; CLC, IU, MH, MIU, Y.

6352 [–] A collection of, private devotions. *For Richard Royston,* 1655. 12°. LT, O, C, LSC, YM; CH, CLC.

6353 [–] —Fifth edition. *By J. F. for R. Royston,* 1664. 12°. L, CP; CLC, MB, NPT.

6354 [–] —Sixth edition. *By R. N. for R. Royston,* 1672. 12°. T.C.I 99. L, O; TU.

6354A [–] —"Sixth" edition. *For R. Royston, and sold by Will. Cademan,* 1672. 12°. CLC, MH, MU, Y.

6355 [–] —Seventh edition. *By J. Grover for R. Royston,* 1676. 12°. T.C.I 241. L, OC; NU, WF, WWC.

6356 — —Eighth edition. *By R. N. for Rich. Royston,* 1681. 12°. L, O, C, BAMB, EN; TSM, Y.

6357 — —Ninth edition. *By W. H. for Luke Meredith,* 1693. 12°. T.C.II 484. L, O, C, CP, ENC; CSU.

6357A —The doctor's last will & testament. [*London*], printed 1641. 4°. C; MH, WF.

6358 —Historia transubstantiationis papalis. *Typis Tho. Roycroft. Apud Hen. Brome,* 1675. 8°. T.C.I 190. L, O, C, EN, DT; BN, CH, CU, MH, NU, WF, Y.

6359 —The history of Popish transubstantiation. *By Andrew Clark for Henry Brome,* 1676. 8°. T.C.I 210. L, O, CT, EN, DT; CH, NC, NU, WF, Y.

6359A — —Second edition. —, 1679. 8°. L, OC, YM; IU, MBP.

6360 —The history of transubstantiation. 1681. 8°. LLL.
—The right reverend Doctor John Cosin, . . . his opinion. 1684. *See* Watson, Richard.

6361 —A scholastical history of the canon. *By R. Norton for Timothy Garthwait,* 1657. 4°. L, O, C, LL, ENC; CLC, CU, MH, NU, WF, Y.

6362 — —Second edition. *By E. Tyler and R. Holt for Robert Pawlett,* 1672. 4°. T.C.I 106. L, O, C, EN, DT; BN, CU, MH, NC, WF, Y.

6363 — —Fourth edition. —, 1683. 4°. T.C.II 21. L, O, CP, LIL, DU; CH, NU, TU, WF.

6363A — —[Anr. ed.] *For R. P. and sold by Abel Swalle,* 1684. 4°. T.C.II 78. L.

6363B —Two letters of. 1686. 8°. L.

6364 **Cosin, Richard.** Conspiracy for pretended Reformation. *Re-printed for Ri. Chiswell,* 1699. 8°. L, O, BAMB, ENC, DT; CH, MBA, NGT, TU, Y.

6365 —Ecclesiæ Anglicanæ politeia. *Oxonii, excudebat L. Lichfield impensis Tho. Fickus, & Joh. Howel,* 1684. fol.* L, O, C, LL, OC; MIU, WF, Y.

6366 **Coste, Pierre.** The life of Lewis, late Prince of Condé. *For T. Goodwin,* 1693. 8°. T.C.II 452. L, O, C, OC, CK; CH, LC, TU, WF, Y.

6366A [**Coster, Robert.**] The diggers mirth. *Printed,* 1659. 8°.* LT.

6367 —A mite cast into the common treasury. [*n.p.,* 1649.] cap., 4°.* LT; MH.

Costes, Gaultier de. *See* La Calprenède, Gaultier de Coste.

6368 **Cotgrave, John.** The English treasury of wit and language. *For Humphrey Moseley,* 1655. 8°. LT, O, CT, DC, ES; CH, CN, LC, MH, WC, Y.

6369 —The muses mistresse. *Printed,* 1660. 8°. O; CH.

6370 —Wits interpreter. *For N. Brooke,* 1655. 8°. LT, O, OC; CH, CLC, CN, MH, WF.

6371 — —Second edition. *For N. Brook,* 1662. 8°. O; CH, MH, TU, WF.

6372 —Third edition. —, 1671. 8°. T.C.I 61. L, O, C, A; CH, MBP, WF, Y.

6373 **Cotgrave, Randle.** A dictionary of barbarous French. *By J. C. for Thomas Basset,* 1679. 4°. L, O, C; LC, Y.

6374 —A French-English dictionary. *By W. H. for Richard Whitaker,* 1650. fol. L, C, OB, MR, E; BN, CN, IU, NP.

6375 — —[Anr. ed.] *By W. H. for Octavain Pulleyn,* 1650. fol. L, OW, BR, MR.

6376 — —[Anr. ed.] *By W. H. for M. M. T. C. and Gabriel Bedell,* 1650. fol. C, OC, CT; CH, Y.

6377 — —[Anr. ed.] *By W. H. for Iohn Williams,* 1650. fol. OC, BR; MBP, NC, TU, WF.

6377A — —[Anr. ed.] *By W. H. for George Lathum,* 1650. fol. WF, W.

6377B — —[Anr. ed.] *By W. H. for Abel Roper,* 1650. fol. MBA.

6377C — —[Anr. ed.] *By W. H. for Humphrey Robinson,* 1650. fol. CK, CT.

6377D — —[Anr. ed.] *By W. H. for Luke Fawne,* 1650. fol. OSA; CN, IU.

6378 —A French and English dictionary. *By William Hunt,* 1660. fol. L, O, C, OM, EN; BN, CSU, CU, WF, Y.

6379 — —[Anr. ed.] *For Anthony Dolle, to be sold by Thomas Williams,* 1673. fol. T.C.I 121. L, C, LL, MR, DT; BN, CLC, CN, LC, MH, TU, Y.

[**Cotton, Charles.**] Book of new epigrams. 1695. *See* Killigrew, Henry.

6380 [–] Burlesque upon burlesque. *For Henry Brome,* 1675. 8°. T.C.I 188. L, O, C, CCH; CH, CN, LC, MH, TU, Y.

6380A — —Second edition. *For Charles Brome,* 1686. 8°. L; CH, WF, Y.

6380B — —"Second" edition. —, 1687. T.C.II 172. O, EN; CN, LC, MH.

6381 —The compleat angler. Part II. *For Richard Marriott, and Henry Brome,* 1676. 8°. L, O, C, DCH; CH, CN, NN, WF, Y.

6382 —The compleat gamester. *By A. M. for R. Cutler, sold by Henry Brome,* 1674. 8°. L, CM; CH, MH, PL, WF, Y.

6383   [–] —Second edition. *For Henry Brome*, 1676. 8°. T.C.I 223. L; CLC, PL, Y.

6384   [–] —"Second" edition. —, 1680. 8°. T.C.I 399. L, O, LVD; IU, NN, WF, Y.

6385   [–] The confinement. A poem. *For C. C.*, 1679. 8°. T.C.I 330. L, O, DCH, EN; CH, MH, NP, WCL.

6386   Entry cancelled.

6386A —Instructions how to play at billiards. 1687. 8°. T.C.II 189. O.

6387   —A panegyrick to the King's most excellent Majesty. *By Tho. Newcomb*, 1660. fol.* L; CH, MH, TU, Y.

6388   —The planters manual. *For Henry Brome*, 1675. 8°. T.C.I 213. L, O, C, OM, E; CH, MBP, NN, WF, Y.

6389   —Poems on several occasions. *For Tho. Basset, Will. Hensman and Tho. Fox*, 1689. 8°. T.C.II 254. L, O, C, EN, DT; CH, CN, LC, MH, TU, WC, Y.

6390   — —[Anr. ed.] *For Tho. Basset, Will. Hinsman and Tho. Fox*, 1689. 8°. C, CT; CH, OCI, NP, Y.

6391   [–] Scarronides: or, Virgile travestie. *By E. Cotes for Henry Brome*, 1664. 8°. L, O, C, E, DT; CH, CU, LC, MH, NN, WF, Y.

6392   [–] Scarronides . . . In imitation. *By E. Cotes for Henry Brome*, 1665. 8°. L, O, CS, GK; CH, MH, TU, WF, Y.

6393   [–] —[Anr. ed.] —, 1667. 8°. L, RPL, M; MH, NP, TU, WF, Y.

6394   [–] —[Anr. ed.] *By J. C. for Henry Brome*, 1670. 8°. T.C.I 51. L, C, CCH, CT; MH, NC, WF, Y.

6395   [–] —[Anr. ed.] *By T. R. for Henry Brome*, 1672. 8°. L; CU, MH, OCI, WF, Y.

6396   [–] —[Anr. ed.] *By T. N. for H. Brome*, 1678. 8°. T.C.I 315. L, BR; CLC, TU, Y.

6397   [–] —[Anr. ed.] *For J. Brome, and sold by Tho. Mercer*, 1682. 8°. L; CLC.

6397A [–] —[Anr. ed.] *By F. L. for C. Brome*, 1691. 8°. T.C.II 312. L, LVD, OC; CLC, NP, Y.

6398   [–] —[Anr. ed.] *For C. Brome*, 1692. 8°. T.C.II 353. O.

6398A [–] —[Anr. ed.] *By J. H. for Chr. Coningsby*, 1692. 8°. DCH; TU, Y.

6398B [–] —"Eighth" edition. *For C. Brome*, 1700. 8°. T.C.III 190. CN, PBL, Y.

6399   [–] The valiant knight: or, the legend of Sʳ Peregrine. *For J. Johnson*, 1663. 4°.* WCL.

6400   —The wonders of the peake. *For Joanna Brome*, 1681. 8°. T.C.I 463. L, O, OM, DT, GK; CH, CN, MH, TU, Y.

6401   — —Second edition. *By J. Wallis for Joanna Brome*, 1683. 8°. L, O, CPE, DCH, A; CH, CU, LC, MH, Y.

6402   — —Third edition. *By W. Everingham and Tho. Whitledge, for Charles Brome*, 1694. 8°. L, C, CE, CK, BR; CLC, IU, MH, OWC, Y.

6403   — —Fourth edition. *For Charles Brome*, 1699. 8°. T.C.III 129. L, O, OC, BAMB, GK; MH, NC, NP, TU, Y.

6404   **Cotton, Clement.** The mirror of martyrs. Sixth edition. *For R. Roberts*, 1685. 12°. T.C.II 152. L, O, C, OB, EN; CH, CLC, NU, Y.

6405   [–] None but Christ. Ninth edition. *For A. K. and are to be sold by Francis Eglesfield*, 1655. 12°. CLC.

6406   —A scripture table. *For John Hancock*, 1682. brs. T.C.II I. L.

6407   **Cotton, John, 1585–1652.** An abstract of laws and government . . . of Christs kingdome. *By M. S. for Livewel Chapman*, 1655. 4°.* O; CN, MH, NU, WF, Y.

6408   [–] An abstract or the lavves of Nevv England. *For F. Coules, and W. Ley*, 1641. 4°.* L, O, OC, CT, DT; CH, CN, LC, MH, NN, Y.

6409   —The bloudy tenent, washed. *By Matthew Symmons for Hannah Allen*, 1647. 4°. L, O, C, DC, ENC; CH, CN, MH, NU, RPJ, Y.

6410   —A brief exposition of the whole book of Canticles. *For Philip Nevil*, 1642. 8°. L, O, C; CLC, MH, NU, RPJ, WF, Y.

6411   — —[Anr. ed.] *By J. Young for Charles Green*, 1648. 8°. L, O, C, LCL, E; CH, LC, MH, NU, Y.

6412   —A brief exposition with practical observations upon the whole book of Canticles. *By T. R. & E. M. for Ralph Smith*, 1655. 8°. L, LCL, CS; CH, LC, MH, NU, Y.

6413   —A brief exposition with practicall observations upon the whole book of Ecclesiastes. *By T. C. for Ralph Smith*, 1654. 8°. L, O, CM, CS, LCL; CH, MH, NU, WF, Y.

6414   — —Second edition. *By W. W. for Ralph Smith*, 1657. 8°. L, O, CS, LCL, OC; MB, MH, NU, RPJ, Y.

6415   —A censure of. *By J. G. for John Stafford*, 1656. 4°. LT, O, C; CH, RPJ, WF.

6416   —Certain queries. *By M. S. for John Allen and Francis Eglesfield*, 1654. 4°.* L, LCL, CM, ENC; CH, MH, NU, RPJ, Y.

6417   —Christ the fountaine of life. *By Robert Ibbitson*, 1651. 4°. C; CH, CN, LC, MH, Y.

6418   — —[Anr. ed.] *By Robert Ibbitson, to be sold by George Calvert*, 1651. 4°. LT, LCL, OC; CS, LC, NU, RPJ, Y.

6419   —The churches resurrection. *By R. O. & G. D. for Henry Overton*, 1642. 4°.* L, O, C, CS, DT; CH, CN, MH, NU, WF, Y.

6419   —A conference. 1646. *See* Cornwell, Francis.

6420   —The controversie concerning liberty of conscience. *For Thomas Banks*, 1646. 4°.* LT, O, CS, EN, DT; CH, MB, MH, RPJ, Y.

6421   — —[Anr. ed.] *By Robert Austin, for Thomas Banks, to be sold at Mrs. Breaches shop*, 1649. 4°.* LT, O; CH, NN, NU, RPJ, WCL.

6422   —A coppy of a letter of. [*London*], *printed*, 1641. 4°.* LT, O, CT, HH, DT; MH, RPJ, WCL, WF, Y.

6423   —The covenant of Gods free grace. *For Matthew Simmons*, 1645. 4°.* LT, O, LSC, LW; MBA, PL, WF.

6424   — —[Anr. ed.] *By M. S. for Iohn Hancock*, 1645. 4°.* L, LCL, CS, E, GH; CH, CN, MH, RPJ, Y.

6425   —The covenant of grace. *By M. S. for Francis Eglesfield and John Allen*, 1655. 8°. L, O, CM; CH, MH, NU, RPJ, Y.

6426   — —[Anr. ed.] *By M. S. for F. Eglesfield and J. Allen*, 1655. 4°. MH, RPJ, Y.

6427   —A defence of. *Oxford, by H: Hall: for T. Robinson*, 1658. 8°. MADAN 2403. L, O, C, LCL, E; CN, LC, MH, NU, Y.

6427   —A discourse about civil government. Cambridge, 1663. *See* Davenport, John.

6428   —The doctrine of the church. *For Samuel Satterthwaite*, 1643. 4°.* O; Y.

6429 ——Second edition. *For Ben: Allen & Sam: Satterthwaite,* 1643. 4°.* L, C, CCC, BP, DT; CN, MHS, NU, RPJ, Y.

6430 ——Third edition. *For Ben: Allen,* 1644. 4°.* L, C, CT, HH, DT; CH, LC, MH, RPJ, Y.

6431 —An exposition upon the thirteenth chapter of the Revelation. *By M. S. for Livewel Chapman,* 1655. 4°. LT, LCL; CN, MB, NU, WF, Y.

6432 ——[Anr. ed.] *For Tim. Smart,* 1656. 4°. LT; CLC, CN, MB, MH, RPJ.

6433 —Gods mercie mixed vvith His ivstice. *By G. M. for Edward Brewster, and Henry Hood,* 1641. 4°. LT, O, CS, CT, LCL; CH, CN, LC, MH, NU, Y.

6434 —God's promise to His plantations. *By William Jones for John Bellamy,* 1634. *Reprinted at Boston in New-England, by Samuel Green; and are to be sold by John Vsher,* 1686. 4°.* EVANS 402. MBA, MH, MHS, V, Y.

6435 —Gospel conversion. *By J. Dawson,* 1646. 4°. LT, WCA; CH, LC, MB, MH, RPJ.

6436 —The grovnds and ends of the baptisme. *By R. C. for Andrew Crooke,* 1647. 4°. LT, O, C, MR, DT; CH, MH, NU, RPJ, Y.

6437 —The keyes of the kingdom of Heaven. *By M. Simmons for Henry Overton and are to be sold at his shop,* 1644. 4°. LT, C, CCL, GH; CH, CN, LC, NU, Y.

6438 ——[Anr. ed.] *By M. Simmons for Henry Overton,* 1644. 4°. LT, O, C, LW, CT; CH, MH, NR, WF, Y.

6439 ——"Second" edition. —, 1644. 4°. L, C, LCL, CS, CT; CH, LC, MH, Y.

6440 ——"Second" edition. *Printed by M. Simmons for Henry Overton,* 1644. 4°. P, DT; MHS.

6441 —A letter of. *Printed at London for Benjamin Allen,* 1643. 4°. L, OB; LC, MB, MH, RPJ, V, Y.

6442 Entry cancelled.

6443 —Milk for babes. *By J. Coe, for Henry Overton,* 1646. 8°.* LT; CH, INU.

6444 —A modest and cleer ansvver. *For H. Overton,* [1642?]. 4°. LT, O, LSC, OB; MB, NU, RPJ.

6445 ——[Anr. ed.] *By R. O. and G. D. for Henry Overton* 1642. 4°. LT, O, C, EN, DT; CN, MH, NU, RPJ, Y.

6446 —Nashauanittue meninnunk. *Cambridge* [*Mass.*]: *printeuoop nashpe Samuel Green, kah Bartholomew Green,* 1691. 8°.* EVANS 550. CS; LC, MH, MWA, NN, Y.

6447 —The new covenant. *By M. S. for Francis Eglesfield & John Allen,* 1654. 4°. L, O, LCL, ENC; CH, MH, NU, RPJ, Y.

6448 —Of the holinesse of church-members. *ptinted* [sic] *by F. N. for Hannah Allen,* 1650. 4°. LT, O, C, GH, DT; CH, LC, MH, NU, RPJ, Y.

6449 —The povvring ovt of the seven vials. *For R. S. and are to be sold at Henry Overtons shop,* 1642. 4°. LT, O, C, LCL, DC; CH, LC, MH, RPJ, Y.

6449A ——[Anr. ed.] *Printed and are to be sold at Henry Overtons shop,* 1642. 4°.

6450 ——[Anr. ed.] *For R. S. to be sold at Henry Overtons shop,* 1645. 4°. L, C, CS, DT; MB, MH, MHS, RPJ, Y.

6451 —A practical commentary, or an exposition. *By R. I. and E. C. for Thomas Parkhurst,* 1656. fol. L, O, C, LCL, E; CH, MH, NU, RPJ, Y.

6452 ——Second edition. *By M. S. for Thomas Parkhurst,* 1658. fol. L, P; CH, CN, LC, MH, NU, Y.

6452A ——"Second" edition. *By M. S. for Elisha Wallis,* 1658. fol. NPT, WF.

6453 —The result of a synod. *By M. S. for John Allen and Francis Eglesfield,* 1654. 4°. L, O, CM, ENC; CH, CN, MH, RPJ, Y.

6454 —The saint's support. *Printed, and are to be sold by Thomas Basset,* 1658. 4°. LT; MH, Y.

6455 —Severall qvestions. *For Thomas Banks,* 1647. 4°.* LT, O, LCL, ENC, DT; CH, MB, MHS, RPJ.

6456 —Singing of psalmes. *By M. S. for Hannah Allen, and John Rothwell,* 1647. 4°. LT, O, C, EN, DT; CH, MH, NPT, NU, RPJ, Y.

6457 ——[Anr. ed.] *For J. R. and H. A.,* 1650. 4°. L, O, C, MR, E; CN, NPT, PL, WF, Y.

6458 —Sixteene questions. *By E. P. for Edward Blackmore,* 1644. 4°.* LT, O, CS, DT; MB, NN, RPJ, WF, Y.

6459 [–] Some treasure fetched out of rubbish. *Printed,* 1660. 4°. LT, O, CT, SP; CH, MH, NU, WF, Y.

6460 —Spiritual milk for babes. *For Peter Parker,* 1668. 4°.* MB.

6461 ——[Anr. ed.] —, 1672. 8°.* PL.

6462 —[Anr. ed.] Spiritual milk for Boston babes. *Cambridg* [*Mass.*]: *by S. G. for Hezekiah Vsher at Boston,* 1656. 4°.* EVANS 42. NN.

6462A ——[Anr. ed.] *For Henry Cripps,* 1657. 8°. OC.

6463 ——[Anr. ed.] *Printed at Boston,* 1684. 4°.* PL.

6464 —A treatise of Mr. Cottons. *By J. D. for Andrew Crook,* 1646. 4°. L, O, P, E, DT; MH, NPT, PL, RPJ, Y.

6465 A treatise of the covenant. Second edition. *By Ja. Cottrel, for John Allen,* 1659. 8°. LT, O, CT, LCL; CN, MB, NU, WF, Y.

6466 ——"Second" edition. *For William Miller,* 1662. 8°. L, LCL; LC.

6467 ——Third edition. *For Peter Parker,* 1671. 8°. L, C, LCL, LW; CH, MH, NPT, NU, RPJ, Y.

6467A ——[Anr. ed.] *Printed and are to be sold by Nath. Crouch,* 1671. 8°. MB.

6468 —The true constitvtion. *For Samuel Satterthwaite,* 1642. 4°.* LT, O, C, LW, HH; CH, MH, NU, PL, RPJ, WF.

6469 —The way of Congregational churches cleared. *By Matthew Simmons, for John Bellamie,* 1648. 4°. LT, O, C, LCL, DT; BN, CH, MH, NU, WF, Y.

6470 —The way of life. *By M. F. for L. Fawne, and S. Gellibrand,* 1641. 4°. L, O, C, LCL, E; CH, CN, MH, NU, WF, Y.

6471 —The way of the churches of Christ in New-England. *By Matthew Simmons,* 1645. 4°. LT, O, C, CT, EN; CH, CN, MH, NU, WF, Y.

6472 ——Second edition. —, 1645. 4°. MH, MHS, RPJ, Y.

6473 **Cotton, John, 1640–1699.** Upon the death of that aged, pious, . . . John Alden. [*Boston,* 1687.] brs. EVANS 426. CH, MBA, MHS.

6473A   **Cotton, John**, 1658–1710. A meet help. *Boston, by B. Green, and J. Allen. Sold by Michael Perry*, 1699. 8°.* MHS.

6473B   **C[otton], Mrs. P[riscilla]**. A briefe description by way of supposition. [*London?* 1659]. cap., 4°.* CLC, MH.

6474   —To the priests and people of England, we discharge our consciences. colop: *Printed at London for Giles Calvert*, 1655. 4°.* LT, O, LF, BBN; PH, PSC.

6475   —A visitation of love unto all people. colop: *For Thomas Simmons*, 1661. cap., 4°.* L, LF, BBN, GU; IE, MH, PH, PL, PSC.

6476   **Cotton, *Sir* Robert Bruce.** An abstract ovt of the records of the Tovver. *For G. Tomlinson, T. A. and A. C.*, [1642]. 4°.* LT, O, C, EC; CH, MH, NC, WF, Y.

6477   [–] An answer made by command of Prince Henry. *By Roger Daniel*, 1655. 8°. L.

6478   —An answer made by Sr. Robert Cotton. *For William Sheares*, 1655. 8°. LT, OM, CE, CCL, CM; CH, CLC, CN, MH, WF, Y.

6479   —An answer to such motives as were offer'd by certain military-men. Second edition. *For Henry Mortlock*, 1665. [*i.e.* 1675]. 8°. L, C, OC; LC, PH, TSM, Y.

6480   ——Second edition —, 1675. 8°. T.C.I 212. L, O, C, CT, DT; CH, LC, MH, NC, WCL.

6481   The antiquity and dignity of Parliaments. *Printed*, 1679. fol.* CCA, EN; CH, CU, MB, MH, NP.

6482   ——[Anr. ed.] *For Norman Nelson*, 1680. fol.* L, LL, CT; MHL, WF, Y.

6482A   —A briefe abstract of the question. *By L. N. & R. C. for Thomas Slater, Novemb. 24*, 1642. 4°.* LT, EC, MR; CLC, Y.

6483–4 Entries cancelled.

6485   —Cottoni posthuma. *By Francis Leach, for Henry Seile*, 1651. 8°. LT, O, C, EN, DT; BN, CH, LC, MH, NN, Y.

6486   ——[Anr. ed.] *For Richard Lowndes, and Matthew Gilli-flower*, 1672. 8°. T.C.I 93. L, O, CS, EN, DT; CH, CU, LC, MH, NC, Y.

6487   ——[Anr. ed.] *By M. C. for C. Harper, to be sold by W. Hensman, and T. Fox*, 1679. 8°. T.C.I 376. L, O, C, LL, AN; CN, LC, MH, NU, Y.

6488   —A discourse of foreign war. *For H. Mortlock*, 1690. 8°. T.C.II 293. L, C, CT, EN; CJC, MH, NC, TU.

6489   —An exact abridgement of the records in the Tower of London. *For William Leake*, 1657. fol. L, O, C, EN, DT; BN, CH, CU, LC, MHL, NU, Y.

6490   ——[Anr. ed.] *For William Leake and John Leake*, 1679. fol. L, CP, CS, BAMB, EN; NCL.

6491   ——[Anr. ed.] *For T. Basset, and C. Harper*, 1689. fol. T.C.II 262. L, LMT, OC; CN, MHL, WSC, Y.

6491A   [–] The field of bloud. *For James Vade*, 1681. 4°.* T.C.I 441. O, C, CS, EN; CH, CLC, Y.

6492   [–] The forme of government of the kingdome of England. *For Tho. Bønkes*, 1642. 4°.* LT, O, C; CN, CSS, LC, MHL, NU, Y.

6493   [–] —[Anr. ed.] 1643. 4°. O.

6494   —The histories of the lives and raignes of Henry the third, and Henry the fourth. *For William Sheares*, 1642. 12°. L, O, C, EN, DT; BN, CH, CU, MH, NU, WF, Y.

6494A   ——[Anr. ed.] —, 1652. 12°. OC, GK.

6495   ——[Anr. ed.] —, 1661. 12°. O; NN, WSC.

6496   ——[Anr. ed.] 1679. 8°. C; IU.

6497   —Seriovs considerations for repressing of the increase of Iesvites. [*London*], printed, 1641. 4°.* L, O, CT, SC, OC; CH, CN, NU, WF, Y.

6498   [–] A short vievv of the long life and reigne of Henry the third. *Printed*, 1641[2]. 4°.* LT, O; NC.

6499   ———Second edition. —, 1641. 4°. LT, C; CH.

6500   ——[Anr. ed.] *By William Bentley for William Shears*, 1651. 8°.* LT, O, C, AN; BN, CH, LC, MH, NU, Y.

6501   —A short view of the reign of King Henry III. *For Richard Janeway*, 1681. 4°.* L, SP; CH, CLC, MH, Y.

6501A   —A speech made by. *For Tho. Horne*, 1690. 4°.* HH; MBA, NC, PU, Y.

6502   —A treatise against recusants. *By Richard Hearn*, 1641. 4°.* LT, O, OCC, EN, DT; CH, CN, MH, NU, WF, Y.

6503   —A treatise, shewing that the soveraignes person is required. [*London*], printed, 1641. 4°.* L, O, C, LCL, LL; CH, CN, LC, MH, NU, Y.

6504   —The troublesome life and raigne of King Henry the Third. *Imprinted at London for George Lindsey*, 1642. 4°.* LT, O, EN; CH, MH, MIU, V, WF, Y.

6505   [–] Warrs with forregen [*sic*] princes. *For William Shears*, 1657. 8°. LT, O, LVF, P; CH, NPT, WF, Y.

6506   **Cotton, Seaborn.** A brief summe of the chief articles. *Cambridg* [*Mass.*]: *by Samuel Green*, 1663. 8°.* EVANS 77. NN.

6507   **Cotton, W.** A new catechisme. *By B. Alsop*, 1648. 8°.* LT.

6508   **Couch, John.** Anabaptistarum scrupuli, or. *By W. D.*, 1650. 4°.* LT.

6508A   —His Majesties miraculous preservation. [*London?* 1660.] brs. L.

6509   **Couch, Robert.** New Englands lamentation for the late firing of the city of London. *Printed at Cambridge in New England, and reprinted at London, at the instance of Mr. Jonathan Ting, for Nathaniel Brooke*, [1666?]. brs. L.

6510   —Praxis Catholica: or, the countryman's universal remedy. *For Robert Harford*, 1680. 8°. L, LSC, LWL, AU; CH, MB, NAM, V, WSG.

6511   **Couchman, Obadiah.** The adamites sermon. [*London*], *for Francis Coules*, 1641. 4°.* L, C.

6512   **Couling, Nicholas.** The saints perfect. *For Giles Calvert*, 1647. 8°.* LT, CT; NU.

6513   —A survey of tyrannie. *By J. M. for John Sweeting*, 1650. 4°.* LT, O, DT; CLC, NU.

6514   —A vvord to the LII London ministers. *Printed*, 1648. 4°.* CT; NU.

Coulton, John. Prognostæ astralis. 1655. *See* Almanacs.

6514A   **Coulton, Richard.** The loyalty of the Church of England. *York, by J. White, and are to be sold by Ro. Clarke*, 1685. 4°.* WCA; NGT, Y.

6515   Council humbly propounded. *By M. Simmons, for H. C.,* 1660. 4°.* LT; CN, NU.

Council of Trent examin'd. 1688. *See* Stillingfleet, Edward, *bp.*

Counsel and directions. 1685. *See* Grenville, Denis.

Counsel for youth. 1650. *See* V., H.

Counsel to the afflicted. 1667. *See* Stockton, Owen.

6516   Counsel to the true English. *For S. Manship,* 1691. 4°.* L, O, CT, AU, DT; CH, NU, Y.

Counsellor Manners his last legacy. 1694. *See* Dare, Josiah.

Counsels of wisdom. 1680. *See* Boutauld, Michael.

Count de Soissons. 1688. *See* Claude, Isaac.

6517   Count Hanlan's downfall. *Dublin, by Joseph Ray for William Winter,* 1681. 4°.* DIX 188. L, O, C, LVF, DI; CH, WF.

Count of Amboise. 1689. *See* Bernard, Catherine.

Count of Gabalis. 1680. *See* Villars, De Montsucon.

6518   The counter bvffe or. . . . *For H. P.,* 1647. 4°.* LT, AN; CLC, NU.

Counter-essay. Edinburgh, 1692. *See* Forrester, Thomas.

Counterfeit bridegroom. 1677. *See* Middleton, Thomas.

6519   The counterfeit bridegroom. [*London,* 1700?] brs. L.

Counterfeit Christian. [*n.p.*], 1674. *See* Penn, William.

6520   The counterfeit court lady. [*London*], *for F. Coles, T. Vere, J. Wright, and J. Clarke,* [1670?]. brs. L; MH, Y.

6520A   The counterfeit Jew. [*Newcastle,* 1653.] 4°.* NU.

Counterfeit lady. 1673. *See* Karman, Francis.

Counterfeits. 1679. *See* Leanerd, John.

Countermine. 1677. *See* Nalson, John.

Covnter-plea. [*n.p.,* 1647.] *See* Prynne, William.

6521   A covnter-plot against Popery. *Printed,* 1642. 4°.* LT, O, CK, DT; CH, CSS, MH, MIU, Y.

6522   The counter-plot; or. *For Henry Brome,* 1680. 4°.* T.C.I 407. L, O, C, HH, DT; CH, MH, NU, WF, Y.

Counter poyson. 1642. *See* Ainsworth, Henry.

Counter-rat. 1684. *See* T., M.

Counter scuffle. 1651. *See* Speed, Robert.

6523   Covnter-votes: or, an arraignment, and conviction of the votes at Oxford. Colop: [*London*], *for Matthew Walbancke,* 1644. cap., 4°.* MADAN 1601. LT, O, HH; MH, Y.

6524   The covnters discovrse with it's varlets discovery. [*London*], *printed,* 1641. 4°.* L, O; CH, WCL, WF, Y.

6524A   The Countess of Roscommon's case. [*London,* 1694.] brs. CH.

Countess of Salisbury. 1683. *See* Argences, d'.

Country almanack. 1676. *See* Almanacs: A. M.

Country captaine. 1649. *See* Newcastle, William Cavendish, *duke of.*

6525   The country club. A poem. *For Walter Kettilby,* 1679. 4°.* T.C.I 350. L, O; CH, CN, MH, WF, Y.

6526   The country committees laid open. [*London*], *printed,* 1649. 4°.* LT, O, HH, BR; CSS, WF.

Country contentments. 1649. *See* Markham, Gervase.

Country conversations. 1694. *See* Wright, James.

6527   The countrey cozen; or, the crafty city dame. [1690?] brs. O.

Country-curate's advice. 1693. *See* Cornwallis, Henry.

6528   A country dialogue between William. [*n.p.,* 1692.] fol. O.

6529   The countrey farmer. [*London*], *for P. Brooksby,* [1675–80]. brs. L, O, CM, HH; MH.

6530   The country farmer's vain-glory. [*London*], *for P. Brooksby, J. Dencon* [*sic*], *J. Blare, and J. Back,* [1688–95]. brs. L, HH, GU.

6530A   The country garland. [*London*], *for P. Brooksby,* 1687. 8°.* CM.

6530B   —[Anr. ed.] —, 1688. 8°.* O.

6531   The country gentleman. *For J. Clark, W. Thackeray, and T. Passinger,* [1655–60]. brs. L, HH; MH.

6532   The country gentleman's notion. *Printed,* 1696. 8°. T.C.II 592. O, CT; CH, MB.

6533   The country gentleman's vade mecum. *For John Harris,* 1699. 8°. T.C.III 175. L, O, C, CT, E; CH, CN, MH, WF, Y.

Countrie girle. 1647. *See* Brewer, Antony.

6534   The country girl's policy. [*London,* 1700?] brs. L.

Country house-wife's garden. 1676. *See* Markham, Gervase.

6535   The country innocence. *For Charles Harper,* 1677. 4°. L; CH, LC, NC, WF.

6536   —[Anr. ed.] [*London,* 1680?] brs. L.

6537   The country lasse. [*London*], *for P. Brooksby, J. Deacon, J. Blare, J. Back,* [1649?]. brs. L.

6538   The country lass for me. [*London*], *for P. Brooksby,* [1680–85]. brs. L, HH; MH.

6539   The country lasse. To a daintie new note. [*London,* 1645?]. brs. L.

6540   The country lass, who left her spinning-wheel. [*London*], *for P. Brooksby, J. Deacon, J. Blare, J. Back,* [1690?]. brs. L, HH.

6540A   The country lasse's good fortune. [*London*], *for J. Millet,* [1691–2.] brs. CM.

6541   The country lawyers maid Joan. [*London*], *for P. Brooksby, J. Deacon, J. Blare, and J. Back,* [1685–92]. brs. L, CM, HH; MH, Y.

6542   The country lovers. [*London*], *for P. Brooksby,* [1672–80]. brs. L, HH; MH, Y.

6542A   The country lovers conquest. [*London*], *for Robert Burton,* [1641–74.] brs. GU.

6542B   The country maiden's lamentation. [*London*], *for Richard Kell,* [1684–94]. brs. O, CM.

6543   The country-maids delight: or, the husbandman's honour made known. [*London*], *for F. Coles, T. Vere, J. Wright, and J. Clarke,* [1690?] brs. O.

The countrey-man's apothecary. 1649. *See* Rondelet, Guillaume.

6544   The country-man's kalender. [*London*], *for P. Brooksby, J. Deacon, J. Blare, J. Back,* [1691.] brs. L.

6545   The covntryman's care. *Printed at London, for T. B.,* 1641. 4°.* LT, M; LC.

6546   The country-mans care in choosing a wife. [*London,* 1672?] brs. L, O, CM, HH; MH, Y.

6547 The country mans case uncased. *Printed*, 1678. *To be sold by John Oliver.* brs. L, EN.

Country-mans catechisme. 1652. *See* Boreman, Robert.
Country-man's companion. [1684.] *See* Tryon, Thomas.

6548 The country-man's complaint, and advice to, the king. Colop: [*London*], *printed*, 1681. brs. L, O, CT, MC; CH, CN, MH, PU, Y.

6549 —[Anr. ed.] [*Edinburgh reprinted,*] 1681. brs. ALDIS 2262. EN, ES.

6549A The country-mans counsellor. *For J. Clark,* [1680.] 12°. CM.

6550 The country-man's delight. [*London*], *for P. Brooksby,* [1672–80]. brs. L, CM, HH; MH.

6550A —[Anr. ed.] [*London*], *for John Wright, John Clarke, William Thackeray, and Thomas Passinger,* [1683.] brs. CM.

6551 The countryman's delight: or, the happy vvooing. [*London,* 1670?] brs. L.

6552 The country-man's fare-wel to London. [*London*], *by A. P. for J. Conniers,* [1665?]. brs. L; MH.

Country-man's guide. 1679. *See* W., W.

6553 The countrey-man's guide. *For P. Brooksby,* 1697. 12°.* Y.

6554 The country-mans lamentation. [*London*], *for C. Passinger,* [1670–80]. brs. L, O, HH, GU.

Country-man's new art of planting. 1652. *See* Brossard, Davy.

6555 The country-mans nevv common-wealth. *For Richard Harper,* 1647. 8°.* LT.

6556 The country mans Paradice. [*London*], *for J. Wright, J. Clark, W. Thackery and T. Passenger,* [1670–82]. brs. HH; MH, Y.

6557 The country-man's petition for a Parliament. *For C. Tebrock,* 1682. brs. L, O, LG; MH, Y.

6558 The countryman's physician. *For Richard Chiswel,* 1680. 8°. T.C.I 417. L, LSC; NN, WSG, WU.

Country-man's recreation. 1654. *See* Barker, Thomas.
Countrey-mans rudiments. Edinburgh, 1699. *See* Belhaven, John Hamilton, *baron.*

6559 The countrey-mans vive le roy. *For J. Jones,* 1660. brs. L.

6560 A country minister's reasons for taking the oaths. *For Randal Taylor,* 1690. 4°.* L, O, CT; WF, Y.

6561 The countrey ministers reflections, on the city-minister's letter. colop: *For E. Reyner and W. Faulkner,* 1688. cap., 4°.* L, O, CT, LIL, MR; CH, MIU, NU, WF.

Country minister's serious advice. Sheffield, 1700. *See* Hough, Edmund.

6562 The country-miser. *For N. Jackson,* 1693. 8°.* I.

6563 The country miss new come in fashion. [*London*], *for E. Oliver,* [1676]. brs. L, O, CM, HH.

6564 —[Anr. ed.] [*London*], *for I. VVright, I. Clarke, VV. Thackeray, and T. Passenger,* [1670–82]. brs. HH; MH.

6565 —[Anr. ed.] *For W. Thackeray, T. Passinger, and W. Whitwood,* [1677?]. brs. L, O, CM.

6565A The country mouse. *For J. Clarke Senior,* 1683. 8°.* CM.

Country-parson's admonition. 1686. *See* Assheton, William.

6566 The country-parson's advice. *For Benj. Tooke,* 1680. 8°. T.C.I 401. L, CS, CT, RPL, EN; CH, CLC.

6567 The country parson's folly. *For J. Bissel,* [1688–95]. brs. L, CM, HH; MH.

6568 The country parson's honest advice. [*London,* 1700?] brs. L, CT; CH, MH, MIU, WF, Y.

Country scuffle. 1693. *See* Ward, Edward.

6569 A countrey song, intituled, The restoration. [*London,* 1661.] brs. LT.

6570 The countreys advice to the late Duke of Monmouth. colop: *By T. M. for the author,* 1685. brs. L, BR, HH; MH.

6571 The countries advice to the city. colop: [*London*], *for Sam. Carr,* 1682. brs. O, CT, MC, HH, EN.

6571A The countries complaint against the aulnagers. [*London?* 169–.] brs. LG.

6572 The countreys plea against tythes. *For S. P.,* 1647. 4°.* LT, O, HH, MR, DT; CH, MH, Y.

Countries sense. 1667. *See* Thomas, William.

6573 The countries vindication, from the aspersions of a late scandalous paper. [*London,* 1679?] cap., fol.* L, O, HH; CH, MBA, MH, NU, WF, Y.

6573A The county of Suffolke divided. *For Christopher Meredith,* 1640. 4°.* L, O; WF.

Covnty of Somerset divided. 1648. *See* Prynne, William.

6574 **Couper, William.** Disputatio juridica. *Edinburgh, heirs of A. Anderson,* 1699. 4°. ALDIS 3838. EN.

6575 Courage crowned with conquest. *For F. Coles, T. Vere, and J. Wright,* 1672. brs. L, O, CM, HH, GU; MH.

6576 Couragious Betty of Chick-Lane. [*London*], *for P. Brooksby, J. Deacon, J. Blare, and J. Back,* [1690?] brs. L.

6577 The couragious cook-maid. [*London*], *for F. Coles, T. Vere, J. Wright, and I. Clarke,* [1670?]. brs. L, HH.

6578 The couragious English boys. [*London*], *for J. Blare,* [1690?] brs. L.

6579 The couragious gallant. [*London*], *for I. Deacon,* [1685–88]. brs. L, HH; MH.

6580 Couragious Jemmy's resolution. [*London*], *for J. Deacon,* [1690?]. brs. L.

6580A Couragious jockey. *Jonah Deacon,* [1685.] brs. CM.

6581 The couragious Loyalists. [*London*], *for I. Deacon* [1683]. brs. L, HH.

6582 The couragious plow-man. *For F. Coles, T. Vere, J. Wright, and J. Clark,* [1670–80]. brs. L, O, HH; MH, WCL.

6583 The couragious seamens loyal health. [*London*], *for J. Back,* [1685–88]. brs. L, O, HH.

6583A The couragious soldiers of the West. [*London*], *for J. Deacon,* [1690.] brs. L.

6583B **Courcelles, Etienne de.** Stephani Curcellæi synopsis ethices. Second edition. *Excudebat M. C. sumptibus H. Dickinson, Cantabrigiæ,* 1684. 8°. L, C, CT, OPE; CU, WF, Y.

Course of lectures. Oxford, 1696. *See* Bray, Thomas.
Court and character. 1650. *See* Weldon, *Sir* Anthony.

6584 The court and kingdom in tears. [*London,* 1694.] brs. L, CM.

6585 The court at Kensington. *Printed,* 1700. fol.* T.C.III 231. LG, CS; CLC, MH, TU, WF, Y.

6586 The court career. [*London*], printed, 1659. 4°.* LT; WF.
Court convert. [*n.p.*], 1698. *See* Waring, Henry.

6587 The court-miss converted. [*London*], *for F. Coles, T. Vere, J. Wright, and J. Clarke*, [1660–70]. brs. L, CM, HH.

6588 The court of curiosities. [*London*], *for P. Brooksby*, [1685]. 8°.* O.

6589 The court of England. Or, the preparation. [*London*], *by A. M. for R. Hayhurst*, 1689. brs. L, O, OC, EN.

6589A The court of honour. [*London*], *by A. Purslow and Tho. Haly*, 1679. 4°.* CN, MH.

6589B The court of justice. *By J. Bradford*, [c. 1700]. 8°. CN, MH, WF.

6590 The court of Neptune burlesqu'd. *Printed, and sold by most Booksellers*, 1700. fol.* L; MH, Y.

6591 The court of Rome. *For Henry Herringman*, 1654. 8°. LT, O, CSSX, DT; CH, CLC, CN, TU, WF, Y.

6591A The court of St. Germains. *Printed*, 1695. 12°. WF, Y.
Covrt of the gentiles. *Oxon*, 1669. *See* Gale, Theophilus.
Court secret. 1689. *See* Bellon, Peter.

6592 **Courten, William.** To the Kings most excellent Majestie, the humble peticion of. [*London*, 1674?] cap., 4°.* L; LUG.

6593 —To the King's . . . Majesty, and . . . his . . . Privy Council; the humble address. [*London*, 1677.] brs. L.

6594 The courteous carman. [*London*], *for F. Coles, T. Vere, J. Wright, J. Clarke, W. Thackeray, T. Passinger*, [1655–80]. brs. L, HH; MH.

6595 —[Anr. ed.] *By and for W. O. to be sold by C. Bates*, [1685]. brs. HH.

6596 **Courthope, Brian.** The case of the coach-makers company. [*London*, 1682.] brs. LG.

6596A The courtier converted. colop: *Bruxelles, printed*, 1686. cap., 4°.* Y.
Courtier's calling. 1675. *See* Caillières, J. de.
Courtiers health. [*n.p.*, 1681.] *See* Taubman, Matthew.

6596B [**Courtilz de Sandras, Gatien de.**] The amorous conquest of the great Alexander. *For R. Bentley and S. Magnes*, 1685. 12°. T.C.II 113. L, CT; CLC, Y.

6597 —The conduct of France. *For William Cademan*, 1684. 8°. T.C.II 60. CE; CLC.

6597A [–] An exact survey of the grand affairs of France. *For William Whitworth*, 1689. 8°. WF.

6597B [–] French intrigues. *For W. Hensman and Tho. Fox*, 12°. T.C.II 103. OC; CH, CN, PL, WF, Y.

6597C [–] The French spy. *For R. Basset*, 1700. 8°. T.C.III 171. L, C; CH, CN, PL, WF, Y.

6598 —The history of the life and actions of . . . Turenne. *By J. B. for Dorman Newman & R. Bentley*, 1686. 8°. L, O, C, DC, OM; CH, CN, MH, WF, Y.

6599 [–] The life of the famous John Baptist Colbert. *For R. Bentley; J. Tonson; H. Bonwick; W. Freeman; and S. Manship*, 1695. 8°. L, CS, CT; CH, CN, MH, WF, Y.

6600 [–] The memoirs of the Count de Rochefort. *By F. L. for James Knapton; Richard Parker; and Tho. Nott*, 1696. 8°. CT; CH, CN, LC, MH, Y.

6600A ——Second edition. *For John Sturton and A. Bosvile*, 1696. 8°. O; MBP, MIU.

6600B [–] The political last testament. *For Charles Brome*, 1695. 8°. T.C.II 527. C, OC, RPL, E, EN; CN, CU, MH, PL, WF, Y.

6601 [–] The political testament of M. Jean Baptist Colbert. *For R. Bentley*, 1695. 8°. L, O, BAMB, EN; CH, MB, WCL, Y.

6602 [**Courtin, Antoine de.**] The rules of civility. *For J. Martyn; and John Starkey*, 1671. 12°. T.C.I 88. L, E; CH, LC, MH.

6603 [–] —Second edition. —, 1673. 12°. T.C.I 138. O; CLC, WF, Y.

6603A [–] —Third edition. —, 1675. 12°. T.C.I 200. L, O, A; MH, NN, WF.

6604 [–] —[Anr. ed.] —, 1678. 12°. T.C.I 322. L, O, C, OC.

6605 [–] —[Anr. ed.] *For R. Chiswell, T. Sawbridge, G. Wells and R. Bently*, 1685. 12°. L, OP, CE, EN; CLC, CU, WF, Y.

6606 [–] A treatise of jealousie. *For W. Freeman*, 1684. 12°. T.C.II 48. L; CLC, CU, TU, Y.

6607 **Courtland, Stephen.** A journal kept by. *Printed and sold by William Bradford New York*, 1693. 4°.* BN.

6608 A courtly ballad of the princely wooing. [*London*, 1675–89.] brs. L, O, HH, GU.

6609 A courtly new ballad. *For F. Coles, T. Vere, and William Gilbertson*, [1670?] brs. L.

6610 The courtly triumph. [*London*, 1689.] brs. HH.

6611 **Courtney, Thomas.** Good newes from Ireland. *Novemb. 21. for T. Wright*, 1642. 4°.* LT; CH, MH, MIU, Y.
Court's apology. 1663. *See* G., L.
Covrts of ivstice. 1642. *See* L., W.

6612 **Covell, William.** A declaration unto the Parliament. *Printed*, 1659. 4°.* O, LUG, OC; CLC, MH, Y.

6613 —A proclamation, to all, of all sorts. [*London*, 1654.] brs. LT, LG.

6614 —The true copy of a letter sent to the Kings. *By J. C. for the author*, [1661]. brs. LT.

6615 **Coven, Stephen.** The militant Christian. *Printed*, 1668. 8°. LCL; MH.

6615A [–] —[Anr. ed.] 1660. 8°. L.
Covenant & alliance. [*n.p.*], 1643. *See* R., J.
Covenant and catechism. 1700. *See* Jacob, Joseph.

6616 A covenant for religion. *For Henry Hutton, Oct. 7*, 1642. 4°.* LT, MR, HH, EN; MH, Y.

6617 The covenant-interest and privilege of believers. *For Jonathan Robinson*, 1675. 8°.* T.C.I 209. CH.
The covenant of grace effectually remembered. 1682. *See* Newcombe, Henry.

6618 The covenant of grace, not absolute. *For Dorman Newman*, 1692. 4°. T.C.II 507. L, OC, CT, LW, EN; MB, NU, WF, Y.

6619 The covenant of life opened. *Edinburgh, by A. A. for Robert Broun*, 1655. 4°. FSF.

6620 Covenant-renouncers. [*London*], 1665. 4°. L.
Covenant to be. 1700. *See* Jacob, Joseph.
Covenant to walk with God. 1646. *See* S., W.

6621 The covenant: with a narrative. *For Thomas Vnderhill*, 1643. 4°.* LT, O, C, LIL, DT; CH, MH, NU, WF, Y.

6621A —[Anr. ed.] *For I. Shirley*, 1643. 4°.* CT.
Covenanter vindicated. 1644. *See* Stuart, Adam.

6622 The covenanters catechisme. *Printed at London by John Raworth,* 1644. 4°.* LT, O, CJ, EN, DT; CH, CLC, MH, NU, WF.

6623 —[Anr. ed.] *By R. R.,* 1647. 4°.* O, SC.

Covenanters plea. 1661. *See* Gataker, Thomas.

6624 Covent Garden drollery. *For James Magnes,* 1672. 8°. MH.

6624A —Second edition. —, 1672, 8°. T.C.I 117. L, O, OW, A; CLC, LC, Y.

6625 [Coventry, Thomas, *baron.*] A perfect and exact direction to all those. *By R. H. for N. Vavasour,* 1641. 8°. L, OC, CS, DK.

6626 Coventry, *Sir* William. A catalogue of books . . . 9 May. [*London*], 1687. 4°.* L, O, HH; MH, JF.

[–] The character of a trimmer. 1688. *See* Halifax, George Savile, *marquis of.*

[–] Englands appeale from the private caballe. 1673. *See* Lisola, Francois Paul, *baron de.*

6627–30 Entries cancelled.

6631 —A letter written to Dr. Burnet. *For Richard Baldwin,* 1685. 4°.* L, O, C, EN, DT; CH, CN, MH, NU, WF, Y.

6632 Covert, Nicholas. The scrivener's guide. *By Charles Harper, and Roger Clavell,* 1695. 8°. T.C.II 558. L, LL; LC.

6633 ——Second edition. *By the assigns of Richard and Edward Atkins, for Charles Harper,* 1700. 8°. L, BAMB; CH, MHL, NN, WF.

6634 The covetous-minded parents. [*London*], *for P. Brooksby, J. Deacon, J. Blare, J. Back,* [1685–92]. brs. L, CM, HH, GU; MH.

6635 The covetous mother. [*London*], *for J. Deacon,* [1685–88]. brs. HH, GU; MH.

6636 Coward, William. Alcali vindicatum: or, the acid opiniator. *For Tim. Childe,* 1698. 8°. T.C.III 40. L, CCA, CS, LWL; HC.

6637 —De fermento. *Excudit J. H. pro T. Bennet,* 1695. 8°. T.C.II 550. L, O, CS, LSC, LWL.

6638 —A Lenten litany. 1698. 8°. L.

6639 Cowell, John, *divine.* A beame of Sabbath-light. [*n.p.*], 1664. 4°. E.

6640 —Divine oracles. *For the authour,* 1664. 4°. O.

6641 Cowell, John, LL.D. The institutes of the lawes of England. *By T. Roycroft for J. Ridley,* 1651. 8°. L, O, C, LL, EN; CH, MHL, NCL, WF, YL.

6642 —Institutiones juris Anglicani. [*Oxoniæ*], *cura & impensis W. Hall pro Ed. Forrest in Oxon,* 1664. 12°. MADAN 2657. L, O, CP, MR, EN; CH, LC, MHI, NCL, YL.

6643 ——[Anr. ed.] *Oxoniæ, excudebat Hen. Hall impensis Ed. Forrest,* 1676. 16°. T.C.I 238. MADAN 3100. L, O, CS, ES, DT; MB, MHL, NCL.

6644 —The interpreter. Third edition. *By F. Leach, to be sold by Hen. Twyford, Tho. Dring, and Io. Place,* 1658. fol. L, CJ, CS, CT, MC; MHL, NCL, TU.

6645 —Νομοθετης. The interpreter. Fourth edition. *By J. Streater, for H. Twyford, G. Sawbridge, J. Place, and T. Basset,* 1672. fol. T.C.I 90. L, LL, LIL, CCA, OC; CH, CU, LC, MH, NU, TU, YL.

6646 ——Fifth edition. *By the assigns of Richard Atkins; and Sir Edward Atkins, for H. Twyford, Tho. Basset, J. Place and H. Sawbridge,* 1684. fol. L, O, CK, LIL, NPL; BN, CH, LC, MHL, NCL, YL.

6647 —The snare broken. *For E. Brewster,* 1677. 8°. T.C.I 280. L, O, C, EN; MHS, MWA, NPT.

6648 [Cowie, John]. Some queries touching excommunication. [*Aberdeen,* 1682.] cap., 4°.* ALDIS 2360. EN; PSC.

6649 Cowley, Abraham. The works of. *By J. M. for Henry Herringman,* 1668. fol. L, O, C, NPL, E; BN, CH, CN, LC, MH, NP, TU, Y.

6650 ——Second edition. —, 1669. fol. T.C.I 11. L, O, C, LG, OM; CN, CU, LC, MH, NC, Y.

6651 ——Third edition. —, 1672. fol. T.C.I 99. L, O, CS, OC, ES; CH, CU, MH, NP, TU, Y.

6652 ——Fourth edition. —, 1674. fol. L, O, C, OB, ENC; CH, CU, MH, TU, Y.

6653 ——Fifth edition. —, 1678. fol. L, O, CT, EN, AU; CLC, MH, NC, TU, WF, Y.

6654 ——Sixth edition. —, 1680. fol. L, O, CT, ELY, EN; CH, CN, MH, TU, Y.

6655 ——Seventh edition. —, 1681. fol. L, O, C, LVD, LCP; CU, MH, NC, TU, WF, Y.

6656 ——[Anr. ed.] —, 1681. 12°. L, O, CK, CT, EN; CH, CLC, MH, TU, WF, Y.

6657 ——"Eighth" edition. *By J. M. for Henry Herringman and are to be sold by Charles Harper and Abel Swalle,* 1684. fol. T.C.II 87. L, O, CT, AM, DT; BN, CH, CN, LC, MH, TU, Y.

6658 ——[Anr. ed.] *By J. M. for H. Herringman, and sold by Jos. Knight and Fra. Saunders,* 1688. fol. L, O, DU, AU; CLC, CU, MH, TU, WF, Y.

6659 ——"Eighth" edition. *For Henry Herringman; to be sold by R. Bentley, J. Tonson, F. Saunders, and T. Bennet,* 1693. fol. L, O, CT, LL, DT; BN, CN, LC, MH, MMO, TU, Y.

6660 ——Ninth edition. *For Henry Herringman; and are to be sold by Jacob Tonson, and Thomas Bennet,* 1700. fol. L, O, C, BQ, EN; CH, LC, MH, NC, TU, WF, Y.

6661 —The second and third parts of the works of. Sixth edition. *For Charles Harper,* 1689. fol. T.C.II 279. L, O, CCC, LVD, LVF; LC, MH, MU, TU, WF.

6662 ——Seventh edition. —, 1700. fol. T.C.III 247. L, O, C, CCH, LWL; CH, LC, MH, Y.

6663 —The second part of the works. Fourth edition. *By Mary Clark, for Charles Harper and Jacob Tonson,* 1681. fol. T.C.II 88. L, O, CT, BR, GK; CH, CLC, MH, TU, WF, Y.

6664 ——"Fourth" edition. —, 1682. 12°. L, O, C, EN; CH, CN, MH, TU, WF, Y.

6664A ——Fifth edition. —, 1684. fol. CPB, TU, WF.

6665 —The third part of the works of. *For Charles Harper,* 1689. fol. T.C.II 275. L, O, CS, GK, DT; MH, TU, WF, Y.

6666 ——Second edition. —, 1700. fol. L, O, C; CH, LC, MH, TU, Y.

[–] Ad populum: or, a lecture. [*n.p.*], 1644. *See* Hausted, Peter.

6667 ——*For Henry Brome,* 1678. 4°.* T.C.I 294. O, LVD, EN; CH Y.

6668   —By Heav'ns, the words by. [*London*, 1660?]. brs. MC.

6669   —Cutter of Coleman-Street. A comedy. *For Henry Herringman*, 1663. 4°. L, O, CK, LVD, DC; CH, MH, NN, TU, WF, Y.

6670   ——[Anr. ed.] *For Henry Herringman, to be sold by R. Bentley, J. Tonson, F. Saunders, and T. Bennet*, 1693. fol.* L; CLC, CN, MH, NP, TU, WF, Y.

6670A   —The learned and loyal Abraham Cowley's definition of a tyrant. *Printed*, 1688. brs. OP; MH, PFL.

        —Essay upon satyr. 1680. *See* title.

6671   —The foure ages of England. [*London*], *printed*, 1648. 8°. L, O; CH, MH, NPT, Y.

6672   ——[Anr. ed.] *By J. C. for Tho. Dring and Joh. Leigh*, 1675. 8°. L, O, GK; CLC, CN, MH, Y.

6673   —The guardian; a comedie. *For John Holden*, 1650. 4°.* L, O, C, LVF, EN; CH, CU, MH, WF, Y.

6673A   [–] An heroick poem upon the late horrid rebellion. *For T. D.*, 1683. 4°.* L, A.

6674   —The mistresse. *For Humphrey Moseley*, 1647. 8°. LT, O, C; CH, MH, TU, WCL, WF, Y.

6675   ——[Anr. ed.] *For Rowland Reynolds*, 1667. 8°. CH, IU, Y.

6676   Entry cancelled.

6677   —Ode, upon the blessed Restoration. *For Henry Herringman*, 1660. 4°.* LT, O, C, CT, E; CH, CU, MH, TU, WF, Y.

6678   —A. Covleii plantarum; libri duo. *Typis J. Flesher, apud Nath. Brooks*, 1662. 8°. L, O, CM, CT; CH, MH, NC, TU, WF, Y.

6679   —A poem on the late civil war. *Printed*, 1679. 4°.* T.C.I 359. L, O, C, CK, DT; CH, MH, TU, WF, Y.

6680   —Abrahami Couleij Angli, poemata Latina. *Typis T. Roycroft, impensis Jo. Martyn*, 1668. 8°. T.C.I 6. L, O, C, EN, DT; CH, CN, LC, MH, NU, TU, Y.

6681   ——Second edition. *Typis M. Clark, impensis Jo. Martyn*, 1678. 8°. T.C.I 336. L, O, CPE, LVD, AU; BN, CH, CN, MH, TU, WF, Y.

        —Poems of. Oxford, 1668. *See* King, William.

6682   —Poems: viz. *For Humphrey Moseley*, 1656. fol. L, O, C, GK; CH, CM, MH, TU, WCL, WF, Y.

6683   —The prologue and epilogue to a comedie, presented, . . . Cambridge. *For James Calvin*, 1642. 4°.* L, O, CK; CH, WF.

6684   —A proposition for the advancement of experimental philosophy. *By J. M. for Henry Herringman*, 1661. 8°. LT, O, C, EN, GK; CH, MH, WF, Y.

6685   —The Puritan and the Papist. *For W. Davis*, 1681/2. 4°.* L, O, EN, DT; CH, CN, NC, NU, TU, WF.

        —A satyre against Separatists. 1642. *See* Hausted, Peter.

6686-7 Entries cancelled.

6688   [–] A satyre. The Puritan and the Papist. [*Oxford, by H. Hall*], *printed*, 1643. 4°.* MADAN 1569. O; CH, Y.

6689   —Six books of plants. 1689. 4°. O; TU.

6690   —A song in Heroick love. [*London?* 1700.] brs. L.

6691   —Songs for one, two, and three voyces. [*Oxford, sold by T. Bowman, and H. Bonwicke, London*, 1677.] fol. T.C.I 319. L.

6692   —A translation of the sixth book of . . . plantarum. *For Samuel Walsall*, 1680. 4°. T.C.I 394. L, O; CH, CN, MH, TU, Y.

6693   —Verses lately written upon several occasions. *For Henry Herringman*, 1663. 8°. L, CT; CH, MB.

6694   —Verses, written upon several occasions. *For Henry Herringman*, 1663. 8°. O, SP, GK; CH, MH, TU, Y.

6695   [–] A vision, concerning His late pretended Highnesse Cromwell. *For Henry Herringman*, 1661. 12°. O, OC; CH, MIU, Y.

6696   —The visions and prophecies concerning England. *For Henry Herringman*, 1661. 12°. LT, O, P, A; CH, CLC, CN, Y.

6697   —Wit and loyalty reviv'd. *For W. Davis*, 1682. 4°. T.C.I 463. L, CT, OC, BAMB, HH; CH, NC, MIU, TU, WF, Y.

Cowling, Nicholas. *See* Couling, Nicholas.

Cowper, William. The anatomy of humane bodies. *Oxford, at the theater, for Sam. Smith and Benj. Walford, London*, 1698. fol. T.C.III 64. L, O, C, E, DT; BN, CH, CU, MH, WF, Y.

6699   —Harmony evangelical. *Hindley*, [1685.] brs. LG.

6700   —Μυοτομια reformata. *For Sam. Smith and Ben. Walford*, 1694. 8°. T.C.II 501. L, O, C, E, GH; CLC, CU, MU, PL, WF.

Cow-ragious castle-combat. 1645. *See* Gower, John.

Cox. *See also* Coxe.

[Cox, Daniel.] Discourse, wherein the interest. 1669. *See* Coxe, Thomas.

6701   C[ox], H. Lisarda: or the travels of love. *For Joseph Knight*, 1690. 8°. CLC, CN, Y.

6701A   **Cox, John.** Articles of Christian faith. *Printed*, 1689. 12°.* LF.

6701B   —An epistle to all the Lord's people. colop: *By Thomas Howkins*, 1685. cap., 4°.* LF.

6701C   —A general epistle to the Christian churches. [*London*], 1683. 4°.* LF.

[Cox, Nicholas.] Account of the late visitation. [*n.p.*, 1688.] *See* Mews, Peter.

6702   —The gentleman's recreation. *By E. Flesher, for Maurice Atkins, and Nicholas Cox*, 1674. 8°. L; CH, MH, WF, Y.

6703   [–] —Second edition. *By J. C. for N. C. to be sold by Tho: Fabian*, 1677. 8°. T.C.I 261. L, O, CS, MC, LWL; CLC, CN, MH, WF, Y.

6704   [–] —Third edition. *London* [*Oxford*], *by Freeman Collins, for Nicholas Cox*, 1686. 8°. T.C.II 152. L; CH, CN.

6705   [–] —"Third" edition. *Sold by Jos. Phillips and Hen. Rodes*, 1686. 8°. MH, WF, Y.

6706   [–] —Fourth edition. *By I. Dawks, for D. Browne; and N. Rolls*, 1697. 8°. L, O, C; NN, VC.

6707   [–] —"Fourth" edition. *By J. Dawks for N. Rolls*, 1697. 8°. CH, CLC, MH, WF, Y.

6707A   [–] —"Fourth" edition. *Printed and sold by I. Carruthers*, 1697. 8°. WU.

6708   [–] The gentleman's recreation. Third part. *By J. C. for N. C.*, [1677]. 8°. O; Y.

6709 [**Cox, Owen.**] The last and truest intelligence from Ireland: being. [*London*], *for A. Wildgoose, October 17.* 1642. 4°.* LT, O, C, EN; IU, Y.

6710 **Cox, Robert.** Actæon and Diana. *By T. Newcomb, for the use of the author Robert Cox,* [1655?]. 4°.* LT, O, OW, EN; CH, MH, WCL, WF.

6711 ——Second edition. *For Edward Archer,* 1656. 4°.* L, OW, EC; CH.

6711A **C[oxcombe], T.** The red-ribbond news from the army. *For M. S.,* 1647. 4°.* LT, O, DT; CLC, MH, WF, Y.

Coxe. See also Cox.

6712 **Coxe, Benjamin.** An after-reconing with Mr. Edwards. *By R. White, for Giles Calvert,* 1646. 4°.* C, LSC; Y.

6713 ——An appendix, to a confession of faith. *Printed,* 1646. 4°.* LT, O, CT, DT; NU, RBU.

6714 Entry cancelled.

6715 ——Some mistaken scriptvres. *By Tho. Paine,* 1646. 4°.* L.

6716 **Coxe, Nehemiah.** A believers triumph. *For Benjamin Alsop,* 1682. 12°. LCL, LSC; CLC, MH.

6717 ——A discourse of the covenants. [*London*], *by J. D. to be sold by Nathaniel Ponder; and Benjamin Alsop,* 1681. 8°. L, O, LW, RB, ENC; NHC, NPT, NU.

6718 ——A sermon preached at the ordination of an elder. *For Tho. Fabian,* 1681. 4°.* T.C.I 448. L, O, C, BAMB, ENC; CH, NHC.

6719 ——Vindiciæ veritatis; or a confutation. *For Nath. Ponder,* 1677. 4°. L, O, BB, MB.

6720 [**Coxe, Sir Richard.**] Aphorisms relating to the kingdom of Ireland. *For Joseph Watts,* 1689. 4°.* L, O, C, LVF, OC, DT; CH, CN, MH, WF, Y.

6721 [–] An essay for the conversion of the Irish. *Dublin, by Joseph Ray,* 1698. 8°.* T.C.III 119. DIX 303. C, RPL, EN, DM, DT; CH.

6722 ——Hibernia Anglicana. *By H. Clark, for Joseph Watts,* 1689. 2 pts. fol. T.C.II 286. L, O, C, EN, DT; BN, CH, CU, LC, MH, Y.

6723 ——Second edition. —, 1692. 2 pts. fol. T.C.II 385. L, O, CT; NP.

6724 [–] Some thoughts on the bill depending. *By J. Darby for Andr. Bell,* 1698. 4°.* L, LUG; CH, CU, MH, TU, WF, Y.

6725 [–] ——[Anr. ed.] *Dublin, by Joseph Ray,* 1698. 4°.* DIX 301. LUG, DI, DK, DN, DT; NC.

6725A ——Whereas the militia. [*Cork,* 1691.] brs. PL.

6726 **Coxe, Sem.** Two sermons . . . preached . . . March 2 & 9 1659. *Dublin, William Bladen,* 1660. 4°. DIX 109. LT.

6727 [**Coxe, Thomas.**] A discourse, wherein the interest of the patient . . . is soberly debated. *For Richard Chiswel,* 1669. 8°. T.C.I 2. L, O, C, AU, DT; CH, WSG, HC.

6728 [–] ——[Anr. ed.] *For C. R.,* 1669. 8°. LWL, CLC; NAM, WF, WSG.

6729 [–] Postscript of a letter written to the Bishop of London. [*Berne,* 1690.] brs. BN.

6730 ——The speech of. *For Richard Baldwin,* [1690.] brs. L, C, MC.

6731 Coy Celia's cruelty. [*London*], *for C. Bates,* [1685?]. brs. HH.

6732 The coy cook-maid. [*London*], *for P. Brooksby,* [1685–88]. brs. L, CM, HH, GU.

6733 ——[Anr. ed.] [*London*], *for E. Brooksby,* [1692?]. brs. L.

6734 Coy Jenny. [*London*], *for J. Deacon,* [1690?]. brs. L.

6734A Coy shepherdess. [*London,* 1670?] *See* P., J.

6734A [**Coyet, Petrus Julius.**] A remonstrance of his sacred royal majesty of Sweden. *By R. Wood for D. Pakeman,* 1659. 4°. LC, Y.

Cozen, John, *bp. See* Cosin, John, *bp.*

Cr., D. Several letters. 1700. *See* Crawford, David.

6735 [**Crab, Roger.**] Dagons-downfall. [*n.p.*], *printed,* 1657. 4°.* LT.

6736 ——The English hermite. *Printed,* 1655. 4°.* LT; CH.

6737 ——Gentle correction for the high-flown backslider. *By I. B.,* 1659. 4°.* CH.

6738 ——A tender salutation. *For I. B.,* 1659. 4°.* CH.

6738A **Crabb, John.** A testimony concerning the works of the living God. *For the author,* 1682. 4°.* LF.

6738B ——[Anr. ed.] *For the author, and are to be sold by John Gain,* 1682. 4°.* LF.

6738C Crack upon crack. [*London*], *for R. J.,* [1680.] cap., fol.* L, O, HH; MBA, TU, Y.

6739 **Crackanthorp, Richard.** Logicæ libri quinque. Second edition. *Typis & impensis Roberti Young,* 1641. 4°. L, O, CT, LW, NPL; CLC, CU, WF, Y.

6740 ————Third edition. *Oxoniæ, typis Lichfieldianis, impensis Johannis Williams* [*London*], 1670. 4°. MADAN 2852. O, LI, OC; CH, IU, MH, WF, Y.

6741 ————Fourth edition. *Oxoniæ, excudebat L. Lichfield & H. Hall, per Johannis Williams* [*London*], 1677. 4°. MADAN 3139. L, OME, CT, E, BQ; LC, NC, TU, Y.

6741A Crackfart & Tony: or, knave and fool. [*London*], *printed,* 1680. 4°.* IU, WF.

6742 **Cradock, Francis.** An expedient for taking away all impositions. *For Henry Seile,* 1660. 4°.* LT, O, CT, EN, DT; CH, CN, MH, NC, Y.

6743 ——Wealth discovered. *By E. C. for A. Seile,* 1661. 4°.* L, O, CM, OC, YM; CH, CU, MH, NC, WF, Y.

6743A [**Cradock, Peter.**] Papers of the treatie at a great meeting. [*London*], *for R. V.,* 1647. 4°.* LT, DT.

6744 **Cradock, Samuel.** The apostolical history. *By A. Maxwell, to be sold by Edward Brewster,* 1672. fol. T.C.I 115. L, O, C, NPL, E; LC, MBA, NU, Y.

6745 ——A brief and plain exposition . . . of the Revelation. *For T. Parkhurst, and J. Robinson,* 1696. 8°. T.C.II 586. L, O, C, CE, LCL; MH, NU, WF, Y.

6746 ——The chief principles of the Christian faith. *For William Grantham, Henry Mortlock and William Miller,* 1668. 4°.* NU.

6747 Entry cancelled.

6748 ——The harmony of the four evangelists. *For Samuel Thompson, and Francis Tyton,* 1668. fol. T.C.I 4. L, O, C, NPL, ES; MH, NPT, NU, WF, Y.

6749 ————[Anr. ed.] *For William Miller,* 1670. fol. ENC; NU, PPT, Y.

6750 ——The history of the Old Testament. *For Thomas Simmons,* 1683. fol. T.C.II 44. L, O, C, E, DT; CU, MBA, NF, NU.

6751 —Knowledge & practice. *By J. Hayes, for John Rothwell*, 1659. 8°. LT, O, LCL, BR, EN; CLC, MU, NPT, TU.

6752 ——[Anr. ed.] *For William Grantham and Will. Miller*, 1664. 8°. E.

6753 ——"Second" edition. —, 1665. 8°. NU, PPT.

6754 ——Third edition. *For William Grantham, Henry Mortlock, and William Miller*, 1673. 8°. T.C.I 143. L, OC, CE, RPL, EN; CH, CLC, NU, WF, Y.

6755 —Renati no possunt totaliter. [*Cambridge*, 1651.] brs. LT.

6756 —A supplement to knowledge and practice. *For Thomas Simmons*, 1679. 4°. T.C.I 357. LCL, LG, OC; CLC, IU, NPT, NU, WF, Y.

6757 **Cradock, Walter.** Divine drops distilled. *By R. W. for Rapha Harford*, 1650. 4°. LT, LCL, AN, CPL; MH, WF.

6758 ——[Anr. ed.] *By R. W. for George Whittington*, 1650. 4°. AN; IU, MH, NPT, NU, Y.

6759 —Glad tydings from Heaven. *By Matthew Simmons*, 1648. 4°. C, LCL, AN; MH, NU.

6760 —Gospel-holinesse. *By M. Simmons, sold by Joseph Blaiklock*, 1651. 8°. L, DC, CPL, AN; MH, NU, PJB.

6761 ——[Anr. ed.] *By M. Simmons, and sold by Hanna Allen*, 1651. 4°. DC; MH, NU.

6762 —Gospel-libertie. *By Matthew Simmons. for Henry Overton*, 1648. 4°. LT, C, LCL, LW, AN; MH, NPT, NU, WF.

6763 —Mount Sion. *Printed*, 1651. 4°. LCL, AN.

6764 —The saints fulnesse of joy. *By Matthew Simmons, for Hannah Allen*, 1646. 4°.* MADAN 1900. L, O, C, EN, DT; CH, NU, WF, Y.

6765 ——[Anr. ed.] *By Matthew Simmons, and are to be sold by George VVhittington*, 1646. 4°.* LT, OCC, CM, LW, AN; CH, MBA, MH, NU, Y.

6766 **Cradock, Zachary.** A sermon preached . . . February 10th 1677. *For Richard Royston*, 1678. 4°.* T.C.I 310. L, O, C, LGI, DT; CH, MIU, NU, PL.

6767 ——Second edition. —, 1678. 4°.* L, O, C, CT, DT; CN, MH, NU, TU, WF, Y.

6768 ——Third edition. —, 1683. 4°.* L, C, LG, OC, OM; NU, RBU.

6769 ——Fourth edition. *For L. Meredith*, 1693. 4°.* T.C.II 433. L, O, C, BAMB; TSM

6770 ——Fifth edition. —, 1695. 4°.* T.C.II 574. L, C, OC, EC, CS; CLC, IU, LC, Y.

6770A [**Crafford, John.**] A new and most exact account of . . . Carolina. *Dublin, for Nathan Tarrant*, 1683. 4°.* NC, NN.

6770B **Craford, Thomas.** Theses. *Edinburgh, heirs of R. Bryson*, 1646. brs. ALDIS 1241. E.

Crafts-mens craft. 1649. *See* B., H.

6770C The crafty barber of Deptford. *For John Clark Junior*, [1685–88.] brs. MH.

6771 The crafty country woman. *For J. Shearer*, [1670?] fol. L.

6772 Craftie Cromwell. [*London*], *printed*, 1648. 4°.* LT, O, C, LVD, OW; CH, MH, Y.

6773 Crafty Kate of Cholchester. [*n.p.*, 1688–95.] brs. HH.

6774 The crafty lady. *For E. Vize*, 1683. 8°. T.C.II 4. L.

6775 The crafty lass of the West. [*London*], *for P. Brooksby, J. Deacon, J. Blare, J. Back*, [1688–92]. brs. HH; MH.

6776 The crafty maid. [*London*], *for P. Brooksby*, [1672–95]. brs. L, O, HH; MH.

Crafty maid of the West. 1672–80. *See* Wade, John.

6777 Entry cancelled.

6778 The crafty maid's approbation. [*London*], *by and for W. O. A. M. and sold by C. Bates*, [1685]. brs. L, O, HH, GU.

6779 The crafty miss. [*London*], *for J. Deacon*, [1684]. brs. L, O, CM, HH.

6780 The crafty whore: or, the mistery and iniquity of bawdy houses. *For Henry Marsh*, 1658. 8°. LT.

6781 The crafty young-man. [1690?] brs. O.

6782 **Cragg, John.** The arraignment, and conviction of Anabaptism. *By T. W. for H. Twyford, N. Brooks, Tho. Dring, J. Place*, 1656. 8°. O, LW, BB, LB, CPL; CLC, CN, NHC, NPT, NU, WF.

6783 —A cabinet of spirituall iewells. *By W. W. for H. Twyford, N. Brooks, T. Dring, J. Place*, 1657. 8°. C, LSC, CPL; CH, MH, NU, WF, Y.

6784 —Englands congratulatorie entertainment. [*London*, 1641.] brs. LT.

6785 —Great Britains prayers. [*London*], *printed*, 1641. 4°.* LT; CH, MH, WF, Y.

6786 —The King's supremacy. *Printed*, 1661. 8°.* LT; Y.

6787 —The light of Gods countenance. *By J. G. for Nath. Webb and Will: Grantham*, 1654. 4°.* L, LSC, AN, CPL.

6788 —A prophecy concerning the Earle of Essex. [*London*], *for John Crag*, 1641. 4°.* LT, SS; CH, WF, Y.

6789 Entry cancelled.

6790 —The royal prerogative vindicated. *By T. R. for H. Twyford, N. Brooke, Tho. Dring, and John Place*, 1661. 8°. LT, O, CS, LCL, CPL; LC, NU, Y.

6791 **Craghead, Robert.** Advice to communicants. *Edinburgh, for William Dickie in Glasgow*, 1695. sixes. ALDIS 3452. L.

6792 ——Second edition. *Glasgow, Robert Sanders*, 1698. sixes. E; LC.

6793 —An answer to a late book, intituled A discourse. *Edinburgh, by the heirs of Andrew Anderson*, 1694. 4°. ALDIS 3366. O, EN, GU, DT, FSF; MHS, PU, WF.

6793A —An answer to the Bishop of Derry's Second admonition. [*Belfast*, 1697.] 4°. BLH, DMA.

6794 [–] A modest apology occasioned. *Glasgow, for the author*, 1696. 8°. ALDIS 3583. EN, GU.

6795 **Cragmile, William.** The King's Bench prisoners thanks to His Majesty. *Printed for and sold by Peter Lillicrap*, 1672. brs. L.

6796 **Craig, John.** An act published by the General Assembly of Scotland. *First printed at Edinburgh by R. VV. and now reprinted at London by B. Alsop and are to be sold by Henry Walker*, 1641. 4°.* EU.

6797 —Methodus figuraram lineis. *Impensis Mosis Pitt*, 1685. 4°.* L, O, C, E, DT; BN, MB, MH, NN, WF.

6798 —Theologiæ Christianæ principia. *Typis Johannis Darby, & impensis Timothei Child*, 1699. 4°.* T.C.III 125. L, C, OM, EN, DT; BN, MBA, MH, NC, NN, WF.

6799 —Tractatus mathematicus. *Prostant apud Sam Smith & Benj. Walford*, 1693. 4°. T.C.II 465. L, O, C, E, EN; BN, CSU, NN, OCI, WF.

6799A **Craig, Mungo.** A lye is no scandal. [*Edinburgh?* 1697.] cap., 8°.* EN.

6800 —A satyr against atheistical deism. *Edinburgh, for Robert Hutchison*, 1696. 4°.* ALDIS 3550. L, EN; CN, MH.

6801 **Craig, Sir Thomas.** Jus feudale tribus libris. *Edingurgi* [sic], *impressum*, 1655. fol. ALDIS 1507. L, O, E, AU, GU; CH, NN, WF, YL.

6802 ——[Anr. ed.] *Impensis societatis stationariorum*, 1655. fol. ALDIS 1508. L, O, CS, EN, DT; BN, CH, LC, MHL, MIU, PU.

6803 ——[Anr. ed.] 1665. fol. ES.

6804 —Scotland's soveraignty. *For Andrew Bell, sold in Edinburgh by T. Brown, A. Henderson, G. Mosman, J. Valens, J. Mackey, Mrs. Ongstone, R. Allen*, 1695. 8°. ALDIS 3453. L, O, C, EN, DT; BN, CH, CLC, MBA, WF, Y.

6804A ——Second edition. *For Andrew Bell*, 1698. 8°. CN, NC.

6805 **Crake, Francis.** A congratulatory poem upon the coronation of William and Mary. colop: *Printed and are to be sold by Randall Taylor*, 1689. fol.* C; CH, Y.

6806 **Crandon, John.** Mr. Baxter's aphorisms exorized. *By Math: Simmons*, 1654. 4°. O, C, OB, LCL, ENC; CH, MH, NU.

6807 ——[Anr. ed.] *By M. S. to be sold by T: Brewster: and L: Chapman*, 1654. 4°. LT, OCC, OM, CS, CT; CH, NPT, PJB.

6808 **Crane, Richard.** An appeal for judgment. *Printed at London*, 1664. brs. LF, BBN; CH, MH, PH.

6809 —The cry of Nevvgate. *Printed*, 1662. 4°.* L, O, C, LF, BBN; CH, MH, PH, WF, Y.

6810 —A few plain words to the officers of the army. *For Thomas Simmons*, 1659. 4°.* O, LF; PH.

6811 [–] A fore-warning and a word. *For Thomas Simmons*, 1660. 4°.* L, O, C, LF, BBN; CH, MH, NU, PH, Y.

6812 —God's holy name magnified. [*London*], printed, 1665. 4°.* L, O, C, OC, BBN; CH, IE, PHS, PSC, Y.

6812A —God's zeal thundered forth. [*London*], printed, 1665. brs. LF; PH.

6813 —A hue and cry after bloodshed. *Printed*, 1662. brs. LF; CH, PH.

6814 —A lamentation over thee, O London. *Printed*, 1665. 4°. L, LF, BBN, EN; MH, PH, PSC, WF, Y.

6815 —A short, but a strict account. *For Thomas Simmons*, 1660. 4°.* L, C, LF, CT, BBN; CLC, MH, NU, PH, PSC, Y.

6816 —Something spoken in vindication. [1660.] brs. L, LF, DT; LC, PH.

6817 —To all you Protestant persecutors. [*London*, 166–?] brs. LF; CH.

6818 **C[rane], T[homas].** Isagoge ad Dei providentiam: or, a prospect. *By A. Maxwell for Edward Brewster*, 1672. 8°. T.C.I 110. L, O, C, LCL, BAMB; CH, NPT, NU, WF, Y.

6819 —Job's assurance of the resurrection. *For Philip Burton in Warrington*, 1690. 4°.* T.C.II 356. L, O, CT; CLC, NU, WF, Y.

6820 Entry cancelled.
[–] Confutation of the Anabaptists. 1644. *See* Bakewell, Thomas.

6821 —The disputes between. *By Gartrude Dawson, to be sold by Gyles Calvert*, 1652. 4°.* LT, O; NHC.

6822 —Four qveries resolved. *For John Hancock*, 1645. 4°.* YM; MH.

6823 —Hæreseo-machia; or, the mischiefe. *By James Young for Charles Green*, 1646. 4°. LT, O, CS, EN, DT; CH, CN, MH, NU, WF, Y.

6824 [–] The teares of Ireland. *By A. N., for Iohn Rothwell*, 1642. 8°. L, O, CT, OC, DT; WF.

6825 —A vindication of a printed paper, entituled, An ordinance. 1646. 8°. E.

6826 **Cranmer, George.** Concerning the nevv chvrch discipline. [*Oxford*], *printed*, 1642. 4°.* MADAN 996. LT, O, C, EN, DT; CH, MH, NU, WF, Y.

6826A —[Anr. ed.] *Oxford*, 1645. 4°.* CH.

6827 **Cranmer, Thomas, abp.** The judgment of. *For John Taylor*, 1689. 4°.* T.C.II 244. L, O, C, EN, DT; MH, NU, PL, WF, Y.

6828 [–] Reformatio legum. *Impensis societatis stationariorum*, 1641. 4°. L, C, LIL, OB, E; BN, MHL, WF, Y.

6829 **Cranwell, Luke.** The holding the bishop. *By A. M. for John Sherley*, 1661. 4°.* LT, ENC.

6830 **C[rashaw], R[ichard].** Carmen Deo nostro, . . . sacred poems. *At Paris, by Peter Targa*, 1652. 4°. LT, O; CH, LC, MH, NPT, WCL, Y.

6831 —The delights of the muses. *By T. W. for H. Moseley*, 1648. 12°. LT, O, OC; MH, NPT, PL, TU, WF, Y.

6832 —Epigrammata sacra selecta . . . Sacred epigrams Englished. *For John Barksdale*, 1682. 8°.* CH.

6833 —A letter from. [1653.] 4°.* LT.

6834 —Richardi Crashawi poemata et epigrammata. Second edition. *Cantabrigiae, ex officina Joan. Hayes*, 1670. 8° LT, O, C, CT, AU; CH, CN, MH, TU, WF, Y.

6835 ——Second edition. *Cantabrigiae, ex officina Joan Hayes*, 1674. 8°. L, C, OM, CPE, GK; BN, CH, NPT, TU, WC.

6836 —Steps to the temple. Sacred poems. *By T. W. for Humphrey Moseley*, 1646. 12°. LT, O, CP, CS, CT; CH, LC, TU, WC, Y.

6837 ——Second edition. *For Humphrey Moseley*, 1648. 12°. LT, O, C, CT, DC; BN, CH, CN, WCL, WF, Y.

6838 ——Third edition. *In the Savoy, by T. N. for Henry Herringman*, 1670. 12°. L, O, OC, OM, CP; CH, CN, MH, NP, WF, Y.

6839 ——"Second" [i.e. fourth] edition. —, 1670. 8°. T.C.I 24. L, O, C, OME, GK; CH, CLC, CN, WC, WF.

6840 ——"Third" edition. *For Richard Bentley, Jacob Tonson, Francis Saunders, and Tho. Bennet*, [1680.] 8°. CH, Y.

6841 **C[rashaw], W[illiam].** The bespotted Iesvite. *Imprinted at London by Bar: Alsop*, 1641[2]. 4°. LT, CS, YM, EN; CH, NU, Y.

6842 Entry cancelled.

6843 —Decimarum & oblationum tabula. A tything table. *By J. T. for Andrew Crook*, 1658. 4°.* L, O, C, CT, EN; CH, MH, NP.

6844 ——[Anr. ed.] —, 1662. 4°.* L, C, LL, OC, YM; MB, MH, MIU, Y.

6845 ——[Anr. ed.] *For Andrew Crook, 1665.* 12°.* L, O, CS, EN, DT; MH, NC, NU, WF.

6846 ——[Anr. ed.] —, *1671.* 4°.* L, C, CCH, LG, LL; CU, MH, NU, WF, Y.

6847 ——[Anr. ed.] —, *1673.* 4°.* L.

6848 ——[Anr. ed.] *For R. Scot, T. Basset, J. Wright, R. Chiswell, 1676.* 4°.* L, O, C, CT, LIL; LC, MH, WF.

6849 ——[Anr. ed.] —, *1683.* 4°.* L, O, C, CS, CT; NC, TU, WF.

6850 [–] Loyola's disloyalty. *By B.A., 1643. Iuly the 4.* 4°. L, LCL, LSC; CH.

6851 **Crasset, Jean.** A new form of meditations. *Printed, 1685.* 8°. L, OC; CN.

6851A ——[Anr. ed.] *For William Grantham, 1685.* 8°. TU.
Crauford. *See also* Crawford; Crawfurd.

6851B [**Crauford, James.**] An abstract of some late characters. *For James Crumpe, 1643.* 4°.* LT, O, YM, E, EN; CH, CU, IU, NU, WF.

6852 —Against vniversal libertie of conscience. *Printed at London for Thomas Vnderhill, 1644.* 4°.* BC.

6853 [–] The history of the house of Esté. *By J. M. for Rich. Chiswell, 1681.* 8°. T.C.I 461. L, C, CT, EN, DT; CH, CN, MBA, PL, WF, Y.

6854 **Crauford, Matthew.** Exercitatio apologetica. [*n.p.*], *1669.* 4°. ENC.

6855 **Craufurd, Thomas.** Amplissimis viris . . . J. Smith. *Edinburgi, by the heirs of R. Bryson, 1646.* brs. ALDIS 1241. E.

6856 —Amplissimis viris . . . J. Stuarto. *Edinburgi, Lithgow, 1650.* brs. ALDIS 1433. E.

6857 —Locorum . . . explicatio. *Edinburgi, impensis D. Trencii, 1664.* 8°. ALDIS 1771. EN.

6858 ——[Anr. ed.] —, *1665.* 8°. ALDIS 1788. L, EN.

6859 —Nobiliss. . . . J. Lauduni. *Edinburgi, R Bryson, 1642.* brs. ALDIS 1066. E.

6860 **Craven, Francis.** Æternalia, or a treatise. *By H. Brugis for R. Northcott, 1677.* 8°. T.C.I 272. L, C, LCL, P; NPT, Y.

6861 —The souls heavenly manna. *For Rich. Northcott, 1679.* 8°. L.

6862 **Craven, Isaac.** The new paradise. *For J. Rothwell, 1658.* 4°.* L, LSC, O; MH, NU, Y.
Crawford. *See also* Craufurd, Crawfurd.
Crawford, earl of. *See* Lindsay, John Lindsay, *17th earl of Crawford, and 1st earl of.*

6863 **Crawford, David.** Courtship a-la-mode. *For J. Barnes and E. Rumbal, 1700.* 4°. L, O, CT, LVD, EN; CH, MH, NC, TU, WF, Y.

6863A —Several letters: containing the amours. *For Job Austin, 1700.* L; CU.
Crawford, Henry. Vox uraniæ. *1676. See* Almanacs.

6864 **Crawford, Laurence.** Irelands ingratitude to the Parliament. *By E. Griffin, 1643[4].* 4°.* LT, C, LVF, OC, HH; CH, MH, NU, WU, Y.
Crawford, William, earl of. *See* Lindsay, William Crawford, *earl of.*
Crawfurd. *See also* Crauford, Crawford.

6865 [**Crawfurd, James.**] A serious expostulation with that party in Scotland. *By J. D. for Richard Chiswell, 1682.* 4°. T.C.I 497. L, O, C, HH, EN; CH, MIU, NU, WF, Y.
Crawshaw, John. *See* Crowshey, John.
Crawshay, John. *See* Crowshey, John.

6865A **Crayford, Robert.** The Christian faith. *For J. Wyat, & T. Norman, 1698.* 8°. CT.

6866 **Creagh, Sir William.** To the right honourable and honourable Lords commissioners. *1684.* 4°.* NC.

6867 [**Creamer, Charles.**] A journey into the country. *For Henry Brome, 1675.* 4°.* T.C.I 205. L, O, C, CT, NPL; CH, CLC, MIU, WF, Y.

6868 **Creamer, Thomas.** A gun-powder-plot in Ireland. *For John Thomas, 1641.* 4°.* LT, C; MH, Y.

6869 The creation of the world. Being the first chapter of Genesis. *By John Hammond, 1646.* brs. LT; MH.

6870 Credible intelligence concerning Captaine Tuthill. [*London*], *by Jane Coe, 1645.* brs. LT.

6871 The credulous virgins complaint. [*London*], *for P. Brooksby*, [1672–95]. brs. L, HH; MH.

6872 **Creech, Thomas.** Catalogue of the library. *Oxford, 20 November, 1700.* 4°. L, O, OC.

6873 **Creed, William.** Judah's purging. *For R. Royston, to be sold by John Courtney in Sarum,* [1660]. 4°.* L, O, CK; WF, Y.

6874 —Judah's return to their allegiance. *By J. C. for Timothy Garthwait, 1660.* 4°.* LT, O, LL; NU.

6875 —The refuter refuted. *For R. Royston, 1660.* 4°. LT, O, CS, E, DT; CLC, MB, NU.
Creed-forgers. *1700. See* Field, John.
Creed of Mr. Hobbes. *1670. See* Tenison, Thomas, *abp.*
Creed of Pope Pius the IV. *1687. See* Altham, Michael.

6876 **Creighton, Robert.** The vanity of the Dissenters plea. *By J. Wallis, for Benj. Tooke, 1682.* 4°.* T.C.I 502. L, O, CS, LW, OCC; CH, NU, PL, WF, Y.

6877 [**Crell, Johann.**] The expiation of a sinner. *By Tho. Harper, and are to be sold by Charles Greene, 1646.* fol. L, O, C, E, DT; CH, NU, V, Y.

6878 [–] The justification of a sinner. *By T. H., 1650.* fol. L, C, OC, P, E; CLC, NU.

6879 [–] A learned and exceeding well-compiled vindication of liberty of religion. [*n.p.*], *printed, 1646.* 8°. LT, C, CT; MBA, NU.

6880 —The two books of. *Printed in Kosmoburg* [*London*], *1665.* 8°. L, O, LCL, LW, EN; CH, CU, MH, NU, PL, WF, Y.

6881 —The unity of God. *Printed, 1691.* 8°. L; NU, WF, Y.

6882 Entry cancelled.

6883 **Creshald, Richard.** A legacy left to the world. *Printed, 1658.* 4°.* L, C, LL, LUG, HH; CLC, MH, MHL, WF, YL.

6884 **Cress, William.** A true copy of the papers that were delivered by. colop: *By Jer. Wilkins,* [1699]. brs. L, CM; CLC.

6885 **Cressener, A.** The vindication of A. Cressener. *For Ric. Chiswell, 1687.* 4°.* T.C.II 270. L, O, C, EN, DT; CH, NU, TU, WF, Y.

6886 **Cressener, Drue.** A demonstration of the first principles. *For Thomas Cockerill,* 1690. 4°. T.C.II 312. L, O, CT, E, DT; NU, WCL, WF.

6887 —The judgments of God. *For Richard Chiswell,* 1689. 4°. T.C.II 248. L, O, C, E, DT; CH, MU, NU, WF, Y.

6888 **Cressener, Robert.** Anti-Baal-Berith justified. *By Tho. Johnson, and are to be sold by Fr. Kirkman, and Hen. Marsh,* 1662. 4°. CH.

6889 **C[ressett], J[ohn].** A copy of a printed letter from. [*London,* 1672.] fol.* L, HH.

6889A **[Cressy, Edmund.]** Captivity improved. *By I. Redmayne,* 1675. 8°. LSC, LW; Y.

6889B [–] Spiritual directions. *By J. Redmayne,* 1676. 8°. L, LSC, YM.

6890 **Cressy, Hugh Paulin.** The church-history of Brittany. [*Rouen*], *printed,* 1668. fol. L, O, C, EN, DT; BN, CH, CU, MH, NU, WF, Y.

6891 —A collection of several treatises in answer to Dr. Stillingfleet. [*n.p.*], 1672. 8°. O, LIL, CS; CN, NU, WF, WG, Y.

6892 [–] Dr. Stillingfleets principles. *Printed at Paris, by the widow of Antonie Christian, and Charles Guillery,* 1671. 8°. L, O, C, LIL; CH, NU, TU, WG, Y.

6893 —The epistle apologetical of S. C. [*London*], *an. Dom.,* 1674. 8°. L, O, LIL, OCC, DT; CLC, CN, NU.

6894 —Exomologesis. *Printed at Paris,* 1647. 12°. L, O, C, DC, YM, EN; BN, CH, MH, NU, WF, Y.

6895 — —Second edition. *Paris, chez Jean Billaine,* 1653. 12°. L, O, OM, CT, DT; BN, CLC, CN, LC, TU, Y.

6896 — —[Anr. ed.] —, 1659. 12°. LC.

6897 Entry cancelled.

6898 —Fanaticism fanatically imputed. [*Douay?*], 1672. 8°. L, O, C, E; BN, CH, CN, NU, TU, WG, Y.

6899 —A non est inventus return'd. [*n.p.*], 1662. 8°. L, O, CS, OC, P; BN, CLC, CN, TU, WF.

6900 —I. Question. Why are you a Catholic? *Printed,* 1686. 4°. L, O, CT, MC, DT; CH, CN, MH, TU, WF, Y.

6901 [–] Reflexions upon the oathes. [*n.p.*], *Printed* 1661. 8°. L, O; CN, NU, WF.

6901A — —[Anr. ed.] [*Douay?* 1690?] 8°. L, LIL, BSM; CN.

6902 —Roman-Catholick doctrines no novelties. [*n.p.*], 1663 [sic]. 8°. L, O, CT, LIL, EN; BN, CH, CU, NU, TU, WG, Y.

6903 —XVI revelations of divine love. *Printed,* 1670. 8°. L, O, CT; NGT, WF.

6904 Entry cancelled.

Creswell, lady, pseud.

6905 Crete wonders foretold. [*London*], *printed,* 1647. 4°.* LT, AN.

6906 **Crew, Isaac.** A speech spoken by. colop: *By Fr. Leach,* 1697. brs. L, LG, MC, EN; Y.

6907 — —[Anr. ed.] *By G. G.,* 1697. brs. PL.

Crew of kind London gossips. 1663. *See* Rowlands, Samuel.

6908 **Crewe, Nathanael, bp.** To the Kings most excellent Majesty the most humble and faithful advice of. [*London,* 1688?] brs. L, C, OC, HH, EN; CH, CN, TU, WF, Y.

6909 —To the reverend the clergy of . . . Durham. [*London,* 1699.] brs. O.

6910 The cryes of England to the Parliament. *For Tho. Vnderhill,* 1653. 4°.* LT; NU.

6911 The cryes of Westminster. [*London,* 1648.] fol.* LT, O; CH.

6912 Crimineel proces, in cas van Hoogverraad. *Gedrukt tot Edenburg in Schotland, by James Warner,* 1688. 4°.* ALDIS 2753. L, O, LL, CT; MIU, NN, WF, Y.

6913 **Crimsal, Richard.** Cupid's soliciter of love. *By Tho. Haly, for Fra. Coles,* 1680. 8°.* O.

6913A — —[Anr. ed.] [*London*], *by J. M. for W. Thackeray, and are to be sold by J. Back,* [1685.] 12°. CM.

6913B The cripples race. [*London?* 1680.] brs. CM.

6914 **[Crisp, Henry.]** Sad news from the county of Kent. *Richard Harper,* 1657. 4°. LT.

6915 **Crisp, Sir Nicholas.** To the right honourable the Commons . . . the humble petition of. [*London,* 1660.] brs. LT.

6916 **C[risp], S[amuel].** Christ alone exalted. *For W. Marshall & H. Barnard,* 1693. 8°. T.C.II 450. L, O, LCL, GU, DT; MH, NU.

6917 [–] Christ exalted, and Dr. Crisp vindicated. *For the author; to be had at Mr. John Marshall's,* 1698. 8°. T.C.III 133. LCL, LW; NU.

6918 [–] Christ made sin. *By J. A. for the author, a son of . . . Tobias Crisp,* 1691. 4°. L, O, CSSX, LG, GU; NU.

6919 —A sermon preach'd . . . 23d of April, 1686. *For Robert Clavell,* 1686. 4°. T.C.II 175. O, C, CT, WCA; NU, WF.

6920 **Crisp, Stephen.** [Works.] A memorable account of the Christian experiences. *Printed and sold by T. Sowle,* 1694. 4°. L, O, E, LF; CH, CN, LC, MH, NU, PH, Y.

6921 —Addresse charitable aux Francois refugiez. *Imprime,* 1688. 4°.* BBN; WF.

6922 —An alarum sounded. [*London*], *printed,* 1671. 4°.* L, CT, LF; CH, MH, PH, PL, Y.

6923 — —[Anr. ed.] —, 1672. 4°.* L, O, C, LF; MH, NU, PSC, WF, Y.

6923A — —"Second" edition. *For T. Northcott,* 1691. 8°. C, LF, LSC.

6924 —A Babylonish opposer of truth. *For Benjamin Clark,* 1681. 4°.* LF, BBN; CH, PH, WF.

6925 —A back-slider reproved. [*London*], *printed,* 1669. 4°.* L, O, LF, BBN; CH, MH, PH, PSC.

6926 —Charitable advice. *By G.L.,* 1688. 4°.* L, O, LF, OC, EN.

6926A —Christ all in all. [*London*], 1700. 12°. LF, BBN.

6927 —Dear and truely beloved in the everlasting seed. 1670. cap., 4°.* LF; CH, PH.

6928 —A description of the Church of Scotland. [*London*], *for M. W.,* 1660. 4°. O, LF; PH, PSC.

6928A —An epistle of tender counsel. [*London*], 1680. 8°.* LF, BBN; PH, PSC.

6929 —An epistle of tender love. [*London*], *printed and sold by A. Sowle,* 1690. 4°. L, O, LF, BBN; CH, MH, PH, Y.

6930 — —[Anr. ed.] *Re-printed and sold by William Bradford at Philadelphia,* 1692. 4°.* EVANS 591. PHS.

6931 —An epistle to Friends. *Printed,* 1666. 4°.* L, O, LF; CH, MH, PH, WF, Y.

6931A — —Second edition. —, 1666. 4°.* LF; CH.

6931B ——Third edition. [*London*], *printed 1666 and re-printed,* 1669. [*i.e.,* 1679.] 4°.* O, LF.

6932 ——"Third" edition. [*London*], *printed 1666, and re-printed,* 1679. 4°. O, LF; PH, PSC.

6933 ——[Anr. ed.] *By Andrew Sowle,* 1683. 4°.* L; BN.

6934 ——Fourth edition. [*London*], *printed 1666, and re-printed,* 1689. 8°. O, LF.

6934A ——"Fourth" edition. *Printed,* 1666, *and re-printed for Thomas Northcott,* 1690. 8°. LF.

6935 [–] An epistle to the monthly, and quarterly meetings of Friends. [*London,* 1692.] brs. L, LF, BBN; PHS.

6936 —A faithful warning and exhortation to Friends. *By John Bringhurst,* 1684. 4°.* L, O, LF, BBN; CH, MH, MU, PH, Y.

6936A ——[Anr. ed.] *Reprinted and sold by William Bradford, at Philadelphia,* 1692. 4°.* EVANS 592. PHS.

6936B —A lamentation over the city of Groninghen. [*London*], 1669. 4°.* PH.

6936C —A new book for children to learn in. 1681. 12°. L.

6937 —A plain path-way opened. [*London*], *printed,* 1668. 4°.* L, LF; CH, MH, PH, PSC, WF, Y.

6938 ——[Anr. ed.] [*London,* 1668]. 4°.* L; MH, PH, PSC, Y.

6939 —The second volume of the sermons. *For Nath. Crouch,* 1693. 8°. L, O, LF; CLC, PH.

6940 ——Second edition. *Printed,* 1697. 8°. LF; NU, PH, PSC.

6941 —Several sermons or declarations of. *For Nath. Crouch,* 1693. 3 v. 12°. T.C.II 506. L, LF; WF.

6941A ——[Anr. ed.] —, 1694. 12°. CLC.

6942 ——Second edition. *For Tho. Northcott,* 1696. 12°. LF; IE, MH, NU, PH, PSC.

6943 —The third and last volume of the sermons of. *For Nath. Crouch,* 1694. 12°. T.C.II 518. L, LF; NU, PSC, WF.
—A warning against the deceit. [*London*], 1677. *See* Frankenburgh, Abraham van.

6944 —De weg tot het koningryk. The way to the kingdom. *t'Amsterdam, buy de wed' van Steven Swart,* 1695. 8°. LF; MH.

6945 —A word in due season. [*London*], 1666. brs. L, LF; PH.

6946 —A word of reproof. *For Thomas Simmons,* 1658. 4°.* L, LF, BBN; MH, PH, Y.

6947 C[risp], T[homas]. Animadversions on George White-head's book. *For John Dunton,* 1694. 4°.* O, C, LF, BBN, GU; CH, MH, PSC, PU, Y.

6948 —Babel's builders. *Printed,* 1681. 4°.* L, O, LF, BBN.

6948A —The counterfeit discovered. [*London,* 1694.] cap., 4°. OC.

6949 —The discovery of the accursed thing. colop: *Printed and are to be sold by John Gwillam,* 1695. cap., 4°.* L, O, CJ, LF, OC; CH, LC, MU.

6950 [–] An essay towards the allaying of George Fox his spirit. colop: *For T. C. and sold by John Gwillim,* 1695. 4°.* L, O, C, LF, BBN; MU, NU, PH, PSC, WF.

6951 —The first part of Babel's-builders unmasking themselves. *Printed, and are to be sold by Enock Prosser,* 1682. 4°.* O, C, LF, CK, CT; NU, PH, PSC, WF, Y.

6952 [–] A just and lawful tryal of the Foxonian chief priests. *For the author; and are to be sold by B. Aylmer,* 1697. 8°. L, O, LF, OC; NU, PSC, RPJ.

6952A The man of sin discovered. [*London?* 1682.] cap., 4°. LSC, OC, CT.

6953 [–] The second part of Babel's-builders. [*n.p.,* 1683?] cap., 4°.* LF, CS; NN, NU.

6953A —The sixth part of Babel's-builders unmaskt. [*London?* 168–.] cap., 4°.* CJ; PH, PSC, Y.

6954 [–] Some considerations (concerning the Quakers). colop: *Printed, and are to be sold by C. Brome,* [1698?]. 4°.* L, LF, OC, CT, BBN; NU, PH, PSC.

6954A [–] The third part of Babel's-builders. Second edition. [*London?* 1682.] 4°.* CJ; MH, PH, PSC.

6955 **Crisp, Tobias.** Christ alone exalted. *By Richard Bishop, at the charge of M. C.,* 1643. 8°. LT, C, CE; MH, NU, Y.

6956 ——[Anr. ed.] 1644. 2 v. 8°. OC, CPE, DC, SC.

6957 ——[Anr. ed.] *For William Marshal,* 1690. 4°. T.C.II 326. L, LCL, LG, LW, DT; MBC, NPT, NU, PL.

6958 ——, Vol. II. [*London*], *printed,* 1643. 8°. LT, CM; NU.

6959 ——, Vol. III. *By M. S. for Henry Overton,* 1648. 8°. LT, CM; NU.

6960 Crispianism unmask'd. *For Richard Baldwin,* 1693. 4°. T.C.II 451. L, O, CT, EN, GU; CLC, CN, NU, Y.

Critica juris. 1661. *See* Plowden, Edmund.

Critical enquiries. 1684. *See* Simon, Richard.

Critical notes on some passages of scripture. 1647. *See* Mann, Nicholas.

Critical scene. 1660. *See* Pearson, John, *ed.*

6960A Critical remarks upon the Adventures of Telemaches. *For H. Rhodes and A. Bell,* 1700. 12°. WF.

6961 [**Crockat, Gilbert**]. The Scotch Presbyterian eloquence. *For Randal Taylor,* 1692. 4°. T.C.II 413. L, O, CT, ENC, GH; CH, NR, NU, Y.

6962 [–] ——Second edition. —, 1693. 4°. L, O, YM, ES; CH, MH, NN, WF, Y.

6963 [–] ——"Second" edition, with additions. —, 1694. 4°. L, OC, CT, EN, DT; CH, CN, MH, NU, WF.

6964 **Crodacott, John.** The vanity and mischief. [*London*], *for A. Kemb, in Southwark,* 1655. 4°. LT, YM, DT; CH, MWA, WF.

6965 **Croese, Gerard.** The general history of the Quakers. *For John Dunton,* 1696. 8°. L, O, CT, EN, DT; CH, CN, MH, NU, PH, WF, Y.

6966 **Croft, Herbert, bp.** The legacy of. *For Charles Harper,* 1679. 4°. T.C.I 339. L, O, C, E, DT; CH, MBA, NU, WF, Y.

6967 ——Second edition. —, 1679. 4°. L, O, C, LIL; CH, CN, NU.

6968 [–] A letter written to a friend concerning Popish idolatrie. *Printed for, and are to be sold by Charles Harper,* 1674. 4°.* T.C.I 189. L, C, OC, BR, P; CH, NC, TU.

6969 ——[Anr. ed.] *For Charles Harper,* 1679. 4°.* T.C.I 340. L, LL, OM, CS, ENC; CN, MH, NU, WF, Y.

6970 [–] The naked truth. [*London*], *printed,* 1675. 4°. L, O, C, EN, DT; BN, CH, CU, MH, NU, WF, Y.

6971 [–] ——Second edition. —, 1680. fol. L, O, CS, BR, HH; CH, CN, WCL, WF, Y.

6972 — —[Anr. ed.] *Printed, and are to be sold by Richard Janeway*, 1689. 4°. O, AU; CH, CN, NU, TU, WF.

6973 —A second call to a farther humiliation. *For Charles Harper*, 1678. 4°. T.C.I 326. L, O, C, LL, EN; CH, MBA, TU, WF, Y.

6974 [–] A sermon preached . . . February 4, 1673/4. *By Andrew Clark, for Charles Harper*, 1674. 4°.* T.C.I 167. L, O, LL, OC, OM; CH, CN, NU, WF, Y.

6975 —A sermon preached . . . April the 12th, 1674. *For Charles Harper*, 1676. 4°.* L, O, C, CPL; CH, MH, NU, Y.

6976 —A short discourse concerning the reading His Majesties late declaration in the churches. *For Charles Harper, and are to be sold by Randal Taylor*, 1688. 4°.* L, O, C, CT, EN; CLC, CN, MH, NU, WF, Y.

6977 —A short narrative of the discovery of a college of Jesuits, at . . . Hereford. *By T. N. for Charles Harper*, 1679. 4°.* L, O, LL, OC, MR; CH, CN, NU, WF, Y.

6978 — —[Anr. ed.] *Reprinted at Dublin*, 1679. 4°.* DIX 168. DT; NC, NGT, Y.

6979 —Some animadversions upon a book intituled The theory of the earth. *For Charles Harper*, 1685. 8°. T.C.II 137. L, O, CT, P, AU; CH, MU, WF, Y.

6979A **Croft, J.** Excerpta antiqua: or a collection. *York*, 1697. 8°. O.

6979B **Croft, Richard.** The wise steward. *By F. Collins for D. T.*, 1697. 8°. L; CLC.

6980 **[Croft, Robert.]** The plea, case, and humble proposals. *Printed, March 30, 1663*. 4°. O; CH, MM, WF.

6981 **Crofton, Zachary.** Altar worship. *For J. Rothwell*, 1661. 12°. L, O, CM, LW, EN; NU, WF.

6982 —'Αναλημψις ανελημφθη, The fastning. *For Ralph Smith*, 1160. [*i.e.* 1660]. 4°. LT, O, C, EN; CH, CN, NU, WF, Y.

6983 — —Second edition. —, 1661. 4°. CCL; CH.

6984 —'Αναλημψις or Saint Peters bonds abide. *For Ralph Smith*, 1660. 4°. L, C, EN, ENC, AU; MIU, WF.

6985 — —Second edition. —, 1660. 4°.* L, O, DT; MH, MIU, NU.

6986 — —Third edition. —, 1660. 4°.* LT, CCH, OCC, HH, E; CH, NPT, Y.

6987 — —Fourth edition. —, 1661. 4°.* L, CCC, LCL, ENC; CH, LC, NU.

6987A [–] Arrest of five unsober men. *For James Nuthal*, 1657. CSS.

6988 [–] Berith anti-Baal. *By M. S. for Ralph Smith, and for Thomas Parkhurst*, 1661. 4°. LT, O, CCC, LVF, EN; CH, NC, NU, WF, Y.

6989 —Bethshemesh clouded. *By A. M. for Joseph Cranford*, 1653. 4°. LT, C, LCL, CK, BR; CLC, MH, NN, NU.

6990 —Catechizing Gods ordinance. *By E. Cotes for Tho. Parkhurst*, 1656. 8°. LT, C; NPT, NU.

6991 — —Second edition. *By R. I. for Tho. Parkhurst*, 1657. 8°. LT, LCL, OC; Y.

6991A —The covenant of grace opened. *By E. T. for Thomas Johnson*, 1661. 8°. CLC.

6992 —A defence against the dread of death. *[London], printed*, 1665. 8°. L, P; NPT, NU, WF.

6992A [–] Excise anotomiz'd. *[London], for Fran. Cossinet*. [1659.] 4°.* LT, LUG; CU, MH, NU, WF, Y.

6993 —Fœlix scelus, querela priorum, . . . or, prospering prophaneness. *For Tho. Parkhurst*, 1660. 8°. LT, LCL, LW; NU.

6994 —Fraterna correptio: or, the saints zeale. *By T. R. and E. M. for Robert Gibbs*, 1655. 8°. L, C, LCL, LSC.

6995 —The hard way to Heaven. *Printed*, 1662. 4°.* L, O, C, LCL, ENC; CH, MH, NU, Y.

[–] Litvrgical considerator. 1661. *See* Firmin, Giles.

6996 —Malice against ministry manifested. *For James Nuthal*, 1657. 4°.* LT, YM; MH.

6997 —The peoples need. *By E. Cotes, for Thomas Parkhurst*, 1657. 4°. LT, O, CCA, CS, ENC; NU, MIU, TU, WF, Y.

6998 [–] Perjury, the proof of forgery. *For James Nuthal*, 1657. 4°.* LT, O, YM; MH, TU, WF, Y.

6999 —The pursuit of peace. *By T. Fawcet for James Nuthall*, 1660. 4°. LT, O.

7000 —Reformation not separation. *[London], printed*, 1662. 4°. L, O, C, LCL, E; CH, MBA, NU, WF, Y.

7000A —Right re-entred. *For James Nuthall*, 1657. 4°.* MH.

7001 —The saints' care. *Printed*, 1671. 8°. T.C.I 70. L, CS, LCL, LW, E; NPT, NU.

7002 —The Scotch covenant newly revived. *Printed*, 1661. 8°.* LT.

7003 [–] A serious review of Presbyters. *For Ralph Smith*, [1661]. 4°.* LT, O, LCL, EN; CH, CU, MH, NU, WF, Y.

7003A —Three treatises. *Printed* 1667. 4°. L, LCL, LW.

7004 —The vertue and value of Baptism. *By D. M. for J. Nuthal*, 1658. 12°. Y.

7004A — —[Anr. ed.] *For Dorman Newman*, 1663. 4°. L, LCL; MH.

7005 **[Crofts, John.]** The copy of a letter sent from the Kings army. *[Cambridge, 1644?]* cap., 4°.* C, CDC.

7006 [–] —[Anr. ed.] *Printed at Cambridge by R. D.*, 1645. 4°.* LT; MH.

7007 **C[rofts], R[obert].** The way to happinesse on earth. *For G. H.*, 1641. 12°. L; CH, CLC, WF.

7007A **[Crofts, William.]** The deliverance. *[London], printed, and are to be sold by R. Baldwin*, 1689. fol.* L, O; CLC, IU, MH, WF, Y.

7007B —Six sonatas or solos. *Printed for and sold by John Walsh & John Hare*, 1700. L.

7007C **[Croiset, Sean.]** A spiritual retreat. *In the year* 1608. 12°. O; CLC, CN, Y.

7007D [–] —[Anr. ed.] 1700. 12°. L, O; CN, NP.

7008 **[Croke, Charles.]** Fortune's uncertainty, or youth's unconstancy. *For Thomas Dring*, 1667. 8°. L, O; CH.

7009 **Croke, Sir George.** An abridgment of. *For John Starkey, Thomas Basset, and Samuel Speed*, 1665. 8°. L, O, C; CH, MIU, WF, YL.

7010 —An exact abridgement of The reports of. *For Tho. Warren and J. Streeter*, 1658. 8°. LT; MIU, WF.

7011 —The first part (though last publish't) of The reports of. *By and for John Field and Tho: Newcomb; also for W. Lee, D. Pakeman, and Gabriel Bedell*, 1661. fol. L, LIL, CT, NPL; LC, YL.

7012 ——[Anr. ed.] *For A.Roper, T.Collins, F.Tyton, J. Place, J.Starkey, and T.Basset,* 1669. fol. T.C.I 11. L, O, CT, LCL, DT; CLC, MB, NCL, WF.

7013 ——Third edition. *By W.Rawlins, S.Roycroft, and H. Sawbridge, assigns of Richard and Edward Atkins, sold by H.Twyford, F.Tyton, H.Herringman, T.Bassett, J. Wright, S.Heyrick, M.Pit, C.Wilkinson, T.Dring, C. Harper, T.Sawbridge, J.Place, G.Collins,* 1683. 3v. fol. T.C.II 35. L, O, C, ES, DT; CH, LC, MB, NP, Y.

7014 —The reports of. *By J.S.,* 1657. fol. L, LMT, DC, E; BBE, LC, NCL, TU, YL.

7015 ——[Anr. ed.] *By R.Hodgkinsonne, sold by William Leake, and Thomas Firby,* 1657. fol. L, CT; LC, MB, WF.

7016 —The second part of The reports of. *By T.Newcomb and W.Godbid, to be sold by John Field,* 1659. fol. L, DC, CT; BBE, LC, MB.

7017 ——Second edition. *For A.Roper, T.Collins, F.Tyton, J.Place, J.Starkey, and T.Bassett,* 1669. fol. L, O, CT, LIL, DT; CLC, BBE, NR, WF.

7018 ——Third edition. *By W.Rawlins, S.Roycroft, and H. Sawbridge, assigns of Richard and Edward Atkins, to be sold by H.Twyford, Fr.Tyton, H.Herringman, T.Basset, J.Wright, S.Heyrick, M.Pit, C.Wilkinson, T. Dring, C.Harper, T.Sawbridge, J.Place, G.Collins,* 1683. fol. T.C.II 35. L, LI, O, C, EN; CH, LC, MB, V.

7019 —The third part (though first publish't,) of The reports of. Second edition. *For A.Roper, T.Collins, F.Tyton, J.Place, J.Starkey, and T.Basset,* 1669. fol. T.C.II L, O, CT, NPL, DT; CLC, WF.

7020 ——Third edition. *By W.Rawlins, S.Roycroft, and H. Sawbridge, assigns of Richard and Edward Atkins; to be sold by H.Twyford, F.Tyton, H.Herringman, J.Starkey, T.Basset, S.Heyrick, J.Wright, M.Pitt, C.Wilkinson, T.Dring, C.Harper, T.Sawbridge, J.Place, and G. Collins,* 1683. fol. T.C.I 410. L, LI, O, C, EN; CH, LC, MB, NR, V.

7021 [**Croke,** *Sir* **Richard.**] The speech of the Recordor of Oxford. colop: *By T.D.,* 1681. brs. L, O; CH, CN, MH, PU.

7022 **Crollius, Oswald.** Bazilica chymica, & praxis . . . or. *For John Starkey, and Thomas Passinger,* 1670. fol. T.C.I 18. O, C, LCS, GU, AU; NP, WF, Y, HC.

7023 —Philosophy reformed. *By M.S. for Lodowick Lloyd,* 1657. 8°. LT, O, C, GU, E; CH, CU, NU, WF, Y.

7024 [**Cromarty, George Mackenzie,** *earl of.*] Additional considerations to these contained in the letter. colop: *[Edinburgh,* 1695.] cap., fol.* ALDIS 3435. LU; WF, Y.

7025 Entry cancelled.

7026 [–] The mistaken advantage. colop: *Edinburgh, by J.Reid,* 1695. cap., 4°. ALDIS 3471. LU, EN, ES; CU, MH, NC, WF, Y.

7027 —A vindication of Robert III. *Edinburgh, by the heirs and successors of Andrew Anderson,* 1695. 4°. ALDIS 3454. L, O, CS, EN, DT; CH, LC, MBP, WF, Y.

7028 **Crompton, Hugh.** Pierides, or the Muses mount. *By J.G. for Charles Webb,* 1658. 4°. LT, O; CH, CLC, MH, Y.

7029 —Poems by. *By E.C. for Tho.Alsop,* 1657. 8°. L; CH.

7030 **Crompton, Richard.** Star-Chamber cases. *By I.O. for Iohn Grove,* 1641. 4°. L, C, OC, HH, DT; CSS, LC, MH, NCL, Y.

7031 [**Crompton, Thomas.**] A true and plenary relation of the great defeat. *For Iohn Franke, Feb. 6, 1642[3].* 4°.* LT, YM, DT.

7032 [**Crompton, William.**] A remedy against superstition. *[London], printed,* 1667. 4°. L, LCL, LW; NPT, NU.

7032A —Sovereign omnipotency. *For Benj. Alsop, to be sold by James Cowsey in Exeter,* 1682. 8°. T.C.I 504. LCL, LSC; CLC.

7033 —An useful tractate. *By J.H. for Philemon Stephens,* 1659. 8°. LT, OC, AU; CLC, NPT, NU.

7034 —A vvilderness of trouble. *By J.D. for J.Robinson,* 1679. 8°. T.C.I 357. O, LCL; MH, NU, WU.

7035 **Cromwel, Richard.** The happy sinner. *For R.Clavell, to be sold by Mich.Johnson, in Leichfield,* 1691. 4°.* L; WCL.

7036 **Cromwell, Elizabeth.** The court & kitchin of. *By Tho. Milbourn, for Randal Taylor,* 1664. 12°. L, CT, MR; CJC, MH.

7037 **Cromwell, Henry.** A proclamation dated May the 9th, 1659. *Dublin,* 1659. brs. DIX 103. C.

7038 —Whereas we take notice that there are sundry apprehensions. *Printed at Dublin by William Bladen,* 1659. *and reprinted at London,* [1659]. brs. LT, O, LG.

7038A **Cromwell, John.** A discourse of spiritual blessings. *By T.S. for Edward Coles in Norwich,* 1685. 8°. T.C.II 93. L; CLC, Y.

7039 **Cromwell, Oliver.** An abstract of a letter from. *For Francis Coles,* 1645. 4°.* MADAN 1772. LT, O; CU, MIU, WF.

7040 —Articles of peace agreed between Oliver . . . and the States General. *By William Du-gard and Henry Hills,* 1654. 4°. LT, C, CCA, CM; WF.

7040A —Articles of peace, friendship & entercourse . . . France. *By H.Hills and J.Field,* 1655. 4°.* LT; CH.

7040B ——[Anr. ed.] *Edinburgh, by Christopher Higgins,* 1655. 4°.* ALDIS 1504. EN; Y.

7040C —Articles of peace, friendship . . . Sweden. *By H.Hills and J.Field,* 1655. 4°.* L; CH.

7040D —Articles of peace, union . . . States General. *By William Du-Gard and Henry Hills,* 1654. 4°. WF.

7041 —The articles signed by His Highness Oliver Cromwell. *For G.Horton,* 1653. brs. STEELE 3022. LT, O, LG.

7042 —Articuli pacis unionis et confœderationis. *Typis Du-Gardianis,* 1654. 4°.* HR, MU, Y.

7043 ——[Anr. ed.] *Typis Guil. Du-Gard & Henr. Hills,* 1654. 4°.* LT, O.

7044 —A brief relation containing an abreviation of the arguments. *[London], printed January,* 1658[9]. 4°.* LT, O, OC, E; CH, NN, NU, WF.

7045 Entry cancelled.

7046 —A collection of all the proclamations, declarations. *By H.Hills,* 1654[5]. fol. L, O, CT, LL; LC, MH, MHL, TU.

7047 —A commission and instructions to Charles Fleetwood. 1653. fol. LT, EN.

7048 —The commission for discoveries. *By Tho. Newcomb,* 1656. 4°.* HH, EN; CH.

7049 —His Highnes's commission under the Great Seal for satisfying the fifths. *By Tho. Newcomb,* 1657. fol.* LT, O, LUG; WF, Y.

7050 —The conclusion of Lieuten: General Cromwells letter. [*London,* 1645.] brs. LT.

7051 —The copy of a letter written by. *For Edward Blackmore, August the 3,* 1643. 4°.* LT, O, CT, SP; CH, MIU, MH, WF.

7052 —A copy of Lieutenant General Crumwels letter. [*London*], *by Robert Ibbitson,* 1648. 4°.* LT, SP; CN.

7053 —A coppie of Lieut. Gen. Cromwels letter. *Octob. 9. London, by Iane Coe,* 1645. 4°.* LT, O, DT; MH, WF.

7054 —A copy of the letter . . . sent to the members. *By M. S. for Tho. Jenner,* 1656. 4°. L, O, MR, YM; CH, CN, MH, WCL, WF, Y.

7054A —Declaratio Oliveri Cromwelli. *Typis Guilielmi Du-Gard,* 1653. 4°. CLC.

7055 —A declaration and order of. *By and for H. Hills, G. Calvert and T. Brewster,* 1653. fol.* L, O, CCA, DT; MH, WF.

7056 —A declaration by the Lord Lieutenant of Ireland. Concerning his resolutions. *Printed at Dublin by William Bladen, and re-printed at London by Robert Ibbitson,* 1649. 4°.* LT, C, LVF, SP; CH, MH, TU.

7057 —A declaration concerning the government. *By R. Wood,* 1653. 4°.* C, MR; NU.

7058 —The declaration of . . . May 9. *For G. Wharton,* 1648. 4°.* LT, AN; WF.

7059 —The declaration of the Lord Governour Cromwel. *For G. Oreton. Aug. 23,* 1649. 4°.* LT, AN.

7060 —A declaration of . . . April the last 1653. *By William Du-Gard,* 1653. brs. STEELE 2993. LT, O, C, LG, LS; MH, NU, Y.

7061 —Declaration of . . . concerning the citizens of London. [*London*], *for R. W.,* 1648. 4°.* LT, HH; CH.

7062 —The declaration of Lieutenant Generall Crumwell concerning the Kingdom of Scotland. *Septemb. 18.* [*London*], *for R. Williamson,* 1648. 4°.* LT, O, HH, EN, DT; MH, NU, WF, Y.

7063 —The declaration of . . . concerning the Kings Majesty. [*London*], *printed, Novemb. 17,* 1648. 4°.* LT; CSS.

7064 [–] The declaration of . . . concerning the Levellers. *Imprinted at London, for G. H., May 14,* 1649, 4°.* LT; CH, MH.

7065 —A declaration of . . . for a collection. colop: *By Henry Hills, and John Field,* 1658. cap., fol.* LT, O, C; MIU, Y.

7066 —A declaration of . . . for a day of publique thanksgiving. *By Henry Hills and John Field,* 1656[7]. fol.* LT, O, CS, LG, HH; CN, MH, NR, WF, Y.

7067 —A declaration of . . . for a day of publick thanksgiving. *By Henry Hills and John Field,* 1658. fol.* LT, O, LW; WF.

7068 — —[Anr. ed.] *Edinburgh, by Christopher Higgins,* 1658. fol.* CH, Y.

7068A —A declaration of . . . for a day of solemn fasting. *By William Du-Gard, and Henry Hills,* 1654. fol.* CJ.

7069 —[Anr. ed.] *By Henry Hills, and John Field,* 1656. fol.* LT, O, CJ, LG; CLC, MH, TU, WF, Y.

7070 — —[Anr. ed.] —, 1656. 4°.* CH.

7071 — —[Anr. ed.] colop: *London, reprinted Edinburgh, by Christopher Higgins,* 1656. 4°.* ALDIS 1538. EN; Y.

7072 —By the Protector. A declaration of . . . for a day . . . 29 April 1658. *By Henry Hills and John Field,* 1658. brs. STEELE 3093. L, LG, LUG, HH, EN.

7073 —A declaration of . . . for a day . . . eighteenth day of May, 1659. *By I. S.,* 1659. fol.* SP; CN, MH, WF, Y.

7074 —A declaration of . . . for the undeceiving of deluded and seduced people. *Printed at Corke, and now reprinted at London by E. Griffin. March 21,* 1650. 4°.* LT, C; CH, MH, WF, Y.

7075 —A declaration of . . . in order to the securing the peace. *By Henry Hills and John Field,* 1655. brs. STEELE 3065. L, O, C, LG, HH; CLC, MB, MH.

7076 —A declaration of . . . inviting persons to send over. *By Henry Hills and John Field,* 1658. brs. STEELE 3096. LT, O, LUG.

7077 —A declaration of . . . inviting the people. *20. March* 1653 *by Henry Hills and William du-Gard,* 1653[4]. brs. STEELE 3027. LT, O, C, LG, DT; CH, MH, NU, Y.

7078 —A declaration of . . . inviting the people . . . 21 November 1655. *By Henry Hills and John Field,* 1655. brs. STEELE 3064. LT, O, C, LG, HH; MB.

7078A —[Anr. ed.] *Dublin, by William Bladen,* 1655. fol.* STEELE 2p 560. L.

7079 — —, 14 March 1655[6]. *By Henry Hills and John Field,* 1655[6]. brs. STEELE 3069. LT, O, C, LG, LS; CN, MH.

7080 —A declaration of . . . setting apart Tuesday the 23. of this present May. *By William du-Gard and Henry Hills,* 1654. brs. STEELE 3037. LT, O, C, HM, DT; CH, CLC, MH, NU.

7081 —A declaration of . . . setting forth. *By Henry Hills and John Field,* 1655. fol.* L, LL, C, MR, HH; CH, LC, MH, NU, Y.

7082 —A declaration of . . . shewing the reasons. *By Henry Hills and John Field,* 1655. 4°.* LT, O, C, OC, CT; CH, CN, MH, TU, WF, Y.

7083 — —[Anr. ed.] *Edinburgh, reprinted by Christopher Higgins,* 1655. 4°.* ALDIS 1511. EN; MH, Y.

7084 — —[Anr. ed.] *Dublin, by William Bladen,* 1655. 4°.* DT.

7085 —A declaration of . . . upon his actual dissolution. *By Robert Wood,* [1655]. 4°.* LT, OC, CS.

7086 Entry cancelled.

7087 —Forasmuch as divers of this nation, . . . 15 March 1651. *Leith, E Tyler,* 1651. brs. STEELE 3p 2065. OCC.

7088 [–] Forasmuch as for many years last past . . . 13 February 1655[6]. *By Henry Hills and John Field,* 1655[6]. brs. STEELE 3067. L, LG, LS, HH.

7089 —Good nevves out of the VVest. *By Matthew Simmons,* 1645. 4°.* LT, O; MH, NN.

7090   [–] Instructions to be observed touching the collection. *By Henry Hills and John Field*, 1655. brs. STEELE 3049. LT, C, CJ, HH; HR, MH.

7091   —The last speech of . . . 12. of this instant September. *By R. Wood*, 1654. 4°.* LT, O, DT; MH, NU, PPT, WF.

7092   —Lieutenant General Cromwel's letter concerning the total routing of the Scots army. *For Edward Husband, August 22*, 1648. 4°.* LT, OC, YM; MH, TU, WF, Y.

7093   —A letter from His Highness the Lord Protector sent into the North. *By Robert Ibbitson*, 1655. 4°.* LT; MH.

7094   —A letter from the Lord General Cromwel, concerning the rendition of the Castle of Edinburgh. *By Edward Husband and John Field*, 1650. 4°.* LT, OC, HH, DT; CLC, CN, Y.

7095   —A letter from the Lord General dated the one and twentieth day of July. *By John Field*, 1651. 4°.* LT, O, HH; CH, CN, NU, WF, Y.

7096   ——September the fourth, 1651. *By John Field*, 1651. 4°.* LT, HH; CN, MH, Y.

7097   —A letter from the Lord General Cromwel from Dunbar: containing a true relation. *By Edward Husband and John Field*, 1650. 4°.* LT, O, HH; CLC, CN, MH, WF, Y.

7098   —A letter from the Lord Lieutenant of Ireland, to . . . Lenthal giving an account. *By John Field for Edward Husband*, 1649. 4°.* LT, O, C, DT; CH, CU, LC, MH, Y.

7099   —A letter from the right honorable, the Lord Lieutenant of Ireland, concerning the surrender of the tovvn of Ross. *By John Field for Edward Husband*, 1649. 4°.* LT, C; CH, MH, WF, WU.

7100   —A letter from the right honorable the Lord Lieutenant of Ireland, to the honorable William Lenthall . . . concerning the surrendring of Enistery. *By John Field for Edward Husband*, 1649. 4°.* LT, C; CH, CN, MH, MIU, Y.

7101   —A letter from the right honourable the Lord Lieutenant of Ireland, to . . . Lenthall . . . concerning the taking and surrendring of Enistery. *By John Field for Edward Husband*, 1649. 4°.* C; CH, CN, MH, MIU.

7102   —A letter from . . . to the honorable William Lenthall . . . relating the good successes. *By Edward Husband and John Field*, 1649[50]. 4°. LT, C, SP; CH, MH, WF, WU.

7103   —A letter from . . . to the honorable William Lenthall . . . relating the several successes. *By Edward Husband and John Field*, 1650. 4°.* LT, O, C, CT; CH, MH, WF, WU, Y.

7104   —A letter from the Lord Generall Cromvvell to the Parliament of England. *Printed at Corcke*, 1650. 4°.* L, EN.

7105   —A letter from the Lord General Cromwel touching the great victory. *By John Field*, 1651. 4°.* LT, HH; CLC, CN, Y.

7106   —A letter sent from . . . to the Marquis of Argyle. *[London], for C. W.*, 1648. 4°.* LT, HH, EN; MH.

7107   —A letter sent to the Generall Assembly of the Kirke of Scotland. *For Hanna Allen*, 1650. 4°.* LT, O, EN, DT; CN, MH, NPT, WF, Y.

7108   —Livetenant [sic] Generall Cromvvels letter sent to the honorable Wm Lenthall. *[London], by T. W. for Ed. Husband*, 1645. Octob. 16, 4°.* LT; CH, MIU, NN, WF.

7109   —Lieut: Generall Cromwells letter to the honorable William Lenthall. *For Edward Husbands, Octob. 20*, 1645. 4°.* L, O, CT, DT; MH, MIU, NU, WF.

7110   ——*For Edward Husband, Octob. 24*, 1645. 4°.* LT, O, C, DT; MH, MIU, WF, Y.

7111   ——*For Edward Husband, August 23*, 1648. 4°.* LT, O, C, CT, HH; CH, MH, NU, WF, Y.

7112   ——*For Edward Husband, Octob. 10*, 1648. 4°.* LT, O, OC, EN; CH, MH, NU, WF.

7113   ——*For Edward Husband, Octob. 19*, 1648. 4°.* LT, O, CT, HH; CH, MH, MIU, WF, Y.

7114   —Lieut: Generall Cromwells letter to the House of Commons. *For Edward Husband, Sept. 18*, 1645. 4°.* LT, O, C, BR, DT; CN, MH, PU, WB, Y.

7114A   ——[Anr. ed.] —*Sept. 22*, 1645. 4°.* BR.

7115   —The Lord Gen. Cromwel's letter: with a narrative. *By Edward Husband and John Field, Aug. 23*, 1650. 4°.* LT, O, C, HH, EN; CH, CN, MH, MIU, WF, Y.

7116   —A letter written by. *By I. M. August 21*, 1648. 4°.* LT, P, YM.

7116A   —Oliver Cromwell's letters to foreign princes. *For John Nutt*, 1700. 4°. T.C.III 200. L, C; CLC, MIU, NU, WF.

7117   —A message sent from His Highness the Lord Protector, to the Great Turk. *For Peter Mitchel*, 1654. 4°.* LT.

7118   —A most learned, conscientious, and devout exercise, *Printed*, 1680. 4°.* T.C.I 460. LT, CT, MR, DT; CH, MH, NU, TU, WF, Y.

7118A   ——[Anr. ed.] *Printed* 1649. 4°.* LT; MM, TSM.

7118B   ——[Anr. ed.] *For Allen Banks*, 1682. 4°.* T.C.I 466. L; MIU.

7119   —Oliver Lord Protector of the Common Wealth . . . [Letters of denization.] 28 February 1655[6]. *[n.p., 1656.]* brs. STEELE 3068. L.

7120   —Oliver Lord Protector of the Commonwealth . . . [South Okendenchurch.] 9 March 1657/8. *[n.p., 1658.]* brs. STEELE 3090. LG.

7121   —An order and declaration of . . . commanding all persons. *By Henry Hills and John Field*, 1655. brs. STEELE 3061. LT, O, LG, HH; MB, MH, Y.

7121A   —An order . . . for . . . additional . . . commissioners. *By Henry Hills and John Field*, 1657. fol.* OC, BR.

7121B   —An order and declaration of . . . for an assessment of sixty thousand pounds . . . 24 June. *By H. Hills and J. Field*, 1655. fol.* CH.

7121C   —[Same title.] . . . 25 Dec. —, 1655. fol.* CH.

7121D   —[Same title.] . . . 24 June. —, 1656. fol.* CH.

7121E   —An order and declaration of . . . for an assessment of three score thousand pounds. *By H. Hills and J. Field*, 1645[5]. fol.* CH, MB.

7121F   —An order and declaration of . . . for continuing the committee. colop: *By Henry Hills and John Field*, 1655. cap., fol.* CH.

7121G   —[Same title.] —, ·1657. fol.* LT; TU, WF.

7121H —An order of . . . for continuing the Committee. colop: *By Henry Hills and John Field, 1657.* fol.* LT.

7122 —An order of . . . for continuing the powers . . . 1 July 1653. *By H. Hills for Calvert, Brewster, and Hills, 1653.* brs. STEELE 3002. LT, LG.

7122A —An order and declaration . . . touching the continuance. colop: *By H. Hills and J. Field, 1654[5].* cap., fol.* CH.

7123 —His Excellencies order to the severall colonels. [*London, 1650.*] cap., 4°. E.

7123A —Ordered by His Highness the Lord Protector. *Edinburgh, by Christopher Higgins, 1656.* brs. ALDIS 1553. EN; Y.

7124 —Ordered by His Highness with . . . 11 May 1654. [*n.p., 1654.*] brs. STEELE 3039. L.

7124A —Orders of. *By H. Hills and John Field, 1635.* fol.* L; CH.

7125 [–] An ordinance against challenges. *By William du-Gard and Henry Hills, 1654.* brs. STEELE 3042. L; CH.

7126 —An ordinance for adjourning part of Easter Term 1654. 6 April 1654. *By Henry Hills and William Du-Gard, 1654.* brs. STEELE 3028. LT, O, C, LS, HH, DT.

7127 —An ordinance for adjourning part of Easter term 1654 . . . 8 April 1654. *By Henry Hills and William Du-Gard, 1654.* brs. STEELE 3031. LT, O, C, LS, HH, DT.

7128 —An ordinance for better amending and keeping in repair the common high-waies. *By Henry Hills and William du-Gard, 1654.* brs. CH.

7129 —An ordinance for erecting courts Baron . . . 12 April 1654. *Leith, reprinted, 1654.* brs. STEELE 3p 2112. EN.

7130 —An ordinance for indempnity to the English Protestants of . . . Minister. *By William du-Gard and Henry Hills, 1654.* brs. L; CH.

7131 ——[Anr. ed.] *Dublin reprinted, W Bladen, 1654.* fol.* STEELE 2p 532. L.

7132 —An ordinance for settling of the estates . . . 12 April 1654. *Leith reprinted, 1654.* fol.* STEELE 3p 2114. EN.

7133 —An ordinance for uniting Scotland . . . 12 April 1654. *Leith reprinted, 1654.* brs. STEELE 3p 2111. ALDIS 1495. ER.

7134 —An ordinance of explanation of a former ordinance . . . high-waies. *By William du-Gard and Henry Hills, 1654.* brs. CH, Y.

7134A —An ordinance of explanation touching treasons. *By William Du-Gard and Henry Hills, 1653[4].* brs. STEELE 3026. LT, O, C, LS, DT; MH, NU.

7135 —An ordinance of pardon and grace . . . 12 April 1654. *Leith, reprinted, 1654.* brs. STEELE 3p 2113. ALDIS 1497. EN, ER, FSF; WF.

7136 —The overthrow of the Scottish army: or a letter sent from. *For John Bellamy, 1648.* 4°.* LT, CT, HH; CH, LC.

7137 —A proclamation by . . . 26 June 1657. *By Henry Hills and John Field, 1657.* brs. STEELE 3082. LT, O, C, LG, LPR; CH, MH, MIU, NR, Y.

7137A ——[Anr. ed.] *Edinburgh, Christopher Higgins, 1657.* brs. MH.

7138 —A proclamation commanding a speedy and due execution. *By Henry Hills and John Field, 1655.* fol.* STEELE 3057. LT, O, C, LG, LPR; MB, MH.

7139 —A proclamation commanding all Papists . . . to depart. *By Henry Hills and John Field, 1657[8].* brs. STEELE 3087. LT, O, CJ, LG, HH; MH.

7140 —A proclamation commanding all Papists . . . to repair. *By Henry Hills and John Field, 1657[8].* brs. STEELE 3088. LT, O, LG, LS, LUG; MH.

7141 —A proclamation commanding all persons. *By Henry Hills and John Field, 1655.* brs. STEELE 3052. LT, O, C, LG, LS; MB, MH.

7142 —A proclamation commanding all persons. *By Henry Hills and John Field, 1656.* fol.* STEELE 3074. LT, C, LG, LL, HH; MH.

7143 —A proclamation concerning the residence. *By Henry Hills and John Field, 1656.* brs. STEELE 3072. LT, C, LS, LUG; MH, TU.

7144 —A proclamation declaring His Highness pleasure. *By Henry Hills and John Field, 1655.* brs. STEELE 3047, LT, O, C, LG, OQ; MB, MH.

7145 —A proclamation declaring that after the first day of August. *By Henry Hills and John Field, 1655.* brs. STEELE 3054. LT, O, C, LG, HH; MB, MH.

7146 —A proclamation declaring the right. *By Henry Hills and John Field, 1657[8].* brs. STEELE 3089. LT; MH.

7147 —A proclamation for appointing of a certain day. *By Henry Hills and John Field, 1658.* brs. STEELE 3094. L, O, LG, LS; Y.

7148 —A proclamation for perfecting the collection. *By Henry Hills and John Field, 1655.* brs. STEELE 3053. LT, C, LG, LS, HH; CLC, MB, MH.

7149 —A proclamation . . . for continuing all persons. *By Henry Hills, 1653.* brs. STEELE 3023. LT, O, C, LG, DT; CLC, MH, NU, Y.

7150 —A proclamation . . . for putting in execution. *By Henry Hills and John Field, 1656.* brs. STEELE 3075. LT, O, LS, LUG, HH; CH, MH, MIU.

7151 —A proclamation for putting the lavvs in execution. *By Henry Hills and John Field, 1655.* brs. STEELE 3056. LT, C, LS, OQ, HH; MB, MH.

7152 —A proclamation for relief of godly ministers. *By Henry Hills and John Field, 1655.* brs. STEELE 3051. LT, O, C, LPR, OQ; CLC, MB, MH.

7153 —A proclamation for the better levying and payment. *By Henry Hills and John Field, 1657[8].* fol.* STEELE 3091. LT, LL, LS, LUG, OQ; MH, Y.

7154 —A proclamation giving encouragement . . . Jamaica *By Henry Hills and John Field, 1655.* brs. STEELE 3059. LG.

7155 —A proclamation giving notice. *By Henry Hills and John Field, 1655.* brs. STEELE 3055. LT, C, LS, HH; MB, MH.

7156 —A proclamation of assistance. *By Henry Hills and John Field, 1658.* brs. STEELE 3097. LT, LS.

7157 —A proclamation of the peace . . . France. *By Henry Hills and Iohn Field*, 1655. brs. STEELE 3062. L, C, LG, LS, HH; MB.

7158 —A proclamation of the peace . . . Portugal. *By Henry Hills and John Field*, 1656[7]. brs. STEELE 3080. LT, LUG, OP.

7159 —A proclamation of the peace . . . Vnited Provinces. *By William du-Gard and Henry Hills*, 1654. brs. STEELE 3034. LT, O, LL, LS, DT; MH, NU.

7160 —A proclamation prohibiting delinquents. *By Henry Hills and John Field*, 1655. brs. STEELE 3058. LT, O, C, LG, LS; MB.

7161 —A proclamation prohibiting horse-races. *By Henry Hills and John Field*, 1654[5]. fol.* STEELE 3046. LT, O, C, LG, HH; CLC, MB, NU.

7161A — —*By Henry Hills and John Field*, 1655. brs. STEELE 3058. MH.

7162 — —*By Henry Hills and John Field*, 1658. brs. STEELE 3092. LT, O, LS.

7163 —A proclamation prohibiting the disturbing of ministers. *By Henry Hills and John Field*, 1654[5]. fol.* STEELE 3045. LT, O, C, LG, HH; CH, CLC, MB, MH, NU.

7164 —Propositions sent in a letter. [*London*], *by Robert Ibbitson*, 1648. 4°.* LT, O; Y.

7165 —Scriptum Dom. Protectoris reipublicæ Angliæ. *Henricus Hills et Iohannes Field*, 1655. 4°. LT, CCA, CT; CH, NPT, WF, Y.

7166 — —Several letters and passages. *By J. Field for Francis Tyton, September 25*, 1650. 4°.* LT, O, C, CT, EN; CN, MH, MIU, TU, WF, Y.

7167 — —[Anr. ed.] *Printed and sold in York by T. Broad, Septem 27*, 1650. 4°.* CH.

7167A — —[Anr. ed.] [*Edinburgh?* 1650.] 4°.* ALDIS 1429. HH, EN.

7168 —Severall letters from Scotland relating the proceedings. *For Robert Ibbitson*, 1650. 4°.* HH; MH.

7169 —The Lord General Cromwel's speech delivered . . . 4 of July, 1653. [*London*], *printed*, 1654. 4°.* LT, O, CS, HH, AN; CH, MH, NU, WF, Y.

7170 —His Highnesse the Lord Protector's speech . . . 12th of September, 1654. *By T. R. and E. M. for G. Sawbridge*, 1654. 4°.* LT, O, EC, HH; CH, LC, MH, NC, TU, Y.

7170A — —The speech of . . . to both Houses. *By Henry Hills and John Field*, [1652.] 4°.* L; CH, WF.

7170B —The speech of His Highness the Lord Protector to the Parliament. *For G. Horton*, 1654. 4°.* LT.

7170C — —[Anr. ed.] *For G. Freeman*, 1654. 4°.* OC; NC, WF.

7171 —His Highness speech to the Parliament . . . 22d. of January, 1654. *By Henry Hills*, 1654[5]. 4°.* LT, O, C, EN, DT; CH, CN, MH, NU, TU, WF, Y.

7172 — —[Anr. ed.] *Reprinted Leith*, 1654. 4°.* EN.

7173 — —[Anr. ed.] *Reprinted in Edinburgh*, 1655. 4°.* ALDIS 1509. LT, EN; Y.

7174 — —[Anr. ed.] *Dublin, by William Bladen*, 1654. 4°.* DIX 93, LW, DK; NL.

7175 —His Highnesse the Lord Protector's speeches to the Parliament. *By T. R. and E. M. for G. Sawbridge*, 1654. 4°. LT, O, C, MR; CH, CN, LC, MH, NU, TU, Y.

7176 —The summe of the charge given in by. [1644.] brs. LT.

7177 —Two letters; one from. [*Newcastle?*], *for J. Chandler*, [1648.] 4°.* CT.

7177A —His Highnesse . . . two speeches. *Printed at London and reprinted at Leigh*, 1654. 4°.* ALDIS 1489. CLC, MIU.

7178 —Whereas by the thirtieth article . . . 24 of May 1654. *By William du-Gard and Henry Hills*, 1654. brs. STEELE 3041. LT, O, LS, HH, DT; CH, MIU.

7178A —Whereas I am informed. *Edinburgh, by Evan Tyler*, 1651. brs. Y.

7179 —Whereas it hath pleased the Parliament . . . 8 November 1651. [*London*, 1651.] brs. STEELE 2955. LT; MH.

7180 —Whereas the enemies of the peace of . . . 23 of May 1654. *By William Du-Gard and Henry Hills*, 1654. brs. STEELE 3040. LT, O, C, LG, DT; MH, MHS, NU.

7181 **Cromwell, Richard.** A declaration of . . . for a day of publique fasting. *By Henry Hills and John Field*, 1658. brs. STEELE 3101. LT, O, LG, LS, HH; MH, Y.

7182 —A declaration of . . . for a day of solemn fasting. *By Henry Hills and John Field*, 1658. brs. STEELE 3103. LT, O, LG, LUG.

7182A — —[Anr. éd.] *Edinburgh, by Christopher Higgins*, 1658. brs. Y.

7183 —A declaration of the Lord Protector and both Houses . . . eighteenth day of May, 1659. *By I. S.*, 1659. 4°.* LT, O; CH, NU, Y.

7184 —The humble petition of. [*London*, 1659.] brs. LT, LS; CH, MH, Y.

7185 —His late Highnes's letter to the Parlament. *By D. Maxwell*, 1656. brs. STEELE 3115. LT, O, C, HH; CU.

7186 —A proclamation about dissolving the Parliament. *By Henry Hills and John Field*, 1659. brs. STEELE 3104. LT, O, LG, LS; MH.

7187 —A proclamation commanding all Papists, . . . to depart. *By Henry Hills and John Field*, 1659. brs. STEELE 3107. LT, O, LS; MH, Y.

7188 —A proclamation commanding all Papists, . . . to repair. *By Henry Hills and John Field*, 1659. brs. STEELE 3106. LT, O, LG, LS; MH, Y.

7189 —A proclamation for the better encouragement of godly ministers. *By Henry Hills and John Field*, 1658. brs. STEELE 3102. LT, O, LG, LS, HH; MH.

7190 —A proclamation signifying His Highness pleasure. *By Henry Hills and John Field*, 1658. brs. STEELE 3100. LT, O, LG, LS, HH; MH.

7191 —The speech of His Highness . . . 27th of January 1658. *By Henry Hills and John Field*, [1659.] 4°.* LT, O, C, LG, EC; CH, CN, MH, NU, TU, WF, Y.

7191A — —[Anr. ed.] *Edinburgh, by Christopher Higgins*, 1659. 4°.* ALDIS 1591. Y.

Cromwell's bloody slaughterhouse. 1660. *See* Gauden, John, *bp.*

7191B **Cromwell, Richard.** The happy sinner. *For R. Clavell, to be sold by Mich. Johnson, on Lerchfield,* 1691. 4°.* L; WCL.

7192   Cromwel's complaint of injustice. colop: *For T. Davis,* 1681. brs. L, O; MH.

7193   Cromwell's conspiracy. *For the author,* 1660. 4°.* LT, O, LVD; CH, LC, Y.

7194   Cromwells panegyrick. [*London*], *printed,* 1647. brs. LT, LS, HH; CH.

7195   Cromwell's recall; or, the petition. *Darby House* [*London*], *printed,* 1649. 4°.* LT, SP; CH, NN, Y.

Crook. *See also* Crooke.

7196 **Crook, John.** An apology for the Quakers. *Printed* 1662. 4°.* L, O, LF, BBN; CH, MH, PH, WF, Y.

7197   —The case of swearing (at all) discussed. *For Robert Wilson,* 1660. 4°.* L, O, C, LF, EN; CH, MH, NU, PH, WF, Y.

7198   [–] Compassion to all the sorrowful. [*London,* 1665.] cap., 4°.* L, O, LF, BBN; MH, PH, PL, PSC, Y.

7199   —The counterfeit convert discovered. [*London,* 1676?] 4°. L, O, LF, BBN; CH, IE, MH, PH, Y.

7200   —The cry of the innocent for justice. [*London*], *printed,* 1662. 4°.* L, O, LF, CT, BBN; CN, MH, NU, PH, WF, Y.

7201   —A declaration of the people of God. colop: *For Thomas Simmons,* 1659. cap., 4°.* L, C, LF, CT, BBN; CH, MH, PH, WF, Y.

7202   —A defence of the true church called Quakers. *For Thomas Simmons,* 1659. 4°. L, O, C, LF, EN; CH, MH, NU, PH, WF.

7203   —An epistle for vnity. *For Robert Wilson,* 1661. 4°.* L, O, C, LF, BBN; CH, MH, PH, WF, Y.

7204   —An epistle of love. *By M. I. and are to be sold by Robert Wilson,* 1660. 4°.* L, O, C, LF, EN; CH, MH, NU, PH, WF, Y.

7205   —An epistle of peace and goodwill. [*London*], 1664. brs. LF, BBN, DT.

7206   —An epistle to all that profess the light. [*London*], *printed,* 1678. 4°.* L, O, C, LF; CH, LC, MH, PH, WF, Y.

7207   — —[Anr. ed.] *By T. Sowle* [1696.] 8°.* MH, PH.

7208   [–] An epistle to all that's young. [*London,* 1672.] cap., 4°.* L, O, LF, BBN, BP; MH, NC, NU, PH, Y.

7209   —An epistle to Friends, for union. colop: *Printed and sold by T. Sowle,* 1698. 8°.* LF, BBN; PH, Y.

7210   —An epistle to young people. [*London,* 1686.] 4°.* L, LF, BBN, BP; CH, IE, MH, PH, Y.

7211   [–] Glad-tydings proclaimed. *Printed,* 1662. 4°.* L, O, LF, BBN; MH, PH, PSC, Y.

7212   —Rebellion rebuked. [*London*], *printed,* 1673. 4°. L, C, LF, BBN; CH, MH, PH, PSC, Y.

7213   —Sixteen reasons drawn from the law of God. *For Robert Wilson,* [1661.] 4°. L, O, LF, WCA, BBN; CH, MH, PH, PSC, WF.

7214   [–] Some reasons why the people called Quakers. [*London*], *printed,* 1665. 4°.* L, LF; WF.

7214A   —To the King and both Houses of Parliament, who have made laws. [*London*], 1664. brs. LF.

7215   —A true and faithful testimony concerning John Samm. *Printed,* 1664. 4°.* L, O, LF, BP; PH, PSC, Y.

7216   —A true information to the nation, from the people called Quakers. [*London*], *printed,* 1664. 4°.* L, LF; CH, MH, PH, PSC, Y.

7217   —Truth's principles. *Printed,* 1662. 4°.* L, OC; CH, PH, PSC, WF.

7218   — —[Anr. ed.] —, 1663. 4°.* LF, DT; CN, PH, PSC, Y.

7219   — —Second edition. *For R. Wilson,* 1663. 4°.* L, LF; WF, Y.

7220   — —Third edition. *Printed,* 1663. *Reprinted and sold by T. Sowle,* 1699. 8°.* L, O, C, LF; NPT, NU, PL, PSC.

7221   — —Fourth edition. —, 1700. 8°.* L, LF.

7222   —Truth's progress. [*London*], *printed,* 1667. 4°. L, O, C, LF, EN; CH, MH, NU, PH, WF, Y.

7223   —Truth's triumph. [*London*], *printed,* 1664. 4°. LF, BBN; PH, PSC.

7224   —Twenty cases of conscience. *For Robert Wilson,* [1667]. 4°.* L, O, C, LF, BP; MH, PH, PSC, Y.

7224A   — —[Anr. ed.] colop: *For Robert Wilson,* 1670. 4°.*. MH.

7225   —Tythes no property. *For Thomas Simmons,* 1659. 4°.* LF, BP; CH, MH, NU, PH, TU.

7225A   —Unrighteousness no plea for truth. *For Thomas Simmons,* 1659. 4°. LF, BBN; PH, PSC.

7226   —The way to a lasting peace. *T. Sowle,* 1697. brs. L, LF, BBN; PH.

7227 **Crook, Samuel.** Τα διαφεροντα, or divine characters. *For A. B. to be sold by Joseph Cranford,* 1658. fol. L, O, LCL, LW, E; CH, CU, MH, MU, NU.

7227A   — —[Anr. ed.] *For Adoniram Byfield,* 1658. fol. LSC, SP; WCL.

7228   —The guide unto true blessedness. Seventh edition. *By Ja. Flesher, to be sold by Richard Royston,* 1650. 12°. C, LCL, LW, BR, DT; NU.

Crooke. *See also* Crook.

7229 **Crooke, Banks.** A sermon preach'd. . . . at the funeral of Mrs. Hannah Bullivant. *For Joseph Wild,* 1698. 4°. T.C.III 90. L, C, BP; NPT, WF, Y.

7230   —Two sermons preach'd. *For Benj. Tooke,* 1695. 4°. L, O, C, LG, OC; NU, WF, Y.

Crooke, *Sir George.* *See* Croke, Sir George.

7231 **Crooke, Helkiah.** Μιχροχοσμογραφια. *By R. C. to be sold by Iohn Clarke,* 1651. fol. L, O; BBE, CJC, CLM, WU, HC.

7232 **Crooke, Unton.** A letter to His Highness the Lord Protector. *By Henry Hills and John Field,* 1654[5]. 4°.* LT; CSS, Y.

7232A   — —[Anr. ed.] *Printed at London, and reprinted in Edinburgh,* 1655. 4°.* Y.

7233   —A second letter. *By Henry Hills and John Field,* 1654[5]. 4°.* LT.

Crooke, William. An almanack. [1652.] *See* Almanacs.

7233A   —Books printed for. [*London?* 1680.] CN.

7234   —A catalogue of such books that are printed for. *Printed,* 1683. 8°.* L, O, SP; CH, CLC, MH, PL, Y.

7234A **Croome, Mr.** At Mr. Croomes, at the sign of the shooe and slop. [*London*, 1677?] brs. L.

7235 [**Croone, William.**] De ratione motus musculorum. *Excudebat J. Hayes, prostant venales apud S. Thomas,* 1664. 4°.* L, O, C, LCP, E, GH; MMO, WSG, HC.

7236 **Croope, J.** Conscience oppression. *Printed,* 1656[7]. 4°. LT, SP; CH.

7237 **Croplie, Thomas.** The resolutions of the army. [*London,* 1648.] brs. LT.

7238 **Cropper, John.** Catalogue of the library. [*London*], 19 *June,* 1693. 4°. L.

Cros, Monsieur de. See LeCroze, Jean Cornand de.

7239 **C[rosbie], J.** Philadelphia or. *For and by Peter Lillicrap,* 1669. 4°.* O; MIU.

7240 **Crosfeild, Robert.** An account of Robert Crosfeild's proceedings in the House of Lords. [*London,* 1692-96?] cap., fol.* L, O, C, LL, HH; CH, MH, PL, WF, Y.

7241 —Brief observations upon the present distresses. [*London,* 1696.] cap., fol.* L, HH.

7242 [–] A dialogue between a modern courtier. colop: [*London*], *printed,* 1696. 4°.* L, O; WF.

7243 —England's glory reviv'd. *Printed,* 1693. 4°. T.C.II 482. L, O, CT; CH, CN, MH, WF, Y.

7244 [–] Great Britain's tears. *Printed,* 1695. 4°.* L, AU; CLC, MH, MM, WF, Y.

7245 [–] Justice perverted. *Printed,* 1695. 4°.* L, C, AU; CH, CN, MH, WF, Y.

7246 [–] Justice the best support. *Printed,* 1697. 4°.* L, O, C, GU; CH, CN, MH, WF, Y.

7247 [–] Truth brought to light. *Printed,* 1694. 4°.* L, O, CCA, EN, GU; CH, CN, MH, NU, WF, Y.

7247A **Crosley, David.** Samson a type of Christ. *For W. Marshall.* 1691. 4°. O, LW.

7248 **Cross, Francis.** Disputatio medica. *Oxoniæ, excudebat H. Hall per R. Davis,* 1668. 12°. MADAN 2797. L, O, CS.

[**Cross, J.**] Account of the life and death of the Blessed Virgin. 1687. *See* Fleetwood, Williaim, bp.

7249 **C[ross], J[ohn]. *alias* More,** An aplogy for the contemplations. *Nath. Thompson,* 1687. 8° OBL, OC, OME, DT; CN.

7250 —Contemplations on the life & glory of Holy Mary. *Paris, anno Domini,* 1685. 8°. L, O, CT, MC, D; CN, TU, WF.

7250A —Philothea's pilgrimage to perfection. *Bruges, by Luke Kerchove,* 1668. 8°. L; O, WARE; CN, WF, Y.

7251 —A sermon preached before Their Sacred Majesties. *By Nath. Thompson,* 1687. 4°.* L, MC; NU, WF.

7252 [**Cross, Nicholas.**] The cynosura. *By I. Redmayne for Thomas Rooks,* 1670. fol. T.C.I 43. L, O, C, WCA, E; CH, CU, MH, WF, Y.

7253 [–] —[Anr. ed.] —, 1679. fol. NU.

7254 —A sermon preach'd . . . 21st day of April, anno 1686. *By Nathaniel Thompson,* 1687. 4°.* L; NU, TU.

7255 —A word to all people. *For the author.* 1661. 4°.* L.

7256 **Crosse, Robert.** Λόγου αλογαὶ, seu, exercitatio theologica. *Oxoniæ, excudebat H. Hall, impensis Th. Robinson,* 1655. 4°.* MADAN 2273. L, O, CT, EN, DT; CH, MH, WF, Y.

7256A **Cross, Thomas.** Nolens volens, or you shall learn. 1695. 8°. O.

7257 **Cross, Walter.** Caleb's spirit parallel'd. *By J. D. for Andrew Bell,* 1697. 4°.* L, LW, BR; MH, WF.

7258 —[Hebrew.] A compend of the covenant. *For Henry Barnard,* 1693. 4°.* T.C.II 585. L, O. LSC, LW, D; Y.

7259 —A discourse on the resurrection. *By John Astwood for Thomas Cockeril,* 1695. 4°.* O, LW; WF.

7260 —An exposition of the second verse of the fourth chapter—Romans. *By J. A. for the author, sold by Tho. Parkhurst,* 1694. 4°. O, LCL, LW, EN, ENC; MH, Y.

7261 —An exposition on the fourth chapter of the Epistle to the Romans. *By J. Astwood for the author,* 1693. 4°.* L, O, LW; NU.

7262 —The instrumentality of faith asserted. *For Tho. Cockerill,* 1695. 4°. O, LW, ENC; NU.

7263 —A specimen of a comment. *By S. Bridge,* 1698. 8°.* L, CT, LW; CH, Y.

7263A ——[Anr. ed.] [*London?* 1700.] 8°.* OC; WF.

7264 —The summ of two sermons. *Printed, and are to be sold by Jonathan Robinson,* 1692. 4°.* L, O, CT, LW, E; CLC, NU, Y.

7265 —The taghmical art. *By S. Bridge, for the author, to be sold by A. and J. Churchill,* 1698. 8°, L, O, CT, LI, EN; CH, MU, NU, WF, Y.

7266 —Two sermons. *By and for John Astwood,* 1695. 4°.* LCL, LW, EC, GU; NU.

7267 The crosses case in Cheapside. [*London*], *for T. U.,* 1642. 4°. LT, LG, CM; CH, MH, WF, Y.

7268 —[Anr. ed.] [*London*], *printed,* 1642. 4°. OC; CH, NU. Crossing of proverbs. [1650?] *See* R., B.

7268A **Crossley, Thomas.** A discovery of false teachers in London. [*London,* 1692.] cap., fol.* C.

7268B **Crossman, Samuel.** An humble plea. *For Henry Mortlock,* 1682. 4°. T.C.I. 470. CPE, BR; CLC, IU, NPT, WF, Y.

7269 —The last testimony and declaration of. [*London,* 1683.] brs. L, O, MC; CH.

7270 —A sermon preached . . . August the 1st. 1676. *Printed,* 1676. 4°.* L, WCA; WF, Y.

7270A —A sermon preached on April xxiii, 1680. *For Charles Allen in Bristol,* 1680. 4°. T.C.I 402. BR, WCA; IU.

7271 —Two sermons. *For Henry Brome, sold by Charles Allen in Bristol,* 1681. 4°. T.C.I 438. O, CPE, BR; CH, IU, WF, Y.

7272 [–] The young man's calling. *By Tho. James, for Nath. Crouch,* 2678. 12°. T.C.I 299. L, O; CN, MH, Y.

7272A [–] —[Anr. ed.] *For N. Crouch,* 1683. 12°. LSC.

7273 [–] —[Anr. ed.] ——, 1685. 12°. T.C.II 25. L.

7274 [–] —[Anr. ed.] —, 1695. 12°. L.

7275 [–] The young-man's divine meditations. 1678. 12°. CN.

7276   —The young man's monitor. *By J. H. to be sold by S. Thompson, and T. Parkhurst,* 1664. 8°. L, O, C, LCL, LSC; CLC, NPT.

7277   The crost couple. [*London*], *for F. Coles, T. Vere, J. Wright, and J. Clarke,* [1690?]. brs. L.

7277A [**Crouch, Humphrey.**] Come buy a mouse-trap. *By Iohn Hammond,* [1647?]. brs. MAU.

7277B —The downfall of pride. *For Francis Grove,* [1656]. brs. O.

7277C —England's jests refin'd and improv'd. Second edition. *For John Harris,* 1687. 12°. T.C.II 180. L; WF.

7277D — —Third edition. —, 1693. 12°. T.C.II 458. L.

7278   —An excellent sonnet of the unfortunate loves, of Hero. [*London*], *for F. Coles, T. Vere, and J. Wright,* [1672?]. brs. L, O, CM, GU.

7279   —A godly exhortation. *For Richard Harper,* 1642. brs. LT.

7279A —The Greeks and Trojans Warrs. *For F. Coles, T. Vere, John Wright and J. Clarke,* 1679? brs. O.

7280   —The heroick history of Guy Earle of Warwick. *For Jane Bell,* 1655. brs. L, EN; Y.

7281   — —[Anr. ed.] *For Edward Brewster,* 1671. 4°.* Y.

7282   — —[Anr. ed.] *For Edward Brewster, to be sold by John Williamson,* 1673. 4°.* CH.

7283   —The Lady Pecunia's journey unto Hell. *For John Clarke,* 1654. brs. LT.

7284   —The mad mans morrice. *For Richard Harper,* [1635–42]. brs. L, HH ,GU.

7285   — —[Anr. ed.] [*London*], *by and for A. M.,* [1670–97]. brs. L, HH; MH.

7286   —A new and pleasant history of unfortunate Hodg of the South. *For T. Locke,* 1655. 8°. O.

7287   —The Parliament of graces. [*London*], *printed,* 1642. 4°.* LT; CLC, TU, Y.

7288   — —[Anr. ed.] [*n.p.*], —, 1643. 4°.* IU.

7288A [–] A pleasant new song that plainly doth show. [*London*], *by M. F. for R. Harper,* [1680–1]. brs. MAU.

7288B —The Welch traveller. *For William Gilbertson,* 1657. 8°. O.

7289   — —*For William Whitwood,* 1671. 8°.* L; Y.

7289A — —[Anr. ed.] 1685. 12°. CM.

7290   **Crouch, John.** Belgica caracteristica, or the Dutch character . . . A poem. *By Edward Crowch,* 1665. 4°.* L.

7291   — —Second edition. —, 1665. 4°.* L; MH.

7291A Census poeticus, the poets tribute. 1663. 4°.* C.

7292   —A congratulation, in honour of the annual festival. [*London,* 1655.] brs. O.

7293   —The Dutch imbergo. *By Edward Crowch,* 1665. 4°.* L; CH.

7294   — —Second edition, —, 1665. 4°.* L; CH, MH.

7295   [–] An elegie, upon the death of . . . Anne, Countesse of Shrewsbury. *Printed,* 1657. 4°.* MH.

7296   —An elegy upon the Marquess of Dorchester. [1680.] brs. L, O; MH, Y.

7297   —An elegie upon the much lamented death of . . . the Earl of Tiveot. *For Tho. Palmer,* 1664. brs. O, HH; MH.

7298   —Flovvers strovved by the muses. *For Francis Kirkman and Henry Marsh,* 1662. 4°.* L; CH, MH, TU.

7299   —Londinenses lacrymæ. *For T. Palmer,* 1666. 4°.* L, O, LG, EN, GH; CH, CLC, CN, MH, Y.

7300   —A mixt poem. *For Thomas Bettertun,* 1660. 4°.* L, C; CH, CN, MH, WF, Y.

7301   — —[Anr. ed.] *For Daniell White,* 1660. 4°.* O.

7302   [–] The muses joy for the recovery of . . . Henretta [sic] Maria. *For Tho. Batterton,* 1661. 4°.* LT, O; CH.

7303   —The muses tears. *For the author,* 1660. 4°.* O; MH, WF.

7303A —Portugallia in portu, Portugall in harbour. *For Richard Hall,* 1662. fol.* NIC.

7304   —Ποτηριον γλυχύπιχρον. Londons bitter-sweet-cup. *By E. Crowch,* 1666. 4°.* L, O, LG, EN; CN, WF, Y.

7305   [–] To His Sacred Majesty: loyall reflections. [*London,* 1660?] fol.* C.

7306   [**Crouch, Nathaniel.**] Admirable curiosities. *By Tho. Snowden, for Natn. Crouch,* 1682. 12°. T.C.II 31. L, O, CS; LC, MH, NP, WF.

7307   [–] —Second edition. *By John Richardson, for Nath. Crouch,* 1684. 12°. T.C.II 57. L, O, CE; MWA.

7308   [–] —Fourth edition. *For Nath. Crouch,* 1685. 8°. L, O, EN; WSC.

7308A [–] — Fifth edition. —, 1697. 12°. LWL.

7309   [–] Ancient and present state of London and Westminster. Third edition. [*London*], 1684. 12°. CHRISTIE-MILLER.

7310   [–] The apprentice's companion. *For T. Mercer,* 1681. 12°. T.C.I 448. L, C, LSC.

7310A [–] —[Anr. ed.] *For Samuel and John Sprint,* 1699. 12°. 12°. T.C.III 95. CLC.

7311   [–] Delightful fables in prose and verse. *For N. Crouch,* 1691. 8°. T.C.II 399. O.

7312   [–] Delights for the ingenious. *For Nath. Crouch,* 1684. 12°. T.C.II 61. L, O, A; CH, CN, CU, Y.

7313   [–] Dwy daith: Gaersalem. *Yn y Mwythig,· John Rhydderch* [*Shrewsbury,* 1690?]. 12°. L.

7314   [–] England's monarchs. *For Nath. Crouch,* 1685. 12°. T.C.II 102. L, O; CLC, CN, MH, PL, Y.

7315   [–] —Second edition. —, 1685. 12°. L, CS, E; NP.

7316   [–] —[Anr. ed.] —, 1691. 12°. T.C.II 358. O, OP; WF.

7317   [–] —[Anr. ed.] —, 1694. 12°. T.C.II 514. L, O, C; PU.

7318   [–] The English acquisitions in Guinea. *For Nath. Crouch,* 1700. 8°. L; MIU, Y.

7319   [–] The English empire in America. *For Nath. Crouch,* 1685. 12°. T.C.II 124. L, CS; CH, CN, MH, NN, WF, Y.

7320   [–] —Second edition. *For Nathaniel Crouch,* 1692. 12°. T.C.II 398. CE, CT; CH, CU, LC, Y.

7321   [–] —Third edition. —, 1698. 12°. L, LVF, CS; MB, NC, NN, PHS.

7321A —The English heroe. *For Nath. Crouch,* 1687. 12°. CH, RPJ, WCL, Y.

7321B [–] —[Anr. ed.] —, 1692. 12°. NN, WF.

7322   [–] —Fourth edition. —, 1695. 12°. T.C.II 532. L; LC, RPJ.

7322A [–] An epitome of all the lives. *By I. Okes, to be sold by Iames Becket,* 1639 [*i.e.,* 1693.] CN, Y.

7323   [-] Extraordinary adventures and discoveries. *By J. Richardson, for Nath. Crouch*, 1683. 12°. L, O; CLC, CN, WF.

7324   [-] —Second edition. *For Nath. Crouch.* 1685. 12°. CLC, LC, MH, MIU.

7325   [-] The famous and renowned history of the worthies. *By W.O. and are to be sold by the booksellers*, [1700]. 4°. WF.

7326   [-] Female excellency, or the ladies glory. *For Nath. Crouch*, 1688. 12°. T.C.II 216. L; CLC, CN, MH, WF, Y.

7327   [-] The general history of earthquakes. 1692. 8°. O.

7328   [-] —[Anr. ed.] *For Nath. Crouch*, 1694. 12°. T.C.II 509. L, O, LNH, C; CN, LC, MIU, WF, Y.

7329   [-] Historical remarques. *For Nath. Crouch*, 1681. 12°. L, O, CT, LVF, A; CH, CLC, MH, PL, Y.

7330   [-] —Third edition. —, 1684. 12°. T.C.II 27. L, O, LG; CH, CLC, CN, MU, WF.

7330A   [-] —Fourth edition. —, 1691. 12°. LU, EN; CLC, MH, PL.

7331   [-] The history of Oliver Cromwel. *For Nath. Crouch*, 1692. 12°. T.C.II 410. L, O; CLC, PAP.

7332   [-] —[Anr. ed.] —, 1693. 12°. T.C.II 453. L, CT, A; WF.

7332A   [-] —Third edition. —, 1698. 12°. L; PL, Y.

7333   [-] The historie of Scotland. *For N. Crouch*, 1696. 12°. T.C.II 568. L.

7334   [-] The history of the House of Orange. *For Nath. Crouch*, 1693. 12°. T.C.II 450. O, CT; MM, PAP, Y.

7335   [-] The history of the kingdom of Ireland. *For Nath. Crouch*, 1693. 12°. T.C.II 509. L, O, CS, A; CH, WF.

7335A   [-] The history of the kingdom of Scotland. *For Nath. Crouch*, 1696. 12°. L, CT.

7336   [-] The history of the kingdoms of Scotland & Ireland. *For Nath. Crouch*, 1685. 12°. T.C.II 102. L, LVF; LC, NP.

7337   [-] The history of the nine worthies. *For Nath. Crouch*, 1687. 12°. T.C.II 193. L, CT; CN, Y.

7338   [-] —[Anr. ed.] —, 1695. 12°. T.C.II 551. MH.

7339   [-] The history of the principality of Wales. *For Nath. Crouch*, 1695. 12°. T.C.II 522. L, C, AN, CPL; LC, NP, PL, WF, Y.

7340   [-] The history of the two late kings. *For Nath. Crouch*, 1693. 12°. T.C.II 453. L, O, CPE, AU; NP, PL, WF.

7341   [-] A journey to Jerusalem. *By T.M. for Nath. Crouch* 1672. 8°. T.C.I 110. L, O, CT, OB; CN, WF.

7342   [-] The kingdom of darkness. *For Nath. Crouch*, 1688. 12°. T.C.II 216. L; WF.

7343-4 Entries cancelled.

7345   [-] Miracles of art and nature. *For William Bowtel*, 1678. 12°. T.C.I 292. L, GU; RPJ, WF, Y.

7345A   [-] The scarlet whore. *For Nath. Crouch*, 1690. 12°. T.C.II 257. CLC.

7346   [-] The secret history, of the four last monarchs of Great Britain. *Printed*, 1691. 12°. O; CH, MB, MM, PL, WF.

7347   [-] —[Anr. ed.] [*London*], 1693. 12°. BR, RPL.

7348   [-] The strange and prodigious religions, customs, . . . of sundry nations. *Printed for and sold by Hen. Rhodes*, 1683. 12°. T.C.I 510. L, O; CLC, MH, Y.

7348A   [-] —Second edition. —, 1688. 12°. T.C.II 235. LSC; MB, Y.

7349   [-] The surprizing miracles of nature and art. *For Nath. Crouch*, 1683. 8°. T.C.II 31. O, GU; CU, MIU, PL, WF, Y.

7350   [-] —Second edition. —, 1685. 12°. LWL; CH, MH, NP.

7350A   — —Third edition. —, 1690. 8°. CLC.

      [-] Two journeys. 1683. *See* Timberlake, Henry.

7351   [-] The unfortunate court favourites. *For Nath. Crouch*, 1695. 12°. T.C.II 523. L, C, CPE; CLC, CN, MH, NC, WF, Y.

7352   [-] Unparallel'd varieties. *For Nath. Crouch*, 1683. 12°. T.C.II 31. L, A; LC.

7353   [-] —Second edition. —, 1685. 12°. L; LC, MH, TU.

7354   [-] —Third edition. —, 1699. 12°. L, O, CCC; CN, LC, Y.

7355   [-] The vanity of the life of man. *For Nath. Crouch*, 1688. 8°.* T.C.II 231. L, O, C.

7355A   [-] —Second edition. —, 1698. 12°. T.C.II 541. L.

7356   [-] A view of the English acquisitions in Guinea. *For Nath. Crouch*, 1686. 12°. T.C.II 144. L; BN, CN, MIU, NN, WF, Y.

7357   [-] The wars in England, Scotland and Ireland. *For Nath. Crouch and John How*, 1681. 12°. L, O, LVF; CH, CN, MH, NN, WF, Y.

7358   [-] —Fourth edition. *For Nath. Crouch*, 1683. 12°. T.C.II 31. L, LG, CS; CLC, MBP, PL, WF, Y.

7359   [-] —Fifth edition. *By J.R. for Nath. Crouch*, 1684. 12°. T.C.II 65. L, O, CS, LCL, LVF; CH, CLC, NP, WF, Y.

7359A   — —Sixth edition. *For Nath. Crouch*, 1697. 12°. T.C.III 8. L; CU, MIU.

7360   [-] Winter-evenings entertainments. *For Nath. Crouch*, 1687. 12°. T.C.II 180. CHRISTIE-MILLER.

7361   [-] Wonderful prodigies of judgement and mercy. *For Nath. Crouch*, 1682. 12°. T.C.II 31. L, O.

7361A   — —[Anr. ed.] —, 1685. 12°. GU; MH, WF.

7361B   [-] —[Anr. ed.] —, 1693. 12°. T.C.II 460. CLC.

7362   [-] —Fifth edition. —, 1699. 12°. L.

7363   [-] Youths divine pastime. Pt. 1. Third edition. *For Nath. Crouch*, 1691. 12°. L.

7364   **Crouch, William.** Status naturæ. [*n.p.*, 1662.] brs. O.

7465   **Crow, Francis.** Mensalia sacra: or, meditations. *For John Dunton*, 1693. 8°. T.C.II 471. L, O, LCL, LW.

7366   —The vanity and impiety. *For John Dunton*, 1690. 12°. T.C.II 338. L, O, LCL; WF.

7367   [**Crowe, William.**] The catalogue of our English writers on the Old and New Testament. Second edition. *By E. Cotes for Thomas Williams*, 1668. 8°. L, O, C, E, DT; CH, CU, LC, MH, NP, Y.

7368   —Elenchus scriptorum. *Typis T.R. impensis authoris, & prostat venalis apud Mosen Pitts*, 1672. 8°. T.C.I 121. L, O, C, EN, DT; CH, MB, NU, WF, Y.

7369   [-] An exact collection or catalogue of our English writers. *By R. Davenport for John Williams*, 1663. 8°. L, O, C, CT, ON; CLC, LC, NC, NU, Y.

7370   **C[rowley], R[obert].** Certain prayers and graces. 1687. 8°. O.

7371 [**Crown, S.**] An anniversary upon the xxxth of January. 1648. Being a poem. *Printed by Nathaniel Butter,* 1650. *But not permitted to be publick till now,* 1660. 8°.* L.

7372 [–] The loyal remembrances. *By R. Wood,* 1650. *But not permitted to be publick till now,* 1660. 4°.* LT, O.

7373 A crowne, a crime. [*London,* 1649.] brs. LT.
Crown and glory. 1676. *See* Nesse, Christopher.

7374 **Crowne, John.** The ambitious statesman. *For William Abington,* 1679. 4°. T.C.I 359. L, O, C, LVD, EN; CH, CN, LC, MH, NP, TU, Y.

7375 — —Second edition. *For R. Bentley and M. Magnes,* 1681. 4°.* T.C.I 446. EN; MH, PU, WF, Y.

7376 —Caligula. *By J. Orme for R. Wellington and sold by Percival Gilborne and Bernard Lintott,* 1698. 4°. T.C.III 65. L, O, C, LVD, EN; CH, CN, LC, MH, NP, TU, Y.

7377 —Calisto. *By Tho: Newcomb for James Magnes and Richard Bentley,* 1675. 4°. T.C.I 218. L, O, C, LVD, EN; CH, CN, LC, MH, NP, TU, Y.

7378 —City politiques. *For R. Bently and Joseph Hindmarsh,* 1683. 4°. T.C.II 17. L, O, C, CS; CH, CN, LC, MH, TU, Y.

7379 — —[Anr. ed.] —, 1688. 4°. L, O, LVD, EN, DT; CH, CN, LC, MH, NC, TU, Y.

7380 —The countrey wit. *By T. N. for James Magnes, and Richard Bentley,* 1675. 4°. T.C.I 236. L, O; CH, CN, LC, MH, TU, Y.

7381 — —[Anr. ed.] *For Thomas Chapman,* 1693. 4°. L, LVD; CU, LC, MH, NP, WF, Y.

7382 [–] Daeneids, or the noble labours. *For Richard Baldwin,* 1692. 4°.* T.C.II 393. L; CLC, CN, MH, TU, Y.

7383 —Darius King of Persia. *For Jos. Knight and Fr. Saunders,* 1688. 4°. T.C.II 231. L, O, C, LVD, EN; CH, CU, LC, MH, TU, Y.

7384 — —[Anr. ed.] *For R. Bentley,* 1688. 4°. L, O, EN; TU, CH; CN, MH, WF, Y.

7385 —The destruction of Jerusalem. *For James Magnes and Richard Bentley,* 1677. 2 pts. 4°. T.C.I 273. L, O, C, EN, DT; CH, CN, LC, MH, TU, Y.

7386 — —[Anr. ed.] *For R. Bentley,* 1693. 4°. L, EN; BN, CN, MH, MU, WF, Y.

7387 —The Cnglish [sic] frier. *For James Knapton,* 1690. 4°. T.C.II 313. L, O, C, LVD, EN; CH, CN, LC, MH, NC, TU, Y.

7388 —Henry the Sixth, the first part. *For R. Bentley, and M. Magnes,* 1681. 4°. T.C.I 462. L, O, LVD, OW, EN; CH, CN, LC, MH, NC, TU, Y.

7389 —Henry the Sixth, the second part. *For R. Bentley and M. Magnes,* 1681. 4°. T.C.I 462. L, O, LVD, EN; CH, CN, MH, NC, TU, WF, Y.

7390 —The history of Charles the Eighth of France. *By T. R. and N. T. for Ambrose Isted,* 1672. 4°. T.C.I 118. L, O, C, LVD, EN; CH, CN, LC, MH, NP, TU, Y.

7391 — —[Anr. ed.] *For A. I. to be sold by Robert Boulter,* 1680. 4°. T.C.I 404. L, OW; LC, MH.

7392 [–] The history of the famous and passionate love. *For R. T.,* 1692. 4°.* L; CH, CLC, MH.

7393 —Juliana. *For Will. Cademan and Will. Birch,* 1671. 4°. T.C.I 87. L, O, LVD, OW, EN; CH, CU, LC, MH, NP, Y.

7394 —The married beau. *For Richard Bentley,* 1694. 4°. T.C.II 511. L, O, LVD, OW, EN; BN, CH, CN, LC, MH, NC, TU, Y.

7395 —The misery of civil-war. *For R. Bentley, and M. Magnes,* 1680. 4°. T.C.I 394. L, O, C, CCA; CH, CN, LC, MH, TU, Y.

7396 —Pandion and Amphigenia. *By I. G. for R. Mills,* 1665. 8°. L, O; CLC, CN, IU, MH, RPB.

7397 —A poem, on the lamented death. *For John Smith,* 1685. 4°.* L, O, C, LVD, CT; CH, CN, MH, TU, WF, Y.

7398 —The prologue and epilogue to the city politiques. colop: *For Thos. Benskins,* 1683. brs. L, O, MC, EN; CH, MH, TU, WF, Y.

7399 —The prologue and epilogue to the new comedy, called, Sir Courtley Nice. colop: *For Tho. Benskin,* 1685. brs. L, O; MH, WF.

7400 [–] The prologue and epilogue to the new comedy, called, The English fryer. colop: *For John Amory, and published by Randal Taylor,* 1690. brs. L.

7401 —The prologue to Calisto. *Printed,* 1675. 4°.* L; CH, CLC, MH, WF.

7402 —Regulus. *For James Knapton,* 1694. 4°. T.C.II 480. L, O, LVD, OW, EN; CH, CN, LC, MH, NN, TU, Y.

7403 [–] See where repenting Cælia lies. [*London,* 1695.] brs. L.

7404 —Sir Courtly Nice. *By H. H. jun. for R. Bently, and Jos. Hindmarsh,* 1685. 4°. T.C.II 147. L, O, LGI; CH, CN, LC, MH, NP, TU, Y.

7405 — —Second edition. *By M. B. for R. Bentley and Jos. Hindmarsh,* 1693. 4°. LC, MH, OC, OW, EN, DT; CN, MIU, WF, Y.

7406 [–] A song in the last new comedy call'd The married beau. [*London*], 1694. brs. MC.

7406A [–] A song made for the entertainment. [*London?* 1698.] fol.* L.

7407 —Three new songs in Sir Courtly Nice. colop: *For John Crouch, and John Smith,* 1685. fol.* L.

7408 —Thyestes. *For R. Bently and M. Magnes,* 1681. 4°. T.C.I 440. L, O, LVD, OW, EN; CH, CN, LC, MH, TU, Y.

7408A [**Crowshey, John.**] The good-husbands jewel. *First printed at York, re-printed at London,* 1651. 8°. LT.

7408AA [–] —Fourth edition. *For Nath. Ekins, to be sold by Francis Newburg at Yorke,* 1656. 8°.* YM; CLC.

7408B [–] —Fifth edition. *Yorke, by Alice Broad, to be sold by Leonard Campleshon,* 1661. 8°.* L.

7408C —"Fifth" edition. *York, by Alice Broad,* 1664. 8°. CT.

7409 **C[rowther], A[rthur Anselm].** The dayly exercise, of the devout Rosarists. *Amsterdam, anno,* 1657. 12°. O, LW; CH, TU, WF.

7409A — —Second edition. 1662. 12°. CLC, CN, WF.

7409B — —Third edition. *Printed* 1673. 12°. L, O; CLC, IU, TU.

7409C — —[Anr. ed.] *For S. Evans in Worcester; sold by H. Sawbridge,* 1684. T.C.II 39. WG, WF.

7409D — —Fourth edition. *Printed,* 1685. 12°. L; CLC, TU.

7409E — —Fifth edition. *For Matthew Turner*, 1688. 8°. L, WARE; CN, IU, TU.

7409F —Jesus, Maria, Joseph. *Antwerp, by William Cesteane*, 1654. 12°. LW; CN.

7410 — —[Anr. ed.] *Printed at Amsterdam*, 1657. 12°. L, CSE, EN; CLC, TU, WF, Y.

7411 — —[Anr. ed.] —, 1663. 8°. L, LW, OC; CLC.

7412 **Crowther, John.** Papers presented to the Parliament. *Printed at London, by Robert Ibbitson*, 1648. 4°.* LT, C; CH, MH, Y.

7413 —The testimony of severall eminent commanders. *For R.L.*, 1648. 4°.* LT, C; CH.

7414 **C[roxton], J[ames].** Q.F.F.Q.S. A new fiction, as wee were. *By J. C. for the author*, 1661. 4°.* LT, LVF; TU.

7414A **Croynes, Josh.** A hundred notable [*sic*] things. *For J. Conyers*, 1686. 8°. CM.

7415 Cruel and barbarous news from Cheapside. [*London*], 1676. 4°. O.

7416 A cruell and blovdy battaile, betwixt the Weymarish. *For Nath: Butter*, 1642. 4°.* LT, O, HH; CN, MH.

7417 A cruel and bloody plot discovered. [*London*], 1660. brs. HH.

7418 The cruel French lady. *Vaughan*, 1673. 4°.* O, LG.

7419 The cruel land-lord. [*London*], *for J.Blare*, [c. 1685]. brs. L, HH; MH.

7419A The cruel midwife. *R. Wier*, 1693. 8°.* L.

7420 The cruel mother. *For W. R.*, 1670. 4°.* L; CLC.

7421 The cruel murtherer, or the treacherous neighbour. [*London*], *for Edward Robinson*, 1673. 4°.* MH.

Cruel subtilty. 1650. *See* Sarpi, Paolo.

7422 The crvell tragedy or inhumane bvtchery. [*London*], *printed*, 1648. 4°.* LT, CS; MIU, Y.

7422A The cruelty of some fighting priests. *For Thomas Simmons*, 1660. 4°.* L, LF, BBN; PH, PSC.

Cruelty of the magistrates. 1655. *See* Smith, Humphry.

Cruelty of the Spaniards. 1658. *See* Davenant, *Sir* William.

7423 **Cruickshank, George.** Disputatio juridica. *Edinburgi, excudebat Jacobus Watson*, 1698. 4°.* ALDIS 3741. EN.

7424 **[Crull, Jodocus.]** The antient and present state of Muscovy. *For A.Roper; and A.Bosvile*, 1698. 8°. L, O, CT, EN, DT; CH, CN, MH, NN, WF, Y.

7425 — —Vol. II. —, 1698. 8°. O, CT, LWL; CH, CN, Y.

7426 —Denmark vindicated. *For Tho. Newborough, and Ed. Mory*, 1694. 8°. T.C.II 513. L, O, C, EN, DT; CH, CU, LC, MH, NC, Y.

7427 —Memoirs of Denmark. *Printed, and sold by John Nutt*, 1700. 8°. L, C, DCH; CLC, IU, MU, WF, Y.

7428 Entry cancelled.

7429 **Crumby, Alexander.** Great news from Ireland, giving an account. colop: *Printed, and sold by R. Janeway*, 1690. brs. Y.

Crums of bread. [*n.p.*, 1652.] *See* Tickell, John.

Crums of comfort. [*n.p.*, 1650?] *See* Sparke, Michael.

—[*n.p.*, 1664.] *See* B., R.

7430 Crums of comfort for the Younge sister. *For P. Brooksby*, 1687. brs. O, CM, HH; MH. Y.

Crumbs of comfort . . . A sermon. [1680?] *See* B., J.

7431 **Crump, John.** The parable of the Great Supper opened. *For Tho. Parkhurst*, 1669. 12°. T.C.I 17. L, LCL, DC, P; CLC, MH, Y.

7431A **Crusius, Thomas Theodorus.** The origine of atheism. *For W. Kettilby*, 1689. 4°.* T.C.II 95. L, O, BAMB, P, A; CH, MM, MU, NN, WF.

7432 **C[ruso], J[ohn].** Castrametation. [sic]. *By R.C. for Andrew Crook*, 1642. 4°. L, O, CS, SC, YM, AU; MU.

7433 —Military instructions. *Cambridge, by Roger Daniel*, 1644. fol. LW, C; LC.

7434 **Cruso, Timothy.** The Christian lover. *By J. B. for J. Salusbury*, 1690. 8°. T.C.II 332. LW; WF.

7435 —The churches plea. *By J. R. for John Salusbury*, 1689. 4°.* L, LW; CH, CLC, NU, WF.

7436 —Discourses upon the rich man and Lazarus. *By S. Bridge, for Tho. Parkhurst*, 1697. 8°. T.C.III 24. L, O, C, LCL; MH, NU, WF, Y.

7437 —The duty and blessing of a tender conscience. *By J. R. for J. Salusbury*, 1691. 12°. T.C.II 367. L, O, C, LW; WF.

7437A —The duty and support of believers. *For Tho. Cockerill*, 1688. 4°.* L; LW; CH, CN.

7437B —An earnest plea for attendance. *For T. Cockerill, snrs. and junrs.*, 1696. 12°.* LW.

7438 —The excellency of the Protestant faith. *By J.R. for John Salusbury*, 1689. 4°.* O, LW, DT; CH, CLC.

7439 —God the guide to youth. *For T. Cockerill*, 1695. 8°. T.C.II 537. LW.

7440 —The mighty wonders of a merciful providence. *For Thomas Cockerill, and John Salisbury*, 1689. 4°.* L, O, LW, EN, ENC; CH, CLC, MH, NU, WF.

7441 —The necessity and advantage of an early victory. *For Thomas Cockerill, and H. Bernard*, 1693. 4°.* L, O, LW; CH, NU, PL, WF.

7442 —The period of humane life determined. *For J. Salusbury*, 1688. 4°.* L, O, C, LW, CT; CH, NPT.

7443 Entry cancelled.

7444 —The three last sermons. *By S. Bridge, for Tho. Parkhurst*, 1698. 8°. L, LCL; MH, WF.

7445 —Twenty-four sermons. *By S.Bridge, for Thomas Parkhurst*, 1699. 8°. L, LCL, LW; MH, NU, WF, Y.

7446 —The usefulnesse of spiritval wisdom. *By J.R. for John Salusbury*, 1689. 4°.* L, O, C, LW; CH, NU, TU, WF, Y.

7447 **C[rutwell], N.** Bristol drollery. *London, for Charles Allen, in Bristol*, 1674. 8°. T.C.I 170. L, BR; CH, MH.

7447A Crux Christi and judgement executed. 1657. 8°. NHC.

7447B **Cruys, Francis.** Ars nova natandi, or, new swimming. *Bristol, by Will. Bonny*, 1698. 4°.* WF.

A cry, a cry. [*n.p.*, 1678.] *See* Mudd, Ann.

Cry against a crying sinne. 1652. *See* Chidley, Samuel.

7448 A cry against oppression & cruelty. *Printed, and are to be sold by William Warwick*, 1663. 4°. LF; CH, PH, PSC.

7449 A cry for a right improvement of all our mercies. *For Tho. Brewster, and Greg: Moule*, 1652. 4°.* LT, LG.

Cry for repentance. 1656. *See* Fox, George.

Cry of blovd. 1654. *See* Musgrave, John.

7449A The cry of blood, or the horrid sin of murther. *Randal Taylor*, 1692. brs. LG; CN, MH.

Cry of innocent blood. [*n.p.*], 1670. *See* Allen, Robert.

Cry of Newgate. 1662. *See* Crane, Richard.

7449B The cry of oppression and cruelty. [*London*, 1677.] 4°.* L, O, BBN; CH, CN, LC, Y.

7449C The cry of oppression continued. [*London*], *printed*, 1676. 4°.* L, BBN; V, Y.

Cry of royal. 1683. *See* Assheton, William.

Cry of Sodom. Cambridge [Mass.], 1674. *See* Danforth, Samuel.

7450 The cry of the innocent & oppressed for justice. *Printed at London*, 1664. 4°.* L, O, C, LF, BBN; CH, LC, MH, NU, PH, PSC, Y.

7451 The cry of the innocent for justice. [*London*], *printed*, 1662. 4°.* L, LF, LL, BBN, EN; CH, CN, MH, PH, WF, Y.

Cry of the just. [*n.p.*, 1660.] *See* Goodaire, Thomas.

Cry of the oppressed. 1656. *See* Benson, Gervase.

Cry of the oppressed. Being. 1691. *See* Pitt, Moses.

Cry of the oppressed by reason. 1659. *See* S., S.

Crying charge. [*London?*], 1649. *See* Douglas, *Lady* Eleanor.

Crying sinnes. 1656. *See* Burrough, Edward.

7452 **Crymes, Thomas.** Parliamentum imperatorium: seu carmine. *Excudebat G. Dawson, renevnt L. Chapman*, 1654. 8°. L, O, DC, P; CH, MH, Y.

Cryptomenysis. 1685. *See* Falconer, John.

7453 [**Crysly, James.**] Good news from Ireland. colop: *For John Dunton*, 1690. brs. L, MC; CH.

7453A [–] —[Anr. ed.] colop: *For Richard Newman*, [1690.] brs. Y.

7453B The cuckold's complaint. [*London*], *for P. Brooksby, J. Deacon, J. Blare, J. Back*, [1689–91.] brs. CM.

7454 The cuckolds dream: or, the comical vision. [1690?]. 4°. brs. O.

7455 The cuckold's lamentation of a bad wife. [*London*], *for P. Brooksby*, [1672–85]. brs. L, O, HH.

7456 The cuckow. [*London*, 1660?] brs. L, O.

7457 The cuckoo of the times. [*London*], *for P. Brooksby*, [1675?]. brs. L, O, HH.

7458 Cuckoo: or the Welsh embassadour's application to the raven. 1691. 4°. L.

7459 The cuckoo's-nest at Westminster, . . . by Mercurius Melancholicus. [*London*], *printed*, 1648. 4°.* LT, O; CH, Y.

7460 **Cudmore, Daniel.** Εὐχοδια. Or, a prayer-song. *By J. C. for William Ley*, 1655. 8°. LT, EN; CH, CN, WF, Y.

7461 — —[Anr. ed.] —, 1657. 8°. LT.

7462 —The history of Ioseph. A poem. *By T. Warren for the use of the author*, 1652. 4°. CH, WF.

7463 **Cudworth, John.** Fides ecclesiæ Anglicanæ. *Oxonii, typis Sheldonianis, impensis Hen. Clements*, 1688. 4°.* L, O, C, OM, SC; BN, NGT, NU, WF, Y.

7464 **Cudworth, Ralph.** Bibliotheca Cudworthiana, sive catlogus. [*London*], 9 Feb., 1690/1. 4°.* L; JF.

7465 —Dantur rationes boni et mali. [*n.p.*, 1651.] brs. LT, O.

7466 —A discovrse concerning the trve notion of the Lords Svpper. *For Richard Cotes*, 1642. 4°. L, O, C, EN, DT; CH, NU, OCI, Y.

7467 — —Second edition. *By J. Flesher for R. Royston*, 1670. 8°. T.C.I 60. L, O, C, E, DT; CN, MH, PL, TU, WF.

7468 — —Third edition. *For R. Royston*, 1676. fol. L, C, OB, EN, AU; BN, CN, MH, NU, PL, WF.

7469 —A sermon preached . . . March 31, 1647. *Cambridge, by Roger Daniel*, 1647. 4°. LT, O, C, LL, DT; CH, MH, NU, WF, Y.

7470 —A sermon preached to the honorable society of Lincolnes-Inne. *By J. Flesher, for R. Royston*, 1664. 4°. O, C, LL, CT, DC; CLC, NU, TU, WF, Y.

7471 —The true intellectual system of the universe: the first part. *For Richard Royston*, 1678. fol. T.C.I 312. L, O, C, EN, DT; BN, CH, CN, MH, TU, WF, Y.

7472 —The union of Christ and the church. *For Richard Bishop*, 1642. 4°.* L, O, C, EN, DT; CH, CU, NU, WF, Y.

7472A [**Cuffe, Henry.**] The ages of mans life. *For Andrew Crook*, 1653. 8°. CU, Y.

7473 [**Cuffe, Maurice.**] Trve nevves from Munster. *For Henry Seyle, Iune 16*, 1642. 4°.* LT, O, C, EC, MR; Y.

7474 **Cuilemborg, Æmilio.** In Wilhelmum Magnum. *Apud H. Mortlock & J. Robinson*, 1695. fol.* O, CT, LW; Y.

7474A [**Cullen, Francis Grant, lord.**] A brief account of the nature. *Edinburgh, by George Mosman*, 1700. 4°. O, C, EN; CU.

7474B [–] A discourse, concerning the execution of the laws. *Edinburgh, by George Mosman*, 1700. 8°. EN, ENC, ES, A; CH, INU, NN, WF.

7475 [–] The loyalist reasons. *Edinburgh, by J: Reid*, 1689. 8°. ALDIS 2890. O, C, EN, FSF.

7475A —Sadducismus debellatus. *H. Newman and A. Bell*, 1698. 4°. O, CT, BAMB, GU, DT; CN, LC, MH, WCL, Y.

7475B [–] A true narrative of the sufferings . . . of a young girle. *Edinburgh, by James Watson*, 1698. 8°. ALDIS 3809. O, EN, AU; CW, CLC, GU; CH, CLC, MH.

7475C The cullies invitation. *For S. Deacon*, [c. 1700]. brs. Y.

7476 **Culman, Leonard.** Sentences for children. *For the company of stationers*, 1658. 8°.* L.

7476A — —[Anr. ed.] *By E. T. for the company of stationers*, 1667. 8°. CP.

7477 —Sententiæ pueriles. *Cantabrigiæ, ex officina Joann. Hayes*, 1676. 8°.* MH.

7477A — —[Anr. ed.] *Typis J. Macock pro societate stationariorum*, 1677. 8°. Y.

7477B **Culme, Arthur.** A diary and relation of passages . . . Dublin. *For Godfrey Emerson*, 1647. 4°. OC.

7477C **Culme, Hugh.** A remonstrance of the beginnings. *August 11. For Godfrey Emerson*, 1642. 4°. O, EC.

7478 **Culmer, Richard.** Cathedrall nevves from Canterbvry. *Printed at London by Rich. Cotes, for Fulk Clifton*, 1644. 4°.* LT, O, CM, CT; CN, NPT, NU, WF, Y.

7479 —Dean and chapter newes. Second edition. *Printed at London, by Richard Cotes*, 1649. 4°.* LT, O, LCL, LW, DT; MH.

7480 [-] Lawles tythe-robbers discovered. *For Thomas New-bery*, 1655. 4°.* LT, O, C, OC, CT; CH, NU, WF, Y.

7481 —The ministers hue and cry. *By Abraham Miller*, 1651. 4°.* LT, O, C, LCL, OC; CH, NU, WF, Y.

7482 —A parish looking-glasse. *By William Miller*, 1657. 4°.* L, O, CCL, CN, WF.

7483 Culmer's crown crackt. colop: *Printed at London*, 1657. 4°.* L.

Culpeper, Sir John. *See* Colepeper John, *baron*.

Culpeper, Nathaniel. Culpeper revived. Cambridge, 1680. *See* Almanacs.

Culpeper, Nicholas. Arts master-piece. *See* Wecker, J. J.

7484 —Culpeper's astrologicall judgment. *For Nath. Brookes* 1655. 8°. L, LCP, LPO, LWL; KT, WSG, HC.

7485 —Catastrophe magnatum, or the fall of monarchie. *For T. Vere and Nath: Brooke*, 1652. 4°. LT, O, CPE, YM; CH, MH, HC.

7486 —Composita: or, a synopsis. *By J. G. for Nath. Brook*, 1655. 8°. LT; HC.

7487 Entry cancelled.

7488 —A directory for midwives. *By Peter Cole*, 1651. 8°. LT, LWL; WSG, HC.

7489 ——[Anr. ed.] *By Peter Cole: and R. Westbrook*, 1653. 8°. HC.

7490 ——Second edition. *By Peter Cole*, 1656. 8°. L.

7491 ——[Anr. ed.] *By Peter Cole, and Edward Cole*, 1660. 8°. HC.

7491A ——[Anr. ed.] *Edinburgh, by George Swinton and James Glen*, 1668. 8°. EN.

7492 ——[Anr. ed.] *By John Streater, to be sold by George Sawbridge*, 1671. 8°. T.C.I 75. LM, LW; CLM, WF, WSG, HC.

7493 ——[Anr. ed.] *For George Sawbridge*, 1675. 8°. LWL, OR; CJC, WSG, HC.

7494 ——[Anr. ed.] —, 1681. 8°. AM; BN, WSG, HC.

7494A ——[Anr. ed.] *For H. Sawbridge*, 1684. 8°. T.C.II 108. LCS, LWL; PBL, HC.

7495 ——[Anr. ed.] *Printed*, 1693. 12°. T.C.II 495. L, AM; HC.

7496 ——[Anr. ed.] —, 1700. 12°. LWL; WSG, HC.

7497 —Culpeper's directory for midwives: or, a guide for women, the second part. *By Peter Cole*, 1662. 8°. CLM, HC.

7498 ——[Anr. ed.] *By J. Streater, to be sold by George Sawbridge*, 1671. 8°. LM; WF, HC.

7499 ——[Anr. ed.] —, 1681. 8°. AM; BN, WSG, HC.

7500 —The English physician. *Printed*, 1652. 12°. L, LNH, LWL; MH, WSG, HC.

7501 ——[Anr. ed.] *By Peter Cole*, 1652. fol. L, LWL, LG; CH, LC, WF, HC.

7501A ——[Anr. ed.] *W. Bentley*, 1652. 12°. LWL.

7502 —The English physitian enlarged. *By Peter Cole*, 1653. 8°. LT, CCL, D; LC, NAM, HC.

7502A ——[Anr. ed.] —, 1655. 8°. CLC.

7503 ——[Anr. ed.] —, 1656. 8°. O, CPE, LCS, LWL, BR, GK; CLC, WF, WS; HC.

7504 ——[Anr. ed.] —, 1661. 8°. L, CPE, LWL; HC.

7504A ——[Anr. ed.] —, 1662. 8°. LWL; HC.

7505 ——[Anr. ed.] —, 1665. 8°. L; BBE, HC.

7506 ——[Anr. ed.] *By John Streater*, 1666. 8°. L, LCS; HC.

7507 ——[Anr. ed.] —, 1669. 8°. L, LWL; CH, WSG, HC.

7508 ——[Anr. ed.] —, 1671. 8°. WSG, HC.

7509 ——[Anr. ed.] *For George Sawbridge*, 1674. 8°. LCS, LWL, OM; CLM, NP.

7510 ——[Anr. ed.] —, 1676. 8°. LWL, AU; CLM, WF, HC.

7511 ——[Anr. ed.] —, 1681. 8°. O, LWL, HH, E, GK; MM, WSG, HC.

7512 ——[Anr. ed.] *For Hannah Sawbridge*, 1683. 8°. L, LSC, GU; BN, CJC, WSG, HC.

7512A ——[Anr. ed.] —, 1684. 8°. CSU, MIU, NAM, NN.

7513 ——[Anr. ed.] *For Hannah Sawbridge, and sold by John Taylor*, 1684. 8°. T.C.II 77. O, LWL, GU; MIU, NAM, HC.

7514 ——[Anr. ed.] *For A. and J. Churchill*, 1695. 8°. T.C.II 541. L, CT, LWL, AU; CLM, MB.

7514A ——[Anr. ed.] —, 1698. 8°. LWL; WF, WSG, HC.

7515 —The English-physician's dayly practice. *J. Conyers*, [c. 1680.] 4°.* LWL.

—Ephemeris. [*London*], 1651. *See* Almanacs.

7516 —Febrilia; or, a treatise of feavers. *N. Brooke*, 1656. 8°. CH, WSG.

7517 —Culpeper's last legacy. *For N. Brooke*, 1655. 8°. LT, O, LWL; CLC, NAM, NN, HC.

7518 ——[Anr. ed.] —, 1657. 12°. CT, LCP, LWL; CH, WSG, WU, HC.

7519 ——[Anr. ed.] —, 1662. 8°. HC.

7520 ——Fourth edition. *By T. Ratcliffe, for Nath. Brooke, and for Ben. Billingsley and Obadiah Blagrave*, 1668. 8°. LWL, DC; CN, WF, WSG, HC.

7521 ——Fifth edition. *For Nath. Brooke, and Obad. Blagrave*, 1671. 8°. T.C.I 68. L, LM, LWL; NAM.

7521A ——"Fifth" edition. *For Nath. Brooke*, 1676. 8°. T.C.I 261. PU. HC.

7521B ——"Fifth" edition. *For Obadiah Blagrave*, 1677. 8°. T.C.I 284. GK; CLM, MH.

7522 ——Sixth edition. *For Obadiah Blagrave*, 1683. 8°. T.C.II 118. L, C, LG, LWL, CK; BN, MIU, NAM, NS, HC.

7523 —Mr. Culpeper's ghost. *For Peter Cole*, 1656. 12°.* CLC, MH, MU, NC, V, WF, HC.

7524 —Opus astrologicum, &c. *By J. Cottrel, for Ri. Moone and Steph. Chatfield*, 1654. 8°. LT, O, OC; MH.

7525 —Pharmacopœia Londinensis. *For Peter Cole*, 1653. fol. L, C, OP, LWL, HH; CLC, MIU, WSG, Y, HC.

7526 ——[Anr. ed.] *By a well-wisher*, 1654. 12°. L, CPE, LCS; CH, CLM, WSG, HC.

7527 ——Sixth edition. *By Peter Cole*, 1654. 4°. LWL, CLM; WF, HC.

7528 ——"Sixth edition" —, 1655. 8°. LWL; HC.

7529 ——"Sixth" edition —, 1656. 8°. HC.

7530 ——"Sixth" edition —, 1659. 8°. L, OB, LCS, LWL, CCA; CH, CJC, WF, WSG, HC.

7531 ——[Anr. ed.] *By Peter Cole and Edward Cole*, 1661. fol. L, O, C, LCP, LCS; CLM.

7532 — —[Anr. ed.] *By John Streater*, 1667. 8°. L, LWL; MH, HC.

7532A — —[Anr. ed.] *By J. Streater for George Sawbridge*, 1669. 8°. LWL, GK; WSG.

7533 — —[Anr. ed.] —, 1672. LWL, CCA, AU; CLM, MU, WSG, HC.

7534 — —[Anr. ed.] *For George Sawbridge*, 1675. 8°. L, C, AU; CH, TU, WSG, HC.

7535 — —[Anr. ed.] —, 1679. 8°. T.C.I 362. CT, LWL; PL, WSG, HC.

7536 — —[Anr. ed.] *For Hanna Sawbridge*, 1683. 8°. T.C.II 55. L, LWL, AN; CLM, NAM, PBL, WF, HC.

7537 — —[Anr. ed.] *For Awnsham and John Churchill*, 1695. 8°. T.C.II 541. L, LCP, LCS, LWL; WSG, HC.

7538 —Physick for the common people. *Edinburgh*, 1664. 8°. LD, S 1772. FSF.

7539 Entry cancelled.

7540 —A physicall directory. *For Peter Cole*, 1649. 4°. LT, O, CT, LM, LWL; LC, WSG, HC.

7541 — —Second edition. —, 1650. fol. CT, LWL, OC, HH; CH, CLM, MH, HC.

7542 — —Third edition. —, 1651. fol. L, LMT, LCP, LWL, AU; CLM, LC, MMO, WF, HC.

7543 —Physical receipts. *For Thomas Howkins*, 1690. 8°.* T.C.II 300. L.

7544 —Culpeper's school of physick. *For N. Brook*, 1659. 4°. LT, C, OW, LWL; MIU, WSG, HC.

7544A — —[Anr. ed.] *G. Blagrave*, 1678. 8°. LWL.

7544B — —[Anr. ed.] *R. Harford*, 1678. 8°. LWL.

7545 — —Second edition. *For O. B. & R. H., sold by Robert Clavel*, 1678. 8°. T.C.I 305. L, LWL, E; CN, LC, WSG, HC.

7546 — —Third edition. *For R. Bently; J. Phillips: H. Rhodes; and J. Taylor*, 1696. 8°. LM, LWL; CLC, WSG, HC.

7547 —Semeiotica Uranica. Or an astrological judgment. *For Nathaniell Brookes*, 1651. 8°. LT, O, LCS, BR; BN, CLC, MH, WSG, HC, JF.

7548 — —Third edition. *For Nath. Brooke*, 1658. 8°. LT; CJC, MMO, Y, HC.

7548A — —Fourth edition. *For N. Brook, and are to be sold by Benj. Billingsley*, 1671. 8°. T.C.I 61. LWL; CH, CLC, NAM, WF, HC.

7549 —Mr. Culpepper's treatise of aurum potabile. *For G. Eversden*, 1656. 12°. L, LCP, LPO, GU; MH, MU, NC, WU.

7549A — —[Anr. ed.] —, 1657. 12°. LWL, GU; PBL, WU.

7550 —Two treatises: the first of blood-letting. *By Peter Cole*, 1663. 12°. L, LCP.

7551 — —Third edition. *By John Streater, to be sold by William Jacob*, 1672. 12°. T.C.I 106. O, C; WF, HC.

7552 [**Culpeper, Sir Thomas, elder.**] A tract against the high rate of vsvrie. *By I. Norton, for Henry Seile*, 1641. 4°.* L, C, LCL, OC, DT; MH, NC, WF, Y.

7553 — —Fourth edition. *By T. Leach, for Christopher Wilkinson*, 1668. 4°.* L, O, C, MR, DT; CH, CU, MH, NC, WF.

7554 **C[ulpeper], T[homas], younger.** The advantages which will manifestly accrue. *By T. L. for Christopher Wilkinson*, 1668. brs. L, LUG; MH, Y.

7555 —A discourse, shewing the many advantages. *By Tho. Leach for Christopher Wilkinson*, 1668. 4°.* L, O, C, LUG, ES; CH, CN, MH, NC, WF, Y.

7556 [–] Essayes or moral discourses. *By H. Bruges for Thomas Proudlove*, 1671. 8°. T.C.I 66. L, O; CLC, CN, CU, MH, WF.

7557 [–] An humble proposal for the relief of debtors. 1671. 4°. C, MRL.

7558 Entry cancelled.

7558 [–] Letter from a gentleman in the country to his friend. 1691. *See* J., H.

7559 —Morall discourses and essayes. *By S. G. for Charles Adams*, 1655. 12°. LT; CH, NPT.

7560 —The necessity of abating usury. *By T. L. for Christopher Wilkinson*, 1670. 4°. T.C.I 39. L, O, C, LG, MR; CH, MH, NC, WF.

7561 [–] Plain English, in a familiar conference. *By T. J. to be sold by Henry Million*, 1673. 4°.* L, O, MR; CH, LC, NC, WF.

7562 [–] Several objections against the reducement of interest, propounded. *Printed* 1671. 4°.* CH, MH, WF.

7563 [–] A short appendix to a late treatise concerning . . . usury. *By Tho. Leach, for Christopher Wilkinson*, 1668. 4°.* L, CK, LLG, CT; CH, CN, MH, NC, WF, Y.

7564 **Culpeper, William.** An heroick poem upon the king. *For Daniel Brown*, 1694. fol.* O, OP; CLC, CU, MH, Y.

7565 Culpeper revived from the grave. [*London*], *printed August*, 1655. 4°.* LT; WSG.

Culros, lady. *See* Melville, Elizabeth.

Cultus evangelicus. 1667. *See* Wilson, John.

7566 **Culverwell, Ezekiel.** A brief ansvver to certain obiections. *By Iohn Dawson*, 1646. 12°.* L, SC; NU, Y.

7567 —A treatise of faith. Eighth edition. *By J. D. for H. Overton to be sold by William Sheares*. 1648. 12°. L, CT, LSC, SC, P; NU, Y.

7568 —The vvay to a blessed estate. *By John Dawson, for Henry Overton*, 1646. 4°.* SC; NU, Y.

7569 **Culverwell, Nathaniel.** An elegant and learned discourse. *By T. R. and E. M. for John Rothwell*, 1652. 4°. LT, C, CT, E, DT; CH, MH, NU, WF, Y.

7570 — —[Anr. ed.] —, 1654. 4°. L, O, C, EN, DT; BN, CLC, CU, NU, TU, WF, Y.

7571 — —[Anr. ed.] *By Tho. Roycroft, for Mary Rothwell*, 1661. 4°. L, O, C, LCL, DT; BN, CU, MH, WF, WU.

7571A — —[Anr. ed.] *By Tho. Roycroft, for William Grantham*, 1661. 4°. CM; Y.

7572 — —[Anr. ed.] *Oxford, for Tho. Williams* [*London*], *to be sold by Henry Dimock, in Oxford*, 1669. 4°. T.C.I II. MADAN 2825. O, CS, SC, AN; LC, MH, MU, NU, Y.

7573 —Spiritual opticks. [*Cambridge*], *by Thomas Buck*, 1651. *To be sold by Anthony Nicholson*. 4°. L, O, C, LCL; CH, NU, Y.

7573A —The white stone. *For John Rothwel*, 1654. 8°. L, O, LW, YM; CLC, Y.

7574 Cum per nuperam dispensandi hac in Academiâ licentiam. [*Oxford*, 1666.] brs. o.

7575 **Cumberland,** . Habitus mentis acquisit sunt. [*n.p.*, 1659.] brs. o.

7576 **Cumberland, Henry Clifford, earl of.** The declaration of. *York: By Robert Barker, and by the assigns of John Bill*, 1642. 4°.* YM; CH.

7577 ——[Anr. ed.] *Printed at York, by Stephen Bukley*, 1642. 4°.* L, O, CT, HH, YM; CH, MH, WF, Y.

7578 ——[Anr. ed.] *Printed at York by Robert Barker, reprinted at London for Iohn Thomas. Septem.* 8, 1642. 4°.* LT, O, CJ, EN, DT; CH, MH, TU.

7579 ——[Anr. ed.] *Printed at Yorke, re-printed at London*, 1642. 4°.* LT, YM; CH.

7580 **Cumberland, Richard, bp.** De legibus naturæ. *Typis E. Flesher, prostat verò apud Nathanaelem Hooke*, 1672. 4°. T.C.I 98. L, O, C, EN, DT; BN, CH, CU, MH, NU, TU, WF, Y.

7581 —An essay towards the recovery of the Jewish measures & weights. *By Richard Chiswell*, 1686. 8°. T.C.II 148. L, O, C, EN, DT; BN, CH, CU, MH, NC, WF, Y.

7582 ——Second edition. *For R. Chiswel, and sold by D. Midwinter, and T. Leigh*, 1699. 8°. T.C.III 101. L, O, C, OC, GU; CN, MH, NP.

7582A [The] Cumberland laddy. [*London*], *for F. Coles, T. Vere, J. Wright, and J. Clarke*, [1674–80.] brs. o.

7582B Cumberland Nelly. [*London*], *by J. Conyers*, [1669?] brs. O, CM.

7583 **Cumming, John.** Sermon preached . . . for the reformation of manners. [*London*], *for Tho. Browne in Shepton Mallet*, 1699. 4°. LCL, BR.

7583A —Sermon preached . . . 5th of March. *For Ra. Simpson and Tho. Brown*, 1695. 4°.* LCL; CH.

7584 **Cunaeus, Petrus.** Petrus Cunaeus of the commonwealth of the Hebrews. *By T. W. for William Lee*, 1653. 12°. LT, O, C, CS; CLC, LC, MH, WF, Y.

Cunctis Christi. 1660. See Fox, George.

Cunctis viam. 1660. See Fox, George.

7585 The cunning Northerne begger. colop: *Printed at London for F. Coules*, [1646–74]. fol. L.

7586 A cvnning plot to divide and destroy. *Printed, and are to be sold by Peter Cole, January* 16, 1643[4]. 4°. LT, O, C, LG, DT; CH, CN, MH, NU, WF, Y.

7587 **Cuninghame, Adam.** Disputatio juridica. *Edinburgh, Mosman*, 1698. 4°. ALDIS 3742. EN.

7588 **Cunninghame, Alexander.** Amplissimis . . . viris D. A. Mure. *Edinburgi, J. Reid*, 1692. brs. ALDIS 3268. E.

7589 [–] The divine right of Episcopacy. *For Randal Taylor*, 1690. 4°.* T.C.II 312. O; NU, Y.

7590 —An essay concerning church government. [*London*], *printed*, 1689. 4°.* L, ON, EN; CH, CN, NU, WWC, Y.

7591 [–]—[Anr. ed.] [*London*], *reprinted*, 1692. 4°.* L, EN; V, Y.

7592 [–] Some questions resolved concerning Episcopal and Presbyterian government in Scotland. *For the author, and are to be sold by Randal Taylor*, 1690. 4°.* L, O, LIL, MR, EN; CH, MH, PL, WF, Y.

7592A **Cunningham, David, bp.** Lease of the tythes. [*London?* 1680.] brs. HH.

7593 **C[unningham], I[ames.]** An essay upon the inscription of Macduff's crosse. *Edinburgh, by the heir of Andrew Anderson*, 1678. 4°.* ALDIS 2118. L, O, HH, EN; MBP, MH, WF, Y.

7593A [–] An humble Service to His sacred Majesty. *Edinburgh, by the heir of Andrew Anderson*, 1683. brs. ALDIS 2383. L, O, EN; MH.

7594 —In Floidum Asaphensum episcopum. *Impressus*, 1685. 4°.* EN; Y.

7595 —Miracula mundi. To the king. *Edinburgh*, 1683. brs. ALDIS 2371. EN; Y.

7595A **Cunninghame, William.** Disputatio juridica. *Edinburgi, ab hæredibus de successoribus A. Anderson*, 1694. 4°.* EN.

Cup for thc citie. [*n.p.*], 1648. See Adis, Henry.

7596 A cup of coffee. *Printed* 1663. brs. L; MH.

7597 A cup of sack prest forth. *By Jane Coe*, 1644. 4°.* LT, C; MBA, MH, TU, WF, Y.

Cupid and death. 1653. See Shirley, James.

Cupid, sung by Mr. Cross. [*London*], 1698. See Powell, George.

7598 Cupids conquest. [*London*], *for J. Deacon*, [1684–85]. brs. HH; MH, Y.

7599 Cupid's court of equity. [*London*], *for P. Brooksby*, [1680–85]. brs. L, HH, GU; MH.

Cupid's court of salutations. [*n.p.*], 1687. See B., W.

Cupids courtesie. [*n.p.*, 1680.] See P., J.

7600 Cvpids covrtesie. [*London*], *for F. Coles, T. Vere, and J. Wright*, [1689]. brs. L, O, HH; MH.

Cupids courtship. 1666. See Mermion, Shackerley.

7601 Cupids delight; or, the two young lovers. [*London*], *for J. Deacon*, [1685?]. brs. L.

7602 Cupids garland set round about with gilded roses. *By E. Crowch, for F. Coles, T. Vere, and J. Wright*, 1674. 4°.* CH.

7602A —[Anr. ed.] [*London*], *for John Clark, William Thackeray, and Thomas Passinger*, [1680?] 8°. CM.

7603 Cupids golden dart. [*London*], *for F. Coles, T. Vere, J. Wright, and J. Clarke*, [1675]. brs. L, O, CM, HH, GU; MH, Y.

7604 Cupid's kindness to constant Coridon. [*London*], *for J. Back*, [1685–88). brs. L, HH.

Cupid's love lessons. 1683. See C., H.

7605 Cupids master-piece. *For John Andrews*, 16[5?]6. 4°.* O.

7606 —[Same title.] [*London*], *by H.B. for J. Clark, W. Thackeray and T. Passenger*, 1685. 4°.* CM.

7607 —[Same title.] *For VV. Thackeray, T. Passenger, and VV. Whitwood*, [1670–77]. brs. L, O, HH; MH, Y.

7608 Cupid's posies For bracelets. *For John Wright*, 1642. 8°.* MH.

7609 —[Anr. ed.] *By E. C. for J. Wright*, 1674. 8°. L.

7609A —[Same title.] *For J. Wright, J. Clarke, W. Thackeray, & T. Passenger*, 1683. 12°.* CM.

7610 Cupid's power. *For Charls Tyus*, 1664. brs. HH.

7611 Cupids revenge. [London], for F. Cole, T. Vere, J. Wright, J. Clark, W. Thackery, T. Passenger, [1660–64]. brs. HH; MH.

7611A —[Anr. ed.] [London], for Philip Brooksby, J. Deacon, J. Blare, and J. Back, [1660–64.] brs. CM.

7612 —[Same title.] [London, 1700?] brs. L, O; CH, MH, MU, WCL, WF.

Cupid's schoole. 1642. See S., W.

7612A Cupid's solicitor of love. By J. M. for W. T., [1680.] 8°. L.

7613 Cupids tragedy. [London], for P. Brooksby, [1680?] brs. L, O, HH; MH.

7614 Cupid's trappan. By and for W. Onley, for A. Milbourn; to be sold by J. Deacon, [1684–95]. brs. L, O, HH, GU.

7614A —[Anr. ed.] By E. Crouch, for F. Coles, T. Vere, and J. Wright, [n.d.] brs. O.

7614B —[Anr. ed.] [London], for F. Coles, T. Vere, J. Wright, and J. Clark, [n.d.] brs. CM.

7614C Cupids tryumph. For W. Thackeray, T. Passenger and W. Whitwood, [1670.] brs. O.

7615 Cupids victory over the virgins hearts. [London], for I. Deacon, [1685–88]. brs. L, O, CM, HH, GU.

Cupid's wanton wiles. [1641–55.] See Price, Laurence.

7616 **Cupif, François.** The blind gvide forsaken. By J. N. for Walter Edmonds, 1641. 8°. C, E.

Cur percussisti: or. 1661. See G., H.

Curate, Jacob, pseud. See Crockat, Gilbert.

7617 The curates conference. [n.p.], printed, 1641. 4°.* LT, CCC, YM; CH, CU, MH, NU, TU, Y.

7618 The curate's queries. [n.p., 1688.] 4°. EN.

7619 A curb for Pegasus. Printed and sold by T. Sowle, 1696. 8°. LF.

7620 A curb for sectaries. Printed, 1641. 4°.* LT, CT, LG, EN; CSS, NPT, NU, WF, Y.

Curcellaeus, Stephenus. See Courcelles, Etienne de.

7621 A cure for the state. [London], printed, 1659. brs. LT; MH.

Cure for the tongue-evill. [n.p.], 1662. See Jordan, Thomas.

Cure of deadly doctrine. [n.p., 1649.] See Graunt, John.

Cure of misprision. 1646. See Younge, Richard.

Cure of prejudice. 1641. See Younge, Richard.

Cvre of the kingdome. [n.p.], 1648. See P., R.

Cureau de la Chambre, M. See La Chambre, M. Cureau de.

7622 [**Curfet,** .] A trve relation of the Scots taking of Cocket Iland. For Andrew Coe, 1644. 4°.* LT, O; CH, CLC, WF, Y.

7622A [**Curio, Cælius Secundus.**] The visions of Pasquin. Printed, and are to be sold by Richard Baldwin, 1689. 4°. T.C.II 258. L, O, C, LIL, P; CPB, MH, NU, TU, WF, Y.

Curiosities in chymistry. 1691. See Gregg, Hugh.

Curious and useful treatise. 1699. See Duillier, Nicolas Fatio de.

7623 A curious collection of books in divinity. [London], 11 June, 1695. 4°. L.

7624 A curious collection of Greek, Latin and English books. [London], 23 February, 1691. 4°. L.

7625 A curious collection of musick-books. [London, 1690.] 4°.* L, O; JF.

7626 At the West-end of Exeter Change. A curious collection of one hundred and odd paintings . . . 19th . . . May. [London, 1690.] 4°.* L.

7627 A curious collection of original paintings, . . . 4th . . . August, 1690. [London], 1690. 4°.* L.

7628 At the West-end of Exeter Change. [Same title] . . . 22th [sic] . . . September. [London, 1690.] 4°.* L.

7629 At the Kings Arms Tavern, will be sold . . . a curious collection of original paintings, . . . 16th of October. [London, 1690.] 4°.* L.

7630 At the Kings-Arms Tavern, . . . will be sold . . . 11th . . . November. A curious collection of original paintings. [London, 1690.] 4°.* L.

7631 At the King-Arms Tavern, . . . a curious collection of original paintings, . . . third . . . March, 1690/91. [London], 1691. 4°.* L.

7632 At the Green Dragon . . . a curious collection of original paintings . . . 24th . . . March [1691]. [London, 1691.] 4°.* L.

7633 At the Kings-Arms Tavern, . . . a curious collection of original paintings, . . . first of April, 1691. [London], 1691. 4°.* L.

7634 A curious collection of original paintings, . . . May the 19th. [London, 1691.] 4°.* L.

7635 —, June the 15th. [London, 1691.] 4°.* L.

7636 At the Two White Posts, . . . 18th . . . a curious collection of original paintings. [London, 1691.] 4°.* L.

7637 A curious collection of original paintings, . . . June the 24th. [London, 1691.] 4°.* L.

7638 At the West End of Exeter Change . . . a curious collection of original paintings, . . . 2d . . . November . . . 1691. [London], 1691. 4°.* L.

7639 —, 18th . . . November, 1691. [London], 1691. 4°.* L.

7640 —, 21, . . . December. [London, 1691.] 4°.* L.

7641 —, 13th . . . January. [London, 1692.] 4°.* L.

7642 —, 24th . . . February. [London, 1692.] 4°.* L.

7643 In the Auction-Room at the West End of Exeter Change . . . a curious collection of original paintings, . . . 15th . . . March. [London, 1692.] 4°.* L.

7644 A curious collection of paintings, . . . 20th . . . May. [London, 1690.] 4°.* L.

7645 —, 4th . . . September. [London, 1690.] 4°.* L.

7646 A curious collection of paintings, . . . 24th . . . September. [London, 1690.] 4°.* L.

7647 A curious collection of paintings, . . . 21st . . . January, 1690. [London], 1691. 4°.* L.

7648 —, 28th . . . January, 1691. [London], 1691. 4°.* L.

7649 —, 10th . . . February, 1691. [London], 1691. 4°.* L.

7650 —, 6th . . . May. [London, 1691.] 4°.* L.

7651 —, 22d. of May. [London, 1691.] cap., 4°.* L.

7652 At the Canary-House, . . . a curious collection of paintings, . . . 8th . . . June, 1691. [London], 1691. 4°.* L.

7653 —, 2d, . . . July. [London, 1691.] 4°.* L.

7654 At the Bell-Tavern . . . a curious collection of paintings; . . . 13th, . . . October, 1691. [London], 1691. 4°.* L.

7655 A curious collection of paintings, . . . 22th [sic] . . . Octob. 1691. [London], 1691. 4°.* L.

7656 —, 27th . . . November, 1691. [London], 1691. 4°.* L.

7657 At the New Auction House . . . 7th, . . . December, . . . a curious collection of paintings. [London, 1691.] brs. L.

7658 A curious collection of paintings, . . . December 11th. [London, 1691.] 4°.* L.

7659 —, 21st of December. [London, 1691.] brs. L.

7660 —, 29th . . . December, 1691. [London], 1691. 4°.* L.

7661 —, 7th . . . January, 1691. [London], 1692. 4°.* L.

7662 —, 13th . . . January, 1691. [London], 1692. 4°.* L.

7663 —, 5th . . . February, 1691. [London], 1692. 4°.* L.

7664 —, 17th . . . March, 1691/92. [London], 1692. 4°.* L.

7665 —, 23th [sic] . . . March. [London, 1692.] 4°.* L.

7666 A curious collection of paintings, and drawings, . . . 14th . . . June, 1689. [London], 1689. 4°.* L.

7667 A curious collection of paintings and limnings, . . . 12th. . . . March, . . . [1691]. [London, 1691.] 4°.* L.

7668 —, 30th . . . March. [London, 1691.] 4°.* L.

7669 A curious collection of paintings, drawings, and prints . . . 31st . . . May, 1689. [London], 1689. 4°.* L.

7670 —, 21st . . . June, 1689. [London], 1689. 4°.* L.

7671 At the West End of Exeter Change . . . a curious collection of pictures, . . . 24th . . . June. [London, 1691.] 4°.* L.

7672 A curious collection of prints and drawings, . . . 12th . . . November. [London, 1690.] 4°.* L.

7673 At the West-end of Exeter Change A curious collection of three hundred and odd paintings . . . 5th . . . May. [London, 1690.] 4°.* L.

7674 —, 2d . . . June. [London, 1690.] 4°.* L.

7675 —, 19th . . . June, 1690. [London], 1690. 4°.* L.

7676 —, 15th . . . July, 1690. [London], 1690. 4°.* L.

7677 Entry cancelled.

7678 Curious enquiries, being six brief discourses. *Printed, and are to be sold by Randal Taylor,* 1688. 4°. T.C.II 209. L, O, LG, LWL; CH, NN, PL, WF, Y.

Curious observations. Dublyn, 1687. *See* Allen, Charles.

7679 **Curle, Walter, bp.** A sermon preached . . . the tenth of May, 1644. *Oxford, by Leonard Lichfield,* 1644. 4°. MADAN 1662. O, DT; CH, NPT.

7680 A currant, 12 Julii, stylo novo, 1642. *For Edward Husbands and John Frank,* 1642. 4°.* LT, EC, DT; CN, Y.

Currie, John. The plain perjury. *Edinburgh,* 1644 [*i.e.,* 1744.]

7681 **Curriehill, Sir John Skene, lord.** De verborum significatione. *By E. G.,* 1641. 4°. L, O, CT, NPL, EN; CLC, CN, MH, WF, YL.

7682 — —[Anr. ed.] *Edinburgh,* 1641. fol.* LGI, LL; MH.

7683 — —[Anr. ed.] *Edinbvrgh, by David Lindsay,* 1681. fol.* ALDIS 2308. O, C, BAMB; BN, MHL, NU, YL.

7684 — —[Anr. ed.] [*Edinburgh*], *A. Smellie,* 1681. fol.* LC, MHL, YL.

7684A A curry-comb for a cocks-comb. colop: *Printed,* 1698. brs. HH; CLC.

7684B A curry-comb turn'd to its right use. colop: 1698. brs. CH.

7685 A curse against Parliament-ale. *Nod-Nol: printed,* 1649. 4°.* LT; CH, CLC, MH.

7686 [**Curson, Henry.**] Compendium of the laws. *By the assigns of Rich. and Edw. Atkins for J. Walthoe,* 1699. 12°, T.C.III 123. L, EN, ES; CN, LC, MHL, NCL, Y.

7687 Cursory remarks upon some late disloyal proceedings. *Printed,* 1699. 4°. T.C.III 143. L, O, AU; CH, MH, TU, WF, Y.

7688 A curtain conference. 1659. brs. L, O.

Curtaine drawne. 1659. *See* Prynne, William.

7689 The curtezan unmasked. *For Henry Marsh,* 1664. 8°.* Y.

7690 **Curtis, Edmond.** A brief relation and exact map of the harbour of New-Castle near Tinmouth-Barre. *For the author, Edmond Curtis,* 1673. brs. L.

7690A **C[urtis], L[angley].** His lamentation on Newgate. [*London*], *for J. Dean,* 1689. brs. O, LG; CH.

7691 [**Curtis, Samuel.**] The lamentable sufferings of the church of God in Dorsetshire. *For Thomas Simmons,* 1659. 4°.* L, LF, BBN; MH, PH, PSC, Y.

7692 **Curtius Rufus, Quintus.** Q. Curtii Rufi de rebus gestis. *Oxonii, typis G. Hall, impensis Edw. Forrest,* 1672. 12°. MADAN 2923. L, O, CT.

7693 — —[Anr. ed.] *Oxonii, excudebat G. Hall, per Tho. Gilbert,* 1672. 12°. MADAN 2924. O; CLC.

7693A — —[Anr. ed.] *Ex officina Joannis Redmayne,* 1672. 8°. CT.

7694 —Historiarum libri. *Sold by D. Newman,* 1684. 12°. T.C.II 119. L, LL.

7695 —The history of the life and death of Alexander the Great. *For E. C.,* 1687. 12°. CH, MH, NN, Y.

7696 [–] The life and death of Alexander the Great. 1661. L; CLC, CU.

7697 — —[Anr. ed.] *By Tho. Johnson for Samuel Speed,* 1670. 8°. T.C.I 39. L, O, OM, EN; CN, NLC, WF.

7697A — —[Anr. ed.] *By J. C. for Samuel Speed,* 1673. 8°. NC, UCLA, Y.

7697B — —[Anr. ed.] *For S. S. and are to be sold by Nich. Cox,* 1674. 8°. T.C.I 156. MH.

7698 —The life of Alexander the Great. *For Gilbert Townly,* 1687. 8°. L; PL, Y.

7698A — —[Anr. ed.] *For Francis Saunders,* 1690. 8°. T.C.II 333. L, O; CLC, CN, NC, PL, Y.

7699 —The ten books of. *By Bernard Alsop,* 1652. 4°. O, LG, CM, CS, LW; CN, NPT, OCI, WF, Y.

7700 **Curtois, John.** A discourse shewing that kings. *For Jo. Hindmarsh,* 1685. 4°.* T.C.II 142. LUG, CT; CH, IU, NU, Y.

7701 —An essay to persuade Christian parents. *For John Knight, in Lincoln,* 1697. 8°. T.C.III I. L.

7702 —A sermon preach'd . . . July xxix. 1683. By J. Play-ford, for Joseph Lawson in Lincoln, and sold by Thomas Sawbridge, and Richard Chiswel, 1684. 4°.* L, O, AN; MBA, WF, Y.

7703 **Curwen, Thomas.** This is an answer to John Wiggan's book. Printed, 1665. 4°. L, LF, BBN; IE, PH, WF.

Cusanus, C. See Khrypffs, Nicolaus.

7704 Custom House, Boston in New England. These may certifie. [Boston, 1688.] brs. MBS.

Customs of the mannor. [n.p., 1660.] See Loveday, Thomas.

7705 **Cuthbert, John.** Proposals humbly offered. [London, 1695.] brs. L, O, LG, LUG; BN.

7706 [**Cutlove, Joseph.**] Two sermons. One from Exod. 20.7. about swearing. By M. Flesher, for Walter Kettilby, 1682. 4°.* L, CT, EC, BAMB; CLC, TSM, WF, Y.

7707 **Cutting, Alexander.** The method proposed by [1690?] brs. L.

7708 [**Cutts, John Cutts, baron.**] La muse de cavalier. For Tho. Fox, 1685. 4°.* T.C.II 159. L, O; CN, CU, Y.

7708A [–] On the death of the Queen. For R. Bentley, 1695. fol.* L, O, CT; CLC, CU, TU, WF, Y.

7709 [–] Poetical exercises. For R. Bentley and S. Magnes, 1687. 8°. L, O, C; CH, CN, MH, WF, Y.

7710 —The right honourable the Lord Cutts his speech to the mayor . . . of Newport. By William Redmayne, 1698. fol.* O, EN; CH.

Cydymaith yr eglwyswr. Mwythig, [1700?] See W., J.

7710A Entry cancelled.

7710B Cynghorion fad. J. Richardson, 1683. 8°. AN.

7710C Cyngor y bugail iw braida. J.B. i'r awdwr, 1700. 8°.* AN.

Cynosura. 1670. See Cross, Nicholas.

7710D Cynthia: with the tragical account. By R. Holt for T. Passinger, and R. Fenner in Canterbury, 1687. 8°. T.C.II 193. MH, MU.

7711 **Cyprian, saint.** Opera. Oxonii, e theatro Sheldoniano, 1682. fol. T.C.I 512. L, O, C, MR, EN; BN, CH, MH, WF, Y.

7711A — —[Anr. ed.] —, 1683. 4°.* Y.

7712 — —Third edition. —, 1700. fol. BN, NU.

7713 —St. Cyprian bishop and martyr, anno 250. Of discipline. For Sam. Keble, 1675. 4°.* T.C.I 198. L, C, CCH, GK; CH, IU, MH, WF.

7714 —Of the unity of the church. Printed at the theater in Oxford, 1681. 4°.* T.C.I 439. L, O, CS, YM, EN; CH, CLC, MH, WF, Y.

7715 [**Cyprien de Gamaches.**] Heaven opened, and the pains. [n.p.], printed, 1663. 8°. O, LW; CH, Y.

7716 —Sure characters. Re-printed at Holy-Rood-House. 1687. 8°. ALDIS 2721. EN; TU.

7717 **Cyrano de Bergerac, Savinien.** The comical history of the states and empires. For Henry Rhodes, 1687. 8°. T.C.II 166. L, C, LVF, E, DT; CH, CN, MH, NC, WF, Y.

7718 —Satyrical characters. For Henry Herringman, 1658. 8°. LT, O, C; CLC, CN, MH, WF, Y.

7719 —Σεμηναρχια. Or, the government of the world in the moon. By J. Cottrel, to be sold by Hum. Robinson, 1659. 16°. L, O, OC; CH, CN, MH, NC, WF, Y.

Cywir daychwelwr. 1657. See Shepard, Thomas.

D

1 **D.** Master D. his counsel. For Benjamin Billingsley, 1672. brs. HH.

D., A. Apostate conscience. 1699. See Docwra, Anne.

—Looking-glass for the Recorder. [n.p., 1682.] See Docwra, Anne.

2 —News from Scotland: or the result of the Generall Assembly. By J.M., [1648]. 4°.* LT, O, LW, HH, EN; Y.

3 —Proposals to supply His Majesty with twelve . . . millions of money. For the author, and sold by Peter Parker, and John Waltho, and John Gouge, 1697. 4°.* L, CCA, CT, GH; CH, MH, NC, WF, Y.

D., A. B. C. Religious demurrer. [n.p., 1649.] See title.

D., B. Controversial discourses. Doway, 1697. See Wilmot, John.

4 —The Essexian triumviri. For James Norris, 1684. 4°.* T.C.II 74. O, CT; CH, CLC, MH.

—Oh! the day. [1660]. See Baker, Daniel.

D., C. Answer to the letter of the Roman. 1688. See Tenison, Thomas, abp.

—An elegy on the death of the queen. 1695. See Darby, Charles.

5 —A letter from a citizen in London. [London, 1698.] brs. LG.

6 —New-England's faction discovered. colop: For I. Hindmarsh, 1690. 4°.* O, GH; CN, LC, MH, RPJ, V.

7 —Novello-mastix, or a scovrge. By I.L. for Christopher Meredith, 1646. 4°.* LT, O, CM, YM, DT; CH, NU, Y.

8 Entry cancelled.

—The reason why. 1694. See Doe, Charles.

9 —A seasonable letter of advice delivered. [London, 1659.] brs. LT.

10 —Some reasons, of the present decay of the practise of physick. Printed, 1675. brs. L.

11 —A true and exact copy of some passionate letters and verses. For N. R., [1692.] 12°. L; CN.

12 —Vindiciæ magistratum. Or, a sober plea. By Henry Hills, to be sold by Thqmas Brewster, 1658. 8°. LT.

D., D. Essay upon projects. 1697. See Defoe, Daniel.

13 —The skillful physician. By Tho. Maxey, for Nath. Ekins, 1656. 12°. L, LCS, LSC.

14 **D., E.** Complaints and queries vpon Englands misery. By J. C., 1659. 4°.* O; CH, WF, Y.

—Consideration and a resolution. 1641. *See* Dering, *Sir* Edward.

15   —The declaration of the officers of the army opened. *Printed*, 1659. 4°. LT, O, OC, SP; CH, LC, MH, TU, WF, Y.

—Innocents no saints. 1658. *See* Dodd, Edward.

16   —A letter to the late Lord Bishop of L. and C. *Printed*, 1699. 4°.* L, O, WCA, SP; MH, NGT, NU, WF.

16A —The pretended high court of justice unbowelled. *For Thomas Hainman*, 1660. 4°.* WF.

17   —A trve relation of the state of the case between the ever honourable Parliament. *By J.C.*, 1659. 4°.* LT, O, C, OC, CCA; CH, CN, MIU, NU, WF, Y.

—Vindication of the historiographer. 1693. *See* Wood, Thomas.

18   **D., Em.** Good nevves from the narrow seas. *For Francis Wright*, [1642.] 4°.* Y.

19   —Nevves from the narrovv seas. *For Francis Wright*, 1642. 4°.* LT, EC.

D., F. Narrative of the settlement. Lovain, 1668. *See* French, Nicholas, *bp.*

20   —A sermon taken out of an Oxford scholar's pocket. *For Tho. Fabian*, 1688. 4°.* T.C.II 222. L, O, OC, WCA, EN; CH, WF, Y.

D., G. Confessio fidei in conventu. Cantabrigiæ, 1656. *See under title.*

21   —Directions for writing. *For J. Stafford*, 1656. obl. 8°. NC.

—Guide to eternal glory. 1685. *See* Wilcox, Thomas.

—Rex meus. 1643. *See* Downham, George.

22   —A seasonable caution, from the North. [*London*, 1682.] 4°.* LF, BP, CS, CT; PH.

—Tryals per pais: or. 1665. *See* Euer, Sampson.

23   —Viro verè pietatis, . . . Joannis Selden. *By Tho. Newcomb*, 1654. brs. LT.

D., H. Historie & policie. 1659. *See* Dawbeny, H.

—Sober and temperate discourse. 1661. *See* Collinges, John.

—Solomon's proverbs. 1676. *See* D'Anvers, Henry.

—Treatise of baptism. 1673. *See* D'Anvers, Henry.

—Two letters of advice. 1672. *See* Dodwell, Henry.

—Vindiciæ academiarum. Oxford, 1654. *See* Ward, Seth, *bp.*

24   Entry cancelled.

D., I. Cleare and evident way. 1650. *See* Keymor, John.

25   —Concordia rara sororum, or a poem upon the late fight at sea. *For J. Ridley*, 1653. 4°.* LT, OC; MH, TU, WF.

26   Entry cancelled.

—English lovers. 1662. *See* Dauncey, John.

27   —Hell's higher court. *Printed*, 1661. 4°.* LT, O, LVD, OW; CH, TU, WF.

—Llyfr y resolusion. 1684. *See* Parsons, Robert.

—Melpomene: or, the muses delight. 1678. *See* Bulteel, John.

28   —A sober caution to the Common Covncell. [*London*], *printed*, 1648. 4°.* LT, HH; MIU.

29   —A true compendious narration. 1665. 4°. O, EN; CLC.

30   —A true relation of a most dreadful fire . . . Udem. *By E. Mallet*, [1685.] brs. O, HH; WF.

D., J. An almanack . . . for . . . 1679. Cambridge [Mass.], 1679. *See* Almanacs: John Danforth.

—Ancient rites. 1672. *See* Davies, John.

—Case of conscience resolved concerning. 1649. *See* Dury, John.

—Civil warres of Great Britain. 1661. *See* Davies, John.

—Considerations concerning the present. 1649. *See* Dury, John.

31   —The coronation of Queen Elizabeth. *For Ben. Hains*, 1680. 4°.* L, O, LG, EN; CH, CU.

—Counsellor Manners his last legacy. 1694. *See* Dare, Josiah.

32   —A discourse concerning the solemne league. [*London*], *printed*, 1661. 4°.* LT, O, HH, EN; CLC, MIU, NU, WF, Y.

—Earnest breathings. 1658. *See* Dury, John.

—Elegie on . . . Alexander Lord Reath. Edinburgh 1698. *See* Donaldson, James.

—Elegie on . . . Umphrey Milne. Edinburgh 1695. *See* Donaldson, James.

—Elegie on . . . William Earl of Crawford. Edinburgh 1698. *See* Donaldson, James.

—Elegy on the usurper O. C. 1681. *See* Dryden, John.

—England's alarum: being. 1693. *See* Dunton, John.

—England's confusion during. 1660. *See* Dauncey, John.

33   —An essay on the fleet riding in the Downes. *By J. C. for R. Robinson*, 1672. brs. L.

—Exact history. 1660. *See* Dauncey, John.

34   —Feed my lambs. *By J. H. for Samuel Richards in Nottingham, and sold by Luke Meredith*, 1686. 8°.* T.C.II 166. L, BAMB.

—Great sacrifice. Antwerp, 1685. *See* Dymock, James.

—History of His Sacred Majesty Charles the II. 1660. *See* Dauncey, John.

—Hymenean essay. [*n.p.*], 1662. *See* Drope, John.

—Iter boreale, or. 1682. *See* Dean, *John*.

35   —A ivdgment, or a definition. [*London*], *printed*, 1641. 4°.* LT, C; MH.

36   Entry cancelled.

—Lawfulnes of mixt-marriage. 1681. *See* Denn, John.

37   —The loyal citizen. *For Walter Davis*, 1682. 4°. L, OC; CH, CN, MBA, TU.

—The mall. 1674. *See* Dryden, John.

38   Entry cancelled.

—Musæ subsecivæ. Cantabrigiæ, 1676. *See* Duport, James.

—Objections against the taking . . . answered. 1650. *See* Dury, John.

—Pharisee's council. 1688. *See* Dormer, John.

39   —The phoenix, sepulchre & cradle. *Printed*, 1691. 4°.* L; Y.

—Pindarique ode: humbly offer'd. 1694. *See* aobb, Samuel.

40   —A Pindaric ode sacred to the memory of . . . Dr. William Sancroft. *By T.B., sold by Randal Taylor*, 1694. fol.* L, O, HH; CN, MH, Y.

41 —A poem upon the Prince of Orange's expedition. 1689. 4°. O, EC, AU; CLC, Y.

—Political and miltary. 1679. *See* Davies, John.

—Profession of the faith. 1642. *See* Davenport, John.

42 —The sacrifice of the new law. *Antverp*, 1685. 12°. LW.

—Second parcel. 1650. *See* Dury, John.

—Secrets of angling. 1652. *See* Dennys, John.

43 —A sermon preached at the funeral of . . . Lady Mary Armyne. *For Nevil Simmons*, 1676. 4°.* T.C.I 216. L, O, C, WCA, BR; CH, TSM, WF, Y.

—Sermon preach'd before Their Majesties. 1687. *See* Dormer, John.

—Short justification. 1681. *See* Dormer, John.

44 —Short meditations on, with a briefe description of . . . Cromwell. colop: *By T.M. for Robert Clavel*, 1661. cap., 4°.* LT.

45 —Speciall newes from Ireland. *For Henry Overton*, 1643. *The first of March*. 4°.* LT, C; Y.

—Strange news from th'Indies. 1652. *See* Darell, John.

—Θρηνοθρίαμβος, sive. *Cantabrigiæ*, 1653. *See* Duport, James.

—True and compendious narration. 1665. *See* Darell, John.

45A —A true and full relation of His Majesty's safe arrival . . . Hague. *For Walter Davis*, 1690. brs. L; CN.

46 —A true narrative of that grand Jesuite father Andrews. *Printed*, 1679. fol.* LT, O, HH, EN, DT; CH, MH, WF, Y.

47 —Upon the most hopeful and ever flourishing sprouts of valour. [*n.p.*], *printed*, 1664. *Reprinted in 1682 by J.D.* brs. L, MC.

—Velitationes polemicæ; or. 1651. *See* Doughty, John.

—Why's? and the how's? 1687. *See* Dormer, John.

48 —A word without doors concerning the bill for succession. [*London*, 1679.] cap., fol.* L, CS, HH, MR, EN; CH, MH, PL, TU, WF.

49 — —[Anr. ed.] [*London*, 1680.] cap., 4°.* L, O, HH, EN; CH, CLC, TU, Y.

50 **D., J. D.** The Popes posie. *For John Crook*, 1663. 4°. L, O, OC, DT; WF.

D., J. O. D. Bradshaw's Ultimum vale. *Oxon*, 1666. *See* Owen, John.

51 **D., L.** A check to debauchery. *For Richard Butt; to be sould by Randal Taylor*, 1692. 12°. NU.

52 An exact relation of the proceedings and transactions. *For Livewell Chapman*, 1654. 4°.* LT, O, C, HH; CH, CN, MH, TU, WF, Y.

53 —A letter from a Protestant of integrity. *For the author*, 1661. 4°. O, C, P, SP; CN.

—New prognostication. Glasgow, 1673. *See* Almanacs.

54 —A Protestants resolution. Sixth edition. *For Samuel Norris*, 1684. 8°. L, O.

55 **D., M.** An account of the arraignment, tryal, escape, and condemnation, of the dog. colop: *For the author, M.D.*, 1682. brs. L, O, LG, EN, DT; CH, MH, TU, Y.

56 —An antidote against the infection of the Jacobites. colop: *By J.D. for Jonathan Robinson*, 1696. fol.* T.C.II 587. L; NN, WF, Y.

—Assurance of the faithfull. 1670. *See* D'Assigny, Marius.

57 —A brief history of the life of Mary Queen of Scots. *For Tho. Cockerill*, 1681. fol. L, O, HH; CH, CN, CPB, WF, Y.

—Charge at the general. 1689. *See* Dayrell, *Sir* Marmaduke.

58 —The declaration and propositions of the navie. *By B. Alsop*, 1648. 4°.* LT, O, LG, AN; MH, MM, Y.

59 —English loyalty; or the case of the oath. colop: *For R.Baldwin*, 1689. brs. O, C, MC, EC, BR; CH, Y.

60 —Friendly advice to Protestants. *For Samuel Heyrick*, 1680. 4°. L, O, P; CH, WF.

61 —A most strange and wonderful, tho' true. 1693. 8°. O.

62 —A present remedy for the poor. *For Jonathan Robinson*, 1700. 4°.* L, O, LUG; MH, NC.

63 —A seasonable advice to all true Protestants. *For T. Fox*, 1679. 4°. L, O, C, WCA, OC; VC, WF, Y.

64 —A short surveigh of the grand case. [*London*], *printed*, 1663. 4°.* L, O, C, GU, DT; MIU, NU, TU, WF, Y.

65 —The subjects desire to see our gracious King Charles. *For H.B.*, 1660. brs. LT.

66 —A true relation of a devilish attempt. *For Jonathan Robinson*, 1679. fol.* L, O; CH, WF.

66A **D., N.** An antidote against melancholy. *By Mer. Melancholicus, to be sold in London and Westminster*, 1661. 4°. LT, O; CH, MH, TU, WF, Y.

66B — —[Anr. ed.] *For John Playford*, 1669. 8°. T.C.II 11. WF.

—Fruit-walls improved. 1699. *See* Fatio de Duiller, Nicolas.

67 —A letter intercepted printed for the use and benefit of the ingeneous reader. *Printed*, 1660. 4°.* LT, OC, HH; LC, MH.

68 —The Protestant conformist. *For Tho. Parkhurst*, 1679. fol.* L, O, C, OC, HH; CH, MM, NU, WF, Y.

69 Entry cancelled.

—Treatise of three conversions. 1688. *See* Parsons, Robert.

70 —A true account of the siege and taking of the famous city of Gran in Humgary. colop: *By E. Mallet*, 1683. brs. L; CH.

71 —Vindiciæ Caroli regis: or, a loyall vindication. [*n.p.*] *Imprinted*, 1644. 4°. LT, O, OC, CPE, DT; CH, MH, NU, TU, WF, Y.

72 —The vertues of coffee. *By W.G. for John Playford*, 1663. 4°.* L.

72A — —[Anr. ed.] *By W. Godbid*, 1663. 4°.* WU.

D., N. F. Fruit-walls improved. 1699. *See* Fatio de Duiller, Nicholas.

73 **D., N. R.** Letter to the most illustrious lord, the Count of Hohenlo. [*London*], *for John Redmayne*, 1664. 4°.* L.

D., P. Another parcell. [*n.p.*], 1648. *See* Nethersole, *Sir* Francis.

74 —The antiquity and honours of the skinner and furrier crafts. [1690?] 4°.* L.

75 —The Hertford letter. *Printed*, 1699. 4°.* L, O, CS, MR; CH, MHL, WF.

76 —A letter from a councellor at law to his client. *Printed*, 1685. 4°.* L, O.

77 —A letter from an English merchant at Amsterdam. *For S. Crouch*, 1695. 4°.* L, LG, EC, GH, GU; CH, LC, MH, NC, Y.

77A ——[Anr. ed.] *Printed*, 1695. 4°.* LUG; MIU.

—Letter to Mr John Goodwin. 1642. *See* Nethersole, *Sir Francis*.

78 —The lives & deaths of the holy apostles. *For Dorman Newman*, 1685. 8°. L; CH, WF.

78A —The Meir of Collingtoun. [*Glasgow?*] *Printed*, 1662. 18°. TU.

79 —[Anr. ed.] —, 1695. 12°. ALDIS 3456. O, EN.

—Parables, reflecting. *Paris*, 1643. *See* Howell, James.

— —[n.p.], 1648. *See* Nethersole, *Sir Francis*.

—Problemes necessary. [*n.p.*], 1648. *See* Nethersole, *Sir Francis*.

—Project for an equitable. [*n.p.*], 1648. *See* Nethersole, *Sir Francis*.

—Strong motive. [*n.p.*], 1648. *See* Nethersole, *Sir Francis*.

D., P. G. True relation of what hath been transacted. 1698. *See* Gaujac, Peter Gally de.

D., R. Bread for the poor. *Exeter*, 1698. *See* Dunning, Richard.

—Candidia, or. 1680. *See* Dixon, Robert.

—An hearty acknowledgment, 1659. *See* Draper, R.

80 —Historical and political observations upon . . . Turkey. *Printed, and are to be sold by J. Smith*, 1683. 12°. T.C.II 51. L; MH.

—Letter to a friend, concerning his. 1692. *See* Davies, Rowland.

81 —On the death of Sir David Falconer. [*n.p.*, 1685.] brs. EN.

82 —On the death of William Sharp. [*n.p.*, 1693.] brs. EN.

—Sacred chronologie. 1648. *See* Drake, Roger.

83 —A satyr against satyrs. *Printed, and are to be sold by Richard Janeway*, 1680. 4°.* L, O; CLC, MH, TU, WF, Y.

84 —Sir Francis Drake revived. *Printed at London, for Nicholas Bourne*, 1653. 4°. LT, O, CT, GH, DT; CLC, LC, MH, WF, Y.

85 —Sixteen antiquæries. [*London*, 1646.] 4°.* LT, O, EN; Y.

85A ——[Anr. ed.] *By R. Cotes for Stephen Bowtell*, 1646. 4°.* CCA, CS.

—Strange and prodigious religions. 1683. *See* Crouch, Nathaniel.

D., S. Astronomical description. *Cambridge* [*Mass.*], 1665. *See* Danforth, Samuel.

85B —Certain assayes propounded. *For Thomas Creake*, 1652. 4°.* CH, MB.

—Cry of Sodom. *Cambridge* [*Mass.*], 1674. *See* Danforth, Samuel.

—New-England almanack. *Cambridge* [*Mass.*], 1685. *See* Almanacs: Samuel Danforth.

85C —The poor English clergyman's complaint. [*London?* 1700.] brs. HH.

86 **D., S. P.** News from the New-Jerusalem. *By G. D. for Giles Calvert*, 1649. 4°. NU.

D., T. Brief manifestation. 1664. *See* Davenport, Thomas.

—Canaan's calamiti. 1677. *See* Dekker, Thomas.

—Catalogue of the lords, knights. 1655. *See* Dring, Thomas.

—Collin's walk. 1690. *See* D'Urfey, Thomas.

—De causa Dei: or. 1678. *See* Danson, Thomas.

—Εἰκὼν τοῦ θηρίου or. [*n.p.*], 1684. *See* Delaune, Thomas.

86A —The enemies fall. *Bristol, by W. Bonny, sold by T. Wall*, 1696. 4°. BR.

87 —Englands anathomy. *For R.E.*, [1653.] 4°.* LT.

—Excellent woman described. 1692. *See* Title.

—Fears and jealousies. [*n.p.*, 1688.] *See* Doolittle, Thomas.

—First part of the pleasant. 1678. *See* Deloney, Thomas.

88 —Food and physick for every householder. *By T. Leech for F. Coles*, 1665. 8°.* L.

89 — —[Anr. ed.] 1666. 8°. O.

—Fool turn'd critick. 1678. *See* D'Urfey, Thomas.

—Garland of good-will. 1678. *See* Deloney, Thomas.

—Gentle craft. 1648. *See* Deloney, Thomas.

90 —The high-way to riches. *Printed*, 1664. brs. L.

—Horse-flesh. 1682. *See* Phillips, John.

—Key to open scripture. 1681. *See* Delaune, Thomas.

91 —A letter from Amsterdam, to J. P. *A. Clark*, 1673. fol.* HH.

92 —A letter from Edenbrough. [*n.p.*, 1681/2.] brs. L, LL.

93 Entry cancelled.

—Pleasant history of Thomas. 1672. *See* Deloney, Thomas.

—Progress of honesty. 1681. *See* D'Urfey, Thomas.

—Protestants answer. 1679. *See* Doolittle, Thomas.

—Psyche debauch'd. 1678. *See* Duffett, Thomas.

—Rebukes for sin. 1667. *See* Doolittle, Thomas.

—Reformed devotions. 1687. *See* Dorrington, Theophilus.

—Royal garland of love. 1674. *See* Deloney, Thomas.

—Thomas of Reading. 1672. *See* Deloney, Thomas.

—Τροπολογία, or, a key. 1681. *See* Delaune, Thomas.

94 —Zions song for young children. *By Jane Bell*, 1650. 8°.* LT.

95 **D., W.** Ἀρνιοβοσχια: or. 1650. 8°. O.

96 — —[Anr. ed.] 1651. 8°. YM.

—Artificial clock-maker. 1696. *See* Derham, William.

—Burnt child. 1675. *See* Denton, William.

—English rudiments. 1663. *See* Dugard, William.

—First days entertainment. 1657. *See* Davenant, *Sir William*.

—Forgetfulness of God. 1683. *See* Disney, William.

—General epistle given forth from. [*n.p.*], 1668. *See* Dewsbury, William.

—In obitum . . . D. Joannis Lauderi. [*Edinburgh*]. 1692. *See* Deniston, Walter.

—Lay-man's answer to the lay-mans opinion. 1687. *See* Darrell, William.

—Lay-mans opinion. [*n.p.*], 1687. *See* Darrell, William.

97 —A letter from a gentleman in the country to his friend at London, concerning a conference. *Printed for, and sold by the booksellers of London and Westminster*, 1698. 4°.* LF, BBN, BP; CH, PH, PSC, Y.

—Letter to the author of the reply. [*n.p.*, 1687.] *See* Darrell, William.

—Life and death of that judicious. 1660. *See* Durham, William.

98   —Mercy triumphant in the conversion of sinner. 1696. 16°. LCL.

—Nil dictum, 1681. *See* Disney, William.

99   —The present interest of England in. *By T. S.*, 1688. 4°.* L, O, LIL, OC, DT; NU, Y.

—Quaker converted. 1690. *See* Dimsdale, William.

—Supplement to the treatise. 1700. *See* Derham, William.

—This for dear Friends in London. [1664]. *See* Dewsbury, William.

—To all nations. 1660. *See* Dewsbury, William.

100   True and remarkable passages from the last of October. *For Fr. Wright*, [1642]. 4°.* LT.

—Word of the Lord, to his. [*n.p.*, 1663.] *See* Dewsbury, William.

    D. E. defeated. 1662. *See* Holden, Samuel.

101   **Daborne, Robert.** The poor mans comfort. *For Rob: Pollard and John Sweeting*, 1655. 4°. L, O, LVD, OW, EN; CH, CN, CU, LC, MH, WF, Y.

    Dacres, R., *pseud.*

    Dade, William. Country-man's kalender. 1684. *See* Almanacs.

    Daeneids, or. 1692. *See* Crowne, John.

101A   **Dafforne, Richard.** The apprentice's time entertainer. Third edition. *By W. Godbid for Robert Horne*, 1670. 4°. T.C.I 22. OC; MH, NP.

101B   —The English merchants companion. Fourth Edition. *For Tho. Horne*, 1700. 4°. MB, NC.

102   —The merchants mirrour. Second edition. *By J. L. for Nicolas Bourn*, 1651. fol. OC; MBP, NC, PU, V, Y.

103   — —Third edition. *By R. H. and J. C. for Nicholas Bourn*, 1660. fol. L; MH, NC, PL, WF.

104   — —[Anr. ed.] *By Miles Flesher for Robert Horne*, 1684. fol. LMT, BAMB; MB, MHL, NC, PL, V.

105   **Daffy, Anthony.** Directions given by mee. [1670?] cap., 4°.* L, O.

106   —Elixir salutis: the choise drink. *For the author, by T. Milbourn*, 1673. 4°.* L, LCS.

106A   — —[Anr. ed.] *For the author, by W. G.*, 1674. 4°.* O.

106B   — —[Anr. ed.] *For the author*, 1675. 4°.* LWL.

106C   —Daffy's original and famous elixir salutis. *By T. Milbourn, for the author*, 1693. 4°.* LWL.

107   —Daffy's original elixir salutis vindicated. [1675?] cap., 4°.* O.

108   **Dagget, George.** The estate of the poor in Sion College London. colop: *For Ric. Chiswell*, 1688. brs. L, O, C, LG, OC; CH, MH, Y.

109   The Dagonizing of Bartholomew Fayre. [*n.p.*, 1647.] brs. LT, O; MH.

    Dagons-downfall. [*n.p.*], 1657. *See* Crab, Roger.

110   Dagon's fall, or the charm broke. colop: [*London*], *for John Smith*, 1681. brs. L, O, MC; CH, CN, WF, Y.

111   Dagon's fall: or the Knight turn'd out of commission. [*n.p.*, 1680.] brs. L, O, CS, HH; CH, CN, MH, TU, WF, Y.

112   Dagon's fall: or, the Whigs lamentation. *By Nath. Thompson*, 1683. brs. CH, MH, TU, WF, Y.

113   **Daillé, Jean.** An apologie for the Reformed churches. *By Th. Buck, Cambridge*, 1653. 8°. LT, O, C, CT, DT; MH, NU, PL, WF, Y.

114   —XLIX sermons. *By R. White, for Tho. Parkhurst*, 1672. fol. T.C.I 95. L, C, LW, CT, E; MB, NP, PL, WF, Y.

115   —La foy fondée . . . Faith grounded upon the Holy Scriptures. *For Benjamin Tooke*, 1675. 8°. T.C.I 204. LCL; NU.

116   Entry cancelled..

117   —Sermons of. *For Tho. Parkhurst*, 1671. fol. L; CLC.

118   —A treatise concerning the right vse of the fathers. *For John Martin*, 1651. 2 pts. 4°. LT, O, C, LL, ENC; CH, MH, NU, WF, Y.

119   — —Second edition. *For John Martin, to be sold by Robert Boulter*, 1675. 2 pts. 4°. T.C.I 199. L, O, C, LL, EN; MH, NU, PL, WF, Y.

    Daily devotions. 1672. *See* Hopton, Susannah.

    Daily exercise, of. *Amsterdam*, 1657. *See* Crowther, Arthur Anselm.

    Daily exercises. *Paris*. 1684. *See* N., N.

    Daily observations. [*n.p.*], 1654. *See* Capell, Arthur Capel, *baron*.

    Daily office for the sick. 1694. *See* Isham, Zacheus.

    Daily practice. 1684. *See* Hammond, Henry.

120   The daily proceedings of His Majesties fleet. *Lonkon* [sic], November 18. *for Joh. Wright*, 1642. 4°.* LT, DT.

    Daily thoughts. 1651. *See* Henshaw, Joseph.

    Daimonomageia. 1665. *See* Drage, William.

    Dainty damsels dream. [1660?] *See* Price, Laurence.

121   A dainty new dialogue between Henry and Elizabeth. *For W. Thackeray, T. Passenger, and W. Whitwood*, [1670–77]. brs. L, CM, HH, GU; MH.

122   A dainty new ditty of a saylor and his love. [1690?] brs. O.

122A   [**Dakins, Thomas.**] A whippe for the custome-house curre. *Printed*, 1653. 4°.* L, O, C, OC; NC.

123   **Dale, John.** The analysis of all the epistles of the New Testament. *Oxford, by Leonard Lichfield*, 1652. 4°. MADAN 2192. LT, O, CT, BR, DC; CLC, CN, NGT, NU, Y.

124   — —[Anr. ed.] *Oxford, by L. L. for E. Forrest and R. Blagrave*, 1657. 8°. MADAN 2334. L, O, CT; WF, Y.

125   **Dale, Robert.** An exact catalogue of the nobility of England. *Printed, and to be sold by Geo. Grafton*, 1697. 8°. T.C.III 25. L, O, C, OM, EN; BN, CH, CU, LC, MH, Y.

126   **Dale, Samuel.** Pharmacologia. *Sumptibus Sam. Smith & Benj. Walford*, 1693. 12°. T.C.II 480. L, O, C, OM, LW; BN, NC, WF, WSG.

127   **Dalerac, François Paulin.** Polish manuscripts: or the secret history of the reign of John Sobieksi. *For H. Rhodes; T. Bennet; A. Bell; T. Leigh and D. Midwinter*, 1700. 8°. T.C.III 213. L, O, OME, EN, GU; CH, CN, LC, PL, Y.

128   **Dalgarno, George.** Ars signorum. *Excudebat J. Hayes, sumptibus authoris*, 1661. 8°. L, O, CS, MR, ES; BN, CH, LC, MH, NN.

128A —Character universalis . . . A new discovery. [*Oxford?* 1657.] brs. L.

129 —Didascalocophus. *Printed at the theater in Oxford,* 1680. 8°. T.C.I 407. MADAN 3263. L, O, LCS, OM, ES; NN, WF, WSG, Y.

129A —News to the whole world. [*Oxford,* 1657.] brs. L.

129B —Omnibus omnino hominibus. [*Oxford?* 1660.] 4°.* L; WF.

129C [–] The possibilitie and great usefulnesse. [*Oxford?* 1658.] brs. L.

130 —Tables of the universal character. [*Oxford, by Leonard Lichfield,* 1657.] brs. MADAN 2335. L, O.

130A [**Dalhusie, John Herman.**] Carmen proseucticon Basiliphili. [*London,* 1689.] fol.* OC, MC; Y.

131 —De regum regnorumque. *Edinburgi, typis hæredis Andreæ Anderson,* 1691. 4°. ALDIS 3140. L, O, E, EN, ES; CH, NC, PL, WF, Y.

131A —Oratio de revolutionibus regnorum. *Edinburgi,* 1692. ALDIS 3218. EN.

132 —The salvation of Protestants asserted. *For James Adamson,* 1689. 4°. T.C.II 244. L, O, C, MC, E; CH, MH, NU, TU, WF, Y.

133 — —[Anr. ed.] *Edinburgh,* 1691. 4°. ALDIS 3141. EN.

134 — —[Anr. ed.] *Dublin, Samuel Lee,* 1694. sixes. DIX 263. O, OB, CD.

135 [**Dalincourt, Pierre.**] A relation of the French kings late expedition. *For John Starkey,* 1669. 12°. T.C.I 5. L, O, P, A; CH, CLC, PL, WF, Y.

136 **Dalison, Sir William.** The reports des divers special cases. *By the assigns of Richard and Edward Atkins, for Samuel Keble, Daniel Brown, Isaac Cleave, and W. Rogers,* 1689. fol. T.C.II 301. L, O, C, LG, LMT, EN; NN, V, WF, Y.

137 **Dallas, George.** System of stiles. *Edinburgh, by the heirs and successors of Andrew Anderson,* 1697. fol. ALDIS 3660. L, LL, EN, ES; CLC, NCL, WF, YL.

       Dallington epitomis'd. 1700. See Stacy, Edmund.

138 [**Dallison, Charles.**] The royalist's defence. [*London,*] *printed,* 1548. 4°. LT, O, C, MR, ES; CH, CN, MH, NU, WF, Y.

139 —Mr. Charles Dallison, Recorder of Lincoln, his speech to the King's Majesty. *For William Gay, August the 3,* 1642. L, O, CCA, LG, EC; WF.

140 Entry cancelled.

141 **Dalmahoy, Sir John.** Unto His Grace, His Majesties high commissioner, . . . the petition of. [*n.p.,* 1691.] brs. O, EN.

       Dalrymple, James. *See* Stair, James Dalrymple, *earl of.*

142 **Dalton, James.** A strange and true relation of a yovng woman possest with the devill. *Imprinted at London by E. P. for Tho. Vere,* 1647. 4°.* LT, O.

143 **Dalton, Michael.** The countrey justice. Sixth edition. *For Richard Best,* 1643. 12°. MC; LC, MHL, NCL.

144 — —[Anr. ed.] *Imprinted at London for the company of stationers,* 1655. fol. L, DC; CH, MHL, NCL, WF.

145 — —[Anr. ed.] —, 1661. fol. L, OB, NPL; LC, MHL, PL, WF.

146 — —[Anr. ed.] *By John Streater, James Flesher, and Henry Twyford, assigns of Richard Atkyns, and Edward Atkyns,* 1666. fol. L, CE, LI; LC, MHL, NCL, PL.

147 — —[Anr. ed.] *By G. Sawbridge, T. Roycroft, and W. Rawlins, assigns of Richard Atkyns, and Edward Atkyns, to be sold by H. Twyford,* 1677. fol. T.C.I 285. L, CJ, CM, SC, YM; BN, CLC, LC, MHL, TU.

148 — —[Anr. ed.] *By H. Sawbridge, S. Roycroft, and W. Rawlins, assigns of R. Atkyns and E Atkyns,* 1682. fol. T.C.I 517. L, CT; CU, LC, MHL, MIU.

149 — —[Anr. d.] *By William Rawlins and Samuel Roycroft, assigns of Richard and Edward Atkyns; to be sold by Samuel Keble,* 1690. fol. T.C.II 307. L, CM, MC; LC, MHL, MIU, NCL, TU.

150 — —[Anr. d.] *To be sold by J. Walthoe, and B. Tooke,* 1697. fol. T.C.III 28. LL, LMT, CK, CT; LC, MBP, MHL, NCL.

151 —Officium vicecomitum. The office and authority of sherrifs. 1662. 4°. O, LG; MIU, NCL, NIC.

152 — —[Anr. ed.] *For H. Twyford, G. Sawbridge, J. Place, J. Bellinger, W. Place, T. Basset, R. Pawlet, C. Wilkinson, T. Dring, W. Jacob, A. Bank, C. Harper, J. Amery, J. Poole, J. Leigh,* 1670. fol. T.C.I 52. LIL, LMT, CP; CH, KT, MHL, NCL, YL.

153 — —[Anr. ed.] *By the assigns of Richard Atkins, and Edward Atkins,* 1682. fol. T.C.I 499. L, CS, MC, EN; CLC, LC, MH, NC, NR.

154 —[Anr. ed.] —, 1700. fol. L, LI, LMT, BAMB; LC, MHL, NCL, V.

       Dammee, Agamemnon Shaglock, *pseud.*

155 The dammee cavalliers warning piece. *For Abraham Everet,* 1643. fol.* LT; MH.

       Dammeeslash, David, *pseud.*

       Damnable heresie. [n.p.], 1672. *See* West, Robert.

156 The damnable principles of the Jesuites. *For Will. Bowtel,* 1679. 4°.* L, O; NU, WF.

157 A damnable treason. [*London*], *for W.B.,* 1641. 4°.* LT, O, CT, EC, BR; CH, MH, NU, WF, Y.

       Damoiselle, 1653. *See* Brome, Richard.

158 [**Damon, John**]. Joyfull newes from Captain Marro in Ireland. [*London*], *for Iohn Wels,* 1642. 4°.* LT, LFEA.

       Damon a pastoral. [n.p.], 1696. *See* G., J.

159 Damon and Celia. [*London*], *for F. Coles, T. Vere, J. Wright, J. Clarke, W. Thackeray, & T. Passenger,* [1655–80]. brs. L, O, HH; MH.

159A The damosels hard shift for a husband. [*London*], *for F. Coles, T. Vere, J. Wright, and J. Clarke,* [1674–79.] brs. O.

160 The damosels tragedy. [*London*], *for J. Back,* [1685–88]. brs. L, HH; MH.

161 **Dampier, William.** A new voyage round the world. *For James Knapton,* 1697. 8°. T.C.III 5. L, O, LI, OM, BR; BN, MH, RPJ, WCL, WF, Y.

162 — —Second edition. —, 1697. 3 v. 8°. T.C.III 17. L, O, LW; CH, MH, NLC, RPJ, WF.

163 — —Third edition. —, 1698. 8°. T.C.III 45. L, CS, EN; CLC, CN, LC, MB, RPJ, V.

164 — —Fourth edition. —, 1699. 8°. T.C.III 113. L, C, CE; BN, CH, NLC, RPJ, WCL, Y.

165 —Voyages and descriptions. Vol. II. *For James Knapton,* 1699. 8°. T.C.III 107. L, O, BR; LC, MH, PL, RPJ, Y.

166 — —Second edition. —, 1700. 8°. T.C.III 201. L; CH, CN, CSU, RPJ.

Danby, Thomas Osborne. *See* Leeds, Thomas Osborn Danby, *duke of.*

Dance machabre. 1653. *See* Coleman, Walter.

Dancing master. 1652. *See* Playford, John.

Dancing-school. 1700. *See* Ward, Edward.

167 **Danckerts, Henrick.** The sea-atlas. *At Amsterdam, by Henry Doncker;* 1660. fol. RPJ.

168 **Dandini, Girolamo.** A voyage to Mount Libanus. [London], *by J. Orme, for A. Roper, and R. Basset,* 1698. 8°. T.C.III 78. L, O, C, CS; CH, MH, TU, WF, Y.

169 **Danes, John.** A light to Lilie. Second edition. *For W. H.,* 1643. 8°. L; BN, Y.

170 The Danes plot discovered. *For Andrew Cro and Marmaduke Boat,* 1642. 4°.* O, CM, EC; CLC, CN, Y.

171 **Danet, Pierre.** A complete dictionary of the Greek and Roman antiquities. *For John Nicholson: Tho. Newborough; and John Bullord: and sold by R. Parker; and B. Tooke,* 1700. 4°. L, O, C, E, DT; CLC, CU, MH, WG, Y.

D[anforth], J[ohn]. Almanack. Cambridge [Mass.], 1679. *See* Almanacs.

171A —A funeral elegy humbly dedicated to . . . Thomas Danforth. [Boston, 1699.] brs. MH.

172 —Kneeling to God. *Boston, by B. Green, & J. Allen. Sold by S. Phillips,* 1697. 24°. EVANS 780. CH, MH, MHS, MWA.

[Danforth, Samuel.] Almanack. Cambridge [Mass.], 1646. *See* Almanacs.

173 —An astronomical description of the late comet. *Cambridge [Mass.]: by Samuel Green,* 1665. 8°.* EVANS 99. L, O; MHS.

174 — —[Anr. ed.] *Printed at Cambridge in New England, and reprinted at London for Peter Parker,* 1666. 8°.* L; NN, RPJ.

175 —A brief recognition of New-Englands errand. *Cambridge [Mass.]: by S. G. and M. J.,* 1671. 4°.* EVANS 160. CH, MB, MHS, MWA, NN, RPJ.

176 —The cry of Sodom. *Cambridge [Mass.], by Marmaduke Johnson,* 1674. 4°.* EVANS 186. MB, MH, MWA, Y.

—New England almanack. Cambridge [Mass.] 1685. *See* Almanacs.

177 The danger and unreasonableness of a toleration. *For Walter Davis,* 1685. 4°.* T.C.II 128. L, O, OCC, CT; CH, MH, MIU, NU, WF.

Danger is over. 1696. *See* G., T.

177A The danger of a comprehension. [London? 1689.] brs. O, HH; INU, MH.

Danger of a total. 1693. *See* Palmer, Charles.

Danger of enthusiasm. 1674. *See* Allen, William.

Danger of mercenary Parliaments. [n.p., 1698.] *See* Toland, John.

178 The danger of pride and ambition. *By H. B. for P. Brooksby,* 1685. 8°.* O; CH.

179 The danger of the Church of England. *For Tho. Bennet, and John Howell,* 1690. 4°.* T.C.II 330. L, O, C, EN, DT; CH, MH, NU, WF, Y.

180 —[Anr. ed.] *A. Baldwin,* 1690. 4°.* L.

Danger of the Protestant religion. 1700. *See* Defoe, Daniel.

Danger of treaties. [n.p., 1644.] *See* Vicars, John.

Danger to England. 1642. *See* Parker, Henry.

181 **Dangerfield, Thomas.** Animadversions upon Mr. John Gadbury's almanack. [London], *published by Langley Curtis,* 1682. fol.* L, O, HH, EN; IU, LC, MH, WF, Y.

182 —Mr. Dangerfield's answer and defence. colop: *For James Dean,* 1685. brs. L, O, HH; INU, MBA.

183 —Tho. Dangerfield's ansvver to a certain scandalous lying pamphlet. *For the author, and are to be sold at Randal Taylor's,* 1680. fol.* L, O, C, EN, DT; CH, CN, MH, NU, WF, Y.

184 — —[Anr. ed.] colop: *For Richard Janeway,* 1680. cap., fol.* L, O, C; CH.

185 —Don Tomazo. *For William Rumbold,* 1680. 8°. L, O, CT, OC, A; CN, MH, NP, Y.

186 —The Grand Impostor defeated. *For Richard Janeway,* 1682. fol.* L, O, CT, OC, HH; CH, MH, TU, WF, Y.

187 —The information of . . . twentieth day of October. *By the assigns of John Bill, Thomas Newcomb, and Henry Hills,* 1680. fol.* L, O, C, EN, DT; BN, CH, MU, NC, TU, Y.

188 — —[Anr. ed.] [Dublin], *re-printed,* 1680. 4°.* DIX 178. C, CD, DT.

188A — —[Same title.] twenty-sixth day of October. *By the assigns of John Bill, Thomas Newcomb, and Henry Hills,* 1680. fol.* MM.

189 [–] The king's evidence justified. colop: *For R. Janeway,* 1679. fol. O; CL, NU.

190 —Dangerfield's memoires. *By J. Bennet for Charles Brome,* 1685. 4°.* T.C.II 128. L, O, C, EN, DT; CH, CN, MH, NU, WF, Y.

191 —More shams still. *For Richard Baldwin,* 1681. 4°.* T.C.I 475. L, O, C, HH, DT; CH, CN, MH, NU, WF, Y.

192 —Mr. Tho. Dangerfeilds particular narrative. *For Henry Hills, John Starkey, Thomas Basset, John Wright, Richard Chiswell, and Samuel Heyrick,* 1679. fol. L, O, C, EN, DT; BN, CH, CN, LC, MH, NU, TU, Y.

193 —Mr. Tho. Dangerfeild's second narrative. *For Thomas Cockerill,* 1680. fol.* L, O, CM, EN, DT; CH, MH, NU, WF, Y.

194 Dangerfields dance. *By J. M.,* 1685. brs. L, O, HH; CH, MH, Y.

194A Dangerfield's ghost to Jefferys. [London? 1689.] brs. MH.

195 A dangerous and blovdy fight upon the coast of Cornwal. *For George Horton,* 1652. 4°.* LT; WF.

196 A dangerous and bloudy plot discovered. *For Richard Wilcocks,* 1648. 4°.* LT; MH.

197 A dangerovs fight at Pembroke Castle. *For R. G.,* 1648. 4°.* LT, AN.

198 Entry cancelled.

Dangerous rule. 1658. *See* Ladyman, Samuel.

199 The dangers of new discipline. [*Oxford*], *for W. R.:* 1642. 4°.* MADAN 1015. LT, O, CJ, DC, DT; CH, CN, MH, NU, Y.

200 [**Daniel, Benjamin.**] True nevves from Cork. *May* 17. *London for F. Rogers,* 1642. 4°.* LT, EC; CN.

200A [**Daniel, Edward.**] Meditations collected and ordered. Second edition. *At Doway, by Baltazar Bellere,* 1663. 12°. O; CLC, CN, PL, Y.

201 [**Daniel, Gabriel.**] A voyage to the world of Cartesius. *Printed, and sold by Thomas Bennet,* 1692. 8°. T.C.II 412. L, CS, MR, E, DT; CH, CN, MH, TU, WF, Y.

202 [–] —Second edition. *For Thomas Bennet,* 1694. 8°. T.C.II 482. L, LL, A; CU, LC, MH, NR, Y.

Daniel, Humphrey. Almanack. [1651.] *See* Almanacs.

202A **Daniel, John.** The birth, life, and death of the Jewish unction. *By F. N.,* 1651. 8°. LT.

203 **Daniel, Richard.** A compendium of the usuall hands of England. [*London,* 1663.] obl. fol. C; CN, MH, MIU.

204 —Daniels copy-book. *For Mathew Collins and Francis Cossinet,* 1664. obl. fol. L, O, LV; CH, CN, IU, NC.

205 — —[Anr. ed.] [*London,* 1680?] obl. fol. L.

205A —Scriptoria Danielis. A writing book. 1681. 8°. OP; CN.

206 **Daniel, Samuel.** Archi-Episcopal priority instituted. [*London*], *printed,* 1642. 4°. LT, O; CH, LC, Y.

207 —The collection of the history of England. Fourth edition. *By E. G. for John Williams,* 1650. fol. L, OB, CE, LGI, E; BN, CH, LC, MH, PL, Y.

208 — —Fifth edition. *By F. Leach for Benj. Tooke and Thomas Sawbridge,* 1685. fol. T.C.II 103. L, LI, C, OME, HH, ES; BN, NC, TU, WF, Y.

209 Daniel Cooper: or, the High-land laddy. [*London*], *for P. Brooksby,* [1695?]. brs. L.

Daniel in the den. 1682. *See* Jay, Stephen.

210 **Dankerman, Cornelius.** Batavia mærens in obitum . . . Mariæ. *For A. Roper and E. Wilkinson,* 1695. brs. CH, MH, NP, WF.

210A **Danks, John.** The captive's returne. [*London*], *printed,* 1680. 4°.* LF; PH.

210B [–] A declaration concerning the people called Quakers. [*London*], 1674. 4°. LF.

210C **Dansie, John.** A mathematical manual. *For J. Moxon,* 1654. 12°. CT.

211 **D[anson], T[homas].** De cavsa Dei: or, a vindication. *For R. Roberts, to be sold by Walter Davis,* 1678. 8°. L, LCL, LW; NU.

211A — —[Anr. ed.] *For Tho. Cockerill,* 1678. 8°. LW, OCC; MB, MH, Y.

212 —A friendly conference between a Paulist and a Galatian. *For Samuel Crouch,* 1694. 8°. L, O, C, LCI, LW; PH, WF.

213 [–] A friendly-debate between Satan and Sherlock. [*London*], *printed,* 1676. 8°. L, O, LCL, CE; MH, NU.

214 —κλητοὶ τετηρημενοι, or the saints persevereance. *For Tho. Parkhurst,* 1672. 8°. T.C.I 110. L, O, CS, LCL; NU.

215 —The Quakers folly made manifest. Second edition. *By J. H. for John Allen,* 1659. 8°. LT, O, CCA, CT, LF; CH.

216 — —Third edition. —, 1664. 8°. O.

217 —The Quakers vvisdom descendeth not from above. *For J. Allen,* 1659. 8°.* LT, CT, BBN; CH, PH.

218 —A synopsis of Quakerism. *Printed,* 1668. 8°. L, O, LCL, LF, BBN; CH, PH, PSC.

219 — —Second edition. —, 1669. 8°. L, O, CT, OC; CLC, WF, Y.

Danverd, John. *See* Danvers, John.

220 **D'Anvers, *Mrs.* Alicia.** Academia, or the humours of the University of Oxford. *Printed and sold by Randal Taylor,* 1691. 4°. T.C.II 360. L, O, OC, EN, DT; CH, CN, MH, WF, Y.

221 —A poem upon His Sacred Majesty, his voyage for Holland. *For Tho. Bever,* 1691. fol.* AU; CH, NN, Y.

222 **D'Anvers, Henry.** Certain qværies concerning liberty of conscience. *For Giles Calvert,* [1649]. 4°.* LT, OC, ENC, DT; CH, NU.

223 —Innocency and truth vindicated. *For Francis Smith,* 1675. 8°. O, C, LCL; CLC, NHC, NU.

224 —Murder will out. *For E. R. and J. R.,* 1689. 4°.* L, C, CT, LCL, HH, A; CN, MH, WF, Y.

225 [–] —[Anr. ed.] [*London,* 1689]. 4°.* OC, EN; CH, NHC, WF, Y.

226 —The mystery of magistracy unveiled. [*London*], 1663. 4°. LCL.

227 —A rejoynder to Mr. Wills's Vindiciæ. [*London*], *For Francis Smith,* 1675. 8°. L, LCL; CH, MH, NHC, NU.

228 —A second reply. *For Francis Smith,* 1675. 8°. L, O, LCL; CH, MH, NC, NHC, NU.

229-30 Entries cancelled.

231 [–] Theopolis, or the city of God. *By T. Ratcliff, and Nat. Thompson, for Nathaniel Ponder,* 1672. 8°. T.C.I 95. L, O; CLC, MH, NU, WF.

232 —A third reply. [*London*], *printed,* 1676. 4°.* L.

233 —A treatise of baptism. *For Francis Smith,* 1673. 8°. T.C.I 142. L, O; CLC, NHC, WF.

234 — —Second edition. —, 1674. 8°. L, O, CS, EN, DT; BN, CU, NHC, NP, NU, Y.

235 — —[Anr. ed.] —, 1675. 8°. T.C.I 182. L, O, CT, LCL, LSC; NHC.

236 —A treatise of laying on of hands. *For Fran. Smith,* 1674. 8°. L, O, LCL, E, DT; CU, LC, NHC, NU, Y.

237 **Danvers, John.** The royal oake. *For G. Horton,* 1660. 4°.* LT, O, CT, LVF, E; CH, MU, NP, WF.

237A — —[Anr. ed.] *Printed at London, and re-printed at Edinburgh by a society of stationers,* 1660. 4°.* ALDIS 1639. EN; Y.

238 — —Fourth edition. *By J. C. for J. J.,* 1660. 4°.* O.

239 Daphne coronalis: a pindarique ode, to . . . James the II. *For Charles Brome,* 1685. 4°. T.C.II 126. O; CH, CLC, WF, Y.

Daphne's complaint. 1678. *See* P., J.

Daphnis and Chloe. 1657. *See* Longus.

240 Daphnis: or, a pastoral elegy upon . . . Mr. Thomas Creech. *For John Deeve,* 1700. fol.* L; CLC, MH, PBL, WF.

241 Entry cancelled.

242   **[Dapper, Olfert.]** Atlas Chinensis. *By Tho. Johnson, for the author,* 1671. fol. L, O, C, OC, DT; BN, CN, CSU, MH, MU, Y.

243   **[Darby, Charles.]** Bacchanalia: or a description of a drunken club. *For Robert Boulter,* 1680. fol.* T.C.I 394. L, O, LG, OC, EC; CH, CN, MH, WF, Y.

244   [–] —[Anr. ed.] —, 1683. fol.* MH, TU.

245   [–] —[Anr. ed.] *Printed and sold by E. Whitlock,* 1698. fol.* T.C.III 65. L; IU.

245A   —An elegy on the death of the Queen. *For John Chamberlain, in St. Edmunds-Bury: to be sold by Peter Parker, and John Whitlock,* 1695. fol.* L, O, OC, OP; CN, MH, WF, Y.

246   **Darcy, Patrick.** An argvment delivered . . . 9. Iunii, 1641. *Printed at Waterford, by Thomas Bourke,* 1643. 4°. L, O.

247   **Dare, Josiah.** Counsellor Manners, his last legacy to his son. *For Edward Gough,* 1673. 8°. T.C.I 134. L, CS, OC, EN, GK; CN, CU, MH, MHL, WF.

247A   — —[Anr. ed.] —, *are or to be sold by Robert Clavee,* 1676. 8°. T.C.I 272. IU.

248   — —[Anr. ed.] *By Tho. Warren for Edward Gough,* 1694. 8°. T.C.II 496. GK; CN, NU.

248A   — —Third edition. *For E. G.; sold by Thomas Shelmerdine,* 1698. 8°. T.C.III 69. L; CLC.

249   — —"Third" edition. *For John Spring and George Conyers,* 1699. 8°. M; WF.

249A   **Darell, John.** East India trade first discovered. 1651. 4°.* L; MH.

250   [–] Mr. Courten's catastrophe and adieu to East India. *By R. I.,* 1652. 4°.* L, LUG.

251   —Strange news from th' Indies. *For Stephen Bowtel,* 1652. 4°.* L, O, CM, LUG, SC; MB, NN, WF, WU.

252   —A true and compendious narration; or (second part of Amboyney). *By T. Mabb for Nathaniel Brooke,* 1665. 4°.* L, O, CT, LUG; CH, MIU, Y.

253   Entry cancelled.

     Darell, William. *See* Darrell, William.

254   **Dares** *Phrygius.* Daretis Phrygii . . . de bello Trojano. *Impensis Thomæ Helder,* 1675. 8°. T.C.I 221. L, O, CT, EC, E; Y.

255–6   Entries cancelled.

257   **Dariot, Claude.** Dariotus redivivus. *For A. Kemb* 1653. 4°. L, O, C, DC, GU; CH, LC, MH, WF, Y.

258   **Darker, John.** A breviary of military discipline. *Printed and sold by D. Brown, T. Fox, and F. Sanders,* 1692. 8°. L, O.

     Darknesse and ignorance. 1659. *See* Howgil, Francis.

     Darkness of atheisme. 1683. *See* Care, Henry.

     Darkness vanquished. 1675. *See* Keach, Benjamin.

259   **Darley, John.** The glory of Chelsey Colledge revived. *For J. Bourn,* 1662. 4°. L, O, LG, MR, EN; CH, MH.

260   **Darling, John.** The carpenters rule made easie. *By R. & W. Leybourn, for John Jones in Worcester,* 1658. 8°. LT, CE.

261   — —Third edition. *For Tho. Sawbridge, and John Jones in Worcester,* 1676. 12°. T.C.I 242. L; NR.

262   — —Fourth edition. *By J. Playford, for Tho. Sawbridge,* 1684. 12°. T.C.II 54. C; Y.

262A   — —Fifth edition. *For George Sawbridge,* 1694. 12°. CLC.

263   **Darrell, Marmaduke.** A charge at the general quarter sessions. *For Randal Taylor,* 1689. 4°. L, LGI, DT; CH.

264   —Mr Darrell's reply to Sir J. Whichcotts pretended answer. [London, 1670?] brs. L.

265   Entry cancelled.

266   **[Darrell, William.]** The lay-mans opinion. [London], *printed,* 1687. 4°.* L, O, C, MC, EN; CH, CLC, NU, WF, Y.

267   —Letter to a lady. [London, 1688.] brs. L, LIL, DT; CH, MIU, Y.

268   —A letter to the author of The reply. colop: *By Henry Hills,* 1687. cap., 4°.* L, OC, E; CH, MIU, NU, WF, Y.

269   —A sermon preached by. [London], 1688. 4°.* MC.

269A   —The vanity of human prospects. *For John and Thomas Lane,* 1688. 4°. HEYTHROP.

270   —A vindication of Saint Ignatius. *For Anthony Boúdet,* 1688. 4°. L, O, LIL, OC, OME; CH, MH, MIU, TU, WF, Y.

270A   **Dartiquenave, Charles.** Augustissimo, potentissimo & clementissimo . . . Carolo II. *Typis E. Tyler & R. Holt,* 1681. fol.* L, O; Y.

271   **Dartmouth, George Legge,** *baron.* To the King's . . . Majesty. [London, 1688.] brs. L, O, C, HH; CH, Y.

272   **Darton,** [Nicholas]. Ecclesia Anglicana. [Oxford, by H. Hall], *printed,* 1649. 4°.* MADAN 2022. O; WF.

273   —The true and absolute bishop. *By Tho. Badger for Humphrey Mosley,* 1641. 4°. L, O, C, LW, EN; MH, NU, WF, Y.

274   **Dary, Michael.** The complete gauger. *For Robert Horne, and Nathanael Ponder,* 1678. 12°. T.C.I 290. L, OC, CE.

274A   —Dary's diary. *By T. F. for George Hurlock,* 1650. 8°. OC.

275   —Gauging epitomized. *By W. Godbid,* 1669. brs. L, O; CLC.

276   —The general doctrine of equation. *For the author,* 1664. 8°.* L, O; CLC.

277   —Interest epitomized. *By William Godbid, for the author, and are to be sold by W. Fisher,* 1677. 8°.* T.C.I 268. O, C, CE, CT; MB, WF, Y.

278   —Dary's miscellanies. *By W. G. and sold by Moses Pitt, Tho. Rookes, and Wil. Birch,* 1669. 8° L, O, C, CT; MU.

279   —A tale of a tub. [London], *for William Shrowsbury,* 1674. brs. L.

     Dash, Jacob, *pseud.*

279A   **Dashfield, John.** A contemplation of mans mortalitie. *Printed at London,* 1649. 4°.* MH, MIU, MWA.

280   **D'Assigny, Marius.** The art of memory. *By J. D. for Andr. Bell,* 1697. 8°. T.C.III 28. L, O, LL, LW, CS; CH, LC, PL, TU, Y.

281   — —Second edition. *For Andr. Bell,* 1699. 8°. L, LCS, CPE, ES; LC, WF, Y.

281A   — —"Second" edition. *Edinburgh, J. Reid,* [c. 1699.] 8°. EN; IU, MWA, NP.

282   —The assurance of the faithfull. *By J. R. for Edward Man,* 1670. 4°.* L; NPT, NU, WF.

283   —The divine art of prayer. *By R. Everingham, to be sold by John Everingham,* 1691. 12°. T.C.II 357. O; NU.

284   — —Second edition. *For T. Cockerill,* 1697. T.C.III 263. LSC.

285   —Rhetorica Anglorum. *Impensis S. & J. Spring, J. Robinson, D. Brown, & A. Bell,* 1699. 8°. L, LL, CCA, CS, EN; MWA.

285A   —Two treatises on the curiosities of old Rome. 1671. 8°. O; MH.

286   **D'Assigny, Samuel.** An antidote against the erroneous. *Dublin, J. B. & S. P.,* 1698. 4°.* DIX 301. O, DT.

287   —A collection of the brave exploits. 1686. 4°. EN; CH.

288   —A short relation of the brave exploits of the Vaudois. *Dublin, John Brent,* 1699. 4°.* DIX 310. L, C, OC, DI, DN; Y.

       Dauborne. *See* Daborn.

       Daughter of Sion. [n.p.], 1677. *See* Fell, Margaret.

       [**Dauncy, John.**] Civil warres of Great Britain, 1661. *See* Davies, John.

289   **Dauncey, John.** A compendious chronicle of the kingdom of Portugal. *By Tho. Johnson, for Francis Kirkman, Henry Brome, and Henry Marsh,* 1661. 8°. L, O, CS, LW, EN; LC, MH, PL, WF, Y.

289A   —The English lovers. *For H. Brome,* 1662, 8°, CN.

289B   — —[Anr. ed.] *For Francis Kirkman, and Henry Marsh,* 1662. 8°. L; WF.

290   —An exact history of the several changes of government in England. *For Simon Miller,* 1660. 8°. LT, O, LG; CLC, CU, LC, MB, MH, Y.

291   [–] The history of His sacred Majesty Charles the II. *For Iames Davies,* 1660. 12°. LT, O, C, EN, DT; CH, CN, MH, NU, WF, Y.

292   [–] —[Anr. ed.] *Cork, reprinted by William Smith,* 1660. 12°. D; CN, MH.

293   [–] The history of the thrice illustrious princess Henrietta Maria. *By E. C. for Philip Chetwind,* 1660. 12°. L, O, LG, EN; WF, Y.

294   —Work for Cooper. [*London,* 1663.] brs. L.

295   **D'Auvergne, Edward.** The history of the campagne in Flanders, for . . . 1695. *For Mat. Wotton and John Newton,* 1696. 4°. L, O, C, HH, MR; CH, CN, TU, WF, Y.

296   — —1696. —, 1696. 4°. T.C.II 601. L, O, CT, OM, HH; CH, CN, TU, WF, Y.

297   — —1697. —, 1698. 4°. T.C.III 53. L, CT, HH; CH, CN, WF, Y.

298   —The history of the campagne in the Spanish Netherlands. *For Matt. Wotton and John Newton,* 1694. 4°. T.C.II 492. L, O, C, HH; EN, CH, CN, PL, TU, WF, Y.

299   —The history of the last campagne. *For John Newton,* 1693. 4°. T.C.II 538. L, O, C, HH; CH, CN, MH, WF, Y.

300   —A relation of the most remarkable transactions. *For Dorman Newman,* 1693. 4°. T.C.II 453. L, O, C, LUS, HH; CH, CN, MH, WF, Y.

301   **Davanzati, Bernardo.** A discourse upon coins. *By J. D. for A. and J. Churchil,* 1696. 4°.* L, O, CT, GH; CLC, CN, LC, MH, NF, Y.

302   **Davenant, Charles.** Circe, a tragedy. *For Richard Tonson,* 1677. 4°. T.C.I 281. L, O, OW, CK, EN; CH, CN, LC, MH, TU, Y.

303   — —Second edition. —, 1685. 4°. L, LVD, CM, HH; CLC, CN, NP, TU, WF, Y.

304   [–] Discourse upon grants and resumptions. *For James Knapton,* 1700. 8°. T.C.III 158. L, O, C, MR, E; CH, CN, LC, MH, NC, Y.

305   [–] —Second edition. —, 1700. 8°. T.C.III 178. L, O, HH, DT; CH, CU, LC, MH, NP, Y.

305A   [–] —Fourth edition. —, 1700. 8°. TU.

306   [–] Discourses on the publick revenues. *For James Knapton,* 1698. 2 v 8°. T.C.III 56. L, O, C, MR, EN; BN, CH, CN, LC, MH, NC, Y.

307   [–] An essay on the East-India-trade. *Printed,* 1696. 8°. L, O, C, MR, DT; CH, CN, MH, NC, WF, Y.

308   [–] —[Anr. ed.] *For J. K.,* [1697.] 8°. O; LC, MU, RPJ, V.

309   [–] An essay upon the probable methods. *For James Knapton,* 1699. 8°. T.C.III 111. L, C, OME, EN, DT; BN, CH, CU, LC, MH, NC, TU, Y.

310   [–] —Second edition. —, 1700. 8°. T.C.III 201. L, LUG, E; CN, LC, MH, PL, Y.

311   [–] An essay upon ways and means. *For Jacob Tonson,* 1695. 8°. L, C, LI, CCA, MR; CH, CN, LC, MH, Y.

312   [–] —Second edition. —, 1695. 8°. L, O, CT, BAMB, DT; MH, MIU, NC, WF.

312A   —Dr. Davenants opinion. [*London,* 1700.] cap. 4°.* NC.

313   [–] The songs in Circe. *For Richard Tonson,* 1677. 4°.* T.C.I 273. L, O, LVD; CH, CLC, CN, WF.

314   **Davenant, John,** *bp.* Animadversions written by. *For Iohn Partridge,* 1641. 8°. L, O, C, EN, DT; BN, CLC, CU, NPT, NU.

315   — —[Anr. ed.] *Cambridge: by Roger Daniel,* 1641. 8°. L, O, C, DC, E; CH, MH, NU, WF, Y.

316   —Dissertatio de morte Christi. *Ex officina Rogeri Danielis, Cantabrigiensis,* 1683. 12°. C, GU; NU, WG.

317   —Dissertationes duæ. [*Cambridge*], *ex officina Rogeri Danielis,* 1650. fol. L, O, C, E, DT; BN, CH, NU, WF, Y.

318   —An exhortation to the restoring of brotherly communion. *By R. B. for Richard Badger and John Williams,* 1641. 8°. L, O, CT, E, DT; CH, MH, NU, WG, Y.

319   [–] Good covnsells for the peace of Reformed churches. *Oxford, by Leonard Lichfield for William Webb,* 1641. 4°. MADAN 997. L, O, CK, EN, DT; CH, NU, WF, Y.

319A   —Vindiciæ. *Typis Guil. Du-Gard,* 1650. 8°. CPE.

320   **Davenant, Sir William.** The works of. *By T. N. for Henry Herringman,* 1673. fol. T.C.I 117. L, O, C, EN, DT; BN, CH, CU, LC, MH, NP, TU, Y.

321   [–] The cruelty of the Spaniards. *For Henry Herringman,* 1658. 4°.* LT, O, LVD, OW; CH, LC, MH, RPJ, WCL, Y.

322   —A discourse upon Gondibert. *Paris* [*London?*], *chez Matthiev Gvillemot,* 1650. 12°. L, O, OC, CS, GU; CH, MH, WCL, WF.

323 —The first days entertainment at Rutland-House. *By J.M. for H.Herringman,* 1657. 8°. LT, O, LG, LVD; CH, TU, WCL, WF, Y.

324 —Gondibert. *By Tho. Newcomb for John Holden,* 1651. 8°. LT, O, C, LVD, EN; CN, LC, MH, TU, Y.

325 — —Second edition. —, 1651. 4°. O, CE, CT, DC, EN; CH, CN, WCL, WF, Y.

326 — —[Anr. ed.] *For John Holden,* 1651. 8°. L, CK, CT; CH, CN, MH, TU, WF, Y.

327 [–] The history of Sʳ Francis Drake. First part. *For Henry Herringman,* 1659. 4°.* LT, O, LVD; CH, CN, LC, MH, RPJ, Y.

328 [–] London, King Charles, his Augusta. *For William Leybourn,* 1648. 4°.* LT, O, LG, LVF; CH, CLC, MH, WF, Y.

329 —Love and honovr. *For Hum: Robinson, and Hum: Moseley,* 1649. 4°.* L, O, C, EN, DT; CH, CN, LC, MH, TU, Y.

330 —Madagascar; with other poems. Second edition. *For Humphrey Moseley,* 1648. 12°. L, O, CT, DC, GK; CH, CN, MH, TU, WF, Y.

331 —The man's the master: a compedy. *In the Savoy, for Henry Herringman,* 1669. 4°. L, O, C, OW, EN; CH, CN, LC, MH, TU, Y.

332 —A panegyrick to His Excellency, the Lord General Monck. *For Henry Herringman,* 1659. brs. LT, O; CH, MH, TU.

333 —Poem, to the King's most sacred Majesty. *For Henry Heringman,* 1663. 4°.* L, OM, CK, CT; CH, MH, TU, WF, Y.

334 —Poem, upon His sacred Majesties most happy return. *For Henry Herringman,* 1660. 4°.* LT, O; CH, CLC, MH, TU, WF, Y.

335 —The preface to Gondibert. *Paris, chez Matthiev Guillemet,* 1650. 8°. MH.

[–] A prologue to His Majesty at the first play presented. 1660. *See* Denham, *Sir John.*

336 [–] The rivals. A comedy. *For William Cademan,* 1668. 4°. T.C.I 3. L, O, C, LVD, EN; CH, MH, TU, WCL, WF, Y.

337 [–] —[Anr. ed.] —, 1669. 4°. IU, LC, WF.

338 —The seventh and last canto of the third book of Gondibert. *For William Miller and Joseph Watts,* 1685. 8°.* T.C.II 114. IU, WC, WF.

339 —The siege of Rhodes . . . *By J.M. for Henry Herringman, at the back of Rutland House,* 1656. 4°. LT, O, C, LVF, OW; CH, CN, MH, TU, WF.

340 — —[Anr. ed., at the Cock-Pit]. —, 1656. 4°. LVD.

341 [–] —Second edition. —, 1659. 4°.* LVD, EN; CH, MB, MH, Y.

342 — —Third edition. *For Henry Herringman,* 1663. 4°. L, O, C, LG, GH; CH, CN, LC, MH, NP, TU, Y.

343 — —Fourth edition. —, 1670. 4°. L, O, OW, CS; CH, CU, MH, TU, WF, Y.

344 —To the honovrale [sic] knights, citizens and burgesses, . . . The humble petition of. *Printed,* 1641. brs. L; TU, Y.

345 —To the honorable knights, citizens, & burgesses of the House of Commons . . . the humble remonstrance of. [*London,* 1641.] brs. L, LG, CJ, LS; CH, TU, WF, Y.

346 Entry cancelled.

347 —Two excellent plays. *For G.Bedel, and T.Collins,* 1665. 8°. L, O, OW, CK, LVD; CH, CU, LC, MH, TU, Y.

348 —The vnfortunate lovers: a tragedie. *By R.H. and are to be sold by Francis Coles,* 1643. 4°. L, O, CT, LVF, A; CH, CLC, MH, WF, Y.

349 — —[Anr. ed.] *For Humphrey Moseley,* 1649. 4°. L, O, LVF; CH, CU, MB, MH.

350 [**Davenport, Christopher.**] An enchiridion of faith. *Printed at Douay,* 1654. 8°. L.

350A — —Second edition. —, 1655. 8°. O, LW, CS, CT; CN, NU, TU.

351 [**Davenport, Francis.**] A cleare vindication of Roman Catholicks. [*n.p.*], 1659. 4°. O.

352 [–] An explanation of the Roman Catholicks belief. [*n.p.*], 1656. 4°. O.

353 [–] —[Anr. ed.] —, 1670. 8°. O.

354 [–] —[Anr. ed.] —, 1673. brs. O.

355 —An historical abstract of Mr. Samuel White. [*London,* 1687/8.] fol.* L, LUG, HH; WF, Y.

356 **Davenport, John.** Another essay. *Cambridge* [*Mass.*]: *by Samuel Green and Marmaduke Johnson,* 1663. 4°. EVANS 78. L; CH, MH, MWA, NN, Y.

357 —A catechisme containing the chief heads . . . for . . . New-Haven. *By John Brudenell, and to be sold by John Allen,* 1659. 8°. LT, O, LW; Y.

358 [–] A discourse about civil government. *Cambridge* [*Mass.*]: *by Samuel Green and Marmaduke Johnson,* 1663. 4°.* EVANS 79. LC, MB, MH, NC, Y.

359 [–] An exhortation to the restoring of brotherly communion. *By R.B. for Richard Badger, and John Williams,* 1641. 12°. LCL, ON, CM; NU.

360 —God's call to His People. *Cambridge* [*Mass.*]: *by S.G. and M.J. for John Vsher of Boston,* 1669. 4°.* EVANS 137. O; CH, MB, MHS, Y.

361 —The knowledge of Christ. *For L.Chapman,* 1653. 4°. L, O, C, OC; CH, MH, NPT, NU, Y.

362 —The power of Congregational churches asserted. *For Rich. Chiswell, to be sold by John Vsher of Boston* [*Mass.*], 1672. 12°. T.C.I 115. L, LCL; MH, NP, NU, V, Y.

363 — —[Anr. ed.] *Printed,* 1672. 12°. L; LC, Y.

364 —The profession of the faith of. *For John Handcock,* 1642. 4°.* LT, O, HH, EN; CH, CN, LC, RPJ, Y.

365 —The saints anchor-hold. *By W.L. for Geo. Hurlock,* 1661. 12°. L, LSC; MB, NPT, WF, Y.

366 — —[Anr. ed.] *For The Guy,* 1682. 12° MM, RPJ, Y.

367 —A sermon preached at the election. [*Cambridge*], *printed,* 1670. 4°.* MB, MH.

368 [–] The witches of Huntingdon. *By W.Wilson, for Richard Clutterbuck,* 1646. 4°.* LT, CT, GU; CH, MH, WF, Y.

369 **Davenport, Robert.** The city night-cap. *By Ja: Cotrell, for Samuel Speed,* 1661. 4°. L, O, LVD, DC, EN; CH, CN, LC, MH, TU, Y.

370 —King Iohn and Matilda. *For Andrew Pennycuicke,* 1655. 4°. L, O, CT, EC, EN; CH, CN, LC, MH, Y.

371 — —[Anr. ed.] *For Richard Gammon, 1662.* 4°. O, C, LVD; CN, WF, Y.

372 **D[avenport], T[homas].** A brief manifestation or the state and case of the Quakers. *Printed at London, 1664.* 4°.* L, LF, O, BBN; CH, MH, MU, PH, Y.

373 —This for the Parliament, counsel, and the officers of the army. *For Thomas Simmons, 1659.* 4°.* LF; CH, CSS, PL.

374 [**David Antiochenus, or Dâ'ud ibn'Umar al-Antâki.**] The nature of the drink kauhi, or coffee. *Oxford, by Henry Hall, 1659.* 8°.* MADAN 2438. LT, O.

David, Cardinal of France, pseud.

375 **David, John.** A testimony against hypocrites. [c. 1686–90.] 4°.* L, O, CJ; PH.

376 David and Bersheba. [*London*], *by and for W.O.,* [1670?]. brs. L.

377 —[Anr. ed.] [*London*], *for W.O. and for A.M. sold by C.Bates,* [1685?]. brs. L.

David and Saul. 1696. *See* B., T.

David's distress. Edinburgh, 1676. *See* Wilson, John.

378 David's three mighties. *Oxford, by Leonard Lychfield, 1643[4].* 4°.* MADAN 1600. LT, O, SP, HH, DT; CH, CN, NU, WF, Y.

379 **D[avidson], T[homas].**] Cantus, songs and fancies. *Printed in Aberdene, by Iohn Forbes, 1662.* 4°. ALDIS 1733. ES; CH.

380 [–]—Second edition. *Aberdene, by Iohn Forbes, 1666.* 4°. ALDIS 1812. L, O, HH, E, AU; CH, MH.

381 [–]—"Second" edition. *Aberdene, by John Forbes, 1666. And are to be sold at Edinburgh, by David Trench.* 4°. ALDIS 1810. HH, AU.

382 [–]—Third edition. *Aberdeen, by Iohn Forbes, 1682.* 4°. ALDIS 2328. L, O, C, EN, GU; CH, CN, LC, MH, WF.

383 [–]—"Third" edition. *Printed in Aberdene by Iohn Forbes, 1682.* 4°. ALDIS 2329. AU.

Davies. *See also* Davyes.

384 [**Davies, Athanasius.**] Tò πνευμα ξωπωρουν or, sparkes of the spirit. *For Edw. Thomas, 1658.* 12°. LT; NU.

385 [–] The Protestants practice. *By M.S. for Lodowyke Lloyd, 1656.* 12°. LT.

Davies, *Lady* Eleanor. *See* Douglas, *Lady* Eleanor.

386 **Davies, James.** A sermon on Ps. Cxix. V. 57. *For Henry Brome, 1679.* 4°.* T.C.I. 340. L, O, C, CS, CT; WF.

387 **Davies, John, *citizen of London.*** An answer to those printed papers. [*London*], *printed, 1641.* 4°.* L.

388 **Davies, John, *of Hereford.*** ψαλμος θέιος. Or a divine psalme. *Printed, and are to be sold by Humphrey Moseley & Andrew Kemb, 1652.* 4°. L.

389 —The writing schoolemaster. *J Maud, 1648.* obl., 8°. LC.

390 — —[Anr. ed.] *Printed, and are to be sold by P.Stent, 1663.* obl., 8°. L, O.

391 — —[Anr. ed.] *By S.Griffin for John Overton, 1667.* obl., 8°. L.

392 **Davies, John, *of Kidwelly.*** The ancient rites, . . . of Durham. *For W.Hensman, 1672.* 8°. T.C.I 89. L, O, C, EN, DT; CLC, MH, PL, WF, Y.

393 —The civil warres of Great Britain and Ireland. *By R.W. for Philip Chetwind, 1661.* fol. L, O, C, EN, DT; CN, MH, TU, WF, Y.

394 [–] —[Anr. ed.] *Glasgow, by Robert Sanders, 1664.* 4°. ALDIS 1768. L, O, C, E, GM; LC, MBA, WCL, Y.

—Epictetus junior. 1670. *See* La Rochfoucauld, François *duc* de.

[–] History of His sacred Majesty Charles the II. 1660. *See* Dauncey, John.

395 [–] A memorial to the learned. *For George Powell and William Powle, 1686.* 8°..T.C.II 170. L, LWL, SP; CH, CV, NC, WF, Y.

[–] New pope. 1677. *See title.*

395A —Political and military observations. [*London, 1677.*] cap., 12°. C; MM.

396 — —[Anr. ed.] *For H.Cox: and H.Bonwick, 1679.* 8°. T.C.I 342. L, O, C; CH, MH, MIU.

396A — —[Anr. ed.] *For Robert Clavel and Jacob Sampson, 1680.* 12°. Y.

397 **Davies, *Sir* John.** England's independency upon the papal power. *By E.Flesher, J.Streater, and H.Twyford, assigns of Richard Atkins and Edward Atkins, 1674.* 4°. T.C.I 169. L, O, C, HH, DT; CH, MIU, NC, Y.

398 —Une exact table al report de. *For James Collins, and Charles Harper, 1677.* fol.* L, C, LG, CS; LC, MH, YL.

399 — —[Anr. ed.] *Dublin; printed, 1677.* fol.* T.C.I 282. DIX 159. L; CLC, MH.

400 [–] Γνωθι σεαυτον. Nosce teipsum: or. *Printed, 1688.* fol. MH, NC, TU, WF.

401 —Historical relations. Second edition. *Dublin, for Samuel Dancer, 1664.* 8°. DIX 126. L, OC, OQ; CH, MIU, PL, WF, Y.

402 — —Third edition. —, *1666.* 8°. DIX 132. L, C, LW, DT.

403 —Jus imponendi vectigalia: or the learning. Second edition. *For Henry Twyford, 1659.* 8°. L, LUG.

404 —Nosce teipsum. *Printed and are to be sold by Edward Brewster and Dorman Newman, 1689.* fol. L, LMT, DT, GK; CH, MH, NLC, WF, Y.

405 —The original, nature, and immortality of the soul. A poem. *For W.Rogers, 1697.* 8°. T.C.III 15. L, O, C, CT, DT; BN, CH, CN, MH, WF, Y.

406 —A perfect abridgment of the eleuen bookes of Reports. *By I.G. for W.Lee, D.Pakeman, and G.Bedell, 1651.* 12°. LT, O, OC; WF.

407 —The question concerning impositions. *By S.G. for Henry Twyford, Exc. Rich. Marriot, 1656.* 8°. L, O, C, LI, MR; CH, LC, MH, NC, Y.

408 —Les reports des cases. *By E.Flesher, J.Streater, and H.Twyford, assigns of Richard Atkyns and Edward Atkyns, 1674. To be sold by George Sawbridge, John Bellinger, Will. Place, Tho. Basset, Rob. Pawlet, Christopher Wilkinson, Tho. Dring, Will. Jacob, Charles Harper, John Leigh, John Amery, John Williams, John Place, John Poole.* fol. T.C.I 183. L, O, C, EN, DT; CN, LC, MHL, WF, YL.

408A — —[Anr. ed.] *Dublin, 1677.* fol. MHL.

409   [–] A work for none but angels. *By M.S. for Tho: Jenner*, 1653. 4°. LT, O, CS, HH; MH, WLC.

410   [–] —[Anr. ed.] —, 1658. 4°.* L, HH; CH, LC, W.

411   **Davies, Rondl.** Profiad yr ysprydion. *Rhydychen [Oxford], gan H.Hall,* 1675. 8°. MADAN 3055. AN; CN.

412   **D[avies], R[owland.]** A letter to a friend, concerning his changing his religion. *For R.Clavell, to be sold by J.North, Dublin,* 1692. 4°.* L, O, DT; CH, CN, MB, WF, Y.

412A   **Davies, *Sir* Thomas.** By the mayor, 17 Nov. *By Andrew Clark,* 1676. brs. L.

412B   — —[Same title.] 7 Dec. —, 1676. brs. L.

412C   **Davila, Enrico Caterino.** The continuation and conclusion of the civill warres of France. *By Ruth Raworth, and are to be sold by Thomas Heath,* 1648. fol. LCL; CCC, CCO; CH, CN, MBP, NHS.

413   —The historie of the civill warres of France. *By R. Raworth, to be sold by W.Lee, D.Pakeman, and G. Bedell,* 1647. fol. L, O, C, ES, DT; BN, CH, CU, MU, NP, TU, WF, Y.

414   — —Second edition. *In the Savoy, by T.N. for Henry Herringman,* 1678. fol. T.C.I 305. L, C, OM, CT, LL; CN, MH, MU, TU, WF, Y.

     Davis. See also Davys.

415   **Davis,**   . Hosanna, before the bishops. *For W.R.,* 1642. 4°.* LT, OC, CT; NU, Y.

416   **Davis, Edward.** Auctio Davisiana, pictuarum vere originalium: or, a collection . . . Novemb. 23, 1691. *[London],* 1691. 4°.* L.

416A   **Davis, Henry.** Practical gaging. *Dublin, by A.Crook and S.Helsham, and are to be sold by William Norman,* 1687. 8°. DIX 372. L (tp. only).

417   **Davis, Hugh.** De jvre vniformitatis ecclesiasticæ: or three books. *By S.Simmons, to be sold by T.Helder, and S.Lowndes,* 1669. fol. 4°. T.C.I 1. L, O, C, LCL, E; MHL, NC, NPT, Y.

418   — —Second edition. *For Giles Widdows,* 1671. 4°. DT; WF.

418A   **Davis, Isaiah.** A sermon at the funeral of . . . Mrs. Margaret Andrewes. *Printed,* 1680. 4°.* Y.

419   **Davis, John.** Certaine and good news from the west of Ireland. *For F.Coule,* 1642. 4°.* LT; WF.

420   —A great discovery of a damnable plot. *By Barnard Alsop,* 1641. 4°.* LT, O.

421   —Σεισμος μεγας. Or, Heaven & earth shaken. *By T. C. for Nathaniel Brooke,* 1655. 8°. LT; NPT.

422   — —[Anr. ed.] —, 1656. 8°. C, CCA, LSC; CLC.

423   **Davis, Nicholas.** The resolutions of those physicians . . . plague. *[London, 1665.]* brs. L, HH.

424-5   Entries cancelled.

426   **Davis, Richard.** Catalogus variorum in quavis lingua & facultate insignium. *[London],* 19 Apr., 1686. fol. L, O, CS, OC, HH; NN, JF.

427   — —Pars secunda. *Oxford,* 4 October, 1686. fol. L, O, OC, WCA; CLC.

428   — —Pars tertia. *Oxford,* June 25: 1688. fol. L, O, LM; Y.

429   — —Pars quarta. *Oxford,* April 11, 1692. 4°. L, O, OP.

430   —Hymns composed on several subjects. *For W.Marshall; and H.Barnard,* 1694. Second edition. sixes L.

431   —On Thursday the 26. of . . . November, 1685. at the Auction-House; . . . part of the stock of Mr. Richard Davis, *[Oxford],* 1685. fol.* L; Y.

432   —A sermon preached at the funeral of Mr. John Bigg. *For Robert Ponder,* 1691. 4°.* L, LCL, LW, AN.

433   —The true spring of gospel sight. *For John Marshall, [1689?].* sixes. L; NU.

434   — —[Anr. ed.] *For H.Barnard,* 1693. 4°.* O, LCL, EN.

435   —Truth and innocency vindicated. *For Nath. and Robert Ponder, to be sold by Randal Taylor, by Mr. Coolidge at Cambridge, Mr. Prior at Colchester, Mr. Noble at St. Edmund's Bury, Mr. Haworth at Ipswich, Northampton, Wellinborow, Kettering, Oundle, Harborow, Litterworth, Upingham, Bedford, Kimbolton and Canterbury, [1692?].* 4°. L, O, LCL, LW, GU.

436   —A vindication of the doctrine of justification. *For William Marshal, and sold by him, and by John Marshal,* 1698. 4°.* T.C.III 63. O, GU.

437   **[Davis, T.]** Strange and terrible nevves from the North, concerning. *For R.G.,* 1648. 4°.* LT; AN.

     Davis, William. Compleat new almanack. *[1687.]* See Almanacs.

438   —The golden farmer's last fareweel. *[London], for P. Brooksby, J.Deacon, J.Blare and J.Back, [1691?].* brs. L.

438A   —Jesus the crucifyed man. *[Philadelphia], for the author,* 1700. 8°. EVANS 908. PHS.

439   **Davison, Thomas.** Christ evidenced. *By J.G. for Robert Clavel,* 1684. 4°.* L, O, C, CS; CH, Y.

440   —The fall of angels. *For R.Clavel,* 1684. 4°. T.C.II 111. L, O, CS; NU.

440A   — —[Anr. ed.] *For R.Clavell, and are to be sold by Joseph Hall, in New-Castle,* 1694. 4°. C; Y.

441   —A sermon preached on the 8 of January. *York: by J. White, for Joseph Hall, in New-Castle upon Tine,* 1688. 4°.* O, CS, WCA, YM; WF.

     [Davors, John.] Secrets of angling. 1652. See Dennys, John.

442   **[Davy, Henry.]** The true copie of a letter sent from an inhabitant of Bridgewater. *For Richard Lownes,* 1643. 4°.* LT, O, HH, BR; CH, MH.

443   **[Davy, John.]** A particular ansvver to a book intituled, The clergy. *By A.Miller for William Leigh,* 1651. 4°. L, OC, P, YM; NU, WF.

444   **Davy, Sarah.** Heaven realiz'd. *[London], printed,* 1670. 8°. L, LCL, AN; BN, CH, NPT.

444A   **Davyes, Thomas.** The tenth worthy. *[London], Oct. 5, [1658.]* brs. LT.

445   **[Davys, John.]** The seamans secrets. Sixth edition. *By Iohn Dawson,* 1643. 4°. O.

446   — —Eighth edition. *By Gertrude Dawson,* 1657. 4°. O, CM, CT; BN.

447   **Davys, Paul.** Adminiculum puerile. *Dublin, for J. Foster,* 1694. 16° DIX 264. DM.

448 **D[awbeny], H[enry]** Historie & policie re-viewed in the heroick transactions of Oliver. *For Nathaniel Brook*, 1659. 8°. LT, O, CM, LVF, GU; CN, CU, MH, NU, Y.

448A [–] The pourtraiture of his royal highness, Oliver. *By T. N., for Edward Thomas*, 1650. 12°. L, O, CM; MH, WF, Y.

449 —A sober and temperate discourse. *For W.A.*, 1661. 12°. LT, O, C, EN, DT; CH, NC, NHC, NU, Y.

450 **Dawes, Lancelot.** Sermons preached upon severall occasions. *For Humphrey Robinson*, 1653. 4°. L, O, CT, YM; NPT, Y.

451 **Dawes, Thomas.** A sermon preach'd . . . March 5. 1694/5. *By F.C. for Gabriel Rogers in Shrewsbury; to be sold by John Whitlock*, 1695. 4°.* L, O, CCA, CT; CH, MIU, WF, Y.

452 [**Dawes, Sir William, abp.**] An anatomy of atheisme. *For Thomas Speed*, 1693. 4°.* T.C.II 480. L; NU.

453 [–] —[Anr. ed.] —, 1694. 4°.* T.C.II 525. L, O, C, DC; CU, MBA, MH, Y.

454 Entry cancelled.

455 —Christianity best propagated. *For Sam. Smith & Benj. Walford, and Tho. Speed*, 1700. 4°.* T.C.III 167. L, C, OC, CT; CH, NU, TU, WF, Y.

455A [–] The duties of the closet. *For T. Speed*, 1695. 12°. T.C.II 547. LSC.

456 —A sermon preach'd . . . Novemb. 5. 1696. *For Thomas Speed*, 1696. 4°.* T.C.II 600. L, O, C, OC, EC; CH, NU, PL, WF, Y.

457 —A sermon preach'd . . . 11th of April. *For Thomas Speed*, 1697. 4°.* T.C.III 21. O, C, CT; CLC, NU, PL, WF, Y.

458 **Dawkins, William.** Affectus. [*n.p.*], 1679. brs. L, O.

459 **Dawson, George.** Origo legum: or, a treatise. *For Richard Chiswell*, 1694. fol. T.C.II 478. L, O, C, EN, DT; BN, CH, CU, NP, WF, YL.

459A **Dawson, John.** XVIII choice sermons. *By T. Badger for Humphrey Mosley*, 1642. 4°. O, CS; CLC, MH, NPT, NU.

459B **Dawson, Richard.** The humble address and remonstrance of. *For the author*, 1661. 4°.* C, LUG, NL; WF.

460 **Day, George.** The communicant's instructor. *For Tho. Parkhurst*, 1700. 12°. T.C.III 166. LCL, LW; NPT, Y.

461 —A persuasive to full communion. *For T. Parkhurst*, 1698. 12°. T.C.III 86. LCL; NPT.

462 Entry cancelled.

463 **Day, Henry.** A thanksgiving-sermon. *For Richard Baldwin*, 1696. 4°.* L, O, CT; WF, Y.

464 **Day, John.** The blind-beggar of Bednal-Green. *For R. Pollard and Tho. Dring*, 1659. 4°. L, O, LVD, OW, EN; CH, CN, MH, TU, WF, Y.

465 —The modest vindication of. *Printed*, 1646. 4°.* LT, O.

466 —The parliament of bees. *For William Lee*, 1641. 4°. L, O, LV, OW, EN; CH, MH, WF, Y.

467 Entry cancelled.

468 —Truth shut out of doors. *For Giles Calvert*, 1653. 4°.* O.

469 **Day, Matthew.** Παρεκβολαί sive excerpta in sex priores Homeri Iliados libros. *Excudebat G.D. sumptibus Gulielmi Sheares*, 1652. 8°. L, C, P, OC, CK; MB.

470 **Day, Richard.** The humble petition or remonstrance of. *By M. Simmons*, 1652. 4°.* LT, C, OC.

471 [**Day, Robert.**] Free thoughts in defence of a future state. *For Dan. Brown, and Andr. Bell*, 1700. 8°. L, O, P, GU, DT; CLC, CU, NU, WF, Y.

472 **Day, William.** An exposition of the book of the prophet Isaiah. *By G.D. and S.G. for Ioshua Kirton*, 1654. fol. L, O, C, CK, P; NU.

473 —A paraphrase and commentary upon the Epistle of Saint Pavl to the Romans. *By S. Griffin for Joshua Kirton*, 1666. fol. L, O, C, OB, YM; NPT, NU, TU.

Day-breaking. 1647. *See* Sheppard, Thomas.

Day-fatality. [*n.p.*, 1679.] *See* Gibbon, John.

474 The [blank] day of [blank] 1644. Received the day and yeare . . . which is to be repaid. [*n.p.*, 1644.] brs. OP.

475 The [blank] day of [blank] 1644. Received the day and yeer . . . which was assessed. [*n.p.*, 1644.] brs. OP.

Day of doom. 1660. *See* Wigglesworth, Michael.

476 The day of the Lord. *By T. W. for J. Crook*, 1654. 4°. L, OC; CU, NU.

Dayrell. *See* Darrell.

De calculo humano. 1696. *See* L., M.

De causa Dei: or. 1678. *See* Danson, Thomas.

De causis errorum. 1645. *See* Herbert of Cherbury, Edward.

477 De fide eivs què ortu, & natura. Second edition. *Apud Petrum Cole*. 1644. 8°. LT.

De fide ejus. 1653. *See* L., T.

De finibus virtutis. Oxford, 1673. *See* Sharrock, Robert.

478 De hodierno statu ecclesiarum. [*n.p.*], 1654. 4°.* L, LCP; MH, NU, WF.

478A —[Anr. ed.] —, 1654. 4°.* L; Y.

De ipsa natura. 1687. *See* Boyle, Robert.

479 De juramento illicito. [*London?* 1660.] brs. L.

De jure maritimo. 1676. *See* Molloy, Charles.

480 De la vertu singuliere du vin rouge. *A Londre; by M. F.*, 1684. 8°.* L.

481 De l'etat present d'Irlande. *Dublin, chez Benjamin Took & John Crooke*, 1681. 4°.* DIX 189. DT.

De linguarum orientalium. 1658. *See* Beveridge, William, bp.

De loco parallelo. Edinburgi, 1656. *See* Colvill, Alexander.

De monarchia absoluta. Oxoniæ, 1659. *See* Bagshawe, Edward.

De morbis capitis; or. 1650. *See* Pem, Robert.

De moribus. Oxoniæ, 1665. *See* Casa, Giovanni della.

De poematum cantu. Oxonii, 1673. *See* Voss, Isaac.

De principiis. 1666. *See* Hobbes, William.

De ratione. 1664. *See* Croone, William.

De rebus Caroli. [*n.p.*], 1644. *See* Wishart, George, bp.

De successionibus. 1699. *See* Hale, Sir Matthew.

De vere inscription. 1691. *See* Ashman, John.

De vera ecclesia. 1698. *See* Garret, Walter.

482 **Deacon, John,** *polemical writer.* An exact history of the life of James Naylor. *For Edward Thomas,* 1657. 4°. LT, C, LF, CCA; NU, PH.

483 [–] The fathers vindicated. *For Ri. Chiswell,* 1697. 8°. L, O, C, CT, LCL; CLC, MBA, WF, Y.

484 [–] The grand imposter examined. *For Henry Brome,* 1656. 4°. LT, O, CT, BR, MR; CH, NU, PSC, TU.

485 [–] —[Anr. ed.] —, 1657. 4°. O; MH, WF.

486 [–] Nayler's blasphemies discovered. *For Simon Waterson,* 1657. 4°. O.

487 —A publick discovery of a secret deceit. *For Jer. Hirons,* 1656. 4°. LT, O, CT; NU, PH.

488 **Deacon, John,** *physician.* The charitable physitian. *By W. G. to be sold by Isaac Pridmore and for the author,* 1657. 8°.* L.

Dead and alive. [1662.] *See* Price, Laurence.

489 The dead man's song. *By and for W. Onley; and A. Milbourn,* [1680–85.] brs. L, O, CM, HH, GU.

489A —[Anr. ed.] *By and for A. M.* [168–?] brs. MH.

489B —[Anr. ed.] [*London*], *for F. Coles, T. Vere, J. Wright, and J. Clarke,* 1675? brs. O.

Dead saint speaking. 1679. *See* Fairfax, John.

490 **Deagent de Saint-Martin, Guichard.** The memoires of. *For Richard Baldwin,* 1690. 12°. T.C.II 312. L, O, C, EN, DT; LC, WF, Y.

490A [–] —[Anr. ed.] *Printed and are to be sold by E. Rumball,* 1700. 12°. MC.

491 **Dean, Edmund.** Spadacrene Anglica: the English spaw. *York, by Tho. Broad,* 1649. 4°.* L, LG; WSG.

492 [**Dean, John.**] The badger in the fox-trap. [*London,* 1681.] cap., fol.* L, O, CT; CH, CN, TU, WF, Y.

492A [–] The hunting of the fox. *For J. D.,* 1682. brs. O; MH.

493 —Iter boreale, or, Tyburn in mourning. *For C. Tebroc,* 1682. brs. L; CH, MH, Y.

A letter from Moscow. colop: *For Tim. Goodwin,* 1699. brs. L, HH; PL, WF.

494 [–] The Lord Russels farewel. [*London*], *for P. Brooksby,* [1683.] brs. CM, HH; MH.

494A [–] The loyal conquest. *For J. Dean,* 1683. brs. L; MH.

494B —Oates's bug-bug-boarding school. 1683. brs. O.

494C ——[Same title.] *For J. Dean,* 1684. brs. O; CLC, MH.

495 [–] The wine cooper's delight. *Printed for the Protestant ballad singers,* [1681]. brs. L.

496 [–] —[Anr. ed.] *For H. L.,* 1681. brs. L, O; MH, TU.

Decm, John, *ship builder.*

497 [**Dean, Richard.**] A copy of a brief treatise of the proper subject. *For the author, to be sold by Thomas Fabian,* 1693. 8°. T.C.II 471. LW; NPT.

497A [–] A declaration of the generals at sea. *By Tho. Newcomb,* [1653]. brs. STEELE 2992. LT, O, LG; MH, Y.

498 **Dean, Samuel.** Positiones nonnullæ physiologicæ. *Abredoniæ, imprimebat Edv. Rabanus,* 1643. 4°.* ALDIS 1077. MURRAY.

499 [**Deane, Thomas.**] The religion of Mar. Luther. *Oxon, by Henry Cruttenden,* 1688. 4°.* L, OC, LIL, CT; CH, CU, MH, NU, WF, Y.

Dear bargain. [n.p., 1688] *See* Johnston, Nathaniel.

Dear friends, the Lord God of heaven. [*London,* 1681.] *See* Billing, Edward.

500 The death and burial of Mistresse Money. *By E. Cotes, and are to be sold by Charles Tyus,* 1664. 8°.* CH.

501 —[Anr. ed.] *By A. Clark, and are to be sold by T. Vere and J. Clark,* 1678. 8°.* CM.

502 Death and the grave. [*London*], 1676/7. brs. MH.

Death, burial, and resurrection. [n.p., 1681.] *See* Whiterson, Edward.

Death consider'd. [1690.] *See* Pierce, Thomas.

Death in a new dress. 1656. *See* F., S.

Death in triumph. 1683. *See* Franklin, Robert.

Death of God's Moses's. 1678. *See* Ll., J.

Death unstung. [n.p., 1700] *See* M., J.

503 Death's master-peece. [*London*], *for Francis Grove,* 1649[50]. 4°.* LT, O, OC; MH.

504 Deaths tryumph dash'd. *Printed,* 1674. brs. L.

505 Death's uncontrollable summons. [*London*], *for P. Brooksby,* [1685]. brs. L, HH, GU.

506 Death's universal summons. *Dublin,* [1650?] 8°.* CLC.

507 The debate at large, between the House of Lords and House of Commons. *For J. Wickins,* 1695. 8°. L, C, LL, LW, EN; CH, CU, LC, MH, NU, Y.

Debate on the justice. 1696. *See* Hill, Samuel.

508 A debate upon the quærie, whether. [*London,* 1689.] cap., fol.* L, O, C, OC, CT; CH, CN, MIU, WF.

509 Debates and resolutions of the French King's council of war. *R. Taylor,* 1693. 4°.* HH; NN.

510 The debates in deposing kings. colop: *For H. I.,* 1688. cap., fol.* L, LG, CT, HH; WF.

De Bathe, Henry. *See* Bathe, Henry de.

Debauched cavalleer. 1642. *See* Lawrence, George.

Debauchee. 1677. *See* Brome, Richard.

511 **Debes, Lucas Jacobson.** Fœroæ, & fœroa reserata: that is a description of. *By F. L. for William Iles,* 1676. 12°. T.C.I 217. L, O, C, EN, DT; CH, CLC, CN, LC, Y.

Debita Deo. 1684. *See* Boyle, Robert.

De Britaine, William. *See* Britaine, William de.

Debtford. *See* Deptford.

Debtors apologie. [n.p.], 1644. *See* Jordan, Thomas.

Debts discharge. 1684. *See* Morton, Charles.

Decad of grievances. [n.p.], 1641. *See* Leighton, Alexander.

512 Decay of trade. A treatise. *Printed at London for John Sweeting,* 1641. 4°.* LT, LUG, EN, DT; CU, NC, NU, WF, Y.

513 The deceased maiden lover. [*London,* 1650?] brs. L.

Deceit and enmity. 1659. *See* Morford, Thomas.

514 The deceived virgin. *For Absalon Chamberlain,* 1684. brs. MC.

Deceiver deceived. 1698. *See* Pix, *Mrs.* Mary.

515 The deceiver deceived. [*London*], *for J. Clark, W. Thackery and T. Passinger,* [1680–5]. brs. L, CM, HH; MH, Y.

Deceivers deceived. 1661. *See* Stone, Samuel.

Decency & order. 1684. *See* Woolley, Charles.

Deceptio visus, 1671. *See* Boursault, Edmé.

516–7 Entries cancelled.

Decimarum & oblationum tabula. 1658. *See* Crashaw, William.

Decisions of divers. 1649. *See* Hall, Joseph, *bp.*

Decius Theophilus, *pseud.*

Declaratio regnorum. 1645. *See* DuMoulin, Louis.

518 A declaration against a crosse petition. *First, printed at Edenburgh and now re-printed at London for I. B.,* 1642[/3.] 4°.* LT, CT; CLC, MU, NU, WF, Y.

519 A declaration against a late dangerous and seditious band. *Printed at Edinburgh by Evan Tyler,* 1646. 4°.* ALDIS 1221. STEELE 3p 1903. LT, EN, AU, GM; MH, NU, WF, Y.

Declaration against all Poperie. [n.p., 1655.] *See* Fox, George.

Declaration against all profession. 1655. *See* Fox, George.

520 A declaration against Anabaptists. *For R. W.,* 1644. 4°.* LT, O, OC; CLC, NU, RPB.

Declaration against Prince Rupert. 1642. *See* B., P.

521 A declaration against the Antinomians. *For Iohn Iones,* 1644. 4°.* LT; MH, NU, WCL, Y.

522 A declaration against the crosse petition. *Edinburgh, by Evan Tyler,* 1643. 4°.* ALDIS 1078. L, CT, E, EN, GM; CH, NU, WF, Y.

Declaration against wigs. [n.p., 1682.] *See* Richardson, Richard.

523 The declaration and address of the gentry of . . . Essex. *For Gabriel Bedell and Thomas Collins,* [1660]. brs. STEELE 3181. LT, LG, HH.

Declaration and an information, 1660. *See* Fell, Margaret.

Declaration and apology. Campbell-town, 1685. *See* Argyle, Archibald, *earl of.*

524 Entry cancelled.

Declaration and appeale. [1655], *See* Frese, James.

525 The declaration and engagement of the army . . . in Ireland. [*Dublin, W. Bladen,* 1660.] brs. STEELE 2p 611. DK.

526 —[Anr. ed.] *London reprinted, W. Godbid,* 1660. brs. STEELE 2p 612. L, O.

527 The declaration and engagement of the commanders, officers, and seamen. *For John Playford, Decem.* 28, 1648. 4°.* LT; CH, MH.

528 The declaration and engagement of the Marquesse of Huntley. *Hagæ, by Samuell Broun,* 1650. brs. L.

529 The declaration and engagement of the officers and souldiers of Col. Ingoldsbies regiment. *By B. A.,* 1649. 4°.* LT; CH, MH, Y.

530 The declaration and ingagement of the Protestant army in . . . Mounster. *Printed at Cork, re-printed at London,* 1648. 4°.* LT, O, OC, CT; CH, CN, MIU.

Declaration and full narrative. 1651. *See* Y., R.

530A A declaration and instructions, for bringing. *Dublin, by W. Bladen,* 1652. 4°.* DM; NC.

531 A declaration and manifestation of the proceedings of both armies. *For Tho. Watson, and Wil. Cook,* 1642. 4°.* LT; WF, Y.

531A The declaration and manifesto of the Protestants of . . . Piedmont. *For T. Salusbury,* 1690. 4°. T.C.II 324. L; CN.

532 The declaration and message sent from the Queen of Bohemiah, . . . to Charles the Second. *Imprinted at London for G. Horton,* 1652. 4°.* LT.

534 A declaration and motive of the persons trusted. *By R. Oulton and G. Dexter for John Wright, May* 6, 1643. brs. LT, LG; MH.

Declaration and proclamation. 1659. *See* Chamberlen, Peter.

534A A declaration and proclamation of the Deputy General. *Dublin,* 1650. 4°.* DM.

535 The declaration and proposals of the citizens of London, concerning. *For John Woolridge,* 1648. 4°.* LT, HH.

536 —[Anr. ed.] *For Richard Cradock,* 1648. 4°.* LT, HH; WF.

537 The declaration and propositions of the lord maior of London. [n.p.], *Decem.* 24 *for Henry Liech,* [1642]. 4°.* LT; Y.

Declaration and propositions of the navie. 1648. *See* D., M.

538 A declartion [sic] and protest of the lords, knights . . . of Chester. *For Thomas Poole,* 1659[60.] brs. LT, O, LG; MH, NC, WF.

539 The declaration and protestation agreed upon by the Grand Iurie. *For G. Badger & R. Marriott,* 1642. brs. STEELE 2240. LT, OC, EC, AN; MH.

540 —*Imprinted at York, by Robert Barker and by the assigns of John Bill,* 1642. brs. STEELE 2238. LT.

541 The declaration and protestation of divers of the knights, gentry, . . . Lincolnshiere. *For Joseph Hunscott,* 19 *July,* 1642. brs. STEELE 2211. LT.

542 The declaration and protestation of divers the knights, gentry, . . . Lincolne. *By A. Norton for Edward Husbands and Iohn Frank,* 1642. brs. STEELE 2201. LT, EC; CH, MH.

Declaration and protestation of the Kings army. 1648. *See* Wilkinson, Jonathan.

Declaration and protestation, of the Parliament of Scotland. 1650. *See* Reynor, William.

543 A declaration and remonstrance of the aldermen. *For George Horton,* 1660. 4°.* L, LG, HH, SP; NU, Y.

544 The declaration and remonstrance, of the earls, lords, viscounts, barons, . . . of Ireland. *For George Sams,* 1662. 4°.* Y.

545 A declaration and remonstrance of the inhabitants of South-Wales. *For J. C.,* 1650. 4°.* LT, AN.

546 The declaration and remonstrance of the King's Majesties loyall subjects. *Printed,* 1648. 4°.* LT.

547 The declaration and remonstrance of the lords, knights and gentry of the covntie of Cornwall. *For Joseph Horton, Octob.* 13, 1642. 4°.* LT, EC; MH.

548 A declaration and remonstrance of the present engagement. *Printed in Edenborough,* 1647. 4°.* ALDIS 1268. LT, OC, YM, E; CH, MH, NU, WF, Y.

549 The declaration and remonstrance of the sea-men. 1653. 4°. MR.

550 A declaration and representation from the forces of
     the Northerne Associations. *For John Benson*, 1647.
     4°.* LT, O, YM; CH, MIU, WF, Y.

551 The declaration and resolution of divers officers and
     souldiers. *London: London [sic], for R.W.*, 1648.
     4°.* LT, OC, HH, AN; CH.

552 The declaration and resolution of many thousands
     citizens of London concerning. *[London], for C.VV.*,
     [1648]. 4°.* LT, OC.

553 The declaration and resolution of the citizens of London.
     For George Horton, 1648. 4°.* LT; Y.

554 The declaration and resolution of the countie of Leicester.
     July 29. for J. Wels [n.p.], 1642. 4°.* LT, LVF, EC;
     MH, Y.

555 The declaration and resolution of the Irish army. *For
     R.W., Aprill 16*, 1649. 4°.* LT, C.

556 The declaration and resolution of the knights, gentry
     . . . of Kent. *For R.W.*, 1648. 4°.* LT, LG, DT; Y.

557 A declaration and resolution of the sheriffes, justices
     of the peace, and other of His Majesties well affected
     subjects, in . . . Flint. *For R.W.*, 1648. 4°.* LT, O,
     AN.

558 The declaration and resolution of the states of Holland.
     For G: Horton, 1652. 4°.* LT; WF.

     Declaration and speech of Colonel Massey. 1650. *See*
     H., J.

559 A declaration and vindication of the lord mayor, alder-
     men and Commons of the city of London . . . 30
     day of April 1660. *By James Flesher, London*, 1660.
     4°.* LT, O, C, HH; CH, CN, MH, NU, TU, WF, Y.

560 A declaration and vindication of the loyal-hearted
     nobility . . . of Kent. *[London], for H.Brome*, 1660.
     brs. LT, LG.

561 A declaration by congregationall societies. *[London],
     by M.Simmons for Henry Overton*, 1647. 4°.* LT, SP;
     MH, NHC, NU, WF, Y.

562 A declaration by direction of the committee at Yorke.
     Printed at Yorke by Tho. Broad, 1645. 4°.* GM; CH.

562A A declaration by severall congregational societies. *By
     Matt: Simmons*, 1647. 4°.* MH.

563 A declaration by the committee of safety. *By Henry
     Hills and John Field*, 1659. fol.* LT, O; MH, Y.

563A Declaration by the general assemblie of the Confederate
     Catholiques. *[Kilkenny*, 1648.] brs. O.

564 A declaration by the masters and professors of New
     Aberdeen. *[n.p.]*, 1660. brs. O.

565 A declaration, by the nobility and gentry of this county
     of York. *[York*, 1688.] brs. STEELE 3908. L, EN; CH.

565A A declaration by the officers in Ireland. *By William
     Bladen, Dublin, reprinted at London by James Cottrel*,
     1660. brs. LT.

566 A declaration by the Presbytery at Bangor. *[n.p.],
     printed*, 1649. 4°.* LT, C, EN, AU.

567 A declaration concerning Colonel H. Marten. 1660.
     4°. L.

     Declaration concerning fasting. 1656. *See* Fox, George.

568 A declaration concerning His Majesties royall person.
     For G.Horton, Ianuary 6, 1647[8]. 4°.* LT, AN.

569 A declaration, concerning the estates. 1643. 4°.* O.

570 A declaration concerning the generall accompts. *By
     Richard Bishop for Laurence Blaiklock*, 1642. fol.* LT,
     O, C, DT; MH, NC, WF, Y.

571 A declaration concerning the government of the three
     nations. *By R. Wood*, 1653. 4°.* LT.

572 A declaration concerning the King, from the citizens
     of London. *For Richard Collings*, 1648. 4°.* LT, O.

573 A declaration concerning the miserable condition of
     Ireland. *[n.p.]*, 1643. 4°.* CHRISTIE-MILLER.

574 A declaration concerning the miserable sufferings of
     the covntrie. *By E. E.*, 1646. 4°.* LT, HH, DT; CLC, WF.

     Declaration concerning the newly invented art. 1648.
     See Petty, *Sir* William.

     Declaration concerning the people. *[n.p.]*, 1674. *See*
     Danks, John.

575 A declaration concerning the publike dispute. *Printed*,
     1645. 4°. LT, O, CS, GU, DT; NHC, NPT, WF.

576 The declaration declared. *[London*, 1648.] 4°.* HH; MIU.

577 Declaration for a free Parliament. *[n.p.*, 1659.] brs. O.

578 A declaration for Ireland. colop: *By Richard Janeway*,
     1689. brs. C, DT.

579 A declaration from His Excellencie Sr Thomas Fairfax,
     and his councell of warre. Concerning their proceed-
     ing. *By M. Simmons, for George Whittington*, 1647.
     4°.* LT, O, C, MR, DT; BN, CH, CN, MH, NU, WF, Y.

580 —[Anr. ed.] *Oxford, by J.Harris and H.Hills*, 1647.
     4°.* MADAN 1960. O, HH; CH, MIU, WF.

581 A declaration from His Excellency Sir Thomas Fairfax,
     and the generall councell of the army, concerning the
     obstructive proceedings. *For C.W.*, 1647. 4°.* LT,
     HH, ENC; CH, WF.

581A —[Anr. ed.] *For G. Whittington*, 1647. 4°.* CT; PT, WF.

582 A declaration from His Excellency Sir Thomas Fairfax,
     and the generall councell of the armie, of their resolu-
     tions. *For George Whittington*, [1648.] 4°.* LT, O, C,
     MR, DT; CH, TU, WF, Y.

583 —[Anr. ed.] *For Edward Husband, Jan. 12*, 1647. 4°.*
     LT, O, HH; CH, MH, WF, Y.

584 A declaration from His Excellencie, with the advice.
     By T.R. & E.M. for R.M., 1649. 4°.* LT; CH, WF,
     Y.

585 A declaration from many thousands of His Majesties
     loyall and faithfull subjects in . . . York. *Printed at
     London for R.W.*, 1648. 4°.* LT, CJ, YM.

586 A declaration from Oxford. *By John Clowes*, 1651.
     4°.* MADAN 2153. O; CH.

587 A declaration from Scotland concerning the advance
     of the Scots army. *For H.Becke*, 1648. 4°.* LT; MH, Y.

588 A declaration from Sir Thomas Fairfax and the army
     . . . concerning the . . . rights and liberties. *For L.
     Chapman and L.Blacklocke*, 1647. 4°.* HH; CH, MIU,
     WF.

589 A declaration from the children of light. *For Giles
     Calvert*, 1655. 4°.* LT, LF, OC, BBN; CH, PH.

590 A declaration from the city of London with instructions. *Printed at London by Robert Ibbitson, 1648.* 4°.* LT; MIU.

591 A declaration from the gentlemen of South Wales. 1648. 4°.* O.

Declaration from the harmless. [n.p., 1660.] *See* For, George.

Declaration from the Isle of Wyght. 1648. *See* Hewat, John.

Declaration from the Lord of Hosts. 1659. *See* Willyer, Lawrence.

592 A declaration from the nobility of the kingdome of Scotland. *For E. Norton, 1647.* 4°.* HH; CLC, Y.

593 A declaration from the nothern [sic] associated counties. *For G. Laurenson, 1648[9].* 4°.* LT, HH, YM.

Declaration from the people called. 1659. *See* Burrough, Edward.

594 A declaration from the people of God, called Quakers. [*London*, 1670?] brs. L, LF, LG; PSC.

595 A declaration from the poor oppressed people of England. [*London*], *printed, 1649.* 4°.* LT, HH; CH, CN, MH, NC, WF, Y.

596 A declaration from the right honourable, the lord major, alderman, and commons of the city of London presented to His Excellency Sir Thomas Fairfax. *Imprinted at London, for Richard Hatfield, 1647.* 4°.* LT, MR; CN.

597 A declaration from the severall respective regiments. *For H.E., November 5, 1647.* 4°.* LT; CH, WF, Y.

598 A declaration in answer to several lying pamphlets. *Printed, 1652.* 4°.* L; NIC.

599 A declaration in answer to some papers of the Scots commissioners. *For John Wright, 1647[8].* 4°. LT, O, GU; MIU, OWC.

Declaration in vindication. 1647. *See* Grene, Giles.

600 A declaration made at Bodmin. *Oxford, Feb. 3, by Laonard Lichfield, 1643[/4].* 4°.* MADAN 1532. L, OCC, DT; WF.

600A —[Anr. ed.] *Bristoll, by Robert Barker and John Bill, 1643.* 4°.* BR.

600B A declaration made by the maior, towne council, . . . Galway. *Kilkenny, 1648.* 4°.* DIX.

601 A declaration made by the rebells in Ireland. *Printed at Waterford by Tho. Bourke: and re-printed at London by R. Austin, for J. T., 1644.* 4°.* LT, O, C, LVF; IU, MH, WF.

602 A declaration of a Congregational church at Tiverton, [*London*], *printed, 1661.* 4°.* LIU.

603 A declaration of a strange and wonderful monster: born. *By Jane Coe, 1646.* 4°.* LT; CH, WF, Y.

604 A declaration of all the passages at the taking of Portsmovth. *For John Sweeting, Septemb. 15, 1642.* 4°.* LT; MH, WF, Y.

604A A declaration of all the water men in and about . . . London. [*London?* 1659.] brs. LG, HH; MH.

Declaration of almighty God. [n.p., 1690.] *See* Burnet, Gilbert, *bp.*

604B A declaration of an happy treatie for peace. *For J. Wright, Febr. 11, 1643.* 4°.* SP; MH, Y.

605 The declaration of Colonel Rich's regiment. *By T.M. for Livewell Chapman, 1659.* 4°.* CCA; NU.

Declaration of divers elders. [n.p., 1651.] *See* Greenhill, William.

606 A declaration of divers gentlemen and others in the principality of Wales. *For R.VV., 1648.* 4°.* LT, AN.

607 A declaration of divers gentlemen of VVales. *For H. Becke, 1648.* 4°.* LT, HH, AN; CH, WF.

608 The declaration of divers well-affected inhabitants of the cities of London. *For R. Baliffe, 1648.* 4°.* LT; CH, MH.

Declaration of Duke Hambleton. [n.p.], 1648. *See* H., A.

Declaration of former passages. [*Cambridge, Mass.*], 1645. *See* Winthrop, John.

609 A declaration of great Lucifer. *Printed in Hell neere Westminster, 1648.* 4°.* LT; CH.

609A A declaration of His Excellency Lord General Fairfax and his councell of warre, delivered. *For John Wright, 1647[8].* 4°.* LT, OC, CT, MR, DT; BN, CH, CU, MBP, WF, Y.

610 A declaration of His Excellencie Lord General Fairfax and his councell of warre . . . shewing the grounds. *For John Partridge, 1648.* 4°.* LT; CH, MH, MU, WF, Y.

610A —[Anr. ed.] *For George Whittington, 1647.* 4°.* TU.

610B —[Anr. ed.] *By John Field for John Partridge, Novemb. 1, 1648.* 4°.* LT, OC; CH, CN, LC, MH, NU, Y.

610C —[Anr. ed.] *For George Horton, 1648.* 4°.* CU, MH.

611 A declaration of His Highnesse the Duke of Yorke his going away from St. Jamses [sic]. *By Robert Ibbitson, 1648.* 4°.* LT; CH, MH.

612 A declaration of His Majesties proceeding. 1642. 4°. O.

Declaration of John Robins. 1651. *See* H., G.

613 A declaration of many thousand well-affected persons. [*London*, 1660.] brs. LT; MH.

614 A declaration of many thousands of the city of Canterbury. *Printed, 1647[8].* 4°.* LT, LG, DT; CN, MH, MIU, Y.

615 A declaration of Old Nick. [*n.p.*], *by George Morgan,* [1660]. brs. LT; MH, MIU.

616 A declaration of peace. 1648. 4°. L.

617 Declaration of several baptized believers. *By G.D. December 29, 1659.* brs. O.

Declaration of several observations. 1646. *See* A., T.

618 A declaration of several of the churches of Christ. *For Livewel Chapman, 1654.* 4°.* LT, LG, OC, E; CH, CU, MH, NU, WF, Y.

619 Declaration of several of the people called Anabaptists. *For Livewel Chapman, 1659.* brs. L, O, LG.

619A —[Anr. ed.] *By Henry Hills, Decemb. 12, 1654.* brs. HH.

620 A declaration of severall officers. *Dublin, by William Bladen, Dec., 1659.* brs. DIX 354. O, OW.

621 A declaration of several officers of the army in Ireland. *Reprinted, for N. Brook, 1659.* brs. STEELE 2p 605a. LT.

622 Declaration of several treasons. 1660. 4°. L.

623   A declaration of Sir John Hotham's proceedings at Hvll. *For George Thomas, Iuly 8, 1642.* 4°.* LT, EC; MH, TU.

624   A declaration of some of the sufferings. [*London*, 1660.] fol. L; RPJ.

625   A declaration of some of those people . . . Anabaptists. *By Thomas Milbourn for Samuel Cleaver*, [1660.] brs. LT.

626   A declaration of some proceedings of Lt. Col. Iohn Lilburn. *For Humphrey Harward*, 1648. 4°. LT, CT, YM; CLC, MH, NU, WF.

Declaration of sundry grievances. 1646. *See* S., I.

627   A declaration of the affections, intentions and resolutions of our brethren in Scotland. *First printed in Scotland and now reprinted at London, for R. Harford, Iune 20th*, 1642. 4°.* LT, O, OC, HH, DT; CSS, MH, NU, WF, Y.

628   The declaration of the armie. [*London*], 1647. 4°.* HH; CU.

629   A declaration of the armie concerning Lieut. Collonel John Lilburn. *Imprinted at London: for G. Horton*, 1652. 4°.* LT.

630   A declaration of the army concerning the apprehending of Major Gen. Overton. *For G. Horton*, 1654[5]. 4°.* LT.

631   The declaration of the armie concerning the city of London. *For R. Williamson*, 1648. 4°.* LT; MH, NN.

632   The declaration of the armie concerning the Kings Majesty. [*London*], 9 Octob., 1648, *for C. W.* 4°.* LT; WF.

633   —[Anr. ed.] *For R. Williamson*, 1648. 4°.* LT; LC, NN.

634   The declaration of the army in Ireland. *Printed at Dublin, and now re-printed at London, by S. Griffin, for John Playford*, 1659[60]. 4°.* L, O, C, LL, HH; CH, CU, MH, WF, Y.

635   A declaration of the army of England upon their march into Scotland . . . 19 Julii, 1650. *By Edward Husband and John Field, July 19*, 1650. 4°.* LT, O, CT, EN, DT; CH, CN, NU, WF, Y.

636   —[Anr. ed.] *Printed at London, and reprinted at Edinburgh, by Evan Tyler*, 1650. 4°.* ALDIS 1407. STEELE 3p 2045. LT, HH, EC, EN; CU, MIU, Y.

637   [Anr. ed.] *Newcastle, by S.B.*, 1650. 4°.* L, NEPL; MH.

638   Entry cancelled.

639   A declaration of the army of the Commonwealth of England. *By Edward Husband and John Field, July 23*, 1650. 4°.* STEELE 3p 2044. LT, O, HH, ER; CH, CN, MH, WF, Y.

640   A declaration of the armie, presented to the Kings Majesty. *For C. W.*, 1648. 4°.* LT; TU.

641   A declaration of the armie to His Excellency the Lord General Cromwel. *Imprinted at London, for John Smithson*, 1652. 4°.* LT.

642   The declaration of the armie under His Excellency Sir Thomas Fairfax. [*London*], *printed*, 1646[7]. 4°.* LT, O, SP; WF, Y.

642A   —[Anr. ed.] —, 1647. 4°.* L, DC; YM, CH.

643   A declaration of the besieged soldiers in . . . Colchester. 1648. 4°.* L, HH.

644   A declaration of the bloudie and unchristian acting of William Star. *For Giles Calvert*, 1649. 4°.* LT; NC.

Declaration of the bountifull. [n.p.], 1669. *See* Forster, Mary.

Declaration of the brethren. Edinburgh, 1658. *See* Wood, James.

644A   A declaration of the brewers at London. [*London*, 1659.] brs. Y.

Declaration of the British. [n.p.], 1648/9. *See* W., R.

645   A declaration of the Christian-free-born subjects. [n.p.], *printed*, 1659. 4°.* LT, O, OC, CCA, CCH; HR, CH, CLC, MH, NC, NU.

646   A declaration of the citizens and inhabitants of the city of Chester. *For Edward Husbands and John Frank, July* 20, 1642. brs. STEELE 2222. LT, O, CCA, LS; CLC, MH.

Declaration of the citizens of Edenborough. 1648. *See* S., T.

647   The declaration of the citizens of London, in answer to the demands. *For G. Horton*, 1648. 4°.* LT.

648   A declaration of the city and county of Gloucester. [1659.] brs. L, LG.

649   A declaration of the commander in chief of the forces in Scotland. *Edinburgh, by Christopher Higgins*, 1659. 4°.* ALDIS 1592. STEELE 3p 2165. LT, O, CCA, OC, EN; MBP, MH, WF, Y.

650   —[Anr. ed.] *Edenburgh, by Christopher Higgins, London reprinted*, 1659. brs. STEELE 3p 2166. LT, LS, CCA; CH, CLC, MBP, MH, Y.

651   A declaration of the commanders and other officers of Colonell Humfrey's regiment. *For Francis Tyton*, 1648. 4°.* LT; CH, MH, WF.

652   A declaration of the commissioners for visitation of universities. *Printed at Leith*, 1653. 4°.* ALDIS 1474. EN; CH, MIU, NU, WF.

653   A declaration of the committee for the militia. [*London*], *for Edward Husbands, October* 18, 1643. 4°.* LT, LG; CH, CN, MH, Y.

654   A declaration of the committee for the safetie of the county of Southampton. [n.p., 1648.] brs. LT, LG.

654A   A declaration of the commons of England. *For G. Horton*, 1652. 4°.* LT.

655   A declaration of the Congregational ministers. *Printed, and are to be sold by the book sellers*, 1699. 4°. T.C.III 170. L, CT, LW; Y.

655A   —Second edition. *For John Hartley*, 1699. 4°. CT; WCA, NU, Y.

656   A declaration of the Cornish-men. [*London*], *for R. W.*, [1648/9]. 4°.* LT, O; MH.

Declaration of the counsel of God's heavenly host. 1662. *See* B., W.

657   A declaration of the council and congregation against plundering. [*Kilkenny*, 1646.] brs. O.

658   A declaration of the counties of Kent and Essex. *By B.A.*, 1648. 4°.* LT, LG, SP.

659 The declaration of the counties of Worcester-shire. By *B.A.*, 1648. 4°.* LT, O.

660 A declaration of the counties of Yorke and Lancaster. *For W. R.*, 1648. 4°.* LT, YM; MH, WF.

661 The declaration of the county of Dorset. [*London*], *printed*, 1648. 4°.* LT, O, DT.

661A A declaration of the county of Hereford. 1642. brs. LT.

662 The declaration of the county of Oxon to . . . Monck. *For John Starkey*, 1660. brs. LT, O, CJ, LG; Y.

662A A declaration of the czars of Muscovy. *For E. Maret, and C. Lucas*, 1689. brs. O.

663 A declaration of the daily grievances of the Catholiques. *For Iohn Thomas*, 1641. 4°.* L, DT; CN, NU, TU, WF.

Declaration of the difference. 1656. *See* Fox, George.

664 A declaration of the engagements, remonstrances, representations, proposals . . . from . . . Fairfax. *By Matthew Simmons*, 1647. 4°. LT, O, C, HH, MR; CH, NPT, WF, Y.

665 A declaration of the English army. [*London*, 1659.] cap., 4°.* LT, HH.

666 A declaration of the English army now in Scotland. *By Edward Husband and John Field, August* 12, 1650. 4°.* LT, O, BP, HH, DT; CH, CN, MH, TU, WF, Y.

Declaration of the faith and order. 1658. *See* Nye, Philip.

667 A declaration of the faithful soldiers of the army. *Printed*, 1659. 4°.* LT, O, C; CH, CN, MH, NU, WF, Y.

668 A declaration of the faithfull sovldiers of the army . . . shewing their resolution to stand by. *Printed*, 1659. 4°.* LT, O, C, OC, HH; CH, CN, MH, NC, NU.

669 The declaration of the free and well-affected people. [*n.p.*], *printed*, 1654[5]. brs. STEELE 3046a. L.

670 A declaration of the free-born people of England. [*n.p.*, 1655.] brs. LT, OC, CT.

670A A declaration of the free-commoners of England. [*London*, 1647.] brs. Y.

671 A declaration of the further proceedings of the English fleet. *For Geor. Horton*, 1653. 4°.* LT, MR.

672 A declaration of the gallant service performed by . . . Hvgh Peters. *For Richard Woodnoth*, 1646. 4°.* LT, SP; CN, MH, OWC, Y.

672A A declaration of the general assemblie of the Confederate Catholicks. Second edition. [*Kilkenny*, 1646.] brs. O.

673 —A declaration of the general council of the officers. *By Henry Hills*, 1659. 4°.* LT, O, CCA, LG, YM; CH, CN, MH, NU, TU, WF, Y.

Declaration of the generals. [1653.] *See* Deane, Richard.

674 A declaration of the gentlemen and inhabitants of the county of Brecknock. *For Edw. Husband, December* 6, 1645. 4°.* LT, CT, AN, DT; WF, Y.

675 The declaration of the genlemen [sic] and others now in armes in . . . Hereford. [*n.p.*, 1648.] brs. LT.

676 The declaration of the gentlemen, free-holders and inhabitants of . . . Bedford. *Printed at London*, 1659[60]. brs. LT, O, LG; MH.

The declaration, of the gentlemen, merchants, and inhabitants of Boston. *Boston* [*Mass.*], 1689. *See* Mather, Cotton.

677 The declaration of the gentry, ministers, free-holders of . . . Lincolne. [*London*], *for H. M.*, 1659[60]. brs. LT, O, LG, CJ; CH, Y.

678 A declaration of the gentry of Somerset-shire. *Royston*, 1660. brs. LG.

678A A declaration of the gentry of the county of Derby. [*London*], 1659[60]. brs. MH, Y.

678B A declaration of the gentry of the county of Gloucester. *Bedell*, 1660. brs. LG.

679 A declaration of the gentry of the county of Kent. *For Gabriel Bedell*, 1660. brs. LT, LG, HH; MIU.

680 The declaration of the gentry, of the county of Norfolk. [*London*, 1660.] brs. LT, O, LG; CH, Y.

680A A declaration of the gentrie of the county of Salop. *Pakeman*, 1660. brs. L, LG.

681 The declaration of the gentrie of the Kings party in . . . Devon. 1660. brs. L, O.

682 A declaration of the gentry of . . . Devon. [*London*, 1660.] brs. L, O, LG; CH, MH, Y.

683 A declaration of the great affaires and matters of consequence. *For I. T.*, [1642]. 4°.* L, O, OC, HH, MR; MH, WF, Y.

684 A declaration of the great and weighty affayres. *For John Thomas*, 1641. 4°.* LT, O; HR, CH, WF.

Declaration of the ground of error. 1657. *See* Fox, George.

684A A declaration of the grounds and reasons, why we the poor inhabitants of . . . Iver. *Brewster*, 1650. brs. LG.

685 A declaration of the grounds and reasons why we the poor inhabitants of . . . VVellingborrow. *For Giles Calvert*, 1650. brs. LT, LG.

686 A declartion [sic] of the heads of severall letters, sent from the committee at York. *For I. T. June* 3, 1642. 4°.* LT, YM; MH.

687 The declaration of the high-sheriffe of York-shire. *By Iohn Clowes*, 1648. 4°.* LT; CH, CLC, NPT, Y.

688 The declaration of the Hollanders concerning the English fleet. *By B.A.*, 1652. 4°.* LT.

Declaration of the Hollanders concerning their joyning. 1648. *See* Vandelet, J.

689 A declaration of the Hollanders tovching the late King. *For D.G.*, 1652. 4°.* LT.

690 Declaration of the horrible treasons. 1679. fol. EN.

690A The declaration of the incorporation of the woollen manufactory at New-Milnes. *Edinburgh, by Mosman*, 1693. brs. LG.

691 The declaration of the kingdomes of England and Scotland, ioyned. *For Iohn Wright, Februar.* 1, 1643[4]. 4°.* LT, O, C, EN, DT; CH, CN, LC, MH, NU, Y.

692 —[Anr. ed.] [*London*], *printed*, [1643]. 12°.* LT, C; PT.

693 —[Anr. ed.] *Edinburgh, by Evan Tyler*, 1644. 4°. ALDIS 1135. STEELE 3p 1813. CT, E, EN, AU; NU.

694 A declaration of the Kings Maiesties army in the north of England. *For R. W.*, 1648. 4°.* LT, CS; AN, MH.

695 A declaration of the Kings most excellent Majesties proceeding with his army at Oxford. *For I. Wright,* 1642[/3]. 4°.* MADAN 1160. LT, SP, DT; CH, MH, MIU, Y.

695A A declaration of the knights and gentlemen of . . . Cornwall. *Seile,* 1660. brs. LG.

696 A declaration of the knights and gentry in the county of Dorset. *Printed,* 1660. brs. LT, O, LG.

697 A declaration of the knights, gentlemen, and freeholders of the county of Surrey. [*London*], *printed,* 1648. 4°.* LT.

698 The declaration of the knights, gentry, and trained bands of . . . Kent. [*London*], *Decemb.* 22 *for J. Banks,* 1642. 4°.* LT, O, LG; CH, MH, MIU, Y.

699 The declaration of the Levellers concerning Prince Charles. *Imprinted at. London, for C.W.* 17 *May,* 1649. 4°.* LT.

700 A declaration of the liberties of the English nation. *For Richard Janeway,* 1681. 4°.* L; CH, LC, MH, Y.

701 A declaration of the Lord Generall and his councel . . . shewing the grounds. *By Hen. Hills and Tho. Brewster,* 1653. 4°.* LT, O, C, E, DT; CH, CU, MH, NU, TU, Y.

702 —[Anr. ed.] *London, reprinted Leith,* 1653. 4°.* EN; WF.

703 Friday, April 22. 1653. The declaration of the Lord Generall, and his councill of officers. [*n.p.,* 1653.] cap., 4°.* LT; Y.

Declaration of the Lord Generall of the army. [*n.p.*], 1646. *See Preston, T.*

704 The declaration of the Lord Lieutenant, the high sheriff . . . of Chester. [*London,* 1688.] brs. L, LG, HH.

705 A declaration of the lord maior, aldermen, . . . of London. *By Richard Cotes, London,* 1647. 4°.* LT, O, OC, BR, MR; CH, CU, NU, TU, WF, Y.

706 A declaration of the lords, and gentry, and others of the provinces of Lemster. [*London*], *by R.W. for Christopher Meredith,* 1644. 4°.* LT, C; WF, Y.

Declaration of the lords, gentlemen. [n.p., 1659.] *See* Delamere, *Sir George Booth.*

707 A declaration of the loyal apprentices of . . . London. *For Nathaniel Frooks,* 1660. brs. Y.

708 A declaration of the loyal resolvtion of . . . Scotland. *For W. Stretton, August,* 6, 1642. 4°.* LT, HH; CU, WF, Y.

709 A declaration of the loyalty of the citizens of London. *For T. Cooke,* 1643. 4°.* LT, HH; NU.

710 A declaration of the maids of the city of London. [*London,* 1659.] brs. LT, O, OC; MH, MIU.

711 A declaration of the marks and fruits, of the false prophets. [*n.p.,* 1655.] cap., 4°.* LT, LF, OC; MH, PH, PSC, WF, Y.

712 A declaration of the most remarkable passages. *For I. T.,* 1642. 4°.* L, O, HH, YM; CH, MH, WF.

713 The declaration of the navie, being the true copie of a letter. [*n.p.,* 1648.] brs. LT; CH.

714 The declaration of the navie; vvith the oath. [*n.p.,* 1648.] brs. LT, CJ.

714A The declaration of the nobility and gentry of . . . Stafford. [*London,* 1688.] brs. L; Y.

715 A declaration of the nobility and gentry of . . . Worcester. [*London*], *for Charles Adams,* 1660. brs. STEELE 3161. LT, LG; Y.

716 A declaration of the nobility and gentry that adhered to the late King. *By Roger Norton,* 1660. brs. LT, LG; CH, MH, Y.

717 The declaration of the nobility, gentry, . . . at Nottingham. [*n.p.,* 1688.] brs. STEELE 3906. L, C, LG, OP, BR; CH, CN, MH, MIU, WF.

718 The declaration of the nobility, gentry, and commonalty at the rendezvous at Nottingham, Nov. 22. 1688. colop: [*London*], *printed,* 1689. 4°.* L, O, OC; CN, MN, Y.

719 —[Anr. ed.] *Reprinted and sold by Samuel Green of Boston,* 1689. brs. EVANS 465. MHS.

720 A declaration of the nobility, gentry, ministry . . . of Kent. [*London,* 1660.] brs. LT, O, LG; MIU, Y.

721 A declaration of the nobilitie, knights & gentry of . . . Oxon. *For Tho. Bassett,* 1660. brs. LT, O, LG, EN.

722 A declaration of the noble resolution of the Earl of Essex. *For T. Banks,* 1642. 4°.* LT; MBP, MH.

723 A declaration of the northern army under . . . Lambert. *By J.M.,* 1648. 4°.* LT; MIU, WF.

724 A declaration of the northerne army with instructions. 1643. 4°. O.

725 —[Anr. ed.] *Printed at York by Thomas Broad, and reprinted at London by Robert Ibbitson,* 1648. 4°.* LT, O, OC, HH; CH, MH, NU, Y.

726 A declaration of the northern counties. *By B. Alsop,* 1647. 4°.* LT, O; CH, CLC, MH, TU.

Declaration of the officers and armies. 1647. *See* Prynne William.

727 A declaration of the officers and company of seamen abord His Majesties ships the Constant Reformation. *Printed at Holland and re-printed at London,* 1648. brs. LT, O, LG, LS; CH, MH, NN.

728 A declaration of the officers and souldiers under the command of Colonell Twisleton. *For John Wright,* 1648. brs. LT, AN.

729 A declaration of the officers belonging . . . Dec. 13. *By John Macock for John Patriridge,* 1648. 4°.* LT, O, HH, YM; CH.

730 A declaration of the officers of the army, inviting the members of the Long Parliament. . . . 6 April, [*i.e.,* May] 1659. *By Henry Hills. for him and William Mountfourt,* 1659. 4°.* LT, O, C, OC, CT; CH, CU, MH, NU, WF, Y.

731 —[Anr. ed.] 6 May, 1659. —, 1659. 4°.* CCA, HH, EN; CLC, MB.

732 A declaration of the officers of the army in Scotland to the churches of Christ. *Edinburgh, by Christopher Higgins,* 1659. 4°.* ALDIS 1593. LT, O, CT, HH, EN; CH, CLC, MIU, PL.

Declaration of the officers of the army opened. 1659. See D., E.

733 The declaration of the officers of the garrison of Hull. For John Playford, March 1, 1649. 4°.* LT, YM, DT; CH, MH, WF, Y.

734 A declaration of the order of the treaty. For R. Smithhurst, 1648. 4°.* LT, O; CLC, MH.

735 A declaration of the peaceable Royallists. Freeman, 1659. brs. L, O, LG.

736 A declaration of the people of England for a free-Parliament. [n.p., 1659.] brs. LT, O, LG, LS; CH, MH.

Declaration of the people of God. 1659. See Crook, John.

737 A declaration of the Philadelphia society. [London, 1699.] cap., 4°.* O.

738 A declaration of the povver of the Lords and Commons. Printed at London by Robert Ibbitson, 1648. Feb. 26: 4°.* LT, O, HH, AN; CH, IU, LC, MH, Y.

739 A declaration of the Presbyterians; concerning His Maiesties royal person. For T. Dacres, 1660. 4°.* LT, O, CCA; WF.

740 A declaration of the present proceedings of the French, Danes. By E. Alsop, 1653. 4°.* LT, O.

Declaration of the present sufferings. 1659. See Burrough, Edward.

741 A declaration of the Princes navie. Imprinted at London, for G. Wharton, May 1, 1649. 4°.* LT, MR; MH.

742 A declaration of the principall pointes of Christian doctrine. At Paris, by Sebastien Cramoisy, 1647. 4°. L, O, CT; CLC, CN, NU, TU, WF.

743 A declaration of the proceedings in the kingdom of Scotland. For R. VV., 1649. 4°.* YM; MBP, MH, Y.

744 A declaration of the proceedings of divers knights, and other gentlemen in Glamorganshire. For I. Coe, and A. Coe, 1647. 4°.* LT, O, AN, DT.

745 A declaration of the proceedings of His Excellency the Lord General Fairfax. Oxford, by H. H. and reprinted at London for John Playford, May 23, 1649. 4°.* MADAN 2014. LT, O; CH, CN, WF, Y.

746 A declaration of the proceedings of His Highnes the Lord Protector; and his reasons. By R. Wood, 1654. 4°.* LT.

747 A declaration of the proceedings of His Highnesse the Prince of Wales. [London], printed, 1648. 4°.* LT, YM; MIU.

748 A declaration of the proceedings of Major General Massey. For G. Horton, 1652. 4°.* LT, LG; WF.

749 A declaration of the proceedings of the army. Oxford, by J. and H., 1647. 4°.* MADAN 1948. O.

749A A declaration of the proceedings of the honourable committee. By T. Pain and M. Simons, 1643. 4°.* MH.

750 A declaration of the proceedings of the Kings Majesty at Carisbrooke. Printed, 1648. 4°.* LT, LVF.

751 A declaration of the proceedings of the new moddel'd army. Printed, 1647. 4°.* LT, O, DT; Y.

752 A declaration of the proceedings of the Parliament & army. For Emanuel Richardson, 1659. 4°.* LT, SP; MH.

753 A declaration of the proceedings of the Prince of VVales, and his coming to the Isle of Jersey. Imprinted at London for R. W. 30 March, 1649. 4°.* LT, O, HH; MH, WF.

754 A declaration of the proceedings of thirteen Christian kings. For G. Horton, 1652. 4°.* LT, O; NN.

755 The declaration of the Protestant army in . . . Munster. Printed at Cork and re-printed at Edinburgh, by Evan Tyler, 1648. 4°.* ALDIS 1322. LT, C, E, EN; Y.

756 A declaration of the Protestant clergie of the city of Dublin. [London], printed July 22, 1647. 4°.* LT, O, MR, DT; CH, MH.

757 The declaration of the Protestant nobility. colop: For Richard Baldwin, 1689. brs. L, O, C; CH.

758 A declaration of the rare exployts of the London souldiers. [n.p.], for William Smith, 1642. 4°.* LT.

Declaration of the reasons and motives. 1689. See Protestant association.

Declaration of the reasons for assisting the Parliament of England. 1643. See Church of Scotland.

759 Entry cancelled.

760 The declaration of the rebels in Scotland. [Edinburgh, 1679.] cap., fol.* ALDIS 2126. L, O, LL, HH; CH, CN, MH, WCL, Y.

761 The declaration of the rebels now in arms in the west of Scotland. [Edinburgh, 1679.] cap., fol.* ALDIS 2265. L, O, LG, MC, HH; CH, CN, MH, TU, WF, Y.

762 Entry cancelled.

763 A declaration of the representations of the officers of the navy. Printed at London, by Robert Ibbitson, 1647. 4°.* LT, MR, DT; CH, CN, MH, Y.

764 A declaration of the right honourable the Lord Major, aldermen, . . . concerning the great and apparent danger. For R. W., 1648. 4°.* LT, O, LG; CLC, CN, Y.

Declaration of the sad. [1660.] See Burrough, Edward.

Declaration of the Scottish armie. 1647. See Wheatly, W.

765 The declaration of the sea commanders and marriners. Printed, 1648. 4°.* LT, O, LG, MR, DT; MIU, NN, WF.

Declaration of the sense. 1696. See Williams, John, bp.

766 Entry cancelled.

767 A declaration of the several treasons, blasphemies and misdemeanors acted, . . . by . . . William Lilly. For Dan. White, 1660. 4°.* L, O, C, HH; CH, CN, MH, WF, Y.

768 The declaration of the states of Holland and Friezland, concerning Prince Charles. Imprinted at London for G. W., May 24, 1649. 4°.* LT; MH.

Declaration of the States of Holland, concerning the King of Scots. 1653. See Ward, John.

769 A declaration of the States of Holland concerning the Parliament of England. For George Horton, 1652. 4°.* LT.

769A   A declaration of the supreme council of the Confederate Catholicks. *Waterford, by Thomas Bourke, 1643.* brs. O.

769B   Declaration of the supreme council of the Confederate Catholicks . . . admonishing. *[Kilkenny, 1648.]* brs. O.

769C   Declaration of the supreme council . . . withdrawing. *[Kilkenny, by Thomas Bourke, 1648.]* brs. O.

770   A declaration of the taking away of Sir William Waller. *[London], printed, 1648.* brs. LT, LG.

Declaration of the tender mercies. [1670?] *See* Wollrich, Humphrey.

771   A declaration of the three deputy-governors of the Isle of Wight. *For R. Smithurst, 1648.* 4°.* LT, O; MH, WF.

772   The declaration of the tower hamblets to the lord maior. *Printed, July 15, 1648.* brs. LT, LG; MH.

773   A declaration of the treaty at Newport. *Imprinted at London for R. VVilliamson, 1648.* 4°.* LT; MH.

774   A declaration of the valiant resolution of the famous prentices. *For Thomas Banks, 1642.* 4°.* LT, LG, HH, BR; CH, MIU, WF, Y.

775   A declaration of the well-affected common-councelmen of . . . London. *For G. Laurenson, Aprill 18, 1649.* 4°.* LT.

776   A declaration of the wel-affected in the county of Buckinghamshire. *[London], printed, 1649.* 4°.* LT; CLC, MH, NU.

777   A declaration of the vvell-affected to the good old cause. *By J. C., 1659.* brs. LT, O, LG; CH, MH, Y.

777A   The declaration of Thomas Lord Fairfax, and the chief. *Johnson, 1659[60].* brs. LG.

777B   The declaration of Thomas Lord Fairfax and the knights. *For G. Horton, 1659.* 4°.* NL.

777C   A declaration on the behalf of the Church of Christ. 1660. CH.

778   A declaration or discovery, of a most horrible plot. *[London], Decemb. 15, for J. Harris, 1642.* 4°.* LT, EC; Y.

779   A declaration, or letters patents of the election of this present King of Poland, John the Third. *For Brabazon Aylmer, 1674.* 4°.* L, CCH; LC, MH, TU, Y.

779A   A declaration or manifesto, wherein. *[London, for E. Blackmore, 1644.]* 4°.* Y.

780   A declaration or remonstrance from the kingdom of Scotland. *For G. Horton, 1647[/8].* 4°.* LT, DT; CN, NU, TU, WF, Y.

781   A declaration or, remonstrance of the office of a prince. *By Iohn Hammond, and Math. Rhodes, 1642.* 4°.* LT, O, EC; CH, MH, Y.

782   A declaration or remonstrance of the state of the kingdome. *For T. P., 1642.* 4°.* O, HH, EN.

783   A declaration or remonstrance, to His Majesties loyal and faithful subjects; touching brokers. *For George Horton, 1660.* 4°.* LT.

784   A declaration or representation of the actions, intentions, and resolutions of divers of the inhabitants of . . . Hartford. *Printed, 1649[50].* 4°.* LT.

785   A declaration, or resolution of the countie of Hereford. *For Tho. Lewes, 1642.* brs. STEELE 2214. L, O, LG, LS; Y.

786   —[Anr. ed.] *Imprinted at London by a printed copie, 1642.* brs. LT, CJ, AN.

Declaration or test. [n.p., 1680.] *See* Penn, William.

787   A declaration presented to the right honourable the Lords and Commons. *Printed at London by Robert Ibbitson, 1648.* 4°.* LT, CM, YM; MH, MIU, WF.

788   A declaration published in the north of England. *For N. Crook, 1659.* 4°.* LT, CCA, HH; CLC, MIU, PL, WF.

789   A declaration published in the Scots army. *For Matthew Walbanck, May 21, 1646.* 4°.* LT, OC, CT, HH, EN; CH, CLC, MH, WF, Y.

790   A declaration sent from severall officers of His Majesties army. *Decemb. 1. by T. F. or L. W., 1642.* 4°.* LT; Y.

791   A declaration sent to the King of France and Spayne. *For I. T., 1642.* 4°.* LT, O, C, LVF, OC; MH, WF, Y.

792   A declaration sent to the Lord Clifford, Earl of Cumberland. *Novemb. 28 by T. F. for L. W., 1642.* 4°.* LT, EC, HH; CH, WF, Y.

793   A declaration set forth by the Lord Lieutenant Generall . . . Barbadoes. *Hagh, by Samuel Broun, 1651.* 4°.* LT.

794   A declaration set forth by the Presbyterians . . . of Kent. *January 12. [London], for F. Brown, 1647.* 4°.* LT, HH, DT; MIU, Y.

795   A declaration shewing the necessity of the Earle of Straffords suffering. *[London], printed, 1641.* 4°.* LT, O, CT, HH, SC; CH, CU, MH, WF, Y.

Declaration to all His Majesties. 1648. *See* N., G.

Declaration to all the world. 1659. *See* Burrough, Edward.

796   Entry cancelled.

797   A declaration to the Commons of England containing thirteen severall reasons. *[London], for H. Hutton, 1643.* 4°.* LT, HH; CH, WF, Y.

Declaration to the English nation. 1649. *See* Clare, Sir Ralph.

Declaration to the free-born. 1654. *See* Lilburne, John.

798   A declaration to the kingdome. *For R. B., 1648.* 4°.* LT, OC, HH; CH, LC, NC, WF.

799   A declaration to the Parliament of the Commonwealth of England of the sufferings. *[n.p., 1659.]* 4°. O.

800   A declaration to the people, concerning the . . . expedition. *For G. & E. Horton, 1659.* brs. LT, C, LG; Y.

800A   A declaration to the powers of England. *Calvert, 1649.* LG.

Declaration to the whole world. 1659. *See* Strutt, James.

801   The declaration; together vvith the petition. *For H. W., 1648.* 4°.* LT; CLC, WF.

801A   A declaration touching His sacred Majesty. *For Bonham Overton, 1660.* 4°. SP.

801B   A declaration touching the weighing of goods. *Samuel Roycroft, 1681.* fol.* L.

802   A declaration wherein is full satisfaction given concerning Sir Edward Deering. [*London*], *by Andrew Coe*, 1644. 4°.* LT; MH, WF, Y.

803   The declarations and humble representations of the officers and souldiers in Colonel Scroops. *For John Partridge*, 1648. 4°.* LT; CH, WF, Y.

Declarations and pleadings. [n.p.], 1684. *See* A., R.

Decollato comite. [n.p., 1641.] *See* Gill, Alexander.

804   The decoy duck. *Printed at London for F. Couls, T. Bates, I. Wright, and T. Banks*, 1642. 4°.* LT, O; CH, CN, MH, NU, WF, Y.

805   The decoy, or, a practice of the Parliaments. [*London*], *printed*, 1648. 4°.* LT, OC; MIU, WF, Y.

Decree made at Rome. 1679. *See* Innocent XI.

806   Decrees and orders of the committee of safety of the commonwealth of Oceana. *Printed*, 1659. 4°.* O; CH, CU, MIU, WF, Y.

807   The decrees of the Parlement of Paris. *For Benj. Tooke*, 1681. 4°.* T.C.I 465. L, O, HH; CH, CLC, NU, Y.

Decreti Oxeniensis. [n.p.], 1696. *See* South, Robert.

Decus & tutamen: or. 1696. *See* H., E.

808   **Dedekind, Friedrich.** Grobianus et Grobiana. Fifth edition. *Ex officina Rogeri Danielis*, 1661. 12°. L, O, CT, E, EC; MH, PL.

809   A deduction wherein is proved. *For Richard Royston*, 1667. 8°. L, O, OC, CT, P; CH, CLC, CU, Y.

810   [**Dee, Arthur.**] Fasciculus chemicus: or chymical collections. *By J. Flesher for Richard Mynne*, 1650. 8°. LT, O, CT, OC, GU; CLC, LC, MH, PL, Y.

811   **Dee, John.** A true & faithful relation of what passed. *By D. Maxwell, for T. Garthwait*, 1659. fol. L, O, C, E, DT; BN, CH, CN, MBP, MH, MMO, NC, WF, HC.

De'el take the war. 1696. *See* D'Urfey, Thomas.

812   A deep sigh breath'd. *For N.V. and J.B.*, 1642. 4°.* LT, O, OC, D, DT; CH, TU, Y.

Deep sighes. [n.p., 1653.]— *See* Fothergill, Thomas.

Deering, *Sir* Edward. *See* Dering, *Sir* Edward.

Defeat of the Barbary fleet. 1657. *See* M., N. N.

Defence and continuation of the discourse concerning the knowledge. 1675. *See* Sherlock, William.

Defence and continuation of the discourse concerning the period. 1678. *See* E., R.

Defence and continuation of the ecclesiastical politie. 1671. *See* Parker, Samuel, *bp.*

Defence and vindication. 1646. *See* Downame, John.

Defence of a book. 1700. *See* Leslie, Charles.

Defence of a brief history. 1691. *See* Biddle, John.

Defence of a treatise. 1643. *See* G., M.

813   A defence of Dr. Oliphant's short discourse. *Edinburgh, by J. W. for Thomas Carruthers*, 1699. 12°.* L.

Defence of Dr. Sherlock's notion. 1694. *See* Sherlocok, William.

Defence of Dr. Sherlock's preservative. 1688. *See* Giles, William.

Defence of Dr. Tenison's sermon. [*n.p.*, 1688.] *See* Tenison, Thomas.

Defence of dramatic poetry. 1698. *See* Settle, Elkanah.

Defence of humane learning. Oxford, 1660. *See* Thurman, Henry.

Defence of Mr. M. H.'s brief enquiry. 1693. *See* Tong, William.

814   A defence of Mr. Toland. *Printed*, 1697. 4°.* T.C.III 42. MR, EN; CH, CN, IU, MB.

814A —[Anr. ed.] *For E. Whitlock*, 1697. 4°.* OV; WF.

Defence of pluralities. 1692. *See* Wharton, Henry.

Defence of Sir Robert Filmer. 1684. *See* Bohun, Edmund.

Defence of some considerations. 1698. *See* Gastrell, Francis, *bp.*

Defence of sundry positions. 1645. *See* Hollingworth, Richard.

Defence of the absolution. [*n.p.*, 1696.] *See* Collier, Jeremy.

Defence of the answer and arguments. Cambridge [Mass.] 1664. *See* Mather, Richard.

Defence of the answer to a paper. [n.p.], 1695. *See* Pullen, Tobias.

Defence of the Arch-bishop's sermon. 1695. *See* Williams, John, *abp.*

Defence of the brief history. 1691. *See* Alix, Perne.

815   A defence of the canon of the New Testament. 1700. 8°. LW.

Defence of the Christian Sabbath. 1695. *See* Wallis, John.

Defence of the church of England. 1691. *See* Welchman, Edward.

Defence of the confuter. 1687. *See* Tully, George.

Defence of the country parson's admonition. 1687. *See* Assheton, William.

Defence of the dean. 1694. *See* Sherlock, William.

Defence of the doctrin. 1688. *See* Warner, John.

Defence of the doctrines. [n.p., 1694.] *See* Bury, Arthur.

816   A defence of the Duke of Buckingham. colop: *For W.C.*, 1685. 4°.* L, O, OCC, A; CH, MIU, NC, WF.

Defence of the Duke of Buckingham's book. 1685. *See* Penn, William.

Defence of the exposition. 1686. *See* Wake, William *abp.*

Defence of the humble remonstrance. 1641. *See* Hall, Joseph, *bp.*

Defence of the innocency. 1680. *See* Warren, John.

Defence of the lawfulnesse. 1645. *See* Barbon, Praisegod.

817   A defence of the liturgy of the Church of England. *For T. Garthwait*, 1661. 12°. LT, OB, YM; CLC, VC.

Defence of the monsters. [1656]. *See* Thomas, William.

Defence of the missionaries arts. 1689. *See* Wake, William, *abp.*

Defence of the orders. 1688. *See* Milbourne, Luke.

Defence of the orindations. 1688. *See* Whitfield, Edmund.

Defence of the papers. 1686. *See* Dryden, John.

818   A defence of the Parliament of 1640. 1698. 4°. L, LVF, BAMB, E; CH, MB.

Defence of the peaceable. Dublin, 1698. *See* Synge, Edward, *abp.*

Defence of the people called Quaker. 1690. *See* Ashby, Richard.

Defence of the plain-man's reply. 1688. *See* Assheton, William.

Defence of the present government. 1689. *See* Claridge, Richard.

Defence of the proceedings. 1691. *See* Harrington, James.

Defence of the profession. 1690. *See* Jenkin, Robert.

Defence of the proposition. 1668. *See* Humfrey, John.

Defence of the Protestant. [n.p.], 1672. *See* Mather, Samuel.

Defence of the report. 1698. *See* Lobb, Stephen.

Defence of the resolution. 1684. *See* Fowler, Edward. *bp.*

Defence of the rights. Oxford, 1690. *See* Langbaine, Gerard.

Defence of the Scots abdicating. [n.p.], 1700. *See* Hodges, James.

Defence of the Scots settlement at Darian. [n.p.], 1699. *See* Foyer, Archibald.

Defence of the Scots settlement at Darien. 1699. *See* Harris, Walter.

Defence of the Scots settlement; with. *Edinburgh*, 1699. *See* Fletcher, Andrew.

Defence of the true church. 1659. *See* Crook, John.

819   A defence of the trve sence and meaning of the words. [n.p.], *printed*, 1641. 12°. LW, CS; NU, WF, Y.

Defence of the vindication of K. Charles. 1699. *See* Wagstaffe, Thomas.

Defence of the vindication of the church. *Edinburgh*, 1694. *See* Rule, Gilbert.

Defence of the vindication of the deprived bishops. 1695. *See* Dodwell, Henry.

Defence of Their Majesties. 1689. *See* S., R.

Defense of true Protestants. 1680. *See* A.

820   Entry cancelled.

Defensative armour. 1680. *See* Collinges, John.

Defense de la nation. 1692. *See* Abbadie, Jacques.

821   Defensio legis: or, the whole state of England inquisited. *By Andrew Clark, sold by W. Cooper*, 1674. 8°. T.C.I 155. LL, CT, P, EN; MH.

822   —[Anr. ed.] *For, and are to be sold by George Savile*, 1674. 8°. L, OC; LC, MIU, NN, PL, Y.

Defensio regia. [*n.p.*], 1649. *See* Saumaise, Claude de.

823   A defensive vindication of the publike liturgy. *By J. R. for R. W.*, 1641. 4°.* L, O, CT, HH, E; CH, NU, WF.

823A   —[Anr. ed.] *By J. R. for R. Whittaker, and I. Williams*, 1641. 4°.* L, OC, CM, CT; CH, MH, MIU, Y.

Defiance against all. [*n.p.*], 1646. *See* Overton, Richard.

824   Defiance to the Dutch. *For T. W.*, 1672. brs. L; MH.

825   The definition of a king. *Printed at London for Thomas Bankes*, [1642]. 4°.* LT; CU, Y.

826   —[Anr. ed.] 1642. 4°.* L; CH, IU, NU, WF, Y.

827   The definition of a Parliament. *For J. F.*, 1642[3]. 4°.* LT; CH, MH, MIU, WF, Y.

827A   [**Defoe, Daniel.**] An account of the late horrid conspiracy. *For J. Humphrys*, 1691. 4°.* L, O, C, LG, CT; CH, MH, NU, WF, Y.

—Account of the societies. 1699. *See* Woodward, Josiah.

827B   [–] The advantages of the present settlement. *For Ric. Chiswell*, 1689. 4°.* L, O, OM, CT, EN; CH, MW, NU, Y.

827C   [–] An answer tto the late K. James's last declaration. *For Richard Baldwin*, 1693. 4°.* T.C.II 466. L, O, OC, MR, DT; CH, MH, NP, NU, Y.

827D   [–] —[Anr. ed.] *Edinburgh, Reprinted* 1693. 4°. ALDIS 3291. O, EN; WF.

827E   [–] —[Anr. ed.] *Dublin, Robert Thornton*, 1693. 4°.* DIX 257. DCA, DT; WF.

827F   [–] —[Anr. ed.] *For Richard Baldwin, and re-printed at Boston in New-England by Benjamin Harris*, 1693. 4°.* Y.

828   [–] An argument shewing, that a standing army, with consent. *For E. Whitlock*, 1698. 4°.* L, O, CT, EC, DT; CLC, CN, MH, TU, WF, Y.

829   [–] A brief reply to the history. *Printed*, 1698. 4°.* L, O, C, EN, DT; CH, CN, MH, TU, WF, Y.

829A   [–] —Second edition. —, 1698. 4°.* C, EN, DT; MB, Y.

829B   [–] The character of the late Dr. Samuel Annesley. *For E. Whitlock*, 1697. 4°.* LW.

830   [–] The compleat mendicant: or, unhappy beggar. *For E. Harris*, 1699. 8°. T.C.III 170. L, O, LW, A; CH, CN, MH, NC, WF, Y.

831   [–] The Englishman's choice. *Printed*, 1694. 4°.* T.C.II 494. L, CT; CLC, MB, Y.

832   —An essay upon projects. *By R. R. for Tho. Cockerill*, 1697. 8°. T.C.III 8. L, O, CT, E, DT; CH, CN, MH, TU, WF, Y.

832A   [–] Essays upon seueral subjects. *By Richard Cotes for Edward Husband*, 1651. 4°.* L, DT; MH, NN, WF, Y.

833   [–] An enquiry into the occasional conformity of dissenters. *Printed*, 1697. 4°.* T.C.III 67. L, O, C, EC, MR; CH, MB, NU, TU, WF, Y.

834   [–] —[Anr. ed.] *Dublin, by J.B. & S.P., for Jacob Milner*, 1698. 4°.* DIX 307. O, C, CD; MB.

835   [–] The interests of the several princes. *Printed*, 1698. 4°.* T.C.III 67. L, O, C; CN, MB, MH, WF, Y.

836   [–] A letter to a dissenter from his friend. colop: *Hague, door Hans Verdraeght*, 1688. 4°.* L, O, CT, LL, EN; CH, MH, NP, NU, Y.

837   [–] A letter to a member of Parliament, shewing. *Oxford for George West, and Henry Clements*, 1699. 4°. T.C.III 125. L, O, OC; CH, MU, NR, VC, Y.

837A   [–] Lex talionis: or, an enquiry. *Printed*, 1698. 4°.* L, O, C; INU, MB, NU, WF.

838   [–] A new discovery of an old intreague. [*London*], *printed*, 1691. 4°.* L, O, LW; IU, LC, MB, MH, Y.

839   [–] The pacificator. A poem. *Printed, and sold by J. Nutt*, 1700. fol.* T.C.III 173. L, O, HH; CLC, MB, TU, Y.

840   [–] The poor man's plea. *For A. Baldwin*, 1698. 4°.* T.C.III 67. L, O, C, CT, E; Y.

841   [–] —Second edition. —, 1698. 4°.* T.C.III 100. L; CLC, MB, MH, NU, PU, TU.

842 [–] —[Anr. ed.] *Printed,* 1698. 4°.* CT; CH, MB, NC, TU, WF.

842A [–] —[Anr. ed.] *For A. Baldwin,* 1699. 4°.* O, LW; WF.

842B [–] —Third edition. —, 1700. 4°.* L, SP.

843 [–] Reasons humbly offer'd for a law. *Printed, and are to be sold by A. Baldwin,* 1700. 4°.* L, O, C, OC, EN; CH, CN, MH, NU, WF, Y.

844 [–] Reflections upon the late great revolution. *For Ric. Chiswell,* 1689. 4°. T.C.II 255. L, O, CT, OC, MR; CH, MB, MIU, NU, WF, Y.

845 [–] Several essays relating to academies. *For Thomas Cockerill,* 1700. 8°. T.C.III 200. Y.

846 [–] The six distinguishing characters. *Printed,* 1700. 4°.* O; CH, CN, LC, MH, Y.

847 [–] Some reflections on a pamphlet lately publish'd, *For E. Whitlock,* 1697. 4°.* L, C, LCL, CT, MR; CH, CN, MH, TU, WF, Y.

848 [–] —Second edition. —, 1697. 4°.* L, CT, MR, EN, DT; CLC, CN, MH, NU, WF, Y.

[–] Speculum crape-gownorum. 1682. *See* Phillips, John.

848A [–] Taxes no charge. *For R. Chiswell,* 1690. 4°.* T.C.II 306. O, C, LV, OM, DT; CH, CN, MH, NC, WF, Y.

849 [–] The true-born Englishman. [*London*], *printed,* 1700. 4°. L; CH, CLC, MH, TU, WCL, Y.

850 [–] The two great questions considered. *By R. T. for A. Baldwin,* 1700. 4°.* L, O, C, EN, DT; HR, CH, CN, LC, MH, NC, Y.

851 [–] The two great questions further considered. *Printed,* 1700. 4°.* L, O, C, CS; CLC, CN, LC, Y.

Defosiwneu priod. [n.p., 1656.] *See* Valentine, Henry.

852 **Degge, Sir Simon.** The parson's counsellor. *For Henry Twyford,* 1676. 8°. L, O, C, DC, MAU; CH, LC, MH, PL, TU.

853 — —Second edition. *By the assigns of Richard and Edward Atkins, for Henry Twyford,* 1677. 8°. T.C.I 239. L, LL, OM, C, YM; MH, MM, TU, YL.

854 — —Third edition. —, 1681. 8°. L, LIL, OC, CE, NPL; CH, CN, LC, MH, NU, TU, Y.

855 — —Fourth edition. *By the assigns of Richard and Edward Atkins for Henry Twyford, to be sold by Dan. Browne, Will. Rogers and Tim. Goodwin,* 1685. 8°. T.C.II 152. L, C, LIL, LG, EN; CH, LC, MH, NCL, Y.

856 — —Fifth edition. *By the assigns of Richard and Edward Atkins, for Richard Sare, and Joseph Hindmarsh,* 1695. 8°. T.C.II 543. L, C, LCL, OC, EN; CLC, LC, MH, NCL, YL.

856A **De Gols, Gerrard.** Samson, or the unhappy lover. *For Robert Battersby,* 1696. 4°.* L; MH.

857 **Degravere, Julius.** Thesaurus remediorum. A treasury. *By G. P.,* 1662. 4°.* L, O, LWL; CH, WSG.

858 **DeGrey, Thomas.** The compleat horse-man. Second edition. *For Thomas Harper and Nicholas Fussell,* 1651. 4°. L, O, CCA, LAS; CLC, PU, TU, Y.

858A — —Third edition. *By J.L., for Humphrey Moseler,* 1656. 4°. L, O, EN, LWL; BBE.

859 — —Fourth edition. *By E. C. and A. C. for Samuel Lowndes,* 1670. 4° T.C.II LM. L, O, C; CH, CJC, CLC, WF, Y.

860 — —Fifth edition. *By J. R. and R. H. for Samuel Lowndes,* 1684. 4°. T.C.II 107. O, OR, LWL, R; LC, Y.

Dei incarnati. 1693. *See* Elys, Edmund.

861 **D[ekker], T[homas].** Canaan's calamitie. *By Tho. James for Edward Thomas,* 1677. 4°. T.C.I 297. L; WF.

862 [–] English villanies. *By E. P. for Nicholas Gamage,* 1648. 4°. L, O; CH, CU, WCL, WF.

863 [–] The shoomakers holiday. *For W. Gilbertson,* 1657. 4°. L, O, EC; CH, LC.

—The young gallants academy. 1674. *See* Vincent, Samuel.

Del teatro Britanico. 1683. *See* Leti, Gregorio.

864 **Delamain, Richard.** The humble presentation of. *By E.G. for I. Wright, and I. Franck,* 1641. brs. LT, O, C, HH; Y.

865 —A table shewing instantly. *By E.G. for I. Wright & I. Franck,* 1641[2]. brs. STEELE 2013. LT, O.

866 **Delamaine, Edward.** God's loud call from Heaven. *By S. Dover,* 1661. 4°.* L, SP.

867 —Suitable comforts for suffering Sion. *By Simon Dover,* 1661. 4°.* LCS, SP, EN; WF.

868 **De La March, John.** A complaint of the false prophet's. *By Thomas Payne to be sold by Humphrey Blunden,* 1641. 4°. LT, O, CT, LCL; CH, MH, NU, WF.

868A —A revelation of the time. [*London*], *by T. Paine, for Ben: Allen,* 1645. 8°. NU.

869 **Delamere, George Booth, baron.** A declaration of Sir George Booth. *For G. Horton,* 1659. 4°.* LT; CH, MH, WF, Y.

870 [–] The declaration of the lords, gentlemen, citizens, freeholders. [*London,* 1659.] brs. STEELE 3124. LT, O, C, LG, HH; MH, Y.

871 —A letter from Sir George Booth. [*London,* 1659.] brs. LT, O, OC, CCA, CJ; CH, MH, Y.

872 —Sir George Booth's letter of the 2d of August 1659. *Printed,* 1659. 4°.* LT, O, C; CN, MIU, WF.

872A —The reply of. *Printed,* 1645. 4°.* Y.

873 **Delamere, Henry Booth, earl of.** The works of. *For John Lawrence, and John Dunton,* 1694. 8°. L, O, CT, EN, DT; CH, CN, NC, WF, Y.

874 —The charge of . . . 11th of October, 1692. *For Richard Baldwin,* 1693. 4°.* L, O, OC, CT, MR; CH, WF, Y.

875 —The charge of . . . 25th day of April, 1693. *For Richard Baldwin,* 1694. 4°.* T.C.II 466. L, O, WCA, MR, DT; CH, CN, WF, Y.

876 —A collection of speeches of. *For Richard Baldwin,* 1694. 4°.* T.C.II 494. L, O; Y.

877 [–] An impartial enquiry into the causes of the present fears. *Printed,* 1692. 4°.* L, O, C, MR, AU; CH, NU, PL, WF, Y.

878 —The late Lord Russel's case. *For Awnsham Churchill,* 1689. fol.* T.C.II 256. L, O, CT, LL, MR; CH, CN, NC, WF, Y.

879 —The Lord Delamere's letter to his tenants. [*n.p.,* 1688.] cap., fol.* O, LL, OC, CS.

880   —Lord Del—r's speech. [*London*, 1688?]. brs. L, O, C, OC, CK, HH; CH, MA, PL, WF, Y.

881   —The speech of . . . March 2, 1680/1. colop: *For John Minshall in Chester, and are to be sold by Langley Curtis*, 1681. cap., fol.* L, O, CM, OC, HH; CH, CN, MBA, WF, Y.

882   —The Earl of Warrington's speech . . . 7 Nov., 1691. *For R. Baldwin*, 1691. cap., fol.* LL, DC, SP.

883   —The speech of . . . April 13. 1692. *For Richard Baldwin*, 1692. 4°.* T.C.II 428. L, O, MR; CH, WF, Y.

884   **Delamore, Thomas de Eschallers.** The English Catholike Christian. *By R. Leybourn*, 1649. 4°.* LT, O.

885   —True old news. *By E. G.*, 1649. 4°.* L, O.

886   **Delamothe, G.** The French alphabet. *By A. Miller, and are to be sold by Tho. Underhill*, 1647. 8°. L, CCH; MIU, WF, Y.

      Delanorosus, Dr. *pseud.*

887   **Delaune, Henry.** Πατριχον δωρον, or a legacy to his sons. *For Henry Seile*, 1651. 8°. L.

888   ——Second edition. *By A. M. for Henry Seile*, 1657. 8°. L, CM, SP; CH, MH, NC, WCL, Y.

889   **Delaune, Thomas.** Angliæ metropolis: or, the present state. *By G. L. for John Harris, and Thomas Howkins*, 1690. 12°. T.C.II 316. L, C, LL, LG, ES; CH, CN, LC, MH, NC, Y.

890   —Compulsion of conscience condemned. *For John How, and Tho. Knowles*, 1683. 4°.* L.

891   —Ειχὼν τδν Θηρίου or the image. [*London*], printed, 1684. 4°.* L, O, C, SP; NHC, NU, WCL, WF, Y.

892   —A narrative of the sufferings of. [*London*], *for the author*, 1684. 4°.* L, O, C, LG; CH, CN, NU, WF, Y.

893   [–] A plea for the Non-Conformists. *For the author*, 1684. 4°. L, C, LCL, LW, EN; CH, NU, WCL, WF, Y.

894   —The present state of London. *By George Larkin for Enoch Prosser and John How*, 1681. 12°. L, O, CT, MR, EN; CH, CN, LC, MH, Y.

894A ——Second edition. *For John How*, 1683. 12°. NS.

894B [–] Proposals about the second volume. [*London*, 1681/2.] fol.* DCH.

895   —Τροπολογία, or, a key. *By John Richardson, and John Darby, for Enoch Prosser*, 1681. fol. T.C.I 457. CS, BB, RB, ENC; MH, NU.

896   ——[Anr. ed.] *By J. R. and J. D. for Enoch Prosser*, 1682. fol. L, O, LCS, GU; MH, NU, Y.

897   —Truth defended. *For the author, to be sold by Francis Smith*, 1677. 8°. LW, O, EN; CLC, WF.

898   —Two letters to Dr. Benjamin Calamy. [*London*, 1683?] cap., 4°.* EN; LC, WF.

      Delavall, John. Heresie and hatred. Philadelphia, 1693. *See* Keith, George.

898A The delectable history of Poore Robin. *For J. Conyers*, [1675.] 8°.* CM.

899   A delectable little history in metter [*sic*]. *Glasgow*, 1695. 8°.* ALDIS 3457. WCL.

900   A delectable little history in metre. *Edinburgh, printed*, 1698. 8°.* ALDIS 3745. L.

      Delectable new ballad. [n.p., 1690?] *See* Burne, Nicol.

Delenda Carthago. [n.p.], 1694. *See* Shaftesbury, Anthony Ashley Cooper, *earl of.*

901   Preston, Novemb. 17, 1646. The deliberate resolution of the ministers of the gospel within . . . Lancaster. *For Luke Favvne, to be sold by Thomas Smith*, 1647. 4°.* LT, LW, MC, MR, DT; NU.

      Deliciæ musicæ. 1695. *See* Playford, Henry.

      Deliciæ Parnassij. *Dublin*, 1700. *See* Rogers, Thomas.

      Delight and pastime. 1697. *See* Miege, Guy.

902   Delightful and ingenious novels. *For Benjamin Crayle*, 1685. 12°. T.C.II 113. CH.

      Delightful fables. 1691. *See* Crouch, Nathaniel.

903   The delightful history of the life & death of that renowned & famous St. Patrick. *For Dorman Newman*, 1685. 16°. T.C.II 113. L, O; CH, CN.

904   Delightful novels. Fourth edition. *For Benjamin Crayle*, 1686. 12°. T.C.II 184. L; CLC.

      Delights for ladies. 1647. *See* Platt, Sir Hugh.

      Delights for the ingenious. 1684. *See* Crouch, Nathaniel.

      Delights of the bottle. [n.p., 1675.] *See* Shadwell, Thomas.

905   Delineation and description of the famous city Offen. *For Joseph Moxon*, 1684. brs. LG; CH.

906   Delineation of a new blazing starre. 1664. brs. O.

907   The delinquent's pasport [*sic*]. [*London*, 1657.] brs. LT.

908   The deliquium: or the grievances of the nation discovered. [n.p., 1681.] brs. L, O, CT, HH; CH, MH, TU, WF, Y.

      The deliverance, a poem. 1689. *See* Crofts, William.

909   The deliverance of the whole hovse of Israel. *By R. Dulton, for Iohn Wright, the younger*, 1641. 4°. L, CCA; CLC, MH, WF.

910   The deliverer in a panegyrick. [n.p.], *printed*, 1660. 4°.* L; CH.

911   **Dell, Jonas.** Christ held forth. *By J. C. for William Learner*, 1646. 8°. LT, E.

912   —Forms the pillars of Antichrist. *For the author*, 1656. 4°. LT.

913   —A voyce from the temple. *For the author*, 1658. 4°. LT, OC, CT, LF, BBN; NU.

914   [**Dell, William.**] Βαπτισμων διδαχή: or, the doctrine of baptisms. *For Giles Calvert*, 1648. 8°.* LT, O, CT, HH; CH, CU, NU, Y.

915   [–] ——[Anr. ed.] —, 1652. 4°.* LT, LCL; CLC, MH, NU, WF, Y.

915A [–] ——[Anr. ed.] *Printed*, 1672. 4°.* CLC, PSC.

916   ——[Anr. ed.] *Printed and sold by T. Sowle*, 1697. 8°. L; NIC, PSC.

916A ——[Anr. ed.] 1698. 8°. CCA.

917   —The building, beauty, teaching. 1651. 8°. LCL, LSL.

918   —The building and glory of the truely Christian and spiritual church. *For G. Calvert*, 1646. 4°.* MADAN 1894. LT, O, HH, EN, DT; CH, CU, MH, NU, Y.

918A ——Second edition. —, 1647. 4°.* C, EN.

919   —Christ's spirit. *For Hen. Cripps and Lod. Lloyd*, 1651. 4°. LT, LCL, LSL, BBN; MH, NU, Y.

920   [–] The city-ministers unmasked. *For Giles Calvert,* 1649. 4°.* LT, O, LG, EN; CN, CU, NU, WF, Y.

921   —The crucified and quickened Christian. *For Giles Calvert,* [1652]. 4°. LT, C, LSC, EN; CH, CU, MH, NU, WF, Y.

922   —The doctrine of the Sabbath. *For Giles Calvert,* 1650. 4°. LT, LCL; CLC, NU, TSM.

923   —The increase of Popery in England. *For Richard Janeway,* 1681. fol. T.C.I 452. L, O, CT, LG, HH, EN; CH, LC, MH, NU, WF, Y.

924   [–] A plain and necessary confutation of divers gross and antichristian errors. *By Robert White, for Giles Calvert,* 1654. 8°. LT, O, CT, LCL; CN, MHC, NU, OCI, WF, Y.

925   —Power from on high. *For Henry Overton,* 1645. 4°. LT, O, LW; CH, CU, MBP, NU, WF, Y.

926   —Right reformation. *By R. White, for Giles Calvert,* 1646. 40pp. 4°. L, O, C, BPL, DT; CH, MH, NU, TU, WF, Y.

927   — —[Anr. ed.] —, 1646. 42 pp. 4°. LT, CJ, CM, D; MH, WF, Y.

928   — —[Anr. ed.] *London, reprinted Edinburgh,* 1650. 4°.* E, EN; NHC.

928A   — —[Anr. ed.] 1651. 4°. LCL, LSL.

929   —Several sermons and discovrses of. *For Giles Calvert,* 1652. 4°. LT, CE, BPL, DT; CH, MH, NU, WF, Y.

930   —The stumbling-stone. *By R. W. for Giles Calvert,* 1653. 4°.* MADAN 2213. LT, O, C, LF, E; CU, MH, NU, PH, TU, WF.

931   —The tryal of spirits. *For Giles Calvert,* 1653. 4°. LT, O, C, LCL, LW; CH, CN, MH, NU, WF, Y.

932   Entry cancelled.

933   — —[Anr. ed.] —, 1660. 4°. L, LCL; MH, NU.

934   — —[Anr. ed.] *Printed and sold by T. Sowle,* [1699]. 8°. T.C.III 169. L, C, LF, AN; IE, MH, PH, WF, Y.

935   Entry cancelled.

936   —Vniformity examined. *By J. Coe for Henry Overton,* 1646. 4°.* E, DT; MIU, MWA, Y.

937   — —[Anr. ed.] *By Matthew Simmons for Henry Overton,* 1646. 4°.* LT, O, LCL, HH; MIU, NU, TU, WF.

938   — —[Anr. ed.] 1651. 4°.* LCL, LSG.

939   —The way of true peace. *For Giles Calvert,* 1649. 4°. LT, O, CCH, BP, EN; CU, NU, PL.

940   — —[Anr. ed.] 1651. 4°. LCL, LSC.

     Della Casa, Giovanni. *See* Casa, Giovanni della.

     Della Valle, Pietro. *See* Valle, Pietro della.

941   **Dellon, Claude.** The history of the Inquisition . . . at Goa. *For James Knapton,* 1688. 4°. T.C.II 223. L, O, LIL, EN, DT; CH, CU, MH, NU, WF, Y.

942   —A voyage to the East Indies. *For D. Browne,* 1698. 8°. T.C.III 93. L, O, C, DT; CLC, CN, LC, RPJ, Y.

943   — —[Anr. ed.] *For D. Browne, A. Roper and T. Leigh,* 1698. 8°. OC; MIU, PL, WF.

944   **D[eloney], T[homas].** The first part of the pleasant and princely history of the gentle craft. *By T. M. for William Thackeray,* 1678. 4°. L.

945   [–] —[Anr. ed.] *By J. Millet, for W. T. to be sold by J. Gilbertson,* [1685]. 4°. CM.

945A   —The garland of delight. *By T. H. for William Thackeray, and Thomas Passenger,* 1681. 12°. CM.

946   —The garland of good-will. *For J. Wright,* 1678. 8°. O.

947   — —[Anr. ed.] *By J. Millet for T. Passenger and J. Deacon,* 1685. 8°. O; CH.

948   — —[Anr. ed.] *By Fr. Clark for George Conyers,* 1688. 8°. O, CM.

949   — —[Anr. ed.] *For G. Conyers,* [c. 1690]. 8°. L, O; CH, CU, WF, Y.

950   Entry cancelled.

951   [–] —[Anr. ed.] [1696?] 8°. L.

952   — —[Anr. ed.] *For G. Conyers,* [1700]. 8°. L, O; CLC, MH, Y.

953   —The gentle craft. Part I. *For John Stafford,* 1648. 4°. L.

954   — —[Anr. ed.] —, 1652. 4°. O.

954A   — —[Anr. ed.] *By G. P. for I. Andrews,* 1660. 4°. MH.

955   — —[Anr. ed.] 1672. 4°. O.

956   [–] The lamentation of Mr. Page's wife. [London], *by and for Alex. Milbourn,* [1670–80]. brs. L, CM, HH, GU.

957   [–] —[Anr. ed.] *By and for W. O. and sold by B. Deacon,* [1685]. brs. HH.

957A   [Anr. ed.] [London, *for F. Coles, T. Vere and I. Wright.* [1676], brs. MH.

957B   [Anr. ed.], [London] *for F. Coles, T. Vere and W. Gilbertson and J. Wright* [1688], brs. MH.

958   [–] A most delightful history of the famous clothier . . . Jack of Newbery. *By H. B. for W. Thackeray,* 1684. 8°. CM.

959   [–] The most rare and excellent history of the Dutches of Suffokls [sic] calamity. [London], *for W. Thackery, J. M. and A. M.,* [1685]. brs. L, CM, HH, GU.

959A   [–] The noble acts newly found. [London], *for F. Coles, T. Vere, & J. Wright,* [1690.] brs. L, O, CM.

960   [–] The pleasant and princely history of the gentlecraft. [1675?] 4°. L, C.

961   [–] —[Anr. ed.] *For H. Rhodes,* [1690]. 4°. L; CH, CN, NC, Y.

962   [–] —Tenth edition [London], *W. Wilde and sold by P. Brooksby, J. Deacon, J. Back, J. Blare, and E. Tracy,* 1696. T.C.II 582. 4°. O; CN.

963   —The pleasant history of Iohn Winchcomb. Eleventh edition. *W. D.,* 1655. 4°. EN.

963A   — —Thirteenth edition. *By E. Crouch, for T. Passenger,* 1672. 4°. O; CN.

964   — —Fourteenth edition. *By W. Wilde, for Thomas Passenger and William Thackeray,* [1680?] 4°. L, CM; CH, NN.

965   [–] —Fifteenth edition. *By Eben. Tracy,* [1700?]. 4°. L, LUG, C; WF.

966   —The pleasant history of Thomas of Reading. *For W. Thackeray,* 1672. 4°. O, CM.

967   —The royal garland of love. *By E. C. for W. T. and are to be sold by John Hose,* 1674. 8°.* L.

968   [–] The Spanish ladies love. [London], *by and for W. O.,* [1670?]. brs. L, HH.

969   [–] [London], *by and for W. O. and A. M. and sold by J. Conyers,* [1688–91]. brs' L, O, CM, HH.

970 [–] —[Anr. ed.] [London], for F. Coles, T. Vere, and W. Gilbertson, [1675], brs. O; GU.

970A Δηλωσις: or, the fundamental articles. By Tho. Milbourn, for R. Clavel, 1697. 4°.* L, CT; WF, Y.

971 The deluded lasses lamentation. [London], for P. Brooksby, J. Deacon, J. Blare, J. Back, [1672]. brs. L, CM, HH, GU; MH.

Deluge: or. 1690. See Ecclestone, Edward.

971A **Delure, Jean.** Lettre à Monsieur Arnaud. Par Jean Brudenell, pour F. Vaillant, 1689. 4°.* O.

Demands already made. 1647. See Prynne, William.

972 The demands and desires of His Excellency the Lord General Fairfax. For John Woolridge, 1648. 4°.* LT, HH, DT.

973 The demands of His Excellency Tho. Lord Fairfax, and the Generall Councell. For R. M., 1648. 4°.* LT, HH; CH, MBP, WF.

974 The demands of Lieutenant-Generall Crumwell [sic]. Imprinted at London, for G. Horton, 1648. 4°.* LT; MH, WF.

975 The demands of the rebels in Ireland. For John Thomas, 1641. 4°.* L, O, C, EC, HH; CH, CLC, MH, WF, Y.

976 The demands, resolutions, and intentions of the army. [London], printed, 1648. 4°.* LT, O.

Demeanour of a good subject. 1681. See Godwyn, Thomas.

977 **Democrates, philosophus.** Aursæ sententiæ. Cantabrigiæ, 1670. 8°. CCA.

Democritus Secundus, pseud.

978 Democritvs turned states-man. Printed, 1656. 4°.* LT, O, C, LG, OC; CH, CN, MH, NU, WF, Y.

Daemon of Burton. 1671. See A., J.

Demonstration how the Latine tongue. 1669. See Brett, Arthur.

Demonstration of family duties. 1643. See Paget, Thomas.

978A A demonstration of the King's right. 1670. brs. MH.

979 A demonstration that farthings are as necessary as bread. [London, 1670?] cap., 4°.* L, OC.

Demonstration that Henry Merrian. 1692. See Feddenian, John.

Demonstration that the church. 1688. See Whitby, Daniel.

Demonstration to the Christians. 1679. See Fox, George.

980 **Demosthenes.** Δημοσθενους λογι εκλεκτοι. Selectæ Demosthenis orationes. Cantabrigiæ, ex officina R. Daniel, 1642. 12°. L, C, DC, CS, WCA.

981 — —[Anr. ed.] —, [c. 1650]. 12°. CS, CT, EC; Y.

982 — —[Anr. ed.] Typis J. Redmayne, 1672. 12°. T.C.I 123. L, O, CT, EC, DT; PL.

983 — —[Anr. ed.] Typis Eliz. Redmayne, 1686. 12°. T.C.II 173. L, O, CT, E; CLC, NC, WF.

984 **[Dempster, George.]** The prodigal returned to Scotland. Edinburgh, in June 1700 by John Reid, and are to be sold at John Vallange's Mrs. Ogstoun's and Thomas Carruther's. 4°.* L, EN, ES, CLC.

985 Entry cancelled.

986 A demvrre to the bill for preventing the growth . . . of heresie. [London, 1646.] cap., 4°.* LT, HH; CU, NHC, NU, Y.

987 Denbigh-Castle surprized. Printed, 1648. 4°.* LT, AN; IU, Y.

Δενδρολογια Dodona's grove. [n.p.], 1644. See Howell, James.

988 **Dendy, Edward.** To the Parlament of the Commonwealth . . . The humble petition of. [London, 1654.] brs. LT; MH.

989 **[Denham, Sir John.]** The anatomy of play. By G. P. for Nicholas Bourne, 1651. 8°.* LT.

990 —Cato major, of old age. A poem. For Henry Herringman, 1669. 8°. T.C.I 2. L, O, C, DT; CH, LC, MH, TU, Y.

991 [–] Certain verses written by severall of the authors friends. Printed, 1653. 8°.* L, CK; CH, CN, MH, Y.

992 [–] —[Anr. ed., "authours."] —, 1653. 8°.* L; WF.

993 [–] Coopers Hill. For Tho. Walkley, 1642. 4°.* LT, O, C, CK, LL; CH, LC, MH, TU, WC, Y.

994 [–] —[Anr. ed.] [Oxford, by H. Hall], printed, 1643. 4°.* MADAN 1570. O, LVD; CH, CN, MH, TU, Y.

995 — —Second edition. For Humphrey Moseley, 1650. 4°.* LT, O, CCA, OC; CH, MH, TU, WF, Y.

996 — —Sixth edition. —, 1655. 4°.* L, O, CE, CK, E; CH, MH, TU, WF, Y.

997 [–] Coopers Hill Latine redditum. Oxonii, e theatro Sheldoniano, 1676. 4°.* MADAN 3101. L, O, CT, OC, BAMB; CLC, CN, CU, TU, Y.

998-1000 Entries cancelled.

[–] Directions to a painter. 1667. See Marvell, Andrew.

1001 [–] The famous battel of the catts. In the Savoy, by T. Newcomb, 1668. 4°.* L, C, LFEA; CH, CN, MH, WF, Y.

1001A [–] —[Anr. ed.] [London] by T. Newcomb, 1686. 4°.* O.

1002 [–] Further advice to a painter. For R. Vaughan, 1673. 4°.* L, O, CT; CLC, LVR, WF, Y.

[–] Gaming-humour considered. 1684. See Morton, Charles.

1002A [–] Mr. Hampden's speech, [London] 1692 brs. LT, O; CH, CU, WF.

1003 —On Mr. Abraham Cowley his death. For H. Herringman, 1667. cap., fol.* O, C; CH, CLC, MH, WF, Y.

1004 [–] A panegyrick on His Excellency the Lord General George Monck. For Richore Marriot, 1659. 4°.* L, O; CH, MH, TU, WF, Y.

1005 —Poems and translations. For H. Herringman, 1668. 8°. L, O, C, LIL, GK; CH, CU, LC, MH, NC, TU, Y.

1006 — —Second edition. By J. M. for H. Herringman, 1671. 8°. L, O, C, CCA; BN, CH, CU, MH, WF, Y.

1007 — —Third edition. By J. M. for H. Herringman; and are to be sold by Jos. Knight and Fr. Saunders, 1684. 8°. T.C.II 105. L, OW, CT, LL, DT; CH, CU, LC, MH, NP.

1008 [–] The prologue to Mrs. Megosdy and the first play. For G. Bedell and T. Collins. 1660. brs. LT, O, LG, HH, MH.

[–] The second advice to a painter. 1667. See Marvell, Andrew.

1009 [-] The sophy. *By Richard Hearne for Thomas Walkley*, 1642. fol. L, O, C, LVD, DC; CH, CU, MH, TU, WF, Y.

1010 — —[Anr. ed.] *By J.M. for H.Herringman*, 1667. 8°. L, O; CU, V, WCL.

1010A — —[Anr. ed.] —, 1671. O; MH, PL, PU, Y.

1011 [-] —[Anr. ed.] *By J.M. for H.Herringman, to be sold by Jos. Knight and Fr. Saunders*, 1684. 8°. O; CN, TU, Y.

1012 [-] The true Presbyterian without disguise. *Printed*, 1661. 4°.* CH, NU.

1013 — —[Anr. ed.] colop: *For J.B.*, 1680. brs. L, O, CT, MC, HH; CH, MH, TU.

Denmark vindicated. 1694. *See* Crull, Jodocus.

1014 **Denne, Henry.** Antichrist vnmasked. *[London], printed*, 1645. 4°. LT, O, CT, ENC, DT; CH, NU, WF, Y.

1015 — —Third edition. *Reprinted at London*, 1646. 8°. L; NH, C.

1015A —A conference between a sick man and a minister. *By Tho. Badger*, 1642. 8°.* L.

1016 — —[Anr. ed.] *For John Svveeting*, 1643. 8°.* O, C, LCL, SP; NHC, NU, Y.

1017 —The doctrine and conversation of John Baptist. *[n.p.]*, 1641. 8°. LCL.

1018 — —[Anr. ed.] *By Tho. Badger*, 1642. 8°. LT, LCL; CLC, NHC.

1019 — —[Anr. ed.] *For John Svveeting*, 1643. 8°. O, C, CM, CT, SP; NU.

1020 —An epistle recommended. *For Francis Smith*, 1660. 4°.* LT, LCL, CSSX, EN; CU, MB, WF.

1020A —Grace, mercy and peace. *Reprinted and sold by Benjamin Needham*, 1696. 12°. NHC, NPT.

1021 —The Levellers designe discovered. *For Francis Tyton*, 1649. 4°.* LT, O; CH, MH, NHC, WF.

1022 —The man of sin discovered. *Printed*, 1645. 4°.* LT, O; CH, NU, Y.

1023 — —[Anr. ed.] *For John Sweeting*, 1646. 4°.* O, GU.

1024 —The Quaker no Papist. *Printed, and are to be sold by Francis Smith*, 1659. 4°.* LT, CSSX, CT, LF, WCA; MU, NHC, Y.

1024A [-] Seven arguments to prove. *Printed*, 1643. 8°.* LCL; Y.

1025 **Denne, John.** Εὐαγγελιον της ειρήνης. The glad tidings. *For John Spring*, 1699. 12°. T.C.III 151. L.

1026 —The lawfulnes of mixt-marriages weighed. *By J.D. for the author to be sold by Thomas Fabian* 1681. 4°.* O; WF Y.

1027 —Truth outweighing error. *For the author, to be sold by F. Smith*, 1673. 8°. T.C.I 146. L, O; CN.

1028 **Dennis, John.** The court of death. *For James Knapton*, 1695. fol.* L, O, C, E; CH, CN, MH, TU, WF, Y.

1029 — —Second edition. —, 1695. fol.* T.C.II 550. CH, CU, TU, Y.

1030 —The impartial critick. *For R.Taylor*, 1693. 4°. T.C.II 441. L, O, LG, CS, LVD; MH, OCI, WCL, WF.

1031 —Iphegenia. *For Richard Parker*, 1700. 4°. L, O, LVD, CS, EN; CH, CN, MH, TU, WF, Y.

1032 [-] The jolly, jolly breeze. *[London], T.Cross*, [1700?]. brs. L; CH.

1033 —Letters upon several occasions. *For Sam. Briscoe* 1696. 8°. L, OM, LW, E, DT; CLC, CU, MH, WF, Y.

1034 —Miscellanies in verse and prose. *For James Knapton* 1693. 8°. T.C.II 465. L, O, C, CS; CLC, MH, NC, TU, Y.

1035 —Miscellany poems. Second edition. *For Sam. Briscoe*, 1697. 8°. L, LVD, LW, OC, CCA; CLC, CU, MH, TU, WF, Y.

1036 [-] Morpheus thou gentle God. *[London, 1700.]* fol.* L.

1037 —The nuptials of Britain's genius and fame. *For R. Parker, Sam. Briscoe; sold by R.Baldwin*, 1697. fol.* L, HH; CLC, IU, MH, PBL, TU.

1038 —A plot and no plot. *For R.Parker, P.Buck, R.Wellington*, [1697]. 4°. L, O, CS, LVD, EN; CH, CN, LC, MH, TU, Y.

1039 [-] Poems in burlesque. *For the booksellers of London and Westminster*, 1692. 4°.* L, O, C, CCA; CH, CN, MH.

1040 —Remarks on a book entituled, Prince Arthur. *For S. Heyrick and R.Sare*, 1696. 8°. L, O, C, EN, DT; CLC, CN, MH, TU, WF, Y.

1041 [-] The reverse. *Printed and sold by John Nutt*, 1700. fol.* L, O, HH; CH, CN, TU, WF, Y.

1041A [-] —Second edition. —, 1700. 4*.° DT.

1042 —Rinaldo and Armida. *For Jacob Tonson*, 1699. 4°. L, O, CCA, LVD, EN; CH, CN, LC, MH, TU, Y.

1043 —The seamens case. *[London, 1698–99.]* cap., fol.* O, LL; CN.

1044 [-] A song in the Plot and no plot. *[London]*, 1697. brs. L, MC.

1045 —The usefulnes of the stage. *For Rich. Parker*, 1698. 8°. L, O, C, LVD, E; CH, CN, MH, TU, WF, Y.

1046 **Denniston, Walter.** Ad amplissimos simul. *[Edinburgh, 1698.]* cap., *. L, O; CN, RPJ.

1047 —Gualteri Dannistoni ad Georgium Buchananum epistola. *Edinburgi, typis Jacobi Vatsoni*, 1700. L, C, E, A; MH.

1048 —Ad Mæcenates suos. *[Edinburgh, 1690?]* brs. ALDIS 3033. EN.

1048A —In annum millesimum septuogenti unum. *Edinburgh*, 1700. TU.

1049 —In obitum ... D. Ioannis Lauderi. *[Edinburgh, 1692.]* brs. ALDIS 3217. EN.

1050 —Nobilissimis, clarissimis & reverendissimis viris. *[Edinburgi, 1690?]* brs. ALDIS 3034. L, E, EN.

1051 **[Denny, Sir William.]** Pelecanicidium: or, the Christian adviser against self-murder. *For Thomas Hucklescott*, 1653. 8°. LT, LSC, MR; CH, CLC, CN.

1051A **D[ennys], J[ohn].** The secrets of angling. *By T.H. for John Harrison, to be sold by Francis Coles*, 1652. 8°. LT; CH, MHS, Y.

1052 **Denshall,** . Le reading del Monsieur. *Excudebat I.C. impensis G.Lee, D.Pakeman, & Gabr. Bedell*, 1662. 4°.* L, O, CT, LL; LC, MH, NCL, YL.

1052A **Dent, Arthur.** Lewybr hyffordd yn cyfarwyddo. *Bennet Griffin*, 1682. 12°. AN, CPL.

1053 —The plain man's pathway. 27th edition. *[n.p.], by J. Young for G.Latham*, 1648. 12°. MH.

1054   —The pain-man's [sic] pathway to Heaven. 1654. 12°.
       LCL, BPL.

1055   —The plaine mans path-way to Heaven. *By R. I. for
       John Wright,* 1664. sixes. L; NN.

1055A ——[Anr. ed.] *By E. C. for J. W. and are to be sold
       by John Williamson,* 1674. 12°. NU.

1056   ——[Anr. ed.] *For John Wright,* 1682. 12°. L.

1057   —The ruine of Rome. *By T. H. and I. Y. for Jo. Water-
       son, to be sold by Charles Greene,* 1644. 8°. E; CLC,
       MH, NU.

1058   ——[Anr. ed.] *For Thomas Harper, for John Waterson,*
       1650. 8°. LW; NU, WG.

1059   ——[Anr. ed.] —, 1656. 8°. LT.

1059A —A sermon of repentance. *By J. Raworth for J. Harison,*
       1642. 8°. L.

1060   **Dent, Edward.** Everlasting blessedness. *For W. Mar-
       shall,* 1692. 4°.* T.C.II 422. L, O, LW; NPT.

1061   **Dent, Henry.** A sober and temperate discourse con-
       cerning the interest. 1661. 4°. LCL.

1062   **Denton, Daniel.** A brief description of New-York.
       For John Hancock, and William Bradley, 1670. 4°.*
       L, OC, CT, GH; CH, LC, MH, NN, RPJ.

1063   [**Denton, Robert.**] Berwick's beauty. *Printed,* 1650.
       8°.* LT, O.

1064   **Denton, William.** The burnt child. *For James Magnes
       and Richard Bentley,* 1675. 4°. T.C.I 212. L, O, C, LIL,
       SC; CH, CLC, NU, WF, Y.

1065   [–] Horæ subsecivæ: or a treatise shewing the original
       grounds. *By R. D. for Tho. Basset, and Ja. Magnes,*
       1664. 4°. L, O, LIL, CS, OC; CH, LC, MH, NU, Y.

1066   —Jus Cæsaris. *For the author, to be sold by John Kersey
       and Henry Faythorn,* 1681. fol. T.C.I 457. L, O, CT,
       HH, E; CH, CN, NPT, WF, Y.

1067   [–] Jus regiminis: being a justification. *Printed,* 1689.
       fol. L, O, BAMB, HH, E; CH, MB, MM, WF.

1068   [–] Some remarks recommended unto ecclesiasticks.
       [*London,* 1690?] cap., fol.* L, OC, BAMB, HH, E; CH,
       MM, WF, Y.

1068A [–] The ungrateful behaviour of the Papists. *For James
       Magnes and Richard Bentley,* 1679. 4°.* L, O, YM; TU.

1068B Denus petition to the Lord General Cromwell. *For
       R. H.,* 1651. 4°.* MH.

1068C Denus to the lyon of England. *For H. Hasilwood,* 1651.
       4°.* MH.
       Deo ecclesiæ. 1693. *See* Snowden, Samuel.
       Deodate. *See* Diodate.

1068D The deplorable case of great numbers of masters.
       [*London?* 1693.] brs. L.

1068E The deplorable case of great numbers of suffering
       subjects. [*London,* 1691.] brs. L.

1069   The deplorable case of many poor widows. [*London,*
       1692?] brs. L.

1070   The deplorable case of the chief and other agents.
       [*London,* 1700?] brs. L, LL; MH.

1071   The deplorable case of the officers, inn-keepers. [*Lon-
       don*], 1679. brs. MC.

1072   Entry cancelled.

1073   The deplorable condition of the assignees of sundry
       goldsmiths. [*London,* 1697.] brs. L, LG.

1074   The deplorable condition of the reduced and discharged
       men. [*London,* c. 1698.] brs. L, O, LL.

1075   Deplorable news from Southwark. [*London*], *for Tho.
       Vere,* [1655?] brs. L.

1076   The deplorable state and condition of the poor French
       Protestants. *For Richard Janeway,* 1681. fol.* O, EN;
       CH, WF, Y.

1076A The deplorable state of the kingdom of Ireland. 1696.
       brs. OC, HH.
       Deplorable tragedy of Floris. 1659. *See* Tooke, George.
       Deploratio mortis. [168–.] *See* H., G.

1077   The deponents. [*London,* 1688?] brs. CH, Y.

1078   The deportment and carriage of the German princess.
       For Nath. Brooke, 1672. 4°.* INU, MH.
       Deposition and farther discovery. [1679.] *See* C.

1079   Depositions at the council chamber in Whitehall. [*Lon-
       don,* 1688.] fol.* LIL.

1080   25th June 1700. The depositions of witnesses. [*London,*
       1700.] fol.* HH.

1081   The Debtford frollick. [*London*], *for P. Brooksby,*
       [1683–95]. brs. L, O, CM, HH.

1082   —[Anr. ed.] [*London*], *for P. Brooksby,* [1680?]. brs. L.

1083   The Debtford plumb cake. *For T. Jackson,* [c. 1700.]
       brs. L.
       Depths of Satan. 1649. *See* Cawdrey, Daniel.

1084   The deputies ghost. [*London*], 1641. brs. L, O.

1085   The deputies of the republick of Amsterdam ... con-
       victed. *For Randal Taylor,* 1684. 4°. L, O, P; CH, MH,
       NU, WF, Y.

1086   [**Derby, Charles Stanley, earl of.**] The Jesuites policy
       to suppress monarchy. [*n.p.*], *printed,* 1669. 12°. C,
       OB, YM; MM.

1087   [–] —[Anr. ed.] *A discipulis sub disciplina J. Wisheart,*
       1670. 12°. E.

1088   [–] —[Anr. ed.] *For William Cademan,* 1678. 4°.*
       T.C.I 332. O, LIL, OC, OM, CT; CH, NU, RPJ, WF, Y.
       [–] Lord Castlemain's ... apology. 1667. *See* Lloyd,
       William, *bp.*

1089   [–] The Protestant religion is a sure foundation. *For
       William Cademan,* 1669. 4°. OCC, CE; CH, WF.

1089A [–] —[Anr. ed.] *Printed,* 1669. 4°. OC; CH, NN, PSC, Y.

1090   — —Second edition. *For William Cademan,* 1671. 4°.
       T.C.I 71. L, O, CT, MC, HH; NU, WF, Y.

1090A [–] Truth-triumphant, in a dialogue. *Printed,* 1669.
       4°. O, OC; CH.

1090B — —[Anr. ed.] —, 1671. 4°. O, LF, OC, YM; PH, PSC.

1091   **Derby, James Stanley, earl of.** A declaration of.
       Printed, 1649. 4°.* LT, MR; CH, WF.

1091A —The Lord Strange his demands. *For Th. Cook,*
       October 8, 1642. 4°.* LT.

1092   —A message sent from. *Printed at York by T. Broad,
       and re-printed for W. R.,* 1649. 4°.* LT.

1092A —Orders concluded by the Lord Strange. [*London*],
       printed, December 29, 1642. 4°.* LT, DT; CH, MA, MH.

1093 —The Earle of Darby's speech on the scaffold. *For Nathaniel Brooks, 1651.* 4°.* LT, CT; CH, MIU, Y.

1093A —A true copy of the Lord Strange his warrant. *Printed, 1642.* brs. LT, LS, EC, GK; MH, Y.

1094 —The true speech delivered on the scaffold by. *For Robert Eles,* [1651]. 4°.* LT, OC, CT; CH, MH.

1095 Darby-shires glory. *For W. Thackeray, T. Passenger, and W. Whitwood,* [1670–77]. brs. HH; MH.

1096 **Derham, Robert.** A brief discourse, proving independency in church government. *For Thomas Bates, 1646.* 4°.* LT, O, HH, CCA, DT; CH, MIU, NU, TU.

1097 —A manuell or, briefe treatise. *For Mathew Walbancke, 1647.* 24°. L, O, C, CT, LI; BN, CU, LC, MH, NU, Y.

1098 **Derham, Samuel.** Hydrologia philosophica; or. *Oxford, by Leon Litchfield for John Howell, 1685.* 8°. L, O, C, CT, DT; CH, LC, PL, MU, Y.

1099 **D[erham], W[illiam].** The artificial clock-maker. *For James Knapton, 1696.* 4°. T.C.II 579. L, O, C, OC, E; CLC, MB, PL, Y.

1100 — —Second edition. —, 1700. 12°. T.C.III 221. L, O, LG, BAMB; CH, CLC, CJC, MH, PL.

1101 Entry cancelled.

1102 **Dering, *Sir* Edward.** The works of. 1659. 8°. LCL.

1103 —A collection of speeches. *Printed, 1642.* 4°. L, C, OM, MR, EN; CLC, CN, MH, NU, WF, Y.

1104 — [Anr. ed.] *By E. G. for F. Eglesfield and Jo, Stafford, 1642.* 4°. LT, O, C, EN, DT; BN, CH, CU, MH, NU, WF, Y.

1105 Entry cancelled.

1106 —A consideration and a resolvtion. *For F. Eglesfeild, 1641.* 4°.* LT, C, CSSX, CT; MH, NN, WF, Y.

1107 — —[Anr. ed.] *By Tho: Paine, for John Stafford, 1641.* 4°.* LT, O, CT, E, DT; CU, MH, NU, TU, WF, Y.

1108 —A declaration by. *By J. Raworth for Philemon Stephens. April 1, 1644.* 4°.* LT, O, C, E, DT; CLC, MH, NU, WF, Y.

1109 —The foure cardinall-vertues. *By Iohn Raworth, for Richard Whitaker, 1641.* 4°. L, O, CT, HH; NU, WF, Y.

1110 —The fower cardinall-vertues. *By I. R. for R. Whitaker, 1641[2].* 4°. LT, LG, DT; CLC, MH, WF.

1111 —Foure speeches made by. *For Francis Coles, 1641.* 4°.* LT, O, CT; BN, MBA, MH, WF, Y.

1112 —A most worthy speech of. *For F. C. and T. B., 1641.* 4°.* L, O, C, HH, EN; CH, MH, TU, WF.

1113 — —[Anr. ed.] *For I. W., 1642.* 4°.* L, O, C, HH, E; CH, MH.

1114 — —[Anr. ed.] *For Iohn Franke, 1642.* 4°.* LT, O, C, LL, DT; CH, CN, MH, NU, TU, WF, Y.

1115 —Περὶ ἰδιο-τροπο-Θυσιας. A discourse of proper sacrifice. *Cambridge, for Francis Englesfield, 1644.* 4°. LT, O, C, LCL, DT; CH, CU, MH, Y.

1115A —Sir Edw. Dering revived. *For L. Chapman, 1660.* 4°. OC, DT; MM, NU, PBL, Y.

1116 —The speeches of. [*London*], *printed, 1641.* 4°.* L, O, C, LVF, WCA; CH, CN, NC, TU, Y.

1117 — —[Anr. ed.] *Printed, 1641.* 4°.* E; MB, MIU, NN, WF, Y.

1118 —Three speeches of. *For J. Stafford, 1641.* 4°.* O, HH, DT; CH, NN, WF, Y.

1119 **Dering, Richard.** Cantica sacra. Ad duas. *Typis Guil. Godbid pro Joh. Playford, 1662.* fol. L, CM; LC.

1120 —Cantica sacra: containing hymns. Second sett. *By W. Godbid, for John Playford, 1674.* fol. T.C.I 170. L; LC, MH.

1121 [**Derodon, David.**] The funeral of the mass. *By Andrew Clark, to be sold by Randal Taylor, 1673.* 8°. T.C.I 153. L, O, LIL, CK, E; CH, NN, NU, WF.

1122 [–] —Second edition. *By T. H. for A. Clarke, and to be sold by Randal Taylor, 1677.* 12°. T.C.I 279. L, LCL, OC; CLC, NP, PL, Y.

1123 [–] —Fourth edition. *For Randal Taylor, 1680.* 8°. T.C.I 409. L, P; CLC, LC, MH, NU.

1123A [–] —[Anr. ed.] *Edinburgh, by W. Carron, sold by G. Shaw, 1680.* 12°. ALDIS 2198. EN, I.

1123B [–] —Fifth edition. *For Randal Taylor, 1685.* 8°. L, RPL.

1123C [–] —Seventh edition. —, 1685. 12°. O, OC, CSSX, CT; CLC, NGT, TU, WF.

1124 [–] —"Third" edition. *Dublin, by J. R., for J. Howes, 1685.* 8°. DIX 210. LW, DM, DW.

1125 [–] —Eleventh edition. *For Randal Taylor, 1685.* 12°. O, CT.

1126 The Derry complaint. *Dublin, 1699.* 4°.* DIX 309. DN.

Desainliens, Claude. *See* Sainliens, Claude de.

1127 **Desborough, John.** A letter sent from . . . December 29, 1659. *By John Streater, and John Macock, 1659.* 4°.* LT, O, HH; MH, NN, WF, Y.

1128 **Desborow, Charles.** The case of. [*London, 1698.*] brs. Y.

1128A —Captain Desborow, by his petition. [*London, 1697.*] brs. Y.

1129 [**Descartes, René.**] A discourse of a method. *By Thomas Newcombe, for John Holden, 1649.* 8°. LT, O, CK, LPO, EN; CLC, CN, WF, WU, HC.

1130 Renati Descartes epistolæ. *Impensis Dunmore, & Octavian Pulleyn, 1668.* 4°. T.C.I 6. L, O, C, E, DT; CLC, CU, MH, NC, WF, Y.

1131 —Ethice. *Impensis N. C. & vendit per W. Davies, 1685.* 8°. T.C.II 147. C, CK, OCC; WG.

1132 —Renatus Des-Cartes excellent compendium of musick. *By Thomas Harper, for Humphrey Moseley, and to be sold at his shop, and by Thomas Heath, 1653.* 4°. LT, O, CT, ELY, E; CLC, CN, LC, MH, Y.

1133 —R. des Cartes meditationes. *H. Eversden, 1664.* 4°. CT, GU.

1133A — —[Anr. ed.] *Excudebat J. F. pro Jona Hart, 1664.* 8°. CK, CT; MB, MIU, NC, Y.

1134 —The passions of the soule. *For A. C. to be sold by J. Martin, and J. Ridley, 1650.* 12°. LT, CK, CS, P, GK; CLC, CU, MH, HC.

1135 — . . . Principia philosophiæ. *Excudebat J. F. pro Jona Hart, 1664.* 8°. L, O, CM; CH, MIU, PL, Y.

1136 —Six metaphysical meditations. *By B. G. for B. Tooke,* 1680. 12°. T.C.I 406. L, C, GU, DT, GK; CLC, CU, MH, WF, Y.

1136A —Specrmene philosophae. *Excudebat J. F. pro. Jone Hert,* 1667. 8°. CM; CLC, MIU, NU.

1137 —The use of the geometrical playing-cards. *Printed and sold by J. Moxon,* 1697. 8°. L; Y.

Descent upon France. 1693. *See* Littleton, Edward.

1138 Descriptio rerum gestarum in expeditione. *Typis E. G.,* 1643. 4°.* LT, LW, SS; CH, CN.

Description and explanation. 1653. *See* Adrichomius, Christian.

1139 A description & plat of the sea-coasts of England. *By M. S. for Tho: Jenner,* 1653. 4°. LT, O, LG, CK, BAMB; CN, MH, WF, Y.

Description and use of a portable instrument. 1685. *See* Gunter, Edmund.

Description and use of a quadrant. 1665. *See* Hewlett, J.

Description and use of the carpenters-rule. 1656. *See* B., J.

Description and use of the planetary systeme. 1674. *See* Streete, Thomas.

1140 The description, causes, and discovery, of symptoms of a church Papist. *For J. T.,* 1642. 4°.* LT.

1141 Description des rejouissances faites pour la naissance du Prince d'Angleterre. *[Londres,* 1688.] 4°. L.

1142 A description of a great sea-storm . . . Florida. *By Thomas Milbourn, for Dorman Newman,* 1671. brs. L; CH.

Description of a plain instrument. 1668. *See* Martindale, Adam.

Description of a prerogative. 1642. *See* B., M.

1143 The description of a strange (and miraculous) fish. [1690?] brs. O.

1144 The description of a town miss. *[London], for F. Coles, T. Vere, J. Wright, and J. Clarke,* [c. 1688]. brs. L, HH; WCL.

1145 A description of a wonderful child which was seen at Naples, 1681. [*n.p.,* 1681.] brs. L.

Description of an annuall vvorld. 1641. *See* Browne, Edward.

1145A A description of Bartholomew-Fair. *[London], for F. Coles, T. Vere, J. Wright, and J. Clarke,* [c. 1680.] brs. HUTH.

1146 A description of Buda. *For T. M. and sold by Will. Benbridge,* 1685. brs. T.C.II 99. O, LG.

1147 A description of Candia. *By J. C. for W. Crook,* 1670. 8°. T.C.I 36. L, O, C, LA, E; CLC, MH, MIU, WF, Y.

Description of France. 1692. *See* S., J.

1148 A description of His Majesties true and loyal subjects. colop: *By J. Wallis for Randall Taylor,* 1682. brs. O, EN; CH.

Description of love. 1653. *See* C., W.

Description of Mr. D—n's funeral. 1700. *See* Brown, Thomas.

Description of New-England. [*n.p.,* 1682.] *See* Seller, John.

1149 A description of old England. *[London], for F. Coles, T. Vere, J. Wright, and J. Clarke,* [1665–70]. brs. O. HH; MH.

1150 Entry cancelled.

1151 A description of Tangier, the country and people adjoyning. *For Samuel Speed,* 1664. 4°. L, O; CH, CN, MH, WF, Y.

1152 A description of the academy. *For Maurice Atkins,* 1673. 4°.* T.C.I 136. L, O, A; CH, CN, TU, WF, Y.

1153 The description of the castle of entertainment. *[London,* 1679?] cap., fol.* L, O; CH, MH.

1154 A description of the ceremonial proceedings . . . James. 1685. brs. O.

1154A —[Same title.] . . . William. *By George Croom,* 1689. brs. O; MH.

1155 A description of the city of London. *By John Overton,* 1676. brs. O.

1156 The description of the coronation of . . . K. James II. colop: *By Nathan Thompson,* 1685. cap., 4°.* L, O, OP; CN, MH.

1156A A description of the covenant of grace. colop: *By K. Astwood,* 1699. brs. PL.

Description of the famous kingdome. 1641. *See* Hartlib, Samuel.

1157 A description of the forme and manner of publick thanksgiving. *By Barnard Alsop,* 1641. 4°.* LT, O, CT, SC; MH, NU.

1158 A description of the four parts of the world. *Edinburgh, reprinted,* 1695. 12°.* FSF.

1159 A description of the four seasons. *Rob. Walton,* [1690?] brs. L.

1160 A description of the funeral solemnities, . . . to honour . . . Turenne. *Printed,* 1675. 4°.* L, O, OCC; CLC, MIU, TU, WF, Y.

Description of the grand signor's seraglio. 1650. *See* Withers, Robert.

Description of the great machines. 1661. *See* Ovid.

Description of the island. 1668. *See* G., E.

Description of the last voyage. 1671. *See* Hardy, John.

1161 A description of the late rebellion in the West. *[London], for P. Brooksby,* [1685]. brs. L, O; MH.

1162 A description of the mines in Cardoganshire. [*n.p.,* 1700?] 12° LPO, OC.

1163 A description of the most glorious and most magnificent arches erected at the Hague. *For P. S. and are to be sold by Richard Baldwin,* 1691. fol.* O, OC, SP; HR, CH, CU, WF.

Description of the office of credit, 1665. *See* Chamberlen, Hugh.

1164 A description of the painting of the theater in Oxford. *Oxford, by L. Lichfield,* 1673. brs. MADAN 2956. O.

1165 A description of the pallace court of Westminster. *[London?* 1700.] brs. L.

1166 A description of the passage of Thomas late Earle of Strafford, over the River of Styx. *[London], printed,* 1641. 4°.* LT, O, CS; CH, CLC, WF, Y.

Description of the province and bay. Edinburgh, 1699. *See* Blackwell, Isaac.

Description of the province of New Albion. [*n.p.*], 1648. *See* Plantagenet, Beauchamp.

1167 A description of the rejoycing, celebrated at Paris. *By Edw: Jones*, 1688. brs. O.

1167A A description of the round-head. *For J. Sweeting*, 1642. 4°.* LT, LG; MH.

1167B A description of the royal schole. [*London*, 1699?] brs. Y.

1168 A description of the sect called the Familie of Love. *Printed*, 1641. 4°.* LT, O, WCA; MIU, WF.

1169 A description of the seven united provinces of Netherland. *For Joseph Moxon, and sold at his shop*, 1673. 4°.* T.C.I 119. L, O, GU; LC, MH, WF, Y.

Description of the seventeen provinces. 1672. *See* Guicciardini, Francesco.

1170 A description of the siege of Basing Castle. *Oxford, by Leonard Lichfield*, 1644[/5]. 4°.* MADAN 1705. LT, O, EN, DT; CH, MH, WF.

Description . . . of the weather glass [*Edinburgh*, 1680?] *See* Sinclair, George.

1171 A description of Tredagh in Ireland. *For Joseph Bowers*, 1689. brs. CH.

1172 A description of Vienna. *For Randolph Taylor*, 1683. brs. T.C.II 45. O; CH.

1173 A description of wanton women. [*London*], *for F. Coles, T. Vere, J. Wright and J. Clarke*, [1690?] brs. O.

1174 **Des-Ecotais, Lewis.** Memoirs of. *By W. Godbid, to be sold by Moses Pitt*, 1677. 8°. T.C.I 285. L, O, C, CCA, CT; CLC, NU.

1174A —Of the facility that there is in loving of God. *For W. Crook*, 1680. 12°. T.C.I 392. OCC.

Description discuss'd. [*n.p.*, 1689.] *See* Collier, Jeremy.

Desfournelles. *pseud. See* Cordemoy, Géraud de.

1175 A designe by Captain Barley, and others, to surprize Carisbrook Castle. *By Robert Ibbitson*, 1648. 4°.* LT; CLC, WF, Y.

Designe for bringing. 1641. *See* Forde, *Sir* Edward.

Designe for plentie. [1652.] *See* Hartlib, Samuel, *ed.*

Design of enslaving. 1689. *See* Ferguson, Robert.

Design of part of the book. 1691. *See* Wollaston, William.

Designe to save the kingdome. 1648. *See* F., S.

1176 The designs and correspondencies of the present committee of estates. *For Edward Husband, August 16*, 1648. 4°.* LT, O, C, CT, HH; CH, CU, NU, WF, Y.

1177 The designs of France against England and Holland discovered. [*n.p.*, 1686.] cap., 4°.* L, O, SP; CH, CU, MH, MIU, WF.

1178 The designe of the rebels in Kent. *By J. C.*, 1648. 4°.* LT, LG; MIU.

1179 Designes un-masqued: or the several reasons. *Southwark. by Henry Hils*, 1648. 4°.* LT, O, LG, OC, DT; MH, Y.

Desires and propositions. [1642.] *See* Mills, John.

1180 The desires, and resolutions of the clvb-men of the counties of Dorset and Wilts. *By Tho. Forcet*, 1645. 4°.* LT, O; CH.

1181 Entry cancelled.

1182 The desires of the commissioners of the kingdom of Scotland; that both Houses. [*n.p.*], *printed*, 1649. 4°.* LT, OC, LSG, E, EN; NU, Y.

1183 The desires of the commissioners for the weekly loane to His Majesties horse. *Printed at Oxford by Leonard Lichfield, Feb. 9*, 1643[/4]. 4°.* MADAN 1533. O, DT; Y.

1184 Entry cancelled.

1185 The desires of the countie of Surrey. *By B.A.*, 1648. 4°.* LT; WF.

1186 Desires propounded to the honourable House of Commons. *By Robert Ibbitson*, 1647. 4°.* LT, SP; CH, MH, WF.

1187 [**Desjardins, Marie Catherine Hortense de, *Mme.* de Villedieu.**] The amours of the Count de Dunois. *For William Cademan*, 1675. 8° T.C.I 226. L; WF, Y.

1187A [–] The annals of love. *For John Starkey*, 1672. 8°. T.C.I 86. L, O; CH, CLC, CN, CU, OCI.

1188 [–] The disorders of love. *For James Magnes and Richard Bentley*, 1677. 12°. T.C.I 290. O; CH, MH.

1188A [–] The husband forced to be jealous. *For H. Herringman*, 1668. 8°. T.C., IL, MO; CLC, CN, MH, MU, WF, Y.

1189 [–] Love's journal. *By Thomas Ratcliffe and Mary Daniel*, 1671. 8°. T.C.I 81. L; CN, CU.

1190 [–] The loves of sundry philosophers. *In the Savoy, by T. N. for H. Herringman and J. Starkey*, 1673. 8°. T.C.I 128. O; CH, CN.

1191 [–] The memoires of the life, and rare adventures of Henrietta Sylvia Moliere. *For William Crook*, 1672. 12°. T.C.I 86. L, O; CN, CU, MH, Y.

1192 [–] —the II, . . . last parts. *By J. C. for W. Crooke*, 1677. 12°. T.C.I 281. L, O; CU, MH, WF, Y.

1193 [–] The unfortunate [sic] heroes. *By T. N. for H. Herringman*, 1679. 8°. T.C.I 369. L; CLC, CN, MH, Y.

1194 [**Desmarets de Saint Sorlin, Jean.**] Ariana. In two parts. Second edition. *By Iohn Dawson for Thomas Walkley*, 1641. fol. L, O, C, CT, A; CLC, CN, MH, WF, Y.

[**Desmos, Raphael.**] *pseud.*

—Merlinus anonymous. 1653. *See* Almanacs.

Desolate state of France. 1697. *See* Souligné, de.

D'Espagne, Jean. *See* Espagnes, Jean, d'. 1675.

1195 The despairing lover. [*London*], *for F. Coles, T. Vere, J. Wright, and J. Clarke*, bis. O.

1196 —[Anr. ed.] *By and for W. O. for A. M. to be sold by J. Deacon*, [1684–95.] brs. L, HH.

1197 The despairing lover. A new song. [*London?* 1682.] brs. O; CH, MH.

1197A The despairing lover's address to Charon. [*London*], *for J. Conyers and J. Bissel*, [1685–88.] brs. O, CM.

1198 The dispairing youths grief. [*London*], *for P. Brooksby*, [1686–8.] brs. L, O; HH; MH, WCL.

1199　**Despautère, Jean.** Artis versificatoriæ compendium. *Glasguæ, excudebat Robertus Sanders*, 1667. 12°.* EN.

1200　——[Anr. ed.] —, 1672. 12°.* EN, GU, GB.

1201　—Ioan. Despauterii Ninivitæ grammaticæ institutionis *Glasguæ, excudebat Robertus Sanders*, 1667. 12°. EN.

1202　——[Anr. ed.] —, 1672. 12°. EN, GU, GB.

1203　——[Anr. ed.] *Edinburgi, excudebat Georgius Swintoun*, 1677. 8°. ALDIS 2098. L, EN; WF.

1203A　——[Anr. ed.] *Edinburgi, excudebat Thomas Brown*, 1677. 8°. L, BP; WF.

1204　——[Anr. ed.] *Edinburgi, excudebat hæres Andreæ Anderson*, 1682. 12°. C.

1204A　——[Anr. ed.] *Edinburgi, excudebat Joannes Reid*, 1684. 12°. ALDIS 2450, L.

1204B　——[Anr. ed.] *Edinburgi*, 1689. 12°. GU.

1205　—Syntaxis. *Glasguæ, excudebat Robertus Sanders*, 1667. 12°. EN.

1206　——[Anr. ed.] —, 1672. 12°. GU.

1207　Entry cancelled.

　　　Despised virgin. 1653. *See* Ll., O.

1208　The destruction of plain dealing. *For J. Deacon*, [1695?] brs. L.

　　　Destruction of Troy. 1663. *See* Lefevre, Raoul.

1209　The detection of a Popish cheat. colop: *Printed at Dublin, and reprinted at London*, 1696. brs. L.

1209A　A detection of dangerous and daily practices. [*London?* 1700.] brs. MH.

1210　A detection of some faults. 1662. 8°. L.

1211　A detection of the falshood in a pamphlet. [*London*], *printed*, 1648. 4°.* LT; MH, Y.

　　　Detection or, discovery. 1641. *See* Harlow, Pedaell.

1212　The detestable designs of France expos'd. *For Robert Clavel*, 1689. 4°.* T.C.II 289. L, O, C, MR, DT; HR, CH, CN, MB, WF, Y.

　　　Δετμα Βασιλιχη: a sermon. 1682. *See* S., T.

　　　Detur pulchriori: or. [*n.p.*], 1658. *See* Vaux, Francis.

　　　Deus, et rex. [1675.] *See* Fisher, Payne.

　　　Deus justificatus: or. 1668. *See* Hallywell, Henry.

1212A　**Devarius, Matthæus.** Liber de Græcæ linguæ particulis. *Apud Robertum Beaumont*, 1657. 12°. L, O; CLC, MB, MH, WF, Y.

1213　**Devenish, Thomas.** Certaine observations concerning the duty of love. *By R. Oulton and G. Dexter, for William Larnar*, 1641[2]. 4°.* LT, OC.

　　　Divell a married man. [*n.p.*, 1647.] *See* Machiavelli, Niccolo.

1214　The devil and broker or a chracter of a pawn broker. *For F.C.*, 1677. 4°.* MH.

1215　The devil and his dam. *Printed*, 1661. brs. L.

1216　The devill and the Parliament. [*London*], *printed*, 1648. 4°.* LT, O; CLC, CN, MB, MH.

1217　The devil and the strumpet. [1700?] 8°. O.

1218　The devil in his dumps. *Printed*, 1647. 4°.* LT, O; CN, MH, NU.

　　　Divell in Kent. 1647. *See* Mowlin, John.

1219　The deviil incarnate. [*Oxford?* 1660/1.] 4°.* MADAN 2551. O.

1220　Devil of a wife. 1686. *See* Jevon, Thomas.

1220　The devil pursued: or, the right saddle laid upon the right mare. *For T. Davies*, 1680. brs. L, O; MH, PU, Y.

1221　The devill seen at St. Albons [sic]. [*London*], *printed*, 1648. 4°.* LT, O; CH.

1221A　The devil to pay at Kensington. *For Nathaniel VVest*, [1700?] brs. HH.

1222　The devil turned Quaker. *For John Andrews*, 1656. 8°.* O.

　　　Devil turn'd round-head. [*n.p.*, 1642.] *See* Taylor, John.

1223　The devil upon dun. Second edition. *Nathaniel Brooke*, 1672. brs. L.

　　　Devil was and is. [*n.p.*, 1682.] *See* Fox, George.

　　　Devilish conspiracy. 1648. *See* Warner, John.

　　　Devil's an asse. 1660. *See* B., T.

1224　The devil's cabinet broke open. *For Henry Marsh*, 1658. 4°.* LT, O, LG, MR; CH, CLC, Y.

1225　The devils cabinet-councell discovered. *By H.Brugis. for Hen. Marsh*, 1660. 8°. LT, CT.

1226　The devils conquest. *For S. Tyus*, [1665.] brs. GU.

　　　Divils cruelty, [1663]. *See* Hammond, Charles.

1227　The divels delvsions. *For Richard Williams at St. Albans*, 1649. 4°.* LT, O.

1227A　The devil's journey to London. *Printed*, 1700. fol.* CH, CLC, MH.

　　　Devil's last legacy. 1642. *See* K., W.

1228　The devil's oak. *For C.Bates*, [1685]. brs. L, HH, GU.

　　　Devils patriarck. 1683. *See* Nesse, Christopher.

1229　The devils reign upon earth. *For Iohn Andrews*, 1655. 8°.* LT.

　　　Devills white boyes. 1644. *See* Brathwaite, Richard.

1230　Devol's [Duval's] last farewell. *For C.Bates*, [1670?] brs. L.

1231　Devon SS. ad general quart. session ... secundo die Octobris ... 1683. *By J.C. and Freeman Collins, and are to be sold by Daniel Brown*, [1683.] brs. O, LF; CH.

1232　—[Same title.] sexto die Octobris. *By Freeman Collins, to be sold by Randal Taylor*, 1685. brs. L, LG; CH.

1233　[**Devonshire, William Cavendish, 1st duke.**] Reasons for His Majesties passing the bill of exclusion. *For J.-W. and sold by Langly Curtis*, 1681. fol* L, C, CT, OP, HH; CH, CN, MH, NC, WF, Y.

1234　[–] The true copy of a paper delivered by the Lord De [blank] to the mayor of Darby. *For John Goodman*, 1688. brs. L, O, C, CK, MC; CH, CN, TU, Y.

1235　The Devonshire ballad. *For the assigns of F.S.*, 1681. brs. L, O, LG; MH, Y.

1236　The Devonshire boys courage. [*London*], *for P.Brooksby, J.Deacon J.Blare and J.Back* [1690]. brs. L, CM, HH, GU.

1237　The Devonshire damsels frollick. [*London*], *for P. Brooksby*, [1685–88]. brs. L, CM, HH, GU.

　　　Devotional poems. 1699. *See* Addison, Lancelot.

　　　Devotions: a daily office. 1699. *See* Isham, Zachary.

　　　Devotions. First part. Roan, 1672. *See* Austin, John.

1238   Devotions for the helpe and assistance. [*Oxford*], *printed*, 1644. 8°. MADAN 1626. L, O; Y.

Devotions in the ancient way. Paris 1668. *See* Austin, John.

1239–41 Entries cancelled.

Devotions of the ancient church. 1660. *See* Bernard, Nicholas.

Devotions: second part. [n.p.], 1675. *See* Austin, John.

1242   Devotions to S. Joseph. [*Paris*], *by T. F.*, 1700. 12°. WF.

Devotions, viz. 1655. *See* Aylett, Robert.

1243   The devouring informers of Bristol, &c. [*London*, 1682.] cap., 4°.* L, LF, BR; NN.

1244   The devouring Quaker. [*London*], *for F. Coles, T. Vere, J. Wright, and J. Clarke*, [1674–79.] brs. O.

Devout Christian. 1672. *See* Patrick, Symon.

Devout communicant assisted. 1671. *See* Seller, Abednego.

1244A The devout communicant exemplifi'd. *For Thomas Dring*, 1671. 12°. T.C.I 55. O; Y.

1244B —Fourth edition. —, 1678. 12°. T.C.I 316. O; NU.

1244C —Fifth edition. —, 1682. 12° T.C.I 468. L.

1244D —[Anr. ed.] —, 1683. 12°. O, LW; CLC.

1244E —Sixth edition. —, 1688. 12°. T.C.II 225. C; NC, Y.

1244F —Seventh edition. —, 1700. 8°. L; WF.

1244G — —[Anr. ed.] *For W. Freeman*, 1700. 8°. WF.

Devout companion. 1688. *See* Seller, Abednego.

1245   Devout meditations. *Edinburgh*, 1672. 12°. L.

1245A Devout reflections on time. *Amsterdam, J. van de Velde*, 1687. 12°. L.

Devout soul. 1644. *See* Hall, Joseph, *bp.*

Devout souls. Early exercise. 1200. *See* Crouch Nathaniel.

Dew of Hermon. 1663. *See* Savage, Henry.

1246   **D'Ewes**, *Sir Simonds*. The bill of foure subsidies. *For John Thomas*, 1641[2]. 4°.* LT, O, C, EN, GK; CLC, NC, NU ,WF, Y.

1247   —A compleat journal of the votes. *For Jonathan Robinson, Jacob Tonson*, 1693. fol. L, LVF, LW, ES; CN, LC, NC, OCI, Y.

1248   — —Second edition. *For Jonathan Robinson, Jacob Tonson, A. and J. Churchill, and John Wyatt*, 1693. fol. T.C.II 431. C, CT, BR; CH, LC, PL, WF, Y.

1249   —The Greeke postscripts of the Epistles to Timothy and Titus. [*London*], *printed*, 1641. 4°.* LT, O, C, EN, DT; CH, MBP, MH, WF, Y.

1250   —The journals of all the Parliaments during the reign of Queen Elizabeth. *For John Starkey*, 1682. fol. T.C.I 486. L, O, CE, EN, DT; BN, CH, LC, MH, NU, Y.

1251   —The primitive practise for preserving truth. *By M. S. for Henry Overton*, 1645. 4°. LT, O, C, EN, DT; CH, MH, NU, TU, Y.

1252   — —Second edition. —, 1645. 4°. L, C, LCL, LW, DT; WF.

1253   —A speech delivered . . . July 7th 1641. [*London*], *printed*, 1641. 4°.* LT, O, CS, EN, DT; CH, CN, MH, NU, WF, Y.

1254   —A speech delivered . . . July 27, 1644. [*London*], *printed*, 1646. 4°.* L, O, HH, P.

1255   —A speech made . . . eleventh of January. *For F. Coles and T. Banks*, 1642. 4°.* LT, O, C, HH, EN; CH, CN, MH, NU, WF, Y.

1256   —Two speeches spoken by. *For Thomas Paybody*, 1642. 4°.* LT, O, C, HH; CH, CN, MH, NU, WF, Y.

1256A **De Witte, Peter.** Catechizing upon the Heidelbergh catechism. *Amsterdam*, 1654. LCL.

1257   **Dewsbury, William.** The breathings of life. *Printed*, 1663. 4°.* L, O, LF, BBN; CH, MH, NU, PH, Y.

1258   —Christ exalted and alone worthy. *For Giles Calvert*, 1656; 4°.* LT, LF, BBN; CH, CU, MH, PH, Y.

1259   —The discovery of mans returne to his first estate. *For Giles Calvert*, 1654. 4°.* LT, O, LF, OC; CH, NU, PH, WF, Y.

1260   — —[Anr. ed.] —, 1655. 4°. L, CT, LF, OC; CH, NU, Y.

1261   — —[Anr. ed.] —, 1656. 4°. L, C, CT, LF; CH, MH, PH, Y.

1262   — —[Anr. ed.] *For Thomas Simmons*, 1659. 4°.* L, CT, LF, EN; CH, Y.

1263   — —[Anr. ed.] *For M. W.*, [1665?]. 8°.* L, O.

1264   —The discovery of the great enmity. *For Giles Calvert, at the West-end . . .*, 1655. 4°.* LT, O, LF, CT, BBN; PH, PSC, WF, Y.

1265   — —[Anr. ed.] *For Giles Calvert, at the West end . . .*, 1655. 4°.* L, C, LF, BBN; CH, CLC, NU, PSC, Y.

1266   —A discovery of the ground. colop: *Printed*, 1655. cap., 4°.* LT, O, LF; CH.

1267   —The faithful testimony of. *Printed and sold by Andrew Sowle*, [1689]. 4°. L, C, LF, CT; CH, MH, NU, PH, WF, Y.

1268   —A general epistle. *By William Dewsberry*. Dear friends. [*London*, 1675.] cap., 4°.* L, C, LF, OC, BBN; CH, MH, MU, NU, PH, Y.

1269   —A general epistle, given forth from the spirit of the Lord. [*London*], *printed*, 1668. 4°.* L, O, LF, CT, BBN; CH, MH, MU, PH, Y.

1270   —A general epistle to be read. *For Benjamin Clark*, 1682. 4°.* L, C, LF, BBN; MH, MU, NU, PH, PSC, Y.

1270A —A general epistle to Friends. [*London*, 1686.] 8°. L, LF, BBN.

1271   —The mighty day of the Lord. *For Giles Calvert*, 1656. 4°.* LT, O, CT, LF, BBN; PH, PSC, Y.

1272   —Several letters written to the saints. *Printed*, 1654. 4°.* LT, LF, BBN; CH, MH, NU, PH, RPJ, WF, Y.

1273   [–] This for dear Friends in London. [*London*, 1664]. cap., 4°.* LF, BBN, BP; CH, MH, PH, Y.

1274   —To all nations, kindreds, languages. *For Robert Wilson*, 1660. 4°. brs. L, CT, LF.

1274A [–] To all the faithfull and suffering members. [*London*, 1664.] brs. L, LF; Y.

1275   [–] [Anr. ed.] colop: *Printed and sold by Andrew Sowle*, 1684. cap., 4°.* L, C, LF; PH.

1276   [–] To all the faithful brethren. colop: *For Thomas Simmons*, 1661. 4°.* L, O, C, LF, EN; MH, MU, NU, PH, WF, Y.

1277   [–] To all the faithfull in Christ. [*London*], *printed*, 1663. 4°.* L, O, C, LF; CH, MH, NU, PH, WF, Y.

1278   [–] —[Anr. ed.] —, 1664. 4°.* L; MH, PSC.

1279   —A true prophecy. *For Giles Calvert*, 1654. 4°.* LT; PH.

1280   — —[Anr. ed.] —, 1655. 4°.* LT, O, CT, LF, OC; CH, MH, PH, PSC, Y.

1281   —The word of the Lord to all children. [*London*], *printed*, 1665. 4°.* L, O, LF, BBN; CH, MH, PH, PSC, Y.

1282   —The word of the Lord to all the inhabitants. [*London*], *printed*, 1666. 4°.* L, O, LF, BBN; CH, MH, NU, PH, WF, Y.

1283   —The word of the Lord, to His beloved citty. [*London*, 1663.*] cap., 4°.* L, O, LF, BBN, BP; CH, MH, MU, PH, Y.

1284   [–] The word of the Lord to His church. [*London*], *printed*, 1666. 4°.* L, C, LF, BBN; CH, IE, MH, PH, WF, Y.

1285   [–] The word of the Lord to Sion. *Printed*, 1664. 4°.* L, LF, OC, BBN; CH, MH, MU, PH, Y.

1286   **Dey, Richard.** The right and legall chvrch-warden. *For Thomas Underhill*, 1643. 4°.* LT, O, DT; MH, NU, WF.

1286A   —The tree of mans life. *To be sold by Ro: Walton*, [1655?] brs. Y.

1287   —Tvvo looks over Lincolne. *By T. Paine and M. Simons*, 1641. 4°.* LT, O, CS, P, DT; CLC, NU, WF, Y.

1288   — —[Anr. ed.] *Printed*, 1641. 4°.* LT, LSC, LW, CT; CH, CU, NU, TU, WF.

   Dia poemata: poetick feet. 1655. *See* Elys, Edmund.

   The Diaboliad. 1677 [1777.]

   Diall, wherein. 1648. *See* Granger, William.

1288A   Dialectica. *Impensis John Martyn*, 1673. 8°. T.C.I 136. O, OC; WG.

   Diallecticon. 1688. *See* Poynet, John.

   Dialling made easy. Oxford, 1692. *See* Edwards, Thomas.

   Dialling universal. 1657. *See* Serle, George.

1288B   A dialogue [between M(ary) and J(ames)]. [*London?* 1688.*] brs. L, OC, C; MH, MIU, TU, Y.

1289   A dialogue about the French government. *For Randal Taylor*, 1690. brs. CH, CN.

   Dialogue, arguing. 1644. *See* Woodward, Hezekiah.

1290   A dialogue at Oxford between a tutor and a gentleman. *For Rich. Janaway*, 1681. 4°.* L, O, C, HH, EN, GU; CH, CN, MH, NU, WF, Y.

   Dialogue between A. and B. 1694. *See* Irvine, Alexander.

1291   A dialogue between a blind-man. *By George Larkin*, 1686. brs. O.

   Dialogue between a blind man. [n.p., 1700.] *See* Standfast, Richard.

1292   A dialogue between a Brovvnist and a Schismatick. *For J. Franklin*, 1643. 4°.* LT, HH; CH, MH.

1292A   A dialogue between a burgermaster and an English gentleman. *By J. Southby*, 1697. 8°.* NC.

   Dialogue between a Christian. 1673. *See* Hicks, Thomas.

1292B   A dialogue between a Churchman. 1689. fol.* O.

   Dialogue between a Conformist. 1668. *See* Estwicke, Nicholas.

   Diaglogue between a country gentleman. 1696. *See* Clement, Simon.

1293   A dialogue between a director of the New East-India company, and one of the committee. *For Andrew Bell*, 1699. 4°.* L, LUG; CH, MH, NC, Y.

   Dialogue between a divine of. 1690. *See* Parkinson, James.

1293A   A dialogue between a gentleman and a lady. *For I. Nutt*, 1694. 8°. T.C.III 99. WF.

1294   A dialogue between a late lord major. *Printed*, 1698. brs. HH.

1295   A dialogue between a living cobler, and the ghost. *For H.B. and C. T.*, 1660. 4°.* LP, HH.

   Dialogue between a modern courtier. [n. p.; 1696.] *See* Baston, Samuel.

1296   A dialogue between a monkey in the Old Bayly. colop: *For John Johnson*, 1681. cap., fol.* L, O, LG; CH, MH, WF, Y.

1297   A dialogue between a new Catholic convert and a Protestant. *By Henry Hills*, 1686. 4°.* L, O, CT, E, DT; CN, LC, MH, MIU, NU, Y.

1298   A dialogue between a Papist. [*London*, 1680?] fol.* L, CT; CN, TU.

   Dialogue between a pastor. 1684. *See* Altham, Michael.

   Dialogue between a Protestant. 1678. *See* H., R.

1299   A dialogue between a Quaker and his neighbour. colop: *For the author*, 1699. brs. L, LG; CN, PL.

   Dialogue between a town sherpes [1710]. *See* D'urter, Thomas.

   Dialogue between a sovldier. 1642. *See* Gilby, Anthony.

1300   A dialogue between a Yorkshire-alderman. colop: *For John Smith*, 1683. brs. L, O; CH, CN.

1300A   A dialogue between a young divine. *For Jonah Deacon*, 1683. 8°. CM.

1300B   A dialogue between Adam and John, . . . of Bristol. [*London*, 169–?] brs. CN.

   Dialogue between alkali. 1698. *See* Emes, Thomas.

1301   A dialogue between an East-Indian Brackmanny. *By Andrew Sowle*, 1683. 8°. L; CH, MH, PL, WF, Y.

1302   A dialogue between an Englishman and a Spaniard. *London*, 1690?] brs. L.

1303   A dialogue between an exchange. colop: *For Richard Janeway*, 1681. cap., fol.* C, LG; MH.

1303A   A dialogue between an exciseman. 1659. brs. L.

1303B   A dialogue between Anthony Earl of Shaftesbury. *By W.P. and are to be sold by W. Davis*, 1683. brs. L, O; MH.

1304   A dialogue between Bowman the Tory. [*London*], *for J. Dean*, 1684. brs. O; CH, CLC, MH, Y.

   Dialogue between claret. 1692. *See* Ames, Richard.

1305   A dialogue between death and Doctor Robert Wyld. *Printed*, 1679. brs. L, O, MC, HH; MH, TU, WF, Y.

1306   A dialogue between Dick and Tom. *Printed and are to be sold by Randal Taylor*, 1689. 4°.* T.C.II 256. L, O, C, LG, EC, AU; CH, MH, NPT, WF, Y.

1307   A dialogue between Dr. Sherlock, the King of France. colop: *Printed*, 1691. brs. O, OC, HH; CH, CN, MU.

1308 A dialogue between Doctor Titus and Bedlows ghost. *For I. S.*, 1688. brs. L; CH.

1309 A dialogue between Duke Lauderdale, and the Lord Danby. [*London*, 1679?] brs. L, O; CH, CN, MH, WF, Y.

1309A A dialogue between Father Gifford. [*London?* 1689.] brs. L.

1310 A dialogue between Father P—rs and William P—n. [*London*, 1687?] cap., 4°.* L, LF, OC; CH, MH, PHS, WF Y.

1310A A dialogue between Father Petre's and the Devil. 1688. 4°.* AU; CH.

1310B A dialogue between fidelity. [*London*], *printed*, 1600. 4°.* WF.

1311 A dialogue between Francisco and Aurelia. colop: *For Randal Taylor*, 1690. cap., 4°.* T.C.II 350. L, O, LG, CS; Y.

Dialogue between George Fox, 1700. *See* Young, Samuel.

1311A A dialogue between George Keith. *Printed*, 1700. 8°.* WF.

1312 A dialogue between Hampton-Court and the Isle of Wight. [*London*], *printed*, 1648. 4°. CH, WF.

1313 A dialogue between Hodge and Heraclitus. [*London*], *J. Davies*, [1682?]. 4°. HH; CH, WF, Y.

Dialogue between Jack and Will. 1697. *See* Ridpath, George.

1314 A dialogue between Iack Ketch and his journey-man. *For J. Dean*, 1683. brs. CH, MH.

Dialogue between K. W. [n.p., 1694.] *See* W., K.

Dialogue between life. 1657. *See* Wates, Richard.

1315 A dialogue between Lod. Muggleton and the Quakers. *For J. C.*, 1677. 4°.* MR; PH.

1316 A dialogue between London & Oxford. colop: *Printed*, 1681. brs. L, O, OC; CH, MH.

1317 A dialogue between Mr. Canterbvry. [*n.p.*], *printed*, 1698. 4°.* NU.

Dialogue between Mr. Merryman. 1690. *See* W., T.

Dialogue between Mr. Prejudice. 1682. *See* Wood, Thomas.

1318 A dialogue between Mistris Macquerella, a suburb bawd. *For Edward Crowch*, 1650. 4°.* LT, O; CLC.

1319 A dialogue between Monmouth-shire, and York-shire. colop: *For W. R.*, 1681. brs. O, CT; CH, CN, MH, MIU, WF, Y.

1320 A dialogue between Pasquin and Porforio, two statues in Rome. [1681]. brs. MH, TU.

1321 A dialogue between Philiater and Momus. *For Walter Kettilby*, 1686. 8°. T.C.II 170. O, C, CT, GK; WSG, HC.

1322 A dialogue between riches, poverty. *For Nehemiah Bradford*, 1659. 4°.* LT; NC, WCL, WF, Y.

1323 A dialogue betweene sacke and six. [*London*], *printed*, 1641[2]. 4°.* LT, LVF; CN, NU.

1323A A dialogue between Satan and a young man. *Thos. Parkhurst*, 1700. brs. CN.

1324 A dialogue between Simeon and Levi. colop: [*n.p.*], 1688. 4°.* LIL, OC; NU.

Dialogue between Sir R. L. 1689. *See* L'Estrange, *Sir* Roger.

Dialogue between Sir Roger. Edinburgh, 1696. *See* Ferguson, Robert.

1325 A dialogue between Sophronius and Philobelgus. The second part. colop: *Printed*, 1692. cap., 4°.* O, CT.

1326 A dialogue between the Arch-B. of C[anterbury]. *For L. P.*, 1688. brs. L, C, LG; MH, NN, TU, Y.

1326A A dialogue between the Bishop of Canterburie. 1641. 4°.* YM.

1326B A dialogue between the Bishop of El—y. [*London*, 1691.] cap., 4°.* L; MH.

1327 A dialogue between the confederate princes. colop: *For H. Hills, and T. Jones*, 1691. cap., 4°.* L, O, SP; CH, CLC, WF, Y.

Dialogue between the crosse. [n.p.], 1641. *See* Peachum, Henry.

1328 A dialogue between the D[uchess] of C[leveland] and the D[uchess] of P[ortsmouth]. colop: *For J. Smith*, [1682.] cap., fol.* O, LS, MC, HH; CH, LC, MH, Y.

Dialogue between the devil. [1649.] *See* Bradshaw, Ellis.

1329 A dialogue, between the Dutchess of Portsmouth and Madam Gwin, at parting. colop: *For J. S.*, 1682. brs. L, O, LS, MC, EN; CH, MH.

1330 A diaologue [*sic*] between the E[arl] of Sh[aftesbury]. colop: *For A. T.*, 1681. brs. L, O, MC; CH, IU, MH, WF, Y.

1331 A dialogue between the Earl of Sh—ry. colop: *For J. S.*, 1682. brs. L, HH; MIU.

Dialogue between the flag. 1696. *See* P., W.

1331A A dialogue between the French King. *For R. Baldwin*, 1687. 8°.* LW; MB.

1332 A dialogue between the ghosts of the two last Parliaments. *For Ap. Baks*, 1681. brs. L, O, EN; MH, TU, WF, Y.

1332A A dialogue between the King of France. *For R. Baldwin*, 1685. 4°.* CH, CN, MIU, Y.

1332B A dialogue between the late King James and the Prince of Conty. *For Richard Baldwin*, 1697. 4°.* CT, LW; MB, WF.

1333 A dialogue between the Pope and a phanatick. *Printed*, 1680. 4°.* L, O, C, EN, DT; CH, CN, MH, NU, TU, WF, Y.

1333A —[Anr. ed.] *For H. Jones*, 1681. 4°.* L, C; CH, CN, MH, MIU, WF.

1333B —revived. *For John Kidgell*, 1681. 4°.* T.C.I 430. L, O, MR, YM; CH, MH, WF.

1334 A dialogue between the Pope and the devil. colop: *For S. J.*, 1681. brs. L, LG; MH.

1335 A dialogue between the two giants in Guildhall, Colebrand and Brandamore. *For the authors*, 6161. 4°.* LT, LG; CH, MH.

Dialogue between Timotheus. 1696. *See* Hill, Henry.

1336 A dialogue between Timothy and Titus. *Printed, and are to be sold by Richard Janeway*, 1689. fol.* T.C.II 247. L, O, C, LG; CH, MIU, NU, WF, Y.

1337 A dialogue between Tom and Dick. [*London*], *printed*, 1680. 4°.* T.C.I 422. L, O, LG, CT, EN; CH, MBP, MH, WF, Y.

1338 A dialogue, between Toney, and the ghost of . . . Stafford. *For P. M.*, 1681. brs. L, O, MC; CH, MH.

1339 A dialogue between two burgesses. colop: *Printed*, 1681. brs. L, O, MC, HH; MBA, MH, Y.

1339A A dialogue between two Church of England-men. [*London?* 1687.] 8°.* TU.

1339B A dialogue between two friends concerning. *For R. Baldwin*, 1690. brs. C.

Dialogue between two friends . . . occasioned. 1689. *See* Kennet, White, *bp.*

1340 A dialogue between two Jesuits. [1680?] cap., fol. O; CH, MBA, MH, WF.

1341 A dialogue between two lovers. [*London*], *for F. Coles, T. Vere, J. Wright, and J. Clark*, [1680?]. brs. L.

1342 A dialogue between two members. [*n.p.*, 1699.] fol.* O.

1343 A dialogue between two Oxford schollars. colop: *Printed for H. H. and T. J.*, 1680. 4°.* L, O, OC; CLC, MIU, WF, Y.

1344 A dialogue between two porters. colop: *For A. Banks*, 1681. brs. L, O, HH, MC; CH, MH, NC, TU, WF, Y.

1345 A dialogue between two young ladies. *Printed*, 1696. 4°.* L; MIU.

1345A —Third edition. —, 1696. 4°.* Y.

1346 A dialogve betvvixt a courtier and a scholler. [*London*, 1642.] cap., 4°.* LT, C, OC, EC, HH; CH, MH, VC, WF, Y.

1347 A dialogve betwixt a horse of warre and a mill-horse. *By Bernard Alsop*, 1643. 4°.* 4°.* LT; CH.

Dialogue betwixt a minister. 1687. *See* Freeman, Samuel.

Dialogue betwixt a Quaker. Aberdeen, [1670]. *See* Mitchell, William.

1348 A dialogue betwixt an excise-man and death. *By I. C.*, 1659. brs. LT.

Dialogue betwixt Cit. 1680. *See* P., E.

1349 A dialogue betwixt H. B.'s ghost. colop: *For J. M.*, [1681]. brs. L, O; CH, MH, NN, TU, Y.

Dialogue betwixt Jack. 1697. *See* Ridpath, George.

1350 A dialogue betwixt Lewis and the devil. *By John Wallis*, [1690.] brs. CN; MH.

Dialogue betwixt London. [1644.] *See* S., T.

1351 A dialogue betwixt Mr. State Rogue. [*London*, 1695.] cap., 4°.* OC, CS, CT, MR; CH, CU, Y.

Dialogue betwixt Philautus. 1681. *See* Fullwood, Francis.

1352 A dialogue betwixt Rattlehead and Roundhead. *For T. G.*, 1641. 4°.* LT, EN; MBP, WF, Y.

1353 A dialogue betwixt Sam. the ferriman of Dochet. *Printed*, 1681. 4°.* L, O, LL, CCC, HH; CH, CU, LC, MH, NU, Y.

1354 A dialogue betwixt Sir George Booth, and Sir John Presbyter. *For William Wild*, 1659. 4°.* LT, OC; MH, MIU, PT.

1355 A dialogue betwixt the devil and the ignoramus doctor. [*London*, 1679?] brs. L, O; MH, WF, Y.

1356 A dialogue betwixt the devil and the Whigs. colop: [*n.p.*], *by N. T.*, 1684. brs. O; CLC, MH.

1357 A dialogue betwixt the ghosts of Charls the I, . . . and Oliver. *Printed*, 1659. 4°.* LT, CT; HR, CH, MH, TU.

1358 A dialogue betwixt three travellers. [*London*], *printed*, 1641. 4°.* LT, O, LG; CN, MH, NN, Y.

1359 A dialogue betwixt Tom and Dick. [*London*, 1660.] brs. LT, O; MH.

1360 A dialogue betwixt two friends, Valentius of Frieland. [*n.p.*], *printed*, 1675. 4°.* SP; WF, Y.

Dialogue betwixt two Protestants. 1685. *See* Rawlet, John.

1361 A dialogue betwixt Whig and Tory. [*London*], *printed*, 1693. 4°.* L, O, C, MR, DT; HR, CLC, MH, NU, TU, WF, Y.

Dialogue by way of question. [*n.p.*, 1693.] *See* Freke, William.

Dialogue concerning a pamphlet. 1698. *See* Hill, Henry.

1362 A dialogue concerning the rights of Her most Christian Majesty. *By Thomas Newcomb*, 1667. 8°. O, OC, CM, CT; CH, CN, CU, WF, Y.

1363 A dialogue concerning the times. [*n.p.*, 1688.] cap., 4°.* L, O, CT, BR, EN; CH, NC, WF, Y.

Dialogue concerning women. 1691. *See* Walsh, William.

1364 A dialogue, containing a compendious discourse concerning the . . . West-Indies. *For R. Lownds*, 1655. 8°.* LT.

1365 Dialogue entre un père et son fils. 1688. 8°. LW.

Dialogue in the last opera. [*London*, 1692.] *See* Settle, Elkanah.

Dialogue of polygamy. 1657. *See* Ochino, Bernardino.

1366 A dialogue or, a dispute betweene the late hangman. [*London*, 1649.] brs. LT.

1367 A dialogue or accidental discourse betwixt Mr. Alderman Abell, and Richard Kilvert. [*London*], *printed*, 1641. 4°.* L, O, LG; MH, TU.

1368 A dialogue or discovrse betweene a Parliament-man. [*London*], *printed*, 4°.* L, O, OC; CH, LC, Y.

Dialogue or, discourse. [*n.p.*], 1647. *See* B., O.

1369 A dialogve or, rather a parley betweene Prince Ruperts dogge. *Printed at London for I. Smith*, 1643. 4°.* LT, O; MH, TU.

1370 Dialogue upon dialogue. colop: *For H. B.*, 1681. cap., fol.* L, O, C, MC; CH, MH, WF, Y.

1371 A dialogue upon the burning of the Pope . . . in effigie. *For Richard Janeway*, 1681. fol.* L, O, LG, OP; CH, MBA, NU, WF.

1372 Dialogues between a lover of peace, and a lover of truth. Part I. *For Joseph Watts*, 1688. 4°.* OCC; NGT, Y.

Dialogues between Philerene. 1688. *See* Watts, Thomas.

Dyalogues in English. 1668. *See* St. Germain, *Sir* Christopher.

1373 Entry cancelled.

Dialogues of the dead. 1685. *See* Fontenelle, Bernard le Bouger.

Dialogues of the dead. 1699. *See* King, William.

1373A Dialogues of the dead: in imitation of Lucian. *For R. C. and are to be sold by J. Nutt,* 1699. 8°.* WF.

Dialogues of William Richworth. Paris, 1648. *See* White, Thomas.

Dialogus anonymi. Oxonii, 1680. *See* Erasmus, Desiderius.

Diana, Dutchess of Mantva. 1679. *See* Carleton, Rowland.

1374 Diana's darling. [*London*], for *J. Conyers,* [before 1679]. brs. L, CM, HH; MH.

Diaphanta: or. [n.p.], 1665. *See* Canes, John Vincent.

Diarium, or journal. 1656. *See* Flecknoe, Richard.

1375 A diary of the siege & surrender of Lymerick. *Dublin, Robert Thornton,* 1692. 4°.* DIX 249. L, LVF, DI, DN, DT; CN.

1376 —[Anr. ed.] *For R. Taylor,* 1692. 4°.* L, O, LW, SP, EN; CH, CU, WF, Y.

1377 A diary of the siege of Athlone. *For Randal Taylor,* 1691. 4°.* L, LG; WF, Y.

1378 A diary of the siege of Colchester. *For John Partridge,* 1648. brs. LT, O; MH.

Diary of the siege of Luxembourg. 1684. *See* Donneau de Vizé, Jean.

1379 A diary or weather-journal kept at [blank]. [1685?] brs. L.

1380 **Dias, John.** Look to it London. [*London,* 1648.] cap., 4°.* LT; CN, MH, WF.

Diatriba de Chaldaicis. Oxonii, 1662. *See* Smith, Thomas.

1380A —The resolutions of the Army. [*London,* 1648]. brs. MH, Y.

Διατριβη περι παιδο-βαπτισμου or. 1654. *See* Horne, John.

Διατριβη wherein. 1647. *See* Simpson, Sidrach.

1381 **Dick, John.** A testimony to the doctrine. [*Edinburgh*], printed, [1684.] 4°. L, EN, ENC; NU, WF.

1382 Dick the plow-man turn'd doctor. [*London*], for *C. Dennisson,* [1685–88]. brs. L, CM, HH; MH.

1383 [**Dickenson, Henry.**] The last true newes from Yorke. *Septemb. 7. London for Iohn Wright,* 1642. 4°.* LT, O, YM; MM, Y.

1384 **Dickenson, Edmund.** Edmundi Dickinsoni de chrysopieia. [*London,* 1687?]. 8°. L, LWL; MH, WSG.

1385 —Delphi Phoenicizantes, sive, tractatus. *Oxoniæ, excudebat H. Hall, impensis Ric. Davis,* 1655. 8°. MADAN 2274. L, O, C, E, DT; BN, CH, CU, MH, WF, Y.

1386 —Epistola. *Oxoniæ, e theatro Sheldoniano,* 1686. 8°. T.C.II 169. L, O, CT, OM, OR; BN, WF, WSG, Y.

1387 **Dickinson, Francisco.** A precious treasury of twenty rare secrets. *For the author,* 1649. 4°.* LT.

1388 **Dickinson, James.** A salutation of love. colop: *Printed and sold by T. Sowle,* 1696. cap., 4°.* L, LF, BBN; CH, MH, PH, PSC.

1389 **Dickinson, Jonathan.** Gods protecting providence. *Printed in Philadelphia by Reinier Jansen,* 1699. 4°. EVANS 863. LF, YB; CH, CN, MH, NN, PHS.

1390 ——Second edition. *Printed in Philadelphia; re-printed in London and sold by T. Sowle,* 1700. 89 pp. 12°. T.C.III 169. L, LF; CN, LC, MU, NN, Y.

1390A ——[Anr. ed.] —, 1700. 85pp. 12°. L; CH, CN, PHS, RPJ, WCL.

1391 **Dickson, David.** A brief explication of the first fifty Psalms. *By T. M. for Ralph Smith,* 1653. 8°. LT, C, LCL, LW, E; MH, NU, PL, PPT, TSM.

1392 ——Second edition. *By T. M. for Thomas Johnson,* 1655. 8°. L, EN, GU; NU, WF, Y.

1393 —A brief explication of the last fifty Psalmes. *By T. R. and E. M. for Ralph Smith,* 1654. 8°. LT, C, LCL, EN, AU; MH, NNG, NU, Y.

1394 ——[Anr. ed.] *By T. R. and E. M. for Joseph Cranford,* 1654. 8°. NU, WF.

1394A ——[Anr. ed.] *By T. R. and E. M. for Tho. Johnson,* 1654. 8°. LW, P; Y.

1395 ——Second edition. *By T. M. for Thomas Johnson,* 1655. 8°. L, O; Y.

1396 —A brief explication of the other fifty Psalmes. *By T. R. & E. M. for Ralph Smith,* 1653. 8°. L, O, C, P, EN; MH, NU, PPT, TU.

1397 ——Second edition. *By T. M. for Thomas Johnson,* 1655. 8°. LT, GU; NU, WF, Y.

1398 —A brief exposition of the evangel of Jesus Christ . . . Matthew. *Printed at Glasgow by George Anderson,* 1647, *to be sold at James Grayes buith, Edinburgh.* 4°. ALDIS 1271. C, GM, FSF.

1399 ——[Anr. ed.] *For Ralph Smith,* 1647. 8°. O, RPL, DT; MH, NU.

1400 ——Third edition. —, 1651. 8°. L, O, LW, E, GU.

1401 —Expositio analytica omnium Apostolicarvm epistolarvm. *Glasguæ, excudebat Georgius Andersonus,* 1645. 4°. ALDIS 1186. L, O, C, EN, ENC; CH, MH, NPT, WF, Y.

1402 ——Second edition. *Glasgva, excudebat Georgius Andersonus & vænuntur ab Andrea Crook & Ægidio Calvert,* 1647. 4°. ALDIS 1270. C, CCA, E.

1403 —An exposition of all St. Pauls epistles. *By R. I. for Francis Eglesfield,* 1659. fol. L, O, C, CS, SC; MH, NPT, WF.

1404 —A short explanation, of the epistle of Paul to the Hebrevves. *Cambridge, by Roger Daniel for Francis Eglesfield,* 1649. 8°, L, O, C, CT, E, DT; CH, NU, Y.

1405 [–] The summe of saving knowledge. *Edinburgh, by George Swintoun, and Thomas Brown, to be sould by James Glen, and David Trench,* 1671. 4°.* NU.

1406 —Thereapeutica sacra. *Edinburgi, excudebat Christophorus Higgins,* 1656. 4°. ALDIS 1539. LW, CCA, E, EN; NU, PL, Y.

1407 ——[Anr. ed.] *Impensis societatis stationiorum,* 1656. 4°. LT, O, C, EN, DT; CH, MH, NPT.

1408 ——[Anr. ed.] *Edinburgh, by Evan Tyler,* 1664. 8°. ALDIS 1773. L, O, C, LW, EN; Y.

1409 ——[Anr. ed.] *Edinburgh, by James Watson,* 1695. 8°. ALDIS 3458. L, GU; MH.

1410 ——Second edition. —, 1697. 8°. ALDIS 3661. L, E, EN; CH, NGT, NP, NU, WF.

1411 [–] True Christian love. *Edinburgh, by Andro Anderson,* 1655. 8°.* ALDIS 1530. L.

1412 [–] Truths victory over error. *Edinburgh,* 1684. 12°. ALDIS 2497. LW, E, EN, ENC; CH, NPT, WF, Y.

1412A [–] ——[Anr. ed.] *Printed,* 1688. 8°. GU.

1413 Dictated thoughts vpon the Presbyterians late petitions. [*London,* 1646.] brs. LT, O, LS, OC; CH, MH, Y.

    Dictionarium etymologicum. 1664. *See* Gouldman, Francis.

    Didascaliæ: Discourses. [n.p.], 1643. *See* Ferret, John.

1414 Diddle, diddle, or. [*London*], *for J. Wroght, J. Clark, W. Thackery, and T. Passenger,* [1672–85]. brs. L, CM, HH, GU.

    Diegerticon ad Britanniam. [n.p., 1666.] *See* Gayton, Edmund.

1414A Diego redivivus. *For Abel Roper,* 1692. 4°.* O; CH, CLC, WF.

1415 **Diemerbroek, Ijsbrand van.** The anatomy of human bodies. *For Edward Brewster,* fol. T.C.II 252. L, O, C, OM, GH; CLC, HC, WSG.

1416 ——[Anr. ed.] *For W. Whitwood,* 1694. fol. C, LCS, LM, LCP, GU; CH, CJC, MMO, NAM, WF, HC.

1417 —Several choice histories. *Matthew Keinton,* 1666. 4°. L, LWL; WF.

    Dieu et mon droit, or a brief historical essay. 166–? *See* P., H.

    Difference abovt church government. 1646. *See* Mayne, Jasper.

1418 The difference between an usurper and a lawfull prince. [*London*], *printed,* 1657. 4°.* LT, OC; CN, MH, NU, WF, Y.

    Difference between the church and court. 1674. *See* Lloyd, William, *bp.*

    Difference between the Church of England. 1687. *See* Williams, John, *bp.*

    Difference betwixt the Protestant. [*n.p.*], 1687. *See* Tenison, Thomas, *abp.*

    Difference of the case. 1683. *See* Clagett, William.

1419 The differences in Scotland stil on foot. *For Robert Leybourn,* 1648. 4°.* LT, C, DT; MH, MIU, NU, WF, Y.

    Differences of the time. Edinburgh, 1679. *See* Forrester, David.

    Difficiles nugæ. 1674. *See* Hale, *Sir* Matthew.

    Digby, George. *See* Bristol, George Digby, *earl of.*

    Digby, John. *See also* Bristol, John, Digby, *earl of.*

1420 [**Digby, John.**] Miracles not ceas'd. 1663. 12°.* O.

1420A [**Digby, Sir Kenelm.**] An answer to the declaration of the House. [*London*], 1648. 4°.* NN, WF.

1421 —Bibliotheca Digbeiana. [*London*], *H. Brome and B. Tooke,* [1680.] 4°. L, O, HH; CH, JF.

1422 [–] Chymical secrets. Second part. *Will. Cooper,* 1682. 12°. T.C.II 16. L, LPO, LWL, GU; CLC, NC, OCI, WU.

1423 Choice and experimented receipts in physick and chirurgery. *For the author,* 1668. 8°. L, C, LCS, LPO, GU; CH, MH, MMO, LC, JF.

1424 ——[Anr. ed.] *For H. Brome,* 1668. 8°. T.C.I 2. O, LWL, E, EN; LC, WU, Y, JF.

1425 ——[Anr. ed.] *By Andrew Clark, for Henry Brome,* 1675. 8°. L, O, C, E, AU; CH, MH, NC, WSG, JF.

1425A —A choice collection of rare chymical secrets. *For the publisher,* 1682. 8°. OCI, WU, Y.

1426 —A choice collection of rare secrets. *By the author, for the publisher, sold by William Cooper,* 1682. 8°. T.C.II 16. LWL, C, HH, GU; MH, OCI, WU, Y.

1426A ——[Anr. ed.] *For the author, to be sold by William Cooper, Henry Farthorne, and John Kersey,* 1682. 8°. WF.

1427 —The closet of . . . opened. *By E. C. for H. Brome,* 1669. 8°. T.C.I 3. L, O, OR, GU; CH, LC, VC, WF, Y.

1428 ——Second edition. *By E. C. & A. C. for H. Brome,* 1671. 8°. T.C.I 61. C, CS; CH, LC, NN, WCL.

1429 ——Third edition. *By H. C. for H. Brome,* 1677. 8°. T.C.I 269. L, C, E, GU, AU; CH, LC, NIC, WU, Y.

1430 [–] A discovrse concerning infallibility in religion. *Printed att* [sic] *Amsterdam,* 1652. 8°. L, O, GU; MMO, PPT.

1431 ——[Anr. ed.] *Printed att* [sic] *Paris, by Peter Targa,* 1652. 8°. L; BN, NNM, JF.

1432 —A discourse concerning the vegetation of plants. *By J. G. for John Dakins,* 1661. 12°. LT, O, C, EN, DT; CH, MH, MMO, PL, Y, JF.

1433 Entry cancelled.

1434 —Institutionum peripateticarum pars theorica. Second edition. *Ex officina R. Whitakeri,* 1647. 12°. CM.

1435 —A late discourse made in a solemne assembly. *For R. Lownes, and T. Davies,* 1658. 12°. L, O, C, EN, GK; CH, MH, MMO, NAE, WF, HC.

1436 ——Second edition. —, 1658. 12°. L, O, C, LCP, GH; CLM, MMO. PBL, Y, JF.

1437 ——Third edition. —, 1660. 12°. L, O, C, GK, GU; OCI, MMO, TU, WF, Y.

1438 ——Fourth edition. *By J. G. to be sold by Octavian Puleyn, jun.,* 1664. 12°. L, O, GU; MB, MH.

1439 —Observations on the 22. stanza . . . Spencer. *For Daniel Frere,* 1643. 8°.* L; NU.

1440 ——[Anr. ed.] —, 1644. 8°.* L, O, CT, DC, GK; CH, CN, MH, WF, Y, JF.

1441 —Observations vpon Religio medici. *By R. C. for Lawrence Chapman and Daniel Frere,* 1643. 8°. O, C; CH, CU, MH, NU, HC.

1442 ——[Anr. ed.] *By R. C. for Daniel Frere,* 1643. 8°. LT, O, CT, OCC, GK; CH, LC, MH, MMO, Y.

1443 ——Second edition. *By F. L. for Lawrence Chapman and Daniel Frere,* 1644. 8°. L, O, CP, CLN, GK; CH, CN, MH, WF, Y.

1444 ——Third edition. *By A. M. for L. C. to be sold by Andrew Crook,* 1659. 8°. L, OB, E, GK; CLC, MH, Y, HC.

1445 —Of bodies, and of mans soul. *By S.G. and B.G. for John Williams,* 1669. 4°. L, O, C, LCS, LL; CH, CU, LC, MH, NP, HC.

1446 Entry cancelled.

1447 [–] The royall apologie. *At Paris, [London], imprinted,* 1648. 4°.* MADAN 1978. LT, O, C, EN, DT; BN, CH, CN, MH, NU, WF, Y.

1448 —Two treatises. In the one of which, the nature of bodies. *At Paris, by Gilles Blaizot,* 1644. fol. L, O, C, E, DT; BN, CH, MH, NU, WF, Y,

1449 — —[Anr. ed.] *For John Williams,* 1645. 4°. L, O, C, AU, BQ; CLC, CN, MH, PL, WF, Y.

1450 [–] —[Anr. ed.] —, 1658. 4°. L, O, C, EN, DT; CSU, MH, MU, NU, WCL, Y.

1451 [–] —[Anr. ed.] —, 1665. 8°. L, O, OME, AU; CN, LC, NAE, TU, HC, JF.

1452 Entry cancelled.

1453 **Digges, Dudley,** *elder.* The compleat ambassador. *By Tho. Newcomb for Gabriel Bedell and Thomas Collins,* 1655. fol. L, O, C, EN, DT; BN, CH, CN, LC, MH, WSC, Y.

1454 **[Digges, Dudley,** *younger.*] An answer to a printed book, intituled, Observations upon. *Printed at Oxford by Leonard Lichfield,* 1642. 4°. MADAN 1078. L, O, C, LG, CT; CH, CU, MH, WF, Y.

1455 [–] —[Anr. ed., vpon.] —, 1642. 4°. MADAN 1079. LT, O, C, EN, DT; CH, MBP, NU, TU, WF, Y.

1456 — —Third edition. *[London],* 1647. 4°. HH.

1457 Entry cancelled.

1458 [–] A discourse of sea-ports. *Printed for and sold by John Nutt,* 1700. 4°.* L, O, LUG; CN, WF, Y.

1459 [–] A review of the observations upon some of His Majesties late answers. *Oxford, by Leonard Lichfield,* 1643. 4°.* MADAN 1313. LT, O, C, CT, DT; CH, CN, MH, NU, WF, Y.

1460 [–] —[Anr. ed.] *Printed at York by Stephen Bulkley,* 1643. 4°.* L, CJ, CT, YM.

1461 —A speech delivered in Parliament by . . . concerning the evill consequences. *For Ioseph Doe,* 1643. 4°.* LT, CT, DT; CLC, MH.

1462 [–] The vnlavvfvlnesse of subjects taking up armes. *[Oxford], printed,* 1643[/4]. 4°. MADAN 1508. L, O, C, E, DT; CH, CN, NU, Y.

1463 [–] —[Anr. ed.] —, 1644. 4°. LT.

1464 — —[Anr. ed.] *[London] printed,* 1644. 4°. L, O, OM, CS, EN; CLC, MH, MIU, NU.

1465 — —[Anr. ed.] —, 1647. 4°. L, O, C, DC, DT; CH, CU, MH, WF, Y.

1466 — —[Anr. ed.] *By Thomas Mabb, for William Sheares,* 1662. 8°. L, C, OC, MC, DT; CH, MH, NC, TU, WF.

1467 — —[Anr. ed.] *By Thomas Mabb for Margaret Sheares,* 1664. 8°. C, LCL; CH, LC, NP.

1467A — —[Anr. ed.] *For Peter Parker,* 1679. 8°. OC, SP; LC, MIU, NC.

1468 **Digges, Leonard.** A booke named Tectonicon. *By Felix Kingston,* 1647. 4°. O, LSH, DCH, DT; MB, NC, WU.

1469 —Tectonicon: briefly shewing. *By Richard Hodgkinsonne,* 1656. 4°. L, O; Y.

1470 —Tetonicon: or the art of measuring. Second edition. *For William Miller,* 1692. 4°. T.C.II 397. L.

1471 **Digges, Thomas.** England's defence. *For F. Haley,* 1680. fol.* T.C.II 386. L, O, C, EN, DT; CH, MH, WCL, WF, Y.

1472 Digiti-lingua; or, the most compendious, . . . way. *For P. Buck,* 1698. 4°.* L, O, C, DT; CLC, WF.

1472A Digitus Dei et vex popvli; or, a panegyrical addresse. *For Henry Marsh,* 1660. 4°.* HH; MIU, PL.

Digitus Dei or God appearing. *[n.p.,* 1676.] *See* Augustine, *saint.*

Digitus Dei; or, God's justice. *Londn [sic],* 1649. *See* Nedham, Marchamont.

Digitus testium, or a dreadful alarm. 1650. *See* Hall, Henry.

Dignity of kingship. 1660. *See* Sheldon, Gilbert.

1473 Dilectis nobis in Christo. 1684. brs. OP.

1474 **[Dilke, Thomas.]** All things seem deaf. *[London],* T. Cross, [1698?]. brs. L.

1475 —The city lady. *For H. Newman,* 1697. 4°. T.C.III 27. L, O, LVD, OW, EN; CH, CU, LC, NC, TU, WCL, Y.

1476 —The lover's luck. *For Henry Playford. and Benj. Tooke,* 1696. 4°. T.C.II 569. L, O, LVD, OW, EN; CH, CN, LC, MH, NC, TU, Y.

1477 — —[Anr. ed.] *For H. Newman,* 1696. 4°. WCL.

1478 —The pretenders. *For Peter Buck,* 1698. 4°. L, O, LVD, LGI, EN; CH, CN, LC, MH, NC, Y.

1479 [–] A song in The city-lady. *[London],* Tho. Cross, [1697]. brs. L.

1480 —XXV select allusions, . . . Part I. *For Peter Buck; and sold by R. Baldwin,* 1698. 4°.* L, MU; MH, Y.

1481 **Dillingham, Theophilus.** Status integritatis. *[n.p.,* 1655.] brs. O.

1482 **Dillingham, William.** Ægyptus triumphata. Poema sacrum. *Typis Milonis Flesher, & prostat apud Ric. Royston,* 1680. T.C.I 371. 4°.* L, O, LW, CS, P; CH, MH, NIC, WF, Y.

1483 —The mystery of iniquity anatomized. *For Jonathan Robinson,* 1689. 4°.* T.C.II 284. L, O, C, OB, P; CLC, MH, TU, WF, Y.

1484 —Poemata varii argumenti. *Typis E. Flesher, prostant apud R. Royston,* 1678. 8°. L, O, C, EN, ENC; BN, CH, CU, MBP, MH, NC, WF, Y.

1485 [–] Protestant certainty. *For Henry Mortlock,* 1689. 4°.* T.C.II 272. L, O, C, LIL, OB; NU, TU, WF, Y.

1486 —Prove all things. *Cambridge, by John Field. To be sold by William Morden,* 1656. 4°. L, O, C, CT, EN; CH, CN, MH, WF, Y.

1487 —A sermon at the funeral of the Lady Elizabeth Alston, . . . Septemb. 10. 1677. *For Jonathan Robinson,* 1678. 4°.* T.C.I 288. L, O, C, CS, BP; CH, CN, WF, Y.

1488 —Vita Laurentii Chadertoni. *Cantabrigiæ, typis academicis, prostant venales apud Tho. Dawson, Sam. Smith & Benj. Walford,* 1700. 8°. L, O, C, ENC, DT; BN, CH, NC, NP, PL, WF.

1489 **Dillon, Edmund.** To the kings most excellent Majesty. The humble petitionary poem of. *Printed*, 1664. 4°.* L; CH, MBA.

1490 Entry cancelled.

1491 The dilucidation of the late commotions of Turkey. *By J. B. and publish'd by Randal Taylor*, 1689. 4°.* L, P, DT; CH, MH, WCL, WF, Y.

1492 Dilivium lachrymarum. A review of the fortunate & unfortunate adventurers. *By R. Taylor*, 1694. 4°.* L, DT; CH, MH, NP, WF, Y.

1493 The dimension of the hollow tree of Hampsted. *By E. Cotes for M. S.*, [1653]. brs. LT.

1494 **D[imsdale], W[illiam].** The Quaker converted. *For J. Robinson*, 1690. 4°.* L, O, LF; MBA, MHS, MU, PH.

1495 Ding dong, or Sr. Pitifull Parliament, on his death-bed. [*London*], *printed*, 1648. 4°.* LT, O, CT; CH, MM, TU, Y.

1496 **Dingley, Robert.** The deputation of angels. *By T. R. for Edw. Dod*, 1654. 8°. LT, LCL, LW, CE, A; MH, NPT, NU, WF, Y.

1497 —Divine opticks. *By J. M. for H. Cripps and L. Lloyd*, 1655. 8°. LT, O, OC; CLC, INU, MH, NPT, NU.

1498 —A glimps of Christ. *By M. Simmons for Thomas Eglesfeild*, 1651. 8°. LT, LCL, LSC, EC; CLC, MH, NPT, NU.

1499 Entry cancelled.

1500 —A sincere believer. 1656. 8°. LCI.

1501 —The spirituall taste described. *By Matthew Simmons*, 1649, 48. 8°. L, O, LCL; CH, MH, NU, WF, Y.

1502 —Vox coeli; or. philosophical, . . . observations. *By M. S. for Henry Cripps*, 1658. 8°. LT, O, C, LCL; CLC, NPT, NU, WF, Y.

1503 [**Dingley, William.**] Poems on several occasions: originals. [*n.p.*], *printed*, 1694. *And are to be sold by most booksellers.* 8°. L, O, CK; CH.

Diocesan churches. 1682. *See* Clarkson, David.

1504 **Diodate, Giovanni.** An answer sent to the ecclesiasti-call assembly. *Genevah* [*Newcastle*]. *Printed*, 1646. 4°.* L, C, E, EN; CN, MH, NU, Y.

1505 ——[Anr. ed.] *Newcastle: by Stephen Bulkley*, 1647. 4°.* LT, O, C, HH, EN; CH, CU, NU, TU, WF.

1506 —Pious and learned annotations. Second edition. *By Miles Flesher, for Nicholas Fussell*, 1648. 8°. L, O, LW, CK, MR; MH, NIC, RBU, Y.

1507 ——Third edition. *By James Flesher, for Nicholas Fussell*, 1651. fol. L, LW, CT, E, DT; CN, MBC, MH, NU, WF, Y.

1508 ——Fourth edition. *By T. Roycroft, for N. Fussell*, 1664. 4°. L, O, C, CT, ENC; MU, NU, WF.

1508A ——"Fourth" edition. *For Nicholas Fussell*, 1664. 4°. OC.

1509 —Pious annotations. 1642. 4°. ENC.

1510 ——[Anr. ed.] *By T. B. for Nicholas Fussell*, 1643. 4°. L, LW, DCH, GU; CH, CN, WF, Y.

1511 —A reply to a letter printed at Newcastle. *By J. C.*, 1646. 4°.* LT, O, C, LG, DT; Y.

1512 **Diodorus Siculus.** The historical library of. *By Edw. Jones for Awnsham and John Churchill, and E. Castle*, 1700. fol. T.C.III 170. L, OME, C, E, DT; CH, LC, MH, WCL, Y.

1513 —The history of. *By John Macock for Giles Calvert*, 1653. fol. L, C, LW, CS, SC; CH, CN, LC, MH, PL, Y.

1514 Entry cancelled.

1515 **Diogenes Laertius.** . . . Περὶ Βίων, . . . de vitis dog-matis. *Impensis Octaviani Pulleyn, typis Tho. Ratcliffe*, 1664. fol. L, O, C, LW, MR; BN, CH, PL, WF, Y.

1516 —The lives, opinions, and remarkable sayings of. vol. I. *For Edward Brewster*, 1688. 8°. T.C.II 206. L, O, C, CS, ES; CH, CU, LC, PL, Y.

1517 ——[Anr. ed.] *For R. Bently, W. Hensman, J. Taylor, and T. Chapman*, 1696. 2 v. 8°. L, O, C, EN, DT; BBE, MH, PL, WF, Y.

Diogenes lanthorne. 1659. *See* Rowlands, Samuel.

1518 **Dion Cassius.** The Emperor Augustus his two speeches. *For J. B.*, 1675. 4°.* O; CH, CLC, MH, WF, Y.

1518A —An oration of Agrippa. *For Livewell Chapman*, 1657. 4°.* LT; NU, Y.

1519 **Dionysius** *Periegetes.* Οικουμενης . . . Orbis descriptio. *Excudebat R. Daniel, impensis Humphredi Robinson*, 1658. 8°. LT, O, C, E, DT, CH, CU, MB, WF, Y.

1520 ——[Anr. ed.] *Apud Joannem Redmayne*, 1668. 8°.* C.

1521 ——[Anr. ed.] *Typis M. Clark, impensis J. Martyn*, 1679. 8°. T.C.I 344. L, CPE, E, ENC, DT; CU, MH, OCI, WCL, Y.

1522 ——[Anr. ed.] *Typis M. Clark, impensis R. Littlebury, R. Scott, T. Sawbridge & G. Wells*, 1688. 8°. L, O, C, LVD, EN; LC, MH, NC, WF, Y.

1523 ——[Anr. ed.] *Oxoniæ, e theatro Sheldoniano, prostant apud S. Smith & B. Walford, Londinensis*, 1697. 8°. T.C.III 14. L, O, C, LVD, MR; CH, LC, MH, NC, Y.

1524 **Dionysius Syrus.** A clear and learned exposition of. *Dublin: by Samuel Lee*, 1695. 4°. L, C, DM.

1525 —The exposition of. *Dublin, for Joseph Wilde*, 1672. 4°. DIX 147. L, O, OB, CT, DI; WF.

Diotrephes catechised. 1646. *See* Prynne, William.

Diotrephes detected. 1658. *See* T., E.

Diotrephes his dialogues. 1661. *See* Womock, Laurence.

Dipper plung'd. [*n.p.*], 1672. *See* Whitehead, George.

1525A A direct road to peace. *For the author*, 1696. 4°.* MM, NU.

1526 A direction for a publick profession. [Cambridge, Mass. *See* Higginson, John.

1527 A direction for the English traviller, by which he shal be inabled to coast about all England and Wales. [*London*], *by Thomas Jenner*, 1643. 12°. L, O, LPO; CH, MH, WF, Y.

1528 ——[Anr. ed.]. *Printed, and are to be sold by John Garrett*, [1677]. 12°. T.C.I 275. L, O, OC; CH, MH, NN, WF.

Directions about preparing. 1669. *See* B., T.

1528A Directions by way of alphabet. *Printed*, 1674. 8°.* MH.

1529 Directions concerning preachers. colop: *John Bill and Christopher Barker*, 1662. cap., fol.* WCL.

1529A —[Anr. ed.] colop: *Charles Bill, Henry Hills and Thomas Newcomb*, 1685. 4°. O, OC, CT, P; CH, CN.

1529B —[Anr. ed.] *Dublin, by Joseph Ray, for Robert Thornton*, 1686. 4°.* DIX 221. C, DT.

Directions concerning the matter. 1671. *See* Arderne, James.

1530 Entry cancelled.

Directions for behaviour [1685]. *See* Seneca Lucius Annoeus.

1531 Directions for brewing malt liquors. *For J. Nutt*, 1700. 12°.* T.C.III 217. L, C; CLC, NN, WF.

1532 Directions for damosels. [*London*], *for J. Deacon*, [1685–88]. brs. L, HH; MH.

Directions for prayer. [n.p., 1686.] *See* Ken, Thomas, *bp*.

1533 Directions for the cure and prevention of the plague. *J. Bill and C. Barker*. 1665. 4°. O, OR.

1534 Directions for the due observation of the Lord's Day. *For Thomas Dring*, 1682. 12°.* T.C.III 2. L.

Directions for the education. 1673. *See* Du Moulin, Peter.

Directions for the Latine tongue. 1681. *See* Merryweather, John.

1535 Directions for the Lords and Commons . . . 19 Aug. 1645. *For J. Wright, August 20, 1645*. 4°.* HH.

Directions for the prevention. 1665. *See* Wharton, Thomas.

Directions for the right receiving. 1679. *See* B., J.

1536 Directions for the use of this famous, admirable and never-failing cordial drink. [*n.p.*, 1673.] brs. O.

Directions for writing. 1656. *See* D., G.

Directions for young students. 1673. *See* Owen, John.

Directions left by a gentleman. 1670. *See* Reeve, Gabriel.

1536A Directions of the committee appointed. [*London*, 1644.] brs. L.

Directions propovnded. 1641. *See* Udall, Ephraim.

1537 Directions shewing how a fit . . . government. 1659. 4°. DT.

Directions to a painter. [*n.p.*], 1667, *See* Marvell, Andrew.

1538 Directions to Fame, about an elegy on . . . Thomas Thynn. *By J. S. and are to be sold by Richard Baldwin*, 1682. 4°.* L, O; CH, MH, TU, WF, Y.

1538A Directions to masters of ships. [*Edinburgh?* 1700.] brs. HH.

1539 Directions to our arch-bishops. *By Charles Bill, and the executrix of Thomas Newcomb*, 1695. 4°.* L, O, C, OC, CT; CLC, MB, NU, WF, Y.

1540 Directions to Robert Earl of Essex. *By A. Norton for Richard Best. October 6*, 1642. 4°.* O, EC, HH, SS; MH, MIU, Y.

1541 Directorium cosmeticum: or. *By George Larkin*, 1684. brs. O.

1542 A directory for church-government. *Edinburgh: by Evan Tyler*, 1647. 4°.* EN; CLC, MM, NU, WF, Y.

1542A —[Anr. ed.] *Edinburgh, by the society of stationers*, 1690. 4°.* ALDIS 3035. EN, GU; AN.

1543 A directory for the female-sex. *By George Larkin*, 1684. brs. L.

1543A —A directory for the publike vvorship of God. *For the good of the Commonwealth*, 1644. 44 pp. 4°.* V.

1544 —[Anr. ed.] *For Evan Tyler, Alexander Fifield, Ralph Smith, and John Field*, 1644[5.] 86 pp. 4°. LT, O, C, MR, EN; CH, CN, LC, TU, WSC, Y.

1545 —[Anr. ed.] —, 1644. 40 pp. 4°.* O, C, CT, CC; CH, MBA, MH, NU, UC; Y.

1546 —[Anr. ed.] —, 1645. 4°. O, C.

1547 —[Anr. ed.] *For the company of stationers*, 1645. 4°. CT, EC; CH, MB, PL.

1548 —[Anr. ed.] *By G.M. and I.F. for the company of stationers*, 1645. 4°.* CSSX, OC; PL, V, TU.

1549 —[Anr. ed.] *Edinburgh: by Evan Tyler*, 1645. 4°. ALDIS 1187. L, O, LCL, E, DT; CLC, NPT, NU, TU.

1550 —[Anr. ed.] *By M.B. and A.M. for the company of stationers*, 1646. 4°.* CT, BR, MR; CLC, MH, NU, PL.

1551 —[Anr. ed.] *By G.M. and J.F. for the company of stationers*, 1646. 4°.* L, O, CT, HH, EN; CN, MIU, TU, Y.

1551A —[Anr. ed.] *By T.R. and E.M. for the company of stationers*, 1651. 4°.* L, C, OCC, CT; WCH; CN, NU, WCL, WF.

1552 —[Anr. ed.] *By J.M. for the company of stationers*, 1652. 4°.* L, DC; NU.

1553 —[Anr. ed.] *By T.R. & E.M. for the company of stationers*, 1656. 4°. NU.

1553A —[Anr. ed.] *By Tho. Ratcliffe, for the company of stationers*, 1660. 4°. CH.

Directory of church-government. 1644. *See* Travers, Walter.

1554 A directory to Christian perfection. *By Matthew Simmons*, 1650. 4°.* LG, OC, CS, CT, DT; CN, NU, TU, WF.

1555 A dirge for the directory. *Oxford, by Leonard Lichfield, of Oxford*, 1645. 4°.* MADAN 1793. LT, O, CE, DT; MM.

Dirgelwch'rai iw ddeall. [1653?] *See* Llwyd, Morgan.

1556 **Dirltoun, *Sir* John Nisbet**. Catalogue of . . . books. *Edinburgh, Mosman*, 1690. 4°. ALDIS 3028. EN.

1557 —Some doubts & questions in the law. *Edinburgh, Mosman*, 1698. fol. ALDIS 3767. L, E, EN, DT; CH, MH, NCL, TU, YL.

1558 **[Dirrecks, Geertruyde Niessen.]** An epistle to be communicated to Friends. [*n.p.*, 1677.] 4°.* LF; MU, NU, PH, PSC.

Dirt wip't off. 1672. *See* Fowler, Edward.

Disbrowe. *See* Desborough, John.

Disce mori, learn to dye. 1662. *See* Sutton, Christopher.

1559 The discipline and order of particular churches. 1699. 8°. O.

1560 The discipline of gathered churches. *For R. Ibbitson*, 1654. 12°. LT.

1561 Discipline pour l'église françoise. *Dublin, Joseph Ray*, 1695. 4°.* DIX 270. DI.

Dis-colliminium or. 1650. *See* Ward, Nathaniel.

Discommendatory verses, on those which are truly commendatory. 1700. *See* Blackmore, *Sir* Richard.

1562 Entry cancelled.

1563   The disconsolate reformado. *Printed*, 1647. 4°.* LT, YM,
        DT; CH, CLC, WF.

1564   The discontented conference betwixt the two great
        associates. [*London*], *printed*, 1641. brs. LT, O, LVF, HH;
        CN, TU, WF.

1565   —[Anr. ed.] —, 1641. fol.* O, HH; CH, Y.

1566   The discontented lady. [1685?]. *See* Urduy, Thomas.

1566A   The disconted [*sic*] lover. *For Richard Harper*, [1643?]
        brs. MH.

1567   The discontented plow-man [*London*], *for F. Coles. T.
        Vere, I. Wright, and I. Clarke*, [1680]. brs. L, O; MH.

        Discorso delle cose. Napoli [*Edinburgh*], 1698. *See*
        Fletcher, Andrew.

        Discours contre. 1685. *See* Tillotson, John.

        Discovrse about a scrvpvlovs. 1684. *See* Calamy, Ben-
        jamin.

        Discourse about ceremonies. 1696. *See* Gailhard, John.

        Discourse about church-unity. 1681. *See* Sherlock,
        William.

        Discourse about civil government. Cambridge [*Mass.*],
        1663. *See* Davenport, John.

1568   A discourse about conscience. *For William Crooke*,
        1684. 4°.* T.C.II 42. L, O, C, OC, OCC; CH, MH, NU,
        WF, Y.

        Discourse about discerning. [n.p.], 1687. *See* Smith,
        Thomas.

        Discourse about edification. 1683. *See* Hascard,
        Gregory.

        Discourse about keeping. 1696. *See* L., E.

1569   A discourse about raising men. *For Richard Baldwin*.
        1696. 4°.* L; CH, MH, WF.

        Discourse about the charge. 1683. *See* Hascard,
        Gregory.

        Discourse about the pretious blood. 1646. *See* Moore,
        Thomas.

        Discourse about trade. [n.p.], 1690. *See* Child, *Sir*
        Josiah.

        Discourse about tradition. 1683. *See* Patrick, Symon,
        bp.

1570   A discourse against profane swearing. *Dublin; for
        Matthew Gunn*, 1698. 4°.* DIX 305. L, DK, DT.

        Discourse against purgatory. 1685. *See* Hartcliffe, John.

        Discourse against transubstantiation. 1675. *See* C., J.

        Discourse against transubstantiation. 1684. *See* Tillot-
        son, John, *abp.*

        Discourse against unequal marriages. 1696. *See* Bufford,
        S.

1571   The discourse and sad complaints betwixt the French-
        man. *By Bernard Alsop*, 1646. 4°.* LT, DT, LFEA.

        Discourse and views. 1663. *See* Berekley, *Sir* William.

1572   A discourse betweene a resolved, and a doubtful
        Englishman. [*London*, 1642.] cap., 4°.* LT, HH; CH,
        CSS, MH, NN, Y.

1573   A discourse between a Romanist and an English-man.
        For R. Janeway, 1681. fol.* T.C.II 475. L, O, GU;
        CH, MH, NU, WF, Y.

1574   A discourse between a statesman. 1681. 4°.* O.

1575   A discourse betwixt Alexander the Great. 1688. 4°.
        EN.

1576   A discourse betwixt Calvin. [n.p.], 1641. 4°. O.

        Discourse (by way of . . .). 1695/6. *See* C., W.

        Discourse concerning a guide. 1683. *See* Tenison,
        Thomas, *abp.*

        Discourse concerning a judge. 1686. *See* Sherlock,
        William.

        Discourse concerning a lumber-office. 1696. *See*
        Morton, Charles.

        Discourse concerning auricular. 1648 [*i.e.*, 1684]. *See*
        Goodman, John.

1577–8 Entries cancelled.

        Discourse concerning banks. [n.p., 1697.] *See* Janssen,
        Sir Theodore.

        Discourse concerning bodily worship. 1650. *See* G., S.

        Discourse concerning conscience. 1684. *See* Sharp, John.

        Discourse concerning divine providence. 1693. *See*
        Smith, Thomas.

        Discourse concerning evangelical love. 1672. *See* Owen,
        John.

1579   A discourse concerning excommunication. *For Tho.
        Parkhurst*, 1680. 4°.* L, MR, EC, P, E; CH, MIU, NU,
        WF, Y.

        Discourse concerning generosity. 1693. *See* Somers,
        John Somers, *lord.*

1580   A discourse concerning God's foreknowledge. *Printed*,
        1697. 8°. DT.

1581   A discourse concerning high treason. *By T.B. for
        Richard Mead*, 1683. fol.* L, O, C, HH, GU; CH, LC,
        MBA, MM, TU, Y.

        Discourse concerning infallibility. Amsterdam, 1652.
        See Digby, *Sir* Kenelm.

        Discourse concerning invocation. 1664. *See* Freeman,
        Samuel.

        Discourse concerning Ireland. 1697/8. *See* Brewster,
        Sir Francis.

        Discourse concerning Lent. 1695. *See* Hooper, George,
        bp.

        Discourse concerning liberty. 1661. *See* Pett, *Sir* Peter.

        Discovrse concerning liturgies. [n.p.], 1662. *See* Owen,
        John.

        Discourse concerning militia's. 1697. *See* Fletcher,
        Andrew.

        Discourse concerning miracles. Antwerp, 1674. *See*
        Worsley, Edward.

        Discourse concerning natural. 1696. *See* Nye, Stephen.

        Discourse concerning penance. 1688. *See* Allix, Pierre.

        Discourse concerning Popish perjurers. 1681. *See*
        Beane, Richard.

        Discourse concerning prayer. 1686. *See* Patrick,
        Symon, *bp.*

        Discourse concerning prayer ex tempore. [n.p.], 1646.
        See Taylor, Jeremy, *bp.*

1582   A discourse concerning prophane swearing. *Dublin,
        by Jos. Ray, for Matthew Gunne*, 1697. 4°.* DIX 292.
        L, LW, C, CD, DW.

Discourse concerning Puritans. [n.p.], 1641. *See* Ley, John.

Discourse concerning schools. 1663. *See* Nedham, Marchemont.

Discourse concerning supreme power. 1680. *See* Monson, *Sir* John.

Discourse concerning the adoration. 1685. *See* Payne, William.

1583 A discourse concerning the affaires of Ireland. *For Giles Calvert*, 1650. cap., 4°.* LT, LFEA; MH, Y.

Discourse concerning the basis. 1667. *See* Theobald, Francis.

Discourse concerning the beauty. 1679. *See* Allestree, Richard.

Discourse concerning the celebration. 1685. *See* Williams, John, *bp.*

Discourse concerning the celibacy. Oxford, 1687. *See* Woodhead, Abraham.

Discourse concerning the devotions. 1685. *See* Stanley, William.

1583A A discourse concerning the divine dreams. 1676. 8°. O.

1584 A discourse concerning the East-India trade. colop: *For Richard Baldwin*, 1693. 4°.* L; NC, WF, Y.

Discourse concerning the Ecclesiastical commission. 1689. *See* Tenison, Thomas, *abp.*

Discourse concerning the engagement. 1650. *See* W., N.

Discourse concerning the execution. Edinburgh, 1700. *See* Cullen, *Sir* Francis Grant.

1585 A discourse concerning the fishery. *For the company of the royal fishery of England*, 1695. 4°.* L, O, MR; CH, CU, MH, NN, WF, Y.

1586 —[Anr. ed.] *Edinburgh reprinted, Mosman*, 1695. 4°.* ALDIS 3459. LUG, EN; Y.

Discourse concerning the foundation. 1688. *See* Merinbourg, Louis.

Discourse concerning the great benefit. [n.p.], 1641. *See* L., I.

1587 Entry cancelled.

Discourse concerning the holy fast. 1686. *See* Francis, William.

Discourse concerning the illegality. 1689. *See* Stillingfleet, Edward, *bp.*

1587A A discourse concerning the invocation. 1684. 4°. O.

Discourse, concerning the interest. 1661. *See* D., H.

Discourse concerning the laws. 1682. *See* Barlow, Thomas, *bp.*

Discourse concerning the love. 1696. *See* Masham, *Lady* Damaris.

Discourse concerning the merit. 1688. *See* Allix, Pierre.

Discourse concerning the nature of idolatry. 1688. *See* Wake, William, *abp.*

1588 A discourse concerning the nature, power, and proper effects. *For J.L. and are to be sold by Richard Baldwin*, 1689. 4°.* T.C.II 276. L, O, C, EN, DT; CH, LC, MH, NC, RPJ, Y.

Discourse concerning the necessity. 1685. *See* Stratford, Nicholas, *bp.*

1589 A discourse concerning the nominal and real Trinitarians. [*London*], *printed*, 1695. 4°.* L, O, OC, BAMB, DT; CH, MH, NU, WF, Y.

Discourse concerning the object. 1685. *See* Sherlock, William.

Discourse concerning the operations. 1678. *See* Clagett, William.

Discourse concerning the original. 1674. *See* Stephens, Edward.

Discourse concerning the period. 1677. *See* Allestree, Richard.

Discourse concerning the precedency. 1664. *See* Howell, James.

Discourse concerning the pretended. 1687. *See* Clagett, William.

Discourse concerning the queries. 1648. *See* H., W.

Discourse concerning the rebellion. 1642. *See* S., M.

Discourse concerning the rise. 1699. *See* Calamy, Edmund.

1589A Discourse concerning the sacrament of extreme unction. 1687. 4°. CCL.

Discourse concerning the second Council. 1688. *See* Comber, Thomas.

Discourse concerning the significance. [n.p., 1689.] *See* Downes, Theophilus.

Discourse concerning the solemne league. [*n.p.*], 1661. *See* D., J.

Discourse concerning the svccesse. 1642. *See* May, Thomas.

Discovrse concerning the trve notion. 1642. *See* Cudworth, Ralph.

Discourse concerning the unity. 1684. *See* Cave, William.

Discourse concerning the unreasonableness. 1689. *See* Stillingfleet, Edward, *bp.*

Discourse concerning the worship of God. 1682. *See* Penton, Stephen.

Discourse concerning the worship of the blessed Virgin. 1686. *See* Clagett, William.

1590 A discourse concerning trade. colop: *Printed and sold by Andrew Sowle*, 1689. cap. 4°.* Y.

Discourse concerning trade. 1689. *See* Child, *Sir* Josiah.

Discourse concerning transubstantiation. 1688. *See* Burnet, Gilbert, *bp.*

Discourse concerning zeal. Dublin, 1700. *See* Hamilton, William.

1591 Entry cancelled.

A discourse, consisting of motives for the enlargement . . . of trade. . . . The first part. *See* Johnson, Thomas.

1592 A discourse discovering some mysteries of our new state. *Oxford, by Leonard Lichfield*, 1645. 4°.* MADAN 1816. LT, O, C, CT, P; CH, MB, NU, WF.

Discourse for a king. 1660. *See* C., W.

1593 A discourse for taking off the tests and penal laws about religion. *Printed, and are to be sold by Randal Taylor*, 1687. 4°. L, O, CT, MC, DT; CH, CU, MH, NU, WF, Y.

Discourse in defence of infants-baptism. 1651. *See* C., G.

Discourse in defense of the Londoners last petition. [1642.] *See* B., H. G. C.

Discourse in derision. [*n.p.*, 1644.] *See* Grantham, Thomas.

Discourse in vindication of Bp. Bramhall. 1673. *See* Parker, Samuel.

1593A A discourse of a citizen of Paris. *For Octavian Pulleyn, junior,* 1665. 4°. CCA, OC, DCH, P; Y.

Discourse of a method. 1649. *See* Descartes, René.

Discourse of a true English-man. 1644. *See* Kilvert, Richard.

Discourse of an unconverted man's enmity. 1700. *See* Howe, John.

Discourse of artificial beauty. 1662. *See* Gauden, John, *bp.*

Discourse of auxiliary beauty. [*n.p.*], 1656. *See* Gauden, John, *bp.*

1594 A discourse of comets. 1684. 8°. LW.

Discourse of conscience. 1685. *See* Sharp, John, *abp.*

1595 A discourse of courage. [*London*], *printed,* 1690. 4°.* L.

1596 —[Anr. ed.] *For S. M.,* 1690. 4°.* L.

Discourse of divine assistance. 1679. *See* Allen, William.

Discourse of duels. 1687. *See* Comber, Thomas.

Discourse of Dunkirk. 1664. *See* Howell, James.

Discourse of earthquakes. 1693. *See* Fleming, Robert *sen.*

Discourse of ecclesiastical politie. 1670. *See* Parker, Samuel, *bp.*

Discourse of eternitie. [1670]. *See* Typing, William.

1597 Entry cancelled.

Discourse of fines. [*n.p.*, 1670.] *See* L., T.

Discourse of fire. 1649. *See* Blaise de Vigenère.

Discourse of friendship. 1672. *See* G., E.

Discourse of God's hearing prayer. 1697. *See* Stafford, Richard.

Discourse of government. Edinburgh, 1698. *See* Fletcher, Andrew.

1598 A discourse of humane reason. *For Awnsham Churchill,* 1690. 8°. T.C.II 314. L, O, CT, OC, DT; CH, NU, WF, Y.

Discourse of husbandrie. 1605 [*i.e.,* 1650]. *See* Weston, *Sir* Richard.

1599 A discourse of infant baptism. *By Thomas Parkhurst,* 1698. 8°. LW, CT; NPT.

1600 Entry cancelled.

Discourse of local motion. 1676. *See* Pardres, Ignace Gaston.

Discourse of miracles upon. 1699. *See* Beverley, Thomas.

Discourse of miracles wrought. Antwerp, 1676. *See* Worsley, Edward.

Discourse of monarchy. 1684. *See* Wilson, John.

Discourse of money. 1696. *See* Briscoe, John.

Discourse of natural and moral impotency. 1671. *See* Truman, Joseph.

Discourse of natural and reveal'd religion. 1691. *See* Nourse, Timothy.

Discourse of patronage. 1675. *See* Cawdrey, Zachery.

Discourse of paying of tithes. 1656. *See* Larkham, Thomas.

Discourse of pluralities. 1680. *See* Hughes, William.

Discourse of profiting. 1683. *See* Patrick, Symon, *bp.*

1601 A discourse of sacriledge. *For Richard Lowndes,* 1641[2]. 4°.* L, O, C, LL, CT; CLC, MH, NU, WF, Y.

Discourse of scandal. 1683. *See* S., S.

1602 A discourse of schism. *For W. Crook,* 1690. 4°.* L, O, C, LW; CH, NU, WF, Y.

Discourse of sea-ports. 1700. *See* Digges, *Sir* Dudley.

Discourse of self-murder. 1692. *See* Pierce, Ezra.

Discourse of subterraneal treasure. 1668. *See* Lawrence, Thomas.

Discourse of taxes. 1689. *See* Petty, *Sir* William.

Discourse of the communion. 1687. *See* Payne, William.

1603 A discourse of the dukedom of Modena. *By J. C. for William Crook,* 1674. 4°.* T.C.I 162. L, O, CT, SC; CH, LC, WF, Y.

1604 A discourse of the duties on merchandize. *Printed,* 1695. 4°.* L, O; CH, CU, LC, MH, RPJ.

Discourse of the empire. 1658. *See* Howell, James.

Discourse of the excellency of Christianity. 1671. *See* Hallywell, Henry.

Discourse of the excellency of the heavenly substance. 1673. *See* Hickes, John.

Discourse of the general notions. 1695. *See* Clement, Simon.

Discourse of the great disingenuity. 1695. *See* Fowler, Edward, *bp.*

Discourse of the growth. 1689. *See* Pett, *Sir* Peter.

Discourse of the Holy Eucharist. 1687. *See* Wake, William, *abp.*

1605 Entry cancelled.

Discourse of the judgements. 1668. *See* Beverley, Thomas.

Discourse of the just antiquity. 1661. *See* D., H.

Discourse of the knowledge. 1657. *See* LcChambre, Cureau de.

1605A A discourse of the lawfulness of compliance. [*London,* 166–?] cap., 4°.* MH.

Discourse of the misery. [*n.p.*, 1697.] *See* Stafford, Richard.

Discourse of the nationall excellencies. 1658. *See* Hawkins, Richard.

Discourse of the nature and obligation. 1662. *See* Stileman, John.

Discourse of the nature, ends. 1673. *See* Allen, William.

Discourse of the nature, offices. 1657. *See* Taylor, Jeremy, *bp.*

Discourse of the nature, series. 1689. *See* Allen, William.

Discourse of the nature, use. 1694. *See* Child, *Sir* Josiah.

Discourse of the necessity of church-guides. [*n.p.*], 1675. *See* Woodhead, Abraham.

1606 A discourse of the necessity of encouraging mechanick industry. *For R. Chiswell*, 1690. 4°.* T.C.II 306. L, O, C, LAS, EN; CH, MH, NC, WF, Y.

Discourse of the original. 1672. *See* Chevalier, Pierre.

Discourse of the peerage. 1679. *See* Barlow, Thomas, *bp.*

Discourse of the Pope's supremacy. 1688. *See* Stratford, Nicholas, *abp.*

1607 Discourse of the Pope's usurped supremacy. 1679. 4°. EN.

Discourse of the real presence. 1686. *See* More, Henry.

Discourse of the religion. 1667. *See* Corbet, John.

1608 A discourse of the repugnancy of sin. *Printed and are to be sold by Edward Millington and William Abington*, 1679. 8°. T.C.I 367. L, OC, LW; CLC, MH, WF.

Discourse of the rise. [n.p.], 1677. *See* Sheridan, Thomas.

Discourse of the sacrifice. 1688. *See* Payne, William.

A discourse of the state ecclesiastical. *See* Downing Calybute.

Discourse of the terrestrial paradise. 1666. *See* Carver, Marmaduke.

Discourse of the truth. 1662. *See* Yelverton, *Sir* Henry.

Discourse of the use. 1687. *See* Gother, John.

Discourse of the vanity. 1673. *See* Radnor, John Robartes, *earl.*

Discourse of things. 1681. *See* Boyle, Robert.

Discourse of toleration. 1668. *See* Perrinchief, Richard.

1609 Discourse of toleration: with some observations. [n.p.], *printed*, 1691. 4°.* OC, BR, HH; LC, MU, NU, Y.

Discourse of trade. 1690. *See* Barbon, Nicholas.

Discourse of trade and coyn. 1697. *See* Pollexfen, John.

1610 A discourse of trade, wherein is plainly discovered. *Printed*, 1675. 4°.* L.

1611 A discourse of women. *For Henry Brome*, 1662. 8°. L, CS; CH, WF.

1611A —[Anr. ed.] *For R. T.*, 1672. 12°. L.

1612 —[Anr. ed.] *For R. T.*, 1673. 12°. T.C.I 153. L; CN, Y.

Discourse on baptism. 1700. *See* Leslie, Charles.

Discourse on the late funds. 1694. *See* Briscoe, John.

Discourse on the memory. Edinburgh, 1665. *See* Burnet, Gilbert, *bp.*

1613 A discourse on the nature of that Episcopacy. 1661. 8°. LW.

1614 Discourse on the rise and power. 1685. 12°. MHL.

Discourse on the woollen manufacture. Dublin, 1698. *See* Hovell, John.

Discourse on water baptism. 1697. *See* Leslie, Charles.

Discourse, opening the nature. 1641. *See* Brooke, Robert.

1615 A discourse or dialogue between the two now potent enemies. *For Thomas Bates*, 1642. 4°.* LT, O, OC; CH, MB, MH, Y.

1616 A discovrse presented to those who seeke the reformation. [*London*], *for W. W. and I. B.*, 1642. 4°.* DC; CH, CN, MH, NU.

Discourse proving by Scripture. 1686. *See* Brinley, John.

Discourse proving from Scripture. 1680. *See* Allestree, Richard.

Discourse proving the divine institution. 1697. *See* Leslie, Charles.

Discourse representing the liberty. 1661. *See* Dury, John.

1617 A discourse shewing in what state. [*London*], *printed*, 1641. 4°.* LT, O, OC, SC, DT; CH, CN, MH, MU, NU, WF, Y.

1618 A discourse, shewing that it is lawfull. *For Joseph Hall in Newcastle-upon-Tyne*, 1689. 4°.* T.C.II 276. L, EN; MM, NU, Y.

1618A —[Anr. ed.] *Printed and sold by R. Baldwin*, 1689. 4°.* DT.

1618B A discourse shewing that it is our duty. 1689. 4°. L.

Discourse shewing that neither temporalitie. 1672. *See* K., E.

Discourse shewing that Protestants. 1687. *See* Beaulieu, Luke de.

1619 A discourse shewing that the Protestant religion is the surest way to Heaven. Dublin, John Brocas, 1700. DIX 318. 16°. DM.

1620 A discourse shewing the great advantages. *Printed*, 1678. 4°.* L, CT, LPO, BR; CN, LC, NC, Y.

Discourse; shewing, who they are. 1698. *See* Leslie, Charles.

Discourse tending to prove. 1642. *See* Barbon, Praisegod.

Discourse touching provision. 1683. *See* Hale, *Sir* Matthew.

Discourse touching Tangiers. 1680. *See* Sheeres, *Sir* Henry.

1621 Entry cancelled.

1622 A discourse touching the addresses. *For J. Hither*, 1682. 4°.* O, C, HH, BP, GU; CH, MH, MIU, NC, WF, Y.

1623 A discourse touching the inconveniences of a long . . . Parliament. [*London?* 1641.] cap., 4°.* Y.

Discourse touching the peace. 1653. *See* Przipcovius, Samuel.

1624 A discourse unto His Royal Highness James. *Edinburgh, by William Caron, to be sold by John Calderwood*, 1680. 4°. ALDIS 2192. EN, FSF; WF, Y.

Discourse upon grants. 1700. *See* Davenant, Charles.

1625 A discourse upon qvestions in debate. [*London*, 1643.] cap., 4°.* LT, DT; CN, CSS, NN, TU.

1626 Entry cancelled.

1627 A discourse upon the greatnesse. 1656. 8°. O.

Discourse upon the passions. 1661. *See* LaChambre, Marin Cureau de.

1628 A discourse vpon the questions in debate. [*London*, 1642.] cap., 4°.* LT, C, HH, MR, DT; CH, MH, NU, WF, Y.

Discourse upon this saying. [1659.] *See* Harrington, James.

1629 A discourse upon usury. *For Samuel Crouch*, 1692. 4°.* T.C.II 414. O, C, LW, CT, A; CLC, MH, NC, WF, Y.

Discourse, wherein the interest. 1669. *See* Coxe, Thomas.

Discourses concerning the ministry. [1660?] *See* Stubbe, Henry.

Discourses on the publick revenues. 1698. *See* Davenant, Charles.

1630 Discourses upon the modern affairs of Europe. [*London*], *printed*, 1680. 4°.* T.C.I 430. L, O, CT, MR; CH, CN, NC, WF, Y.

Discourses upon trade. 1691. *See* North, *Sir* Dudley.

Discoverer discovered. 1695. *See* Penington, Edward.

1630A The discoverer uncovered. *Printed*, 1649. 4°. CN, CSS.

Discoverer. VVherein. 1649. *See* Canne, John.

Discoveries of the day-dawning. 1661. *See* Perrot, John.

1631 A discovery after some search of the sinnes of the ministers. [*Leith*], *printed* [*by E. Tyler*], 1651. 4°.* ALDIS 1439. EN; Y.

Discoverie for division. 1653. *See* Dymcock, Cressy.

1632 The discovery made by Captain Mark Baggot. colop: *For James Partridge*, 1691. brs. L.

1633 A discovery made by His Highnesse the Lord Protector. [*London*], *for Tho. Vere, and Will. Gilbertson*, [1658]. 8°.* LT.

Discovery of a great and wicked conspiracie. 1642. *See* Norwich, George Goring, *baron*.

1634 The discovery of a great plot. *Jan: 8. London, for And: Coe*, 1644. 4°.* CH, NU, WF, Y.

1635 —1648. 4°.* O.

1636 A discovery of a horrible and bloody treason. *For Iohn Thomas*, 1641. 4°.* LT, C, LG, AN; WF, Y.

1637 The discovery of a late and bloody conspiracie at Edenburgh. *For Iohn Thomas*, 1641. 4°.* LT, O, C; CH, CN, MH, NU, WF, Y.

Discovery of a new world. [1644.] *See* Healy, John.

Discovery of a swarme. 1641. *See* Taylor, John.

1638 A discovery of audacious insolence. *By Tho. Snowden, for Edward Giles in Norwich*, 1691. 4°.* O.

1639 The discovery of Captain Bury. [*London*], *printed*, 1679. 4°.* O, LIL; CN, NU, Y.

Discovery of charity. 1654. *See* Williamson, R.

1640 A discovery of divers sorts of asses. *July 8. London for Iohn Powel*, 1642. 4°.* LT, C, CJ.

Discovery of divine mysteries. 1700. *See* B., C.

Discovery of faith. 1653. *See* Farnworth, Richard.

Discovery of Fonseca. Dublin. 1682. *See* S., J.

Discoverie of London obstinacie. [*n.p.*], 1643. *See* Spelman, *Sir* John.

1641 The discovery of malignants. [*London*, 1643.] cap., 4°.* LT, O, C, HH; MH, NU, WF.

1642 A discovery of many, great, and bloudy robberies. *Printed at London for Iohn Thomas*, 1641. 4°.* LT; NU, Y.

1643 A discovery of new light. [*n.p.*], *Printed*, 1641. 8°.* O; WF.

Discovery of new worlds. 1688. *See* Fontenelle, Bernard Le Bovier de.

1644 A discovery of one sham more. [*London*], *for Benj. Tooke*, 1681. fol.* L, O, OC, CS, HH; CH, CN, TU, WF, Y.

Discovery of Sathan. [*n.p.*], 1668. *See* West, Robert.

Discovery of silk-worms. 1650. *See* Williams, Edward.

1645 A discovery of six women-preachers, . . . in Middlesex, Kent. [*London*], *printed*, 1641. 4°.* LT, O, OC, LP, E; CH, MH, NU, Y.

1646 A discovery of some fruits of the profession. colop: *For Thomas Simmons*, 1656. cap., 4°.* LT, LF, OC; CH, MU.

1647 A discovery of some plots of Lucifer. *For T. Brewster*, 1656. 12°. LT.

1648 A discovery of some sins of the ministry. *Printed*, 1661. 8°.* LT.

Discovery of subterraneal treasure. 1653. *See* Plattes, Gabriel.

Discovery of the accursed thing. [*n.p.*, 1695.] *See* Crisp, Thomas.

1649 A discovery of the arch-whore. [*London*, 1642.] brs. LT, LS, EC.

Discovery of the beasts. [*n.p.*], 1641. *See* *W., I.

1650 Entry cancelled.

Discovery of the education. 1659. *See* Sammon, Edward.

Discovery of the falsehood. 1649. *See* J., T.

Discovery of the first wisdom. 1656. *See* Nayler, James.

1651 A discovery of the great fantasie. *By T. P. and M. S.*, 1642. 4°.* LT, DT; CH, CSS.

1652 Entry cancelled.

Discovery of the groundlesness. 1675. *See* Sergeant, John.

1653 A discoverie of the hellish plot. *For Iohn Greensmith*, 1642. 4°.* LT, C; CSU, MH, WF, Y.

1654 A discovery of the intentions of the army, under . . . Fairfax. [*London*, 1648.] brs. LT; MH.

1655 A discovery of the Iesuits trumpery. *For Henry Gosson*, [1642?]. brs. LT.

1656 A discovery of the ivglings and deceitfvll impostvres. *By G. M.*, 1643. 1 pl., 6 pp. 4°.* LT, DT; CH, NU, WF, Y.

1657 —[Anr. ed.] —, 1643. 4 ll. 4°.* LT, O; V.

Discovery of the most dangerous dead faith. [1642.] *See* Eaton, John.

Discovery of the person. 1679. *See* Nesse, Christopher.

1658 The discovery of the Popish plot. *Printed*, 1679. 4°.* L, O, C, MR, ENC; CH, MH, NU, WF, Y.

Discovery of the priests [London, 1660.] *See* Simpson, William.

Discovery of the rebels. [*n.p.*], 1643. *See* Vicars, John.

1658A A discovery of the Savoy plot. *Th. Linsey*, 1689. brs. CN.

1659 A discovery of the society. *For R. Royston*, 1658. 8°.* O, C; Y.

Discovery of the state of Ireland. Dublin, 1666. *See* Davies, *Sir* John.

Discovery of the trecherous attempts of the Cavaliers. 1643. *See* Hutchinson, John.

Discovery of the true. 1658. *See* S., S.

1660 A discovery of theisme. *For Chares Brome*, 1698. 8°. T.C.III 64. CT; CH, MM, Y.

1661 A discoverie of treason. *Octob. 29, by R.A. and A.C. for G. Smith*, 1642. 4°.* LT, LG, EC, SP; NU, WU.

Discoverie of truth. [n.p.], 1645. *See* H., P.

Discovery of truth and falsehood. 1653. *See* Farnworth, Richard.

1662 A discoverie of 29. sects here in London. [*London*], *printed*, 1641. 4°.* LT, LG, CJ; CLC, MH, NHC, NU.

Discovery of two unclean spirits. 1657. *See* Holder, Anthony.

Discovery of witches. 1647. *See* Hopkins, Matthew.

Discovery, or, certaine observations. [n.p.], 1657. *See* M., J.

1663 Discovery or declaration. *Printed in the year*, 1660. 4°. CH, WF.

Discovery to the prayse. [n.p.], 1641. *See* O'Connor, William.

1664 A discoverie, what God, the supreme judge, ... hath caused to bee manifested. [*London*], *printed*, 1643. 4°.* LT, CM; MH, NU.

Discreet and ivdiciovs discovrse. 1642. *See* P., R.

1665 Entry cancelled.

Discussion of Mr. Frye's tenents. [n.p., 1650.] *See* Cheynell, Francis.

Discussion of the first. 1689. *See* Hooper, George, *bp.*

1666 The disdainful virgin led captive. [*London*], *for J. Jordan*, [1690]. brs. L.

1667 The disease of the house. *Nod. Nol* [*London*], *printed*, 1649. 4°.* LT; CH, CN, WF.

1668 The diseased maiden lover. [*London*], *for F. Coles, T. Vere, and J. Wright*, [1655–80]. brs. L, O, CM, HH.

Diseases of the times. [1642.] *See* Taylor, John.

Disingag'd survey. 1650. *See* Dury, John.

1669 The disloyal favourite. *For W. Thackeray, T. Passinger, and W. Whitwood*, [1679?]. brs. L, HH; MH, Y.

1670 The disloyal forty & forty one. colop: *For T.B.*, 1680. fol.* L, O, MC, EN; CH, CN, MH, WF, Y.

1670A A dismal account of the burning of our solemn league. [*London*, 1662.] brs. NU.

1671 The dismal ruine of Athlone. *Dublin, at the Post Office*, [1697]. brs. DIX 288. DN.

1671A **Disney, Gervase.** Some remarkable passages in the holy life. *By J.D. for Jonathan Robinson*, 1692. 8°. L; CLC, CN, MH, WF, Y.

1672 **D[isney], W[illiam].** Forgetfulness of God. *For Jacob Sampson*, 1681. 8°. AU; NC.

1672A ——[Anr. ed.] *For Thomas Simmons*, 1683. 8°. T.C.II 3. Y.

1672B —Nil dictum quod non dictum prius or the case. *By A.B. for F.T. to be sold by Thomas Fox*, 1681. 8°. L, O, CCH, CT, EN; CN, NU.

1672C ——[Anr. ed.] *By A.B. for F.T.*, 1681. 8°. L, CT; CH, WF, Y.

1672D —A warning to traytors. *By E.Mallet*, 1685. fol.* MH.

1673 The disorders of Basset, a novel. *For John Newton*, 1688. 12°. L; CN.

Disorders of love. 1677. *See* Desjardins, Marie Catherine Hortense de.

Dispensary. 1699. *See* Garth, *Sir* Samuel.

1674 The dispersed vnited. [*London*], *printed*, 1659. 4°.* LT, O, HH; CH, CN, MH, NU, WF, Y.

Display of tyranny. 1689. *See* Oates, Titus.

1675 The displaying of the life-guards colours. *Printed*, 1648. 4°.* LT, O; CH, MH, WF, Y.

Disputatio de pace. 1653. *See* Hales, John.

Disputatio inauguralis. 1688. *See* Brathwait, Richard.

Disputation at Winchcombe. Oxford, [1653]. *See* Barksdale, Clement.

1676 A disputation betwixt the Devill and the Pope. *Printed*, 1642. 4°.* LT; MH, Y.

Disputation concerning church-members. 1659. *See* Mather, Richard.

1677 A disputation: proving, that it is not convenient. *Printed*, 1679. 4°.* L, O, CS, SC; CH, MH, NU, WF, Y.

Disputation with Mr Gunning. 1658. *See* White, Thomas.

Dispute against the English. [n.p.], 1660. *See* Gellespie, George.

1678 A dispute betwixt an atheist and a Christian. *Printed*, 1646. 8°. LT.

1679 A dispvte betwixt two clergie-men upon the roade. [*London*], *for A.H.*, 1651. 4°.* O.

Disquisitio. Eleutheropoli, 1650. *See* Hales, John.

Disquisition about the final causes. 1689. *See* Boyle, Robert.

Disquisition upon our Saviour's sanction. 1685. *See* Beverly, Thomas.

Disquisitiones criticae. 1684. *See* Simon, Richard.

Dis-satisfaction satisfied. 1654. *See* G., J.

1680 The dissatisfied subject. [*London*], *for P.Brooksby, J. Deacon, J.Blare, J.Back*, [1688–92]. brs. L, CM, HH.

Dissection of all governments. 1649. *See* J., W.

Dissenter from those. 1696. *See* S., M.

1681 The Dissenter truely described. colop: *For N. Thompson*, 1681. brs. L, O, OC; CH, CN, MH, WF, Y.

1682 The Dissenter unmask'd: being some reflections upon ... the Dissenters. *For the author*, 1691. 4°.* O, C, MR; CH.

1683 The Dissenter unmaskt, with respect to the two plots. colop: *For J.Cripps*, 1683. cap., fol.* L, O, OC; CH, MBA, MIU, PU, Y.

1684 The Dissenters address, to His Majesty. colop: *For J.D.*, 1683. brs. O, OC; CH, Y.

1685 The Dissenters case. *By H.C. sold by Richard Baldwin*, 1689. 4°.* CT; LC.

1686 The Dissenters case in relation to the bill. [1700?] brs. L.

1687 The Dissenters diescription [*sic*] of true loyalty. *Printed, and sold by Andrew Sowle*, [1687]. brs. O; Y.

1688 The Dissenters guide. *Printed for, and are to be sold by Richard Janeway*, 1683. 4°.* L, O, CS; CH, MH, Y.

1689 Entry cancelled.

Dissenting casuist. 1682. *See* Wood, Thomas.

Dissertatio de pace. 1653. *See* Przipcovius, Samuel.

Dissertatio theoretico-practica. 1700. *See* B., A.

Dissertation concerning the antiquity. 1696. *See* Hill, Joseph.

Dissertation concerning the pre-existency. 1684. *See* P., C.

Dissertation upon water-baptism. 1700. *See* Salmon, William.

1690 The dissolution of the Parliament in Scotland Novemb. 19, 1641. *For John Wright,* 1641. 4°.* LT, CT, HH, EN; MBP, NIC, WSG, Y.

Disswasive from conformity. 1675. *See* Stubbe, Henry.

Dissuasive from Popery. Dublin, 1681. *See* B., A.

Dissvasive from the errours. 1646. *See* Baillie, Robert.

1691 The distiller of London. *For Tho. Huntington and Wil. Nealand,* 1652. Sixes. LT, O, LPO, LWL; NAM.

1692 —*By Robert Paske, for the company of distillers,* 1668. fol. L, LG; Y.

1693 —*By Sarah Paske, for the company of distillers,* 1698. fol. L, C, LG; MH.

1694 A distinct and faithful accompt of all the receipts. *By Hen. Hills and John Field,* 1658. fol. LT, CS; CH, WF, Y.

Distinction between real. 1696. *See* Sherlock, William.

Distinction between the phanatick. 1660. *See* Fox, George.

Distinction between true liberty. [n.p., 1685.] *See* Fox, George.

Distinction betwixt the two suppers. [n.p.], 1685. *See* Fox, George.

1694A The distracted damsel. [London], *for J. Clark,* [1680.] brs. O.

1695 Distracted Englands lamentation. *For Richard Harper,* 1646. 4°.* LT.

1696 The distracted maid's lamentation. [London, 1700?] brs. L.

Distracted state. 1651. *See* Tatham, John.

1697 The distracted young-mans answer. *For P. Pelcomb,* [1686–89]. brs. L, CM, HH.

1698 The distractions of our times. *Printed,* 1642. 4°.* L, CJ, CT; CH, MH, MIU.

1698A —[Anr. ed.] —, 1643. 4°.* O, C, CJ; CH, CU, NU, Y.

1699 The distressed case of the people called Quakers. *For Benjamin Clark,* 1682. 4°.* L, LF; CH, MH, PH, WF.

1700 [The] distressed child, or the cruel uncle. [1700?] 8°. O.

1701 The distressed damsels. [London], *for P. Brooksby, J. Deacon, J. Blare, J. Back,* [c. 1691]. brs. L, O, HH, GU.

1701A The distressed damosels downfall. *For F. Coles, T. Vere, J. Wright, and J. Clarke,* [1674–79.] brs. O.

1702 The distressed estate of the city of Dublin. *For John Thomas,* 1641. 4°. L, O, C.

1702A The distressed gentlewoman. [London], *for P. Brooksby, J. Deacon, J. Blare, J. Back,* [1691.] brs. CM.

1703 The distressed mother. *For J. Beuvet,* [1690?] brs. L.

1704 —[London], *for P. Brooksby, J. Deacon, J. Blare, J. Back,* [1692?]. brs. L, CM, HH; WCL.

Distressed oppressed condition. [n.p., 1655.] *See* M., G.

1705 The distressed pilgrim. *For W. Thackeray, T. Passenger, and W. Whitwood,* [1670–77]. brs. L, O, HH; MH.

Distressed virgin. [1655.] *See* Parker, Martin.

1705A The distressed Welshman. *By and for T. Norris,* [1700.] 12°.* L, CM.

1705B The disturbed ghost. *For Phillip Brooksby,* [1674.] brs. O.

1706 **Ditton, George.** Symbolvm apostolicvm. *By Thomas Harper, to be sold by John Courtney, in Salisbury,* 1650. brs. LT.

Diurnall and particula [sic]. [n.p., 1642.] *See* P., I.

Diurnall occurrences. 1641. *See* England, Parliament.

Divrnall occvrrences, truly relating. [1642.] *See* G., H.

Diurnall of dangers. [1642.] *See* Jordan, Thomas.

Diurnall of sea designes. 1642. *See* H., W.

Divrnal of true proceedings. 1642. *See* Sampson, Lat.

1707 July, 18. A diurnall out of the North. colop: *By T. Fawcet, for D. C. July 18,* 1642. cap., 4°.* LT, O, EC.

Diurnal speculum. 1696. *See* Bockett, John.

1708 Westminster, 26 Dec. 1688. Divers of the members. colop: *By John Starkey, Awnsham and William Churchill,* 1688. cap., fol.* L, O; CH, CLC, Y.

1709 Divers papers from the army viz Marshall Generall Skippons speech. *For Hanna Allen,* 1647. 4°.* LT, O, HH, BR; CH, MH, NU, WF, Y.

Divers papers presented. 1645. *See* Scotland, Parliament.

1710 Divers questions upon His Majesties last answer, concerning the militia. *For Ioseph Hunscott,* 1 *March,* 1641[2]. brs. STEELE 2002. L, LG, CT, EC, BR; MH.

1710A Divers reasons against lightening the coin. [London, 1690.] brs. NC.

1711 Divers remarkable occurrences that have hapned in the Tower. *For Nath: Butter, Iuky 8,* 1642. 4°.* LT, LFEA.

1712 Divers remarkable passages concerning the originall and progresse of the present action in Essex. [London], *printed,* 1684. 4°.* LT, O; CH, Y.

1713 Divers remarkable passages of God's good providence. *For I. Wright, Iune 3,* 1643. 4°.* LT, DT.

1714 Divers serious cautions. *For John Johnson* [1659]. brs. O; MH.

Dives and Lazarus. 1677. *See* J., R.

Divine and immediate revelation. 1685. *See* K., G.

1715 Divine and moral discourses on divers subjects. *For Samuel Keble,* 1693. 12°. T.C.II 448. O.

Divine Astrea. [1697]. *See* Settle, Elkanah.

Divine balsam. 1642. *See* L., I.

1716 The divine banquet. *For N. Crouch,* 1686. 8°. T.C.II 155. L.

1717 —[Anr. ed.] *For Nath. Crouch,* 1696. 8°. L, O; CLC, NN, WF.

1718 Entry cancelled.

Divine blossomes. 1657. *See* Cockin, Francis.

Divine breathings. 1672. *See* Sherman, Thomas.

Divine catastrophe. 1652. *See* Weldon, *Sir* Anthony.

Divine considerations. 1676. *See* Halsey, James.

1719 Divine consolations for mourners. [n.p.], *printed,* 1664. 4°. DT; MWA.

Divine contemplations. 1648. *See* Isaacson, Henry.

Divine dialogues. 1668. *See* More, Henry.

1720 The divine dreamer: or, a short treatise. *[London]*, *printed*, 1641. 4°.* LT, O, CT; CH, NU, PU, WF.

Divine eloquence. 1694. *See* Norwood, Cornelius.

1720A Divine examples of God's severe judgments. *For T. C. and sold by William Miller*, 1672. brs. L; MH.

1721 Divine fire-works. Or, some sparkles. *[London, 1657.]* brs. LT.

Divine history. 1670. *See* Gott, Samuel.

Divine horn-book. 1688. *See* L., H.

Divine hymns. 1695. *See* C., R.

Divine immediate revelation. 1684. *See* Keith, George.

Divine institution. 1697. *See* Leslie, Charles.

1722 Divine light, manifesting the love of God. *[London]*, *printed*, 1646. 4°.* LT, O; CH, NU, Y.

Divine light of Christ. 1692. *See* Whitehead, George.

Divine love. 1677. *See* Powell, Vavasor.

Divine meditations and contemplations. 1641. *See* R., G.

Divine meditations grounded. York, 1650. *See* Llewellin, Edward.

Divine meditations on. 1653. *See* Waterhouse, Edward.

Divine meditations; or. 1700. *See* Liddell, George.

Divine meditations upon. 1682. *See* Waller, *Sir* William.

Divine meditations, written. 1641. *See* Wake, *Sir* Isaac.

Divine observations. Evrope, 1646. *See* Overton, Richard.

1723 A diuin oade. *By F.L.*, 1641[2]. brs. LT, LS.

1724 A divine pater-noster. *For Thomas Underhill*, [1642]. brs. LT.

1725 Entry cancelled.

1726 Divine physick for devout souls. *For R. I. to be sold by Sam. Speed*, 1662. 4°.* O, HH, MR.

Divine physician. [n.p.], 1676. *See* Harris John.

1727 A divine poem. *For William Marshall*, 1682. brs. CH, MH.

Divine poem. [London], 1684. *See* Wells, Mary.

1728 A divine poem of Christs fulness. *For John Andrews*, 1660. brs. L.

1729 A divine poem; or, glad tidings. 1698. 8°. MR.

1730 Divine poems upon the inexhaustible goodness. *By George Croom*, 1686, vrs. O; MH.

Divine poems. Oxon, 1658. *See* Elys, Edmund.

1731 A divine prayer necessary. *[London]*, *printed*, 1641. 4°.* HH, SP, E; CSS, MIU, WF.

1732 The divine right and irresistibility of kings. Oxford, *by Leonard Lichfield*, 1645. 4°.* MADAN 1845. O, HH, EN, DT; CH, MIU, Y.

1733-4 Entries cancelled.

Divine right of episcopacy. 1690. *See* Cuningham, Alexander.

1735 The divine right of the gospel ministry. 1654. 4°. LW; MWA.

Divine right of kings. [n.p., 1680] *See* P., W.

Divine services. 1663. *See* Clifford, James.

Divine teachings. 1649. *See* Coppe, Abiezer.

1736 The divine unity once more asserted. *[London]*, *printed*, 1697. 4°.* L, OC, CCH, EC, DT; CH, MH, RPB, WF, Y.

Divine wooer. 1673. *See* Horne, John.

1737 Divinity and philosophy dissected. *Amsterdam*, *printed*, 1644. 4°. LT, O; NU, WF.

Divinity no enemy. [1653.] *See* Swadlin, Thomas.

Divinity of Christ. 1669. *See* Whitehead, George.

Divinity of the Trinity. 1654. *See* Brayne, John.

Division divided. 1646. *See* Bridges, Walter.

1738 The division of the county of Essex. *For John Wright*, 1648. 4°.* L, O, CM, SP, HH; CLC, WF.

1739 The division of the county of Middlesex. 1647. 4°. BC.

1740 The division of the county of Surrey. *By A.M. for Christopher Meredith*, 1648. 4°.* LT, O, OC; MH.

1741 The division viol. *[n.p.]*, 1667. obl., 4°. GU.

1742 The division-violin. *Printed, and sold by John Playford*, 1685. obl., 4°. T.C.II 47. L, O.

1743 The division violin. *[London, Henry Playford*, 1695.]* obl., 4°. L.

Divisions of the church. 1642. *See* Taylor, John.

1744 **Dix, Henry.** The art of brachygraphy. Third edition. *For T.B. to be sold by the author*, 1641. 12°. L, CM.

1745 **D[ixon], R[obert].** Candidia. *By S. Roycroft for Robert Clavell*, 1683. 4°. T.C.II 47. L, O, LVD, GU; CH, CN, MH, WF, Y.

1746 —The degrees of consanguinity. *By T.R. and N.T. for Benjamin Took*, 1674. 12°. T.C.I 198. L, O, C, LWL, E; CLC, NU, WF, Y.

1747 —The doctrine of faith. *By William Godbid*, 1668. 4°. L, P, YM; WF.

1748 —The nature of the two testaments. *By Tho. Roycroft for the author*, 1676. fol. T.C.I 250. L, O, C, YM; MH, NPT, WF.

1748A —A sermon preached ... December 22, 1680. *By S. Roycroft, for Robert Clavel*, 1681. 4°. CLC, WF.

1748B —A short essay of modern divinity. *By S.R. for R. Clavell*, 1681. 4°. CLC, NPT, WF, Y.

1749 **[Dixon, Roger.]** Advice for the poor by way of cure. *[London, 1665.]* cap., 4°.* L.

1750 —Consultum sanitatis, a directory to health. *Printed*, 1663. 8°.* L.

1750A —A directory for the poor. *[London]*, 19 June, 1665. brs. HH.

Dobbing, Anthony. *See* Dopping, Anthony.

1751 **Dobson, Edward.** The declaration, vindication, and protestation of. Bristoll *[London]*, *printed*, 1644. 4°.* LT, LG.

1752 —XIV articles of treason. Oxford *by Leonard Lichfield, for Edward Dobson*, 1643. 4°.* MADAN 1297. LT, O, CJ, CS, A; CH, MH, MIU, Y.

1753 **[Dobson, John.]** Dr. Pierce his preaching confuted. *[London, 1663.]* 4°.* MADAN 2624. O.

1754 [–] Queries upon queries. 1662/3. 4°.* LL.

1755 [–] —Third edition. *[London]*, *for R. Royston*, [1663.]* 4°.* L, C, OC, CJ; CH, MH, NU, WF, Y.

1756 —A sermon preacht . . . 5th day of August, [1670]. *For R.Royston*, 1670. 4°.* T.C.I 54. L, O, C, CT, E; CH, IU, WF, Y.

1757 **Dochant, George.** A new catechism. *Printed*, 1653[4]. 4°.* LT.

1758 The doctor and beggar-wench. [*London*], *for J.Back*, [1685–88]. brs. HH.

1759 Dr. B . . . t's farewell, confessor to the late King of Poland. 1683. brs. O; CH, CN.

Dr. Burnett's reflections. 1688. *See* Northleigh, John.

1760 The doctor degraded, of the reward of deceit. *By George Groom*, 1685. brs. CH, MH.

1761 Dr. Dorislaw's ghost. colop: *By R.I. for T.Hinde, and N.Brooke*, 1652. fol.* LT; MH.

1762 Doctor Hannes dissected. [*London*, 1700?] fol. L.

Doctor Hill's funeral-sermon. 1654. *See* Hasselwood, Henry.

1763 Doctor Lamb's darling: or, strange and terrible news from Salisbury. *For G.Horton*, 1653. 4°.* LT, O; MH.

Doctor Merry-man. 1671. *See* Rowlands, Samuel.

1763A Dr. Oats last farewell to England. *For I.Dean* [1683]. brs. CLC, MH.

Dr. Oate's narrative. 1680. *See* Phillips, John.

1764 Dr. Otes his vindication. *By T.Dawks*, 1680. brs. L, LS.

1764A —[Anr. ed.] *Printed*, 1680. brs. L; MH.

Dr. Pierce his preaching. [n.p., 1663.] *See* Dobson, John.

Dr. Pierce his preaching exemplified. [n.p.], 1663. *See* G., N.

1765 Doctor Popes wish. 1693. brs. O.

1765A Dr. Robert Wild's last legacie. *For A.B.*, [1679?]. brs. L, O; CN, MH, TU, Y.

Dr. Sherlock sifted. 1687. *See* Sabran, Lewis.

1765B Dr. Sherlock vindicated. colop: *Printed*, 1690. brs. C; PL.

1765C —[Anr. ed.] —, *and reprinted at Edinburgh*, 1691. brs. L.

Dr. Sherlock's case. 1691. *See* Collier, John.

Dr. Sherlock's preservative. 1688. *See* Sabran, Lewis.

1766 Dr. Sherlock's two kings of Brainford. *Printed*, 1690. 4°.* L, CCA, CT, MR; MH, NU, WF, Y.

1767 —[Anr. ed.] *For the author, and are to be sold by Rich. Humpheries*, 1691. 4°.* L, O, CT, HH, EN; CH, CN, MH, WF, Y.

Doctor Stillingfleet against Doctor Stillingfleet. [n.p.], 1671. *See* Warner, John.

Dr. Stillingfleets principles. Paris, 1671. *See* Cressy, Hugh Paulin.

Dr Stillingfleet's principles. [n.p.], 1673. *See* Warner, John.

1767A Dr. Wild's echo. [*London*, 1663?] brs. L.

1768 Doctor Wild's squibs return'd. *For J.R.*, 1672. brs. L, LL; CH.

Doctors in all faculties. [n.p., 1687.] *See* Oxford University.

1768A The doctors last will and testament. [*London*], *printed*, 1641. 4°.* MH, WF.

1769 The doctor's medicines and counsel. [1680.] brs. O.

Doctor's physician. 1685. *See* Fremont d'Ablancourt, Nicoles.

Doctorum virorum elogia. 1671. *See* Thou, Jacques Auguste de.

Doctresse. 1656. *See* Bunworth, Richard.

Doctrina placitandi, ou. 1677. *See* Euer, Samson.

Doctrinæ antiquæ. 1654. *See* La Haye, Carolus de.

Doctrinæ sphæricæ. Oxoniæ, 1662. *See* Brancker, Thomas.

Doctrine and discipline. 1643. *See* Milton, John.

Doctrine and practice. 1686. *See* Stillingfleet, Edward.

1769A The doctrine of baptism reduced. 1648. 4°. O.

1770 22th. The doctrine of Christ's glorious kingdom. [*London*], 1672. cap., 4°.* L, O.

Doctrine of devils. 1676. *See* Orchard, N.

1771 Entry cancelled.

Doctrine of non-resistance. 1689. *See* Bohun, Edmond.

Doctrine of passive obedience. [n.p., 1689.] *See* Hickes, George.

Doctrine of perfection. 1663. *See* Whitehouse, John.

Doctrine of schism. 1672. *See* Fullwood, Francis.

Doctrine of surds. 1680. *See* Moore, Jonas.

1772 The doctrine of the Bible. *By Rob. Young, for E. Brewster*, 1642. 4°. NU.

1772A —[Anr. ed.] *By M.Bell for Edward Brewster*, 1646. 12°. L; Y.

1772B —[Anr. ed.] *For Edw. Brewster*, 1649. 12°. CT; CLC.

1772C —[Anr. ed.] *For J.Wright*, 1649. 12°. L; WF.

1772D —[Anr. ed.] —, 1652. 12°. L.

1773 —[Anr. ed.] 1656. 12°. C.

1773A —[Anr. ed.] *For E.Brewster and J.Wright*, 1679. 12°. T.C.I 388. L.

1773B —Thirty-first edition. *For E.Brewster, and M.Wotton*, 1698. 12°. T.C.III 103. L.

1774 The doctrine of the Catholick church. *For Richard Baldwin*, 1697. 4°.* L, LW, EC, BAMB, DT; CH, MH, PW, WF, Y.

Doctrine of the Church of England, concerning the independency. 1697. *See* Dodwell, Henry.

Doctrine of the Church of England, concerning the Lord's Day. 1683. *See* Smith, John.

Doctrine of the Church of England, established. [n.p.], 1642. *See* Ingoldsby, William.

Doctrine of the Fathers. 1695. *See* Braddocke, John.

Doctrine of the Holy Trinity. 1694. *See* Bury, Arthur.

Doctrine of the light. [n.p., 1658.] *See* Howet, Henoch.

1775 The doctrine of the Presbyterians. *Printed*, 1647. 8°.* OC, CT.

The doctrine of the Sabbath. *See* Dell, William.

Doctrine of the sphere. 1680. *See* Flamsteed, John.

Doctrine of the Synod. [*n.p.*, 1650.] *See* Twisse, William.

Doctrine of the trinity. 1687. *See* Stillingfleet, Edward.

1776 The doctrine of unitie. [*London*, 1643.] cap., 4°.* LT, O, LG, CCL, WF.

Doctrines and practices. 1686. *See* Stillingfleet, Edward.

1777 **D[ocwra, Anne.]** An apostate conscience exposed. *Printed and sold by T. Sowle,* 1699. 8°. LF, LSC, BBN; PH.

1777A —A brief discovery of the work of the enemy. 1683. fol. CT, BBN, BP.

1778 [–] An epistle of love and good advice. [*London,* 1683.] cap., 4°.* L, C, LF, BBN; CH, MH, MU, PH, WF, Y.

1779 —A looking-glass for the recorder. [*London,* 1682.] cap., 4°.* L, O, C, CT, LF; CH, MH, PH, PSC, Y.

1780 —The second part of an apostate-conscience exposed. *Printed and sold by T. Sowle,* 1700. 8°.* L, LF, BBN; PSC.

1781 [–] Spiritual community, vindicated. [*London,* 1687]. 4°.* LF, BBN; CH, MU.

1782 **Docwra, William.** An advertisement on the behalf of. [*n.p.,* 1689.] brs. L, O.

1782A —The practical method of conveyance of letters. [*London?* 1682.] cap., fol.* LG.

1782B —The practical method of the penny-post. colop: *By George Larkin,* 1681. cap., fol.* L, OC, LG, DCH.

1782C **[Dod, John.]** An extemporary sermon upon malt. [*London*] 1690. cap., 4°.* Y.

1783 —Old Mr Dod's sayings. *By A. Maxwell,* 1667. brs. O.

1784 — —[Anr. ed.] —, 1671. brs. L.

1784A — —[Anr. ed., *Cambridge, Mass, by Marmaduke, Johnson,* 1677, 4°.* EVANS 174. LC, MWA.

1785 — —[Anr. ed.] *By A. P. and T. H. for T. Passinger,* 1678. 8°.* L, O.

1785A — —[Anr. ed.] *By A. Maxwell,* 1680. 16°.* EN.

1786 — —[Anr. ed.] —, 1681. brs. L.

1786A — —[Anr. ed.] *Glasgow, by Robert Sanders,* 1699. 4°.* WF.

1786B —A plain and familiar exposition of the ten Commandments. Nineteenth edition. *By W. Leybourn for Andrew Kemb,* 1662. 4°. NU.

1786C —Sayings of. [*London?* 1700.] brs. L.

1787 —A second sheet of old Mr. Dod's sayings. *For William Miller,* 1670. brs. L.

1788 —Ten sermons tending chifly to the fitting of men. *By S. Griffin for W. Lee,* 1661. 8°. L, C, LW; IU.

1789 —Ymadroddion hen Mr. Dod. *Printiedig yn Llundain gan Tho. Whitledge a W. Everingham,* 1693. brs. MC, AN, CPL; MH.

1789A — —[Anr. ed.] [*London,* 1688.] cap., 4°.* AN.
Dod, or Chathan. The beloved. 1653. *See* Rogers, John.

1790 **D[odd], E[dward].** Innocents no saints. *For Francis Tyton,* 1658. 4°.* LT, LF.

1791 **Doddridge, John.** The antiquity and power of Parliaments. *For William Leake, and John Leake,* 1679. 8°. L, O; CN, WF.

1792 —A compleat parson. *For Iohn Grove,* 1641. 4°. L, O, C, EN, DT; CU, MH, NC, WF, Y.

1793 —Honors pedigree. *For William Sheares,* 1652. 8°. L, O, CCA, AN; CH, MIU, NU, Y.

1794 —Judge Dodaridge [*sic*], his law of nobility. *For L. Chapman,* 1658. 8°. L, O, C, LL, DT; CN, MHL, MU, WF, Y.

1795 —Judge Doddridges reading of advowsons. *For Laur. Chapman,* 1663. 4°. L, P.

1796 —The several opinions of sundry learned antiquaries. *For William Leake,* 1658. 8°. LT, O, CT, ES, DT; BN, CH, CN, LC, MH, NU, YL.

1797 — —[Anr. ed.] *By F. L. for Matt. Gillyflower,* 1685. 12°. L, OC, DT; BN, CH, CN, LC, MB.

1798 Entry cancelled.
Δωδεχαμηνο-διεταϛ-γραφη. 1652. *See* Almanacs Thomas Dunster.

1799 **[Dodson, Jeremiah.]** The preachers precept. *By E. Cotes for the author,* 1665. 4°.* L, O; LCL, NU.

1800 —A sermon preached . . . November, 20th. 1688. *By W. Wilde,* 1688. 4°.* L, LG; WF.

1801 **Dodson, William.** The designe for the perfect draining of . . . the fens. *By R. Wood, to be sold by Henry Twiford and by Richard Marriot,* 1665. 4°.* L, O, C, CT, LPO; MH, WF.

1801A **Dodsworth, Christopher.** Mr. Christopher Dodsworth's proceedings. [*London,* 1690.] brs. NC.
Dodsworth, Roger. Monasticon Anglicanum. *See* Dugdale, William.

1802 **Dodwell, Henry.** An account of the fundamental principle of Popery. *For Benj. Tooke,* 1688. 4°.* C, LCL, OC, CPE, EN; TU, Y.

1803 —An answer to six queries. *For Benj. Tooke,* 1688. 4°.* L, C, LCL, CPE, EN; NU, WF, Y.

1804 [–] Concerning the case of taking the new oath. [*London,* 1689.] cap., 4°.* O, C, OC, HH, MR; CH, NU, WF, Y.

1804A —De geographorum aetati & scriptis dissertationes. *Oxoniae e theatro Sheldoniano,* 1698. 8°. CCH.

1804B —De jure laicorum sacerdotali. 1635 [1685]. L, O, CT; MWA, WG, Y.

1805 [–] A defence of the vindication of the deprived bishops. *Printed,* 1695. 4°. L, O, CT, EN, DT; CN, LC, MH, NU, Y.

1806 —A discourse concerning Sanchoniathon's Phœnician history. *By M. Clark, for B. Tooke,* 1681. 8°. T.C.I 418. L, C, LCL, MR, DT; BN, CLC, NU, TU, WF, Y.

1807 — —[Anr. ed.] *For Benjamin Tooke, to be sold by Walter Kettilby,* 1691. 8°. OC, CE, D; CH, NU, TU, Y.

1808 —A discourse concerning the one altar. *For Benj. Tooke,* 1683. 8°. T.C.I 502. L, O, CS, E, DT; BN, CH, NU, PBL, WF, Y.

1809 —Dissertationes Cyprianicæ. [*Oxon,* 1682.] fol. L, OB, C, EC, EN; CH, NGT.

1810 — —[Anr. ed.] *Oxoniæ, e theatro Sheldoniano,* 1684. 8°. T.C.II 127. L, O, C, EN, DT; BN, CU, MH, NU, Y.

1811 — —[Anr. ed.] *Oxonii,* [1700]. fol. MR; BN.

1812 —Dissertationes in Irenæum. *Oxoniæ, e theatro Sheldoniano,* 1689. 8°. T.C.II 288. L, C, OB, EN, DT; BN, CLC, MH, NU, PL, WF, Y.

1813 [–] The doctrine of the Church of England, concerning the independency. *Printed,* 1697. 4°. L, O, CT, EN, DT; CH, CN, MH, NU, WF, Y.

1814 Entry cancelled.

1815   [–] Prælectiones academicæ. Oxonii, e theatro Sheldoniano: væneunt in officina Benj. Tooke, Londinensis, 1692.
8°. T.C.II 425. L, O, CK, EN, DT; CH, CU, LC, MH, NP,
Y.

1816   [–] Reflexions on a pamphlet, entitled, Remarks. By
T. Snowden for John Everingham, 1698. 4°.* L, C, OC,
EC, BAMB; MIU, WF.

1817   —A reply to Mr. Baxter's pretended confutation. For
Benj. Tooke, 1681. 8°. T.C.I 426. L, O, C, E, DT; NC,
NU, PU, WF, Y.

1818   —Separation of churches. For Benjamin Tooke, 1679.
4°. T.C.I 339. L, O, C, EN, DT; BN, CH, CN, MH, NU,
WF, Y.

1819   [–] Some considerations of present concernment. By
T. R. for Benj. Tooke, 1675. 8°. T.C.I 186. L, O, C,
EN, DT; CH, IU, TSM, WF, Y.

1820   —A treatise concerning the lawfulness of instrumental
music. For W. Hawes, London, and Henry Clements,
in Oxford, and W. Burton, at Tiverton, 1700. 8°.
T.C.III 182. L, O, C, LW, E; CN, LC, MH, NU, Y.

1821   — —Second edition. For William Haws, 1700. 8°.
T.C.III 247. L, C, LCL, OC, DT; CH, LC, MH, WF, Y.

1822   —Two letters of advice. Dublin, by Benjamin Tooke, to
be sold by Joseph Wilde, 1672. 8°. T.C.I 116. DIX 144.
L, O, C, E, DT; CH, MH, NC, NU, Y.

1823   [–] —Second edition. By M. C. for Benjamin Tooke,
1680. 8°. T.C.I 422. L, O, C, LL, E; CLC, NU, PL, WF, Y.

1824   — —Third edition. For B. Tooke, to be sold by Walter
Kettilby, 1691. 8°. T.C.II 362. L, O, CT, EN, DT; CH,
CU, TU, WF, Y.

1824A   — —"Third" edition. For Benjamin Tooke, and sold
by Samuel Simpson, and Richard Green, Cambridge,
1691. 8°. CH.

1825   —Two short discourses. For Benj. Tooke, 1676. 8°. T.C.I
256. L, O, C, E, DT; CH, NP, NU, Y.

1826   — —[Anr. ed.] —, 1688. 4°. T.C.II 245. L, O, C, EN,
DT; CH, MH, TU, WF, Y.

1827   [–] A vindication of the deprived bishops. Printed,
1692. 4°. L, O, C, EN, DT; CH, LC, MH, NU, Y.

1827A   **Doe, Charles.** A collection of experience. [1700.] 12°.
L, O.

1827B   —The reason why not infant sprinkling. 1694. 12°. L,
MHS.

1827C   — —Fourth edition, 1694. 12°. LCL.

Dogerell, Owen, pseud.

1828   **Doggett, Thomas.** The country-wake. For Sam. Briscoe, sold by R. Wellington, R. Parker, 1696. 4°. L,
LGI, HH, EN; CH, CN, MH, NC, TU, WF, Y.

1829   —[Anr. ed.] —, [1697]. 4°. L, O, OW, A; CH, CU, MH,
TU, WF, Y.

1829A   **Doglioni, Giovanni Nicolo.** The recovery of lost
time. For W. Crook, 1676. 4°.* Y.

1830   A dog's elegy, or Rvpert's tears. Printed at London, for
G. B. July 27, 1644. 4°.* LT, EN; Y.

1830A   **Dolaeus, Johan.** Systema medinale. For T. Passinger,
T. Sawbridge, and T. Flesher, 1686. 8°. T.C.II 167.
LCP, LCS, LWL; CLC, NAM, MIU, WF, Y.

1831   **Dolben, John, bp.** A sermon preached . . . March 24.
1664/5. For Timothy Garthwait, 1665. 4°. L, O, CT,
LL, DC; CH, MIU, WF, Y.

1832   —A sermon preached . . . June 20th. 1665. By A,
Maxwell for Timothy Garthwait, 1655. 4°.* L, O, LG,
CT, YM; WF, Y.

1833   —A sermon preached . . . Aug. 14. 1666. For Timothy
Garthwait, 1666. 4°.* L, LG, CT, DC, YM; CH, MBA,
MIU, NU, WF, Y.

1834   **Dole, Dorcas.** Once more a warning. [London], printed,
1683. 4°.* L, LF; MU, PL.

1834A   — —[Anr. ed.] —, 1684. 4°.* L, C, LF, OC, BR; MH, PH.

1835   —A salutation and seasonable exhortation. By John
Bringhurst, 1682/3. brs. LF, BBN; MH.

1835A   — —Second edition. Printed and sold by T. Sowle,
1700. 8°.* L, LF; CLC, MU, PH, Y.

1836   —A salutation of my endeared love. colop: By John
Bringhurst, 1685. cap., 4°.* L, O, LF, BBN, BR; CH,
NR, PH, WF, Y.

1836A   — —[Anr. ed.] [London, 1685?] 4°.* PL, PSC, Y.

Doleful dance. [n.p., 1655–80]. See Hill, Thomas.

Dolefull fall of Andrew Sall. [n.p.], 1674. See French,
Nicholas, bp.

1837   The doleful lamentation of Cheap-side Crosse. For F.
C. and T.B., 1641. 4°.* LT, O, CT, LG, LP; CH, LC,
MH, NU, Y.

1838   The doleful lamentation of Thomas Dangerfield. For
J. Huzzey, 1685. brs. O, HH; MH, Y.

1839   Dolefvll newes from Edinborough. [London], for William Field, 1641. 4°.* LT; MH, WF, Y.

Doleful newes from Ireland. 1642. See S., P.

Doleman, R., pseud. See Parsons, Robert.

1840   Dolly and Molly. [London], for P. Brookby [sic], [1672–95].
brs. L, O, HH; MH, Y.

Dolor, ac voluptas. 1660. See W., T.

1841   Dolvs an virtvs? Or, an answer. For Henry Brome, 1668.
4°.* L, O, C, OC, HH; CH, MH, NU, WF, Y.

1842   Domestick devotions. By J. Playford for William
Shrowsbery, 1683. 8°. T.C.II 37. L, O, CS.

1843   Dominium maris: or, the dominion of the sea. By William Du Gard, 1652. 4°.* LT, O, ES; CSB, MH, NC, WF.

Dominus est Deus. Oxford, 1690. See Elys Edmund.

Domus sadica. 1653. See Macedo, Francisco de.

1843A   **Domvile, Sir Thomas.** To the honourable knights
. . . the humble petition. [London, 1690.] brs. L.

Don Carlos: or. 1674. See Saint-Réal, Cesar Vischard
de.

1844   Don Henrique de Castro. Or, the conquest of the
Indies. By R.E. for R. Bentley and S. Magnes, [1686].
12°. T.C.II 156. L; CLC, CN, WF.

Don Juan Lamberto, or. 1661. See Montelion,

1845   Don Pedro de Quixot, or in English the right reverend
Hugh Peters. For T. Smith, 1660. brs. LT; MH.

1845A   Don Quixot redivivus encountering a barns-door.
For the company of informers, 1673. 4°.* LCL; CH, MIU.

1846   Don Samuel Crispe. [London, for H. Marsh], 1660. 4°.*
L, O.

1847 Don Sebastian King of Portugal. *For R. Bentley and S. Magnes*, 1683. 12°. T.C.II 27. L; CLC, CN, MH, WF, Y.

1848 Entry cancelled.

Don Zara del Fogo. 1656. *See* Holland, Samuel.

1849 **D[onaldson], J[ames.]** Elegie on . . . Alexander Lord Reath. [*Edinburgh, J. Reid?*], 1698. brs. ALDIS 3743. EN, ES.

1850 —Elegie on the much to be lamented death, & loss of the right honourable—William Earl of Crawfoord. [*Edinburgh, J. Reid?*], 1698. brs. ALDIS 3744. ES.

1851 —Elegie on the much to be lamented death of the worthy—Umphrey Milne. [*Edinburgh, J. Reid?*], 1695. brs. ALDIS 3455. ES.

1852 —Husbandry anatomized. *Edinburgh*, 1696. 12°. ALDIS 3553. ES.

1853 ——[Anr. ed.] *Edinburgh, by John Reid*, 1697–8. 8°. ALDIS 3662. L, R, EN, FSF; CH, NC, PL, WF, Y.

1853A [–] A letter to a member of Parliament from a wel-wisher. [*Edinburgh?* 1697.] cap., 4°.* L, OP, EN; MU, WF, Y.

1853B —Overtures for regulating . . . linnen. *Edinburgh, John Reid*, 1700. 8°.* LUG.

1854 [–] A pick-tooth for swearers. *Edinburgh, by John Reid*, 1698. 4°.* ALDIS 3769. L, EN, ES; CH, WCL.

1855 [–] Postscript to husbandry anatomiz'd. *Edinburgh, by John Reid*, 1698. 8°.* ALDIS 3772. L, FSF; NC, WDA, Y.

1856 [–] The undoubted art of thriving. *Edinburgh, by John Reid*, 1700. 4°. L, EN; CH, MH, NC, RPJ, Y.

Donation of Canaan. 1677. *See* L., S.

Doncker. *See* Danckerts.

1857 [**Done, John.**] A miscellanea of morall, theologicall, . . . sentances. [*London*], *for Iohn Sweeting*, 1650. 8°. O, SP.

1858 **Donne, John.** Βιαθαναος. *By John Dawson*, [1644]. 4°. KEYNES 47. L, O, C, LI, ENC; CH, CU, LC, MH, NP, MMO, TU, Y.

1859 ——[Anr. ed.] *For Humphrey Moseley*, 1648. 4°. KEYNES 48. LT, O, CT, EN, DT; BN, CH, LC, MH, NU, Y.

1860 ——Second edition. *Printed*, 1700. 8°. T.C.III 178. KEYNES 49. L, O, C, OC, EN; CU, MH, NU, WF, Y.

1861 —Essayes in divinity. *By T. M. for Richard Marriott*, 1651. 12°. KEYNES 50. LT, O, C, CT, ES; CH, CN, MH, WF, Y.

1862 —Fifty sermons, . . . The second volume. *By Ja. Flesher for M. F. J. Marriot, and R. Royston*, 1649. fol. KEYNES 30. L, O, C, LP, EN; CH, CU, MH, TU, WF, Y.

1863 —Ignatius his conclave. *Printed at London*, 1653. 4°. KEYNES 10. O, LCL, ES; MH, NU, Y.

1864 —Letters to severall persons of honour. *By J. Flesher, for Richard Marriot*, 1651. 4°. KEYNES 55. LT, O, CT, LVD, EN; CH, CN, LC, MH, TU, Y.

1865 ——Second edition. *By J. Flesher, and are to be sold by John Sweeting*, 1654. 4°. KEYNES 56. L, O, CT, CC, GK; BN, CH, CU, MH, TU, WF, Y.

1866 —Paradoxes, problemes, essayes, characters. *By T. N. for Humphrey Moseley*, 1652. 12°. KEYNES 45. LT, C, LW, ENC, GK; CH, MH, NU, WCL, Y.

1867 ——[Anr. ed.] —, 1652. 12°. KEYNES 46. L, O, OC, ES, GK; CN, MH, WF.

1868 —Poems. Fourth edition. *By M. F. for John Marriot*, 1649. 8°. KEYNES 81. GK; CH, IU, MH, Y.

1869 ——Fifth edition. *For John Marriot, and are to be sold by Richard Marriot*, 1650. 8°. KEYNES 82. L, OC, CE, LW, E; BN, CH, MH, WC, WF, Y.

1870 ——Sixth edition. *By J. Flesher, and are to be sold by John Sweeting*, 1654. 8°. KEYNES 83. L, O, C, DT, GK; CH, CU, MH, TU, WF, Y.

1871 —Seventh edition. *In the Savoy, by T. N. for Henry Herringman*, 1669. 8°. KEYNES 84. L, O, CT, LI, DT; BN, CH, CU, MH, TU, WF, Y.

1872 —XXVI. sermons. The third volume. *By T. N. for James Magnes*, 1660/1. fol. KEYNES 31. L, O, C, LP, GK; CN, MH, OCI, Y.

1873 ——[Anr. ed.] *By Thomas Newcomb*, 1661. fol. KEYNES 32. L, GK; CU, WF.

1874 ——[Anr. ed.] *At the charge of Dr. Donne*, 1661. fol. KEYNES 320. GK; Y.

1875 **Donne, John, jr.** Dr. Donne's last will and testament. [*London*], *printed February 23*, 1662. brs. KEYNES 272. L, O, CT; MH, Y.

1876 ——[Anr. ed.] *Printed*, 1663. 4°. GK; MH.

1877 —Donne's satyr. *By R. W. for M. Wright*, 1662. 8°. KEYNES 271. L; MH, MIU.

1877A [–] To the right honorable the Lord Chancellor, the humble Peter Hon of Covent Garden. [*London*, 1661]. brs. O.

1878 [**Donneau de Vizé, Jean.**] A diary of the siege of Luxembourg. *By J. G. for D. Brown; to be sold by W. Davis*, 1864. 4°. T.C.II 96. L, O, MR, EN, DT; CH, MIU, NC, WF, Y.

1879 **Doolittle, Samuel.** The righteous man's hope. *For Thomas Cockerill*, 1693. 8°. T.C.II 451. L, O, C, LW, CPE; NGT, WF.

1880 —A sermon occasioned . . . by the late earthquake . . . eighth of September, 1692. *By J. R. for J. Salusbury*, 1692. 4°.* T.C.II 451. L, O, CT, LW; Y.

1880A **Doolittle, Thomas.** A call to delaying sinners. Sixth edition. *For H. Newman*, 1698. 12°. EN.

1880B ——[Anr. ed.] *Boston in N.B., by Bartholomew Green, & John Allen, for Benjamin Eliot*, 1700. 12°. MHS.

1880C —Captives bound in chains. *By A. M. for Tho. Parkhurst*, 1674. 8°. O, YM; MH, NN, Y.

1881 —Catechism made practical. 1688. 8°. LCL.

1882 —Catechizing necessary for the ignorant. *Printed and are to be sold by Tho. Parkhurst*, 1692. 8°.* O.

1883 —Earthquakes explained. *For John Salusbury*, 1693. 8°. T.C.II 427. L, O, C, LG, LPO; CJC, MB, RPJ, WF, Y.

1883A ——[Anr. ed.], *Boston, by Benjamin Harris*, 1693, 8°. EVANS 634. LC.

1884 —Fears and jealousies ceas'd. [*London*, 1688.] 4°.* L, LIL, OC; CH, MU, NC, WF, Y.

1885 —The Lords last sufferings shewed in the Lords-Supper. *For John Dunton*, 1682. 12°. T.C.I 458. L, LCL, LW, GU; MH.

1886 —Love to Christ, necessary. *For Tho. Cockerill, 1692.* 8°. T.C.II 421. LW; NU.

1887 — —[Anr. ed.] —, 1693. 8°. L, O, C, LCL; WF, Y.

1888 —The mourner's directory. *By J.A. for Tho. Cockeril,* 1693. 8°. T.C.II 451. L, O, C, CPE; CLC, MH, NU, WF, Y.

1888A — —[Anr. ed.] 1695. 8°. LCL.

1889 —A plain method of catechizing. *By John Astwood, for the author, to be had at the author's house,* 1698. 8°. L, LCL, AN, ENC; PPT, Y.

1890 — —Third edition. *By K.Astwood for the author to be had at the author's house* 1699. 8°. L ENC; NU, WF.

1891 — —Fourth edition. *For T.Parkhurst,* 1700. 12°. T.C.III 205. LSC, LW.

1892 —Rebukes for sin. *Printed, and are to be sold by Dorman Newman,* 1667. 12°. L, LCL; CLC, MIU, NPT, WF.

1893 —The saints convoy. *For John Lawrence,* 1698. 8°. T.C.III 90. L, O, LCL, LW; MH, NPT, NU.

1894 —The saints mansions. *For John Lawrence,* 1698. 8°. L; NPT, NU.

1895 —[Hebrew] Or, a serious enquiry. *By R.I. for J. Johnson, to be sold by A.Brewster,* 1666. 8°. L, O, C, LCP, LG; CLC, CN, NU, WF, WSG.

1896 [–] A spiritual antidote. *Printed,* 1665. 8°. O, OB, LW, LWL; CN.

1897 — —Second edition. *By R.I. for Tho. Passenger,* 1667. 8°. L, O, C, LCL, YM; MIU, NGT, WF.

1898 —The swearer silenced. *By J.Astwood for Jonathan Greenwood, to be sold by Tho. Parkhurst,* 1689. 12°. T.C.II 237. L, O; WF.

1899 —A treatise concerning the Lords Supper. *By R.I. for Joshua Johnson, to be sold by William Adderton,* 1667. 12°. O; CLC.

1899A — —Sixth edition. *By Thomas Ratcliffe and Mary Daniel for Edward Thomas,* 1671. 12°. AN.

1899B — —Seventh edition. *By E.Crowch for G.Calvert and S.Sprint,* 1678. 12°. NPT.

1900 — —Ninth edition. *By Fr. Leach, for G.Calvert,* 1675. 12°. L, O.

1901 — —Eleventh edition. *For G.Calvert, and S.Sprint,* 1680. 12°. L; CLC, MH, NPT.

1902 — —Twelfth edition. *For G.Calvert and R.Simpson.* 1681. 12°. LCL, LW; CLC.

1902A — —Thirteenth edition. *By J.A. for G.Calvert and Ralph Simpson, and S.Sprint,* 1683. 12°. Y.

1902B — —Fourteenth edition. —, 1687. 12°. CPE; MH, WF.

1903 — —Fifteenth edition. *By J.Astwood for Ralph Simpson,* 1689. 12°. NU.

1903A — —"Fifteenth" edition. *For Edward Mory,* 1690. 12°. MH, NPT, WF.

1904 — —Nineteenth edition. *For Ralph Simpson,* 1697. 12°. L.

1904A — —Twentieth edition. —, 1700. 12°. O.

1905 — —"Nineteenth" edition. *Boston: reprinted by B.Green and J.Allen, for Benjamin Eliot,* 1700. 8°. EVANS 909. INU, MB, MWA.

1905A — —[Anr. ed.] *Boston, by B.Green and J.Allen for Samuel Phillips,* 1700. 8°. MWA, UCLA, WCL.

1906 —The young man's instructer [sic]. *For Thomas Parkhurst,* 1673. 8°. T.C.I 140. L, O, C, LW, E; CH, MIU, WF, Y.

1907 Doomes-day: or, the great day. *For W.Ley,* 1647. 4°.* LT, O; CH, NR, NU.

1908 A door of hope: or, a call and declaration. [*London,* 1661?] cap., 4°.* LT.

Door of salvation opened. 1648. *See* B., R.

[Same title.] 1665. *See* Passenger, T.

Door of truth opened. 1645. *See* Calamy, Edmund.

Door opened. 1667. *See* Nayler, James.

1909 A door opening into Christian religion. *Printed,* 1662. 8°. NU, Y.

1910 [**Dopping, Anthony, bp.**] The case of the Dissenters of Ireland. *Dublin, Joseph Ray,* 1695. fol.* DIX 267. DT.

1911 —A form of reconciliation. *Dublin, Andw. Crook,* 1691. 16°. DIX 246. DM.

1912 Entry cancelled.

1913 —A sermon preached . . . November, 18, 1693. *Dublin, by Joseph Ray,* 1694. 4°.* DIX 260. L, C, DI, DT.

1914 —Speech of. *For B. Took, and sold by Randal Taylor,* 1690. brs. L, MC, HH.

1915 —The speech of. *Printed at London, and reprinted at Edinburgh, by the heir of Andrew Anderson,* 1690. brs. ALDIS 3036. L, EN; MH.

1916 —A speech spoken by the Bishop of Meath . . . July the 7th, 1690. colop: *Dublin, by Andrew Crook assignee of Benjamin Tooke,* [1690]. brs. DIX 241. C, DN; MH, Y.

1917 —Tractatus de visitationibus Episcopalibus. *Dublin, Jo. Brocas and Cornelius Carter,* 1696. 8°. T.C.II 602. DIX 282. O, CS, CD, LLP, DT.

1918 **Dorchester, Henry Pierpoint, marquess of.** The Lord Marquesse of Dorchesters letter to the Lord Roos. *Printed,* 1660. 4°.* L, O, C; MIU, OWC, TU.

1919 —The reasons why. [*London*], *printed the 20th of March,* [1660]. brs. LT, O; CH.

1919A —My lord Newarks speech to the trained bands. *By Edward Griffin,* 1642. 4°.* LT, O, EC; CLC, MH, MU, TU, Y.

1920 —A true and perfect copy of a letter written by. [*London,* 1660.] brs. LT; MH, Y.

1921 —Two speeches spoken. *Printed,* 1641. 4°.* LT, O, C, OC, DT; CH, CN, MH, NU, WF, Y.

1922 **Dormer, John.** The respondents case. [*London?* 1700.] brs. L.

1923 [**Dormer, John, alias Huddleston.**] The new plot of the Papists: by which they designed. *For Robert Harford,* 1679. fol.* L, O, C, MR, E; CH, Y.

1924 [–] The new plot of the Papists to transform traitors. *Printed,* 1679. 4°.* L, O, DC; CH, MH, NU, WF, Y.

1925 [–] —[Anr. ed.] *Dublin, reprinted,* 1679. 4°.* DIX 173. C, DT.

1926 —The Pharisee's council. *By Mary Thompson for the author,* 1688. 4°.* L.

1927 —A sermon of judgment. *By Nat. Thompson*, 1687. 4°.* O, MC; NU, Y.

1928 —A sermon preach'd before Their Majesties ... November 17th. 1686. *By Nat. Thompson*, 1687. 4°.* L, O, CT, MC, SC; NU, TU, WF.

1928A [–] Usury explain'd. *By D.L.*, 1695/6. 8°. L, O, C; CJC, MH, NC, WF, Y.

1929 —The why's? and the how's? *By Nat. Thompson*, 1687. 4°.* L, O, MC; NU, RPB.

1929A [**Dormer, P.**] Monarchia triumphans, or, the super-eminency. *Printed* 1666. 4°.* MH.

1930 **Dorney, Henry.** Divine contemplations. *By James Rawlins, for John Wright*, 1684. 12°. L; CLC, LC, MH, WF, Y.

1931 **Dorney, John.** A brief and exact relation of the most materiall and remarkeable [sic] passages. *For Tomas [sic] Vnderhill*, 1643. 4°.* LT, O, LUS, SP; CH, MH, WF, Y.

1932 —Certain speeches. *By A.M. for Tho. Vnderhill*, 1653. 8°. L, O; CLC, MH, TU, WF, Y.

1933 —City of Glouc. At a common council ... [22 Aug. 1656]. *[London]*, 1656. brs. L.

1934 **Dornford, Robert.** Gospel-light. *By R.W. for Francis Tyton*, 1652. 12°. LT; CLC.

1935 —Gospel-mysterie. *By R.W. for Francis Tyton*, 1652. 12°. LT; WF.

1935A **Dorotheus Siculus.** The origine of atheism. 1689. 4°. O.

1935B **Dorrill, Robert.** Captain Dorrill's answer to Mr. Littleton's letter. *[London? 1695.]* brs. MH.

1935C **Dorrington, Theophilus.** Arweiniwr catrefol i'r iawn. *J.R. dros B. Aylmer*, 1700. 8°. AN.

1935D —Consolations addressed to a friend. *For John Wyatt*, 1695. 8°. T.C.II 555. CT; CLC, MH, PL.

—Excellent woman described. 1692. *See* DuBosc, Jacques.

1936 —A familiar guide to the right and profitable receiving of the Lord's Supper. *By J.H. for Brab. Aylmer*, 1695. 12°. T.C.II 517. L, O, CS; CLC.

1937 ——Fifth edition. *For Brab. Aylmer*, 1700. 12°. L, O.

1938 —Family devotions. Volume I. *For John Wyat*, 1693. 8°. T.C.II 451. L, O, CS, OC.

1938A ——Second edition. —, 1696. 8°. T.C.II 583. D.

1939 ——Volume II. *For John Wyat*, 1694. 8°. T.C.II 491. L, O, CS, OC.

1940 ——The third and fourth volumes. *For John Wyat*, 1695. 8°. T.C.II 555. L, OC, CT, D; PL.

1941 ——Volume IV. *For John Wyat*, 1695. 8°. L.

1942 ——The honour due to the civil magistrate. *For John Wyat*, 1696. 4°.* T.C.II 577. L, O, C, LW, CT; CLC, NU, WF, Y.

1943 —Instruction familiere. *Pour Brabazon Aylmer*, 1699. sixes. L.

1944 —Observations concerning the present state of the religion. *For John Wyat*, 1699. 8°. T.C.III 107. L, O, CT, EN, DT; BN, CLC, NC, NU, WF, Y.

1945 [–] Reform'd devotions. *For Joseph Watts*, 1686. 12°. T.C.II 163. 8C, OM.

1946 ——Second edition. *By J.A. for Joseph Watts*, 1687. 12°. T.C.II 184. O, CT; CLC, NU, WF.

1947 [–] —Third edition. *By H. Clark, for Richard Cumberland*, 1693. 12°. T.C.II 458. C, OC, ELY.

1948 [–] —Fourth edition. —, 1696. 12°. T.C.II 594. L; Y.

1949 [–] —Fifth edition. *For A. Roper and R. Basset*, 1700. 12°. L, O, BAMB; NNG.

1950 —The right use of an estate. *For Thomas Cockerill*, 1683. 4°. T.C.II 12. L, O, C, LW, CT; CN, MH, V, WF, Y.

1951 **Dorset, Edward Sackville,** *earl of.* The Earl of Dorset his speech for propositions of peace. *Printed*, 1642. [/3]. 4°.* MADAN 1200. LT, O, C, HH, DT; CH, MH, NC, Y.

1952 —Two speeches spoken. *First printed at Oxford by Leonard Lichfield, and now re-printed at London for Edward Hartley, [1642/3]*. 4°.* MADAN 1155. LT, O; CLC, MH, WF, Y.

1953 The Dorset-shire damosel. *[London], for J. Deacon, [1684–95]*. brs. L, CM, HH; WCL.

1954 The Dorset-shire lovers. *For P. Brooksby, [1688–92]*. brs. HH; MH.

Dose for Chamberlain. 1661. *See* Cook, William.

1954A The doting Athenians imposing questions. *[London, 1692.]* brs. CM; TU.

Doting doctor. *[n.p.]*, 1655. *See* E., N.

1955 The doting old dad. *[London], for P. Brooksby, [1685–88]*. brs. L, HH; MH.

1955A The double deliverance. *By R. Taylor*, 1690. fol.* T.C.II 347. CH, MH, Y.

Double descent. 1692. *See* Ames, Richard.

1956 The double list, containing. colop: *For A. Roper and E. Wilkenson*, 1695. cap., fol.* O; CLC, Y.

Double proposal. 1695/6. *See* Whately, Thomas.

Double writing. *[n.p., 1648.]* *See* Petty, *Sir* William.

Doubtful Robin. *[n.p., 1676–85.]* *See* Browne, Tobia.

Doubting virgin. *[n.p., 1680.]* *See* Browne, Tobias.

1957 The doubting virgins satisfaction. *[London], for P. Brooksby, [1680?]*. brs. L, O.

Doubts concerning the Roman infallibility. 1687. *See* Maurice, Henry.

1958 **Douch, John.** Englands jubilee: or, her happy return. *For R.R., and are to be sold by Tho. Miller*, 1660. 4°.* LT, C; CH, WF.

1959 **Doughty, John.** Analecta sacra. *Typis Guil. Godbid, impensis Ro. Littlebury*, 1658. 8°. L, O, C, LW, E; MH, NPT, WF, Y.

1960 ——Pars posterior. *Excudebat R.W. sumptibus Joannis Baker*, 1660. 8°. LT, C, CT, EC, ELY.

1961 [–] The kings cavse. *[London], printed*, 1644. 45pp.s 4°.* LT, O, DC, HH, DT; MB, WF.

1962 [–] —[Anr. ed.] 47 pp. *[Oxford, by H. Hall]*, printed, 1644. 4°. MADAN 1558. O, OC, EC, HH; CH, CLC, WF, Y.

1963 —Velitationes polemicæ; or polemicall short discussions. *By W.H. to be sold by Robert Littlebury*, 1651. 8°. O, C, CS, P, ENC; Y.

1964 — —[Anr. ed.] —, 1652. 8°. L, C, LCL, E, DT; CH, CN, MH, NU, WF.

1965 — —[Anr. ed.] 1660. 8°. DT.

1966 [**Doughty, Thomas.**] A true relation of the carriage of a party of horse. For R. W., 1646. 4°.* LT; MH.ʿ

1967 [**Douglas,** *Lady* **Eleanor.**] Amend, amend; Gods kingdome is at hand. [London, 1643.] 4°.* HINDLE 6. L; CH, CN.

1968 [–] And without proving what we say. [n.p., 1648?] cap., 4°.* HINDLE 33. L; MH, WF.

1969 —Apocalyps, chap. 11. Its accomplishment. [n.p., 164–?] cap., 4°.* HINDLE 52. O; MH, WF.

1970 [–] Apocalypsis Jesu Christi. [n.p.], printed, 1644. 4°.* HINDLE 10. L.

1971 —The Lady Eleanor, her appeale. [n.p.], printed, 1641. 4°.* HINDLE 4. LT; CSS, MH.

1972 —The Lady Eleanor her appeal. [n.p.], printed, 1646. 4°.* HINDLE 25. O, A.

1972A [–] The appearance. [London], printed, 1650. 4°.* WF.

1972B —The arraignment. [London], printed, 1650. 4°.* WF.

1973 [–] As not unknowne, this petition. [n.p., 1644/5.] brs. HINDLE 14. LT, OW; MH, WF.

1974 [–] Before the Lords second coming. [n.p.], printed, 1650. 4°.* HINDLE 43. LT; WF.

1975 [–] The benediction. [n.p.], printed, 1651. 4°.* HINDLE 46a. O, C; CH, CN, MH, WF, Y.

1976 [–] The benidiction. I have an errand. [n.p.], printed, 1651. 4°.* HINDLE 46b. L, O, C; WF, Y.

1977 [–] The benediction. I have an errand. [n.p.], printed, 1651. 4°.* HINDLE 46c. L; MH, WF.

1978 [–] Bethlehem signifying the house of bread. [n.p.], printed, 1652. 4°.* HINDLE 51. O; MH, WF.

1979 —The bill of excommunication. [n.p.], printed, 1649. 4°.* HINDLE 40. L; WF.

1980 [–] The blasphemous charge against Her. [n.p.], printed, 1649. 4°.* HINDLE 37. L; WF.

1981 [–] —Second edition ["her" for "Her".]. [n.p.], printed, 1649. 4°.* HINDLE 38. OW; MH.

1982 —The brides preparation. [London], printed March, 1644[5]. 4°.* HINDLE 15. LT, DT; WF.

1982A [–] The crying charge. Ezekiel. 22. [London], printed, 1649. 4°.* MH, WF.

1983 —The day of ivdgements modell. [London], printed, 1646. 4°.* HINDLE 23. LT, O, SP; CLC, MH.

1984 [–] The dragons blasphemous charge. [n.p.], printed, 1651. 4°.* L; MH.

1985 [–] Elijah the Tishbite's supplication. [n.p.], printed, 1650. 4°.* HINDLE 44. LT; WF.

1986 [–] The everlasting gospel. [n.p.], printed, Decem., 1649. 4°.* HINDLE 36. O; MH, WF.

1987 —The excommunication out of paradice. [n.p.], printed, 1647. 4°.* HINDLE 27. L, O, OC; MH, WF.

1988 [–] Ezekiel, Cap. 2. [n.p., 164–?] cap., 4°.* HINDLE 53. O; MH, WF.

1988A [–] Ezekiel the prohpet explained. [London? 1679.] 4°.* WF.

1989 —For the blessed feast of Easter. [n.p.], printed, 1646. 4°.* HINDLE 22. L; WF, Y.

1989A [–] For the most honorable states. Printed, 1649. 4°.* WF.

1989B —For the right noble, Sir Balthazar Gerbier. Printed, 1649. 4°.* WF.

1990 [–] For Whitsun Tyds last feast. [n.p.], printed, 1645. 4°.* HINDLE 17. OW; WF.

1991 —From the Lady Eleanor, her blessing. [London], printed, 1644. 4°.* HINDLE 9. LT; WF.

1991A [–] The gatehouse salutation from. [London], printed, 1646. 4°.* MH, WF.

1992 —Given to the Elector Prince Charles of the Rhyne. Amsterdam: by Frederick Stam., 1633. [i.e. 1648]. 4°.* HINDLE 29. OW; MH.

1993 — —[Anr. ed., "Charls."] —, 1633 [i.e. 1651]. 4°.* HINDLE 48. L, O; MH, WF.

1994 —Great Brittains visitation. [London], printed, 1645. 4°.* HINDLE 18. L.

1995 —Hells destruction. [n.p.], printed, 1651. 4°.* HINDLE 45. O; MH, WF.

1996 —I am the first, and the last. [n.p., 1644/5.] cap., 4°.* HINDLE 13. LT.

1996A [–] Je le tien. The general restitution. [London], printed, 1646. 4°.* WF.

1996B —The Lady Eleanor Douglas, dowager, her iubilees. [London, 1650.] 4°.* WF.

1996C —The mystery of general redemption. [London], printed, 1647. 4°.* MH, WF.

1997 —The new Jerusalem at hand. [n.p.], printed, 1649. 4°.* HINDLE 34. L, OW; MH, WF.

1998 [–] The new proclamation, in ansvver. Printed, 1649. 4°.* HINDLE 39. L.

1999 —Of errors ioyned vvith Gods word. [London], printed, 1645. 4°.* HINDLE 16. L.

1999A —Of the general great days approach. [London], printed, 1648. 4°.* WF.

2000 —Of times and seasons. [n.p.], printed, 1651. 4°.* HINDLE 49. L; WF.

2001 [–] A prayer or petition for peace. [London], printed, 1644. 4°.* HINDLE 11. L; NF.

2002 [–] —Second edition. —, 1645. 4°.* HINDLE 19. L.

2003 [–] —[Anr. ed.] —, 1645. [i.e. 1647]. 4°.* HINDLE 28. L.

2004 —A prophesie of the last day. Printed, 1645. 4°.* HINDLE 20. L.

2005 —Prophetia de die. Excudebat Tho. Paine, 1644. 4°.* DT.

2005A [–] Reader, the heavy hour. [London], 1648. cap., 4°.* WF.

2006 —The Lady Eleanor her remonstrance. [n.p.], printed, 1648. 4°.* HINDLE 30. L, O.

2007 —The restitution of prophecy. [n.p.], printed, 1651. 4°. HINDLE 47. O; MH, WF.

2008 [–] The restitvtion of reprobates. [London], printed, 1644. 4°.* HINDLE 8. LT; WF.

2009 —The revelation interpreted. [London], printed, 1646. 4°.* HINDLE 24. L, SP; WF.

2010 [–] Samsons fall. Printed, 1642. [i.e. 1649]. 4°.* HINDLE 42. L; WF.

2011 —Samsons legacie. [n.p., 1642.] 4°, DT.

2012 —The [second] co[mming of Our] Lo[rd]. *Printed,* 1645. 4°.* HINDLE 21. L.

2012A —The serpents excommunication. [*London*], *printed,* 1651. 4°.* MH, WF.

2012AA —A sign given tnem. *Printed, 1644. Reprinted, 1649.* 4°.* WF.

2012B —Sions lamentation. [*London*], *printed* 1649. 4°.* O; MH.

2013 —The star to the vvise. *Printed,* 1643. 4°.* HINDLE 7. LT, O; WF.

2014 —Strange and vvonderful prophesies. *For Robert Ibbitson,* 1649. 4°.* HINDLE 35. LT, O, OW; CH, MBP, MH, NC.

2015 [–] To the most honorable the High Covrt of Parliament assembled. &c. My Lords; ther's a time. [*n.p.,* 1643.] cap., 4°.* HINDLE 5. LT, HH; Y.

2016 [–] Tobits book; a lesson. [*London*], *printed,* 1652. 4°.* HINDLE 50. L; MH, WF.

2017 [–] Wherefore to prove the thing. [*n.p.,* 1648.] cap., 4°.* HINDLE 32. L; WF.

2018 —The vvord of God. [*London*], *printed,* 1644. 4°.* HINDLE 12. L, OW, DT.

2019 —The writ of restitution. [*n.p.*], *printed,* 1648. 4°.* HINDLE 31. L; MH, WF.

2020 [–] Zach. 12. And they shall look. [*n.p.,* 1649?] cap., 4°.* HINDLE 41. L, O.

2021 **Douglas, George.** Disputatio juridica. *Edinburgh, heirs of A. Anderson,* 1699. 4°. ALDIS 3841. EN.

Douglas, James. See also Queensberry, James Douglas, duke of.

2022 —Great news from Athlone. [1690.] brs. L.

2023 —A strange and wonderful prophesie of. *By J.C.,* 1651. 4°.* LT; MH.

2024 —Strange news from Scotland. *By J.C.,* 1651. 4°.* LT, EN, HH; WF.

2025 **[Douglas, Robert.]** Copie of a letter from the commission of the General Assembly. *Printed at Edinburgh by Evan Tyler,* 1647. 4°.* BN.

2026 [–] The form and order of the coronation . . . Januarie, 1651. *Aberdeen, by James Brown,* 1651. 4°.* ALDIS 1441. L, HH, E, AU, GU; CN, MB.

2027 [–] —[Anr. ed.] *Aberdene,* —, 1651. 4°.* ALDIS 1442. L, C, HH, EN, AU; CN, MH, PL, WF, Y.

2028 [–] —[Anr. ed.] —, 1651. 4°.* ALDIS 1443. LT, O, HH, FSF; CH, MB, MIU, Y.

2029 [–] —[Anr. ed.] —, 1651. 8°. ALDIS 1444. L, O, HH, EN, AU; MH, Y.

2030 [–] —[Anr. ed.] *According to the copie printed,* 1651. 4°.* HH, D; NU, PL.

2030A [–] —[Anr. ed.] *Aberdene, by James Brown,* 1660. 4°.* ALDIS 1643. EN.

2030B [–] —[Anr. ed.] *Aberdene, by James Brown, and reprinted at London,* 1660. 4°.* L, O, C, LCL, HH; NU, TU, WF, Y.

2031 [–] —[Anr. ed.] *Aberdene, imprinted by James Brown* [1651]; *and-reprinted at London, to be sold by Edward Thomas,* 1660. 4°.* L, O, HH, EN, ENC; MM, TU, WF.

2032 [–] —[Anr. ed.] *Printed,* 1660. 4°.* L, O, CT, HH, ES; CLC, CN, LC, MH, TU, VC, Y.

2033 [–] —[Anr. ed.] *Aberdeen printed, and Edinburgh, reprinted by John Reid,* 1700. 8°. FSF.

2034 [–] A phenix, or, the solemn league. *Edinburgh, printed,* [1662]. 12°. ALDIS 2776. L, EN, FSF; CH, CN, NU, MB, TU, WF, Y.

2035 Entry cancelled.

2036 —Master Dowglasse his sermon. [*Edinburgh,* 1661.] 4°.* LSC, ES; CLC.

2037 — —[Anr. ed.] *Printed,* 1661. 4°.* L, O, E; CLC, MH, WF.

2038 [–] A short information and brotherly exhortation to our brethren. colop: *Aberdene by James Brown,* [1651]. cap., 4°.* ALDIS 1453. E, EN.

[Douglas, Thomas.] Jerubbal. Or, a vindication. 1668. See Brown, Robert.

2039 [–] Μαρτυριον χριστιανόν, . . . or a Christian and sober testimony. *For the author,* 1664. 4°. O, CT, LG, LW; CH, MIU, PL.

2040 —Θεανορωπος: or. *For H.C. and T.P.,* 1661. 4°. L, LW, LCL, WCA; NU, WF.

2041 Entry cancelled.

2042 **Douglas, William.** Academiarvm vindiciæ. *Aberdoniæ, exudebat Yzcibus Brunus,* 1659. 4°. ALDIS 1594. O, E, EN, AU; MH.

2043 —Oratio panegyrica. *Edinburgi, ex officina societatis stationariorum,* 1660. 4°. ALDIS 1641. HH, E, EN, ES, AU; CH, CLC, CN.

2044 —The stable trveths of the Kirk. *Aberdene, by J.B. in March,* 1660. ALDIS 1642. L, HH, E, EN, AU.

2045 —Vindiciæ Psalmodiæ. *Aberdoniæ, excudebat Jacobus Brunus,* 1657. ALDIS 1566. 4°. L, HH, E, EN, AU; CLC, NPT, Y.

2046 —Vindiciæ veritatis. *Aberdoniæ, excudebat Jacobus Brounus,* 1655. 4°. ALDIS 1516. HH, E, EN, AU; NPT, Y.

2047 **Dove, Henry.** Albiana. A poem. *For Daniel Dring, and sold by John Whitlock,* 1695. fol.* T.C.II 559. O, C, LVF, E; CLC, MH, TU, WF, Y.

2048 —A sermon preached . . . November 5. 1680. *By M.C. for H.Brome, and Benj. Tooke,* 1680. 4°.* T.C.I 413. L, O, C, LL, EN; CH, MH, NU, TU, WF, Y.

2049 —A sermon preached . . . feast of S. Michael, 1682. *For Benj. Tooke,* 1682. 4°.* T.C.I 502. L, O, C, DC, DT; CH, MH, NU, TU, WF, Y.

2050 —A sermon preached . . . January 25. 1684/5. *For Benjamin Tooke,* 1685. 4°.* T.C.II 122. L, O, C, OM, CT; CH, MH, TU, WF, Y.

2051 —A sermon preached . . . Decemb. 2. 1686. *For Benj. Tooke,* 1687. 4°.* T.C.II 186. L, O, C, CT, DT; CH, CU, WF, Y.

2052 —A sermon preached before the Queen, . . . February the fifteenth, 1690/1. *By T.M. for Robert Clavel,* 1691. 4°.* T.C.II 356. L, O, C, OM, EN; CN, NU, WF, Y.

Dove, Jonathan. Almanack. Cambridge, 1641. *See* Almanacs.

2053   **[Dover, John.]** The Roman generalls. *For Samuel Herrick,* 1667. 4°. L, O, C, OW; CH, CN, TU, WF, Y.

2054   **Dowcet, Abraham.** A declaration delivered. *For A. H.,* 1648. 4°.* LT, O; CH, MH, MB, MIU, Y.

2055   **Dowdall, Gerard.** Mr. Dowdall's just and sober vindication. *For Gerard Dowdell,* 1681. 12°. LW, CE, EN; CN, WF.

2055A   **Dowdall, Henry.** The speech of. [*London,* 1689.] brs. MH.

2055B   **Dowdall, Katherine.** To the honourable the knights. [*Dublin, c.* 1695.] brs. DI.

Do-well, *pseud.*

2056   **Dowell, John.** The Leviathan heretical. *Oxon, by L. Lichfield, to be sold by A. Stephens,* 1683. sixes. T.C.II 32. L, O, CT, OM.

2057   [–] The triumph of Christianity. *By F. Grantham, for R. R., and sold by Hugh Ellis,* 1683. 8°. T.C.II 18. L; CH, NU, RPB, WF, Y.

Dowglas. *See* Douglas.

2057A   **Downame, George,** *bp.* An apostolicall injunction. *By M. O.,* 1644. 4°.* Y.

2058   —A briefe summe of divinitie. Third edition. [*Oxford, by H. Hall*], *for W. Webb in Oxford and W. Graves in Cambridge,* 1652. 8°. MADAN 2193. O; NU.

2059   —The covenant of grace. *By John Macock for Ralph Smith,* 1647. 12°. C, LW, CM; CLC, MH, NU.

2060   —The dcotrine of practicall praying. *By W. H. for Nicolas Bourne,* 1656. 4°. O, CCH, LSC.

2061   Entry cancelled.

2062   **[Downame, John.]** Annotations upon all the books. *By John Legatt and John Raworth,* 1645. fol. L, CS, BR, YM, GU; CH, CU, LC, MB, NPT.

2063   [–] —Second edition. *By John Legatt,* 1651. fol. L, C, OB, E, DT; CH, NC, NP, NU, Y.

2064   [–] —Third edition. *By Evan Tyler,* 1657. fol. L, C, OC, P, DT; MH, NN, PBL, WF, Y.

2065   —A briefe concordance. *For N. Bourne and R. Young,* 1642. 8°. L, O, C; CH, NN.

2066   — —[Anr. ed.] *For N. Bourne and J. Young, and sold by Charles Green,* 1646. 8°. L, LW, OC; NN, PU, WF, Y.

2067   — —[Anr. ed.] *By William Du-Gard for Nicolas Bourn, sold by Edward Dod & Nathaniel Ekins,* 1652. 8°. L, C, CT; CLC, CN, IU, NN, WF.

2068   — —[Anr. ed.] *By W. Du-Gard for N. Bourn,* 1654. 12°. L, O, C; CLC, MIU, NPT.

2069   — —[Anr. ed.] *By James Flesher for Nicolas Bourn,* 1659. 12°. L; NN.

2070   — —[Anr. ed.] *By James Flesher for Thomas Clark,* 1663. 12°. I; NN.

2071   — —[Anr. ed.] *For Robert Horn,* 1671. 12°. T.C.I 92. L, O, C, LSC; LC, NC, V, Y.

2072   — —[Anr. ed.] *For Tho. Horne,* 1688. 12°. L, O, AN.

2072A   — —[Anr. ed.] —, 1689. 12°. PL, TU.

2073   — —[Anr. ed.] —, 1696. 12°. CCL, E, SA.

2074   [–] A defence and vindication of the right of tithes. *By George Miller,* 1646. 4°.* LT, O, C, OC, CT; CH, CN, MH, NU, WF, Y.

2075   [–] The second volume of annotations. Third edition. *By Evan Tyler,* 1657. fol. L, P.

2076   —Spiritual physick. *Glasgow, by Robert Sanders,* 1673. 12°. ALDIS 1986. HG, ECS, EN, GU.

2077   —A treatise tending to direct the weak Christian. *For Philemon Stephens,* 1645. 8°. L, O, P, ENC; CU, NPT, NU, Y.

2078   **[Downe, Thomas.]** The first principles of the oracles of God. *For John Hancock,* 1677. 8°. L, O, LCL, AU.

2079   **Downe, William Dudie, 1st visc.** Catalogus bibliotheca. [*London*], 1680. 4°. L, OP.

2080   **Downes, Henry.** The excellency of publick charity. *For Charles Harper,* 1697. 4°.* T.C.III 11. L, O, CT, OM, EC; MBA, NU, WF.

2081   **Downes, John.** A true and humble representation of. [*London,* 1660.] brs. L.

2082   **[Downes, Theophilus.]** A discourse concerning the signification of allegiance. [*London,* 1689.] cap., 4°.* L, C, OC, CT, EN; CH, WF, Y.

2083   [–] An examination of the arguments drawn from Scripture. *Printed,* 1691. 4°. L, OM, CT, MR, EN; CH, MB, NU, WF, Y.

Downfal of Anti-Christ. 1644. *See* Carpenter, Richard.

Downfall of Babylon. [1643.] *See* R., S.

2084   The downe-fall of Dagon. [*London*], *for Thomas Wilson,* 1643. 4°.* LT, O, LG, LP, HH; CH, Y.

2085   —[Anr. ed.] *Printed at London,* 1653. 4°.* LT; CH.

2086   The dovvnfall of greatnesse. [*London*], *printed,* 1641. 4°.* LT, O, CS, YM, D; CH, Y.

2087   The dovvnfall of Mercurius Britannicus. [*London*], *printed,* 1660. brs. LT.

Downfall of pride. 1656. *See* Crouch, Humphrey.

2088   The dovvnefall of temporizing poets. [*London*], *printed,* 1641. 4°.* LT, C, LG, WCA, A; CH, CN, MH, Y.

2089   The down-fall of the ark. *Printed,* 1661. brs. L; MH.

2090   The downfall of the bailiffs. *For Thomas Grumbleton,* 1675. 4°.* LUG; Y.

2091   The downfall of the Chancery. [*n.p.,* 1684.] brs. L.

2092   The downfall of the fifth monarchy. *For John Andrews,* 1657. 8°.* LT, OC.

Downfall of the pretended. [*n.p.,* 1641.] *See* Fenwick, John.

2092A   The downfall of the Rump. [*London?* 1660.] brs. L.

2093   The downfal of the Whiggs. [*London*], *for J. Dean,* [1679–82]. brs. O, HH; CH.

2093A   —[Anr. ed.] *For Tho. Johnson,* 1682. brs. O.

2094   The downfal of the Whiggs: or, their lamentation. [1680?] brs. O.

2095   The downfal of William Grismond. [*London*], *for F. Coles, T. Vere, and I Wright,* [1675?]. brs. L, O.

2096   —[Anr. ed.] [*London*], *for A. M. VV. O. and Tho. Thackeray,* [1680–88]. brs. L, HH, GU.

2096A **D[ownham], G[eorge].** Rex mevs est deus, or, a sermon. *Printed,* 1642[3]. 4°.* LT, O, CS, DT; CH, MH, WF.

2097 **[Downie, Robert.]** Scotorum elogivm seu ὑπομνημα. *Abredoniæ, imprimebat Edvardus Rabanus,* 1641. 4°.* ALDIS 1019. AU.

2098 **[Downing, Calybute.]** An appeale to every impartiall iudicious, and godly reader. *For Francis Coules and Henry Twyford,* 1641[2]. 4°.* LT, CPE, HH, DT; IU, MH, WCL, WF, Y.

2099 [–] The cleere antithesis. *For Francis Coules, and Henry Twyford,* 1644. 4°.* LT, O, LCL, EC; NU.

2100 [–] —[Anr. ed.] —, 1645. 4°.* L; NPT.

2101 —Considerations toward a peaceable reformation. *By Richard Hearn,* 1641. 4°.* LT, O, CT, LCL, E; CH, MH, NU, TU, WF, Y.

2102 —A discovrse vpon the interest of England. *By Richard Hearn,* 1641. 4°.* LT, O, CCA, CS; CH, CN, MH, NU, WF, Y.

2103 —A discovrsive coniectvre. *By Richard Hearne, for Iohn Partridge,* 1641. 4°.* LT, O, C, EN, DT; HR, CH, CN, MH, NU, WF, Y.

2104 —A discoverie of the false grounds. *By Ric. Hearn, to be sold by Thomas Bates,* 1641. 4°. LT, O, CCC, SC, EN; CH, CN, MH, NU, WF, Y.

2105 —A sermon preached ... 1 September 1640. *By E. G. for Iohn Rothwell,* 1641. 4°.* LT, O, C, OC, DT; CH, CLC, NU, WF, Y.

2106 **Downing, *Sir* George.** A discourse written by. *By J. M.,* 1664. 4°.* L, O, CT, OC; CH, MB, NS, TU, WF, Y.

2107 — —[Anr. ed.] *For Dorman Newman, and John Luttone,* 1672. 12°. T.C.I 123. L, O, CS, CT, EN; MB, MH, NS, RPJ.

2108 — —[Anr. ed.] *For John Luttone,* 1672. 12°. T.C.I 112. L, CS, CT, EN; BN, CH, MH, PL, WCL, WF, Y.

2109 —A reply of. *Printed,* 1665. 4°. L, O, C, CT, DT; CH, CN, LC, MH, NN, RPJ, Y.

2110 [–] A true relation of the progress of the Parliaments forces in Scotland. *By William Du-Gard,* 1651. 4°.* LT, O, HH, EN; CH, CN, MH, Y.

2111 The down-right country-man. [*London*], *for P. Brooksby,* [1672–95]. brs. L, O, HH; MH, Y.
Dovvn-right dealing. [*n.p.*], 1647. *See* Howell, James.

2112 Down-right Dick of the West. [*London*], *for J. Deacon,* [1685?] brs. L, CM.

2113 The dovvn right wooing. [*London*], *for W. Thackeray,* [1680]. brs. L.
Down-ight [sic] wooing of honest John. [1685]. *See* W., E.

2114 **[Doyley, Edward.]** A narrative of the great success God hath been pleased to give ... Jamaica. *By Henry Hills, and John Field,* 1658. 4°.* LT, O, OR, CT; MY, RPJ, V.

2115 A dozen of principall points. [*London,* 1648.] cap., 4°.* LT, OC, CJ; MH.

2116 **Drabicius, Nicolaus.** Several visions. *Printed,* 1664. 4° * NU.

Draconica: or. 1687. *See* Care, Henry.

2117 **[Drage, William.]** Daimonomageia: a small treatise. *By J. Dover,* 1665. 4°.* L, LWL, MR, GU; MH, NIC, PT.

2118 —Physical experiments. *For Simon Miller,* 1668. 4°. LPO, E; MH.

2118A —A physical nosonomy. *By J. Dover for the author,* 1664. 4°. LSC; MH, NU, WSG.

2118B — —[Anr. ed.] *By J. Dover, and are to be sold by R. Tomlins and Geo. Calvert,* 1665. 4°. L; WSG.

2119 Πυρετολογία sive. *Excudebat J. S. in usum authoris,* 1665. 8°. L, C, CCL, LCS; WF.

2119A **[Draghi, Giovanni Battista.]** An ode to the King. *For R. Bentley,* 1684. 4°.* WF, Y.

2120 —Six select suites of lessons for the harpsichord. [*London,* 1700?] fol. L.
Dragon missionaire: or. [*n.p.*], 1686. *See* Jurieu, Pierre.
Dragons blasphemous charge. [*n.p.*], 1651. *See* Douglas, *Lady* Eleanor.

2121 The dragon's forces totally routed. [*London,* 1660.] brs. LT.

2122 **Drake, *Sir* Francis.** Sir Francis Drake revived. *Printed at London for Nicholas Bourne,* 1655. 4°. L, O, CT, E, DT; CH, CN, LC, MB, NN, RPJ, Y.

2122A —The voyages and travels of. [*London*], *by W. O. for E. Brooksby,* [c. 1650.] 4°.* NN.

2122B — —[Anr. ed.] [*London*], *by C.B. for J.F. and sold by E. Tracy,* [1652.] 4°. L; CH, RPJ.

2123 — —[Anr. ed.] *By M.H. and I.M. for P. Brooksby,* 1683. 4°.* T.C.II 20. OR.

2124 **[Drake, James.]** The antient and modern stages survey'd. *For Abel Roper,* 1699. 8°. L, O, LVF, EN, DT; CH, CN, MH, NU, TU, WF, Y.

2125 [–] The sham-lawyer. *For Abel Roper,* 1697. 4°. L, O; CH, LC, MB, MH, WF.
[–] A short history of the last Parliament. 1699. *See* Blackmore, *Sir* Richard.
[Drake, *Mrs.* Judith.] Essay in defence. 1696. *See* Astell, Mary.

2126 **Drake, Nathaniel.** A sermon against bribery. *For Walter Kettilby, and Francis Hildyard in York,* 1695. 4°.* L, SC, BAMB, YM; NU, WF.

2127 —A sermon against false weights. *By W. Onley, for A. Bosvile; and N. Simmons, in Sheffield,* 1697. 4°.* L, O, CS, CT; NPT, WF.

2128 **Drake, Roger.** The bar, against free admission. *For Philip Chetwind,* 1656. 8°. LT, O, LCL, LW, YM; NPT, NU.

2129 —A boundary to the holy mount. *By A.M. for St. Bowtell,* 1653. 12°. LT, LCL, LW, ENC.

2130 — —[Anr. ed.] *By Abraham Miller,* 1653. 8°. LT, LW, OC, CM; CLC, NPT, NU, Y.

2131 —Sacred chronologie, drawn. *By James and Joseph Moxon, for Stephen Bowtell,* 1648. 4°. LT, O, C, CT, P; MB, NPT, WF.

2132 —R. D. . . . Vindiciæ. Contra animadversiones. *Excudebant R.O. & G.D. pro Johanne Rothwell,* 1641. 4°. L, O, C, LM, GH; MH.

2133   **Drake, Samuel.** Θεοῦ διάκογος, or the civil deacon's sacred power. *For William Grantham*, 1670. 4°.* T.C.I 34. L, CS, YM; MIU.

2134   —Totvm hominis; or, the decalogue. *For William Grantham*, 1670. 4°.* L, CS, WCA; CH, IU, MIU, NU.

2135   [**Drake, *Sir* William.**] The Long Parliament revived. *For the author*, 1660. 4°.* LT, O; Y.

2136   [-] —[Anr. ed.] *For the author and are to be sold at the Black-Spread Eagle*, 1661. 4°.* LT, O, C, MR, EN; CU, MBP, NU, PL, Y.

2137   [-] —[Anr. ed.] *For the author, to be sold at the Castle and Lion*, 1661. 4°.* L, LG, OC, CJ, CT; CH, CN, MH, WF, Y.

2138   —Sir William Drake his speech . . . November 10. 1641. *For W. L.*, 1641. 4°.* LT, C, HH; CH, LC, MH, WF, Y.

2138A   **Draper, R.** An hearty acknowledgement. 1659. 4°.* L.

2138B   Drapers-hall, October the 11th 1695. We whose names, [*London*], 1695. brs. LG.

2139   **Drapes, Edward.** Gospel-glory. *For Francis Tyton*, 1649. 4°. LT, O; MH, NHC, NPT.

2140   —A plain and faithfvll discovery of a beame in Master Edwards his eye. [*London*] *printed and are to be sold by William Larner*, 1646. 4°.* LT, O, GU; CH, NHC, WF, Y.

2141   The draught of an act for county registers. 1652/3. fol. O, EN.

2142   A draught of a bill for an act to enable their Majesties to . . . employ any of their Protestants subjects [*London*, 1695.] brs. O; CH.

2143   **Draxe, Thomas.** Bibliotheca scholastica . . . or, a treasury. *Excudebat S. G. impensis Jos. Kirton*, 1654. 8°. L, O, EC, P, BR; MWA, NN, NPT, WF, Y.

2144   —Calliepeia, or a rich store-house. *By M. F. for Richard Whittaker*, 1643. 8°. L, C, CM, CP, DC; CLC, CU, MH, NC, PL, Y.

2144A   — —[Anr. ed.] *By S. G. for J. Kirton*, 1662. 8°. DC; MWA.

2145   **Drayton, Michael.** England's heroical epistles. *For S. Smethwick, and sold by Benjamin Crayle*, 1689. 8°. T.C.II 295. Y.

2145A   — —[Anr. ed.] *For S. Smethwick and R. Gilford*, [1695?] 8°. L, C, CT; CH, CN, LC, NU, TU, Y.

2146   — —[Anr. ed.] *For J. Conyers*, 1697. 8°. L, EN; Y.

2147   **Drayton, Thomas.** An answer according to truth. *Printed*, 1655. 4°. O, C, CT.

2148   —The proviso or condition. *By Tho. Newcomb*, 1657. 4°. LT, O, WCA, DT; NU, WF, Y.

2148A   A dreadful account of a barbarous bloudy murther . . . Mr. Cymball. *For R. Lyford*, 1695. brs. CN.

       Dreadful account of a more terrible earthquake, 1693. *See* B., W.

2149   Dreadful account of the horrid murther of Mr. Tilly. *Printed, and are to be sold by Randal Taylor*, 1694. brs. O.

2150   The dreadful and most prodigious tempest. *For Will. Gilbertson*, 1659. 4°.* L; MIU.

       Dreadful, and terrible day. [n.p., 1665.] *See* Bayly, William.

       Dreadful and terrible voice. [1660.] *See* S., R.

2151   The dreadful apparition. [*London*], *for J. Jordan*, 1680. brs. L, O; CLC, MH.

       Dreadful character of a drunkard. [n.p.], 1678. *See* Hart, John.

2152   The dreadful danger of sacriledge. [*London*, 1652.] brs. LT.

2152A   Dreadful news from Hackney Marsh. *For Alex: Milbourn*, 1690. brs. MH.

       Dreadful news from Limerick. 1694. *See* H., J.

2153   Dreadful news from Southwark. [*London*, 1679?] cap., fol.* O, LG, HH; CH, MH.

2153A   Dreadful news from Taunton Dean. [*London*, 1700?] 4°. BR.

2154   Dreadfull nevves from Wiltshire. [*London*], *for Iohn Smith*, 1642. 4°.* LT.

       Dreadful prognostication. [n.p.], 1649. *See* Wing, Vincent.

2154A   A dreadful relation, of the cruel, bloudy, and the most inhumane massacre. *For Iohn Andrews*, 1655. brs. L.

2155   A dreadful warning to lewd livers. [*London*], *for P. Brooksby*, [1682?]. brs. L.

2156   A dreame: or nevves from Hell. *Printed in Sicilia on the back-side of the Cyclopean Mountaines*, 1641. [*London*]. 4°.* L, OC, YM; CH, LC, MH, TU, WF, Y.

2157   The dream. Weary'ed with business. [*London*, 1688]. cap., 8°.* L, O, EN; CH, CN, MH, WF, Y.

2158   Dregs of drollery, or old poetry in its ragges. *Printed*, 1660. 4°.* CH.

2159   **Drelincourt, Charles.** Catechism. *For the author, sold by Edward Castle*, 1698. 12°. T.C.III 73. CT.

2159A   —Catechisme ou instruction familiere. *Par B. G. et se vend chez Daniel du Chemin*, 1697. 8°. Y.

2160   —The Christians defence. *By T. N. for John Starkey*, 1675. 8°. T.C.I 209. O; CLC, CU, NU, Y.

2160A   — —Second edition. *For John Starkey*, 1682. 8°. EN; KU, Y.

2160B   — —Third edition. *By F. C. for R. Clavell, J. Robinson; and A. and J. Churchill*, 1692. 8°. T.C.II 415. P, RPL; MBA, PL, WG.

2160C   [-] A collection of texts of Scripture. *For Samuel Norman*, 1686. 12°. L, C; CH, CLC, CN; MH, NU, WF.

2160D   [-] —[Anr. ed.] *For W. Booker*, 1688. 12°. L, C.

2160E   — —[Anr. ed.] *For Awnsham Churchill*, 1688. 12°. OC, CS, AN.

2161   —The Protestant's self-defence; or, a discourse. 1685. 12°. LCL, LW.

2162   —The Protestants triumph. *By D. Maxwel for Tho. Parkhurst*, 1664. 8°. L, O, P, ENC; NU, WF, Y.

2163   **Drelincourt, Peter.** A speech made. *Dublin, by Joseph Ray, for William Mendey*, 1682. 4°.* DIX 193. L, O, C, DK, DT; MH.

2164   **Dremelius, Gerhard.** A true copy of the letter that was sent by. Colop: *By J. Wilkins*, 1700. brs. L.

2165 **Drew, John.** The Northern subscribers plea. *By R.I. to be sold by John Wright*, 1651. 4°. LT; WF.

2166 —A serious addresse to Samuel Oates. *For John Bartlet*, 1649. 4°.* LT, O, LF, NM, DT; CH, NHC, NPT.

2167 **Drewrey, N.** The vindication of the separate brethren. *Printed*, 1641[2]. 4°.* LT, O, CT, OC, HH; CH, CU, CN, WF, Y.

2168 **Drexel, Jeremy.** The Christians zodiake. *William Willson*, 1647. 24°. L, O, C, OB, CT; CLC, WF.

2169 —Considerations of Drexelius upon eternitie. *Cambridge, by Roger Daniel*, 1641. 24°. CH, MH.

2170 — —[Anr. ed.] —, 1646. 24°. O, C; IU.

2171 — —[Anr. ed.] —, 1650. 12°. L, C, EN.

2172 — —[Anr. ed.] *By Roger Daniel; to be sold by John Williams*, 1654. 12°. C; CH, MH.

2173 — —[Anr. ed.] *By Roger Daniel*, 1658. 12°. L; CU, Y.

2174 — —[Anr. ed.] *By Iohn Redmayne, for Thomas Rooks*, 1663. 12°. C, CK; CLC, NPT, PU, Y.

2175 — —[Anr. ed.] *Cambridge, by Roger Daniel. To be sould by Tho. Rooks [London]*, 1666. 12°. C; WF.

2176 — —[Anr. ed.] *By A.M. for Thomas Rooks*, 1672. 12° L, O, C, LCL, ENC; CLC, WG.

2177 — —[Anr. ed.] *By I.R. for Thomas Rooks*, 1675. 12°. L; CLC.

2178 — —[Anr. ed.] *By J.R. for Richard Chiswel, and to be sold by Samuel Tidmarsh*, 1684. 12°. T.C.II 120. L; CLC, CN.

2179 — —[Anr. ed.] *For Richard Chiswell, to be sold by Richard Parker*, 1689. 12°. T.C.II 279. L, CSE, EN; CLC, NPT, NU.

2180 — —[Anr. ed.] *For Richard Chiswell*, 1694. 12°. L, C; CU, LC, MM, Y.

2181 — —[Anr. ed.] *For Rich. Chiswell, and sold by Percivall Gilbourne; and William Davis*, 1699. 12°. T.C.III 120. L, O, LW, EN; INU.

2181A — —[Anr. ed.] *By S.Bridge, for H. Walwyn*, 1699. 12°. L, LSC, CSE; CLC.

2182 —Ystyriaethau Drexelivs ar dragywydd oldeb. *Rhydychen [Oxford], gan Hen. Hall tros Rich. Davis*, 1661. 12°. MADAN 2552. L, O, AN, CPL; MH.

2183 —The forerunner of eternity. *By J.N. to be sold by John Sweeting*, 1642. 12°. L, O; Y.

2184 —The hive of devotion. *For R. Best*, 1647. 12°. L; CLC.

2184A —A pleasant and profitable treatise of Hell. *[London], printed*, 1668. 8°. L, O, WARE; IU, LC.

2185 —A right intention the rule. *For Iasp. Emery*, 1641. 12°. L, O, C, CT, P; CLC, WF, Y.

2185A — —[Anr. ed.] —, 1655. 12°. LSC; CLC.

2186 —A spiritual repository. *For R.B.*, 1676. 12°. L, C, CT.

2187 **D[ring], T[homas].** A catalogue of the lords, knights, and gentlemen. *For Thomas Dring*, 1655. 8°. L, O, C, MR, EN; CH, CN, MH, TU, WF, Y.

2187A Droytwich case. *[London? 1687.]* brs. CH.

2188 **Drope, Francis.** A short and sure guide . . . fruit-trees. *Oxford, [by W. Hall], for Ric. Davis*, 1672. 8°. T.C.I 104. MADAN 2925. L, O, C, OC; CH, MH, WDA, WF, Y.

2189 **D[rope], J[ohn].** An hymenaean essay; or. *[n.p.]*, 1662. 4°.* L, O; MH.

2190 [–] Upon the most hopefull and ever-flourishing sprouts of valour. *[Oxford, by W. Hall], printed*, 1664. brs. MADAN 2658. O.

2191 [–] —[Anr. ed.] —, 1666. brs. MADAN 2740. L, O.

2192 — —[Anr. ed.] *[Oxford], printed*, 1664. *Reprinted*, 1682. brs. L.

Drops of myrrhe. 1654. *See* Master, William.

Drudge. 1673. *See* Le Pays, René.

2193 **Drummond, William.** Anagram of His Excellency . . . George Monck. *[London, 1600.]* brs. LT, HH.

2194 — Breviuscula, & compendiuscula, tellatio. *Edinburgi, re-printat*, 1684. 4°.* FSF.

2195 —Forth feasting. 1656. 8°. EN.

2196 —The history of Scotland. *By Henry Hills for Rich. Tomlins and himself*, 1655. fol. L, O, C, E, DT; BN, CH, CN, MH, WF, Y.

2197 — —[Anr. ed.] *For Tho. Fabian*, [1680]. 8°. O, C, CM, LI, DT; PL.

2198 — —Second edition. —, 1681. 8°. L, OM, LLL, MR, EN; CH, CU, TU.

2199 — —"Second" edition. —, 1682. 8°. T.C.I 445. L, LW, RPL, EN, DT; BN, CLC, CN, LC, MBA.

2200 —The most elegant and elaborate poems. *For William Rands*, 1659. 8°. L, O, CT, RPL, EN; CH, CN, MH, WF, Y.

2201 —Poems. Third edition. *By W.H., sold in the company of stationers*, 1656. 8°. L, O, EN, ES, I; CH, CN, MH, WC, WF.

2202 — —"Third" edition. *For Richard Tomlins*, 1656. 8°. L, CT, E; CH, CN, MH, WF, Y.

2203 [–] Polemo-Midinia carmen maccaronicum. *[Aberdeen, 1650.]* cap., 4°.* ALDIS 1147. L, EN; MH.

2204 — —[Anr. ed.] *Oxonii, e theatro Sheldoniano*, 1691. 4°.* L, O, C, CT, EN; BN, CH, CN, NN, WF, Y.

2205 The drunkard forewarn'd. *For William Sceales*, 1680. 4°.* WF.

2205A —[Anr. ed.] —, 1682. 4°.* L.

2206 The drunkards character. *[London, 1646.]* brs. LT.

2206A The Drury-Lane monster. *For J. Roberts*, [1690?] brs. TU.

2207 **Dryden, John.** The works of. *Printed, and are to be sold by Jacob Tonson*, 1691. 4v. 4°. MACD 106a. OW.

2208 — —[Anr. ed.] *For Jacob Tonson*, 1693. 4v. 4°. MACD 106b. O; CLC, MH, WF (3, 4), Y.

2209 — —[Anr. ed.] —, 1694. 4v. 4°. MACD 106c. LLL, DT; CLC, MH, WF.

2210 —The first [second, third, fourth] volume of the works of. *For Jacob Tonson*, 1695. 4°. MACD 106e. L, OB, E; CCC, CLC, WF, Y.

2211 —The dramatick works of. *For R.Bentley*, 1695. 3v. 8°. MACD 106f. MH, NF, WF.

2212 [–] Absalom and Achitophel. A poem. *For J. T. and are to be sold by W. Davis*, 1681. fol.* MACD 12a i–iv. L, O, C, LVD, MR; CH, CU, MH, TU, WF, Y.

2213 [–] Absalom and Achitophel. A poem, with all the additions. [*Dublin*, 1681.] 4°.* MACD 12b. O; WF.

2214 [–] Absalom and Achitophel. A poem. The second edition. [*Dublin*, 1681.] 4°.* MACD 12c. L, C, E, DT; CH, CLC, Y.

2215 — —"Second" edition. *For J. T. and are to be sold by W. Davis*, 1681. fol.* MACD 12d. L, O, CSSX; CH, CN, MH, WF, Y.

2216 — —"Second" edition. —, 1681. 4°.* MACD 12e. L, O, CT, LVD, DC; CH, CU, MH, MIU, WF, Y.

2217 [–] —"Second" edition. [*London*], *for J. T. to be sold by W. Davis*, 1681. fol.* MACD 12e ii WF.

2218 [–] —Third edition. —, 1682. 4°.* MACD 12f. L, O, C, LVD; CLC, CU, MH, NU, TU, WF, Y.

2219 [–] —Fourth edition. —, 1682. MACD 12g. 4°.* L, O, CT, MR, EN; CH, CN, MH, TU, WF, Y.

2220 [–] —Fifth edition. *For Jacob Tonson*, 1682. fol.* MACD 12h. L, O, C, CS, HH; CLC, CN, MH, TU, WF, Y.

2221 [–] Absalon et Achitophel. Carmine Latino heroico. *Oxon, typis Lichfieldianis prostant apud Ricardum Davis*, 1682. 4°.* MACD 12j. L, O, C, LVD, A; CH, CN, MH, TU, WF, Y.

2222 [–] Absalon et Achitophel. Poema Latino . . . carmine donatum. *Oxon, typis Lichfieldianis, prostant apud Johannem Crosley*, 1682. 4°.* MACD 12k. L, O, C, CT, EN; CH, MH, TU, WF, Y.

2223 Entry cancelled.
—, *pseud.* The address of . . . to His Highness. 1689. *See title.*

2224 —Albion and Albanius: an opera. *For Jacob Tonson*, 1685. fol.* MACD 88a. L, O, CS, OC, HH; CH, CU, LC, MH, TU, WF, Y.

2225 [–] —Second edition. *For the author, to be sold at the door of the Royal Theater; and by William Nott*, 1687. fol. MACD 88b. L, O, CM, E, GU; CH, LC, MB, MH, WF.

2226 — —"Second" edition. *For Jacob Tonson*, 1691. 4°.* MACD 88c. L, O, OW, LVD, DT; BN, CN, MH, MU, TU, WF, Y.

2227 — —Third edition. —, 1691. 4°.* CH, Y.

2228 —Alexander's feast; or. *For Jacob Tonson*, 1697. fol.* MACD 34. L, O, C, LVD, DT; CH, MH, TU, WCL, WF, Y.

2229 —All for love. *In the Savoy: by Tho. Newcomb, for Henry Herringman*, 1678. 4°. MACD 82a. L, O, CK, EN, DT; BN, CH, CN, MH, TU, WF, Y.

2230 — —Second edition. *In the Savoy: for H. Herringman, and sold by R. Bently, J. Tonson, F. Saunders, and T. Bennet*, 1692. 4°. MACD 82b. L, O, LVD, C, EN; BN, CH, CN, MH, TU, WF, Y.

2231 — —[Anr. ed.] *By Tho. Warren, for Henry Herringman, and sold by R. Bentley, J. Tonson, F. Saunders, and T. Bennet*, 1696. 4°. MACD 82c. L, O, CT, EN; CH, CN, MH, TU, WF, Y.

2232 —Amboyna: a tragedy. *By T. N. for Henry Herringman*, 1673. 4°. T.C.I 151. MACD 79a. L, O, C, EN, DT; BN, CH, CN, MH, TU, WF, Y.

2233 — —Second edition. *For Henry Herringman, and are to be sold by Richard Bentley*, 1691. 4°. T.C.II 387. MACD 79b. L, O, CK, EN, DT; CH, CN, MH, TU, WF, Y.

2234 —Amphitryon. *For J. Tonson; and M. Tonson*, 1690. 4°. MACD 90ai. L, O, OW, CT, EN; CH, LC, MH, WF, Y.

2235 — —Second edition. —, 1691. 4°. MACD 90aii. L, O, LVD, OM, OW; CH, CN, MBP, MH, TU, WF, Y.

2236 — —"Second" edition. *For Jacob Tonson*, 1694. 4°. MACD 90b. L, O, OW, EN, DT; CH, CN, MH, TU, WF, Y.

2237 [–] The annual miscellany: for the year 1694. *By R. E. for Jacob Tonson*, 1694. 8°. MACD 46a. L, O, C, OC, DT; CH, CN, MH, TU, WF, Y.

2238 —Annus mirabilis: the year. *For Henry Herringman*, 1667. 8°. MACD 9ai. L, O, C, LG, CT; CH, CN, MH, TU, WF, Y.

2239 — —[Anr. ed.] —, 1668. 8°. MACD 9b. O, LSC, OW, EN; CLC, CU, MH, WF.

2240 — —[Anr. ed.] *For Henry Herringman, and sold by Jacob Tonson*, 1688. 4°. MACD 9c. L, O, C, E, DT; CH, CN, MH, MU, TU, WF, Y.

2241 —The assignation. *By T. N. for Henry Herringman.* 1673. 4°. T.C.I 121. MACD 78a. L, O, OW, CK, DT; BN, CH, CN, MH, TU, WF, Y.

2242 — —Second edition. —, 1678. 4°. MACD 78b. L, O, CT, LVD, EN; CH, CN, MH, TU, WF, Y.

2243 — —Third edition. *For Richard Bently, Jacob Tonson, Francis Saunders, and Thomas Bennet*, 1692. 4°. MACD 78c. L, O, LVF, EN, DT; BN, CH, CN, MH, TU, WF, Y.

2244 —Astræa redux. A poem. *By J. M. for Henry Herringman*, 1660. fol.* MACD 5a. LT, O, C, OM, LVF; BN, CH, CLC, MH, WF, Y.

2245 —Aureng-Zebe; a tragedy. *By T. N. for Henry Herringman*, 1676. 4°. T.C.I 236. MACD 80a. L, O, LVD, C, EN; BN, CH, CN, MH, TU, WF, Y.

2246 — —Second edition. *By J. M. for Henry Herringman, to be sold by Jos. Knight and F. Saunders*, 1685. 4°. MACD 80b. L, O, OW, EN; CH, CU, MH, TU, WF, Y.

2247 — —Third edition. *For Henry Herringman*, 1690. 4°. MACD 80c. O, C; CLC, CN, MH, WF, Y.

2248 — —Fourth edition. *For Henry Herringman; and sold by R. Bentley, J. Tonson, F. Saunders, and T. Bennet*, 1692. 4°. MACD 80d. L, O, OW, EN, DT; BN, LC, MH, TU, WF, Y.

2249 — —Fifth edition. —, 1694. 4°. MACD 80e. L, O, LVF, DT; BN, CH, CN, MH, TU, WF, Y.

2250 — —Sixth edition. *By Tho. Warren, for Henry Herringman; and sold by J. Tonson, F. Saunders, and T. Bennet*, 1699. 4°. MACD 80f. L, O, C; CLC, MB, MH, TU, WF.

2251 —Britannia rediviva; a poem. *For J. Tonson*, 1688. 14 pp. fol.* MACD 27a. L, O, CS, EN, DT; CH, CN, MH, TU, WF, Y.

2252 — —[Anr. ed.] *Holy-Rood-House, re-printed by Mr. P. B. Enginier*, 1688. 4°.* ALDIS 2755. MACD 27b. L, OW, EN; CH, MH, WF, Y.

2253 — —[Anr. ed.] *For J. Tonson*, 1688 [c. 1691]. 20 pp. 4°.* MACD 27C. L, O, DC, EN, DT; CH, CU, MH, TU, WF, Y.

2254 —Cleomenes. *For Jacob Tonson*, 1692. 4°. MACD 92. L, O, CT, EN, DT; CH, CU, MH, TU, WF, Y.

2255 —A collection of new songs. *Sould by I. Walsh*, [1700]. fol.* L; MH.

2255A [–] The conjuror's song and the Indian queen. [*London*] 1700, 4°.* L.

2256 —The conquest of Granada. *In the Savoy, by T. N. for Henry Herringman*, 1672. 4°. T.C.I 96. MACD 76a. L, O, LVD, CK; CH, CU, MH, TU, WF, Y.

2257 — —Second edition. *By T. N. for Henry Herringman*, 1673. MACD 76b. L, O, C, EN, DT; CH, CN, MH, TU, WF, Y.

2258 — —Third edition. *By H. Hills, for Henry Herringman*, 1678. 4°. MACD 76C. L, O, LVD, OC; CLC, CU, MH, TU, WF, Y.

2259 — —Fourth edition. *By J. M. for Henry Herringman, and are to be sold by Joseph Knight and Francis Saunders*, 1687. 4°. MACD 76d. L, O, OW, EN; CLC, CU, MH, TU, WF, Y.

2260 — —Fifth edition. *For Henry Herringman; and sold by R. Bentley, J. Tonson, F. Saunders, and T. Bennet*, 1695. 4°. MACD 76e. L, O, C, DT; CN, LC, MH, NC, TU, WF, Y.

2261 [–] A defence of the papers written by the late king. *By H. Hills*, 1686. 4°. MACD 133. L, O, C, E, DT; CH, CN, MH, NU, TU, WF, Y.

2261A —A dialogue and secular masque in The Pilgrim. *For Benjamin Tooke*, 1700. 4°.* MB, PU, WCL.

2262 —Don Sebastian. *For Jo. Hindmarsh*, 1690. 4°. T.C.II 301. MACD 89a. L, O, CS, LVD, EN; CH, CN, MH, TU, WF, Y.

2263 — —Second edition. —, 1692. 4°. 4°. L, O, C, LVD, DT; CH, CN, MH, NC, TU, WF, Y.

2264 —The Duke of Guise. A tragedy. *By T. H. for R. Bentley and J. Tonson*, 1683. 4°. MACD 87a. L, O, C, LVD, EN; CH, CN, MH, TU, WF, Y.

2265 — —Second edition. *By R. E. for R. Bentley and J. Tonson*, 1687. 4°. MACD 87b. L, O, LVD, OW, DT; CH, CN, MH, TU, WF, Y.

2266 — —[Anr. ed.] *For Jacob Tonson*, 1699. 4°. MACD 87C. L, C; CLC, MH, TU, WF, Y.

2267 — —[Anr. ed.] *For R. Wellington and E. Rumball*, 1699. 4°. MACD 87d. L, O, OW, CT, EN; CLC, MH, TU, WF, Y.

2268 —An elegy on the usurper O. C. *For J. Smith*, 1681. brs. MACD 3b. L, O, LVD, MC, HH; CLC, CN, MH, WF, Y.

2269 — —[Anr. ed.] [*Dublin?*], *reprinted*, 1682. 4°.* MACD 3c. E, DT; MH, TU, WCL, Y.

2270 —Eleonora: a panegyrical poem. *For Jacob Tonson*, 1692. 4°.* MACD 29. L, O, C, EN, DT; CH, CN, MH, TU, WF, Y.

2271 [–] The epilogue spoken to the king. [*Oxford, by L. Lichfield, jun.*, 1681.] brs. MACD 95. OC; CLC.

2272 —The epilogue. Writ by Mr. Dreyden. *For Rich. Royston*, [1680]. brs. MACD 95a. L, O; CLC, Y.

2273 —An evening's love. *In the Savoy, by T. N. for Henry Herringman*, 1671. 4°. T.C.I 66. MACD 75a. L, O, CS, EN, DT; CH, CN, MH, TU, WF, Y.

2274 — —Second edition. —, 1671. 4°. MACD 75b. L, O, OC, EN; CH, CN, MH, TU, WF, Y.

2275 — —[Anr. ed.] —, 1675. 4°. MACD 75C. O; CLC, MH, WF, Y.

2276 — —Fourth edition. *For Henry Herringman, and are to be sold by Richard Bentley*, 1691. 4°. T.C.II 387. MACD 75d. L, O, C, OW, DT; BN, CH, CU, MH, TU, WF, Y.

2277 [–] Examen poeticum: being the third part of miscellany poems. *By R. E. for Jacob Tonson*, 1693. 8°. MACD 45a. L, O, CT, LCP, DT; CH, CN, MH, TU, WF, Y.

2278 —Fables ancient and modern. *For Jacob Tonson*, 1700. fol. MACD 37a. L, O, C, E, DT; CH, MH, TU, WF, Y.

2279 [–] For Iris I sigh. [*London*], *for Ch. Bates*, [1690]. brs. L.

2280 [–] The happy shepheard. [*London*], *for C. Bates*, [1695?]. brs. L.

2281 [–] The hind and the panther. *For Jacob Tonson*, 1687. 4°. MACD 24. L, O, C, MR, EN; CH, CN, MH, TU, WF, Y.

2282 [–] —[Anr. ed.] *Holy-Rood-House: re-printed by James Watson*, 1687. 4°. ALDIS 2691. MACD 24b. L, O, EN; CLC, WF.

2283 [–] —[Anr. ed.] *Dublin, reprinted by Andrew Crook and Samuel Helsham*, 1687. 4°. DIX 226. MACD 24c. O, C, CD, DT; CH, CLC, MH, WF, Y.

2284 [–] —Second edition. *For Jacob Tonson*, 1687. 4°. MACD 24d. L, O, C, MR; BN, CU, MH, NU, WF, Y.

2285 [–] —Third edition. —, 1687. 4°. MACD 24e. L, O, C, DC, DT; CH, CU, MH, TU, WF, Y.

2286 [–] His Majesties declaration defended. *For T. Davies*, 1681. fol.* MACD 129. L, O, OC; CH, MH, TU, WCL, WF, Y.

2287 [–] I see she flyes me. [*London, T. Cross*, 1695?] brs. L.

2288 —The Indian emperour. *By J. M. for H. Herringman*, 1667. 4°. MACD 69a. L, O; CH, MH, TU, WF, Y.

2289 — —Second edition. *For H. Herringman*, 1668. 4°. MACD 69b. L, O, LVD, OC, EN; CH, MH, RPJ, TU, WF, Y.

2290 — —Third edition. —, 1670. 4°. MACD 69c. L, O, C, DT; BN, CCC, CN, TU, WF, Y.

2291 — —"Third" edition, emperor. —, 1670. 4°. MACD 69d. L, O; BN, CH, CN, MH, TU, WF, Y.

2292 — —Fourth edition. —, 1681. 4°. MACD 69e. O, OW, EN; CH, LC, MH, MU, TU, Y.

2293 — —Fifth edition. *For H. Herringman, and are to be sold by Joseph Knight, and Francis Saunders*, 1686. 4°. MACD 69f. L, O, EN; CH, CN, MH, TU, WF, Y.

2294 — —Sixth edition. *For Henry Herringman, to be sold by R. Bentley, J. Tonson, F. Saunders, and T. Bennet*, 1692. 4°. MACD 69g. L, O, OW; CH, CN, MH, TU, WF, Y.

2295 — —Seventh edition. *By T. Warren for Henry Herring-man, and are to be sold by T. Bentley, J. Tonson, F. Saunders, and T. Bennet,* 1694. 4°. MACD 69h. L, O, EN, DT; BN, CLC, CU, MH, TU, WF, Y.

2296 — —Eighth edition. —, 1696. 4°. MACD 69i. L, O, C, EN; CLC, CN, MH, TU, WF, Y.

2296A — —[Anr. ed.] —, 1696. 4°. MACD 69j–k. CLC, MH, NIC, TU, WF.

2296B — —[Anr. ed.] *For J. Tonson and sold by J. Knapton, G. Strahan and E. Sanger,* 1700. 4°. CH.

2297 —The kind keeper. *For R. Bentley, and M. Magnes,* 1680. 4°. T.C.I 370. MACD 85a. L, O, LVF, OW, CK; BN, CH, CN, MH, TU, WF, Y.

2298 — —Second edition. —, 1690. 4°. T.C.II 325. MACD 85b. L, O, LVD, EN, DT; BN, CH, CN, MH, TU, WF, Y.

2299 —King Arthur. *For Jacob Tonson,* 1691. 4°. MACD 91a. L, O, CK, EN, DT; CH, CN, MH, TU, WF, Y.

2300 — —Second edition. —, 1695. 4°. MACD 91b. L, O, CS, CT, EN; CH, CN, MH, TU, WF, Y.

—Letters upon several occasions. 1696. *See* Dennis, John.

2301 [–] Love and jealousie: or a song in The Duke of Guies. *For P. Brooksby,* 1683. brs. CH.

2302 —Love triumphant. *For Jacob Tonson,* 1694. 4°. MACD 93a. L, O, CT, ES, DT; BN, CH, CN, MH, TU, WF, Y.

2303 [–] Mac Flecknoe, or a satyr. *For D. Green,* 1682. 4°.* MACD 14a. L, O, C, CCO; CH, MH, TU, WF, Y.

2304 [–] —[Anr. ed.] *For Jacob Tonson,* 1692. 4°. MACD 14b. L, O, DC, EN; CCL, MU, WF, Y.

2305 —The mall. *For William Cademan,* 1674. 8°. T.C.I 170. MACD 144. L, O, EN; CH, CU, MH, TU, WF, Y.

2306 —Marriage a-la-mode. *By T. N. for Henry Herring-man,* 1673. 4°. T.C.I 141. MACD 77a. L, O, CK, EN, DT; BN, CH, CN, MH, TU, WF, Y.

2307 — —Second edition. *By T. N. for Henry Herringman, sold by Joseph Knight, and Francis Saunders,* 1684. 4°. T.C.II 64. MACD 77b. L, O, LVF, OW, DT; CH, CN, MH, TU, WF, Y.

2308 — —[Anr. ed.] [*n.p.*], 1687. 4°. OW.

2309 — —Third edition. *In the Savoy: by Edw. Jones, for Henry Herringman, and are to be sold by R. Bentl[e]y,* 1691. 4°. T.C.II 387. MACD 77c. L, O, CT, EN, DT; BN, CH, MH, TU, WF, Y.

2310 — —[Anr. ed.] *In the Savoy: by Edw. Jones, for Henry Herringman, and are to be sold by J. Tonson, F. Saunders, and T. Bennet,* 1698. 4°. MACD 77d. L, O, C; CH, CU, MH, TU, WF, Y.

2311 [–] The medall. A satyre. *For Jacob Tonson,* 1682. 4°.* MACD 13a. L, O, C, MR, E; CH, CU, MH, NC, TU, WF, Y.

2312 [–] —[Anr. ed.] *Edinburgh, re-printed,* 1682. 4°.* ALDIS 2338. MACD 13b. L, O, C, EN; MH, Y.

2313 [–] —[Anr. ed.] *Dublin, reprinted for Robert Thornton,* 1682. 4°.* DIX 197. MACD 13c. O, DI, DK; CH, LC, MH, WF, Y.

2314 [–] Miscellany poems. Containing. *For Jacob Tonson,* 1684. 8°. MACD 24ai. L, O, C, OC, CT; CH, CN, MH, TU, WF, Y.

2315 [–] —[Anr. ed.] *For Thomas Chapman,* 1688. 8°. MACD 42a ii. TU, WF.

2316 —Miscellany poems: in two parts. Second edition. *For Jacob Tonson,* 1692. 8°. MACD 42b i. DT; MH, TU, WF, Y.

2317 — —"Second" edition. *For Jacob Tonson, to be sold by Joseph Hindmarsh,* 1692. 8°. MACD 42b ii. L, O, LW, E; CCL, CLC, CN, WF.

2318 [–] The mistaken husband. *For J. Magnes and R. Bentley,* 1675. 4°. T.C.I 219. MACD 145. L, O, CT, EN; CH, CN, MH, TU, WF, Y.

2318A — A new song in the dramatick opera [*London*], 1692. brs. L.

2318B —A new song in the play call'd The Spanish fryer [*London*] *T. Cross* [1696]. brs. L.

2319 [–] A new song, sung in The Spanish frier. [*London,* 1690.] brs. L; WF, Y.

2320 [–] Notes and observations on The Empress of Morocco. *Printed,* 1674. 4°. T.C.I 197. MACD 128. L, O, LG, OC, CT; BN, CH, CN, MH, NC, TU, WF.

2321 —An ode, on the death of Mr. Henry Purcell. *By J. Heptinstall, for Henry Playford,* 1696. fol.* T.C.II 589 MACD 32a. L, LLL, OC, CS; CH, CN, MH, TU, WF, Y.

2322 —Oedipus: a tragedy. *For R. Bentley and M. Magnes,* 1679. 4°. T.C.I 350. MACD 83a. L, O, CK, LVD, EN; BN, CH, CN, MH, TU, WF, Y.

2323 — —Second edition. *For Richard Bentley,* 1682. 4°. T.C.I 516. MACD 83b. L, O, LLL, LVF, OC; CH, CU, MH, TU, WF, Y.

2324 — —Third edition. —, 1687. 4°. T.C.II 190. MACD 83c. L, O, OW, EN; CH, CU, MH, TU, WF, Y.

2325 — —Fourth edition. —, 1692. 4°. MACD 83d. L, O, LVD, EN, DT; BN, CH, CU, MH, TU, WF, Y.

2326 — —Fifth edition. *For Tho. Chapman,* [1696]. 4°. MACD 83e. L, O, CT, EN; CH, MH, TU, WF, Y.

2327 —Of dramatick poesie. *For Henry Herringman,* 1668. 4°. MACD 127a. L, O, C, LVD, EN; BN, CH, CN, MH, TU, WF, Y.

2328 — —Second edition. —, 1684. 4°. T.C.II 64. MACD 127b i. L, O, DT, GK; CH, CU, MH, TU, WF, Y.

2329 — —[Anr. ed.] *By T. Warren for Henry Herringman, to be sold by R. Bentley, J. Tonson, F. Saunders, and T. Bennet,* 1693. 4°. MACD 127c. L, O, C, EN, DT; CH, CU, MH, MU, TU, WF, Y.

2330 —A poem upon the death of His late Highness, Oliver. *For William Wilson,* 1659. 4°.* MACD 3f. L, O, CK, DC, DT; CH, CU, MH, TU, WF, Y.

2331 [–] A poem upon the death of the late usurper. *For S. H.,* 1687. 4°.* MACD 3e. L, O, CT; BN, CH, CN, MH, WF, Y.

2332 —The prologue and epilogue to The History of Bacon in Virginia. colop: *For Jacob Tonson,* 1689. fol.* MACD 105. O, C; CLC, CN.

2332A —The prologue and epilogue to the last new play, Constantine. [*London*], *for C. Tebroc,* 1683. brs. MACD 102A. CH, CLC, MH, WF.

2333 [–] A prologue spoken at Mithridates. colop: *For J. Sturton*, [1682]. brs. MACD 96. L, O; CH, CLC, MH, Y.

2334 [–] Prologue to a new play, call'd The disappointment. colop: *For E. Lucy*, 1684. brs. MACD 103. O; CH, CLC, Y.

2335 —Prologue to His Royal Highness. *For J. Tonson*, 1682. brs. MACD 98a. L, O, LG; CH, CLC, MH, TU, WF, Y.

2336 — —[Anr. ed.] —, [1682]. brs. MACD 98b. L, O, EN; CH, CLC, MH, Y.

2337 —A prologue to the Dutchess, on her return. colop: [*London*], *for Jacob Tonson*, 1682. cap., brs. MACD 99. L, O, CT, HH, EN; CH, CLC, LC, MH, WF.

2338 —Prologue, to The Duke of Guise. colop: *For Jacob Tonson*, 1683. cap., fol.* MACD 101. L, O, OW, HH; CH, CLC, MH, TU, WF, Y.

2339 —Prologue. To the king and queen. colop: *For Jacob Tonson*, 1683. fol.* MACD 100. L, O, C, HH; CH, LC, MH, TU, WF, Y.

2340 —Prologue to the opera. [*London*, 1687?] brs. MACD 104. L; CH, WF.

2341 —A prologue written by. colop: *For J. Tonson*, [1682]. brs. MACD 97. L, O, CS, CT; CH, CN, MH, TU, WF, Y.

2342 —Religio laici or a laymans faith. A poem. *For Jacob Tonson*, 1682. 4°.* MACD 16a i–ii. L, O, C, EN, DT; BN, CH, CN, MH, MMO, TU, WF, Y.

2343 — —[Anr. ed.] —, [1682]. 4°.* MACD 16a iii. O.

2344 — —Second edition. —, 1682. 4°.* MACD 16b. L, O, OC, OW, CT; CH, CLC, MH, TU, WF, Y.

2345 — —Third edition. —, 1683. 4°.* MACD 16c. L, O, CS, DT, GK; CH, CU, MH, TU, WF, Y.

2346 [–] The rival ladies. *By W. W. for Henry Heringman*, 1664. 4°. MACD 67a. L, O, LVD, OW, CK; CH, CN, MH, TU, WF, Y.

2347 — —Second edition. *For H. Herringman*, 1669. 4°. MACD 67b. L, O, CT; CH, CU, MH, TU, WF, Y.

2348 — —Third edition. *By T. N. for Henry Herringman*, 1675. 4°. MACD 67c. L, O, CT, LVD, EN; BN, CH, CU, MH, NC, TU, WF, Y.

2349 — —Fourth edition. *By T. W. for H. Herringman, and are to be sold by R. Bentley, J. Tonson, F. Saunders, and T. Bennet*, 1693. 4°. MACD 67d. L, O, C, EN, DT; CH, CN, MH, TU, WF, Y.

[–] Satyr to his muse. 1682. *See* Shadwell, Thomas.

2350 [–] The second part of Absalom. *For Jacob Tonson*, 1682. fol.* MACD 15a. L, O, LG, LL, CT; CH, CN, MH, WF, Y.

2351 [–] —Second edition. —, 1682. fol.* MACD 15b. L, C, LVD, HH; CLC, CN, MH, TU, WC, WF.

2352 [–] —*Dublin, for Robert Thornton*, 1682. 4°.* MACD 15c. WF.

2353 —Secret-love. *For Henry Herringman*, 1668. 4°. MACD 70a. L, O, OW, CK, CS; CH, MH, NN, TU, WF, Y.

2354 — —Second edition. —, 1669. 4°. MACD 70b. L, O, CT, LVD, DT; BN, CH, CU, MH, TU, WF, Y.

2355 — —Third edition. *By J. M. for Henry Herriman*, 1675. 4°. Y.

2356 — —Fourth edition. —, 1679. 4°. MACD 70c. L, O, CK, LVD, EN; CH, CU, MH, TU, WF, Y.

2357 — —Fifth edition. *For Henry Herringman, and are to be sold by Richard Bentley*, 1691. 4°. T.C.II 387. MACD 70d. L, O, OW, EN, DT; BN, CH, CN, MH, TU, WF, Y.

2358 — —Sixth edition. *By T. Warren for Henry Herringman, to be sold by Jacob Tonson, Francis Saunders, and Thomas Bennet*, 1698. 4°. MACD 70e. L, O, C, EN; CLC, CU, MH, TU, WF, Y.

2358A — —[Anr. ed.] — *and K. Bentley*, 1698. 4°. NIC, Y.

2359 [–] Sʳ Martin Mar-all. *For H. Herringman*, 1668. 4°. T.C.I 3. MACD 71a. L, O, CK, LVF, EN; CH, CU, MH, TU, WF, Y.

2360 [–] —Second edition. —, 1668. 4°. MACD 71b. L, O; CCL, CN, TU, WF, Y.

2361 [–] —[Anr. ed.] —, 1669. 4°. MACD 71bn. L, O, DT; CH, CN, LC, MH, WF.

2362 [–] —Third edition. —, 1678. 4°. MACD 71c. L, O, LVD, OC, EN; CH, CN, MH, TU, WF, Y.

2363 — —Fourth edition. *For Henry Herringman, and are to be sold by Francis Saunders*, 1691. 4°. T.C.II 373. MACD 71d. L, O, C, EN, DT; BN, CH, CN, MH, TU, WF, Y.

2364 — —Fifth edition. *By T. Warren for Henry Herringman, to be sold by R. Bentley, J. Tonson, F. Saunders, and T. Bennet*, 1697. 4°. MACD 71e. L, O, EN; CH, MH, TU, WF, Y.

2365 —A song for Sᵗ Cecilia's Day, 1687. [*London*], *for T. Dring*, 1687. brs. MACD 25. L.

2365A [–] A song in the Indian queen [*London*, 1695?], brs. L.

2365B [–] A song in The Spanish frier. [*London*, 1698.] brs. CLC.

2365C [–] A song set to musick [*London*, 1692], brs. CH.

2365D [–] A song sung by Mrs. Aliffin ... Tyrannick love. [*London*, 1698.] brs. L; CLC.

2366 [–] The songs in Amphitryon. *By J. Hoptons for Jacob Tonson*. 1690. 4°. L, O, LVD, LVF; CLC, MB, MBP, TU, WF, Y.

2367 [–] The songs in The Indian queen. *By J. Heptinstall; to be sold by John May and for John Hudgebutt*, 1695 fol.* L, GU; CLC, LC, NN, WF.

2368 —The Spanish Fryar. *For Richard Tonson and Jacob Tonson*, 1681. 4°. T.C.I 451. MACD 86a. L, O, LVD, OW, CK; BN, CH, CN, MH, TU, WF, Y.

2369 — —Second edition. —, 1686. 4°. MACD 86b. L, O, CCA, LVD, EN; CH, CN, MH, TU, WF, Y.

2370 — —Third edition. —, 1690. 4°. MACD 86c. L, O, CT, EN, DT; BN, CH, CN, MH, TU, WF, Y.

2371 — —Fourth edition. *For E. Tonson, and Jacob Tonson*, 1695. 4°. MACD 86d. L, O, C, DT; BN, CH, MH, NC, TU, WF, Y.

2372 —The state of innocence. *By T. N. for Henry Herringman*, 1677. 4°. T.C.I 266. MACD 81a. L, O, C, OW, EC; BN, CH, CN, MH, TU, WF, Y.

2373 — —Second edition. —, 1677. 4°. CH.

2374 — —Third edition. *By H.H. for Henry Herringman,* 1678. 4°.* MACD 81b. L, O, EN; CH, CN, MH, TU, WF, Y.

2375 — —[Anr. ed.] *By H.H. for Henry Herringman, to be sold by Joseph Knight, and Francis Saunders,* 1684. 4°.* T.C.II 105. MACD 81c–e. L, O, LG, LVD, GK; CLC, MH, WF, Y.

2376 — —Fifth edition. *By J.M. for Henry Herringman, to be sold by Abel Roper,* 1690. 4°.* MACD 81f. L, O, OW, EN, DT; CH, CU, MH, TU, WF, Y.

2377 — —Sixth edition. *For Henry Herringman, and are to be sold by Abel Roper,* 1692. 4°.* MACD 81g. L, O, LVF, EN; BN, CH, MH, TU, WF, Y.

2378 — —Seventh edition. *For Hen. Herringman, and are to be sold by J. Tonson, F. Saunders, and T. Bennet,* 1695. 4°. MACD 81h. L, O, EN; CH, CU, MH, TU, WF, Y.

2379 [–] Sylvæ: or, the second part of poetical miscellanies. *For Jacob Tonson,* 1685. 8°. MACD 43ai. L, O, CS, OC, GK; CH, CN, MH, TU, WF, Y.

2380 [–] —Second edition. —, 1692. 8°. MACD 43b. MH, TU, WF, Y.

2381 [–] —"Second" edition. —, 1693. 8°. MACD 43bn. O, WCA; MB, WF, Y.

2382 —Three poems. Second edition. *By William Wilson,* 1659. *And reprinted for R. Baldwin,* 1682. 4°. MACD 3d. T.C.I 490. L, O, CT, LG, LVD; CH, CN, MH, TU, WF, Y.

2383 —Threnodia Augustalis: a funeral-Pindarique poem. *For Jacob Tonson,* 1685. 4°.* MACD 20a. L, O, CT, OC, OM; BN, CH, CN, MH, TU, WF, Y.

2384 — —Second edition. —, 1685. 4°.* MACD 20b. L, O, CT, DC, DT; CH, CN, MH, TU, WF, Y.

2385 — —[Anr. ed.] *Dublin, reprinted by Joseph Ray, for Robert Thornton,* 1685. 4°.* DIX 210. MACD 20c. C, LVD, DM, DT; CH, MH.

2386 —To His Sacred Majesty. A panegyrick. *For Henry Herringman,* 1661. fol.* MACD 6ai. LT, O, C, OW; CH, MH, TU, WCL, WF, Y.

2387 —To My Lord Chancellor presented on New-years-day. *For Henry Herringman,* 1662. fol.* MACD 7. L, O, C, LVD, OW; CH, CLC, MH, WF.

2388 —Troilus and Cressida. *For Jacob Tonson, and Abel Swall,* 1679. 4°. MACD 84a i. L, O, C, CK, LLL; BN, CH, CN, MH, TU, WF, Y.

2389 — —[Anr. ed.] *For Abel Swall, and Jacob Tonson,* 1679. 4°. MACD 84a ii. L, O, CT, LVF, DT; BN, CH, CN, MH, TU, WF, Y.

2390 — —[Anr. ed.] *For Jacob Tonson,* 1679 [i.e., 1692]. 4°. MACD 84b. CLC, MB, MH, TU, WF.

2391 — —[Anr. ed.] *By I. Dawks, for Jacob Tonson,* 1695. 4°. MACD 84c. L, O, CT, EN; BN, CH, CN, MH, TU, WF, Y.

2392 —A trve coppy of the epilogue to Constantine the Great. *For J. Tonson,* 1684. brs. MACD 102b. CH, CLC, MH, WF.

2393 —Tyrannick love. *For H. Herringman,* 1670. 4°. T.C.I 56. MACD 74a. L, O, CT, LUS, EN; CH, CU, MH, TU, WF, Y.

2394 — —Second edition. —, 1672. 4°. MACD 74b. L, O, LVF, OM, DT; BN, CH, CU, MH, TU, WF, Y.

2395 — —Third edition. —, 1677. 4°. MACD 74c. L, O, C, LVD, EN; CLC, CU, MH, TU, WF, Y.

2396 — —Fourth edition. *For H. Herringman, to be sold by Joseph Knight, and Francis Saunders,* 1686. 4°. MACD 74d. L, O, LVD, OW, EN; CH, CN, MH, TU, WF, Y.

2396A — —[Anr. ed.] —, 1694. 4°. MH, WF.

2397 — —Fifth edition. *For Henry Herringman, and are to be sold by R. Bently, J. Tonson, F. Saunders, and T. Bennet,* 1695. 4°. MACD 74e. L, O, DT; CH, CN, MH, TU, WF, Y.

2398 —The vindication: or the parallel. *For Jacob Tonson,* 1683. 4°. MACD 130. L, O, C, EN, DT; CH, CN, MH, TU, WF, Y.

2399 —The wild gallant. *In the Savoy, by Tho. Newcomb, for H. Herringman,* 1669. 4°. T.C.I 10. MACD 72a. L, O, CT, EN, DT; BN, CN, MH, TU, WF, Y.

2400 — —[Anr. ed.] *In the Savoy, by Tho. Newcomb, for H. Heringman,* 1669. 4°. MACD 72b. L, O, CK, EN; CH, MH, TU, WF, Y.

2401 — —Second edition. *By H. Hills, for H. Herringman,* 1684. 4°. T.C.II 64. MACD 72c. L, O, C, LVD, EN; CH, CN, MH, TU, WF, Y.

2402 — —Third edition. *By T. Warren for Henry Herringman, and are to be sold by R. Bentley, J. Tonson, F. Saunders, and T. Bennet,* 1694. 4°. MACD 72d. L, O, CK, ES, DT; BN, CH, CU, MH, TU, WF, Y.

2403 —, *jr.* The husband his own cuckold. *For J. Tonson,* 1696. 4°. L, O, LVD, OW, EN; CH, CN, MH, TU, WF, Y.

2404 [Du Bail, Louis Moreau, *sieur*.] The famous Chinois. *By E.O. for Thomas Dring,* 1669. 8°. T.C.I 13. L; CH, CN, V, Y.

2405 Du Bartas, Guillaume de Saluste. Divine weekes and workes. *By Robert Young,* 1641. fol. L, O, CT, MR, DT; CH, CN, MH, WF, Y.

2405A — —[Anr. ed.] —, *and are to bee sold by William Hope,* 1641. fol. OC.

2405B Dublin. An act of the Lord Mayor. *Dublin, by Joseph Ray,* [1681.] fol.* DIX 189. DI.

2406 Du Bois, Nicholas. Fuga peccati. *Typis Guil. Downing,* 1677. 12°. CM, E; Y.

Du Bois de la Cour, *pseud*. See Filleau de la Chaise, Jean.

2407 [Du Bosc, Jacques.] The accomplished woman. *For Gabriel Bedell and Tho. Collins,* 1656. 12°. T.C.I 76. LT; CH, WCL, WF, Y.

2407A [–] —Second edition. *For Tho. Collins and John Ford,* 1671. 12°. M; CN.

2407B [–] The excellent woman described. *For J. Watts,* 1692. 8°. L, O, CT, M; CH, CU, LC, MH, Y.

2407C [–] —[Anr. ed.] *For John Wyat,* 1695. 8°. L, CT, M; CN, MH, WF, Y.

2408 Dubourdieu, Isaac. Discourse of obedience. *For Samuel Lowndes,* 1684. 4°. O, WCA, DT; CLC.

2409 **Dubourdieu, Jean Armand.** An historical dissertation upon the Thebean Legion. *For R.Bentley,* 1696. 8°. T.C.II 589. L, O, C, EN, DT; BN, CH, CLC, TU, WF, Y.

2409A —Sermon prononcé la veille des funerailles de la Reyne. *Se vend chez la veuve Maret,* 1695. 4°. L; WF.

2410 [–] A true copy of a project for the reunion. colop: *For Randal Taylor,* 1685. cap., fol.* L, O, CS, HH, DT; CH, NU, PL, WF, Y.

2411 [**Dubreuil, Jean.**] Perspective practical. *By H.Lloyd, and sold by Robert Pricke,* 1672. 4°. T.C.I 111. L, C; CL; CLC, PL, TU, Y.

2412 [–] —[Anr. ed.] *For Robert Pricke; and are to be sold by S.Sprint,* 1698. 4°. L; CH, CLC, PU, WF, W.

2413 **Du Brez, Guy.** Johannes Becoldus redivivus: or, the English Quaker. *Printed for, and are to be sold by John Allen:* 1659. 8°. LT, CCA, CS, CT.

2414 Entry cancelled.

2415 [**Du Cambout de Pont Château, Sebastian Joseph.**] The moral practice of the Jesuites. *For Simon Miller,* 1670. 12°. T.C.I 37. L, O, C, P, DT; CH, NU, TU, WF, Y.

2416 [–] —[Anr. ed.] —, 1671. 12°. LIL; CLC.

2417 **Du Chastelet de Luzancy, Hippolite.** A conference between an orthodox Christian. *By Tho. Warren for Thomas Bennet,* 1698. 8°. T.C.III 52. L, O, CT, EC, GU; NU, WF, Y.

2417A —A panegyrick to the memory of His Grace Frederick. *For R. Bentley,* 1690. 8°.* T.C.II 338. L, C, CT; CH, MH, WF, Y.

2418 —Reflexions on the Council of Trent. *Oxford, at the theater,* 1677. 4°. MADAN 3144. L, O, C, LW, DT; CH, WF, Y.

2418A — —[Anr. ed.] — *to be had there, and in London at Simon Millers,* 1677. 4°. L, OC.

2419 — —[Anr. ed.] *Oxford, at the theater, to be sold by Moses Pit, Peter Parker, William Leak, and Thomas Guy,* 1679. 4°. MADAN 3214. L, CT; CN, MIU, NU.

2420 —Remarks on several late writings. *By Tho. Warren, for Thomas Bennet,* 1696. 8°. O, CT, LW, EC, DT; CLC, NU, WG.

2421 —Sermon du. *A Londres, se vendent chez Moyse Pitt,* 1675. 4°.* L, O, LW; NU, WF.

2422 —A sermon preached . . . July 11. *By W. Godbid, to be sold by Moses Pitt,* 1675. 4°.* T.C.I 215. L, O, CS, OC, WCA; CN, WF, Y.

2423 — —Second edition. —, 1676. 4°. T.C.I 231. L, O, C, EC, EN; CH, IU, MH, NN, TU.

2423A —A sermon preached . . . June 2, 1697. *By E. Holt for Tho. Bennet,* 1697. 4°. L, OC, LW; IU.

2423B —A treatise against irreligion. *By E. W. and are to be sold by Hen. Bonwicke,* 1678. 8°. T.C.I 308. L, LSC, OC, P, WF.

Dutchess of Malfi. 1678. *See* Webster, John.

2424 The Dutchess of Mazarines farewel. [*London*], *for Langley Curtiss,* 1680. brs. CN, MH, PU, TU, Y.

2425 The Dutchess of Monmouths lamentation. colop: *By J. Millitt,* 1683. fol.* L, O, EN; CH, CLC, MH, Y.

2425A —[Anr. ed.] *For J. Deacon,* 1683. brs. L.

2426 The Dutchess of Portsmouths and Count Coningsmarks farvvel. colop: *For J. Bayly,* 1682. brs. L, O, EN; CH, MH, NN, Y.

'2426A The Dutchess of Portsmouths farwel. *For J. Clarke, W. Thackeray, and T. Passinger,* [1685.] brs. L.

2427 **Duck, Sir Arthur.** De usu & authoritate juris civilis Romanorum. *Typis Richardi Hodgkinsonne,* 1653. 8°. LT, O, C, E, DT; MH, NCL.

2428 — —[Anr. ed.] Impensis Thomae Dring & venales prostant apud Johannem Dunmore, 1679. 12°. T.C.I 338. L, C, LL, EN, DT; MH, NCL, TU, WF, YL.

2429 — —[Anr. ed.] —, 1689. L, O, CS, EN, DT; CH, CLC, LC, NCL, WF.

2430 —The life of Henry Chichele. *For Ri. Chiswell,* 1699. 8°. T.C.III 154. L, O, C, EN, DT; CH, CU, MBA, NU, WF, Y.

Duckers duck'd. 1700. *See* Young, Samuel.

2430A **Ducket, Charles.** Sparks from the golden altar. *By T. C. for Joseph Blacklock,* 1660. 8°. L, LSC; CH, CLC, MH, WF.

2430B **Duckett, Thomas.** The messenger of profit. *By T. Forcet,* 1649. 4°.* MH, Y.

2431 —To the right honble Lords, . . . the humble petition of. [*London,* 1646.] cap., 4°.* L; WF.

2432 **Du Clos, Samuel Cotreau, *sieur.*** Observations on the mineral waters of France. *For Henry Faithorne, and John Kersey,* 1684. 8°. T.C.II 71. L, O, C, LCP, GU; CLC, HC.

2433 — —[Anr. ed.] —, 1685. 8°. OM.

2434 — —[Anr. ed.] —, 169–? 12°. LM. [trimmed]

2435 [**Du Coignet, Pierre.**] Anti-Cotton. *Printed, and are to be sold by Randal Taylor,* 1689. 4°. L, O, CCA, OC, BAMB; CH, MBA, NU, PL, WF, Y.

2436 **Ducros, Simon.** A letter from. *Printed,* 1693. 4°.* L; CN, NU, WF.

2437 — —[Anr. ed.] *For Abel Roper,* 1693. 8°.* L, O, C, LW, EN; CH, MIU, Y.

Ductor historicus: or. 1698. *See* Hearne, Thomas.

Ducy, Sir Simon. *See* D'Ewes, Sir Simon.

2438 **Dudley, Dud.** Dud Dudley's metallum martis. *By T. M. for the author,* 1665. 8°. L, OR; NN.

2439 **Dudley, Sir Gamaliel.** A trve copy of Colonel Sr Gamaliel Dvdley's letter. *Oxford, by Leonord Lichfield,* 1644[/5]. 4°.* MADAN 1736. O, C, YM; WF, Y.

Dudley, Joseph. Almanack. Cambridge [Mass.], 1668. *See* Almanacs.

2440 —The speech of . . . May 17, 1686. *Boston, Pierce for Phillips,* 1691. LPR.

[**Dudley, Thomas.**] Massachusetts or. Boston, 1696. *See* Scottow, Joshua, *ed.*

Due correction. Oxford, 1656. *See* Wallis, John.

Due order. 1680. *See* Hookes, Ellis.

2441 The dve right of tithes examined. *For Thomas Pierrepont,* 1654. 4°.* LT.

2442 [**Duffet, Thomas**]. Amintor's lamentation. [*London*], *for P. Brooksby,* [1676]. brs. L, O, HH.

2443 [-] The amorous old-woman. *For Simon Neale, and B. Tooth*, 1674. 4°. T.C.I 170. L, O, EN; LC, MH, NC, Y.

2443A [-] —[Anr. ed.] *For Simon Neale*, 1674. 4°. CH, CLC, CN.

2444 —Beauties triumph. *Printed*, 1676. 4°.* L, O, CS; CH, CN, CU, WF, Y.

2445 [-] The bleeding lover. *[London], for J. Clarke, W. Thackeray, and T. Passenger*, [1676-80]. brs. L, O, HH.

2446 [-] The Empress of Morocco. *For Simon Neale*, 1674. 4°. T.C.I 170. L, O, OW, ES; CH, CN, LC, MH, TU, Y.

2447 [-] The fond lady, a comedy. *For Simon Neale*, 1684. 4°.* L, O; CH, MB, NP, WF.

2448 —The mock-tempest. *For William Cademan*, 1675. 4°. T.C.I 197. L, O, CT, OW, EN; CH, LC, MH, NC, TU, Y.

2449 —New poems, songs, prologues and epilogues. *For Nicholas Woolfe*, 1676. 8°. T.C.I 236. L, O, OW; CH, LC, MH, WF, Y.

2450 —New songs, and poems, a-la-mode at Court. *For Nicholas Woolfe*, 1677. 8°. L; CH.

2451 [-] The prologue to the last new play A duke and no duke. colop: *By Geo. Croom*, 1684. brs. L, O; CH, CLC, MH.

2452 —Psyche debauch'd. *For John Smith*, 1678. 4°. L, O, OW; CH, WF, Y.

2453 —The Spanish rogue. *For William Cademan*, 1674. 4°. T.C.I 163. L, O, CT, OW, EN; CH, CN, LC, MH, TU, Y.

2454 [Dufour, Sylvestre.] The manner of making of coffee, tea, and chocolate. 1685. 12°. L, O, CS, LWL, GH; BN, CH, LC, MH, PBL, Y.

2455 [-] Moral instructions of a father. *For W. Crook*, 1683. T.C.II 51. LSC; RPJ, Y.

2456 [Du Four de Longuerue, Louis.] An historical treatise written by an author of the communion . . . touching transubstantiation. Second edition. *For Richard Chiswell*, 1687. 4°. L, O, HH, E, EN; CN, MH, NPT, PL, Y.

2456A [-] Traitté d'un autheur. *Ches B. Griffin, pour Jean Cailloué*, 1686. 12°. O, OC, LSC, CJ.

2457 [-] A treatise written by an author. *For Richard Chiswell*, 1687. 4°. T.C.II 272. L, C, CT, HH, DT; CH, CLC, NU, TU, Y.

2458 Du Fresnoy, Charles Alphonse. De arte graphica. The art of painting. *By J. Heptinstall, for W. Rogers*, 1695. 4°. T.C.II 560. L, O, C, EN, DT; CH, CN, LC, MH, TU, Y.

2459 [Dugard, Samuel.] The marriages of cousin germans. *Oxford, by Hen: Hall for Thomas Bovvman*, 1673. 8°. T.C.I 153. MADAN 2973. L, O, C, CT, EN; CLC, CU, MH, NU, WF, Y.

2460 [-] Περι Πολυπαιδιας Or, a discourse concerning the having many children. *For W. Rogers*, 1695. 8°. L, O, LWL, OC; CH, MH, NC, WF, Y.

2461 —The true nature of the divine law. *For Jos. Watts*, 1687. 8°. T.C.II 192. L, LSC, LW, P; CLC, NPT, NU, WF.

2462 Dugard, Thomas. The change: or, the blind eye opened. *By G. M. for George Edwards*, 1641. 12°. LW; Y.

2463 —Death and the grave. *By William Du-gard*, 1649. 4°. L, O, CT, BC; CH, CLC, MH, WF, Y.

2463A —Philobasileus. *Printed and are to be sold by Edward Brewster*, 1664. 8°. L; CH.

2464 Du-Gard, William. The English rudiments of the Latine tongue. *By W. D. to bee sold by Francis Eglesfield*, 1656. 4°. LT, LG.

2464A —[Anr. ed.] *By H. L. and R. V. and are to be sold by Francis Eglesfield*, 1660. 8°. Y.

2465 — —[Anr. ed.] *By John Redmayne, for Francis Eglesfield*, 1665. 8°. O.

2465A — —[Anr. ed.] *For Francis Eglesfield*, 1673. 8°. T.C.I 99. EC.

2465B — —[Anr. ed.] *By A. and I. Dawks, for Awnsham and John Churchill*, 1693. 8°. Y.

2466 —Græcæ grammaticas rudimenta. *Typis authoris, veneunt apud Andr. Crook*, 1654. 8°. C, LW, ELY; PL, Y.

2466A —An humble remonstrance. *Printed*, 1661. 4°.* L.

2467 —Lexicon Græci Testamenti alphabeticum. *Typis Henrici Lloyd*, 1660. 8°. L, C; LC.

2468 —Rhetorices elementa. *Typis autoris*, 1648. 12°. LG.

2469 — —Second edition. *Typis authoris. Veneunt apud Fr. Eglesfield*, 1651. 8°. C; NC.

2469A — —Third edition. —, 1653. 8°. CCA.

2470 — —Fifth edition. —, 1657. 8°. C; LC, WF.

2470A — —Seventh edition. *Typis I. Redmayne, impensis Francisci Eglesfield*, 1673. 8°.* T.C.I 138. L.

2470B — —Eighth edition. —, 1676. 8°. PL.

2470C — —Ninth edition. —, 1679. 8°. IU, WF, Y.

2470D — —Tenth edition. *Typis Eliz. Redmayne impensis Francisci Eglesfield prostent venales apud Randal Taylor*, 1686. 8°. CLC, MHS.

2470E — —Eleventh edition. *Excudebat Eliz. Redmayne, pro Randal Taylor*, 1694. 8°.* L; PL.

2471 Dugdale, John. A catalogue of the nobility of England. *For Robert Clavell*, 1685. brs. T.C.II 115. L, O, LG, HH.

2472 Dugdale, Richard. A narrative of the wicked plots. *By T. B. to be sold by Robert Clavel*, 1679. fol.* L, O, C, LG, EN; CH, NU, TU, WF, Y.

2473 —A narrative of unheard of Popish cruelties. *For John Hancock*, 1680. fol.* T.C.I 382. L, O, CT, MR, EN; CH, CN, NU, PL, WF.

2474 Dugdale, Stephen. The further information of. *For Thomas Parkhurst: and Thomas Simmons*, 1680. fol.* T.C.I 421. L, O, C, EN, DT; CH, CN, LC, MH, NC, Y.

2475 —The information of. *By the assigns of John Bill, Thomas Newcomb, and Henry Hills*, 1680. fol.* L, O, C, EN, DT; BN, CH, CN, MH, WF, Y.

2476 — —[Anr. ed.] *Reprinted at Dublin*, 1680. 4°.* DIX 177. L, O, CD, DT; Y.

2477 Dugdale, Sir William. The antient usage. *Oxford, at the theater, for Rich. Davis*, 1682. 8°. T.C.I 475. L, O, C, E, DT; BBE, MIU, Y.

2477A ——[Anr. ed.] *Oxford, at the theater for Moses Pitt,* 1682. 8°. OC; MB, MN, NP.

2478 ——Second edition. *Oxford, at the theater for Moses Pitt, and sold by Samuel Smith,* 1682. 12°. T.C.I 489. L, O, CSSX, HH, ES; BN, CH, CU, LC, MH, Y.

2479 —The antiquities of Warwickshire. *By Thomas Warren,* 1656. fol. L, O, CE, ES, DT; BN, CH, CLC, CN, MH, WF, Y.

2480 —The baronage of England. *By Tho. Newcomb for Abel Roper, John Martin, and Henry Herringman,* 1675-76. 2v. fol. T.C.I 210. L, O, C, EN, DT; CH, CN, LC, MH, NC, Y.

2480A [–] A full relation of the passage. *Printed at Oxford by Leonard Lichtrek,* 1645. 4°. MADAN 1766. LT, O, LG, HH; CH, CN, MH, WF, Y.

2480B [–] —[Anr. ed.] *Bristol, by Robert Barker and John Bill,* 1645. 4°. DT.

2481 —The history of imbanking and drayning . . . fenns and marshes. *By Alice Warren,* 1662. fol. L, O, C, EN, DT; CH, LC, MH, NC, Y.

2482 —The history of St. Pauls Cathedral. *By Tho. Warren,* 1658. fol. L, O, C, ES, DT; BN, CH, LC, MH, NU, Y.

2483 —Monasticon Anglicanum. *Typis Richardi Hodgkinsonne,* 1655. O, C, LL, EN, DT; BN, CH, CN, MH, WF, Y.

2484 —Monastici Anglicani: volumen alterum. *Typis Aliciæ Warren,* 1661. fol. O, C, LM, HH, EN; BN, CH, CN, MH, NU, WF.

2485 —Monastici Anglicani, volumen secundus. *Typis A. W. prostant apud R. Scott,* 1673. fol. CSSX, CT; CLC, CPB, NC, WF.

2486 —Monastici Anglicani, volumen tertium. *In the Savoy: excudebat Tho. Newcomb, & prostant venales Ab. Roper, Joh. Martin & Hen. Herringman,* 1673. fol. T.C.I 136. L, CT, NPL, ES, DT; CLC, CN, MH, NU, WF, Y.

2487 ——[Anr. ed.] *Prostant apud R. Scott,* 1683. fol. CT.

2487A ——Second edition. *Impensis Christopheri Wilkinson, Thomæ Dring, & Caroli Harper,* 1682. fol. T.C.I 496. LG, OC, SC, CT, DT; BN, TU, WCL.

2487B —Monasticon Anglicanum . . . epitomized in English. *For Sam. Keble; Hen. Rhodes,* 1693. fol. T.C.II 476. L, O, C, LG, E; CH, CN, NC, TU, WF, Y.

2488 —Origines juridiciales or historical memorials of the English laws. *By F. and T. Warren, for the author,* 1666. fol. L, O, C, E, DT; CH, CLC, MH, NCL, WF.

2489 ——Second edition. *In the Savoy, by Tho. Newcomb for Abel Roper, John Martin and Henry Herringman,* 1671. fol. T.C.I 90. L, O, CS, ES, DT; CH, CN, LC, MH, NP, Y.

2490 ——Third edition. *For Christop. Wilkinson, Tho. Dring and Charles Harper,* 1680. fol. T.C.I 410. L, O, CM, EN, DT; BN, CH, LC, MH, NCL, Y.

2491 —A perfect copy of all summons. *By S. R. for Robert Clavell,* 1685. fol. T.C.II 145. L, O, C, EN, DT; BN, CH, CN, LC, MH, NP, NU, Y.

2492 —A short view of the late troubles in England. *Oxford, at the theater for Moses Pitt, London,* 1681. fol. T.C.I 439. L, O, C, EN, DT; BN, CH, CN, LC, MH, NU, Y.

2493 **Dugres, Gabriel.** Dialogi Gallico-Anglico-Latini. Second edition. *Oxoniæ, excudebat Leon. Lichfield: veneunt apud Thom. Robinson,* 1652. 8°. MADAN 2194. L, O, SC; BN, WF.

2494 ——Third edition. *Oxoniæ, exc. A. Lichfield,* 1660. 8°. MADAN 2490. L, O, OC, CCA; CH, CLC.

2495 —Jean Arman Du Plessis, Duke of Richelieu, . . . his life. *By Tho. Fawcet,* 1643. 8°. LT, O; CLC.

2496 **Du Hamel, Jean Baptiste.** De consensu veteris et novæ philosophiæ. *Oxoniæ, excudebat W. Hall impensis Joh. Crosley & Amos Curteyne,* 1669. 8°. MADAN 2826. O, CT, E, ELY, YM; NC, WF, Y.

2497-8 Entries cancelled.

2499 [–] Philosophia vetus et nova. Fourth edition. *For G. Wells, and A. Swalle,* 1685. 12°. T.C.II 139. L, O, CM, E, DT; CH, PL, WF, Y.

2500 **Duke, Francis.** An answer to some of the principle Quakers. *By T. N. for Miles Michel the younger,* 1660. 4°. L, O, LF, CT, SC; PH.

2501 —The fulnesse and freenesse of Gods grace. [Part 1.] *By Richard Oulton and Gregory Dexter,* 1642. 4°. LT, O; MH, NPT, WF.

2502 —The fulness and freeness of Gods grace . . . In two parts. *By Thomas Newcomb, for John Clark,* 1655. 4°. LT, O, LCL, OC, EN; MH, NPT.

2503 —The fulness and freeness of Gods grace. Third part. *By T. N. for Wil. Milward, and Miles Michael,* 1656. 4°. LT, LF, OC, SC; NPT.

2504 **[Duke, Richard.]** An epithalamium upon the marriage of Capt. William Bedloe. *[London,* 1679?] brs. L, CT; CN, MBA, MIU, TU, WF.

2505 [–] Floriana. A pastoral. colop: *For Samuel Cooke,* 1681. fol.* L, O; CH, CN, TU, WF, Y.

2505A [–] Funeral tears upon the death of Captain William Bedloe. *[London,* 1680]. brs. L, O, OP, HH; CH, CLC, CN, MH, Y.

2505B [–] —[Anr. ed.] *For J. Vade,* 1681. brs. CN, MH, PU, WF.

2505C [–] A panegyrick upon Oates. *[London,* 1679]. brs. L, O; CH, CN, MH, WF, Y.

Duke and no duke. 1685. *See* Cokayne. *Sir* Aston.

2506 Duke Dangerfield declaring how he represented the Duke of Mon—. colop: *For J. Smith,* 1685. brs. L, O, HH.

2507 Duke Hamiltons conditions. *[London], for R. B.,* 1648. 4°.* LT, DT; MH.

2508 Duke Hamilton's ghost, or. *Printed,* 1659. 4°.* LT, OC; CLC, TU.

Duke of Monmouth, and Earl of Essex. [n.p., 1680.] *See* N., C.

2509 The Duke of Monmouth's case. colop: *For J. C.,* 1682. brs. L, O, MC; CH, CN, MH, TU, WF, Y.

2510 —colop: *For E. C.,* 1682. brs. CH.

2511 The Duke of Monmouth's kind answer. *[London], for Tho. Wright,* 1683. fol. O, EN; CLC, MH, TU.

2512 The Duke of Monmouth's lamentation. *[London], for P. Brooksby,* [168–]. brs. L.

C0390

2512A The Duke of Monmouths triumph. *For I. Dean*, 1683. brs. L; MH.

2513 The Duke of Norfolk's case: or the doctrine. [*London*], *printed*, 1688. fol. L, O, C, EN, DT; CH, NU, WF, Y.

2514 The Duke of Norfolk's case: with. [*London*, 1699], brs. L, LL; MIU.

2515 —[*Anr. ed.*] *By Jer. Wilkins*, 1700. brs. LL, OC, HH, EN.

2516 The Duke's daughter's cruelty. *For J. Deacon*, [1688–95]. brs. L, CM, HH.

2517 **Dulany, Edmund.** A sermon preached . . . on Ash-Wednesday. *Dublin, for James Malone*, 1689. 4°.* DIX 374. C, DM.

2517A Dulcedo ex acerbis. Sound doctrine. [*London?* 1700.] cap., 4°.* L.

2518 Dullman turn'd doctor. [*London*, 1648.] cap., 4°.* LT.

2519 Dum spiro spero. An humble representation . . . woollen manufactures, *Printed*, 1700. 4°.* L, LUG; MH, NC, PU, WF, Y.

2519A **Du Maresq, Richard.** Sermon prêché . . . 28me de Novemb. 1675. *Par J. M. pour Moyse Pitt*, 1675. 4°.* SP, EN.

2520 **Du May, Lewis.** A discourse historical and political of the War of Hungary. *Glasgow, by Robert Sanders*, 1669. 8°. ALDIS 1859. L, C, E, EN, GM.

2521 —The estate of the empire, . . . of Germany. *By R. Norton, for R. Royston*, 1664. 8°. L, LW, OM, CM, SC; CH, CLC, LC, NC, Y.

2522 — —[*Anr. ed.*] *By J. Macock for Richard Royston*, 1676. 8°. T.C.I 217. L, O, C, EN, DT; CLC, CN, PL, TU, WF, Y.

2523 The dumb lady. [*London*], *for P. Brookby* [sic], [1682–90]. brs. L, O, CM, HH; MH.

2524 The dumb maid. *By and for W. O. A. M. to be sold by C. Bates*, [1678]. brs. L, HH, GU; MH.

2525 The dumb maid. [*London*], *for F. Coles, T. Vere, I. Wright, J. Clarke, W. Thackeray, and T. Passinger*, [1675?]. brs. L.

Dumb speech: or. 1646. *See* Spencer, Benjamin.

Dumbritons castle. [*n.p.*, 1643.] *See* C., A. B.

2526 **Dumont, Jean, *baron de Carlscroon*.** A new voyage to the Levant. *By T. H. for M. Gillyflower, T. Goodwin, M. Wotton, J. Walthoe, and R. Parker*, 1696. 8°. L, C, OC, EN, DT; CH, LC, MH, TU, Y.

2527 **[Dumont, Joseph.]** The reasons for which an ecclesiastick of the Romanish church hath left the errors. *Printed*, 1681. 4°.* CH.

2528 **Du Moulin, Louis.** Amplissimo senatui academico. [*Oxford*, 1660.] brs. MADAN 2491. O.

2529 —Apologia pro epistola. *Typis E. G. pro T. W.*, 1641. 4°. C, CT, P, EN, DT.

2530 —An appeal of all the Non-Conformists. *For Richard Janeway*, 1681. 4°.* T.C.I 420. L, O, C, CT, YM; CH, MH, NU, WF, Y.

2531 [–] ᾿Αυτομαχια or, the self-contradiction. *Printed*, 1643. 4°. LT, O, HH, DT; CH, CN, NC, NPT, NU.

2532 —Conformité de la conduite de ceux qu'on appelle communement Independans. 1680. 8°. ENC; Y.

2533 —The conformity of the discipline. *For Richard Janeway*, 1680. 4°. T.C.I 402. L, LW, EN; CLC, MH, NU, Y.

2534 [–] Consilium de reformanda ecclesia Anglicana. *Typis E. G.*, 1642. 4°. L, WCA; NU.

2535 [–] —[*Anr. ed.*] —, 1643. 4°. LT, O, CS, P; WF.

2536 —Corollarium. *Excudebat R. Daniel prostat apud Samuelem Thomson*, 1657. 8°. C, OC, CT, DT; BN.

2537 — . . . De fidei partibus . . . dissertatio. *Typis Abrahami Miller*, 1653. 12°. O, C, DT; CLC.

2538 [–] Declaratio regnorum. *Excudebat Edw. Griffin*, 1645. 4°.* L, O, CS, ES; MH, NN, NU, WF.

2539 —Declaratory considerations. 1679. 4°. O, SP, DT; CN, MH.

2540 — . . . Epistola ad amicum. *Excudebat R. Daniel: prostat apud Samuelem Thomson*, 1658. 12°. LT, O, LW, E; BN, BBE, MU.

2541 [–] Jugulum causæ, seu nova, unica, compendiaria, 1671. 8°. T.C.I 74. L, O, C, P, ENC; CLC, NP, WF, Y.

2542 —The last words of. *For Rich. Royston*, 1680. 4°.* T.C., I 420, L, O, C, CT, DT; CH, CN, NU, WF, Y.

2543 —Moral reflections. *For Richard Janeway*, 1680. 4°.* T.C.I 402. L, CT, BAMB, EN; CH, MH, NU, WF, Y.

2544 [–] Motions to this present Parliament. [*London*], *printed*, 1641. 4°.* CCA; NU.

2545 —Of the right of churches. *By R. D. to be sold by Sa. Thomson*, 1658. 8°. LT, O, C, E, DT; NU.

2546 —Oratio auspicalis. *Oxoniæ, excudebat L. Lichfield*, 1652. 4°.* MADAN 2186. LT, O, C, CT; E; BN, WF, Y.

2547 —Papæ ultrajectinus. *Apud Thomam Roycrof*, 1668. 4°. L, O, CS, ENC, DT; BN, CH, CLC, Y.

2548 —Paraenesis ad aedificatores imperii in imperio. *Excudebat R. Daniel, prostat apud Samuelem Thomson*, 1656. 8°. LT, O, C, E, DT; BN, MH, Y.

2549 [–] Patronus bonæ fidei. [*London*], *typus N. B. apud I. P.*, 1672. 8°. L, O, CT, LW, ENC; BN, CLC, MBA, MH, NU, Y.

2549A —Les pensées de. 1680. 16°. L.

2550 —Philadelphvs vapulans. *Excudebat Milo Flesher, impensis Nathanielis Butter*, 1641. 4°. L, O, CT, OCC, DT; MB, NU, Y.

2551 —The povver of the Christian magistrate. *By G. Dawson, for Francis Eglesfield*, 1650. 8°. LT, O, C, LW, ENC; NU, WF, Y.

2552 —Proposals and reasons. *By Iohn Redmayne*, 1659. 4°.* L, O, CT, HH; CH, CLC, MH, NU, WF, Y.

2553 —A short and true account of the several advances. *Printed*, 1680. 4°. L, O, C, EN, DT; CH, MH, NU, WF, Y.

2553A [–] A sober and unpassionate reply. *For Richard Janeway*, 1680. 4°.* LLL; INU, MBA.

2554 —La tyrannie des préjugez. *Pour l'autheur*, 1678. 12°. L, CS; BN, CH, NPT, Y.

2554A [–] The understanding Christians duty. *By T. C. for D. White*, 1660. 12°. LW.

2555 [–] Vox populi, expressed in xxxv. motions. [London], printed, 1641. 4°.* L, O, CT, MR, E; CN, CSS, MH, NU, WF, Y.

2556 **[Du Moulin, Peter, younger.]** A calm answer to a violent discourse of N. N. For Henry Brome, 1677. 4°.* T.C.I 274. L, O, C, LIL, OC; CH, CLC, MH, NU, WF, Y.

2557 [–] Directions for the education of a young prince. For H. Brome, 1673. 12°. T.C.I 120. L, O, M; IU, MH.

2557A —Ecclesiae gemitus, [London], anno Dom. 1649. 4°. L, O, C, CT, MR; MH, NHC, Y.

2558 —The great loyalty. Printed, 1673. 4°.* L, O, CT, HH, YM; CH, LC, MH, NU, TU, WF.

2559 [–] A letter to a person of quality, concerning the fines. Printed, 1668. 4°.* O, LL; CLC, NU, WF.

2560 —Of peace and contentment. For Humphrey Moseley, 1657. 8°. LT, O, C, LCL, LW; NU.

2561 —Petri Molinæi P. F. παρεργα. Poematvm libri tres. Cantabrigiæ, excudebat Joann. Hayes, 1670. Impensis Joannis Creed, 8°. L, O, C, CT, EN; BN, CLC, CN, NU, WF, Y.

2562 ——[Anr. ed.] Cantabrigiæ, excudebat Joann. Hayes, 1671. Impensis Joannis Creed. 8°. T.C.I 59. L, C, CT; CLC, MH, WF, Y.

2563 — . . . Παρεργων incrementum. Cantabrigiæ, excudebat Joann. Hayes, 1671. Impensis Joannis Creeed. 8°. T.C.I 73. L, CS, OCC, CT, LVD; WF, Y.

2564 —A replie to a person of honour. For Henry Brome, 1675. 4°.* T.C.I 205. L, O, C, CT, EN; MBA, NU, TU, WF, Y.

2565 —The ruine of Papacy. For Robert Harford, 1678. 8°. L, P.

2566 —A sermon preach'd . . . Sept. 14. 1669. For J. Morgan, 1669. 4°.* L, O; CH, LLC, RPB.

2567 —A sermon preached . . . October 17. MDCLXXII. For Henry Brome, 1672. 4°.* T.C.I 116. L, O, C, LL, CT; CH, NU, WF, Y.

2568 —Ten sermons. For Rich. Royston, 1684. 8°. T.C.II 80. LCL, P; CLC, MH, NU, PPT.

2569 —A treatise of peace. Second edition. By A. Clark for John Sims, 1671. 8°. T.C.I 68. L, C, CS, E; CLC, CN, NPT, NU, Y.

2570 ——Third edition. By R. White for John Sims, 1678. 8°. T.C.I 295. L, C, CE, YM; CU, WF.

2570A ——[Anr. ed.] By R. White, for Samuel Tidmarsh, 1679. 8°. OM, CM, CT; MM, Y.

2571 —A vindication of the sincerity. By I. Redmayne, for John Crook, 1664. 4°. L, O, CT, EN, DT; BN, CH, MH, NU, WF, Y.

2572 ——Second edition. For John Crook, 1667. 4°. SC, E, EN; MU, TU.

2573 ——Third edition. —, 1668. 4°. C, LMT, DC, DT; MH, MIU, NNG.

2574 ——Fourth edition. For B. T. to be sold by Henry Bonwick, 1679. 4°. L, O, C, LIL, DT; BN, MBA, NC, NU, Y.

2574A ——"Fourth" edition. For Benjamin Took, 1679. 4°. C; CH, WF.

2575 —A week of soliloquies. For H. Moseley, 1657. 12°. O.

2576 ——[Anr. ed.] For H. Brome, 1677. 12°. T.C.I 294. O, C, YM; MH.

2577 ——[Anr. ed.] For H. Brome, D. Newman, and T. Cockerill, 1679. 12°. T.C.I 377. L; CLC, NU, Y.

2578 ——[Anr. ed.] For D. Newman, T. Cockerill, and Ch. Brome, 1692. 12°. L, C, LW; NU.

2579 **Du Moulin, Pierre.** The anatomie of the masse. By J. B. for Humphrey Robinson, 1641. 12°. L, O, C, OM, GU; CN, NU, WF, Y.

2580 —The anatomie of the messe [sic]. Edinburgh, J. Bryson, 1641. 4°. ALDIS 1000. CK, SA.

[–] Anti-Cotton. 1689. See Du Coignet, Pierre.

2581 [–] The Capuchin; or, the Pharisaisme. For James Collins, 1675. 8°. NU, Y.

2582 —The Capucin treated. For Henry Marsh, 1665. 8°. L, O, P, LCL; CLC.

2583 —The elements of logick. Oxford, by Henry Hall, 1647. 8°. MADAN 1964. O.

2584 —Heraclitus, or mans looking-glass. For Henry Seile, 1652. 12°. O, C.

2585 [–] The history of the English & Scotch Presbytery. Printed in Villa Franca, [London], 1659. 8°. LT, O, C, DC, E; BN, CN, NU, WF, Y.

2586 [–] —Second edition. —, 1660. 8°. L, LW, OC, YM, EN; BN, CH, NU, TU, WF, Y.

2587 —A learned treatise of traditions. For Humphrey Robinson, 1641. 8°. O, C, LLL, OB, E; CN, Y.

2588 —The love of God. Printed at York by Tho: Broad for the author, 1656. 4°.* L; MH, WF.

2589 —The masse in Latine and English. By S. B. for R. S., [1641]. 8°. L.

2590 ——[Anr. ed.] By Stephen Bulkley, for Robert Somer and Thomas Cowley, 1641. 8°. O, C; NU, WF.

2591 ——[Anr. ed.] By Steven Bulkley, to be sold by Rob: Somer, and Tho: Cowley, 1641. 8°. O, E; CH, LC, NU, WF, Y.

2592 [–] The monk's hood pull'd off. For James Collins, 1671. 8°. T.C.I 88. L, O, P; BN, CH, CN, NU, WF, Y.

2593 —The novelty of popery, opposed. By Robert White, to be sold by Francis Tyton, 1662. fol. O, C; MIU.

2594 ——[Anr. ed.] By Robert White, 1664. fol. O, C, LW, P, DT; NU, RPB.

2595 —The papal tyranny, as it was exercised. For H. Brome, 1674. 4°. T.C.I 162. L, O, C, CT, MC; CH, NPT, NU, WF, Y.

2596 —A short view of the chief points. For Benjamin Tooke, 1680. 8°. T.C.I 39. O, LSC, SP; NC.

2596A ——[Anr. ed.] —, 1686. 8°. L, O, C, OC, CT; NGT, WF, Y.

2597 **Dunbar, David.** The theologicall key. Printed, 1646. 4°. O, DC; NU.

2598 **[Dunbar, William.]** Cogitations upon death. Fourth edition. Aberdeen, by John Forbes, 1681. 8°.* ALDIS 2259. HH.

2599 [–] —Sixth edition. Edinburgh, printed, 1688. 8°.* EN.

2599A **[Duncombe, Giles.]** Scutum regele. The royal buckler. 1660. 8°. L, O, C, P, CT; CH, CN, HH, NU, WF, Y.
—Tryals per pais; or. 1665. *See* Euer, Sampson.

2600 **Duncome, William.** Forgetfulness of God. 1683. 8°. LCL.

2601 **Duncon, Eleazar.** Eleazaris Dunconi: . . . de adoratione. [*Cambridge?*], 1660. 12°. L, O, C, CS, YM; WF.

2602 —De adoratione Dei versus altare: or that pious and devout ceremony of bowing. *Printed, to be sold by Timothy Garthwait*, [1661]. 4°.* LT, O, OC, CT, LL; NU, WWC, Y.

2603 —Of worshipping God towards the altar. *Printed, to to be sold by Timothy Garthwait*, 1660[JI]. 4°.* L, LL, HH; CH, MH, NU.

2603A **[Duncon, John.]** An essay of afflictions. 1647. 8°. O.

2604 —The holy life and death of . . . Letice, Vi-Countess Falkland. Third edition. *For Rich: Royston*, 1653. 12°. L, O, C, CT, MR; CH, WF, Y.

2605 [–] The retvrnes of spiritual comfort and girief. *For Rich: Royston*, 1648. 12°. L, O, C, LSC, OCC; CH, TU, WF, Y.

2606 — —Second edition. —, 1649. 12°. L, O, C, LVF, OC; CH, NPT, NU.

2607 **Duncon, Samuel.** Several proposals. *Printed at London, by James Cottrel*, 1659. 4°.* LT.

2608 —Several propositions of pvblick concernment. *By I. C.*, 1652. 4°.* LT; Y.

2609 **Duncomb, George.** Abraham's faith. *For Tim. Goodwin*, 1697. 4°.* L, O, OC, BAMB.

2610 **Duncomb, Thomas.** The great efficacy. *By John Winter, for William Cadman*, 1671. 4°.* T.C.I 54. L, O, OC, CS, WCA; MH, NU, WF, Y.

2611 **Dundas, David.** Disputatio juridica. *Edinburgh, heirs of A. Anderson*, 1698. 4°. ALDIS 3842. EN.

2612 **Dundas, William.** A few words of truth. [*London*], *printed*, 1673. 4°.* L, O, C, BBN, EN; MH, MU, PH, WF, Y.

2613 **D[unning], R[ichard].** Bread for the poor. *Exeter, by Samuel Darker, for Charles Yeo, John Pearse, and Philip Bishop*, 1698. 4°.* L, O, OC; MH, NC, Y.

2614 —A plain and easie method; shewing how the office *Printed*, 1685. 4°.* O.

2615 —[Anr. ed.] —, 1686. 4°.* L; CH, NC.
Dunois, countess. *See* Aulnoy.

2615A **Duns, J., Scotus.** Idiota's: or, Duns contemplations. *Printed at Paris*, 1662. 12°. L.

2616 **Dunstan, John.** Catalogue of library. [*London*], 7 Sept., 1693. 4°. L.

2617 **Dunstar, Samuel.** Anglia rediviva; being a full description. *For T. Bennet*, 1699. 12°. T.C.III 155. L, O, LVF, EN; CH, CU, LC.
Dunster, Thomas. Δωδεκαμηνο. 1652. *See* Almanacs.

2618 **Dunstervill, Edward.** A sermon at the funerall of . . . Sir Simon Harcourt, . . . Mar. 31. 1642. *For Richard Badger*, 1642. 4°.* LT, O; MH, Y.

2619 **Dunstervile, Thomas.** A declaration concerning state-farthings. [*London*], *the author*, 1654. 4°.* LT, C, LUG; Y.

2620 **Dunton, John.** The art of living incognito. Part I. *For the author, to be sold by A. Baldwin*, 1700. 4°. L, LCL; BN, CH, CLC, CN, MH, Y.

2621 —The case of. *Printed, and are to be sold by A. Baldwin*, 1700. 4°.* MB, MHL, Y.

2621A [–] A congratulatory poem to the ministers sons. *By J. A. for John Dunton*, 1682. brs. O, MC; CH, MH, PU, Y.

2622 —The Dublin scuffle. *For the author, and are to be sold by A. Baldwin*, 1699. 8°. L, O, C, EN, DT; CH, CLC, LC, MH, WF, Y.

2623 —England's alarum: being an account. *For Thomas Parkhurst*, 1693. 4°.* T.C.II 463. L, O, C, CT, EN; CLC, Y.

2624 [–] An essay proving that we shall know our friends in Heaven. *Printed and are to be sold by E. Whitlock*, 1698. 8°. L, LCL, OC; CU, MH, MM, RPB, WF.

2625 —Heavenly pastime. *For John Dunton*, 1685. 12°. L, O.

2626 — —Second edition. —, 1685. 12°. L, C; LC.

2627 —The house of weeping. *For John Dunton*, 1682. 12°. T.C.II 12. L, C.

2628 —An hue and cry after conscience. *For John Dunton*, 1685. 12°. T.C. 123. L.

2629 [–] The informer's doom. *For John Dunton*, 1683. 8°. T.C.II 19. L, LG; MH.

2630 [–] A mourning-ring. In memory. Second edition. *For John Dunton*, 1692. 12°. T.C.II 463. L, O, C, LIC; CH, LC, Y.

2631 [–] The parable of the top-knots. colop: *For R. Newcome*, 1691. fol.* L; CH, Y.

2632 —The pilgrim's guide. *For John Dunton*, 1684. 12°. L; CN, MH, WF.

2632A —A poem upon the death of her late Majesty Queen Mary. *For Richard Baldwin*, 1695. * CH, CN, MH, TU, WF, Y.

2632B —Reflections on Mr. Dunton's leaving his wife. [*London*, 1700?] cap., fol.* MB.
[–] Religio bibliopolæ. 1691. *See* Bridgwater, Benjamin.

2633 —Dunton's remains. *For J. Dunton*, 1684. 8°. T.C.II 38. L, O, OB, P; CH, CN, LC, VC, Y.

2633A — —Second edition. —, 1684. 8°. LC.

2633B [–] A seasonable address to the right hon. the Lord Mayor. [*London*, 1680.] cap., 4°.* L, C, MC, HH; CH, CN, MH, WF, Y.

2634 [–] The visions of the soul. *For John Dunton*, 1692. 8°. T.C.II 390. L, O; CH, CN, MH, WF, Y.

2634A [–] A voyage round the world. *For Richard Newcome*, 1691. 8°. T.C.II 338. L, O, LG; CN, LC, MB.

2635 [–] The young-students-library. *For John Dunton*, 1692. fol. T.C.II 483. L, O, C, HH, EN; CH, LC, MH, NU, PL, Y.

2635A Duo panegyrici; Cromwello scripti Londini. [*London*], 1654. 4°.* MH, WF.

2636 Duorum unitas or the agreement. [n.p., 1666.] cap., 4°.* NU.

2637 **Du Perron, Jacques Davy, *cardinal*.** The copy of a letter sent from. [*London*], *printed*, 1641. 4°.* LT, O, BR, WCA, SP; CLC, CN, MH, TU, Y.

2638 —Lvthers alcoran. [*n.p.*], *imprinted*, 1642. 8°. LSC; CH, NU.

2639 —A warning to the Parliament. *For R. W.*, 1647. 4°.* LT, O, LG; CH, CLC, MH, WF.

2640 **Dupin, Louis Ellies.** A compleat history of the canon. *For H. Rhodes, T. Bennet, A. Bell, D. Midwinter, and T. Leigh*, 1699–1700. 2v. fol. L, O, C, E, DT; CLC, NU, OCI, TU, WF, Y.

2641 —De antiqua ecclesiæ. *Abel Swal*, 1691. 4°. LIL, DT; BBE, NU, WF.

2641A —The evangelical history. *For Abel Swalle and T. Childe*, 1694. 8°. T.C.II 507. L, O, MC; CH, Y.

2642 — —Second edition. *For A. Swall and T. Child*, 1696. 8°. T.C.II 595. CS, CT, ELY, DT; WF.

2642A — —Part the second. *For A. Swall and T. Childs*, 1696. 8°. OC.

2643 —A new history. *For Abel Swalle and T. Childe*, 1692. fol. O, CS, NPL, ES, DT; CH, CN, MH, VC.

2644 — —Second edition. —, 1693. 13v. fol. T.C.II 440. L, O, C, LI, YM, DT; CH, CU, NU, PL, WF.

2645 — —Third edition. *London and Oxford*, 1696–1725. fol. C, LL, MR, E, DT; NU, PL, WF, Y.

2646 —Proposals for printing by subscription Bibliotheca patrum. [*London*, 1692.] cap., fol.* O.

2647 **Dupin, Nicholas.** Proposals . . . to all the parishes . . . to set the poor to work. colop: *Printed*, 1698. cap., fol.* L; Y.

2648 **Duport, James.** Δαβίδης ἔμμετρος, sive metaphrasis. *Cantabrigiæ, excudebat Iohannes Field*, 1666. 4°. L, O, C, LW, OC; BN, CH, MH, NU, WF, Y.

2649 — —[Anr. ed.] *Typis Andr. Clark, impensis Richardi Chiswell*, 1674. 8°. T.C.I 191. L, C, LW, OME, DU; CH, CLC, NR, NU, Y.

2650 —Evangelical politie. *Cambridge: by John Field*, 1660. 4°.* L, O, C, LP, ENC; MH, MWA, NU, WF, Y.

2651 —Homeri . . . gnomologia. *Cantabrigiæ, excudebat J. Field*, 1660. 4°. L, O, C, LVF, EN; BN, CH, CU, MH, WF, Y.

2652 —Musæ subsecivæ, seu poetica stromata. *Cantabrigiæ, ex officina Joann. Hayes*, 1676. 8°. T.C.I 272. L, O, C, LL, EN; CH, CN, MH, WF, Y.

2653 — —[Anr. ed.] *Ex officina S. Buckley*, 1696. 8°. BN, CH, CLC.

2653A —Poemata. *For R. Clavell*, 1678. 8°. T.C.I 321. P; WF.

2654 —Σολομων ἔμμετρος, sive tres libri Solomonis scilicet. *Cantabrigiæ, ex officina Rogeri Danielis*, 1646. 8°. L, O, C, LL, E; BN, CH, CN, NU, WF, Y.

2655 —Three sermons. *For Henry Brome*, 1676. 4°. T.C.I 233. L, O, C, CT, DC; CH, CN, NU, WF, Y.

2656 —Θρηνοθριαμβος, sive liber Job graeco carmine redditus. *Cantabrigiæ, apud T. Buck*, 1653. 8°. L, C, CT, NPL, DU; BN.

2657 — —Second edition. *Cantabrigiæ, apud Thomam Buck*, 1653. *Veneunt ibidem per Guilielmum Graves*, 8°. O, OC, CM, EC; LC, PL, Y.

2658 **Duppa, Brian, *bp*.** Angels rejoicing. *For Rich: Royston*, 1648. 4°.* LT, O, C, CT, DT; CH, NU, TU, WF, Y.

2658 [–] Daily devotions. 1672. *See* Hopton, Susannah.

2659 [–] A guide for the penitent. *By James Flesher, for Richard Royston*, 1660. 8°. LT.

2660 —Holy rules and helps. *For J. Collins*, 1674. 12°. T.C.I 162. C; MH.

2661 — —[Anr. ed.] *For W. Hensman*, 1675. 12°. L, CT; Y.

2662 — —[Anr. ed.] —, 1679. 12°. L, C, CSE; CLC, Y.

2663 — —Fourth edition. —, 1683. 12°. L, C; WF.

2663A — —Fifth edition. —, 1690. 12°. OC.

2663B — —Second part. *For J. Collins*, 1673. 12°. L, O; MH.

2664 [–] A prayer of thanksgiving for His Majesties late victory. [*London*, 1643.] brs. MADAN 1465. LT, OC; MH, Y.

2665 [–] Private formes of prayer. *Oxford, by Leonard Lichfield*, 1645. 8°. MADAN 1818. LT, O, CM, OC; CH, MB, MH, Y.

2665A [–] —[Anr. ed.] *By Tho. Mabb and to be sold by William Not*, 1660. 8°. CH.

2666 —The soules soliloquie. *For R. Royston*, 1648. 4°.* LT, O, C, CT, DT; BN, CH, NU, TU, WF, Y.

2666A [–] Two letters the one being sent. *For Ed. Husbands, and Iohn Francke*, 1642. 4°.* LT, O, AN, DT; CH, WF, Y.

2667 [–] Two prayers; one for the safety of His Majesties person. *Oxford, by Leonard Lichfield*, 1644. 4°.* MADAN 1648. L, O; TU.

2668 **DuPrat, .** Catalogue of library. [*London*], 2 *May*, 1699. 4°. L.

2668A [**Du Pré, *abbe*.**] The monk unvail'd. *For Jonathan Edwin*, 1678. 8°. T.C.I 293. O, SP; CH, NU, WF, Y.

2669 **Duquesne, Abraham.** A new voyage to the East Indies. *For Daniel Dring*, 1696. 8°. T.C.II 588. L, O, C, LAD, ES; CU, LC, MH.

2669 Durable legacy. 1681. *See* Brooke, Humphrey.

2670 **Durant, John.** Altum silentium: or, silence the duty of saints. *By J. Streater*, 1659. 8°. LT; Y.

2671 —The Christian's compass. *By T. L. for the author*, 1658. 8°. L; NU, Y.

2672 —A cluster of grapes. *By L. C. to bee sold by H. Hartlocke*, 1660. 8°. LT, DC; MH, NPT, WU.

2673 —Comfort & counsell for dejected soules. *Printed at London by R. I. for Hannah Allen*, 1651. 8°. LT, LCL; CH, NPT, NU, Y.

2674 — —[Anr. ed.] *For R. I. to be sold by Tho. Newberry*, 1653. 8°. LT; MH, NPT, Y.

2675 — —Fourth edition. *For R. I. to be sold by Charles Tyus*, 1658. 8°. LT, O; MH, NPT, WF.

2676 —A discovery of glorious love. *By R. I. for Hannah Allen*, 1650. 8°. CLC, MH, NU.

2677 — —[Anr. ed.] *For R. I. to be sold by W. Gilbertson*, 1655. 8°. O, C, YM; NPT, WG.

2678 —The salvation of the saints. *By R. I. for Livewell Chapman*, 1653. 8°. LT, LCL; CH, MH, MBP, NPT, NU.

2678A —Sips of sweetness. *By M.S. for Hanna Allen,* 1649. 8°. YM; CLC, MH.

2679 — —Second edition. *For R.I. to be sold by Wil. Gilbertson,* 1652. 8°. O, LW.

2680 — —Third edition. *For R.I. to be sold by H. Mortlock, and J.Simms,* 1662. 12°. LCL, LW; CH, MH, NU, WF.

2681 —The spiritual sea-man. *For L.Chapman,* 1655. 12°. LT.

2681A **Durant, John,** *student.* Art and nature joyn. *For Sam Clark,* 1697. 8°. L.

2682 **Durant, William.** The false Jew. 1659. 4°. LCL.

2682A **Durante de Gualdo, Castore.** A family-herbal. Second edition. *For W.Crook,* 1689. 12°. L; RPJ, WSG.

2682B —A treasure of health. *For William Crook,* 1686. 12°. LG, LL, OM, CS; CLC, WF, WSG, HC.

2682C **[Du Refuge, Eustache.]** The accomplish'd courtier. *For Thomas Dring,* 1658. 8°. LT, O, P; CN, WF, Y.

2683 [–] Arcana aulica: or Walsingham's manual. *For James Yong,* 1652. 12°. L, O, C, DC, OC; CH, MH.

2684 — —[Anr. ed.] *By M.Gillyflower,* 1655. 12°. LC, WCL, Y.

2685 — —[Anr. ed.] *By T.C. sold by Iohn Wright,* 1655. 12°. LT, O, CM, E, M; WF.

2686 — —[Anr. ed.] *For Matthew Gillyflower,* 1694. 12°. L, O, OC, CK; CH, CN, MIU, LC, Y.

2686A [–] The art of complaisance. *For John Starkey,* 1673. 12°. T.C.I 142. L, O; CN, CSU, LC, MH, NC, Y.

2686B [–] —Second edition. —, 1677. 12°. T.C.I 278. L, O, C, M; CH, MH, MU, WF.

2687 **Durel, Jean.** Historia rituum sanctæ. *Typis Guliel. Godbid,* [sic] *prostant apud Guliel. Wells & Rob. Scott,* 1672. 4°. NU.

2687A [–] La liturgie. *Dublin, par Jean Crooke, & se vendent chez Sam. Dancer,* 1660. 12°. C.

2687B [–] —[Anr. ed.] *Par Jean Bill,* 1661. 12°. OC, CN.

2688 [–] —[Anr. ed.] *Pour Iean Dunmore & Octavian Pulleyn le Ieune,* 1667. 12°. L, O, OC; BN, CH, IU, WF.

2688A [–] —"Second" edition. *Pour Robert Scott,* 1677. 12°. MB, PL.

2689 [–] —[Anr. ed.] *Pour Robert Scott, & se vend chez Geo. Wells & S.Carr,* 1678. 12°. T.C.I 291. OC; CN, NGT, WF, Y.

2690 [–] —[Anr. ed.] *Par R.E. pour R.Bentley & S.Magnes,* 1683. 12°. T.C.I 517. L, OC, YM; CLC, CN, NU, RPJ.

2691 [–] —[Anr. ed.] *Par R.Everingham, & se vend chez R. Bentley & M.Magnes,* 1688. 12°. L, C; MB.

2691A [–] —[Anr. ed.] —, 1689. 8°. L; MB.

2691B [–] —[Anr. ed.] *Par R.Everingham, & se vend chez R.Bentley,* 1695. 12°. T.C.II 590. L, O, C, NL, EC; MB, NGT.

2692 —The liturgy of the Church of England. *For R.Royston,* 1662. 4°. L, O, C, EN, DT; CH, MH, NU, WF, Y.

2693 — —Second edition. *By J.L. for Luke Meredith,* 1688. 4°. T.C.II 205. L, O, CS, OC, DT; CH, WF, Y.

2694 —Sanctæ ecclesiæ Anglicanæ. *Typis Guliel Godbid, prostant apud Guliel. Wells & Rob. Scott,* 1669. 4°. T.C.I 15. L, O, C, EN, DT; BN, CN, MB, NU, WF, Y.

2695 —A view of the government. *By J.G. for R.Royston,* 1662. 4°. L, O, C, EN, DT; CH, MH, PL, WF, Y.

Duresme, Thomas. *See* Morton, Thomas, *bp.*

2695A **Duret, Noël.** Novæ motuum cælestivm ephemerides. *Apud Johannem Benson,* 1647. fol. CLC.

2696 —Supplementi tabularum Richelienarum pars prima. 1647. fol. E.

Durette, François. *See* Parrain de Durette, François.

2697 **[D'Urfey, Thomas].** Advice to the city. [*London*], *for Jos. Hindmarsh,* 1682. brs. L, O; MH, WF, Y.

2697A [–] Advice to the ladies of London. *For J.Back* [1686–88]. brs. L, CM, HH.

2698 —Ah how sweet. [*London*], *Tho. Cross,* [1700?]. brs. L.

2699 —Albion's blessing. *By W.Onley, for Robert Battersby, and Thomas Cater,* 1698. fol.* L, LVF; MH.

2699A —Amoret and Phillis. *For J.Hose,* [167–?] brs. O; LC.

2700 —The banditti. *By J.B. for R.Bentley, and J.Hindmarsh,* 1686. 4°. T.C.II 179. L, O, C, LVD, EN; CH, CN, LC, MH, NC, Y.

2701 [–] Beauty's cruelty. [*London*], *for P.Brooksby, J.Deacon, J.Back, J.Blare,* [1685–88]. brs. L, O, CM, HH, GU.

2702 [–] Bonny Dundee. [*London*], *for C.Bates,* [1685–88]. brs. L, HH; WF.

2703 [–] Butler's ghost: or Hudibras. The fourth part. *For Joseph Hindmarsh,* 1682. 8°. T.C.I 485. L, O, C, LVD, EN; CH, CN, LC, MH, NC, TU, Y.

2704 [–] The call to the races. [*London*], *for P.Brooksby, J. Deacon, J.Blare, J.Back,* [1685–88]. brs. L, HH.

2704A [–] —[Anr. ed.] [*London*], *for C.Bates,* [c. 1685.] brs. L.

2705 —The campaigners. *For A.Baldwin,* 1698. 4°. L, O, LVD, EN, ES; CH, CN, LC, MH, TU, Y.

2706 [–] A carrouse to the Emperor. [*London*], *for P.Brooksby,* [1683]. brs. L, CM, HH; MH.

2707 —Celemene pray tell me. [*London*], *Thos. Cross,* [1700?]. fol. L.

2708 —A choice collection of new songs. *For H.Playford,* 1699. fol.* T.C.III 124. MH.

2709 [–] Choice new songs. *By John Playford, for Joseph Hindmarsh,* 1684. fol. T.C.II 99. L, CM, GU; CH, CLC, LC, MIU.

2710 —Collin's walk through London. *For Rich. Parker, and Abel Roper,* 1690. 8°. L, O, CT, LG, EN; CH, CN, LC, MH, Y.

2711 — —[Anr. ed.] *For John Bullard,* 1690. 8°. L; CH, CU, TU, Y.

2712 —The comical history of Don Quixote . . . Part I. *For Samuel Briscoe,* 1694. 4°. L, O, C, EN, DT; CH, CN, LC, MH, Y.

2713 — —Part the second. *For S.Briscoe, and H.Newman,* 1694. 4°. T.C.II 525. L, O, C, LVD, EN; CH, CN, LC, MH, Y.

2714 — —The third part. *For Samuel Briscoe,* 1696. 4°. L, O, C, LVD, EN; CH, CN, LC, MH, Y.

2715 —A common-wealth of women. *For R.Bentley, and J. Hindmarsh,* 1686. 4°. T.C.II 147. L, O, C, LVD, EN; CH, CN, MH, TU, WF, Y.

2716 —A compleat collection of Mr D'Urfeys songs and odes. *For Joseph Hindmarsh*, 1687. 8°. T.C.II 200. DT; CN, MH.

2717 [–] The constant lover. [*London*], *for J. Conyers*, [1685–88]. brs. L, O, HH.

2718 —The country farmer, a song. [*London*, 1700?] brs. L.

2719 —Crown your bowles. [*London*, 1700?] brs. L; CH.

2719A [–] De'el take the war. *T. Moore*, 1696. brs. C.

2719B [–] A dialogue between a town sharper. [*London*, 1700], brs. L.

2719C [–] A dialogue supposed to be between a eunuch boy. [*London*, 1698.] cap., fol.* L.

2719D [–] The discontented lady. [*London*] *for G. Bates* [1685?], brs. L, HH.

2720 —An elegy upon the late blessed monarch King Charles II. *For Jo. Hindmarsh*, 1685. fol.* T.C.II 127. L, O, OB; CH, CN, MH, TU, WF, Y.

2721 [–] An essay towards the theory of the intelligible world. . . . Part III. Second edition. [*London*], *printed one thousand seven hundred, &c.* 8°. L, C, OB, OC, ES; CH, CN, MH, WF, Y.

2722 —The famous history of the rise and fall of Massaniello. *For John Nutt*, 1700–1699. 4°. T.C.III 157. L, O, C, LVD, EN; CH, CN, LC, MH, NC, Y.

2722A [–] The fishermans-song. [*London*, 1700.] brs. L.

2723 —Fly from my sight. [*London*], *Tho. Cross*, [1698]. fol. L.

2724 —A fond husband. *By T.N. for James Magnes and Rich. Bentley*, 1677. 4°. L, LVD, OW; CH, CU, LC, MH, WF, Y.

2725 — —Second edition. —, 1677. 4°. WF.

2726 — —"Second" edition. *By R.E. for James Magnes and Rich. Bentley*, 1678. 4°. L, EN; CH, CN, LC, MH, TU, Y.

2727 — —[Anr. ed.] *By R.E. for R.Bentley & S.Magnes*, 1685. 4°. L, O, LG, EN, DT; CU, MH, NN, WF, Y.

2728 —The fool turn'd critick. *For James Magnes and Richard Bentley*, 1678. 4°. T.C.I 320. L, O, CK, LVD, EN; CH, CN, LC, MH, TU, Y.

2729 —A fool's preferment. [*London*], *for Jos. Knight, and Fra. Saunders*, 1688. 4°. L, O, LVD, EN, DT; CH, CN, LC, MH, TU, Y.

2730 —Gloriana. A funeral pindarique poem. *For Samuel Briscoe*, 1695. 4°.* L, C, CT; CH, CLC, CN, MH, Y.

2731 [–] The gowlin: or, a pleasant fancy. [*London*], *for I. Wright, I. Clark, W. Thackeray, and T. Passinger*, [1678–82]. brs. L, O, CM, HH.

2732 [–] I burn, I burn. [*London*], 1694. brs. MC.

2733 [–] I burn. A song in Don Quixote. [*London*, *T. Cross*, 1697?] brs. L.

2734 [–] —[Anr. ed.] [*London*, 1700?] fol.* L; CH.

2735 —The injured princess. *For R.Bentley and M.Magnes*, 1682. 4°. T.C.I 485. L, O, LVD; CH, CN, MH, TU, WF, Y.

2736 —The intrigues at Versailles. *For F. Saunders, P.Buck, R.Parker, and H.Newman*, 1697. 4°. T.C.III 27. L, O, C, LVD, EN; CH, CN, LC, TU, Y.

2737 [–] The joys of vertuous love. [*London*], *for C. Dennisson*, [1685–88]. brs. L, CM, HH.

2738 [–] The kind lady. [*London*], *for J. Conyers*, [1683]. brs. L, CM, HH; WCL.

2739 [–] The King's health. *For Jos. Hindmarsh*, 1682 L, brs. L. OP.

2739A [–] —[Anr. ed.] 1687. brs. CH.

2740 —Love for money. *For J. Hindmarsh, Abel Roper, to be sold by Randal Taylor*, 1691. 4°. L, C, LVD, EN; CH, MBI, WF, Y.

2741 — —[Anr. ed.] *For Abel Roper, sold by Randal Taylor*, 1691. 4°. L, O, CPE, OW, EN; CH, CN, LC, MH, NC, Y.

2742 — —[Anr. ed.] *For A.Roper, and E.Wilkinson, and J.Hindmarsh*, 1696. 4°. L, O, LVF, EN; CSU, CU, LC, MH, TU, Y.

2742A [–] The mad dialogue. Sung. [*London?* 1700.] cap., fol.* L.

2743 —Madame Fickle. *By T.N. for James Magnes and Rich. Bentley*, 1677. 4°. L, O, C, LVD, EN; CH, CN, MH, NC, TU, WCL, Y.

2743A — —[Anr. ed.] 1679. 4°. CCA.

2744 — —[Anr. ed.] *For R.Bentley*, 1682. 4°. T.C.I 516. L, O; CN, LC, MH, WF, Y.

2745 — —[Anr. ed.] —, 1691. 4°. T.C.II 387. L, C, EN; CLC, CN, MH, PU, WF, Y.

2746 —Maiden fresh as a rose. [*London*], 1693. brs. MC.

2747 [–] The maiden-warrier. [*London*], *for P.Brooksby*, [1689]. brs. L, CM, HH, GU; MH.

2748 [–] The malecontent; a satyr. *For Joseph Hindmarsh*, 1648. fol.* T.C.II 47. L, O, LL, HH, ES; CH, CN, MH, NC, TU, Y.

2749 —The marriage-hater match'd. *For Richard Bentley*, 1692. 4°. T.C.II 343. L, O, OW; CH, CU, LC, MH, MU, NC.

2749A — —[Anr. ed.] *For Richard Parker and S.Briscoe*, 1692. 4°. L, LG; CH, LC, MB, NP, Y.

2750 — —[Anr. ed.] *For R.Bentley, R.Parker and S.Briscoe*, 1693. 4°. T.C.II 480. O, LVD, EN; CLC, CN, LC, MH, TU, Y.

2751 —A new collection of songs and poems. *For Joseph Hindmarsh*, 1683. 8°. T.C.I 508. L; CLC, LC, MH.

2751A —A new lottery designed. *For Joseph Hindmarsh*, 1689. brs. L, O; CLC, MH.

2751B [–] The New-market song. [*London?* 1684.] brs. O; CLC.

2751C [–] —[Anr. ed.] *Printed*, 1684. brs. O; MH.

2752 —A new opera, call'd Cinthia and Endimion. *By W. Onley, for Sam. Briscoe, and R. Wellington*, 1697. 4°. L, O, OW, LVD, EN; CH, CN, MH, WCL, WF, Y.

2752A — —Second edition. —, 1697. 4°. CH, CN, NIC, Y.

2753 —New operas with comic stories. *For Joseph Hindmarsh*, 1681. fol. CHRISTIE-MILLER.

2754 —New poems. *For J.Bullord, and A.Roper*, 1690. 8°. T.C.II 288. L, O, EC, ES; CH, CLC, MH, WF, Y.

2755 —A new song sung by Mrs. Hudson in . . . Richmond heiress. [*London*], 1693. brs. MC.

2756   —New songs in the third part of The comical history of Don Quixote. *For Samuel Briscoe,* 1696. fol.* L, O; CLC, LC, MB.

2757   [–] The Northern ditty. [*London*], *for P. Brooksby, J. Deacon, J. Blare, J. Back,* [1692?] brs. L, GU.

2757A   —The nurses song in the campaigners. [*London,* 1691?], brs. CH.

2758   —An ode, for the anniversary feast . . . St. Cæcilia. colop: *For Henry Playford,* 1700. brs. CN, Y.

2758A   —An ode on the anniversary of the Queens birth. *Printed,* 1690. fol.* MIU, PU, Y.

2759   [–] Phyllis has such charming graces. [*London*], *T. Cross,* [1698?] brs. L.

2759A   —A Pindarick ode, on New-Year's-Day. *For Abel Roper,* 1691. fol.* CH, CN, Y.

2760   —A Pindarick poem on the royal navy. *Printed and are to be sold by Randall Taylor,* 1691. fol.* L; CH, CN, MH, PU, Y.

2761   —A Pindaric poem upon the fleet. [*London*], *sold by Randall Taylor,* 1692. fol.* CLC, MH.

2762   —A poem congratulatory on the birth of the young prince. *For Joseph Knight and Francis Saunders,* 1688. 4°.* T.C.II 231. L, O, C, AU, EN; CH, MH, TU, WF, Y.

2763   [–] Pretty Kate of Edenborough. [*London*], *for P. Brooksby,* [1672–85]. brs. L, O, CM, HH.

2764   —The progress of honesty. *For Joseph Hindmarsh,* 1681. fol.* T.C.I 418. L, O, C, CT, HH; CH, CN, LC, MH, TU, Y.

2765   — —Second edition. —, 1681. 4°.* T.C.I 446. L, O, CS, DT; MIU, PU, WF, Y.

2766   [–] Prologue to A commonwealth of women. colop: *For R. Bentley, to be sold by R. Baldwin,* 1685. brs. L, O; MH.

2767   —A prologue to a new play, called The royallist. [*London,* 1682.] brs. L, O, EN; CH, MH, PU, WF, Y.

2768   —The prologue to Mr. Lacy's new play, Sir Hercules Buffoon. colop: *For Joseph Hindmarsh,* 1684. brs. L, O, MC; CH, CLC, Y.

2769   —The Richmond heiress. *For Samuel Briscoe,* 1693. 4°. T.C.II 480. L, O, LVD, OW, EN; CH, CN, LC, MH, NC, TU, Y.

2769A   — —Second edition. —, 1694. 4°. CK.

2770   —The royalist. *For Jos. Hindmarsh,* 1682. 4°. T.C.I 485. L, O, C, LVD, EN; CH, CN, LC, MH, TU, Y.

2771   [–] The Scotch lad's moan. [*London*], *for P. Brooksby,* [1685–88]. brs. L, CM, HH.

2772   [–] The Scotch lasses constancy. colop: [*London*], *by T. H. for P. Brooksby,* 1682. brs. L, O, CM, HH; CH, MH.

2773   —A Scotch song. [*London*], *T. Cross,* [1698?]. brs. L; CH.

2773A   [–] A Scotch-song in the second part of . . . Don Quixote. [*London,* 1697], brs. L.

2774   [–] The Scotch wedding. [*London*], *for P. Brooksby,* [1676–95]. brs. L, O, HH, GU.

2775   —The second collection of new songs. *By William Pearson, for Henry Playford,* 1699. fol* T.C.III 14°. HARDING.

2776   —Several new songs. *By J. Playford, for Joseph Hindmarsh,* 1684. fol.* T.C.II 61. L, O; CH, LC, TU.

2777   —The siege of Memphis. *For W. Cadman,* 1676. 4°. T.C.I 255. L, O, LVD, OW; CH, CN, LC, MH, TU, Y.

2778   —Sir Barnaby Whigg. *By A. G. and J. P. for Joseph Hindmarsh,* 1681. 4°. T.C.I 463. L, O, LVD, OW, EN; CH, CN, LC, MH, TU, WCL, Y.

2779   —A song in The campaigners. [*London,* 1698.] brs. L, MC; CH.

2780   [–] A song in the first part of Don Quixote. [*London*], 1694. brs. L, MC.

2781   [–] A song in the last new comedy, call'd The Marriage hater match'd. [*London*], 1692. brs. MC.

2781A   —A song in the play called The Richmond heiress. [*London?* 1695.] brs, L, Y.

2782   [–] A song in the third part of Don Quixote. [*London*], 1696. brs. L, MC.

2783   —The songs to the new play of Don Quixote. Part the first. *By J. Heptinstall for Samuel Briscoe,* 1694. fol.* L, BR, GU; CH, CU, MB, WF, Y.

2784   —The songs to the new play of Don Quixote. As they are sung . . . Part the first. *By J. Heptinstall for Samuel Briscoe,* 1694. fol.* CH, LC, MB, Y.

2785   —The songs to the new play of Don Quixote . . . Part the second. *By J. Heptinstall for Samuel Briscoe,* 1694. fol.* L, O, GU; CH, LC, MB, WF, Y.

2786   —Squire Oldsapp. *For James Magnes and Richard Bentley,* 1679. 4°. T.C.I 330. L, O, LVD, OW, EN; CH, CN, LC, MH, NC, TU, Y.

2786A   [–] State and ambition. [*London*], *for Philip Brooksby,* [1684.] brs. O, CM; MH.

2786B   —Stories, moral. *By Fr. Leach,* 1691. 8°. CH, LC, MIU.

2787   —A storm at sea. [*London,* 1700?] brs. L.

2788   —A third collection of new songs. *By J. P. for Joseph Hindmarsh,* 1685. fol.* T.C.II 125. L, O, HH, DT; CH, CN, LC.

2789   —Trick for trick. *For Langley Curtiss,* 1678. 4°. T.C.I 320. L, O, LVD, OW, EN; CH, CN, LC, WF, Y.

2789A   [–] The triennial mayor. *For Will. Griffits,* 1691. 4°.* O, LG; CH, IU, MH, WF, Y.

2789B   [–] A two-part song. [*London?* 1700]. cap., fol.* L; CH.

2789C   —Virtumnus Flora you that bless. [*London?* 1698]. brs., fol.* L.

2790   —The virtuous wife. *In the Savoy: by T. N. for R. Bentley, and M. Magnes,* 1680. 4°. T.C.I 370. L, O, CCA, LVD, EN; CH, CN, LC, MH, TU, Y.

2791   [–] The Whig's exaltation. *By Nath. Thompson,* 1682. brs. L, O; CH, MH, Y.

2792   [–] Whilst wretched fools. [*London,* 1700.] brs. L.

2792A   [–] The Winchester wedding. *For P. Brooksby,* [1670.] fol.* CM; WCL.

2793   [–] —[Anr. ed.] *For J. Deacon,* [1685–92]. L, HH; MH.

2794   [–] A word in season: or, now or never. [*London*], *for J. Wright, J. Clark, W. Thackeray, and T. Passenger,* [1683]. brs. L, CM, HH; MH.

2795   **Durham, James.** The blessedness of the death. [*Glasgow, Sanders*], *printed,* 1681. 8°. EN, ECS, A; NP, NU, Y.

2796 — —Second edition. [*Edinburgh, Anderson*], *printed*, 1682. 8°. L, ES, FSF.

2796A — —[Anr. ed.] *Glasgow, R. Sanders*, 1682. 12°. EN.

2797 — —Third edition. *Edinburgh, heir of Andrew Anderson*, 1684. 12°. CHRISTIE.

2798 — —[Anr. ed.] *Edinburgh, by the heirs and successors of Andrew Anderson*, 1694. 12°. EN.

2799 —Christ crucified. *Edinburgh, by the heir of Andrew Anderson*, 1683. 4°. EN, GU; BN, NPT, NU.

2800 — —Second edition. —, 1686. 4°. EN, ENC.

2801 — —Third edition. —, 1700. 4°. EN; CLC.

2802 —Clavis cantici: or, an exposition. *Edinburgh, by George Swintoun and James Glen*, 1668. 4°. ALDIS 1841. L, E, EN, ENC; CH, IU, NU, Y.

2803 — —Second edition. *By J. W. for Dorman Newman*, 1669. 4°. T.C.I 12. L, O, C, LCL, GU; CLC, IU, NP, WF, Y.

2804 — —Fourth edition. *Glasgow, by Robert Sanders*, 1688. 4°. ALDIS 2756. L, GM, GU; CLC.

2805 —A commentarie upon the Book of the Revelation. *Edinburgh, by Christopher Higgins*, 1658. fol. ALDIS 1575. L, E, EN, DT; PL, WF, Y.

2806 — —Second edition. *For the company of stationers*, 1658. fol. L, CCA, MC, AU.

2807 — —Third edition. *Amsterdam, by John Fredericksz Stam*, 1660. fol. L, O, LW, AU; BN, CU, NU, PPT, Y.

2808 — —Fourth edition. *Edinburgh, by the heir of Andrew Anderson*, 1680. 4°. ALDIS 2193. T.C.I 408. L, LCL, GU; IU LL, PL, WF.

2809 — —Fifth edition. *Glasgow, by Robert Sanders*, 1680. 4°. ALDIS 2194. C, EN, ECS, GU, GM; CH, MH, NPT, PPT.

2810 —The dying man's testament. *Edinburgh, by Christopher Higgins*, 1659. 8°. ALDIS 1595. L, O, E, EN, GU; CN, MH, NU, Y.

2811 — —Second edition. *For the company of stationers*, 1659. 8°. LT, AU, EN; CH.

2812 — —Third edition. *Edinburgh, by the heir of Andrew Anderson*, 1680. 8°. T.C.I 435. ALDIS 2195. L, C, ENC, GU, EN; NPT, NU, WF, Y.

2813 — —Fourth edition. *Edinburgh, by William Carron, for John Cairnes*, 1680. 8°. ALDIS 2196. L, OCC, EN; NP, NU, PPT, Y.

2814 —The great corruption of subtile self. *Edinburgh, by the heir of Andrew Anderson*, 1686. 12°. ALDIS 2639. EN, GU; WF, Y.

2814A —The great gain. *Edinburgh, by the heir of A. Anderson*, 1685. 12°. EN, GU; WF, Y.

2815 —Heaven upon earth. *Edinburgh, by the heir of Andrew Anderson*, 1685. 8°. ALDIS 2543. LW, E, EN, ENC, GU; NPT, NU.

2816 —The law unsealed. *Edinburgh, by the heir of Andrew Anderson*, 1676. 4°. ALDIS 2075. EN, GU, I.

2817 — —Second edition. *Glasgow, by Robert Sanders*, 1676. 4°. ALDIS 2076. L, EN, GM.

2818 — —Third edition. *Edinburgh, by the heir of Andrew Anderson, to be sold by James Dunlop in Glasgow*, 1676. 8°. L, LW, GU.

2819 — —Fourth edition. *Edinburgh, by the heir of Andrew Anderson*, 1676. 8°. L, LW; MWA, NU.

2820 — —Fifth edition. *Glasgow, by Robert Sanders*, 1677. 8°. ALDIS 2099. L, ENC; WF, Y.

2821 —The Parliaments commission: delivered. colop: [*London*], *by R. Austin, and A. Coe*, 1643. cap., 4°.* LT; NU, WF, Y.

2822 —A practical exposition of the X. commandments. *For Dorman Newman*, 1675. 4°. T.C.I 225. L, O, C, LW, EN; CH, MH, NU, WF, Y.

2823 — —Second "addition." *Glasgow, Robert Sanders*, 1676. 4°. L, E, EN, GU; NU, PPT, Y.

2824 Entry cancelled.

2825 — —Fourth edition. *Edinburgh, by the heir of Andrew Anderson*, 1676. 8°. ALDIS 2075. L, I.

2826 — —Fifth edition. *Glasgow, Robert Sanders*, 1677. 8°. L, AU.

2827 —The unsearchable riches of Christ. *Glasgow, by Robert Sanders*, 1685. 12°. EN, GU.

2828 — —Second edition. —, 1695. 12°. ALDIS 3460. WF.

2829 — —Third edition. *Edinburgh, heirs and successors of Andrew Anderson*, 1696. 12°. CHRISTIE.

2830 **Durham, William.** Encouragement to charity. *For Matthew Gilliflower*, 1679. 4°.* L, O, OC; CH, WF, Y.

2831 —The life and death of that judicious divine, . . . Robert Harris. *For S.B. to be sold by J. Bartlet*, 1660. 8°. L, O, OC, CT, E; CLC, INU, NU, WF, Y.

2831A — —[Anr. ed.] *For H. Brome*, 1662. 8°. L.

2832 —Maran-Atha: the second advent. *By T. Maxey, for M. M. G. Bedell, and T. Collins*, 1652. 4°. LT, LW, CT, WCA, EN; CLC, NU, MB, WF, Y.

2833 —A sermon preached . . . August the 30th, 1670. *By T. R. for Samuel Gellibrand*, 1671. 4°.* T.C.I 54. L, O, CS, CT, WCA; MBA, NU, WF, Y.

2834 —A sermon preached . . . 21th. of November, 1675. *By T. R. for Edward Gellibrand*, 1676. 4°.* T.C.I 226. L, O, WCA; NU, TSM, WF, Y.

Durret, Natalis. *See* Duret, Noël.

2835 [**Dury, John.**] A briefe relation of that which hath been lately attempted. *By I. R. for Andrew Crooke*, 1641. 4°. L, P, BR, YM; CSS, MH, MIU, NU.

2836 —A case of conscience, concerning. *By Francis Neile for Richard Wodenothe*, 1650. 4°. LT, O, C, EN, DT; CH, CU, NU, Y.

2837 —A case of conscience resolved: concerning. *By R. L. for R. W.*, 1649. 4°.* LT, O, C, LCL, E; CH, CU, MH, NU, WF, Y.

2838 —A case of conscience, whether it be lawful to admit Jews. *For Richard Wodenothe*, 1656. 4°.* LT, LW, OC, YM, LC, NIU, NN.

2839 —Certaine considerations shewing the necessity. [*London*], *for Wil. Hope*, 1642. 4°.* O, C, HH, DT; MH, NU, WF, Y.

2840 —Concordiæ inter evangelicos. [*London*], 1654[5]. 4°.* LT, O.

2841 —Conscience eased. *For T.H.*, 1651. 4°.* LT, O, CCO, EN, DT; CH, CN, MH, NU, WF, Y.

2842 —Considerations concerning the present engagement. *By John Clowes for Richard Wodenoth*, 1649. 4°.* LT, O, OC, CCH, DT; CN, MH, NU, TU, Y.

2843 ——Second edition. —, 1650. 4°.* L, O, LCL, LG, OC; CLC, MBP, MIU, WF.

2844 ——Third edition. *By J.C. for Richard Wodenothe*, 1650. 4°.* L, O, OC; CH, MBP, MH, NU, Y.

2845 ——Fourth edition. *By R.L. for Richard Wodenothe*, 1650. 4°.* L, O; MIU, NU.

2846 Entry cancelled.

2847 —Consvltatio theologica. *Exudebat G.M. pro. Andrea Crooke*, 1641. 4°.* O, E, EN, DT; BN, NPC, NU, Y.

2848 [–] The copy of a letter vvritten to Mr. Alexander Hinderson. *Printed*, 1643. 4°.* LT, O, CT, OC, DT; CH, MH, NU, WF, Y.

2849 —A copy of Mr John Duries letter. *By G.M. for Thomas Underhill*, 1643. 4°.* LT, O, HH, E; MU, NU, WF, Y.

2850 —A declaration of. *Printed*, 1660. 4°.* LW, YM; MU, NU, WF.

2851 —A demonstration of the necessity. *For Richard Wodnothe*, 1654. 4°. L, CJ, YM, DT; NN, NU, WF.

2852 Entry cancelled.

2853 [–] A discourse representing the liberty of conscience. *For Nathaniel Brook*, 1661. 8°. O, SP; MH.

2854 [–] A disingag'd survey. *For John Wright*, 1650. 4°.* LT, O, OC, YM, DT; CH, MH, NU, TU, WF.

2855 —The earnest breathings. *For T.Underhill*, 1658. 4°. L; BN, NU.

2856 —An earnest plea. *For Richard Wodenothe*, 1654. 4°. LT, C, OME, YM, DT; NU, Y.

2857 —The effect of Master Dury's negotiation. [*London*, 1657?] cap., 4°.* L, OC, YM; CH, NU, TU, WF, Y.

2858 —Epistola veridica ad homines. *Excusum*, 1659[60]. 4°.* LT, O, CJ; WF, Y.

2859 —An epistolary discourse. *For Charles Greene*, 1644. 4°.* LT, O, C, EN, DT; CLC, MH, NU, WF, Y.

2860 —Epistolica dissertatio. [*London*]. 1641. 4°.* MAU, E; NU.

2861 Entry cancelled.

2862 [–] Gospel-commvnion. *For Richard Wodenothe*, 1654. 4°.* LCL; CH, NU, TU.

2863 Entry cancelled.

2864 [–] The interest of England in the Protestant cause. *Printed*, 1659. 4°.* O, YM; CH, CN, NC, NU, Y.

2865 [–] Irenicum: in quo casus. *Impensis Richardi Wodenothe*, 1654. 4°.* L, O, C, DT; CH, NU, MB, WF.

2866 [–] ——[Anr. ed.] —, 1654. 4°.* NU.

2867 —Israels call to march ovt of Babylon. *By G.M. for Tho. Vnderhill*, 1646. 4°. LT, O, C, EN, DT; BN, CH, MH, NU, WF, Y.

2868 —Jvst re-proposals. *By R.L. for Richard Wodenothe*, 1650. 4°.* L, O, C, OM, DT; CLC, CN, MH, NU, Y.

2868A ——[Anr. ed.] *By J.C. for Richard Wodenothe*, 1650. 4°.* LT, O, C, OC; CLC, CN, MH, MIU, WF.

2869 —Lettre de. *S. Thomson*, 1658. 12°. BN.

2870 [–] Madam, although my former freedom. [*London*, 1645.] cap., 4°.* LT.

2871 [–] Madam, ever since I had a resolution. [*London*, 1645.] cap., 4°.* LT.

2872 —A memoriall concerning peace ecclesiasticall. *For W. Hope*, 1641. 4°.* LT, O, C, EN, DT; CH, LC, NU, WF, Y.

2873 —A model of church-government. *By T.R. and E.M. for John Bellamy*, 1647. 4°. LT, O, C, EN, DT; CH, MH, NU, WF, Y.

2874 —A motion tending to the pvblick good. *By P.L. for Michael Sparke senior*, 1642. 4°. L, YM, DT; NU, WF.

2875 [–] Motives to induce the Protestant princes. *For William Hope*, 1641. 4°.* LT, E, DT; MH, NU, WF.

2876 —Objections against the taking of the engagement answered. *By John Clowes, for Richard Wodenothe*, 1650. 8°.* LT, O, YM, EN, DT; CLC, MIU, NU, Y.

2876A —Pacis evangelicæ. *Excudebat R.Daniel, prostat apud Samuelem Thoman*, 1657. 8°.* CM.

2877 —A peace-maker. *By R.Cotes for Iohn Bellamy*, 1648. 4°.* LT, O, CT, E, DT; CH, CLC, NU.

2878 —John Dury his Petition to the honourable House of Commons. *Printed*, 1641. 4°.* LT, O, CT, EN, DT; CN, LC, NPT, NU, Y.

2879 ——[Anr. ed.] *For William Hope*, 1642. 4°.* O, C, LCL, HH, DT; CLC, MH, NU, WF.

2880 —John Dury his petition. *Printed*, 1651. 4°.* NU.

2881 [–] The plain way of peace. *For Fr. Tyton*, 1669. 8°.* LT, O; NU.

2882 —The reformed librarie-keeper. *By William Du-Gard, to bee sold by Rob. Littleberrie*, 1650. 12°. L, O, CM; CLC, MH.

2883 —The reformed school. *By R.D. for Richard Wodnothe*, [1649?]. 12°. L, O, CM.

2884 ——[Anr. ed.] *By William Du-Gard*, 1651. 12°. O, LCL, GU; MB, NN, Y.

2885 [–] The reformed spiritvall husbandman. *For Richard Wodenothe*, 1652. 4°.* L, C, CT; CH, NU, WF, HC.

2886 —A seasonable discourse written by. *For R.Woodnothe*, 1649. 4°.* LT, CT, YM; WF, Y.

2887 —A second parcel of objections. *By Will. Du-Gard*, 1650. 4°. O, EN, DT; NU, Y.

2888 —A summarie account. *For the author*, 1657. 4°.* L, LCL; CH, CN, MH, NU, TU, WF, Y.

2889 —A summary discourse. *Cambridge: by Roger Daniel*, 1641. 4°. LT, O, C, CT, E; CH, MH, NU, Y.

2890 [–] A summarie platform. *For Richard Wodenothe*, 1654. 4°.* L, O, C, YM, DT; NU, Y.

2891 —Syllabus documentorum. [*London*, 1656.] 4°.* L, YM; NU.

2892 —The time-serving Proteus. [*London*], *printed*, 1650. 4°.* L, O, DT.

2893 Entry cancelled.

2894 —The unchanged, constant. *By J.Clowes, for Richard Wodenothe*, 1650. 4°.* LT, O, DT; MH, NU, WF.

The Dutch annotations. *See* Haak, Theodore.

2895 The Dutch armado. *For Thomas Palmer*, 1665. brs. L.

Dutch bloody almanack. 1653. *See* Almanacs.

2896   The Dutch boare dissected. *Printed*, 1665. brs. L.
2896A The Dutch bribe, a ballad. [*London?* 1700.] brs. MH.
2897   The Dutch design anatomized. *Printed, and are to be sold by Randal Taylor*, 1688. 4°.* L, CE, CT, AU; CLC, MH, MIU, WF, Y.
2898   The Dutch drawn to the life. *For Tho. Johnson, and H. Marsh*, 1664. 12°. L, O, LUG, EN; CH, CN, MH, WF, Y.
       Dutch fortune teller. [*n.p.*], 1677. *See* Booker, John.
2899   The Dutch gazette: or, the sheet of wild-fire. *By T. Leach*, 1666. brs. L, HH.
2900   The Dutch-gards farewell to England. *Printed*, 1699. brs. MC; LC.
2900A Dutch ingratitude exemplified. [*London*], *printed*, 1672/3. brs. MM.
       Dutch-mans pedigree. 1653. *See* F., D.
2901   The Dutch-men's reasons. *Amsterdam* [*London*], 1693. brs. EN.
2902   The Dutch miller. [1675] brs. O.
2903   The Dutch Nebuchadnezzar. [*London*], 1666. 4°. O.
2904   The Dutch remonstrance. [*London*], *by S. and B.G., and are to be sold by R.C.*, [1672]. 4°.* T.C.I 118. L, C, LG, CT, MR; HR, CH, MH, NC, WF, Y.
2905   The Dutch rogue. *By A.M. for G. Hill*, 1683. 12°. T.C.II 28. O; CH, CLC.
2906   The Dutch storm. *By J. Mottershed*, 1665. brs. L.
2907   The Dutch-tutor. *For William Fisher*, [1660]. 8°. LT, CM.
2907A —[Same title.] *By E. Cotes for W. Fisher*, 1669. 8°. L; PU.
       Dutch way of toleration. 1698. *See* Baron, William.
       Dutch whore. [*n.p.*], 1690. *See* Trumbill, Joseph.
       Dutchess. *See* Duchess.
2907B The duties of such as wish. [*Edinburgh*], *printed*, 1659. 4°.* Y.
       Duties of the closet. 1695. *See* Dawes, *Sir* William.
       Dutiful advice. 1650. *See* Raleigh, *Sir* Walter.
2908   The dutiful sons complaint. *For Thomas Newborough*, 1690. 4°.* L, O, C, OC, CT; CH, LC, MM, NU, WF.
2909   **Du Trieu, Philippus.** Manuductio ad logicam. *Oxoniæ, typis & impensis Guil. Hall, prostant Venales apud F. Oxlad & S. Pocock*, 1662. 8°. MADAN 2589. L, O, OC; MH, MB, NC, Y.
2909A ——[Anr. ed.] *Oxoniæ, typis L. Lichfield pro T. Bowman*, 1678. 8°. MADAN 3173. O, OA, CM, OC; IU, Y.
2909B **Dutton, John.** John Dutton alias Prince Duttons farewel to Temple-bar. *For the author*, 1694. 4°.* LG; WF.
       Duty and interest united. 1695. *See* Alsop, Vincent.
       Duty and support. 1688. *See* Cruso, Timothy.
       Duty of allegiance. 1691. *See* Kettlewell, John.
2910   The duty of children to their parents. *Sam & Will. Keble*, [1680?]. brs. L.
2911   The duty of Dissenters. *Printed and sold by George Larkin*, 1689. 4°.* MM, NU.
2911A The duty of everyone that intends to be saved. *For Simon Miller*, 1669. 12°. LSC; NU.
       Duty of servants. 1685. *See* Lucas, Richard.

2912   The dutie of Sir Francis Wortley. [*London*], *by R.O. for F.W.*, 1641. 4°.* LT.
2913   The duty of subjects reinforc'd. colop: *For Robert Clavell*, 1685. cap., fol.* L, O, LG, CS; CH, MB, PU, Y.
2914   —[Anr. ed.] *Reprinted Edinburgh, by the heir of Andrew Anderson*, 1685. fol. ALDIS 2544. EN.
2915   **Du Vair, Guillaume.** The morall philosophy of the Stoicks. *For Henry Mortlock*, 1664. 8°. L, O, CS, OM, E; CH, LC, NC, WF, Y.
2916   ——[Anr. ed.] —, 1667. 8°. L, C, CK, CS, P; CLC, CN, CU, NP, Y.
2917   ——[Anr. ed.] —, 1671. 8°. O, C, ES; CH, MH, WF, Y.
2918   Entry cancelled.
       Duval, Claude. The memoires of. 1670. *See* Pope, Walter.
2919   **Du Val, Pierre.** Geographia universalis: the present state. *By H. Clark, for F. Pearse, to be sold by Benjamin Cox*, 1685. 8°. T.C.II 137. L, C, OM, GU; CH, CN, LC, MH, V.
2920   ——Second edition. *For T. Newborough*, 1691. 8°. T.C.II 396. L, O, CE, CT, EN; CLC, V, Y.
2920A [–] A geographical dictionary. *By J.C. to be sold by Henry Brome*, 1662. 8°. O; WF.
2920B [–] —Second edition. *By A.M. for Henry Brome*, 1676. 12°. T.C.I 240. O, OC, CS, DC.
2920C [–] —Third edition. *By M.C. for Henry Brome*, 1678. 12°. T.C.I 316. L; MIU, PL.
2920D [–] —Fourth edition. *By S.R. for Henry Brome*, 1681. 12°. T.C.I 447. CPE; CN, PL.
2920E [–] —Fifth edition. *For Charles Brome and sold by Benj. Crayle*, 1687. 12°. T.C.II 196. O; Y.
2920F [–] —[Anr. ed.] 1693. 12°. DRS.
       Du Veil, C. M. *See* Veil, Charles Maric de.
2921   **Du Verger.** Du Vergers hvmble reflections. *Printed at London*, 1657. 8°. L, O; BN, CH, Y.
2921A [**Du Vignan, sieur des Joannots.**] A new account of the present condition of the Turkish affairs. 1688. 12°. L, RPL; CN, NN, WF.
2922   [–] The Turkish secretary. *By J.B. and sold by Jo. Hindmarsh, and Randal Taylor*, 1688. 4°. L, O, SP, P, A; CH, CLC, WF.
2923   Dux bonis omnibus appellans. The swans welcome to, His Royall Highness the duke. [*n.p.*, 1679.] cap., fol.* O, C, CT; CH, Y.
2924   Dux redux: or, Londons thanksgiving. *By T.M. for Richard Head*, 1672. brs. L.
       Dwy daith: Gaersalem. Mwythig, [1690?]. *See* Crouch, Nathaniel.
2925   **Dyer, Sir James.** An exact abridgement. *For Matthew Walbancke, and John Place*, 1651. 8°. L, O, C, LL, OC; CH, WF.
2926   —Les reports. *By John Streater, Eliz. Flesher, and Henry Twyford, assignes of Richard and Edward Atkyns, to be sold by George Sawbridge*, 1672. fol. LIL, CJ; BN, LC.

2927 — —[Anr. ed.] *By W. Rawlins, S. Roycroft, and M. Flesher, assigns of Richard and Edward Atkins. For Samuel Keble,* 1688. fol. L, O, C, LL, EN; CH, LC, MHL, TU, YL.

2928 Entry cancelled.

2929 —Three learned readings. *For W. Lee, M: Walbancke, D. Pakeman, and G. Bedell,* 1648. 4°. LT, O, C, LL, LGI; MH, NU, WF, YL.

2930 **Dyer, William.** Dyer's works, viz. *Printed,* 1671. 12°. L.

2930A — —[Anr. ed.] —, 1675. 12°. L.

2930B — —[Anr. ed.] —, 1676. 12°. CLC, Y.

2931 —A cabinet of jewels. *[London], printed,* 1663. 8°. L, C, LCL; NGT.

2932 — —[Anr. ed.] —, 1664. 12°. L, O, C, LW; WF.

2933 — —[Anr. ed.] *For Elizabeth Calvert,* 1668. 12°. NU.

2933A — —[Anr. ed.] *Printed,* 1676. 12°. Y.

2934 — —[Anr. ed.] *Glasgow,* 1679. 12°. MURRAY.

2935 —Christ's famous titles. *Printed,* 1663. 8°. L.

2936 — —[Anr. ed.] *For the author,* 1666. 8°. L, LW.

2937 — —[Anr. ed.] *Cambridge [Mass.] by M. J. for Edmund Ranger and Joseph Farnham in Boston,* 1672. 8°. CH.

2937A — —[Anr. ed.] *For the author,* 1673. 12°. Y.

2938 — —[Anr. ed.] —, 1675. 12°. L, C.

2939 — —[Anr. ed.] *Glasgow, by Robert Sanders,* 1675. 8°. ALDIS 2051. I.

2940 — —[Anr. ed.] *Printed,* 1676. 12°. L, LCL; PH.

2940A — —[Anr. ed.] *Edinburgh, by the heir of A. Anderson,* 1677. 12°. EN.

2940B — —[Anr. ed.] *For the author,* 1679. 12°. Y.

2940C — —[Anr. ed.] *Glasgow, R. Sanders,* 1684. 8°. EN.

2941 — —[Anr. ed.] *Printed,* 1687. 12°. L, AN; NPT, NU.

2941A — —[Anr. ed.] *For Henry Nelme,* 1698. 12°. NU.

2942 —Christ's voice to London. *For E. Calvert,* 1666. 8°. L, LG, LW; CLC.

2942A — —[Anr. ed.] *[London], printed,* 1666. 8°. LW.

2943 — —[Anr. ed.] *For Eliz. Calvert, and Matthias Walker,* 1668. 12°. NU.

2944 — —[Anr. ed.] *[London], printed,* 1670. 12°. L, C; CLC, Y.

2945 — —[Anr. ed.] *Glasgow,* 1679. 12°. MURRAY.

2946 —Desire of all nations. *Glasgow, [Sanders,* 1679]. 12°. MURRAY.

2947 —Heaven upon earth. *For Thomas and Nath. Crouch jun.,* 1697. 12°. T.C.III 2. LCL; NU.

2947A —Holy and profitable sayings of. *[London,* 1680.] brs. O; MH.

2948 —Mount Sion. *For Nath. Crouch,* 1689. 12°. T.C.II 246. L, LCL; CLC, WF.

2948A —To the King's most excellent majesty. The humble petition. *[London?* 1670.] cap., fol.* L.

2949 The dyers destiny. *[London], for J. Blare,* [1685–88]. brs. L, O, HH; MH, Y.

2950 The dying Christians friendly advice. *[London], for C. Dennisson,* [1685–89]. 8°. L, CM; MH.

2950A The dying Christian's pious exhortation. *By H. Brugrs for J. Wright, J. Clark, W. Thackerary, and T. Passinger,* 1685, 8° CLC.

Dying fathers living legacy. *[n.p.],* 1660. *See* S., F.

Dying infants. 1699. *See* Acton, Samuel.

2951 The dying lovers complaint. *[London], for F. Cole, T. Vere, J. Wright, J. Clark, W. Thackery and T. Passenger,* [c. 1680–85]. brs. L, HH.

2952 The dying lover's last farewel. *For J. Conyers,* [1688–91]. brs. HH.

2953 The dying lovers reprieve. *[London], for F. Coles, T. Vere, J. Wright, and J. Clarke,* [1680–85]. brs. L, O, HH; MH, Y.

2954 The dying man's assistant. *For J. Lawrence,* 1697. 12°. T.C.II 599. C, LW.

Dying man's destiny. 1682. *See* Nicholetts, Charles.

2955 The dying man's good counsel. *John Back,* [1680]. brs. O.

Dying man's last legacy. 1685. *See* G., F.

Dying man's last sermon. 1662. *See* Hart, John.

2956 Entry cancelled.

Dying speeches, letters and prayers, 1680. *See* Tudchin, John 1675.

2957 The dying speeches of several excellent persons. *Printed,* 1689. 4°.* L, C, HH, YM; CH, MH, TU, WF, Y.

2958 The dying tears of a panitent sinner. *[London], for F. Coles, T. Vere, J. Wright, J. Clarke, W. Thackeray, and T. Passinger* [1675]. brs. L, O, HH, GU.

Dying tears of a true lover. *[n.p.,* 1675.] *See* Hill, Hugh.

2959 **Dyke, Daniel.** The mystery of selfe-deceiving. *By Richard Bishop,* 1642. 4°. L, O, CCA, CS, DT; CU, IU, NN, Y, PJB.

[–] Quakers appeal answered. 1674. *See* Kiffen, William.

[Dyke, Jeremiah.] Burning bush. Edinburgh, 1679. *See* Hart, John.

2959A —The righteous mans conversation. *For T. Pierrepont,* 1652. 8°. EN.

2960 —The righteous man's honor. 1641. 8°. LCL, CS; MWA.

2960A — —[Anr. ed.] *By R. H. for I. Rothwell,* 1643. 8°. L.

2961 —A worthy communicant. *By J. Raworth, for Luke Fawn,* 1642. 8°. O; Y.

2962 — —[Anr. ed.] —, 1645. 8°. L, O, LI; MH, NPT, NU, Y.

2963 — —[Anr. ed.] *By J. Macock for Luke Favvn,* 1652. 8°. L, CS; NIA, Y.

2963A — —[Anr. ed.] —, 1657. 8°. YM; CLC, LC.

2964 — —[Anr. ed.] *For Luke Fawn,* 1661. 8°. L, LSC.

2964A — —[Anr. ed.] *By J. M. for Nathaniel Ranew, and Johnathan Robinson,* 1667. 8°. NL.

2964B — —[Anr. ed.] —, 1675. 12°. T.C.I 185. LCL.

2965 — —Sixteenth edition. *For N. Ranew and J. Robinson,* 1680, brs. T.C.I 399. LW.

2966 — —Seventeenth edition. *For Jonathan Robinson, A. and J. Churchill, J. Taylor, and J. Wyat,* 1696. 12°. T.C.II 607. L, LCL; Y.

2967 **Dykes, Oswald.** Good manners for schools. *By J. Rawlins, for John Place,* 1700. brs. L, M.

2968 **Dykes, Patrick.** Grammatica Latina. *Edinburgi, excudebat hæres Andreæ Anderson,* 1679. 8°. ALDIS 2153. L.

2969 — —[Anr. ed.] —, 1685. 12°. ALDIS 2545. L, C.

2970 Entry cancelled.

2970A **[Dymock, Cressy.]** An essay for advancement of husbandry-learning. *By Henry Hills,* 1651. 4°.* L, LAS, LUG, R; CH, LC, MH, NC, Y.

2971 [–] An invention of engines of motion. *By I. C. for Richard Woodnoth,* 1651. 4°.* L, CT, LUG, R, SP; CH, LC, MH, WF.

2972 **[Dymock, James.]** The great sacrifice of the new law. *[n.p.], printed,* 1676. 8°. L, O, RPL, YM; CN, NU, TU, WF, Y.

2973 — —Fourth edition. *Antwerp, for G. W.,* 1685. 12°. L, O, OC, P; TU.

2973A — —Fifth edition. *Antwerp, for B. W.* 1686, 12°. CM.

2974 — [–] [Anr. ed.] *[Scotland?], printed,* 1686. 12°. EN.

2975 — —Eighth edition. *For Matthew Turner,* 1687. 12°. L, O; CH, CN, TU, WF, WG.

2976 **Dymock, Thomas.** Englands dust and ashes raked up. *[London], printed,* 1648. 4°. LT, O, LVF, DC, OB; CH, CN, LC, NU, Y.

2977 **[Dyot, Richard.]** Litchfield to be surrendred. *By Bernard Alsop. July 6.* 1646. 4°.* LT, DT.

2978 **Dyve, *Sir* Lewis.** A letter from. *[London], printed,* 1648. 4°.* LT, O, CT; CH, WF.

2979 — —[Anr. ed.] *Hagve, by Samuell Broun,* 1650. 4°. LT, O, C, SC, DT; CH, MH, MU, WF, Y.

E

E., A. Catechistical discourses. *Paris,* 1654. *See* Errington, Anthony.

1 —The mischief of dissensions. *For John Kidgell,* 1681. 4°.* T.C.I 427. O, LW, SP, DT; NU.

2 —The watch-mans lanthorn. *By T. R. for Nath. Ekins,* 1655. O; VC.

3 **E., A. B. C. D.** Novembris monstrum. Or Rome brought to bed in England. *By F. L. for Iohn Burroughs,* 1641. 12°. L; MH.

4 **E., B.** A new dictionary of the terms . . . of the canting crew. *For W. Hawes, P. Gilbourne, and W. Davis,* 1699. 8°. L; MH, Y.

5 — —[Anr. ed.] —[1699]. 8°. L, HH; CH, CN, PL, WF, Y.

E., C. Civil right. 1650. *See* Elderfield, Christopher.

—Gentile sinner. *Oxford,* 1660. *See* Ellis, Clement.

6 —A letter to the Lord General Monck. [1660.] brs. O; CH, MH.

E., D. Letter unto a person of honour. 1662. *See* Bagshaw, Edward, *jr.*

—New prognostication. *Glasgow,* 1670. *See* Almanacs.

7 **E., E.** An abstract of some letters. *For Henry Overton,* 1679. 8°. O; WF.

—Alphabet. 1656. *See* Elys, Edmund.

—Answer to six arguments. 1696. *See* Elys, Edmund.

—Bishops downefall. *[n.p.],* 1642. *See* Elys, Edmund.

—Dia poemata: poetick feet. 1655. *See* Elys, Edmund.

—Divine poems. *Oxon,* 1658. *See* Elys, Edmund.

—Great pressures. 1681. *See* Everard, Edmond.

8 —The late prosperous proceedings of the Protestant army in Ireland. *April 12. for John Wright,* 1643. 4°.* LT, O; CH, CLC, CSU, Y.

9 —Londons choice of citizens. *[London,* 1679.] cap., fol.* L, O, C, OP, HH; MH, WF.

—Pressure and grievances. 1681. *See* Everard, Edmund.

E., F. Christian information. 1664. *See* Ellington, Francis.

—Few words to all who. *[n.p.],* 1665. *See* Ellington, Francis.

—Propugnaculum pietatis. *[n.p.],* 1667. *See* English, Francis.

—Saint's Ebenezer. 1667. *See* English, Francis.

E., F. J. Clear looking-glass. *[London]* 1652. *See* Sir Eyston, Bernard Francis.

9A —An exact survey of divine . . . faith. *Printed at Louvain by Peter Sassenus,* 1673. 12°. Y.

E., G. Answer to the eighth chapter. 1687. *See* Taylor, James.

—Frauds of Romish monks. 1691. *See* Gavin, Antoine.

—Spiritual Quaker. *[n.p.,* 1655.] *See* Emmot, George.

E., H. Encyclical epistle. *[n.p.,* 1660.] *See* Ellis, Humphrey.

10 —The jury-man charged. *Printed,* 1664. 4°.* L, O, C, OC, BBN; MH, NU, PSC, WF, Y.

—Presbytery popish. 1661. *See* Edmonds, Hugh.

E., I. Anabaptists ground-work. 1644. *See* Etherington, John.

11 —The land of promise. *By F. L. for I. W. the younger,* 1641. 4°.* LT, DT.

12 —The propheticall intelligencer. *by M. Simmons, and are to be sold by John Hancocke,* 1647. 4°.* LT; CH, NU, WF.

13 —The two olive trees. *By Matthew Simmons,* 1645. 4°.* LT, YM, EN, DT; CH, NU, TU.

13A **E., J.** Baptisms in their verity. *[London], M. Simmons,* 1678. 8°.* L.

—Epigrams upon the paintings. 1700. *See* Elsum, John.

—Fumifugium. 1661. *See* Evelyn, John.

14 —Grammaticus analyticus, or the analytical grammarian. *By Thomas Milbourn, for W. Bradley,* 1670. T.C.I 43. EN; Y.

—Great day. 1648. *See* Eachard, John.

14A —The great deliverance. *By M.C.*, 1652. 8°. O.
—History of the three late. [*n.p.*], 1669. *See* Evelyn, John.
—Indian dialogues. *Cambridge, Mass.*, 1671. *See* Eliot, John.
—Logick primer. [n.p.], 1672. *See* Eliot. John.

15 —A narrative of the cause and manner of the imprisonment of the Lords. *Amsterdam*, 1677. 4°.* L, O, CJ, SP; CH, MH, WF, Y.

15A —The office of enteries. [*London?* 1657.] brs. LG.
—Publick employment. 1667. *See* Evelyn, John.
—Sculptura: or. 1662. *See* Evelyn, John.

16 —A soveraign counter-poyson. *Printed at Louain*, 1674. 8°. DT.
—State of France. 1652. *See* Evelyn, John.
—Sylva, or. 1664. *See* Evelyn, John.

17 —A use of the exhortation to the London apprentices. [1659?] brs. L.

17A **E., L.** The Popish net broken. [*London*], *printed*, 1687. 8°. CLC.

18 **E., N.** The confident questionist questioned. *For Tho. Newberry*, 1658. 4°. LT, SP.

18A —A dialogue betwixt a Conformist. [*London*], *printed*, 1668. 4°.* O, OC, LW; CH, NU.

19 —The doting doctor. [*London*], *printed*, 1655. 4°.* CH.

20 —The great question: or, how religion. *For John Southby, and sold by Randal Taylor*, 1690. 4°.* T.C.II 371. L, LW, HH, CLC, D; MH, WF, Y.

21 ——[Anr. ed.] —, 1691. 4°. L, O, HH, SP; CH, CLC, CN, NU.

22 —The truth of our bad newes from Exeter. *For John Rothwell, May* 24, 1643. 4°.* LT, A; CH.

22A **E., O.** A moderate answer to a pamphlet lately set forth. *Printed at London*, 1646. 4°.* MIU.

E., P. First sermon. 1686. *See* Ellis, Philip.

23 —A helpe to discourse: or, more merriment. Thirteenth edition. *By M.B. for I.B. to be sold by A. Crooke*, 1648. 12°. L; WF.

24 ——Fourteenth edition. *By E.T. for Andrew Crook*, 1654. 8°. L, O.

25 ——Fifteenth edition. *By J.M. for Andrew Crooke*, 1663. 8°. E, A; WF.

25A ——Sixteenth edition. *By S.G. for Andrew Crook*, 1667. 12°. WF.

25B ——Seventeenth edition. *By J.R. for R.Scot, T.Basset, J.Wright, & R.Chiswell*, 1682. 12°. T.C.I 515. L, O.

26 **E., R.** An ansvver to a letter, written out of the country. *Printed*, 1643. 4°.* LT, O, CT; MH.

27 —A defence and continuation of the discourse concerning the period of humane life. *For E.Wyer*, 1678. 8°. T.C.I 294. L, O, C, LWL, E; CH.
—Discourse concerning the period. 1677. *See* Allestree, Richard.

28 —A letter directed to Master Bridgeman. *For Joseph Hunscott*, 1641. brs. L, O, OC, CT, BR; Y.

28A ——[Anr. ed.] *Printed*, 1641. brs. EC.

28B ——[Anr. ed.] *For Joseph Hunscott*, 1642. brs. C, LG, CT, EC.

29 —A letter to a friend concerning the bill for resuming the forfeited estates in Ireland. colop: *For the author*, 1700. fol.* HH; Y.

30 —A letter vvritten out of the country to Mr Iohn Pym. [*Oxford*], *for W.Webb*, 1642[/3]. 4°.* MADAN 1226. LT, O, CT, BR, DT; CH, CLC, MIU, WF, Y.

31 —A perfect diurnall of the proceedings in Hartfordshire. [*London*], *for W.M. Septemb.* 1, 1642. 4°.* LT.

32 —A scriptural catechism. *By H.C. for Moses Pitt*, 1676. 8°. T.C.I 251. L, O, C, OC, CS; CH, WF.

33 ——Second edition. *For Moses Pitt*, 1678. 8°. T.C.I 306. L, CT, AU.

34 ——Third edition. —. 1682. 8°. T.C.I 499. L, OCC, P.

35 ——[Anr. ed.] *For Cave Pullein*, 1686. 8°. CT; Y.

36 ——[Anr. ed.] *For Richard Cumberland*, 1696. 8°. T.C.II 582. CT; NU.

37 —Strange and wonderful visions. 1693. 8°. O.

E., S. A briefe abstract of the kings letters to the queene. 1648. *See* Charles I.
—Doctrina placitandi, ou. 1677. *See* Euer, Samson.

38 —A friendly check to Dr. Bastwick. *For Tho. Vnderhill*, 1645. 4°.* LT, LCL, E; CH, CN, NU, WF, Y.

39 —Further quæries upon the present state. [*Boston*, 1690.] 4°.* EVANS 507. CHW.

40 —A letter from a person of honour in France. *For Thomas Pool*, 1659[/60]. brs. LT, O, LG, LS; MH, MIU, Y.

41 —The toutch-stone of mony and commerce. *At the authors charge*, [1654]. 4°.* L, SP, EN; MH, WF, Y.
—Tryals per pais: or. 1665. *See* Euer, Sampson.
—Unkinde desertor. [n.p.], 1676. *See* French, Nicholas, bp.

E., T. An account of tythes in general. [*London*, 1678.] *See* Ellwood, Thomas.
—Dialling made easy. Oxford, 1692. *See* Edwards, Thomas.
—Dialogue between alkali. 1698. *See* Emes, Thomas.

42 Entry cancelled.
—Some considerations. 1675. *See* Boyle, Robert.
—Two charges. 1650. *See* Edgar, Thomas.

E., W. Anti-Haman or. [n.p.], 1679. *See* Warner, John.
—Flash of lightning [1653]. *See* Erbery, William.
—Jack Pudding: or. 1654. *See* Erbery, William.
—Mad man's plea. 1653. *See* Erbery, William.

43 —Melius inquirendum; or, an impartial enquiry. colop: *For G.L.*, 1688. cap., fol.* O, OC, MC, HH; CH, WF.
—A tutor to astrologic. [1657.] *See* Eland, William.

44 —A vindication of the ministers of Christ. *For John Pike of Shaftsbury*, 1673. 4°. L.
—Wretched people. 1653. *See* Erbery, William.

45 **E., Y.** A caveat for the Protestant clergy. [*n.p.*], 1671. 8°. O; CLC.

45A The E. of Shaftesbury's expedient. *Langley Curtis*, 1684.* CH, WF.

45B **Eachard, John.** Dr. Eachards works. Part II. *By B.M. for Walter Kettilby*, 1697. 8°. OC.

46 —The axe, against siu [sic] and error. *By Matthew Simmons, and are to be sold by John Hancock,* 1646. 4°. LT, O, C, ENC, DT; NU, RPB, WF, Y.

47 [–] A free and impartial inquiry into the causes. *By J.M. for Richard Royston,* 1673. 12°. L, O, C, LCL, AU; NU.

48 —Good nevves for all. Christian souldiers. *By Matthew Simmons,* 1645. 4°.* LT, O, CM, DT; CH.

49 —The great day at the dore. *Printed at London by Matthew Simmons,* 1648. 4°.* O, DT; CU, MH, NU.

50 [–] The grounds & occasions of the contempt of the clergy. *By W.Godbid for N.Brooke,* 1670. 8°. T.C.I 57. L, O, C, DC, EN; BN, CH, CN, WF, Y.

51 [–] —[Anr. ed.] *By W.G. for N.B.,* 1671. 8°. DT.

52 [–] —Eighth edition. *By E.Tyler and R.Holt for Nath. Brooke,* 1672. 8°. T.C.I 114. L, O, CT, LVF, OME; CLC, MH, MIU.

53 [–] —Ninth edition. *By R.H. for Obadiah Blagrave,* 1685. 8°. T.C.II 119. L, O, OC, CT, DT; CH, MH, NU, TU, WF.

54 — —Tenth edition. *For R.Bentley, J.Phillips, H.Rhodes, and J.Taylor,* 1696. 8°. T.C.II 572. ENC.

55 [–] —"Tenth" edition. *For E.Blagrave,* 1696. 8°. L, OC, BR, DT; BN, CLC, MBA, NU, PBL.

56 — —[Anr. ed.] *For J.Phillips,* 1698. 8°. L, C, LL, RPL, DT, V.

57 [–] Mr. Hobb's state of nature considered. *By E.T. and R.H. for Nath. Brooke,* 1672. 8°. T.C.I 97. L, O, CK, CT, LCL; CH, CU, NU, PL, Y.

57A [–] —Second edition. —, 1672. 8°. L, CS, CT; CN, MH, NV, TU, WF.

58 [–] —Third edition. *By R.Holt, for Obadiah Blagrave,* 1685. 8°. L, CT, DT; MH, NU, TU, WF, Y.

59 [–] —Fourth edition. *For E.Blagrave,* 1696. 8°. L, C, OC, CT, ENC; BN, CU, LV, MBA, NU, PBL, TSM.

60 [–] Some observations upon the ansvver to an enqviry. *For N.Brooke,* 1671. 8°. T.C.I 73. L, O, C, LL, EN; BN, CH, CN, NU, TU, Y.

61 [–] —Fourth edition. *By E.Tyler and R.Holt, for N. Brooke,* 1672. 8°. L, O, CS, CT; CLC, MH, MIU.

62 [–] —Fifth edition. *By R.Holt, for Obadiah Blagrave,* 1685. 8°. L, O, CT, DT; CLC, MH, MU, NU, TU, WF.

63 [–] —Sixth edition. *For E.Blagrave,* 1696. 8°. L, OC, BR, ENC, DT; CU, MBA, NU, PBL, Y.

64 [–] Some opinions of Mr Hobbs considered. *By J.Macock for Walter Kettilby,* 1673. 8°. T.C.I 142. L, O, C, CT, DT; CH, CN, LC, MH, NU, Y.

65 [–] A vindication of the clergy, from the contempt. *By Andr. Clark for Hen. Brome,* 1672. 8°. T.C.I 88. L, O, C, DC, E; CH, MIU, NGT, NU, WF.

66 [–] —Second edition. *For C.Brome,* 1686. 8°. T.C.II 161. O.

Eachard, Laurence. *See* Echard, Laurence.

Eagle-trussers elegie. 1660. *See* Tooke, George.

67 **Eames, John.** A poem. Being an essay. *For Henry Herringman,* 1666. fol.* L; HR, MU.

68 **[Earbery, Matthias.]** An answer to a book entituled, Tractatus. *For Charles Brome,* 1697. 8°. O, OB.

69 —Deism examin'd. *For Charles Brome,* 1697. 8°. T.C.III 12. L, C, CS, CT; MH, PU, Y.

70 The Earl Marshal's order touching the habits of the peeresses. colop: *In the Savoy: by Edward Jones,* 1688. brs. L, O, MC; CH, Y.

71 The Earl of Carberyes pedigree. *[London], printed,* 1646. 4°.* LT, AN.

71A The Earl of Cleveland's bill. *[London,* 1666?] brs. L.

71B The Earl of Cleveland his case. *[London,* 1666?] brs. L.

72 The Earle of Corkes victorie. *For John Greensmith,* 13 Dec. 1641. 4°.* LT, O; MH.

73 The Earle of Essex his desires to the Parliament. *[London], for T.Thomson,* 1642. August 15. 4°.* LT; MH, NU.

74 The Earle of Essex his loyaltie and love. *For G.K. Oct.* 20. 1642. 4°.* LT; MH.

75 The Earl of Exeter with divers other lords and gentlemen are proprietors and owners. *[London?* 1661.] brs. L, LUG.

Earl of Glamorgans negotiations. 1645. *See* Worcester, Edward Somerset, *earl of.*

76 The Earl of Maclesfeld's case. *[London?* 1698.] cap. fol.* LUG.

Earle of Melfort's letter. [n.p., 1689.] *See* Burnet, Gilbert.

77 The Earl of P——'s speech to the House of Peers. colop: *Printed and sold,* [1690?] brs. Y.

78 The Earle of Pembrokes last speech. *Printed,* 1650. 4°.* LT, AN.

79 The Earle of Pembroke's speech in the House of Peeres. *Printed,* 1648. 4°.* LT, O, C, MR; CH, CN, MBP, WF, Y.

79A —[Anr. ed.] —, 1648. 4°.* LT, AN; CH, CLC.

79B —[Anr. ed.] *[London,* 1690.] cap., fol.* CH.

79C —[Anr. ed.] colop: *[London], re-printed in the year* 1693, *for the Duke of Bolton,* 1693. brs. Y.

80 The Earl of Pembrookes speech to Nol-Cromwell. *Nod-Nol, printed,* 1649. 4°.* LT; CH.

80A The Earl of Pembroke's speech to the House of Peers. colop: *Printed,* 1647. cap., 4°.* LG, HH; CH, CN.

81 The Earl of Shaftsbury's grand-jury vindicated. colop: *For R.Baldwyn,* 1682. brs. L, O, HH; CH, MH, MHL, TU, WF, Y.

81A The Earl of Shaftesbury's loyalty revived. *For Richard Baldwin,* 1681. brs. O.

82 The Earle of Strafford characterized in a letter. *[London], anno Dom.* 1641. 4°.* L, O, LG, CT, HH; CH, CLC, MIU, WF, Y.

83 The Earle of Strafford his ellegiack poem. *[London],* 1641. brs. L; MH.

84 The Earle of Straffords ghost. *For G.Bishop, August* 22, 1644. 4°.* LT, CS; CH, MH, MM, WF.

85 The Earle of Warwickes gloriovs victory. *For J.Horton, June* 15. 1642. 4°.* LT; MBP, MH, WF, Y.

86 The Earl of Warwicks surrender of the ordinance. *For Richard Best,* 1645. 4°.* LT, O; WF.

87 **[Earle, John.]** The character of a tavern. *For D.A.,* 1675. 4°.* LG.

88 —Microcosmographie. Ninth edition. *By W.Bentley, for William Sheres,* 1650. 12°. L, O; CN.

89 [–] —[Anr. ed.] —, 1650. 60 12°. L, O; WF.

90 [–] —[Anr. ed.] —, 1650. 72 12°. L; WF, Y.

91 [–] —"Ninth" edition. *By Thomas Ratcliffe, and Thomas Daniel*, 1660. 12°. NU.

92 [–] —Tenth edition. *By R. D. for P. C.*, 1664. 12°. L, OB.

93 — —Eleventh edition. *By T. Radcliffe and T. Daniel for Philip Chetwind*, 1669. 12°. L, O, C; MH, WF.

94 [–] A trve description of the pot-companion poet. *For R. W.* 1642. 4°.* LT.

Early piety. 1689. *See* Mather, Cotton.

Earnest and compassionate suit. 1691. *See* Wetenhall, Edward.

Earnest and humble invitation. 1684. *See* I., T.

Earnest breathings. 1658. *See* Dury, John.

95 An earnest call to family-catechising. *By J. W. for John Dunton*, 1693. 12°. T.C.II 463. L, O.

Earnest call to the people. [n.p.], 1692. *See* Elys, Edmund.

96 An earnest call to those Nonconformists. *Printed, and are to be sold by Randal Taylor*, 1691. 8°.* T.C.II 367. L.

Earnest exhortation for. 1647. *See* H., T.

97 An earnest exhortation from a minister. *Worcester*, [1700?]. 8°. L.

98 An earnest exhortation to a trve Ninivitish repentance. *By T. P. and M. S. to be sold by Ben. Allen*, 1643. 4°.* LT, DT; CH.

98A —[Anr. ed.] *For Ben. Allen*, 1644. 12°.* WF, Y.

98B The earnest petition of many thousand knights. 1648. 4°.* O.

98C An earnest request to Mr. John Standish. *Printed*, 1676. 4°. LG, CS, CT; CLC.

Earth twice shaken. 1693/4. *See* R., J. D.

99 The earthquake Naples. *Boston, N.E. reprinted by B. Green. February 21.* 1694. 5. brs. EVANS 715. CH, MHS.

99A **Eason, Laurence.** A guide to salvation. *Bruges, by Luke Kerchove*, 1673. 4°. C, HEYTHORP; CN, TU.

99B The East-India and Guinny-trade. [*London?* 1690.] brs. L; NC.

99C **East India Company.** Abstract of regulations. [*London?* 1694.] brs. MH.

100 —An answer of the committee of seventeen, representing the East-India Company. colop: *Amsterdam, by Paul Matthewson, and reprinted*, [*London*], *by Langely* [sic] *Curtis*, [1683?]. brs. O.

100A —Answer to all the material objections. [*London?* 1699.] cap., fol.* L; CU, Y.

100AA —At a court of committees . . . holden the eighteenth day of December, 1667. [*London*, 1667.] brs. MH.

100AB —[Same title.] [*London*, 1680.] brs. MIU.

100AC —[Same title.] holden the 10th day of August, 1683. [*London*, 1683.] brs. MH.

100ACA[–] —At a general court of adventurers. [*London*, 1694], brs. MH.

100AD —By-laws, constitutions, orders and rules. [*London*, 1700]. fol. L, O.

100B —By-laws proposed by the government. 1695. brs. O.

100BA —The court of committees for the East-India Company. [*London*, 1695.] brs. MH.

100C —The East India companies charter. [*London*, 1686].· fol.* MH.

100CA —For sale at the East-India-House. [*London*, 1675.] cap., 4°.* MIU.

100D —General courts of elections to be holden. [*London*, 1691] brs. MH.

100E —A list of the names of all the adventurers. [*London?* 1691.] fol.* RPJ, Y.

100EA —A list of the names of all the members. [*London?* 1700.] cap., fol.* MIU.

100EB —A list of the names of the governour. [*London?* 1685.] brs. HH.

100F —The petition and remonstrance of the governour. *For Nicholas Bourne*, 1641. 4°.* L, LG, LUG, P, MR, EN; CU, MH, NU, LC, Y.

100G — —[Anr. ed.] *Printed*, 1641. 4°.* L, O, C, LUG; CH, MB, MIU, WF, Y.

100H —The petition of. colop: *By Thomas Braddyll and Robert Everingham*, 1691. brs. PL, Y.

100I —To all people to whom. [*London*, 1696.] brs. MH, NN.

100J —To the right honourable . . . citizens . . . The answer of. [*London*, 1688]. cap., fol.* L; Y.

100K — —[Anr. ed.] The East India Company's answer. [*London*, 1688]. brs. L; KU, WF.

100L —You do sincerely promise and swear. [*London?* 169–.] brs. MH.

101 The East-India stock in the companies books. [*London*, 169? .] brs. L, O.

East-India-trade a most profitable. 1677. *See* Papillon, Thomas.

102 The East-India trade: a true narration. [*London*, 1641?] cap., 4°.* L, LUG; EN, MHS.

103 The East-India trade. Being a jewel. [*London*, 1693.] cap., fol.* L; WF, Y.

104 The East India trade being lately proposed. [*London*, 1694.] brs. L; WF.

Easter not mis-timed. 1664. *See* Pell, John.

Easter-reckoning. [n.p., 1653.] *See* Farnworth, Richard.

105 The Easter wedding. [*London*], *for C. Dennisson*, [1685–88]. brs. L, O, CM, HH.

106 **Eastern Counties Association.** Cambridge. tricesimo die Aprilis anno Dom. 1643. It is this day ordered by the committee of the Association. [*London*], *April 21*, 1643. brs. CD.

107 **Easton, Thomas.** A sermon preach'd . . . 27th day of [June] . . . 1692. *For Tho. Bennet*, 1692. 4°.* T.C.II 418. L, O, C; CLC.

107A An easie and profitable order in filling of ground. [n.p., 165–?] cap., 4°.* R. LC; MH.

108 An easie method for satisfaction. *Printed, to be sold by Richard Baldwin*, 1691. 4°.* OC, BAMB, D; CH, CN, MH, WF, Y.

109 Easie method for the manning of His Majesties fleet. 1695. LUS.

109A An easy method of supporting . . . a public academy. [*London?* 1696.] brs. L.

109B An easie way to get money. *For the society of informers*, 1671. 4°. OC.

110 An easie way to tame a shrew. [*London*], *for P. Brooksby*, [1672–90]. brs. HH; MH.

111 The eating of blood vindicated. *For H. Shepheard, and W. Ley*, 1646. 4°.* LT, DT; CN, MH, NN.

112 [**Eaton, John.**] The discovery of the most dangerous dead faith. *By J. Hart, & sold by John Lewis*, [1642]. 4°. L, LCL.

113 — —[Anr. ed.] *By R. Bishop for William Adderton*, 1642. 12°. L, O, LCL.

114 — —"Second" edition. —, 1642. 12°. L, DC; NPT.

115 —The honey-combe of free justification by Christ alone. *By R.B. at the charge of Robert Lancaster*, 1642. 4°. L, O, LCL, LW, ENC; CLC, MH, NPT, NU, PL, Y.

116 **Eaton, Nathanael.** De fastis Anglicis, ... being a treble series of epigrams. *By H.L.* 1661. 8°. L, O.

117 —Μηνο-εξεολογια; or a treatise of moneths. *By J. Macock, or ſthe company of stationers*, 1657. 8°. O, CT, E.

118 **Eaton, Samuel.** A defence of sundry positions. *By Matthew Simmons, for Henry Overton*, 1645. 4°. LT, O, LCL, EN, DT; CH, MBA, Y.

119 —, —. [Anr. ed.] —, 1646. 4°. LT, LCL, DT; CLC, MH.

120 —The defence of sundry position & Scriptures for the Congregational-way. Second edition. *By Matthew Simmons, for Henry Overton*, 1646. 4°. L; NU, RPJ.

121 —A friendly debate on a weighty subject. *By T. N. for Gyles Calvert*, 1650. 4°. LT, O; NU.

122 —A just apologie for the church of Duckenfeild. *By M. S. for Henry Overton*, 1647. 4°.* O, C, GU.

123 —The mystery of God incarnate. *For Henry Cripps, and Lodowick Lloyd*, 1650. 8°. LT, LCL, LW, DT; MH, NPT, NU, WF.

124 —The oath of allegiance. *By Peter Cole*, 1650. 4°. LT, LCL, DT; NU, Y.

125 —The Quakers confuted. *By R. White for Thomas Brewster*, 1654. 4°. LT, O, CJ, LCL, LF; MU, PL, NU, PSC.

126 —A vindication, or further confirmation. *For Henry Cripps and Lodowick Lloyd*, 1651. 8°. L, C, LSC, LW; MH, NPT, Y.

Eau de mer douce. 1683. *See* Fitzgerald, Robert.

126A **Ebbs, Joyce.** The last speech, confession & prayer. *For G. Chambers*, 1662. 4°. OC.

Ebenezer. 1675. *See* Okeley, William.

126B Eben-Ezer. A full and exact relation. *For T. W.* 1644. 4°.* LT, O, CCL; BBE, MH, MIU, WF.

Eben-Ezer, as a thankfull remembrance. 1643. *See* P., T.

Ecce homo; the little Parliament. 1644. *See* Walker, Henry.

127 Ecce the New Testament of our lords and saviours, the House of Commons. [*London*], *printed*, 1648. 4°.* LT, O, LVF, P; MIU, TU, WF, Y.

[**Eccles, F.**] Christian information. 1664. *See* Ellington, Francis.

127A **Eccles, John.** Theater musick. *Sould by I: Walsh*, [1698.] DUC.

128 **Eccles, Solomon.** In the year 59 ... the presence of the Lord God was felt within me. *For M.W.* 1659. 4°.* L, CT; PH.

129 —A musick-lector. *Printed*, 1667. 4°.* L, O, CT, LG, BBN; CH, LC, MH, MU, NU, Y.

129A —The Quaker's challeng. [*London?* 1668.] cap., 4°.* L, OC; MU, PH, PSC.

130 —Signes are from the Lord. 1663. brs. L, BBN; CH, PSC.

131 **Eccles, William.** Reasons for the taking off. [*London?* 1700] brs. L; WF, Y.

Ecclesia enucleata. 1684. *See* Chauncy, Isaac.

Ecclesia & factio. 1698. *See* Ward, Edward.

132 Ecclesia et reformatio. A dialogue. 1698. 8°.* L, LG, EN; MH.

Ecclesia gemens: or. 1677. *See* Lee, Samuel.

133 Ecclesia restaurata. *For Henry Brome*, 1677. fol.* L, O, LG; MH.

Ecclesia reviviscens. 1691. *See* Jones, William.

134 Entry cancelled.

135 Ecclesiæ Anglicanæ filii collatio. *Oxonii, typis Lichfield-ianis*, 1690. 8°.* L, O.

Ecclesiæ gemitus. 1649. *See* DuMoulin, Peter.

Ecclesiastica methermeneutica. 1652. *See* Homes, Nathaniel.

136 The ecclesiasticall discipline of the Reformed churches in France. *By E.P. for Nicholas Bourne*, 1642. 4°. LT, O, C, LL, EN; CH, NU, WSC, Y.

137 —[Anr. ed.] *For J. Bourne*, 1662. 4°. MB, NPT, WF.

Ecclesiastical history epitomized. 1682. *See* Shirley, John.

Ecclesiastical history of France. 1676. *See* G., G.

Ecclesiasticum: or. 1690. *See* Chauncy, Isaac.

Eccleston, Christodolus, *pseud.*

138 **Eccleston, Edward.** The cataclysm. An opera. *For T. M. and sold by Iohn Holford*, 1685. 4°. T.C.II 114. C; CH, LC, WCL.

139 [–] The deluge: or, the destruction. *For James Knapton*, 1690. 4°. T.C.II 322. L.

140 —Noah's flood. *By M. Clark, and sold by B. Tooke*, 1679. 4°. T.C.I 370. L, O, CCA, CT; CH, CN, MH, WF, Y.

141 [**Eccleston, Theodor.**] A brief representation of the Quakers' case of not-swearing. [*London,* 1694.] cap., 4°.* L, O, LL, BBN; MH, PH.

141A —An epistle by way of encouragement. *By T. Sowle*, 1693. 4°.* PSC.

142 **Echard, Laurence.** An exact description of Ireland. *For Tho. Salusbury*, 1691. 16°. T.C.II 369. L, O, C, MR, DT; CH, CN, WF, Y.

143 [–] Flanders: or, the Spanish Netherlands. *For Tho. Salusbury*, 1691. 12°. T.C.II 380. O.

144 [–] —Second edition. —, 1692. 12°. L, CT; INU, WF.

144A —The gazetteer's. *For Tho. Salusbury*, 1692. sixes. CH, IU, PU, Y.

145 — —Second edition. —, 1693. sixes. T.C.II 410. O; CN.

146 ——Third edition. —, 1695. sixes. L, O, C, CT; WF.

146A ——Fourth edition. *For John Nicholson*, 1700. 12°.
L, CPE; CH, NIC, Y.

147 —The hainousness of injustice. *For M. Wotton*, 1698.
4°.* T.C.III 106. OC, CT, EC; WF, Y.

148 —A most compleat compendium of geography. *For
Thomas Salusbury*, 1691. 12°. T.C.II 359. L, CCA, CCH;
PL, WF.

149 ——Second edition. *For Tho. Salusbury*, 1691. 8°.
T.C.II 388. L, O, C; CH, CLC, INU, Y.

149A ——Third edition. —, 1693. 12°. T.C.II 444. OC; Y.

150 ——Fourth edition. *For J. Salusbury*, 1697. 12°. L, O,
CS, CT; CL, CLC, CN.

150A ——Fifth edition. *For John Nicholson*, [1700.] 12°. CH, NN,
PBM, RPB.

151 —The Roman history. *For M. Gillyflower; J. Tonson;
H. Bonwick; and R. Parker*. 1695. 8°. T.C.II 548. L, C,
LCP, CCH, ELY; CLC.

152 ——Second edition. *By T. Hodgkin, —*, 1696. 8°. C,
OC; MB, MU, NHS, Y.

153 ——Third edition. —, 1697. 8°. L, O, EN; PL, WF.

154 ——Fourth edition. —, 1699. 8°. T.C.III 146. L, O, CE,
EN, DT; IU, PL, RPB, Y.

155 —The Roman history. Vol. II. *By T. H. for M. Gillyflower; J. Tonson; H. Bonwick; and R. Parker*, 1698.
8°. L, O, C, OC, ELY; PL, WF.

156 ——Second edition. *By T. Hodgkin, for M. Gillyflower, H. Bonwick, J. Tonson, W. Freeman, T. Goodwin, M. Wotton, J. Walthoe, S. Manship, R. Parker,
and B. Tooke*, 1699. 8°. CS, EN, DT; MB, Y.

157 An eccho to the plea for limited monarchy. *By T. M.
for William Shears*, 1660. 4°.* LT, SP.

157A Echo's echo. [*London?* 1672.] cap., fol.* L.

Ecchoes from the sixth trumpet. [n.p., 1666.] *See* Wither,
George.

Eclaircissements. 1687. *See* Jurieu, Pierre.

157B Eclectical chiliasm, or a discourse. *For the author, and
sold by C. Brome*, 1700. 8°. T.C.III 159. O; CLC, MH.

158 Eclogs or, pastorals on several arguments. *For Joseph
Collier*. 1682. 4°.* L.

158A The ecstasie. *For Tho. Parkhurst*, 1689. 8°. PL.

159 **Edelen, Philip.** The Christians hope. *For R. Thrale*,
1653. 8°.* LT, O, CM, SP; MH, MWA.

160 **E[dgar], T[homas].** Two charges, as they were delivered by. *For Matthew Walbancke*, 1650. 4°.* LT,
O, C, LVF, DT; CH, CLC, LC, MH, MHL.

An edict in the Roman law. [*London?* 1688.] *See* Burnet,
Gilbert, *bp.*

Edifying wonder. *Glasgow*, 1668. *See* Simpson.

160B **Edinburgh.** By the Provost, baillies. *Edinburgh*, 1659.
brs. Y.

160C —Edinburgh, Ianuary 23, 1655. Forsameikle, as there
hath been. [*Edinburgh*, 1655/6.] brs. Y.

160D **Edinburgh, Town Council.** Act anent women-
servants. [*Edinburgh*, 1699.] brs. ALDIS 3820. L, HH, ES,
FSF.

161 —Act of the Town Council of Edinburgh, . . . 6 Nov.
Edinburgh, 1689. brs. STEELE 3p 2855. ALDIS 2851. ES.

162 —Act of Town Council . . . 21 May. Against beggars.
Edinburgh, 1675. brs. ALDIS 2040. HH.

163 —Act of Town Council . . . 30 March. Cleansing.
Edinburgh, heir of A. Anderson, 1687. brs. ALDIS 2681.
HH, ES.

164 —Acts of the Town Council of Edinburgh. *Edinburgh.
[by the heir of Andrew Anderson]*, 1678. fol.* ALDIS
2114. L, HH, ES; CH.

165 **Edinburgh University.** Academiæ Edinburgenae gratulatio ob . . . Caroli II. *Edinburgi, excudebat Gideon
Lithgo*, 1661. 4°.* ALDIS 1682. O, E, EN.

166 —An advertisement. These are to give notice. [*Edinburgh, by the heir of Andrew Anderson*, 1680.] brs.
ALDIS 2183. L, E, EN.

167 —Q. F. Fq; S. Juvenes lycei . . . 21 July 1673. [*Edinburgh, by Andrew Anderson?* 1673.] brs. ALDIS 1997. E.

168 —Q. F. fq; S. Monet hoc programma . . . 9 Nov.
1674. [*Edinburgh*, 1674.] brs. ALDIS 2035. E.

169 —Q. F. F. Q. S. Noverint universi. [*Edinburgh, by the
heir of Andrew Anderson*], 1681. brs. ALDIS 2303. E.

170 —Q. F. Fq; S. Sciant omnes divinis. [*Edinburgh*, 1675.]
brs. ALDIS 2062. E.

171 —Senatus Edinburgenus, academiæ [*Edinburgh*, 1680?]
brs. ALDIS 2225. E.

171A —Theses & problemata philosophica. *Edinburgi, excudebat hæres Andræ Anderson*, 1679. brs. ALDIS 2177. HH, E.

172 Edinburgh, first May one thousand six hundred and
seventy four. The which day. [*Edinburgh*, 1674.]
cap., fol.* L, HH, EN.

173 Edinburghs joy for His Majesties coronation. [*Edinburgh*], 1661. 4°. ALDIS 1696. EN.

174 **Edlyn, Richard.** Observationes astrologicae or an
astrologicall discourse. *By T. W. to be sold by Richard
Blome.* [1659.] 8°. LT.

175 ——[Anr. ed.] *For Samuell Speed*, 1659. 8°. O, C, LWL;
CLC, LC, MU, WF.

176 ——[Anr. ed.]. *For B. Billingsly and O. Blagrave*, 1668.
8°. L, AN; IU.

177 —Prae-nuncius sydereus: an astrological treatise. *By
J. G. for Nath: Brook*, 1664. 4°. L, O; CH, WF, Y.

177A Edmond Pickering painter . . . is now removed. [*London*,
1681.] brs. O.

177B **Edmonds, David.** A sharp arrow darted. *By T. H.*,
1652. 8°.* DT.

178 **[Edmonds, Edward].** A reviving vvord from the quick
and the dead. *For Giles Calvert*, 1657. 4°. LT, O, LCL; NU,
WF, Y.

178A **Edmonds, Hugh.** The censors censured. *For R.
Stephens*, 1661. 4°. LSC.

178B —Presbytery popish, not episcopacy. *For Philemon
Stephens*, 1661. 4°.* L; MH, MIU, PPT, WF.

178C **Edmondson, Christopher.** The pilgrims saying. *For
Randal Taylor, to be sold at his house; and by Rich.
Burton in Preston*, [1664?] 12°. MB.

179 **[Edmondson, William.]** A letter of examination. [*London*], *printed*, 1672. 4°.* L, O, CT; PH, PSC, Y.

180 **[Edmundson, Henry.]** Comes facundus in via. The fellow-traveller. *For Hum. Robinson*, 1658. 8°. LT, C, OP, MR; CH, CN, MH, WF.

181 [–] The fellow-traveller through city and countrey. [*n.p.*], 1658. 8°. O; CH.

182 —*Συν Θεω*. Homonyma et synonyma. *Oxoniæ excudebat. W. H. per R. Davis*, 1661. 8°. MADAN 2553. O.

183 —*Συν Θεω*. Lingua linguarum. The natural language of languages. *By T. Roycroft, for Humfrey Robinson*, 1655. 8°. O, SP; MB, MBP, MH, WF.

184 — —[Anr. ed.] *Printed*, 1658. 8°. LT, EN; WF, Y.

Edovardus confessor. 1688. *See* Gibbon, John.

The education of young gentlewomen. 1699. *See* Fenela, French.

185 **Edward, VI.** K. Edward the VIth his own arguments. *By J. D. for Jonathan Robinson*, 1682. 8°. T.C.I 497. L, O, LW, CK, ENC; CH, CN, MH, NU, WF, Y.

186 —A letter of. *Printed*, 1641. 4°.* LT, CSS, MH, NU, Y.

187 **Edward, Robert.** The doxology approven. *Edinburgh, by the heir of Andrew Anderson*, 1683. 8°. ALDIS 2376. L, EN, ENC, I; CLC.

188 Edward Littleton, Lord Keeper of the Great Seale of England, . . . escape from the Parliament. *For T. H.* 1642. 4°.* LT, CCO, EC, SP, YM; CH, WF, Y.

189 Entry cancelled.

190 **[Edwards,   .]** A treatise concerning the plague and the pox. *By Gartrude Dawson*, 1652. 4°. C, CCA, LWL, OR; HC.

191 **[Edwards, Charles.]** An afflicted man's testimony. [*London*, 1691.] 8°.* L, O; Y.

192 —Fatherly instructions. 1686. 8°. L, AN.

—Y Ffydd ddiffuant.

193 — —Second edition. *Rhydychen* [*Oxford*] *by H. Hall, sold in Wrexham, Llanfyllin, &c.*, 1671. 8°. MADAN 2886. O, AN.

194 — —Third edition. *Preintiedig yn Rhydychen, gan Hen: Hall*. 1677. 8°. MADAN 3140. L, AN; Y.

194A —[Hanes y ffydd.] [*Rhydychen* (*Oxford*), *Henry Hall*, 1666?] 8°. CPL. AN.

195 —Hebraismorum Cambro-Britannicorum specimen. [*London*, 1675.] fol.* L, O, CT, AN; CH.

195A [–] Some omissions and mistakes in the . . . Bible. [*London?* 1672]. cap., fol.* L, AN.

196 **Edwards, George.** Reverendis et eruditis viris. [*Oxford, by George Edwards*, 1674.] fol.* MADAN 2997. O; Y.

[Edwards, Henry,] Preparative to studie. 1641. *See* Heywood, Thomas.

197 **Edwards, John.** Brief remarks upon Mr. Whiston's new theory. *For J. Robinson, and J. Wyat*, 1697. 8°. L, CS; MB, WF, Y.

198 —A brief vindication of the fundamental articles. *For J. Robinson, and J. Wyat*, 1697. 8°. T.C.III 21. L, O, CE, LCL, NPL; Y.

199 [–] Cometomantia. A discourse of comets. *For Brab. Aylmer*, 1684. 8°. T.C.II 49. L, O, C, LWL, EO; CLC, MH, V, WF, HC.

200 —Concio et determinatio. *Cantabrigiæ, typs academicis, impensis Edmundi Jeffery*, 1700. 8°. T.C.III 186. L, OM, CS, CT, EC; MH, MWA, WF.

201 —A demonstration of the existence and providence of God. *By J. D. for Jonathan Robinson, and John Wyat*, 1696. 8°. T.C.II 578. L, O, C, NPL, DT; CLC, MH, NU, WF, Y.

202 —A discourse concerning the authority. *Printed; and sold by Richard Wilkin*, 1693–95. 3v. 8°. T.C.II 475. L, O, C, E, DT; CLC, MBA, NPT, NU, WF, Y.

202A — —[Anr. ed.] *By J. D. for Jonathan Robinson and John Wyat*, 1694-5. 8°. PL.

203 — —Second edition. *By J. D. for Jonathan Robinson, and John Wyat*. 1696. 8°. T.C.II 499. L, ENC; MBA, NPT, PL.

204 —The eternal and intrinsick reasons. *Cambridge, at the university press, for Edmund Jeffery*, 1699. 4°.* T.C.III 152. L, O, C, LW, CT; CU, MBA, NU, WF.

205 — —[Anr. ed.] —, 1700. 8°. T.C.III 181. OM, CS; CH, CLC, Y.

206 —A farther enquiry into several remarkable texts. *For J. Robinson, J. Everingham, and J. Wyat*, 1692. 8°. T.C.II 422. L, O, C, NPL, E; CLC, CU, MB, NU, WF.

207 — —Second edition. *Printed, and sold by Richard Wilkin*, 1694. 8°. T.C.II 530. L, O, LCL, OM, DT; CH, IU, MH, Y.

208 —An enquiry into four remarkable texts. *Cambridge, by J. Hayes; for W. Graves*, 1692. 4°. T.C.II 400. L, O, C, NPL, E; CH, NU, TU, WF, Y.

208A — —Second edition. —, 1694. 8°. LCL.

209 —The plague of the heart. *Cambridge: by John Field, for Edmund Beechinoe*, 1665. 4°. L, O, CS, CSSX, WCA; MIU.

210 —*Πολυποικλος σοφρια*. A compleat history. *For Daniel Brown, Jonath. Robinson, Andrew Bell, John Wyat, and E. Harris*. 1699. 2 v. 8°. T.C.III 135. L, O, C, E, DT; CH, CU, MBP, NU, Y.

211 —Sermons on special occasions. *For Jonathan Robinson, and John Wyat*, 1698. 8°. T.C.III 51. L, O, CT, NPL, RPL; CLC, MB, NU, WF, Y.

212 —The Socinian creed. *For J. Robinson, and J. Wyat*, 1697. 8°. T.C.II 600. L, O, CS, LCL, E; CH, MB, NU, WF, Y.

213 Entry cancelled

214 —Socinianism unmask'd. *For J. Robinson, and J. Wyat*, 1696. 8°. T.C.II 577. L, O, CT, NPL, E; CH, MH, NU, WF.

215 —Some thoughts concerning the several causes. *For J. Robinson, and J. Wyat*, 1695. 8°. L, O, CT, E, DT; CH, MH, NU, WF, Y.

216 **Edwards, Jonathan.** A preservative against Socinianism. The first part. *Oxon. At the theater for Henry Clements*, 1693. 4°. T.C.II 473. L, O, CT, DU, ES; CH, CLC, MBA, WF, Y.

217 — —Second edition. —, 1693. 4°. OM, C, AN; NU.

218 — —Third edition. —, 1698. 4°. L, O, C, LW, DT; BBE, CLC, NU, WSC, Y.

219 —A preservative against Socinianism. Second part. *Oxon, at the theater for H. Clements, 1694.* 4°. O, C, CT, DU, ES; NU, WF.

219A —— Second edition. —, *1698.* 4°. O; CLC, PPT, Y.

220 —A preservative against Socinianism. The third part. *Oxon., at the theater for H. Clements, 1697.* 4°. L, O, CT, ES, DT; CLC, MH, NU, WF, Y.

221 [–] Remarks upon a book lately published by Dr. Will. Sherlock. *Oxford, at the theater, 1695. To be sold by H. Clements.* 4°. L, O, C, LP, MR; CLC, CN, NU, WF, Y.

222 **Edwards, Thomas.** Antapologia. *By G. M. for John Bellamie, 1644.* 4°. LT, O, C, ENC, DT; CLC, LC, MH, RPJ, Y.

223 ——[Anr. ed.] *By G. M. for Ralph Smith, 1644.* 4°. LT, CT, LW, HH; BN, CH, MIU, NU, WCL, WF.

224 ——[Anr. ed.] *By T. R. and E. M. for Ralph Smith, 1646.* 4°. L, LVF, OM, EN, ES; MH, NU, RPJ.

224A ——[Anr. ed.] *By T. R. and E. M. for John Bellamie, 1646.* 4°. EC, OCC; MH.

225 —The casting down. First part. *By T. R. and E. M. for George Calvert, 1647.* 4°. LT, O, CT, EN, DT; CH, CU, MH, NU, WF, Y.

226 —Dialling made easy. *Oxford, by L. Lichfield, for Sam. Clarke, 1692.* 8°. L, O, OC, OCC; CSB, PL, Y.

227 —The first and second part of Gangraena. *By T. R. and E. M. for Ralph Smith, 1646.* 4°. C, LVF, LW, ENC; CN, MH, NPT, NU, Y.

228 —Gangræna: or a catalogue. *For Ralph Smith, 1646.* 4°. LT, O, C, EN, DT; MH, NU, RPJ, WF, Y.

229 —— Second edition. —, *1646.* 4°. L, O, C, OM, EN; CH, CU, MH, PH, Y.

230 —— Third edition. —, *1646.* 4°. L, CJ, CS, EN, DT; CN, MBA, NHC, Y.

231 —The paraselene dismantled. *Printed and sold by Will. Marshal, and John Marshal, 1699.* 4°. T.C.III 195. L, LCL, LF, LW, ENC; CH, NPT, NU, PH, WF.

232 —A plain and impartial enquiry. *For William Marshall, 1693.* 4°. T.C.II 450. L, O, C, GU, DT; MH, NPT, WF.

233 —Reasons against the independent government. *By Richard Cotes for Jo. Bellamie, & Ralph Smith, 1641.* 4°. LT, O, LCL, E, DT; CH, CN, NU, WF, Y.

234 —The second part of Gangraena. *By T. R. and E. M. for Ralph Smith, 1646.* 4°. LT, O, C, EN, DT; CH, CLE, MH, WF, Y.

235 —— Third edition. *1646.* 4°. C, DT; CN.

236 —A short review of some reflections. *For Will. Marshall, 1693.* 4°.* T.C.II 474. L, O, C, GU; NPT, WF.

237 —The third part of Gangraena. *For Ralph Smith, 1646.* 4°. LT, O, CT, EN, DT; CH, MH, NU, WF, Y.

238 [–] To His Sacred Majesty, Charles the Second, on his happy return. [*London, 1660.*] fol.* LT, O; Y.

238A [–] To the high court of Parliament. A dilemma. *By Matthew Simmons for Henry Overton, 1646.* 4°.* LT, CT, HH, DT; CH, IU, MH, Y.

239 **Edzard, Johann Ezdras.** The finger of God. *By F. Collins, for James Knapton, 1696.* 4°.* T.C.II 576. L, C, CT; WF.

240 **Edzard, Sebastian.** Jacobi patriarchæ. *Prostant apud Thomam Bennet, 1698.* 8°. T.C.III 80. L, CT; RPB.

241 **Eedes, John.** The orthodox doctrine. *For Henry Cripps and Lodowick Lloyd, 1654.* 4°. LT, O; TSM, WF.

241A [**Eedes, Judith.**] A warning to all the inhabitants of the earth. colop: *By J. B. for the authour, 1659, cap.,* 4°.* CT; CH.

241B **Eedes, Nicholas.** One blow at the feet. *For the author, and are to be sold by J. Gwillim; and Edw. Swaine, 1693.* 4°. CS, LF; PSC.

241C **Eedes, Richard.** Christ exalted. *By A. W. to be sold by John Shirley and Tho. Underhill and Samuel Tompson, 1659.* 8°. L, P, LSC, LW; CLC, NPT, Y.

242 —Great Britains resurrection. *By Ja. Cottrel, for Henry Fletcher, 1660.* 4°.* LT, CT.

243 —Great salvation by Jesvs Christ. *By T. W. for the author, 1659.* 8°. LCL, LW; NPT, NU, TU.

243A Earn'ghe extraction. *By Robert Wood* [1646.] 4°.* MIU, NN, NU.

244 The effect of all letters read. *Novemb. 23. For John Cave, 1642.* 4°.* LT, HH.

244A The effect of what was spoken by Sir John Lowther. *For Randal Taylor, 1689.* cap., fol.* L, O, C; CH.

244B An effectual method to raise money. [*London? 1696.*] brs. L; MH.

Effectual prescription. Oxford, 1691. *See* Prince, Thomas.

Effigies amoris. 1682. *See* Waring, Robert.

245 **Egan, Anthony.** The book of rates. *For Benjamin Southwood, 1673.* 4°.* L, O, C, OC, YM; CH, MH, TU, WF.

246 ——[Anr. ed.] —, *1674.* 4°.* T.C.I 163. L, O, C, ENC, DT; CH, MBP, NC, WF, Y.

247 —— "Second" edition. *For Isaac Cleave, 1678.* 4°.* T.C.I 306. L, C, CK, NPL, EN; NU, WF.

248 —The Franciscan convert: ... preached in London. *For Robert Clavel, 1673.* 4°.* T.C.I 132. L, O, C, LIL, EN; CH, MH, NU, WF, Y.

249 —The Franciscan convert; ... preached at St. Maudlins. *Dublin, 1673.* 4°.* DT.

250 [–] The Papists designs detected. *For John Leigh, 1678.* 4°.* O, C, CCH, LIL; CH, NU, PL, WF.

251 —The Romanists designs detected. *For John Leigh, 1674.* 4°.* T.C.I 164. L, O, C, OM, EN; CH, MH, NU, Y.

251A [**Egerton, Sarah Fyge.**] The female advocate, *By H. C. from John Taylor, 1681.* 4°.* T.C.II 170. L, O; H, CN, CU, PL.

251B [–] —Second edition. —, *1687.* 4°.* T.C.II 183. CH, OCI.

252 [**Egerton, Stephen.**] A briefe method of catechizing. Forty-fourth edition. *By T. Forcet, for Humphrey Robinson, 1644.* 4°. O; NPT, NU, Y.

252A [–] [Anr. ed.] *Printed, 1671.* 8°. OC.

252B **Egerton, Thomas.** Certaine observations. *For Matthew VValbanck; for Henry Twyford, and John Place, 1651.* L, O, C, LGI, LL; CH, CU, MHL, NCL, Y.

252C —The privileges and prerogatives. *For Henry Sheapheard, 1641.* 4°.* L, O, C, LL, DT; CH, MHL, WCL, WF, Y.

253 Εγκυκλοχορεια; or universal motion. 4°. 1662. LG, LL; MH.

253A [**Eglesfield, Francis.**] The life and reigne of . . . Charles the II. By R. Daniel for Francis Eglesfield, 1660. 12° L; MH.

254 [–] Monarchy revived, in the most illustrious Charles the Second. By R. Daniel for Francis Eglesfield, 1661. 12°. LT; MH.

254A **Eglesfield, James.** The saints sacred laver. By Thomas Harper, 1646. 8°.* CLC.

255 **Eglisham, George.** A declaration to the kingdome of England. For Geo: Horton, 1648. 4°.* LT, HH; NAM, WF, Y.

256 —The fore-runner of revenge. Printed at London, 1642. 4°.* LT, O, C, LCL, EN; CH, CN, MH, NU, TU, WF, Y.

256A Eglurhddbyrr ar catechism. Matth. *Wootton, 1699. 8°. L.

Ehrer Kynd, pseud.

257 Eight and thirty queries. For Richard Andrews, 1659. 4°.* LT; HR, MH, MIU, WF.

258 Eight antiqueries in answer. For Giles Calvert, 1647. 4°.* LT, O, DT; CH, CLC, MH, NU, Y.

259 Eight propositions concerning the Kings Majestie. Imprinted at Oxford by Leonard Lichfield, and re-printed at London, 1648. 4°.* MADAN 1963. LT, HH; CH, MH, WF, WU.

Eight propositions of the desires of the commissioners. 1648. See Church of Scotland.

VIII qveries. 1647. See Prynne, William.

260 Eight reasons for baptizing infants. Printed, 1649. 4°.* LT.

261 Eight resolutions to eight queries. [n.p., 1647.] 4°.* L, O; CH.

262 Eight speeches spoken. For Peter Cole, 1642. 4°.* LT, O, CT, HH, E; CH, CN, MH, WF, Y.

262A — —[Anr. ed.] For George Lindsey, October 13, 1642. 4°.* CCA, SP, D; TU, Y.

262B — —[Anr. ed.] For Francis Coles and Thomas Bates, 1642. 4°.* LSE, OC,

Eight very serious. 1646. See C., R.

262C Eighteen court quæries. 1649. 4°.* O.

263 Eighteen new court-quæries. Printed, 1659. 4°.* LT, O, LG, CSSX, HH; CH, CN, MH, NU, WF, Y.

264 Eighteene propositions by way of questions from the high court. Printed at London for Iohn Watson, 1642. 4°.* LT, CK, EC; CH, MH, NU, TU, WF, Y.

265 Eighteene queries, extreame needfull to be debated. For C. H., 1647. 4°.* LT, O, HH; CN, CU, MH, WF, Y.

265A The eighth collection of papers. Printed, and are to be sold by Rich. Janeway, 1689. 4°.* L, O, CM, HH, DT; MBA, NU, RPJ, WF, Y.

265B —[Anr. ed.] Printed, 1689. 4°.* L, C, OC; CH, NU, TU, WF, Y.

Eighth day. 1661. See Beling, Sir Richard.

266 The eighth liberal science: or a new found-art . . . of drinking. By B. A. 1650. 8°.* LT.

Eighth part of the Christian-Quaker. [n.p., 1682.] See Rogers, William.

Εικων ακλαστως the image. [n.p.], 1651. See Jane, Joseph, bp.

267 Ε᾿ικων α᾿λ᾿ θινη The povrtraitvre of truths . . . majesty. By Thomas Paine, and are to be sold by George Whittington, 1649. 4°. ALMACK p. 74. LT, O, CT, EC; CH, CN, MH, NU, TU, WF, Y.

Εικων βασιλικη, or an image. 1660. See Oxenden, Henry.

Ε᾿ικὼν βασιλικη or, the true pourtraiture. 1660. See F., R.

268 Ε᾿ικὼν βασιλικὴ. The povrtraictvre of His Sacred Maiestie. [London], 1648. 12°. ALMACK 1. MADAN 1. L, O, CS, AN; CH, CN, MH, TU, Y.

269 —Second edition. For R. Royston, 1648. 12°. ALMACK 1 note. C; CH, PL.

270 —[Anr. ed.] [London], 1648. 12°. ALMACK 2. MADAN 1. L, O, CF, LLL, EC; CH, CLC, TU, Y, MH.

271 —[Anr. ed.] [London], 1648. 8°. ALMACK 3. MADAN 2. O, EC; TU.

272 —[Anr. ed.] [London], 1648. 8°. ALMACK 4. MADAN 2. L, O, C, OC; MH, WF, Y.

273 —[Anr. ed.] [London], 1648. 8°. ALMACK 5. MADAN 3. L, O, C, LG, OC, CT; BBE, CLC, MH.

274 —[Anr. ed.] [London], 1648. ALMACK 6. MADAN 3. O, C; CH, Y.

275 —[Anr. ed., pourtraicture.] [London], printed, 1648. 8°. ALMACK 7. MADAN 11–12. L, O, C; CU, MH, WCL, Y.

276 —[Anr. ed., pourtracture.] [London], reprinted in R. M., 1648. 12°. ALMACK 8. MADAN 13. L, O, C, CT, LVD; CN, CU, MH, V, Y.

277 —[Anr. ed., pourtraicture.] [London], reprinted in R. M., 1648. 12°. ALMACK 9. MADAN 14. L, O, C, OC; MH, Y.

278 —[Anr. ed., pourtraicture.] [London], printed, 1648. 12°. ALMACK 10. MADAN 4. L, O, C; MH, Y.

279 —[Anr. ed., pourtraicture.] [London], printed, 1648. 12°. ALMACK 11, MADAN 5. L, O, C, DC; MH, TU.

280 —[Anr. ed., pourtraicture, Maiesty.] [London], printed, 1648. 12°. ALMACK 12. MADAN 6. L, O, C, ELY; MH, Y.

281 —[Anr. ed.] [London], 1648. 12°. ALMACK 13. MADAN 7. L, O, C, CPL; MH, WF.

282 —[Anr. ed.] [London], 1648. 12°. ALMACK 14. MADAN 7. L, O, C, CPL; Y.

283 —[Anr. ed., Majestie.] [London], 1648. 8°. ALMACK 15. MADAN 21. L, O, C, I; MH, TU, Y.

284 —[Anr. ed., povtraictvre.] [London], 1648. ALMACK 16. MADAN 18. O, WF.

285 —[Anr. ed., pourtraicture.] [London], printed, 1648. 24°. ALMACK 17. MADAN 20. O, C; Y.

286 —[Anr. ed.] [London] printed, 1648. 12°. ALMACK 18. MADAN, 19. L, C, OC.

287 —[Anr. ed.] [London] reprinted in R. M. for James Young, 1648. ALMACK 24. O.

288 —[Anr. ed., pourtracture.] [London], printed, 1648. 12°. ALMACK 25. MADAN 16. O, AN; MH, WF, Y.

289 —[Anr. ed., pourtraicture.] Hage, by Samuell Brown, 1649. 8°. ALMACK 26. MADAN 37. L, O, C, CLC.

290 —[Anr. ed., pourtraicture.] [*London by H. Hills*], 1649. 12°. ALMACK 27. MADAN 17. O, C, OC; MH, Y.

291 —[Anr. ed., pourtraicture, Maiesty.] *Corck, by Peter de Pienne*, 1649. 12°. ALMACK p. iii. L, O, C.

292 —[Anr. ed.] *At Paris*, 1649. 8°. ALMACK 28. MADAN 40. O, C, ON; MH.

293 —[Anr. ed., Maiesty.] [*London*], *printed*, 1649. 8°. ALMACK 29. MADAN 18. O.

294 —"Second" edition. *Hage, by Samuel Broun*, 1649. 12°. ALMACK 30. MADAN 38. O, C, CPL, HH, E; MB.

295 —[Anr. ed., pourtraicture, Majesty.] [*London*], 1649. 12°. ALMACK 31. MADAN 61. L, O, C; MH, NU.

296 —[Anr. ed.] [*London*], *printed*, 1649. 12°. ALMACK 32. MADAN 10. O, C.

297 —[Anr. ed.] [*London*], *printed*, 1649. 12°. ALMACK 33. MADAN 28. O, C; CH, CLC, MH, Y.

298 —[Anr. ed., pourtracture.] [*London*], *printed*, 1649. 12°. ALMACK 34. MADAN 8. L, O.

299 —[Anr. ed., pourtracture.] *Printed at London*, [*by Thos. Newcomb?*], 1649. 12°. ALMACK 35. MADAN 8. L, O, C.

300 —[Anr. ed., pourtraiture, Majesty.] [*London*], 1649. 12°. ALMACK 36. MADAN 30. L, C.

301 —[Anr. ed., pourtracture, Majestie.] [*London*], *re-printed for John Williams*, 1649. 12°. ALMACK 37. MADAN 34. L, O, C.

302 —[Anr. ed.] [*London*], *reprinted for John Williams*, 1649. 12°. ALMACK 38. MADAN 33. L, O, C, OC, OP.

303 —[Anr. ed., Maiestie.] [*London*], *reprinted*, 1649. 12°. ALMACK 39. MADAN 32. L, O, C; CH, MBE.

304 —[Anr. ed., pourtraicture, Maiesty.] *For R. Royston*, 1649. 24°. ALMACK 40. MADAN 63. L, O, C; CH, MH, Y.

305 —[Anr. ed., Majestie.] [*London*], *printed*, 1649. 12°. ALMACK 41. MADAN 23. L, MH.

306 —[Anr. ed., pourtraicture, Majestie.] [*London*], 1649. 8°. ALMACK 42. MADAN 26. L, O, C; CH, RPJ, Y.

307 —[Anr. ed.] [*London*], 1649. 8°. ALMACK 43. MADAN 25. L, O, C, CK, EC; MH, NU, TU, Y.

308 —[Anr. ed.] [*London*], 1649. 8°. ALMACK 44. MADAN 26. L, O, C, CPE; CH, TU, WF, Y.

309 —[Anr. ed.] [*London*], 1649. 8°. ALMACK 46. MADAN 27. O, C, OC, CK; CH, Y.

310 —[Anr. ed., porvtraictvre.] [*London*], 1649. 8°. ALMACK 47. MADAN 62. O, C, GK; MH, PL, TSM.

311 —[Anr. ed., porvtraictvre.] [*London*], 1649. 8°. ALMACK 48. MADAN 62. MH, WF, WWC, Y.

312 Εἰκὼν βασιλικὴ δευτέρα. The pourtraicture. [*London*], *printed*, 1694. 8°. ALMACK p. 82. L, C, OC, CT, EN; CLC, CN, MBP, NU, WF, Y.

313 Εἰκὼν βροτολοιγου: or, the picture of Titus Oates. 1697. 4°.* L, CT, HH, BR; INU, MIU, NLC.

313A —Second edition. *Printed*, 1657. 4°.* CT.

314 Εικων η πιστη or, the faithfull pourtraicture. [*London*], *printed*, 1649. 4°. ALMACK p. 74. LT, CS, EC, EN, DT; CH, MH, NU, TU, WF, Y.

Εἰκὼν τοῦ Θυρίου. [n.p.], 1684. *See* Delaune, Thomas.

Eikonoclastes. 1649. *See* Milton, John.

315 Εἰρηνικον, a poeme. *For Luke Fawne*, 1656. 4°.* LT, O, OC; CLC, MH, NHC, WF.

Ἐιρηνικον: or a peaceable. [n.p.], 1665. *See* Sherwin, William.

Εἰρηικον or a treatise. 1660. *See* Gell, Robert.

Εἰρηνομαχια. The agreement. 1652. *See* Goodwin, John.

Εἰσαγωγη: sive. 1656. *See* Shirley, James.

315A [**Eizat, Sir Edward.**] Apollo mathematicus: or the art. [*London*], 1695. 8°. L, C, LCP, ENC, GU; NMU, WSG, WU.

316 —Melius inquirendum: or, an answer. *Edinburgh, for J. Vallange*, 1699. 8°. ALDIS 3869. EN, FSF; TU.

317 [–] A modest examination of a late pamphlet entituled, Apollo. [*Edinburgh*], *printed*, 1696. 4°.* ALDIS 3584. L, O, E, EN; MM.

Εκοκυβαλαυρον: or. 1652. *See* Urquhart, Sir Thomas.

El, M. List of the names of the members. [n.p., 1648.] *See* Elsynge, Henry.

—Second centurie. [n.p., 1648.] *See* Elsynge; Henry.

Eland, William. Hemerologium astronomicum. 1656. *See* Almanacs.

318 —A tutor to astrologie. *By Joseph Moxon*, [1657]. 12°. LT, O; WF.

318A — —Sixth edition. *For Ioseph Moxon*, 1670. 12°. T.C.I 32. WF.

319 — —Seventh edition. *Printed and sold by J. Moxon*, 1694. Sixes. L, LWL; Y.

320 **Elborough, Robert.** London's calamity. *By M. S. for Dorman Newman*, 1666. 4°.* L, O, LG, LP, DT; CH, MH, NU, WF, Y.

321 **Elborow, Thomas.** An exposition of the Book of Common-Prayer. *For T. Garthwait*, 1663. 8°. C, OB, CS, CT, P; CLC, IU.

322 —An exposition upon the latter part of the Common-Prayer-Book. *By J. W. for Joseph Clark*, 1672. 8°. T.C.I 115. L, O, CS, CT; CLC.

322A —A guide to the humble. *For Henry Brome*, 1675. 8°. T.C.I 146. CLC, UCLA.

323 —A prospect of the primitive Christianity. *In the Savoy, by Tho. Newcomb for William Grantham*, 1668. WCA, 8°. LW, OC, WCA, YM, E; NU, Y.

324 —The reasonableness of our Christian service. *For the author*, 1677. 8°. L; CLC, IU.

324A — —[Anr. ed.] *For Richard Chiswell*, 1678. 8°. T.C.I 288. DT.

325 **Elcock, Ephraim.** Animadversions on a book called A plea. *By John Clowes, for Richard Wodnothe*, 1651. 4°. LT, O, LVF, LCL, DT; LC, Y.

325A **Elder, William.** The modish penman. [*London*], *sold by Chr. Coningsby*, [1691?] T.C.II 360. LV, OP; CN.

325B —Useful examples for youth. [*London? 1700.*] CM.

325C —The young man's companion. [*London, sold by Rob. Vincent & Chr. Coningsby*, [1695.] L.

326 **E[lderfield], C[hristopher].** The civil right of tythes. *By Tho. Newcomb, for John Holden*, 1650. 4°. L, C, LL, E, DT; CH, MH, NU, Y.

327 — —[Anr. ed.]—, 1650. 4°. O, OB; LC, MHL, WF.

328 — —[Anr. ed.] *For John Wright*, 1653. 4°.* L, C, CSSX, SP; MH, NC.

328A —Cuique suum. *For H. Herringman*, 1654. LSC.

329 —Of regeneration. *By Tho. Newcomb*, 1653. 4°. O, CS, LCL, LL, OC; CLC.

330 The elders dreame. [*London*], *printed*, 1647. 4°.* LT; CH, MH.

331 **Eldred, William.** The gvnners glasse. *By T. Forcet for Robert Boydel*, 1646[7]. 4°. LT, O, OC, GU; LCLA.

332 — —[Anr. ed.] —, 1647, 4°. LT.

Eleanor, *Lady*. *See* Douglas, *Lady* Eleanor.

332A **Eleazar, bar Isajah.** A brief compendium. *Printed*, 1652. 4°.* LT, O, CT, OC, EN; NU, WF.

333 —A vindication of the Christian Messiah. *By Gartrude Dawson*, 1653. 4°. L, O, CS, EN, DT; MH, NPT, NU, WF, Y.

334 Electa thargumico-rabbinica. 1658. E.

334A Election at the Merchant-Taylors' school. [*London*, 1682.] brs. L.

334B The election of Pope Alexander VIII. *Richard Baldwin*, 1689. brs. L.

Elegantiæ poeticæ. Oxonii, 1679. *See* Blumerel, Johannes.

334C An elegiack acrostick upon . . . Mr. Joseph Caryl. *For Benj. Hurlock*, [1672.] brs. MH.

Elegiack essay humbly offered. 1699. *See* Browne, M.

Elegiack essay upon the death of Thomas Gouge. 1700. *See* M., J.

335 An elegiack essay upon the decease of the groomporter. *For R. Basset*, 1700. fol.* T.C.III 173. INU, MH.

Elegiack memoriall. 1653. *See* Tw., Th.

Elegiack poem in memory of William Whitmore. 1684. *See* W., F. N.

336 Elegiack verses upon the death of Captain Thomas Harman. *Printed*, 1677. brs. L; MH.

337 An elegiacall commemoration of the pious life . . . of Mr. Josjah Shvte. *Printed*, 1643. 4°.* LT, O; WF, Y.

337A An elegiacal poem humbly suffered to . . . Gilbert. *For D. M.*, 1677. brs. MH.

Elegies. 1660. *See* Lovelace, Dudley Posthumous.

338 Elegies celebrating the happy memory of Sr. Horatio Veere. *By T. Badger, for Christopher Meredith*, 1642. 8°. LT, O; CH, MH.

338A Elegies of old age. *For B. Crayle*, 1688. 8°. CLC.

339 Elegies on the death of that worthy . . . John Hampden. *By Luke Norton, for I. T. October 16*, 1643. 4°.* LT; MH.

340 Elegies on the much lamented death of the honourable and worthy patriot, Francis Pierepont. [*London*], *printed*, 1659. CH.

Elegies on the much lamented death of . . . Mountrath. Dublin, 1661. *See* Jones, John.

341 An elogy against occasion requires upon the Earl of Shaftsbury. colop: *For Ab. Green*, 1681. brs. L, O, MC; CH, MH, NU, TU, WF, Y.

Elegy, an acrostick. 1673. *See* R., S.

Elogie, and epitaph, consecrated. [n.p.], 1649. *See* H., F.

342 An elegie, and epitaph for Mistris Abigail Sherard. [*London*, 1648.] brs. LT.

343 An elegie and epitaph on that glorious saint, . . . King Charles I. *For J. Williams*, 1661. 4°.* LT, CS; CLC, MH, NU, PL, WF.

344 An elegie and epitaph, upon the right honourable the Lord Francis Villars. *Printed at London*, 1648. brs. LT.

345 An elegy and funeral oration upon the death of Richard Lingard. 1671. fol. O.

346 An elegy, consecrated to the inestimable memory of . . . Charles the First. *By R. W. for R. G.*, 1660. brs. LT; MH.

347 An elegy humbly offered to the memory of the reverend father in God Doctor Humphry Henchman. [*London*, 1675.] brs. L; MH.

348 An elegie in commemoration of Madam Ellenor Gwinn. *By D. Mallet*, 1687. brs. O; MH.

349 An elegy in commemoration of Sr Edmund Saunders. *For Langly Curtes* [sic], 1683. brs. L, OP; MH.

350 An elegy in commemoration of the right honourable James Earl of Salisbury. *For Langly Curtis*, 1683. brs. L, O; CH, MH.

351 An elegy in commemoration of the right worshipful Sir William Scroggs. *By J. Grantham*, 1683. brs. L, O; CH, MH.

352 An elegy in commemoration of . . . Talmash. *Edinburgh*, 1694. brs. ALDIS 3368. EN.

352A An elegie in memorie . . . of Sir Henry Mervyn. [*London?* 1646.] brs. L.

Elegy, in memory of that famous, . . . Doctor Oldsworth. [n.p., 1649]. *See* F., W.

353 An elegy, in memory of that reverend divine, Mr. Edmond Calamy. [*n.p.*, 1666.] brs. LS.

353A An elegy occasioned by the death of . . . Samuel Smith. *For J. Read*, 1698. brs. MH.

Elegie offered up. 1646. *See* C., I.

Elegie on . . . Alexander Lord Reath. [*Edinburgh*], 1698. *See* Donaldson, James.

354 Elegie on . . . death, of . . . Captain George Melvil. *Edinburgh, J. Reid*, 1699. brs. ALDIS 3844. ES.

355 An elegy on Captain William Harman. *Printed*, 1678. brs. L; MH.

356 An elegie on Coronel [sic] Blood. *By J. S.*, 1680. brs. L, MC; MH, Y.

Elegy on Her Grace. 1684. *See* Arwaker, Edmund.

Elegy on His Grace. 1695. *See* Tate, Nahum.

356A An elegie on his grace the illustrious Charles Stuart, Duke of Richmond. [*London*], *for Philip Brooksby*, 1673. brs. L.

356B An elegy on his much honoured . . . John Collings. *For Tho. Parkhurst*, 1691. brs. MH.

357 An elegy on James Scot, late Duke of Monmouth. *For C. W. to be sold by Walter Davis*, 1685. brs. O, HH; MH.

357A An elegy on Lodowick Muggleton. [*London*], *for E. O.*, [1698.] brs. MH.

Elegy on Mr. Francis Bampfield. 1684. *See* T., W.

358 An elegy on Mrs. Alicia Lisle. *For J. M. to be sold by Randal Taylor*, [1685]. brs. O, HH; MH.

Elegy on Sir George Jeffereys. 1689. *See* H., N.

359   An elegy on Sir Thomas Armstrong. *For J. S.*, 1684. brs. o; CLC.

360   An elegie on ... Sir Thomas Armstrong. *Edinburgh. by the heir of A. Anderson*, 1684. brs. ALDIS 2451. EN,

Elegy on that faithful and laborious ... Francis Bampfield. 1684. *See* S., J.

361   An elegy on that famous oracle of law, ... Sᵗ Matthew Hale. *For Ben. Harris*, 1677. brs. L, O; MH.

362   An elegy on that famous sea-commander Michael de Ruyter. *For William Whitwood*, 1676. brs. L; MH.

Elegy on that grand example of loyalty. 1673. *See* W., S.

363   An elegy on that great example ... Edvvard Earl of Sandvvich. *For Philip Brooksby*, [1672]. brs. L; MH.

363A An elegie on that great example ... the Countess dowager of Thanet. *For D. M.*, 1676. brs. MH.

364   An elegy on that illustrious and high-born Prince Rupert. *For Langley Curtis*, 1682. brs. L, O; MH, WF, Y.

365   An elegie on that incomparable example ... William Whitmore. *For L. C.*, 1678. brs. L; MH.

366   An elegie on that reverend and learned minister ... Mr. William Jenkins. *By George Larkin*, [1685]. brs. L; MH.

367   The elegy on that reverend presbyter Mr. William Jenkins. *[London], sold by Walter Davis*, 1685. brs. L, O, HH; CH.

368   An elegy on that worthy and famous actor, Mr. Charles Hart. *[London], by Nath. Thompson*, 1683. brs. L, OC; MH.

369   An elegy on the death of Algernon Sidney. *By George Croom*, 1683. brs. L, O; CH, MH.

369A An elegy on the death of Denzil Ld Holles. *[London? 1680]*. brs. L; CN, MH, TU.

Elegy on the death of Dr. Sanderson. 1663. *See* H., J.

370   An elegy on the death of Dr. Thomas Saffold. *For A. Turner*, 1691. brs. L, O; MH.

370A An elegie on the death of ... Gilbert. *For John Smith*, 1677. brs. MH.

371   Elegy on the death of Her Highness Mary. *For Edward Husband*, 1660. brs. L; MH.

Elegy on the death of her late sacred majesty Mary. York, 1695. *See* R., J. L.

Elegy on the death of His Grace. 1690. *See* F., J.

372   An elegy on the death of His Sacred Majesty, King Charles the II. *By J. Millet, for W. Thackeray*, 1685. brs. L; MH, WF, Y.

372A An elegy on the death of James Hoare, Esq. *[London? 1696.]* brs. MH.

373   An elegy on the death of ... John Lake. 1689. brs. L.

Elgy on the death of Mr. James Bristow. Oxford, 1667. *See* Palmer, Edward.

Elegie on the death of ... Mr. James Janeway. 1674. *See* S., J.

374   An elegy on the death of Mr Nalton. *For the author*, 1663. 4°. GK.

375   An elegy on the death of ... Mr. Stephen Charnock. *[n.p.]*, 1680. brs. CHRISTIE-MILLER.

Elgie on the death of Mr. William Dunlop. [n.p., 1700.] *See* Paul, James.

376   An elegy on the death of Mr. William Sherwood. *For A. B.*, 1699. brs. L; CH.

377   An elegie on the death of Mrs Rebecca Palmer. *[n.p., 1667.]* brs. L; MH.

378   An elegy on the death of ... Richard, Earl of Arran. *Dublin*, 1685. brs. L.

Elegie on the death of ... Robert Blake. 1657. *See* C., R.

379   An elegie on the death of Sir Charles Lucas. *[London, 1648.]* brs. LT; MH.

380   An elegy on the death of Sir Edmond Saunders. *For J. Norris*, 1683. brs. L, O; CH, MH, PU.

381   —[Anr. ed.] *[London] for I. Deacon*, [1683]. brs. O; CH, MH, PU.

382   An elegy on the death of Sir Joseph Sheldon. *For T. Haly*, 1681. brs. L, O, LG; MH, Y.

383   An elegy on the death of Sir Nathanael Hern. *[n.p., 1679.]* brs. L, O; MH, Y.

384   An elegy on the death of Sir William Turner. *For George Croom*, [1693]. brs. L; MH.

385   An elegy on the death of that brave sea-commander, Reer-Admiral Garter. *For Richard Baldwin*, 1692. brs. L.

386   An elegy on the death of that eminent minister ... Mr. George Cokayn. *Printed, and are to be sold by Richard Baldwin*, 1691. brs. L.

387   An elegy on the death of that eminent minister ... Nathaniel Partridge. *By J. How, and sold by John Pattman*, 1684. brs. O; MH.

388   An elegie on the death of that late incomparable poet Robert Wild. *[n.p., 1679.]* brs. O; MH, WF.

388A An elegy on the death of that learned and pious farmer Mr. John Gibbon. *[London 1663]*. brs. MH.

389   An elegy on the death of that learned, pious, ... Richard Baxter. *For Richard Baldwin*, 1691. brs. L.

390   An elegy on the death of that learned ... Doctor John Owen. *For Richard Janeway*, 1683. brs. L, O; MH.

391   An elegy on the death of that learned and famous physician Dr. Richard Lower. *For E. Reyner*, 1691. brs. O.

Elegy on the death of that most laborious ... John Norcot. 1676. *See* Keach, Benjamin.

392   An elegie on the death of that most noble and herocik knight, Sir Charles Lucas. *[London, 1648.]* brs. LT; CH, MH.

393   An elegy on the death of that much lamented ... reverend Mr. Ralph Venning. *Printed*, 1674. brs. L; MH.

Elegy on the death of that painted montster. [1677.] *See* W., W.

393A An elegy on the death of that reverend divine ... Mr. John Turnor. *For Richard Baldwin*, 1692. brs. MH.

394 An elegy on the death of that worthy prelate, . . . Dr. John Lake. *For Sam. Keble,* 1689. brs. L, O.

394A An elegy on the death of the author of the characters. [*London,* 1695.] brs. L.

395 An elegy on the death of the Duke of Cambridge. *By T. D. for H. Brome,* 1678. brs. L.

Elegy on the death of the honourable Mr. Robert Boyle. Oxford, 1692. *See* Morgan, Matthew.

396 An elegy on the death of the late honourable George Lord Dartmouth. *For David Sley,* 1691. brs. L.

Elogie on the death of the learned . . . Sir George Mackenzie. [n.p., 1691.] *See* A., R.

396A An elegy on the death of the Lord Chief Justice Hales. [*London*], *for the author,* 1677. brs. MH.

397 An elegy on the death of the Lord Russel. *For P. Brooksby,* 1683. brs. L; CH.

398 An elegy on the death of the most illustrious Lord, the Earl of St. Albans. [*London*], *for I. Deacon,* 1684. brs. L, O; CH, MH.

398A An elegie on the death of the most reverend . . . Gilbert. *For John Smith,* 1677. brs. MH.

398B An elegie on the death of the most serene . . . Henrietta-Maria. *By and for Thomas Ratcliffe and Thomas Daniel,* 1669. brs. MH.

399 An elegy on the death of the old East-India Company. *For the author,* 1699. fol.* L, O, HH; MH.

400 An elegy on the death of the plot. colop: *For E. P.,* 1681. brs. L, O, CT, MC; CH, MH, TU, WF, Y.

Elegy on the death of the Queen. 1695. *See* Darby, Charles.

401 An elegy on the death of the reverend and pious Mr. Thoma Wadsworth. [*London,* 1676.] brs. L; MH.

402 An elegy on the death of the reverend, . . . William Bell. *By T. Moore, & J. Ashburne, for Joseph Roberts,* 1683. brs. L, O; CH, MH.

403 An elegy on the death of the right honourable Heneage Lord Finch. [*London*], *for J. Deacon,* 1682. brs. L, O; CH, MH, Y.

404 An elegy on the death of the right honourable John Earl of Radnor, Viscount Bodmin, and Baron of Truro. *By E. Mallet,* 1685. brs. O, HH; CH.

405 An elegy on the death of the right honble. Richard Butler. *Dublin, printed,* 1685. brs. DIX 215. L.

406 An elegy on the death of the Rt. Hon. Robert Blake. *John Bartlett,* 1657. brs. L.

407 An elegy on the death of the right honourable Spencer, Earle of Northampton. [*Oxford,* 1643.] cap., 4°.* MADAN 1355. LT, HH; MH, Y.

408 An elegy on the death of the right noble Prince Henry Howard. [*London*], *for I. Deacon,* 1684. brs. L, O; CH, MH.

408A An elegy on the death of the right worshipful Sir Thomas Pilkington. [*London,* 1691.] brs. L.

409 An elegy of the death of the truly reverend . . . Stephen Charnock. *By J. A. for Thomas Cockerill,* 1680. brs. O; MH, Y.

410 An elegy on the death of Thomas Beddingfield. *By George Croom,* 1684. brs. L, O; MH, Y.

411 An elegy on the death of Thomas Merry. [n.p., 1682.] brs. L; MH, PU.

412 An elegy on the death of trade. *Printed,* 1698. 4°.* L; CU.

413 An elegy on the death of William late Viscount Stafford. *For William Miller,* 1681. brs. L, O; MH.

414 An elegy on the death of William Lord Russel. [*London*], *by Nath. Thompson,* 1683. brs. L; CH, MH.

Elegy on the deplorable . . . death, of . . . Charles the II. 1685. *See* K., P.

415 An elegie on the Earl of Essex. *For J. Smith,* 1683. brs. L, O, LG, EN; CH, MH.

416 —[Anr. ed.] *Edinburgh, by the heir of A. Anderson,* 1683. brs. ALDIS 2377. EN, A.

417 An elegie on the famous and renowned Lady, . . . Madam Mary Carlton. *For Samuel Speed,* 1673. brs. L.

417A An elegy on the glorious death of Col. John Okey. *Printed,* 1662. brs. MH.

417B An elegy on the lamented death of Miss Edwards. *T. Davis,* [1700?] brs. L.

418 An elegy on the lamented death of the most illustrious princess, Anne. [n.p., 1671.] brs. L; MH.

419 An elegy on the late Duke of Monmouth. *By E. Mallet,* [1685]. brs. O, HH; CH, MH.

420 An elegy on the learned and zealous minister . . . Christopher Fowler. *Printed,* 1677. brs. L, O; MH.

421 An elegy on the Lord Viscount Stafford. [n.p.], *for T. Benskin,* [1680.] brs. O; MH.

422 An elegie on the meekest of men. [*London*], *printed,* 1649. 4°.* LT, O, CT, LVF; CH, CN, LC, MH, Y.

423 An elegie on the miraculously learned, . . . Bishop of Armagh. *By Francis Leach,* 1656. 4°.* LT.

423A An elegy on the modern heroe, Redmon ô Hanlon. [*London?* 1681.] brs. O; CH, MH.

Elegy on the most accomplished Elizabeth Hurne. [n.p.], 1983 [i.e. 1683]. *See* B.

424 An elegie, on the most barbarous, . . . murder . . . Sir Charles Lvcas. *Printed,* 1648. 4°.* LT, O, OC; CH, PL, TU, WF, Y.

424A An elegy on the most execrable murther of the Clun. *Edward Crouch,* 1664, brs. L.

425 An elegy on the most lamented of princes King Charles the Second. *By Elizabeth Mallet,* 1685. brs. L; MH, Y.

Elegy on the most noble James, Earl of Annandale. [n.p., 1659.] *See* S., T.

426 An elegie on the most reverend father in God VVilliam Lord Arch-bishop of Canterbury. [*Oxford, by L. Lichfield*], *printed,* 1644[/5]. 4°.* MADAN 1731. LT, O, CT, YM; CH, MH, TU, WF, Y.

426A An elegy on the much-bewailed death of . . . Mr. Alexander Carmichel. *For B. H.,* 1676. brs. MH.

Elegy on the much lamented death of Ezerell Tonge. 1681. *See* Tonge, Simson.

426B An elegy on the much lamented death of His Grace, the Duke of Beauford. *By J. Wilkins,* 1700. brs. MH.

427 An elegy on the much lamented death of Mr. Samuel Loveday. *For Francis Smith*, 1677. brs. L; MH.

428 An elegy on the much lamented death of that late reverend . . . Dr. William Bates. *Printed, and sold by A. Baldwin*, 1699. brs. L.

428A An elegy on the much lamented death of the reverend . . . Edward Stillingfleet. *Printed and sold by J. Bradford*, 1699. brs. L.

428B An elegy on the much lamented death of the reverend Mr. Joseph Caryl. [London, 1672.] brs. MH.

429 An elegy on the much lamented death of, Thomas Jekyll. [n.p., 1698.] brs. HH.

430 An elegy on the much lamented Sir William Waller. [London], *by N. T.*, 1683. brs. L; CH, MH, WF.

Elegy on the much-to-be-deplored death of . . . Nathaniel Collins. Boston, [Mass.], 1685. *See* Mather, Cotton.

431 An elegie on the never to be forgotten Sir Thomas Armstrong. *For William Bateman*, [1684]. brs. L, O, HH, EN; CH, MH.

432 An elegy on the renowned memory of . . . Edward [Reynolds]. [London, 1676.] brs. L; MH.

433 An elegy on the reverend and learned divine, D^r. Lazarus Seaman. [London, 1675.] brs. L; MH.

434 An elegy on the right honourable Anthony Earl of Shaftsbury. *Printed*, 1683. brs. L, O, HH; CLC, MH.

435 —[Anr. ed.] *For Langley Curtis*, 1683. brs. L, MH.

436 —[same title, parody.] —, 1683. brs. L, O, HH.

436A An elegy on the right honourable Sir John Chapman. *For Randall Taylor*, 1688/9. brs. MH.

437 An elegy on the right honourable William Earl of Pembrook. *By E. Mallet*, 1683. brs. L; MH.

438 An elegy on the right reverend father in God, Humphrey [Henchman]. *For J. Coniers*, 1675. brs. L; MH.

439 An elegie on the right worshipful Sir Edmund-Bury Godfrey. *For Ben. Harris*, 1678. brs. L; MH.

440 An elegy on the timely death of John Warner. [London, 1648.] brs. LT.

441 An elegy on the truly honoured and greatly beloved Sir William Jones. *For Langley Curtis*, 1682. brs. L, O; MH, PU.

442 An elegy on the truly honourable, . . . Lady, Countesse of Devonshire. [London, 1670?] brs. L, O; MH.

442A An elegy on the unfortunate . . . deaths of . . . Schombers. *For T. Clark*. [1690.] brs. MH.

442B An elegie on the untimely and much lamented death of Mistress Ann Gray. 1656. brs. L.

443 Elegie on the untimely death of . . . Francis, Lord Villiers. [London, 1648.] brs. LT, O; MH.

Elegy on the usurper O. C. 1681. *See* Dryden, John.

443A An elegy on the (very little) lamented death of old Father Peter's. *Printed*, 1699. brs. MH.

443B An elegy on the young man's poker. [London? 1690.] brs. L.

Elegie on . . . Umphrey Milne. [Edinburgh], 1695. *See* Donaldson, James.

443C Elegy on White-hall. *J. Harris*, 1698. brs. LC; MH.

Elegie on . . . William Earl of Crawford. [Edinburgh], 1698. *See* Donaldson, James.

444 An elegy, or a sign for the sufferings of King Charles. [1649?] brs. L.

444A An elegy or, copy of verses. *By Tho. James for Benjamin Harris*, 1678. brs. LW; MH.

445 An elegy or, final farewel to Sir John Fenwick. *Printed and sold by J. Bradford*, 1697. brs. L.

445A An elegy sacred to the immortall memory of . . . Henry Ireton. *By J. C. and T. W.*, 1652. brs. MH.

446 An elegie sacred to the immortall memory of . . . John Pym. [London], *for Lawrence Chapman*, 1643. brs. LT; Y.

447 An elegy, sacred to the memory of our most Gracious Soveraigne Lord King Charles. [London, 1649.] brs. LT; WF.

Elegie sacred to the memory of Sir Edmund-bury Godfrey. 1678. *See* Care, Henry.

448 An elegy to commemorate, and lament, the death of . . . S^r. John Micklevvaite. *For William Miller*, 1682. brs. L, O; MH.

448A An elegy, to the heroick and eternal memory of . . . Edward Henry. *Printed*, 1694. brs. MH.

449 An elegie to the indeared memory of . . . Lazarus Seaman. *For D. M.*, 1675. brs. L; MH.

450 An elegie to the memory of Richard Earl of Tyrconnell. [n.p., 1691.] brs. EN.

451 An elegy to the memory of the right houorable [sic] Thomas Earl of Ossory. [n.p., 1680.] brs. L, O; CH, MH, WCL.

451A An elegy to the memory of . . . William Juxon. [London? 1663.] brs. MH.

452 An elegie upon Dr Tho. Fuller. *Printed*, 1661. brs. O; MH.

453 An elegie upon Edward Fitz-Harris. *For Thomas Snowden*, 1681. brs. L, O; MH, PU, Y.

454 An elegy upon George Gyfford. 1686. brs. O.

Elegy upon . . . Henry Gorge. 1674. *See* C., J.

455 An elegy upon His late Majesty (of blessed memory) King Charles the Second. *By J. Millet*, 1684/5. brs. L; MH.

456 An elegy upon Marsh's. [London], *printed*, 1675. brs. L; MH.

457 An elegy upon Mr. Hobbes. [London], *printed*, 1680. brs. L; MH.

458 An elegie upon Mr. Thomas Hobbes. [London], *printed*, 1679. brs. L, OP; CH, MH.

458A An elegie upon several eminent divines lately deceased. *For D. M.*, 1678. brs. MH.

458B An elegie upon that great minister of state Anthony Earl of Shaftsbury. colop: *For Iohn Dunton*, 1683. brs. O; CH, MH.

459 An elogy upon that never to be forgotten matron, old Maddam Gwinn. [n.p., 1679.] brs. L, O, OP; MH.

460 An elegy upon that perfidious bankrupt . . . M^r. J. H[unter]. *By A. B. for C. D.*, 1694. brs. L.

461 An elegy upon that renowned hero and cavalier the Lord Capel. *By H. Hills jun. for W. Davis,* 1683. brs. L; CH, MH, PU.

462 An elegie upon the death, and in commemoration of . . . John, Lord Wilmot. *Printed,* 1680. brs. L, O, CK; MH.

Elegie, upon the death of . . . Anne, Countesse of Shrewsbury. 1657. *See* Crouch, John.

Elegy upon the death of Dr. Annesley. 1697. *See* Defoe, Daniel.

Elegie vpon the death of . . . Earle of Essex. 1646. *See* Mercer, William.

Elegy upon the death of Eliz. Hoyle. York, [1644.] *See* F., J.

463 An elegy upon the death of George Lord Jefferies. *By G. Croom,* 1689. brs. O; MH.

464 An elegie upon the death of King Charles. [*London,* 1649?] brs. CH.

465 An elegy upon the death of Major John Ashton. *By G. C. for W. Rayner,* 1691. brs. MH.

466 An elegy, upon the death of Monsieur St. Ruth. *For W. Rayner,* 1691. brs. HH.

466A An elegy upon the death of Mr. Francis Holcroft. *By Will. Marshall,* 1691/2. brs. MH.

466B An elegy upon the death of Mr. Mason. [*London*], *for A. Milbourn,* 1692. brs. MH.

467 An elegy upon the death of Mr. William Lilly. *For Obadiah Blagrave,* 1681. brs. L; MH.

467A An elegy upon the death of Mrs. A. Behn. *By E. J.,* 1689. brs. MH.

Elegy upon the death of my Lord Francis Villiers. [n.p., 1648.] *See* Marvell, Andrew.

468 An elegie upon the death of my pretty infant-cousin, Mris. Jane Gabry. *Printed,* 1672. brs. L.

An elegie upon the death of Our Dread Soveraign Lord King Charls. [*London,* 1649.] *See* Gregory, Francis.

469 An elegy upon the death of Pope Innocent the XI. *Printed* 1689. brs. EN; MH.

469A An elegy upon the death of Sᵣ. William Davenant. [*London,* 1668.] brs. O; MH.

469B An elegy upon the death of that able . . . Samuel Sowthen. [*London?* 1665.] brs. MH.

469C An elegy upon the death of that faithful servant . . . John Wells. *For B. H.,* 1676. brs. MH.

Elegie upon the death of that famous . . . James Renwick. 1688. *See* Shields, Alexander.

469D An elegy upon the death of that most eminent . . . Jeremy Ives. *For B. H.,* Oct. 25, 1675. brs. MH.

470 An elegy upon the death of that renowned Prince Rupert. [*London*], *for I. Deacon,* 1682. brs. L; MH.

471 [Elegy?] upon the death of that reverend and aged man of God, Mr. Samuel Arnold. [*Boston, Mass.,* 1693.] brs. LC.

472 An elegy upon the death of that worthy gentleman Collonel Edward Cook. [n.p., 1684.] brs. L; CH, MH.

473 An elegie upon the death of the mirrovr of magnanamity, . . . Robert Lord Brooke. *For H. O.,* 1642. brs. LT, HH.

473A An elegy upon the death of the most eminent disputant Mr. Jeremy Ives. [*London*] *for B. W.,* Oct. 20, 1675. brs. MH.

Elegy upon the death of the most excellent poet Mr. Iohn Cleaveland. [n.p., 1658.] *See* Vaux, Francis.

Elegie upon the death of the most illustrivs . . . Gustavus Adolphvs. [n.p., 1642.] *See* R., I.

474 An elegy upon the death of the most illustrious princess Heneretta. Dutchess of Orleance. [*London*], *for John Clark,* [1670.] brs. L; MH.

474A —[Anr. ed.] *By E. Crowel for T. Passenger,* 1670. brs. MH.

Elegie upon the death of the most incomparable Mʳˢ Katharine Phillips. [1664]. *See* C., J.

474B An elegy upon the death of the much lamented . . . Doctor Thomson. *Printed,* 1677. brs. MH.

474C An elegy upon the death of the reverend Dr. Sandcroft. *By William Downing* [1699]. brs. MH.

Elegie vpon the death of the renowned, Sir Iohn Sutlin. [n.p.], 1642. *See* Norris, William.

475 An elligie upon the death of the right honourable Robert Devereux, late Earle of Essex. *By Iohn Hammond,* [1646]. brs. LT; MH.

475A An elegy upon the death of the right honourable Sir John Shorter. *By D. Mallet,* 1688. brs. MH.

Elegie upon the death of the thrice noble generall, Richard Dean. 1653. *See* R., J.

476 An elegie upon the death of Thomas Earle of Strafford. [n.p.], 1641. CHRISTIE-MILLER.

477 An elegy upon the death of two eminent ministers. *For B. H.* 1676. brs. L; MH.

478 —[Anr. ed.] *For E. N.* 1676. brs. L.

479 An elegy upon the decease of the most incomparable pious lady, the Princess Elizabeth. [*London*], *printed* 1650[1]. 4°.* LT; CLC.

480 An elegie upon the Earl of Angus. [*Edinburgh?* 1692.] brs. E.

Elegie upon the Earle of Essex's funerall. [n p., 1646.] *See* W., J.

Elegie upon the honourable Colonel Thomas Rainsbrough. [n.p., 1648.] *See* T., J.

480A An elegie upon the most eminently famous . . . Thomas late Earl of Cleveland. *By S. C.,* 1667. brs. MH.

481 An egley [sic] upon the most execrable murther of Mᵣ Clun. *By Edward Crowch,* [1664.] brs. L; MH.

482 An elegy upon the most illustrious and high born Prince Rupert. *For Tho. Benskin,* 1682. brs. L, O; CH, MH, WF.

Elegie upon the most incomparable K. Charles the I. [n.p., 1649]. *See* King, Henry, *bp.*

483 An elegy upon the most ingenious Mr. Henry Care. *By George Larkin,* [1688]. brs. O; MH.

Elegie upon the most lamented death of . . . Essex. [n.p., 1646.] *See* G., C.

484 An elegie upon the most pious and eminent, Doctor John Hewitt. [*London,* 1658.] brs. LT, O; MH.

484A An elegy upon the most pious and incomparable Princesse Mary, Queene. *John Whitlock*, 1694. brs. O.

485 An elegy upon the much lamented death of . . . Henry Wilkinson. [*London*, 1675.] brs. L; MH.

486 An elegie vpon the much lamented death of . . . John Pym. [*London*, 1643.] brs. LT, BR; Y.

487 An elegie upon the much lamented death of . . . Lord Brooke. [*London*], *by Robert Austin and Andrew Coe*, 1643. brs. LT, O.

Elegie upon the never satisfactorily deplored death of . . . Iohn Cleaveland. 1658. *See Pecke, Thomas.*

487A An elegy upon the Philadelphian society. [*London*, 1698?] brs. MB.

488 An elegy upon the renowned hero and cavalier, the Lord Capel. *By H. Hills, jun. for W. Davis*, 1683. br. L.

489 An elegy, upon the right honourable Richard Earle of Arran. *Dublin, by Andrew Crook and Samuel Helsham, to be sold by Samuel Helsham and by William Norman*, [1685]. brs. DIX 215. L.

490 An elegie upon the truly worthy, and ever-to-be-remembred . . . Captain Will. Bedlow. *For Langley Curtis*, 1680. brs. L, O, HH; MH.

491 An elegy upon the unfortunate death of Captain William Bedloe. *For John Gay*, 1680. brs. L, O, OP; MH.

Elegy vpon the vnhappy losse of the noble Earle of Essex. 1646. *See Twyss, Thomas.*

492 An eligie [sic] upon the universally-lamented death of . . . Prince, Henry Duke of Gloucester. *For Thomas Parkhurst*, [1660]. brs. LT, HH.

493 An elegie, with an accrostick . . . James Janeway. *For Thomas Cockeril*, 1674. brs. L; MH.

Elementa arithmeticæ. *Oxoniæ*, 1698. *See Wells, Edward.*

Elementa opticæ. 1651. *See Powell, Thomas.*

494 The elements of vvater-drawing. *By Tho. Leach, for Henry Brome*, [1660]. 4°. L, O, C.

495 The elements or principles of geometrie. *By J. P. for Samuel Crouch, Richard Mount, and Awnsham Churchill*, 1684. 8°. T.C.II 84. O, C, DT.

495A —[Anr. ed.] *By A. Gibbon and J. Playford, for John Sellers*, [1684]. 8°. WF.

Ελεοθριαμβος: being. 1698. *See G., T.*

Ελεοθριαμβος, or. 1677. *See Lee, Samuel.*

495B The elephants speech to the citzens. *Printed*, 1675. 4°.* MH.

Eleutheria, or. 1698. *See Mather, Cotton.*

Eleutherius, Philodemius, *pseud.*

496 The 11 members iustification. [*n.p.*, 1660.] brs. HH.

496A Eleven queries humbly tendered . . . East-India silks. [*London?* 1697.] brs. L, C; MH.

497 XI. qveries propounded and answered. *Printed at Oxford, and reprinted at London*, 1642[/3]. 4°.* MADAN 1237. LT, O, CT, DT; CH, CLC, NU, WF, Y.

498 Eleventh collection of papers relating to the present juncture. *Printed, to be sold by Richard Janeway*, 1689. 4°.* L, C, CM, BR, DT; CH, CN, NU, PL, WF, Y.

498A **Elsore, Walter.** Apret of the state of the case. [*London*, 1649]. brs. LT.

498B —To the supreme authority . . . the humble petition of. [*London*, 1659.] brs. O.

499 Eliana, a new romance. *By T. R. for Peter Dring*, 1661. fol. L, O, CT; CN, IU, MH, Y.

499A **Elias, John.** A true and strange relation of the travels . . . of four . . . Quakers. *For L. W.*, 1674. 4°.* LF; PH.

Elijah the Tishbite's supplication. [*n.p.*], 1650. *See Douglas, Lady Eleanor.*

500 Elijahs fiery-chariot. *For Thomas Rooks*, 1659. 8°. LT.

501 **Eliot, Sir John.** Sir Iohn Eliot, his grave and learned speech. *For V. V.*, 1641. 4°.* LT, O, C, EN, DT; CH, NU, TU, WF, Y.

502 Entry cancelled.

503 **Eliot, John.** A brief answer to a small book. *Boston, by John Foster*, 1679. 8°.* EVANS 266. NN.

504 —A brief narrative. *For John Allen*, 1671. 4°.* L, C, LW; CH, CN, LC, RPJ, WCL, Y.

505 —The Christian commonvvealth. *For Livewell Chapman*, [1659]. 4°. LT, O; CH, LC, MB, NN, RPJ, Y.

506 —Christiane oonoowae sampoowaonk. A Christian. [*Cambridge, Mass., by Samuel Green*, 166–?] brs. EVANS 58. E.

507 — —[Anr. ed.] [—, 1670.] brs. EVANS 147. MCL.

508 —Communion of churches. *Cambridge* [*Mass.*]: *by Marmaduke Johnson*, 1665. 8°.* EVANS 101. O; CH, NN.

509 —The dying speeches of several Indians. [*Cambridge, Mass., by Samuel Green*, 1683?] *EVANS 340. NN.

510 [–] A further accompt of the progresse of the gospel. *By M. Simmons for the corporation of New-England*, 1659. 4°. L, O, LW; CH, LC, MH, NN, RPJ.

511 — —[Anr. ed.] *By John Macock*, 1660. 4°. L, O, LW; CN, LC, RPJ, Y.

—The glorious progress of the gospel. 1649. *See Winslow, Edward.*

512 —The harmony of the gospels. *Boston* [*Mass.*]; *by John Foster*, 1678. 4°. EVANS 246. L; LC, MB, MH, NU, RPJ.

513 —Indian dialogues. *Printed at Cambridge* [*Mass.*], 1671. 8°. EVANS 161. O; NN.

514 —The Indian grammar begun. *Cambridge* [*Mass.*]: *by Marmaduke Johnson*, 1666. 4°. EVANS 106. L, O, CT, E, ES; MBA, MH, MWA, NN, RPJ.

515 —The Indian primer. *Cambridge* [*Mass.*], *printed*, 1669. EVANS 138. 8°. E; MWA.

516 — —[Anr. ed.] [*Cambridge, Mass.: by Samuel Green*, 1687?] EVANS 427. 8°. MHS.

517 —A late and further manifestation. *By M. S.*, 1655. 4°.* L, O, LW, OC; CH, CN, LC, MH, RPJ, WCL, Y.

518 —The logick primer. [*Cambridge, Mass.*], *by M. J.*, 1672. 12°. EVANS 166. L.

519 [–] New Englands first fruits. *By R. O. and G. D. for Henry Overton*, 1643. 4°.* LT, O, OC, CM; CH, CN, LC, MH, NN, Y.

520 —Tears of repentance. *By Peter Cole*, 1653. 4°. LT, C, LW, E, GH; CH, LC, NN, RPJ, WCL, Y.

521 — —Second edition. —, 1653. 4°. RPJ.

522 — —Third edition. —, 1653. 4°. LT; CN, PL, RPJ.

523 **Eliot, John, M.D.** Mr. John Eliot . . . his last speech . . . March 9, 1694. colop: *Edinburgh, by George Mosman*, 1694. cap., 4°.* ALDIS 3369. L, E, EN; WF.

524 **Eliot, John,** *poet.* Choyce poems. *For Henry Brome*, 1661. 8°. CLC, MH.

Elise or innocencie guilty. 1655. *See* Camus, Jean Pierre, *bp.*

Elisha succeeding Elijah. 1646. *See* B., N.

524A [–] Poems consisting of epistles & epigrams. *For Henry Brome*, 1658. 8°. LT; CH, CN.

524B [–] Poems or epigrams, satyrs. *For Henry Brome*, 1658. 8°. L.

525 Elixir magnum stomachicum or, the great cordial. [*London*, 1690?] brs. L.

526 Eliza's babes: or the virgins offering. *By M. S. for Laurence Blaiklock*, 1652. 8°. LT; IU.

526A **Elizabeth,** *queen of Bohemia.* The declaration of . . . concerning her coming. *For H. Blundell,* Dec. 14, 1642. 4°.* NU.

527 — —The Queen of Bohemia, her desires and propositions. *For I. White, Septembdr* 24, 1642. 4°.* LT; WF.

528 **Elizabeth, Queen.** The golden speech of. *By Tho. Milbourn,* [1659]. brs. LT, O.

528A — —[Anr. ed.] *Dublin,* [1698.] 4°.* DN.

529 —Injunctions given by the Queenes Majestie. [*London*], *printed,* 1641. LIL, OC, CS, P, EN; CH, CN, MB, MH, WF.

530 —The last speech and thanks of. *Printed,* 1671. fol.* L, O, C, HH, MR; CH, NU, PL, Y.

531 —A most excellent and remarkabl speech. *For Humphrey Richardson, Ianuary* 28, 1643. 4°.* LT, DT; CH, WF, Y.

532 —Queen Elizabeth's opinion concerning the transubstantiation. *For F. E.,* 1688. brs. L, O, OC, OP, HH.

533 —A speech made by. colop: *By D. Mallet,* 1688. brs. L, O, C; WF.

534 —Qveene Elizabeths speech to her last Parliament. [*London*, 1642.] 4°.* LT, C, WCA.

535 — —[Anr. ed.] *For Edward Husband, March* 16. 1647[8]. 4°.* LT, DT; CH, Y.

536 **Elkes, Richard.** Approved medicines. *For Robert Ibbitson, to be sold by Tho: Vere,* 1651. 8°.* LT.

537 **Ellesby, James.** The doctrine of passive obedience. *For William Crooke,* 1685. 4°.* T.C.II 112. L, O, C, YM, CT; CH, CN, IU, NGT, WF.

538 —The great danger. *For W. Crook,* 1693. 4°. T.C.II 422. L, CT, LW, WCA; CH, WF.

539-40 Entries cancelled.

Ellesmere, Thomas Egerton. *See* Egerton, Thomas.

541 **E[llington], F[rancis].** Christian information concerning these last times. *Printed,* 1664. 4°.* L, O, C, BBN; CH, MH, NC, PH, WF, Y.

542 —A few words to all who professe. [*London*], *printed,* 1665. 4°. L, O, BBN; CH, MH, PH, PSC, Y.

543 **Elliot, Adam.** A modest vindication of Titus Oates. *For the author, to be sold by Joseph Hindmarsh.* 1682. fol. T.C.I 509. L, O, CT, MR, EN; CH, CN, NU, WF, Y.

543A —A vindication of Dr. Titus Oates. *By T. Snowden, for the author,* 1683. 4°.* CH.

544 **Elliot, George.** The atheist answered. *By E. C. for Thomas Sare,* [1675?]. brs. L.

545 —An English duel or three to three. [*London*], *printed,* 1666. brs. LS.

546 —Great Brittain's beauty. *For E. Horton,* 1671. brs. L.

547 —London's lamentation: or, godly sorrow. [*London,* 1665.] brs. L.

548 —Londons looking-glass. *Printed,* 1665. brs. L.

548A **Elliott, John.** The grace of God asserted. *For Thos. Northcott,* 1695. 8°. L, BBN; PHS.

548B —The saving grace of God owned. *For Thomas Northcott,* 1693. 8°. L.

549 —To the right honourable the Parliament . . . The humble petition of. [*London,* 1650?] brs. L.

550 **Ellis, Clement.** A catechism wherein the learner. *For Sam. Richards in Nottingham,* 1674. 8°. C.

550A — —[Anr. ed.] *For Th. Guy,* 1674. 8°. T.C.I 185. Y.

551 —The Christian hearer's first lesson. *For W. Rogers,* 1694. 4°. T.C.II 517. L, O, CJ, CT, DT; NGT, PL, TU, WF, Y.

552 —Christianity in short. *Printed and sold by Henry Hills,* [1682]. 8°.* T.C.I 493. L; Y.

552A — —[Anr. ed.] *For Samuel Richards, in Nottingham,* 1682. 12°. NGT.

552B — —[Anr. ed.] 1693. 8°. LW; WF.

553 — —[Anr. ed.] 1699. 8°. O, LCL, RPL; NC.

554 —The communicant's guide. *For John Baker,* 1685. 12°. T.C.II 124. NU, WF.

555 —The folly of atheism. *Printed, and are to be sold by William Rogers, and Thomas Elis in Mansfield,* 1692. 8°. T.C.II 390. L, O, C, LL, CE; CLC, MH, NU.

556 —The Gentile sinner. *Oxford, by Henry Hall for Edward & John Forrest,* 1660. 8°. MADAN 2492. L, O, C, OCC; CU, MH, TU, WF, Y.

556A —[Anr. ed.] *Oxford, by A. and L. Lichfield, for Edward and John Forrest,* 1661. 8°. MADAN 2492n. L; Y.

557 — —Second edition. *Oxford, by A. & L. Lichfield, for E. & J. Forrest,* 1661. 8°. MADAN 2554. L, O, OM, M; CN, NN, Y.

558 — —Third edition. —, 1664. 8°. MADAN 2659. L, O, C, CT, NPL; LC, NPT, NU, Y.

559 — —Fourth edition. *Oxford, by Henry Hall for Edward and John Forrest,* 1668. 8°. MADAN 2798. L, O, C, CE, CK; CH, CU, TU, VC, Y.

560 — —Fifth edition. *Oxford, by Henry Hall for Tho. Gilbert,* 1672. 8°. MADAN 2926. L, O; CLC, NN, PL, Y.

561 — —Sixth edition. *Oxford, by H. Hall for R. Davis & E. Forrest,* 1679. 12°. MADAN 3209. L, O, CPE, OB, M; CLC, MBA, NC, WF, Y.

562 — —Seventh edition. *Oxford, for Ric. Davis, to be sold by L. Meredith,* 1690. 12°. T.C.II 325. L, O.

563 [–] Justifying faith. *For William Crook*, 1679. 12°. T.C.I 326. O, CS; CH.

564 [–] The lambs of Christ. *Printed, to be sold by W. Rogers; and Tho. Elis, in Mansfield*, 1692. 12°. T.C.II 390. L, O, LW.

565 [–] A letter to a friend, reflecting on some passages. *For William Rogers*, 1687. 4°.* T.C.II 285. L, O, C, E, DT; CH, MH, TU, WF, Y.

566 —The necessity of serious consideration. *Printed and sold by William Rogers, and Thomas Elis in Mansfield*, 1691. 8°. T.C.II 376. O, CT, OC; MWA, PL, Y.

566A — —Second edition. —, 1699. 8°. T.C.III 165. NU.

567 [–] Piæ juventuti sacrum. An elegie. [*Oxford, by H. Hall*], *printed*, 1658. 4°.* MADAN 2382. O; IU.

568 [–] The Protestant resolved. *For William Rogers*, 1688. 4°. T.C.II 285. L, O, C, E, DT; CLC, MH, NU, TU, Y.

569 [–] —Second edition. —, 1688. 4°. L, O, LIL, CT, E; MH, NU, WF, Y.

570 [–] The reflecter's defence. *For William Rogers*, 1688. 4°. T.C.II 285. L, O, C, MC, DT; CH, MH, NU, TU, WF, Y.

571 —Religion & loyalty inseperable. *For William Rogers; and Clement Elis, in Mansfield*, 1691. 4°.* T.C.II 329. L, CSSX, CT; MH, NGT, WF, Y.

571A —Rest for the heavy-laden. *By J. Heptinstall for L. Meredith*, 1686. 12°. T.C.II 156. CT; Y.

572 —The right foundation of quietness. *For John Baker*, 1684. 8°. T.C.II 91. O, SP; CLC, NU, WF, Y.

573 —A sermon preached on the 29th of May 1661. *Oxford, by Henery Hall, for Edward and John Forrest*, 1661. 4°. MADAN 2555. L, O, C, DT; MM, NPT, NU, WF.

573A —The summe of Christianity. *For Will Rogers*, 1696. 12°. T.C.II 584. OC, CT.

574 — —[Anr. ed.] —, 1699. 8°.* T.C.III 133. LW.

575 [–] To the King's most excellent Majesty: on his happie and miraculous return. colop: *By James Cottrel, for James Cottrel, for Humphrey Robinson*, 1660. fol* LT.

576 [–] The vanity of scoffing. *For R. Royston*, 1674. 4°.* T.C.I 180. L, O, C, CT, HH; CH, CN, NU, WF, Y.

577 **Ellis, Edward.** A sudden and cloudy messenger. *For the author*, 1649[50]. 4°.* LT, DT.

578 **Ellis, Humphrey.** Pseudo christus, or a true. *For L. Fawn*, 1649. 4°. CM; MH.

579 — —[Anr. ed.] *By John Macock, for Luke Fawn*, 1650. 4°. LT, O, CT, LWL, DT; CH, CU, MH, NU, WF, Y.

580 —Two sermons. *By R. L. for Luke Fawne*, 1647. 4°. O, C, LCL; MH, MM.

581 **Ellis, John.** Articulorum xxxix . . . Defensio. Second edition. *Cantabrigiæ, ex officina Johann. Hayes*. 1694. *Impensis Hen. Dickinson, et prostant venales apud S. Smith, Lond.* 12°. T.C.II 493. L, O, C, CT, DT; CH, NGT, PL, WF, Y.

582 —Bellum in Idumæos. *Excudebat Felix Kingston, & prostat apud Eliseum Morgan*, 1641. 8°.* O, CT, E, DT.

583 —Clavis fidei. *Oxonii, excudebat Henricus Hall, impensis Guil: Webb*, 1642. 8°. MADAN 1284. O, OC; Y.

584 — —[Anr. ed.] —, 1643. 8°. MADAN 1571. L, O, CM, CS, CT.

585 — —[Anr. ed.] *Cambridge, by John Field*, 1668. 8°. O, C, CS, LCL, ELY.

586 — —[Anr. ed.] *Cambridge, J. Creed*, 1669. 8°. O; BN.

587 —A defense of the thirty nine articles. *For H. Bonwicke, T. Goodwin, M. Wotton, S. Manship, and B. Tooke*, 1700. 12°. T.C.III 169. L, O, LIC, OB; CH, LC, NU, WF, Y.

588 —Defensio fidei; seu responsio. *Typis Roberti White, & sumptibus Johannis Symmes*. 1660. 12°. LT; CLC.

588A — —Letter reflecting on some passages. 1687. 4°. CPE.

589 —The pastor and the clerks. *For Elisha Wallis*, 1659. 8°. LT, O, OC.

590 —S. Austin imitated. *By W. Godbid, to be sold by Timothy Garthwait*, 1662. 4°. L, O, C, LCL, YM; CLC, CU, NU, WF, Y.

591 — —A sermon preached . . . Jan. 4, 1698/9. *For John Richards in Nottingham; and sold by J. Robinson*, 1699. 8°. T.C.III 106. EC.

592 —The sole path to a sound peace. *By John Raworth, for George Latham, and John Rothwell*, 1643. 4°. LT, O, C, EN, DT; CH, MH, NU, TU, WF, Y.

593 —Vindiciæ Catholicæ. *For Henry Overton*, 1647. 4°. LT, O, CT, EN, DT; LC, MH, NU, WF, Y.

594 **Ellis, Philip.** The fifth sermon. *By Henry Hills*, 1686. 4°.* L, O, MC, EN, DT; CH, NU, WF.

595 —The first sermon. *By Henry Hills*, 1686. 4°.* L, O, CT, EN, DT; CH, CN, MH, NU, WF, Y.

596 —The fourth sermon. *By Henry Hills*. 1686. 4°.* L, O, CS, EN, DT; CH, MH, NU, WF, Y.

597 —Second sermon preach'd . . . November 1, 1685. *By Henry Hills*, 1686. 4°.* L, O, C, EN, DT; CH, MH, NU, WF, Y.

598 —A sermon preach'd . . . November the 13, 1686. *By H. Hills*, 1686. 4°.* L, O, MC, EN, DT; BN, CLC, MH, TU.

599 —A sermon preach'd . . . fifth of December, 1686. *By Henry Hills*, 1686. 4°.* L, O, EN, DT; HR, MH, NU.

600 —A sermon preach'd before the king and queen. *By Henry Hills*, 1687. 4°.* O, EN, DT; TU.

601 —A sermon preached befor the Queen Dowager, . . . St. Stephen's day. *By Henry Hills*, 1687. 4°.* EN, DT; MH, Y.

602 —Sixth sermon. *By Henry Hills*, 1686. 4°.* L, O, CT, EN, DT; CH, MH, NU, TU, WF, Y.

603 —The third sermon. *By Henry Hills*, 1686. 4°.* L, O, CT, DT, EN; CH, CN, MH, NU, WF, Y.

604 —Two sermons. *By Henry Hills*, 1686. 4°.* L, O, C, EN, DT; CH, CN, MH, NU, TU, WF, Y.

605 **[Ellis, Thomas.]** An exact and full relation of the last fight. *For Ben. Allen, July 5.* 1644. 4°.* LT, O; CH, CLC, WF, Y.

606 [–] The traytors unvailed. [*London*], *printed*, 1661. 4°.* LT; MIU, WF.

607 **Ellis, Tobias.** The English school. Fifth edition. *By John Darby, for the author*, 1680. 4°. L, WF.

608 —The kingdom of God opened. [*London*], *by T. N. for H. Mortlock*, 1678. 8°. T.C.I 300. L, O, CE, YM; WF, Y.

609 — —[Anr. ed.] *Oxford, by Leon. Lichfield, to be sold by Francis Oxlad and Robert Gibs*, 1683. 8°. LCL; NPT, WF.

609A —The poors English spelling book. *Oxford, by Leon. Lichfield, for the author*, 1684. 4°. NC, NN.

609B —The royal catholick English school. Fifth edition. *By J. D. to be sold by Tho. Hawkins,* 1685. 8°. LSC.

609C —The true English school. *Oxford, by Leon. Lichfield for the author,* 1684. 4°. PRF.

609D ——[Anr. ed.] *For the author, and are to be sold by W. Freeman,* 1691. 4°. T.C.II 340. L.

610 **Ellison, Nathanael.** The magistrates obligation. *By W. B. for Richard Randell, in Newcastle upon Tyne; and sold by Luke Meredith,* 1700. 4°.* T.C.III 153. L, C, OCC, BAMB; CLC, MU, WF, Y.

610A **Ellway, Thomas.** A two part song. [*London,* 1700.] brs. L; WF.

611 **Ellwood, Thomas.** An account from Wickham. [*London*], printed, 1689. 4°. L, O.

611A ——An account of tythes. [*London?* 1700.] cap., 8°.* L, O; MH, PH, PSC, PU.

612 —An alarm to the priests. colop: *For Robert Wilson,* 1660. 4°. L, O, C, BBN; CH, NU, PH, WF, Y.

613 —An ansvver to George Keith's narrative. *Printed and sold by T. Sowle,* 1696. 8°. L, O, C, LG; CH, CN, NU, RPJ, WF, Y.

614 —Thomas Ellwood's answer to so much of Leonard Key's late printed sheet. [*n.p.,* 1693.] brs. L, OP, BBN.

615 —An antidote against the infection of William Roger's book. *For Benjamin Clark,* 1682. 4°. C, OC; IE, NU, PH, PSC, Y.

616 —A caution to constables. *For William Skeate,* 1683. 4°.* L, O, C, BBN; CH, PH, PSC, WF, Y.

617 —Deceit discovered. 1693. brs. L, BBN; PH.

618 —A discourse concerning riots. *For Thomas Howkins,* 1683. 4°.* L, O, LCL, LW; MH, PH, PSC, WF, Y.

618A ——[Anr. ed.] *For Benjamin Clark,* 1683. 4°.* CH, PH, PSC.

619 —An epistle to Friedns [sic]. [*n.p.,* 1686.] cap., 4°.* L; MH, PH, Y.

620 —An epistle to Friends, briefly. *Printed (and sold) by T. Sowle,* 1694. 8°. L; CH, CN, LC, PH, RPJ.

620A —A fair examination of a foul paper. *By T. Sowle,* 1693. 4°. BBN; MBA, PH.

621 —Forgery no Christianity. [*London*], printed, 1674. 8°. L, OC; BN, PH.

622 —The foundation of tythes shaken. [*London*], printed, 1678. 8°. L, LCL,-LUG; BN, CH, LC, NU, PH, WF, Y.

622A —A fresh pursuit. [*London?* 1674]. brs. PSC.

623 —A further discovery. *By T. Sowle,* 1694. 8°. BBN; CH, CN, LC, PH, RPJ, WF.

624 —A reply to an ansvver, lately published to a book. [*London*], *printed, and sold by T. Sowle,* 1691. 4°. L, O, BBN; MH, MU, NU, PSC, WF, Y.

625 —Rogero mastix. A rod for William Rogers. *Printed,* 1685. 4°.* L, OC, BBN; PH, PSC, Y.

626 —A seasonable disswasive from persecution. *For William Skeate,* 1683. 4°.* L, C, BBN; CH, PH, PSC, WF, Y.

627 —Several kinds. *For Charles Brome,* 1698. 8°. CT.

628 [–] A sober reply, on behalf of the people called Quakers. *Printed, and sold by T. Sowle,* 1699. 4°.* L, O, LF, BAMB; PH, PHS, PSC, WF, Y.

628A [–] —Second edition. —, 1700. 4°.* PH, PSC.

629 —Trvth defended. *Printed and sold by T. Sowle,* 1695. 8°. L, BBN; CN, NU, PH, PSC, RPJ.

630 —Truth prevailing. [*London*], *printed,* 1676. 8°. L, C; CH, IE, PH, PSC, WF.

631 [**Ellyson, John.**] Hereticks, sectaries, and schismaticks. *Printed,* 1647. 4°.* L, O, HH, YM, E; MIU, NU, WF.

632 [**Ellyson, Thomas.**] The shepherds letters. *Printed,* 1646. 4°.* LT; LC, MIU.

633 —The shepheard of Easeington his letters. [*London,* 1647.] 4°. ENC.

633A —To his highness, Oliver . . . the petition of. [*London,* 1655.] cap., 4°.* CT; Y.

634 **Ellythorp, Sebastian.** A testimony. *Printed, and sold by T. Sowle,* 1692. 4°.* L, BBN; CLC, MH, PH, PSC.

634A **Elmy.** At the Blew-ball in Sir William Pritchards rents. [*London?* 1700.] brs. L.

Elogium heroinum: or. 1651. *See* Gerbier, Charles.

635 The eloquent master of languages. *Hamburg, Thomas van Wiering,* 1693. 8°. L, O; MH.

Elphinstone, John. *See also* Balmerino, John Eliphinstone, 2nd baron.

636 **Elphinstone, John.** Disputatio juridica. *Edinburgi, ex Officina typographicâ hæredum Andreæ Anderson,* 1699. 4°.* ALDIS 3845. EN, ES.

637 Ελπις και ειρηνη. *By J. L. for H. Bonwicke,* 1692. 8°. O; MU.

638 **Elshotz, Johann Sigismund.** The curious distillatory. *By J. D. for Robert Boulter,* 1677. 8°. T.C.I 273. L, O, C, LCP, GU; CLC, WF, WSG, WU, JF.

639 [**Elsing, Christopher**]. The testimony of severall eminent commanders. *For R.L.,* 1648. 4°.* OC, HH; CH.

639A **Elslyot, Thomas.** The lambe still pursuing the wolfe. [*London*], 1651. 4°.* MH.

640 —The lamb taking of the woolf. *Printed,* 1652. 4°.* LT; CH, CLC, MH, WF, Y.

640A —The martial horse, or power. [*London*], *imprinted,* 1652. 4°.* MH, Y.

641 —The true mariner. *Imprinted at London,* 1652. 4°.* LT.

642 [**Elson, Mary**] A tender and Christian testimony to young people. [*London,* 1685.] 4°.* L, LF; MH, PH, PSC, Y.

642A **Elston, John.** A sermon preached . . . Septemb. 14. *For R. Clavell,* 1680. 4°.* L.

642B ——[Anr. ed.] *By S. Roycroft for Charles Yeo, in Exeter,* 1681. 4°.* EC; LC, MM, Y.

643 **E[lsum], J[ohn].** Epigrams upon the paintings of the most eminent masters. *For Dan. Brown, and G. Strahan.* 1700. 8°. L, O, LG, OC; CH, CU, MB, TU, WF, Y.

644 **Elsynge, Henry.** The ancient and present manner. Second edition. *For Samuel Speed,* 1663. 8°. L, LW, CCA, CT, SC; BN, CH, MH, MHL, Y.

645 —The ancient method and manner of holding Parliaments. *By S. G. for Daniel Pakeman,* 1660. 8°. L, C, LI, OC; CH, CN, MHL, NCL, WF.

645A ——Third edition. *For S. S. and to be sold by Tho. Dring,* 1675. 12°. T.C.I 206. L, C, LVF, OM, LGI; CN, LC, MH, PBM, PL.

646   ——Fourth edition. *For Tho. Dring*, 1679. 12°. L, O, CK, EC; CH, MBP, MHL, NU, WF, Y.

647   —A list of the names of the members of the House of Commons. [*London*, 1648.] brs. LT, O; CH, PL.

648   ——[Anr. ed.] [*London*], printed, 1648. 4°.* LT, O, CM, HH; CH, CLC, MIU, WF.

649   —The method of passing bills. *By F.L. for Matt. Gilliflower*, 1685. 12°.* L, O, OC, DT; BN, CH, CN, LC.

650   [–] A second centurie (of such of the aldermen, . . .). [*London*, 1648.] brs. LT, O, C, LG, OC; WF.

650A **Elton, Edward.** Gods holy minde. *By C. M. sold by John Walker*, 1648. 4°. L, LSC, CS; CLC, NU.

651   —The great mystery of godlinesse. *By J.L. for Christopher Meredith*, 1653. fol. L, LCL; CLC, MH, PL.

651A —A plaine and easie exposition upon the Lords Prayer. *For Christopher Meredith*, 1647. 8°. CLC, NU.

652   —Three excellent and pious treatises. *By J.L. for Christopher Meredith*. 1653. fol. L, LCL, CS, OW; CLC, MH.

653 **Elton, Richard.** The compleat body of the art military. *By Robert Leybourn*, 1650. fol. L, O; CH, MBA, Y.

654   ——Second edition. *By R. & W. Leybourn*, 1659. fol. L, O, C, LUS, CT; CLC, MH, MU, NB, Y.

655   ——[Anr. ed.] *For W.L. to be sold by Henry Brome, and Thomas Basset*. 1668. fol. T.C.I 3. L, O, LG; CN, MBA, PL, WF, Y.

     Elvira. 1667. *See* Bristol, George Digby, *2nd earl.*

656 **Elwood, Thomas.** The case of. [*London*, 1659.] brs. LT.

656A **Elys, Edmund.** Ad Samuelem Parkerum. *Typis A. G. & J.P. pro R. Clavell*, 1680. 8°. T.C.I 395. LW.

657   —Admonition to Doctor Burges. *By Matthew Inman, for James Magnes*, 1661. 4°.* O.

658   —An alphabet of elegiack groans, . . . John Fortescue. *For Tho. Heath*, 1656. 4°.* LT; CU.

659   —Amor Dei lux animæ. *Excusum sumptibus R.C.* 1670. 4°.* O, CS; CH.

660   —Anglia rediviva. [*Oxford, by Henry Hall*], printed, 1660. 4°.* MADAN 2493. L, O; CLC, MH.

661   ——[Anr. ed.] *Oxon., exc. H.Hall*, 1662. fol.* MADAN 2590. O.

662   —Animadversions upon a late discourse concerning divinity. [*London*, 1695.] cap., 4°.* O, CT.

663   [–] Animadversions upon some passages in a book. *Sold by Richard Baldwin*, 1690. 8°.* T.C.II 332. O, CT; Y.

663A [–] An answer to six arguments. *For W. Marshall, and I. Marshall*, 1698. 8°. T.C.III 73. CT, BAMB.

664   —The bishops downefall or the prelats snare! [*London*], *for G. Thompson*, 1642. 4°.* LT; CH, MH, WF, Y.

665   [–] A clergy-man of the Church of England. *By Randal Taylor*, 1688. brs. L, O.

666   [–] Dei incarnati vindiciæ. *For S.Smith*, 1693. 4°. T.C.II 426. O, CS, P; CN, IU.

667   —Dia poemata: poetick feet. *By J.G. for Philip Briggs*, 1655. 8°. LT; MH, WF, Y.

667A ——[Anr. ed.] [*London*], printed, 1655. 4°. MH.

668   —Divine poems. With a short description. *Oxon, by H. Hall for R. Blagrave*, 1658. 8°. MADAN 2383. LT, O; CLC, MH, NPT.

669   ——[Anr. ed.] *By T.Lock for the use of the author*, 1659. 4°. CH.

670   [–] Dominus est Deus. *Oxford*, 1690. 8°. O.

671   [–] An earnest call to the people of England. [*London*], printed, 1692. 8°.* O.

672   —Ecclesiæ Anglicanæ Presbyteri cogitata ulteriora. *Typis Th. Newcomb*. 1679. 8°.* O.

673   [–] ʹΕπιγραμματα. *For James Collins*, 1668. 4°.* L, CS.

674   —An epistle to the truly religious and loyal gentry. *Printed*, 1687. 4°.* O, C, LIL; CN.

674A [–] An exclamation against an apology. 1670. 4°. L.

675   [–] An exclamation to all those that love the Lord Jesus. *For Robert Clavel*, 1670. 4°.* L, CS.

675A —George Keith his saying. That the light within. colop: *Printed and sold by T. Sowle*, 1697. 4°.* IE, PHS, PSC, RPJ.

675B —Ioannis Miltoni sententiae potestati adversantis refutatio. *Typis J. M. Impemsis R. Wilkin*, 1699. 4°.* CH.

676   —A letter from. [*London*, 1693.] cap., 4°.* O, BR; PSC.

677   —A letter to the author of a book, entituled, An answer to W.P.'s key. *For Thomas Northcott*, 1695. 4°. O; IE, PH.

678   [–] A letter to the author of a book, entitvled, Considerations. [*London*, 1694.] cap., 4°.* O.

678A —A letter to the honourable Sir Robert Howard. *For Richard Wilkin*, 1696. 4°.* CH.

679   [–] The letter torn in pieces. *By T.J. to be sold by Nich. Hooper*, 1692. 4°.* O; CN, WF.

680   —Letters to Mr. Hvghes. *For R. Royston*, 1660. 4°.* NU.

681   —Miscellanea. [*Oxford, by H. Hall*], 1658. 12°. MADAN 2384. LT.

682   ——[Anr. ed.] *Oxoniæ, excudebat Hen. Hall, impensis Tho. Robinson*, 1662. 4°. MADAN 2591. L, O; CLC, MH, NU.

682A [–] Observations on several books. *Printed for and sold by Will. Marshall*, 1700. 8°. T.C.III 195. Y.

683   —Omnes qui audiunt evangelium. [*Oxford*], 1662. 4°.* MADAN 2592. O.

684   ——[Anr. ed.] *Ex officina S. Streater, & prostant venales apud R. Clavel*, 1677. 8°.* T.C.I 291. L, O, CS, P; CLC.

684A —The opinion of Mr. Perkins. *Oxford, by A.L.*, 1660. 4°.* MADAN 2494. Y.

685   —Polemica Christiana: or, an earnest contending. [*London*], printed, 1696. 4°.* O.

686   —The quiet soule. *Oxford, by H.H. for T. Robinson*, 1659. 4°.* MADAN 2439. L, O; Y.

687   —Reflections upon a pamphlet. [*London*, 1695.] cap., 4°.* L, O; PH.

687A —Reflections upon a passage. [*London?* 1698.] cap., 4°.* IE.

688   [–] Reflections upon several passages. [*London*], printed, 1692. 8°.* O.

688A [–]—[Anr. ed.] [*London*, 1698]. cap., 4°.* Y.

689   —Reflections upon some passages. colop: *Printed and sold by T. Sowle*, 1698. cap., 4°.* L, O; IE, PH, PL, Y.

690   ——[Anr. ed.] [*London*, 1699.] 4°.* L, O; PH, PHS, PSC, Y.

691   ——[Anr. ed.] *Printed and sold by T. Sowle*, 1700. 4°.* O; IE, PH, PSC.

692   —Reflections upon some scandalous passages. [*London*], printed, 1693. 4°.* CT; Y.

692A —A refutation of some of the false conceits. *For and sold by Will. Marshall & John Marshall*, 1697. 8°.* T.C.III 4. L, LW.

693 —The second epistle to the truly religious. *For the author*, 1687. 4°.* L, O, LIL, OC; MH, NGT, NU, Y.

694 —A second letter. *For Thomas Northcott*, 1697. 4°. O.

695 —Some reflections upon Francis Bugg's book. [*London*, 1699.] cap., 4°.* L; PH, PSC.

695A —Summum bonum. *Prostant apud Henricum Faithorne & Johannem Kersey*, 1681. 8°. T.C.I 444. CLC, Y.

696 —Three letters. *For T. Northcott*, 1694. 4°. O; PSC.

696A —To all persons that have any sense. [*London*, 1698.] cap., 4°.* PH, PSC.

697 —Edmund Elys his vindication of himself. *Printed and sold by T. Sowle*, 1697. 4°. L; IE, PHS.

698 —A vindication of the doctrine concerning the light within. *Printed and sold by T. Sowle*, 1699. 4°. L; CH, MH, PH, PSC, RPJ.

699 [–] A vindication of the honour of King Charles I. [*London*], printed, 1691. 8°.* O.

700 —Vindiciæ quorundam Roberti Barclaii noematum. [*London*], *for T. N.*, 1693. 4°.* L, O; PH.

Elysii campi, a paradice. 1671. *See* Wyne, Robert.

An embassage from the Kings. 1654. *See* Blake, William.

701 Embassage from the Prince of Orange. [*n.p.*], 1642. 4°. LVF.

Embassies from . . . Charles II. 1669. *See* M., G.

Emblem of a virtuous woman. [n.p., 1650.] *See* F., E.

Emblem of ingratitude. 1672. *See* Beaumont.

701A An emblem of mortalitie. [*London*], *by A. M. for P. Brooksby* [1687?]. brs. MH.

702 The emblem of our King. *Edinburgh, by John Reid*, 1700. 4°.* L, EN; RPB, Y.

703 An embleme of the times. *By R.A.*, 1647. brs. LT.

Emblems. 1658. *See* Hall, John.

703A Emblemeta ametorre, *Conte, chez l'amoureux*. [1700?]. 8°. L; CH, CN, LC, MIU, Y.

704 Emblems divine, moral, natural. and historical. *By J. C. for Will: Miller and Fra: Haley*, 1673. 8°. T.C.I 127. CH, MH.

704A Emblems for the King and Queen. *For H. Newman*, 1695. brs. T.C.II 560. MH.

705 **Emeris.** A panegyrick upon William III. *London, reprinted Edinburgh, Watson*, 1669. 4°. ALDIS 3846. EN, AU.

706 **Emerson, John.** The vvorld prospect. *By E.P. for Nicholas Gamage*, 1646. 8°. LT.

707 **Emes, Thomas.** The atheist turn'd deist. *Printed*, 1698. 8°. T.C.III 52. L, O, CT, LW, GU; CH, NPT, NU, PHS, Y.

708 —A dialogue between alkali and acid. *For Rich. Cumberland & T. Speed*, 1698. 8°. T.C.III 94. L, O, CT, LWL, GH; NAM, NN, WSG.

709 ——Second edition. *For Thomas Speed*, 1699. 8°. T.C.III 130. LCS, CCA, GU; WF, HC.

710 —A letter to a gentleman concerning alkali and acid. *For Tho. Speed*, 1700. 8°. T.C.III 185. L, C, LCS, LG, GH; NAM.

711 Emilia. *For the author*, 1672. 8°. L, O, LVD; CH, CU, IU, MB, V.

Emiliane, Gabriel d', pseud. *See* Gavin, Antoine.

712 [**Emitie, Thomas.**] A new remonstrance from Ireland. *For George Tomlinson*, 1642. 4°.* LT, C, EC.

713 **Emlyn, Thomas.** A sermon preached . . . October the 4th, 1698. *Dublin, by Andrew Crook, for Math. Gunne, and Josiah Shaw*, 1698. 4°.* DIX 299. L, C, DI, DN, DT.

713A —A sermon preached before the Societies. *Printed Dublin, reprinted London, sold by W. Marshall*, [1700.] 8°.* T.C.III 196. CM, CT; WF.

Emmanuel manifested. 1655. *See* C., A.

713B **Emmerton, John.** The case of. [*London*, 1680.] cap., fol.* L; MH.

714 **Emmot, George.** A northern blast. *For R. Lambert, in York*, 1655. 4°.* LT; Y.

714A —The spiritual Quaker. [*London*, 1655?] cap., 4°.* PH.

Emperor. *See also* Leopold I, *of Germany*.

715–6 Entries cancelled.

717 The emperor, King, noble, and beggar. *By R.I. for Samuel Rand*, 1650. brs. MH.

Empress of Morocco. 1674. *See* Duffet, Thomas.

718 το 'εν 'αρχη: or, an exercitation upon a momentous question in divinity. *Printed*, 1675. 4°. L, LW, BAMB; MH, MIU, NU, Y.

719 The enchanted lover. [*London*], *for P. Brooksby*, [1672]. brs. L, CM, HH; MH.

719A The inchanted tower. 1662. 4°. CN.

720 Enchiridion legum: A discourse. *By Elizabeth Flesher, John Streater, and Henry Twyford, assigns of Richard Atkins & Edw. Atkins. To be sold by G.S., H.T., J.P., W.P., J.B., T.B., R.P., C.W., T.D., W.J., C.H., J.L., J.A., J.W., & J.P.*, 1673. 8°. T.C.I 159. L, O, C, OC, CP; CH, MBA, MHL, WF, Y.

721 —[Anr. ed.] —, 1683. 8°. L, C, LL.

Enchiridion metaphysicum. 1671. *See* More, Henry.

Enchiridion medicinæ. 1662. *See* B., E.

Enchiridion of faith. Douay, 1655. *See* Davenport, Christopher.

Enchiridion of fortification. [1645.] *See* Stone, Nicholas.

Echyridion physicæ 1651. *See* Espagne, Jean, d'.

722 Enchiridium epigrammatum Latino-Anglicum. *By R: Hodgkinsonne (for the author)*, 1654. 8°. LT, O; CH, LC, MH, RPJ, Y.

Encomiastick or. 1658. *See* Tooke, George.

722A An encomium on the Indian and African Company's undertaking. [*London? 1700.*] brs. HH.

723 An encomium on the reverend and valiant Mr. George Walker. colop: *For J. Green*, 1689. brs. O; MH, Y.

Encomium, or congratulatory poem. 1674. *See* G., T.

724 An encouragement for the charitable. [*London*, 1700.] brs. LUG.

725 Encouragements to builders and planters of Little Yarmouth. *For Samuel Speed*, 1668. brs. L, O.

725A An encyclical epistle, sent to their brethren. [*London*, 1660.] 4°.* L; CN, TU.

End of one wonder. 1651. *See* Brague, Thomas.

End to controversie. Doway, 1654. *See Bayly, Thomas.*

725B An end to the controversy. *For Richard Welington,* 1697. 8°. T.C.III 12. WF.

726 An endeavour after further union. [*London*], printed, 1692. 4°.* L, O, C, E.

727 An endevovr after the reconcilement of that long debated . . . difference. *By M. S. for John Bellamy,* 1648. 4°. LT, O, LSC, CM; CH, CU, NU, WF, Y.

Endeavor for peace. 1680. *See Hughes, William.*

Endeavour to rectify. 1671. *See Truman, Joseph.*

728 **Enderbie, Percie.** Cambria triumphans. *For Andrew Crooke,* 1661. fol. L, O, C, MR, DT; CH, CN, MBP, MH, WF, Y.

729 Endlesse queries. *Printed,* 1659. 4°.* LT, DT; CH, CLC, MH, WF.

730 Entry cancelled.

Enemies fall. Bristol, 1696. *See D., T.*

Enerratio methodica. [n.p.], 1678. *See Starkey, George.*

731 Enfield Common. [*London*], *for Charles Bates,* [1695?]. brs. L, HH.

732 The ingagement and declaration of the Grand-Iury, freeholders, and other inhabitants of . . . Essex. [*London*], printed 1648. 4°.* LT, O, CJ; CH, MH, MIU, Y.

733 Entry cancelled.

734 The ingagement and resolvtion of the principall gentlemen of the county of Salop. [*Oxford, by L. Lichfield*], 1642. brs. STEELE 2320. MADAN 1103. L, O; CLC.

735 An engagement of the Lords and Commons that went to the army. [*London*], printed, 1647. 4°.* LT, HH; CH, MH, WF, Y.

736 The engagement or declaration of the officers. [*London*], printed May 19, 1648. 4°.* LT, O, HH; CH, MIU.

Engagement vindicated. 1650. *See B., T.*

Engelland wie stehts. 1688. *See Burnet, Gilbert.*

737 [**Engel, Johann.**] Εσοπτρον Αστρολογικου. Astrologicall opticks. *For John Allen, and R. Moon,* [1655]. 8°. LT, LWL; CLC, WF.

738 Den Engleschen bokkum. *Gedrukt by James Warner,* 1688. 4°.* L, DT; MIU.

739 **England, John.** Man's sinfulness. *By J. Heptinstall, for John Sprint, and sold by John Miller in Sherborne, and Thomas Wall in Bristol,* 1700. 8°. T.C.III 185. LCL, BAMB; CH, MB, MH, NU, WF.

ENGLAND: Army Council

740 —Orders established the 14th . . . January. *For Edward Husband,* Jan. 26, 1646 [7]. 4°.* O, CT, CDC, HH; CH, CLC, LC, WF.

741 —A particular charge or impeachment. *For George Whittington,* 1647. 4°.* LT, O, C, LG, AN; CH, CN, MIU, NU, WF, Y.

741A ——[Anr. ed.] *Printed,* 1647. 4°.* LG, OC, YM, AN, DT.

ENGLAND: Commissioners for Ecclesiastical Causes

742 —The reports of . . . 4 November 1686. *In the Savoy, T. Newcomb,* 1686. brs. STEELE 3838. L, LPO, HH.

ENGLAND: Committee of Safety

743 —By the Committee of Safety. . . . A proclamation declaring the continuance of justices. *By Henry Hills and John Field,* [1659]. brs. STEELE 3133. LT, O, LUG, LS; MH.

744 —A proclamation forasmuch as this Committee. *By Henry Hills and John Field.* [1659]. brs. LT, LUG; MH.

745 —A proclamation inhibiting all meetings. *By Henry Hills and John Field,* 1659. brs. STEELE 3134. LT, O, LG, LS, HH; MH.

746 —A proclamation prohibiting the contrivance. *By Henry Hills and John Field,* [1659]. brs. STEELE 3137. L, O, LG, LS, LUG; MH.

747 —A proclamation requiring the departure. *By Henry Hills and John Field,* 1659. brs. STEELE 3140. LT, O, LG, LS; MH.

748 —A proclamation touching the summoning of a Parliament. *By Henry Hills and John Field,* 1659. brs. STEELE 3139. LT, O, C, LG, LS; CH, MH.

749-54 Entries cancelled.

ENGLAND: Council of State

755 —An additional instruction vnto Josias Berners. *For Giles Calvert, Thomas Brewster, and by and for Henry Hills,* 1653. brs. STEELE 3003. LT, O, LG.

756 —By His Excellency the Lord General and the Council of State. Whereas information is given. *For Giles Calvert, Thomas Brewster, and for Henry Hills,* 1653. brs. LT, O, LG; Y.

757 —Saturday April 22, 1654. By the Council at White-Hall. Whereas. *By Will du-Gard and Hen. Hills,* 1654. brs. LT, O, LG; CH, NU.

758 —By the . . . . A proclamation . . . the Council of State being informed. *By Abel Roper and Tho. Collins,* [1660.] brs. LT, O, LL; MH, Y.

759 —A proclamation. The Council of State being intrusted. [*London*], *by Abel Roper, and Tho: Collins,* [1660]. brs. LT, O, LG; MH, Y.

760 —A proclamation. The Council of State having received. *By Abel Roper and Tho. Collins,* [1660]. brs. LT, LG; MH.

761 —A proclamation. Whereas by an act of the last Parliament. [*London*], *by Abel Roper, and Tho: Collins,* [1660]. brs. LT, C, LG; MH, Y.

762 —A proclamation. Whereas Colonel John Lambert. *By Abel Roper and Tho. Collins,* [1660]. brs. LT, O, LG; MH.

763 —A proclamation. Whereas several officers reduced. *By Abel Roper and Thomas Collins,* [1660]. brs. LT, O, LG; MH.

764 —A proclamation. Whereas the Council of State hath received. *By Abel Roper and Tho. Collins,* [1660]. brs. LT, LG; MH.

765 —A proclamation. Whereas the Council of State is given. *By Abel Roper and Tho. Collins,* [1660]. brs. LT; MH, Y.

766 —A proclamation. Whereas the Council of State is informed. *By Abel Roper and Thomas Collins,* [1660]. brs. LT, O, LG, OP; MH, Y.

767 —A proclamation. Whereas the Parliament . . . dissolved, and the care. [London], *by Abel Roper, and Tho: Collins,* [1660]. brs. LT, O, C, LG; MH, Y.

768 —A proclamation. Whereas the Parliament . . . dissolved, and the enemies. [London], *by Abel Roper, and Thomas Collins,* [1660]. brs. LT, O, C, LG.

769 —appointed by authority of Parliament. Whereas for the encouragement of sea-men. *By Henry Hills for him, Giles Calvert, and Thomas Brewster,* 1653. brs. LT, O.

770 Entry cancelled.

771 —The Council of State taking notice. *By Henry Hills,* [1653]. brs. STEELE 3019. LT, O; NU, WF.

772 —By vertue of instructions received from the . . . Councell of State. [London, 1650.] brs. LT.

773 —The Councel having read the petition . . . 30 March 1653. [London, 1653.] brs. STEELE 2990. LT.

774 —The Council of State taking notice . . . 10 December 1653. *By Henry Hills,* [1653]. brs. STEELE 3019. LT, O, LG, HH; MH.

775 —A declaration from the General and Council of State, . . . 11 June 1653. *For Giles Calvert, Henry Hills, & Thomas Brewster,* 1653. brs. STEELE 2996. LT, O, LG; CH, NU, Y.

775A —13 Feb. 1655[6]. Forasmuch as for many years. 1655[6]. brs. STEELE 3067. OP.

776 —Forasmuch as this Court did apprehend . . . 27 July 1648. *By Richard Cotes, London,* 1648. brs. STEELE 2783. LT, HH.

777 —An instrvction unto Josias Bervers. *For Giles Calvert, Henry Hills, and Thomas Brewster,* 1653. brs. STEELE 2998. LT, O, LG.

778 —Instructions to be observed by the several iustices. *For Edward Husband,* 1649. brs. STEELE 2884. LT, O, LG, LUG.

779 — —[Anr. ed.] [London, 1649.] brs. STEELE 2885. O, LUG; WF.

779A —An order and determination of. *Calvert,* 1653. brs. STEELE 3000. LG.

780 —The Parliament having lately . . . 12 November 1653. *By Henry Hills,* 1653. brs. STEELE 3014. LT, OQ, LG, HH; MH.

781 —A proclamation . . . Whitehall: 17 March 1659[60]. *By Abel Roper & Thomas Collins,* [1660]. brs. STEELE 3166. LT, O, LS, LUG, HH.

782 —A proclamation. . . . Whitehal: 17 March 1659[60]. [London], —, [1660]. brs. STEELE 3168. L, O, C, LS, LUG; MH.

783 — —[Anr. ed.] —, [1660]. fol.* STEELE 3170. L, O, LS, LUG; HH, MH.

783A —A proclamation—24 March 1659 [60]. —, [1660]. fol.* STEELE 3174. L, O, LS.

784 —A proclamation . . . 28 March 1660. —, [1660]. brs. STEELE 3175. LT, O, LS, LUG, OP.

785 — —[Anr. ed.] —, [1660]. brs. STEELE 3176. LT, O, LS.

786 —A proclamation . . . 11 April 1660. —, [1660]. brs. STEELE 3178. LT, LS.

787 —A proclamation . . . 13 April 1660. —, [1660]. brs. STEELE 3179. LT, O, LPR, LS; MH.

788 —A proclamation . . . 13 Aprill 1660. —, [1660]. fol.* STEELE 3180. LT, LS; WF.

789 —A proclamation . . . 21 April 1660. —, [1660]. brs. STEELE 3182. LT, CT, LS, HH; Y.

790 — —[Anr. ed.] —, [1660]. brs. STEELE 3183. LT, LS.

791 —That Doctor Homes have the sole . . . 29 November 1653. [London, 1653.] brs. STEELE 3015. LT.

792 —That the Commissioners for removing . . . 16 June 1653. *For Giles Calvert, Henry Hills, & Edward Brewster,* 1653. brs. STEELE 2999. LT, LG, HH.

793 —To the Honourable the knights, citizens and burgesses, in Parliament assembled, —the humble petition of the members of the Common Council. colop: *By Thomas Braddyll and Robert Everingham,* 1690. brs. E; CH, RPJ, Y.

794 —Whereas for the encouragement of sea-men. *By Henry Hills, for Henry Hills, Giles Calvert and Edward Brewster,* 1653. brs. STEELE 3011. LT, O, LG, OQ, HH.

795 —Whereas the Council hath been . . . 18 May 1653. [London, 1653.] brs. STEELE 2995. L, LPR.

795A — —Whereas the late Parliament dissolved. *Dublin, by William Bladen,* 1653. brs. STEELE 2 p525. PL.

ENGLAND: General Council of Officers

796 —The agreement of the General Council of Officers. *By Henry Hills,* 1659. brs. STEELE 3141. LT, O.

ENGLAND: King in Council

796A —At the court at Kensington. [London, 1700.] cap., fol.* Y.

797 —At the Court at Whitehall, for the preventing tumultuous . . . 7 April 1680. *By John Bill,* 1680. brs. STEELE 3711. L, O, C, LG, HH, DT; CH, Y.

798 —At the court. For the preventing tumultuous. *By the assigns of John Bill, and by Henry Hills & Thomas Newcomb,* 1682. brs. STEELE 3734. L, O, C, LG, DT; CH, MH.

799 —At the court. For the preventing tumultuous . . . 6 November 1685. *By the assigns of John Bill,* 1685. brs. STEELE 3824. L, O, LG, MC, HH; CH, Y.

800 —At the Court. His Majesty being desirous that . . . 26 March 1684. *By the assigns of John Bill, and by Henry Hills and Thomas Newcomb,* 1683. brs. STEELE 3758. L, O, C, LG, LS; CH.

801 —His Majesty being informed that there . . . 24 July 1668. [London], *J. Flesher,* [1668]. brs. STEELE 3516. L, LPC, CCA.

802 —His Majesty being informed, that . . . 13 October 1680. *By John Bill,* 1680. brs. STEELE 3719. L, LPC, HH.

803 —At the court at Whitehall, Dec the nineteenth. His Majesty being willing, by . . . 19 December 1679. *By John Bill, and by Henry Hills, and Thomas Newcomb,* 1679. brs. L, O, C, LG, DT; CH, MH, Y.

804 —His Majesty, by and with the . . . 22 March 1664[5]. *By John Bill and Christopher Barker,* 1664[5]. brs. STEELE 3414. L, OQ, LPR, LS, HH.

805 —At the Court at Whitehall, . . . His Majesty by and with . . . 10 May, 1672. [London, 1672.] brs. CH.

806   —At the Court at White-hall, . . . His Majesty having
      been informed . . . 13 July 1682. *For C. Read*, 1682. brs.
      STEELE 3733. L, LG, MC, HH, DT; CH.

807   —His Majesty having taken notice . . . 11 September
      1667. *In the Savoy, by the assigns of John Bill and Christo-
      pher Barker*, 1667. brs. STEELE 3504. L, OQ, C, LG, LPR; CH.

808   —At the Court at Whitehall, . . . His Majesty minding to
      secure all . . . 19 December 1684. *By the assigns of John
      Bill, and by Henry Hills, and Thomas Newcomb*, 1684.
      brs. STEELE 3763. L, O, C, LG, MC; CH, MH.

809   —At the Court at Whitehall . . . His Majesty was this day
      pleased . . . 3 February 1674/5. *By the assigns of John Bill
      and Christopher Barker*, 1674/5. cap., fol.* STEELE 3608.
      L, O, C, MC, DT; CH, MH, Y.

810   ——[Anr. ed.] *Dublin, B. Tooke*, 1674[5]. brs. STEELE 2
      p. 855. DK, DPR.

811   —At the Court at Whitehall, . . . His Majesty was this day
      pleased . . . 2 November 1678. *By John Bill, Christopher
      Barker, Thomas Newcomb, and Henry Hills*, 1678. brs.
      STEELE 3661. L, O, C, LG, HH; CH, MH.

812   —The humble petition of divers of . . . 11 February
      1684[5]. [*London*, 1684/5.] brs. STEELE 3782. HH.

813   —At the Court at Whitehall, . . . It is ordered by His
      Majesty in . . . 15 May 1672. [*London*], *by Andrew Clark*,
      1672. cap., fol.* STEELE 3568. L, LG, LS, OC, HH; CH, MH.

814   —It is this day ordered by His . . . 30 November 1660.
      [*London*, 1660.] brs. STEELE 3269. C; MH, Y.

815   —It is this day ordered . . . that His Majesties . . . 4 May
      1688. *By John Bill, Henry Hills, & Thomas Newcomb*,
      1688. brs. STEELE 3865. L.

816   —It was this day ordered . . . 2 March 1665/6. *By John
      Bill and Christopher Barker*, 1665/6. brs. STEELE 3456. L,
      OP, OQ, DT.

817   —An order made by the Lord Mayor . . . 8 May 1667.
      [*London*], *J. Flesher* [1667]. brs. STEELE 3492. L, LG, HH.

818   —Right trusty and welbeloved . . . 22 August 1662.
      J Flesher, [1662]. brs. STEELE 3367. L, LS.

819   —Rules and orders to be observed by all justices. *By
      John Bill and Christopher Barker*, 1666. fol.* STEELE 3461.
      L, O, LPR, LS, DT.

820   —At the Court at Whitehall, . . . there having been lately
      presented. *By John Bill, Christopher Barker, Thomas
      Newcomb, and Henry Hills*, 1678/9. cap., fol.* STEELE
      3677. L, O, C, LG, DT; CH, MH, WF.

821   —There having been lately presented . . . 17 January
      1678/9. *Dublin, B. Took*, 1678[9]. brs. STEELE 2p. 900.
      CT, ORM; CH, MH.

822   —Upon reading this day at the board . . . 26 March 1672.
      *In the Savoy, by the assigns of John Bill and Christopher
      Barker*, 1672. brs. STEELE 3560. L.

823   —Upon reading this day at the . . . 24 November 1676.
      By the Assigns of John Bill and Christopher Barker, 1676.
      brs. STEELE 3634. L, O, C, LG, OQ.

824   —We greet you well, being tender . . . 13 October.
      [*London*, 1660.] brs. STEELE 3264. LT.

825   —Whereas a petition was this day . . . 22 November
      1682. [*London*, 1682.] brs. STEELE 3735. L.

826   ——[Anr. ed.] [*London*], *S.Roycroft*, 1682. brs. STEELE
      3736. HH.

827   —Whereas by an Act of Parliament . . . 29 June 1662.
      [*London*, 1662.] brs. STEELE 3363. L, O, LPR.

828   —At the Court at Whitehall, . . . whereas by an order in
      Council . . . 21 April 1680. *By John Bill, Christopher
      Barker, Thomas Newcomb, and Henry Hills*, 1680. brs.
      STEELE 3714. L, LG, LPC, HH; CH.

829   —At the Court at Whitehall, . . . whereas by His Majesties
      proclamation . . . 30 December 1668. *In the Savoy, by
      the assigns of John Bill and Christopher Barker*, 1668. brs.
      STEELE 3523. L, C, OQ, LG, LPC; CH.

830   —Whereas by Our order, bearing date the tenth . . . 24
      April 1695. *By John Bill & the executrix of Thomas
      Newcomb*, 1695. brs. STEELE 4151. L, LG, LPC, LPR, LS.

831   —At the Court at   Whitehall, . . . whereas by the grace
      and blessing of . . . 9 January 1683[4]. *By the assigns of
      John Bill, and by Henry Hills and Thomas Newcomb*,
      1683[4]. brs. STEELE 3755. L, O, C, LG, OQ; CH, MH, NAM,
      WCL.

832   —Whereas by the late act of uniformity . . . 16 February
      1684[5]. *By the assigns of John Bill*, 1684[5]. brs. STEELE
      3785. L, O, LG, MC, DT; CH, MH, Y.

833   —Whereas by the late act of uniformity . . . 29 June 1688.
      By John Bill, and by Henry Hills, and Thomas Newcomb,
      1688. brs. STEELE 3868. L, O, LG, LPC, MC; WF.

834   —Whereas by the late act of uniformity . . . 16 February
      1688[9] *By John Bill and Thomas Newcomb*, 1688[9].
      brs. STEELE 3966. L, O, LG, LPR, EN; Y.

835   —At the Court at Whitehall, . . . whereas by the late
      address of . . . 6 June 1673. *By the assigns of John Bill and
      Christopher Barker*, 1673. brs. STEELE 3581. L, O, C, LG,
      LS; CH, NC.

836   ——[Anr. ed.] *Edinburgh reprinted A.Anderson*, 1673. brs.
      STEELE 3p 2370. HH; Y.

837   —At the Court at Whitehall, . . . whereas complaint was
      this day . . . 7 November 1683. *By the assigns of John
      Bill, and by Henry Hills, and Thomas Newcomb*, 1683.
      brs. STEELE 3754. L, O, C, LG, MC; CH, WF.

838   —Whereas divers scandalous untruths and . . . 25 Sep-
      tember. [*London*, 1660.] brs. STEELE 3258. L.

839   —At the Court at Whitehall, . . . whereas His Excellency
      the Herr . . . 28 November 1677. *By John Bill*, 1677.
      brs. STEELE 3644. L, O, C, LG, HH; CH, MH.

840   —At the Court at Whitehall, . . . whereas His Majesty
      and this board . . . 3 October, 1676. *By the assigns of
      John Bill, and Christopher Barker*, 1676. brs. L; CH.

840A —[Anr. ed.] *Edinburgh, re-printed by the heir of Andrew
      Anderson*, 1676. brs. Y.

841   —At the Court at Whitehall, . . . whereas His Majesty
      and this board . . . 6 December 1678. *By John Bill,
      Christopher Barker, Thomas Newcomb, and Henry Hills*,
      1678. cap., fol.* STEELE 3671. L, O, C, LG, DT; CH, MH.

842   —At the Court at Whitehall, . . . whereas His Majesty by
      His . . . 19 November 1678. *By John Bill, Christopher
      Barker, Thomas Newcomb, and Henry Hills*, 1678. brs.
      STEELE 3665. L, O, C, LG, DT; CH, Y.

843   ——[Anr. ed.] *Dublin, B. Took,* 1678. brs. STEELE 2p 893.
      ORM.

844   —Whereas His Majesty did the . . . 15 May 1672. *Edin-
      burgh, re-printed by Evan Tyler,* 1672. brs. ALDIS 1957.
      STEELE 3p 2357. HH; CH, Y.

845· —Whereas His Majesty hath . . . 24 October. *By John
      Bill, Christopher Barker, Thomas Newcomb, and Henry
      Hills,* 1678. brs. STEELE 3658. L, O, LPC, DT; CH.

846   —At the Court at Whitehall, . . . whereas His Majesty
      hath . . . 31 January 1678/9. *By John Bill, Christopher
      Barker, Thomas Newcomb, and Henry Hills,* 1678/9. brs.
      STEELE 3682. L, O, C, LG, DT; CH, MH.

847   —Whereas His Majesty taking notice of the daily in-
      fringement of the act of Parliament. [*London,* 1669?]
      brs. CH.

848   —Whereas in the charters, patents, or grants made . . . 17
      October 1688. *By John Bill, and by Henry Hills, and
      Thomas Newcomb,* 1688. brs. STEELE 3884. L, LG, OP, HH;
      WF.

849   —At the Court at Whitehall, . . . whereas information
      hath . . . 16 April 1680. *By John Bill, Christopher Barker,
      Thomas Newcomb, and Henry Hills,* 1680. brs. STEELE
      3712. L, O, C, LG, HH; CH, WF.

850   —At the Court at Whitehall, . . . whereas it has been
      represented . . . 13 December 1682. *By the assigns of
      John Bill, and by Henry Hills and Thomas Newcomb,*
      1682. brs. STEELE 3737. L, O, LG, LPC, HH; CH, Y.

851   —Whereas it hath been represented . . . 26 March 1686.
      By Charles Bill, Henry Hills, and Thomas Newcomb,
      1686. cap., fol.* STEELE 3830. L, O, LG, MC, DT; CH.

852   —Whereas it hath pleased God in . . . 19 August 1670.
      [*London, J. Flesher,* 1670.] brs. STEELE 3538. L, HH; MH.

853   —At the Court at Whitehall, . . . whereas it is generally
      reported . . . 25 June 1667. *In the Savoy, by the assigns of
      John Bill and Christopher Barker,* 1667. brs. STEELE 3494.
      L, OQ, LPC, LPR, HH; CH, MH.

854   —Whereas our game in and about our palace . . . 8 July
      1689. *By John Bill and Thomas Newcomb,* 1689. brs.
      STEELE 4018. L, LG, LPC, LPR; Y.

855   —Whereas since the expiration of . . . 16 February 1680[1].
      *By the Assigns of John Bill, Thomas Newcomb, and Henry
      Hills,* 1680[1]. cap., fol.* STEELE 3726. L, C, LG, LS, HH;
      MIU.

856   —At the Court at Whitehall, . . . whereas the considera-
      tion of the . . . 3 May 1672. [*London*], *by Andrew Clark,*
      1672. cap., fol.* STEELE 3567. L, LG, LS, OP, HH; CH.

857   —At the Court at Whitehall, . . . whereas the kings most
      excellent . . . 3 January 1678/9. *By John Bill, Christopher
      Barker, Thomas Newcomb, and Henry Hills,* 1678/9. brs.
      STEELE 3674. L, O, LPC, MC, DT; CH, Y.

858   —At the Court at Hampton-Court, . . . whereas the right
      honourable . . . 13 June 1683. *By the assigns of John Bill,
      and by Henry Hills and Thomas Newcomb,* 1683. brs.
      STEELE 3741. L, O, C, LG, DT; CH.

859   —Whereas there have risen of late . . . 8 November, 1671.
      [*London,* 1671]. brs. STEELE 3553. L.

ENGLAND: Laws, statutes

860   —An abridgement of the statutes made in the thirteenth
      . . . Charles the Second. *Printed,* 1661. 8°.* L; CH.

861   —An abridgment: or, a summary account of all the
      statute laws . . . made against Jesuites. *Printed in the
      year,* 1666. 4°.* L; CH, MHL, PL, WF.

861A —An abstract of all such acts of Parliament . . . Admiralty
      1663. 12°. LAD.

861B ——[Same title.] *By S. Bridge,* 1697. 8°. RPJ, WF.

862   —An abstract of all the penal-laws now in force. *For
      John Starkey,* 1679. 4°.* L, O, CS, LL, WCA; CH, NU, WF, Y.

862A —An abstract of all the penal laws touching . . . religion.
      1688. L, O, GU.

863   —An abstract of all the statute laws . . . recusants. *For
      John Starkey,* 1675. 4°.* L, O; CH, WF.

863A —An abstract of an act of Parliament for the encrease.
      [*London?* 1695]. brs. MH.

864   —An abstract of such parts of several statutes relating to
      silks called alamodes. [*London,* 1699.] brs. L, LL.

864A —An abstract of the acts for annuities. [*London,* 1698.]
      cap., 4°.* L; Y.

865   —·An abstract of the acts of Parliament. For officers and
      soldiers to set up . . . trades. *For Samuel Hill,* 1699. brs.
      NC.

866   —An abstract of the laws already in force against pro-
      faneness. *Printed and sold by R. Baldwin,* 1698. 4°.*
      T.C.III 76. C; CN, LC.

867   —An abstract of the laws in force against forestallers . . .
      of corn. *By William Downing,* 1698. brs. MC.

868   —An abstract of the laws now in force against popery.
      colop: *For J. H.,* 1688. brs. L; CH, WF, Y.

869   —An abstract of the penal laws against immorality. *By
      William Downing,* 1698. brs. MC, SP; LC, TU, WF.

870   —An abstract of the penal laws against immortality [*sic*].
      By T. B. & sold by E. Baldwin, 1698. brs. L.

870A —An abstract of the penal laws against profaneness. 1700.
      4°.* O.

871   —An abstract of those laws commanded by the Queen's
      . . . Majesty. *Tho. Braddey,* 1691. brs. L, LL.

871A —All the statutes now in force . . . bankrupts. *By the
      assigns of R. and E. Atkins for J. Walthoe,* 1695. 8°. LC.

871B —Articles of enquiries for surveying the bishops-lands.
      By R. Cotes for John Bellamy, 1647. 4°.* BR; CLC, MIU.

872   —A briefe declaration of all the penall stattuts. *For J. T.,*
      1643. 4°.* LT, CK, HH; CH, MH, MIU.

873   —A collection of acts and ordinances. *By Henry Hills and
      John Field,* 1658. fol. L, O, C, LVF, E; CH, CN, MH, NU,
      WF, Y.

874   —Collection of acts made in the Parliament . . . 17 Sept–
      26 June. *By Henry Hills and John Field,* 1657. fol. NU.

874A —A collection of all the acts, memorials & letters. *By H.
      Hills, to be sold by Walter Kettilby,* 1679. 8°. T.C.I 349.
      MHL, PL.

875   —A collection of all the acts of Parliament. *For Jo. Hind-
      marsh,* 1693. 4°.* C, CS, HH, E, EN; CN, NU, WF, Y.

876   —A collection of all the proclamations. 1654. fol. L, LMT; MIU.

877   —A collection of all the publicke orders. 1643. fol. E.

878   —A collection of all the publicke orders ordinances and declarations. *By T. W. for Ed: Husband,* 1646. fol. MADAN 1908. LT, O, C, LG, HH; CH, CN, LC, MH, NU, Y.

879   ——[Anr. ed.] 1658. fol. LMT.

880   —A collection of all the statutes at large. *In the Savoy, by the assigns of John Bill and Christopher Barker,* 1647. fol. LC.

881   ——[Anr. ed.] —, 1667. fol. L, C, CCA, CT; CN, LC.

882   —A collection of all the statutes. *By the assigns of John Bill and Christopher Barker,* 1670. fol. L, C, CS, LUG, E; LC.

883   —A collection of all the statutes now in force. *By C. Bill, and the executrix of T. Newcomb,* 1696 8°. LUG; CN, MH.

883A —[Anr. ed.] —, 1697. 8°. L; MH, MIU, WF.

883B —[Anr. ed.] —, 1699. 8°. LUG, CS; CN, LC, MH, MHL.

884   —A collection of all the statutes now in use. *By the assigns of John Bill and Christopher Barker; for John Streater, James Flesher, and Henry Twyford, assigns of Richard Atkyns, and Edward Atkyns,* 1670. fol. T.C.I 45. L, O, C, OME; MHL, Y.

885   —[Anr. ed.] *By the assigns of John Bill & Christopher Barker,* 1700 fol. LC, Y.

885A —A collection of all the statutes relating to the excise. *By the assigns of John Bill, and Christopher Barker,* 1676. 12°. MH, WF.

885B ——[Anr. ed.] *By the assigns of John Bill, and by Henry Hills and Thomas Newcomb,* 1683. 12°. WF.

886   —A collection of certaine statutes. 1643. 4°. DT; MHL.

887   ——[Anr. ed.] *By Robert White,* 1644. 4°.* LT, O, C, LSC; CH, MH, NU, WF, Y.

888   —A collection of declarations, treaties. *By J. Flesher for R. Royston.* 1662. fol. LG, LL, HH; CH, CLC, Y.

889   —A collection of several acts of Parliaments. *By John Field,* 1651. *and are to be sold by W. Lee, D. Pakeman, and G. Bedell.* fol. L, LUG, DT; CH, CN, MU.

890   ——[Anr. ed.] *By John Field, and are to be sold by W. Lee, D. Pakeman, and G. Bedell,* 1653. fol. AN; CH, MBA, NCL.

891   ——[Anr. ed.] *Printed,* 1657. 4°. MADAN 2324. O, C, LIC; MH, MHL.

892   —A collection of several statutes in force. 1644. 4°. EN.

893   Entry cancelled.

894   —A collection of such statutes as do enjoyn the observation of Lent. *For R. Pawley,* 1660/1. brs. LT; CH.

895   —A collection of such statutes. *By H. Hills, jun., for R. Taylor,* 1685. 4°.* HH; CH, MM.

896   —A collection of sundry statutes. *For the company of stationers, John Bill, and Christopher Barker,* 1661. fol. L, CCC, LI; LC, MHL.

897   —A collection of the severall acts, ordinances, & orders. *By John Macock, and Gartrude Dawson,* 1655. fol. C, LS, LUG, ES; MH, MHL, NN, Y.

898   —A collection of the statutes. *By John Streater, James Flesher, and Henry Twyford, assigns of Richard Atkyns and Edward Atkyns,* 1667. fol. L, O, LL; BN, CLC, LC, MHL, NU, Y.

899   —A compendious abridgement of all statutes. *For Robert Pawley,* 1661. 12°. L; CH, LC, WF, YL.

900   —A compendious abridgment of all the publick acts. *By J. Streater,* 1663. cap., 8°. C; WF.

901   —A continuation of the abridgment. *By Charles Bill, and the executrix of Tho. Newcomb, and by W. Rawlins and S. Roycroft,* 1699. 8°. T.C.III 137. L, LL; CH, NCL, YL.

902   —An exact abridgment of all the statutes in force. [Hughes.] *For J. Starkey, and T. Basset,* 1663. L, O, C; CH, LC, NCL, NN; WF.

903   ——[Anr. ed.] *By John Bill and Christopher Barker,* 1664. 8°. L, P.

904   ——[Same title. Manby.] *By Henry Twyford, John Streater, and Elizabeth Flesher, assigns of Richard Atkins and Edward Atkins: to be sold by the said H. Twyford,* 1674. 8°. T.C.I 173. L, O, C; LC.

905   ——[Same title. Wingate.] Second edition. *By R. & W. Leybourn, to be sold by Henry Twiford, and Roger Wingate,* 1655. 8°. L, O, C, E, BR; LC, MIU, NCL.

905A ——Third edition. *By T. R. for Henry Twyford, and Tho. Dring,* 1657. 8°. MM.

906   ——"Third" edition. *By John Streater, James Flesher, and Henry Twyford, assigns of Richard Atkyns, and Edward Atkyns,* 1666. 8°. L; LC, MH, MIU, Y.

907   ——Fourth edition. *By John Streater, James Flesher, and Henry Twyford, assigns of R. Atkyns, and E. Atkyns. To be sold by George Sawbridge, John Place, John Bellinger, William Place, Thomas Basset, Robert Pawlet, Ch. Wilkinson, Th. Dring, Will. Jacob, Allan Banks, Charles Harper, John Amery, John Poole, John Leigh,* 1670. 8°. T.C.I 53. L, CS, LSC; CN, LC, MH, TU.

908   ——Fifth edition. [London], *by John Streater, Eliz. Flesher, and Henry Twyford, assigns of R. Atkins and E. Atkins. To be sold by George Sawbridge, John Bellinger, William Place, Tho. Basset, Robert Pawlet, Ch. Wilkinson, Th. Dring, Wil. Jacob, Charles Harper, John Amery, John Leigh, John Williams, John Place, and John Pool,* 1675. 8°. O, LW, OBL, LW; CLC, MIU, PL.

909   ——Sixth edition. *By the assigns of J. Bill, T. Newcomb, and H. Hills. G. Sawbridge, W. Rawlins, and S. Roycroft, assigns of R. Atkyns and E. Atkyns. To be sold by G. Sawbridge, H. Twyford, F. Tyton, J. Bellinger, T. Basset, R. Pawlet, S. Heyrick, J. Wright, R. Chiswel, C. Wilkinson, T. Dring, C. Harper, J. Amery, J. Place, R. Tonson, J. Harrison, H. Tonson, and J. Poole,* 1681. 8°. T.C.I 446. L, O, DC, OM, DT; CLC, MHL, MIU, PL.

910   ——Seventh edition. *By the assigns of J. Bill, H. Hills, and T. Newcomb. And by the assigns of R. Atkins and E. Atkins. Sold by Tho. Dring, and Char. Harper,* 1684. 8°. L, LL, CCA, DC, MC; MHL, NCL, WF, YL.

911   ——Eighth edition. *By the assigns of the king's printers and by the assigns of R. Atkins and E. Atkins. To be sold by Charles Harper, William Crooke, and Richard Tonson,* 1689. 8°. T.C.II 265. L, C, LMT, OC, BR; LC, MH, NU, Y.

912   ——Ninth edition. *By His Majesties printers, and by the assigns of R. Atkins and E. Atkins;* 1700. 8°. L, O, C, DT; CH, LC, MH, NCL, PL, Y.

913   — —[Washington.] *By the assigns of the kings printers, and by the assigns of R. Atkins and E. Atkins. To be sold by M. Gilliflower, S. Keble, D. Brown, W. Rogers, T. Woodwin, A. Churchill and J. Walthoe,* 1694. 8°. T.C.II 523. L, CS, BR; BBE, PL, WF.

914   — —Second edition. *By the assigns of the kings printers and by the assigns of R. and E. Atkyns. To be sold by H. Mortlock, R. Chiswell, C. Harper, S. Keble, A. Churchill, J. Walthoe, and B. Took,* 1696. 8°. T.C.II 590. L, C, LL, LSC, DC; LC, NCL, WG.

914A   — —[Anr. ed.] —, 1699. 8°. T.C.III 137. L; CH, MIU.

915   — —An exact abridgment of publick acts. [Hughes.] *By T. R. for H. Twyford, T. Dring, and J. Place,* 1657. 4°. LT, O, C, LIL, DC; CH, LC, MH, YL.

916   —Five special orders. *Nov. 26. London, for Iohn Wright,* 1642. 4°.* LT, O, LG, HH, DT; CLC, MA, NU, WF, Y.

916A   —An index or abridgement of the acts. *Edinburgh, by John Reid,* 1685. 12°. ALDIS 2527. Y.

916B   —Index vectigalium or, an abbreviated collection of the laws. *By John Macock, for Godfrey Richards.* 1670. fol. T.C.I 72. L, O; MH, WF.

917   —The law of England touching His Majesties four principal seals. *For Dan. Brown,* 1696. 12°. T.C.II 573. CT.

918   —The lawes against witches and conivration. *For R. W.,* 1645. 4°.* LT, MR; MB, MH.

918A   —The laws and acts of Parliament. *Reprinted at Edinburgh by Evan Tyler,* 1647. 4°. ALDIS 1258. CH, L, OP; CLC, WF.

918B   —A necessary abstract of the laws relating to the militia. *For Robert Vincent,* 1691. 8°. L, OP; CLC.

919   —A perfect abstract of all the laws. *By George Sawbridge, Thomas Roycroft and Will. Rawlins, assigns of Richard Atkins and Edward Atkins: for William Jacob,* 1677. fol.* L, OC, HH, EC; CH, CN, WF, Y.

919A   —A plain abridgment of several statutes. *[London, 169–?]* brs. LG.

920   —The rates of merchandizes. *For Lawrence Blaiklock,* 1642. 8°. O, LL; LC, MHk Y.

921   — —[Anr. ed.] 1657. 8°. LC.

922   — —[Anr. ed.] *By Edward Husbands, and Thomas Newcomb,* 1660. fol. LT, O, LG; MH, MIU.

923   —The rates of the excise and new-impost. *By Richard Cotes and T. Newcomb,* 1649. fol. O.

923A   —Rules and instructions for the tare of goods. *Printed,* 1663. 8°. MH.

923B   — —[Anr. ed.] —, 1667. 8°.* CJ.

923C   —The several statutes by force. *By Robert White,* 1661. 4°.* LT, O, OB.

923D   —A statute against drunkenness. *[London,* 1643.] brs. LT.

923E   —The statutes at large. *By the assigns of John Bill and Christopher Barker,* 1676. fol. T.C.I 260. L, C, OB, LCP, LL; BN, CH, NR, QF.

923F   — —[Anr. ed.] *By the assigns of John Bill, Thomas Newcombe and Henry Hills,* 1611. fol. L, LTL, OM, CM, EN; CN, LC, MH, MIU, NU.

923G   — —[Anr. ed.] —, 1684. fol. L, O, WCA; BN, MHL, NN, PL, WF, YL.

923H   — —[Anr. ed.] *By Charles Bill and the executrix of Thomas Newcomb,* 1695. fol. L, O, OC, CK; LC, PL.

924   —A summary account of all the statute-laws against Jesuites. *For John Starkey,* 1673. 4°.* T.C.I 142. DT; CH, MIU, NU, WF.

925   —A table of publick and private acts. colop: *By the assigns of J. Bill and C. Barker,* 1677. brs. LC, Y.

926   —A table of the publick and private acts. *[London,* 1678.] cap., fol.* Y.

926A   —The tenth chapter of the statute made. *Printed,* 1666. 4°.* MM.

ENGLAND: Lord Chancellor

927   —An ordinance made . . . 18 July 1666. *[London,* 1666.] STEELE 3465. L, HH.

ENGLAND: Lords Commissioners

928   —An order for the observance and execution of the statute. *Oxford, L. Lichfield,* 1644. brs. STEELE 2579. O.

929   — —[Anr. ed.] —, 1645. brs. STEELE 2615. O.

930   —Oxford, 4. Die Junij. 1646. An order of the Lords and governour, for the better direction of the overseers. *Printed at Oxford by Leonard Lichfield,* 1646. brs. STEELE 2657. MADAN 1870. O.

ENGLAND: Lords Justices

931   —Order of their Excellencies the Lord Justices in Council, . . . 24. of November, 1698. colop: *Boston [Mass.], by Bartholomew Green and John Allen,* 1699. fol.* EVANS 864. MHL, MHS.

931A   —A proclamation. *For Henry Shepheard,* 1641[2]. 4°.* LT, HH; WF.

932   — —28 May 1696. *By John Bill and the executrix of Thomas Newcomb,* 1696. brs. STEELE 4197. L, LG, LPC, LPR, LS.

933   — —17 July 1696. — 1696. brs. STEELE 4199. L, LPC, LPR.

934   — —10 August 1696. —, 1696. brs. STEELE 4200. L, LCP, LPR, LS.

935   — —[Anr. ed.] — 1696. brs. STEELE 4202. L, LPC, LPR.

936   — —10 September 1696. —, 1696. brs. STEELE 4206. L, LPC, LPR, HH; MH.

937   — —24 September 1696. —, 1696. brs. STEELE 4208. L, LG, LPC, LPC, LPR, LS.

938   — —6 May 1697. —, 1697. brs. STEELE 4225. L, LG, LPC, LPR, LS; MH.

939   — —7 May 1697. —, 1697. brs. STEELE 4226. L, LG, LPC, LPR, LS; MH.

940   — —27 May 1697. —, 1697. brs. STEELE 4227. L, LG, LPC, LPR.

941   — —30 July 1697. —, 1697. brs. STEELE 4229. L, LPC, LPR, LS, HH; MH.

942   — —17 September 1697. —, 1697. brs. STEELE 4231. L, LPR, HH.

942A   — —24 September 1697. —, 1697. brs. STEELE 4232. L, LC, LPC, LPR, HH; MH.

943 ——21 October 1697. —, 1697. brs. STEELE 4234. L, LG, LPR, HH; MH.

944 ——11 November 1697. —, 1697. brs. STEELE 4238. L, LPC, LPR, LS.

945 ——9 August 1698. —, 1698. brs. STEELE 4251. L, LPC, LPR; Y.

946 ——3 November 1698. —, 1698. brs. STEELE 4255. L, LPC, LPR, LS.

947 —A proclamation declaring the Parliament. —, 1696. brs. STEELE 4195. L, LG, LPC, LPR, LS; MH.

948 —A proclamation for a general fast . . . 23 May 1695. —, 1695. brs. STEELE 4155. L, O, LPC, LPR, ES.

949 ——23 May 1696. —, 1696. brs. STEELE 4196. L, LG, LPC, LPR.

950 —A proclamation for a publick thanksgiving. —, 1695. brs. STEELE 5149. L, LG, LPC, MC, ES.

950A —A proclamation for apprehending and securing . . . John Robert. *By Charles Bill, and the executrix of Thomas Newcomb,* 1695. brs. STEELE 4156. L, LG, LS, HH.

951 —A proclamation for apprehending William Berkenhead. —, 1696. brs. STEELE 4203. L, O, LG, LPC, LPR, HH.

952 —A proclamation for publishing the peace . . . French. —, 1697. brs. STEELE 4233. L, O, LG, LPC, LPR; WF.

953 ——[Anr. ed.] *Edinburgh, by the heirs & successors of A. Anderson,* 1697. brs. STEELE 3p 3132. L.

954 —A proclamation, for putting in execution. *By John Bill and the executrix of Thomas Newcomb,* 1698. brs. STEELE 4252. L, LPC, LPR, LS, ES.

955 —A proclamation for putting the laws, —, 1698. brs. STEELE 4253. L, LPC, LPR, OC; MH.

955A —A proclamation. Whereas by proclamation. *C. Bill,* 1696. brs. STEELE 4208. OP.

956 —Whereas by reason of the recoining . . . 2 July 1696. —, 1696. brs. STEELE 4198. L, LG, LPC, LPR, LS.

957 —Whereas divers of His Majesty's subjects . . . 2 November 1697. —, brs. STEELE 4235. L, LG, LPR; Y.

958 ——8 November 1697. —, 1697. brs. STEELE 4237. L, LG, LPR, LS; CH.

ENGLAND: Parliament

958A —An abstract of an act for importing. colop: *By Charles Bill and the executrix of Thomas Newcomb,* 1696. brs. OC; MH.

958B —An abstract of so much of the act for establishing. [London, 1696?] fol.* MH.

958C —An abstract of the act for granting an aid. colop: *By Charles Bill and the executrix of Thomas Newcomb,* 1696. fol.* PL, Y.

958D —An abstract of the act for granting to His Majesty an aid. colop: *By Charles Bill and the executrix of Thomas Newcomb,* 1698. fol.* PL.

958E —An abstract of the act . . . for granting to His Majesty certain duties. *By Charles Bill, and the executrix of Tho. Newcomb. Sold by J. Walthoe* 1695. 4°.* L, OC; MH, WF.

959 —An abstract of the act for granting to His Majesty the sum. colop: *By Charles Bill, and the executrix of Thomas Newcomb,* 1698. fol.* O; MH, PL.

959A ——[Anr. ed.] —, 1699. fol.* PL.

960 —An abstract of the act made in the 5th and 6th years. *By Charles Bill, and executrix of Tho. Newcomb; and sold by J. Walthoe,* 1694. 4°.* L, OC; CH, MH, WF, Y.

960A —An abstract of the act made Anno VI° & VII° Guliemi III. *By Charles Bill and the executrix of Thomas Newcomb, and sold by Robert Vincent and Joshua Brixey,* 1695. 4°.* OC; MH, WF.

960B —An abstract of the bill intituled An act for relief. [*London?* 1696.] cap., 4°.* MH.

961 —An abstract of the bill now depending. [*London,* 1664?] brs. L.

962 —An abstract of the proceedings in Parliament in the time of Edward the 3. *For Fr. Coles,* 1642. 4°.* O, MR, HH; CSS, MH, WF, Y.

963 —An abstract of the several acts. *By Charles Bill, and the executrix of Thomas Newcomb,* 1700. fol.* L, OC, DC; JF.

964 —An account at large, of the proceedings at the Sessions-House . . . 24 of November 1681. colop: *For Roger Evens,* 1681. cap., fol.* L, O, EC; CH, WF, Y.

965 —An account of some transactions in this present Parliament. [*London,* 1690?]* LL, EN; CH, TU.

966 —An account of the proceedings of the Lords and Commons. *For W. D.,* 1688. brs. L, OC, CK, MC; MIU.

967 —An accompt of transactions mannaged by the Lords and Commons. *Printed at London by Robert Ibbitson,* 1648. *Feb. 12.* 4°.* LT; CH, MH, MHL.

968 —An act against delinquents. colop: *By John Field and Henry Hills,* 1659. cap., fol.* LT; MH, Y.

969 Entry cancelled.

970 —An act against the raising of moneys. *By John Field,* 1659. fol.* LT; MH, Y.

971 —An act against vagrants. colop: *By Henry Hills and John Field,* 1657. cap., fol.* LT, O, C, HH; CH, MH, NU, WF, Y.

972 ——[Anr. ed.] *Edinburgh, Christopher Higgins,* 1657. fol.* ALDIS 1559. EN.

973 —An act agreed upon at the treaty, . . . October 9, 1648. [*London*], *by Robert Ibbitson,* 1648. 4°.* LT, O, HH; Y.

974 —An act and declaration for putting the lawes. *By John Streater, and John Macock,* 1659. fol.* LT; CH, MH.

975 —An act and declaration of the Parliament . . . touching a pamphlet. *By Edward Husband and John Field,* 1650. brs. STEELE 2910. LT, O, C, LG, HH; MH, NU, Y.

976 —An act and declaration touching several acts. *By Hen. Hills and Iohn Field,* 1657. fol.* LT, O, C, BR, HH; CH, MH, NU, WF, Y.

976A ——[Anr. ed.] *Edinburgh, re-printed by Christopher Higgins,* 1657. fol.* L.

976B —Act anent the aliment of poor prisoners. *By Jr. Wilkins,* 1700. brs. LU.

977 —An act appointing commissioners for sequestrations. *By John Field,* 1659. fol.* LT; MH.

978 —An act appointing commissioners for the government. *By John Streater*, [1659]. brs. STEELE 3132. LT, LG, LS, LUG; MH.

979 —An act appointing judges for the Admiralty . . . 19 May 1659. *By John Field*, 1659. brs. STEELE 3113. LT, LG, LS, LUG, OQ; MH.

980 —An act appointing judges of the Admiralty. 19 July 1659. *By John Field*, 1659. brs. STEELE 3119. L, LUG, LV; MH.

981 —An act appointing Thursday the last day of February, 1649. *For Edward Husband and John Field*, 1949[50]. brs. STEELE 2888. LT, O, C, LG, OQ; Y.

982 —An act appointing Thursday the thirteenth of June, 1650. *By Edward Husband and Iohn Field*, 1650. brs. STEELE 2897. LT, C, LG, OQ, LUG, HH; MH, NU.

983 —An act concerning bonds for custome. *By Richard Cotes and Thomas Newcombe*, 1649. brs. STEELE 2857. L.

984 —An act concerning the militia's. *By John Field*, 1651. brs. STEELE 2942. LT, LG, LUG, OQ, HH; MH, Y.

985 —An act constituting Major-General Philip Skippon. *By Edward Husband and John Field*, 1650. brs. STEELE 2901. LT, C, LG, OQ, HH; CH, MH, NU, Y.

986 —An act declaring and constituting the people of England. *For E. Husband*, 21 May, 1649. brs. STEELE 2849. L, C, BR; MB, MH.

987 ——[Anr. ed.] *For Edward Husband*, 1649. brs. STEELE 2850. L, C, HH; CN, TU, Y.

988 —An act enabling such commissioners of sewers. *By John Field*, 1659. brs. STEELE 3111. LT, LG, LS, LUG, OQ; MH.

989 —An act enabling the commissioners. *By John Field*, 1651. brs. STEELE 2951. LT, LG, LUG, NN, HH; CH, MH, Y.

990 ——[Anr. ed.] —, 1659. fol.* LT; MH.

991 —An act enabling the militia of the city of London. *By Richard Cotes*, 1650. brs. STEELE 2900. LT; CN.

992 —An act establishing the povvers of Lord Admiral. *By John Field*, 1650[1]. brs. STEELE 2925. LT, LG, LUG, OQ, HH; NU, Y.

993 —An act for a day of publique thanksgiving. *By John Field for Edward Husband*, 1649. brs. STEELE 2875. LT, O, C, LG, HH; CH, MH, Y.

994 —An act for a free and voluntary present. *By John Bill and Christopher Barker*, 1661. fol.* OC, HH.

994A —An act for a grant to Their Majesties. *By Charles Bill and Thomas Newcomb*, 1689. fol.* OC.

995 —An act for a seal of the Parliament. *By Edward Husband and John Field*, 1650[1]. brs. STEELE 2923. LT, O, LG, OQ, HH; CLC, MH, NU, Y.

996 —An act for an assessment of. *By John Streater, and John Macock*, 1659. fol. LT; MH.

997 —An act for an assessment upon England. *By Hen: Hills and John Field*, 1657. fol. LT, O, HH, AN; CH, MH, NCL, WF, Y.

998 —An act for an assessment . . . upon England . . . for three years. *By Henry Hills and Iohn Field*, 1657. fol.* L, O, OC, CT, HH; CH, MBP, MH, WF, Y.

999 Entry cancelled.

1000 —An act for appointing commissioners. colop: *By John Field*, 1659. cap., fol.* LT; MH, Y.

1001 —An act for approbation. *By John Streater, and John Macock*, 1659. fol.* LT, OC; CH, MB, MH, Y.

1002 —An act for authorizing Colonel Blake. *For Edw. Husband*, March 5, 1648. brs. O; MIU, TU.

1003 —An act for better regulation of courts. *James Flesher*, 1669. 4°. CT.

1004 —An act for bringing in the revenue. *By John Streater, and John Macock*, 1659. fol.* LT; CH, MH, WF.

1004A —An act for charging of tobacco. [London, 1650.] brs. NN, RPJ.

1005 —An act for confirmation of judicial proceedings. *By John Bill and Christopher Barker*, 4660. fol.* LT, OC; MH.

1006 —An act for confirmation of the sale of the lands . . . of Sir Iohn Stowel. *By John Field*, 1653. brs. STEELE 3010. LT, O, LG, OQ, DT; MH.

1007 —An act for confirming and establishing the administration of goods and chattels of Sir William Godolphin. colop: *By Charles Bill, and the executrix of Thomas Newcomb*, 1700. cap., fol.* L; CH.

1007A —An act for constituting a committee for the army. *By John Streater and John Macock*, 1659. fol.* MH.

1008 —An act for constituting commissioners. *By John Field*, 1653. brs. STEELE 3017. LT, O, LG, HH; MH.

1009 ——[Anr. ed.] —, 1659. fol.* LT; MH.

1010 ——[Anr. ed.] *By John Streater, and John Macock*, 1659[/60]. fol.* LT; MH.

1011 —An act for continuance of a former act. *By Edward Husband and John Field*, 1650[1]. brs. STEELE 2924. LT, LG, LS, OQ, HH; CU, MH, Y.

1012 —An act for continuance of the imposition. *By John Field*, 1652[3]. brs. STEELE 2989. L, OQ, HH; Y.

1013 —An act for continuation of the act for redemption of captives . . . 31 March 1652. *By John Field*, 1652. brs. STEELE 2964. LT, LG, OQ, HH; Y.

1014 ——21 December 1652. *By John Field*, 1652. brs. STEELE 2980. LT.

1015 —An act for continuation of the act for removing all Papists. *By John Field*, 1650. brs. STEELE 2928. LT, LG, LUG, OQ, HH; MH, NU, WF, Y.

1016 —An act for continuing and establishing the subsidie. *By Henry Hills, and John Field*, 1657. fol.* LT, O, C, CT, HH; CH, CN, MH, WF, Y.

1017 ——[Anr. ed.] *Edinburgh: re-printed by Christopher Higgins*, 1657. fol.* EN.

1018 —An act for continuing John Bradshaw . . . first of April, 1652. *By John Field*, 1652. brs. STEELE 2965. LT, HH; MH, Y.

1019 ——[Same title.] 1 January 1652[3]. *By John Field*, 1652[3]. brs. STEELE 2983. LT, O, LG, HH; MH, Y.

1020 ——[Same title.] 8 April 1653. *By John Field*, 1653. brs. STEELE 2991. L.

1021 —An act for continuing of the excise. *By John Bill and Christopher Barker*, 1660. fol.* LT; MH.

1022 —An act for continuing the commissioners. *By John Field*, 1652. brs. STEELE 2977. LT, O, LG, HH; Y.

1023 —An act for continuing the High Court of Justice. *By John Field*, 1651. brs. STEELE 2953. LT, LG, LUG, HH; MH, NU, Y.

1024 —An act for continuing the jurisdiction. *By John Field*, 1651. brs. STEELE 2930. LT, LG, LUG, OQ, HH; Y.

1025 —An act for continuing the powers of commissioners. *By John Field*, 1653. brs. STEELE 3013. LT, LG, LUG, OQ; MH, Y.

1026 —An act for continuing the priviledges . . . of Lancaster. *By John Field*, 1653. brs. STEELE 3008. LT, LG, LUG, HH; MH, Y.

1027 —An act for continuing two former acts. *By Edward Husband and Iohn Field*, 1650. brs. STEELE 2919. LT, LG, LUG, OQ, HH; MH.

1028 ——[Anr. ed.] *By John Field*, 1651. brs. STEELE 2960. L, HH.

1029 —An act for disabling delinquents to bear office. colop: *By John Field*, 1652. CH.

1030 —An act for discovering, convicting, and repressing of Popish recusants. *By Henry Hills and John Field*, 1657. fol.* LT, O, C, BR, HH; CH, MH, NU, WF, Y.

1030A ——[Anr. ed.] *Edinburgh, by Christopher Higgins*, 1657. fol.* L.

1031 —An act for dissolving the Parliament. *By John Streater, and John Macock*, 1659. fol.* LT, SP; MH, WF, Y.

1032 —An act for enabling and authorising certain persons to be justices. colop: *By John Field*, 1659. fol.* LT; CH, MH, Y.

1033 —An act for enabling judges. *By John Field*, 1659. fol.* LT; MH.

1033A —An act for erecting a new parish. *By the assigns of John Bill and Henry Hills and Thomas Newcomb*, 1685. fol.* L, OC.

1034 —An act for establishing the coronation oath. [*London*, 1689.] 4°.* L, MR; WF.

1035 —An act for explanation of certain clauses. *By John Streater, and John Macock*, 1659. fol.* LT, C; MH.

1036 —An act for further continuance of the customs. *By John Streater*, 1659. fol.* LT; MH, Y.

1037 —An act for further impowring the commissioners. *By John Field*, 1652. brs. STEELE 2975. LT, LG, OQ, HH; MH, Y.

1037A —An act for granting a royal aid. *By John Bill and Christopher Barker*, 1664. fol.* OC.

1037B —An act for granting a supply. *By John Bill, Christopher Barker, and Henry Hill*, 1678. fol.* OC.

1037C —An act for granting an aid. *By Charles Bill and Thomas Newcomb*, 1690. fol.* OC.

1037D —An act for granting to Their Majesties an aid. *By Charles Bill and the executrix of Thomas Newcomb*, 1693. fol.* OC.

1038 —An act for holding an assize for . . . Lancaster. *By John Field*, 1659. fol.* LT; MH.

1039 —An act for householders. *By John Field*, 1659. fol.* LT, C; CH, MH.

1040 —An act for impresting of seamen. *By John Field and Henry Hills*, 1659. fol.* LT; MH.

1041 —An act for impresting seamen. Die veneris 28 Februarii, 1650. *By John Field*, 1650[1]. fol.* CH.

1042 —An act for indempnifying of sucn persons. *By Hen: Hills and John Field*, 1657. fol.* LT, O, C, HH; CH, MH, NU, WF, Y.

1042A ——[Anr. ed.] *Edinburgh, re-printed by Christopher Higgins*, 1657. fol.* L.

1042B —An act for indempnity and free pardon. *J. Field and H. Hills*, 1659. fol.* LT.

1043 —An act for keeping and celebrating the twenty third of October. *For Robert Clavell*, 1680. 4°.* L, O, C, OC; Y.

1044 —An act for laying impositions. *In the Savoy*, 1671. fol. C; MH.

1045 —An act for laying several duties upon low wines. 1696. E.

1046 —An act for limiting and setling the prices for vvines. *By Henry Hills, and John Field*, 1657. fol.* LT, O, C, HH; CH, MH, NU, TU, WF, Y.

1047 ——[Anr. ed.] *Edinburgh: re-printed by Christopher Higgins*, 1657. fol.* FSF.

1048 —An act for making the collectors receipts. *Dublin: by Andrew Crook*, 1697. fol.* L.

1048A —An act for ministers and payment of thythes. *By John Streater, and John Macock*, 1659. fol.* CH, MH, Y.

1048B —An act for more effectual suppressing prophane cursing. *C. Bill*, 1697. brs. OP.

1048C —[Anr. ed.] For preventing frauds. *Busby*, 1685. 4°.* EVANS 794. MWA.

1049 —An act for punishing of such persons. colop: *By Henry Hills and Iohn Field*, 1657. fol.* LT, O, C, HH; CH, MH, NU, WF, Y.

1049A ——[Anr. ed.] *Edinburgh, Christopher Higgins*, 1657. fol. STEELE 3p 2158. ALDIS 1561. EN.

1050 —An act for putting in execution. *By John Bill and Christopher Barker*, 1660. fol.* LT; CH, MH.

1051 —An act for quiet enjoying of sequestred parsonages. colop: *By Hen: Hills and John Field*, 1657. cap., fol.* LT, O, C, BR, HH; CH, CN, MH, NU, WF, Y.

1052 ——[Anr. ed.] colop: *Edinburgh, re-printed by Christopher Higgins*, 1657. cap., fol.* FSF.

1052A —An act for raising £584,978.2.2 1/2 for . . . ships of war. *By the assigns of John Bill and Christopher Barker*, 1677. fol.* OC.

1053 —An act for raising moneys by a poll. *In the Savoy, by the assigns of John Bill and Christopher Higgins*, 1666. fol.* C, OC.

1054 —An act for raising of fifteen thousand pounds . . . in Scotland. *By Henry Hills and John Field*, 1657. fol.* LT, O, HH, E; CH, MBP, MH, WF, Y.

1055 ——[Anr. ed.] *Edinburgh, re-printed by Christopher Higgins*, 1657. fol.* L; CH, MH.

1056 —An act for raising sevenscore thousand pounds. *By John Bill and Christopher Barker*, 1660. fol.* LT; MH.

1057 —An act for raising the sum of 1238750 £. 1673. fol. C, CS.

1058   —An act for recognizing King William and Queen Mary. *By Charles Bill and Thomas Newcomb*, 1690. fol.* OC.

1058A   — —[Anr. ed.] *Edinburgh, re-printed*, 1690. brs. L, HH, EN.

1059   —An act for recovery of publique debts. *By John Streater, and John Macock*, 1659. fol.* LT; MH, TU.

1059A   —An act for reliefe of religious . . . people. *By John Field*, 1650. fol.* WF.

1059B   —An act for remedying the ill state of the coyn. *By Charles Bill and the executrix of Thomas Newcomb*, 1695. fol.* OC.

1060   —The act for remedying the ill state of the coyn of this kingdom enacts, that all. *For E. Whitlock*, 1696. brs. L, CT, GH; MH, TU, Y.

1061   —The act for remedying the ill state of the coin of the kingdom, enacts; that the several. colop: *For E. Whitlock*, [1696]. brs. L, CJ; MH, TU.

1062   —An act for removing and preventing all questions. *By John Bill and Christopher Barker*, 1660. fol.* LT; MH.

1062A   — —[Anr. ed.] *Edinburgh, reprinted*, 1689. 4°.* L, EN.

1063   —An act for renouncing and disanulling . . . Charls Stuart. colop: *By Henry Hills and John Field*, 1656[7]. fol.* STEELE 3076. LT, O, LG, LPR, HH; CN, WF, Y.

1064   —An act of renouncing and disanulling the pretended title of Charls Stuart. *By Henry Hills and John Field*, 1657. fol.* L, O, C, CJ, HH; CH, MBP, MH, NU, WF, Y.

1065   —An act for repeal of two acts. *By John Streater and John Macock*, 1659[60]. fol.* LT; MH, TU, Y.

1065A   —An act for reviving an act for impresting seamen. *By John Streater and John Macock*, 1659. brs. MH.

1065B   —An act for reviving an act impowering judges for probate. *By John Field*, 1659. brs. STEELE 3118. LT, LUG, LV; MH.

1066   —An act for reviving and continuing of several acts. *By John Field*, 1651. brs. STEELE 2943. L, LG, LUG, OQ, HH.

1067   —An act for satisfying Lieutenant-Colonel John Lilburn. [*London*, 1650.] brs. STEELE 2908. LT.

1067A   —An act for securing the peace. *Dublin, reprinted by Benjamin Tooke and John Crooke to be sold by Mary Crooke and Andrew Crooke*, 1681. fol.* DIX 189. DN, DT.

1068   —An act for sequestrations. *By John Field*, 1659. fol.* LT; MH, Y.

1069   —An act for setling the militia for . . . London. *By John Field and Henry Hills*, 1659. fol.* LT, CS; MH.

1070   —An act for setling the milita for . . . Southwark. *By John Field and Henry Hills*, 1659. fol.* LT; MH, Y.

1071   —An act for setling the militia in England. *By John Field*, 1659. fol.* LT, C, OC, CJ, CM; MH.

1072   —An act for setling the militia of . . . Westminster. *By John Field and Henry Hills*, 1659. fol.* LT; MH.

1073   —An act for setling the militia within England. *By John Streater, and John Macock*, 1659. fol. LT; MH, Y.

1074   —An act for setling the militia within . . . Tower of London. *By John Field and Henry Hills*, 1659. fol.* LT; MH, Y.

1074A   —An act for settling the revenue on His Majesty. *By the assigns of John Bill and by Henry Hills, and Thomas Newcomb*, 1685. fol. O, OC; MH, WF.

1075   —An act for setting apart a day of solemn fasting . . . 23 April 1649. *For Edward Husband*, [1649]. brs. STEELE 2845. LT, O, LG, OQ, HH; MH, WF, Y.

1076   — —[Anr. ed.] *For E. Scobell*, 1649. fol.* O.

1076A   —An act for setting apart Friday the four and twentieth day of October. *By John Field*, 1656. fol.* SP, AN.

1077   —An act for setting apart VVednesday the thirteenth day of October, 1652. *By John Field*, 1652. brs. STEELE 2974. LT, O, LG, HH; NU, Y.

1078   —An act for stating and determining the accompts of such officers. *By John Field*, 1652. fol. C; CH.

1079   —An act for stating the accompts of the general officers. colop: *For Edward Husband*, 1649. fol. C; CH.

1079A   —An act for subscribing the engagement. *For Edward Husband*, 1649. fol.* C, LG.

1080   —An act for supplying and explaining. *By John Bill and Christopher Barker*, 1660. fol.* LT, CS; MH.

1081   —An act for suppressing the detestable sins of incest. *By John Field*, 1650. 8°. CH.

1081A   —An act for taking and receiving the accompts. *By William Larner, Octob. 15.* 1649. 4°.* C, OC; CH, MH.

1082   —An act for taking away fines. *By John Field*, 1653. brs. STEELE 3004. LT, O, LG, OQ, HH; MH.

1083   —An act for taking away the court of wards. *By John Bill*, 1660[1]. fol.* LT.

1084   —An act for taking away the fee of damage cleere. *By Edward Husband and John Field*, 1650. brs. STEELE 2922. LT, O, LG, OQ, HH; NU, Y.

1085   —An act for taking the accompts. *By John Streater, and John Macock*, 1659[/60]. fol.* LT; MH.

1086   —An act for the abolishing the kingly office. *For Edward Husband, March 19,* 1648[9]. fol.* STEELE 2833. LT, O, C, LG, HH; CH, MH, NU, WCL, Y.

1086A   — —[Anr. ed.] [*London*, 1648.] cap., fol.* L; NU.

1087   —An act for the adjournment of this present Parliament. *By Hen: Hills and John Field*, 1657. fol.* LT, O, C, CT, HH; CH, CU, MH, WF, Y.

1087A   — —[Anr. ed.] *Edinburgh, Higgins*, 1657. fol.* ALDIS 1562. EN.

1088   —An act for the admitting of the six counties. *For Edward Husband*, 1649.* C, AN.

1089   —An act for the apprehension of Thomas Cook Esq. *By John Field*, 1650[1]. brs. STEELE 2929. LT, LG, LUG, OQ, HH.

1089A   —An act for the appropriating the rectories of Llanrhayader. *By John Bill, Thomas Newcomb, and Henry Hills*, 1679. fol.* OC.

1090   —An act for the ascertaining the time of payment. *By John Field*, 1652. brs. STEELE 2979. LT, O, LG, OQ, HH; CLC, Y.

1090A   —An act for the assembling and holding of Parliaments. *By John Bill and Christopher Barker*, 1664. fol.* MH, Y.

1091 —An act for the assuring, confirming and setling of lands . . . in Ireland. *By Henry Hills and John Field,* 1657. fol.* LT, O, C, HH; CH, MH, NU, WF, Y.

1091A ——[Anr. ed.] *Edinburgh, reprinted by C.Higgins,* 1657. fol.* L.

1092 —An act for the attainder of the rebels in Ireland. *By Henry Hills and John Field,* 1657. fol.* LT, O, C, HH; CH, MH, NU, WF, Y.

1092A ——[Anr. ed.] *Edinburgh, reprinted by C.Higgins,* 1657. fol.* L.

1093 —An act for the better advancement of the gospel. colop: *By Edward Husband and John Field,* 1649. fol. C; CH.

1094 —An act for the better observation of the Lords-Day. *By Hen: Hills and John Field,* 1657. fol.* LT, O, C, OC, HH; CH, MH, NU, WF, Y.

1094A ——[Anr. ed.] *Edinburgh, by Christopher Higgins,* 1657. fol.* L.

1095 —An act for the better ordering the selling of wines. *By John Bill,* 1660[1]. fol. LT, OC, E.

1095A —An act for the better packing of butter. *Edward Husband & Iohn Field,* 1649. fol.* L; Y.

1096 —An act for the better payment of augmentations. *By Edward Husband and Iohn Field,* 1650. brs. STEELE 2899. LT, O, C, LG, HH; NU.

1097 —An act for the better preventing and suppressing of prophane swearing. *By Edward Husband and Iohn Field,* 1650. brs. STEELE 2902. L; CH, MH, Y.

1098 —An act for the better propagating and preaching. *By Edward Husband and John Field,* 1649. 4°.* O, C, AN.

1099 ——[Anr. ed.] *For Francis Tyton,* 1650. AN.

1100 —An act for the better suppressing of theft. *By Hen: Hills and John Field,* 1657. fol.* LT, O, C, HH; CH, MH, NU, WF, Y.

1100A ——[Anr. ed.] *Edinburgh, re-printed by Christopher Higgins,* 1657. fol.* L.

1101 —An act for the confirmation of the treaty . . . between . . . England and Scotland. *Oxford, re-printed by Leonard Lichfield,* 1643. 4°.* O, C, CT, HH; CH.

1102 —An act for the confirming and restoring of ministers. *By John Bill and Christopher Barker,* 1660. fol.* LT, OC; MH, TU, WF.

1103 —An act for the continuance of judicatories. *By John Field,* 1652. brs. STEELE 2976. LT, LG, OQ, HH; Y.

1104 —An act for the continuance of process. *By John Macock, and Francis Tyton,* 1660. fol.* LT; MH.

1105 —An act for the continuance of the customs. *By John Field,* 1652[3]. brs. STEELE 2988. LT, LG, OQ, HH; KU, MH, Y.

1106 ——[Anr. ed.] —, 1659. fol.* LT; MH, Y.

1107 ——[Anr. ed.] *By John Streater, and John Macock,* 1659[60]. fol.* LT; MH, Y.

1107A —An act for the continuing the jurisdiction of the . . . Admiralty. *J.Field,* 1651. brs. LT.

1108 —An act for the encouraging & increasing. *By John Bill and Christopher Barker,* 1660. fol.* LT, OC; MH, RPJ, WF.

1108A —An act for the establishing articles . . . navies. [*London*], *by order of the principal officers . . . Navy,* 1666. brs. L.

1109 —An act for the exportation of several commodities. *By Henry Hills and Iohn Field,* 1656. fol.* STEELE 3079. LT, O, C, LG, ES; CH, CN, MBP, MIU.

1110 ——[Anr. ed.] colop: *By Hen: Hills and John Field,* 1656 [7] fol.* LUG, MH, MIU, WF.

1111 —An act for the further relief of His Majesties armie. colop: *By Robert Barker, and by the assigns of John Bill,* 1641. fol. in 4°. LT, O, OC.

1112 —An act for the impresting of soldiers. 1651. fol.* L.

1113 —An act for the improvement of the revenue. colop: *By Hen: Hills and John Field,* 1657. cap., fol.* LT, O, C; CH, MH, NU, WF, Y.

1114 —An act for the more certain and constant supply. *By Henry Hills and John Field,* 1659. fol.* LT, O, LG, OC.

1115 —An act for the more effectual preserving the kings person. *By John Bill and Christopher Barker,* 1678. fol.* C, OC, HH; CN.

1116 Entry cancelled.

1117 ——[Anr. ed.] *Dublin, by Benjamin Took, to be sold by Mary Crook,* 1678. fol.* C.

1117A —An act for the more effectual restraining. [*London?* 1691.] cap., 4°.* Y.

1117B —An act for the necessary maintenance of . . . dreining. [*London?* 1661.] brs. L; MH.

1118 —An act for the observation of a day of publique fasting. *By John Field,* 1652. brs. STEELE 2970. LT, LG, OQ, HH; MH, NU, Y.

1119 —An act for the preventing of the multiplicity of buildings. *By Henry Hills and Iohn Field,* 1657. fol.* LT, O, C, HH; CH, MH, NU, WF, Y.

1120 —An act for the regulating of the trade of bay-making. *By John Bill and Christopher Barker,* 1660. fol.* LT.

1120A —An act for the relief and release. *By Charles Bill and Thomas Newcomb,* 1690. fol.* L.

1121 —An act for the relief of creditors. *By Iohn Field,* 1653. fol.* C; CH, WCL, Y.

1122 —An act for the security of His Highness the Lord Protector. colop: *By Henry Hills and John Field,* 1656. fol.* STEELE 3077. LT, O, LG, LPR, ES.

1123 ——[Anr. ed.] —, 1657. fol.* L, O, C, CJ, HH; CH, CN, NU, WF, Y.

1123A —An act for the settling of Ireland. *J.Field,* 1652. 4°.* L.

1123B ——[Anr. ed.] *Re-printed at Dublin by Wil. Bladen,* 1652. 4°.* DIX 91. LW, DN, DT.

1123C ——[Anr. ed.] *Waterford, by Peter de Pienne,* 1652. 4°.* DN.

1124 —An act for the setling of the postage. *By Henry Hills and John Field,* 1657. fol.* L, C, LG, HH; CH, MBP, MH, MIU, Y.

1125 —An act for the setting apart a day. *By Edward Husband and Iohn Field,* 1650. brs. STEELE 2903. L, AN.

1126 —An act for the settling the militia for . . . London. *By John Streater, and John Macock,* 1659[/60]. fol.* LT, O, AN; MH, Y.

1127 —An act for the speedie and effectuall reducing. 1641. fol. O, DT.

1128 —An act for the speedy bringing in of second moyeties. *By John Field*, 1659. fol.* LT; MH.

1129 —An act for the speedy disbanding of the army. *By John Bill and Christopher Barker*, 1660. fol.* LT, OC; CH, MH.

1130 —An act for the speedie provision of money. *By Robert Barker: and by the assigns of John Bill*, 1641. fol.* LT, O.

1130A ——[Anr. ed.] *By John Bill and Christopher Barker*, 1660. fol.* OC; MH, WF.

1131 —An act for the taking away of purveyance. *By Hen: Hills and Iohn Field*, 1657. fol.* LT, O, C, CT, HH; CH, MBP, MH, WF, Y.

1132 ——[Anr. ed.] *Edinburgh, re-printed by Christopher Higgins*, 1657. fol.* L, EN.

1133 —An act for the taking away the court of wards. *By Henry Hills and John Field*, 1656. brs. STEELE 3078. LT, O, LG, HH, ES; CN.

1134 ——[Anr. ed.] —, 1657. fol.* L, O, CJ, HH; CH, MH, NU, WF, Y.

1135 —An act for the tryal of Sir John Stowel. *By Edward Husband and Iohn Field*, 1650. fol.* C, AN; MIU.

1136 —An act for the uniformity of publick prayers. *London, printed, Edinburgh re-printed*, 1662. 4°.* MH.

1137 —An act for turning the books of the law. *By Edward Husband and Iohn Field*, 1650. brs. STEELE 2917. L.

1138 —An act giving licence for transporting fish. colop: *By Henry Hills and John Field*, 1657. fol.* LT, O, C, HH; CH, LC, MH, TU, Y.

1139 ——[Anr. ed.] colop: *Edinburgh, re-printed by Christopher Higgins*, 1657. cap., fol.* EN.

1140 —An act impowering judges for probate. *By John Field*, 1659. brs. STEELE 3112. LT, LG, LS, LUG, OQ; MH.

1141 —An act impowring the commissioners. *By John Field*, 1652[3], brs. STEELE 2982. LT, O, LG, HH; CH, MH, Y.

1142 —An act making void the acts. *By John Streater, and John Macock*, 1659[/60]. fol.* LT; MH.

1143 —An act of assessment. *By John Field and Henry Hills*, 1659. fol.* LT, C; MH, Y.

1144 —An act of free and general pardon, indemnity, and oblivion. *By John Bill and Christopher Barker*, 1660. fol.* L, OC; CH, CLC, MH, WF.

1144A ——[Anr. ed.] *Edinburgh, by a society of stationers*, 1660. 4°.* CT.

1145 —An act of indempnity. *By John Field and Henry Hills*, 1659. fol.* LT, C; CH, MH, Y.

1146 —The act of Parliament of the 27th. of Queen Elizabeth. [*London*], *printed* 1679. fol.* L, O, C, SP, HH; CH, CU, MH, WF, Y.

1147 —An act of this present Parliament, for the alteration of several names. colop: *For Edward Husband, Jan. 30*, 1648. fol.* L, C, BR; CLC, MB, MIU.

1147A —The act of tonnage and poundage. *By the assigns of John Bill and Christopher Barker*, 1675. 12°. L, CM; MH, MIU, WF.

1147B ——[Same title.] *By the assigns of John Bill and by Henry Hills and Thomas Newcomb*, 1682. MIU.

1148 ——[Same title.] *By Charles Bill and Thomas Newcomb*, 1689. 4°. L; CH, LC, MH, NC, Y.

1149 —An act prohibiting correspondence. *By John Field*, 1651. brs. STEELE 2941. LT, O, CJ, LG, HH; CH, MH, NU, WF, Y.

1149A —An act prohibiting the importing of any wines. *E. Husband*, 1649. brs. MH.

1150 —An act prohibiting the proclaiming of any person. colop: *For Edward Husband, Jan. 31*, 1648. cap., 4°. L, HH; MH, TSM, TU.

1150A ——[Anr. ed.] colop: *By John Field for Edward Husband*, 1649. 4°. L, O; CLC, MH, Y.

1151 —An act prohibiting to brew for sale any ale. *For Edward Husband*, 1649. brs. STEELE 2872. LT, LG, OQ, HH.

1152 —An act repealing the power formerly given to the Lord Admiral. colop: *For Edward Husband, Febr. 24*, 1648[9]. fol.* C; CH.

1152A —An act to enable . . . Liverpool . . . to build a church. *By Charles Bill and the executrix of Thomas Newcomb*, 1699. fol.* OC.

1153 —An act to enable their Majesties to dispense with the statute of 25 Car. 2. [*London*, 1690?] brs. Y.

1153A —An act to encourage to bringing in plate. [*London*, 1696.] brs. MH.

1153B —An act to prevent exactions of the occupiers of locks. 1695. fol.* O.

1154 —An act to prevent malicious maiming. *In the Savoy, by the assigns of John Bill and Christopher Barker*, 1670/71. fol.* L, HH; MH.

1154A —An act to prevent the destroying . . . bastard children. *S. Roycroft*, 1680. brs. L.

1155 —An act to prevent the killing of deer. *By John Field*, 1651. brs. STEELE 2938. LT, O, LG, LUG, HH; Y.

1155A —An act to retain the Queens Majesties subjects. [*London*, 1662.] cap., 4°.* HUTH.

1156 —An act touching a common-gaole. [*London*, 1651.] brs. L.

1157 —An act touching idiots and lunatiques. *By John Field*, 1653. brs. STEELE 3009. L, O, LG, OQ, HH; MH, NU, Y.

1158 —An act touching the moneys and coyns of England. *By Edward Husband and John Field*, 1649. brs. STEELE 2862. LT.

1159 ——[Anr. ed.] [*London*], *for E. Husband*, 1649. brs. STEELE 2863. L, LG, HH; MH.

1160 —An act which His Maiesty hath promised His Royall word to passe. *By Robert Ibbitson*, [1648]. brs. LT, O, HH.

1161 —An act with instructions to the commissioners. *By John Field*, 1651. brs. STEELE 2944. LT, LG, OQ, HH, AN; MH, Y.

1162 —Acts and ordinances. Beginning with acts made . . . 1648. The second part. *By Henry Hills and John Field*, 1657. fol. CH, NU.

1162A —Acts done and past in the third session of the second triennial Parliament. *Edinburgh, by Evan Tyler*, 1649. fol. ALDIS 1348. L; MH, WF.

1163 —Acts for the utter abolishing of bishops. *For Thomas Watson*, 1643. 4°.* LT, DT; MH, MIU, WF, Y.

1163A —Acts for tonnage. *By the assigns of J. Bill, and Chr. Barker*, 1671. 8°. OP; MM.

1164 —The acts made in the first Parliament of . . . Charles the First. *Edinburgh, reprinted,* 1674. ALDIS 2011. C, E, EN.

1165 ——[Anr. ed.] *Edinburgh, by David Lindsay,* 1683. 12°. ALDIS 2364. MBA, Y.

1166 —Acts of Parliament now in force, establishing the religion of the Church of England. *For Robert Pawley,* 1660. 4°.* LT, O, LL; CH, MH, NU, WF, Y.

1167 —Acts of Parliament passed in the year 1685. 1685. fol. O.

1168 —An additional act for bringing in all arrear. colop: *By John Field and Henry Hills,* 1659. cap., fol.* LT; MH, Y.

1169 —An additional act for more speedy effecting. *By J. Field,* 1650. fol.* C, E; MH.

1170 —An additionall act for sequestrations. *By John Streater, and John Macock,* 1659. fol.* LT; MH.

1170A —An additional act for the setting the militia. *J. Field* OC, HH; MH, WF, Y.

1171 —An additional act for the better improvement. *By Henry Hills and John Field,* 1657. fol. LT, O, C; CH, CN, LC, MH, NU, Y.

1171A ——[Anr. ed.] *Edinburgh, re-printed by Christopher Higgins,* 1657. fol.* L.

1172 —An additional act for the better observation of the Lords-Day. *By John Field,* 1650. 8°.* CJ; CH.

1173 —An additional article to the laws of war. *By John Field,* 1653. brs. STEELE 3012. LT, O, LG, OQ, HH; MH, WF, Y.

1174 —Additionall articles of the Lords and Commons. *By Richard Cotes and John Raworth,* [1643]. 4°.* LT, O, CJ, HH; LC, MA, MH, WF, Y.

1175 —Additionall directions of the Lords and Commons . . . for the billeting. *For John Wright,* 1647[8]. brs. STEELE 2740. LT, O; CLC, MH, Y.

1175A —An additionall instruction unto J. Berners. *Giles Calvert,* 1653. brs. LT.

1176 —An additionall ordinance of the Lords and Commons assembled . . . concerning dayes and recreation, . . . 28 Junii, 1647. *For John Wright,* 1647. 4°.* LT, OC, LUG, HH; CH, MH, NU, WF, Y.

1177 —An additionall ordinance of the Lords & Commons . . . for the better taking and expediting the accompts . . . Junii 26, 1645. *By T.W. for Ed. Husband,* 1645. 4°.* LT, O, C, BR, HH; CH, MA, MH, WF, Y.

1178 —An additionall ordinance of the Lords and Commons . . . for the better regulating and speedy bringing in . . . 25 August, 1648. *Imprinted at London for John Wright,* 1648. 4°.* LT, O, CT, HH; MH, WF, Y.

1178A —An additional ordnance for the excise. 1644. fol.* CJ, AN, DT.

1179 —An additionall ordinance of the Lords and Commons . . . for the explaining and enlarging . . . 5 Junii, 1648. *Imprinted at London for John Wright,* 1648. 4°.* LT, C, OC, HH; CH, CLC, MH, WF, Y.

1179A —An additionall ordinance of the Lords and Commons . . . for the explanation and better execution. *By R. Cotes for Iohn Bellamie,* 1648. 4°.* MH.

1180 —An additional ordinance of the Lords and Commons . . . for the more full indempnity . . . 5 Junii, 1647. [*London*], *by T.W. for Edw. Husband,* 1647. 4°.* LT, OC, HH; CH, CLC, MH, WF, Y.

1181 ——[Anr. ed.] *Printed at London, for John Wright,* 1647. brs. STEELE 2694. LT, O, C, EN; CLC, MHL, WF, Y.

1182 —An additional ordinance of the Lords and Commons . . . for the true payment of tithes . . . 9 August, 1647. *For John Wright,* 1647. 4°.* LT, O, C, BR, HH; CH, MH, NU, TU, WF, Y.

1183 —An additional ordinance of the Lords and Commons . . . to a former ordinance of the 19. of February. *For Edw. Husbands.* October 29, 1644. 4°.* LT, O, EN; CH, MH, TU, WF, Y.

1184 —An additionall ordinance of the Lords and Commons . . . to enable Sir Thomas Middleton. *For Edward Husbands,* Feb. 21. 1644. 4°.* LT, O, LG, AN; CH, MA, MH, WF, Y.

1185 —The address of the Lords spiritual and temporal . . . 15° Martii, 1688. *By James Partridge, Matthew Gillyflower, and Samuel Heyrick,* 1688[9]. brs. L, O, C, OP, HH; CH, WF, Y.

1186 ——8th March, 1688/9. *By James Partridge, Matthew Gillyflower, and Samuel Heyrick,* 1688/9. fol.* L, O, C, CT, HH; CH, CN, MH, PL, TU, WF, Y.

1187 ——eigth of March, 1688/9 [Anr. ed.] *London, reprinted Edinburgh,* 1689. brs. ALDIS 2855. L, EN; CN, Y.

1188 ——16° Aprilis, 1689. colop: *In the Savoy, by Edward Jones, for James Partridge, Matthew Gillyflower, and Samuel Heyrick,* 1689. brs. L, O, C, BR, HH; CN, MH, PL, WF, Y.

1189 ——16 April 1689 [Anr. ed.] *Edinburgh, re-printed,* 1689. brs. STEELE 3p 2804. ALDIS 2856. L, HH, ES.

1190 ——[Anr. ed.] *Printed at London, and re-printed at Edinburgh,* 1689. 4°.* HH, FSF; CLC, Y.

1191 ——18 Novembris 1692. *In the Savoy, by Edw. Jones,* 1692. fol.* L, HH; CN, PL.

1192 ——[Anr. ed.] *Edinburgh, re-printed by the heir of Andrew Anderson,* 1692. brs. ALDIS 3213. L, E.

1193 ——23rd February 1692[3]. *In the Savoy, by Edw. Jones,* 1693. fol.* L, C, HH; RPJ, WF, Y.

1193A ——9th of . . . March 1692. colop: —, 1692/3. cap., fol.* L, C; PL, RPJ, WF, Y.

1194 ——to . . . the Prince of Orange; . . . 22° Januarii 1688/9. *For James Partridge and Matthew Gyllyflower,* [1688/9]. brs. O, C, LUG, HH; CH, CN, PL, WF.

1195 —Address to His Majesty by the Parliament . . . 5 Aug. [*Edinburgh,* 1698.] brs. ALDIS 3730. HH, EN; MH, MIU.

1196 —The addresses of the Lords and Commons . . . May the 23d, 1685. *Edinburgh, by the heir of Andrew Anderson,* 1685. brs. ALDIS 2528. EN; CH, MH.

1197 —The advice and direction of both Hovses. August 19. *Printed at London for John Wright,* 1642. 4°.* LT, O, HH, EC, AN; MH, MHL, TU, WF, Y.

1198 —The agreement between the commissioners of Parliament, and His Excellencie Sr. Thomas Fairfax. *For Robert White,* 1647. 4°.* LT, O, YM; CH, CU, MH, Y.

1199 —All ordinances and orders, for the better observation of the Lords-Day, . . . 9 Decemb. 1646. *For Edw. Husband, Feb. the 18, 1646[7]. 4°.** LT, O, C, HH, EN; CH, MH, NU, WF, Y.

1199A —All the acts, ordinances and orders. *For John Wright* [1652.] 4°.* MR; MH.

1200 —All the ordinances and declarations of the Lords and Commons . . . for the assessing. *Printed at London for R.Dunscomb, Februar. 14, 1642[3]. 4°.** LT, O, C, LG, DT; CH, CSS, LC, MH, Y.

1200A — —for the indempnity. *For John Wright, 1647. 4°.** MH.

1201 —All the ordinances of the Lords and Commons . . . for the true payments of tythes. *For John Wright,* [1652.] 4°.* LL, CT; Y.

1201A — —[Anr. ed.] *For John Wright, 1649. 4°.** NIC.

1202 —All the several ordinances and orders, made by the Lords and Commons. *For Edward Husbands, Decem. 4, 1643. 4°.** L, O, C, EC, HH; CH, MA, MH, NU, Y.

1202A — —[Anr. ed.] —, 1644. 4°.* LG, CCA, CT, OC; CLC, MH, MIU, Y.

1203 — —[Anr. ed.] —, *June 22, 1644. 4°.** L, O, BR, HH; CH, CLC, MH.

1204 — —[Anr. ed.] *For Iohn Wright. August 19, 1644. 4°.** LT; CH, MA, MH, Y.

1205 — —[Anr. ed.] *For Lawrence Blaiklock, 1645. 4°.** CT, BR, HH; CLC, MH.

1206 — —[Anr. ed.] *For Ed. Husband, 1646. 4°.* L, O, OC, CCA, HH; CH, MH, NU, WF.

1207 — —[Anr. ed.] —, 1648, 4°. O, OC; CU, MH.

1208 — —[Anr. ed.] 1650. 4°. C, BP, AN; CLC, TU.

1209 —All the several ordinances, and votes. 1645. 4°. EN.

1209A —All the several ordinances, declarations & orders. *Wright, 1657.* LG.

1210 —All the several ordinances, directions and votes of the Lords and Commons. *Imprinted at London, for Iohn Wright, 1645[6]. 4°.** L, C, BR, HH; CH, NU, WF, Y.

1211 — —[Anr. ed.] —, 1646. 4°.* O, OC, OP, CT; MH, MB, PL, V, WF, Y.

1212 —Another declaration from both Houses of Parliament: sent to His Majesty, March 22. 1641[2]. *By R. Oulton & G. Dexter, 1641[2]. 4°.** LT, O, C, EC, DT; MB, MBP, MH, WF, Y.

1213 — —March 23, 1641[2]. *By R. Oulton & G. Dexter, 1641[2]. 4°.** O, LG, LVF, HH; CH, CN, LC, MH, Y.

1214 — —[Anr. ed.] *Edinburgh,* [R.Bryson], *1642. 4°.** ALDIS 1027. C, E, EN; Y.

1215 —Another declaration of the Lords and Commons . . . concerning svbscriptions. *By Luke Norton and Iohn Field, for Edward Husbands and Iohn Franck. July 6, 1642. 4°.** LT, O, CT, BP, EC; CH, LC, MH, NC, Y.

1216 — —Julii 5, 1642. *By Luke Norton and Iohn Field, for Edward Husbands and Iohn Franck. July 7, 1642. 4°.** L, BR, HH; CH, MH, NU, TU, WF, Y.

1217 — —[Anr. ed.] *For N.Allen, 7 July, 1642. 4°.** CCL; CH, CSS, MH.

1217A —Another message sent to the Kings . . . from both Houses. *For John Thomas, 1642. 4°.** LT; CLC, MH.

1217B —Another order for contributions. *For Edw. Husbands, 1693. 8°.** Y.

1218 —An answer from both Houses of Parliament, to a declaration. *For B.A., 1647. 4°.** LT, OC, HH; CN.

1219 —The answer of both Houses of Parliament, presented to His Majestie at York, the ninth of May, 1642. *By Robert Barker, and by the assignes of John Bill, 1642. 4°.** LT, O, LL, CT, HH; CH, CN, MH, WF, Y.

1219A — —[Anr. ed.] *York, by Robert Barker, and by the assignes of John Bill, 1642. 4°.** L, CF; MH.

1219B — —[Anr. ed.] *For I.T., 1642. 4°.** OWC.

1220 —An ansvver of both Houses of Parliament to His Majesties last message. *For H. Becke, 1648. 4°.** LT; MH.

1221 —The answer of both Hovses of Parliament to His Majesties message of the 12. of November. *Printed at Oxford by Leonard Lichfield, 1642. 4°.** MADAN 1086. L, O, BR, DT; CLC, MH, TU, WF, Y.

1222 —The answer of both Houses of Parliament to the kings message, sent . . . the 16th of March. 1641. *By E. G. for I. Wright, 1642. 4°.** L, O, C, CT, DT; CSS, MH, NU, WF.

1223 Entry cancelled.

1224 —The answer of the Lords and Commons assembled . . . to several papers of the commissioners . . . 14 April, 1646. *For Edward Husband, April 16. 1646. 4°.** LT, C, MR, E, EN; CH, CU, LC, MH, NU, TU, Y.

1225 —The ansvver of the Lords and Commons to the Essex petition. *By B.A., 1648. 4°.** LT; Y.

1226 —The ansvver of the Lords and Commons . . . to the peitition of the knights, . . . of Sussex. [*London,* 1648.] brs. LT.

1227 —The answer of the Parliament of England, to a paper, . . . 20 Semptem. 1650. *By Edward Husband and John Field, 1650. 4°.** LT, O, C, LL, EN; CH, CU, MH, WF, Y.

1228 —The answer of the Parliament of the Commonwealth of England to three papers. *By John Field, 1652.* 4°.* LT, O, C, LL, BR; CH, MH, NU, PL, WF, Y.

1229 —Articles and acts of Parliament: taken out of the records. *For Theophilus Bourne, 1642. 4°.** LT, EC, HH, DT; NU, WF.

1230 —Articles exhibited in Parliament, against Master Iohn Sqvire . . . August 7th. 1641. [*London*], *printed, 1641.* 4°. LT, O, LG, HH, YM; CH, MH, NU, WF, Y.

1230A —Articles exhibited in the Parliament, Against William Beale. [*London*], *printed 1641. 4°.** L, O, OC, E, DT; CN, MH, NU, WF, Y.

1231 —The articles of cessation of the Lords and Commons. *Printed at Oxford by Leonard Lichfield, March 25, 1643.* 4°.* MADAN 1290. O, DT; CN, MH, MIU, NU, Y.

1232 — —March 22, 1642[3]. *Oxford, March 25. by Leonard Lichfield,* [*London*], *reprinted for R. Royston, 1643. 4°.** LT, O, C, OC, HH; CH, MH, MHL, WF, Y.

1233 — —[Anr. ed.] *Printed at Oxford, and reprinted at Shrewsbury, 1643. 4°.** LT.

1234 —Articles of impeachment exhibited in Parliament against Spencer Earle of Northamp. *July,* 1. *London, by T. F. for J.Y., 1642. 4°.** LT, SP; CH, LC, MH. WF, Y.

1235   —The articles or charge exhibited in Parliament against Sir Francis Windebanck. [*London*], *printed*, 1641. 4°.* LT, O, CT, HH; CH, CU, NU, TU, WF, Y.

1236   —Association. Whereas there has been a horrid and detestable conspiracy. [*Boston, Mass.*, 1699?] brs. CH.

1237   —Anno Regni Willielmi et Mariae, . . . primo. On the twenty third day of February, . . . 1688. *By Charles Bill and Thomas Newcomb*, 1688. fol.* L; CH, Y.

1237A   — —[Anr. ed.] — *and re-printed at Edinburgh*, 1689. fol.* MIU.

1238   —At a Parliament begun and holden at Westminster the 22d of January, . . . an act for reversing the attainder of Henry Cornish. [*London*, 1689.] brs. Y.

1239   —At the Committee of Lords and Commons appointed by ordinance. *For Ed. Husband*, 1645. brs. LT; MH.

1240   —At the Committee of Lords and Commons, for advance of money, . . . [*London*, 1642.] cap., brs. STEELE 2315. LT, EC; MH.

1241   — —[Anr. ed.] [*London*, 1642.] cap., brs. STEELE 2317. LT, LG; MH, MHS.

1242   — —15 December 1642. *For R. Dunscomb*, 2 Jan. 1642/3. brs. STEELE 2324. LT, LU.

1243   — —[Anr. ed.] [*London*, 1643.] brs. STEELE 2430. LT; MH.

1244   — —[Anr. ed.] [*London*, 1643.] brs. STEELE 2473. LT; MH.

1244A   — —[Anr. ed., Octobris 6. 1643.] [*London*, 1643.] brs. MH.

1245   —At the Committee of Lords and Commons . . . for securing eighty thousand pounds. *For E. Husband*, 1645. brs. STEELE 2612. LT; MH.

1246   —At the Parliament begun at Westminster the third day of November, anno Dom. 1640. *By Robert Barker: and by the assignes of John Bill*, 1641. 4°.* O; CLC, MM, NU.

1246A   — —[Anr. ed.] —, 1642. 4°.* MM.

1246B   — —[Anr. ed.] —, *re-printed at Dublin by W. Bladen*, 1652. 4°.* DIX 90. DK.

1247   —At the Parliament begun at Westminster, the five and twentieth day of April, . . . 1660. *Edinburgh by a society of stationers*, 1660. 4°.* ALDIS 1622. C, HH, EN; CH, CLC, MH, Y.

1247A   — —[Anr. ed.] *By John Bill and Christopher Barker*, 1660. fol.* CS; MH, WF.

1247B   — —[Anr. ed.] —, *reprinted at Dublin by William Bladen*, 1660. fol.* DIX 107, DT.

1248   —At the Parliament begun at Westminster the eighth day of May, anno Dom. 1661. *Printed*, 1662. 4°.* CH, CN, MH, Y.

1249   — —[Anr. ed.] *Printed at London, and re-printed at Edinburgh*, 1662. 4°.* FSF.

1249A   — —[Anr. ed.] *By John Bill and Christopher Barker*, 1664. fol. L; Y.

1250   — —[Anr. ed.] *In the Savoy, by the assigns of John Bill and Christopher Barker*, 1670. fol. L, HH; CH, CN, MH, WF.

1250A   — —[Anr. ed.] *By John Bill, Christopher Barker, Thomas Newcomb, and Henry Hills*, 1678. fol. L, O, CS; CH, MH, WCL, WF.

1250B   — —[Anr. ed.] *Dublin, by Benjamin Took; and are to be sold by Mary Crook*, 1678. 8°.* DIX 162. DI, DK, DT.

1251   —At the Parliament begun . . . two and twentieth day of November, . . . 1695. *By Charles Bill, and the executrix of Thomas Newcomb*, 1696. fol.* L; CH, MHL,Y.

1251A   — —[Anr. ed.] *By Charles Bill, and reprinted in Dublin*, 1698. fol.* DIX 299. DN.

1252   —At the Parliament begun at Westminster the four and twentieth day of August . . . 1698. *By Charles Bill and the executrix of Thomas Newcomb*, 1699. 4°. L; CH, MHL, MIU.

1252A   — —[Anr. ed.] —; *and re-printed by John Brocas, Dublin*, 1699. 4°.* DIX 309. CD, DI, DK, DT.

1252B   — —[Anr. ed.] *London, printed; and reprinted in Dublin for Matt. Gunn*, 1700. 4°.* DIX 316. CD, DI, DN.

1252C   — —[Anr. ed.] *Reprinted in Dublin, by John Brocas, for Jacob Millner, and Patrick Campbell*, 1700. 8°. DIX 316. DN, DT.

1253   —At a Parliament. *Printed at London, and re-printed at Edinburgh*, 1700. 4°.* EN; WF.

1254   — —[Anr. ed.] *London, by Charles Bill, and the executrix of Thomas Newcomb, reprinted at Boston in New England by Bartholomew Green & John Allen*, 1696. 4°.* EVANS 741. MHS, MWA, Y.

1255   —Be it enacted and ordained by autho . . . 25 April 1650. [*London*, 1650.] brs. STEELE 2895. HH.

1256   —Be it enacted by this present Parliament . . . 14 May 1659. *By John Field*, 1659. brs. STEELE 3110. LT, OQ; MH.

1257   —Be it ordained and it is ordained by . . . 28 May 1647. [*London*], *for E. Husband*, 8 June, 1647. brs. STEELE 2689. L, LG; CLC, MH.

1258   —Be it ordained by the Lords and Commons . . . that John Towse. *By Richard Cotes and John Raworth*, 1644. brs. STEELE 2592. LT, LG.

1259   —Be it ordained by the Lords and Commons . . . 20 September 1647. *For J. Wright*, 1647. brs. STEELE 2731. L, LG; MH.

1260   —Be it ordained . . . that John Bradshaw. *For J. Wright*, 1648. brs. STEELE 2773. HODGKIN.

1261   —Be it ordained . . . that the declaration of the twenty foure . . . be null and void. *For Thomas Vere*, 1647. brs. MH, Y.

1262   —A bill for the establishment of a court-merchant in London. colop: *By Iohn Redmayne*, 1659. cap., 4°.* L; WF, Y.

1263   —A brief of an act of Parliament. [*London?* 1644.] 4°.* C.

1264   —By authority of the Parliament of the Commonwealth of England, these are to command. *By Iohn Field*, 1651. brs. STEELE 2935. L; Y.

1264A   —By the commissioners of the Parliament . . . for ordering and managing affairs in Scotland. *Printed at Leith by Evan Tyler*, 1651. brs. Y.

1265   —By the committee of the Lords and Commons for the safety of king and kingdome. *Septem. 23. London, by John Partridge*, 1642. brs. STEELE 2262. LT; MH.

1266   —By the knights citizens and burgesses in Parliament assembled. It is this day ordered, . . . 14 April 1666. *Dublin, J. Crook*, 1666. brs. STEELE 2p 758. DPR.

1267 ——3 August 1666. *Dublin, J. Crook,* 1666. brs. STEELE 2p 765. LS, DPR.

1268 —By the Lords and Commons . . . instructions rules and directions. colop: *For Edward Husbands,* 1645. fol.* STEELE 2617. LT, O, LG; CH, CLC, MA.

1269 —By the Lords and others His Majesties Commissions. An order for the observance and execution of the statute. *Printed at Oxford by Leonard Lichfield,* 1644. brs. MADAN 1671. O.

1270 —By vertue of an ordinance of both. [*London,* 1643.] brs. STEELE 2505. L.

1271 —A catalogue and collection of all those ordinances. *By William Du-Gard, and Henry Hills,* 1654. fol. L, LG, LUG, DT; CH, MH, NU, WF, Y.

1271A —Certain acts of Parliament. *Oxford, L. L[ichfield],* 1681. fol.* WCL.

1271B —August 6. Certaine observations of both Houses. *For John Wright,* 1642. 4°.* BR; Y.

1272 —Certain propositions made by the High Covrt of Parliament. *For John Francke, October 21,* 1642. 4°.* LT, LG, EC; CN, WF, Y.

1273 —Certaine propositions of both Houses . . . concerning the raising of horse. *For T. P.,* [1642]. 4°.* BP, SP; BBE, CN, MH, Y.

1274 ——[Anr. ed.] *For Ioseph Hunscott,* 1642. 4°.* LT, O, C, OC; CN, CSS, MH, WF, Y.

1275 ——[Anr. ed.] *For E. Husbands and J. Franck,* 1642. 4°.* L, BR, HH, YM; CH, MH, MIU, Y.

1276 ——[Anr. ed.] [*London*], *are to be sold at the Hospitall Gate in Smith-Field,* 1642. 4°.* Y.

1276A ——[Anr. ed.] *For Tho. Winter,* 1642. 4°.* EC; MH.

1276B ——[Anr. ed.] *For Edward Blackmore,* 1642. 4°.* O, CJ; CN, WF.

1276C ——[Anr. ed.] *Gaye,* 1642. LSE.

1277 —Charissimis consanguineis nostris Hen. Com. Huntington. *For Iohn Wright,* 1642. brs. STEELE 2197. LT, O, HH; CH.

1278 —Charles by the grace of God King of England . . . 18 January. [*London*], 1647 [8]. brs. STEELE 2744. L.

1279 Entry cancelled.

1279A —A collection of orders, votes, debates, . . . Danby. 1679. fol. LL, OC.

1280 —A collection of some memorable and weighty transactions in Parliament. *Printed,* 1695. 4°.* L, OC, SP; CH, CN, MH, TU, WF, Y.

1280A ——[Anr. ed.] —, 1697. 4°.* CT.

1281 —A collection of the debates and proceedings in Parliament, in 1694, and 1695. *Printed,* 1695. 4°. L, C, OC, HH, EN; CH, CN, MH, NCL, WF, Y.

1282 ——[Anr. ed] —, 1695. 4°. L, C, OC; CH, MH, WF, Y.

1283 —Committee appointed by Parliament for the navy and customes. *By J. R. for J. Hunscott, July 12,* 1643. brs. STEELE 2454. LT.

1284 —The copies of such bills. *For E. Husbands, July 19,* 1643. 4°. CCA, CT; WF.

1285 —A copy of a letter, from the members of both Houses . . . to the Earle of Essex. *Oxford by Leonard Lichfield,* 1643. 4°.* MADAN 1524. LT, O, C, LSC, DT; CH, CN, MH, WF, Y.

1285A ——[Anr. ed.] —, 1643. 4°.* MADAN 1525. O; Y.

1285B ——[Anr. ed.] *Bristoll, by R. Barker and J. Bill,* 1643. 4°.* BR.

1286 —The coppy of a letter sent by the Lords and Commons . . . to the committees . . . October 23. 1641. *For Iohn Thomas,* 1641. 4°.* LT, O, HH; OWC, Y.

1287 —Copy of the orders for repealing of several acts. colop: *Boston in New-England by Bartholomew Green, and John Allen,* 1697. 4°.* EVANS 217. LPR; MWA, NN.

1288 —A copie of the petition of both Houses of Parliament . . . 1° Martii 1641[2]. *By Robert Barker, and by the assignes of John Bill,* 1641[2]. 4°.* LT, CT, EC, BR, HH; CLC, CN, MH, TU, WF, Y.

1288A —The debate at large. [*London*], *for J. Wickins,* 1623. 8°. L, C, LL, LW, EN; CH, CU, LL, MH, WU, Y.

1289 —Declaratio Parliamenti Angliae de expectiore. *Typis Carl, Du-gard,* 1656. 4°.* C; HR.

1290 —Parliamenti Angliae declaratio: in quâ res numperum gestae. *Apud Franciscum Tytonium, Mensis Martii 22°,* 1648. 4°.* LT, C, CJ, CT, HH; CH, NU, WF, Y.

1291-3 Entries cancelled.

1294 A declaration . . . 13 February 1688/9. *Edinburgh, reprinted* [*heir of A. Anderson*], 1689. brs. STEELE 3p 2771. HH, ER.

1295 —The declaration and desires of the Lords and Commons . . . to the subjects of Scotland. *Decemb. 29.* [*London*], *for Richard West,* 1642. 4°.* CN, MH, WF, Y.

1296 —A declaration and narrative of the proceedings of the Parliament of England, touching the message and letters of credence. *Imprinted at London, for G. Horton,* 1651. 4°.* LT.

1297 —A declaration and ordinance of the Lords and Commons . . . for new loans . . . 30 Januar. 1642[3]. *By J. R. for Edw. Husbands, Feb. 2,* 1642[3]. 4°.* LT, O, C, OC, HH; CH, LC, MH, TU, WF, Y.

1298 ——[Anr. ed.] [*London,* 1643] brs. STEELE 2357. LT, O, C, LPR, LS.

1299 —A declaration and ordinance of the Lords and Commons . . . for the associating of the severall counties. *By J. R. for Edw. Husbands, Feb. 3,* 1642[3]. 4°.* LT, CT, HH, DT; MA, MH, WF.

1300 —A declaration and ordinance . . . for the better preventing of spyes. 1643. 4°.* O, EC, EN; Y.

1300A ——[Anr. ed.] [*London*], *for Edward Husbands, October 23,* 1643. 4°.* MADAN 1479. L; MA, Y.

1301 —A declaration and ordinance of the Lords and Commons . . . for the better securing and setling of the peace of . . . Kent. *For I. Wright, June 1,* 1643. 4°.* LT, O, HH, SP; CLC, MA, MH, MIU, WF.

1302 —A declaration and ordinance of the Lords and Commons . . . for the seizing and sequestring of the estates. *For Edward Husbands, March 31,* 1643. 4°.* LT, O, OC, MR, DT; CH, CN, MH, NU, WF, Y.

1302A — —[Anr. ed.] *For I. Wright and I. Franke, Aprill* 1, 1643. 4°.* L, BR; CLC.

1303 —A declaration and ordinance of the Lords and Commons . . . for the sequestering the estates. *For Edward Husband,* 1648. brs. STEELE 2802. LT, LG; MIU.

1304 —A declaration and ordinance of the Lords and Commons . . . for the speedy raising of a body of horse. *For Edward Husbands. July* 27, [1643.] 4°.* LT, O, C, LG, EN; CH, MBP, MH, WF, Y.

1305 —The declaration and ordinance of the Lords and Commons . . . touching the Great Seale. [*London*], *for Edward Husbands, November* 11, 1643. 4°.* LT, O, HH, EN; CN, MH, MIU, NU, WF, Y.

1306 — —[Anr. ed.] *For Edward Husbands, November,* 13, 1643. 4°.* CCA, HH, E; CH, CLC, CU, LC, Y.

1307 — —[Anr. ed.] *Printed at Oxford by Leonard Lichfield, Nov.* 21, 1643. 4°.* MADAN 1491. LT, O, CF, CT, YM; CH, MH, MIU, Y.

1307A — —[Anr. ed.] *Bristoll, by Robert Barker and John Bill,* 1643. 4°.* O, OC.

1308 —The declaration and petition of both Houses . . . June 22. *June* 27, *London, for I. Tompson, and A. Coe,* 1642. 4°.* L, O, BR, OC, SP; CLC, CN, MH, PL, Y.

1309 —A declaration and protestation of the Lords and Commons . . . Octob. 22, 1642. *Octob.* 23. *London, for Iohn Wright,* 1642. 4°.* LT, O, CCA, BR, HH; CN, CSS, LC, MH, NPT.

1310 — —[Anr. ed.] *For I. Wright, Octob.* 24, 1642. 4°.* L, C, EC, HH, EN; CSS, CU, MH, NU, WF, Y.

1310A — —[Anr. ed.] *For I. Wright, Octob.* 25, 1642. 4°.* CJ; MH, WF.

1310B — —[Anr. ed.] —, *and reprinted for W. Lee,* 1642. 4°.* CT.

1311 —A declaration and protestation of the Lords and Commons . . . wherein (amongst divers . . .) Octob. 22, 1642. *By L. N. for E. Husbands and J. Frank,* 1642.* O, C, LL, HH; Y.

1312 — —[Anr. ed.] *For Edward Blackmore, Octob.* 25, 1642. 4°.* CH, CN.

1313 —A declaration and resolution of the Lords and Commons . . . concerning His Majesties late proclamation. *August* 15. *London, for Edward Husbands and Iohn Franck,* 1642. 4°.* LT, C, CT, EC; CSS, MH, NU, Y.

1314 — —[Anr. ed.] *By L. N. and I. F. for Edward Husbands and John Franck, August* 15, 1642. 4°.* L, CJ, BR, SP; CH, CN, PL, TU, Y.

1315 — —[Anr. ed.] *By F. Leach for Edward Husbands, and John Franck, August* 15, 1642. 4°.* L, O, C, LW, HH; MH, TU, WF, Y.

1316 — —[Anr. ed.] *For John Wright, August* 15, 1642. 4°.* HH; CH, MH.

1317 — —[Anr. ed.] *August* 15. *London, for Edward Blackmore,* 1642. 4°.* OC; CN, MH, NU, WF.

1318 — —[Anr. ed.] *For Iospeh Hunscott,* 1642. 4°.* LT.

1319 — —[Anr. ed.] *For Edward Husbands and John Franck, September* 23, 1642. 4°.* CJ, HH; CN, MHL, NU.

1320 —A declaration and resolution of the Lords and Commons . . . in answer to the Scots declaration. *For Edward Husbands and John Franck, September* 23, 1642. 4°.* LT, EC, HH; CH, MBP, MH, WF, Y.

1321 — —[Anr. ed.] *Septemb.* 23. *London, for John Wright,* [1642]. 4°.* L, O, CJ, CT, HH; NU, TU, Y.

1322 — —[Anr. ed.] *June* 6. *London for I. H.,* [1643]. 4°.* LT, C, MR, EN; MH, MIU, Y.

1323 — —[Anr. ed.] *For John Wright, Septemb.* 23, [1644]. 4°.* HH; MIU.

1324 —The declaration and several votes of both Houses of Parliament. 1642. 4°. C, EN; MH.

1325 —The declaration and votes of both Houses of Parliament, concerning the magazine at Hull. *By Fr. Leach,* 1642. 4°.* O; NU.

1325A — —[Anr. ed.] *For John Wright,* 1642. 4°.* CN, MB, MH.

1326 — —[Anr. ed.] *By Robert Barker: and the assignes of John Bill,* 1642. 4°.* LT, C, OC, EC, DT; CH, MH, MHL, WF, Y.

1326A — —[Anr. ed.] *York, by Robert Barker, and by the assignes of John Bill,* 1642. 4°.* CF; YM.

1327 —A declaration and votes of the Lords and Commons . . . concerning some scruple . . . Decemb. 7, 1642. *Decem.* 8. *London, for John Wright,* 1642. 4°.* LT, O, LL, HH, DT; MA, MH, WF, Y.

1328 —The declaration and votes of the Lords and Commons . . . concerning the late treaty . . . Octob. 4, 1642. *October* 5. [*London*], *for Iohn Wright,* 1642. 4°.* LT, O, OC, EC, HH; CH, CLC, MH, WF, Y.

1329 — —[Anr. ed.] *For John Wright, October* 6. 1642. 4°.* C, CCA, OC, HH; MHL.

1330 —A declaration by the Lords and Commons . . . declaring that none shall aprehend. *For Francis Leach,* [1642]. brs. STEELE 2219. LT, O, LS, HH.

1331 —A declaration concerning the present treaty of peace. *For J. H. and Hen. Hutton,* 1643. 4°.* LT; CH, PL, WF, Y.

1332 —La declaration des Seigneurs & Communes . . . touchant les escrites des commissaires d'Escosse. *Par Tho: Forcet,* 1648. 4°. LT; WF, Y.

1333 Entry cancelled.

1334 —La declaration du Parlement d'Angleterre: contenant les motifs. *Imprimé,* 1649. 4°.* L, C, CS; Y.

1335 —Declaration du Parlement d'Angleterre, touchant les efforts. *A Londres, par Matthieu Simmons,* 1649. 4°. HR, LC.

1336 —La declaration du Parlement de la republique d'Angleterre, sur les affaires. *A Londres, par Guil. Du-Gard,* 1652. 4°. LNC; HR, CH, MH, WF.

1336A —A declaration from both Houses of Parliament . . . 9 of March, 1641. *Printed,* 1641. 4°.* CCA; MH.

1337 —A declaration from both Houses of Parliament . . . 12 Martii, 1642. *By R. Oulton & G. Dexter,* 1642. 4°.* L, SP, E; CLC, WF, Y.

1337A — —[Anr. ed.] *Printed,* 1642. 4°.* CH, MH, Y.

1338 — —May 17. [*n.p.*] *May* 20, *for I. Tomson, and A. Coe,* 1642. 4°.* LT, O.

1339 —A declaration in answer to some papers. *For John Wright*, 1647. 4°. LT, O, GU; MIU, OWC.

1339A —A declaration of both Houses . . . 12 May 1642. *For J. Hunscott, 16 May*, 1642. brs. STEELE 2127. LT, O, LS.

1340 —The declaration of both Hovses . . . concerning His Majesties letter. *For Joseph Hunscot and Iohn Wright, 16 Iune*, 1642. brs. STEELE 2180. LT, O, CT, LG, HH; MH, WF.

1341 —A declaration of both Houses of Parliament, concerning the affairs of Ireland. *For Joseph Hunscott*, 1641[2]. 4°.* LT, O, C, EC, HH; CH, CU, LC, MH, Y.

1342 —A declaration of both Houses of Parliament, in answer to His Majesties last message. [*London*], *May 5, for Joseph Hunscott*, 1642. 4°.* LT, O, CT, BR, HH; CLC, CN, LC, MH, Y.

1343 ——[Anr. ed.] *For Edward Husbands, June 17*, 1642. 4°.* L, O, OC, HH; CH, MH.

1344 —A declaration of both Houses of Parliament sent to the well-affected brethren. [*London*], *for Tho. Nelson, Novemb.* 17, 1642. 4°.* LT; MIU.

1345 —Declaration of both Houses of Parliament, shewing the necessity of a present subscription. *18 Jan.*, 1642[3]. brs. STEELE 2345. L, O, LG; MH.

1346 —A declaration of both Hovses of Parliament shewing the necessity of a present subscription. *Printed at London for R. Dunscomb, Januar.* 23, 1642. 4°.* LT, HH, BR, DT; CSS, MH, NC, WF, Y.

1347 —The declaration of both Houses of Parliament, to the Kings. *For I. Weight* [*sic*], 1643. 4°.* HH; NU.

1347A —A declaration of both Houses, touching the government. 1647. brs. CJ.

1348 —A declaration of the Lords and Commons . . . Martis ult. Februarii, 1642. The Lords. *March* 1. *London, for Iohn Wright*, 1642[3]. brs. STEELE 2378. LT, LS, HH; CH, Y.

1349 —A declaration of the Lords and Commons . . . die Mercurii 10. May 1643. Whereas. *For Iohn Wright*, 1643. brs. STEELE 2420. LT; CH, MH, Y.

1350 —A declaration of the Lords and Commons die Lunae 8 Septemb. 1645. Whereas. *For John Wright, 9 Septemb.*, 1645. brs. STEELE 2629. LT, AN.

1351 —A declaration of the Lords and Commons . . . die Martis 30. Martii 1647. That the two Houses. *Printed at London, for John Wright*, 1647. brs. STEELE 2686. LT, O, LG, LS; MH, WF, Y.

1352 —A declaration of the Lords and Commons . . . die Veneris 13 Octob. 1648. *For John Wright*, 1648. brs. STEELE 2799. LT, O, LG; CH, MH.

1353 —A declaration of the Lords and Commons . . . Die Veneris 15. Decemb. 1648. *For John Wright*, 1648. brs. STEELE 2807. LT, O, HH; MH, MIU.

1354 —The declaration of the Lords and Commons . . . 13th of February, 1688/9. colop: [*London*], *printed* 1689. fol.* L, LL, OC, OP, HH; CH, CLC, WF, Y.

1355 ——[Anr. ed.] colop: [*Edinburgh*], *re-printed* 1689. brs. ALDIS 2579. EN; Y.

1356 —A declaration of the Lords & Commons against George Lord Goring. *For Edward Husband, June* 15, 1648. 4°.* LT, LG; CLC, MH, MIU, NU, WF.

1357 —A declaration of the Lords and Commons . . . concerning a late difference. *March* 24. *for John Wright*, 1642[3]. 4°.* LT, O, C, HH, DT; CH, MH, NU, WF, Y.

1358 —A declaration of the Lords and Commons . . . concerning a late proclamation. *For Iohn Wright, Iune 2*, 1643. 4°.* LT, O, HH, DT; CH, MH, NU, WF, Y.

1359 —A declaration of the Lords and Commons . . . concerning a personall treaty. *For J.J.*, 1648. 4°.* LT.

1359A —A declaration of the Lords and Commons . . . concerning a printed paper. *For Iohn Francke, and Edward Husbands*, 1642. 4°.* CN, MBP, MHL.

1360 —A declaration of the Lords and Commons . . . concering an illegall vvritt. *By A. Norton for Edw. Husbands and Iohn Franke, June 20*, 1642. 4°.* L, O, OC, CCA; CH, MH, Y.

1361 —A declaration of the Lords and Commons . . . concerning an insolent letter. *For John Wright, 14 Septemb.*, 1642. 4°.* LT, O, LL, HH, DT; CH, MH, NR, WF, Y.

1362 —A declaration of the Lords and Commons . . . concerning coales and salt. *Jan.* 13. *London for T. S.*, [1643]. 4°.* LT, O; CSS, MH, WF, Y.

1363 —A declaration of the Lords and Commons concerning divers well-affected persons. *For Edward Husbands and John Franck, Novemb.*, 16, 1642. 4°. LT, O, LG, HH, DT; CN, CSS, MH, WF, Y.

1364 —A declaration of the Lords and Commons . . . concerning diverse well affected persons . . . of London. [*London*, 1642.] brs. STEELE 2305. LT, LG, LS, EC.

1365 —A declaration of the Lords and Commons . . . concerning His Majesties advancing with his army . . . 15 Octob. 1642. *For I. Wright, Octob.* 17, 1642. 4°.* LT, C, LL, HH, EN; CH, CN, CSS, MH, NU, Y.

1366 ——[Anr. ed.] *Octob.* 17. *London, for John Wright*, 1642. 4°.* L, O, OC, CCA, CJ; CH, MBP, MH, TU, WF.

1367 ——[Anr. ed.] *For Edw. Husbands and I. Franke, Octob.* 18, 1642. 4°.* LT, O, LG, YM, HH; CLC, MH, MHL, WF, Y.

1368 —A declaration of the Lords and Commons . . . concerning His Maiesties late proclamation. *Lomdon* [*sic*]. *Decemb.* 31, *for T. Frank*, 1642. 4°.* LT, DT; MH, Y.

1369 ——[Anr. ed.] *For Iohn Wright, April.* 23, 1644. 4°.* LT, O, HH, SP; CH, MH, V, WF, Y.

1370 —A declaration of the Lords and Commons . . . concerning His Maiesties letter . . . Mercvrii. 15 [Junii] 1642. *For Joseph Hunscott and John Wright*, 1642. 4°.* L, OC, CT, HH, DT; CLC, CSS, MH, WF.

1370A ——[Anr. ed.] *For Tho. Winter and T. Hewer*, 1642. 4°.* MBP.

1371 —A declaration of the Lords and Commons . . . concerning His Maiesties proclamation of May 27. *By A. Norton for Edward Husbands, Iune 8*, 1642. 4°.* LT, CCA, CT, BR, YM; CH, CN, MBP, MH, TU, WF.

1371A ——[Anr. ed.] *For Joseph Hunscott*, 1642. 4°.* OC, CCA, CJ.

1371B ——[Anr. ed.] *For William Gaye, June 8*, 1642. 4°.* CF; CSS.

1372 ——[Anr. ed.] *For Joseph Hunscott and John Wright*, 1642. 4°.* L, O, CJ, EN, DT; CSS, MH, NU, WF, Y.

1372A ——[Anr. ed.] *For Jos. Hunscott and J. Wright*, 1642. 4°.* L, O, CM, EC, HH; CH, MH, MHL, WF.

1373 —A declaration of the Lords and Commons . . . concerning His Majesties proclamation. *For Tho. Banks, Novemb. 4*, 1642. 4°.* LT, O, HH; CLC, CN, MH, RPJ, Y.

1374 —A declaration of the Lords and Commons . . . concerning His Majesties proclamation. *For Iohn Wright. January 23*, 1642[3]. 4°.* LT, O, HH, YM; CLC, CSS, MH. WF, Y.

1375 —A declaration of the Lords and Commons . . . concerning His Maiesties proclamation. *For T. Wright*, 1643. 4°.* LT, LG, OC, CT, HH; CN, MBP, MH, NU, Y.

1376 —A declaration of the Lords and Commons . . . concerning His Majesty's severall messages . . . 5 Maii 1642. *For I. T.*, 1642. 4°.* L, O, C, OC; CN, MH, Y.

1377 ——[Anr. ed.] *For John Wright*, 1642. 4°.* L, O, CM, EC, BR; CLC, MBP, MH, TU, WF, Y.

1377A ——[Anr. ed.] *For Math. Rhodes*, 1642. 4°.* OC; MH.

1378 —A declaration of the Lords and Commons . . . concerning prisoners in the Island of Jersey. *For John Wright*, 1645. brs. CH.

1379 —A declaration of the Lords and Commons . . . concerning soldiers that resort. *For Edward Husband. Octob. 23.* 1647. 4°. MH.

1380 —A declaration of the Lords and Commons . . . concerning the abuses. *For E. Husbands and I. Franck, Septemb. 3*, 1642. 4°.* O, C, HH; CU, LC, MH, MHL, Y.

1381 ——[Anr. ed.] *By Luke Norton and John Field, for E. Husband and J. Franck, September 3*, 1642. 4°.* L, CT.

1382 —A declaration of the Lords and Commons . . . concerning the commission. [*London*, 1642.] 4°.* O.

1383 —A declaration of the Lords and Commons . . . concerning the disbanding of the army. *For John Wright*, 1647. 4°.* LT, O, C, HH, EN; CH, LC, MH, MHL, Y.

1384 —The declaration of the Lords and Commons . . . concerning the Earl of Stamford. *By E. G. for C. Latham and T. Creake*, 1942 (*i.e.*, 1642). brs. STEELE 2231. LT, O, LG, HH; MH.

1385 —A declaration of the Lords and Commons . . . concerning the estates, rent, . . . Cambridge. *For F. Constable, and Iohn Wright, January 8*, 1643[4]. 4°.* LT, O, C, YM, EN; CH, CN, MH, WF, Y.

1386 —A declaration of the Lords and Commons . . . conncerning [*sic*] the Kings Majesty. *By Robert Ibbitson*, 1647. 4°.* L, CJ; MH, WF, Y.

1387 —A declaration of the Lords and Commons . . . concerning the Kings Majesty. *For R. W.*, 1648. 4°.* LT; CSS, MH, MHL, NU.

1388 —A declaration of the Lords and Commons . . . concerning the late treaty of peace in Cheshire. *Ian. 9.* [*London*], *for I. Wright*, 1642[3]. 4°.* LT, O, C, EN, DT; CLC, CSS, MH, WF, Y.

1389 —A declaration of the Lords and Commons . . . concerning the late valorous and acceptable service. *Novemb 1. London, for John Wright*, 1642. 4°.* LT, LG, EN.

1390 ——[Anr. ed.] *Novemb. 12. London, for John Wright*, 1642. 4°.* LT, O, EC, HH; CH, MH, NU, WF, Y.

1391 —A declaration of the Lords and Commons . . . concerning the miserable distractions. *For Edward Husband, and John Frank, July 13*, 1642. 4°.* LT, O, C, LL, HH; CLC, MH, NU, WF, Y.

1392 —A declaration of the Lords and Commons . . . concerning the papers of the Scots Commissioners. *For Edward Husband, March 13*, 1647[8]. 4°. LT, O, C, MR, EN; CH, CU, MH, NU, WF, Y.

1393 —A declaration of the Lords and Commons . . . concerning the particular causes of this division. *Iuly 8. London, by T. F. for S. F.* 1642. 4°.* LT, O; CSS, NU, Y.

1394 —A declaration of the Lords and Commons . . . concerning the present lamentable, and miserable condition of Ireland. *By George Miller, June 24*, 1643. 4°.* LT, O, C, OC, HH; CH, MH, MIU, WF.

1395 —The declaration of the Lords and Commons . . . concerning the present lamentable estate . . . of Ireland. *For I. Wright, Inne* [*sic*] *17*, 1643. 4°.* LT, O, C; CH, CU, WF, Y.

1396 —A declaration of the Lords and Commons . . . concerning the preservation of Hull. *July, the 13, London, for Iohn Wright*, 1642. 4°.* LT, YM; CSS, MH.

1397 —A declaration of the Lords and Commons . . . concerning the pressing necessities. *For Iohn Wright, January, 10.* 1642[3]. 4°.* LT, O, C, BR, HH; CLC, MBP, MH, WF, Y.

1398 —A declaration of the Lords and Commons . . . concerning the publishing. *For Ed. Husbands and Jo. Franck*, 1642. *July 6.* brs. STEELE 2212. LT, O, LS, CT, EC; MH.

1399 —A declaration of the Lords and Commons . . . concerning the reducing of the late revolted ships. *Imprinted at London for John Wright*, 1648. 4°.* LT, HH, BR, MR; CH, MH, MIU, WF, Y.

1400 —A declaration of the Lords and Commons . . . concerning the regulating of great inconveniencies. [*London*], *by John Field, for Edward Husbands and John Franck. Nov. 10,* [1642]. STEELE 2303. LT, O, HH, DT; CN, MH, WF, Y.

1401 —A declaration of the Lords and Commons . . . concerning the tryall of the king. [*London*], *for I. VVhite* [1649]. 4°.* LT, O, YM, SP; MH, WF, Y.

1402 —The declaration of the Lords and Commons . . . concerning their endeavours. *Printed at Oxford by Leonard Lichfield*, 1643[4]. 4°.* MADAN 1563. LT, O, CT, EC, EN; CH, MH, PL, WF, Y.

1403 ——[Anr. ed.] *Bristoll, R. Barker and J. Bill*, 1644. 4°.* HH, EN.

1404 —A declaration of the Lords and Commons declaring a full explanation . . . Decemb. 5. *For Ed. Husbands and John Francks, Decemb.* 8, 1642. 4°.* O, HH, DT; MA.

1405 —A declaration of the Lords and Commons . . . declaring John Webster. *For Edward Husbands, Julii* 13, 1644. brs. STEELE 2578. LT, O, LG, LPR, HH; MH, Y.

1406 —The declaration of the Lords and Commons . . . directed to the high sheriffe of . . . Essex. *For Joseph Hunscot and Iohn Wright,* 1642. brs. STEELE 2190. LT, O, LG, HH; Y.

1407 ——[Anr. ed.] *For J. H. 20 June,* 1642. brs. STEELE 2192. O, LG, LS.

1408 —A declaration of the Lords and Commons . . . exhorting to the duty of repentance. *Jan.* 30. *London for T. S.,* 1643[4]. 4°.* LT, C; MH, WF, Y.

1409 —A declaration of the Lords and Commons . . . for making void. *For Edward Husband, June 9,* [1647]. brs. STEELE 2696. LT, O, LG, HH; MH, Y.

1410 —A declaration of the Lords and Commons . . . for payment of our brethren of Scotland. *For Edw. Husband,* [1646]. brs. STEELE 2667. LT, O, LG; MH.

1411 —A declaration of the Lords and Commons . . . for the appeasing and quietting. *Septemb.* 3. *London for Iohn Wright,* 1642. 4°.* LT, C, HH, AN, DT; CH, CN, MH, NU, WF, Y.

1412 —A declaration of the Lords and Commons . . . for the association. [*London*], *Ian.* 10. *for I. Wright,* 1642[3]. 4°.* LT, O, CT, HH, DT; CSS, MH, NU, WF, Y.

1413 —A declaration of the Lords and Commons . . . for the defence and preservation of Hertfordshire. *For J. Wright,* 1642[3]. brs. STEELE 2339. LT, LG, LS; MH.

1414 —A declaration of the Lords and Commons . . . for the disarming of all Popish recusants. *By A. N. for Ed. Husbands. and I. Franke, August* 24, 1642. 4°.* LT, O, BR, YM, DT; MH, WF.

1415 ——[Anr. ed.] *By E. G. for Ed. Husbands and I. Franke, August* 25, 1642. 4°.* O, LG, HH; OWC, PT, WF, Y.

1416 —A declaration of the Lords and Commons . . . for the incouragement of all such apprentices. [*London*], *Novemb.* 8. *for John Wright,* 1642. 4°.* LT, O, CT, LG, DT; CSS, CU, MH, WF, Y.

1417 —A declaration of the Lords and Commons . . . for the Kings Majesties speedy coming. *For Edward Husband, August* 2, 1647. brs. STEELE 2719. LT, O, LG.

1418 ——[Anr. ed.] *For J. Wright,* 1647. brs. STEELE 2720. HODGKIN.

1419 —A declaration of the Lords and Commons . . . for the preservation and safety of the kingdom, and . . . Hull. *By Luke Norton and John Field for Edward Husbands and John Franck, July* 12, 1642. 4°.* O, HH, EC, DT; CH, CN, MH, WF.

1419A ——[Anr. ed.] —, *July* 13, 1642. 4°.* L; CLC, MH, WF.

1420 —A declaration of the Lords and Commons . . . for the prevention of a most horrid, . . . designe. *Ian.* 30. [*London*], *for John Wright,* 1642[/3]. 4°.* LT, O, CT, HH, DT; CLC, MH, Y.

1421 —A declaration of the Lords and Commons . . . for the protecting of all those . . . *September* 8, 1642. *By L. Norton and J. Field for E. Husband and J. Franck, Septemb.* 9, 1642. 4°.* L, O, LL, HH; MH, Y.

1422 —A declaration of the Lords and Commons . . . for the protection of Sir George Chudleigh. *Decemb.* 21. *London, for Iohn Wright,* 1642. brs. STEELE 2330. LT, O, LG, LS, HH; MH.

1422A —A declaration of the Lords and Commons . . . for the protection of Sir William Brereton. *For J. Wright,* 1642. brs. MH.

1423 —A declaration of the Lords and Commons . . . for the raising of all power. *August* 9. *London for Edward Husbands, and Iohn Franck,* 1642. 4°.* LT, O, C, BR, HH; CLC, MH, WF.

1424 ——[Anr. ed.] *By L. N. and I. F. for Edward Husbands and John Franck, August* 9, 1642. 4°.* L, C, OC, BR, HH; CH, CLC, MH, PL, Y.

1425 ——[Anr. ed.] *For Thomas Banks and William Ley,* [1642.] 4°.* O, LL, HH, EN, DT; CLC, CN, TU, WF, Y.

1426 ——[Anr. ed.] *For John Wright, Aug.* 10, 1642. 4°.* L, O, C, BR, HH; MH, TU, WF.

1427 ——[Anr. ed.] *York, R. Barker and by the assignes of J. Bill,* 1642. 4°.* L, C, CF, HH; CLC, MH, WF.

1428 ——[Anr. ed.] *Reprinted at Oxford by Leonard Lichfield,* 1642. 4°.* MADAN 1021. O, HH, DT; CSS, Y.

1429 —A declaration of the Lords and Commons . . . for the raising of forces. *For Edw. Husbands, and Joh. Franks,* 1642. 4°.* LT, O, C, HH, DT; CH, CN, CSS, MH, WF.

1430 —A declaration of the Lords and Commons . . . for the speedy putting this city. *For I. Wright. Octob.* 27, 1642. 4°.* LT, O, CCA, OC, HH; CH, CU, MH, NU, WF, Y.

1431 ——[Anr. ed.] *Printed at London for T. Smith,* 1642. 4°.* L, CC, BR, HH; CH, MHL, WF.

1432 —A declaration of the Lords and Commons . . . for the speedy setting forth of a fleet. *March* 14, *printed at London for John Wright,* 1642[3]. brs. STEELE 2389. LT, O, HH.

1433 —A declaration of the Lords and Commons . . . for the suppressing of all tumultuous assemblies. *Imprinted at London for John Wright,* 1648. 4°.* LT, O, BR, YM, HH; CH, MH, MIU, WF.

1434 ——[Anr. ed.] *For E. Husband,* 23 *May,* 1648. brs. STEELE 2762. L, LG.

1435 —The declaration of the Lords and Commons . . . for the suppressing of divers Papists. *For I. T. Novemb.* 25, 1642. 4°.* LT, O, C, HH, DT; MIU, WF.

1436 ——[Anr. ed.] *For I. Thomas, Novemb.* 25, 1642. 4°.* HH, YM; CH, MH, MIU, WF, Y.

1437 —A declaration of the Lords and Commons . . . for the vindication of Ferdinando Lord Fairefax. [*London*], *Feb.* 4, *for John Wright,* 1642. 4°.* LT, O, DT; CH, CN, MH, NU, WF.

1438 ——[Anr. ed.] *For John Franke, February* 4, 1642[3]. 4°.* HH; MH, Y.

1438A —A declaration of the Lords and Commons . . . fully pardoning divers officers. *For J. Wright, March 6. 1644[5].* STEELE 2603. brs. LT, O, LG.

1439 —A declaration of the Lords and Commons . . . in answer, to a letter sent from His Majestie . . . 20 Junii, 1642. *For Joseph Hunscott, 1642.* 4°.* LT, O, CCA, HH, DT; CH, CSS, MH, WF, Y.

1440 —A declaration of the Lords and Commons . . . in answer to a petition presented . . . Octob. 22, 1642. *For John Dam, Novemb. 1, 1642.* 4°.* LT.

1441 —A declaration of the Lords and Commons . . . in answer to a proclamation. *For Lawrence Blaiklock, 1642.* 4°.* LT, O, HH; CSS, MH, NR, WF, Y.

1442 —A declaration of the Lords and Commons . . . in answer to His Majesties declaration. *For Edward Husbands, and John Franke, 1642.* 4°.* LT, O, CC, EN, DT; CSS, LC, MH, MHL, Y.

1442A —A declaration of the Lords and Commons . . . in answer to His Majesties letter. *For John Wright, 1642.* LG, CF.

1443 —A declaration of the Lords and Commons . . . in answer to the kings declaration concerning Hull. *For Ioseph Hunscot, and Iohn Wright, May 26, 1642.* 4°.* O, C, CT, SP, EN; CSS, MH, MHL, WF, Y.

1444 —A declaration of the Lords and Commons . . . in commendation of the inhabitants of . . . Manchester. *For Tho. Underhill, 1642.* brs. STEELE 2273. LT, LG; MH.

1445 —A declaration of the Lords and Commons . . . of their proceedings. *Printed at Oxford, by Leonard Lichfield, 1643[/4].* 4°.* MADAN 1560. LT, O, C, EC, HH; CH, CU, MH, NU, WF, Y.

1445A ——[Anr. ed.] —, 1643. *And reprinted at Dublin by Robert Hughes, [1664].* 4°.* C.

1446 —The declaration of the Lords and Commons . . . or. Five severall passages of state. *For Ioseph Hunscot and Iohn Wright, 1642.* 4°.* L, O, C, HH, DT; CLC, CN, MH, TU, WF, Y.

1447 —The declaration of the Lords and Commons . . . presented to Their Highnesses. colop: [London], *printed, 1689.* cap., fol* L, O, OC, DC; CH, MB, WF, Y.

1448 —The declaration of the Lords and Commons . . . sent to His Majesties Privie Council. *Edinburgh, by Evan Tyler, 1643.* 4°.* ALDIS 1080. C, CT, E, AU; Y.

1449 —A declaration of the Lords and Commons . . . sent to the generall Assembly of the Church of Scotland. *September 1. 1642. London, for Richard Best.* fol.* O, HH, DT; CN, MH, NU, WF, Y.

1449A ——[Anr. ed.] *By A. N. for Richard Lownds, 1642.* fol.* L, CJ, CT; MH.

1450 —A declaration of the Lords and Commons . . . setting forth the grounds. *August 3. London, for Edward Husbands, and Iohn Franck, 1642.* 4°.* LT, O, C, EC, EN; CH, CN, LC, MH, NU, TU, Y.

1451 ——[Anr. ed.] *For T. Banks and W. Lee, 1642.* 4°.* O, HH; MH.

1452 ——[Anr. ed.] *For John Wright, August 3, 1642.* 4°.* L, O, C, EC, HH; CH, CLC, CSS, MH, TU.

1453 —A declaration of the Lords and Commons . . . setting forth the innumerable plots. *For Henry Fowler, Septem. 24, 1642.* 4°.* LT, O, HH, DT; MH, NPT, NU, WF, Y.

1454 —A declaration of the Lords and Commons . . . setting forth the several plots. *For Edward Husbands, 1643.* 4°.* LT, YM; CH, MH, MHL, WF, Y.

1455 —A declaration of the Lords and Commons . . . shevving the imminent danger. *[London], for John Frank, Jan. 26, 1642[3].* 4°.* LT, O, CT, BR, DT; CH, CN, LC, MH, WF.

1456 Entry cancelled.

1457 —A declaration of the Lords and Commons . . . shewing the present designe. *For Iohn Wright, Octob. 2, 1643.* 4°.* LT, O, C, HH, SP; CH, CN, MH, WF, Y.

1458 —A declaration of the Lords and Commons . . . shewing the reasons why they cannot consent. *Aprill 19 for John Wright, 1643.* 4°.* MADAN 1325. LT, O, C; CH, MH, NU, WF, Y.

1459 —A declaration of the Lords and Commons . . . straightly charging and forbidding all in-keepers. *For Edw. Husbands, Aprill 7, 1643.* 4°.* LT, MR; MH, WF.

1460 —A declaration of the Lords and Commons . . . the Lords . . . taking into their serious consideration. *Printed at London, for John Wright, 1647.* brs. STEELE 2727. LT, LG, HH; CH, MH.

1461 —A declaration of the Lords and Commons . . . that all colonels. *For John Wright, November 6, 1643.* 4°.* LT, O; MA, TU, Y.

1462 —A declaration of the Lords and Commons . . . that all such persons. *[London], Decemb. 3. for Iohn Wright, 1642.* 4°.* LT, OC, HH; CH, MH, NC, WF, Y.

1463 —A declaration of the Lords and Commons . . . that no ships, barques. *[London], Ian. 16. for John Wright, 1642.* 4°.* LT, O, C, DT; CH, MH, Y.

1464 ——[Anr. ed.] *For Lawrence Blaiklocke, Jan. 16, 1642[3].* 4°.* HH; WF.

1465 —A declaration of the Lords and Commons . . . that none shall be elected. *Printed at London, for John Wright, 1647.* brs. STEELE 2729. LT, LG, HH; CH, MH.

1465A —A declaration of the Lords and Commons . . . that the severall judges. *March 1. For John Wright, 1642.* brs. CT.

1466 —A declaration of the Lords and Commons . . . that the sheriffes of London. *March 11. Printed at London, for John Wright, 1642[3].* brs. STEELE 2380. LT, LG, HH; CH, MH, Y.

1467 —A declaration of the Lords and Commons . . . that whatsoever souldier. *August 29, London for Iohn Wright, 1642.* 4°.* LT, O, C, HH, DT; CLC, MH, NU, WF, Y.

1468 —A declaration of the Lords and Commons . . . the Lords and Commons taking into consideration. *For John Wright, 11 July, 1643.* brs. STEELE 2453. LT, EN; CH, MH, Y.

1469 —A declaration of the Lords and Commons . . . to dispence with divers persons. *For I. Wright, [1642].* brs. STEELE 2282. HH.

1470 —A declaration of the Lords and Commons . . . to the high and mighty Lords, the states of the United Provinces. *By A. N. for Richard Best, October 8, 1642.* 4°.* LT, O, HH, DT; CH, MH, NU, WF, Y.

1471 —The declaration of the Lords and Commons . . . to the subjects of Scotland. *Printed at Oxford by Leonard Lichfield, 1642.* 4°.* MADAN 1117. LT, O, CT, EN, DT; CH, CN, MH, WF, Y.

1472 ——[Anr. ed.] *Printed at York by Stephen Bulkley, 1642.* 4°.* YM.

1473 —A declaration of the Lords and Commons . . . to the whole kingdome. *For John Wright, 1646.* 4°.* LT, O, LUG, HH, EN; LC, MH, TU, WF, Y.

1474 —A declaration of the Lords and Commons . . . vpon information received. *July 30. For I. Wright, 1642.* 4°.* LT, O, LG, EC; MH, MHL, Y.

1475 —A declaration of the Lords and Commons . . . upon the statute of 5 H. 4. *For Edw. Husbands and John Frank, 1642.* 4°.* LT, O, C, LL, DT; CU, CSS, LC, MH, NU, Y.

1476 —A declaration of the Lords and Commons . . . whereas the king. *For Edward Husbands and John Franck, 1642.* brs. STEELE 2247. LT, LS, BR; MH.

1476A ——[Anr. ed.] *York, by Robert Barker; and by the assigns of John Bill, 1642.* brs. Y.

1477 —A declaration of the Lords and Commons . . . whereby the good subiects. *August 22. Printed at London, for Iohn Wright, 1642.* 4°.* LT, O, CT, HH, DT; CH, CLC, MH, WF, Y.

1478 —The declaration of the Lords and Commons . . . willing, that no messenger. *July 28. London, for John Wright, 1642.* 4°.* O, CJ, HH, SS; CH, CLC, MH, WF, Y.

1479 —A declaration of the Lords and Commons . . . with additions. *By L. N. and J. F. for E. Husbands and J. Franck, July 28, 1642.* brs. STEELE 2232. LT; MB.

1480 ——[Anr. ed.] *By A. N. for E. Husbands and J. Franck, [1642.]* brs. STEELE 2233. LS, EC.

1481 ——[Anr. ed.] *By E. G. for Edward Husbands and Iohn Franck, 1642.* brs. STEELE 2234. O; MH.

1482 —A declaration of the Lords and Commons . . . with instrvctions for the Lords Lieutenants. *For Henry Overton, 1642[3].* 4°.* LT, O, CT, HH, DT; CSS, MH, WF, Y.

1483 —A declaration of the Lords and Commons . . . with the additionall reasons, last presented. *For Ioseph Hunscott, 1641[2].* 4°.* LT, O, C, CT, OC; CLC, CN, LC, MH, NU.

1484 ——[Anr. ed.] *For Iohn Wright and I. Franke, 1641.* 4°.* O; LC, MBP, MH, Y.

1484A ——[Anr. ed.] *Printed, 1641.* 4°.* O, CCL, OC, EC; CH, CLC, MH.

1484B ——[Anr. ed.] *[London], printed, 1641.* 4°.* O, CJ; MH.

1485 ——[Anr. ed.] *For F. C. and T. B., 1641.* 4°.* L; CH, CLC, CSS.

1486 —A declaration of the Lords and Commons . . . with the advice and concurrence of the Commissioners. *For Edward Husbands, March 29, 1644.* 4°.* HH; Y.

1486A ——[Anr. ed.] —*March 30, 1644.* 4°.* LT, O, CT, E, EN; CH, MH, NU, WF, Y.

1487 —A declaration of the Lords and Commons . . . with the resolutions of both Houses. *For Edward Husband, Jan. 18, 1647[8].* 4°.* LT, C, HH, SP; CH, CU, MH, WF, Y.

1488 —A declaration of the Lords and Commons . . . with their resolution, . . . Decemb. 17. 1642. *[London], for John Wright, Decemb. 19, 1642.* 4°.* L, O, C, CT, HH; CN, CSS, MH, Y.

1489 —The declaration of the Lords spiritual and temporal, and Commons. *For James Partridge, Matthew Gillyflower, and Samuel Heyrick, 1689.* fol.* L, O, C, EC, HH; CH, CN, MH, PL, Y.

1490 —A declaration of the members of Parliament, lately dissolved. *[London, 1655.]* brs. STEELE 3044a. LT, CCA.

1491 —A declaration of the Parliament assembled at Westminster. January 23. 1659. *By John Streater and John Macock, 1659[60].* 4°.* LT, O, C, HH, LL; CH, CU, MH, TU, WF, Y.

1492 ——[Anr. ed.] *Reprinted Edinburgh, by Christopher Higgins, 1660.* 4°.* ALDIS 1640. EN; WF, Y.

1493 —A declaration of the Parliament for a day of thanksgiving. colop: *By John Field, 1659.* cap., fol.* LT, O, CJ; MH.

1494 —A declaration of the Parliament of England . . . 27 Septemb. 1649. *By John Field for Edward Husband, 1649.* 4°.* O, HH, YM.

1495 ——Junii 26, 1650. *By William Du-Gard, 1650.* 4°.* HH, YM; Y.

1496 ——7th of May 1659. *By John Field, 1659.* brs. STEELE 3108. LT, O, CCA, LG, LS; MB, MH, Y.

1497 ——7 July 1659. *By John Field and Henry Hills, 1659.* brs. STEELE 3117. LT, LG, LS, LU, OQ; MH.

1498 —A declaration of the Parlament (sic) of England, concerning their late endeavors. *For Matthew Simmons, 1649.* 4°.* LT, O, CT, HH, EN; HR, CH, CN, MH, NU, WF, Y.

1499 —A declaration of the Parliament of England, expressing the grounds. *For Edward Husband, March 22. 1648.* 4°.* LT, O, C, MR, EN; CH, MH, NU, TU, WF, Y.

1500 Entry cancelled.

1501 —A declaration of the Parliament of England, in answer to the late letters. *For Edward Husband, Febr. 22. 1648[9].* 4°.* LT, O, CS, MH, E; CH, LC, MH, NU, TU, Y.

1502 —A declaration of the Parliament of England, in order to the uniting of Scotland. *By John Field, 1652.* brs. STEELE 2963. L, LG, HH, AU.

1503 —A declaration of the Parliament of England, in vindication of their proceedings. *By John Field for Edward Husband, 1649.* 4°.* LT, O, C, EN, DT; CH, CN, MH, NU, WF, Y.

1504 Entry cancelled.

1505 —A declaration of the Parlament [sic] of England, upon the marching of the armie into Scotland. *By William Du-Gard, 1650.* 4°.* STEELE 3p 2041. LT, O, C, E, EN; HR, CH, CN, MH, NU, TU, WF, Y.

1506 —A declaration of the Parliament of England . . . whereas by a clause. *By John Field and Henry Hills, [1659.]* brs. L.

1507 —A declaration of the Parliament of England, written to the high and mighty lords, . . . of the Low-Countreys. *For Lawrence Blaiklocke*, 1645. 4°.* LT, O, C, HH, SP; HR, CH, CN, LC, MH, Y.

1508 —A declaration of the Parliament of the Commonwealth of England. colop: *By John Field*, 1653. cap., 4°.* L; NR, NU.

1508A —A declaration of the Parliament of the Commonwealth of England, concerning the settlement. *By John Field*, 1651. brs. L.

1508B ——[Anr. ed.] *Printed at Leith by Evan Tyler*, 1651. brs. Y.

1509 ——[Anr. ed.] *For Robert Ibbitson*, 1652. 4°.* LT, HH; Y.

1510 —A declaration of the Parliament of the Commonwealth . . . for a time of publique thanksgiving. *By John Field*, 1653. brs. STEELE 3005. LT, O, LG, LUG; MH, Y.

1511 —A declaration of the Parliament of the Commonwealth of England, relating to the affairs. *By Iohn Field*, 1652. 4°. LT, O, C, MR, E; HR, CH, CU, MH, WF, Y.

1511A ——[Anr. ed.] *Printed at Leith by Evan Tyler*, 1652. 4°.* Y.

1512 —A declaration of the several proceedings of both Houses of Parliament. *For Edward Husband, June 5*, 1648. 4°.* LT, OC, SP; CH, MHL, MIU, WF, Y.

1513 —A declaration of the several votes and resolutions agreed upon. *Iune 14, for Iohn Thomas*, 1642. 4°.* LT, O, CJ, YM, HH; CH, MH, PL, WF, Y.

1514 —A declaration or ordinance of the Lords and commons . . . concerning the seizing of horses. *For Edward Husbands, June 10*, 1643. 4°.* LT, C, LG, LUG, E; CH, MH. NC, Y.

1515 —A declaration or ordinance of the Lords and Commons . . . concerning the taking of horses. [*London*], *May 11. for John Wright*, 1643. 4°.* LT, O, C, HH, DT; MA, MH, NU, WF, Y.

1516 —A declaration or ordinance of the Lords and Commons . . . that the committee for the militia. *For Iohn Wright, April 13*, 1642. 4°.* LT, C, EN, DT; CH, CN, MH, WF, Y.

1516A ——[Anr. ed.] —, 1643. 4°.* MH.

1517 —The declaration or remonstrance of the Lords and Commons . . . with divers depositions and letters . . . 19 Maii 1942. *For Joseph Hunscott and John Wright*, 1642. 4°. LT, O, C, LL, EN; CH, CN, CSS, MH, NU, WF, Y.

1518 —A declaration or remonstrance of the state of the kingdom. [*London*], *for T.P.*, 1642. 4°. LT, O, CT, SP, YM; CSS, MH, WF.

1519 —A declaration. The Lords and Commons . . . having received. *By John Macock, and Francis Tyton*, 1660. brs. STEELE 3186. LT, LG, LS.

1519A ——[Anr. ed.] *Husbands & Newcomb*, [1660.] brs. STEELE 3187. L, O, C, MC, DT.

1519B —A Declaration. The Lords and Commons . . . Taking into their consideration. *By Edward Husbands and Thomas Newcomb* [1660.] brs. STEELE 3210. L, O, LG, LPR, LS; MH.

1520 —The declaration, votes, and order of assistance of both Houses. *By Robert Barker; and by the assignes of John Bill*, 1642. 4°.* LT, O, CT, LL, HH; CH, CN, MH, NU, WF, Y.

1521 —The declarations of both Houses of Parliament. *May, 16, London, for Joseph Hunscott*, 1642. brs. STEELE 2127. LT, O, CJ, LG, LS.

1521A —Depositions taken the 22d of October, *Edinburgh*, 1688. cap., fol.* ALDIS 2757. L, EN.

1522 —The desire and advice of the Lords and Commons . . . February, 21, 1642[3]. *Printed at Oxford by Leonard Lichfield, February 24, 1642[/3]*. 4°.* MADAN 1253. LT, O, CT, HH; CH, MH, TU, WF, Y.

1523 —Directions of the Lords and Commons . . . after advice had with the Assembly of Divines, . . . Presbyteriall-government. That . . . electing. *For Iohn Wright, August 20*, 1645. 4°.* LT, O, CT, E, DT; CH, MH, NU, PL, WF, Y.

1524 ——[Anr. ed.] —, 1645. 4°.* L, CJ; NPT, WF, Y.

1525 —The diurnall occvrrences of every dayes proceedings. *By R.H. and are to be sold by William Cooke*, 1641. 4°. LT, C, DC, HH, DT; CH, CN, LC, MHL, NU, Y.

1526 —The diurnall occurrences, or dayly proceedings of both Houses, . . . third of November, 1640, to — 1641. *For William Cooke*, 1641. 4°. LT, O, C, HH, EN; CH, CN, CU, MH, WF.

1527 —Divers depositions and letters. 1642. CJ.

1528 —Divers orders set forth by both the honorable House [*sic*]. *For F. Coles and T.B.*, 1641[2]. 4°.* LT, O; CH, LC, MH, WF, Y.

1529 —Eight speciall orders of the Lords and Commons. *For Edward Husbands, June 2*, 1643. 4°.* LT, O, HH, EN, DT; CH, MH, NU, WF, Y.

1529A —Eighteen propositions by way of questions. *For Iohn Watson*, 1642. 4°.* LT, CK, EC; CH, MH, NU, TL, WF, Y.

1529B —An engagement of the Lords and Commons. [*London*], *printed*, 1647. 4°.* LT, HH; CH, CN, MH, WF, Y.

1530 —An exact and true collection of the weekly passages, from the first of January last, to this sixteenth of February. *By B.A., to be sold by W.H.*, [1645]. 4°.* LT, EN; CN.

1531 —An exact collection of all orders, votes, debates and conferences. *For Francis Smith*, 1679. fol.* L, O, C, LL, HH; CH, MBP, MH, WF, Y.

1532 —An exact collection of all remonstrances. *For Edward Husbands, T.Warren, R.Best*, 1642. 4°. MADAN 1332. L, O, BR, E, AU; CH, LC, MHL, NU, TU, Y.

1533 ——[Anr. ed.] *For Edward Husbands, T.Warren, R.Best*, 1643. 4°. LT, O, C, LVF, HH; CH, CN, LC, MH, NU, TU, Y.

1534 —Expresse commands from both the honourable Houses. *For Robert Cotton*, 1641[2]. 4°.* LT, O, EC, HH, DT; CH, MIU, NU, WF, Y.

1535 —An extract of some proceedings in Parliament, relating to the East-India Company. [*London*, 1694.] brs. L, O, LUG; MH, WF, Y.

1536 —Five orders and ordinance of Parliament, for payment. *For Edward Husband*, 1647. brs. STEELE 2702. LT, O; MH.

1537 —For the better satisfaction of the kingdome. *By Richard Cotes* [1647.] brs. STEELE 2721. LT, O.

1538 —Die Martis 8. Junii 1647. Forasmuch as the feasts of the nativity. *For John Wright*, 1647. brs. STEELE 2695. LT, O, LG, HH; MH, Y.

1539 —The form of church-government to be used. *Imprinted at London for John Wright*, 1648. 4°.* LT, O, C, EN, DT; CH, MH, NU, TU, WF, Y.

1540 — —[Anr. ed.] *By W. Wilson, for John Wright*, 1642. 12°. Y.

1540A —Fourtie articles. *For T. Bates*, 1641. 4°.* LW; Y.

1541 —The four bills sent to the king to the Isle of Wight. *For Edward Husband, March 20*, 1647[8]. 4°.* LT, O, HH, LW, DT; CH, CN, MH, NU, TU, WF, Y.

1542 —Foure orders of great consequence of the Lords and Commons. *May 17. London, for R. B.*, 1643. 4°.* LT, O, C, HH; CLC, MA, MH, NC, Y.

1543 —Fovre ordinances of the Lords and Commons . . . concerning the weekly assessment. *For Edw. Husbands, Aprill.* 14, 1643. 4°.* LT, O, C, BR, DT; CH, CLC, MH, WF.

1543A — —[Anr. ed.] —, *May* 10. 1643. 4°.* LUG, OC; MH.

1543B — —[Anr. ed.] —, 1643. 4°.* CT.

1544 —Four ordinances of the Lords and Commons . . . for raising moneys for Sir Thomas Fairfax army. *For Edw. Husbands, January 23*, 1645[6]. 4°.* LT, O, HH; CLC, MH, NC, WF, Y.

1545 —Fovre ordinances of the Lords and Commons, viz. the 1. for raising . . . horse. *For Edward Husbands, March 18*, 1645. 4°.* LT, LG, HH; CH, MA, MH, WF.

1546 — —[Anr. ed.] *For John Wright*, [1647]. 4°.* HH, LSE.

1547 —Four special orders. *For Edward Husband, October.* 30, 1646. 4°.* LT, HH; LC.

1548 —XIIII orders voted by . . . Parliament. *[London], for Samuell Horton*, 1641. 4°.* LT, EC; NU, WF, Y.

1549 —A further additional act for relief. *By John Field*, 1652. brs. STEELE: 2967. LT, LG, OQ, HH; CH, MH, Y.

1550 —A general advertisement. *Novemb. 26, for John Hanson*, 1642. 4°.* LT; WF.

1551 —The humble address of the right honourable the Lords . . . and Commons. *By Charles Bill and the executrix of Thomas Newcomb*, 1695. fol.* L; CH, RPJ.

1551A — —[Same title.] —, 1695. fol.* RPJ, WF.

1551B — —[Same title.] —, 1696. fol.* RPJ.

1551C — —[Anr. ed.] *Edinburgh*, 1696. fol.* ALDIS 3569. L, EN.

1551D — —[Same title.] *By Charles Bill and the executrix of Thomas Newcomb*, 1697. fol.* RPJ.

1551E — —[Same title.] —, 1698. fol.* RPJ.

1551F — —[Same title.] —, 1699. fol.* RPJ.

1551G — —[Same title.] —, 1700. fol.* RPJ, Y.

1552 —The humble advice, petition and reasons of the Lords and Commons . . . why part of the terme ought not be removed to Oxford. *Printed*, 1643. 4°.* LT, O; CH, CN, MH, TU, Y.

1553 —The humble ansvver of the Lords and Commons . . . August 27, 1642. *For J. Wright, August 30*, 1642. 4°.* L, O, CF, CJ, HH; CLC, MH, MHL, NR, Y.

1553A —The humble answer of the Lords and Commons . . . to the message. *York, by Robert Barker: and by the assignes of John Bill*, 1642. brs. CF.

1553B —The humble desires and propositions for a safe and well-grounded peace. *For Edw. Husbands, Dec. 13*, 1644. 4°.* MADAN 1697. LT, O, CT, EN, DT; CH, LC, MBP, MH, NU, Y.

1553C — —[Anr. ed.] *Edinburgh*, 1644. 4°.* ALDIS 1139. EN.

1553D — —[Anr. ed.] *[London], by Edward Husbands, Oct. 13*, 1645. 4°.* MADAN 1698. LT, O, HH; CN, LC, MBP, Y.

1554 —The humble desires and propositions of the Lords and Commons . . . third of February, 1642[3]. *By Robert Barker and by the assigns of J. Bill*, 1642[3]. 4°.* L, CJ, HH; CLC, MBP, MHL, WF.

1555 — —Feb. 6, 1642[3]. *For Edward Husbands, Febr. 7*, 1642[3]. 4°.* YM, BAMB; CSS, MH, MHL, TU.

1556 — —[Anr. ed.] *For John Wright, Feb. 8*, 1642. 4°.* OC, CJ, CT, HH; CN.

1557 — —8 Feb. 1642. *For Thomas Bancks*, 1642. 4°.* L, HH; WF.

1558 — —[Anr. ed.] *By Robert Barker: and by the assigns of John Bill*, 1642. 4°.* LT, C.

1559 — —10 December. 1644. *For Edw. Husbands, Dec. 13*, 1644. 4°.* O, HH; LC, MH, Y.

1560 —The humble desires and propositions of the Lords and Commons . . . for a treaty. *Oxford, by Leonard Lichfield, and re-printed at London, March 8*, 1642[/3]. 4°.* MADAN 1266. O, CM, CT, EN; WF, Y.

1561 —The humble desires and propositions of the Lords and Commons . . . presented . . . February 1. 1642. *Feb. 7 [London], for Iohn Wright*, 1642[/3]. 4°.* MADAN 1220.* O, CM, HH; CSS, Y.

1561A — —[Anr. ed.] *York, by Stephen Bulkeley*, 1642. 4°.* CF.

1562 —The humble desires and propositions of the Lords and Commons . . . tendered . . . . 1. February, 1642. *Printed at Oxford by Leonard Lichfield, February 4*, 1642[/3]. 4°.* MADAN 1219. O, EN; CH, MH, WF, Y.

1563 — —[Anr. ed.] *By Robert Barker; and by the assignes of John Bill*, 1642[/3]. 4°.* MADAN 1222. L, O, CT, OC; CH, MH, NU, TU, WF.

1564 —The humble desires and propositions for a safe and well-grounded peace, . . . together with an order. *[London], for Edward Husbands, Oct. 13*, 1645. 4°.* MADAN 1698. LT, O, HH; CN, LC, MBP, Y.

1565 —The humble petition and advice of both Houses of Parliament, with, xix propositions. *[London], for I. Hunscott, and I. Wright*, 1642. 4°.* LT, O, OC, CT; CN, CSS, MH, WF, Y.

1566 —The humble petition and advice presented unto His Highness . . . by . . . Parliament. *By Henry Hills and Iohn Field*, 1657. fol.* LT, O, C, HH, E; CH, CN, MH, NU, TU, WF, Y.

1567 — —[Anr. ed.] *Edinburgh. re-printed for Christopher Higgins*, 1657. fol.* ALDIS 1567. EN; CH.

1568   —The humble petition and declaration of both Houses. *For Iohn Wright, 1641.* 4°.* L, O, OC, YM; CSS, MBP, MH, WF, Y.

1568A   —The humble petition and propositions of the Lords and Commons . . . February 3. 1642. *Oxford, by Leonard Lichfield, 1642.* 4°.* MADAN 1221. SP; Y.

1569   ——[Anr. ed.] [*London, 1642/3.*] 4°.* MADAN 1222.** EC, SP.

1569A   —The humble petition and resolution of both . . . to the Kings . . . March 1, 1641. *For Iohn Wright and John Frank* [1641]. 4°.* L, LW; CH, CSS, MH, WF, Y.

1570   —The humble petition of both Hovses of Parliament presented to His Majesty on the 24th of November. *Printed at Oxford by Leonard Lichfield, 1642.* 4°.* MADAN 1091. O, CM, BR, EN, DT; CN, MBP, MH, TU, Y.

1571   ——[Anr. ed.] *Printed at Oxford by Leonard Lichfield, 1642.* 4°.* MADAN 1092. LT, O, OC, CM, CT; CH, CN, NU, WF.

1572   —The humble petition of the Lords and Commons . . . [16 February 1641–2]. *For J. Hunscott, 18 Feb., 1641*[2]. cap., brs. STEELE 1992. LT, O, OC.

1573   ——seventeenth of June, 1642. *Cambridge, by Roger Daniel, 1642.* 4°.* L, CM, CT, HH; Y.

1573A   ——[Anr. ed.] *York, by Robert Barker, and by the assignes of John Bill, 1642.* 4°.* C, CF, YM; MH, WF.

1574   ——18 Iune 1642. *By R. Bishop for Edw. Husbands and Iohn Francke, Iune the 21, 1642.* 4°.* LT, CCA, HH, SP; MH, WF.

1575   —The humble petition of the Lords and Commons, concerning this message. *For J. Hunscott, 22 February,* [1642]. brs. STEELE 1997. LT, O, HH.

1576   —The humble petition of the Lords and Commons assembled in Parliament, presented to His Majestie at York . . . 26 of March, 1642. *York, by Robert Barker, and by the assignes of John Bill 1642.* 4°.* YM; CH, CLC, CSS, MH.

1577   —The humble petition of the Lords and Commons assembled in Parliament, presented to His Majestie at York, 18 April. *York: by Robert Barker, and by the assigns of John Bill, 1642.* 4°.* O, C, HH, YM; CH, CLC, MH, WF.

1578   ——[Anr. ed.] *Reprinted at Oxford, by Leonard Lichfield, 1642.* 4°.* MADAN 1009. O; CSS, HW, WF, Y.

1579   —The humble petition of the Lords and Commons . . . presented to the Kings Majesty. *Decemb 30* [*London*], *for Richard West, 1642.* 4°.* LT, CT, HH, SP; CLC, WF.

1580   —The hvmble petition of the Lords and Commons . . . sent to His Excellence Robert Earle of Essex. *For Edw. Husbands, and Iohn Francke, 1642.* 4°.* LT, C, OC, BR; CH, CN, MH, WF, Y.

1581   ——[Anr. ed.] *For J. Wright, Sept. 27, 1642.* 4°.* L, OC; CH, MBP, MH, TU.

1582   —The humble petition of the Lords and Commons assembled in Parliament, sent to His Majestie at York . . . 14 April, 1642. *York: by Robert Barker, and by the assigns of John Bill, 1642.* 4°.* LT, C, CF, CT, YM; CH, MH, WF.

1582A   ——[Same title.] *By R. Bishop for Edw. Husbands and Iohn Franke, Iune the 21, 1642.* 4°.* LT, CJ, EC, YM; MBP.

1582B   —The humble petition of the Lords and Commons . . . to His Majesty. *Printed at Oxford by Leonard Lichfield, 1642.* 4°.* MADAN 1075. Y.

1583   —The humble petition of the Lords and Commons to the king, for leave to remove the magazine at Hull. *By Robert Barker; and by the assignes of John Bill, 1642.* 4°.* LT, O, C, HH, EN; CH, CN, MH, NU, WF, Y.

1583A   ——[Anr. ed.] *By T.P. for T.B.,* [1642.] 4°.* C, OC, EC; MB, WF.

1584   —The hvmble petition of the Lords and Commons . . . to the kings. *For Christopher Latham, and T. Creake, 1642.* 4°.* LT, O, CT, EC, SP; CH, CN, MH, NU, WF, Y.

1585   —The hvmble petition of the Lords and Commons to the kings most excellent Majesty. For a pacification. *Iulii 15, 1642. For T. Winter, and T. Hewer,* [1642]. 4°.* CCA, YM; CH, CLC, CN, MH.

1585A   ——[Anr. ed.] *For John Wright, 1642.* 4°.* L, OC, EC, SP; CLC, MH.

1585B   ——[Anr. ed.] *For N. Allen, 1642.* 4°.* LSE, EC, YM.

1586   —The humble petition of the Lords and Commons assembled in Parliament unto His Majesty . . . to decline his intended journey into Ireland. *By A. N. for John Franck, 1642.* 4°.* L, O, YM; CLC, MBP, MH, NU, WF.

1586A   ——[Anr. ed.] *By T. Paine for T. Bankes, 1642.* 4°.* L, SP.

1587   —The humble representation and petition of . . . Parliament, concerning Romish priests and Jesuits. *By John Bill and Christopher Barker, 1663.* fol.* L, C, LL, OC, HH; CH, CLC, MH, WF, Y.

1587A   ——[Anr. ed.] — *and reprinted at Dublin for Samuel Dancer, 1663.* fol.* DIX 121. DK.

1587B   ——[Anr. ed.] *Edinburgh, reprinted by Evan Tyler, 1663.* fol.* CT.

1588   —Instructions agreed on by a committee. *For Edw. Husbands, Aprill 11. 1643.* 4°.* LT, O, LG, BR; MA, MH, WF.

1588A   ——[Anr. ed.] —, *June 19, 1643.* 4°.* MH.

1589   —Instructions agreed upon by the Lords and Commons. *By R. O. and G. D. for Henry Overton, 1642.* 4°.* LT, O, CT, DT; CLC, CN, MH, NU, WF, Y.

1590   ——[Anr. ed.] [*London*], *by A. N. for R. Best, Octob. 5, 1642.* 4°.* LT, O, CT, EC, EN; CH, MH, WF.

1591   —Instrvctions agreed upon by the Lords and Commons . . . for Sir William Brereton. *For Iohn Wright, Ian. 11, 1642*[3]. 4°.* LT, CS, CT; CH, MH.

1592   —Instructions agreed upon in Parliament for Commissioners. *By Henry Hills and John Field, 1657.* fol.* LT, O, C, LUG, E; CH, MH, NR, WF, Y.

1593   —Instructions and directions made by the trustees. *By John Field, 1653.* brs. STEELE 3016. L, OQ.

1593A   —Instructions for the trustees. *R. Coates, 1649.* fol.* L, HH.

1594   —Instructions how and in what manner the said vow. *For E. Husbands,* [1643]. brs. STEELE 2450. L.

1595   —Instructions lately agreed on, . . . 16th day of May, 1660. *For Robert Clavel, 1660.* 4°.* LT, C, HH; CH, CN, MH, NU, WF, Y.

1596 —Instrvctions of the Lords and Commons . . . for the right honourable Francis Lord Willoughby. Septemb. 30. *For J. B. to be sold by John Wright, 1642.* 4°.* LT, O, C, OC, HH; CN, MH, WF.

1597 ——[Anr. ed.] *By J.F. for E. Husbands and J. Franck, October 24, 1642.* 4°.* HH.

1598 —It is declared by the Lords and Commons. *Imprinted at London, by Robert Barker and by the assigns of John Bill, 1642.* brs. STEELE 2092. LT, LG, LS, CT, EC.

1599 —It is desired by the clerks and gentlemen. [*London, 1643.*] brs. LT.

1600 —It is this day ordained and declared . . . that no person be permitted to preach. *For John Wright, 1645.* brs. STEELE 2611. LT, O, HH; CH, MH, WF, Y.

1601 —Die Sabbati 16. Januarii, 1640. It is this day ordered. *Imprinted at London by Robert Barker, and by the assigns of John Bill, 1641.* brs. STEELE 1887. LT; MHS, Y.

1602 —Die Lunae, 3. Ianuar. 1641. It is this day ordered. [*London*], *for Tho. Bates, 1641.* brs. LT.

1603 —It is this day ordered and ordained . . . that the serjeants and councellors at law. *For Edward Husbands, 1644.* brs. CH, MH.

1604 —It is this day ordered by the committees of both . . . 5 October 1641. *Imprinted at London by Robert Barker and by the assigns of John Bill, 1641.* brs. STEELE 1894. LT, O, CJ, OQ; MH, Y.

1605 —It is this day ordered by the Lords and . . . 20 Maii. 1642. *For Joseph Hunscott, 1642.* brs. STEELE 2143. LT, O, LS, BR; CH, MH.

1606 ——[Anr. ed.] *For I. T., 1642.* brs. STEELE 2145. LT, O, HH, EN.

1607 —Die Sabbati 4° Junij, 1642. It is this day ordered by the Lords and Commons. *For Edward Husbands, June 6, 1642.* brs. STEELE 2168. LT, O, LS, EC; CH, MH, Y.

1608 —Die Lvnae. October, 4. 1642. It is this day ordered by the Lords and Commons. *Imprinted at London by L. N. for E. Husbands and I. Frank, 1642.* brs. STEELE 2272. LT, EC, HH; MH.

1609 —Die Lunae 24 October 1642. It is this day ordered by the Lords and Commons. *For William Larnar, 1[642].* brs. STEELE 2281. LT.

1610 —Die Jovii. 23. Martii. 1643. It is this day ordered by Lords and . . . 23 March 1643. *For John Wright, 1643.* brs. STEELE 2392. LT, EC; MH.

1611 —Die Veneris 5°, Maij. 1643. It is this day ordered. *For Thomas Underhill, May 9, 1643.* brs. LT; WF.

1612 —It is this day ordered by the Lords and Commons . . . 4 October 1642. *By L. N. for Edward Husbands and Iohn Frank, 1642.* brs. STEELE 2272. L, HH.

1613 —It is this day ordered by the Lords and Commons . . . 15 October 1642. *For I. Wright, 1642.* cap., brs. STEELE 2276. O, HH.

1614 —2. Novemb. 1642. It is this day ordered. *For John Wright, 1642.* brs. CH.

1615 —It is this day ordered by the Lords and . . . 3 February 1642[3]. *For R. Dunscomb, 11 Feb., 1642[3].* brs. STEELE 2362. LT, LS.

1616 —Die Martis 12 Martii 1643[4]. It is this day ordered by the Lords and Commons . . . that the Lord Maior of London. [*London, 1644.*] cap., 4°.* LT, SP.

1617 —It is this day ordered by the Lords and . . . 5 May 1643. *For T. Vnderhill, 9 May, 1643.* brs. STEELE 2419. LT.

1618 —It is this day ordered by the Lords and . . . 17 June 1643. *For E. Husbands, [1643].* brs. STEELE 2439. L.

1619 —Die Sabbath: 24, Junii 1643. It is this day ordered. *Printed at London for John Wright 26 June, 1643.* brs. STEELE 2447. LT; CH, MH.

1620 ——[Anr. ed.] *For John Wright 26 June, 1643.* brs. STEELE 2448. LT; MH.

1621 —It is this day ordered by the Lords and . . . 24 May 1645. *For E. Husband, 9 Sept., 1645.* cap., brs. STEELE 2618. L, HH; MH.

1621A —It is this day resolved. *By L. N. and J. F. for Husbands & Franck, 12 July, 1642.* brs. STEELE 2213. O; WF.

1621B —The joynt resolvtions and declaration. [*London*], *printed, 1649.* 4°.* LT, CT; CM, CU.

1621C —A joyfull message sat. *August 8., for I. H. and T. Rider, [1672.]* 4°.* LT, O, DT.

1622 —The last message and resolution of both Houses of Parliament. 1642. 4°. O, YM.

1623 —The late letters from both Houses of Parliament concerning their purpose. *Printed at Oxford by Leonard Lichfield, 1642.* 4°* MADAN 1070. O, CT, BR, EN; CN, MH, Y.

1624 ——[Anr. ed.] *Printed at Oxford, and and [sic] now reprinted at London for R. Royston, 1642.* 4°.* LT, O, CM, EC, HH; CH, MH, MHL, WF, Y.

1625 —A letter sent by order of both Houses of Parliament, to the high sheriffe of every shire. *For Iohn Franke, 1642.* 4°.* LT, C, EC, DT; CH, CU, MH, WF, Y.

1626 —A letter sent from both Houses . . . to all the high-sheriffs. *March 11. London, for Ioseph Hunscott, 1641[2].* brs. STEELE 2001. LT, LG, HH.

1627 —A letter sent from both Houses . . . to His Excellence, the Earle of Essex. [*London*], *for Joh. Franc. Octob, 11, 1642.* 4°.* LT, SP; CH.

1628 —A letter sent from the Speakers of both Houses . . . with several votes. *By M.B. 31 Aug., 1648.* 4°.* LT, OC; CH, MH, TU, WF, Y.

1629 —The Lords and Commons assembled in . . . 25 April 1643. [*London, 1643*] brs. STEELE 2414. L, EN.

1630 —The Lords and Commons assembled in . . . out of the deep sense. [*London, 1643.*] brs. STEELE 2458. LT; MH, Y.

1631 —The Lords and Commons assembled . . . do declare, that by reason of . . . 5 May 1660. *By Edward Husbands and Thomas Newcomb, [1660].* brs. STEELE 3185. LT, O, C, LG, DT; MH, WF.

1632 —The Lords and Commons assembled . . . do hereby order and declare, . . . 11 May 1660. *By Edward Husbands and Thomas Newcomb, [1660].* brs. STEELE 3201. LT, O, C, LG, EN, DT; MH.

1633 ——[Anr. ed.] *Macock & Tyton, 1660.* cap., brs. STEELE 3202. O, LPR, LUG.

1634 —The Lords and Commons . . . doe approve of the late action. *For John Wright*, 1647. brs. STEELE 2724. LT; MH.

1635 —The Lords and Commons do declare. *Imprinted at London by Robert Barker, and by the assigns of John Bill*, 1642. brs. STEELE 2071. LT, O, CJ, HH; MH, Y.

1635A —The Lords and Commons do declare, May 20. *For Joseph Hunscott*, 1642. brs. OC, CJ, EC.

1635B —Monday May 7. 1660. The Lords and Commons . . . having received several informations. *By Edward Husbands and Thomas Newcomb*, [1660]. brs. STEELE 3187. C, LG, CJ; CH, CLC, MH.

1636 —The Lords and Commons having seene a printed paper. *For John Wright*, 1647. cap., brs. STEELE 2717. LT, O.

1637 —The Lords and Commons having well accepted. *For John Wright*, 1647. brs. STEELE 2706. LT; MH, Y.

1638 —The Lords and Commons in Parliament assembled, having certain information. *For Edward Husbands*, 1644. brs. CH, MH.

1639 —The Lords and Commons in Parliament do conceive. *Imprinted at London by L.N. for E. Husbands and I. Frank*, 1642. brs. STEELE 2270. LT, EC; MH.

1640 —The Lords and Commons in Parliament having received certain notice. *For Edward Husbands, October 24*, 1643. brs. STEELE 2504. LT.

1641 Entry cancelled.

1642 —The Lords and Commons taking into consideration . . . 3 August 1647. [*London*, 1647.] brs. STEELE 2723. HH.

1643 —The Lords and Commons . . . taking into their consideration. [*London, March* 1645.] brs. STEELE 2605. LT.

1644 —Many remarkable passages from both Houses . . . Parliament. *For T. Ryder*, 1642. 4°.* LT; CLC, WF, Y.

1645 —A message agreed upon by both Houses . . . 1 Novemb. 1648. *For R. Smithurst*, 1648. 4°.* LT, HH; CN, MH, WF.

1646 —A message agreed upon by the Lords and Commons. *For R.W.*, 1648. 4°.* LT, AN.

1647 —The message and resolution of both Houses . . . March 2, 1641. *By T. S. for J. Thomas*, 1641. 4°.* LT, C, LG; CU, LC, MH, NU, Y.

1648 —A message from a Committee of both Houses . . . to the Spanish ambassador. *February 18. London, for Joseph Hunscott*, 1641[2]. brs. STEELE 1993. LT, O, LG, LS.

1648A ——[Anr. ed.] *Reprinted at Dublin*, 1641[2]. 4°.* L.

1649 —A message from both Houses of Parliament, sent to the king and queenes majesties. *Febr. 22. London for Ioseph Hunscott*, 1641[2]. 4°.* LT, O, EC, HH; CN, CSS, MH, WF, Y.

1649A ——[Anr. ed.] *For John Wright. Febr.* 21, 1642. 4°l* MH.

1650 —A message from both Houses of Parliament sent to the Kings . . . at Yorke. *March 28, 1642. By E.G. for I. Wright*, 1641[2]. 4°.* L, O, CJ, EC, HH, EN; CH, CN, MB, WF, Y.

1651 ——[Anr. ed.] *For Francis Coules*, 1642. 4°.* HH; CH, CLC.

1652 ——[Anr. ed.] *Printed at London. for F. Coules, ond* [sic] *Tho. Banks*, 1642. 4°.* O, C.

1653 ——[Anr. ed.] *For John Wright*, 1642. 4°.* LT, HH, DT; MH, WF.

1654 —A message from both Houses of Parliament unto His Majestie, concerning the prince. *By Robert Barker: and by the assignes of John Bill*, 1641[2]. 4°.* LT, O, C, LG, CJ; CH, CN, MH, WF, Y.

1655 ——[Anr. ed.] *For John Tompson*, 1641[2]. 4°.* L; CSS.

1655A —The message of both Houses. *By Robert Barker; and by the assignes of John Bill*, 1642. 4°.* Y.

1656 —A message of the Lords and Commons . . . to His Majesty, now at his Court, at Holmby. *For George Duglasse, March 4, 1647*. 4°.* LT; NPT, Y.

1657 —A message ordered by both Houses of Parliament to be sent to the kings. *For V, V.*, 1647. 4°.* LT, C, CM, HH.

1658 —A message sent from both Houses . . . 16 of March. *For Iohn Franke*, 1642. 4°.* LT, O, C, EN, DT; CN, MBP, MH, WF, Y.

1659 —A message sent from both Houses. *Imprinted at London, for Nehemiah Wilson*, 1648. 4°.* LT, HH; MH.

1660 —A message sent from both Houses of Parliament, to the Kings Majesty, on Friday last. *For R. Snithurst*, 1648. 4°.* LT, C; CH, CU.

1660A —A message sent to the King from both Houses . . . 15 Novemb. 1648. *For H.Becke*, 1648. 4°.* LT, O, YM; CN, MH, WF, Y.

1661 —A message sent unto His Majesty, by a speciall committee of both Houses. *For Joseph Hunscott*, 1641[2]. brs. STEELE 2004. LT, O, CT, LS; MH, Y.

1662 —A message to the King's Majesty from both Houses. *Printed at London, by R.I.*, 1647. 4°.* LT, HH, SP; CH, MH, WF, Y.

1662A —More ordinances and orders of the Lords and Commons. *For Iohn Wright*, 1646. 4°.* CT; MH, MIU, Y.

1663 —A new declaration from both Houses . . . May 17. 1642. *For W.G., May the* 20, 1642. brs. STEELE 2140. LT, C, CT; MH.

1664 ——[Anr. ed.] *For J. Hunscott, 20 May*, 1642. brs. STEELE 2141. L, O, LG, LS, HH.

1664A —A new declaration of both Houses . . . Die Jovis 12. Maii 1642. May 16. *For John Wright*, 1642. 4°.* LI, CSS.

1665 —A new declaration of both Houses . . . sent to the Kings . . . sixteenth of March. *For Iohn Franke*, 1642. 4°.* L, EC; MH.

1666 —A new declaration of the Lords and Commons. *By A.N. for Edw. Husbands and Iohn Franck, June* 21, 1642. 4°.* HH; CH.

1667 ——[Anr. ed.] *By E.G. for Edward Husbands and John Franck*, 1642. 4°.* O, LG, HH; CH, MH, MHL, MIU, Y.

1668 ——[Anr. ed.] *For E. Husbands and J.Franck, June* 21, [1642]. 4°.* L, O, CJ, EC, DT; CH, CN, MH, WF, Y.

1669 ——[Anr. ed.] *For W.Gay*, 1642. 4°.* CSS.

1669A ——[Anr. ed.] *For Thomas Androes*, 1642. 4°.* CT, EC.

1670 —New propositions agreed upon by the Lords and Commons. *For G.W.*, 1648. 4°.* LT; MH.

1670A —New propositions propounded. *By T. F. for F. S., July* 15, 1672. 4°.* LT, HH, YM; CLC.

1671 —New votes of both Houses of Parliament, the 20th of May, 1642. *Printed, May* 24, 1642. 4°.* L, O, HH, YM; CH, WF.

1672 —The new votes of Parliament for the further securing. *For G.W.,* 1642. brs. STEELE 2130. LS, EC, BR; MH.

1673 —Nineteen propositions. *Cambridge, R.Daniel,* 1642. 4°. CT.

1674 —XIX propositions made by both Houses. *York, by Robert Barker, and by the assignes of John Bill,* 1642. 4°. L, C, CT, HH, YM; CN, MH, TU.

1675 — —[Anr. ed.] *Printed the fourth of June for W. Gaye,* 1642. 4°.* EC, YM, HH; WF, Y.

1676 Entry cancelled.

1677 —An order and declaration. Whereas . . . 17 May 1660. *By Edward Husbands and Thomas Newcomb,* [1660]. brs. STEELE 3204. LT, O, C, LG, DT; MH, WF.

1678 —An order and ordinance of Parliament, for punishing such of the trained-bands. *R. Cotes,* 1648. brs. STEELE 2417. HH.

1679 —Order by the Committee appointed by Parliament for the Navy and Customes. *By J. R. for Joseph Hunscott, July* 12, 1643. brs. LS.

1680 —Order by the Committee of Lords & Commons for repayment of the loan. [*London,* 1644.] brs. LS.

1681 —An order for the six regiments to advance towards Reading. [*London,* 1643.] brs. STEELE 2494. LT, LG.

1682 —An order for the speedy raising of money . . . 7 October 1643. [*London,* 1643.] brs. STEELE 2495. LT, LG, LS; MH.

1683 —An order from the Committee, that eleven thousand three hundred horse . . . into Ireland. *For W. R.,* 1642. 4°.* LT, O; Y.

1684 —An order from the High Court of Parliament, which was read . . . 19, day of December, 1641. *For William Bowden,* 1641. 4°.* LT, LG, LP; CLC, Y.

1685 —An order made by both Houses of Parliament, for the bringing in of corne. *For Joseph Hunscott,* 1641[2]. brs. STEELE 1963. LT, LUG; Y.

1686 —An order made by both Houses of Parliament, to prevent the going over of Popish commanders into Ireland. *For Joseph Hunscott,* 1641[2]. brs. STEELE 1970. LT, O, LS, LUG, EC; WF, Y.

1687 —An order made in Parliament concerning the suppressing of those men. *For F. Leach and F. Coles,* 1642. 4°.* LT, O, CM; MH, WF.

1688 —The order of assistance given to the committees of both Houses. *By Robert Barker: and by the assignes of John Bill,* 1642. brs. STEELE 2093. LT, O, CT, LS, HH; MH.

1689 —An order of both Houses . . . for a publick thansgiving. [*London,* 1644.] brs. LG.

1690 —An order of both Houses of Parliament, for encovragement of volvntiers. *By L.N. and J.E. for E. Husbands and J. Franck, Iuly* 28, 1642. brs. STEELE 2226. LT, O, HH, EC, AN; CH, MH.

1691 —An order of Parliament, for a thanksgiving. *By Edward Husband and John Field,* 1650. brs. STEELE 2911. LT, O, C, LG, HH; MH, NU, WF, Y.

1692 —An order of Parliament for the putting in due execution. *By Richard Cotes,* 1643. 4°.* LT, O, EN; MH, WF.

1693 —An order of Parliament for setting apart Tuesday. *By John Field,* 1653. brs. STEELE 2987. HH; Y.

1694 —An order of Parliament, with the consent of His Highness the Lord Protector, for a day of publike thanksgiving. *By Henry Hills and John Field,* 1657. fol.* LT, LG, HH, E; CLC, LC, MH, RPJ, Y.

1695 —An order of the committee of the Lords and Commons. *For George Calvert,* 1648. 4°.* LT, C, LG, HH; MH, WF, Y.

1696 —An order of the Committee of the Lords and Commons at Guildhall for the defence. *For I. Iackson, G. Tomlinson, & T. Homer,* 4 *Nov.,* 1642. brs. STEELE 2292. L, O, LS, EC; CH, MH.

1697 — —[Anr. ed.] *For I. Iackson, G. Tomlinson, and T. Homer,* 1642. Novemb, 5. brs. STEELE 2293. LT, HH.

1698 Entry cancelled.

1698A —An order of the house of Parliament concerning the gathering in . . . May 6, 1642. *By A. N. for Iohn Franck* [1642]. brs. STEELE 2115. MH.

1699 —An order of the Lords and Commons . . . concerning all officers. *For E. Husband,* 8 *Feb.,* 1646[7]. brs. STEELE 2671. L, O, LPR, LS; MH.

1700 — —[Anr. ed.] *For Edw. Husband, Febr.* 8, [1647]. brs. STEELE 2672. LT; CH.

1701 —An order of the Lords and Commons . . . concerning all Papists. *For E. Husband,* 2 *April,* 1646. brs. STEELE 2649. O.

1702 —An order of the Lords and Commons . . . concerning His Maiesties forrests. *For John Wright,* 1642. brs. STEELE 2126. LT, LG, LS, LUG, EC; MH.

1703 —An order of the Lords and Commons . . . concerning Ireland. *Dublin,* 12 *November,* 1641. brs. STEELE 2p 347. DPR.

1703A —An order of the Lords and Commons concerning the chusing. *For J. Wright,* [1647.] brs. OP.

1704 —An order of the Lords and Commons for a day of publike thanksgiving. *For John Wright,* 1646. brs. MC.

1705 —An order of the Lords and Commons for a day of thanksgiving. *For John Wright,* 1645. brs. MC.

1705A —An order of the Lords and Commons for a publick thanksgiving. *For J. Partridge and M. Gillyflower,* [1689.] brs. STEELE 3953. C; WF.

1706 —An order of the Lords and Commons . . . for all Papists. *For Edward Husband, December* 14, 1646. brs. STEELE 2673. LT, O, LG; CH, MH.

1707 —An order of the Lords and Commons . . . for publishing the ordinance of sequestration . . . 26 Septemb. *For Iohn Wright,* 1643. brs. STEELE 2488. LT, HH, EN; CH.

1708 —An order of the Lords and Commons . . . for putting in due execution. *For Edward Husband, March* 24, 1646[7]. brs. STEELE 2685. LT, O; MH.

1709   —An order of the Lords and Commons . . . for setling and manageing. *For Edward Husbands, Aprill. the 21,* 1645. brs. STEELE 2610. LT, O, HH; MH.

1709A   —An order of the Lords and Commons for suppressing of publique play-houses. *For Edward Husband,* 1647. brs. LG; WF.

1710   —Order of the Lords and Commons for the Committee of Safety. *By J. F. for E. Husbands and J. Franck,* [1642]. brs. LS.

1711   —An order of the Lords and Commons for the regulating of printing. *For I. Wright, Iune 16,* 1643. 4°.* LT, O, CT, DT; CH, MH, NU, WF, Y.

1712   —An order of the Lords and Commons . . . for the relief . . . of the Protestants in Ireland. *Jan. 4. London, for T. Wright,* 1643. 4°.* LT; CH, MH.

1713   —An order of the Lords and Commons for the restraint of passage from Oxford. *18 Octob.* 1643. *For John Wright,* 1643. cap., brs. CH.

1714   —An order of the Lords and Commons for the taking away of the Court of Wards. [*London*], *for Edward Husband; February 27,* 1645[6]. brs. STEELE 2644. LT, O, LL, HH; MH, Y.

1715   —An order of the Lords and Commons . . . that the judges and justices. *For Joseph Hunscott, and John Wright,* 1642. *July 21.* brs. STEELE 2230. LT, O, CCA, LS, HH; MH, MIU.

1716   —An order of the Lords and Commons to set apart a day. *For John Wright, 21 March,* 1645. brs. MC.

1717   —An order of the Lords and Commons . . . to the sheriff of the County of Lancaster. *For J. Hunscott,* 1642. brs. STEELE 2157. LS, EN; MH.

1717A   —An order of the Lords and Commons . . . whereas commissions of array. 1642. brs. STEELE 2230. OP.

1718   —An order of the Parliament touching the extraordinary rate of coals. *By John Field,* 1652. brs. STEELE 2978. LT, LG, OQ, HH; MH, Y.

1718A   —Ordered by both Houses of Parliament that this table. [*London?* 1641]. brs. HH; MH.

1719   —Ordered by the Lords and Commons in. [*London,* 1642.] brs. STEELE 2102. L; MH.

1720   ——[Die Martis 26. April. 1642]. *Imprinted at London, by Robert Barker: and by the assignes of John Bill,* 1642. brs. STEELE 2091. LT, CT.

1721   ——2 May 1646. [*London,* 1646.] brs. STEELE 2652. L.

1722   ——[Die Veneris 11 Junii. 1647]. *For Iohn Wright,* 1647. brs. STEELE 2698. LT, O; MH.

1723   ——[Anr. ed.] *For John Wright,* 1647. brs. STEELE 2699. LT, O, HH; CLC.

1724   ——[Die Mecurii 16. Junii 1647]. *For John Wright,* 1647. brs. STEELE 2703. LT, O; CH, MH, Y.

1725   ——27 January 1647[8]. *For E. Husband, 28 Jan.,* 1647[8]. brs. STEELE 2747. L; MH.

1726   ——[Die Lunae, 6. Martii, 1647]. [*London,* 1648.] brs. STEELE 2749. LT.

1727   ——[Die Jovis, 22 Junii, 1648]. *For Iohn Wright,* 1648. brs. STEELE 2770. LT; MH.

1728   ——[Die Sabbathi 8 Julii 1648]. *For John Wright,* 1648. brs. STEELE 2774. LT.

1729   ——[Anr. ed.] [*London,* 1648.] brs. STEELE 2775. LT.

1730   ——[Die Mercurii 9. Maii, 1660]. *By John Macock, and Francis Tyton,* 1660. brs. STEELE 3199. LT, O, LG.

1731   ——[Die Jovis, 17. May 1660]. *By John Macock and Francis Tyton,* 1660. brs. STEELE 3206. LT; MH.

1732   ——[Anr. ed.] *By Edward Husbands & Thomas Newcomb,* [1660]. brs. STEELE 3207. L, O, C, MC, DT; MH.

1733   —Ordered by the Lords and Commons now . . . 21 June 1660. *By John Bill & Christopher Barker,* 1660. brs. STEELE 3232. L, O, C, LG, DT; MH.

1733A   ——Die Veneris, 17 Decemb. 1647. Ordered by the Lords and Commons . . . that all committees of sequestrations. *For John Wright,* 1647. brs. L; MH.

1733B   ——Die Jivis, 22 Jan'y, 1648, ordered by the Lords and Commons . . . that Richard Osborne may come. *For John Wright,* 1648. brs. STEELE 2770. LT; MH.

1734   —Die Mercurij 16. Aprill, 1645. Ordered by the Lords and Commons . . . that the Lord Major of the city of London. [*London,* 1645.] brs. LT.

1735   —Die Veneris, 28 August. 1646. Ordered by the Lords and Commons . . . that Tuesday, . . . eight day of September. *For John Wright,* 1646. brs. STEELE 2663. LT, O, MC; MH.

1736   —Die Martis, 17 Septembr, 1650. Ordered by the Parliament. *By Edward Husband and John Field,* 1650. brs. STEELE 2912. L, C.

1737   —Tuesday, September 20. 1659. Ordered by the Parliament, that all masters. *By John Field,* 1659. brs. STEELE 3130. LT, O, LUG; MH.

1738   —Saturday, January 7, 1659. Ordered by the Parliament, that all mayors. *By John Streater, and John Macock,* 1659[60]. brs. LT, O; MH.

1739   —Ordered . . . that all the rents and profits . . . 26 May 1649. *R. Cotes,* [1649]. brs. STEELE 2853. O.

1740   —Ordered . . . that all treasurers, . . . 25 October 1649. *By I. Field for E. Husband,* 1649. brs. STEELE 2881. L, O.

1741   —Ordered . . . that in regard of the late . . . 21 April 1648. [*London,* 1648.] brs. STEELE 2755. O.

1741A   —Ordered . . . that it be referred. *By Iohn Field,* 1659. brs. Y.

1742   —Ordered by the Parliament, that no forces. *By John Streater, and John Macock,* 1659. brs. LT, LUG.

1743   —Ordered . . . that no pass or license . . . 14 April 1649. *By J. Field for E. Husband,* 1649. brs. STEELE 2843. HODGKIN.

1744   —Ordered . . . that such of the persons . . . 7 May 1649. [*London,* 1649.] brs. STEELE 2846. O, LU.

1745   —Ordered . . . that the boursers and treasurers . . . 21 April 1648. [*London,* 1648.] brs. STEELE 2754. O.

1746   —Ordered . . . that the generall be required. *For J. Wright,* 1647. brs. STEELE 2701. O, LPR; MH.

1747   —Ordered . . . that the ministers. *By John Field,* 1652. brs. MH, MIU, NU, Y.

1748   —Ordered . . . that the officers. *By John Field,* 1650[1]. brs. LT, LUG· MH.

1749 —Ordered . . . that the proceedings. *By John Field*, 1659. brs. LT, LUG; MH, Y.

1749A —Ordered . . . that the troops. *By Iohn Field*, 1659. brs. Y.

1749B —Ordered . . . that this act be forthwith printed. *Waterford, by Peter de Pienne*, 1652. 4°.* DN.

1750 —Ordered . . . that Thursday come . . . 23 August 1648. *For J. Wright*, 1648. brs. STEELE 2788. HODGKIN.

1751 —Ordered . . . that Thursday come . . . 2 September 1648. *For J. Wright*, 1648. brs. STEELE 2790. HODGKIN.

1752 —Ordered . . . that Thursday shall be three . . . 21 March 1645[6]. [*London*, 1646.] brs. STEELE 2647a. MC.

1753 —Ordered . . . that Wednesday. *By John Field*, 1659. brs. L.

1754 —Ordered that it be, and it is hereby. *For John Wright*, 1646. brs. STEELE 2653. LT, O, OC; MH.

1755 —Orders conceived and approved by the committee. [*London, September*, 1644.] brs. STEELE 2584. LT, HH.

1756 —Orders conceived and published. *By James Flesher*, [1665]. 4°.* L, O, HH.

1757 —Orders from the High Court of Parliament, for the setling of these kingdomes. *For V.V.*, 1641. 4°.* LT; CN, WF, Y.

1758 —Orders from the High Court of Parliament for the voting of the new bill. [*London*], *printed*, 1641. 4°.* L, CT, HH, SP; CH, LC, MB, Y.

1759 —Orders of the Lords and Commons . . . for the regulating. *August 19. London, for Iohn Wright*, 1642. brs. STEELE 2249. LT, O, LS, OC, EC; MH.

1760 —Orders presented to His Majesty by advice of the Lords & Commons. *Printed at Oxford, by Leonard Lichfield*, 1644. 4°.* MADAN 1622. L, LG; CH, WF, Y.

1760A —Orders, proceedings, punishments, and privileges. *For Miles Mitchell junior*, 1661. 12°. L; MIU.

1761 —Orders, votes, and declarations agreed upon by the High Court of Parliament this present moneth of January. *Ian. 27 for T.VVright*, 1643. 4°.* LT; CH, MH, WF, Y.

1762 —An ordinance against challenges. *June 29, 1654. By William du-Gard and Henry Hills*, 1654. 4°.* STEELE 3042. L; CH, TU, WF.

1763 —An ordinance and declaration of both Houses of Parliament sent to the Lord Maior of London. *For Iohn Hawes*, 1642. 4°.* LT, O.

1764 —An ordinance and declaration of the Lords and Commons . . . 21 Septemb. 1643. *For John Wright, Sept. 23*, 1643. 4°.* HH.

1765 —An ordinance and declaration of the Lords and Commons . . . allowing and authorizing. *Octob. 21 London for I. Wright*, 1642. 4°.* LT, C, LL, MR, DT; CH, CN, MH, NC, WF, Y.

1765A —An ordinance and declaration of the Lords and Commons . . . authorizing Colonell Walter Long. *Husbands*, 1643. 4°.* LSE; MH.

1766 —An ordinance and declaration of the Lords and Commons . . . for re-establishing the duty of excise. *For John Wright, August 30*, 1647. 4°.* LT, O, HH, EN; MH, WF.

1767 —The ordinance and declaration of the Lords and Commons, for the assessing of all such. *Decemb. 1*, [*London*], *for I. Wright*, 1642. 4ll. 4°.* L, O, C, BR, HH; CN, CSS, LC, MH, NU, Y.

1768 ——[Anr. ed.] *London, for I. Wright, Decemb. 1*, 1642. 8ll. 4°.* LT, LG, LU, OC; MH, MHL.

1769 ——[Anr. ed.] *For Ed. Blackmore, Decemb. 1*, 1642. 4°.* L, O, LG, HH; CN, MA.

1770 ——[Anr. ed.] *Printed at Oxford by Leonard Lichfield, Dec. 8*, 1642. 4°.* MADAN 1106. L, O, CT, HH, BR; CH, LC, MHL, WF, Y.

1771 ——[Anr. ed.] *Oxford Decemb. 8. By Leonard Lichfield*, 1642. 4°.* MADAN 1108. LT, CJ, CM, HH; MH, WF, Y.

1771A ——[Anr. ed.] *For R.D. Decemb. 17*, 1642. 4°.* O; CN, MA, MH, Y.

1772 —An ordinance and declaration of the Lords and Commons . . . for the raising, maintaining, . . . 30 Martii. 1644. [*London*], *for John Wright. April 1*, 1644. 4°.* LT, O, SC, SP; MA, MH, MHL, WF, Y.

1773 —An ordinance and declaration of the Lords and Commons . . . one for the speedy setting forth. *Printed at London for T.S. April 6*, 1644. 4°.* LT, O, MR; CLC, Y.

1774 —An ordinance and declaration of the Lords and Commons . . . that no person. [*London*], *Decemb. 21. for Iohn Wright*, 1643. 4°.* LT, O, LG; CH, MA, MHL.

1774A ——[Anr. ed.] *By Richard Cotes*, 1644. 4°.* MA, MH.

1775 —An ordinance and declaration of the Lords and Commons . . . that the Lord Major. *For I. Wright, March 8*, 1642[3]. 4°.* L, OC, CT, HH, DT; CH, CN, MH, NC, WF, Y.

1776 —An ordinance and declaration of the Lords and Commons . . . that the Lord Major. [*London*], *Aprill 25. for John Wright*, 1643. 4°.* LT, O; MA, MH, Y.

1777 —An ordinance and declaration of the Lords and Commons . . . touching the sallery. *For Iohn Wright, Septemb. 19*, 1643. 4°.* LT, DT; CLC, MH, NU, WF, Y.

1778 —An ordinance by the Lords and Commons . . . enabling all persons. *For Laurence Blaiklocke*, 1643. 4°.* LT, MR; CH, CLC, MA, NU, Y.

1779 —An ordinance by the Lords and Commons . . . for the preservation. *By R. Olten and G. Dexter, for Henry Overton*, 1642. 4°.* LT, O; CH, CLC, MH, MIU.

1780 ——18 Novemb. 1643. *For Edw. Husbands*, 1643. 4°.* LT, O, C, HH; CH, MA, WF, Y.

1781 —An ordinance declaratory . . . 3 Augusti, 1644. *By Richard Cotes and John Raworth*, 1644. 4°.* LG, LUG, HH; Y.

1782 —An ordinance for adjourning part of Eastern Term, 1654 . . . April 6, 1654. *By Henry Hills and William du-Gard*, 1654. brs. STEELE 3028. LT, O, C, LL, DT; MH, Y.

1783 ——April 8. 1654. *By William du-Gard, and Henry Hills*, 1654. brs. STEELE 3031. LT, O, C, HH, DT; MH, Y.

1784 —An ordinance for repealing of the former ordinance for setling the militia. *For J. Wright*, 1648. brs. STEELE 2810. WF.

1785 —An ordinance for repealing the former ordinance for . . . Lancaster. *For J. Wright*, 1648. brs. STEELE 2809. HODGKIN.

1786 —An ordinance for the better raysing and levying of mariners. *For I. Wright, February 4, 1642[3].* brs. STEELE 2361. LT, LS, EC, HH; CH, MH.

1786A —An ordinance for the setling of the yeerly summe. [*London*, 1645.] cap., 4°.* OC; MH.

1787 —An ordinance from His Maiesty, and both Hovses. *By R. O. and G. D. for F. Coules,* [1642]. 4°.* LT, C, EC; MH, WF.

1788 —An ordinance from His Majesty and both Houses . . . for the ordering of the militia. *For John Wright,* 1642. 4°.* L, CT, BR, HH, DT; CH, MB, MH, WF, Y.

1789 —An ordinance made and agreed by the Lords and Commons of Parliament the 28th day of August 1641. *By Robert Barker, and by the assignes of John Bill,* 1641. 4°.* LT, O, CT, BR, HH; CH, MH, NU, WF, Y.

1790 —An ordinance, made by the Lords and Commons . . . for the better and more speedy execution. *For Robert Dunscomb, Decemb.* 17, 1642. brs. STEELE 2323. LT, O, LS; MA, MB, MH.

1791 — —[Anr. ed.] —, *January* 2, 1642[3]. brs. LT.

1792 — —[Anr. ed.] [*London,* 1643.] brs. LG; CH, MH.

1793 —An ordinance of both Houses of Parliament, for the safeguard of the Parliament. *February* 18. *London, for Joseph Hunscott,* 1641[2]. brs. STEELE 1989. L, O, CT, LS, OC; MIU, Y.

1794 —An ordinance of both Houses of Parliament, for the speedy raising and levying of money. *For Edward Husbands, August* 4, 1643. 4°.* LT, O, OC, BR; MA, MH, Y.

1794A —An ordinance of explanation and further enlargement. *For Laurence Blaikelocke, Aug.* 21, 1643. 4°.* LT, O, C; CH, CN, MH, WF, Y.

1795 —An ordinance of Parliament, concerning the subsidie. *By T. Badger for Lawrence Blaikelock,* 1642. 8°.* O, LG, LL; CSS, LC, MH, WF, Y.

1795A — —[Anr. ed.] *For Lawrence Blaikelock,* 1642. 4°.* OP, BR.

1795B — —[Anr. ed.] —, 1643. 4°.* O, LUG; CLC, CSS, MH.

1796 —An ordinance of Parliament for a day of publike thanksgiving. *By Robert Barker and the assignes of John Bill,* 1641. brs. STEELE 1882. LT, O, LS, EN; Y.

1797 — —[Anr. ed.] *Imprinted at London by Robert Barker: and by the assignes of John Bill,* 1641. brs. LT, CJ.

1797A —An ordinance of Parliament, for the continuance of the subsidy. *L. Blaikelock,* 1642. 4°.* MH.

1797B —An ordinance of Parliament: for the leavying of moneys. *R. Cotes and R. Raworth,* 1643. 4°. CT.

1798 —An ordinance of Parliament, whereby a Committee . . . 1 Julii. 1645. [*London,* 1645.] brs. STEELE 2622. LT; CH, LC.

1798A —An ordinance of Parliament; with instructions. *For E. Husbands,* [1644]. 4°. CT.

1799 —An ordinance of the Lords and Commons . . . 17 Augusti, 1643. *For J. Wright, Aug.* 18, 1643. 4°.* HH.

1800 — —26 January 1642[3]. *Printed at London, for Iohn Wright,* 1642[3]. brs. STEELE 2354. LT, O, HH.

1801 —An ordinance of the Lords and Commons . . . after advice had . . . 2 Octob. 1644. *For Ralph Smith,* 1644. 4°.* LT, O, C, MR, E; CH, MH, NC, WF, Y.

1802 —An ordinance of the Lords & Commons . . . against unlicensed or scandalous pamphlets. *For Edward Husband, Sept.* 30, 1647. 4°.* LT, O, CT, HH; NR, NU.

1802A —An ordinance of the Lords and Commons . . . appointing a comptroll. *By Rich. Cotes, and R. Raworth,* 1645. 4°.* MH.

1803 —An ordinance of the Lords and Commons . . . authorizing commissioners. *For Matthew Walbancke,* 1646. 4°.* LT, O, HH; MA, MH, WF.

1804 —An ordinance of the Lords and Commons . . . authorizing Robert Earl of Warwick. *For Edward Husband, August* 22, 1648. brs. STEELE 2786. LT; CH.

1805 —An ordinance of the Lords and Commons . . . authorizing the commissioners. *For Humphrey Tuckey,* 1644. brs. STEELE 2526. LT, O, OP, HH; MH, Y.

1806 —An ordinance of the Lords and Commons . . . authorizing the committee. *For John Wright,* 25. *April,* 1645. 4°.* LT, LG, HH; CH, MH, MHL, NC, Y.

1807 — —[Anr. ed.] *For Edward Husband, Sept.* 28, 1647. 4°.* LT, O, OC, HH; CH, CLC, MH, WF, Y.

1808 —An ordinance of the Lords and Commons . . . authorizing the committee of Lords and Commons for the army, . . . 9 Januarii, 1648. *Imprinted at London for John Wright,* 1648[9]. 4°.* LT, O, HH; CH, MH.

1809 —An ordinance of the Lords and Commons . . . being a weekly assesment upon . . . Northampton. *For Iohn Wright, Octob.* 14, 1644. 4°.* LT, HH; CH.

1810 —An ordinance of the Lords and Commons . . . being an exhortation. *For John Wright, Febr.* 11, 1644[5]. brs. STEELE 2599. LT, LG, HH; Y.

1811 —An ordinance of the Lords and Commons . . . commanding all officers. *For Edw. Husbands,* 1644[5]. brs. STEELE 2601. LT, LG, LS.

1812 —An ordinance of the Lords and Commons . . . commanding all Papists, . . . 9 Julii, 1647. *For John Wright,* 1647. 4°.* LT, O, C, LG, HH; CH, CN, MH, WF, Y.

1813 —An ordinance of the Lords and Commons . . . concerning a new excise upon allum. *For John Wright, July* 10, 1644. 4°.* LT, O, LG, HH, EN; CH, LC, MH, WF, Y.

1814 —An ordinance of the Lords and Commons . . . concerning sequestred books. *For Edward Husband, Sept.* 28, 1647. brs. STEELE 2732. LT, LPR, HH.

1814A —An ordinance of the Lords and Commons . . . concerning suspention from the sacrament. *For John Wright,* 1675. brs. LIC, OP.

1815 —An ordinance of the Lords and Commons . . . concerning the arch-bishop of Canterbury. *May* 19, for *John Wright,* 1643. 4°.* L, O; MH, MIU, NGT, NU.

1816 —An ordinance of the Lords and Commons . . . concerning the associating of . . . Hertford. *For John Partridge, Sept.* 20, 1643. 4°.* LT, O; CH, MH, WF, Y.

1817 —An ordinance of the Lords and Commons . . . concerning the association. *By G. M. for Christopher Meredith,* 1643. 4°.* LT, O, AN, EN, DT; MH.

1818 —An ordinance of the Lords and Commons . . . concerning the company of merchants trading into France: . . . 19 Octob. 1648. *Imprinted at London, for John Wright*, 1648. 4°.* LT, LUG, MR, HH; CH, MH, NC.

1819 —An ordinance of the Lords and Commons . . . concerning the Dutchy seale of Lancaster. *For Edward Husbands, Septemb.* 4, 1645. 4°.* LT, O, HH; CH, MA, WF.

1820 —An ordinance of the Lords and Commons . . . concerning the election. [*London*], *by Richard Cotes*, [1648]. brs. STEELE 2811. LT, O, HH.

1820A —An ordinance of the Lords and Commons . . . concerning the excise of flesh. *By Richard Cotes and John Raworth*, 1643. brs. OC, BR.

1821 —An ordinance of the Lords and Commons . . . concerning the excise of tobacco . . . 17 Octob. 1643. *By Richard Cotes and John Raworth*, 1643. 4°.* O, LUG, HH; LC, MH, WF.

1822 ——[Anr. ed.] —, [1643]. 4°.* L, HH, DT; NC, NN, RPJ.

1823 —An ordinance of the Lords and Commons . . . concerning the growth. *For Edw. Husband*, [1646(7)]. brs. STEELE 2679 L, C; Y.

1824 ——[Anr. ed.] *For John Wright*, 1646[/7]. 4°.* LT, O, CJ, E, AU; CH, MH, NU, WF.

1825 —An ordinance of the Lords and Commons . . . concerning the late rebellious insurrection in . . . Kent. [*London*], *August* 17, *for John Wright*, 1643. 4°.* LT, LG, SP; CH, CN, MH, Y.

1826 —An ordinance of the Lords and Commons . . . concerning the militia . . . 19 July 1643. [*London*, 1643.] brs. STEELE 2459. L.

1827 —An ordinance of the Lords and Commons . . . concerning the names of the committee. [*London*], *for Edward Husbands, August* 14, [1643]. 4°.* LT, CT, DT; CH, CN, MH, WF, Y.

1828 —An ordinance of the Lords and Commons . . . concerning the proceedings of divers ill-affected persons. [*London*], *for Edw. Husbands, Iuly* 11, 1643. 4°.* LT, O, CT, AN, DT; MA, MH, Y.

1829 —An ordinance of the Lords and Commons . . . concerning those. *For Edward Husbands, Novemb.* 14, 1645. 4°.* LT, O, C, HH, EN; MA, MH, WF, Y.

1830 —An ordinance of the Lords and Commons . . . constituting a committee. [*London*], *by T. W. for Ed. Husband, Iune the* 26, 1645. 4°.* LT, O, HH; CH, MA.

1831 —An ordinance of the Lords and Commons . . . constituting and appointing Sergeant Major Generall Richard Brown, . . . 8 Junii, 1644. *For Matthew Walbanck, June* 10, 1644. 4°.* MADAN 1651. LT, O, HH; CH, MA, MHL ,WF, Y.

1832 —An ordinance of the Lords and Commons . . . containing certaine instructions. *For Iohn Wright*, 1645. 4°.* LT, O; MA, MH, Y.

1833 —An ordinance of the Lords and Commons . . . declaring, that it shall and may be lawfull for all foreigners. *For Iohn Wright, August* 31, 1644. 4°.* LT, O, C, MR, HH; CH, MH, NC, WF, Y.

1834 —An ordinance declaring that the offenses herein mentioned. *London, reprinted Leith*, 1653. 4°. ALDIS 1481. E, EN.

1835 —An ordinance of the Lords and Commons . . . declaring the causes. *For Iohn Wright, Octob.* 19, 1643. 4°.* LT, C; MA, MH.

1836 ——[Anr. ed.] *Printed* 27 *Octob.*, 1643. 4°.* LT, OC, CM, HH; CH, MH, NU, WF.

1837 —An ordinance of the Lords and Commons . . . directing the payment of all duties. *December* 28 [*London*], *for John Wright*, 1643. brs. STEELE 2518. LT, LPR, LS; MA, Y.

1838 ——[Anr. ed.] *For John Wright*, 1644. brs. STEELE 2519. L; CH, Y.

1839 —An ordinance of the Lords and Commons . . . enabling all persons approved of by Parliament, to set forth sips [*sic*]. *For L. Blaiklock, Ian.* 20, [1643]. 4°.* L, O, MR, SP; CH, MH, NU, Y.

1840 ——[Anr. ed.] *For Laurence Blaiklocke*, 1643. 4°.* L; CH, NC, WF.

1841 —An ordinance of the Lords and Commons . . . enabling commissioners. *By T. W. for Ed. Husband*, 1645. 4°.* LT, HH; MA, MH, Y.

1841A ——[Anr. ed.] *By I. F. for Ed. Husband*, 1645. 4°.* CLC, MH, WF.

1842 —An ordinance of the Lords and Commons . . . enabling the commissioners. *By L. N. for Laurence Blaiklock, March* 13, 1644. brs. STEELE 2535. LT.

1843 —An ordinance of the Lords and Commons . . . enabling the committee at Goldsmiths Hall. *Iune the* 13. *by T. W. for Ed. Husband*, 1645. 4°.* MADAN 1789. LT, HH; WF, Y.

1844 —An ordinance of the Lords and Commons enabling the committee of Oxon, Bucks, and Barks, . . . 10 Maii 1645. [*London*, 1645.] brs. CH.

1845 —An ordinance of the Lords and Commons . . . enabling the committee of Southampton. *By T. W. for Ed. Husband, Iune the* 14, 1645. 4°.* LT, O; CH, MA, MH, WF.

1846 —An ordinance of the Lords and Commons . . . enabling the committee of the County of Worcester. *For John Wright*, 1648. brs. STEELE 2792. LT, HH.

1847 —An ordinance of the Lords and Commons . . . inabling the Lord Maior. *For John Wright*, 12. *May*, 1645. 4°.* LT, LG; CH, MA, MH, WF, Y.

1848 —An ordinance of the Lords and Commons . . . inabling the militia. *By Richard Cotes*, 1647. 4°.* LT, O; CH, CN, MH, WF, Y.

1849 —An ordinance of the Lords and Commons . . . exhorting all . . . good subjects . . . 15 Feb. 1642[3]. *Feb:* 16. *for John Wright*, 1642[3]. 4°.* LT, O, C, OC, HH; CH, MH, NU, WF, Y.

1850 —An ordinance of the Lords and Commons . . . explaining the former ordinance. *For Iohn Wright, Aug.* 26, 1643. 4°.* EC, DT; MA, MH, NC, WF, Y.

1851 —An ordinance of the Lords and Commons . . . for a committee of militia. *For Edward Husband, Sept.* 11, 1647. 4°.* LT, C, LG, HH; CN, MH, MHL, Y.

1852 —An ordinance of the Lords and Commons . . . for a monethly charge. *Printed at London for Edward Husbands.* April 8, 1645. 4°.* LT, O, HH; CH, MA, MH, WF, Y.

1853 —An ordinance of the Lords and Commons . . . for a new impost or excise upon herring. [*London*], *for Laurence Blaiklock, August 27,* [1644]. 4°.* LT, O; CH, MA, MH, WF, Y.

1854 —An ordinance of the Lords and Commons . . . for advancing by way of loane. [*London*], *by T. W. for Edw. Husband,* 1645. 4°.* LT, O, HH, YM; CH, LC, MH, TU, WF, Y.

1855 Entry cancelled.

1856 —An ordinance of the Lords and Commons for an assessment of seventy thousand pounds. *By Edward Husband and Thomas Newcomb,* [1660]. fol. LT; CH, MH.

1857 —An ordinance of the Lords and Commons . . . for and concerning one tenth part. [*London*], *for Edward Husbands, November 20,* 1643. 4°.* LT; MA, MH, MHL, WF, Y.

1858 —An ordinance of the Lords and Commons . . . for appointing a solemne day. [*London*], *for Edward Husbands, April 4.* 1644. 4°.* LT, C, EC, HH; MH, MHL, NU, WF, Y.

1859 —An ordinance of the Lords & Commons . . . for appointing and authorizing Thomas Andrews. *For Edward Husband, April 10,* 1647[8]. 4°.* LT, C, OC, HH; MH, Y.

1860 —An ordinance of the Lords and Commons . . . for appointing the speakers. *For Edward Husband, Novemb. 2,* 1646. 4°.* LT, O, LL, HH; CH, CN, LC, MH, WF, Y.

1861 —An ordinance of the Lords and Commons . . . for assessing of all such members. *Octob.* 11. *for R. Dunscomb,* 1643. 4°.* LT, C, DT; MA, MH, MHL, NC, WF.

1862 —An ordinance of the Lords and Commons . . . for associating of the counties of Pembroke, . . . 8 Junii, 1644. [*London*], *for Edward Husbands, Iune 14,* 1644. 4°.* LT, O, HH, YM, AN; CH, MA, MHL, WF, Y.

1863 —An ordinance of the Lords and Commons . . . for bringing in of the arrears. *For Iohn Wright,* 1646. 4°.* MH, Y.

1864 —An ordinance of the Lords and Commons . . . for bringing in the arrears. *For Edw. Husbands. Dec.* 28, 1644. 4°.* LT, O, LG; MA, MH.

1865 ——[Same title.] 12 *Octob.* 1647. *For John Wright,* 1647. 4°.* LT, O, HH, OC, YM; CH, CLC, WF, Y.

1866 —An ordinance of the Lords and Commons . . . for charging and taxing. *For Edward Husband, Aprill 2,* 1645. 4°.* L, O, HH; CH, MA, MH, MHL, WF, Y.

1867 —An ordinance of the Lords and Commons . . . for compositions for wardships. [*London,* 1645.] brs. STEELE 2635. O.

1868 —An ordinance of the Lords and Commons . . . for, constituting a committee. *Imprinted at London for John Wright,* 1647[8]. 4°.* LT, O, LG; CN, MH, NU.

1869 —An ordinance of the Lords and Commons . . . for constituting and appointing. *For Ed. Husband, December 2,* 1645. 4°.* LT, O, HH; CH, MA, WF, Y.

1870 —An ordinance of the Lords and Commons . . . for constituting and setling of the committee. *For John Wright,* 1647. 4°.* LT, O, HH, OC; CH, CN, MH, MHL, Y.

1871 ——2 *Septembi,* 1647. *For John Wright,* 1647. 4°.* LT, O, LG, HH; CN, MH, NC.

1872 —An ordinance of the Lords and Commons . . . for constituting commissioners. [*London*], *by T. W. for Ed. Husband, May the first,* 1645. 4°.* LT, LG; CH, MH, MIU, Y.

1873 —An ordinance of the Lords and Commons . . . for constituting commissioners . . . for . . . Kent. [*London*], *for T. W. for Ed. Husband, Iune the 10,* 1645. 4°.* LT, LG; MA, MH, MIU, WF, Y.

1874 —An ordinance of the Lords and Commons . . . for constituting of Major Generall Philip Skippon. *Imprinted at London for John Wright,* 1648. 4°.* LT, LG; CLC, MH, MIU, WF, Y.

1875 —An ordinance of the Lords and Commons . . . for continuance of the assessements. *For Edward Husband, Aug.* 20, 1645. 4°.* L, O, HH; CH, MA, MH.

1876 —An ordinance of the Lords and Commons . . . for continuance of the excise. *By Richard Cotes and John Raworth,* [1644]. brs. STEELE 2556. LT.

1877 ——[Anr. ed.] *By Rich. Cotes, and Jo. Raworth,* 1644. 4°.* LT, CT, LG, HH; MA, MH, Y.

1878 —An ordinance of the Lords and Commons for continuance of the former ordinance for four moneths. [*London,* 1644.] cap., 4°.* CH.

1879 —An ordinance of the Lords and Commons . . . for continuance of the subsidy. *For Laurence Blaiklock,* 1644[5]. 4°.* L, O, LUG, OP, HH; CH, CLC, MA, MH, WF.

1880 ——[Anr. ed.] [*London, for E. Husbands,* 1645.] fol.* STEELE 2600a. MC.

1881 —An ordinance for continuation of an act, . . . 20 March, 1653[4]. *By William du-Gard and Henry Hills,* 1653[4]. fol.* HH; WF.

1882 —An ordinance of the Lords and Commons . . . for continuing of the duty. [*London,* 1647.] brs. STEELE 2688. L.

1883 —An ordinance of the Lords and Commons . . . for disabling delinquents. *For Edward Husband, Octob.* 5, 1647. 4°.* LT, O, OC, HH, MR; CH, MH, WF, Y.

1884 —An ordinance of the Lords and Commons . . . for disbanded sovldiers. *For Ed. Husbands,* [1647]. brs. STEELE 2713. L, LPR, HH; CH, MH.

1885 —An ordinance of the Lords and Commons . . . for enabling a committee. *For Iohn Wright,* 1647[8]. brs. STEELE 2745. LT; MIU.

1886 —An ordinance of the Lords and Commons . . . for, enabling commissioners in the county of Wilts . . . 6 Septemb. 1648. *Imprinted at London for John Wright,* 1648. 4°.* LT, HH; CH, CLC, MH.

1887 —An ordinance of the Lords & Commons . . . for establishing commissioners of Lords and Commons. *For Edward Husband, February 8,* 1646[7]. 4°.* LT, O, BR, HH; BN, CH, MH, NU, WF.

1888 —An ordinance of the Lords and Commons . . . for every second Tuesday. [*London*, 1647.] brs. STEELE 2700. L; MH.

1889 —An ordinance of the Lords and Commons . . . for excluding such members. *For Edward Husbands. Iuly 9, 1644.* 4°.* LT, C, HH; CH, MA, MH, WF, Y.

1890 —An ordinance of the Lords and Commons . . . for execution of martiall law. [*London*], *for Edward Husbands, August 17.* [1644]. 4°.* LT, O, LG, SP; CH, MH, TU, WF, Y.

1890A —An ordinance of the Lords and Commons . . . for exempting the University of Cambridge. *For John Wright, 1645.* 4°.* CM; MH.

1891 —An ordinance of the Lords and Commons . . . for explanation. [*London*, 1643.] 4°.* O, C, OC, EC, HH; CH, CN, MH, MIU.

1892 —An ordinance of the Lords and Commons . . . for freeing and dischargeing the vintners. [*London*], *by T. W. for Ed. Husband, May the 12, 1645.* 4°.* LT, LG; CH, MA, WF, Y.

1893 —An ordinance of the Lords and Commons . . . for further addition of power. *Decemb. 20. London for John Partridge, 1643.* 4°.* LT, O, OC; MH.

1894 —An ordinance of the Lords and Commons . . . for giving power to all the classicall presbyteries . . . 10 Novemb. 1645. *For John Wright, 12 Novemb., 1645.* 4°.* LT, O, C, MR, E; CH, MH, NU, WF, Y.

1895 —An ordinance of the Lords and Commons . . . for keeping of scandalous persons from the Sacrament. *For Edw. Husband, March 16, 1645*[6]. 4°.* LT, O, C, MR, EN; CH, CU, LC, MH, NU, Y.

1895A ——[Anr. ed.] —, 1646. 4°.* L, O, C, MR, HH; CLC, MH, TU, WF, Y.

1896 —An ordinance of the Lords and Commons . . . for making the Covent-Garden. *For William Beesley, 1646.* 4°.* L, HH; MA.

1897 —An ordinance of the Lords and Commons . . . for master sollicitors. *For Mathew Walebancke, May 30, 1644.* 4°.* LT, BR, HH; MA, MH, WF, Y.

1897A —An ordinance of the Lords and Commons . . . for mitigation of the excise. *By R. Cotes and J. Raworth, 1644.* 4°.* LUG, CT.

1898 —An ordinance of the Lords and Commons . . . for prevention of adiournment . . . 30 April 1644. *Imprinted at London, for Iohn Wright, 1644.* brs. STEELE 2561. LT, O.

1899 —An ordinance of the Lords and Commons . . . for prevention of the adjournment. *Imprinted at London, for L. Baiklocke* [sic], *1643*[4]. brs. STEELE 2525. LT, LG, LS.

1900 —An ordinance of the Lords and Commons . . . for providing of draught-horses. *Printed at London for Edward Husbands. March 15, 1644*[5]. 4°.* LT, O, LG, HH; CH, MA, MH, WF.

1901 —An ordinance of the Lords and Commons . . . for putting all delinquents. *Printed at London for John Wright, 1648.* 4°.* LT, O; CH, CN, MH, MIU, NU, WF.

1902 —An ordinance of the Lords and Commons . . . for putting malignants. *Imprinted at London for John Wright, 1648.* 4°.* STEELE 2764. LT, C; CLC, CN, MH, NU, WF, Y.

1903 —An ordinance of the Lords and Commons . . . for putting the associated counties of Suffolk. *For Edward Husbands, Iuly 5, 1644.* 4°.* LT, O, CJ, CT, HH; CH, MA, MH, WF, Y.

1904 —An ordinance of the Lords and Commons . . . for putting the County of Surrey. *For Edw. Husbands, Jul. 3, 1645.* 4°.* LT, O, HH; CH, MA, MH, WF, Y.

1905 —An ordinance of the Lords and Commons . . . for raising an army of horse and foot . . . 12 July 1644. *For Edward Husbands, July 15, 1644.* 4°.* LT, O, HH, AN; CH, MH, NC, WF, Y.

1906 —An ordinance of the Lords and Commons . . . for raising and maintaining of forces. *Printed at London, for Edw. Husbands, Febr. 17, 1644*[/5]. 4°.* LT, O, CT, LL, HH; CH, MH, NC, WF, Y.

1907 ——[Anr. ed.] [*London*], *for Edward Husband, Feb. 17, 1644*[5]. 4°.* OC, SP, YM; CH, CLC, WF.

1907A ——[Anr. ed.] *By T. W. for Ed. Husband, 1645.* 4°.* MH, PT.

1908 —An ordinance of the Lords and Commons . . . for raysing and maintaining of horse. [*London*], *for Edward Husbands, 1644. May 13.* 4°.* LT, OC, SP, AN; MA, MH, WF, Y.

1909 ——[Anr. ed.] —, *May 24, 1644.* 4°.* LT.

1910 ——[Anr. ed.] *For Edward Husbands. Sept. 23,* [1644]. 4°.* LT, O, C, HH; CH, CN, WF.

1911 —An ordinance of the Lords and Commons . . . for raising fifty thousand pounds. *For Edward Husband, Jan. 31, 1647*[8]. 4°.* LT, O, C, OC; CH, MH, MIU, Y.

1911A ——[Anr. ed.] *For John Wright, 1647.* 4°.* O, C, OC; MH.

1912 —An ordinance of the Lords & Commons . . . for raising moneys to be imployed. *For Edward Husband, March 23, 1647*[8]. 4°.* LT, O, C, LL, HH; CH, MH, NC, WF, Y.

1913 —An ordinance of the Lords and Commons . . . for raising of fourscore thousand pounds. *For Edw. Husband, October 23, 1644.* 4°.* LT, O, C, OC, BR; CH, MH, MIU, WF, Y.

1914 —An ordinance of the Lords and Commons . . . for raising of twenty thousand pounds. *For Edward Husband, Febr. 24, 1646*[7]. 4°.* LT, O, C, OC, EN; CH, MH, NU, WF, Y.

1915 —An ordinance of the Lords and Commons . . . for regulating the University of Cambridge. *For John Wright, 1645*[6]. 4°.* LT, O, CS, CT, HH; WF.

1916 —An ordinance of the Lords and Commons . . . for reimbursing of Captaine William Edwards. *For J. Wright, 1644.* 4°.* LT; PT.

1917 —An ordinance of the Lords and Commons . . . for reliefe of maymed souldiers. *For Edward Husband, 1647.* brs. STEELE 2690. L; WF.

1917A —An ordinance of the Lords and Commons . . . for reliefe of the counties of Oxon. *By Richard Cotes, 1645.* 4°.* SP.

1918 —An ordinance of the Lords and Commons . . . for reliefe of the subiect. *Printed at London, for Edw. Husbands,* 1644. brs. STEELE 2566. LT, O, HH; CH, MH, Y.

1919 —An ordinance of the Lords and Commons . . . for removing obstructions . . . 17 Martis, 1647[8]. *Imprinted at London for John Wright,* 1647[8]. 4°.* LT, O, C, BR, HH; MH, MIU, WF.

1919A ——[Anr. ed.] *By R. Cotes for J. Bellamy,* 1647. 4°.* L; MH.

1919B ——2 Decemb. 1647. *For John Wright,* 1647. 4°.* L, OC; MH.

1920 Entry cancelled.

1921 —An ordinance of the Lords and Commons . . . for saving harmless . . . such persons. *For Edward Husband, May 22,* 1647. 4°.* LT, C, HH; CH, MH, TU, WF, Y.

1922 —An ordinance of the Lords and Commons . . . for securing of all those . . . 13 Maii, 1647. *For John Wright,* 1647. 4°.* LT, O, CM, OC, HH; MH, MHL, WF, Y.

1923 —An ordinance of the Lords and Commons . . . for securing of the eighty thousand pounds. *Printed at London for Edward Husbands. April 2,* 1645. 4°.* LT, O, HH, SP; CH, CLC, MH, MHL, WF, Y.

1924 —An ordinance of the Lords and Commons . . . for sending forth five regiments. *Printed at London, by Richard Cotes,* 1644. brs. STEELE 2588. LT, O, HH; MH.

1924A —An ordinance of the Lords and Commons . . . for sequestration of the estates. *For John Wright,* 1648. 4°.* CT; WF, Y.

1925 —An ordinance of the Lords and Commons . . . for setling of the militia . . . Hereford. *For John Wright,* 1648. brs. STEELE 2763. LT, LG; CH, CN, MH, Y.

1926 ——23 Maii, 1648. *For John Wright,* 1648. 4°.* LT, HH; MIU, WF.

1927 —An ordinance of the Lords and Commons . . . for setling of the militia of . . . Southwarke. *Imprinted at London for John Wright,* 1648. 4°.* LT; CN, MIU, WF, Y.

1928 —An ordinance of the Lords and Commons . . . for setling the jurisdiction of the Court Admiralty . . . 12 April, 1648. *Imprinted at London for John Wright,* 1648. 4°.* LT, MR, HH; CH, CLC, MH, TU, WF.

1929 —An ordinance of the Lords and Commons . . . for setling the militia. *By Robert Ibbitson in Smithfield,* 1648. 4°.* MIU.

1930 —An ordinance of the Lords and Commons . . . for taking and receiving of the accompts. [*London*], *for Edw. Husbands, Febr. 24,* 1643[4]. 4°.* LT, O, C, BR; CH, MH, NC, WF, Y.

1931 —An ordinance of the Lords and Commons . . . for taking away the fifth part. *For Edward Husband, Septemb. 11,* 1645. brs. STEELE 2630. LT, HH; Y.

1932 —An ordinance of the Lords and Commons . . . for taking, stating and determining the accompts. *For Edward Husband, Septemb. 5,* 1648. 4°.* LT, O, OC, HH; CH, CLC, MH, Y.

1933 —An ordinance of the Lords and Commons . . . for the advance of thirty one thousand pounds. *By Rich. Cotes,* 1645. 4°.* LT, O, LUG, HH; CLC, MA, MH, WF.

1934 —An ordinance of the Lords and Commons . . . for the advancing of monies. *By George Miller,* 1646. 4°.* LT, OC; WF, Y.

1935 —An ordinance of the Lords and Commons, . . . for the appointing . . . of Henry Brooke, . . . 13 Sept. 1644. *For Tho. Underhill,* 1644. 4°.* O, HH.

1936 —An ordinance of the Lords and Commons . . . for the appointment of Col. Gower. *By Iane Coe, June 19,* 1647. 4°.* LT, OC, HH; MH, MHL, Y.

1937 —An ordinance of the Lords and Commons . . . for the apprehending and bringing. *For John Wright, May 9,* 1645. brs. STEELE 2613a. LT, O, LG; CH, MH.

1938 —An ordinance of the Lords and Commons . . . for the associating five counties in North-VVales . . . 9 August, 1648. *For John Wright,* 1648. 4°.* LT, O, HH, AN; MIU.

1939 —An ordinance of the Lords and Commons . . . for the associating the counties of Wilts. [*London*], *for Edward Husbands, August 22,* [1644]. 4°.* LT, O, CT, BR, HH; CH, MA, WF, Y.

1940 —An ordinance of the Lords and Commons . . . for the associating the severall counties of York. *For Edw. Husbands, Jun. 24,* 1645. 4°.* LT, O, CJ, HH; CH, MA, WF.

1941 —An ordinance of the Lords and Commons . . . for the better execution of the former ordinances for sequestration. [*London*], *for Laurence Blaiklock, May 27,* 1644. 4°.* LT, O, CCA, EN; MH, NC, NU, WF, Y.

1942 —An ordinance of the Lords and Commons . . . for the better levying and receiving of moneyes. *For R. Dunscomb, February 11,* 1642[3]. brs. STEELE 2364. LT, O, CJ, LG, HH; CH, MH, WF, Y.

1943 —An ordinance of the Lords and Commons . . . for the better observation . . . 24 August, 1642. *For Laurence Blaiklock,* 1642. 4°.* O, C, HH, GU; CH, CN, MH, NU, WF.

1944 ——[Same title.] *For Edward Husbands, April. 10,* 1644. 4°.* STEELE 2552. LT, O, C, OC, HH; CH, MH, NU, WF, Y.

1945 ——[Same title.] 20 Decembris. 1646. *For Edward Husbands,* 1646. brs. STEELE 2669. LT, O, LG; MH.

1946 —An ordinance of the Lords and Commons . . . for the better observing. [*London,* 1642.] brs. STEELE 2250. HH.

1947 —An ordinance of the Lords & Commons . . . for the better payment of tythes. *For Edward Husband, April 24,* 1648. 4°.* LT, O, BR, HH; CH, MH, MHL, MIU, WF.

1948 —An ordinance of the Lords and Commons . . . for the better raising, leavying, and impresting of mariners. [*London*], *for L. Blaiklock, Ian. 15,* [1643]. 4°.* LT, O, MR; MH, WF, Y.

1949 —An ordinance of the Lords and Commons . . . for the better regulating and ordering. *Imprinted at London for John Wright,* 1648. 4°.* LT; CH, CN, MH, NU, WF, Y.

1950 —An ordinance of the Lords and Commons . . . for the better securing and setling the peace. *Printed at London for R. D.,* 1643. 4°.* LT, DT; MH.

1950A —An ordinance of the Lords and Commons . . . for the better security. *By R. Cotes, for John Bellamy,* 1647. 4°.* L, O; MH.

1951 —An ordinance of the Lords and Commons . . . for the bringing in the arreares. *Imprinted at London for John Wright*, 1648. 4°.* LT, LG, SP; CN, MH, MIU, WF.

1952 —An ordinance of the Lords and Commons . . . for the calling of an assembly. *For I. Wright, June* 13. 1643. 4°.* LT, O, CJ, HH, EN; CH, CN, MH, NU, WF, Y.

1953 ——[Anr. ed.] *For J. Rothwel*, 1658. 4p. 4°.* D; CH, NU, PPT, V, WF, Y.

1954 ——[Anr. ed.] *For J. Rothwel*, 1658. 12p. 4°.* LT, OC, BR, DT; CN, NGT, NU, TU.

1955 —An ordinance of the Lords and Commons . . . for the chusing of common-councell-men . . . 18 Decemb. 1648. *Imprinted at London for John Wright*, 1648. 4°.* LT, O, HH; CLC, CN, MH, MHL, WF.

1956 —An ordinance of the Lords and Commons . . . for the constant reliefe . . . 17 Dec. 1647. *For Iohn Wright*, 1647. 4°.* LT, O, LG, LUG, HH; MH, WF, Y.

1957 —An ordinance of the Lords and Commons . . . for the constituting and appointing of Sergeant-Major Generall Phillip Skippon. *[London]*, *by T. W. for Edw. Husband*, 1645. 4°.* LT, O, BR; MA, WF.

1958 —An ordinance of the Lords and Commons . . . for, the constituting and setling of the committee. *Imprinted at London for John Wright*, 1648. 4°.* LT, O, BR, SP; CH, CN, MH, MIU, WF, Y.

1959 —An ordinance of the Lords and Commons . . . for the constituting of Sir Nathaniel Brent jvdge. *For Edw. Husbands, Novem.* 5, 1644. 4°.* LT, O, LG; CH, CLC, WF.

1960 —An ordinance of the Lords and Commons . . . for the continuance and maintenance of the alms-houses. *By Henry Hills and John Field*, 1655. brs. NU.

1961 —An ordinance of the Lords and Commons . . . for, the continuance of the assessement of 60000 li per mensem . . . 6 Octob. 1648. *Imprinted at London for John Wright*, 1648. 4°.* LT, O, HH; CH, CLC, MHL, WF.

1962 —An ordinance of the Lords and Commons . . . for the continuance of the monethly assessment. *For Iohn Wright*, 16 August, 1645. brs. STEELE 2624. LT; CH.

1963 —An ordinance of the Lords and Commons . . . for the continuance of the weekly assessment. *For Iohn Wright*, 1646. 4°.* O, C, OC; MH, WF.

1963A —An ordinance of the Lords and Commons . . . for the continuance of tonnage. *For John Wright*, 1646. brs. OP; MH.

1964 —An ordinance of the Lords and Commons . . . for the contribution of the value of one meale a weeke. *For John Wright, March* 28, 1644. 4°.* LT, O, C, SP; CH, CN, MH, NC, WF, Y.

1965 —An ordinance of the Lords and Commons . . . for the county of Lancaster. *For Edward Husband, Sept.* 5, 1645. 4°.* LT, HH; CH, MA, WF, Y.

1966 —An ordinance of the Lords and Commons . . . for the cutting and felling of wood. *For Iohn Wright, Octob.* 3, 1643. 4°.* LT, O, C, HH, DT; CH, MH, NC, WF, Y.

1967 —An ordinance of the Lords and Commons . . . for the discharging of the members. *For I. Wright, April* 5, 1645. 4°.* LT, O, HH; CH, MH, NC, WF, Y.

1968 —An ordinance of the Lords and Commons . . . for the due and orderly receiving. *[London]*, *for I. Wright*, 1643. fol.* STEELE 2480. L.

1969 —An ordinance of the Lords and Commons . . . for the inabling of Sir William Brereton . . . 26 Martii. 1644. *[London]*, *for John Wright. March* 29, 1644. 4°.* LT, O, C, SP; MA, MH, MHL, Y.

1970 —An ordinance of the Lords and Commons . . . for the enabling the committee. *For John Wright*, 1647. 4°.* LT, OC, BR, HH; CN, MH, Y.

1971 —An ordinance of the Lords and Commons . . . for the enabling the committees. *For Edward Husbands, Iuly* 6, 1644. 4°.* LT, EN; WF, Y.

1972 —An ordinance of the Lords and Commons for the enabling the committees herein named. *[London, 1644.]* cap., 4°.* CH.

1973 —An ordinance of the Lords and Commons . . . for the incouragement and security. *Printed at London by Richard Cotes*, 1644. brs. STEELE 2550. LT, O, LG; MA, MH, Y.

1974 —An ordinance of the Lords and Commons . . . for the erecting and maintaining of a garrison. *For John Partridge, Decemb.* 20. 1643. 4°.* LT, O, LSE, EC; CLC, LC, MH, WF.

1975 —An ordinance of the Lords and Commons . . . for the establishing certaine rules. *For Iohn Wright. Septemb.* 2, 1644. 4°.* LT, LUG, HH, SP; CLC, MH, MHL, NC, Y.

1976 —An ordinance of the Lords and Commons . . . for the establishing of the subsidy . . . 16 Decem. 1647. *For Lawrence Blaiklocke*, 1647. 4°.* LT, O, C, HH; MH, WF.

1976A —An ordinance of the Lords and Commons . . . for the executing the ordinance. *For Edward Husband, September* 3, 1645. brs. MH.

1977 —An ordinance of the Lords and Commons . . . for the explanation of a former ordinance. *For Edward Husbands, Iuly* 11, 1644. 4°.* LT, C, OC, BR; CH, MA, MH, WF, Y.

1978 —An ordinance of the Lords and Commons . . . for the explanation of the weekly assessment. *Aprill* 13. *for John Wright*, 1643. 4°.* LT, O, C, LG, LUG; CH, CN, LC, MH, WF, Y.

1978A —An ordinance of the Lords and Commons . . . for the freeing and discharging of all rents. *[London, 1644.]* brs. CH.

1979 —An ordinance of the Lords and Commons . . . for the further ascertaining of the arrears. *For Edward Husband, April* 24, 1648. 4°.* LT; MH, MHL, MIU, MM.

1980 ——[Anr. ed.] *For John Wright*, 1648. 4°.* L, OC; WF.

1981 —An ordinance of the Lords and Commons . . . for the further continuance. *For Edw. Husband, May* 9, 1646. 4°.* LT, O, HH, YM; CH, CLC, MH, WF.

1982 —An ordinance of the Lords and Commons, for the further inlargement. *For Edward Husbands, Novemb.* 11, 1643. 4°.* LT, LG; MA, MHL, NU.

1983 —An ordinance of the Lords and Commons . . . for the further supply of the British army in Ireland 27 Sept. 1645. *[London, 1645.]* cap., 4°.* CH.

1984 —An ordinance of the Lords and Commons . . . for the indempnifying and saving . . . 4 Aprill, 1648. *Imprinted at London for John Wright*, 1648. 4°.* LT, LG, OC, HH; CH, MH, MIU, WF.

1985 —An ordinance of the Lords and Commons . . . for the indempnity. *For John Wright*, 1647. 4°.* O, MR; CH, MH, NU, WF.

1986 —An ordinance of the Lords and Commons . . . for the levying and collecting of money. *Printed at London by Richard Cotes*, 1645. 4°.* LT, HH, SP; NC, WF, Y.

1987 —An ordinance of the Lords and Commons . . . for the leavying of moneys. *By Richard Cotes and Ruth Raworth*, 1643. 4°.* L, OC, CJ, CT, HH; CH, LC, NH, WF, Y.

1988 ——[Anr. ed.] *For Edward Husbands, Septemb.* 11, 1643. 4°.* LT, O, HH, BP, DT; CLC, CN, MA, NC, WF, Y.

1989 —An ordinance of the Lords and Commons . . . for the maintenance and pay of the garrisons of Newport Pagnel. *For Edward Husband, Septemb.* 4, 1645. 4°.* LT, O, BP, HH; CH, MA, MH, MHL, WF, Y.

1990 —An ordinance of the Lords and Commons . . . for the maintaining of the forces of the seven associated counties. *[London], for Edward Husbands*, 1644. *May* 14. 4°.* LT, O; MA, MH, WF, Y.

1991 ——[Anr. ed.] *For Edward Husbands, October* 10, 1644. 4°.* LT, O; CH, MH.

1992 —An ordinance of the Lords and Commons . . . for the making of salt-peter. *[London], for Edward Husbands, April* 5, 1644. 4°.* LT, O, HH, SP; CH, MB, MH, WF, Y.

1993 —An ordinance of the Lords and Commons . . . for the making void all commissions. *Imprinted at London for John Wright*, 1645. 4°.* LT, O; MA, Y.

1994 —An ordinance of the Lords and Commons . . . for the monthly taxing. *For Edward Husband, Aug.* 12, 1645. 4°.* LT, O, HH; MA, MH, WF, Y.

1995 —An ordinance of the Lords and Commons . . . for the more effectuall puting in execution the directory. *[London], by T. W. for Edw. Husband*, 1645. 4°.* LT, O, CT, HH, E; CH, CU, MH, NU, WF, Y.

1996 —[Anr. ed.] *By T. W. for Edw. Husband*, 1646. 4°.* L, OC, CT, EC, BR; CH, MH, PL.

1997 ——[Anr. ed.] *For John Wright*, 1646. 4°.* O, C, OC, HH; MH, MIU, PL.

1998 —An ordinance of the Lords and Commons . . . for the more speedy getting in of the monies. *Printed at London by Richard Cotes*, 1645. 4°.* LT, OC.

1999 —An ordinance of the Lords and Commons . . . for the more speedy raising of the monies. *By Richard Cotes*, 1643. 4°.* LT, O, LG; CH, CN, MH, NU, Y.

1999A —An ordinance of the Lords and Commons . . . for the more speedy satisfying the moneys. *By R. Cotes, for John Bellamy* [1648]. 4°.* BR; CH, MH.

1999B —An ordinance of the Lords and Commons . . . for the ordination of ministers pro tempore. *For Ralph Smith*, 1644. 4°.* LT, C; Y.

2000 —An ordinance of the Lords and Commons . . . for the ordination of ministers. *For John Wright*, 31 *Aug.*, 1646. 4°.* LT, O, C, MR, EN; CH, MH, NU, PL, WF, Y.

2001 —An ordinance of the Lords and Commons . . . for the present raising of one and thirty thousand pounds. *By Richard Cotes*, 1645. 4°.* LT, HH; WF.

2002 —An ordinance of the Lords and Commons . . . for the present setling (wihtout further delay). *Imprinted at London for John Wright*, 1646. 4°.* L, O, C, OC, MR; CN, MH, NU, WF, Y.

2003 ——[Anr. ed.] *For Iohn Wright*, 1646. 4°. LT, O, C, BR, EN; CH, MH, NPT, PL, WF, Y.

2004 —An ordinance of the Lords and Commons . . . for the prohibiting the transportation. *Imprinted at London for John Wright*, 1647[8]. 4°.* LT, O, LUG, SP; NC, WF, Y.

2005 —An ordinance of the Lords and Commons . . . for the provision of turff. *For Edward Husbands, July* 20, 1644. 4°.* LT, O, C, HH; CH, CLC, MA, MH, WF.

2006 —An ordinance of the Lords and Commons . . . for the punishing of blasphemies. *Imprinted at London for John Wright*, 1648. 4°.* LT, O, C, HH, E; CH, CU, MH, NU, WF, Y.

2007 ——[Anr. ed.] *For Edward Husband*, 1648. 4°.* L, EN; CLC, CU, NU, MIU.

2007A —An ordinance of the Lords and Commons . . . for the punishing of such souldiers. *For Edward Husband*, 1645. brs. MH.

2008 —An ordinance of the Lords and Commons . . . for the putting out of the cities . . . 17. Decemb. 1647. *[London, 1648.]* brs. STEELE 2739. LT; WF.

2009 ——[Anr. ed.] *For John Wright*, 1647. 4°.* LT, O, BR, HH; CN, MH, MIU, WF, Y.

2009A —An ordinance of the Lords and Commons . . . for the raising and collecting of ten thousand pounds. *For Lawrence Blaiklock, July* 15. 1645. 4°.* MA, Y.

2010 —An ordinance of the Lords and Commons . . . for the raising and levying. *Printed at London for Edw. Husbands, Feb.* 24, 1644[5]. 4°.* LT, O, OC, CT, HH; CH, CN, MH, NU, WF, Y.

2011 —An ordinance of the Lords and Commons . . . for the raising and securing of 42000. li. . . . 3 Junii, 1647. *For John Wright*, 1647. 4°.* LT, O, LG, OC, HH; MH, MHL, WF, Y.

2012 —An ordinance of the Lords and Commons . . . for the raising of a monthly summe upon . . . Derby. *By F. Neile for Tho. Underhill*, 1645. 4°.* LT; CN.

2013 —An ordinance of the Lords and Commons . . . for the raising of a new loan. *[London], for Edw. Husbands. Febr.* 19, 1643[4]. 4°.* LT, O, LG, EN; CH, MH, MHL, WF, Y.

2014 —An ordinance of the Lords and Commons . . . for the raysing of five hundred horse. *By Richard Cotes*, 1645. 4°.* LT, C, LG, HH; CN, MA, MH, WF, Y.

2015 —An ordinance of the Lords and Commons . . . for the raising of horse. *By Richard Cotes*, 1645[6]. 4°.* LT, OC, LG, HH; CN, MH, TU, WF, Y.

2016 —An ordinance of the Lords and Commons . . . for the raising of money to pay. *By Richard Cotes*, 1644. 4°.* L, O, LG, SP; CH, MH, NC, Y.

2017 —An ordinance of the Lords and Commons . . . for the raising of moneys. *Printed at London for Laurence Blaiklock, Jan.* 30, 1644[5]. 4°.* LT, O; CH, MA, MH, Y.

2018 —An ordinance of the Lords and Commons . . . for the raising of moneys for maintaining. *For Edward Husband, Aug.* 19, 1645. 4°.* LT; MA.

2019 ——[Anr. ed.] *For E. Husbands,* 1645. brs. STEELE 2614. CT, HH; MH, Y.

2020 —An ordinance of the Lords and Commons . . . for the raising of monies to be imployed . . . 23 Junii, 1647. *For John Wright,* 1647. 4°.* LT, O, HH, SP, YM; CH, MH, MHL, NC, WF, Y.

2020A ——[Anr. ed.] *For E. Husband,* 1647. 4°.* BR.

2021 —An ordinance of the Lords and Commons . . . for the raising of 66666 £. 13s. 4d. *For Laurence Blaikelocke, Octob.* 27, 1643. 4°.* LT, O, C, OC, HH; CH, MH, NC, WF, Y.

2022 ——[Anr. ed.] *By Richard Cotes,* 1644. 4°.* LT, O, EC, HH; MA, MH, TU, Y.

2022A —An ordinance of the Lords and Commons . . . for the raising of thirtie two thousand pounds. *By Richard Cotes,* 1645. 4°.* MH.

2023 —An ordinance of the Lords and Commons . . . for the raising of twenty thousand pounds. *By T. W. for Ed. Husband,* 1645. 4°.* LT, O, HH; CH, CLC, MA, WF, Y.

2024 —An ordinance of the Lords and Commons . . . for the redressing. *For John Wright,* 1648. brs. STEELE 2756. LT, O, LG, HH; CLC, MH, Y.

2025 —An ordinance of the Lords and Commons . . . for the regulating of the rates on . . . tobacco. *By Richard Cotes, & John Raworth,* 1644. brs. LT, O, CJ, LUG; CH, LC, MH, NN, RPJ, WF.

2025A —An ordinance of the Lords and Commons . . . for the reliefe and employment of the poor. *J. Wright,* 1647. 4°.* MH.

2026 —An ordinance of the Lords and Commons . . . for the reliefe and maintenance of sicke . . . souldiers. *For John Wright, November.* 2, 1643. 4°.* LT, O; MA, MH, Y.

2027 —An ordinance of the Lords and Commons . . . for the reliefe of the counties of Oxon. *By T. W. for Ed. Husband,* 1645. 4°.* LT, O, HH; CH, CLC, MA, MH, Y.

2028 —An ordinance of the Lords and Commons . . . for the reliefe of the distressed clergy. *For J. Wright,* 19 Sept. 1643. brs. STEELE 2479. L.

2029 —An ordinance of the Lords and Commons . . . for the reliefe of the distressed Protestants. *For John Wright,* 1647. 4°.* LT, O, C; MH, Y.

2030 —An ordinance of the Lords and Commons . . . for the relieving of all persons over rated by the ordinance. *March* 10. 1642. *London, for Edw. Husbands.* 4°.* LT, CT, BR, DT; CH, MIU, NU, WF, Y.

2031 ——[Anr. ed.] *For George Lindsey,* 1647[8]. 4°.* LT, O, CT, HH; MH.

2032 —An ordinance of the Lords and Commons . . . for the repairing of churches. *Imprinted at London for John Wright,* 1647. 12°.* LT, O, C, BR, MR; CH, MH, NU, WF, Y.

2033 —An ordinance of the Lords and Commons . . . for the safety and defence of the kingdom. *For Ioseph Hunscott,* 1641. 4°.* LT, O, C, OC, HH; CH, LC, MH, NU, TU, Y.

2034 ——[Anr. ed.] *For Joseph Hunscott,* 1642. 4°.* L; CSS, WF.

2035 ——[Anr. ed.] *For Richard Best,* 1642. 4°.* O, HH, DT; CLC, Y.

2036 —An ordinance of the Lords and Commons . . . for the sale of parcel of the lands. *For Edward Husband,* [1646]. 4°.* L.

2037 —An ordinance of the Lords and Commons . . . for the securing those apprentices. [London], *for Edward Husbands, September* 26, 1643. 4°.* LT, LG, HH, DT; CLC, MA, OWC.

2038 —An ordinance of the Lords and Commons . . . for the selling of the lands. *For John Wright, Novemb.* 18, 1646. 4°.* LT, O, C, MR, EN; CH, LC, MH, NU, Y.

2038A ——[Anr. ed.] *For J. Bellamie,* 1646. 4°.* L, BP, AN; CH, CLC, MH, Y.

2039 —An ordinance of the Lords and Commons . . . for the setling the militia. *Imprinted at London for John Wright,* 1648. 4°.* LT, O; CH, CN, MH, WF, Y.

2040 —An ordinance of the Lords and Commons . . . for the setting forth ships of warre. *For Laurence Blaiklock, Septemb.* 2, 1645. brs. STEELE 2627. LT, HH.

2041 —An ordinance of the Lords and Commons . . . for the sleighting and demolishing of severall garrisons . . . 6 August, 1646. *For Iohn Wright,* 1646. 4°.* LT, C, HH, SP; MH.

2042 —An ordinance of the Lords and Commons . . . for the speedy constituting of Sir Nathaniel Brent, . . . 4 Novemb. 1644. *For Iohn Wright, Novemb.* 6, 1644. 4°.* O, CT, HH; CH, MA, MH, WF.

2043 —An ordinance of the Lords and Commons . . . for the speedy dividing . . . 29 Januarii 1647[8]. *Imprinted at London for John Wright,* 1647[8]. 4°.* LT, O, C, MR, E; CH, MH, NPT, WF, Y.

2043A ——[Anr. ed.] *For Edward Husband,* 1647 [8]. 4°.* HH; MH.

2044 —An ordinance of the Lords and Commons . . . for the speedy establishing. *For Iohn Wright,* 4 April, 1646. 4°.* LT, O, C, HH, EN; CLC, CN, LC, MA, MH, Y.

2045 —An ordinance of the Lords and Commons . . . for the speedy establishing of a court martiall. *For Iohn Wright. August* 19, 1644. 4°.* LT, O, CS, HH; CH, MH, MHL, WF, Y.

2046 —An ordinance of the Lords and Commons . . . for the speedy getting in the arrears. *By Richard Cotes,* 1648. 4°.* LT; CH, CLC, CN, WF, Y.

2047 —An ordinance of the Lords and Commons . . . for the speedy pressing of 20 000 souldiers. *August* 17. *London, for John Wright,* 1643. 4°.* LT, CS, CT; CLC, MA, Y.

2048 —An ordinance of the Lords and Commons . . . for the speedy raising and impresting of men. [London], *for Edward Husbands, August* 11, [1643]. 4°.* LT, O, OC, BR, HH; CH, CN, MH, WF, Y.

2049 ——[Anr. ed.] *Fot* [sic] *Edward Husband, Febr.* 28, 1645. 4°.* LT, O, C, OC, HH; CH, CN, MH, WF, Y.

2050 —An ordinance of the Lords and Commons for the speedy raising and levying of money . . . February22, 1642. For Edw. Husband, 1643. 4°.* LT, O, C, OC, HH; CH, CSS, MH, NU, Y.

2051 —An ordinance of the Lords and Commons . . . for the speedy raising and leavying of money. For Edward Husbands, May 11, 1643. 4°.* LT, O, LG, BR, HH; CH, CN, LC, MH, Y.

2052 —An ordinance of the Lords and Commons . . . for the speedy raising and levying of moneyes. For John Wright, July 27, 1643. 4°.* LT, O, OC, EC, HH; CLC, MH, MIU, NC, WF, Y.

2052A ——[Anr. ed.] For Edward Husbands, August 4. 1643. 4°.* OC, EC; CLC, MH, Y.

2053 ——[Anr. ed.] For Iohn Wright. October 14, 1644. 4°.* LT, O, LG, SP; CH, MA, MH, Y.

2054 —An ordinance of the Lords and Commons . . . for the speedy raising and maintaining of a competent number of horse . . . 15 Iulii 1644. For Iohn Wright, July 17, 1644. 4°.* LT; CH, MA, MH.

2055 —An ordinance of the Lords and Commons . . . for the speedy raising of foure hundred and fifty pounds weekly. Aprill 1. for John Wright, 1643. 4°.* LT, O, EC; CH, CN, MH, NC, WF.

2056 —An ordinance of the Lords and Commons . . . for the speedy raising of fourteene thousand pounds. By L. N. for Edward Husbands, October 12, 1643. 4°.* LT, BR; CH, MH, NU, WF, Y.

2057 —An ordinance of the Lords and Commons . . . for the speedy raising of monies. [London], for Edward Husbands, March 28, 1644. 4°.* LT, O, CT, HH; MA, MH, NU, WF, Y.

2058 ——[Anr. ed.] For Edward Husbands, June 4, 1644. 4°.* L, O; CH.

2059 —An ordinance of the Lords and Commons . . . for the speedy raising of money in the Easterne Association. Imprinted at London for John Wright, 13. August, 1645. 4°.* LT, O, HH; MA, WF, Y.

2060 ——[Anr. ed.] By T.W. for Edw. Husband, 13. August, 1645. 4°.* CH.

2061 —An ordinance of the Lords and Commons . . . for the speedy raising of one thousand dragoons. [London], for Edward Husbands, August 15, [1643]. 4°.* LT; MA, MH, WF.

2062 —An ordinance of the Lords and Commons . . . for the speedy sending out the auxiliaries. By R.Cotes, 1644. brs. STEELE 2575. L; MH.

2063 —An ordinance of the Lords and Commons . . . for the speedy setting forth. For Iohn Wright, Decemb. 12, 1642. 4°.* LT, O, OC, MR, DT; CLC, MA, MH, WF, Y.

2064 —An ordinance of the Lords and Commons . . . for the speedy supply of monies . . . 18 August, 1643. Printed at London by Richard Cotes, 1643. 4°.* LT, O, LG, HH; MA, MH, NU, WF, Y.

2065 —An ordinance of the Lords and Commons . . . for the true payment of tythes. For Iohn Wright, Novemb. 9, 1644. 4°.* LT, O, C, HH, EN; CH, MH, NU, TU, WF, Y.

2065A ——[Anr. ed.] For John Wright, 8 Novemb. 1644. 4°.* O, OC, CT; CLC.

2066 ——[Anr. ed.] —, 1648. 4°.* LT, C, CM; CLC, MH, WF, Y.

2067 —An ordinance of the Lords and Commons . . . for the upholding the government. [London, 1643.] brs. STEELE 2499. LT, LPR, LUG; MH.

2068 ——[Anr. ed.] March 11, 1643. London, for Edward Husbands, 1643[4]. 4°.* LT, O, HH, MR; CH, LC, MH, NC, WF, Y.

2069 —An ordinance of the Lords and Commons . . . for the utter demolishing, . . . monvments. [London], for Edward Husbands, August 29, [1643]. 4°.* L, O, CT, HH, AN; CH, CN, MHL, WF, Y.

2069A ——[Anr. ed.] —, October 11, 1643. 4°.* CLC, MH, V.

2070 —An ordinance of the Lords and Commons . . . for the utter suppression and abolishing of all stage-playes . . . 11 Februarii, 1647[8]. Imprinted at London for John Wright, 1647[8]. 4°.* LT, O, LG, HH; CH, MH, WCL, WF, Y.

2071 —An ordinance of the Lords and Commons . . . for the visitation and reformation of the Universitie of Oxford. For John Wright, 1647. 4°. MADAN 1920. LT, O, LG, MR; CH, CN, MH, WF, Y.

2072 —An ordinance of the Lords and Commons . . . for Thursday next to be a day of thanksgiving. For Ed. Husband, Iune the 17, 1645. 4°.* LT, O, LG, HH; CH, MH, WF.

2073 —An ordinance of the Lords and Commons . . . for twenty thousand pounds. For Edward Husband, March 10, 1645[6]. brs. STEELE 2645. LT, HH, EN; MH.

2074 —An ordinance of the Lords & Commons . . . for uniting certain churches. For Edward Husband, April 10, 1647[8]. 4°.* LT, AN; WF.

2075 —An ordinance of the Lords and Commons . . . for upholding the government . . . 7 March 1643-4. [London, 1644, reprinted, 1660.] brs. STEELE 2540. LPR.

2076 —An ordinance of the Lords and Commons . . . giving power to the committee of the militia. Imprinted at London for John Wright 16 Jan. 1645[6]. 4°.* LT, O, LG, HH; MA, MHL, WF.

2077 —An ordinance of the Lords and Commons . . . giving security. For Edward Husband, Octob. 12, 1647. 4°.* LT, O, HH, OC, EC; CLC, MH, V, WF.

2078 —An ordinance of the Lords and Commons . . . giving Sir Tho. Fairfax power. For Edward Husband, Iune the 12, 1645. brs. STEELE 2620. LT, HH; Y.

2079 —An ordinance of the Lords and Commons . . . inhibiting the importation of currans. For Laurence Blaiklock, 1642. brs. STEELE 2254. LT, LPR, LS, EC; MH.

2080 —An ordinance of the Lords and Commons . . . prohibiting the importation of whale-oyle. For John Wright, 7. May, 1645. brs. STEELE 2613. LT; CH.

2081 —An ordinance of the Lords and Commons . . . shewing that all brewers. For John Wright, October 18, 1643. 4°.* LT, LG; CH, CN, NC, Y.

2082   —An ordinance of the Lords and Commons . . . shewing that all His Majesties, the Queenes, and Princes honours. *For Iohn Wright,* 1643. 4°.* LT, O, HH, DT; CH, MH, NU, WF, Y.

2083   —An ordinance of the Lords and Commons . . . that all delinquents. *Printed at London, for John Wright,* 1647. brs. STEELE 2730. LT, HH; CH, MH.

2084   —An ordinance of the Lords and Commons . . . that all the temporall livings. [*London*], *Iune 13. for Iohn Wright,* 1643. 4°.* LT, O, CT; CH, CN, MH, NU, WF.

2085   —An ordinance of the Lords and Commons . . . that from henceforth. *Printed at London, for John Wright,* 1647. brs. STEELE 2728. LT, LG, LUG, HH; MH, Y.

2086   —An ordinance of the Lords and Commons . . . that no wharfinger, woodmonger. *Feb. 23.* [*London*], *for John Wright,* 1642[3]. 4°.* LT, O, CT, LUG, HH; CSS, MA, MH, WF.

2087   —An ordinance of the Lodrs [*sic*] and Commons . . . that the committee for the militia. *For John Wright, Inne* [*sic*] 17, 1644. 4°.* LT, O, OC, HH; CH, MH, NU, WF, Y.

2088   —An ordinance of the Lords and Commons . . . that the committee for the militia of London shall have power. *Printed at London for Edward Husbands, Febr. 28,* 1644[5]. 4°.* LT, LG, HH; CH, MH, TU, WF, Y.

2089   Entry cancelled.

2090   —An ordinance of the Lords and Commons . . . to appoint and enable committees. *For Edward Husbands. Iune 27,* 1644. 4°.* LT, O, OC; CH, CN, MH, WF, Y.

2091   —An ordinance of the Lords and Commons . . . to command all Papists. *Printed at London by Ric. Cotes,* 1646. 4°.* LT, O; CH, CN, MH, WF, Y.

2092   ——[Anr. ed.] —, 1646. 4°.* LT, HH.

2093   —An ordinance of the Lords and Commons . . . to inable the associated counties. *For R. B.,* 1644. 4°.* LT, O.

2094   —An ordinance of the Lords and Commons . . . to inable the committee of the militia. *For John Wright,* 1647. 4°.* LT, O, LG, OC; CH, CN, MH, WF, Y.

2095   —An ordinance of the Lords and Commons . . . to inable the right honourable, Edward, Earle of Manchester . . . *March 6.* 1643. *For Edward Husbands,* 1643[4]. 4°.* LT, O, CT; CH, NC.

2096   ——[Anr. ed.] *By L. N. for Edward Husbands,* 1643. 4°.* LT, EC; CN, MA, MH, WF.

097   —An ordinance of the Lords and Commons . . . to prevent the coming over. *For Edward Husbands, Septemb.* 12, 1643. 4°.* LT, O, HH; CSU, MA, MH.

097A   —An ordinance of the Lords and Commons . . . together with rules and directions . . . Lords Supper. 20 *October for John Wright,* 1645. 4°.* C, OC.

2098   ——[Anr. ed.] *Imprinted at London for John Wright,* 21 *Octob.,* 1645. 4°.* L, O, C, MR, EN; CH, MH, NC, TU, WF, Y.

2099   ——[Anr. ed.] *For John Wright,* 1645. 4°.* LT, C, CT, HH, MR; CH, MA, MH, NU, V.

2100   —-An ordinance of the Lords and Commons . . . touching the excise. *By Rich. Cotes and Joh. Raworth,* 1643[4]. 4°.* LT, O, CCA, HH, EN; CLC, LC, MH, NC, Y.

2100A ——[Anr. ed.] —, 1644. 4°.* MH, MHL.

2101   —An ordinance of the Lords and Commons . . . whereby all vintners. *By Richard Cotes and John Raworth,* 1643. *Novemb.* 8. 4°.* LT, LG, HH; LC, MH, NC, Y,

2102   ——[Anr. ed.] —, 1643. brs. STEELE 2506. LT, CT; CLC.

2103   —An ordinance of the Lords and Commons . . . whereby commissioners are appointed. *June 2.* [*London*], *for Iohn Wright,* 1643. 4°.* LT, O, LUG, HH; CH, NC, NU, WF, Y.

2104   —An ordinance of the Lords and Commons . . . whereby Robert Earle of Warwicke. *For Iohn Wright, Novemb.* 3, 1643. 4°.* LT, O; CH, CN, RPJ, WF.

2105   —An ordinance of the Lords and Commons . . . whereby Sir George Vane. *For Iohn Wright,* 1645[6]. 4°.* LT, O; MH, Y.

2106   —An ordinance of the Lords and Commons . . . whereby the commissioners named. *For Iohn Wright, May 23,* 1643. 4°.* LT, EC, BR; MA, MH, WF, Y.

2107   —An ordinance of the Lords and Commons . . . wherein the county of Lincolne is added. *For Iohn Wright, Septemb.* 22, 1643. 4°.* LT, O, EC, DT; CH, MA, WF.

2108   —An ordinance of the Lords and Commons . . . with an exhortation. *Yorke: by Th. Broad, Septem.* 26, 1644. 4°.* YM.

2109   —An ordinance of the Lords and Commons . . . with an oath or covenant. *For John Wright,* 1634 (i.e. 1643). 4°.* LT, O, C; CH, CN, LC, MH, NC, NU, Y.

2109A ——[Anr. ed.] —, 1643. 4°.* LSE; TU, WF, Y.

2110   —An ordinance of the Lords and Commons . . . with instrvctions. [*London*], *for E. Husbands,* [1644?]. 4°. STEELE 2528. LT, O, C, LS, MR; CH, CN, LC, NU, Y.

2111   —An ordinance of the Lords and Commons . . . with instrvctions for the taking of the Leagve and Covenant. [*London*], *for E. Husbands,* 1643. 4°.* LT, OC, EC, GK; MH, NC, NU, WF, Y.

2112   —An ordinance of the Lords and Commons . . . with the names of the knights. *For Iohn Wright, May 4,* 1643. 4°.* LT, O, C, AN, DT; CH, MH, NC, WF, Y.

2113   —An ordinance or declaration of the Lords and Commons . . . concerning a commission. *May 26.* [*London*], *for Iohn Wright,* 1643. 4°.* LT, O, HH; MH, Y.

2114   —An ordinance or declaration of the Lords and Commons, . . . for the encouragement of adventurers. *For John Wright, July.* 15, 1643. 4°.* LT, O, C, LVF, OC; CH, CN, MH, NU, Y.

2115   —An ordinance or declaration of the Lords and Commons . . . shewing that all the regiments of foot, . . . 23 Septemb. 1642. *For Iohn Wright,* 24 *Septemb.,* 1642. 4°.* LT, O, C, LG, HH; CH, CN, LC, MH, NU, Y.

2115A —An ordinance to prohibit the transporting of wooll. [*London,* 1648.] cap., 8°.* OP.

2116   —An ordinance with several propositions of the Lords and Commons . . . 5 Jun. 1643. *For I. Wright, June 8,* 1643. 4°.* LT, O, HH, DT; CH, CN, MH, WF, Y.

2117   —An ordination and declaration of both Houses . . . sent to the Lord Maior. *For Iohn Hawes,* 1642. 4°.* LT, O, OC, EC, EN; NU, WF.

2118   —A paper received by His Maiesty from the Com-
        mittee of both Houses. *Printed at Oxford, by Leonard
        Lichfield*, 1643. 4°.* MADAN 1326. LT, O, C; CH, CLC,
        MH, WF, Y.

2119   —The Parliament being desirous . . . 27 February
        1659[60]. *By John Streater and John Macock*, 1659[60].
        brs. STEELE 3160. LT, O, LG, LUG; MH.

2120   —The Parliament doth declare, that the recognition of
        the government. *By William du-Gard and Henry Hills*,
        1654. brs. STEELE 3044. LT, O, LPR, HH; MB, NU.

2121   —The Parliament doth resolve and declare. *By John
        Field*, 1659. brs. STEELE 3109. LT, O, LS, OQ; MH.

2122   —The Parliament for divers weighty . . . 25 February,
        1659[60]. *By John Streater and John Macock*, 1659[60].
        cap., brs. STEELE 3158. LT, O, LG; MH.

2123   —The Parliament having received intelli-. *For Edward
        Husband*, 5 June, 1649. cap. STEELE 2855. HH.

2124   —The Parliament having received intelligence. *By John
        Field*, 1651. STEELE 2949. OP, HH; MH, Y.

2125   —The Parliament of Englands message to the Queen of
        Sweden. *Imprinted at London for James Nichols*, 1652.
        4°.* LT.

2126   —The Parliament's agreement for a personall treaty
        with the king. *By B. Alsop*, 1647. 4°.* LT, O, HH; CH,
        WF.

2127   —The Parliament's answer to His Majesties two letters.
        For Edward Husband, Jan. 17, 1646. 4°.* LT, O, C, HH;
        CH, MH, NPT, WF, Y.

2128   —The Parliaments answer, to the armies proposals. *By
        John Redmayne*, 1659. 4°.* L, O, CS, OC; CH, MH, NU,
        WF, Y.

2129   —The Parliaments answer to the two petitions of the
        countie of Buckingham. [*London*], *for H.F.*, 1641[2].
        4°.* L, HH, DT; Y.

2130   ——[Anr. ed.] [*London*], *printed* 13 *of January*, 1642. 4°.*
        LT, C, SP; WF.

2131   —The Parliament's care for the citie of London. [*Lon-
        don*], *for Iohn Hamon*, 1642. 4°.* LT.

2132   —The Parliaments censvre on Sir Richard Gvrney. *For
        Iohn Cave*. August 13, 1642. 4°.* LT, LG, CCO, CJ, EC;
        MH, Y.

2133   —The Parliaments censure to the Jesuites. *For H. Blunon*,
        1642. 4°.* L, O, HH; WF, Y.

2134   —The Parliaments declaration concerning the Kings
        most excellent Majesty. [*London*], *August* 3, *for R.
        VVilliams*, 1642. 4°.* LT.

2135   —The Parliaments desire and resolution concerning the
        Prince. *Jun.* 3. *for J. Greensmith, and A. Coe*, 1642. 4°.*
        LT, O, YM, EN; MH, WF.

2135A   —The Parliaments desires to the Earl of Warwicke. *For
        Iohn Smith*, July 21 [1642]. 4°.* L, O; MH.

2136   —The Parliaments determination. *Iuly* 4. *London. by
        T.F. for N.O.*, 1641. 4°.* L, O; MH, WF, Y.

2137   —The Parliaments directions to the Protestants in Ire-
        land. *For I. H.*, 1641. brs. LT, EC; Y.

2137A   —The Parliaments instructions, agreed on. *For J. Han-
        sott [sic]*, August 16, 1642. 4°.* L, CJ; WF.

2138   —The Parliaments instructions to the Earl of Essex. *For
        H. Bland. September* 20, 1642. 4°.* LT; MH, MIU.

2139   —The Parliaments last order. *July 27. London, for I.
        Watson*, [1642]. 4°.* LT, O, YM.

2140   —The Parliaments letter to the King of France. *For
        Henry Deymour, October* 1, 1642. 4°.* LT; MH.

2141   —The Parliaments message to the King at Yorke. [*Lon-
        don*], *print d Danniel Hopson*, 1642. 4°.* LT, O, YM; Y.

2142   —The Parliaments protestation. *For Ioseph Horton*, 1642.
        4°.* LT, C, CCA, YM.

2143   —The Parliaments reply to the Kings Majesties answer
        . . . 29 Ianuary, 1641. *Printed*, 1641[2]. 4°.* O, HH; CH,
        CN, MH, WF, Y.

2144   —The Parliaments resolution concerning the kings de-
        termination. *By T. F. for T. Bankes*, 1642. 4°.* O.

2145   —The Parliaments resolution, concerning the Kings . . .
        Maiesty. *By T. F. for N. R. June* 23, 1642. 4°.* L, CCA,
        YM; CH, MH, MHL, WF.

2145A   ——[Anr. ed.] *By T. Favvcet*, 1642. *June,* 23. 4°.* L, OC,
        CJ, EC; WF, Y.

2146   —The Parliaments resolution, concerning the kings pro-
        clamation. [*London*], *August* 22. *for J. Horton*, [1642].
        4°.* LT; MH.

2147   —The Parliaments resolvtion concerning the sending of
        Sir Thomas Barrington. [*London*], *for Tho. Willet.
        Augvst* 27, 1642. 4°.* L; MH, Y.

2148   —The Parliaments resolvtion concerning the volvntiers.
        [*London*], *July*. 30, *for Thomas Baley*, 1642. 4°.* LT;
        CH, MH, MIU, Y.

2149   —The Parliaments resolution, for the speedy sending an
        army. *For G. Tomlinson*, 1642. 4°.* LT; MH, PT, WF.

2150   ——The Parliaments resolution to raise forces to suppresse.
        By Tho. Fawcet. Iuly 22, 1642. 4°.* LT, CJ; CLC, WF.

2151   —The Parliaments resolution to the citizens of London.
        For R. West, Dec. 17, 1642. 4°.* O, LG, EN; MH.

2152   —The Parliaments vindication of Iohn Pym. *For John
        Bull*, 1643. 4°.* LT, EC, BR; MIU, Y.

2153   —A particular of the several victories and the occasions
        of . . . thanksgiving appointed by both Houses. *For
        Edward Husband, August* 28, 1648. 4°.* LT, O, YM, AN,
        HH; CH, MIU, NU.

2154   —The petition and articles exhibited in Parliament
        against Dr. Fvller. *Printed*, 1641. 4°.* LT, C, LW, HH,
        SP; CH, NU, WF, Y.

2155   —The petition and articles exhibited in Parliament
        against Doctor Heywood. *Printed*, 1641. 4°.* LT, O,
        EN; CH, CLC, NU, WF, Y.

2156   —The petition and articles exhibited in Parliament
        against Iohn Pocklington. *Imprinted at London*, 1641.
        4°.* LT, O, CS, BP; WF, Y.

2157   —The petition and articles or severall charge [*sic*] exhi-
        bited in Parliament against Edward Finch. *Sould by R.
        Harford*, 1641. 4°.* LT, O, LG, HH; CN, NU, TU, WF, Y.

2158   —The petition and articles, or severall charge exhibited
        in Parliament against John Pocklington. *For L. C.*,
        1641. 4°.* O, CS, LW, BP, EN; CLC, MH, WF, Y.

2159 —The petition and reasons of both Houses. *For R. Har-ford,* 1642. 4°.* LT, O, C, HH; CH, CN, MH, WF, Y.

2159A —The petition and reasons of the Lords and Commons . . . to decline his intended journey into Ireland. *For I.T.,* 1642. 4°.* L, YM.

2160 —The petition of both Houses of Parliament, presented . . . March 26, 1642. *For A.C.,* 1642. 4°.* O, CCA, YM, EN, DT; CLC, MH, NU, TU.

2161 ——[Anr. ed.] *Printed at London, for Francis Cowles, and Thomas Banks,* 1642. 4°.* OC, HH; CSS.

2162 ——[Anr. ed.] *For John Wright,* 1642. 4°.* L, O, C, BR, HH; MH, OWC, WF.

2163 ——[Anr. ed.] *For R. West,* 1642. 4°.* MH, WF.

2163A ——[Anr. ed.] *For J. Thomas,* 1642. 4°.* CN, WF.

2164 ——[Anr. ed.] *By Robert Barker, and by the assignes of John Bill,* 1642. 4°.* LT, O, C, LL, HH; CH, CN, MH, WF, Y.

2165 ——23. of May 1642. *York: by Robert Barker: and by the assignes of John Bill,* 1642. 4°.* O, CF; MH, WF.

2166 ——[Anr. ed.] *Printed first at York, and now reprinted at London, by A.N. for Edward Husbands,* 1642. 4°.* O, LL, YM, EN; CLC.

2167 ——[Anr. ed.] *Imprinted at York, and reprinted at London, for Richard Lownes,* 1642. 4°.* L, O, OC, SP; CH, MH, MIU, WF, Y.

2168 —The petition of both Houses of Parliament to His Majestie concerning his intended going to Ireland. *For Joseph Hunscott,* 1642. 4°.* O, CM, HH, DT; CH, MH, WF, Y.

2169 —The petition of right: exhibited. *Printed at London for George Lindesay, to bee sold by Iohn Gyles,* 1642. Iune 8. 4°.* L; CSS.

2170 —The petition of rights. *For M. Walbancke and L. Chapman,* 1642. 4°.* L; CN, CSS.

2171 —The petition of the Lords and Commons . . . 16 day of Jvly. *By A. Norton, for Mathew Walbancke and Richard Lownds,* 1642. 4°.* OC, CCA, SP, HH; CN, MH, OWC, Y.

2172 ——[Anr. ed.] *By Edward Griffin,* 1642. 4°.* CCO, SP, HH; CH, CSS, MH, MHL, WF.

2173 ——[Anr. ed.] *By F. Leach, for M. Walbancke and R. Lownds,* 1642. 4°.* HH; MB.

2174 ——[Anr. ed.] *By Robert Barker: and by the assigns of John Bill.* 1642. 4°.* LT, O, CT, HH, EN; CH, CN, MH, NU, TU, Y.

2174A ——[Anr. ed.] *York, —,* 1642. 4°.* L, CF, YM; MH, WF.

2175 ——[Anr. ed.] *Edinburgh, by Evan Tyler,* 1642. 4°.* ALDIS 1048. E, EN.

2176 —The petition of the Lords and Commons assembled . . . presented to His Majestie at Beverley. *Reprinted at Oxford by Leonard Lichfield,* 1642. 4°.* MADAN 1014. HH, AN; Y.

2176A ——[Anr. ed.] *Cambridge, by R. Daniel,* 1642. 4°.* CJ, CM, CS, CT; MH.

2177 —The petition of the Lords and Commons of Parliament assembled at Oxford, presented. *Printed at Oxford, by Leonard Lichfield,* 1644. 4°.* MADAN 1610. L, O, CJ, EC, HH; CLC, CN, MH, WF, Y.

2178 —The petition of the Lords and Commons. *Bristoll, by R. Barker and J. Bill,* 1644. 4°.* HH.

2179 —The petition of the Lords and Commons presented to His Majestie, . . . April 18, 1642. *By Robert Barker: and by the assignes of John Bill,* 1642. 4°.* LT, O, C, E, DT; CH, CN, MH, NU, TU, WF, Y.

2179A ——[Anr. ed.] *For Robert Williamson,* 1642. 4°.* SP; MH.

2179B ——[Anr. ed.] *For I.T.,* 1642. 4°.* L; MH.

2179C ——[Anr. ed.] *Printed at Edinburgh,* 1642. 4°.* ALDIS 1047. EN; Y.

2180 —The petition of the Lords and Commons . . . presented to the Kings. *For Iohn Thomas,* 1641. 4°.* LT, O, CT; WF, Y.

2181 —A petition presented to the Kings Majesty at York, the first of April. *For J. Hunscott,* 13 *April,* 1642. brs. STEELE 2067. L, O.

2182 —A petition sent to His Majestie from . . . Parliament. *For Tho: Banks, Novemb.* 8, 1642. 4°.* LT, O, EC, HH; MH, WF, Y.

2183 —The petitions and reasons of both Houses. *For R. Herford,* 1642. CH.

2184 —The proceedings of the Parliament upon the petition and appeal of John Primat. 1651. fol. MIU.

2185 —The proceedings, votes, resolves, and acts of . . . the Rump. *For John Thomason,* 1660. fol.* LT, O; CH, CN, MH, MIU, WF.

2186 —Die Sabbathi 23 Ianuarii 1646. A proclamation. *For John Wright,* 1646. brs. STEELE 2677. HH; RPJ.

2187 ——[8 May]. *By Edward Husbands and Thomas Newcomb,* [1660]. brs. STEELE 3190. LT, O, C, EN, DT; WF.

2188 ——[13 February 1689]. *Edinburgh, reprinted,* 1689. brs. STEELE 3p 2772. HH, EN.

2189 Entry cancelled.

2190 —A proclamation although it can no way be doubted. *By Edward Husbands and Thomas Newcomb,* [May, 1660]. brs. LT, O, C; CH, MB, MH, WF.

2191 —A proclamation by His Highness and the Parliament. Whereas the knights. *By Henry Hills and Iohn Field,* 1657. brs. LT; CH, MIU, WF, Y.

2192 —A proclamation commanding all Jesuits. *By Iohn Field,* 1652[3]. brs. STEELE 2984. LT, LG, LS, HH; NU, Y.

2193 Entry cancelled.

2194 —A proclamation for the discovery and apprehending of Charls Stuart. *By John Field,* 1651. brs. STEELE 2952. LT, LG, LS, LUG; CH, NU.

2195 —A proclamation for tryall of the king. *By Robert Ibbitson,* 1648[9]. 4°.* LT, O, MR, HH, SP; CH, WF, Y.

2196 —A proclamation of both Houses . . . for proclaiming of His Majesty king. *By John Macock, and Francis Tyton,* 1660. brs. STEELE 3188. LT, O, CT, HH, DT; MH.

2197 ——[Anr. ed.] *Edinburgh, by Christopher Higgins,* 1660. brs. ALDIS 1657. STEELE 3p 2171. EN, FSF; Y.

2198 —A proclamation of the Parliament of the Commonwealth, . . . declaring Charls Stuart. *By John Field,* 1651. brs. STEELE 2947. LT, O, LG, LS, MC; CH, MH, NU, WF.

2199 —A proclamation touching the kings audit. [*London,* 1643.] brs. STEELE 2521. LPC.

2200 —Propositions agreed upon by both Houses. *For V. V.,* 1647. 4°.* LT, HH; MH, WF, Y.

2201 —Propositions and orders, by the Lords and Commons . . . for bringing in of money . . . 10 June 1642. *By R. B. for Edward Husbands and I. F.,* 1642. 4°.* L, O, C, BR, EN; CN, CSS, MH, NC, Y.

2202 ——[Anr. ed.] *For Edward Husbands and I. F.,* 1642. 4°.* L, BP, SP; Y.

2202A ——[Anr. ed.] *For John Thomas,* 1642. 4°.* L; MIU, CF.

2203 —Propositions from the Parliament. *For C. L. and L. F.,* 1647. 4°.* LT, O, HH; Y.

2204 —Propositions made by both Houses . . . 2 Junii, 1642. *By E. G. for Christopher Latham,* 1642. 4°.* O, LL, EC, DT; CH, MH, NU, WF, Y.

2205 —Propositions made by both Houses of Parliament, to the Kings Maiesty, for a reconciliation. *By Edward Griffin for Christopher Latham,* 1642. 4°.* LT, OC; MIU, WF, Y.

2206 ——[Anr. ed.] *For Anthony Vincent,* 1642. 4°.* LSE, SP.

2207 —Propositions of peace propounded . . . November 5. *By T. Favvcet for J. R.,* 1642. 4°.* L, CJ, HH, EN; CH, CN, MH, WF, Y.

2208 ——[Anr. ed.] *Novemb. 7. for Thomas Holt,* 1642. 4°.* LT, BR; MH.

2209 —The propositions of the Lords and Commons . . . for a safe and well-grounded peace . . . 15 Julii 1646. *For Iohn Wright,* 17 Iuly, 1646. 4°.* LT, O, CT, HH, EN; CH, CN, LC, MH, NU, Y.

2210 ——29 August, 1648. *Imprinted at London, for John Wright,* 1648. 4°.* LT, HH; CH, CN, MH, NPT, Y.

2211 —The protestation made by the Parliament the third day of May, . . . 1641. *[London], printed anno,* 1641. 4°.* L, CCA, LL, YM; CH, MH, TU, WF, Y.

2212 —Questions resolved upon by both Houses. *For J. Wright,* [1642]. brs. STEELE p 2008. L, O, HH.

2213 ——[Anr. ed.] *For Joseph Hunscott,* 1641[2]. brs. L, CJ, OC, EC, BR; MH, Y.

2213A —The rates of the excise and new-impost set. *R. Cotes and T. Newcomb,* 1649. 4°.* MH.

2214 —The reasons of the Lords and Commons in Parliament, why they cannot agree. *Printed at Oxford by Leonard Lichfield,* 1643. 25 pp. 4°.* MADAN 1309. LT, O, CT, HH; CN, MH, NU, WF, Y.

2215 ——[Anr. ed.] —, 1643. 8 pp. 4°.* MADAN 1310. LT, O, CJ, CT; CLC, MH, Y.

2216 —Regni argumenta consilij. *For John Place,* 1659. NU, Y.

2217 —A remonstrance and declaration of the Lords and Commons. *[London], for G. Tomlingson,* 1642. 4°.* L, O, EC, HH; WF, Y.

2218 Entry cancelled.

2219 —A remonstrance of the Lords and Commons . . . or, the reply . . . November 2. 1642. *For R. B. and R. L.,* 1642. 4°.* O, HH, YM; CN, CSS, Y.

2220 ——[Anr. ed.] *For I. Wright, Novemb.* 3, 1642. 4°. LT, O, CT, BR, HH; CH, LC, MHL, WF, Y.

2221 ——[Anr. ed.] —, *Novemb.* 3, 1642. 4°. CCA, LL, EC, DT; CH, CN, MH, NU, Y.

2221A —A remonstrance of the state of the Kingdom . . . 15 December 1641. *For Ioseph Hunscott,* 1641. 4°.* LT, O, CCA, HH, DT; CH, CN, NU, RPJ, WF, Y.

2221B ——[Anr. ed.] *Printed,* 1641. 4°.* O, C; CH, LC, PL, TU, Y.

2221C ——[Anr. ed.] *For Ioseph Hunscott,* 1641. 4°. LT, O, C; CH, CLC, MH, WF, Y.

2221D ——[Anr. ed.] *Imprinted first at London, and reprinted at Edinburgh, by Robert Young and Evan Tyler,* 1641. 4°.* ALDIS 1017. E, D, EN; NU, Y.

2221E ——[Anr. ed.] *For Henry Fowler, Septem.* 13, 1642. 4°.* L, BR, HH; CH, CLC, MH, Y.

2222 —A remonstrance of the state of the kingdom, agreed on by the Lords and Commons . . . 19 May, 1642. *For Iohn Bartlet,* 1642. 4°.* L, C, OC, CS; CH, CN, MH, WF, Y.

2223 ——[Anr. ed.] *For F. C.,* 1642. 4°.* O, C, CJ, HH, DT; CH, MH, NU, PL, WF.

2223A ——[Anr. ed.] *For T. Paybody,* 1642. 4°. CT; WF.

2223B ——[Anr. ed.] *For Thomas Bates,* 1642. 4°. CCA.

2224 —A remonstrance or declaration of the Lords and Commons . . . shewing the imminent danger. *For F. I. May the first,* 1643. 4°.* O, CT; CH, CLC, MH, Y.

2225 —A remonstrance or the declaration of the Lords and Commons . . . 26. of May, 1642. In answer. *By T. P. and M. S. for John Owen,* 1642. June 18. 4°.* L; CH, CSS, MH.

2226 ——[Anr. ed.] *For Iohn Franke,* 1642. 4°.* LT, O, CT, E, DT; CH, CN, MH, NU, WF, Y.

2226A ——[Anr. ed.] *For E. Paxton and T. P.,* 1642. 4°.* O, CS; MH.

2227 ——[Anr. ed.] *By A. N. for Iohn Franke,* 1742 [i.e. 1642]. 4°.* L, C, LW, OC; CLC, MH, Y.

2227A ——[Anr. ed.] of [*sic*] the declaration. *For Richard Lownds,* 1642. 4°.* L, O, CJ, CT, EN; CH, CLC, MH, WF, Y.

2228 —A remonstrance presented to His Maiestie by the Parliament in June, ann. Dom. 1628. colop: *By T. P. and M. S. for John Owen, Septemb.* 2. 1642. cap., 4°.* LT, C, EC; MH, WF.

2229 ——[Anr. ed.] *[London, 1643.]* cap., 4°.* LT, O, C, CT; MH, Y.

2230 —A replication of the Lords and Commons . . . 28 July, 1642. *Iuly 29. London, for Iohn Wright,* 1642. 4°.* LT, O, CT, HH, DT; CN, CU, MH, WF, Y.

2230A ——[Anr. ed.] *For Nathaniel Allen,* 1642. 4°.* L, O, OC.

2231 —The report of the commissioners appointed by Parliament to enquire into the Irish forfeitures. *For Edw. Jones, and Tim. Goodwin,* 1700. fol.* L, O, C, EN, DT; CH, MH, RPJ, WF, Y.

2231A ——[Anr. ed.] *Printed,* 1700. 4°.* OC.

2232 ——[Anr. ed.] *By Edw. Jones; and re-printed in Dublin, by John Brocas,* 1700. fol.* L, DT; CH, TU, WF, Y.

2232A —Reports past the committee. *By Richard Cotes,* 1649. 4°.* LT, OC, LG, LUG, HH.

2233 —The resolution and votes of the Parliament of England concerning Major Generall Brown. *Aprill* 10. *London, for R. W.,* 2649 [i.e. 1649]. 4°.* LT, HH; MH.

2234 —The resolvtion of of [sic] both Hovses of Parliament, concerning a pacification. *For John Hanson, Novemb.* 9. 1642. 4°.* LT, EN; WF, Y.

2235 —The resolution of both Houses of Parliament: concerning the Kings Majesties last letter. *For R. B.,* 1647. 4°.* LT, O, HH; CH, CLC.

2236 —Resolution of both Houses of Parliament touching the government & liturgy of the church. *For R. H.,* [1642]. brs. LS.

2237 —The resolvtion of the Lords and Commons . . . to the kings most excellent Maiestie. *[London], for Iohn Smith,* 1642. 4°.* LT, O, YM; CLC.

2237A —Resolutions of Parliament, touching delinquents. colop: *By John Field for Edward Husband,* 1649. cap., 4°.* L, BR; Y.

2237B —Friday, March the 16th 1659. Resolved, &c. That Friday, the sixth day of April. *By John Streater and John Macock,* 1660. brs. LUG; MH.

2238 —Tuesday the 27th. of December 1659. Resolved, &c. That on the fifth day of January next. *By John Streater,* 1659. brs. LT; MH.

2239 —Die Martis, 6° Augusti, 1650. Resolved, &c. That the Parliament. *By Edward Husband and John Field,* 1650. brs. L, LG, LUG, HH.

2240 —Thursday, April 26. 1660. Resolved by the Lords and Commons. *By John Macock, and Francis Tyton,* 1660. brs. LT.

2241 —Die Martis 29, Februarii, 1647[8]. Resolved by the Lords and Commons . . . that no person or persons. *Imprinted at London for John Wright,* 1647[8]. brs. LT; CH, MH.

2242 —Die Lunae, 16 Septemb. 1644. Resolved by the Lords and Commons . . . that one of the articles. *For I. Wright, Septemb.* 16, 1644. brs. STEELE 2583. LT; MH.

2243 —Die Veneris, 20. Feb. 1645[6]. Resolved by the Lords and Commons . . . that there bee. *[London], by Richard Cotes,* 1645. brs. LT, C, OP, HH, SP; MIU.

2243A ——[Anr. ed.] *For John Wright,* 1645. brs. OC.

2244 —Diae Veneris 12 May, 1648. Resolved by the Lords and Commons, that Wednesday next. *For Iohn Wright,* 1648. brs. STEELE 2760. LT, AN.

2245 —Die Mercurii, 7 Maii 1650. Resolved by the Parliament. *By Edward Husband and Iohn Field,* 1650. brs. LT, C, LUG, E; MH, Y.

2246 —Die Veneris, 6 Decembr. 1650. Resolved by the Parliament. *By Edward Husband and Iohn Field,* 1650. brs. LT, LUG; Y.

2247 —Thursday the 17th of July, 1651. Resolved by the Parliament. *By John Field,* [1651]. brs. LT, OP, LUG; CLC.

2248 —Monday the first of September, 1651. Resolved by the Parliament. *By John Field,* 1651. brs. LT, OP, LUG; CLC, MH, NU, Y.

2249 —Wednesday the eighteenth of August, 1652. Resolved by the Parliament, that the Parliament doth declare. *By John Field,* 1652. brs. LUG, OP; CH, MB.

2250 —Friday the four and twentieth day of December, 1652. Resolved by the Parliament. *By John Field,* 1652. brs. LT; MH.

2251 —Tuesday the fifth of September, 1654. Resolved by the Parliament. *By John Field,* 1655. brs. STEELE 3043. LT, O.

2252 —Munday, January 2. 1659. Resolved by the Parliament. *By John Streater, and John Macock,* 1659[60]. brs. LT, O, LG; MH.

2253 —Friday 22 of July, 1659. Resolved by the Parliament. *By John Field,* 1659. brs. STEELE 3120. LT, O, LG, LUG; MH.

2254 —Resolved by the Parliament, that . . . 12 December 1651. *[London,* 1651.] brs. STEELE 2957. L.

2255 —Resolved by the Parliament, that all primers. *By John Field,* 1651. brs. STEELE 2937. L, LUG, HH; MB, MH, NU.

2256 —Die Veneris, 15 Novemb. 1650. Resolved by the Parliament, that all sums. *By Edward Husband and Iohn Field,* 1650. brs. STEELE 2915. L, LUG; MIU.

2257 —Resolved by the Parliament that such delinquents. *By John Field,* 1651. brs. STEELE 2962. OQ, HH; Y.

2258 —Die Martis, 9° Aprilis, 1650. Resolved by the Parliament, that the arms of the late king be taken down. *By Edward Husband and John Field,* 1650. brs. STEELE 2893. LT, O, C, OQ, HH; Y.

2259 —Resolved by the Parliament, that the markets. *By John Field,* 1652. brs. STEELE 2981. LT, LUG, HH; NU, Y.

2260 —Friday, the 27th of June, 1651. Resolved, that the Parliament doth declare. *By John Field,* 1651. brs. LT, LUG; MH, Y.

2261 —Monday June 27th 1659. Resolved, that this Parliament. *By John Field and Henry Hills,* 1659. brs. LT, LUG; MH.

2262 —Thursday, January 5. 1659[60]. Resolved, that upon the whole matter. *By John Streater, and John Macock,* 1659[60]. brs. LT, O; MH.

2263 —Tuesday the 27th of May, 1651. Resolved upon the question. *By John Field,* 1651. brs. LT, O, LUG; Y.

2264 —Die Mercurii, 9. May 1660. Resolved upon the question. *By John Macock, and Francis Tyton,* 1660. brs. STEELE 3196. LT, OP; CH, WF.

2264A ——[Anr. ed.] *By Edward Husbands and Thomas Newcomb,* 1660. brs. LG; MH.

2265 —Die Dominico 8 Aug. 1641. Resolved upon the question by both Houses. *Imprinted at London by Robert Barker, and by the assignes of John Bill,* 1641. brs. STEELE 1880. LT, O, CJ, LPR; Y.

2265A —Die Sabbathi, viz. 18 Juni, 1642. Resolved upon the question, by the Lords and Commons. *[London,* 1642]. brs. MH, Y.

2266 —Die Lunae 5 Iunii, 1648. Resolved upon the question, by the Lords and Commons . . . that the fifth and twentieth part. *Imprinted at London for John Wright,* 1648. brs. STEELE 2768. LT; MH.

2267 —Die Lunae 28. Junii 1647. Resolved upon the question by the Lords and Commons . . . that they do declare. *For John Wright,* 1647. brs. CH, MH, Y.

2268 —Thursday, February 23. 1659. Resolved upon the question by the Parliament, that all the militias. *By John Streater, and John Macock,* 1659[60]. brs. LT, LUG.

2269 —Die Jovis. 8 Novembr. 1649. Resolved upon the question by the Parliament, that such person. *By John Field for Edward Husband,* [1649]. brs. STEELE 2883. L, O, HH; CH.

2270 —Die Martis 26. April. 1642. Resolved upon the question, that Sir Iohn Hotham. *Imprinted at London by Robert Barker: and by the assignes of Iohn Bill,* 1642. brs. STEELE 2090. LT, CT, E C.

2271 Entry cancelled.

2272 —Die Martis, 23 Julii, 1650. Resolves of Parliament. *By Edward Husband and Iohn Field,* 1650. brs. LT.

2273 Entry cancelled.

2274 —Resolves of Parliament, concerning rates. *By Edward Husband and Iohn Field,* 1650. brs. STEELE 2914. LT, O, LUG, OQ, LU, HH; MH, NU, Y.

2275 —Resolves of Parliament, concerning such delinquents. *By Edward Husband and Iohn Field,* 1650. brs. STEELE 2905. LT, O, C, OQ, HH; MH, NU.

2276 ——[Anr. ed.] *Iohn Field,* 1650. brs. STEELE 2907. L.

2277 —Resolves of Parliament, for the suspending. *By Edward Husband and Iohn Field,* 1650. brs. STEELE 2904. LT, O, C, OQ, HH; CH, NU, WF, Y.

2278 —Resolves of Parliament, touching the Lord Generals taking. *By Edward Husband & John Field,* 1649[50]. brs. STEELE 2889. LT, O, C, OQ, HH; MH, NU, Y.

2279 —Resolves of Parliament touching the subscribing. *By John Field for Edward Husband,* 1649. fol.* STEELE 2877. LT, CT, LPR, HH; MH, NU, TU, Y.

2280 —Returne from the Parliament of England, to the commissioners. *Edinburgh, by Evan Tyler,* 1642. 4°.* ALDIS 1055. L, O, CT, EC, EN; CH, NU, WF, Y.

2281 Entry cancelled.

2282 —The rules and directions of the Lords and Commons. *Printed at London for John Wright,* 1647. 8°.* LT, C; CH, PL.

2283 —Rules and instrvctions to the muster-masters. *For Edward Husband,* 1645. brs. STEELE 2616. LT; CH, CLC.

2284 —A sacred vow and covenant taken by the Lords and Commons. *For Edward Husbands, June 12,* 1643. LT, O, CJ, EN, DT; CH, CN, MH, NU, TU, WF, Y.

2285 —Scriptum Parlamenti reipublicae Angliae de iis quae ad hac repubicum . . . Belgii. *Typis Du-Gardianis,* 1652. 4°. LT; HR, CH, WF, Y.

2286 —A second declaration of the Lords and Commons . . . of the whole proceedings. *For Edward Husband, Sept.* 18, 1645. 4°.* LT, O, MR, HH, A; CH, CN, MH, NC, WF, Y.

2287 —A second remonstrance or, declaration of the Lords and Commons . . . concerning the commission of array. *For Iohn Wright, and Richard Best, Ianuary 18,* 1642[3]. 4°.* LT, O, CT, HH, DT; CH, CN, LC, MH, Y.

2288 —Dia Savado 24. de Febrero 1643/4. Los Senores y Communos del Parlamento. [*London,* 1644.] brs. STEELE p2532. LT.

2288A —Several acts and ordinances. *For Edward Husband,* 1649. 4°. L; WF.

2289 —The severall answers of both Houses of Parliament to the city petition. *For Iohn Wright,* 1641[2]. 4°. SP; CH, Y.

2289A —Several draughts of acts. *J. Field,* 1653. fol. L, EN.

2290 —Severall orders and votes of both Houses. *Printed at London by Robert Ibbitson,* 1647. 4°.* LT, O, SP; CH, CN, MH, WF, Y.

2291 —The severall ordinances and declarations of the Lords and Commons assembled in Parliament. *For John Bellamy,* 1646. 4°. L, CT, BP, BR; CH, MH, TU, WF, Y.

2292 ——[Anr. ed.] *By R. Cotes, for John Bellamy,* 1648. 4°. L, LUG, CSE; CH, NU.

2292A —Severall ordinances of the Lords and Commons . . . concerning the sale of bishops-lands. *By R. Cotes for John Bellamy,* 1647. 4°.* L; MH.

2293 —Several ordinances of the Lords and Commons . . . for the abolishing of archbishops. *By Richard Cotes,* 1649. 4°. LSC; MH, NU, WF.

2294 —Severall ordinances of the Lords and Commons . . . for the disbanding . . . 24 Decemb. 1647. *Imprinted at London for John Wright,* 1647. 4°.* LT, O, C, MR, HH; CH, MH, NU, WF, Y.

2295 —Die Veneris, Februarii, 1649: several passages in a book printed, entituled, a fiery flying roll. *By Edward Husband and John Field,* 1649[50]. brs. STEELE 2887. LT, O, C, OQ, HH; MH, WF, Y.

2296 —The severall petitions and messages of Parliment. *By Robert Barker and by the assignes of John Bill,* 1641[2]. 4°.* L, CS, CT, SC; CH, CN, MH, WF, Y.

2297 —Several proceedings of Parliament. colop: *By John Field,* 1653. 4°. CH.

2298 —Several votes and orders of the House of Parliament, die Martis 23. October, 1649. *By Richard Cotes.* 1649. brs. STEELE 2880. LT, LPR; MH.

2299 —The severall votes and resolution of both Houses . . . 16. of March 1641[2]. *For F. C. and T. B.,* brs. STEELE 2047. L.

2300 ——[Anr. ed.] *For John Franck,* 1641[/2]. brs. STEELE 2048. L, O, LS, CJ.

2301 —The severall votes and resolutions of both Houses of Parliament, concerning the kings last message. *Printed at London for Rich. Harper and I.G.,* 1641[2]. 4°.* LT, O, CF; CH, MH, WF.

2302 —Die Martis 17. Maii. 1642. Severall votes of Parliament concerning Sergeant Major Generall Skippon. *For Joseph Hunscott, May 23,* 1642. brs. LS, CCA, EC; CH, MH, Y.

2302A —Several votes of the Lords and Commons concerning His Majesties message. *For Francis Kit, Aug.* 30, 1642. 4°.* LSE, OC.

2303 —Several votes of the Lords & Commons . . . concerning such as take up arms. *For Edward Husband. June 24,* 1648. 4°.* LT; CH, MH, MIU, WF, Y.

2304 —Severall votes of the Lords and Commons . . . declaring what forces. *For Iohn Wright, Iune 1,* 1647. 4°.* LT, OC, HH, AN; CN, MH, WF.

2305 —Severall votes, orders & ordinances of the Lords and Commons. *For R. Smithurst*, 1648. 4°.* LT; CH, MH, WF.

2306 —Severall votes resolved upon by both Houses. *March 16. London, for Ioseph Hunscott*, 1641[2]. brs. STEELE 2036. L, O, CT, BR, HH; WF, Y.

2307 ——[Anr. ed.] *For Ioseph Huncott, 26 Mar.*, 1641[2]. brs. STEELE 2038. L, O, LG; WF.

2307A —Six severall orders of the Lords and Commons. *By E. P. for T. S. July* 18, 1643. 4°.* LT; CN, MH, MIU, WF, Y.

2308 —Sixteene propositions in Parliament. *For I. T.*, 1642. 4°.* LT, LL, EC, HH; CH, MH, NU, TU, WF.

2309 —Speeches and passages of this great and happy Parliament. *For William Cooke*, 1641. 4°.* LT, O, C, E, DT; CH, CN, MH, NU, WF, Y.

2310 —A subsidie granted to the king, of tunnage. *By Robert Barker; and by the assigns of John Bill*, 1641. 4°.* LT.

2311 ——[Anr. ed.] *For L. Blaiklock*, 1642. 4°.* O, LL.

2312 ——[Anr. ed.] *For Lawrence Blaiklock*, 1642. 8°.* LG, O, OP, BR; LC, MH, WF, Y.

2313 ——[Anr. ed.] *For L. Blaiklock, and T. Hewer*, 1653. 12°. L, LUG; CH, LC, MH, NC, WF, Y.

2313A ——[Anr. ed.] *By S. Griffin, for T. Hewer*, 1657. 12°. L, LUG; MH.

2314 ——[Anr. ed.] *By John Bill and Christopher Barker*, 1660. fol.* LT, DC, GU; LC, MH, WF, Y.

2315 ——[Anr. ed.] *By Chr. Barker*, 1661. 12°. LUG, CLC, Y.

2315A ——[Anr. ed.] *By the assigns of John Bill and Christopher Barker*, 1667. 12°. L, LUG, CJ; MH, WF.

2316 —The substance of a conference . . . of both Hovses . . . October 27. 1641. [London], printed, 1641. 4°.* LT, O, OC, HH, EN; CSS, MH, NU, TU, Y.

2317 —A supplement to the collection of the debates. *Printed*, 1695. C, MR, EN; MIU.

2317A —Anno regni Jacobi II . . . a table of the statutes printed and not printed. *By the assigns of John Bill and by Henry Hills, and Thomas Newcomb*, 1685. fol.* O, OC; MH.

2317B —A table of the statutes publick and private. [London], 1696.] fol.* OC.

2317C —The ten yeeres proceedings. *Printed*, 1652. MM.

2318 —That all and every such poor person. *By J. Field for E. Husband*, 1649. brs. STEELE 2874. LT.

2319 —That all and every the ministers . . . 9 May 1660. *Macock & Tyton*, 1660. brs. STEELE 3196. LT, O, LS, HH, DT.

2320 ——[Anr. ed.] *By Edward Husbands and Thomas Newcomb*, [1660]. brs. STEELE 3197. L, O, C, LPR, DT.

2321 —That all masters and governors of . . . 20 September 1659. *By John Field*, 1659. brs. STEELE 3130. LT, O, LU, LV.

2322 —That all mayors, justices of the peace, . . . 7 January 1659[60]. *By John Streater & John Macock*, 1659[60]. brs. STEELE 3147. LT, LU.

2323 —That all officers who were in Com- . . . 2 January 1659[60]. *By John Streater & John Macock*, 1659[60]. brs. STEELE 3145. LT, O, LU, LV.

2324 Entry cancelled.

2325 —That all recognizances for the peace. *By John Field*, 1651. brs. STEELE 2932. LT, O, LU, OQ, HH.

2326 Entry cancelled.

2327 —That all such delinquents who having. *By Edward Husband and John Field*, 1650. brs. STEELE 2896. LT, O, LU, OQ, HH.

2328 Entry cancelled.

2329 —That all the militias in the re- . . . 23 February 1659[60]. *Streater & Macock*, 1659[60]. brs. STEELE 3157. LT, LU.

2330 —That Friday, the sixth day of April, . . . 16 March 1659[60]. *Streater & Macock*, 1660. brs. STEELE 3165. L, LU.

2331 —That no captain shall absent himself . . . 6 December 1650. *By Edward Husband and John Field*, 1650. brs. STEELE 2918. LT, LU, HH.

2332 —That no forces shall be raised, but . . . 27 December 1659. *By John Streater & John Macock.* 1659. brs. STEELE 3143. LT, O, LU, LV.

2333 —That no person or persons whatsoever. *For J. Wright*, 1647[8]. brs. STEELE 2748. LT, LPR, HH.

2334 —That no petition against any . . . 5 September 1654. *By John Field*, 1655[4]. brs. STEELE 3043. LT, O, LPR.

2335 —That on the fifth day of January next . . . 27 December 1659. *J. Streater*, 1659. brs. STEELE 3142. LT, O, LU, LV.

2336-9 Entries cancelled.

2340 —That the fair usually held and kept. *By John Field*, [1651]. brs. STEELE 2936. LT, LU, HH.

2341 —That the members of Parliament who . . . 22 July 1659. *By John Field*, 1659. brs. STEELE 3120. LT, O, LU.

2342 —That the ministers in the several. *By John Field*, 1652[3]. brs. STEELE 2986. L.

2343 —That the officers belonging to the recruits. *By John Field*, 1650[1]. brs. STEELE 2926. LT, O, LU, OQ, HH.

2344 —That the Parliament doth declare . . . 6 August 1650. *By Edward Husband and Iohn Field*, 1650. brs. STEELE 2909. L, LU, HH; WF.

2345 ——27 June 1651. *By John Field*, 1651. brs. STEELE 2934. LT, OQ, LU, HH.

2346 ——18 August 1652. *By John Field*, 1652. brs. STEELE 2973. L.

2347 —That the proceedings of the commissioners . . . 27 August 1659. *By John Field*, 1659. brs. STEELE 3128. LT, O, LU, LV.

2348 —That the reports of all such fines as have . . . 23 May, 1649. *R. Cotes*, 1649. brs. STEELE 2852. LT.

2349 —That the several commissioners for the . . . 1 March 1659[60]. *Streater & Macock*, 1659[60]. brs. STEELE 3162. L.

2350 —That there bee forthwith a choice made. [*London*], *R. Cotes*, 1645[6]. brs. STEELE 2642. LT, HH.

2351 —That this day fortnight be set . . . 26 April 1660. *Macock & Tyton*, 1660. brs. STEELE 3184. LT.

2352 —That this Parliament doth declare . . . 27 June 1659. *Field & Hills*, 1659. brs. STEELE 3116. LT, O, LS, LU, LV.

2353 —That upon the whole matter of the report . . . 5 January 1659[60]. *Streater & Macock, 1659[60].* brs. STEELE 3146. LT, O.

2354 —That Wednesday the 31 of August 1659 . . . 26 July 1659. *By John Field, 1659.* brs. STEELE 3121. L, HH.

2355 —That whatsoever person or persons have. *By John Field, 1651.* brs. STEELE 2950. LT, LU, HH.

2356 —Three declarations of the Lords and Commons . . . the one, declaring. *For Edward Husband, July 12, 1648.* 4°.* LT, HH; CH, CN, MH, WF, Y.

2357 —Three declarations: I, of the Parliament. *First printed at York, reprinted, September 17, 1642.* 4°.* L, O, OC, DT; CN, MH, Y.

2358 —Three ordinances, declarations and votes . . . 20 Decemb. 1642. *For Iohn Wright, Decemb. 22, 1642.* 4°.* LT, O, SC, CJ, HH; CSS, MA, MH, WF.

2359 Entry cancelled.

2360 —Three ordinances of the Lords and Commons . . . containing the names of divers knights. *For Iohn Wright, May 19, 1643.* 4°.* LT, O, LG, DT; MA, MH, OWC, WF.

2361 —Three ordinances of the Lords and Commons . . . first for the regulating of the excise. *August 5. [London] for John Wright, 1644.* 4°.* LT, O, C, HH, EN; CH, MA, NC, WF, Y.

2362 —Three ordinances of the Lords and Commons . . . for defraying the sallaries. *For John Wright. 17. Decemb., 1647.* 4°.* LT, O, C, OC, HH; CH, MH, NU, WF.

2363 —Three ordinances of the Lords & Commons . . . for impowering Major General Skippon . . . 13 Julii, 1648. *For Edward Husband, July 14, 1648.* 4°.* LT, HH; CH, CN, MH, NU, WF, Y.

2364-5 Entries cancelled.

2366 —Three ordinances of the Lords and Commons . . . for the better observation. *For I. Wright, Decemb. 21, 1644.* 4°.* LT, O, C, LG; CH, MH, NU, WF, Y.

2367 —Three ordinances of the Lords and Commons . . . one, concerning the trained bands *[London], for John Wright, March 5, 1644.* 4°.* LT, O, HH; CH, CN, NU, WF, Y.

2368 —Three ordinances of the Lords and Commons . . . the first for keeping in godly ministers . . . 23 August, 1647. *For John Wright, 1647.* 4°.* LT, O, OC, HH; CLC, MH, MIU, NU.

2369 —Three ordinances of the Lords and Commons . . . the first, for regulating the excize. *For John Wright, Octob. 7, 1644.* 4°.* LT, O, HH; CH, MH, NU, WF, Y.

2370 —Three ordinances of the Lords and Commons: . . . viz. I. an ordinance. *Printed at London, for Edw. Husbands, Feb. 11, 1644[5].* 4°.* LT, O, C, HH; MA, NAM.

2371 —To the Kings most excellent Majesty, the humble answer of the Lords and Commons . . . 11. Sept. 1642. *September 17. For Iohn Wright, 1642.* 4°.* L, O, C, OC, EC; CH, CN, MH, NU, WF, Y.

2372 —To the Kings most excellent Majesty: the humble desires of the High Court of Parliament. *July 23. London for A. Coe, [1642].* 4°.* LT; MHL.

2373 —To the Kings most excellent Majesty: the humble petition of the Lords and Commons. *[London], for F. Coules. September 27. 1642.* 4°.* O, CJ; TU.

2374 ——[Anr. ed.] *For John Wright, Nov. 12, 1642.* 4°.* OC, BR; CSS.

2375 —To the Kings most excellent Majesty: the humble petition of the Lords and Commons . . . delivered at Colebrook, 10 Nov. 1642. *[London, 1642.]* brs. STEELE 2291. LT, O, LL; Y.

2376 —To the Kings most excellent Majesty; the humble petition of the Lords and Commons . . . touching the proceedings against the Lord Kimbolton. *Feb. 18. London, for Joseph Hunscott, 1641[2].* brs. STEELE 1992. LT, O, LS, EC; CH, MH, Y.

2377 —To the Kings most excellent Maiestie. The humble remonstrance and petition of the Lords and Commons. *[London], imprinted, 1641.* brs. STEELE 1906. LT, LS, DT; MH.

2377A —A true and compleat list of the Lords Spiritual and Temporal. *By Tho. Newcomb, and sold by Tho. Basset, 1685.* brs. O, LS, MC; TU, Y.

2378 —The true ansvver of the Parliament to the petition of the Lord Major. *For R. W., 1648.* 4°.* LT; CLC, MBP.

2378A —A true collection of speeches and passages. *For L. Chapman, 1659.* 4°. L, CT; CN.

2379 —True copies of the present associations. *[London], for John Everingham, and sold by E. Whitlock, [1696.* 4°.* T.C.II 592. LCS; MB, TSM.

2380 —A true coppy of the instructions agreed upon. *[London], for F. Coules. 1642. Octob. 5.* brs. LM, SS; WF.

2381 ——[Anr. ed.] *[London], for Fr. Coles, 1642. Octob. 6.* 4°.* LT, LG, CJ; CH, CSS, MH, Y.

2382 —A true narrative of the proceedings in Parliament. *By John Redmayne, 1659.* 4°. LT, O, LW, SP; CH, CN, MH, WF, Y.

2382A —Twenty eight propositions made by both Houses. *For William Lee, Iune the 20, 1642.* 4°.* MH.

2383 —Two acts I. An act for reviving two statutes. *Dublin, by Andrew Crook, 1695.* fol.* L.

2384 —Two acts, I. an act for taking away the writt. *Dublin, by Andrew Crook, 1695.* fol.* L.

2385 —Two acts I. An act to take away damage clear. *Dublin, re-printed by Andrew Crook, 1695.* fol.* L.

2385A —Two acts of Parliament. *Dublin, re-printed by Richard Wilde, 1695.* DT.

2386 —Two declarations of the Lords and Commons . . . one for the re-payment. *Aprill 7. for John Wright, 1643.* 4°.* LT, O, C, LG, LUG; CH, MH, WF, Y.

2387 —Two declarations of the Lords and Commons . . . one, Iuly 12. *For E. Husbands and I. Franck, 1642.* 4°.* O, C, OC, BR, HH; MH, NU, WF.

2388 —Two declarations of the Lords and Commons . . . the first, to the convention of the estates. *Printed at London, for John Bellamie and Ralph Smith, 1643.* 4°.* LT, C, SP, DT; CN, MH, NU, WF, Y.

2389 —Two declarations of the Lords and Commons . . . the former, being a full narration. *For John Burroughes,* 1642. 4°.* L, CCA, SP, YM; CSS, MH, Y.

2390 —Two declarations of the Lords and Commons . . . the one concerning His Majesties late proclamation. *For Edward Blackmore, August* 16. 1642. 4°. CCA, CT, BR, SP; CSS, MH, MHL, WF.

2391 —Two declarations of the Lords and Commons . . . the one, concerning the releasing of diverse worthy ministers. *September* 9. *London for Iohn Wright,* 1642. 4°.* LT, O, C, CJ, HH; CH, CN, MBP, MH, WF.

2392 —Two declarations of the Lords and Commons . . . the one, for the preservation and safety of the kingdome. *By R.O. & G.D. for Joseph Hunscott,* 1642. 4°.* LT, CJ, LSC; LC, MH.

2393 —Two declarations of the Lords and Commons . . . the one, for the raising of all power. *[London], Decemb.* 10. *by R. Austin and A. Coe,* 1642. 4°.* LT, YM; CSS, MH, Y.

2394 —Two declarations of the Parliament of the Commonwealth . . . concerning Scotland. *By John Field,* 1652. 4°.* LT, O, HH; MH, MM.

2395 —Two orders of Parliament concerning the apprehending of thieves. *By Edward Husband and John Field,* 1650[1]. brs. STEELE 2921. LT, O, LUG, OQ, HH; NU.

2396 —Two orders of Parliament: the one, appointing the giving. *By John Field for Edward Husbands,* [1649]. brs. STEELE 2883. LT, O, C, OQ, HH; CH, MH, NU, Y.

2397 —Two orders of the Lords and Commons . . . concerning a committee of citizens. *Decem.* 5. *for Iohn Wright,* [London], 1642. 4°.* LT, O, C, LL, DT; MH, Y.

2397A —Two orders; the one to all high sheriffes. *By E. Griffin, for Christopher Latham,* 1642. brs. STEELE 2156. LT; MH, WF, Y.

2398 —Two ordinances of the Lords and Commons . . . 26 *July, for Matthew Walbanck,* 1647. brs. STEELE 2718. LT, O, HH; Y.

2399 —Two ordinances of the Lords and Commons . . . concerning the trained bands. *May* 4. *[London], for John Wright,* 1643. 4°.* LT, O, LG, DT; CH, MH, NU, WF, Y.

2400 —Two ordinances of the Lords and Commons. First, for the regulating of the excise. *[London], August* 5. *for John Wright,* 1644. 4°.* LG; CH.

2401 —Die Mercurii, 29 Januarii, 1644. Two ordinances of the Lords and Commons . . . for continuation of the severall ordinances of excise. *[London,* 1645.] brs. STEELE 2597. LT.

2402 ——[Anr. ed.] *By Richard Cotes and John Raworth,* [1645]. 4°.* LT, O.

2403 —Die Martis, 23. Maii, 1648. Two ordinances of the Lords and Commons . . . for putting all delinquents. *[London,* 1648.] brs. STEELE 2765. LT, HH.

2404 —Two ordinances of the Lords and Commons for the assessing all men. *For Iohn Wright, Ianuary* 17, 1642[3]. 4°.* LT, O, DT; CSS, MH, WF, Y.

2405 —Two ordinances of the Lords and Commons . . . for the better execution. *[London], L. Blaiklock, May* 27, 1644. 4°.* HH.

2406 —Two ordinances of the Lords and Commons . . . for the maintenance of some preaching ministers. *For John Wright, Decemb.* 29, 1645. 4°.* LT, O, YM; CH, MA, WF.

2407 —Two ordinances of the Lords and Commons . . . for the reliefe and maintenance of maimed souldiers. *For John Wright,* 1647. 4°.* LT, O; CH, MH, WF.

2408 —Two ordinances of the Lords and Commons . . . for the speedy demolishing of all organs, images. *For John Wright, May* 11, 1644. 4°.* LT, C, BR; CH, CN, LC, NU, Y.

2408A ——[Anr. ed.] *For Edward Husband,* 1645. 4°.* LSE, BP.

2409 —Two ordinances of the Lords and Commons . . . one commanding that no officer. *For Iohn Wright, 26 Octob.,* 1644. 4°.* LT, O, HH, SP; CH, MH, NC, WF, Y.

2410 —Two ordinances of the Lords and Commons . . . one concerning 23000 li. *May* 9. *[London], for John Wright,* 1643. 4°.* LT, O, LG; CH, MH, NU, WF, Y.

2411 —Two ordinances of the Lords and Commons . . . one for the abolishing of archbishops. *For John Wright, Octob.* 14, 1646. 4°.* LT, O, C, HH, EN; CH, LC, MH, NU, Y.

2412 —Two ordinances of the Lords and Commons . . . one for the constant recruiting. *For Iohn Wright, Jan.* 24, 1643[4]. 4°.* LT, O, C, HH; CH, LC, MH, WF, Y.

2413 —Two ordinances of the Lords and Commons . . . one for the Lord Major of the city of London. *Printed at London by Robert Ibbitson,* 1647. 4°.* LT, O, HH; CH, MH, PT, WF.

2414 —Two ordinances of the Lords and Commons . . . one for the raising six thousand pounds. *Imprinted at London for John Wright,* 1648. 4°.* LT, O, C, HH; CH, MH, MIU, NU, WF.

2415 —Two ordinances of the Lord and Commons one, that that all sellers of wines. *For Iohn Wright, Octob.* 10, 1643. 4°.* LT, O; CH, MA, MH, WF.

2416 —Two ordinances of the Lords and Commons . . . one, that the committee at Haberdashers Hall. *[London], Iune* 3. *for Iohn Wright,* 1643. 4°.* LT, O; MA, MH, WF, Y.

2417 —Two ordinances of the Lords and Commons . . . the first, for the appointing the House of Sr Richard Gurnie. *By R. Cotes, for John Bellamy,* 1646. 4°.* L, O, C, LSC, EN; MH, NU, WF, Y.

2418 —Two ordinances of the Lords and Commons . . . the one dated November 2. 1643. *For John Wright,* 1645. 4°.* LT, O; MH, WCL.

2419 —Two ordinances of the Lords and Commons . . . the one, for compositions for wardships. *For Edward Husband, Novemb.* 7, 1645. 4°.* LT, EC, HH; CH, MH, TU, WF, Y.

2420 —Two ordinances of the Lords and Commons . . . the one, for exempting the University of Cambridge. *For John Wright.* 14. *April,* 1645. 4°.* LT, O, C, HH; CH, MA, MH, WF.

2421 —Two ordinances of the Lords and Commons . . . the one, for raising monies. [*London*], *by T. W. for Ed. Husband, May the 29*, 1645. 4°.* MADAN 1783. LT, O, HH; MA, Y.

2422 —Two ordinances of the Lords and Commons . . . the one, for the enabling of the commissioners. *For Iohn Wright, April. 7*, 1645. 4°.* LT, O, OC, HH, EN; CN, MH, WF, Y.

2423 —Two ordinances of the Lords and Commons . . . the one for the speedy raising and levying of money. *For Edw. Husbands*, 1643. 4°.* LT, HH, BR; CH, CLC, WF.

2424 —Two ordinances of the Lords and Commons . . . the one, giving power to the committee. *For John Wright, 4 Novemb.*, 1645. 4°.* LT, O, OC, HH, E; CH, LC, MH, WF, Y.

2424A ——[Anr. ed.] *By T. W. for Edw. Husband*, 1645. 4°.* O, HH; MH.

2424B ——[Anr. ed.] *For Iohn Wright*, 1646. 4°.* MH, NU.

2425 —Two ordinances of the Lords & Commons . . . the one of the 16 of October, 1648. *For Edward Husband, Nov.* 16, 1648. 4°.* L, HH; CH, MH, MHL, Y.

2426 —Two ordinances of the Lords and Commons . . . the one, that the severall persons of the committees. *Imprinted at London for John Wright, 7. August*, 1645. 4°.* LT, O, HH, SP; CH, MA, MH, WF, Y.

2427 —Tvvo ordinances of the Lords and Commons . . . viz. one concerning eight hundred horse. *For Edward Husband, Sept. 27*, 1645. 4°.* LT, O, HH; CLC, MA, MH, WF, Y.

2428 —Two ordinances of the Lords and Commons, viz. the first enabling the committee. [*London*], *for Edward Husbands. November* 10, 1643. 4°.* LT, O, C, MR; MA, MH, WF, Y.

2428A —Two ordinances or declarations. *R. Cotes and R. Raworth*, 1647. 4°.* L.

2429 —Two petitions of the Lords and Commons to His Majestie, *Febr.* 2, 1641[2]. *By Robert Barker, and by the assignes of John Bill*, 1641[2]. 4°.* LT, O, C, LVF, HH; CH, CN, MH, WF, Y.

2429A ——[Anr. ed.] *Reprinted*, 1641. 4°.* O, SP; Y.

2430 —Two speeches made by the speakers. *Printed at London, by Robert Ibbitson*, 1647. 4°.* LT, OC, LG, HH; CH, CLC, TU, WF, Y.

2431 —The unanimous vote and resolution of both Houses . . . 13 May. *R. Hodgkinson*, 1661. brs. STEELE 3302. L, O.

2432 —Upon report from the committee for suppressing licentious and impious practices. *By Edward Husband and John Field*, 1650. brs. STEELE 2913. LT, O, C, OQ, HH; CN, NU, Y.

2433 —The vote of both Houses of Parliament; vpon the discovering. *For Peter Cole, Ianuary* 22, [1644]. 4°.* LT, O; CH, NU.

2434 —A vote of the Parliament touching delinquents. *By Edward Husband and John Field*, 1650. brs. STEELE 2892. LT, O, C, LUG, HH; CH, MH, NU, Y.

2435 —The votes agreed on by the Lords and Commons concerning a treaty. *Printed at Oxford by Leonard Lichfield, March* 7, 1642[/3]. 4°.* MADAN 1264. L, O, OC, CM, CT; MH, TU, Y.

2436 ——[Anr. ed.] [*London*], *printed*, 1642. 4°.* O, OC, DT; MH, MHL, NU, Y.

2437 ——[Anr. ed.] *By Robert Barker; and by the assignes of John Bill*, 1642[3]. 4°.* LT, HH; CH, CN, MH, WF, Y.

2438 —The votes and declaartion [*sic*] of the Lords and Commons . . . April 26. [*London*], *for John Wels*, 1642. 4°.* HH, YM; CH, WF, Y.

2439 —Votes and declarations of both Houses . . . 12 July 1642. [*London*], *for F. L. and W. G. Iuly* 14, 1642. 4°.* O; NU, Y.

2439A ——[Anr. ed.] *For Francis Leach and William Gay*, 1642. *July* 14. 4°.* OC; Y.

2440 —The votes and farther proceedings. *Dublin, by Benjamin Took; to be sold by Samuel Helsham*, 1685. fol.* L.

2441 —The votes and proceedings in Parliament for bringing the king. *By B. A.*, 1648. 4°.* LT; CLC.

2442 —Votes concerning the post-master. *For H: Blunden, August* 22, 1642. 4°.* LT, EC, BR; WF.

2443 —Votes. Die Martis. 12, July. 1642. That an army be forthwith raised. [*London*], *by T. P. and M. S.*, [1642]. brs. STEELE 2220. EC, BR, LS; CH, MH.

2444 —Votes in Parliament for seting of the kingdome. *By B. A.*, 1648. 4°.* LT; CN, Y.

2445 —Votes in Parliament. 1 That the carrying the king prisoner. *For R. A.*, 1648. 4°.* LT, C; WF.

2446 —The votes of both Houses of Parliament, the 20. of May, 1642. *For Ioseph Hunscot, and Iohn Wright, May* 24, 1642. 4°.* LT, O, C, LL, YM; CH, NC, WF, Y.

2446A ——[Anr. ed.] *For Ioseph Hunscott*, 1642. brs. EC; Y.

2447 ——[Anr. ed.] *For J. Hunscott*, [1642]. 4°.* L, EC, LSC, HH, DT; CLC, WF.

2447A ——[Anr. ed.] *For T. Bankes*, 1642. 4°.* CT.

2448 —Votes of both Houses of Parliament: with sundry articles, . . . 28 Maii, 1642. *By E. Griffin, for Cristopher Latham*, 1642. 4°.* LT, O, C, HH, DT; CH, MH, TU, Y.

2449 ——[Anr. ed.] *For Joseph Hunscott*, 1642. brs. EC; MH, MHS.

2449A ——[Anr. ed.] *For Iohn Thomas*, 1642. 4°.* CJ.

2450 —The votes of Parliament. Die Iovis xij Maij 1642. *For I. F.*, 1642. brs. STEELE 2131. LT, O.

2451 —Votes of Parliament for setting apart a day . . . 9 February 1652[3]. *By John Field*, 1652[3]. brs. STEELE 2985. LT, OP; MH, Y.

2452 —Votes of Parliament for setting the poor on work. *By John Field*, 1652. brs. STEELE 2969. LT, O, OQ, HH; MH, NU.

2453 —Votes of Parliament touching the book . . . Racovian catechism. *By John Field*, 1652. brs. STEELE 2966. LT, O, OQ, HH; NU, Y.

2454 —Votes of Parliament touching the excise of beer. *By John Field*, 1651. brs. STEELE 2958. LT, HH; MH, Y.

2455 —The votes of the high court. *For T. B. and A. E.*, 1643. 4°.* LT; Y.

2456 —The votes of the Lord & Commons . . . touching no farther address . . . 17 Februarii, 1647[8]. *For Edward Husband, Feb. 18, 1647[8].* 4°.* L, O, CCA, MR, HH; CH, CN, MH, WF, Y.

2457 —The votes of the Lords and Commons upon the propositions for . . . reducing of . . . Ireland. colop: *By D. M.,* 1689. brs. O, OC, MC; CH.

2458 —The votes of the Parliament . . . declaring all persons offering violence. *For I. F.,* 1642. brs. LT, LS; CH, MH, Y.

2458A —Votes, resolves and orders. [*London?* 1660.] brs. HH.

2459 —The vow and covenant appointed by the Lords and Commons. *For Edward Husbands,* [1642]. brs. L, CCA; MIU.

2460 ——[Anr. ed.] *Sould by Thomas Ienner,* [1643?]. brs. CH, Y.

2461 ——[Anr. ed.] *For Iohn Wright, Iune 22,* 1643. 4°.* LT, C, LG, HH, EN; MHL, WF, Y.

2462 ——[Anr. ed.] *For Edward Husbands, 29 Junii,* 1643. 4°.* STEELE 2436. LT, O, C, HH, DT; MIU, NU, Y.

2462A ——[Anr. ed.] —, *July* 1, 1643. brs. L; Y.

2463 —Wee your Majesties loyall subjects, the Lords . . . 2 August 1647. *R.Cotes,* 1647. brs. STEELE 2722. L, LPR.

2464 ——[Anr. ed.] *For John Bright,* 1647. brs. CN, Y.

2465 —Whatsoever dangers are threatned or feared. *For J. Wright,* 1648. brs. STEELE 2757. LT, LG; MH.

2466 —Whereas an ordinance was lately made by . . . 4 October 6143. *For L.Blaiklock,* 1643. brs. STEELE 2489. L.

2467 —Whereas both Houses of Parliament, have . . . 21 February 1644[5]. *For L.Blaikock,* 1644[5]. brs. STEELE 2600. LG, HH; MH.

2468 —Whereas by an ordinance of Parliament, bearing date. [*London,* 1649.] brs. LT.

2469 —Whereas by an ordinance of this present Parliament. *Printed at London for John Wright,* 1647. *December the first.* brs. STEELE 2734. LT, LG.

2470 —Whereas divers innovations. *Imprinted at London by Robert Barker: and by the assigns of John Bill,* 1641. brs. STEELE 1886. LT, O, LG, LS.

2471 —Whereas divers malignants. *For John Wright,* 1646. brs. STEELE 2661. LT, O; MH.

2472 —Whereas divers persons have beene assessed. *August 28. London for John Wright,* 1643. brs. STEELE 2470. LT, O.

2473 —Whereas divers statutes were made, viz. [*London,* 1644.] brs. LT.

2474 —Whereas divers well-affected persons, citizens. [*London,* 1642.] brs. STEELE 2304. LT.

2475 —Whereas for divers yeeres there hath not been any election, (28. August. 1645). *For Iohn Wright,* 1645. brs. CH.

2476 —Die Jovis, 1. Junii, 1643. Whereas in the ordinance of both Houses. [*London,* 1643.] cap., 4°.* LUG, OC, EC, AN, HH; CLC, MB, MH, WF.

2477 —Die Veneris 15 Septem. 1643. Whereas in times of common danger. *For Edward Husbands,* [1643]. brs. STEELE 2477. LT, LS.

2478 —Die Jovis 13. Januarii. 1641. Whereas information hath been given. *Imprinted at London by Robert Barker, and by the assigns of John Bill,* 1641. brs. STEELE 1938. LT, O, BR, HH; Y.

2479 ——[Anr. ed.] 1641. brs. STEELE 1939. L, LS.

2480 —Whereas information is given . . . 3 September 1659. *By John Field,* 1659. brs. STEELE 3129. LT, O, LS, LUG, LV; MH.

2481 —Die Jovis 2. Junij, 1642. Whereas it doth appear to the Lord and Commons. *For Joseph Hunscott,* 1642. brs. STEELE 2158. LT, O, LS, HH; MH, MHS.

2481A —Whereas it has pleased Almighty God to vouchsafe a miraculous deliverance. *For James Partridge, Matthew Gillyflower and Samuel Heyrick,* 1689. fol.* L, DC.

2481B —Die Mercurii, Novemb. 9, 1642. Whereas it is found that great inconvenience. *For Edw. Husbands and I. Franck,* 1642. brs. MH.

2482 —Whereas it is ordained in the ordinance. *For E. Husband, 8 Mar.,* 1642[3]. brs. STEELE 2381. L; MH.

2483 —Whereas it is very well known what. [*London,* 1645.] brs. STEELE 2633. L.

2484 —By the Parliament. Whereas John Lambert Esq; being. *By John Streater, and John Macock,* 1659[60]. brs. STEELE 3152. LT, O, LG; MH.

2485 —Die Mercurii, 4 Jan. 1642. Whereas many of the trained bands. *April 6. London, for John Wright,* 1643. brs. STEELE 2342. LT.

2486 —Die Lunae 29. Novemb. 1641. Whereas severall certificates. *Imprinted at London by Robert Barker; and by the assigns of John Bill,* 1641. brs. STEELE 1898. LT, LPR, DT.

2487 —Die Veneris, Decemb. 16. 1642. Whereas severall ordinances of both Houses. [*London,* 1642.] brs. STEELE 2328. LT; CH, MA.

2488 —Whereas some doubts have been raised . . . 19 December 1644. *For J.Wright,* 1644. brs. STEELE 2594. HH.

2489 —Die Jovis 24°. Martii 1641. Whereas the bill of tonnage. *For F.Coles and T.Bankes,* 1642. brs. STEELE 2061. LT, LG.

2490 —The 21. of August, 1643. Whereas the committee for the militia in the city of London. *Printed at London, by Richard Cotes,* 1643. brs. STEELE 2469. LT, LG, HH; MH.

2491 —Die Sabbathi. 30. Sept. 1643. Whereas the companies of London. *For John Wright,* 1643. brs. STEELE 2487. LT, LG; CH.

2492 —Februar. 18. 1642. Whereas the Lords and Commons of both Houses of Parliament, made request. [*London,* 1643.] brs. LT; MA, MH.

2493 —Die Jovis, 21 Martii, 1643. Whereas the Lords and Commons by an ordinance. *March 23, London for John Wright,* 1643[4]. brs. STEELE 2545. LT, LS; MH, Y.

2494 —Die Martis, 11. Iulii, 1648. Whereas the Lords and Commons . . . have been necessitated. *By R.Cotes, and R.Raworth,* 1648. brs. STEELE 2776. LT.

2495 —Whereas the old and implacable . . . 9 August 1659. *By John Field,* 1659. brs. STEELE 3125. L, O, LG, LS, HH; MH, MIU.

2496 —Whereas the several plantations in Virginia. *For John Wright*, 1646. brs. STEELE 2677. LT; CH.

2496A —Die Martis, 20 Maii, 1643. Whereas there are many and grave abuses. [*London*, 1643]. brs. MH.

2497 —Die Lunae 14 April 1645. Whereas there are many and great abuses. *For Laurence Blaiklock*, 1645. brs. STEELE 2608. L.; CH, LC, WF.

2498 —Whereas Thomas Andrewes, John Fowke, . . . 18 September 1643. *For Laurence Blaikelock*, 1644. brs. STEELE 2478. L; CH, LC.

2499 —Die Mercurii, 2. November, 1642. Whereas wee the Lords and Commons. *By J.F. for E. Husbands and J. Franck*, [1642]. brs. STEELE 2289. LT, O, EC; MH.

2500 ——[Anr. ed.] *For Iohn Wright*, 1642. brs. CH, MH.

2501 Entry cancelled.

ENGLAND: PARLIAMENT, HOUSE OF COMMONS

2502 —An abstract of proceedings of the House of Commons, in relation to the East-India Company. [*London*, 1698.] cap., fol.* L, O.

2503 —An account of some transactions in the honourable House of Commons. *Printed*, 1693. 4°.* L; MH, MIU, WF, Y.

2504 —An act of the Commons . . . for the adjourning of part of the term of Hilary. *For Edward Husband, Jan.* 16, 1648[9]. brs. STEELE 2819. LT, O, C, LG, HH; CH, MB, MH, WF, Y.

2505 —An act of the Commons . . . for the keeping a day of humiliation. *For Edward Husband, March* 20, 1648[9]. brs. STEELE 2835. LT, O, OQ, HH; CH, MB, MH, NU, Y.

2506 —An act of the Commons . . . for the relief, and imployment of the poor. *By Richard Cotes*, 1649. 4°.* LT, O, C, GU, DT; WF, Y.

2506A ——[Anr. ed.] *By John Field for Edward Husband*, 1649. 4°.* NU.

2506B ——[Anr. ed.] *By Richard Cotes*, 1650. 4°.* LG, LW.

2507 —Die Mercurii 17. Januarii. 1648. An act of the Commons . . . for the setling of the militia. *By Richard Cotes*, 1648[9]. 4°.* LT, O, LG, CCO; MH, TU, Y.

2508 —An act of the Commons . . . for the speedy raising and levying. *By Richard Cotes, and Thomas Newcombe*, 1649. fol.* L, C; MB.

2509 —An act of the Commons . . . touching the regulating of the officers of the navy. *For Edward Husband, Jan.* 18, 1648[9]. 4°.* LT, O, C, OC; MH, MHL, WF, Y.

2509A —An act of the Commons . . . whereas by ordinance. [1648.] brs. OP.

2509B —An act of the Commons . . . with further instructions. *By Richard Cotes*, 1649. fol.* MH.

2510 —An act prohibiting the importing of any vvines, wool. *For Edward Husband*, 1649. brs. STEELE 2867. LT, O, LG, HH; LC, MH.

2511 ——[Anr. ed.] *By Edward Husband and Iohn Field*, 1650. brs. STEELE 2868. L, HH; CH, Y.

2511A —An act touching the first 4,000,000. colop: *By John Field for Edward Husband*, 1648. fol.* L, BR; CLC.

2512 —Acts of accusation and impeachment of the House of Commons, . . . against William Pierce. *For G. Thomlinson*, 1642. 4°. L.

2513 —The Commons address against the Duke of Lauderdail, . . . May 9. 1679. [*London?* 1679.] cap., fol.* L, O, C, LL, HH; MB, MH, WF, Y.

2514 —The address of the honourable the House of Commons: . . . 25th day of April, 1689. *By Charles Bill, and Thomas Newcomb*, 1689. fol.* L, O, C, OC; CH, MB, PL, WF, Y.

2515 ——[Anr. ed.] *Edinburgh, re-printed*, 1689. brs. ALDIS 2854. L, EN.

2516 —The address of the House of Commons to the king. *Edinburgh, re-printed by the heir of Andrew Anderson*, 1692. brs. ALDIS 3213. L, E.

2517 ——[Anr. ed.] *London, reprinted Edinburgh*, 1695. fol. ALDIS 3437. EN.

2517A —Another order for contributions. *For Edw. Husbands, Aprill* 27, 1643. 4°.* LT, O; WF, Y.

2518 —Another order of the Commons . . . concerning coals. *For Edw. Husbands, April* 21, 1643. 4°.* LT, O, HH, DT; CH, MH, NC, NU, Y.

2519 —The ansvver of the Commons, to a petition, in the name. [*London*], *printed*, 1648. 4°.* LT, C, HH; MH, NU, WF, Y.

2520 —The answer of the Commons . . . to the Scots commissioners papers . . . 28 November 1646. *For Edward Husband, December* 4, 1646. 4°. LT, O, C, EN, DT; CH, CU, MH, NU, TU, WF, Y.

2520A —The answer of the House of Commons. Decemb. 20. *For Richard West*, 1642. 4°.* LT, LG, HH, DT; MIU, Y.

2521 —Articles of accusation, exhibited by the Commons . . . against Sr John Bramston. [*London*], *for I. H.*, 1641. 4°. L, O, CT, LG, EN, DT; CH, CN, LC, MH, NU, Y.

2522 ——[Anr. ed.] [*London*], *printed*, 1641. 4°.* LT, O, LG, CT, BR; CH, MH, TU, WF, Y.

2523 —Articles of impeachment by the Commons . . . against Sir Thomas Gardiner. *For Tho: Walkley, May* 23, 1642. 4°.* LT, O, LG, OC, DT; CH, CN, NU, WF.

2524 ——[Anr. ed.] *For John Thomas Bates, May* 23, 1642. 4°.* L; Y.

2524A ——[Anr. ed.] *Printed, May* 23, 1642. 4°.* LT, O, LSC; CSS, MBP, MHL.

2525 —Articles of impeachment of the Commons, . . . against Matthew Wren. [*London*], *printed*, 1641. 4°.* LT, O, CP, P, EN; CN, CSS, LC, MH, TU, Y.

2526 ——[Anr. ed.] —, 1641. 4°.* L, CT; NU.

2527 —Articles of the Commons . . . in maintenance of their accusation, against William Laud. [*London*], *Jan.* 19. *for John Wright*, 1643[4]. 4°.* LT, O, CT, E, DT; CH, MH, NU, TU, WF, Y.

2528 —The articles or, charge exhibited in Parliament against D. Cozens. *Printed*, 1641. 4°.* O, C, LG, BR, HH; CH, MH, NU, TU, Y.

2529 —Die Martis 28 Septemb. 1641. At the Committee appointed by the Commons. *Imprinted at London by Robert Barker; and by the assigns of John Bill*, 1641. brs. STEELE 1893. L, LS, OQ, CT; Y.

2530 —At the Committee of the House of Commons. [*London*, 1642.] brs. STEELE 1927. L.

2531 —Primo die Novembris, 1648. At the committee of the House of Commons appointed for the consideration. *By Rich. Cotes*, 1648. brs. LT.

2532 —The bill for regulating abuses. [*London?* 1679.] cap., fol.* O, HH; MBA, MH, WF, Y.

2533 —The bill of attainder, . . . against Thomas Earle of Strafford. [*London*], *for J.A.*, 1641. 4°.* L, LG, OC, HH; CH, MH, NU, WF, Y.

2533A — —[Anr. ed.] [*London*], printed, 1641. 4°.* Y.

2533B —A breif collection of some forgotten votes of the Commons. *Printed*, 1647. brs. LT.

2534 —By the Commons . . . in the whole management. *By Richard Cotes*, 1648. brs. LT; MH.

2535 —By the right honourable the House of Commons. Die Lunae, 3. Januar. 1641. *Printed at London*, 1641. brs. L, CT.

2535A —Certificate of what hath been done. *By Robert Barker and by the assignes of John Bill*, 1641. brs. STEELE 1900. LT, LPR, DT.

2536 —The charge drawne up . . . against Sir Richard Gurnet. *For J.Smith, July 12*, 1642. 4°.* O, LG, OC, SP; MM, OWC.

2537 —The charge of the Commons of England, against Charls Stuart, . . . Jan. 20, 1648[9]. *For Rapha Harford*, 1648[9]. 4°.* LT, O, C, GH, DT; CH, CN, MH, NU, WF, Y.

2538 —A collection of the substance of several speeches and debates. *For Francis Smith*, 1681. fol.* L, O, C, EN, DT; CH, LC, MH, NU, TU, Y.

2539 —A committee appointed by the Commons . . . to consider of such grievances as have been promised . . . 8 Januarii 1647. *For Edward Husband, Jan. 11*, 1647[8]. 4°.* LT, O, OC, HH, DT; MH, WF, Y.

2539A —Die Sabbathi, 27. May, 1643. The Commons being informed. *For Edw: Husbands, May 29*, 1643. brs. CH.

2540 —A complaint of the House of Commons, and resolution. *Printed at York, by Stephen Bulkley*, 1642. 4°.* YM.

2541 —The copie of an order agreed upon in the House of Commons vpon Friday the eighteenth of Iune. [*London*], *printed*, 1641. brs. STEELE 1860. LT, O, CT; MH.

2542 — —[Anr. ed.] [*London*], *printed*, 1641. brs. STEELE 1861. LT, LG, LUG, MC; MH.

2543 —A copy of the association agreed upon by the honourable House of Commons, . . . 24th of February, 1695/6. [*London*, 1696.] brs. CH.

2544 —A coppy of the Journal-book of the House of Commons. *Printed*, 1680. 8°. L, O, C, CT, EN; CH, CU, NU, WF, Y.

2544A —A copy of two journal books. *Printed*, 1680. 8°. MIU, WF.

2545 —The debates in the honourable House of Commons, . . . March 21. 1680. *For John Peacock*, 1681. fol.* L, O, CCA, CT, SP, EN; CH, CN, MH, WF, Y.

2546 —The debates in the House of Commons assembled at Oxford the twenty first of March, 1680. colop: *For R. Baldwin*, 1681. cap., fol.* L, O, C, MR, GU; CH, CN, MH, TU, WF, Y.

2546A — —[Anr. ed.] *Dublin, reprinted*, 1681. 4°.* C.

2547 —The debates of the House of Commons . . . touching His Majesties concessions. *For R. Smithurst*, 1648. 4°.* LT, C, HH, DT; CH, MIU, OWC.

2548 —The declaration agreed upon by the committee of the . . . Commons. [*London, for Joseph Hunscott*, 1641/2.] brs. STEELE 1920. L, O, LG, LPR, HH; MH, Y.

2549 Entry cancelled.

2550 —A declaration of the Commons . . . made September the 9th 1641. *By Robert Barker; and by the assignes of John Bill*, 1641. 4°.* LT, O, CT, EN, DT; CH, CN, MH, NU, WF, Y.

2551 — —[Anr. ed.] *Edinburgh, R. & J.Bryson*, 1641. 4°.* ALDIS 999. EN.

2552 —A declaration of the Commons . . . against a scandalous book. *For Edward Husband, March 29*, 1649. brs. STEELE 2839. LT, O, LG; MB, MH, MIU.

2553 —A declaration of the Commons . . . against all such persons . . . 31 Decemb. 1646. *For Edward Husband, January 2*, 1646[7]. 4°.* LT, LW, OC, BR, DT; MH, MHL, NU, WF, Y.

2554 — —[Anr. ed.] *For E. Husband*, [1647]. brs. STEELE 2675. L, LG; MH.

2555 —Declaration of the Commons concerning false rumours. *By L. N. for E. Husbands and J. Frank, Decemb. 17*, 1642. 4°.* L, O, OC, HH, DT; MA, Y.

2556 —A declaration of the Commons . . . concerning the jurisdiction. *For Edward Husband*, 1648[9]. 4°.* LT, O, MR; CH, MH, TU, Y.

2557 —A declaration of the Commons . . . concerning the rise and progresse of the grand rebellion in Ireland. *For Edw. Husbands, Iuly 25*, 1643. 4°. LT, O, C, EN, DT; CH, CN, LC, MH, NU, Y.

2558 —A declaration of the Commons . . . declaring all persons. *For Edward Husband*, 1649. brs. STEELE 2866. LT, O, C, LG, LPR; CH, MH, MIU, WF, Y.

2559 —A declaration of the Commons of England . . . expressing their reasons and grounds . . . 11 Februarii 1647. *For Edward Husband, Feb. 15*, 1647[8]. 4°.* LT, O, C, HH, DT; CH, CN, MH, NU, WF, Y.

2559A — —[Anr. ed.] —, *reprinted at Kilkenny*, 1648. 4°.* DN.

2560 —A declaration of the Commons of England . . . expressing their reasons for the adnulling and vacating. *For Edward Husband, Jan. 18*, 1648[9]. 4°.* LT, O, C, HH, DT; CH, MH, NPT, WF, Y.

2561 —A declaration of the Commons . . . for bringing to condigne punishment. *For Richard Best, October, 10*, 1642. 4°.* LT, C, BR, HH, DT; CH, CN, MH, WF, Y.

2562   —A declaration of the Commons . . . of their true intentions. [*London*], *for Edward Husband, April 18,* 1646. 4°.* LT, C, OC, HH, EN; CH, LC, MH, NU, Y.

2563   —A declaration of the Commons . . . that the ayd and assistance of the Lord Generall, Lord Fairfax. *For Edw. Husbands, July 18,* 1643. 4°.* LT, LG, CS; CN, MA, MH, Y.

2564   —A declaration of the Commons . . . upon two letters sent by Sir John Brooks. *May 10. London, for Edw. Husbands,* 1643. 4°.* LT, O, C, HH, DT; CH, LC, MH, NU, Y.

2565   —A declaration of the House of Commons . . . declaring I. that the people are under God. *By Robert Ibbitson,* 1648. 4°.* LT, C, SP; CLC, MH, NU.

2566   —A declaration of the honourable House of Commons, in answer to the Scotch papers. *For Humphrey Harwood,* 1648. 4°. LT, O, CCA, P, EN; CH, MH, NU, WF, Y.

2567   —A declaration of the Hovse of Commons in vindication of divers members . . . *Julii* 21. 1642. *By Luke Norton and John Field, for Edward Husbands and Iohn Franck, July 22,* 1642. 4°.* LT, O, CS, LG, HH; CN, MH, NU, WF, Y.

2568   —A declaration of the Hovse of Commons tovching the late breach. *For Ioseph Hunscott,* 1642. brs. STEELE 1941. LT, O, CM, ES, DT; MH, Y.

2569   —A declaration of the House of Commons, touching the breach of their priviledges. *For Fr. Coules, and T. Bankes,* 1641[2]. 4°.* LT, C, EN; CH, MH, MHL.

2570   —A declaration of the proceedings of the honourable committee of the House of Commons, at Merchant-Taylors Hall. *By T. Pain and M. Simons,* 1643. 4°.* LT; CH, CN, NU, WF, Y.

2571   —A declaration. The Commons . . . do declare. *By Edward Husbands & Thomas Newcomb,* [1660]. brs. STEELE 3195. LT, O, C, LPR, DT; MH, Y.

2572   —Depositions and articles against Thomas Earle of Strafford, Feb. 16, 1640. [*London*], *printed,* 1640[1]. 4°.* L, LL, YM, E; CH, CU, MIU, TU, WF, Y.

2572A   — —[Anr. ed.] *Printed,* 1641. 4°. MIU, VC.

2573   —A disclaimer and answer of the Commons of England. *By G. M.,* 1643. 4°.* LT, O, CT, HH; CH, CN, MH, NU, WF, Y.

2574   —An exact collection of the debates of the House of Commons. *For R. Clavel, J. Robinson, and A. Churchil,* 1689, 8°. T.C.II 250. L, C, OB, E, DT; BN, CU, MH, NU, PL, WF, Y.

2574A   — —[Anr. ed.] *For R. Baldwin,* 1689. 8°. CM, EC; MIU, PL, TU.

2575   —An exact collection of the most considerable debates. *For R. Baldwin,* 1681. 8°. T.C.I 453. L, C, LL, OC, EN; BN, CH, CN, LC, MH, WF, Y.

2575A   —Exceeding joyfull propositions. *Decemb.* 23, *for I. H. and William Crumwell,* 1642. 4°.* LT, HH; MBP, MIU, Y.

2576   —The faithful register; or, the debates. *Printed,* [1689]. 8°. L, C, OC, BR; CH, CN, LC, MH, MIU, Y.

2577   —Forasmuch as the charge of conducting . . . 21 June 1644. [*London,* 1644.] brs. STEELE 2577. L.

2577A   —Four special orders and a declaration. *For Edward Husband, October 30,* 1646. 4°.* LT, OC; CH, LC, MH, WF, Y.

2578   —From the Committee of sequestrations, . . . 28 September 1643. [*London,* 1643.] brs. STEELE 2485. LT.

2579   —The House of Commons taking into . . . 20 July 1643. [*London,* 1643.] brs. STEELE 2460. L.

2580   —The House of Commons, upon late information received from their armies in Ireland. *For Edward Husbands,* [1644]. brs. STEELE 2581. LT, O; CH.

2581   —The humble address of the House of Commons. *By John Leake for T. Goodwin and T. Cockerill,* 1696. brs. SP; CN, WF.

2582   — —[Anr. ed.] *Reprinted Edinburgh, by the heirs and successors of Andrew Anderson,* 1696. brs. ALDIS 3567. L, EN.

2583   — —[Anr. ed.] *Edinburgh, by the heirs and successors of Andrew Anderson,* 1697. brs. ALDIS 3672. HH, EN.

2583A   — —[Anr. ed.] —, 1698. brs. L.

2584   — —[Anr. ed.] *For Edward Jones and Timothy Goodwin,* 1699. brs. L, LG, MC; PL, WF.

2585   — —[Anr. ed.] *Edinburgh, by the heirs and successors of Andrew Anderson,* 1699. brs. ALDIS 3856. EN, FSF.

2586   —The hvmble answer of the honourable House of Commons to the kings. *For Iohn Franke,* 1641[2]. brs. STEELE 1981. LT, O; MH.

2587   —The humble petition of the House of Commons. If Charles thou wilt. colop: *Printed at Oxford by Leonard Lichfield,* [1643]. 4°.* MADAN 1459. LT, O.

2587A   —The humble representation of. colop: *Printed and sold by John Leake,* 1694. brs. SP; PL.

2587B   —An impeachment of high treason . . . Lord Strange. *Septemb.* 17, *for John Wright,* 1642. 4°.* LT, EC; CH, LN, MH, WF, Y.

2588   —In order to the safety of the Parliament . . . 2 July 1646. *R. Cotes,* 1646. brs. STEELE 2659. L.

2589   —In the whole management . . . 18 July 1648. *R. Cotes,* 1648. brs. STEELE 2782. LT; MH.

2589A   —Instructions and directions from the . . . Commons. *For Laurence Blaiklocke,* 1642. 4°.* MH, WF.

2589B   —Instructions for deputy lieutenants. *By A. Norton for Edw. Husbands and Iohn Franke, June 16,* 1642. 4°.* LT; CN.

2589C   — —[Anr. ed.] —, *June 17,* 1642. 4°.* OC, BR; CH, MH, MU, Y.

2589D   — —[Anr. ed.] *By L. N. and J. F. for Edward Husbands and Iohn Franke, June 17,* 1642. brs. STEELE 2183. LT, LS, EC, HH; MH, MIU, WF, Y.

2590   —Instructions from the honourable House of Commons . . . to the committee in Kent. *For Thomas Cook, August 13,* 1642. 4°.* LT, O, CJ, OC; MH, MIU, OWC, Y.

2590A   —It is ordered by the House of Commons that the persons named. *For Edw: Husbands, April 22,* 1643. brs. CH.

2591   —It is this day ordered by the Commons . . . 7 August 1641. *By Robert Barker & by the assigns of John Bill,* 1641. brs. STEELE 1875. L, HH, BR.

2592   — —2 June 1642. [*London*], *for Ioseph Hunscott,* 1642. brs. STEELE 2159. LT, LS; MH, MHS.

2593 —Die Martis 3 Augusti, 1642. —. [London, 1642.] brs. STEELE 2236. LT; MH.

2594 ——27 March 1643. [London, 1643.] brs. STEELE: 2397. L, LS, ES; MH.

2595 Entry cancelled.

2596 ——23 February 1643[4]. [London, 1644.] brs. STEELE 2531. L, LG.

2597 ——17 June 1644. [London, 1644.] brs. STEELE 2574. L.

2598 ——25 March 1644. [London, 1644.] brs. STEELE 2548. L.

2599 —Die Lunae 10. Martii, 1644[5]. —. [London, 1645.] brs. STEELE 2604. LT; MH.

2600 —Die Veneris, 27° Junij, 1645. —. [London, 1645.] brs. LT.

2601 —Die Lunae, 8. Junij, 1646. —. [London, 1646.] brs. STEELE 2658. LT.

2602 —7. Decemb. 1643. It is this day ordered by the Commons . . . that Master Marshall. For Edward Husbands, [1643]. brs. CH.

2603 —Die Martis, Aug. 27. 1644. It is this day ordered by the Commons . . . that Master Speaker shall have power to grant passes. [London, 1645.] brs. STEELE 2582. LT; CH.

2604 —Die Martis, Junii 24. 1645. It is this day ordered by the Commons that the ensignes and cornetts sent up. For Edward Husband, 1645. brs. STEELE 2621. LT; CH.

2605 Entry cancelled.

2606 —It is this day ordered by the Commons . . . that whatsoever prisoner. For Edward Husbands, October 31, 1643. brs. CH.

2607 —It is this day ordered by the Commons House of Parliament, that such particular persons. For Edward Husbands, April 15, 1643. brs. CH, MH.

2608 —6 Septemb. 1643. It is this day ordered by the Commons House of Parliament, that the Deputy-lieutenants. For Edward Husbands, [1643]. brs. CH.

2609 —Die Mercurii 5° Maii. 1641. It is this day ordered by the House. . . . By Robert Barker & by the assigns of John Bill, 1641. brs. STEELE 1844. LT, LS, O, CM, BR; CH, Y.

2610 ——[Anr. ed.] Printed at London by Robert Barker, and reprinted at Edinburgh by Robert Bryson, 1641. brs. MH, MHS.

2611 ——[Anr. ed.] Imprinted at London by Robert Barker: and by the assignes of John Bill, 1641. brs. STEELE 1849. LT, O, CJ, OC.

2612 ——[Anr. ed.] [London], for J. Aston, 1641. brs. STEELE 1848. LT.

2613 ——[Anr. ed.] [London], by R. Oulton & G. Dexter, [1641]. brs. STEELE 1854. LG, DT; Y.

2613A ——[Anr. ed.] [London, 1641.] brs. EC.

2614 ——14 July 1641. By Robert Barker & by the assigns of John Bill, 1641. brs. STEELE 1867. L, O, LG, YM, BR.

2615 ——19 August 1643. By L. N. for E. Husbands, 1643. brs. STEELE 2468. LT.

2616 —It is this day ordered that publike thankes . . . 2 February 1643[4]. For Robert Bostock, 1643[4]. brs. STEELE 2527. LT.

2617 —Die Lunae, 3 Januar. 1641. It is this day ordered upon the question. [London], for T. Bates, 1641[2]. brs. STEELE 1917. LT, O, OQ; Y.

2617A —A journal of the proceedings. Printed at Rome, 1674. 4°.* L, O; WF.

2617B —A joyfull message sent. By J. H. and T. Ryder, July 9, 1672. 4°.* LT, EC; CLC, Y.

2618 —A letter concerning Colonel Monk's surprizing . . . Carrickfergus. For E. Husband, 30 Sept. 1648. brs. STEELE 2798. LT.

2619 —A letter directed to Master Bridgeman. For Joseph Hunscott, 1641[2]. brs. STEELE 1932. LT, O.

2620 ——[Anr. ed.] Printed, 1642. brs. STEELE 1933. L, C.

2621 —A letter from the House of Commons . . . to the right honourable and right reverend, the Lords. For Edward Husband, August 8, 1648. 4°.* LT, C, HH, EN, AU; CH, MH, NU, WF, Y.

2622 —A letter to the kings most excellent Majesty from the Commons. By Edward Husbands and Thomas Newcomb, 1660. fol.* L, O, OC, GU; CH, WF, Y.

2623 ——[Anr. ed.] Edinburgh reprinted by Christopher Higgins, 1660. brs. STEELE 3184b. L; Y.

2624 —The message from the Hovse of Commons . . . February 23, 1642[3]. By E. Griffin, 1642[3]. 4°.* L, O, HH; MIU, OWC, WF, Y.

2624A —A message sent. [London], for John Iones, August 22, 1642. 4°.* LT, O; WF.

2624B —My lord, we the Commons. [London? 1679.] brs. L, HH.

2625 —The narrative & reasons of the honorable House of Commons concerning the tryal. Printed, 1679. 4°.* L, O, CJ; CH, CN, MH, MIU, WF.

2626 —The narrative and reasons which were delivered by the . . . Commons . . . touching the trials. Printed, 1679. fol. L, O, DT; CH, CN, LC, MHL, Y.

2627 ——[Anr. ed.] [London, 1679.] cap., fol. L; CLC, TU.

2628 —A new declaration concerning the king, from the Commons. [London], for L. VVhite, [1649]. 4°.* LT, YM, SP; CH.

2629 Entry cancelled.

2630 —The opinion of the Parliament, about religion, twenty years ago. colop: For William Crook, 1682. fol.* T.C.1 511. L, O, OC, HH, EN; CH, MB, MH, WF.

2631 —An order and declaration of the Commons . . . that, no person . . . 19 Decemb. 1644. Printed at London by Richard Cotes, 1644. 4°.* LT, O, LG, OC, HH; MH.

2631A —The order and forme for church-goverment [sic]. [London], printed, 1641. 4°.* L, O, CT, LW, EC; CSS, MH, NU, WF.

2632 —Order by the Commons . . . that the inhabitants of the severall counties shall have power to assemble. [London, 1642.] brs. LS.

2633 —An order concerning the price of coales. By Richard Cotes, 1643. brs. STEELE 2434. LT; MH.

2634 —An order for a charitable contribution for the relief of maymed souldiers. By Edw. Husbands and Joh. Frank, 1642. brs. STEELE 2335. LT, LG; MH.

2635   —An order from the Hovse of Commons . . . for the
       protection and rescuing of any member . . . Jan 6.
       1641. By Tho: Paine, 1641. 4°.* L, O, CM, BR, DT; CH,
       MH, NU, WF, Y.

2636   —An order from the House of Commons vnto the
       sheriffes of each county. For William Gay, 1642. brs.
       STEELE 2064. LT, LS; MH, Y.

2637   —An order made by the committees of the House of
       Commons . . . Oct 19. 1641. For Iohn Thomas, 1641.
       4°.* L, CT, HH; CH, MH, MIU, WF, Y.

2638   —Die Sabbati 28. Ianua: 1642. An order made by the
       Commons. By Jo: Field, for Edw: Husbands. Febr. 6,
       1642[3]. brs. STEELE 2355. LT, O, LG; Y.

2639   —An order made by the honourable House of Com-
       mons. Die Sabbati, 29. Januarii. 1641. It is ordered that
       the master and wardens of the company of stationers.
       [London, 1641.] brs. LT.

2640   —An order made by the House of Commons, for the
       establishing of preaching lecturers . . . Septemb. 8,
       1641. By B. Alsop, 1641. 4°.* LT, O, C, BR, EN; CSS, MH,
       MIU, WF, Y.

2641   ——[Anr. ed.] May 28. London, for I.T., 1642. 4°.* L, O,
       E; MH, NU, WF.

2642   —An order made by the House of Commons for the
       removal of the Comunion table. [London], by Robert
       Barker and by the assignes of John Bill, 1641. brs. LT; Y.

2643   —An order of the Commons . . . concerning all such
       persons. For Edward Husband, December 18, 1645. brs.
       STEELE 2638. LT, LG.

2644   —An order of the Commons Hovse of Parliament; con-
       cerning the restitution. Novemb. 26 [London], for L.
       Wright, 1642. brs. STEELE 2308. LT, MC; CH, MA, MH.

2645   —An order of the Commons . . . concerning the re-
       turning, in writing, . . . the names. For Edward Hus-
       bands, Decemb. 2, 1643. 4°.* LT, O; CH, CN, MH, NU,
       WF, Y.

2646   —An order of the Commons . . . enabling the severall
       committees. For Edw. Husband, November 22, 1645.
       4°.* LT, O, HH, GK; CH, MA, WF, Y.

2647   —An order of the Commons . . . enabling the visitors.
       For Edward Husband April 24, 1648. brs. STEELE 2753;
       MADAN 1979. LT, O; CH, MH, MIU, Y.

2648   —An order of the Commons . . . for limitation of the
       committee. For Edward Husband, [1646]. brs. STEELE
       2662. LT.

2649   —An order of the Commons . . . for taking off the
       priviledge. For Edward Husband, Jan. 6, 1647[8]. 4°.*
       LT, O, OC; CH, CN, MH, MHL, Y.

2650   —An order of the Commons . . . for the dismantling the
       garrison of Darby. For I.P., 1646. 4°.* LT, O, SP, DT;
       CLC, MH, Y.

2651   —An order of the Commons . . . for the removall out of
       . . . London. For Edward Husbands, May 28, 1644. brs.
       STEELE 2567. LT, O, HH; CH, MH, Y.

2652   —An order of the Commons assembled in Parliament,
       forbidding any person whatsoever that is come from
       Oxford. By Richard Cotes, 1646. 4°.* MADAN 1893.
       LT, DT; CN, MH, MHL, Y.

2653   —An order of the House of Commons against arresting.
       For Tho. Bates, 1641. brs. MC.

2654   —An order of the House of Commons, declaring the
       high breach of priviledge of Parliament. For Joseph
       Hunscott, 1642. 4°.* LT, O, CJ, BR, DT; CN, MH, NU,
       WF, Y.

2655   —An order of the House of Commons for printing the
       preamble. [London], by Robert Barker and by the assignes
       of John Bill, 1641. LT; Y.

2656   —An order of the House of Commons, for the speedy
       bringing in. For J. Wright, 1646. brs. STEELE 2651. L;
       MH.

2657   —An order of the House of Parliament concerning the
       gathering in of the pole-moneys. [London], by A.N.
       for Iohn Franck, [1642]. brs. STEELE 2115. LT.

2658   —An order of the right honourable the Commons . . .
       for appointing a committee. By Richard Cotes, [1648].
       brs. STEELE 2771. LT, O, LG, HH; CH.

2659   —Ordered by the Commons . . . that in regard those
       souldiers. [London, 1645.] brs. LT.

2660   —Die Jovis, 8. Julii, 1646. Ordered by the Commons
       assembled in. [London, 1646.] brs. STEELE 2660. LT, HH;
       MH.

2661   —Die Lunae, 29 Novemb. 1647. —. For Edward Hus-
       band. Decemb. 1, 1647. brs. STEELE 2736. LT, LPR.

2662   —Die Martis, 4 April. 1648. —. —, April 6. 1648. brs.
       STEELE: 2752. LT, HH; MH.

2663   ——30 August 1648. [London], for E. Husband, 21 Sept.,
       1648. brs. STEELE 2789. HODGKIN.

2664   —Die Sabbathi, 14 Aprilis, 1649. —. For Edward Hus-
       band, April 17. 1649. brs. STEELE 2841. LT, O, C, LUG,
       HH; MB, MH.

2665   —Die Sabbathi, 9 Junii, 1649. —. —, 1649. brs. STEELE
       2856. LT, O, C, HH; MB, MH, Y.

2666   —Die Veneris, 6 Julii, 1649. —. —, July 7, 1649. brs.
       STEELE 2859. LT, C, HH; MB, MH.

2666A —Die Sabbathi, 26 Maii 1649. Ordered by the Com-
       mons . . . that all the rents. By Richard Cotes, [1649].
       brs. STEELE 2853. O; MH.

2667   —Ordered by the Commons . . . that no master of com-
       mander. By J. Field for E. Husband, 1649. brs. STEELE
       2832. LU, O; CH, MH.

2668   —Ordered by the Commons assembled . . . that it be
       referred. For Edward Husband, 1646. brs. STEELE 2664.
       LT.

2669   —Ordered by the Commons . . . that it bee referred to
       the committee . . . to issue warrants. By Richard Cotes,
       1649. brs. CH.

2670   —Ordered by the Commons . . . that the petition of the
       eldership . . . 31 March 1648. [London, 1648.] brs.
       STEELE 2751. CANTERBURY, LG.

2671   —Ordered by the Commons . . . that this day fortnight . . . 27 July 1648. *For E. Husband*, 1648. brs. STEELE 2784. HODGKIN.

2672   —Ordered that the adventurers. [*London*, 1643.] brs. LT.

2673   —Ordered (upon the question) by the . . . that the several committees. *For Edward Husband*, 1648. brs. STEELE 2750. LT; CH.

2674   —The orders from the Hovse of Commons for the abolishing of superstition. *By B. Alsop*, 1641. 4°.* LT, O, C, E, DT; CSS, MH, NU, WF, Y.

2675   —The orders, proceedings, punishments and priviledges of the Commons. [*London*], *printed*, 1641. 4°.* L, OC, CT, EN, DT; CH, LC, MH, NU, Y.

2676   —An ordinance and declaration of the Commons . . . that no person within the city. *By Richard Cotes*, 19 *Decemb.*, 1644. 4°.* LL; Y.

2677   —An ordinance of the Commons . . . for a bill. *By C. A. Dublin*, 1647. 4°.* LT, O.

2678   —An ordinance of the Commons . . . in vindication of Thomas Brown. *For Edw. Husbands. May* 17, 1643. 4°.* LT, O, C; MH, NU, Y.

2679   —The Commons petition to the king, in defence of Mr. Pym. *For William Bond*, 1641[2]. 4°.* LT, O, LVF, HH, DT; CLC, CN, MIU, WF, Y.

2680   —A petition of the House of Commons, which accompanied the declaration . . . presented to His Majesty. *Printed*, 1641. 4°.* O, CT, LL, HH, DT; CH, MH, WF, Y.

2681   ——[*Anr. ed.*] *Printed at London, and re-printed at Edinburgh*, [1641]. 4°.* ALDIS 1012. E; Y.

2682   —The petition of the members of the House of Commons, who are accused by the army. *For Ralph Smith*, 1647. 4°.* O; CH.

2682A   —A petition sent to the Kings . . . maiestie. *For B. W.*, 1641. 4°.* LT, O, LUG, EC, BR; CH, CLC, NU, WF, Y.

2683   —The proceedings in the House of Commons touching the impeachment of . . . Clarendon. [*London*], *printed* 1700. 8°. MU, Y.

2684   ——Second edition. —, 1700. 8°. O, CS, MR, HH, EN; CH, CN, LC, NCL.

2685   —Proceedings of the honourable House of Commons, who met at Oxford, March 21. 1680/1. *For John Peacock*, 1681. fol.* L, O, C, CCA, CT; CH, CLC, MH, WF, Y.

2686   —The proceedings of the House of Commons, at Oxford, Lun. 21° die Martii, 168° [*sic*]. [*London*, 1680/1.] cap., fol.* L, SP; CH, CLC, MH, WF, Y.

2687   Entry cancelled.

2688   —A proposition or a message sent the 31 of Decemb. 1641. *By Robert Barker and by the assigns of John Bill*, 1641[2]. 4°.* LT, O, CH, HH, DT; CH, CN, MH, WF, Y.

2689   —The protestation made by the House of Commons, May 5, 1641. 1641. brs. O, DT.

2690   —The protestation wch the knights, citizens, and burgesses, in ye Commons . . . made, ye 3° of May, 1642. [*London*, 1642.] brs. CH, Y.

2691   —A publike declaration and protestation of the secured and secluded members. [*London*, 1649.] brs. STEELE 2829. LT, O, LPR, HH.

2691A   —Questions propounded to Mr. Herbert. *For Iohn Frank*, 1641[2]. 4°.* LT, O, HH; CLC, MH, MU, NU, WF, Y.

2692   —Qvestions propounded to the assembly of divines . . . April ult, 1646. *For Edward Husband, May 4, 1646.* 4°.* LT, O, CT, EN, DT; MH, NPT, NU, TU, WF.

2692A   —The rates of merchandizes. *For L. Blaiklock*, 1642. 8°. LUG, OP.

2693   —The reasons & narrative of proceedings betwixt the two Houses. [*London*, 1679.] fol.* L, O, C, CS, OP; CH, CLC, TU, WF.

2694   ——[*Anr. ed.*] *Printed*, 1679. fol.* L, O, C, BR, HH; CH, LC, MH, NU, WCL, Y.

2695   —The reasons of the House of Commons, to stay . . . 14 . . . 15 July. [*London*], 1641. brs. STEELE 1868. LT; MH, WF.

2696   —Reasons of the House of Commons why bishops ought not to have votes. [*London*, 1641.] brs. STEELE 1858. LT, OC, LG, E; CH, MH, WF.

2697   —The reasons which the House of Commons deliver'd at a conference. [*London*, 169-.] cap., fol.* Y.

2698   —A record of some vvorthie proceedings: in the honorable, wise, and faithfvll Hovse of Commons. [*London*], *printed*, 1641. 4°.* L, O, CT, LL, HH; CH, LC, MH, NU, TU, Y.

2699   —A relation of the transactions of the commands. 1642. 4°. O.

2699A   —A relation touching the present state . . . of Ireland. *By E. G., for Richard Best*, 1641[2]. 4°.* LT, OC, MR, EN; CH, CN, LC, MH, Y.

2700   —22 April, 1647. Remedies for removing some obstructions. *For Edward Husband, April*, 30, 1647. 4°.* LT, OC, MR, HH, E; MB, NU, TU, WF, Y.

2701   —A remonstrance of the Commons in Parliament concerning the present state. [*London*], *June* 10, *for Robert Bird*, 1643. 4°.* LT, O; MH, MHL, WF, Y.

2702   —The remonstrance of the Commons of England. [*Oxford*], *printed*, 1642[/3]. 4°.* MADAN 1261. O, HH, DT; LC, OWC, WF, Y.

2703   ——[*Anr. ed.*] [*London*], *printed*, 1643. 4°.* LT, O, HH, EN, DT; CH, MH, NU, WF, Y.

2704   —A remonstrance of the state of the kingdom. *For Ioseph Hunscutt*, 1641. 4°.* LT, O, C, BR, HH; CH, CN, MH, RPJ, WF.

2704A   ——[*Anr. ed.*] *Printed*, 1641. 4°.* L, O, C, CDC, BR, HH; CH, CLC, CN, Y.

2704AA   ——[*Anr. ed.*] *Re-printed at Edinburgh by Robert Young and Evan Tyler*, 1641. 4°.* ALDIS 1017. EN; NU, Y.

2704AB   ——[*Anr. ed.*] *Edinburgh, R. B. & J. B.*, 1641. 4°.* ALDIS 1018. E, EN.

2704B   —A report of the committee of the charge against Matthew Wren. [*London*], *printed*, 1641. 4°.* L, O, EN; LC, MIU.

2705   —The report of the committee of the House of Commons, to whom the petition of the Royal Lustring-Company. *Printed, and are to be sold by E. Whitlock*, 1698. fol. L, C, LUG, CCA; MH, WF.

2706 —The resolutions of the House of Commons, concerning the kings answere to the militia, Feb. 28, 1641[2]. *For L. B,* 1641[2]. brs. STEELE 2003. LT.

2707 —Resolutions of the House of Commons concerning the prices of wines. [*London*, 1641.] brs. LS.

2708 —Thursday November 15, 1660. Resolved and declared by the Commons. *By John Bill,* 1660. brs. LT, O, C, LG, LUG.

2709 —Resolved by the Commons assembled . . . Resolved, &c. that Charles Stuart. *By Richard Cotes,* 1649. brs. NU.

2710 —Die Sabbathi, 19. Maii, 1649. Resolved, &c. that all such delinquents. *By Richard Cotes,* 1649. brs. LT.

2711 —Die Martis, 8 Decemb. 1646. Resolved, &c. that no committee-man. *By Richard Cotes,* 1646. brs. LT, O.

2712 —Die Martis 10 Novemb. 1646. Resolved, &c. that the committee of sequestrations. *By Richard Cotes,* 1646. brs. LT, O; CH, MH.

2713 —Resolved, &c. that the court of wards and liveries (20. Septemb.). [*London,* 1645.] brs. CH.

2714 —Die Martis, 3 Octobr. 1649. Resolved by the Commons. *By John Field for Edward Husband,* 1649. brs. LT, LG, OP.

2714A —Friday, September 7, 1660. Resolved by the Commons . . . that no moneys. *By John Bill and Christopher Barker,* 1660. brs. STEELE 3252. O, LG, LUG; MH.

2715 —Die Mercurii, 14 Martii, 1648. Resolved by the Commons . . . that Sir Iohn Stowell. *By R.Cotes,* 1649. brs. STEELE 2831. LT, O, BR; CH, MH.

2716 —Resolved . . . that all persons . . . 4 August 1648. *For E. Husband,* 5 *August,* 1648. brs. STEELE 2785. HODGKIN.

2717 —Resolved . . . that the members of this House . . . 8 May 1660. *By Edward Husbands and Thomas Newcomb,* [1660]. brs. STEELE 3194. O.

2718 —Die Mercurii, 25 Julii, 1649. Resolved upon the question by the Commons. *For Edward Husband, July 26,* 1649. brs. STEELE 2865. LT, O, C, LUG.

2719 —Die Veneris, 31 Augusti, 1649. Resolved (upon the question) by the Commons. *By John Field,* 1649. brs. STEELE 2869. LT, O, LUG, OQ; CH, MH, Y.

2720 —Resolved upon the question by the . . . 25 November 1661. *R. Hodgkinson,* 1661. brs. STEELE 3338. L.

2721 —Die Veneris 30 Julii. 1641. Resolved upon the question, that this house. [*London,* 1641.] brs. LT, O; MH.

2722 —Resolved upon the question: to provide for. [*London,* 1642.] brs. STEELE 2171 L, OC; MH.

2723 —Resolves of the Commons assembled . . . concerning such ministers. *For Edward Husband, July 10,* 1649. brs. STEELE 2861. LT, O, C, BR, HH; CH, MH, Y.

2724 —The sentence of the House of Commons, vpon Mr. Henry Darell. *For E. Husbands and I. Franck,* Oct. 18, 1642. 4°.* LT, CT, BR, HH, DT; CLC, WF.

2724A —Severall acts of the Commons . . . for the abolishing of deanes. *By Richard Cotes,* 1649. 4°.* L, O; MH, NGT, WF.

2725 —The several debates of the House of Commons, in the reign of . . . James II. . . . *Printed,* 1697. 4°.* L, C, MR; CH, CN, MH, WF, Y.

2726 —The several debates of the House of Commons pro & contra, . . . establishment of militia. *Printed,* 1689. 8°. L, CT, OC, LW, P; CH, CN, MH, WF, Y.

2727 —Several orders of the Commons . . . 1 September 1645. *For E. Husband 22 Iune,* 1647. brs. STEELE 2628. LT.

2728 ——5 June 1647. *For E. Husband, 22 Iune,* 1647. brs. STEELE 2693. LT.

2729 —Several orders of the Commons . . . viz. I. For receiving complaints. *For Edward Husband, Iune 22,* 1647. brs. STEELE 2691. LT, O, HH; MH.

2729A —Several propositions presented from the House of Commons to the Lords. *For Iohn Bull, June 7,* 1642. 4°.* L, O, EC, HH, BR; CH, MH, WF, Y.

2730 —Severall votes and resolutions of the Commons. *For M. W.,* 1648. 4°.* LT.

2731 —Several votes of the Commons . . . against certain papers. *For Edward Husband, Nov. 25,* 1647. 4°. LT, OC, EC; CH, MH, WF, Y.

2732 —Several votes of the Commons . . . concerning delinquents. *For Edward Husband, Dec. 17,* 1646. 4°.* CH, MH.

2733 —Several votes of the Commons . . . concerning such members. *For Edward Husband, Iuly 10,* 1647. brs. STEELE 2712. LT, LG, HH; MH.

2734 —The substance of the clause offered to the Land-Bank-Bill. [*London,* 1696?] fol.* L.

2735 —Die Lunae, 28 Junii, 1647. That it be referred to the commissioners. *By Richard Cotes and Ruth Raworth,* 1647. brs. STEELE 2709. LT, HH; MH.

2736 ——29 December 1659. *Streater & Macock,* 1659. brs. STEELE 3144. L, O.

2737 —That no committee-men, sequestrator, . . . 8 December 1646. *R. Cotes,* 1646. brs. STEELE 2670. L; MH.

2738 —That no moneys due to any of . . . 7 September 1660. *By John Bill and Christopher Barker,* 1660. brs. STEELE 3252. L, O, LS, HH.

2739 —That Sir John Stowell knight be proceeded. *R. Cotes,* 1649. brs. STEELE 2831. LT, O, LPR; CH.

2740 —That the committee of sequestrations. *R. Cotes,* 1646. brs. STEELE 2666. L, O; MH.

2741 —That the priviledge of this House, in . . . 15 November 1660. *By John Bill,* 1660. brs. STEELE 3268. LT, O, C, DT.

2742 —That this House doth conceive. [*London,* 1641.] brs. STEELE 1874. LT, O.

—To the Kings most excellent majestie, the humble petition. 1642[3]. *See* Scotland. Estates.

2743 —To the Kings most excellent Maiesty, the humble petition of the Commons of the late Parliament, and others. [*London*], *printed,* 1643. 4°.* LT, O, SP; WF, Y.

2744 —To the right honourable Sir Patience Ward knight, Lord Mayor . . . the humble petition of the Commons . . . June 27. 1681. colop: *For R. Baldwyn,* 1681. brs. Y.

2745 —A true and exact list of those persons nominated and recommended by . . . Commons. *For Iohn Franke, 1641*[2]. brs. STEELE 1986. LT, O, LG; MH.

2746 —A true and perfect collection of all messages, addresses, &c. from the House of Commons. *Printed, 1680.* fol. L, O, CCA, BR, EN; CH, CN, MH, WF, Y.

2747 —The true copie of an act, or, declaration of that honourable House of Commons, . . . Decemb. 24. 1641. *For T.B.*, 1641. 4°.* LT, O, OC, HH, DT; CH, CN, MH, NU, WF, Y.

2748 —True copy of the journal-book of the last Parliament. *Printed, 1680.* 8°. L, O, C, P, DT; CH, CN, LC, MH, WF.

2748A —True extract out of the Commons journal. *Printed, 1678.* 4°.* L, LUG, SP; CLC, PL, WF, Y.

2748B —Two acts. *By Richard Cotes & Thomas Newcomb, 1649.* fol.* MB.

2749 —Two declarations of the Commons — . . . the one concerning the court of wards. *For Edw. Husband, January 3, 1645*[6]. 4°.* LT, O, HH, EN, DT; CH, CLC, MH.

2750 —Two orders of the Commons . . . concerning soldiers. *For Edward Husband, June 23, 1647.* brs. STEELE 2707. LT, O, C, HH; MH.

2751 —Two orders of the Commons . . . of great consequence. *For Edw. Husbands, March 30, 1643.* 4°.* LT, O, C, OC, DT; CN, MH, NU, WF, Y.

2752 —Two speciall orders made by the House of Commons . . . the one prohibiting. *For John Franck, Januar. 17, 1642*[3]. brs. STEELE 2351. LT, O, LG, HH; CH, CCC, MH.

2753 —Two votes of the Commons . . . declaring the forces. *For Edward Husband, July 24, 1648.* brs. STEELE 2779. LT, O, C; CH, MH, Y.

2754 —The vote in the House of Commons made July 26. *Printed at London, by Robert Ibbitson, 1647.* 4°.* LT, O, OC; CH, CN, MH, Y.

2755 —A vote of the Commons House . . . 13 May. *R. Hodgkinson, 1661.* brs. STEELE 3303. L.

2756 —Votes, die Martis 2 [14] July, 1642. Resolved. *[London], by T.P. and M.S.*, [1642]. brs. STEELE 2220. L, O, LG.

2757 —Votes and addresses of the honourable House of Commons . . . March 29. 1673. *[London, 1673.]* cap., 4°.* L, O, C, MR; CH, CN, MH, NU, WF, Y.

2758 —The votes and orders of the . . . House fo Commons, . . . upon reading His Majesties gracious declaration. *By John Bill and Christopher Barker, 1662*[3]. fol.* L, O, C, LL, HH; CH, MM, WF, Y.

2759 —Votes and resolves of the Commons House . . . 15 July. *By R.Hodgkinson, 1661.* brs. STEELE 3313. L, LL; CH, MH, Y.

2760 —Votes &c of the honourable House of Commons: Febr. 25. &c. 1662. *[London, 1663.]* 4°.* L, CS, CT, EC, WCA; CH, MH, NU, WF, Y.

2761 —Votes of the honorable House of Commons against protection. *In the Savoy, T.Newcomb, 1670.* brs. STEELE 3542. L.

2762 —Votes of the honourable the Commons . . . in favour of Protestant Dissenters. *For Francis Smith,* [1680]. brs. L, O, SP; PL.

2763 —The votes of the honourable House of Commons, in vindication. *By R.R.*, 1647. brs. STEELE 2708. LT, O, HH; CH, MH.

2764 —Votes of the House of Commons. *By Thomas Braddyll and Robert Everingham,* 1692. fol. CCA; MM.

2765 —Votes of the House of Commons, at Oxford. colop: *For Gabriel Kunholt, published by Langley Curtis,* [1681.] L, O, C, CCA; CH, MBA, MH.

2765A ——[Anr. ed.] *[Dublin, 1681.]* cap., 4°.* C, DT.

2766 —Votes of the House of Commons for divers of their members. *Printed at London by Robert Ibbitson, 1647.* 4°.* LT, OC, HH, DT; MH, WF.

2766A —Votes of the House of Commons, perused and signed. *By the assigns of John Bill, Thomas Newcomb, and Henry Hills,* 1680. fol.* O, C, OC, CM, BR; CH, MH, PL, WCL, WF, Y.

2766B ——[Anr. ed.] *[Dublin], reprinted,* 1680. 4°. C, DT.

2767 —The votes of the House of Commons upon His Majesties last message. *[London], for R. Smithurst,* 1648. 4°.* LT, O; CH, CU, MH.

2768 —The votes of the House. Or the dayly proceedings in Parliament . . . 21 of February . . . March 16. 1650. *By Iohn Redmayne, 1659*[60]. 4°. LT, YM.

2769 —Wee the Commons in Parliament . . . 17 July 1648. *For J. Wright,* 1648. brs. STEELE 2781. HODGKIN.

2770 —Whereas by an order of the House of Commons, bearing date the 3d day of October, 1649. *[London, 1649.]* brs. LT.

2771 —Whereas by an ordinance of . . . September 1648. *[London, 1648.]* brs. STEELE 2796a. MC.

2772 —Whereas by an ordinance of Parliament . . . 13 January 1648[9]. *[London, 1649.]* brs. STEELE 2818. LT.

2773 —Whereas by order of the House of Commons. *[London, 1643.]* brs. LT.

2774 —Whereas by reason of the long and . . . 19 June 1644. *[London, 1644.]* brs. STEELE 2576. L.

2775 —Whereas by speciall order of the House of Commons. *London, 1645.]* brs. STEELE 2623. LT.

2776 —Whereas divers debenters signed by the . . . 12 July 1648. *For J.Wright,* 1648. brs. STEELE 2778. HODGKIN.

2777 —Whereas divers summes of money . . . 11 February 1642[3]. *[London, 1642*[3].] brs. STEELE 2368. LPR.

2778 —Whereas His most excellent Majestie. *By Christopher Barker and by the assignes of John Bill,* 1641. brs. STEELE 1910. L, LS, CT, OP; Y.

2779 —Die Lunae 7mo. November, 1642. Whereas in these times. *For R.Oulton & G.Dexter,* 1642. brs. STEELE 2297. LT, LS, EC; MH.

2780 —Die Martis, 21. Februarii, 1642[3]. —. *For John Wright,* 1642[3]. brs. STEELE 2374. LT, LS, CT, HH.

2781 —Whereas it doth appear to this House. *Imprinted at London by Robert Barker, and by the assigns of John Bill,* 1641. brs. STEELE 1892. LT, O, LPR, LS, DT.

2782 —Whereas the Lords and Commons in Parliament . . . 24 April 1643. *For Edward Husband,* [1643]. brs. STEELE 2412. HH; CH.

2783 —Whereas the maimed soldiers and. *By John Bill,* 1660. brs. STEELE 3272. LT, LUG, MC, HH, DT.

2784 —Whereas there are many poore, sick and . . . 13 June 1644. [*London,* 1644.] brs. STEELE 2573. HH.

2785 —Whereas there was an act made. [*London,* 169–.] brs. L; WF.

2786 —Die Sabbathi September 24, 1642. Whereas, this Kingdome. *By L. N. for E. Husbands and Iohn Frank,* 1642. brs. STEELE 3268. LT, EC, HH; MH.

2787 —Whereas Thursday next is by former order. *R. Coles,* 1675[/6]. brs. STEELE 2646. LT.

ENGLAND: PARLIAMENT, HOUSE OF LORDS

2787A —After debate about the printing. [*London,* 1641]. brs. STEELE 1888. LT, C, LG.

2788 —The agreement of the House of Lords, during this session. [*London,* 1690.] brs. L, OC, HH; CH, WF.

2789 —Articles of impeachment in the High Court of Parliament against the nine Lords. July I. [*London*], *for J. Tompson, and A. Coe,* 1642. 4°.* OC; NU.

2790 —By the Lords spiritual and temporal, . . . 25 December 1688. *By John Starkey and Awnsham & William Churchill,* 1688. brs. STEELE 3937. L, O, HH, EN, DM; CH, CN, WF.

2791 ——[Anr. ed.] *For A. & W. Churchill,* 1688. brs. STEELE 3938. O, HH.

2791A —The censure of the Earl of Berkshire. *For J. Johnson, Septemb.* 20. 1642. 4°.* LT, C, LFEA; Y.

2791B —Certain orders . . . plague. *For Robert Barker, and for the assigns of John Bill,* 1641. brs. STEELE 188. LT, O, LPR; WSG, Y.

2791C ——[Anr. ed.] *By Richard Cotes,* 1646. brs. STEELE 1894. LT, O.

2792 —A command from the House of Peers. 1642. 4°. O.

2793 —A conference desired by the Lords. *By A. N. for Mathew Walbancke, and Richard Best,* 1642. 4°. L, O, C, EN, DT; BN, CH, LC, MH, NU, TU, Y.

—Declaration and protestation of the peers. [*London,* 1649.] *See* Prynne, William.

2794 —A declaration of the Lords . . . 11 December 1688. *In the Savoy, by Edward Jones,* 1688. brs. STEELE 3918. L, O, CCA, LG, LS; CH, WF, Y.

2795 —A declaration of the Lords . . . concerning the committee. *For John Wright,* 1646[7]. brs. STEELE 2678. LT, O, LG, LUG, HH; MH, Y.

2796 —The declaration of the Lords spiritual and . . . 11 December 1688. *Edinburgh reprinted* [*heir of A. Anderson*], 1688. brs. STEELE 3p 2752; ALDIS 2754. L, HH, EN, ER; CH.

2797 —An exact collection of all orders, votes. *For F. Smith,* 1679. fol. OP.

2798 —Forasmuch as many writs of error be now. *For Iohn Wright,* 1646. brs. STEELE 2656. LT, O, HH; CH, MH.

2799 —Forasmuch as upon writs of error returnable . . . 13 December 1661. *By John Bill and Christopher Barker,* 1661. brs. STEELE 3345. L, O, HH; MH, Y.

2800 —The House this day reading the names . . . 27 January 1696[7]. *By Charles Bill & the executrix of Thomas Newcomb,* 1698. brs. STEELE 4220. L, LPR.

2800A —The humble address . . . 7 March 1694. *By Charles Bill and the executrix of Thomas Newcomb,* 1694. fol.* L, OC, SP, TU, WF.

2800B ——[Same title.] 31 Dec. 1694. —, 1694. fol.* L, OC.

2800C ——[Same title.] 16 Feb. 1697. —, 1697. fol.* OC.

2800D ——[Same title.] 6 Feb. 1698. —, 1698. fol.* OP, SP; WF.

2801 —The humble address of the Lords spiritual and temporal to His Majesty, in relation to the petition of Charles Desborow. *For C. Desborow,* 1699. 4°.* L, O, OC; CH, LC, RPJ.

2801A —The humble address of the right honorable the Lords . . . eighth day of December, 1693. *By Charles Bill and the executrix of Thomas Newcomb,* 1693. fol. CM.

2802 ——[Same title.] sixteenth of December, 1695. —, 1695. fol.* L, HH; CH, NC, Y.

2803 ——[Same title.] —, 1696. fol. L, SP; CN.

2804 ——[Anr. ed.] *Printed at London, and re-printed at Edinburgh,* 1696. fol.* ALDIS 3569. SCOTT.

2805 ——[Same title.] *By Charles Bill and the executrix of Thomas Newcomb,* 1700. fol.* L, DC, EC, LUG; WF.

2805A ——[Anr. ed.] *Edinburgh, re-printed by the heirs and successors of Andrew Anderson,* 1700. brs. L; MIU.

2805B ——[Anr. ed.] *Dublin,* 1700. brs. DT.

2806 —The humble answer of the House of Peers to His Majesties gracious letter and declaration. *By John Macock, and Francis Tyton,* 1660. 4°.* LT, O, C, LG; CLC, MH, NU, TU, WF, Y.

2807 —It is this day ordered by the Lords . . . 9 September 1641. *By Christopher Barker & the assigns of John Bill,* 1641. brs. STEELE 1887. L, LS, OP, OQ.

2808 ——11 June 1642. *For Joseph Hunscott, and Iohn Wright,* 1642. brs. STEELE 2173. LT, O, LS, EC; MH.

2809 Entry cancelled.

2810 ——12 May 1660. *By John Macock, and Francis Tyton,* 1660. brs. STEELE 3203. LT, O, LG, HH.

2811 ——23 April 1679. *By John Bill, Thomas Newcomb, & Henry Hills,* 1679. brs. STEELE 3685. L, O, C, LPC, OQ; CH, MH, WF, Y.

2812 ——5 May 1679. *By John Bill, Thomas Newcomb, and Henry Hills,* 1679. brs. STEELE 3690. L, O, C, LG, DT; CH, MH, WF.

2813 ——4 July 1698. *By Charles Bill and the executrix of Thomas Newcomb,* 1698. brs. STEELE 4248. L, LPR.

2814 —A letter from the Lords at Oxford. *Oxford, March 1, by Leonard Lichfield,* 1643[/4]. 4°.* MADAN 1542. O, HH; MBP, WF.

2814A —A list of the House of Lords. *For Nathaniel Ponder and Michael Davis in Oxford,* 1681. brs. OC.

2815 —The Lords . . . do order and appoint this . . . 22 January 1645[6]. [*London,* 1646.] brs. STEELE 2640a. MC.

2816 —The Lords in Parliament assembled . . . 5 March 1646[7]. *For J. Wright,* 1646[7]. brs. STEELE 2682. LT; MH.

2817 ——20 May 1661. *By John Bill and Christopher Barker,* 1661. brs. STEELE 3306. L, O, LG, LUG, HH.

2818 —The Lords in Parliament taking notice . . . 22 December 1660. *By John Bill,* 1660. brs. STEELE 3275. L, O, LG, HH, DT.

2819 ——26 July 1661. *By John Bill and Christopher Barker,* 1661. brs. STEELE 3315. L, O, HH.

2820 —The Lords spiritual and temporal . . . 20 February 1662[3]. *By John Bill and Christopher Barker,* 1662[3]. brs. STEELE 3379. L.

2821 —Die Jovis 24° Martii 1663. The Lords spiritual and temporal. *By John Bill and Christopher Barker,* 1663. brs. STEELE 3396. L, LPR, LS, DT; MH.

2822 ——25 November 1664. *By John Bill and Christopher Barker,* 1664. brs. STEELE 3406. L, HH, DT; MH.

2822A ——[Same title.] 25 December 1688. *By John Starkey, and Awnsham and William Churchill,* 1688. brs. OC.

2823 ——[Anr. ed.] [*Edinburgh, by the heir of Andrew Anderson,* 1688.] STEELE 3p 2759; ALDIS 2919. HH, EN, ES.

2824 ———[Anr. ed.] *Edinburgh, re-printed by John Reid,* 1689. brs. STEELE 3p 2760; ALDIS 2918. HH; Y.

2825 —Die Veneris, 5 March, 1646. The Lords . . . taking into their consideration the multitude of beggars. *Printed at London for John Wright,* 1646[7]. brs. LT.

2826 —Order by the Lords in Parliament that all private petitions be deferred. *By E.G. for John Wright,* 1642. brs. LS.

2827 —An order of the House of Peers, limiting the time. *By John Bill, Christopher Barker, Thomas Newcomb, and Henry Hills,* 1678. brs. STEELE 3652. L, O, C, LG, DT; CH, MH, WF.

2828 —The order of the House of the Lords for the calling in . . . vox Hiberniae. *By R.B. for Philemon Stephens,* 1641[2]. fol.* LT, HH.

2829 —Oxford, 12. de Maij. 1645. An order of the Lords. *Printed at Oxford by Leonard Lichfield,* 1645. brs. MADAN 1776. O.

2830 Entry cancelled.

2831 —An order of the Lords deferring all private business. [*London*], *by Robert Barker and the assignes of John Bill,* 1641. brs. LT.

2832 —An order of the Lords . . . for a publick thanksgiving. *For James Partridge & Matthew Gyllyflower,* (1688/9). brs. STEELE 3953. O, OQ, HH; PL, WF, Y.

2833 —An order of the Lords, for the better direction of the overseers. *Printed at Oxford by Leonard Lichfield,* 1644. brs. STEELE 2580; MADAN 1673. O.

2834 —An order of the Lords . . . for the due putting in execution. *Printed at London for John Wright,* 1646[7]. brs. STEELE 2684. LT, O; Y.

2835 —An order of the Lords . . . for the not-observing. *In the Savoy, by Edward Jones & for James Partridge, Matthew Gillyflower, and Samuel Heyrick,* 1688[9]. brs. STEELE 3955. L, O; CH, Y.

2836 —An order of the Lords . . . for the punishing of Anabaptists . . . 22 December 1646. *For Iohn Wright,* 1646. 4°.* LT, O, LG, OC, HH; MH, MIU, NHC, NU.

2836A —An order of the Lords . . . that all Papists . . . 22 December 1688. *For Awnsham and William Churchill,* 1688. brs. STEELE 3933. L, O, LS, EN, DM; CH, CN.

2837 —Ordered by the Lords in Parliament, that these particulars shall be forthwith printed. *For Joseph Hunscott and John Wright,* 1642. brs. STEELE 2182. LT, LS, LG, EC; MH, Y.

2838 —Ordered by the Lords spiritual and . . . 22 November 1680. *By the assigns of John Bill,* 1680. brs. STEELE 3721. L, O, C, HH, DT; CH.

2839 ——3 December 1680. *By the assigns of John Bill, Thomas Newcomb and Henry Hills,* 1680. brs. STEELE 3723 L, O, C, LG, DT; CH, MH, WF, Y.

2840 ——[Die Sabbathi 15° Jun., 1689]. *By Charles Bill & Thomas Newcomb,* 1689. brs. STEELE 4015. L, LG, LPC, LPR, OQ; CH, CLC, MH, WF, Y.

2841 —The proposals of the right honourable the Lords. *Edinburgh reprinted,* 1688. fol.* STEELE 3p 2750; ALDIS 2811. EN; WF.

2842 —Propositions delivered by the Lords at a conference. *Printed at London by Robert Ibbitson,* 1647. 4°.* LT, OC, YM, DT; MH, Y.

2843 —The protestation of the Lords upon rejecting the impeachment . . . Fitz-Harris. colop: *For Francis Smith,* 1681. brs. L, O, C, CT, HH; CH, CN, MH, TU, WCL, Y.

2844 Entry cancelled.

2845 —The report from the committee of safety. *For Iohn Wright,* 1643. brs. STEELE 2472. LT; WF.

2846 —Severall votes and orders of the House of Peeres. *For R.J.,* 1648. 4°.* LT, HH; CU, MH.

2847 —Some passages of the House of Lords. [*London,* 1693.] cap., 4°.* CT, MR; CH, Y.

2848 —To the Kings most excellent Majesty . . . the humble petition . . . of all the bishops. *For Joseph Hunscott,* 1641. brs. LT, O, CT, LG; CH, Y.

2849 —To the Kings most excellent Majesty, the humble petition of the Lords. *For E.Jones,* 1688. brs. STEELE 3901. L, O, LS, OQ, EN; CH, WF, Y.

2850 ——[Anr. ed.] *For T.Pyke,* 1688. brs. STEELE 3903. L, O, C, LS, HH; CLC, MH, Y.

2851 —A true account of the proceedings before the House of Lords. 1692. fol. L, O, EN; CN.

2852 —Two iudgements of the Lords. *For John Wright,* 1647. 4°.* LT, LG, DT.

2853 —Two orders; the one: to all high sheriffes. *Printed at London, by E.Griffin for Christopher Latham* 1642. brs. STEELE 2156. LT, O, C, HH; Y.

2854 —Two several addresses from the House of Peeres . . . 9th of October, 1690. *For Timothy Goodwin,* 1690. fol.* CCA, HH; CH, RPJ, WF.

2855 —Two votes concerning the king. *By John Bill and Christopher Barker,* 1660. brs. STEELE 3231. LT, O, LG, LS, DT.

2856 —Upon complaint made to this House . . . [9 December]. *By Charles Bill and the executrix of John Bill,* 1698. brs. STEELE 4257. LPR; MH.

2857 ——[23 November]. —, 1699. brs. STEELE 4268. LPR; MH.

2858 —Upon complaint this day made by the. *By John Macock and Francis Tyton*, 1660. brs. STEELE 3208. LT, O, LG, HH, DT; CH, MH, Y.

2858A ——[Anr. ed.] *Edinburgh, re-printed by Christopher Higgins*, 1660. brs. Y.

2859 —Upon reading the order of this House . . . 13 October 1690. *By John Bill & Thomas Newcomb*, 1690. brs. STEELE 4053. L, LG, LPC, LPR, OQ; WF.

2860 —Upon reading the petition of William Earl of Bedford. *By Iohn Bill, and Christopher Barker*, 1661. brs. STEELE 3304. L.

2861 —Upon reading this day in the House. *By Charles Bill and Thomas Newcomb*, 1690. brs. STEELE 4033. L, O, C, LG, MC, Y.

2862 —Upon report from the Lords committees . . . 3 December 1661. *By John Bill and Christopher Barker*, 1661. brs. STEELE 3341. L, HH; MH, Y.

2863 ——13 June 1660. *By John Macock and Francis Tyton*, 1660. brs. STEELE 3227. LPR.

2864 ——17 December 1660. *By John Bill*, 1660. brs. STEELE 3271. L, O, C, LG, HH; MH.

2865 —Upon report this day made. *By John Macock, and Francis Tyton*, 1660. brs. STEELE 3200. LT.

2865A —We conceive such an order. *J. Bill & C. Barker*, 1663. brs. L.

2866 —We, Peers of the realm, assembled with some . . . 14 December 1688. *In the Savoy: by Edward Jones*, 1688. brs. STEELE 3927. L, O, C, OP, HH; CH, WF, Y.

2867 —Wee the Peers of this realm, being assembled . . . 12th day of December, 1688. *In the Savoy: by Edward Jones*, 1688. brs. STEELE 3921. L, O, C, OC, HH; CN, MH, WF, Y.

2867A —Whereas provision is made. *For J. Wright*, 1646. brs. STEELE 2681. LT, O.

2868 —Whereas the House was this day informed . . . 30 June 1660. *By John Bill and Christopher Barker*, 1660. brs. STEELE 3233. L, LG, LS, DT; MH, WF.

2869 —Whereas the Lords in Parliament assembled. *For J. Wright*, 1646[7]. brs. STEELE 2680. LT, O, LG, HH; MH.

2870 —Whereas the Lords in Parliament, have this. *For J. Hunscott*, 18 May, 1642. brs. STEELE 2139. L, O, EC; MH.

2871 —Whereas the Lords in the Upper House. *Imprinted at London by Robert Barker: and by the assigns of John Bill*, 1641[2]. brs. STEELE 2044. LT, LS.

2872 —Die Iovis 5° Maii. 1642. Whereas the Lords in the Upper. *By E. G. for J. Wright*, 1642. brs. STEELE 2111. LT.

2873 —Whereas upon the Lords finding. *Imprinted at London by Robert Barker: and by the assigns of John Bill*, 1641. brs. STEELE 1897. LT.

2874 —Whereas upon the Lords meeting after their late. *By Robert Barker and by the assigns of John Bill*, 1641. brs. STEELE 1895. O, LS, OQ.

2875 —The whole proceedings in the House of Lords upon the bill of attainder. [*London*, 1696?] CN.

2876 —The whole series of all that hath been transacted . . . Popish plot. *By J. Redmayne*, 1681. fol. L, CM, EN, GU, DT; CN, MBP, MH, NU, TU.

2876A ——[Anr. ed.] *Printed*, 1681. 8°. L; PL.

ENGLAND: PRIVY COUNCIL.

2877 —Wednesday February 13. 1655. At the Council at Whitehall. Forasmuch. *By Henry Hills and Iohn Field*, 1655. brs. L.

2878 —Tuesday the five and twentieth of August, 1657. At the Council at White-hall, His Highness and the Council. *By Henry Hills and John Field*, 1657. brs. LT, LUG.

2879 —Thursday the thirteenth of August, 1657. At the Council at White-hall. His Highness the Lord Protector. *By Henry Hills and John Field*, 1657. brs. LT, LUG.

2880 —Thursday the tenth of September, 1657. —. —, 1657. brs. LT, LG, LUG, CJ.

2881 —Saturday 13th of June, 1657. At the Council at Whitehal. Whereas in an act made. colop: *By Henry Hills and Iohn Field*, 1657. cap., fol.* LT; WF.

2882 —At the Council-Chamber in Whitehall, Monday the 22th. of October, 1688. This day an extraordinary Council met. colop: *By Charles Bill, Henry Hills, and Thomas Newcomb*, 1688. cap., fol.* L, O, C, CS, DC; CH, MBA, WF, Y.

2882A ——[Anr. ed.] *Edinburgh, re-printed by the heir of Andrew Anderson*, 1688. fol.* Y.

2882B ——[Anr. ed.] *Dublin, re-printed by Andrew Crook and Samuel Helsham, assigns of Benj. Tooke*, 1688. 4°.* DIX 228. CD, DN.

2883 —Thursday June 16, 1653. At the Councill of State at White-hall, ordered. *For Giles Calvert, Hen. Hills, and Tho. Brewster*, 1653. brs. LT, O.

2884 —Tuesday 29 Novemb. 1653. At the Council of State at Whitehall. Ordered that Doctor Homes. [*London*, 1653.] brs. LT.

2885 —At the Council of State at White-Hall, the Parliament having lately intrusted. *By Henry Hills*, 1653. brs. LT, O; NU.

2886 —At the Councel of State at White Hall. Whereas divers of the inhabitants. [*London*, 1653.] cap., fol.* LT.

2887 —At the Court at Hampton-Court the 28th day of July 1681. colop: *By the assigns of John Bill, Thomas Newcomb and Henry Hills*, 1681. cap., fol.* L, O, C; CH, NU, WF, Y.

2888 —At the Court at White-Hall, August the 14, 1663. Present. colop: *By John Bill and Christopher Barker*, 1663. fol.* L; CH, CN.

2889 —At the Court at White Hall January 2, 1671/2. colop: *In the Savoy, by the assigns of John Bill, and Christopher Barker*, 1671/2. fol.* O; CH.

2890 —At the Court at Whitehall the eighth of May 1667. [*London*], *by James Flesher*, 1667. brs. L.

2890A —At the court at Whitehall the 16th of February 1680. *By the assigns of John Bill, Thomas Newcomb, and Henry Hills*, 1680. fol.* MH.

2891   —At the Court at Whitehall, April the sixteenth, 1680. *By John Bill, Thomas Newcomb, and Henry Hills, 1680.* brs. L; WF.

2892   —At the Court at Whitehall, November the 22th, 1682. [*London*, 1682.] brs. L.

2893   —At the Court at Whitehall, the 20th of July, 1683. colop: *By the assigns of John Bill: and by Henry Hills, and Thomas Newcomb,* 1683. fol.* L, O, C; CH, MH, RPJ, WF, Y.

2893A   —At the Court at Whitehall, 12th of February, 1684. [*London*, 1684.] brs. OC.

2894   —At the Court at Whitehall. The sixteenth of February, 1684. *By the assigns of John Bill, and by Henry Hills, and Thomas Newcomb,* 1684. brs. O, OP; CH.

2895   —At the Court at Whitehall the nineteenth of December 1684. *By the assigns of John Bill: and by Henry Hills, and Thomas Newcomb,* 1684. brs. L, O; CH, WF.

2896   —At the Court at Whitehall, the 26th day of March 1686. *By Charles Bill, Henry Hills, and Thomas Newcomb,* 1686. brs. L.

2897   —At the Court at White-Hall. March 18th, 1687/8. colop: *By Samuel Roycroft, London,* [1688.] cap., fol.* Y.

2898   —At the Court at Whitehall, the 29th of June, 1688. *By Charles Bill, Henry Hills, and Thomas Newcomb,* 1688. brs. O, OP; CH, WF, Y.

2899   —At the Court at Whitehall, the sixteenth day of February, 1688. *By Charles Bill and Thomas Newcomb,* 1688[9]. brs. L, O, OC, OP; CH, TSM.

2900   —At the Court at Whitehall the 29th day of December, 1694. [*London*, 1694.] brs. LG, CM.

2901   —A Common-Councell holden in the Chamber of the Guildhall of the city of London, the 21 day of May 1660. [*London*], *by James Flesher,* 1660. 4°.* C; NU.

2902   —A Common Council holden the 29. of Decemb. 1659. To this Common Council was presented. [*London*, 1659.] brs. LT.

2903   —Depositions made upon the birth . . . Prince of Wales. [*London*], *printed,* 8°.* LI, L; WF, Y.

2904   —20. November, 1644. For the better encouragement. *Printed at Oxford by Leonard Lichfield,* 1644. brs. STEELE 2591; MADAN 1693. O.

2905   —His Highness and the Council, calling . . . 25 August 1657. *By Henry Hills and Field,* 1657. brs. STEELE 3085. L.

2906   —His Highness the Lord Protector and His . . . 13 August 1657. *By Henry Hills and Field,* 1657. brs. STEELE 3084. L, O.

2907   ——10 September 1657. —, 1657. brs. STEELE 3086. L.

2908   —It was this day ordered by Her Majesty in Council . . . 10 October 1692. *By Charles Bill and the executrix of Thomas Newcomb,* 1692. brs. STEELE 4105. L, LPC, LPR, OQ.

2909   —A letter from the Councel of officers at Whitehall to Colonel Lilburne. *Leith,* 1653. 4°.* STEELE 3p 2100a; ALDIS 1478. EN; WF.

2910   —A message sent from the Lords of His Majesties most honourable Privie Counsaile. *Oxford, by Leonard Lichfield,* 1642. 4°.* MADAN 1120. LT, O, OC; CLC, CSS, MH, WF.

2911   —An order and declaration of the Council of State, concerning the determination. *For Giles Calvert, Henry Hills, and Thomas Brewster,* 1653. brs. STEELE 3000. LT, O, LPR, HH.

2912   —An order and declaration of His Highness the Lord Protector and His Privy Council, appointing a committee. colop: *By Henry Hills and John Field,* 1658. cap., fol.* LT.

2913   —An order of His Excellency the Lord General Cromvvell, and the Council of State, for continuing the powers. *For Giles Calvert, Thomas Brewster, and by and for Henry Hills,* 1653. brs. LT, O.

2913A   —Order of their excellencies . . . Nov. 24. 1690. *Boston,* 1690. fol.* EVANS 864. MWA.

2914   —Orders and instrvctions from the Lords of the Kings Majesties Privie Councell. *For Matthew Walbancke, May 23, 1646.* 4°.* MADAN 1867. LT, O, OC; COC, Y.

2915   —The several declarations, together with the several depositions made in Council . . . 22d of October, 1688. *Printed,* [1688]. 4°.* L, E; CH, Y.

2916   ——[Anr. ed.] *Printed, and sold by the booksellers,* 1688. 4°.* L; CH, CU, MBP, MU, Y.

2917   Entry cancelled.

2918   —Whereas a peace is made, concluded. *Du-Gard & Hills,* 1654. brs. STEELE 3033. L, O, OQ, DT; MH, MIU.

2919   ——22 April 1654. *Leith,* 1654. brs. STEELE 3p 2115. HH, ES.

2920   —Whereas by a former order of the second of July . . . 19 August 1645. *Oxford, L.Lichfield,* [1645]. brs. STEELE 2626. O.

2921   —Whereas by the late act of uniformity . . . 29 December 1694. *By Charles Bill and the executrix of Thomas Newcomb,* 1694. brs. STEELE 4145. L, LPC, LPR.

2922   —Whereas it hath pleased Almighty God . . . [6 February, 1684/5]. *By the assigns of John Bill, and by Henry Hills, and Thomas Newcomb,* 1684[5]. cap., brs. STEELE 3764. L, O, LG, MC, DT; CH, CLC, MH, TSM.

2922A   ——[Anr. ed.] *Edinburgh, by the heir of Andrew Anderson,* 1685. brs. STEELE 3p 2580. EN, ER.

2923   —Whereas it hath pleased God. *By I.Field for E.Husband,* 1649. brs. STEELE 2873. O.

2924   —Whereas it hath pleased the most wise God, in His providence, to take out of this world . . . Oliver. *By Henry Hills and Iohn Field,* 1658. brs. STEELE 3098. LT, O, LG, LS, HH; Y.

2925   —Whereas it is informed . . . 8 July 1664. [*Edinburgh, E. Tyler,* 1664.] brs. STEELE 3p 2271. AU, ER.

2926   —Whereas the late Parliament dissolving. *By Henry Hills,* 1653. brs. STEELE 3020. LT, O, C, LG, DT; CLC, WF.